THE
COMPLETE BOOK
OF THE
BRITISH
CHARTS
SINGLES & ALBUMS

BY TONY BROWN
JON KUTNER & NEIL WARWICK

WITH A FOREWORD BY
PAUL GAMBACCINI

OMNIBUS PRESS

One afternoon in 1973 this *Rolling Stone* reporter interviewed Tim Rice and Andrew Lloyd Webber at Tim's London home concerning the film of *Jesus Christ Superstar*. The occasion proved to be important to me far beyond the pages of the paper. I had begun personal relationships which continue to this day. And while waiting for the duo to finish their conversation with the project's publicist, the first bona fide public relations person I had ever met, I noticed two items in Tim's house that thrilled me.

The first was a pinball machine. I thought it a wonderful demonstration of priorities that someone had spent royalties from a hit musical on a pin table. I also noticed a copy of Joel Whitburn's privately printed guide to the American Hot 100, 1955–1969. I was very excited by this discovery, thinking that Tim and I might well have the only two copies in the country. One day the following week I was back at Oxford University feeling bored. I wondered what I would like to work on other than academic essays and my singles review column. I remembered that in researching my first *Rolling Stone* cover story, an interview with Elton John and Bernie Taupin, I could not find a reference book containing all the chart positions of Elton's UK hits. I called Tim on a whim and asked him, "Do you think there's room for a British Joel Whitburn?" He replied, "Yes, and I know someone who will publish it." That five-second exchange began our 23-year relationship as co-authors.

It turned out, however, that the company Tim thought would publish the book would not. His brother Jo came up with the idea to go to the firm that eventually did print our ten editions of *British Hit Singles* and 21 other related books. In 1975 I returned from a trip to the States to find that our trio had become a quartet with the addition of the Rice brothers' pal, Mike Read. There we were, a foursome of young men who never played a round of golf but instead churned out chart books. Like Tim's pinball machine, that demonstrated our priorities.

We were all pleased when the first edition appeared in 1977. Ironically, this was the year that I stopped writing regularly for *Rolling Stone*. I would not be needing the book for research on the paper after all! But by now I had my own show on Radio 1, and it was handy for my programmes.

Radio 1 picked up on the book as a competition prize, a gesture I thought friendly and perhaps useful in shifting a few copies. I had no idea how useful it would be. The regular on-air exposure brought the book to the attention of chart buffs across the country. There were more of us than we had ever dreamed, an entire class of human beings I call chartologists. They were chart followers, invariably young men, who had previously lived in isolation and were inspired by the success of *British Hit Singles* to communicate with us. They kept tabs on the weekly UK, and sometimes US, charts, and loved lists so much they often kept tables of their own favourite singles. In 1983 I met such a young man face-to-face. He looked at me and said, "You're Paul Gambaccini," a fact I could not deny. This was my introduction to Tony Brown, chartologist par excellence. Tony succeeded Nick Todd as our assistant on the chart books and proved to truly be "one of us". He loved the subject, retained the most obscure yet fascinating facts, and thought hours of hard labour on chart tabulation was his idea of fun. I always thought that Tony would be our natural successor as author of a chart book.

And now he is.

The volume in your hands is the result of a couple of years' work by Tony and his colleagues. I am looking forward to it as much as you, for I have always believed Tony Brown is the future of chartology.

Paul Gambaccini

SINGLES:

Like A Rolling Stone	**Bob Dylan**
Hey Jude	**The Beatles**
All The Way	**Frank Sinatra**
At The Hop	**Danny & The Juniors**
Unchanged Melody	**Righteous Brothers**
Stardust	**Nat 'King' Cole**
My Girl	**The Temptations**
Nothing Compares 2 U	**Sinead O'Connor**
If I Could Turn Back The Hands Of Time	**R. Kelly**
Losing My Religion	**R.E.M.**

ALBUMS:

Revolver	**The Beatles**
Sgt. Pepper's Lonely Hearts Club Band	**The Beatles**
Tapestry	**Carole King**
Bringing It All Back Home	**Bob Dylan**
What's Going On	**Marvin Gaye**
Songs In The Key Of Life	**Stevie Wonder**
Abbey Road	**The Beatles**
Blood On The Tracks	**Bob Dylan**
Frank Sinatra Sings For Only The Lonely	
The Circle Game	**Tom Rush**

- The charts used to compile this book are taken from the following sources:

Singles:	*New Musical Express*	(15 November 1952 – 5 March 1960);
	Record Retailer/Music Week	(12 March 1960 – 1 January 2000).
EPs:	*Record Retailer*	(12 March 1960 – 2 December 1967).
Albums:	*Melody Maker*	(8 November 1958 – 5 March 1960);
	Record Retailer/Music Week	(12 March 1960 – 1 January 2000).
Compilation Albums:	*Music Week*	(14 January 1989 – 1 January 2000).

- All dates refer to the Saturday of the relevant week, not necessarily the date of the magazine's publication nor the date each chart was first announced.

- Artists are ordered alphabetically and under each artist is a list of their hit singles, followed by EPs, then albums.

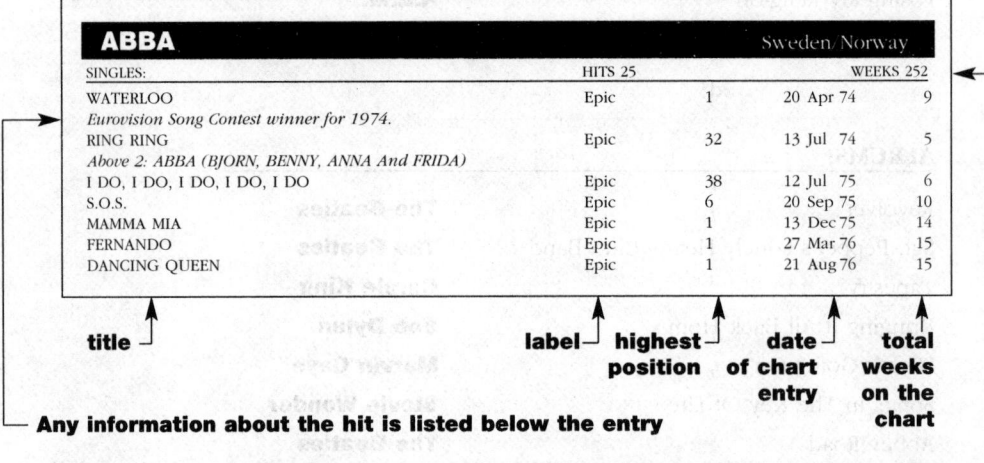

ABBA				Sweden/Norway
SINGLES:		HITS 25		WEEKS 252
WATERLOO	Epic	1	20 Apr 74	9
Eurovision Song Contest winner for 1974.				
RING RING	Epic	32	13 Jul 74	5
Above 2: ABBA (BJORN, BENNY, ANNA And FRIDA)				
I DO, I DO, I DO, I DO, I DO	Epic	38	12 Jul 75	6
S.O.S.	Epic	6	20 Sep 75	10
MAMMA MIA	Epic	1	13 Dec 75	14
FERNANDO	Epic	1	27 Mar 76	15
DANCING QUEEN	Epic	1	21 Aug 76	15

title ⌐   label⌐ highest⌐   date⌐   total
                         position   of chart   weeks
                                    entry   on the
Any information about the hit is listed below the entry   chart

Each artist has hits and weeks totals at the top of the listing ⌐

- Re-mixes and re-issues are classed as the same hit as the original while re-recordings are considered new hits.

- If the credit on the release is different to the main artist credit, then this is also highlighted below the hit.

- Any albums that appeared in the compilation chart, but where an artist had a major credit (i.e. featured on 50% or more of the tracks), are listed under the artist concerned, in chronological   order and within the list of albums.

- Each time a single enters the chart, it is given a separate listing, detailing date, highest position etc.

  EPs, however, are accumulated totals and often include several re-entries.

- Album totals are also accumulated, but re-entries are given a separate listing in the following Circumstances:

  If an album reaches its highest position six months or more after its original chart run.

  If an album has a chart life of more than 10 years.

  If an album is re-issued on a different label, or if on the same label, it has been given a new catalogue number.

- In the case of duets and collaborations, the following criteria have been selected to define when a hit is attributed to the artists involved:

  The words, 'and', 'versus', 'meets' between each artist defines an equal collaboration. Each artist has the hit listed under their name.

  (e.g. Elton John and Kiki Dee; 808 State vs UB40; Man 2 Man meets Man Parrish)

  An equal collaboration of more than three artists warrants a separate entry in the book.

  (e.g. All For Love is listed three times, under Bryan Adams, Rod Stewart and Sting; while Diana Ross, Marvin Gaye, Stevie Wonder and Smokey Robinson are considered a separate recording entity for Pops We Love You).

  If an artist credit includes 'featuring', 'with' or 'presents', then the hit is considered to be by the first named artist, and latter artist(s) are guests on the recording. If the credit reflects just one guest act, it is classed as a hit for both. More than one, and the hit is only listed under the first artist.

  (e.g. A hit by Puff Daddy featuring Mase would be listed under each named artist; while a hit by Puff Daddy and the Family featuring the Notorious B.I.G. and Mase, is only listed under Puff Daddy's entry).

  Artists who have collaborated on four or more hit singles are considered a regular recording act and have their own separate entry.

  (e.g. Ike and Tina Turner's hits are not combined with Tina Turner's solo output.)

  Artists who record an album together are also considered a separate act, but only if all named have charted solo material too.

  (e.g. McAlmont and Butler's hits are listed separately from their solo work, but Daniel O'Donnell and Mary Duff's album is to be found under Daniel O'Donnell listing, because Mary Duff has not charted in her own right and the pair have charted fewer than four singles together.)

CONTENTS

A — UK

SINGLES:	HITS 6			WEEKS 6
FOGHORN	Tycoon	63	7 Feb 98	1
NUMBER ONE	Tycoon	47	11 Apr 98	1
SING-A-LONG	Tycoon	57	27 Jun 98	1
SUMMER ON THE UNDERGROUND	Tycoon	72	24 Oct 98	1
OLD FOLKS	Tycoon	54	5 Jun 99	1
I LOVE LAKE TAHOE	Tycoon	59	21 Aug 99	1
ALBUMS:	**HITS 1**			**WEEKS 1**
MONKEY KONG	Tycoon	62	28 Aug 99	1

A+ — US

SINGLES:	HITS 1			WEEKS 9
ENJOY YOURSELF	Universal	5	13 Feb 99	9

Samples Walter Murphy And The Big Apple Band's A Fifth Of Beethoven.

A vs B — UK/Greece

SINGLES:	HITS 1			WEEKS 1
RIPPED IN 2 MINUTES	Positiva	49	9 May 98	1

Amalgam of Jomanda's Make My Body Work and Bug Kann's Made In 2 Minutes.

A-HA — Norway

SINGLES:	HITS 18			WEEKS 131
TAKE ON ME	Warner Brothers	2	28 Sep 85	19
THE SUN ALWAYS SHINES ON TV	Warner Brothers	1	28 Dec 85	12
TRAIN OF THOUGHT	Warner Brothers	8	5 Apr 86	8
HUNTING HIGH AND LOW	Warner Brothers	5	14 Jun 86	10
I'VE BEEN LOSING YOU	Warner Brothers	8	4 Oct 86	7
CRY WOLF	Warner Brothers	5	6 Dec 86	9
MANHATTAN SKYLINE	Warner Brothers	13	28 Feb 87	6
THE LIVING DAYLIGHTS	Warner Brothers	5	4 Jul 87	9

From the James Bond film of the same name.

STAY ON THESE ROADS	Warner Brothers	5	26 Mar 88	6
THE BLOOD THAT MOVES THE BODY	Warner Brothers	25	18 Jun 88	4
TOUCHY!	Warner Brothers	11	27 Aug 88	7
YOU ARE THE ONE	Warner Brothers	13	3 Dec 88	10
CRYING IN THE RAIN	Warner Brothers	13	13 Oct 90	7
I CALL YOUR NAME	Warner Brothers	44	15 Dec 90	5
MOVE TO MEMPHIS	Warner Brothers	47	26 Oct 91	2
DARK IS THE NIGHT	Warner Brothers	19	5 Jun 93	4
ANGEL	Warner Brothers	41	18 Sep 93	3
SHAPES THAT GO TOGETHER	Warner Brothers	27	26 Mar 94	3
ALBUMS:	**HITS 6**			**WEEKS 143**
HUNTING HIGH AND LOW	Warner Brothers	2	9 Nov 85	78
SCOUNDREL DAYS	Warner Brothers	2	18 Oct 86	29
STAY ON THESE ROADS	Warner Brothers	2	14 May 88	19
EAST OF THE SUN, WEST OF THE MOON	Warner Brothers	12	3 Nov 90	4
HEADLINES AND DEADLINES - THE HITS OF A-HA	Warner Brothers	12	16 Nov 91	10
MEMORIAL BEACH	Warner Brothers	17	26 Jun 93	3

A.B.'S — Japan

ALBUMS:	HITS 1			WEEKS 2
DEJA VU	Street Sounds	80	14 Apr 84	2

12" single not eligible for the singles chart.

A.D.A.M. featuring AMY — France

SINGLES:	HITS 1			WEEKS 11
ZOMBIE	Eternal	16	1 Jul 95	11

A.K.A. — UK

SINGLES:	HITS 1			WEEKS 2
WARNING	RCA	43	12 Oct 96	2

Re-works the riff from an old reggae standard also titled Warning.

A.S.A.P. — UK

SINGLES:	HITS 2			WEEKS 4
SILVER AND GOLD	EMI	60	14 Oct 89	2
DOWN THE WIRE	EMI	67	3 Feb 90	2
ALBUMS:	**HITS 1**			**WEEKS 1**
SILVER AND GOLD	EMI	70	4 Nov 89	1

A.T.F.C. presents ONEPHATDEEVA — UK/US

SINGLES:	HITS 1			WEEKS 5
IN AND OUT OF MY LIFE	Defected	11	30 Oct 99	5

Samples Adeva's In And Out Of My Life with Fatboy Slim's Right Here Right Now.

A.T.G.O.C. — Italy

SINGLES:	HITS 1			WEEKS 2
REPEATED LOVE	Wonderboy	38	21 Nov 98	2

A*TEENS — Sweden

SINGLES:	HITS 2			WEEKS 9
MAMMA MIA	Stockholm	12	4 Sep 99	5
SUPER TROUPER	Stockholm	21	11 Dec 99	4

AALIYAH — US

SINGLES:	HITS 13			WEEKS 32
BACK AND FORTH	Jive	16	2 Jul 94	5
(AT YOUR BEST) YOU ARE LOVE	Jive	27	15 Oct 94	2

Originally recorded by the Isley Brothers on their 1976 album Harvest For The World.

AGE AIN'T NOTHING BUT A NUMBER	Jive	32	11 Mar 95	2
DOWN WITH THE CLIQUE	Jive	33	13 May 95	2

Above 3: AALIYAH (AH-LEE-YAH).

THE THING I LIKE	Jive	33	9 Sep 95	2
I NEED YOU TONIGHT	Big Beat	66	3 Feb 96	1

Above hit: JUNIOR M.A.F.I.A. featuring AALIYAH.

IF YOUR GIRL ONLY KNEW	Atlantic	21	24 Aug 96	2
GOT TO GIVE IT UP	Atlantic	37	23 Nov 96	2

Features Slick Rick.

IF YOUR GIRL ONLY KNEW [RI] / ONE IN A MILLION	Atlantic	15	24 May 97	3
4 PAGE LETTER	Atlantic	24	30 Aug 97	2
THE ONE I GAVE MY HEART TO / HOT LIKE FIRE	Atlantic	30	22 Nov 97	2
JOURNEY TO THE PAST	Atlantic	22	18 Apr 98	3

From the film 'Anastasia'.

ARE YOU THAT SOMEBODY?	Atlantic	11	12 Sep 98	4

From the film 'Dr. Dolittle'.

ALBUMS:	HITS 2			WEEKS 9
AGE AIN'T NOTHING BUT A NUMBER	Jive	23	23 Jul 94	6
ONE IN A MILLION	Atlantic	33	7 Sep 96	3

ABBA — Sweden/Norway

SINGLES:	HITS 25			WEEKS 252
WATERLOO	Epic	1	20 Apr 74	9

Eurovision Song Contest winner in 1974.

RING RING	Epic	32	13 Jul 74	5

Above 2: ABBA (BJORN, BENNY, ANNA and FRIDA).

I DO, I DO, I DO, I DO, I DO	Epic	38	12 Jul 75	6
SOS	Epic	6	20 Sep 75	10

Only example of a palindromic artist and title.

KNOWING ME, KNOWING YOU	Epic	1	26 Feb 77	
MAMMA MIA	Epic	1	13 Dec 75	14
FERNANDO	Epic	1	27 Mar 76	15
DANCING QUEEN	Epic	1	21 Aug 76	15
MONEY, MONEY, MONEY	Epic	3	20 Nov 76	12
THE NAME OF THE GAME	Epic	1	22 Oct 77	12
TAKE A CHANCE ON ME	Epic	1	4 Feb 78	10
SUMMER NIGHT CITY	Epic	5	16 Sep 78	9
CHIQUITITA	Epic	2	3 Feb 79	9
DOES YOUR MOTHER KNOW	Epic	4	5 May 79	9
ANGELEYES / VOULEZ-VOUS	Epic	3	14 Jul 79	11
GIMME, GIMME, GIMME (A MAN AFTER MIDNIGHT)	Epic	3	20 Oct 79	12
I HAVE A DREAM	Epic	2	15 Dec 79	10
THE WINNER TAKES IT ALL	Epic	1	2 Aug 80	10
SUPER TROUPER	Epic	1	15 Nov 80	12
LAY ALL YOUR LOVE ON ME	Epic	7	18 Jul 81	7
ONE OF US	Epic	3	12 Dec 81	10
HEAD OVER HEELS	Epic	25	20 Feb 82	7
THE DAY BEFORE YOU CAME	Epic	32	23 Oct 82	6
UNDER ATTACK	Epic	26	11 Dec 82	8
THANK YOU FOR THE MUSIC	Epic	33	12 Nov 83	6
DANCING QUEEN [RI]	Polydor	16	5 Sep 92	5

ALBUMS:	HITS 15			WEEKS 786
WATERLOO	Epic	28	8 Jun 74	2

Above hit: ABBA (BJORN, BENNY, ANNA and FRIDA).

ABBA	Epic	13	31 Jan 76	10
GREATEST HITS	Epic	1	10 Apr 76	130

ARRIVAL	*Epic*	1	*27 Nov 76*	92
THE ALBUM	*Epic*	1	*4 Feb 78*	61
VOULEZ-VOUS	*Epic*	1	*19 May 79*	43
GREATEST HITS VOLUME 2	*Epic*	1	*10 Nov 79*	63
SUPER TROUPER	*Epic*	1	*22 Nov 80*	43
THE VISITORS	*Epic*	1	*19 Dec 81*	21
THE SINGLES – THE FIRST TEN YEARS	*Epic*	1	*20 Nov 82*	22
THANK YOU FOR THE MUSIC	*Epic*	17	*19 Nov 83*	12
ABSOLUTE ABBA	*Telstar*	70	*19 Nov 88*	7
GOLD – GREATEST HITS	*Polydor*	1	*3 Oct 92*	206
MORE ABBA GOLD – MORE ABBA HITS	*Polydor*	14	*5 Jun 93*	14
LOVE STORIES	*Polydor*	51	*7 Nov 98*	2
GOLD – GREATEST HITS [RE]	*Polydor*	1	*30 Jan 99*	49
Longest gap between separate runs at No.1.				
MORE ABBA GOLD - MORE ABBA HITS [RE]	*Polydor*	13	*7 Aug 99*	9

ABBACADABRA
UK

SINGLES:	HITS 1			WEEKS 1
DANCING QUEEN	*PWL International*	57	*5 Sep 92*	1

Russ ABBOT
UK

SINGLES:	HITS 3			WEEKS 22
A DAY IN THE LIFE OF VINCE PRINCE [M]	*EMI*	61	*6 Feb 82*	1
A DAY IN THE LIFE OF VINCE PRINCE [M] [RE]	*EMI*	75	*20 Feb 82*	1
ATMOSPHERE	*Spirit*	7	*29 Dec 84*	13
ALL NIGHT HOLIDAY	*Spirit*	20	*13 Jul 85*	7
ALBUMS:	**HITS 2**			**WEEKS 16**
RUSS ABBOT'S MADHOUSE	*Ronco*	41	*5 Nov 83*	7
I LOVE A PARTY	*K-Tel*	12	*23 Nov 85*	9

Gregory ABBOTT
US

SINGLES:	HITS 1			WEEKS 13
SHAKE YOU DOWN	*CBS*	6	*22 Nov 86*	13
ALBUMS:	**HITS 1**			**WEEKS 5**
SHAKE YOU DOWN	*CBS*	53	*10 Jan 87*	5

ABC
UK

SINGLES:	HITS 18			WEEKS 93
TEARS ARE NOT ENOUGH	*Neutron*	19	*31 Oct 81*	8
POISON ARROW	*Neutron*	6	*20 Feb 82*	11
THE LOOK OF LOVE	*Neutron*	4	*15 May 82*	11
ALL OF MY HEART	*Neutron*	5	*4 Sep 82*	8
THE LOOK OF LOVE [RE]	*Neutron*	71	*15 Jan 83*	1
THAT WAS THEN BUT THIS IS NOW	*Neutron*	18	*5 Nov 83*	4
S.O.S.	*Neutron*	39	*21 Jan 84*	5
HOW TO BE A MILLIONAIRE	*Neutron*	49	*10 Nov 84*	4
BE NEAR ME	*Neutron*	26	*6 Apr 85*	4
VANITY KILLS	*Neutron*	70	*15 Jun 85*	1
OCEAN BLUE	*Neutron*	51	*18 Jan 86*	3
WHEN SMOKEY SINGS	*Neutron*	11	*6 Jun 87*	10
Tribute to Smokey Robinson.				
THE NIGHT YOU MURDERED LOVE	*Neutron*	31	*5 Sep 87*	8
KING WITHOUT A CROWN	*Neutron*	44	*28 Nov 87*	3
ONE BETTER WORLD	*Neutron*	32	*27 May 89*	4
THE REAL THING	*Neutron*	68	*23 Sep 89*	1
THE LOOK OF LOVE (1990 MIX) [RM]	*Neutron*	68	*14 Apr 90*	1
LOVE CONQUERS ALL	*Parlophone*	47	*27 Jul 91*	2
SAY IT	*Parlophone*	42	*11 Jan 92*	3
STRANGER THINGS	*Blatant*	57	*22 Mar 97*	1
ALBUMS:	**HITS 7**			**WEEKS 90**
THE LEXICON OF LOVE	*Neutron*	1	*3 Jul 82*	50
BEAUTY STAB	*Neutron*	12	*26 Nov 83*	13
HOW TO BE A ZILLIONAIRE	*Neutron*	28	*26 Oct 85*	3
ALPHABET CITY	*Neutron*	7	*24 Oct 87*	10
UP	*Neutron*	58	*28 Oct 89*	1
ABSOLUTELY	*Neutron*	7	*21 Apr 90*	12
Compilation.				
ABRACADABRA	*Parlophone*	50	*24 Aug 91*	1

Paula ABDUL
US

SINGLES:	HITS 11			WEEKS 67
STRAIGHT UP	*Siren*	3	*4 Mar 89*	13
FOREVER YOUR GIRL	*Siren*	24	*3 Jun 89*	6
KNOCKED OUT	*Siren*	45	*19 Aug 89*	3
Original release reached No. 98 in 1988.				

(IT'S JUST) THE WAY THAT YOU LOVE ME	Siren	74	2 Dec 89	1
OPPOSITES ATTRACT	Siren	2	7 Apr 90	13
Above hit: Paula ABDUL (duet with the WILD PAIR).				
KNOCKED OUT [RM]	Virgin America	21	21 Jul 90	5
Remixed by Shep Pettibone.				
COLD HEARTED	Virgin America	46	29 Sep 90	3
RUSH RUSH	Virgin America	6	22 Jun 91	11
THE PROMISE OF A NEW DAY	Virgin America	52	31 Aug 91	2
VIBEOLOGY	Virgin America	19	18 Jan 92	6
WILL YOU MARRY ME?	Virgin America	73	8 Aug 92	1
MY LOVE IS FOR REAL	Virgin	28	17 Jun 95	3
Features vocals by Ofra Haza.				
ALBUMS:	**HITS 4**		**WEEKS 51**	
FOREVER YOUR GIRL	Siren	5	15 Apr 89	21
FOREVER YOUR GIRL [RE]	Siren	3	12 May 90	18
SHUT UP AND DANCE (THE DANCE MIXES)	Virgin America	40	10 Nov 90	2
SPELLBOUND	Virgin America	4	27 Jul 91	9
HEAD OVER HEELS	Virgin	61	1 Jul 95	1

ABI   UK

SINGLES:	**HITS 1**		**WEEKS 2**	
COUNTING THE DAYS	Kuku	44	13 Jun 98	2

ABIGAIL   UK

SINGLES:	**HITS 1**		**WEEKS 4**	
SMELLS LIKE TEEN SPIRIT	Klone	29	16 Jul 94	4

Colonel ABRAMS   US

SINGLES:	**HITS 4**		**WEEKS 35**	
TRAPPED	MCA	3	17 Aug 85	23
THE TRUTH	MCA	53	7 Dec 85	3
I'M NOT GONNA LET YOU	MCA	24	8 Feb 86	7
HOW SOON WE FORGET	MCA	75	15 Aug 87	2

ABSOLUTE   US

SINGLES:	**HITS 2**		**WEEKS 3**	
I BELIEVE	AM:PM	38	18 Jan 97	2
Above hit: ABSOLUTE featuring Suzanne PALMER.				
CATCH ME	AM:PM	69	14 Mar 98	1

ABSOLUTELY FABULOUS - See PET SHOP BOYS

AC/DC   Australia/UK

SINGLES:	**HITS 26**		**WEEKS 125**	
ROCK 'N' ROLL DAMNATION	Atlantic	24	10 Jun 78	9
HIGHWAY TO HELL	Atlantic	56	1 Sep 79	4
TOUCH TOO MUCH	Atlantic	29	2 Feb 80	9
WHOLE LOTTA ROSIE	Atlantic	36	28 Jun 80	8
DIRTY DEEDS DONE DIRT CHEAP	Atlantic	47	28 Jun 80	3
HIGH VOLTAGE (LIVE VERSION)	Atlantic	48	28 Jun 80	3
IT'S A LONG WAY TO THE TOP (IF YOU WANNA ROCK 'N' ROLL)	Atlantic	55	28 Jun 80	3
YOU SHOOK ME ALL NIGHT LONG	Atlantic	38	13 Sep 80	6
ROCK 'N' ROLL AIN'T NOISE POLLUTION	Atlantic	15	29 Nov 80	8
LET'S GET IT UP	Atlantic	13	6 Feb 82	6
FOR THOSE ABOUT TO ROCK (WE SALUTE YOU)	Atlantic	15	3 Jul 82	6
GUNS FOR HIRE	Atlantic	37	29 Oct 83	4
NERVOUS SHAKEDOWN	Atlantic	35	4 Aug 84	5
DANGER	Atlantic	48	6 Jul 85	4
SHAKE YOUR FOUNDATIONS	Atlantic	24	18 Jan 86	5
WHO MADE WHO	Atlantic	16	24 May 86	5
YOU SHOOK ME ALL NIGHT LONG [RI]	Arista	46	30 Aug 86	4
HEATSEEKER	Atlantic	12	16 Jan 88	6
THAT'S THE WAY I WANNA ROCK N ROLL	Atlantic	22	2 Apr 88	5
THUNDERSTRUCK	Atco	13	22 Sep 90	5
MONEYTALKS	Atco	36	24 Nov 90	3
ARE YOU READY	Atco	34	27 Apr 91	3
HIGHWAY TO HELL (LIVE) [RR]	Atco	14	17 Oct 92	4
DIRTY DEEDS DONE DIRT CHEAP (LIVE) [RR]	Atco	68	6 Mar 93	1
Above 2 are live recordings from Donnington, 1991.				
BIG GUN	Atco	23	10 Jul 93	3
HARD AS A ROCK	Atlantic	33	30 Sep 95	2
HAIL CAESAR	East West	56	11 May 96	1
ALBUMS:	**HITS 13**		**WEEKS 251**	
LET THERE BE ROCK	Atlantic	17	5 Nov 77	5
POWERAGE	Atlantic	26	20 May 78	9
IF YOU WANT BLOOD YOU'VE GOT IT	Atlantic	13	28 Oct 78	58

HIGHWAY TO HELL	*Atlantic*	8	*18 Aug 79*	32
BACK IN BLACK	*Atlantic*	1	*9 Aug 80*	40
FOR THOSE ABOUT TO ROCK WE SALUTE YOU	*Atlantic*	3	*5 Dec 81*	29
FLICK OF THE SWITCH	*Atlantic*	4	*3 Sep 83*	9
FLY ON THE WALL	*Atlantic*	7	*13 Jul 85*	10
WHO MADE WHO	*Atlantic*	11	*7 Jun 86*	12

Original soundtrack to the film 'Maximum Overdrive'.

BLOW UP YOUR VIDEO	*Atlantic*	2	*13 Feb 88*	14
THE RAZOR'S EDGE	*Atco*	4	*6 Oct 90*	18
AC/DC LIVE	*Atco*	5	*7 Nov 92*	7

Live recordings from Donnington, 1991.

BALLBREAKER	*East West*	6	*7 Oct 95*	8

ACADEMY of ANCIENT MUSIC conducted by Christopher HOGWOOD — UK

ALBUMS:	HITS 1		WEEKS 2	
VIVALDI'S THE FOUR SEASONS	*L'Oiseau Lyre*	85	*16 Mar 85*	2

ACADEMY OF ST MARTIN IN THE FIELDS - See Neville MARRINER and the ACADEMY OF ST MARTIN IN THE FIELDS

ACCEPT — Germany

ALBUMS:	HITS 4		WEEKS 5	
RESTLESS AND WILD	*Heavy Metal International*	98	*7 May 83*	2
METAL HEART	*Portrait*	50	*30 Mar 85*	1
KAIZOKU-BAN	*Portrait*	91	*15 Feb 86*	1
RUSSIAN ROULETTE	*Portrait*	80	*3 May 86*	1

ACE — UK

SINGLES:	HITS 1		WEEKS 10	
HOW LONG	*Anchor*	20	*9 Nov 74*	10

ACE OF BASE — Sweden

SINGLES:	HITS 12		WEEKS 100	
ALL THAT SHE WANTS	*London*	1	*8 May 93*	16
WHEEL OF FORTUNE	*London*	20	*28 Aug 93*	6
HAPPY NATION	*London*	42	*13 Nov 93*	3
THE SIGN	*London*	2	*26 Feb 94*	16
DON'T TURN AROUND	*London*	5	*11 Jun 94*	11
HAPPY NATION [RI]	*London*	40	*15 Oct 94*	3
LIVING IN DANGER	*London*	18	*14 Jan 95*	4
LUCKY LOVE	*London*	20	*11 Nov 95*	5
BEAUTIFUL LIFE	*London*	15	*27 Jan 96*	6
LIFE IS A FLOWER	*London*	5	*25 Jul 98*	11
CRUEL SUMMER	*London*	8	*10 Oct 98*	5
ALWAYS HAVE, ALWAYS WILL	*London*	12	*19 Dec 98*	10
EVERYTIME IT RAINS	*London*	22	*17 Apr 99*	4

ALBUMS:	HITS 4		WEEKS 45	
HAPPY NATION	*London*	21	*19 Jun 93*	7
HAPPY NATION [RE]	*London*	1	*26 Mar 94*	31

Repackaged with additional track.

THE BRIDGE	*London*	66	*2 Dec 95*	1
FLOWERS	*London*	15	*22 Aug 98*	5
SINGLES OF THE 90'S	*Polydor*	62	*27 Nov 99*	1

Compilation.

Richard ACE — Jamaica

SINGLES:	HITS 1		WEEKS 2	
STAYIN' ALIVE	*Blue Inc.*	66	*2 Dec 78*	2

ACEN — UK

SINGLES:	HITS 1		WEEKS 4	
TRIP II THE MOON	*Production House*	38	*8 Aug 92*	3
TRIP II THE MOON (KALEIDOSCOPIKLIMAX) [RM]	*Production House*	71	*10 Oct 92*	1

Tracy ACKERMAN - See Q

ACT — UK/Germany

SINGLES:	HITS 1		WEEKS 2	
SNOBBERY AND DECAY	*ZTT*	60	*23 May 87*	2

ACT ONE — US

SINGLES:	HITS 1		WEEKS 6	
TOM THE PEEPER	*Mercury*	40	*18 May 74*	6

ADAM and the ANTS - See Adam ANT

Arthur ADAMS
US

SINGLES:	HITS 1			WEEKS 5
YOU GOT THE FLOOR	RCA	38	24 Oct 81	5

Bryan ADAMS
Canada

(See also Various Artists: Films – Original Soundtracks 'Robin Hood: Prince Of Thieves'.)

SINGLES:	HITS 32			WEEKS 219
RUN TO YOU	A&M	11	12 Jan 85	12
SOMEBODY	A&M	35	16 Mar 85	7
HEAVEN	A&M	38	25 May 85	5
SUMMER OF '69	A&M	42	10 Aug 85	7
IT'S ONLY LOVE	A&M	29	2 Nov 85	6
Above hit: Bryan ADAMS and Tina TURNER.				
CHRISTMAS TIME	A&M	55	21 Dec 85	2
THIS TIME	A&M	41	22 Feb 86	7
STRAIGHT FROM THE HEART	A&M	51	12 Jul 86	3
HEAT OF THE NIGHT	A&M	50	28 Mar 87	2
HEARTS ON FIRE	A&M	57	20 Jun 87	3
VICTIM OF LOVE	A&M	68	17 Oct 87	2
(EVERYTHING I DO) I DO IT FOR YOU	A&M	1	29 Jun 91	24
From the film 'Robin Hood (Prince Of Thieves)'.				
CAN'T STOP THIS THING WE STARTED	A&M	12	14 Sep 91	6
THERE WILL NEVER BE ANOTHER TONIGHT	A&M	32	23 Nov 91	3
(EVERYTHING I DO) I DO IT FOR YOU [RE]	A&M	73	28 Dec 91	1
THOUGHT I'D DIED AND GONE TO HEAVEN	A&M	8	22 Feb 92	7
ALL I WANT IS YOU	A&M	22	18 Jul 92	5
DO I HAVE TO SAY THE WORDS?	A&M	30	26 Sep 92	3
PLEASE FORGIVE ME	A&M	2	30 Oct 93	16
ALL FOR LOVE	A&M	2	15 Jan 94	13
From the film 'The Three Musketeers'.				
Above hit: Bryan ADAMS, Rod STEWART and STING.				
HAVE YOU EVER REALLY LOVE A WOMAN?	A&M	4	22 Apr 95	9
Featuring guitarist Paco De Lucia & taken from the film 'Juan De Marco'.				
ROCK STEADY	Capitol	50	11 Nov 95	2
Above hit: Bonnie RAITT and Bryan ADAMS.				
THE ONLY THING THAT LOOKS GOOD ON ME IS YOU	A&M	6	1 Jun 96	7
LET'S MAKE A NIGHT TO REMEMBER	A&M	10	24 Aug 96	8
STAR	A&M	13	23 Nov 96	4
I FINALLY FOUND SOMEONE	A&M	10	8 Feb 97	7
From the film 'The Mirror Has Two Faces'.				
Above hit: Barbra STREISAND and Bryan ADAMS.				
18 TILL I DIE	A&M	22	19 Apr 97	3
BACK TO YOU	A&M	18	20 Dec 97	7
I'M READY	A&M	20	21 Mar 98	4
Above 2 are live recordings for MTV from New York's Hammersmith Ballroom, 26 Sep 97.				
ON A DAY LIKE TODAY	A&M	13	10 Oct 98	5
WHEN YOU'RE GONE	Mercury	3	12 Dec 98	19
Above hit: Bryan ADAMS Featuring Melanie C.				
CLOUD #9	A&M	6	15 May 99	9
THE BEST OF ME	A&M	47	18 Dec 99	1

ALBUMS:	HITS 11			WEEKS 357
RECKLESS	A&M	7	2 Mar 85	115
YOU WANT IT, YOU GOT IT	A&M	78	24 Aug 85	5
Originally released in 1981.				
CUTS LIKE A KNIFE	A&M	21	15 Mar 86	6
Originally released in 1983.				
INTO THE FIRE	A&M	10	11 Apr 87	21
WAKING UP THE NEIGHBOURS	A&M	1	5 Oct 91	54
SO FAR SO GOOD	A&M	1	20 Nov 93	52
Compilation.				
LIVE! LIVE! LIVE!	A&M	17	6 Aug 94	4
Live recordings from Wercher, Belgium during the summer of '88.				
18 TIL I DIE	A&M	1	22 Jun 96	40
UNPLUGGED	A&M	19	13 Dec 97	19
Live recordings from New York's Hammersmith Ballroom, 26 Sep 97.				
ON A DAY LIKE TODAY	A&M	11	31 Oct 98	35
Repackaged, May 99 to include Chicane remix (hit single version) of Cloud #9.				
THE BEST OF ME	A&M	12	27 Nov 99	6
Compilation.				

Cliff ADAMS SINGERS
UK

SINGLES:	HITS 1			WEEKS 2
THE LONELY MAN THEME	Pye International	39	30 Apr 60	2
Used in the Strand cigarettes commercial.				
Above hit: CLIFF ADAMS ORCHESTRA.				

ALBUMS:	HITS 4			WEEKS 20
SING SOMETHING SIMPLE	Pye	18	16 Apr 60	1
SING SOMETHING SIMPLE [RE]	Pye	15	18 Feb 61	3
SING SOMETHING SIMPLE	Pye Golden Guinea	15	24 Nov 62	2
SING SOMETHING SIMPLE '76	Warwick	23	20 Nov 76	8
SING SOMETHING SIMPLE	Ronco	39	25 Dec 82	6

Title taken from the BBC Radio 2 show. All albums are different recordings.

Gayle ADAMS   US

SINGLES:	HITS 1			WEEKS 1
STRETCH'IN OUT	Epic	64	26 Jul 80	1

Marie ADAMS - See Johnny OTIS with Marie ADAMS

Oleta ADAMS   US

SINGLES:	HITS 9			WEEKS 36
RHYTHM OF LIFE	Fontana	52	24 Mar 90	2
RHYTHM OF LIFE [RE]	Fontana	56	3 Nov 90	3
GET HERE	Fontana	4	12 Jan 91	12
Originally recorded by Brenda Russell.				
YOU'VE GOT TO GIVE ME ROOM / RHYTHM OF LIFE [RI]	Fontana	49	13 Apr 91	3
CIRCLE OF ONE	Fontana	73	29 Jun 91	1
Original release reached No. 95 in 1990.				
DON'T LET THE SUN GO DOWN ON ME	Fontana	33	28 Sep 91	5
WOMAN IN CHAINS	Fontana	57	25 Apr 92	1
Adams was not credited on the original release in 1989.				
Above hit: TEARS FOR FEARS featuring Oleta ADAMS.				
I JUST HAD TO HEAR YOUR VOICE	Fontana	42	10 Jul 93	3
NEVER KNEW LOVE	Fontana	22	7 Oct 95	3
RHYTHM OF LIFE - THE REMIXES [RM]	Fontana	38	16 Dec 95	2
Remixed by Reverend Jefferson.				
WE WILL MEET AGAIN	Mercury	51	10 Feb 96	1
ALBUMS:	HITS 3			WEEKS 34
CIRCLE OF ONE	Fontana	49	26 May 90	2
CIRCLE OF ONE [RE]	Fontana	1	2 Mar 91	24
EVOLUTION	Fontana	10	7 Aug 93	7
MOVING ON	Fontana	59	4 Nov 95	1

ADAMSKI   UK

SINGLES:	HITS 8			WEEKS 39
N-R-G	MCA	12	20 Jan 90	6
KILLER	MCA	1	7 Apr 90	18
Vocals by Seal.				
THE SPACE JUNGLE	MCA	7	8 Sep 90	8
FLASHBACK JACK	MCA	46	17 Nov 90	2
NEVER GOIN' DOWN (INCORPORATING FUTURE FREAK) / BORN TO BE ALIVE!	MCA	51	9 Nov 91	2
Above hit: ADAMSKI + Jimi POLO / ADAMSKI + SOHO.				
GET YOUR BODY!	MCA	68	4 Apr 92	1
Above hit: ADAMSKI featuring Nina HAGEN.				
BACK TO FRONT	MCA	63	4 Jul 92	1
ONE OF THE PEOPLE	ZTT	56	11 Jul 98	1
Vocals by Gerideau.				
Above hit: ADAMSKI'S THING.				
ALBUMS:	HITS 2			WEEKS 17
LIVEANDIRECT	MCA	65	9 Dec 89	1
LIVEANDIRECT [RE]	MCA	47	17 Feb 90	11
Re-released.				
DOCTOR ADAMSKI'S MUSICAL PHARMACY	MCA	8	13 Oct 90	5

Barry ADAMSON   UK

ALBUMS:	HITS 1			WEEKS 1
OEDIPUS SCHMOEDIPUS	Mute	51	10 Aug 96	1

ADDAMS and GEE   UK

SINGLES:	HITS 1			WEEKS 1
CHUNG KUO (REVISITED)	Debut	72	20 Apr 91	1

Original by Vangelis, from the album China.

ADDIS BLACK WIDOW   US

SINGLES:	HITS 1			WEEKS 2
INNOCENT	Mercury	42	3 Feb 96	2

Samples Running For Your Love by Brothers Johnson.

ADDRISI BROTHERS US

SINGLES:		HITS 1		WEEKS 3
GHOST DANCER	Scotti Brothers	57	6 Oct 79	3

King Sunny ADE and his AFRICAN BEATS Nigeria

ALBUMS:		HITS 1		WEEKS 1
SYNCHRO SYSTEM	Island	93	9 Jul 83	1

ADEVA US

SINGLES:		HITS 15		WEEKS 66
RESPECT	Cooltempo	17	14 Jan 89	9
MUSICAL FREEDOM (MOVING ON UP)	Cooltempo	22	25 Mar 89	8
Above hit: Paul SIMPSON featuring ADEVA.				
WARNING!	Cooltempo	17	12 Aug 89	8
I THANK YOU	Cooltempo	17	21 Oct 89	7
Originally recorded by Sam and Dave in 1968.				
BEAUTIFUL LOVE	Cooltempo	57	16 Dec 89	5
TREAT ME RIGHT	Cooltempo	62	28 Apr 90	2
RING MY BELL	Cooltempo	20	6 Apr 91	5
Above hit: Monie LOVE Vs ADEVA.				
IT SHOULD'VE BEEN ME	Cooltempo	48	19 Oct 91	3
Original by Gladys Knight and the Pips reached No. 40 in the US in 1968.				
DON'T LET IT SHOW ON YOUR FACE	Cooltempo	34	29 Feb 92	4
UNTIL YOU COME BACK TO ME	Cooltempo	45	6 Jun 92	3
I'M THE ONE FOR YOU	Cooltempo	51	17 Oct 92	2
RESPECT '93 [RM]	Network	65	11 Dec 93	1
Remixed by Mental Instrum.				
TOO MANY FISH	Virgin	34	27 May 95	2
WHADDA U WANT (FROM ME)	Virgin	36	18 Nov 95	2
Above 2: Frankie KNUCKLES featuring ADEVA.				
DO WATCHA DO	Avex UK	54	6 Apr 96	1
Above hit: HYPER GO GO and ADEVA.				
I THANK YOU [RM]	Cooltempo	37	4 May 96	2
Remixed by Love To Infinity and Dancing Divas.				
DO WATCHA DO [RM]	Distinct'ive	60	12 Apr 97	1
Remixed by K-Klass.				
Above hit: HYPER GO GO and ADEVA.				
WHERE IS THE LOVE? / THE WAY THAT YOU FEEL	Distinct'ive	54	26 Jul 97	1
Backing vocals Incognito and Rachel Macfarlane.				
ALBUMS:		HITS 1		WEEKS 24
ADEVA	Cooltempo	6	9 Sep 89	24

ADICTS UK

SINGLES:		HITS 1		WEEKS 1
BAD BOY	Razor	75	14 May 83	1
ALBUMS:		HITS 1		WEEKS 1
SOUND OF MUSIC	Razor	99	4 Dec 82	1

ADIEMUS UK/South Africa

SINGLES:		HITS 1		WEEKS 2
ADIEMUS	Venture	48	14 Oct 95	2
From the Delta Airlines TV commercial.				
ALBUMS:		HITS 3		WEEKS 22
SONGS OF SANCTUARY	Venture	38	1 Jul 95	4
SONGS OF SANCTUARY [RE]	Venture	35	3 Feb 96	8
ADIEMUS II - CANTATA MUNDI	Venture	15	1 Mar 97	9
Above hit: Miriam STOCKLEY/LONDON PHILHARMONIC ORCHESTRA conducted: Karl JENKINS.				
ADIEMUS III - DANCES OF TIME	Venture	58	24 Oct 98	1

Larry ADLER US

SINGLES:		HITS 1		WEEKS 2
THE MAN I LOVE	Mercury	27	30 Jul 94	2
Above hit: Larry ADLER and Kate BUSH.				
ALBUMS:		HITS 1		WEEKS 18
THE GLORY OF GERSHWIN	Mercury	2	6 Aug 94	18
Features Peter Gabriel, Elton John, Kate Bush among others.				
Above hit: Larry ADLER and VARIOUS ARTISTS.				

ADONIS (featuring 2 PUERTO RICANS, a BLACKMAN and a DOMINICAN) US

SINGLES:		HITS 1		WEEKS 4
NO WAY BACK / DO IT PROPERLY ("NO WAY BACK' ")	London	47	13 Jun 87	4
Featuring 2 Puerto Ricans etc. not credited on the label for No Way Back.				

ADORABLE
UK

ALBUMS:	HITS 1			WEEKS 1
AGAINST PERFECTION	Creation	70	13 Mar 93	1

ADRENALIN M.O.D.
US

SINGLES:	HITS 1			WEEKS 5
O-O-O	MCA	49	8 Oct 88	5

ADULT NET
UK/US

SINGLES:	HITS 1			WEEKS 2
WHERE WERE YOU	Fontana	66	10 Jun 89	2

Original by the Grassroots reached No. 28 in the US in 1966.

ADVENTURES
UK

SINGLES:	HITS 6			WEEKS 24
ANOTHER SILENT DAY	Chrysalis	71	15 Sep 84	2
SEND MY HEART	Chrysalis	62	1 Dec 84	4
FEEL THE RAINDROPS	Chrysalis	58	13 Jul 85	3
BROKEN LAND	Elektra	20	9 Apr 88	10
DROWNING IN THE SEA OF LOVE	Elektra	44	2 Jul 88	4
RAINING ALL OVER THE WORLD	Polydor	68	13 Jun 92	1
ALBUMS:	HITS 2			WEEKS 11
THE SEA OF LOVE	Elektra	30	21 May 88	10
TRADING SECRETS WITH THE MOON	Elektra	64	17 Mar 90	1

ADVENTURES OF STEVIE V
US

SINGLES:	HITS 3			WEEKS 22
DIRTY CASH	Mercury	2	21 Apr 90	13
BODY LANGUAGE (MONEY TALKS)	Mercury	29	29 Sep 90	5
JEALOUSY	Mercury	58	2 Mar 91	3
DIRTY CASH [RM]	Avex Trax	69	27 Sep 97	1

Remixed by Todd Terry.
Above hit: ADVENTURES OF STEVIE V featuring NAZLYN.

ADVERTS
UK

SINGLES:	HITS 2			WEEKS 11
GARY GILMORE'S EYES	Anchor	18	27 Aug 77	7
Refers to the death-row criminal who offered to donate his eyes to science.				
NO TIME TO BE 21	Bright	34	4 Feb 78	4
ALBUMS:	HITS 1			WEEKS 1
CROSSING THE RED SEA WITH THE ADVERTS	Bright	38	11 Mar 78	1

AEROSMITH
US

SINGLES:	HITS 16			WEEKS 85
DUDE (LOOKS LIKE A LADY)	Geffen	45	17 Oct 87	5
ANGEL	Geffen	69	16 Apr 88	2
LOVE IN AN ELEVATOR	Geffen	13	9 Sep 89	8
DUDE (LOOKS LIKE A LADY) [RI]	Geffen	20	24 Feb 90	5
RAG DOLL	Geffen	42	14 Apr 90	4
THE OTHER SIDE	Geffen	46	1 Sep 90	2
LIVIN' ON THE EDGE	Geffen	19	10 Apr 93	4
EAT THE RICH	Geffen	34	3 Jul 93	3
From the film of the same name.				
CRYIN'	Geffen	17	30 Oct 93	6
AMAZING	Geffen	57	18 Dec 93	3
SHUT UP AND DANCE	Geffen	24	2 Jul 94	4
SWEET EMOTION	Columbia	74	20 Aug 94	1
From the film 'Dazed And Confused'.				
CRAZY/BLIND MAN	Geffen	23	5 Nov 94	4
FALLING IN LOVE (IS HARD ON THE KNEES)	Columbia	22	8 Mar 97	4
HOLE IN MY SOUL	Columbia	29	21 Jun 97	2
PINK	Columbia	38	27 Dec 97	2
I DON'T WANT TO MISS A THING	Columbia	4	12 Sep 98	20
From the film 'Armageddon'.				
PINK [RI]	Columbia	13	26 Jun 99	6
Re-released to coincide with their Wembley gig with Lenny Kravitz, 26 Jun 99.				
ALBUMS:	HITS 6			WEEKS 107
PERMANENT VACATION	Geffen	37	5 Sep 87	14
PUMP	Geffen	3	23 Sep 89	24
GET A GRIP	Geffen	2	1 May 93	38
BIG ONES	Geffen	7	12 Nov 94	16
Compilation.				
PUMP [RE]	Geffen	50	4 Mar 95	2
Re-released at mid-price.				

NINE LIVES	Columbia	4	22 Mar 97	11
A LITTLE SOUTH OF SANITY	Geffen	36	31 Oct 98	2

Live recordings from their 92/94 and 98/98 tours.

AFGHAN WHIGS   UK

ALBUMS:		HITS 2		WEEKS 3
GENTLEMEN	Blast	58	16 Oct 93	1
BLACK LOVE	Mute	41	23 Mar 96	2

AFRICAN BUSINESS   Italy

SINGLES:		HITS 1		WEEKS 1
IN ZAIRE	Urban	73	17 Nov 90	1

AFRO CELT SOUND SYSTEM   UK/Ireland/Africa

ALBUMS:		HITS 2		WEEKS 5
VOLUME I - SOUND MAGIC	Realworld	59	27 Jul 96	2
VOLUME 2: RELEASE	Realworld	38	8 May 99	3

AFTER DARK   UK

ALBUMS:		HITS 1		WEEKS 5
LATE NIGHT SAX	EMI TV	18	3 Feb 96	5

Sax interpretations of classic hits.

AFTER 7   US

SINGLES:		HITS 1		WEEKS 3
CAN'T STOP	Virgin America	54	3 Nov 90	3

AFTER THE FIRE   UK

SINGLES:		HITS 3		WEEKS 12
ONE RULE FOR YOU	CBS	40	9 Jun 79	6
LASER LOVE	CBS	62	8 Sep 79	2
DER KOMMISSAR	CBS	47	9 Apr 83	4

Originally recorded by Falco.

ALBUMS:		HITS 3		WEEKS 4
LASER LOVE	CBS	57	13 Oct 79	1
80 F	Epic	69	1 Nov 80	1
BATTERIES NOT INCLUDED	CBS	82	3 Apr 82	2

AFTERSHOCK   US

SINGLES:		HITS 1		WEEKS 8
SLAVE TO THE VIBE	Virgin America	11	21 Aug 93	8

AGE OF CHANCE   UK

SINGLES:		HITS 3		WEEKS 13
KISS	FON	50	17 Jan 87	6
WHO'S AFRAID OF THE BIG BAD NOISE!	Virgin	65	30 May 87	2
HIGHER THAN HEAVEN	Virgin	53	20 Jan 90	5

AGE OF LOVE   Italy/Belgium

SINGLES:		HITS 1		WEEKS 6
THE AGE OF LOVE - THE REMIXES	React	17	5 Jul 97	4

Originally released in 1990 and 1992.

THE AGE OF LOVE [RM]	React	38	19 Sep 98	2

Remixed by Brainbug and Johnny Vicious.

AGENT 00   UK

SINGLES:		HITS 1		WEEKS 1
THE MAGNIFICENT	Inferno	65	7 Mar 98	1

Samples Dave & Ansil Collins' Double Barrel.

AGENT PROVOCATEUR   UK

SINGLES:		HITS 1		WEEKS 1
AGENT DAN	Epic	49	22 Mar 97	1

AGNELLI and NELSON   UK

SINGLES:		HITS 2		WEEKS 8
EL NINO	Xtravaganza	21	15 Aug 98	4
EVERYDAY	Xtravaganza	17	11 Sep 99	4

Christina AGUILERA — US

SINGLES:		HITS 1		WEEKS 17	
GENIE IN A BOTTLE		RCA	50	11 Sep 99	5
Import.					
GENIE IN A BOTTLE		RCA	1	16 Oct 99	12
ALBUMS:		**HITS 1**		**WEEKS 3**	
CHRISTINA AGUILERA		RCA	21	30 Oct 99	3

AHEAD OF OUR TIME ORCHESTRA – See COLDCUT

AHMAD — US

SINGLES:		HITS 1		WEEKS 2	
BACK IN THE DAY		Giant	64	9 Jul 94	2

Alyn AINSWORTH and his Orchestra – See Des O'CONNOR; Frankie VAUGHAN

AIR (FRENCH BAND) — France

SINGLES:		HITS 3		WEEKS 10	
SEXY BOY		Virgin/Sam	13	21 Feb 98	4
KELLY WATCH THE STARS		Virgin	18	16 May 98	3
Single is tribute to Kelly from the 1970s TV series 'Charlie's Angels'.					
ALL I NEED		Virgin	29	21 Nov 98	3
ALBUMS:		**HITS 2**		**WEEKS 43**	
MOON SAFARI		Virgin	6	31 Jan 98	39
PREMIERS SYMPTOMES		Virgin	12	18 Sep 99	4
This was their first release in France.					
Above hit: AIR.					

AIR SUPPLY — UK/Australia

SINGLES:		HITS 3		WEEKS 17	
ALL OUT OF LOVE		Arista	11	27 Sep 80	11
EVEN THE NIGHTS ARE BETTER		Arista	44	2 Oct 82	4
GOODBYE		Giant	66	20 Nov 93	2

AIRHEAD — UK

SINGLES:		HITS 3		WEEKS 10	
FUNNY HOW		Korova	57	5 Oct 91	3
COUNTING SHEEP		Korova	35	21 Dec 91	5
RIGHT NOW		Korova	50	7 Mar 92	2
ALBUMS:		**HITS 1**		**WEEKS 7**	
BOING!		Korova	29	1 Feb 92	7

AIRSCAPE — Belgium/Holland

(See also Balearic Bill.)

SINGLES:		HITS 3		WEEKS 5	
PACIFIC MELODY		Xtravaganza	27	9 Aug 97	2
AMAZON CHANT		Xtravaganza	46	29 Aug 98	1
Featured on BBC1 TV's 'Grandstand'.					
L'ESPERANZA		Xtravaganza	33	4 Dec 99	2

Laurel AITKEN and the UNITONE — Jamaica/Cuba

SINGLES:		HITS 1		WEEKS 3	
RUDI GOT MARRIED		I-Spy	60	17 May 80	3

AKABU – See Gary CLAIL ON-U SOUND SYSTEM

Jewel AKENS — US

SINGLES:		HITS 1		WEEKS 8	
THE BIRDS AND THE BEES		London	29	27 Mar 65	8

AKIN — UK

SINGLES:		HITS 1		WEEKS 1	
STAY RIGHT HERE		WEA	60	14 Jun 97	1

ALABAMA – See Lionel RICHIE

ALABAMA 3 — UK

SINGLES:		HITS 2		WEEKS 3	
SPEED AT THE SOUND OF LONELINESS		El-e-mental	72	22 Nov 97	1
AIN'T GOIN' TO GOA		El-e-mental	40	11 Apr 98	2
Original release reached No. 98 in 1996.					

Roberto ALAGNA/Angela GHEORGIU — Italy/Romania

ALBUMS:	HITS 1			WEEKS 5
DUETS & ARIAS	EMI Classics	42	18 May 96	5

ALANA - See MK

ALARM — UK

SINGLES:	HITS 16			WEEKS 64
68 GUNS	I.R.S.	17	24 Sep 83	7
WHERE WERE YOU HIDING WHEN THE STORM BROKE	I.R.S.	22	21 Jan 84	6
THE DECEIVER	I.R.S.	51	31 Mar 84	4
THE CHANT HAS JUST BEGUN	I.R.S.	48	3 Nov 84	4
ABSOLUTE REALITY	I.R.S.	35	2 Mar 85	6
STRENGTH	I.R.S.	40	28 Sep 85	4
SPIRIT OF 76	I.R.S.	22	18 Jan 86	5
KNIFE EDGE	I.R.S.	43	26 Apr 86	3
RAIN IN THE SUMMERTIME	I.R.S.	18	17 Oct 87	5
RESCUE ME	I.R.S.	48	12 Dec 87	2
PRESENCE OF LOVE (LAUGHARNE)	I.R.S.	44	20 Feb 88	3
SOLD ME DOWN THE RIVER / YN GYMREAG	I.R.S.	43	16 Sep 89	3
Yn Gymreag only listed for week of 16 Sep 89.				
A NEW SOUTH WALES / THE ROCK	I.R.S.	31	4 Nov 89	5
Above hit: ALARM featuring the MORRISTON ORPHEUS MALE VOICE CHOIR / ALARM.				
LOVE DON'T COME EASY	I.R.S.	48	3 Feb 90	3
UNSAFE BUILDING 1990	I.R.S.	54	27 Oct 90	2
RAW	I.R.S.	51	13 Apr 91	2
ALBUMS:	HITS 7			WEEKS 29
DECLARATION	I.R.S.	6	25 Feb 84	11
STRENGTH	I.R.S.	18	26 Oct 85	6
EYE OF THE HURRICANE	I.R.S.	23	14 Nov 87	4
ELECTRIC FOLKLORE LIVE	I.R.S.	62	5 Nov 88	2
CHANGE	I.R.S.	13	30 Sep 89	3
STANDARDS	I.R.S.	47	24 Nov 90	1
RAW	I.R.S.	33	4 May 91	2

Morris ALBERT — Brazil

SINGLES:	HITS 1			WEEKS 10
FEELINGS	Decca	4	27 Sep 75	10

ALBERTA — UK

SINGLES:	HITS 1			WEEKS 3
YOYO BOY	RCA	48	26 Dec 98	3

ALBERTO Y LOST TRIOS PARANOIAS — UK

SINGLES:	HITS 1			WEEKS 5
HEADS DOWN NO NONSENSE MINDLESS BOOGIE	Logo	47	23 Sep 78	5

Al ALBERTS - See FOUR ACES

ALCATRAZ — US

SINGLES:	HITS 1			WEEKS 4
GIVE ME LUV	AM:PM	12	17 Feb 96	4

ALDA — Iceland

SINGLES:	HITS 2			WEEKS 14
REAL GOOD TIME	Wildstar	7	29 Aug 98	7
GIRLS NIGHT OUT	Wildstar	20	26 Dec 98	7

John ALDISS - See LONDON PHILHARMONIC CHOIR

Cali ALEMAN - See Tito PUENTE Jr. and the LATIN RHYTHM featuring Tito PUENTE, INDIA and Cali ALEMAN

ALENA — Jamaica

SINGLES:	HITS 1			WEEKS 5
TURN IT AROUND	Wonderboy	14	13 Nov 99	5

ALESSANDRA - See DJAIMIN featuring ALESSANDRA

ALESSI — US

SINGLES:	HITS 1			WEEKS 11
OH, LORI	A&M	8	11 Jun 77	11

ALEX PARTY

UK/Italy

SINGLES:		HITS 3		WEEKS 28	
ALEX PARTY (SATURDAY NIGHT PARTY)	Cleveland City Imports	49	18 Dec 93	6
SATURDAY NIGHT PARTY (READ MY LIPS) [RE]	Cleveland City Imports	29	28 May 94	4

Although same catalogue number was used, it was issued with different title.

DON'T GIVE ME YOUR LIFE	Systematic	2	18 Feb 95	13
WRAP ME UP	Systematic	17	18 Nov 95	3
READ MY LIPS [RM]	Systematic	28	19 Oct 96	2

A vocal remix of Saturday Night Party.

Jeff ALEXANDER CHOIR - See Mario LANZA

ALEXANDER BROTHERS

UK

EPS:		HITS 1		WEEKS 1	
NOBDODY'S CHILD	Pye	20	5 Mar 66	1
ALBUMS:		HITS 1		WEEKS 1	
THESE ARE MY MOUNTAINS	Pye Golden Guinea	29	10 Dec 66	1

ALEXIA

Italy

SINGLES:		HITS 3		WEEKS 15	
UH LA LA LA	Dance Pool	10	21 Mar 98	9
GIMME LOVE	Dance Pool	17	13 Jun 98	4
THE MUSIC I LIKE	Dance Pool	31	10 Oct 98	2

ALFI and HARRY

US

See also David Seville.

SINGLES:		HITS 1		WEEKS 5	
THE TROUBLE WITH HARRY	London	15	24 Mar 56	5

From the film of the same name.

John ALFORD

UK

SINGLES:		HITS 3		WEEKS 12	
SMOKE GETS IN YOUR EYES	Love This	13	17 Feb 96	5

Originally recorded by Paul Whiteman.

BLUE MOON / ONLY YOU	Love This	9	25 May 96	4

Originally recorded by the Glen Gray Orchestra in 1933.

IF / KEEP ON RUNNING	Love This	24	23 Nov 96	3

ALI

UK

SINGLES:		HITS 2		WEEKS 2	
LOVE LETTERS	Wild Card	63	23 May 98	1

Theme to the US sitcom 'Days Of Our Lives'.

FEELIN' YOU	Wild Card	63	24 Oct 98	1

Tatyana ALI

US

SINGLES:		HITS 3		WEEKS 18	
DAYDREAMIN'	MJJ	6	14 Nov 98	5

Features rappers Lord Tariq and Peter Gunz.

BOY YOU KNOCK ME OUT	MJJ	3	13 Feb 99	8

Samples Bobby Caldwell's What You Won't Do For Love.
Above hit: Tatyana ALI featuring Will SMITH.

BOY YOU KNOCK ME OUT [RE]	MJJ	69	15 May 99	1
EVERYTIME	MJJ	20	19 Jun 99	4
ALBUMS:		HITS 1		WEEKS 4	
KISS THE SKY	MJJ	41	20 Feb 99	4

ALI and FRAZIER

UK

SINGLES:		HITS 1		WEEKS 4	
UPTOWN TOP RANKING	Arista	33	7 Aug 93	4

ALIBI

UK

SINGLES:		HITS 2		WEEKS 2	
I'M NOT TO BLAME	Urgent	51	15 Feb 97	1
HOW MUCH I FEEL	Urgent	58	7 Feb 98	1

ALICE COOPER - See Alice COOPER

ALICE DEEJAY

Holland

SINGLES:		HITS 2		WEEKS 21	
BETTER OFF ALONE	Positiva	2	31 Jul 99	16

Above hit: DJ JURGEN presents ALICE DEEJAY.

BACK IN MY LIFE	Positiva	4	4 Dec 99	5

ALICE IN CHAINS | | | | US

SINGLES:	HITS 6			WEEKS 14
WOULD?	Columbia	19	23 Jan 93	3
THEM BONES	Columbia	26	20 Mar 93	3
ANGRY CHAIR	Columbia	33	5 Jun 93	2
DOWN IN A HOLE	Columbia	36	23 Oct 93	2
GRIND	Columbia	23	11 Nov 95	2
HEAVEN BESIDE YOU	Columbia	35	10 Feb 96	2
ALBUMS:	HITS 4			WEEKS 22
DIRT	Columbia	42	24 Oct 92	13
JAR OF FLIES/SAP	Columbia	4	5 Feb 94	5

Jar Of Flies is a 7-track mini-LP. Sap is a 4-track EP.

ALICE IN CHAINS	Columbia	37	18 Nov 95	2
MTV UNPLUGGED	Columbia	20	10 Aug 96	2

Live recordings from Brooklyn, 10 Apr 96.

ALIEN SEX FIEND | | | | UK

ALBUMS:	HITS 1			WEEKS 1
MAXIMUM SECURITY	Anagram	100	12 Oct 85	1

ALIEN VOICES featuring the THREE DEGREES | | | | UK/US

See also Three Degrees.

SINGLES:	HITS 1			WEEKS 2
LAST CHRISTMAS	Wildstar	54	26 Dec 98	2

ALISHA | | | | US

SINGLES:	HITS 1			WEEKS 2
BABY TALK	Total Control	67	25 Jan 86	2

ALISHA'S ATTIC | | | | UK

SINGLES:	HITS 7			WEEKS 42
I AM, I FEEL	Mercury	14	3 Aug 96	10
ALISHA RULES THE WORLD	Mercury	12	2 Nov 96	6
INDESTRUCTIBLE	Mercury	12	15 Mar 97	6
AIR WE BREATHE	Mercury	12	12 Jul 97	6
THE INCIDENTALS	Mercury	13	19 Sep 98	7
WISH I WERE YOU	Mercury	29	9 Jan 99	5
BARBARELLA	Mercury	34	17 Apr 99	2
ALBUMS:	HITS 2			WEEKS 46
ALISHA RULES THE WORLD	Mercury	14	23 Nov 96	43
ILLUMINA	Mercury	15	17 Oct 98	3

ALL ABOUT EVE | | | | UK

SINGLES:	HITS 13			WEEKS 47
IN THE CLOUDS	Mercury	47	31 Oct 87	5
WILD HEARTED WOMAN	Mercury	33	23 Jan 88	4
EVERY ANGEL	Mercury	30	9 Apr 88	5
MARTHA'S HARBOUR	Mercury	10	30 Jul 88	8
WHAT KIND OF FOOL	Mercury	29	12 Nov 88	4
ROAD TO YOUR SOUL	Mercury	37	30 Sep 89	4
DECEMBER	Mercury	34	16 Dec 89	5
SCARLET	Mercury	34	28 Apr 90	2
FAREWELL MR. SORROW	Mercury	36	15 Jun 91	2
STRANGE WAY	Vertigo	50	10 Aug 91	3
THE DREAMER	Vertigo	41	19 Oct 91	2
PHASED [EP]	MCA	38	10 Oct 92	2

Lead track: Phased.

SOME FINER DAY	MCA	57	28 Nov 92	1
ALBUMS:	HITS 4			WEEKS 37
ALL ABOUT EVE	Mercury	7	27 Feb 88	29
SCARLET AND OTHER STORIES	Mercury	9	28 Oct 89	4
TOUCHED BY JESUS	Vertigo	17	7 Sep 91	3
ULTRAVIOLET	MCA	46	7 Nov 92	1

ALL BLUE | | | | UK

SINGLES:	HITS 1			WEEKS 1
PRISONER	WEA	73	21 Aug 99	1

ALL-4-ONE | | | | US

SINGLES:	HITS 3			WEEKS 23
SO MUCH IN LOVE	Atlantic	60	2 Apr 94	1

Originally recorded by the Tymes.

I SWEAR	Atlantic	2	18 Jun 94	18
Originally recorded by John Michael Montgomery.				
SO MUCH IN LOVE [RM]	Atlantic	49	19 Nov 94	2
Remixed by Tim O'Brien.				
I CAN LOVE YOU LIKE THAT	Atlantic	33	15 Jul 95	2
Originally recorded by John Michael Montgomery.				
ALBUMS:	**HITS 1**			**WEEKS 5**
ALL-4-ONE	Atlantic	25	23 Jul 94	5

ALL SAINTS
UK/Canada

SINGLES:	**HITS 5**			**WEEKS 68**
I KNOW WHERE IT'S AT	London	4	6 Sep 97	8
NEVER EVER	London	1	22 Nov 97	24
UNDER THE BRIDGE / LADY MARMALADE	London	1	9 May 98	14
Lady Marmalade originally recorded by Eleventh Hour.				
BOOTIE CALL	London	1	12 Sep 98	11
WAR OF NERVES	London	7	5 Dec 98	11
ALBUMS:	**HITS 1**			**WEEKS 63**
ALL SAINTS	London	2	6 Dec 97	63

ALL SEEING I
UK

SINGLES:	**HITS 3**			**WEEKS 17**
BEAT GOES ON	ffrr	11	28 Mar 98	7
Sampled vocals from a version by Buddy Rich and his 12 year old daughter.				
WALK LIKE A PANTHER	ffrr	10	23 Jan 99	7
Above hit: ALL SEEING I featuring Tony CHRISTIE.				
1ST MAN IN SPACE	ffrr	28	18 Sep 99	3
Vocals by Phil Oakey (Human League).				
ALBUMS:	**HITS 1**			**WEEKS 1**
PICKLED EGGS & SHERBET	ffrr	45	2 Oct 99	1

ALL STAR CHOIR - See Donna SUMMER

ALL STAR HIT PARADE
UK

(See also entries for each artist.)

SINGLES:	**HITS 2**			**WEEKS 16**
ALL STAR HIT PARADE [M]	Decca	2	30 Jun 56	9
6 song medley over 2 sides. Artists credited: Dave King, Lita Roza, David Whitfield, Dickie Valentine, Joan Regan, Winifred Atwell.				
ALL STAR HIT PARADE NO. 2 [M]	Decca	15	27 Jul 57	7
6 song medley over 2 sides. Artists credited: Johnston Brothers, Billy Cotton, Jimmy Young, Max Bygraves, Beverly Sisters, Tommy Steele.				

ALL STARS - See Louis ARMSTRONG

ALL STARS - See PRINCE BUSTER and ALL STARS

ALL SYSTEMS GO
UK

SINGLES:	**HITS 1**			**WEEKS 2**
POP MUZIK	Unique	63	18 Jun 88	2

Richard ALLAN
UK

SINGLES:	**HITS 1**			**WEEKS 1**
AS TIME GOES BY	Parlophone	43	26 Mar 60	1

Steve ALLAN
UK

SINGLES:	**HITS 1**			**WEEKS 2**
TOGETHER WE ARE BEAUTIFUL	Creole	67	27 Jan 79	1
TOGETHER WE ARE BEAUTIFUL [RE]	Creole	70	10 Feb 79	1

Donna ALLEN
US

SINGLES:	**HITS 4**			**WEEKS 27**
SERIOUS	Portrait	8	18 Apr 87	12
JOY AND PAIN	BCM	10	3 Jun 89	10
REAL	Epic	34	21 Jan 95	2
From the film 'The Specialist'.				
SATURDAY	AM:PM	29	11 Oct 97	3
Original release was an instrumental reaching No. 110 in 1996.				
Above hit: EAST 57TH ST featuring Donna ALLEN.				

Keith ALLEN - See BLACK GRAPE; FAT LES

Patrick ALLEN - See Kevin PEEK and Rick WAKEMAN

Ed ALLEYNE-JOHNSON
UK

ALBUMS:	**HITS 1**			**WEEKS 1**
ULTRAVIOLET	Equation	68	18 Jun 94	1

Mose ALLISON   US

ALBUMS:		HITS 1		WEEKS 1
MOSE ALIVE	*Atlantic*	30	*4 Jun 66*	1

ALLISONS   UK

SINGLES:		HITS 3		WEEKS 27
ARE YOU SURE	*Fontana*	2	*25 Feb 61*	16
UK's Eurovision entry in 1961, it came 2nd.				
WORDS	*Fontana*	34	*20 May 61*	5
LESSONS IN LOVE	*Fontana*	30	*17 Feb 62*	6
Originally recorded by Cliff Richard.				

ALLMAN BROTHERS BAND   US

ALBUMS:		HITS 2		WEEKS 4
BROTHERS AND SISTERS	*Warner Brothers*	42	*6 Oct 73*	3
THE ROAD GOES ON FOREVER	*Capricorn*	54	*6 Mar 76*	1

ALLNIGHT BAND   UK

SINGLES:		HITS 1		WEEKS 3
THE JOKER (THE WIGAN JOKER)	*Casino Classics*	50	*3 Feb 79*	3
Originally recorded by Butch Baker.				

ALLURE   US

SINGLES:		HITS 2		WEEKS 8
HEAD OVER HEELS	*Epic*	18	*14 Jun 97*	3
Samples MC Shan's The Bridge.				
Above hit: ALLURE featuring NAS.				
ALL CRIED OUT	*Epic*	12	*10 Jan 98*	5
Originally recorded by Lisa Lisa and Cult Jam.				
Above hit: ALLURE featuring 112.				

ALMIGHTY   UK/Canada

SINGLES:		HITS 11		WEEKS 22
WILD AND WONDERFUL	*Polydor*	50	*30 Jun 90*	2
FREE 'N' EASY	*Polydor*	35	*2 Mar 91*	2
DEVIL'S TOY	*Polydor*	36	*11 May 91*	2
LITTLE LOST SOMETIMES	*Polydor*	42	*29 Jun 91*	2
ADDICTION	*Polydor*	38	*3 Apr 93*	2
OUT OF SEASON	*Polydor*	41	*29 May 93*	2
OVER THE EDGE	*Polydor*	38	*30 Oct 93*	2
WRENCH	*Chrysalis*	26	*24 Sep 94*	2
JONESTOWN MIND	*Chrysalis*	26	*14 Jan 95*	3
ALL SUSSED OUT	*Chrysalis*	28	*16 Mar 96*	2
DO YOU UNDERSTAND	*Raw Power*	38	*25 May 96*	1
ALBUMS:		**HITS 5**		**WEEKS 13**
BLOOD, FIRE AND LIVE	*Polydor*	62	*20 Oct 90*	1
SOUL DESTRUCTION	*Polydor*	22	*30 Mar 91*	4
POWERTRIPPIN'	*Polydor*	5	*17 Apr 93*	4
CRANK	*Chrysalis*	15	*8 Oct 94*	2
JUST ADD LIFE	*Chrysalis*	34	*30 Mar 96*	2

Marc ALMOND   UK

(See also Soft Cell.)

SINGLES:		HITS 24		WEEKS 101
BLACK HEART	*Some Bizzare*	49	*2 Jul 83*	3
Above hit: MARC and the MAMBAS.				
THE BOY WHO CAME BACK	*Some Bizzare*	52	*2 Jun 84*	5
YOU HAVE	*Some Bizzare*	57	*1 Sep 84*	3
I FEEL LOVE [M]	*Forbidden Fruit*	3	*20 Apr 85*	12
Above hit: BRONSKI BEAT/Marc ALMOND.				
STORIES OF JOHNNY	*Some Bizzare*	23	*24 Aug 85*	5
LOVE LETTER	*Some Bizzare*	68	*26 Oct 85*	3
Features the Westminster City School Choir.				
THE HOUSE IS HAUNTED (BY THE ECHO OF YOUR LAST GOODBYE)	*Some Bizzare*	55	*4 Jan 86*	3
Vocals by Sally Timms.				
A WOMAN'S STORY	*Some Bizzare*	41	*7 Jun 86*	5
Originally recorded by Cher in 1976.				
Above hit: Marc ALMOND and the WILLING SINNERS.				
RUBY RED	*Some Bizzare*	47	*18 Oct 86*	3
MELANCHOLY ROSE	*Some Bizzare*	71	*14 Feb 87*	1
TEARS RUN RINGS	*Parlophone*	26	*3 Sep 88*	7
BITTER SWEET	*Parlophone*	40	*5 Nov 88*	3
SOMETHING'S GOTTEN HOLD OF MY HEART	*Parlophone*	1	*14 Jan 89*	12
Above hit: Marc ALMOND featuring special guest star Gene PITNEY.				

ONLY THE MOMENT	Parlophone	45	8 Apr 89	2
A LOVER SPURNED	Parlophone	29	3 Mar 90	4
THE DESPERATE HOURS	Parlophone	45	19 May 90	2
JACKY	Some Bizzare	17	28 Sep 91	6
MY HAND OVER MY HEART	Some Bizzare	33	11 Jan 92	5
THE DAYS OF PEARLY SPENCER	Some Bizzare	4	25 Apr 92	7
Originally recorded by David McWilliams.				
WHAT MAKES A MAN A MAN (LIVE)	Some Bizzare	60	27 Mar 93	2
Live recording from the Royal Albert Hall.				
ADORED AND EXPLORED	Some Bizzare	25	13 May 95	3
THE IDOL	Some Bizzare	44	29 Jul 95	2
CHILD STAR	Some Bizzare	41	30 Dec 95	1
YESTERDAY HAS GONE	EMI Premier	58	28 Dec 96	1
Original by Little Anthony and the Imperials.				
YESTERDAY HAS GONE [RE]	EMI Premier	69	11 Jan 97	1
Above hit: P.J. PROBY; Marc ALMOND featuring the MY LIFE STORY ORCHESTRA.				
ALBUMS:	**HITS 10**			**WEEKS 39**
UNTITLED	Some Bizzare	42	16 Oct 82	4
TORMENT AND TOREROS	Some Bizzare	28	20 Aug 83	5
Above 2: MARC and the MAMBAS.				
VERMIN IN ERMINE	Some Bizzare	36	10 Nov 84	2
Above hit: Marc ALMOND and the WILLING SINNERS.				
STORIES OF JOHNNY	Some Bizzare	22	5 Oct 85	3
MOTHER FIST AND HER FIVE DAUGHTERS	Some Bizzare	41	18 Apr 87	2
Above hit: Marc ALMOND and the WILLING SINNERS.				
THE STARS WE ARE	Parlophone	41	8 Oct 88	4
THE STARS WE ARE [RE]	Parlophone	68	4 Mar 89	1
Repackaged with additional track.				
ENCHANTED	Parlophone	52	16 Jun 90	1
MEMORABILIA – THE SINGLES	Mercury	8	1 Jun 91	13
Includes both Almond's solo and group material.				
Above hit: SOFT CELL Marc ALMOND.				
TENEMENT SYMPHONY	Some Bizzare	48	26 Oct 91	1
TENEMENT SYMPHONY [RE]	Some Bizzare	39	16 May 92	2
FANTASTIC STAR	Some Bizzare	54	9 Mar 96	1

ALOOF   UK

SINGLES:	**HITS 4**			**WEEKS 6**
ON A MISSION	Cowboy	64	19 Sep 92	1
WISH YOU WERE HERE . . .	East West	61	18 May 96	1
ONE NIGHT STAND	East West	30	30 Nov 96	2
WISH YOU WERE HERE . . . [RI]	East West	43	1 Mar 97	1
WHAT I MISS THE MOST	East West	70	29 Aug 98	1

Herb ALPERT and the TIJUANA BRASS   US

SINGLES:	**HITS 11**			**WEEKS 106**
THE LONELY BULL (EL SOLO TORRO)	Stateside	22	5 Jan 63	9
SPANISH FLEA	Pye International	3	11 Dec 65	20
TIJUANA TAXI	Pye International	37	26 Mar 66	4
CASINO ROYALE	A&M	27	29 Apr 67	14
THIS GUY'S IN LOVE WITH YOU	A&M	3	6 Jul 68	16
THIS GUY'S IN LOVE WITH YOU [RE-1ST]	A&M	46	29 Mar 69	1
THIS GUY'S IN LOVE WITH YOU [RE-2ND]	A&M	49	12 Apr 69	1
THIS GUY'S IN LOVE WITH YOU [RE-3RD]	A&M	50	10 May 69	1
Above 4: Herb ALPERT.				
WITHOUT HER	A&M	36	21 Jun 69	5
Originally recorded by Harry Nilsson.				
JERUSALEM	A&M	47	12 Dec 70	1
JERUSALEM [RE]	A&M	42	2 Jan 71	2
RISE	A&M	13	13 Oct 79	13
ROTATION	A&M	46	19 Jan 80	3
KEEP YOUR EYE ON ME – SPECIAL MIX	Breakout	19	21 Mar 87	9
DIAMONDS	Breakout	27	6 Jun 87	7
Features vocals by Janet Jackson and Lisa Keith.				
Above 4: Herb ALPERT.				
ALBUMS:	**HITS 16**			**WEEKS 322**
GOING PLACES	Pye	5	29 Jan 66	22
WHIPPED CREAM AND OTHER DELIGHTS	Pye	2	23 Apr 66	42
WHAT NOW MY LOVE	Pye	18	28 May 66	12
GOING PLACES [RE]	Pye	4	13 Aug 66	116
Re-issued on the A&M label from 29 Jul 67.				
S.R.O.	Pye	5	11 Feb 67	26
WHAT NOW MY LOVE [RI]	A&M	19	15 Jul 67	5
SOUNDS LIKE	A&M	21	15 Jul 67	10
NINTH	A&M	26	3 Feb 68	19
BEAT OF THE BRASS	A&M	4	29 Jun 68	21
WARM	A&M	30	9 Aug 69	4

17

THE BRASS ARE COMIN'	A&M	40	14 Mar 70	1
GREATEST HITS	A&M	8	30 May 70	27
DOWN MEXICO WAY	A&M	64	27 Jun 70	1
AMERICA	A&M	45	13 Nov 71	1
40 GREATEST	K-Tel	45	12 Nov 77	2
RISE	A&M	37	17 Nov 79	7
KEEP YOUR EYE ON ME	Breakout	79	4 Apr 87	3
THE VERY BEST OF HERB ALPERT	A&M	34	28 Sep 91	3

Above 3: Herb ALPERT.

ALPHAVILLE · Germany

SINGLES:	HITS 1			WEEKS 13
BIG IN JAPAN	WEA International	8	18 Aug 84	13

Gerald ALSTON · US

SINGLES:	HITS 1			WEEKS 1
ACTIVATED	RCA	73	15 Apr 89	1

ALT · UK/Ireland/New Zealand

ALBUMS:	HITS 1			WEEKS 1
ALTITUDE	Parlophone	67	24 Jun 95	1

ALTERED IMAGES · UK

SINGLES:	HITS 8			WEEKS 60
DEAD POP STARS	Epic	67	28 Mar 81	2
HAPPY BIRTHDAY	Epic	2	26 Sep 81	17
I COULD BE HAPPY	Epic	7	12 Dec 81	12
SEE THOSE EYES	Epic	11	27 Mar 82	7
PINKY BLUE	Epic	35	22 May 82	6
DON'T TALK TO ME ABOUT LOVE	Epic	7	19 Mar 83	7
BRING ME CLOSER	Epic	29	28 May 83	6
LOVE TO STAY	Epic	46	16 Jul 83	3
ALBUMS:	HITS 3			WEEKS 40
HAPPY BIRTHDAY	Epic	26	19 Sep 81	21
PINKY BLUE	Epic	12	15 May 82	10
BITE	Epic	16	25 Jun 83	9

ALTERN 8 · UK

SINGLES:	HITS 8			WEEKS 34
INFILTRATE 202	Network	28	13 Jul 91	7
ACTIV 8 (COME WITH ME)	Network	3	16 Nov 91	9
FREQUENCY	Network	41	8 Feb 92	1
EVAPOR 8	Network	6	11 Apr 92	6

Above hit: ALTERN 8 guest vocal P.P. ARNOLD.

HYPNOTIC ST-8	Network	16	4 Jul 92	4
SHAME (HARDCORE MIX)	Network	74	10 Oct 92	1

Remix of Evelyn King's original.
Above hit: ALTERN 8 vs Evelyn KING.

BRUTAL-8-E	Network	43	12 Dec 92	5
EVERYBODY	Network	58	3 Jul 93	1
ALBUMS:	HITS 1			WEEKS 4
FULL ON..MASK HYSTERIA	Network	11	25 Jul 92	4

ALTHIA and DONNA · Jamaica

SINGLES:	HITS 1			WEEKS 11
UP TOWN TOP RANKING	Lightning	1	24 Dec 77	11

Originally recorded by Trinity as Three Piece Suite. Uptown Top Ranking is a Jamaican slang term for showing off in the city.

ALVIN and the CHIPMUNKS - See CHIPMUNKS

ALY-US · US

SINGLES:	HITS 1			WEEKS 2
FOLLOW ME	Cooltempo	43	21 Nov 92	2

Shola AMA · UK

SINGLES:	HITS 7			WEEKS 46
YOU MIGHT NEED SOMEBODY	WEA	4	19 Apr 97	14

Original by Turley Richards in 1980.

YOU'RE THE ONE I LOVE	WEA	3	30 Aug 97	8
WHO'S LOVING MY BABY	WEA	13	29 Nov 97	7
MUCH LOVE	WEA	17	21 Feb 98	3

SOMEDAY I'LL FIND YOU	EMI	28	11 Apr 98	3

[AA] listed with I've Been To A Marvellous Party by the Divine Comedy. From the Noel Coward commemorative album Twentieth Century Blues.
Above hit: Shola AMA with Craig ARMSTRONG.

TABOO	WEA	10	17 Apr 99	8

Above hit: GLAMMA KID featuring Shola AMA.

STILL BELIEVE	WEA	26	6 Nov 99	3
ALBUMS:	**HITS 1**		**WEEKS 32**	
MUCH LOVE	WEA	6	13 Sep 97	32

Eddie AMADOR — US

SINGLES:	**HITS 1**		**WEEKS 2**	
HOUSE MUSIC	Pukka	37	24 Oct 98	2

AMAZULU — UK

SINGLES:	**HITS 6**		**WEEKS 57**	
EXCITABLE	Island	12	6 Jul 85	13
DON'T YOU JUST KNOW IT	Island	15	23 Nov 85	11

Original by Huey 'Piano' Smith reached No. 9 in the US in 1958.

THE THINGS THE LONELY DO	Island	43	15 Mar 86	6
TOO GOOD TO BE FORGOTTEN	Island	5	31 May 86	13
MONTEGO BAY	Island	16	13 Sep 86	9
MONY MONY	EMI	38	10 Oct 87	5
ALBUMS:	**HITS 1**		**WEEKS 1**	
AMAZULU	Island	97	6 Dec 86	1

AMBASSADORS OF FUNK featuring M.C. MARIO — UK

(See also Simon Harris.)

SINGLES:	**HITS 1**		**WEEKS 8**	
SUPERMARIOLAND	Living Beat	8	31 Oct 92	8

Based upon the theme to the Nintendo game of the same name.

AMBER - See STARS ON 54

AMEN CORNER — UK

SINGLES:	**HITS 6**		**WEEKS 67**	
GIN HOUSE BLUES	Deram	12	29 Jul 67	10
THE WORLD OF BROKEN HEARTS	Deram	24	14 Oct 67	6
BEND ME SHAPE ME	Deram	3	20 Jan 68	12

Originally recorded by the Models.

HIGH IN THE SKY	Deram	6	3 Aug 68	13
(IF PARADISE IS) HALF AS NICE	Immediate	1	1 Feb 69	11
HELLO SUZIE	Immediate	4	28 Jun 69	10

Originally recorded by Roy Wood.

(IF PARADISE IS) HALF AS NICE [RI]	Immediate	34	14 Feb 76	5
ALBUMS:	**HITS 2**		**WEEKS 8**	
ROUND AMEN CORNER	Deram	26	30 Mar 68	7
EXPLOSIVE COMPANY	Immediate	19	1 Nov 69	1

AMEN! UK — UK/Greece

SINGLES:	**HITS 2**		**WEEKS 6**	
PASSION	Feverpitch	15	8 Feb 97	4
PEOPLE OF LOVE	Feverpitch	36	28 Jun 97	2

AMERICA — US/UK

SINGLES:	**HITS 3**		**WEEKS 20**	
A HORSE WITH NO NAME	Warner Brothers	49	18 Dec 71	2
A HORSE WITH NO NAME [RE]	Warner Brothers	3	8 Jan 72	11
VENTURA HIGHWAY	Warner Brothers	43	25 Nov 72	4
YOU CAN DO MAGIC	Capitol	59	6 Nov 82	3
ALBUMS:	**HITS 4**		**WEEKS 22**	
AMERICA	Warner Brothers	14	22 Jan 72	13
HOMECOMING	Warner Brothers	21	9 Dec 72	5
HAT TRICK	Warner Brothers	41	10 Nov 73	3
HISTORY - AMERICA'S GREATEST HITS	Warner Brothers	60	7 Feb 76	1

AMERICAN BREED — US

SINGLES:	**HITS 1**		**WEEKS 6**	
BEND ME SHAPE ME	Stateside	24	10 Feb 68	6

AMERICAN MUSIC CLUB — US

SINGLES:	**HITS 2**		**WEEKS 4**	
JOHNNY MATHIS' FEET	Virgin	58	24 Apr 93	2

WISH THE WORLD AWAY		*Virgin*	46	*10 Sep 94*	2
ALBUMS:		**HITS 2**			**WEEKS 3**
MERCURY		*Virgin*	41	*27 Mar 93*	2
SAN FRANCISCO		*Virgin*	72	*24 Sep 94*	1

AMES BROTHERS with Hugo WINTERHALTER and his Orchestra · US

SINGLES:		**HITS 1**			**WEEKS 6**
THE NAUGHTY LADY OF SHADY LANE		*His Master's Voice*	6	*5 Feb 55*	6

AMIL Of MAJOR COINZ – See JAY-Z

AMIRA · US

SINGLES:		**HITS 1**			**WEEKS 3**
MY DESIRE		*VC Recordings*	51	*13 Dec 97*	1
Vocals by Amira Rahseed.					
MY DESIRE [RM]		*VC Recordings*	46	*8 Aug 98*	2
Remixed by Club Asylum.					

AMNESIA – See Frank O'MOIRAGHI featuring AMNESIA

Johnny AMOBI – See Jason DONOVAN

AMOS · UK

SINGLES:		**HITS 5**			**WEEKS 12**
ONLY SAW TODAY/INSTANT KARMA [M]		*Positiva*	48	*3 Sep 94*	2
LET LOVE SHINE		*Positiva*	31	*25 Mar 95*	2
CHURCH OF FREEDOM		*Positiva*	54	*7 Oct 95*	1
STAMP!		*Positiva*	11	*12 Oct 96*	5
ARGENTINA		*Positiva*	30	*31 May 97*	2
Above 2: Jeremy HEALY and AMOS.					

Tori AMOS · US

SINGLES:		**HITS 14**			**WEEKS 64**
SILENT ALL THESE YEARS		*East West*	51	*23 Nov 91*	3
CHINA		*East West*	51	*1 Feb 92*	2
WINTER		*East West*	25	*21 Mar 92*	4
CRUCIFY		*East West*	15	*20 Jun 92*	6
SILENT ALL THESE YEARS [RI]		*East West*	26	*22 Aug 92*	4
CORNFLAKE GIRL		*East West*	4	*22 Jan 94*	6
PRETTY GOOD YEAR		*East West*	7	*19 Mar 94*	4
PAST THE MISSION		*East West*	31	*28 May 94*	3
Vocals by Trent Reznor of Nine Inch Nails.					
GOD		*East West*	44	*15 Oct 94*	2
CAUGHT A LITE SNEEZE		*East West*	20	*13 Jan 96*	3
TALULA		*East West*	22	*23 Mar 96*	2
HEY JUPITER / PROFESSIONAL WIDOW		*East West*	20	*3 Aug 96*	9
Professional Widow mixed by Armand Van Helden.					
BLUE SKIES		*Perfecto*	26	*9 Nov 96*	2
Above hit: BT featuring Tori AMOS.					
PROFESSIONAL WIDOW (IT'S GOT TO BE BIG) [RI]		*East West*	1	*11 Jan 97*	10
SPARK		*Atlantic*	16	*2 May 98*	3
GLORY OF THE 80'S		*Atlantic*	46	*13 Nov 99*	1
ALBUMS:		**HITS 5**			**WEEKS 49**
LITTLE EARTHQUAKES		*East West*	14	*18 Jan 92*	23
UNDER THE PINK		*East West*	1	*12 Feb 94*	13
BOYS FOR PELE		*East West*	2	*3 Feb 96*	6
FROM THE CHOIRGIRL HOTEL		*Atlantic*	6	*16 May 98*	5
TO VENUS AND BACK		*Atlantic*	22	*2 Oct 99*	2
Comprises a studio set and live recordings from her 1998 'Plugged' tour.					

AMPS · US

SINGLES:		**HITS 1**			**WEEKS 1**
TIPP CITY		*4AD*	61	*21 Oct 95*	1
ALBUMS:		**HITS 1**			**WEEKS 1**
PACER		*4AD*	60	*11 Nov 95*	1

AMY – See A.D.A.M. featuring AMY

ANADIN BROTHERS – See DOCTOR and the MEDICS

AND WHY NOT? · UK

SINGLES:		**HITS 3**			**WEEKS 18**
RESTLESS DAYS (SHE SCREAMS OUT LOUD)		*Island*	38	*14 Oct 89*	7
THE FACE		*Island*	13	*13 Jan 90*	8
SOMETHING YOU GOT		*Island*	39	*21 Apr 90*	3

ALBUMS:		HITS 1		WEEKS 3	
MOVE YOUR SKIN	Island	24	10 Mar 90	3	

Angry ANDERSON
Australia

SINGLES:		HITS 1		WEEKS 13	
SUDDENLY (THE WEDDING THEME FROM NEIGHBOURS)	Food For Thought	3	19 Nov 88	13	

Played at the marriage of Scott (Jason Donovan) and Charlene (Kylie Minogue).

Carl ANDERSON
US

SINGLES:		HITS 1		WEEKS 4	
BUTTERCUP	Streetwave	49	8 Jun 85	4	

Carleen ANDERSON
US

SINGLES:		HITS 6		WEEKS 17	
NERVOUS BREAKDOWN	Circa	27	12 Feb 94	4	
MAMA SAID	Circa	26	28 May 94	4	
TRUE SPIRIT	Circa	24	13 Aug 94	3	
LET IT LAST	Circa	16	14 Jan 95	3	
MAYBE I'M AMAZED	Circa	24	7 Feb 98	2	
WOMAN IN ME	Circa	74	25 Apr 98	1	

ALBUMS:		HITS 3		WEEKS 7	
DUSKY SAPPHO [EP]	Circa	38	13 Nov 93	1	
TRUE SPIRIT	Circa	12	18 Jun 94	4	
BLESSED BURDEN	Circa	51	2 May 98	2	

Gillian ANDERSON - See HAL featuring Gillian ANDERSON

Ian ANDERSON
UK

ALBUMS:		HITS 1		WEEKS 1	
WALK INTO LIGHT	Chrysalis	78	26 Nov 83	1	

John ANDERSON BIG BAND
UK

SINGLES:		HITS 1		WEEKS 5	
GLENN MILLER MEDLEY [M]	Modern	63	21 Dec 85	2	
GLENN MILLER MEDLEY [M] [RE]	Modern	61	11 Jan 86	3	

John ANDERSON ORCHESTRA
Ireland

ALBUMS:		HITS 1		WEEKS 5	
PAN PIPES - ROMANCE OF IRELAND	MCA	56	25 Nov 95	5	

Jon ANDERSON
UK

(See also Anderson Bruford Wakeman Howe; Jon and Vangelis.)

ALBUMS:		HITS 3		WEEKS 19	
OLIAS OF SUNHILLOW	Atlantic	8	24 Jul 76	10	
SONG OF SEVEN	Atlantic	38	15 Nov 80	3	
ANIMATION	Polydor	43	5 Jun 82	6	

Laurie ANDERSON
US

SINGLES:		HITS 1		WEEKS 6	
O SUPERMAN	Warner Brothers	2	17 Oct 81	6	

ALBUMS:		HITS 2		WEEKS 8	
BIG SCIENCE	Warner Brothers	29	1 May 82	6	
MISTER HEARTBREAK	Warner Brothers	93	10 Mar 84	2	

Leroy ANDERSON and his POPS CONCERT ORCHESTRA
US

SINGLES:		HITS 1		WEEKS 4	
FORGOTTEN DREAMS	Brunswick	28	29 Jun 57	1	
FORGOTTEN DREAMS [RE-1ST]	Brunswick	30	13 Jul 57	1	
FORGOTTEN DREAMS [RE-2ND]	Brunswick	24	7 Sep 57	2	

Lynn ANDERSON
US

SINGLES:		HITS 1		WEEKS 20	
ROSE GARDEN	CBS	3	20 Feb 71	20	

Originally recorded by Joe South.

ALBUMS:		HITS 1		WEEKS 1	
ROSE GARDEN	CBS	45	17 Apr 71	1	

Moira ANDERSON
UK

See also Harry Secombe and Moira Anderson.

SINGLES:		HITS 1		WEEKS 2	
HOLY CITY	Decca	43	27 Dec 69	2	

ALBUMS:		HITS 1		WEEKS 1
THESE ARE MY SONGS	Decca	50	20 Jun 70	1

ANDERSON BRUFORD WAKEMAN HOWE   UK
(See also Jon Anderson; Steve Howe; Rick Wakeman.)

SINGLES:		HITS 1		WEEKS 2
BROTHER OF MINE	Arista	63	24 Jun 89	2

ALBUMS:		HITS 1		WEEKS 6
ANDERSON BRUFORD WAKEMAN HOWE	Arista	14	8 Jul 89	6

Peter ANDRE   UK

SINGLES:		HITS 10		WEEKS 83
TURN IT UP	Mushroom	64	10 Jun 95	1
MYSTERIOUS GIRL	Mushroom	53	16 Sep 95	2

Though Bubbler Ranx was credited on the re-issue, he was not credited on this release.

ONLY ONE	Mushroom	16	16 Mar 96	3
ONLY ONE [RE]	Mushroom	69	13 Apr 96	1
MYSTERIOUS GIRL [RI]	Mushroom	2	1 Jun 96	18

Above hit: Peter ANDRE featuring BUBBLER RANX.

FLAVA	Mushroom	1	14 Sep 96	9
I FEEL YOU	Mushroom	1	7 Dec 96	9
I FEEL YOU [RE-1ST]	Mushroom	65	1 Mar 97	1
NATURAL	Mushroom	6	8 Mar 97	8
I FEEL YOU [RE-2ND]	Mushroom	74	15 Mar 97	1
NATURAL [RE-1ST]	Mushroom	58	10 May 97	1
NATURAL [RE-2ND]	Mushroom	68	24 May 97	2
ALL ABOUT US	Mushroom	3	9 Aug 97	8

Features rapper Little Bo Peep.

ALL ABOUT US [RE]	Mushroom	75	1 Nov 97	1
LONELY	Mushroom	6	8 Nov 97	5
LONELY [RE]	Mushroom	68	3 Jan 98	4
ALL NIGHT ALL RIGHT	Mushroom	16	24 Jan 98	4

Samples A Taste Of Honey's Boogie Oogie Oogie.
Above hit: Peter ANDRE featuring Warren G.

KISS THE GIRL	Mushroom	9	25 Jul 98	5

From the Walt Disney film 'The Little Mermaid'.

ALBUMS:		HITS 2		WEEKS 27
NATURAL	Mushroom	1	12 Oct 96	23
TIME	Mushroom	28	29 Nov 97	4

Chris ANDREWS   UK

SINGLES:		HITS 5		WEEKS 36
YESTERDAY MAN	Decca	3	9 Oct 65	15
TO WHOM IT CONCERNS	Decca	13	4 Dec 65	10
SOMETHING ON MY MIND	Decca	45	16 Apr 66	1
SOMETHING ON MY MIND [RE]	Decca	41	30 Apr 66	2
WHAT'CHA GONNA DO NOW	Decca	40	4 Jun 66	4
STOP THAT GIRL	Decca	36	27 Aug 66	4

Eamonn ANDREWS with Ron GOODWIN and his Orchestra and Chorus   Ireland

SINGLES:		HITS 1		WEEKS 3
THE SHIFTING WHISPERING SANDS	Parlophone	18	21 Jan 56	3

Originally recorded by Billy Vaughn and his Orchestra.

Julie ANDREWS   UK
(See also Various Artists: Films – Original Soundtracks 'Mary Poppins', 'The Sound Of Music', 'Thoroughly Modern Millie', 'Star!'; Stage Cast – Broadway 'My Fair Lady'; Studio Cast 'The King And I'.)

ALBUMS:		HITS 1		WEEKS 5
LOVE ME TENDER	Peach River	63	16 Jul 83	5

ANEKA   UK

SINGLES:		HITS 2		WEEKS 16
JAPANESE BOY	Hansa	1	8 Aug 81	12
LITTLE LADY	Hansa	50	7 Nov 81	4

Dave ANGEL   UK

SINGLES:		HITS 1		WEEKS 1
TOKYO STEALTH FIGHTER	Fourth & Broadway	58	2 Aug 97	1

Simone ANGEL   Holland

SINGLES:		HITS 1		WEEKS 1
LET THIS FEELING	A&M	60	13 Nov 93	1

ANGELETTES
				UK
SINGLES:	**HITS 1**		**WEEKS 5**	
DON'T LET HIM TOUCH YOU	Decca	35	13 May 72	5

ANGELHEART
				UK
SINGLES:	**HITS 2**		**WEEKS 2**	
COME BACK TO ME	Hi-Life	68	6 Apr 96	1
Above hit: ANGELHEART featuring Rochelle HARRIS.				
I'M STILL WAITING	Hi-Life	74	22 Mar 97	1
Above hit: ANGELHEART featuring Aletia BOURNE.				

ANGELIC UPSTARTS
				UK
SINGLES:	**HITS 7**		**WEEKS 30**	
I'M AN UPSTART	Warner Brothers	31	21 Apr 79	8
TEENAGE WARNING	Warner Brothers	29	11 Aug 79	6
NEVER 'AD NOTHIN'	Warner Brothers	52	3 Nov 79	4
OUT OF CONTROL	Warner Brothers	58	9 Feb 80	3
WE GOTTA GET OUT OF THIS PLACE	Warner Brothers	65	22 Mar 80	2
LAST NIGHT ANOTHER SOLDIER	Zonophone	51	2 Aug 80	4
KIDS ON THE STREET	Zonophone	57	7 Feb 81	3
ALBUMS:	**HITS 4**		**WEEKS 20**	
TEENAGE WARNING	Warner Brothers	29	18 Aug 79	7
WE'VE GOTTA GET OUT OF THIS PLACE	Warner Brothers	54	12 Apr 80	3
2,000,000 VOICES	Zonophone	32	27 Jun 81	3
ANGELIC UPSTARTS	Zonophone	27	26 Sep 81	7

Bobby ANGELO and the TUXEDOS
				UK
SINGLES:	**HITS 1**		**WEEKS 6**	
BABY SITTIN'	His Master's Voice	30	12 Aug 61	6

ANGELS
				US
SINGLES:	**HITS 1**		**WEEKS 1**	
MY BOYFRIEND'S BACK	Mercury	50	5 Oct 63	1

ANGELS OF LIGHT - See PSYCHIC TV

ANGELWITCH
				UK
SINGLES:	**HITS 1**		**WEEKS 1**	
SWEET DANGER	EMI	75	7 Jun 80	1

ANIMAL
				US
SINGLES:	**HITS 1**		**WEEKS 3**	
WIPE OUT	BMG Kidz	38	23 Jul 94	3

ANIMAL NIGHTLIFE
				UK
SINGLES:	**HITS 4**		**WEEKS 22**	
NATIVE BOY (UPTOWN)	Inner Vision	60	13 Aug 83	3
MR. SOLITARE	Island	25	18 Aug 84	12
LOVE IS JUST THE GREAT PRETENDER '85	Island	28	6 Jul 85	6
PREACHER, PREACHER	Island	67	5 Oct 85	1
ALBUMS:	**HITS 1**		**WEEKS 6**	
SHANGRI-LA	Island	36	24 Aug 85	6

ANIMALS
				UK
SINGLES:	**HITS 15**		**WEEKS 147**	
BABY LET ME TAKE YOU HOME	Columbia	21	18 Apr 64	8
THE HOUSE OF THE RISING SUN	Columbia	1	27 Jun 64	12
Originally recorded by Josh White.				
I'M CRYING	Columbia	8	19 Sep 64	10
DON'T LET ME BE MISUNDERSTOOD	Columbia	3	6 Feb 65	9
Originally recorded by Nina Simone.				
BRING IT ON HOME TO ME	Columbia	7	10 Apr 65	11
Original by Sam Cooke reached No. 13 in the US in 1962.				
WE'VE GOTTA GET OUT OF THIS PLACE	Columbia	2	17 Jul 65	12
IT'S MY LIFE	Columbia	7	30 Oct 65	11
INSIDE-LOOKING OUT	Decca	12	19 Feb 66	8
DON'T BRING ME DOWN	Decca	6	4 Jun 66	8
HELP ME GIRL	Decca	14	29 Oct 66	10
WHEN I WAS YOUNG	MGM	45	17 Jun 67	3
GOOD TIMES	MGM	20	9 Sep 67	11
SAN FRANCISCAN NIGHTS	MGM	7	21 Oct 67	10
Above 4: Eric BURDON and the ANIMALS.				

SKY PILOT	*MGM*	40	*17 Feb 68*	3
Above hit: Eric BURDON.				
RING OF FIRE	*MGM*	35	*18 Jan 69*	5
Above hit: Eric BURDON and the ANIMALS.				
THE HOUSE OF THE RISING SUN [RI]	*RAK*	25	*7 Oct 72*	6
THE HOUSE OF THE RISING SUN [RI] [RE]	*RAK*	11	*18 Sep 82*	10
ALBUMS:	**HITS 4**			**WEEKS 86**
THE ANIMALS IS HERE	*Columbia*	3	*9 Jan 65*	37
THE ANIMALS ARE BACK	*Columbia*	8	*23 Oct 65*	14
ANIMAL TRACKS	*Columbia*	7	*17 Sep 66*	4
EPS:	**HITS 3**			**WEEKS 55**
THE ANIMALS	*Columbia*	6	*14 Nov 64*	20
ANIMAL TRACKS	*Columbia*	6	*22 May 65*	26
THE MOST OF THE ANIMALS	*Columbia*	4	*16 Apr 66*	20
ANIMALISMS	*Decca*	4	*28 May 66*	17
THE MOST OF THE ANIMALS [RI]	*Music For Pleasure*	18	*25 Sep 71*	3

ANIMOTION   US/UK

SINGLES:	**HITS 1**			**WEEKS 12**
OBSESSION	*Mercury*	5	*11 May 85*	12

Paul ANKA   Canada

SINGLES:	**HITS 14**			**WEEKS 134**
DIANA	*Columbia*	1	*10 Aug 57*	25
Written about his baby sitter Diana Ayoub.				
I LOVE YOU, BABY	*Columbia*	3	*9 Nov 57*	15
TELL ME THAT YOU LOVE ME	*Columbia*	25	*9 Nov 57*	2
Above 2 entries were separate sides of the same release, each had its own chart run.				
YOU ARE MY DESTINY	*Columbia*	6	*1 Feb 58*	13
CRAZY LOVE	*Columbia*	26	*31 May 58*	1
MIDNIGHT	*Columbia*	26	*27 Sep 58*	1
(ALL OF A SUDDEN) MY HEART SINGS	*Columbia*	10	*31 Jan 59*	13
Originally recorded by Johnnie Johnson.				
LONELY BOY	*Columbia*	3	*11 Jul 59*	17
From the film 'Girl's Town'.				
PUT YOUR HEAD ON MY SHOULDER	*Columbia*	7	*31 Oct 59*	12
IT'S TIME TO CRY	*Columbia*	28	*27 Feb 60*	1
From the film 'Girl's Town'.				
PUPPY LOVE	*Columbia*	33	*2 Apr 60*	4
IT'S TIME TO CRY [RI]	*Columbia*	47	*16 Apr 60*	1
PUPPY LOVE [RI]	*Columbia*	37	*7 May 60*	3
HELLO YOUNG LOVERS	*Columbia*	44	*17 Sep 60*	1
LOVE ME WARM AND TENDER	*RCA*	19	*17 Mar 62*	11
A STEEL GUITAR AND A GLASS OF WINE	*RCA*	41	*28 Jul 62*	4
Above hit: Paul ANKA with Ray ELLIS and his Orchestra.				
'YOU'RE' HAVING MY BABY	*United Artists*	6	*28 Sep 74*	10
Duet with Odia Coates.				

ANNETTE – See VARIOUS ARTISTS (EPs) 'The Further Adventures Of North – More Underground Dance EP'

ANNIHILATOR   UK

ALBUMS:	**HITS 1**			**WEEKS 1**
NEVER, NEVERLAND	*Roadrunner*	48	*11 Aug 90*	1

ANOTHER LEVEL   UK

SINGLES:	**HITS 7**			**WEEKS 77**
BE ALONE NO MORE	*Northwestside*	6	*28 Feb 98*	9
FREAK ME	*Northwestside*	1	*18 Jul 98*	12
GUESS I WAS A FOOL	*Northwestside*	5	*7 Nov 98*	13
I WANT YOU FOR MYSELF	*Northwestside*	2	*23 Jan 99*	8
Chart also credits Ghostface Killah.				
BE ALONE NO MORE [RM]	*Northwestside*	11	*10 Apr 99*	9
Remixed by Cutfather and Joe. CD2 has Holding Back The Years as the first track. Charity record in aid of Capital Radio's Help A London Child.				
Above hit: ANOTHER LEVEL featuring JAY Z.				
FROM THE HEART	*Northwestside*	6	*12 Jun 99*	10
From the film 'Notting Hill'.				
FROM THE HEART [RE]	*Northwestside*	74	*28 Aug 99*	1
SUMMERTIME	*Northwestside*	7	*4 Sep 99*	7
Above hit: ANOTHER LEVEL featuring TQ.				
BOMB DIGGY	*Northwestside*	6	*13 Nov 99*	8
Used as the theme music for Channel 4's 'North Hollywood High'.				
ALBUMS:	**HITS 2**			**WEEKS 40**
ANOTHER LEVEL	*Northwestside*	13	*21 Nov 98*	25
NEXUS . . .	*Northwestside*	7	*25 Sep 99*	15

Adam ANT

UK

SINGLES:		HITS 22			WEEKS 199
KINGS OF THE WILD FRONTIER	CBS	48	2 Aug 80	5
DOG EAT DOG	CBS	4	11 Oct 80	16
ANTMUSIC	CBS	2	6 Dec 80	18
YOUNG PARISIANS	Decca	9	27 Dec 80	13
Originally released in 1978.				
CARTROUBLE	Do It	33	24 Jan 81	9
Originally released in 1980.				
ZEROX	Do It	45	24 Jan 81	9
Originally released in 1979.				
KINGS OF THE WILD FRONTIER [RE]	CBS	2	21 Feb 81	13
STAND AND DELIVER	CBS	1	9 May 81	15
PRINCE CHARMING	CBS	1	12 Sep 81	12
ANT RAP	CBS	3	12 Dec 81	10
Above 10: ADAM and the ANTS.				
DEUTSCHER GIRLS	E'G	13	27 Feb 82	6
From the 1977 film 'Jubilee'.				
Above hit: Original ADAM and the ANTS.				
THE ANTMUSIC (EP) (THE B-SIDES) [EP]	Do It	46	13 Mar 82	4
Lead track: Friends.				
Above hit: ADAM and the ANTS.				
GOODY TWO SHOES	CBS	1	22 May 82	11
FRIEND OR FOE	CBS	9	18 Sep 82	8
DESPERATE BUT NOT SERIOUS	CBS	33	27 Nov 82	7
PUSS 'N BOOTS	CBS	5	29 Oct 83	11
STRIP	CBS	41	10 Dec 83	6
APOLLO 9	CBS	13	22 Sep 84	8
VIVE LE ROCK	CBS	50	13 Jul 85	4
ROOM AT THE TOP	MCA	13	17 Feb 90	7
CAN'T SET RULES ABOUT LOVE	MCA	47	28 Apr 90	2
WONDERFUL	EMI	32	11 Feb 95	3
GOTTA BE A SIN	EMI	48	3 Jun 95	2
ALBUMS:		HITS 10			WEEKS 157
KINGS OF THE WILD FRONTIER	CBS	1	15 Nov 80	66
DIRK WEARS WHITE SOX	Do It	16	17 Jan 81	29
PRINCE CHARMING	CBS	2	14 Nov 81	21
Above 3: ADAM and the ANTS.				
FRIEND OR FOE	CBS	5	23 Oct 82	12
STRIP	CBS	20	19 Nov 83	8
VIVE LE ROCK	CBS	42	14 Sep 85	3
MANNERS AND PHYSIQUE	MCA	19	24 Mar 90	3
ANTMUSIC – THE VERY BEST OF ADAM ANT	Arcade	6	28 Aug 93	11
Includes both solo and group material. From 26 Mar 94, album was repackaged with a live CD.				
WONDERFUL	EMI	24	15 Apr 95	2
THE VERY BEST OF ADAM AND THE ANTS	Columbia	56	3 Apr 99	2
Above hit: ADAM and the ANTS.				

ANT and DEC

UK

SINGLES:		HITS 14			WEEKS 81
TONIGHT I'M FREE	XSRhythm	62	18 Dec 93	3
Above hit: PJ and DUNCAN (BYKER GROVE).				
WHY ME?	XSRhythm	27	23 Apr 94	4
Above hit: PJ and DUNCAN (A.K.A. ANT and DECLAN).				
LET'S GET READY TO RHUMBLE	XSRhythm	9	23 Jul 94	11
IF I GIVE YOU MY NUMBER	XSRhythm	15	8 Oct 94	7
ETERNAL LOVE	XSRhythm	12	3 Dec 94	9
OUR RADIO ROCKS	XSRhythm	15	25 Feb 95	5
Above 4: PJ and DUNCAN A.K.A.				
STUCK ON U	Telstar	12	29 Jul 95	5
U KRAZY KATZ	XSRhythm	15	14 Oct 95	4
Features Jamiroquai's brass section.				
PERFECT	Telstar	16	2 Dec 95	7
STEPPING STONE	Telstar	11	30 Mar 96	5
Originally recorded by Paul Revere and the Raiders In 1966.				
Above 4: PJ and DUNCAN.				
BETTER WATCH OUT	Telstar	10	24 Aug 96	4
Above hit: The Cult Of . . . ANT and DEC.				
WHEN I FALL IN LOVE	Telstar	12	23 Nov 96	8
SHOUT	Telstar	10	15 Mar 97	5
Features Andy Bell of Erasure on backing vocals and samples Walk On The Wild Side by Lou Reed.				
FALLING	Telstar	14	10 May 97	
ALBUMS:		HITS 3			WEEKS 31
PSYCHE – THE ALBUM	XSRhythm	5	19 Nov 94	20
TOP KATZ – THE ALBUM	Telstar	46	18 Nov 95	8
Above 2: PJ and DUNCAN				
THE CULT OF ANT & DEC	Telstar	15	24 May 97	3

Mark ANTHONI – See FIRE ISLAND

Billie ANTHONY with Eric JUPP and his Orchestra — UK

SINGLES:	HITS 1			WEEKS 16
THIS OLE HOUSE	Columbia	4	16 Oct 54	16

Marc ANTHONY — US

SINGLES:	HITS 2			WEEKS 7
RIDE ON THE RHYTHM	Atlantic	71	5 Oct 91	1
Above hit: Little Louie VEGA and Marc ANTHONY.				
RIDE ON THE RHYTHM [RI]	Atlantic	70	23 May 92	1
Above hit: Louie VEGA and Marc ANTHONY.				
RIDE ON THE RHYTHM [RM]	Perfecto Red	36	31 Jan 98	2
Remixed by Mr. Roy.				
Above hit: "Little" LOUIE and Marc ANTHONY.				
I NEED TO KNOW	Columbia	28	13 Nov 99	3

Ray ANTHONY and his Orchestra — US

SINGLES:	HITS 1			WEEKS 2
DRAGNET	Capitol	7	5 Dec 53	1
DRAGNET [RE]	Capitol	11	9 Jan 54	1
Originally recorded by Henry Mancini.				

Richard ANTHONY — France

SINGLES:	HITS 2			WEEKS 15
WALKING ALONE	Columbia	37	14 Dec 63	5
IF I LOVED YOU	Columbia	48	4 Apr 64	1
From the film 'Carousel'.				
IF I LOVED YOU [RE]	Columbia	18	25 Apr 64	9
EPS:	HITS 2			WEEKS 11
RICHARD ANTHONY	Columbia	18	2 May 64	1
WALKIN' ALONE	Columbia	6	11 Jul 64	10

Truth ANTHONY – See Ronny JORDAN

ANTHRAX — US

SINGLES:	HITS 10			WEEKS 37
I AM THE LAW	Island	32	28 Feb 87	5
INDIANS	Island	44	27 Jun 87	4
I'M THE MAN (DEF UNCENSORED VERSION)	Island	20	5 Dec 87	6
MAKE ME LAUGH	Island	26	10 Sep 88	3
ANTI-SOCIAL	Island	44	18 Mar 89	3
IN MY WORLD	Island	29	1 Sep 90	2
GOT THE TIME	Island	16	5 Jan 91	4
Originally recorded by Joe Jackson.				
BRING THE NOISE	Island	14	6 Jul 91	5
Above hit: ANTHRAX featuring Chuck D from PUBLIC ENEMY.				
ONLY	Elektra	36	8 May 93	3
BLACK LODGE	Elektra	53	11 Sep 93	2
ALBUMS:	HITS 6			WEEKS 23
AMONG THE LIVING	Island	18	18 Apr 87	5
STATE OF EUPHORIA	Island	12	24 Sep 88	4
PERSISTENCE OF TIME	Island	13	8 Sep 90	5
ATTACK OF THE KILLER BS	Island	13	20 Jul 91	5
SOUND OF WHITE NOISE	Elektra	14	29 May 93	3
VOLUME 8 - THE THREAT IS REAL!	Ignition	73	1 Aug 98	1

ANTI-NOWHERE LEAGUE

SINGLES:	HITS 3			WEEKS 10
STREETS OF LONDON	WXYZ	48	23 Jan 82	5
I HATE . . . PEOPLE	WXYZ	46	20 Mar 82	3
WOMAN	WXYZ	72	3 Jul 82	2
ALBUMS:	HITS 2			WEEKS 12
WE ARE . . . THE LEAGUE	WXYZ	24	22 May 82	11
LIVE IN YUGOSLAVIA	Identity	88	5 Nov 83	1

ANTI-PASTI — UK

SINGLES:	HITS 1			WEEKS 1
DON'T LET 'EM GRIND YOU DOWN EP (EXTRACTS FROM THE EDINBURGH LIVE NITE [EP]	Superville	70	5 Dec 81	1
Live recordings with one side for each group, there is no actual track listing.				
Above hit: EXPLOITED / ANTI-PASTI.				

ALBUMS:	HITS 1			WEEKS 7
THE LAST CALL	Rondelet	31	15 Aug 81	7

ANTICAPPELLA

Italy/UK

SINGLES:	HITS 4			WEEKS 12
$\sqrt[2]{231}$	PWL Continental	24	16 Nov 91	4
EVERYDAY	PWL Continental	45	18 Apr 92	2
MOVE YOUR BODY	Media	21	25 Jun 94	3
Above hit: ANTICAPPELLA (featuring MC FIXX IT)				
EXPRESS YOUR FREEDOM	Media	31	1 Apr 95	2
$\sqrt[2]{231}$ [RM] / MOVE YOUR BODY [RI]	Media	54	25 May 96	1
Remixed by Ben Keen and Paul Thompson.				

ANTONIA – See BOMB THE BASS

Miki ANTONY

UK

SINGLES:	HITS 1			WEEKS 7
IF IT WASN'T FOR THE REASON THAT I LOVE YOU	Bell	27	3 Feb 73	7

ANUNA and the RTE CONCERT ORCHESTRA - See Bill WHELAN

A1

UK/Norway

SINGLES:	HITS 3			WEEKS 24
BE THE FIRST TO BELIEVE	Columbia	6	3 Jul 99	9
SUMMERTIME OF OUR LIVES	Columbia	5	11 Sep 99	6
SUMMERTIME OF OUR LIVES [RE]	Columbia	62	13 Nov 99	2
EVERYTIME / READY OR NOT	Columbia	3	20 Nov 99	7
ALBUMS:	HITS 1			WEEKS 5
HERE WE COME	Columbia	20	4 Dec 99	5

APACHE INDIAN

UK

SINGLES:	HITS 10			WEEKS 33
FE REAL	Ten Records	33	28 Nov 92	3
[AA] listed with Just Wanna Know by Maxi Priest.				
Above hit: Maxi PRIEST and APACHE INDIAN.				
ARRANGED MARRIAGE	Island	16	2 Jan 93	6
CHOK THERE	Island	30	27 Mar 93	4
NUFF VIBES [EP]	Island	5	14 Aug 93	10
Lead track: Caste System, though Boom Shack A Lak received more airplay.				
MOVIN' ON	Island	48	23 Oct 93	2
A response to the election of a right wing candidate to Tower Hamlets council.				
WRECKX SHOP	MCA	26	7 May 94	2
Above hit: WRECKX 'N' EFFECT (featuring APACHE INDIAN).				
MAKE WAY FOR THE INDIAN	Island	29	11 Feb 95	2
Above hit: APACHE INDIAN and Tim DOG.				
RAGGAMUFFIN GIRL	Island	31	22 Apr 95	2
Above hit: APACHE INDIAN with Frankie PAUL.				
LOVIN' (LET ME LOVE YOU)	Coalition	53	29 Mar 97	1
Vocals by Sameera Singh.				
REAL PEOPLE	Coalition	66	18 Oct 97	1
ALBUMS:	HITS 1			WEEKS 2
NO RESERVATIONS	Island	36	6 Feb 93	2

APHEX TWIN

UK

(See also Polygon Window.)

SINGLES:	HITS 6			WEEKS 12
DIGERIDOO	R&S	55	9 May 92	2
ON	Warp	32	27 Nov 93	3
VENTOLIN	Warp	49	8 Apr 95	1
GIRL/BOY [EP]	Warp	64	26 Oct 96	1
Lead track: Girl Boy. With 6 tracks, it should have qualified as an entry to the album charts.				
COME TO DADDY	Warp	36	18 Oct 97	2
WINDOWLICKER	Warp	16	3 Apr 99	3
Above hit: APHEXTWIN.				
ALBUMS:	HITS 4			WEEKS 8
SELECTED AMBIENT WORKS VOLUME II	Warp	11	19 Mar 94	3
CLASSICS	R&S	24	11 Feb 95	2
Compilation of early tracks.				
. . . I CARE BECAUSE YOU DO	Warp	24	6 May 95	2
RICHARD D. JAMES ALBUM	Warp	62	16 Nov 96	1

APHRODITE'S CHILD | | | Greece

SINGLES:		HITS 1		WEEKS 7
RAIN AND TEARS	Mercury	29	9 Nov 68	7

APOLLO FOUR FORTY | | | UK

SINGLES:		HITS 10		WEEKS 46
ASTRAL AMERICA	Stealth Sonic	36	22 Jan 94	2
LIQUID COOL (THEME FROM CRYONIC SUSPENSION)	Stealth Sonic	35	5 Nov 94	2
(DON'T FEAR) THE REAPER	Stealth Sonic	35	25 Mar 95	2
Above 3: APOLLO 440.				
KRUPA	Stealth Sonic	23	27 Jul 96	4
Tribute to jazz drummer Gene Krupa.				
KRUPA [RE]	Stealth Sonic	24	28 Sep 96	4
AIN'T TALKIN' 'BOUT DUB	Stealth Sonic	7	15 Feb 97	7
Samples Van Halen's Ain't Talking About Love.				
RAW POWER	Stealth Sonic	32	5 Jul 97	3
RENDEZ-VOUS 98	Epic	12	11 Jul 98	6
Theme to ITV's sports coverage of the World Cup 1998.				
Above hit: Jean Michel JARRE and APOLLO FOUR FORTY.				
LOST IN SPACE (THEME)	Stealth Sonic	94	8 Aug 98	9
From the film of the same name.				
STOP THE ROCK	Stealth Sonic	10	28 Aug 99	6
Vocals by Mary Mary (former lead singer with Gaye Bykers On Acid). Based on Status Quo's Caroline.				
HEART GO BOOM	Stealth Sonic	57	27 Nov 99	1
ALBUMS:		HITS 2		WEEKS 4
ELECTRO GLIDE IN BLUE	Stealth Sonic	62	15 Mar 97	1
GETTIN' HIGH ON YOUR OWN SUPPLY	Stealth Sonic	20	18 Sep 99	3

APOLLO presents - See HOUSE OF VIRGINISM

APOLLO 2000 | | | UK

ALBUMS:		HITS 1		WEEKS 3
OUT OF THIS WORLD	Telstar	43	27 Apr 96	3
Instrumental music from science fiction films and TV.				

Carmine APPICE - See Jeff BECK, Tim BOGERT and Carmine APPICE

Stan APPLEBAUM and His ORCHESTRA - See Neil SEDAKA

Kim APPLEBY | | | UK

(See also Mel and Kim.)

SINGLES:		HITS 7		WEEKS 31
DON'T WORRY	Parlophone	2	3 Nov 90	10
G.L.A.D.	Parlophone	10	9 Feb 91	6
MAMA	Parlophone	19	29 Jun 91	8
IF YOU CARED	Parlophone	44	19 Oct 91	3
LIGHT OF THE WORLD	Parlophone	41	31 Jul 93	2
BREAKAWAY	Parlophone	56	13 Nov 93	1
FREE SPIRIT	Parlophone	51	12 Nov 94	1
ALBUMS:		HITS 1		WEEKS 13
KIM APPLEBY	Parlophone	23	8 Dec 90	13

APPLEJACKS | | | UK

SINGLES:		HITS 3		WEEKS 29
TELL ME WHEN	Decca	7	7 Mar 64	13
LIKE DREAMERS DO	Decca	20	13 Jun 64	11
Written by Lennon/McCartney.				
THREE LITTLE WORDS (I LOVE YOU)	Decca	23	17 Oct 64	5

APPLES | | | UK

SINGLES:		HITS 1		WEEKS 1
EYE WONDER	Epic	75	23 Mar 91	1

Charlie APPLEWHITE with Victor YOUNG and his Orchestra and Chorus | | US

SINGLES:		HITS 1		WEEKS 1
BLUE STAR	Brunswick	20	24 Sep 55	1
Theme to the TV series 'The Medic'.				

Helen APRIL - See John DUMMER and Helen APRIL

APRIL WINE | | | Canada

SINGLES:		HITS 2		WEEKS 9
I LIKE TO ROCK	Capitol	41	15 Mar 80	5
JUST BETWEEN YOU AND ME	Capitol	52	11 Apr 81	4

ALBUMS:		HITS 2		WEEKS 8	
HARDER . . . FASTER	Capitol	34	15 Mar 80	5
THE NATURE OF THE BEAST	Capitol	48	24 Jan 81	3

AQUA
Denmark/Norway

SINGLES:		HITS 5		WEEKS 68	
BARBIE GIRL	Universal	1	25 Oct 97	24
DOCTOR JONES	Universal	1	7 Feb 98	14
BARBIE GIRL [RE]	Universal	66	25 Apr 98	2
TURN BACK TIME	Universal	1	16 May 98	10
From the film 'Sliding Doors'.				
MY OH MY	Universal	6	1 Aug 98	9
MY OH MY [RE]	Universal	66	17 Oct 98	2
GOOD MORNING SUNSHINE	Universal	18	26 Dec 98	7

ALBUMS:		HITS 1		WEEKS 47	
AQUARIUM	Universal	6	15 Nov 97	47

AQUA MARINA - See F.A.B.

AQUARIAN DREAM
US

SINGLES:		HITS 1		WEEKS 1	
YOU'RE A STAR	Elektra	67	24 Feb 79	1

ARAB STRAP
UK

SINGLES:		HITS 3		WEEKS 3	
THE GIRLS OF SUMMER [EP]	Chemikal Underground	74	13 Sep 97	1
Lead track: Hey! Fever.				
HERE WE GO / TRIPPY	Chemikal Underground	48	4 Apr 98	1
Trippy credits Tremendon O'Hare.				
(AFTERNOON) SOAPS	Chemikal Underground	74	10 Oct 98	1

ALBUMS:		HITS 1		WEEKS 2	
PHILOPHOBIA	Chemikal Underground	37	2 May 98	2

ARCADIA
UK

SINGLES:		HITS 3		WEEKS 13	
ELECTION DAY	Parlophone Odean Series	7	26 Oct 85	7
Includes narration by Grace Jones.				
THE PROMISE	Parlophone Odean Series	37	25 Jan 86	4
THE FLAME	Parlophone Odean Series	58	26 Jul 86	2

ALBUMS:		HITS 1		WEEKS 10	
SO RED THE ROSE	Parlophone Odean Series	30	7 Dec 85	10

Tasmin ARCHER
UK

SINGLES:		HITS 6		WEEKS 37	
SLEEPING SATELLITE	EMI	1	12 Sep 92	15
SLEEPING SATELLITE [RE]	EMI	67	2 Jan 93	2
IN YOUR CARE	EMI	16	20 Feb 93	6
LORDS OF THE NEW CHURCH	EMI	26	29 May 93	4
ARIENNE	EMI	30	21 Aug 93	4
SHIPBUILDING	EMI	40	8 Jan 94	4
Sleeve also gives title as an EP.				
ONE MORE GOOD NIGHT WITH THE BOYS	EMI	45	23 Mar 96	2

ALBUMS:		HITS 1		WEEKS 42	
GREAT EXPECTATIONS	EMI	8	31 Oct 92	42

ARCHIES
US

SINGLES:		HITS 1		WEEKS 26	
SUGAR, SUGAR	RCA Victor	1	11 Oct 69	26
Originally written for and rejected by the Monkees.				

Jann ARDEN
Canada

SINGLES:		HITS 1		WEEKS 2	
INSENSITIVE	A&M	40	13 Jul 96	2
From the film 'Bed Of Roses'.				

Tina ARENA
Australia

SINGLES:		HITS 7		WEEKS 31	
CHAINS	Columbia	6	15 Apr 95	11
HEAVEN HELP MY HEART	Columbia	25	12 Aug 95	5
SHOW ME HEAVEN	Columbia	29	2 Dec 95	3
SORRENTO MOON (I REMEMBER)	Columbia	22	3 Aug 96	4
WHISTLE DOWN THE WIND	Really Useful	24	27 Jun 98	5
From the Andrew Lloyd Webber/Jim Steinman musical of the same name.				

IF I WAS A RIVER	*Columbia*	43	*24 Oct 98*	2
BURN	*Columbia*	47	*13 Mar 99*	1
ALBUMS:	**HITS 1**		**WEEKS 15**	
DON'T ASK	*Columbia*	11	*20 May 95*	15

ARGENT   UK

(See also San Jose featuring Rodriguez Argentina; Silsoe.)

SINGLES:	**HITS 3**		**WEEKS 27**	
HOLD YOUR HEAD UP	*Epic*	5	*4 Mar 72*	12
TRAGEDY	*Epic*	34	*10 Jun 72*	7
GOD GAVE ROCK AND ROLL TO YOU	*Epic*	18	*24 Mar 73*	8
ALBUMS:	**HITS 2**		**WEEKS 9**	
ALL TOGETHER NOW	*Epic*	13	*29 Apr 72*	8
IN DEEP	*Epic*	49	*31 Mar 73*	1

ARIEL   UK

SINGLES:	**HITS 1**		**WEEKS 2**	
LET IT SLIDE	*Deconstruction*	57	*27 Mar 93*	2

ARIEL   UK

SINGLES:	**HITS 1**		**WEEKS 1**	
DEEP (I'M FALLING DEEPER)	*Wonderboy*	47	*21 Jun 97*	1

Originally released in 1992 on the Pilot Music label.

ARIZONA featuring ZEITIA   UK

SINGLES:	**HITS 1**		**WEEKS 1**	
I SPECIALIZE IN LOVE	*Union*	74	*12 Mar 94*	1

Ship's Company and Royal Marine Band Of H.M.S. ARK ROYAL   UK

SINGLES:	**HITS 1**		**WEEKS 6**	
THE LAST FAREWELL	*BBC*	46	*23 Dec 78*	6

Conductor: W.O. Keith Whittall.

ARKARNA   UK

SINGLES:	**HITS 2**		**WEEKS 3**	
HOUSE ON FIRE	*WEA*	33	*25 Jan 97*	2
SO LITTLE TIME	*WEA*	46	*2 Aug 97*	1

Joan ARMATRADING   UK

SINGLES:	**HITS 10**		**WEEKS 53**	
LOVE AND AFFECTION	*A&M*	10	*16 Oct 76*	9
ROSIE	*A&M*	49	*23 Feb 80*	5
ME MYSELF I	*A&M*	21	*14 Jun 80*	11
ALL THE WAY FROM AMERICA	*A&M*	54	*6 Sep 80*	3
I'M LUCKY	*A&M*	46	*12 Sep 81*	5
NO LOVE	*A&M*	50	*16 Jan 82*	5
DROP THE PILOT	*A&M*	11	*19 Feb 83*	10
TEMPTATION	*A&M*	65	*16 Mar 85*	2
MORE THAN ONE KIND OF LOVE	*A&M*	75	*26 May 90*	1
WRAPPED AROUND HER	*A&M*	56	*23 May 92*	2
ALBUMS:	**HITS 14**		**WEEKS 193**	
JOAN ARMATRADING	*A&M*	12	*4 Sep 76*	27
SHOW SOME EMOTION	*A&M*	6	*1 Oct 77*	11
TO THE LIMIT	*A&M*	13	*14 Oct 78*	10
ME MYSELF I	*A&M*	5	*24 May 80*	23
WALK UNDER LADDERS	*A&M*	6	*12 Sep 81*	29
THE KEY	*A&M*	10	*12 Mar 83*	14
TRACK RECORD	*A&M*	18	*26 Nov 83*	32
SECRET SECRETS	*A&M*	14	*16 Feb 85*	12
SLEIGHT OF HAND	*A&M*	34	*24 May 86*	6
THE SHOUTING STAGE	*A&M*	28	*16 Jul 88*	10
HEARTS AND FLOWERS	*A&M*	29	*16 Jun 90*	4
THE VERY BEST OF JOAN ARMATRADING	*A&M*	9	*16 Mar 91*	11
SQUARE THE CIRCLE	*A&M*	34	*20 Jun 92*	2
WHAT'S INSIDE	*RCA*	48	*10 Jun 95*	2

ARMIN   Holland

SINGLES:	**HITS 1**		**WEEKS 1**	
BLUE FEAR	*Xtravaganza*	45	*14 Feb 98*	1

ARMOURY SHOW · UK

SINGLES:	HITS 3			WEEKS 6
CASTLES IN SPAIN	*Parlophone*	69	*25 Aug 84*	2
WE CAN BE BRAVE AGAIN	*Parlophone*	66	*26 Jan 85*	1
LOVE IN ANGER	*Parlophone*	63	*17 Jan 87*	3
ALBUMS:	HITS 1			WEEKS 1
WAITING FOR THE FLOODS	*Parlophone*	57	*21 Sep 85*	1

Craig ARMSTRONG – See Shola AMA

Louis ARMSTRONG · US

(See also Various Artists: Films – Original Soundtracks 'The Five Pennies'.)

SINGLES:	HITS 8			WEEKS 93
TAKES TWO TO TANGO	*Brunswick*	6	*20 Dec 52*	10
A THEME FROM THE THREEPENNY OPERA (MACK THE KNIFE)	*Philips*	8	*14 Apr 56*	11
TAKE IT SATCH [EP]	*Philips*	29	*16 Jun 56*	1
Lead track: Tiger Rag. First hit single released in a picture sleeve.				
THE FAITHFUL HUSSAR	*Philips*	27	*14 Jul 56*	2
MACK THE KNIFE (THE THEME FROM THE THREEPENNY OPERA) [RI]	*Philips*	24	*7 Nov 59*	1
Above 4: Louis ARMSTRONG and his ALL STARS.				
HELLO, DOLLY!	*London*	4	*6 Jun 64*	14
From the musical of the same name.				
Above hit: Louis ARMSTRONG and the ALL STARS.				
WHAT A WONDERFUL WORLD / CABARET	*His Master's Voice*	1	*10 Feb 68*	29
Cabaret listed from 17 Feb 68.				
Above hit: Louis ARMSTRONG ORCHESTRA and CHORUS/Louis ARMSTRONG and his ALL STARS.				
THE SUNSHINE OF LOVE	*Stateside*	41	*29 Jun 68*	7
WHAT A WONDERFUL WORLD [RI]	*A&M*	53	*16 Apr 88*	5
From the film 'Good Morning Vietnam'.				
WE HAVE ALL THE TIME IN THE WORLD	*EMI*	3	*19 Nov 94*	11
Originally from the James Bond film 'On Her Majesty's Secret Service', re-issued after its inclusion in a Guinness TV commercial.				
WE HAVE ALL THE TIME IN THE WORLD [RE]	*EMI*	66	*18 Mar 95*	2
ALBUMS:	HITS 7			WEEKS 29
SATCHMO PLAYS KING OLIVER	*Audio Fidelity*	20	*22 Oct 60*	1
JAZZ CLASSICS	*Ace Of Hearts*	20	*28 Oct 61*	1
HELLO DOLLY	*London*	11	*27 Jun 64*	6
WHAT A WONDERFUL WORLD	*Stateside*	37	*16 Nov 68*	3
THE VERY BEST OF LOUIS ARMSTRONG	*Warwick*	30	*20 Feb 82*	3
THE ULTIMATE COLLECTION	*Bluebird*	48	*21 May 94*	3
WE HAVE ALL THE TIME IN THE WORLD – THE VERY BEST OF LOUIS ARMSTRONG	*EMI*	10	*17 Dec 94*	12

ARMY OF LOVERS · Sweden/France

SINGLES:	HITS 3			WEEKS 12
CRUCIFIED	*Ton Son Ton*	47	*17 Aug 91*	5
OBSESSION	*Ton Son Ton*	67	*28 Dec 91*	1
CRUCIFIED [RI]	*Ton Son Ton*	31	*15 Feb 92*	5
RIDE THE BULLET	*Ton Son Ton*	67	*18 Apr 92*	1

ARNEE and the TERMINATERS · UK

SINGLES:	HITS 1			WEEKS 7
I'LL BE BACK	*Epic*	5	*24 Aug 91*	7

ARNIE'S LOVE · US

SINGLES:	HITS 1			WEEKS 3
I'M OUT OF YOUR LIFE	*Streetwave*	67	*26 Nov 83*	3

David ARNOLD · UK

SINGLES:	HITS 3			WEEKS 13
PLAY DEAD	*Island*	12	*23 Oct 93*	6
From the film 'The Young Americans'.				
Above hit: BJORK and David ARNOLD.				
ON HER MAJESTY'S SECRET SERVICE	*East West*	7	*18 Oct 97*	5
Above hit: PROPELLERHEADS/David ARNOLD.				
DIAMONDS ARE FOREVER	*East West*	39	*22 Nov 97*	2
Above hit: David McALMONT/David ARNOLD.				
ALBUMS:	HITS 2			WEEKS 10
INDEPENDENCE DAY [OST]	*RCA Victor*	71	*17 Aug 96*	1
SHAKEN AND STIRRED	*East West*	11	*1 Nov 97*	9
Reworked James Bond themes.				

Eddy ARNOLD
US

SINGLES:		HITS 3			WEEKS 21
MAKE THE WORLD GO AWAY	RCA Victor	8	19 Feb 66	17
I WANT TO GO WITH YOU	RCA Victor	49	28 May 66	1
I WANT TO GO WITH YOU [RE]	RCA Victor	46	11 Jun 66	2
IF YOU WERE MINE MARY	RCA Victor	49	30 Jul 66	1

P.P. ARNOLD
US

SINGLES:		HITS 7			WEEKS 47
THE FIRST CUT IS THE DEEPEST	Immediate	18	6 May 67	10
THE TIME HAS COME	Immediate	47	5 Aug 67	2
(IF YOU THINK) YOU'RE GROOVY	Immediate	41	27 Jan 68	4
ANGEL OF THE MORNING	Immediate	29	13 Jul 68	11
BURN IT UP	Rhythm King	14	24 Sep 88	10
Above hit: BEATMASTERS with P.P. ARNOLD.				
EVAPOR 8	Network	6	11 Apr 92	6
Above hit: ALTERN 8 Guest Vocal P.P. ARNOLD.				
IT'S A BEAUTIFUL THING	MCA	12	28 Feb 98	4
Above hit: OCEAN COLOUR SCENE with PP ARNOLD.				

ARPEGGIO
US

SINGLES:		HITS 1			WEEKS 3
LOVE AND DESIRE	Polydor	63	31 Mar 79	3

ARRESTED DEVELOPMENT
US

SINGLES:		HITS 4			WEEKS 39
TENNESSEE	Cooltempo	46	16 May 92	4
TENNESSEE [RE]	Cooltempo	54	11 Jul 92	3
PEOPLE EVERYDAY	Cooltempo	2	24 Oct 92	14
Originally recorded by Sly & The Family Stone.				
MR. WENDAL / REVOLUTION	Cooltempo	4	9 Jan 93	9
TENNESSEE [RI]	Cooltempo	18	3 Apr 93	6
EASY MY MIND	Cooltempo	33	28 May 94	3

ALBUMS:		HITS 3			WEEKS 40
3 YEARS, 5 MONTHS AND 2 DAYS IN THE LIFE OF ARRESTED DEVELOPMENT	Cooltempo	3	31 Oct 92	34
Title refers to the time it took for the band to get a recording contract.				
UNPLUGGED	Cooltempo	40	10 Apr 93	3
ZINGALAMDUNI	Cooltempo	16	18 Jun 94	3

Steve ARRINGTON
US

SINGLES:		HITS 2			WEEKS 19
FEEL SO REAL	Atlantic	5	27 Apr 85	10
DANCIN' IN THE KEY OF LIFE	Atlantic	21	6 Jul 85	8
DANCIN' IN THE KEY OF LIFE [RE]	Atlantic	75	7 Sep 85	1

ALBUMS:		HITS 1			WEEKS 11
DANCIN' IN THE KEY OF LIFE	Atlantic	41	13 Apr 85	11

ARRIVAL
UK

SINGLES:		HITS 2			WEEKS 20
FRIENDS	Decca	8	10 Jan 70	9
Originally recorded by Terry Reid.				
I WILL SURVIVE	Decca	16	6 Jun 70	11

ARROLA - See RUFF DRIVERZ

ARROW
Montserrat

SINGLES:		HITS 2			WEEKS 15
HOT-HOT-HOT	Cooltempo	59	28 Jul 84	5
LONG TIME	London	30	13 Jul 85	7
HOT HOT HOT [RM]	The Hit Label	38	3 Sep 94	3
Remixed by Les Adams.				

ARROWS
US

SINGLES:		HITS 2			WEEKS 16
TOUCH TOO MUCH	RAK	8	25 May 74	9
MY LAST NIGHT WITH YOU	RAK	25	1 Feb 75	7

ARSENAL F.C.
UK

SINGLES:		HITS 3			WEEKS 15
GOOD OLD ARSENAL	Pye	16	8 May 71	7
Above hit: ARSENAL 1ST TEAM SQUAD.				

SHOUTING FOR THE GUNNERS	London	34	15 May 93	3

Above hit: ARSENAL F.A. CUP FINAL SQUAD '93 featuring Tippa IRIE and Peter HUNNINGDALE.

HOT STUFF	Grapevine	9	23 May 98	5

ART COMPANY — Holland

SINGLES:	HITS 1		WEEKS 11	
SUSANNA	Epic	12	26 May 84	11

ART OF NOISE — UK

SINGLES:	HITS 12		WEEKS 65	
CLOSE (TO THE EDIT)	ZTT	8	24 Nov 84	19
MOMENTS IN LOVE / BEAT BOX	ZTT	51	13 Apr 85	4

Beat Box originally reached No. 92 in 1984.

LEGS	China	69	9 Nov 85	1
PETER GUNN	China	8	22 Mar 86	9

Above hit: ART OF NOISE featuring Duane EDDY.

PARANOIMIA	China	12	21 Jun 86	9

Above hit: ART OF NOISE with Max HEADROOM.

DRAGNET	China	60	18 Jul 87	4
KISS	China	5	29 Oct 88	7

Above hit: ART OF NOISE featuring Tom JONES.

YEBO!	China	63	12 Aug 89	3

Above hit: ART OF NOISE featuring MAHLATHINI and the MAHOTELLA QUEENS.

ART OF LOVE	China	67	16 Jun 90	1
INSTRUMENTS OF DARKNESS (ALL OF US ARE ONE PEOPLE)	China	45	11 Jan 92	5
SHADES OF PARANOIMIA	China	53	29 Feb 92	2

Homage to the French poet Charles Baudelaire. Includes narration by John Hurt.
Above hit: ART OF NOISE Your Forecaster: RAKIM.

ALBUMS:	HITS 4		WEEKS 37	
(WHO'S AFRAID OF?) THE ART OF NOISE	ZTT	27	3 Nov 84	17
IN VISIBLE SILENCE	China	18	26 Apr 86	15
IN NO SENSE/NONSENSE	China	55	10 Oct 87	2
THE BEST OF THE ART OF NOISE	China	55	3 Dec 88	3

ART OF TRANCE — UK

SINGLES:	HITS 1		WEEKS 3	
MADAGASGA	Platipus	69	31 Oct 98	1
MADAGASCAR [RM]	Platipus	48	7 Aug 99	2

Remixed by Ferry Corsten.

ARTEMESIA — Holland

(See also Ethics; Moving Melodies; Subliminal Cuts.)

SINGLES:	HITS 1		WEEKS 3	
BITS + PIECES	Hooj Choons	46	15 Apr 95	2
BITS + PIECES [RE]	Hooj Choons	75	23 Sep 95	1

ARTFUL DODGER — UK

SINGLES:	HITS 1		WEEKS 4	
RE-REWIND THE CROWD SAY BO SELECTA	Relentless	2	11 Dec 99	4

Neil ARTHUR — UK

SINGLES:	HITS 1		WEEKS 2	
I LOVE I HATE	Chrysalis	50	5 Feb 94	2

ARTIST – See PRINCE

ARTISTS UNITED AGAINST APARTHEID — Multi-National

SINGLES:	HITS 1		WEEKS 8	
SUN CITY	Manhattan	21	23 Nov 85	8

Charity assembly for the Africa Fund.

ASCENSION — UK

SINGLES:	HITS 1		WEEKS 1	
SOMEONE	Perfecto	55	5 Jul 97	1

ASH — UK

SINGLES:	HITS 8		WEEKS 34	
KUNG FU	Infectious	57	1 Apr 95	1
GIRL FROM MARS	Infectious	11	12 Aug 95	5
ANGEL INTERCEPTOR	Infectious	14	21 Oct 95	4

GOLDFINGER	*Infectious*	5	*27 Apr 96*	5
OH YEAH	*Infectious*	6	*6 Jul 96*	7
OH YEAH [RE]	*Infectious*	69	*28 Sep 96*	1
A LIFE LESS ORDINARY	*Infectious*	10	*25 Oct 97*	5
From the film of the same name.				
JESUS SAYS	*Infectious*	15	*3 Oct 98*	4
WILD SURF	*Infectious*	31	*5 Dec 98*	2
ALBUMS:	**HITS 2**		**WEEKS 30**	
1977	*Infectious*	1	*18 May 96*	26
NU-CLEAR SOUNDS	*Infectious*	7	*17 Oct 98*	4

Leslie ASH - See QUENTIN and ASH

ASHA
Italy

SINGLES:	**HITS 1**		**WEEKS 2**	
J.J. TRIBUTE	*Ffrreedom*	38	*8 Jul 95*	2
Tribute to Janis Joplin.				

ASHAYE
UK

SINGLES:	**HITS 1**		**WEEKS 3**	
DON'T STOP TIL YOU GET ENOUGH (MICHAEL JACKSON MEDLEY) [M]	*Record Shack*	45	*15 Oct 83*	3

John ASHER
UK

SINGLES:	**HITS 1**		**WEEKS 6**	
LET'S TWIST AGAIN	*Creole*	14	*15 Nov 75*	6

ASHFORD and SIMPSON
UK

SINGLES:	**HITS 3**		**WEEKS 22**	
IT SEEMS TO HANG ON	*Warner Brothers*	48	*18 Nov 78*	4
SOLID	*Capitol*	3	*5 Jan 85*	15
BABIES	*Capitol*	56	*20 Apr 85*	3
ALBUMS:	**HITS 1**		**WEEKS 6**	
SOLID	*Capitol*	42	*16 Feb 85*	6

ASHTON, GARDNER AND DYKE
UK

SINGLES:	**HITS 1**		**WEEKS 14**	
THE RESURRECTION SHUFFLE	*Capitol*	3	*16 Jan 71*	14

ASIA
UK

SINGLES:	**HITS 3**		**WEEKS 13**	
HEAT OF THE MOMENT	*Geffen*	46	*3 Jul 82*	5
ONLY TIME WILL TELL	*Geffen*	54	*18 Sep 82*	3
DON'T CRY	*Geffen*	33	*13 Aug 83*	5
ALBUMS:	**HITS 3**		**WEEKS 50**	
ASIA	*Geffen*	11	*10 Apr 82*	38
ALPHA	*Geffen*	5	*20 Aug 83*	11
ASTRA	*Geffen*	68	*14 Dec 85*	1

ASIA BLUE
UK

SINGLES:	**HITS 1**		**WEEKS 2**	
ESCAPING	*Atomic*	50	*27 Jun 92*	2

ASIAN DUB FOUNDATION
UK

SINGLES:	**HITS 3**		**WEEKS 4**	
FREE SATPAL RAM	*ffrr*	56	*21 Feb 98*	1
In 1986 Satpal Ram was attacked by six fascists, he fought back, killing one and is serving a life sentence.				
BUZZIN'	*ffrr*	31	*2 May 98*	2
BLACK WHITE	*ffrr*	52	*4 Jul 98*	1
ALBUMS:	**HITS 1**		**WEEKS 3**	
RAFI'S REVENGE	*ffrr*	20	*23 May 98*	3

ASSEMBLY
UK

SINGLES:	**HITS 1**		**WEEKS 10**	
NEVER NEVER	*Mute*	4	*12 Nov 83*	10

ASSOCIATES
UK

SINGLES:	**HITS 7**		**WEEKS 47**	
PARTY FEARS TWO	*Associates*	9	*20 Feb 82*	10
CLUB COUNTRY	*Associates*	13	*8 May 82*	10
18 CARAT LOVE AFFAIR / LOVE HANGOVER	*Associates*	21	*7 Aug 82*	8
Love Hangover no longer listed from 28 Aug 82.				

THOSE FIRST IMPRESSIONS	*WEA*	43	*16 Jun 84*	6
WAITING FOR THE LOVEBOAT	*WEA*	53	*1 Sep 84*	4
BREAKFAST	*WEA*	49	*19 Jan 85*	6
HEART OF GLASS	*WEA*	56	*17 Sep 88*	3
ALBUMS:	**HITS 3**		**WEEKS 28**	
SULK	*Associates*	10	*22 May 82*	20
PERHAPS	*WEA*	23	*16 Feb 85*	7
WILD AND LONELY	*Circa*	71	*31 Mar 90*	1

ASSOCIATION
US

SINGLES:	**HITS 1**		**WEEKS 8**	
TIME FOR LIVIN'	*Warner Brothers*	23	*25 May 68*	8

Rick ASTLEY
UK

SINGLES:	**HITS 12**		**WEEKS 91**	
NEVER GONNA GIVE YOU UP	*RCA*	1	*8 Aug 87*	18
WHENEVER YOU NEED SOMEBODY	*RCA*	3	*31 Oct 87*	12
Originally recorded by Ochi Brown in 1985.				
WHEN I FALL IN LOVE / MY ARMS KEEP MISSING YOU	*RCA*	2	*12 Dec 87*	10
When I Fall In Love listed only until 9 Jan 88 after which My Arms Keep Missing You was the *side listed. When I Fall In Love originally recorded by Doris Day.*				
TOGETHER FOREVER	*RCA*	2	*27 Feb 88*	9
SHE WANTS TO DANCE WITH ME	*RCA*	6	*24 Sep 88*	10
TAKE ME TO YOUR HEART	*RCA*	8	*26 Nov 88*	10
HOLD ME IN YOUR ARMS	*RCA*	10	*11 Feb 89*	8
CRY FOR HELP	*RCA*	7	*26 Jan 91*	7
MOVE RIGHT OUT	*RCA*	58	*30 Mar 91*	2
NEVER KNEW LOVE	*RCA*	70	*29 Jun 91*	1
THE ONES YOU LOVE	*RCA*	48	*4 Sep 93*	2
HOPELESSLY	*RCA*	33	*13 Nov 93*	2
ALBUMS:	**HITS 3**		**WEEKS 62**	
WHENEVER YOU NEED SOMEBODY	*RCA*	1	*28 Nov 87*	34
HOLD ME IN YOUR ARMS	*RCA*	8	*10 Dec 88*	19
FREE	*RCA*	9	*2 Mar 91*	9

ASTRO TRAX TEAM featuring Shola PHILLIPS
UK

SINGLES:	**HITS 1**		**WEEKS 1**	
THE ENERGY (FEEL THE VIBE)	*Satellite*	74	*24 Oct 98*	1

ASWAD
UK

SINGLES:	**HITS 16**		**WEEKS 80**	
CHASING FOR THE BREEZE	*Island*	51	*3 Mar 84*	3
54-46 (WAS MY NUMBER)	*Island*	70	*6 Oct 84*	3
Originally recorded by the Maytals.				
DON'T TURN AROUND	*Island*	1	*27 Feb 88*	12
Original version by Tina Turner.				
GIVE A LITTLE LOVE	*Mango*	11	*21 May 88*	8
Original version by Bucks Fizz.				
SET THEM FREE	*Mango*	70	*24 Sep 88*	2
BEAUTY'S ONLY SKIN DEEP	*Mango*	31	*1 Apr 89*	6
ON AND ON	*Mango*	25	*22 Jul 89*	8
Original by Stephen Bishop reached No. 11 in the US in 1977.				
NEXT TO YOU	*Mango*	24	*18 Aug 90*	6
SMILE	*Mango*	53	*17 Nov 90*	2
Above hit: ASWAD featuring Sweetie IRIE.				
TOO WICKED [EP]	*Mango*	61	*30 Mar 91*	2
Lead track: Best Of My Love.				
HOW LONG	*Polydor*	31	*31 Jul 93*	5
Above hit: YAZZ and ASWAD.				
DANCE HALL MOOD	*Bubblin'*	48	*9 Oct 93*	2
SHINE	*Bubblin'*	5	*18 Jun 94*	14
WARRIORS	*Bubblin'*	33	*17 Sep 94*	3
YOU'RE NO GOOD	*Bubblin'*	35	*18 Feb 95*	3
IF I WAS	*Bubblin'*	58	*5 Aug 95*	1
ALBUMS:	**HITS 9**		**WEEKS 60**	
NOT SATISFIED	*CBS*	50	*24 Jul 82*	6
LIVE AND DIRECT	*Island*	57	*10 Dec 83*	16
REBEL SOULS	*Island*	48	*3 Nov 84*	2
TO THE TOP	*Simba*	71	*28 Jun 86*	3
DISTANT THUNDER	*Mango*	10	*9 Apr 88*	15
RENAISSANCE	*Stylus*	52	*3 Dec 88*	8
TOO WICKED	*Mango*	51	*29 Sep 90*	2
RISE AND SHINE	*Bubblin'*	38	*9 Jul 94*	5
GREATEST HITS	*Bubblin'*	20	*12 Aug 95*	3

Gali ATARI – See MILK and HONEY featuring Gali ATARI

ATB
Germany

SINGLES:	HITS 2			WEEKS 34
(9PM) 'TIL I COME	Data	68	13 Mar 99	1
Australian import.				
9PM (TILL I COME)	Club Tools	72	22 May 99	3
German import.				
9PM (TILL I COME)	DanceNet	63	19 Jun 99	1
9PM (TILL I COME) [RE]	Club Tools	47	19 Jun 99	2
9PM (TILL I COME) [RM]	Sound Of Ministry	1	3 Jul 99	15
Remixed by Andre 'ATB' Tanneberger.				
DON'T STOP	Club Tools	61	9 Oct 99	2
Import. Vocals by Yolanda Rivera.				
DON'T STOP [RM]	Sound Of Ministry	3	23 Oct 99	9
DON'T STOP [RM] [RE]	Sound Of Ministry	74	1 Jan 00	1

ATHLETICO SPIZZ 80
UK

ALBUMS:	HITS 1			WEEKS 5
DO A RUNNER	A&M	27	26 Jul 80	5

Chet ATKINS
US

(See also Chet Atkins and Mark Knopfler.)

SINGLES:	HITS 1			WEEKS 2
TEENSVILLE	RCA	46	19 Mar 60	1
TEENSVILLE [RE]	RCA	49	7 May 60	1
EPS:	**HITS 1**			**WEEKS 1**
GUITAR GENIUS	RCA Victor	19	21 Dec 63	1
ALBUMS:	**HITS 3**			**WEEKS 5**
THE OTHER CHET ATKINS	RCA	20	18 Mar 61	1
CHET ATKINS' WORKSHOP	RCA	19	17 Jun 61	1
CARIBBEAN GUITAR	RCA Victor	17	25 Feb 63	3

Chet ATKINS and Mark KNOPFLER
US

(See also Chet Atkins; Mark Knopfler.)

ALBUMS:	HITS 1			WEEKS 11
NECK AND NECK	CBS	41	24 Nov 90	11

Rowan ATKINSON
UK

ALBUMS:	HITS 1			WEEKS 9
LIVE IN BELFAST	Arista	44	7 Feb 81	9

ATLANTA RHYTHM SECTION
US

SINGLES:	HITS 1			WEEKS 4
SPOOKY	Polydor	48	27 Oct 79	4
Originally recorded by Mike Sharpe.				

ATLANTIC OCEAN
Holland

SINGLES:	HITS 3			WEEKS 14
WATERFALL	Eastern Bloc	22	19 Feb 94	6
BODY IN MOTION	Eastern Bloc	15	2 Jul 94	4
MUSIC IS A PASSION	Eastern Bloc	59	26 Nov 94	1
Vocals by Farida and Rowetta.				
WATERFALL [RI]	Eastern Bloc	21	30 Nov 96	3

ATLANTIC STARR
US

SINGLES:	HITS 8			WEEKS 48
GIMME YOUR LUVIN'	A&M	66	9 Sep 78	3
SILVER SHADOW	A&M	41	29 Jun 85	6
ONE LOVE	A&M	58	7 Sep 85	4
SECRET LOVERS	A&M	10	15 Mar 86	12
IF YOUR HEART IS'NT IN IT	A&M	48	24 May 86	4
ALWAYS	Warner Brothers	3	13 Jun 87	14
ONE LOVER AT A TIME	Warner Brothers	57	12 Sep 87	3
EVERYBODY'S GOT SUMMER	Arista	36	27 Aug 94	2
ALBUMS:	**HITS 3**			**WEEKS 19**
AS THE BAND TURNS	A&M	64	15 Jun 85	3
THE ARTISTS VOLUME 2	Street Sounds	45	13 Jul 85	4
Compilation album with tracks by each artist.				
Above hit: Luther VANDROSS/Teddy PENDERGRASS/CHANGE/ATLANTIC STARR.				
ALL IN THE NAME OF LOVE	Warner Brothers	48	11 Jul 87	12

ATMOSFEAR
UK

SINGLES:		HITS 1		WEEKS 7
DANCING IN OUTER SPACE	MCA	46	17 Nov 79	7

ATOMIC KITTEN
UK

SINGLES:		HITS 1		WEEKS 4
RIGHT NOW	Innocent	10	11 Dec 99	4

ATOMIC ROOSTER
UK

SINGLES:		HITS 2		WEEKS 25
TOMORROW NIGHT	B&C	11	6 Feb 71	12
DEVIL'S ANSWER	B&C	4	10 Jul 71	13
ALBUMS:		HITS 3		WEEKS 13
ATOMIC ROOSTER	B&C	49	13 Jun 70	1
DEATH WALKS BEHIND YOU	Charisma	12	16 Jan 71	8
IN HEARING OF ATOMIC ROOSTER	Pegasus	18	21 Aug 71	4

Winifred ATWELL and her 'Other Piano'
UK

(See also All Star Hit Parade.)

SINGLES:		HITS 15		WEEKS 117
BRITTANNIA RAG	Decca	11	13 Dec 52	1
BRITTANNIA RAG [RE]	Decca	5	10 Jan 53	5
CORONATION RAG	Decca	12	16 May 53	1
CORONATION RAG [RE]	Decca	5	30 May 53	5
FLIRTATION WALTZ	Decca	12	26 Sep 53	1
FLIRTATION WALTZ [RE-1ST]	Decca	10	10 Oct 53	1
FLIRTATION WALTZ [RE-2ND]	Decca	12	7 Nov 53	1
LET'S HAVE A PARTY [M]	Philips	2	5 Dec 53	9
RACHMANINOFF'S 18TH VARIATION ON A THEME BY PAGANINI	Philips	9	24 Jul 54	7
From the film 'The Story Of Three Loves'.				
Above hit: Winifred ATWELL with Wally STOTT and his Orchestra (and re-entry below).				
RACHMANINOFF'S 18TH VARIATION ON A THEME BY PAGANINI [RE]	Philips	19	2 Oct 54	2
LET'S HAVE A PARTY [M] [RE]	Philips	14	27 Nov 54	6
LET'S HAVE ANOTHER PARTY [M]	Philips	1	27 Nov 54	8
LET'S HAVE A DING DONG [M]	Decca	3	5 Nov 55	10
THE POOR PEOPLE OF PARIS	Decca	1	17 Mar 56	16
PORT-AU-PRINCE	Decca	18	19 May 56	6
Above hit: Winifred ATWELL and Frank CHACKSFIELD.				
THE LEFT BANK (C'EST A HAMBOURG)	Decca	14	21 Jul 56	7
MAKE IT A PARTY [M]	Decca	7	27 Oct 56	12
LETS ROCK 'N' ROLL [M]	Decca	28	23 Feb 57	2
LETS ROCK 'N' ROLL [M] [RE]	Decca	24	16 Mar 57	2
LET'S HAVE A BALL [M]	Decca	4	7 Dec 57	6
THE SUMMER OF THE SEVENTEENTH DOLL	Decca	24	8 Aug 59	2
PIANO PARTY [M]	Decca	10	28 Nov 59	7

AU PAIRS
UK

ALBUMS:		HITS 2		WEEKS 10
PLAYING WITH A DIFFERENT SEX	Human	33	6 Jun 81	7
SENSE AND SENSUALITY	Kamera	79	4 Sep 82	3

AUDIOWEB
UK

SINGLES:		HITS 8		WEEKS 12
SLEEPER	Mother	74	14 Oct 95	1
YEAH?	Mother	73	9 Mar 96	1
INTO MY WORLD	Mother	42	15 Jun 96	1
SLEEPER [RI]	Mother	50	19 Oct 96	2
BANKROBBER	Mother	19	15 Feb 97	2
FAKER	Mother	70	24 May 97	1
POLICEMAN SKANK . . . (THE STORY OF MY LIFE)	Mother	21	25 Apr 98	2
PERSONAL FEELING	Mother	65	4 Jul 98	1
TEST THE THEORY	Mother	56	20 Feb 99	1
ALBUMS:		HITS 1		WEEKS 1
AUDIOWEB	Mother	70	9 Nov 96	1

Brian AUGER – See Julie DRISCOLL, Brian AUGER and the TRINITY

AURA – See POPPERS present AURA

AURORA
UK

SINGLES:		HITS 1		WEEKS 1
HEAR YOU CALLING	Additive	71	5 Jun 99	1
Vocals by Sally Anne Marsh.				

AURRA   US

SINGLES:	HITS 2			WEEKS 18
LIKE I LIKE IT	10 Records	51	4 May 85	5
YOU AND ME TONIGHT	10 Records	12	19 Apr 86	8
LIKE I LIKE IT [RM]	10 Records	43	21 Jun 86	5

Remixed by Timmy Reggisford and Boyd Jarvis.

Adam AUSTIN   UK

SINGLES:	HITS 1			WEEKS 1
CENTERFOLD	Power Station	41	13 Feb 99	1

David AUSTIN   UK

SINGLES:	HITS 1			WEEKS 3
TURN TO GOLD	Parlophone	68	21 Jul 84	3

Patti AUSTIN   US

(See also Quincy Jones.)

SINGLES:	HITS 2			WEEKS 11
BABY, COME TO ME	Qwest	11	12 Feb 83	10
Above hit: Patti AUSTIN and James INGRAM.				
I'LL KEEP YOUR DREAMS ALIVE	Ammi	68	5 Sep 92	1
Above hit: George BENSON and Patti AUSTIN.				
ALBUMS:	HITS 1			WEEKS 1
EVERY HOME SHOULD HAVE ONE	Qwest	99	26 Sep 81	1

AUTECHRE   UK

SINGLES:	HITS 1			WEEKS 1
BASSCAD [EP]	Warp	56	7 May 94	1

Various mixes of the track Basscadetmxs spread over 3 10"/1 CD formats.

AUTEURS   UK

SINGLES:	HITS 5			WEEKS 9
LENNY VALENTINO	Hut	41	27 Nov 93	2
CHINESE BAKERY	Hut	42	23 Apr 94	2
BACK WITH THE KILLER [EP]	Hut	45	6 Jan 96	3
Lead track: Unsolved Child Murder.				
LIGHT AIRCRAFT ON FIRE	Hut	58	24 Feb 96	1
THE RUBETTES	Hut	66	3 Jul 99	1
ALBUMS:	HITS 3			WEEKS 4
NEW WAVE	Hut	35	6 Mar 93	2
NOW I'M A COWBOY	Hut	27	21 May 94	1
AFTER MURDER PARK	Hut	53	16 Mar 96	1

AUTUMN   UK

SINGLES:	HITS 1			WEEKS 6
MY LITTLE GIRL	Pye	37	16 Oct 71	6

Peter AUTY - See SNOWMAN

Frankie AVALON   US

SINGLES:	HITS 4			WEEKS 15
GINGER BREAD	His Master's Voice	30	11 Oct 58	1
VENUS	His Master's Voice	16	25 Apr 59	6
WHY	His Master's Voice	20	23 Jan 60	4
DON'T THROW AWAY ALL THOSE TEARDROPS	His Master's Voice	37	30 Apr 60	4

AVALON BOYS - See LAUREL and HARDY

AVERAGE WHITE BAND   UK

SINGLES:	HITS 7			WEEKS 47
PICK UP THE PIECES	Atlantic	6	22 Feb 75	9
CUT THE CAKE	Atlantic	31	26 Apr 75	4
QUEEN OF MY SOUL	Atlantic	23	9 Oct 76	7
WALK ON BY	RCA Victor	46	28 Apr 79	5
WHEN WILL YOU BE MINE	RCA	49	25 Aug 79	5
LET'S GO ROUND AGAIN	RCA	12	26 Apr 80	11
FOR YOU FOR LOVE	RCA	46	26 Jul 80	4
LET'S GO ROUND AGAIN [RM]	The Hit Label	56	26 Mar 94	2
Remixed by CCN.				
ALBUMS:	HITS 6			WEEKS 50
AVERAGE WHITE BAND	Atlantic	6	1 Mar 75	14
CUT THE CAKE	Atlantic	28	5 Jul 75	4
SOUL SEARCHING TIME	Atlantic	60	31 Jul 76	1

I FEEL NO FRET	*RCA Victor*	15	*10 Mar 79*	15
SHINE	*RCA*	14	*31 May 80*	13
LET'S GO ROUND AGAIN – THE BEST OF THE AVERAGE WHITE BAND	*The Hit Label*	38	*2 Apr 94*	3

Kevin AVIANCE   US

SINGLES:		**HITS 1**		**WEEKS 1**
DIN DA DA	*Distinct'ive*	65	*13 Jun 98*	1

Originally recorded by George Krantz.

AVONS   UK

SINGLES:		**HITS 4**		**WEEKS 22**
SEVEN LITTLE GIRLS SITTING IN THE BACK SEAT	*Columbia*	3	*14 Nov 59*	13
WE'RE ONLY YOUNG ONCE	*Columbia*	49	*9 Jul 60*	1
WE'RE ONLY YOUNG ONCE [RE]	*Columbia*	45	*23 Jul 60*	1
FOUR LITTLE HEELS	*Columbia*	45	*29 Oct 60*	2
FOUR LITTLE HEELS [RE]	*Columbia*	49	*3 Dec 60*	1
RUBBER BALL	*Columbia*	30	*28 Jan 61*	4

AWAKENING – See MISTA E featuring the AWAKENING

AWESOME   UK

SINGLES:		**HITS 2**		**WEEKS 2**
RUMOURS	*Universal*	58	*8 Nov 97*	1
CRAZY	*Universal*	63	*21 Mar 98*	1

AWESOME 3   UK

SINGLES:		**HITS 2**		**WEEKS 8**
HARD UP	*A&M*	55	*8 Sep 90*	3
DON'T GO	*Citybeat*	75	*3 Oct 92*	1
DON'T GO '94 [RM-1ST]	*Citybeat*	45	*4 Jun 94*	2
Remixed by Mark and Adrian Luvdup.				
DON'T GO [RM-2ND]	*XL Recordings*	27	*26 Oct 96*	2

Remixed by Dancing Divas.
Above hit: AWESOME 3 featuring Julie McDERMOTT.

Hoyt AXTON   US

SINGLES:		**HITS 1**		**WEEKS 4**
DELLA AND THE DEALER	*Young Blood*	48	*7 Jun 80*	4

AXUS   UK

SINGLES:		**HITS 1**		**WEEKS 1**
ABACUS (WHEN I FALL IN LOVE)	*INCredible*	62	*26 Sep 98*	1

Roy AYERS   US

SINGLES:		**HITS 4**		**WEEKS 13**
GET ON UP, GET ON DOWN	*Polydor*	41	*21 Oct 78*	4
HEAT OF THE BEAT	*Polydor*	43	*13 Jan 79*	5
Above hit: Roy AYERS/Wayne HENDERSON.				
DON'T STOP THE FEELING	*Polydor*	56	*2 Feb 80*	3
EXPANSIONS	*Soma Recordings*	68	*16 May 98*	1
Above hit: Scott GROOVES featuring Roy AYERS.				
ALBUMS:		**HITS 1**		**WEEKS 2**
YOU MIGHT BE SURPRISED	*CBS*	91	*26 Oct 85*	2

AYLA   Germany

SINGLES:		**HITS 1**		**WEEKS 3**
AYLA	*Positiva*	22	*4 Sep 99*	3

Original release on the Additive label reached No. 198 in 1998.

Mitchell AYRES' ORCHESTRA – See Perry COMO

Pam AYRES   UK

ALBUMS:		**HITS 2**		**WEEKS 29**
SOME OF ME POEMS AND SONGS	*Galaxy*	13	*27 Mar 76*	23
SOME MORE OF ME POEMS AND SONGS	*Galaxy*	23	*11 Dec 76*	6

Live recordings from the Queen Elizabeth Hall, London, 22 Sep 76.

AZ   US

SINGLES:		**HITS 1**		**WEEKS 1**
SUGARHILL	*Cooltempo*	67	*30 Mar 96*	1

AZ YET
US

SINGLES:	HITS 2			WEEKS 10
LAST NIGHT	LaFace	21	1 Mar 97	3
From the film 'The Nutty Professor'.				
HARD TO SAY I'M SORRY	LaFace	7	21 Jun 97	7
Above hit: AZ YET featuring Peter CETERA.				

Charles AZNAVOUR
France

SINGLES:	HITS 2			WEEKS 29
THE OLD FASHIONED WAY (LES PLAISIRS DEMODES)	Barclay	50	22 Sep 73	1
THE OLD FASHIONED WAY (LES PLAISIRS DEMODES) [RE-1ST]	Barclay	38	20 Oct 73	12
SHE	Barclay	1	22 Jun 74	14
Theme from the ITV series 'Seven Faces Of Woman'.				
THE OLD FASHIONED WAY (LES PLAISIRS DEMODES) [RE-2ND]	Barclay	47	27 Jul 74	2
ALBUMS:	HITS 3			WEEKS 21
AZNAVOUR SINGS AZNAVOUR VOLUME 3	Barclay	23	29 Jun 74	1
A TAPESTRY OF DREAMS	Barclay	9	7 Sep 74	13
HIS GREATEST LOVE SONGS	K-Tel	73	2 Aug 80	1

AZTEC CAMERA
UK

SINGLES:	HITS 11			WEEKS 74
OBLIVIOUS	Rough Trade	47	19 Feb 83	6
WALK OUT TO THE WINTER	Rough Trade	64	4 Jun 83	4
OBLIVIOUS [RI]	WEA	18	5 Nov 83	11
ALL I NEED IS EVERYTHING / JUMP	WEA	34	1 Sep 84	6
Jump listed from 22 Sep 84.				
HOW MEN ARE	WEA	25	13 Feb 88	9
SOMEWHERE IN MY HEART	WEA	3	23 Apr 88	14
WORKING IN A GOLDMINE	WEA	31	6 Aug 88	5
DEEP & WIDE & TALL	WEA	55	8 Oct 88	3
Original release reached No. 79 in 1987.				
THE CRYING SCENE	WEA	70	7 Jul 90	3
GOOD MORNING BRITAIN	WEA	19	6 Oct 90	8
Above hit: AZTEC CAMERA and Mick JONES.				
SPANISH HORSES	WEA	52	18 Jul 92	3
DREAM SWEET DREAMS	WEA	67	1 May 93	2
ALBUMS:	HITS 6			WEEKS 80
HIGH LAND, HARD RAIN	Rough Trade	22	23 Apr 83	18
KNIFE	WEA	14	29 Sep 84	6
LOVE	WEA	49	21 Nov 87	12
LOVE [RE]	WEA	10	23 Apr 88	31
STRAY	WEA	22	16 Jun 90	7
DREAMLAND	WEA	21	29 May 93	2
THE BEST OF AZTEC CAMERA	warner.esp	36	7 Aug 99	4

AZURE
Italy

SINGLES:	HITS 1			WEEKS 2
MAMA USED TO SAY	Inferno	56	25 Apr 98	2

AZYMUTH
Brazil

SINGLES:	HITS 1			WEEKS 8
JAZZ CARNIVAL	Milestone	19	12 Jan 80	8

Bob AZZAM and his Orchestra
Egypt

SINGLES:	HITS 1			WEEKS 14
MUSTAPHA	Decca	23	28 May 60	14

B

Derek B
UK

SINGLES:	HITS 3			WEEKS 15
GOODGROOVE	Music Of Life	16	27 Feb 88	6
BAD YOUNG BROTHER	Tuff Audio	16	7 May 88	6
WE'VE GOT THE JUICE	Tuff Audio	56	2 Jul 88	3
ALBUMS:	HITS 1			WEEKS 9
BULLET FROM A GUN	Tuff Audio	11	28 May 88	9

Eric B. and RAKIM · UK

(See also Rakim.)

SINGLES:		HITS 6		WEEKS 26	
PAID IN FULL (THE COLD CUT REMIX)	Fourth & Broadway	15	7 Nov 87	6
MOVE THE CROWD	Fourth & Broadway	53	20 Feb 88	2
I KNOW YOU GOT SOUL (THE DOUBLE TROUBLE REMIX)	Cooltempo	13	12 Mar 88	6

Original release reached No. 76 in 1987.

FOLLOW THE LEADER	MCA	21	2 Jul 88	5
MICROPHONE FIEND	MCA	74	19 Nov 88	1
FRIENDS	MCA	21	12 Aug 89	6

Above hit: Jody WATLEY with Eric B. and RAKIM.

ALBUMS:		HITS 4		WEEKS 10	
PAID IN FULL	Fourth & Broadway	85	12 Sep 87	4
FOLLOW THE LEADER	MCA	25	6 Aug 88	4
LET THE RHYTHM HIT 'EM	MCA	58	7 Jul 90	1
DON'T SWEAT THE TECHNIQUE	MCA	73	11 Jul 92	1

Howie B · UK

SINGLES:		HITS 3		WEEKS 4	
ANGELS GO BALD: TOO	Polydor	36	19 Jul 97	2
SWITCH	Polydor	62	18 Oct 97	1
TAKE YOUR PARTNER BY THE HAND	Polydor	74	11 Apr 98	1

Above hit: Howie B featuring Robbie ROBERTSON.

ALBUMS:		HITS 1		WEEKS 1	
TURN THE DARK OFF	Polydor	58	9 Aug 97	1

Jazzie B - See Maxi PRIEST; SOUL II SOUL

Jon B · US

SINGLES:		HITS 1		WEEKS 2	
THEY DON'T KNOW	Epic	32	17 Oct 98	2

Lisa B · US

SINGLES:		HITS 3		WEEKS 9	
GLAM	ffrr	49	12 Jun 93	2
FASCINATED	London	35	25 Sep 93	3
YOU AND ME	ffrr	39	8 Jan 94	4

Lorna B - See DJ SCOTT featuring Lorna B; ZERO VU featuring Lorna B

Melanie B · UK

SINGLES:		HITS 2		WEEKS 17	
I WANT YOU BACK	Virgin	1	26 Sep 98	9

From the film 'Why Do Fools Fall In Love'.
Melanie B featuring Missy "Misdemeanor" ELLIOTT

WORD UP	Virgin	14	10 Jul 99	7

From the film 'Austin Powers – The Spy Who Shagged Me'.
Above hit: Melanie G.

WORD UP [RE]	Virgin	71	25 Sep 99	1

Sandy B · US

SINGLES:		HITS 3		WEEKS 8	
FEEL LIKE SINGIN'	Nervous	60	20 Feb 93	1

Originally recorded by Tak Tix.

MAKE THE WORLD GO ROUND	Champion	73	18 May 96	1
MAKE THE WORLD GO ROUND [RM]	Champion	35	24 May 97	2

Remixed by Deep Dish.

AIN'T NO NEED TO HIDE	Champion	60	8 Nov 97	1
MAKE THE WORLD GO ROUND [RM] [RI]	Champion	20	28 Feb 98	3

Stevie B · US

SINGLES:		HITS 1		WEEKS 9	
BECAUSE I LOVE YOU (THE POSTMAN SONG)	Polydor	6	23 Feb 91	9

Tairrie B · US

SINGLES:		HITS 1		WEEKS 2	
MURDER SHE WROTE	MCA	71	1 Dec 90	2

B.A.D. - See BIG AUDIO DYNAMITE

B B and Q BAND · US

SINGLES:		HITS 4		WEEKS 15	
ON THE BEAT	Capitol	41	18 Jul 81	5

GENIE	Cooltempo	40	6 Jul 85	4
Above hit: BROOKLYN BRONX and QUEENS (B.B.& Q.).				
DREAMER	Cooltempo	35	20 Sep 86	5
Above hit: BB + Q BROOKLYN BRONX and QUEENS.				
RICCOCHET	Cooltempo	71	17 Oct 87	1
Above hit: B B and Q.				

B.B.E.   France/Italy

SINGLES:	HITS 4			WEEKS 20
SEVEN DAYS AND ONE WEEK	Positiva	3	28 Sep 96	9
Title refers to how long track took to make.				
FLASH	Positiva	5	29 Mar 97	5
DESIRE	Positiva	19	14 Feb 98	3
DEEPER LOVE (SYMPHONIC PARADISE)	Positiva	19	30 May 98	3
ALBUMS:	**HITS 1**			**WEEKS 2**
GAMES	Positiva	60	28 Feb 98	2

B BOYS   US

ALBUMS:	HITS 1			WEEKS 1
CUTTIN' HERBIE	Street Sounds	90	28 Jan 84	1

B-CREW featuring Barbara TUCKER, Ultra NATE, DAJAE, MONE   US

SINGLES:	HITS 1			WEEKS 1
PARTAY FEELING	Positiva	45	20 Sep 97	1

B.E.F.   UK/US

SINGLES:	HITS 1			WEEKS 5
FAMILY AFFAIR	Ten Records	37	27 Jul 91	5
Originally recorded by Sly and the Family Stone.				
Above hit: B.E.F. featuring Lalah HATHAWAY.				

B-52'S   US

SINGLES:	HITS 10			WEEKS 61
ROCK LOBSTER	Island	37	11 Aug 79	5
GIVE ME BACK MY MAN	Island	61	9 Aug 80	3
SONG FOR A FUTURE GENERATION	Island	63	7 May 83	2
ROCK LOBSTER [RI] / PLANET CLARE	Island	12	10 May 86	7
Planet Clare listed from 17 May 86.				
LOVE SHACK	Reprise	2	3 Mar 90	13
ROAM	Reprise	17	19 May 90	7
CHANNEL Z	Reprise	61	18 Aug 90	2
GOOD STUFF	Reprise	21	20 Jun 92	6
TELL IT LIKE IT T-I-IS	Reprise	61	12 Sep 92	3
(MEET) THE FLINTSTONES	MCA	3	9 Jul 94	12
From the film 'The Flintstones'.				
Above hit: BC-52'S.				
LOVE SHACK 99 [RM]	Reprise	66	30 Jan 99	1
Remixed by Mike Koglin and Vanessa Quinones (Espiritiu).				
ALBUMS:	**HITS 9**			**WEEKS 69**
THE B-52'S	Island	22	4 Aug 79	12
WILD PLANET	Island	18	13 Sep 80	4
THE PARTY MIX ALBUM	Island	36	11 Jul 81	5
MESOPOTAMIA	EMI	18	27 Feb 82	6
WHAMMY!	Island	33	21 May 83	4
BOUNCING OFF THE SATELLITES	Island	74	8 Aug 87	2
COSMIC THING	Reprise	75	29 Jul 89	1
COSMIC THING [RE]	Reprise	8	31 Mar 90	26
THE BEST OF THE B-52'S - DANCE THIS MESS AROUND	Island	36	14 Jul 90	3
GOOD STUFF	Reprise	8	11 Jul 92	6

B.G. THE PRINCE OF RAP   Germany

SINGLES:	HITS 1			WEEKS 2
TAKE CONTROL OF THE PARTY	Columbia	71	18 Jan 92	2

B M EX   UK

(See also Sasha.)

ALBUMS:	HITS 1			WEEKS 2
APPOLONIA / FEEL THE DROP	Union City	17	30 Jan 93	2
12" double-pack single. Four mixes of Appolonia, two of Feel The Drop.				

B.M.R. Featuring FELICIA — Germany/UK

SINGLES:	HITS 1			WEEKS 2	
CHECK IT OUT (EVERYBODY)	*Almo Sounds*	29	*1 May 99*	2
Samples MFSB's TSOP.

B.M.U. (BLACK MEN UNITED) — US/UK

SINGLES:	HITS 1			WEEKS 2	
U WILL KNOW	*Mercury*	23	*18 Feb 95*	2
From the film 'Jason's Lyric'.

B-MOVIE — UK

SINGLES:	HITS 2			WEEKS 7	
REMEMBRANCE DAY	*Deram*	61	*18 Apr 81*	3
NOWHERE GIRL	*Some Bizzare*	67	*27 Mar 82*	4

B REAL, Busta RHYMES, COOLIO, LL COOL J and METHOD MAN — US

SINGLES:	HITS 1			WEEKS 6	
HIT 'EM HIGH (THE MONSTARS' ANTHEM)	*Atlantic*	8	*5 Apr 97*	6
From the film 'Space Jam'.

B.T. EXPRESS — US

SINGLES:	HITS 2			WEEKS 11	
EXPRESS	*Pye International*	34	*29 Mar 75*	6
DOES IT FEEL GOOD / GIVE UP THE FUNK (LET'S DANCE)	*Calibre*	52	*26 Jul 80*	4
EXPRESS [RM]	*PWL*	67	*23 Apr 94*	1
Remixed by Mother.

B-TRIBE — Spain

SINGLES:	HITS 1			WEEKS 4	
¡FIESTA FATAL!	*East West*	64	*25 Sep 93*	4

B.V.S.M.P. — US

SINGLES:	HITS 1			WEEKS 12	
I NEED YOU	*Debut*	3	*23 Jul 88*	12

B*WITCHED — UK

(See also Steps Tina Cousins Cleopatra B*Witched Billie.)

SINGLES:	HITS 6			WEEKS 70	
C'EST LA VIE	*Glow Worm*	1	*6 Jun 98*	19
ROLLERCOASTER	*Glow Worm*	1	*3 Oct 98*	15
TO YOU I BELONG	*Glow Worm*	1	*19 Dec 98*	12
BLAME IT ON THE WEATHERMAN	*Glow Worm*	1	*27 Mar 99*	9
TO YOU I BELONG [RE]	*Glow Worm*	64	*27 Mar 99*	2
JESSE HOLD ON	*Glow Worm*	4	*16 Oct 99*	10
I SHALL BE THERE	*Glow Worm*	13	*18 Dec 99*	3
*Above hit: B*WITCHED featuring LADYSMITH BLACK MAMBAZO.*

ALBUMS:	HITS 2			WEEKS 46	
B*WITCHED	*Glow Worm*	3	*24 Oct 98*	36
AWAKE AND BREATHE	*Glow Worm*	5	*30 Oct 99*	10

BABE INSTINCT — UK

SINGLES:	HITS 1			WEEKS 2	
DISCO BABES FROM OUTER SPACE	*Positiva*	21	*16 Jan 99*	2

BABES IN TOYLAND — US

ALBUMS:	HITS 2			WEEKS 3	
FONTANELLE	*Southern*	24	*5 Sep 92*	2
PAINKILLERS	*Southern*	53	*3 Jul 93*	1

Alice BABS — Sweden

SINGLES:	HITS 1			WEEKS 1	
AFTER YOU'VE GONE	*Fontana*	43	*17 Aug 63*	1
Originally recorded by Henry Burr and Albert Campbell in 1918.

BABY ANIMALS — Australia

ALBUMS:	HITS 1			WEEKS 1	
BABY ANIMALS	*Imago*	70	*14 Mar 92*	1

BABY BUMPS
UK

SINGLES:		HITS 1			WEEKS 4
BURNING	*Delirious*		17	*8 Aug 98*	4

Samples the Trammps' Disco Inferno.

BABY D
UK

SINGLES:		HITS 6			WEEKS 40
DESTINY	*Production House*		69	*18 Dec 93*	1
CASANOVA	*Production House*		67	*23 Jul 94*	1
LET ME BE YOUR FANTASY	*Systematic*		1	*19 Nov 94*	14

Original release reached No. 87 in 1992.

(EVERYBODY'S GOT TO LEARN SOMETIME) I NEED YOUR LOVING	*Systematic*		3	*3 Jun 95*	12
SO PURE	*Systematic*		3	*13 Jan 96*	7
TAKE ME TO HEAVEN	*Systematic*		15	*6 Apr 96*	5
ALBUMS:		HITS 1			WEEKS 5
DELIVERANCE	*Systematic*		5	*10 Feb 96*	5

BABY DC featuring IMAJIN
US

SINGLES:		HITS 1			WEEKS 1
BOUNCE, ROCK, SKATE, ROLL	*Jive*		45	*24 Apr 99*	1

BABY JUNE
UK

SINGLES:		HITS 1			WEEKS 1
HEY! WHAT'S YOUR NAME	*Arista*		75	*15 Aug 92*	1

BABY O
US

SINGLES:		HITS 1			WEEKS 5
IN THE FOREST	*Calibre*		46	*26 Jul 80*	5

BABY ROOTS
UK

SINGLES:		HITS 1			WEEKS 1
ROCK ME BABY	*ZYX*		71	*1 Aug 92*	1

BABYBIRD
UK

SINGLES:		HITS 7			WEEKS 32
GOODNIGHT	*Echo*		28	*10 Aug 96*	2
YOU'RE GORGEOUS	*Echo*		3	*12 Oct 96*	16
CANDY GIRL	*Echo*		14	*1 Feb 97*	3
CORNERSHOP	*Echo*		37	*17 May 97*	2
BAD OLD MAN	*Echo*		31	*9 May 98*	2
IF YOU'LL BE MINE	*Echo*		28	*22 Aug 98*	4
BACK TOGETHER	*Echo*		22	*27 Feb 99*	3
ALBUMS:		HITS 2			WEEKS 14
UGLY BEAUTIFUL	*Echo*		9	*2 Nov 96*	12

Compilation from 5 earlier albums.

THERE'S SOMETHING GOING ON	*Echo*		28	*5 Sep 98*	2

BABYFACE
US

(See also Jay-Z.)

SINGLES:		HITS 5			WEEKS 21
ROCK BOTTOM	*Epic*		50	*9 Jul 94*	4
WHEN CAN I SEE YOU	*Epic*		35	*1 Oct 94*	3
THIS IS FOR THE LOVER IN YOU	*Epic*		12	*9 Nov 96*	5

Above hit: BABYFACE featuring LL COOL J, Jody WATLEY, Howard HEWETT and Jeffrey DANIELS.

EVERYTIME I CLOSE MY EYES	*Epic*		13	*8 Mar 97*	4

Features Mariah Carey on backing vocals and Kenny G on sax.

HOW COME, HOW LONG	*Epic*		10	*19 Jul 97*	5

Above hit: BABYFACE featuring Stevie WONDER.

ALBUMS:		HITS 1			WEEKS 5
THE DAY	*Epic*		34	*16 Nov 96*	5

BABYLON ZOO
UK

SINGLES:		HITS 4			WEEKS 20
SPACEMAN	*EMI*		1	*27 Jan 96*	14

Featured in the Levi's Jeans TV commercial.

ANIMAL ARMY	*EMI*		17	*27 Apr 96*	3
THE BOY WITH THE X-RAY EYES	*EMI*		32	*5 Oct 96*	2
ALL THE MONEY'S GONE	*EMI*		46	*6 Feb 99*	1
ALBUMS:		HITS 1			WEEKS 5
THE BOY WITH THE X-RAY EYES	*EMI*		6	*17 Feb 96*	5

BABYS
US/UK

SINGLES:		HITS 1			WEEKS 3
ISN'T IT TIME	Chrysalis		45	21 Jan 78	3

BACCARA
Spain

SINGLES:		HITS 2			WEEKS 26
YES SIR, I CAN BOOGIE	RCA Victor		1	17 Sep 77	17
SORRY I'M A LADY	RCA Victor		8	14 Jan 78	9
ALBUMS:		**HITS 1**			**WEEKS 6**
BACCARA	RCA Victor		26	4 Mar 78	6

Burt BACHARACH his Orchestra and Chorus
US

SINGLES:		HITS 2			WEEKS 12
TRAINS AND BOATS AND PLANES	London		4	22 May 65	11
TOLEDO	Mercury		72	1 May 99	1
Above hit: Elvis COSTELLO with Burt BACHARACH.					
ALBUMS:		**HITS 5**			**WEEKS 46**
HIT MAKER-BURT BACHARACH	London		3	22 May 65	18
CASINO ROYALE [OST]	RCA Victor		35	22 Jul 67	1
Includes tracks by Herb Alpert and Dusty Springfield.					
REACH OUT	A&M		52	28 Nov 70	3
PORTRAIT IN MUSIC	A&M		5	3 Apr 71	22
PAINTED FROM MEMORY	Mercury		32	10 Oct 98	2
Above hit: Elvis COSTELLO with Burt BACHARACH.					

BACHELORS
Ireland

SINGLES:		HITS 17			WEEKS 187
CHARMAINE	Decca		6	26 Jan 63	19
Originally recorded by Mantovani.					
FARAWAY PLACES	Decca		36	6 Jul 63	3
WHISPERING	Decca		18	31 Aug 63	10
Originally recorded by Paul Whiteman in 1920.					
DIANE	Decca		1	25 Jan 64	19
Originally recorded by Nat Shilkret Orchestra in 1928.					
I BELIEVE	Decca		2	21 Mar 64	17
RAMONA	Decca		4	6 Jun 64	13
Originally recorded by Gene Austin.					
I WOULDN'T TRADE YOU FOR THE WORLD	Decca		4	15 Aug 64	16
NO ARMS CAN EVER HOLD YOU	Decca		7	5 Dec 64	12
TRUE LOVE FOR EVERMORE	Decca		34	3 Apr 65	6
MARIE	Decca		9	22 May 65	12
Originally recorded by Tommy Dorsey in 1940.					
IN THE CHAPEL IN THE MOONLIGHT	Decca		27	30 Oct 65	10
Originally recorded by Shep Fields in 1936.					
HELLO, DOLLY!	Decca		38	8 Jan 66	4
From the musical of the same name.					
THE SOUND OF SILENCE	Decca		3	19 Mar 66	13
CAN I TRUST YOU	Decca		26	9 Jul 66	7
WALK WITH FAITH IN YOUR HEART	Decca		22	3 Dec 66	9
OH HOW I MISS YOU	Decca		30	8 Apr 67	8
MARTA	Decca		20	8 Jul 67	9
EPS:		**HITS 4**			**WEEKS 98**
BACHELORS VOLUME 2	Decca		7	14 Mar 64	30
BACHELORS	Decca		5	21 Mar 64	22
BACHELORS' HITS	Decca		1	5 Dec 64	32
BACHELORS' HITS VOLUME 2	Decca		9	8 Jan 66	14
ALBUMS:		**HITS 8**			**WEEKS 103**
THE BACHELORS AND 16 GREAT SONGS	Decca		2	27 Jun 64	44
MORE GREAT SONG HITS FROM THE BACHELORS	Decca		15	9 Oct 65	6
HITS OF THE SIXTIES	Decca		12	9 Jul 66	9
BACHELORS' GIRLS	Decca		24	5 Nov 66	8
GOLDEN ALL TIME HITS	Decca		19	1 Jul 67	7
WORLD OF THE BACHELORS	Decca		8	14 Jun 69	18
WORLD OF THE BACHELORS VOLUME 2	Decca		11	23 Aug 69	7
25 GOLDEN GREATS	Warwick		38	22 Dec 79	4

Randy BACHMAN - See BUS STOP

Tal BACHMAN
Canada

SINGLES:		HITS 1			WEEKS 2
SHE'S SO HIGH	Columbia		30	30 Oct 99	2

BACHMAN-TURNER OVERDRIVE

Canada

SINGLES:	HITS 2			WEEKS 18
YOU AIN'T SEEN NOTHING YET	Mercury	2	16 Nov 74	12
Written about Randy Bachman's brother Gary who stuttered.				
ROLL ON DOWN THE HIGHWAY	Mercury	22	1 Feb 75	6
ALBUMS:	HITS 1			WEEKS 13
NOT FRAGILE	Mercury	12	14 Dec 74	13

BACK TO THE PLANET

UK

SINGLES:	HITS 2			WEEKS 2
TEENAGE TURTLES	Parallel	52	10 Apr 93	1
DAYDREAM	Parallel	52	4 Sep 93	1
ALBUMS:	HITS 1			WEEKS 2
MIND AND SOUL COLLABORATORS	Parallel	32	18 Sep 93	2

BACKBEAT BAND

US

SINGLES:	HITS 2			WEEKS 5
MONEY	Virgin	48	26 Mar 94	3
Original by Barrett Strong reached No. 23 in the US in 1960.				
MONEY [RE]	Virgin	73	23 Apr 94	1
PLEASE MR. POSTMAN	Virgin	69	14 May 94	1
Original by the Marvelettes reached No. 1 in the US in 1961.				
ALBUMS:	HITS 1			WEEKS 2
BACKBEAT [OST]	Virgin	39	16 Apr 94	2
Film chronicles the early days of the Beatles.				

BACKROOM BOYS - See CHAS and DAVE

BACKSTREET BOYS

US

SINGLES:	HITS 10			WEEKS 111
WE'VE GOT IT GOIN' ON	Jive	54	28 Oct 95	1
I'LL NEVER BREAK YOUR HEART	Jive	42	16 Dec 95	3
GET DOWN (YOU'RE THE ONE FOR ME)	Jive	14	1 Jun 96	8
WE'VE GOT IT GOIN' ON [RI]	Jive	3	24 Aug 96	7
I'LL NEVER BREAK YOUR HEART [RI]	Jive	8	16 Nov 96	8
QUIT PLAYING GAMES (WITH MY HEART)	Jive	2	18 Jan 97	10
ANYWHERE FOR YOU	Jive	4	29 Mar 97	6
ANYWHERE FOR YOU [RE-1ST]	Jive	72	31 May 97	1
ANYWHERE FOR YOU [RE-2ND]	Jive	70	14 Jun 97	1
EVERYBODY (BACKSTREET'S BACK)	Jive	3	2 Aug 97	11
AS LONG AS YOU LOVE ME	Jive	3	11 Oct 97	19
ALL I HAVE TO GIVE	Jive	2	14 Feb 98	12
I WANT IT THAT WAY	Jive	1	15 May 99	14
LARGER THAN LIFE	Jive	5	30 Oct 99	10
ALBUMS:	HITS 3			WEEKS 95
BACKSTREET BOYS	Jive	12	21 Sep 96	19
BACKSTREET'S BACK	Jive	2	23 Aug 97	44
MILLENNIUM	Jive	2	29 May 99	32

BAD BOYS INC.

UK

SINGLES:	HITS 6			WEEKS 31
DON'T TALK ABOUT LOVE	A&M	19	14 Aug 93	5
WHENEVER YOU NEED SOMEONE	A&M	26	2 Oct 93	3
WALKING ON AIR	A&M	24	11 Dec 93	6
MORE TO THIS WORLD	A&M	8	21 May 94	7
TAKE ME AWAY (I'LL FOLLOW YOU)	A&M	15	23 Jul 94	6
LOVE HERE I COME	A&M	26	17 Sep 94	4
ALBUMS:	HITS 1			WEEKS 6
BAD BOYS INC	A&M	13	18 Jun 94	6

BAD COMPANY

UK

SINGLES:	HITS 3			WEEKS 23
CAN'T GET ENOUGH	Island	15	1 Jun 74	8
GOOD LOVIN' GONE BAD	Island	31	22 Mar 75	6
FEEL LIKE MAKIN' LOVE	Island	20	30 Aug 75	9
ALBUMS:	HITS 6			WEEKS 87
BAD COMPANY	Island	3	15 Jun 74	25
STRAIGHT SHOOTER	Island	3	12 Apr 75	27
RUN WITH THE PACK	Island	4	21 Feb 76	12
BURNIN' SKY	Island	17	19 Mar 77	7
DESOLATION ANGELS	Swan Song	10	17 Mar 79	9
ROUGH DIAMONDS	Swan Song	15	28 Aug 82	6

BAD ENGLISH UK/US

SINGLES:	HITS 1			WEEKS 3
WHEN I SEE YOU SMILE	Epic	61	25 Nov 89	3
ALBUMS:	**HITS 2**			**WEEKS 2**
BAD ENGLISH	Epic	74	16 Sep 89	1
BACKLASH	Epic	64	19 Oct 91	1

BAD MANNERS UK

SINGLES:	HITS 12			WEEKS 111
NE-NE NA-NA NA-NA NU-NU	Magnet	28	1 Mar 80	14
Originally recorded by Dicky Doo and the Dont's.				
LIP UP FATTY	Magnet	15	14 Jun 80	14
SPECIAL BREW	Magnet	3	27 Sep 80	13
LORRAINE	Magnet	21	6 Dec 80	12
JUST A FEELING	Magnet	13	28 Mar 81	9
CAN CAN	Magnet	3	27 Jun 81	13
WALKING IN THE SUNSHINE	Magnet	10	26 Sep 81	9
BUONA SERA / DON'T BE ANGRY	Magnet	34	21 Nov 81	9
Sleeve gives title as an EP: Special 'R'N'B' Party Four.				
GOT NO BRAINS	Magnet	44	1 May 82	5
MY GIRL LOLLIPOP (MY BOY LOLLIPOP)	Magnet	9	31 Jul 82	7
SAMSON AND DELILAH	Magnet	58	30 Oct 82	3
THAT'LL DO NICELY	Magnet	49	14 May 83	3
ALBUMS:	**HITS 5**			**WEEKS 44**
SKA 'N' B	Magnet	34	26 Apr 80	13
LOONEE TUNES	Magnet	36	29 Nov 80	12
GOSH IT'S BAD MANNERS	Magnet	18	24 Oct 81	12
FORGING AHEAD	Magnet	78	27 Nov 82	1
THE HEIGHT OF BAD MANNERS	Telstar	23	7 May 83	6
Compilation.				

BAD NEWS UK

SINGLES:	HITS 1			WEEKS 5
BOHEMIAN RHAPSODY	EMI	44	12 Sep 87	5
ALBUMS:	**HITS 1**			**WEEKS 1**
BAD NEWS	EMI	69	24 Oct 87	1

BAD RELIGION US

SINGLES:	HITS 1			WEEKS 2
21ST CENTURY (DIGITAL BOY)	Columbia	41	11 Feb 95	2

BAD SEEDS – See Nick CAVE and the BAD SEEDS

BAD YARD CLUB – See David MORALES

Angelo BADALAMENTI with Julee CRUISE and VARIOUS ARTISTS Italy

(See also Booth and the Bad Angel.)

ALBUMS:	HITS 1			WEEKS 25
MUSIC FROM 'TWIN PEAKS' [OST-TV]	Warner Brothers	27	17 Nov 90	25

Wally BADAROU France

SINGLES:	HITS 1			WEEKS 6
CHIEF INSPECTOR	Fourth & Broadway	46	19 Oct 85	6

BADDIEL and SKINNER and the LIGHTNING SEEDS UK

SINGLES:	HITS 2			WEEKS 28
THREE LIONS (THE OFFICIAL SONG OF THE ENGLAND FOOTBALL TEAM)	Epic	1	1 Jun 96	15
Official anthem for England's football team in Euro 96				
3 LIONS '98 [RR]	Epic	1	20 Jun 98	13
Re-recorded for the 1998 World Cup in France.				

BADFINGER UK

(See also Various Artists (EPs) 'The Apple EP'.)

SINGLES:	HITS 3			WEEKS 34
COME AND GET IT	Apple	4	10 Jan 70	11
From the film 'Magic Christian'. Originally recorded by the Beatles.				
NO MATTER WHAT	Apple	5	9 Jan 71	12
DAY AFTER DAY	Apple	10	29 Jan 72	11
Features George Harrison on guitar and Leon Russell on piano.				

BADLANDS UK

ALBUMS:	HITS 2			WEEKS 3
BADLANDS	WEA	39	24 Jun 89	2
VOODOO HIGHWAY	Atlantic	74	22 Jun 91	1

BADLY DRAWN BOY

				UK
SINGLES:		HITS 1		WEEKS 2
ONCE AROUND THE BLOCK	*Twisted Nerve*	46	*4 Sep 99*	2

BADMAN

				UK
SINGLES:		HITS 1		WEEKS 3
MAGIC STYLE	*Citybeat*	61	*2 Feb 91*	3

Erykah BADU

				US
SINGLES:		HITS 5		WEEKS 13
ON & ON	*Universal*	12	*19 Apr 97*	4
NEXT LIFETIME	*Universal*	30	*14 Jun 97*	3
APPLE TREE	*Universal*	47	*29 Nov 97*	1
ONE	*Elektra*	23	*11 Jul 98*	3
Above hit: Busta RHYMES (featuring Erykah BADU).				
YOU GOT ME	*MCA*	31	*6 Mar 99*	2
Above hit: ROOTS featuring Erykah BADU.				
ALBUMS:		HITS 1		WEEKS 25
BADUIZM	*MCA*	17	*1 Mar 97*	25

Joan BAEZ

				US
SINGLES:		HITS 6		WEEKS 47
WE SHALL OVERCOME	*Fontana*	26	*8 May 65*	10
THERE BUT FOR FORTUNE	*Fontana*	8	*10 Jul 65*	12
Originally recorded by Phil Ochs.				
IT'S ALL OVER NOW, BABY BLUE	*Fontana*	22	*4 Sep 65*	8
FAREWELL ANGELINA	*Fontana*	35	*25 Dec 65*	3
FAREWELL ANGELINA [RE]	*Fontana*	49	*22 Jan 66*	1
PACK UP YOUR SORROWS	*Fontana*	50	*30 Jul 66*	1
THE NIGHT THEY DROVE OLD DIXIE DOWN	*Vanguard*	6	*9 Oct 71*	12
Originally recorded by the Band.				
EPS:		HITS 4		WEEKS 97
DON'T THINK TWICE, IT'S ALRIGHT	*Fontana*	10	*17 Apr 65*	23
SILVER DAGGER AND OTHER THINGS	*Philips*	3	*17 Apr 65*	33
WITH GOD ON OUR SIDE	*Fontana*	1	*26 Mar 66*	36
A HARD RAIN'S GONNA FALL	*Fontana*	7	*2 Jul 66*	5
ALBUMS:		HITS 6		WEEKS 88
JOAN BAEZ IN CONCERT VOLUME 2	*Fontana*	15	*18 Jul 64*	4
JOAN BAEZ NUMBER 5	*Fontana*	3	*15 May 65*	27
JOAN BAEZ	*Fontana*	9	*19 Jun 65*	13
JOAN BAEZ IN CONCERT VOLUME 2 [RE]	*Fontana*	8	*10 Jul 65*	15
FAREWELL ANGELINA	*Fontana*	5	*27 Nov 65*	23
JOAN BAEZ ON VANGUARD	*Vanguard*	15	*19 Jul 69*	5
FIRST TEN YEARS	*Vanguard*	41	*3 Apr 71*	1

Carol BAILEY

				UK
SINGLES:		HITS 1		WEEKS 2
FEEL IT	*Multiply*	41	*25 Feb 95*	2

Philip BAILEY

				US
SINGLES:		HITS 2		WEEKS 20
EASY LOVER	*CBS*	1	*9 Mar 85*	12
Above hit: Philip BAILEY (Duet with Phil COLLINS).				
WALKING ON THE CHINESE WALL	*CBS*	34	*18 May 85*	8
ALBUMS:		HITS 1		WEEKS 17
CHINESE WALL	*CBS*	29	*30 Mar 85*	17

Merril BAINBRIDGE

				Australia
SINGLES:		HITS 1		WEEKS 1
MOUTH	*Gotham*	51	*7 Dec 96*	1

Adrian BAKER

				UK
SINGLES:		HITS 1		WEEKS 8
SHERRY	*Magnet*	10	*19 Jul 75*	8

Anita BAKER

				US
SINGLES:		HITS 5		WEEKS 22
SWEET LOVE	*Elektra*	13	*15 Nov 86*	10
CAUGHT UP IN THE RAPTURE	*Elektra*	51	*31 Jan 87*	5
GIVING YOU THE BEST THAT I GOT	*Elektra*	55	*8 Oct 88*	3
TALK TO ME	*Elektra*	68	*30 Jun 90*	2
BODY AND SOUL	*Elektra*	48	*17 Sep 94*	2

ALBUMS:		HITS 4		WEEKS 81	
RAPTURE	Elektra	53	3 May 86	6
RAPTURE [RE]	Elektra	13	9 Aug 86	41
GIVING YOU THE BEST THAT I GOT	Elektra	9	29 Oct 88	20
COMPOSITIONS	Elektra	7	14 Jul 90	9
RHYTHM OF LOVE	Elektra	14	24 Sep 94	5

Arthur BAKER and the BACKBEAT DISCIPLES   US

SINGLES:		HITS 2		WEEKS 7	
IT'S YOUR TIME	Breakout	64	20 May 89	2

Above hit: Arthur BAKER and the BACKBEAT DISCIPLES (featuring Shirley LEWIS).

THE MESSAGE IS LOVE	Breakout	38	21 Oct 89	5

Above hit: Arthur BAKER and the BACKBEAT DISCIPLES featuring Al GREEN.

George BAKER SELECTION   UK

SINGLES:		HITS 1		WEEKS 10	
PALOMA BLANCA	Warner Brothers	10	6 Sep 75	10

Ginger BAKER'S AIR FORCE   UK

(See also Baker-Gurvitz Army.)

ALBUMS:		HITS 1		WEEKS 1	
GINGER BAKER'S AIR FORCE	Polydor	37	13 Jun 70	1

Hylda BAKER and Arthur MULLARD   UK

SINGLES:		HITS 1		WEEKS 6	
YOU'RE THE ONE THAT I WANT	Pye	22	9 Sep 78	6

BAKER-GURVITZ ARMY   UK

(See also Ginger Baker's Air Force; Adrian Gurvitz.)

ALBUMS:		HITS 1		WEEKS 5	
BAKER-GURVITZ ARMY	Vertigo	22	22 Feb 75	5

BALAAM AND THE ANGEL   UK

SINGLES:		HITS 1		WEEKS 2	
SHE KNOWS	Virgin	70	29 Mar 86	2
ALBUMS:		HITS 1		WEEKS 2	
THE GREATEST STORY EVER TOLD	Virgin	67	16 Aug 86	2

Long John BALDRY   UK

SINGLES:		HITS 4		WEEKS 36	
LET THE HEARTACHES BEGIN	Pye	1	11 Nov 67	13
WHEN THE SUN COMES SHINING THRU	Pye	29	31 Aug 68	7
MEXICO	Pye	15	26 Oct 68	8
IT'S TOO LATE NOW	Pye	21	1 Feb 69	8

BALEARIC BILL   Belgium/Holland

(See also Airscape.)

SINGLES:		HITS 1		WEEKS 2	
DESTINATION SUNSHINE	Xtravaganza	36	2 Oct 99	2

Edward BALL   UK

SINGLES:		HITS 2		WEEKS 2	
THE MILL HILL SELF HATE CLUB	Creation	57	20 Jul 96	1
LOVE IS BLUE	Creation	59	22 Feb 97	1

Kenny BALL and his JAZZMEN   UK

SINGLES:		HITS 14		WEEKS 136	
SAMANTHA	Pye Jazz Today	13	25 Feb 61	15

From the film 'High Society'.
Above hit: Lonnie DONEGAN presents – Kenny BALL and his JAZZMEN.

I STILL LOVE YOU ALL	Pye Jazz Today	24	13 May 61	6
SOMEDAY (YOU'LL BE SORRY)	Pye Jazz Today	28	2 Sep 61	6

Above 3 has sub credit: Vocal: Kenny BALL.

MIDNIGHT IN MOSCOW	Pye Jazz Today	2	11 Nov 61	21

Based on a Russian song Padmeskoveeye Vietchera.

MARCH OF THE SIAMESE CHILDREN	Pye Jazz Today	4	17 Feb 62	13

From the film 'The King And I'.

THE GREEN LEAVES OF SUMMER	Pye	7	19 May 62	14

From the film 'The Alamo'.

SO DO I	Pye Jazz Today	14	25 Aug 62	8
THE PAY-OFF (A MOI DE PAYER)	Pye Jazz Today	23	20 Oct 62	6

Above hit: Kenny BALL and his JAZZMEN; Clarinet-Dave JONES.

SUKIYAKI	*Pye Jazz Today*	10	*19 Jan 63*	13
CASABLANCA	*Pye Jazz Today*	21	*27 Apr 63*	11
RONDO (BASED ON MOZART'S RONDO A LA TURK)	*Pye Jazz Today*	24	*15 Jun 63*	8
ACAPULCO 1922	*Pye Jazz Today*	27	*24 Aug 63*	6
HELLO DOLLY	*Pye Jazz Today*	30	*13 Jun 64*	7
WHEN I'M SIXTY-FOUR	*Pye*	43	*22 Jul 67*	2
Originally recorded by the Beatles..				
EPS:	**HITS 2**		**WEEKS 67**	
KENNY'S BIG FOUR	*Pye*	3	*2 Dec 61*	24
KENNY BALL'S HIT PARADE	*Pye*	5	*3 Mar 62*	43
ALBUMS:	**HITS 2**		**WEEKS 50**	
THE BEST OF BALL, BARBER AND BILK	*Pye Golden Guinea*	1	*25 Aug 62*	24
Above hit: Kenny BALL, Chris BARBER and Mr. Acker BILK.				
KENNY BALL'S GOLDEN HITS	*Pye Golden Guinea*	4	*7 Sep 63*	26
Above hit: Kenny BALL..				

Michael BALL   UK

(See also Various Artists: Stage Cast – London 'Aspects Of Love'; Studio Cast 'Leonard Bernstein's West Side Story'.)

SINGLES:	**HITS 10**		**WEEKS 39**	
LOVE CHANGES EVERYTHING	*Really Useful*	2	*28 Jan 89*	14
From the musical 'Aspects Of Love'.				
THE FIRST MAN YOU REMEMBER	*Really Useful*	68	*28 Oct 89*	2
Above hit: Michael BALL and Diana MORRISON.				
IT'S STILL YOU	*Polydor*	58	*10 Aug 91*	2
ONE STEP OUT OF TIME	*Polydor*	20	*25 Apr 92*	7
UK's Eurovision entry in 1992, it came 2nd.				
IF I CAN DREAM [EP]	*Polydor*	51	*12 Dec 92*	1
Lead track: If I Can Dream.				
IF I CAN DREAM [EP] [RE]	*Polydor*	68	*26 Dec 92*	1
SUNSET BOULEVARD	*Polydor*	72	*11 Sep 93*	1
FROM HERE TO ETERNITY	*Columbia*	36	*30 Jul 94*	3
THE LOVERS WE WERE	*Columbia*	63	*17 Sep 94*	2
THE ROSE	*Columbia*	42	*9 Dec 95*	4
Theme from the TV series 'The Ladykillers'. Original by Bette Midler reached No. 3 in the US in 1980.				
(SOMETHING INSIDE) SO STRONG	*Columbia*	40	*17 Feb 96*	2
ALBUMS:	**HITS 8**		**WEEKS 74**	
MICHAEL BALL	*Polydor*	1	*30 May 92*	10
ALWAYS	*Polydor*	3	*17 Jul 93*	11
ONE CAREFUL OWNER	*Columbia*	7	*13 Aug 94*	6
THE BEST OF MICHAEL BALL	*PolyGram TV*	25	*19 Nov 94*	7
FIRST LOVE	*Columbia*	4	*27 Jan 96*	6
THE MUSICALS	*PolyGram TV*	20	*16 Nov 96*	10
THE MOVIES	*PolyGram TV*	13	*7 Nov 98*	17
THE VERY BEST OF MICHAEL BALL IN CONCERT AT THE ROYAL ALBERT HALL / CHRISTMAS	*Universal Music TV*	18	*20 Nov 99*	7
Double album package.				

BALTIMORA   Ireland

SINGLES:	**HITS 1**		**WEEKS 12**	
TARZAN BOY	*Columbia*	3	*10 Aug 85*	12

Charli BALTIMORE   US

SINGLES:	**HITS 1**		**WEEKS 4**	
MONEY	*Epic*	12	*1 Aug 98*	4
Remake of the O'Jays' 'For The Love Of Money'; from the film 'Woo'.				

BAM-BAM   US

SINGLES:	**HITS 1**		**WEEKS 2**	
GIVE IT TO ME	*Serious*	65	*19 Mar 88*	2

Afrika BAMBAATAA   US

(See also Time Zone featuring John Lydon and Afrika Bambaataa.)

SINGLES:	**HITS 6**		**WEEKS 32**	
PLANET ROCK	*Polydor*	53	*28 Aug 82*	3
THE RENEGADES OF FUNK	*Tommy Boy*	30	*10 Mar 84*	4
Above 2: Afrika BAMBAATAA and the SOUL SONIC FORCE.				
UNITY (PART 1 - THE THIRD COMING)	*Tommy Boy*	49	*1 Sep 84*	5
Above hit: Afrika BAMBAATAA and the Godfather of Soul – James BROWN.				
RECKLESS	*EMI*	17	*27 Feb 88*	8
Above hit: Afrika BAMBAATAA and FAMILY featuring UB40.				
JUST GET UP AND DANCE	*EMI USA*	45	*12 Oct 91*	3

| GOT TO GET UP [RM] | Multiply | 22 | 17 Oct 98 | 4 |

Remixes by Tall Paul and Loop Da Loop.
Above hit: Afrika BAMBAATAA vs. CARPE DIEM.

| AFRIKA SHOX | Hard Hands | 7 | 18 Sep 99 | 5 |

Above hit: LEFTFIELD. BAMBAATAA.

BAMBOO   UK

SINGLES:	HITS 2			WEEKS 12
BAMBOOGIE	VC Recordings	2	17 Jan 98	10

Featured in the Bud Ice TV commercial.

| THE STRUTT | VC Recordings | 36 | 4 Jul 98 | 2 |

BANANARAMA   UK

SINGLES:	HITS 26			WEEKS 202
IT AIN'T WHAT YOU DO IT'S THE WAY THAT YOU DO IT	Chrysalis	4	13 Feb 82	10

Originally recorded by Jimmy Lunceford.
Above hit: FUN BOY THREE with BANANARAMA.

| REALLY SAYING SOMETHING (HE WAS REALLY SAYIN' SOMETHIN') | Deram | 5 | 10 Apr 82 | 10 |

Originally recorded by the Velvelettes.
Above hit: BANANARAMA and the FUN BOY THREE.

SHY BOY	London	4	3 Jul 82	11
CHEERS THEN	London	45	4 Dec 82	7
NA NA HEY HEY KISS HIM GOODBYE	London	5	26 Feb 83	10
CRUEL SUMMER	London	8	9 Jul 83	10
ROBERT DE NIRO'S WAITING	London	3	3 Mar 84	11
ROUGH JUSTICE	London	23	26 May 84	7
HOT LINE TO HEAVEN	London	58	24 Nov 84	2
DO NOT DISTURB	London	31	24 Aug 85	6
VENUS	London	8	31 May 86	13
MORE THAN PHYSICAL	London	41	16 Aug 86	5
TRICK OF THE NIGHT	London	32	14 Feb 87	5
I HEARD A RUMOUR	London	14	11 Jul 87	9
LOVE IN THE FIRST DEGREE / MR. SLEAZE	London	3	10 Oct 87	12

Mr. Sleaze listed from 24 Oct 87.

I CAN'T HELP IT	London	20	9 Jan 88	6
I WANT YOU BACK	London	5	9 Apr 88	10
LOVE, TRUTH AND HONESTLY	London	23	24 Sep 88	8
NATHAN JONES	London	15	19 Nov 88	9
HELP	London	3	25 Feb 89	9

In aid of Comic Relief.
Above hit: BANANARAMA LA NA NEE NEE NOO NOO.

| CRUEL SUMMER (SWING BEAT VERSION) [RM] | London | 19 | 10 Jun 89 | 6 |

Remixed by Atkins, Atkins and Trottman.

ONLY YOUR LOVE	London	27	28 Jul 90	4
PREACHER MAN	London	20	5 Jan 91	6
LONG TRAIN RUNNING	London	30	20 Apr 91	5
MOVIN' ON	London	24	29 Aug 92	5
LAST THING ON MY MIND	London	71	28 Nov 92	2
MORE, MORE, MORE	London	24	20 Mar 93	4
ALBUMS:	HITS 7			WEEKS 97
DEEP SEA SKIVING	London	7	19 Mar 83	16
BANANARAMA	London	16	28 Apr 84	11
TRUE CONFESSIONS	London	46	19 Jul 86	5
WOW!	London	26	19 Sep 87	26
THE GREATEST HITS COLLECTION	London	3	22 Oct 88	37
POP LIFE	London	42	25 May 91	1
PLEASE YOURSELF	London	46	10 Apr 93	1

BANCO DE GAIA   UK

ALBUMS:	HITS 2			WEEKS 4
MAYA	Ultimate	34	12 Mar 94	2
LAST TRAIN TO LHASA	Planet Dog	31	13 May 95	2

Lhasa is the capital of Tibet.

BAND   US/Canada

SINGLES:	HITS 2			WEEKS 18
THE WEIGHT	Capitol	21	21 Sep 68	9

Single shows full credit as Jamie Robbie Robertson-Rick Danko-Richard Manuel-Gartha
*   Hudson-Leyon Helm-(The Band).*

RAG MAMA RAG	Capitol	16	4 Apr 70	9
ALBUMS:	HITS 4			WEEKS 23
THE BAND	Capitol	25	31 Jan 70	11
STAGE FRIGHT	Capitol	15	3 Oct 70	6
CAHOOTS	Capitol	41	27 Nov 71	1

THE LAST WALTZ [OST]	*Warner Brothers*	39	*6 May 78*	4
Live recordings from their final concert at the Winterland, San Francisco, 25 Nov 76. Features guests Eric Clapton, Bob Dylan, Neil Diamond, Joni Mitchell, Van Morrison, Ringo Starr, Muddy Waters and Neil Young.				
THE BAND [RE]	*Capitol*	41	*30 Aug 97*	1
Re-released. Charted after being featured on BBC1 TV's 'Classic Albums' series.				

BAND A.K.A.
US

SINGLES:	HITS 2			WEEKS 12
GRACE	*Epic*	41	*15 May 82*	5
JOY	*Epic*	24	*5 Mar 83*	7

BAND AID
International

SINGLES:	HITS 2			WEEKS 26
DO THEY KNOW IT'S CHRISTMAS?	*Mercury*	1	*15 Dec 84*	13
DO THEY KNOW IT'S CHRISTMAS? [RE]	*Mercury*	3	*7 Dec 85*	7
DO THEY KNOW IT'S CHRISTMAS? [RR]	*PWL/Polydor*	1	*23 Dec 89*	6
Above hit: BAND AID II.				

BAND OF GOLD
Holland

SINGLES:	HITS 1			WEEKS 11
LOVE SONGS ARE BACK AGAIN [M]	*RCA*	24	*14 Jul 84*	11
9 track medley of ballads.				

BANDERAS
UK

SINGLES:	HITS 2			WEEKS 16
THIS IS YOUR LIFE	*London*	16	*23 Feb 91*	10
SHE SELLS	*London*	41	*15 Jun 91*	6
ALBUMS:	HITS 1			WEEKS 3
RIPE	*London*	40	*13 Apr 91*	3

BANDITS - See Billy COTTON and his BAND

BANDWAGON - See Johnny JOHNSON and the BANDWAGON

Honey BANE
UK

SINGLES:	HITS 2			WEEKS 8
TURN ME ON TURN ME OFF	*Zonophone*	37	*24 Jan 81*	5
BABY LOVE	*Zonophone*	58	*18 Apr 81*	3

BANG
UK

SINGLES:	HITS 1			WEEKS 2
YOU'RE THE ONE	*RCA*	74	*6 May 89*	2

BANGLES
US

SINGLES:	HITS 11			WEEKS 94
MANIC MONDAY	*CBS*	2	*15 Feb 86*	12
Written by Prince under the pseudonym Christopher.				
IF SHE KNEW WHAT SHE WANTS	*CBS*	31	*26 Apr 86*	7
Originally recorded by Jules Shear.				
GOING DOWN TO LIVERPOOL	*CBS*	56	*5 Jul 86*	3
Original release reached No. 79 in 1985. Originally recorded by Katrina and the Waves.				
WALK LIKE AN EGYPTIAN	*CBS*	3	*13 Sep 86*	19
WALKING DOWN YOUR STREET	*CBS*	16	*10 Jan 87*	6
FOLLOWING	*CBS*	55	*18 Apr 87*	3
HAZY SHADE OF WINTER	*Def Jam*	11	*6 Feb 88*	10
From the film 'Less Than Zero'. Original by Simon and Garfunkel reached No. 13 in the US in 1966.				
IN YOUR ROOM	*CBS*	35	*5 Nov 88*	6
ETERNAL FLAME	*CBS*	1	*18 Feb 89*	18
BE WITH YOU	*CBS*	23	*10 Jun 89*	8
I'LL SET YOU FREE	*CBS*	74	*14 Oct 89*	1
WALK LIKE AN EGYPTIAN [RI]	*CBS*	73	*9 Jun 90*	1
ALBUMS:	HITS 4			WEEKS 97
ALL OVER THE PLACE	*CBS*	86	*16 Mar 85*	1
DIFFERENT LIGHT	*CBS*	30	*15 Mar 86*	14
DIFFERENT LIGHT [RE]	*CBS*	3	*4 Oct 86*	33
EVERYTHING	*CBS*	5	*10 Dec 88*	26
GREATEST HITS	*CBS*	4	*9 Jun 90*	19
GREATEST HITS [RI]	*Columbia*	37	*7 May 94*	4
Re-released at mid-price.				

Tony BANKS
UK

SINGLES:		HITS 1			WEEKS 1
SHORTCUT TO SOMEWHERE	Charisma	75	18 Oct 86	1
Above hit: FISH and Tony BANKS.				

ALBUMS:		HITS 2			WEEKS 7
A CURIOUS FEELING	Charisma	21	20 Oct 79	5
THE FUGITIVE	Charisma	50	25 Jun 83	2

BANNED
UK

SINGLES:		HITS 1			WEEKS 6
LITTLE GIRL	Harvest	36	17 Dec 77	6
Original by Syndicate Of Sound reached No. 8 in the US in 1966.				

Buju BANTON
Jamaica

(See also Jamaica United.)

SINGLES:		HITS 1			WEEKS 1
MAKE MY DAY	Mercury	72	7 Aug 93	1

Pato BANTON
UK

SINGLES:		HITS 5			WEEKS 37
BABY COME BACK	Virgin	1	1 Oct 94	18
Above hit: Pato BANTON featuring Ali and Robin CAMPBELL of UB40.				
THIS COWBOY SONG	A&M	15	11 Feb 95	6
Above hit: STING (featuring Pato BANTON).				
BUBBLING HOT	Virgin	15	8 Apr 95	7
Above hit: Pato BANTON with RANKING ROGER.				
SPIRITS IN THE MATERIAL WORLD	MCA	36	20 Jan 96	2
From the film 'Ace Ventura When Nature Calls'.				
Above hit: Pato BANTON with STING.				
GROOVIN'	I.R.S.	14	27 Jul 96	4
Above hit: Pato BANTON and the REGGAE REVOLUTION.				

BAR-CODES featuring Alison BROWN
UK

SINGLES:		HITS 1			WEEKS 1
SUPERMARKET SWEEP	Blanca Casa	72	17 Dec 94	1
With M.C. Dale (Winton), from ITV show of the same name.				

BAR-KAYS
US

SINGLES:		HITS 3			WEEKS 15
SOUL FINGER	Stax	33	26 Aug 67	7
SHAKE YOUR RUMP TO THE FUNK	Mercury	41	22 Jan 77	4
SEXOMATIC	Club	51	12 Jan 85	4

Chris BARBER'S JAZZ BAND
UK

SINGLES:		HITS 3			WEEKS 30
PETITE FLEUR	Pye Nixa	3	14 Feb 59	22
Originally recorded by Sidney Bechet.				
Above hit: Chris BARBER'S JAZZ BAND; Clarinet Solo – Monty SUNSHINE.				
PETITE FLEUR [RE]	Pye Nixa	22	1 Aug 59	2
LONESOME (SI TU VOIS MA MERE)	Columbia	27	10 Oct 59	2
Above hit: Chris BARBER'S JAZZ BAND featuring Monty SUNSHINE.				
REVIVAL	Columbia	50	6 Jan 62	2
REVIVAL [RE]	Columbia	43	3 Feb 62	2

EPS:		HITS 1			WEEKS 1
BARBERS BEST VOLUME 1	Decca	11	25 Jun 60	1

ALBUMS:		HITS 6			WEEKS 88
CHRIS BARBER BAND BOX NUMBER 2	Columbia	17	24 Sep 60	1
ELITE SYNCOPATIONS	Columbia	18	5 Nov 60	1
THE BEST OF CHRIS BARBER	Ace Of Clubs	17	12 Nov 60	1
Above 3: Chris BARBER.				
THE BEST OF BARBER AND BILK VOLUME 1	Pye Golden Guinea	4	27 May 61	43
THE BEST OF BARBER AND BILK VOLUME 2	Pye Golden Guinea	8	11 Nov 61	18
Above 2: Chris BARBER and Mr. Acker BILK.				
THE BEST OF BALL, BARBER AND BILK	Pye Golden Guinea	1	25 Aug 62	24
Above hit: Kenny BALL, Chris BARBER and Mr. Acker BILK.				

BARBRA and NEIL - See Barbra STREISAND; Neil DIAMOND

BARCLAY JAMES HARVEST
UK

SINGLES:		HITS 4			WEEKS 9
LIVE [EP]	Polydor	49	2 Apr 77	1
Lead track: Rock 'N Roll Star.				
LIVE [EP] [RE]	Polydor	49	16 Apr 77	1

LOVE ON THE LINE	Polydor	63	26 Jan 80	2
LIFE IS FOR LIVING	Polydor	61	22 Nov 80	3
JUST A DAY AWAY	Polydor	68	21 May 83	2
ALBUMS:	**HITS 10**			**WEEKS 42**
BARCLAY JAMES HARVEST LIVE	Polydor	40	14 Dec 74	2
TIME HONOURED GHOST	Polydor	32	18 Oct 75	3
OCTOBERON	Polydor	19	23 Oct 76	4
GONE TO EARTH	Polydor	30	1 Oct 77	7
BARCLAY JAMES HARVEST XII	Polydor	31	21 Oct 78	2
TURN OF THE TIDE	Polydor	55	23 May 81	2
A CONCERT FOR THE PEOPLE (BERLIN)	Polydor	15	24 Jul 82	11
RING OF CHANGES	Polydor	36	28 May 83	4
VICTIMS OF CIRCUMSTANCE	Polydor	33	14 Apr 84	6
FACE TO FACE	Polydor	65	14 Feb 87	1

BARDO   UK

SINGLES:	**HITS 1**			**WEEKS 8**
ONE STEP FURTHER	Epic	2	10 Apr 82	8

UK's Eurovision entry in 1982, it came 7th.

Bobby BARE – See Bill PARSONS

BAREFOOT MAN   Germany

SINGLES:	**HITS 1**			**WEEKS 7**
BIG PANTY WOMAN	Plaza	21	5 Dec 98	7

BARENAKED LADIES   Canada

SINGLES:	**HITS 4**			**WEEKS 12**
ONE WEEK	Reprise	5	20 Feb 99	8
IT'S ALL BEEN DONE	Reprise	28	15 May 99	2
CALL AND ANSWER	Reprise	52	24 Jul 99	1
From the film 'EDtv'.				
BRIAN WILSON (2000)	Reprise	73	11 Dec 99	1
First appeared on the 1993 album Gordon.				
ALBUMS:	**HITS 2**			**WEEKS 17**
MAYBE YOU SHOULD DRIVE	Reprise	57	27 Aug 94	1
STUNT	Reprise	20	6 Mar 99	16

Daniel BARENBOIM – See John WILLIAMS

Gary BARLOW   UK

SINGLES:	**HITS 6**			**WEEKS 47**
FOREVER LOVE	RCA	1	20 Jul 96	16
From the film 'The Leading Man'.				
LOVE WON'T WAIT	RCA	1	10 May 97	7
Co-written with Madonna.				
LOVE WON'T WAIT [RE-1ST]	RCA	64	26 Jul 97	1
SO HELP ME GIRL	RCA	11	26 Jul 97	7
Originally recorded by Joe Diffie.				
LOVE WON'T WAIT [RE-2ND]	RCA	67	9 Aug 97	1
SO HELP ME GIRL [RE]	RCA	64	20 Sep 97	4
OPEN ROAD	RCA	7	15 Nov 97	5
STRONGER	RCA	16	17 Jul 99	4
FOR ALL THAT YOU WANT	RCA	24	9 Oct 99	2
ALBUMS:	**HITS 2**			**WEEKS 27**
OPEN ROAD	RCA	1	7 Jun 97	26
TWELVE MONTHS, ELEVEN DAYS	RCA	35	23 Oct 99	1

BARNBRACK   UK

SINGLES:	**HITS 1**			**WEEKS 7**
BELFAST	Homespun	45	16 Mar 85	7

Jimmy BARNES and INXS   Australia

(See also INXS.)

SINGLES:	**HITS 1**			**WEEKS 8**
GOOD TIMES	Atlantic	18	26 Jan 91	8

From the film 'The Lost Boys'. Originally recorded by the Easybeats.

Richard BARNES   UK

SINGLES:	**HITS 2**			**WEEKS 10**
TAKE TO THE MOUNTAINS	Philips	35	23 May 70	6
GO NORTH	Philips	49	24 Oct 70	1
GO NORTH [RE]	Philips	38	7 Nov 70	3

Kathy BARNET – See Claude FRANCOIS; girl vocal: Kathy BARNET

Gary BARNICLE – See BIG FUN; SONIA

BAROCK-AND-ROCK ENSEMBLE   Germany

EPS:	HITS 1			WEEKS 12
EINE KLEINE BEATLEMUSIK	HMV	4	29 May 65	12

BARRACUDAS   UK/US

SINGLES:	HITS 1			WEEKS 6
SUMMER FUN	EMI-Wipe Out	37	16 Aug 80	6

Syd BARRETT   UK

ALBUMS:	HITS 1			WEEKS 1
MADCAP LAUGHS	Harvest	40	7 Feb 70	1

Amanda BARRIE and Johnny BRIGGS – See CORONATION STREET CAST

J.J. BARRIE   Canada

SINGLES:	HITS 1			WEEKS 11
NO CHARGE	Power Exchange	1	24 Apr 76	11

Original by Melba Montgomery reached No. 39 in the US in 1974.

Ken BARRIE   UK

SINGLES:	HITS 1			WEEKS 15
POSTMAN PAT	Post Music	44	10 Jul 82	8

Theme from the Children's BBC TV series.

POSTMAN PAT [RE-1ST]	Post Music	54	25 Dec 82	3
POSTMAN PAT [RE-2ND]	Post Music	59	24 Dec 83	4

BARRON KNIGHTS   UK

SINGLES:	HITS 13			WEEKS 95
CALL UP THE GROUPS [M]	Columbia	3	11 Jul 64	13
COME TO THE DANCE	Columbia	42	24 Oct 64	2
POP GO THE WORKERS [M]	Columbia	5	27 Mar 65	13
MERRY GENTLE POPS [M]	Columbia	9	18 Dec 65	7
UNDER NEW MANAGEMENT [M]	Columbia	15	3 Dec 66	9

Above 5: BARRON KNIGHTS with Duke D'MOND.

AN OLYMPIC RECORD [M]	Columbia	35	26 Oct 68	4
LIVE IN TROUBLE [M]	Epic	7	29 Oct 77	11
A TASTE OF AGGRO [M]	Epic	3	2 Dec 78	10
FOOD FOR THOUGHT [M]	Epic	46	8 Dec 79	6
THE SIT SONG	Epic	44	4 Oct 80	4

Spoof of dog trainer Barbara Woodhouse.

NEVER MIND THE PRESENTS [M]	Epic	17	6 Dec 80	8
BLACKBOARD JUMBLE [M]	Epic	52	5 Dec 81	5

All medleys listed above are parodies of contemporary hits.

BUFFALO BILL'S LAST SCRATCH	Epic	49	19 Mar 83	3

ALBUMS:	HITS 3			WEEKS 22
NIGHT GALLERY	Epic	15	2 Dec 78	13
TEACH THE WORLD TO LAUGH	Epic	51	1 Dec 79	4
JUST A GIGGLE	Epic	45	13 Dec 80	5

Joe BARRY   US

SINGLES:	HITS 1			WEEKS 1
I'M A FOOL TO CARE	Mercury	49	26 Aug 61	1

Originally recorded by Les Paul and Mary Ford.

John BARRY   UK

(See also Russ Conway; Adam Faith.)

SINGLES:	HITS 10			WEEKS 79
HIT AND MISS	Columbia	10	5 Mar 60	13

Above hit: John BARRY SEVEN plus FOUR.

BEAT FOR BEATNIKS	Columbia	40	30 Apr 60	2

Above hit: John BARRY and his Orchestra.

HIT AND MISS [RE]	Columbia	45	11 Jun 60	1
NEVER LET GO	Columbia	49	16 Jul 60	1
BLUEBERRY HILL	Columbia	34	20 Aug 60	3

Above 2 entries were separate sides of the same release, each had its own chart run.
Above 2: John BARRY ORCHESTRA.

WALK DON'T RUN	Columbia	49	10 Sep 60	1
WALK DON'T RUN [RE]	Columbia	11	24 Sep 60	13
BLACK STOCKINGS	Columbia	27	10 Dec 60	9
THE MAGNIFICENT SEVEN	Columbia	48	4 Mar 61	1

From the film of the same name.

THE MAGNIFICENT SEVEN [RE-1ST]	Columbia	45	18 Mar 61	2

THE MAGNIFICENT SEVEN [RE-2ND]	Columbia	50	8 Apr 61	1
THE MAGNIFICENT SEVEN [RE-3RD]	Columbia	47	10 Jun 61	1
Above 7: John BARRY SEVEN.				
CUTTY SARK	Columbia	35	28 Apr 62	2
THE JAMES BOND THEME	Columbia	13	3 Nov 62	11
From the film 'Doctor No'.				
FROM RUSSIA WITH LOVE	Ember	44	23 Nov 63	1
From the James Bond film of the same name.				
FROM RUSSIA WITH LOVE [RE]	Ember	39	21 Dec 63	2
Above 4: John BARRY SEVEN and ORCHESTRA.				
THEME FROM "THE PERSUADERS"	CBS	13	11 Dec 71	15
From the TV series.				
EPS:	**HITS 1**			**WEEKS 25**
THE JOHN BARRY SOUND	Columbia	4	25 Feb 61	25
Above hit: John BARRY 7 + 4.				
ALBUMS:	**HITS 7**			**WEEKS 32**
JAMES BOND 007 – GOLDFINGER [OST]	United Artists	14	31 Oct 64	5
Includes title track by Shirley Bassey.				
THE PERSUADERS [OST-TV]	CBS	18	29 Jan 72	9
JAMES BOND 007 – A VIEW TO A KILL [OST]	Parlophone	81	22 Jun 85	1
Includes title track by Duran Duran.				
OUT OF AFRICA [OST]	MCA	81	26 Apr 86	2
JAMES BOND 007 – THE LIVING DAYLIGHTS [OST]	Warner Brothers	57	1 Aug 87	6
Includes tracks by A-ha and Pretenders.				
DANCES WITH WOLVES [OST]	Epic	45	20 Apr 91	8
THE BEYONDNESS OF THINGS	Decca	67	8 May 99	1
Above hit: ENGLISH CHAMBER ORCHESTRA Conducted by John BARRY.				

Len BARRY   US

SINGLES:	**HITS 2**			**WEEKS 24**
1-2-3	Brunswick	3	6 Nov 65	14
LIKE A BABY	Brunswick	10	15 Jan 66	10

Michael BARRYMORE   UK

SINGLES:	**HITS 1**			**WEEKS 4**
TOO MUCH FOR ONE HEART	EMI	25	16 Dec 95	4

Lionel BART   UK

SINGLES:	**HITS 1**			**WEEKS 3**
HAPPY ENDINGS (GIVE YOURSELF A PINCH)	EMI	68	25 Nov 89	1
Featured in the Abbey National TV commercial.				
HAPPY ENDINGS (GIVE YOURSELF A PINCH) [RE]	EMI	71	23 Dec 89	2
EPS:	**HITS 1**			**WEEKS 1**
BART FOR BART'S SAKE	Decca	20	26 Mar 60	1

BART and HOMER - See SIMPSONS

BAS NOIR   US

SINGLES:	**HITS 1**			**WEEKS 1**
MY LOVE IS MAGIC	10 Records	73	11 Feb 89	1

Rob BASE and D.J. E-Z ROCK   US

SINGLES:	**HITS 3**			**WEEKS 19**
IT TAKES TWO	Citybeat	24	16 Apr 88	6
GET ON THE DANCE FLOOR	Supreme	14	14 Jan 89	7
IT TAKES TWO [RE]	Citybeat	49	4 Mar 89	3
JOY AND PAIN	Supreme	47	22 Apr 89	3
Features rap by Omar Chandler.				

BASEMENT BOYS - See Ultra NATE

BASEMENT JAXX   UK

SINGLES:	**HITS 4**			**WEEKS 26**
FLY LIFE	Multiply	19	31 May 97	3
RED ALERT	XL Recordings	5	1 May 99	10
Samples Locksmith's Far Beyond.				
RENDEZ-VU	XL Recordings	4	14 Aug 99	8
JUMP N' SHOUT	XL Recordings	12	6 Nov 99	5
Vocals by Slarta John and Madman Swyli.				
Above hit: BASEMENT JAXX Featuring SLARTA JOHN.				
ALBUMS:	**HITS 1**			**WEEKS 22**
REMEDY	XL Recordings	4	22 May 99	22

BASIA
Poland

SINGLES:		HITS 3			WEEKS 9
PROMISES (FRENCH MIX)	Epic	48	23 Jan 88		4
TIME AND TIDE	Epic	61	28 May 88		3
DRUNK ON LOVE	Epic	41	14 Jan 95		2
ALBUMS:		HITS 2			WEEKS 4
TIME AND TIDE	Portrait	61	13 Feb 88		3
LONDON WARSAW NEW YORK	Epic	68	3 Mar 90		1

Count BASIE and his Orchestra
US

(See also Frank Sinatra and Count Basie and his Orchestra.)

ALBUMS:		HITS 1			WEEKS 1
CHAIRMAN OF THE BOARD	Columbia	17	16 Apr 60		1

Toni BASIL
US

SINGLES:		HITS 2			WEEKS 16
MICKEY	Radialchoice	2	6 Feb 82		12
Originally recorded by Racey (as Kitty).					
NOBODY	Radialchoice	52	1 May 82		4
ALBUMS:		HITS 1			WEEKS 16
WORD OF MOUTH	Radialchoice	15	6 Feb 82		16

Fontella BASS
US

SINGLES:		HITS 2			WEEKS 15
RESCUE ME	Chess	11	4 Dec 65		10
RECOVERY	Chess	32	22 Jan 66		5

Sid BASS' ORCHESTRA – See FOUR ESQUIRES – vocal with the Sid BASS' ORCHESTRA

BASS BOYZ
UK

(See also Pianoman.)

SINGLES:		HITS 1			WEEKS 1
GUNZ AND PIANOZ	Polydor	74	28 Sep 96		1
Based around the guitar riff from Sweet Child Of Mine by Guns N'Roses.					

BASS BUMPERS
Germany/UK

SINGLES:		HITS 2			WEEKS 4
RUNNIN'	Vertigo	68	25 Sep 93		1
THE MUSIC'S GOT ME	Vertigo	25	5 Feb 94		3

BASS JUMPERS
Holland

SINGLES:		HITS 1			WEEKS 1
MAKE UP YOUR MIND	Pepper	44	13 Feb 99		1

BASS-O-MATIC
UK

SINGLES:		HITS 4			WEEKS 19
IN THE REALM OF THE SENSES	Virgin	66	12 May 90		3
FASCINATING RHYTHM	Virgin	9	1 Sep 90		11
EASE ON BY	Virgin	61	22 Dec 90		4
FUNKY LOVE VIBRATIONS	Virgin	71	3 Aug 91		1
ALBUMS:		HITS 1			WEEKS 2
SET THE CONTROLS FOR THE HEART OF THE BASS	Virgin	57	13 Oct 90		2

Shirley BASSEY
UK

SINGLES:		HITS 30			WEEKS 326
THE BANANA BOAT SONG	Philips	8	16 Feb 57		10
FIRE DOWN BELOW	Philips	30	24 Aug 57		1
Inspired by the film 'Fire Down Below'.					
YOU, YOU ROMEO	Philips	29	7 Sep 57		2
Above 2 entries were separate sides of the same release, each had its own chart run.					
AS I LOVE YOU	Philips	27	20 Dec 58		2
From the film 'The Big Beat'. Originally recorded by Carmen McCrae.					
KISS ME, HONEY HONEY, KISS ME	Philips	3	27 Dec 58		17
AS I LOVE YOU [RE]	Philips	1	10 Jan 59		17
Above 6: Shirley BASSEY with Wally STOTT and his Orchestra.					
WITH THESE HANDS	Columbia	38	2 Apr 60		2
WITH THESE HANDS [RE-1ST]	Columbia	31	23 Apr 60		2
WITH THESE HANDS [RE-2ND]	Columbia	41	14 May 60		2
AS LONG AS HE NEEDS ME	Columbia	2	6 Aug 60		30
From the musical 'Oliver!'.					

BASSEY

Title	Label	Pos	Date	Wks
YOU'LL NEVER KNOW	Columbia	6	13 May 61	17

Originally recorded by Dick Haymes in 1943.
Above 5: Shirley BASSEY with the Rita WILLIAMS SINGERS and Geoff LOVE and his Orchestra.

| REACH FOR THE STARS / CLIMB EV'RY MOUNTAIN | Columbia | 1 | 29 Jul 61 | 16 |

Climb Ev'ry Mountain from the musical 'The Sound Of Music'; it was not listed from 30 Sep 61.
Above hit: Shirley BASSEY with Geoff LOVE and his Orchestra.

| REACH FOR THE STARS [RE] | Columbia | 40 | 25 Nov 61 | 2 |
| I'LL GET BY (AS LONG AS I HAVE YOU) | Columbia | 10 | 25 Nov 61 | 8 |

Originally recorded by Ruth Etting.
Above hit: Shirley BASSEY with the WILLIAMS SINGERS and Geoff LOVE and his Orchestra.

| TONIGHT | Columbia | 21 | 17 Feb 62 | 8 |

From the film/show 'West Side Story'.
Above hit: Shirley BASSEY and the Rita WILLIAMS SINGERS with Geoff LOVE and his Orchestra.

| AVE MARIA | Columbia | 31 | 28 Apr 62 | 4 |

Ave Maria is a Catholic form of address to the Virgin Mary.

| FAR AWAY | Columbia | 24 | 2 Jun 62 | 13 |

From the musical 'Blitz'.
Above hit: Shirley BASSEY with Geoff LOVE and his Orchestra.

| WHAT NOW MY LOVE? | Columbia | 5 | 1 Sep 62 | 17 |

Above hit: Shirley BASSEY with Nelson RIDDLE and his Orchestra.

| WHAT KIND OF FOOL AM I? | Columbia | 47 | 2 Mar 63 | 2 |

From the show 'Stop The World I Want To Get Off'.
Above hit: Shirley BASSEY with Frank BARBER and his Orchestra.

| I (WHO HAVE NOTHING) (UNO DEI TANTI) | Columbia | 6 | 28 Sep 63 | 20 |

Original by Ben E. King reached No. 29 in the US in 1963.

MY SPECIAL DREAM (THEME FROM "THE VICTORS")	Columbia	32	25 Jan 64	7
GONE	Columbia	36	11 Apr 64	5
GOLDFINGER	Columbia	21	17 Oct 64	9

From the James Bond film of the same name.

| NO REGRETS (NON JE NE REGRETTE RIEN) | Columbia | 39 | 22 May 65 | 4 |

Originally recorded by Edith Piaf.

| BIG SPENDER | United Artists | 21 | 14 Oct 67 | 15 |

From 'Sweet Charity'.

| SOMETHING | United Artists | 4 | 20 Jun 70 | 21 |

Written by George Harrison.

| THE FOOL ON THE HILL | United Artists | 48 | 2 Jan 71 | 1 |

Originally written and recorded by the Beatles.

| SOMETHING [RE] | United Artists | 50 | 23 Jan 71 | 1 |
| (WHERE DO I BEGIN) LOVE STORY | United Artists | 34 | 27 Mar 71 | 9 |

From the film 'Love Story'.

| FOR ALL WE KNOW | United Artists | 46 | 7 Aug 71 | 1 |

From the film 'Lovers And Other Strangers'.

| FOR ALL WE KNOW [RE] | United Artists | 6 | 21 Aug 71 | 23 |
| DIAMONDS ARE FOREVER | United Artists | 38 | 15 Jan 72 | 6 |

From the James Bond film of the same name.

NEVER, NEVER, NEVER (GRANDE, GRANDE, GRANDE)	United Artists	8	3 Mar 73	18
NEVER, NEVER, NEVER (GRANDE, GRANDE, GRANDE) [RE]	United Artists	48	14 Jul 73	1
THE RHYTHM DIVINE	Mercury	54	22 Aug 87	2

Backing vocals by Billy Mackenzie (The Associates).
Above hit: YELLO featuring Shirley BASSEY.

| 'DISCO' LA PASSIONE | East West | 41 | 16 Nov 96 | 1 |

From the film 'La Passione'.
Above hit: Chris REA/Shirley BASSEY.

| HISTORY REPEATING | Wall Of Sound | 19 | 20 Dec 97 | 7 |

Above hit: PROPELLERHEADS featuring Miss Shirley BASSEY.

| WORLD IN UNION | Decca | 35 | 23 Oct 99 | 3 |

Official ITV theme of the 1999 Rugby World Cup. Features The Morriston Rugby Club Choir and the City of Prague Philharmonic Orchestra.
Above hit: Shirley BASSEY, Bryn TERFEL and the BLACK MOUNTAIN MALE CHORUS.

EPS:	HITS 5			WEEKS 78
FABULOUS MISS BASSEY	Columbia	5	22 Oct 60	15
AS LONG AS HE NEEDS ME	Columbia	3	21 Jan 61	57
FABULOUS SHIRLEY BASSEY NO. 2	Columbia	15	18 Feb 61	2
SHIRLEY NO. 2	Columbia	15	2 Dec 61	3
DYNAMIC SHIRLEY BASSEY	Columbia	15	28 Nov 64	1

ALBUMS:	HITS 33			WEEKS 293
FABULOUS SHIRLEY BASSEY	Columbia	12	28 Jan 61	2

Originally released in 1959.

SHIRLEY	Columbia	9	25 Feb 61	10
SHIRLEY BASSEY	Columbia	14	17 Feb 62	11
LET'S FACE THE MUSIC	Columbia	12	15 Dec 62	7

Above hit: Shirley BASSEY with the NELSON RIDDLE ORCHESTRA.

| SHIRLEY BASSEY AT THE PIGALLE | Columbia | 15 | 4 Dec 65 | 7 |

I'VE GOT A SONG FOR YOU	United Artists	26	27 Aug 66	1
TWELVE OF THOSE SONGS	Columbia	38	17 Feb 68	3
THE GOLDEN HITS OF SHIRLEY BASSEY	Columbia	28	7 Dec 68	40
LIVE AT THE TALK OF THE TOWN	United Artists	38	11 Jul 70	6
SOMETHING	United Artists	5	29 Aug 70	28
SOMETHING ELSE	United Artists	7	15 May 71	9
BIG SPENDER	Sunset	27	2 Oct 71	8
IT'S MAGIC	Starline	32	30 Oct 71	1
Above 2 were budget releases.				
THE FABULOUS SHIRLEY BASSEY	Music For Pleasure	48	6 Nov 71	1
WHAT NOW MY LOVE	Music For Pleasure	17	4 Dec 71	5
THE SHIRLEY BASSEY COLLECTION	United Artists	37	8 Jan 72	1
I CAPRICORN	United Artists	13	19 Feb 72	11
AND I LOVE YOU SO	United Artists	24	25 Nov 72	9
NEVER NEVER NEVER	United Artists	10	2 Jun 73	10
THE SHIRLEY BASSEY SINGLES ALBUM	United Artists	2	15 Mar 75	23
GOOD, BAD BUT BEAUTIFUL	United Artists	13	1 Nov 75	7
LOVE, LIFE AND FEELINGS	United Artists	13	15 May 76	5
THOUGHTS OF LOVE	United Artists	15	4 Dec 76	9
YOU TAKE MY HEART AWAY	United Artists	34	25 Jun 77	5
25TH ANNIVERSARY ALBUM	United Artists	3	4 Nov 78	12
THE MAGIC IS YOU	United Artists	40	12 May 79	5
LOVE SONGS	Applause	48	17 Jul 82	5
I AM WHAT I AM	Towerbell	25	20 Oct 84	18
Above hit: Shirley BASSEY with the LONDON SYMPHONY ORCHESTRA.				
KEEP THE MUSIC PLAYING	Freestyle	25	18 May 91	7
THE BEST OF SHIRLEY BASSEY	Dino	27	5 Dec 92	5
SHIRLEY BASSEY SINGS ANDREW LLOYD WEBBER	Premier	34	4 Dec 93	5
SHIRLEY BASSEY SINGS THE MOVIES	PolyGram TV	24	11 Nov 95	9
THE SHOW MUST GO ON	PolyGram TV	47	9 Nov 96	8
Compilation to coincide with her 60th birthday.				

BASSHEADS — UK

SINGLES:	HITS 4			WEEKS 19
IS THERE ANYBODY OUT THERE?	Deconstruction	5	16 Nov 91	8
BACK TO THE OLD SCHOOL	Deconstruction	12	30 May 92	4
WHO CAN MAKE ME FEEL GOOD?	Deconstruction	38	28 Nov 92	2
START A BRAND NEW LIFE (SAVE ME)	Deconstruction	49	28 Aug 93	2
IS THERE ANYBODY OUT THERE? [RI]	Deconstruction	24	15 Jul 95	3

BATES — Germany

SINGLES:	HITS 1			WEEKS 1
BILLIE JEAN	Virgin	67	3 Feb 96	1

Mike BATT (with the NEW EDITION) — UK

(See also Justin Hayward with Mike Batt and the London Philharmonic Orchestra.)

SINGLES:	HITS 1			WEEKS 8
SUMMERTIME CITY	Epic	4	16 Aug 75	8

BAUHAUS — UK

SINGLES:	HITS 8			WEEKS 35
KICK IN THE EYE	Beggars Banquet	59	18 Apr 81	3
THE PASSION OF LOVERS	Beggars Banquet	56	4 Jul 81	2
KICK IN THE EYE – SEARCHING FOR SATORI [EP]	Beggars Banquet	45	6 Mar 82	4
Lead track: Kick In The Eye (Searching For Satori).				
SPIRIT	Beggars Banquet	42	19 Jun 82	5
ZIGGY STARDUST	Beggars Banquet	15	9 Oct 82	7
LAGARTIJA NICK	Beggars Banquet	44	22 Jan 83	4
SHE'S IN PARTIES	Beggars Banquet	26	9 Apr 83	6
THE SINGLES 1981-1983 [EP]	Beggars Banquet	52	29 Oct 83	4
Lead track: The Passion Of Lovers. 6 track 12" only release featuring their first 6 hits.				
ALBUMS:	HITS 5			WEEKS 24
IN THE FLAT FIELD	4AD	72	15 Nov 80	1
MASK	Beggars Banquet	30	24 Oct 81	5
THE SKY'S GONE OUT	Beggars Banquet	4	30 Oct 82	6
BURNING FROM THE INSIDE	Beggars Banquet	13	23 Jul 83	10
1979-1983	Beggars Banquet	36	30 Nov 85	2

Les BAXTER his Chorus and Orchestra — US

SINGLES:	HITS 1			WEEKS 9
UNCHAINED MELODY	Capitol	10	14 May 55	9
From the film 'Unchained'.				

BAY CITY ROLLERS   UK

SINGLES:		HITS 12			WEEKS 113	
KEEP ON DANCING	Bell		9	18 Sep 71		13
Jonathan King is actually the vocalist on this hit. Originally recorded by Avantis in 1963.						
REMEMBER (SHA-LA-LA)	Bell		6	9 Feb 74		12
Some copies only show title as 'Remember'.						
SHANG-A-LANG	Bell		2	27 Apr 74		10
SUMMERLOVE SENSATION	Bell		3	27 Jul 74		10
ALL OF ME LOVE ALL OF YOU	Bell		4	12 Oct 74		10
BYE BYE BABY	Bell		1	8 Mar 75		16
Original by the Four Seasons reached No. 12 in the US in 1965.						
GIVE A LITTLE LOVE	Bell		1	12 Jul 75		9
MONEY HONEY	Bell		3	22 Nov 75		9
Originally recorded by the Drifters.						
LOVE ME LIKE I LOVE YOU	Bell		4	10 Apr 76		6
I ONLY WANNA BE WITH YOU	Bell		4	11 Sep 76		9
IT'S A GAME	Arista		16	7 May 77		6
Originally recorded by String Driven Thing.						
YOU MADE ME BELIEVE IN MAGIC	Arista		34	30 Jul 77		3
ALBUMS:		HITS 5			WEEKS 127	
ROLLIN'	Bell		1	12 Oct 74		62
ONCE UPON A STAR	Bell		1	3 May 75		37
WOULDN'T YOU LIKE IT	Bell		3	13 Dec 75		12
DEDICATION	Bell		4	25 Sep 76		12
IT'S A GAME	Arista		18	13 Aug 77		4

Duke BAYSEE   UK

SINGLES:		HITS 2			WEEKS 6	
SUGAR SUGAR	Bell		30	3 Sep 94		4
DO YOU LOVE ME?	Double Dekker		46	21 Jan 95		2

BBC CONCERT ORCHESTRA/BBC SYMPHONY CHORUS Conducted by Stephen JACKSON   UK

SINGLES:		HITS 1			WEEKS 3	
ODE TO JOY (FROM BEETHOVEN SYMPHONY NO. 9)	Virgin		36	22 Jun 96		3
BBC-TV theme to the European Football Championships, 1996.						

BBC SYMPHONY ORCHESTRA, SINGERS and SYMPHONY CHORUS   UK

EPS:		HITS 1			WEEKS 1	
PLANET SUITE – MARS AND JUPITER	HMV		14	26 Mar 60		1
Above hit: BBC SYMPHONY ORCHESTRA.						
ALBUMS:		HITS 3			WEEKS 7	
LAST NIGHT OF THE PROMS	Philips		36	4 Oct 69		1
Above hit: Colin DAVIS conducting the BBC SYMPHONY ORCHESTRA, SINGERS and CHORUS.						
HIGHLIGHTS OF THE LAST NIGHT OF THE PROMS '82	K-Tel		69	11 Dec 82		5
Above hit: BBC SYMPHONY ORCHESTRA, SINGERS and SYMPHONY CHORUS conducted by James LOUGHRAN.						
ELGAR/PAYNE: SYMPHONY NO. 3	NMC		44	28 Feb 98		1
Above hit: BBC SYMPHONY ORCHESTRA conducted by Andrew DAVIS.						

BBC WELSH SYMPHONY ORCHESTRA and CHORUS - See Aled JONES

BBD - See BELL BIV DEVOE

BBG   UK

SINGLES:		HITS 4			WEEKS 10	
SNAPPINESS	Urban		28	28 Apr 90		5
Samples Soul II Soul's Happiness.						
Above hit: BBG featuring Dina TAYLOR.						
SOME KIND OF HEAVEN	Urban		65	11 Aug 90		2
LET THE MUSIC PLAY	MCA		46	23 Mar 96		1
Above hit: BBG featuring ERIN.						
SNAPPINESS [RM]	Hi-Life		50	18 May 96		1
Remixed by Bob and Tony Newland.						
JUST BE TONIGHT	Hi-Life		45	5 Jul 97		1
Above hit: BBG featuring ERIN.						

BBM   UK

SINGLES:		HITS 1			WEEKS 2	
WHERE IN THE WORLD	Virgin		57	6 Aug 94		2
ALBUMS:		HITS 1			WEEKS 4	
AROUND THE NEXT DREAM	Virgin		9	18 Jun 94		4

BBMAK

UK

SINGLES:	HITS 1		WEEKS 2	
BACK HERE	Telstar	37	28 Aug 99	2

BC-52's – See B-52'S

BE-BOP DELUXE

UK

SINGLES:	HITS 2		WEEKS 13	
SHIPS IN THE NIGHT	Harvest	23	21 Feb 76	8
HOT VALVES [EP]	Harvest	36	13 Nov 76	5
Lead track: Maid In Heaven.				
ALBUMS:	**HITS 4**		**WEEKS 28**	
SUNBURST FINISH	Harvest	17	31 Jan 76	12
MODERN MUSIC	Harvest	12	25 Sep 76	6
LIVE! IN THE AIR AGE	Harvest	10	6 Aug 77	5
DRASTIC PLASTIC	Harvest	22	25 Feb 78	5

BEACH BOYS

US

SINGLES:	HITS 30		WEEKS 281	
SURFIN' U.S.A.	Capitol	34	3 Aug 63	7
Adapted lyrics to Chuck Berry's Sweet Little Sixteen.				
I GET AROUND	Capitol	7	11 Jul 64	13
WHEN I GROW UP (TO BE A MAN)	Capitol	44	31 Oct 64	2
WHEN I GROW UP (TO BE A MAN) [RE]	Capitol	27	21 Nov 64	5
DANCE DANCE DANCE	Capitol	24	23 Jan 65	6
HELP ME RHONDA	Capitol	27	5 Jun 65	10
CALIFORNIA GIRLS	Capitol	26	4 Sep 65	8
BARBARA ANN	Capitol	3	19 Feb 66	10
Original by the Regents reached No. 13 in the US in 1961. Dean Torrence of Jan & Dean and Glen Campbell on backing vocals.				
SLOOP JOHN B	Capitol	2	23 Apr 66	15
GOD ONLY KNOWS	Capitol	2	30 Jul 66	14
GOOD VIBRATIONS	Capitol	1	5 Nov 66	13
Glen Campbell on lead guitar.				
THEN I KISSED HER	Capitol	4	6 May 67	11
HEROES AND VILLANS	Capitol	8	26 Aug 67	9
WILD HONEY	Capitol	29	25 Nov 67	6
DARLIN'	Capitol	11	20 Jan 68	14
FRIENDS	Capitol	25	11 May 68	7
DO IT AGAIN	Capitol	1	27 Jul 68	14
BLUEBIRDS OVER THE MOUNTAIN	Capitol	33	28 Dec 68	5
I CAN HEAR MUSIC	Capitol	10	1 Mar 69	13
Originally recorded by Ellie Greenwich.				
BREAK AWAY	Capitol	6	14 Jun 69	11
COTTONFIELDS	Capitol	5	16 May 70	17
CALIFORNIA SAGA/CALIFORNIA	Reprise	37	3 Mar 73	5
GOOD VIBRATIONS [RI]	Capitol	18	3 Jul 76	7
ROCK AND ROLL MUSIC	Reprise	36	10 Jul 76	4
HERE COMES THE NIGHT	Caribou	37	31 Mar 79	8
LADY LYNDA	Caribou	6	16 Jun 79	11
SUMAHAMA	Caribou	45	29 Sep 79	4
THE BEACH BOYS MEDLEY [M]	Capitol	47	29 Aug 81	4
WIPEOUT	Urban	2	22 Aug 87	12
Above hit: FAT BOYS and the BEACH BOYS.				
KOKOMO	Elektra	25	19 Nov 88	9
From the film 'Cocktail'.				
WOULDN'T IT BE NICE	Capitol	58	2 Jun 90	1
DO IT AGAIN [RI]	Capitol	61	29 Jun 91	2
FUN FUN FUN	PolyGram TV	24	2 Mar 96	4
Above hit: STATUS QUO with the BEACH BOYS.				
EPS:	**HITS 4**		**WEEKS 108**	
FUN, FUN, FUN	Capitol	19	29 Aug 64	1
FOUR BY THE BEACH BOYS	Capitol	11	14 Nov 64	8
THE BEACH BOY HITS	Capitol	1	14 May 66	82
GOD ONLY KNOWS	Capitol	3	12 Nov 66	17
ALBUMS:	**HITS 29**		**WEEKS 564**	
SURFIN' USA	Capitol	17	25 Sep 65	7
BEACH BOYS PARTY	Capitol	3	19 Feb 66	14
BEACH BOYS TODAY	Capitol	6	16 Apr 66	25
PET SOUNDS	Capitol	2	9 Jul 66	39
SUMMER DAYS (AND SUMMER NIGHTS!!)	Capitol	4	16 Jul 66	22
BEST OF THE BEACH BOYS	Capitol	2	12 Nov 66	142
SURFER GIRL	Capitol	13	11 Mar 67	14
BEST OF THE BEACH BOYS VOLUME 2	Capitol	3	21 Oct 67	39
SMILEY SMILE	Capitol	9	18 Nov 67	8

WILD HONEY	Capitol	7	16 Mar 68	15
FRIENDS	Capitol	13	21 Sep 68	8
BEST OF THE BEACH BOYS VOLUME 3	Capitol	8	23 Nov 68	12
20/20	Capitol	3	29 Mar 69	10
GREATEST HITS	Capitol	5	19 Sep 70	30
SUNFLOWER	Stateside	29	5 Dec 70	6
SURF'S UP	Stateside	15	27 Nov 71	7
CARL AND THE PASSIONS/SO TOUGH	Reprise	25	24 Jun 72	1
HOLLAND	Reprise	20	17 Feb 73	7
20 GOLDEN GREATS	Capitol	1	10 Jul 76	86
15 BIG ONES	Reprise	31	24 Jul 76	3
THE BEACH BOYS LOVE YOU	Reprise	28	7 May 77	1
LA (LIGHT ALBUM)	Caribou	32	21 Apr 79	6
KEEPING THE SUMMER ALIVE	Caribou	54	12 Apr 80	3
THE VERY BEST OF THE BEACH BOYS	Capitol	1	30 Jul 83	17
THE BEACH BOYS	Caribou	60	22 Jun 85	2
SUMMER DREAMS – 28 CLASSIC TRACKS	Capitol	2	23 Jun 90	27
THE BEST OF THE BEACH BOYS	Capitol	25	1 Jul 95	6
First compilation to feature all their Top 30 hits.				
PET SOUNDS [RI]	Fame	70	16 Sep 95	2
GREATEST HITS	EMI	28	11 Jul 98	4
ENDLESS HARMONY SOUNDTRACK	Capitol	56	19 Sep 98	1
Previously unreleased live tracks, demos, remixes and alternative recordings.				

Walter BEASLEY   US

SINGLES:	HITS 1			WEEKS 3
I'M SO HAPPY	Urban	70	23 Jan 88	3

BEASTIE BOYS   US

SINGLES:	HITS 12			WEEKS 58
(YOU GOTTA) FIGHT FOR YOUR RIGHT (TO PARTY)	Def Jam	11	28 Feb 87	11
NO SLEEP TILL BROOKLYN	Def Jam	14	30 May 87	7
SHE'S ON IT	Def Jam	10	18 Jul 87	8
GIRLS / SHE'S CRAFTY	Def Jam	34	3 Oct 87	4
PASS THE MIC	Grand Royal	47	11 Apr 92	2
FROZEN METAL HEAD [EP]	Grand Royal	55	4 Jul 92	1
Lead track: Jimmy James.				
GET IT TOGETHER / SABOTAGE	Grand Royal	19	9 Jul 94	4
SURE SHOT	Grand Royal	27	26 Nov 94	3
..INTERGALACTIC..	Grand Royal	5	4 Jul 98	7
THE BODY MOVIN'	Grand Royal	15	7 Nov 98	4
THE BODY MOVIN' [RE]	Grand Royal	69	16 Jan 99	1
REMOTE CONTROL / 3 MCS & 1 DJ	Grand Royal	21	29 May 99	3
ALIVE	Grand Royal	28	18 Dec 99	3
Samples I'm Still #1 by Boogie Down Productions.				
ALBUMS:	**HITS 6**			**WEEKS 86**
LICENSE TO ILL	Def Jam	7	31 Jan 87	40
PAUL'S BOUTIQUE	Capitol	44	5 Aug 89	2
ILL COMMUNICATION	Grand Royal	10	4 Jun 94	15
ROOT DOWN [EP]	Grand Royal	23	10 Jun 95	2
3 mixes of Root Down and 7 tracks recorded live on their European tour.				
THE IN SOUND FROM WAY OUT!	Grand Royal	45	6 Apr 96	1
Includes B-sides, alternative versions and unreleased material.				
HELLO NASTY	Grand Royal	1	18 Jul 98	21
ANTHOLOGY – THE SOUNDS OF SCIENCE	Grand Royal	36	4 Dec 99	5
Rarities and unreleased tracks packaged with an 80 page booklet.				

BEAT   UK

(See also Various Artists (EPs) 'The 2 Tone EP'.)

SINGLES:	HITS 13			WEEKS 92
TEARS OF A CLOWN / RANKING FULL STOP	2-Tone	6	8 Dec 79	11
HANDS OFF . . . SHE'S MINE	Go-Feet	9	23 Feb 80	9
MIRROR IN THE BATHROOM	Go-Feet	4	3 May 80	9
BEST FRIEND / STAND DOWN MARGARET (DUB)	Go-Feet	22	16 Aug 80	9
TOO NICE TO TALK TO	Go-Feet	7	13 Dec 80	11
DROWNING / ALL OUT TO GET YOU	Go-Feet	22	18 Apr 81	8
DOORS OF YOUR HEART	Go-Feet	33	20 Jun 81	6
HIT IT	Go-Feet	70	5 Dec 81	2
SAVE IT FOR LATER	Go-Feet	47	17 Apr 82	4
JEANETTE	Go-Feet	45	18 Sep 82	3
I CONFESS	Go-Feet	54	4 Dec 82	3
CAN'T GET USED TO LOSING YOU	Go-Feet	3	30 Apr 83	11
ACKEE 1-2-3	Go-Feet	54	2 Jul 83	4
MIRROR IN THE BATHROOM [RM]	Go-Feet	44	27 Jan 96	2
Remixed by Mark "Spike" Stent.				

ALBUMS:		HITS 5			WEEKS 73
JUST CAN'T STOP IT		Go-Feet	3	31 May 80	32
WHA'PPEN		Go-Feet	3	16 May 81	18
SPECIAL BEAT SERVICE		Go-Feet	21	9 Oct 82	6
WHAT IS BEAT? (THE BEST OF THE BEAT)		Go-Feet	10	11 Jun 83	13
BPM . . . THE VERY BEST OF THE BEAT		Go-Feet	13	10 Feb 96	4

BEAT BOYS – See Gene VINCENT

BEAT SYSTEM UK

SINGLES:		HITS 2			WEEKS 3
WALK ON THE WILD SIDE		Fourth & Broadway	63	3 Mar 90	2
TO A BRIGHTER DAY (O'HAPPY DAY)		London	70	18 Sep 93	1

BEATLES UK

SINGLES:	HITS 32			WEEKS 456
LOVE ME DO	Parlophone	17	13 Oct 62	18
PLEASE PLEASE ME	Parlophone	2	19 Jan 63	18
FROM ME TO YOU	Parlophone	1	20 Apr 63	21
MY BONNIE	Polydor	48	8 Jun 63	1
First released in 1962.				
Above hit: Tony SHERIDAN and the BEATLES.				
SHE LOVES YOU	Parlophone	1	31 Aug 63	31
The best selling single of all-time in the UK until 1977.				
I WANT TO HOLD YOUR HAND	Parlophone	1	7 Dec 63	21
CAN'T BUY ME LOVE	Parlophone	1	28 Mar 64	14
SHE LOVES YOU [RE-1ST]	Parlophone	42	11 Apr 64	2
I WANT TO HOLD YOUR HAND [RE-1ST]	Parlophone	48	16 May 64	1
AIN'T SHE SWEET	Polydor	29	13 Jun 64	6
CAN'T BUY ME LOVE [RE-1ST]		47	11 Jul 64	1
A HARD DAY'S NIGHT	Parlophone	1	18 Jul 64	13
From the film of the same name.				
I FEEL FINE	Parlophone	1	5 Dec 64	13
TICKET TO RIDE	Parlophone	1	17 Apr 65	12
HELP!	Parlophone	1	31 Jul 65	14
From the film of the same name.				
DAY TRIPPER / WE CAN WORK IT OUT	Parlophone	1	11 Dec 65	12
PAPERBACK WRITER	Parlophone	1	18 Jun 66	11
YELLOW SUBMARINE / ELEANOR RIGBY	Parlophone	1	13 Aug 66	13
PENNY LANE / STRAWBERRY FIELDS FOREVER	Parlophone	2	25 Feb 67	11
ALL YOU NEED IS LOVE	Parlophone	1	15 Jul 67	13
Song featured on the BBC TV show 'Our World', 25 Jun 67 as part of a live global TV				
satelitte link-up.				
HELLO, GOODBYE	Parlophone	1	2 Dec 67	12
MAGICAL MYSTERY TOUR (DOUBLE EP) [EP]	Parlophone	2	16 Dec 67	12
6 tracks from the TV film. Lead track: Magical Mystery Tour.				
LADY MADONNA	Parlophone	1	23 Mar 68	8
HEY JUDE	Apple	1	7 Sep 68	16
GET BACK	Apple	1	26 Apr 69	17
Above hit: BEATLES with Billy PRESTON.				
THE BALLAD OF JOHN AND YOKO	Apple	1	7 Jun 69	14
SOMETHING / COME TOGETHER	Apple	4	8 Nov 69	12
LET IT BE	Apple	2	14 Mar 70	9
LET IT BE [RE]	Apple	43	24 Oct 70	1
YESTERDAY	Apple	8	13 Mar 76	7
Originally written for but turned down by Billy J.Kramer.				
PAPERBACK WRITER [RE]	Parlophone	23	27 Mar 76	5
HEY JUDE [RE]	Apple	12	27 Mar 76	7
STRAWBERRY FIELDS FOREVER [RE-1ST]	Parlophone	32	3 Apr 76	3
GET BACK [RE-1ST]	Apple	28	3 Apr 76	5
Above hit: BEATLES with Billy PRESTON.				
HELP! [RE]	Parlophone	37	10 Apr 76	3
Though the entries in 1976 had the same catalogue numbers, they were re-issued with green and				
black sleeves.				
BACK IN THE U.S.S.R.	Parlophone	19	10 Jul 76	6
SGT. PEPPER'S LONELY HEARTS CLUB BAND/WITH A LITTLE				
HELP FROM MY FRIENDS [M]	Parlophone	63	7 Oct 78	3
BEATLES MOVIE MEDLEY [M]	Parlophone	10	5 Jun 82	9
7 track medley from their films.				
LOVE ME DO [RE-1ST]	Parlophone	4	16 Oct 82	7
All re-entries from this date were released to mark the 20th anniversary of their original issue.				
PLEASE PLEASE ME [RE]	Parlophone	29	22 Jan 83	4
FROM ME TO YOU [RE]	Parlophone	40	23 Apr 83	4
SHE LOVES YOU [RE-2ND]	Parlophone	45	3 Sep 83	3
I WANT TO HOLD YOUR HAND [RE-2ND]	Parlophone	62	26 Nov 83	2
CAN'T BUY ME LOVE [RE-2ND]	Parlophone	53	31 Mar 84	2
A HARD DAY'S NIGHT [RE]	Parlophone	52	21 Jul 84	2
I FEEL FINE [RE]	Parlophone	65	8 Dec 84	1

TICKET TO RIDE [RE]	Parlophone	70	20 Apr 85	2
YELLOW SUBMARINE / ELEANOR RIGBY [RE]	Parlophone	63	30 Aug 86	1
STRAWBERRY FIELDS FOREVER / PENNY LANE [RE-2ND]	Parlophone	65	28 Feb 87	2
ALL YOU NEED IS LOVE [RE]	Parlophone	47	18 Jul 87	3
HELLO, GOODBYE [RE]	Parlophone	63	5 Dec 87	1
LADY MADONNA [RE]	Parlophone	67	26 Mar 88	1
HEY JUDE [RE-2ND]	Apple	52	10 Sep 88	2
GET BACK [RE-2ND]	Apple	74	22 Apr 89	1
Above hit: BEATLES with Billy PRESTON.				
LOVE ME DO [RE-2ND]	Parlophone	53	17 Oct 92	1
30th Anniversary re-issue.				
BABY IT'S YOU	Apple	7	1 Apr 95	6
Recorded at the BBC on 1 Jun 63 for 'Pop Go The Beatles'.				
BABY IT'S YOU [RE]	Apple	71	8 Jul 95	1
FREE AS A BIRD	Apple	2	16 Dec 95	8
First new recording in 25 years. Written by John Lennon in 1977.				
REAL LOVE	Apple	4	16 Mar 96	7
John Lennon's vocal from circa 1979.				

EPS:	HITS 12		WEEKS 392	
TWIST AND SHOUT	Parlophone	1	20 Jul 63	64
THE BEATLES' HITS	Parlophone	1	21 Sep 63	43
THE BEATLES (NO. 1)	Parlophone	2	9 Nov 63	29
ALL MY LOVING	Parlophone	1	8 Feb 64	44
LONG TALL SALLY	Parlophone	1	4 Jul 64	37
Last song the Beatles ever performed at their final concert at Candlestick Park, San Francisco.				
A HARD DAY'S NIGHT	Parlophone	1	14 Nov 64	30
A HARD DAY'S NIGHT VOLUME 2	Parlophone	8	9 Jan 65	17
BEATLES FOR SALE	Parlophone	1	10 Apr 65	47
BEATLES FOR SALE (NO. 2)	Parlophone	5	12 Jun 65	24
THE BEATLES' MILLION SELLERS	Parlophone	1	11 Dec 65	26
YESTERDAY	Parlophone	1	12 Mar 66	13
NOWHERE MAN	Parlophone	4	16 Jul 66	18

ALBUMS:	HITS 30		WEEKS 1240	
PLEASE PLEASE ME	Parlophone	1	6 Apr 63	70
WITH THE BEATLES	Parlophone	1	30 Nov 63	51
A HARD DAY'S NIGHT	Parlophone	1	18 Jul 64	38
BEATLES FOR SALE	Parlophone	1	12 Dec 64	46
HELP!	Parlophone	1	14 Aug 65	37
RUBBER SOUL	Parlophone	1	11 Dec 65	42
REVOLVER	Parlophone	1	13 Aug 66	34
A COLLECTION OF BEATLES' OLDIES	Parlophone	7	10 Dec 66	34
SGT. PEPPER'S LONELY HEARTS CLUB BAND	Parlophone	1	3 Jun 67	148
The best selling album of all time in the UK.				
MAGICAL MYSTERY TOUR	Capitol	31	13 Jan 68	2
US import.				
THE BEATLES (THE WHITE ALBUM)	Apple	1	7 Dec 68	22
YELLOW SUBMARINE	Apple	3	1 Feb 69	10
Above hit: BEATLES featuring the George MARTIN ORCHESTRA.				
ABBEY ROAD	Apple	1	4 Oct 69	81
LET IT BE	Apple	1	23 May 70	59
A HARD DAY'S NIGHT [RE-1ST]	Parlophone	30	16 Jan 71	1
HELP! [RE-1ST]	Parlophone	33	24 Jul 71	2
Above 2 were re-released with new catalogue numbers.				
THE BEATLES 1962-1966	Apple	3	5 May 73	114
THE BEATLES 1967-1970	Apple	2	5 May 73	106
ROCK 'N' ROLL MUSIC	Parlophone	11	26 Jun 76	15
THE BEATLES TAPES	Polydor	45	21 Aug 76	1
THE BEATLES AT THE HOLLYWOOD BOWL	Parlophone	1	21 May 77	17
LOVE SONGS	Parlophone	7	17 Dec 77	17
RARITIES	Parlophone	71	3 Nov 79	1
BEATLES BALLADS	Parlophone	40	15 Nov 80	5
THE BEATLES 1962-1966 [RE-1ST]	Apple	37	20 Dec 80	34
THE BEATLES 1967-1970 [RE-1ST]	Apple	66	20 Dec 80	7
BEATLES BALLADS [RE]	Parlophone	17	29 Aug 81	11
20 GREATEST HITS	Parlophone	10	30 Oct 82	30
A HARD DAY'S NIGHT [RE-2ND]	Parlophone	30	7 Mar 87	4
PLEASE PLEASE ME [RE]	Parlophone	32	7 Mar 87	4
WITH THE BEATLES [RE-1ST]	Parlophone	40	7 Mar 87	2
BEATLES FOR SALE [RE]	Parlophone	45	7 Mar 87	2
REVOLVER [RE-1ST]	Parlophone	55	9 May 87	6
Includes re-entry in 1997.				
RUBBER SOUL [RE-1ST]	Parlophone	60	9 May 87	4
Includes re-entry in 1997.				
HELP! [RE-2ND]	Parlophone	61	9 May 87	2
SGT. PEPPER'S LONELY HEARTS CLUB BAND [RE-1ST]	Parlophone	3	6 Jun 87	16
THE BEATLES (THE WHITE ALBUM) [RE-1ST]	Apple	18	5 Sep 87	2
YELLOW SUBMARINE [RE]	Apple	60	5 Sep 87	1
Above hit: BEATLES featuring the George MARTIN ORCHESTRA.				

MAGICAL MYSTERY TOUR [RI]	Parlophone	52	3 Oct 87	1
ABBEY ROAD [RE-1ST]	Apple	30	31 Oct 87	2
LET IT BE [RE]	Apple	50	31 Oct 87	1
All re-entries/re-issues listed above were available for the first time on CD.				
PAST MASTERS VOLUME 2	Parlophone	46	19 Mar 88	1
PAST MASTERS VOLUME 1	Parlophone	49	19 Mar 88	1
SGT. PEPPER'S LONELY HEARTS CLUB BAND[RE-2ND]	Parlophone	6	20 Jun 92	33
Re-promoted to celebrate the 25th anniversary of its release. Includes re-entries through to 1999.				
THE BEATLES 1962-1966 [RE-2ND]	Apple	3	2 Oct 93	24
THE BEATLES 1967-1970 [RE-2ND]	Apple	4	2 Oct 93	24
Above 2 were available for the first time on CD.				
LIVE AT THE BBC	Apple	1	10 Dec 94	20
Compilation of songs recorded by the BBC during 1963-65.				
ANTHOLOGY 1	Apple	2	2 Dec 95	10
ANTHOLOGY 2	Apple	1	30 Mar 96	12
ANTHOLOGY 3	Apple	4	9 Nov 96	11
Above 3 are collections of out-takes, demos or previously unreleased songs.				
ABBEY ROAD [RE-2ND]	Apple	42	8 Mar 97	9
WITH THE BEATLES [RE-2ND]	Parlophone	72	22 Mar 97	1
REVOLVER [RE-2ND]	Parlophone	46	11 Apr 98	6
RUBBER SOUL [RE-2ND]	Parlophone	62	25 Apr 98	1
YELLOW SUBMARINE SONGTRACK [OST]	Parlophone	8	25 Sep 99	5
Now includes all Beatles songs from the film less tracks by the George Martin Orchestra.				

BEATMASTERS   UK

SINGLES:	HITS 7		WEEKS 47	
ROK DA HOUSE	Rhythm King	5	9 Jan 88	11
Original release reached No. 79 in 1987.				
Above hit: BEATMASTERS featuring the COOKIE CREW.				
BURN IT UP	Rhythm King	14	24 Sep 88	10
Above hit: BEATMASTERS with P.P. ARNOLD.				
WHO'S IN THE HOUSE (THE HIP HOUSE ANTHEM)	Rhythm King	8	22 Apr 89	9
Above hit: BEATMASTERS with MERLIN.				
HEY DJ/I CAN'T DANCE (TO THAT MUSIC YOUR PLAYING) /SKA TRAIN	Rhythm King	7	12 Aug 89	11
Backing vocals: Claudia Fontaine. I Can't Dance originally recorded by Martha and the Vandellas.				
Above hit: BEATMASTERS featuring Betty BOO.				
WARM LOVE	Rhythm King	51	2 Dec 89	2
Above hit: BEATMASTERS featuring Claudia FONTAINE.				
BOULEVARD OF BROKEN DREAMS	Rhythm King	62	21 Sep 91	1
DUNNO WHAT IT IS (ABOUT YOU)	Rhythm King	43	16 May 92	3
Original release reached No. 82 in 1991.				
Above hit: BEATMASTERS featuring Elaine VASSELL.				
ALBUMS:	HITS 1		WEEKS 10	
ANYWAYAWANNA	Rhythm King	30	1 Jul 89	10

BEATRICE - See Mike KOGLIN

BEATS INTERNATIONAL   UK

(See also Norman Cook.)

SINGLES:	HITS 6		WEEKS 30	
DUB BE GOOD TO ME	Go.Beat	1	10 Feb 90	13
Above hit: BEATS INTERNATIONAL featuring LINDY.				
WON'T TALK ABOUT IT	Go.Beat	9	12 May 90	7
BURUNDI BLUES	Go.Beat	51	15 Sep 90	3
Features vocals by Janet Kay.				
ECHO CHAMBER	Go.Beat	60	2 Mar 91	2
THE SUN DOESN'T SHINE	Go.Beat	66	21 Sep 91	2
IN THE GHETTO	Go.Beat	44	23 Nov 91	3
ALBUMS:	HITS 1		WEEKS 15	
LET THEM EAT BINGO	Go.Beat	17	14 Apr 90	15

BEAUTIFUL PEOPLE   UK

SINGLES:	HITS 1		WEEKS 1	
IF 60'S WERE 90'S	Essential	74	28 May 94	1
Features Jimi Hendrix samples.				

BEAUTIFUL SOUTH   UK

SINGLES:	HITS 23		WEEKS 145	
SONG FOR WHOEVER	Go! Discs	2	3 Jun 89	11
YOU KEEP IT ALL IN	Go! Discs	8	23 Sep 89	8
I'LL SAIL THIS SHIP ALONE	Go! Discs	31	2 Dec 89	8
A LITTLE TIME	Go! Discs	1	6 Oct 90	14
MY BOOK	Go! Discs	43	8 Dec 90	6
LET LOVE SPEAK UP ITSELF	Go! Discs	51	16 Mar 91	2

OLD RED EYES IS BACK	Go! Discs	22	11 Jan 92	6
WE ARE EACH OTHER	Go! Discs	30	14 Mar 92	3
BELL BOTTOMED TEAR	Go! Discs	16	13 Jun 92	5
36D	Go! Discs	46	26 Sep 92	2
GOOD AS GOLD	Go! Discs	23	12 Mar 94	5
EVERYBODY'S TALKIN'	Go! Discs	12	4 Jun 94	8
Originally recorded by Fred Neil.				
PRETTIEST EYES	Go! Discs	37	3 Sep 94	3
ONE LAST LOVE SONG	Go! Discs	14	12 Nov 94	5
PRETENDERS TO THE THRONE	Go! Discs	18	18 Nov 95	4
ROTTERDAM	Go! Discs	5	12 Oct 96	9
DON'T MARRY HER	Go! Discs	8	14 Dec 96	10
BLACKBIRD ON THE WIRE	Go! Discs	23	29 Mar 97	5
LIARS' BAR	Go! Discs	43	5 Jul 97	1
Featuring the Black Dyke Mills Band.				
PERFECT 10	Go! Discs	2	3 Oct 98	14
DUMB	Go! Discs	16	19 Dec 98	7
DUMB [RE]	Go! Discs	72	13 Mar 99	1
HOW LONG'S A TEAR TAKE TO DRY?	Go! Discs	12	20 Mar 99	6
THE TABLE	Go! Discs	47	10 Jul 99	2
Features the London Community Gospel Choir.				
ALBUMS:	**HITS 7**			**WEEKS 261**
WELCOME TO THE BEAUTIFUL SOUTH	Go! Discs	2	4 Nov 89	26
CHOKE	Go! Discs	2	10 Nov 90	22
0898: BEAUTIFUL SOUTH	Go! Discs	4	11 Apr 92	17
MIAOW	Go! Discs	6	9 Apr 94	24
CARRY ON UP THE CHARTS – THE BEST OF THE BEAUTIFUL SOUTH	Go! Discs	1	19 Nov 94	89
BLUE IS THE COLOUR	Go! Discs	1	2 Nov 96	46
QUENCH	Go! Discs	1	24 Oct 98	37

BEAVIS and BUTT-HEAD – See CHER

Gilbert BECAUD   France

SINGLES:	**HITS 1**			**WEEKS 12**
A LITTLE LOVE AND UNDERSTANDING	Decca	10	29 Mar 75	12

BECK   US

SINGLES:	**HITS 8**			**WEEKS 25**
LOSER	Geffen	15	5 Mar 94	6
Samples Walking On Guilded Splinters by Dr John.				
WHERE IT'S AT	Geffen	35	29 Jun 96	2
Samples Get Up And Dance by Mantronix.				
DEVILS HAIRCUT	Geffen	22	16 Nov 96	2
Samples Out Of Sight by Them.				
THE NEW POLLUTION	Geffen	14	8 Mar 97	5
SISSYNECK	Geffen	30	24 May 97	2
From the film 'Feather In Your Cap'.				
DEADWEIGHT	Geffen	23	8 Nov 97	3
From the film 'A Life Less Ordinary'.				
TROPICALIA	Geffen	39	19 Dec 98	2
SEXX LAWS	Geffen	27	20 Nov 99	3
ALBUMS:	**HITS 4**			**WEEKS 66**
MELLOW GOLD	Geffen	41	2 Apr 94	4
O-DE-LAY	Geffen	18	6 Jul 96	10
O-DE-LAY [RE]	Geffen	17	11 Jan 97	41
MUTATIONS	Geffen	24	14 Nov 98	6
MIDNITE VULTURES	Geffen	19	4 Dec 99	5

Jeff BECK   UK

(See also Jeff Beck, Tim Bogert and Carmine Appice.)

SINGLES:	**HITS 6**			**WEEKS 57**
HI-HO SILVER LINING	Columbia	14	25 Mar 67	14
TALLYMAN	Columbia	30	5 Aug 67	3
LOVE IS BLUE (L'AMOUR EST BLEU)	Columbia	23	2 Mar 68	7
GOO GOO BARABAJAGAL (LOVE IS HOT)	Pye	12	12 Jul 69	9
Some issues only had title listed as 'Barabajagal'.				
Above hit: DONOVAN and Jeff BECK GROUP.				
HI HO SILVER LINING [RI]	RAK	17	4 Nov 72	11
I'VE BEEN DRINKING	RAK	27	5 May 73	6
First released in 1968.				
Above hit: Jeff BECK GROUP Vocal: Rod STEWART.				
HI HO SILVER LINING [RI] [RE]	RAK	62	9 Oct 82	4
PEOPLE GET READY	Epic	49	7 Mar 92	3
Originally recorded by Curtis Mayfield.				
Above hit: Jeff BECK and Rod STEWART.				

ALBUMS:		HITS 5		WEEKS 12
COSA NOSTRA BECK – OLA	Columbia	39	13 Sep 69	1
WIRED	CBS	38	24 Jul 76	5
THERE AND BACK	Epic	38	19 Jul 80	4
FLASH	Epic	83	17 Aug 85	1
WHO ELSE?	Epic	74	27 Mar 99	1

Jeff BECK, Tim BOGERT and Carmine APPICE   UK

ALBUMS:		HITS 1		WEEKS 3
JEFF BECK, TIM BOGERT & CARMINE APPICE	Epic	28	28 Apr 73	3

Robin BECK   Canada

SINGLES:		HITS 1		WEEKS 13
THE FIRST TIME	Mercury	1	22 Oct 88	13

A Coca-Cola TV commercial theme.

Peter BECKETT – See Barry GRAY ORCHESTRA

Shelton BECTON – See Frankie KNUCKLES

BEDAZZLED   UK

SINGLES:		HITS 1		WEEKS 1
SUMMER SONG	Columbia	73	4 Jul 92	1

BEDLAM   UK

SINGLES:		HITS 1		WEEKS 1
DA-FORCE	Playola	68	6 Feb 99	1

Samples the Real Thing's Can You Feel The Force.

BEDLAM AGO GO   UK

SINGLES:		HITS 1		WEEKS 1
SEASON NO. 5	Sony S2	57	4 Apr 98	1

BEDROCK   UK

SINGLES:		HITS 3		WEEKS 7
FOR WHAT YOU DREAM OF	Stress	25	1 Jun 96	3
SET IN STONE / FORBIDDEN ZONE	Stress	71	12 Jul 97	1
HEAVEN SCENT	Bedrock	35	6 Nov 99	3

From the film 'Trainspotting'.
Above hit: John DIGWEED and Nick MUIR present BEDROCK featuring KYO (aka Carole LEEMING).
Above hit: John DIGWEED and Nick MUIR present BEDROCK.

BEDROCKS   UK

SINGLES:		HITS 1		WEEKS 7
OB-LA-DI, OB-LA-DA	Columbia	20	21 Dec 68	7

Written and originally recorded by the Beatles.

Celi BEE and the BUZZY BUNCH   US

SINGLES:		HITS 1		WEEKS 1
HOLD YOUR HORSES, BABE	TK	72	17 Jun 78	1

BEE GEES   UK

(See also Various Artists: Films – Original Soundtracks 'Saturday Night Fever'; 'Sgt. Pepper's Lonely Hearts Club Band'; 'Stayin' Alive'.)

SINGLES:		HITS 37		WEEKS 349
NEW YORK MINING DISASTER 1941	Polydor	12	29 Apr 67	10
TO LOVE SOMEBODY	Polydor	50	15 Jul 67	1
TO LOVE SOMEBODY [RE]	Polydor	41	29 Jul 67	4
MASSACHUSETTS (THE LIGHTS WENT OUT IN)	Polydor	1	23 Sep 67	17
WORLD	Polydor	9	25 Nov 67	16
WORDS	Polydor	8	3 Feb 68	10
JUMBO / THE SINGER SANG HIS SONG	Polydor	25	30 Mar 68	7
I'VE GOTTA GET A MESSAGE TO YOU	Polydor	1	10 Aug 68	15
FIRST OF MAY	Polydor	6	22 Feb 69	11
TOMORROW, TOMORROW	Polydor	23	7 Jun 69	8
DON'T FORGET TO REMEMBER	Polydor	2	16 Aug 69	15
I.O.I.O.	Polydor	49	28 Mar 70	1
LONELY DAYS	Polydor	33	5 Dec 70	9
MY WORLD	Polydor	16	29 Jan 72	9
RUN TO ME	Polydor	9	22 Jul 72	10
JIVE TALKIN'	RSO	5	28 Jun 75	11

Originally written for, but turned down by, Otis Redding.
Above 2: BEE GEES featuring Barry GIBB, Maurice GIBB and Colin PETERSON.
Above hit: BEE GEES featuring Barry and Maurice GIBB.

YOU SHOULD BE DANCING	*RSO*	5	*31 Jul 76*	10
LOVE SO RIGHT	*RSO*	41	*13 Nov 76*	4
HOW DEEP IS YOUR LOVE	*RSO*	3	*29 Oct 77*	15
Originally written for Yvonne Elliman.				
STAYIN' ALIVE	*RSO*	4	*4 Feb 78*	12
NIGHT FEVER	*RSO*	1	*15 Apr 78*	20
Above 3 from the film 'Saturday Night Fever'.				
STAYIN' ALIVE [RE]	*RSO*	63	*13 May 78*	6
TOO MUCH HEAVEN	*RSO*	3	*25 Nov 78*	13
TRAGEDY	*RSO*	1	*17 Feb 79*	10
LOVE YOU INSIDE OUT	*RSO*	13	*14 Apr 79*	9
SPIRITS (HAVING FLOWN)	*RSO*	16	*5 Jan 80*	7
SOMEONE BELONGING TO SOMEONE	*RSO*	49	*17 Sep 83*	4
From the film 'Stayin' Alive'.				
YOU WIN AGAIN	*Warner Brothers*	1	*26 Sep 87*	15
E.S.P.	*Warner Brothers*	51	*12 Dec 87*	5
ORDINARY LIVES	*Warner Brothers*	54	*15 Apr 89*	3
ONE	*Warner Brothers*	71	*24 Jun 89*	1
SECRET LOVE	*Warner Brothers*	5	*2 Mar 91*	11
PAYING THE PRICE OF LOVE	*Polydor*	23	*21 Aug 93*	5
FOR WHOM THE BELLS TOLLS	*Polydor*	4	*27 Nov 93*	14
HOW TO FALL IN LOVE PART 1	*Polydor*	30	*16 Apr 94*	4
ALONE	*Polydor*	5	*1 Mar 97*	9
I COULD NOT LOVE YOU MORE	*Polydor*	14	*21 Jun 97*	3
STILL WATERS (RUN DEEP)	*Polydor*	18	*8 Nov 97*	3
IMMORTALITY	*Epic*	5	*18 Jul 98*	12
Above hit: Celine DION with special guests the BEE GEES.				
ALBUMS:	**HITS 16**			**WEEKS 359**
BEE GEES FIRST	*Polydor*	8	*12 Aug 67*	26
HORIZONTAL	*Polydor*	16	*24 Feb 68*	15
IDEA	*Polydor*	4	*28 Sep 68*	18
ODESSA	*Polydor*	10	*5 Apr 69*	1
BEST OF THE BEE GEES	*Polydor*	7	*8 Nov 69*	22
CUCUMBER CASTLE	*Polydor*	57	*9 May 70*	2
SPIRITS HAVING FLOWN	*RSO*	1	*17 Feb 79*	33
BEE GEES GREATEST	*RSO*	6	*10 Nov 79*	25
LIVING EYES	*RSO*	73	*7 Nov 81*	8
E.S.P.	*Warner Brothers*	5	*3 Oct 87*	24
ONE	*Warner Brothers*	29	*29 Apr 89*	3
THE VERY BEST OF THE BEE GEES	*Polydor*	8	*17 Nov 90*	46
HIGH CIVILZATION	*Warner Brothers*	24	*6 Apr 91*	5
SIZE ISN'T EVERYTHING	*Polydor*	23	*25 Sep 93*	13
THE VERY BEST OF THE BEE GEES [RE]	*Polydor*	6	*22 Feb 97*	60
STILL WATERS	*Polydor*	2	*22 Mar 97*	19
LIVE ONE NIGHT ONLY	*Polydor*	4	*19 Sep 98*	39
Live recordings from the MGM Grand, Las Vegas, November 97.				

Sir Thomas BEECHAM – See ORCHESTRE NATIONALE DE LA RADIO DIFFUSION FRANCAISE conducted by Sir Thomas BEECHAM

BEENIE MAN   Jamaica

SINGLES:	**HITS 3**			**WEEKS 7**
DANCEHALL QUEEN	*Island Jamaica*	70	*20 Sep 97*	1
From the film 'Dancehall Queen'.				
Above hit: Chevelle FRANKLYN featuring BEENIE MAN.				
WHO AM I (ZIM-ZIMMA)	*Greensleeves*	10	*7 Mar 98*	5
FOUNDATION	*Jetstar*	69	*8 Aug 98*	1
Should not have charted as its track listing violated chart rules.				
Above hit: BEENIE MAN and the TAXI GANG.				

Lou BEGA   Germany

SINGLES:	**HITS 2**			**WEEKS 21**
MAMBO NO. 5 (A LITTLE BIT OF . . .)	*Lautstark*	31	*7 Aug 99*	4
German import.				
MAMBO NO. 5 (A LITTLE BIT OF . . .)	*RCA*	1	*4 Sep 99*	15
Theme to Channel 4's cricket coverage.				
I GOT A GIRL	*RCA*	55	*18 Dec 99*	2
ALBUMS:	**HITS 1**			**WEEKS 2**
A LITTLE BIT OF MAMBO	*RCA*	50	*18 Sep 99*	2

BEGGAR and CO.   UK

SINGLES:	**HITS 2**			**WEEKS 15**
(SOMEBODY) HELP ME OUT	*Ensign*	15	*7 Feb 81*	10
MULE (CHANT NO. 2)	*RCA*	37	*12 Sep 81*	5
Backing by Spandau Ballet.				

BEGINNING OF THE END | | | | US

SINGLES:		HITS 1		WEEKS 6
FUNKY NASSAU	Atlantic	31	23 Feb 74	6

BEIJING SPRING | | | | UK

SINGLES:		HITS 2		WEEKS 5
I WANNA BE IN LOVE AGAIN	MCA	43	23 Jan 93	3
SUMMERLANDS	MCA	53	8 May 93	2

BEL CANTO | | | | UK

SINGLES:		HITS 1		WEEKS 1
WE'VE GOT TO WORK IT OUT	Good Groove	65	14 Oct 95	1

Harry BELAFONTE | | | | US

SINGLES:		HITS 7		WEEKS 87
BANANA BOAT SONG (DAY-O)	His Master's Voice	2	2 Mar 57	18
Above hit: Harry BELAFONTE with Tony SCOTT'S ORCHESTRA and Chorus and Millard THOMAS, guitar.				
ISLAND IN THE SUN	RCA	3	15 Jun 57	25
SCARLET RIBBONS	His Master's Voice	18	7 Sep 57	6
Originally recorded by Jo Stafford.				
Above hit: Harry BELAFONTE and Millard THOMAS.				
MARY'S BOY CHILD	RCA	1	2 Nov 57	12
LITTLE BERNADETTE	RCA	16	23 Aug 58	7
Above hit: BELAFONTE.				
MARY'S BOY CHILD [RE-1ST]	RCA	10	29 Nov 58	6
THE SON OF MARY	RCA	18	13 Dec 58	4
MARY'S BOY CHILD [RE-2ND]	RCA	30	12 Dec 59	1
THERE'S A HOLE IN THE BUCKET	RCA	32	23 Sep 61	2
Harry BELAFONTE and ODETTA				
THERE'S A HOLE IN THE BUCKET [RE]	RCA	34	14 Oct 61	6
EPS:		HITS 2		WEEKS 2
SCARLET RIBBONS	RCA	18	16 Apr 60	1
BELAFONTE AT CHRISTMAS TIME	RCA	18	9 Dec 61	1

Archie BELL and the DRELLS | | | | US

SINGLES:		HITS 5		WEEKS 33
(THERE'S GONNA BE) A SHOWDOWN	Atlantic	36	27 Jan 73	5
THE SOUL CITY WALK	Philadelphia International	13	8 May 76	10
EVERYBODY HAVE A GOOD TIME	Philadelphia International	43	11 Jun 77	4
DON'T LET LOVE GET YOU DOWN	Portrait	49	28 Jun 86	4

Freddie BELL and the BELL BOYS | | | | US

SINGLES:		HITS 1		WEEKS 10
GIDDY-UP-A DING DONG	Mercury	4	29 Sep 56	10

Maggie BELL | | | | UK

SINGLES:		HITS 2		WEEKS 12
HAZELL	Swan Song	37	15 Apr 78	3
Theme from the Thames TV series of the same name.				
HAZELL [RE]	Swan Song	74	13 May 78	1
HOLD ME	Swan Song	11	17 Oct 81	8
Above hit: B.A. ROBERTSON and Maggie BELL.				

William BELL | | | | US

SINGLES:		HITS 3		WEEKS 22
A TRIBUTE TO A KING	Stax	31	1 Jun 68	7
A tribute to Otis Redding.				
PRIVATE NUMBER	Stax	8	23 Nov 68	14
Above hit: Judy CLAY and William BELL.				
HEADLINE NEWS	Absolute	70	26 Apr 86	1

BELL and JAMES | | | | US

SINGLES:		HITS 1		WEEKS 3
LIVIN' IT UP (FRIDAY NIGHT)	A&M	68	31 Mar 79	1
LIVIN' IT UP (FRIDAY NIGHT)[RE]	A&M	59	14 Apr 79	2

BELL BIV DEVOE | | | | US

(See also Janet Jackson; Luther Vandross.)

SINGLES:		HITS 3		WEEKS 16
POISON	MCA	19	30 Jun 90	11
DO ME	MCA	56	22 Sep 90	3

SOMETHING IN YOUR EYES	MCA	60	9 Oct 93	2
ALBUMS:	**HITS 1**		**WEEKS 5**	
POISON	MCA	35	1 Sep 90	5

BELL BOOK AND CANDLE   Germany

SINGLES:	**HITS 1**		**WEEKS 1**	
RESCUE ME	Logic	63	17 Oct 98	1

BELLAMY BROTHERS   US

SINGLES:	**HITS 3**		**WEEKS 29**	
LET YOUR LOVE FLOW	Warner Brothers	7	17 Apr 76	12
SATIN SHEETS	Warner Brothers	43	21 Aug 76	3
IF I SAID YOU HAVE A BEAUTIFUL BODY WOULD YOU HOLD IT AGAINST ME	Warner Brothers	3	11 Aug 79	14
ALBUMS:	**HITS 1**		**WEEKS 6**	
BELLAMY BROTHERS	Warner Brothers	21	19 Jun 76	6

Regina BELLE   US

SINGLES:	**HITS 2**		**WEEKS 13**	
GOOD LOVIN'	CBS	73	21 Oct 89	1
A WHOLE NEW WORLD (ALADDIN'S THEME)	Columbia	12	11 Dec 93	12
From the Walt Disney film 'Aladdin'.				
Above hit: Regina BELLE and Peabo BRYSON.				
ALBUMS:	**HITS 2**		**WEEKS 5**	
ALL BY MYSELF	CBS	53	1 Aug 87	4
STAY WITH ME	CBS	62	16 Sep 89	1

BELLE and the DEVOTIONS   UK

SINGLES:	**HITS 1**		**WEEKS 8**	
LOVE GAMES	CBS	11	21 Apr 84	8
UK's Eurovision entry in 1984, it came 7th.				

BELLE AND SEBASTIAN   UK

SINGLES:	**HITS 3**		**WEEKS 5**	
DOG ON WHEELS	Jeepster	59	24 May 97	1
LAZY LINE PAINTER JANE	Jeepster	41	9 Aug 97	2
3.. 6.. 9 SECONDS OF LIGHT [EP]	Jeepster	32	25 Oct 97	2
Lead track: A Century Of Fakers.				
ALBUMS:	**HITS 2**		**WEEKS 10**	
THE BOY WITH THE ARAB STRAP	Jeepster	12	19 Sep 98	6
TIGERMILK	Jeepster	13	24 Jul 99	4
Originally released in 1996 on the Electric Honey label.				

La BELLE EPOQUE   France

SINGLES:	**HITS 1**		**WEEKS 14**	
BLACK IS BLACK	Harvest	48	27 Aug 77	1
BLACK IS BLACK [RE]	Harvest	2	10 Sep 77	13

BELLE STARS   UK

SINGLES:	**HITS 7**		**WEEKS 42**	
IKO IKO	Stiff	35	5 Jun 82	6
Originally recorded by James 'Sugarboy' Crawford as Jock-O-Mo.				
THE CLAPPING SONG	Stiff	11	17 Jul 82	9
MOCKINGBIRD	Stiff	51	16 Oct 82	3
SIGN OF THE TIMES	Stiff	3	15 Jan 83	11
SWEET MEMORY	Stiff	22	16 Apr 83	9
INDIAN SUMMER	Stiff	52	13 Aug 83	2
80'S ROMANCE	Stiff	71	14 Jul 84	1
ALBUMS:	**HITS 1**		**WEEKS 12**	
THE BELLE STARS	Stiff	15	5 Feb 83	12

BELLINI   Brazil/Thailand/Indonesia/Germany

SINGLES:	**HITS 1**		**WEEKS 7**	
SAMBA DE JANEIRO	Virgin	8	27 Sep 97	7
Melody based on Airto Moreira's 'Celebration Suit'.				

BELLY   US

SINGLES:	**HITS 4**		**WEEKS 9**	
FEED THE TREE	4AD	32	23 Jan 93	3
GEPETTO	4AD	49	10 Apr 93	2
NOW THEY'LL SLEEP	4AD	28	4 Feb 95	2
SEAL MY FATE	4AD	35	22 Jul 95	2

ALBUMS:		HITS 2			WEEKS 13	
STAR		4AD	2	13 Feb 93		10
KING		4AD	6	25 Feb 95		3

Pierre BELMONDE
France

ALBUMS:		HITS 1			WEEKS 10	
THEMES FOR DREAMS		K-Tel	13	7 Jun 80		10

BELMONTS - See DION

BELOVED
UK

SINGLES:		HITS 10			WEEKS 47	
THE SUN RISING		WEA	26	21 Oct 89		7
HELLO		WEA	19	27 Jan 90		7
YOUR LOVE TAKES ME HIGHER		East West	39	24 Mar 90		3
Original release reached No. 91 in 1989.						
TIME AFTER TIME		East West	46	9 Jun 90		4
IT'S ALRIGHT NOW		East West	48	10 Nov 90		3
SWEET HARMONY		East West	8	23 Jan 93		10
YOU'VE GOT ME THINKING		East West	23	10 Apr 93		4
OUTERSPACE GIRL		East West	38	14 Aug 93		2
SATELLITE		East West	19	30 Mar 96		3
EASE THE PRESSURE		East West	43	10 Aug 96		2
THE SUN RISING [RI]		East West	31	30 Aug 97		2

ALBUMS:		HITS 4			WEEKS 31	
HAPPINESS		East West	14	3 Mar 90		14
BLISSED OUT		East West	38	1 Dec 90		2
CONSCIENCE		East West	2	20 Feb 93		12
X		East West	25	20 Apr 96		3

BELTRAM
US

SINGLES:		HITS 2			WEEKS 4	
ENERGY FLASH [EP]		R&S	52	28 Sep 91		2
Lead track: Energy Flash.						
THE OMEN		R&S	53	7 Dec 91		2
Above hit: PROGRAM 2 BELTRAM.						

Pat BENATAR
US

SINGLES:		HITS 9			WEEKS 53	
LOVE IS A BATTLEFIELD		Chrysalis	49	21 Jan 84		5
WE BELONG		Chrysalis	22	12 Jan 85		9
LOVE IS A BATTLEFIELD [RI]		Chrysalis	17	23 Mar 85		10
SHADOWS OF THE NIGHT		Chrysalis	50	15 Jun 85		4
Original release reached No. 83 in 1983.						
INVINCIBLE (THEME FROM 'THE LEGEND OF BILLIE JEAN')		Chrysalis	53	19 Oct 85		3
SEX AS A WEAPON		Chrysalis	67	15 Feb 86		3
ALL FIRED UP		Chrysalis	19	2 Jul 88		10
DON'T WALK AWAY		Chrysalis	42	1 Oct 88		5
ONE LOVE		Chrysalis	59	14 Jan 89		3
SOMEBODY'S BABY		Chrysalis	48	30 Oct 93		1

ALBUMS:		HITS 9			WEEKS 84	
PRECIOUS TIME		Chrysalis	30	25 Jul 81		7
GET NERVOUS		Chrysalis	73	13 Nov 82		6
LIVE FROM EARTH		Chrysalis	60	15 Oct 83		5
Live recordings (except for 2 studio tracks).						
TROPICO		Chrysalis	31	17 Nov 84		25
IN THE HEAT OF THE NIGHT		Chrysalis	98	24 Aug 85		1
SEVEN THE HARD WAY		Chrysalis	69	7 Dec 85		4
BEST SHOTS		Chrysalis	6	7 Nov 87		19
WIDE AWAKE IN DREAMLAND		Chrysalis	11	16 Jul 88		14
TRUE LOVE		Chrysalis	40	4 May 91		3

David BENDETH
Canada

SINGLES:		HITS 1			WEEKS 5	
FEEL THE REAL		Sidewalk	44	8 Sep 79		5

BENELUX and Nancy DEE
Belgium/Luxembourg/Holland

SINGLES:		HITS 1			WEEKS 4	
SWITCH		Scope	52	25 Aug 79		4

Eric BENET
US

SINGLES:		HITS 2			WEEKS 4	
SPIRITUAL THANG		Warner Brothers	62	22 Mar 97		1

71

GEORGY PORGY	Warner Brothers	28	1 May 99	3

Original by Toto reached No. 48 in the US in 1978.
Above hit: Eric BENET featuring Faith EVANS.

ALBUMS:	HITS 1			WEEKS 1
A DAY IN THE LIFE	Warner Brothers	67	15 May 99	1

Addell BENJAMIN - See 2 FOR JOY

Nigel BENN - See PACK featuring Nigel BENN

BENNET UK

SINGLES:	HITS 2			WEEKS 3
MUM'S GONE TO ICELAND	Roadrunner	34	22 Feb 97	2
SOMEONE ALWAYS GETS THERE FIRST	Roadrunner	69	3 May 97	1

Original release reached No. 145 in 1996.

Boyd BENNETT and his ROCKETS (Vocal by BIG MOE) US

SINGLES:	HITS 1			WEEKS 2
SEVENTEEN	Parlophone	16	24 Dec 55	2

Chris BENNETT - See MUSIC MACHINE

Cliff BENNETT and the REBEL ROUSERS UK

SINGLES:	HITS 3			WEEKS 23
ONE WAY LOVE	Parlophone	9	3 Oct 64	9
I'LL TAKE YOU HOME	Parlophone	42	6 Feb 65	3

Above 2 originally recorded by the Drifters.

GOT TO GET YOU INTO MY LIFE	Parlophone	6	13 Aug 66	11

Originally written and recorded by the Beatles.

ALBUMS:	HITS 1			WEEKS 3
DRIVIN' ME WILD	Music For Pleasure	25	22 Oct 66	3

Peter E. BENNETT with the CO-OPERATION CHOIR UK

SINGLES:	HITS 1			WEEKS 1
THE SEAGULL'S NAME WAS NELSON	RCA Victor	45	7 Nov 70	1

Tony BENNETT US

SINGLES:	HITS 8			WEEKS 61
STRANGER IN PARADISE	Philips	1	16 Apr 55	16

From the show 'Kismet'.
Above hit: Tony BENNETT with Percy FAITH and his Orchestra and Chorus.

CLOSE YOUR EYES	Philips	18	17 Sep 55	1
COME NEXT SPRING	Philips	29	14 Apr 56	1
TILL	Philips	35	7 Jan 61	2

Incorrectly listed on the chart as a double A-side with Serenata.

THE GOOD LIFE	CBS	27	20 Jul 63	13
IF I RULED THE WORLD	CBS	40	8 May 65	5

Above hit: Tony BENNETT with the Will BRONSON CHORUS conducted by Don
COSTA.

(I LEFT MY HEART) IN SAN FRANCISCO	CBS	46	29 May 65	2
(I LEFT MY HEART) IN SAN FRANCISCO [RE-1ST]	CBS	40	2 Oct 65	5
(I LEFT MY HEART) IN SAN FRANCISCO [RE-2ND]	CBS	25	11 Dec 65	7
THE VERY THOUGHT OF YOU	CBS	21	25 Dec 65	9

Above hit: Tony BENNETT featuring Bobby HACKETT.

EPS:	HITS 3			WEEKS 72
TONY BENNETT	CBS	5	4 Dec 65	19
TILL	CBS	7	21 May 66	6
THE BEST OF BENNETT	CBS	2	7 Jan 67	47

ALBUMS:	HITS 7			WEEKS 67
I LEFT MY HEART IN SAN FRANCISCO	CBS	20	29 May 65	1
I LEFT MY HEART IN SAN FRANCISCO [RE]	CBS	13	4 Dec 65	13
A STRING OF TONY'S HITS	CBS	9	19 Feb 66	13
TONY'S GREATEST HITS	CBS	14	10 Jun 67	24
TONY MAKES IT HAPPEN	CBS	31	23 Sep 67	3
FOR ONCE IN MY LIFE	CBS	29	23 Mar 68	5
THE VERY BEST OF TONY BENNETT - 20 GREATEST HITS	Warwick	23	26 Feb 77	4
THE ESSENTIAL TONY BENNETT	Columbia	49	28 Nov 98	4

Gary BENSON UK

SINGLES:	HITS 1			WEEKS 8
DON'T THROW IT ALL AWAY	State	20	9 Aug 75	8

George BENSON US

(See also George Benson and Earl Klugh.)

SINGLES:		HITS 22		WEEKS 143	
SUPERSHIP	CTI	30	25 Oct 75	6	
Above hit: George 'Bad' BENSON.					
NATURE BOY	Warner Brothers	26	4 Jun 77	6	
THE GREATEST LOVE OF ALL	Arista	27	24 Sep 77	7	
From the film 'The Greatest'.					
LOVE BALLAD	Warner Brothers	29	31 Mar 79	9	
Original by L.T.D. reached No. 20 in the US in 1976.					
GIVE ME THE NIGHT	Warner Brothers	7	26 Jul 80	10	
LOVE X LOVE	Warner Brothers	10	4 Oct 80	8	
WHAT'S ON YOUR MIND	Warner Brothers	45	7 Feb 81	5	
LOVE ALL THE HURT AWAY	Arista	49	19 Sep 81	3	
Above hit: Aretha FRANKLIN and George BENSON.					
TURN YOUR LOVE AROUND	Warner Brothers	29	14 Nov 81	11	
NEVER GIVE UP ON A GOOD THING	Warner Brothers	14	23 Jan 82	10	
LADY LOVE ME (ONE MORE TIME)	Warner Brothers	11	21 May 83	10	
FEEL LIKE MAKIN' LOVE	Warner Brothers	28	16 Jul 83	7	
IN YOUR EYES	Warner Brothers	7	24 Sep 83	10	
Co-written by Dan Hill.					
INSIDE LOVE (SO PERSONAL)	Warner Brothers	57	17 Dec 83	5	
20/20	Warner Brothers	29	19 Jan 85	9	
BEYOND THE SEA (LA MER)	Warner Brothers	60	20 Apr 85	3	
KISSES IN THE MOONLIGHT	Warner Brothers	60	16 Aug 86	4	
SHIVER	Warner Brothers	19	29 Nov 86	9	
TEASER	Warner Brothers	45	14 Feb 87	4	
LET'S DO IT AGAIN	Warner Brothers	56	27 Aug 88	3	
I'LL KEEP YOUR DREAMS ALIVE	Ammi	68	5 Sep 92	1	
Above hit: George BENSON and Patti AUSTIN.					
SEVEN DAYS	MCA	22	11 Jul 98	3	
Above hit: Mary J. BLIGE featuring George BENSON.					
ALBUMS:		HITS 14		WEEKS 274	
IN FLIGHT	Warner Brothers	19	19 Mar 77	23	
WEEKEND IN L.A.	Warner Brothers	47	18 Feb 78	1	
LIVING INSIDE YOUR LOVE	Warner Brothers	24	24 Mar 79	14	
GIVE ME THE NIGHT	Warner Brothers	3	26 Jul 80	40	
THE GEORGE BENSON COLLECTION	Warner Brothers	19	14 Nov 81	35	
IN YOUR EYES	Warner Brothers	3	11 Jun 83	53	
20/20	Warner Brothers	9	26 Jan 85	19	
THE LOVE SONGS	K-Tel	1	19 Oct 85	26	
WHILE THE CITY SLEEPS . .	Warner Brothers	13	6 Sep 86	27	
TWICE THE LOVE	Warner Brothers	16	10 Sep 88	10	
TENDERLY	Warner Brothers	52	8 Jul 89	3	
MIDNIGHT MOODS - THE LOVE COLLECTION	Telstar	25	26 Oct 91	12	
THAT'S RIGHT	GRP	61	29 Jun 96	1	
ESSENTIALS . . . THE VERY BEST OF GEORGE BENSON	warner.esp/Jive	8	25 Apr 98	10	

George BENSON and Earl KLUGH UK/US

(See also George Benson.)

ALBUMS:		HITS 1		WEEKS 6	
COLLABORATION	Warner Brothers	47	11 Jul 87	6	

BENTLEY RHYTHM ACE UK

SINGLES:		HITS 1		WEEKS 4	
BENTLEYS GONNA SORT YOU OUT!	Parlophone	17	6 Sep 97	4	
ALBUMS:		HITS 1		WEEKS 5	
BENTLEY RHYTHM ACE	Skint	13	24 May 97	5	

Brook BENTON US

SINGLES:		HITS 4		WEEKS 18	
ENDLESSLY	Mercury	28	11 Jul 59	2	
KIDDIO	Mercury	42	8 Oct 60	3	
Originally recorded by Teddy Randazzo.					
KIDDIO [RE]	Mercury	41	5 Nov 60	3	
FOOLS RUSH IN (WHERE ANGELS FEAR TO TREAD)	Mercury	50	18 Feb 61	1	
THE BOLL WEEVIL SONG	Mercury	30	15 Jul 61	9	
Originally recorded by Dave Bartholomew.					

BENZ UK

SINGLES:		HITS 5		WEEKS 9	
BOOM ROCK SOUL	RCA	62	16 Dec 95	2	
URBAN CITY GIRL	Hacktown	31	16 Mar 96	3	
MISS PARKER	RCA	35	25 May 96	2	

IF I REMEMBER	Hendricks	59	29 Mar 97	1
ON A SUN-DAY	Hendricks	73	9 Aug 97	1

Ingrid BERGMAN – See Dooley WILSON with the voices of Humphrey BOGART and Ingrid BERGMAN

BERLIN   US

SINGLES:	HITS 3			WEEKS 39
TAKE MY BREATH AWAY (LOVE THEME FROM "TOP GUN")	CBS	1	25 Oct 86	15
From the film 'Top Gun'.				
YOU DON'T KNOW	Mercury	39	17 Jan 87	6
LIKE FLAMES	Mercury	47	14 Mar 87	3
TAKE MY BREATH AWAY (LOVE THEME FROM "TOP GUN") [RE]	CBS	52	20 Feb 88	3
TAKE MY BREATH AWAY (LOVE THEME FROM "TOP GUN") [RI]	CBS	3	13 Oct 90	12
Re-Issued after the first showing of 'Top Gun' on British TV.				
ALBUMS:	HITS 1			WEEKS 11
COUNT THREE AND PRAY	Mercury	32	17 Jan 87	11

BERLIN PHILHARMONIC ORCHESTRA – See Herbert VON KARAJAN conducting the BERLIN PHILHARMONIC ORCHESTRA

Shelley BERMAN   US

ALBUMS:	HITS 1			WEEKS 4
INSIDE SHELLEY BERMAN	Capitol	12	19 Nov 60	4

Elmer BERNSTEIN   US

SINGLES:	HITS 1			WEEKS 11
STACCATO'S THEME	Capitol	4	19 Dec 59	10
STACCATO'S THEME [RE]	Capitol	40	12 Mar 60	1
EPS:	HITS 1			WEEKS 1
STACCATO	Capitol	6	12 Mar 60	1

Orchestra and Chorus conducted by Leonard BERNSTEIN   US

(See also Various Artists: Studio Cast 'West Side Story'.)

SINGLES:	HITS 1			WEEKS 4
AMERICA – THE OFFICIAL 1994 BBC WORLD CUP THEME	Deutsche Grammophon	44	2 Jul 94	4
ALBUMS:	HITS 1			WEEKS 2
BERNSTEIN IN BERLIN – BEETHOVEN SYMPHONY NO. 9	Deutsche Grammophon	54	10 Feb 90	2

BERRI   UK

SINGLES:	HITS 2			WEEKS 22
THE SUNSHINE AFTER THE RAIN	Ffrreedom	26	26 Nov 94	6
Above hit: NEW ATLANTIC/U4EA featuring BERRI.				
THE SUNSHINE AFTER THE RAIN [RI]	Ffrreedom	4	2 Sep 95	11
SHINE LIKE A STAR	Ffrreedom	20	2 Dec 95	5

LaKiesha BERRI   US

SINGLES:	HITS 1			WEEKS 1
LIKE THIS AND LIKE THAT	Adept	54	5 Jul 97	1

Chuck BERRY   US

SINGLES:	HITS 11			WEEKS 91
SCHOOL DAY (RING! RING! GOES THE BELL)	Columbia	24	22 Jun 57	2
SCHOOL DAY (RING! RING! GOES THE BELL) [RE]	Columbia	24	13 Jul 57	2
SWEET LITTLE SIXTEEN	London	16	26 Apr 58	5
GO, GO, GO	Pye International	38	13 Jul 63	6
LET IT ROCK / MEMPHIS TENNESSEE	Pye International	6	12 Oct 63	13
RUN RUDOLPH RUN	Pye International	36	21 Dec 63	6
NADINE (IS IT YOU)	Pye International	27	15 Feb 64	6
NADINE (IS IT YOU) [RE]	Pye International	43	4 Apr 64	1
NO PARTICULAR PLACE TO GO	Pye International	3	9 May 64	12
YOU NEVER CAN TELL	Pye International	23	22 Aug 64	8
THE PROMISED LAND	Pye International	26	16 Jan 65	6
MY DING-A-LING	Chess	1	28 Oct 72	17
Originally recorded by Dave Bartholomew in 1952. Backing musicians are the Average White Band.				
REELIN' AND ROCKIN'	Chess	18	3 Feb 73	7
EPS:	HITS 5			WEEKS 68
CHUCK BERRY	Pye International	7	5 Oct 63	14
CHUCK AND BO	Pye International	6	5 Oct 63	22
CHUCK AND BO, VOLUME 2	Pye International	15	30 Nov 63	2
Above 2: Chuck BERRY and Bo DIDDLEY.				
THE BEST OF CHUCK BERRY	Pye International	5	8 Feb 64	25
CHUCK AND BO, VOLUME 3	Pye International	12	15 Feb 64	5
Above hit: Chuck BERRY and Bo DIDDLEY.				

ALBUMS:		HITS 6		WEEKS 53	
CHUCK BERRY	Pye International	12	25 May 63	16
CHUCK BERRY ON STAGE	Pye International	6	5 Oct 63	11
MORE CHUCK BERRY	Pye International	9	7 Dec 63	8
THE LATEST AND GREATEST	Pye International	8	30 May 64	7
YOU NEVER CAN TELL	Pye International	18	3 Oct 64	2
MOTORVATIN'	Chess	7	12 Feb 77	9

Dave BERRY   UK

SINGLES:		HITS 8		WEEKS 76	
MEMPHIS TENNESSEE	Decca	19	21 Sep 63	13
Above hit: Dave BERRY and the CRUISERS.				
MY BABY LEFT ME	Decca	41	11 Jan 64	1
Originally recorded by Arthur 'Bigboy' Cruddup.				
MY BABY LEFT ME [RE]	Decca	37	25 Jan 64	8
BABY IT'S YOU	Decca	24	2 May 64	6
THE CRYING GAME	Decca	5	8 Aug 64	12
ONE HEART BETWEEN TWO	Decca	41	28 Nov 64	2
LITTLE THINGS	Decca	5	27 Mar 65	12
Original by Bobby Goldsboro reached No. 13 in the US in 1965.				
THIS STRANGE EFFECT	Decca	37	24 Jul 65	6
Written by Ray Davies of the Kinks.				
MAMA	Decca	5	2 Jul 66	16
Originall by B.J.Thomas reached No. 22 in the US in 1966.				
EPS:		HITS 1		WEEKS 6	
CAN I GET IT FROM YOU	Decca	12	10 Jul 65	6

Mike BERRY   UK

SINGLES:		HITS 6		WEEKS 51	
TRIBUTE TO BUDDY HOLLY	His Master's Voice	24	14 Oct 61	6
DON'T YOU THINK IT'S TIME	His Master's Voice	6	5 Jan 63	12
MY LITTLE BABY	His Master's Voice	34	13 Apr 63	7
Above 3: Mike BERRY with the OUTLAWS.				
THE SUNSHINE OF YOUR SMILE	Polydor	9	2 Aug 80	12
Originally recorded by John McCormack in 1916. Produced by Chas Hodges of Chas & Dave.				
IF I COULD ONLY MAKE YOU CARE	Polydor	37	29 Nov 80	9
MEMORIES	Polydor	55	5 Sep 81	5
EPS:		HITS 1		WEEKS 4	
A TRIBUTE TO BUDDY HOLLY	HMV	17	31 Aug 63	4
Above hit: Mike BERRY with the OUTLAWS.				
ALBUMS:		HITS 1		WEEKS 3	
THE SUNSHINE OF YOUR SMILE	Polydor	63	24 Jan 81	3

Nick BERRY   UK

SINGLES:		HITS 3		WEEKS 24	
EVERY LOSER WINS	BBC	1	4 Oct 86	11
EVERY LOSER WINS [RE]	BBC	72	27 Dec 86	2
HEARTBEAT	Columbia	2	13 Jun 92	8
Theme from the Yorkshire TV series of the same name.				
LONG LIVE LOVE	Columbia	47	31 Oct 92	3
ALBUMS:		HITS 2		WEEKS 8	
NICK BERRY	BBC	99	20 Dec 86	1
NICK BERRY	Columbia	28	21 Nov 92	7
Identically titled albums are different.				

Adele BERTEI – See JELLYBEAN

BEST COMPANY   UK

SINGLES:		HITS 1		WEEKS 1	
DON'T YOU FORGET ABOUT ME	ZYX	65	27 Mar 93	1

BEST SHOT   UK

SINGLES:		HITS 1		WEEKS 2	
UNITED COLOURS	East West	64	5 Feb 94	2

BETA BAND   UK

ALBUMS:		HITS 2		WEEKS 3	
THE THREE E.P.S	Regal	35	10 Oct 98	1
12 track set bringing together tracks from their limited edition EPs.				
THE BETA BAND	Regal	18	3 Jul 99	2

BEVERLEY-PHILLIPS ORCHESTRA UK

ALBUMS:		HITS 1		WEEKS 9	
GOLD ON SILVER	Warwick	22	9 Oct 76		9

BEVERLEY SISTERS UK

(See also All Star Hit Parade.)

SINGLES:		HITS 6		WEEKS 34	
I SAW MOMMY KISSING SANTA CLAUS	Philips	11	28 Nov 53		1
I SAW MOMMY KISSING SANTA CLAUS [RE]	Philips	6	12 Dec 53		4
WILLIE CAN	Decca	23	14 Apr 56		4
I DREAMED	Decca	24	2 Feb 57		2
Above hit: BEVERLEY SISTERS with the Roland SHAW ORCHESTRA.					
THE LITTLE DRUMMER BOY	Decca	6	14 Feb 59		13
LITTLE DONKEY	Decca	14	21 Nov 59		7
GREEN FIELDS	Columbia	48	25 Jun 60		1
GREEN FIELDS [RE]	Columbia	29	9 Jul 60		2
EPS:		HITS 1		WEEKS 2	
THE BEVS FOR CHRISTMAS	Decca	11	24 Dec 60		2

Frankie BEVERLY – See MAZE featuring Frankie BEVERLY

BEYOND UK

SINGLES:		HITS 1		WEEKS 1	
RAGING [EP]	Harvest	68	21 Sep 91		1
Lead track: Great Indifference.					

BIBLE UK

SINGLES:		HITS 2		WEEKS 8	
GRACELAND	Chrysalis	51	20 May 89		4
Released in 1986, reached No. 87; a year later it peaked at No. 86.					
HONEY BE GOOD	Ensign	54	26 Aug 89		4
ALBUMS:		HITS 2		WEEKS 2	
EUREKA	Chrysalis	71	4 Jun 88		1
THE BIBLE	Ensign	67	7 Oct 89		1

BIDDU ORCHESTRA UK

SINGLES:		HITS 3		WEEKS 13	
SUMMER OF '42	Epic	14	2 Aug 75		8
RAIN FOREST	Epic	39	17 Apr 76		4
JOURNEY TO THE MOON	Epic	41	11 Feb 78		1

BIG APPLE BAND – See Walter MURPHY and the BIG APPLE BAND

BIG AUDIO DYNAMITE UK/US

SINGLES:		HITS 6		WEEKS 27	
E = MC^2	CBS	11	22 Mar 86		9
MEDICINE SHOW	CBS	29	7 Jun 86		5
C'MON EVERY BEATBOX	CBS	51	18 Oct 86		3
V. THIRTEEN	CBS	49	21 Feb 87		5
JUST PLAY MUSIC!	CBS	51	28 May 88		3
LOOKING FOR A SONG	Columbia	68	12 Nov 94		2
Above hit: BIG AUDIO.					
ALBUMS:		HITS 6		WEEKS 43	
THIS IS BIG AUDIO DYNAMITE	CBS	27	16 Nov 85		27
NO. 10 UPPING STREET	CBS	11	8 Nov 86		8
TIGHTEN UP VOLUME 88	CBS	33	9 Jul 88		3
MEGATOP PHOENIX	CBS	26	16 Sep 89		3
KOOL-AID	CBS	55	3 Nov 90		1
THE GLOBE	Columbia	63	17 Aug 91		1
Above 2: BIG AUDIO DYNAMITE II.					

BIG BAD HORNS – See LITTLE ANGELS

BIG BAM BOO UK/Canada

SINGLES:		HITS 1		WEEKS 2	
SHOOTING FROM MY HEART	MCA	61	28 Jan 89		2

BIG BEN UK

SINGLES:		HITS 1		WEEKS 1	
MILLENNIUM CHIMES	London	73	1 Jan 00		1
Donation from sales goes towards the Children's Promise – The Millennium Final Hour Appeal.					

BIG BEN BANJO BAND · UK

SINGLES:		HITS 2			WEEKS 6
LET'S GET TOGETHER NO. 1 [M]	Columbia	6	11 Dec 54	4
LET'S GET TOGETHER AGAIN – NO. 1 [M]	Columbia	19	10 Dec 55	1
LET'S GET TOGETHER AGAIN – NO. 1 [M] [RE]	Columbia	18	31 Dec 55	1
ALBUMS:		**HITS 1**			**WEEKS 1**
MORE MINSTREL MELODIES	Columbia	20	17 Dec 60	1

BIG BOPPER · US

SINGLES:		HITS 1			WEEKS 8
CHANTILLY LACE	Mercury	30	27 Dec 58	1
CHANTILLY LACE [RE]	Mercury	12	10 Jan 59	7

BIG BOSS STYLUS presents RED VENOM · UK

SINGLES:		HITS 1			WEEKS 1
LET'S GET IT ON	All Around The World	72	31 Jul 99	1

BIG C - See Alex WHITCOMBE and BIG C

BIG COUNTRY · UK

SINGLES:		HITS 23			WEEKS 103
FIELDS OF FIRE (400 MILES)	Mercury	10	26 Feb 83	12
IN A BIG COUNTRY	Mercury	17	28 May 83	7
CHANCE	Mercury	9	3 Sep 83	9
WONDERLAND	Mercury	8	21 Jan 84	8
EAST OF EDEN	Mercury	17	29 Sep 84	6
WHERE THE ROSE IS SOWN	Mercury	29	1 Dec 84	7
JUST A SHADOW	Mercury	26	19 Jan 85	4
LOOK AWAY	Mercury	7	12 Apr 86	8
THE TEACHER	Mercury	28	21 Jun 86	4
ONE GREAT THING	Mercury	19	20 Sep 86	6
HOLD THE HEART	Mercury	55	29 Nov 86	2
KING OF EMOTION	Mercury	16	20 Aug 88	5
KING OF EMOTION [RE]	Mercury	74	1 Oct 88	1
BROKEN HEART (THIRTEEN VALLEYS)	Mercury	47	5 Nov 88	4
PEACE IN OUR TIME	Mercury	39	4 Feb 89	3
SAVE ME	Mercury	41	12 May 90	3
HEART OF THE WORLD	Mercury	50	21 Jul 90	2
REPUBLICAN PARTY REPTILE [EP]	Vertigo	37	31 Aug 91	2
Lead track: Republican Party Reptile.				
BEAUTIFUL PEOPLE	Vertigo	72	19 Oct 91	1
ALONE	Compulsion	24	13 Mar 93	3
SHIPS (WHERE WERE YOU?)	Compulsion	29	1 May 93	3
I'M NOT ASHAMED	Transatlantic	69	10 Jun 95	1
YOU DREAMER	Transatlantic	68	9 Sep 95	1
FRAGILE THING	Track Record	69	21 Aug 99	1
Above hit: BIG COUNTRY (featuring Eddi READER).				
ALBUMS:		**HITS 10**			**WEEKS 148**
THE CROSSING	Mercury	3	6 Aug 83	80
STEELTOWN	Mercury	1	27 Oct 84	21
THE SEER	Mercury	2	12 Jul 86	16
PEACE IN OUR TIME	Mercury	9	8 Oct 88	6
THROUGH A BIG COUNTRY - GREATEST HITS	Mercury	2	26 May 90	17
NO PLACE LIKE HOME	Vertigo	28	28 Sep 91	2
THE BUFFALO SKINNERS	Compulsion	25	3 Apr 93	2
WITHOUT THE AID OF A SAFETY NET (LIVE)	Compulsion	35	18 Jun 94	1
Live recordings from 1993/94.				
WHY THE LONG FACE	Transatlantic	48	24 Jun 95	2
ECLECTIC	Transatlantic	41	24 Aug 96	1
Live recordings from Dingwall's, London, March 96.				

BIG DADDY · US

SINGLES:		HITS 1			WEEKS 8
DANCING IN THE DARK [EP]	Making Waves	21	9 Mar 85	8
Lead track: I Right The Songs, though Dancing In The Dark received more airplay.				

BIG DADDY KANE · US

SINGLES:		HITS 3			WEEKS 6
RAP SUMMARY / WRATH OF KANE	Cold Chillin'	52	13 May 89	2
SMOOTH OPERATOR	Cold Chillin'	65	26 Aug 89	1
AIN'T NO STOPPIN' US NOW	Cold Chillin'	44	13 Jan 90	3
ALBUMS:		**HITS 1**			**WEEKS 3**
IT'S A BIG DADDY THING	Cold Chillin'	37	30 Sep 89	3

BIG DISH
UK

SINGLES:		HITS 1			WEEKS 5
MISS AMERICA	*East West*	37	*12 Jan 91*		5
ALBUMS:		**HITS 2**			**WEEKS 3**
SWIMMER	*Virgin*	85	*11 Oct 86*		1
SATELLITES	*East West*	43	*23 Feb 91*		2

BIG FUN
UK

SINGLES:		HITS 5			WEEKS 33
BLAME IT ON THE BOOGIE	*Jive*	4	*12 Aug 89*		11
CAN'T SHAKE THE FEELING	*Jive*	8	*25 Nov 89*		9
HANDFUL OF PROMISES	*Jive*	21	*17 Mar 90*		6
YOU'VE GOT A FRIEND	*Jive*	14	*23 Jun 90*		6

Charity record in aid of Childline.
Above hit: BIG FUN and SONIA featuring Gary BARNACLE on saxophone.

HEY THERE LONELY GIRL	*Jive*	62	*4 Aug 90*		1
ALBUMS:		**HITS 1**			**WEEKS 11**
A POCKETFUL OF DREAMS	*Jive*	7	*12 May 90*		11

BIG MOE – See Boyd BENNETT and his ROCKETS (Vocal by BIG MOE)

BIG MOUNTAIN
US

SINGLES:		HITS 2			WEEKS 15
BABY, I LOVE YOUR WAY	*RCA*	2	*4 Jun 94*		14

From the film 'Reality Bites'.

SWEET SENSUAL LOVE	*Giant*	51	*24 Sep 94*		1

BIG ROOM GIRL featuring Darryl PANDY
UK/US

(See also Darryl Pandy.)

SINGLES:		HITS 1			WEEKS 2
RAISE YOUR HANDS	*VC Recordings*	40	*20 Feb 99*		2

BIG SOUND AUTHORITY
UK

SINGLES:		HITS 2			WEEKS 12
THIS HOUSE (IS WHERE YOUR LOVE STANDS)	*Source*	21	*19 Jan 85*		9
A BAD TOWN	*Source*	54	*8 Jun 85*		3

BIG SUPREME
UK

SINGLES:		HITS 2			WEEKS 5
DON'T WALK	*Polydor*	58	*20 Sep 86*		3
PLEASE YOURSELF	*Polydor*	64	*14 Mar 87*		2

BIG THREE
UK

SINGLES:		HITS 2			WEEKS 17
SOME OTHER GUY	*Decca*	37	*13 Apr 63*		7
BY THE WAY	*Decca*	22	*13 Jul 63*		10
EPS:		**HITS 1**			**WEEKS 17**
AT THE CAVERN	*Decca*	6	*14 Dec 63*		17

BIG TIME CHARLIE
UK

SINGLES:		HITS 1			WEEKS 2
ON THE RUN	*Inferno*	22	*23 Oct 99*		2

Samples Ecstasy's Touch And Go.

Barry BIGGS
Jamaica

SINGLES:		HITS 6			WEEKS 46
WORK ALL DAY	*Dynamic*	38	*28 Aug 76*		5
SIDE SHOW	*Dynamic*	3	*4 Dec 76*		16

Originally recorded by Blue Magic.

YOU'RE MY LIFE	*Dynamic*	36	*23 Apr 77*		4
THREE RING CIRCUS	*Dynamic*	22	*9 Jul 77*		8

Originally recorded by Blue Magic.

WHAT'S YOUR SIGN GIRL	*Dynamic*	55	*15 Dec 79*		7
WIDE AWAKE IN A DREAM	*Dynamic*	44	*20 Jun 81*		6

Ivor BIGGUN
UK

SINGLES:		HITS 2			WEEKS 15
THE WINKER'S SONG (MISPRINT)	*Beggars Banquet*	22	*2 Sep 78*		12

Above hit: Ivor BIGGUN and the RED NOSED-BURGLARS.

BRAS ON 45 (FAMILY VERSION)	*Dead Badger*	50	*12 Sep 81*		3

Spoof of the Stars On 45 hits.
Above hit: Ivor BIGGUN and the D-KUPS.

BIKINI KILL/HUGGY BEAR — US/UK

COMPILATION ALBUMS:		HITS 1		WEEKS 2	
YEAH YEAH YEAH YEAH / OUR TROUBLED YOUTH	Catcall	12	20 Mar 93		2

Listed on the compilation chart, one side by Bikini Kill, the other by Huggy Bear.

BILBO — UK

SINGLES:		HITS 1		WEEKS 7	
SHE'S GONNA WIN	Lightning	42	26 Aug 78		7

Mr. Acker BILK — UK

SINGLES:		HITS 12		WEEKS 172	
SUMMER SET	Columbia	5	23 Jan 60		20
Above hit: Mr. Acker BILK and his PARAMOUNT JAZZ BAND.					
GOODBYE SWEET PRINCE	Melodisc	50	11 Jun 60		1
Above hit: Mister Acker BILK.					
WHITE CLIFFS OF DOVER	Columbia	30	20 Aug 60		9
BUONA SERA	Columbia	7	10 Dec 60		18
THAT'S MY HOME	Columbia	7	15 Jul 61		17
Sub credit: (Vocal Mr. Acker BILK)					
STARS AND STRIPES FOREVER / CREOLE JAZZ	Columbia	22	4 Nov 61		10
Above 4: Mr. Acker BILK and his PARAMOUNT JAZZ BAND.					
STRANGER ON THE SHORE	Columbia	2	2 Dec 61		55
Theme from the BBC TV series of the same name. Originally called 'Jenny'.					
Above hit: Mr. Acker BILK with the Leon YOUNG STRING CHORALE.					
FRANKIE AND JOHNNY	Columbia	42	17 Mar 62		2
From the film 'It's Trad Dad'.					
GOTTA SEE BABY TONIGHT	Columbia	24	28 Jul 62		9
Above 2: Mr. Acker BILK and his PARAMOUNT JAZZ BAND (Vocal by Mr. Acker BILK).					
LONELY	Columbia	14	29 Sep 62		11
From the film 'Band Of Thieves'.					
A TASTE OF HONEY	Columbia	16	26 Jan 63		9
Above 2: Mr. Acker BILK with the Leon YOUNG STRING CHORALE.					
ARIA	Pye	5	21 Aug 76		11
Above hit: Acker BILK, his clarinet and strings.					

EPS:		HITS 11		WEEKS 134	
ACKER'S AWAY	Columbia	16	26 Mar 60		2
MR. ACKER BILK REQUESTS VOLUME 2	Pye	11	2 Apr 60		8
MR. ACKER BILK MARCHES ON	Pye	12	7 May 60		2
MR. ACKER BILK SINGS	Pye	15	11 Jun 60		1
SEVEN AGES OF ACKER	Columbia	6	5 Nov 60		23
CLARINET JAMBOREE	Columbia	19	4 Mar 61		1
Above hit: Mr. Acker BILK and Terry LIGHTFOOT.					
SEVEN AGES OF ACKER VOLUME 2	Columbia	9	18 Mar 61		12
ACKER NO. 1	Columbia	6	26 Aug 61		5
ACKER NO. 2	Columbia	11	13 Jan 62		7
FOUR HITS AND A MISTER	Columbia	2	14 Apr 62		56
BAND OF THIEVES	Columbia	6	29 Sep 62		17

ALBUMS:		HITS 12		WEEKS 161	
SEVEN AGES OF ACKER	Columbia	6	19 Mar 60		6
ACKER BILK'S OMNIBUS	Pye	14	9 Apr 60		3
ACKER	Columbia	17	4 Mar 61		1
GOLDEN TREASURY OF BILK	Columbia	11	1 Apr 61		6
THE BEST OF BARBER AND BILK VOLUME 1	Pye Golden Guinea	4	27 May 61		43
THE BEST OF BARBER AND BILK VOLUME 2	Pye Golden Guinea	8	11 Nov 61		18
Above 2: Chris BARBER and Mr. Acker BILK.					
STRANGER ON THE SHORE	Columbia	6	26 May 62		28
THE BEST OF BALL, BARBER AND BILK	Pye Golden Guinea	1	25 Aug 62		24
Above hit: Kenny BALL, Chris BARBER and Mr. Acker BILK.					
A TASTE OF HONEY	Columbia	17	4 May 63		4
THE ONE FOR ME	Pye	38	9 Oct 76		6
SHEER MAGIC	Warwick	5	4 Jun 77		8
EVERGREEN	Warwick	17	11 Nov 78		14

BILL — UK

SINGLES:		HITS 1		WEEKS 1	
CAR BOOT SALE	Mercury	73	23 Oct 93		1

Character featured on Steve Wright's BBC Radio 1 afternoon show.

BILLIE - See H2O featuring BILLIE

BILLIE — UK

(See also Steps Tina Cousins Cleopatra B*Witched Billie.)

SINGLES:		HITS 4		WEEKS 48	
BECAUSE WE WANT TO	Innocent	1	11 Jul 98		12

GIRLFRIEND	Innocent	1	17 Oct 98	10
SHE WANTS YOU	Innocent	3	19 Dec 98	11
GIRLFRIEND [RE]	Innocent	71	2 Jan 99	2
SHE WANTS YOU [RE]	Innocent	54	13 Mar 99	2
HONEY TO THE BEE	Innocent	3	3 Apr 99	9
HONEY TO THE BEE [RE]	Innocent	70	26 Jun 99	2
ALBUMS:	**HITS 1**		**WEEKS 23**	
HONEY TO THE B	Innocent	14	31 Oct 98	23

BIMBO JET
France

| **SINGLES:** | **HITS 1** | | **WEEKS 10** | |
| EL BIMBO | EMI | 12 | 26 Jul 75 | 10 |

BINARY FINARY
UK

SINGLES:	**HITS 1**		**WEEKS 9**	
1998	Positiva	24	10 Oct 98	3
1999 [RM]	Positiva	11	28 Aug 99	6
Remix of 1998 by Kaycee.				

Umberto BINDI
Italy

| **SINGLES:** | **HITS 1** | | **WEEKS 1** | |
| IL NOSTRO CONCERTO (OUR CONCERTO) | Oriole | 47 | 12 Nov 60 | 1 |

BIOHAZARD
US

SINGLES:	**HITS 2**		**WEEKS 4**	
TALES FROM THE HARD SIDE	Warner Brothers	47	9 Jul 94	2
HOW IT IS	Warner Brothers	62	20 Aug 94	2
Vocals by Sen Dog of Cypress Hill.				
ALBUMS:	**HITS 2**		**WEEKS 2**	
STATE OF THE WORLD ADDRESS	Warner Brothers	72	14 May 94	1
MATA LEAO	Warner Brothers	72	8 Jun 96	1

La BIONDA
Italy

| **SINGLES:** | **HITS 1** | | **WEEKS 4** | |
| ONE FOR YOU ONE FOR ME | Philips | 54 | 7 Oct 78 | 4 |

BIOSPHERE
Norway

SINGLES:	**HITS 1**		**WEEKS 2**	
NOVELTY WAVES	Apollo	51	29 Apr 95	2
Featured in a Levi's Jeans TV commerical.				
ALBUMS:	**HITS 1**		**WEEKS 1**	
PATASHNIK	Apollo	50	5 Mar 94	1

BIRDLAND
UK

SINGLES:	**HITS 5**		**WEEKS 7**	
HOLLOW HEART	Lazy	70	1 Apr 89	1
PARADISE	Lazy	70	8 Jul 89	1
SLEEP WITH ME	Lazy	32	3 Feb 90	3
ROCK AND ROLL NIGGER	Lazy	47	22 Sep 90	1
EVERYBODY NEEDS SOMEBODY	Lazy	44	2 Feb 91	1
ALBUMS:	**HITS 1**		**WEEKS 1**	
BIRDLAND	Lazy	44	2 Mar 91	1

BIRDS
UK

| **SINGLES:** | **HITS 1** | | **WEEKS 1** | |
| LEAVING HERE | Decca | 45 | 29 May 65 | 1 |

Jane BIRKIN and Serge GAINSBOURG
UK/France

SINGLES:	**HITS 1**		**WEEKS 34**	
JE T'AIME . . . MOI NON PLUS	Fontana	2	2 Aug 69	11
JE T'AIME . . . MOI NON PLUS [RI-1ST]	Major Minor	1	4 Oct 69	14
Major Minor picked up license after Fontana deleted the release.				
JE T'AIME . . . MOI NON PLUS [RI-2ND]	Antic	31	7 Dec 74	9
Above hit: Serge GAINSBOURG and Jane BIRKIN.				

BIRTHDAY PARTY
Australia

| **ALBUMS:** | **HITS 1** | | **WEEKS 3** | |
| JUNKYARD | 4AD | 73 | 24 Jul 82 | 3 |

BIS
UK

SINGLES:		HITS 7		WEEKS 9
THE SECRET VAMPIRE SOUNDTRACK [EP]	Chemikal Underground	25	30 Mar 96	2
Lead track: Kandy Pop.				
BIS VS. THE D.I.Y. CORPS [EP]	Teen-C	45	22 Jun 96	1
Lead track: This Is Fake D.I.Y.				
ATOM POWERED ACTION! [EP]	Wiiija	54	9 Nov 96	1
Lead track: Starbright Boy.				
SWEET SHOP AVENGERZ	Wiiija	46	15 Mar 97	1
EVERYBODY THINKS THEY'RE GOING TO GET THEIRS	Wiiija	64	10 May 97	1
EURODISCO	Wiiija	37	14 Nov 98	2
ACTION AND DRAMA	Wiiija	50	27 Feb 99	1
ALBUMS:		HITS 1		WEEKS 1
THE NEW TRANSISTOR HEROES	Wiiija	55	19 Apr 97	1

Elvin BISHOP
US

SINGLES:		HITS 1		WEEKS 4
FOOLED AROUND AND FELL IN LOVE	Capricorn	34	15 May 76	4
Uncredited vocals by Mickey Thomas of Starship.				

Stephen BISHOP
US

ALBUMS:		HITS 1		WEEKS 3
GREIG AND SCHUMANN PIANO CONCERTOS	Philips	34	1 Apr 72	3

BITI - See DEGREES OF MOTION featuring BITI

BIZARRE INC
UK

SINGLES:		HITS 7		WEEKS 49
PLAYING WITH KNIVES	Vinyl Solution	43	16 Mar 91	5
SUCH A FEELING	Vinyl Solution	13	14 Sep 91	9
PLAYING WITH KNIVES [RM-1ST]	Vinyl Solution	4	23 Nov 91	8
I'M GONNA GET YOU	Vinyl Solution	3	3 Oct 92	12
I'M GONNA GET YOU [RE]	Vinyl Solution	72	2 Jan 93	1
TOOK MY LOVE	Vinyl Solution	19	27 Feb 93	5
Above 3: BIZARRE INC featuring Angie BROWN.				
KEEP THE MUSIC STRONG	Mercury	33	23 Mar 96	2
SURPRISE	Mercury	21	6 Jul 96	3
Guest vocals by Julie Driscoll.				
GET UP SUNSHINE STREET	Mercury	45	14 Sep 96	2
PLAYING WITH KNIVES [RM-2ND]	Vinyl Solution	30	13 Mar 99	2
Remixed by Tarrrentella and Al Scott.				
ALBUMS:		HITS 1		WEEKS 2
ENERGIQUE	Vinyl Solution	41	7 Nov 92	2

BIZZ NIZZ
US/Belgium

SINGLES:		HITS 1		WEEKS 11
DON'T MISS THE PARTYLINE	Cooltempo	7	31 Mar 90	11

BIZZI
UK

SINGLES:		HITS 1		WEEKS 1
BIZZI'S PARTY	Parlophone	62	6 Dec 97	1

BJORK
Iceland

SINGLES:		HITS 16		WEEKS 69
OOOPS	ZTT	42	27 Apr 91	3
Above hit: 808 STATE featuring BJORK.				
HUMAN BEHAVIOUR	One Little Indian	36	19 Jun 93	2
VENUS AS A BOY	One Little Indian	29	4 Sep 93	4
PLAY DEAD	Island	12	23 Oct 93	6
From the film 'The Young Americans'.				
Above hit: BJORK and David ARNOLD.				
BIG TIME SENSUALITY	One Little Indian	17	4 Dec 93	8
VIOLENTLY HAPPY	One Little Indian	13	19 Mar 94	4
ARMY OF ME	One Little Indian	10	6 May 95	5
ISOBEL	One Little Indian	23	26 Aug 95	3
IT'S OH SO QUIET	One Little Indian	4	25 Nov 95	15
Originally recorded by Betty Hutton in 1948.				
HYPERBALLAD	One Little Indian	8	24 Feb 96	4
POSSIBLY MAYBE	One Little Indian	13	9 Nov 96	3
I MISS YOU	One Little Indian	36	1 Mar 97	2
BACHELORETTE	One Little Indian	21	20 Dec 97	5
HUNTER	One Little Indian	44	17 Oct 98	1
ALARM CALL	One Little Indian	33	12 Dec 98	2
ALL IS FULL OF LOVE	One Little Indian	24	19 Jun 99	2

ALBUMS	HITS 3			WEEKS 120
DEBUT	One Little Indian	3	17 Jul 93	69
Repackaged with additional track from 25 Dec 93. Includes re-entries through to 1999.				
POST	One Little Indian	2	24 Jun 95	37
Initial copies were withdrawn on first day of sale due to an uncleared sample of 'Mass Observation' by Scanner.				
POST / TELEGRAM [RE]	One Little Indian	59	7 Dec 96	1
Telegram was a remix album, sales were combined.				
HOMOGENIC	One Little Indian	4	4 Oct 97	13

BJORN, BENNY, ANNA and FRIDA – See ABBA

BJORN AGAIN   Australia

SINGLES:	HITS 3			WEEKS 8
ERASURE-ISH – (A LITTLE RESPECT / STOP!)	M&G	25	24 Oct 92	3
SANTA CLAUS IS COMING TO TOWN	M&G	55	12 Dec 92	4
FLASHDANCE . . . WHAT A FEELING	M&G	65	27 Nov 93	1

BLACK   UK

SINGLES:	HITS 8			WEEKS 35
WONDERFUL LIFE	Ugly Man	72	27 Sep 86	1
SWEETEST SMILE	A&M	8	27 Jun 87	10
WONDERFUL LIFE [RR]	A&M	8	22 Aug 87	9
PARADISE	A&M	38	16 Jan 88	3
THE BIG ONE	A&M	54	24 Sep 88	4
NOW YOU'RE GONE	A&M	66	21 Jan 89	2
FEEL LIKE CHANGE	A&M	56	4 May 91	2
HERE IT COMES AGAIN	A&M	70	15 Jun 91	1
WONDERFUL LIFE [RR] [RI]	PolyGram TV	42	5 Mar 94	3
Featured in TV commercials for Standard Life Assurance and Cadbury's.				

ALBUMS:	HITS 3			WEEKS 29
WONDERFUL LIFE	A&M	3	26 Sep 87	23
COMEDY	A&M	32	29 Oct 88	4
BLACK	A&M	42	1 Jun 91	2

Bill BLACK'S COMBO   US

SINGLES:	HITS 2			WEEKS 8
WHITE SILVER SANDS	London	50	10 Sep 60	1
Originally recorded by Don Rondo.				
DON'T BE CRUEL	London	32	5 Nov 60	7

Cilla BLACK   UK

SINGLES:	HITS 21			WEEKS 194
LOVE OF THE LOVED	Parlophone	35	19 Oct 63	6
Written by Lennon/McCartney.				
ANYONE WHO HAD A HEART	Parlophone	1	8 Feb 64	17
Originally recorded by Dionne Warwick.				
YOU'RE MY WORLD (IL MIO MONDO)	Parlophone	1	9 May 64	17
IT'S FOR YOU	Parlophone	7	8 Aug 64	10
Written by Lennon/McCartney.				
YOU'VE LOST THAT LOVIN' FEELIN'	Parlophone	2	16 Jan 65	9
I'VE BEEN WRONG BEFORE	Parlophone	17	24 Apr 65	8
LOVE'S JUST A BROKEN HEART	Parlophone	5	15 Jan 66	11
ALFIE	Parlophone	9	2 Apr 66	12
From the film of the same name.				
DON'T ANSWER ME	Parlophone	6	11 Jun 66	10
A FOOL AM I (DIMMELO PARLAMI)	Parlophone	13	22 Oct 66	9
WHAT GOOD AM I?	Parlophone	24	10 Jun 67	7
I ONLY LIVE TO LOVE YOU	Parlophone	26	2 Dec 67	11
STEP INSIDE LOVE	Parlophone	8	16 Mar 68	9
Written by Lennon/McCartney.				
WHERE IS TOMORROW?	Parlophone	39	15 Jun 68	3
SURROUND YOURSELF WITH SORROW	Parlophone	3	15 Feb 69	12
CONVERSATIONS	Parlophone	7	12 Jul 69	12
IF I THOUGHT YOU'D EVER CHANGE YOUR MIND	Parlophone	20	13 Dec 69	9
SOMETHING TELLS ME (SOMETHING'S GONNA HAPPEN TONIGHT)	Parlophone	3	20 Nov 71	14
Theme from her BBC1 TV show.				
BABY WE CAN'T GO WRONG	EMI	36	2 Feb 74	6
THROUGH THE YEARS	Columbia	54	18 Sep 93	1
HEART AND SOUL	Columbia	75	30 Oct 93	1
Above hit: Cilla BLACK and Dusty SPRINGFIELD.				

EPS:	HITS 3			WEEKS 29
ANYONE WHO HAD A HEART	Parlophone	5	25 Apr 64	17
IT'S FOR YOU	Parlophone	12	17 Oct 64	8
CILLA'S HITS	Parlophone	6	17 Sep 66	4

ALBUMS:		HITS 7			WEEKS 63
CILLA	Parlophone	5	13 Feb 65		11
CILLA SINGS A RAINBOW	Parlophone	4	14 May 66		15
SHER-OO	Parlophone	7	13 Apr 68		11
THE BEST OF CILLA BLACK	Parlophone	21	30 Nov 68		11
SWEET INSPIRATION	Parlophone	42	25 Jul 70		4
THE VERY BEST OF CILLA BLACK	Parlophone	20	29 Jan 83		9
THROUGH THE YEARS	Columbia	41	2 Oct 93		2

Album released to mark her 30th year in showbusiness.

Frank BLACK   US

SINGLES:		HITS 3			WEEKS 4
HEADACHE	4AD	53	21 May 94		1
MEN IN BLACK	Dragnet	37	20 Jan 96		2
I DON'T WANT TO HURT YOU (EVERY SINGLE TIME)	Dragnet	63	27 Jul 96		1

ALBUMS:		HITS 4			WEEKS 8
FRANK BLACK	4AD	9	20 Mar 93		3
TEENAGER OF THE YEAR	4AD	21	4 Jun 94		2
THE CULT OF RAY	Dragnet	39	3 Feb 96		2
FRANK BLACK AND THE CATHOLICS	Play It	61	16 May 98		1

Above hit: Frank BLACK and the CATHOLICS.

Jeanne BLACK   US

SINGLES:		HITS 1			WEEKS 4
HE'LL HAVE TO STAY	Capitol	41	25 Jun 60		4

Answer version to Jim Reeves' He'll Have To Go.

Mary BLACK   Ireland

ALBUMS:		HITS 4			WEEKS 10
THE HOLY GROUND	Grapevine	58	3 Jul 93		2
CIRCUS	Grapevine	16	16 Sep 95		4
SHINE	Grapevine	33	29 Mar 97		3
SPEAKING WITH THE ANGEL	Grapevine	63	28 Aug 99		1

Stanley BLACK and his Orchestra - See David WHITFIELD

BLACK AND WHITE ARMY   UK

SINGLES:		HITS 1			WEEKS 2
BLACK & WHITE ARMY (BRING THE PRIDE BACK HOME)	Toon	26	23 May 98		2

The official F.A. Cup song for Newcastle United.

BLACK BOX   Italy

SINGLES:		HITS 11			WEEKS 74
RIDE ON TIME	Deconstruction	1	12 Aug 89		22
I DON'T KNOW ANYBODY ELSE	Deconstruction	4	17 Feb 90		8
EVERYBODY EVERYBODY	Deconstruction	16	2 Jun 90		8
FANTASY (REMIXED)	Deconstruction	5	3 Nov 90		11
THE TOTAL MIX [M]	Deconstruction	12	15 Dec 90		8
Mix of their hits.					
STRIKE IT UP	Deconstruction	16	6 Apr 91		8
OPEN YOUR EYES	Deconstruction	48	14 Dec 91		4
ROCKIN' TO THE MUSIC	Deconstruction	39	14 Aug 93		2
NOT ANYONE	Mercury	31	24 Jun 95		2
I GOT THE VIBRATION / A POSITIVE VIBRATION	Manifesto	21	20 Apr 96		3
Samples Love Hangover by Diana Ross.					
NATIVE NEW YORKER	Manifesto	46	22 Feb 97		1
Above 2: BLACKBOX.					

ALBUMS:		HITS 1			WEEKS 30
DREAMLAND	Deconstruction	14	5 May 90		30

BLACK CONNECTION   Italy

SINGLES:		HITS 2			WEEKS 3
GIVE ME RHYTHM	Xtravaganza	32	14 Mar 98		2
I'M GONNA GET YA BABY	Xtravaganza	62	24 Oct 98		1

BLACK CROWES   US

SINGLES:		HITS 11			WEEKS 28
HARD TO HANDLE	Def American	45	1 Sep 90		5
TWICE AS HARD	Def American	47	12 Jan 91		3
JEALOUS AGAIN / SHE TALKS TO ANGELS	Def American	70	22 Jun 91		1
HARD TO HANDLE [RI]	Def American	39	24 Aug 91		4
SEEING THINGS	Def American	72	26 Oct 91		1
REMEDY	Def American	24	2 May 92		3
STING ME	Def American	42	26 Sep 92		2

HOTEL ILLNESS	*Def American*	47	*28 Nov 92*	3
HIGH HEAD BLUES / A CONSPIRACY	*American Recordings*	25	*11 Feb 95*	2
WISER TIME	*American Recordings*	34	*22 Jul 95*	2
ONE MIRROR TOO MANY	*American Recordings*	51	*27 Jul 96*	1
KICKING MY HEART AROUND	*American Recordings*	55	*7 Nov 98*	1
ALBUMS:	**HITS 5**		**WEEKS 27**	
SHAKE YOUR MONEY MAKER	*Def American*	36	*24 Aug 91*	11
THE SOUTHERN HARMONY AND MUSICAL COMPANION	*Def American*	2	*23 May 92*	7
AMORICA	*American Recordings*	8	*12 Nov 94*	4
THREE SNAKES AND ONE CHARM	*American Recordings*	17	*3 Aug 96*	3
BY YOUR SIDE	*Columbia*	34	*23 Jan 99*	2

BLACK DIAMOND   US

SINGLES:	**HITS 1**		**WEEKS 1**	
LET ME BE	*Systematic*	56	*17 Sep 94*	1

BLACK DOG   UK

SINGLES:	**HITS 1**		**WEEKS 1**	
BABYLON	*warner.esp*	65	*3 Apr 99*	1

Above hit: BLACK DOG featuring Ofra HAZA.

ALBUMS:	**HITS 1**		**WEEKS 2**	
SPANNERS	*Warp*	30	*28 Jan 95*	2

BLACK DUCK   UK

SINGLES:	**HITS 1**		**WEEKS 5**	
WHIGGLE IN LINE	*Flying South*	33	*17 Dec 94*	5

Based around Whigfield's Saturday Night.

BLACK EYED PEAS   US

SINGLES:	**HITS 1**		**WEEKS 1**	
JOINTS AND JAM	*Interscope*	53	*10 Oct 98*	1

BLACK GORILLA   UK

SINGLES:	**HITS 1**		**WEEKS 6**	
GIMME DAT BANANA	*Response*	29	*27 Aug 77*	6

BLACK GRAPE   UK

SINGLES:	**HITS 7**		**WEEKS 25**	
REVEREND BLACK GRAPE	*Radioactive*	9	*10 Jun 95*	5
IN THE NAME OF THE FATHER	*Radioactive*	8	*5 Aug 95*	4
KELLY'S HEROES	*Radioactive*	17	*2 Dec 95*	5
FAT NECK	*Radioactive*	10	*25 May 96*	3
ENGLAND'S IRIE	*Radioactive*	6	*29 Jun 96*	4

Above hit: BLACK GRAPE featuring Joe STRUMMER and Keith ALLEN.

GET HIGHER	*Radioactive*	24	*1 Nov 97*	3
MARBLES	*Radioactive*	46	*7 Mar 98*	1
ALBUMS:	**HITS 2**		**WEEKS 46**	
IT'S GREAT WHEN YOU'RE STRAIGHT . . . YEAH	*Radioactive*	1	*19 Aug 95*	39
STUPID STUPID STUPID	*Radioactive*	11	*22 Nov 97*	7

BLACK LACE   UK

SINGLES:	**HITS 10**		**WEEKS 83**	
MARY ANN	*EMI*	42	*31 Mar 79*	4

UK's Eurovision entry in 1979, it came 7th.

SUPERMAN (GIOCA JOUER)	*Flair*	9	*24 Sep 83*	18

Originally recorded by Phil Charles as 'The Joker'.

AGADOO	*Flair*	2	*30 Jun 84*	30

Originally recorded by the Saragossa Band in 1981.

DO THE CONGA	*Flair*	10	*24 Nov 84*	9
EL VINO COLLAPSO	*Flair*	42	*1 Jun 85*	5
I SPEAKA DA LINGO	*Flair*	49	*7 Sep 85*	4
THE HOKEY-COKEY	*Flair*	31	*7 Dec 85*	6
WIG WAM BAM	*Flair*	63	*20 Sep 86*	3
I AM THE MUSIC MAN	*Flair*	52	*26 Aug 89*	3
AGADOO [RR]	*N.O.W.*	64	*22 Aug 98*	1
ALBUMS:	**HITS 3**		**WEEKS 26**	
PARTY PARTY – 16 GREAT PARTY ICEBREAKERS	*Telstar*	4	*8 Dec 84*	14
PARTY PARTY 2	*Telstar*	18	*7 Dec 85*	6
PARTY CRAZY	*Telstar*	58	*6 Dec 86*	6

BLACK MACHINE   France/Nigeria

SINGLES:	**HITS 1**		**WEEKS 5**	
HOW GEE	*London*	17	*9 Apr 94*	5

BLACK MAGIC: A LIL' LOUIS PAINTING   US

(See also Lil' Louis.)

SINGLES:		HITS 1		WEEKS 2
FREEDOM (MAKE IT FUNKY)	*Positiva*	41	*1 Jun 96*	2

BLACK MOUNTAIN MALE CHORUS - See Shirley BASSEY; Bryn TERFEL

BLACKOUT   UK

SINGLES:		HITS 1		WEEKS 1
GOTTA HAVE HOPE	*Multiply*	46	*27 Mar 99*	1

Original release reached No. 139 in 1997. Samples 2001: A Space Odyssey.

BLACK RIOT   US

SINGLES:		HITS 1		WEEKS 3
A DAY IN THE LIFE / WARLOCK	*Champion*	68	*3 Dec 88*	3

A Day In The Life not listed until 10 Dec 88.

BLACK, ROCK and RON   US

ALBUMS:		HITS 1		WEEKS 1
STOP THE WORLD	*Supreme*	72	*22 Apr 89*	1

BLACK SABBATH   UK

SINGLES:		HITS 9		WEEKS 70
PARANOID	*Vertigo*	4	*29 Aug 70*	18
NEVER SAY DIE	*Vertigo*	21	*3 Jun 78*	8
HARD ROAD	*Vertigo*	33	*14 Oct 78*	4
NEON KNIGHTS	*Vertigo*	22	*5 Jul 80*	9
PARANOID [RI]	*NEMS*	14	*16 Aug 80*	12
DIE YOUNG	*Vertigo*	41	*6 Dec 80*	7
MOB RULES	*Vertigo*	46	*7 Nov 81*	4
TURN UP THE NIGHT	*Vertigo*	37	*13 Feb 82*	5
HEADLESS CROSS	*I.R.S.*	62	*15 Apr 89*	1
TV CRIMES	*I.R.S.*	33	*13 Jun 92*	2

ALBUMS:		HITS 22		WEEKS 214
BLACK SABBATH	*Vertigo*	8	*7 Mar 70*	42
PARANOID	*Vertigo*	1	*26 Sep 70*	27
MASTER OF REALITY	*Vertigo*	5	*21 Aug 71*	13
BLACK SABBATH VOLUME 4	*Vertigo*	8	*30 Sep 72*	10
SABBATH BLOODY SABBATH	*WWA*	4	*8 Dec 73*	11
SABOTAGE	*NEMS*	7	*27 Sep 75*	7
WE SOLD OUR SOUL FOR ROCK 'N' ROLL	*NEMS*	35	*7 Feb 76*	5
TECHNICAL ECSTASY	*Vertigo*	13	*6 Nov 76*	6
NEVER SAY DIE	*Vertigo*	12	*14 Oct 78*	6
HEAVEN AND HELL	*Vertigo*	9	*26 Apr 80*	22
BLACK SABBATH LIVE AT LAST	*NEMS*	5	*5 Jul 80*	15
Live recordings from 1975.				
PARANOID [RI]	*NEMS*	54	*27 Sep 80*	2
MOB RULES	*Mercury*	12	*14 Nov 81*	14
LIVE EVIL	*Vertigo*	13	*22 Jan 83*	11
BORN AGAIN	*Vertigo*	4	*24 Sep 83*	7
SEVENTH STAR	*Vertigo*	27	*1 Mar 86*	5
Above hit: BLACK SABBATH featuring Tony IOMMI.				
THE ETERNAL IDOL	*Vertigo*	66	*28 Nov 87*	1
HEADLESS CROSS	*I.R.S.*	31	*29 Apr 89*	2
TYR	*I.R.S.*	24	*1 Sep 90*	3
DEHUMANIZER	*I.R.S.*	28	*4 Jul 92*	2
CROSS PURPOSES	*I.R.S.*	41	*12 Feb 94*	1
FORBIDDEN	*I.R.S.*	71	*17 Jun 95*	1
REUNION	*Epic*	41	*31 Oct 98*	1

Live recordings from the NEC, Birmingham, 5 Dec 97 plus 2 studio tracks.

BLACK SCIENCE ORCHESTRA   UK

ALBUMS:		HITS 1		WEEKS 1
WALTERS ROOM	*Junior Boy's Own*	68	*3 Aug 96*	1

BLACK SHEEP   US

SINGLES:		HITS 1		WEEKS 1
WITHOUT A DOUBT	*Mercury*	60	*19 Nov 94*	1

BLACK SLATE   UK/Jamaica

SINGLES:		HITS 2		WEEKS 15
AMIGO	*Ensign*	9	*20 Sep 80*	9
BOOM BOOM	*Ensign*	51	*6 Dec 80*	6

BLACK STAR LINER | | | | UK

ALBUMS:		HITS 1			WEEKS 1
YEMEN CUTTA CONNECTION	EXP		66	7 Sep 96	1

BLACK UHURU | | | | Jamaica

SINGLES:		HITS 2			WEEKS 9
WHAT IS LIFE?	Island		56	8 Sep 84	6
THE GREAT TRAIN ROBBERY	Real Authentic Sound		62	31 May 86	3
ALBUMS:		HITS 4			WEEKS 22
RED	Island		28	13 Jun 81	13
BLACK UHURU	Virgin		81	22 Aug 81	2
CHILL OUT	Island		38	19 Jun 82	6
ANTHEM	Island		90	25 Aug 84	1

Band of the BLACK WATCH | | | | UK

SINGLES:		HITS 2			WEEKS 22
SCOTCH ON THE ROCKS	Spark		8	30 Aug 75	14
DANCE OF THE CUCKOOS (THE "LAUREL & HARDY" THEME)	Spark		37	13 Dec 75	8
ALBUMS:		HITS 1			WEEKS 13
SCOTCH ON THE ROCKS	Spark		11	7 Feb 76	13

BLACK WIDOW | | | | UK

ALBUMS:		HITS 1			WEEKS 2
SACRIFICE	CBS		32	4 Apr 70	2

Tony BLACKBURN | | | | UK

SINGLES:		HITS 2			WEEKS 7
SO MUCH LOVE	MGM		31	27 Jan 68	4
IT'S ONLY LOVE	MGM		41	29 Mar 69	3

Above hit: Tony BLACKBURN with the MAJORITY.

BLACKBYRDS | | | | US

SINGLES:		HITS 1			WEEKS 6
WALKING IN RHYTHM	Fantasy		23	31 May 75	6

BLACKFOOT | | | | US

SINGLES:		HITS 2			WEEKS 5
FOUR FROM BLACKFOOT [EP]	Atco		43	6 Mar 82	4
Lead track: Dry County.					
SEND ME AN ANGEL	Atco		66	18 Jun 83	1
ALBUMS:		HITS 4			WEEKS 22
MARAUDER	Atco		38	18 Jul 81	12
HIGHWAY SONG – BLACKFOOT LIVE	Atco		14	11 Sep 82	6
SIOGO	Atlantic		28	21 May 83	3
VERTICAL SMILES	Atco		82	29 Sep 84	1

J. BLACKFOOT | | | | US

SINGLES:		HITS 1			WEEKS 4
TAXI	Allegiance		48	17 Mar 84	4

BLACKFOOT SUE | | | | UK

SINGLES:		HITS 2			WEEKS 15
STANDING IN THE ROAD	Jam		4	12 Aug 72	10
SING DON'T SPEAK	Jam		36	16 Dec 72	5

BLACKGIRL | | | | US

SINGLES:		HITS 1			WEEKS 3
90'S GIRL	RCA		23	16 Jul 94	3

Features rap from Menton 'Peanut' Smith.

Honor BLACKMAN – See Patrick MacNEE and Honor BLACKMAN

Ritchie BLACKMORE'S RAINBOW – See RAINBOW

BLACKNUSS featuring Stephen SIMMONDS-ADL-Richie PASTA-MULADOE | | Sweden

SINGLES:		HITS 1			WEEKS 1
DINAH	Arista		56	28 Jun 97	1

BLACKSTREET | | | | US

SINGLES:		HITS 14			WEEKS 70
BABY BE MINE	MCA		37	19 Jun 93	3

Above hit: BLACKSTREET featuring Teddy RILEY.

BOOTI CALL	Interscope	56	13 Aug 94	1
Features rapper Antwone Dickey – T-Pirate.				
U BLOW MY MIND	Interscope	39	11 Feb 95	2
JOY	Interscope	56	27 May 95	2
NO DIGGITY	Interscope	9	19 Oct 96	7
Above hit: BLACKSTREET (featuring DR. DRE).				
GET ME HOME	Def Jam	11	8 Mar 97	5
Based on Eugene Wilde's Gotta Get You Home Tonight.				
Above hit: Foxy BROWN featuring BLACKSTREET.				
DON'T LEAVE ME	Interscope	6	26 Apr 97	10
Samples 2 Pac's I Ain't Mad At Cha.				
FIX	Interscope	7	27 Sep 97	5
Samples Grandmaster Flash's The Message. Features Slash (Guns N' Roses) and Ol' Dity Bastard (Wu-Tang Clan).				
(MONEY CAN'T) BUY ME LOVE	Interscope	18	13 Dec 97	6
I GET LONELY	Virgin	5	4 Apr 98	7
Above hit: JANET (featuring BLACKSTREET).				
THE CITY IS MINE	Northwestside	38	27 Jun 98	2
Above hit: JAY-Z featuring BLACKSTREET.				
TAKE ME THERE	Interscope	7	12 Dec 98	9
From the film 'The Rugrats Movie'.				
Above hit: BLACKSTREET and MYA featuring MASE and BLINKY BLINK.				
GIRLFRIEND / BOYFRIEND	Interscope	11	17 Apr 99	7
This is just one song title. Rap by Ja Rule and Eve.				
Above hit: BLACKSTREET featuring JANET.				
GET READY	Puff Daddy	32	10 Jul 99	4
Samples Shalamar's A Night To Remember.				
Above hit: MASE (featuring BLACKSTREET).				
ALBUMS:	**HITS 3**			**WEEKS 36**
BLACKSTREET	Interscope	35	9 Jul 94	6
ANOTHER LEVEL	Interscope	26	21 Sep 96	26
FINALLY	Interscope	27	3 Apr 99	4

Charles BLACKWELL – See Michael COX; Billie DAVIS; Rita PAVONE; Mike SARNE

Roger BLACKWELL and his Orchestra - See LITTLE RICHARD

BLACKWELLS   US

SINGLES:	**HITS 1**			**WEEKS 2**
LOVE OR MONEY	London	46	20 May 61	2

BLAGGERS I.T.A.   UK

SINGLES:	**HITS 3**			**WEEKS 7**
STRESS	Parlophone	56	12 Jun 93	2
OXYGEN	Parlophone	51	9 Oct 93	2
ABANDON SHIP	Parlophone	48	8 Jan 94	3

BLAHZAY BLAHZAY   US

SINGLES:	**HITS 1**			**WEEKS 1**
DANGER	Mercury	56	2 Mar 96	1

Vivian BLAINE   US

SINGLES:	**HITS 1**			**WEEKS 1**
BUSHEL AND A PECK	Brunswick	12	11 Jul 53	1

BLAIR   UK

SINGLES:	**HITS 2**			**WEEKS 5**
HAVE FUN, GO MAD!	Mercury	37	2 Sep 95	3
LIFE?	Mercury	44	6 Jan 96	2
Theme to the BBC childrens TV show 'Dear Dilemma'.				

BLAIR and ANOUCHKA - See Terry HALL

Howard BLAKE conducting the SINFONIA OF LONDON, Narration: Bernard CRIBBINS   UK

(See also Snowman.)

ALBUMS:	**HITS 1**			**WEEKS 12**
THE SNOWMAN	CBS	89	22 Dec 84	2
THE SNOWMAN [RE-1ST]	CBS	78	14 Dec 85	6
THE SNOWMAN [RE-2ND]	CBS	54	12 Dec 87	4

Peter BLAKE   UK

SINGLES:	**HITS 1**			**WEEKS 4**
LIPSMACKIN' ROCK 'N ROLLIN'	Pepper/United Artists	40	8 Oct 77	4
Featured in a TV commercial for Pepsi.				

BLAME | | | | | UK

SINGLES:	HITS 1			WEEKS 2	
MUSIC TAKES YOU	Moving Shadow	48	11 Apr 92		2

BLAMELESS | | | | | UK

SINGLES:	HITS 3			WEEKS 5	
TOWN CLOWNS	China	56	4 Nov 95		1
BREATHE (A LITTLE DEEPER)	China	27	23 Mar 96		3
SIGNS . . .	China	49	1 Jun 96		1

BLANCMANGE | | | | | UK

SINGLES:	HITS 10			WEEKS 71	
GOD'S KITCHEN / I'VE SEEN THE WORD	London	65	17 Apr 82		2
FEEL ME	London	46	31 Jul 82		5
LIVING ON THE CEILING	London	7	30 Oct 82		14
WAVES	London	19	19 Feb 83		9
BLIND VISION	London	10	7 May 83		8
THAT'S LOVE, THAT IT IS	London	33	26 Nov 83		8
DON'T TELL ME	London	8	14 Apr 84		10
THE DAY BEFORE YOU CAME	London	22	21 Jul 84		8
WHAT'S YOUR PROBLEM	London	40	7 Sep 85		5
I CAN SEE IT	London	71	10 May 86		2
ALBUMS:	HITS 3			WEEKS 57	
HAPPY FAMILIES	London	30	9 Oct 82		38
MANGE TOUT	London	8	26 May 84		17
BELIEVE YOU ME	London	54	26 Oct 85		2

Billy BLAND | | | | | US

SINGLES:	HITS 1			WEEKS 10	
LET THE LITTLE GIRL DANCE	London	15	21 May 60		10

BLANK and JONES | | | | | Germany

SINGLES:	HITS 1			WEEKS 3	
CREAM	Deviant	24	26 Jun 99		3

BLAQUE IVORY | | | | | US

SINGLES:	HITS 1			WEEKS 3	
808	Columbia	31	3 Jul 99		3

BLAST featuring V.D.C. | | | | | Italy

SINGLES:	HITS 2			WEEKS 5	
CRAYZY MAN	MCA	22	18 Jun 94		3
PRINCES OF THE NIGHT	MCA	40	12 Nov 94		2

BLEACH BOYS - See WIZZARD

Memphis BLEEK featuring JAY-Z | | | | | US

(See also Jay-Z.)

SINGLES:	HITS 1			WEEKS 1	
WHAT YOU THINK OF THAT	Roc-A-Fella	58	4 Dec 99		1

Samples Keith Mansfield's High Velocity.

BLESSID UNION OF SOULS | | | | | US

SINGLES:	HITS 2			WEEKS 6	
I BELIEVE	EMI	29	27 May 95		5
LET ME BE THE ONE	EMI	74	23 Mar 96		1

BLESSING | | | | | UK

SINGLES:	HITS 2			WEEKS 13	
HIGHWAY 5	MCA	42	11 May 91		6
HIGHWAY 5 '92 [RM]	MCA	30	18 Jan 92		6
SOUL LOVE	MCA	73	19 Feb 94		1

Above hit: BLESSING featuring Cutty RANKS.

Archie BLEYER and his Orchestra - See Bill HAYES

Mary J. BLIGE | | | | | US

SINGLES:	HITS 19			WEEKS 78	
REAL LOVE	MCA	68	28 Nov 92		2
REMINISCE	MCA	31	27 Feb 93		4
YOU REMIND ME	MCA	48	12 Jun 93		3
REAL LOVE [RM]	MCA	26	28 Aug 93		4

Remixed by Blacksmith and the Funky Mob.

YOU DON'T HAVE TO WORRY	Uptown	36	4 Dec 93	2
From the film 'Who's The Man'. Samples Papa Don't Take No Mess by James Brown.				
MY LOVE	Uptown	29	14 May 94	3
BE HAPPY	Uptown	30	10 Dec 94	4
Samples You're Too Good To Me by Curtis Mayfield.				
I'M GOIN' DOWN	Uptown	12	15 Apr 95	4
Originally recorded by Rose Royce in 1978.				
I'LL BE THERE FOR YOU/YOU'RE ALL I NEED TO GET BY [M]	Def Jam	10	29 Jul 95	5
Above hit: METHOD MAN featuring Mary J. BLIGE.				
MARY JANE (ALL NIGHT LONG)	Uptown	17	30 Sep 95	4
(YOU MAKE ME FEEL LIKE A) NATURAL WOMAN	Uptown	23	16 Dec 95	3
Originally recorded by Carole King.				
NOT GON' CRY	Arista	39	30 Mar 96	2
From the film 'Waiting To Exhale'.				
CAN'T KNOCK THE HUSTLE	Northwestside	30	1 Mar 97	2
Above hit: JAY-Z featuring Mary J. BLIGE.				
LOVE IS ALL WE NEED	MCA	15	17 May 97	4
Samples 'Moonchild' by Rick James.				
EVERYTHING	MCA	6	16 Aug 97	9
Based on Diana Ross and Marvin Gaye's 'You Are Everything'.				
MISSING YOU	MCA	19	29 Nov 97	3
MISSING YOU [RE-1ST]	MCA	72	3 Jan 98	1
MISSING YOU [RE-2ND]	MCA	74	31 Jan 98	1
SEVEN DAYS	MCA	22	11 Jul 98	3
Above hit: Mary J. BLIGE featuring George BENSON.				
AS	Epic	4	13 Mar 99	10
Originally recorded by Stevie Wonder's on his 1976 album Songs In The Key Of Life.				
Above hit: George MICHAEL – Mary J. BLIGE.				
ALL THAT I CAN SAY	MCA	29	21 Aug 99	3
DEEP INSIDE	MCA	42	11 Dec 99	2
Samples Elton John's Bennie And The Jets.				
ALBUMS:	**HITS 4**		**WEEKS 42**	
WHAT'S THE 411?	MCA	53	20 Mar 93	1
MY LIFE	Uptown	59	17 Dec 94	3
SHARE MY WORLD	MCA	8	26 Apr 97	32
MARY	MCA	5	28 Aug 99	6

BLIND FAITH   UK

ALBUMS:	**HITS 1**		**WEEKS 10**	
BLIND FAITH	Polydor	1	13 Sep 69	10

BLIND MELON   US

SINGLES:	**HITS 4**		**WEEKS 13**	
TONES OF HOME [EP]	Capitol	62	12 Jun 93	2
Lead track: Tones Of Home.				
NO RAIN	Capitol	17	11 Dec 93	6
CHANGE	Capitol	35	9 Jul 94	3
GALAXIE	Capitol	37	5 Aug 95	2
ALBUMS:	**HITS 2**		**WEEKS 4**	
BLIND MELON	Capitol	53	22 Jan 94	3
SOUP	Capitol	48	19 Aug 95	1

BLINK   Ireland

SINGLES:	**HITS 1**		**WEEKS 1**	
HAPPY DAY	Parlophone	57	16 Jul 94	1

BLINK 182   US

SINGLES:	**HITS 1**		**WEEKS 2**	
WHAT'S MY AGE AGAIN?	MCA	38	2 Oct 99	2

BLINKY BLINK - See BLACKSTREET

BLITZ   UK

ALBUMS:	**HITS 1**		**WEEKS 3**	
VOICE OF A GENERATION	No Future	27	6 Nov 82	3

Brandon BLOCK - See BLOCKSTER; GRIFTERS featuring TALL PAUL and Brandon BLOCK

BLOCKSTER   UK

SINGLES:	**HITS 2**		**WEEKS 11**	
YOU SHOULD BE ...	Sound Of Ministry	3	16 Jan 99	9
GROOVELINE	Sound Of Ministry	18	24 Jul 99	2

BLODWYN PIG UK

ALBUMS:	HITS 2			WEEKS 11
AHEAD RINGS OUT	Island	9	16 Aug 69	4
GETTING TO THIS	Chrysalis	8	25 Apr 70	7

Kristine BLOND Denmark

SINGLES:	HITS 1			WEEKS 3
LOVE SHY	Reverb	22	11 Apr 98	3

BLONDIE US/UK

SINGLES:	HITS 16			WEEKS 169
DENIS (DENEE)	Chrysalis	2	18 Feb 78	14
Original by Randy and the Rainbows reached No. 10 in the US in 1963.				
(I'M ALWAYS TOUCHED BY YOUR) PRESENCE DEAR	Chrysalis	10	6 May 78	9
PICTURE THIS	Chrysalis	12	26 Aug 78	11
HANGING ON THE TELPHONE	Chrysalis	5	11 Nov 78	12
Originally recorded by Jack Lee.				
HEART OF GLASS	Chrysalis	1	27 Jan 79	12
SUNDAY GIRL	Chrysalis	1	19 May 79	13
DREAMING	Chrysalis	2	29 Sep 79	8
UNION CITY BLUE	Chrysalis	13	24 Nov 79	10
ATOMIC	Chrysalis	1	23 Feb 80	9
CALL ME	Chrysalis	1	12 Apr 80	9
From the film 'An American Gigolo'.				
THE TIDE IS HIGH	Chrysalis	1	8 Nov 80	12
Originally recorded by the Paragons.				
RAPTURE	Chrysalis	5	24 Jan 81	8
ISLAND OF LOST SOULS	Chrysalis	11	8 May 82	9
WAR CHILD	Chrysalis	39	24 Jul 82	4
DENIS (THE '88 REMIX) [RM]	Chrysalis	50	3 Dec 88	3
Remixed by Danny D.				
CALL ME [RM]	Chrysalis	61	11 Feb 89	2
Remixed by Ben Liebrand.				
ATOMIC: REMIXES [RM]	Chrysalis	19	10 Sep 94	4
HEART OF GLASS [RM]	Chrysalis	15	8 Jul 95	3
UNION CITY BLUE [RM]	Chrysalis	31	28 Oct 95	2
Above 3 remixed by Diddy.				
MARIA	Beyond	1	13 Feb 99	12
NOTHING IS REAL BUT THE GIRL	Beyond	26	12 Jun 99	3

ALBUMS:	HITS 12			WEEKS 340
PLASTIC LETTERS	Chrysalis	10	4 Mar 78	54
PARALLEL LINES	Chrysalis	1	23 Sep 78	105
BLONDIE	Chrysalis	75	10 Mar 79	1
Originally released in 1977.				
EAT TO THE BEAT	Chrysalis	1	13 Oct 79	38
AUTOAMERICAN	Chrysalis	3	29 Nov 80	16
THE BEST OF BLONDIE	Chrysalis	4	31 Oct 81	40
THE HUNTER	Chrysalis	9	5 Jun 82	12
ONCE MORE INTO THE BLEACH	Chrysalis	50	17 Dec 88	4
Remix album of Debbie Harry's solo and group material.				
Above hit: Debbie HARRY and BLONDIE.				
THE COMPLETE PICTURE – THE VERY BEST OF DEBORAH HARRY AND BLONDIE	Chrysalis	3	16 Mar 91	22
Above hit: Deborah HARRY and BLONDIE.				
BEAUTIFUL – THE REMIX ALBUM	Chrysalis	25	29 Jul 95	2
ATOMIC – THE VERY BEST OF BLONDE	EMI	12	25 Jul 98	13
ATOMIC/ATOMIX – THE VERY BEST OF BLONDIE [RE]	EMI	12	20 Feb 99	18
Repackaged with remix album.				
NO EXIT	Beyond	3	27 Feb 99	15

BLOOD, SWEAT AND TEARS US

SINGLES:	HITS 1			WEEKS 6
YOU'VE MADE ME SO VERY HAPPY	CBS	35	3 May 69	6
Originally recorded by Brenda Holloway.				

ALBUMS:	HITS 3			WEEKS 21
CHILD IS THE FATHER TO THE MAN	CBS	40	13 Jul 68	1
BLOOD SWEAT AND TEARS	CBS	15	12 Apr 69	8
BLOOD SWEAT AND TEARS 3	CBS	14	8 Aug 70	12

BLOODHOUND GANG US

SINGLES:	HITS 1			WEEKS 1
WHY'S EVERYBODY ALWAYS PICKIN' ON ME?	Geffen	56	23 Aug 97	1

Major Denis BLOODNOK, 43RD DESERTERS (Rtd.) – See GOONS

BLOODSTONE

SINGLES:		HITS 1		US WEEKS 4
NATURAL HIGH	Decca	40	18 Aug 73	4

Bobby BLOOM

SINGLES:		HITS 2		US WEEKS 24
MONTEGO BAY	Polydor	3	29 Aug 70	14
MONTEGO BAY [RE-1ST]	Polydor	42	12 Dec 70	3
MONTEGO BAY [RE-2ND]	Polydor	47	9 Jan 71	2
HEAVY MAKES YOU HAPPY	Polydor	31	9 Jan 71	5

BLOOMSBURY SET

SINGLES:		HITS 1		UK WEEKS 3
HANGING AROUND WITH THE BIG BOYS	Stiletto	56	25 Jun 83	3

Tanya BLOUNT

SINGLES:		HITS 1		US WEEKS 1
I'M GONNA MAKE YOU MINE	Polydor	69	11 Jun 94	1

Kurtis BLOW

SINGLES:		HITS 6		US WEEKS 23
CHRISTMAS RAPPIN'	Mercury	30	15 Dec 79	6
THE BREAKS	Mercury	47	11 Oct 80	4
PARTY TIME (THE GO-GO EDIT)	Club	67	16 Mar 85	1
SAVE YOUR LOVE (FOR # 1)	Club	66	15 Jun 85	2
Above hit: RENE and ANGELA with Kurtis BLOW.				
IF I RULED THE WORLD	Club	24	18 Jan 86	8
I'M CHILLIN'	Club	64	8 Nov 86	2

BLOW MONKEYS

SINGLES:		HITS 10		UK WEEKS 46
DIGGING YOUR SCENE	RCA	12	1 Mar 86	10
WICKED WAYS	RCA	60	17 May 86	2
IT DOESN'T HAVE TO BE THIS WAY	RCA	5	31 Jan 87	8
OUT WITH HER	RCA	30	28 Mar 87	6
(CELEBRATE) THE DAY AFTER YOU	RCA	52	30 May 87	2
Above hit: BLOW MONKEYS with Curtis MAYFIELD.				
SOME KIND OF WONDERFUL	RCA	67	15 Aug 87	1
THIS IS YOUR LIFE	RCA	70	6 Aug 88	2
THIS IS YOUR LIFE [RM]	RCA	32	8 Apr 89	5
CHOICE?	RCA	22	15 Jul 89	6
SLAVES NO MORE	RCA	73	14 Oct 89	2
Above 2: BLOW MONKEYS featuring Sylvia TELLA.				
SPRINGTIME FOR THE WORLD	RCA	69	26 May 90	2
ALBUMS:		HITS 4		WEEKS 27
ANIMAL MAGIC	RCA	21	19 Apr 86	8
SHE WAS ONLY A GROCER'S DAUGHTER	RCA	20	25 Apr 87	8
WHOOPS! THERE GOES THE NEIGHBOURHOOD	RCA	46	11 Feb 89	2
CHOICES – THE SINGLES COLLECTION	RCA	5	26 Aug 89	9

BLOWING FREE

ALBUMS:		HITS 2		UK WEEKS 14
SAX MOODS	Dino	6	29 Jul 95	13
SAX MOODS – VOLUME 2	Dino	70	30 Nov 96	1

BLU PETER

SINGLES:		HITS 1		UK WEEKS 1
TELL ME WHAT YOU WANT / JAMES HAS KITTENS	React	70	21 Mar 98	1

BLUE

SINGLES:		HITS 1		UK WEEKS 8
GONNA CAPTURE YOUR HEART	Rocket	18	30 Apr 77	8

Babbity BLUE

SINGLES:		HITS 1		UK WEEKS 2
DON'T MAKE ME (FALL IN LOVE WITH YOU)	Decca	48	13 Feb 65	2

Barry BLUE

(See also Cry Sisco!)

SINGLES:		HITS 5		UK WEEKS 48
DANCIN' (ON A SATURDAY NIGHT)	Bell	2	28 Jul 73	15
Originally recorded by Lynsey De Paul.				

DO YOU WANNA DANCE?	*Bell*	7	*3 Nov 73*	12	
SCHOOL LOVE	*Bell*	11	*2 Mar 74*	9	
MISS HIT AND RUN	*Bell*	26	*3 Aug 74*	7	
HOT SHOT	*Bell*	23	*26 Oct 74*	5	

BLUE ADONIS featuring LIL' MISS MAX   Belgium

SINGLES:	**HITS 1**			**WEEKS 3**
DISCO COP	*Serious*	27	*17 Oct 98*	3

BLUE AEROPLANES   UK

SINGLES:	**HITS 2**			**WEEKS 3**
JACKET HANGS	*Ensign*	72	*17 Feb 90*	1
. . . AND STONES	*Ensign*	63	*26 May 90*	2
ALBUMS:	**HITS 3**			**WEEKS 5**
SWAGGER	*Ensign*	54	*24 Feb 90*	1
BEATSONGS	*Ensign*	33	*17 Aug 91*	3
LIFE MODEL	*Beggars Banquet*	59	*12 Mar 94*	1

BLUE AMAZON   UK

SINGLES:	**HITS 1**			**WEEKS 1**
AND THEN THE RAIN FALLS	*Sony*	53	*17 May 97*	1

BLUE BAMBOO   Belgium

SINGLES:	**HITS 1**			**WEEKS 4**
ABC AND D . . .	*Escapade*	23	*3 Dec 94*	4

BLUE CAPS – See Gene VINCENT

BLUE FEATHER   Holland

SINGLES:	**HITS 1**			**WEEKS 4**
LET'S FUNK TONIGHT	*Mercury*	50	*3 Jul 82*	4

BLUE FLAMES – See Georgie FAME

BLUE HAZE   UK

SINGLES:	**HITS 1**			**WEEKS 6**
SMOKE GETS IN YOUR EYES	*A&M*	32	*18 Mar 72*	6

Originally recorded by Paul Whiteman in 1933.

BLUE MELONS   UK

SINGLES:	**HITS 1**			**WEEKS 1**
DO WAH DIDDY DIDDY (THE WIGGLE MIX)	*Fundamental*	70	*8 Jun 96*	1

BLUE MERCEDES   UK

SINGLES:	**HITS 3**			**WEEKS 18**
I WANT TO BE YOUR PROPERTY	*MCA*	23	*10 Oct 87*	11
SEE WANT MUST HAVE	*MCA*	57	*13 Feb 88*	2
LOVE IS THE GUN	*MCA*	46	*23 Jul 88*	5

BLUE MINK   UK

SINGLES:	**HITS 7**			**WEEKS 83**
MELTING POT	*Philips*	3	*15 Nov 69*	15
GOOD MORNING FREEDOM	*Philips*	10	*28 Mar 70*	10
OUR WORLD	*Philips*	17	*19 Sep 70*	9
THE BANNER MAN	*Regal Zonophone*	3	*29 May 71*	14
STAY WITH ME	*Regal Zonophone*	11	*11 Nov 72*	13
STAY WITH ME [RE]	*Regal Zonophone*	43	*17 Feb 73*	2
BY THE DEVIL (I WAS TEMPTED)	*EMI*	26	*3 Mar 73*	9
RANDY	*EMI*	9	*23 Jun 73*	11

BLUE MURDER   US

ALBUMS:	**HITS 1**			**WEEKS 3**
BLUE MURDER	*Geffen*	45	*6 May 89*	3

BLUE NILE   UK

SINGLES:	**HITS 3**			**WEEKS 4**
THE DOWNTOWN LIGHTS	*Linn*	67	*30 Sep 89*	1
HEADLIGHTS ON THE PARADE	*Linn*	72	*29 Sep 90*	1
SATURDAY NIGHT	*Linn*	50	*19 Jan 91*	2
ALBUMS:	**HITS 3**			**WEEKS 10**
A WALK ACROSS THE ROOFTOPS	*Linn*	80	*19 May 84*	2
HATS	*Linn*	12	*21 Oct 89*	4
PEACE AT LAST	*Warner Brothers*	13	*22 Jun 96*	4

BLUE NOTES - See Neil YOUNG

BLUE OYSTER CULT

			US	
SINGLES:	HITS 1		**WEEKS 14**	
(DON'T FEAR) THE REAPER	CBS	16	20 May 78	14
ALBUMS:	HITS 8		**WEEKS 40**	
AGENTS OF FORTUNE	CBS	26	3 Jul 76	10
SPECTURES	CBS	60	4 Feb 78	1
SOME ENCHANTED EVENING	CBS	18	28 Oct 78	4
Live recordings.				
MIRRORS	CBS	46	18 Aug 79	5
CULTOSAURUS ERECTUS	CBS	12	19 Jul 80	7
FIRE OF UNKNOWN ORIGIN	CBS	29	25 Jul 81	7
EXTRATERRESTRIAL LIVE	CBS	39	22 May 82	5
THE REVOLUTION BY NIGHT	CBS	95	19 Nov 83	1

BLUE PEARL

			UK/US	
SINGLES:	HITS 6		**WEEKS 29**	
NAKED IN THE RAIN	Big Life	4	7 Jul 90	13
LITTLE BROTHER	Big Life	31	3 Nov 90	5
(CAN YOU) FEEL THE PASSION	Big Life	14	11 Jan 92	6
MOTHER DAWN	Big Life	50	25 Jul 92	2
FIRE OF LOVE	Logic	71	27 Nov 93	1
Above hit: JUNGLE HIGH with BLUE PEARL.				
NAKED IN THE RAIN '98 [RR]	Malarky	22	4 Jul 98	2
ALBUMS:	HITS 1		**WEEKS 2**	
NAKED	Big Life	58	1 Dec 90	2

BLUE RONDO A LA TURK

			UK	
SINGLES:	HITS 2		**WEEKS 9**	
ME AND MR. SANCHEZ	Diable Noir	40	14 Nov 81	4
KLACTOVEESEDSTEIN	Diable Noir	50	13 Mar 82	5
ALBUMS:	HITS 1		**WEEKS 2**	
CHEWING THE FAT	Diable Noir	80	6 Nov 82	2

BLUE ZOO

			UK	
SINGLES:	HITS 3		**WEEKS 17**	
I'M YOUR MAN	Magnet	55	12 Jun 82	3
CRY BOY CRY	Magnet	13	16 Oct 82	10
(I JUST CAN'T) FORGIVE AND FORGET	Magnet	60	28 May 83	4

BLUEBELLS

			UK	
SINGLES:	HITS 6		**WEEKS 49**	
CATH	London	62	12 Mar 83	2
SUGAR BRIDGE (IT WILL STAND)	London	72	9 Jul 83	1
I'M FALLING	London	11	24 Mar 84	12
YOUNG AT HEART	London	8	23 Jun 84	12
CATH [RI] / WILL SHE ALWAYS BE WAITING	London	38	1 Sep 84	7
ALL I AM (IS LOVING YOU)	London	58	9 Feb 85	3
YOUNG AT HEART [RI]	London	1	27 Mar 93	12
Featured in the Volkswagen TV commercial.				
ALBUMS:	HITS 2		**WEEKS 15**	
SISTERS	London	22	11 Aug 84	10
THE BLUEBELLS - THE SINGLES COLLECTION	London	27	17 Apr 93	5

BLUEBOY

			UK	
SINGLES:	HITS 2		**WEEKS 16**	
REMEMBER ME	Pharm	8	1 Feb 97	13
SANDMAN	Sidewalk	25	23 Aug 97	3
Samples Undisputed Truth's You + Me = Love.				

BLUES BAND

			UK	
SINGLES:	HITS 1		**WEEKS 2**	
THE BLUES BAND [EP]	Arista	68	12 Jul 80	2
Lead tack: Maggie's Farm.				
ALBUMS:	HITS 3		**WEEKS 18**	
OFFICIAL BOOTLEG ALBUM	Arista	40	8 Mar 80	9
READY	Arista	36	18 Oct 80	6
ITCHY FEET	Arista	60	17 Oct 81	3

BLUES BROTHERS

US

SINGLES:	HITS 1			WEEKS 8
EVERYBODY NEEDS SOMEBODY TO LOVE	*Atlantic*	12	*7 Apr 90*	8

[AA] listed with Think by Aretha Franklin. Originally recorded by Solomon Burke.

ALBUMS:	HITS 1			WEEKS 26
THE BLUES BROTHERS [OST]	*Atlantic*	64	*11 Apr 87*	18

Features tracks by James Brown, Ray Charles and Aretha Franklin.

THE BLUES BROTHERS [OST] [RE]	*Atlantic*	59	*3 Sep 88*	8
COMPILATION ALBUMS:	**HITS 1**			**WEEKS 80**
THE BLUES BROTHERS [OST]	*Atlantic*	9	*21 Jan 89*	37

Relegated to the Compilation chart as it included tracks by other artists.

THE BLUES BROTHERS [OST] [RE]	*Atlantic*	4	*20 Jan 90*	43

BLUESBREAKERS – See John MAYALL

BLUETONES

UK

SINGLES:	HITS 8			WEEKS 35
ARE YOU BLUE OR ARE YOU BLIND?	*Superior Quality Recordings*	31	*17 Jun 95*	2
BLUETONIC	*Superior Quality Recordings*	19	*14 Oct 95*	3
SLIGHT RETURN	*Superior Quality Recordings*	2	*3 Feb 96*	8

Originally released in 1994.

CUT SOME RUG / CASTLE ROCK	*Superior Quality Recordings*	7	*11 May 96*	5
CUT SOME RUG / CASTLE ROCK [RE]	*Superior Quality Recordings*	73	*20 Jul 96*	1
MARBLEHEAD JOHNSON	*Superior Quality Recordings*	7	*28 Sep 96*	6
SOLOMON BITES THE WORM	*Superior Quality Recordings*	10	*21 Feb 98*	3
IF. . .	*Superior Quality Recordings*	13	*9 May 98*	5
SLEAZY BED TRACK	*Superior Quality Recordings*	35	*8 Aug 98*	2
ALBUMS:	**HITS 2**			**WEEKS 41**
EXPECTING TO FLY	*Superior Quality Recordings*	1	*24 Feb 96*	25
RETURN TO THE LAST CHANCE SALOON	*Superior Quality Recordings*	10	*21 Mar 98*	16

Colin BLUNSTONE

UK

(See also Neil MacArthur.)

SINGLES:	HITS 6			WEEKS 30
SAY YOU DON'T MIND	*Epic*	15	*12 Feb 72*	9

Originally recorded by Denny Laine.

I DON'T BELIEVE IN MIRACLES	*Epic*	31	*11 Nov 72*	6
HOW COULD WE DARE TO BE WRONG	*Epic*	45	*17 Feb 73*	2
WHAT BECOMES OF THE BROKEN HEARTED?	*Stiff*	13	*14 Mar 81*	10

Above hit: Dave STEWART guest vocals Colin BLUNSTONE.

TRACKS OF MY TEARS	*PRT*	60	*29 May 82*	2
OLD AND WISE	*Arista*	74	*15 Jan 83*	1

Above hit: Alan PARSONS PROJECT: lead vocals by Colin BLUNSTONE.

BLUR

UK

SINGLES:	HITS 22			WEEKS 122
SHE'S SO HIGH	*Food*	48	*27 Oct 90*	3
THERE'S NO OTHER WAY	*Food*	8	*27 Apr 91*	8
BANG	*Food*	24	*10 Aug 91*	4
POPSCENE	*Food*	32	*11 Apr 92*	2
FOR TOMORROW	*Food*	28	*1 May 93*	4
CHEMICAL WORLD	*Food*	28	*10 Jul 93*	4
SUNDAY SUNDAY	*Food*	26	*16 Oct 93*	3
GIRLS AND BOYS	*Food*	5	*19 Mar 94*	7
TO THE END	*Food*	16	*11 Jun 94*	5

Features Laetitia from Stereolab on backing vocals.

PARKLIFE	*Food*	10	*3 Sep 94*	7

Above hit: BLUR starring Phil DANIELS.

END OF A CENTURY	*Food*	19	*19 Nov 94*	3
COUNTRY HOUSE	*Food*	1	*26 Aug 95*	11
COUNTRY HOUSE	*Food*	57	*9 Sep 95*	1

Sales of 7" format which, due to chart eligibility rules, was listed separately.

THE UNIVERSAL	*Food*	5	*25 Nov 95*	9
STEREOTYPES	*Food*	7	*24 Feb 96*	5
CHARMLESS MAN	*Food*	5	*11 May 96*	6
BEETLEBUM	*Food*	1	*1 Feb 97*	5
SONG 2	*Food*	2	*19 Apr 97*	5
BEETLEBUM [RE]	*Food*	59	*26 Apr 97*	2
ON YOUR OWN	*Food*	5	*28 Jun 97*	5
M.O.R.	*Food*	15	*27 Sep 97*	3
TENDER	*Food*	2	*6 Mar 99*	10
COFFEE + TV	*Food*	11	*10 Jul 99*	7
NO DISTANCE LEFT TO RUN	*Food*	14	*27 Nov 99*	3

ALBUMS:		HITS 6		WEEKS 271	
LEISURE	Food		7	7 Sep 91	12
Includes re-entries through to 1999.					
MODERN LIFE IS RUBBISH	Food		15	22 May 93	14
PARKLIFE	Food		1	7 May 94	106
Includes re-entries through to 1999.					
THE GREAT ESCAPE	Food		1	23 Sep 95	47
BLUR	Food		1	22 Feb 97	65
13	Food		1	27 Mar 99	27

BOB and EARL
US

SINGLES:		HITS 1		WEEKS 13	
HARLEM SHUFFLE	Island		7	15 Mar 69	13

BOB and MARCIA
Jamaica

SINGLES:		HITS 2		WEEKS 25	
YOUNG, GIFTED AND BLACK	Harry J		5	14 Mar 70	12
Originally recorded by Nina Simone and features Boris Gardiner on bass.					
PIED PIPER	Trojan		11	5 Jun 71	13

BOBBYSOCKS
Sweden/Norway

SINGLES:		HITS 1		WEEKS 4	
LET IT SWING	RCA		44	25 May 85	4
Eurovision Song Contest winner for Norway in 1985.					

Su Su BOBIEN – See MASS SYNDICATE featuring Su Su BOBIEN

Andrea BOCELLI
Italy

SINGLES:		HITS 3		WEEKS 19	
TIME TO SAY GOODBYE (CON TE PARTIRO)	Coalition		2	24 May 97	14
Above hit: Sarah BRIGHTMAN and Andrea BOCELLI.					
CANTO DELLA TERRA	Polydor		25	25 Sep 99	4
AVE MARIA	Philips		65	18 Dec 99	1
With the Coro Di Voci Bianche Dell'Arcum (Chorus Master: Paulo Lucci). Ave Maria is a					
Catholic form of address to the Virgin Mary.					
Above hit: Andrea BOCELLI and the ORCHESTRA E CORO DELL'ACCADEMIA					
NAZIONALE DI SANTA CECILIA conducted by Myung-Whun CHUNG.					

ALBUMS:		HITS 5		WEEKS 57	
ROMANZA	Philips		6	31 May 97	12
ARIA - THE OPERA ALBUM	Philips		33	9 May 98	5
VIAGGIO ITALIANO	Philips		55	13 Feb 99	3
SOGNO	Insieme		4	10 Apr 99	30
SACRED ARIAS	Philips		20	20 Nov 99	7
With the Orchestra dell'Accademia Nazionale di Santa Cecila conducted by Myung-Whun					
Chung.					

Karen BODDINGTON and Mark WILLIAMS
Australia

SINGLES:		HITS 1		WEEKS 1	
HOME AND AWAY	First Night		73	2 Sep 89	1

BODINES
UK

ALBUMS:		HITS 1		WEEKS 1	
PLAYED	Pop		94	29 Aug 87	1

BODY COUNT
US

SINGLES:		HITS 2		WEEKS 4	
BORN DEAD	Virgin		28	8 Oct 94	2
NECESSARY EVIL	Virgin		45	17 Dec 94	2

ALBUMS:		HITS 1		WEEKS 2	
BORN DEAD	Virgin		15	17 Sep 94	2

BODYSNATCHERS
UK

SINGLES:		HITS 2		WEEKS 12	
LETS DO ROCK STEADY	2-Tone		22	15 Mar 80	9
EASY LIFE	2-Tone		50	19 Jul 80	3

Humphrey BOGART – See Dooley WILSON with the Voices of Humphrey BOGART and Ingrid BERGMAN

Tim BOGERT – See Jeff BECK, Tim BOGERT and Carmine APPICE

Suzy BOGGUSS
US

ALBUMS:		HITS 1		WEEKS 1	
SOMETHING UP MY SLEEVE	Liberty		69	25 Sep 93	1

Hamilton BOHANNON — US

SINGLES:	HITS 6			WEEKS 38
SOUTH AFRICAN MAN	*Brunswick*	22	*15 Feb 75*	8
DISCO STOMP	*Brunswick*	6	*24 May 75*	12
FOOT STOMPIN' MUSIC	*Brunswick*	23	*5 Jul 75*	6
HAPPY FEELING	*Brunswick*	49	*6 Sep 75*	3
LET'S START THE DANCE	*Mercury*	56	*26 Aug 78*	4
LET'S START TO DANCE AGAIN	*London*	49	*13 Feb 82*	5

BOILING POINT — US

SINGLES:	HITS 1			WEEKS 6
LET'S GET FUNKTIFIED	*Bang*	41	*27 May 78*	6

Marc BOLAN – See T. REX

C.J. BOLLAND — UK

(See also Ravesignal III.)

SINGLES:	HITS 3			WEEKS 10
SUGAR IS SWEETER	*Internal*	11	*5 Oct 96*	5
THE PROPHET	*ffrr*	19	*17 May 97*	3
IT AIN'T GONNA BE ME	*Essential Recordings*	35	*3 Jul 99*	2

Samples Samuel L. Jackson's vocal from the film 'Jackie Brown'. The track is from the film 'Human Traffic'.

ALBUMS:	HITS 1			WEEKS 2
THE ANALOGUE THEATRE	*Internal*	43	*26 Oct 96*	2

BOLSHOI — UK

ALBUMS:	HITS 1			WEEKS 1
LINDY'S PARTY	*Beggars Banquet*	100	*3 Oct 87*	1

Michael BOLTON — US

SINGLES:	HITS 18			WEEKS 113
HOW AM I SUPPOSED TO LIVE WITHOUT YOU	*CBS*	3	*17 Feb 90*	10
HOW CAN WE BE LOVERS	*CBS*	10	*28 Apr 90*	10
WHEN I'M BACK ON MY FEET AGAIN	*CBS*	44	*21 Jul 90*	5
LOVE IS A WONDERFUL THING	*Columbia*	23	*20 Apr 91*	8
TIME, LOVE AND TENDERNESS	*Columbia*	28	*27 Jul 91*	7
WHEN A MAN LOVES A WOMAN	*Columbia*	8	*9 Nov 91*	9
STEEL BARS	*Columbia*	17	*8 Feb 92*	6

Co-written by Bob Dylan.

| MISSING YOU KNOW | *Columbia* | 28 | *9 May 92* | 4 |

Above hit: Michael BOLTON featuring Kenny G.

| TO LOVE SOMEBODY | *Columbia* | 16 | *31 Oct 92* | 6 |
| DRIFT AWAY | *Columbia* | 18 | *26 Dec 92* | 5 |

Originally recorded by Dobie Gray.

REACH OUT I'LL BE THERE	*Columbia*	37	*13 Mar 93*	4
SAID I LOVED YOU, BUT I LIED	*Columbia*	15	*13 Nov 93*	8
SOUL OF MY SOUL	*Columbia*	32	*26 Feb 94*	3
LEAN ON ME	*Columbia*	14	*14 May 94*	7
CAN I TOUCH YOU … THERE?	*Columbia*	6	*9 Sep 95*	9
A LOVE SO BEAUTIFUL	*Columbia*	27	*2 Dec 95*	5

Originally recorded by Roy Orbison.

| SOUL PROVIDER | *Columbia* | 35 | *16 Mar 96* | 3 |
| THE BEST OF LOVE / GO THE DISTANCE | *Columbia* | 14 | *8 Nov 97* | 4 |

Go The Distance from the Walt Disney film 'Hercules'.

ALBUMS:	HITS 9			WEEKS 226
SOUL PROVIDER	*CBS*	4	*17 Mar 90*	72
THE HUNGER	*CBS*	44	*11 Aug 90*	5
TIME, LOVE AND TENDERNESS	*Columbia*	2	*18 May 91*	57
TIMELESS (THE CLASSICS)	*Columbia*	3	*10 Oct 92*	24
THE ONE THING	*Columbia*	4	*27 Nov 93*	24
GREATEST HITS 1985-1995	*Columbia*	2	*30 Sep 95*	30
ALL THAT MATTERS	*Columbia*	20	*22 Nov 97*	7
MY SECRET PASSION - THE ARIAS	*Sony Classical*	25	*2 May 98*	5
TIMELESS - THE CLASSICS VOLUME 2	*Columbia*	50	*4 Dec 99*	2

BOMB THE BASS — UK

SINGLES:	HITS 10			WEEKS 50
BEAT DIS	*Rhythm King*	2	*20 Feb 88*	9
MEGABLAST / DON'T MAKE ME WAIT	*Mister-ron*	6	*27 Aug 88*	9

Above hit: BOMB THE BASS featuring MERLIN and ANTONIA / BOMB THE BASS featuring LORRAINE.

| SAY A LITTLE PRAYER | *Rhythm King* | 10 | *26 Nov 88* | 10 |

Above hit: BOMB THE BASS featuring MAUREEN.

WINTER IN JULY	*Rhythm King*	7	*27 Jul 91*	9
THE AIR YOU BREATHE	*Rhythm King*	52	*9 Nov 91*	3
KEEP GIVING ME LOVE	*Rhythm King*	62	*2 May 92*	2
BUG POWDER DUST	*Stoned Heights*	24	*1 Oct 94*	3
Above hit: BOMB THE BASS featuring Justin WARFIELD.				
DARKHEART	*Stoned Heights*	35	*17 Dec 94*	3
Above hit: BOMB THE BASS featuring SPIKEY TEE.				
1 TO 1 RELIGION	*Stoned Heights*	53	*1 Apr 95*	1
Above hit: BOMB THE BASS featuring CARLTON.				
SANDCASTLES	*Fourth & Broadway*	54	*16 Sep 95*	1
Above hit: BOMB THE BASS featuring Bernard FOWLER.				
ALBUMS:	**HITS 3**		**WEEKS 16**	
INTO THE DRAGON	*Rhythm King*	18	*22 Oct 88*	10
UNKNOWN TERRITORY	*Rhythm King*	19	*31 Aug 91*	4
CLEAR	*Fourth & Broadway*	22	*15 Apr 95*	2

BOMBALURINA   UK

SINGLES:	**HITS 2**		**WEEKS 20**	
ITSY BITSY TEENY WEENY YELLOW POLKA DOT BIKINI	*Carpet*	1	*28 Jul 90*	13
SEVEN LITTLE GIRLS (SITTING IN THE BACKSEAT)	*Carpet*	18	*24 Nov 90*	7
Above hit: BOMBALURINA featuring Timmy MALLETT.				
ALBUMS:	**HITS 1**		**WEEKS 5**	
HUGGIN' AN'A KISSIN'	*Polydor*	55	*15 Dec 90*	5
Above hit: BOMBALURINA featuring Timmy MALLETT.				

BOMBERS   Canada

SINGLES:	**HITS 2**		**WEEKS 10**	
(EVERYBODY) GET DANCIN'	*Flamingo*	37	*5 May 79*	7
LET'S DANCE	*Flamingo*	58	*18 Aug 79*	3

BON JOVI   US

(See also Jon Bon Jovi.)

SINGLES:	**HITS 25**		**WEEKS 182**	
HARDEST PART IS THE NIGHT	*Vertigo*	68	*31 Aug 85*	1
YOU GIVE LOVE A BAD NAME	*Vertigo*	14	*9 Aug 86*	10
LIVIN' ON A PRAYER	*Vertigo*	4	*25 Oct 86*	15
WANTED DEAD OR ALIVE	*Vertigo*	13	*11 Apr 87*	7
NEVER SAY GOODBYE	*Vertigo*	21	*15 Aug 87*	5
BAD MEDICINE	*Vertigo*	17	*24 Sep 88*	7
BORN TO BE MY BABY	*Vertigo*	22	*10 Dec 88*	7
I'LL BE THERE FOR YOU	*Vertigo*	18	*29 Apr 89*	7
LAY YOUR HANDS ON ME	*Vertigo*	18	*26 Aug 89*	6
LIVING IN SIN	*Vertigo*	35	*9 Dec 89*	6
KEEP THE FAITH	*Jambco*	5	*24 Oct 92*	6
BED OF ROSES	*Jambco*	13	*23 Jan 93*	6
IN THESE ARMS	*Jambco*	9	*15 May 93*	7
I'LL SLEEP WHEN I'M DEAD	*Jambco*	17	*7 Aug 93*	5
I BELIEVE	*Jambco*	11	*2 Oct 93*	6
DRY COUNTY	*Jambco*	9	*26 Mar 94*	6
ALWAYS	*Jambco*	2	*24 Sep 94*	18
PLEASE COME HOME FOR CHRISTMAS	*Jambco*	7	*17 Dec 94*	6
SOMEDAY I'LL BE SATURDAY NIGHT	*Jambco*	7	*25 Feb 95*	7
PLEASE COME HOME FOR CHRISTMAS [RE]	*Jambco*	46	*4 Mar 95*	4
THIS AIN'T A LOVE SONG	*Mercury*	6	*10 Jun 95*	9
SOMETHING FOR THE PAIN	*Mercury*	8	*30 Sep 95*	7
LIE TO ME	*Mercury*	10	*25 Nov 95*	8
THESE DAYS	*Mercury*	7	*9 Mar 96*	6
HEY GOD	*Mercury*	13	*6 Jul 96*	5
REAL LIFE	*Reprise*	21	*10 Apr 99*	5
From the film 'EDtv'.				
ALBUMS:	**HITS 7**		**WEEKS 372**	
BON JOVI	*Vertigo*	71	*28 Apr 84*	3
7800° FAHRENHEIT	*Vertigo*	28	*11 May 85*	12
SLIPPERY WHEN WET	*Vertigo*	6	*20 Sep 86*	123
NEW JERSEY	*Vertigo*	1	*1 Oct 88*	47
KEEP THE FAITH	*Jambco*	1	*14 Nov 92*	70
CROSS ROAD - THE BEST OF BON JOVI	*Jambco*	1	*22 Oct 94*	67
THESE DAYS	*Mercury*	1	*1 Jul 95*	50

Jon BON JOVI   US

(See also Bon Jovi.)

SINGLES:	**HITS 5**		**WEEKS 27**	
BLAZE OF GLORY	*Vertigo*	13	*4 Aug 90*	8
From the film 'Young Guns II', also features Jeff Beck on guitar and Randy Jackson on bass.				
MIRACLE	*Vertigo*	29	*10 Nov 90*	5

MIDNIGHT AT CHELSEA	Mercury	4	14 Jun 97	7
QUEEN OF NEW ORLEANS	Mercury	10	30 Aug 97	4
JANIE, DON'T TAKE YOUR LOVE TO TOWN	Mercury	13	15 Nov 97	3
ALBUMS:	**HITS 2**		**WEEKS 41**	
BLAZE OF GLORY/YOUNG GUNS II [OST]	Vertigo	2	25 Aug 90	23
DESTINATION ANYWHERE	Mercury	2	28 Jun 97	18

Graham BOND
UK

| **ALBUMS:** | **HITS 1** | | **WEEKS 2** | |
| SOLID BOND | Warner Brothers | 40 | 20 Jun 70 | 2 |

Ronnie BOND
UK

| **SINGLES:** | **HITS 1** | | **WEEKS 5** | |
| IT'S WRITTEN ON YOUR BODY | Mercury | 52 | 31 May 80 | 5 |

Featured in a Levi's Jeans TV commercial.

Gary U.S. BONDS
US

SINGLES:	**HITS 6**		**WEEKS 39**	
NEW ORLEANS	Top Rank	16	21 Jan 61	11
QUARTER TO THREE	Top Rank	7	22 Jul 61	13

Above 2: U.S. BONDS

| THIS LITTLE GIRL | EMI America | 43 | 30 May 81 | 6 |

Originally recorded by Bruce Springsteen.

| JOLE BLON | EMI America | 51 | 22 Aug 81 | 3 |

Originally recorded by Moon Mullican in 1947.
Above hit: Gary U.S. BONDS with Bruce SPRINGSTEEN.

IT'S ONLY LOVE	EMI America	43	31 Oct 81	3
SOUL DEEP	EMI America	59	17 Jul 82	3
ALBUMS:	**HITS 2**		**WEEKS 8**	
DEDICATION	EMI America	43	22 Aug 81	3
ON THE LINE	EMI America	55	10 Jul 82	5

BONE
UK

| **SINGLES:** | **HITS 1** | | **WEEKS 1** | |
| WINGS OF LOVE | Deconstruction | 55 | 2 Apr 94 | 1 |

BONE THUGS-N-HARMONY
US

SINGLES:	**HITS 4**		**WEEKS 22**	
1ST OF THA MONTH	Epic	32	4 Nov 95	2
THA CROSSROADS	Epic	8	10 Aug 96	11

Samples the Isley Brothers' Make Me Say It Again.

| 1ST OF THA MONTH [RI] | Epic | 15 | 9 Nov 96 | 4 |
| DAYS OF OUR LIVEZ | East West America | 37 | 15 Feb 97 | 2 |

From the film 'Set It Off'.

| LOOK INTO MY EYES | Epic | 16 | 26 Jul 97 | 3 |

From the film 'Batman And Robin'.

ALBUMS:	**HITS 2**		**WEEKS 4**	
E.1999 ETERNAL	Epic	39	31 Aug 96	3
THE ART OF WAR	Epic	42	9 Aug 97	1

Elbow BONES and the RACKETEERS
US

| **SINGLES:** | **HITS 1** | | **WEEKS 9** | |
| A NIGHT IN NEW YORK | EMI America | 33 | 14 Jan 84 | 9 |

Produced by Kid Creole (August Darnell).

BONEY M
Jamaica/Antilles/Montserrat

| **SINGLES:** | **HITS 17** | | **WEEKS 169** | |
| DADDY COOL | Atlantic | 6 | 18 Dec 76 | 13 |

Originally recorded by the Rays.

SUNNY	Atlantic	3	12 Mar 77	10
MA BAKER	Atlantic	2	25 Jun 77	13
BELFAST	Atlantic	8	29 Oct 77	13
RIVERS OF BABYLON / BROWN GIRL IN THE RING	Atlantic	1	29 Apr 78	40

Brown Girl in The Ring listed from 5 Aug 78 and the song climbed back to No. 2. Rivers of Babylon originally recorded by the Melodians; Brown Girl In The Ring originally recorded by Exuma.

RASPUTIN	Atlantic	2	7 Oct 78	10
MARY'S BOY CHILD/OH MY LORD [M]	Atlantic	1	2 Dec 78	8
PAINTER MAN	Atlantic	10	3 Mar 79	6
HOORAY HOORAY, IT'S A HOLI – HOLIDAY	Atlantic	3	28 Apr 79	9
GOTTA GO HOME/EL LUTE	Atlantic	12	11 Aug 79	11

El Lute listed from 29 Sep 79.

| I'M BORN AGAIN | Atlantic | 35 | 15 Dec 79 | 7 |
| MY FRIEND JACK | Atlantic | 57 | 26 Apr 80 | 5 |

Originally recorded by the Smoke.

CHILDREN OF PARADISE	*Atlantic*	66	*14 Feb 81*	2
WE KILL THE WORLD (DON'T KILL THE WORLD)	*Atlantic*	39	*21 Nov 81*	5
MEGAMIX [M] / MARY'S BOY CHILD [RM]	*Ariola*	52	*24 Dec 88*	3
BONEY M MEGAMIX [M]	*Arista*	7	*5 Dec 92*	9

Both Megamixes are different.

BROWN GIRL IN THE RING (REMIX '93) [RM]	*Arista*	38	*17 Apr 93*	3
MA BAKER / SOMEBODY SCREAM [M]	*Logic*	22	*8 May 99*	2

Chorus of Ma Baker is sampled.
Above hit: BONEY M vs HORNY UNITED

ALBUMS:	HITS 7		WEEKS 140	
TAKE THE HEAT OFF ME	*Atlantic*	40	*23 Apr 77*	15
LOVE FOR SALE	*Atlantic*	60	*6 Aug 77*	1
NIGHT FLIGHT TO VENUS	*Atlantic*	1	*29 Jul 78*	65
OCEANS OF FANTASY	*Atlantic*	1	*29 Sep 79*	18
THE MAGIC OF BONEY M	*Atlantic*	1	*12 Apr 80*	26
THE BEST OF 10 YEARS – 32 SUPERHITS	*Stylus*	35	*6 Sep 86*	5
THE GREATEST HITS	*Telstar*	14	*27 Mar 93*	10

BONFIRE
Germany

ALBUMS:	HITS 1		WEEKS 1	
POINT BLANK	*MSA*	74	*21 Oct 89*	1

Graham BONNET
UK

SINGLES:	HITS 2		WEEKS 15	
NIGHT GAMES	*Vertigo*	6	*21 Mar 81*	11
LIAR	*Vertigo*	51	*13 Jun 81*	4

ALBUMS:	HITS 1		WEEKS 3	
LINE UP	*Vertigo*	62	*7 Nov 81*	3

Graham BONNEY with Johnny SCOTT and his Orchestra
UK

SINGLES:	HITS 1		WEEKS 8	
SUPER GIRL	*Columbia*	19	*26 Mar 66*	8

BONO
Ireland

SINGLES:	HITS 4		WEEKS 25	
IN A LIFETIME	*RCA*	20	*25 Jan 86*	5

Above hit: CLANNAD / additional vocals: BONO.

IN A LIFETIME [RI]	*RCA*	17	*10 Jun 89*	7

Above hit: CLANNAD (guest vocal: BONO).

I'VE GOT YOU UNDER MY SKIN	*Island*	4	*4 Dec 93*	9

[AA] listed with Stay (Faraway, So Close) by U2. It was not available on the 2nd CD format.
Above hit: Frank SINATRA with BONO.

IN THE NAME OF THE FATHER	*Island*	46	*9 Apr 94*	2

From the film of the same name.
Above hit: BONO and Gavin FRIDAY.

NEW DAY	*Columbia*	23	*23 Oct 99*	2

Official Single of the Net Aid concert, 9 Oct 99 at London, New York, Geneva. Charity record
in aid of NetAid, Wyclef Jean Foundation and War Child.
Above hit: Wyclef JEAN featuring BONO.

BONZO DOG DOO-DAH BAND
UK

SINGLES:	HITS 1		WEEKS 14	
I'M THE URBAN SPACEMAN	*Liberty*	5	*9 Nov 68*	14

Produced by Paul McCartney under the pseudonym Apollo C. Vermouth.

ALBUMS:	HITS 3		WEEKS 4	
DOUGHNUT IN GRANNY'S GREENHOUSE	*Liberty*	40	*18 Jan 69*	1
TADPOLES	*Liberty*	36	*30 Aug 69*	1
THE HISTORY OF THE BONZOS	*United Artists*	41	*22 Jun 74*	2

Betty BOO
UK

SINGLES:	HITS 7		WEEKS 55	
HEY DJ/I CAN'T DANCE (TO THAT MUSIC YOUR PLAYING) / SKA TRAIN	*Rhythm King*	7	*12 Aug 89*	11

Backing vocals: Claudia Fontaine. I Can't Dance originally recorded by Martha and the
Vandellas.
Above hit: BEATMASTERS featuring Betty Boo.

DOIN' THE DO	*Rhythm King*	7	*19 May 90*	12

Samples Reparata and the Delrons' Captain Of Your Ship.

WHERE ARE YOU BABY?	*Rhythm King*	3	*11 Aug 90*	10
24 HOURS	*Rhythm King*	25	*1 Dec 90*	8
LET ME TAKE YOU THERE	*WEA*	12	*8 Aug 92*	8

Samples the Four Top's It's All In The Game.

I'M ON MY WAY	*WEA*	44	*3 Oct 92*	3
HANGOVER	*WEA*	50	*10 Apr 93*	3

ALBUMS:		HITS 2			WEEKS 25
BOOMANIA	Rhythm King	4	22 Sep 90	24
GRRR! IT'S BETTY BOO	WEA	62	24 Oct 92	1

BOO RADLEYS   UK

SINGLES:		HITS 12			WEEKS 27
DOES THIS HURT? / BOO! FOREVER	Creation	67	20 Jun 92	1
WISH I WAS SKINNY	Creation	75	23 Oct 93	1
BARNEY (. . . AND ME)	Creation	48	12 Feb 94	2
LAZARUS	Creation	50	11 Jun 94	2
Original reached No. 76 in 1992.				
WAKE UP BOO!	Creation	9	11 Mar 95	8
FIND THE ANSWER WITHIN	Creation	37	13 May 95	3
IT'S LULU	Creation	25	29 Jul 95	2
FROM THE BENCH AT BELVIDERE	Creation	24	7 Oct 95	2
WHAT'S IN THE BOX? (SEE WHATCHA GOT)	Creation	25	17 Aug 96	2
C'MON KIDS	Creation	18	19 Oct 96	2
RIDE THE TIGER	Creation	38	1 Feb 97	1
FREE HUEY	Creation	54	17 Oct 98	1
The Huey in the song is Huey Newton, a prominent member of the Black Panther movement in the 1960s.				

ALBUMS:		HITS 5			WEEKS 29
EVERYTHING'S ALRIGHT FOREVER	Creation	55	4 Apr 92	1
GIANT STEPS	Creation	17	28 Aug 93	4
WAKE UP!	Creation	1	8 Apr 95	21
C'MON KIDS	Creation	20	21 Sep 96	2
KINGSIZE	Creation	62	31 Oct 98	1

BOO-YAA T.R.I.B.E.   US

SINGLES:		HITS 2			WEEKS 6
PSYKO FUNK	Fourth & Broadway	43	30 Jun 90	3
ANOTHER BODY MURDERED	Epic	26	6 Nov 93	3
From the film 'Judgment Night'.				
Above hit: FAITH NO MORE and BOO-YAA TRIBE.				

ALBUMS:		HITS 1			WEEKS 1
NEW FUNKY NATION	Fourth & Broadway	74	14 Apr 90	1

BOOGIE BOX HIGH   UK

SINGLES:		HITS 1			WEEKS 11
JIVE TALKIN'	Hardback	7	4 Jul 87	11
Vocals by George Michael.				

BOOGIE DOWN PRODUCTIONS   US

SINGLES:		HITS 1			WEEKS 2
MY PHILOSOPHY / STOP THE VIOLENCE	Jive	69	4 Jun 88	2

ALBUMS:		HITS 3			WEEKS 9
BY ALL MEANS NECESSARY	Jive	38	18 Jun 88	3
GHETTO MUSIC: THE BLUEPRINT OF HIP HOP	Jive	32	22 Jul 89	4
EDUTAINMENT	Jive	52	25 Aug 90	2

BOOKER T. and the M.G.s   US

SINGLES:		HITS 4			WEEKS 43
SOUL LIMBO	Stax	30	14 Dec 68	9
Theme to BBC TV's cricket coverage.				
TIME IS TIGHT	Stax	4	10 May 69	18
From the film 'Uptight'.				
SOUL CLAP '69	Stax	35	30 Aug 69	4
GREEN ONIONS	Atlantic	7	15 Dec 79	12
Originally released in 1962.				

EPS:		HITS 1			WEEKS 1
R&B WITH BOOKER T VOL. 2	Atlantic	19	27 Feb 65	1

ALBUMS:		HITS 2			WEEKS 5
GREEN ONIONS	London	11	25 Jul 64	4
MCLEMORE AVENUE	Stax	70	11 Jul 70	1

BOOM BOOM ROOM   UK

SINGLES:		HITS 1			WEEKS 1
HERE COMES THE MAN	Fun After All	74	8 Mar 86	1

BOOMTOWN RATS   Ireland

SINGLES:		HITS 14			WEEKS 123
LOOKING AFTER NO. 1	Ensign	11	27 Aug 77	9
MARY OF THE 4TH FORM	Ensign	15	19 Nov 77	9

SHE'S SO MODERN	Ensign	12	15 Apr 78	11
LIKE CLOCKWORK	Ensign	6	17 Jun 78	13
RAT TRAP	Ensign	1	14 Oct 78	15
I DON'T LIKE MONDAYS	Ensign	1	21 Jul 79	12
Written about San Diego schoolgirl Brenda Spencer who shot two people because she didn't like Mondays.				
DIAMOND SMILES	Ensign	13	17 Nov 79	10
SOMEONE'S LOOKING AT YOU	Ensign	4	26 Jan 80	9
BANANA REPUBLIC	Ensign	3	22 Nov 80	11
THE ELEPHANTS GRAVEYARD (GUILTY)	Mercury	26	31 Jan 81	6
NEVER IN A MILLION YEARS	Mercury	62	12 Dec 81	4
HOUSE ON FIRE	Mercury	24	20 Mar 82	8
TONIGHT	Mercury	73	18 Feb 84	1
DRAG ME DOWN	Mercury	50	19 May 84	3
I DON'T LIKE MONDAYS [RI]	Vertigo	38	2 Jul 94	2
ALBUMS:	**HITS 6**			**WEEKS 96**
BOOMTOWN RATS	Ensign	18	17 Sep 77	11
TONIC FOR THE TROOPS	Ensign	8	8 Jul 78	44
THE FINE ART OF SURFACING	Ensign	7	3 Nov 79	26
MONDO BONGO	Mercury	6	24 Jan 81	7
V DEEP	Mercury	64	3 Apr 82	5
LOUDMOUTH – THE BEST OF THE BOOMTOWN RATS AND BOB GELDOF	Vertigo	10	9 Jul 94	3
Includes solo and group material.				
Above hit: BOOMTOWN RATS and Bob GELDOF.				

Clint BOON EXPERIENCE!   UK

SINGLES:	**HITS 1**			**WEEKS 1**
WHITE NO SUGAR	Artful	61	6 Nov 99	1
Original release on the Rabid Badger label reached No. 84 in 1998.				

Daniel BOONE   UK

SINGLES:	**HITS 2**			**WEEKS 25**
DADDY DON'T YOU WALK SO FAST	Penny Farthing	17	14 Aug 71	15
BEAUTIFUL SUNDAY	Penny Farthing	48	1 Apr 72	1
BEAUTIFUL SUNDAY [RE]	Penny Farthing	21	15 Apr 72	9

Debby BOONE   US

SINGLES:	**HITS 1**			**WEEKS 3**
YOU LIGHT UP MY LIFE	Warner Brothers	48	24 Dec 77	3
From the film of the same name. Originally recorded by Kacey Cisyk.				

Pat BOONE   US

SINGLES:	**HITS 26**			**WEEKS 308**
AIN'T THAT A SHAME	London	7	19 Nov 55	9
I'LL BE HOME	London	1	28 Apr 56	22
Originally recorded by the Flamingos.				
LONG TALL SALLY	London	27	28 Jul 56	3
I ALMOST LOST MY MIND	London	14	18 Aug 56	7
Originally recorded by Ivory Joe Hunter.				
LONG TALL SALLY [RE]	London	18	25 Aug 56	4
FRIENDLY PERSUASION (THEE I LOVE)	London	3	8 Dec 56	21
From the film 'Friendly Persuasion'.				
AIN'T THAT A SHAME [RE]	London	22	12 Jan 57	2
I'LL BE HOME [RE]	London	19	12 Jan 57	2
DON'T FORBID ME	London	2	2 Feb 57	16
WHY BABY WHY	London	17	27 Apr 57	7
LOVE LETTERS IN THE SAND	London	2	6 Jul 57	21
Whistling by Neil Sedaka. Originally recorded by Ted Black.				
REMEMBER YOU'RE MINE / THERE'S A GOLD MINE IN THE SKY	London	5	28 Sep 57	18
There's A Gold Mine In Sky only listed for its first chart week.				
Above 2: Pat BOONE with Billy VAUGHN'S ORCHESTRA.				
APRIL LOVE	London	7	7 Dec 57	23
From the film of the same name.				
WHITE CHRISTMAS	London	29	14 Dec 57	1
Above hit: Pat BOONE with Mort LINDSEY and his Orchestra and the Artie MALVERN SINGERS.				
A WONDERFUL TIME UP THERE	London	2	5 Apr 58	17
IT'S TOO SOON TO KNOW	London	7	12 Apr 58	12
Above 2 entries were separate sides of the same release, each had its own chart run. Originally recorded by the Orioles.				
SUGAR MOON	London	6	28 Jun 58	12
Originally recorded by Collins and Harlan.				
IF DREAMS CAME TRUE	London	16	30 Aug 58	11
GEE, BUT IT'S LONELY	London	30	6 Dec 58	1
Written by Phil Everly.				
I'LL REMEMBER TONIGHT	London	28	17 Jan 59	1
From the film 'Mardi Gras'.				

I'LL REMEMBER TONIGHT [RE-1ST]	*London*	21	*7 Feb 59*	1
I'LL REMEMBER TONIGHT [RE-2ND]	*London*	18	*21 Feb 59*	7
WITH THE WIND AND THE RAIN IN YOUR HAIR	*London*	21	*11 Apr 59*	3
FOR A PENNY	*London*	28	*23 May 59*	3
FOR A PENNY [RE]	*London*	19	*27 Jun 59*	6
TWIXT TWELVE AND TWENTY	*London*	18	*1 Aug 59*	6
TWIXT TWELVE AND TWENTY [RE]	*London*	26	*19 Sep 59*	1
WALKING THE FLOOR OVER YOU	*London*	40	*25 Jun 60*	2
Originally recorded by Ernest Tubb in 1941.				
WALKING THE FLOOR OVER YOU [RE-1ST]	*London*	46	*16 Jul 60*	1
WALKING THE FLOOR OVER YOU [RE-2ND]	*London*	39	*6 Aug 60*	2
MOODY RIVER	*London*	18	*8 Jul 61*	10
JOHNNY WILL	*London*	4	*9 Dec 61*	13
Written by Paul Evans.				
I'LL SEE YOU IN MY DREAMS	*London*	27	*17 Feb 62*	9
QUANDO, QUANDO, QUANDO	*London*	41	*26 May 62*	4
Originally recorded by Tony Renis.				
SPEEDY GONZALES	*London*	2	*14 Jul 62*	19
Originally recorded by Dave Dante.				
THE MAIN ATTRACTION	*London*	12	*17 Nov 62*	11
From the film of the same name.				

EPS:	HITS 1		WEEKS 5	
JOURNEY TO THE CENTRE OF THE EARTH [OST]	*London*	8	*12 Mar 60*	5

ALBUMS:	HITS 4		WEEKS 12	
STARDUST	*London*	10	*22 Nov 58*	1
HYMNS WE HAVE LOVED	*London*	12	*28 May 60*	2
HYMNS WE LOVE	*London*	14	*25 Jun 60*	1
PAT BOONE ORIGINALS	*ABC*	16	*24 Apr 76*	8

BOOT ROOM BOYZ – See LIVERPOOL FOOTBALL CLUB

Duke BOOTEE – See Melle MEL

BOOTH and the BAD ANGEL   US/UK

(See also Angelo Badalamenti.)

SINGLES:	HITS 2		WEEKS 4	
I BELIEVE	*Fontana*	25	*22 Jun 96*	3
FALL IN LOVE WITH ME	*Mercury*	57	*11 Jul 98*	1
From the film 'Martha Meet Frank, Daniel & Laurence'.				
Above hit: BOOTH and the BAD ANGEL featuring Tim BOOTH of JAMES.				

ALBUMS:	HITS 1		WEEKS 2	
BOOTH AND THE BAD ANGEL	*Fontana*	35	*13 Jul 96*	2

Ken BOOTHE   Jamaica

SINGLES:	HITS 2		WEEKS 22	
EVERYTHING I OWN	*Trojan*	1	*21 Sep 74*	12
CRYING OVER YOU	*Trojan*	11	*14 Dec 74*	10

BOOTHILL FOOT-TAPPERS   UK

SINGLES:	HITS 1		WEEKS 3	
GET YOUR FEET OUT OF MY SHOES	*Go! Discs*	64	*14 Jul 84*	3

BOOTSY'S RUBBER BAND   US

SINGLES:	HITS 1		WEEKS 3	
BOOTZILLA	*Warner Brothers*	43	*8 Jul 78*	3

BOOTZILLA ORCHESTRA – See Malcolm McLAREN

Victor BORGE   Denmark

EPS:	HITS 1		WEEKS 2	
PHONETIC PUNCTUATION	*Philips*	15	*7 Jan 61*	2

BOSS   US

(See also David Morales.)

SINGLES:	HITS 1		WEEKS 1	
CONGO	*Cooltempo*	54	*27 Aug 94*	1

BOSTON   US

SINGLES:	HITS 2		WEEKS 13	
MORE THAN A FEELING	*Epic*	22	*29 Jan 77*	8
DON'T LOOK BACK	*Epic*	43	*7 Oct 78*	5

ALBUMS:	HITS 4		WEEKS 44	
BOSTON	*Epic*	11	*5 Feb 77*	20
DON'T LOOK BACK	*Epic*	9	*9 Sep 78*	10

BOSTON [RE]	Epic	58	4 Apr 81	2
Re-released with a different catalogue number.				
THIRD STAGE	MCA	37	18 Oct 86	11
WALK ON	MCA	56	25 Jun 94	1

Eve BOSWELL with Glenn SOMERS and his ORCHESTRA — Hungary

SINGLES:		HITS 1		WEEKS 13
PICKIN' A - CHICKEN	Parlophone	9	31 Dec 55	7
PICKIN' A - CHICKEN [RE-1ST]	Parlophone	16	3 Mar 56	3
PICKIN' A - CHICKEN [RE-2ND]	Parlophone	20	7 Apr 56	3

La BOUCHE — US

SINGLES:		HITS 3		WEEKS 12
SWEET DREAMS	Bell	63	24 Sep 94	1
BE MY LOVER	Arista	27	15 Jul 95	4
FALLING IN LOVE	Arista	43	30 Sep 95	2
BE MY LOVER [RI]	Arista	25	2 Mar 96	4
SWEET DREAMS [RI]	Arista	44	7 Sep 96	1

Judy BOUCHER — UK

SINGLES:		HITS 2		WEEKS 23
CAN'T BE WITH YOU TONIGHT	Orbitone	2	4 Apr 87	14
YOU CAUGHT MY EYE	Orbitone	18	4 Jul 87	9
ALBUMS:		HITS 1		WEEKS 1
CAN'T BE WITH YOU TONIGHT	Orbitone	95	25 Apr 87	1

Peter BOUNCER - See SHUT UP AND DANCE

BOUNCING CZECKS featuring Charlene DUCALL — UK

SINGLES:		HITS 1		WEEKS 1
I'M A LITTLE CHRISTMAS CRACKER	RCA	72	29 Dec 84	1

BOUNTY KILLER (featuring COCOA BROVAZ, Nona HENDRYX and FREE) — Jamaica

SINGLES:		HITS 1		WEEKS 1
IT'S A PARTY	Edel	65	27 Feb 99	1
Additional vocals by Mr. Gentleman and DaNaCeE.				

BOURGEOIS TAGG — US

SINGLES:		HITS 1		WEEKS 6
I DON'T MIND AT ALL	Island	35	6 Feb 88	6

BOURGIE BOURGIE — UK

SINGLES:		HITS 1		WEEKS 4
BREAKING POINT	MCA	48	3 Mar 84	4

Toby BOURKE with George MICHAEL — UK

(See also George Michael.)

SINGLES:		HITS 1		WEEKS 4
WALTZ AWAY DREAMING	Aegean	10	7 Jun 97	4
Dedicated to George Michael's late mother.				

Aletia BOURNE - See ANGELHEART

BOW WOW WOW — UK

SINGLES:		HITS 9		WEEKS 54
C'30, C'60, C'90, G0	EMI	34	26 Jul 80	7
The first cassette single released.				
YOUR CASSETTE PET [EP]	EMI	58	6 Dec 80	6
Cassette only release. Lead track: Louis Quatorze, which was listed on its own for the chart of 6 Dec 80.				
W.O.R.K. (N.O. NAH NO! NO! MY DADDY DON'T)	EMI	62	28 Mar 81	3
PRINCE OF DARKNESS	RCA	58	15 Aug 81	4
CHIHUAHUA	RCA	51	7 Nov 81	4
GO WILD IN THE COUNTRY	RCA	7	30 Jan 82	13
SEE JUNGLE! (JUNGLE BOY) / (I'M A) TV SAVAGE	RCA	45	1 May 82	3
I WANT CANDY	RCA	9	5 Jun 82	8
Originally recorded by the Strangeloves. Reached No. 12 in the US in 1965.				
LOUIS QUATORZE [RI]	RCA	66	31 Jul 82	2
The lead track from the Your Cassette Pet [EP].				
DO YOU WANNA HOLD ME?	RCA	47	12 Mar 83	4
ALBUMS:		HITS 2		WEEKS 38
SEE JUNGLE! SEE JUNGLE! GO JOIN YOUR GANG YEAH CITY ALL OVER! GO APE CRAZY	RCA	26	24 Oct 81	32
I WANT CANDY	EMI	26	7 Aug 82	6

BOWA featuring MALA
US

SINGLES:	HITS 1			WEEKS 1
DIFFERENT STORY	Dead Dead Good	64	7 Dec 91	1

David BOWIE
UK

SINGLES:	HITS 61			WEEKS 439
SPACE ODDITY	Philips	48	6 Sep 69	1
SPACE ODDITY [RE]	Philips	5	20 Sep 69	13
STARMAN	RCA Victor	10	24 Jun 72	11
JOHN, I'M ONLY DANCING	RCA Victor	12	16 Sep 72	10
THE JEAN GENIE	RCA Victor	2	9 Dec 72	13
DRIVE-IN SATURDAY (SEATTLE – PHOENIX)	RCA Victor	3	14 Apr 73	10
LIFE ON MARS?	RCA Victor	3	30 Jun 73	13
THE LAUGHING GNOME	Deram	6	15 Sep 73	12
Originally released in 1967.				
SORROW	RCA Victor	3	20 Oct 73	15
REBEL REBEL	RCA Victor	5	23 Feb 74	7
ROCK 'N' ROLL SUICIDE	RCA Victor	22	20 Apr 74	7
DIAMOND DOGS	RCA Victor	21	22 Jun 74	6
KNOCK ON WOOD	RCA Victor	10	28 Sep 74	6
Above 3: BOWIE.				
YOUNG AMERICANS	RCA Victor	18	1 Mar 75	7
Features backing vocals by Luther Vandross and David Sanborn on saxophone.				
FAME	RCA Victor	17	2 Aug 75	8
Co written and backing vocals by John Lennon.				
SPACE ODDITY [RI]	RCA Victor Maximillion	1	11 Oct 75	10
GOLDEN YEARS	RCA Victor	8	29 Nov 75	10
Above hit: BOWIE.				
TVC 15	RCA Victor	33	22 May 76	4
SOUND AND VISION	RCA Victor	3	19 Feb 77	11
Backing vocals by Mary Hopkin.				
HEROES	RCA Victor	24	15 Oct 77	8
BEAUTY AND THE BEAST	RCA Victor	39	21 Jan 78	3
BREAKING GLASS [EP]	RCA Victor	54	2 Dec 78	7
Lead track: Breaking Glass.				
BOYS KEEP SWINGING	RCA Victor	7	5 May 79	10
D.J.	RCA Victor	29	21 Jul 79	5
JOHN, I'M ONLY DANCING (AGAIN)(1975)/JOHN, I'M ONLY DANCING (1972) [RR]	RCA	12	15 Dec 79	8
ALABAMA SONG	RCA	23	1 Mar 80	5
ASHES TO ASHES	RCA	1	16 Aug 80	10
FASHION	RCA	5	1 Nov 80	12
SCARY MONSTERS (AND SUPER CREEPS)	RCA	20	10 Jan 81	6
UP THE HILL BACKWARDS	RCA	32	28 Mar 81	6
UNDER PRESSURE	EMI	1	14 Nov 81	11
Above hit: QUEEN and David BOWIE.				
WILD IS THE WIND	RCA	24	28 Nov 81	10
BAAL'S HYMN [EP]	RCA	29	6 Mar 82	5
From the BBC TV production of Berthold Brecht's 'Baal' in which Bowie took title role.				
Lead track: Baal's Hymn.				
CAT PEOPLE (PUTTING OUT FIRE)	MCA	26	10 Apr 82	6
From the film of the same name.				
PEACE ON EARTH / LITTLE DRUMMER BOY [M]	RCA	3	27 Nov 82	8
Recorded in 1977 on Bing Crosby's Christmas TV show.				
Above hit: David BOWIE and Bing CROSBY.				
LET'S DANCE	EMI America	1	26 Mar 83	14
CHINA GIRL	EMI America	2	11 Jun 83	8
Originally recorded by Iggy Pop.				
MODERN LOVE	EMI America	2	24 Sep 83	8
Features Stevie Ray Vaughan on guitar.				
WHITE LIGHT/WHITE HEAT	RCA	46	5 Nov 83	3
BLUE JEAN	EMI America	6	22 Sep 84	8
TONIGHT	EMI America	53	8 Dec 84	4
Backing vocals by Tina Turner.				
THIS IS NOT AMERICA (THE THEME FROM "THE FALCON AND THE SNOWMAN")	EMI America	14	9 Feb 85	7
From the film 'The Falcon And The Snowman'.				
Above hit: David BOWIE/Pat METHENY GROUP.				
LOVING THE ALIEN	EMI America	19	8 Jun 85	6
LOVING THE ALIEN [RE]	EMI America	67	27 Jul 85	1
DANCING IN THE STREET	EMI America	1	7 Sep 85	12
Above hit: David BOWIE and Mick JAGGER.				
ABSOLUTE BEGINNERS	Virgin	2	15 Mar 86	9
From the film of the same name.				
UNDERGROUND	EMI America	21	21 Jun 86	6
From the film 'Labyrinth'.				
WHEN THE WIND BLOWS	Virgin	44	8 Nov 86	4
From the film of the same name.				

DAY-IN DAY-OUT	EMI America	17	4 Apr 87	6
TIME WILL CRAWL	EMI America	33	27 Jun 87	4
NEVER LET ME DOWN	EMI America	34	29 Aug 87	6
FAME 90 (GASS MIX) [RM]	EMI USA	28	7 Apr 90	4

Remixed by Jon Gass. From the film 'Pretty Woman'.

REAL COOL WORLD	Warner Brothers	53	22 Aug 92	1

Theme from the film 'Cool World'.

JUMP THEY SAY	Arista	9	27 Mar 93	6
BLACK TIE WHITE NOISE	Arista	36	12 Jun 93	2

Above hit: David BOWIE featuring Al B. SURE!

MIRACLE GOODNIGHT	Arista	40	23 Oct 93	2
BUDDHA OF SUBURBIA	Arista	35	4 Dec 93	3

Theme from the BBC TV series of the same name.
Above hit: David BOWIE (featuring Lenny KRAVITZ on guitar).

THE HEARTS FILTHY LESSON	RCA	35	23 Sep 95	2
STRANGERS WHEN WE MEET / THE MAN WHO SOLD THE WORLD (LIVE)	RCA	39	2 Dec 95	2
HALLO SPACEBOY	RCA	12	2 Mar 96	4

Duet with the Pet Shop Boys.

LITTLE WONDER	RCA	14	8 Feb 97	3
DEAD MAN WALKING	RCA	32	26 Apr 97	2
SEVEN YEARS IN TIBET	RCA	61	30 Aug 97	1

From the film of the same name.

I CAN'T READ	Velvet	73	21 Feb 98	1

From the film 'The Ice Storm'.

THURSDAY'S CHILD	Virgin	16	2 Oct 99	3
UNDER PRESSURE [RM]	Parlophone	14	18 Dec 99	3

Remixed by Queen, Joshua J. Macrae and Justin Shirley-Smith.
Above hit: QUEEN + David BOWIE.

ALBUMS:		HITS 35		WEEKS 927
THE RISE AND FALL OF ZIGGY STARDUST AND THE SPIDERS FROM MARS	RCA Victor	5	1 Jul 72	106
HUNKY DORY	RCA Victor	3	23 Sep 72	69
THE MAN WHO SOLD THE WORLD	RCA Victor	26	25 Nov 72	22

Originally released in April 71 with 'dress' cover sleeve.

SPACE ODDITY	RCA Victor	17	25 Nov 72	37

Originally titled David Bowie when released on the Philips label in 1969.

ALADDIN SANE	RCA Victor	1	5 May 73	47
PIN-UPS	RCA Victor	1	3 Nov 73	21
DIAMOND DOGS	RCA Victor	1	8 Jun 74	17
DAVID LIVE	RCA Victor	2	16 Nov 74	12

Live recordings from The Tower, Philadelphia, during his 1974 "Diamond Dogs" tour.

YOUNG AMERICANS	RCA Victor	2	5 Apr 75	12
STATION TO STATION	RCA Victor	5	7 Feb 76	16
CHANGESONEBOWIE	RCA Victor	2	12 Jun 76	28

Compilation.

LOW	RCA Victor	2	29 Jan 77	18
HEROES	RCA Victor	3	29 Oct 77	18
STAGE	RCA Victor	5	14 Oct 78	10
LODGER	RCA Victor	4	9 Jun 79	17
SCARY MONSTERS AND SUPER CREEPS	RCA	1	27 Sep 80	32
THE VERY BEST OF DAVID BOWIE	K-Tel	3	10 Jan 81	20
HUNKY DORY [RI-1ST]	RCA International	32	17 Jan 81	51

Peak position reached in 1983.

THE RISE AND FALL OF ZIGGY STARDUST AND THE SPIDERS FROM MARS [RI-1ST]	RCA International	33	31 Jan 81	62

Peak position reached in 1983.

CHANGESTWOBOWIE	RCA	24	28 Nov 81	17

Compilation.

ALADDIN SANE [RI-1ST]	RCA International	49	6 Mar 82	24

Peak position reached in 1983.

RARE	RCA	34	15 Jan 83	11
LET'S DANCE	EMI America	1	23 Apr 83	56
PIN-UPS [RI-1ST]	RCA International	57	30 Apr 83	15
THE MAN WHO SOLD THE WORLD [RI-1ST]	RCA International	64	30 Apr 83	8
DIAMOND DOGS [RI-1ST]	RCA International	60	14 May 83	14
HEROES [RI]	RCA International	75	11 Jun 83	8
LOW [RI-1ST]	RCA International	85	11 Jun 83	5
GOLDEN YEARS	RCA	33	20 Aug 83	5
ZIGGY STARDUST – THE MOTION PICTURE	RCA	17	5 Nov 83	6
FAME AND FASHION (BOWIE'S ALL TIME GREATEST HITS)	RCA	40	28 Apr 84	6
LOVE YOU TILL TUESDAY	Deram	53	19 May 84	4
TONIGHT	EMI America	1	6 Oct 84	19
NEVER LET ME DOWN	EMI America	6	2 May 87	16
CHANGESBOWIE	EMI	1	24 Mar 90	29

Compilation.

HUNKY DORY [RI-2ND]	EMI	39	14 Apr 90	3

Includes re-entry in 1997.

SPACE ODDITY [RI]	EMI	64	14 Apr 90	1
THE MAN WHO SOLD THE WORLD [RI-2ND]	EMI	66	14 Apr 90	1

THE RISE AND FALL OF ZIGGY STARDUST AND THE SPIDERS				
FROM MARS [RI-2ND]	EMI	25	23 Jun 90	4
ALADDIN SANE [RI-2ND]	EMI	43	28 Jul 90	1
PIN-UPS [RI-2ND]	EMI	52	28 Jul 90	1
DIAMOND DOGS [RI-2ND]	EMI	67	27 Oct 90	3
Includes re-entry in 1997.				
YOUNG AMERICANS [RI]	EMI	54	4 May 91	1
STATION TO STATION [RI]	EMI	57	4 May 91	1
LOW [RI-2ND]	EMI	64	7 Sep 91	1
All re-issues listed above were available for the first time on CD and included bonus tracks.				
BLACK TIE WHITE NOISE	Arista	1	17 Apr 93	11
THE SINGLES COLLECTION	EMI	9	20 Nov 93	15
SANTA MONICA '72	Trident	74	7 May 94	1
OUTSIDE	RCA	8	7 Oct 95	4
EARTHLING	RCA	6	15 Feb 97	4
THE BEST OF 1969/1974	EMI	13	8 Nov 97	10
THE BEST OF 1974/1979	EMI	39	2 May 98	2
HOURS . . .	Virgin	5	16 Oct 99	5

George BOWYER and William McCLINTOCK BUNBURY — UK

SINGLES:		HITS 1		WEEKS 2
GUARDIANS OF THE LAND	BOYS	33	22 Aug 98	2
Song is a defence of fox hunting. Backing fiddle and banjo playing by the Pedigrees.				

BOX TOPS — US

SINGLES:		HITS 3		WEEKS 33
THE LETTER	Stateside	5	16 Sep 67	12
CRY LIKE A BABY	Bell	15	23 Mar 68	12
SOUL DEEP	Bell	22	23 Aug 69	9

BOXCAR WILLIE — US

ALBUMS:		HITS 1		WEEKS 12
KING OF THE ROAD	Warwick	5	31 May 80	12

BOY GEORGE — UK

(See also Jesus Loves You; Culture Club.)

SINGLES:		HITS 13		WEEKS 46
EVERYTHING I OWN	Virgin	1	7 Mar 87	9
KEEP ME IN MIND	Virgin	29	6 Jun 87	4
SOLD	Virgin	24	18 Jul 87	5
TO BE REBORN	Virgin	13	21 Nov 87	7
LIVE MY LIFE	Virgin	62	5 Mar 88	2
NO CLAUSE 28	Virgin	57	18 Jun 88	3
DON'T CRY	Virgin	60	8 Oct 88	2
DON'T TAKE MY MIND ON A TRIP	Virgin	68	4 Mar 89	2
THE CRYING GAME	Spaghetti	22	19 Sep 92	4
From the film of the same name.				
MORE THAN LIKELY	Gee Street	40	12 Jun 93	3
Above hit: PM DAWN featuring BOY GEORGE.				
FUNTIME	Virgin	45	1 Apr 95	2
Originally recorded by Iggy Pop.				
IL ADORE	Virgin	50	1 Jul 95	2
SAME THING IN REVERSE	Virgin	56	21 Oct 95	1
ALBUMS:		HITS 4		WEEKS 14
SOLD	Virgin	29	27 Jun 87	6
AT WORST . . . THE BEST OF BOY GEORGE & CULTURE CLUB	Virgin	24	2 Oct 93	5
Also includes Jesus Loves You tracks.				
Above hit: BOY GEORGE/CULTURE CLUB.				
THE DEVIL IN SISTER GEORGE	Virgin	26	12 Mar 94	2
Remix album.				
Above hit: BOY GEORGE/JESUS LOVES YOU/CULTURE CLUB.				
CHEAPNESS AND BEAUTY	Virgin	44	3 Jun 95	1

BOY MEETS GIRL — US

SINGLES:		HITS 1		WEEKS 13
WAITING FOR A STAR TO FALL	RCA	9	3 Dec 88	13
ALBUMS:		HITS 1		WEEKS 1
REEL LIFE	RCA	74	4 Feb 89	1

BOY WUNDA – See PROGRESS presents The BOY WUNDA

Max BOYCE — UK

ALBUMS:		HITS 7		WEEKS 105
LIVE AT TREORCHY	One Up	21	5 Jul 75	32
WE ALL HAD DOCTORS' PAPERS	EMI	1	1 Nov 75	17

THE INCREDIBLE PLAN	EMI	9	20 Nov 76	12
THE ROAD AND THE MILES	EMI	50	7 Jan 78	3
LIVE AT TREORCHY [RE]	One Up	42	11 Mar 78	6
Re-released with a different catalogue number.				
I KNOW COS I WAS THERE	EMI	6	27 May 78	14
NOT THAT I'M BIASED	EMI	27	13 Oct 79	13
ME AND BILLY WILLIAMS	EMI	37	15 Nov 80	8

Jimmy BOYD   US

SINGLES:	HITS 2		WEEKS 22	
TELL ME A STORY	Philips	5	9 May 53	15
Features accompaniment by Norman Luboff and Carl Fischer on piano.				
Above hit: Jimmy BOYD-Frankie LAINE.				
TELL ME A STORY [RE]	Philips	12	12 Sep 53	1
I SAW MOMMY KISSING SANTA CLAUS	Columbia	3	28 Nov 53	6

Jacqueline BOYER   France

SINGLES:	HITS 1		WEEKS 2	
TOM PILLIBI	Columbia	33	30 Apr 60	2
Eurovision Song Contest winner in 1960.				

BOYS   US

SINGLES:	HITS 2		WEEKS 5	
DIAL MY HEART	Motown	61	12 Nov 88	2
CRAZY	Motown	57	29 Sep 90	3
ALBUMS:	HITS 1		WEEKS 1	
THE BOYS	NEMS	50	1 Oct 77	1

BOYSTOWN GANG   US

SINGLES:	HITS 3		WEEKS 20	
AIN'T NO MOUNTAIN HIGH ENOUGH/REMEMBER ME [M]	WEA	46	22 Aug 81	6
CAN'T TAKE MY EYES OFF YOU	ERC	4	31 Jul 82	11
Original by Frankie Valli reached No. 2 in the US in 1967.				
SIGNED, SEALED, DELIVERED (I'M YOURS)	ERC	50	9 Oct 82	3

BOYZ II MEN   US

SINGLES:	HITS 12		WEEKS 81	
END OF THE ROAD	Motown	1	5 Sep 92	21
From the film 'Boomerang'.				
MOTOWNPHILLY	Motown	23	19 Dec 92	6
Rap is by Michael Bivins of Bell Biv Devoe.				
IN THE STILL OF THE NITE (I'LL REMEMBER)	Motown	27	27 Feb 93	4
From the film 'The Jacksons – An American Dream'.				
I'LL MAKE LOVE TO YOU	Motown	5	3 Sep 94	12
ON BENDED KNEE	Motown	20	26 Nov 94	3
I'LL MAKE LOVE TO YOU [RE]	Motown	57	24 Dec 94	3
THANK YOU	Motown	26	22 Apr 95	3
Samples La-Di-Da-Di by Doug E.Fresh.				
WATER RUNS DRY	Motown	24	8 Jul 95	3
ONE SWEET DAY	Columbia	6	9 Dec 95	11
Song spent 16 weeks at No. 1 in the US.				
Above hit: Mariah CAREY and BOYZ II MEN.				
HEY LOVER	Def Jam	17	20 Jan 96	4
Based on Michael Jackson's Lady In My Life.				
Above hit: LL COOL J featuring BOYZ II MEN.				
4 SEASONS OF LONELINESS	Motown	10	20 Sep 97	6
A SONG FOR MAMA	Motown	34	6 Dec 97	2
CAN'T LET HER GO	Motown	23	25 Jul 98	3
ALBUMS:	HITS 3		WEEKS 28	
COOLEYHIGHHARMONY	Motown	7	31 Oct 92	18
II	Motown	17	24 Sep 94	5
EVOLUTION	Motown	12	4 Oct 97	5

BOYZONE   Ireland

SINGLES:	HITS 16		WEEKS 205	
LOVE ME FOR A REASON	Polydor	2	10 Dec 94	13
KEY TO MY LIFE	Polydor	3	29 Apr 95	8
SO GOOD	Polydor	3	12 Aug 95	6
FATHER AND SON	Polydor	2	25 Nov 95	16
Originally recorded by Cat Stevens.				
COMING HOME NOW	Polydor	4	9 Mar 96	9
WORDS	Polydor	1	19 Oct 96	14
A DIFFERENT BEAT	Polydor	1	14 Dec 96	10
A DIFFERENT BEAT [RE-1ST]	Polydor	74	1 Mar 97	1
A DIFFERENT BEAT [RE-2ND]	Polydor	62	15 Mar 97	4

ISN'T IT A WONDER	Polydor	2	22 Mar 97	7
ISN'T IT A WONDER [RE]	Polydor	44	17 May 97	7
PICTURE OF YOU	Polydor	2	2 Aug 97	18
From the film 'Bean: The Movie'.				
BABY CAN I HOLD YOU / SHOOTING STAR	Polydor	2	6 Dec 97	14
Baby Can I Hold You was originally recorded by Tracy Chapman in 1988. Shooting Star from the film 'Hercules'.				
ALL THAT I NEED	Polydor	1	2 May 98	10
ALL THAT I NEED [RE]	Polydor	49	18 Jul 98	4
NO MATTER WHAT	Polydor	1	15 Aug 98	15
From the musical 'Whistle Down The Wind'. At the request of Polydor, the single was removed from chart while at No. 34.				
I LOVE THE WAY YOU LOVE ME	Polydor	2	5 Dec 98	13
WHEN THE GOING GETS TOUGH	Polydor	1	13 Mar 99	14
Charity record in aid of Comic Relief.				
YOU NEEDED ME	Polydor	1	22 May 99	12
WHEN THE GOING GETS TOUGH [RE]	Polydor	57	17 Jul 99	2
YOU NEEDED ME [RE]	Polydor	60	28 Aug 99	3
EVERY DAY I LOVE YOU	Polydor	3	4 Dec 99	5
ALBUMS:	**HITS 4**			**WEEKS 167**
SAID AND DONE	Polydor	1	2 Sep 95	58
A DIFFERENT BEAT	Polydor	1	9 Nov 96	24
WHERE WE BELONG	Polydor	1	6 Jun 98	55
BY REQUEST	Polydor	1	12 Jun 99	30

BRAD US

SINGLES:	**HITS 1**			**WEEKS 1**
20TH CENTURY	Epic	64	26 Jun 93	1
ALBUMS:	**HITS 1**			**WEEKS 1**
SHAME	Epic	72	15 May 93	1

James Dean BRADFIELD - See 808 STATE; MANIC STREET PREACHERS

Scott BRADLEY UK

SINGLES:	**HITS 1**			**WEEKS 1**
ZOOM	Hidden Agenda	61	15 Oct 94	1
Backing vocals by Motown session singer Pat Lewis.				

Paul BRADY UK

SINGLES:	**HITS 1**			**WEEKS 1**
THE WORLD IS WHAT YOU MAKE IT	Mercury	67	13 Jan 96	1
Theme from the ITV series 'Faith In The Future'.				
ALBUMS:	**HITS 1**			**WEEKS 1**
TRICK OR TREAT	Fontana	62	6 Apr 91	1

Billy BRAGG UK

(See also Billy Bragg and Wilco.)

SINGLES:	**HITS 12**			**WEEKS 51**
BETWEEN THE WARS [EP]	Go! Discs	15	16 Mar 85	6
Lead track: Between The Wars.				
DAYS LIKE THESE	Go! Discs	43	28 Dec 85	5
LEVI STUBBS TEARS [EP]	Go! Discs	29	28 Jun 86	6
Lead track; Levi Stubbs Tears.				
GREETINGS TO THE NEW BRUNETTE	Go! Discs	58	15 Nov 86	2
Above hit: Billy BRAGG with Johnny MARR and Kirsty MacCOLL.				
SHE'S LEAVING HOME	Childline	1	14 May 88	11
Charity record in aid of Childline. [AA] listed with With A Little Help From My Friends by Wet Wet Wet.				
Above hit: Billy BRAGG with Cara TIVEY.				
WAITING FOR THE GREAT LEAP FORWARDS	Go! Discs	52	10 Sep 88	3
WON'T TALK ABOUT IT	Go.Beat	29	8 Jul 89	6
Above hit: Norman COOK featuring Billy BRAGG.				
SEXUALITY	Go! Discs	27	6 Jul 91	5
YOU WOKE UP MY NEIGHBOURHOOD	Go! Discs	54	7 Sep 91	2
ACCIDENT WAITING TO HAPPEN [EP]	Go! Discs	33	29 Feb 92	3
Lead track: Accident Waiting To Happen.				
UPFIELD	Cooking Vinyl	46	31 Aug 96	1
THE BOY DONE GOOD	Cooking Vinyl	55	17 May 97	1
ALBUMS:	**HITS 10**			**WEEKS 83**
LIFE'S A RIOT WITH SPY VS SPY	Go! Discs	32	21 Jan 84	15
BREWING UP WITH BILLY BRAGG	Go! Discs	16	20 Oct 84	21
LIFE'S A RIOT WITH SPY VS SPY [RE]	Go! Discs	30	2 Feb 85	15
TALKING WITH THE TAXMAN ABOUT POETRY	Go! Discs	8	4 Oct 86	8
BACK TO BASICS	Go! Discs	37	13 Jun 87	4
WORKERS' PLAYTIME	Go! Discs	17	1 Oct 88	4

THE INTERNATIONALE	*Utility*	34	*12 May 90*	4
DON'T TRY THIS AT HOME	*Go! Discs*	8	*28 Sep 91*	6
WILLIAM BLOKE	*Cooking Vinyl*	16	*21 Sep 96*	3
BLOKE ON BLOKE	*Cooking Vinyl*	72	*28 Jun 97*	1
Album of rarities and previously unavailable tracks.				
REACHING TO THE CONVERTED	*Cooking Vinyl*	41	*11 Sep 99*	2
Compilation of rarities, B-sides and live recordings.				

Billy BRAGG and WILCO — UK/US

(See also Billy Bragg; Wilco.)

ALBUMS:		HITS 1		WEEKS 2
MERMAID AVENUE	*Elektra*	34	*11 Jul 98*	2

BRAIDS — US

SINGLES:		HITS 1		WEEKS 3
BOHEMIAN RHAPSODY	*Atlantic*	21	*2 Nov 96*	3
From the film 'High School High'.				

BRAINBUG — Italy

SINGLES:		HITS 2		WEEKS 7
NIGHTMARE	*Positiva*	11	*3 May 97*	5
BENEDICTUS / NIGHTMARE [RI]	*Positiva*	24	*22 Nov 97*	2

BRAINCHILD — Germany

SINGLES:		HITS 1		WEEKS 2
SYMMETRY C	*Multiply*	31	*30 Oct 99*	2
Originally released in 1992.				

Wilfred BRAMBELL and Harry H. CORBETT — UK

SINGLES:		HITS 1		WEEKS 12
STEPTOE & SON AT BUCKINGHAM PALACE	*Pye*	25	*30 Nov 63*	12
Live recording from the Royal Variety Performance of 1963.				
EPS:		HITS 2		WEEKS 36
FACTS OF LIFE FROM STEPTOE AND SON	*Pye*	4	*8 Jun 63*	28
WAGES OF SIN	*Pye*	10	*21 Dec 63*	8
ALBUMS:		HITS 3		WEEKS 34
STEPTOE AND SON	*Pye*	4	*23 Mar 63*	28
STEPTOE AND SON	*Pye Golden Guinea*	14	*11 Jan 64*	5
Both albums are different.				
MORE JUNK	*Pye*	19	*14 Mar 64*	1

Bekka BRAMLETT – See Joe COCKER

BRAN VAN 3000 — Canada

SINGLES:		HITS 1		WEEKS 13
DRINKING IN L.A.	*Capitol*	34	*6 Jun 98*	2
DRINKING IN L.A. [RI]	*Capitol*	3	*21 Aug 99*	11
Featured in the Rolling Rock beer TV commercial.				

BRAND NEW HEAVIES — UK/US

SINGLES:		HITS 15		WEEKS 66
NEVER STOP	*ffrr*	43	*5 Oct 91*	3
DREAM COME TRUE	*ffrr*	24	*15 Feb 92*	4
ULTIMATE TRUNK FUNK – THE EP [EP]	*ffrr*	19	*18 Apr 92*	6
Lead track: Never Stop, a remix by David Morales of their first hit.				
DON'T LET IT GO TO YOUR HEAD	*ffrr*	24	*1 Aug 92*	4
Originally recorded by Jean Carn.				
STAY THIS WAY	*ffrr*	40	*19 Dec 92*	5
Remix of a track from the Ultimate Trunk Funk EP.				
Above 5: BRAND NEW HEAVIES featuring N'Dea DAVENPORT.				
DREAM ON DREAMER	*ffrr*	15	*26 Mar 94*	4
BACK TO LOVE	*ffrr*	23	*11 Jun 94*	4
MIDNIGHT AT THE OASIS	*ffrr*	13	*13 Aug 94*	6
SPEND SOME TIME	*ffrr*	26	*5 Nov 94*	4
CLOSE TO YOU	*ffrr*	38	*11 Mar 95*	3
From the film 'Pret A Porter'.				
SOMETIMES	*ffrr*	11	*12 Apr 97*	5
YOU ARE THE UNIVERSE	*ffrr*	21	*28 Jun 97*	4
YOU'VE GOT A FRIEND	*ffrr*	9	*18 Oct 97*	8
SHELTER	*ffrr*	31	*10 Jan 98*	4
SATURDAY NITE	*ffrr*	35	*11 Sep 99*	2
ALBUMS:		HITS 6		WEEKS 103
BRAND NEW HEAVIES	*ffrr*	25	*14 Mar 92*	16
Repackaged from 29 Aug 92.				

HEAVY RHYME EXPERIENCE VOLUME 1	*ffrr*	38	*5 Sep 92*	2
Features various rappers.				
BROTHER SISTER	*ffrr*	4	*16 Apr 94*	48
ORIGINAL FLAVA	*Acid Jazz*	64	*12 Nov 94*	1
Album of early Brand New Heavies material.				
SHELTER	*ffrr*	5	*3 May 97*	33
TRUNK FUNK – THE BEST OF THE BRAND NEW HEAVIES	*ffrr*	13	*25 Sep 99*	3

BRAND X — UK

ALBUMS:	HITS 2		WEEKS 6	
MOROCCAN ROLL	*Charisma*	37	*21 May 77*	5
IS THERE ANYTHING ABOUT?	*CBS*	93	*11 Sep 82*	1

Johnny BRANDON with the PHANTOMS — UK

SINGLES:	HITS 2		WEEKS 12	
TOMORROW	*Polygon*	8	*12 Mar 55*	6
TOMORROW [RE]	*Polygon*	16	*30 Apr 55*	2
Above hit: Johnny BRANDON with the PHANTOMS and the Norman WARREN				
MUSIC.				
DON'T WORRY	*Polygon*	18	*2 Jul 55*	4

BRANDY — US

SINGLES:	HITS 6		WEEKS 52	
I WANNA BE DOWN	*Atlantic*	44	*10 Dec 94*	3
I WANNA BE DOWN [RI]	*Atlantic*	36	*3 Jun 95*	3
SITTIN' UP IN MY ROOM	*Arista*	30	*3 Feb 96*	4
From the film 'Waiting To Exhale'.				
THE BOY IS MINE	*Atlantic*	2	*6 Jun 98*	20
Above hit: BRANDY and MONICA.				
TOP OF THE WORLD	*Atlantic*	2	*10 Oct 98*	8
Above hit: BRANDY featuring MASE.				
HAVE YOU EVER?	*Atlantic*	13	*12 Dec 98*	8
TOP OF THE WORLD [RE]	*Atlantic*	61	*9 Jan 99*	1
Above hit: BRANDY featuring MASE.				
ALMOST DOESN'T COUNT	*Atlantic*	15	*19 Jun 99*	5
ALBUMS:	HITS 1		WEEKS 31	
NEVER S-A-Y NEVER	*Atlantic*	19	*20 Jun 98*	31

Laura BRANIGAN — US

SINGLES:	HITS 3		WEEKS 33	
GLORIA	*Atlantic*	6	*18 Dec 82*	13
Originally recorded by Umberto Tozzi.				
SELF CONTROL	*Atlantic*	5	*7 Jul 84*	17
THE LUCKY ONE	*Atlantic*	56	*6 Oct 84*	3
ALBUMS:	HITS 2		WEEKS 18	
SELF CONTROL	*Atlantic*	16	*18 Aug 84*	14
HOLD ME	*Atlantic*	64	*24 Aug 85*	4

BRASS CONSTRUCTION — US

SINGLES:	HITS 8		WEEKS 35	
MOVIN'	*United Artists*	23	*3 Apr 76*	6
HA CHA CHA (FUNKTION)	*United Artists*	37	*5 Feb 77*	5
MUSIC MAKES YOU FEEL LIKE DANCING	*United Artists*	39	*26 Jan 80*	6
WALKIN' THE LINE	*Capitol*	47	*28 May 83*	3
WE CAN WORK IT OUT	*Capitol*	70	*16 Jul 83*	2
PARTYLINE	*Capitol*	56	*7 Jul 84*	4
INTERNATIONAL	*Capitol*	70	*27 Oct 84*	2
GIVE AND TAKE	*Capitol*	62	*9 Nov 85*	3
MOVIN' – 1988 [RM]	*Syncopate*	24	*28 May 88*	4
Remixed by Phil Harding.				
ALBUMS:	HITS 2		WEEKS 12	
BRASS CONSTRUCTION	*United Artists*	9	*20 Mar 76*	11
RENEGADES	*Capitol*	94	*30 Jun 84*	1

BRAT — UK

SINGLES:	HITS 1		WEEKS 8	
CHALK DUST – THE UMPIRE STRIKES BACK	*Hansa*	19	*10 Jul 82*	8

BRAVADO — UK

SINGLES:	HITS 1		WEEKS 3	
HARMONICA MAN	*Peach*	37	*18 Jun 94*	3
Harmonica playing is by world harmonica champion Paul Lamb.				

BRAVO ALL STARS
UK/US/Germany

SINGLES:	HITS 1			WEEKS 2
LET THE MUSIC HEAL YOUR SOUL	Edel	36	29 Aug 98	2

Profits to Nordoff Robbins Music Therapy.

Los BRAVOS
Spain/Germany

SINGLES:	HITS 2			WEEKS 24
BLACK IS BLACK	Decca	2	2 Jul 66	13
I DON'T CARE	Decca	16	10 Sep 66	11
ALBUMS:	HITS 1			WEEKS 1
BLACK IS BLACK	Decca	29	8 Oct 66	1

Dhar BRAXTON
US

SINGLES:	HITS 1			WEEKS 8
JUMP BACK (SET ME FREE)	Fourth & Broadway	32	31 May 86	8

Toni BRAXTON
US

SINGLES:	HITS 8			WEEKS 72
ANOTHER SAD LOVE SONG	LaFace	51	18 Sep 93	2
BREATHE AGAIN	LaFace	2	15 Jan 94	12
ANOTHER SAD LOVE SONG [RI]	LaFace	15	2 Apr 94	8
YOU MEAN THE WORLD TO ME	LaFace	30	9 Jul 94	5
LOVE SHOULDA BROUGHT YOU HOME	LaFace	33	3 Dec 94	3
YOU'RE MAKIN ME HIGH	LaFace	7	13 Jul 96	11
UN-BREAK MY HEART	LaFace	2	2 Nov 96	19

Backing vocals by Shanice.

I DON'T WANT TO	LaFace	9	24 May 97	8
HOW COULD AN ANGEL BREAK MY HEART	LaFace	22	8 Nov 97	4

Above hit: Toni BRAXTON with Kenny G.

ALBUMS:	HITS 2			WEEKS 114
TONI BRAXTON	LaFace	4	29 Jan 94	33
SECRETS	LaFace	53	29 Jun 96	3

This chart run was from import sales.

SECRETS [RE]	LaFace	10	27 Jul 96	78

Peak position reached on 25 Jan 97.

BRAXTONS
US

SINGLES:	HITS 3			WEEKS 7
SO MANY WAYS	Atlantic	32	1 Feb 97	2

From the film 'High School High'.

THE BOSS	Atlantic	31	29 Mar 97	3
SLOW FLOW	Atlantic	26	19 Jul 97	2

BREAD
US

SINGLES:	HITS 5			WEEKS 46
MAKE IT WITH YOU	Elektra	5	1 Aug 70	14
BABY I'M-A WANT YOU	Elektra	14	15 Jan 72	10
EVERYTHING I OWN	Elektra	32	29 Apr 72	6
THE GUITAR MAN	Elektra	16	30 Sep 72	9
LOST WITHOUT YOUR LOVE	Elektra	27	25 Dec 76	7
ALBUMS:	HITS 8			WEEKS 198
ON THE WATERS	Elektra	34	26 Sep 70	5
BABY I'M A-WANT YOU	Elektra	9	18 Mar 72	19
THE BEST OF BREAD	Elektra	7	28 Oct 72	100
THE BEST OF BREAD VOLUME 2	Elektra	48	27 Jul 74	1
LOST WITHOUT YOUR LOVE	Elektra	17	29 Jan 77	6
THE SOUND OF BREAD	Elektra	1	5 Nov 77	46
THE COLLECTION - THE VERY BEST OF BREAD AND DAVID GATES	Telstar	84	28 Nov 87	2

Above hit: BREAD and David GATES.

DAVID GATES AND BREAD: ESSENTIALS	warner.esp/Jive	9	5 Jul 97	19

Above hit: David GATES and BREAD.
Above 2 albums include Gates solo and group recordings.

BREAK MACHINE
US

SINGLES:	HITS 3			WEEKS 32
STREET DANCE	Record Shack	3	4 Feb 84	14
BREAK DANCE PARTY	Record Shack	9	12 May 84	8
BREAK DANCE PARTY [RE]	Record Shack	65	14 Jul 84	2
ARE YOU READY	Record Shack	27	11 Aug 84	8
ALBUMS:	HITS 1			WEEKS 16
BREAK MACHINE	Record Shack	17	9 Jun 84	16

BREAKBEAT ERA | UK

SINGLES:	HITS 2			WEEKS 4	
BREAKBEAT ERA	XL Recordings	38	18 Jul 98		2
ULTRA-OBSCENE	XL Recordings	48	21 Aug 99		2
ALBUMS:	**HITS 1**			**WEEKS 2**	
ULTRA OBSCENE	XL Recordings	31	11 Sep 99		2

BREAKFAST CLUB | US

SINGLES:	HITS 1			WEEKS 3	
RIGHT ON TRACK	MCA	54	27 Jun 87		3

Julian BREAM | UK

ALBUMS:	HITS 1			WEEKS 2	
THE ULTIMATE GUITAR COLLECTION	RCA Victor	66	27 Apr 96		2

Compilation covering the period 1955–1983.

BREATHE | UK

SINGLES:	HITS 4			WEEKS 27	
HANDS TO HEAVEN	Siren	4	30 Jul 88		12
JONAH	Siren	60	22 Oct 88		3
HOW CAN I FALL?	Siren	48	3 Dec 88		7
DON'T TELL ME LIES	Siren	45	11 Mar 89		5
ALBUMS:	**HITS 1**			**WEEKS 5**	
ALL THAT JAZZ	Siren	22	8 Oct 88		5

Freddy BRECK | Germany

SINGLES:	HITS 1			WEEKS 4	
SO IN LOVE WITH YOU	Decca	44	13 Apr 74		4

BRECKER BROTHERS | US

SINGLES:	HITS 1			WEEKS 5	
EAST RIVER	Arista	34	4 Nov 78		5

BREEDERS | US/UK

SINGLES:	HITS 4			WEEKS 6	
SAFARI [EP]	4AD	69	18 Apr 92		1
Lead track: Do You Love Me Now.					
CANNONBALL [EP]	4AD	40	21 Aug 93		3
Lead track: Cannonball.					
DIVINE HAMMER	4AD	59	6 Nov 93		1
HEAD TO TOE [EP]	4AD	68	23 Jul 94		1
10" only release. Lead track: Head To Toe.					
ALBUMS:	**HITS 2**			**WEEKS 8**	
POD	4AD	22	9 Jun 90		3
LAST SPLASH	4AD	5	11 Sep 93		5

BREEKOUT KREW | US

SINGLES:	HITS 1			WEEKS 3	
MATT'S MOOD	London	51	24 Nov 84		3

Ann BREEN | Ireland

SINGLES:	HITS 1			WEEKS 2	
PAL OF MY CRADLE DAYS	Homespun	69	19 Mar 83		1
PAL OF MY CRADLE DAYS [RE]	Homespun	74	7 Jan 84		1

BRENDON | UK

SINGLES:	HITS 1			WEEKS 9	
GIMME SOME	Magnet	14	19 Mar 77		9

Originally recorded by Jimmy Bo Horne.

Maire BRENNAN | Ireland

SINGLES:	HITS 2			WEEKS 12	
AGAINST THE WIND	RCA	64	16 May 92		2
SALTWATER	Xtravaganza	6	5 Jun 99		10
Based around Clannad's Theme From Harry's Game.					
Above hit: CHICANE (featuring Maire BRENNAN of CLANNAD).					
ALBUMS:	**HITS 1**			**WEEKS 2**	
MAIRE	RCA	53	13 Jun 92		2

Rose BRENNAN — Ireland

SINGLES:	HITS 1			WEEKS 9
TALL DARK STRANGER	Philips	31	9 Dec 61	9

Walter BRENNAN with the Johnny MANN SINGERS — US

SINGLES:	HITS 1			WEEKS 3
OLD RIVERS	Liberty	38	30 Jun 62	3

Tony BRENT — UK

SINGLES:	HITS 8			WEEKS 52
WALKIN' TO MISSOURI	Columbia	9	20 Dec 52	2
Above hit: Tony BRENT with Norrie PARAMOR, his Chorus and Orchestra.				
MAKE IT SOON	Columbia	9	3 Jan 53	4
WALKIN' TO MISSOURI [RE]	Columbia	7	10 Jan 53	5
GOT YOU ON MY MIND	Columbia	12	24 Jan 53	1
MAKE IT SOON [RE]	Columbia	9	14 Mar 53	3
CINDY OH CINDY	Columbia	16	1 Dec 56	6
CINDY OH CINDY [RE]	Columbia	30	9 Feb 57	1
DARK MOON	Columbia	17	29 Jun 57	14
Originally recorded by Bonny Guitar.				
Above 3: Tony BRENT with Eric JUPP and his Orchestra.				
THE CLOUDS WILL SOON ROLL BY	Columbia	24	1 Mar 58	3
THE CLOUDS WILL SOON ROLL BY [RE]	Columbia	20	10 May 58	2
GIRL OF MY DREAMS	Columbia	16	6 Sep 58	7
Above hit: Tony BRENT with Eric JUPP and his Orchestra.				
WHY SHOULD I BE LONELY ?	Columbia	24	25 Jul 59	4

Bernard BRESSLAW — UK

(See also Michael Medwin, Bernard Bresslaw, Alfie Bass and Leslie Fyson.)

SINGLES:	HITS 1			WEEKS 11
MAD PASSIONATE LOVE	His Master's Voice	6	6 Sep 58	11

Adrian BRETT — UK

ALBUMS:	HITS 1			WEEKS 11
ECHOES OF GOLD	Warwick	19	10 Nov 79	11

Paul BRETT — UK

ALBUMS:	HITS 1			WEEKS 7
ROMANTIC GUITAR	K-Tel	24	19 Jul 80	7

Teresa BREWER — US

SINGLES:	HITS 5			WEEKS 53
LET ME GO LOVER	Vogue Coral	9	12 Feb 55	10
Originally recorded by Joan Weber.				
Above hit: Teresa BREWER with the LANCERS.				
A TEAR FELL	Vogue Coral	2	14 Apr 56	15
A SWEET OLD FASHIONED GIRL	Vogue Coral	3	14 Jul 56	15
NORA MALONE	Vogue Coral	26	11 May 57	2
HOW DO YOU KNOW IT'S LOVE	Coral	21	25 Jun 60	11

BRIAN and MICHAEL (BURKE and JERK) — UK

SINGLES:	HITS 1			WEEKS 19
MATCHSTALK MEN AND MATCHSTALK CATS AND DOGS (LOWRY'S SONG)	Pye	1	25 Feb 78	19

BRICK — US

SINGLES:	HITS 1			WEEKS 4
DAZZ	Bang	36	5 Feb 77	4

Edie BRICKELL and the NEW BOHEMIANS — US

SINGLES:	HITS 3			WEEKS 10
WHAT I AM	Geffen	31	4 Feb 89	7
CIRCLE	Geffen	74	27 May 89	1
GOOD TIMES	Geffen	40	1 Oct 94	2
Features vocals by Barry White.				
Above hit: Edie BRICKELL.				

ALBUMS:	HITS 3			WEEKS 19
SHOOTING RUBBERBANDS AT THE STARS	Geffen	25	4 Feb 89	17
GHOST OF A DOG	Geffen	63	10 Nov 90	1
PICTURE PERFECT MORNING	Geffen	59	3 Sep 94	1
Above hit: Edie BRICKELL.				

113

Alicia BRIDGES — US

SINGLES:	HITS 1		WEEKS 11	
I LOVE THE NIGHT LIFE (DISCO 'ROUND)	*Polydor*	32	*11 Nov 78*	10
I LOVE THE NIGHTLIFE (DISCO 'ROUND) [RM]	*Mother*	61	*8 Oct 94*	1

From the film 'The Adventures Of Priscilla Queen Of The Desert'. Remixed by the Rapino Brothers.

Johnny BRIGGS – See CORONATION STREET CAST

BRIGHOUSE and RASTRICK BRASS BAND — UK

SINGLES:	HITS 1		WEEKS 13	
THE FLORAL DANCE	*Transatlantic*	2	*12 Nov 77*	13
ALBUMS:	HITS 1		WEEKS 11	
FLORAL DANCE	*Logo*	10	*28 Jan 78*	11

Bette BRIGHT — UK

SINGLES:	HITS 1		WEEKS 5	
HELLO, I AM YOUR HEART	*Korova*	50	*8 Mar 80*	5

Originally recorded by Dennis Linde.

Sarah BRIGHTMAN — UK

(See also Andrew Lloyd Webber; Various Artists: Stage Cast – London 'The Phantom Of The Opera'; Television – Soundtracks 'Song And Dance'.)

SINGLES:	HITS 13		WEEKS 98	
I LOST MY HEART TO A STARSHIP TROOPER	*Ariola Hansa*	6	*11 Nov 78*	14
Above hit: Sarah BRIGHTMAN and HOT GOSSIP.				
THE ADVENTURES OF THE LOVE CRUSADER	*Ariola Hansa*	53	*7 Apr 79*	5
Above hit: Sarah BRIGHTMAN and the STARSHIP TROOPERS.				
HIM	*Polydor*	55	*30 Jul 83*	4
Above hit: Sarah BRIGHTMAN and the ROYAL PHILHARMONIC ORCHESTRA.				
PIE JESU	*His Master's Voice*	3	*23 Mar 85*	8
Above hit: Sarah BRIGHTMAN and Paul MILES-KINGSTON; WINCHESTER CATHEDRAL CHOIR Director, Martin NEARY, James LANCELOT – Organ; ENGLISH CHAMBER ORCHESTRA conducted by Lorin MAAZEL.				
THE PHANTOM OF THE OPERA	*Polydor*	7	*11 Jan 86*	10
Above hit: Sarah BRIGHTMAN and Steve HARLEY.				
ALL I ASK OF YOU	*Polydor*	3	*4 Oct 86*	16
Above hit: Cliff RICHARD and Sarah BRIGHTMAN with the ROYAL PHILHARMONIC ORCHESTRA conducted by David CADDICK.				
WISHING YOU WERE SOMEHOW HERE AGAIN	*Polydor*	7	*10 Jan 87*	11
Above 3 from the musical 'The Phantom Of The Opera'. [AA] listed with The Music Of The Night by Michael Crawford.				
AMIGOS PARA SIEMPRE (FRIENDS FOR LIFE)	*Really Useful*	11	*11 Jul 92*	11
The theme to the Barcelona 1992 Olympic Games. *Above hit: Jose CARRERAS and Sarah BRIGHTMAN.*				
TIME TO SAY GOODBYE (CON TE PARTIRO)	*Coalition*	2	*24 May 97*	14
Above hit: Sarah BRIGHTMAN and Andrea BOCELLI.				
WHO WANTS TO LIVE FOREVER	*Coalition*	45	*23 Aug 97*	1
JUST SHOW ME HOW TO LOVE YOU	*Coalition*	54	*6 Dec 97*	2
Above hit: Sarah BRIGHTMAN and the LONDON SYMPHONY ORCHESTRA featuring Jose CURA.				
STARSHIP TROOPERS	*Coalition*	58	*14 Feb 98*	1
Featuring re-recorded vocals from Brightman's first hit. *Above hit: UNITED CITIZEN FEDERATION featuring Sarah BRIGHTMAN.*				
EDEN	*Coalition*	68	*13 Feb 99*	1
ALBUMS:	HITS 3		WEEKS 25	
THE SONGS THAT GOT AWAY	*Really Useful*	48	*17 Jun 89*	2
THE UNEXPECTED SONGS – SURRENDER	*Really Useful*	45	*11 Nov 95*	2
Album of Andrew Lloyd Webber songs.				
TIMELESS	*Coalition*	2	*14 Jun 97*	21
Recorded with the London Philharmonic Orchestra.				

BRIGHTON AND HOVE ALBION F.C. – See SEAGULLS – BRIGHTON and HOVE ALBION FOOTBALL CLUB

BRILLIANT — UK

SINGLES:	HITS 3		WEEKS 13	
IT'S A MAN'S MAN'S MAN'S WORLD	*Food*	58	*19 Oct 85*	5
LOVE IS WAR	*Food*	64	*22 Mar 86*	4
SOMEBODY	*Food*	67	*2 Aug 86*	4
ALBUMS:	HITS 1		WEEKS 1	
KISS THE LIPS OF LIFE	*Food*	83	*20 Sep 86*	1

Danielle BRISEBOIS — US

SINGLES:	HITS 1		WEEKS 1	
GIMME LITTLE SIGN	*Epic*	75	*9 Sep 95*	1

Johnny BRISTOL
US

SINGLES:		HITS 2			WEEKS 16
HANG ON IN THERE BABY		MGM	3	24 Aug 74	11
MY GUY – MY GIRL [M]		Atlantic	39	19 Jul 80	5
Above hit: Amii STEWART and Johnny BRISTOL.					
ALBUMS:		HITS 1			WEEKS 7
HANG ON IN THERE BABY		MGM	12	5 Oct 74	7

BROCK LANDARS
UK

SINGLES:		HITS 1			WEEKS 2
S.M.D.U.		Parlophone	49	11 Jul 98	2
Samples Blur's Song 2 and Prodigy's Smack My Bitch Up. Acronym for Smack My Dick Up.					

BRODSKY QUARTET – See Elvis COSTELLO and the ATTRACTIONS

BROKEN ENGLISH
UK

SINGLES:		HITS 2			WEEKS 13
COMIN' ON STRONG		EMI	18	30 May 87	10
LOVE ON THE SIDE		EMI	69	3 Oct 87	3

June BRONHILL and Thomas ROUND
UK/Australia

ALBUMS:		HITS 1			WEEKS 1
LILAC TIME		His Master's Voice	17	18 Jun 60	1

BRONSKI BEAT
UK

(See also Jimmy Somerville.)

SINGLES:		HITS 7			WEEKS 78
SMALLTOWN BOY		Forbidden Fruit	3	2 Jun 84	13
WHY?		Forbidden Fruit	6	22 Sep 84	10
IT AIN'T NECESSARILY SO		Forbidden Fruit	16	1 Dec 84	11
I FEEL LOVE [M]		Forbidden Fruit	3	20 Apr 85	12
Above hit: BRONSKI BEAT/Marc ALMOND.					
HIT THAT PERFECT BEAT		Forbidden Fruit	3	30 Nov 85	14
COME ON, COME ON		Forbidden Fruit	20	29 Mar 86	7
Sleeve reads 'C'mon! C'mon!'.					
CHA CHA HEELS		Arista	32	1 Jul 89	7
Above hit: Eartha KITT and BRONSKI BEAT.					
SMALLTOWN BOY (1991 REMIX) [RM]		London	32	2 Feb 91	4
Above hit: Jimmy SOMERVILLE with BRONSKI BEAT.					
ALBUMS:		HITS 3			WEEKS 65
THE AGE OF CONSENT		Forbidden Fruit	4	20 Oct 84	53
HUNDREDS AND THOUSANDS		Forbidden Fruit	24	21 Sep 85	6
TRUTHDARE DOUBLEDARE		Forbidden Fruit	18	10 May 86	6

Will BRONSON CHORUS – See Tony BENNETT

Jet BRONX and the FORBIDDEN
UK

SINGLES:		HITS 1			WEEKS 1
AIN'T DOIN' NOTHIN'		Lightning	49	17 Dec 77	1

Michael BROOK – See Nusrat Fateh Ali KHAN/Michael BROOK

BROOK BROTHERS
UK

SINGLES:		HITS 5			WEEKS 35
WARPAINT		Pye	5	1 Apr 61	14
Above hit: BROOK BROTHERS with the Tony HATCH GROUP.					
AIN'T GONNA WASH FOR A WEEK		Pye	13	26 Aug 61	10
Originally recorded by Eddie Hodges.					
HE'S OLD ENOUGH TO KNOW BETTER		Pye	37	27 Jan 62	1
WELCOME HOME, BABY		Pye	33	18 Aug 62	6
TROUBLE IS MY MIDDLE NAME		Pye	38	23 Feb 63	4

Bruno BROOKES – See Liz KERSHAW and Bruno BROOKES

BROOKLYN BOUNCE
Germany

SINGLES:		HITS 1			WEEKS 1
THE MUSIC'S GOT ME		Club Tools	67	30 May 98	1

BROOKLYN BRONX and QUEENS – See B B and Q BAND

Elkie BROOKS
UK

SINGLES:		HITS 13			WEEKS 91
PEARL'S A SINGER		A&M	8	2 Apr 77	9
Originally recorded by Dino and Sembello.					

115

SUNSHINE AFTER THE RAIN	A&M	10	20 Aug 77	9
Originally recorded by Carole King.				
LILAC WINE	A&M	16	25 Feb 78	7
Originally recorded by Eartha Kitt.				
ONLY LOVE CAN BREAK YOUR HEART	A&M	43	3 Jun 78	5
Original by Neil Young reached No. 33 in the US in 1970.				
DON'T CRY OUT LOUD	A&M	12	11 Nov 78	11
THE RUNAWAY	A&M	50	5 May 79	5
FOOL IF YOU THINK IT'S OVER	A&M	17	16 Jan 82	10
OUR LOVE	A&M	43	1 May 82	5
NIGHTS IN WHITE SATIN	A&M	33	17 Jul 82	5
GASOLINE ALLEY	A&M	52	22 Jan 83	5
NO MORE THE FOOL	Legend	5	22 Nov 86	16
Originally recorded by Russ Ballard.				
BREAK THE CHAIN	Legend	55	4 Apr 87	3
WE'VE GOT TONIGHT	Legend	69	11 Jul 87	1
ALBUMS:	**HITS 15**		**WEEKS 223**	
TWO DAYS AWAY	A&M	16	18 Jun 77	20
SHOOTING STAR	A&M	20	13 May 78	13
LIVE AND LEARN	A&M	34	13 Oct 79	6
PEARLS	A&M	2	14 Nov 81	79
PEARLS II	A&M	5	13 Nov 82	25
MINUTES	A&M	35	14 Jul 84	7
SCREEN GEMS	EMI	35	8 Dec 84	11
NO MORE THE FOOL	Legend	5	6 Dec 86	23
THE VERY BEST OF ELKIE BROOKS	Telstar	10	27 Dec 86	18
BOOKBINDER'S KID	Legend	57	11 Jun 88	3
INSPIRATIONS	Telstar	58	18 Nov 89	3
ROUND MIDNIGHT	Castle Communications	27	13 Mar 93	4
NOTHIN' BUT THE BLUES	Castle Communications	58	16 Apr 94	2
AMAZING	Carlton Premiere	49	13 Apr 96	2
Re-recordings of her greatest hits.				
Above hit: Elkie BROOKS with the ROYAL PHILHARMONIC ORCHESTRA.				
THE VERY BEST OF ELKIE BROOKS	PolyGram TV	23	15 Mar 97	7
Both Best Of albums are different.				

Garth BROOKS
				US
SINGLES:	**HITS 6**		**WEEKS 15**	
SHAMELESS	Capitol	71	1 Feb 92	1
THE RED STROKES / AIN'T GOING DOWN (TILL THE SUN COMES UP)	Liberty	13	22 Jan 94	5
STANDING OUTSIDE THE FIRE	Liberty	28	16 Apr 94	4
THE DANCE / FRIENDS IN LOW PLACES	Capitol	36	18 Feb 95	3
SHE'S EVERY WOMAN	Capitol	55	17 Feb 96	1
LOST IN YOU	Capitol	70	13 Nov 99	1
Chris Gaines is a fictional character played by Brooks in the film 'The Lamb'.				
Above hit: Garth BROOKS as Chris GAINES.				
ALBUMS:	**HITS 6**		**WEEKS 48**	
ROPIN' THE WIND	Capitol	41	15 Feb 92	2
IN PIECES	Capitol	2	12 Feb 94	11
Label changed to Liberty from 26 Feb 94.				
THE HITS	Liberty	11	24 Dec 94	21
FRESH HORSES	Capitol	22	2 Dec 95	6
SEVENS	Capitol	34	13 Dec 97	7
DOUBLE LIVE	Capitol	57	28 Nov 98	1
Live recordings made between 1991–98.				

Mel BROOKS
				US
SINGLES:	**HITS 1**		**WEEKS 10**	
TO BE OR NOT TO BE (THE HITLER RAP)	Island	12	18 Feb 84	10
From the film 'To Be Or Not To Be'.				

Meredith BROOKS
				US
SINGLES:	**HITS 3**		**WEEKS 13**	
BITCH	Capitol	6	2 Aug 97	10
I NEED	Capitol	28	6 Dec 97	2
WHAT WOULD HAPPEN	Capitol	49	7 Mar 98	1
ALBUMS:	**HITS 1**		**WEEKS 10**	
BLURRING THE EDGES	Capitol	5	23 Aug 97	10

Nigel BROOKS SINGERS
				UK
ALBUMS:	**HITS 2**		**WEEKS 17**	
SONGS OF JOY	K-Tel	5	29 Nov 75	16
20 ALL TIME EUROVISION FAVOURITES	K-Tel	44	5 Jun 76	1

Norman BROOKS · Canada

SINGLES:	HITS 1			WEEKS 1
A SKY-BLUE SHIRT AND A RAINBOW TIE	London	17	13 Nov 54	1

BROS · UK

SINGLES:	HITS 11			WEEKS 84
WHEN WILL I BE FAMOUS?	CBS	62	5 Dec 87	2
WHEN WILL I BE FAMOUS? [RE]	CBS	2	9 Jan 88	13
DROP THE BOY	CBS	2	19 Mar 88	10
I OWE YOU NOTHING	CBS	1	18 Jun 88	11
Original release reached No. 80 in 1987.				
I QUIT	CBS	4	17 Sep 88	8
CAT AMONG THE PIGEONS / SILENT NIGHT	CBS	2	3 Dec 88	8
TOO MUCH	CBS	2	29 Jul 89	7
CHOCOLATE BOX	CBS	9	7 Oct 89	6
SISTER	CBS	10	16 Dec 89	6
Dedicated to their sister who died in a car crash.				
MADLY IN LOVE	CBS	14	10 Mar 90	4
ARE YOU MINE?	Columbia	12	13 Jul 91	5
TRY	Columbia	27	21 Sep 91	4
ALBUMS:	**HITS 3**			**WEEKS 69**
PUSH	CBS	2	9 Apr 88	54
THE TIME	CBS	4	28 Oct 89	13
CHANGING FACES	Columbia	18	12 Oct 91	2

BROTHER BEYOND · UK

SINGLES:	HITS 10			WEEKS 58
HOW MANY TIMES	EMI	62	4 Apr 87	3
CHAIN-GANG SMILE	Parlophone	57	8 Aug 87	3
CAN YOU KEEP A SECRET?	Parlophone	56	23 Jan 88	4
THE HARDER I TRY	Parlophone	2	30 Jul 88	14
HE AIN'T NO COMPETITION	Parlophone	6	5 Nov 88	10
BE MY TWIN	Parlophone	14	21 Jan 89	6
CAN YOU KEEP A SECRET? (89 MIX) [RM]	Parlophone	22	1 Apr 89	5
Remixed by Phil Harding.				
DRIVE ON	Parlophone	39	28 Oct 89	4
WHEN WILL I SEE YOU AGAIN	Parlophone	43	9 Dec 89	5
TRUST	Parlophone	53	10 Mar 90	2
THE GIRL I USED TO KNOW	Parlophone	48	19 Jan 91	2
ALBUMS:	**HITS 2**			**WEEKS 24**
GET EVEN	Parlophone	9	26 Nov 88	23
TRUST	Parlophone	60	25 Nov 89	1

BROTHER BROWN featuring FRANK'EE · Denmark

SINGLES:	HITS 1			WEEKS 4
UNDER THE WATER	ffrr	18	2 Oct 99	4
Vocals by Marie Frank.				

BROTHERHOOD · UK

SINGLES:	HITS 1			WEEKS 1
ONE SHOT / NOTHING IN PARTICULAR	Bite It	55	27 Jan 96	1
ALBUMS:	**HITS 1**			**WEEKS 1**
ELEMENTALZ	Bite It	50	17 Feb 96	1

BROTHERHOOD OF MAN · UK

SINGLES:	HITS 10			WEEKS 97
UNITED WE STAND	Deram	10	14 Feb 70	9
WHERE ARE YOU GOING TO MY LOVE	Deram	22	4 Jul 70	10
SAVE YOUR KISSES FOR ME	Pye	1	13 Mar 76	16
UK's Eurovision entry in 1976, it came 1st.				
MY SWEET ROSALIE	Pye	30	19 Jun 76	7
OH BOY (THE MOOD I'M IN)	Pye	8	26 Feb 77	12
ANGELO	Pye	1	9 Jul 77	12
FIGARO	Pye	1	14 Jan 78	11
BEAUTIFUL LOVER	Pye	15	27 May 78	12
MIDDLE OF THE NIGHT	Pye	41	30 Sep 78	6
LIGHTNING FLASH	EMI	67	3 Jul 82	2
ALBUMS:	**HITS 4**			**WEEKS 40**
LOVE AND KISSES FROM	Pye	20	24 Apr 76	8
B FOR BROTHERHOOD	Pye	18	12 Aug 78	9
BROTHERHOOD OF MAN	K-Tel	6	7 Oct 78	15
BROTHERHOOD OF MAN SING 20 NUMBER ONE HITS	Warwick	14	29 Nov 80	8

BROTHERLOVE – See PRATT and McLAIN with BROTHERLOVE

BROTHERS

				UK
SINGLES:		HITS 1		WEEKS 9
SING ME	Bus Stop	8	29 Jan 77	9

BROTHERS FOUR

				US
SINGLES:		HITS 1		WEEKS 2
GREENFIELDS	Philips	49	25 Jun 60	1
GREENFIELDS [RE]	Philips	40	9 Jul 60	1

BROTHERS IN RHYTHM

				UK
SINGLES:		HITS 2		WEEKS 12
SUCH A GOOD FEELING	Fourth & Broadway	64	16 Mar 91	2
SUCH A GOOD FEELING [RI]	Fourth & Broadway	14	14 Sep 91	8
FOREVER AND A DAY	Stress	51	30 Apr 94	2
Above hit: BROTHERS IN RHYTHM present CHARVONI.				

BROTHERS JOHNSON

				US
SINGLES:		HITS 6		WEEKS 34
STRAWBERRY LETTER 23	A&M	35	9 Jul 77	5
AIN'T WE FUNKIN' NOW	A&M	43	2 Sep 78	6
RIDE-O-ROCKET	A&M	50	4 Nov 78	4
STOMP	A&M	6	23 Feb 80	12
LIGHT UP THE NIGHT	A&M	47	31 May 80	4
THE REAL THING	A&M	50	25 Jul 81	3
ALBUMS:		HITS 3		WEEKS 22
BLAM!!	A&M	48	19 Aug 78	8
LIGHT UP THE NIGHT	A&M	22	23 Feb 80	12
WINNERS	A&M	42	18 Jul 81	2

BROTHERS LIKE OUTLAW featuring Alison EVELYN

				UK
SINGLES:		HITS 1		WEEKS 1
GOOD VIBRATIONS	Gee Street	74	23 Jan 93	1

Edgar BROUGHTON BAND

				UK
SINGLES:		HITS 2		WEEKS 10
OUT DEMONS OUT	Harvest	39	18 Apr 70	5
APACHE DROPOUT [M]	Harvest	49	23 Jan 71	1
APACHE DROPOUT [M] [RE-1ST]	Harvest	35	6 Feb 71	2
APACHE DROPOUT [M] [RE-2ND]	Harvest	35	13 Mar 71	1
APACHE DROPOUT [M] [RE-3RD]	Harvest	33	27 Mar 71	1
ALBUMS:		HITS 2		WEEKS 6
SING BROTHER SING	Harvest	18	20 Jun 70	4
THE EDGAR BROUGHTON BAND	Harvest	28	5 Jun 71	2

Angie BROWN – See BIZARRE INC; MOTIV 8

Arthur BROWN – See CRAZY WORLD OF ARTHUR BROWN

Bobby BROWN

				US
SINGLES:		HITS 14		WEEKS 123
DON'T BE CRUEL	MCA	42	6 Aug 88	7
MY PREROGATIVE	MCA	6	17 Dec 88	17
DON'T BE CRUEL [RM]	MCA	13	25 Mar 89	8
EVERY LITTLE STEP	MCA	6	20 May 89	9
ON OUR OWN	MCA	4	15 Jul 89	9
From the film 'Ghostbusters II'.				
ROCK WIT'CHA	MCA	33	23 Sep 89	6
RONI	MCA	21	25 Nov 89	7
THE FREE STYLE MEGA-MIX [M]	MCA	14	9 Jun 90	7
Mix of his earlier hits.				
SHE AIN'T WORTH IT	London	12	30 Jun 90	9
Above hit: Glenn MEDEIROS (featuring Bobby BROWN).				
HUMPIN' AROUND	MCA	19	22 Aug 92	6
GOOD ENOUGH	MCA	41	17 Oct 92	4
THAT'S THE WAY LOVE IS	MCA	56	19 Jun 93	2
SOMETHING IN COMMON	MCA	16	22 Jan 94	5
Above hit: Bobby BROWN (Duet with Whitney HOUSTON).				
TWO CAN PLAY THAT GAME	MCA	38	25 Jun 94	3
TWO CAN PLAY THAT GAME [RE]	MCA	3	1 Apr 95	12
HUMPIN' AROUND [RM]	MCA	8	8 Jul 95	6
Remixed by K Klass.				
MY PREROGATIVE [RM]	MCA	17	14 Oct 95	3
Remixed by Joe T. Vannelli.				
EVERY LITTLE STEP [RM]	MCA	25	3 Feb 96	2
Remixed by CJ Mackintosh.				

FEELIN' INSIDE	MCA	40	22 Nov 97	1
ALBUMS:	**HITS 5**		**WEEKS 65**	
DON'T BE CRUEL	MCA	3	28 Jan 89	41
KING OF STAGE	MCA	40	5 Aug 89	6
DANCE! . . . YA KNOW IT!	MCA	26	2 Dec 89	10
BOBBY	MCA	11	5 Sep 92	5
TWO CAN PLAY THAT GAME	MCA	24	5 Aug 95	3

Compilation (mainly remixes of hit singles).

Carl BROWN – See DOUBLE TROUBLE

Dennis BROWN   Jamaica

SINGLES:	**HITS 3**		**WEEKS 18**	
MONEY IN MY POCKET	Lightning	14	3 Mar 79	9
LOVE HAS FOUND ITS WAY	A&M	47	3 Jul 82	6
HALFWAY UP, HALFWAY DOWN	A&M	56	11 Sep 82	3
ALBUMS:	**HITS 1**		**WEEKS 6**	
LOVE HAS FOUND ITS WAY	A&M	72	26 Jun 82	6

Diana BROWN and Barrie K. SHARPE   UK

SINGLES:	**HITS 4**		**WEEKS 11**	
THE MASTERPLAN	ffrr	39	2 Jun 90	6
SUN WORSHIPPERS (POSITIVE THINKING)	ffrr	61	1 Sep 90	2
LOVE OR NOTHING	ffrr	71	23 Mar 91	1
EATING ME ALIVE	ffrr	53	27 Jun 92	2

Errol BROWN   UK

SINGLES:	**HITS 2**		**WEEKS 10**	
PERSONAL TOUCH	WEA	25	4 Jul 87	8
BODY ROCKIN'	WEA	51	28 Nov 87	2

Foxy BROWN   US

(See also Nas Escobar, Foxy Brown, AZ and Nature present the Firm featuring Dawn Robinson; Jay-Z.)

SINGLES:	**HITS 6**		**WEEKS 20**	
TOUCH ME TEASE ME	Def Jam	26	21 Sep 96	3

From the film 'The Nutty Professor'.
Above hit: CASE featuring Foxy BROWN.

GET ME HOME	Def Jam	11	8 Mar 97	5

Based on Eugene Wilde's Gotta Get You Home Tonight.
Above hit: Foxy BROWN featuring BLACKSTREET.

AIN'T NO PLAYA	Northwestside	31	10 May 97	2

Above hit: JAY-Z featuring Foxy BROWN.

I'LL BE	Def Jam	9	21 Jun 97	5

Samples Rene And Angela's I'll Be Good and Blondie's Rapture.
Above hit: Foxy BROWN featuring JAY Z.

BIG BAD MAMMA	Def Jam	12	11 Oct 97	3

From the film 'How To Be A Player'.
Above hit: Foxy BROWN featuring DRU HILL.

HOT SPOT	Def Jam	31	13 Mar 99	2
ALBUMS:	**HITS 1**		**WEEKS 1**	
CHYNA DOLL	Def Jam	51	6 Feb 99	1

Gloria D. BROWN   US

SINGLES:	**HITS 1**		**WEEKS 3**	
THE MORE THEY KNOCK THE MORE I LOVE YOU	10 Records	57	8 Jun 85	3

Horace BROWN   US

SINGLES:	**HITS 3**		**WEEKS 7**	
TASTE YOUR LOVE	Uptown	58	25 Feb 95	1
ONE FOR THE MONEY	Motown	12	18 May 96	4
THINGS WE DO FOR LOVE	Motown	27	12 Oct 96	2
ALBUMS:	**HITS 1**		**WEEKS 1**	
HORACE BROWN	Motown	48	6 Jul 96	1

Ian BROWN   UK

SINGLES:	**HITS 5**		**WEEKS 20**	
MY STAR	Polydor	5	24 Jan 98	4
CORPSES	Polydor	14	4 Apr 98	4

Backing vocals by Noel Gallagher.

CAN'T SEE ME	Polydor	21	20 Jun 98	3
BE THERE	Mo Wax	8	20 Feb 99	6

Above hit: UNKLE featuring Ian BROWN.

LOVE LIKE A FOUNTAIN	Polydor	23	6 Nov 99	3

ALBUMS:		HITS 2			WEEKS 26
UNFINISHED MONKEY BUSINESS	Polydor	4	14 Feb 98	24
GOLDEN GREATS	Polydor	14	20 Nov 99	2

Jackie BROWN - See Anthony STEEL with the RADIO REVELLERS and Jackie BROWN and his Music

James BROWN
US

SINGLES:		HITS 18			WEEKS 103
PAPA'S GOT A BRAND NEW BAG	London	25	25 Sep 65	7
I GOT YOU	Pye International	29	26 Feb 66	6
IT'S A MAN'S MAN'S MAN'S WORLD	Pye International	13	18 Jun 66	9
Above 3: James BROWN and the FAMOUS FLAMES.				
GET UP I FEEL LIKE BEING A SEX MACHINE	Polydor	32	10 Oct 70	7
HEY AMERICA !	Mojo	47	27 Nov 71	3
GET UP OFFA THAT THING	Polydor	22	18 Sep 76	6
Sub credit: James Brown – Minister Of New New Super Heavy Funk.				
BODYHEAT	Polydor	36	29 Jan 77	4
Sub credit: James Brown – Brand New Sound.				
RAPP PAYBACK (WHERE IZ MOSES ?)	RCA	39	10 Jan 81	5
BRING IT ON . . . BRING IT ON	Sonet	45	2 Jul 83	4
UNITY (PART 1 – THE THIRD COMING)	Tommy Boy	49	1 Sep 84	5
Above hit: Afrika BAMBAATAA and the Godfather Of Soul – James BROWN.				
FROGGY MIX [M]	Boiling Point	50	27 Apr 85	3
Megamix of 12 songs.				
GET UP I FEEL LIKE BEING A SEX MACHINE [RI-1ST]	Boiling Point	47	1 Jun 85	5
LIVING IN AMERICA	Scotti Brothers	5	25 Jan 86	10
From the film 'Rocky IV'.				
GET UP I FEEL LIKE BEING A SEX MACHINE [RI-1ST] [RE]	Boiling Point	46	1 Mar 86	4
GRAVITY	Scotti Brothers	65	18 Oct 86	2
SHE'S THE ONE	Urban	45	30 Jan 88	3
THE PAYBACK MIX PART ONE [M]	Urban	12	23 Apr 88	6
Mixed by Coldcut.				
I'M REAL	Scotti Brothers	31	4 Jun 88	4
Above hit: James BROWN with FULL FORCE.				
I GOT YOU (I FEEL GOOD) [RI]	A&M	52	23 Jul 88	
[AA] listed with Nowhere To Run by Martha Reeves and the Vandellas.				
GET UP (I FEEL LIKE BEING A) SEX MACHINE [RI-2ND]	Polydor	69	16 Nov 91	2
I GOT YOU (I FEEL GOOD) [RM]	FBI	72	24 Oct 92	1
Above hit: James BROWN v DAKEYNE.				
CAN'T GET ANY HARDER	Polydor	59	17 Apr 93	2
FUNK ON AH ROLL	Eagle	40	17 Apr 99	2
Samples his own track, Hot Pants.				

ALBUMS:		HITS 4			WEEKS 51
GRAVITY	Scotti Brothers	85	18 Oct 86	3
THE BEST OF JAMES BROWN – THE GODFATHER OF SOUL	K-Tel	17	10 Oct 87	21
I'M REAL	Scotti Brothers	27	25 Jun 88	5
SEX MACHINE – THE VERY BEST OF JAMES BROWN	Polydor	19	16 Nov 91	22

Jennifer BROWN
Sweden

SINGLES:		HITS 1			WEEKS 1
TUESDAY AFTERNOON	RCA	57	1 May 99	1

Joanne BROWN - See Tony OSBORNE SOUND featuring Joanne BROWN

Jocelyn BROWN
US

(See also Todd Terry.)

SINGLES:		HITS 16			WEEKS 58
SOMEBODY ELSE'S GUY	Fourth & Broadway	13	21 Apr 84	9
I WISH YOU WOULD	Fourth & Broadway	51	22 Sep 84	3
LOVE'S GONNA GET YOU	Warner Brothers	70	15 Mar 86	1
ALWAYS THERE	Talkin Loud	6	29 Jun 91	9
Above hit: INCOGNITO featuring Jocelyn BROWN.				
SHE GOT SOUL	A&M	57	14 Sep 91	3
Above hit: JAMESTOWN featuring Jocelyn BROWN.				
DON'T TALK JUST KISS	Tug	3	7 Dec 91	11
Above hit: RIGHT SAID FRED guest vocal Jocelyn BROWN.				
TAKE ME UP	A&M	61	20 Mar 93	1
Above hit: SONIC SURFERS featuring Jocelyn BROWN.				
NO MORE TEARS (ENOUGH IS ENOUGH)	Bell	13	11 Jun 94	7
Above hit: Kym MAZELLE and Jocelyn BROWN.				
GIMME ALL YOUR LOVIN'	Bell	22	8 Oct 94	3
Above hit: Jocelyn BROWN and Kym MAZELLE.				
IT'S ALRIGHT, I FEEL IT!	Talkin Loud	26	10 May 97	2
I AM THE BLACK GOLD OF THE SUN	Talkin Loud	31	25 Oct 97	2
Originally recorded by Minnie Riperton's band the Rotary Connection.				
Above 2: NUYORICAN SOUL featuring Jocelyn BROWN.				

Abba's 'Lay All Your Love On Me' was the first hit to be available only as a 12" single. (LFI)

*At 68 years old **Louis Armstrong** is the oldest male soloist to top the singles chart. (LFI)*

***AC/DC** have scored a record 27 hits without reaching the Top 10. (LFI)*

***Aqua** were the first act from outside the UK to have their first three hits top the chart. (LFI)*

Winifred Atwell *was the first black female artist to reach No.1. (LFI)*

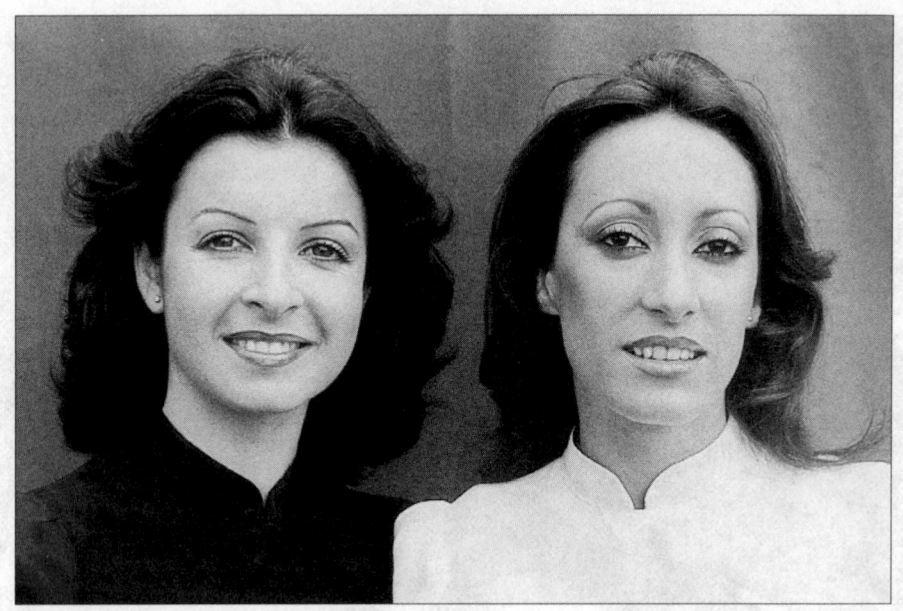

*The first female duo to top the chart was **Baccara**. (LFI)*

B*Witched *were the first act to have their first four singles enter the chart at the top. (LFI)*

*When 'I Want To Hold Your Hand' replaced 'She Loves You' at No.1, **The Beatles** became the first act to enjoy consecutive chart toppers. (LFI)*

Harry Belafonte was the first black male soloist to top the chart. (LFI)

*The Millennium Chimes by **Big Ben** clocks in at a mere 1 minute 22 seconds, making it the shortest 'song' in the book.*

The Bee Gees *have written 36 UK Top 10 hits. (LFI)*

On 11th October 1986 **Nick Berry**'s 'Every Loser Wins' rocketed from No.66 to No.4; it remains the biggest jump within the chart in history. (LFI)

Blondie *are the only American group to have No.1 hits in the '70s, '80s and '90s. (LFI)*

HAPPINESS	S3	45	22 Nov 97	1
Above hit: KAMASULTRA featuring Jocelyn BROWN.				
FUN	INCredible	33	2 May 98	2
Above hit: DA MOB featuring Jocelyn BROWN.				
AIN'T NO MOUNTAIN HIGH ENOUGH	INCredible	35	29 Aug 98	2
I BELIEVE	Playola	62	27 Mar 99	1
Above hit: JAMESTOWN featuring Jocelyn BROWN.				
IT'S ALL GOOD	INCredible	54	3 Jul 99	1
Above hit: DA MOB featuring Jocelyn BROWN.				

Joe BROWN and the BRUVVERS — UK

SINGLES:	HITS 11			WEEKS 92
THE DARKTOWN STRUTTERS BALL	Decca	34	19 Mar 60	6
Originally recorded by Original Dixieland Jazz Band.				
SHINE	Pye	33	28 Jan 61	6
Above hit: Joe BROWN.				
WHAT A CRAZY WORLD WE'RE LIVING IN	Piccadilly	37	13 Jan 62	2
Recorded during his act at the Granada, Woolwich.				
A PICTURE OF YOU	Piccadilly	2	19 May 62	19
YOUR TENDER LOOK	Piccadilly	31	15 Sep 62	6
IT ONLY TOOK A MINUTE	Piccadilly	6	17 Nov 62	13
THAT'S WHAT LOVE WILL DO	Piccadilly	3	9 Feb 63	14
IT ONLY TOOK A MINUTE [RE]	Piccadilly	50	23 Feb 63	1
NATURE'S TIME FOR LOVE	Piccadilly	26	29 Jun 63	6
SALLY ANN	Piccadilly	28	28 Sep 63	9
WITH A LITTLE HELP FROM MY FRIENDS	Pye	32	2 Jul 67	4
HEY MAMA	Ammo	33	14 Apr 73	6
Above 2: Joe BROWN.				
EPS:	HITS 1			WEEKS 1
JOE BROWN HIT PARADE	Piccadilly	20	28 Sep 63	1
Above hit: Joe BROWN.				
ALBUMS:	HITS 2			WEEKS 47
A PICTURE OF YOU	Pye Golden Guinea	3	1 Sep 62	39
JOE BROWN - LIVE	Piccadilly	14	25 May 63	8
Above hit: Joe BROWN.				

Karen BROWN - See DJs RULE

Kathy BROWN — US

SINGLES:	HITS 2			WEEKS 6
TURN ME OUT	Stress	44	25 Nov 95	2
Original release reached No. 86 in 1994.				
TURN ME OUT (TURN TO SUGAR) [RM]	ffrr	35	20 Sep 97	3
Remixed by The Sol Brothers.				
Above 2: PRAXIS featuring Kathy BROWN.				
JOY	Azuli	63	10 Apr 99	1

Miquel BROWN — US

SINGLES:	HITS 2			WEEKS 7
HE'S A SAINT, HE'S A SINNER	Record Shack	68	18 Feb 84	4
CLOSE TO PERFECTION	Record Shack	63	24 Aug 85	3

Peter BROWN — US

SINGLES:	HITS 2			WEEKS 9
DO YA WANNA GET FUNKY WITH ME	TK	43	11 Feb 78	4
DANCE WITH ME	TK	57	17 Jun 78	5
Above hit: Peter BROWN – Special background vocals: Betty WRIGHT.				

Polly BROWN — UK

SINGLES:	HITS 1			WEEKS 5
UP IN A PUFF OF SMOKE	GTO	43	14 Sep 74	5

Roy 'Chubby' BROWN — UK

SINGLES:	HITS 2			WEEKS 22
LIVING NEXT DOOR TO ALICE (WHO THE F**K IS ALICE?)	N.O.W.	64	13 May 95	2
Above hit: SMOKIE featuring Roy Chubby BROWN.				
LIVING NEXT DOOR TO ALICE (WHO THE F**K IS ALICE?) [RE]	N.O.W.	3	26 Aug 95	17
ROCKIN' GOOD CHRISTMAS	PolyStar	51	21 Dec 96	3
ALBUMS:	HITS 2			WEEKS 8
TAKE FAT AND PARTY	PolyStar	29	25 Nov 95	7
FAT OUT OF HELL	PolyStar	67	7 Dec 96	1

Sam BROWN | | | | | UK

SINGLES:		HITS 5			WEEKS 35
STOP	A&M		52	11 Jun 88	3
STOP [RE]	A&M		4	4 Feb 89	12
CAN I GET A WITNESS?	A&M		15	13 May 89	7
WITH A LITTLE LOVE	A&M		44	3 Mar 90	4
KISSING GATE	A&M		23	5 May 90	8
JUST GOOD FRIENDS	The Dick Brothers		63	26 Aug 95	1
Above hit: FISH featuring Sam BROWN.					
ALBUMS:		HITS 2			WEEKS 30
STOP!	A&M		4	11 Mar 89	18
APRIL MOON	A&M		38	14 Apr 90	12

Sharon BROWN | | | | | US

SINGLES:		HITS 1			WEEKS 11
I SPECIALIZE IN LOVE	Virgin		38	17 Apr 82	9
I SPECIALIZE IN LOVE [RM]	Deep Distraxion		62	26 Feb 94	2
Remixed by Tommy D & Paul Gotel.					

BROWN SAUCE | | | | | UK

SINGLES:		HITS 1			WEEKS 12
I WANNA BE A WINNER	BBC		15	12 Dec 81	12

Duncan BROWNE | | | | | UK

SINGLES:		HITS 2			WEEKS 8
JOURNEY	RAK		23	19 Aug 72	6
THEME FROM TRAVELLING MAN	Towerbell		68	22 Dec 84	2
From the Granada TV series.					

Jackson BROWNE | | | | | US

SINGLES:		HITS 3			WEEKS 14
STAY	Asylum		12	1 Jul 78	11
IN THE SHAPE OF A HEART	Elektra		66	18 Oct 86	2
EVERYWHERE I GO	Elektra		67	25 Jun 94	1
ALBUMS:		HITS 8			WEEKS 37
THE PRETENDER	Asylum		26	4 Dec 76	5
RUNNING ON EMPTY	Asylum		28	21 Jan 78	7
HOLD OUT	Asylum		44	12 Jul 80	5
LAWYERS IN LOVE	Asylum		37	13 Aug 83	7
LIVES IN THE BALANCE	Asylum		36	8 Mar 86	7
WORLD IN MOTION	Elektra		39	17 Jun 89	2
I'M ALIVE	Elektra		35	6 Nov 93	3
LOOKING EAST	Elektra		47	9 Mar 96	1

Ronnie BROWNE – See SCOTTISH RUGBY TEAM with Ronnie BROWNE

Tom BROWNE | | | | | US

SINGLES:		HITS 3			WEEKS 24
FUNKIN' FOR JAMAICA (N.Y.)	Arista		10	19 Jul 80	11
THIGHS HIGH (GRIP YOUR HIPS AND MOVE)	Arista		45	25 Oct 80	5
FUNGI MAMA (BEBOPAFUNKADISCOLYPSO)	Arista		58	30 Jan 82	4
FUNKIN' FOR JAMAICA (1991 REMIX) [RM]	Arista		45	11 Jan 92	4

BROWNS | | | | | US

SINGLES:		HITS 1			WEEKS 13
THE THREE BELLS (LES TROIS CLOCHES)	RCA		6	19 Sep 59	13

BROWNSTONE | | | | | US

SINGLES:		HITS 5			WEEKS 24
IF YOU LOVE ME	MJJ Productions		8	1 Apr 95	12
GRAPEVYNE	MJJ Productions		16	15 Jul 95	4
I CAN'T TELL YOU WHY	MJJ Productions		27	23 Sep 95	2
Originally recorded by the Eagles.					
5 MILES TO EMPTY	Epic		12	17 May 97	4
KISS AND TELL	Epic		21	27 Sep 97	2
ALBUMS:		HITS 2			WEEKS 16
FROM THE BOTTOM UP	MJJ Productions		18	29 Apr 95	13
STILL CLIMBING Epic			19	31 May 97	3

BROWNSVILLE STATION | | | | | US

SINGLES:		HITS 1			WEEKS 6
SMOKIN' IN THE BOY'S ROOM	Philips		27	2 Mar 74	6

Dave BRUBECK QUARTET — US

SINGLES:	HITS 3			WEEKS 30
TAKE FIVE	Fontana	6	28 Oct 61	15
IT'S A RAGGY WALTZ	Fontana	36	10 Feb 62	3
UNSQUARE DANCE	CBS	14	19 May 62	12
EPS:	HITS 2			WEEKS 41
BRUBECK IN EUROPE	Fontana	15	26 Mar 60	1
TAKE FIVE	Fontana	4	30 Sep 61	40
Above 2: Dave BRUBECK.				
ALBUMS:	HITS 2			WEEKS 17
TIME OUT	Fontana	11	25 Jun 60	1
TIME FURTHER OUT	Fontana	12	7 Apr 62	16
Above hit: Dave BRUBECK.				

Jack BRUCE — UK

ALBUMS:	HITS 1			WEEKS 9
SONGS FOR A TAILOR	Polydor	6	27 Sep 69	9

Tommy BRUCE and the BRUISERS — US

(See also Bruisers.)

SINGLES:	HITS 3			WEEKS 21
AIN'T MISBEHAVIN'	Columbia	3	28 May 60	16
Originally recorded by Fats Waller.				
BROKEN DOLL	Columbia	36	10 Sep 60	4
BABETTE	Columbia	50	24 Feb 62	1
Above hit: Tommy BRUCE.				

Claudia BRUCKEN — Germany

SINGLES:	HITS 2			WEEKS 2
ABSOLUT(E)	Island	71	11 Aug 90	1
KISS LIKE ETHER	Island	63	16 Feb 91	1

BRUISERS — UK

(See also Tommy Bruce and the Bruisers.)

SINGLES:	HITS 1			WEEKS 7
BLUE GIRL	Parlophone	31	10 Aug 63	6
BLUE GIRL [RE]	Parlophone	47	28 Sep 63	1

Frank BRUNO — UK

SINGLES:	HITS 1			WEEKS 4
EYE OF THE TIGER	RCA	28	23 Dec 95	4

BRUNO and LIZ and the RADIO 1 POSSE – See Liz KERSHAW and Bruno BROOKES

Tyrone BRUNSON — US

SINGLES:	HITS 1			WEEKS 5
THE SMURF	Epic	52	25 Dec 82	5

Dora BRYAN — UK

SINGLES:	HITS 1			WEEKS 6
ALL I WANT FOR CHRISTMAS IS A BEATLE	Fontana	20	7 Dec 63	6

Kelle BRYAN — UK

SINGLES:	HITS 1			WEEKS 4
HIGHER THAN HEAVEN	Mercury	14	2 Oct 99	4

Anita BRYANT — US

SINGLES:	HITS 2			WEEKS 6
PAPER ROSES	London	49	28 May 60	1
PAPER ROSES [RE-1ST]	London	45	2 Jul 60	1
PAPER ROSES [RE-2ND]	London	24	16 Jul 60	2
MY LITTLE CORNER OF THE WORLD	London	48	8 Oct 60	2

Peabo BRYSON — US

(See also Peabo Bryson and Roberta Flack.)

SINGLES:	HITS 3			WEEKS 22
BEAUTY AND THE BEAST	Epic	9	16 May 92	7
From the Walt Disney film of the same name.				
Above hit: Celine DION and Peabo BRYSON.				
BY THE TIME THIS NIGHT IS OVER	Arista	56	17 Jul 93	3
Above hit: Kenny G with Peabo BRYSON.				

| A WHOLE NEW WORLD (ALADDIN'S THEME) | Columbia | 12 | 11 Dec 93 | 12 |

From the Walt Disney film 'Aladdin'.
Above hit: Regina BELLE and Peabo BRYSON.

Peabo BRYSON and Roberta FLACK   US

(See also Peabo Bryson; Roberta Flack; Roberta Flack and Donny Hathaway.)

SINGLES:	HITS 1			WEEKS 13
TONIGHT I CELEBRATE MY LOVE	Capitol	2	20 Aug 83	13
ALBUMS:	HITS 1			WEEKS 10
BORN TO LOVE	Capitol	15	17 Sep 83	10

BT   US

SINGLES:	HITS 8			WEEKS 23
EMBRACING THE SUNSHINE	East West	34	18 Mar 95	2
LOVING YOU MORE	Perfecto	28	16 Sep 95	2
LOVING YOU MORE [RM]	Perfecto	14	10 Feb 96	3

Above 2: BT featuring Vincent COVELLO.

| BLUE SKIES | Perfecto | 26 | 9 Nov 96 | 2 |

Above hit: BT featuring Tori AMOS.

FLAMING JUNE	Perfecto	19	19 Jul 97	4
LOVE, PEACE AND GREASE	Perfecto	41	29 Nov 97	1
FLAMING JUNE [RI]	Perfecto	28	10 Jan 98	4
REMEMBER	Perfecto	27	18 Apr 98	2
GODSPEED	Renaissance Music	54	21 Nov 98	1
MERCURY AND SOLACE	Headspace	38	9 Oct 99	2

Above hit: BT featuring vocals by Jan JOHNSTON.

ALBUMS:	HITS 2			WEEKS 5
IMA	Perfecto	45	21 Oct 95	4
ESCM	Perfecto	35	4 Oct 97	1

BUBBLER RANX - See Peter ANDRE

BUBBLEROCK - See Jonathan KING

BUCCANEER - See PHOEBE ONE featuring RED RAT, GOOFY and BUCCANEER

Catherine BUCHANAN - See JELLYBEAN

Roy BUCHANAN   US

SINGLES:	HITS 1			WEEKS 3
SWEET DREAMS	Polydor	40	31 Mar 73	3

Originally recorded by Don Gibson.

Kenny "Dope" presents the BUCKETHEADS   US

SINGLES:	HITS 2			WEEKS 16
THE BOMB (THESE SOUNDS FALL INTO MY MIND)	Positiva	5	4 Mar 95	13

Samples Chicago's Streetplayer.

| GOT MYSELF TOGETHER | Positiva | 12 | 20 Jan 96 | 3 |

Samples Brass Construction's Movin'.

ALBUMS:	HITS 1			WEEKS 1
ALL IN THE MIND	Positiva	74	27 Jan 96	1

Lindsey BUCKINGHAM   US

SINGLES:	HITS 1			WEEKS 7
TROUBLE	Mercury	31	16 Jan 82	7
ALBUMS:	HITS 1			WEEKS 1
OUT OF THE CRADLE	Mercury	51	8 Aug 92	1

Jeff BUCKLEY   US

SINGLES:	HITS 2			WEEKS 3
LAST GOODBYE	Columbia	54	27 May 95	2
EVERYBODY HERE WANTS YOU	Columbia	43	6 Jun 98	1
ALBUMS:	HITS 2			WEEKS 10
GRACE	Columbia	50	27 Aug 94	6
SKETCHES FOR MY SWEETHEART THE DRUNK	Columbia	7	23 May 98	4

Compilation including his final session recordings.

BUCKS FIZZ   UK

SINGLES:	HITS 20			WEEKS 150
MAKING YOUR MIND UP	RCA	1	28 Mar 81	12

UK's Eurovision entry in 1981, it came 1st.

PIECE OF THE ACTION	RCA	12	6 Jun 81	9
ONE OF THOSE NIGHTS	RCA	20	15 Aug 81	10
THE LAND OF MAKE BELIEVE	RCA	1	28 Nov 81	16

MY CAMERA NEVER LIES	*RCA*	1	*27 Mar 82*	8
NOW THOSE DAYS ARE GONE	*RCA*	8	*19 Jun 82*	9
IF YOU CAN'T STAND THE HEAT	*RCA*	10	*27 Nov 82*	11
RUN FOR YOUR LIFE	*RCA*	14	*12 Mar 83*	7
WHEN WE WERE YOUNG	*RCA*	10	*18 Jun 83*	8
LONDON TOWN	*RCA*	34	*1 Oct 83*	6
RULES OF THE GAME	*RCA*	57	*17 Dec 83*	6
TALKING IN YOUR SLEEP	*RCA*	15	*25 Aug 84*	9
GOLDEN DAYS	*RCA*	42	*27 Oct 84*	4
I HEAR TALK	*RCA*	34	*29 Dec 84*	8
YOU AND YOUR HEART SO BLUE	*RCA*	43	*22 Jun 85*	4
MAGICAL	*RCA*	57	*14 Sep 85*	3
NEW BEGINNING (MAMBA SEYRA)	*Polydor*	8	*7 Jun 86*	10
LOVE THE ONE YOU'RE WITH	*Polydor*	47	*30 Aug 86*	3
KEEP EACH OTHER WARM	*Polydor*	45	*15 Nov 86*	4
HEART OF STONE	*RCA*	50	*5 Nov 88*	3
ALBUMS:	**HITS 6**			**WEEKS 80**
BUCKS FIZZ	*RCA*	14	*8 Aug 81*	28
ARE YOU READY?	*RCA*	10	*8 May 82*	23
HAND CUT	*RCA*	17	*19 Mar 83*	13
GREATEST HITS	*RCA*	25	*3 Dec 83*	13
I HEAR TALK	*RCA*	66	*24 Nov 84*	2
THE WRITING ON THE WALL	*Polydor*	89	*13 Dec 86*	1

BUCKSHOT LEFONQUE — US

SINGLES:	**HITS 1**			**WEEKS 1**
ANOTHER DAY	*Columbia*	65	*6 Dec 97*	1

Harold BUDD, Elizabeth FRASER, Robin GUTHRIE and Simon RAYMONDE — UK

ALBUMS:	**HITS 1**			**WEEKS 2**
THE MOON AND THE MELODIES	*4AD*	46	*22 Nov 86*	2

Roy BUDD — UK

SINGLES:	**HITS 1**			**WEEKS 1**
THE THEME FROM GET CARTER	*Cinephile*	68	*10 Jul 99*	1
ALBUMS:	**HITS 1**			**WEEKS 1**
GET CARTER [OST]	*Cinephile*	68	*19 Sep 98*	1

First UK release of the original 1970 film soundtrack.

BUDGIE — UK

SINGLES:	**HITS 1**			**WEEKS 2**
KEEPING A RENDEZVOUS	*RCA*	71	*3 Oct 81*	2
ALBUMS:	**HITS 4**			**WEEKS 10**
IN FOR THE KILL	*MCA*	29	*8 Jun 74*	3
BANDOLIER	*MCA*	36	*27 Sep 75*	4
NIGHT FLIGHT	*RCA*	68	*31 Oct 81*	2
DELIVER US FROM EVIL	*RCA*	62	*23 Oct 82*	1

BUFFALO TOM — US

SINGLES:	**HITS 1**			**WEEKS 5**
GOING UNDERGROUND	*Ignition*	6	*23 Oct 99*	5

[AA] listed with Carnation by Liam Gallagher and Steve Cradock. From the Jam tribute album Fire & Skill.

ALBUMS:	**HITS 3**			**WEEKS 5**
LET ME COME OVER	*Situation Two*	49	*14 Mar 92*	1
(BIG RED LETTER DAY)	*Beggars Banquet*	17	*9 Oct 93*	3
SLEEPY EYED	*Beggars Banquet*	31	*22 Jul 95*	1

BUG KANN and the PLASTIC JAM — UK

SINGLES:	**HITS 1**			**WEEKS 2**
MADE IN TWO MINUTES	*Optimum Dance*	70	*31 Aug 91*	1

Above hit: BUG KANN and the PLASTIC JAM featuring Patti LOW and DOOGIE.

MADE IN TWO MINUTES [RM]	*PWL*	64	*26 Feb 94*	1

BUGGLES — UK

SINGLES:	**HITS 4**			**WEEKS 28**
VIDEO KILLED THE RADIO STAR	*Island*	1	*22 Sep 79*	11

The first video shown on MTV in America. Originally recorded by Bruce Wooley.

LIVING IN THE PLASTIC AGE	*Island*	16	*26 Jan 80*	8
CLEAN, CLEAN	*Island*	38	*5 Apr 80*	5
ELSTREE	*Island*	55	*8 Nov 80*	4

125

ALBUMS:	HITS 1			WEEKS 6	
THE AGE OF PLASTIC	Island	27	16 Feb 80		6

James BULLER
UK

SINGLES:	HITS 1			WEEKS 1	
CAN'T SMILE WITHOUT YOU	BBC Music	51	6 Mar 99		1

From the BBC TV series 'Sunburn'. Originally recorded by David Martin.

B. BUMBLE and the STINGERS
US

SINGLES:	HITS 1			WEEKS 26	
NUT ROCKER	Top Rank	1	21 Apr 62		15

Based upon Tchaikovsky's Nutcracker Suite. Originally recorded by Jack B. Nimble and the Quicks.

NUT ROCKER [RI]	Stateside	19	3 Jun 72		11

BUMP
UK

SINGLES:	HITS 1			WEEKS 5	
I'M RUSHING	Good Boy	40	4 Jul 92		4
I'M RUSHIN' 95 [RM]	Deconstruction	45	11 Nov 95		1

Remixed by David Valentine.

BUMP and FLEX
UK

SINGLES:	HITS 1			WEEKS 1	
LONG TIME COMING	Heat Recordings	73	23 May 98		1

Originally released in 1997.

BUNKER KRU/HARLEQUIN 4'S
US

SINGLES:	HITS 1			WEEKS 4	
SET IT OFF (BUNKER '88 MIX)	Champion	55	19 Mar 88		4

Original release reached No. 78 in 1986.

Emma BUNTON – See TIN TIN OUT

Eric BURDON and WAR
UK

(See also Animals; War.)

ALBUMS:	HITS 1			WEEKS 2	
ERIC BURDON DECLARES WAR	Polydor	50	3 Oct 70		2

Geoffrey BURGON
UK

SINGLES:	HITS 1			WEEKS 4	
BRIDESHEAD THEME	Chrysalis	48	26 Dec 81		4

From the Granada ITV series.

ALBUMS:	HITS 1			WEEKS 12	
BRIDESHEAD REVISITED [OST-TV]	Chrysalis	50	21 Nov 81		12

Keni BURKE
US

SINGLES:	HITS 2			WEEKS 4	
LET SOMEBODY LOVE YOU	RCA	59	27 Jun 81		3
RISIN' TO THE TOP	RCA	70	18 Apr 92		1

Original release reached No. 96 in 1987.

Jean-Jacques BURNEL
UK

(See also Dave Greenfield and Jean-Jacques Burnel.)

ALBUMS:	HITS 1			WEEKS 5	
EUROMAN COMETH	United Artists	40	21 Apr 79		5

Hank C. BURNETTE
Sweden

SINGLES:	HITS 1			WEEKS 8	
SPINNING ROCK BOOGIE	Sonet	21	30 Oct 76		8

Johnny BURNETTE
US

SINGLES:	HITS 5			WEEKS 48	
DREAMIN'	London	5	1 Oct 60		16
YOU'RE SIXTEEN	London	3	14 Jan 61		12

Originally called You're 13.

LITTLE BOY SAD	London	12	15 Apr 61		12
GIRLS	London	37	12 Aug 61		5
CLOWN SHOES	Liberty	35	19 May 62		3

Rocky BURNETTE
US

SINGLES:		HITS 1		WEEKS 7
TIRED OF TOEIN' THE LINE	EMI	58	17 Nov 79	7

Features Dave Edmunds on guitar.

Jerry BURNS
UK

SINGLES:		HITS 1		WEEKS 1
PALE RED	Columbia	64	25 Apr 92	1

Ray BURNS
UK

SINGLES:		HITS 2		WEEKS 19
MOBILE	Columbia	4	12 Feb 55	13

Above hit: Ray BURNS with Eric JUPP and his Orchestra.

THAT'S HOW A LOVE SONG WAS BORN	Columbia	14	27 Aug 55	6

Above hit: Ray BURNS with the CORONETS.

Malandra BURROWS
UK

SINGLES:		HITS 3		WEEKS 10
JUST THIS SIDE OF LOVE	Yorkshire Television Entertainment	11	1 Dec 90	8

From the Yorkshire TV series 'Emmerdale'.

CARNIVAL IN HEAVEN	warner.esp	49	18 Oct 97	1
DON'T LEAVE ME	warner.esp	54	29 Aug 98	1

Jenny BURTON
US

SINGLES:		HITS 1		WEEKS 2
BAD HABITS	Atlantic	68	30 Mar 85	2

BURUNDI STEIPHENSON BLACK
Burundi/France

SINGLES:		HITS 1		WEEKS 14
BURUNDI BLACK	Barclay	31	13 Nov 71	14

BUS STOP
UK/Jamaica

SINGLES:		HITS 3		WEEKS 18
KUNG FU FIGHTING	All Around The World	8	23 May 98	11

Samples Douglas' original vocal.
Above hit: BUS STOP featuring Carl DOUGLAS.

YOU AIN'T SEEN NOTHING YET	All Around The World	22	24 Oct 98	4

Featured in the ITV series 'Gladiators', accompanying a game called Vertigo.
Above hit: BUS STOP featuring Randy BACHMAN.

JUMP	All Around The World	23	10 Apr 99	3

BUS75 – See WHALE

Lou BUSCH and his Orchestra
US

(See also Joe 'Fingers' Carr.)

SINGLES:		HITS 1		WEEKS 17
ZAMBESI	Capitol	2	28 Jan 56	17

BUSH
UK

SINGLES:		HITS 5		WEEKS 11
MACHINEHEAD	Interscope	48	8 Jun 96	2
SWALLOWED	Interscope	7	1 Mar 97	5
GREEDY FLY	Interscope	22	7 Jun 97	2
BONEDRIVEN	Interscope	49	1 Nov 97	1
THE CHEMICALS BETWEEN US	Trauma	46	4 Dec 99	1
ALBUMS:		HITS 3		WEEKS 17
SIXTEEN STONE	Atlantic	42	15 Jun 96	3
RAZORBLADE SUITCASE	Interscope	4	1 Feb 97	12
THE SCIENCE OF THINGS	Polydor	28	6 Nov 99	2

Kate BUSH
UK

SINGLES:		HITS 26		WEEKS 168
WUTHERING HEIGHTS	EMI	1	11 Feb 78	12
WUTHERING HEIGHTS [RE]	EMI	75	13 May 78	1
THE MAN WITH THE CHILD IN HIS EYES	EMI	6	10 Jun 78	11
HAMMER HORROR	EMI	44	11 Nov 78	6
WOW	EMI	14	17 Mar 79	10
KATE BUSH ON STAGE [EP]	EMI	10	15 Sep 79	9

Lead track: Them Heavy People. Live recordings from a benefit concert at Hammersmith Odeon, London, 12 May 79.

BREATHING	EMI	16	26 Apr 80	7
BABOOSHKA	EMI	5	5 Jul 80	10
ARMY DREAMERS	EMI	16	4 Oct 80	9

DECEMBER WILL BE MAGIC AGAIN	EMI	29	6 Dec 80	7
SAT IN YOUR LAP	EMI	11	11 Jul 81	7
THE DREAMING	EMI	48	7 Aug 82	3
RUNNING UP THAT HILL	EMI	3	17 Aug 85	11
CLOUDBUSTING	EMI	20	26 Oct 85	6
HOUNDS OF LOVE	EMI	18	1 Mar 86	5
THE BIG SKY	EMI	37	10 May 86	3
DON'T GIVE UP	Virgin	9	1 Nov 86	11
Above hit: Peter GABRIEL and Kate BUSH.				
EXPERIMENT IV	EMI	23	8 Nov 86	4
THE SENSUAL WORLD	EMI	12	30 Sep 89	5
THIS WOMAN'S WORK	EMI	25	2 Dec 89	5
LOVE AND ANGER	EMI	38	10 Mar 90	3
ROCKET MAN (I THINK IT'S GOING TO BE A LONG, LONG TIME)	Mercury	12	7 Dec 91	8
RUBBERBAND GIRL	EMI	12	18 Sep 93	5
MOMENTS OF PLEASURE	EMI	26	27 Nov 93	3
THE RED SHOES	EMI	21	16 Apr 94	3
THE MAN I LOVE	Mercury	27	30 Jul 94	2
Above hit: Larry ADLER and Kate BUSH.				
AND SO IS LOVE	EMI	26	19 Nov 94	2
ALBUMS:	**HITS 8**			**WEEKS 278**
THE KICK INSIDE	EMI	3	11 Mar 78	70
LIONHEART	EMI	6	25 Nov 78	36
NEVER FOR EVER	EMI	1	20 Sep 80	23
THE DREAMING	EMI	3	25 Sep 82	10
HOUNDS OF LOVE	EMI	1	28 Sep 85	51
THE WHOLE STORY	EMI	1	22 Nov 86	53
Compilation.				
THE SENSUAL WORLD	EMI	2	28 Oct 89	20
THE RED SHOES	EMI	2	13 Nov 93	15

BUSTER   UK

SINGLES:	**HITS 1**			**WEEKS 1**
SUNDAY	RCA Victor	49	19 Jun 76	1

Sam BUTERA and the WITNESSES – See Louis PRIMA

Bernard BUTLER   UK

(See also McAlmont and Butler.)

SINGLES:	**HITS 4**			**WEEKS 9**
STAY	Creation	12	17 Jan 98	4
NOT ALONE	Creation	27	28 Mar 98	3
A CHANGE OF HEART	Creation	45	27 Jun 98	1
YOU MUST GO ON	Creation	44	23 Oct 99	1
ALBUMS:	**HITS 2**			**WEEKS 9**
PEOPLE MOVE ON	Creation	11	18 Apr 98	8
FRIENDS AND LOVERS	Creation	43	6 Nov 99	1

Gerry BUTLER STRINGS – See WHITE PLAINS

Jonathan BUTLER   US

SINGLES:	**HITS 2**			**WEEKS 18**
IF YOU'RE READY (COME GO WITH ME)	Jive	30	25 Jan 86	7
Above hit: Ruby TURNER featuring Jonathan BUTLER.				
LIES	Jive	18	8 Aug 87	11
ALBUMS:	**HITS 2**			**WEEKS 14**
JONATHAN BUTLER	Jive	12	12 Sep 87	11
MORE THAN FRIENDS	Jive	29	4 Feb 89	3

BUTTERSCOTCH   UK

SINGLES:	**HITS 1**			**WEEKS 11**
DON'T YOU KNOW (SHE SAID HELLO)	RCA Victor	17	2 May 70	11

BUTTHOLE SURFERS   US

SINGLES:	**HITS 1**			**WEEKS 1**
PEPPER	Capitol	59	5 Oct 96	1
ALBUMS:	**HITS 2**			**WEEKS 2**
PIOUHGD	Rough Trade	68	16 Mar 91	1
INDEPENDENT WORM SALOON	Capitol	73	3 Apr 93	1

BUZZCOCKS   UK

SINGLES:	**HITS 9**			**WEEKS 53**
WHAT DO I GET?	United Artists	37	18 Feb 78	3
I DON'T MIND	United Artists	55	13 May 78	2

LOVE YOU MORE	*United Artists*	34	*15 Jul 78*	6
EVER FALLEN IN LOVE (WITH SOMEONE YOU SHOULDN'T'VE)	*United Artists*	12	*23 Sep 78*	11
PROMISES	*United Artists*	20	*25 Nov 78*	10
EVERYBODY'S HAPPY NOWADAYS	*United Artists*	29	*10 Mar 79*	6
HARMONY IN MY HEAD	*United Artists*	32	*21 Jul 79*	6
SPIRAL SCRATCH [EP]	*New Hormones*	31	*25 Aug 79*	6

Lead track: Breakdown.
Above hit: BUZZCOCKS with Howard DEVOTO.

ARE EVERYTHING / WHY SHE'S A GIRL FROM THE CHAINSTORE	*United Artists*	61	*6 Sep 80*	3

Why She's A Girl From The Chainstore listed from 13 Sep 80.

ALBUMS:		**HITS 3**		**WEEKS 23**
ANOTHER MUSIC IN A DIFFERENT KITCHEN	*United Artists*	15	*25 Mar 78*	11
LOVE BITES	*United Artists*	13	*7 Oct 78*	9
A DIFFERENT KIND OF TENSION	*United Artists*	26	*6 Oct 79*	3

BY ALL MEANS   US

SINGLES:		**HITS 1**		**WEEKS 2**
I SURRENDER TO YOUR LOVE	*Fourth & Broadway*	65	*18 Jun 88*	2
ALBUMS:		**HITS 1**		**WEEKS 1**
BY ALL MEANS	*Fourth & Broadway*	80	*16 Jul 88*	1

Max BYGRAVES   UK

(See also All Star Hit Parade.)

SINGLES:		**HITS 18**		**WEEKS 131**
COWPUNCHER'S CANTATA [M]	*His Master's Voice*	11	*15 Nov 52*	1
COWPUNCHER'S CANTATA [M] [RE-1ST]	*His Master's Voice*	8	*3 Jan 53*	1
COWPUNCHER'S CANTATA [M] [RE-2ND]	*His Master's Voice*	6	*24 Jan 53*	5
COWPUNCHER'S CANTATA [M] [RE-3RD]	*His Master's Voice*	10	*7 Mar 53*	1
THE GANG THAT SANG HEART OF MY HEART	*His Master's Voice*	7	*15 May 54*	8

Above hit: Max BYGRAVES and vocal quartet.

GILLY GILLY OSSENFEFFER KATZENELLENBOGEN BY THE SEA	*His Master's Voice*	7	*11 Sep 54*	7

Above hit: Max BYGRAVES with CHILDREN'S CHORUS.

GILLY GILLY OSSENFEFFER KATZENELLENBOGEN BY THE SEA [RE]	*His Master's Voice*	20	*6 Nov 54*	1
MISTER SANDMAN	*His Master's Voice*	16	*22 Jan 55*	1

Originally recorded by Vaughan Monroe.

MEET ME ON THE CORNER	*His Master's Voice*	2	*19 Nov 55*	11
THE BALLAD OF DAVY CROCKETT	*His Master's Voice*	20	*18 Feb 56*	1

Above hit: Max BYGRAVES with CHILDREN'S CHORUS.

OUT OF TOWN	*His Master's Voice*	18	*26 May 56*	7
HEART	*Decca*	14	*6 Apr 57*	8

Above hit: Max BYGRAVES with Malcolm LOCKYER and his Orchestra.

TULIPS FROM AMSTERDAM / YOU NEED HANDS	*Decca*	3	*3 May 58*	25

Tulips From Amsterdam listed from 10.May 58.
Above hit: Max BYGRAVES with Eric RODGERS and his Orchestra / Max BYGRAVES with the CLARKE BROTHERS and Eric RODGERS and his Orchestra.

LITTLE TRAIN / GOTTA HAVE RAIN	*Decca*	28	*23 Aug 58*	2

Little Train from the film 'A Cry From The Streets'.

(I LOVE TO PLAY) MY UKELELE	*Decca*	19	*3 Jan 59*	4
JINGLE BELL ROCK	*Decca*	7	*19 Dec 59*	4

Original by Bobby Helms reached No. 6 in the US in 1957.

FINGS AIN'T WOT THEY USED T'BE	*Decca*	5	*12 Mar 60*	15

Originally recorded by Lionel Bart.

CONSIDER YOURSELF	*Decca*	50	*30 Jul 60*	1
THE BELLS OF AVIGNON	*Decca*	36	*3 Jun 61*	5

Above hit: Max BYGRAVES with the CORONA CHILDREN.

YOU'RE MY EVERYTHING	*Pye*	50	*22 Feb 69*	1
YOU'RE MY EVERYTHING [RE]	*Pye*	34	*8 Mar 69*	3
DECK OF CARDS	*Pye*	13	*6 Oct 73*	15
WHITE CHRISTMAS	*Parkfield*	71	*9 Dec 89*	4

ALBUMS:		**HITS 12**		**WEEKS 176**
SING ALONG WITH MAX	*Pye*	4	*23 Sep 72*	44
SING ALONG WITH MAX VOLUME 2	*Pye*	11	*2 Dec 72*	23
SINGALONGAMAX VOLUME 3	*Pye*	5	*5 May 73*	30
SINGALONGAMAX VOLUME 4	*Pye*	7	*29 Sep 73*	12
SINGALONGPARTY SONG	*Pye*	15	*15 Dec 73*	6
YOU MAKE ME FEEL LIKE SINGING A SONG	*Pye*	39	*12 Oct 74*	3
SINGALONGAXMAS	*Pye*	21	*7 Dec 74*	6
100 GOLDEN GREATS	*Ronco*	3	*13 Nov 76*	21
LINGALONGAMAX	*Ronco*	39	*28 Oct 78*	5
THE SONG AND DANCE MEN	*Pye*	67	*16 Dec 78*	1
SINGALONGAWARYEARS	*Parkfield Music*	5	*19 Aug 89*	19
SINGALONGAWARYEARS VOLUME 2	*Parkfield*	33	*25 Nov 89*	6

BYKER GROOOVE!   UK

SINGLES:		**HITS 1**		**WEEKS 3**
LOVE YOUR SEXY . . . !!	*Groove*	48	*24 Dec 94*	3

Charlie BYRD - See Stan GETZ and Charlie BYRD

Debra BYRD - See Barry MANILOW

Donald BYRD   US

SINGLES:	HITS 1			WEEKS 6
LOVE HAS COME AROUND / LOVING YOU	Elektra	41	26 Sep 81	6
ALBUMS:	HITS 1			WEEKS 3
LOVE BYRD	Elektra	70	10 Oct 81	3

Gary BYRD and the GB EXPERIENCE   US

SINGLES:	HITS 1			WEEKS 9
THE CROWN	Motown	6	23 Jul 83	9

Features vocals by and co written with Stevie Wonder.

BYRDS   US

SINGLES:	HITS 6			WEEKS 52
MR. TAMBOURINE MAN	CBS	1	19 Jun 65	14
Originally recorded by Bob Dylan.				
ALL I REALLY WANT TO DO	CBS	4	14 Aug 65	10
TURN! TURN! TURN! (TO EVERYTHING THERE IS A SEASON)	CBS	26	13 Nov 65	8
Lyrics adapted from the Book Of Ecclesiastes by Pete Seeger.				
EIGHT MILES HIGH	CBS	24	7 May 66	9
YOU AIN'T GOING NOWHERE	CBS	45	8 Jun 68	3
Written by Bob Dylan.				
CHESTNUT MARE	CBS	19	13 Feb 71	8
EPS:	HITS 2			WEEKS 5
THE TIMES THEY ARE A' CHANGIN'	CBS	15	19 Feb 66	4
EIGHT MILES HIGH	CBS	8	15 Oct 66	1
ALBUMS:	HITS 10			WEEKS 42
MR. TAMBOURINE MAN	CBS	7	28 Aug 65	12
TURN, TURN, TURN	CBS	11	9 Apr 66	5
5TH DIMENSION	CBS	27	1 Oct 66	2
YOUNGER THAN YESTERDAY	CBS	37	22 Apr 67	4
THE NOTORIOUS BYRD BROTHERS	CBS	12	4 May 68	11
DR. BYRDS AND MR HYDE	CBS	15	24 May 69	1
BALLAD OF EASY RIDER	CBS	41	14 Feb 70	1
UNTITLED	CBS	11	28 Nov 70	4
BYRDS	Asylum	31	14 Apr 73	1
HISTORY OF THE BYRDS	CBS	47	19 May 73	1

David BYRNE   UK

(See also Brian Eno and David Byrne.)

ALBUMS:	HITS 3			WEEKS 9
REI MOMO	Sire	52	21 Oct 89	2
UH-OH	Luaka Bop	26	14 Mar 92	5
DAVID BYRNE	Luaka Bop	44	4 Jun 94	2

Ed BYRNES   US

SINGLES:	HITS 1			WEEKS 8
KOOKIE, KOOKIE (LEND ME YOUR COMB)	Warner Brothers	27	7 May 60	8

From '77 Sunset Strip'.
Above hit: Ed BYRNES and Connie STEVENS with the Big Sound of Don RALKE.

EPS:	HITS 1			WEEKS 1
KOOKIE	Warner Brothers	20	25 Mar 61	1

BYSTANDERS   UK

SINGLES:	HITS 1			WEEKS 1
98.6	Piccadilly	45	11 Feb 67	1

C

Melanie C   UK

SINGLES:	HITS 3			WEEKS 30
WHEN YOU'RE GONE	Mercury	3	12 Dec 98	19
Above hit: Bryan ADAMS featuring Melanie C.				
GOIN' DOWN	Virgin	4	9 Oct 99	4
GOIN' DOWN [RE]	Virgin	64	13 Nov 99	2
NORTHERN STAR	Virgin	4	4 Dec 99	5

ALBUMS:		HITS 1		WEEKS 10	
NORTHERN STAR	*Virgin*	10	*30 Oct 99*	10	

Roy C
US

SINGLES:		HITS 1		WEEKS 24	
SHOTGUN WEDDING	*Island*	6	*23 Apr 66*	11	
SHOTGUN WEDDING [RI]	*UK*	8	*25 Nov 72*	13	

C&C MUSIC FACTORY
US

SINGLES:		HITS 10		WEEKS 53	
GONNA MAKE YOU SWEAT (EVERYBODY DANCE NOW)	*CBS*	3	*15 Dec 90*	12	
HERE WE GO	*Columbia*	20	*30 Mar 91*	7	
THINGS THAT MAKE YOU GO HMMM . . .	*Columbia*	4	*6 Jul 91*	11	
Above 3: C&C MUSIC FACTORY (featuring Freedom WILLIAMS).					
JUST A TOUCH OF LOVE (EVERYDAY)	*Columbia*	31	*23 Nov 91*	3	
Above hit: C&C MUSIC FACTORY featuring Zelma DAVIS.					
PRIDE (IN THE NAME OF LOVE)	*Columbia*	15	*18 Jan 92*	5	
A DEEPER LOVE	*Columbia*	15	*14 Mar 92*	5	
Above 2: CLIVILLES and COLE.					
KEEP IT COMIN' (DANCE TIL YOU CAN'T DANCE NO MORE)	*Columbia*	34	*3 Oct 92*	3	
From the film 'Buffy The Vampire Slayer'.					
Above hit: C&C MUSIC FACTORY featuring Q UNIQUE and Deborah COOPER.					
DO YOU WANNA GET FUNKY	*Columbia*	27	*27 Aug 94*	3	
I FOUND LOVE / TAKE A TOKE	*Columbia*	26	*18 Feb 95*	2	
The 12" format of Take A Toke featured Martha Wash.					
Above hit: C & C MUSIC FACTORY featuring Zelma DAVIS / C & C MUSIC					
FACTORY featuring TRILOGY.					
I'LL ALWAYS BE AROUND	*MCA*	42	*11 Nov 95*	2	
Above hit: C+C MUSIC FACTORY.					

ALBUMS:		HITS 2		WEEKS 14	
GONNA MAKE YOU SWEAT	*Columbia*	8	*9 Feb 91*	13	
GREATEST REMIXES VOLUME 1	*Columbia*	45	*28 Mar 92*	1	
Above hit: CLIVILLES and COLE.					

C.C.S.
UK

SINGLES:		HITS 5		WEEKS 55	
WHOLE LOTTA LOVE	*RAK*	13	*31 Oct 70*	13	
The theme to the BBC 1's 'Top Of The Pops' in the 1970s.					
WALKING	*RAK*	7	*27 Feb 71*	16	
TAP TURNS ON THE WATER	*RAK*	5	*4 Sep 71*	13	
BROTHER	*RAK*	25	*4 Mar 72*	8	
THE BAND PLAYED THE BOOGIE	*RAK*	36	*4 Aug 73*	5	

ALBUMS:		HITS 1		WEEKS 5	
C.C.S.	*RAK*	23	*8 Apr 72*	5	

C.J. and CO.
US

SINGLES:		HITS 1		WEEKS 2	
DEVIL'S GUN	*Atlantic*	43	*30 Jul 77*	2	

C.L.S.
US

SINGLES:		HITS 1		WEEKS 1	
CAN YOU FEEL IT?	*Satellite*	46	*30 May 98*	1	

C.O.D.
US

SINGLES:		HITS 1		WEEKS 2	
IN THE BOTTLE	*Streetwave*	54	*14 May 83*	2	

ÇA VA ÇA VA
UK

SINGLES:		HITS 2		WEEKS 8	
WHERE'S ROMEO?	*Regard*	49	*18 Sep 82*	5	
BROTHER BRIGHT	*Regard*	65	*19 Feb 83*	3	

Montserrat CABALLE – See Placido DOMINGO, Jose CARRERAS and Montserrat CABALLE; Freddie MERCURY and Montserrat CABALLE

CABANA
Brazil

SINGLES:		HITS 1		WEEKS 1	
BAILANDO CON LOBOS	*Hi-Life*	65	*15 Jul 95*	1	

CABARET VOLTAIRE
UK

SINGLES:		HITS 4		WEEKS 8	
DON'T ARGUE	*Parlophone*	69	*18 Jul 87*	2	
HYPNOTISED	*Parlophone*	66	*4 Nov 89*	2	

KEEP ON	Parlophone	55	12 May 90	2
EASY LIFE	Parlophone	61	18 Aug 90	2
ALBUMS:	HITS 5		WEEKS 11	
2 X 45	Rough Trade	98	26 Jun 82	1
THE CRACKDOWN	Some Bizzare	31	13 Aug 83	5
MICRO-PHONIES	Some Bizzare	69	10 Nov 84	1
DRINKING GASOLINE	Some Bizzare	71	3 Aug 85	2
THE COVENANT, THE SWORD AND THE ARM OF THE LAW	Some Bizzare	57	26 Oct 85	2

CABLE   UK

SINGLES:	HITS 1		WEEKS 2	
FREEZE THE ATLANTIC	Infectious	44	14 Jun 97	2

CACIQUE   UK

SINGLES:	HITS 1		WEEKS 1	
DEVOTED TO YOU	Diamond Duel	69	1 Jun 85	1

CACTUS WORLD NEWS   Ireland

SINGLES:	HITS 3		WEEKS 7	
YEARS LATER	MCA	59	8 Feb 86	3
WORLDS APART	MCA	58	26 Apr 86	3
THE BRIDGE	MCA	74	20 Sep 86	1
ALBUMS:	HITS 1		WEEKS 2	
URBAN BEACHES	MCA	56	24 May 86	2

David CADDICK – See Michael CRAWFORD

CADETS with Eileen REED Lead vocal   Ireland

SINGLES:	HITS 1		WEEKS 1	
JEALOUS HEART	Pye	42	5 Jun 65	1

Susan CADOGAN   UK

SINGLES:	HITS 2		WEEKS 19	
HURT SO GOOD	Magnet	4	5 Apr 75	12
Originally recorded by Katie Love.				
LOVE ME BABY	Magnet	22	19 Jul 75	7

Athena CAGE – See Keith SWEAT

Al CAIOLA and his Orchestra   US

SINGLES:	HITS 1		WEEKS 6	
THEME FROM 'THE MAGNIFICENT SEVEN'	His Master's Voice / London	34	17 Jun 61	6
From 24 Jun 61 sales were combined for issues on both the HMV and London labels.				

CAKE   US

SINGLES:	HITS 3		WEEKS 6	
THE DISTANCE	Capricorn	22	22 Mar 97	3
I WILL SURVIVE	Capricorn	29	31 May 97	2
NEVER THERE	Capricorn	66	1 May 99	1
ALBUMS:	HITS 1		WEEKS 2	
FASHION NUGGET	Capricorn	53	5 Apr 97	2

J.J. CALE   US

ALBUMS:	HITS 6		WEEKS 24	
TROUBADOUR	Island	53	2 Oct 76	1
5	Shelter	40	25 Aug 79	6
SHADES	Shelter	44	21 Feb 81	7
GRASSHOPPER	Shelter	36	20 Mar 82	5
NUMBER 8	Mercury	47	24 Sep 83	3
NUMBER 10	Silvertone	58	26 Sep 92	2

John CALE – See Lou REED

CALIBRE CUTS   Multi National

SINGLES:	HITS 1		WEEKS 2	
CALIBRE CUTS [M]	Calibre	75	17 May 80	2
16 track montage of 13 singles plus 3 re-makes of hit titles.				

CALIFORNIA SUNSHINE   Israel/Italy

SINGLES:	HITS 1		WEEKS 1	
SUMMER '89	Perfecto Fluoro	56	16 Aug 97	1

CALL
US

SINGLES:	HITS 1			WEEKS 6
LET THE DAY BEGIN	*MCA*	42	*30 Sep 89*	6

Maria CALLAS
Greece

ALBUMS:	HITS 2			WEEKS 8
THE MARIA CALLAS COLLECTION	*Stylus*	50	*20 Jun 87*	7
DIVA - THE ULTIMATE COLLECTION	*EMI*	61	*24 Feb 96*	1

Terry CALLIER
US

(See also Beth Orton.)

SINGLES:	HITS 1			WEEKS 1
LOVE THEME FROM SPARTACUS	*Talkin Loud*	57	*23 May 98*	1

Constantine CALLINICOS - See Mario LANZA

Eddie CALVERT (The Man with the Golden Trumpet) with Norrie PARAMOR and his Orchestra
UK

SINGLES:	HITS 7			WEEKS 80
OH, MEIN PAPA	*Columbia*	1	*19 Dec 53*	21
Originally recorded by Lys Assia.				
CHERRY PINK (AND APPLE BLOSSOM WHITE)	*Columbia*	1	*9 Apr 55*	21
STRANGER IN PARADISE	*Columbia*	14	*14 May 55*	4
From the musical 'Kismet'.				
JOHN AND JULIE	*Columbia*	6	*30 Jul 55*	11
From the film of the same name.				
ZAMBESI	*Columbia*	18	*10 Mar 56*	1
ZAMBESI [RE]	*Columbia*	13	*24 Mar 56*	6
MANDY (THE PANSY)	*Columbia*	9	*8 Feb 58*	14
LITTLE SERENADE (PICCOLISSIMA SERENATA)	*Columbia*	28	*21 Jun 58*	2

Donnie CALVIN - See ROCKERS REVENGE featuring Donnie CALVIN

CAMEL
UK

ALBUMS:	HITS 8			WEEKS 47
THE SNOW GOOSE	*Decca*	22	*24 May 75*	13
MOON MADNESS	*Decca*	15	*17 Apr 76*	6
RAIN DANCES	*Decca*	20	*17 Sep 77*	8
BREATHLESS	*Decca*	26	*14 Oct 78*	1
I CAN SEE YOUR HOUSE FROM HERE	*Decca*	45	*27 Oct 79*	3
NUDE	*Decca*	34	*31 Jan 81*	7
THE SINGLE FACTOR	*Decca*	57	*15 May 82*	5
STATIONARY TRAVELLER	*Decca*	57	*21 Apr 84*	4

CAMEO
US

SINGLES:	HITS 9			WEEKS 66
SHE'S STRANGE	*Club*	37	*31 Mar 84*	8
ATTACK ME WITH YOUR LOVE	*Club*	65	*13 Jul 85*	2
SINGLE LIFE	*Club*	15	*14 Sep 85*	10
SHE'S STRANGE [RI]	*Club*	22	*7 Dec 85*	8
A GOODBYE	*Club*	65	*22 Mar 86*	2
WORD UP	*Club*	3	*30 Aug 86*	13
CANDY	*Club*	27	*29 Nov 86*	9
BACK AND FORTH	*Club*	11	*25 Apr 87*	9
SHE'S MINE	*Club*	35	*17 Oct 87*	4
YOU MAKE ME WORK	*Club*	74	*29 Oct 88*	1
ALBUMS:	HITS 3			WEEKS 47
SINGLE LIFE	*Club*	66	*10 Aug 85*	12
WORD UP	*Club*	7	*18 Oct 86*	34
MACHISMO	*Club*	86	*26 Nov 88*	1

Andy CAMERON
UK

SINGLES:	HITS 1			WEEKS 8
ALLY'S TARTAN ARMY	*Klub*	6	*4 Mar 78*	8
A tribute to the Scottish World Cup football squad.				

Tony CAMILLO'S BAZUKA
US

SINGLES:	HITS 1			WEEKS 5
DYNOMITE	*A&M*	28	*31 May 75*	5

CAMISRA
UK

SINGLES:	HITS 3			WEEKS 12
LET ME SHOW YOU	*VC Recordings*	5	*21 Feb 98*	8
FEEL THE BEAT	*VC Recordings*	32	*11 Jul 98*	2
CLAP YOUR HANDS	*VC Recordings*	34	*22 May 99*	2

CAMOUFLAGE featuring 'MYSTI' | | | | UK

SINGLES:		HITS 1		WEEKS 3
BEE STING	State	48	24 Sep 77	3

CAMP LO | | | | US

SINGLES:		HITS 1		WEEKS 1
LUCHINI AKA (THIS IS IT)	ffrr	74	16 Aug 97	1

Ali CAMPBELL | | | | UK

(See also Pato Banton.)

SINGLES:		HITS 3		WEEKS 18
THAT LOOK IN YOUR EYE	Kuff	5	20 May 95	10
Features vocals by Pamela Starks.				
LET YOUR YEAH BE YEAH	Kuff	25	26 Aug 95	4
SOMETHIN' STUPID	Kuff	30	9 Dec 95	4
Above hit: Ali and Kibibi CAMPBELL.				
ALBUMS:		**HITS 1**		**WEEKS 11**
BIG LOVE	Kuff	6	17 Jun 95	11

Ali and Robin CAMPBELL of UB40 - See Pato BANTON

Danny CAMPBELL and SASHA | | | | UK

SINGLES:		HITS 1		WEEKS 1
TOGETHER	ffrr	57	31 Jul 93	1

Don CAMPBELL - See GENERAL SAINT

Ellie CAMPBELL | | | | UK

SINGLES:		HITS 2		WEEKS 4
SWEET LIES	Jive	42	3 Apr 99	1
SO MANY WAYS	Jive	26	14 Aug 99	3

Ethna CAMPBELL | | | | UK

SINGLES:		HITS 1		WEEKS 11
THE OLD RUGGED CROSS	Philips	33	27 Dec 75	11

Glen CAMPBELL | | | | US

(See also Bobbie Gentry and Glen Campbell.)

SINGLES:		HITS 9		WEEKS 84
WICHITA LINEMAN	Ember	7	1 Feb 69	13
GALVESTON	Ember	14	10 May 69	10
TRY A LITTLE KINDNESS	Capitol	45	7 Feb 70	2
HONEY COME BACK	Capitol	4	9 May 70	19
EVERYTHING A MAN COULD EVER NEED	Capitol	32	26 Sep 70	5
IT'S ONLY MAKE BELIEVE	Capitol	4	21 Nov 70	14
DREAM BABY (HOW LONG MUST I DREAM)	Capitol	39	27 Mar 71	3
RHINESTONE COWBOY	Capitol	4	4 Oct 75	12
Originally recorded by Larry Weiss.				
SOUTHERN NIGHTS	Capitol	28	26 Mar 77	6
Originally recorded by Allan Toussaint.				
ALBUMS:		**HITS 9**		**WEEKS 184**
GLEN CAMPBELL LIVE	Capitol	16	31 Jan 70	14
TRY A LITTLE KINDNESS	Capitol	37	30 May 70	10
THE GLEN CAMPBELL ALBUM	Capitol	16	12 Dec 70	5
GLEN CAMPBELLS GREATEST HITS	Capitol	8	27 Nov 71	113
RHINESTONE COWBOY	Capitol	38	25 Oct 75	9
20 GOLDEN GREATS	Capitol	1	20 Nov 76	27
SOUTHERN NIGHTS	Capitol	51	23 Apr 77	1
THE COMPLETE GLEN CAMPBELL	Stylus	47	22 Jul 89	4
MY HITS AND LOVE SONGS	Capitol	50	2 Oct 99	1

Ian CAMPBELL FOLK GROUP | | | | UK

SINGLES:		HITS 1		WEEKS 5
THE TIMES THEY ARE A CHANGIN'	Transatlantic	42	13 Mar 65	2
THE TIMES THEY ARE A CHANGIN' [RE-1ST]	Transatlantic	47	3 Apr 65	1
THE TIMES THEY ARE A CHANGIN' [RE-2ND]	Transatlantic	46	17 Apr 65	2

Jo Ann CAMPBELL | | | | US

SINGLES:		HITS 1		WEEKS 3
MOTORCYCLE MICHAEL	His Master's Voice	41	10 Jun 61	3

Junior CAMPBELL | UK

SINGLES:	HITS 2			WEEKS 18
HALLELUJAH FREEDOM	Deram	10	14 Oct 72	9
SWEET ILLUSION	Deram	15	2 Jun 73	9

Kibibi CAMPBELL – See Ali CAMPBELL

Naomi CAMPBELL | UK

SINGLES:	HITS 1			WEEKS 3
LOVE AND TEARS	Epic	40	24 Sep 94	3

Backing vocals by Chrissie Hynde.

Pat CAMPBELL | Ireland

SINGLES:	HITS 1			WEEKS 5
THE DEAL	Major Minor	31	15 Nov 69	5

Stan CAMPBELL | UK

SINGLES:	HITS 1			WEEKS 3
YEARS GO BY	WEA	65	6 Jun 87	3

Tevin CAMPBELL | US

SINGLES:	HITS 1			WEEKS 2
TELL ME WHAT YOU WANT ME TO DO	Qwest	63	18 Apr 92	2

CAM'RON featuring MASE | US

SINGLES:	HITS 1			WEEKS 4
HORSE & CARRIAGE	Epic	12	19 Sep 98	4

CAN | Germany

SINGLES:	HITS 1			WEEKS 10
I WANT MORE	Virgin	26	28 Aug 76	10

CANDIDO | US

SINGLES:	HITS 1			WEEKS 3
JINGO	Excaliber	55	18 Jul 81	3

Originally recorded by Michael Olatunji.

CANDLEWICK GREEN | UK

SINGLES:	HITS 1			WEEKS 8
WHO DO YOU THINK YOU ARE?	Decca	21	23 Feb 74	8

CANDY FLIP | UK

SINGLES:	HITS 2			WEEKS 14
STRAWBERRY FIELDS FOREVER	Debut	3	17 Mar 90	10
THIS CAN BE REAL (SMALLER)	Debut	60	14 Jul 90	4

CANDY GIRLS | UK

SINGLES:	HITS 3			WEEKS 10
FEE FI FO FUM	VC Recordings	23	30 Sep 95	4
WHAM BAM	VC Recordings	20	24 Feb 96	4
Above 2: CANDY GIRLS featuring SWEET PUSSY PAULINE.				
I WANT CANDY	Feverpitch	30	7 Dec 96	2

Original by the Strangeloves reached No. 11 in the US in 1965.
Above hit: CANDY GIRLS featuring Valerie MALCOLM.

CANDYLAND | UK

SINGLES:	HITS 1			WEEKS 1
FOUNTAIN O' YOUTH	Non Fiction	72	9 Mar 91	1

CANDYSKINS | UK

SINGLES:	HITS 3			WEEKS 4
MRS HOOVER	Ultimate	65	19 Oct 96	1
MONDAY MORNING	Ultimate	34	8 Feb 97	2
HANG MYSELF ON YOU	Ultimate	65	3 May 97	1

CANIBUS | US

SINGLES:	HITS 2			WEEKS 3
SECOND ROUND K.O.	Universal	35	27 Jun 98	2

Features boxer Mike Tyson on backing vocals.

HOW COME	Interscope	52	10 Oct 98	1

From the film 'Bulworth'.
Above hit: Youssou N'DOUR and CANIBUS.

ALBUMS:	HITS 1		WEEKS 1	
CAN-I-BUS	Universal	43	19 Sep 98	1

CANNED HEAT
US

SINGLES:	HITS 4		WEEKS 41	
ON THE ROAD AGAIN	Liberty	8	27 Jul 68	15
GOING UP THE COUNTRY	Liberty	19	4 Jan 69	10

Based around Bull Doze Blues by Henry Thomas.

LET'S WORK TOGETHER	Liberty	2	17 Jan 70	15

Original by Wilbert Harrison reached No. 32 in the US in 1970.

SUGAR BEE	Liberty	49	11 Jul 70	1
ALBUMS:	HITS 4		WEEKS 40	
BOOGIE WITH CANNED HEAT	Liberty	5	29 Jun 68	21
CANNED HEAT COOKBOOK	Liberty	8	14 Feb 70	12

Compilation.

CANNED HEAT '70 CONCERT	Liberty	15	4 Jul 70	3

Live recordings from European shows.

FUTURE BLUES	Liberty	27	10 Oct 70	4

Freddie CANNON
US

SINGLES:	HITS 6		WEEKS 54	
TALLAHASSEE LASSIE	Top Rank	17	15 Aug 59	8

Co-written by Freddie's mother.
Above hit: Freddy CANNON.

WAY DOWN YONDER IN NEW ORLEANS	Top Rank	3	2 Jan 60	18

Originally recorded by Layton & Johnson.

CALIFORNIA HERE I COME	Top Rank	25	5 Mar 60	2

Originally recorded by Al Jolson.

INDIANA	Top Rank	42	19 Mar 60	1

Above 2 entries were separate sides of the same release, each had its own chart run.

CALIFORNIA HERE I COME [RE]	Top Rank	46	26 Mar 60	1
THE URGE	Top Rank	18	21 May 60	10
MUSKRAT RAMBLE	Top Rank	32	22 Apr 61	5
PALISADES PARK	Stateside	20	30 Jun 62	9

Above 3: Freddy CANNON with Frank SLAY and his Orchestra.

ALBUMS:	HITS 1		WEEKS 11	
THE EXPLOSIVE FREDDY CANNON	Top Rank	1	27 Feb 60	11

Above hit: Freddy CANNON.

Jim CAPALDI
UK

SINGLES:	HITS 2		WEEKS 17	
IT'S ALL UP TO YOU	Island	27	27 Jul 74	6
LOVE HURTS	Island	4	25 Oct 75	11

Originally recorded by Roy Orbison.

CAPERCAILLIE
UK

SINGLES:	HITS 2		WEEKS 3	
A PRINCE AMONG ISLANDS [EP]	Survival	39	23 May 92	2

Music from the TV programme 'A Prince Among Islands'. Lead track: Coisich A Ruin (Walk My Beloved).

DARK ALAN (AILEIN DUINN)	Survival	65	17 Jun 95	1

From the film 'Rob Roy'.

ALBUMS:	HITS 4		WEEKS 8	
SECRET PEOPLE	Arista	40	25 Sep 93	3
CAPERCAILLIE	Survival	61	17 Sep 94	1
TO THE MOON	Survival	41	4 Nov 95	1
BEAUTIFUL WASTELAND	Survival	55	20 Sep 97	2

CAPPADONNA
US

SINGLES:	HITS 1		WEEKS 1	
TRIUMPH	Loud	46	16 Aug 97	1

Above hit: WU-TANG CLAN (featuring CAPPADONNA).

ALBUMS:	HITS 1		WEEKS 1	
THE PILLAGE	Epic	43	4 Apr 98	1

CAPPELLA
UK/Italy

SINGLES:	HITS 12		WEEKS 68	
PUSH THE BEAT/BAUHAUS	Fast Globe	60	9 Apr 88	2

One song title, not a double 'A' side.

HELYOM HALIB	Music Man	11	6 May 89	9
HOUSE ENERGY REVENGE	Music Man	73	23 Sep 89	1

EVERYBODY	ffrr	66	27 Apr 91	1
TAKE ME AWAY	PWL Continental	25	18 Jan 92	5

Above hit: CAPPELLA featuring Loleatta HOLLOWAY.

U GOT 2 KNOW	Internal Dance	6	3 Apr 93	11
U GOT 2 KNOW REVISITED [RM]	Internal Dance	43	14 Aug 93	3

Remixed by Paul Newman & Craig Daniel Michael Yefet.

U GOT 2 LET THE MUSIC	Internal Dance	2	23 Oct 93	12
MOVE ON BABY	Internal Dance	7	19 Feb 94	7
U & ME	Internal Dance	10	18 Jun 94	7
MOVE IT UP / BIG BEAT	Internal Dance	16	15 Oct 94	6
TELL ME THE WAY	Systematic	17	16 Sep 95	3
BE MY BABY	Nukleuz	53	6 Sep 97	1
ALBUMS:	**HITS 1**			**WEEKS 9**
U GOT 2 KNOW	Internal Dance	10	26 Mar 94	9

CAPRICCIO   UK

SINGLES:	**HITS 1**			**WEEKS 2**
EVERYBODY GET UP	Defected	44	27 Mar 99	2

Samples Jazzy Dee's Get On Up.

CAPRICE   US

SINGLES:	**HITS 1**			**WEEKS 3**
OH YEAH	Virgin	24	4 Sep 99	3

CAPRICORN   Belgium

SINGLES:	**HITS 1**			**WEEKS 1**
20HZ (NEW FREQUENCIES)	R&S	73	29 Nov 97	1

Tony CAPSTICK-CARLTON MAIN/FRICKLEY COLLIERY BAND   UK

SINGLES:	**HITS 1**			**WEEKS 8**
CAPSTICK COMES HOME / THE SHEFFIELD GRINDER	Dingle's	3	21 Mar 81	8

CAPTAIN and TENNILLE   US

SINGLES:	**HITS 4**			**WEEKS 24**
LOVE WILL KEEP US TOGETHER	A&M	32	2 Aug 75	5

Originally recorded by Neil Sedaka.

THE WAY I WANT TO TOUCH YOU	A&M	28	24 Jan 76	6
YOU NEVER DONE IT LIKE THAT	A&M	63	4 Nov 78	3
DO THAT TO ME ONE MORE TIME	Casablanca	7	16 Feb 80	10
ALBUMS:	**HITS 1**			**WEEKS 6**
MAKE YOUR MOVE	Casablanca	33	22 Mar 80	6

CAPTAIN BEAKY and His BAND - See Keith MICHELL

CAPTAIN BEEFHEART and his MAGIC BAND   US

ALBUMS:	**HITS 5**			**WEEKS 16**
TROUT MASK REPLICA	Straight	21	6 Dec 69	1
LICK MY DECALS OFF BABY	Straight	20	23 Jan 71	10
MIRROR MAN	Buddah	49	29 May 71	1
THE SPOTLIGHT KID	Reprise	44	19 Feb 72	2
ICE CREAM FOR CROW	Virgin	90	18 Sep 82	2

CAPTAIN HOLLYWOOD PROJECT   US/Germany

(See also Twenty 4 Seven featuring Captain Hollywood.)

SINGLES:	**HITS 4**			**WEEKS 12**
ONLY WITH YOU	Pulse 8	67	27 Mar 93	1
MORE AND MORE	Pulse 8	23	6 Nov 93	6

Originally reached No. 113 in 1992.

IMPOSSIBLE	Pulse 8	29	5 Feb 94	3
ONLY WITH YOU [RI]	Pulse 8	61	11 Jun 94	1
FLYING HIGH	Pulse 8	58	1 Apr 95	1

CAPTAIN SENSIBLE   UK

SINGLES:	**HITS 5**			**WEEKS 31**
HAPPY TALK	A&M	1	26 Jun 82	8

Backing vocals by the Dolly Mixtures. Originally recorded by Juanita Hall.

WOT!	A&M	26	14 Aug 82	7
GLAD IT'S ALL OVER/ DAMNED ON 45 [M]	A&M	6	24 Mar 84	10
THERE ARE MORE SNAKES THAN LADDERS	A&M	57	28 Jul 84	5
THE HOKEY COKEY	Have A Nice Day	71	10 Dec 94	1

Charity record in aid of Great Ormond Street Children's Hospital.

ALBUMS:	**HITS 1**			**WEEKS 3**
WOMEN AND CAPTAIN FIRST	A&M	64	11 Sep 82	3

Irene CARA | | | | | US

SINGLES:	HITS 3			WEEKS 33	
FAME	RSO	1	3 Jul 82	16
OUT HERE ON MY OWN	RSO	58	4 Sep 82	3
Above 2 from the film 'Fame'.				
FLASHDANCE ... WHAT A FEELING	Casablanca	2	4 Jun 83	14
From the film 'Flashdance'.				

CARAMBA | | | | | Sweden

SINGLES:	HITS 1			WEEKS 6	
FEDORA (I'LL BE YOUR DAWG)	Billco	56	12 Nov 83	6

CARAVAN | | | | | UK

ALBUMS:	HITS 2			WEEKS 2	
CUNNING STUNTS	Decca	50	30 Aug 75	1
BLIND DOG AT ST. DUNSTAN'S	BTM	53	15 May 76	1

CARAVELLES | | | | | UK

SINGLES:	HITS 1			WEEKS 13	
YOU DON'T HAVE TO BE A BABY TO CRY	Decca	6	10 Aug 63	13

CARCASS | | | | | UK

ALBUMS:	HITS 2			WEEKS 2	
HEARTWORK	Earache	67	6 Nov 93	1
SWANSONG	Earache	68	6 Jul 96	1

CARDIGANS | | | | | Sweden

SINGLES:	HITS 10			WEEKS 66	
CARNIVAL	Stockholm	72	17 Jun 95	1
SICK & TIRED	Stockholm	34	30 Sep 95	3
CARNIVAL [RE]	Stockholm	35	2 Dec 95	2
RISE & SHINE	Stockholm	29	17 Feb 96	2
Their debut release in Sweden.				
LOVEFOOL	Stockholm	21	21 Sep 96	4
BEEN IT	Stockholm	56	7 Dec 96	1
LOVEFOOL [RI]	Stockholm	2	3 May 97	13
From the film 'Romeo & Juliet'.				
YOUR NEW CUCKOO	Stockholm	35	6 Sep 97	2
MY FAVOURITE GAME	Stockholm	14	17 Oct 98	18
ERASE/REWIND	Stockholm	7	6 Mar 99	9
One song.				
HANGING AROUND	Stockholm	17	24 Jul 99	4
BURNING DOWN THE HOUSE	Gut	7	25 Sep 99	7
Originally recorded by Talking Heads on their 1983 album Speaking In Tongues.				
Above hit: Tom JONES and the CARDIGANS.				

ALBUMS:	HITS 3			WEEKS 59	
LIFE	Stockholm	51	8 Jul 95	9
FIRST BAND ON THE MOON	Stockholm	18	12 Oct 96	10
GRAN TURISMO	Stockholm	27	31 Oct 98	4
GRAN TURISMO [RE]	Stockholm	8	9 Jan 99	36

CARE | | | | | UK

SINGLES:	HITS 1			WEEKS 4	
FLAMING SWORD	Arista	48	12 Nov 83	4

Mariah CAREY | | | | | US

SINGLES:	HITS 24			WEEKS 220	
VISION OF LOVE	CBS	9	4 Aug 90	12
LOVE TAKES TIME	CBS	37	10 Nov 90	8
SOMEDAY	Columbia	38	26 Jan 91	5
THERE'S GOT TO BE A WAY	Columbia	54	1 Jun 91	3
EMOTIONS	Columbia	17	5 Oct 91	9
CAN'T LET GO	Columbia	20	11 Jan 92	7
MAKE IT HAPPEN	Columbia	17	18 Apr 92	5
I'LL BE THERE	Columbia	2	27 Jun 92	9
Uncredited duet with Trey Lorenz.				
DREAMLOVER	Columbia	9	21 Aug 93	10
HERO	Columbia	7	6 Nov 93	15
WITHOUT YOU	Columbia	1	19 Feb 94	14
Originally recorded by Badfinger.				
ANYTIME YOU NEED A FRIEND	Columbia	8	18 Jun 94	10
ENDLESS LOVE	Epic	3	17 Sep 94	10
Above hit: Luther VANDROSS and Mariah CAREY.				
ALL I WANT FOR CHRISTMAS IS YOU	Columbia	2	10 Dec 94	7

ENDLESS LOVE [RE-1ST]	*Epic*	70	*7 Jan 95*	2
ENDLESS LOVE [RE-2ND]	*Epic*	55	*4 Feb 95*	4
ALL I WANT FOR CHRISTMAS IS YOU [RE]	*Columbia*	59	*11 Mar 95*	1
FANTASY	*Columbia*	4	*23 Sep 95*	11
Samples Tom Tom Club's Genius Of Love.				
ONE SWEET DAY	*Columbia*	6	*9 Dec 95*	11
Song spent 16 weeks at No.1 in the US.				
Above hit: Mariah CAREY and BOYZ II MEN.				
OPEN ARMS	*Columbia*	4	*17 Feb 96*	6
Original by Journey reached No. 2 in the US in 1982.				
ALWAYS BE MY BABY	*Columbia*	3	*22 Jun 96*	10
HONEY	*Columbia*	3	*6 Sep 97*	8
Samples The Body Rock by Treacherous.				
BUTTERFLY	*Columbia*	22	*13 Dec 97*	6
MY ALL	*Columbia*	4	*13 Jun 98*	8
WHEN YOU BELIEVE (FROM THE PRINCE OF EGYPT)	*Columbia*	4	*19 Dec 98*	11
From the film 'The Prince Of Egypt'.				
Above hit: Mariah CAREY and Whitney HOUSTON.				
WHEN YOU BELIEVE (FROM THE PRINCE OF EGYPT) [RE]	*Columbia*	68	*27 Mar 99*	2
I STILL BELIEVE	*Columbia*	16	*10 Apr 99*	7
Original by Brenda K. Starr reached No. 13 in the US in 1988.				
HEARTBREAKER	*Columbia*	5	*6 Nov 99*	9
Samples Stacy Lattisaw's Attack Of The Name Game.				
Above hit: Mariah CAREY featuring JAY-Z.				

ALBUMS:	**HITS 9**		**WEEKS 287**	
MARIAH CAREY	*CBS*	6	*15 Sep 90*	40
EMOTIONS	*Columbia*	4	*26 Oct 91*	40
MTV UNPLUGGED [EP]	*Columbia*	3	*18 Jul 92*	10
Live recordings for the TV station, 16 Mar 92.				
MUSIC BOX	*Columbia*	1	*11 Sep 93*	77
MERRY CHRISTMAS	*Columbia*	32	*19 Nov 94*	7
DAYDREAM	*Columbia*	1	*7 Oct 95*	46
BUTTERFLY	*Columbia*	2	*20 Sep 97*	27
#1S	*Columbia*	10	*28 Nov 98*	32
Compilation.				
RAINBOW	*Columbia*	8	*13 Nov 99*	8

CARL - See CLUBHOUSE

Belinda CARLISLE   US

SINGLES:	**HITS 23**		**WEEKS 145**	
HEAVEN IS A PLACE ON EARTH	*Virgin*	1	*12 Dec 87*	14
I GET WEAK	*Virgin*	10	*27 Feb 88*	9
CIRCLE IN THE SAND	*Virgin*	4	*7 May 88*	11
MAD ABOUT YOU	*I.R.S.*	67	*6 Aug 88*	3
WORLD WITHOUT YOU	*Virgin*	34	*10 Sep 88*	6
LOVE NEVER DIES . . .	*Virgin*	54	*10 Dec 88*	5
LEAVE A LIGHT ON	*Virgin*	4	*7 Oct 89*	10
Features slide guitar by George Harrison.				
LA LUNA	*Virgin*	38	*9 Dec 89*	6
RUNAWAY HORSES	*Virgin*	40	*24 Feb 90*	5
VISION OF YOU	*Virgin*	41	*26 May 90*	4
(WE WANT) THE SAME THING	*Virgin*	6	*13 Oct 90*	10
SUMMER RAIN	*Virgin*	23	*22 Dec 90*	10
VISION OF YOU [RE]	*Virgin*	71	*20 Apr 91*	1
LIVE YOUR LIFE BE FREE	*Virgin*	12	*28 Sep 91*	7
DO YOU FEEL LIKE I FEEL?	*Virgin*	29	*16 Nov 91*	4
HALF THE WORLD	*Virgin*	35	*11 Jan 92*	4
LITTLE BLACK BOOK	*Virgin*	28	*29 Aug 92*	5
BIG SCARY ANIMAL	*Virgin*	12	*25 Sep 93*	6
LAY DOWN YOUR ARMS	*Virgin*	27	*27 Nov 93*	6
IN TOO DEEP	*Chrysalis*	6	*13 Jul 96*	7
ALWAYS BREAKING MY HEART	*Chrysalis*	8	*21 Sep 96*	6
LOVE IN THE KEY OF C	*Chrysalis*	20	*30 Nov 96*	3
CALIFORNIA	*Chrysalis*	31	*1 Mar 97*	2
Beach Boy Brian Wilson is on backing vocals.				
ALL GOD'S CHILDREN	*Virgin*	66	*27 Nov 99*	1

ALBUMS:	**HITS 7**		**WEEKS 160**	
HEAVEN ON EARTH	*Virgin*	4	*2 Jan 88*	53
RUNAWAY HORSES	*Virgin*	4	*4 Nov 89*	39
HEAVEN ON EARTH [RE]	*Virgin*	46	*15 Jun 91*	1
Re-released at mid-price.				
LIVE YOUR LIFE BE FREE	*Virgin*	7	*26 Oct 91*	16
THE BEST OF BELINDA VOLUME 1	*Virgin*	1	*19 Sep 92*	35
REAL	*Virgin*	9	*23 Oct 93*	5
A WOMAN AND A MAN	*Chrysalis*	12	*5 Oct 96*	5
A PLACE ON EARTH - THE GREATEST HITS	*Virgin*	15	*13 Nov 99*	6

Bob CARLISLE | | | | US

SINGLES:		HITS 1			WEEKS 2
BUTTERFLY KISSES	Jive		56	30 Aug 97	2

Sara CARLSON – See MANIC MC'S featuring Sara CARLSON

CARLTON | | | | UK

SINGLES:		HITS 2			WEEKS 3
LOVE AND PAIN	3 Stripe		56	16 Feb 91	2
1 TO 1 RELIGION	Stoned Heights		53	1 Apr 95	1

Above hit: BOMB THE BASS featuring CARLTON.

Carl CARLTON | | | | US

SINGLES:		HITS 1			WEEKS 8
SHE'S A BAD MAMA JAMA (SHE'S BUILT, SHE'S STACKED)	20th Century		34	18 Jul 81	8

Larry CARLTON – See Mike POST

CARLTON MAIN/FRICKLEY COLLIERY BAND – See Tony CAPSTICK-CARLTON MAIN/FRICKLEY COLLIERY BAND

CARMEL | | | | UK

SINGLES:		HITS 3			WEEKS 19
BAD DAY	London		15	6 Aug 83	9
MORE, MORE, MORE	London		23	11 Feb 84	7
SALLY	London		60	14 Jun 86	3
ALBUMS:		HITS 3			WEEKS 11
CARMEL 6-TRACK [EP]	Red Flame		94	1 Oct 83	2
THE DRUM IS EVERYTHING	London		19	24 Mar 84	8
THE FALLING	London		88	27 Sep 86	1

Eric CARMEN | | | | US

SINGLES:		HITS 1			WEEKS 7
ALL BY MYSELF	Arista		12	10 Apr 76	7
ALBUMS:		HITS 1			WEEKS 1
ERIC CARMEN	Arista		58	15 May 76	1

Tracey CARMEN – See RUTHLESS RAP ASSASSINS

Ian CARMICHAEL | | | | UK

EPS:		HITS 1			WEEKS 3
HOUSE AT POOH CORNER	HMV		10	23 Dec 61	3

Jean CARN – See Bobby M featuring Jean CARN

Kim CARNEGIE | | | | UK

SINGLES:		HITS 1			WEEKS 1
JAZZ RAP	Best		73	19 Jan 91	1

Kim CARNES | | | | US

SINGLES:		HITS 3			WEEKS 15
BETTE DAVIES EYES	EMI America		10	9 May 81	9

Originally recorded by Jackie De Shannon.

DRAW OF THE CARDS	EMI America		49	8 Aug 81	4
VOYEUR	EMI America		68	9 Oct 82	2
ALBUMS:		HITS 1			WEEKS 16
MISTAKEN IDENTITY	EMI America		26	20 Jun 81	16

CARNIVAL featuring. R.I.P. vs. RED RAT – See R.I.P. PRODUCTIONS; RED RAT

Renato CAROSONE and His SEXTET | | | | Italy

SINGLES:		HITS 1			WEEKS 1
TORERO - CHA CHA CHA	Parlophone		25	5 Jul 58	1

CAROUSEL – ORIGINAL SOUNDTRACK – See VARIOUS ARTISTS: FILMS – ORIGINAL SOUNDTRACKS

CARPE DIEM – See Afrika BAMBAATAA

Mary Chapin CARPENTER | | | | US

SINGLES:		HITS 3			WEEKS 6
HE THINKS HE'LL KEEP HER	Columbia		71	20 Nov 93	1
ONE COOL REMOVE	Columbia		40	7 Jan 95	3

Above hit: Shawn COLVIN with Mary Chapin CARPENTER.

SHUT UP AND KISS ME	Columbia		35	3 Jun 95	2
ALBUMS:		HITS 3			WEEKS 8
STONES IN THE ROAD	Columbia		26	29 Oct 94	5

| A PLACE IN THE WORLD | Columbia | 36 | 2 Nov 96 | 2 |
| PARTY DOLL AND OTHER FAVORITES | Columbia | 65 | 5 Jun 99 | 1 |

Compilation includes live recordings.

CARPENTERS

US

SINGLES:	HITS 19		WEEKS 173	
THEY LONG TO BE CLOSE TO YOU	A&M	6	5 Sep 70	18

Originally recorded by Richard Chamberlain.

| WE'VE ONLY JUST BEGUN | A&M | 28 | 9 Jan 71 | 7 |
| SUPERSTAR / FOR ALL WE KNOW | A&M | 18 | 18 Sep 71 | 13 |

Superstar originally recorded by Delaney & Bonnie & Friends and Eric Clapton as Groupie (Superstar).

| MERRY CHRISTMAS DARLING | A&M | 45 | 1 Jan 72 | 1 |
| GOODBYE TO LOVE / I WON'T LAST A DAY WITHOUT YOU | A&M | 9 | 23 Sep 72 | 16 |

I Won't Last A Day Without You listed on 23 Sep 72 (at No. 49). From 30 Sep 72 only Goodbye To Love was listed.

YESTERDAY ONCE MORE	A&M	2	7 Jul 73	17
TOP OF THE WORLD	A&M	5	20 Oct 73	18
JAMBALAYA (ON THE BAYOU) / MR. GUDER	A&M	12	2 Mar 74	11

Mr. Guder listed from 16 Mar 74.

| I WON'T LAST A DAY WITHOUT YOU [RI] | A&M | 32 | 8 Jun 74 | 5 |
| PLEASE MR POSTMAN | A&M | 2 | 18 Jan 75 | 12 |

Original by the Marvelettes reached No. 1 in the US in 1961.

ONLY YESTERDAY	A&M	7	19 Apr 75	10
SOLITAIRE	A&M	32	30 Aug 75	5
SANTA CLAUS IS COMIN' TO TOWN	A&M	37	20 Dec 75	4

Originally recorded by George Hall in 1934.

| THERE'S A KIND OF HUSH (ALL OVER THE WORLD) | A&M | 22 | 27 Mar 76 | 6 |

Originally recorded by New Vaudeville Band.

| I NEED TO BE IN LOVE | A&M | 36 | 3 Jul 76 | 5 |
| CALLING OCCUPANTS OF INTERPLANETARY CRAFT (THE RECOGNIZED ANTHEM OF WORLD CONTACT DAY) | A&M | 9 | 8 Oct 77 | 9 |

Originally recorded by Klaatu.

SWEET, SWEET SMILE	A&M	40	11 Feb 78	4
MAKE BELIEVE IT'S YOUR FIRST TIME	A&M	60	22 Oct 83	3
MERRY CHRISTMAS DARLING [RI] / (THEY LONG TO BE) CLOSE TO YOU [RI]	A&M	25	8 Dec 90	5
RAINY DAYS AND MONDAYS	A&M	63	13 Feb 93	2

Released to commemorate 10th anniversary of Karen's death.

| TRYIN' TO GET THE FEELING AGAIN | A&M | 44 | 24 Dec 94 | 2 |

First recorded in 1975 and re-discovered in 1991.

ALBUMS:	HITS 18		WEEKS 590	
CLOSE TO YOU	A&M	23	23 Jan 71	82
THE CARPENTERS	A&M	12	30 Oct 71	36
TICKET TO RIDE	A&M	20	15 Apr 72	3
A SONG FOR YOU	A&M	13	23 Sep 72	37
NOW AND THEN	A&M	2	7 Jul 73	65
THE SINGLES 1969–1973	A&M	1	26 Jan 74	116

Includes re-entry in 1983.

| HORIZON | A&M | 1 | 28 Jun 75 | 27 |
| TICKET TO RIDE [RI] | Hamlet | 35 | 23 Aug 75 | 2 |

Re-released at mid-price.

A KIND OF HUSH	A&M	3	3 Jul 76	15
LIVE AT THE PALLADIUM	A&M	28	8 Jan 77	3
PASSAGE	A&M	12	8 Oct 77	12
THE SINGLES 1974–1978	A&M	12	2 Dec 78	20
MADE IN AMERICA	A&M	12	27 Jun 81	10
VOICE OF THE HEART	A&M	6	15 Oct 83	19
YESTERDAY ONCE MORE	EMI	10	20 Oct 84	26
THE SINGLES 1969–1973 [RE]	A&M	24	13 Jan 90	9
THE SINGLES 1974–1978 [RE]	A&M	42	13 Jan 90	7
LOVELINES	A&M	73	13 Jan 90	1
ONLY YESTERDAY – RICHARD & KAREN CARPENTER'S GREATEST HITS	A&M	1	31 Mar 90	82
INTERPRETATIONS	A&M	29	15 Oct 94	10

Album of cover versions.

| LOVE SONGS | A&M | 47 | 22 Nov 97 | 8 |

Joe 'Fingers' CARR

US

SINGLES:	HITS 1		WEEKS 5	
PORTUGUESE WASHERWOMAN	Capitol	20	30 Jun 56	5

Linda CARR

US

SINGLES:	HITS 2		WEEKS 12	
HIGHWIRE	Chelsea	15	12 Jul 75	8

Above hit: Linda CARR and the LOVE SQUAD.

| SOLD MY ROCK 'N' ROLL (GAVE IT FOR FUNKY SOUL) | Spark | 36 | 5 Jun 76 | 4 |

Above hit: LINDA and the FUNKY BOYS.

Pearl **CARR** – See Teddy JOHNSON and Pearl CARR

Suzi CARR   US

SINGLES:		HITS 1		WEEKS 1
ALL OVER ME	Cowboy	45	8 Oct 94	1

Valerie CARR with Hugo PERETTI and his Orchestra   US

SINGLES:		HITS 1		WEEKS 2
WHEN THE BOYS TALK ABOUT THE GIRLS	Columbia	29	5 Jul 58	1
WHEN THE BOYS TALK ABOUT THE GIRLS [RE]	Columbia	30	19 Jul 58	1

Vikki CARR   US

SINGLES:		HITS 3		WEEKS 26
IT MUST BE HIM (SEUL SUR SON E TOILE)	Liberty	2	3 Jun 67	20
THERE I GO (SE PER TE C'E SOLTANTO QUELL'UOMO)	Liberty	50	2 Sep 67	1
WITH PEN IN HAND	Liberty	43	15 Mar 69	1
Originally recorded by Bobby Goldsboro.				
WITH PEN IN HAND [RE-1ST]	Liberty	39	29 Mar 69	2
WITH PEN IN HAND [RE-2ND]	Liberty	40	3 May 69	2
ALBUMS:		HITS 2		WEEKS 12
WAY OF TODAY	Liberty	31	22 Jul 67	2
IT MUST BE HIM	Liberty	12	12 Aug 67	10

Raffaella CARRA   Italy

SINGLES:		HITS 1		WEEKS 12
DO IT, DO IT AGAIN	Epic	9	15 Apr 78	12

Paul CARRACK   UK

SINGLES:		HITS 4		WEEKS 18
WHEN YOU WALK IN THE ROOM	Chrysalis	48	16 May 87	5
DON'T SHED A TEAR	Chrysalis	60	18 Mar 89	3
EYES OF BLUE	I.R.S.	40	6 Jan 96	4
HOW LONG?	I.R.S.	32	6 Apr 96	5
EYES OF BLUE [RI]	I.R.S.	45	24 Aug 96	1
ALBUMS:		HITS 1		WEEKS 7
BLUE VIEWS	I.R.S.	55	3 Feb 96	7

José CARRERAS   Spain

(See also Placido Domingo, Diana Ross and José Carreras; Placido Domingo, José Carreras and Montserrat Caballe; 3 Tenors: José Carreras, Placido Domingo, Luciano Pavarotti; Various Artists: Studio Cast 'West Side Story, South Pacific'.)

SINGLES:		HITS 1		WEEKS 11
AMIGOS PARA SIEMPRE (FRIENDS FOR LIFE)	Really Useful	11	11 Jul 92	11
The official theme to the Barcelona 1992 Olympic Games.				
Above hit: Jose CARRERAS and Sarah BRIGHTMAN.				
ALBUMS:		HITS 7		WEEKS 35
JOSÉ CARRERAS COLLECTION	Stylus	90	1 Oct 88	4
JOSÉ CARRERAS SINGS ANDREW LLOYD WEBBER	WEA	42	23 Dec 89	6
THE ESSENTIAL JOSÉ CARRERAS	Philips	24	23 Feb 91	9
HOLLYWOOD GOLDEN CLASSICS	East West	47	6 Apr 91	3
AMIGOS PARA SIEMPRE (FRIENDS FOR LIFE)	East West	53	8 Aug 92	4
WITH A SONG IN MY HEART	Teldec	73	16 Oct 93	1
PASSION	Erato	21	3 Feb 96	8

Tia CARRERE   US

SINGLES:		HITS 1		WEEKS 6
BALLROOM BLITZ	Reprise	26	30 May 92	6
From the film 'Wayne's World'.				

Jim CARREY   US

SINGLES:		HITS 1		WEEKS 3
CUBAN PETE	Columbia	31	21 Jan 95	3
From the film 'The Mask'.				

CARRIE   UK/US/Australia

SINGLES:		HITS 2		WEEKS 2
MOLLY	Island	56	14 Mar 98	1
CALIFORNIA SCREAMIN'	Island	55	9 May 98	1

Dina CARROLL   UK

SINGLES:		HITS 13		WEEKS 97
IT'S TOO LATE	Mercury	8	2 Feb 91	14
Above hit: QUARTZ introducing Dina CARROLL.				

NAKED LOVE (JUST SAY YOU WANT ME)	*Mercury*	39	*15 Jun 91*	3
Above hit: QUARTZ and Dina CARROLL.				
AIN'T NO MAN	*A&M*	16	*11 Jul 92*	8
SPECIAL KIND OF LOVE	*A&M*	16	*10 Oct 92*	5
SO CLOSE	*A&M*	20	*5 Dec 92*	8
THIS TIME	*A&M*	23	*27 Feb 93*	6
EXPRESS	*A&M*	12	*15 May 93*	6
DON'T BE A STRANGER	*A&M*	3	*16 Oct 93*	13
THE PERFECT YEAR	*A&M*	5	*11 Dec 93*	11
From the musical 'Sunset Boulevard'.				
ESCAPING	*Mercury*	3	*28 Sep 96*	8
ONLY HUMAN	*Mercury*	33	*21 Dec 96*	4
ONE, TWO, THREE	*Mercury*	16	*24 Oct 98*	4
WITHOUT LOVE	*Manifesto*	13	*24 Jul 99*	7
ALBUMS:	**HITS 2**			**WEEKS 76**
SO CLOSE	*A&M*	2	*30 Jan 93*	63
ONLY HUMAN	*Mercury*	2	*26 Oct 96*	13

Jimmy CARROLL and his Orchestra - See Frankie LAINE; Guy MITCHELL

Ronnie CARROLL   UK

SINGLES:	**HITS 7**			**WEEKS 50**
WALK HAND IN HAND	*Philips*	13	*28 Jul 56*	8
Above hit: Ronnie CARROLL with Wally STOTT and his Orchestra.				
THE WISDOM OF A FOOL	*Philips*	20	*30 Mar 57*	2
Originally recorded by Annette Klooger with the Ted Heath Band.				
FOOTSTEPS	*Philips*	36	*2 Apr 60*	3
RING-A-DING GIRL	*Philips*	46	*24 Feb 62*	3
ROSES ARE RED (MY LOVE)	*Philips*	3	*4 Aug 62*	16
IF ONLY TOMORROW (COULD BE LIKE TODAY)	*Philips*	33	*17 Nov 62*	4
SAY WONDERFUL THINGS	*Philips*	6	*9 Mar 63*	14
All 6 above: Ronnie CARROLL with Wally STOTT and his Orchestra and Chorus.				

Jasper CARROTT   UK

SINGLES:	**HITS 1**			**WEEKS 15**
FUNKY MOPED / MAGIC ROUNDABOUT	*DJM*	5	*16 Aug 75*	15
ALBUMS:	**HITS 8**			**WEEKS 66**
RABBITS ON AND ON	*DJM*	10	*18 Oct 75*	7
CARROTT IN NOTTS	*DJM*	56	*6 Nov 76*	1
THE BEST OF JASPER CARROTT	*DJM*	38	*25 Nov 78*	13
THE UNRECORDED JASPER CARROTT	*DJM*	19	*20 Oct 79*	15
BEAT THE CARROTT	*DJM*	13	*19 Sep 81*	16
CARROTT'S LIB	*DJM*	80	*25 Dec 82*	3
THE STUN (CARROTT TELLS ALL)	*DJM*	57	*19 Nov 83*	8
COSMIC CARROTT	*Portrait*	66	*7 Feb 87*	3

CARS   US

SINGLES:	**HITS 5**			**WEEKS 51**
MY BEST FRIEND'S GIRL	*Elektra*	3	*11 Nov 78*	10
The first single released on picture disc.				
JUST WHAT I NEEDED	*Elektra*	17	*17 Feb 79*	10
LET'S GO	*Elektra*	51	*28 Jul 79*	4
SINCE YOU'RE GONE	*Elektra*	37	*5 Jun 82*	4
DRIVE	*Elektra*	5	*29 Sep 84*	11
DRIVE [RE]	*Elektra*	4	*3 Aug 85*	12
Re-entered after its airing at Live Aid.				
ALBUMS:	**HITS 5**			**WEEKS 72**
CARS	*Elektra*	29	*2 Dec 78*	15
CANDY-O	*Elektra*	30	*7 Jul 79*	6
HEARTBEAT CITY	*Elektra*	27	*6 Oct 84*	15
HEARTBEAT CITY [RE]	*Elektra*	25	*27 Jul 85*	15
THE CARS GREATEST HITS	*Elektra*	27	*9 Nov 85*	19
DOOR TO DOOR	*Elektra*	72	*5 Sep 87*	2

Aaron CARTER   US

SINGLES:	**HITS 4**			**WEEKS 24**
CRUSH ON YOU	*Ultra Pop*	9	*29 Nov 97*	8
CRAZY LITTLE PARTY GIRL	*Ultra Pop*	7	*7 Feb 98*	6
I'M GONNA MISS YOU FOREVER	*Ultra Pop*	24	*28 Mar 98*	5
SURFIN' USA	*Ultra Pop*	18	*4 Jul 98*	5
ALBUMS:	**HITS 1**			**WEEKS 8**
AARON CARTER	*Ultra Pop*	12	*28 Feb 98*	8

Clarence CARTER
US

SINGLES:		HITS 1			WEEKS 13
PATCHES	Atlantic	2	10 Oct 70	13

Originally recorded by Chairmen Of The Board.

CARTER – THE UNSTOPPABLE SEX MACHINE
UK

SINGLES:		HITS 13			WEEKS 46
BLOODSPORTS FOR ALL	Rough Trade	48	26 Jan 91	2
SHERIFF FATMAN	Big Cat	23	22 Jun 91	7
AFTER THE WATERSHED (EARLY LEARNING THE HARD WAY)	Chrysalis	11	26 Oct 91	5
RUBBISH	Big Cat	14	11 Jan 92	5
THE ONLY LIVING BOY IN NEW CROSS	Big Cat	7	25 Apr 92	5
DO RE ME, SO FAR SO GOOD	Chrysalis	22	4 Jul 92	3
THE IMPOSSIBLE DREAM	Chrysalis	21	28 Nov 92	3
LEAN ON ME I WON'T FALL OVER	Chrysalis	16	4 Sep 93	3
LENNY AND TERENCE	Chrysalis	40	16 Oct 93	2
GLAM ROCK COPS	Chrysalis	24	12 Mar 94	3
LET'S GET TATTOOS	Chrysalis	30	19 Nov 94	3
THE YOUNG OFFENDER'S MUM	Chrysalis	34	4 Feb 95	3
BORN ON THE 5TH OF NOVEMBER	Chrysalis	35	30 Sep 95	2
ALBUMS:		**HITS 8**			**WEEKS 40**
30 SOMETHING	Rough Trade	8	2 Mar 91	9
101 DAMNATIONS	Big Cat	29	21 Sep 91	6
30 SOMETHING [RI]	Chrysalis	21	1 Feb 92	4
1992 – THE LOVE ALBUM	Chrysalis	1	16 May 92	9
POST HISTORIC MONSTERS	Chrysalis	5	18 Sep 93	4
STARRY EYED AND BOLLOCK NAKED	Chrysalis	22	26 Mar 94	2
WORRY BOMB	Chrysalis	9	18 Feb 95	3
STRAW DONKEY . . . THE SINGLES	Chrysalis	37	14 Oct 95	2
A WORLD WITHOUT DAVE	Cooking Vinyl	73	5 Apr 97	1

6 track mini-LP.

CARTER TWINS
Ireland

SINGLES:		HITS 1			WEEKS 1
THE TWELFTH OF NEVER / TOO RIGHT TO BE WRONG	RCA	61	8 Mar 97	1

Junior CARTIER
UK

(See also Money Mafia.)

SINGLES:		HITS 1			WEEKS 1
WOMEN BEAT THEIR MEN	Nucamp	70	6 Nov 99	1

Samples Dominatrix's The Dominatrix Sleeps Tonight.

CARTOONS
Denmark

SINGLES:		HITS 3			WEEKS 30
WITCH DOCTOR	Flex	2	3 Apr 99	13
DOODAH!	Flex	7	19 Jun 99	11
AISY WAISY	Island	16	4 Sep 99	5
DOODAH! [RE]	Flex	73	16 Oct 99	1
ALBUMS:		**HITS 1**			**WEEKS 14**
TOONAGE	Flex	17	17 Apr 99	14

Sam CARTWRIGHT – See VOLCANO

CARVELLS
UK

SINGLES:		HITS 1			WEEKS 4
THE L.A. RUN	Creole	31	26 Nov 77	4

CASCADES
US

SINGLES:		HITS 1			WEEKS 16
RHYTHM OF THE RAIN	Warner Brothers	5	2 Mar 63	16

CASE featuring Foxxy BROWN
US

SINGLES:		HITS 1			WEEKS 3
TOUCH ME TEASE ME	Def Jam	26	21 Sep 96	3

From the film 'The Nutty Professor'.

Natalie CASEY
UK

SINGLES:		HITS 1			WEEKS 1
CHICK CHICK CHICKEN	Polydor	72	7 Jan 84	1

Plays Carol Groves in Channel 4 Soap 'Hollyoaks'. Youngest artist to have a chart hit at the age of 3.

Johnny CASH US

SINGLES:		HITS 5			WEEKS 59
IT AIN'T ME BABE	CBS		28	5 Jun 65	8
Originally recorded by Bob Dylan.					
A BOY NAMED SUE	CBS		4	6 Sep 69	19
Originally recorded by Shel Silverstein.					
WHAT IS TRUTH	CBS		21	23 May 70	11
A THING CALLED LOVE	CBS		4	15 Apr 72	13
Originally recorded by Jerry Reed.					
Above hit: Johnny CASH and the EVANGEL TEMPLE CHOIR.					
A THING CALLED LOVE [RE]	CBS		48	22 Jul 72	1
ONE PIECE AT A TIME	CBS		32	3 Jul 76	7
Above hit: Johnny CASH and the TENNESSEE THREE.					

EPS:		HITS 1			WEEKS 2
MEAN AS HELL	CBS		8	4 Jun 66	2

ALBUMS:		HITS 17			WEEKS 290
EVERYBODY LOVES A NUT	CBS		28	23 Jul 66	1
FROM SEA TO SHINING SEA	CBS		40	4 May 68	1
OLD GOLDEN THROAT	CBS		37	6 Jul 68	2
JOHNNY CASH AT FOLSOM PRISON	CBS		8	24 Aug 68	53
JOHNNY CASH AT SAN QUENTIN	CBS		2	23 Aug 69	114
Above 2 are live recordings at the respective prisons. Johnny Cash at San Quentin was also a TV soundtrack for a Granada ITV documentary.					
GREATEST HITS VOLUME 1	CBS		23	4 Oct 69	25
HELLO I'M JOHNNY CASH	CBS		6	7 Mar 70	16
THE WORLD OF JOHNNY CASH	CBS		5	15 Aug 70	31
THE JOHNNY CASH SHOW	CBS		18	12 Dec 70	6
MAN IN BLACK	CBS		18	18 Sep 71	7
JOHNNY CASH	Hallmark		43	13 Nov 71	2
A THING CALLED LOVE	CBS		8	20 May 72	11
STAR PORTRAIT	CBS		16	14 Oct 72	7
ONE PIECE AT A TIME	CBS		49	10 Jul 76	3
THE BEST OF JOHNNY CASH	CBS		48	9 Oct 76	2
ITCHY FEET	CBS		36	2 Sep 78	4
THE MAN IN BLACK - DEFINITIVE COLLECTION	Columbia		15	27 Aug 94	5

Pat CASH - See John McENROE and Pat CASH with the FULL METAL RACKETS

CASHFLOW US

SINGLES:		HITS 1			WEEKS 8
MINE ALL MINE / PARTY FREAK	Club		15	24 May 86	8

ALBUMS:		HITS 1			WEEKS 3
CASHFLOW	Club		33	28 Jun 86	3

CASHMERE US

SINGLES:		HITS 2			WEEKS 11
CAN I	Fourth & Broadway		29	19 Jan 85	8
WE NEED LOVE	Fourth & Broadway		52	23 Mar 85	3

ALBUMS:		HITS 1			WEEKS 5
CASHMERE	Fourth & Broadway		63	2 Mar 85	5

CASINO UK

SINGLES:		HITS 2			WEEKS 2
SOUND OF EDEN	Worx		52	17 May 97	1
ONLY YOU	POW!		72	10 Jul 99	1

CASINOS US

SINGLES:		HITS 1			WEEKS 7
THEN YOU CAN TELL ME GOODBYE	President		28	25 Feb 67	7
Originally recorded by John D. Loudermilk.					

David CASSIDY US

(See also Partridge Family.)

SINGLES:		HITS 11			WEEKS 109
COULD IT BE FOREVER / CHERISH	Bell		2	8 Apr 72	17
Cherish was originally recorded by the Association and reached No. 1 in the US in 1966.					
HOW CAN I BE SURE	Bell		1	16 Sep 72	11
Original by the Young Rascals reached No. 4 in the US in 1967.					
ROCK ME BABY	Bell		11	25 Nov 72	9
I AM A CLOWN / SOME KIND OF A SUMMER	Bell		3	24 Mar 73	12
DAYDREAMER / THE PUPPY SONG	Bell		1	13 Oct 73	15
IF I DIDN'T CARE	Bell		9	11 May 74	8
Originally recorded by Inkspots.					

PLEASE PLEASE ME	*Bell*	16	*27 Jul 74*	6
Live recording.				
I WRITE THE SONGS / GET IT UP FOR LOVE	*RCA Victor*	11	*5 Jul 75*	8
I Write The Songs originally recorded by Bruce Johnston.				
DARLIN'	*RCA Victor*	16	*25 Oct 75*	8
THE LAST KISS	*Arista*	6	*23 Feb 85*	9
Backing vocals by George Michael.				
ROMANCE (LET YOUR HEART GO)	*Arista*	54	*11 May 85*	6
ALBUMS:	**HITS 6**			**WEEKS 94**
CHERISH	*Bell*	2	*20 May 72*	43
ROCK ME BABY	*Bell*	2	*24 Feb 73*	20
DREAMS ARE NUTHIN' MORE THAN WISHES	*Bell*	1	*24 Nov 73*	13
CASSIDY LIVE	*Bell*	9	*3 Aug 74*	7
THE HIGHER THEY CLIMB	*RCA Victor*	22	*9 Aug 75*	5
ROMANCE	*Arista*	20	*8 Jun 85*	6

CASSIUS   France

SINGLES:	**HITS 3**			**WEEKS 12**
CASSIUS 99	*Virgin*	7	*23 Jan 99*	7
Samples Donna Summer's Love Is Just A Breath Away.				
FEELING FOR YOU	*Virgin*	16	*15 May 99*	4
Samples Gwen McCrae's All The Love That I'm Giving.				
LA MOUCHE	*Virgin*	53	*20 Nov 99*	1
Title is French for the fly. Single is based around the Scientist's hit The Bee.				
ALBUMS:	**HITS 1**			**WEEKS 2**
1999	*Virgin*	28	*6 Feb 99*	2

CAST   UK

SINGLES:	**HITS 11**			**WEEKS 54**
FINETIME	*Polydor*	17	*15 Jul 95*	4
ALRIGHT	*Polydor*	13	*30 Sep 95*	4
SANDSTORM	*Polydor*	8	*20 Jan 96*	5
WALKAWAY	*Polydor*	9	*30 Mar 96*	7
FLYING	*Polydor*	4	*26 Oct 96*	5
FREE ME	*Polydor*	7	*5 Apr 97*	6
FREE ME [RE]	*Polydor*	64	*21 Jun 97*	1
GUIDING STAR	*Polydor*	9	*28 Jun 97*	6
LIVE THE DREAM	*Polydor*	7	*13 Sep 97*	5
I'M SO LONELY	*Polydor*	14	*15 Nov 97*	3
BEAT MAMA	*Polydor*	9	*8 May 99*	5
MAGIC HOUR	*Polydor*	28	*7 Aug 99*	3
ALBUMS:	**HITS 3**			**WEEKS 116**
ALL CHANGE	*Polydor*	7	*28 Oct 95*	67
MOTHER NATURE CALLS	*Polydor*	3	*26 Apr 97*	42
MAGIC HOUR	*Polydor*	6	*29 May 99*	7

CAST FROM CASUALTY   UK

SINGLES:	**HITS 1**			**WEEKS 6**
EVERLASTING LOVE	*warner.esp*	5	*14 Mar 98*	6

CAST OF THE NEW ROCKY HORROR SHOW   UK

SINGLES:	**HITS 1**			**WEEKS 1**
THE TIMEWARP	*Damm It Janet*	57	*12 Dec 98*	1

Roy CASTLE with Wally STOTT and his ORCHESTRA   UK

SINGLES:	**HITS 1**			**WEEKS 3**
LITTLE WHITE BERRY	*Philips*	40	*24 Dec 60*	3

CASUALS   UK

SINGLES:	**HITS 2**			**WEEKS 26**
JESAMINE	*Decca*	2	*17 Aug 68*	18
Originally recorded by the Bystanders.				
TOY	*Decca*	30	*7 Dec 68*	8

Elaine CASWELL - See Joe JACKSON

CAT   UK

SINGLES:	**HITS 1**			**WEEKS 4**
TONGUE TIED	*EMI*	17	*23 Oct 93*	4

146

CATATONIA
UK

(See also Space.)

SINGLES:		HITS 12		WEEKS 46
SWEET CATATONIA	Blanco Y Negro	61	3 Feb 96	1
LOST CAT	Blanco Y Negro	41	4 May 96	1
YOU'VE GOT A LOT TO ANSWER FOR	Blanco Y Negro	35	7 Sep 96	2
BLEED	Blanco Y Negro	46	30 Nov 96	1
Original release on the Nursery label in 1995 reached No. 158.				
I AM THE MOB	Blanco Y Negro	40	18 Oct 97	2
MULDER AND SCULLY	Blanco Y Negro	3	31 Jan 98	10
ROAD RAGE	Blanco Y Negro	5	2 May 98	8
STRANGE GLUE	Blanco Y Negro	11	1 Aug 98	6
GAME ON	Blanco Y Negro	33	7 Nov 98	2
DEAD FROM THE WAIST DOWN	Blanco Y Negro	7	10 Apr 99	8
LONDINIUM	Blanco Y Negro	20	24 Jul 99	3
KARAOKE QUEEN	Blanco Y Negro	36	13 Nov 99	2
ALBUMS:		HITS 3		WEEKS 112
WAY BEYOND BLUE	Blanco Y Negro	40	12 Oct 96	1
INTERNATIONAL VELVET	Blanco Y Negro	1	14 Feb 98	86
EQUALLY CURSED AND BLESSED	Blanco Y Negro	1	24 Apr 99	23
WAY BEYOND BLUE [RE]	Blanco Y Negro	32	24 Apr 99	2

CATCH
UK

SINGLES:		HITS 1		WEEKS 1
FREE (C'MON)	ffrr	70	17 Nov 90	1

CATCH
UK

SINGLES:		HITS 2		WEEKS 6
BINGO	Virgin	23	11 Oct 97	4
DIVE IN	Virgin	44	21 Feb 98	2

CATHERINE WHEEL
UK

SINGLES:		HITS 10		WEEKS 12
BLACK METALLIC [EP]	Fontana	68	23 Nov 91	1
Lead track: Black Metallic.				
BALLOON	Fontana	59	8 Feb 92	1
I WANT TO TOUCH YOU	Fontana	35	18 Apr 92	2
30 CENTURY MAN	Fontana	47	9 Jan 93	2
Cover of a Scott Walker song from his 1969 album Scott 3.				
CRANK	Fontana	66	10 Jul 93	1
SHOW ME MARY	Fontana	62	16 Oct 93	1
WAYDOWN	Fontana	67	5 Aug 95	1
DELICIOUS	Chrysalis	53	13 Dec 97	1
MA SOLITUDA	Chrysalis	53	28 Feb 98	1
BROKEN NOSE	Chrysalis	48	2 May 98	1
ALBUMS:		HITS 3		WEEKS 3
FERMENT	Fontana	36	29 Feb 92	1
CHROME	Fontana	58	31 Jul 93	1
ADAM AND EVE	Chrysalis	53	16 May 98	1

CATHOLICS – See Frank BLACK

Lorraine CATO
UK

SINGLES:		HITS 2		WEEKS 3
HOW CAN YOU TELL ME IT'S OVER?	Columbia	46	6 Feb 93	2
I WAS MADE TO LOVE YOU	MCA	41	3 Aug 96	1

CATS
UK

SINGLES:		HITS 1		WEEKS 2
SWAN LAKE	BAF	48	12 Apr 69	1
SWAN LAKE [RE]	BAF	50	24 May 69	1

CATS U.K.
UK

SINGLES:		HITS 1		WEEKS 8
LUTON AIRPORT	WEA	22	6 Oct 79	8
The catch phrase from the Lorraine Chase Campari TV commercial.				

Nick CAVE and the BAD SEEDS
Australia/Germany

SINGLES:		HITS 7		WEEKS 10
STRAIGHT TO YOU / JACK THE RIPPER	Mute	68	11 Apr 92	1
WHAT A WONDERFUL WORLD	Mute	72	12 Dec 92	1
Above hit: Nick CAVE and Shane MacGOWAN.				
DO YOU LOVE ME?	Mute	68	9 Apr 94	1

WHERE THE WILD ROSES GROW	Mute	11	14 Oct 95	4
Above hit: Nick CAVE and the BAD SEEDS + Kylie MINOGUE.				
HENRY LEE	Mute	36	9 Mar 96	1
Above hit: Nick CAVE and PJ HARVEY and the BAD SEEDS.				
INTO MY ARMS	Mute	53	22 Feb 97	1
(ARE YOU) THE ONE THAT I'VE BEEN WAITING FOR?	Mute	67	31 May 97	1
ALBUMS:	**HITS 11**			**WEEKS 24**
FROM HER TO ETERNITY	Mute	40	2 Jun 84	3
Above hit: Nick CAVE featuring the BAD SEEDS.				
THE FIRST BORN IS DEAD	Mute	53	15 Jun 85	1
KICKING AGAINST THE PRICKS	Mute	89	30 Aug 86	1
TENDER PREY	Mute	67	1 Oct 88	1
THE GOOD SON	Mute	47	28 Apr 90	1
HENRY'S DREAM	Mute	29	9 May 92	2
LIVE SEEDS	Mute	67	18 Sep 93	1
LET LOVE IN	Mute	12	30 Apr 94	2
MURDER BALLADS	Mute	8	17 Feb 96	5
THE BOATMAN'S CALL	Mute	22	15 Mar 97	3
THE BEST OF NICK CAVE AND THE BAD SEEDS	Mute	11	23 May 98	4

CAVEMAN UK

SINGLES:	**HITS 1**			**WEEKS 2**
I'M READY	Profile	65	9 Mar 91	2
ALBUMS:	**HITS 1**			**WEEKS 2**
POSITIVE REACTION	Profile	43	13 Apr 91	2

CECIL UK

SINGLES:	**HITS 2**			**WEEKS 2**
HOSTAGE IN A FROCK	Parlophone	68	25 Oct 97	1
THE MOST TIRING DAY	Parlophone	69	28 Mar 98	1

CELEDA UK

SINGLES:	**HITS 2**			**WEEKS 5**
MUSIC IS THE ANSWER (DANCIN' AND PRANCIN')	Twisted UK	36	5 Sep 98	3
Above hit: Danny TENAGLIA + CELEDA.				
BE YOURSELF	Twisted UK	61	12 Jun 99	1
MUSIC IS THE ANSWER '99 (DANCIN' AND PRANCIN') [RM]	Twisted UK	50	23 Oct 99	1
Remixed by Future Shock.				
Above hit: Danny TENAGLIA + CELEDA.				

CELETIA UK

SINGLES:	**HITS 2**			**WEEKS 3**
REWIND	Big Life	29	11 Apr 98	2
RUNAWAY SKIES	Big Life	66	8 Aug 98	1

CELTIC SPIRIT UK

ALBUMS:	**HITS 1**			**WEEKS 1**
CELTIC DREAMS	PolyGram TV	62	31 Jan 98	1

CENTORY US

SINGLES:	**HITS 1**			**WEEKS 1**
POINT OF NO RETURN	EMI	67	17 Dec 94	1

CENTRAL LINE UK

SINGLES:	**HITS 6**			**WEEKS 30**
(YOU KNOW) YOU CAN DO IT	Mercury	67	31 Jan 81	3
WALKING INTO SUNSHINE	Mercury	42	15 Aug 81	10
DON'T TELL ME	Mercury	55	30 Jan 82	3
YOU'VE SAID ENOUGH	Mercury	58	20 Nov 82	3
NATURE BOY	Mercury	21	22 Jan 83	8
SURPRISE SURPRISE	Mercury	48	11 Jun 83	3
ALBUMS:	**HITS 1**			**WEEKS 5**
BREAKING POINT	Mercury	64	13 Feb 82	5

CERRONE France

SINGLES:	**HITS 3**			**WEEKS 21**
LOVE IS 'C' MINOR	Atlantic	31	5 Mar 77	4
SUPERNATURE	Atlantic	8	29 Jul 78	12
Features Stephanie De Sykes and Madeline Bell (Blue Mink) on vocals.				
JE SUIS MUSIC	CBS	39	13 Jan 79	4
SUPERNATURE [RM]	Encore	66	10 Aug 96	1
Remixed by the Candy Girls.				

ALBUMS:	HITS 1			WEEKS 1
SUPERNATURE	Atlantic	60	30 Sep 78	1

A CERTAIN RATIO
UK

SINGLES:	HITS 1			WEEKS 3
WON'T STOP LOVING YOU	A&M	55	16 Jun 90	3
Original release reached No. 96 in 1989.				

ALBUMS:	HITS 1			WEEKS 3
SEXTET	Factory	53	30 Jan 82	3

CERYS of CATATONIA – See Tom JONES; SPACE

Peter CETERA
US

SINGLES:	HITS 2			WEEKS 20
GLORY OF LOVE (THEME FROM KARATE KID PT. II)	Full Moon	3	2 Aug 86	13
From the film 'The Karate Kid Part II'.				
HARD TO SAY I'M SORRY	LaFace	7	21 Jun 97	7
Above hit: AZ YET featuring Peter CETERA.				

ALBUMS:	HITS 1			WEEKS 4
SOLITUDE/SOLITAIRE	Full Moon	56	13 Sep 86	4

Frank CHACKSFIELD and His Orchestra
UK

SINGLES:	HITS 6			WEEKS 41
LITTLE RED MONKEY	Parlophone	10	4 Apr 53	3
Above hit: Frank CHACKSFIELD'S TUNESMITHS with Jack JORDAN (clavioline).				
TERRY'S THEME FROM "LIMELIGHT"	Decca	2	23 May 53	24
From the film 'Limelight'.				
EBB TIDE	Decca	9	13 Feb 54	2
Originally recorded by Robert Maxwell.				
IN OLD LISBON	Decca	15	25 Feb 56	4
PORT-AU-PRINCE	Decca	18	19 May 56	6
Above hit: Winifred ATWELL and Frank CHACKSFIELD.				
THE DONKEY CART	Decca	26	1 Sep 56	2

CHAIRMEN OF THE BOARD
US

SINGLES:	HITS 10			WEEKS 78
GIVE ME JUST A LITTLE MORE TIME	Invictus	3	22 Aug 70	13
YOU'VE GOT ME DANGLING ON A STRING	Invictus	5	14 Nov 70	13
EVERYTHING'S TUESDAY	Invictus	12	20 Feb 71	9
PAY TO THE PIPER	Invictus	34	15 May 71	7
CHAIRMAN OF THE BOARD	Invictus	48	4 Sep 71	2
WORKING ON A BUILDING OF LOVE	Invictus	20	15 Jul 72	8
ELMO JAMES	Invictus	21	7 Oct 72	7
I'M ON MY WAY TO A BETTER PLACE	Invictus	38	16 Dec 72	1
I'M ON MY WAY TO A BETTER PLACE [RE]	Invictus	30	6 Jan 73	6
FINDERS KEEPERS	Invictus	21	23 Jun 73	9
LOVER BOY	EMI	56	13 Sep 86	3
Above hit: CHAIRMEN OF THE BOARD featuring GENERAL JOHNSON.				

CHAKACHAS
Belgium

SINGLES:	HITS 2			WEEKS 8
TWIST TWIST	RCA	48	13 Jan 62	1
JUNGLE FEVER	Polydor	29	27 May 72	7

George CHAKIRIS
US

SINGLES:	HITS 1			WEEKS 1
HEART OF A TEENAGE GIRL	Triumph	49	4 Jun 60	1

CHAKKA BOOM BANG
Holland

SINGLES:	HITS 1			WEEKS 1
TOSSING AND TURNING	Hooj Choons	57	20 Jan 96	1

CHAKRA
UK

SINGLES:	HITS 3			WEEKS 4
I AM	WEA	24	18 Jan 97	2
Originally released in 1996.				
HOME	WEA	46	23 Aug 97	1
LOVE SHINES THROUGH	WEA	67	23 Oct 99	1
Vocals by Kate Cameron.				

Sue CHALONER
UK

SINGLES:	HITS 1			WEEKS 1
MOVE ON UP	Pulse 8	64	22 May 93	1

Richard CHAMBERLAIN | US

SINGLES:		HITS 4		WEEKS 36	
THEME FROM DR. KILDARE (THREE STARS WILL SHINE TONIGHT)	*MGM*	12	*9 Jun 62*	10
LOVE ME TENDER	*MGM*	15	*3 Nov 62*	11
HI-LILI, HI-LO	*MGM*	20	*23 Feb 63*	9
Originally recorded by Leslie Caron.				
TRUE LOVE	*MGM*	30	*20 Jul 63*	6
ALBUMS:		HITS 1		WEEKS 8
RICHARD CHAMBERLAIN SINGS	*MGM*	8	*16 Mar 63*	8

CHAMELEON | UK

SINGLES:		HITS 1		WEEKS 2
THE WAY IT IS	*Stress*	34	*18 May 96*	2
First released through DMC in 1995.				

CHAMELEONS | US

ALBUMS:		HITS 2		WEEKS 4
WHAT DOES ANYTHING MEAN? BASICALLY	*Statik*	60	*25 May 85*	2
STRANGE TIMES	*Geffen*	44	*20 Sep 86*	2

CHAMPAIGN | US

SINGLES:		HITS 1		WEEKS 13
HOW 'BOUT US	*CBS*	5	*9 May 81*	13
ALBUMS:		HITS 1		WEEKS 4
HOW 'BOUT US	*CBS*	38	*27 Jun 81*	4

CHAMPIONS - See MANCHESTER UNITED FOOTBALL SQUAD

CHAMPS | US

SINGLES:		HITS 2		WEEKS 10
TEQUILA	*London*	5	*5 Apr 58*	9
TOO MUCH TEQUILA	*London*	49	*19 Mar 60*	1

CHAMPS BOYS | France

SINGLES:		HITS 1		WEEKS 6
TUBULAR BELLS	*Philips*	41	*19 Jun 76*	6

CHANCE - See SUNKIDS featuring CHANCE

Gene CHANDLER | US

SINGLES:		HITS 4		WEEKS 29
NOTHING CAN STOP ME	*Soul City*	41	*8 Jun 68*	4
GET DOWN	*20th Century*	11	*3 Feb 79*	11
WHEN YOU'RE NUMBER 1	*20th Century*	43	*1 Sep 79*	5
DOES SHE HAVE A FRIEND?	*20th Century*	28	*28 Jun 80*	9

George CHANDLER - See OLYMPIC RUNNERS

CHANELLE | US

SINGLES:		HITS 1		WEEKS 9
ONE MAN	*Cooltempo*	16	*11 Mar 89*	8
ONE MAN [RM]	*Deep Distraxion*	50	*10 Dec 94*	1
Remixed by Joey Musaphia.				

CHANGE | US

SINGLES:		HITS 7		WEEKS 43
A LOVER'S HOLIDAY / THE GLOW OF LOVE	*WEA*	14	*28 Jun 80*	8
SEARCHING	*WEA*	11	*6 Sep 80*	10
CHANGE OF HEART	*WEA*	17	*2 Jun 84*	10
YOU ARE MY MELODY	*WEA*	48	*11 Aug 84*	4
LET'S GO TOGETHER	*Cooltempo*	37	*16 Mar 85*	7
OH WHAT A FEELING	*Cooltempo*	56	*25 May 85*	2
MUTUAL ATTRACTION	*Cooltempo*	60	*13 Jul 85*	2
ALBUMS:		HITS 3		WEEKS 27
CHANGE OF HEART	*WEA*	34	*19 May 84*	17
TURN ON THE RADIO	*Cooltempo*	39	*27 Apr 85*	6
THE ARTISTS VOLUME 2	*Street Sounds*	45	*13 Jul 85*	4
Compilation album with tracks by each artist.				
Above hit: Luther VANDROSS / Teddy PENDERGRASS / CHANGE / ATLANTIC.				
STARR				

CHANGING FACES | US

SINGLES:		HITS 5		WEEKS 12
STROKE YOU UP	*Atlantic*	43	*24 Sep 94*	3

G.H.E.T.T.O.U.T.		*Atlantic*	10	*26 Jul 97*	5
I GOT SOMEBODY ELSE		*Atlantic*	42	*1 Nov 97*	1
TIME AFTER TIME		*Atlantic*	35	*4 Apr 98*	2
Above hit: CHANGING FACES (featuring JAY-Z).					
SAME TEMPO		*A&M*	53	*1 Aug 98*	1
From the film 'The Players Club'.					

CHANNEL X — Belgium

SINGLES:	HITS 1				WEEKS 1
GROOVE TO MOVE		*PWL Continental*	67	*14 Dec 91*	1

Bruce CHANNEL — US

SINGLES:	HITS 2				WEEKS 28
HEY! BABY		*Mercury*	2	*24 Mar 62*	12
Features Delbert McClinton on harmonica.					
KEEP ON		*Bell*	12	*29 Jun 68*	16

CHANSON — US

SINGLES:	HITS 1				WEEKS 7
DON'T HOLD BACK		*Ariola*	33	*13 Jan 79*	7

CHANTAYS — US

SINGLES:	HITS 1				WEEKS 14
PIPELINE		*London*	16	*20 Apr 63*	14

CHANTER SISTERS — UK

SINGLES:	HITS 1				WEEKS 5
SIDESHOW		*Polydor*	43	*17 Jul 76*	5

CHAOS — UK

SINGLES:	HITS 1				WEEKS 2
FAREWELL MY SUMMER LOVE		*Arista*	55	*3 Oct 92*	2

Harry CHAPIN — US

SINGLES:	HITS 1				WEEKS 5
W.O.L.D.		*Elektra*	34	*11 May 74*	5

Michael CHAPMAN — UK

ALBUMS:	HITS 1				WEEKS 1
FULLY QUALIFIED SURVIVOR		*Harvest*	45	*21 Mar 70*	1

Simone CHAPMAN - See ILLEGAL MOTION featuring Simone CHAPMAN

Tracy CHAPMAN — US

SINGLES:	HITS 2				WEEKS 15
FAST CAR		*Elektra*	5	*11 Jun 88*	12
CROSSROADS		*Elektra*	61	*30 Sep 89*	3
ALBUMS:	HITS 3				WEEKS 168
TRACY CHAPMAN		*Elektra*	1	*21 May 88*	75
CROSSROADS		*Elektra*	1	*14 Oct 89*	16
MATTERS OF THE HEART		*Elektra*	19	*9 May 92*	3
TRACY CHAPMAN [RE-1ST]		*Elektra*	19	*2 Apr 94*	74
Re-released at mid-price. Chart position reached in 1999.					

CHAPTERHOUSE — UK

SINGLES:	HITS 2				WEEKS 3
PEARL		*Dedicated*	67	*30 Mar 91*	1
MESMERISE		*Dedicated*	60	*12 Oct 91*	2
ALBUMS:	HITS 1				WEEKS 3
WHIRLPOOL		*Dedicated*	23	*11 May 91*	3

CHAQUITO ORCHESTRA — UK

SINGLES:	HITS 1				WEEKS 1
NEVER ON SUNDAY (JAMIAS LE DIMANCHE)		*Fontana*	50	*29 Oct 60*	1
ALBUMS:	HITS 2				WEEKS 2
THIS IS CHAQUITO		*Fontana*	36	*24 Feb 68*	1
Above hit: CHAQUITO and QUEDO BRASS.					
THRILLER THEMES		*Philips*	48	*4 Mar 72*	1

CHARGED GBH — UK

SINGLES:	HITS 2				WEEKS 5
NO SURVIVORS		*Clay*	63	*6 Feb 82*	2

GIVE ME FIRE	Clay	69	20 Nov 82	3
ALBUMS:	**HITS 1**			**WEEKS 6**
CITY BABY ATTACKED BY RATS	Clay	17	14 Aug 82	6

CHARLATANS   UK

SINGLES:	**HITS 19**			**WEEKS 69**
THE ONLY ONE I KNOW	Situation Two	9	2 Jun 90	9
THEN	Situation Two	12	22 Sep 90	5
OVER RISING	Situation Two	15	9 Mar 91	5
INDIAN ROPE	Dead Dead Good	57	17 Aug 91	1
ME. IN TIME	Situation Two	28	9 Nov 91	3
WEIRDO	Situation Two	19	7 Mar 92	4
TREMELO SONG [EP]	Situation Two	44	18 Jul 92	2
Lead track: Tremelo Song.				
CAN'T GET OUT OF BED	Beggars Banquet	24	5 Feb 94	3
I NEVER WANT AN EASY LIFE IF ME AND HE WERE EVER TO GET THERE	Beggars Banquet	38	19 Mar 94	1
Limited edition boxed CD.				
JESUS HAIRDO	Beggars Banquet	48	2 Jul 94	2
Title taken from quote in Douglas Couplan's Novel 'Shampoo Planet'.				
CRASHIN' IN	Beggars Banquet	31	7 Jan 95	2
JUST LOOKIN / BULLET COMES	Beggars Banquet	32	27 May 95	3
JUST WHEN YOU'RE THINKIN' THINGS OVER	Beggars Banquet	12	26 Aug 95	3
ONE TO ANOTHER	Beggars Banquet	3	7 Sep 96	6
NORTH COUNTRY BOY	Beggars Banquet	4	5 Apr 97	5
Recorded before the death of keyboardist Rob Collins the previous year.				
HOW HIGH	Beggars Banquet	6	21 Jun 97	5
NORTH COUNTRY BOY [RE]	Beggars Banquet	74	21 Jun 97	1
TELLIN' STORIES	Beggars Banquet	16	1 Nov 97	3
FOREVER	Universal	12	16 Oct 99	3
MY BEAUTIFUL FRIEND	Universal	31	18 Dec 99	3
ALBUMS:	**HITS 7**			**WEEKS 97**
SOME FRIENDLY	Situation Two	1	20 Oct 90	17
BETWEEN 10TH AND 11TH	Situation Two	21	4 Apr 92	4
UP TO OUR HIPS	Beggars Banquet	8	2 Apr 94	3
THE CHARLATANS	Beggars Banquet	1	9 Sep 95	13
TELLIN' STORIES	Beggars Banquet	1	3 May 97	28
MELTING POT	Beggars Banquet	4	7 Mar 98	25
Compilation made up of live favourites and rare alternative mixes.				
US AND US ONLY	Universal	2	30 Oct 99	7

CHARLENE   US

SINGLES:	**HITS 1**			**WEEKS 12**
I'VE NEVER BEEN TO ME	Motown	1	15 May 82	12
Originally recorded by Nancy Wilson.				
ALBUMS:	**HITS 1**			**WEEKS 4**
I'VE NEVER BEEN TO ME	Motown	43	17 Jul 82	4

Don CHARLES   UK

SINGLES:	**HITS 1**			**WEEKS 5**
WALK WITH ME MY ANGEL	Decca	39	24 Feb 62	5
Originally recorded by John Leyton.				

Don CHARLES presents the SINGING DOGS   Denmark

SINGLES:	**HITS 1**			**WEEKS 4**
PAT-A-CAKE, PAT-A-CAKE/THREE BLIND MICE/JINGLE BELLS [M] / OH SUSANNA	Pye Nixa	13	26 Nov 55	4
Chart reflects the entry only as 'The Singing Dogs'.				
The above entry only lists both sides.				

Ray CHARLES   US

(See also Quincy Jones.)

SINGLES:	**HITS 16**			**WEEKS 123**
GEORGIA ON MY MIND	His Master's Voice	47	3 Dec 60	1
Originally recorded by Hoagy Carmichael.				
GEORGIA ON MY MIND [RE]	His Master's Voice	24	17 Dec 60	7
HIT THE ROAD JACK	His Master's Voice	6	21 Oct 61	12
Originally recorded by Percy Mayfield.				
Above hit: Ray CHARLES and his Orchestra. Vocal by Ray CHARLES with the RAELETS.				
I CAN'T STOP LOVING YOU	His Master's Voice	1	16 Jun 62	17
Originally recorded by Don Gibson.				
YOU DON'T KNOW ME	His Master's Voice	9	15 Sep 62	13
Originally recorded by Eddy Arnold.				
YOUR CHEATING HEART	His Master's Voice	13	15 Dec 62	8
Originally recorded by Hank Williams.				
Above hit: Ray CHARLES with the Jack HALLORAN SINGERS.				

DON'T SET ME FREE	His Master's Voice	37	30 Mar 63	3

Above hit: Ray CHARLES and his Orchestra with the RAELETTES featuring Margie HENDRIX.

TAKE THESE CHAINS FROM MY HEART	His Master's Voice	5	18 May 63	20

Originally recorded by Hank Williams.
Above hit: Ray CHARLES with the Jack HALLORAN SINGERS.

NO ONE	His Master's Voice	35	14 Sep 63	7
BUSTED	His Master's Voice	21	2 Nov 63	10

Originally recorded by Johnny Cash.
Above hit: Ray CHARLES and his Orchestra.

NO ONE TO CRY TO	His Master's Voice	38	26 Sep 64	3
MAKIN' WHOOPEE	His Master's Voice	42	23 Jan 65	4
CRYIN' TIME	His Master's Voice	50	12 Feb 66	1
TOGETHER AGAIN	His Master's Voice	48	23 Apr 66	1

Above 2 originally recorded by Buck Owens.

HERE WE GO AGAIN	His Master's Voice	38	8 Jul 67	1
HERE WE GO AGAIN [RE]	His Master's Voice	45	22 Jul 67	2
YESTERDAY	Stateside	44	23 Dec 67	4
ELEANOR RIGBY	Stateside	36	3 Aug 68	9
EPS:	**HITS 2**		**WEEKS 41**	
I CAN'T STOP LOVING YOU	HMV	10	12 Jan 63	36
TAKE THESE CHAINS FROM MY HEART	HMV	16	21 Sep 63	5
ALBUMS:	**HITS 7**		**WEEKS 45**	
MODERN SOUNDS IN COUNTRY AND WESTERN MUSIC	His Master's Voice	6	28 Jul 62	16
MODERN SOUNDS IN COUNTRY AND WESTERN MUSIC VOLUME 2	His Master's Voice	15	23 Feb 63	5
GREATEST HITS	His Master's Voice	16	20 Jul 63	5
GREATEST HITS VOLUME 2	Stateside	24	5 Oct 68	8
HEART TO HEART – 20 HOT HITS	London	29	19 Jul 80	5
COLLECTION	Westmoor	36	24 Mar 90	3
RAY CHARLES – THE LIVING LEGEND	Arcade	48	13 Mar 93	3

Ray CHARLES SINGERS - See Perry COMO

Suzette CHARLES   US

SINGLES:	**HITS 1**		**WEEKS 2**	
FREE TO LOVE AGAIN	RCA	58	21 Aug 93	2

Tina CHARLES   UK

SINGLES:	**HITS 7**		**WEEKS 63**	
I LOVE TO LOVE (BUT MY BABY LOVES TO DANCE)	CBS	1	7 Feb 76	12
LOVE ME LIKE A LOVER	CBS	28	1 May 76	7
DANCE LITTLE LADY DANCE	CBS	6	21 Aug 76	13
DR. LOVE	CBS	4	4 Dec 76	10

Originally recorded by the Electric Dolls.

RENDEZVOUS	CBS	27	14 May 77	6
LOVE BUG – SWEETS FOR MY SWEET [M]	CBS	26	29 Oct 77	4
I'LL GO WHERE YOUR MUSIC TAKES ME	CBS	27	11 Mar 78	8
I LOVE TO LOVE (TEENAGE MIX) [RM]	Disco Mix Club	67	30 Aug 86	3
ALBUMS:	**HITS 1**		**WEEKS 7**	
HEART 'N' SOUL	CBS	35	3 Dec 77	7

CHARLES and EDDIE   US

SINGLES:	**HITS 4**		**WEEKS 30**	
WOULD I LIE TO YOU?	Capitol	1	31 Oct 92	17
N.Y.C. (CAN YOU BELIEVE THIS CITY?)	Capitol	33	20 Feb 93	5
HOUSE IS NOT A HOME	Capitol	29	22 May 93	4
24-7-365	Capitol	38	13 May 95	4
ALBUMS:	**HITS 1**		**WEEKS 15**	
DUOPHONIC	Capitol	19	12 Dec 92	15

Dick CHARLESWORTH and his CITY GENTS   UK

SINGLES:	**HITS 1**		**WEEKS 1**	
BILLY BOY	Top Rank	43	6 May 61	1

CHARLOTTE   UK

SINGLES:	**HITS 4**		**WEEKS 4**	
QUEEN OF HEARTS	Big Life	54	12 Mar 94	1
BE MINE	Parlophone	59	2 May 98	1
SKIN	Parlophone Rhythm Series	56	29 May 99	1
SOMEDAY	Parlophone Rhythm Series	74	4 Sep 99	1

CHARME | | | | US

SINGLES:		HITS 1		WEEKS 2
GEORGY PORGY	RCA	68	17 Nov 84	2

Originally recorded by Toto.

CHARO and the SALSOUL ORCHESTRA | | | | US

SINGLES:		HITS 1		WEEKS 4
DANCE A LITTLE BIT CLOSER	Salsoul	44	29 Apr 78	4

CHARVONI – See BROTHERS IN RHYTHM

CHAS and DAVE | | | | UK

(See also Tottenham Hotspur FA Cup Final Squad.)

SINGLES:		HITS 10		WEEKS 66
STRUMMIN' / I'M IN TROUBLE	EMI	52	11 Nov 78	3

I'm In Trouble listed from 18 Nov 78.
Above hit: CHAS and DAVE with ROCKNEY.

GERTCHA	EMI	20	26 May 79	8
THE SIDEBOARD SONG (GOT MY BEER IN THE SIDEBOARD HERE)	EMI	55	1 Sep 79	3
RABBIT	Rockney	8	29 Nov 80	11

Above 3 and Margate used in the Courage Best Bitter TV commercials.

STARS OVER 45 [M]	Rockney	21	12 Dec 81	8

Medley of sing-a-long songs from the early 20th century.

AIN'T NO PLEASING YOU	Rockney	2	13 Mar 82	11
MARGATE	Rockney	46	17 Jul 82	4
LONDON GIRLS	Rockney	63	19 Mar 83	3
MY MELANCHOLY BABY	Rockney	51	3 Dec 83	6
SNOOKER LOOPY	Rockney	6	3 May 86	9

Vocals by snooker stars Stevie Davis, Tony Griffiths, Tony Meo, Dennis Taylor and Willie Thorne.
Above hit: MATCHROOM MOB with CHAS and DAVE.

ALBUMS:		HITS 9		WEEKS 101
CHAS AND DAVE'S CHRISTMAS JAMBOREE BAG	Warwick	25	5 Dec 81	15
MUSTN'T GRUMBLE	Rockney	35	17 Apr 82	11
JOB LOT	Rockney	59	8 Jan 83	15
CHAS AND DAVE'S KNEES UP – JAMBOREE BAG NUMBER 2	Rockney	7	15 Oct 83	17
WELL PLEASED	Rockney	27	11 Aug 84	10
CHAS AND DAVE'S GREATEST HITS	Rockney	16	17 Nov 84	10
CHAS AND DAVE'S CHRISTMAS JAMBOREE BAG [RI]	Rockney	87	15 Dec 84	1
JAMBOREE BAG NUMBER 3	Rockney	15	9 Nov 85	13
CHAS AND DAVE'S CHRISTMAS CAROL ALBUM	Telstar	37	13 Dec 86	4
STREET PARTY	Telstar	3	29 Apr 95	5

50-track medley of war songs, released in time for the 50th anniversary of VE day.
Above hit: CHAS 'N' DAVE.

Ingrid CHAVEZ – See Riuichi SAKAMOTO; David SYLVIAN

CHEAP TRICK | | | | US

SINGLES:		HITS 3		WEEKS 14
I WANT YOU TO WANT ME	Epic	29	5 May 79	9
WAY OF THE WORLD	Epic	73	2 Feb 80	2
IF YOU WANT MY LOVE	Epic	57	31 Jul 82	3
ALBUMS:		HITS 3		WEEKS 15
CHEAP TRICK AT BUDOKAN	Epic	29	24 Feb 79	9
DREAM POLICE	Epic	41	6 Oct 79	5
ONE ON ONE	Epic	95	5 Jun 82	1

Oliver CHEATHAM | | | | US

SINGLES:		HITS 1		WEEKS 5
GET DOWN SATURDAY NIGHT	MCA	38	2 Jul 83	5

CHECK 1-2 – See Craig McLACHLAN

Chubby CHECKER | | | | US

SINGLES:		HITS 10		WEEKS 112
THE TWIST	Columbia	49	24 Sep 60	1

Originally recorded by Hank Ballard and the Midnighters.

THE TWIST [RE-1ST]	Columbia	44	8 Oct 60	1
PONY TIME	Columbia	27	1 Apr 61	6

Originally recorded by Don Covay and the Goodtimers.

LET'S TWIST AGAIN	Columbia	37	19 Aug 61	3
LET'S TWIST AGAIN [RE-1ST]	Columbia	2	30 Dec 61	27
THE TWIST [RE-2ND]	Columbia	14	13 Jan 62	10

SLOW TWISTIN'	Columbia	23	7 Apr 62	8
TEACH ME TO TWIST	Columbia	45	21 Apr 62	1
Above hit: Chubby CHECKER; Bobby RYDELL.				
DANCIN' PARTY	Columbia	19	11 Aug 62	13
LET'S TWIST AGAIN [RE-2ND]	Columbia	46	25 Aug 62	1
LET'S TWIST AGAIN [RE-3RD]	Columbia	49	15 Sep 62	3
LIMBO ROCK	Cameo-Parkway	32	3 Nov 62	10
JINGLE BELL ROCK	Cameo-Parkway	40	22 Dec 62	3
Above hit: Bobby RYDELL and Chubby CHECKER.				
WHAT DO YA SAY	Cameo-Parkway	37	2 Nov 63	4
LET'S TWIST AGAIN [RI] / THE TWIST [RI]	London	5	29 Nov 75	10
THE TWIST (YO, TWIST)	Urban	2	18 Jun 88	11
Above hit: FAT BOYS (lead vocal: Chubby CHECKER).				
EPS:	**HITS 2**			**WEEKS 46**
KING OF THE TWIST	Columbia	3	17 Mar 62	43
DANCING PARTY	Cameo Parkway	17	2 Feb 63	3
ALBUMS:	**HITS 2**			**WEEKS 7**
TWIST WITH CHUBBY CHECKER	Columbia	13	27 Jan 62	4
FOR TWISTERS ONLY	Columbia	17	3 Mar 62	3

CHECKMATES LTD. featuring Sonny CHARLES   US

SINGLES:	**HITS 1**			**WEEKS 8**
PROUD MARY	A&M	30	15 Nov 69	8

Judy CHEEKS   US

SINGLES:	**HITS 4**			**WEEKS 15**
SO IN LOVE (THE REAL DEAL)	Positiva	27	13 Nov 93	3
REACH	Positiva	17	7 May 94	4
THIS TIME/RESPECT	Positiva	23	4 Mar 95	2
YOU'RE THE STORY OF MY LIFE / AS LONG AS YOU'RE GOOD TO ME	Positiva	30	17 Jun 95	3
REACH [RM]	Positiva	22	13 Jan 96	3
Remixed by Dancing Divaz.				

CHEETAHS   UK

SINGLES:	**HITS 2**			**WEEKS 6**
MECCA	Philips	36	3 Oct 64	3
Originally recorded by Gene Pitney.				
SOLDIER BOY	Philips	39	23 Jan 65	3

CHEF   US

(See also Isaac Hayes.)

SINGLES:	**HITS 1**			**WEEKS 13**
CHOCOLATE SALTY BALLS (P.S. I LOVE YOU)	Columbia	1	26 Dec 98	13

CHELSEA FOOTBALL TEAM   UK

SINGLES:	**HITS 3**			**WEEKS 20**
BLUE IS THE COLOUR	Penny Farthing	5	26 Feb 72	12
NO ONE CAN STOP US NOW	RCA	23	14 May 94	3
BLUE DAY	WEA	22	17 May 97	5
Above hit: SUGGS and CO. featuring the CHELSEA TEAM.				

CHEMICAL BROTHERS   UK

SINGLES:	**HITS 9**			**WEEKS 47**
LEAVE HOME	Junior Boy's Own	17	17 Jun 95	4
LIFE IS SWEET	Junior Boy's Own	25	9 Sep 95	3
Features vocals by Tim Burgess of the Charlatans.				
LOOPS OF FURY [EP]	Junior Boy's Own	13	27 Jan 96	1
Lead track: Loops Of Fury.				
SETTING SUN	Virgin	1	12 Oct 96	7
Features vocals by Noel Gallagher of Oasis.				
BLOCK ROCKIN' BEATS	Virgin	1	5 Apr 97	6
Vocals by Schooly D.				
BLOCK ROCKIN' BEATS [RE]	Virgin	69	28 Jun 97	1
ELEKTROBANK	Virgin	17	20 Sep 97	4
HEY BOY HEY GIRL	Virgin	3	12 Jun 99	10
LET FOREVER BE	Virgin	9	14 Aug 99	7
Vocals by Noel Gallagher.				
OUT OF CONTROL	Virgin	21	23 Oct 99	4
Vocal and guitar by Bernard Summer (New Order) and additional vocals by Bobby Gillespie (Primal Scream).				
ALBUMS:	**HITS 3**			**WEEKS 93**
EXIT PLANET DUST	Junior Boy's Own	9	8 Jul 95	41

DIG YOUR OWN HOLE	*Virgin*	1	*19 Apr 97*	27
SURRENDER	*Virgin*	1	*3 Jul 99*	25

CHEQUERS · UK

SINGLES:	HITS 2			WEEKS 10
ROCK ON BROTHER	*Creole*	21	*18 Oct 75*	5
HEY MISS PAYNE	*Creole*	32	*28 Feb 76*	5

CHER · US

(See also Cher, Chrissie Hynde and Neneh Cherry with Eric Clapton; Sonny and Cher; Various Artists: Films – Original Soundtracks 'Mermaids'.)

SINGLES:	HITS 29			WEEKS 211
ALL I REALLY WANT TO DO	*Liberty*	9	*21 Aug 65*	10
BANG BANG (MY BABY SHOT ME DOWN)	*Liberty*	3	*2 Apr 66*	12
I FEEL SOMETHING IN THE AIR	*Liberty*	43	*6 Aug 66*	2
SUNNY	*Liberty*	32	*24 Sep 66*	5
GYPSYS, TRAMPS AND THIEVES	*MCA*	4	*6 Nov 71*	13
Originally titled Gypsies, Tramps and White Trash.				
DARK LADY	*MCA*	36	*16 Feb 74*	3
DARK LADY [RE]	*MCA*	45	*16 Mar 74*	1
I FOUND SOMEONE	*Geffen*	5	*19 Dec 87*	10
Written and produced by Michael Bolton.				
WE ALL SLEEP ALONE	*Geffen*	47	*2 Apr 88*	5
IF I COULD TURN BACK TIME	*Geffen*	6	*2 Sep 89*	14
JUST LIKE JESSE JAMES	*Geffen*	11	*13 Jan 90*	11
HEART OF STONE	*Geffen*	43	*7 Apr 90*	5
YOU WOULDN'T KNOW LOVE	*Geffen*	55	*11 Aug 90*	3
THE SHOOP SHOOP SONG (IT'S IN HIS KISS)	*Epic*	1	*13 Apr 91*	15
From the film 'Mermaids'. Originally recorded by Ramona King.				
LOVE AND UNDERSTANDING	*Geffen*	10	*13 Jul 91*	8
SAVE UP ALL YOUR TEARS	*Geffen*	37	*12 Oct 91*	5
Robin Beck's original reached No. 84 in 1989.				
LOVE HURTS	*Geffen*	43	*7 Dec 91*	5
COULD'VE BEEN YOU	*Geffen*	31	*18 Apr 92*	4
OH NO NOT MY BABY	*Geffen*	33	*14 Nov 92*	4
MANY RIVERS TO CROSS (LIVE FROM THE MIRAGE)	*Geffen*	37	*16 Jan 93*	3
WHENEVER YOU'RE NEAR	*Geffen*	72	*6 Mar 93*	1
I GOT YOU BABE	*Geffen*	35	*15 Jan 94*	3
Beavis and Butt-Head are cartoon characters from MTV.				
Above hit: CHER with BEAVIS and BUTT-HEAD.				
WALKING IN MEMPHIS	*WEA*	11	*28 Oct 95*	7
ONE BY ONE	*WEA*	7	*20 Jan 96*	9
Originally recorded by Jo Jo and the Real People in 1987.				
NOT ENOUGH LOVE IN THE WORLD	*WEA*	31	*27 Apr 96*	2
Originally recorded by Don Henley from his album Building The Perfect Beast.				
THE SUN AIN'T GONNA SHINE ANYMORE	*WEA*	26	*17 Aug 96*	3
BELIEVE	*WEA*	1	*31 Oct 98*	26
STRONG ENOUGH	*WEA*	5	*6 Mar 99*	10
BELIEVE [RE]	*WEA*	59	*8 May 99*	2
ALL OR NOTHING	*WEA*	12	*19 Jun 99*	7
DOV'E L'AMOURE	*WEA*	21	*6 Nov 99*	3
EPS:	HITS 1			WEEKS 1
THE HITS OF CHER	*Liberty*	10	*22 Oct 66*	1
ALBUMS:	HITS 9			WEEKS 277
ALL I REALLY WANT TO DO	*Liberty*	7	*2 Oct 65*	9
SONNY SIDE OF CHER	*Liberty*	11	*7 May 66*	11
CHER	*Geffen*	26	*16 Jan 88*	22
HEART OF STONE	*Geffen*	15	*22 Jul 89*	13
HEART OF STONE [RE-1ST]	*Geffen*	7	*30 Dec 89*	47
HEART OF STONE [RE-2ND]	*Geffen*	43	*27 Apr 91*	22
Re-released at mid-price. Chart position reached in 1992.				
LOVE HURTS	*Geffen*	1	*29 Jun 91*	51
CHER'S GREATEST HITS: 1965–1992	*Geffen*	1	*21 Nov 92*	33
IT'S A MAN'S WORLD	*WEA*	10	*18 Nov 95*	18
Tracks on the album were all originally written and performed by men.				
BELIEVE	*WEA*	7	*7 Nov 98*	44
THE GREATEST HITS	*WEA/Universal Music TV*	7	*20 Nov 99*	7

CHER, Chrissie HYNDE and Neneh CHERRY with Eric CLAPTON · UK/US/Sweden

(See also Cher; Neneh Cherry; Eric Clapton.)

SINGLES:	HITS 1			WEEKS 8
LOVE CAN BUILD A BRIDGE	*London*	1	*18 Mar 95*	8

In aid of Comic Relief. Originally recorded by the Judds in 1990.

CHERI
US

SINGLES:		HITS 1		WEEKS 9
MURPHY'S LAW	Polydor	13	19 Jun 82	9

CHEROKEES
UK

SINGLES:		HITS 1		WEEKS 5
SEVEN DAFFODILS	Columbia	33	5 Sep 64	5

CHERRELLE
US

SINGLES:		HITS 5		WEEKS 26
SATURDAY LOVE	Tabu	6	28 Dec 85	11
Above hit: CHERRELLE with Alexander O'NEAL.				
WILL YOU SATISFY?	Tabu	57	1 Mar 86	3
NEVER KNEW LOVE LIKE THIS	Tabu	26	6 Feb 88	7
Above hit: Alexander O'NEAL featuring CHERRELLE.				
AFFAIR	Tabu	67	6 May 89	2
SATURDAY LOVE (FEELIN' LUV MIX) [RM]	Tabu	55	24 Mar 90	2
Remixed by Olimar and D.J. Shapps.				
Above hit: CHERRELLE with Alexander O'NEAL.				
BABY COME TO ME	One World Entertainment	56	2 Aug 97	1
Above hit: Alexander O'NEAL and CHERRELLE.				
ALBUMS:		HITS 1		WEEKS 9
HIGH PRIORITY	Tabu	17	25 Jan 86	9

Don CHERRY
US

SINGLES:		HITS 1		WEEKS 11
BAND OF GOLD	Philips	6	11 Feb 56	11
Above hit: Don CHERRY with Ray CONNIFF and his Orchestra.				

Eagle-Eye CHERRY
Sweden

SINGLES:		HITS 3		WEEKS 22
SAVE TONIGHT	Polydor	6	4 Jul 98	13
FALLING IN LOVE AGAIN	Polydor	8	14 Nov 98	8
PERMANENT TEARS	Polydor	43	20 Mar 99	1
ALBUMS:		HITS 1		WEEKS 29
DESIRELESS	Polydor	3	1 Aug 98	29

Neneh CHERRY
Sweden

(See also Cher, Chrissie Hynde and Neneh Cherry with Eric Clapton.)

SINGLES:		HITS 11		WEEKS 88
BUFFALO STANCE	Circa	3	10 Dec 88	13
MANCHILD	Circa	5	20 May 89	10
KISSES ON THE WIND	Circa	20	12 Aug 89	6
INNA CITY MAMMA	Circa	31	23 Dec 89	7
I'VE GOT YOU UNDER MY SKIN	Circa	25	29 Sep 90	5
From the Red, Hot and Blue album to benefit AIDS research.				
MONEY LOVE	Circa	23	3 Oct 92	4
BUDDY X	Circa	35	19 Jun 93	3
Samples Juicy's Sugar Free. Features rap by the Notorious B.I.G.				
7 SECONDS	Columbia	3	25 Jun 94	21
Above hit: Youssou N'DOUR (featuring Neneh CHERRY).				
7 SECONDS [RE]	Columbia	54	24 Dec 94	4
WOMAN	Hut	9	3 Aug 96	7
Based on James Brown's It's A Man's World.				
KOOTCHI	Hut	38	14 Dec 96	2
FEEL IT	Hut	68	22 Feb 97	1
A tribute to her father.				
BUDDY X 99 [RM]	4 Liberty	15	6 Nov 99	5
Remixed produced by B. Simms. Additional vocals by PSG.				
Above hit: DREEM TEEM 'v' Neneh CHERRY.				
ALBUMS:		HITS 3		WEEKS 49
RAW LIKE SUSHI	Circa	2	17 Jun 89	43
HOMEBREW	Circa	27	7 Nov 92	2
MAN	Hut	16	14 Sep 96	4

Maurice CHEVALIER and Hayley MILLS
France/UK

(See also Hayley Mills.)

EPS:		HITS 1		WEEKS 1
IN SEARCH OF THE CASTAWAYS [OST]	Decca	18	9 Feb 63	1

CHI-LITES
US

SINGLES:	HITS 9			WEEKS 89
(FOR GOD'S SAKE) GIVE MORE POWER TO THE PEOPLE	MCA	32	28 Aug 71	6
HAVE YOU SEEN HER	MCA	3	15 Jan 72	12
OH GIRL	MCA	14	27 May 72	9
HOMELY GIRL	Brunswick	5	23 Mar 74	13
I FOUND SUNSHINE	Brunswick	35	20 Jul 74	5
TOO GOOD TO BE FORGOTTEN	Brunswick	10	2 Nov 74	11
HAVE YOU SEEN HER? [RI]/OH GIRL [RI]	Brunswick	5	21 Jun 75	9
IT'S TIME FOR LOVE	Brunswick	5	13 Sep 75	10
YOU DON'T HAVE TO GO	Brunswick	3	31 Jul 76	11
CHANGING FOR YOU	R&B	61	13 Aug 83	3

CHIC
US

SINGLES:	HITS 10			WEEKS 90
DANCE, DANCE, DANCE (YOWSAH, YOWSAH, YOWSAH)	Atlantic	6	26 Nov 77	12
EVERYBODY DANCE	Atlantic	9	1 Apr 78	11
LE FREAK	Atlantic	7	18 Nov 78	16
Backing vocals by Luther Vandross.				
I WANT YOUR LOVE	Atlantic	4	24 Feb 79	11
GOOD TIMES	Atlantic	5	30 Jun 79	11
MY FORBIDDEN LOVER	Atlantic	15	13 Oct 79	8
MY FEET KEEP DANCING	Atlantic	21	8 Dec 79	9
HANGIN'	Atlantic	64	12 Mar 83	1
JACK LE FREAK [RM]	Atlantic	19	19 Sep 87	6
CHIC MEDLEY [M]	Atlantic	58	14 Jul 90	2
Above hit: MEGACHIC.				
CHIC MYSTIQUE	Warner Brothers	48	15 Feb 92	3
ALBUMS:	**HITS 4**			**WEEKS 47**
COMPILATION ALBUMS:	**HITS 1**			**WEEKS 6**
C'EST CHIC	Atlantic	2	3 Feb 79	24
RISQUE	Atlantic	29	18 Aug 79	12
THE BEST OF CHIC	Atlantic	30	15 Dec 79	8
FREAK OUT	Telstar	72	5 Dec 87	3
Compilation of hits from the two groups.				
Above hit: CHIC and SISTER SLEDGE.				
CHIC AND ROSE ROYCE - THEIR GREATEST HITS - SIDE BY SIDE	Dino	8	27 Jul 91	6
LP contained two different recording acts and was thus ineligible for the main album chart.				
Above hit: ROSE ROYCE and CHIC.				

CHICAGO
US

SINGLES:	HITS 7			WEEKS 81
I'M A MAN	CBS	8	10 Jan 70	11
25 OR 6 TO 4	CBS	7	18 Jul 70	13
IF YOU LEAVE ME NOW	CBS	1	9 Oct 76	16
BABY, WHAT A BIG SURPRISE	CBS	41	5 Nov 77	3
HARD TO SAY I'M SORRY	Full Moon	4	21 Aug 82	15
HARD HABIT TO BREAK	Full Moon	8	27 Oct 84	13
YOU'RE THE INSPIRATION	Full Moon	14	26 Jan 85	10
ALBUMS:	**HITS 10**			**WEEKS 121**
CHICAGO TRANSIT AUTHORITY	CBS	9	27 Sep 69	14
Above hit: CHICAGO TRANSIT AUTHORITY.				
CHICAGO	CBS	6	4 Apr 70	27
CHICAGO 3	CBS	31	3 Apr 71	1
CHICAGO 5	CBS	24	30 Sep 72	2
CHICAGO X	CBS	21	23 Oct 76	11
CHICAGO 16	Full Moon	44	2 Oct 82	9
LOVE SONGS	TV Records	42	4 Dec 82	8
CHICAGO 17	Full Moon	24	1 Dec 84	20
THE HEART OF CHICAGO	Reprise	15	25 Nov 89	14
THE HEART OF CHICAGO [RE]	Reprise	6	19 Feb 94	11
Re-released at mid-price.				
THE HEART OF CHICAGO - 1967-1997	Reprise	21	13 Feb 99	4
Updated version of their 1989 compilation.				

CHICANE
UK

(See also Disco Citizens.)

SINGLES:	HITS 5			WEEKS 29
OFFSHORE	Xtravaganza	14	21 Dec 96	7
SUNSTROKE	Xtravaganza	21	14 Jun 97	3
OFFSHORE '97 [RM]	Xtravaganza	17	13 Sep 97	4
Remixed by Anthony Pappa.				
Above hit: CHICANE with POWER CIRCLE.				
LOST YOU SOMEWHERE	Xtravaganza	35	20 Dec 97	3

STRONG IN LOVE	Xtravaganza	32	10 Oct 98	2
Above hit: CHICANE featuring MASON.				
SALTWATER	Xtravaganza	6	5 Jun 99	10
Based on Clannad's Theme From Harry's Game.				
Above hit: CHICANE (featuring Maire BRENNAN of CLANNAD).				

ALBUMS:	HITS 1		WEEKS 1	
FAR FROM THE MADDENING CROWDS	Xtravaganza	49	1 Nov 97	1

CHICKEN SHACK
UK

SINGLES:	HITS 2		WEEKS 19	
I'D RATHER GO BLIND	Blue Horizon	14	10 May 69	13
Originally recorded by Etta James.				
TEARS IN THE WIND	Blue Horizon	29	6 Sep 69	6

ALBUMS:	HITS 2		WEEKS 9	
FORTY BLUE FINGERS FRESHLY PACKED	Blue Horizon	12	22 Jun 68	8
OK KEN?	Blue Horizon	9	15 Feb 69	1

CHICKEN SHED
UK

SINGLES:	HITS 1		WEEKS 6	
I AM IN LOVE WITH THE WORLD	Columbia	15	27 Dec 97	6
Charity record with proceeds to Diana, Princess Of Wales Memorial Fund.				

CHICORY TIP
UK

SINGLES:	HITS 3		WEEKS 34	
SON OF MY FATHER	CBS	1	29 Jan 72	13
Originally recorded by Georgio.				
WHAT'S YOUR NAME	CBS	13	20 May 72	8
GOOD GRIEF CHRISTINA	CBS	17	31 Mar 73	13

CHIEFTAINS
Ireland

(See also James Galway and the Chieftains; Van Morrison and the Chieftains.)

SINGLES:	HITS 1		WEEKS 3	
I KNOW MY LOVE	RCA Victor	37	12 Jun 99	3
Above hit: CHIEFTAINS featuring the CORRS.				

ALBUMS:	HITS 2		WEEKS 13	
THE LONG BLACK VEIL	RCA	17	4 Feb 95	9
TEARS OF STONE	RCA Victor	36	6 Mar 99	4

CHIFFONS
US

SINGLES:	HITS 3		WEEKS 40	
HE'S SO FINE	Stateside	16	13 Apr 63	12
ONE FINE DAY	Stateside	29	20 Jul 63	6
SWEET TALKIN' GUY	Stateside	31	28 May 66	8
SWEET TALKIN' GUY [RI]	London	4	18 Mar 72	14

CHILD
UK

SINGLES:	HITS 3		WEEKS 22	
WHEN YOU WALK IN THE ROOM	Ariola Hansa	38	29 Apr 78	5
IT'S ONLY MAKE BELIEVE	Ariola Hansa	10	22 Jul 78	12
ONLY YOU (AND YOU ALONE)	Ariola Hansa	33	28 Apr 79	5

Jane CHILD
Canada

SINGLES:	HITS 1		WEEKS 8	
DON'T WANNA FALL IN LOVE	Warner Brothers	22	12 May 90	8

CHILDLINERS
UK/US/Australia

SINGLES:	HITS 1		WEEKS 6	
THE GIFT OF CHRISTMAS	London	9	16 Dec 95	6
In aid of the charity Childline.				

CHILDREN FOR RWANDA
UK

SINGLES:	HITS 1		WEEKS 2	
LOVE CAN BUILD A BRIDGE	East West	57	10 Sep 94	2
Proceeds to Rwandan aid charities. Originally recorded by the Judds in 1990.				

CHILDREN OF THE NIGHT
UK

SINGLES:	HITS 1		WEEKS 2	
IT'S A TRIP (TUNE IN, TURN ON, DROP OUT)	Jive	52	26 Nov 88	2

CHILDREN OF THE REVOLUTION - See KLF

CHILDREN'S CHORUS - See Max BYGRAVES; Guy MITCHELL

Toni CHILDS
US

SINGLES:		HITS 1			WEEKS 4
DON'T WALK AWAY	A&M		53	25 Mar 89	4
ALBUMS:		**HITS 1**			**WEEKS 1**
UNION	A&M		73	22 Apr 89	1

CHILL FAC-TORR
US

SINGLES:		HITS 1			WEEKS 8
TWIST (ROUND 'N' ROUND)	Phillyworld		37	2 Apr 83	8

CHILLI featuring CARRAPICHO
US/Ghana/Brazil

SINGLES:		HITS 1			WEEKS 1
TIC, TIC TAC	Arista		59	20 Sep 97	1

Song has its own dance, the Boi Bumba.

CHIMES
UK

SINGLES:		HITS 5			WEEKS 28
1-2-3	CBS		60	19 Aug 89	3
HEAVEN	CBS		66	2 Dec 89	2
HEAVEN [RE]	CBS		69	6 Jan 90	3
I STILL HAVEN'T FOUND WHAT I'M LOOKING FOR	CBS		6	19 May 90	9
TRUE LOVE	CBS		48	28 Jul 90	3
HEAVEN [RI]	CBS		24	29 Sep 90	6
LOVE COMES TO MIND	CBS		49	1 Dec 90	2
ALBUMS:		**HITS 1**			**WEEKS 19**
THE CHIMES	CBS		17	23 Jun 90	19

CHIMIRA
South Africa

SINGLES:		HITS 1			WEEKS 1
SHOW ME HEAVEN	Neoteric		70	6 Dec 97	1

CHINA BLACK
UK

SINGLES:		HITS 4			WEEKS 35
SEARCHING	Wild Card		4	16 Jul 94	16
Originally released in 1992.					
STARS	Wild Card		19	29 Oct 94	7
SEARCHING [RE]	Wild Card		54	17 Dec 94	4
ALMOST SEE YOU (SOMEWHERE)	Wild Card		31	11 Feb 95	2
SWING LOW SWEET CHARIOT	PolyGram TV		15	3 Jun 95	6

The England Rugby World Cup Squad's theme tune.
Above hit: LADYSMITH BLACK MAMBAZO featuring CHINA BLACK.

ALBUMS:		HITS 1			WEEKS 4
BORN	Wild Card		27	11 Mar 95	4

CHINA CRISIS
UK

SINGLES:		HITS 11			WEEKS 66
AFRICAN AND WHITE	Inevitable		45	7 Aug 82	5
CHRISTIAN	Virgin		12	22 Jan 83	9
TRAGEDY AND MYSTERY	Virgin		46	21 May 83	6
WORKING WITH FIRE AND STEEL	Virgin		48	15 Oct 83	5
WISHFUL THINKING	Virgin		9	14 Jan 84	8
HANNA HANNA	Virgin		44	10 Mar 84	3
BLACK MAN RAY	Virgin		14	30 Mar 85	9
KING IN A CATHOLIC STYLE (WAKE UP)	Virgin		19	1 Jun 85	9
YOU DID CUT ME	Virgin		54	7 Sep 85	3
ARIZONA SKY	Virgin		47	8 Nov 86	4
BEST KEPT SECRET	Virgin		36	24 Jan 87	5
ALBUMS:		**HITS 6**			**WEEKS 68**
DIFFICULT SHAPES AND PASSIVE RHYTHMS SOME PEOPLE THINK IT'S FUN TO ENTERTAIN	Virgin		21	20 Nov 82	18
WORKING WITH FIRE AND STEEL - POSSIBLE POP SONGS VOLUME 2	Virgin		20	12 Nov 83	16
FLAUNT THE IMPERFECTION	Virgin		9	11 May 85	22
WHAT PRICE PARADISE?	Virgin		63	6 Dec 86	6
DIARY OF A HOLLOW HORSE	Virgin		58	13 May 89	2
CHINA CRISIS COLLECTION - THE VERY BEST OF CHINA CRISIS	Virgin		32	15 Sep 90	4

CHINA DRUM
UK

SINGLES:		HITS 4			WEEKS 4
CAN'T STOP THESE THINGS	Mantra		65	2 Mar 96	1
LAST CHANCE	Mantra		60	20 Apr 96	1
FICTION OF LIFE	Mantra		65	9 Aug 97	1
SOMEWHERE ELSE	Mantra		74	27 Sep 97	1

ALBUMS:	HITS 1			WEEKS 1	
GOOSEFAIR	*Mantra*	53	*11 May 96*		1

Jonny CHINGAS — US

SINGLES:	HITS 1			WEEKS 6	
PHONE HOME	*CBS*	43	*19 Feb 83*		6

CHIPMUNKS — US

(See also David Seville.)

SINGLES:	HITS 3			WEEKS 12	
RAGTIME COWBOY JOE	*London*	11	*25 Jul 59*		8
Above hit: David SEVILLE and the CHIPMUNKS.					
ACHY BREAKY HEART	*Epic*	53	*19 Dec 92*		3
Above hit: ALVIN and the CHIPMUNKS (with special guest Billy Ray CYRUS).					
MACARENA	*Sony Wonder*	65	*14 Dec 96*		1
Above hit: LOS DEL CHIPMUNKS.					

CHIPPENDALES — UK/US

SINGLES:	HITS 1			WEEKS 4	
GIVE ME YOUR BODY	*XSRhythm*	28	*31 Oct 92*		4

George CHISHOLM - See Clinton FORD; JOHNSTON BROTHERS

CHOIR OF NEW COLLEGE OXFORD/Edward HIGGINBOTTOM — UK

ALBUMS:	HITS 2			WEEKS 7	
AGNUS DEI	*Erato*	49	*12 Oct 96*		5
AGNUS DEI II	*Erato*	57	*18 Apr 98*		2

CHOPS-EMC and EXTENSIVE — UK

SINGLES:	HITS 1			WEEKS 1	
ME' ISRAELITES	*Faze 2*	60	*8 Aug 92*		1

CHORDETTES — US

SINGLES:	HITS 3			WEEKS 25	
MR. SANDMAN	*Columbia*	11	*18 Dec 54*		8
Originally recorded by Vaughan Monroe.					
BORN TO BE WITH YOU	*London*	8	*1 Sep 56*		9
LOLLIPOP	*London*	6	*19 Apr 58*		8
Original by Ronald and Ruby reached No. 20 in the US in the same year.					

CHORDS — UK

SINGLES:	HITS 5			WEEKS 17	
NOW IT'S GONE	*Polydor*	63	*6 Oct 79*		2
MAYBE TOMORROW	*Polydor*	40	*2 Feb 80*		5
SOMETHING'S MISSING	*Polydor*	55	*26 Apr 80*		3
THE BRITISH WAY OF LIFE	*Polydor*	54	*12 Jul 80*		3
IN MY STREET	*Polydor*	50	*18 Oct 80*		4
ALBUMS:	HITS 1			WEEKS 3	
SO FAR AWAY	*Polydor*	30	*24 May 80*		3

CHORUS GIRLS with the PLAYBOYS - See Dorothy PROVINE

CHRIS and JAMES — UK

SINGLES:	HITS 3			WEEKS 3	
CALM DOWN (BASS KEEPS PUMPIN')	*Stress*	74	*17 Sep 94*		1
FOX FORCE FIVE	*Stress*	71	*4 Nov 95*		1
CLUB FOR LIFE '98	*Stress*	66	*7 Nov 98*		1

Neil CHRISTIAN — UK

SINGLES:	HITS 1			WEEKS 10	
THAT'S NICE	*Strike*	14	*9 Apr 66*		10

Roger CHRISTIAN — UK

SINGLES:	HITS 1			WEEKS 3	
TAKE IT FROM ME	*Island*	63	*30 Sep 89*		3

CHRISTIANS — UK

(See also Christians, Holly Johnson, Paul McCartney, Gerry Marsden, Stock Aitken Waterman.)

SINGLES:	HITS 12			WEEKS 77	
FORGOTTEN TOWN	*Island*	22	*31 Jan 87*		11
HOOVERVILLE (AND THEY PROMISED US THE WORLD)	*Island*	21	*13 Jun 87*		10
WHEN THE FINGERS POINT	*Island*	34	*26 Sep 87*		7

IDEAL WORLD	Island	14	5 Dec 87	13
BORN AGAIN	Island	25	23 Apr 88	7
HARVEST FOR THE WORLD	Island	8	15 Oct 88	7
WORDS	Island	18	23 Dec 89	8
I FOUND OUT	Island	56	7 Apr 90	2
GREENBACK DRIVE	Island	63	15 Sep 90	2
WHAT'S IN A WORD	Island	33	5 Sep 92	5
FATHER	Island	55	14 Nov 92	2
THE BOTTLE	Island	39	6 Mar 93	3
ALBUMS:	**HITS 4**			**WEEKS 96**
THE CHRISTIANS	Island	2	31 Oct 87	68
COLOUR	Island	1	27 Jan 90	17
HAPPY IN HELL	Island	18	10 Oct 92	3
THE BEST OF THE CHRISTIANS	Island	22	20 Nov 93	8

CHRISTIANS, Holly JOHNSON, Paul McCARTNEY, Gerry MARSDEN and STOCK AITKEN WATERMAN — UK

(See also Christians; Gerry and the Pacemakers; Holly Johnson; Paul McCartney; Stock Aitken Waterman.)

SINGLES:	**HITS 1**			**WEEKS 7**
FERRY 'CROSS THE MERSEY	PWL	1	20 May 89	7

CHRISTIE — UK

SINGLES:	**HITS 3**			**WEEKS 37**
YELLOW RIVER	CBS	1	2 May 70	22
Song was originally intended for the Tremeloes.				
SAN BERNADINO	CBS	49	10 Oct 70	1
SAN BERNADINO [RE]	CBS	7	24 Oct 70	13
IRON HORSE	CBS	47	25 Mar 72	1

David CHRISTIE — France

SINGLES:	**HITS 1**			**WEEKS 12**
SADDLE UP	KR	9	14 Aug 82	12

John CHRISTIE — Australia

SINGLES:	**HITS 1**			**WEEKS 6**
HERE'S TO LOVE (AULD LANG SYNE)	EMI	24	25 Dec 76	6

Lou CHRISTIE — US

SINGLES:	**HITS 4**			**WEEKS 35**
LIGHTNIN' STRIKES	MGM	11	26 Feb 66	8
RHAPSODY IN THE RAIN	MGM	37	30 Apr 66	2
I'M GONNA MAKE YOU MINE	Buddah	2	13 Sep 69	17
SHE SOLD ME MAGIC	Buddah	25	27 Dec 69	8

Tony CHRISTIE — UK

SINGLES:	**HITS 6**			**WEEKS 54**
LAS VEGAS	MCA	21	9 Jan 71	9
I DID WHAT I DID FOR MARIA	MCA	2	8 May 71	17
(IS THIS THE WAY TO) AMARILLO	MCA	18	20 Nov 71	13
Originally recorded by Neil Sedaka.				
AVENUES AND ALLEYWAYS	MCA	37	10 Feb 73	4
DRIVE SAFELY DARLIN'	MCA	35	17 Jan 76	4
From the TV series 'The Protectors'.				
WALK LIKE A PANTHER	ffrr	10	23 Jan 99	7
Above hit: ALL SEEING I featuring Tony CHRISTIE.				
ALBUMS:	**HITS 4**			**WEEKS 10**
I DID WHAT I DID FOR MARIA	MCA	37	24 Jul 71	1
WITH LOVING FEELING	MCA	19	17 Feb 73	2
TONY CHRISTIE – LIVE	MCA	33	31 May 75	3
BEST OF TONY CHRISTIE	MCA	28	6 Nov 76	4

Shawn CHRISTOPHER — US

SINGLES:	**HITS 3**			**WEEKS 11**
ANOTHER SLEEPLESS NIGHT	Arista	74	22 Sep 90	1
Above hit: Mike 'Hitman' WILSON featuring Shawn CHRISTOPHER.				
ANOTHER SLEEPLESS NIGHT [RI]	Arista	50	4 May 91	4
DON'T LOSE THE MAGIC	Arista	30	21 Mar 92	5
MAKE MY LOVE	BTB	57	2 Jul 94	1

CHRON GEN — UK

ALBUMS:	**HITS 1**			**WEEKS 3**
CHRONIC GENERATION	Secret	53	3 Apr 82	3

CHUBBY CHUNKS · UK

SINGLES:	HITS 2			WEEKS 2
TESTAMENT 4	Cleveland City	52	4 Jun 94	1
Above hit: CHUBBY CHUNKS VOLUME II.				
I'M TELLIN YOU	Cleveland City	61	29 May 99	1
Re-recording of Testament 1 from 1993, with added vocals.				
Above hit: KENTISH MAN presents CHUBBY CHUNKS featuring Kim RUFFIN.				

CHUCKS · UK

SINGLES:	HITS 1			WEEKS 7
LOO-BE-LOO	Decca	22	26 Jan 63	7

CHUMBAWAMBA · UK

SINGLES:	HITS 5			WEEKS 31
ENOUGH IS ENOUGH	One Little Indian	56	18 Sep 93	2
Above hit: CHUMBAWAMBA and CREDIT TO THE NATION.				
TIMEBOMB	One Little Indian	59	4 Dec 93	1
TUBTHUMPING	EMI	2	23 Aug 97	20
AMNESIA	EMI	10	31 Jan 98	5
TOP OF THE WORLD (OLE, OLE, OLE)	EMI	21	13 Jun 98	3
ALBUMS:	**HITS 3**			**WEEKS 10**
ANARCHY	One Little Indian	29	7 May 94	2
SWINGIN' WITH RAYMOND	One Little Indian	70	4 Nov 95	1
TUBTHUMPER	EMI	19	13 Sep 97	7

Myung- Whun CHUNG - See Andrea BOCELLI

CHUPITO · Spain

SINGLES:	HITS 1			WEEKS 2
AMERICAN PIE	Eternal	54	23 Sep 95	2

Charlotte CHURCH · UK

SINGLES:	HITS 1			WEEKS 2
JUST WAVE HELLO	Sony Classical	31	25 Dec 99	2
With the London Symphony Orchestra. Featured in the Ford Global TV commercial.				
ALBUMS:	**HITS 2**			**WEEKS 26**
VOICE OF AN ANGEL	Sony Classical	4	21 Nov 98	20
CHARLOTTE CHURCH	Sony Classical	8	27 Nov 99	6

Sir Winston CHURCHILL · UK

ALBUMS:	HITS 1			WEEKS 8
THE VOICE OF CHURCHILL	Decca	6	13 Feb 65	8

CHYNA - See INCOGNITO

CICCONE YOUTH - See SONIC YOUTH

CICERO · UK

SINGLES:	HITS 3			WEEKS 12
LOVE IS EVERYWHERE	Spaghetti	19	18 Jan 92	8
THAT LOVING FEELING	Spagetti	46	18 Apr 92	3
HEAVEN MUST HAVE SENT YOU BACK TO ME	Spagetti	70	1 Aug 92	1

CINDERELLA · US

SINGLES:	HITS 4			WEEKS 7
GYPSY ROAD	Vertigo	54	6 Aug 88	2
DON'T KNOW WHAT YOU GOT (TIL IT'S GONE)	Vertigo	54	4 Mar 89	2
SHELTER ME	Vertigo	55	17 Nov 90	2
HEARTBREAK STATION	Vertigo	63	27 Apr 91	1
ALBUMS:	**HITS 2**			**WEEKS 8**
LONG COLD WINTER	Vertigo	30	23 Jul 88	6
HEARTBREAK STATION	Vertigo	36	1 Dec 90	2

CINDY and the SAFFRONS · UK

SINGLES:	HITS 1			WEEKS 3
PAST, PRESENT AND FUTURE	Stilletto	56	15 Jan 83	3
Originally recorded by The Shangrila's.				

CINERAMA · UK

SINGLES:	HITS 1			WEEKS 1
KERRY KERRY	Cooking Vinyl	71	18 Jul 98	1

Gigliola CINQUETTI — Italy

SINGLES:	HITS 2			WEEKS 27
NON HO L'ETA' PER AMARTI	Decca	17	25 Apr 64	17
Eurovision Song Contest winner for 1964.				
GO (BEFORE YOU BREAK MY HEART)	CBS	8	4 May 74	10
Italian Eurovision entry in 1974, it came 2nd.				

CIRCA featuring DESTRY — UK/US

SINGLES:	HITS 1			WEEKS 1
SUN SHINING DOWN	Inferno	70	27 Nov 99	1
Vocals by Destry Spigner.				

CIRCUIT — UK

SINGLES:	HITS 1			WEEKS 3
SHELTER ME	Cooltempo	44	20 Jul 91	2
Original release reached No. 82 in 1990.				
SHELTER ME [RI]	Pukka	50	1 Apr 95	1

CIRRUS — UK

SINGLES:	HITS 1			WEEKS 1
ROLLIN' ON	Jet	62	30 Sep 78	1

CITY BOY — UK

SINGLES:	HITS 3			WEEKS 20
5.7.0.5.	Vertigo	8	8 Jul 78	12
WHAT A NIGHT	Vertigo	39	28 Oct 78	5
THE DAY THE EARTH CAUGHT FIRE	Vertigo	67	15 Sep 79	3

Gary CLAIL ON-U SOUND SYSTEM — UK

SINGLES:	HITS 5			WEEKS 19
BEEF	RCA	64	14 Jul 90	2
Above hit: Gary CLAIL ON-U SOUND SYSTEM featuring Bim SHERMAN.				
HUMAN NATURE	Perfecto	10	30 Mar 91	9
ESCAPE	Perfecto	44	8 Jun 91	3
Above hit: Gary CLAIL ON-U SOUND SYSTEM (additional vocals By AKABU).				
WHO PAYS THE PIPER?	Perfecto	31	14 Nov 92	3
THESE THINGS ARE WORTH FIGHTING FOR	Perfecto	45	22 May 93	2
ALBUMS:	HITS 1			WEEKS 2
THE EMOTIONAL HOOLIGAN	Perfecto	35	4 May 91	2

CLAIRE and FRIENDS — UK

SINGLES:	HITS 1			WEEKS 11
IT'S 'ORRIBLE BEING IN LOVE (WHEN YOU'RE 8½)	BBC	13	7 Jun 86	11
From BBC1 TV's 'Saturday Superstore'.				

CLANCY BROTHERS and Tommy MAKEM — Ireland

ALBUMS:	HITS 1			WEEKS 5
ISN'T IT GRAND BOYS?	CBS	22	16 Apr 66	5

CLANNAD — Ireland

SINGLES:	HITS 5			WEEKS 29
THEME FROM HARRY'S GAME	RCA	5	6 Nov 82	10
Theme from the ITV series 'Harry's Game'.				
NEW GRANGE	RCA	65	2 Jul 83	1
ROBIN (THE HOODED MAN)	RCA	42	12 May 84	5
Theme from the TV series 'Robin Of Sherwood'.				
IN A LIFETIME	RCA	20	25 Jan 86	5
Above hit: CLANNAD/ additional vocals: BONO.				
IN A LIFETIME [RI]	RCA	17	10 Jun 89	7
Above hit: CLANNAD (guest vocal: BONO).				
BOTH SIDES NOW	MCA	74	10 Aug 91	1
Above hit: CLANNAD and Paul YOUNG.				
ALBUMS:	HITS 11			WEEKS 150
MAGICAL RING	RCA	26	2 Apr 83	21
LEGEND (MUSIC FROM ROBIN OF SHERWOOD)	RCA	16	12 May 84	14
MAGICAL RING [RE]	RCA	91	2 Jun 84	1
Re-released.				
LEGEND (MUSIC FROM ROBIN OF SHERWOOD) [RE]	RCA	15	16 Mar 85	26
MACALLA	RCA	33	26 Oct 85	24
SIRIUS	RCA	34	7 Nov 87	4
ATLANTIC REALM [OST-TV]	BBC	41	4 Feb 89	3
PAST PRESENT	RCA	5	6 May 89	23
Re-released.				

ANAM	RCA	14	20 Oct 90	7
BANBA	RCA	5	15 May 93	11
PAST PRESENT [RE]	RCA	55	16 Sep 95	3
Re-released.				
LORE	RCA	14	6 Apr 96	7
THE ULTIMATE COLLECTION	RCA	46	31 May 97	4
LANDMARKS	RCA	34	11 Apr 98	2

Jimmy CLANTON — US

SINGLES:	HITS 1			WEEKS 1
ANOTHER SLEEPLESS NIGHT	Top Rank	50	23 Jul 60	1
Written by Neil Sedaka.				

Eric CLAPTON — UK

(See also Cher, Chrissie Hynde and Neneh Cherry with Eric Clapton; Derek and the Dominos.)

SINGLES:	HITS 22			WEEKS 119
COMIN' HOME	Atlantic	16	20 Dec 69	9
Above hit: DELANEY and BONNIE and FRIENDS featuring Eric CLAPTON.				
I SHOT THE SHERIFF	RSO	9	27 Jul 74	9
Originally recorded by Bob Marley & the Wailers.				
SWING LOW SWEET CHARIOT	RSO	19	10 May 75	9
KNOCKIN' ON HEAVEN'S DOOR	RSO	38	16 Aug 75	4
LAY DOWN SALLY	RSO	39	24 Dec 77	6
PROMISES	RSO	37	21 Oct 78	7
I SHOT THE SHERIFF [RI]	RSO	64	5 Jun 82	2
THE SHAPE YOU'RE IN	Duck	75	23 Apr 83	1
FOREVER MAN	Warner Brothers	51	16 Mar 85	4
EDGE OF DARKNESS	BBC	65	4 Jan 86	3
Theme from the BBC TV series of the same name.				
Above hit: Eric CLAPTON with Michael KAMEN.				
BEHIND THE MASK	Duck	15	17 Jan 87	11
Originally recorded by the Yellow Magic Orchestra.				
TEARING US APART	Duck	56	20 Jun 87	3
Above hit: Eric CLAPTON and Tina TURNER.				
BAD LOVE	Duck	25	27 Jan 90	7
Backing vocals by Phil Collins.				
NO ALIBIS	Duck	53	14 Apr 90	3
WONDERFUL TONIGHT	Duck	30	16 Nov 91	7
Live recording from the Royal Albert Hall, London.				
TEARS IN HEAVEN	Reprise	50	8 Feb 92	3
From the film 'Rush'. Written about his dead son Connor.				
TEARS IN HEAVEN [RE]	Reprise	5	7 Mar 92	9
RUNAWAY TRAIN	Rocket	31	1 Aug 92	4
Above hit: Elton JOHN and Eric CLAPTON.				
IT'S PROBABLY ME	A&M	30	29 Aug 92	5
From the film 'Lethal Weapon 3'.				
Above hit: STING with Eric CLAPTON.				
LAYLA (ACOUSTIC)	Duck	45	3 Oct 92	3
MOTHERLESS CHILD	Duck	63	15 Oct 94	1
CHANGE THE WORLD	Reprise	18	20 Jul 96	5
From the film 'Phenomenon'.				
MY FATHER'S EYES	Duck	33	4 Apr 98	2
CIRCUS	Duck	39	4 Jul 98	2
First performed at Clapton's MTV Unplugged concert.				

ALBUMS:	HITS 24			WEEKS 508
BLUES BREAKERS	Decca	6	30 Jul 66	17
Above hit: John MAYALL with Eric CLAPTON.				
ERIC CLAPTON	Polydor	17	5 Sep 70	8
HISTORY OF ERIC CLAPTON	Polydor	20	26 Aug 72	6
461 OCEAN BOULEVARD	RSO	3	24 Aug 74	19
THERE'S ONE IN EVERY CROWD	RSO	15	12 Apr 75	8
E.C. WAS HERE	RSO	14	13 Sep 75	6
NO REASON TO CRY	RSO	8	11 Sep 76	7
SLOWHAND	RSO	23	26 Nov 77	13
BACKLESS	RSO	18	9 Dec 78	12
JUST ONE NIGHT	RSO	3	10 May 80	12
ANOTHER TICKET	RSO	18	7 Mar 81	8
TIME PIECES - THE BEST OF ERIC CLAPTON	RSO	20	24 Apr 82	13
MONEY & CIGARETTES	Duck	13	19 Feb 83	17
BACKTRACKIN'	Starblend	29	9 Jun 84	16
BEHIND THE SUN	Duck	8	23 Mar 85	14
AUGUST	Duck	3	6 Dec 86	42
THE CREAM OF ERIC CLAPTON	Polydor	3	26 Sep 87	98
Above hit: Eric CLAPTON and CREAM.				
JOURNEYMAN	Duck	2	18 Nov 89	34
24 NIGHTS	Duck	17	26 Oct 91	7
Live recordings from the Royal Albert Hall, London, 1990.				

UNPLUGGED	Duck	2	12 Sep 92	90
TIME PIECES – THE BEST OF ERIC CLAPTON [RE]	RSO	58	6 Mar 93	1
Re-released at mid-price.				
THE CREAM OF ERIC CLAPTON [RE-1ST] / THE BEST OF ERIC CLAPTON	Polydor	25	10 Jul 93	6
The re-package The Best Of Eric Clapton listed from 17 Jul 93.				
Above hit: Eric CLAPTON and CREAM.				
FROM THE CRADLE	Duck	1	24 Sep 94	18
A collection of old Blues numbers.				
AUGUST [RE]	Duck	38	4 Mar 95	4
Re-released at mid-price.				
PILGRIM	Duck	6	21 Mar 98	15
THE CREAM OF ERIC CLAPTON [RE-2ND]	Polydor	52	18 Apr 98	5
Re-released.				
Above hit: Eric CLAPTON and CREAM.				
BLUES	Polydor	52	26 Jun 99	2
Includes studio and live recordings from 1970–80.				
CLAPTON CHRONICLES – THE BEST OF ERIC CLAPTON	Duck	6	30 Oct 99	10

Dave CLARK FIVE   UK

SINGLES:	**HITS 22**			**WEEKS 174**
DO YOU LOVE ME	Columbia	30	5 Oct 63	6
Originally recorded by the Contours.				
GLAD ALL OVER	Columbia	1	23 Nov 63	19
BITS AND PIECES	Columbia	2	22 Feb 64	11
CAN'T YOU SEE THAT SHE'S MINE	Columbia	10	30 May 64	11
THINKING OF YOU BABY	Columbia	26	15 Aug 64	4
ANYWAY YOU WANT IT	Columbia	25	24 Oct 64	5
EVERYBODY KNOWS	Columbia	37	16 Jan 65	4
REELIN' AND ROCKIN'	Columbia	24	13 Mar 65	8
COME HOME	Columbia	16	29 May 65	8
CATCH US IF YOU CAN	Columbia	5	17 Jul 65	11
OVER AND OVER	Columbia	45	13 Nov 65	4
Originally recorded by Bobby Day.				
LOOK BEFORE YOU LEAP	Columbia	50	21 May 66	1
YOU GOT WHAT IT TAKES	Columbia	28	18 Mar 67	8
EVERYBODY KNOWS	Columbia	2	4 Nov 67	14
Song is different from their 1965 hit.				
NO ONE CAN BREAK A HEART LIKE YOU	Columbia	28	2 Mar 68	7
THE RED BALLOON	Columbia	7	21 Sep 68	11
Originally recorded by Raymond Froggatt.				
LIVE IN THE SKY	Columbia	39	30 Nov 68	6
PUT A LITTLE LOVE IN YOUR HEART	Columbia	31	25 Oct 69	4
Originally recorded by Jackie De Shannon.				
GOOD OLD ROCK 'N' ROLL [M]	Columbia	7	6 Dec 69	12
Originally recorded by Cat Mother and the All Night News Boys.				
EVERYBODY GET TOGETHER	Columbia	8	7 Mar 70	8
Originally recorded by the Youngbloods.				
HERE COMES SUMMER	Columbia	44	4 Jul 70	3
MORE GOOD OLD ROCK 'N ROLL [M]	Columbia	34	7 Nov 70	6
GLAD ALL OVER [RI]	EMI	37	1 May 93	3
EPS:	**HITS 3**			**WEEKS 35**
THE DAVE CLARK FIVE	Columbia	3	18 Jan 64	24
THE HITS OF THE DAVE CLARK FIVE	Columbia	20	23 Jan 65	1
WILD WEEKEND	Columbia	10	25 Sep 65	10
ALBUMS:	**HITS 4**			**WEEKS 31**
A SESSION WITH THE DAVE CLARK FIVE	Columbia	3	18 Apr 64	8
CATCH US IF YOU CAN	Columbia	8	14 Aug 65	8
25 THUMPING GREAT HITS	Polydor	7	4 Mar 78	10
GLAD ALL OVER AGAIN	EMI	28	17 Apr 93	5

Dee CLARK   US

SINGLES:	**HITS 2**			**WEEKS 9**
JUST KEEP IT UP (AND SEE WHAT HAPPENS)	London	26	3 Oct 59	1
RIDE A WILD HORSE	Chelsea	16	11 Oct 75	8

Gary CLARK   UK

SINGLES:	**HITS 3**			**WEEKS 8**
WE SAIL ON THE STORMY WATERS	Circa	34	30 Jan 93	4
FREEFLOATING	Circa	50	3 Apr 93	3
MAKE A FAMILY	Circa	70	19 Jun 93	1
ALBUMS:	**HITS 1**			**WEEKS 2**
TEN SHORT SONGS ABOUT LOVE	Circa	25	8 May 93	2

Loni CLARK
US

SINGLES:	HITS 3			WEEKS 6
RUSHING	A&M	37	5 Jun 93	2
U	A&M	28	22 Jan 94	3
Shortest title for a hit single.				
LOVE'S GOT ME ON A TRIP SO HIGH	A&M	59	17 Dec 94	1

Louis CLARK - See ROYAL PHILHARMONIC ORCHESTRA

Petula CLARK
UK

SINGLES:	HITS 27			WEEKS 247
THE LITTLE SHOEMAKER (LES PETIT CORDONNIER)	Polygon	12	12 Jun 54	1
Above hit: Petula CLARK with Malcolm LOCKYER and his Orchestra.				
THE LITTLE SHOEMAKER (LES PETIT CORDONNIER) [RE]	Polygon	7	26 Jun 54	9
MAJORCA	Polygon	12	19 Feb 55	4
Above hit: Petula CLARK with Laurie JOHNSON and his Orchestra.				
MAJORCA [RE]	Polygon	18	26 Mar 55	1
Above hit: Petula CLARK with Laurie JOHNSON and his Orchestra.				
SUDDENLY THERE'S A VALLEY	Pye Nixa	7	26 Nov 55	10
Originally recorded by Gogi Grant.				
WITH ALL MY HEART	Pye Nixa	4	27 Jul 57	18
Originally recorded by Jodie Sands.				
Above 2: Petula CLARK with Tony OSBORNE and his Orchestra.				
ALONE	Pye Nixa	8	16 Nov 57	12
Above hit: Petula CLARK with the Kim DRAKE ORCHESTRA and the Beryl STOTT GROUP.				
BABY LOVER	Pye Nixa	12	1 Mar 58	7
Above hit: Petula CLARK with the Peter KNIGHT ORCHESTRA with the Beryl STOTT GROUP.				
SAILOR	Pye	1	28 Jan 61	15
Original by Lolita reached No. 5 in the US in 1960.				
SOMETHING MISSING (L'ABSENT)	Pye	44	15 Apr 61	1
From the film 'Top Hat'.				
Above 2: Petula CLARK; Peter KNIGHT ORCHESTRA.				
ROMEO	Pye	3	15 Jul 61	15
MY FRIEND THE SEA	Pye	7	18 Nov 61	13
I'M COUNTING ON YOU	Pye	41	10 Feb 62	2
YA YA TWIST	Pye	14	30 Jun 62	11
YA YA TWIST [RE]	Pye	45	22 Sep 62	2
CASANOVA / CHARIOT	Pye	39	4 May 63	7
Above hit: Petula CLARK with the Henry MAYER ORCHESTRA (on Casanova only).				
DOWNTOWN	Pye	2	14 Nov 64	15
I KNOW A PLACE	Pye	17	13 Mar 65	8
YOU'D BETTER COME HOME	Pye	44	14 Aug 65	3
ROUND EVERY CORNER	Pye	43	16 Oct 65	3
YOU'RE THE ONE	Pye	23	6 Nov 65	9
MY LOVE	Pye	4	12 Feb 66	9
A SIGN OF THE TIMES	Pye	49	23 Apr 66	1
I COULDN'T LIVE WITHOUT YOUR LOVE	Pye	6	2 Jul 66	11
THIS IS MY SONG	Pye	1	4 Feb 67	14
From the film 'A Countess From Hong Kong'. Written by Charlie Chaplin.				
DON'T SLEEP IN THE SUBWAY	Pye	12	27 May 67	11
THE OTHER MAN'S GRASS (IS ALWAYS GREENER)	Pye	20	16 Dec 67	9
KISS ME GOODBYE	Pye	50	9 Mar 68	1
THE SONG OF MY LIFE	Pye	41	30 Jan 71	1
THE SONG OF MY LIFE [RE]	Pye	32	13 Feb 71	11
I DON'T KNOW HOW TO LOVE HIM	Pye	47	15 Jan 72	1
I DON'T KNOW HOW TO LOVE HIM [RE]	Pye	49	29 Jan 72	1
DOWNTOWN '88 [RM]	PRT	10	19 Nov 88	11
Remixed by Peter Slaghuis.				
EPS:	HITS 2			WEEKS 12
DOWNTOWN	Pye	12	20 Feb 65	6
THIS IS MY SONG	Pye	6	29 Apr 67	6
ALBUMS:	HITS 6			WEEKS 43
I COULDN'T LIVE WITHOUT YOUR LOVE	Pye	11	30 Jul 66	10
HIT PARADE	Pye	18	4 Feb 67	13
COLOUR MY WORLD	Pye	16	18 Feb 67	9
THESE ARE MY SONGS	Pye	38	7 Oct 67	3
THE OTHER MAN'S GRASS IS ALWAYS GREENER	Pye	37	6 Apr 68	1
20 ALL TIME GREATEST	K-Tel	18	5 Feb 77	7

Roland CLARK - See Armand VAN HELDEN

Dave CLARKE
UK

SINGLES:	HITS 3			WEEKS 6
RED THREE [EP]	Bush	45	30 Sep 95	2
Lead Track: Thunder.				

SOUTHSIDE	*Bush*	34	*3 Feb 96*	2
NO ONE'S DRIVING	*Bush*	37	*15 Jun 96*	2
ALBUMS:	**HITS 1**		**WEEKS 2**	
ARCHIVE ONE	*Bush*	36	*17 Feb 96*	2

Gilby CLARKE   US

ALBUMS:	**HITS 1**		**WEEKS 1**	
PAWNSHOP GUITARS	*Virgin*	39	*6 Aug 94*	1

John Cooper CLARKE   UK

SINGLES:	**HITS 1**		**WEEKS 3**	
¡ GIMMIX ! PLAY LOUD	*Epic*	39	*10 Mar 79*	3
ALBUMS:	**HITS 2**		**WEEKS 9**	
SNAP CRACKLE AND BOP	*Epic*	26	*19 Apr 80*	7
ZIP STYLE METHOD	*Epic*	97	*5 Jun 82*	2

Rick CLARKE   UK

SINGLES:	**HITS 1**		**WEEKS 2**	
I'LL SEE YOU ALONG THE WAY	*WA*	63	*30 Apr 88*	2

Sharon Dee CLARKE – See F.P.I. PROJECT; SERIOUS ROPE

Stanley CLARKE   US

ALBUMS:	**HITS 1**		**WEEKS 2**	
ROCKS PEBBLES AND SAND	*Epic*	42	*12 Jul 80*	2

CLARKE BROTHERS – See Max BYGRAVES

CLASH   UK

SINGLES:	**HITS 18**		**WEEKS 135**	
WHITE RIOT	*CBS*	38	*2 Apr 77*	3
COMPLETE CONTROL	*CBS*	28	*8 Oct 77*	2
CLASH CITY ROCKERS	*CBS*	35	*4 Mar 78*	4
(WHITE MAN) IN HAMMERSMITH PALAIS	*CBS*	32	*24 Jun 78*	7
TOMMY GUN	*CBS*	19	*2 Dec 78*	10
ENGLISH CIVIL WAR (JOHNNY COMES MARCHING HOME)	*CBS*	25	*3 Mar 79*	6
THE COST OF LIVING [EP]	*CBS*	22	*19 May 79*	8
Lead track: I Fought The Law.				
LONDON CALLING	*CBS*	11	*15 Dec 79*	10
BANKROBBER	*CBS*	12	*9 Aug 80*	10
THE CALL UP	*CBS*	40	*6 Dec 80*	6
HITSVILLE UK	*CBS*	56	*24 Jan 81*	4
THE MAGNIFICENT SEVEN	*CBS*	34	*25 Apr 81*	5
THIS IS RADIO CLASH	*CBS*	47	*28 Nov 81*	6
KNOW YOUR RIGHTS	*CBS*	43	*1 May 82*	3
ROCK THE CASBAH	*CBS*	30	*26 Jun 82*	10
SHOULD I STAY OR SHOULD I GO / STRAIGHT TO HELL	*CBS*	17	*25 Sep 82*	9
THIS IS ENGLAND	*CBS*	24	*12 Oct 85*	5
I FOUGHT THE LAW	*CBS*	29	*12 Mar 88*	5
LONDON CALLING [RI-1ST]	*CBS*	46	*7 May 88*	3
RETURN TO BRIXTON	*CBS*	57	*21 Jul 90*	2
SHOULD I STAY OR SHOULD I GO [RI]	*Columbia*	1	*2 Mar 91*	9
Featured in a Levi's jeans TV commercial.				
ROCK THE CASBAH [RI]	*Columbia*	15	*13 Apr 91*	6
LONDON CALLING [RI-2ND]	*Columbia*	64	*8 Jun 91*	2
ALBUMS:	**HITS 9**		**WEEKS 112**	
CLASH	*CBS*	12	*30 Apr 77*	16
GIVE 'EM ENOUGH ROPE	*CBS*	2	*25 Nov 78*	14
LONDON CALLING	*CBS*	9	*22 Dec 79*	20
SANDINISTA	*CBS*	19	*20 Dec 80*	9
COMBAT ROCK	*CBS*	2	*22 May 82*	23
CUT THE CRAP	*CBS*	16	*16 Nov 85*	3
THE STORY OF THE CLASH – VOLUME 1	*CBS*	7	*2 Apr 88*	10
THE STORY OF THE CLASH – VOLUME 1 [RI]	*Columbia*	13	*30 Mar 91*	10
THE SINGLES COLLECTION	*Columbia*	68	*16 Nov 91*	2
FROM HERE TO ETERNITY	*Columbia*	13	*16 Oct 99*	3
Live recordings from 1977–1982. Released to coincide with the airing of a BBC TV documentary about the band, 'Westway To The World' on 2 Oct 99.				
LONDON CALLING [RE]	*Columbia*	63	*16 Oct 99*	1
THE STORY OF THE CLASH – VOLUME 1 [RE]	*Columbia*	70	*16 Oct 99*	1

CLASS ACTION featuring Chris WILTSHIRE   US

SINGLES:	**HITS 1**		**WEEKS 3**	
WEEKEND	*Jive*	49	*7 May 83*	3

CLASSICS IV | | US

SINGLES:	HITS 1			WEEKS 1
SPOOKY	*Liberty*	46	*2 Mar 68*	1

Originally recorded by Mike Sharpe.

CLASSIX NOUVEAUX | | UK

SINGLES:	HITS 7			WEEKS 34
GUILTY	*Liberty*	43	*28 Feb 81*	7
TOKYO	*Liberty*	67	*16 May 81*	3
INSIDE OUTSIDE	*Liberty*	45	*8 Aug 81*	5
NEVER AGAIN (THE DAYS TIME ERASED)	*Liberty*	44	*7 Nov 81*	4
IS IT A DREAM	*Liberty*	11	*13 Mar 82*	9
BECAUSE YOU'RE YOUNG	*Liberty*	43	*29 May 82*	4
THE END . . . OR THE BEGINNING?	*Liberty*	60	*30 Oct 82*	2
ALBUMS:	**HITS 2**			**WEEKS 6**
NIGHT PEOPLE	*Liberty*	66	*30 May 81*	2
LA VERITE	*Liberty*	44	*24 Apr 82*	4

CLAWFINGER | | Norway/Sweden

SINGLES:	HITS 1			WEEKS 1
WARFAIR	*East West*	54	*19 Mar 94*	1

Judy CLAY and William BELL | | US

(See also William Bell.)

SINGLES:	HITS 1			WEEKS 14
PRIVATE NUMBER	*Stax*	8	*23 Nov 68*	14

Richard CLAYDERMAN | | France

(See also Richard Clayderman and James Last.)

ALBUMS:	HITS 14			WEEKS 189
RICHARD CLAYDERMAN	*Decca*	2	*13 Nov 82*	64
THE MUSIC OF RICHARD CLAYDERMAN	*Decca*	21	*8 Oct 83*	28
THE MUSIC OF LOVE	*Decca*	28	*24 Nov 84*	21
RICHARD CLAYDERMAN - CHRISTMAS	*Decca*	53	*1 Dec 84*	5
THE CLASSIC TOUCH	*Decca*	17	*23 Nov 85*	18

Above hit: Richard CLAYDERMAN with the ROYAL PHILHARMONIC ORCHESTRA.

HOLLYWOOD AND BROADWAY	*Decca*	28	*22 Nov 86*	9
SONGS OF LOVE	*Decca*	19	*28 Nov 87*	13
A LITTLE NIGHT MUSIC	*Decca Delphine*	52	*3 Dec 88*	5
THE LOVE SONGS OF ANDREW LLOYD WEBBER	*Decca Delphine*	18	*25 Nov 89*	10
MY CLASSIC COLLECTION	*Decca*	29	*24 Nov 90*	7
THE VERY BEST OF RICHARD CLAYDERMAN	*Decca Delphine*	47	*14 Nov 92*	5

Above 2: Richard CLAYDERMAN with the ROYAL PHILHARMONIC ORCHESTRA.

THE CARPENTERS COLLECTION	*PolyGram TV*	65	*25 Nov 95*	2
THE BEST OF RICHARD CLAYDERMAN	*Decca Delphine*	73	*20 Dec 97*	1
. . . WITH LOVE	*Music Collection*	62	*18 Sep 99*	1

Richard CLAYDERMAN and James LAST | | France/Germany

(See also Richard Clayderman; James Last.)

ALBUMS:	HITS 2			WEEKS 22
TOGETHER AT LAST	*Decca Delphine*	14	*9 Nov 91*	15
IN HARMONY	*Polydor*	28	*19 Nov 94*	7

Adam CLAYTON and Larry MULLEN | | Ireland

SINGLES:	HITS 1			WEEKS 12
THEME FROM MISSION: IMPOSSIBLE	*Mother*	7	*15 Jun 96*	12

Merry CLAYTON | | US

SINGLES:	HITS 1			WEEKS 1
YES	*RCA*	70	*21 May 88*	1

From the film 'Dirty Dancing'.

CLAYTOWN TROUPE | | UK

SINGLES:	HITS 2			WEEKS 3
WAYS OF LOVE	*Island*	57	*16 Jun 90*	2
WANTED IT ALL	*EMI USA*	74	*14 Mar 92*	1
ALBUMS:	**HITS 1**			**WEEKS 1**
THROUGH THE VEIL	*Island*	72	*21 Oct 89*	1

Johnny CLEGG and SAVUKA
UK/South Africa

SINGLES:	HITS 1			WEEKS 1
SCATTERLINGS OF AFRICA	EMI	75	16 May 87	1

CLEOPATRA
UK

(See also Steps Tina Cousins Cleopatra B*Witched Billie.)

SINGLES:	HITS 4			WEEKS 28
CLEOPATRA'S THEME	WEA	3	14 Feb 98	10
LIFE AIN'T EASY	WEA	4	16 May 98	7
I WANT YOU BACK	WEA	4	22 Aug 98	7
A TOUCH OF LOVE	WEA	24	6 Mar 99	4
ALBUMS:	HITS 1			WEEKS 4
COMIN' ATCHA!	WEA	20	6 Jun 98	4

CLICK
US

SINGLES:	HITS 1			WEEKS 1
SCANDALOUS	Jive	54	29 Jun 96	1

Jimmy CLIFF
Jamaica

SINGLES:	HITS 4			WEEKS 33
WONDERFUL WORLD, BEAUTIFUL PEOPLE	Trojan	6	25 Oct 69	13
VIETNAM	Trojan	47	14 Feb 70	1
VIETNAM [RE]	Trojan	46	28 Feb 70	2
WILD WORLD	Island	8	8 Aug 70	12
Originally recorded by Cat Stevens.				
I CAN SEE CLEARLY NOW	Columbia	23	19 Mar 94	5
From the film 'Cool Runnings'.				

Buzz CLIFFORD
US

SINGLES:	HITS 1			WEEKS 13
BABY SITTIN' BOOGIE	Fontana	17	4 Mar 61	13

Linda CLIFFORD
US

SINGLES:	HITS 2			WEEKS 12
IF MY FRIENDS COULD SEE ME NOW	Curtom	50	10 Jun 78	5
BRIDGE OVER TROUBLED WATER	RSO	28	5 May 79	7

CLIMAX BLUES BAND
UK

SINGLES:	HITS 1			WEEKS 9
COULDN'T GET IT RIGHT	BTM	10	9 Oct 76	9
ALBUMS:	HITS 1			WEEKS 1
GOLD PLATED	BTM	56	13 Nov 76	1

Simon CLIMIE
UK

SINGLES:	HITS 1			WEEKS 2
SOUL INSPIRATION	Epic	60	19 Sep 92	2

CLIMIE FISHER
UK

SINGLES:	HITS 6			WEEKS 44
LOVE CHANGES (EVERYTHING)	EMI	67	5 Sep 87	2
Originally intended for Rod Stewart.				
RISE TO THE OCCASION	EMI	10	12 Dec 87	11
LOVE CHANGES (EVERYTHING) [RM]	EMI	2	12 Mar 88	12
THIS IS ME	EMI	22	21 May 88	5
I WON'T BLEED FOR YOU	EMI	35	20 Aug 88	4
LOVE LIKE A RIVER	EMI	22	24 Dec 88	7
FACTS OF LOVE	EMI	50	23 Sep 89	3
ALBUMS:	HITS 2			WEEKS 38
EVERYTHING	EMI	14	13 Feb 88	36
COMING IN FOR THE KILL	EMI	35	21 Oct 89	2

Patsy CLINE
US

SINGLES:	HITS 3			WEEKS 17
SHE'S GOT YOU	Brunswick	43	28 Apr 62	1
HEARTACHES	Brunswick	31	1 Dec 62	5
CRAZY	MCA	14	8 Dec 90	11
First released 1961. A previous re-issue reached No. 79 in 1987. Originally recorded by Willie Nelson.				
ALBUMS:	HITS 4			WEEKS 28
SWEET DREAMS	MCA	18	19 Jan 91	10
DREAMING . . .	Platinum Musix	55	19 Jan 91	4

| THE DEFINITIVE PATSY CLINE 1932-1963 | Arcade | 11 | 5 Sep 92 | 8 |
| THE VERY BEST OF PATSY CLINE | MCA | 21 | 6 Jul 96 | 6 |

Above 4 are all compilations.

George CLINTON   US

(See also Ice Cube; Xavier featuring George Clinton and Bootsy Collins.)

SINGLES:		HITS 2		WEEKS 7
LOOPZILLA	Capitol	57	4 Dec 82	5
DO FRIES GO WITH THAT SHAKE	Capitol	57	26 Apr 86	2

CLIVILLES and COLE - See C&C MUSIC FACTORY

CLOCK   UK

SINGLES:		HITS 15		WEEKS 70
HOLDING ON	Media	66	30 Oct 93	1
Vocals by Ann-Marie Smith. Samples the 49ers' Move Your Feet.				
THE RHYTHM	Media	28	21 May 94	2
KEEP THE FIRES BURNING	Media	36	10 Sep 94	3
AXEL F / KEEP PUSHIN'	Media	7	4 Mar 95	9
WHOOMPH! (THERE IT IS)	Media	4	1 Jul 95	9
EVERYBODY	Media	6	26 Aug 95	5
IN THE HOUSE	Media	23	18 Nov 95	3
HOLDING ON 4 U [RR]	Media	27	24 Feb 96	2
Vocals by O.D.C. MC and Tinka.				
OH WHAT A NIGHT	Media	13	7 Sep 96	10
IT'S OVER	Media	10	22 Mar 97	5
U SEXY THING	Media	11	18 Oct 97	9
THAT'S THE WAY (I LIKE IT)	Media	11	17 Jan 98	4
ROCK YOUR BODY	Media	30	11 Jul 98	3
BLAME IT ON THE BOOGIE	Media	16	28 Nov 98	4
SUNSHINE DAY	Power Station	58	31 Jul 99	1
ALBUMS:		HITS 2		WEEKS 4
IT'S TIME . . .	Media	27	23 Sep 95	2
ABOUT TIME 2	Media	56	5 Apr 97	2

Rosemary CLOONEY   US

SINGLES:		HITS 7		WEEKS 81
HALF AS MUCH	Columbia	3	15 Nov 52	9
Originally recorded by Hank Williams.				
Above hit: Rosemary CLOONEY with Percy FAITH and his Orchestra.				
MAN (UH - HUH)	Philips	7	6 Feb 54	5
[AA] listed with Woman (Uh – Huh) by Jose Ferrer.				
THIS OLE HOUSE	Philips	1	9 Oct 54	18
Originally recorded by Stuart Hamblen.				
Above hit: Rosemary CLOONEY with Buddy COLE and his Orchestra.				
MAMBO ITALIANO	Philips	1	18 Dec 54	16
Above hit: Rosemary CLOONEY and the MELLOMEN.				
WHERE WILL THE DIMPLE BE?	Philips	6	21 May 55	13
Above hit: Rosemary CLOONEY and the MELLOMEN with the Buddy COLE QUARTET Bass solo: Thurl RAVENSCROFT.				
HEY THERE	Philips	4	1 Oct 55	11
From the film 'The Pajama Game'. Originally recorded by John Raitt. (Bonnie Raitt's father).				
Above hit: Rosemary CLOONEY with Buddy COLE and his Orchestra.				
MANGOS	Philips	25	30 Mar 57	2
Above hit: Rosemary CLOONEY with Frank COMSTOCK.				
MANGOS [RE]	Philips	17	27 Apr 57	7

CLOUD   UK

SINGLES:		HITS 1		WEEKS 1
ALL NIGHT LONG / TAKE IT TO THE TOP	UK Champagne	72	31 Jan 81	1

CLOUT   South Africa

SINGLES:		HITS 1		WEEKS 15
SUBSTITUTE	Carrere	2	17 Jun 78	15
Originally recorded by the Righteous Brothers.				

CLUB NOUVEAU   US

SINGLES:		HITS 1		WEEKS 12
LEAN ON ME	Warner Brothers	3	21 Mar 87	12

CLUB 69   Austria/US

SINGLES:		HITS 2		WEEKS 6
LET ME BE YOUR UNDERWEAR	ffrr	33	5 Dec 92	5
ALRIGHT	Twisted UK	70	14 Nov 98	1
Above hit: CLUB 69 featuring Suzanne PALMER.				

CLUBHOUSE
Italy

SINGLES:		HITS 7		WEEKS 40	
DO IT AGAIN / BILLIE JEAN [M]	Island	11	23 Jul 83	6
SUPERSTITION / GOOD TIMES [M]	Island	59	3 Dec 83	3
Above 2: CLUB HOUSE.				
I'M A MAN/YE KE YE KE [M]	Music Man	69	1 Jul 89	3
DEEP IN MY HEART	ffrr	59	20 Apr 91	2
DEEP IN MY HEART [RE]	ffrr	55	22 Jun 91	2
LIGHT MY FIRE	PWL International	59	4 Sep 93	1
Above hit: CLUB HOUSE featuring CARL.				
LIGHT MY FIRE [RE-1ST]	PWL International	45	13 Nov 93	5
LIGHT MY FIRE [RE-2ND]	PWL International	53	25 Dec 93	6
LIGHT MY FIRE [RM]	PWL	7	30 Apr 94	8
Remixed by Cappella.				
LIVING IN THE SUNSHINE	PWL Continental	21	23 Jul 94	3
NOWHERE LAND	PWL International	56	11 Mar 95	1
Above 3: CLUBHOUSE featuring CARL.				

CLUBZONE
UK/Germany

SINGLES:		HITS 1		WEEKS 1	
HANDS UP	Logic	50	19 Nov 94	1

CLUELESS
US

SINGLES:		HITS 1		WEEKS 1	
DON'T SPEAK	ZYX	61	5 Apr 97	1

Jeremy CLYDE – See Chad STUART and Jeremy CLYDE

CLYDE VALLEY STOMPERS
UK

SINGLES:		HITS 1		WEEKS 8	
PETER AND THE WOLF	Parlophone	25	11 Aug 62	8

CO-CO
UK

SINGLES:		HITS 1		WEEKS 7	
BAD OLD DAYS	Ariola Hansa	13	22 Apr 78	7
UK's Eurovision entry in 1978, it came 11th.				

CO-OPERATION CHOIR – See Peter BENNETT with the CO-OPERATION CHOIR

CO.RO featuring TARLISA
Germany

SINGLES:		HITS 1		WEEKS 1	
BECAUSE THE NIGHT	ZYX	61	12 Dec 92	1

COAL CHAMBER
US

ALBUMS:		HITS 1		WEEKS 2	
CHAMBER MUSIC	Roadrunner	21	18 Sep 99	2

COAST TO COAST
UK

SINGLES:		HITS 2		WEEKS 22	
(DO) THE HUCKLEBUCK	Polydor	5	31 Jan 81	15
Originally recorded by Paul Williams.				
LET'S JUMP THE BROOMSTICK	Polydor	28	23 May 81	7

COASTERS
US

SINGLES:		HITS 5		WEEKS 32	
SEARCHIN'	London	30	28 Sep 57	1
YAKETY YAK	London	12	16 Aug 58	8
CHARLIE BROWN	London	6	28 Mar 59	12
POISON IVY	London	15	31 Oct 59	7
SORRY BUT I'M GONNA HAVE TO PASS	Atlantic	41	9 Apr 94	4
Featured in the Volkswagen TV commercial. Originally released in 1958.				

Odia COATES – See Paul ANKA

Luis COBOS
Spain

SINGLES:		HITS 1		WEEKS 2	
TURANDOT 'NESSUM DORMA'	Epic	59	16 Jun 90	2
Above hit: Luis COBOS featuring Placido DOMINGO.				

ALBUMS:		HITS 1		WEEKS 1	
OPERA EXTRAVAGANZA	Epic	72	21 Apr 90	1
Sleeve credits The Royal Philharmonic Orchestra, Chorus Royal Opera House, the London Symphony Orchestra, conductor Luis Cobos.				

Eddie COCHRAN | US

SINGLES:	HITS 9			WEEKS 90
SUMMERTIME BLUES	London	18	8 Nov 58	6
C'MON EVERYBODY	London	6	14 Mar 59	13
Originally titled Lets Get Together.				
SOMETHIN' ELSE	London	22	17 Oct 59	3
HALLELUJAH, I LOVE HER SO	London	28	23 Jan 60	1
Originally recorded by Ray Charles.				
HALLELUJAH, I LOVE HER SO [RE]	London	22	6 Feb 60	3
THREE STEPS TO HEAVEN	London	1	14 May 60	15
SWEETIE PIE	London	38	8 Oct 60	3
LONELY	London	41	5 Nov 60	1
A-side was Sweetie Pie but not listed on this entry.				
WEEKEND	London	15	17 Jun 61	16
JEANNIE, JEANNIE, JEANNIE	London	31	2 Dec 61	4
Originally recorded by Jimmie Madden.				
MY WAY	Liberty	23	27 Apr 63	10
SUMMERTIME BLUES [RI]	Liberty	34	27 Apr 68	8
C'MON EVERYBODY [RI]	Liberty	14	13 Feb 88	7
Featured in the Levi's Jeans TV commercial.				
EPS:	HITS 3			WEEKS 51
SOMETHIN' ELSE	London	6	7 May 60	11
C'MON EVERYBODY	London	2	18 Jun 60	38
NEVER TO BE FORGOTTEN	Liberty	18	16 Feb 63	2
ALBUMS:	HITS 6			WEEKS 47
SINGING TO MY BABY	London	19	30 Jul 60	1
EDDIE COCHRAN MEMORIAL ALBUM	London	9	1 Oct 60	12
CHERISHED MEMORIES	Liberty	15	12 Jan 63	3
EDDIE COCHRAN MEMORIAL ALBUM [RI]	Liberty	11	20 Apr 63	18
SINGING TO MY BABY [RI]	Liberty	20	19 Oct 63	1
VERY BEST OF EDDIE COCHRAN	Liberty	34	9 May 70	3
THE EDDIE COCHRAN SINGLES ALBUM	United Artists	39	18 Aug 79	6
C'MON EVERYBODY	Liberty	53	16 Apr 88	3

Brenda COCHRANE | UK

ALBUMS:	HITS 2			WEEKS 14
THE VOICE	Polydor	14	14 Apr 90	11
IN DREAMS	Polydor	55	6 Apr 91	3

Tom COCHRANE | Canada

SINGLES:	HITS 1			WEEKS 2
LIFE IS A HIGHWAY	Capitol	62	27 Jun 92	2

COCK ROBIN | US

SINGLES:	HITS 1			WEEKS 12
THE PROMISE YOU MADE	CBS	28	31 May 86	12

Joe COCKER | UK

SINGLES:	HITS 15			WEEKS 89
MARJORINE	Regal Zonophone	48	25 May 68	1
WITH A LITTLE HELP FROM MY FRIENDS	Regal Zonophone	1	5 Oct 68	13
Originally recorded by the Beatles.				
DELTA LADY	Regal Zonophone	10	27 Sep 69	11
Written and originally recorded by Leon Russell about Rita Coolidge.				
THE LETTER	Regal Zonophone	39	4 Jul 70	6
I'M SO GLAD I'M STANDING HERE TODAY	MCA	61	26 Sep 81	3
Above hit: CRUSADERS, featured vocalist Joe COCKER.				
UP WHERE WE BELONG	Island	7	15 Jan 83	13
From the film 'An Officer And A Gentleman'. Originally recorded by Buffy Saint-Marie.				
Above hit: JOE COCKER and Jennifer WARNES.				
UNCHAIN MY HEART	Capitol	46	14 Nov 87	4
WHEN THE NIGHT COMES	Capitol	65	13 Jan 90	2
FEELS LIKE FOREVER	Capitol	25	7 Mar 92	5
NOW THAT THE MAGIC HAS GONE	Capitol	28	9 May 92	6
UNCHAIN MY HEART [RM]	Capitol	17	4 Jul 92	6
Remixed by Chris Lord-Alge.				
WHEN THE NIGHT COMES [RI]	Capitol	61	21 Nov 92	3
THE SIMPLE THINGS	Capitol	17	13 Aug 94	5
TAKE ME HOME	Capitol	41	22 Oct 94	3
Above hit: Joe COCKER featuring Bekka BRAMLETT.				
LET THE HEALING BEGIN	Capitol	32	17 Dec 94	5
HAVE A LITTLE FAITH	Capitol	67	23 Sep 95	2
DON'T LET ME BE MISUNDERSTOOD	Parlophone	53	12 Oct 96	1

ALBUMS:		HITS 9			WEEKS 66
MAD DOGS AND ENGLISHMEN		*A&M*	16	*26 Sep 70*	8
JOE COCKER / WITH A LITTLE HELP FROM MY FRIENDS		*Double Back*	29	*6 May 72*	4
Re-issue of albums originally released in 1969.					
A CIVILISED MAN		*Capitol*	100	*30 Jun 84*	1
NIGHT CALLS		*Capitol*	25	*11 Apr 92*	14
THE LEGEND – THE ESSENTIAL COLLECTION		*PolyGram TV*	4	*27 Jun 92*	20
HAVE A LITTLE FAITH		*Capitol*	9	*17 Sep 94*	15
ORGANIC		*Parlophone*	49	*26 Oct 96*	1
Re-recorded versions of Cocker's songs.					
GREATEST HITS		*EMI*	24	*20 Feb 99*	2
NO ORDINARY WORLD		*Parlophone*	63	*23 Oct 99*	1

COCKEREL CHORUS UK

SINGLES:		HITS 1			WEEKS 12
NICE ONE CYRIL		*Young Blood*	14	*24 Feb 73*	12

COCKNEY REBEL - See Steve HARLEY and COCKNEY REBEL

COCKNEY REJECTS UK

SINGLES:		HITS 6			WEEKS 22
I'M NOT A FOOL		*EMI*	65	*1 Dec 79*	2
BADMAN		*EMI*	65	*16 Feb 80*	3
THE GREATEST COCKNEY RIP-OFF		*Zonophone*	21	*26 Apr 80*	7
I'M FOREVER BLOWING BUBBLES		*Zonophone*	35	*17 May 80*	5
WE CAN DO ANYTHING		*Zonophone*	65	*12 Jul 80*	2
WE ARE THE FIRM		*Zonophone*	54	*25 Oct 80*	3

ALBUMS:		HITS 3			WEEKS 17
GREATEST HITS VOLUME 1		*Zonophone*	22	*15 Mar 80*	11
GREATEST HITS VOLUME 2		*Zonophone*	23	*25 Oct 80*	3
GREATEST HITS VOLUME 3 (LIVE AND LOUD)		*Zonophone*	27	*18 Apr 81*	3

COCO UK

SINGLES:		HITS 1			WEEKS 2
I NEED A MIRACLE		*Positiva*	39	*8 Nov 97*	2

El COCO US

SINGLES:		HITS 1			WEEKS 4
COCOMOTION		*Pye International*	31	*14 Jan 78*	4

COCOA BROVAZ - See BOUNTY KILLER (featuring COCOA BROVAZ, Nona HENDRYX and FREE)

COCONUTS US

SINGLES:		HITS 1			WEEKS 3
DID YOU HAVE TO LOVE ME LIKE YOU DID		*EMI America*	60	*11 Jun 83*	3

COCTEAU TWINS UK

SINGLES:		HITS 13			WEEKS 25
PEARLY-DEWDROPS DROPS		*4AD*	29	*28 Apr 84*	5
AIKEA-GUINEA		*4AD*	41	*30 Mar 85*	3
TINY DYNAMINE [EP]		*4AD*	52	*23 Nov 85*	2
Lead track: Pink Orange Red.					
ECHOES IN A SHALLOW BAY [EP]		*4AD*	65	*7 Dec 85*	1
Lead track: Great Spangled Fritillary.					
LOVE'S EASY TEARS		*4AD*	53	*25 Oct 86*	1
ICEBLINK LUCK		*4AD*	38	*8 Sep 90*	3
EVANGELINE		*Fontana*	34	*2 Oct 93*	1
WINTER WONDERLAND / FROSTY THE SNOWMAN		*Fontana*	58	*18 Dec 93*	1
BLUEBEARD		*Fontana*	33	*26 Feb 94*	2
TWINLIGHTS [EP]		*Fontana*	59	*7 Oct 95*	1
Lead track: Rilkean Heart.					
OTHERNESS [EP]		*Fontana*	59	*4 Nov 95*	1
Lead track: Feet Like Fins.					
TISHBITE		*Fontana*	34	*30 Mar 96*	2
VIOLAINE		*Fontana*	56	*20 Jul 96*	1

ALBUMS:		HITS 7			WEEKS 45
HEAD OVER HEELS		*4AD*	51	*29 Oct 83*	15
TREASURE		*4AD*	29	*24 Nov 84*	8
VICTORIALAND		*4AD*	10	*26 Apr 86*	7
BLUE BELL KNOLL		*4AD*	15	*1 Oct 88*	4
HEAVEN OR LAS VEGAS		*4AD*	7	*29 Sep 90*	5
FOUR-CALENDAR CAFE		*Fontana*	13	*30 Oct 93*	3
MILK & KISSES		*Fontana*	17	*27 Apr 96*	3

CODE RED — UK

SINGLES:		HITS 5		WEEKS 7	
I GAVE YOU EVERYTHING	Polydor	50	6 Jul 96	1
THIS IS OUR SONG	Polydor	59	16 Nov 96	1
CAN WE TALK . . .	Polydor	29	14 Jun 97	2
Original by Tevin Campbell reached No. 92 in 1993.				
IS THERE SOMEONE OUT THERE?	Polydor	34	9 Aug 97	2
WHAT WOULD YOU DO IF . . . ?	Polydor	55	4 Jul 98	1

COFFEE — US

SINGLES:		HITS 2		WEEKS 13	
CASANOVA	De-Lite	13	27 Sep 80	10
Originally recorded by Ruby Andrews.				
SLIP AND DIP / I WANNA BE WITH YOU	De-Lite	57	6 Dec 80	3

Alma COGAN — UK

SINGLES:		HITS 18		WEEKS 110	
BELL BOTTOM BLUES	His Master's Voice	4	20 Mar 54	9
Originally recorded by Teresa Brewer.				
LITTLE THINGS MEAN A LOT	His Master's Voice	11	28 Aug 54	2
LITTLE THINGS MEAN A LOT [RE-1ST]	His Master's Voice	19	9 Oct 54	1
LITTLE THINGS MEAN A LOT [RE-2ND]	His Master's Voice	18	23 Oct 54	2
I CAN'T TELL A WALTZ FROM A TANGO	His Master's Voice	6	4 Dec 54	11
Originally recorded by Patti Page.				
DREAMBOAT	His Master's Voice	1	28 May 55	16
THE BANJO'S BACK IN TOWN	His Master's Voice	17	24 Sep 55	1
GO ON BY	His Master's Voice	16	15 Oct 55	4
Above 2 entries were separate sides of the same release, each had its own chart run.				
TWENTY TINY FINGERS	His Master's Voice	17	17 Dec 55	1
Majority of singles listed above featured an Orchestra conducted by Frank Cordell.				
NEVER DO A TANGO WITH AN ESKIMO	His Master's Voice	6	24 Dec 55	5
Above 2 entries were separate sides of the same release, each had its own chart run.				
WILLIE CAN	His Master's Voice	13	31 Mar 56	8
Above hit: Alma COGAN with Desmond LANE – penny whistle.				
(THE SAME THINGS HAPPEN WITH) THE BIRDS AND THE BEES	His Master's Voice	25	14 Jul 56	4
WHY DO FOOLS FALL IN LOVE	His Master's Voice	22	11 Aug 56	3
Above 2 entries were separate sides of the same release, each had its own chart run.				
Above 2: Alma COGAN with vocal group and Orchestra.				
IN THE MIDDLE OF THE HOUSE	His Master's Voice	26	3 Nov 56	1
IN THE MIDDLE OF THE HOUSE [RE]	His Master's Voice	20	24 Nov 56	3
YOU, ME AND US	His Master's Voice	18	19 Jan 57	6
WHATEVER LOLA WANTS (LOLA GETS)	His Master's Voice	26	30 Mar 57	2
THE STORY OF MY LIFE	His Master's Voice	25	1 Feb 58	2
SUGARTIME	His Master's Voice	16	15 Feb 58	10
SUGARTIME [RE]	His Master's Voice	30	3 May 58	1
LAST NIGHT ON THE BACK PORCH	His Master's Voice	27	24 Jan 59	2
Above 3: Alma COGAN with the Michael SAMMES SINGERS.				
WE GOT LOVE	His Master's Voice	26	19 Dec 59	4
Above hit: Alma COGAN with the Don RIDDELLE SINGERS.				
DREAM TALK	His Master's Voice	48	14 May 60	1
THE TRAIN OF LOVE	His Master's Voice	27	13 Aug 60	5
Above 2: Alma COGAN with the Michael SAMMES SINGERS.				
COWBOY JIMMY JOE	Columbia	37	22 Apr 61	6
Above hit: Alma COGAN with Geoff LOVE and his Orchestra and the Rita WILLIAMS SINGERS.				

Shaye COGAN — US

SINGLES:		HITS 1		WEEKS 1	
MEAN TO ME	MGM	40	26 Mar 60	1
Originally recorded by Ruth Etting.				

Izhar COHEN and the 'ALPHA-BETA' — Israel

SINGLES:		HITS 1		WEEKS 7	
A-BA-NI-BI	Polydor	20	13 May 78	7
Eurovision Song Contest winner in 1978.				

Leonard COHEN — Canada

ALBUMS:		HITS 10		WEEKS 150	
SONGS OF LEONARD COHEN	CBS	18	31 Aug 68	12
SONGS OF LEONARD COHEN [RE]	CBS	13	26 Apr 69	59
SONGS FROM A ROOM	CBS	2	3 May 69	26
SONGS OF LOVE AND HATE	CBS	4	24 Apr 71	18
NEW SKIN FOR THE OLD CEREMONY	CBS	24	28 Sep 74	3
DEATH OF A LADIES' MAN	CBS	35	10 Dec 77	5
VARIOUS POSITIONS	CBS	52	16 Feb 85	6

I'M YOUR MAN	CBS	48	27 Feb 88	13
GREATEST HITS	CBS	99	6 Aug 88	1
THE FUTURE	Columbia	36	5 Dec 92	3
COHEN LIVE	Columbia	35	6 Aug 94	4

Live recordings dating from 1988–93.

Marc COHN
US

SINGLES:	HITS 3			WEEKS 15
WALKING IN MEMPHIS	Atlantic	66	25 May 91	4
SILVER THUNDERBIRD	Atlantic	54	10 Aug 91	3
WALKING IN MEMPHIS [RI]	Atlantic	22	12 Oct 91	5
WALK THROUGH THE WORLD	Atlantic	37	29 May 93	3
ALBUMS:	**HITS 2**			**WEEKS 23**
MARC COHN	Atlantic	27	29 Jun 91	20
THE RAINY SEASON	Atlantic	24	12 Jun 93	3

COLA BOY
UK

| SINGLES: | HITS 1 | | | WEEKS 7 |
| 7 WAYS TO LOVE | Arista | 8 | 6 Jul 91 | 7 |

COLDCUT
UK

| SINGLES: | HITS 9 | | | WEEKS 38 |
| DOCTORIN' THE HOUSE | Ahead Our Our Time | 6 | 20 Feb 88 | 9 |

Above hit: COLDCUT featuring YAZZ and the PLASTIC POPULATION.

| STOP THIS CRAZY THING | Ahead Our Our Time | 21 | 10 Sep 88 | 7 |

Above hit: COLDCUT featuring Junior REID and the AHEAD OF OUR TIME ORCHESTRA.

| PEOPLE HOLD ON | Ahead Our Our Time | 11 | 25 Mar 89 | 9 |

Above hit: COLDCUT featuring Lisa STANSFIELD.

MY TELPHONE	Ahead Our Our Time	52	3 Jun 89	2
COLDCUT'S CHRISTMAS BREAK	Ahead Our Our Time	67	16 Dec 89	3
FIND A WAY	Ahead Our Our Time	52	26 May 90	2

Above hit: COLDCUT featuring QUEEN LATIFAH.

DREAMER	Arista	54	4 Sep 93	2
AUTUMN LEAVES	Arista	50	22 Jan 94	2
MORE BEATS + PIECES	Ninja Tune	37	16 Aug 97	2
ALBUMS:	**HITS 2**			**WEEKS 5**
WHAT'S THAT NOISE	Ahead Our Our Time	20	29 Apr 89	4
LET US PLAY!	Ninja Tune	33	20 Sep 97	1

COLDJAM featuring GRACE
US

| SINGLES: | HITS 1 | | | WEEKS 2 |
| LAST NIGHT A DJ SAVED MY LIFE | Big Wave | 64 | 28 Jul 90 | 2 |

Andy COLE
UK

| SINGLES: | HITS 1 | | | WEEKS 1 |
| OUTSTANDING | WEA | 68 | 18 Sep 99 | 1 |

Buddy COLE QUARTET – See Rosemary CLOONEY; Johnnie RAY

Cozy COLE
US

| SINGLES: | HITS 1 | | | WEEKS 1 |
| TOPSY | London | 29 | 6 Dec 58 | 1 |

George COLE – See Dennis WATERMAN

Lloyd COLE
UK

SINGLES:	HITS 15			WEEKS 62
PERFECT SKIN	Polydor	71	26 May 84	1
PERFECT SKIN [RE]	Polydor	26	9 Jun 84	8
FOREST FIRE	Polydor	41	25 Aug 84	6
RATTLESNAKES	Polydor	65	17 Nov 84	2
BRAND NEW FRIEND	Polydor	19	14 Sep 85	8
LOST WEEKEND	Polydor	17	9 Nov 85	7
CUT ME DOWN	Polydor	38	18 Jan 86	4
MY BAG	Polydor	46	3 Oct 87	4
JENNIFER SHE SAID	Polydor	31	9 Jan 88	5
FROM THE HIP [EP]	Polydor	59	23 Apr 88	2

Lead track: From The Hip.
Above 10: Lloyd COLE and the COMMOTIONS.

NO BLUE SKIES	Polydor	42	3 Feb 90	4
DON'T LOOK BACK	Polydor	59	7 Apr 90	3
SHE'S A GIRL AND I'M A MAN	Polydor	55	31 Aug 91	2
SO YOU'D LIKE TO SAVE THE WORLD	Fontana	72	25 Sep 93	2

LIKE LOVERS DO	Fontana	24	16 Sep 95	3

A collaboration with former Commotion guitarist Neil Clark.

SENTIMENTAL FOOL	Fontana	73	2 Dec 95	1

ALBUMS:	HITS 9		WEEKS 92	
RATTLESNAKES	Polydor	13	20 Oct 84	30
EASY PIECES	Polydor	5	30 Nov 85	18
MAINSTREAM	Polydor	9	7 Nov 87	20
1984–1989	Polydor	14	8 Apr 89	7

Above 4: Lloyd COLE and the COMMOTIONS.

LLOYD COLE	Polydor	11	3 Mar 90	6
DON'T GET WEIRD ON ME BABE	Polydor	21	28 Sep 91	3
BAD VIBES	Fontana	38	23 Oct 93	2
LOVE STORY	Fontana	27	7 Oct 95	2
THE COLLECTION	Mercury	24	23 Jan 99	4

MJ COLE   UK

SINGLES:	HITS 1		WEEKS 2	
SINCERE	AM:PM	38	23 May 98	2

Nat 'King' COLE   US

(See also Nat King Cole/The George Shearing Quintet.)

SINGLES:	HITS 30		WEEKS 235	
SOMEWHERE ALONG THE WAY	Capitol	3	15 Nov 52	7
BECAUSE YOU'RE MINE	Capitol	6	20 Dec 52	2
FAITH CAN MOVE MOUNTAINS	Capitol	11	3 Jan 53	1

Above 2 entries were separate sides of the same release, each had its own chart run.

FAITH CAN MOVE MOUNTAINS [RE-1ST]	Capitol	12	17 Jan 53	2
BECAUSE YOU'RE MINE [RE-1ST]	Capitol	10	24 Jan 53	1
FAITH CAN MOVE MOUNTAINS [RE-2ND]	Capitol	10	7 Feb 53	1
BECAUSE YOU'RE MINE [RE-2ND]	Capitol	11	14 Feb 53	1
PRETEND	Capitol	2	25 Apr 53	18
CAN'T I	Capitol	9	15 Aug 53	3

Above hit: Nat "King" COLE and Billy MAY and His Orchestra.

MOTHER NATURE AND FATHER TIME	Capitol	7	19 Sep 53	7
CAN'T I [RE-1ST]	Capitol	6	19 Sep 53	4
CAN'T I [RE-2ND]	Capitol	10	31 Oct 53	1
TENDERLY	Capitol	10	17 Apr 54	1
SMILE	Capitol	2	11 Sep 54	14
MAKE HER MINE	Capitol	11	9 Oct 54	2

Above 2 entries were separate sides of the same release, each had its own chart run.

A BLOSSOM FELL	Capitol	3	26 Feb 55	10
MY ONE SIN (IN LIFE)	Capitol	18	27 Aug 55	1
MY ONE SIN (IN LIFE) [RE]	Capitol	17	17 Sep 55	1
DREAMS CAN TELL A LIE	Capitol	10	28 Jan 56	9
TOO YOUNG TO GO STEADY	Capitol	8	12 May 56	14

From the film 'Strip For Action'.
Nat "King" COLE with the Music of Nelson RIDDLE.

LOVE ME AS IF THERE WERE NO TOMORROW	Capitol	24	15 Sep 56	2
LOVE ME AS IF THERE WERE NO TOMORROW [RE]	Capitol	11	6 Oct 56	13
WHEN I FALL IN LOVE	Capitol	2	20 Apr 57	20

Originally recorded by Doris Day.

WHEN ROCK AND ROLL COME TO TRINIDAD	Capitol	28	6 Jul 57	1
MY PERSONAL POSSESSION	Capitol	21	19 Oct 57	2

The majority of hits above also had the credit 'Orchestra conducted by Nelson Riddle'.
Above hit: Nat "King" COLE and the FOUR KNIGHTS with Nelson RIDDLE's Music.

STARDUST	Capitol	24	26 Oct 57	2

Originally recorded by Irving Mills.

YOU MADE ME LOVE YOU	Capitol	22	30 May 59	3

Originally recorded by Al Jolson in 1913.

MIDNIGHT FLYER	Capitol	27	5 Sep 59	1
MIDNIGHT FLYER [RE]	Capitol	23	19 Sep 59	3
TIME AND THE RIVER	Capitol	29	13 Feb 60	1
TIME AND THE RIVER [RE-1ST]	Capitol	23	27 Feb 60	3
TIME AND THE RIVER [RE-2ND]	Capitol	47	2 Apr 60	1
THAT'S YOU	Capitol	10	28 May 60	8

Nat King COLE with the music of Nelson RIDDLE.

JUST AS MUCH AS EVER	Capitol	18	12 Nov 60	10
THE WORLD IN MY ARMS	Capitol	36	4 Feb 61	10
LET TRUE LOVE BEGIN	Capitol	29	18 Nov 61	10
BRAZILIAN LOVE SONG (ANDORHINA PRETA)	Capitol	34	24 Mar 62	4
THE RIGHT THING TO SAY	Capitol	42	2 Jun 62	4
RAMBLIN' ROSE	Capitol	5	29 Sep 62	14
DEAR LONELY HEARTS	Capitol	37	22 Dec 62	3
WHEN I FALL IN LOVE [RI]	Capitol	4	12 Dec 87	7
UNFORGETTABLE	Elektra	19	22 Jun 91	8

Above hit: Natalie COLE with Nat 'King' COLE.

THE CHRISTMAS SONG (CHESTNUTS ROASTING ON AN OPEN FIRE)	Capitol	69	14 Dec 91	2
Originally recorded by Mel Torme.				
LET'S FACE THE MUSIC AND DANCE	EMI	30	19 Mar 94	3
Featured in an Allied Dunbar TV Commercial.				

EPS:	HITS 3		WEEKS 94	
LOVE IS THE THING	Capitol	2	28 May 60	23
UNFORGETTABLE	Capitol	2	15 Oct 60	62
TENDERLY	Capitol	9	22 Apr 61	9

ALBUMS:	HITS 10		WEEKS 126	
STRING ALONG WITH NAT 'KING' COLE	Encore	12	19 Aug 61	9
UNFORGETTABLE NAT 'KING' COLE	Capitol	11	27 Mar 65	8
THE BEST OF NAT 'KING' COLE	Capitol	5	7 Dec 68	18
THE BEST OF NAT 'KING' COLE VOLUME 2	Capitol	39	5 Dec 70	2
WHITE CHRISTMAS	Music for Pleasure	45	27 Nov 71	1
Budget compilation.				
Above hit: Nat 'King' COLE and Dean MARTIN.				
20 GOLDEN GREATS	Capitol	1	8 Apr 78	30
20 GREATEST LOVE SONGS	Capitol	7	20 Nov 82	26
20 GOLDEN GREATS [RI]	EMI	66	19 Dec 87	7
CHRISTMAS WITH NAT 'KING' COLE	Stylus	25	26 Nov 88	9
THE UNFORGETTABLE NAT 'KING' COLE	EMI	23	23 Nov 91	9
THE ULTIMATE COLLECTION	EMI	26	20 Nov 99	7

Nat King COLE/The George SHEARING QUINTET   US

(See also Nat 'King' Cole; George Shearing Quintet with Strings.)

SINGLES:	HITS 1		WEEKS 14	
LET THERE BE LOVE	Capitol	11	21 Jul 62	14

ALBUMS:	HITS 1		WEEKS 7	
NAT KING COLE SINGS AND THE GEORGE SHEARING QUINTET PLAYS	Capitol	8	20 Oct 62	7

Natalie COLE   US

(See also Johnny Mathis and Natalie Cole.)

SINGLES:	HITS 11		WEEKS 87	
THIS WILL BE	Capitol	32	11 Oct 75	5
JUMP START	Manhattan	44	8 Aug 87	8
PINK CADILLAC	Manhattan	5	26 Mar 88	12
Originally recorded by Bruce Springsteen.				
EVERLASTING	Manhattan	28	25 Jun 88	6
JUMP START [RI]	Manhattan	36	20 Aug 88	5
I LIVE FOR YOUR LOVE	Manhattan	23	26 Nov 88	14
Original release reached No. 86 in 1987.				
MISS YOU LIKE CRAZY	EMI USA	2	15 Apr 89	15
REST OF THE NIGHT	EMI USA	56	22 Jul 89	2
STARTING OVER AGAIN	EMI USA	56	16 Dec 89	4
WILD WOMEN DO	EMI USA	16	21 Apr 90	7
From the film 'Pretty Woman'.				
UNFORGETTABLE	Elektra	19	22 Jun 91	8
Originally recorded by her father Nat 'King' Cole.				
Above hit: Natalie COLE with Nat 'King' COLE.				
THE VERY THOUGHT OF YOU	Elektra	71	16 May 92	1

ALBUMS:	HITS 4		WEEKS 49	
EVERLASTING	Manhattan	62	7 May 88	4
GOOD TO BE BACK	EMI-USA	10	20 May 89	12
UNFORGETTABLE – WITH LOVE	Elektra	11	27 Jul 91	29
TAKE A LOOK	Elektra	16	26 Jun 93	4

Paula COLE   US

SINGLES:	HITS 2		WEEKS 9	
WHERE HAVE ALL THE COWBOYS GONE?	Warner Brothers	15	28 Jun 97	8
I DON'T WANT TO WAIT	Warner Brothers	43	1 Aug 98	1
From the film 'City Of Angels'.				

ALBUMS:	HITS 1		WEEKS 1	
THIS FIRE	Warner Brothers	60	26 Jul 97	1

COLETTE – See SISTER BLISS with COLETTE

John Ford COLEY – See ENGLAND DAN and John Ford COLEY

COLLAGE   US/Canada/Philippines

SINGLES:	HITS 1		WEEKS 5	
ROMEO WHERE'S JULIET?	MCA	46	21 Sep 85	5

COLLAPSED LUNG
UK

SINGLES:		HITS 1		WEEKS 8	
LONDON TONIGHT / EAT MY GOAL	Deceptive	31	22 Jun 96		3
Eat My Goal was used in the TV commercial for Coca Cola during the Euro '96 football championships.					
EAT MY GOAL [RI]	Deceptive	18	30 May 98		5

Albert COLLINS - See Gary MOORE

Bootsy COLLINS - See XAVIER featuring George CLINTON and Bootsy COLLINS

Dave and Ansil COLLINS
Jamaica

SINGLES:		HITS 2		WEEKS 27	
DOUBLE BARREL	Technique	1	27 Mar 71		15
MONKEY SPANNER	Technique	7	26 Jun 71		12
ALBUMS:		HITS 1		WEEKS 2	
DOUBLE BARREL	Trojan	41	7 Aug 71		2

Edwyn COLLINS
UK

SINGLES:		HITS 5		WEEKS 25	
PALE BLUE EYES	Swamplands	72	11 Aug 84		2
Above hit: Paul QUINN and Edwyn COLLINS.					
EXPRESSLY [EP]	Setanta	42	12 Nov 94		3
Lead track: A Girl Like You.					
A GIRL LIKE YOU [RI]	Setanta	4	17 Jun 95		14
KEEP ON BURNING	Setanta	45	2 Mar 96		2
THE MAGIC PIPER (OF LOVE)	Setanta	32	2 Aug 97		3
From the film 'Austin Powers'.					
ADIDAS WORLD	Setanta	71	18 Oct 97		1
ALBUMS:		HITS 2		WEEKS 9	
GORGEOUS GEORGE	Setanta	8	22 Jul 95		8
I'M NOT FOLLOWING YOU	Setanta	55	13 Sep 97		1

Felicia COLLINS - See LUKK featuring Felicia COLLINS

Jeff COLLINS
UK

SINGLES:		HITS 1		WEEKS 8	
ONLY YOU	Polydor	40	18 Nov 72		8

Judy COLLINS
US

SINGLES:		HITS 3		WEEKS 86	
BOTH SIDES NOW	Elektra	14	17 Jan 70		11
Originally recorded by Joni Mitchell.					
AMAZING GRACE	Elektra	5	5 Dec 70		32
AMAZING GRACE [RE-1ST]	Elektra	48	24 Jul 71		1
AMAZING GRACE [RE-2ND]	Elektra	40	4 Sep 71		7
AMAZING GRACE [RE-3RD]	Elektra	50	20 Nov 71		1
AMAZING GRACE [RE-4TH]	Elektra	48	18 Dec 71		2
AMAZING GRACE [RE-5TH]	Elektra	20	22 Apr 72		19
AMAZING GRACE [RE-6TH]	Elektra	46	9 Sep 72		2
AMAZING GRACE [RE-7TH]	Elektra	49	23 Dec 72		3
SEND IN THE CLOWNS	Elektra	6	17 May 75		8
Originally recorded by Glynis Johns.					
ALBUMS:		HITS 3		WEEKS 18	
WHALES AND NIGHTINGALES	Elektra	37	10 Apr 71		2
JUDITH	Elektra	7	31 May 75		12
AMAZING GRACE	Telstar	34	14 Dec 85		4

Michelle COLLINS
UK

SINGLES:		HITS 1		WEEKS 3	
SUNBURN	BBC Music	28	27 Feb 99		3
Theme from the BBC TV series of the same name.					

Phil COLLINS
UK

(See also Various Artists: Films - Original Soundtracks 'Buster'.)

SINGLES:		HITS 29		WEEKS 226	
IN THE AIR TONIGHT	Virgin	2	17 Jan 81		10
I MISSED AGAIN	Virgin	14	7 Mar 81		8
IF LEAVING ME IS EASY	Virgin	17	30 May 81		8
THRU' THESE WALLS	Virgin	56	23 Oct 82		2
YOU CAN'T HURRY LOVE	Virgin	1	4 Dec 82		16
DON'T LET HIM STEAL YOUR HEART AWAY	Virgin	45	19 Mar 83		5
Above hit: Phil COLLINS with the Martyn FORD ORCHESTRA.					

AGAINST ALL ODDS (TAKE A LOOK AT ME NOW)	Virgin	2	7 Apr 84	14
From the film 'Against All Odds'.				
SUSSUDIO	Virgin	12	26 Jan 85	9
EASY LOVER	CBS	1	9 Mar 85	12
Above hit: Philip BAILEY (duet with Phil COLLINS).				
ONE MORE NIGHT	Virgin	4	13 Apr 85	9
TAKE ME HOME	Virgin	19	27 Jul 85	9
SEPARATE LIVES	Virgin	4	23 Nov 85	13
From the film 'White Nights'.				
Above hit: Phil COLLINS and Marilyn MARTIN.				
IN THE AIR TONIGHT ('88 REMIX) [RM]	Virgin	4	18 Jun 88	9
This remix had an identical catalogue number to the original. Remixed by Phil Collins and Hugh Padgham.				
A GROOVY KIND OF LOVE	Virgin	1	3 Sep 88	13
Originally recorded by Patti Labelle and the Bluebells.				
TWO HEARTS	Virgin	6	26 Nov 88	11
Above 2 from the film 'Buster'.				
ANOTHER DAY IN PARADISE	Virgin	2	4 Nov 89	11
I WISH IT WOULD RAIN DOWN	Virgin	7	27 Jan 90	9
SOMETHING HAPPENED ON THE WAY TO HEAVEN	Virgin	15	28 Apr 90	7
THAT'S JUST THE WAY IT IS	Virgin	26	28 Jul 90	5
HANG IN LONG ENOUGH	Virgin	34	6 Oct 90	3
DO YOU REMEMBER (LIVE)	Virgin	57	8 Dec 90	5
HERO	Atlantic	56	15 May 93	3
Above hit: David CROSBY featuring Phil COLLINS.				
BOTH SIDES OF THE STORY	Virgin	7	30 Oct 93	5
BOTH SIDES OF THE STORY [RE]	Virgin	61	1 Jan 94	1
EVERYDAY	Virgin	15	15 Jan 94	5
WE WAIT AND WE WONDER	Virgin	45	7 May 94	2
DANCE INTO THE LIGHT	Face Value	9	5 Oct 96	6
IT'S IN YOUR EYES	Face Value	30	14 Dec 96	4
WEAR MY HAT	Face Value	43	12 Jul 97	2
TRUE COLORS	Virgin	26	7 Nov 98	4
YOU'LL BE IN MY HEART	Walt Disney	17	6 Nov 99	6
From the Walt Disney film 'Tarzan'.				
ALBUMS:	**HITS 8**		**WEEKS 796**	
FACE VALUE	Virgin	1	21 Feb 81	274
HELLO, I MUST BE GOING!	Virgin	2	13 Nov 82	135
NO JACKET REQUIRED	Virgin	1	2 Mar 85	176
HELLO, I MUST BE GOING! [RE]	Virgin	48	16 Jul 88	28
Re-released at mid-price. Chart position reached in 1990.				
BUT SERIOUSLY	Virgin	1	2 Dec 89	72
SERIOUS HITS . . . LIVE!	Virgin	2	17 Nov 90	50
Live recordings from the 1990 Serious Tour.				
BOTH SIDES	Virgin	1	20 Nov 93	21
DANCE INTO THE LIGHT	Face Value	4	2 Nov 96	13
HITS	Virgin	1	17 Oct 98	27

Rodger COLLINS — US

SINGLES:	**HITS 1**		**WEEKS 6**	
YOU SEXY SUGAR PLUM (BUT I LIKE IT)	Fantasy	22	3 Apr 76	6

Willie COLLINS — US

SINGLES:	**HITS 1**		**WEEKS 4**	
WHERE YOU GONNA BE TONIGHT?	Capitol	46	28 Jun 86	4
ALBUMS:	**HITS 1**		**WEEKS 1**	
WHERE YOU GONNA BE TONIGHT?	Capitol	97	14 Jun 86	1

Michel COLOMBIER – See Pierre HENRY/Michel COLOMBIER

Willie COLON — US

SINGLES:	**HITS 1**		**WEEKS 7**	
SET FIRE TO ME	A&M	41	28 Jun 86	7

COLOR ME BADD — US

SINGLES:	**HITS 6**		**WEEKS 31**	
I WANNA SEX YOU UP	Giant	1	18 May 91	14
From the film 'New Jack City'.				
ALL 4 LOVE	Giant	5	3 Aug 91	10
I ADORE MI AMOR	Giant	44	12 Oct 91	2
I ADORE MI AMOR [RI]	Giant	59	9 Nov 91	2
HEARTBREAKER	Giant	58	22 Feb 92	1
TIME AND CHANCE	Giant	62	20 Nov 93	1
CHOOSE	Giant	65	16 Apr 94	1
ALBUMS:	**HITS 1**		**WEEKS 22**	
C.M.B.	Giant	3	24 Aug 91	22

COLORADO
UK

SINGLES:	HITS 1			WEEKS 3
CALIFORNIA DREAMING	Pinnacle	45	21 Oct 78	3

COLOSSEUM
UK

ALBUMS:	HITS 4			WEEKS 14
COLOSSEUM	Fontana	15	17 May 69	1
VALENTYNE SUITE	Vertigo	15	22 Nov 69	2
DAUGHTER OF TIME	Vertigo	23	5 Dec 70	5
COLOSSEUM LIVE	Bronze	17	26 Jun 71	6

COLOURBOX
UK

ALBUMS:	HITS 1			WEEKS 2
COLOURBOX	4AD	67	24 Aug 85	2

COLOURFIELD
UK

SINGLES:	HITS 4			WEEKS 18
THE COLOUR FIELD	Chrysalis	43	21 Jan 84	4
Above hit: COLOUR FIELD.				
TAKE	Chrysalis	70	28 Jul 84	1
THINKING OF YOU	Chrysalis	12	26 Jan 85	10
CASTLES IN THE AIR	Chrysalis	51	13 Apr 85	3
ALBUMS:	HITS 2			WEEKS 8
VIRGINS AND PHILISTINES	Chrysalis	12	4 May 85	7
DECEPTION	Chrysalis	95	4 Apr 87	1

COLOURS featuring Stephen EMMANUEL and ESKA
UK

SINGLES:	HITS 1			WEEKS 1
WHAT U DO	Inferno	51	27 Feb 99	1

Alice COLTRANE – See Carlos SANTANA and Alice COLTRANE

COLUMBIA PICTURES ORCHESTRA – See Morris STOLOFF conducting the Columbia PICTURES ORCHESTRA

COLUMBO presents IN FULL ROCK-A-PHONIC SOUND featuring OOE
UK

SINGLES:	HITS 1			WEEKS 1
ROCKABILLY BOB	V2	59	15 May 99	1

Shawn COLVIN
US

SINGLES:	HITS 6			WEEKS 12
I DON'T KNOW WHY	Columbia	62	27 Nov 93	1
ROUND OF BLUES	Columbia	73	12 Feb 94	1
EVERY LITTLE THING HE DOES IS MAGIC	Columbia	65	3 Sep 94	2
ONE COOL REMOVE	Columbia	40	7 Jan 95	3
Above hit: Shawn COLVIN with Mary Chapin CARPENTER.				
I DON'T KNOW WHY [RI]	Columbia	52	12 Aug 95	1
From the film 'Clockwork Mice'.				
GET OUT OF THIS HOUSE	Columbia	70	15 Mar 97	1
SUNNY CAME HOME	Columbia	29	30 May 98	3
ALBUMS:	HITS 1			WEEKS 1
COVER GIRL	Columbia	67	17 Sep 94	1

COMETS – See Bill HALEY and his COMETS

COMIC RELIEF
UK

ALBUMS:	HITS 1			WEEKS 8
COMIC RELIEF PRESENTS UTTERLY UTTERLY LIVE!	WEA	10	10 May 86	8

COMING OUT CREW
US

SINGLES:	HITS 1			WEEKS 1
FREE GAY AND HAPPY	Out On Vinyl	50	18 Mar 95	1
Vocals by Sabrina Johnston.				

COMMENTATORS
UK

SINGLES:	HITS 1			WEEKS 7
N-N-NINETEEN NOT OUT	Oval	13	22 Jun 85	7
A pastiche of Paul Hardcastle's 19.				

COMMITMENTS
Ireland

SINGLES:	HITS 1			WEEKS 1
MUSTANG SALLY	MCA	63	30 Nov 91	1

ALBUMS:		HITS 2			WEEKS 141
THE COMMITMENTS [OST]	MCA	4	26 Oct 91	130
THE COMMITMENTS VOLUME 2	MCA	13	25 Apr 92	11

COMMODORES

US

SINGLES:		HITS 16			WEEKS 121
MACHINE GUN	Tamla Motown	20	24 Aug 74	11
THE ZOO (THE HUMAN ZOO)	Tamla Motown	44	23 Nov 74	2
EASY	Motown	9	2 Jul 77	10
BRICK HOUSE / SWEET LOVE	Motown	32	8 Oct 77	6
TOO HOT TA TROT / ZOOM	Motown	38	11 Mar 78	4
FLYING HIGH	Motown	37	24 Jun 78	7
THREE TIMES A LADY	Motown	1	5 Aug 78	14
JUST TO BE CLOSE TO YOU	Motown	62	25 Nov 78	4
SAIL ON	Motown	8	25 Aug 79	10
STILL	Motown	4	3 Nov 79	11
WONDERLAND	Motown	40	19 Jan 80	4
LADY (YOU BRING ME UP)	Motown	56	1 Aug 81	5
OH NO	Motown	44	21 Nov 81	3
NIGHTSHIFT	Motown	3	26 Jan 85	14
ANIMAL INSTINCT	Motown	74	11 May 85	1
GOIN' TO THE BANK	Polydor	43	25 Oct 86	4
EASY [RI]	Motown	15	13 Aug 88	11
ALBUMS:		HITS 10			WEEKS 129
COMMODORES LIVE!	Motown	60	13 May 78	1
NATURAL HIGH	Motown	8	10 Jun 78	23
GREATEST HITS	Motown	19	2 Dec 78	16
MIDNIGHT MAGIC	Motown	15	18 Aug 79	25
HEROES	Motown	50	28 Jun 80	5
IN THE POCKET	Motown	69	18 Jul 81	5
LOVE SONGS	K-Tel	5	14 Aug 82	28
NIGHTSHIFT	Motown	13	23 Feb 85	10
THE VERY BEST OF COMMODORES – 16 CLASSIC TRACKS	Telstar	25	9 Nov 85	13
THE VERY BEST OF THE COMMODORES	Motown	26	6 May 95	3

COMMON featuring Chantay SAVAGE

US

SINGLES:		HITS 1			WEEKS 1
REMINDING ME (OF SEF)	Epic	59	8 Nov 97	1

COMMUNARDS

UK

(See also Jimmy Somerville.)

SINGLES:		HITS 8			WEEKS 76
YOU ARE MY WORLD	London	30	12 Oct 85	8
Above hit: COMMUNARDS/Jimmy SOMERVILLE – Richard COLES.				
DISENCHANTED	London	29	24 May 86	5
DON'T LEAVE ME THIS WAY	London	1	23 Aug 86	14
Above hit: COMMUNARDS with Sarah Jane MORRIS.				
SO COLD THE NIGHT	London	8	29 Nov 86	10
YOU ARE MY WORLD ('87) [RM]	London	21	21 Feb 87	6
TOMORROW	London	23	12 Sep 87	7
NEVER CAN SAY GOODBYE	London	4	7 Nov 87	11
Originally recorded by the Jackson 5.				
FOR A FRIEND	London	28	20 Feb 88	7
THERE'S MORE TO LOVE	London	20	11 Jun 88	8
ALBUMS:		HITS 2			WEEKS 74
COMMUNARDS	London	7	2 Aug 86	45
RED	London	4	17 Oct 87	29

Perry COMO

US

SINGLES:		HITS 23			WEEKS 323
DON'T LET THE STARS GET IN YOUR EYES	His Master's Voice	1	17 Jan 53	15
Originally recorded by Slim Willet.				
Above hit: Perry COMO with the RAMBLERS.				
WANTED	His Master's Voice	4	5 Jun 54	14
Above hit: Perry COMO with Hugo WINTERHALTER'S ORCHESTRA and				
CHORUS.				
IDLE GOSSIP	His Master's Voice	3	26 Jun 54	15
Above hit: Perry COMO with Hugo WINTERHALTER and his Orchestra.				
WANTED [RE]	His Master's Voice	18	2 Oct 54	1
PAPA LOVES MAMBO	His Master's Voice	16	11 Dec 54	1
Above hit: Perry COMO and the Ray CHARLES SINGERS.				
TINA MARIE	His Master's Voice	24	31 Dec 55	1
Above hit: Perry COMO and the Ray CHARLES SINGERS with Mitchell AYRES and				
his Orchestra.				
JUKE BOX BABY	His Master's Voice	22	28 Apr 56	6

HOT DIGGITY (DOG ZIGGITY BOOM)	His Master's Voice	4	26 May 56	13
Above hit: Perry COMO with Mitchell AYRES and his Orchestra and the Ray CHARLES				
SINGERS.				
MORE	His Master's Voice	10	22 Sep 56	11
GLENDORA	His Master's Voice	18	29 Sep 56	6
Above 2 entries were separate sides of the same release, each had its own chart run.				
MORE [RE]	His Master's Voice	29	15 Dec 56	1
Above 3: Perry COMO and the Ray CHARLES SINGERS with Mitchell AYRES and his				
Orchestra.				
MAGIC MOMENTS	RCA	1	8 Feb 58	17
CATCH A FALLING STAR	RCA	9	8 Mar 58	10
Above 2 entries were separate sides of the same release, each had its own chart run.				
KEWPIE DOLL	RCA	9	10 May 58	7
I MAY NEVER PASS THIS WAY AGAIN	RCA	15	31 May 58	8
MOON TALK	RCA	17	6 Sep 58	13
LOVE MAKES THE WORLD GO 'ROUND (YEAH, YEAH)	RCA	6	8 Nov 58	14
MANDOLINS IN THE MOONLIGHT	RCA	13	22 Nov 58	12
Above 2 entries were separate sides of the same release, each had its own chart run.				
TOMBOY	RCA	10	28 Feb 59	12
I KNOW	RCA	13	11 Jul 59	16
DELAWARE	RCA	3	27 Feb 60	14
Above 10: Perry COMO with Mitchell AYRES ORCHESTRA and the Ray CHARLES				
SINGERS.				
CATERINA	RCA	37	12 May 62	4
Above hit: Perry COMO with the Ray CHARLES SINGERS; Mitchell AYRES and his				
Orchestra.				
CATERINA [RE]	RCA	45	16 Jun 62	2
IT'S IMPOSSIBLE	RCA Victor	4	30 Jan 71	23
I THINK OF YOU	RCA Victor	14	15 May 71	11
AND I LOVE YOU SO	RCA Victor	3	21 Apr 73	31
Originally recorded by Don McLean.				
FOR THE GOOD TIMES	RCA Victor	7	25 Aug 73	27
Originally recorded by Kris Kristofferson.				
WALK RIGHT BACK	RCA Victor	33	8 Dec 73	10
AND I LOVE YOU SO [RE]	RCA Victor	40	12 Jan 74	4
I WANT TO GIVE (AHORA QUE SOY LIBRE)	RCA Victor	31	25 May 74	6
EPS:	**HITS 1**			**WEEKS 1**
YOU'LL NEVER WALK ALONE	RCA	20	18 Jun 60	1
ALBUMS:	**HITS 8**			**WEEKS 191**
DEAR PERRY	RCA	6	8 Nov 58	5
COMO'S GOLDEN RECORDS	RCA	4	31 Jan 59	5
IT'S IMPOSSIBLE	RCA Victor	13	10 Apr 71	13
AND I LOVE YOU SO	RCA Victor	1	7 Jul 73	109
Peak position reached on 26 Jan 74.				
PERRY	RCA Victor	26	24 Aug 74	3
MEMORIES ARE MADE OF HITS	RCA Victor	14	19 Apr 75	16
40 GREATEST HITS	K-Tel	1	25 Oct 75	34
FOR THE GOOD TIMES	Telstar	41	3 Dec 83	6

COMPAGNONS DE LA CHANSON — France

SINGLES:	**HITS 1**			**WEEKS 3**
THE THREE BELLS (THE JIMMY BROWN SONG)	Columbia	27	10 Oct 59	1
THE THREE BELLS (THE JIMMY BROWN SONG) [RE]	Columbia	21	24 Oct 59	2

COMPULSION — Ireland/Holland

ALBUMS:	**HITS 1**			**WEEKS 1**
COMFORTER	One Little Indian	59	9 Apr 94	1

COMSAT ANGELS — UK

SINGLES:	**HITS 1**			**WEEKS 2**
INDEPENDENCE DAY	Jive	75	21 Jan 84	1
INDEPENDENCE DAY [RE]	Jive	71	4 Feb 84	1
ALBUMS:	**HITS 3**			**WEEKS 9**
SLEEP NO MORE	Polydor	51	5 Sep 81	5
FICTION	Polydor	94	18 Sep 82	2
LAND	Jive	91	8 Oct 83	2

Frank COMSTOCK - See Rosemary CLOONEY

CON FUNK SHUN — US

SINGLES:	**HITS 1**			**WEEKS 2**
BURNIN' LOVE	Club	68	19 Jul 86	2

CONCEPT

SINGLES:		HITS 1		US WEEKS 6
MR. D.J.	*Fourth & Broadway*	27	*14 Dec 85*	6

CONFEDERATES - See Elvis COSTELLO and the ATTRACTIONS

CONGREGATION

SINGLES:		HITS 1		UK WEEKS 14
SOFTLY WHISPERING I LOVE YOU	*Columbia*	4	*27 Nov 71*	14
Originally recorded by David and Jonathan.				

CONGRESS

SINGLES:		HITS 1		UK WEEKS 4
40 MILES	*Inner Rhythm*	26	*26 Oct 91*	4

Arthur CONLEY

SINGLES:		HITS 2		US WEEKS 15
SWEET SOUL MUSIC	*Atlantic*	7	*29 Apr 67*	14
FUNKY STREET	*Atlantic*	46	*13 Apr 68*	1

Jud CONLON'S RHYTHMAIRES and ORCHESTRA - See Bing CROSBY

CONNELLS

SINGLES:		HITS 1		US WEEKS 11
'74-'75	*TNT*	14	*12 Aug 95*	8
'74-'75 [RE]	*TNT*	21	*16 Mar 96*	3
ALBUMS:		**HITS 1**		**WEEKS 2**
RING	*London*	36	*9 Sep 95*	2

Harry CONNICK Jr.

SINGLES:		HITS 3		US WEEKS 11
RECIPE FOR LOVE / IT HAD TO BE YOU	*Columbia*	32	*25 May 91*	6
Recipe For Love originally reached No. 86 in 1990. It Had To Be You from the film 'When Harry Met Sally' and originally recorded by Isham Jones.				
WE ARE IN LOVE	*Columbia*	62	*3 Aug 91*	2
BLUE LIGHT, RED LIGHT (SOMEONE'S THERE)	*Columbia*	54	*23 Nov 91*	3
ALBUMS:		**HITS 5**		**WEEKS 67**
WE ARE IN LOVE	*CBS*	17	*22 Sep 90*	27
Re-issued on the Columbia label from 12 Jan 91.				
WE ARE IN LOVE [RI]	*Columbia*	7	*25 May 91*	19
BLUE LIGHT, RED LIGHT	*Columbia*	16	*26 Oct 91*	11
25	*Columbia*	35	*30 Jan 93*	2
FOREVER FOR NOW	*Columbia*	32	*12 Jun 93*	5
SHE	*Columbia*	21	*27 Aug 94*	3

Ray CONNIFF

US

(See also Don Cherry; Frankie Laine; Guy Mitchell; Johnnie Ray.)

ALBUMS:		HITS 11		WEEKS 96
IT'S THE TALK OF THE TOWN	*Philips*	15	*28 May 60*	1
'S AWFUL NICE	*Philips*	13	*25 Jun 60*	1
HI-FI COMPANION ALBUM	*Philips*	3	*26 Nov 60*	44
MEMORIES ARE MADE OF THIS	*Philips*	14	*20 May 61*	4
'S WONDERFUL 'S MARVELLOUS	*CBS*	18	*29 Dec 62*	3
WE WISH YOU A MERRY CHRISTMAS	*CBS*	12	*29 Dec 62*	1
HI-FI COMPANION ALBUM [RI]	*CBS*	24	*16 Apr 66*	4
SOMEWHERE MY LOVE	*CBS*	34	*9 Sep 67*	3
HIS ORCHESTRA, HIS CHORUS, HIS SINGERS, HIS SOUND	*CBS*	1	*21 Jun 69*	16
BRIDGE OVER TROUBLED WATER	*CBS*	30	*23 May 70*	14
LOVE STORY	*CBS*	34	*12 Jun 71*	1
I'D LIKE TO TEACH THE WORLD TO SING	*CBS*	17	*19 Feb 72*	4

Billy CONNOLLY

SINGLES:		HITS 4		UK WEEKS 31
D.I.V.O.R.C.E.	*Polydor*	1	*1 Nov 75*	10
Live recording from the Apollo, Glasgow. A parody of the Tammy Wynette hit.				
NO CHANCE (NO CHARGE)	*Polydor*	24	*17 Jul 76*	5
Parody of the J.J. Barrie hit.				
IN THE BROWNIES	*Polydor*	38	*25 Aug 79*	7
Parody of the Village People hit In The Navy.				
SUPER GRAN (THEME)	*Stiff*	32	*9 Mar 85*	9
Theme from the Tyne Tees TV series 'Super Gran'.				
ALBUMS:		**HITS 8**		**WEEKS 108**
SOLO CONCERT	*Transatlantic*	8	*20 Jul 74*	33

COP YER WHACK OF THIS	Polydor	10	18 Jan 75	29
WORDS AND MUSIC	Transatlantic	34	20 Sep 75	10
GET RIGHT INTAE HIM	Polydor	6	6 Dec 75	14
ATLANTIC BRIDGE	Polydor	20	11 Dec 76	9
RAW MEAT FOR THE BALCONY	Polydor	57	28 Jan 78	3
THE PICK OF BILLY CONNOLLY	Polydor	23	5 Dec 81	8
BILLY AND ALBERT	10 Records	81	5 Dec 87	2

CONQUERING LION   UK

SINGLES:	HITS 1			WEEKS 1
CODE RED ('94 REMIX)	Mango	53	8 Oct 94	1

Includes samples from Supercat and Reggie Stepper.

Leena CONQUEST and HIP HOP FINGER   US

SINGLES:	HITS 1			WEEKS 1
BOUNDARIES	Naturalresponse	67	18 Jun 94	1

Jess CONRAD   UK

SINGLES:	HITS 3			WEEKS 13
CHERRY PIE	Decca	39	2 Jul 60	1
MYSTERY GIRL	Decca	44	28 Jan 61	1
MYSTERY GIRL [RE]	Decca	18	11 Feb 61	9
PRETTY JENNY	Decca	50	13 Oct 62	2

CONSOLIDATED   US

ALBUMS:	HITS 1			WEEKS 1
BUSINESS OF PUNISHMENT	London	53	30 Jul 94	1

CONSORTIUM   UK

SINGLES:	HITS 1			WEEKS 9
ALL THE LOVE IN THE WORLD	Pye	22	15 Feb 69	9

Ann CONSUELO – See SUBTERRANIA featuring Ann CONSUELO

CONTOURS   US

SINGLES:	HITS 1			WEEKS 6
JUST A LITTLE MISUNDERSTANDING	Tamla Motown	31	24 Jan 70	6

CONTRABAND   Germany/US

SINGLES:	HITS 1			WEEKS 2
ALL THE WAY FROM MEMPHIS	Impact American	65	20 Jul 91	2

CONTROL   UK

SINGLES:	HITS 1			WEEKS 5
DANCE WITH ME (I'M YOUR ECSTASY)	All Around The World	17	2 Nov 91	5

CONVERT   Belgium

SINGLES:	HITS 2			WEEKS 7
NIGHTBIRD	A&M	39	11 Jan 92	4
ROCKIN' TO THE RHYTHM	A&M	42	29 May 93	2
NIGHTBIRD [RM]	Wonderboy	45	31 Jan 98	1

Remixed by Tin Tin Out.

Russ CONWAY   UK

SINGLES:	HITS 20			WEEKS 179
PARTY POPS [M]	Columbia	24	30 Nov 57	5
GOT A MATCH	Columbia	30	30 Aug 58	1

The week Got A Match charted, Yakety Yak by the Coasters was inadvertently omitted. The mistake allowed Russ Conway to sneak in at No.30.

MORE PARTY POPS [M]	Columbia	10	29 Nov 58	7
THE WORLD OUTSIDE (THEME FROM THE WARSAW CONCERTO)	Columbia	24	24 Jan 59	1

Above hit: Russ CONWAY with Geoff LOVE and his Orchestra and the Rita WILLIAMS SINGERS.

SIDE SADDLE	Columbia	1	21 Feb 59	30
THE WORLD OUTSIDE (THEME FROM THE WARSAW CONCERTO) [RE]	Columbia	24	07 Mar 59	3

Above hit: Russ CONWAY with Geoff LOVE and his Orchestra and the Rita WILLIAMS SINGERS.

ROULETTE	Columbia	1	16 May 59	19
CHINA TEA	Columbia	5	22 Aug 59	13
SNOW COACH	Columbia	7	14 Nov 59	9
MORE AND MORE PARTY POPS [M]	Columbia	5	21 Nov 59	8
ROYAL EVENT	Columbia	15	5 Mar 60	8
FINGS AIN'T WOT THEY USED T'BE	Columbia	47	23 Apr 60	1
LUCKY FIVE	Columbia	14	21 May 60	9

PASSING BREEZE	Columbia	16	1 Oct 60	10
Above hit: Russ CONWAY with Tony OSBORNE and his Orchestra.				
EVEN MORE PARTY POPS [M]	Columbia	27	26 Nov 60	9
PEPE	Columbia	19	21 Jan 61	9
Above hit: Russ CONWAY with John BARRY and his Orchestra.				
PABLO	Columbia	45	27 May 61	2
Above hit: Russ CONWAY with Tony OSBORNE and his Orchestra.				
SAY IT WITH FLOWERS	Columbia	23	26 Aug 61	10
Above hit: Dorothy SQUIRES/Russ CONWAY with Tony OSBORNE and his Orchestra.				
TOY BALLOONS	Columbia	7	2 Dec 61	11
LESSON ONE	Columbia	21	24 Feb 62	7
ALWAYS YOU AND ME	Columbia	33	1 Dec 62	4
Majority of the above hits had the credit 'accompaniment directed by Geoff Love'.				
Above hit: Russ CONWAY with Geoff LOVE and his Orchestra.				
ALWAYS YOU AND ME [RE]	Columbia	35	5 Jan 63	3
EPS:	**HITS 5**			**WEEKS 25**
TIME TO CELEBRATE	Columbia	17	9 Apr 60	3
ANOTHER SIX	Columbia	12	13 Aug 60	5
ROCKING HORSE COWBOY	Columbia	12	29 Oct 60	3
MORE PARTY POPS	Columbia	7	24 Dec 60	8
MY CONCERTO FOR YOU NO. 2	Columbia	11	29 Apr 61	6
ALBUMS:	**HITS 7**			**WEEKS 69**
PACK UP YOUR TROUBLES	Columbia	9	22 Nov 58	5
SONGS TO SING IN YOUR BATH	Columbia	8	2 May 59	10
FAMILY FAVOURITES	Columbia	3	19 Sep 59	16
TIME TO CELEBRATE	Columbia	3	19 Dec 59	7
MY CONCERTO FOR YOU	Columbia	5	26 Mar 60	17
PARTY TIME	Columbia	7	17 Dec 60	11
RUSS CONWAY PRESENTS 24 PIANO GREATS	Ronco	25	23 Apr 77	3

CONWAY BROTHERS US

SINGLES:	**HITS 1**			**WEEKS 10**
TURN IT UP	10 Records	11	22 Jun 85	10

Ry COODER US

(See also Ali Farka Toure and Ry Cooder.)

ALBUMS:	**HITS 5**			**WEEKS 40**
BOP TILL YOU DROP	Warner Brothers	36	11 Aug 79	9
BORDER LINE	Warner Brothers	35	18 Oct 80	6
THE SLIDE AREA	Warner Brothers	18	24 Apr 82	12
GET RHYTHM	Warner Brothers	75	14 Nov 87	3
BUENA VISTA SOCIAL CLUB	World Circuit	44	5 Jul 97	10
Collaboration with veteran Cuban musicians.				

Martin COOK – See Richard DENTON and Martin COOK

Norman COOK UK

(See also Fatboy Slim; Mighty Dub Katz.)

SINGLES:	**HITS 2**			**WEEKS 10**
WON'T TALK ABOUT IT / BLAME IT ON THE BASSLINE	Go.Beat	29	8 Jul 89	6
Above hit: Norman COOK featuring Billy BRAGG / Norman COOK featuring M.C. WILDSKI.				
FOR SPACIOUS LIES	Go.Beat	48	21 Oct 89	4
Above hit: Norman COOK featuring LESTER.				

Peter COOK and Dudley MOORE UK

SINGLES:	**HITS 2**			**WEEKS 15**
GOODBYEEE	Decca	18	19 Jun 65	10
Above hit: Peter COOK and Dudley MOORE with the Dudley MOORE TRIO.				
THE BALLAD OF SPOTTY MULDOON	Decca	34	17 Jul 65	5
Above hit: Peter COOK with the Dudley MOORE TRIO.				
EPS:	**HITS 1**			**WEEKS 3**
BY APPOINTMENT	Decca	18	29 Jan 66	3
ALBUMS:	**HITS 3**			**WEEKS 34**
ONCE MOORE WITH COOK	Decca	25	21 May 66	1
DEREK AND CLIVE LIVE	Island	12	18 Sep 76	25
COME AGAIN	Virgin	18	24 Dec 77	8

Brandon COOKE featuring Roxanne SHANTE US

(See also Roxanne Shante.)

SINGLES:	**HITS 1**			**WEEKS 3**
SHARP AS A KNIFE	Club	45	29 Oct 88	3

Sam COOKE   US

SINGLES:	HITS 8			WEEKS 82
YOU SEND ME	London	29	18 Jan 58	1
ONLY SIXTEEN	His Master's Voice	23	15 Aug 59	4
WONDERFUL WORLD	His Master's Voice	27	9 Jul 60	8
CHAIN GANG	RCA	9	1 Oct 60	11
CUPID	RCA	7	29 Jul 61	14
TWISTIN' THE NIGHT AWAY	RCA Victor	6	10 Mar 62	14
ANOTHER SATURDAY NIGHT	RCA Victor	23	18 May 63	12
FRANKIE AND JOHNNY	RCA Victor	30	7 Sep 63	6
WONDERFUL WORLD [RI]	RCA	2	22 Mar 86	11
Featured in the Levi's Jeans TV commercial.				
ANOTHER SATURDAY NIGHT [RI]	RCA Victor	75	10 May 86	1
ALBUMS:	**HITS 1**			**WEEKS 27**
THE MAN AND HIS MUSIC	RCA	8	26 Apr 86	27

COOKIE CREW   UK

SINGLES:	HITS 5			WEEKS 31
ROK DA HOUSE	Rhythm King	5	9 Jan 88	11
Original release reached No. 79 in 1987.				
Above hit: BEATMASTERS featuring the COOKIE CREW.				
BORN THIS WAY (LET'S DANCE)	ffrr	23	7 Jan 89	5
GOT TO KEEP ON	ffrr	17	1 Apr 89	9
COME ON AND GET SOME	ffrr	42	15 Jul 89	3
SECRETS (OF SUCCESS)	ffrr	53	27 Jul 91	3
Above hit: COOKIE CREW featuring Danny D.				
ALBUMS:	**HITS 1**			**WEEKS 4**
BORN THIS WAY!	London	24	6 May 89	4

COOKIES   US

SINGLES:	HITS 1			WEEKS 1
CHAINS	London	50	12 Jan 63	1

COOL, the FAB and the GROOVY present Quincy JONES   UK

(See also Quincy Jones.)

SINGLES:	HITS 1			WEEKS 1
SOUL BOSSA NOVA	Manifesto	47	1 Aug 98	1
Originally released by Quincy Jones in 1962. Featured in the Nike TV commercial.				

COOL DOWN ZONE   UK

SINGLES:	HITS 1			WEEKS 4
HEAVEN KNOWS	10 Records	52	30 Jun 90	4

COOL JACK   Italy

SINGLES:	HITS 1			WEEKS 1
JUS' COME	AM:PM	44	9 Nov 96	1

COOL NOTES   UK

SINGLES:	HITS 6			WEEKS 28
YOU'RE NEVER TOO YOUNG	Abstract Dance	42	18 Aug 84	5
I FORGOT	Abstract Dance	63	17 Nov 84	2
SPEND THE NIGHT	Abstract Dance	11	23 Mar 85	9
IN YOUR CAR	Abstract Dance	13	13 Jul 85	9
HAVE A GOOD FOREVER . . .	Abstract Dance	73	19 Oct 85	1
INTO THE MOTION	Abstract Dance	66	17 May 86	2
ALBUMS:	**HITS 1**			**WEEKS 2**
HAVE A GOOD FOREVER . . .	Abstract Dance	66	9 Nov 85	2

Rita COOLIDGE   US

(See also Kris Kristofferson and Rita Coolidge.)

SINGLES:	HITS 4			WEEKS 24
WE'RE ALL ALONE	A&M	6	25 Jun 77	13
Originally recorded by Boz Scaggs.				
(YOUR LOVE HAS LIFTED ME) HIGHER AND HIGHER	A&M	49	15 Oct 77	1
(YOUR LOVE HAS LIFTED ME) HIGHER AND HIGHER [RE]	A&M	48	29 Oct 77	1
WORDS	A&M	25	4 Feb 78	8
ALL TIME HIGH	A&M	75	25 Jun 83	1
Theme song from the James Bond film 'Octopussy'.				
ALBUMS:	**HITS 3**			**WEEKS 40**
ANYTIME ANYWHERE	A&M	6	6 Aug 77	28
LOVE ME AGAIN	A&M	51	8 Jul 78	1
THE VERY BEST OF RITA COOLIDGE	A&M	6	14 Mar 81	11

COOLIO US

(See also B Real, Busta Rhymes, Coolio, LL Cool J and Method Man; Quincy Jones.)

SINGLES:		HITS 9		WEEKS 56
FANTASTIC VOYAGE	Tommy Boy	41	23 Jul 94	2
Originally recorded by Lakeside.				
I REMEMBER	Tommy Boy	73	15 Oct 94	1
Samples Float On by the Floaters.				
GANGSTA'S PARADISE	Tommy Boy	1	28 Oct 95	20
From the film 'Dangerous Minds'. Samples Stevie Wonder's Pastime Paradise.				
Above hit: COOLIO featuring L.V.				
TOO HOT	Tommy Boy	9	20 Jan 96	6
Kool And The Gang's JT Taylor re-recorded his vocal sample for this hit.				
1, 2, 3, 4 (SUMPIN' NEW)	Tommy Boy	13	6 Apr 96	7
Samples Wikka Wrap by the Evasions.				
IT'S ALL THE WAY LIVE (NOW)	Tommy Boy	34	17 Aug 96	2
From the film 'Eddie'. Originally recorded by Lakeside.				
THE WINNER	Atlantic	53	7 Jun 97	1
From the film 'Space Jam'.				
C U WHEN U GET THERE	Tommy Boy	3	19 Jul 97	12
From the film 'Nothing To Lose'. Song based on Pacelbel's 'Canon'.				
Above hit: COOLIO featuring 40 THEVZ.				
OOH LA LA	Tommy Boy	14	11 Oct 97	5
Samples Grace Jones' Pull Up To The Bumper.				
ALBUMS:		HITS 3		WEEKS 27
IT TAKES A THIEF	Tommy Boy	67	29 Oct 94	1
GANGSTA'S PARADISE	Tommy Boy	18	18 Nov 95	24
MY SOUL	Tommy Boy	28	13 Sep 97	2

Alice COOPER US

SINGLES:		HITS 19		WEEKS 104
SCHOOL'S OUT	Warner Brothers	1	15 Jul 72	12
ELECTED	Warner Brothers	4	7 Oct 72	10
HELLO HURRAY	Warner Brothers	6	10 Feb 73	12
NO MORE MR. NICE GUY	Warner Brothers	10	21 Apr 73	10
TEENAGE LAMENT '74	Warner Brothers	12	19 Jan 74	7
(NO MORE) LOVE AT YOUR CONVENIENCE	Warner Brothers	44	21 May 77	2
HOW YOU GONNA SEE ME NOW	Warner Brothers	61	23 Dec 78	6
SEVEN AND SEVEN IS (LIVE VERSION)	Warner Brothers	62	6 Mar 82	3
FOR BRITAIN ONLY / UNDER MY WHEELS (LIVE)	Warner Brothers	66	8 May 82	2
HE'S BACK (THE MAN BEHIND THE MASK)	MCA	61	18 Oct 86	2
FREEDOM	MCA	50	9 Apr 88	3
POISON	Epic	2	29 Jul 89	11
BED OF NAILS	Epic	38	7 Oct 89	5
HOUSE OF FIRE	Epic	65	2 Dec 89	2
HEY STOOPID	Epic	21	22 Jun 91	6
LOVE'S A LOADED GUN	Epic	38	5 Oct 91	2
FEED MY FRANKENSTEIN	Epic	27	6 Jun 92	3
From the film 'Wayne's World'.				
LOST IN AMERICA	Epic	22	28 May 94	3
IT'S ME	Epic	34	23 Jul 94	2
ALBUMS:		HITS 17		WEEKS 127
KILLER	Warner Brothers	27	5 Feb 72	18
SCHOOL'S OUT	Warner Brothers	4	22 Jul 72	20
LOVE IT TO DEATH	Warner Brothers	28	9 Sep 72	7
BILLION DOLLAR BABIES	Warner Brothers	1	24 Mar 73	23
MUSCLE OF LOVE	Warner Brothers	34	12 Jan 74	4
WELCOME TO MY NIGHTMARE	Anchor	19	15 Mar 75	8
ALICE COOPER GOES TO HELL	Warner Brothers	23	24 Jul 76	7
LACE AND WHISKY	Warner Brothers	33	28 May 77	3
FROM THE INSIDE	Warner Brothers	68	23 Dec 78	3
FLUSH THE FASHION	Warner Brothers	56	17 May 80	3
SPECIAL FORCES	Warner Brothers	96	12 Sep 81	1
DADA	Warner Brothers	93	12 Nov 83	1
CONSTRICTOR	MCA	41	1 Nov 86	2
RAISE YOUR FIST AND YELL	MCA	48	7 Nov 87	3
TRASH	Epic	2	26 Aug 89	12
HEY STOOPID	Epic	4	13 Jul 91	3
THE LAST TEMPTATION	Epic	6	18 Jun 94	5

Deborah COOPER - See C&C MUSIC FACTORY

Tommy COOPER UK

SINGLES:		HITS 1		WEEKS 3
DON'T JUMP OFF THE ROOF DAD	Palette	40	1 Jul 61	2
DON'T JUMP OFF THE ROOF DAD [RE]	Palette	50	22 Jul 61	1

Julian COPE
UK

SINGLES:		HITS 15		WEEKS 59	
SUNSHINE PLAYROOM	Mercury	64	19 Nov 83	1
THE GREATNESS AND PERFECTION OF LOVE	Mercury	52	31 Mar 84	5
WORLD SHUT YOUR MOUTH	Island	19	27 Sep 86	8
TRAMPOLENE	Island	31	17 Jan 87	6
EVE'S VOLCANO (COVERED IN SIN)	Island	41	11 Apr 87	5
CHARLOTTE ANNE	Island	35	24 Sep 88	6
5 O'CLOCK WORLD	Island	42	21 Jan 89	4
Originally recorded by the Vogues.				
CHINA DOLL	Island	53	24 Jun 89	2
BEAUTIFUL LOVE	Island	32	9 Feb 91	6
EAST EASY RIDER	Island	51	20 Apr 91	3
HEAD	Island	57	3 Aug 91	2
WORLD SHUT YOUR MOUTH [RI]	Island	44	8 Aug 92	3
FEAR LOVES THIS PLACE	Island	42	17 Oct 92	2
TRY TRY TRY	Echo	24	12 Aug 95	3
I COME FROM ANOTHER PLANET, BABY	Echo	34	27 Jul 96	2
PLANETARY SIT-IN (EVERY GIRL HAS YOUR NAME)	Echo	34	5 Oct 96	1
ALBUMS:		**HITS 10**		**WEEKS 35**	
WORLD SHUT YOUR MOUTH	Mercury	40	3 Mar 84	4
"FRIED"	Mercury	87	24 Nov 84	1
SAINT JULIAN	Island	11	14 Mar 87	10
MY NATION UNDERGROUND	Island	42	29 Oct 88	2
PEGGY SUICIDE	Island	23	16 Mar 91	7
FLOORED GENIUS – THE BEST OF JULIAN COPE AND THE TEARDROP EXPLODES	Island	22	15 Aug 92	3
Includes his solo and group material.				
Above hit: Julian COPE and the TEARDROP EXPLODES.				
JEHOVAHKILL	Island	20	31 Oct 92	2
AUTOGEDDON	Echo	16	16 Jul 94	3
JULIAN COPE PRESENTS 20 MOTHERS	Echo	20	9 Sep 95	2
INTERPRETER	Echo	39	26 Oct 96	1

Imani COPPOLA
US

SINGLES:		HITS 1		WEEKS 3	
LEGEND OF A COWGIRL	Columbia	32	28 Feb 98	3

Frank CORDELL and his Orchestra
UK

SINGLES:		HITS 1		WEEKS 4	
SADIE'S SHAWL (SANTIE SE KOPDOEK)	His Master's Voice	29	25 Aug 56	2
THE BLACK BEAR	His Master's Voice	44	18 Feb 61	2

Louise CORDET
France

SINGLES:		HITS 1		WEEKS 13	
I'M JUST A BABY	Decca	13	7 Jul 62	13

CORDUROY
UK

ALBUMS:		HITS 1		WEEKS 1	
OUT OF HERE	Acid Jazz	73	8 Oct 94	1

Chris CORNELL
US

SINGLES:		HITS 1		WEEKS 1	
CAN'T CHANGE ME	A&M	62	23 Oct 99	1
ALBUMS:		**HITS 1**		**WEEKS 1**	
EUPHORIA MORNING	A&M	31	2 Oct 99	1

Don CORNELL
US

SINGLES:		HITS 2		WEEKS 23	
HOLD MY HAND	Vogue	1	4 Sep 54	21
From the film 'Susan Slept Here'.				
STRANGER IN PARADISE	Vogue Coral	19	23 Apr 55	2
Above hit: Don CORNELL with the Roland SHAW ORCHESTRA.				

Lyn CORNELL
UK

SINGLES:		HITS 1		WEEKS 9	
NEVER ON SUNDAY	Decca	30	22 Oct 60	9

CORNERSHOP
UK

SINGLES:		HITS 2		WEEKS 16	
BRIMFUL OF ASHA	Wiiija	60	30 Aug 97	1

BRIMFUL OF ASHA [RI]	*Wiiija*	1	*28 Feb 98*	12

Though the main track is a re-issue, it was the B-side Norman Cook remix that was more popular.

SLEEP ON THE LEFT SIDE	*Wiiija*	23	*16 May 98*	3
ALBUMS:	HITS 1		WEEKS 15	
WHEN I WAS BORN FOR THE 7TH TIME	*Wiiija*	17	*20 Sep 97*	15

Charlotte CORNWELL – See Julie COVINGTON, Charlotte CORNWELL, Rula LENSKA, Sue JONES-DAVIES

Hugh CORNWELL   UK

SINGLES:	HITS 2		WEEKS 3	
FACTS + FIGURES	*Virgin*	61	*24 Jan 87*	2
ANOTHER KIND OF LOVE	*Virgin*	71	*7 May 88*	1
ALBUMS:	HITS 1		WEEKS 1	
WOLF	*Virgin*	98	*18 Jun 88*	1

CORO DE MUNJES DEL MONASTERIO BENEDICTINO DE SANTO DOMINGO DE SILOS   Spain

(Popularly known as the Monks Chorus Silos.)

ALBUMS:	HITS 2		WEEKS 28	
CANTO GREGORIANO	*EMI Classics*	7	*5 Mar 94*	25
CANTO NOEL	*EMI Classics*	53	*17 Dec 94*	3

CORONA   Brazil/Italy

SINGLES:	HITS 5		WEEKS 44	
THE RHYTHM OF THE NIGHT	*WEA*	2	*10 Sep 94*	14
THE RHYTHM OF THE NIGHT [RE]	*WEA*	55	*31 Dec 94*	4
BABY BABY	*Eternal*	5	*8 Apr 95*	8
TRY ME OUT	*Eternal*	6	*22 Jul 95*	10
I DON'T WANNA BE A STAR	*Eternal*	22	*23 Dec 95*	6
MEGAMIX [M]	*Eternal*	36	*22 Feb 97*	2

Megamix of previous 4 hits.

ALBUMS:	HITS 1		WEEKS 7	
THE RHYTHM OF THE NIGHT	*Eternal*	18	*20 May 95*	7

CORONA SCHOOL CHILDREN – See Max BYGRAVES; Norman VAUGHAN

CORONATION STREET CAST featuring Bill WADDINGTON (Percy Sugden) / Amanda BARRIE and Johnny BRIGGS (Alma & Mike Baldwin)   UK

SINGLES:	HITS 1		WEEKS 3	
THE CORONATION STREET SINGLE: – ALWAYS LOOK ON THE BRIGHT SIDE OF LIFE / SOMETHING STUPID	*EMI Premier*	35	*16 Dec 95*	3

CORONETS   UK

SINGLES:	HITS 2		WEEKS 7	
THAT'S HOW A LOVE SONG WAS BORN	*Columbia*	14	*27 Aug 55*	6

Above hit: Ray BURNS with the CORONETS.

TWENTY TINY FINGERS	*Columbia*	20	*26 Nov 55*	1

Above hit: CORONETS with Eric JUPP and his Orchestra.

CORRIES   UK

ALBUMS:	HITS 2		WEEKS 5	
SCOTTISH LOVE SONGS	*Fontana*	46	*9 May 70*	4
SOUND OF PIBROCH	*Columbia*	39	*16 Sep 72*	1

Briana CORRIGAN   UK

SINGLES:	HITS 1		WEEKS 2	
LOVE ME NOW	*East West*	48	*11 May 96*	2

CORROSION OF CONFORMITY   US

ALBUMS:	HITS 1		WEEKS 1	
WISEBLOOD	*Columbia*	43	*14 Sep 96*	1

CORRS   Ireland

SINGLES:	HITS 9		WEEKS 60	
RUNAWAY	*Atlantic*	49	*17 Feb 96*	2
RUNAWAY [RE]	*Atlantic*	60	*7 Dec 96*	1
LOVE TO LOVE YOU / RUNAWAY [RI]	*Atlantic*	62	*1 Feb 97*	1

Re-issue of Runaway is a slightly longer version than the original chart entry.

ONLY WHEN I SLEEP	*Atlantic*	58	*25 Oct 97*	1
I NEVER LOVED YOU ANYWAY	*Atlantic*	43	*20 Dec 97*	2
WHAT CAN I DO	*Atlantic*	53	*28 Mar 98*	1

DREAMS	Atlantic	6	16 May 98	10
WHAT CAN I DO [RM]	Atlantic	3	29 Aug 98	11
Remixed by Tin Tin Out.				
SO YOUNG	Atlantic	6	28 Nov 98	13
RUNAWAY [RM]	Atlantic	2	27 Feb 99	11
Remixed by Tin Tin Out.				
I KNOW MY LOVE	RCA Victor	37	12 Jun 99	3
Above hit: CHIEFTAINS featuring the CORRS.				
RADIO	Atlantic	18	11 Dec 99	4
ALBUMS:	**HITS 3**		**WEEKS 199**	
FORGIVEN, NOT FORGOTTEN	Atlantic	36	2 Mar 96	47
TALK ON CORNERS	Atlantic	7	1 Nov 97	15
TALK ON CORNERS [RE]	Atlantic	1	21 Mar 98	88
Peak position reached on 27 Jun 98.				
FORGIVEN, NOT FORGOTTEN [RE]	Atlantic	2	16 Jan 99	43
UNPLUGGED	Atlantic	7	27 Nov 99	6
Recorded for MTV at Ardmore Studios, Co. Wicklow, Ireland, 5 Oct 99.				

Vladimir COSMA — Hungary

SINGLES:	**HITS 1**		**WEEKS 1**	
DAVID'S SONG (MAIN THEME FROM "KIDNAPPED")	Decca	64	14 Jul 79	1
Theme from the ITV series 'Kidnapped'.				
Above hit: Arranged and conducted by Vladimir COSMA.				
ALBUMS:	**HITS 1**		**WEEKS 3**	
MISTRAL'S DAUGHTER [OST-TV]	Carrere	53	1 Feb 86	3
Above hit: Conducted by Vladimir COSMA featuring Nana MOUSKOURI.				

COSMIC BABY — Germany

SINGLES:	**HITS 1**		**WEEKS 1**	
LOOPS OF INFINITY	Logic	70	26 Feb 94	1
ALBUMS:	**HITS 1**		**WEEKS 1**	
THINKING ABOUT MYSELF	Logic	60	23 Apr 94	1

COSMOS — UK

SINGLES:	**HITS 1**		**WEEKS 1**	
SUMMER IN SPACE	Island Blue	49	18 Sep 99	1
Vocals by David Laudat.				

Don COSTA and his Orchestra and Chorus — US

(See also Paul Anka; Tony Bennett; Lloyd Price.)

SINGLES:	**HITS 1**		**WEEKS 10**	
NEVER ON SUNDAY	London	27	15 Oct 60	9
From the film of the same name.				
NEVER ON SUNDAY [RE]	London	41	24 Dec 60	1

Elvis COSTELLO and the ATTRACTIONS — UK

SINGLES:	**HITS 35**		**WEEKS 179**	
WATCHING THE DETECTIVES	Stiff	15	5 Nov 77	11
Above hit: Elvis COSTELLO.				
(I DON'T WANT TO GO TO) CHELSEA	Radar	16	11 Mar 78	10
PUMP IT UP	Radar	24	13 May 78	10
RADIO RADIO	Radar	29	28 Oct 78	7
OLIVER'S ARMY	Radar	2	10 Feb 79	12
ACCIDENTS WILL HAPPEN	Radar	28	12 May 79	8
I CAN'T STAND UP FOR FALLING DOWN	F-Beat	4	16 Feb 80	8
Originally recorded by Sam & Dave.				
HIGH FIDELITY	F-Beat	30	12 Apr 80	5
NEW AMSTERDAM	F-Beat	36	7 Jun 80	6
Above hit: Elvis COSTELLO.				
CLUBLAND	F-Beat	60	20 Dec 80	4
A GOOD YEAR FOR THE ROSES	F-Beat	6	3 Oct 81	11
Originally recorded by George Jones.				
SWEET DREAMS	F-Beat	42	12 Dec 81	8
Originally recorded by Don Gibson.				
I'M YOUR TOY	F-Beat	51	10 Apr 82	3
Originally recorded by the Flying Burrito Brothers as Hot Burrito #1.				
Above hit: Elvis COSTELLO and the ATTRACTIONS with the ROYAL PHILHARMONIC ORCHESTRA.				
YOU LITTLE FOOL	F-Beat	52	19 Jun 82	3
MAN OUT OF TIME	F-Beat	58	31 Jul 82	2
FROM HEAD TO TOE	F-Beat	43	25 Sep 82	4
PARTY PARTY	A&M	48	11 Dec 82	6
From the film of the same name. Features Gary Barnacle on tenor and baritone sax & Annie Whitehead on Trombone.				
Above hit: Elvis COSTELLO and the ATTRACTIONS with the ROYAL GUARD HORNS.				

PILLS AND SOAP *Above hit: IMPOSTER.*	IMP	16	*11 Jun 83*	4
EVERYDAY I WRITE THE BOOK	F-Beat	28	*9 Jul 83*	8
LET THEM ALL TALK *Above hit: Elvis COSTELLO and the ATTRACTIONS with the TKO HORNS.*	F-Beat	59	*17 Sep 83*	2
PEACE IN OUR TIME *Above hit: IMPOSTER.*	Imposter	48	*28 Apr 84*	3
I WANNA BE LOVED / TURNING THE TOWN RED *Turning The Town Red from the Granda TV series 'Scully'.*	F-Beat	25	*16 Jun 84*	6
THE ONLY FLAME IN TOWN	F-Beat	71	*25 Aug 84*	2
GREEN SHIRT	F-Beat	71	*4 May 85*	1
GREEN SHIRT [RE]	F-Beat	68	*18 May 85*	1
DON'T LET ME BE MISUNDERSTOOD *Above hit: COSTELLO SHOW featuring the CONFEDERATES.*	F-Beat	33	*1 Feb 86*	4
TOKYO STORM WARNING	IMP	73	*30 Aug 86*	1
VERONICA *Co-written by Paul McCartney.*	Warner Brothers	31	*4 Mar 89*	6
BABY PLAYS AROUND [EP] *Lead track: Baby Plays Around.*	Warner Brothers	65	*20 May 89*	1
THE OTHER SIDE OF SUMMER	Warner Brothers	43	*4 May 91*	4
SULKY GIRL	Warner Brothers	22	*5 Mar 94*	3
13 STEPS LEAD DOWN *Above 5: Elvis COSTELLO.*	Warner Brothers	59	*30 Apr 94*	1
LONDON'S BRILLIANT PARADE [EP] *Lead track: London's Brilliant Parade.*	Warner Brothers	48	*26 Nov 94*	2
IT'S TIME	Warner Brothers	58	*11 May 96*	1
TOLEDO *Above hit: Elvis COSTELLO with Burt BACHARACH.*	Mercury	72	*1 May 99*	1
SHE *From the film 'Notting Hill'. Features the London Symphony Orchestra.* *Above hit: Elvis COSTELLO.*	Mercury	19	*31 Jul 99*	8
SHE [RE]	Mercury	57	*9 Oct 99*	2

ALBUMS:		HITS 22		WEEKS 218
MY AIM IS TRUE	Stiff	14	*6 Aug 77*	12
THIS YEAR'S MODEL *Above 2: Elvis COSTELLO.*	Radar	4	*1 Apr 78*	14
ARMED FORCES	Radar	2	*20 Jan 79*	28
GET HAPPY!	F-Beat	2	*23 Feb 80*	14
TRUST	F-Beat	9	*31 Jan 81*	7
ALMOST BLUE	F-Beat	7	*31 Oct 81*	18
IMPERIAL BEDROOM	F-Beat	6	*10 Jul 82*	12
PUNCH THE CLOCK	F-Beat	3	*6 Aug 83*	13
GOODBYE CRUEL WORLD	F-Beat	10	*7 Jul 84*	10
THE BEST OF ELVIS COSTELLO – THE MAN	Telstar	8	*20 Apr 85*	17
KING OF AMERICA *Above hit: COSTELLO SHOW.*	F-Beat	11	*1 Mar 86*	9
BLOOD AND CHOCOLATE	Imp	16	*27 Sep 86*	5
SPIKE	Warner Brothers	5	*18 Feb 89*	16
GIRLS GIRLS GIRLS *Compilation. Other formats not available on vinyl have different track listing.*	Demon	67	*28 Oct 89*	1
MIGHTY LIKE A ROSE *Above 3: Elvis COSTELLO.*	Warner Brothers	5	*25 May 91*	6
THE JULIET LETTERS *Above hit: Elvis COSTELLO and the BRODSKY QUARTET.*	Warner Brothers	18	*30 Jan 93*	3
BRUTAL YOUTH	Warner Brothers	2	*19 Mar 94*	5
THE BEST OF ELVIS COSTELLO – THE MAN [RI]	Demon	50	*19 Mar 94*	8
THE VERY BEST OF ELVIS COSTELLO AND THE ATTRACTIONS	Demon	57	*12 Nov 94*	2
KOJAK VARIETY *Title refers to a brand of lager sold in Barbados.* *Above hit: Elvis COSTELLO.*	Warner Brothers	21	*27 May 95*	2
KING OF AMERICA [RI] *Re-issued with additional tracks.* *Above hit: COSTELLO SHOW.*	Demon	71	*12 Aug 95*	1
ALL THIS USELESS BEAUTY	Warner Brothers	28	*25 May 96*	3
PAINTED FROM MEMORY *Above hit: Elvis COSTELLO with Burt BACHARACH.*	Mercury	32	*10 Oct 98*	2
THE VERY BEST OF ELVIS COSTELLO *Above hit: Elvis COSTELLO.*	Universal Music TV	4	*14 Aug 99*	10

Billy COTTON and His BAND
UK

(See also All Star Hit Parade.)

SINGLES:		HITS 3		WEEKS 25
IN A GOLDEN COACH (THERE'S A HEART OF GOLD) *Above hit: Billy COTTON and his BAND with Doreen STEPHENS and CHORUS.*	Decca	3	*2 May 53*	10
I SAW MOMMY KISSING SANTA CLAUS *Above hit: Billy COTTON and his BAND featuring the MILL GIRLS and the* *BANDITS.*	Decca	11	*19 Dec 53*	3

FRIENDS AND NEIGHBOURS	Decca	12	1 May 54	1
Above hit: Billy COTTON and his BAND featuring the BANDITS (and re-entry below).				
FRIENDS AND NEIGHBOURS [RE]	Decca	3	15 May 54	11

Mike COTTON JAZZMEN — UK

SINGLES:	HITS 1		WEEKS 4	
SWING THAT HAMMER	Columbia	36	22 Jun 63	4

John COUGAR – See John Cougar MELLENCAMP

COUGARS — UK

SINGLES:	HITS 1		WEEKS 8	
SATURDAY NIGHT AT THE DUCK POND	Parlophone	33	2 Mar 63	8

Phil COULTER — Ireland

ALBUMS:	HITS 2		WEEKS 15	
SEA OF TRANQUILITY	K-Tel Ireland	46	13 Oct 84	14
From 27 Oct 84 it got an official release in the UK.				
PHIL COULTER'S IRELAND	K-Tel	86	18 May 85	1

COUNCIL COLLECTIVE — UK/US

SINGLES:	HITS 1		WEEKS 6	
SOUL DEEP (PART 1)	Polydor	24	22 Dec 84	6
Charity record with proceeds to striking miners and the widow of taxi driver David Wilkie (killed when a concrete block was dropped on his car).				

COUNTING CROWS — US

SINGLES:	HITS 7		WEEKS 11	
MR. JONES	Geffen	28	30 Apr 94	2
ROUND HERE	Geffen	70	9 Jul 94	1
RAIN KING	Geffen	49	15 Oct 94	3
ANGELS OF THE SILENCES	Geffen	41	19 Oct 96	1
A LONG DECEMBER	Geffen	62	14 Dec 96	1
DAYLIGHT FADING	Geffen	54	31 May 97	1
A LONG DECEMBER [RE]	Geffen	68	20 Dec 97	1
HANGINAROUND	Geffen	46	30 Oct 99	1
ALBUMS:	HITS 4		WEEKS 49	
AUGUST AND EVERYTHING AFTER	Geffen	16	12 Mar 94	38
RECOVERING THE SATELLITES	Geffen	4	26 Oct 96	4
ACROSS A WIRE - LIVE IN NEW YORK	Geffen	27	25 Jul 98	4
Consists of 2 discs divided between live recordings for MTV and the other of acoustic versions.				
THIS DESERT LIFE	Geffen	19	13 Nov 99	3

COUNTRYMEN — UK

SINGLES:	HITS 1		WEEKS 2	
I KNOW WHERE I'M GOING	Piccadilly	45	5 May 62	2

COURSE — Holland

SINGLES:	HITS 3		WEEKS 15	
READY OR NOT	The Brothers	5	19 Apr 97	7
AIN'T NOBODY	The Brothers	8	5 Jul 97	6
BEST LOVE	The Brothers	51	20 Dec 97	2

Tina COUSINS — UK

(See also Steps Tina Cousins Cleopatra B*Witched Billie.)

SINGLES:	HITS 5		WEEKS 22	
MYSTERIOUS TIMES	Multiply	2	15 Aug 98	12
Above hit: SASH! featuring Tina COUSINS.				
PRAY	Jive	20	21 Nov 98	3
KILLIN' TIME	Jive	15	27 Mar 99	4
FOREVER	Jive	45	10 Jul 99	2
ANGEL	Jive	46	9 Oct 99	1
ALBUMS:	HITS 1		WEEKS 1	
KILLING TIME	Jive	50	24 Jul 99	1

Don COVAY — US

SINGLES:	HITS 1		WEEKS 6	
IT'S BETTER TO HAVE (AND DON'T NEED)	Mercury	29	7 Sep 74	6

Vincent COVELLO – See BT

COVENTRY CITY F.A. CUP SQUAD — UK

SINGLES:		HITS 1		WEEKS 2	
GO FOR IT!	Sky Blue	61	23 May 87		2

COVER GIRLS — US

SINGLES:		HITS 1		WEEKS 4	
WISHING ON A STAR	Epic	38	1 Aug 92		4

David COVERDALE — UK

(See also Coverdale Page; Whitesnake.)

ALBUMS:		HITS 1		WEEKS 1	
NORTHWINDS	Purple	78	27 Feb 82		1

COVERDALE PAGE — UK

(See also David Coverdale; Jimmy Page and Robert Plant; Jimmy Page.)

SINGLES:		HITS 2		WEEKS 3	
TAKE ME FOR A LITTLE WHILE	EMI	29	3 Jul 93		2
TAKE A LOOK AT YOURSELF	EMI	43	23 Oct 93		1

ALBUMS:		HITS 1		WEEKS 8	
COVERDALE PAGE	EMI	4	27 Mar 93		8

Julie COVINGTON — UK

(See also Julie Covington, Charlotte Cornwell, Rula Lenska, SueJones-Davies; Various Artists: Studio Cast 'Evita'.)

SINGLES:		HITS 2		WEEKS 29	
DON'T CRY FOR ME ARGENTINA	MCA	1	25 Dec 76		15
From the musical 'Evita'.					
ONLY WOMEN BLEED	Virgin	12	3 Dec 77		11
Original by Alice Cooper reached No. 12 in the US in 1975.					
DON'T CRY FOR ME ARGENTINA [RE]	MCA	63	15 Jul 78		3

Julie COVINGTON, Charlotte CORNWELL, Rula LENSKA, Sue JONES-DAVIES — UK

(See also Julie Covington; Various Artists: Television – Soundtracks 'Rock Follies'.)

SINGLES:		HITS 1		WEEKS 6	
O.K?	Polydor	10	21 May 77		6
From the ITV series 'Rock Follies II'.					

COWBOY JUNKIES — US

ALBUMS:		HITS 2		WEEKS 7	
THE CAUTION HORSES	RCA	33	24 Mar 90		4
BLACK EYED MAN	RCA	21	15 Feb 92		3

COWBOY TIMMY – See MR. HANKY POO

Patrick COWLEY – See SYLVESTER

Carl COX — UK

SINGLES:		HITS 7		WEEKS 19	
I WANT YOU (FOREVER)	Perfecto	23	28 Sep 91		7
DOES IT FEEL GOOD TO YOU	Perfecto	35	8 Aug 92		3
Above hit: DJ Carl COX.					
THE PLANET OF LOVE	Perfecto	44	6 Nov 93		2
Above hit: Carl COX CONCEPT.					
TWO PAINTINGS AND A DRUM [EP]	Edel	24	9 Mar 96		2
Lead track: Phoebus Apollo.					
SENSUAL SOPHIS-TI-CAT / THE PLAYER	Edel	25	8 Jun 96		2
THE LATIN THEME	Edel	52	12 Dec 98		1
PHUTURE 2000	Worldwide Ultimation	40	22 May 99		2

ALBUMS:		HITS 1		WEEKS 4	
AT THE END OF THE CLICHE	Edel:	23	15 Jun 96		4

Deborah COX — US

SINGLES:		HITS 4		WEEKS 8	
SENTIMENTAL	Arista	34	11 Nov 95		3
WHO DO U LOVE	Arista	31	24 Feb 96		3
Backing vocals by Danny Madden.					
IT'S OVER NOW	Arista	49	31 Jul 99		1
Samples Harold Melvin and the Blue Notes' Bad Luck.					
NOBODY'S SUPPOSED TO BE HERE	Arista	55	9 Oct 99		1

Michael COX — UK

SINGLES:		HITS 2		WEEKS 15	
ANGELA JONES	Triumph	7	11 Jun 60		13
Originally recorded by John D.Loudermilk.					

ALONG CAME CAROLINE	His Master's Voice	41	22 Oct 60	2

Above 2: Michael COX; Charles BLACKWELL'S ORCHESTRA.

Peter COX · UK

SINGLES:	HITS 3			WEEKS 6
AIN'T GONNA CRY AGAIN	Chrysalis	37	2 Aug 97	2
IF YOU WALK AWAY	Chrysalis	24	15 Nov 97	2
WHAT A FOOL BELIEVES	Chrysalis	39	20 Jun 98	2
ALBUMS:	HITS 1			WEEKS 1
PETER COX	Chrysalis	64	29 Nov 97	1

Graham COXON · UK

ALBUMS:	HITS 1			WEEKS 2
THE SKY IS TOO HIGH	Transcopic	31	22 Aug 98	2

CRACKER · US

SINGLES:	HITS 2			WEEKS 9
LOW	Virgin	43	28 May 94	4
GET OFF THIS	Virgin	41	23 Jul 94	3
LOW [RE]	Virgin	54	3 Dec 94	2
ALBUMS:	HITS 1			WEEKS 2
KEROSENE HAT	Virgin	44	25 Jun 94	2

Sarah CRACKNELL · UK

SINGLES:	HITS 1			WEEKS 1
ANYMORE	Gut	39	14 Sep 96	1

CRADLE OF FILTH · UK

ALBUMS:	HITS 1			WEEKS 1
CRUELTY AND THE BEAST	Music For Nations	48	16 May 98	1

Steve CRADOCK - See Liam GALLAGHER and Steve CRADOCK

Floyd CRAMER · US

SINGLES:	HITS 3			WEEKS 24
ON THE REBOUND	RCA	1	15 Apr 61	14
SAN ANTONIO ROSE	RCA	36	22 Jul 61	8
Originally recorded by Bob Wills and the Texas Playboys.				
HOT PEPPER	RCA	46	25 Aug 62	2

CRAMPS · US

SINGLES:	HITS 2			WEEKS 4
CAN YOUR PUSSY DO THE DOG?	Big Beat	68	9 Nov 85	1
BIKINI GIRLS WITH MACHINE GUNS	Enigma	35	10 Feb 90	3
ALBUMS:	HITS 4			WEEKS 13
OFF THE BONE	Illegal	44	25 Jun 83	4
SMELL OF FEMALE	Ace	74	26 Nov 83	2
A DATE WITH ELVIS	Big Beat	34	1 Mar 86	6
STAY SICK!	Ensign	62	24 Feb 90	1

CRANBERRIES · Ireland

(See also Jah Wobble's Invaders Of The Heart.)

SINGLES:	HITS 10			WEEKS 50
LINGER	Island	74	27 Feb 93	1
LINGER [RI]	Island	14	12 Feb 94	11
DREAMS	Island	27	7 May 94	5
ZOMBIE	Island	14	1 Oct 94	6
ODE TO MY FAMILY	Island	26	3 Dec 94	6
I CAN'T BE WITH YOU	Island	23	11 Mar 95	5
RIDICULOUS THOUGHTS	Island	20	12 Aug 95	3
From the film 'Butterfly Kiss'.				
SALVATION	Island	13	20 Apr 96	5
FREE TO DECIDE	Island	33	13 Jul 96	3
PROMISES	Island US	13	17 Apr 99	4
ANIMAL INSTINCT	Island US	54	17 Jul 99	1
ALBUMS:	HITS 4			WEEKS 188
EVERYBODY ELSE IS DOING IT, SO WHY CAN'T WE?	Island	64	13 Mar 93	1
EVERYBODY ELSE IS DOING IT, SO WHY CAN'T WE? [RE]	Island	1	12 Mar 94	85
NO NEED TO ARGUE	Island	2	15 Oct 94	78
TO THE FAITHFUL DEPARTED	Island	2	11 May 96	19
BURY THE HATCHET	Island US	7	1 May 99	5

Les CRANE
US

SINGLES:	HITS 1			WEEKS 14
DESIDERATA	Warner Brothers	7	19 Feb 72	14

Whitfield CRANE - See MOTORHEAD

CRANES
UK

SINGLES:	HITS 2			WEEKS 2
JEWEL	Dedicated	29	25 Sep 93	1
SHINING ROAD	Dedicated	57	3 Sep 94	1
ALBUMS:	HITS 2			WEEKS 2
WINGS OF JOY	Dedicated	52	28 Sep 91	1
FOREVER	Dedicated	40	8 May 93	1

CRASH TEST DUMMIES
Canada

SINGLES:	HITS 3			WEEKS 20
MMM MMM MMM MMM	RCA	2	23 Apr 94	11
AFTERNOONS AND COFFEESPOONS	RCA	23	16 Jul 94	5
THE BALLAD OF PETER PUMPKINHEAD	RCA	30	15 Apr 95	4
From the film 'Dumb And Dumber'.				
Above hit: CRASH TEST DUMMIES featuring Ellen REID.				
ALBUMS:	HITS 1			WEEKS 23
GOD SHUFFLED HIS FEET	RCA	2	14 May 94	23

CRASS
UK

ALBUMS:	HITS 1			WEEKS 2
CHRIST THE ALBUM	Crass	26	28 Aug 82	2

Beverley CRAVEN
UK

SINGLES:	HITS 6			WEEKS 33
PROMISE ME	Epic	3	20 Apr 91	13
HOLDING ON	Epic	32	20 Jul 91	7
WOMAN TO WOMAN	Epic	40	5 Oct 91	5
MEMORIES	Epic	68	7 Dec 91	2
LOVE SCENES	Epic	34	25 Sep 93	4
MOLLIE'S SONG	Epic	61	20 Nov 93	2
ALBUMS:	HITS 3			WEEKS 67
BEVERLEY CRAVEN	Epic	3	2 Mar 91	52
LOVE SCENES	Epic	4	9 Oct 93	13
MIXED EMOTIONS	Epic	46	12 Jun 99	2

Billy CRAWFORD
Philippines

SINGLES:	HITS 1			WEEKS 2
URGENTLY IN LOVE	V2	48	10 Oct 98	2

Jimmy CRAWFORD
UK

SINGLES:	HITS 2			WEEKS 11
LOVE OR MONEY	Columbia	49	10 Jun 61	1
I LOVE HOW YOU LOVE ME	Columbia	18	18 Nov 61	10
Originally recorded by the Paris sisters.				

Michael CRAWFORD
UK

(See also Various Artists: Stage Cast – London 'The Phantom Of The Opera'.)

SINGLES:	HITS 2			WEEKS 14
THE MUSIC OF THE NIGHT	Polydor	7	10 Jan 87	11
[AA] listed with Wishing You Were Somehow Here Again by Sarah Brightman.				
Above hit: Michael CRAWFORD with the ROYAL PHILHARMONIC ORCHESTRA conducted by David CADDICK.				
THE MUSIC OF THE NIGHT [RR]	Columbia	54	15 Jan 94	3
Above 2 from the musical 'The Phantom Of The Opera'.				
Above hit: Barbra STREISAND (duet with Michael CRAWFORD).				
ALBUMS:	HITS 7			WEEKS 73
SONGS FROM STAGE AND SCREEN	Telstar	12	28 Nov 87	13
Above hit: Michael CRAWFORD and the LONDON SYMPHONY ORCHESTRA.				
WITH LOVE	Telstar	31	2 Dec 89	7
MICHAEL CRAWFORD PERFORMS ANDREW LLOYD WEBBER	Telstar	3	9 Nov 91	36
Above hit: Michael CRAWFORD and the ROYAL PHILHARMONIC ORCHESTRA.				
A TOUCH OF MUSIC IN THE NIGHT	Telstar	12	13 Nov 93	11
THE LOVE SONGS ALBUM	Telstar	64	19 Nov 94	3
ON EAGLE'S WINGS	Atlantic	65	21 Nov 98	2
THE MOST WONDERFUL TIME OF THE YEAR	Telstar TV	69	25 Dec 99	1

Randy CRAWFORD
US

(See also Crusaders.)

SINGLES:		HITS 12		WEEKS 75	
LAST NIGHT AT DANCELAND	Warner Brothers	61	21 Jun 80	2
ONE DAY I'LL FLY AWAY	Warner Brothers	2	30 Aug 80	11
YOU MIGHT NEED SOMEBODY	Warner Brothers	11	30 May 81	13
Originally recorded by Turley Richards.				
RAINY NIGHT IN GEORGIA	Warner Brothers	18	8 Aug 81	9
Written by Tony Joe White and originally recorded by Brook Benton.				
SECRET COMBINATION	Warner Brothers	48	31 Oct 81	3
IMAGINE	Warner Brothers	60	30 Jan 82	1
Live recording.				
Above hit: Randy CRAWFORD; accompanied by YELLOW JACKETS.				
IMAGINE [RE]	Warner Brothers	75	13 Feb 82	1
ONE HELLO	Warner Brothers	48	5 Jun 82	4
HE REMINDS ME	Warner Brothers	65	19 Feb 83	2
NIGHTLINE	Warner Brothers	51	8 Oct 83	4
ALMAZ	Warner Brothers	4	29 Nov 86	17
DIAMANTE	London	44	18 Jan 92	7
Above hit: ZUCCHERO with Randy CRAWFORD.				
GIVE ME THE NIGHT	WEA	60	15 Nov 97	1
ALBUMS:		HITS 9		WEEKS 151	
NOW WE MAY BEGIN	Warner Brothers	10	28 Jun 80	16
SECRET COMBINATION	Warner Brothers	2	16 May 81	60
WINDSONG	Warner Brothers	7	12 Jun 82	17
NIGHTLINE	Warner Brothers	37	22 Oct 83	4
MISS RANDY CRAWFORD – THE GREATEST HITS	K-Tel	10	13 Oct 84	17
ABSTRACT EMOTIONS	Warner Brothers	78	28 Jun 86	1
ABSTRACT EMOTIONS [RE]	Warner Brothers	14	31 Jan 87	9
THE LOVE SONGS	Telstar	27	10 Oct 87	13
RICH AND POOR	Warner Brothers	63	21 Oct 89	1
THE VERY BEST OF RANDY CRAWFORD	Dino	8	27 Mar 93	13

Robert CRAY BAND
US

SINGLES:		HITS 2		WEEKS 5	
RIGHT NEXT DOOR (BECAUSE OF ME)	Mercury	50	20 Jun 87	4
BABY LEE	Silvertone	65	20 Apr 96	1
Featured in a TV commercial for Lee Jeans.				
Above hit: John Lee HOOKER with Robert CRAY.				
ALBUMS:		HITS 7		WEEKS 53	
FALSE ACCUSATIONS	Demon	68	12 Oct 85	1
STRONG PERSUADER	Mercury	41	15 Nov 86	11
STRONG PERSUADER [RE]	Mercury	34	13 Jun 87	17
DON'T BE AFRAID OF THE DARK	Mercury	13	3 Sep 88	12
MIDNIGHT STROLL	Mercury	19	29 Sep 90	7
Above hit: Robert CRAY BAND with the MEMPHIS HORNS.				
I WAS WARNED	Mercury	29	12 Sep 92	3
Above hit: Robert CRAY.				
SHAME AND SIN	Mercury	48	16 Oct 93	1
SOME RAINY MORNING	Mercury	63	20 May 95	1
Above hit: Robert CRAY.				

CRAZY ELEPHANT
US

SINGLES:		HITS 1		WEEKS 13	
GIMME GIMME GOOD LOVIN'	Major Minor	12	24 May 69	13

CRAZY HORSE - See Ian McNABB; Neil YOUNG

CRAZY WORLD OF ARTHUR BROWN
UK

SINGLES:		HITS 1		WEEKS 14	
FIRE!	Track	1	29 Jun 68	14
ALBUMS:		HITS 1		WEEKS 16	
THE CRAZY WORLD OF ARTHUR BROWN	Track	2	6 Jul 68	16

CRAZYHEAD
UK

(See also Various Artists (EPs) 'The Food Christmas EP 1989'.)

SINGLES:		HITS 2		WEEKS 4	
TIME HAS TAKEN IT'S TOLL ON YOU	Food	65	16 Jul 88	2
HAVE LOVE, WILL TRAVEL [EP]	Food	68	25 Feb 89	2
Lead track: Have Love, Will Travel.				

CREAM
UK

SINGLES:		HITS 7		WEEKS 59	
WRAPPING PAPER	Reaction	34	22 Oct 66	6

I FEEL FREE	*Reaction*	11	*17 Dec 66*	12
STRANGE BREW	*Reaction*	17	*10 Jun 67*	9
ANYONE FOR TENNIS (THE SAVAGE SEVEN THEME)	*Polydor*	40	*8 Jun 68*	3
SUNSHINE OF YOUR LOVE	*Polydor*	25	*12 Oct 68*	7
WHITE ROOM	*Polydor*	28	*18 Jan 69*	8
BADGE	*Polydor*	18	*12 Apr 69*	10
BADGE [RI]	*Polydor*	42	*28 Oct 72*	4
ALBUMS:	**HITS 9**		**WEEKS 291**	
FRESH CREAM	*Reaction*	6	*24 Dec 66*	19
DISRAELI GEARS	*Reaction*	5	*18 Nov 67*	42
WHEELS OF FIRE (SINGLE: IN THE STUDIO)	*Polydor*	7	*17 Aug 68*	13
WHEELS OF FIRE (DOUBLE: LIVE AND STUDIO)	*Polydor*	3	*17 Aug 68*	26
Live recordings from the Fillmore West in San Francisco.				
GOODBYE	*Polydor*	1	*15 Mar 69*	28
THE BEST OF CREAM	*Polydor*	6	*8 Nov 69*	34
LIVE CREAM	*Polydor*	4	*4 Jul 70*	15
LIVE CREAM VOLUME 2	*Polydor*	15	*24 Jun 72*	5
THE CREAM OF ERIC CLAPTON [RE-1ST] / THE BEST OF ERIC CLAPTON	*Polydor*	3	*26 Sep 87*	98
	Polydor	25	*10 Jul 93*	6
The re-package The Best Of Eric Clapton listed from 17 Jul 93.				
THE CREAM OF ERIC CLAPTON [RE-2ND]	*Polydor*	52	*18 Apr 98*	5
Re-released.				
Above hit: Eric CLAPTON and CREAM.				

CREATION
UK

SINGLES:	**HITS 2**		**WEEKS 3**	
MAKING TIME	*Planet*	49	*9 Jul 66*	1
PAINTER MAN	*Planet*	36	*5 Nov 66*	2

CREATURES
UK

SINGLES:	**HITS 5**		**WEEKS 27**	
MAD EYED SCREAMER	*Polydor*	24	*3 Oct 81*	7
Sleeve gives title as an EP: Wild Things.				
MISS THE GIRL	*Wonderland*	21	*23 Apr 83*	7
RIGHT NOW	*Wonderland*	14	*16 Jul 83*	10
Originally recorded by Mel Torme.				
STANDING THERE	*Wonderland*	53	*14 Oct 89*	2
SAY	*Sioux*	72	*27 Mar 99*	1
ALBUMS:	**HITS 1**		**WEEKS 9**	
FEAST	*Wonderland*	17	*28 May 83*	9

CREDIT TO THE NATION
UK

SINGLES:	**HITS 6**		**WEEKS 11**	
CALL IT WHAT YOU WANT	*One Little Indian*	57	*22 May 93*	3
ENOUGH IS ENOUGH	*One Little Indian*	56	*18 Sep 93*	2
Above hit: CHUMBAWAMBA and CREDIT TO THE NATION.				
TEENAGE SENSATION	*One Little Indian*	24	*12 Mar 94*	3
SOWING THE SEEDS OF HATRED	*One Little Indian*	72	*14 May 94*	1
LIAR LIAR	*One Little Indian*	60	*22 Jul 95*	1
TACKY LOVE SONG	*Chrysalis*	60	*12 Sep 98*	1
Samples Radiohead's High And Dry.				
ALBUMS:	**HITS 1**		**WEEKS 3**	
TAKE DIS	*One Little Indian*	20	*9 Apr 94*	3

CREEDENCE CLEARWATER REVIVAL
UK

SINGLES:	**HITS 9**		**WEEKS 94**	
PROUD MARY	*Liberty*	8	*31 May 69*	13
BAD MOON RISING	*Liberty*	1	*16 Aug 69*	15
GREEN RIVER	*Liberty*	19	*15 Nov 69*	11
DOWN ON THE CORNER	*Liberty*	31	*14 Feb 70*	6
TRAVELIN' BAND	*Liberty*	8	*4 Apr 70*	12
UP AROUND THE BEND	*Liberty*	3	*20 Jun 70*	12
TRAVELIN' BAND [RE]	*Liberty*	46	*4 Jul 70*	1
LONG AS I CAN SEE THE LIGHT	*Liberty*	20	*5 Sep 70*	9
HAVE YOU EVER SEEN THE RAIN	*Liberty*	36	*20 Mar 71*	6
SWEET HITCH-HIKER	*United Artists*	36	*24 Jul 71*	8
BAD MOON RISING [RI]	*Epic*	71	*2 May 92*	1
ALBUMS:	**HITS 7**		**WEEKS 65**	
GREEN RIVER	*Liberty*	20	*24 Jan 70*	6
WILLY AND THE POOR BOYS	*Liberty*	10	*28 Mar 70*	24
BAYOU COUNTRY	*Liberty*	62	*2 May 70*	1
COSMO'S FACTORY	*Liberty*	1	*12 Sep 70*	15
PENDULUM	*Liberty*	23	*23 Jan 71*	12
GREATEST HITS	*Fantasy*	35	*30 Jun 79*	5
THE CREEDENCE COLLECTION	*Impression*	68	*19 Oct 85*	2

Kid CREOLE and the COCONUTS — US

(See also Coconuts.)

SINGLES:		HITS 8		WEEKS 58
ME NO POP I	Ze	32	13 Jun 81	7
Above hit: Kid CREOLE and the COCONUTS present Coati MUNDI.				
I'M A WONDERFUL THING, BABY	Ze	4	15 May 82	11
STOOL PIGEON	Ze	7	24 Jul 82	9
ANNIE, I'M NOT YOUR DADDY	Ze	2	9 Oct 82	8
DEAR ADDY	Ze	29	11 Dec 82	7
Sleeve gives title as an EP: Christmas In B'Dilli Bay.				
THERE'S SOMETHING WRONG IN PARADISE	Island	35	10 Sep 83	5
THE LIFEBOAT PARTY	Ze	49	19 Nov 83	4
THE SEX OF IT	CBS	29	14 Apr 90	5
I'M A WONDERFUL THING, BABY [RM]	Island	60	10 Apr 93	2
Remixed by Brothers In Rhythm.				
ALBUMS:		HITS 4		WEEKS 54
TROPICAL GANGSTERS	Ze	3	22 May 82	40
FRESH FRUIT IN FOREIGN PLACES	Ze	99	26 Jun 82	1
DOPPELGANGER	Island	21	17 Sep 83	6
CRE-OLE (BEST OF KID CREOLE AND COCONUTS)	Island	21	15 Sep 84	7

CRESCENDO — UK/US

SINGLES:		HITS 1		WEEKS 5
ARE YOU OUT THERE	ffrr	20	23 Dec 95	5

CRESTERS - See Mike SAGER and CRESTERS

CREW-CUTS — Canada

SINGLES:		HITS 2		WEEKS 29
SH-BOOM (LIFE COULD BE A DREAM)	Mercury	12	2 Oct 54	9
EARTH ANGEL	Mercury	4	16 Apr 55	20
Originally recorded by the Penguins.				
Above hit: CREW-CUTS with David CARROLL and his Orchestra.				

Bernard CRIBBINS — UK

(See also Howard Blake conducting the Sinfonia of London, Narration: Bernard Cribbins.)

SINGLES:		HITS 3		WEEKS 29
THE HOLE IN THE GROUND	Parlophone	9	17 Feb 62	13
RIGHT, SAID FRED	Parlophone	10	7 Jul 62	10
GOSSIP CALYPSO	Parlophone	25	15 Dec 62	6

CRICKETS — US

(See also Buddy Holly; Bobby Vee and the Crickets.)

SINGLES:		HITS 12		WEEKS 97
THAT'LL BE THE DAY	Vogue Coral	1	28 Sep 57	14
OH, BOY	Coral	3	28 Dec 57	15
THAT'LL BE THE DAY [RE]	Vogue Coral	29	11 Jan 58	1
MAYBE BABY	Coral	4	15 Mar 58	10
THINK IT OVER	Coral	11	26 Jul 58	7
LOVE'S MADE A FOOL OF YOU	Coral	26	25 Apr 59	1
LOVE'S MADE A FOOL OF YOU [RE]	Coral	30	9 May 59	1
WHEN YOU ASK ABOUT LOVE	Coral	27	16 Jan 60	1
MORE THAN I CAN SAY	Coral	42	14 May 60	1
BABY MY HEART	Coral	33	28 May 60	4
Above 2 entries were separate sides of the same release, each had its own chart run.				
DON'T EVER CHANGE	Liberty	5	23 Jun 62	13
MY LITTLE GIRL	Liberty	17	26 Jan 63	9
DON'T TRY TO CHANGE ME	Liberty	37	8 Jun 63	4
YOU'VE GOT LOVE	Coral	40	16 May 64	6
Above hit: Buddy HOLLY and the CRICKETS.				
(THEY CALL HER) LA BAMBA	Liberty	21	4 Jul 64	10
EPS:		HITS 2		WEEKS 6
FOUR MORE	Coral	7	18 Jun 60	5
IT'S SO EASY	Coral	18	20 Jan 62	1
ALBUMS:		HITS 1		WEEKS 7
IN STYLE WITH THE CRICKETS	Coral	13	25 Mar 61	7

CRIMINAL ELEMENT ORCHESTRA - See Wally JUMP JR. and the CRIMINAL ELEMENT

CRISPY and COMPANY — US

SINGLES:		HITS 2		WEEKS 11
BRAZIL	Creole	26	16 Aug 75	5
GET IT TOGETHER	Creole	21	27 Dec 75	6
Above hit: CRISPY and CO.				

CRITTERS

US

SINGLES:		HITS 1			WEEKS 5
YOUNGER GIRL	London		38	2 Jul 66	5

Originally recorded by Lovin' Spoonful.

Tony CROMBIE and his ROCKETS

UK

(See also Ray Ellington with Tony Crombie, his Orchestra and Chorus.)

SINGLES:		HITS 1			WEEKS 2
TEACH YOU TO ROCK / SHORT'NIN' BREAD ROCK	Columbia		25	20 Oct 56	2

Bing CROSBY

US

(See also Various Artists: Films – Original Soundtracks 'High Society'.)

SINGLES:		HITS 12			WEEKS 97
THE ISLE OF INNISFREE	Brunswick		3	15 Nov 52	12

Above hit: Bing CROSBY with John Scott TROTTER and his Orchestra.

ZING A LITTLE ZONG	Brunswick		10	6 Dec 52	2

From the film 'Just For You'.
Above hit: Bing CROSBY and Jane WYMAN with Jud CONLON'S RHYTHMAIRES and ORCHESTRA.

SILENT NIGHT, HOLY NIGHT	Brunswick		8	20 Dec 52	2

Above hit: Bing CROSBY; vocal with the Max TERR CHOIR and John Scott TROTTER and his Orchestra.

CHANGING PARTNERS	Brunswick		10	20 Mar 54	1

Above hit: Bing CROSBY with Jud CONLON'S RHYTHMAIRES

CHANGING PARTNERS [RE-1ST]	Brunswick		9	3 Apr 54	1
CHANGING PARTNERS [RE-2ND]	Brunswick		11	24 Apr 54	1
COUNT YOUR BLESSINGS INSTEAD OF SHEEP	Brunswick		18	8 Jan 55	1
COUNT YOUR BLESSINGS INSTEAD OF SHEEP [RE]	Brunswick		11	22 Jan 55	2
STRANGER IN PARADISE	Brunswick		17	30 Apr 55	2
IN A LITTLE SPANISH TOWN	Brunswick		22	28 Apr 56	3

Originally recorded by Paul Whiteman in 1927.

TRUE LOVE	Capitol		4	24 Nov 56	27

From the film 'High Society'.
Above hit: Bing CROSBY and Grace KELLY.

AROUND THE WORLD	Brunswick		5	25 May 57	15

From the film 'Around The World In Eighty Days'.

THAT'S WHAT LIFE IS ALL ABOUT	United Artists		41	9 Aug 75	4

Above hit: Bing CROSBY with the Peter MOORE ORCHESTRA.

WHITE CHRISTMAS	MCA		5	3 Dec 77	7

Originally released in 1942. It was the best selling single in the world until the release of Elton John's 'Candle In The Wind' in 1997.

PEACE ON EARTH / LITTLE DRUMMER BOY [M]	RCA		3	27 Nov 82	8

Recorded in 1977 on Bing Crosby's Christmas TV show.
Above hit: David BOWIE and Bing CROSBY.

TRUE LOVE [RI]	Capitol		70	17 Dec 83	3

Above hit: Bing CROSBY and Grace KELLY.

| WHITE CHRISTMAS [RI-1ST] | MCA | | 69 | 21 Dec 85 | 2 |
| WHITE CHRISTMAS [RE-2ND] | MCA | | 29 | 19 Dec 98 | 4 |

EPS:		HITS 1			WEEKS 6
MERRY CHRISTMAS, PART 1	Columbia		9	3 Dec 60	6

ALBUMS:		HITS 9			WEEKS 45
JOIN BING AND SING ALONG	Warner Brothers		7	8 Oct 60	11
WHITE CHRISTMAS	MCA		45	21 Dec 74	3
THAT'S WHAT LIFE IS ALL ABOUT	United Artists		28	20 Sep 75	6
LIVE AT THE LONDON PALLADIUM	K-Tel		9	5 Nov 77	2

Live recordings from the theatre in London.

THE BEST OF BING	MCA		41	5 Nov 77	7
SEASONS	Polydor		25	17 Dec 77	7
SONGS OF A LIFETIME	Philips		29	5 May 79	3
CHRISTMAS WITH BING CROSBY	Telstar		66	14 Dec 91	3
THE BEST OF BING CROSBY	MCA		59	23 Nov 96	3

David CROSBY

US

(See also Crosby, Stills, Nash and Young.)

SINGLES:		HITS 1			WEEKS 3
HERO	Atlantic		56	15 May 93	3

Above hit: David CROSBY featuring Phil COLLINS.

ALBUMS:		HITS 1			WEEKS 7
IF ONLY I COULD REMEMBER MY NAME	Atlantic		12	24 Apr 71	7

CROSBY, STILLS, NASH and YOUNG

US/UK

(See also David Crosby; Graham Nash and David Crosby; Graham Nash; Steven Stills; Stephen Stills' Manassas; Stills-Young Band, Neil Young.)

SINGLES:		HITS 2			WEEKS 12
MARRAKESH EXPRESS	Atlantic		17	16 Aug 69	9

Above hit: CROSBY, STILLS and NASH.

AMERICAN DREAM	Atlantic	55	21 Jan 89	3
ALBUMS:	**HITS 6**			**WEEKS 94**
CROSBY, STILLS AND NASH	Atlantic	25	23 Aug 69	5
Above hit: CROSBY, STILLS and NASH.				
DEJA VU	Atlantic	5	30 May 70	61
FOUR-WAY STREET	Atlantic	5	22 May 71	12
SO FAR	Atlantic	25	21 Sep 74	6
CSN	Atlantic	23	9 Jul 77	9
Above hit: CROSBY, STILLS and NASH.				
LOOKING FORWARD	Reprise	54	6 Nov 99	1

CROSS UK/US

SINGLES:	**HITS 1**			**WEEKS 1**
COWBOYS AND INDIANS	Virgin	74	17 Oct 87	1
ALBUMS:	**HITS 1**			**WEEKS 2**
SHOVE IT	Virgin	58	6 Feb 88	2

Christopher CROSS US

SINGLES:	**HITS 4**			**WEEKS 27**
RIDE LIKE THE WIND	Warner Brothers	69	19 Apr 80	1
SAILING	Warner Brothers	48	14 Feb 81	6
ARTHUR'S THEME (BEST THAT YOU CAN DO)	Warner Brothers	56	17 Oct 81	4
From the film 'Arthur'.				
ARTHUR'S THEME (BEST THAT YOU CAN DO) [RE]	Warner Brothers	7	9 Jan 82	11
ALL RIGHT	Warner Brothers	51	5 Feb 83	5
ALBUMS:	**HITS 2**			**WEEKS 93**
CHRISTOPHER CROSS	Warner Brothers	14	21 Feb 81	77
ANOTHER PAGE	Warner Brothers	4	19 Feb 83	16

Lynn CROUCH – See QWILO and FELIX DA HOUSECAT featuring Lynn CROUCH

Sheryl CROW US

SINGLES:	**HITS 16**			**WEEKS 77**
LEAVING LAS VEGAS	A&M	66	18 Jun 94	1
ALL I WANNA DO	A&M	4	5 Nov 94	13
STRONG ENOUGH	A&M	33	11 Feb 95	4
From the film 'Kalifornia'.				
CAN'T CRY ANYMORE	A&M	33	27 May 95	3
RUN, BABY, RUN	A&M	24	29 Jul 95	4
Originally reached No. 92 in 1994.				
WHAT I CAN DO FOR YOU	A&M	43	11 Nov 95	1
IF IT MAKES YOU HAPPY	A&M	9	21 Sep 96	6
EVERYDAY IS A WINDING ROAD	A&M	12	30 Nov 96	6
HARD TO MAKE A STAND	A&M	22	29 Mar 97	3
A CHANGE WOULD DO YOU GOOD	A&M	8	12 Jul 97	5
HOME	A&M	25	18 Oct 97	2
TOMORROW NEVER DIES	A&M	12	13 Dec 97	9
From the James Bond film of the same name.				
MY FAVORITE MISTAKE	A&M	9	12 Sep 98	6
THERE GOES THE NEIGHBORHOOD	A&M	19	5 Dec 98	7
ANYTHING BUT DOWN	A&M	19	6 Mar 99	4
SWEET CHILD O' MINE	Columbia	30	11 Sep 99	3
From the film 'Big Daddy'.				
ALBUMS:	**HITS 3**			**WEEKS 157**
TUESDAY NIGHT MUSIC CLUB	A&M	68	12 Feb 94	1
TUESDAY NIGHT MUSIC CLUB [RE]	A&M	8	26 Nov 94	54
Peak position reached on 3 June 95.				
SHERYL CROW	A&M	5	12 Oct 96	70
THE GLOBE SESSIONS	A&M	2	3 Oct 98	32

CROWD Multi-National

SINGLES:	**HITS 1**			**WEEKS 11**
YOU'LL NEVER WALK ALONE	Spartan	1	1 Jun 85	11

CROWDED HOUSE Australia/New Zealand/US

SINGLES:	**HITS 13**			**WEEKS 64**
DON'T DREAM IT'S OVER	Capitol	27	6 Jun 87	8
CHOCOLATE CAKE	Capitol	69	22 Jun 91	1
FALL AT YOUR FEET	Capitol	17	2 Nov 91	7
WEATHER WITH YOU	Capitol	7	29 Feb 92	9
FOUR SEASONS IN ONE DAY	Capitol	26	20 Jun 92	5
IT'S ONLY NATURAL	Capitol	24	26 Sep 92	4
DISTANT SUN	Capitol	19	2 Oct 93	6
NAILS IN MY FEET	Capitol	22	20 Nov 93	4
LOCKED OUT	Capitol	12	19 Feb 94	4

FINGERS OF LOVE		Capitol	25	11 Jun 94	3
PINEAPPLE HEAD		Capitol	27	24 Sep 94	3
INSTINCT		Capitol	12	22 Jun 96	4
NOT THE GIRL YOU THINK YOU ARE		Capitol	20	17 Aug 96	3
DON'T DREAM IT'S OVER [RI]		Capitol	25	9 Nov 96	2
ALBUMS:	**HITS 3**			**WEEKS 181**	
WOODFACE		Capitol	34	13 Jul 91	4
WOODFACE [RE]		Capitol	6	29 Feb 92	82
TOGETHER ALONE		Capitol	4	23 Oct 93	32
RECURRING DREAM – THE VERY BEST OF CROWDED HOUSE		Capitol	1	6 Jul 96	63

CROWN HEIGHTS AFFAIR
US

SINGLES:	**HITS 5**			**WEEKS 34**	
GALAXY OF LOVE		Mercury	24	19 Aug 78	10
I'M GONNA LOVE YOU FOREVER		Mercury	47	11 Nov 78	4
DANCE LADY DANCE		Mercury	44	14 Apr 79	4
YOU GAVE ME LOVE		De-Lite	10	3 May 80	12
YOU'VE BEEN GONE		De-Lite	44	9 Aug 80	4
ALBUMS:	**HITS 1**			**WEEKS 3**	
DREAM WORLD		Philips	40	23 Sep 78	3

Julee CRUISE
US

(See also Angelo Badalamenti with Julee Cruise and Various Artists.)

SINGLES:	**HITS 3**			**WEEKS 14**	
FALLING		Warner Brothers	7	10 Nov 90	11
From the TV series 'Twin Peaks'.					
ROCKIN' BACK INSIDE MY HEART		Warner Brothers	66	2 Mar 91	2
IF I SURVIVE		Distinct'ive	52	11 Sep 99	1
Above hit: HYBRID featuring Julee CRUISE.					

CRUISERS - See Dave BERRY.

CRUSADERS
US

SINGLES:	**HITS 3**			**WEEKS 16**	
STREET LIFE		MCA	5	18 Aug 79	11
Vocals by Randy Crawford.					
I'M SO GLAD I'M STANDING HERE TODAY		MCA	61	26 Sep 81	3
Above hit: CRUSADERS, featured vocalist Joe COCKER.					
NIGHT LADIES		MCA	55	7 Apr 84	2
ALBUMS:	**HITS 4**			**WEEKS 30**	
STREET LIFE		MCA	10	21 Jul 79	16
RHAPSODY AND BLUE		MCA	40	19 Jul 80	5
STANDING TALL		MCA	47	12 Sep 81	5
GHETTO BLASTER		MCA	46	7 Apr 84	4

CRUSH
UK

SINGLES:	**HITS 2**			**WEEKS 3**	
JELLYHEAD		Telstar	50	24 Feb 96	2
LUV'D UP		Telstar	45	3 Aug 96	1

Bobby CRUSH
UK

SINGLES:	**HITS 1**			**WEEKS 4**	
BORSALINO		Philips	37	4 Nov 72	4
ALBUMS:	**HITS 2**			**WEEKS 12**	
BOBBY CRUSH		Philips	15	25 Nov 72	7
THE BOBBY CRUSH INCREDIBLE DOUBLE DECKER PARTY 101 GREAT SONGS		Warwick	53	18 Dec 82	5

CRY BEFORE DAWN
Ireland

SINGLES:	**HITS 1**			**WEEKS 2**	
WITNESS FOR THE WORLD		Epic	67	17 Jun 89	2

CRY FREEDOM (solo voice: Thuli DUMAKUDE) /
CRY FREEDOM (solo voices: George FENTON, Jonas GWANGWA)
UK/South Africa

SINGLES:	**HITS 1**			**WEEKS 1**	
THE FUNERAL (SEPTEMBER 25, 1977) / CRY FREEDOM		MCA	75	2 Jan 88	1
From the film 'Cry Freedom'.					

CRY OF LOVE
US

SINGLES:	**HITS 1**			**WEEKS 1**	
BAD THING		Columbia	60	15 Jan 94	1

CRY SISCO! — UK

SINGLES:	HITS 1			WEEKS 9
AFRO DIZZI ACT	Escape	42	2 Sep 89	8
AFRO DIZZI ACT [RE]	Escape	70	20 Jan 90	1

CRYIN' SHAMES — UK

SINGLES:	HITS 1			WEEKS 7
PLEASE STAY	Decca	26	2 Apr 66	7

Originally recorded by Drifters.

CRYSTAL METHOD — US

SINGLES:	HITS 3			WEEKS 4
(CAN'T YOU) TRIP LIKE I DO	Epic	39	11 Oct 97	2

From the film 'Spawn'.
Above hit: FILTER and the CRYSTAL METHOD.

KEEP HOPE ALIVE	Sony S2	71	7 Mar 98	1

Title inspired by Jesse Jackson's speech at the 1992 Democratic party convention.

COMIN' BACK	Sony S2	73	8 Aug 98	1

CRYSTAL PALACE FC 1990 FA CUP FINAL SQUAD featuring the "FAB FOUR" — UK

SINGLES:	HITS 1			WEEKS 2
GLAD ALL OVER / WHERE EAGLES FLY	Parkfield	50	12 May 90	2

CRYSTALS — US

SINGLES:	HITS 4			WEEKS 54
HE'S A REBEL	London	19	24 Nov 62	13

Originally recorded by Vicki Carr.

DA DOO RON RON	London	5	22 Jun 63	16
THEN HE KISSED ME	London	2	21 Sep 63	14
I WONDER	London	36	7 Mar 64	3
DA DOO RON RON [RI]	Warner Spector	15	19 Oct 74	8

EPS:	HITS 1			WEEKS 1
DA DOO RON RON	London	18	1 Feb 64	1

CSILLA — Hungary

SINGLES:	HITS 1			WEEKS 1
MAN IN THE MOON	Worx	69	13 Jul 96	1

CUBAN BOYS — UK

SINGLES:	HITS 1			WEEKS 2
COGNOSCENTI VS INTELLIGENTSIA	EMI	4	25 Dec 99	2

Samples the Hamsterdance website and Roger Miller's Whistle Stop.

CUBIC 22 — Belgium

SINGLES:	HITS 1			WEEKS 7
NIGHT IN MOTION	XL Recordings	15	22 Jun 91	7

CUD — UK

SINGLES:	HITS 8			WEEKS 16
OH NO WON'T DO [EP]	A&M	49	19 Oct 91	2

Lead track: Oh No Won't Do.

THROUGH THE ROOF	A&M	44	28 Mar 92	2
RICH AND STRANGE	A&M	24	30 May 92	3
PURPLE LOVE BALLOON	A&M	27	15 Aug 92	3
ONCE AGAIN	A&M	45	10 Oct 92	1
NEUROTICA	A&M	37	12 Feb 94	2
STICKS AND STONES	A&M	68	2 Apr 94	1
ONE GIANT LOVE	A&M	52	3 Sep 94	2

ALBUMS:	HITS 2			WEEKS 2
ASQUARIUS	A&M	30	11 Jul 92	1
SHOWBIZ	A&M	46	23 Apr 94	1

CUDDLES – See Keith HARRIS and ORVILLE

CUFF-LINKS — US

SINGLES:	HITS 2			WEEKS 30
TRACY	MCA	4	29 Nov 69	16
WHEN JULIE COMES AROUND	MCA	10	14 Mar 70	14

Lead vocals by Rupert Holmes.

CULPRITS – See Craig McLACHLAN

CULT
UK

SINGLES:	HITS 15			WEEKS 80
RESURRECTION JOE	Beggars Banquet	74	22 Dec 84	2
SHE SELLS SANCTUARY	Beggars Banquet	15	25 May 85	17
SHE SELLS SANCTUARY [RE]	Beggars Banquet	61	28 Sep 85	2
RAIN	Beggars Banquet	17	5 Oct 85	8
REVOLUTION	Beggars Banquet	30	30 Nov 85	7
LOVE REMOVAL MACHINE	Beggars Banquet	18	28 Feb 87	7
LIL' DEVIL	Beggars Banquet	11	2 May 87	7
WILD FLOWER	Beggars Banquet	24	22 Aug 87	2
This entry was based on sales of a 7" doublepack.				
WILD FLOWER	Beggars Banquet	30	29 Aug 87	4
FIRE WOMAN	Beggars Banquet	15	1 Apr 89	4
EDIE (CIAO BABY)	Beggars Banquet	32	8 Jul 89	5
SUN KING / EDIE (CIAO BABY) [RI]	Beggars Banquet	39	18 Nov 89	2
SWEET SOUL SISTER	Beggars Banquet	42	10 Mar 90	4
WILD HEARTED SON	Beggars Banquet	40	14 Sep 91	2
HEART OF SOUL	Beggars Banquet	51	29 Feb 92	1
SHE SELLS SANCTUARY (MCMXCIII REMIXES) [RM]	Beggars Banquet	15	30 Jan 93	4
Remixes by Youth/Butch Vig/J.G. Thilwell.				
COMING DOWN	Beggars Banquet	50	8 Oct 94	1
STAR	Beggars Banquet	65	7 Jan 95	1
ALBUMS:	**HITS 8**			**WEEKS 85**
THE SOUTHERN DEATH CULT	Beggars Banquet	43	18 Jun 83	3
Above hit: SOUTHERN DEATH CULT.				
DREAMTIME	Beggars Banquet	21	8 Sep 84	8
LOVE	Beggars Banquet	4	26 Oct 85	22
ELECTRIC	Beggars Banquet	4	18 Apr 87	27
SONIC TEMPLE	Beggars Banquet	3	22 Apr 89	11
CEREMONY	Beggars Banquet	9	5 Oct 91	4
PURE CULT	Beggars Banquet	1	13 Feb 93	8
Compilation.				
THE CULT	Beggars Banquet	21	22 Oct 94	2

CULTURE
Jamaica

ALBUMS:	HITS 1			WEEKS 1
TWO SEVENS CLASH	Lightning	60	1 Apr 78	1

CULTURE BEAT
UK/US/Germany

SINGLES:	HITS 8			WEEKS 46
(CHERRY LIPS) DER ERDBEERMUND	Epic	55	3 Feb 90	3
MR. VAIN	Epic	1	7 Aug 93	15
GOT TO GET IT	Epic	4	6 Nov 93	11
ANYTHING	Epic	5	15 Jan 94	8
WORLD IN YOUR HANDS	Epic	20	2 Apr 94	4
INSIDE OUT	Epic	32	27 Jan 96	2
CRYING IN THE RAIN	Epic	29	15 Jun 96	2
TAKE ME AWAY	Epic	52	28 Sep 96	1
ALBUMS:	**HITS 1**			**WEEKS 10**
SERENITY	Dance Pool	13	25 Sep 93	10

CULTURE CLUB
UK

(See also Boy George.)

SINGLES:	HITS 13			WEEKS 119
DO YOU REALLY WANT TO HURT ME	Virgin	1	18 Sep 82	18
TIME (CLOCK OF THE HEART)	Virgin	3	27 Nov 82	12
CHURCH OF THE POISON MIND	Virgin	2	9 Apr 83	9
KARMA CHAMELEON	Virgin	1	17 Sep 83	20
VICTIMS	Virgin	3	10 Dec 83	10
IT'S A MIRACLE	Virgin	4	24 Mar 84	9
Above 4 feature backing vocals from Helen Terry.				
THE WAR SONG	Virgin	2	6 Oct 84	8
THE MEDAL SONG	Virgin	32	1 Dec 84	4
THE MEDAL SONG [RE]	Virgin	74	5 Jan 85	1
MOVE AWAY	Virgin	7	15 Mar 86	7
GOD THANK YOU WOMAN	Virgin	31	31 May 86	5
I JUST WANNA BE LOVED	Virgin	4	31 Oct 98	10
YOUR KISSES ARE CHARITY	Virgin	25	7 Aug 99	4
COLD SHOULDER / STARMAN	Virgin	43	27 Nov 99	2
ALBUMS:	**HITS 8**			**WEEKS 163**
KISSING TO BE CLEVER	Virgin	5	16 Oct 82	59
COLOUR BY NUMBERS	Virgin	1	22 Oct 83	56
WAKING UP WITH THE HOUSE ON FIRE	Virgin	2	3 Nov 84	13
FROM LUXURY TO HEARTACHE	Virgin	10	12 Apr 86	6
THIS TIME: THE FIRST FOUR YEARS	Virgin	8	18 Apr 87	10

AT WORST. . .THE BEST OF BOY GEORGE & CULTURE CLUB	*Virgin*	24	*2 Oct 93*	5

Also includes Jesus Loves You tracks.
Above hit: BOY GEORGE/CULTURE CLUB.

GREATEST MOMENTS	*Virgin*	15	*21 Nov 98*	13
DON'T MIND IF I DO	*Virgin*	64	*4 Dec 99*	1

Smiley CULTURE · UK

SINGLES:	HITS 3		WEEKS 13	
POLICE OFFICER	*Fashion*	12	*15 Dec 84*	10
COCKNEY TRANSLATION	*Fashion*	71	*6 Apr 85*	1
SCHOOLTIME CHRONICLE	*Polydor*	59	*13 Sep 86*	2

Larry CUNNINGHAM and the MIGHTY AVONS · Ireland

SINGLES:	HITS 1		WEEKS 11	
TRIBUTE TO JIM REEVES	*King*	40	*12 Dec 64*	8

Includes words and music from 4 songs (3 hits) recorded by Jim Reeves.

TRIBUTE TO JIM REEVES [RE]	*King*	46	*27 Feb 65*	3

CUPID'S INSPIRATION · UK

SINGLES:	HITS 2		WEEKS 19	
YESTERDAY HAS GONE	*Nems*	4	*22 Jun 68*	11

Originally recorded by Little Anthony and the Imperials.

MY WORLD	*Nems*	33	*5 Oct 68*	8

Jose CURA – See Sarah BRIGHTMAN

Mike CURB CONGREGATION – See Little Jimmy OSMOND

CURE · UK

SINGLES:	HITS 26		WEEKS 144	
A FOREST	*Fiction*	31	*12 Apr 80*	8
PRIMARY	*Fiction*	43	*4 Apr 81*	6
CHARLOTTE SOMETIMES	*Fiction*	44	*17 Oct 81*	4
THE HANGING GARDEN	*Fiction*	34	*24 Jul 82*	4
LET'S GO TO BED	*Fiction*	44	*27 Nov 82*	4
LET'S GO TO BED [RE]	*Fiction*	75	*8 Jan 83*	1
THE WALK	*Fiction*	12	*9 Jul 83*	8
THE LOVE CATS	*Fiction*	7	*29 Oct 83*	11
THE CATERPILLAR	*Fiction*	14	*7 Apr 84*	7
IN BETWEEN DAYS	*Fiction*	15	*27 Jul 85*	10
CLOSE TO ME	*Fiction*	24	*21 Sep 85*	8
BOYS DON'T CRY	*Fiction*	22	*3 May 86*	6
WHY CAN'T I BE YOU?	*Fiction*	21	*18 Apr 87*	5
CATCH	*Fiction*	27	*4 Jul 87*	6
JUST LIKE HEAVEN	*Fiction*	29	*17 Oct 87*	5
HOT HOT HOT!!!	*Fiction*	45	*20 Feb 88*	3
LULLABY	*Fiction*	5	*22 Apr 89*	6
LOVESONG	*Fiction*	18	*2 Sep 89*	7
PICTURES OF YOU	*Fiction*	24	*31 Mar 90*	6
NEVER ENOUGH	*Fiction*	13	*29 Sep 90*	5
CLOSE TO ME [RM]	*Fiction*	13	*3 Nov 90*	5
HIGH	*Fiction*	8	*28 Mar 92*	3
HIGH [RM]	*Fiction*	44	*11 Apr 92*	1
FRIDAY I'M IN LOVE	*Fiction*	6	*23 May 92*	7
A LETTER TO ELISE	*Fiction*	28	*17 Oct 92*	2
THE 13TH	*Fiction*	15	*4 May 96*	2
MINT CAR	*Fiction*	31	*29 Jun 96*	2
GONE!	*Fiction*	60	*14 Dec 96*	1
WRONG NUMBER	*Fiction*	62	*29 Nov 97*	1

Features Reeves Gabrels (Tin Machine) on guitar.

ALBUMS:	HITS 19		WEEKS 200	
THREE IMAGINARY BOYS	*Fiction*	44	*2 Jun 79*	3
17 SECONDS	*Fiction*	20	*3 May 80*	10
FAITH	*Fiction*	14	*25 Apr 81*	8
PORNOGRAPHY	*Fiction*	8	*15 May 82*	9
BOYS DON'T CRY	*Fiction*	77	*3 Sep 83*	5

Chart position reached in 1994.

JAPANESE WHISPERS: SINGLES NOV 82 – NOV 83	*Fiction*	26	*24 Dec 83*	14
THE TOP	*Fiction*	10	*12 May 84*	10
CONCERT – THE CURE LIVE	*Fiction*	26	*3 Nov 84*	4
THE HEAD ON THE DOOR	*Fiction*	7	*7 Sep 85*	13
BOYS DON'T CRY [RE]	*Fiction*	71	*10 May 86*	2
STANDING ON A BEACH – THE SINGLES	*Fiction*	4	*31 May 86*	35

CD format was titled Staring At The Sea.

KISS ME KISS ME KISS ME	*Fiction*	6	*6 Jun 87*	15
DISINTEGRATION	*Fiction*	3	*13 May 89*	26
MIXED UP	*Fiction*	8	*17 Nov 90*	17

ENTREAT	*Fiction*	10	*6 Apr 91*	5
WISH	*Fiction*	1	*2 May 92*	13
SHOW	*Fiction*	29	*25 Sep 93*	2
PARIS	*Fiction*	56	*6 Nov 93*	1
WILD MOOD SWINGS	*Fiction*	9	*18 May 96*	6
GALORE - THE SINGLES 1987-1997	*Fiction*	37	*15 Nov 97*	2

CURIOSITY KILLED THE CAT
UK

SINGLES:	**HITS 8**			**WEEKS 58**
DOWN TO EARTH	*Mercury*	3	*13 Dec 86*	18
ORDINARY DAY	*Mercury*	11	*4 Apr 87*	7
MISFIT	*Mercury*	7	*20 Jun 87*	9
Original release reached No. 76 in 1986.				
FREE	*Mercury*	56	*19 Sep 87*	2
NAME AND NUMBER	*Mercury*	14	*16 Sep 89*	9
HANG ON IN THERE BABY	*RCA*	3	*25 Apr 92*	10
I NEED YOUR LOVIN'	*RCA*	47	*29 Aug 92*	2
GIMME THE SUNSHINE	*RCA*	73	*30 Oct 93*	1
Above 3: CURIOSITY.				
ALBUMS:	**HITS 2**			**WEEKS 27**
KEEP YOUR DISTANCE	*Mercury*	1	*9 May 87*	24
GETAHEAD	*Mercury*	29	*4 Nov 89*	3

CURLS - See Paul EVANS

Chantal CURTIS
France

SINGLES:	**HITS 1**			**WEEKS 3**
GET ANOTHER LOVE	*Pye International*	51	*14 Jul 79*	3

T.C. CURTIS backing vocals by GALAXY
Jamaica

SINGLES:	**HITS 1**			**WEEKS 4**
YOU SHOULD HAVE KNOWN BETTER	*Hot Melt*	50	*23 Feb 85*	4

CURVE
UK

SINGLES:	**HITS 7**			**WEEKS 14**
THE BLINDFOLD [EP]	*AnXious*	68	*16 Mar 91*	1
Lead track: Ten Little Girls.				
COAST IS CLEAR	*AnXious*	34	*25 May 91*	3
CLIPPED	*AnXious*	36	*9 Nov 91*	2
FAIT ACCOMPLI	*AnXious*	22	*7 Mar 92*	3
HORROR HEAD	*AnXious*	31	*18 Jul 92*	2
BLACKERTHREETRACKER [EP]	*AnXious*	39	*4 Sep 93*	2
Lead track: Missing Link.				
COMING UP ROSES	*Universal*	51	*16 May 98*	1
ALBUMS:	**HITS 3**			**WEEKS 6**
DOPPELGANGER	*Anxious*	11	*21 Mar 92*	3
RADIO SESSIONS	*Anxious*	72	*19 Jun 93*	1
CUCKOO	*Anxious*	23	*25 Sep 93*	2

CURVED AIR
UK

SINGLES:	**HITS 1**			**WEEKS 12**
BACK STREET LUV	*Warner Brothers*	4	*7 Aug 71*	12
ALBUMS:	**HITS 3**			**WEEKS 32**
AIR CONDITIONING	*Warner Brothers*	8	*5 Dec 70*	21
CURVED AIR	*Warner Brothers*	11	*9 Oct 71*	6
PHANTASMAGORIA	*Reprise*	20	*13 May 72*	5

CUT 'N' MOVE
Denmark

SINGLES:	**HITS 2**			**WEEKS 4**
GIVE IT UP	*EMI*	61	*2 Oct 93*	2
I'M ALIVE	*EMI*	49	*9 Sep 95*	2

Frankie CUTLASS
US

SINGLES:	**HITS 1**			**WEEKS 1**
THE CYPHER: PART 3	*Epic*	59	*5 Apr 97*	1

Adge CUTLER and the WURZELS - See WURZELS

CUTTING CREW
UK/Canada

SINGLES:	**HITS 4**			**WEEKS 37**
(I JUST) DIED IN YOUR ARMS	*Siren*	4	*16 Aug 86*	12
I'VE BEEN IN LOVE BEFORE	*Siren*	31	*25 Oct 86*	9
I'VE BEEN IN LOVE BEFORE [RE]	*Siren*	70	*10 Jan 87*	1
ONE FOR THE MOCKINGBIRD	*Siren*	52	*7 Mar 87*	5

I'VE BEEN IN LOVE BEFORE [RM]	Siren	24	21 Nov 87	8
Mixed by Steve Thompson and Michael Barbiero.				
(BETWEEN A) ROCK AND A HARD PLACE	Siren	66	22 Jul 89	2
ALBUMS:	**HITS 1**		**WEEKS 6**	
BROADCAST	Siren	41	29 Nov 86	6

CYBERSONIK   US

SINGLES:	**HITS 1**		**WEEKS 1**	
TECHNARCHY	Champion	73	10 Nov 90	1

Johnny CYMBAL   UK

SINGLES:	**HITS 1**		**WEEKS 10**	
MR. BASS MAN	London	24	16 Mar 63	10

CYPRESS HILL   US

SINGLES:	**HITS 8**		**WEEKS 34**	
INSANE IN THE BRAIN	Columbia	32	31 Jul 93	4
WHEN THE SH** GOES DOWN	Columbia	19	2 Oct 93	4
I AIN'T GOIN' OUT LIKE THAT	Columbia	15	11 Dec 93	7
INSANE IN THE BRAIN [RI]	Columbia	21	26 Feb 94	4
LICK A SHOT	Columbia	20	7 May 94	3
THROW YOUR SET IN THE AIR	Columbia	15	7 Oct 95	3
ILLUSIONS	Columbia	23	17 Feb 96	2
TEQUILA SUNRISE	Columbia	23	10 Oct 98	2
DR. GREENTHUMB	Columbia	34	10 Apr 99	2
INSANE IN THE BRAIN [RM]	INCredible	19	26 Jun 99	3
Remixed by Jason Nevins.				
Above hit: Jason NEVINS vs. CYPRESS HILL.				
ALBUMS:	**HITS 4**		**WEEKS 61**	
BLACK SUNDAY	Columbia	13	7 Aug 93	49
CYPRESS HILL III (TEMPLES OF BOOM)	Columbia	11	11 Nov 95	5
UNRELEASED & REVAMPED [EP]	Columbia	29	24 Aug 96	4
Consists of tracks previously unreleased.				
IV	Columbia	25	17 Oct 98	3

Billy Ray CYRUS   US

SINGLES:	**HITS 4**		**WEEKS 18**	
ACHY BREAKY HEART	Mercury	3	25 Jul 92	10
Originally recorded by the Marci Brothers as Don't Tell My Heart.				
COULD'VE BEEN ME	Mercury	24	10 Oct 92	4
THESE BOOTS ARE MADE FOR WALKIN'	Mercury	63	28 Nov 92	1
ACHY BREAKY HEART [RR]	Epic	53	19 Dec 92	3
Above hit: ALVIN and the CHIPMUNKS (with Special Guest Billy Ray CYRUS).				
ALBUMS:	**HITS 1**		**WEEKS 10**	
SOME GAVE ALL	Mercury	9	29 Aug 92	10

Holger CZUKAY – See David SYLVIAN

D

Chuck D   US

SINGLES:	**HITS 2**		**WEEKS 6**	
BRING THE NOISE	Island	14	6 Jul 91	5
Above hit: ANTHRAX featuring Chuck D from PUBLIC ENEMY.				
NO	Mercury	55	26 Oct 96	1

Danny D – See COOKIE CREW; D-MOB

Dimples D   US

SINGLES:	**HITS 1**		**WEEKS 10**	
SUCKER DJ	FBI	17	17 Nov 90	10
Recorded in 1983 and samples the TV theme 'I Dream Of Jeannie'.				

Longsy D's HOUSE SOUND   UK

SINGLES:	**HITS 1**		**WEEKS 7**	
THIS IS SKA	Big One	56	4 Mar 89	7

Nikki D   US

SINGLES:	**HITS 2**		**WEEKS 6**	
MY LOVE IS SO RAW	Def Jam	34	6 May 89	5
Above hit: Alyson WILLIAMS featuring NIKKI-D.				
DADDY'S LITTLE GIRL	Def Jam	75	30 Mar 91	1

Vicky "D"
US

SINGLES:		HITS 1			WEEKS 6
THIS BEAT IS MINE	*Virgin/Sam*	42	*13 Mar 82*		6

D.B.M.
Germany

SINGLES:		HITS 1			WEEKS 3
DISCOBEATLEMANIA [M]	*Atlantic*	45	*12 Nov 77*		3

D. B. M. and T.
UK

SINGLES:		HITS 1			WEEKS 8
MR. PRESIDENT	*Fontana*	33	*1 Aug 70*		8

D.BO GENERAL – See URBAN SHAKEDOWN featuring Micky FINN

D-INFLUENCE
UK

SINGLES:		HITS 5			WEEKS 10
GOOD LOVER	*East West America*	46	*20 Jun 92*		2
GOOD LOVER [RI]	*East West America*	61	*27 Mar 93*		1
Samples Eleanore Mills' Mr. Right.					
MIDNITE	*East West America*	58	*24 Jun 95*		1
HYPNOTIZE	*Echo*	33	*16 Aug 97*		2
MAGIC	*Echo*	45	*11 Oct 97*		1
ROCK WITH YOU	*Echo*	30	*5 Sep 98*		3
ALBUMS:		HITS 1			WEEKS 1
LONDON	*Echo*	56	*25 Oct 97*		1

D.J.H. featuring STEFY
Italy

SINGLES:		HITS 3			WEEKS 14
THINK ABOUT . . .	*RCA*	22	*16 Feb 91*		6
Samples Aretha Franklin's Rock-A-Lott.					
I LIKE IT	*RCA*	16	*13 Jul 91*		7
MOVE YOUR LOVE	*RCA*	73	*19 Oct 91*		1
Also samples Aretha Franklin's Rock-A-Lott.					

D-KUPS – See Ivor BIGGUN

D'LUX
UK

SINGLES:		HITS 1			WEEKS 1
LOVE RESURRECTION	*Logic*	58	*22 Jun 96*		1

D'MENACE
UK

SINGLES:		HITS 1			WEEKS 3
DEEP MENACE (SPANK)	*Inferno*	20	*8 Aug 98*		3

D-MOB
UK

SINGLES:		HITS 7			WEEKS 48
WE CALL IT ACIEED	*ffrr*	3	*15 Oct 88*		12
Above hit: D. MOB (featuring Gary HAISMAN).					
IT IS TIME TO GET FUNKY	*ffrr*	9	*3 Jun 89*		10
Above hit: D. MOB featuring L.R.S. and D.C. SAROME.					
C'MON AND GET MY LOVE	*ffrr*	15	*21 Oct 89*		10
Above hit: D MOB introducing Cathy DENNIS.					
PUT YOUR HANDS TOGETHER	*London*	7	*6 Jan 90*		8
Above hit: D. MOB featuring NUFF JUICE.					
THAT'S THE WAY OF THE WORLD	*ffrr*	48	*7 Apr 90*		3
Above hit: D MOB featuring Cathy DENNIS.					
WHY	*ffrr*	23	*12 Feb 94*		3
Above hit: D-MOB with Cathy DENNIS.					
ONE DAY	*ffrr*	41	*3 Sep 94*		2
Vocals by Steven Dante.					
Above hit: Danny D presents D:MOB					
ALBUMS:		HITS 1			WEEKS 11
A LITTLE BIT OF THIS, A LITTLE BIT OF THAT	*ffrr*	46	*11 Nov 89*		11

D*NOTE
UK

SINGLES:		HITS 2			WEEKS 2
WAITING HOPEFULLY	*VC Recordings*	46	*12 Jul 97*		1
LOST AND FOUND	*VC Recordings*	59	*15 Nov 97*		1

D.O.P.
UK

SINGLES:		HITS 2			WEEKS 2
STOP STARTING TO START STOPPING [EP]	*Hi-Life*	58	*3 Feb 96*		1
Lead track: Gusta.					

GROOVY BEAT	Hi-Life	54	13 Jul 96	1

Originally released in 1992.

D.O.S.E. featuring Mark E. SMITH — UK

SINGLES:		HITS 1		WEEKS 1
PLUG MYSELF IN	Coliseum	50	23 Mar 96	1

D:REAM — UK

SINGLES:		HITS 8		WEEKS 74
U R THE BEST THING	FXU	72	4 Jul 92	1
THINGS CAN ONLY GET BETTER	Magnet	24	30 Jan 93	5
U R THE BEST THING [RM-1ST]	Magnet	19	24 Apr 93	8
UNFORGIVEN	Magnet	29	31 Jul 93	3
STAR / I LIKE IT	Magnet	26	2 Oct 93	4
THINGS CAN ONLY GET BETTER [RM]	Magnet	1	8 Jan 94	16
U R THE BEST THING [RM-2ND]	Magnet	4	26 Mar 94	10

Remixed by Paul Oakenfold and Steve Osborne.

TAKE ME AWAY	Magnet	18	18 Jun 94	5
BLAME IT ON ME	Magnet	25	10 Sep 94	5
SHOOT ME WITH YOUR LOVE	Magnet	7	8 Jul 95	7
PARTY UP THE WORLD	Magnet	20	9 Sep 95	6
THE POWER (OF ALL THE LOVE IN THE WORLD)	Magnet	40	11 Nov 95	1
THINGS CAN ONLY GET BETTER [RM] [RI]	Magnet	19	3 May 97	3

Used as a Labour party anthem in the 1997 general election.

ALBUMS:		HITS 2		WEEKS 41
D:REAM ON VOLUME 1	Magnet	44	30 Oct 93	3
D:REAM ON VOLUME 1 [RE]	Magnet	5	5 Feb 94	34

Re-packaged.

WORLD	Magnet	5	30 Sep 95	4

D.S.M. — US

SINGLES:		HITS 1		WEEKS 4
WARRIOR GROOVE	10 Records	68	7 Dec 85	4

D-SHAKE — Holland

SINGLES:		HITS 2		WEEKS 8
YAAAH / TECHNO TRANCE	Cooltempo	20	2 Jun 90	6
MY HEART, THE BEAT	Cooltempo	42	2 Feb 91	2

D-TEK — UK

SINGLES:		HITS 1		WEEKS 1
DROP THE ROCK [EP]	Positiva	70	6 Nov 93	1

Lead track: Drop The Rock.

D-TRAIN — US

SINGLES:		HITS 4		WEEKS 36
YOU'RE THE ONE FOR ME	Epic	30	6 Feb 82	8
WALK ON BY	Epic	44	8 May 82	6
MUSIC	Prelude	23	7 May 83	7
KEEP GIVING ME LOVE	Prelude	65	16 Jul 83	2
YOU'RE THE ONE FOR ME (LABOUR OF LOVE MIX) [RM]	Prelude	15	27 Jul 85	11
MUSIC [RM]	Prelude	62	12 Oct 85	2

Above 2 remixed by Paul Hardcastle.

ALBUMS:		HITS 1		WEEKS 4
D-TRAIN	Epic	72	8 May 82	4

DA BRAT — US

(See also Lil' Kim.)

SINGLES:		HITS 2		WEEKS 3
FUNKDAFIED	Columbia	65	22 Oct 94	1
SOCKIT2ME	East West	33	29 Nov 97	2

Above hit: Missy Misdemeanor ELLIOTT featuring DA BRAT.

DA CLICK — UK

SINGLES:		HITS 2		WEEKS 8
GOOD RHYMES	ffrr	14	16 Jan 99	6

Based around Chic's Good Times.

WE ARE DA CLICK	ffrr	38	29 May 99	2

Samples Tom Browne's Funkin' For Jamaica.

DA FOOL
UK

SINGLES:	HITS 1			WEEKS 2
NO GOOD (FORMERLY KNOWN AS "MEET HIM AT THE BLUE OYSTER BAR")	ffrr	38	16 Jan 99	2
Samples SIL's Blue Oyster.				

Ricardo DA FORCE
UK

SINGLES:	HITS 3			WEEKS 14
PUMP UP THE VOLUME	Stress	51	18 Mar 95	2
Above hit: GREED featuring Ricardo DA FORCE.				
STAYIN' ALIVE	All Around the World	2	16 Sep 95	11
Above hit: N-TRANCE featuring Ricardo DA FORCE.				
WHY?	ffrr	58	31 Aug 96	1

DA HOOL
Germany

SINGLES:	HITS 2			WEEKS 7
MEET HER AT THE LOVE PARADE	Manifesto	15	14 Feb 98	4
BORA BORA	Manifesto	35	22 Aug 98	3
Bora Bora is an island 150 miles northwest at Tahiti.				

DA LENCH MOB
US

SINGLES:	HITS 1			WEEKS 2
FREEDOM GOT AN A.K.	East West America	51	20 Mar 93	2

DA MOB featuring Jocelyn BROWN
US

(See also Jocelyn Brown.)

SINGLES:	HITS 2			WEEKS 3
FUN	INCredible	33	2 May 98	2
IT'S ALL GOOD	INCredible	54	3 Jul 99	1

DA TECHNO BOHEMIAN
Holland

SINGLES:	HITS 1			WEEKS 1
BANGIN' BASS	Hi-Life	63	25 Jan 97	1

Paul DA VINCI
UK

SINGLES:	HITS 1			WEEKS 8
YOUR BABY AIN'T YOUR BABY ANYMORE	Penny Farthing	20	20 Jul 74	8

Terry DACTYL and the DINOSAURS
UK

(See also Jona Lewie.)

SINGLES:	HITS 2			WEEKS 16
SEASIDE SHUFFLE	UK	2	15 Jul 72	12
ON A SATURDAY NIGHT	UK	45	13 Jan 73	4
Label has minor credit 'featuring John G. Lewis'.				

DADA
US

SINGLES:	HITS 1			WEEKS 1
DOG	I.R.S.	71	4 Dec 93	1

DADDY FREDDY - See Simon HARRIS

DADDY'S FAVOURITE
UK

SINGLES:	HITS 1			WEEKS 3
I FEEL GOOD THINGS FOR YOU	Go.Beat	44	21 Nov 98	2
Samples Patrice Rushen's Haven't You Heard.				
I FEEL GOOD THINGS FOR YOU [RI]	Go.Beat	50	9 Oct 99	1

DAFFY DUCK featuring the GROOVE GANG
Germany

SINGLES:	HITS 1			WEEKS 3
PARTY ZONE	WEA	58	6 Jul 91	3

DAFT PUNK
France

SINGLES:	HITS 4			WEEKS 13
DA FUNK / MUSIQUE	Virgin	7	22 Feb 97	5
AROUND THE WORLD	Virgin	5	26 Apr 97	5
BURNIN'	Virgin	30	4 Oct 97	2
REVOLUTION 909	Virgin	47	28 Feb 98	1

ALBUMS:	HITS 1			WEEKS 15
HOMEWORK	Virgin	8	1 Feb 97	15

Gigi D'AGOSTINO - See R.A.F.

Etienne DAHO - See SAINT ETIENNE

DAINTEES - See Martin STEPHENSON and the DAINTEES

DAISY CHAINSAW   UK

SINGLES:	HITS 2			WEEKS 6
LOVE YOUR MONEY	Deva	26	18 Jan 92	5
Chart for 18 Jan 92 listed the EP title: Lovesick Pleasure.				
PINK FLOWER / ROOM ELEVEN	Deva	65	28 Mar 92	1
ALBUMS:	**HITS 1**			**WEEKS 1**
ELEVENTEEN	Deva	62	10 Oct 92	1

DAJAE - See B-CREW featuring Barbara TUCKER, Ultra NATE, DAJAE, MONE; Junior SANCHEZ featuring DAJAE

DAKEYNE - See James BROWN; TINMAN

DAKOTAS   UK
(See also Billy J. Kramer with the Dakotas.)

SINGLES:	HITS 1			WEEKS 13
THE CRUEL SEA	Parlophone	18	13 Jul 63	13
EPS:	**HITS 1**			**WEEKS 1**
MEET THE DAKOTAS	Parlophone	19	14 Dec 63	1

Jim DALE   UK

SINGLES:	HITS 3			WEEKS 22
BE MY GIRL	Parlophone	2	12 Oct 57	16
Originally recorded by Don Fox.				
JUST BORN (TO BE YOUR BABY)	Parlophone	27	11 Jan 58	1
CRAZY DREAM	Parlophone	24	18 Jan 58	2
Above 2 entries were separate sides of the same release, each had its own chart run.				
SUGARTIME	Parlophone	25	8 Mar 58	3

DALE and GRACE   US

SINGLES:	HITS 1			WEEKS 2
I'M LEAVING IT UP TO YOU	London	42	11 Jan 64	2

DALE SISTERS   US

SINGLES:	HITS 1			WEEKS 6
MY SUNDAY BABY (UN TELEGRAMA)	Ember	36	25 Nov 61	6

DALEK I   UK

ALBUMS:	HITS 1			WEEKS 2
COMPASS KUMPAS	Backdoor	54	9 Aug 80	2

DALI'S CAR   UK

SINGLES:	HITS 1			WEEKS 2
THE JUDGEMENT IS THE MIRROR	Paradox	66	3 Nov 84	2
ALBUMS:	**HITS 1**			**WEEKS 1**
THE WAKING HOUR	Paradox	84	1 Dec 84	1

Roger DALTREY   UK

SINGLES:	HITS 8			WEEKS 46
GIVING IT ALL AWAY	Track	5	14 Apr 73	11
I'M FREE	Ode	13	4 Aug 73	10
Above hit: Roger DALTREY with LONDON SYMPHONY ORCHESTRA and				
ENGLISH CHAMBER CHOIR conducted by David MEASHAM.				
WRITTEN ON THE WIND	Polydor	46	14 May 77	2
FREE ME	Polydor	39	2 Aug 80	6
WITHOUT YOUR LOVE	Polydor	55	11 Oct 80	4
Above 2 from the film 'McVicar'.				
WALKING IN MY SLEEP	WEA International	56	3 Mar 84	3
AFTER THE FIRE	10 Records	50	5 Oct 85	5
UNDER A RAGING MOON	10 Records	43	8 Mar 86	5
Features 7 different drummers including Roger Taylor, Cozy Powell, Stewart Copeland and Zak				
Starkley.				
ALBUMS:	**HITS 4**			**WEEKS 24**
RIDE A ROCK HORSE	Polydor	14	26 Jul 75	10
ONE OF THE BOYS	Polydor	45	4 Jun 77	1
McVICAR [OST]	Polydor	39	23 Aug 80	11
UNDER A RAGING MOON	10 Records	52	2 Nov 85	2

Glen DALY   UK

ALBUMS:	HITS 1			WEEKS 2
GLASGOW NIGHT OUT	Golden Guinea	28	20 Nov 71	2

DAMAGE — UK

SINGLES:	HITS 6			WEEKS 33
ANYTHING	Big Life	68	20 Jul 96	1
Features US rapper Little Caesar from the Junior M.A.F.I.A. collective.				
LOVE II LOVE	Big Life	12	12 Oct 96	6
FOREVER	Big Life	6	14 Dec 96	9
LOVE GUARANTEED	Big Life	7	22 Mar 97	6
WONDERFUL TONIGHT	Big Life	3	17 May 97	8
Originally recorded by Eric Clapton in 1977.				
LOVE GUARANTEED [RE]	Big Life	73	14 Jun 97	1
LOVE LADY	Big Life	33	9 Aug 97	2
ALBUMS:	HITS 1			WEEKS 12
FOREVER	Big Life	13	19 Apr 97	12

Carolina DAMAS - See SUENO LATINO featuring Carolina DAMAS

Bobby D'AMBROSIO featuring Michelle WEEKS — US

SINGLES:	HITS 1			WEEKS 3
MOMENT OF MY LIFE	Ministry Of Sound	23	2 Aug 97	3
Originally recorded by Inner Life in 1982.				

DAMIAN — UK

SINGLES:	HITS 2			WEEKS 26
THE TIME WARP II (BRAND NEW VERSION)	Jive	51	26 Dec 87	6
The dance routine from 'the Rocky Horror Show'. Original release reached No. 94 in 1986.				
THE TIME WARP 2 (BRAND NEW VERSION) [RI]	Jive	64	27 Aug 88	3
THE TIME WARP (PWL REMIX) [RM]	Jive	7	19 Aug 89	13
Remixed by Peter Hammond.				
WIG WAM BAM	Jive	49	16 Dec 89	4

DAMNED — UK

SINGLES:	HITS 15			WEEKS 77
LOVE SONG	Chiswick	20	5 May 79	8
SMASH IT UP	Chiswick	35	20 Oct 79	5
I JUST CAN'T BE HAPPY TODAY	Chiswick	46	1 Dec 79	5
THE HISTORY OF THE WORLD	Chiswick	51	4 Oct 80	4
FRIDAY THE THIRTEENTH [EP]	Stale One	50	28 Nov 81	4
Lead track: Disco Man.				
LOVELY MONEY	Bronze	42	10 Jul 82	4
THANKS FOR THE NIGHT	Plus One	43	9 Jun 84	4
GRIMLY FIENDISH	MCA	21	30 Mar 85	7
THE SHADOW OF LOVE (EDITION PREMIERE)	MCA	25	22 Jun 85	8
IS IT A DREAM "WILD WEST END MIX"	MCA	34	21 Sep 85	4
ELOISE	MCA	3	8 Feb 86	9
ELOISE [RE]	MCA	72	19 Apr 86	1
ANYTHING	MCA	32	22 Nov 86	4
GIGOLO	MCA	29	7 Feb 87	3
ALONE AGAIN OR	MCA	27	25 Apr 87	6
IN DULCE DECORUM	MCA	72	28 Nov 87	1
ALBUMS:	HITS 8			WEEKS 54
DAMNED DAMNED DAMNED	Stiff	36	12 Mar 77	10
MACHINE GUN ETIQUETTE	Chiswick	31	17 Nov 79	5
THE BLACK ALBUM	Chiswick	29	29 Nov 80	3
THE BEST OF THE DAMNED	Big Beat	43	28 Nov 81	12
STRAWBERRIES	Bronze	15	23 Oct 82	4
PHANTASMAGORIA	MCA	11	27 Jul 85	17
ANYTHING	MCA	40	13 Dec 86	2
LIGHT AT THE END OF THE TUNNEL	MCA	87	12 Dec 87	1

Kenny DAMON — US

SINGLES:	HITS 1			WEEKS 1
WHILE I LIVE	Mercury	45	21 May 66	1

Vic DAMONE — US

SINGLES:	HITS 3			WEEKS 22
AN AFFAIR TO REMEMBER (OUR LOVE AFFAIR)	Philips	29	7 Dec 57	1
Originally recorded by Carmen Cavallaro & his Orchestra.				
AN AFFAIR TO REMEMBER (OUR LOVE AFFAIR) [RE]	Philips	30	1 Feb 58	1
ON THE STREET WHERE YOU LIVE	Philips	1	10 May 58	17
From the musical 'My Fair Lady'.				
Above hit: Vic DAMONE with Percy FAITH and his Orchestra and Chorus.				
THE ONLY MAN ON THE ISLAND	Philips	24	2 Aug 58	3
Above hit: Vic DAMONE with Frank DE VOL and his Orchestra.				

ALBUMS:		HITS 2		WEEKS 8	
NOW!		*RCA International*	28	*25 Apr 81*	7
VIC DAMONE SINGS THE GREAT SONGS		*Cameo*	87	*2 Apr 83*	1

DAN-I
UK

SINGLES:		HITS 1		WEEKS 9	
MONKEY CHOP		*Island*	30	*10 Nov 79*	9

DANA
UK

SINGLES:		HITS 8		WEEKS 75	
ALL KINDS OF EVERYTHING		*Rex*	1	*4 Apr 70*	15
Eurovision Song Contest winner for Ireland in 1970.					
ALL KINDS OF EVERYTHING [RE]		*Rex*	47	*25 Jul 70*	1
WHO PUT THE LIGHTS OUT		*Rex*	14	*13 Feb 71*	11
PLEASE TELL HIM THAT I SAID HELLO		*GTO*	8	*25 Jan 75*	14
IT'S GONNA BE A COLD COLD CHRISTMAS		*GTO*	4	*13 Dec 75*	6
NEVER GONNA FALL IN LOVE AGAIN		*GTO*	31	*6 Mar 76*	4
Originally recorded by Eric Carmen.					
FAIRYTALE		*GTO*	13	*16 Oct 76*	16
SOMETHING'S COOKING IN THE KITCHEN		*GTO*	44	*31 Mar 79*	5
I FEEL LOVE COMIN' ON		*Creole*	66	*15 May 82*	3
ALBUMS:		HITS 1		WEEKS 3	
EVERYTHING IS BEAUTIFUL		*Warwick*	43	*27 Dec 80*	3

DANA INTERNATIONAL
Israel

SINGLES:		HITS 1		WEEKS 4	
DIVA		*Dance Pool*	11	*27 Jun 98*	4
Eurovision Song Contest winner in 1998.					

DANCE CONSPIRACY
UK

SINGLES:		HITS 1		WEEKS 1	
DUB WAR		*XL Recordings*	72	*3 Oct 92*	1

DANCE FLOOR VIRUS
Italy

SINGLES:		HITS 1		WEEKS 2	
MESSAGE IN A BOTTLE		*Epic*	49	*21 Oct 95*	2

DANCE 2 TRANCE
Germany

SINGLES:		HITS 3		WEEKS 8	
P.OWER OF A.MERICAN N.ATIVES		*Logic*	25	*24 Apr 93*	4
TAKE A FREE FALL		*Logic*	36	*24 Jul 93*	3
WARRIOR		*Logic*	56	*4 Feb 95*	1

Evan DANDO – See Kirsty MacCOLL

Suzanne DANDO
UK

ALBUMS:		HITS 1		WEEKS 1	
SHAPE UP AND DANCE WITH SUZANNE DANDO		*Lifestyle*	87	*17 Mar 84*	1

DANDY WARHOLS
US

SINGLES:		HITS 3		WEEKS 8	
EVERY DAY SHOULD BE A HOLIDAY		*Capitol*	29	*28 Feb 98*	2
NOT IF YOU WERE THE LAST JUNKIE ON EARTH		*Capitol*	13	*2 May 98*	4
BOYS BETTER		*Capitol*	36	*8 Aug 98*	3
ALBUMS:		HITS 1		WEEKS 8	
COME DOWN		*Capitol*	16	*16 May 98*	8

DANDYS
UK

SINGLES:		HITS 2		WEEKS 2	
YOU MAKE ME WANT TO SCREAM		*Artificial*	71	*14 Mar 98*	1
ENGLISH COUNTRY GARDEN		*Artificial*	57	*30 May 98*	1

D'ANGELO
US

(See also Genius/GZA.)

SINGLES:		HITS 4		WEEKS 9	
BROWN SUGAR		*Cooltempo*	24	*28 Oct 95*	3
CRUISIN'		*Cooltempo*	31	*2 Mar 96*	2
Original by Smokey Robinson reached No. 4 in the US in 1979.					
LADY		*Cooltempo*	21	*15 Jun 96*	2
BREAK UPS 2 MAKE UPS		*Def Jam*	33	*22 May 99*	2
Above hit: METHOD MAN featuring D'ANGELO.					

ALBUMS:		HITS 1		WEEKS 2
BROWN SUGAR	Cooltempo	57	28 Oct 95	2

DANGER DANGER   US

SINGLES:		HITS 3		WEEKS 5
MONKEY BUSINESS	Epic	42	8 Feb 92	2
I STILL THINK ABOUT YOU	Epic	46	28 Mar 92	2
COMIN' HOME	Epic	75	13 Jun 92	1

Charlie DANIELS BAND   US

SINGLES:		HITS 1		WEEKS 10
THE DEVIL WENT DOWN TO GEORGIA	Epic	14	22 Sep 79	10
ALBUMS:		**HITS 1**		**WEEKS 1**
MILLION MILE REFLECTIONS	Epic	74	10 Nov 79	1

Jeffrey DANIELS – See BABYFACE

Phil DANIELS – See BLUR

Johnny DANKWORTH and his Orchestra   UK

SINGLES:		HITS 2		WEEKS 33
EXPERIMENTS WITH MICE	Parlophone	7	23 Jun 56	12
AFRICAN WALTZ	Columbia	9	25 Feb 61	21

DANNII – See Dannii MINOGUE

DANNY and the JUNIORS   US

SINGLES:		HITS 1		WEEKS 19
AT THE HOP	His Master's Voice	3	18 Jan 58	14
Originally written as Do The Bop.				
AT THE HOP [RI]	ABC	39	10 Jul 76	5

DANNY WILSON   UK

SINGLES:		HITS 3		WEEKS 28
MARY'S PRAYER	Virgin	42	22 Aug 87	7
MARY'S PRAYER [RM]	Virgin	3	2 Apr 88	11
Remixed by Paul Staveley and issued with the same catalogue number as the previous entry.				
THE SECOND SUMMER OF LOVE	Virgin	23	17 Jun 89	9
NEVER GONNA BE THE SAME	Virgin	69	16 Sep 89	1
ALBUMS:		**HITS 3**		**WEEKS 11**
MEET DANNY WILSON	Virgin	65	30 Apr 88	5
BEEBOP MOPTOP	Virgin	24	29 Jul 89	5
SWEET DANNY WILSON	Virgin	54	31 Aug 91	1

DANSE SOCIETY   UK

SINGLES:		HITS 2		WEEKS 5
WAKE UP	Society	61	27 Aug 83	3
HEAVEN IS WAITING	Society	60	5 Nov 83	2
ALBUMS:		**HITS 1**		**WEEKS 4**
HEAVEN IS WAITING	Society	39	11 Feb 84	4

DANSKI and DJ DELMUNDO present VENGABOYS – See VENGABOYS

Steven DANTE   UK

(See also D-Mob.)

SINGLES:		HITS 2		WEEKS 16
THE REAL THING	Chrysalis	13	26 Sep 87	10
Above hit: JELLYBEAN featuring Steven DANTE.				
I'M TOO SCARED	Cooltempo	34	9 Jul 88	6
ALBUMS:		**HITS 1**		**WEEKS 1**
FIND OUT	Cooltempo	87	3 Sep 88	1

Tonja DANTZLER   US

SINGLES:		HITS 1		WEEKS 1
IN AND OUT OF MY LIFE	ffrr	66	17 Dec 94	1

DANY – See DOUBLE DEE (featuring DANY)

DANZIG   US

SINGLES:		HITS 1		WEEKS 1
MOTHER	American	62	14 May 94	1

DAPHNE

				US
SINGLES:	HITS 1		WEEKS 1	
CHANGE	Stress	71	9 Dec 95	1

Terence Trent D'ARBY

				US
SINGLES:	HITS 11		WEEKS 77	
IF YOU LET ME STAY	CBS	7	14 Mar 87	13
WISHING WELL	CBS	4	20 Jun 87	11
DANCE LITTLE SISTER (PART ONE)	CBS	20	10 Oct 87	7
SIGN YOUR NAME	CBS	2	9 Jan 88	10
TO KNOW SOMEONE DEEPLY IS TO KNOW SOMEONE SOFTLY	CBS	55	20 Jan 90	3
DO YOU LOVE ME LIKE YOU SAY?	Columbia	14	17 Apr 93	6
DELICATE	Columbia	14	19 Jun 93	6
Above hit: Terence Trent D'ARBY featuring DES'REE.				
SHE KISSED ME	Columbia	16	28 Aug 93	7
LET HER DOWN EASY	Columbia	18	20 Nov 93	7
HOLDING ON TO YOU	Columbia	20	8 Apr 95	6
VIBRATOR	Columbia	57	5 Aug 95	1
ALBUMS:	HITS 4		WEEKS 96	
INTRODUCING THE HARDLINE ACCORDING TO TERENCE TRENT D'ARBY	CBS	1	25 Jul 87	65
NEITHER FISH NOR FLESH	CBS	12	4 Nov 89	5
SYMPHONY OR DAMN	Columbia	4	15 May 93	19
TERENCE TRENT D'ARBY'S VIBRATOR	Columbia	11	29 Apr 95	5
INTRODUCING THE HARDLINE ACCORDING TO TERENCE TRENT D'ARBY [RI]	Columbia	53	16 Sep 95	2

Richard DARBYSHIRE

				UK
SINGLES:	HITS 3		WEEKS 7	
COMING BACK FOR MORE	Chrysalis	41	20 Aug 88	3
Above hit: JELLYBEAN featuring Richard DARBYSHIRE.				
THIS I SWEAR	Dome	50	24 Jul 93	3
WHEN ONLY LOVE WILL DO	Dome	54	12 Feb 94	1

DARE

				UK
SINGLES:	HITS 4		WEEKS 7	
THE RAINDANCE	A&M	62	29 Apr 89	2
ABANDON	A&M	71	29 Jul 89	2
Original release reached No. 99 in 1988.				
WE DON'T NEED A REASON	A&M	52	10 Aug 91	2
REAL LOVE	A&M	67	5 Oct 91	1
ALBUMS:	HITS 1		WEEKS 1	
BLOOD FROM STONE	A&M	48	14 Sep 91	1

Matt DAREY presents MASH UP

				UK
SINGLES:	HITS 1		WEEKS 3	
LIBERATION (TEMPTATION - FLY LIKE AN ANGEL)	Incentive	19	9 Oct 99	3

Bobby DARIN

				US
SINGLES:	HITS 17		WEEKS 162	
SPLISH SPLASH	London	28	2 Aug 58	1
SPLISH SPLASH [RE]	London	18	16 Aug 58	6
QUEEN OF THE HOP	London	24	10 Jan 59	2
DREAM LOVER	London	1	30 May 59	19
MACK THE KNIFE	London	1	26 Sep 59	16
MACK THE KNIFE [RE-1ST]	London	30	23 Jan 60	1
LA MER (BEYOND THE SEA)	London	8	30 Jan 60	11
Originally recorded by Charles Trenet.				
MACK THE KNIFE [RE-2ND]	London	50	12 Mar 60	1
CLEMENTINE	London	8	2 Apr 60	12
LA MER (BEYOND THE SEA) [RE]	London	40	23 Apr 60	2
BILL BAILEY WON'T YOU PLEASE COME HOME	London	36	2 Jul 60	1
Originally recorded by Arthur Collins in 1902.				
BILL BAILEY WON'T YOU PLEASE COME HOME [RE]	London	34	16 Jul 60	1
LAZY RIVER	London	2	18 Mar 61	13
Originally recorded by Hoagy Carmichael.				
NATURE BOY	London	24	8 Jul 61	7
Originally recorded by Dick Haymes and the Song Spinners.				
YOU MUST HAVE BEEN A BEAUTIFUL BABY	London	10	14 Oct 61	11
Originally recorded by Bing Crosby.				
THEME FROM "COME SEPTEMBER"	London	50	28 Oct 61	1
Above hit: Bobby DARIN and his Orchestra.				
MULTIPLICATION	London	5	23 Dec 61	13
Above 2 from the film 'Come September'.				
THINGS	London	2	21 Jul 62	17

IF A MAN ANSWERS	Capitol	24	6 Oct 62	6
From the film 'If A Man Answers'.				
BABY FACE	London	40	1 Dec 62	4
Originally recorded by Al Jolson in 1949.				
EIGHTEEN YELLOW ROSES	Capitol	37	27 Jul 63	4
IF I WERE A CARPENTER	Atlantic	9	15 Oct 66	12
DREAM LOVER [RI] / MACK THE KNIFE [RI]	Lightning	64	14 Apr 79	1
EPS:	**HITS 1**		**WEEKS 9**	
THAT'S ALL	London	6	19 Mar 60	9
ALBUMS:	**HITS 3**		**WEEKS 15**	
THIS IS DARIN	London	4	19 Mar 60	8
THAT'S ALL	London	15	9 Apr 60	1
THE LEGEND OF BOBBY DARIN - HIS GREATEST HITS	Stylus	39	5 Oct 85	6

DARIO G
UK

SINGLES:	**HITS 3**		**WEEKS 31**	
SUNCHYME	Eternal	2	27 Sep 97	18
Samples Dream Academy's Life In A Northern Town.				
CARNAVAL DE PARIS	Eternal	5	20 Jun 98	9
SUNMACHINE	Eternal	17	12 Sep 98	4
Based around David Bowie's Memory Of A Free Festival, from the Space Oddity album.				
ALBUMS:	**HITS 1**		**WEEKS 4**	
SUNMACHINE	Eternal	26	11 Jul 98	4

DARK STAR
UK

SINGLES:	**HITS 1**		**WEEKS 1**	
ABOUT 3AM	Harvest	50	26 Jun 99	1

DARKMAN
UK

SINGLES:	**HITS 4**		**WEEKS 8**	
YABBA DABBA DOO	Wild Card	49	14 May 94	2
WHO'S THE DARKMAN?	Wild Card	46	20 Aug 94	2
YABBA DABBA DOO [RM]	Wild Card	37	3 Dec 94	2
Remixed by Paul Waller and Seamus Haji.				
BRAND NEW DAY	Wild Card	74	21 Oct 95	1
REPUTATIONS (JUST BE GOOD TO ME)	WEA	75	14 Nov 98	1
Above hit: Andrea GRANT featuring DARKMAN.				

DARLING BUDS
UK

SINGLES:	**HITS 6**		**WEEKS 20**	
BURST	Epic	50	8 Oct 88	5
HIT THE GROUND	Epic	27	7 Jan 89	5
LET'S GO ROUND THERE	Epic	49	25 Mar 89	4
YOU'VE GOT TO CHOOSE	Epic	45	22 Jul 89	3
TINY MACHINE	Epic	60	2 Jun 90	2
SURE THING	Epic	71	12 Sep 92	1
ALBUMS:	**HITS 1**		**WEEKS 3**	
POP SAID	Epic	23	18 Feb 89	3

Guy DARRELL
UK

SINGLES:	**HITS 1**		**WEEKS 13**	
I'VE BEEN HURT	Santa Ponsa	12	18 Aug 73	13
Originally recorded in 1966.				

James DARREN
US

SINGLES:	**HITS 4**		**WEEKS 25**	
BECAUSE THEY'RE YOUNG	Pye International	29	13 Aug 60	7
GOODBYE CRUEL WORLD	Pye International	28	16 Dec 61	9
Originally recorded by Gloria Shayne.				
HER ROYAL MAJESTY	Pye International	36	31 Mar 62	3
CONSCIENCE	Pye International	30	23 Jun 62	6

DARTS
UK

SINGLES:	**HITS 12**		**WEEKS 117**	
DADDY COOL/THE GIRL CAN'T HELP IT [M]	Magnet	6	5 Nov 77	13
Originally recorded by the Rays/Little Richard.				
COME BACK MY LOVE	Magnet	2	28 Jan 78	12
Originally recorded by the Wrens.				
THE BOY FROM NEW YORK CITY	Magnet	2	6 May 78	13
Original by the Ad-Libs reached No. 8 in the US in 1965.				
IT'S RAINING	Magnet	2	5 Aug 78	11
DON'T LET IT FADE AWAY	Magnet	18	11 Nov 78	11
GET IT	Magnet	10	10 Feb 79	9

DUKE OF EARL	Magnet	6	21 Jul 79	11
Originally recorded by Gene Chandler.				
CAN'T GET ENOUGH OF YOUR LOVE	Magnet	43	20 Oct 79	6
REET PETITE	Magnet	51	1 Dec 79	7
LET'S HANG ON	Magnet	11	31 May 80	14
PEACHES	Magnet	66	6 Sep 80	3
WHITE CHRISTMAS / SH-BOOM (LIFE COULD BE A DREAM)	Magnet	48	29 Nov 80	7
ALBUMS:	**HITS 4**			**WEEKS 57**
DARTS	Magnet	9	3 Dec 77	22
EVERYONE PLAY DARTS	Magnet	12	3 Jun 78	18
AMAZING DARTS	Magnet	8	18 Nov 78	13
DART ATTACK	Magnet	38	6 Oct 79	4

DAS EFX
US

SINGLES:	**HITS 2**			**WEEKS 5**
CHECK YO SELF	Fourth & Broadway	36	7 Aug 93	4
Above hit: ICE CUBE featuring DAS EFX.				
RAP SCHOLAR	East West America	42	25 Apr 98	1
Above hit: DAS EFX featuring REDMAN.				

N'Dea DAVENPORT
US

(See also Brand New Heavies.)

SINGLES:	**HITS 2**			**WEEKS 3**
TRUST ME	Cooltempo	34	11 Sep 93	2
Above hit: GURU featuring N'Dea DAVENPORT.				
BRING IT ON	V2	52	20 Jun 98	1

Anne-Marie DAVID
France

SINGLES:	**HITS 1**			**WEEKS 9**
WONDERFUL DREAM	Epic	13	28 Apr 73	9
Eurovision Song Contest winner for Luxembourg in 1973.				

F.R. DAVID
France

SINGLES:	**HITS 2**			**WEEKS 13**
WORDS	Carrere	2	2 Apr 83	12
MUSIC	Carrere	71	18 Jun 83	1
ALBUMS:	**HITS 1**			**WEEKS 6**
WORDS	Carrere	46	7 May 83	6

DAVID and JONATHAN
UK

SINGLES:	**HITS 2**			**WEEKS 22**
MICHELLE	Columbia	11	15 Jan 66	6
Originally recorded by the Beatles.				
LOVERS OF THE WORLD UNITE	Columbia	7	9 Jul 66	16

DAVID DEVANT AND HIS SPIRIT WIFE
UK

SINGLES:	**HITS 2**			**WEEKS 2**
GINGER	Kindness	54	5 Apr 97	1
THIS IS FOR REAL	Kindness	61	21 Jun 97	1
ALBUMS:	**HITS 1**			**WEEKS 1**
WORK, LOVELIFE, MISCELLANEOUS	Kindness	70	5 Jul 97	1

Jim DAVIDSON
UK

SINGLES:	**HITS 1**			**WEEKS 4**
WHITE CHRISTMAS / TOO RISKY	Scratch	52	27 Dec 80	4

Paul DAVIDSON
Jamaica

SINGLES:	**HITS 1**			**WEEKS 10**
MIDNIGHT RIDER	Tropical	10	27 Dec 75	10
Originally recorded by the Allman Brothers.				

Hutch DAVIE ORCHESTRA - See Linda SCOTT

Dave DAVIES
UK

SINGLES:	**HITS 2**			**WEEKS 17**
DEATH OF A CLOWN	Pye	3	22 Jul 67	10
SUZANAH'S STILL ALIVE	Pye	20	9 Dec 67	7

Ray DAVIES - See Ken THORNE and his Orchestra

Windsor DAVIES as B.S.M. WILLIAMS and Don ESTELLE as GUNNER SUGDEN (LOFTY) — UK

SINGLES:	HITS 2			WEEKS 16	
WHISPERING GRASS	EMI		1	17 May 75	12
Originally recorded by Inkspots.					
PAPER DOLL	EMI		41	25 Oct 75	4
Above hit: Don ESTELLE and Windsor DAVIES.					
ALBUMS:	HITS 1			WEEKS 8	
SING LOFTY	EMI		10	10 Jan 76	8
Above hit: Don ESTELLE and Windsor DAVIES.					

Andrew DAVIS – See BBC SYMPHONY ORCHESTRA, SINGERS and SYMPHONY CHORUS

Billie DAVIS — UK

SINGLES:	HITS 4			WEEKS 33	
WILL I WHAT	Parlophone		18	1 Sep 62	10
Above hit: Mike SARNE featuring Billie DAVIS with the Charles BLACKWELL ORCHESTRA.					
TELL HIM	Decca		10	9 Feb 63	12
HE'S THE ONE	Decca		40	1 Jun 63	3
I WANT YOU TO BE MY BABY	Decca		33	12 Oct 68	8

Billy DAVIS, JR. – See Marilyn McCOO and Billy DAVIS, JR.

Carl DAVIS and the ROYAL LIVERPOOL PHILHARMONIC ORCHESTRA and CHOIR — UK

ALBUMS:	HITS 1			WEEKS 4	
PAUL McCARTNEY'S LIVERPOOL ORATORIO	EMI Classics		36	19 Oct 91	4

Colin DAVIS – See BBC SYMPHONY ORCHESTRA, SINGERS and SYMPHONY CHORUS

Darlene DAVIS — US

SINGLES:	HITS 1			WEEKS 5	
I FOUND LOVE	Serious		55	7 Feb 87	5

John DAVIS and the MONSTER ORCHESTRA — US

SINGLES:	HITS 1			WEEKS 2	
AIN'T THAT ENOUGH FOR YOU	Miracle		70	10 Feb 79	2

Mac DAVIS — US

SINGLES:	HITS 2			WEEKS 22	
BABY DON'T GET HOOKED ON ME	CBS		29	4 Nov 72	6
IT'S HARD TO BE HUMBLE	Casablanca		27	15 Nov 80	16

Miles DAVIS — US

ALBUMS:	HITS 5			WEEKS 7	
BITCHES BREW	CBS		71	11 Jul 70	1
YOU'RE UNDER ARREST	CBS		88	15 Jun 85	1
TUTU	Warner Brothers		74	18 Oct 86	2
AMANDLA	Warner Brothers		49	3 Jun 89	2
THE VERY BEST OF MILES DAVIS	Columbia		64	5 Oct 96	1
Released to commemorate the 5th anniversary of his death.					

Richie DAVIS – See SHUT UP AND DANCE

Roy DAVIS JR. featuring Peven EVERETT — US

SINGLES:	HITS 1			WEEKS 4	
GABRIEL	XL Recordings		22	1 Nov 97	4

Ruth DAVIS – See Bo KIRKLAND and Ruth DAVIS

Sammy DAVIS JR. — US

SINGLES:	HITS 8			WEEKS 37	
SOMETHING'S GOTTA GIVE	Brunswick		19	30 Jul 55	2
SOMETHING'S GOTTA GIVE [RE]	Brunswick		11	20 Aug 55	5
LOVE ME OR LEAVE ME	Brunswick		8	10 Sep 55	6
Originally recorded by Ruth Etting. Above 2 entries were separate sides of the same release, each had its own chart run.					
THAT OLD BLACK MAGIC	Brunswick		16	1 Oct 55	1
Originally recorded by Glenn Miller.					
HEY THERE	Brunswick		19	8 Oct 55	1
From the film 'The Pajama Game'. Originally recorded by John Raitt (Bonnie Raitt's father).					
LOVE ME OR LEAVE ME [RE]	Brunswick		18	5 Nov 55	2
IN A PERSIAN MARKET	Brunswick		28	21 Apr 56	1
ALL OF YOU	Brunswick		28	29 Dec 56	1
Above 8: Sammy DAVIS.					

HAPPY TO MAKE YOUR ACQUAINTANCE	Brunswick	46	18 Jun 60	1
Above hit: Sammy DAVIS JR. and Carmen McRAE.				
WHAT KIND OF FOOL AM I / GONNA BUILD A MOUNTAIN	Reprise	26	24 Mar 62	8
ME AND MY SHADOW	Reprise	20	15 Dec 62	7
Above hit: Frank SINATRA and Sammy DAVIS Jnr.				
ME AND MY SHADOW [RE]	Reprise	47	9 Feb 63	2
EPS:	**HITS 2**		**WEEKS 3**	
STARRING SAMMY DAVIS, VOLUME 1	Brunswick	20	30 Jul 60	1
SAMMY DAVIS JR. IMPERSONATING	Reprise	18	31 Aug 63	2
ALBUMS:	**HITS 1**		**WEEKS 1**	
SAMMY DAVIS JR. AT THE COCONUT GROVE	Reprise	19	13 Apr 63	1

Skeeter DAVIS   US

SINGLES:	**HITS 1**		**WEEKS 13**	
THE END OF THE WORLD	RCA Victor	18	16 Mar 63	13

Spencer DAVIS GROUP   UK

SINGLES:	**HITS 10**		**WEEKS 71**	
I CAN'T STAND IT	Fontana	47	5 Nov 64	3
Original by the Soul Sisters.				
EVERY LITTLE BIT HURTS	Fontana	43	27 Feb 65	2
EVERY LITTLE BIT HURTS [RE]	Fontana	41	20 Mar 65	1
STRONG LOVE	Fontana	50	12 Jun 65	1
STRONG LOVE [RE]	Fontana	44	26 Jun 65	3
KEEP ON RUNNING	Fontana	1	4 Dec 65	14
SOMEBODY HELP ME	Fontana	1	26 Mar 66	10
Above 2 originally recorded by Jackie Edwards.				
WHEN I COME HOME	Fontana	12	3 Sep 66	9
GIMMIE SOME LOVING	Fontana	2	5 Nov 66	12
I'M A MAN	Fontana	9	28 Jan 67	7
TIME SELLER	Fontana	30	12 Aug 67	5
MR. SECOND CLASS	United Artists	35	13 Jan 68	4
EPS:	**HITS 2**		**WEEKS 34**	
YOU PUT THE HURT ON ME	Fontana	4	23 Oct 65	27
SITTIN' AND THINKIN'	Fontana	3	21 May 66	7
ALBUMS:	**HITS 3**		**WEEKS 47**	
THEIR FIRST LP	Fontana	6	8 Jan 66	9
THE SECOND ALBUM	Fontana	3	22 Jan 66	18
AUTUMN '66	Fontana	4	10 Sep 66	20

T.J. DAVIS - See FULL MONTY ALLSTARS featuring T.J. DAVIS

Zelma DAVIS - See C&C MUSIC FACTORY

DAVIS PINCKNEY PROJECT - See GO GO LORENZO and the DAVIS PINCKNEY PROJECT

DAWN   US

SINGLES:	**HITS 6**		**WEEKS 109**	
CANDIDA	Bell	9	16 Jan 71	11
KNOCK THREE TIMES	Bell	1	10 Apr 71	27
WHAT ARE YOU DOING SUNDAY	Bell	3	31 Jul 71	12
TIE A YELLOW RIBBON ROUND THE OLE OAK TREE	Bell	1	10 Mar 73	39
SAY, HAS ANYBODY SEEN MY SWEET GYPSY ROSE	Bell	12	4 Aug 73	15
TIE A YELLOW RIBBON ROUND THE OLE OAK TREE [RE]	Bell	41	5 Jan 74	1
WHO'S IN THE STRAWBERRY PATCH WITH SALLY	Bell	37	9 Mar 74	4
Above 4: DAWN featuring Tony ORLANDO.				
ALBUMS:	**HITS 1**		**WEEKS 2**	
GOLDEN RIBBONS	Bell	46	4 May 74	2

DAWN OF THE REPLICANTS   UK

SINGLES:	**HITS 2**		**WEEKS 2**	
CANDLEFIRE	East West	52	7 Feb 98	1
HOGWASH FARM (THE DIESEL HANDS E.P.) [EP]	East West	65	4 Apr 98	1
Lead track: Hogwash Farm (Re-Built).				
ALBUMS:	**HITS 1**		**WEEKS 1**	
ONE HEAD, TWO ARMS, TWO LEGS	East West	62	28 Feb 98	1

Julie DAWN - See Cyril STAPLETON and his Orchestra

Liz DAWN - See Joe LONGTHORNE

Dana DAWSON   US

SINGLES:	**HITS 4**		**WEEKS 14**	
3 IS FAMILY	EMI	9	15 Jul 95	8
GOT TO GIVE ME LOVE	EMI	27	28 Oct 95	2

SHOW ME	EMI	28	4 May 96	3
HOW I WANNA BE LOVED	EMI	42	20 Jul 96	1

Bobby DAY · US

SINGLES:		HITS 1		WEEKS 2
ROCKIN' ROBIN	London	29	8 Nov 58	2

Darren DAY · UK

SINGLES:		HITS 3		WEEKS 7
YOUNG GIRL	Bell	42	8 Oct 94	2
SUMMER HOLIDAY MEDLEY [M]	RCA	17	8 Jun 96	4

Backing vocals by Cliff Richard. From the musical 'Summer Holiday'.

HOW CAN I BE SURE?	EastCoast	71	9 May 98	1
ALBUMS:		**HITS 1**		**WEEKS 1**
DARREN DAY	EastCoast	62	18 Apr 98	1

Doris DAY · US

SINGLES:		HITS 14		WEEKS 146
SUGAR BUSH	Columbia	8	15 Nov 52	2

Above hit: Doris DAY and Frankie LAINE with Carl FISCHER'S ORCHESTRA and the Norman LUBOFF CHOIR.

MY LOVE AND DEVOTION	Columbia	10	22 Nov 52	2

Above hit: Doris DAY with Percy FAITH and his Orchestra.

SUGAR BUSH [RE]	Columbia	8	6 Dec 52	6
MA SAYS PA SAYS	Columbia	12	4 Apr 53	1
FULL TIME JOB	Columbia	11	18 Apr 53	1

Above 2 entries were separate sides of the same release, each had its own chart run.

LET'S WALK THAT-A-WAY	Philips	4	25 Jul 53	14

Above 3: Doris DAY and Johnnie RAY with Paul WESTON and his Orchestra.

SECRET LOVE	Philips	1	3 Apr 54	29
THE BLACK HILLS OF DAKOTA	Philips	7	28 Aug 54	8

Above 2 from the film 'Calamity Jane'.

IF I GIVE MY HEART TO YOU	Philips	4	2 Oct 54	11

Above hit: Doris DAY with the MELLOMEN.

READY, WILLING AND ABLE	Philips	7	9 Apr 55	9

From the film 'Young At Heart'.
Above hit: Doris DAY with Buddy COLE and his Orchestra.

LOVE ME OR LEAVE ME	Philips	20	10 Sep 55	1

Originally recorded by Ruth Etting.

I'LL NEVER STOP LOVING YOU	Philips	17	22 Oct 55	2
I'LL NEVER STOP LOVING YOU [RE]	Philips	19	26 Nov 55	1

Above hit: Doris DAY with Percy FAITH and his Orchestra.

WHATEVER WILL BE, WILL BE (QUE SERA, SERA)	Philips	1	30 Jun 56	22

From the film 'The Man Who Knew Too Much'.

A VERY PRECIOUS LOVE	Philips	16	14 Jun 58	11

From the film 'Marjorie Morningstar'.

EVERYBODY LOVES A LOVER	Philips	25	16 Aug 58	3
EVERYBODY LOVES A LOVER [RE]	Philips	27	27 Sep 58	1

Above 4: Doris DAY with Frank DE VOL and his Orchestra.

MOVE OVER DARLING	CBS	8	14 Mar 64	16

From the film of the same name.

MOVE OVER DARLING [RI]	CBS	45	18 Apr 87	6

Featured in the Pretty Polly tights TV commercial.

EPS:		**HITS 1**		**WEEKS 6**
PILLOW TALK	Philips	11	19 Mar 60	6
ALBUMS:		**HITS 5**		**WEEKS 36**
20 GOLDEN GREATS	Warwick	12	6 Jan 79	11
A PORTRAIT OF DORIS DAY	Stylus	32	11 Nov 89	9
GREATEST HITS	Telstar	14	6 Nov 93	12
THE LOVE ALBUM	Vision	64	10 Dec 94	3
THE MAGIC OF THE MOVIES	Columbia	63	20 Nov 99	1

Inaya DAY – See Harry 'Choo Choo' ROMERO presents Inaya DAY

Patti DAY · US

SINGLES:		HITS 1		WEEKS 1
RIGHT BEFORE MY EYES	Debut	69	9 Dec 89	1

DAY ONE · UK

SINGLES:		HITS 1		WEEKS 1
I'M DOIN' FINE	Melankolic	68	13 Nov 99	1

DAYEENE · Sweden

SINGLES:		HITS 1		WEEKS 1
AND IT HURTS	Pukka	63	17 Jul 99	1

Taylor DAYNE — US

SINGLES:	HITS 10			WEEKS 54
TELL IT TO MY HEART	Arista	3	23 Jan 88	13
PROVE YOUR LOVE	Arista	8	19 Mar 88	10
I'LL ALWAYS LOVE YOU	Arista	41	11 Jun 88	7
WITH EVERY BEAT OF MY HEART	Arista	53	18 Nov 89	2
I'LL BE YOUR SHELTER	Arista	43	14 Apr 90	5
LOVE WILL LEAD YOU BACK	Arista	69	4 Aug 90	1
CAN'T GET ENOUGH OF YOUR LOVE	Arista	14	3 Jul 93	8
I'LL WAIT	Arista	29	16 Apr 94	3
ORIGINAL SIN (THEME FROM THE SHADOW)	Arista	63	4 Feb 95	1
From the film 'The Shadow'.				
SAY A PRAYER	Arista	58	18 Nov 95	1
TELL IT TO MY HEART [RM]	Arista	23	13 Jan 96	3
Remixed by T-Empo.				
ALBUMS:	HITS 1			WEEKS 17
TELL IT TO MY HEART	Arista	24	5 Mar 88	17

DAYTON — US

SINGLES:	HITS 1			WEEKS 1
THE SOUND OF MUSIC	Capitol	75	10 Dec 83	1

DAZZ BAND — US

SINGLES:	HITS 1			WEEKS 12
LET IT ALL BLOW	Motown	12	3 Nov 84	12

D'BORA — US

SINGLES:	HITS 3			WEEKS 4
DREAM ABOUT YOU	Polydor	75	14 Sep 91	1
GOING ROUND	Vibe	40	1 Jul 95	2
GOOD LOVE REAL LOVE	MCA/Music Plant	58	30 Mar 96	1

Nino DE ANGELO — Germany

SINGLES:	HITS 1			WEEKS 5
GUARDIAN ANGEL	Carrere	57	21 Jul 84	5

DE BOS — Holland

SINGLES:	HITS 1			WEEKS 1
ON THE RUN	Jive	51	25 Oct 97	1

Chris DE BURGH — Ireland

SINGLES:	HITS 14			WEEKS 71
DON'T PAY THE FERRYMAN	A&M	48	23 Oct 82	5
HIGH ON EMOTION	A&M	44	12 May 84	5
THE LADY IN RED	A&M	1	12 Jul 86	14
FATAL HESITATION	A&M	44	20 Sep 86	4
A SPACEMAN CAME TRAVELLING / THE BALLROOM OF ROMANCE	A&M	40	13 Dec 86	5
THE LADY IN RED [RE]	A&M	74	21 Feb 87	1
THE SIMPLE TRUTH (A CHILD IS BORN)	A&M	69	12 Dec 87	2
THE SIMPLE TRUTH (A CHILD IS BORN) [RE]	A&M	55	2 Jan 88	1
MISSING YOU	A&M	3	29 Oct 88	12
TENDER HANDS	A&M	43	7 Jan 89	6
THIS WAITING HEART	A&M	59	14 Oct 89	3
THE SIMPLE TRUTH: CAMPAIGN FOR KURDISH REFUGEES [RI]	A&M	36	25 May 91	2
Charity record for the Red Cross campaign for the protection of war victims.				
SEPARATE TABLES	A&M	30	11 Apr 92	4
BLONDE HAIR, BLUE JEANS	A&M	51	21 May 94	1
THE SNOWS OF NEW YORK	A&M	60	9 Dec 95	1
SO BEAUTIFUL	A&M	29	27 Sep 97	4
WHEN I THINK OF YOU	A&M	59	18 Sep 99	1
ALBUMS:	HITS 15			WEEKS 276
BEST MOVES	A&M	65	12 Sep 81	4
THE GETAWAY	A&M	30	9 Oct 82	16
MAN ON THE LINE	A&M	11	19 May 84	24
THE VERY BEST OF CHRIS DE BURGH	Telstar	6	29 Dec 84	70
SPANISH TRAIN AND OTHER STORIES	A&M	78	24 Aug 85	3
INTO THE LIGHT	A&M	2	7 Jun 86	59
CRUSADER	A&M	72	4 Oct 86	1
FLYING COLOURS	A&M	1	15 Oct 88	30
FROM A SPARK TO A FLAME - THE VERY BEST OF CHRIS DE BURGH	A&M	4	4 Nov 89	29
HIGH ON EMOTION - LIVE FROM DUBLIN	A&M	15	22 Sep 90	6
POWER OF TEN	A&M	3	9 May 92	10
THIS WAY UP	A&M	5	28 May 94	6
BEAUTIFUL DREAMS	A&M	33	18 Nov 95	8

THE LOVE SONGS	A&M	8	11 Oct 97	7
QUIET REVOLUTION	A&M	23	2 Oct 99	3

DE CASTRO SISTERS with Skip MARTIN and his Orchestra — Cuba

SINGLES:	HITS 1			WEEKS 1
TEACH ME TONIGHT	London	20	12 Feb 55	1

Originally recorded by Janet Brace.

DE-CODE featuring Beverli SKEETE — UK

SINGLES:	HITS 1			WEEKS 1
WONDERWALL / SOME MIGHT SAY	Neoteric	69	18 May 96	1

Etienne DE CRECY — France

SINGLES:	HITS 1			WEEKS 1
PRIX CHOC	Different	60	28 Mar 98	1

DE FUNK featuring F45 — UK

SINGLES:	HITS 1			WEEKS 1
PLEASURE LOVE	INCredible	49	25 Sep 99	1

Features guitar sample from Earth, Wind And Fire's September.

Lennie DE ICE — UK

SINGLES:	HITS 1			WEEKS 1
WE ARE I.E.	Distinct'ive	61	17 Apr 99	1

DE LA SOUL — US

(See also Jungle Brothers.)

SINGLES:	HITS 12			WEEKS 57
ME MYSELF AND I	Big Life	22	8 Apr 89	8
SAY NO GO	Big Life	18	8 Jul 89	7
EYE KNOW	Big Life	14	21 Oct 89	7

Samples Otis Redding's (Sittin' On) The Dock Of The Bay.

THE MAGIC NUMBER / BUDDY	Big Life	7	23 Dec 89	8

Buddy no longer listed from 14 Jan 90, hit peaked at No. 8.
Above hit: DE LA SOUL / DE LA SOUL featuring the JUNGLE BROTHERS,
*   Monie LOVE, QUEEN LATIFAH and Q-TIP.*

MAMMA GAVE BIRTH TO THE SOUL CHILDREN	Gee Street	14	24 Mar 90	7

Above hit: QUEEN LATIFAH + DE LA SOUL.

RING RING RING (HA HA HEY)	Big Life	10	27 Apr 91	7
A ROLLER SKATING JAM NAMED "SATURDAYS"	Big Life	22	3 Aug 91	5
KEEPIN' THE FAITH	Big Life	50	23 Nov 91	2
BREAKADAWN	Big Life	39	18 Sep 93	3

Samples Michael Jackson's I Can't Help It.

FALLIN'	Epic	59	2 Apr 94	1

From the film 'Judgement Night'. Samples Tom Petty's Free Fallin'.
Above hit: TEENAGE FANCLUB and DE LA SOUL.

STAKES IS HIGH	Tommy Boy	55	29 Jun 96	1
4 MORE	Tommy Boy	52	8 Mar 97	1

Recreates Sharon Redd's Never Give You Up.
Above hit: DE LA SOUL featuring ZHANE.

ALBUMS:	HITS 4			WEEKS 72
3 FEET HIGH AND RISING	Big Life	27	25 Mar 89	12
3 FEET HIGH AND RISING [RE]	Big Life	13	15 Jul 89	44

Peak position reached on 27 Jan 90.

DE LA SOUL IS DEAD	Big Life	7	25 May 91	11
BUHLOONE MINDSTATE	Big Life	37	9 Oct 93	2
STAKES IS HIGH	Tommy Boy	42	13 Jul 96	1
3 FEET HIGH AND RISING [RI]	Tommy Boy	17	9 Oct 99	2

Donna DE LORY — US

SINGLES:	HITS 1			WEEKS 1
JUST A DREAM	MCA	71	24 Jul 93	1

Waldo DE LOS RIOS — Argentina

SINGLES:	HITS 1			WEEKS 16
MOZART SYMPHONY NO. 40 IN G MINOR K550 1ST MOVEMENT (ALLEGRO MOLTO)	A&M	5	10 Apr 71	16
ALBUMS:	HITS 1			WEEKS 26
SYMPHONIES FOR THE SEVENTIES	A&M	6	1 May 71	26

Vincent DE MOOR — Holland

SINGLES:	HITS 1			WEEKS 1
FLOWTATION	XL Recordings	54	16 Aug 97	1

Lynsey DE PAUL

UK

SINGLES:	HITS 7			WEEKS 54
SUGAR ME	MAM	5	19 Aug 72	11
GETTING A DRAG	MAM	18	2 Dec 72	8
WON'T SOMBODY DANCE WITH ME	MAM	14	27 Oct 73	7
OOH I DO	Warner Brothers	25	8 Jun 74	6
NO HONESTLY	Jet	7	2 Nov 74	11
From the ITV series of the same name.				
MY MAN AND ME	Jet	40	22 Mar 75	4
ROCK BOTTOM	Polydor	19	26 Mar 77	7
UK's Eurovision entry in 1977, it came 2nd.				
Above hit: Lynsey DE PAUL and Mike MORAN.				

Tullio DE PISCOPO

Italy

SINGLES:	HITS 1			WEEKS 4
STOP BAJON . . . PRIMAVERA	Greyhound	58	28 Feb 87	4

Manitas DE PLATA

Spain

ALBUMS:	HITS 1			WEEKS 1
FLAMENCO GUITAR	Philips	40	29 Jul 67	1

Rebecca DE RUVO

Sweden

SINGLES:	HITS 1			WEEKS 1
I CAUGHT YOU OUT	Arista	72	1 Oct 94	1

Teri DE SARIO

US

SINGLES:	HITS 1			WEEKS 5
AIN'T NOTHING GONNA KEEP ME FROM YOU	Casablanca	52	2 Sep 78	5

Stephanie DE SYKES

UK

SINGLES:	HITS 2			WEEKS 17
BORN WITH A SMILE ON MY FACE	Bradley's	2	20 Jul 74	10
Above hit: Stephanie DE SYKES (with RAIN).				
WE'LL FIND OUR DAY	Bradley's	17	19 Apr 75	7

DE VANTE – See VARIOUS ARTISTS (EPs) 'Dangerous Minds EP'

Tony DE VIT

UK

(See also Various Artists (EPs) 'Trade EP 2'.)

SINGLES:	HITS 4			WEEKS 9
BURNING UP	Icon	25	4 Mar 95	3
HOOKED	Labello Dance	28	12 Aug 95	2
Above hit: 99TH FLOOR ELEVATORS featuring Tony DE VIT.				
TO THE LIMIT	Xplode	44	9 Sep 95	2
I'LL BE THERE	Labello Dance	37	30 Mar 96	2
Vocals by Lorraine.				
Above hit: 99TH FLOOR ELEVATORS featuring Tony DE VIT.				

Frank DE VOL and his Orchestra – See Vic DAMONE; Doris DAY

DEACON BLUE

UK

SINGLES:	HITS 19			WEEKS 111
DIGNITY	CBS	31	23 Jan 88	8
WHEN WILL YOU MAKE MY TELEPHONE RING	CBS	34	9 Apr 88	7
Original release reached No. 86 in 1987.				
CHOCOLATE GIRL	CBS	43	16 Jul 88	7
REAL GONE KID	CBS	8	15 Oct 88	13
WAGES DAY	CBS	18	4 Mar 89	6
FERGUS SINGS THE BLUES	CBS	14	20 May 89	6
LOVE AND REGRET	CBS	28	16 Sep 89	5
QUEEN OF THE NEW YEAR	CBS	21	6 Jan 90	5
FOUR BACHARACH AND DAVID SONGS [EP]	CBS	2	25 Aug 90	9
Lead track: I'll Never Fall In Love Again.				
YOUR SWAYING ARMS	Columbia	23	25 May 91	4
TWIST AND SHOUT	Columbia	10	27 Jul 91	9
CLOSING TIME	Columbia	42	12 Oct 91	3
COVER FROM THE SKY	Columbia	31	14 Dec 91	4
YOUR TOWN	Columbia	14	28 Nov 92	8
WILL WE BE LOVERS	Columbia	31	13 Feb 93	4
ONLY TENDER LOVE	Columbia	22	24 Apr 93	4
HANG YOUR HEAD [EP]	Columbia	21	17 Jul 93	3
Lead track: Hang Your Head.				
I WAS RIGHT AND YOU WERE WRONG	Columbia	32	2 Apr 94	3

DIGNITY [RR]	Columbia	20	28 May 94	3
The original version first issued in 1987.				

ALBUMS:	**HITS 7**		**WEEKS 216**	
RAINTOWN	CBS	33	6 Jun 87	18
RAINTOWN [RE]	CBS	14	16 Jul 88	59
WHEN THE WORLD KNOWS YOUR NAME	CBS	1	15 Apr 89	54
OOH LAS VEGAS	CBS	3	22 Sep 90	8
FELLOW HOODLUMS	Columbia	2	15 Jun 91	27
WHATEVER YOU SAY, SAY NOTHING	Columbia	4	13 Mar 93	10
OUR TOWN – THE GREATEST HITS OF DEACON BLUE	Columbia	1	16 Apr 94	38
WALKING BACK HOME	Columbia	39	23 Oct 99	2

DEAD CAN DANCE
Australia

ALBUMS:	**HITS 2**		**WEEKS 3**	
INTO THE LABYRINTH	4AD	47	25 Sep 93	1
SPIRITCHASER	4AD	43	29 Jun 96	2

DEAD DRED
UK

SINGLES:	**HITS 1**		**WEEKS 2**	
DRED BASS	Moving Shadow	60	5 Nov 94	2

DEAD END KIDS
UK

SINGLES:	**HITS 1**		**WEEKS 10**	
HAVE I THE RIGHT	CBS	6	26 Mar 77	10

DEAD KENNEDYS
US

SINGLES:	**HITS 2**		**WEEKS 9**	
KILL THE POOR	Cherry Red	49	1 Nov 80	3
TOO DRUNK TO FUCK	Cherry Red	36	30 May 81	6

ALBUMS:	**HITS 2**		**WEEKS 8**	
FRESH FRUIT FOR ROTTING VEGETABLES	Cherry Red	33	13 Sep 80	6
GIVE ME CONVENIENCE	Alternative Tentacles	84	4 Jul 87	2

DEAD OR ALIVE
UK

SINGLES:	**HITS 10**		**WEEKS 70**	
THAT'S THE WAY (I LIKE IT)	Epic	22	24 Mar 84	9
YOU SPIN ME ROUND (LIKE A RECORD)	Epic	1	1 Dec 84	23
LOVER COME BACK TO ME	Epic	11	20 Apr 85	8
IN TOO DEEP	Epic	14	29 Jun 85	8
MY HEART GOES BANG (GET ME TO THE DOCTOR)	Epic	23	21 Sep 85	6
BRAND NEW LOVER	Epic	31	20 Sep 86	4
SOMETHING IN MY HOUSE	Epic	12	10 Jan 87	7
HOOKED ON LOVE	Epic	69	4 Apr 87	1
TURN AROUND AND COUNT 2 TEN	Epic	70	3 Sep 88	1
COME HOME WITH ME BABY	Epic	62	22 Jul 89	2

ALBUMS:	**HITS 3**		**WEEKS 22**	
SOPHISTICATED BOOM BOOM	Epic	29	28 Apr 84	3
YOUTHQUAKE	Epic	9	25 May 85	15
MAD, BAD AND DANGEROUS TO KNOW	Epic	27	14 Feb 87	4

DEADLY SINS
UK/Italy

SINGLES:	**HITS 1**		**WEEKS 2**	
WE ARE GOING ON DOWN	Ffrreedom	45	30 Apr 94	2

Hazell DEAN
UK

SINGLES:	**HITS 11**		**WEEKS 71**	
EVERGREEN / JEALOUS LOVE	Proto	63	18 Feb 84	3
SEARCHIN'	Proto	6	21 Apr 84	15
Original release reached No. 76 in 1983.				
WHATEVER I DO (WHEREVER I GO)	Proto	4	28 Jul 84	11
BACK IN MY ARMS (ONCE AGAIN)	Proto	41	3 Nov 84	4
NO FOOL (FOR LOVE)	Proto	41	2 Mar 85	5
THEY SAY IT'S GONNA RAIN	Parlophone	58	12 Oct 85	4
WHO'S LEAVING WHO	EMI	4	2 Apr 88	11
Originally recorded by Anne Murray.				
MAYBE (WE SHOULD CALL IT A DAY)	EMI	15	25 Jun 88	6
TURN IT INTO LOVE	EMI	21	24 Sep 88	7
LOVE PAINS	Lisson	48	26 Aug 89	4
BETTER OFF WITHOUT YOU	Lisson	72	23 Mar 91	1

ALBUMS:	**HITS 1**		**WEEKS 3**	
ALWAYS	EMI	38	22 Oct 88	3

Jimmy DEAN | | | | US

SINGLES:		HITS 2		WEEKS 17
BIG BAD JOHN	Philips	2	28 Oct 61	13
LITTLE BLACK BOOK	CBS	33	10 Nov 62	4

Letitia DEAN and Paul MEDFORD | | | | UK

SINGLES:		HITS 1		WEEKS 7
SOMETHING OUTA NOTHING	BBC	12	25 Oct 86	7

Syd DEAN and his Band - See STARGAZERS

DEAR JON | | | | UK

SINGLES:		HITS 1		WEEKS 1
ONE GIFT OF LOVE	MDMC	68	22 Apr 95	1

Beaten into second place by Gina G in the contest to represent the UK at Eurovision.

DEATH IN VEGAS | | | | UK

SINGLES:		HITS 2		WEEKS 2
DIRT	Concrete	61	2 Aug 97	1
Original release reached No. 88 in 1996.				
ROCCO	Concrete	51	1 Nov 97	1
ALBUMS:		**HITS 2**		**WEEKS 4**
DEAD ELVIS	Concrete	52	29 Mar 97	1
THE CONTINO SESSIONS	Concrete	19	25 Sep 99	3

Named after the band's studio.

DEBARGE | | | | US

SINGLES:		HITS 2		WEEKS 17
RHYTHM OF THE NIGHT	Gordy	4	6 Apr 85	14
From the film 'The Last Dragon'.				
YOU WEAR IT WELL	Gordy	54	21 Sep 85	3
Above hit: El DEBARGE with DEBARGE.				
ALBUMS:		**HITS 1**		**WEEKS 2**
RHYTHM OF THE NIGHT	Gordy	94	25 May 85	2

Chico DEBARGE | | | | US

SINGLES:		HITS 1		WEEKS 1
IGGIN' ME	Universal	50	14 Mar 98	1

El DEBARGE | | | | US

(See also DeBarge; Quincy Jones.)

SINGLES:		HITS 1		WEEKS 2
WHO'S JOHNNY ("SHORT CIRCUIT" THEME)	Gordy	60	28 Jun 86	2

From the film 'Short Circuit'.

Diana DECKER | | | | US

SINGLES:		HITS 1		WEEKS 10
POPPA PICCOLINO	Columbia	2	24 Oct 53	8
POPPA PICCOLINO [RE]	Columbia	5	9 Jan 54	2

Dave DEE | | | | UK

(See also Dave Dee, Dozy, Beaky, Mick and Tich.)

SINGLES:		HITS 1		WEEKS 4
MY WOMAN'S MAN	Fontana	42	14 Mar 70	4

Dave DEE, DOZY, BEAKY, MICK and TICH | | | | UK

(See also D. B. M. and T.; Dave Dee.)

SINGLES:		HITS 13		WEEKS 141
YOU MAKE IT MOVE	Fontana	26	25 Dec 65	8
HOLD TIGHT!	Fontana	4	5 Mar 66	17
HIDEAWAY	Fontana	10	11 Jun 66	11
BEND IT!	Fontana	2	17 Sep 66	12
SAVE ME	Fontana	4	10 Dec 66	10
TOUCH ME, TOUCH ME	Fontana	13	11 Mar 67	9
OKAY!	Fontana	4	20 May 67	11
ZABADAK!	Fontana	3	14 Oct 67	14
THE LEGEND OF XANADU	Fontana	1	17 Feb 68	12
LAST NIGHT IN SOHO	Fontana	8	6 Jul 68	11
THE WRECK OF THE 'ANTOINETTE'	Fontana	14	5 Oct 68	9
DON JUAN	Fontana	23	8 Mar 69	9
SNAKE IN THE GRASS	Fontana	23	17 May 69	8

EPS:	HITS 1		WEEKS 3	
LOOS OF ENGLAND	Fontana	8	4 Mar 67	3
ALBUMS:	HITS 2		WEEKS 15	
DAVE DEE, DOZY, BEAKY, MICK AND TICH	Fontana	11	2 Jul 66	10
IF MUSIC BE THE FOOD OF LOVE . . . PREPARE FOR INDIGESTION	Fontana	27	7 Jan 67	5

Jazzy DEE
US

SINGLES:	HITS 1		WEEKS 5	
GET ON UP	Laurie	53	5 Mar 83	5

Joey DEE and the STARLITERS
US

SINGLES:	HITS 1		WEEKS 8	
PEPPERMINT TWIST	Columbia	33	10 Feb 62	8

Kiki DEE
UK

SINGLES:	HITS 10		WEEKS 79	
AMOUREUSE	Rocket	13	10 Nov 73	13
Originally recorded by Veronique Sanson.				
I GOT THE MUSIC IN ME	Rocket	19	7 Sep 74	8
Originally recorded by Sabrina Lory.				
(YOU DON'T KNOW) HOW GLAD I AM	Rocket	33	12 Apr 75	4
Originally recorded by Nancy Wilson. Some labels only show title as How Glad I Am.				
Above 2: Kiki DEE BAND.				
DON'T GO BREAKING MY HEART	Rocket	1	3 Jul 76	14
Above hit: Elton JOHN and Kiki DEE.				
LOVING AND FREE / AMOUREUSE [RI]	Rocket	13	11 Sep 76	8
Amoureuse listed from 11 Sep 76 for 2 weeks and 9 Oct 76 for 4 weeks.				
FIRST THING IN THE MORNING	Rocket	32	19 Feb 77	5
CHICAGO	Rocket	28	11 Jun 77	4
[AA] listed with Bite Your Lip (Get Up and Dance) by Elton John.				
STAR	Ariola	13	21 Feb 81	10
PERFECT TIMING	Ariola	66	23 May 81	3
TRUE LOVE	Rocket	2	20 Nov 93	10
Above hit: Elton JOHN – duet with Kiki DEE.				
ALBUMS:	HITS 3		WEEKS 11	
KIKI DEE	Rocket	24	26 Mar 77	5
PERFECT TIMING	Ariola	47	18 Jul 81	4
THE VERY BEST OF KIKI DEE	Rocket	62	9 Apr 94	2

Nancy DEE – See BENELUX and Nancy DEE

DEE – TAH
Chile

SINGLES:	HITS 2		WEEKS 10	
RELAX	ffrr	11	26 Sep 98	8
Samples Dire Straits' Why Worry.				
EL PARAISCO RICO	ffrr	39	1 May 99	2
Based around Madonna's La Isla Bonita.				

DEEE-LITE
US/Russia/Japan

SINGLES:	HITS 6		WEEKS 30	
GROOVE IS IN THE HEART / WHAT IS LOVE?	Elektra	2	18 Aug 90	13
Bootsy Collins on backing vocals on Groove Is In The Heart. What Is Love? listed from 25 Aug 90.				
POWER OF LOVE / DEEE-LITE THEME	Elektra	25	24 Nov 90	7
HOW DO YOU SAY . . . LOVE / GROOVE IS IN THE HEART (BOOTSIFIED TO THE NTH MIX) [RM]	Elektra	52	23 Feb 91	2
GOOD BEAT / RIDING ON THROUGH	Elektra	53	27 Apr 91	3
RUNAWAY	Elektra	45	13 Jun 92	3
PICNIC IN THE SUMMERTIME	Elektra	43	30 Jul 94	2
ALBUMS:	HITS 2		WEEKS 19	
WORLD CLIQUE	Elektra	14	8 Sep 90	18
INFINITY WITHIN	Elektra	37	4 Jul 92	1

DEEJAY PUNK-ROC
US

SINGLES:	HITS 4		WEEKS 5	
DEAD HUSBAND	Independiente	71	21 Mar 98	1
MY BEATBOX	Independiente	43	9 May 98	1
FAR OUT	Independiente	43	8 Aug 98	2
ROC-IN-IT	Independiente	59	20 Feb 99	1
Above hit: DEEJAY PUNK-ROC vs ONYX.				
ALBUMS:	HITS 1		WEEKS 1	
CHICKENEYE	Independiente	47	30 May 98	1

DEEJAY SVEN – See M.C. MIKER 'G' and DEEJAY SVEN

Carol DEENE | | | | UK

SINGLES:	HITS 4			WEEKS 25
SAD MOVIES	His Master's Voice	44	28 Oct 61	3
NORMAN	His Master's Voice	24	27 Jan 62	8
Above two originally recorded by John D.Loudermilk.				
JOHNNY GET ANGRY	His Master's Voice	32	7 Jul 62	4
Above hit: Carol DEENE with the Michael SAMMES SINGERS.				
SOME PEOPLE	His Master's Voice	25	25 Aug 62	10
From the film of the same name.				

Scotti DEEP | | | | US

SINGLES:	HITS 1			WEEKS 1
BROOKLYN BEATS	Extravaganza	67	15 Mar 97	1

DEEP BLUE | | | | UK

SINGLES:	HITS 1			WEEKS 2
THE HELICOPTER TUNE	Moving Shadow	68	16 Apr 94	2

DEEP BLUE SOMETHING | | | | US

SINGLES:	HITS 2			WEEKS 17
BREAKFAST AT TIFFANY'S	Interscope	55	6 Jul 96	2
BREAKFAST AT TIFFANY'S [RE]	Interscope	1	21 Sep 96	12
JOSEY	Interscope	27	7 Dec 96	3
ALBUMS:	HITS 1			WEEKS 5
HOME	Interscope	24	5 Oct 96	5

DEEP C | | | | UK

SINGLES:	HITS 2			WEEKS 3
AFRICAN REIGN	M&G	75	19 Jan 91	1
CHILL TO THE PANIC	M&G	73	8 Jun 91	2
Above hit: DEEP C featuring DEZZ the DEZZ and SHOLA.				

DEEP CREED 94 | | | | US

(See also Armand Van Helden.)

SINGLES:	HITS 1			WEEKS 1
CAN U FEEL IT	Eastern Bloc	59	7 May 94	1

DEEP DISH | | | | US

SINGLES:	HITS 2			WEEKS 4
STAY GOLD	Deconstruction	41	26 Oct 96	1
STRANDED	Deconstruction	60	1 Nov 97	1
THE FUTURE OF THE FUTURE (STAY GOLD) [RM]	Deconstruction	31	3 Oct 98	2
Remixed by Ben Watt / David Morales and includes vocals by Tracy Thorn.				
Above hit: DEEP DISH with EVERYTHING BUT THE GIRL.				
ALBUMS:	HITS 1			WEEKS 2
JUNK SCIENCE	Deconstruction	37	18 Jul 98	2

DEEP FEELING | | | | UK

SINGLES:	HITS 1			WEEKS 5
DO YOU LOVE ME	Page One	45	25 Apr 70	1
DO YOU LOVE ME [RE]	Page One	34	9 May 70	4

DEEP FOREST | | | | France

SINGLES:	HITS 4			WEEKS 14
SWEET LULLABY	Columbia	10	5 Feb 94	6
DEEP FOREST	Columbia	20	21 May 94	4
SAVANNA DANCE	Columbia	28	23 Jul 94	2
MARTA'S SONG	Columbia	26	24 Jun 95	2
Vocals by Marta Sebestyen. From the film 'Pret-A-Porter'.				
ALBUMS:	HITS 3			WEEKS 17
DEEP FOREST	Columbia	15	26 Feb 94	11
BOHEME	Columbia	12	3 Jun 95	5
COMPARSA	Columbia	60	31 Jan 98	1

DEEP PURPLE | | | | UK

SINGLES:	HITS 13			WEEKS 85
BLACK NIGHT	Harvest	2	15 Aug 70	21
STRANGE KIND OF WOMAN	Harvest	8	27 Feb 71	12
FIREBALL	Harvest	15	13 Nov 71	13
NEVER BEFORE	Purple	35	1 Apr 72	6
SMOKE ON THE WATER	Purple	21	16 Apr 77	7

NEW LIVE AND RARE [EP] Lead track: Black Night (Live Version).	Purple	31	15 Oct 77	4
NEW LIVE AND RARE VOL. II [EP] Lead track: Burn (Edited Version).	Purple	45	7 Oct 78	3
BLACK NIGHT [RI]	Harvest	43	2 Aug 80	6
NEW LIVE AND RARE VOLUME 3 [EP] Lead track: Smoke On The Water.	Harvest	48	1 Nov 80	3
PERFECT STRANGERS	Polydor	48	26 Jan 85	3
KNOCKING AT YOUR BACK DOOR / PERFECT STRANGERS [RI]	Polydor	68	15 Jun 85	1
HUSH	Polydor	62	18 Jun 88	2
KING OF DREAMS	RCA	70	20 Oct 90	1
LOVE CONQUERS ALL	RCA	57	2 Mar 91	2
BLACK NIGHT [RM] Released to coincide with 25th anniversary of the Deep Purple In Rock album. Remixed by Roger Glover.	EMI	66	24 Jun 95	1

ALBUMS:	HITS 23		WEEKS 278	
CONCERTO FOR GROUP AND ORCHESTRA Live recordings from the Royal Albert Hall on 15 Sep 70 with the Royal Philharmonic Orchestra conducted by Malcolm Arnold.	Harvest	26	24 Jan 70	4
DEEP PURPLE IN ROCK	Harvest	4	20 Jun 70	68
FIREBALL	Harvest	1	18 Sep 71	25
MACHINE HEAD	Purple	1	15 Apr 72	24
MADE IN JAPAN Live recordings from Tokyo and Osako on 16 & 17 Aug 72.	Purple	16	6 Jan 73	14
WHO DO WE THINK WE ARE	Purple	4	17 Feb 73	11
BURN	Purple	3	2 Mar 74	21
STORM BRINGER	Purple	6	23 Nov 74	12
24 CARAT PURPLE	Purple	14	5 Jul 75	17
COME TASTE THE BAND	Purple	19	22 Nov 75	4
DEEP PURPLE LIVE Live recordings from their 1975 European tour.	Purple	12	27 Nov 76	6
THE MARK II PURPLE SINGLES	Purple	24	21 Apr 79	6
DEEPEST PURPLE	Harvest	1	19 Jul 80	15
IN CONCERT Live recordings from 1970–72.	Harvest	30	13 Dec 80	8
DEEP PURPLE LIVE IN LONDON Recorded in 1974 for the BBC.	Harvest	23	4 Sep 82	5
PERFECT STRANGERS	Polydor	5	10 Nov 84	15
THE ANTHOLOGY	Harvest	50	29 Jun 85	3
THE HOUSE OF BLUE LIGHT	Polydor	10	24 Jan 87	9
NOBODY'S PERFECT	Polydor	38	16 Jul 88	2
SLAVES AND MASTERS	RCA	45	3 Nov 90	2
THE BATTLE RAGES ON …	RCA	21	7 Aug 93	3
PURPENDICULAR	RCA	58	17 Feb 96	1
MADE IN JAPAN [RI] Re-issued with bonus CD of 3 encores.	EMI	73	31 Jan 98	1
30: VERY BEST OF DEEP PURPLE	EMI	39	24 Oct 98	2

DEEP RIVER BOYS with Sid PHILLIPS and his Orchestra   US

SINGLES:	HITS 1		WEEKS 1	
THAT'S RIGHT	His Master's Voice	29	8 Dec 56	1

Rick DEES and his CAST OF IDIOTS   US

SINGLES:	HITS 1		WEEKS 9	
DISCO DUCK Features duck noises by Ken Pruitt.	RSO	6	18 Sep 76	9

DEF LEPPARD   UK

SINGLES:	HITS 24		WEEKS 112	
WASTED	Vertigo	61	17 Nov 79	3
HELLO AMERICA	Vertigo	45	23 Feb 80	4
PHOTOGRAPH	Vertigo	66	5 Feb 83	3
ROCK OF AGES	Vertigo	41	27 Aug 83	4
ANIMAL	Bludgeon Riffola	6	1 Aug 87	9
POUR SOME SUGAR ON ME	Bludgeon Riffola	18	19 Sep 87	6
HYSTERIA	Bludgeon Riffola	26	28 Nov 87	5
HYSTERIA [RE]	Bludgeon Riffola	74	9 Jan 88	1
ARMAGEDDON IT (THE ATOMIC MIX)	Bludgeon Riffola	20	9 Apr 88	5
LOVE BITES	Bludgeon Riffola	11	16 Jul 88	8
ROCKET	Bludgeon Riffola	15	11 Feb 89	7
LET'S GET ROCKED	Bludgeon Riffola	2	28 Mar 92	7
MAKE LOVE LIKE A MAN	Bludgeon Riffola	12	27 Jun 92	5
HAVE YOU EVER NEEDED SOMEONE SO BAD	Bludgeon Riffola	16	12 Sep 92	5
HEAVEN IS	Bludgeon Riffola	13	30 Jan 93	5
TONIGHT	Bludgeon Riffola	34	1 May 93	3
TWO STEPS BEHIND From the film 'Last Action Hero'.	Bludgeon Riffola	32	18 Sep 93	4

ACTION	Bludgeon Riffola	14	15 Jan 94	5
WHEN LOVE & HATE COLLIDE	Bludgeon Riffola	2	14 Oct 95	10
SLANG	Bludgeon Riffola	17	4 May 96	5
WORK IT OUT	Bludgeon Riffola	22	13 Jul 96	3
ALL I WANT IS EVERYTHING	Bludgeon Riffola	38	28 Sep 96	2
BREATHE A SIGH	Bludgeon Riffola	43	30 Nov 96	1
PROMISES	Bludgeon Riffola	41	24 Jul 99	1
GOODBYE	Bludgeon Riffola	54	9 Oct 99	1
ALBUMS:	**HITS 9**		**WEEKS 187**	
ON THROUGH THE NIGHT	Vertigo	15	22 Mar 80	8
HIGH 'N' DRY	Vertigo	26	25 Jul 81	8
PYROMANIA	Vertigo	18	12 Mar 83	8
HYSTERIA	Bludgeon Riffola	1	29 Aug 87	101
ADRENALIZE	Bludgeon Riffola	1	11 Apr 92	30
RETRO ACTIVE	Bludgeon Riffola	6	16 Oct 93	5
VAULT – THE GREATEST HITS 1980-1995	Bludgeon Riffola	3	4 Nov 95	14
SLANG	Bludgeon Riffola	5	25 May 96	8
EUPHORIA	Bludgeon Riffola	11	26 Jun 99	5

DEFINITION OF SOUND
UK

SINGLES:	**HITS 9**		**WEEKS 26**	
WEAR YOUR LOVE LIKE HEAVEN	Circa	17	9 Mar 91	9
NOW IS TOMORROW	Circa	46	1 Jun 91	4
Above hit: DEFINITION OF SOUND (vocals by Elaine VASSELL).				
MOIRA JANE'S CAFE	Circa	34	8 Feb 92	4
WHAT ARE YOU UNDER	Circa	68	19 Sep 92	1
CAN I GET OVER	Circa	61	14 Nov 92	2
BOOM BOOM	Fontana	59	20 May 95	1
Track based around a piano sample of the Moody Blues' Go Now.				
PASS THE VIBES	Fontana	23	2 Dec 95	3
CHILD	Fontana	48	24 Feb 96	1
HERE WE GO	Freskanova	45	24 Jul 99	1
Above hit: FREESTYLERS featuring DEFINITION OF SOUND.				
ALBUMS:	**HITS 1**		**WEEKS 3**	
LOVE AND LIFE	Circa	38	29 Jun 91	3

DEFTONES
US

SINGLES:	**HITS 2**		**WEEKS 3**	
MY OWN SUMMER (SHOVE IT)	Maverick	29	21 Mar 98	2
BE QUITE AND DRIVE (FAR AWAY)	Maverick	50	11 Jul 98	1
ALBUMS:	**HITS 1**		**WEEKS 1**	
AROUND THE FUR	Maverick	56	8 Nov 97	1

DEGREES OF MOTION featuring BITI
US

SINGLES:	**HITS 3**		**WEEKS 21**	
DO YOU WANT IT RIGHT NOW	ffrr	31	25 Apr 92	5
Originally recorded by Taylor Dayne.				
SHINE ON	ffrr	43	18 Jul 92	3
Above hit: DEGREES OF MOTION featuring BITI with Kit WEST.				
SOUL FREEDOM – FREE YOUR SOUL	ffrr	64	7 Nov 92	1
SHINE ON [RM]	ffrr	8	19 Mar 94	8
DO YOU WANT IT RIGHT NOW [RM]	ffrr	26	25 Jun 94	4
Above 2 remixed by Richie Jones.				
Above hit: DEGREES OF MOTION.				

DEICIDE
US

ALBUMS:	**HITS 1**		**WEEKS 1**	
ONCE UPON THE CROSS	Roadrunner	66	13 May 95	1

DEJA
US

SINGLES:	**HITS 1**		**WEEKS 1**	
SERIOUS	10 Records	75	29 Aug 87	1

DEJA VU
UK

SINGLES:	**HITS 1**		**WEEKS 1**	
WHY? WHY? WHY?	Cowboy	57	5 Feb 94	1

Desmond DEKKER and the ACES
Jamaica

SINGLES:	**HITS 6**		**WEEKS 71**	
007 (SHANTY TOWN)	Pyramid	14	15 Jul 67	11
Some labels credit simply 007.				
ISRAELITES	Pyramid	1	22 Mar 69	14
First reggae song to top the UK chart.				
IT MIEK	Pyramid	7	28 Jun 69	11

ISRAELITES [RE]	Pyramid	45	5 Jul	69	1
PICKNEY GAL	Pyramid	42	10 Jan	70	3
YOU CAN GET IT IF YOU REALLY WANT	Trojan	2	22 Aug	70	15
ISRAELITES [RI]	Cactus	10	10 May	75	9
SING A LITTLE SONG	Cactus	16	30 Aug	75	7

Above 4: Desmond DEKKER.

ALBUMS:	**HITS 1**			**WEEKS 4**	
THIS IS DESMOND DEKKER	Trojan	27	5 Jul	69	4

Above hit: Desmond DEKKER.

DEL AMITRI
UK

SINGLES:	**HITS 16**			**WEEKS 69**	
KISS THIS THING GOODBYE	A&M	59	19 Aug	89	2
NOTHING EVER HAPPENS	A&M	11	13 Jan	90	9
KISS THIS THING GOODBYE [RI]	A&M	43	24 Mar	90	4
MOVE AWAY JIMMY BLUE	A&M	36	16 Jun	90	6
SPIT IN THE RAIN	A&M	21	3 Nov	90	6
ALWAYS THE LAST TO KNOW	A&M	13	9 May	92	7
BE MY DOWNFALL	A&M	30	11 Jul	92	4
JUST LIKE A MAN	A&M	25	12 Sep	92	4
WHEN YOU WERE YOUNG	A&M	20	23 Jan	93	3
HERE AND NOW	A&M	21	18 Feb	95	4
DRIVING WITH THE BRAKES ON	A&M	18	29 Apr	95	4
ROLL TO ME	A&M	22	8 Jul	95	4
TELL HER THIS	A&M	32	28 Oct	95	2
NOT WHERE IT'S AT	A&M	21	21 Jun	97	3
SOME OTHER SUCKER'S PARADE	A&M	46	6 Dec	97	1
DON'T COME HOME TOO SOON (OFFICIAL TEAM SCOTLAND SONG					
WORLD CUP '98)	A&M	15	13 Jun	98	4
CRY TO BE FOUND	Mercury	40	5 Sep	98	2

ALBUMS:	**HITS 5**			**WEEKS 105**	
WAKING HOURS	A&M	6	24 Feb	90	44
CHANGE EVERYTHING	A&M	2	13 Jun	92	20
TWISTED	A&M	3	11 Mar	95	25
SOME OTHER SUCKER'S PARADE	A&M	6	12 Jul	97	5
THE BEST OF DEL AMITRI - HATFUL OF RAIN	Mercury	5	19 Sep	98	11

Also released at same time was an album of B-sides, ineligible for the chart because of its low price.

DE'LACY
US

SINGLES:	**HITS 2**			**WEEKS 16**	
HIDEAWAY	Deconstruction	9	2 Sep	95	10
THAT LOOK	Deconstruction	19	31 Aug	96	4
HIDEAWAY 1998 [RM]	Deconstruction	21	14 Feb	98	2

Remixed by Nu Birth.

ALBUMS:	**HITS 1**			**WEEKS 1**	
HIDEAWAY	Slip'n'Slide	53	1 Jul	95	1

Doublepack 12" single featuring 4 mixes.

DELAGE
UK

SINGLES:	**HITS 1**			**WEEKS 2**	
ROCK THE BOAT	PWL/Polydor	63	15 Dec	90	2

DELAKOTA
UK

SINGLES:	**HITS 3**			**WEEKS 3**	
THE ROCK	Go.Beat	60	18 Jul	98	1
C'MON CINCINNATI	Go.Beat	55	19 Sep	98	1

Above hit: DELAKOTA featuring Rose SMITH.

555	Go.Beat	42	13 Feb	99	1

ALBUMS:	**HITS 1**			**WEEKS 1**	
ONE LOVE	Go.Beat	58	3 Oct	98	1

DELANEY and BONNIE and FRIENDS
US

SINGLES:	**HITS 1**			**WEEKS 9**	
COMIN' HOME	Atlantic	16	20 Dec	69	9

Above hit: DELANEY and BONNIE and FRIENDS featuring Eric CLAPTON.

ALBUMS:	**HITS 1**			**WEEKS 3**	
ON TOUR	Atlantic	39	6 Jun	70	3

DELEGATION
UK

SINGLES:	**HITS 2**			**WEEKS 7**	
WHERE IS THE LOVE (WE USED TO KNOW)	State	22	23 Apr	77	6
YOU'RE BEEN DOING ME WRONG	State	49	20 Aug	77	1

DELERIUM
Canada

SINGLES:	HITS 1			WEEKS 1
SILENCE	Nettwerk	73	12 Jun 99	1

Vocals by Sarah McLachlan.

DELFONICS
US

SINGLES:	HITS 3			WEEKS 23
DIDN'T I (BLOW YOUR MIND THIS TIME)	Bell	43	10 Apr 71	1
DIDN'T I (BLOW YOUR MIND THIS TIME) [RE]	Bell	22	24 Apr 71	8
LA-LA MEANS I LOVE YOU	Bell	19	10 Jul 71	10
READY OR NOT HERE I COME (CAN'T HIDE THE LOVE)	Bell	41	16 Oct 71	4

DELGADOS
UK

SINGLES:	HITS 1			WEEKS 1
PULL THE WIRES FROM THE WALL	Chemikal Underground	69	23 May 98	1
ALBUMS:	HITS 1			WEEKS 1
PELOTON	Chemikal Underground	56	20 Jun 98	1

DELIRIOUS?
UK

SINGLES:	HITS 4			WEEKS 11
WHITE RIBBON DAY	Furious?	41	1 Mar 97	2
DEEPER	Furious?	20	17 May 97	3
PROMISE	Furious?	20	26 Jul 97	2
DEEPER [RI]	Furious?	36	15 Nov 97	2
SEE THE STAR	Furious?	16	27 Mar 99	2
ALBUMS:	HITS 2			WEEKS 5
KING OF FOOLS	Furious?	13	28 Jun 97	3
MEZZAMORPHIS	Furious?	25	24 Apr 99	2

'DELIVERANCE' SOUNDTRACK
US

SINGLES:	HITS 1			WEEKS 7
DUELLING BANJOS	Warner Brothers	17	31 Mar 73	7

From the film 'Deliverance'. Originally recorded by Arthur 'Guitar Boogie' Smith in 1955 as the Feuding Banjos.

DELLS
US

SINGLES:	HITS 1			WEEKS 9
MEDLEY: (a) SING A RAINBOW (b) LOVE IS BLUE [M]	Chess	15	19 Jul 69	9

DELTA – See David MORALES

DELUXE
US

SINGLES:	HITS 1			WEEKS 1
JUST A LITTLE MORE	Unyque	74	18 Mar 89	1

DEM 2
UK

SINGLES:	HITS 1			WEEKS 2
DESTINY	Locked On	58	24 Oct 98	2

DEMOLITION MAN – See PRIZNA featuring the DEMOLITION MAN

DEMON
UK

ALBUMS:	HITS 2			WEEKS 5
THE UNEXPECTED GUEST	Carrere	47	14 Aug 82	3
THE PLAGUE	Clay	73	2 Jul 83	2

D'EMPRESS – See 187 LOCKDOWN

Chaka DEMUS and PLIERS
Jamaica

SINGLES:	HITS 8			WEEKS 55
TEASE ME	Mango	3	12 Jun 93	15
SHE DON'T LET NOBODY	Mango	4	18 Sep 93	10

Originally recorded by Curtis Mayfield.

TWIST AND SHOUT	Mango	1	18 Dec 93	13

Above hit: Chaka DEMUS and PLIERS with JACK RADICS and TAXI GANG.

MURDER SHE WROTE	Mango	27	12 Mar 94	4
I WANNA BE YOUR MAN	Mango	19	18 Jun 94	6
GAL WINE	Mango	20	27 Aug 94	4

This was their first release as a duo in 1992.

TWIST AND SHOUT [RE]	Mango	67	1 Apr 95	1
EVERY KINDA PEOPLE	Island Jamaica	47	31 Aug 96	1
EVERY LITTLE THING SHE DOES IS MAGIC	Virgin	51	30 Aug 97	1

ALBUMS:		HITS 1			WEEKS 30	
TEASE ME		*Mango*	26	*10 Jul 93*		10
TEASE ME [RE]		*Mango*	1	*29 Jan 94*		20
Repackaged with additional track.						

Terry DENE with the Malcolm LOCKYER GROUP — UK

SINGLES:		HITS 3			WEEKS 20	
A WHITE SPORT'S COAT (AND A PINK CARNATION)		*Decca*	18	*8 Jun 57*		6
START MOVIN' (IN MY DIRECTION)		*Decca*	15	*20 Jul 57*		8
A WHITE SPORT'S COAT (AND A PINK CARNATION) [RE]		*Decca*	30	*27 Jul 57*		1
STAIRWAY OF LOVE		*Decca*	16	*17 May 58*		5

DENISE and JOHNNY — UK

SINGLES:		HITS 1			WEEKS 12	
ESPECIALLY FOR YOU		*RCA*	3	*26 Dec 98*		10
Backing vocals by Steps. Charity record in aid of BBC's Children In Need.						
ESPECIALLY FOR YOU [RE]		*RCA*	53	*10 Apr 99*		2

Cathy DENNIS — UK

SINGLES:		HITS 13			WEEKS 68	
C'MON AND GET MY LOVE		*ffrr*	15	*21 Oct 89*		10
Above hit: D MOB introducing Cathy DENNIS.						
THAT'S THE WAY OF THE WORLD		*ffrr*	48	*7 Apr 90*		3
Above hit: D MOB featuring Cathy DENNIS.						
TOUCH ME (ALL NIGHT LONG)		*Polydor*	5	*4 May 91*		10
JUST ANOTHER DREAM		*Polydor*	13	*20 Jul 91*		7
First release reached No. 93 in 1989 then No. 95 in 1990.						
TOO MANY WALLS		*Polydor*	17	*5 Oct 91*		7
EVERYBODY MOVE		*Polydor*	25	*7 Dec 91*		8
YOU LIED TO ME		*Polydor*	34	*29 Aug 92*		4
IRRESISTIBLE		*Polydor*	24	*21 Nov 92*		6
FALLING (THE PM DAWN VERSION)		*Polydor*	32	*6 Feb 93*		2
WHY		*ffrr*	23	*12 Feb 94*		3
Above hit: D-MOB with Cathy DENNIS.						
WEST END PAD		*Polydor*	25	*10 Aug 96*		2
WATERLOO SUNSET		*Polydor*	11	*1 Mar 97*		5
WHEN DREAMS TURN TO DUST		*Polydor*	43	*21 Jun 97*		1
ALBUMS:		HITS 2			WEEKS 35	
MOVE TO THIS		*Polydor*	3	*10 Aug 91*		31
INTO THE SKYLINE		*Polydor*	8	*23 Jan 93*		4

Jackie DENNIS — UK

SINGLES:		HITS 2			WEEKS 10	
LA DEE DAH		*Decca*	4	*15 Mar 58*		9
Originally recorded by Billie and Lillie.						
THE PURPLE PEOPLE EATER		*Decca*	29	*28 Jun 58*		1

Stefan DENNIS — Australia

SINGLES:		HITS 2			WEEKS 8	
DON'T IT MAKE YOU FEEL GOOD		*Sublime*	16	*6 May 89*		7
THIS LOVE AFFAIR		*Sublime*	67	*7 Oct 89*		1

DENNISONS — UK

SINGLES:		HITS 2			WEEKS 13	
(COME ON) BE MY GIRL		*Decca*	46	*17 Aug 63*		6
WALKING THE DOG		*Decca*	36	*9 May 64*		7

Sandy DENNY — UK

ALBUMS:		HITS 1			WEEKS 2	
THE NORTH STAR GRASSMAN AND THE RAVENS		*Island*	31	*2 Oct 71*		2

Richard DENTON and Martin COOK — UK

SINGLES:		HITS 1			WEEKS 7	
THEME FROM 'HONG KONG BEAT'		*BBC*	25	*15 Apr 78*		7
From the BBC1 TV series.						

John DENVER — US

(See also Placido Domingo and John Denver.)

SINGLES:		HITS 1			WEEKS 13	
ANNIE'S SONG		*RCA Victor*	1	*17 Aug 74*		13
ALBUMS:		HITS 16			WEEKS 228	
ROCKY MOUNTAIN HIGH		*RCA Victor*	11	*17 Mar 73*		15

POEMS, PRAYERS AND PROMISES	RCA Victor	19	2 Jun 73	5
RHYMES AND REASONS	RCA Victor	21	23 Jun 73	5
THE BEST OF JOHN DENVER	RCA Victor	7	30 Mar 74	69
BACK HOME AGAIN	RCA Victor	3	7 Sep 74	29
AN EVENING WITH JOHN DENVER	RCA Victor	31	22 Mar 75	4

Live recordings from the Universal City Amphitheater, California.

WIND SONG	RCA Victor	14	11 Oct 75	21
LIVE IN LONDON	RCA Victor	2	15 May 76	29

Live recordings from the London Palladium during the week of 29 Mar 76.

SPIRIT	RCA Victor	9	4 Sep 76	11
BEST OF JOHN DENVER VOLUME 2	RCA Victor	9	19 Mar 77	9
I WANT TO LIVE	RCA Victor	25	11 Feb 78	5
JOHN DENVER	RCA Victor	68	21 Apr 79	1
IT'S ABOUT TIME	RCA	90	22 Oct 83	2
JOHN DENVER - COLLECTION	Telstar	20	1 Dec 84	11
ONE WORLD	RCA	91	23 Aug 86	3
THE ROCKY MOUNTAIN COLLECTION	RCA	19	22 Mar 97	9

Karl DENVER — UK

SINGLES:	HITS 12		WEEKS 127	
MARCHETA	Decca	8	24 Jun 61	20
MEXICALI ROSE	Decca	8	21 Oct 61	11

Originally recorded by Bing Crosby.

WIMOWEH	Decca	4	27 Jan 62	17
NEVER GOODBYE	Decca	9	24 Feb 62	18
A LITTLE LOVE, A LITTLE KISS	Decca	19	9 Jun 62	10
BLUE WEEK-END	Decca	33	22 Sep 62	5
CAN YOU FORGIVE ME	Decca	32	23 Mar 63	8
INDIAN LOVE CALL	Decca	32	15 Jun 63	8
STILL	Decca	13	24 Aug 63	15
MY WORLD OF BLUE	Decca	29	7 Mar 64	6
LOVE ME WITH ALL YOUR HEART	Decca	37	6 Jun 64	6
LAZYITIS - ONE ARMED BOXER	Factory	46	9 Jun 90	3

Above hit: HAPPY MONDAYS and Karl DENVER.

EPS:	HITS 2		WEEKS 29	
BY A SLEEPY LAGOON	Decca	2	15 Sep 62	20
KARL DENVER HITS	Decca	7	24 Nov 62	9

ALBUMS:	HITS 1		WEEKS 27	
WIMOWEH	Ace Of Clubs	7	23 Dec 61	27

DEODATO arranged and conducted by Eumir DEODATO — US

SINGLES:	HITS 1		WEEKS 9	
ALSO SPRACH ZARATHUSTRA (2001)	CTI	7	5 May 73	9

DEPARTMENT S — UK

SINGLES:	HITS 2		WEEKS 13	
IS VIC THERE?	RCA	22	4 Apr 81	10

Chart incorrectly lists Demon label.

GOING LEFT RIGHT	Stiff	55	11 Jul 81	3

DEPECHE MODE — UK

SINGLES:	HITS 35		WEEKS 226	
DREAMING OF ME	Mute	57	4 Apr 81	4
NEW LIFE	Mute	11	13 Jun 81	15
JUST CAN'T GET ENOUGH	Mute	8	19 Sep 81	10
SEE YOU	Mute	6	13 Feb 82	10
THE MEANING OF LOVE	Mute	12	8 May 82	8
LEAVE IN SILENCE	Mute	18	28 Aug 82	10
GET THE BALANCE RIGHT!	Mute	13	12 Feb 83	8
EVERYTHING COUNTS	Mute	6	23 Jul 83	11
LOVE IN ITSELF . 2	Mute	21	1 Oct 83	7
PEOPLE ARE PEOPLE	Mute	4	24 Mar 84	10
MASTER AND SERVANT	Mute	9	1 Sep 84	9
SOMEBODY / BLASPHEMOUS RUMOURS	Mute	16	10 Nov 84	6

From 17 Nov 84 titles were listed in reverse. Somebody was not available on a second 7" format.

SHAKE THE DISEASE	Mute	18	11 May 85	9
IT'S CALLED A HEART	Mute	18	28 Sep 85	4
STRIPPED	Mute	15	22 Feb 86	5
A QUESTION OF LUST	Mute	28	26 Apr 86	5
A QUESTION OF TIME	Mute	17	23 Aug 86	6
STRANGELOVE	Mute	16	9 May 87	5
NEVER LET ME DOWN AGAIN	Mute	22	5 Sep 87	4
BEHIND THE WHEEL	Mute	21	9 Jan 88	5
LITTLE 15	Mute	60	28 May 88	2

Import.

EVERYTHING COUNTS [RR]	Mute	22	25 Feb 89	7
Live recording.				
PERSONAL JESUS	Mute	13	9 Sep 89	8
Above hit: DM				
ENJOY THE SILENCE	Mute	6	17 Feb 90	9
POLICY OF TRUTH	Mute	16	19 May 90	6
WORLD IN MY EYES	Mute	17	29 Sep 90	6
I FEEL YOU	Mute	8	27 Feb 93	7
WALKING IN MY SHOES	Mute	14	8 May 93	4
CONDEMNATION [EP]	Mute	9	25 Sep 93	4
Lead track: Condemnation.				
IN YOUR ROOM	Mute	8	22 Jan 94	4
BARREL OF A GUN	Mute	4	15 Feb 97	4
IT'S NO GOOD	Mute	5	12 Apr 97	5
HOME	Mute	23	28 Jun 97	4
USELESS	Mute	28	1 Nov 97	2
ONLY WHEN I LOSE MYSELF	Mute	17	19 Sep 98	3
ALBUMS:	**HITS 12**		**WEEKS 177**	
SPEAK AND SPELL	Mute	10	14 Nov 81	33
A BROKEN FRAME	Mute	8	9 Oct 82	11
CONSTRUCTION TIME AGAIN	Mute	6	3 Sep 83	12
SOME GREAT REWARD	Mute	5	6 Oct 84	12
THE SINGLES 81-85	Mute	6	26 Oct 85	22
BLACK CELEBRATION	Mute	4	29 Mar 86	11
MUSIC FOR THE MASSES	Mute	10	10 Oct 87	4
101	Mute	5	25 Mar 89	8
VIOLATOR	Mute	2	31 Mar 90	30
SONGS OF FAITH AND DEVOTION	Mute	1	3 Apr 93	16
ULTRA	Mute	1	26 Apr 97	11
THE SINGLES 86>98	Mute	5	10 Oct 98	6
THE SINGLES 81-85 [RE]	Mute	57	7 Nov 98	1
Re-released with a new catalogue number.				

DEPTH CHARGE
UK

SINGLES:	HITS 1		WEEKS 1	
LEGEND OF THE GOLDEN SNAKE	DC Recordings	75	29 Jul 95	1

DER DRITTE RAUM
Germany

SINGLES:	HITS 1		WEEKS 1	
HALE BOPP	Additive	75	4 Sep 99	1

Van DER TOORN - See PAPPA BEAR featuring Van DER TOORN

DEREK and the DOMINOS
UK

SINGLES:	HITS 1		WEEKS 21	
LAYLA	Polydor	7	12 Aug 72	11
LAYLA [RI]	RSO	4	6 Mar 82	10
ALBUMS:	**HITS 1**		**WEEKS 1**	
DEREK AND THE DOMINOS IN CONCERT	RSO	36	24 Mar 73	1

Kevin DESIMONE - See Barry MANILOW

DESIRELESS
France

SINGLES:	HITS 1		WEEKS 19	
VOYAGE VOYAGE	CBS	53	31 Oct 87	6
VOYAGE VOYAGE [RM]	CBS	5	14 May 88	13
Remixed by Pete Hammond and Peter Waterman.				

DESIYA featuring Melissa YIANNAKOU
UK

SINGLES:	HITS 1		WEEKS 1	
COMIN' ON STRONG	Black Market	74	1 Feb 92	1

DESKEE
UK

SINGLES:	HITS 2		WEEKS 3	
LET THERE BE HOUSE	Big One	52	3 Feb 90	2
DANCE, DANCE	Big One	74	8 Sep 90	1

DES'REE
UK

SINGLES:	HITS 10		WEEKS 72	
FEEL SO HIGH	Dusted Sound	51	31 Aug 91	5
FEEL SO HIGH [RI]	Dusted Sound	13	11 Jan 92	7
MIND ADVENTURES	Dusted Sound	43	21 Mar 92	3
WHY SHOULD I LOVE YOU?	Dusted Sound	44	27 Jun 92	3
DELICATE	Columbia	14	19 Jun 93	6
Above hit: Terence Trent D'ARBY featuring DES'REE.				

YOU GOTTA BE	Dusted Sound	20	9 Apr 94	7
I AIN'T MOVIN'	Dusted Sound	44	18 Jun 94	3
LITTLE CHILD	Dusted Sound	69	3 Sep 94	1
YOU GOTTA BE [RI]	Dusted Sound	14	11 Mar 95	8
LIFE	Dusted Sound	8	20 Jun 98	15
WHAT'S YOUR SIGN?	Dusted Sound	19	7 Nov 98	4
YOU GOTTA BE 1999 MIX [RM]	Dusted Sound	10	3 Apr 99	8

Featured in the Ford Focus TV commercial. Remixed by Brian Tench.

AIN'T NO SUNSHINE	Universal	42	16 Oct 99	2

Original by Bill Withers reached No. 3 in the US in 1971.
Above hit: LADYSMITH BLACK MAMBAZO featuring DES'REE.

ALBUMS:	HITS 3		WEEKS 27	
MIND ADVENTURES	Dusted Sound	26	29 Feb 92	5
I AIN'T MOVIN'	Dusted Sound	13	21 May 94	6
SUPERNATURAL	Dusted Sound	16	11 Jul 98	16

DESTINY'S CHILD
UK

SINGLES:	HITS 6		WEEKS 35	
NO NO NO	Columbia	5	28 Mar 98	8

Above hit: DESTINY'S CHILD (featuring Wyclef JEAN).

WITH ME	Columbia	19	11 Jul 98	3

Above hit: DESTINY'S CHILD (featuring JD).

SHE'S GONE	Columbia	24	7 Nov 98	3

Above hit: Matthew MARSDEN (featuring DESTINY'S CHILD).

GET ON THE BUS	East West	15	23 Jan 99	5

From the film 'Why Do Fools Fall In Love'.
Above hit: DESTINY'S CHILD (featuring TIMBALAND).

BILLS, BILLS, BILLS	Columbia	6	24 Jul 99	9
BUG A BOO	Columbia	9	30 Oct 99	7

ALBUMS:	HITS 2		WEEKS 25	
DESTINY'S CHILD	Columbia	45	14 Mar 98	3
THE WRITING'S ON THE WALL	Columbia	12	7 Aug 99	22

DESTROYERS - See George THOROGOOD and the DESTROYERS

DESTRY - See CIRCA featuring DESTRY; ZOO EXPERIENCE - featuring DESTRY

Marcella DETROIT
US

SINGLES:	HITS 3		WEEKS 16	
I BELIEVE	London	11	12 Mar 94	8
AIN'T NOTHING LIKE THE REAL THING	London	24	14 May 94	4

Above hit: Marcella DETROIT and Elton JOHN.

I'M NO ANGEL	London	33	16 Jul 94	4

ALBUMS:	HITS 1		WEEKS 5	
JEWEL	London	15	9 Apr 94	5

DETROIT EMERALDS
US

SINGLES:	HITS 4		WEEKS 44	
FEEL THE NEED IN ME	Janus	4	10 Feb 73	15
YOU WANT IT, YOU GOT IT	Westbound	12	5 May 73	9
I THINK OF YOU	Westbound	27	11 Aug 73	9
FEEL THE NEED [RR]	Atlantic	12	18 Jun 77	11

DETROIT SPINNERS
US

(See also Rappin-4-Tay.)

SINGLES:	HITS 10		WEEKS 89	
IT'S A SHAME	Tamla Motown	20	14 Nov 70	11

Above hit: MOTOWN SPINNERS.

COULD IT BE I'M FALLING IN LOVE	Atlantic	11	21 Apr 73	11
GHETTO CHILD	Atlantic	7	29 Sep 73	10
THEN CAME YOU	Atlantic	29	19 Oct 74	6

Above hit: Dionne WARWICKE and the DETROIT SPINNERS.

THE RUBBERBAND MAN	Atlantic	16	11 Sep 76	11
WAKE UP SUSAN	Atlantic	29	29 Jan 77	6
COULD IT BE I'M FALLING IN LOVE [EP]	Atlantic	32	7 May 77	3

Lead track: Could It Be I'm Falling In Love. (This is a re-issue.)

WORKING MY WAY BACK TO YOU	Atlantic	1	23 Feb 80	14

Although not credited on the label, it is also known and was listed on the chart as a medley with
  Forgive Me Girl.

BODY LANGUAGE	Atlantic	40	10 May 80	7
MEDLEY: a. CUPID; b. I'VE LOVED YOU FOR A LONG TIME [M]	Atlantic	4	28 Jun 80	10

ALBUMS:	HITS 1		WEEKS 3	
DETROIT SPINNERS' SMASH HITS	Atlantic	37	14 May 77	3

DEUCE

SINGLES:				UK
	HITS 4			**WEEKS 23**
CALL IT LOVE	London	11	21 Jan 95	10
I NEED YOU	London	10	22 Apr 95	5
Beaten into third place by Gina G and Dear Jon in the contest to represent the UK at Eurovision.				
ON THE BIBLE	London	13	19 Aug 95	6
NO SURRENDER	Love This	29	29 Jun 96	2
ALBUMS:	**HITS 1**			**WEEKS 2**
ON THE LOOSE!	London	18	9 Sep 95	2

dEUS

SINGLES:				Belgium
	HITS 6			**WEEKS 7**
HOTELLOUNGE (BE THE DEATH OF ME)	Island	55	11 Feb 95	1
THEME FROM TURNPIKE [EP]	Island	68	13 Jul 96	1
Lead track: Theme From Turnpike.				
LITTLE ARITHMETICS	Island	44	19 Oct 96	2
ROSES	Island	56	15 Mar 97	1
INSTANT STREET	Island	49	24 Apr 99	1
SISTER DEW	Island	62	3 Jul 99	1
ALBUMS:	**HITS 1**			**WEEKS 1**
THE IDEAL CRASH	Island	64	3 Apr 99	1

William DEVAUGHN

SINGLES:				US
	HITS 2			**WEEKS 10**
BE THANKFUL FOR WHAT YOU GOT	Chelsea	31	6 Jul 74	5
BE THANKFUL FOR WHAT YOU GOT [RR]	EMI	44	20 Sep 80	5

Sidney DEVINE

SINGLES:				UK
	HITS 1			**WEEKS 1**
SCOTLAND FOR EVER	Philips	48	1 Apr 78	1
ALBUMS:	**HITS 2**			**WEEKS 11**
DOUBLE DEVINE	Philips	14	10 Apr 76	10
DEVINE TIME	Philips	49	11 Dec 76	1

DEVO

SINGLES:				UK
	HITS 5			**WEEKS 23**
(I CAN'T GET ME NO) SATISFACTION	Stiff	41	22 Apr 78	8
JOCKO HOMO	Stiff	62	13 May 78	3
BE STIFF	Stiff	71	12 Aug 78	1
COME BACK JONEE	Virgin	60	2 Sep 78	4
WHIP IT	Virgin	51	22 Nov 80	7
ALBUMS:	**HITS 4**			**WEEKS 22**
Q: ARE WE NOT MEN? A: NO WE ARE DEVO	Virgin	12	16 Sep 78	7
DUTY NOW FOR THE FUTURE	Virgin	49	23 Jun 79	6
FREEDOM OF CHOICE	Virgin	47	24 May 80	5
NEW TRADITIONALISTS	Virgin	50	5 Sep 81	4

Howard DEVOTO

(See also Buzzcocks.)

ALBUMS:				UK
	HITS 1			**WEEKS 2**
JERKY VERSIONS OF THE DREAM	Virgin	57	6 Aug 83	2

DEXY'S MIDNIGHT RUNNERS

SINGLES:				UK
	HITS 11			**WEEKS 93**
DANCE STANCE	Oddball Productions	40	19 Jan 80	6
GENO	Late Night Feelings	1	22 Mar 80	14
THERE THERE MY DEAR	Late Night Feelings	7	12 Jul 80	9
PLAN B	Parlophone	58	21 Mar 81	2
SHOW ME	Mercury	16	11 Jul 81	9
Above hit: DEXYS MIDNIGHT RUNNERS.				
THE CELTIC SOUL BROTHERS	Mercury	45	20 Mar 82	4
COME ON EILEEN	Mercury	1	3 Jul 82	17
Above 2: DEXYS MIDNIGHT RUNNERS and the EMERALD EXPRESS.				
JACKIE WILSON SAID (I'M IN HEAVEN WHEN YOU SMILE)	Mercury	5	2 Oct 82	7
Originally recorded by Van Morrison.				
LET'S GET THIS STRAIGHT (FROM THE START) / OLD	Mercury	17	4 Dec 82	9
THE CELTIC SOUL BROTHERS (MORE, PLEASE, THANK YOU) [RR]	Mercury	20	2 Apr 83	6
Above 3: Kevin ROWLAND and DEXYS MIDNIGHT RUNNERS.				
BECAUSE OF YOU	Mercury	13	22 Nov 86	10
Theme from the BBC1 TV comedy series 'Brush Strokes'.				
Above hit: Kevin ROWLAND featuring DEXY'S MIDNIGHT RUNNERS.				

ALBUMS:		HITS 5		WEEKS 79
SEARCHING FOR THE YOUNG SOUL REBELS	Parlophone	6	26 Jul 80	10
TOO-RYE-AY	Mercury	2	7 Aug 82	46
Above hit: Kevin ROWLAND and DEXYS MIDNIGHT RUNNERS.				
GENO	EMI	79	26 Mar 83	2
Originally released in 1980.				
DON'T STAND ME DOWN	Mercury	22	21 Sep 85	6
THE VERY BEST OF DEXY'S MIDNIGHT RUNNERS	Mercury	12	8 Jun 91	15

DEZZ the DEZZ and SHOLA - See DEEP C

Tony DI BART   UK

SINGLES:		HITS 4		WEEKS 19
THE REAL THING	Cleveland City Blues	1	9 Apr 94	12
Original release reached No. 83 in 1993.				
DO IT	Cleveland City Blues	21	20 Aug 94	4
WHY DID YA	Cleveland City Blues	46	20 May 95	1
TURN YOUR LOVE AROUND	Cleveland City Blues	66	2 Mar 96	1
THE REAL THING [RM]	Cleveland City	51	17 Oct 98	1
Remixed by Mellonheads.				

Gregg DIAMOND BIONIC BOOGIE   US

SINGLES:		HITS 1		WEEKS 3
CREAM (ALWAYS RISES TO THE TOP)	Polydor	61	20 Jan 79	3

Jim DIAMOND   UK

SINGLES:		HITS 4		WEEKS 30
I SHOULD HAVE KNOWN BETTER	A&M	1	3 Nov 84	13
I SLEEP ALONE AT NIGHT	A&M	72	2 Feb 85	1
REMEMBER I LOVE YOU	A&M	42	18 May 85	5
HI HO SILVER	A&M	5	22 Feb 86	11
Theme from the ITV series 'Boon'.				

ALBUMS:		HITS 1		WEEKS 5
JIM DIAMOND	PolyGram TV	16	22 May 93	5

Neil DIAMOND   US

SINGLES:		HITS 13		WEEKS 121
CRACKLIN' ROSIE	Uni	3	7 Nov 70	17
SWEET CAROLINE	Uni	8	20 Feb 71	11
I AM . . . I SAID	Uni	4	8 May 71	12
SONG SUNG BLUE	Uni	14	13 May 72	13
IF YOU KNOW WHAT I MEAN	CBS	35	14 Aug 76	4
BEAUTIFUL NOISE	CBS	13	23 Oct 76	9
DESIREE	CBS	39	24 Dec 77	6
YOU DON'T BRING ME FLOWERS	CBS	5	25 Nov 78	12
Originally by Neil Diamond on his 1977 album I'm Glad You're Here With Me Tonight.				
Above hit: BARBRA and NEIL.				
FOREVER IN BLUE JEANS	CBS	16	3 Mar 79	12
LOVE ON THE ROCKS	Capitol	17	15 Nov 80	12
HELLO AGAIN	Capitol	51	14 Feb 81	4
Above 2 from the film 'The Jazz Singer'.				
HEARTLIGHT	CBS	47	20 Nov 82	7
MORNING HAS BROKEN	Columbia	36	21 Nov 92	2

ALBUMS:		HITS 33		WEEKS 571
TAP ROOT MANUSCRIPT	Uni	19	3 Apr 71	12
GOLD	Uni	23	3 Apr 71	11
STONES	Uni	18	11 Dec 71	14
MOODS	Uni	7	5 Aug 72	19
HOT AUGUST NIGHT	Uni	32	12 Jan 74	2
Live recordings from the Greek Theatre, Los Angeles, 24 Aug 72.				
JONATHAN LIVINGSTON SEAGULL [OST]	CBS	35	16 Feb 74	1
RAINBOW	MCA	39	9 Mar 74	5
HIS 12 GREATEST HITS	MCA	13	29 Jun 74	78
SERENADE	CBS	11	9 Nov 74	14
BEAUTIFUL NOISE	CBS	10	10 Jul 76	26
LOVE AT THE GREEK	CBS	3	12 Mar 77	32
Live recordings from the Greek Theatre, Los Angeles, Aug 76.				
HOT AUGUST NIGHT [RI]	MCA	60	6 Aug 77	1
I'M GLAD YOU'RE HERE WITH ME TONIGHT	CBS	16	17 Dec 77	12
20 GOLDEN GREATS	MCA	2	25 Nov 78	26
YOU DON'T BRING ME FLOWERS	CBS	15	6 Jan 79	23
SEPTEMBER MORN	CBS	14	19 Jan 80	11
THE JAZZ SINGER [OST]	Capitol	3	22 Nov 80	110
LOVE SONGS	MCA	43	28 Feb 81	6
THE WAY TO THE SKY	CBS	39	5 Dec 81	13
12 GREATEST HITS VOLUME 2	CBS	32	19 Jun 82	8

HEARTLIGHT	CBS	43	13 Nov 82	10
THE VERY BEST OF NEIL DIAMOND	K-Tel	33	10 Dec 83	11
PRIMITIVE	CBS	7	28 Jul 84	10
HEADED FOR THE FUTURE	CBS	36	24 May 86	8
HOT AUGUST NIGHT II	CBS	74	28 Nov 87	4
Live recordings from the Greek Theatre, Los Angeles.				
THE BEST YEARS OF OUR LIVES	CBS	55	25 Feb 89	3
THE BEST YEARS OF OUR LIVES [RE]	CBS	42	18 Nov 89	3
LOVESCAPE	Columbia	36	9 Nov 91	13
THE GREATEST HITS 1966-1992	Columbia	1	4 Jul 92	30
20 GOLDEN GREATS [RE]	MCA	48	25 Jul 92	3
Re-released with a new catalogue number.				
THE CHRISTMAS ALBUM	Columbia	50	28 Nov 92	6
UP ON THE ROOF – SONGS FROM THE BRILL BUILDING	Columbia	28	9 Oct 93	10
TENNESSEE MOON (THE NASHVILLE COLLECTION)	Columbia	12	17 Feb 96	13
A collaboration with Nashville country stars.				
THE BEST OF NEIL DIAMOND	MCA	68	25 May 96	1
THE ULTIMATE COLLECTION	Sony TV/MCA	5	31 Aug 96	20
THE MOVIE ALBUM – AS TIME GOES BY	Columbia	68	14 Nov 98	2
Live recordings, conducted by Elmer Bernstein.				

DIAMOND HEAD
UK

SINGLES:	HITS 1			WEEKS 2
IN THE HEAT OF THE NIGHT	MCA	67	11 Sep 82	2
ALBUMS:	**HITS 2**			**WEEKS 9**
BORROWED TIME	MCA	24	23 Oct 82	5
CANTERBURY	MCA	32	24 Sep 83	4

DIAMONDS
Canada

SINGLES:	HITS 1			WEEKS 17
LITTLE DARLIN'	Mercury	3	1 Jun 57	17
Originally by the Gladiolas reached No. 51 in the US in 1957.				

DIANA - See Diana ROSS

DICK and DEEDEE
US

SINGLES:	HITS 1			WEEKS 3
THE MOUNTAIN'S HIGH	London	37	28 Oct 61	3

Charles DICKENS
UK

SINGLES:	HITS 1			WEEKS 8
THAT'S THE WAY LOVE GOES	Pye	37	3 Jul 65	8

Gwen DICKEY
US

(See also Rose Royce.)

SINGLES:	HITS 3			WEEKS 10
CAR WASH	Swanyard	72	27 Jan 90	2
AIN'T NOBODY (LOVES ME BETTER)	X-Clusive	21	2 Jul 94	4
Sleeve reflects artist credits in reverse.				
Above hit: Gwen DICKEY and K.W.S.				
WISHING ON A STAR	Northwestside	13	14 Feb 98	4
Above hit: JAY-Z featuring Gwen DICKEY.				

Neville DICKIE
UK

SINGLES:	HITS 1			WEEKS 10
THE ROBIN'S RETURN	Major Minor	33	25 Oct 69	7
THE ROBIN'S RETURN [RE]	Major Minor	43	20 Dec 69	3

DICKIES
US

SINGLES:	HITS 6			WEEKS 28
SILENT NIGHT	A&M	47	16 Dec 78	4
BANANA SPLITS (THE TRA LA LA SONG)	A&M	7	21 Apr 79	8
PARANOID	A&M	45	21 Jul 79	6
NIGHTS IN WHITE SATIN	A&M	39	15 Sep 79	5
FAN MAIL	A&M	57	16 Feb 80	3
GIGANTOR	A&M	72	19 Jul 80	2
ALBUMS:	**HITS 2**			**WEEKS 19**
THE INCREDIBLE SHRINKING DICKIES	A&M	18	17 Feb 79	17
DAWN OF THE DICKIES	A&M	60	24 Nov 79	2

Bruce DICKINSON
UK

SINGLES:	HITS 8			WEEKS 23
TATTOOED MILLIONAIRE	EMI	18	28 Apr 90	5
ALL THE YOUNG DUDES	EMI	23	23 Jun 90	5

DIVE! DIVE! DIVE!	EMI	45	25 Aug 90	2
(I WANT TO BE) ELECTED	London	9	4 Apr 92	5

Mr. Bean is a character played by comedian Rowan Atkinson.
Above hit: MR. BEAN and SMEAR CAMPAIGN (featuring Bruce DICKINSON).

TEARS OF THE DRAGON	EMI	28	28 May 94	2
SHOOT ALL THE CLOWNS	EMI	37	8 Oct 94	2
BACK FROM THE EDGE	Raw Power	68	13 Apr 96	1
ACCIDENT OF BIRTH	Raw Power	54	3 May 97	1
ALBUMS:	**HITS 5**		**WEEKS 15**	
TATTOOED MILLIONAIRE	EMI	14	19 May 90	9
BALLS TO PICASSO	EMI	21	18 Jun 94	3
SKUNKWORKS	Raw Power	41	9 Mar 96	1
ACCIDENT OF BIRTH	Raw Power	53	24 May 97	1
THE CHEMICAL WEDDING	Air Raid	55	26 Sep 98	1

Barbara DICKSON   UK

SINGLES:	**HITS 6**		**WEEKS 49**	
ANSWER ME	RSO	9	17 Jan 76	7
ANOTHER SUITCASE IN ANOTHER HALL	MCA	18	26 Feb 77	7

From the musical 'Evita'.

CARAVAN SONG	Epic	41	19 Jan 80	7

Above hit: Song from the film "CARAVANS" featuring Barbara DICKSON.

JANUARY FEBRUARY	Epic	11	15 Mar 80	10
IN THE NIGHT	Epic	48	14 Jun 80	2
I KNOW HIM SO WELL	RCA	1	5 Jan 85	16

From the musical 'Chess'.
Above hit: Elaine PAIGE and Barbara DICKSON.

ALBUMS:	**HITS 14**		**WEEKS 143**	
MORNING COMES QUICKLY	RSO	58	18 Jun 77	1
THE BARBARA DICKSON ALBUM	Epic	7	12 Apr 80	12
YOU KNOW IT'S ME	Epic	39	16 May 81	6
ALL FOR A SONG	Epic	3	6 Feb 82	38
TELL ME IT'S NOT TRUE 'FROM THE MUSICAL BLOOD BROTHERS'	Legacy	100	24 Sep 83	1
HEARTBEATS	Epic	21	23 Jun 84	8
THE BARBARA DICKSON SONGBOOK	K-Tel	5	12 Jan 85	19
GOLD	K-Tel	11	23 Nov 85	18
THE VERY BEST OF BARBARA DICKSON	Telstar	78	15 Nov 86	8
THE RIGHT MOMENT	K-Tel	39	29 Nov 86	8
COMING ALIVE AGAIN	Telstar	30	6 May 89	7
DON'T THINK TWICE IT'S ALL RIGHT	Columbia	32	15 Aug 92	5
THE BEST OF ELAINE PAIGE AND BARBARA DICKSON	Telstar	22	28 Nov 92	9

Above hit: Elaine PAIGE and Barbara DICKSON.

PARCEL OF ROGUES	Castle Communication	30	5 Mar 94	3

DICTATORS   US

SINGLES:	**HITS 1**		**WEEKS 2**	
SEARCH AND DESTROY	Asylum	49	17 Sep 77	1

Originally recorded by Iggy Pop.

SEARCH AND DESTROY [RE]	Asylum	50	1 Oct 77	1

Bo DIDDLEY   US

SINGLES:	**HITS 2**		**WEEKS 10**	
PRETTY THING	Pye International	34	12 Oct 63	6
HEY GOOD LOOKIN'	Chess	39	20 Mar 65	4
EPS:	**HITS 3**		**WEEKS 29**	
CHUCK AND BO	Pye International	6	5 Oct 63	22
CHUCK AND BO, VOLUME 2	Pye International	15	30 Nov 63	2
CHUCK AND BO, VOLUME 3	Pye International	12	15 Feb 64	5

Above 3: Chuck BERRY and Bo DIDDLEY.

ALBUMS:	**HITS 4**		**WEEKS 16**	
BO DIDDLEY	Pye International	11	5 Oct 63	8
BO DIDDLEY IS A GUNSLINGER	Pye	20	9 Nov 63	1
BO DIDDLEY RIDES AGAIN	Pye International	19	30 Nov 63	1
BO DIDDLEY'S BEACH PARTY	Pye	13	15 Feb 64	6

DIDDY   UK

SINGLES:	**HITS 1**		**WEEKS 3**	
GIVE ME LOVE	Positiva	52	19 Feb 94	1
GIVE ME LOVE [RM]	Feverpitch	23	12 Jul 97	2

Remixed by Diddy.

DIESEL PARK WEST
UK

(See also Various Artists (EPs) 'The Food Christmas EP 1989'.)

SINGLES:		HITS 6		WEEKS 15	
ALL THE MYTHS ON SUNDAY	Food		66	4 Feb 89	2
LIKE PRINCES DO	Food		58	1 Apr 89	3
WHEN THE HOODOO COMES	Food		62	5 Aug 89	2
FALL TO LOVE	Food		48	18 Jan 92	3
BOY ON TOP OF THE NEWS	Food		58	21 Mar 92	2
GOD ONLY KNOWS	Food		57	5 Sep 92	3
ALBUMS:		HITS 2		WEEKS 3	
SHAKESPEARE ALABAMA	Food		55	11 Feb 89	2
DECENCY	Food		57	15 Feb 92	1

DIFFORD and TILBROOK
UK

SINGLES:		HITS 1		WEEKS 2	
LOVE'S CRASHING WAVES	A&M		57	30 Jun 84	2
ALBUMS:		HITS 1		WEEKS 3	
DIFFORD AND TILBROOK	A&M		47	14 Jul 84	3

DIGABLE PLANETS
US

SINGLES:		HITS 1		WEEKS 2	
REBIRTH OF SLICK (COOL LIKE DAT)	Elektra		67	13 Feb 93	2

DIGITAL DREAM BABY
UK

SINGLES:		HITS 1		WEEKS 4	
WALKING IN THE AIR (FROM THE SNOWMAN)	Columbia		49	14 Dec 91	4

Dance remix of Walking In The Air by the Snowman.

DIGITAL EXCITATION
Belgium

SINGLES:		HITS 1		WEEKS 2	
PURE PLEASURE	R&S		37	29 Feb 92	2

DIGITAL ORGASM
Belgium

SINGLES:		HITS 3		WEEKS 14	
RUNNING OUT OF TIME	Dead Dead Good		16	7 Dec 91	9
STARTOUCHERS	DDG International		31	18 Apr 92	3
MOOG ERUPTION	DDG International		62	25 Jul 92	2

DIGITAL UNDERGROUND
US

SINGLES:		HITS 1		WEEKS 4	
SAME SONG	Big Life		52	16 Mar 91	4
ALBUMS:		HITS 2		WEEKS 2	
SEX PACKETS	BCM		59	7 Apr 90	1
DOOWUTCHYALIKE / PACKET MAN	BCM		59	30 Jun 90	1

12"/CD single too long to be eligible for the singles charts.

John DIGWEED – See BEDROCK

DILEMMA
Italy

SINGLES:		HITS 1		WEEKS 1	
IN SPIRIT	ffrr		42	6 Apr 96	1

First released in 1991.

Ricky DILLARD – See Farley "Jackmaster" FUNK

Richard DIMBLEBY
UK

ALBUMS:		HITS 1		WEEKS 5	
THE VOICE OF RICHARD DIMBLEBY	Music For Pleasure		14	4 Jun 66	5

Paolo DINI – See F.P.I. PROJECT

Mark DINNING
US

SINGLES:		HITS 1		WEEKS 4	
TEEN ANGEL	MGM		37	12 Mar 60	3
TEEN ANGEL [RE]	MGM		42	9 Apr 60	1

Written by Mark's sister Jeannie.

DINOSAUR JR
US

SINGLES:		HITS 7		WEEKS 13	
THE WAGON	Blanco Y Negro		49	2 Feb 91	2
GET ME	Blanco Y Negro		44	14 Nov 92	1
START CHOPPIN	Blanco Y Negro		20	30 Jan 93	3

*Worldwide, **Garth Brooks** was the biggest selling recording artist of the '90s. (LFI)*

Bow Wow Wow were named in honour of the HMV dog Nipper.

All 16 of Boyzone's single releases to date have reached the Top 5. (LFI)

Eddie Calvert was the first chart-topping artist to write a No.1 hit for someone else (Vera Lynn's 'My Son My Son'). (LFI)

Mariah Carey's total of 14 American No.1 hits is bettered only be The Beatles and Elvis. (LFI)

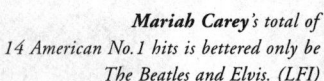

'My Best Friend's Girl' by the *Cars* was the first hit available on a 7" pictures disc. (LFI)

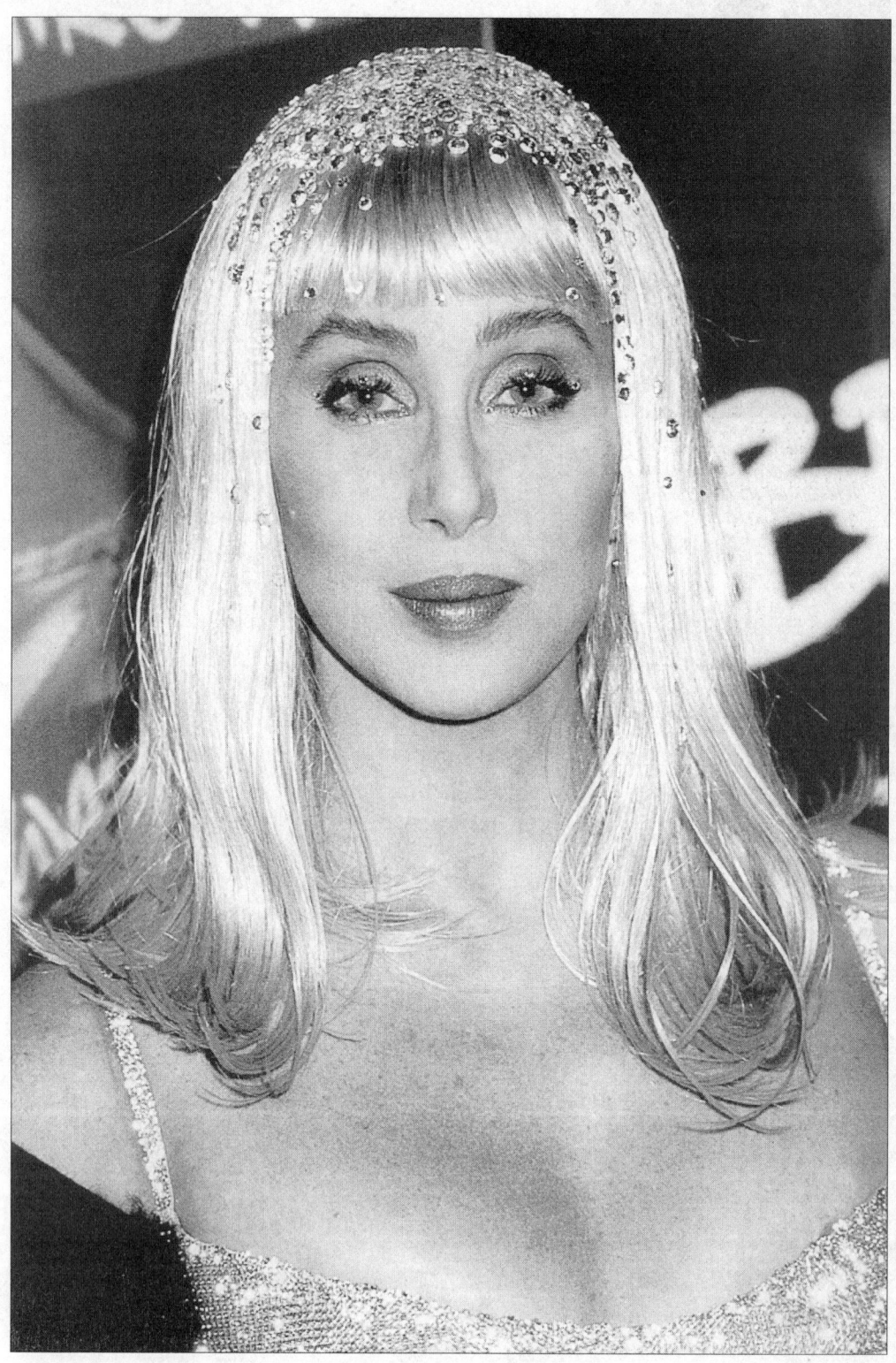

*The oldest female soloist to top the singles chart is **Cher**, who was 52 years old when 'Believe' reached No.1 in 1998. (LFI)*

Lonnie Donegan's *Gamblin' Man*
was the first live single to top
the chart. (LFI)

Nat King Cole's *'When I Fall*
In Love' reached No.2 in 1957;
it returned to the Top 10
30 years and 8 months later.
(LFI)

Eric Clapton; *there was a record gap of 28 years and 13 weeks between Eric's first charted album and his first No.1.*
(LFI)

At 1 minute 17 seconds, **Duane Eddy**'s *'Some Kinda Earthquake' is the shortest single to make the US chart; the UK release, however, is 26 seconds longer. (Decca Records)*

Jason Donovan *is the only artist to top the chart with a song from a show in which he appeared. (LFI)*

Erasure *took their name from the David Lynch film* Eraserhead. *(LFI)*

*The longest hit song title belongs to **The Faces**. (Harry Goodwin)*

OUT THERE	Blanco Y Negro	44	12 Jun 93	2
FEEL THE PAIN	Blanco Y Negro	25	27 Aug 94	3
I DON'T THINK SO	Blanco Y Negro	67	11 Feb 95	1
TAKE A RUN AT THE SUN	Blanco Y Negro	53	5 Apr 97	1
ALBUMS:	**HITS 3**			**WEEKS 7**
GREEN MIND	Blanco Y Negro	36	2 Mar 91	2
WHERE YOU BEEN	Blanco Y Negro	10	20 Feb 93	3
WITHOUT A SOUND	Blanco Y Negro	24	10 Sep 94	2

DIO   UK/US

SINGLES:	**HITS 7**			**WEEKS 22**
HOLY DIVER	Vertigo	72	20 Aug 83	2
RAINBOW IN THE DARK	Vertigo	46	29 Oct 83	3
WE ROCK	Vertigo	42	11 Aug 84	3
MYSTERY	Vertigo	34	29 Sep 84	4
ROCK 'N' ROLL CHILDREN	Vertigo	26	10 Aug 85	6
HUNGRY FOR HEAVEN	Vertigo	72	2 Nov 85	1
HUNGRY FOR HEAVEN [RI]	Vertigo	56	17 May 86	2
I COULD HAVE BEEN A DREAMER	Vertigo	69	1 Aug 87	1
ALBUMS:	**HITS 6**			**WEEKS 48**
HOLY DIVER	Vertigo	13	11 Jun 83	15
THE LAST IN LINE	Vertigo	4	21 Jul 84	14
SACRED HEART	Vertigo	4	7 Sep 85	6
INTERMISSION	Vertigo	22	5 Jul 86	5
DREAM EVIL	Vertigo	8	22 Aug 87	5
LOCK UP THE WOLVES	Vertigo	28	26 May 90	3

DION   US

SINGLES:	**HITS 4**			**WEEKS 35**
A TEENAGER IN LOVE	London	28	27 Jun 59	2
Above hit: DION and the BELMONTS.				
LONELY TEENAGER	Top Rank	47	21 Jan 61	1
RUNAROUND SUE	Top Rank	11	4 Nov 61	9
THE WANDERER	His Master's Voice	10	17 Feb 62	12
THE WANDERER [RI]	Philips	16	22 May 76	9
KING OF THE NEW YORK STREETS	Arista	74	19 Aug 89	2
ALBUMS:	**HITS 1**			**WEEKS 5**
20 GOLDEN GREATS	K-Tel	31	12 Apr 80	5
Above hit: DION and the BELMONTS.				

Celine DION   Canada

SINGLES:	**HITS 21**			**WEEKS 216**
BEAUTY AND THE BEAST	Epic	9	16 May 92	7
From the Walt Disney film of the same name.				
Above hit: Celine DION and Peabo BRYSON.				
IF YOU ASKED ME TO	Epic	60	4 Jul 92	2
LOVE CAN MOVE MOUNTAINS	Epic	46	14 Nov 92	2
IF YOU ASKED ME TO [RE]	Epic	57	26 Dec 92	3
WHERE DOES MY HEART BEAT NOW	Epic	72	3 Apr 93	1
Originally released in 1991.				
THE POWER OF LOVE	Epic	4	29 Jan 94	10
MISLED	Epic	40	23 Apr 94	3
THINK TWICE	Epic	1	22 Oct 94	31
ONLY ONE ROAD	Epic	8	20 May 95	8
TU M'AIMES ENCORE (TO LOVE ME AGAIN)	Epic	7	9 Sep 95	9
MISLED [RI]	Epic	15	2 Dec 95	6
FALLING INTO YOU	Epic	10	2 Mar 96	10
BECAUSE YOU LOVED ME (THEME FROM "UP CLOSE & PERSONAL")	Epic	5	1 Jun 96	16
From the film 'Up Close And Personal'.				
IT'S ALL COMING BACK TO ME NOW	Epic	3	5 Oct 96	14
ALL BY MYSELF	Epic	6	21 Dec 96	10
Based on Rachmaninoff's Piano Concerto composed around 1892.				
ALL BY MYSELF [RE]	Epic	58	15 Mar 97	3
CALL THE MAN	Epic	11	28 Jun 97	6
TELL HIM	Columbia	3	15 Nov 97	15
Above hit: Barbra STREISAND / Celine DION.				
THE REASON	Epic	11	20 Dec 97	8
MY HEART WILL GO ON (LOVE THEME FROM TITANIC)	Epic	1	21 Feb 98	20
From the film 'Titanic'.				
IMMORTALITY	Epic	5	18 Jul 98	12
Above hit: Celine DION with special guests the BEE GEES.				
I'M YOUR ANGEL	Epic	3	28 Nov 98	13
Above hit: Celine DION and R. KELLY.				
TREAT HER LIKE A LADY	Epic	29	10 Jul 99	3
THAT'S THE WAY IT IS	Epic	12	11 Dec 99	4

ALBUMS:		HITS 11		WEEKS 333
THE COLOUR OF MY LOVE	Epic	10	5 Mar 94	4
THE COLOUR OF MY LOVE [RE]	Epic	1	24 Dec 94	105
UNISON	Epic	56	16 Sep 95	2
Originally released in 1991.				
D'EUX - THE FRENCH ALBUM	Epic	7	7 Oct 95	9
FALLING INTO YOU	Epic	1	23 Mar 96	113
UNISON [RE]	Epic	55	19 Oct 96	1
LIVE A PARIS	Epic	53	9 Nov 96	1
Live recordings from the Zenith Theatre, Paris, Autumn 1995.				
C'EST POUR VIVRE	Nectar Masters	49	15 Mar 97	3
French recordings from 1983-87.				
LET'S TALK ABOUT LOVE	Epic	1	29 Nov 97	73
S'IL SUFFISAIT D'AIMER	Epic	17	19 Sep 98	4
CELINE DION	Epic	70	26 Sep 98	2
First released 1992.				
THESE ARE SPECIAL TIMES	Epic	20	14 Nov 98	10
ALL THE WAY . . . A DECADE OF LOVE SONGS	Epic	1	27 Nov 99	6
Compilation plus 7 new tracks.				

Kathryn DION – See 2 FUNKY 2 featuring Kathryn DION

DIONNE				Canada
SINGLES:		HITS 1		WEEKS 2
COME GET MY LOVIN'	Citybeat	69	23 Sep 89	2

Wasis DIOP featuring Lena FIAGBE				Senegal/UK
SINGLES:		HITS 1		WEEKS 2
AFRICAN DREAM	Mercury	44	10 Feb 96	2

DIPPY – See Keith HARRIS and ORVILLE

DIRE STRAITS				UK
SINGLES:		HITS 18		WEEKS 119
SULTANS OF SWING	Vertigo	8	10 Mar 79	11
LADY WRITER	Vertigo	51	28 Jul 79	6
ROMEO AND JULIET	Vertigo	8	17 Jan 81	11
SKATEAWAY	Vertigo	37	4 Apr 81	5
TUNNEL OF LOVE	Vertigo	54	10 Oct 81	3
PRIVATE INVESTIGATIONS	Vertigo	2	4 Sep 82	8
TWISTING BY THE POOL	Vertigo	14	22 Jan 83	7
Sleeve gives title as an EP: Dance Play.				
LOVE OVER GOLD (LIVE) / SOLID ROCK (LIVE)	Vertigo	50	18 Feb 84	3
SO FAR AWAY	Vertigo	20	20 Apr 85	6
MONEY FOR NOTHING	Vertigo	4	6 Jul 85	16
Features vocals by Sting.				
BROTHERS IN ARMS	Vertigo	16	26 Oct 85	13
WALK OF LIFE	Vertigo	2	11 Jan 86	11
YOUR LATEST TRICK	Vertigo	26	3 May 86	6
Royalties from this single donated to Great Ormond Street Hospital.				
SULTANS OF SWING [RI]	Vertigo	62	5 Nov 88	1
CALLING ELVIS	Vertigo	21	31 Aug 91	4
HEAVY FUEL	Vertigo	55	2 Nov 91	2
ON EVERY STREET	Vertigo	42	29 Feb 92	2
THE BUG	Vertigo	67	27 Jun 92	1
ENCORES [EP]	Vertigo	31	22 May 93	3
Live recordings, lead track: Your Latest Trick.				
ALBUMS:		HITS 11		WEEKS 1129
DIRE STRAITS	Vertigo	5	22 Jul 78	130
Includes re-entries through to 1988.				
COMMUNIQUE	Vertigo	5	23 Jun 79	32
MAKING MOVIES	Vertigo	4	25 Oct 80	249
LOVE OVER GOLD	Vertigo	1	2 Oct 82	198
Above 2 include re-entries through to 1988.				
ALCHEMY - DIRE STRAITS LIVE	Vertigo	3	24 Mar 84	163
BROTHERS IN ARMS	Vertigo	1	25 May 85	203
Includes re-entries through to 1994.				
MONEY FOR NOTHING	Vertigo	1	29 Oct 88	64
ON EVERY STREET	Vertigo	1	21 Sep 91	35
ON THE NIGHT	Vertigo	4	22 May 93	7
LIVE AT THE BBC	Windsong	71	8 Jul 95	1
Various sessions recorded for Radio 1 in 1978.				
BROTHERS IN ARMS [RE]	Vertigo	19	15 Jun 96	21
LOVE OVER GOLD [RE]	Vertigo	66	15 Jun 96	2
DIRE STRAITS [RE]	Vertigo	69	15 Jun 96	2

MAKING MOVIES [RE]	*Vertigo*	70	*15 Jun 96*	2
Above 4 were digitally remastered.				
SULTANS OF SWING - THE VERY BEST OF DIRE STRAITS	*Vertigo*	6	*31 Oct 98*	20

DIRECKT — UK
(See also E-Lustrious.)

SINGLES:	HITS 1		WEEKS 2	
TWO FATT GUITARS (REVISITED)	*UFG*	36	*13 Aug 94*	2

DIRECT DRIVE — UK

SINGLES:	HITS 2		WEEKS 3	
ANYTHING?	*Polydor*	67	*26 Jan 85*	2
A.B.C. (FALLING IN LOVE'S NOT EASY)	*Boiling Point*	75	*4 May 85*	1

DIRTY ROTTEN SCOUNDRELS - See Lisa STANSFIELD

DISCHARGE — UK

SINGLES:	HITS 1		WEEKS 3	
NEVER AGAIN	*Clay*	64	*24 Oct 81*	3
ALBUMS:	HITS 1		WEEKS 5	
HEAR NOTHING, SEE NOTHING, SAY NOTHING	*Clay*	40	*15 May 82*	5

DISCIPLES OF SOUL - See LITTLE STEPHEN

DISCO ANTHEM — Holland

SINGLES:	HITS 1		WEEKS 2	
SCREAM	*Sweat*	47	*18 Jun 94*	2
Samples Daryl Pandy's vocals from Love Can't Turn Around by Farley Jackmaster Funk.				

DISCO CITIZENS — UK

SINGLES:	HITS 3		WEEKS 5	
RIGHT HERE RIGHT NOW	*Deconstruction*	40	*22 Jul 95*	2
FOOTPRINT	*Xtravaganza*	34	*12 Apr 97*	2
NAGASAKI BADGER	*Xtravaganza*	56	*4 Jul 98*	1

DISCO EVANGELISTS — UK

SINGLES:	HITS 1		WEEKS 2	
DE NIRO	*Positiva*	59	*8 May 93*	2

DISCO TEX and the SEX-O-LETTES — US

SINGLES:	HITS 2		WEEKS 22	
GET DANCIN'	*Chelsea*	8	*23 Nov 74*	12
I WANNA DANCE WIT' CHOO (DOO DAT DANEE)	*Chelsea*	6	*26 Apr 75*	10
Features backing vocals by Jocelyn Brown.				

DISPOSABLE HEROES OF HIPHOPRISY — US

SINGLES:	HITS 2		WEEKS 7	
TELEVISION, THE DRUG OF THE NATION	*Fourth & Broadway*	57	*4 Apr 92*	2
LANGUAGE OF VIOLENCE	*Fourth & Broadway*	68	*30 May 92*	1
TELEVISION, THE DRUG OF THE NATION [RE]	*Fourth & Broadway*	44	*19 Dec 92*	4
ALBUMS:	HITS 1		WEEKS 3	
HYPOCRISY IS THE GREATEST LUXURY	*Fourth & Broadway*	40	*16 May 92*	3

Sacha DISTEL — France

SINGLES:	HITS 1		WEEKS 27	
RAIN DROPS KEEP FALLING ON MY HEAD	*Warner Brothers*	50	*10 Jan 70*	1
From the film 'Butch Cassidy and the Sundance Kid'. Originally recorded by B.J.Thomas.				
RAIN DROPS KEEP FALLING ON MY HEAD [RE-1ST]	*Warner Brothers*	10	*24 Jan 70*	20
RAIN DROPS KEEP FALLING ON MY HEAD [RE-2ND]	*Warner Brothers*	43	*27 Jun 70*	4
RAIN DROPS KEEP FALLING ON MY HEAD [RE-3RD]	*Warner Brothers*	47	*1 Aug 70*	1
RAIN DROPS KEEP FALLING ON MY HEAD [RE-4TH]	*Warner Brothers*	44	*15 Aug 70*	1
ALBUMS:	HITS 1		WEEKS 14	
SACHA DISTEL	*Warner Brothers*	21	*2 May 70*	14

DIVA — Norway

SINGLES:	HITS 2		WEEKS 2	
THE SUN ALWAYS SHINES ON TV	*East West*	53	*7 Oct 95*	1
EVERYBODY (MOVE YOUR BODY)	*East West*	44	*20 Jul 96*	1

DIVA SURPRISE featuring Georgia JONES — US/Spain

SINGLES:	HITS 1		WEEKS 2	
ON THE TOP OF THE WORLD	*Positiva*	29	*14 Nov 98*	2

DIVE   UK

SINGLES:		HITS 1		WEEKS 1
BOOGIE	WEA	35	21 Feb 98	1

DIVERSIONS   UK

SINGLES:		HITS 1		WEEKS 3
FATTIE BUM-BUM	Gull	34	20 Sep 75	3

Features sax solo by Lene Lovich.

DIVINE   US

SINGLES:		HITS 5		WEEKS 24
LOVE REACTION	Design Communications	65	15 Oct 83	2
YOU THINK YOU'RE A MAN	Proto	16	14 Jul 84	10
I'M SO BEAUTIFUL	Proto	52	20 Oct 84	2
WALK LIKE A MAN	Proto	23	27 Apr 85	7
TWISTIN' THE NIGHT AWAY	Proto	47	20 Jul 85	3

DIVINE   US

SINGLES:		HITS 1		WEEKS 1
LATELY	Red Ant	52	16 Oct 99	1

DIVINE COMEDY   UK

SINGLES:		HITS 10		WEEKS 33
SOMETHING FOR THE WEEKEND	Setanta	14	29 Jun 96	5
BECOMING MORE LIKE ALFIE	Setanta	27	24 Aug 96	2
THE FROG PRINCESS	Setanta	15	16 Nov 96	2
EVERYBODY KNOWS (EXCEPT YOU)	Setanta	14	22 Mar 97	4

Features 30 piece orchestra conducted by Christopher Austin.

I'VE BEEN TO A MARVELLOUS PARTY	EMI	28	11 Apr 98	3

[AA] listed with Someday I'll Find You by Shola Ama. From the Noel Coward commemorative album Twentieth Century Blues.

GENERATION SEX	Setanta	19	26 Sep 98	3
THE CERTAINTY OF CHANCE	Setanta	49	28 Nov 98	1
NATIONAL EXPRESS	Setanta	8	6 Feb 99	7
THE POP SINGER'S FEAR OF THE POLLEN COUNT	Setanta	17	21 Aug 99	4

Originally appeared on their 1993 album Liberation.

GIN SOAKED BOY	Setanta	38	13 Nov 99	2
ALBUMS:		**HITS 4**		**WEEKS 39**
CASANOVA	Setanta	48	11 May 96	9
A SHORT ALBUM ABOUT LOVE	Setanta	13	22 Feb 97	6

Orchestral love songs recorded on 19 Oct 96 at the Shepherd's Bush Empire with the Brunel Ensemble.

FIN DE SIECLE	Setanta	9	12 Sep 98	14
A SECRET HISTORY – THE BEST OF THE DIVINE COMEDY	Setanta	3	11 Sep 99	10

DIVINE WORKS   Europe

(See also Sacred Spirit.)

ALBUMS:		HITS 1		WEEKS 2
DIVINE WORKS	Virgin	43	16 Aug 97	2

DIVINYLS   Australia

SINGLES:		HITS 1		WEEKS 12
I TOUCH MYSELF	Virgin America	10	18 May 91	12
ALBUMS:		**HITS 1**		**WEEKS 1**
DIVINYLS	Virgin America	59	20 Jul 91	1

DIXIE CHICKS   US

SINGLES:		HITS 2		WEEKS 6
THERE'S YOUR TROUBLE	Epic	26	3 Jul 99	5
READY TO RUN	Epic	53	6 Nov 99	1
ALBUMS:		**HITS 2**		**WEEKS 8**
WIDE OPEN SPACE	Epic	29	3 Jul 99	6

Originally released in 1998.

FLY	Epic	38	11 Sep 99	2

DIXIE CUPS   US

SINGLES:		HITS 2		WEEKS 16
CHAPEL OF LOVE	Pye International	22	20 Jun 64	8
IKO IKO	Red Bird	23	15 May 65	8

Originally recorded by James 'Sugarboy' Crawford as Jock-O-Mo.

DIXIE HUMMINGBIRDS – See Paul SIMON

DIZZY HEIGHTS
UK

SINGLES:	HITS 1			WEEKS 4	
CHRISTMAS RAPPING	Polydor	49	18 Dec 82	4

D.J. BOBO
Switzerland

SINGLES:	HITS 2			WEEKS 4	
EVERYBODY	PWL	47	24 Sep 94	2
LOVE IS ALL AROUND	Avex UK	49	17 Jun 95	2

DJ Carl COX – See Carl COX

DJ DADO
Italy

SINGLES:	HITS 4			WEEKS 9	
X-FILES	ZYX	8	6 Apr 96	6
Dance version of theme to the TV series.				
COMING BACK	Ffrreedom	63	14 Mar 98	1
GIVE ME LOVE	VC Recordings	59	11 Jul 98	1
Above hit: DJ DADO vs Michelle WEEKS.				
READY OR NOT	Chemistry	51	8 May 99	1
Above hit: DJ DADO and Simone JAY.				

DJ DISCIPLE
US

SINGLES:	HITS 1			WEEKS 1	
ON THE DANCEFLOOR	Mother	67	12 Nov 94	1

DJ DUKE
US

SINGLES:	HITS 2			WEEKS 7	
BLOW YOUR WHISTLE	ffrr	15	8 Jan 94	5
TURN IT UP (SAY YEAH)	ffrr	31	16 Jul 94	2

D.J. E-Z ROCK – See Rob BASE and D.J. E-Z ROCK

DJ ERIC presents
UK

SINGLES:	HITS 1			WEEKS 2	
WE ARE LOVE	Distinct'ive	37	13 Feb 99	2
Samples Daryl Hall and John Oates' I Can't Go For That (No Can Do) and Alexander Hope's Brothers & Sisters.				

DJ FAST EDDIE
US

SINGLES:	HITS 4			WEEKS 15	
CAN U DANCE	Champion	71	11 Apr 87	2
Above hit: Kenny "Jammin" JASON and "Fast" Eddie SMITH.				
CAN U DANCE [RE]	Champion	67	14 Nov 87	2
HIP HOUSE / I CAN DANCE	DJ International	47	21 Jan 89	4
YO YO GET FUNKY	DJ International	54	11 Mar 89	3
Label credit: Fast Eddie.				
GIT ON UP	DJ International	49	28 Oct 89	4
Above hit: EAST EDDIE featuring SUNDANCE.				

DJ FLAVOURS
UK

SINGLES:	HITS 1			WEEKS 4	
YOUR CARESS (ALL I NEED)	All Around the World	19	11 Oct 97	4
Samples Pacha's One Kiss.				

DJ HYPE
UK

(See also Various Artists (EPs) 'Subplates Volume 1 EP'.)

SINGLES:	HITS 1			WEEKS 1	
SHOT IN THE DARK	Suburban Base	63	20 Mar 93	1
ALBUMS:	**HITS 1**			**WEEKS 1**	
NEW FRONTIERS [EP]	Parousia	56	30 Aug 97	1
Above hit: DJ HYPE presents GANJA KRU.				

DJ JAZZY JEFF and the FRESH PRINCE – See JAZZY JEFF and the FRESH PRINCE

DJ JEAN
Holland

SINGLES:	HITS 1			WEEKS 11	
THE LAUNCH	AM:PM	2	11 Sep 99	11

DJ JURGEN presents ALICE DEEJAY – See ALICE DEEJAY

DJ KOOL
US

SINGLES:	HITS 1			WEEKS 7	
LET ME CLEAR MY THROAT	American Recordings	8	22 Feb 97	7
Guest rapper is Doug E Fresh. Samples Kool and the Gang's Hollywood Swingin'.				

DJ KRUSH | | | | Japan

SINGLES:	HITS 2			WEEKS 2
MEISO	Mo Wax	52	16 Mar 96	1
ONLY THE STRONG SURVIVE	Mo Wax	71	12 Oct 96	1
ALBUMS:	**HITS 2**			**WEEKS 2**
BAD BROTHERS	Island	58	3 Sep 94	1

Mixes of Ronny Jordan material by DJ Krush.
Above hit: Ronny JORDAN meets DJ KRUSH.

MEISO	Mo Wax	64	11 Nov 95	1

DJ LUCK and MC NEAT | | | | UK

SINGLES:	HITS 1			WEEKS 2
A LITTLE BIT OF LUCK	Red Rose	17	25 Dec 99	2

DJ MANTA | | | | Holland

SINGLES:	HITS 1			WEEKS 1
HOLDING ON	A&M	47	9 Oct 99	1

Samples Orchestral Manoeuvres In The Dark's Maid Of Orleans (The Waltz Joan Of Arc).

DJ MIKO | | | | Italy

SINGLES:	HITS 1			WEEKS 10
WHAT'S UP	Systematic	6	13 Aug 94	10

Features female vocalist Louise Gard.

DJ MILANO featuring Samantha FOX | | | | Italy

(See also Samantha Fox.)

SINGLES:	HITS 1			WEEKS 2
SANTA MARIA	All Around the World	31	28 Mar 98	2

Rap by Eagle E.

DJ MISJAH and DJ TIM | | | | Holland

SINGLES:	HITS 1			WEEKS 3
ACCESS	Ffrreedom	16	23 Mar 96	3

DJ MUGGS - See TRICKY

DJ POWER | | | | Italy

SINGLES:	HITS 1			WEEKS 2
EVERYBODY PUMP	Cooltempo	46	7 Mar 92	2

DJ PROFESSOR | | | | Italy

SINGLES:	HITS 4			WEEKS 6
WE GOTTA DO IT	Fourth & Broadway	57	10 Aug 91	2

Above hit: DJ PROFESSOR and Francesco ZAPPALA.

ROCK ME STEADY	PWL Continental	49	28 Mar 92	2
ROCKIN' ME	Citra	56	8 Oct 94	1

Above hit: PROFESSOR.

WALKIN' ON UP	Nuklenz	64	1 Mar 97	1

Above hit: DJ PROF-X-OR.

DJ QUICKSILVER | | | | Turkey

SINGLES:	HITS 3			WEEKS 29
BELLISSIMA	Positiva	4	5 Apr 97	17
FREE	Positiva	7	6 Sep 97	7
PLANET LOVE	Positiva	12	21 Feb 98	5
ALBUMS:	**HITS 1**			**WEEKS 3**
QUICKSILVER	Positiva	26	7 Mar 98	3

DJ QUIK - See TONY! TONI! TONE!

DJ RAP | | | | UK

SINGLES:	HITS 3			WEEKS 5
BAD GIRL	Higher Ground	32	4 Jul 98	2
GOOD TO BE ALIVE	Higher Ground	36	17 Oct 98	2
EVERYDAY GIRL	Higher Ground	47	3 Apr 99	1

DJ SAKIN and FRIENDS | | | | Germany

SINGLES:	HITS 2			WEEKS 18
PROTECT YOUR MIND (FOR THE LOVE OF A PRINCESS)	Positiva	4	20 Feb 99	10

Samples James Horner's For The Love Of A Princess (from the film 'Braveheart').

PROTECT YOUR MIND (FOR THE LOVE OF A PRINCESS) [RE]	Positiva	71	8 May 99	1

| NOMANSLAND (DAVID'S SONG) | Positiva | 14 | 5 Jun 99 | 7 |

Samples the theme from the 1970s TV show 'The Adventures Of David Belfour'.

DJ SCOT PROJECT   Germany

SINGLES:	HITS 1		WEEKS 1
Y (HOW DEEP IS YOUR LOVE)	Perfecto Mainline	57	14 Feb 98	1

DJ Doc SCOTT   UK

SINGLES:	HITS 1		WEEKS 2
N.H.S. [EP]	Absolute	64	1 Feb 92	2

Lead track: Surgery.

DJ SCOTT featuring Lorna B   UK

SINGLES:	HITS 2		WEEKS 5
DO YOU WANNA PARTY	Steppin' Out	36	28 Jan 95	3

Originally released in 1994.

| SWEET DREAMS | Steppin' Out | 37 | 1 Apr 95 | 2 |

DJ SEDUCTION   UK

SINGLES:	HITS 2		WEEKS 8
HARDCORE HEAVEN/YOU AND ME	Ffrreedom	26	22 Feb 92	5
COME ON	Ffrreedom	37	11 Jul 92	3

DJ SHADOW   US

SINGLES:	HITS 5		WEEKS 7
WHAT DOES YOUR SOUL LOOK LIKE	Mo Wax	59	25 Mar 95	1
MIDNIGHT IN A PERFECT WORLD	Mo Wax	54	14 Sep 96	1
STEM	Mo Wax	74	9 Nov 96	1
HIGH NOON	Mo Wax	22	11 Oct 97	2
CAMEL BOBSLED RACE	Mo Wax	62	20 Dec 97	1

24 minute megamix of 7 DJ Shadow tracks mixed by DJ Q-Bert.

| WHAT DOES YOUR SOUL LOOK LIKE (PART 1) [RM] | Mo Wax | 54 | 24 Jan 98 | 1 |

Remixed by Peshay and DJ Die.

ALBUMS:	HITS 1		WEEKS 3
ENDTRODUCING	Mo Wax	17	28 Sep 96	3

DJ SUPREME   UK

SINGLES:	HITS 4		WEEKS 11
THA WILDSTYLE	Distinct'ive	39	5 Oct 96	2

Samples The Badman Is Robbin' by Hijack.

| THA WILDSTYLE [RM] | Distinct'ive | 24 | 3 May 97 | 2 |

Remixed by Klubbheads.

| ENTER THE SCENE | Distinct'ive | 49 | 6 Dec 97 | 1 |

Above hit: DJ SUPREME vs the RHYTHM MASTERS.

| THA HORNS OF JERICHO | All Around the World | 29 | 21 Feb 98 | 2 |
| UP TO THE WILDSTYLE [RR] | All Around The World | 10 | 16 Jan 99 | 4 |

Above hit: PORN KINGS vs DJ SUPREME.

DJ TAUCHER   Germany

SINGLES:	HITS 1		WEEKS 1
CHILD OF THE UNIVERSE (SANVEAN)	Additive	74	8 May 99	1

DJ TIM – See DJ MISJAH and DJ TIM

DJAIMIN featuring ALESSANDRA   Switzerland

SINGLES:	HITS 1		WEEKS 2
GIVE YOU	Cooltempo	45	19 Sep 92	2

DJPC   Belgium

SINGLES:	HITS 1		WEEKS 5
INSSOMNIAK	Hype	62	26 Oct 91	4
INSSOMNIAK [RM]	Hype	64	29 Feb 92	1

DJ'S RULE   Canada

SINGLES:	HITS 1		WEEKS 2
GET INTO THE MUSIC	Distinct'ive	72	2 Mar 96	1
GET INTO THE MUSIC [RI]	Distinct'ive	65	5 Apr 97	1

Above hit: DJ'S RULE feauring Karen BROWN.

DJ'S UNITE – See VARIOUS ARTISTS (EPs) 'Fourplay Volume 1 EP'

DJUM DJUM – See LEFTFIELD

Boris DLUGOSCH presents BOOOM
US/Germany

SINGLES:		HITS 2			WEEKS 4
KEEP PUSHIN'	Manifesto		41	7 Dec 96	2
HOLD YOUR HEAD UP HIGH	Positiva		23	13 Sep 97	2

Duke D'MOND - See BARRON KNIGHTS

DMX
US

SINGLES:		HITS 1			WEEKS 2
SLIPPIN'	Def Jam		30	15 May 99	2

Samples Grover Washington Jr.'s Moonstream.

DNA
UK

SINGLES:		HITS 5			WEEKS 29
TOM'S DINER	A&M		2	28 Jul 90	10

DNA remix of a 1987 Suzanne Vega hit.
Above hit: DNA featuring Suzanne VEGA.

LA SERENISSIMA	Raw Bass		34	18 Aug 90	8
REBEL WOMAN	DNA		42	3 Aug 91	4

Samples David Bowie's Rebel Rebel.
Above hit: DNA rap performed by Jazzi P.

CAN YOU HANDLE IT	EMI		17	1 Feb 92	5

Above hit: DNA featuring Sharon REDD.

BLUE LOVE (CALL MY NAME)	EMI		66	9 May 92	2

Above hit: DNA featuring Joe NYE.

Carl DOBKINS
US

SINGLES:		HITS 1			WEEKS 1
LUCKY DEVIL	Brunswick		44	2 Apr 60	1

Anita DOBSON
UK

SINGLES:		HITS 2			WEEKS 13
ANYONE CAN FALL IN LOVE	BBC		4	9 Aug 86	9

Above hit: Anita DOBSON and the Simon MAY ORCHESTRA.

TALKING OF LOVE	Parlophone		43	18 Jul 87	4

DOCTOR and the MEDICS
UK

SINGLES:		HITS 3			WEEKS 25
SPIRIT IN THE SKY	I.R.S.		1	10 May 86	15
BURN	I.R.S.		29	9 Aug 86	6
WATERLOO	I.R.S.		45	22 Nov 86	4

Above hit: DOCTOR and the MEDICS with Roy WOOD starring the ANADIN
BROTHERS.

ALBUMS:		HITS 1			WEEKS 3
LAUGHING AT THE PIECES	I.R.S.		25	21 Jun 86	3

DR. ALBAN
Nigeria

SINGLES:		HITS 6			WEEKS 28
IT'S MY LIFE	Logic		2	5 Sep 92	12
ONE LOVE	Logic		45	14 Nov 92	2
SING HALLELUJAH!	Logic		16	10 Apr 93	8
LOOK WHO'S TALKING	Logic		55	26 Mar 94	3
AWAY FROM HOME	Logic		42	13 Aug 94	2
SWEET DREAMS	Logic		59	29 Apr 95	1

Above hit: SWING featuring DR. ALBAN.

DR. BARNARDO'S CHILDREN - See Joan REGAN

DR. DRE
US

(See also Scarface.)

SINGLES:		HITS 8			WEEKS 37
NUTHIN' BUT A 'G' THANG / LET ME RIDE	Death Row		31	22 Jan 94	3

Original release reached No. 81 in 1993. Nuthin' But A 'G' Thang features vocals by Snoop
Doggy Dog.

DRE DAY	Death Row		59	3 Sep 94	2
NATURAL BORN KILLAZ	Death Row		45	15 Apr 95	2

From the film 'Murder Was The Case'.
Above hit: DR. DRE and ICE CUBE.

KEEP THEIR HEADS RINGIN'	Priority		25	10 Jun 95	4

From the film 'Friday'.

CALIFORNIA LOVE	Death Row		6	13 Apr 96	8

Samples Zapp's So Ruff So Tuff and Joe Cocker's Woman To Woman.
Above hit: 2PAC featuring DR DRE.

NO DIGGITY	Interscope	9	19 Oct 96	7
Above hit: BLACKSTREET (featuring DR. DRE).				
ZOOM	Interscope	15	11 Jul 98	3
From the film 'Bulworth'.				
Above hit: DR. DRE LL COOL J.				
GUILTY CONSCIENCE	Interscope	5	14 Aug 99	8
Samples the track Go Home Pigs. From the film 'Getting Straight'.				
Above hit: EMINEM featuring DR. DRE.				
ALBUMS:	**HITS 1**			**WEEKS 2**
2001	Interscope	48	27 Nov 99	2

DR. FEELGOOD   UK

SINGLES:	**HITS 6**			**WEEKS 29**
SNEAKIN' SUSPICION	United Artists	47	11 Jun 77	3
SHE'S A WIND UP	United Artists	34	24 Sep 77	5
DOWN AT THE DOCTORS	United Artists	48	30 Sep 78	5
Originally recorded by Mickey Jupp.				
MILK AND ALCOHOL	United Artists	9	20 Jan 79	9
Co-written by Nick Lowe.				
AS LONG AS THE PRICE IS RIGHT	United Artists	40	5 May 79	6
PUT HIM OUT OF YOUR MIND	United Artists	73	8 Dec 79	1
ALBUMS:	**HITS 6**			**WEEKS 33**
MALPRACTICE	United Artists	17	18 Oct 75	6
STUPIDITY	United Artists	1	2 Oct 76	9
Live recordings. Side 1 from Sheffield City Hall 23 May 76, side 2 from Southend Kursaal 8 Nov 75.				
SNEAKIN' SUSPICION	United Artists	10	4 Jun 77	6
BE SEEING YOU	United Artists	55	8 Oct 77	3
PRIVATE PRACTICE	United Artists	41	7 Oct 78	5
AS IT HAPPENS	United Artists	42	2 Jun 79	4

DR. HOOK   US

SINGLES:	**HITS 10**			**WEEKS 105**
SYLVIA'S MOTHER	CBS	2	24 Jun 72	13
Originally recorded by Shel Silverstein.				
Above hit: DR HOOK and the MEDICINE SHOW.				
A LITTLE BIT MORE	Capitol	2	26 Jun 76	14
IF NOT YOU	Capitol	5	30 Oct 76	11
MORE LIKE THE MOVIES	Capitol	14	25 Mar 78	10
Originally recorded by Shel Silverstein.				
WHEN YOU'RE IN LOVE WITH A BEAUTIFUL WOMAN	Capitol	1	22 Sep 79	17
BETTER LOVE NEXT TIME	Capitol	8	5 Jan 80	8
SEXY EYES	Capitol	4	29 Mar 80	9
YEARS FROM NOW	Capitol	47	23 Aug 80	6
SHARING THE NIGHT TOGETHER	Capitol	43	8 Nov 80	4
Originally recorded by Dobie Gray.				
GIRLS CAN GET IT	Mercury	40	22 Nov 80	5
WHEN YOU'RE IN LOVE WITH A BEAUTIFUL WOMAN [RI]	Capitol	44	1 Feb 92	4
A LITTLE BIT MORE [RI]	EMI	47	6 Jun 92	4
ALBUMS:	**HITS 9**			**WEEKS 157**
A LITTLE BIT MORE	Capitol	5	26 Jun 76	42
MAKING LOVE AND MUSIC	Capitol	39	29 Oct 77	4
PLEASURE AND PAIN	Capitol	47	27 Oct 79	6
SOMETIMES YOU WIN	Capitol	14	17 Nov 79	44
RISING	Mercury	44	29 Nov 80	5
DR. HOOK'S GREATEST HITS	Capitol	2	6 Dec 80	28
DR. HOOK LIVE IN THE UK	Capitol	90	14 Nov 81	1
COMPLETELY HOOKED - THE BEST OF DR. HOOK	Capitol	3	13 Jun 92	19
LOVE SONGS	EMI	8	13 Feb 99	8

DR. JOHN   US

ALBUMS:	**HITS 1**			**WEEKS 3**
ANUTHA ZONE	Parlophone	33	27 Jun 98	3

DR. MOUTHQUAKE - See E-ZEE POSSEE

DR. OCTAGON   US

SINGLES:	**HITS 1**			**WEEKS 1**
BLUE FLOWERS	Mo Wax	66	7 Sep 96	1

DOCTOR SPIN   UK

SINGLES:	**HITS 1**			**WEEKS 8**
TETRIS	Carpet	6	3 Oct 92	8
Theme to the Nintendo computer game.				

Ken DODD — UK

SINGLES:		HITS 19			WEEKS 233
LOVE IS LIKE A VIOLIN	Decca	8	9 Jul 60		18
ONCE IN EVERY LIFETIME	Decca	28	17 Jun 61		7
ONCE IN EVERY LIFETIME [RE-1ST]	Decca	47	12 Aug 61		1
ONCE IN EVERY LIFETIME [RE-2ND]	Decca	31	26 Aug 61		10
PIANISSIMO	Decca	21	3 Feb 62		15
STILL	Columbia	35	31 Aug 63		10
Originally recorded by Bill Anderson.					
Above hit: Ken DODD with Geoff LOVE and his Orchestra.					
EIGHT BY TEN	Columbia	22	8 Feb 64		11
HAPPINESS	Columbia	31	25 Jul 64		13
SO DEEP IS THE NIGHT	Columbia	31	28 Nov 64		7
TEARS	Columbia	1	4 Sep 65		24
THE RIVER (LE COLLINE SONO IN FIORE)	Columbia	3	20 Nov 65		14
PROMISES	Columbia	6	14 May 66		14
Above 3: Ken DODD with Geoff LOVE and his Orchestra.					
MORE THAN LOVE	Columbia	14	6 Aug 66		11
Above hit: Ken DODD with Johnny PEARSON and his Orchestra.					
IT'S LOVE (IN UN FIORE)	Columbia	36	29 Oct 66		7
Above hit: Ken DODD with Brian FAHEY and his Orchestra.					
LET ME CRY ON YOUR SHOULDER	Columbia	11	21 Jan 67		10
Above hit: Ken DODD with Geoff LOVE and his Orchestra.					
TEARS WON'T WASH AWAY THESE HEARTACHES	Columbia	22	2 Aug 69		11
BROKENHEARTED	Columbia	15	5 Dec 70		9
BROKENHEARTED [RE]	Columbia	38	13 Feb 71		1
WHEN LOVE COMES ROUND AGAIN (L'ARCA DI NOE)	Columbia	19	10 Jul 71		16
JUST OUT OF REACH (OF MY TWO EMPTY ARMS)	Columbia	29	18 Nov 72		11
THINK OF ME (WHEREVER YOU ARE)	EMI	21	29 Nov 75		8
HOLD MY HAND	Images	44	26 Dec 81		5
EPS:		HITS 3			WEEKS 19
STILL	Columbia	18	22 Feb 64		1
DODDY AND THE DIDDY MEN	Columbia	4	25 Dec 65		17
DIDDYNESS	Columbia	8	7 Jan 67		1
ALBUMS:		HITS 4			WEEKS 36
TEARS OF HAPPINESS	Columbia	6	25 Dec 65		12
HITS FOR NOW AND ALWAYS	Columbia	14	23 Jul 66		11
FOR SOMEONE SPECIAL	Columbia	40	14 Jan 67		1
20 GOLDEN GREATS OF KEN DODD	Warwick	8	29 Nov 80		12

DODGY — UK

SINGLES:		HITS 11			WEEKS 41
LOVEBIRDS	A&M	65	8 May 93		2
I NEED ANOTHER [EP]	A&M	67	3 Jul 93		2
Lead track: I Need Another.					
THE MELOD-E.P. [EP]	A&M	53	6 Aug 94		1
Lead track: Melodies Haunt You.					
STAYING OUT FOR THE SUMMER	A&M	38	1 Oct 94		2
SO LET ME GO FAR	A&M	30	7 Jan 95		3
MAKING THE MOST OF	A&M	22	11 Mar 95		3
Above hit: DODGY with the KICK HORNS.					
STAYING OUT FOR THE SUMMER (SUMMER '95) [RM]	A&M	19	10 Jun 95		5
IN A ROOM	A&M	12	8 Jun 96		6
GOOD ENOUGH	A&M	4	10 Aug 96		8
IF YOU'RE THINKING OF ME	A&M	11	16 Nov 96		4
FOUND YOU	A&M	19	15 Mar 97		3
EVERY SINGLE DAY	A&M	32	26 Sep 98		2
ALBUMS:		HITS 4			WEEKS 54
THE DODGY ALBUM	A&M	75	5 Jun 93		1
HOMEGROWN	A&M	43	5 Nov 94		1
HOMEGROWN [RE]	A&M	28	24 Jun 95		13
FREE PEACE SWEET	A&M	7	29 Jun 96		38
ACE A'S + KILLER B'S	A&M	55	17 Oct 98		1

DOG EAT DOG — US

SINGLES:		HITS 2			WEEKS 7
NO FRONTS – THE REMIXES	Roadrunner	64	19 Aug 95		1
NO FRONTS – THE REMIXES [RE]	Roadrunner	9	3 Feb 96		5
ISMS	Roadrunner	43	13 Jul 96		1
ALBUMS:		HITS 1			WEEKS 2
PLAY GAMES	Roadrunner	40	27 Jul 96		2

Tim DOG — US

SINGLES:		HITS 2			WEEKS 3
BITCH WITH A PERM	Dis-stress	49	29 Oct 94		1

MAKE WAY FOR THE INDIAN	Island	29	11 Feb 95	2

Above hit: APACHE INDIAN and Tim DOG.

Nate DOGG – See Warren G

DOGS D'AMOUR
UK

SINGLES: HITS 6 — WEEKS 15

HOW COME IT NEVER RAINS	China	44	4 Feb 89	3
SATELLITE KID	China	26	5 Aug 89	3
TRAIL OF TEARS	China	47	14 Oct 89	3
VICTIMS OF SUCCESS	China	36	23 Jun 90	3
EMPTY WORLD	China	61	15 Sep 90	1
ALL OR NOTHING	China	53	19 Jun 93	1

ALBUMS: HITS 6 — WEEKS 12

IN THE DYNAMITE JET SALOON	China	97	22 Oct 88	1
A GRAVEYARD OF EMPTY BOTTLES	China	16	25 Mar 89	4
ERROL FLYNN	China	22	30 Sep 89	3
STRAIGHT	China	32	6 Oct 90	2
DOG'S HITS AND THE BOOTLEG ALBUM	China	58	7 Sep 91	1
...MORE UNCHARTERED HEIGHTS OF DISGRACE	China	30	15 May 93	1

Ken DOH
UK

SINGLES: HITS 1 — WEEKS 7

NAKASAKI EP (I NEED A LOVER TONIGHT) [EP]	ffrr	7	30 Mar 96	7

Various mixes of the track I Need A Lover Tonight.

DOKKEN
UK

ALBUMS: HITS 1 — WEEKS 1

BACK FOR THE ATTACK	Elektra	96	21 Nov 87	1

Joe DOLAN
Ireland

SINGLES: HITS 4 — WEEKS 40

MAKE ME AN ISLAND	Pye	3	28 Jun 69	18
TERESA	Pye	20	1 Nov 69	7
MAKE ME AN ISLAND [RE]	Pye	48	8 Nov 69	1
YOU'RE SUCH A GOOD LOOKING WOMAN	Pye	17	28 Feb 70	13
I NEED YOU	Pye	43	17 Sep 77	1

Thomas DOLBY
UK

SINGLES: HITS 9 — WEEKS 51

EUROPA AND THE PIRATE TWINS	Parlophone	48	3 Oct 81	3
WINDPOWER	Venice In Peril	31	14 Aug 82	8
SHE BLINDED ME WITH SCIENCE	Venice In Peril	49	6 Nov 82	4

Features vocals from Dr. Magnus Pike.

SHE BLINDED ME WITH SCIENCE [RI]	Venice In Peril	56	16 Jul 83	4
HYPERACTIVE!	Parlophone Odean Series	17	21 Jan 84	9
I SCARE MYSELF	Parlophone Odean Series	46	31 Mar 84	5

Originally recorded by Dan Hicks and his Hot Licks.

AIRHEAD	Manhattan	53	16 Apr 88	3
CLOSE BUT NO CIGAR	Virgin	22	9 May 92	5
I LOVE YOU GOODBYE	Virgin	36	11 Jul 92	4
SILK PYJAMAS	Virgin	62	26 Sep 92	2
HYPERACTIVE! [RI]	Parlophone	23	22 Jan 94	4

ALBUMS: HITS 4 — WEEKS 29

THE GOLDEN AGE OF WIRELESS	Venice In Peril	65	22 May 82	10
THE FLAT EARTH	Parlophone	14	18 Feb 84	14
ALIENS ATE MY BUICK	Manhattan	30	7 May 88	3
ASTRONAUTS AND HERETICS	Virgin	35	8 Aug 92	2

Joe DOLCE MUSIC THEATRE
US

SINGLES: HITS 1 — WEEKS 10

SHADDAP YOU FACE	Epic	1	7 Feb 81	10

DOLL
UK

SINGLES: HITS 1 — WEEKS 8

DESIRE ME	Beggars Banquet	28	13 Jan 79	8

DOLLAR
UK

SINGLES: HITS 14 — WEEKS 128

SHOOTING STAR	Carrere	14	11 Nov 78	12
WHO WERE YOU WITH IN THE MOONLIGHT	Carrere	14	19 May 79	12
LOVE'S GOTTA HOLD ON ME	Carrere	4	18 Aug 79	13
I WANNA HOLD YOUR HAND	Carrere	9	24 Nov 79	14
TAKIN' A CHANCE ON YOU	WEA	62	25 Oct 80	3

HAND HELD IN BLACK AND WHITE	*WEA*	19	*15 Aug 81*	12
MIRROR MIRROR (MON AMOUR)	*WEA*	4	*14 Nov 81*	17
RING RING	*Carrere*	61	*20 Mar 82*	2
GIVE ME BACK MY HEART	*WEA*	4	*27 Mar 82*	9
VIDEOTHEQUE	*WEA*	17	*19 Jun 82*	10
GIVE ME SOME KINDA MAGIC	*WEA*	34	*18 Sep 82*	6
WE WALKED IN LOVE	*Arista*	61	*16 Aug 86*	4
O L'AMOUR	*London*	7	*26 Dec 87*	11
Originally recorded by Erasure.				
IT'S NATURE'S WAY (NO PROBLEM)	*London*	58	*16 Jul 88*	3

ALBUMS: **HITS 3** **WEEKS 28**

SHOOTING STARS	*Carrere*	36	*15 Sep 79*	8
THE VERY BEST OF DOLLAR	*Carrere*	31	*24 Apr 82*	9
THE DOLLAR ALBUM	*WEA*	18	*30 Oct 82*	11

DOLORES – See CRANBERRIES; Jah WOBBLE'S INVADERS OF THE HEART

Placido DOMINGO
Spain

(See also Placido Domingo and John Denver; Placido Domingo, Diana Ross and José Carreras; Placido Domingo, José Carreras and Montserrat Caballe; Andrew Lloyd Webber; 3 Tenors: José Carreras, Placido Domingo, Luciano Pavarotti; Dionne Warwick Placido Domingo.)

SINGLES: **HITS 2** **WEEKS 11**

TILL I LOVED YOU	*CBS*	24	*27 May 89*	9
Above hit: Placido DOMINGO and Jennifer RUSH.				
TURANDOT 'NESSUM DORMA'	*Epic*	59	*16 Jun 90*	2
Above hit: Luis COBOS featuring Placido DOMINGO.				

ALBUMS: **HITS 8** **WEEKS 57**

MY LIFE FOR A SONG	*CBS*	31	*21 May 83*	8
PLACIDO DOMINGO COLLECTION	*Stylus*	30	*27 Dec 86*	14
GREATEST LOVE SONGS	*CBS*	63	*23 Apr 88*	2
THE ESSENTIAL DOMINGO	*Deutsche Grammophon*	20	*17 Jun 89*	8
GOYA . . . A LIFE IN A SONG	*CBS*	36	*17 Jun 89*	4
BE MY LOVE . . . AN ALBUM OF LOVE	*EMI*	14	*24 Nov 90*	12
THE BROADWAY I LOVE	*East West*	45	*7 Dec 91*	6
Above hit: Placido DOMINGO with the LONDON SYMPHONY ORCHESTRA conducted by Eugene KOHN.				
DOMINGO: ARIAS AND SPANISH SONGS	*Deutsche Grammophon*	47	*13 Jun 92*	3

Placido DOMINGO, José CARRERAS and Montserrat CABALLE
Spain/Italy

(See also José Carreras; Placido Domingo; Freddie Mercury and Montserrat Caballe.)

ALBUMS: **HITS 1** **WEEKS 3**

FROM THE OFFICAL BARCELONA GAMES CEREMONY	*RCA Red Seal*	41	*8 Aug 92*	3

Placido DOMINGO and John DENVER
Spain/US

(See also John Denver; Placido Domingo.)

SINGLES: **HITS 1** **WEEKS 9**

PERHAPS LOVE	*CBS*	46	*12 Dec 81*	9
Above hit: Placido DOMINGO and John DENVER, vocal duet – John DENVER, guitar.				

ALBUMS: **HITS 1** **WEEKS 21**

PERHAPS LOVE	*CBS*	17	*28 Nov 81*	21

Placido DOMINGO, Diana ROSS and José CARRERAS
Spain/US

(See also José Carreras; Placido Domingo; Diana Ross.)

ALBUMS: **HITS 1** **WEEKS 2**

CHRISTMAS IN VIENNA	*Sony Classical*	71	*25 Dec 93*	2
Live recordings from the Rathaus, Vienna, 21 Dec 92.				

DOMINO
US

SINGLES: **HITS 2** **WEEKS 6**

GETTO JAM	*Outburst*	33	*22 Jan 94*	4
SWEET POTATOE PIE	*Outburst*	42	*14 May 94*	2

Fats DOMINO
UK

SINGLES: **HITS 20** **WEEKS 110**

I'M IN LOVE AGAIN	*London*	28	*28 Jul 56*	1
I'M IN LOVE AGAIN [RE]	*London*	12	*18 Aug 56*	13
BLUEBERRY HILL	*London*	26	*1 Dec 56*	1
Originally recorded by Glenn Miller.				
BLUEBERRY HILL [RE]	*London*	6	*22 Dec 56*	14
AIN'T THAT A SHAME	*London*	23	*26 Jan 57*	2
HONEY CHILE	*London*	29	*2 Feb 57*	1
BLUE MONDAY	*London*	23	*30 Mar 57*	1

I'M WALKIN'	*London*	19	20 Apr 57	7
BLUE MONDAY [RE]	*London*	30	20 Apr 57	1
VALLEY OF TEARS	*London*	25	20 Jul 57	1
THE BIG BEAT	*London*	20	29 Mar 58	4
SICK AND TIRED	*London*	26	5 Jul 58	1
Originally recorded by Guy Lombardo.				
MARGIE	*London*	18	23 May 59	5
Originally recorded by Eddie Cantor.				
I WANT TO WALK YOU HOME	*London*	14	17 Oct 59	5
BE MY GUEST	*London*	11	19 Dec 59	8
BE MY GUEST [RE]	*London*	19	20 Feb 60	4
COUNTRY BOY	*London*	19	19 Mar 60	11
WALKING TO NEW ORLEANS	*London*	19	23 Jul 60	10
THREE NIGHTS A WEEK	*London*	45	12 Nov 60	2
MY GIRL JOSEPHINE	*London*	32	7 Jan 61	4
IT KEEPS RAININ'	*London*	49	29 Jul 61	1
WHAT A PARTY	*London*	43	2 Dec 61	1
JAMBALAYA	*London*	41	31 Mar 62	1
RED SAILS IN THE SUNSET	*His Master's Voice*	34	2 Nov 63	6
BLUEBERRY HILL [RI]	*United Artists*	41	24 Apr 76	5
ALBUMS:	**HITS 1**		**WEEKS 1**	
VERY BEST OF FATS DOMINO	*Liberty*	56	16 May 70	1

DOMINOS - See Billy WARD and the DOMINOES

DON-E
UK

SINGLES:	**HITS 3**		**WEEKS 8**	
LOVE MAKES THE WORLD GO ROUND	*Fourth & Broadway*	18	9 May 92	6
PEACE IN THE WORLD	*Fourth & Broadway*	41	25 Jul 92	1
Single was removed from the chart when evidence of hyping was uncovered.				
DELICIOUS	*Mushroom*	52	28 Feb 98	1
Above hit: Deni HINES featuring DON-E.				

DON PABLO'S ANIMALS
Italy

SINGLES:	**HITS 1**		**WEEKS 10**	
VENUS	*Rumour*	4	19 May 90	10

Lonnie DONEGAN
UK

(See also Miki and Griff.)

SINGLES:	**HITS 30**		**WEEKS 321**	
ROCK ISLAND LINE	*Decca*	8	7 Jan 56	13
Sub credit: (Lonnie Donegan-guitar and vocal; Chris Barber-bass; Beryl Bryden-washboard).				
Originally recorded by Leadbelly.				
ROCK ISLAND LINE [RE-1ST]	*Decca*	16	14 Apr 56	3
STEWBALL	*Pye Nixa*	27	21 Apr 56	1
LOST JOHN / STEWBALL	*Pye Nixa*	2	28 Apr 56	17
Stewball was only listed from 12 May 56 for 3 weeks, peaking at No. 7.				
ROCK ISLAND LINE [RE-2ND]	*Decca*	19	12 May 56	6
LONNIE DONEGAN SKIFFLE SESSION [EP]	*Pye Nixa*	20	7 Jul 56	2
Lead track: Railroad Bill.				
Above 6: Lonnie DONEGAN SKIFFLE GROUP.				
BRING A LITTLE WATER, SYLVIE / DEAD OR ALIVE	*Pye Nixa*	7	8 Sep 56	12
Dead Or Alive listed from 15 Sep 56. Bring A Little Water Sylvie originally recorded by				
Leadbelly.				
LONNIE DONEGAN SHOWCASE [LP]	*Pye Nixa*	26	22 Dec 56	3
8 track LP, first track: Wabash Cannonball.				
BRING A LITTLE WATER, SYLVIE / DEAD OR ALIVE [RE]	*Pye Nixa*	30	12 Jan 57	1
DON'T YOU ROCK ME DADDY-O	*Pye Nixa*	4	19 Jan 57	17
CUMBERLAND GAP	*Pye Nixa*	1	6 Apr 57	12
PUTTIN' ON THE STYLE / GAMBLIN' MAN	*Pye Nixa*	1	8 Jun 57	19
Gamblin' Man listed from 22 Jun 57 and had first credit. Both sides are live recordings from the				
London Palladium, 9 May 57. Some copies have Putting rather than Puttin'.				
MY DIXIE DARLING	*Pye Nixa*	10	12 Oct 57	15
Originally recorded by the Carter Family.				
JACK O' DIAMONDS	*Pye Nixa*	14	21 Dec 57	7
THE GRAND COOLIE DAM	*Pye Nixa*	6	12 Apr 58	15
From the film 'Six Five Special'. Title on some copies is Grand Coulee Dam. Originally recorded				
by Woody Guthrie.				
SALLY DON'T YOU GRIEVE / BETTY, BETTY, BETTY	*Pye Nixa*	11	12 Jul 58	7
Sally Don't You Grieve originally recorded by Woody Guthrie.				
LONESOME TRAVELLER	*Pye Nixa*	28	27 Sep 58	1
LONNIE'S SKIFFLE PARTY [M]	*Pye Nixa*	23	15 Nov 58	5
TOM DOOLEY	*Pye Nixa*	3	22 Nov 58	14
DOES YOUR CHEWING GUM LOSE ITS FLAVOUR (ON THE BEDPOST OVERNIGHT)	*Pye Nixa*	3	7 Feb 59	12
Live recording from the New Theatre, Oxford, 13 Dec 58. Originally recorded by Ernest Hare				
& Billy Jones in 1924.				

FORT WORTH JAIL	Pye Nixa	14	9 May 59	5
BATTLE OF NEW ORLEANS	Pye	2	27 Jun 59	16
Recorded at the Bristol Hippodrome. Originally recorded by Jimmie Driftwood.				
SAL'S GOT A SUGAR LIP	Pye	13	12 Sep 59	4
Recorded at the Royal Aquarium, Great Yarmouth.				
SAN MIGUEL	Pye	19	5 Dec 59	4
Above 18: Lonnie DONEGAN and his SKIFFLE GROUP.				
MY OLD MAN'S A DUSTMAN (BALLAD OF A REFUSE DISPOSAL OFFICER)	Pye	1	26 Mar 60	13
Live recording from the Gaumont Cinema, Doncaster.				
Above hit: Lonnie DONEGAN and his Group.				
I WANNA GO HOME (THE WRECK OF THE JOHN "B")	Pye	5	28 May 60	17
Above hit: Lonnie DONEGAN; Wally STOTT ORCHESTRA.				
LORELEI	Pye	10	27 Aug 60	8
LIVELY	Pye	13	26 Nov 60	9
Above hit: Lonnie DONEGAN and his Group.				
VIRGIN MARY	Pye	27	10 Dec 60	5
HAVE A DRINK ON ME	Pye	8	13 May 61	15
MICHAEL, ROW THE BOAT / LUMBERED	Pye	6	2 Sep 61	11
From 14 Oct 61, Lumbered no longer listed on the chart. Recorded at the Winter Gardens Pavilion Theatre, Blackpool.				
Above 2: Lonnie DONEGAN and his Group.				
THE COMANCHEROS	Pye	14	20 Jan 62	10
THE PARTY'S OVER	Pye	9	7 Apr 62	12
From the musical 'Bells Are Ringing'.				
PICK A BALE OF COTTON	Pye	11	18 Aug 62	10
Originally recorded by Leadbelly.				
Above hit: Lonnie DONEGAN and his Group.				

EPS:	HITS 1		WEEKS 8	
YANKEE DOODLE DONEGAN	Pye Nixa	8	1 Oct 60	8

ALBUMS:	HITS 3		WEEKS 29	
GOLDEN AGE OF DONEGAN	Pye Golden Guinea	3	1 Sep 62	23
GOLDEN AGE OF DONEGAN VOLUME 2	Pye Golden Guinea	15	9 Feb 63	3
PUTTING ON THE STYLE	Chrysalis	51	25 Feb 78	3

Tanya DONELLY

US

SINGLES:	HITS 2		WEEKS 2	
PRETTY DEEP	4AD	55	30 Aug 97	1
THE BRIGHT LIGHT	4AD	64	6 Dec 97	1

ALBUMS:	HITS 1		WEEKS 1	
LOVESONGS FOR UNDERDOGS	4AD	36	20 Sep 97	1

Ral DONNER

US

SINGLES:	HITS 1		WEEKS 10	
YOU DON'T KNOW WHAT YOU'VE GOT (UNTIL YOU LOSE IT)	Parlophone	25	23 Sep 61	10

DONOVAN

UK

SINGLES:	HITS 11		WEEKS 100	
CATCH THE WIND	Pye	4	27 Mar 65	13
COLOURS	Pye	4	5 Jun 65	12
TURQUOISE	Pye	30	13 Nov 65	6
SUNSHINE SUPERMAN	Pye	2	10 Dec 66	11
Features Jimmy Page on guitar.				
MELLOW YELLOW	Pye	8	11 Feb 67	8
Backing vocals by Paul McCartney.				
THERE IS A MOUNTAIN	Pye	8	28 Oct 67	11
JENNIFER JUNIPER	Pye	5	24 Feb 68	11
HURDY GURDY MAN	Pye	4	1 Jun 68	10
ATLANTIS	Pye	23	7 Dec 68	8
GOO GOO BARABAJAGAL (LOVE IS HOT)	Pye	12	12 Jul 69	9
Some issues only had title listed as Barabajagal.				
Above hit: DONOVAN and Jeff BECK GROUP.				
JENNIFER JUNIPER	Fontana	68	1 Dec 90	1
Above hit: SINGING CORNER meets DONOVAN.				

EPS:	HITS 2		WEEKS 36	
THE UNIVERSAL SOLDIER	Pye	1	21 Aug 65	30
DONOVAN, VOLUME ONE	Pye	12	5 Mar 66	6

ALBUMS:	HITS 7		WEEKS 73	
WHAT'S BIN DID AND WHAT'D BIN HID	Pye	3	5 Jun 65	16
FAIRY TALE	Pye	20	6 Nov 65	2
SUNSHINE SUPERMAN	Pye	25	8 Jul 67	7
UNIVERSAL SOLDIER	Marble Arch	5	14 Oct 67	18
A GIFT FROM A FLOWER TO A GARDEN	Pye	13	11 May 68	14
OPEN ROAD	Dawn	30	12 Sep 70	4
COSMIC WHEELS	Epic	15	24 Mar 73	12

Jason DONOVAN   Australia

(See also Various Artists: Stage Cast – London 'Joseph and the Amazing Technicolor Dreamcoat'.)

SINGLES:		HITS 17			WEEKS 137
NOTHING CAN DIVIDE US	PWL		5	10 Sep 88	12
ESPECIALLY FOR YOU	PWL		1	10 Dec 88	14
Above hit: Kylie MINOGUE and Jason DONOVAN.					
TOO MANY BROKEN HEARTS	PWL		1	4 Mar 89	13
SEALED WITH A KISS	PWL		1	10 Jun 89	10
EVERY DAY (I LOVE YOU MORE)	PWL		2	9 Sep 89	9
WHEN YOU COME BACK TO ME	PWL		2	9 Dec 89	11
HANG ON TO YOUR LOVE	PWL		8	7 Apr 90	7
ANOTHER NIGHT	PWL		18	30 Jun 90	5
RHYTHM OF THE RAIN	PWL		9	1 Sep 90	6
I'M DOING FINE	PWL		22	27 Oct 90	6
R.S.V.P.	PWL		17	18 May 91	5
ANY DREAM WILL DO	Really Useful		1	22 Jun 91	12
From the musical 'Joseph and the Amazing Technicolor Dreamcoat'.					
HAPPY TOGETHER	PWL		10	24 Aug 91	6
JOSEPH MEGA-REMIX [M]	Really Useful		13	7 Dec 91	8
From the musical 'Joseph and the Amazing Technicolor Dreamcoat'.					
Above hit: Jason DONOVAN with the ORIGNAL LONDON CAST featuring Linzi					
HATELEY, David EASTER and Johnny AMOBI.					
MISSION OF LOVE	Polydor		26	18 Jul 92	4
AS TIME GOES BY	Polydor		26	28 Nov 92	6
ALL AROUND THE WORLD	Polydor		41	7 Aug 93	3
ALBUMS:		HITS 4			WEEKS 99
TEN GOOD REASONS	PWL		1	13 May 89	54
BETWEEN THE LINES	PWL		2	9 Jun 90	26
GREATEST HITS	PWL		9	28 Sep 91	17
ALL AROUND THE WORLD	Polydor		27	11 Sep 93	2

DOOBIE BROTHERS   US

SINGLES:		HITS 6			WEEKS 45
LISTEN TO THE MUSIC	Warner Brothers		29	9 Mar 74	7
TAKE ME IN YOUR ARMS (ROCK ME A LITTLE WHILE)	Warner Brothers		29	7 Jun 75	5
WHAT A FOOL BELIEVES	Warner Brothers		31	17 Feb 79	10
WHAT A FOOL BELIEVES [RE]	Warner Brothers		72	5 May 79	1
MINUTE BY MINUTE	Warner Brothers		47	14 Jul 79	4
WHAT A FOOL BELIEVES [RI]	Warner Brothers		57	24 Jan 87	3
Above hit: DOOBIE BROTHERS featuring Michael McDONALD.					
THE DOCTOR	Capitol		73	29 Jul 89	2
LONG TRAIN RUNNIN'	Warner Brothers		7	27 Nov 93	10
First released 1974, but never charted. Remixed twice, No.125 in 1990 and No. 76 in 1993.					
This entry was remixed by Sure Is Pure.					
LISTEN TO THE MUSIC [RM]	Warner Brothers		37	14 May 94	3
Remixed by Motiv8.					
ALBUMS:		HITS 5			WEEKS 30
WHAT WERE ONCE VICES ARE NOW HABITS	Warner Brothers		19	30 Mar 74	10
STAMPEDE	Warner Brothers		14	17 May 75	11
TAKIN' IT TO THE STREETS	Warner Brothers		42	10 Apr 76	2
LIVING ON THE FAULT LINE	Warner Brothers		25	17 Sep 77	5
ONE STEP CLOSER	Warner Brothers		53	11 Oct 80	2

DOOLALLY   UK

(See also Shanks & Bigfoot.)

SINGLES:		HITS 1			WEEKS 16
STRAIGHT FROM THE HEART	Locked On		20	14 Nov 98	6
Vocals by Sharon Woolf.					
STRAIGHT FROM THE HEART [RE]	Locked On		63	2 Jan 99	4
STRAIGHT FROM THE HEART [RI]	Locked On		9	7 Aug 99	6

DOOLEYS   UK

SINGLES:		HITS 10			WEEKS 83
THINK I'M GONNA FALL IN LOVE WITH YOU	GTO		13	13 Aug 77	10
LOVE OF MY LIFE	GTO		9	12 Nov 77	11
DON'T TAKE IT LYIN' DOWN	GTO		60	13 May 78	3
A ROSE HAS TO DIE	GTO		11	2 Sep 78	11
Originally recorded by the Ryders.					
HONEY I'M LOST	GTO		24	10 Feb 79	9
WANTED	GTO		3	16 Jun 79	14
THE CHOSEN FEW	GTO		7	22 Sep 79	11
LOVE PATROL	GTO		29	8 Mar 80	7
BODY LANGUAGE	GTO		46	6 Sep 80	4
AND I WISH	GTO		52	10 Oct 81	3

ALBUMS:	HITS 3			WEEKS 27
THE BEST OF THE DOOLEYS	GTO	6	30 Jun 79	21
THE CHOSEN FEW	GTO	56	3 Nov 79	4
FULL HOUSE	GTO	54	25 Oct 80	2

Val DOONICAN
Ireland

SINGLES:	HITS 14			WEEKS 143
WALK TALL	Decca	3	17 Oct 64	21
THE SPECIAL YEARS	Decca	7	23 Jan 65	12
I'M GONNA GET THERE SOMEHOW	Decca	25	10 Apr 65	5
THE SPECIAL YEARS [RE]	Decca	49	24 Apr 65	1
ELUSIVE BUTTERFLY	Decca	5	19 Mar 66	12
WHAT WOULD I BE	Decca	2	5 Nov 66	17
MEMORIES ARE MADE OF THIS	Decca	11	25 Feb 67	12
TWO STREETS	Decca	39	27 May 67	4
IF THE WHOLE WORLD STOPPED LOVIN'	Pye	3	21 Oct 67	19
YOU'RE THE ONLY ONE	Pye	37	24 Feb 68	4
NOW	Pye	43	15 Jun 68	2
IF I KNEW THEN WHAT I KNOW NOW	Pye	14	26 Oct 68	13
RING OF BRIGHT WATER	Pye	48	26 Apr 69	1
MORNING	Philips	12	4 Dec 71	13
HEAVEN IS MY WOMAN'S LOVE	Philips	34	10 Mar 73	6
HEAVEN IS MY WOMAN'S LOVE [RE]	Philips	47	28 Apr 73	1

EPS:	HITS 2			WEEKS 44
GREEN SHADES OF VAL DOONICAN	Decca	1	20 Feb 65	39
DOONICAN'S IRISH STEW	Decca	4	28 May 66	5

ALBUMS:	HITS 11			WEEKS 170
LUCKY 13 SHADES OF VAL DOONICAN	Decca	2	12 Dec 64	27
GENTLE SHADES OF VAL DOONICAN	Decca	5	3 Dec 66	52
VAL DOONICAN ROCKS BUT GENTLY	Pye	1	2 Dec 67	23
VAL	Pye	6	30 Nov 68	11
THE WORLD OF VAL DOONICAN	Decca	2	14 Jun 69	31
SOUNDS GENTLE	Pye	22	13 Dec 69	9
THE MAGIC OF VAL DOONICAN	Philips	34	19 Dec 70	3
THIS IS VAL DOONICAN	Philips	40	27 Nov 71	1
I LOVE COUNTRY MUSIC	Philips	37	22 Feb 75	2
SOME OF MY BEST FRIENDS ARE SONGS	Philips	29	21 May 77	5
SONGS FROM MY SKETCH BOOK	Parkfield	33	24 Mar 90	6

DOOP
Holland

SINGLES:	HITS 1			WEEKS 12
DOOP	Citybeat	1	12 Mar 94	12

Based on the Charleston.

DOORS
US

SINGLES:	HITS 4			WEEKS 42
LIGHT MY FIRE	Elektra	49	19 Aug 67	1
HELLO I LOVE YOU, WON'T YOU TELL ME YOUR NAME?	Elektra	15	31 Aug 68	12
RIDERS ON THE STORM	Elektra	50	16 Oct 71	1
RIDERS ON THE STORM [RE]	Elektra	22	30 Oct 71	10
RIDERS ON THE STORM [RI-1ST]	Elektra	33	20 Mar 76	5
HELLO I LOVE YOU [RI]	Elektra	71	3 Feb 79	2
BREAK ON THROUGH	Elektra	64	27 Apr 91	2
LIGHT MY FIRE [RI]	Elektra	7	1 Jun 91	8
RIDERS ON THE STORM [RI-2ND]	Elektra	68	10 Aug 91	1

ALBUMS:	HITS 11			WEEKS 93
WAITING FOR THE SUN	Elektra	16	28 Sep 68	10
MORRISON HOTEL	Elektra	12	11 Apr 70	8
ABSOLUTELY LIVE	Elektra	69	26 Sep 70	1
Live recordings from New York's Felt Forum, January 70.				
L.A. WOMAN	Elektra	28	31 Jul 71	3
WEIRD SCENES INSIDE THE GOLD MINE	Elektra	50	1 Apr 72	1
ALIVE, SHE CRIED	Elektra	36	29 Oct 83	5
From lost tapes discovered in an LA warehouse.				
LIVE AT THE HOLLYWOOD BOWL	Elektra	51	4 Jul 87	3
Live recordings from the Hollywood Bowl, Los Angeles, 5 Jul 68.				
THE DOORS [OST]	Elektra	11	6 Apr 91	17
Only the CD format contains material by other artists.				
Above hit: DOORS and Jim MORRISON and VARIOUS ARTISTS.				
THE BEST OF THE DOORS	Elektra	17	20 Apr 91	18
THE DOORS	Elektra	43	20 Apr 91	12
L.A. WOMAN [RE]	Elektra	73	20 Apr 91	1
IN CONCERT	Elektra	24	1 Jun 91	5
THE DOORS [RE]	Elektra	70	9 Apr 94	1
THE BEST OF THE DOORS [RE]	Elektra	37	21 Mar 98	8
Above 2 re-released at mid-price.				

DOPE SMUGGLAZ
UK

SINGLES:		HITS 2		WEEKS 5	
THE WORD	Perfecto	62	5 Dec 98	1
Based around Frankie Valli's Grease.					
DOUBLE DOUBLE DUTCH	Perfecto	15	7 Aug 99	4

Charlie DORE
UK

SINGLES:		HITS 1		WEEKS 2	
PILOT OF THE AIRWAVES	Island	66	17 Nov 79	2

DO'REEN – See SOUL II SOUL

DOROTHY
UK

SINGLES:		HITS 1		WEEKS 5	
WHAT'S THAT TUNE?	RCA	31	9 Dec 95	5
(DOO DOO, DOO DOO, DOO-DOO-DOO-DOO-DOO-DOO . . .)					
Dance version of the theme tune from LWT's 'Blind Date'.					

Lee DORSEY
US

SINGLES:		HITS 4		WEEKS 36	
GET OUT OF MY LIFE, WOMAN	Stateside	22	5 Feb 66	7
CONFUSION	Stateside	38	7 May 66	6
WORKING IN THE COAL MINE	Stateside	8	13 Aug 66	11
HOLY COW	Stateside	6	29 Oct 66	12
EPS:		HITS 1		WEEKS 4	
YOU'RE BREAKIN' ME UP	Stateside	7	3 Sep 66	4
ALBUMS:		HITS 1		WEEKS 4	
NEW LEE DORSEY	Stateside	34	17 Dec 66	4

Marc DORSEY
US

SINGLES:		HITS 1		WEEKS 1	
IF YOU REALLY WANNA KNOW	Jive	58	19 Jun 99	1

Tommy DORSEY ORCHESTRA starring Warren COVINGTON
US

SINGLES:		HITS 1		WEEKS 19	
TEA FOR TWO CHA CHA	Brunswick	3	18 Oct 58	19

DOUBLE
Switzerland

SINGLES:		HITS 2		WEEKS 10	
THE CAPTAIN OF HER HEART	Polydor	8	25 Jan 86	9
DEVIL'S BALL	Polydor	71	5 Dec 87	1
ALBUMS:		HITS 1		WEEKS 4	
BLUE	Polydor	69	8 Mar 86	4

DOUBLE DEE (featuring DANY)
Italy

SINGLES:		HITS 1		WEEKS 4	
FOUND LOVE	Epic	63	1 Dec 90	2
FOUND LOVE [RM]	Sony	33	25 Nov 95	2
Remixed by Strike.					

DOUBLE 99
UK

(See also R.I.P. Productions.)

SINGLES:		HITS 1		WEEKS 9	
RIPGROOVE	Satellite	31	31 May 97	3
RIP GROOVE [RM]	Satellite	14	1 Nov 97	6
Remixes by Karl 'Tuff Enough' Brown & Matt 'Jam' Lamont.					
Above hit: DOUBLE 99 featuring TOP CAT.					

007 – See also RED RAW featuring 007

DOUBLE SIX
UK

SINGLES:		HITS 2		WEEKS 2	
REAL GOOD	Multiply	66	19 Sep 98	1
BREAKDOWN	Multiply	59	12 Jun 99	1
Vocals by Steve Eusebe.					

DOUBLE TROUBLE
UK

SINGLES:		HITS 5		WEEKS 35	
JUST KEEP ROCKIN'	Desire	11	27 May 89	12
Above hit: DOUBLE TROUBLE and the REBEL MC.					
STREET TUFF	Desire	3	7 Oct 89	14
Above hit: REBEL MC DOUBLE TROUBLE.					

TALK BACK	*Desire*	71	*12 May 90*	1
Above hit: DOUBLE TROUBLE vocals by Janette SEWELL.				
LOVE DON'T LIVE HERE ANYMORE	*Desire*	21	*30 Jun 90*	6
Above hit: DOUBLE TROUBLE vocals – Janette SEWELL voice-overs – Carl BROWN.				
RUB-A-DUB	*Desire*	66	*15 Jun 91*	2
ALBUMS:	**HITS 1**		**WEEKS 1**	
AS ONE	*Desire*	73	*4 Aug 90*	1

DOUBLE YOU?
Italy

SINGLES:	**HITS 1**		**WEEKS 3**	
PLEASE DON'T GO	*ZYX*	41	*2 May 92*	3

Rob DOUGAN
UK

SINGLES:	**HITS 1**		**WEEKS 1**	
FURIOUS ANGELS	*Cheeky*	62	*4 Apr 98*	1

Carl DOUGLAS
Jamaica

(See also Bus Stop.)

SINGLES:	**HITS 3**		**WEEKS 28**	
KUNG FU FIGHTING	*Pye*	1	*17 Aug 74*	13
DANCE THE KUNG FU	*Pye*	35	*30 Nov 74*	5
RUN BACK	*Pye*	25	*3 Dec 77*	10

Carol DOUGLAS
US

SINGLES:	**HITS 1**		**WEEKS 4**	
NIGHT FEVER	*Gull*	66	*22 Jul 78*	4
From the film 'Saturday Night Fever'.				

Craig DOUGLAS
UK

SINGLES:	**HITS 11**		**WEEKS 113**	
A TEENAGER IN LOVE	*Top Rank*	13	*13 Jun 59*	11
ONLY SIXTEEN	*Top Rank*	1	*8 Aug 59*	15
PRETTY BLUE EYES	*Top Rank*	4	*23 Jan 60*	15
Originally recorded by Steve Lawrence.				
HEART OF A TEENAGE GIRL	*Top Rank*	10	*30 Apr 60*	9
OH! WHAT A DAY	*Top Rank*	43	*13 Aug 60*	1
A HUNDRED POUNDS OF CLAY	*Top Rank*	9	*22 Apr 61*	9
Originally recorded by Gene McDaniels.				
TIME	*Top Rank*	9	*1 Jul 61*	14
Originally recorded by Jerry Jackson.				
WHEN MY LITTLE GIRL IS SMILING	*Top Rank*	9	*24 Mar 62*	13
OUR FAVOURITE MELODIES	*Columbia*	9	*30 Jun 62*	10
Originally recorded by Gary Criss.				
Above 4: Craig DOUGLAS with Harry ROBINSON and his Orchestra.				
OH, LONESOME ME	*Decca*	15	*20 Oct 62*	12
TOWN CRIER	*Decca*	36	*2 Mar 63*	4
ALBUMS:	**HITS 1**		**WEEKS 2**	
CRAIG DOUGLAS	*Top Rank*	17	*6 Aug 60*	2

Johnny DOUGLAS and his Orchestra - See JOHNSTON BROTHERS; Joan REGAN; Dickie VALENTINE

DOVE
Ireland

SINGLES:	**HITS 1**		**WEEKS 2**	
DON'T DREAM	*ZTT*	37	*11 Sep 99*	2

DOVES
UK

SINGLES:	**HITS 1**		**WEEKS 1**	
HERE IT COMES	*Casino*	73	*14 Aug 99*	1

DOWLANDS
UK

SINGLES:	**HITS 1**		**WEEKS 7**	
ALL MY LOVING	*Oriole*	33	*11 Jan 64*	7
Originally recorded by the Beatles.				

DOWN
US

ALBUMS:	**HITS 1**		**WEEKS 1**	
NOLA	*Atlantic*	68	*30 Sep 95*	1

Robert DOWNEY Jr.
US

SINGLES:	**HITS 1**		**WEEKS 1**	
SMILE	*Epic*	68	*30 Jan 93*	1
From the film 'Chaplin'.				

Don DOWNING
US

SINGLES:	HITS 1			WEEKS 10
LONELY DAYS LONELY NIGHTS	*People*	32	*10 Nov 73*	10

Will DOWNING
US

SINGLES:	HITS 7			WEEKS 35
A LOVE SUPREME	*Fourth & Broadway*	14	*2 Apr 88*	10
Originally recorded by John Coltrane.				
IN MY DREAMS	*Fourth & Broadway*	34	*25 Jun 88*	6
FREE	*Fourth & Broadway*	58	*1 Oct 88*	5
WHERE IS THE LOVE	*Fourth & Broadway*	19	*21 Jan 89*	7
Above hit: Mica PARIS and Will DOWNING.				
TEST OF TIME	*Fourth & Broadway*	67	*28 Oct 89*	2
COME TOGETHER AS ONE	*Fourth & Broadway*	48	*24 Feb 90*	4
THERE'S NO LIVING WITHOUT YOU	*Fourth & Broadway*	67	*18 Sep 93*	1
ALBUMS:	HITS 3			WEEKS 28
WILL DOWNING	*Fourth & Broadway*	20	*26 Mar 88*	23
COME TOGETHER AS ONE	*Fourth & Broadway*	36	*18 Nov 89*	2
A DREAM FULFILLED	*Fourth & Broadway*	43	*6 Apr 91*	3

DOWNSIDE ABBEY MONKS and CHOIRBOYS
UK

ALBUMS:	HITS 2			WEEKS 6
THE ABBEY	*Virgin*	54	*2 Nov 96*	5
GREGORIAN MOODS	*Virgin*	59	*3 Jan 98*	1

Lamont DOZIER – See HOLLAND-DOZIER featuring Lamont DOZIER

Charlie DRAKE
UK

SINGLES:	HITS 5			WEEKS 37
SPLISH SPLASH	*Parlophone*	7	*9 Aug 58*	11
VOLARE	*Parlophone*	28	*25 Oct 58*	2
MR. CUSTER	*Parlophone*	12	*29 Oct 60*	12
Originally recorded by Larry Verne.				
MY BOOMERANG WON'T COME BACK	*Parlophone*	14	*7 Oct 61*	11
PUCKWUDGIE	*Columbia*	47	*1 Jan 72*	1

Kim DRAKE – See Petula CLARK; Lance FORTUNE; David MacBETH – Kim DRAKE MUSIC – Beryl STOTT GROUP; Gary MILLER

DRAMATIS
UK

SINGLES:	HITS 2			WEEKS 8
LOVE NEEDS NO DISGUISE	*Beggars Banquet*	33	*5 Dec 81*	7
Above hit: Gary NUMAN and DRAMATIS.				
I CAN SEE HER NOW	*Rocket*	57	*13 Nov 82*	1

Rusty DRAPER
US

SINGLES:	HITS 1			WEEKS 4
MULE SKINNER BLUES	*Mercury*	39	*13 Aug 60*	4
Originally recorded by Jimmie Rodgers.				

DREAD ZEPPELIN
US

SINGLES:	HITS 2			WEEKS 3
YOUR TIME IS GONNA COME	*I.R.S.*	59	*1 Dec 90*	1
STAIRWAY TO HEAVEN	*I.R.S.*	62	*13 Jul 91*	2
ALBUMS:	HITS 1			WEEKS 2
UN-LED-ED	*I.R.S.*	71	*11 Aug 90*	2

DREADZONE
UK

SINGLES:	HITS 7			WEEKS 15
ZION YOUTH	*Virgin*	49	*6 May 95*	2
CAPTAIN DREAD	*Virgin*	49	*29 Jul 95*	2
MAXIMUM [EP]	*Virgin*	56	*23 Sep 95*	2
Lead track: Fight the Power 95.				
LITTLE BRITAIN	*Virgin*	20	*6 Jan 96*	6
LIFE LOVE & UNITY	*Virgin*	56	*30 Mar 96*	1
EARTH ANGEL	*Virgin*	51	*10 May 97*	1
MOVING ON	*Virgin*	58	*26 Jul 97*	1
ALBUMS:	HITS 2			WEEKS 5
SECOND LIGHT	*Virgin*	37	*10 Jun 95*	4
BIOLOGICAL RADIO	*Virgin*	45	*9 Aug 97*	1

DREAM ACADEMY
UK

SINGLES:	HITS 2			WEEKS 10
LIFE IN A NORTHERN TOWN	*Blanco Y Negro*	15	*30 Mar 85*	8

THE LOVE PARADE		Blanco Y Negro	68	14 Sep 85	2
ALBUMS:	**HITS 1**			**WEEKS 2**	
THE DREAM ACADEMY		Blanco Y Negro	58	12 Oct 85	2

DREAM FREQUENCY
					UK
SINGLES:	**HITS 5**			**WEEKS 12**	
LOVE, PEACE AND HARMONY		Citybeat	71	12 Jan 91	2
FEEL SO REAL		Citybeat	23	25 Jan 92	5
TAKE ME		Citybeat	39	25 Apr 92	3
Above 2: DREAM FREQUENCY featuring Debbie SHARP.					
GOOD TIMES / THE DREAM		Citybeat	67	21 May 94	1
YOU MAKE ME FEEL MIGHTY REAL		Citybeat	65	10 Sep 94	1

DREAM THEATER
					US
ALBUMS:	**HITS 1**			**WEEKS 1**	
AWAKE		East West	65	15 Oct 94	1

DREAM WARRIORS
					Canada
SINGLES:	**HITS 3**			**WEEKS 19**	
WASH YOUR FACE IN MY SINK		Fourth & Broadway	16	14 Jul 90	8
MY DEFINITION OF A BOOMBASTIC JAZZ STYLE		Fourth & Broadway	13	24 Nov 90	8
LUDI		Fourth & Broadway	39	2 Mar 91	3
ALBUMS:	**HITS 1**			**WEEKS 7**	
AND NOW THE LEGACY BEGINS		Fourth & Broadway	18	16 Feb 91	7

DREAM WEAVERS
					US
SINGLES:	**HITS 1**			**WEEKS 18**	
IT'S ALMOST TOMORROW		Brunswick	1	11 Feb 56	18

DREAMHOUSE
					UK
SINGLES:	**HITS 1**			**WEEKS 2**	
STAY		Chase	62	3 Jun 95	2

DREAMKEEPER
					UK
ALBUMS:	**HITS 1**			**WEEKS 1**	
SPIRIT OF RELAXATION		Flute	71	9 Aug 97	1

DREEM TEEM
					UK
SINGLES:	**HITS 2**			**WEEKS 9**	
THE THEME		Deconstruction	34	13 Dec 97	4
BUDDY X 99		4 Liberty	15	6 Nov 99	5
Remixed by B. Simms. Additional vocals by PSG.					
Above hit: DREEM TEEM 'v' Neneh CHERRY.					

Eddie DRENNON and B.B.S. UNLIMITED
					US
SINGLES:	**HITS 1**			**WEEKS 6**	
LET'S DO THE LATIN HUSTLE		Pye International	20	28 Feb 76	6

Alan DREW
					UK
SINGLES:	**HITS 1**			**WEEKS 2**	
ALWAYS THE LONELY ONE		Columbia	48	28 Sep 63	2

DRIFTERS - See Cliff RICHARD

DRIFTERS
					US
SINGLES:	**HITS 19**			**WEEKS 176**	
DANCE WITH ME		London	17	9 Jan 60	4
DANCE WITH ME [RE]		London	35	12 Mar 60	1
SAVE THE LAST DANCE FOR ME		London	2	5 Nov 60	18
I COUNT THE TEARS		London	28	18 Mar 61	6
WHEN MY LITTLE GIRL IS SMILING		London	31	7 Apr 62	3
I'LL TAKE YOU HOME		London	37	12 Oct 63	5
UNDER THE BOARDWALK		Atlantic	45	26 Sep 64	4
AT THE CLUB		Atlantic	35	10 Apr 65	7
COME ON OVER TO MY PLACE		Atlantic	40	1 May 65	5
BABY WHAT I MEAN		Atlantic	49	4 Feb 67	1
AT THE CLUB [RI]		Atlantic	39	25 Mar 72	1
AT THE CLUB [RI] / SATURDAY NIGHT AT THE MOVIES [RE]		Atlantic	3	8 Apr 72	19
COME ON OVER TO MY PLACE [RI]		Atlantic	9	26 Aug 72	11
LIKE SISTER AND BROTHER		Bell	7	4 Aug 73	12
KISSIN' IN THE BACK ROW OF THE MOVIES		Bell	2	15 Jun 74	13
DOWN ON THE BEACH TONIGHT		Bell	7	12 Oct 74	9

LOVE GAMES	*Bell*	33	*8 Feb 75*	6
THERE GOES MY FIRST LOVE	*Bell*	3	*6 Sep 75*	12
CAN I TAKE YOU HOME LITTLE GIRL	*Bell*	10	*29 Nov 75*	10
HELLO HAPPINESS	*Bell*	12	*13 Mar 76*	8
Originally recorded by Claude Francois.				
EVERY NITE'S A SATURDAY NIGHT WITH YOU	*Bell*	29	*11 Sep 76*	7
YOU'RE MORE THAN A NUMBER IN MY LITTLE RED BOOK	*Arista*	5	*18 Dec 76*	12
SAVE THE LAST DANCE FOR ME [RI] /WHEN MY LITTLE GIRL IS SMILING [RI]	*Lightning*	69	*14 Apr 79*	2
ALBUMS:	**HITS 7**		**WEEKS 92**	
GOLDEN HITS	*Atlantic*	27	*18 May 68*	7
GOLDEN HITS [RE]	*Atlantic*	26	*10 Jun 72*	8
Re-released with a new catalogue number.				
24 ORIGINAL HITS	*Atlantic*	2	*8 Nov 75*	34
LOVE GAMES	*Bell*	51	*13 Dec 75*	1
THE VERY BEST OF THE DRIFTERS	*Telstar*	24	*18 Oct 86*	15
STAND BY ME (THE ULTIMATE COLLECTION)	*Atlantic*	14	*14 Mar 87*	8
The Drifters are only on 3 tracks.				
THE VERY BEST OF BEN E. KING AND THE DRIFTERS	*Telstar*	15	*20 Oct 90*	16
THE VERY BEST OF BEN E. KING AND THE DRIFTERS	*Warner.esp/ Global TV*	41	*7 Nov 98*	3
Above 2 albums are different.				
Above 3: Ben E. KING and the DRIFTERS.				

Julie DRISCOLL, Brian AUGER and the TRINITY — UK

SINGLES:	**HITS 1**		**WEEKS 16**	
THIS WHEEL'S ON FIRE	*Marmalade*	5	*20 Apr 68*	16
Originally recorded by Bob Dylan.				
ALBUMS:	**HITS 1**		**WEEKS 13**	
OPEN	*Marmalade*	12	*8 Jun 68*	13
Above hit: Julie DRISCOLL and the Brian AUGER TRINITY.				

DRIVER 67 — UK

SINGLES:	**HITS 1**		**WEEKS 12**	
CAR 67	*Logo*	7	*23 Dec 78*	12

DRIZA-BONE — US

SINGLES:	**HITS 5**		**WEEKS 18**	
REAL LOVE	*Fourth & Broadway*	16	*22 Jun 91*	8
CATCH THE FIRE	*Fourth & Broadway*	54	*26 Oct 91*	2
PRESSURE	*Fourth & Broadway*	33	*23 Apr 94*	2
BRIGHTEST STAR	*Fourth & Broadway*	45	*15 Oct 94*	2
REAL LOVE [RR]	*Fourth & Broadway*	24	*4 Mar 95*	4
ALBUMS:	**HITS 1**		**WEEKS 1**	
CONSPIRACY	*Fourth & Broadway*	72	*19 Nov 94*	1

Frank D'RONE — US

SINGLES:	**HITS 1**		**WEEKS 6**	
STRAWBERRY BLONDE (THE BAND ROCKED ON)	*Mercury*	24	*24 Dec 60*	6

DRU HILL — US

SINGLES:	**HITS 7**		**WEEKS 42**	
TELL ME	*Fourth & Broadway*	30	*15 Feb 97*	3
From the film 'Eddie'.				
IN MY BED	*Fourth & Broadway*	16	*10 May 97*	3
BIG BAD MAMMA	*Def Jam*	12	*11 Oct 97*	3
From the film 'How To Be A Player'.				
Above hit: Foxy BROWN featuring DRU HILL.				
5 STEPS	*Island Black Music*	22	*6 Dec 97*	3
Above hit: DRU HILL.				
HOW DEEP IS YOUR LOVE	*Island Black Music*	9	*24 Oct 98*	7
Above hit: DRU HILL (featuring REDMAN).				
HOW DEEP IS YOUR LOVE [RE]	*Island Black Music*	75	*16 Jan 99*	1
Above hit: DRU HILL (featuring REDMAN).				
THESE ARE THE TIMES	*Island Black Music*	4	*6 Feb 99*	6
WILD WILD WEST	*Columbia*	2	*10 Jul 99*	16
Samples Stevie Wonder' I Wish. From the film of the same name.				
Above hit: Will SMITH (featuring DRU HILL).				
ALBUMS:	**HITS 1**		**WEEKS 7**	
ENTER THE DRU	*Island Black Music*	42	*7 Nov 98*	7

DRUGSTORE — UK/US/Brazil

SINGLES:	**HITS 3**		**WEEKS 5**	
FADER	*Honey*	72	*10 Jun 95*	1

EL PRESIDENT *Features vocals from Thom Yorke of Radiohead.*	Roadrunner	20	*2 May 98*	3
SOBER	Roadrunner	68	*4 Jul 98*	1
ALBUMS:	**HITS 2**		**WEEKS 3**	
DRUGSTORE	Honey	31	*8 Apr 95*	2
WHITE MAGIC FOR LOVERS	Roadrunner	45	*16 May 98*	1

DRUM CLUB
UK

SINGLES:	**HITS 1**		**WEEKS 1**	
SOUND SYSTEM	Butterfly	62	*6 Nov 93*	1
ALBUMS:	**HITS 1**		**WEEKS 1**	
DRUMS ARE DANGEROUS	Butterfly	53	*20 Aug 94*	1

DRUM THEATRE
UK

SINGLES:	**HITS 2**		**WEEKS 8**	
LIVING IN THE PAST	Epic	67	*15 Feb 86*	2
ELDORADO	Epic	44	*17 Jan 87*	6

DRUPI
Italy

SINGLES:	**HITS 1**		**WEEKS 12**	
VADO VIA	A&M	17	*1 Dec 73*	12

DSK
UK

SINGLES:	**HITS 1**		**WEEKS 4**	
WHAT WOULD WE DO / READ MY LIPS *Read My Lips listed from 7 Sep 91, once single had dropped to No. 51.*	Boys Own Productions	46	*31 Aug 91*	3
WHAT WOULD WE DO? [RM] *Remixed by Industry Standard.*	Fresh	55	*22 Nov 97*	1

DTI
US

SINGLES:	**HITS 1**		**WEEKS 1**	
KEEP THIS FREQUENCY CLEAR	Premiere UK	73	*16 Apr 88*	1

DTOX
UK

SINGLES:	**HITS 1**		**WEEKS 1**	
SHATTERED GLASS	Vitality	75	*21 Nov 92*	1

John DU CANN
UK

SINGLES:	**HITS 1**		**WEEKS 6**	
DON'T BE A DUMMY *Featured in the Levi's Jeans TV commercial.*	Vertigo	33	*22 Sep 79*	6

John DU PREZ - See MODERN ROMANCE

DUB PISTOLS
UK

SINGLES:	**HITS 1**		**WEEKS 1**	
CYCLONE *Vocals by rapper: T.K. Lawrence.*	Concrete	63	*10 Oct 98*	1

DUB WAR
UK

SINGLES:	**HITS 4**		**WEEKS 5**	
STRIKE IT	Earache	70	*3 Jun 95*	1
ENEMY MAKER	Earache	41	*27 Jan 96*	2
CRY DIGNITY	Earache	59	*24 Aug 96*	1
MILLION DOLLAR LOVE	Earache	73	*29 Mar 97*	1

DUBLINERS
Ireland

SINGLES:	**HITS 5**		**WEEKS 45**	
SEVEN DRUNKEN NIGHTS	Major Minor	7	*1 Apr 67*	17
BLACK VELVET BAND *Originally recorded by the Kinsfolk Folk Group.*	Major Minor	15	*2 Sep 67*	15
MAIDS. WHEN YOU'RE YOUNG. NEVER WED AN OLD MAN	Major Minor	43	*23 Dec 67*	3
THE IRISH ROVER	Stiff	8	*28 Mar 87*	8
JACK'S HEROES / WHISKEY IN THE JAR *Above 2: POGUES and the DUBLINERS.*	Pogue Mahone	63	*16 Jun 90*	2
ALBUMS:	**HITS 5**		**WEEKS 88**	
A DROP OF THE HARD STUFF	Major Minor	5	*13 May 67*	41
BEST OF THE DUBLINERS	Transatlantic	25	*9 Sep 67*	11
MORE OF THE HARD STUFF	Major Minor	8	*7 Oct 67*	23
DRINKIN' AND COURTIN'	Major Minor	31	*2 Mar 68*	3
THE DUBLINERS 25 YEARS CELEBRATION	Stylus	43	*25 Apr 87*	10

DUBSTAR | | | | UK |

SINGLES:	HITS 7			WEEKS 25
STARS	Food	40	8 Jul 95	3
ANYWHERE	Food	37	30 Sep 95	3
NOT SO MANIC NOW	Food	18	6 Jan 96	5
STARS [RI]	Food	15	30 Mar 96	6
ELEVATOR SONG – THE MIXES	Food	25	3 Aug 96	2
NO MORE TALK	Food	20	19 Jul 97	3
CATHEDRAL PARK	Food	41	20 Sep 97	1
I WILL BE YOUR GIRLFRIEND	Food	28	7 Feb 98	2
ALBUMS:	**HITS 2**			**WEEKS 20**
DISGRACEFUL	Food	33	21 Oct 95	5
DISGRACEFUL [RE]	Food	30	6 Apr 96	13
GOODBYE	Food	18	4 Oct 97	2

Anne DUDLEY - See TRAVIS

Mary DUFF - See Daniel O'DONNELL

DUFFO | | | | Australia |

SINGLES:	HITS 1			WEEKS 2
GIVE ME BACK ME BRAIN	Beggars Banquet	60	24 Mar 79	2

Stephen 'Tin Tin' DUFFY | | | | UK |

SINGLES:	HITS 3			WEEKS 24
HOLD IT	Curve	55	9 Jul 83	4
Above hit: TINTIN.				
KISS ME	10 Records	4	2 Mar 85	11
Original release reached No. 78 in 1984.				
ICING ON THE CAKE	10 Records	14	18 May 85	9
ALBUMS:	**HITS 1**			**WEEKS 7**
THE UPS AND DOWNS	10 Records	35	20 Apr 85	7

DUKE | | | | UK |

SINGLES:	HITS 1			WEEKS 5
SO IN LOVE WITH YOU	Encore	66	25 May 96	1
SO IN LOVE WITH YOU [RI]	Pukka	22	26 Oct 96	4

George DUKE | | | | US |

SINGLES:	HITS 1			WEEKS 6
BRAZILIAN LOVE AFFAIR	Epic	36	12 Jul 80	6
ALBUMS:	**HITS 1**			**WEEKS 4**
BRAZILIAN LOVE AFFAIR	Epic	33	26 Jul 80	4

DUKES - See Steve EARL

DUKES | | | | UK |

SINGLES:	HITS 2			WEEKS 13
MYSTERY GIRL	WEA	47	17 Oct 81	7
THANK YOU FOR THE PARTY	WEA	53	1 May 82	6
Above hit: DUKES (BUGATTI and MUSKER).				

Candy DULFER | | | | Holland |

(See also David A. Stewart.)

ALBUMS:	HITS 2			WEEKS 11
LILY WAS HERE	AnXious	6	24 Feb 90	12
Above hit: David A. STEWART featuring Candy DULFER.				
SAXUALITY	RCA	60	4 Aug 90	2
SINGLES:	**HITS 2**			**WEEKS 14**
SAXUALITY	RCA	27	18 Aug 90	9
SAX-A-GO-GO	Ariola	56	13 Mar 93	2

Thuli DUMAKUDE - See CRY FREEDOM

John DUMMER and Helen APRIL | | | | UK |

SINGLES:	HITS 1			WEEKS 3
BLUE SKIES	Speed	54	28 Aug 82	3

Sly DUNBAR and Robert SHAKESPEARE - See SLY and ROBBIE

DUNBLANE | | | | UK |

SINGLES:	HITS 1			WEEKS 15
KNOCKIN' ON HEAVEN'S DOOR / THROW THESE GUNS AWAY	BMG	1	21 Dec 96	15
Recorded in memory of the children murdered in the Dunblaine shooting in March '96.				

Johnny DUNCAN and the BLUE GRASS BOYS

US

SINGLES:		HITS 3			WEEKS 20
LAST TRAIN TO SAN FERNANDO	Columbia		2	27 Jul 57	17
BLUE, BLUE HEARTACHE	Columbia		27	26 Oct 57	1
FOOTPRINTS IN THE SNOW	Columbia		27	30 Nov 57	1
FOOTPRINTS IN THE SNOW [RE]	Columbia		28	4 Jan 58	1

David DUNDAS

UK

SINGLES:		HITS 2			WEEKS 14
JEANS ON	Air		3	24 Jul 76	9
Featured in the Brutus Jeans TV commercial.					
ANOTHER FUNNY HONEYMOON	Air		29	9 Apr 77	5

DUNE - See Quincy JONES

Errol DUNKLEY

Jamaica

SINGLES:		HITS 2			WEEKS 14
O.K. FRED	Scope		11	22 Sep 79	11
Originally recorded by John Holt.					
SIT DOWN AND CRY	Scope		52	2 Feb 80	3

Clive DUNN

UK

SINGLES:		HITS 1			WEEKS 28
GRANDAD	Columbia		1	28 Nov 70	27
GRANDAD [RE]	Columbia		50	26 Jun 71	1

Simon DUPREE and the BIG SOUND

UK

SINGLES:		HITS 2			WEEKS 16
KITES	Parlophone		9	25 Nov 67	13
FOR WHOM THE BELL TOLLS	Parlophone		43	6 Apr 68	3
ALBUMS:		**HITS 1**			**WEEKS 1**
WITHOUT RESERVATIONS	Parlophone		39	19 Aug 67	1

DURAN DURAN

UK

SINGLES:		HITS 29			WEEKS 221
PLANET EARTH	EMI		12	21 Feb 81	11
CARELESS MEMORIES	EMI		37	9 May 81	7
GIRLS ON FILM	EMI		5	25 Jul 81	11
MY OWN WAY	EMI		14	28 Nov 81	11
HUNGRY LIKE THE WOLF	EMI		5	15 May 82	12
SAVE A PRAYER	EMI		2	21 Aug 82	9
RIO	EMI		9	13 Nov 82	11
IS THERE SOMETHING I SHOULD KNOW?	EMI		1	26 Mar 83	9
UNION OF THE SNAKE	EMI		3	29 Oct 83	7
UNION OF THE SNAKE [RE]	EMI		66	24 Dec 83	4
NEW MOON ON MONDAY	EMI		9	4 Feb 84	7
THE REFLEX	EMI		1	28 Apr 84	14
THE WILD BOYS	Parlophone		2	3 Nov 84	14
A VIEW TO A KILL	Parlophone		2	18 May 85	16
Theme from the James Bond film of the same name.					
NOTORIOUS	EMI		7	1 Nov 86	6
NOTORIOUS [RE]	EMI		73	3 Jan 87	1
SKIN TRADE	EMI		22	21 Feb 87	6
MEET EL PRESIDENTE	EMI		24	25 Apr 87	5
I DON'T WANT YOUR LOVE	EMI		14	1 Oct 88	5
ALL SHE WANTS IS	EMI		9	7 Jan 89	5
DO YOU BELIEVE IN SHAME?	EMI		30	22 Apr 89	4
Above 3: DURANDURAN.					
BURNING THE GROUND [M]	EMI		31	16 Dec 89	5
Medley of earlier hits.					
VIOLENCE OF SUMMER (LOVE'S TAKING OVER)	Parlophone		20	4 Aug 90	4
SERIOUS	Parlophone		48	17 Nov 90	3
ORDINARY WORLD	Parlophone		6	30 Jan 93	9
COME UNDONE	Parlophone		13	10 Apr 93	8
TOO MUCH INFORMATION	Parlophone		35	4 Sep 93	3
PERFECT DAY	Parlophone		28	25 Mar 95	4
Cover of a Lou Reed track from his 1973 album Transformer.					
WHITE LINES (DON'T DO IT)	Parlophone		17	17 Jun 95	4
OUT OF MY MIND	Virgin		21	24 May 97	2
From the film 'The Saint'.					
ELECTRIC BARBARELLA	EMI		23	30 Jan 99	3
ALBUMS:		**HITS 12**			**WEEKS 393**
DURAN DURAN	EMI		3	27 Jun 81	118
RIO	EMI		2	22 May 82	109
SEVEN AND THE RAGGED TIGER	EMI		1	3 Dec 83	47

ARENA	Parlophone	6	24 Nov 84	31
Live recordings from their 1984 world tour.				
NOTORIOUS	EMI	16	6 Dec 86	16
BIG THING	EMI	15	29 Oct 88	5
Above hit: DURANDURAN.				
DECADE	EMI	5	25 Nov 89	15
LIBERTY	Parlophone	8	1 Sep 90	4
DURAN DURAN (THE WEDDING ALBUM)	Parlophone	4	27 Feb 93	23
DECADE [RI]	Parlophone	66	24 Sep 94	1
THANK YOU	Parlophone	12	8 Apr 95	3
Album of cover versions.				
GREATEST	EMI	15	21 Nov 98	20
STRANGE BEHAVIOUR	EMI	70	27 Mar 99	1
12" versions and remixes.				

Jimmy DURANTE — US

SINGLES:	**HITS 1**		**WEEKS 1**	
MAKE SOMEONE HAPPY	Warner Brothers	69	14 Dec 96	1

Deanna DURBIN — Canada

ALBUMS:	**HITS 1**		**WEEKS 4**	
THE BEST OF DEANNA DURBIN	MCA	84	30 Jan 82	4

Tyler DURDEN – See DUST BROTHERS (Michael SIMPSON and John KING) featuring Tyler DURDEN

Judith DURHAM — Australia

(See also Seekers.)

SINGLES:	**HITS 1**		**WEEKS 5**	
THE OLIVE TREE	Columbia	33	17 Jun 67	5
ALBUMS:	**HITS 2**		**WEEKS 14**	
CARNIVAL OF HITS	EMI	7	23 Apr 94	12
Above hit: Judith DURHAM and the SEEKERS.				
MONA LISAS	EMI Premier	46	30 Mar 96	2

Ian DURY and the BLOCKHEADS — UK

SINGLES:	**HITS 6**		**WEEKS 55**	
WHAT A WASTE	Stiff	9	29 Apr 78	12
Above hit: Ian DURY and the BLOCKHEADS and JANKEL and JENNER and LATHAM.				
HIT ME WITH YOUR RHYTHM STICK	Stiff	1	9 Dec 78	15
Above hit: IAN and the BLOCKHEADS.				
REASONS TO BE CHEERFUL, PART 3	Stiff	3	4 Aug 79	8
I WANT TO BE STRAIGHT	Stiff	22	30 Aug 80	7
SUEPERMAN'S BIG SISTER	Stiff	51	15 Nov 80	3
HIT ME WITH YOUR RHYTHM STICK [RM-1ST]	Stiff	55	25 May 85	4
Remixed by Paul Hardcastle.				
PROFOUNDLY IN LOVE WITH PANDORA	EMI	45	26 Oct 85	5
Theme from the ITV series 'The Secret Diary Of Adrian Mole'.				
Above hit: Ian DURY.				
HIT ME WITH YOUR RHYTHM STICK '91 [RM-2ND]	Flying	73	27 Jul 91	1
ALBUMS:	**HITS 7**		**WEEKS 122**	
NEW BOOTS AND PANTIES!!	Stiff	5	22 Oct 77	90
Above hit: Ian DURY.				
DO IT YOURSELF	Stiff	2	2 Jun 79	18
LAUGHTER	Stiff	48	6 Dec 80	4
LORD UPMINSTER	Polydor	53	10 Oct 81	4
4,000 WEEKS HOLIDAY	Polydor	54	4 Feb 84	2
Above hit: Ian DURY and the MUSIC STUDENTS.				
MR. LOVE PANTS	Ronnie Harris	57	11 Jul 98	2
REASONS TO BE CHEERFUL - THE VERY BEST OF IAN DURY AND THE BLOCKHEADS	EMI	40	9 Oct 99	2

DUST BROTHERS (Michael SIMPSON and John KING) featuring Tyler DURDEN — US

SINGLES:	**HITS 1**		**WEEKS 1**	
THIS IS YOUR LIFE – MUSIC FROM FIGHT CLUB	Restless	60	11 Dec 99	1
From the film 'The Fight Club'. Features vocals by Brad Pitt.				

DUST JUNKYS — UK

SINGLES:	**HITS 3**		**WEEKS 5**	
(NONSTOPOPERATION)	Polydor	47	15 Nov 97	2
WHAT.TIME.IS.IT.?	Polydor	39	28 Feb 98	2
NOTHIN' PERSONAL	Polydor	62	16 May 98	1
Samples Oh Well by Fleetwood Mac.				

ALBUMS:		HITS 1		WEEKS 2	
DONE AND DUSTED	Polydor		35	21 Mar 98	2

Slim DUSTY with Dick CARR and his BUSHLANDERS
Australia

SINGLES:		HITS 1		WEEKS 15	
A PUB WITH NO BEER	Columbia		3	31 Jan 59	15

Ondrea DUVERNEY – See HUSTLERS CONVENTION featuring Dave LAUDAT and Ondrea DUVERNEY

DWEEB
UK

SINGLES:		HITS 2		WEEKS 2	
SCOOBY DOO	Blanco Y Negro		63	22 Feb 97	1
OH YEAH, BABY	Blanco Y Negro		70	7 Jun 97	1

Bob DYLAN
US

(See also Bob Dylan and the Grateful Dead.)

SINGLES:		HITS 18		WEEKS 136	
TIMES THEY ARE A-CHANGIN'	CBS		9	27 Mar 65	11
SUBTERRANEAN HOMESICK BLUES	CBS		9	1 May 65	9
MAGGIE'S FARM	CBS		22	19 Jun 65	8
LIKE A ROLLING STONE	CBS		4	21 Aug 65	12
Features Al Kooper (from Blood Sweat & Tears) on organ.					
POSITIVELY 4TH STREET	CBS		8	30 Oct 65	12
CAN YOU PLEASE CRAWL OUT YOUR WINDOW	CBS		17	29 Jan 66	5
ONE OF US MUST KNOW (SOONER OR LATER)	CBS		33	16 Apr 66	5
RAINY DAY WOMEN NOS. 12 & 35	CBS		7	14 May 66	8
I WANT YOU	CBS		16	23 Jul 66	9
I THREW IT ALL AWAY	CBS		30	17 May 69	6
LAY LADY LAY	CBS		5	13 Sep 69	12
Written for his wife at the time Sarah Lowndres.					
WATCHING THE RIVER FLOW	CBS		24	10 Jul 71	9
KNOCKIN' ON HEAVEN'S DOOR	CBS		14	6 Oct 73	9
HURRICANE	CBS		43	7 Feb 76	4
BABY STOP CRYING	CBS		13	29 Jul 78	11
IS YOUR LOVE IN VAIN?	CBS		56	28 Oct 78	3
DIGNITY	Columbia		33	20 May 95	2
LOVE SICK	Columbia		64	11 Jul 98	1

EPS:		HITS 3		WEEKS 57	
BOB DYLAN	CBS		3	3 Jul 65	41
ONE TOO MANY MORNINGS	CBS		8	19 Feb 66	8
MR. TAMBOURINE MAN	CBS		4	15 Oct 66	8

ALBUMS:		HITS 39		WEEKS 598	
THE FREEWHEELIN' BOB DYLAN	CBS		11	23 May 64	17
THE TIMES THEY ARE A-CHANGIN'	CBS		15	11 Jul 64	6
ANOTHER SIDE OF BOB DYLAN	CBS		8	21 Nov 64	19
THE FREEWHEELIN' BOB DYLAN [RE]	CBS		1	13 Mar 65	32
THE TIMES THEY ARE A-CHANGIN' [RE]	CBS		4	20 Mar 65	14
BOB DYLAN	CBS		13	8 May 65	6
BRINGING IT ALL BACK HOME	CBS		1	15 May 65	29
HIGHWAY 61 REVISITED	CBS		4	9 Oct 65	15
BLONDE ON BLONDE	CBS		3	20 Aug 66	15
GREATEST HITS	CBS		6	14 Jan 67	82
JOHN WESLEY HARDING	CBS		1	2 Mar 68	29
NASHVILLE SKYLINE	CBS		1	17 May 69	42
SELF PORTRAIT	CBS		1	11 Jul 70	15
NEW MORNING	CBS		1	28 Nov 70	18
MORE BOB DYLAN GREATEST HITS	CBS		12	25 Dec 71	15
PAT GARRETT & BILLY THE KID [OST]	CBS		29	29 Sep 73	11
Only 3 tracks are included with his vocals, though he wrote the soundtrack and appeared in the film as outlaw Alias.					
PLANET WAVES	Island		7	23 Feb 74	8
BEFORE THE FLOOD	Asylum		8	13 Jul 74	7
Live recordings from the January & February 74 US tour. Supported by the Band.					
BLOOD ON THE TRACKS	CBS		4	15 Feb 75	16
THE BASEMENT TAPES	CBS		8	26 Jul 75	10
DESIRE	CBS		3	31 Jan 76	35
HARD RAIN	CBS		3	9 Oct 76	7
Live recordings from Forth Worth, Texas and Fort Collins, Colarado.					
STREET LEGAL	CBS		2	1 Jul 78	20
BOB DYLAN AT BUDOKAN	CBS		4	26 May 79	19
Live recordings from Japan 1 March 78.					
SLOW TRAIN COMING	CBS		2	8 Sep 79	13
SAVED	CBS		3	28 Jun 80	8
SHOT OF LOVE	CBS		6	29 Aug 81	8
INFIDELS	CBS		9	12 Nov 83	12

REAL LIVE	CBS	54	15 Dec 84	2
Live recordings from his Summer 1984 European tour.				
EMPIRE BURLESQUE	CBS	11	22 Jun 85	6
KNOCKED OUT LOADED	CBS	35	2 Aug 86	5
GREATEST HITS [RE]	CBS	99	23 Apr 88	1
Re-released at mid-price.				
DOWN IN THE GROOVE	CBS	32	25 Jun 88	3
OH MERCY	CBS	6	14 Oct 89	7
UNDER THE SKY	CBS	13	29 Sep 90	3
THE BOOTLEG SERIES VOLUMES 1-3	Columbia	32	13 Apr 91	5
GOOD AS I BEEN TO YOU	Columbia	18	14 Nov 92	3
WORLD GONE WRONG	Columbia	35	20 Nov 93	2
UNPLUGGED	Columbia	10	29 Apr 95	5
Recorded for MTV on 17 Nov 94.				
GREATEST HITS [RI]	Columbia	47	23 Sep 95	2
THE BEST OF BOB DYLAN	Columbia	6	14 Jun 97	18
TIME OUT OF MIND	Columbia	10	11 Oct 97	6
LIVE AT THE ROYAL ALBERT HALL	Legacy	19	24 Oct 98	2
Live recordings actually from Manchester's Free Trade Hall in the mid 1960s.				

Bob DYLAN and the GRATEFUL DEAD | US

(See also Bob Dylan; Grateful Dead.)

ALBUMS:	HITS 1			WEEKS 3
DYLAN AND THE DEAD	CBS	38	18 Feb 89	3

DYNAMIX II featuring: TOO TOUGH TEE | US

SINGLES:	HITS 1			WEEKS 4
JUST GIVE THE DJ A BREAK	Cooltempo	50	8 Aug 87	4

DYNASTY | US

SINGLES:	HITS 3			WEEKS 20
I DON'T WANT TO BE A FREAK (BUT I CAN'T HELP MYSELF)	Solar	20	13 Oct 79	13
I'VE JUST BEGUN TO LOVE YOU	Solar	51	9 Aug 80	4
DOES THAT RING A BELL	Solar	53	21 May 83	3

DYNASTY OF TWO featuring ROWETTA – See VARIOUS ARTISTS (EPs) 'The Further Adventures Of North - More Underground Dance EP'

Ronnie DYSON | US

SINGLES:	HITS 1			WEEKS 6
WHEN YOU GET RIGHT DOWN TO IT	CBS	34	4 Dec 71	6
Originally recorded by Barry Mann.				

E

Katherine E | US

SINGLES:	HITS 2			WEEKS 7
I'M ALRIGHT	Dead Dead Good	41	6 Apr 91	5
THEN I FEEL GOOD	PWL Continental	56	18 Jan 92	2

Lizz E - See FRESH 4 (CHILDREN OF THE GHETTO) featuring Lizz E

Sheila E | US

SINGLES:	HITS 1			WEEKS 9
THE BELLE OF ST. MARK	Warner Brothers	18	23 Feb 85	9

E-LUSTRIOUS | UK

(See also Direkt.)

SINGLES:	HITS 2			WEEKS 2
DANCE NO MORE	MOS	58	15 Feb 92	1
Above hit: E-LUSTRIOUS featuring Deborah FRENCH.				
IN YOUR DANCE	UFG	69	2 Jul 94	1

E-MALE | UK

SINGLES:	HITS 1			WEEKS 1
WE ARE E-MALE	East West	44	31 Jan 98	1

E-MOTION | UK

SINGLES:	HITS 2			WEEKS 7
THE NAUGHTY NORTH & THE SEXY SOUTH	Sound Proof	20	3 Feb 96	3

I STAND ALONE	*Sound Proof*	60	*17 Aug 96*	1
THE NAUGHTY NORTH & THE SEXY SOUTH [RI]	*Sound Proof*	17	*26 Oct 96*	3

E – ROTIC US/Germany

SINGLES:	HITS 1		WEEKS 2	
MAX DON'T HAVE SEX WITH YOUR EX	*Stip*	45	*3 Jun 95*	2

E-17 – See EAST 17

E-SMOOVE featuring Latanza WATERS UK/US

SINGLES:	HITS 1		WEEKS 1	
DEJA VU	*AM:PM*	63	*15 Aug 98*	1

E STREET BAND – See Bruce SPRINGSTEEN

E-TYPE Sweden

SINGLES:	HITS 1		WEEKS 1	
THIS IS THE WAY	*Ffrreedom*	53	*23 Sep 95*	1

E.U. – See SALT-N-PEPA

E.V.E. UK/US

SINGLES:	HITS 2		WEEKS 5	
GROOVE OF LOVE	*MCA*	30	*1 Oct 94*	3
GOOD LIFE	*MCA*	39	*28 Jan 95*	2

E'VOKE UK

SINGLES:	HITS 2		WEEKS 6	
RUNAWAY	*Ffrreedom*	30	*25 Nov 95*	3
ARMS OF LOREN	*Manifesto*	25	*24 Aug 96*	3

E.Y.C. US

SINGLES:	HITS 7		WEEKS 36	
FEELIN' ALRIGHT	*MCA*	16	*11 Dec 93*	8
THE WAY YOU WORK IT	*MCA*	14	*5 Mar 94*	7
NUMBER ONE	*MCA*	27	*14 May 94*	5
BLACK BOOK	*MCA*	13	*30 Jul 94*	6
ONE MORE CHANCE	*MCA*	25	*10 Dec 94*	6
OOH-AH-AA (I FEEL IT)	*MCA*	33	*23 Sep 95*	2
IN THE BEGINNING	*MCA*	41	*2 Dec 95*	2
ALBUMS:	HITS 1		WEEKS 5	
EXPRESS YOURSELF CLEARLY	*MCA*	14	*16 Apr 94*	5

E-Z ROLLERS UK

SINGLES:	HITS 1		WEEKS 3	
WALK THIS LAND	*Moving Shadow*	18	*24 Apr 99*	3
From the film 'Lock, Stock And Two Smoking Barrels'.				

E-ZEE POSSEE UK

SINGLES:	HITS 4		WEEKS 16	
EVERYTHING STARTS WITH AN 'E'	*More Protein*	69	*26 Aug 89*	1
Sleeve shows title as Everything Begins With An 'E'.				
LOVE ON LOVE	*More Protein*	59	*20 Jan 90*	3
Above hit: E-ZEE POSSEE featuring DR. MOUTHQUAKE.				
EVERYTHING STARTS WITH AN 'E' [RE]	*More Protein*	15	*17 Mar 90*	8
THE SUN MACHINE	*More Protein*	62	*30 Jun 90*	3
BREATHING IS E-ZEE	*More Protein*	72	*21 Sep 91*	1
Above hit: E-ZEE POSSEE featuring Tara NEWLEY.				

EAGLES US

SINGLES:	HITS 9		WEEKS 51	
ONE OF THESE NIGHTS	*Asylum*	23	*9 Aug 75*	7
LYIN' EYES	*Asylum*	23	*1 Nov 75*	7
TAKE IT TO THE LIMIT	*Asylum*	12	*6 Mar 76*	7
NEW KID IN TOWN	*Asylum*	20	*15 Jan 77*	7
HOTEL CALIFORNIA	*Asylum*	8	*16 Apr 77*	10
PLEASE COME HOME FOR CHRISTMAS	*Asylum*	30	*16 Dec 78*	5
Originally recorded by Charles Brown.				
HEARTACHE TONIGHT	*Asylum*	40	*13 Oct 79*	5
Co-written by Bob Seger.				
THE LONG RUN	*Elektra*	66	*1 Dec 79*	2
LOVE WILL KEEP US ALIVE	*Geffen*	52	*13 Jul 96*	1
ALBUMS:	HITS 10		WEEKS 379	
ON THE BORDER	*Asylum*	28	*27 Apr 74*	9

DESPERADO	*Asylum*	39	*12 Jul 75*	9
ONE OF THESE NIGHTS	*Asylum*	8	*12 Jul 75*	40
THEIR GREATEST HITS 1971-1975	*Asylum*	2	*6 Mar 76*	77
HOTEL CALIFORNIA	*Asylum*	2	*25 Dec 76*	61
THE LONG RUN	*Asylum*	4	*13 Oct 79*	16
LIVE	*Asylum*	24	*22 Nov 80*	13
Compiled from onstage recordings during the 1970s.				
THE BEST OF EAGLES	*Asylum*	10	*18 May 85*	24
HOTEL CALIFORNIA [RE]	*Asylum*	56	*28 Feb 87*	8
Includes re-entries through to 1996. Peak position reached in 1994.				
THE BEST OF EAGLES [RE-1ST]	*Asylum*	8	*13 Aug 88*	41
THE BEST OF EAGLES [RE-2ND]	*Asylum*	15	*30 Apr 94*	8
Re-released at mid-price.				
THE VERY BEST OF THE EAGLES	*Elektra*	4	*23 Jul 94*	51
Includes re-entries through to 1999.				
HELL FREEZES OVER	*Geffen*	28	*19 Nov 94*	11
ONE OF THESE NIGHTS [RE]	*Asylum*	57	*11 Mar 95*	1
Re-released at mid-price.				
HELL FREEZES OVER [RE]	*Geffen*	18	*13 Jul 96*	10

Robert EARL
UK

SINGLES:	HITS 3			WEEKS 27
I MAY NEVER PASS THIS WAY AGAIN	*Philips*	14	*26 Apr 58*	13
MORE THAN EVER (COME PRIMA)	*Philips*	26	*25 Oct 58*	2
MORE THAN EVER (COME PRIMA) [RE]	*Philips*	28	*22 Nov 58*	2
THE WONDERFUL SECRET OF LOVE	*Philips*	17	*14 Feb 59*	10

Above 3: Robert EARL with Wally STOTT and his Orchestra and Chorus.

Charles EARLAND
US

SINGLES:	HITS 1			WEEKS 5
LET THE MUSIC PLAY	*Mercury*	46	*19 Aug 78*	5

Steve EARLE
US

SINGLES:	HITS 2			WEEKS 7
COPPERHEAD ROAD	*MCA*	45	*15 Oct 88*	6
JOHNNY COME LATELY	*MCA*	75	*31 Dec 88*	1
ALBUMS:	HITS 7			WEEKS 20
EXIT O	*MCA*	77	*4 Jul 87*	2
COPPERHEAD ROAD	*MCA*	42	*19 Nov 88*	8
THE HARD WAY	*MCA*	22	*7 Jul 90*	4
SHUT UP AND DIE LIKE AN AVIATOR	*MCA*	62	*19 Oct 91*	1

Above 2: Steve EARLE and the DUKES.

I FEEL ALRIGHT	*Transatlantic*	44	*23 Mar 96*	3
EL COROZON	*Warner Brothers*	59	*18 Oct 97*	1
THE MOUNTAIN	*Grapevine*	51	*6 Mar 99*	1

Above hit: Steve EARLE and the Del McCOURY BAND.

EARLY MUSIC CONSORT, directed by David MUNROW
UK

SINGLES:	HITS 1			WEEKS 1
HENRY VIII SUITE: THE SIX WIVES OF HENRY VIII [OST-TV] [EP]	*BBC*	49	*3 Apr 71*	1

Lead track: Fanfare, Passomezo Du Roy, Gaillard De Escosse. This was the theme and incidental music from the six plays written for BBC-TV.

EARTH, WIND AND FIRE
US

(See also Various Artists: Films – Original Soundtracks 'Sgt. Pepper's Lonely Hearts Club Band'.)

SINGLES:	HITS 17			WEEKS 128
SATURDAY NITE	*CBS*	17	*12 Feb 77*	9
FANTASY	*CBS*	14	*11 Feb 78*	10
JUPITER	*CBS*	41	*13 May 78*	5
MAGIC MIND	*CBS*	75	*29 Jul 78*	1
MAGIC MIND [RE]	*CBS*	54	*12 Aug 78*	4
GOT TO GET YOU INTO MY LIFE	*CBS*	33	*7 Oct 78*	7
Originally recorded by the Beatles.				
SEPTEMBER	*CBS*	3	*9 Dec 78*	13
BOOGIE WONDERLAND	*CBS*	4	*12 May 79*	13
Above hit: EARTH, WIND AND FIRE with the EMOTIONS.				
AFTER THE LOVE HAS GONE	*CBS*	4	*28 Jul 79*	10
STAR	*CBS*	16	*6 Oct 79*	8
CAN'T LET GO	*CBS*	46	*15 Dec 79*	7
IN THE STONE	*CBS*	53	*8 Mar 80*	3
LET ME TALK	*CBS*	29	*11 Oct 80*	5
BACK ON THE ROAD	*CBS*	63	*20 Dec 80*	4
LET'S GROOVE	*CBS*	3	*7 Nov 81*	13
I'VE HAD ENOUGH	*CBS*	29	*6 Feb 82*	6
FALL IN LOVE WITH ME	*CBS*	47	*5 Feb 83*	4

SYSTEM OF SURVIVAL	CBS	54	7 Nov 87	3
SEPTEMBER 99 [RM]	INCredible	25	31 Jul 99	3

Remixed by Phats and Small.

ALBUMS:	HITS 10		WEEKS 171	
ALL 'N' ALL	CBS	13	21 Jan 78	23
THE BEST OF EARTH WIND AND FIRE VOLUME 1	CBS	6	16 Dec 78	42
I AM	CBS	5	23 Jun 79	41
FACES	CBS	10	1 Nov 80	6
RAISE!	CBS	14	14 Nov 81	22
POWERLIGHT	CBS	22	19 Feb 83	7
THE ARTISTS VOLUME 1	Street Sounds	65	9 Mar 85	4

Compilation album with tracks by each artist.
Above hit: EARTH WIND AND FIRE/Jean CARN/ROSE ROYCE.

THE COLLECTION – 24 ESSENTIAL HITS	K-Tel	5	10 May 86	13
THE VERY BEST OF EARTH, WIND AND FIRE	Telstar	40	28 Nov 92	6
BOOGIE WONDERLAND – THE VERY BEST OF EARTH, WIND AND FIRE [RE]	Telstar	29	28 Sep 96	4

Repackage of The Very Best Of Earth, Wind And Fire.

THE ULTIMATE COLLECTION	Columbia	34	7 Aug 99	3

EARTHLING
UK

SINGLES:	HITS 2		WEEKS 2	
ECHO ON MY MIND PART II	Cooltempo	61	14 Oct 95	1
BLOOD MUSIC [EP]	Cooltempo	69	1 Jun 96	1

Lead track: 1st Transmission.

ALBUMS:	HITS 1		WEEKS 1	
RADAR	Cooltempo	66	3 Jun 95	1

Features guest female vocalist Segun.

EAST 57TH ST featuring Donna ALLEN
UK

SINGLES:	HITS 1		WEEKS 3	
SATURDAY	AM:PM	29	11 Oct 97	3

Originally recorded by Norma Jean. Original release in instrumental form reached No. 110 in 1996.

EAST OF EDEN
UK

SINGLES:	HITS 1		WEEKS 12	
JIG-A-JIG	Deram	7	17 Apr 71	12
ALBUMS:	HITS 1		WEEKS 2	
SNAFU	Deram	29	14 Mar 70	2

EAST 17
UK

SINGLES:	HITS 18		WEEKS 170	
HOUSE OF LOVE	London	10	29 Aug 92	9
GOLD	London	28	14 Nov 92	4
GOLD [RE]	London	64	19 Dec 92	4
DEEP	London	5	30 Jan 93	10
SLOW IT DOWN	London	13	10 Apr 93	7
WEST END GIRLS	London	11	26 Jun 93	7
IT'S ALRIGHT	London	3	4 Dec 93	14
AROUND THE WORLD	London	3	14 May 94	13
STEAM	London	7	1 Oct 94	8
STAY ANOTHER DAY	London	1	3 Dec 94	15
LET IT RAIN	London	10	25 Mar 95	7
STAY ANOTHER DAY [RE]	London	64	6 May 95	1
HOLD MY BODY TIGHT	London	12	17 Jun 95	7
THUNDER	London	4	4 Nov 95	14

Above hit: E.17.

DO U STILL?	London	7	10 Feb 96	7
SOMEONE TO LOVE	London	16	10 Aug 96	8

Above hit: EAST 7EVENTEEN.

IF YOU EVER	London	2	2 Nov 96	15

Original by Shai reached No.2 in the US in 1992.
Above hit: EAST SEVENTEEN featuring GABRIELLE.

HEY CHILD	London	3	18 Jan 97	5

Written for Mortimer's daughters Atlanta and Ocean.
Above hit: EAST SEVENTEEN.

EACH TIME	Telstar	2	14 Nov 98	10
BETCHA CAN'T WAIT	Telstar	12	13 Mar 99	5

Above 2: E-17.

ALBUMS:	HITS 5		WEEKS 102	
WALTHAMSTOW	London	1	27 Feb 93	14
WALTHAMSTOW [RE]	London	16	17 Jul 93	19

Repackaged with additional track.

STEAM	London	3	29 Oct 94	36
UP ALL NIGHT	London	7	25 Nov 95	15
AROUND THE WORLD – THE JOURNEY SO FAR	London	3	16 Nov 96	16

Compilation.

RESURRECTION	*Telstar*	43	*28 Nov 98*	2

Above hit: E-17.

EAST SIDE BEAT — Italy

SINGLES:	HITS 3		WEEKS 18	
RIDE LIKE THE WIND	*ffrr*	3	*30 Nov 91*	11
ALIVE AND KICKING	*ffrr*	26	*19 Dec 92*	6
YOU'RE MY EVERYTHING	*ffrr*	65	*29 May 93*	1

David EASTER – See Jason DONOVAN

EASTERHOUSE — UK

ALBUMS:	HITS 1		WEEKS 1	
CONTENDERS	*Rough Trade*	91	*28 Jun 86*	1

Sheena EASTON — UK

SINGLES:	HITS 14		WEEKS 103	
MODERN GIRL	*EMI*	56	*5 Apr 80*	3
9 TO 5	*EMI*	3	*19 Jul 80*	15
MODERN GIRL [RE]	*EMI*	8	*9 Aug 80*	12
ONE MAN WOMAN	*EMI*	14	*25 Oct 80*	6
TAKE MY TIME	*EMI*	44	*14 Feb 81*	5
WHEN HE SHINES	*EMI*	12	*2 May 81*	8
FOR YOUR EYES ONLY	*EMI*	8	*27 Jun 81*	13
From the James Bond film of the same name.				
JUST ANOTHER BROKEN HEART	*EMI*	33	*12 Sep 81*	8
YOU COULD HAVE BEEN WITH ME	*EMI*	54	*5 Dec 81*	3
MACHINERY	*EMI*	38	*31 Jul 82*	5
WE'VE GOT TONIGHT	*Liberty*	28	*12 Feb 83*	7
Above hit: Kenny ROGERS and Sheena EASTON.				
THE LOVER IN ME	*MCA*	15	*21 Jan 89*	8
DAYS LIKE THIS	*MCA*	43	*18 Mar 89*	3
101	*MCA*	54	*15 Jul 89*	2
THE ARMS OF ORION	*Warner Brothers*	27	*18 Nov 89*	5
Above hit: PRINCE with Sheena EASTON.				
ALBUMS:	HITS 5		WEEKS 27	
TAKE MY TIME	*EMI*	17	*31 Jan 81*	9
YOU COULD HAVE BEEN WITH ME	*EMI*	33	*3 Oct 81*	6
MADNESS, MONEY AND MUSIC	*EMI*	44	*25 Sep 82*	4
BEST KEPT SECRET	*EMI*	99	*15 Oct 83*	1
THE LOVER IN ME	*MCA*	30	*4 Mar 89*	7

EASTSIDE CONNECTION — US

SINGLES:	HITS 1		WEEKS 3	
YOU'RE SO RIGHT FOR ME	*Creole*	44	*8 Apr 78*	3

Clint EASTWOOD — US

(See also Various Artists: Films – Original Soundtracks 'Paint Your Wagon'.)

SINGLES:	HITS 1		WEEKS 2	
I TALK TO THE TREES	*Paramount*	18	*7 Feb 70*	2

From the film 'Paint Your Wagon'. [AA] listed with Wand'rin' Star by Lee Marvin.

Clint EASTWOOD and GENERAL SAINT — UK

SINGLES:	HITS 1		WEEKS 3	
LAST PLANE (ONE WAY TICKET)	*MCA*	51	*29 Sep 84*	3
ALBUMS:	HITS 2		WEEKS 3	
TWO BAD DJ	*Greensleeves*	99	*6 Feb 82*	2
STOP THAT TRAIN	*Greensleeves*	98	*28 May 83*	1

EASY RIDERS – See Frankie LAINE

EASYBEATS — Australia

SINGLES:	HITS 2		WEEKS 24	
FRIDAY ON MY MIND	*United Artists*	6	*29 Oct 66*	15
HELLO, HOW ARE YOU	*United Artists*	20	*13 Apr 68*	9

EAT — UK/US

SINGLES:	HITS 1		WEEKS 1	
BLEED ME WHITE	*Fiction*	73	*12 Jun 93*	1

EAT STATIC — UK

SINGLES:	HITS 3		WEEKS 3	
HYBRID	*Planet Dog*	41	*22 Feb 97*	1

INTERCEPTOR	*Planet Dog*	44	*27 Sep 97*	1
CONTACT . . .	*Planet Dog*	67	*27 Jun 98*	1
ALBUMS:	**HITS 3**			**WEEKS 5**
ABDUCTION	*Ultimate*	62	*15 May 93*	1
IMPLANT	*Planet Dog*	13	*25 Jun 94*	3
SCIENCE OF THE GODS	*Planet Dog*	60	*25 Oct 97*	1

Dedicated to Jon Pertwee and Timothy Leary.

Cleveland EATON   US

SINGLES:	**HITS 1**			**WEEKS 6**
BAMA BOOGIE WOOGIE	*Gull*	35	*23 Sep 78*	6

EAV (ERSTE ALLGEMEINE VERUNSICHERUNG)   Austria

SINGLES:	**HITS 1**			**WEEKS 4**
BA-BA-BANKROBBERY (ENGLISH VERSION??)	*Columbia*	63	*27 Sep 86*	4

EAZY-E   US

SINGLES:	**HITS 1**			**WEEKS 3**
JUST TAH LET U KNOW	*Epic*	30	*6 Jan 96*	3
ALBUMS:	**HITS 1**			**WEEKS 1**
STR8 OFF THA STREETZ OF MUTHAPHUKKIN COMPTON	*Epic*	66	*10 Feb 96*	1

Bernard EBBINGHOUSE and his Orchestra - See Cliff RICHARD

ECHO and the BUNNYMEN   UK

(See also England United.)

SINGLES:	**HITS 17**			**WEEKS 85**
RESCUE	*Korova*	62	*17 May 80*	1
CROCODILES	*Korova*	37	*18 Apr 81*	4
A PROMISE	*Korova*	49	*18 Jul 81*	4
THE BACK OF LOVE	*Korova*	19	*29 May 82*	7
THE CUTTER	*Korova*	8	*22 Jan 83*	8
NEVER STOP	*Korova*	15	*16 Jul 83*	7
THE KILLING MOON	*Korova*	9	*28 Jan 84*	6
SILVER	*Korova*	30	*21 Apr 84*	5
SEVEN SEAS	*Korova*	16	*14 Jul 84*	7
BRING ON THE DANCING HORSES	*Korova*	21	*19 Oct 85*	7
THE GAME	*WEA*	28	*13 Jun 87*	4
LIPS LIKE SUGAR	*WEA*	36	*1 Aug 87*	4
PEOPLE ARE STRANGE	*WEA*	29	*20 Feb 88*	5
PEOPLE ARE STRANGE [RI]	*East West*	34	*2 Mar 91*	4
From the film 'The Lost Boys'.				
NOTHING LASTS FOREVER	*London*	8	*28 Jun 97*	6
I WANT TO BE THERE WHEN YOU COME	*London*	30	*13 Sep 97*	2
DON'T LET IT GET YOU DOWN	*London*	50	*8 Nov 97*	1
RUST	*London*	22	*27 Mar 99*	3
ALBUMS:	**HITS 9**			**WEEKS 99**
CROCODILES	*Korova*	17	*26 Jul 80*	6
HEAVEN UP HERE	*Korova*	10	*6 Jun 81*	16
PORCUPINE	*Korova*	2	*12 Feb 83*	17
OCEAN RAIN	*Korova*	4	*12 May 84*	26
SONGS TO LEARN AND SING	*Korova*	6	*23 Nov 85*	15
ECHO AND THE BUNNYMEN	*WEA*	4	*18 Jul 87*	9
BALLYHOO - THE BEST OF ECHO AND THE BUNNYMEN	*Korova*	59	*21 Jun 97*	1
EVERGREEN	*London*	8	*26 Jul 97*	7
WHAT ARE YOU GOING TO DO WITH YOUR LIFE?	*London*	21	*17 Apr 99*	2

ECHOBEATZ   UK

SINGLES:	**HITS 1**			**WEEKS 5**
MAS QUE NADA	*Eternal*	10	*25 Jul 98*	5

Dance version of the track featured in the Nike TV commercial.

ECHOBELLY   UK

SINGLES:	**HITS 8**			**WEEKS 16**
INSOMNIAC	*Fauve*	47	*2 Apr 94*	1
I CAN'T IMAGINE THE WORLD WITHOUT ME	*Fauve*	39	*2 Jul 94*	2
CLOSE . . . BUT	*Fauve*	59	*5 Nov 94*	1
GREAT THINGS	*Fauve*	13	*2 Sep 95*	3
KING OF THE KERB	*Fauve*	25	*4 Nov 95*	3
DARK THERAPY	*Fauve*	20	*2 Mar 96*	3
THE WORLD IS FLAT	*Epic*	31	*23 Aug 97*	2
HERE COMES THE BIG RUSH	*Epic*	56	*8 Nov 97*	1
ALBUMS:	**HITS 3**			**WEEKS 28**
EVERYONE'S GOT ONE	*Fauve*	8	*3 Sep 94*	3

ON	*Fauve*	4	*30 Sep 95*	24
LUSTRA	*Epic*	47	*22 Nov 97*	1

Billy ECKSTINE | | | US

SINGLES:	HITS 3			WEEKS 48
NO ONE BUT YOU	*MGM*	3	*13 Nov 54*	17
From the film 'Flame And The Flesh'.				
PASSING STRANGERS	*Mercury*	22	*28 Sep 57*	2
Above hit: Billy VAUGHAN and Billy ECKSTINE.				
GIGI	*Mercury*	8	*14 Feb 59*	14
From the film of the same name.				
PASSING STRANGERS [RI]	*Mercury*	20	*15 Mar 69*	15
Above hit: Billy VAUGHAN and Billy ECKSTINE.				

ECLIPSE | | | Italy

SINGLES:	HITS 1			WEEKS 4
MAKES ME LOVE YOU	*Azuli*	25	*14 Aug 99*	4
Samples Sister Sledge's Thinking Of You.				

EDDIE and the HOT RODS | | | UK

SINGLES:	HITS 5			WEEKS 26
LIVE AT THE MARQUEE [EP]	*Island*	43	*11 Sep 76*	5
Lead Track: 96 Tears.				
TEENAGE DEPRESSION	*Island*	35	*13 Nov 76*	4
I MIGHT BE LYING	*Island*	44	*23 Apr 77*	3
DO ANYTHING YOU WANNA DO	*Island*	9	*13 Aug 77*	10
Above hit: RODS.				
QUIT THIS TOWN	*Island*	36	*21 Jan 78*	4
ALBUMS:	**HITS 3**			**WEEKS 5**
TEENAGE DEPRESSION	*Island*	43	*18 Dec 76*	1
LIFE ON THE LINE	*Island*	27	*3 Dec 77*	3
THRILLER	*Island*	50	*24 Mar 79*	1

EDDY | | | UK

SINGLES:	HITS 1			WEEKS 2
SOMEDAY	*Positiva*	49	*9 Jul 94*	2

Duane EDDY | | | US

SINGLES:	HITS 22			WEEKS 202
REBEL-ROUSER	*London*	19	*6 Sep 58*	10
Above hit: Duane EDDY and his twangy guitar.				
CANNONBALL	*London*	22	*3 Jan 59*	4
Above hit: Duane EDDY, his "twangy" guitar and the REBELS.				
PETER GUNN	*London*	6	*20 Jun 59*	10
Originally recorded by Henry Mancini.				
YEP!	*London*	17	*25 Jul 59*	5
Above 2 entries were separate sides of the same release, each had its own chart run.				
FORTY MILES OF BAD ROAD	*London*	11	*5 Sep 59*	9
PETER GUNN [RE]	*London*	27	*12 Sep 59*	1
SOME KIND-A EARTHQUAKE	*London*	12	*19 Dec 59*	5
BONNIE CAME BACK	*London*	12	*20 Feb 60*	11
SHAZAM!	*London*	4	*30 Apr 60*	13
BECAUSE THEY'RE YOUNG	*London*	2	*23 Jul 60*	18
Above 2 from the film 'Because They're Young'.				
KOMMOTION	*London*	13	*12 Nov 60*	10
PEPE	*London*	2	*14 Jan 61*	14
From the film of the same name.				
THEME FROM DIXIE	*London*	7	*22 Apr 61*	10
RING OF FIRE	*London*	17	*24 Jun 61*	10
DRIVIN' HOME	*London*	30	*16 Sep 61*	4
CARAVAN	*Parlophone*	42	*7 Oct 61*	3
Originally recorded by Duke Ellington.				
DEEP IN THE HEART OF TEXAS	*RCA*	19	*26 May 62*	8
Originally recorded by Alvino Rey & his Orchestra.				
BALLAD OF PALADIN	*RCA*	10	*25 Aug 62*	10
(DANCE WITH THE) GUITAR MAN	*RCA*	4	*10 Nov 62*	16
BOSS GUITAR	*RCA Victor*	27	*16 Feb 63*	8
Above 2: Duane EDDY and the REBELETTES.				
LONELY BOY LONELY GUITAR	*RCA Victor*	35	*1 Jun 63*	4
YOUR BABY'S GONE SURFIN'	*RCA Victor*	49	*31 Aug 63*	1
PLAY ME LIKE YOU PLAY YOUR GUITAR	*GTO*	9	*8 Mar 75*	9
Above hit: Duane EDDY and the REBELETTES.				
PETER GUNN	*China*	8	*22 Mar 86*	9
Above hit: ART OF NOISE featuring Duane EDDY.				

EPS:		HITS 5		WEEKS 37	
YEP!	*London*	16	*30 Jul 60*	2
TWANGY	*London*	4	*10 Dec 60*	30
BECAUSE THEY'RE YOUNG	*London*	17	*18 Feb 61*	1
THE LONELY ONE	*London*	16	*20 May 61*	1
PEPE	*London*	10	*1 Jul 61*	3
ALBUMS:		**HITS 9**		**WEEKS 88**	
HAVE TWANGY GUITAR WILL TRAVEL	*London*	6	*6 Jun 59*	3
SPECIALLY FOR YOU	*London*	6	*31 Oct 59*	8
THE TWANG'S THE THANG	*London*	2	*19 Mar 60*	25
SONGS OF OUR HERITAGE	*London*	13	*26 Nov 60*	5
A MILLION DOLLARS' WORTH OF TWANG	*London*	5	*1 Apr 61*	19
A MILLION DOLLARS' WORTH OF TWANG VOLUME 2	*London*	18	*9 Jun 62*	1
TWISTIN' AND TWANGIN'	*RCA*	8	*21 Jul 62*	12
TWANGY GUITAR – SILKY STRINGS	*RCA Victor*	13	*8 Dec 62*	11
DANCE WITH THE GUITAR MAN	*RCA Victor*	14	*16 Mar 63*	4

Nelson EDDY
US

EPS:		HITS 1		WEEKS 1	
INDIAN LOVE CALL	*RCA*	12	*23 Apr 60*	1

EDDY and the SOULBAND
US

SINGLES:		HITS 1		WEEKS 7	
THEME FROM SHAFT	*Club*	13	*23 Feb 85*	7

Randy EDELMAN
US

SINGLES:		HITS 4		WEEKS 18	
CONCRETE AND CLAY	*20th Century*	11	*6 Mar 76*	7
THE UPTOWN, UPTEMPO WOMAN	*20th Century*	25	*18 Sep 76*	7
YOU	*20th Century*	49	*15 Jan 77*	2
NOBODY MADE ME	*Rocket*	60	*17 Jul 82*	2

EDELWEISS
Austria

SINGLES:		HITS 1		WEEKS 10	
BRING ME EDELWEISS	*WEA*	5	*29 Apr 89*	10
Tune based on Abba's S.O.S.				

EDEN
UK/Australia

SINGLES:		HITS 1		WEEKS 2	
DO U FEEL 4 ME	*Logic*	51	*6 Mar 93*	2

Lyn EDEN - See SMOKIN BEATS featuring Lyn EDEN

EDISON LIGHTHOUSE
UK

SINGLES:		HITS 2		WEEKS 13	
LOVE GROWS (WHERE MY ROSEMARY GOES)	*Bell*	1	*24 Jan 70*	12
Originally recorded by Jeff Barry.				
IT'S UP TO YOU PETULA	*Bell*	49	*30 Jan 71*	1

EDMONTON SYMPHONY ORCHESTA - See PROCOL HARUM

Dave EDMUNDS
UK

(See also Rockpile.)

SINGLES:		HITS 12		WEEKS 93	
I HEAR YOU KNOCKING	*MAM*	1	*21 Nov 70*	14
Originally recorded by Smiley Lewis.				
Above hit: Dave EDMUND'S ROCKPILE.				
BABY I LOVE YOU	*Rockfield*	8	*20 Jan 73*	13
BORN TO BE WITH YOU	*Rockfield*	5	*9 Jun 73*	12
I KNEW THE BRIDE	*Swan Song*	26	*2 Jul 77*	8
GIRLS TALK	*Swan Song*	4	*30 Jun 79*	11
Originally recorded by Elvis Costello and the Attractions.				
QUEEN OF HEARTS	*Swan Song*	11	*22 Sep 79*	9
CRAWLING FROM THE WRECKAGE	*Swan Song*	59	*24 Nov 79*	4
SINGING THE BLUES	*Swan Song*	28	*9 Feb 80*	8
ALMOST SATURDAY NIGHT	*Swan Song*	58	*28 Mar 81*	3
Originally recorded by John Fogerty.				
THE RACE IS ON	*Swan Song*	34	*20 Jun 81*	6
Originally recorded by George Jones.				
Above hit: Dave EDMUNDS and the STRAY CATS.				
SLIPPING AWAY	*Arista*	60	*26 Mar 83*	4
Written and produced by Jeff Lynne.				
KING OF LOVE	*Capitol*	68	*7 Apr 90*	1
Features Brian Setzer on backing vocals and Lee Rocker (both of the Stray Cats) on bass.				

ALBUMS:		HITS 4		WEEKS 21
REPEAT WHEN NECESSARY	Swan Song	39	23 Jun 79	12
TWANGIN'	Swan Song	37	18 Apr 81	4
DE 7	Arista	60	3 Apr 82	3
INFORMATION	Arista	92	30 Apr 83	2

Alton EDWARDS   Zimbabwe

SINGLES:		HITS 1		WEEKS 9
I JUST WANNA (SPEND SOME TIME WITH YOU)	Streetwave	20	9 Jan 82	9

Dennis EDWARDS   US

SINGLES:		HITS 1		WEEKS 10
DON'T LOOK ANY FURTHER	Gordy	45	24 Mar 84	5
Above hit: Dennis EDWARDS featuring Siedah GARRETT.				
DON'T LOOK ANY FURTHER [RE]	Gordy	55	20 Jun 87	5
ALBUMS:		HITS 1		WEEKS 1
DON'T LOOK ANY FURTHER	Gordy	91	14 Apr 84	1

Doreen EDWARDS - See T-EMPO

Rupie EDWARDS   Jamaica

SINGLES:		HITS 2		WEEKS 16
IRE FEELINGS (SKANGA)	Cactus	9	23 Nov 74	10
LEGO SKANGA	Cactus	32	8 Feb 75	6

Todd EDWARDS   US

ALBUMS:		HITS 1		WEEKS 1
SAVED MY LIFE	ffrr	69	24 Aug 96	1
12" single, too long to be eligible for the singles chart.				

Tommy EDWARDS   US

SINGLES:		HITS 2		WEEKS 18
IT'S ALL IN THE GAME	MGM	1	4 Oct 58	17
Co-writer Carl Sigman was Vice President of the United States from 1925–1929. Originally recorded in 1951.				
MY MELANCHOLY BABY	MGM	29	8 Aug 59	1
Originally recorded by Walter Van Brunt in 1915.				
EPS:		HITS 1		WEEKS 1
THE WAYS OF LOVE	MGM	15	16 Apr 60	1

EEK-A-MOUSE   Jamaica

ALBUMS:		HITS 1		WEEKS 3
SKIDIP	Greensleeves	61	14 Aug 82	3

EELS   US

SINGLES:		HITS 5		WEEKS 16
NOVOCAINE FOR THE SOUL	Dreamworks	10	15 Feb 97	5
SUSAN'S HOUSE	Dreamworks	9	17 May 97	5
YOUR LUCKY DAY IN HELL	Dreamworks	35	13 Sep 97	2
LAST STOP: THIS TOWN	Dreamworks	23	26 Sep 98	3
CANCER FOR THE CURE	Dreamworks	60	12 Dec 98	1
ALBUMS:		HITS 2		WEEKS 31
BEAUTIFUL FREAK	Dreamworks	5	8 Feb 97	27
ELECTRO-SHOCK BLUES	Dreamworks	12	3 Oct 98	4

EFUA   UK

SINGLES:		HITS 1		WEEKS 5
SOMEWHERE	Virgin	42	3 Jul 93	5

EGG   UK

SINGLES:		HITS 1		WEEKS 1
GETTING AWAY WITH IT	Indochina	58	30 Jan 99	1

EGGS ON LEGS   UK

SINGLES:		HITS 1		WEEKS 1
COCK A DOODLE DO IT	Avex UK	42	23 Sep 95	1
Theme from Channel 4's 'The Big Breakfast "Eggs On Legs" ' tour.				

EGYPTIAN EMPIRE   UK

SINGLES:		HITS 1		WEEKS 2
THE HORN TRACK	Ffrreedom	61	24 Oct 92	2

EIFFEL 65 | | | | Italy

SINGLES:		HITS 1		WEEKS 20
BLUE [DA BA DEE]	Logic	39	21 Aug 99	5
Import.				
BLUE [DA BA DEE]	Eternal	1	25 Sep 99	15

18 WHEELER | | | | UK

SINGLES:		HITS 1		WEEKS 1
STAY	Creation	59	15 Mar 97	1

EIGHTH WONDER | | | | UK

SINGLES:		HITS 4		WEEKS 25
STAY WITH ME	CBS	65	2 Nov 85	2
I'M NOT SCARED	CBS	7	20 Feb 88	13
Written by the Pet Shop Boys.				
CROSS MY HEART	CBS	13	25 Jun 88	8
BABY BABY	CBS	65	1 Oct 88	2
ALBUMS:		HITS 1		WEEKS 4
FEARLESS	CBS	47	23 Jul 88	4

801 | | | | UK

ALBUMS:		HITS 1		WEEKS 2
801 LIVE	Island	52	20 Nov 76	2

808 STATE | | | | UK

SINGLES:		HITS 15		WEEKS 70
PACIFIC	ZTT	10	18 Nov 89	9
THE EXTENDED PLEASURE OF DANCE [EP]	ZTT	56	31 Mar 90	1
12" vinyl release only. Lead track: Ancodia.				
THE ONLY RHYME THAT BITES	ZTT	10	2 Jun 90	10
TUNES SPLITS THE ATOM	ZTT	18	15 Sep 90	7
Above 2: MC TUNES versus 808 STATE.				
CUBIK / OLYMPIC	ZTT	10	10 Nov 90	10
Cubik first appeared on the Extended Pleasure Of Dance EP.				
IN YER FACE	ZTT	9	16 Feb 91	6
OOOPS	ZTT	42	27 Apr 91	3
Above hit: 808 STATE featuring BJORK.				
LIFT / OPEN YOUR MIND	ZTT	38	17 Aug 91	4
TIME BOMB / NIMBUS	ZTT	59	29 Aug 92	1
ONE IN TEN	ZTT	17	12 Dec 92	8
Above hit: 808 STATE UB40.				
PLAN 9	ZTT	50	30 Jan 93	2
10 X 10	ZTT	67	26 Jun 93	1
BOMBADIN	ZTT	67	13 Aug 94	1
BOND	ZTT	57	29 Jun 96	1
LOPEZ (METAPHORICALLY)	ZTT	20	8 Feb 97	2
Above hit: 808 STATE via the PROPELLERHEADS, Brian ENO and themselves; viva! the guest vocals of James Dean BRADFIELD.				
PACIFIC 808:98 [RM] / CUBIK [RI]	ZTT	21	16 May 98	3
Remixed by Grooverider.				
THE ONLY RHYME THAT BITES 99 [RI]	ZTT	53	6 Mar 99	1
Though billed as a remix, the lead track is just a longer version of the original.				
Above hit: MC TUNES vs 808 STATE.				
ALBUMS:		HITS 4		WEEKS 20
NINETY	ZTT	57	16 Dec 89	5
EX:EL	ZTT	4	16 Mar 91	10
GORGEOUS	ZTT	17	13 Feb 93	3
808:88:98	ZTT	40	30 May 98	2

88.3 featuring Lisa MAY | | | | UK

SINGLES:		HITS 1		WEEKS 1
WISHING ON A STAR	Urban Gorilla	61	15 Jul 95	1

EINSTEIN – See AMBASSADORS OF FUNK featuring M.C. MARIO; Simon HARRIS; TECHNOTRONIC; SNAP!

EL MARIACHI | | | | US

SINGLES:		HITS 1		WEEKS 2
CUBA	ffrr	38	9 Nov 96	2

ELASTICA | | | | UK

SINGLES:		HITS 3		WEEKS 11
LINE UP	Deceptive	20	12 Feb 94	3
CONNECTION	Deceptive	17	22 Oct 94	4
WAKING UP	Deceptive	13	25 Feb 95	4
Based on the Stranglers' No More Heroes.				

ALBUMS:	HITS 1		WEEKS 25
ELASTICA	*Deceptive*	1	*25 Mar 95* 25

ELATE
UK

SINGLES:	HITS 1		WEEKS 2
SOMEBODY LIKE YOU	*VC Recordings*	38	*26 Jul 97* 2

Samples Clannad's Theme From Harry's Game.

Donnie ELBERT
US

SINGLES:	HITS 3		WEEKS 29
WHERE DID OUR LOVE GO	*London*	8	*8 Jan 72* 10
I CAN'T HELP MYSELF	*Avco*	11	*26 Feb 72* 10
A LITTLE PIECE OF LEATHER	*London*	27	*29 Apr 72* 9

ELECTRA
UK

SINGLES:	HITS 2		WEEKS 7
JIBARO	*ffrr*	54	*6 Aug 88* 3
IT'S YOUR DESTINY / AUTUMN LOVE	*ffrr*	51	*30 Dec 89* 4

Autumn Love listed from 13 Jan 90.

ELECTRAFIXION
UK

SINGLES:	HITS 4		WEEKS 6
ZEPHYR	*Spacejunk*	47	*19 Nov 94* 2
LOWDOWN	*Spacejunk*	54	*9 Sep 95* 2
NEVER	*Spacejunk*	58	*4 Nov 95* 1
SISTER PAIN	*Spacejunk*	27	*16 Mar 96* 1
ALBUMS:	HITS 1		WEEKS 2
BURNED	*Spacejunk*	38	*7 Oct 95* 2

ELECTRASY
UK

SINGLES:	HITS 3		WEEKS 7
LOST IN SPACE	*MCA*	60	*13 Jun 98* 1
MORNING AFTERGLOW	*MCA*	19	*5 Sep 98* 4
BEST FRIEND'S GIRL	*MCA*	41	*28 Nov 98* 2
ALBUMS:	HITS 1		WEEKS 1
BEAUTIFUL INSANE	*MCA*	48	*26 Sep 98* 1

ELECTRIBE 101
UK/Germany

SINGLES:	HITS 3		WEEKS 15
TELL ME WHEN THE FEVER ENDED	*Mercury*	32	*28 Oct 89* 5
TALKING WITH MYSELF	*Mercury*	23	*24 Feb 90* 5
YOU'RE WALKING	*Mercury*	50	*22 Sep 90* 3
TALKING WITH MYSELF '98 [RM]	*Manifesto*	39	*10 Oct 98* 2

Remixed by Canny.

ALBUMS:	HITS 1		WEEKS 3
ELECTRIBAL MEMORIES	*Mercury*	26	*20 Oct 90* 3

ELECTRIC BOYS
Sweden

ALBUMS:	HITS 1		WEEKS 1
GROOVUS MAXIMUS	*Vertigo*	61	*6 Jun 92* 1

ELECTRIC LIGHT ORCHESTRA
UK

SINGLES:	HITS 29		WEEKS 255
10538 OVERTURE	*Harvest*	9	*29 Jul 72* 8
ROLL OVER BEETHOVEN	*Harvest*	6	*27 Jan 73* 10
SHOWDOWN	*Harvest*	12	*6 Oct 73* 10
MA-MA-MA-BELLE	*Warner Brothers*	22	*9 Mar 74* 8
EVIL WOMAN	*Jet*	10	*10 Jan 76* 8
STRANGE MAGIC	*Jet*	38	*3 Jul 76* 3
LIVIN' THING	*Jet*	4	*13 Nov 76* 12
ROCKARIA!	*Jet*	9	*19 Feb 77* 9
TELEPHONE LINE	*Jet*	8	*21 May 77* 10
TURN TO STONE	*Jet*	18	*29 Oct 77* 12
MR. BLUE SKY	*Jet*	6	*28 Jan 78* 11
WILD WEST HERO	*Jet*	6	*10 Jun 78* 14
SWEET TALKIN' WOMAN	*Jet*	6	*7 Oct 78* 9
THE ELO EP [EP]	*Jet*	34	*9 Dec 78* 8

EP of old releases. Lead track: Can't Get It Out Of My Head.

SHINE A LITTLE LOVE	*Jet*	6	*19 May 79* 10
THE DIARY OF HORACE WIMP	*Jet*	8	*21 Jul 79* 9
DON'T BRING ME DOWN	*Jet*	3	*1 Sep 79* 9
CONFUSION / LAST TRAIN TO LONDON	*Jet*	8	*17 Nov 79* 10
I'M ALIVE	*Jet*	20	*24 May 80* 9

XANADU	*Jet*	1	*21 Jun 80*	11
Above hit: Olivia NEWTON-JOHN/ELECTRIC LIGHT ORCHESTRA.				
ALL OVER THE WORLD	*Jet*	11	*2 Aug 80*	8
DON'T WALK AWAY	*Jet*	21	*22 Nov 80*	10
Above 4 from the film 'Xanadu'.				
HOLD ON TIGHT	*Jet*	4	*1 Aug 81*	12
Above hit: ELO.				
TWILIGHT	*Jet*	30	*24 Oct 81*	7
HERE IS THE NEWS / TICKET TO THE MOON	*Jet*	24	*9 Jan 82*	8
Here Is the News listed from 16 Jan 82.				
Above hit: ELO.				
ROCK 'N' ROLL IS KING	*Jet*	13	*18 Jun 83*	9
SECRET MESSAGES	*Jet*	48	*3 Sep 83*	3
CALLING AMERICA	*Epic*	28	*1 Mar 86*	7
HONEST MEN	*Telstar*	60	*11 May 91*	1
Above hit: ELECTRIC LIGHT ORCHESTRA PART TWO.				
ALBUMS:	**HITS 15**		**WEEKS 402**	
ELECTRIC LIGHT ORCHESTRA	*Harvest*	32	*12 Aug 72*	4
ELECTRIC LIGHT ORCHESTRA II	*Harvest*	35	*31 Mar 73*	1
A NEW WORLD RECORD	*Jet*	6	*11 Dec 76*	100
OUT OF THE BLUE	*Jet*	4	*12 Nov 77*	108
Above 2 albums were on the Jet label when first released but had United Artists catalogue numbers. From 1978 they were re-issued with Jet catalogue numbers.				
THREE LIGHT YEARS	*Jet*	38	*6 Jan 79*	9
Boxed set of On the Third Day/Eldorado/Face the Music, 3 uncharted early ELO albums.				
DISCOVERY	*Jet*	1	*16 Jun 79*	46
ELO'S GREATEST HITS	*Jet*	7	*1 Dec 79*	18
XANADU [OST]	*Jet*	2	*19 Jul 80*	17
Album divided with one side by each artist.				
Above hit: Olivia NEWTON-JOHN/ELECTRIC LIGHT ORCHESTRA.				
TIME	*Jet*	1	*8 Aug 81*	32
SECRET MESSAGES	*Jet*	4	*2 Jul 83*	15
BALANCE OF POWER	*Epic*	9	*15 Mar 86*	12
THE GREATEST HITS	*Telstar*	23	*16 Dec 89*	12
THE VERY BEST OF THE ELECTRIC LIGHT ORCHESTRA [RE]	*Telstar*	28	*20 Oct 90*	9
Repackage of The Greatest Hits.				
ELECTRIC LIGHT ORCHESTRA PART TWO	*Telstar*	34	*1 Jun 91*	4
Above hit: ELECTRIC LIGHT ORCHESTRA PART TWO.				
THE VERY BEST OF THE ELECTRIC LIGHT ORCHESTRA	*Dino*	4	*2 Jul 94*	11
LIGHT YEARS – THE VERY BEST OF ELECTRIC LIGHT ORCHESTRA	*Epic*	60	*8 Nov 97*	4

ELECTRIC PRUNES US

SINGLES:	**HITS 2**		**WEEKS 5**	
I HAD TOO MUCH TO DREAM (LAST NIGHT)	*Reprise*	49	*11 Feb 67*	1
GET ME TO THE WORLD ON TIME	*Reprise*	42	*13 May 67*	4

ELECTRIC WIND ENSEMBLE UK

ALBUMS:	**HITS 1**		**WEEKS 9**	
HAUNTING MELODIES	*Nouveau Music*	28	*18 Feb 84*	9

ELECTRONIC UK

SINGLES:	**HITS 8**		**WEEKS 36**	
GETTING AWAY WITH IT	*Factory*	12	*16 Dec 89*	9
Vocals by Neil Tennant (Pet Shop Boys).				
GET THE MESSAGE	*Factory*	8	*27 Apr 91*	7
FEEL EVERY BEAT	*Factory*	39	*21 Sep 91*	4
DISAPPOINTED	*Parlophone*	6	*4 Jul 92*	5
FORBIDDEN CITY	*Parlophone*	14	*6 Jul 96*	4
FOR YOU	*Parlophone*	16	*28 Sep 96*	2
SECOND NATURE	*Parlophone*	35	*15 Feb 97*	2
Keyboardist is Karl Bartos from Kraftwerk. Denise Johnson provides backing vocals.				
VIVID	*Parlophone*	17	*24 Apr 99*	3
ALBUMS:	**HITS 3**		**WEEKS 24**	
ELECTRONIC	*Factory*	2	*8 Jun 91*	16
RAISE THE PRESSURE	*Parlophone*	8	*20 Jul 96*	5
TWISTED TENDERNESS	*Parlophone*	9	*8 May 99*	3

ELECTRONICA'S Holland

SINGLES:	**HITS 1**		**WEEKS 8**	
THE ORIGINAL BIRD DANCE	*Polydor*	22	*19 Sep 81*	8

ELECTROSET UK

SINGLES:	**HITS 2**		**WEEKS 4**	
HOW DOES IT FEEL? (THEME FROM TECHNO BLUES)	*ffrr*	27	*21 Nov 92*	3
Based on Blue Monday by New Order.				

SENSATION	Ffrreedom	69	15 Jul 95	1

Based on New Sensation by INXS.

ELEGANTS — US

SINGLES:	HITS 1		WEEKS 2	
LITTLE STAR	His Master's Voice	25	27 Sep 58	2

ELEPHANT'S MEMORY - See John LENNON

ELEVATION — UK

SINGLES:	HITS 1		WEEKS 1	
CAN U FEEL IT	Nova	62	23 May 92	1

ELEVATORMAN — UK

SINGLES:	HITS 2		WEEKS 4	
FUNK AND DRIVE	Wired	37	14 Jan 95	3
FIRED UP	Wired	44	1 Jul 95	1

Danny ELFMAN — US

ALBUMS:	HITS 1		WEEKS 6	
BATMAN [OST]	Warner Brothers	45	19 Aug 89	6

ELGINS — US

SINGLES:	HITS 2		WEEKS 20	
HEAVEN MUST HAVE SENT YOU	Tamla Motown	3	1 May 71	13
PUT YOURSELF IN MY PLACE	Tamla Motown	28	9 Oct 71	7

ELIAS and his ZIG-ZAG JIVE FLUTES — South Africa

SINGLES:	HITS 1		WEEKS 14	
TOM HARK	Columbia	2	26 Apr 58	14

Theme to the TV series 'The Killing Stone'. Tom Hark is South African slang for a police van.

Yvonne ELLIMAN — US

SINGLES:	HITS 5		WEEKS 44	
I DON'T KNOW HOW TO LOVE HIM	MCA	47	29 Jan 72	1

From the musical 'Jesus Christ Superstar'. This was a maxi-single of which only 2 tracks were listed, this, and Superstar by Murray Head with the Trinidad Singers.
Above hit: Yvonne ELLIMAN/VARIOUS ARTISTS.

LOVE ME	RSO	6	6 Nov 76	13

Originally recorded by the Bee Gees.

HELLO STRANGER	RSO	26	7 May 77	5
I CAN'T GET YOU OUTA MY MIND	RSO	17	13 Aug 77	13
IF I CAN'T HAVE YOU	RSO	4	6 May 78	12

From the film 'Saturday Night Fever'.

Duke ELLINGTON — US

SINGLES:	HITS 1		WEEKS 4	
SKIN DEEP	Philips	7	6 Mar 54	4

Above hit: Duke ELLINGTON and his Orchestra (featuring Louis BELLSON, drums).

ALBUMS:	HITS 1		WEEKS 2	
NUT CRACKER SUITE	Philips	11	8 Apr 61	2

Lance ELLINGTON — UK

SINGLES:	HITS 1		WEEKS 1	
LONELY (HAVE WE LOST OUR LOVE)	RCA	57	21 Aug 93	1

Ray ELLINGTON with Tony CROMBIE, his Orchestra and Chorus — UK

SINGLES:	HITS 1		WEEKS 4	
THE MADISON	Ember	41	17 Nov 62	2
THE MADISON [RE]	Ember	36	22 Dec 62	2

Bern ELLIOTT and the FENMEN — UK

SINGLES:	HITS 2		WEEKS 22	
MONEY	Decca	14	23 Nov 63	13

Original by Barrett Strong reached No. 23 in the US in 1960.

NEW ORLEANS	Decca	24	21 Mar 64	9
EPS:	HITS 1		WEEKS 5	
BERN ELLIOTT AND THE FENMEN	Decca	10	18 Jan 64	5

Joe ELLIOTT - See Mick RONSON

Missy "Misdemeanor" ELLIOTT
US

(See also Lil' Kim; Nicole; Timbaland.)

SINGLES:		HITS 7		WEEKS 25	
THE RAIN (SUPA DUPA FLY)	East West	16	30 Aug 97	3
Based around Ann Peebles' I Can't Stand the Rain.					
SOCKIT2ME	East West	33	29 Nov 97	2
Above hit: Missy Misdemeanor ELLIOTT featuring DA BRAT.					
BEEP ME 911	East West America	14	25 Apr 98	3
Above hit: Missy Misdemeanor ELLIOTT (featuring 702 and MAGOO).					
HIT 'EM WITH DA HEE	East West America	25	22 Aug 98	3
Above hit: Missy Misdemeanor ELLIOTT featuring LIL' KIM and MOCHA.					
I WANT YOU BACK	Virgin	1	26 Sep 98	9
Above hit: Melanie B featuring Missy "Misdemeanor" ELLIOTT.					
5 MINUTES	East West America	72	21 Nov 98	1
Above 2 from the film 'Why Do Fools Fall In Love'.					
Above hit: LIL 'MO featuring Missy "Misdemeanor" ELLIOTT.					
ALL N MY GRILL	Elektra	20	25 Sep 99	4
Above hit: Missy Misdemeanor ELLIOTT featuring MC SOLAAR.					
ALBUMS:		HITS 1		WEEKS 2	
DA REAL WORLD	Elektra	40	10 Jul 99	2

Greg ELLIS - See Reva RICE and Greg ELLIS

Joey B. ELLIS
US

SINGLES:		HITS 2		WEEKS 10	
GO FOR IT! (HEART AND FIRE)	Capitol	20	16 Feb 91	8
From the film 'Rocky V'.					
Above hit: "ROCKY V" featuring Joey B. ELLIS and Tynetta HARE.					
THOUGHT U WERE THE ONE FOR ME	Capitol	58	18 May 91	2

Ray ELLIS and his Orchestra - See Johnny MATHIS; Frankie VAUGHAN

Shirley ELLIS
US

SINGLES:		HITS 2		WEEKS 17	
THE CLAPPING SONG	London	6	8 May 65	13
THE CLAPPING SONG [EP]	MCA	59	8 Jul 78	4
Lead track: The Clapping Song.					

ELLIS, BEGGS and HOWARD
UK

SINGLES:		HITS 1		WEEKS 8	
BIG BUBBLES, NO TROUBLES	RCA	59	2 Jul 88	3
BIG BUBBLES, NO TROUBLES [RE]	RCA	41	11 Mar 89	5
Though listed as a re-entry with same catalogue number, there was also a re-mixed version available.					

Ben ELTON
UK

ALBUMS:		HITS 1		WEEKS 2	
MOTORMOUTH	Mercury	86	14 Nov 87	2

EMBRACE
UK

SINGLES:		HITS 6		WEEKS 24	
FIREWORKS [EP]	Hut	34	17 May 97	2
Lead track: The Last Gas.					
ONE BIG FAMILY [EP]	Hut	21	19 Jul 97	3
Lead track: One Big Family.					
ALL YOU GOOD GOOD PEOPLE [EP]	Hut	8	8 Nov 97	4
Lead track: All You Good Good People.					
COME BACK TO WHAT YOU KNOW	Hut	6	6 Jun 98	8
MY WEAKNESS IS NONE OF YOUR BUSINESS	Hut	9	29 Aug 98	4
HOOLIGAN	Hut	18	13 Nov 99	3
ALBUMS:		HITS 1		WEEKS 21	
THE GOOD WILL OUT	Hut	1	20 Jun 98	21

EMERALD EXPRESS - See DEXY'S MIDNIGHT RUNNERS

Keith EMERSON
UK

(See also Emerson, Lake and Palmer; Emerson, Lake and Powell.)

SINGLES:		HITS 1		WEEKS 5	
HONKY TONK TRAIN BLUES	Manticore	21	10 Apr 76	5
Originally recorded by Meade Lux Lewis.					

EMERSON, LAKE and PALMER   UK

(See also Keith Emerson; Emerson, Lake and Powell; Greg Lake.)

SINGLES:		HITS 1		WEEKS 13	
FANFARE FOR THE COMMON MAN	Atlantic		2	4 Jun 77	13
ALBUMS:		**HITS 9**		**WEEKS 135**	
EMERSON, LAKE AND PALMER	Island		4	5 Dec 70	28
TARKUS	Island		1	19 Jun 71	17
PICTURES AT AN EXHIBITION	Island		3	4 Dec 71	5
Live recordings from the City Hall, Newcastle, 26 Mar 71					
TRILOGY	Island		2	8 Jul 72	29
BRAIN SALAD SURGERY	Manticore		2	22 Dec 73	17
WELCOME BACK MY FRIENDS TO THE SHOW THAT NEVER ENDS – LADIES AND GENTLEMEN: EMERSON, LAKE AND PALMER	Manticore		5	24 Aug 74	5
Live recordings.					
WORKS	Atlantic		9	9 Apr 77	25
WORKS VOLUME 2	Atlantic		20	10 Dec 77	5
Above 2 were essentially solo recordings.					
LOVE BEACH	Atlantic		48	9 Dec 78	4

EMERSON, LAKE and POWELL   UK

(See also Keith Emerson; Emerson, Lake and Powell; Cozy Powell.)

ALBUMS:		HITS 1		WEEKS 5	
EMERSON, LAKE AND POWELL	Polydor		35	14 Jun 86	5

Dick EMERY   UK

SINGLES:		HITS 2		WEEKS 8	
IF YOU LOVE HER	Pye		32	1 Mar 69	4
YOU ARE AWFUL (BUT I LIKE YOU)	Pye		43	13 Jan 73	4

EMF   UK

SINGLES:		HITS 10		WEEKS 50	
UNBELIEVABLE	Parlophone		3	3 Nov 90	13
I BELIEVE	Parlophone		6	2 Feb 91	7
CHILDREN	Parlophone		19	27 Apr 91	5
LIES	Parlophone		28	31 Aug 91	3
UNEXPLAINED [EP]	Parlophone		18	2 May 92	4
Lead track: Getting Through.					
THEY'RE HERE	Parlophone		29	19 Sep 92	3
IT'S YOU	Parlophone		23	21 Nov 92	3
PERFECT DAY	Parlophone		27	25 Feb 95	3
I'M A BELIEVER	Parlophone		3	8 Jul 95	8
Above hit: EMF and REEVES and MORTIMER.					
AFRO KING	Parlophone		51	28 Oct 95	1
ALBUMS:		**HITS 3**		**WEEKS 22**	
SCHUBERT DIP	Parlophone		3	18 May 91	19
STIGMA	Parlophone		19	10 Oct 92	2
CHA CHA CHA	Parlophone		30	18 Mar 95	1

EMILIA   Sweden

SINGLES:		HITS 2		WEEKS 14	
BIG BIG WORLD	Universal		5	12 Dec 98	13
GOOD SIGN	Universal		54	1 May 99	1

EMINEM   US

SINGLES:		HITS 2		WEEKS 20	
MY NAME IS	Interscope		2	10 Apr 99	11
Samples Labi Siffre's I Got The.					
MY NAME IS [RE]	Interscope		68	24 Jul 99	1
GUILTY CONSCIENCE	Interscope		5	14 Aug 99	8
Samples the track Go Home Pigs. From the film 'Getting Straight'.					
Above hit: EMINEM featuring DR. DRE.					
ALBUMS:		**HITS 1**		**WEEKS 29**	
THE SLIM SHADY LP	Interscope		12	24 Apr 99	29
Available as an explicit vocal or clean version.					

EMMA   UK

SINGLES:		HITS 1		WEEKS 6	
GIVE A LITTLE LOVE BACK TO THE WORLD	Big Wave		33	28 Apr 90	6
UK's Eurovision entry in 1990, it came 6th.					

Ivor EMMANUEL   UK

EPS:		HITS 1		WEEKS 5	
LAND OF SONG	Delyse		13	21 Jan 61	5

Stephen EMMANUEL – See COLOURS featuring Stephen EMMANUEL and ESKA

EMMIE
UK

SINGLES:		HITS 1			WEEKS 8
MORE THAN THIS	Manifesto		5	23 Jan 99	8

An EMOTIONAL FISH
Ireland

SINGLES:		HITS 1			WEEKS 5
CELEBRATE	East West		46	23 Jun 90	5
ALBUMS:		**HITS 1**			**WEEKS 3**
AN EMOTIONAL FISH	East West		40	25 Aug 90	3

EMOTIONS
US

SINGLES:		HITS 3			WEEKS 28
BEST OF MY LOVE	CBS		4	10 Sep 77	10
I DON'T WANNA LOSE YOUR LOVE	CBS		40	24 Dec 77	5
BOOGIE WONDERLAND	CBS		4	12 May 79	13
Above hit: EARTH, WIND AND FIRE with the EMOTIONS.					

EMPIRION
UK

SINGLES:		HITS 2			WEEKS 2
NARCOTIC INFLUENCE	XL Recordings		64	6 Jul 96	1
BETA	XL Recordings		75	21 Jun 97	1

EN VOGUE
US

SINGLES:		HITS 12			WEEKS 81
HOLD ON	Atlantic		5	5 May 90	11
LIES	Atlantic		44	21 Jul 90	4
MY LOVIN'	East West America		69	4 Apr 92	3
MY LOVIN' [RE]	East West America		4	9 May 92	9
GIVING HIM SOMETHING HE CAN FEEL	East West America		44	15 Aug 92	3
Originally recorded by Aretha Franklin as Something He Can Feel.					
FREE YOUR MIND / GIVING HIM SOMETHING HE CAN FEEL [RI]	East West America		16	7 Nov 92	8
GIVE IT UP, TURN IT LOOSE	East West America		22	16 Jan 93	4
LOVE DON'T LOVE YOU	East West America		64	10 Apr 93	1
RUNAWAY LOVE	East West America		36	9 Oct 93	3
WHATTA MAN	ffrr		7	19 Mar 94	10
Originally recorded by Linda Lyndell.					
Above hit: SALT 'N' PEPA with EN VOGUE.					
DON'T LET GO (LOVE)	East West America		5	11 Jan 97	16
From the film 'Set It Off'. Backing vocals by Mariah Carey, saxophone by Kenny G.					
WHATEVER	East West America		14	14 Jun 97	5
TOO GONE, TOO LONG	East West America		20	6 Sep 97	3
HOLD ON [RM]	East West America		53	28 Nov 98	1
Remixed by Tuff Jam.					
ALBUMS:		**HITS 4**			**WEEKS 52**
BORN TO SING	Atlantic		23	2 Jun 90	13
FUNKY DIVAS	East West America		26	23 May 92	10
FUNKY DIVAS [RE]	East West America		4	16 Jan 93	19
EV3	East West America		9	28 Jun 97	8
BEST OF EN VOGUE	East West America		39	31 Oct 98	2

ENCORE
France

SINGLES:		HITS 1			WEEKS 4
LE DISC JOCKEY	Sum		12	14 Feb 98	4

ENERGISE
UK

SINGLES:		HITS 1			WEEKS 1
REPORT TO THE DANCEFLOOR	Network		69	16 Feb 91	1

ENERGY 52
Germany

SINGLES:		HITS 1			WEEKS 7
CAFE DEL MAR	Hooj Choons		51	8 Mar 97	1
CAFE DEL MAR '98 [RI]	Hooj Choons		12	25 Jul 98	6
Though listed as a remix, the lead track of the CD format is a straight re-issue.					

ENERGY ORCHARD
Ireland

SINGLES:		HITS 2			WEEKS 6
BELFAST	MCA		52	27 Jan 90	4
SAILORTOWN	MCA		73	7 Apr 90	2
ALBUMS:		**HITS 1**			**WEEKS 2**
ENERGY ORCHARD	MCA		53	12 May 90	2

Harry ENFIELD | | | UK

SINGLES:	HITS 1		WEEKS 7
LOADSAMONEY (DOIN' UP THE HOUSE)	Mercury	4	7 May 88 7

ENGLAND DAN and John Ford COLEY | | | US

SINGLES:	HITS 2		WEEKS 12
I'D REALLY LOVE TO SEE YOU TONIGHT	Atlantic	26	25 Sep 76 7
LOVE IS THE ANSWER	Big Tree	45	23 Jun 79 5
Originally recorded by Utopia.			

ENGLAND RUGBY WORLD CUP SQUAD - See UNION

ENGLAND SISTERS | | | UK

SINGLES:	HITS 1		WEEKS 1
HEARTBEAT	His Master's Voice	33	19 Mar 60 1

ENGLAND SUPPORTERS BAND | | | UK

SINGLES:	HITS 1		WEEKS 2
THE GREAT ESCAPE	V2	46	27 Jun 98 2

ENGLAND UNITED | | | UK

SINGLES:	HITS 1		WEEKS 11
(HOW DOES IT FEEL TO BE) ON TOP OF THE WORLD	London	9	13 Jun 98 9
The official song of the 1998 England World Cup Team.			
Above hit: ENGLAND UNITED : ECHO & THE BUNNYMEN, OCEAN			
COLOUR SCENE, SPACE, SPICE GIRLS.			
(HOW DOES IT FEEL TO BE) ON TOP OF THE WORLD [RE]	London	61	22 Aug 98 2

ENGLAND WORLD CUP SQUAD | | | UK

SINGLES:	HITS 5		WEEKS 46
BACK HOME	Pye	1	18 Apr 70 16
Above hit: ENGLAND WORLD CUP SQUAD "70".			
BACK HOME [RE]	Pye	46	15 Aug 70 1
THIS TIME (WE'LL GET IT RIGHT) / ENGLAND, WE'LL FLY THE FLAG	England	2	10 Apr 82 13
WE'VE GOT THE WHOLE WORLD AT OUR FEET / WHEN WE ARE FAR FROM HOME	Columbia	66	19 Apr 86 2
Above hit: ENGLAND WORLD CUP SQUAD 1986.			
ALL THE WAY	MCA	64	21 May 88 2
Above hit: ENGLAND FOOTBALL TEAM with the 'Sound' Of STOCK, AITKEN and WATERMAN			
WORLD IN MOTION . . .	Factory	1	2 Jun 90 12
New Order and the England World Cup Squad for Italia 1990.			
Above hit: ENGLANDNEWORDER.			
ALBUMS:	HITS 2		WEEKS 18
THE WORLD BEATERS SING THE WORLD BEATERS	Pye	4	16 May 70 8
Above hit: ENGLAND FOOTBALL WORLD CUP SQUAD 1970.			
THIS TIME	K-Tel	37	15 May 82 10

ENGLAND'S BARMY ARMY | | | UK

SINGLES:	HITS 1		WEEKS 1
COME ON ENGLAND!	Wildstar	45	12 Jun 99 1
A reworking of Booker T. & the MGs' Soul Limbo by supporters of the England World Cup cricket squad.			

Kim ENGLISH | | | US

SINGLES:	HITS 4		WEEKS 7
NITE LIFE	Hi-Life	35	23 Jul 94 2
TIME FOR LOVE	Hi-Life	48	4 Mar 95 1
I KNOW A PLACE	Hi-Life	52	9 Sep 95 1
NITE LIFE [RM]	Hi-Life	35	30 Nov 96 2
Remixed by J.T. Vannelli.			
SUPERNATURAL	Hi-Life	50	26 Apr 97 1

Scott ENGLISH | | | US

SINGLES:	HITS 1		WEEKS 10
BRANDY	Horse	12	9 Oct 71 10

ENGLISH CHAMBER CHOIR - See Roger DALTREY; Rick WAKEMAN

ENGLISH CHAMBER ORCHESTRA
UK

(See also Nigel Kennedy; Andrew Lloyd Webber; Kiri Te Kanawa; John Williams.)

ALBUMS:	HITS 1			WEEKS 1
THE BEYONDNESS OF THINGS	Decca	67	8 May 99	1

Above hit: ENGLISH CHAMBER ORCHESTRA conducted by John BARRY.

ENIAC - See NOVY Vs. ENIAC

ENIGMA
UK

SINGLES:	HITS 2			WEEKS 15
AIN'T NO STOPPING - DISCO MIX '81 [M]	Creole	11	23 May 81	8
I LOVE MUSIC [M]	Creole	25	8 Aug 81	7

Above 2 are segued tracks of disco hits.

ALBUMS:	HITS 1			WEEKS 3
AIN'T NO STOPPIN'	Creole	80	5 Sep 81	3

ENIGMA
Romania/Germany

SINGLES:	HITS 9			WEEKS 45
SADNESS PART 1	Virgin International	1	15 Dec 90	12
MEA CULPA PART II	Virgin International	55	30 Mar 91	3
PRINCIPLES OF LUST	Virgin International	59	10 Aug 91	2
THE RIVERS OF BELIEF	Virgin International	68	11 Jan 92	2
RETURN TO INNOCENCE	Virgin	3	29 Jan 94	14
THE EYES OF TRUTH	Virgin	21	14 May 94	4
AGE OF LONELINESS	Virgin	21	20 Aug 94	5

From the film 'Sliver'.

BEYOND THE INVISIBLE	Virgin	26	25 Jan 97	2
T.N.T. FOR THE BRAIN	Virgin	60	19 Apr 97	1

ALBUMS:	HITS 3			WEEKS 130
MCMXC A.D.	Virgin International	1	22 Dec 90	57
MCMXC A.D. [RI]	Virgin	38	22 Jan 94	26
THE CROSS OF CHANGES	Virgin	1	19 Feb 94	35
LE ROI EST MORT, VIVE LE ROI!	Virgin	12	7 Dec 96	12

Brian ENO
UK

(See also 808 State; Brian Eno and David Byrne; Brian Eno and Jah Wobble.)

ALBUMS:	HITS 5			WEEKS 7
HERE COME THE WARM JETS	Island	26	9 Mar 74	2
MUSIC FOR FILMS	Polydor	55	21 Oct 78	1
AMBIENT 4 ON LAND	E'G	93	8 May 82	1
NERVE NET	Opal	70	12 Sep 92	1
WAH WAH	Fontana	11	24 Sep 94	2

Though credited, Eno is more the producer/remixer on the album. Consists of re-workings/alternate versions/studio jams recorded by James at the same time as their Laid album.
Above hit: JAMES and Brian ENO.

Brian ENO and David BYRNE
UK

(See also David Byrne; Brian Eno.)

ALBUMS:	HITS 1			WEEKS 8
MY LIFE IN THE BUSH OF GHOSTS	E'G	29	21 Feb 81	8

Brian ENO and Jah WOBBLE
UK

(See also Brian Eno; Jah Wobble's Invaders Of The Heart.)

ALBUMS:	HITS 1			WEEKS 1
SPINNER	All Saints	71	14 Oct 95	1

Music composed by Eno and remixed by Wobble. Several tracks are from the film 'Glitterbug'.

ENRICO - See Marc VAN DALE with ENRICO

Jocelyn ENRIQUEZ - See STARS ON 54: Ultra NATE, AMBER, Jocelyn ENRIQUEZ

ENTOMBED
Sweden

ALBUMS:	HITS 1			WEEKS 1
TO RIDE, SHOOT STRAIGHT AND SPEAK THE TRUTH	Threeman Recordings	75	15 Mar 97	1

ENUFF Z'NUFF
US

ALBUMS:	HITS 1			WEEKS 1
STRENGTH	Atco	56	13 Apr 91	1

ENYA
Ireland

SINGLES:	HITS 10			WEEKS 59
ORINOCO FLOW (SAIL AWAY)	WEA	1	15 Oct 88	13

EVENING FALLS . . .	*WEA*	20	*24 Dec 88*	4
STORMS IN AFRICA (PART II)	*WEA*	41	*10 Jun 89*	4
CARIBBEAN BLUE	*WEA*	13	*19 Oct 91*	7
HOW CAN I KEEP FROM SINGING?	*WEA*	32	*7 Dec 91*	5
BOOK OF DAYS	*WEA*	10	*1 Aug 92*	6
From the film 'Far and Away'.				
THE CELTS	*WEA*	29	*14 Nov 92*	4
ANYWHERE IS	*WEA*	7	*18 Nov 95*	12
ON MY WAY HOME	*WEA*	26	*7 Dec 96*	2
ONLY IF . . .	*WEA*	43	*13 Dec 97*	2
ALBUMS:	**HITS 5**		**WEEKS 256**	
ENYA [OST-TV]	*BBC*	69	*6 Jun 87*	4
Music from the TV series 'The Celts'.				
WATERMARK	*WEA*	5	*15 Oct 88*	92
SHEPHERD MOONS	*WEA*	1	*16 Nov 91*	90
THE CELTS [RI]	*WEA*	10	*28 Nov 92*	19
Repackaged version of her debut album. Includes re-entry in 1998.				
THE MEMORY OF TREES	*WEA*	5	*2 Dec 95*	24
PAINT THE SKY WITH STARS – THE BEST OF ENYA	*WEA*	4	*15 Nov 97*	27

EON   UK

SINGLES:	**HITS 1**		**WEEKS 1**	
FEAR: THE MINDKILLER [EP]	*Vinyl Solution*	63	*17 Aug 91*	1
Lead track: Fear (Prologue).				

EPMD   US

SINGLES:	**HITS 1**		**WEEKS 1**	
STRICTLY BUSINESS	*Parlophone*	43	*15 Aug 98*	1
Samples Eric Clapton's I Shot the Sheriff.				
Above hit: MANTRONIK vs EPMD.				
ALBUMS:	**HITS 1**		**WEEKS 1**	
BUSINESS AS USUAL	*Def Jam*	69	*16 Feb 91*	1
Above hit: E.P.M.D.				

EQ – See VARIOUS ARTISTS (EPs) 'Fourplay Volume 1 EP'

EQUALS   UK/Guyana

SINGLES:	**HITS 8**		**WEEKS 69**	
I GET SO EXCITED	*President*	44	*24 Feb 68*	4
BABY COME BACK	*President*	50	*4 May 68*	1
BABY COME BACK [RE]	*President*	1	*18 May 68*	17
LAUREL AND HARDY	*President*	35	*24 Aug 68*	5
SOFTLY SOFTLY	*President*	48	*30 Nov 68*	3
MICHAEL AND THE SLIPPER TREE	*President*	24	*5 Apr 69*	7
VIVA BOBBY JOE	*President*	6	*2 Aug 69*	14
RUB A DUB DUB	*President*	34	*27 Dec 69*	7
BLACK SKIN BLUE EYED BOYS	*President*	9	*19 Dec 70*	11
ALBUMS:	**HITS 2**		**WEEKS 10**	
UNEQUALLED EQUALS	*President*	10	*18 Nov 67*	9
EQUALS EXPLOSION	*President*	32	*9 Mar 68*	1

ERASURE   UK

SINGLES:	**HITS 25**		**WEEKS 201**	
WHO NEEDS LOVE LIKE THAT	*Mute*	55	*5 Oct 85*	2
SOMETIMES	*Mute*	2	*25 Oct 86*	17
IT DOESN'T HAVE TO BE	*Mute*	12	*28 Feb 87*	9
VICTIM OF LOVE	*Mute*	7	*30 May 87*	9
THE CIRCUS	*Mute*	6	*3 Oct 87*	10
SHIP OF FOOLS	*Mute*	6	*5 Mar 88*	8
CHAINS OF LOVE	*Mute*	11	*11 Jun 88*	7
A LITTLE RESPECT	*Mute*	4	*1 Oct 88*	10
CRACKERS INTERNATIONAL [EP]	*Mute*	2	*10 Dec 88*	13
Lead track: Stop!				
DRAMA!	*Mute*	4	*30 Sep 89*	8
YOU SURROUND ME	*Mute*	15	*9 Dec 89*	9
BLUE SAVANNAH	*Mute*	3	*10 Mar 90*	10
STAR	*Mute*	11	*2 Jun 90*	7
CHORUS	*Mute*	3	*29 Jun 91*	9
LOVE TO HATE YOU	*Mute*	4	*21 Sep 91*	9
AM I RIGHT?	*Mute*	15	*7 Dec 91*	6
AM I RIGHT? [RM]	*Mute*	22	*11 Jan 92*	3
The remix entry was a 2nd 12"/CD format. As chart rules allowed only 4 formats, it was listed separately.				
BREATH OF LIFE	*Mute*	8	*28 Mar 92*	6

ABBA-ESQUE [EP]	*Mute*	1	*13 Jun 92*	12
Lead track: Lay All Your Love On Me, though all 4 tracks received airplay. Take A Chance On Me featured a rap by MC Kinky.				
WHO NEEDS LOVE (LIKE THAT) [RM]	*Mute*	10	*7 Nov 92*	4
Remixed by Dave Bascombe and Erasure.				
ALWAYS	*Mute*	4	*23 Apr 94*	9
RUN TO THE SUN	*Mute*	6	*30 Jul 94*	5
I LOVE SATURDAY	*Mute*	20	*3 Dec 94*	6
STAY WITH ME	*Mute*	15	*23 Sep 95*	4
FINGERS & THUMBS (COLD SUMMER'S DAY)	*Mute*	20	*9 Dec 95*	3
IN MY ARMS	*Mute*	13	*18 Jan 97*	4
DON'T SAY YOUR LOVE IS KILLING ME	*Mute*	23	*8 Mar 97*	4
ALBUMS:	**HITS 9**		**WEEKS 315**	
WONDERLAND	*Mute*	71	*14 Jun 86*	7
THE CIRCUS	*Mute*	6	*11 Apr 87*	107
THE INNOCENTS	*Mute*	1	*30 Apr 88*	78
WILD!	*Mute*	1	*28 Oct 89*	48
CHORUS	*Mute*	1	*26 Oct 91*	25
POP! – THE FIRST 20 HITS	*Mute*	1	*28 Nov 92*	26
I SAY I SAY I SAY	*Mute*	1	*28 May 94*	15
ERASURE	*Mute*	14	*4 Nov 95*	5
COWBOY	*Mute*	10	*12 Apr 97*	4

ERIC and BILLY - See S-EXPRESS

ERIC and the GOOD GOOD FEELING | UK

(See also S-Express.)

SINGLES:	**HITS 1**		**WEEKS 1**	
GOOD GOOD FEELING	*Equinox*	73	*3 Jun 89*	1

ERIK | UK

SINGLES:	**HITS 3**		**WEEKS 5**	
LOOKS LIKE I'M IN LOVE AGAIN	*PWL Sanctuary*	46	*10 Apr 93*	2
Above hit: KEY WEST featuring ERIK.				
GOT TO BE REAL	*PWL International*	42	*29 Jan 94*	2
WE GOT THE LOVE	*PWL International*	55	*1 Oct 94*	1

ERIN - See BBG; SHUT UP AND DANCE

EROTIC DRUM BAND | Canada

SINGLES:	**HITS 1**		**WEEKS 3**	
LOVE DISCO STYLE	*Scope*	47	*9 Jun 79*	3

ERUPTION | UK

SINGLES:	**HITS 2**		**WEEKS 21**	
I CAN'T STAND THE RAIN	*Atlantic*	5	*18 Feb 78*	11
Originally recorded by Ann Peebles. Some copies do not credit Precious Wilson.				
Above hit: ERUPTION featuring Precious WILSON.				
ONE WAY TICKET	*Atlantic*	9	*21 Apr 79*	10
Originally recorded by Neil Sedaka.				

Nas ESCOBAR - See Nas ESCOBAR, Foxy BROWN, AZ and NATURE present the FIRM featuring Dawn ROBINSON

ESCORTS | UK

SINGLES:	**HITS 1**		**WEEKS 2**	
THE ONE TO CRY	*Fontana*	49	*4 Jul 64*	2

ESCRIMA | UK

SINGLES:	**HITS 2**		**WEEKS 4**	
TRAIN OF THOUGHT	*Ffrreedom*	36	*11 Feb 95*	2
Features a sample from King Bee's Back By Dope Demand.				
DEEPER	*Hooj Choons*	27	*7 Oct 95*	2

ESKA - See COLOURS featuring Stephen EMMANUEL and ESKA

ESKIMOS AND EGYPT | UK

SINGLES:	**HITS 2**		**WEEKS 4**	
FALL FROM GRACE	*One Little Indian*	51	*13 Feb 93*	2
UK – USA	*One Little Indian*	52	*29 May 93*	2

ESPIRITU | UK/France

SINGLES:	**HITS 4**		**WEEKS 10**	
CONQUISTADOR	*Heavenly*	47	*6 Mar 93*	2
LOS AMERICANOS	*Heavenly*	45	*7 Aug 93*	2
BONITA MANANA	*Columbia*	50	*20 Aug 94*	1
ALWAYS SOMETHING THERE TO REMIND ME	*WEA*	14	*25 Mar 95*	5
Above hit: TIN TIN OUT featuring ESPIRITU.				

ESSENCE | | | UK

SINGLES:	HITS 1			WEEKS 2
THE PROMISE	*Innocent*	27	*21 Mar 98*	2

ESSEX | | | US

SINGLES:	HITS 1			WEEKS 5
EASIER SAID THAN DONE	*Columbia*	41	*10 Aug 63*	5

David ESSEX | | | UK

SINGLES:	HITS 25			WEEKS 199
ROCK ON	*CBS*	3	*18 Aug 73*	11
LAMPLIGHT	*CBS*	7	*10 Nov 73*	15
AMERICA	*CBS*	32	*11 May 74*	5
GONNA MAKE YOU A STAR	*CBS*	1	*12 Oct 74*	17
STARDUST	*CBS*	7	*14 Dec 74*	10
From the film of the same name.				
ROLLING STONE	*CBS*	5	*5 Jul 75*	7
HOLD ME CLOSE	*CBS*	1	*13 Sep 75*	10
IF I COULD	*CBS*	13	*6 Dec 75*	8
CITY LIGHTS	*CBS*	24	*20 Mar 76*	4
COMING HOME	*CBS*	24	*16 Oct 76*	6
COOL OUT TONIGHT	*CBS*	23	*17 Sep 77*	6
STAY WITH ME BABY	*CBS*	45	*11 Mar 78*	5
OH WHAT A CIRCUS	*Mercury*	3	*19 Aug 78*	11
BRAVE NEW WORLD	*CBS*	55	*21 Oct 78*	3
Above hit: featuring the vocal performance of David ESSEX from Jeff WAYNE'S "THE WAR OF THE WORLDS".				
IMPERIAL WIZARD	*Mercury*	32	*3 Mar 79*	8
SILVER DREAM MACHINE	*Mercury*	4	*5 Apr 80*	11
From the film 'Silver Dream Racer'.				
HOT LOVE	*Mercury*	57	*14 Jun 80*	4
ME AND MY GIRL (NIGHT-CLUBBING)	*Mercury*	13	*26 Jun 82*	10
A WINTER'S TALE	*Mercury*	2	*11 Dec 82*	10
THE SMILE	*Mercury*	52	*4 Jun 83*	4
TAHITI	*Mercury*	8	*27 Aug 83*	11
From the musical 'Mutiny On The Bounty'.				
YOU'RE IN MY HEART	*Mercury*	67	*26 Nov 83*	2
YOU'RE IN MY HEART [RE]	*Mercury*	59	*17 Dec 83*	4
FALLING ANGELS RIDING	*Mercury*	29	*23 Feb 85*	7
MYFANWY	*Arista*	41	*18 Apr 87*	7
From the musical 'Betjeman'.				
TRUE LOVE WAYS	*PolyGram TV*	38	*26 Nov 94*	3
Above hit: David ESSEX and Catherine Zeta JONES.				

ALBUMS:	HITS 20			WEEKS 178
ROCK ON	*CBS*	7	*24 Nov 73*	22
DAVID ESSEX	*CBS*	2	*19 Oct 74*	24
ALL THE FUN OF THE FAIR	*CBS*	3	*27 Sep 75*	20
ON TOUR	*CBS*	51	*5 Jun 76*	1
OUT ON THE STREET	*CBS*	31	*30 Oct 76*	9
GOLD AND IVORY	*CBS*	29	*8 Oct 77*	4
THE DAVID ESSEX ALBUM	*CBS*	29	*6 Jan 79*	7
IMPERIAL WIZARD	*Mercury*	12	*31 Mar 79*	9
HOT LOVE	*Mercury*	75	*12 Jul 80*	1
STAGE-STRUCK	*Mercury*	31	*19 Jun 82*	15
THE VERY BEST OF DAVID ESSEX	*TV Records*	37	*27 Nov 82*	11
MUTINY (STUDIO CAST RECORDING)	*Mercury*	39	*15 Oct 83*	4
This show was not staged until 1985.				
Above hit: David ESSEX, Frank FINLAY and VARIOUS ARTISTS.				
THE WHISPER	*Mercury*	67	*17 Dec 83*	6
CENTRE STAGE	*K-Tel*	82	*6 Dec 86*	4
HIS GREATEST HITS	*Mercury*	13	*19 Oct 91*	13
COVER SHOT	*PolyGram TV*	3	*10 Apr 93*	8
BACK TO BACK	*PolyGram TV*	33	*22 Oct 94*	2
MISSING YOU	*PolyGram TV*	26	*9 Dec 95*	9
A NIGHT AT THE MOVIES	*PolyGram TV*	14	*17 May 97*	5
Features the Royal Philharmonic Orchestra.				
GREATEST HITS	*PolyGram TV*	31	*13 Jun 98*	4

Gloria ESTEFAN | | | US

SINGLES:	HITS 31			WEEKS 204
DR. BEAT	*Epic*	6	*11 Aug 84*	14
BAD BOY	*Epic*	16	*17 May 86*	11
Above 2: MIAMI SOUND MACHINE.				
ANYTHING FOR YOU	*Epic*	10	*16 Jul 88*	16
1-2-3	*Epic*	9	*22 Oct 88*	9
RHYTHM IS GONNA GET YOU	*Epic*	16	*17 Dec 88*	9

1-2-3 [RE]	Epic	72	31 Dec 88	1
CAN'T STAY AWAY FROM YOU	Epic	7	11 Feb 89	12

Originally reached No. 88 in 1988.
Above 5: Gloria ESTEFAN and MIAMI SOUND MACHINE.

DON'T WANNA LOSE YOU	Epic	6	15 Jul 89	10
OYE MI CANTO (HEAR MY VOICE)	Epic	16	16 Sep 89	8
GET ON YOUR FEET	Epic	23	25 Nov 89	7
HERE WE ARE	Epic	23	3 Mar 90	6
CUTS BOTH WAYS	Epic	49	26 May 90	5
COMING OUT OF THE DARK	Epic	25	26 Jan 91	5

Backing vocals by Jon Secada and Betty Wright.

SEAL OUR FATE	Epic	24	6 Apr 91	7
REMEMBER ME WITH LOVE	Epic	22	8 Jun 91	6
LIVE FOR LOVING YOU	Epic	33	21 Sep 91	5
ALWAYS TOMORROW	Epic	24	24 Oct 92	4
MIAMI HIT MIX [M] / CHRISTMAS THROUGH YOUR EYES	Epic	8	12 Dec 92	9

Medley of 5 earlier hits. Christmas Through Your Eyes listed from 19 Dec 92.

I SEE YOUR SMILE	Epic	48	13 Feb 93	2
GO AWAY	Epic	13	3 Apr 93	6
MI TIERRA	Epic	36	3 Jul 93	3
IF WE WERE LOVERS / CON LOS ANOS QUE ME QUEDAN	Epic	40	14 Aug 93	3
MONTUNO	Epic	55	18 Dec 93	2
TURN THE BEAT AROUND	Epic	21	15 Oct 94	6

From the film 'The Specialist'. Original by Vicki Sue Robinson reached No. 10 in the US in 1976.

HOLD ME, THRILL ME, KISS ME	Epic	11	3 Dec 94	10

Originally recorded by Harry Noble and his Orchestra.

EVERLASTING LOVE	Epic	19	18 Feb 95	5
HOLD ME, THRILL ME, KISS ME [RE]	Epic	68	18 Mar 95	1
REACH	Epic	15	25 May 96	6

The official anthem of the Atlanta 1996 Olympic Games.

REACH [RE-1ST]	Epic	68	3 Aug 96	1
REACH [RE-2ND]	Epic	55	17 Aug 96	1
YOU'LL BE MINE (PARTY TIME)	Epic	18	24 Aug 96	3

Performed at the closing ceremony of the 1996 Olympic Games.

I'M NOT GIVING YOU UP	Epic	28	14 Dec 96	3
HEAVEN'S WHAT I FEEL	Epic	17	6 Jun 98	4
OYE	Epic	33	10 Oct 98	2
DON'T LET THIS MOMENT END	Epic	28	16 Jan 99	2

Above 2: GLORIA!

ALBUMS:		HITS 9		WEEKS 245
ANYTHING FOR YOU	Epic	1	19 Nov 88	54

Originally released in 1987 with title 'Let It Loose'.
Above hit: Gloria ESTEFAN and MIAMI SOUND MACHINE.

CUTS BOTH WAYS	Epic	1	5 Aug 89	64
INTO THE LIGHT	Epic	2	16 Feb 91	36
GREATEST HITS	Epic	2	14 Nov 92	47
MI TIERRA	Epic	11	10 Jul 93	11
HOLD ME, THRILL ME, KISS ME	Epic	5	29 Oct 94	19

Album of cover versions.

ABRIENDO PUERTAS	Epic	70	21 Oct 95	1
DESTINY	Epic	12	15 Jun 96	9
GLORIA!	Epic	16	13 Jun 98	4

Don ESTELLE and Windsor DAVIES - See Windsor DAVIES as B.S.M. WILLIAMS and Don ESTELLE as GUNNER SUGDEN

Deon ESTUS
US

SINGLES:		HITS 2		WEEKS 7
MY GUY, MY GIRL [M]	Sedition	63	25 Jan 86	3

Above hit: Amii STEWART and Dion ESTUS.

HEAVEN HELP ME	Mika	41	29 Apr 89	4

Features backing vocals by George Michael.

ETA
Denmark

SINGLES:		HITS 1		WEEKS 5
CASUAL SUB (BURNING SPEAR)	East West	28	28 Jun 97	3
CASUAL SUB (BURNING SPEAR) [RI]	East West Dance	28	31 Jan 98	2

ETERNAL
UK

SINGLES:		HITS 15		WEEKS 134
STAY	EMI	4	2 Oct 93	9

Originally recorded by Glenn Jones in 1990.

SAVE OUR LOVE	EMI	8	15 Jan 94	7
JUST A STEP FROM HEAVEN	EMI	8	30 Apr 94	10
SO GOOD	EMI	13	20 Aug 94	7
OH BABY I . . .	EMI	4	5 Nov 94	13
CRAZY	EMI	15	24 Dec 94	7

POWER OF A WOMAN	EMI	5	21 Oct 95	8
I AM BLESSED	EMI	7	9 Dec 95	12
GOOD THING	EMI	8	9 Mar 96	6
SOMEDAY	EMI	4	17 Aug 96	9
From the film 'The Hunchback of Notre Dame'.				
SECRETS	EMI	9	7 Dec 96	7
DON'T YOU LOVE ME	EMI	3	8 Mar 97	7
I WANNA BE THE ONLY ONE	EMI	1	31 May 97	15
Above hit: ETERNAL featuring BeBe WINANS.				
ANGEL OF MINE	EMI	4	11 Oct 97	13
WHAT'CHA GONNA DO	EMI	16	30 Oct 99	4
ALBUMS:	**HITS 4**		**WEEKS 163**	
ALWAYS & FOREVER	EMI	9	11 Dec 93	16
ALWAYS & FOREVER [RE]	EMI	2	7 May 94	60
Peak position reached on 7 Jan 95.				
POWER OF A WOMAN	EMI	6	11 Nov 95	31
BEFORE THE RAIN	EMI	3	29 Mar 97	29
GREATEST HITS	EMI	2	1 Nov 97	27

ETHER
UK

SINGLES:	**HITS 1**		**WEEKS 1**	
WATCHING YOU	Parlophone	74	28 Mar 98	1

Melissa ETHERIDGE
US

ALBUMS:	**HITS 2**		**WEEKS 2**	
BRAVE AND CRAZY	Island	63	30 Sep 89	1
NEVER ENOUGH	Island	56	9 May 92	1

ETHICS
Holland

(See also Artemesia; Movin' Melodies; Subliminal Cuts.)

SINGLES:	**HITS 1**		**WEEKS 5**	
TO THE BEAT OF THE DRUM (LA LUNA)	VC Recordings	13	25 Nov 95	5
Song was originally released by Movin' Melodies.				

ETHIOPIANS
Jamaica

SINGLES:	**HITS 1**		**WEEKS 6**	
TRAIN TO SKAVILLE	Rio	40	16 Sep 67	6

Tony ETORIA
UK

SINGLES:	**HITS 1**		**WEEKS 8**	
I CAN PROVE IT	GTO	21	4 Jun 77	8

EUROGROOVE
UK

SINGLES:	**HITS 3**		**WEEKS 7**	
MOVE YOUR BODY	Avex UK	29	20 May 95	2
DIVE TO PARADISE	Avex UK	31	5 Aug 95	2
IT'S ON YOU (SCAN ME)	Avex UK	25	21 Oct 95	2
MOVE YOUR BODY [RM]	Avex UK	44	3 Feb 96	1
Remixed by Boyz With Pride.				

EUROPE
Sweden

SINGLES:	**HITS 7**		**WEEKS 48**	
THE FINAL COUNTDOWN	Epic	1	1 Nov 86	15
ROCK THE NIGHT	Epic	12	31 Jan 87	9
CARRIE	Epic	22	18 Apr 87	8
SUPERSTITIOUS	Epic	34	20 Aug 88	5
I'LL CRY FOR YOU	Epic	28	1 Feb 92	5
HALFWAY TO HEAVEN	Epic	42	21 Mar 92	4
THE FINAL COUNTDOWN 2000 [RR]	Epic	39	25 Dec 99	2
New Millennium Mix.				
ALBUMS:	**HITS 3**		**WEEKS 43**	
THE FINAL COUNTDOWN	Epic	9	22 Nov 86	37
OUT OF THIS WORLD	Epic	12	17 Sep 88	5
PRISONERS IN PARADISE	Epic	61	19 Oct 91	1

EUROPEANS
UK

ALBUMS:	**HITS 1**		**WEEKS 1**	
LIVE	A&M	100	11 Feb 84	1

EURYTHMICS
UK

SINGLES:	**HITS 25**		**WEEKS 204**	
NEVER GONNA CRY AGAIN	RCA	63	4 Jul 81	3
LOVE IS A STRANGER	RCA	54	20 Nov 82	5

SWEET DREAMS (ARE MADE OF THIS)	*RCA*	2	*12 Feb 83*	14
LOVE IS A STRANGER [RE]	*RCA*	6	*9 Apr 83*	8
WHO'S THAT GIRL?	*RCA*	3	*9 Jul 83*	10
RIGHT BY YOUR SIDE	*RCA*	10	*5 Nov 83*	11
HERE COMES THE RAIN AGAIN	*RCA*	8	*21 Jan 84*	8
SEX CRIME (NINETEEN EIGHTY-FOUR)	*Virgin*	4	*3 Nov 84*	13
From the film 'Nineteen-Eighty Four'.				
JULIA	*Virgin*	44	*19 Jan 85*	4
WOULD I LIE TO YOU?	*RCA*	17	*20 Apr 85*	8
THERE MUST BE AN ANGEL (PLAYING WITH MY HEART)	*RCA*	1	*6 Jul 85*	13
Features harmonica playing by Stevie Wonder.				
SISTERS ARE DOIN' IT FOR THEMSELVES	*RCA*	9	*2 Nov 85*	11
Above hit: EURYTHMICS and Aretha FRANKLIN.				
IT'S ALRIGHT (BABY'S COMING BACK)	*RCA*	12	*11 Jan 86*	8
WHEN TOMORROW COMES	*RCA*	30	*14 Jun 86*	6
THORN IN MY SIDE	*RCA*	5	*6 Sep 86*	11
THE MIRACLE OF LOVE	*RCA*	23	*29 Nov 86*	9
MISSIONARY MAN	*RCA*	31	*28 Feb 87*	4
BEETHOVEN (I LOVE TO LISTEN TO)	*RCA*	25	*24 Oct 87*	5
SHAME	*RCA*	41	*26 Dec 87*	6
I NEED A MAN	*RCA*	26	*9 Apr 88*	5
YOU HAVE PLACED A CHILL IN MY HEART	*RCA*	16	*11 Jun 88*	8
REVIVAL	*RCA*	26	*26 Aug 89*	6
DON'T ASK ME WHY	*RCA*	25	*4 Nov 89*	6
THE KING AND QUEEN OF AMERICA	*RCA*	29	*3 Feb 90*	5
ANGEL	*RCA*	23	*12 May 90*	6
LOVE IS A STRANGER [RI]	*RCA*	46	*9 Mar 91*	3
SWEET DREAMS (ARE MADE OF THIS) '91 [RM]	*RCA*	48	*16 Nov 91*	2
I SAVED THE WORLD TODAY	*RCA*	11	*16 Oct 99*	6
ALBUMS:	**HITS 11**			**WEEKS 442**
SWEET DREAMS (ARE MADE OF THIS)	*RCA*	3	*12 Feb 83*	59
TOUCH	*RCA*	1	*26 Nov 83*	48
TOUCH DANCE	*RCA*	31	*9 Jun 84*	5
Remixes of four tracks from Touch.				
1984 (FOR THE LOVE OF BIG BROTHER) [OST]	*Virgin*	23	*24 Nov 84*	17
BE YOURSELF TONIGHT	*RCA*	3	*11 May 85*	80
REVENGE	*RCA*	3	*12 Jul 86*	52
SAVAGE	*RCA*	7	*21 Nov 87*	33
WE TOO ARE ONE	*RCA*	1	*23 Sep 89*	32
GREATEST HITS	*RCA*	1	*30 Mar 91*	98
Includes re-entries through to 1999.				
SWEET DREAMS (ARE MADE OF THIS) [RE]	*RCA*	64	*15 Jun 91*	1
Re-released at mid-price.				
EURYTHMICS LIVE 1983-1989	*RCA*	22	*27 Nov 93*	7
PEACE	*RCA*	4	*30 Oct 99*	10

EUSEBE

				UK
SINGLES:	**HITS 1**			**WEEKS 3**
SUMMERTIME HEALING	*Mama's Yard*	32	*26 Aug 95*	3

EVANGEL TEMPLE CHOIR - See Johnny CASH

Faith EVANS

				US
(See also A Tribe Called Quest.)				
SINGLES:	**HITS 5**			**WEEKS 33**
YOU USED TO LOVE ME	*Puff Daddy*	42	*14 Oct 95*	2
I'LL BE MISSING YOU	*Puff Daddy*	1	*28 Jun 97*	21
Sleeve gives title as an EP:Tribute To the Notorious B.I.G. Based on the Police's Every Breath You Take.				
Above hit: PUFF DADDY and Faith EVANS (featuring 112).				
LOVE LIKE THIS	*Puff Daddy*	24	*14 Nov 98*	4
Samples Chic's Chic Cheer.				
GEORGY PORGY	*Warner Brothers*	28	*1 May 99*	3
Original by Toto reached No.48 in the US in 1978.				
Above hit: Eric BENET featuring Faith EVANS.				
ALL NIGHT LONG	*Puff Daddy*	23	*1 May 99*	3
Samples Unlimited Touch's I Hear Music In The Street.				
Above hit: Faith EVANS (featuring PUFF DADDY).				
ALBUMS:	**HITS 1**			**WEEKS 1**
KEEP THE FAITH	*Puff Daddy*	69	*7 Nov 98*	1

Maureen EVANS

				UK
SINGLES:	**HITS 5**			**WEEKS 37**
THE BIG HURT	*Oriole*	26	*23 Jan 60*	2
Above hit: Maureen EVANS with Norman PERCIVAL and his Orchestra.				
LOVE KISSES AND HEARTACHES	*Oriole*	44	*19 Mar 60*	1

PAPER ROSES		Oriole	40	4 Jun 60	5
LIKE I DO		Oriole	3	1 Dec 62	18
I LOVE HOW YOU LOVE ME		Oriole	34	29 Feb 64	10
I LOVE HOW YOU LOVE ME [RE]		Oriole	50	16 May 64	1

Paul EVANS
US

SINGLES:	**HITS 3**			**WEEKS 14**	
SEVEN LITTLE GIRLS SITTING IN THE BACK SEAT		London	25	28 Nov 59	1
Above hit: Paul EVANS and the CURLS.					
MIDNITE SPECIAL		London	41	2 Apr 60	1
HELLO, THIS IS JOANNIE (THE TELEPHONE ANSWERING MACHINE SONG)		Spring	6	16 Dec 78	12

EVASIONS
UK

SINGLES:	**HITS 1**			**WEEKS 8**	
WIKKA WRAP		Groove	20	13 Jun 81	8
Spoof take-off of Alan Whicker against the tune of Tom Browne's Funkin' For Jamaica.					

Alison EVELYN - See BROTHERS LIKE OUTLAW featuring Alison EVELYN

EVERCLEAR
US

SINGLES:	**HITS 3**			**WEEKS 5**	
HEARTSPARK DOLLARSIGN		Capitol	48	1 Jun 96	2
SANTA MONICA (WATCH THE WORLD DIE)		Capitol	40	31 Aug 96	2
EVERYTHING TO EVERYONE		Capitol	41	9 May 98	1
ALBUMS:	**HITS 1**			**WEEKS 1**	
SO MUCH FOR THE AFTERGLOW		Capitol	63	14 Mar 98	1

Betty EVERETT
US

SINGLES:	**HITS 2**			**WEEKS 14**	
GETTING MIGHTY CROWDED		Fontana	29	16 Jan 65	7
IT'S IN HIS KISS (THE SHOOP SHOOP SONG)		President	34	2 Nov 68	7

Kenny EVERETT
UK

SINGLES:	**HITS 2**			**WEEKS 12**	
CAPTAIN KREMMEN (RETRIBUTION)		DJM	32	12 Nov 77	4
Captain Kremmen was a fictional character in Everett's Capital Radio show.					
Above hit: Kenny EVERETT and Mike VICKERS.					
SNOT RAP		RCA	9	26 Mar 83	8
Sid Snot and Cupid Stunt were 2 characters from his BBC TV show.					
Above hit: Kenny EVERETT featuring Sid SNOT and Cupid STUNT.					

Peven EVERETT - See Roy DAVIS JR. featuring Peven EVERETT

EVERLAST
US

SINGLES:	**HITS 2**			**WEEKS 3**	
WHAT IT'S LIKE		Tommy Boy	34	27 Feb 99	2
ENDS		Tommy Boy	47	3 Jul 99	1
Samples Wu Tang Clan's C.R.E.A.M.					
ALBUMS:	**HITS 1**			**WEEKS 1**	
WHITEY FORD SINGS THE BLUES		Tommy Boy	65	13 Mar 99	1

Phil EVERLY
US

SINGLES:	**HITS 3**			**WEEKS 24**	
LOUISE		Capitol	47	6 Nov 82	6
SHE MEANS NOTHING TO ME		Capitol	9	19 Feb 83	9
Above hit: Phil EVERLY / Cliff RICHARD.					
ALL I HAVE TO DO IS DREAM		EMI	14	10 Dec 94	6
[AA] listed with the re-issue of Miss You Nights by Cliff Richard.					
Above hit: Cliff RICHARD (with Phil EVERLY).					
ALL I HAVE TO DO IS DREAM [RE]		EMI	58	25 Feb 95	3
ALBUMS:	**HITS 1**			**WEEKS 1**	
PHIL EVERLY		Capitol	61	7 May 83	1

EVERLY BROTHERS
US

SINGLES:	**HITS 29**			**WEEKS 345**	
BYE BYE, LOVE		London	6	13 Jul 57	16
WAKE UP LITTLE SUSIE		London	2	9 Nov 57	13
ALL I HAVE TO DO IS DREAM / CLAUDETTE		London	1	24 May 58	21
Claudette listed from 31 May 58. Originally written and recorded by Roy Orbison.					
BIRD DOG		London	2	13 Sep 58	16
PROBLEMS		London	6	24 Jan 59	12
TAKE A MESSAGE TO MARY		London	29	23 May 59	1

POOR JENNY	*London*	14	*30 May 59*	11
Above 2 entries were separate sides of the same release, each had its own chart run.				
TAKE A MESSAGE TO MARY [RE-1ST]	*London*	27	*20 Jun 59*	1
TAKE A MESSAGE TO MARY [RE-2ND]	*London*	20	*4 Jul 59*	8
('TIL) I KISSED YOU	*London*	2	*12 Sep 59*	15
The Crickets on backing vocals.				
LET IT BE ME	*London*	13	*13 Feb 60*	6
Originally recorded by Jill Corey in 1957.				
LET IT BE ME [RE]	*London*	26	*2 Apr 60*	4
CATHY'S CLOWN	*Warner Brothers*	1	*16 Apr 60*	18
The first release on the Warner Brothers label.				
WHEN WILL I BE LOVED	*London*	4	*16 Jul 60*	16
LUCILLE / SO SAD (TO WATCH GOOD LOVE GO BAD)	*Warner Brothers*	4	*24 Sep 60*	15
LIKE STRANGERS	*London*	11	*17 Dec 60*	10
EBONY EYES / WALK RIGHT BACK	*Warner Brothers*	1	*11 Feb 61*	16
Ebony Eyes only listed on 11 Feb 61. Both sides listed for the next 3 weeks. From 11 Mar 61 Walk Right Back had first credit and from 1 Apr 61 it was the only side listed.				
TEMPTATION	*Warner Brothers*	1	*17 Jun 61*	15
Originally recorded by Bing Crosby.				
MUSKRAT / DON'T BLAME ME	*Warner Brothers*	20	*7 Oct 61*	6
Don't Blame Me only listed from 14 Oct 61 for 4 weeks. Originally recorded by Ethel Merman in 1933.				
CRYING IN THE RAIN	*Warner Brothers*	6	*20 Jan 62*	15
HOW CAN I MEET HER	*Warner Brothers*	12	*19 May 62*	10
NO ONE CAN MAKE MY SUNSHINE SMILE	*Warner Brothers*	11	*27 Oct 62*	11
(SO IT WAS . . . SO IT IS) SO IT WILL ALWAYS BE	*Warner Brothers*	23	*23 Mar 63*	11
IT'S BEEN NICE (GOODNIGHT)	*Warner Brothers*	26	*15 Jun 63*	5
From the film 'Just For Fun'.				
THE GIRL SANG THE BLUES	*Warner Brothers*	25	*19 Oct 63*	9
THE FERRIS WHEEL	*Warner Brothers*	22	*18 Jul 64*	10
GONE GONE GONE	*Warner Brothers*	36	*5 Dec 64*	7
THAT'LL BE THE DAY	*Warner Brothers*	30	*8 May 65*	4
THE PRICE OF LOVE	*Warner Brothers*	2	*22 May 65*	14
I'LL NEVER GET OVER YOU	*Warner Brothers*	35	*28 Aug 65*	5
LOVE IS STRANGE	*Warner Brothers*	11	*23 Oct 65*	9
Originally recorded by Micky and Sylvia.				
IT'S MY TIME	*Warner Brothers*	39	*11 May 68*	6
ON THE WINGS OF A NIGHTINGALE	*Mercury*	41	*22 Sep 84*	9
EPS:	**HITS 4**		**WEEKS 13**	
THE EVERLY BROTHERS – NO. 5	*London*	7	*7 May 60*	6
THE EVERLY BROTHERS	*London*	15	*23 Jul 60*	1
THE EVERLY BROTHERS – NO. 4	*London*	8	*23 Jul 60*	5
THE EVERLY BROTHERS – NO. 6	*London*	20	*9 Jun 62*	1
ALBUMS:	**HITS 12**		**WEEKS 123**	
IT'S EVERLY TIME	*Warner Brothers*	2	*2 Jul 60*	23
FABULOUS STYLE OF THE EVERLY BROTHERS	*London*	4	*15 Oct 60*	11
A DATE WITH THE EVERLY BROTHERS	*Warner Brothers*	3	*4 Mar 61*	14
INSTANT PARTY	*Warner Brothers*	20	*21 Jul 62*	1
ORIGINAL GREATEST HITS	*CBS*	7	*12 Sep 70*	16
THE VERY BEST OF THE EVERLY BROTHERS	*Warner Brothers*	43	*8 Jun 74*	1
WALK RIGHT BACK WITH THE EVERLYS	*Warner Brothers*	10	*29 Nov 75*	10
LIVING LEGENDS	*Warwick*	12	*9 Apr 77*	10
LOVE HURTS	*K-Tel*	31	*18 Dec 82*	10
EVERLY BROTHERS REUNION CONCERT – LIVE AT THE ROYAL ALBERT HALL	*Impression*	47	*7 Jan 84*	6
Live recordings from 23 Sep 83.				
THE EVERLY BROTHERS	*Mercury*	36	*3 Nov 84*	4
LOVE HURTS [RE]	*K-Tel*	22	*29 Dec 84*	12
THE GOLDEN YEARS OF THE EVERLY BROTHERS – THEIR 24 GREATEST HITS	*Warner Brothers*	26	*29 May 93*	5

EVERTON FOOTBALL CLUB UK

SINGLES:	**HITS 2**		**WEEKS 8**	
HERE WE GO	*Columbia*	14	*11 May 85*	5
Above hit: EVERTON 1985 (the OFFICIAL TEAM RECORD).				
ALL TOGETHER NOW	*MDMC*	24	*20 May 95*	3
Features vocals by Keith Mullen of the Farm.				

EVERYTHING BUT THE GIRL UK

SINGLES:	**HITS 19**		**WEEKS 93**	
EACH AND EVERYONE	*Blanco Y Negro*	28	*12 May 84*	7
MINE	*Blanco Y Negro*	58	*21 Jul 84*	2
NATIVE LAND	*Blanco Y Negro*	73	*6 Oct 84*	2
COME ON HOME	*Blanco Y Negro*	44	*2 Aug 86*	7
DON'T LEAVE ME BEHIND	*Blanco Y Negro*	72	*11 Oct 86*	2
THESE EARLY DAYS	*Blanco Y Negro*	75	*13 Feb 88*	1
I DON'T WANT TO TALK ABOUT IT	*Blanco Y Negro*	3	*9 Jul 88*	9
DRIVING	*Blanco Y Negro*	54	*27 Jan 90*	2

COVERS [EP]	Blanco Y Negro	13	22 Feb 92	6
Lead track: Love Is Strange.				
THE ONLY LIVING BOY IN NEW YORK [EP]	Blanco Y Negro	42	24 Apr 93	5
Lead track: The Only Living Boy In New York. Originally recorded by Simon and Garfunkel.				
I DIDN'T KNOW I WAS LOOKING FOR LOVE [EP]	Blanco Y Negro	72	19 Jun 93	1
Lead track: I Didn't Know I Was Looking For Love.				
ROLLERCOASTER [EP]	Blanco Y Negro	65	4 Jun 94	1
Lead track: Rollercoaster.				
MISSING	Blanco Y Negro	69	20 Aug 94	1
MISSING [RM]	Blanco Y Negro	3	28 Oct 95	22
Remixed by Todd Terry.				
WALKING WOUNDED	Virgin	6	20 Apr 96	6
WRONG	Virgin	8	29 Jun 96	7
SINGLE	Virgin	20	5 Oct 96	3
DRIVING [RM]	Blanco Y Negro	36	7 Dec 96	2
Remixed by Todd Terry.				
BEFORE TODAY	Virgin	25	1 Mar 97	2
THE FUTURE OF THE FUTURE (STAY GOLD) [RM]	Deconstruction	31	3 Oct 98	2
Remixed by Ben Watt and David Morales, it features Thorn's vocals.				
Above hit: DEEP DISH with EVERYTHING BUT THE GIRL.				
FIVE FATHOMS	Virgin	27	25 Sep 99	3
ALBUMS:	**HITS 11**		**WEEKS 131**	
EDEN	Blanco Y Negro	14	16 Jun 84	22
LOVE NOT MONEY	Blanco Y Negro	10	27 Apr 85	9
BABY THE STARS SHINE BRIGHT	Blanco Y Negro	22	6 Sep 86	9
IDLEWILD	Blanco Y Negro	13	12 Mar 88	9
IDLEWILD [RE]	Blanco Y Negro	21	6 Aug 88	6
Repackaged with additional track.				
THE LANGUAGE OF LIFE	Blanco Y Negro	10	17 Feb 90	6
WORLDWIDE	Blanco Y Negro	29	5 Oct 91	5
HOME MOVIES – THE BEST OF EVERYTHING BUT THE GIRL	Blanco Y Negro	5	22 May 93	8
AMPLIFIED HEART	Blanco Y Negro	20	25 Jun 94	15
WALKING WOUNDED	Virgin	4	18 May 96	27
THE BEST OF EVERYTHING BUT THE GIRL	Blanco Y Negro	23	9 Nov 96	12
TEMPERAMENTAL	Virgin	16	9 Oct 99	3

EVOLUTION
UK

SINGLES:	**HITS 5**		**WEEKS 12**	
LOVE THING	Deconstruction	32	20 Mar 93	2
EVERYBODY DANCE	Deconstruction	19	3 Jul 93	5
EVOLUTIONDANCE PART ONE [EP]	Deconstruction	52	8 Jan 94	3
Lead track: Escape To Alcatraz.				
LOOK UP TO THE LIGHT	Deconstruction	55	4 Nov 95	1
YOUR LOVE IS CALLING	Deconstruction	60	19 Oct 96	1

EX PISTOLS
UK

(See also Sex Pistols.)

SINGLES:	**HITS 1**		**WEEKS 2**	
LAND OF HOPE AND GLORY	Virgin	69	2 Feb 85	2

EXCITERS
US

SINGLES:	**HITS 2**		**WEEKS 7**	
TELL HIM	United Artists	46	23 Feb 63	1
REACHING FOR THE BEST	20th Century	31	4 Oct 75	6

EXETER BRAMDEAN BOYS' CHOIR
UK

SINGLES:	**HITS 1**		**WEEKS 3**	
REMEMBERING CHRISTMAS [EP]	Golden Sounds	46	18 Dec 93	3
Lead track: No Room At The Inn. Charity record in aid of the Bosnian Children Appeal and the Bramdean Chapel Foundation Trust.				

EXILE
US

SINGLES:	**HITS 3**		**WEEKS 18**	
KISS YOU ALL OVER	RAK	6	19 Aug 78	12
HOW CAN THIS GO WRONG	RAK	67	12 May 79	2
HEART AND SOUL	RAK	54	12 Sep 81	4

EXODUS
US

ALBUMS:	**HITS 1**		**WEEKS 1**	
FABULOUS DISASTER	Music For Nations	67	11 Feb 89	1

EXOTERIX
UK

SINGLES:	**HITS 2**		**WEEKS 2**	
VOID	Positiva	58	24 Apr 93	1
SATISFY MY LOVE	Union	62	5 Feb 94	1

EXOTICA featuring Itsy FOSTER | | | | UK/Italy

SINGLES:		HITS 1			WEEKS 1
THE SUMMER IS MAGIC '95	Polydor	68	16 Sep 95	1

EXPLOITED | | | | | UK

SINGLES:		HITS 4			WEEKS 13
DOGS OF WAR	Secret	63	18 Apr 81	4
DEAD CITIES	Secret	31	17 Oct 81	5
DON'T LET 'EM GRIND YOU DOWN EP (EXTRACTS FROM THE EDINBURGH LIVE NITE [EP]	Superville	70	5 Dec 81	1

One side of single for each group. There is no actual track listing.
Above hit: EXPLOITED / ANTI-PASTI.

ATTACK	Secret	50	8 May 82	3
ALBUMS:		HITS 3			WEEKS 26
PUNK'S NOT DEAD	Secret	20	16 May 81	11
EXPLOITED LIVE	Superville	52	14 Nov 81	3
TROOPS OF TOMORROW	Secret	17	19 Jun 82	12

EXPOSE | | | | | US

SINGLES:		HITS 1			WEEKS 1
I'LL NEVER GET OVER YOU (GETTING OVER ME)	Arista	75	28 Aug 93	1

EXPRESS OF SOUND | | | | | Italy

SINGLES:		HITS 1			WEEKS 1
REAL VIBRATION (WANT LOVE)	Positiva	45	2 Nov 96	1

Originally released in 1995.

EXPRESSOS | | | | | UK

SINGLES:		HITS 2			WEEKS 5
HEY GIRL	WEA	60	21 Jun 80	3
TANGO IN MONO	WEA	70	14 Mar 81	2

EXTREME | | | | | US

SINGLES:		HITS 9			WEEKS 46
GET THE FUNK OUT	A&M	19	8 Jun 91	7
MORE THAN WORDS	A&M	2	27 Jul 91	11
DECADENCE DANCE	A&M	36	12 Oct 91	3
HOLE HEARTED	A&M	12	23 Nov 91	7
SONG FOR LOVE	A&M	12	2 May 92	6
REST IN PEACE	A&M	13	5 Sep 92	5
STOP THE WORLD	A&M	22	14 Nov 92	2
TRAGIC COMIC	A&M	15	6 Feb 93	4
HIP TODAY	A&M	44	11 Mar 95	1
ALBUMS:		HITS 3			WEEKS 75
EXTREME II PORNOGRAFFITTI	A&M	12	1 Jun 91	61
III SIDES TO EVERY STORY	A&M	2	26 Sep 92	11
WAITING FOR THE PUNCHLINE	A&M	10	11 Feb 95	3

EYES CREAM | | | | | Italy

SINGLES:		HITS 1			WEEKS 1
FLY AWAY (BYE BYE)	Accolade	53	16 Oct 99	1

Samples Sylvester's You Make Me Fell Mighty Real.

F

Adam F | | | | | UK

SINGLES:		HITS 2			WEEKS 6
CIRCLES	Positiva	20	27 Sep 97	3
MUSIC IN MY MIND	Positiva	27	7 Mar 98	3
ALBUMS:		HITS 1			WEEKS 1
COLOURS	Positiva	47	15 Nov 97	1

F.A.B. | | | | | UK

SINGLES:		HITS 3			WEEKS 11
THUNDERBIRDS ARE GO	Brothers Organisation	5	7 Jul 90	8

Above hit: F.A.B. featuring M.C. PARKER.

| THE PRISONER | Brothers Organisation | 56 | 20 Oct 90 | 2 |

Above hit: F.A.B. featuring MC NUMBER 6.

THE STINGRAY MEGAMIX	Brothers Organisation	66	1 Dec 90	1

Above hit: F.A.B. featuring AQUA MARINA.

ALBUMS:		HITS 1		WEEKS 3
POWER THEMES 90	Telstar	53	10 Nov 90	3

F.P.I. PROJECT — Italy

SINGLES:		HITS 3		WEEKS 17
GOING BACK TO MY ROOTS / RICH IN PARADISE	Rumour	9	9 Dec 89	12

Re-issued from 27 Jan 90 with new vocals by Sharon Dee Clarke on Going Back To My Roots.
Above hit: F.P.I. PROJECT present RICH IN PARADISE featuring vocals of Paolo DINI.

EVERYBODY (ALL OVER THE WORLD)	Rumour	65	9 Mar 91	3
COME ON (AND DO IT)	Synthetic	59	7 Aug 93	1
EVERYBODY ALL OVER THE WORLD [RM]	99 North	67	13 Mar 99	1

Remixed by Dillon and Dickins.
Above hit: FPI PROJECT.

FAB! — Ireland

SINGLES:		HITS 1		WEEKS 1
TURN AROUND	Break Records 2000	59	1 Aug 98	1

Shelley FABARES — US

SINGLES:		HITS 1		WEEKS 4
JOHNNY ANGEL	Pye International	41	28 Apr 62	4

Backing vocals by the Blossoms.

FABIAN — US

SINGLES:		HITS 1		WEEKS 1
HOUND DOG MAN	His Master's Voice	46	12 Mar 60	1

FABULOUS BAKER BOYS — UK

SINGLES:		HITS 1		WEEKS 2
OH BOY	Multiply	34	15 Nov 97	2

Originally released in 1992.

FABULOUS FLEE-RAKKERS — UK

SINGLES:		HITS 1		WEEKS 13
GREEN JEANS	Triumph	23	21 May 60	13

FACE – See David MORALES

FACES — UK

SINGLES:		HITS 5		WEEKS 46
STAY WITH ME	Warner Brothers	6	18 Dec 71	14
CINDY INCIDENTALLY	Warner Brothers	2	17 Feb 73	9
POOL HALL RICHARD / I WISH IT WOULD RAIN (WITH A TRUMPET)	Warner Brothers	8	8 Dec 73	11
YOU CAN MAKE ME DANCE, SING OR ANYTHING (EVEN TAKE THE DOG FOR A WALK, MEND A FUSE, FOLD AWAY THE IRONING BOARD, OR ANY OTHER DOMESTIC SHORT COMINGS)	Warner Brothers	12	7 Dec 74	9

Above hit: FACES/Rod STEWART.

THE FACES [EP]	Riva	41	4 Jun 77	3

Lead track: Memphis.

ALBUMS:		HITS 7		WEEKS 57
FIRST STEP	Warner Brothers	45	4 Apr 70	1
LONG PLAYER	Warner Brothers	31	8 May 71	7
A NOD'S AS GOOD AS A WINK ... TO A BLIND HORSE	Warner Brothers	2	25 Dec 71	22
OOH-LA-LA	Warner Brothers	1	21 Apr 73	13
OVERTURE AND BEGINNERS	Mercury	3	26 Jan 74	7

Above hit: Rod STEWART and the FACES.

THE BEST OF THE FACES	Riva	24	21 May 77	6
THE BEST OF ROD STEWART AND THE FACES 1971-1975	Mercury	58	7 Nov 92	1

Features both Rod Stewart's solo and group material.
Above hit: Rod STEWART and the FACES.

FACTORY OF UNLIMITED RHYTHM — Jamaica

SINGLES:		HITS 1		WEEKS 1
THE SWEETEST SURRENDER	Kuff	59	1 Jun 96	1

Donald FAGEN — US

SINGLES:		HITS 1		WEEKS 2
TOMORROW'S GIRLS	Reprise	46	3 Jul 93	2
ALBUMS:		HITS 2		WEEKS 25
THE NIGHTFLY	Warner Brothers	44	30 Oct 82	16
KAMAKIRIAD	Reprise	3	5 Jun 93	9

Joe FAGIN
UK

SINGLES:	HITS 2			WEEKS 20
THAT'S LIVING ALRIGHT	Towerbell	3	7 Jan 84	11
The original A-side was Breakin' Away though this was not listed on the charts.				
BACK WITH THE BOYS AGAIN / GET IT RIGHT	Towerbell	53	5 Apr 86	9
Above 2: From the Central ITV series 'Auf Wiedersehen, Pet'.				

Brian FAHEY and his Orchestra - See Ken DODD

Yvonne FAIR
US

SINGLES:	HITS 1			WEEKS 11
IT SHOULD HAVE BEEN ME	Tamla Motown	5	24 Jan 76	11
Originally recorded by Kim Weston in 1963.				

FAIR WEATHER
UK

SINGLES:	HITS 1			WEEKS 12
NATURAL SINNER	RCA Victor	6	18 Jul 70	12

FAIRGROUND ATTRACTION
UK

SINGLES:	HITS 4			WEEKS 27
PERFECT	RCA	1	16 Apr 88	13
FIND MY LOVE	RCA	7	30 Jul 88	10
A SMILE IN A WHISPER	RCA	75	19 Nov 88	1
CLARE	RCA	49	28 Jan 89	3
ALBUMS:	**HITS 2**			**WEEKS 54**
THE FIRST OF A MILLION KISSES	RCA	2	28 May 88	52
AY FOND KISS	RCA	55	30 Jun 90	2

FAIRPORT CONVENTION
UK

SINGLES:	HITS 1			WEEKS 9
SI TU DOIS PARTIR (IF YOU GOTTA GO, GO NOW)	Island	21	26 Jul 69	8
SI TU DOIS PARTIR (IF YOU GOTTA GO, GO NOW) [RE]	Island	49	27 Sep 69	1
ALBUMS:	**HITS 6**			**WEEKS 41**
UNHALFBRICKING	Island	12	2 Aug 69	8
LIEGE AND LIEF	Island	17	17 Jan 70	15
FULL HOUSE	Island	13	18 Jul 70	11
ANGEL DELIGHT	Island	8	3 Jul 71	5
RISING FOR THE MOON	Island	52	12 Jul 75	1
RED AND GOLD	New Routes	74	28 Jan 89	1

Andy FAIRWEATHER LOW
UK

SINGLES:	HITS 2			WEEKS 18
REGGAE TUNE	A&M	10	21 Sep 74	8
WIDE EYED AND LEGLESS	A&M	6	6 Dec 75	10

Adam FAITH
UK

SINGLES:	HITS 24			WEEKS 252
WHAT DO YOU WANT?	Parlophone	1	21 Nov 59	19
POOR ME	Parlophone	1	23 Jan 60	18
SOMEONE ELSE'S BABY	Parlophone	2	16 Apr 60	13
JOHNNY COMES MARCHING HOME / MADE YOU	Parlophone	5	2 Jul 60	13
Johnny Comes Marching Home from the film 'Never Let Go'; Made You from the film 'Beat Girl'.				
HOW ABOUT THAT!	Parlophone	4	17 Sep 60	14
Above 2: Adam FAITH with John BARRY and his Orchestra.				
LONELY PUP (IN A CHRISTMAS SHOP)	Parlophone	4	19 Nov 60	11
Above hit: Adam FAITH with the Children.				
WHO AM I? / THIS IS IT	Parlophone	5	11 Feb 61	14
This Is It had first billing for the first 2 weeks, and from 11 Mar 61 it was no longer listed.				
EASY GOING ME	Parlophone	12	29 Apr 61	10
DON'T YOU KNOW IT?	Parlophone	12	22 Jul 61	10
THE TIME HAS COME	Parlophone	4	28 Oct 61	14
From the film 'What A Whopper'.				
LONESOME	Parlophone	12	20 Jan 62	9
AS YOU LIKE IT	Parlophone	5	5 May 62	15
Above 2: Adam FAITH with John BARRY and his Orchestra.				
DON'T THAT BEAT ALL	Parlophone	8	1 Sep 62	11
Above hit: Adam FAITH with Johnny KEATING and his Orchestra.				
BABY TAKE A BOW	Parlophone	22	15 Dec 62	6
Though not billed, single had accompaniment directed by Johnny Keating.				
WHAT NOW	Parlophone	31	2 Feb 63	5
WALKIN' TALL	Parlophone	23	13 Jul 63	6
Above 2: Adam FAITH with Johnny KEATING and his Orchestra.				

THE FIRST TIME	Parlophone	5	21 Sep 63	13
Written by Chris Andrews.				
WE ARE IN LOVE	Parlophone	11	14 Dec 63	12
IF HE TELLS YOU	Parlophone	25	14 Mar 64	9
I LOVE BEING IN LOVE WITH YOU	Parlophone	33	30 May 64	6
Above 4: Adam FAITH with the ROULETTES.				
A MESSAGE TO MARTHA (KENTUCKY BLUEBIRD)	Parlophone	12	28 Nov 64	11
STOP FEELING SORRY FOR YOURSELF	Parlophone	23	13 Feb 65	6
SOMEONE'S TAKEN MARIA AWAY	Parlophone	34	19 Jun 65	5
Above 2: Adam FAITH with the ROULETTES.				
CHERYL'S GOIN' HOME	Parlophone	46	22 Oct 66	2
Originally recorded by Bob Lind.				

EPS:	**HITS 4**			**WEEKS 95**
ADAM'S HIT PARADE	Parlophone	1	17 Sep 60	77
ADAM NO. 1	Parlophone	4	11 Mar 61	13
ADAM FAITH NO. 1	Parlophone	12	17 Mar 62	4
A MESSAGE TO MARTHA – FROM ADAM	Parlophone	17	13 Mar 65	1

ALBUMS:	**HITS 5**			**WEEKS 46**
ADAM	Parlophone	6	19 Nov 60	36
BEAT GIRL [OST]	Columbia	11	11 Feb 61	3
Includes tracks featuring the John Barry Seven and the John Barry Orchestra.				
ADAM FAITH	Parlophone	20	24 Mar 62	1
FAITH ALIVE	Parlophone	19	25 Sep 65	1
20 GOLDEN GREATS	Warwick	61	19 Dec 81	3
MIDNIGHT POSTCARDS	PolyGram TV	43	27 Nov 93	2

Horace FAITH   Jamaica

SINGLES:	**HITS 1**			**WEEKS 10**
BLACK PEARL	Trojan	13	12 Sep 70	10
Originally recorded by Sonny Charles.				

Percy FAITH and his Orchestra   Canada

(See also Tony Bennett; Rosemary Clooney; Vic Damone; Doris Day; Frankie Laine; Johnnie Ray.)

SINGLES:	**HITS 1**			**WEEKS 31**
THE THEME FROM "A SUMMER PLACE"	Philips	2	5 Mar 60	31
Originally recorded by Hugo Winterhalter and his Orchestra. From the film of the same name.				

FAITH BROTHERS   UK

SINGLES:	**HITS 2**			**WEEKS 6**
THE COUNTRY OF THE BLIND	Siren	63	13 Apr 85	3
A STRANGER ON HOME GROUND	Siren	69	6 Jul 85	3

ALBUMS:	**HITS 1**			**WEEKS 1**
EVENTIDE	Siren	66	9 Nov 85	1

FAITH HOPE and CHARITY   US

SINGLES:	**HITS 1**			**WEEKS 4**
JUST ONE LOOK	RCA Victor	38	31 Jan 76	4

FAITH HOPE and CHARITY   UK

SINGLES:	**HITS 1**			**WEEKS 3**
BATTLE OF THE SEXES	WEA	53	23 Jun 90	3

FAITH NO MORE   US

SINGLES:	**HITS 16**			**WEEKS 65**
WE CARE A LOT	Slash	53	6 Feb 88	3
EPIC	Slash	37	10 Feb 90	4
FROM OUT OF NOWHERE	Slash	23	14 Apr 90	6
FALLING TO PIECES	Slash	41	14 Jul 90	3
EPIC [RI]	Slash	25	8 Sep 90	5
MIDLIFE CRISIS	Slash	10	6 Jun 92	5
A SMALL VICTORY	Slash	29	15 Aug 92	5
A SMALL VICTORY [RM]	Slash	55	12 Sep 92	1
Remixed by Youth.				
EVERYTHING'S RUINED	Slash	28	21 Nov 92	3
I'M EASY / BE AGGRESSIVE	Slash	3	16 Jan 93	7
I'M EASY / BE AGGRESSIVE [RE]	Slash	75	13 Mar 93	1
ANOTHER BODY MURDERED	Epic	26	6 Nov 93	3
From the film 'Judgement Night'.				
Above hit: FAITH NO MORE and BOO-YAA TRIBE.				
DIGGING THE GRAVE	Slash	16	11 Mar 95	4
RICOCHET	Slash	27	27 May 95	2
EVIDENCE	Slash	32	29 Jul 95	3
ASHES TO ASHES	Slash	15	31 May 97	3
LAST CUP OF SORROW	Slash	51	16 Aug 97	1

THIS TOWN AIN'T BIG ENOUGH FOR BOTH OF US	Roadrunner	40	13 Dec 97	2

Above hit: SPARKS vs. FAITH NO MORE.

ASHES TO ASHES [RI]	Slash	29	17 Jan 98	3
I STARTED A JOKE	Slash	49	7 Nov 98	1

Originally recorded by the Bee Gees.

ALBUMS: HITS 6 — WEEKS 74

THE REAL THING	Slash	30	17 Feb 90	35
LIVE AT THE BRIXTON ACADEMY	Slash	20	16 Feb 91	4
ANGEL DUST	Slash	2	20 Jun 92	25
KING FOR A DAY, FOOL FOR A LIFETIME	Slash	5	25 Mar 95	6
ALBUM OF THE YEAR	Slash	7	21 Jun 97	3
WHO CARES A LOT? - THE GREATEST HITS	Slash	37	21 Nov 98	1

Sales of CD doublepack only due to chart rules. The standard release only reached No. 93.

Marianne FAITHFULL — UK

SINGLES: HITS 7 — WEEKS 59

AS TEARS GO BY	Decca	9	15 Aug 64	13

Originally recorded by Rolling Stones.

COME AND STAY WITH ME	Decca	4	20 Feb 65	13

Written by Jackie De Shannon.

THIS LITTLE BIRD	Decca	6	8 May 65	11

Originally recorded by John D. Loudermilk.

SUMMER NIGHTS	Decca	10	24 Jul 65	10
YESTERDAY	Decca	36	6 Nov 65	4
IS THIS WHAT I GET FROM LOVING YOU?	Decca	43	11 Mar 67	2
THE BALLAD OF LUCY JORDAN	Island	48	24 Nov 79	6

Originally recorded by Shel Silverstein.

EPS: HITS 1 — WEEKS 19

GO AWAY FROM MY WORLD	Decca	4	19 Jun 65	19

ALBUMS: HITS 6 — WEEKS 19

COME MY WAY	Decca	12	5 Jun 65	7
MARIANNE FAITHFULL	Decca	15	5 Jun 65	2
BROKEN ENGLISH	Island	57	24 Nov 79	3
DANGEROUS ACQUAINTANCES	Island	45	17 Oct 81	4
A CHILD'S ADVENTURE	Island	99	26 Mar 83	1
STRANGE WEATHER	Island	78	8 Aug 87	2

FAITHLESS — UK

SINGLES: HITS 7 — WEEKS 50

SALVA MEA (SAVE ME)	Cheeky	30	5 Aug 95	2
INSOMNIA	Cheeky	27	9 Dec 95	2
DON'T LEAVE	Cheeky	34	23 Mar 96	2
INSOMNIA [RI]	Cheeky	3	26 Oct 96	13
SALVA MEA [RM]	Cheeky	9	21 Dec 96	7

Additional vocals by Collette.

REVERENCE	Cheeky	10	26 Apr 97	3
DON'T LEAVE [RI]	Cheeky	21	15 Nov 97	2

From the film 'A Life Less Ordinary'.

GOD IS A DJ	Cheeky	6	5 Sep 98	8
TAKE THE LONG WAY HOME	Cheeky	15	5 Dec 98	6
BRING MY FAMILY BACK	Cheeky	14	1 May 99	5

From the film 'Forces Of Nature'.

ALBUMS: HITS 2 — WEEKS 20

REVERENCE	Cheeky	26	23 Nov 96	13

Sales were combined with Irreverence, a remix CD.

SUNDAY 8PM	Cheeky	10	3 Oct 98	7

FALCO — Austria

SINGLES: HITS 4 — WEEKS 26

ROCK ME AMADEUS	A&M	1	22 Mar 86	15

Tribute to composer Wolfgang Amadeus Mozart.

VIENNA CALLING	A&M	10	31 May 86	8
JEANNY	A&M	68	2 Aug 86	1
THE SOUND OF MUSIK	WEA	61	27 Sep 86	2

ALBUMS: HITS 1 — WEEKS 15

FALCO 3	A&M	32	26 Apr 86	15

FALL — UK

SINGLES: HITS 14 — WEEKS 25

MR. PHARMACIST	Beggars Banquet	75	13 Sep 86	1
HEY! LUCIANI	Beggars Banquet	59	20 Dec 86	1
THERE'S A GHOST IN MY HOUSE	Beggars Banquet	30	9 May 87	4
HIT THE NORTH	Beggars Banquet	57	31 Oct 87	5
VICTORIA	Beggars Banquet	35	30 Jan 88	3

BIG NEW PRINZ / JERUSALEM	*Beggars Banquet*	59	*26 Nov 88*	2
TELEPHONE THING	*Cog Sinister*	58	*27 Jan 90*	1
WHITE LIGHTNING	*Cog Sinister*	56	*8 Sep 90*	2
FREE RANGE	*Cog Sinister*	40	*14 Mar 92*	1
WHY ARE PEOPLE GRUDGEFUL?	*Permanent*	43	*17 Apr 93*	1
BEHIND THE COUNTER [EP]	*Permanent*	75	*25 Dec 93*	1
Lead track: Behind The Counter.				
15 WAYS	*Permanent*	65	*30 Apr 94*	1
THE CHISELLERS	*Jet*	60	*17 Feb 96*	1
MASQUERADE	*Artful*	69	*21 Feb 98*	1
ALBUMS:	**HITS 15**			**WEEKS 32**
HEX EDUCATION HOUR	*Kamera*	71	*20 Mar 82*	3
THE WONDERFUL AND FRIGHTENING WORLD OF . . .	*Beggars Banquet*	62	*20 Oct 84*	2
THIS NATION'S SAVING GRACE	*Beggars Banquet*	54	*5 Oct 85*	2
BEND SINISTER	*Beggars Banquet*	36	*11 Oct 86*	3
THE FRENZ EXPERIMENT	*Beggars Banquet*	19	*12 Mar 88*	4
I AM KURIOUS, ORANJ	*Beggars Banquet*	54	*12 Nov 88*	2
SEMINAL LIVE	*Beggars Banquet*	40	*8 Jul 89*	2
EXTRICATE	*Cog Sinister*	31	*3 Mar 90*	3
458489 A-SIDES	*Beggars Banquet*	44	*15 Sep 90*	2
Compilation.				
SHIFT-WORK	*Cog Sinister*	17	*4 May 91*	2
CODE: SELFISH	*Cog Sinister*	21	*28 Mar 92*	1
INFOTAINMENT SCAN	*Permanent*	9	*8 May 93*	3
MIDDLE CLASS REVOLT	*Permanent*	48	*14 May 94*	1
CEREBRAL CAUSTIC	*Permanent*	67	*11 Mar 95*	1
THE LIGHT USER SYNDROME	*Jet*	54	*22 Jun 96*	1

Harold FALTERMEYER
Germany

SINGLES:	**HITS 2**			**WEEKS 23**
AXEL F	*MCA*	62	*23 Mar 85*	4
AXEL F [RE]	*MCA*	2	*1 Jun 85*	18
"FLETCH" THEME	*MCA*	74	*24 Aug 85*	1
All singles from the film' Beverly Hills Cop'.				

Agnetha FALTSKOG
Sweden

SINGLES:	**HITS 3**			**WEEKS 12**
THE HEAT IS ON	*Epic*	35	*28 May 83*	6
WRAP YOUR ARMS AROUND ME	*Epic*	44	*13 Aug 83*	5
CAN'T SHAKE LOOSE	*Epic*	63	*22 Oct 83*	1
ALBUMS:	**HITS 3**			**WEEKS 17**
WRAP YOUR ARMS AROUND ME	*Epic*	18	*11 Jun 83*	13
EYES OF A WOMAN	*Epic*	38	*4 May 85*	3
I STAND ALONE	*WEA*	72	*12 Mar 88*	1

Georgie FAME
UK

(See also Mondo Kane featuring Dee Lewis and Coral Gordon Guest star Georgie Fame.)

SINGLES:	**HITS 13**			**WEEKS 115**
YEH, YEH	*Columbia*	1	*19 Dec 64*	12
Originally recorded by Jon Hendricks.				
IN THE MEANTIME	*Columbia*	22	*6 Mar 65*	8
LIKE WE USED TO BE	*Columbia*	33	*31 Jul 65*	7
SOMETHING	*Columbia*	23	*30 Oct 65*	7
GETAWAY	*Columbia*	1	*25 Jun 66*	11
Above 5: Georgie FAME and the BLUE FLAMES.				
SUNNY	*Columbia*	13	*24 Sep 66*	8
SITTING IN THE PARK	*Columbia*	12	*24 Dec 66*	10
Above hit: Georgie FAME and the BLUE FLAMES.				
BECAUSE I LOVE YOU	*CBS*	15	*25 Mar 67*	8
TRY MY WORLD	*CBS*	37	*16 Sep 67*	5
THE BALLAD OF BONNIE AND CLYDE	*CBS*	1	*16 Dec 67*	13
PEACEFUL	*CBS*	16	*12 Jul 69*	9
SEVENTH SON	*CBS*	25	*13 Dec 69*	7
ROSETTA	*CBS*	11	*10 Apr 71*	10
Above hit: FAME and PRICE, PRICE and FAME TOGETHER.				
EPS:	**HITS 4**			**WEEKS 48**
RHYTHM AND BLUES AT THE FLAMINGO	*Columbia*	8	*16 Jan 65*	13
Live recordings from the Flamingo club in Soho, London.				
FATS FOR FAME	*Columbia*	15	*5 Jun 65*	2
GETAWAY	*Columbia*	7	*10 Dec 66*	7
GEORGIE FAME	*CBS*	2	*10 Jun 67*	26
ALBUMS:	**HITS 5**			**WEEKS 72**
FAME AT LAST	*Columbia*	15	*17 Oct 64*	8
SWEET THINGS	*Columbia*	6	*14 May 66*	22
SOUND VENTURE	*Columbia*	9	*15 Oct 66*	9

HALL OF FAME	*Columbia*	12	*11 Mar 67*	18
TWO FACES OF FAME	*CBS*	22	*1 Jul 67*	15

FAMILY
UK

SINGLES:	HITS 4			WEEKS 44
NO MULE'S FOOL	*Reprise*	29	*1 Nov 69*	7
STRANGE BAND: THE WEAVERS ANSWER	*Reprise*	11	*22 Aug 70*	12
IN MY OWN TIME	*Reprise*	4	*17 Jul 71*	13
BURLESQUE	*Reprise*	13	*23 Sep 72*	12
ALBUMS:	HITS 7			WEEKS 41
MUSIC IN THE DOLLS HOUSE	*Reprise*	35	*10 Aug 68*	3
FAMILY ENTERTAINMENT	*Reprise*	6	*22 Mar 69*	3
A SONG FOR ME	*Reprise*	4	*7 Feb 70*	13
ANYWAY	*Reprise*	7	*28 Nov 70*	7
FEARLESS	*Reprise*	14	*20 Nov 71*	2
BANDSTAND	*Reprise*	15	*30 Sep 72*	10
IT'S ONLY A MOVIE	*Raft*	30	*29 Sep 73*	3

FAMILY – See Afrika BAMBAATAA

FAMILY – See PUFF DADDY

FAMILY CAT
UK

SINGLES:	HITS 3			WEEKS 5
AIRPLANE GARDENS / ATMOSPHERIC ROAD	*Dedicated*	69	*28 Aug 93*	1
WONDERFUL EXCUSE	*Dedicated*	48	*21 May 94*	2
GOLDENBOOK	*Dedicated*	42	*30 Jul 94*	2
ALBUMS:	HITS 1			WEEKS 1
FURTHEST FROM THE SUN	*Dedicated*	55	*4 Jul 92*	1

FAMILY DOGG
UK

SINGLES:	HITS 1			WEEKS 14
A WAY OF LIFE	*Bell*	6	*31 May 69*	14

FAMILY FOUNDATION
UK

SINGLES:	HITS 1			WEEKS 4
XPRESS YOURSELF	*380 PEW*	42	*13 Jun 92*	4

FAMILY STAND
US

SINGLES:	HITS 1			WEEKS 13
GHETTO HEAVEN	*Atlantic*	10	*31 Mar 90*	11
GHETTO HEAVEN [RM]	*Perfecto Red*	30	*17 Jan 98*	2
Remixed by Jeff Ishmael.				
ALBUMS:	HITS 1			WEEKS 3
CHAIN	*Atlantic*	52	*19 May 90*	3

FAMOUS FLAMES – See James BROWN

FANTASTIC FOUR
US

SINGLES:	HITS 1			WEEKS 4
B.Y.O.F. (BRING YOUR OWN FUNK)	*Atlantic*	62	*24 Feb 79*	4

FANTASTICS
US

SINGLES:	HITS 1			WEEKS 12
SOMETHING OLD, SOMETHING NEW	*Bell*	9	*27 Mar 71*	12

FANTASY U.F.O.
UK

SINGLES:	HITS 2			WEEKS 6
FANTASY	*XL Recordings*	56	*29 Sep 90*	3
MIND, BODY, SOUL	*East West*	50	*10 Aug 91*	3
Above hit: FANTASY U.F.O. featuring Jay GROOVE.				

FAR CORPORATION
UK/US/Germany

SINGLES:	HITS 1			WEEKS 11
STAIRWAY TO HEAVEN	*Arista*	8	*26 Oct 85*	11
Originally recorded by Led Zeppelin.				

Sonny FARAR and his Banjo Band – See STARGAZERS

Don FARDON
UK

SINGLES:	HITS 2			WEEKS 22
BELFAST BOY	*Young Blood*	32	*18 Apr 70*	5
INDIAN RESERVATION	*Young Blood*	3	*10 Oct 70*	17
Originally recorded by John D. Loudermilk.				

FARGETTA — UK/Italy

SINGLES:	HITS 2			WEEKS 3
MUSIC	Synthetic	34	23 Jan 93	2
Above hit: FARGETTA and Anne-Marie SMITH.				
THE MUSIC IS MOVING	Arista	74	10 Aug 96	1

Chris FARLOWE — UK

SINGLES:	HITS 6			WEEKS 36
THINK	Immediate	49	29 Jan 66	1
THINK [RE]	Immediate	37	12 Feb 66	2
OUT OF TIME	Immediate	1	25 Jun 66	13
RIDE ON BABY	Immediate	31	29 Oct 66	7
Above 3 originally recorded by Rolling Stones.				
MY WAY OF GIVING IN	Immediate	48	18 Feb 67	1
Originally recorded by Small Faces.				
MOANIN'	Immediate	46	2 Jul 67	2
Originally recorded by Art Blakey and the Jazz Messengers.				
HANDBAGS AND GLADRAGS	Immediate	33	16 Dec 67	6
OUT OF TIME [RI]	Immediate	44	27 Sep 75	4
EPS:	HITS 1			WEEKS 13
FARLOWE IN THE MIDNIGHT HOUR	Immediate	6	15 Jan 66	13
ALBUMS:	HITS 2			WEEKS 3
14 THINGS TO THINK ABOUT	Immediate	19	2 Apr 66	1
THE ART OF CHRIS FARLOWE	Immediate	37	10 Dec 66	2

FARM — UK

SINGLES:	HITS 9			WEEKS 54
STEPPING STONE / FAMILY OF MAN	Produce	58	5 May 90	4
GROOVY TRAIN	Produce	6	1 Sep 90	10
ALL TOGETHER NOW	Produce	4	8 Dec 90	12
SINFUL! (SCARY JIGGIN' WITH DOCTOR LOVE)	Siren	28	13 Apr 91	5
Above hit: Pete WYLIE (and the FARM).				
DON'T LET ME DOWN	Produce	36	4 May 91	3
MIND	Produce	31	24 Aug 91	4
LOVE SEE NO COLOUR	Produce	58	14 Dec 91	4
RISING SUN	End Product	48	4 Jul 92	3
DON'T YOU WANT ME	End Product	18	17 Oct 92	5
Track from the NME 40th Anniversary album 'Ruby Trax'.				
LOVE SEE NO COLOUR [RI]	End Product	35	2 Jan 93	4
ALBUMS:	HITS 1			WEEKS 17
SPARTACUS	Produce	1	16 Mar 91	17

FARMER'S BOYS — UK

SINGLES:	HITS 4			WEEKS 17
MUCK IT OUT!	EMI	48	9 Apr 83	6
FOR YOU	EMI	66	30 Jul 83	3
IN THE COUNTRY	EMI	44	4 Aug 84	5
PHEW WOW	EMI	59	3 Nov 84	3
ALBUMS:	HITS 1			WEEKS 1
GET OUT AND WALK	EMI	49	29 Oct 83	1

John FARNHAM — Australia

SINGLES:	HITS 1			WEEKS 17
YOU'RE THE VOICE	Wheatley	6	25 Apr 87	17
ALBUMS:	HITS 1			WEEKS 9
WHISPERING JACK	RCA	35	11 Jul 87	9

FARRAR – See MARVIN, WELCH and FARRAR

Joanne FARRELL — US

SINGLES:	HITS 1			WEEKS 2
ALL I WANNA DO	Big Beat	40	24 Jun 95	2

Joe FARRELL — US

SINGLES:	HITS 1			WEEKS 4
NIGHT DANCING	Warner Brothers	57	16 Dec 78	4

Dionne FARRIS — US

SINGLES:	HITS 2			WEEKS 6
I KNOW	Columbia	47	18 Mar 95	2
I KNOW [RE]	Columbia	41	27 May 95	3

HOPELESS	Columbia	42	7 Jun 97	1
From the film 'Love Jones'.				

Gene FARROW with the G. F. BAND — UK

SINGLES:	HITS 2		WEEKS 8	
MOVE YOUR BODY	Magnet	33	1 Apr 78	5
MOVE YOUR BODY [RE]	Magnet	67	13 May 78	1
DON'T STOP NOW	Magnet	71	5 Aug 78	1
DON'T STOP NOW [RE]	Magnet	74	19 Aug 78	1

FASCINATIONS — US

SINGLES:	HITS 1		WEEKS 6	
GIRLS ARE OUT TO GET YOU	Mojo	32	3 Jul 71	6

FASHION — UK

SINGLES:	HITS 3		WEEKS 12	
STREETPLAYER (MECHANIK)	Arista	46	3 Apr 82	5
LOVE SHADOW	Arista	51	21 Aug 82	5
EYE TALK	Epic	69	18 Feb 84	2
ALBUMS:	HITS 2		WEEKS 17	
FABRIQUE	Arista	10	3 Jul 82	16
TWILIGHT OF IDOLS	De Stijl	69	16 Jun 84	1

Susan FASSBENDER — UK

SINGLES:	HITS 1		WEEKS 8	
TWILIGHT CAFE	CBS	21	17 Jan 81	8

FAST EDDIE - See DJ FAST EDDIE

FASTBALL — US

SINGLES:	HITS 1		WEEKS 5	
THE WAY	Hollywood	21	3 Oct 98	5

FASTER PUSSYCAT — US

ALBUMS:	HITS 2		WEEKS 3	
WAKE ME WHEN IT'S OVER	Elektra	35	16 Sep 89	2
WHIPPED!	Elektra	58	22 Aug 92	1

FASTWAY — UK

SINGLES:	HITS 1		WEEKS 1	
EASY LIVIN'	CBS	74	2 Apr 83	1
ALBUMS:	HITS 1		WEEKS 2	
FASTWAY	CBS	43	30 Apr 83	2

FAT BOYS — US

SINGLES:	HITS 4		WEEKS 29	
JAIL HOUSE RAP	Sultra	63	4 May 85	2
WIPEOUT	Urban	2	22 Aug 87	12
Above hit: FAT BOYS and the BEACH BOYS.				
THE TWIST (YO, TWIST)	Urban	2	18 Jun 88	11
Original by Hank Ballard and the Midniters reached No. 28 in the US in 1960.				
Above hit: FAT BOYS (Lead Vocal: Chubby CHECKER).				
LOUIE LOUIE	Urban	46	5 Nov 88	4
Originally recorded by Richard Berry and the Pharoahs in 1957.				
ALBUMS:	HITS 2		WEEKS 5	
CRUSHIN'	Urban	49	3 Oct 87	4
COMING BACK HARD AGAIN	Urban	98	30 Jul 88	1

FAT LADY SINGS — Ireland

SINGLES:	HITS 1		WEEKS 2	
DRUNKARD LOGIC	East West	56	17 Jul 93	2
ALBUMS:	HITS 1		WEEKS 1	
TWIST	East West	50	18 May 91	1

FAT LARRY'S BAND — US

SINGLES:	HITS 4		WEEKS 26	
CENTER CITY	WMOT	31	2 Jul 77	5
BOOGIE TOWN	Fantasy	46	10 Mar 79	4
Above hit: FLB.				
LOOKIN' FOR LOVE TONIGHT	Fantasy	46	18 Aug 79	6
Above hit: FAT LARRY'S BAND (FLB).				
ZOOM	WMOT	2	18 Sep 82	11

ALBUMS:		HITS 1			WEEKS 4
BREAKIN' OUT	WMOT		58	9 Oct 82	4

FAT LES UK

SINGLES:		HITS 2			WEEKS 17
VINDALOO	Telstar		2	20 Jun 98	12
NAUGHTY CHRISTMAS (GOBLIN IN THE OFFICE)	Turtleneck:		21	19 Dec 98	5

FATBACK BAND US

SINGLES:		HITS 9			WEEKS 67
YUM, YUM (GIMME SOME)	Polydor		40	6 Sep 75	6
(ARE YOU READY) DO THE BUS STOP	Polydor		18	6 Dec 75	10
(DO THE) SPANISH HUSTLE	Polydor		10	21 Feb 76	7
PARTY TIME	Polydor		41	29 May 76	4
NIGHT FEVER	Spring		38	14 Aug 76	4
DOUBLE DUTCH	Spring		31	12 Mar 77	4
BACKSTROKIN'	Spring		41	9 Aug 80	9
Above hit: FATBACK.					
I FOUND LOVIN'	Master Mix		49	23 Jun 84	4
GIRLS ON MY MIND	Atlantic		69	4 May 85	2
Above hit: FATBACK.					
I FOUND LOVIN' [RM] + [RE-1ST]	Important & Master Mix		55	6 Sep 86	5
Sales were combined for the original and the remix.					
I FOUND LOVIN' [RE-2ND]	Master Mix		7	5 Sep 87	12
ALBUMS:		HITS 2			WEEKS 7
RAISING HELL	Polydor		19	6 Mar 76	6
FATBACK LIVE	Start		80	4 Jul 87	1
Above hit: FATBACK.					

FATBOY SLIM UK

(See also Norman Cook; Mighty Dub Katz.)

SINGLES:		HITS 7			WEEKS 45
GOING OUT OF MY HEAD / MICHAEL JACKSON	Skint		57	3 May 97	1
EVERYBODY NEEDS A 303	Skint		34	1 Nov 97	2
THE ROCKAFELLER SKANK	Skint		6	20 Jun 98	10
Samples the Just Brothers' Sliced Tomatoes.					
GANGSTA TRIPPIN	Skint		3	17 Oct 98	8
PRAISE YOU	Skint		1	16 Jan 99	12
Samples Camille Yarborough's Take Yo Praise.					
RIGHT HERE RIGHT NOW	Skint		2	1 May 99	10
BADDER BADDER SCHWING	Eye Q		34	1 May 99	2
Above hit: Freddy FRESH (featuring FATBOY SLIM).					
ALBUMS:		HITS 2			WEEKS 58
BETTER LIVING THROUGH CHEMISTRY	Skint		69	28 Sep 96	3
YOU'VE COME A LONG WAY, BABY	Skint		1	31 Oct 98	55

FATHER ABRAHAM and the SMURFS - See SMURFS

FATHER ABRAPHART and the SMURPS - See Jonathan KING

FATHER Colm KILCOYNE - See POPE JOHN PAUL II

FATIMA MANSIONS Ireland

SINGLES:		HITS 4			WEEKS 11
EVIL MAN	Radioactive		59	23 May 92	1
1000%	Radioactive		61	1 Aug 92	3
EVERYTHING I DO (I DO IT FOR YOU)	Columbia		7	19 Sep 92	6
[AA] listed with Theme From M.A.S.H. (Suicide Is Painless) by Manic Street Preachers. Both were tracks from the NME 40th Anniversary album 'Ruby Trax'.					
THE LOYALISER	Kitchenware		58	6 Aug 94	1
ALBUMS:		HITS 1			WEEKS 1
VALHALLA AVENUE	Radioactive		52	6 Jun 92	1

FEAR FACTORY US

SINGLES:		HITS 1			WEEKS 1
CARS	Roadrunner		57	9 Oct 99	1
Includes vocals by Gary Numan.					
ALBUMS:		HITS 3			WEEKS 4
DEMANUFACTURE	Roadrunner		27	1 Jul 95	1
REMANUFACTURE - CLONING TECHNOLOGY	Roadrunner		22	14 Jun 97	1
Tracks from Demanufacture, remixed by Rhys Fulber, DJ Dano, Kingsize and Junkie XL.					
OBSOLETE	Roadrunner		20	8 Aug 98	2

Phil FEARON
UK
(See also T.C. Curtis.)

SINGLES:	HITS 9			WEEKS 63
DANCING TIGHT	Ensign	4	23 Apr 83	11
WAIT UNTIL TONIGHT (MY LOVE)	Ensign	20	30 Jul 83	8
Above 2: GALAXY featuring Phil FEARON.				
FANTASY REAL	Ensign	41	22 Oct 83	6
WHAT DO I DO?	Ensign	5	10 Mar 84	10
EVERYBODY'S LAUGHING	Ensign	10	14 Jul 84	10
YOU DON'T NEED A REASON	Ensign	42	15 Jun 85	4
Above 4: Phil FEARON and GALAXY.				
THIS KIND OF LOVE	Ensign	70	27 Jul 85	3
Above hit: Phil FEARON and GALAXY featuring Dee GALDES.				
I CAN PROVE IT	Ensign	8	2 Aug 86	9
Originally recorded by Tony Etoria.				
AIN'T NOTHING BUT A HOUSE PARTY	Ensign	60	15 Nov 86	2
ALBUMS:	HITS 2			WEEKS 9
PHIL FEARON AND GALAXY	Ensign	8	25 Aug 84	8
THIS KIND OF LOVE	Ensign	98	14 Sep 85	1
Above 2: Phil FEARON and GALAXY.				

FEEBI – See T-EMPO

FEEDER
UK

SINGLES:	HITS 9			WEEKS 16
TANGERINE	Echo	60	8 Mar 97	1
CEMENT	Echo	53	10 May 97	1
CRASH	Echo	48	23 Aug 97	1
HIGH	Echo	24	18 Oct 97	2
SUFFOCATE	Echo	37	28 Feb 98	1
DAY IN DAY OUT	Echo	31	3 Apr 99	2
INSOMNIA	Echo	22	12 Jun 99	3
YESTERDAY WENT TOO SOON	Echo	20	21 Aug 99	3
PAPERFACES	Echo	41	20 Nov 99	2
ALBUMS:	HITS 2			WEEKS 4
POLYTHENE	Echo	65	31 May 97	1
YESTERDAY WENT TOO SOON	Echo	8	11 Sep 99	3

Wilton FELDER
US

SINGLES:	HITS 2			WEEKS 7
INHERIT THE WIND	MCA	39	1 Nov 80	5
Lead vocals by Bobby Womack.				
(NO MATTER HOW HIGH I GET) I'LL STILL BE LOOKIN' UP TO YOU	MCA	63	16 Feb 85	2
Above hit: Wilton FELDER featuring Bobby WOMACK and introducing Alltrinna GRAYSON.				
ALBUMS:	HITS 1			WEEKS 3
SECRETS	MCA	77	23 Feb 85	3
Above hit: Wilton FELDER featuring Bobby WOMACK and introducing Alltrina GRAYSON.				

FELICIA – See B.M.R. featuring FELICIA

Jose FELICIANO
US

SINGLES:	HITS 2			WEEKS 23
LIGHT MY FIRE	RCA Victor	6	21 Sep 68	16
AND THE SUN WILL SHINE	RCA Victor	25	18 Oct 69	7
Originally recorded by The Bee Gees.				
ALBUMS:	HITS 4			WEEKS 40
FELICIANO	RCA Victor	6	2 Nov 68	36
JOSE FELICIANO	RCA Victor	29	29 Nov 69	2
10 TO 23	RCA Victor	38	14 Feb 70	1
FIREWORKS	RCA Victor	65	22 Aug 70	1

FELIX
UK

SINGLES:	HITS 3			WEEKS 29
DON'T YOU WANT ME	Deconstruction	6	8 Aug 92	11
IT WILL MAKE ME CRAZY	Deconstruction	11	24 Oct 92	6
Vocals by Steele.				
STARS	Deconstruction	29	22 May 93	3
DON'T YOU WANT ME [RM-1ST]	Deconstruction	10	12 Aug 95	5
Remixed by Patrick Prins.				
DON'T YOU WANT ME ('96 PUGILIST MIX) [RM-2ND]	Deconstruction	17	19 Oct 96	4
Featured in the Tango Blackcurrant TV commercial. Remixed by Tom Hayes.				

ALBUMS:		HITS 1		WEEKS 4	
FELIX #1	*Deconstruction*		26	*10 Apr 93*	4

Julie FELIX

US

SINGLES:		HITS 2		WEEKS 19	
EL CONDOR PASA (IF I COULD)	*RAK*		19	*18 Apr 70*	11
Originally recorded by Simon And Garfunkel.					
HEAVEN IS HERE	*RAK*		22	*17 Oct 70*	8
EPS:		HITS 1		WEEKS 6	
SONGS FROM THE FROST REPORT	*Fontana*		5	*13 Aug 66*	6
ALBUMS:		HITS 1		WEEKS 4	
CHANGES	*Fontana*		27	*10 Sep 66*	4

FELLY – See TECHNOTRONIC

FEMME FATALE

US

SINGLES:		HITS 1		WEEKS 2	
FALLING IN AND OUT OF LOVE	*MCA*		69	*11 Feb 89*	2

FENDERMEN

US

SINGLES:		HITS 1		WEEKS 9	
MULE SKINNER BLUES	*Top Rank*		50	*20 Aug 60*	1
Originally recorded by Jimmie Rodgers in 1931.					
MULE SKINNER BLUES [RE-1ST]	*Top Rank*		37	*3 Sep 60*	2
MULE SKINNER BLUES [RE-2ND]	*Top Rank*		32	*1 Oct 60*	6

George FENTON – See Cry Freedom

Peter FENTON

UK

SINGLES:		HITS 1		WEEKS 3	
MARBLE BREAKS IRON BENDS	*Fontana*		46	*12 Nov 66*	3
Originally recorded by Drafi.					

Shane FENTON and the FENTONES

UK

(See also Fentones; Alvin Stardust.)

SINGLES:		HITS 4		WEEKS 28	
I'M A MOODY GUY	*Parlophone*		22	*28 Oct 61*	8
WALK AWAY	*Parlophone*		38	*3 Feb 62*	5
IT'S ALL OVER NOW	*Parlophone*		29	*7 Apr 62*	7
CINDY'S BIRTHDAY	*Parlophone*		19	*14 Jul 62*	8
Originally recorded by Johnny Crawford.					

FENTONES

UK

(See also Shane Fenton and the Fentones.)

SINGLES:		HITS 2		WEEKS 4	
THE MEXICAN	*Parlophone*		41	*21 Apr 62*	3
THE BREEZE AND I	*Parlophone*		48	*29 Sep 62*	1

Sheila FERGUSON

US

SINGLES:		HITS 1		WEEKS 1	
WHEN WILL I SEE YOU AGAIN	*XSRhythm*		60	*5 Feb 94*	1

FERKO STRING BAND

US

SINGLES:		HITS 1		WEEKS 2	
ALABAMA JUBILEE	*London*		20	*13 Aug 55*	2
Originally recorded by Arthur Collins and Byron Harlan in 1915.					

Luisa FERNANDEZ

Spain

SINGLES:		HITS 1		WEEKS 8	
LAY LOVE ON YOU	*Warner Brothers*		31	*11 Nov 78*	8

Pamela FERNANDEZ

US

SINGLES:		HITS 2		WEEKS 3	
KICKIN' IN THE BEAT	*Ore*		43	*17 Sep 94*	2
LET'S START OVER / KICKIN' IN THE BEAT [RM]	*Ore*		59	*3 Jun 95*	1
Kickin' In the Beat remixed by Todd Terry.					

FERRANTE and TEICHER

US

SINGLES:		HITS 2		WEEKS 18	
THEME FROM 'THE APARTMENT'	*London*		44	*20 Aug 60*	1
Title originally called Jealous Lover in 1949.					

THEME FROM "EXODUS" | | London | | 6 | 11 Mar 61 | 17
Issued on HMV during chart run when United Artists changed UK outlets. Both labels listed on the chart from 10 Jun 61. The HMV label reads title as Exodus (Theme From "Exodus").

Ibrahim FERRER — Cuba

ALBUMS:	HITS 1			WEEKS 3
BUENA VISTA SOCIAL CLUB PRESENTS . . .	World Circuit	42	5 Jun 99	3

Jose FERRER — US

SINGLES:	HITS 1			WEEKS 3
WOMAN (UH – HUH)	Philips	7	20 Feb 54	3

[AA] listed with Man (Uh – Huh) by Rosemary Clooney.

Tony FERRINO — UK

SINGLES:	HITS 1			WEEKS 2
HELP YOURSELF / BIGAMY AT CHRISTMAS	RCA	42	23 Nov 96	2

Bryan FERRY — UK

SINGLES:	HITS 22			WEEKS 133
A HARD RAIN'S A-GONNA FALL	Island	10	29 Sep 73	9

Originally recorded by Bob Dylan.

THE 'IN' CROWD	Island	13	25 May 74	6
SMOKE GETS IN YOUR EYES	Island	17	31 Aug 74	8

Originally recorded by Paul Whiteman in 1933.

YOU GO TO MY HEAD	Island	33	5 Jul 75	3
LET'S STICK TOGETHER (LET'S WORK TOGETHER)	Island	4	12 Jun 76	10

Originally recorded by Wilbert Harrison.

EXTENDED PLAY [EP]	Island	7	7 Aug 76	9

Lead track: Price Of Love.

THIS IS TOMORROW	Polydor	9	5 Feb 77	9
TOKYO JOE	Polydor	15	14 May 77	7
WHAT GOES ON	Polydor	67	13 May 78	2
SIGN OF THE TIMES	Polydor	37	5 Aug 78	8
SLAVE TO LOVE	E'G	10	11 May 85	9
DON'T STOP THE DANCE	E'G	21	31 Aug 85	7
WINDSWEPT	E'G	46	7 Dec 85	3
IS YOUR LOVE STRONG ENOUGH	E'G	22	29 Mar 86	7
THE RIGHT STUFF	Virgin	37	10 Oct 87	6
KISS AND TELL	Virgin	41	13 Feb 88	5

From the film 'Bright Lights Big City'.

LET'S STICK TOGETHER WESTSIDE '88 REMIX [RM]	E'G	12	29 Oct 88	7
THE PRICE OF LOVE: THE R&B '89 REMIX [RM]	E'G	49	11 Feb 89	3

Above 2 remixed by Bruce Lampcov and Rhett Davies.

HE'LL HAVE TO GO	E'G	63	22 Apr 89	1
I PUT A SPELL ON YOU	Virgin	18	6 Mar 93	5
WILL YOU LOVE ME TOMORROW	Virgin	23	29 May 93	5
GIRL OF MY BEST FRIEND	Virgin	57	4 Sep 93	2
YOUR PAINTED SMILE	Virgin	52	29 Oct 94	1
MAMOUNA	Virgin	57	11 Feb 95	1

ALBUMS:	HITS 13			WEEKS 308
THESE FOOLISH THINGS	Island	5	3 Nov 73	42
ANOTHER TIME, ANOTHER PLACE	Island	4	20 Jul 74	25
LET'S STICK TOGETHER	Island	19	2 Oct 76	5
IN YOUR MIND	Polydor	5	5 Mar 77	17
THE BRIDE STRIPPED BARE	Polydor	13	30 Sep 78	5
BOYS AND GIRLS	E'G	1	15 Jun 85	44
STREET LIFE – 20 GREAT HITS	E'G	1	26 Apr 86	77

Above hit: Bryan FERRY ROXY MUSIC.

BETE NOIRE	Virgin	9	14 Nov 87	16
THE ULTIMATE COLLECTION	E'G	6	19 Nov 88	27

Above hit: Bryan FERRY and ROXY MUSIC.

TAXI	Virgin	2	3 Apr 93	14
MAMOUNA	Virgin	11	17 Sep 94	4
THE ULTIMATE COLLECTION [RI]	Virgin	26	17 Sep 94	8

Above hit: Bryan FERRY and ROXY MUSIC.

MORE THAN THIS – THE BEST OF BRYAN FERRY AND ROXY MUSIC	Virgin	15	4 Nov 95	15

Above hit: Bryan FERRY and ROXY MUSIC.

AS TIME GOES BY	Virgin	16	6 Nov 99	9

Collection of songs from the 1930s.

FERRY AID — International

SINGLES:	HITS 1			WEEKS 7
LET IT BE	The Sun	1	4 Apr 87	7

Proceeds to the Sun's Zeebrugge Disaster Fund.

FEVER featuring Tippa IRIE — UK

SINGLES:	HITS 1			WEEKS 1
STAYING ALIVE 95	Telstar	48	8 Jul 95	1

F45 – See DE FUNK featuring F45

FFWD — UK/Germany

ALBUMS:	HITS 1			WEEKS 1
FFWD	Inter	48	13 Aug 94	1

Lena FIAGBE — UK

SINGLES:	HITS 5			WEEKS 13
YOU COME FROM EARTH	Mother	69	24 Jul 93	1
Above hit: LENA.				
GOTTA GET IT RIGHT	Mother	20	23 Oct 93	5
WHAT'S IT LIKE TO BE BEAUTIFUL	Mother	52	16 Apr 94	3
VISIONS	Mother	48	25 Jun 94	2
AFRICAN DREAM	Mercury	44	10 Feb 96	2
Above hit: Wasis DIOP featuring Lena FIAGBE.				

Karel FIALKA — UK

SINGLES:	HITS 2			WEEKS 12
THE EYES HAVE IT	Blueprint	52	17 May 80	4
HEY MATTHEW	I.R.S.	9	5 Sep 87	8
Features Karel's step-son Matthew.				

FIAT LUX — UK

SINGLES:	HITS 2			WEEKS 4
SECRETS	Polydor	65	28 Jan 84	3
BLUE EMOTION	Polydor	59	17 Mar 84	1

FICTION FACTORY — UK

SINGLES:	HITS 2			WEEKS 11
(FEELS LIKE) HEAVEN	CBS	6	14 Jan 84	9
GHOST OF LOVE	CBS	64	17 Mar 84	2

FIDDLER'S DRAM — UK

SINGLES:	HITS 1			WEEKS 9
DAYTRIP TO BANGOR (DIDN'T WE HAVE A LOVELY TIME)	Dingle's	3	15 Dec 79	9

FIDELFATTI featuring RONNETTE — Italy

SINGLES:	HITS 1			WEEKS 1
JUST WANNA TOUCH ME	Urban	65	27 Jan 90	1
Original release reached No. 88 in 1989.				

Brad FIEDEL — Germany

ALBUMS:	HITS 1			WEEKS 7
TERMINATOR 2 [OST]	Varese Sarabande	26	31 Aug 91	7

Billy FIELD — Australia

SINGLES:	HITS 1			WEEKS 3
YOU WEREN'T IN LOVE WITH ME	CBS	67	12 Jun 82	3

Ernie FIELD'S ORCHESTRA — US

SINGLES:	HITS 1			WEEKS 8
IN THE MOOD	London	13	26 Dec 59	8
Originally recorded by Glenn Miller in 1939.				

Gracie FIELDS — UK

SINGLES:	HITS 2			WEEKS 15
AROUND THE WORLD	Columbia	8	1 Jun 57	8
From the film 'Around the World In 80 Days'.				
Above hit: Gracie FIELDS with Tony OSBORNE and his Orchestra and Chorus.				
AROUND THE WORLD [RE]	Columbia	24	3 Aug 57	1
LITTLE DONKEY	Columbia	30	7 Nov 59	1
Above hit: Gracie FIELDS with the Rita WILLIAMS SINGERS.				
LITTLE DONKEY [RE]	Columbia	21	21 Nov 59	5
EPS:	HITS 1			WEEKS 1
OUR GRACIE SINGS COMEDY SONGS	HMV	16	26 Nov 60	1

ALBUMS:		HITS 1		WEEKS 3
THE GOLDEN YEARS	Warwick	48	20 Dec 75	3

Richard 'Dimples' FIELDS
US

SINGLES:		HITS 1		WEEKS 4
I'VE GOT TO LEARN TO SAY NO!	Epic	56	20 Feb 82	4

FIELDS OF THE NEPHILIM
UK

SINGLES:		HITS 5		WEEKS 9
BLUE WATER	Situation Two	75	24 Oct 87	1
MOONCHILD	Situation Two	28	4 Jun 88	3
PSYCHONAUT	Situation Two	35	27 May 89	3
FOR HER LIGHT	Beggars Banquet	54	4 Aug 90	1
SUMERLAND (DREAMED)	Beggars Banquet	37	24 Nov 90	1

ALBUMS:		HITS 4		WEEKS 9
DAWNRAZOR	Situation Two	62	30 May 87	2
THE NEPHILIM	Situation Two	14	17 Sep 88	3
ELIZIUM	Beggars Banquet	22	6 Oct 90	2
EARTH INFERNO	Beggars Banquet	39	6 Apr 91	2

FIERCE
UK

SINGLES:		HITS 3		WEEKS 15
RIGHT HERE RIGHT NOW	Wildstar	25	9 Jan 99	5
DAYS LIKE THAT	Wildstar	11	15 May 99	5
SO LONG	Wildstar	15	14 Aug 99	5

ALBUMS:		HITS 1		WEEKS 2
RIGHT HERE RIGHT NOW	Wildstar	27	28 Aug 99	2

5TH DIMENSION
US

SINGLES:		HITS 2		WEEKS 21
MEDLEY: AQUARIUS/LET THE SUNSHINE IN (THE FLESH FAILURES) [M]	Liberty	11	19 Apr 69	12
From the musical 'Hair'.				
WEDDING BELL BLUES	Liberty	16	17 Jan 70	9
Originally recorded by Laura Nyro.				

52ND STREET
UK

SINGLES:		HITS 3		WEEKS 13
TELL ME (HOW IT FEELS)	10 Records	54	2 Nov 85	5
YOU'RE MY LAST CHANCE	10 Records	49	11 Jan 86	4
I CAN'T LET YOU GO	10 Records	57	8 Mar 86	4

ALBUMS:		HITS 1		WEEKS 1
CHILDREN OF THE NIGHT	10 Records	71	19 Apr 86	1

53RD & 3RD featuring the SOUND OF SHAG - See Jonathan KING

FILTER
US

SINGLES:		HITS 1		WEEKS 2
(CAN'T YOU) TRIP LIKE I DO	Epic	39	11 Oct 97	2
From the film 'Spawn'.				
Above hit: FILTER and the CRYSTAL METHOD.				

ALBUMS:		HITS 1		WEEKS 1
TITLE OF RECORD	Reprise	75	4 Sep 99	1

FINAL CUT - See TRUE FAITH and Bridgette GRACE with FINAL CUT

FINE YOUNG CANNIBALS
UK

SINGLES:		HITS 11		WEEKS 81
JOHNNY COME HOME	London	8	8 Jun 85	13
BLUE	London	41	9 Nov 85	6
SUSPICIOUS MINDS	London	8	11 Jan 86	9
FUNNY HOW LOVE IS	London	58	12 Apr 86	4
EVER FALLEN IN LOVE	London	9	21 Mar 87	10
SHE DRIVES ME CRAZY	London	5	7 Jan 89	11
GOOD THING	London	7	15 Apr 89	8
From the film 'Tin Men'.				
DON'T LOOK BACK	London	34	19 Aug 89	4
I'M NOT THE MAN I USED TO BE	London	20	18 Nov 89	8
I'M NOT SATISFIED	London	46	24 Feb 90	3
THE FLAME	ffrr	17	16 Nov 96	3
SHE DRIVES ME CRAZY [RI]	ffrr	36	11 Jan 97	2

ALBUMS:		HITS 4		WEEKS 107
FINE YOUNG CANNIBALS	London	11	21 Dec 85	27
THE RAW AND THE COOKED	London	1	18 Feb 89	66

THE RAW AND THE REMIX	*London*	61	*15 Dec 90*	1

Remixed tracks from The Raw And The Cooked.
Above hit: FYC.

THE FINEST	*ffrr*	10	*23 Nov 96*	13

FINITRIBE
UK

SINGLES:	HITS 2		WEEKS 2	
FOREVERGREEN	*One Little Indian*	51	*11 Jul 92*	1
BRAND NEW	*ffrr*	69	*19 Nov 94*	1

FINK BROTHERS
UK

SINGLES:	HITS 1		WEEKS 4	
MUTANTS IN MEGA CITY ONE	*Zarjazz*	50	*9 Feb 85*	4

Frank FINLAY - See David ESSEX

FINN
New Zealand

SINGLES:	HITS 2		WEEKS 5	
SUFFER NEVER	*Parlophone*	29	*14 Oct 95*	3
ANGEL'S HEAP	*Parlophone*	41	*9 Dec 95*	2
ALBUMS:	HITS 1		WEEKS 3	
FINN	*Parlophone*	15	*28 Oct 95*	3

Micky FINN - See URBAN SHAKEDOWN featuring Micky FINN

Neil FINN
New Zealand

SINGLES:	HITS 2		WEEKS 3	
SHE WILL HAVE HER WAY	*Parlophone*	26	*13 Jun 98*	2
SINNER	*Parlophone*	39	*17 Oct 98*	1
ALBUMS:	HITS 1		WEEKS 11	
TRY WHISTLING THIS	*Parlophone*	5	*27 Jun 98*	11

Tim FINN
New Zealand

SINGLES:	HITS 2		WEEKS 6	
PERSUASION	*Capitol*	43	*26 Jun 93*	3
HIT THE GROUND RUNNING	*Capitol*	50	*18 Sep 93*	3
ALBUMS:	HITS 1		WEEKS 2	
BEFORE AND AFTER	*Capitol*	29	*10 Jul 93*	2

Elisa FIORILLO
US

SINGLES:	HITS 2		WEEKS 14	
WHO FOUND WHO	*Chrysalis*	10	*28 Nov 87*	10

Above hit: JELLYBEAN featuring Elisa FIORILLO.

HOW CAN I FORGET YOU	*Chrysalis*	50	*13 Feb 88*	4

FIRE INC. - See Jim STEINMAN

FIRE ISLAND
UK

(See also Heller and Farley Project.)

SINGLES:	HITS 4		WEEKS 7	
IN YOUR BONES / FIRE ISLAND	*Boy's Own Productions*	66	*8 Aug 92*	1
THERE BUT FOR THE GRACE OF GOD	*Junior Boy's Own*	32	*12 Mar 94*	3

Originally recorded by Kid Creole and the Coconuts.
Above hit: FIRE ISLAND featuring: LOVE NELSON.

IF YOU SHOULD NEED A FRIEND	*Junior Boy's Own*	51	*4 Mar 95*	1

Originally recorded by Blaze in 1987.
Above hit: FIRE ISLAND featuring Mark ANTHONI.

SHOUT TO THE TOP	*JBO*	23	*11 Apr 98*	2

Above hit: FIRE ISLAND featuring Loleatta HOLLOWAY.

FIREBALLS
US

SINGLES:	HITS 2		WEEKS 17	
QUITE A PARTY	*Pye International*	29	*29 Jul 61*	9
SUGAR SHACK	*London*	45	*16 Nov 63*	4

Above hit: Jimmy GILMER and the FIREBALLS.

SUGAR SHACK [RE]	*London*	46	*21 Dec 63*	4

FIREHOUSE
US

SINGLES:	HITS 2		WEEKS 2	
DON'T TREAT ME BAD	*Epic*	71	*13 Jul 91*	1
WHEN I LOOK INTO YOUR EYES	*Epic*	65	*19 Dec 92*	1

309

FIRM
SINGLES:	HITS 2				UK WEEKS 21
ARTHUR DALEY ('E'S ALRIGHT)	Bark	14	17 Jul 82	9
Arthur Daley is character from the Thames ITV series 'Minder'.				
STAR TREKKIN'	Bark	1	6 Jun 87	12
Novelty single based around characters from 'Star Trek'.				

FIRM
ALBUMS:	HITS 2			UK WEEKS 8
THE FIRM	Atlantic	15	2 Mar 85	5
MEAN BUSINESS	Atlantic	46	5 Apr 86	3

Nas ESCOBAR, Foxy BROWN, AZ and NATURE present the FIRM featuring Dawn ROBINSON
US
(See also AZ; Foxy Brown; Nas.)

SINGLES:	HITS 1			WEEKS 3
FIRM BIZ	Columbia	18	29 Nov 97	3

FIRST CHOICE
SINGLES:	HITS 2			UK WEEKS 21
ARMED AND EXTREMELY DANGEROUS	Bell	16	19 May 73	10
SMARTY PANTS	Bell	9	4 Aug 73	11

FIRST CIRCLE
ALBUMS:	HITS 1			US WEEKS 2
BOY'S NIGHT OUT	EMI America	70	2 May 87	2

FIRST CLASS
SINGLES:	HITS 1			UK WEEKS 10
BEACH BABY	UK	13	15 Jun 74	10

FIRST EDITION – See Kenny ROGERS

FIRST LIGHT
SINGLES:	HITS 2			UK WEEKS 5
EXPLAIN THE REASONS	London	65	21 May 83	3
WISH YOU WERE HERE	London	71	28 Jan 84	2

FIRSTBORN
SINGLES:	HITS 1			Ireland WEEKS 1
THE MOOD CLUB	Independiente	69	19 Jun 99	1
From the film 'Human Traffic'.				

Carl FISCHER – See Doris DAY; Frankie LAINE.

FISCHER-Z
SINGLES:	HITS 2			UK WEEKS 7
THE WORKER	United Artists	53	26 May 79	5
SO LONG	United Artists	72	3 May 80	2
ALBUMS:	HITS 1			WEEKS 1
WORD SALAD	United Artists	66	23 Jun 79	1

FISH
SINGLES:	HITS 10			UK WEEKS 20
SHORTCUT TO SOMEWHERE	Charisma	75	18 Oct 86	1
Above hit: FISH and Tony BANKS.				
STATE OF MIND	EMI	32	28 Oct 89	3
BIG WEDGE	EMI	25	6 Jan 90	4
A GENTLEMAN'S EXCUSE ME	EMI	30	17 Mar 90	3
INTERNAL EXILE	Polydor	37	28 Sep 91	2
CREDO	Polydor	38	11 Jan 92	2
SOMETHING IN THE AIR	Polydor	51	4 Jul 92	2
LADY LET IT LIE	The Dick Brothers	46	16 Apr 94	1
FORTUNES OF WAR	The Dick Brothers	67	1 Oct 94	1
JUST GOOD FRIENDS	The Dick Brothers	63	26 Aug 95	1
Above hit: FISH featuring Sam BROWN.				
ALBUMS:	HITS 8			WEEKS 17
VIGIL IN A WILDERNESS OF MIRRORS	EMI	5	10 Feb 90	6
INTERNAL EXILE	Polydor	21	9 Nov 91	3
SONGS FROM THE MIRROR	Polydor	46	30 Jan 93	2
SUITS	The Dick Brothers	18	11 Jun 94	2
YANG	The Dick Brothers	52	16 Sep 95	1

YIN	*The Dick Brothers*	58	*16 Sep 95*	1
Above 2 feature remixes/re-recordings of Marillion and solo material.				
SUNSETS ON EMPIRE	*The Dick Brothers*	42	*31 May 97*	1
RAINGODS WITH ZIPPOS	*Roadrunner*	57	*1 May 99*	1

FISHBONE
US

SINGLES:	HITS 2		WEEKS 3	
EVERYDAY SUNSHINE / FIGHT THE YOUTH	*Columbia*	60	*1 Aug 92*	2
SWIM	*Columbia*	54	*28 Aug 93*	1
ALBUMS:	**HITS 1**		**WEEKS 1**	
THE REALITY OF MY SURROUNDINGS	*Columbia*	75	*13 Jul 91*	1

Cevin FISHER
US

SINGLES:	HITS 3		WEEKS 7	
THE FREAKS COME OUT	*Sound Of Ministry*	34	*3 Oct 98*	2
Above hit: Cevin FISHER'S BIG BREAK.				
(YOU GOT ME) BURNING UP	*Wonderboy*	14	*20 Feb 99*	4
Samples Loleatta Holloway's Love Sensation.				
Above hit: Cevin FISHER featuring Loleatta HOLLOWAY.				
MUSIC SAVED MY LIFE	*Sm:)e Communications*	67	*7 Aug 99*	1

Eddie FISHER
US

SINGLES:	HITS 9		WEEKS 105	
OUTSIDE OF HEAVEN	*His Master's Voice*	1	*3 Jan 53*	16
EVERYTHING I HAVE IS YOURS	*His Master's Voice*	12	*24 Jan 53*	1
EVERYTHING I HAVE IS YOURS [RE]	*His Master's Voice*	8	*7 Feb 53*	4
Above 3: Eddie FISHER with Hugo WINTERHALTER's ORCHESTRA and CHORUS.				
DOWNHEARTED	*His Master's Voice*	3	*2 May 53*	1
Above hit : Eddie FISHER with Hugo WINTERHALTER and his Orchestra.				
OUTSIDE OF HEAVEN [RE]	*His Master's Voice*	12	*2 May 53*	1
Above hit: Eddie FISHER with Hugo WINTERHALTER's ORCHESTRA and CHORUS.				
I'M WALKING BEHIND YOU	*His Master's Voice*	1	*23 May 53*	18
Above hit: Eddie FISHER with Hugo WINTERHALTER and his Orchestra and Sally SWEETLAND.				
WISH YOU WERE HERE	*His Master's Voice*	8	*7 Nov 53*	9
From the musical of the same name.				
Above hit : Eddie FISHER with Hugo WINTERHALTER and his Orchestra.				
OH MY PAPA (O MEIN PAPA)	*His Master's Voice*	9	*23 Jan 54*	1
Above hit: Eddie FISHER with Hugo WINTERHALTER's ORCHESTRA and CHORUS.				
OH MY PAPA (O MEIN PAPA) [RE-1ST]	*His Master's Voice*	11	*6 Feb 54*	1
OH MY PAPA (O MEIN PAPA) [RE-2ND]	*His Master's Voice*	10	*27 Feb 54*	1
OH MY PAPA (O MEIN PAPA) [RE-3RD]	*His Master's Voice*	11	*13 Mar 54*	1
I NEED YOU NOW	*His Master's Voice*	16	*30 Oct 54*	2
Above hit: Eddie FISHER with Hugo WINTERHALTER and his Orchestra.				
I NEED YOU NOW [RE-1ST]	*His Master's Voice*	13	*20 Nov 54*	7
I NEED YOU NOW [RE-2ND]	*His Master's Voice*	19	*22 Jan 55*	1
(I'M ALWAYS HEARING) WEDDING BELLS	*His Master's Voice*	5	*19 Mar 55*	11
CINDY, OH CINDY	*His Master's Voice*	5	*24 Nov 56*	16
Above 2: Eddie FISHER with Hugo WINTERHALTER's ORCHESTRA and CHORUS.				

Mark FISHER (featuring Dotty GREEN)
UK

SINGLES:	HITS 1		WEEKS 2	
LOVE SITUATION	*Total Control*	59	*29 Jun 85*	2

Toni FISHER
US

SINGLES:	HITS 1		WEEKS 1	
THE BIG HURT	*Top Rank*	30	*13 Feb 60*	1
First hit to use a phasing gimmick.				

Martin FISHLEY – See PRESSURE DROP featuring Constantine WEIR and Martin FISHLEY

FITS OF GLOOM
UK/Italy

SINGLES:	HITS 2		WEEKS 4	
HEAVEN	*MCA*	47	*4 Jun 94*	2
THE POWER OF LOVE	*Media*	49	*5 Nov 94*	2
Above hit: FITS OF GLOOM featuring Lizzy MACK.				

Ella FITZGERALD
US

SINGLES:	HITS 6		WEEKS 29	
THE SWINGIN' SHEPHERD BLUES	*His Master's Voice*	15	*24 May 58*	5
Above hit: Ella FITZGERALD and her SHEPHERDS.				

BUT NOT FOR ME	His Master's Voice	25	17 Oct 59	2
From the film of the same name.				
BUT NOT FOR ME [RE]	His Master's Voice	29	26 Dec 59	1
MACK THE KNIFE	His Master's Voice	19	23 Apr 60	9
HOW HIGH THE MOON	His Master's Voice	46	8 Oct 60	1
From the film 'Two For The Show'. Originally recorded by Benny Goodman.				
Above 2: Ella FITZGERALD with the Paul SMITH QUARTET.				
DESAFINADO (SLIGHTLY OUT OF TUNE)	Verve	38	24 Nov 62	4
DESAFINADO (SLIGHTLY OUT OF TUNE) [RE]	Verve	41	29 Dec 62	2
CAN'T BUY ME LOVE	Verve	34	2 May 64	5

EPS:	HITS 3			WEEKS 7
WITH A SONG IN MY HEART	HMV	10	11 Jun 60	3
MOODS OF ELLA	HMV	17	13 Aug 60	1
ELLA SINGS IRVING BERLIN	HMV	17	27 Aug 60	3

ALBUMS:	HITS 7			WEEKS 43
ELLA SINGS GERSHWIN	Brunswick	13	11 Jun 60	3
ELLA AT THE OPERA HOUSE	Columbia	16	18 Jun 60	1
ELLA SINGS GERSHWIN VOLUME 5	His Master's Voice	18	23 Jul 60	2
THE INCOMPARABLE ELLA	Polydor	40	10 May 80	7
A PORTRAIT OF ELLA FITZGERALD	Stylus	42	27 Feb 88	10
ESSENTIAL ELLA	PolyGram TV	35	19 Nov 94	14
Recordings from 1956 and 1960.				
FOREVER ELLA	Verve/PolyGram TV	19	23 Mar 96	6

Scott FITZGERALD

UK

SINGLES:	HITS 2			WEEKS 12
IF I HAD WORDS	Pepper/United Artists	3	14 Jan 78	10
Above hit: Scott FITZGERALD and Yvonne KEELY (with the ST. THOMAS MORE SCHOOL CHOIR).				
GO	PRT	52	7 May 88	2
UK's Eurovision entry in 1988, it came 2nd.				

FIVE

UK

SINGLES:	HITS 7			WEEKS 76
SLAM DUNK (DA FUNK)	RCA	10	13 Dec 97	9
WHEN THE LIGHTS GO OUT	RCA	4	14 Mar 98	9
GOT THE FEELIN'	RCA	3	20 Jun 98	13
Above 3: 5.				
EVERYBODY GET UP	RCA	2	12 Sep 98	12
Samples Joan Jett and the Blackhearts' I Love Rock and Roll.				
UNTIL THE TIME IS THROUGH	RCA	2	28 Nov 98	12
IF YA GETTIN' DOWN	RCA	2	31 Jul 99	12
Samples Indeep's Last Night A DJ Saved My Life.				
KEEP ON MOVIN'	RCA	1	6 Nov 99	9

ALBUMS:	HITS 2			WEEKS 43
FIVE	RCA	1	4 Jul 98	36
INVINCIBLE	RCA	4	20 Nov 99	7

FIVE PENNY PIECE

UK

ALBUMS:	HITS 2			WEEKS 6
MAKING TRACKS	Columbia	37	24 Mar 73	1
KING COTTON	EMI	9	3 Jul 76	5

FIVE SMITH BROTHERS

UK

SINGLES:	HITS 1			WEEKS 1
I'M IN FAVOUR OF FRIENDSHIP	Decca	20	23 Jul 55	1

FIVE STAR

UK

SINGLES:	HITS 21			WEEKS 140
ALL FALL DOWN	Tent	15	4 May 85	12
LET ME BE THE ONE	Tent	18	20 Jul 85	9
LOVE TAKE OVER	Tent	25	14 Sep 85	9
R.S.V.P.	Tent	45	16 Nov 85	5
SYSTEM ADDICT	Tent	3	11 Jan 86	11
CAN'T WAIT ANOTHER MINUTE	Tent	7	12 Apr 86	10
Originally recorded by Lewis.				
FIND THE TIME	Tent	7	26 Jul 86	10
RAIN OR SHINE	Tent	2	13 Sep 86	11
IF I SAY YES	Tent	15	22 Nov 86	9
STAY OUT OF MY LIFE	Tent	9	7 Feb 87	8
THE SLIGHTEST TOUCH	Tent	4	18 Apr 87	9
WHENEVER YOU'RE READY	Tent	11	22 Aug 87	6
STRONG AS STEEL	Tent	16	10 Oct 87	7
SOMEWHERE SOMEBODY	Tent	23	5 Dec 87	6
ANOTHER WEEKEND	Tent	18	4 Jun 88	4

ROCK MY WORLD	*Tent*	28	*6 Aug 88*	4
THERE'S A BRAND NEW WORLD	*Tent*	61	*17 Sep 88*	2
LET ME BE YOURS	*Tent*	51	*19 Nov 88*	3
WITH EVERY HEARTBEAT	*Tent*	49	*8 Apr 89*	2
TREAT ME LIKE A LADY	*Tent*	54	*10 Mar 90*	2
HOT LOVE	*Tent*	68	*7 Jul 90*	1
ALBUMS:	**HITS 5**		**WEEKS 153**	
LUXURY OF LIFE	*Tent*	24	*3 Aug 85*	21
LUXURY OF LIFE [RE]	*Tent*	12	*4 Jan 86*	49
SILK AND STEEL	*Tent*	1	*30 Aug 86*	58
BETWEEN THE LINES	*Tent*	7	*26 Sep 87*	17
ROCK THE WORLD	*Tent*	17	*27 Aug 88*	5
GREATEST HITS	*Tent*	53	*21 Oct 89*	3

FIVE THIRTY — UK

SINGLES:	**HITS 4**		**WEEKS 4**	
ABSTAIN	*East West*	75	*4 Aug 90*	1
13TH DISCIPLE	*East West*	67	*25 May 91*	1
SUPERNOVA	*East West*	75	*3 Aug 91*	1
YOU [EP]	*East West*	72	*2 Nov 91*	1
Lead track: You.				
ALBUMS:	**HITS 1**		**WEEKS 1**	
BED	*East West*	57	*31 Aug 91*	1

5000 VOLTS — UK

SINGLES:	**HITS 2**		**WEEKS 18**	
I'M ON FIRE	*Philips*	4	*6 Sep 75*	9
DOCTOR KISS - KISS	*Philips*	8	*24 Jul 76*	9
Vocals by Linda Kelly.				

FIXX — UK

SINGLES:	**HITS 2**		**WEEKS 8**	
STAND OR FALL	*MCA*	54	*24 Apr 82*	4
RED SKIES	*MCA*	57	*17 Jul 82*	4
ALBUMS:	**HITS 2**		**WEEKS 7**	
SHUTTERED ROOM	*MCA*	54	*22 May 82*	6
REACH THE BEACH	*MCA*	91	*21 May 83*	1

FKW — UK

SINGLES:	**HITS 4**		**WEEKS 8**	
NEVER GONNA GIVE YOU UP	*PWL International*	48	*2 Oct 93*	2
SEIZE THE DAY	*PWL International*	45	*11 Dec 93*	2
JINGO	*PWL International*	30	*5 Mar 94*	3
THIS IS THE WAY	*PWL International*	63	*4 Jun 94*	1

Roberta FLACK — US

(See also Peabo Bryson and Roberta Flack; Roberta Flack and Donny Hathaway.)

SINGLES:	**HITS 5**		**WEEKS 44**	
THE FIRST TIME EVER I SAW YOUR FACE	*Atlantic*	14	*27 May 72*	14
Originally recorded by Peter, Paul & Mary in 1962. Featured in the Clint Eastwood film 'Play Misty For Me'.				
KILLING ME SOFTLY WITH HIS SONG	*Atlantic*	6	*17 Feb 73*	14
Originally recorded by Lori Leiberman in 1972. Inspired by a Don McLean concert.				
FEEL LIKE MAKIN' LOVE	*Atlantic*	34	*24 Aug 74*	7
DON'T MAKE ME WAIT TOO LONG	*Atlantic*	44	*30 Aug 80*	7
UH-UH OOH OOH LOOK OUT (HERE IT COMES)	*Atlantic*	72	*29 Jul 89*	2
ALBUMS:	**HITS 4**		**WEEKS 28**	
FIRST TAKE	*Atlantic*	47	*15 Jul 72*	2
KILLING ME SOFTLY	*Atlantic*	40	*13 Oct 73*	2
ROBERTA FLACK'S GREATEST HITS	*K-Tel*	35	*31 Mar 84*	14
SOFTLY WITH THESE SONGS - THE BEST OF ROBERTA FLACK	*Atlantic*	7	*19 Feb 94*	10

Roberta FLACK and Donny HATHAWAY — US

(See also Peabo Bryson and Roberta Flack; Roberta Flack.)

SINGLES:	**HITS 3**		**WEEKS 22**	
WHERE IS THE LOVE	*Atlantic*	29	*5 Aug 72*	7
THE CLOSER I GET TO YOU	*Atlantic*	42	*6 May 78*	4
Above hit: Roberta FLACK with Donny HATHAWAY.				
BACK TOGETHER AGAIN	*Atlantic*	3	*17 May 80*	11
ALBUMS:	**HITS 1**		**WEEKS 7**	
ROBERTA FLACK AND DONNY HATHAWAY	*Atlantic*	31	*7 Jun 80*	7

FLAJ - See GETO BOYS featuring FLAJ

FLAMING LIPS

				US
SINGLES:	HITS 3			WEEKS 4
THIS HERE GIRAFFE	Warner Brothers	72	9 Mar 96	1
RACE FOR THE PRIZE	Warner Brothers	39	26 Jun 99	2
WAITIN' FOR A SUPERMAN	Warner Brothers	73	20 Nov 99	1
ALBUMS:	HITS 1			WEEKS 2
THE SOFT BULLETIN	Warner Brothers	39	29 May 99	2

FLAMINGOS

				US
SINGLES:	HITS 1			WEEKS 5
THE BOOGALOO PARTY	Philips	26	7 Jun 69	5

Originally released in 1966.

Michael FLANDERS with the Michael SAMMES SINGERS

				UK
SINGLES:	HITS 1			WEEKS 3
THE LITTLE DRUMMER BOY	Parlophone	20	28 Feb 59	2
THE LITTLE DRUMMER BOY [RE]	Parlophone	24	18 Apr 59	1

FLASH AND THE PAN

				Australia
SINGLES:	HITS 2			WEEKS 15
AND THE BAND PLAYED ON (DOWN AMONG THE DEAD MEN)	Ensign	54	23 Sep 78	4
WAITING FOR A TRAIN	Easybeat	7	21 May 83	11
ALBUMS:	HITS 1			WEEKS 1
PAN-ORAMA	Easybeat	69	16 Jul 83	2

Lester FLATT and Earl SCRUGGS

				US
SINGLES:	HITS 1			WEEKS 6
FOGGY MOUNTAIN BREAKDOWN	CBS & Mercury	39	18 Nov 67	6

Sales of two different recordings (CBS from 1965, Mercury from 1949) were combined. Theme from the film 'Bonnie and Clyde'.

Fogwell FLAX and the ANKLE BITERS from FREEHOLD JUNIOR SCHOOL

				UK
SINGLES:	HITS 1			WEEKS 2
ONE-NINE FOR SANTA	EMI	68	26 Dec 81	2

FLB – See FAT LARRY'S BAND

FLEETWOOD MAC

				UK/US
SINGLES:	HITS 25			WEEKS 223
BLACK MAGIC WOMAN	Blue Horizon	37	13 Apr 68	7
NEED YOUR LOVE SO BAD	Blue Horizon	31	20 Jul 68	13
ALBATROSS	Blue Horizon	1	7 Dec 68	20
MAN OF THE WORLD	Immediate	2	19 Apr 69	14
NEED YOUR LOVE SO BAD [RI]	Blue Horizon	32	26 Jul 69	6
NEED YOUR LOVE SO BAD [RI] [RE]	Blue Horizon	42	13 Sep 69	3
OH WELL	Reprise	2	4 Oct 69	16
THE GREEN MANALISHI (WITH THE TWO PRONG CROWN)	Reprise	10	23 May 70	12
ALBATROSS [RI]	CBS	2	12 May 73	15
SAY YOU LOVE ME	Reprise	40	13 Nov 76	4
GO YOUR OWN WAY	Warner Brothers	38	19 Feb 77	4
DON'T STOP	Warner Brothers	32	30 Apr 77	5
DREAMS	Warner Brothers	24	9 Jul 77	9
YOU MAKE LOVING FUN	Warner Brothers	45	22 Oct 77	2
RHIANNON	Reprise	46	11 Mar 78	3
Originally released in 1976.				
TUSK	Warner Brothers	6	6 Oct 79	10
SARA	Warner Brothers	37	22 Dec 79	8
GYPSY	Warner Brothers	46	25 Sep 82	3
OH DIANE	Warner Brothers	9	18 Dec 82	15
BIG LOVE	Warner Brothers	9	4 Apr 87	12
SEVEN WONDERS	Warner Brothers	56	11 Jul 87	4
LITTLE LIES	Warner Brothers	5	26 Sep 87	12
FAMILY MAN	Warner Brothers	54	26 Dec 87	5
EVERYWHERE	Warner Brothers	4	2 Apr 88	10
ISN'T IT MIDNIGHT	Warner Brothers	60	18 Jun 88	2
AS LONG AS YOU FOLLOW	Warner Brothers	66	17 Dec 88	3
SAVE ME	Warner Brothers	53	5 May 90	3
IN THE BACK OF MY MIND	Warner Brothers	58	25 Aug 90	3
ALBUMS:	HITS 17			WEEKS 826
FLEETWOOD MAC	Blue Horizon	4	2 Mar 68	37
Above hit: Peter GREEN'S FLEETWOOD MAC.				
MR. WONDERFUL	Blue Horizon	10	7 Sep 68	11
THE PIOUS BIRD OF GOOD OMEN	Blue Horizon	18	30 Aug 69	4
Compilation.				

THEN PLAY ON	Reprise	6	4 Oct 69	11
KILN HOUSE	Reprise	39	10 Oct 70	2
GREATEST HITS	CBS	36	19 Feb 72	11
FLEETWOOD MAC	Reprise	23	6 Nov 76	19
RUMOURS	Warner Brothers	1	26 Feb 77	402
Peak position reached on 28 Jan.78. Includes re-entries through to 1987.				
TUSK	Warner Brothers	1	27 Oct 79	26
FLEETWOOD MAC LIVE	Warner Brothers	31	13 Dec 80	9
MIRAGE	Warner Brothers	5	10 Jul 82	39
TANGO IN THE NIGHT	Warner Brothers	1	25 Apr 87	100
Peak position reached on 31 Oct 87.				
RUMOURS [RE-1ST]	Warner Brothers	28	9 Jan 88	41
GREATEST HITS [RE]	CBS	81	14 May 88	2
Repackaged.				
GREATEST HITS	Warner Brothers	3	3 Dec 88	31
The 2 Greatest Hits albums are different.				
BEHIND THE MASK	Warner Brothers	1	21 Apr 90	21
TANGO IN THE NIGHT [RE]	Warner Brothers	28	2 Apr 94	14
Re-released at mid-price. Chart position reached in 1995.				
GREATEST HITS [RE]	Warner Brothers	38	30 Apr 94	21
Repackaged at mid-price.				
LIVE AT THE BBC	Essential	48	23 Sep 95	2
Recorded for the BBC between 1967–69.				
GREATEST HITS [RI]	Columbia	73	23 Sep 95	1
TIME	Warner Brothers	47	21 Oct 95	1
THE DANCE	Reprise	15	6 Sep 97	10
Compilation with 4 new tracks.				
RUMOURS [RE-2ND]	Warner Brothers	18	6 Sep 97	9
Charted after being featured on BBC1 TV's 'Classic Albums' series.				

FLEETWOODS   US

SINGLES:	HITS 1			WEEKS 8
COME SOFTLY TO ME	London	6	25 Apr 59	8

John '00' FLEMING   UK

SINGLES:	HITS 1			WEEKS 1
LOST IN EMOTION	React	74	25 Dec 99	1

La FLEUR   Holland

SINGLES:	HITS 1			WEEKS 4
BOOGIE NIGHTS	Proto	51	30 Jul 83	4

KC FLIGHTT   US

SINGLES:	HITS 1			WEEKS 4
PLANET E	RCA	48	1 Apr 89	4

Dread FLIMSTONE and the NEW TONE AGE FAMILY   US

SINGLES:	HITS 1			WEEKS 1
FROM THE GHETTO	Urban	66	30 Nov 91	1

Berni FLINT   UK

SINGLES:	HITS 2			WEEKS 11
I DON'T WANT TO PUT A HOLD ON YOU	EMI	3	19 Mar 77	10
SOUTHERN COMFORT	EMI	48	23 Jul 77	1
ALBUMS:	**HITS 1**			**WEEKS 6**
I DON'T WANT TO PUT A HOLD ON YOU	EMI	37	2 Jul 77	6

FLINTLOCK   UK

SINGLES:	HITS 1			WEEKS 5
DAWN	Pinnacle	30	29 May 76	5

FLIPMODE SQUAD (Starring Busta RHYMES, BABY SHAM, RAH DIGGA and SPLIFF STAR)   US

(See also Busta Rhymes.)

SINGLES:	HITS 1			WEEKS 1
CHA CHA CHA	Elektra	54	31 Oct 98	1

FLOATERS   US

SINGLES:	HITS 1			WEEKS 11
FLOAT ON	ABC	1	23 Jul 77	11
ALBUMS:	**HITS 1**			**WEEKS 8**
FLOATERS	ABC	17	20 Aug 77	8

FLOCK
UK

ALBUMS:		HITS 1		WEEKS 2	
FLOCK	*CBS*		59	2 May 70	2

A FLOCK OF SEAGULLS
UK

SINGLES:		HITS 7		WEEKS 46	
I RAN	*Jive*		43	27 Mar 82	6
SPACE AGE LOVE SONG	*Jive*		34	12 Jun 82	6
WISHING (IF I HAD A PHOTOGRAPH OF YOU)	*Jive*		10	6 Nov 82	12
NIGHTMARES	*Jive*		53	23 Apr 83	3
TRANSFER AFFECTION	*Jive*		38	25 Jun 83	5
THE MORE YOU LIVE, THE MORE YOU LOVE	*Jive*		26	14 Jul 84	11
WHO'S THAT GIRL? SHE'S GOT IT	*Jive*		66	19 Oct 85	3
ALBUMS:		HITS 3		WEEKS 59	
A FLOCK OF SEAGULLS	*Jive*		32	17 Apr 82	44
LISTEN	*Arista*		16	7 May 83	10
THE STORY OF A YOUNG HEART	*Jive*		30	1 Sep 84	5

FLOORPLAY
UK

SINGLES:		HITS 1		WEEKS 1	
AUTOMATIC	*Perfecto*		50	27 Jan 96	1

FLOWER POT MEN
UK

SINGLES:		HITS 1		WEEKS 12	
LET'S GO TO SAN FRANCISCO	*Deram*		4	26 Aug 67	12

FLOWERED UP
UK

(See also Various Artists (EPs) 'The Fred EP'.)

SINGLES:		HITS 5		WEEKS 17	
IT'S ON	*Heavenly*		54	28 Jul 90	4
PHOBIA	*Heavenly*		75	24 Nov 90	1
TAKE IT	*London*		34	11 May 91	4
IT'S ON [RI] / EGG RUSH	*London*		38	17 Aug 91	3
WEEKENDER	*Heavenly*		20	2 May 92	5
ALBUMS:		HITS 1		WEEKS 3	
A LIFE WITH BRIAN	*London*		23	7 Sep 91	3

Mike FLOWERS POPS
UK

SINGLES:		HITS 3		WEEKS 14	
WONDERWALL	*London*		2	30 Dec 95	7
WONDERWALL [RE]	*London*		52	13 Apr 96	2
LIGHT MY FIRE / PLEASE RELEASE ME	*London*		39	8 Jun 96	2
DON'T CRY FOR ME ARGENTINA	*Love This*		30	28 Dec 96	3

Eddie FLOYD
US

SINGLES:		HITS 3		WEEKS 29	
KNOCK ON WOOD	*Atlantic*		50	4 Feb 67	1
KNOCK ON WOOD [RE]	*Atlantic*		19	4 Mar 67	17
RAISE YOUR HAND	*Stax*		42	18 Mar 67	3
THINGS GET BETTER	*Stax*		31	12 Aug 67	8
ALBUMS:		HITS 1		WEEKS 5	
KNOCK ON WOOD	*Stax*		36	29 Apr 67	5

FLUFFY
UK

SINGLES:		HITS 2		WEEKS 2	
HUSBAND	*Parkway*		58	17 Feb 96	1
NOTHING	*Virgin*		52	5 Oct 96	1

FLUKE
UK

SINGLES:		HITS 9		WEEKS 20	
SLID	*Circa*		59	20 Mar 93	1
ELECTRIC GUITAR	*Circa*		58	19 Jun 93	2
Samples Jimi Hendrix's Crosstown Traffic.					
GROOVY FEELING	*Circa*		45	11 Sep 93	3
BUBBLE	*Circa*		37	23 Apr 94	2
BULLET	*Circa*		23	29 Jul 95	3
TOSH	*Circa*		32	16 Dec 95	3
ATOM BOMB	*Circa*		20	16 Nov 96	3
Song is featured on the WipeOut2 2097 Game for Playstation.					
ABSURD	*Circa*		25	31 May 97	2
SQUIRT	*Circa*		46	27 Sep 97	1

ALBUMS:		HITS 3		WEEKS 3
SIX WHEELS ON MY WAGON	Circa	41	23 Oct 93	1
Live recordings.				
OTO	Circa	44	19 Aug 95	1
RISOTTO	Circa	45	11 Oct 97	1

FLUSH - See SLADE

FLUX FIDDLERS - See John LENNON

A FLUX OF PINK INDIANS · UK

ALBUMS:		HITS 1		WEEKS 2
STRIVE TO SURVIVE CAUSING LEAST SUFFERING POSSIBLE	Spiderleg	79	5 Feb 83	2

FLYING LIZARDS · UK

SINGLES:		HITS 2		WEEKS 16
MONEY	Virgin	5	4 Aug 79	10
Original by Barrett Strong reached No. 23 in the US in 1960.				
TV	Virgin	43	9 Feb 80	6
ALBUMS:		HITS 1		WEEKS 3
FLYING LIZARDS	Virgin	60	16 Feb 80	3

FLYING PICKETS · UK

SINGLES:		HITS 3		WEEKS 20
ONLY YOU	10 Records	1	26 Nov 83	11
First a cappella song to top the chart.				
(WHEN YOU'RE) YOUNG AND IN LOVE	10 Records	7	21 Apr 84	8
Originally recorded by the Marvelettes.				
WHO'S THAT GIRL	10 Records	71	8 Dec 84	1
ALBUMS:		HITS 2		WEEKS 22
LIVE AT THE ALBANY EMPIRE	VAM	48	17 Dec 83	11
LOST BOYS	10 Records	11	9 Jun 84	11

Jerome FLYNN - See ROBSON and JEROME

FM · UK

SINGLES:		HITS 5		WEEKS 11
FROZEN HEART	Portrait	64	31 Jan 87	2
Original release reached No. 92 in 1985.				
LET LOVE BE THE LEADER	Portrait	71	20 Jun 87	2
BAD LUCK	Epic	54	5 Aug 89	4
SOMEDAY (YOU'LL COME RUNNING)	CBS	64	7 Oct 89	2
EVERYTIME I THINK OF YOU	Epic	73	10 Feb 90	1
ALBUMS:		HITS 2		WEEKS 3
INDISCREET	Portrait	76	20 Sep 86	1
TOUGH IT OUT	Epic	34	14 Oct 89	2

FOCUS · Holland

SINGLES:		HITS 2		WEEKS 21
HOCUS POCUS	Polydor	20	20 Jan 73	10
SYLVIA	Polydor	4	27 Jan 73	11
ALBUMS:		HITS 5		WEEKS 65
MOVING WAVES	Polydor	2	11 Nov 72	34
FOCUS 3	Polydor	6	2 Dec 72	15
FOCUS AT THE RAINBOW	Polydor	23	20 Oct 73	5
HAMBURGER CONCERTO	Polydor	20	25 May 74	5
FOCUS	Polydor	23	9 Aug 75	6

FOG · US

SINGLES:		HITS 1		WEEKS 4
BEEN A LONG TIME	Columbia	44	19 Feb 94	2
BEEN A LONG TIME [RM]	Pukka	27	6 Jun 98	2
Remixed by Full Intention.				

Dan FOGELBERG · US

SINGLES:		HITS 1		WEEKS 4
LONGER	Full Moon	59	15 Mar 80	4
ALBUMS:		HITS 1		WEEKS 3
PHOENIX	Full Moon	42	29 Mar 80	3

John FOGERTY · US

ALBUMS:		HITS 1		WEEKS 11
CENTERFIELD	Warner Brothers	48	16 Feb 85	11

Ben FOLDS FIVE

US

SINGLES:		HITS 5			WEEKS 12
UNDERGROUND	Caroline	37	14 Sep 96	2
BATTLE OF WHO COULD CARE LESS	Epic	26	1 Mar 97	3
KATE	Epic	39	7 Jun 97	2
BRICK	Epic	26	18 Apr 98	3
ARMY	Epic	28	24 Apr 99	2
ALBUMS:		HITS 3			WEEKS 6
WHATEVER AND EVER AMEN	Epic	30	15 Mar 97	3
NAKED BABY PHOTOS	Virgin	65	24 Jan 98	1
Compilation of live versions/out-takes from 1994–98.				
THE UNAUTHORIZED BIOGRAPHY OF REINHOLD MESSNER	Epic	22	8 May 99	2
Messner was the first mountaineer to scale Everest without oxygen.				

Ellen FOLEY

US

ALBUMS:		HITS 2			WEEKS 3
NIGHT OUT	Epic	68	17 Nov 79	1
SPIRIT OF ST. LOUIS	Epic	57	4 Apr 81	2

FOLK IMPLOSION

US

SINGLES:		HITS 1			WEEKS 1
NATURAL ONE	London	45	15 Jun 96	1
From the film 'Kids'.				

Jane FONDA

US

ALBUMS:		HITS 2			WEEKS 51
JANE FONDA'S WORKOUT RECORD	CBS	7	29 Jan 83	47
JANE FONDA'S WORKOUT RECORD: NEW AND IMPROVED	CBS	60	22 Sep 84	4

Claudia FONTAINE – See BEATMASTERS

Wayne FONTANA

UK

(See also Wayne Fontana and the Mindbenders.)

SINGLES:		HITS 4			WEEKS 31
IT WAS EASIER TO HURT HER	Fontana	36	11 Dec 65	6
COME ON HOME	Fontana	16	23 Apr 66	12
GOODBYE BLUEBIRD	Fontana	49	27 Aug 66	1
PAMELA, PAMELA	Fontana	11	10 Dec 66	12

Wayne FONTANA and the MINDBENDERS

UK

(See also Wayne Fontana; Mindbenders.)

SINGLES:		HITS 6			WEEKS 45
HELLO JOSEPHINE	Fontana	46	13 Jul 63	2
STOP LOOK AND LISTEN	Fontana	37	30 May 64	4
UM, UM, UM, UM, UM, UM	Fontana	5	10 Oct 64	15
THE GAME OF LOVE	Fontana	2	6 Feb 65	11
IT'S JUST A LITTLE BIT TOO LATE	Fontana	20	19 Jun 65	7
SHE NEEDS LOVE	Fontana	32	2 Oct 65	6
EPS:		HITS 2			WEEKS 20
UM, UM, UM, UM, UM, UM	Fontana	7	12 Dec 64	19
THE GAME OF LOVE	Fontana	19	15 May 65	1
ALBUMS:		HITS 1			WEEKS 1
WAYNE FONTANA AND THE MINDBENDERS	Fontana	18	20 Feb 65	1

FOO FIGHTERS

US

SINGLES:		HITS 9			WEEKS 27
THIS IS A CALL	Roswell	5	1 Jul 95	4
I'LL STICK AROUND	Roswell	18	16 Sep 95	3
FOR ALL THE COWS	Roswell	28	2 Dec 95	2
BIG ME	Roswell	19	6 Apr 96	3
MONKEY WRENCH	Roswell	12	10 May 97	4
EVERLONG	Roswell	18	30 Aug 97	3
MY HERO	Roswell	21	31 Jan 98	2
WALKING AFTER YOU	Elektra	20	29 Aug 98	3
[AA] listed with Beacon Light by Ween. From the film 'The X Files'.				
LEARN TO FLY	RCA	21	30 Oct 99	3
ALBUMS:		HITS 3			WEEKS 33
FOO FIGHTERS	Roswell	3	8 Jul 95	17
THE COLOUR AND THE SHAPE	Roswell	3	24 May 97	12
THERE IS NOTHING LEFT TO LOSE	RCA	10	13 Nov 99	4

FOOL BOONA | | | | UK

SINGLES:		HITS 1		WEEKS 1
POPPED!!	VC Recordings	52	10 Apr 99	1

Contains re-recorded samples from Iggy Pop's The Passenger.

FOOL'S GARDEN | | | | Germany

SINGLES:		HITS 1		WEEKS 4
LEMON TREE	Encore	61	25 May 96	1
LEMON TREE [RI]	Encore	26	3 Aug 96	3

FOR REAL | | | | US

SINGLES:		HITS 2		WEEKS 2
YOU DON'T KNOW NOTHIN'	A&M	54	1 Jul 95	1
LIKE I DO	Arista	45	12 Jul 97	1

Steve FORBERT | | | | US

ALBUMS:		HITS 2		WEEKS 3
ALIVE ON ARRIVAL	Epic	56	9 Jun 79	1
JACK RABBIT SLIM	Epic	54	24 Nov 79	2

Bill FORBES | | | | UK

SINGLES:		HITS 1		WEEKS 1
TOO YOUNG	Columbia	29	16 Jan 60	1

FORCE M.D.'S | | | | US

SINGLES:		HITS 1		WEEKS 9
TENDER LOVE	Tommy Boy	23	12 Apr 86	9

From the film 'Krush Groove'.

FORCE and STYLES featuring Kelly LLORENNA | | | | UK

(See also Kelly Llorenna.)

SINGLES:		HITS 1		WEEKS 1
HEART OF GOLD	Diverse	55	25 Jul 98	1

Baby FORD | | | | UK

SINGLES:		HITS 4		WEEKS 16
OOCHY KOOCHY (F.U. BABY YEAH YEAH)	Rhythm King	58	10 Sep 88	6
CHIKKI CHIKKI AHH AHH	Rhythm King	75	24 Dec 88	1
CHIKKI CHIKKI AHH AHH [RE]	Rhythm King	54	7 Jan 89	3
CHILDREN OF THE REVOLUTION	Rhythm King	53	17 Jun 89	4
BEACH BUMP	Rhythm King	68	17 Feb 90	2

Clinton FORD | | | | UK

SINGLES:		HITS 4		WEEKS 25
OLD SHEP	Oriole	27	24 Oct 59	1
TOO MANY BEAUTIFUL GIRLS (AND NOT ENOUGH TIME)	Oriole	48	19 Aug 61	1
FANLIGHT FANNY	Oriole	22	10 Mar 62	10

Above hit: Clinton FORD with the George CHISHOLM ALL-STARS.

RUN TO THE DOOR	Piccadilly	25	7 Jan 67	13
ALBUMS:		HITS 1		WEEKS 4
CLINTON FORD	Oriole	16	26 May 62	4

Emile FORD and the CHECKMATES | | | | US

SINGLES:		HITS 8		WEEKS 89
WHAT DO YOU WANT TO MAKE THOSE EYES AT ME FOR?	Pye Nixa	1	31 Oct 59	26

Originally recorded by Ada Jones and Billy Murray in 1917.

ON A SLOW BOAT TO CHINA	Pye	3	6 Feb 60	15

Originally recorded by Kay Kyser in 1948.

YOU'LL NEVER KNOW WHAT YOU'RE MISSIN' 'TIL YOU TRY	Pye	12	28 May 60	9
THEM THERE EYES	Pye	18	3 Sep 60	16

Above hit: Emile FORD; Johnny KEATING MUSIC; Babs KNIGHT GROUP.

COUNTING TEARDROPS	Pye	4	10 Dec 60	12

Originally recorded by Barry Mann.

WHAT AM I GONNA DO	Pye	33	4 Mar 61	6
HALF OF MY HEART	Piccadilly	50	20 May 61	1
HALF OF MY HEART [RE]	Piccadilly	42	24 Jun 61	3
I WONDER WHO'S KISSING HER NOW	Piccadilly	43	10 Mar 62	1

Originally recorded by Ada Reeve and Harry Woodruff in 1909.

EPS:		HITS 1		WEEKS 23
EMILE	Pye	1	9 Apr 60	23

Tennessee Ernie FORD
US

SINGLES:	HITS 3				WEEKS 42
GIVE ME YOUR WORD	Capitol	1		22 Jan 55	24
SIXTEEN TONS	Capitol	1		7 Jan 56	11
Originally recorded by Merle Travis.					
THE BALLAD OF DAVY CROCKETT	Capitol	3		14 Jan 56	7
From the film 'Davy Crockett, King Of The Wild Frontier'.					

Lita FORD
UK

SINGLES:	HITS 3				WEEKS 7
KISS ME DEADLY	RCA	75		17 Dec 88	1
CLOSE MY EYES FOREVER	Dreamland	47		20 May 89	3
Above hit: Lita FORD (Duet with Ozzy OSBOURNE).					
SHOT OF POISON	RCA	63		11 Jan 92	3
ALBUMS:	HITS 3				WEEKS 4
DANCIN' ON THE EDGE	Vertigo	96		26 May 84	1
STILETTO	RCA	66		23 Jun 90	1
DANGEROUS CURVES	RCA	51		25 Jan 92	2

Martyn FORD ORCHESTRA
UK

(See also Phil Collins.)

SINGLES:	HITS 1				WEEKS 3
LET YOUR BODY GO DOWNTOWN	Mountain	38		14 May 77	3

Mary FORD – See Les PAUL and Mary FORD

Penny FORD
US

SINGLES:	HITS 2				WEEKS 7
DANGEROUS	Total Experience	43		4 May 85	5
Above hit: Pennye FORD.					
DAYDREAMING	Columbia	43		29 May 93	2

Julia FORDHAM
UK

SINGLES:	HITS 5				WEEKS 32
HAPPY EVER AFTER	Circa	27		2 Jul 88	9
WHERE DOES THE TIME GO?	Circa	41		25 Feb 89	5
I THOUGHT IT WAS YOU	Circa	64		31 Aug 91	2
LOVE MOVES (IN MYSTERIOUS WAYS)	Circa	19		18 Jan 92	9
From the film 'The Butcher's Wife'.					
I THOUGHT IT WAS YOU [RM]	Circa	45		30 May 92	3
DIFFERENT TIME DIFFERENT PLACE	Circa	41		30 Apr 94	3
I CAN'T HELP MYSELF	Circa	62		23 Jul 94	1
ALBUMS:	HITS 4				WEEKS 36
JULIA FORDHAM	Circa	41		18 Jun 88	16
JULIA FORDHAM [RE]	Circa	20		18 Mar 89	6
PORCELAIN	Circa	13		21 Oct 89	5
SWEPT	Circa	33		2 Nov 91	3
SWEPT [RE]	Circa	46		7 Mar 92	3
Repackaged.					
FALLING FORWARD	Circa	21		21 May 94	3

FOREIGNER
US

SINGLES:	HITS 11				WEEKS 78
FEELS LIKE THE FIRST TIME	Atlantic	39		6 May 78	6
COLD AS ICE	Atlantic	24		15 Jul 78	10
Above 2 originally released in 1977.					
HOT BLOODED	Atlantic	42		28 Oct 78	3
BLUE MORNING, BLUE DAY	Atlantic	45		24 Feb 79	4
URGENT	Atlantic	54		29 Aug 81	4
Features Junior Walker on saxophone.					
JUKE BOX HERO	Atlantic	48		10 Oct 81	4
WAITING FOR A GIRL LIKE YOU	Atlantic	8		12 Dec 81	13
URGENT [RI]	Atlantic	45		8 May 82	5
I WANT TO KNOW WHAT LOVE IS	Atlantic	1		8 Dec 84	16
Features Tom Bailey of the Thompson Twins on keyboards and Jennifer Holliday on backing vocals.					
THAT WAS YESTERDAY	Atlantic	28		6 Apr 85	6
COLD AS ICE [RM]	Atlantic	64		22 Jun 85	2
SAY YOU WILL	Atlantic	71		19 Dec 87	4
WHITE LIE	Arista	58		22 Oct 94	1
ALBUMS:	HITS 8				WEEKS 126
DOUBLE VISION	Atlantic	32		26 Aug 78	5
4	Atlantic	5		25 Jul 81	62
RECORDS: THE BEST OF FOREIGNER	Atlantic	58		18 Dec 82	11

AGENT PROVOCATEUR	*Atlantic*	1	*22 Dec 84*	32
INSIDE INFORMATION	*Atlantic*	64	*19 Dec 87*	7
UNUSUAL HEAT	*Atlantic*	56	*6 Jul 91*	1
THE VERY BEST OF FOREIGNER	*Atlantic*	19	*2 May 92*	7
MR. MOONLIGHT	*Arista*	59	*12 Nov 94*	1

FORMATIONS   US

SINGLES:		HITS 1		WEEKS 11
AT THE TOP OF THE STAIRS	*Mojo*	50	*31 Jul 71*	1
AT THE TOP OF THE STAIRS [RE]	*Mojo*	28	*14 Aug 71*	10

George FORMBY with the Beryl STOTT CHORUS   UK

SINGLES:		HITS 1		WEEKS 3
HAPPY GO LUCKY ME / BANJO BOY	*Pye*	40	*23 Jul 60*	3

FORREST   US

SINGLES:		HITS 3		WEEKS 20
ROCK THE BOAT	*CBS*	4	*26 Feb 83*	10
FEEL THE NEED IN ME	*CBS*	17	*14 May 83*	8
ONE LOVER (DON'T STOP THE SHOW)	*CBS*	67	*17 Sep 83*	2

Sharon FORRESTER   Jamaica

SINGLES:		HITS 1		WEEKS 1
LOVE INSIDE	*ffrr*	50	*11 Feb 95*	1

FORTE - See FUGEES

Lance FORTUNE   UK

SINGLES:		HITS 2		WEEKS 18
BE MINE (ALLE MADCHEN WOLLEN KUSSEN)	*Pye*	4	*20 Feb 60*	13
THIS LOVE I HAVE FOR YOU	*Pye*	26	*7 May 60*	5

Above hit: Lance FORTUNE; Kim DRAKE MUSIC.

FORTUNES   UK

SINGLES:		HITS 5		WEEKS 65
YOU'VE GOT YOUR TROUBLES	*Decca*	2	*10 Jul 65*	14

Originally recorded by David and Jonathan.

HERE IT COMES AGAIN	*Decca*	4	*9 Oct 65*	14
THIS GOLDEN RING	*Decca*	15	*5 Feb 66*	9

Originally recorded by Cook & Greenaway.

FREEDOM COME, FREEDOM GO	*Capitol*	6	*11 Sep 71*	17
STORM IN A TEACUP	*Capitol*	7	*29 Jan 72*	11

Originally recorded by Lynsey De Paul.

40 THEVZ - See COOLIO

45 KING   US

SINGLES:		HITS 1		WEEKS 6
THE KING IS HERE / THE 900 NUMBER	*Trax*	60	*28 Oct 89*	5
THE 900 NUMBER [RE]	*Trax*	73	*11 Aug 90*	1

49ERS   Italy

SINGLES:		HITS 6		WEEKS 27
TOUCH ME	*Fourth & Broadway*	3	*16 Dec 89*	13

Samples Alisha Warren's recording of the same song title.

DON'T YOU LOVE ME	*Fourth & Broadway*	12	*17 Mar 90*	6
GIRL TO GIRL	*Fourth & Broadway*	31	*9 Jun 90*	3
GOT TO BE FREE	*Fourth & Broadway*	46	*6 Jun 92*	2
THE MESSAGE	*Fourth & Broadway*	68	*29 Aug 92*	1
ROCKIN' MY BODY	*Media*	31	*18 Mar 95*	2

Above hit: 49ERS featuring Ann-Marie SMITH.

ALBUMS:		HITS 1		WEEKS 5
THE 49ERS	*Fourth & Broadway*	51	*10 Mar 90*	5

Itsy FOSTER - See EXOTICA featuring Itsy FOSTER

Lawrence FOSTER - See LONDON SYMPHONY ORCHESTRA

FOSTER and ALLEN   Ireland

SINGLES:		HITS 6		WEEKS 47
A BUNCH OF THYME	*Ritz*	18	*27 Feb 82*	11
OLD FLAMES	*Ritz*	51	*30 Oct 82*	8
MAGGIE	*Ritz*	27	*19 Feb 83*	9
I WILL LOVE YOU ALL OF MY LIFE	*Ritz*	49	*29 Oct 83*	6

Title on label: I Will Love You All My Life.

JUST FOR OLD TIME'S SAKE	*Ritz*	47	*30 Jun 84*	6
AFTER ALL THESE YEARS	*Ritz*	43	*29 Mar 86*	7
ALBUMS:	**HITS 22**			**WEEKS 190**
COMPILATION ALBUMS:	**HITS 1**			**WEEKS 18**
MAGGIE	*Ritz*	72	*14 May 83*	6
I WILL LOVE YOU ALL OF MY LIFE	*Ritz*	71	*5 Nov 83*	6
THE VERY BEST OF FOSTER AND ALLEN	*Ritz*	18	*17 Nov 84*	18
AFTER ALL THESE YEARS	*Ritz*	82	*29 Mar 86*	2
REMINISCING	*Stylus*	11	*25 Oct 86*	15
LOVE SONGS – THE VERY BEST OF FOSTER AND ALLEN VOLUME 2	*Ritz*	92	*27 Jun 87*	1
REFLECTIONS	*Stylus*	16	*10 Oct 87*	16
REMEMBER YOU'RE MINE	*Stylus*	16	*30 Apr 88*	15
THE WORLDS OF FOSTER AND ALLEN	*Stylus*	21	*1 Oct 88*	15
Album consisted only of solo recordings, thus it was eligible for the compilation chart from 1989.				
THE WORLDS OF FOSTER AND ALLEN	*Stylus*	16	*14 Jan 89*	3
This is an entry in the compilation chart.				
THE MAGIC OF FOSTER AND ALLEN (THEIR GREATEST HITS)	*Stylus*	29	*28 Oct 89*	12
FOSTER AND ALLEN'S CHRISTMAS COLLECTION	*Stylus*	40	*9 Dec 89*	4
Chart shows title as 'The Foster And Allen Christmas Album'.				
SOUVENIRS	*Telstar*	15	*10 Nov 90*	12
THE CHRISTMAS COLLECTION	*Telstar*	44	*8 Dec 90*	4
MEMORIES	*Telstar*	18	*2 Nov 91*	11
HEART STRINGS	*Telstar*	37	*31 Oct 92*	10
BY REQUEST	*Telstar*	14	*23 Oct 93*	12
SONGS WE LOVE TO SING	*Telstar*	41	*5 Nov 94*	9
100 GOLDEN GREATS	*Telstar*	30	*4 Nov 95*	12
SOMETHING SPECIAL – 100 GOLDEN LOVE SONGS	*Telstar*	46	*2 Nov 96*	10
SHADES OF GREEN	*Telstar*	55	*26 Apr 97*	2
BEST FRIENDS	*Telstar TV*	36	*15 Nov 97*	8
GREATEST HITS	*Telstar TV*	52	*12 Dec 98*	4
ONE DAY AT A TIME	*Telstar TV*	61	*25 Dec 99*	1

FOTHERINGAY UK

ALBUMS:	**HITS 1**			**WEEKS 6**
FOTHERINGAY	*Island*	18	*11 Jul 70*	6

FOUNDATIONS UK

SINGLES:	**HITS 6**			**WEEKS 57**
BABY, NOW THAT I'VE FOUND YOU	*Pye*	1	*30 Sep 67*	16
BACK ON MY FEET AGAIN	*Pye*	18	*27 Jan 68*	10
ANY OLD TIME YOU'RE SAD AND LONELY	*Pye*	48	*4 May 68*	1
ANY OLD TIME YOU'RE SAD AND LONELY [RE]	*Pye*	50	*18 May 68*	1
BUILD ME UP BUTTERCUP	*Pye*	2	*23 Nov 68*	15
Co-written by Mike D'Abo from Manfred Mann.				
IN THE BAD, BAD OLD DAYS (BEFORE YOU LOVED ME)	*Pye*	8	*15 Mar 69*	10
BORN TO LIVE, BORN TO DIE	*Pye*	46	*13 Sep 69*	3
BUILD ME UP BUTTERCUP [RI]	*Sequal*	71	*12 Dec 98*	1
From the film 'There's Something About Mary'.				

FOUNTAINS OF WAYNE US

SINGLES:	**HITS 5**			**WEEKS 7**
RADIATION VIBE	*Atlantic*	32	*22 Mar 97*	2
SINK TO THE BOTTOM	*Atlantic*	42	*10 May 97*	1
SURVIVAL CAR	*Atlantic*	53	*26 Jul 97*	1
I WANT AN ALIEN FOR CHRISTMAS	*Atlantic*	36	*27 Dec 97*	2
DENISE	*Atlantic*	57	*20 Mar 99*	1
ALBUMS:	**HITS 1**			**WEEKS 1**
FOUNTAINS OF WAYNE	*Atlantic*	67	*7 Jun 97*	1

FOUR ACES US

SINGLES:	**HITS 7**			**WEEKS 40**
THREE COINS IN THE FOUNTAIN	*Brunswick*	5	*31 Jul 54*	5
From the film of the same name.				
THREE COINS IN THE FOUNTAIN [RE]	*Brunswick*	17	*23 Oct 54*	1
MISTER SANDMAN	*Brunswick*	9	*8 Jan 55*	5
Originally recorded by Vaughan Monroe.				
STRANGER IN PARADISE	*Brunswick*	6	*21 May 55*	6
LOVE IS A MANY SPLENDOURED THING	*Brunswick*	2	*19 Nov 55*	13
From the film of the same name.				
A WOMAN IN LOVE	*Brunswick*	19	*20 Oct 56*	3
Above 6: FOUR ACES featuring Al ALBERTS.				
FRIENDLY PERSUASION (THEE I LOVE)	*Brunswick*	29	*5 Jan 57*	1
From the film of the same name.				
THE WORLD OUTSIDE (THEME FROM WARSAW CONCERTO)	*Brunswick*	18	*24 Jan 59*	6

FOUR BUCKETEERS
UK

SINGLES:	HITS 1			WEEKS 6
THE BUCKET OF WATER SONG	CBS	26	3 May 80	6

From the ITV children's show 'Tiswas'.

FOUR ESQUIRES – vocal with the Sid BASS' ORCHESTRA
US

SINGLES:	HITS 1			WEEKS 2
LOVE ME FOREVER	London	23	1 Feb 58	2

4 HERO
UK

SINGLES:	HITS 3			WEEKS 5
COMBAT DANCING [EP]	Reinforced	73	24 Nov 90	2

Only the lead track Mr. Kirk's Nightmare was listed on 1 Dec 90.

COOKIN' UP YAH BRAIN	Reinforced	59	9 May 92	2
STAR CHASERS	Talkin Loud	41	15 Aug 98	1
ALBUMS:	HITS 1			WEEKS 6
TWO PAGES	Talkin Loud	38	25 Jul 98	6

400 BLOWS
UK

SINGLES:	HITS 1			WEEKS 4
MOVIN'	Illuminated	54	29 Jun 85	4

FOUR JAYS - See Billy FURY

FOUR KESTRELS - See Billy FURY

FOUR KNIGHTS
US

SINGLES:	HITS 2			WEEKS 13
I GET SO LONELY (WHEN I DREAM ABOUT YOU)	Capitol	5	5 Jun 54	7
I GET SO LONELY (WHEN I DREAM ABOUT YOU) [RE]	Capitol	10	31 Jul 54	4
MY PERSONAL POSSESSION	Capitol	21	19 Oct 57	2

Above hit: Nat "King" COLE and the FOUR KNIGHTS with Nelson RIDDLE's MUSIC.

FOUR LADS
Canada

SINGLES:	HITS 3			WEEKS 23
FAITH CAN MOVE MOUNTAINS	Columbia	7	20 Dec 52	2

Above hit: Johnnie RAY and the FOUR LADS.

FAITH CAN MOVE MOUNTAINS [RE]	Columbia	9	10 Jan 53	1
RAIN, RAIN, RAIN	Philips	8	23 Oct 54	16

Above hit: Frankie LAINE and the FOUR LADS with the Buddy COLE QUARTET.

STANDING ON THE CORNER	Philips	34	30 Apr 60	4

From the musical 'The Most Happy Fella'.

4 NON BLONDES
US

SINGLES:	HITS 2			WEEKS 19
WHAT'S UP?	Interscope	2	19 Jun 93	17
SPACEMAN	Interscope	53	16 Oct 93	2
ALBUMS:	HITS 1			WEEKS 18
BIGGER, BETTER, FASTER, MORE!	Interscope	4	17 Jul 93	18

4 OF US
Ireland

SINGLES:	HITS 2			WEEKS 6
SHE HITS ME	Columbia	35	27 Feb 93	4
I MISS YOU	Columbia	62	1 May 93	2
ALBUMS:	HITS 1			WEEKS 1
MAN ALIVE	Columbia	64	20 Mar 93	1

FOUR PENNIES
UK

SINGLES:	HITS 6			WEEKS 56
DO YOU WANT ME TO	Philips	47	18 Jan 64	1
DO YOU WANT ME TO [RE]	Philips	49	8 Feb 64	1
JULIET	Philips	1	4 Apr 64	15

The flip side, Tell Me Girl (What Are You Gonna Do), was initially promoted as the A-side.

I FOUND OUT THE HARD WAY	Philips	14	18 Jul 64	11
BLACK GIRL	Philips	20	31 Oct 64	12
UNTIL IT'S TIME FOR YOU TO GO	Philips	19	9 Oct 65	11

Originally recorded by Buffy St Marie.

TROUBLE IS MY MIDDLE NAME	Philips	32	19 Feb 66	5
EPS:	HITS 1			WEEKS 15
SPIN WITH THE PENNIES	Philips	6	1 Aug 64	15
ALBUMS:	HITS 1			WEEKS 5
TWO SIDES OF FOUR PENNIES	Philips	13	7 Nov 64	5

FOUR PREPS

US

SINGLES:		HITS 3			WEEKS 23
BIG MAN	Capitol	2	14 Jun 58		13
BIG MAN [RE]	Capitol	22	20 Sep 58		1
GOT A GIRL	Capitol	28	28 May 60		6
GOT A GIRL [RE]	Capitol	47	16 Jul 60		1
MORE MONEY FOR YOU AND ME [M]	Capitol	39	4 Nov 61		2

FOUR SEASONS

US

SINGLES:		HITS 17			WEEKS 151
SHERRY	Stateside	8	6 Oct 62		16
BIG GIRLS DON'T CRY	Stateside	13	19 Jan 63		10
WALK LIKE A MAN	Stateside	12	30 Mar 63		12
AIN'T THAT A SHAME	Stateside	38	29 Jun 63		3
Above 4: 4 SEASONS.					
RAG DOLL	Philips	2	29 Aug 64		13
LET'S HANG ON!	Philips	4	20 Nov 65		16
WORKING MY WAY BACK TO YOU	Philips	50	2 Apr 66		3
OPUS 17 (DON'T YOU WORRY 'BOUT ME)	Philips	20	4 Jun 66		9
I'VE GOT YOU UNDER MY SKIN	Philips	12	1 Oct 66		11
Originally recorded by Ray Noble and his Orchestra in 1936.					
TELL IT TO THE RAIN	Philips	37	14 Jan 67		5
Above 6: 4 SEASONS featuring the "Sound" Of Frankie VALLI.					
THE NIGHT	Mowest	7	19 Apr 75		9
Originally released in 1972.					
Above hit: Frankie VALLI and the FOUR SEASONS.					
WHO LOVES YOU	Warner Brothers	6	20 Sep 75		9
DECEMBER, 1963 (OH, WHAT A NIGHT)	Warner Brothers	1	31 Jan 76		10
The song's original year was 1933, and it was about the repeal of prohibition in the US.					
SILVER STAR	Warner Brothers	3	24 Apr 76		9
WE CAN WORK IT OUT	Warner Brothers	34	27 Nov 76		4
RHAPSODY	Warner Brothers	37	18 Jun 77		3
DOWN THE HALL	Warner Brothers	34	20 Aug 77		5
DECEMBER, 1963 (OH, WHAT A NIGHT) [RM]	BR	49	29 Oct 88		4
Remixed by Ben Liebrand.					
Above hit: Frankie VALLI and the FOUR SEASONS.					

ALBUMS:		HITS 8			WEEKS 64
SHERRY	Stateside	20	6 Jul 63		1
EDIZIOBE D'ORO	Philips	11	10 Apr 71		7
THE BIG ONES	Philips	37	20 Nov 71		1
THE FOUR SEASONS STORY	Private Stock	20	6 Mar 76		8
WHO LOVES YOU	Warner Brothers	12	6 Mar 76		17
GREATEST HITS	K-Tel	4	20 Nov 76		6
THE COLLECTION – THE 20 GREATEST HITS	Telstar	38	21 May 88		9
CD format is titled The 22 Greatest Hits.					
THE VERY BEST OF FRANKIE VALLI AND THE FOUR SEASONS	PolyGram TV	7	7 Mar 92		15
Above 2 contain Frankie Valli's solo and group material.					
Above 2: Frankie VALLI and the FOUR SEASONS.					

FOUR SHEPHERD BOYS - See Michael HOLLIDAY

4 THE CAUSE

US

SINGLES:		HITS 1			WEEKS 9
STAND BY ME	RCA	12	10 Oct 98		9

FOUR TOPS

US

(See also Supremes and the Four Tops.)

SINGLES:		HITS 27			WEEKS 298
I CAN'T HELP MYSELF	Tamla Motown	23	3 Jul 65		9
IT'S THE SAME OLD SONG	Tamla Motown	34	4 Sep 65		8
LOVING YOU IS SWEETER THAN EVER	Tamla Motown	21	23 Jul 66		12
Co-written by Stevie Wonder.					
REACH OUT I'LL BE THERE	Tamla Motown	1	15 Oct 66		16
STANDING IN THE SHADOWS OF LOVE	Tamla Motown	6	14 Jan 67		8
BERNADETTE	Tamla Motown	8	1 Apr 67		10
7-ROOMS OF GLOOM	Tamla Motown	12	17 Jun 67		9
YOU KEEP RUNNING AWAY	Tamla Motown	26	14 Oct 67		7
WALK AWAY RENEE	Tamla Motown	3	16 Dec 67		11
Original by Left Banke reached No. 5 in the US in 1966.					
IF I WERE A CARPENTER	Tamla Motown	7	16 Mar 68		11
YESTERDAY'S DREAMS	Tamla Motown	23	24 Aug 68		15
I'M IN A DIFFERENT WORLD	Tamla Motown	27	16 Nov 68		13
WHAT IS A MAN	Tamla Motown	16	31 May 69		11
DO WHAT YOU GOTTA DO	Tamla Motown	11	27 Sep 69		11
I CAN'T HELP MYSELF [RI]	Tamla Motown	10	21 Mar 70		11
IT'S ALL IN THE GAME	Tamla Motown	5	30 May 70		14

IT'S ALL IN THE GAME [RE]	*Tamla Motown*	48	*12 Sep 70*	2
STILL WATER (LOVE)	*Tamla Motown*	10	*3 Oct 70*	10
STILL WATER (LOVE) [RE]	*Tamla Motown*	44	*19 Dec 70*	2
JUST SEVEN NUMBERS (CAN STRAIGHTEN OUT MY LIFE)	*Tamla Motown*	36	*1 May 71*	5
SIMPLE GAME	*Tamla Motown*	3	*25 Sep 71*	11

Originally recorded by Moody Blues.

BERNADETTE [RI]	*Tamla Motown*	23	*11 Mar 72*	7
WALK WITH ME TALK WITH ME DARLING	*Tamla Motown*	32	*5 Aug 72*	6
KEEPER OF THE CASTLE	*Probe*	18	*18 Nov 72*	9
SWEET UNDERSTANDING LOVE	*Probe*	29	*10 Nov 73*	10
WHEN SHE WAS MY GIRL	*Casablanca*	3	*17 Oct 81*	10
DON'T WALK AWAY	*Casablanca*	16	*19 Dec 81*	11
TONIGHT I'M GONNA LOVE YOU ALL OVER	*Casablanca*	43	*6 Mar 82*	4
BACK TO SCHOOL AGAIN	*RSO*	62	*26 Jun 82*	2

From the film 'Grease 2'.

REACH OUT, I'LL BE THERE [RM]	*Motown*	11	*23 Jul 88*	9
INDESTRUCTIBLE [RM]	*Arista*	55	*17 Sep 88*	4

Above 2: remixed by Phil Harding and Ian Curnow.
Above hit: FOUR TOPS featuring Smokey ROBINSON.

LOCO IN ACAPULCO	*Arista*	7	*3 Dec 88*	13

From the film 'Buster'.

INDESTRUCTIBLE	*Arista*	30	*25 Feb 89*	7

This was actually the original US recording, it charted after the UK mix. Smokey Robinson was only credited on the back of the sleeves of both releases.
Above hit: FOUR TOPS featuring Smokey ROBINSON.

EPS:	**HITS 2**			**WEEKS 97**
THE FOUR TOPS	*Tamla Motown*	2	*29 Oct 66*	58
FOUR TOPS HITS	*Tamla Motown*	1	*11 Mar 67*	39

ALBUMS:	**HITS 11**			**WEEKS 244**
FOUR TOPS ON TOP	*Tamla Motown*	9	*19 Nov 66*	23
FOUR TOPS LIVE!	*Tamla Motown*	4	*11 Feb 67*	72

Live recordings from the Roostertail in Detroit.

REACH OUT	*Tamla Motown*	4	*25 Nov 67*	34
FOUR TOPS GREATEST HITS	*Tamla Motown*	1	*20 Jan 68*	67
YESTERDAY'S DREAMS	*Tamla Motown*	37	*8 Feb 69*	1
STILL WATERS RUN DEEP	*Tamla Motown*	29	*27 Jun 70*	8
FOUR TOPS' GREATEST HITS VOLUME 2	*Tamla Motown*	25	*27 Nov 71*	10
THE FOUR TOPS STORY 1964-72	*Tamla Motown*	35	*10 Nov 73*	5
THE BEST OF THE FOUR TOPS	*K-Tel*	13	*13 Feb 82*	13
THEIR GREATEST HITS	*Telstar*	47	*8 Dec 90*	6
THE SINGLES COLLECTION	*PolyGram TV*	11	*19 Sep 92*	5

4MANDU
UK

SINGLES:	**HITS 3**			**WEEKS 6**
THIS IS IT	*Arista*	45	*29 Jul 95*	3
DO IT FOR LOVE	*Arista*	45	*17 Feb 96*	2
BABY DON'T GO	*Arista*	47	*15 Jun 96*	1

FOURMOST
UK

SINGLES:	**HITS 6**			**WEEKS 64**
HELLO LITTLE GIRL	*Parlophone*	9	*14 Sep 63*	17
I'M IN LOVE	*Parlophone*	17	*28 Dec 63*	12

Above 2 written by Lennon & McCartney.

A LITTLE LOVING	*Parlophone*	6	*25 Apr 64*	13
HOW CAN I TELL HER	*Parlophone*	33	*15 Aug 64*	4
BABY I NEED YOUR LOVING	*Parlophone*	24	*28 Nov 64*	12
GIRLS GIRLS GIRLS	*Parlophone*	33	*11 Dec 65*	6

Originally recorded by the Coasters.

EPS:	**HITS 1**			**WEEKS 5**
FOURMOST SOUND	*Parlophone*	15	*29 Feb 64*	5

4-SKINS
UK

ALBUMS:	**HITS 1**			**WEEKS 4**
THE GOOD, THE BAD AND THE 4-SKINS	*Secret*	80	*17 Apr 82*	4

14-18
UK

SINGLES:	**HITS 1**			**WEEKS 4**
GOOD-BYE-EE	*Magnet*	33	*1 Nov 75*	4

Bernard FOWLER - See BOMB THE BASS

FOX
UK

SINGLES:	**HITS 3**			**WEEKS 29**
ONLY YOU CAN	*GTO*	3	*15 Feb 75*	11
IMAGINE ME IMAGINE YOU	*GTO*	15	*10 May 75*	8

S-S-S-SINGLE BED	GTO	4	10 Apr 76	10
ALBUMS:	**HITS 1**			**WEEKS 8**
FOX	GTO	7	17 May 75	8

Noosha FOX
UK

SINGLES:	**HITS 1**			**WEEKS 6**
GEORGINA BAILEY	GTO	31	12 Nov 77	6

Samantha FOX
UK

SINGLES:	**HITS 13**			**WEEKS 73**
TOUCH ME (I WANT YOUR BODY)	Jive	3	22 Mar 86	10
DO YA DO YA (WANNA PLEASE ME)	Jive	10	28 Jun 86	7
HOLD ON TIGHT	Jive	26	6 Sep 86	5
I'M ALL YOU NEED	Jive	41	13 Dec 86	6
NOTHING'S GONNA STOP ME NOW	Jive	8	30 May 87	9
I SURRENDER (TO THE SPIRIT OF THE NIGHT)	Jive	25	25 Jul 87	7
I PROMISE YOU (GET READY)	Jive	58	17 Oct 87	3
TRUE DEVOTION	Jive	62	19 Dec 87	3
NAUGHTY GIRLS (NEED LOVE TOO)	Jive	31	21 May 88	5
LOVE HOUSE	Jive	32	19 Nov 88	6
I ONLY WANNA BE WITH YOU	Jive	16	28 Jan 89	8
I WANNA HAVE SOME FUN	Jive	63	17 Jun 89	2
SANTA MARIA	All Around the World	31	28 Mar 98	2

Rap by Eagle E.
Above hit: DJ MILANO featuring Samantha FOX.

ALBUMS:	**HITS 3**			**WEEKS 18**
TOUCH ME	Jive	17	26 Jul 86	10
SAMANTHA FOX	Jive	22	1 Aug 87	6
I WANNA HAVE SOME FUN	Jive	46	18 Feb 89	2

Bruce FOXTON
UK

SINGLES:	**HITS 3**			**WEEKS 9**
FREAK	Arista	23	30 Jul 83	5
THIS IS THE WAY	Arista	56	29 Oct 83	3
IT MAKES ME WONDER	Arista	74	21 Apr 84	1
ALBUMS:	**HITS 1**			**WEEKS 4**
TOUCH SENSITIVE	Arista	68	12 May 84	4

Charlie FOXX - See Inez FOXX

Inez FOXX
US

SINGLES:	**HITS 2**			**WEEKS 8**
HURT BY LOVE	Sue	40	25 Jul 64	3
MOCKINGBIRD	United Artists	36	22 Feb 69	2

Above hit: Inez and Charlie FOXX.

MOCKINGBIRD [RE]	United Artists	33	22 Mar 69	3

John FOXX
UK

SINGLES:	**HITS 7**			**WEEKS 31**
UNDERPASS	Metal Beat	31	26 Jan 80	8
NO-ONE DRIVING	Metal Beat	32	29 Mar 80	4

Also available as a double single with the same catalogue number as the standard 7".

BURNING CAR	Metal Beat	35	19 Jul 80	7
MILES AWAY	Metal Beat	51	8 Nov 80	3
EUROPE AFTER THE RAIN	Metal Beat	40	29 Aug 81	5
ENDLESSLY	Virgin	66	2 Jul 83	3
YOUR DRESS	Virgin	61	17 Sep 83	1
ALBUMS:	**HITS 4**			**WEEKS 17**
METAMATIX	Metal Beat	18	2 Feb 80	7
THE GARDEN	Metal Beat	24	3 Oct 81	6
THE GOLDEN SECTION	Virgin	27	8 Oct 83	3
IN MYSTERIOUS WAYS	Virgin	85	5 Oct 85	1

FRAGGLES
UK/US

SINGLES:	**HITS 1**			**WEEKS 8**
FRAGGLE ROCK THEME	RCA	33	18 Feb 84	8

Theme from the Children's ITV series of the same name.

ALBUMS:	**HITS 1**			**WEEKS 4**
FRAGGLE ROCK	RCA	38	21 Apr 84	4

FRAGMA
Germany/Spain

SINGLES:	**HITS 1**			**WEEKS 6**
TOCA ME	Positiva	11	25 Sep 99	6

Roddy FRAME — UK

SINGLES:	HITS 1		WEEKS 2	
REASON FOR LIVING	*Independiente*	45	*19 Sep 98*	2
ALBUMS:	**HITS 1**		**WEEKS 1**	
THE NORTH STAR	*Independiente*	55	*3 Oct 98*	1

Peter FRAMPTON — UK

(See also Various Artists: Films – Original Soundtracks 'Sgt.Pepper's Lonely Hearts Club Band'.)

SINGLES:	HITS 4		WEEKS 24	
SHOW ME THE WAY	*A&M*	10	*1 May 76*	12
BABY I LOVE YOUR WAY	*A&M*	43	*11 Sep 76*	5
DO YOU FEEL LIKE WE DO	*A&M*	39	*6 Nov 76*	4
Above 3 are live recordings.				
I'M IN YOU	*A&M*	41	*23 Jul 77*	3
ALBUMS:	**HITS 2**		**WEEKS 49**	
FRAMPTON COMES ALIVE	*A&M*	6	*22 May 76*	39
Live recordings from the Winterland, San Francisco. Biggest selling live album of all time.				
I'M IN YOU	*A&M*	19	*18 Jun 77*	10

Connie FRANCIS — US

SINGLES:	HITS 23		WEEKS 244	
WHO'S SORRY NOW	*MGM*	1	*5 Apr 58*	25
Originally recorded by Isham Jones in 1923.				
I'M SORRY I MADE YOU CRY	*MGM*	11	*28 Jun 58*	10
Originally recorded by Henry Burr in 1918.				
STUPID CUPID / CAROLINA MOON	*MGM*	1	*23 Aug 58*	19
Carolina Moon had first credit on the charts of 22 Aug 58 and 29 Aug 58. Stupid Cupid originally recorded by Neil Sedaka, Carolina Moon originally recorded by Gene Austin in 1929.				
I'LL GET BY	*MGM*	19	*1 Nov 58*	6
Originally recorded by Ruth Etting in 1929.				
FALLIN'	*MGM*	20	*22 Nov 58*	5
Above 2 entries were separate sides of the same release, each had its own chart run.				
YOU ALWAYS HURT THE ONE YOU LOVE	*MGM*	13	*27 Dec 58*	7
MY HAPPINESS	*MGM*	4	*14 Feb 59*	14
Originally recorded by Jon and Sondra Steele in 1948.				
Above hit: Connie FRANCIS: David ROSE and his Orchestra.				
MY HAPPINESS [RE]	*MGM*	30	*30 May 59*	1
LIPSTICK ON YOUR COLLAR	*MGM*	3	*4 Jul 59*	16
PLENTY GOOD LOVIN'	*MGM*	18	*12 Sep 59*	6
AMONG MY SOUVENIRS	*MGM*	11	*5 Dec 59*	10
Originally recorded by Paul Whiteman in 1928.				
VALENTINO	*MGM*	27	*19 Mar 60*	8
MAMA / ROBOT MAN	*MGM*	2	*21 May 60*	19
Robot Man listed from 4 Jun 60.				
EVERYBODY'S SOMEBODY'S FOOL	*MGM*	5	*20 Aug 60*	13
MY HEART HAS A MIND OF ITS OWN	*MGM*	3	*5 Nov 60*	15
MANY TEARS AGO	*MGM*	12	*14 Jan 61*	9
WHERE THE BOYS ARE / BABY ROO	*MGM*	5	*18 Mar 61*	14
Baby Roo had first billing on 18 Mar 61, and from 13 May 61 was no longer listed. Where the Boys Are written by Neil Sedaka and from the film of same name.				
BREAKIN' IN A BRAND NEW BROKEN HEART	*MGM*	12	*17 Jun 61*	11
TOGETHER	*MGM*	6	*16 Sep 61*	11
Originally recorded by Paul Whiteman in 1928.				
BABY'S FIRST CHRISTMAS	*MGM*	30	*16 Dec 61*	4
DON'T BREAK THE HEART THAT LOVES YOU	*MGM*	39	*28 Apr 62*	3
VACATION	*MGM*	10	*4 Aug 62*	9
I'M GONNA BE WARM THIS WINTER	*MGM*	48	*22 Dec 62*	1
MY CHILD	*MGM*	26	*12 Jun 65*	6
JEALOUS HEART	*MGM*	44	*22 Jan 66*	2
Originally recorded by Al Morgan in 1949.				
EPS:	**HITS 2**		**WEEKS 17**	
HEARTACHES	*MGM*	14	*7 Jan 61*	2
FIRST LADY OF RECORD	*MGM*	7	*21 Jan 61*	15
ALBUMS:	**HITS 4**		**WEEKS 31**	
ROCK 'N' ROLL MILLION SELLERS	*MGM*	12	*26 Mar 60*	1
CONNIE'S GREATEST HITS	*MGM*	16	*11 Feb 61*	3
20 ALL TIME GREATS	*Polydor*	1	*18 Jun 77*	22
First solo female to top the album chart.				
THE SINGLES COLLECTION	*PolyGram TV*	12	*24 Apr 93*	5

Jill FRANCIS — UK

SINGLES:	HITS 1		WEEKS 1	
MAKE LOVE TO ME	*Glady Wax*	70	*3 Jul 93*	1

Claude FRANCOIS; Girl vocal: Kathy BARNET
France

SINGLES:	HITS 1			WEEKS 4
TEARS ON THE TELEPHONE	Bradley's	35	10 Jan 76	4

Joe FRANK – See HAMILTON, Joe FRANK and REYNOLDS

FRANK AND WALTERS
Ireland

SINGLES:	HITS 4			WEEKS 13
HAPPY BUSMAN	Setanta	49	21 Mar 92	2
THIS IS NOT A SONG	Setanta	46	12 Sep 92	3
AFTER ALL	Setanta	11	9 Jan 93	5
FASHION CRISIS HITS NEW YORK	Setanta	42	17 Apr 93	3
ALBUMS:	HITS 1			WEEKS 1
TRAINS, BOATS AND PLANES	Setanta	36	7 Nov 92	1

FRANKE
UK

(See also Our Tribe/One Tribe/O.T. Quartet.)

SINGLES:	HITS 1			WEEKS 2
UNDERSTAND THIS GROOVE	China	60	7 Nov 92	2

FRANK'EE – See BROTHER BROWN featuring FRANK'EE

FRANKIE GOES TO HOLLYWOOD
UK

SINGLES:	HITS 7			WEEKS 137
RELAX	ZTT	1	26 Nov 83	48
Reached No. 1 on 28 Jan 84, it dropped down the chart and climbed back to No. 2 on 7 Jul 84.				
TWO TRIBES	ZTT	1	16 Jun 84	20
Features the voice of Patrick Allen.				
TWO TRIBES [RE]	ZTT	73	10 Nov 84	1
THE POWER OF LOVE	ZTT	1	1 Dec 84	11
RELAX [RE]	ZTT	58	16 Feb 85	4
THE POWER OF LOVE [RE]	ZTT	64	23 Feb 85	1
WELCOME TO THE PLEASURE DOME	ZTT	2	30 Mar 85	11
RAGE HARD	ZTT	4	6 Sep 86	7
WARRIORS (OF THE WASTELAND)	ZTT	19	22 Nov 86	8
WATCHING THE WILDLIFE	ZTT	28	7 Mar 87	6
RELAX [RI]	ZTT	5	2 Oct 93	7
WELCOME TO THE PLEASUREDOME [RM]	ZTT	18	20 Nov 93	3
This is the original 7" mix before the 1985 single release was remixed.				
THE POWER OF LOVE [RI]	ZTT	10	18 Dec 93	7
TWO TRIBES [RM]	ZTT	16	26 Feb 94	3
Remixed by Fluke.				
ALBUMS:	HITS 3			WEEKS 94
WELCOME TO THE PLEASUREDOME	ZTT	1	10 Nov 84	58
LIVERPOOL	ZTT	5	1 Nov 86	13
BANG! - GREATEST HITS OF FRANKIE GOES TO HOLLYWOOD	ZTT	4	30 Oct 93	15
WELCOME TO THE PLEASUREDOME [RE-1ST]	ZTT	24	18 Feb 95	5
Re-released at mid-price.				
WELCOME TO THE PLEASUREDOME [RE-2ND]	ZTT	16	10 Jul 99	3

Aretha FRANKLIN
US

SINGLES:	HITS 29			WEEKS 182
RESPECT	Atlantic	10	10 Jun 67	14
Written by Otis Redding and features King Curtis on saxophone.				
BABY I LOVE YOU	Atlantic	39	26 Aug 67	4
CHAIN OF FOOLS / SATISFACTION	Atlantic	43	23 Dec 67	2
Chain Of Fools features Joe South on guitar.				
SATISFACTION [RE]	Atlantic	37	13 Jan 68	5
(SWEET SWEET BABY) SINCE YOU'VE BEEN GONE	Atlantic	47	16 Mar 68	1
THINK	Atlantic	26	25 May 68	9
I SAY A LITTLE PRAYER	Atlantic	4	10 Aug 68	14
Originally recorded by Dionne Warwick.				
DON'T PLAY THAT SONG	Atlantic	13	22 Aug 70	11
SPANISH HARLEM	Atlantic	14	2 Oct 71	9
ANGEL	Atlantic	37	8 Sep 73	5
UNTIL YOU COME BACK TO ME (THAT'S WHAT I'M GONNA DO)	Atlantic	26	16 Feb 74	8
Co-written by Stevie Wonder.				
WHAT A FOOL BELIEVES	Arista	46	6 Dec 80	7
LOVE ALL THE HURT AWAY	Arista	49	19 Sep 81	3
Above hit: Aretha FRANKLIN and George BENSON.				
JUMP TO IT	Arista	42	4 Sep 82	5
GET IT RIGHT	Arista	74	23 Jul 83	2
FREEWAY OF LOVE	Arista	68	13 Jul 85	3

SISTERS ARE DOIN' IT FOR THEMSELVES	RCA	9	2 Nov 85	11

Above hit: EURYTHMICS and Aretha FRANKLIN.

WHO'S ZOOMIN' WHO	Arista	11	23 Nov 85	14
ANOTHER NIGHT	Arista	54	22 Feb 86	6
FREEWAY OF LOVE [RE]	Arista	51	10 May 86	3
JUMPIN' JACK FLASH	Arista	58	25 Oct 86	3

From the film of the same name and produced by Keith Richards.

I KNEW YOU WERE WAITING (FOR ME)	Epic	1	31 Jan 87	9

Co-written by Simon Climie of Climie Fisher.
Above hit: Aretha FRANKLIN and George MICHAEL.

JIMMY LEE	Arista	46	14 Mar 87	4
THROUGH THE STORM	Arista	41	6 May 89	3

Above hit: Aretha FRANKLIN and Elton JOHN.

IT ISN'T, IT WASN'T, IT AIN'T NEVER GONNA BE	Arista	29	9 Sep 89	5

Label only credits Aretha Franklin.
Above hit: ARETHA and WHITNEY.

THINK [RR]	Atlantic	31	7 Apr 90	2

[AA] listed with Everybody Needs Somebody To Love by the Blues Brothers. From the film 'The Blues Brothers'.

EVERYDAY PEOPLE	Arista	69	27 Jul 91	1
A DEEPER LOVE	Arista	5	12 Feb 94	7

From the film 'Sister Act 2: Back In The Habit'.

WILLING TO FORGIVE	Arista	17	25 Jun 94	7
A ROSE IS STILL A ROSE	Arista	22	9 May 98	4
HERE WE GO AGAIN	Arista	68	26 Sep 98	1
ALBUMS:	**HITS 10**			**WEEKS 76**
I NEVER LOVED A MAN	Atlantic	36	12 Aug 67	2
LADY SOUL	Atlantic	25	13 Apr 68	18
ARETHA NOW	Atlantic	6	14 Sep 68	11
WHO'S ZOOMIN' WHO?	Arista	49	18 Jan 86	12
THE FIRST LADY OF SOUL	Stylus	89	24 May 86	1
ARETHA	Arista	51	8 Nov 86	13
THROUGH THE STORM	Arista	46	3 Jun 89	1
GREATEST HITS 1980-1994	Arista	27	19 Mar 94	3
QUEEN OF SOUL - THE VERY BEST OF ARETHA FRANKLIN	Atlantic	20	29 Oct 94	5
GREATEST HITS	Global Television	38	21 Nov 98	10

Erma FRANKLIN   US

SINGLES:	**HITS 1**			**WEEKS 10**
(TAKE A LITTLE) PIECE OF MY HEART	Epic	9	10 Oct 92	10

Featured in the Levi's Jeans TV commercial.

Rodney FRANKLIN   US

SINGLES:	**HITS 1**			**WEEKS 9**
THE GROOVE	CBS	7	19 Apr 80	9
ALBUMS:	**HITS 1**			**WEEKS 2**
YOU'LL NEVER KNOW	CBS	64	24 May 80	2

Chevelle FRANKLYN featuring BEENIE MAN   Jamaica

SINGLES:	**HITS 1**			**WEEKS 1**
DANCEHALL QUEEN	Island Jamaica	70	20 Sep 97	1

From the film of the same name.

FRANTIC FIVE – See Don LANG

FRANTIQUE   US

SINGLES:	**HITS 1**			**WEEKS 12**
STRUT YOUR FUNKY STUFF	Philadelphia International	10	11 Aug 79	12

Elizabeth FRASER – See Harold BUDD, Elizabeth FRASER, Robin GUTHRIE and Simon RAYMONDE; FUTURE SOUND OF LONDON; Ian McCULLOCH.

Wendy FRASER – See Patrick SWAYZE featuring Wendy FRASER

FRASH   UK

SINGLES:	**HITS 1**			**WEEKS 1**
HERE I GO AGAIN	PWL International	69	18 Feb 95	1

FRAZIER CHORUS   UK

SINGLES:	**HITS 6**			**WEEKS 14**
DREAM KITCHEN	Virgin	57	4 Feb 89	3
TYPICAL!	Virgin	53	15 Apr 89	2
SLOPPY HEART	Virgin	73	15 Jul 89	1
CLOUD 8	Virgin	52	9 Jun 90	3
NOTHING	Virgin	51	25 Aug 90	3
WALKING ON AIR	Virgin	60	16 Feb 91	2

ALBUMS:	HITS 2		WEEKS 2	
SUE	*Virgin*	56	*20 May 89*	1
RAY	*Virgin*	66	*16 Mar 91*	1

FREAK OF NATURE
US/Denmark

ALBUMS:	HITS 1		WEEKS 1	
GATHERING OF FREAKS	*Music For Nations*	66	*1 Oct 94*	1

FREAK POWER
UK/Canada

SINGLES:	HITS 4		WEEKS 20	
TURN ON, TUNE IN, COP OUT	*Fourth & Broadway*	29	*16 Oct 93*	5
RUSH	*Fourth & Broadway*	62	*26 Feb 94*	2
TURN ON, TUNE IN, COP OUT [RI]	*Fourth & Broadway*	3	*18 Mar 95*	9
Featured in the Levi's Jeans 'Taxi' TV commercial.				
NEW DIRECTION	*Fourth & Broadway*	60	*8 Jun 96*	1
NO WAY	*Deconstruction*	29	*9 May 98*	3
ALBUMS:	HITS 1		WEEKS 5	
DRIVE-THRU BOOTY	*Fourth & Broadway*	11	*15 Apr 95*	5

FREAKY REALISTIC
UK/Japan

SINGLES:	HITS 2		WEEKS 3	
KOOCHIE RYDER	*Frealism*	52	*3 Apr 93*	2
LEONARD NIMOY	*Polydor*	71	*3 Jul 93*	1

FREAKYMAN
Holland

SINGLES:	HITS 1		WEEKS 1	
DISCOBUG '97	*Xtravaganza*	68	*27 Sep 97*	1
Originally released in 1996.				

Stan FREBERG
US

SINGLES:	HITS 3		WEEKS 5	
SH-BOOM (LIFE COULD BE A DREAM)	*Capitol*	15	*20 Nov 54*	2
Above hit: Stan FREBERG with the TOADS featuring Jessie WHITE Music by Billy MAY with the TOADS.				
ROCK ISLAND LINE / HEARTBREAK HOTEL	*Capitol*	24	*28 Jul 56*	1
Above hit: Stan FREBERG and his SNIFFLE GROUP Interruptions by Peter LEEDS / Stan FREBERG Echo by MAMMOTH CAVE.				
ROCK ISLAND LINE / HEARTBREAK HOTEL [RE]	*Capitol*	29	*11 Aug 56*	1
THE OLD PAYOLA ROLL BLUES	*Capitol*	40	*14 May 60*	1
Above hit: Stan FREBERG with the TOADS featuring Jessie WHITE Music by Billy MAY with the TOADS.				

John FRED and his PLAYBOY BAND
US

SINGLES:	HITS 1		WEEKS 12	
JUDY IN DISGUISE (WITH GLASSES)	*Pye International*	3	*6 Jan 68*	12
Title based on Lucy In The Sky With Diamonds.				

FREDDIE and the DREAMERS
UK

SINGLES:	HITS 9		WEEKS 85	
IF YOU GOTTA MAKE A FOOL OF SOMEBODY	*Columbia*	3	*11 May 63*	14
Original by James Ray reached No. 22 in the US in 1962.				
I'M TELLIN' YOU NOW	*Columbia*	2	*10 Aug 63*	11
YOU WERE MADE FOR ME	*Columbia*	3	*9 Nov 63*	15
OVER YOU	*Columbia*	13	*22 Feb 64*	11
I LOVE YOU BABY	*Columbia*	16	*16 May 64*	8
JUST FOR YOU	*Columbia*	41	*18 Jul 64*	3
I UNDERSTAND	*Columbia*	5	*7 Nov 64*	15
A LITTLE YOU	*Columbia*	26	*24 Apr 65*	5
THOU SHALT NOT STEAL	*Columbia*	44	*6 Nov 65*	3
EPS:	HITS 3		WEEKS 14	
IF YOU GOTTA MAKE A FOOL OF SOMEBODY	*Columbia*	8	*19 Oct 63*	11
SONGS FROM THE FILM "WHAT A CRAZY WORLD"	*Columbia*	15	*8 Feb 64*	2
OVER YOU	*Columbia*	17	*4 Jul 64*	1
ALBUMS:	HITS 1		WEEKS 26	
FREDDIE AND THE DREAMERS	*Columbia*	5	*9 Nov 63*	26

FREDERIK – See NINA and FREDERIK

Dee FREDRIX
UK

SINGLES:	HITS 2		WEEKS 5	
AND SO I WILL WAIT FOR YOU	*East West*	56	*27 Feb 93*	4
DIRTY MONEY	*East West*	74	*3 Jul 93*	1

FREE
UK

SINGLES:	HITS 5		WEEKS 75	
ALL RIGHT NOW	Island	2	6 Jun 70	16
MY BROTHER JAKE	Island	4	1 May 71	11
LITTLE BIT OF LOVE	Island	13	27 May 72	10
WISHING WELL	Island	7	13 Jan 73	10
ALL RIGHT NOW [RE]	Island	15	21 Jul 73	9
FREE [EP]	Island	11	18 Feb 78	7
Lead track: All Right Now (re-issue).				
FREE [EP] [RE]	Island	57	23 Oct 82	3
ALL RIGHT NOW [RM]	Island	8	9 Feb 91	9
Featured in the Wrigley's Chewing Gum TV commercial. Remixed by Bob Clearmountain.				
ALBUMS:	HITS 7		WEEKS 71	
FIRE AND WATER	Island	2	11 Jul 70	18
HIGHWAY	Island	41	23 Jan 71	10
FREE LIVE!	Island	4	26 Jun 71	12
FREE AT LAST	Island	9	17 Jun 72	9
HEARTBREAKER	Island	9	3 Feb 73	7
THE FREE STORY	Island	2	16 Mar 74	6
THE BEST OF FREE – ALL RIGHT NOW	Island	9	2 Mar 91	9

FREE - See BOUNTY KILLER (featuring COCOA BROVAZ, Nona HENDRYX and FREE) Wyclef JEAN; QUEEN; QUEEN LATIFAH

FREE SPIRIT
UK

SINGLES:	HITS 1		WEEKS 1	
NO MORE RAINY DAYS	Columbia	68	13 May 95	1
Vocals by Elaine Vassel.				

FREE THE SPIRIT
UK

ALBUMS:	HITS 3		WEEKS 42	
PAN PIPE MOODS	PolyGram TV	2	4 Feb 95	26
PAN PIPES MOODS TWO	PolyGram TV	18	4 Nov 95	11
PAN PIPE MOODS IN PARADISE	PolyGram TV	26	25 May 96	5

FREEEZ
UK

SINGLES:	HITS 5		WEEKS 48	
KEEP IN TOUCH	Calibre	49	7 Jun 80	3
SOUTHERN FREEEZ	Beggars Banquet	8	7 Feb 81	11
FLYING HIGH	Beggars Banquet	35	18 Apr 81	5
I.O.U.	Beggars Banquet	2	18 Jun 83	15
POP GOES MY LOVE	Beggars Banquet	26	1 Oct 83	6
I.O.U. (THE ULTIMATE MIXES – '87) [RM]	Citybeat	23	17 Jan 87	6
Above hit: FREEEZ featuring John ROCCA.				
SOUTHERN FREEEZ [RM]	Total Control	63	30 May 87	2
ALBUMS:	HITS 2		WEEKS 18	
SOUTHERN FREEEZ	Beggars Banquet	17	7 Feb 81	15
GONNA GET YOU	Beggars Banquet	46	22 Oct 83	3

FREEFALL featuring Jan JOHNSTON
UK/US

SINGLES:	HITS 1		WEEKS 1	
SKYDIVE	Stress	75	28 Nov 98	1

FREEFALL featuring PSYCHOTROPIC
UK/Australia

SINGLES:	HITS 1		WEEKS 1	
FEEL SURREAL	ffrr	63	27 Jul 91	1

FREESTYLERS
UK

SINGLES:	HITS 3		WEEKS 5	
B-BOY STANCE	Freskanova	23	7 Feb 98	3
Above hit: FREESTYLERS featuring TENOR FLY.				
WARNING	Freskanova	68	14 Nov 98	1
Above hit: FREESTYLERS featuring NAVIGATOR.				
HERE WE GO	Freskanova	45	24 Jul 99	1
Additional vocals by Navigator.				
Above hit: FREESTYLERS featuring DEFINITION OF SOUND.				
ALBUMS:	HITS 1		WEEKS 3	
WE ROCK HARD	Freskanova	33	15 Aug 98	3

FREHLEY'S COMET
US

ALBUMS:	HITS 1		WEEKS 1	
SECOND SIGHTING	Atlantic	79	18 Jun 88	1

FREIHEIT
Germany

SINGLES:		HITS 1			WEEKS 9
KEEPING THE DREAM ALIVE	CBS	14	17 Dec 88	9

Debbie FRENCH – See Joey NEGRO

Deborah FRENCH – See E-LUSTRIOUS

Nicki FRENCH
UK

SINGLES:		HITS 3			WEEKS 16
TOTAL ECLIPSE OF THE HEART	Bags Of Fun	54	15 Oct 94	1
TOTAL ECLIPSE OF THE HEART [RE]	Bags Of Fun	5	14 Jan 95	12
FOR ALL WE KNOW	Bags Of Fun	42	22 Apr 95	2
DID YOU EVER REALLY LOVE ME?	Love This	55	15 Jul 95	1

FREQUENCY 9 – See VARIOUS ARTISTS (EPs) 'The Further Adventures Of North – More Underground Dance EP'

Doug E. FRESH and the GET FRESH CREW
US

SINGLES:		HITS 1			WEEKS 11
THE SHOW	Cooltempo	7	9 Nov 85	11

Freddy FRESH
US

SINGLES:		HITS 2			WEEKS 3
BADDER BADDER SCHWING	Eye Q	34	1 May 99	2
Above hit: Freddy FRESH (featuring FATBOY SLIM).				
WHAT IT IS	Eye Q	63	31 Jul 99	1

FRESH 4 (CHILDREN OF THE GHETTO) featuring Lizz E
UK

SINGLES:		HITS 1			WEEKS 9
WISHING ON A STAR	10 Records	10	7 Oct 89	9

FRESH PRINCE – See JAZZY JEFF and the FRESH PRINCE

FRESHIES
UK

SINGLES:		HITS 1			WEEKS 3
I'M IN LOVE WITH THE GIRL ON A CERTAIN MANCHESTER MEGASTORE CHECKOUT DESK	MCA	54	14 Feb 81	3
Original copies on the Razz record label credited the title as I'm In Love With A Girl On A Certain Virgin Manchester Megastore Checkout Desk.				

Matt FRETTON
UK

SINGLES:		HITS 1			WEEKS 5
IT'S SO HIGH	Chrysalis	50	11 Jun 83	5

FREUR
UK

SINGLES:		HITS 1			WEEKS 4
DOOT DOOT	CBS	59	23 Apr 83	4

Glenn FREY
US

SINGLES:		HITS 2			WEEKS 20
THE HEAT IS ON (FROM 'BEVERLY HILLS COP')	MCA	12	2 Mar 85	12
From the film 'Beverly Hills Cop'.				
SMUGGLER'S BLUES	BBC	22	22 Jun 85	8
From the BBC TV series 'Miami Vice'.				

ALBUMS:		HITS 1			WEEKS 9
THE ALLNIGHTER	MCA	31	6 Jul 85	9

FRIDA
Norway

SINGLES:		HITS 2			WEEKS 12
I KNOW THERE'S SOMETHING GOING ON	Epic	43	21 Aug 82	7
Production and drums by Phil Collins.				
TIME	Epic	45	17 Dec 83	5
Above hit: FRIDA and B.A. ROBERTSON.				

ALBUMS:		HITS 2			WEEKS 8
SOMETHING'S GOING ON	Epic	18	18 Sep 82	7
SHINE	Epic	67	20 Oct 84	1

Gavin FRIDAY – See BONO

Ralph FRIDGE
Germany

SINGLES:		HITS 1			WEEKS 1
PARADISE	Additive	68	24 Apr 99	1

Dean FRIEDMAN | US

SINGLES:	HITS 3			WEEKS 22	
WOMAN OF MINE	Lifesong	52	3 Jun 78		5
LUCKY STARS	Lifesong	3	23 Sep 78		10
This is a duet with female vocalist Denise Marser.					
LYDIA	Lifesong	31	18 Nov 78		7
ALBUMS:	**HITS 1**			**WEEKS 14**	
WELL, WELL, SAID THE ROCKING CHAIR	Lifesong	21	21 Oct 78		14

FRIENDS AGAIN | UK

SINGLES:	HITS 1			WEEKS 3	
THE FRIENDS AGAIN [EP]	Mercury	59	4 Aug 84		3
Lead track: Lullaby No. 2 Love On Board.					

FRIENDS OF MATTHEW | UK

SINGLES:	HITS 1			WEEKS 1	
OUT THERE	Serious	61	10 Jul 99		1
Originally released on Pulse-8 Records in 1991. Vocals by Sally Kemp.					

FRIGID VINEGAR | UK

SINGLES:	HITS 1			WEEKS 1	
DOGMONAUT 2000 (IS THERE ANYBODY OUT THERE?)	Gut	53	21 Aug 99		1
Samples Les Reed's brass arrangement of It's Not Unusual.					

FRIJID PINK | US

SINGLES:	HITS 1			WEEKS 16	
THE HOUSE OF THE RISING SUN	Deram	4	28 Mar 70		16

Robert FRIPP | UK

(See also David Sylvian and Robert Fripp.)

ALBUMS:	HITS 1			WEEKS 1	
EXPOSURE	Polydor	71	12 May 79		1

FROG CHORUS – See Paul McCARTNEY

Jane FROMAN | US

SINGLES:	HITS 1			WEEKS 4	
I WONDER	Capitol	14	18 Jun 55		4

FRONT 242 | US/Belgium

SINGLES:	HITS 1			WEEKS 1	
RELIGION	RRE	46	1 May 93		1
ALBUMS:	**HITS 3**			**WEEKS 3**	
TYRANNY FOR YOU	RRE	49	2 Feb 91		1
06:21:03:11 UP EVIL	RRE	44	22 May 93		1
05:22:09:12 OFF	RRE	46	4 Sep 93		1

Bernard FROST – See Francis ROSSI

Christian FRY | UK

SINGLES:	HITS 2			WEEKS 3	
YOU GOT ME	Mushroom	45	14 Nov 98		2
WON'T YOU STAY	Mushroom	48	3 Apr 99		1

FSOL – See FUTURE SOUND OF LONDON

FUGAZI | US

ALBUMS:	HITS 4			WEEKS 6	
STEADY DIET OF NOTHING	Dischord	63	21 Sep 91		1
IN ON THE KILLTAKER	Dischord	24	19 Jun 93		2
RED MEDICINE	Dischord	18	13 May 95		2
END HITS	Dischord	47	25 Apr 98		1

FUGEES (REFUGEE CAMP) | US

SINGLES:	HITS 6			WEEKS 58	
FU-GEE-LA	Columbia	21	6 Apr 96		5
Samples Ooh La La La by Teena Marie.					
KILLING ME SOFTLY	Columbia	1	8 Jun 96		20
READY OR NOT	Columbia	1	14 Sep 96		12
Samples Enya's Song For Bodecia.					
NO WOMAN, NO CRY	Columbia	2	30 Nov 96		9
Features Bob Marley's son Steve.					

RUMBLE IN THE JUNGLE	Mercury	3	15 Mar 97	8

Samples Abba's The Name Of The Game. From the film 'When We Were Kings'.
Above hit: FUGEES featuring A TRIBE CALLED QUEST, Busta RHYMES and FORTE.

THE SWEETEST THING	Columbia	18	6 Sep 97	4

Rap by John Forte. From the film 'Love Jones'.
Above hit: REFUGEE CAMP ALLSTARS featuring Lauryn HILL.

ALBUMS:	HITS 2		WEEKS 72	
THE SCORE	Columbia	2	30 Mar 96	70

Peak position reached on 5 Oct 96.

THE BOOTLEG VERSIONS	Columbia	55	7 Dec 96	2

Mini album features mixes from their first album 'Blunted On Reality'.

FULL CIRCLE — US

SINGLES:	HITS 1		WEEKS 5	
WORKIN' UP A SWEAT	EMI America	41	7 Mar 87	5

FULL FORCE — US

SINGLES:	HITS 3		WEEKS 32	
I WONDER IF I TAKE YOU HOME	CBS	53	4 May 85	6

Above hit: LISA LISA and CULT JAM with FULL FORCE.

I WONDER IF I TAKE YOU HOME [RE]	CBS	12	3 Aug 85	11
ALICE, I WANT YOU JUST FOR ME!	CBS	9	21 Dec 85	11
I'M REAL	Scotti Brothers	31	4 Jun 88	4

Above hit: James BROWN with FULL FORCE.

ALBUMS:	HITS 1		WEEKS 1	
LISA LISA AND CULT JAM WITH FULL FORCE	CBS	96	21 Sep 85	1

Above hit: LISA LISA and CULT JAM with FULL FORCE.

FULL INTENTION — UK

SINGLES:	HITS 4		WEEKS 7	
AMERICA (I LOVE AMERICA)	Stress	32	6 Apr 96	2
UPTOWN DOWNTOWN	Stress	61	10 Aug 96	1
SHAKE YOUR BODY (DOWN TO THE GROUND)	Sugar Daddy	34	26 Jul 97	2
AMERICA (I LOVE AMERICA) [RE]	Stress	56	22 Nov 97	1
YOU ARE SOMEBODY	Sugar Daddy	75	6 Jun 98	1

FULL MONTY — UK

SINGLES:	HITS 1		WEEKS 1	
THE FULL MONTY MONSTER MIX [M]	RCA Victor	62	12 Sep 98	1

Medley of 3 tracks from the film.

FULL MONTY ALLSTARS featuring T.J. DAVIS — UK

SINGLES:	HITS 1		WEEKS 1	
BRILLIANT FEELING	Arista	72	27 Jul 96	1

Bobby FULLER FOUR — US

SINGLES:	HITS 1		WEEKS 4	
I FOUGHT THE LAW	London	33	16 Apr 66	4

Originally recorded by the Crickets, and features Barry White on drums.

FUN BOY THREE — UK

SINGLES:	HITS 8		WEEKS 70	
THE LUNATICS (HAVE TAKEN OVER THE ASYLUM)	Chrysalis	20	7 Nov 81	12
IT AIN'T WHAT YOU DO IT'S THE WAY THAT YOU DO IT	Chrysalis	4	13 Feb 82	10

Originally recorded by Jimmy Lunceford.
Above hit: FUN BOY THREE with BANANARAMA.

REALLY SAYING SOMETHING (HE WAS REALLY SAYIN' SOMETHIN')	Deram	5	10 Apr 82	10

Originally recorded by the Velvelettes.
Above hit: BANANARAMA and the FUN BOY THREE.

THE TELEPHONE ALWAYS RINGS	Chrysalis	17	8 May 82	9
SUMMERTIME	Chrysalis	18	31 Jul 82	8
THE MORE I SEE (THE LESS I BELIEVE)	Chrysalis	68	15 Jan 83	1
TUNNEL OF LOVE	Chrysalis	10	5 Feb 83	10
OUR LIPS ARE SEALED	Chrysalis	7	30 Apr 83	10

ALBUMS:	HITS 2		WEEKS 40	
THE FUN BOY THREE	Chrysalis	7	20 Mar 82	20
WAITING	Chrysalis	14	19 Feb 83	20

FUN DA MENTAL — UK

ALBUMS:	HITS 1		WEEKS 1	
SIEZE THE TIME	Nation	74	25 Jun 94	1

FUN LOVIN' CRIMINALS
US

SINGLES:		HITS 8		WEEKS 24	
THE GRAVE AND THE CONSTANT	Chrysalis	72	8 Jun 96	1
SCOOBY SNACKS	Chrysalis	22	17 Aug 96	3
THE FUN LOVIN' CRIMINAL	Chrysalis	26	16 Nov 96	3
KING OF NEW YORK	Chrysalis	28	29 Mar 97	3
I'M NOT IN LOVE / SCOOBY SNACKS [RI]	Chrysalis	12	5 Jul 97	5
LOVE UNLIMITED	Chrysalis	18	15 Aug 98	4
Tribute to Barry White.				
BIG NIGHT OUT	Chrysalis	29	17 Oct 98	2
Samples Tom Petty's American Girl and Marshall Tucker Band's Can't You See.				
KOREAN BODEGA	Chrysalis	15	8 May 99	3

ALBUMS:		HITS 3		WEEKS 96	
COME FIND YOURSELF	Chrysalis	10	13 Jul 96	28
COME FIND YOURSELF [RE]	Chrysalis	7	28 Jun 97	41
100% COLOMBIAN	Chrysalis	3	5 Sep 98	23
MIMOSA	Chrysalis	37	11 Dec 99	4

Farley "Jackmaster" FUNK
US

SINGLES:		HITS 2		WEEKS 16	
LOVE CAN'T TURN AROUND	DJ International	10	23 Aug 86	12
Above hit: Farley "Jackmaster" FUNK and Jessie SAUNDERS.				
AS ALWAYS	Champion	49	11 Feb 89	2
Above hit: Farley 'Jackmaster' FUNK Presents Ricky DILLARD.				
LOVE CAN'T TURN AROUND [RM]	4 Liberty	40	14 Dec 96	2
Above hit: Farley 'Jackmaster' FUNK featuring Darryl PANDY.				

FUNK JUNKEEZ
US

SINGLES:		HITS 1		WEEKS 1	
GOT FUNK	Evocative	57	21 Feb 98	1

FUNK MASTER
UK

SINGLES:		HITS 1		WEEKS 12	
IT'S OVER	Master-Funk	8	18 Jun 83	12

FUNKADELIC
US

(See also Scott Grooves.)

SINGLES:		HITS 1		WEEKS 12	
ONE NATION UNDER A GROOVE	Warner Brothers	9	9 Dec 78	12

ALBUMS:		HITS 1		WEEKS 5	
ONE NATION UNDER A GROOVE	Warner Brothers	56	23 Dec 78	5

FUNKAPOLITAN
UK

SINGLES:		HITS 1		WEEKS 7	
AS THE TIME GOES BY	London	41	22 Aug 81	7

FUNKDOOBIEST
US

SINGLES:		HITS 2		WEEKS 6	
WOPBABALUBOP	Epic	37	11 Dec 93	4
BOW WOW WOW	Epic	34	5 Mar 94	2

ALBUMS:		HITS 1		WEEKS 1	
BROTHAS DOOBIE	Epic	62	15 Jul 95	1

FUNKSTAR DE LUXE - See Bob MARLEY and the WAILERS

FUNKY CHOAD featuring Nick SKITZ
Australia/Italy

SINGLES:		HITS 1		WEEKS 1	
THE ULTIMATE	ffrr	51	29 Aug 98	1

FUNKY GREEN DOGS
US

SINGLES:		HITS 4		WEEKS 6	
FIRED UP!	Twisted UK	17	12 Apr 97	3
THE WAY	Twisted UK	43	28 Jun 97	1
UNTIL THE DAY	Twisted UK	75	20 Jun 98	1
BODY	Twisted UK	46	27 Feb 99	1

FUNKY POETS
US

SINGLES:		HITS 1		WEEKS 1	
BORN IN THE GHETTO	Epic	72	7 May 94	1

FUNKY WORM
UK

SINGLES:	HITS 3		WEEKS 14	
HUSTLE! (TO THE MUSIC . . .)	FON	13	30 Jul 88	8
THE SPELL!	FON	61	26 Nov 88	3
U + ME = LOVE	FON	46	20 May 89	3

FUREYS and Davey ARTHUR
Ireland

SINGLES:	HITS 2		WEEKS 14	
WHEN YOU WERE SWEET SIXTEEN	Ritz	14	10 Oct 81	11
Originally recorded by George C. Gaskin in 1900.				
I WILL LOVE YOU (EVERYTIME WHEN WE ARE GONE)	Ritz	54	3 Apr 82	3
Above hit: FUREYS.				

ALBUMS:	HITS 4		WEEKS 38	
WHEN YOU WERE SWEET SIXTEEN	Ritz	99	8 May 82	1
GOLDEN DAYS	K-Tel	17	10 Nov 84	19
AT THE END OF THE DAY	K-Tel	35	26 Oct 85	11
FUREYS FINEST	Telstar	65	21 Nov 87	7

FURIOUS FIVE - See GRANDMASTER FLASH and the FURIOUS FIVE; Melle MEL

FURNITURE
UK

SINGLES:	HITS 1		WEEKS 10	
BRILLIANT MIND	Stiff	21	14 Jun 86	10

Billy FURY
UK

SINGLES:	HITS 29		WEEKS 281	
MAYBE TOMORROW	Decca	22	28 Feb 59	3
MAYBE TOMORROW [RE]	Decca	18	28 Mar 59	6
MARGO	Decca	28	27 Jun 59	1
COLLETTE	Decca	9	12 Mar 60	10
THAT'S LOVE	Decca	19	28 May 60	11
Above hit: Billy FURY with the FOUR JAYS.				
WONDEROUS PLACE	Decca	25	24 Sep 60	9
A THOUSAND STARS	Decca	14	21 Jan 61	10
DON'T WORRY	Decca	40	29 Apr 61	2
Above hit: Billy FURY and the FOUR KESTRELS.				
HALFWAY TO PARADISE	Decca	3	13 May 61	23
Original by Tony Orlando reached No. 39 in the US in 1961.				
JEALOUSY	Decca	2	9 Sep 61	12
Originally recorded by Frankie Laine in 1951.				
I'D NEVER FIND ANOTHER YOU	Decca	5	16 Dec 61	15
LETTER FULL OF TEARS	Decca	32	17 Mar 62	6
LAST NIGHT WAS MADE FOR LOVE	Decca	4	5 May 62	16
ONCE UPON A DREAM	Decca	7	21 Jul 62	13
From the film 'Play It Cool'.				
BECAUSE OF LOVE	Decca	18	27 Oct 62	14
LIKE I'VE NEVER BEEN GONE	Decca	3	16 Feb 63	15
WHEN WILL YOU SAY I LOVE YOU	Decca	3	18 May 63	12
IN SUMMER	Decca	5	27 Jul 63	11
SOMEBODY ELSE'S GIRL	Decca	18	5 Oct 63	7
DO YOU REALLY LOVE ME TOO (FOOLS ERRAND)	Decca	13	4 Jan 64	10
I WILL	Decca	14	2 May 64	12
Originally recorded by Vic Dana.				
IT'S ONLY MAKE BELIEVE	Decca	10	25 Jul 64	10
I'M LOST WITHOUT YOU	Decca	16	16 Jan 65	10
Originally recorded by Teddy Randazzo.				
IN THOUGHTS OF YOU	Decca	9	24 Jul 65	11
RUN TO MY LOVIN' ARMS	Decca	25	18 Sep 65	7
Originally recorded by Jay and the Americans.				
I'LL NEVER QUITE GET OVER YOU	Decca	35	12 Feb 66	5
GIVE ME YOUR WORD	Decca	27	6 Aug 66	7
LOVE OR MONEY	Polydor	57	4 Sep 82	5
DEVIL OR ANGEL	Polydor	58	13 Nov 82	4
FORGET HIM	Polydor	59	4 Jun 83	4

EPS:	HITS 3		WEEKS 91	
PLAY IT COOL	Decca	2	9 Jun 62	45
BILLY FURY HITS	Decca	8	10 Nov 62	30
BILLY FURY AND THE TORNADOS	Decca	2	25 May 63	16
Above hit: Billy FURY and the TORNADOS.				

ALBUMS:	HITS 6		WEEKS 51	
THE SOUND OF FURY	Decca	18	4 Jun 60	2
HALFWAY TO PARADISE	Ace Of Clubs	5	23 Sep 61	9
BILLY	Decca	6	11 May 63	21
WE WANT BILLY	Decca	14	26 Oct 63	2
Live recordings, also features the Tornados.				

THE BILLY FURY HIT PARADE	*Decca*	44	*19 Feb 83*	15
THE ONE AND ONLY BILLY FURY	*Polydor*	56	*26 Mar 83*	2

FUSE   Canada
(See also Plastik Man.)

ALBUMS:		HITS 1		WEEKS 1
DIMENSION INTRUSION	*Warp*	63	*19 Jun 93*	1

FUSED   Sweden

SINGLES:		HITS 1		WEEKS 1
THIS PARTY SUCKS!	*Columbia*	64	*20 Mar 99*	1

FUTURE BREEZE   Germany

SINGLES:		HITS 1		WEEKS 1
WHY DON'T YOU DANCE WITH ME	*AM:PM*	50	*6 Sep 97*	1

FUTURE FORCE   UK/US

SINGLES:		HITS 1		WEEKS 1
WHAT YOU WANT	*AM:PM*	47	*17 Aug 96*	1

FUTURE SOUND OF LONDON   UK

SINGLES:		HITS 7		WEEKS 22
PAPUA NEW GUINEA	*Jumpin' & Pumpin'*	22	*23 May 92*	6
CASCADE	*Virgin*	27	*6 Nov 93*	3
EXPANDER	*Jumpin' & Pumpin'*	72	*30 Jul 94*	1
LIFEFORMS	*Virgin*	14	*13 Aug 94*	3
Above hit: FSOL with vocals by Elizabeth FRASER.				
FAR-OUT SON OF LUNG AND THE RAMBLINGS OF A MADMAN	*Virgin*	22	*27 May 95*	3
MY KINGDOM	*Virgin*	13	*26 Oct 96*	3
Samples Mary Hopkin's vocals from Vangelis' Rachel's Song.				
WE HAVE EXPLOSIVE	*Virgin*	12	*12 Apr 97*	3
Soundtrack to the Playstation's Wipeout 2097 computer game.				
ALBUMS:		HITS 5		WEEKS 10
ACCELERATOR	*Jumpin' & Pumpin'*	75	*18 Jul 92*	1
LIFEFORMS	*Virgin*	6	*4 Jun 94*	5
ISDN	*Virgin*	62	*17 Dec 94*	1
Recorded from live radio broadcasts transmitted down from ISDN phonelines from their studio.				
ISDN (REMIX)	*Virgin*	44	*17 Jun 95*	1
DEAD CITIES	*Virgin*	26	*9 Nov 96*	2

FUZZBOX - See WE'VE GOT A FUZZBOX AND WE'RE GONNA USE IT

FUZZBUBBLE - See PUFF DADDY

FYC - See FINE YOUNG CANNIBALS

Leslie FYSON - See Michael MEDWIN, Bernard BRESSLAW, Alfie BASS and Leslie FYSON

G

Andy G'S STARSKY and HUTCH ALLSTARS featuring HUGGY BEAR   UK

SINGLES:		HITS 1		WEEKS 1
STARSKY & HUTCH - THE THEME	*Virgin*	51	*3 Oct 98*	1
Song is dance reworking of the 1970s TV theme.				

Bobby G   UK

SINGLES:		HITS 1		WEEKS 12
BIG DEAL (THEME FROM THE BBC TV SERIES)	*BBC*	75	*1 Dec 84*	1
BIG DEAL (THEME FROM THE BBC TV SERIES) [RE-1ST]	*BBC*	65	*15 Dec 84*	5
BIG DEAL (THEME FROM THE BBC TV SERIES) [RE-2ND]	*BBC*	46	*19 Oct 85*	6

Gina G   Australia

SINGLES:		HITS 6		WEEKS 51
OOH AAH . . . JUST A LITTLE BIT	*Eternal*	1	*6 Apr 96*	23
UK's Eurovision entry in 1996, it came 7th.				
OOH AAH . . . JUST A LITTLE BIT [RE-1ST]	*Eternal*	62	*21 Sep 96*	1
OOH AAH . . . JUST A LITTLE BIT [RE-2ND]	*Eternal*	64	*5 Oct 96*	1
I BELONG TO YOU	*Eternal*	6	*9 Nov 96*	11
FRESH!	*Eternal*	6	*22 Mar 97*	7
TI AMO	*Eternal*	11	*7 Jun 97*	5
GIMME SOME LOVE	*Eternal*	25	*6 Sep 97*	2
EVERY TIME I FALL	*Eternal*	52	*15 Nov 97*	1

ALBUMS:		HITS 1		WEEKS 4	
FRESH!	Eternal		12	5 Apr 97	4

Kenny G   US

SINGLES:		HITS 7		WEEKS 26	
HI! HOW YA DOIN'?	Arista		70	21 Apr 84	3
WHAT DOES IT TAKE (TO WIN YOUR LOVE)	Arista		64	30 Aug 86	2
SONGBIRD	Arista		22	4 Jul 87	7
MISSING YOU KNOW	Columbia		28	9 May 92	4
Above hit: Michael BOLTON featuring Kenny G.					
FOREVER IN LOVE	Arista		47	24 Apr 93	3
BY THE TIME THIS NIGHT IS OVER	Arista		56	17 Jul 93	3
Above hit: Kenny G with Peabo BRYSON.					
HOW COULD AN ANGEL BREAK MY HEART	LaFace		22	8 Nov 97	4
Above hit: Toni BRAXTON with Kenny G.					

ALBUMS:		HITS 6		WEEKS 58	
G FORCE	Arista		56	17 Mar 84	5
DUOTONES	Arista		28	8 Aug 87	5
MONTAGE	Arista		32	14 Apr 90	7
BREATHLESS	Arista		4	15 May 93	27
THE MOMENT	Arista		19	19 Oct 96	9
GREATEST HITS	Arista		38	13 Dec 97	5

Warren G   US

SINGLES:		HITS 8		WEEKS 59	
REGULATE	Death Row		5	23 Jul 94	14
From the film 'Above The Rim'. Samples Michael McDonald's I Keep Forgettin'.					
Above hit: Warren G and Nate DOGG.					
THIS DJ	RAL		12	12 Nov 94	5
THIS DJ [RE]	RAL		68	31 Dec 94	2
DO YOU SEE	RAL		29	25 Mar 95	2
Samples Junior's Mama Used To Say.					
WHAT'S LOVE GOT TO DO WITH IT	Interscope		2	23 Nov 96	12
Above hit: Warren G featuring Adina HOWARD.					
I SHOT THE SHERIFF	Def Jam		2	22 Feb 97	8
SMOKIN' ME OUT	Def Jam		14	31 May 97	5
Cover of the Isley Brothers' Coolin' Me Out from their 1978 album Shakedown.					
Above hit: Warren G featuring Ron ISLEY.					
PRINCE IGOR	Def Jam		15	10 Jan 98	7
Based on music composed by Borodin.					
Above hit: RAPSODY: Warren G and SISSEL.					
ALL NIGHT ALL RIGHT	Mushroom		16	24 Jan 98	4
Samples A Taste Of Honey's Boogie Oogie Oogie.					
Above hit: Peter ANDRE featuring Warren G.					

ALBUMS:		HITS 2		WEEKS 10	
REGULATE . . . G FUNK ERA	RAL		25	6 Aug 94	6
TAKE A LOOK OVER YOUR SHOULDER (REALITY)	Def Jam		20	8 Mar 97	4

G.B.H. - See CHARGED G.B.H.

G-CLEFS   US

SINGLES:		HITS 1		WEEKS 12	
I UNDERSTAND (JUST HOW YOU FEEL)	London		17	2 Dec 61	12
Originally recorded by the Four Tunes in 1954.					

G NATION featuring ROSIE   UK

SINGLES:		HITS 1		WEEKS 1	
FEEL THE NEED	Cooltempo		58	9 Aug 97	1

G.O.S.H.   UK

SINGLES:		HITS 1		WEEKS 11	
THE WISHING WELL	MSS		22	28 Nov 87	11
G.O.S.H. stands for 'Great Ormond Street Help'. Charity record for the hospital's Wishing Well appeal.					

G.Q.   US

SINGLES:		HITS 1		WEEKS 6	
DISCO NIGHTS-(ROCK FREAK)	Arista		42	10 Mar 79	6

G.S.P.   UK

SINGLES:		HITS 1		WEEKS 3	
THE BANANA SONG	Yoyo		37	3 Oct 92	3

G.T.O.   UK
(See also Technohead; Tricky Disco.)

SINGLES:		HITS 3		WEEKS 7
PURE	Cooltempo	57	4 Aug 90	3
LISTEN TO THE RHYTHM FLOW / BULLFROG	React	72	7 Sep 91	2
ELEVATION	React	59	2 May 92	2

G.T.R.   UK

ALBUMS:		HITS 1		WEEKS 4
GTR	Arista	41	19 Jul 86	4

G.U.N. – See GUN

G.U.S. (FOOTWEAR) BAND and the MORRISTOWN ORPHEUS CHOIR   UK

ALBUMS:		HITS 1		WEEKS 1
LAND OF HOPE AND GLORY	Columbia	54	3 Oct 70	1

Eric GABLE   US

SINGLES:		HITS 1		WEEKS 1
PROCESS OF ELIMINATION	Epic	63	19 Mar 94	1

Peter GABRIEL   UK

SINGLES:		HITS 19		WEEKS 112
SOLSBURY HILL	Charisma	13	9 Apr 77	9
GAMES WITHOUT FRONTIERS	Charisma	4	9 Feb 80	11
Features uncredited vocals by Kate Bush.				
NO SELF CONTROL	Charisma	33	10 May 80	6
BIKO	Charisma	38	23 Aug 80	3
SHOCK THE MONKEY	Charisma	58	25 Sep 82	5
I DON'T REMEMBER	Charisma	62	9 Jul 83	3
WALK THROUGH THE FIRE	Virgin	69	2 Jun 84	3
From the film 'Against All Odds'.				
SLEDGEHAMMER	Virgin	4	26 Apr 86	16
DON'T GIVE UP	Virgin	9	1 Nov 86	11
Above hit: Peter GABRIEL and Kate BUSH.				
BIG TIME	Virgin	13	28 Mar 87	7
Features the Police's Stewart Copeland on drums.				
RED RAIN	Virgin	46	11 Jul 87	3
BIKO [RR]	Virgin	49	21 Nov 87	6
Live recording from the Blossom Music Centre, Cleveland, 27 Jul 87.				
SHAKIN' THE TREE	Virgin	61	3 Jun 89	3
Above hit: Youssou N'DOUR and Peter GABRIEL.				
SOLSBURY HILL [RI] / SHAKING THE TREE [RI]	Virgin	57	22 Dec 90	4
Above hit: Peter GABRIEL / Peter GABRIEL and Youssou N'DOUR.				
DIGGING IN THE DIRT	Virgin	24	19 Sep 92	4
STEAM	Realworld	10	16 Jan 93	7
BLOOD OF EDEN	Realworld	43	3 Apr 93	4
KISS THAT FROG	Realworld	46	25 Sep 93	3
LOVETOWN	Epic	49	25 Jun 94	2
From the film 'Philadelphia'.				
SW LIVE [EP]	Realworld	39	3 Sep 94	2
Lead track: Red Rain. Live recording from Palasport Nouvo, Modena, Italy, 16+17 Nov 93.				

ALBUMS:		HITS 11		WEEKS 202
PETER GABRIEL	Charisma	7	12 Mar 77	19
PETER GABRIEL	Charisma	10	17 Jun 78	8
PETER GABRIEL	Charisma	1	7 Jun 80	18
PETER GABRIEL	Charisma	6	18 Sep 82	16
All 4 self-titled albums above are different.				
PETER GABRIEL PLAYS LIVE	Charisma	8	18 Jun 83	9
BIRDY [OST]	Charisma	51	30 Mar 85	3
SO	Virgin	1	31 May 86	76
PASSION	Virgin	29	17 Jun 89	5
SHAKING THE TREE	Virgin	11	1 Dec 90	15
Compilation. CD format also has the credit '16 Golden Greats', while the vinyl format has '12 Golden Greats'.				
US	Realworld	2	10 Oct 92	29
SECRET WORLD LIVE	Realworld	10	10 Sep 94	4
Live recordings from Modena, Italy, Nov 93.				

GABRIELLE   UK

SINGLES:		HITS 10		WEEKS 91
DREAMS	Go.Beat	1	19 Jun 93	15
GOING NOWHERE	Go.Beat	9	2 Oct 93	7
I WISH	Go.Beat	26	11 Dec 93	5
BECAUSE OF YOU	Go.Beat	24	26 Feb 94	5

GIVE ME A LITTLE MORE TIME	Go.Beat	5	24 Feb 96	18
FORGET ABOUT THE WORLD	Go.Beat	23	22 Jun 96	5
IF YOU REALLY CARED	Go.Beat	15	5 Oct 96	5
IF YOU EVER	London	2	2 Nov 96	15

Original by Shai reached No. 2 in the US in 1992.
Above hit: EAST SEVENTEEN featuring GABRIELLE.

WALK ON BY	Go.Beat	7	1 Feb 97	8
SUNSHINE	Go.Beat	9	9 Oct 99	8
ALBUMS:	**HITS 3**			**WEEKS 54**
FIND YOUR WAY	Go.Beat	9	30 Oct 93	22
GABRIELLE	Go.Beat	11	8 Jun 96	30
RISE	Go.Beat	25	30 Oct 99	2

Yvonne GAGE   US

SINGLES:	**HITS 1**			**WEEKS 4**
DOIN' IT IN A HAUNTED HOUSE	Epic	45	16 Jun 84	4

Danni'elle GAHA   Australia

SINGLES:	**HITS 3**			**WEEKS 7**
STUCK IN THE MIDDLE	Epic	68	1 Aug 92	2
DO IT FOR LOVE	Epic	52	27 Feb 93	2
SECRET LOVE	Epic	41	12 Jun 93	3

Billy and Sarah GAINES   US

SINGLES:	**HITS 1**			**WEEKS 1**
I FOUND SOMEONE	Expansion	48	14 Jun 97	1

Originally released in 1991.

Chris GAINES – See Garth BROOKS.

Rosie GAINES   US

SINGLES:	**HITS 3**			**WEEKS 15**
I WANT U	Motown	70	11 Nov 95	1
CLOSER THAN CLOSE	Big Bang	4	31 May 97	12
I SURRENDER	Big Bang	39	29 Nov 97	2

Serge GAINSBOURG and Jane BIRKIN – See Jane BIRKIN and Serge GAINSBOURG

GALA   Italy

SINGLES:	**HITS 3**			**WEEKS 24**
FREED FROM DESIRE	Big Life	2	19 Jul 97	14
LET A BOY CRY	Big Life	11	6 Dec 97	8
COME INTO MY LIFE	Big Life	38	22 Aug 98	2

GALAXY featuring Phil FEARON – See Phil FEARON

Dee GALDES – See Phil FEARON

Eve GALLAGHER   UK

SINGLES:	**HITS 4**			**WEEKS 8**
LOVE COME DOWN	More Protein	61	1 Dec 90	3
LOVE COME DOWN [RE]	More Protein	68	29 Dec 90	1
YOU CAN HAVE IT ALL	Cleveland City	43	15 Apr 95	2
LOVE COME DOWN [RR]	Cleveland City	57	28 Oct 95	1
HEARTBREAK	React	44	6 Jul 96	1

Above hit: MRS WOOD featuring Eve GALLAGHER.

Liam GALLAGHER and Steve CRADOCK   UK

SINGLES:	**HITS 1**			**WEEKS 5**
CARNATION	Ignition	6	23 Oct 99	5

[AA] listed with Going Underground by Buffalo Tom. From the Jam tribute album Fire & Skill.

Rory GALLAGHER   UK

ALBUMS:	**HITS 10**			**WEEKS 43**
RORY GALLAGHER	Polydor	32	29 May 71	2
DEUCE	Polydor	39	4 Dec 71	1
LIVE! IN EUROPE	Polydor	9	20 May 72	15
BLUE PRINT	Polydor	12	24 Feb 73	7
TATTOO	Polydor	32	17 Nov 73	3
IRISH TOUR '74	Polydor	36	27 Jul 74	2
CALLING CARD	Chrysalis	32	30 Oct 76	1
TOP PRIORITY	Chrysalis	56	22 Sep 79	4
STAGE STRUCK	Chrysalis	40	8 Nov 80	3
JINX	Chrysalis	68	8 May 82	5

GALLAGHER and LYLE
UK

SINGLES:	HITS 4			WEEKS 27
I WANNA STAY WITH YOU	A&M	6	28 Feb 76	9
HEART ON MY SLEEVE	A&M	6	22 May 76	10
BREAKAWAY	A&M	35	11 Sep 76	4
EVERY LITTLE TEARDROP	A&M	32	29 Jan 77	4
ALBUMS:	**HITS 2**			**WEEKS 44**
BREAKAWAY	A&M	6	28 Feb 76	35
LOVE ON THE AIRWAYS	A&M	19	29 Jan 77	9

Patsy GALLANT
Canada

SINGLES:	HITS 1			WEEKS 9
FROM NEW YORK TO L.A.	EMI	6	10 Sep 77	9

GALLIANO
UK

SINGLES:	HITS 6			WEEKS 14
SKUNK FUNK	Talkin Loud	41	30 May 92	2
PRINCE OF PEACE	Talkin Loud	47	1 Aug 92	3
JUS' REACH (RECYCLED)	Epic	66	10 Oct 92	2
LONG TIME GONE	Talkin Loud	15	28 May 94	3
Originally recorded by Crosby, Stills, Nash and Young in 1971.				
TWYFORD DOWN	Talkin Loud	37	30 Jul 94	2
EASE YOUR MIND	Talkin Loud	45	27 Jul 96	2
ALBUMS:	**HITS 2**			**WEEKS 15**
A JOYFUL NOISE UNTO THE CREATOR	Talkin Loud	28	20 Jun 92	3
THE PLOT THICKENS	Talkin Loud	7	11 Jun 94	12

GALLON DRUNK
UK

ALBUMS:	HITS 1			WEEKS 1
FROM THE HEART OF TOWN	Clawfist	67	13 Mar 93	1

James GALWAY
Ireland

(See also Cleo Laine and James Galway; James Galway and Henry Mancini with the National Philharmonic Orchestra; James Galway and the Chieftains.)

SINGLES:	HITS 1			WEEKS 13
ANNIE'S SONG	RCA Red Seal	3	27 May 78	13
Above hit: James GALWAY, Flute: NATIONAL PHILHARMONIC ORCHESTRA; Charles GERHART, conductor.				
ALBUMS:	**HITS 8**			**WEEKS 75**
THE MAGIC FLUTE OF JAMES GALWAY	RCA Red Seal	43	27 May 78	6
THE MAN WITH THE GOLDEN FLUTE	RCA Red Seal	52	1 Jul 78	3
JAMES GALWAY PLAYS SONGS FOR ANNIE	RCA Red Seal	7	9 Sep 78	40
SONGS OF THE SEASHORE	Solar	39	15 Dec 79	6
THE JAMES GALWAY COLLECTION	Telstar	41	18 Dec 82	8
MASTERPIECES - THE ESSENTIAL FLUTE OF JAMES GALWAY	RCA Victor	30	17 Apr 93	5
I WILL ALWAYS LOVE YOU	RCA Victor	59	18 Feb 95	2
CLASSICAL MEDITATIONS	RCA Victor	45	20 Jul 96	5
1 of 2 albums released on the same day. The other, The Celtic Minstrel, entered at No.168.				

James GALWAY and the CHIEFTAINS
UK/Ireland

(See also Chieftains; James Galway.)

ALBUMS:	HITS 1			WEEKS 5
JAMES GALWAY AND THE CHIEFTAINS IN IRELAND	RCA Red Seal	32	28 Mar 87	5

James GALWAY and Henry MANCINI with the NATIONAL PHILHARMONIC ORCHESTRA
UK/US

(See also James Galway; Henry Mancini and his Orchestra.)

ALBUMS:	HITS 1			WEEKS 6
IN THE PINK	RCA Red Seal	62	8 Dec 84	6

GAMBAFREAKS featuring Paco RIVAZ
Italy

SINGLES:	HITS 1			WEEKS 1
INSTANT REPLAY	Evocative	57	12 Sep 98	1

GAMBLE - See PHILADELPHIA INTERNATIONAL ALL STARS: Lou RAWLS, Billy PAUL, Archie BELL, Teddy PENDERGRASS, O'JAYS, Dee Dee SHARP, GAMBLE

GANG OF FOUR
UK

SINGLES:	HITS 2			WEEKS 5
AT HOME HE'S A TOURIST	EMI	58	16 Jun 79	3
I LOVE A MAN IN UNIFORM	EMI	65	22 May 82	2

ALBUMS:		HITS 3			WEEKS 9
ENTERTAINMENT	EMI	45	13 Oct 79		3
SOLID GOLD	EMI	52	21 Mar 81		2
SONGS OF THE FREE	EMI	61	29 May 82		4

GANG STARR
US

SINGLES:		HITS 4			WEEKS 8
JAZZ THING	CBS	66	13 Oct 90		2
TAKE A REST	Cooltempo	63	23 Feb 91		1
LOVESICK	Cooltempo	50	25 May 91		3
2 DEEP	Cooltempo	67	13 Jun 92		2

ALBUMS:		HITS 4			WEEKS 9
STEP IN THE ARENA	Cooltempo	36	26 Jan 91		3
HARD TO EARN	Cooltempo	29	12 Mar 94		3
MOMENT OF TRUTH	Cooltempo	43	11 Apr 98		1
FULL CLIP: A DECADE OF GANG STARR	Cooltempo	47	7 Aug 99		2

GANJA KRU - See DJ HYPE

GANT
UK

SINGLES:		HITS 1			WEEKS 1
SOUND BWOY BURIAL / ALL NIGHT LONG	Positiva	67	27 Dec 97		1

GAP BAND
US

SINGLES:		HITS 12			WEEKS 82
OOPS UP SIDE YOUR HEAD	Mercury	6	12 Jul 80		14
PARTY LIGHTS	Mercury	30	27 Sep 80		8
BURN RUBBER ON ME (WHY YOU WANNA HURT ME)	Mercury	22	27 Dec 80		11
HUMPIN'	Mercury	36	11 Apr 81		6
YEARNING FOR YOUR LOVE	Mercury	47	27 Jun 81		4
EARLY IN THE MORNING	Mercury	55	5 Jun 82		3
OUTSTANDING	Total Experience	68	19 Feb 83		2
SOMEDAY	Total Experience	17	31 Mar 84		8
JAMMIN' IN AMERICA	Total Experience	64	23 Jun 84		2
BIG FUN	Total Experience	4	13 Dec 86		12
HOW MUSIC CAME ABOUT (BOP B DA B DA DA)	Total Experience	61	14 Mar 87		2
OOPS UPSIDE YOUR HEAD ('87 MIX) [RM]	Club	20	11 Jul 87		8
Remixed by Lonnie Simmons and Rudy Taylor.					
I'M GONNA GIT YOU SUCKA	Arista	63	18 Feb 89		2

ALBUMS:		HITS 1			WEEKS 3
GAP BAND 8	Total Experience	47	7 Feb 87		3

GARBAGE
UK/US

SINGLES:		HITS 11			WEEKS 54
SUBHUMAN	Mushroom	50	19 Aug 95		1
ONLY HAPPY WHEN IT RAINS	Mushroom	29	30 Sep 95		3
QUEER	Mushroom	13	2 Dec 95		4
STUPID GIRL	Mushroom	4	23 Mar 96		7
Samples Train In Vain by the Clash.					
MILK	Mushroom	10	23 Nov 96		7
Though credited on the chart, Tricky's contribution was only as a remixer of a secondary track of the CD.					
Above hit: GARBAGE featuring TRICKY.					
MILK [RE]	Mushroom	74	18 Jan 97		1
PUSH IT	Mushroom	9	9 May 98		5
I THINK I'M PARANOID	Mushroom	9	18 Jul 98		5
SPECIAL	Mushroom	15	17 Oct 98		4
Samples The Pretenders' The Talk Of The Town.					
WHEN I GROW UP	Mushroom	9	6 Feb 99		7
YOU LOOK SO FINE	Mushroom	19	5 Jun 99		4
THE WORLD IS NOT ENOUGH	Radioactive	11	27 Nov 99		6
Theme from the James Bond film of the same name.					

ALBUMS:		HITS 2			WEEKS 162
GARBAGE	Mushroom	6	14 Oct 95		99
VERSION 2.0	Mushroom	1	23 May 98		63

Jan GARBAREK
Norway

ALBUMS:		HITS 1			WEEKS 1
VISIBLE WORLD	ECM	69	4 May 96		1

Adam GARCIA
Australia

SINGLES:		HITS 1			WEEKS 5
NIGHT FEVER	Polydor	15	16 May 98		5
From the musical 'Saturday Night Fever'.					

Scott GARCIA featuring MC STYLES
UK

SINGLES:		HITS 1			WEEKS 3
A LONDON THING	Connected		29	1 Nov 97	3

Originally released in 1996.

Boris GARDINER
Jamaica

SINGLES:		HITS 4			WEEKS 38
ELIZABETHAN REGGAE	Duke		48	17 Jan 70	1

*Original copies credited Byron Lee as the artist (he recorded the B-side). This entry and for the first 4
weeks of the re-entry, the charts credited him instead of Boris Gardner.*
Above hit: Boris GARDNER.

ELIZABETHAN REGGAE [RE]	Duke		14	31 Jan 70	13
I WANNA WAKE UP WITH YOU	Revue		1	26 Jul 86	15

Originally recorded by Mac Davis in 1980.

YOU'RE EVERYTHING TO ME	Revue		11	4 Oct 86	8

Some copies of the above 2 hits have his surname as Gardner.

THE MEANING OF CHRISTMAS	Revue		69	27 Dec 86	1

Paul GARDINER
UK

SINGLES:		HITS 1			WEEKS 4
STORMTROOPER IN DRAG	Beggars Banquet		49	25 Jul 81	4

Features vocals by Gary Numan.

Art GARFUNKEL
US

(See also Simon and Garfunkel.)

SINGLES:		HITS 3			WEEKS 37
I ONLY HAVE EYES FOR YOU	CBS		1	13 Sep 75	11

Originally recorded by Ben Selvin in 1934.

BRIGHT EYES	CBS		1	3 Mar 79	19

From the film 'Watership Down'.

SINCE I DON'T HAVE YOU	CBS		38	7 Jul 79	7

Originally recorded by the Skyliners.

ALBUMS:		HITS 7			WEEKS 64
ANGEL CLARE	CBS		14	13 Oct 73	7
BREAKAWAY	CBS		7	1 Nov 75	10
WATER MARK	CBS		25	18 Mar 78	5
FATE FOR BREAKFAST	CBS		2	21 Apr 79	20
SCISSORS CUT	CBS		51	19 Sep 81	3
THE ART GARFUNKEL ALBUM	CBS		12	17 Nov 84	13
THE VERY BEST OF ART GARFUNKEL – ACROSS AMERICA	Virgin		35	14 Dec 96	6

Judy GARLAND
US

SINGLES:		HITS 1			WEEKS 2
THE MAN THAT GOT AWAY	Philips		18	11 Jun 55	2
EPS:		HITS 1			WEEKS 3
MAGGIE MAY	Capitol		18	5 Dec 64	3
ALBUMS:		HITS 1			WEEKS 3
JUDY AT CARNEGIE HALL	Capitol		13	3 Mar 62	3

Errol GARNER
US

ALBUMS:		HITS 1			WEEKS 1
CLOSE UP IN SWING	Philips		20	14 Jul 62	1

Laurent GARNIER
France

SINGLES:		HITS 1			WEEKS 1
CRISPY BACON	F. Communications		60	15 Feb 97	1

Lee GARRETT
US

SINGLES:		HITS 1			WEEKS 7
YOU'RE MY EVERYTHING	Chrysalis		15	29 May 76	7

Leif GARRETT
US

SINGLES:		HITS 2			WEEKS 14
I WAS MADE FOR DANCIN'	Scotti Brothers		4	20 Jan 79	10
FEEL THE NEED	Scotti Brothers		38	21 Apr 79	4

Lesley GARRETT
UK

SINGLES:		HITS 1			WEEKS 10
AVE MARIA	Internal Affairs		16	6 Nov 93	10

*Duet with leukaemia sufferer Thompson was broadcast on BBC TV's 'Hearts Of Gold' on 26
Sep 93. Ave Maria is a Catholic form of address to the Virgin Mary.*
Above hit: Lesley GARRETT with Amanda THOMPSON.

ALBUMS:		HITS 6			WEEKS 36
AVE MARIA - THE ALBUM	Telstar	25	12 Feb 94	7
SOPRANO IN RED	Silva Classics	59	18 Nov 95	8
SOPRANO IN HOLLYWOOD	Silva Classics	53	19 Oct 96	4
Features the BBC Concert Orchestra and includes songs from the 1930s/40s.				
THE SOPRANO'S GREATEST HITS	Silva Classics	53	18 Oct 97	2
Recorded with the Royal Philharmonic Orchestra.				
A SOPRANO INSPIRED	Conifer Classics	48	22 Nov 97	7
LESLEY GARRETT	BBC	34	14 Nov 98	8

Siedah GARRETT - See Dennis EDWARDS; Michael JACKSON

David GARRICK
UK

SINGLES:		HITS 2			WEEKS 16
LADY JANE	Piccadilly	28	11 Jun 66	7
Originally recorded by the Rolling Stones.				
DEAR MRS. APPLEBEE	Piccadilly	22	24 Sep 66	9
Originally recorded by Flip Cartridge.				

GARY'S GANG
US

SINGLES:		HITS 3			WEEKS 18
KEEP ON DANCIN'	CBS	8	24 Feb 79	10
LET'S LOVEDANCE TONIGHT	CBS	49	2 Jun 79	4
KNOCK ME OUT	Arista	45	6 Nov 82	4

Barbara GASKIN - See Dave STEWART

GAT DECOR
UK

SINGLES:		HITS 1			WEEKS 10
PASSION	Effective	29	16 May 92	4
PASSION [RM]	Way Of Life	6	9 Mar 96	6
The theme to BBC1 TV's 'Ski Sunday'. Remixed by Northern Scum and new vocals by Beverli Skeete.				

David GATES
US

SINGLES:		HITS 1			WEEKS 2
TOOK THE LAST TRAIN	Elektra	50	22 Jul 78	2
ALBUMS:		**HITS 4**			**WEEKS 25**
NEVER LET HER GO	Elektra	32	31 May 75	1
GOODBYE GIRL	Elektra	28	29 Jul 78	3
THE COLLECTION - THE VERY BEST OF BREAD AND DAVID GATES	Telstar	84	28 Nov 87	2
Above hit: BREAD and David GATES.				
DAVID GATES AND BREAD: ESSENTIALS	Warner.esp/Jive	9	5 Jul 97	19
Above 2 albums include Gates' solo and group recordings.				
Above hit: David GATES and BREAD.				

GAY DAD
UK

SINGLES:		HITS 3			WEEKS 8
TO EARTH WITH LOVE	London	10	30 Jan 99	4
JOY!	London	22	5 Jun 99	3
OH JIM	London	47	14 Aug 99	1
ALBUMS:		**HITS 1**			**WEEKS 3**
LEISURE NOISE	London	14	19 Jun 99	3

GAY GORDON and the MINCE PIES
UK

SINGLES:		HITS 1			WEEKS 5
THE ESSENTIAL WALLY PARTY MEDLEY [M]	Lifestyle	60	6 Dec 86	5

Marvin GAYE
US

(See also Marvin Gaye and Tammi Terrell; Diana Ross and Marvin Gaye; Diana Ross, Marvin Gaye, Smokey Robinson and Stevie Wonder.)

SINGLES:		HITS 14			WEEKS 114
ONCE UPON A TIME	Stateside	50	1 Aug 64	1
Above hit: Marvin GAYE and Mary WELLS.				
HOW SWEET IT IS	Stateside	49	12 Dec 64	1
LITTLE DARLIN' (I NEED YOU)	Tamla Motown	50	1 Oct 66	1
IT TAKES TWO	Tamla Motown	16	28 Jan 67	11
Above hit: Marvin GAYE and Kim WESTON.				
I HEARD IT THROUGH THE GRAPEVINE	Tamla Motown	1	15 Feb 69	15
Originally recorded by Smokey Robinson & the Miracles.				
TOO BUSY THINKING ABOUT MY BABY	Tamla Motown	5	26 Jul 69	16
ABRAHAM, MARTIN AND JOHN	Tamla Motown	9	9 May 70	14
Originally recorded by Dion.				
SAVE THE CHILDREN	Tamla Motown	41	11 Dec 71	6

LET'S GET IT ON	Tamla Motown	31	22 Sep 73	7
GOT TO GIVE IT UP	Motown	7	7 May 77	10
SEXUAL HEALING	CBS	4	30 Oct 82	14
MY LOVE IS WAITING	CBS	34	8 Jan 83	5
SANCTIFIED LADY	CBS	51	18 May 85	4
I HEARD IT THROUGH THE GRAPEVINE [RI]	Motown	8	26 Apr 86	8
Featured in the Levi's 501 jeans TV commercial.				
LUCKY LUCKY ME	Motown	67	14 May 94	1

EPS:	**HITS 1**			**WEEKS 8**
ORIGINALS FROM MARVIN GAYE	Tamla Motown	3	15 Apr 67	8

ALBUMS:	**HITS 12**			**WEEKS 127**
GREATEST HITS	Tamla Motown	40	16 Mar 68	1
LET'S GET IT ON	Tamla Motown	39	10 Nov 73	1
I WANT YOU	Tamla Motown	22	15 May 76	5
THE BEST OF MARVIN GAYE	Tamla Motown	56	30 Oct 76	1
IN OUR LIFETIME	Motown	48	28 Feb 81	4
MIDNIGHT LOVE	CBS	10	20 Nov 82	16
GREATEST HITS	Telstar	13	12 Nov 83	61
The two Greatest Hits albums are different.				
DREAM OF A LIFETIME	CBS	46	15 Jun 85	4
LOVE SONGS	Telstar	69	12 Nov 88	9
Compilation, one side for each artist.				
Above hit: Marvin GAYE and Smokey ROBINSON.				
LOVE SONGS	Telstar	39	3 Nov 90	5
THE VERY BEST OF MARVIN GAYE	Motown	3	9 Apr 94	19
Includes re-entry in 1999.				
WHAT'S GOING ON?	Motown	69	24 Jul 99	1
Originally released in 1971.				

Marvin GAYE and Tammi TERRELL   US

(See also Marvin Gaye.)

SINGLES:	**HITS 6**			**WEEKS 61**
IF I COULD BUILD MY WHOLE WORLD AROUND YOU	Tamla Motown	41	20 Jan 68	7
AIN'T NOTHIN' LIKE THE REAL THING	Tamla Motown	34	15 Jun 68	7
YOU'RE ALL I NEED TO GET BY	Tamla Motown	19	5 Oct 68	19
YOU AIN'T LIVIN' TILL YOU'RE LOVIN'	Tamla Motown	21	25 Jan 69	8
GOOD LOVIN' AIN'T EASY TO COME BY	Tamla Motown	26	7 Jun 69	7
GOOD LOVIN' AIN'T EASY TO COME BY [RE]	Tamla Motown	48	2 Aug 69	1
THE ONION SONG	Tamla Motown	9	15 Nov 69	12
Female vocal on the above two was actually Valerie Simpson, due to Terrell's ill health.				

ALBUMS:	**HITS 1**			**WEEKS 4**
GREATEST HITS	Tamla Motown	60	22 Aug 70	4

GAYE BYKERS ON ACID   UK

SINGLES:	**HITS 1**			**WEEKS 2**
GIT DOWN (SHAKE YOUR THANG)	Virgin	54	31 Oct 87	2

ALBUMS:	**HITS 1**			**WEEKS 1**
DRILL YOUR OWN HOLE	Virgin	95	14 Nov 87	1

Crystal GAYLE   US

SINGLES:	**HITS 2**			**WEEKS 28**
DON'T IT MAKE MY BROWN EYES BLUE	United Artists	5	12 Nov 77	14
TALKING IN YOUR SLEEP	United Artists	11	26 Aug 78	14

ALBUMS:	**HITS 3**			**WEEKS 25**
WE MUST BELIEVE IN MAGIC	United Artists	15	21 Jan 78	7
WHEN I DREAM	United Artists	25	23 Sep 78	8
THE CRYSTAL GAYLE SINGLES ALBUM	United Artists	7	22 Mar 80	10

Michelle GAYLE   UK

SINGLES:	**HITS 7**			**WEEKS 52**
LOOKING UP	RCA	11	7 Aug 93	6
SWEETNESS	RCA	4	24 Sep 94	16
I'LL FIND YOU	RCA	26	17 Dec 94	7
FREEDOM	RCA	16	27 May 95	6
HAPPY JUST TO BE WITH YOU	RCA	11	26 Aug 95	7
Samples Chic's Good Times.				
DO YOU KNOW	RCA	6	8 Feb 97	6
SENSATIONAL	RCA	14	26 Apr 97	4
Based on For The Love Of You by the Isley Brothers.				

ALBUMS:	**HITS 2**			**WEEKS 13**
MICHELLE GAYLE	RCA	30	22 Oct 94	10
SENSATIONAL	RCA	17	10 May 97	3

Roy GAYLE – See MIRAGE

GAYLE and GILLIAN

Australia

SINGLES:		HITS 2		WEEKS 2	
MAD IF YA DON'T!	Mushroom	75	3 Jul 93	1
WANNA BE YOUR LOVER	Mushroom	62	19 Mar 94	1

Gloria GAYNOR

US

SINGLES:		HITS 7		WEEKS 72	
NEVER CAN SAY GOODBYE	MGM	2	7 Dec 74	13
REACH OUT, I'LL BE THERE	MGM	14	8 Mar 75	8
ALL I NEED IS YOUR SWEET LOVIN'	MGM	44	9 Aug 75	3
HOW HIGH THE MOON	MGM	33	17 Jan 76	4
Originally recorded by Les Paul and Mary Ford in 1951.				
I WILL SURVIVE	Polydor	1	3 Feb 79	15
LET ME KNOW (I HAVE A RIGHT)	Polydor	32	6 Oct 79	7
I AM WHAT I AM (FROM 'LA CAGE AUX FOLLES')	Chrysalis	13	24 Dec 83	12
From the stage show.				
I WILL SURVIVE [RM]	Polydor	5	26 Jun 93	10
Remixed by Phil Kelsey.				
ALBUMS:		HITS 3		WEEKS 17	
NEVER CAN SAY GOODBYE	MGM	32	8 Mar 75	8
LOVE TRACKS	Polydor	31	24 Mar 79	7
THE POWER OF GLORIA GAYNOR	Stylus	81	16 Aug 86	2

GAZ

US

SINGLES:		HITS 1		WEEKS 4	
SING SING	Salsoul	60	24 Feb 79	4

GAZZA

UK

SINGLES:		HITS 2		WEEKS 14	
FOG ON THE TYNE (REVISITED)	Best	2	10 Nov 90	9
Above hit: GAZZA and LINDISFARNE.				
GEORDIE BOYS (GAZZA RAP)	Best	31	22 Dec 90	5

J. GEILS BAND

US

SINGLES:		HITS 4		WEEKS 20	
ONE LAST KISS	EMI America	74	9 Jun 79	1
CENTERFOLD	EMI America	3	13 Feb 82	9
FREEZE-FRAME	EMI America	27	10 Apr 82	7
ANGEL IN BLUE	EMI America	55	26 Jun 82	3
ALBUMS:		HITS 1		WEEKS 15	
FREEZE-FRAME	EMI America	12	27 Feb 82	15

Bob GELDOF

Ireland

SINGLES:		HITS 4		WEEKS 15	
THIS IS THE WORLD CALLING	Mercury	25	1 Nov 86	5
LOVE LIKE A ROCKET	Mercury	61	21 Feb 87	3
THE GREAT SONG OF INDIFFERENCE	Mercury	15	23 Jun 90	6
CRAZY	Vertigo	65	7 May 94	1
Backing vocals by Sting.				
ALBUMS:		HITS 3		WEEKS 10	
DEEP IN THE HEART OF NOWHERE	Mercury	79	6 Dec 86	1
THE VEGETARIANS OF LOVE	Mercury	21	4 Aug 90	6
LOUDMOUTH – THE BEST OF THE BOOMTOWN RATS AND BOB GELDOF	Vertigo	10	9 Jul 94	3
Includes both solo and group material.				
Above hit: BOOMTOWN RATS and Bob GELDOF.				

GEM – See OUR TRIBE/ONE TRIBE/O.T. QUARTET

GEMINI

UK

SINGLES:		HITS 3		WEEKS 7	
EVEN THOUGH YOU BROKE MY HEART	EMI	40	30 Sep 95	3
STEAL YOUR LOVE AWAY	EMI	37	10 Feb 96	2
COULD IT BE FOREVER	EMI	38	29 Jun 96	2

GEMS FOR JEM

UK

SINGLES:		HITS 1		WEEKS 2	
LIFTING ME HIGHER	Box 21	28	6 May 95	2
Samples Evelyn Thomas' High Energy.				

GEN X – See GENERATION X

GENE

SINGLES:	HITS 11			UK WEEKS 22	
BE MY LIGHT, BE MY GUIDE	Costermonger	54	13 Aug 94	1	
SLEEP WELL TONIGHT	Costermonger	36	12 Nov 94	2	
HAUNTED BY YOU	Costermonger	32	4 Mar 95	2	
OLYMPIAN	Costermonger	18	22 Jul 95	2	
FOR THE DEAD	Costermonger	14	13 Jan 96	3	
FIGHTING FIT	Polydor	22	2 Nov 96	2	
WE COULD BE KINGS	Polydor	17	1 Feb 97	2	
WHERE ARE THEY NOW?	Polydor	22	10 May 97	2	
SPEAK TO ME SOMEONE	Polydor	30	9 Aug 97	2	
AS GOOD AS IT GETS	Polydor	23	27 Feb 99	2	
FILL HER UP	Polydor	36	24 Apr 99	2	
ALBUMS:	HITS 4			WEEKS 14	
OLYMPIAN	Costermonger	8	1 Apr 95	6	
TO SEE THE LIGHTS	Costermonger	11	3 Feb 96	3	
DRAWN TO THE DEEP END	Polydor	8	1 Mar 97	3	
REVELATIONS	Polydor	25	13 Mar 99	2	

GENE AND JIM ARE INTO SHAKES

SINGLES:	HITS 1			UK WEEKS 2	
SHAKE! (HOW ABOUT A SAMPLING, GENE?)	Rough Trade	68	19 Mar 88	2	

GENE LOVES JEZEBEL

SINGLES:	HITS 4			UK WEEKS 7	
SWEETEST THING	Beggars Banquet	75	29 Mar 86	1	
HEARTACHE	Beggars Banquet	71	14 Jun 86	2	
THE MOTION OF LOVE	Beggars Banquet	56	5 Sep 87	3	
GORGEOUS	Beggars Banquet	68	5 Dec 87	1	
ALBUMS:	HITS 2			WEEKS 5	
DISCOVER	Beggars Banquet	32	19 Jul 86	4	
HOUSE OF DOLLS	Beggars Banquet	81	24 Oct 87	1	

GENERAL DEGREE - See Richie STEPHENS featuring GENERAL DEGREE

GENERAL LEVY

SINGLES:	HITS 2			UK WEEKS 13	
MONKEY MAN	London	75	4 Sep 93	1	
INCREDIBLE	Renk	39	18 Jun 94	3	
Above hit: M-BEAT featuring GENERAL LEVY.					
INCREDIBLE [RM]	Renk	8	10 Sep 94	9	

GENERAL PUBLIC

SINGLES:	HITS 2			UK WEEKS 4	
GENERAL PUBLIC	Virgin	60	10 Mar 84	3	
I'LL TAKE YOU THERE	Epic	73	2 Jul 94	1	
From the film 'Threesome'.					

GENERAL SAINT

(See also Clint Eastwood and General Saint.)

SINGLES:	HITS 2			UK WEEKS 6	
OH CAROL!	Copasetic	54	2 Apr 94	5	
Above hit: GENERAL SAINT featuring Don CAMPBELL.					
SAVE THE LAST DANCE FOR ME	Copasetic	75	6 Aug 94	1	
Above hit: SAINT and CAMPBELL.					

GENERATION X

SINGLES:	HITS 7			UK WEEKS 31	
YOUR GENERATION	Chrysalis	36	17 Sep 77	4	
READY STEADY GO	Chrysalis	47	11 Mar 78	3	
KING ROCKER	Chrysalis	11	20 Jan 79	9	
VALLEY OF THE DOLLS	Chrysalis	23	7 Apr 79	7	
FRIDAYS ANGELS	Chrysalis	62	30 Jun 79	2	
DANCING WITH MYSELF	Chrysalis	62	18 Oct 80	2	
DANCING WITH MYSELF [EP]	Chrysalis	60	24 Jan 81	4	
Lead track: Dancing With Myself.					
Above 2: GEN X.					
ALBUMS:	HITS 2			WEEKS 9	
GENERATION X	Chrysalis	29	8 Apr 78	4	
VALLEY OF THE DOLLS	Chrysalis	51	17 Feb 79	5	

GENERATOR
Holland

SINGLES:		HITS 1			WEEKS 1
WHERE ARE YOU NOW?		Tidy Trax	60	23 Oct 99	1
Originally released on the Polar State label in 1998.					

GENESIS
UK

SINGLES:		HITS 29			WEEKS 187
I KNOW WHAT I LIKE (IN YOUR WARDROBE)		Charisma	21	6 Apr 74	7
YOUR OWN SPECIAL WAY		Charisma	43	26 Feb 77	3
SPOT THE PIGEON [EP]		Charisma	14	28 May 77	7
Lead track: Match Of The Day.					
FOLLOW YOU FOLLOW ME		Charisma	7	11 Mar 78	13
MANY TOO MANY		Charisma	43	8 Jul 78	5
TURN IT ON AGAIN		Charisma	8	15 Mar 80	10
DUCHESS		Charisma	46	17 May 80	5
MISUNDERSTANDING		Charisma	42	13 Sep 80	5
ABACAB		Charisma	9	22 Aug 81	8
Title is the chord sequence of the song.					
KEEP IT DARK		Charisma	33	31 Oct 81	4
MAN ON THE CORNER		Charisma	41	13 Mar 82	5
3 X 3 [EP]		Charisma	10	22 May 82	8
Lead track: Paperlate.					
MAMA		Charisma	4	3 Sep 83	10
THAT'S ALL		Charisma	16	12 Nov 83	11
ILLEGAL ALIEN		Charisma	46	11 Feb 84	3
ILLEGAL ALIEN [RE]		Charisma	70	10 Mar 84	1
INVISIBLE TOUCH		Virgin	15	31 May 86	8
IN TOO DEEP (FROM THE FILM 'MONA LISA')		Virgin	19	30 Aug 86	9
LAND OF CONFUSION		Virgin	14	22 Nov 86	12
TONIGHT, TONIGHT, TONIGHT		Virgin	18	14 Mar 87	6
THROWING IT ALL AWAY		Virgin	22	20 Jun 87	8
NO SON OF MINE		Virgin	6	2 Nov 91	6
NO SON OF MINE [RE]		Virgin	70	4 Jan 92	1
I CAN'T DANCE		Virgin	7	11 Jan 92	9
HOLD ON MY HEART		Virgin	16	18 Apr 92	5
JESUS HE KNOWS ME		Virgin	20	25 Jul 92	7
INVISIBLE TOUCH (LIVE) [RR]		Virgin	7	21 Nov 92	4
TELL ME WHY		Virgin	40	20 Feb 93	3
CONGO		Virgin	29	27 Sep 97	2
SHIPWRECKED		Virgin	54	13 Dec 97	1
NOT ABOUT US		Virgin	66	7 Mar 98	1

ALBUMS:		HITS 21			WEEKS 485
FOXTROT		Charisma	12	14 Oct 72	7
GENESIS LIVE		Charisma	9	11 Aug 73	10
SELLING ENGLAND BY THE POUND		Charisma	3	20 Oct 73	21
NURSERY CRYME		Charisma	39	11 May 74	1
THE LAMB LIES DOWN ON BROADWAY		Charisma	10	7 Dec 74	6
A TRICK OF THE TRAIL		Charisma	3	28 Feb 76	39
WIND AND WUTHERING		Charisma	7	15 Jan 77	22
SECONDS OUT		Charisma	4	29 Oct 77	17
. . . AND THEN THERE WERE THREE . . .		Charisma	3	15 Apr 78	32
DUKE		Charisma	1	5 Apr 80	30
ABACAB		Charisma	1	26 Sep 81	27
THREE SIDES LIVE		Charisma	2	12 Jun 82	19
Live recordings apart from the fourth side, which contains studio cuts from 1979–81.					
GENESIS		Charisma	1	15 Oct 83	51
NURSERY CRYME [RE]		Charisma	68	31 Mar 84	1
Repackaged.					
TRESPASS		Charisma	98	21 Apr 84	1
Originally released in 1970.					
INVISIBLE TOUCH		Charisma	1	21 Jun 86	96
WE CAN'T DANCE		Virgin	1	23 Nov 91	61
LIVE - THE WAY WE WALK VOLUME 1: THE SHORTS		Virgin	3	28 Nov 92	18
LIVE - THE WAY WE WALK VOLUME 2: THE LONGS		Virgin	1	23 Jan 93	9
CALLING ALL STATIONS		Virgin	2	13 Sep 97	7
ARCHIVE 1967-75		Virgin	35	4 Jul 98	1
4 CD box set containing a live version of The Lamb Lies Down On Broadway and live tracks/B-sides and demos.					
TURN IT ON AGAIN - THE HITS		Virgin	4	6 Nov 99	9

Lee A. GENESIS - See Bob SINCLAR featuring Lee A. GENESIS

GENEVA
UK

SINGLES:		HITS 5			WEEKS 8
NO ONE SPEAKS		Nude	32	26 Oct 96	2
INTO THE BLUE		Nude	26	8 Feb 97	2
TRANQUILLIZER		Nude	24	31 May 97	2

BEST REGRETS	*Nude*	38	*16 Aug 97*	1
DOLLARS IN THE HEAVENS	*Nude*	59	*27 Nov 99*	1
ALBUMS:	**HITS 1**		**WEEKS 2**	
FURTHER	*Nude*	20	*21 Jun 97*	2

GENEVEVE
UK

SINGLES:	**HITS 1**		**WEEKS 1**	
ONCE	*CBS*	43	*7 May 66*	1

GENIUS/GZA
US

SINGLES:	**HITS 1**		**WEEKS 2**	
COLD WORLD	*Geffen*	40	*2 Mar 96*	2

Above hit: GENIUS/GZA featuring D'ANGELO and INSPEKTAH DECK A.K.A.
ROLLIE FINGERS.

ALBUMS:	**HITS 2**		**WEEKS 2**	
LIQUID SWORDS	*Geffen*	73	*2 Dec 95*	1
BENEATH THE SURFACE	*MCA*	56	*10 Jul 99*	1

Jackie GENOVA
UK

ALBUMS:	**HITS 1**		**WEEKS 2**	
WORK THAT BODY	*Island*	74	*21 May 83*	2

Bobbie GENTRY
US

(See also Bobbie Gentry and Glen Campbell.)

SINGLES:	**HITS 3**		**WEEKS 34**	
ODE TO BILLY JOE	*Capitol*	13	*16 Sep 67*	11
I'LL NEVER FALL IN LOVE AGAIN	*Capitol*	1	*30 Aug 69*	19

Originally recorded by Dionne Warwick.

RAINDROPS KEEP FALLING ON MY HEAD	*Capitol*	40	*21 Feb 70*	4
ALBUMS:	**HITS 1**		**WEEKS 1**	
TOUCH 'EM WITH LOVE	*Capitol*	21	*25 Oct 69*	1

Bobbie GENTRY and Glen CAMPBELL
US

(See also Glen Campbell; Bobbie Gentry.)

SINGLES:	**HITS 1**		**WEEKS 14**	
ALL I HAVE TO DO IS DREAM	*Capitol*	3	*6 Dec 69*	14
ALBUMS:	**HITS 1**		**WEEKS 1**	
BOBBIE GENTRY AND GLEN CAMPBELL	*Capitol*	50	*28 Feb 70*	1

GEORDIE
UK

SINGLES:	**HITS 4**		**WEEKS 35**	
DON'T DO THAT	*Regal Zonophone*	32	*2 Dec 72*	7
ALL BECAUSE OF YOU	*EMI*	6	*17 Mar 73*	13
CAN YOU DO IT	*EMI*	13	*16 Jun 73*	9
ELECTRIC LADY	*EMI*	32	*25 Aug 73*	6

Lowell GEORGE
US

ALBUMS:	**HITS 1**		**WEEKS 1**	
THANKS BUT I'LL EAT IT HERE	*Warner Brothers*	71	*21 Apr 79*	1

Robin GEORGE
UK

SINGLES:	**HITS 1**		**WEEKS 2**	
HEARTLINE	*Bronze*	68	*27 Apr 85*	2
ALBUMS:	**HITS 1**		**WEEKS 3**	
DANGEROUS MUSIC	*Bronze*	65	*2 Mar 85*	3

Sophia GEORGE
Jamaica

SINGLES:	**HITS 1**		**WEEKS 11**	
GIRLIE GIRLIE	*Winner*	7	*7 Dec 85*	11

GEORGIA SATELLITES
US

SINGLES:	**HITS 3**		**WEEKS 8**	
KEEP YOUR HANDS TO YOURSELF	*Elektra*	69	*7 Feb 87*	1
BATTLESHIP CHAINS (KICK 'N' LICK REMIX)	*Elektra*	44	*16 May 87*	4
HIPPY HIPPY SHAKE	*Elektra*	63	*21 Jan 89*	3
ALBUMS:	**HITS 2**		**WEEKS 9**	
GEORGIA SATELLITES	*Elektra*	52	*7 Feb 87*	7
OPEN ALL NIGHT	*Elektra*	39	*2 Jul 88*	2

GEORGIE PORGIE

			US	
SINGLES:	HITS 2		WEEKS 2	
EVERYBODY MUST PARTY	*Vibe*	61	*12 Aug 95*	1
TAKE ME HIGHER	*MCA/Music Plant*	61	*4 May 96*	1

GEORGIO

			US	
SINGLES:	HITS 1		WEEKS 3	
LOVER'S LANE	*Motown*	54	*20 Feb 88*	3

Danyel GERARD

			France	
SINGLES:	HITS 1		WEEKS 12	
BUTTERFLY	*CBS*	11	*18 Sep 71*	12

Charles GERHARDT – See James GALWAY.

GERIDEAU

			US	
SINGLES:	HITS 2		WEEKS 2	
BRING IT BACK 2 LUV	*Fruittree*	65	*27 Aug 94*	1
Above hit: PROJECT featuring GERIDEAU.				
MASQUERADE	*Inferno*	63	*4 Jul 98*	1

GERRY and the PACEMAKERS

			UK	
SINGLES:	HITS 9		WEEKS 114	
HOW DO YOU DO IT?	*Columbia*	1	*16 Mar 63*	18
Originally written for Adam Faith.				
I LIKE IT	*Columbia*	1	*1 Jun 63*	15
YOU'LL NEVER WALK ALONE	*Columbia*	1	*12 Oct 63*	19
From the film 'Carousel'. Also the terrace chant for Liverpool FC.				
I'M THE ONE	*Columbia*	2	*18 Jan 64*	15
DON'T LET THE SUN CATCH YOU CRYING	*Columbia*	6	*18 Apr 64*	11
Originally recorded by Louise Cordet.				
IT'S GONNA BE ALL RIGHT	*Columbia*	24	*5 Sep 64*	7
FERRY CROSS THE MERSEY	*Columbia*	8	*19 Dec 64*	13
From the film of the same name.				
I'LL BE THERE	*Columbia*	15	*27 Mar 65*	9
Originally recorded by Bobby Darin.				
WALK HAND IN HAND	*Columbia*	29	*20 Nov 65*	7
EPS:	HITS 4		WEEKS 49	
HOW DO YOU DO IT?	*Columbia*	2	*13 Jul 63*	35
YOU'LL NEVER WALK ALONE	*Columbia*	8	*22 Feb 64*	8
I'M THE ONE	*Columbia*	11	*18 Apr 64*	5
DON'T LET THE SUN CATCH YOU CRYING	*Columbia*	15	*10 Oct 64*	1
ALBUMS:	HITS 2		WEEKS 29	
HOW DO YOU LIKE IT?	*Columbia*	2	*26 Oct 63*	28
FERRY ACROSS THE MERSEY	*Columbia*	19	*6 Feb 65*	1

GET READY

			UK	
SINGLES:	HITS 1		WEEKS 1	
WILD, WILD WEST	*Mega*	65	*3 Jun 95*	1

GETO BOYS featuring FLAJ

			US	
SINGLES:	HITS 1		WEEKS 1	
THE WORLD IS A GHETTO	*Virgin*	49	*11 May 96*	1

Stan GETZ

(See also Stan Getz and Charlie Byrd.)

			US	
SINGLES:	HITS 1		WEEKS 16	
THE GIRL FROM IPANEMA (GAROTA DE IPANEMA)	*Verve*	29	*25 Jul 64*	10
Above hit: Stan GETZ Joao GILBERTO vocal by Astrud GILBERTO.				
THE GIRL FROM IPANEMA [RI]	*Verve*	55	*25 Aug 84*	6
Above hit: Astrud GILBERTO.				

Stan GETZ and Charlie BYRD

(See also Stan Getz.)

			US	
SINGLES:	HITS 1		WEEKS 13	
DESAFINADO	*His Master's Voice*	11	*10 Nov 62*	13
ALBUMS:	HITS 1		WEEKS 7	
JAZZ SAMBA	*Verve*	15	*23 Feb 63*	7

Angela GHEORGIU – See Roberto ALAGNA/Angela GHEORGIU

GHOST DANCE

UK

SINGLES:	HITS 1		WEEKS 2	
DOWN TO THE WIRE	Chrysalis	66	17 Jun 89	2

GHOSTFACE KILLAH

US

SINGLES:	HITS 1		WEEKS 4	
ALL THAT I GOT IS YOU	Epic Street	11	12 Jul 97	4

Samples the Jackson 5's Maybe Tomorrow.

ALBUMS:	HITS 1		WEEKS 2	
IRONMAN	Epic	38	9 Nov 96	2

Andy GIBB

UK

SINGLES:	HITS 4		WEEKS 30	
I JUST WANNA BE YOUR EVERYTHING	RSO	26	25 Jun 77	7
SHADOW DANCING	RSO	42	13 May 78	6
AN EVERLASTING LOVE	RSO	10	12 Aug 78	10
(OUR LOVE) DON'T THROW IT ALL AWAY	RSO	32	27 Jan 79	7

ALBUMS:	HITS 1		WEEKS 9	
SHADOW DANCING	RSO	15	19 Aug 78	9

Barry GIBB

UK

SINGLES:	HITS 1		WEEKS 10	
GUILTY	CBS	34	6 Dec 80	10

Above hit: Barbra STREISAND and Barry GIBB.

ALBUMS:	HITS 1		WEEKS 2	
NOW VOYAGER	Polydor	85	20 Oct 84	2

Robin GIBB

UK

SINGLES:	HITS 3		WEEKS 21	
SAVED BY THE BELL	Polydor	2	12 Jul 69	16
SAVED BY THE BELL [RE]	Polydor	49	15 Nov 69	1
AUGUST OCTOBER	Polydor	45	7 Feb 70	3
ANOTHER LONELY NIGHT IN NEW YORK	Polydor	71	11 Feb 84	1

Steve GIBBONS BAND

UK

SINGLES:	HITS 2		WEEKS 14	
TULANE	Polydor	12	6 Aug 77	10
EDDY VORTEX	Polydor	56	13 May 78	4

ALBUMS:	HITS 1		WEEKS 3	
CAUGHT IN THE ACT	Polydor	22	22 Oct 77	3

Georgia GIBBS

US

SINGLES:	HITS 2		WEEKS 2	
TWEEDLEE DEE	Mercury	20	23 Apr 55	1

Above hit: Georgia GIBBS with Glenn OSSER and his Orchestra.

KISS ME ANOTHER	Mercury	24	14 Jul 56	1

Debbie GIBSON

US

(See also Various Artists: Stage Cast – London 'Grease'.)

SINGLES:	HITS 11		WEEKS 70	
ONLY IN MY DREAMS	Atlantic	54	26 Sep 87	5
SHAKE YOUR LOVE	Atlantic	7	23 Jan 88	8
ONLY IN MY DREAMS [RE]	Atlantic	11	19 Mar 88	7
OUT OF THE BLUE	Atlantic	19	7 May 88	7
FOOLISH BEAT	Atlantic	9	9 Jul 88	9
STAYING TOGETHER	Atlantic	53	15 Oct 88	2
LOST IN YOUR EYES	Atlantic	34	28 Jan 89	7
ELECTRIC YOUTH	Atlantic	14	29 Apr 89	8
WE COULD BE TOGETHER	Atlantic	22	19 Aug 89	8
ANYTHING IS POSSIBLE	Atlantic	51	9 Mar 91	2
SHOCK YOUR MAMA	Atlantic	74	3 Apr 93	1
YOU'RE THE ONE THAT I WANT	Epic	13	24 Jul 93	6

From the musical 'Grease'.
Above hit: Craig McLACHLAN and Debbie GIBSON.

ALBUMS:	HITS 3		WEEKS 52	
OUT OF THE BLUE	Atlantic	26	30 Jan 88	35
ELECTRIC YOUTH	Atlantic	8	11 Feb 89	16
ANYTHING IS POSSIBLE	Atlantic	69	30 Mar 91	1

Don GIBSON

US

SINGLES:	HITS 2			WEEKS 16
SEA OF HEARTBREAK	RCA	14	2 Sep 61	13
LONESOME NUMBER ONE	RCA	47	3 Feb 62	3
ALBUMS:	HITS 1			WEEKS 10
COUNTRY NUMBER ONE	Warwick	13	22 Mar 80	10

Wayne GIBSON

UK

SINGLES:	HITS 2			WEEKS 13
KELLY	Pye	48	5 Sep 64	2
Originally recorded by Del Shannon.				
UNDER MY THUMB	Pye Disco Demand	17	23 Nov 74	11
Originally recorded by the Rolling Stones.				

GIBSON BROTHERS

Martinique

SINGLES:	HITS 6			WEEKS 54
CUBA	Island	41	10 Mar 79	9
OOH! WHAT A LIFE	Island	10	21 Jul 79	12
QUE SERA MI VIDA (IF YOU SHOULD GO)	Island	5	17 Nov 79	11
CUBA [RI] / BETTER DO IT SALSA	Island	12	23 Feb 80	9
MARIANA	Island	11	12 Jul 80	10
MY HEART'S BEATING WILD (TIC TAC TIC TAC)	Stiff	56	9 Jul 83	3
ALBUMS:	HITS 1			WEEKS 3
ON THE RIVIERA	Island	50	30 Aug 80	3

GIDEA PARK

UK

SINGLES:	HITS 2			WEEKS 19
BEACH BOY GOLD [M]	Stone	11	4 Jul 81	13
SEASONS OF GOLD [M]	Polo	28	12 Sep 81	6
Above 2 medleys are of Beach Boys and Four Seasons songs.				

GIFTED

UK

SINGLES:	HITS 1			WEEKS 1
DO I	Perfecto	60	23 Aug 97	1

GIGOLO AUNTS

US

SINGLES:	HITS 2			WEEKS 4
MRS. WASHINGTON	Fire	74	23 Apr 94	1
WHERE I FIND MY HEAVEN	Fire	29	13 May 95	3
From the film 'Dumb And Dumber'. Originally released in 1994.				

Astrud GILBERTO – See Stan GETZ

Joao GILBERTO – See Stan GETZ

Donna GILES

US

SINGLES:	HITS 1			WEEKS 4
AND I'M TELLING YOU I'M NOT GOING	Ore	43	13 Aug 94	2
AND I'M TELLING YOU I'M NOT GOING [RM]	Ore	27	10 Feb 96	2
From the film 'Dreamgirls'. Remixed by Stonebridge and Nick Nice.				

Johnny GILL

US

SINGLES:	HITS 4			WEEKS 12
WRAP MY BODY TIGHT	Motown	57	23 Feb 91	2
SLOW AND SEXY	Epic	17	28 Nov 92	7
Above hit: Shabba RANKS (featuring Johnny GILL).				
THE FLOOR	Motown	53	17 Jul 93	1
A CUTE, SWEET, LOVE ADDICTION	Motown	46	29 Jan 94	2
ALBUMS:	HITS 1			WEEKS 3
PROVOCATIVE	Motown	41	19 Jun 93	3

Vince GILL – See Amy GRANT; Barbra STREISAND

GILLAN

UK

(See also Ian Gillan.)

SINGLES:	HITS 8			WEEKS 46
SLEEPING ON THE JOB	Virgin	55	14 Jun 80	3
TROUBLE	Virgin	14	4 Oct 80	6
MUTUALLY ASSURED DESTRUCTION	Virgin	32	14 Feb 81	5
NEW ORLEANS	Virgin	17	21 Mar 81	10
NO LAUGHING IN HEAVEN	Virgin	31	20 Jun 81	6
NIGHTMARE	Virgin	36	10 Oct 81	6

RESTLESS	Virgin	25	23 Jan 82	7
LIVING FOR THE CITY	Virgin	50	4 Sep 82	3
ALBUMS:	**HITS 6**		**WEEKS 53**	
CHILD IN TIME	Polydor	55	17 Jul 76	1
Above hit: Ian GILLAN BAND.				
MR. UNIVERSE	Acrobat	11	20 Oct 79	6
GLORY ROAD	Virgin	3	16 Aug 80	12
FUTURE SHOCK	Virgin	2	25 Apr 81	13
DOUBLE TROUBLE	Virgin	12	7 Nov 81	15
MAGIC	Virgin	17	2 Oct 82	6

Ian GILLAN UK

(See also Gillan.)

ALBUMS:	**HITS 1**		**WEEKS 1**	
NAKED THUNDER	Teldec	63	28 Jul 90	1

GILLETTE - See 20 FINGERS

Stuart GILLIES UK

SINGLES:	**HITS 1**		**WEEKS 10**	
AMANDA	Philips	13	31 Mar 73	10

Jimmy GILMER and the FIREBALLS - See FIREBALLS

David GILMOUR UK

ALBUMS:	**HITS 2**		**WEEKS 18**	
DAVID GILMOUR	Harvest	17	10 Jun 78	9
ABOUT FACE	Harvest	21	17 Mar 84	9

James GILREATH US

SINGLES:	**HITS 1**		**WEEKS 10**	
LITTLE BAND OF GOLD	Pye International	29	4 May 63	10

Jim GILSTRAP US

SINGLES:	**HITS 1**		**WEEKS 11**	
SWING YOUR DADDY	Chelsea	4	15 Mar 75	11

Gordon GILTRAP UK

SINGLES:	**HITS 2**		**WEEKS 10**	
HEARTSONG	Electric	21	14 Jan 78	7
Occasionally used as the BBC's Holiday programme theme.				
FEAR OF THE DARK	Electric	58	28 Apr 79	3
Above hit: Gordon GILTRAP BAND.				
ALBUMS:	**HITS 1**		**WEEKS 7**	
PERILOUS JOURNEY	Electric	29	18 Feb 78	7

GIN BLOSSOMS US

SINGLES:	**HITS 4**		**WEEKS 12**	
HEY JEALOUSY	Fontana	24	5 Feb 94	5
FOUND OUT ABOUT YOU	Fontana	40	16 Apr 94	3
TIL I HEAR IT FROM YOU	A&M	39	10 Feb 96	2
From the film 'Empire'.				
FOLLOW YOU DOWN	A&M	30	27 Apr 96	2
ALBUMS:	**HITS 2**		**WEEKS 6**	
NEW MISERABLE EXPERIENCE	Fontana	53	26 Feb 94	4
CONGRATULATIONS, I'M SORRY	A&M	42	24 Feb 96	2

GINUWINE US

SINGLES:	**HITS 5**		**WEEKS 22**	
PONY	Epic	16	25 Jan 97	6
TELL ME DO U WANNA	Epic	16	24 May 97	3
WHEN DOVES CRY	Epic	10	6 Sep 97	5
HOLLER	Epic	13	14 Mar 98	4
Additional vocals by Maria Wallace.				
WHAT'S SO DIFFERENT?	Epic	10	13 Mar 99	4
Samples the Monkees' Valleri.				
ALBUMS:	**HITS 2**		**WEEKS 2**	
GINUWINE ... THE BACHELOR	Epic	74	28 Mar 98	1
100% GINUWINE	Epic	42	27 Mar 99	1

GIORGIO - See Giorgio MORODER

GIPSY KINGS

France

SINGLES:		HITS 1		WEEKS 2	
HITS MEDLEY [M]	Columbia	53	3 Sep 94	2
Medley of 5 previous uncharted single releases.					
ALBUMS:		HITS 5		WEEKS 65	
GIPSY KINGS	Telstar	16	15 Apr 89	29
MOSAIQUE	Telstar	27	25 Nov 89	13
ESTE MUNDO	Columbia	19	13 Jul 91	7
GREATEST HITS	Columbia	11	6 Aug 94	11
VOLARE - THE VERY BEST OF THE GIPSY KINGS	Columbia	20	24 Jul 99	5

Martine GIRAULT

UK

SINGLES:		HITS 2		WEEKS 7	
REVIVAL	ffrr	53	29 Aug 92	2
REVIVAL [RI-1ST]	ffrr	37	30 Jan 93	3
BEEN THINKING ABOUT YOU	RCA	63	28 Oct 95	1
REVIVAL [RI-2ND]	RCA	61	1 Feb 97	1

GIRL

UK

SINGLES:		HITS 1		WEEKS 3	
HOLLYWOOD TEASE	Jet	50	12 Apr 80	3
ALBUMS:		HITS 2		WEEKS 6	
SHEER GREED	Jet	33	9 Feb 80	5
WASTED YOUTH	Jet	92	23 Jan 82	1

GIRLFRIEND

UK

SINGLES:		HITS 2		WEEKS 5	
TAKE IT FROM ME	Arista	47	30 Jan 93	4
GIRL'S LIFE	Arista	68	15 May 93	1

GIRLS AT OUR BEST

UK

ALBUMS:		HITS 1		WEEKS 3	
PLEASURE	Happy Birthday	60	7 Nov 81	3

GIRLSCHOOL

UK

SINGLES:		HITS 5		WEEKS 25	
RACE WITH THE DEVIL	Bronze	49	2 Aug 80	6
ST. VALENTINE'S DAY MASSACRE [EP]	Bronze	5	21 Feb 81	8
Lead track: Please Don't Touch.					
Above hit: HEADGIRL (MOTORHEAD and GIRLSCHOOL).					
HIT AND RUN	Bronze	32	11 Apr 81	6
C'MON LET'S GO	Bronze	42	11 Jul 81	3
WILDLIFE [EP]	Bronze	58	3 Apr 82	2
Lead track: Don't Call It Love.					
ALBUMS:		HITS 4		WEEKS 23	
DEMOLITION	Bronze	28	5 Jul 80	10
HIT 'N' RUN	Bronze	5	25 Apr 81	6
SCREAMING BLUE MURDER	Bronze	27	12 Jun 82	6
PLAY DIRTY	Bronze	66	12 Nov 83	1

Junior GISCOMBE - See JUNIOR

GLADEZZ - See SOUND OF ONE featuring GLADEZZ

GLADIATORS

UK

SINGLES:		HITS 1		WEEKS 1	
THE BOYS ARE BACK IN TOWN	RCA	70	30 Nov 96	1
Title music to ITV's 5th series of 'Gladiators'.					
COMPILATION ALBUMS:		HITS 1		WEEKS 10	
GLADIATORS - THE ALBUM	PolyGram TV	11	28 Nov 92	10
Above entry was in the compilation chart.					

GLAM

Italy

SINGLES:		HITS 1		WEEKS 2	
HELL'S PARTY	Six6	42	1 May 93	2

GLAM METAL DETECTIVES

UK

SINGLES:		HITS 1		WEEKS 2	
EVERYBODY UP!	ZTT	29	11 Mar 95	2
Theme from the BBC2 TV series 'Glam Metal Detectives'.					

GLAMMA KID

UK

SINGLES:		HITS 3		WEEKS 15	
FASHION 98	WEA		49	21 Nov 98	1
TABOO	WEA		10	17 Apr 99	8
Above hit: GLAMMA KID featuring Shola AMA.					
WHY	WEA		10	27 Nov 99	6
Includes vocals by Marcelle Duprey.					

GLASGOW RANGERS FOOTBALL CLUB

UK

SINGLES:		HITS 1		WEEKS 2	
GLASGOW RANGERS (NINE IN A ROW)	Gers		54	4 Oct 97	2

GLASS TIGER

Canada

SINGLES:		HITS 3		WEEKS 18	
DON'T FORGET ME (WHEN I'M GONE)	Manhattan		29	18 Oct 86	9
Backing vocals by Bryan Adams.					
SOMEDAY	Manhattan		66	31 Jan 87	2
MY TOWN	EMI		33	26 Oct 91	7
Vocals by Rod Stewart.					

Mayson GLEN ORCHESTRA - See Paul HENRY and the Mayson GLEN ORCHESTRA

GLENN and CHRIS

UK

SINGLES:		HITS 1		WEEKS 8	
DIAMOND LIGHTS	Record Shack		12	18 Apr 87	8

GLIDE - See VARIOUS ARTISTS (EPs) 'Fourplay Volume 1 EP'

Gary GLITTER

UK

SINGLES:		HITS 23		WEEKS 170	
ROCK AND ROLL PART 1 / ROCK AND ROLL PART 2	Bell		2	10 Jun 72	15
Part 2 was listed on the chart from 24 Jun 72.					
I DIDN'T KNOW I LOVED YOU (TILL I SAW YOU ROCK AND ROLL)	Bell		4	23 Sep 72	11
DO YOU WANNA TOUCH ME? (OH YEAH!)	Bell		2	20 Jan 73	11
HELLO! HELLO! I'M BACK AGAIN	Bell		2	7 Apr 73	14
I'M THE LEADER OF THE GANG (I AM!)	Bell		1	21 Jul 73	12
I LOVE YOU LOVE ME LOVE	Bell		1	17 Nov 73	14
REMEMBER ME THIS WAY	Bell		3	30 Mar 74	8
ALWAYS YOURS	Bell		1	15 Jun 74	9
OH YES! YOU'RE BEAUTIFUL	Bell		2	23 Nov 74	10
LOVE LIKE YOU AND ME	Bell		10	3 May 75	6
DOING ALL RIGHT WITH THE BOYS	Bell		6	21 Jun 75	7
PAPA OOM MOW MOW	Bell		38	8 Nov 75	5
Originally recorded by the Rivingtons.					
YOU BELONG TO ME	Bell		40	13 Mar 76	5
IT TAKES ALL NIGHT LONG	Arista		25	22 Jan 77	6
A LITTLE BOOGIE WOOGIE IN THE BACK OF MY MIND	Arista		31	16 Jul 77	5
GARY GLITTER [EP]	GTO		57	20 Sep 80	3
Lead track: I'm The Leader Of The Gang (I Am). This and the other tracks are all re-issues.					
AND THEN SHE KISSED ME	Bell		39	10 Oct 81	5
ALL THAT GLITTERS [M]	Bell		48	5 Dec 81	5
DANCE ME UP	Arista		25	23 Jun 84	5
ANOTHER ROCK AND ROLL CHRISTMAS	Arista		7	1 Dec 84	7
AND THE LEADER ROCKS ON [M]	EMI		58	10 Oct 92	2
THROUGH THE YEARS	EMI		49	21 Nov 92	3
HELLO, HELLO, I'M BACK AGAIN (AGAIN!) [RR]	Carlton Sounds		50	16 Dec 95	2
Sleeve gives title as an EP: By Public Demand.					
ALBUMS:		HITS 5		WEEKS 100	
GLITTER	Bell		8	21 Oct 72	40
TOUCH ME	Bell		2	16 Jun 73	33
REMEMBER ME THIS WAY	Bell		5	29 Jun 74	14
GARY GLITTER'S GREATEST HITS	Bell		33	27 Mar 76	5
MANY HAPPY RETURNS - THE HITS	EMI		35	14 Nov 92	8

GLITTER BAND

UK

SINGLES:		HITS 7		WEEKS 60	
ANGEL FACE	Bell		4	23 Mar 74	10
JUST FOR YOU	Bell		10	3 Aug 74	8
LET'S GET TOGETHER AGAIN	Bell		8	19 Oct 74	8
GOODBYE MY LOVE	Bell		2	18 Jan 75	9
THE TEARS I CRIED	Bell		8	12 Apr 75	8
LOVE IN THE SUN	Bell		15	9 Aug 75	8
PEOPLE LIKE YOU AND PEOPLE LIKE ME	Bell		5	28 Feb 76	9
ALBUMS:		HITS 3		WEEKS 17	
HEY	Bell		13	14 Sep 74	12

ROCK 'N' ROLL DUDES	Bell	17	3 May 75	4
GREATEST HITS	Bell	52	19 Jun 76	1

GLOBAL COMMUNICATION
UK

SINGLES:	**HITS 1**		**WEEKS 1**	
THE WAY / THE DEEP	Dedicated	51	11 Jan 97	1

GLORIA! – See Gloria ESTEFAN

GLOVE
UK

SINGLES:	**HITS 1**		**WEEKS 3**	
LIKE A ANIMAL	Wonderland	52	20 Aug 83	3
ALBUMS:	**HITS 1**		**WEEKS 3**	
BLUE SUNSHINE	Wonderland	35	17 Sep 83	3

GLOWORM
UK/US

SINGLES:	**HITS 2**		**WEEKS 17**	
I LIFT MY CUP	Pulse 8	20	6 Feb 93	4
CARRY ME HOME	Go! Discs	9	14 May 94	11
I LIFT MY CUP [RI]	Pulse 8	46	6 Aug 94	2

GO-BETWEENS
Australia

ALBUMS:	**HITS 2**		**WEEKS 2**	
TALLULAH	Beggars Banquet	91	13 May 87	1
16 LOVER'S LANE	Beggars Banquet	81	10 Sep 88	1

GO GO LORENZO and the DAVIS PINCKNEY PROJECT
US

SINGLES:	**HITS 1**		**WEEKS 8**	
YOU CAN DANCE IF YOU WANT TO	Boiling Point	46	6 Dec 86	8

GO-GO'S
US

SINGLES:	**HITS 3**		**WEEKS 10**	
OUR LIPS ARE SEALED	I.R.S.	47	15 Jun 82	6
COOL JERK	I.R.S.	60	26 Jan 91	1
THE WHOLE WORLD LOST IT'S HEAD	I.R.S.	29	18 Feb 95	3

Single was issued as a double-A side with Our Lips Are Sealed, though not listed on the chart as such.

ALBUMS:	**HITS 2**		**WEEKS 4**	
VACATION	I.R.S.	75	21 Aug 82	3
RETURN TO THE VALLEY OF THE GO-GO'S	I.R.S.	52	18 Mar 95	1

Compilation of singles, live tracks and B-sides with 3 new tracks.

GO WEST
UK

SINGLES:	**HITS 12**		**WEEKS 85**	
WE CLOSE OUR EYES	Chrysalis	5	23 Feb 85	14
CALL ME	Chrysalis	12	11 May 85	10
GOODBYE GIRL	Chrysalis	25	3 Aug 85	7
DON'T LOOK DOWN – THE SEQUEL	Chrysalis	13	23 Nov 85	10
TRUE COLOURS	Chrysalis	48	29 Nov 86	7
I WANT TO HEAR IT FROM YOU	Chrysalis	43	9 May 87	3
THE KING IS DEAD	Chrysalis	67	12 Sep 87	2
THE KING OF WISHFUL THINKING	Chrysalis	18	28 Jul 90	10
FAITHFUL	Chrysalis	13	17 Oct 92	6
WHAT YOU WON'T DO FOR LOVE	Chrysalis	15	16 Jan 93	5

Original by Bobby Caldwell reached No. 8 in the US in 1979.

STILL IN LOVE	Chrysalis	43	27 Mar 93	3
TRACKS OF MY TEARS	Chrysalis	16	2 Oct 93	5
WE CLOSE OUR EYES '93 [RM]	Chrysalis	40	4 Dec 93	3

Remixed by Tom Lord Alge.

ALBUMS:	**HITS 4**		**WEEKS 119**	
GO WEST / BANGS AND CRASHES	Chrysalis	8	13 Apr 85	83

Peak position reached on 8 Mar 86. Bangs and Crashes was a remix album listed from 31 May 86, sales were combined.

DANCING ON THE COUCH	Chrysalis	19	6 Jun 87	5
INDIAN SUMMER	Chrysalis	13	14 Nov 92	16
ACES AND KINGS – THE BEST OF GO WEST	Chrysalis	5	16 Oct 93	15

GOATS
US

SINGLES:	**HITS 1**		**WEEKS 2**	
AAAH D YAAA / TYPICAL AMERICAN	Columbia	53	29 May 93	2

Typical American only listed on 5 Jun 93 once it had dropped to No. 65.

ALBUMS:	**HITS 1**		**WEEKS 1**	
NO GOATS, NO GLORY	Columbia	58	27 Aug 94	1

GOD MACHINE

US

SINGLES:	HITS 1			WEEKS 2
HOME	Fiction	65	30 Jan 93	2
ALBUMS:	HITS 1			WEEKS 1
SCENES FROM THE SECOND STOREY	Fiction	55	20 Feb 93	1

GODFATHERS

UK

ALBUMS:	HITS 2			WEEKS 3
BIRTH, SCHOOL, WORK, DEATH	Epic	80	13 Feb 88	2
MORE SONGS ABOUT LOVE AND HATE	Epic	49	20 May 89	1

GODIEGO

US/Japan

SINGLES:	HITS 2			WEEKS 11
THE WATER MARGIN	BBC	37	15 Oct 77	4

Theme sung in English from the BBC1 TV series of the same name. [AA] listed with Pete Mac Junior's Japanese version.

GANDHARA	BBC	56	16 Feb 80	7

Theme from the BBC TV series 'Monkey'.

GODLEY and CREME

UK

SINGLES:	HITS 3			WEEKS 36
UNDER YOUR THUMB	Polydor	3	12 Sep 81	11
WEDDING BELLS	Polydor	7	21 Nov 81	11
CRY	Polydor	19	30 Mar 85	11
CRY [RE]	Polydor	66	16 Aug 86	3
ALBUMS:	HITS 4			WEEKS 34
CONSEQUENCES	Mercury	52	19 Nov 77	1

Above hit: Kevin GODLEY and Lol CRÈME.

L	Mercury	47	9 Sep 78	2
ISMISM	Polydor	29	17 Oct 81	13
CHANGING FACES – THE VERY BEST OF 10CC AND GODLEY AND CREME	ProTV	4	29 Aug 87	18

Above hit: 10CC and GODLEY and CRÈME.

GOD'S PROPERTY From Kirk FRANKLIN'S NU NATION

US

SINGLES:	HITS 1			WEEKS 1
STOMP	B-rite Music	60	22 Nov 97	1

Based around Funkadelic's One Nation Under A Groove.

Andrew GOLD

US

SINGLES:	HITS 4			WEEKS 36
LONELY BOY	Asylum	11	2 Apr 77	9

Backing vocals by Linda Ronstadt.

NEVER LET HER SLIP AWAY	Asylum	5	25 Mar 78	13
HOW CAN THIS BE LOVE	Asylum	19	24 Jun 78	10
THANK YOU FOR BEING A FRIEND	Asylum	42	14 Oct 78	4
ALBUMS:	HITS 1			WEEKS 7
ALL THIS AND HEAVEN TOO	Asylum	31	15 Apr 78	7

Brian and Tony GOLD - See RED DRAGON with Brian and Tony GOLD

GOLD BLADE

UK

SINGLES:	HITS 1			WEEKS 1
STRICTLY HARDCORE	Ultimate	64	22 Mar 97	1

GOLDBUG

UK

SINGLES:	HITS 1			WEEKS 5
WHOLE LOTTA LOVE	Acid Jazz	3	27 Jan 96	5

Samples the Pearl & Dean cinema tune called Asteroid.

GOLDEN EARRING

Holland

SINGLES:	HITS 2			WEEKS 16
RADAR LOVE	Track	7	8 Dec 73	13
RADAR LOVE [RR]	Polydor	44	8 Oct 77	3

Live recording.
Above hit: GOLDEN EARRING 'LIVE'.

ALBUMS:	HITS 1			WEEKS 4
MOONTAN	Track	24	2 Feb 74	4

GOLDEN GIRLS

UK

SINGLES:	HITS 1			WEEKS 3
KINETIC	Distinct'ive	38	3 Oct 98	2

Original release reached No. 86 in 1993.

KINETIC '99 [RM]	*Distinct'ive*	56	*4 Dec 99*	1

Remixed by Commie.

GOLDIE

UK

SINGLES:	**HITS 1**			**WEEKS 11**
MAKING UP AGAIN	*Bronze*	7	*27 May 78*	11

GOLDIE

UK

SINGLES:	**HITS 5**			**WEEKS 16**
INNER CITY LIFE	*ffrr*	49	*3 Dec 94*	2

Above hit: GOLDIE Presents METALHEADS.

ANGEL	*ffrr*	41	*9 Sep 95*	3
INNER CITY LIFE [RI]	*ffrr*	39	*11 Nov 95*	2

All three entries above feature vocals by Diane Charlamagne (of Urban Cookie Collective).

DIGITAL	*ffrr*	13	*1 Nov 97*	3

Above hit: GOLDIE featuring KRS ONE.

TEMPER TEMPER	*ffrr*	13	*24 Jan 98*	4

Features Noel Gallagher on vocal and guitar.

BELIEVE	*ffrr*	36	*18 Apr 98*	2

Samples Loose Ends' Hanging On A String.

ALBUMS:	**HITS 2**			**WEEKS 16**
TIMELESS	*ffrr*	7	*19 Aug 95*	12
SATURNZ RETURN	*ffrr*	15	*14 Feb 98*	4

GOLDIE and the GINGERBREADS

US

SINGLES:	**HITS 1**			**WEEKS 5**
CAN'T YOU HEAR MY HEARTBEAT?	*Decca*	25	*27 Feb 65*	5

Originally recorded by John Leyton.

Bobby GOLDSBORO

US

SINGLES:	**HITS 3**			**WEEKS 47**
HONEY	*United Artists*	2	*20 Apr 68*	15

Originally recorded by Bob Shane.

SUMMER (THE FIRST TIME)	*United Artists*	9	*4 Aug 73*	10
HELLO, SUMMERTIME	*United Artists*	14	*3 Aug 74*	10

Featured in the Coca-Cola TV commercial.

HONEY [RI]	*United Artists*	2	*29 Mar 75*	12

Glen GOLDSMITH

UK

SINGLES:	**HITS 4**			**WEEKS 24**
I WON'T CRY	*Reproduction*	34	*7 Nov 87*	7
DREAMING	*Reproduction*	12	*12 Mar 88*	11
WHAT YOU SEE IS WHAT YOU GET	*Reproduction*	33	*11 Jun 88*	5
SAVE A LITTLE BIT	*Reproduction*	73	*3 Sep 88*	1
ALBUMS:	**HITS 1**			**WEEKS 9**
WHAT YOU SEE IS WHAT YOU GET	*RCA*	14	*23 Jul 88*	9

GOMEZ

UK

SINGLES:	**HITS 6**			**WEEKS 13**
78 STONE WOBBLE	*Hut*	44	*11 Apr 98*	1
GET MYSELF ARRESTED	*Hut*	45	*13 Jun 98*	1
WHIPPIN' PICCADILLY	*Hut*	35	*12 Sep 98*	3
BRING IT ON	*Hut*	21	*10 Jul 99*	3
RHYTHM & BLUES ALIBI	*Hut*	18	*11 Sep 99*	3
WE HAVEN'T TURNED AROUND	*Hut*	38	*27 Nov 99*	2
ALBUMS:	**HITS 2**			**WEEKS 70**
BRING IT ON	*Hut*	11	*25 Apr 98*	58

Peak position reached on 3 Oct 98. Mercury Music Price winner of 1998.

LIQUID SKIN	*Hut*	2	*25 Sep 99*	12

Leroy GOMEZ – See SANTA ESMERALDA and Leroy GOMEZ

GOMPIE

Holland

SINGLES:	**HITS 1**			**WEEKS 12**
ALICE (WHO THE X IS ALICE?) (LIVING NEXT DOOR TO ALICE)	*Habana*	34	*20 May 95*	5
ALICE (WHO THE X IS ALICE?) (LIVING NEXT DOOR TO ALICE) [RE]	*Habana*	17	*02 Sep 95*	7

GONZALEZ

UK/US

SINGLES:	**HITS 1**			**WEEKS 11**
HAVEN'T STOPPED DANCING YET	*Sidewalk*	15	*31 Mar 79*	11

Written by Marc Bolan's girlfriend Gloria Jones.

GOO GOO DOLLS
US

SINGLES:	HITS 2			WEEKS 4	
IRIS	Reprise	50	1 Aug 98	1
From the film 'City Of Angels'.				
SLIDE	Hollywood	43	27 Mar 99	1
IRIS [RI]	Hollywood	26	17 Jul 99	2
ALBUMS:	HITS 1			WEEKS 1	
DIZZY UP THE GIRL	Hollywood	47	31 Jul 99	1

GOOD GIRLS
US

SINGLES:	HITS 1			WEEKS 1	
JUST CALL ME	Motown	75	24 Jul 93	1

Jack GOOD – See LORD ROCKINGHAM'S XI

GOODBYE MR. MACKENZIE
UK

SINGLES:	HITS 5			WEEKS 13	
GOODBYE MR. MACKENZIE	Capitol	62	20 Aug 88	2
THE RATTLER	Capitol	37	11 Mar 89	6
GOODWILL CITY / I'M SICK OF YOU	Capitol	49	29 Jul 89	2
LOVE CHILD	Parlophone	52	21 Apr 90	2
BLACKER THAN BLACK	Parlophone	61	23 Jun 90	1
ALBUMS:	HITS 2			WEEKS 4	
GOOD DEEDS AND DIRTY RAGS	Capitol	26	22 Apr 89	3
HAMMER AND TONGS	Radioactive	61	16 Mar 91	1
Original release was due in 1990 on the Parlophone label, but was not issued.				

GOODFELLAZ
US

SINGLES:	HITS 1			WEEKS 2	
SUGAR HONEY ICE TEA	Wild Card	25	10 May 97	2

GOODIES
UK

SINGLES:	HITS 5			WEEKS 38	
THE INBETWEENIES / FATHER CHRISTMAS DO NOT TOUCH ME	Bradley's	7	7 Dec 74	9
THE FUNKY GIBBON / SICK-MAN BLUES	Bradley's	4	15 Mar 75	10
BLACK PUDDING BERTHA (THE QUEEN OF NORTHERN SOUL)	Bradley's	19	21 Jun 75	7
NAPPY LOVE / WILD THING	Bradley's	21	27 Sep 75	6
MAKA A DAFT NOISE FOR CHRISTMAS	Bradley's	20	13 Dec 75	6
ALBUMS:	HITS 1			WEEKS 11	
THE NEW GOODIES LP	Bradley's	25	8 Nov 75	11

Cuba GOODING
US

SINGLES:	HITS 1			WEEKS 2	
HAPPINESS IS JUST AROUND THE BEND	London	72	19 Nov 83	2
Originally recorded by Brian Auger.				

Benny GOODMAN
US

ALBUMS:	HITS 1			WEEKS 1	
BENNY GOODMAN TODAY	Decca	49	3 Apr 71	1

GOODMEN
Holland

SINGLES:	HITS 1			WEEKS 19	
GIVE IT UP	F/freedom	23	7 Aug 93	5
GIVE IT UP [RE]	F/freedom	5	9 Oct 93	14

Ron GOODWIN and his Orchestra
UK

(See also Eammon Andrews; Dick James; Glen Mason.)

SINGLES:	HITS 2			WEEKS 24	
THE THEME FROM THE FILM "LIMELIGHT"	Parlophone	3	16 May 53	23
BLUE STAR (THE MEDIC THEME)	Parlophone	20	29 Oct 55	1
ALBUMS:	HITS 1			WEEKS 1	
LEGEND OF THE GLASS MOUNTAIN	Studio Two	49	2 May 70	1

GOODY GOODY
US

SINGLES:	HITS 1			WEEKS 5	
#1 DEE JAY	Atlantic	55	2 Dec 78	5

GOOFY – See Phoebe ONE featuring RED RAT, GOOFY and BUCCANEER (MAIN STREET CREW)

GOOMBAY DANCE BAND
Germany/Montserrat

SINGLES:	HITS 2			WEEKS 16	
SEVEN TEARS	Epic	1	27 Feb 82		12
SUN OF JAMAICA	Epic	50	15 May 82		4
ALBUMS:	HITS 1			WEEKS 9	
SEVEN TEARS	Epic	16	10 Apr 82		9

GOONS
UK

(See also Harry Secombe, Peter Sellers and Spike Milligan.)

SINGLES:	HITS 2			WEEKS 30	
I'M WALKING BACKWARDS FOR CHRISTMAS / THE BLUEBOTTLE BLUES	Decca	4	30 Jun 56		10

The Bluebottle Blues listed from 14 Jul 56.
Above hit: GOONS with Nick RAUCHEN conducting the BALL'S POND ROAD Near "The ONE-IN-HARMONY" / GOONS with Maurice PONKE and his Orchestre Fromage.

| THE YING TONG SONG / BLOODNOK'S ROCK'N'ROLL CALL | Decca | 3 | 15 Sep 56 | | 10 |

Bloodnok's Rock'n'Roll Call had first credit for the week 15 Sep 56.
Above hit: GOONS with Maurice PONKE and his Orchestre Fromage / GOONS featuring Major Dennis BLOODNOK, 43rd Deserters (Rtd.), with Roland ROCKCAKE and his WHOLLY ROLLERS directed by Maestro PONKE.

YING TONG SONG [RI]	Decca	9	21 Jul 73		10
ALBUMS:	HITS 3			WEEKS 31	
BEST OF THE GOONS SHOWS	Parlophone	8	28 Nov 59		14
BEST OF THE GOONS SHOWS VOLUME 2	Parlophone	11	17 Dec 60		6
LAST GOON SHOW OF ALL	BBC	8	4 Nov 72		11

Coral GORDON – See MONDO KANE featuring Dee LEWIS and Coral GORDON Guest star Georgie FAME

Lonnie GORDON
US

SINGLES:	HITS 6			WEEKS 23	
(I'VE GOT YOUR) PLEASURE CONTROL	ffrr	60	24 Jun 89		3

Above hit: Simon HARRIS featuring Lonnie GORDON.

HAPPENIN' ALL OVER AGAIN	Supreme	4	27 Jan 90		10
BEYOND YOUR WILDEST DREAMS	Supreme	48	11 Aug 90		2
IF I HAVE TO STAND ALONE	Supreme	68	17 Nov 90		1
GONNA CATCH YOU	Supreme	32	4 May 91		5
LOVE EVICTION	Xplode	32	7 Oct 95		2

Above hit: QUARTZ LOCK featuring Lonnie GORDON.

Leslie GORE
US

SINGLES:	HITS 2			WEEKS 20	
IT'S MY PARTY	Mercury	9	22 Jun 63		12

Originally recorded by Helen Shapiro.

| MAYBE I KNOW | Mercury | 20 | 26 Sep 64 | | 8 |

Martin L. GORE
UK

ALBUMS:	HITS 1			WEEKS 1	
COUNTERFEIT [EP]	Mute	51	24 Jun 89		1

GORKY'S ZYGOTIC MYNCI
UK

SINGLES:	HITS 6			WEEKS 6	
PATIO SONG	Fontana	41	9 Nov 96		1
DIAMOND DEW	Fontana	42	29 Mar 97		1
YOUNG GIRLS & HAPPY ENDINGS / DARK NIGHT	Fontana	49	21 Jun 97		1
SWEET JOHNNY	Fontana	60	6 Jun 98		1
LET'S GET TOGETHER (IN OUR MINDS)	Fontana	43	29 Aug 98		1
SPANISH DANCE TROUPE	Mantra	47	2 Oct 99		1
ALBUMS:	HITS 2			WEEKS 2	
BARAFUNDLE	Fontana	46	19 Apr 97		1
GORKY 5	Fontana	67	12 Sep 98		1

Eydie GORME
US

SINGLES:	HITS 4			WEEKS 33	
LOVE ME FOREVER	His Master's Voice	21	25 Jan 58		5
YES MY DARLING DAUGHTER	CBS	10	23 Jun 62		9
BLAME IT ON THE BOSSA NOVA	CBS	32	2 Feb 63		6
I WANT TO STAY HERE	CBS	3	24 Aug 63		13

Above hit: STEVE and EYDIE.

Luke GOSS and the BAND OF THIEVES
UK

SINGLES:	HITS 2			WEEKS 3	
SWEETER THAN THE MIDNIGHT TRAIN	Sabre	52	12 Jun 93		2
GIVE ME ONE MORE CHANCE	Sabre	68	21 Aug 93		1

*The first female artist to top the LP listings was **Connie Francis**. (LFI)*

The Gap Band *took their name from the initials of three streets in their hometown of Tulsa in* *Oklahoma: Greenwood, Archer & Pine. (LFI)*

Peter Frampton's Frampton Comes Alive *is the biggest selling live album of all time. (A&M Records)*

'Oh Mein Papa', in versions by
Eddie Fisher (above) and Eddie
Calvert, was the first song to chart
as an instrumental and with vocals.
(LFI)

Judy Garland was the first artist to
have just one hit on each of the singles,
EPs and albums charts. (LFI)

Bill Haley & The Comets were the first American group to top the British charts. (LFI)

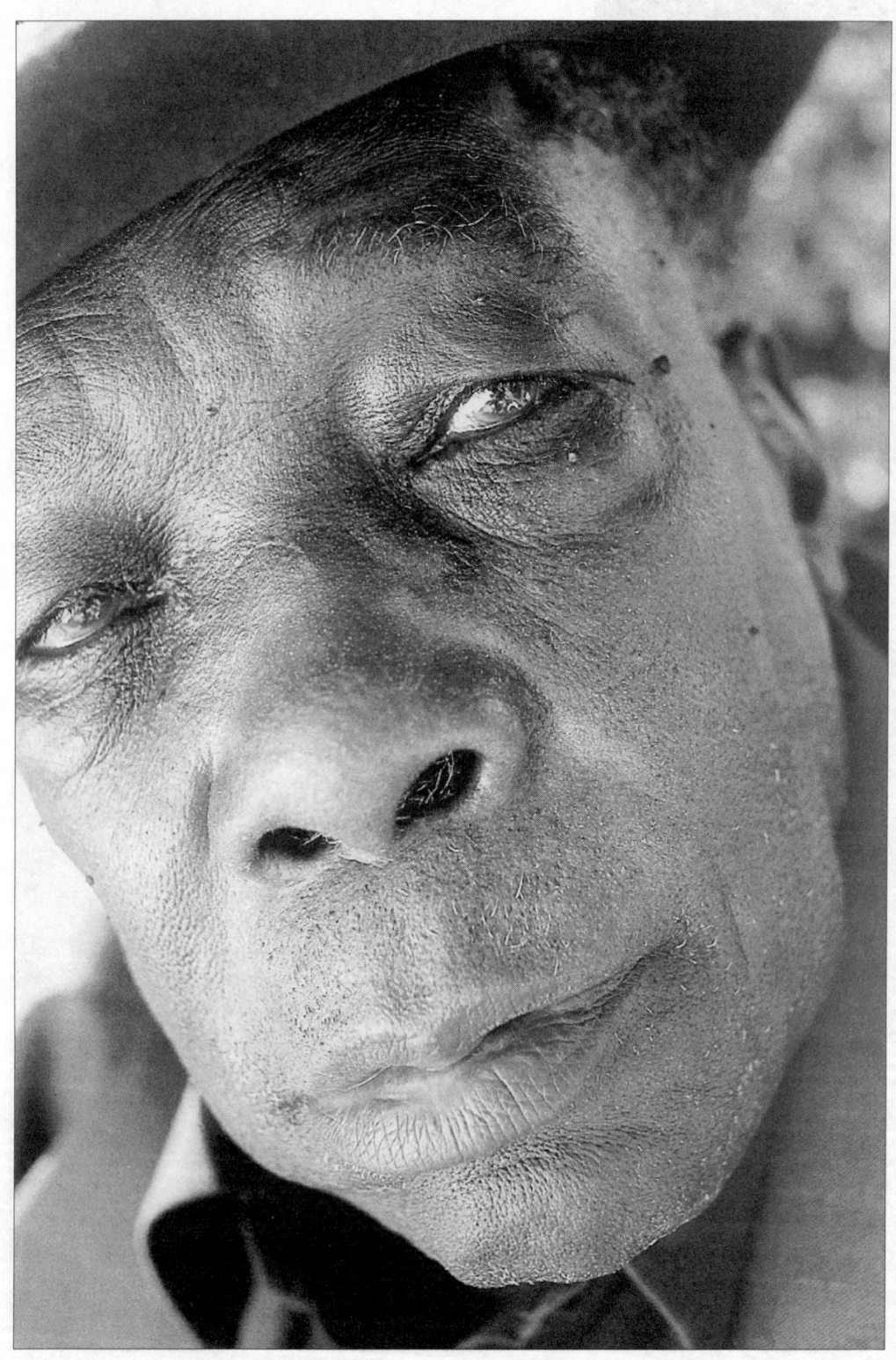

When **John Lee Hooker**'s 'Don't Look Back' charted in 1997, the 79-year-old bluesman became the oldest artist to reach the album chart. (LFI)

Buddy Holly's 'It Doesn't Matter Anymore' was the first posthumous No.1 hit. (Decca Records)

Janet and Michael Jackson *are the only artists to take seven hit singles from three consecutive albums. (LFI)*

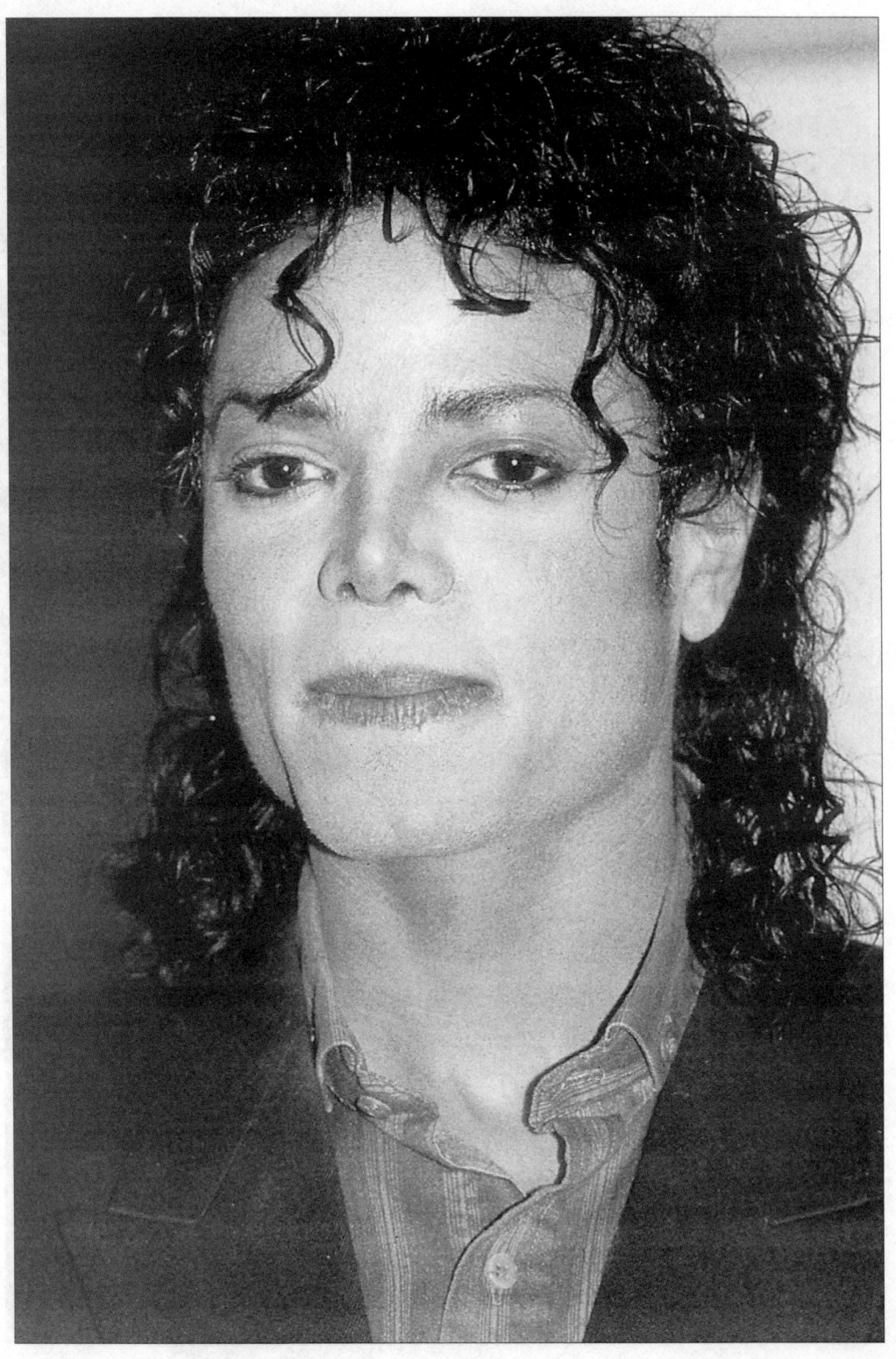

The biggest selling single of all time is **Elton John**'*s re-recorded version of 'Candle In The Wind'. (LFI)*

Matt GOSS — UK

SINGLES:		HITS 2			WEEKS 5
THE KEY	Atlas		40	26 Aug 95	2
IF YOU WERE HERE TONIGHT	Atlas		23	27 Apr 96	3

Donald GOULD - See UNITED KINGDOM SYMPHONY ORCHESTRA conducted by Donald GOULD

Nigel GOULDING - See Abigail MEAD and Nigel GOULDING

Graham GOULDMAN — UK

SINGLES:		HITS 1			WEEKS 4
SUNBURN	Mercury		52	23 Jun 79	4

From the film of the same name.

GOURYELLA — Holland

SINGLES:		HITS 2			WEEKS 9
GOURYELLA	Code Blue		15	10 Jul 99	7
WALHALLA	Code Blue		27	4 Dec 99	2

Vocals by Rachiel Spier.

GRACE — UK

SINGLES:		HITS 6			WEEKS 24
NOT OVER YET	Perfecto		6	8 Apr 95	8
Originally released in 1993.					
I WANT TO LIVE	Perfecto		30	23 Sep 95	2
Written by Gavin Friday and originally intended for Bono.					
SKIN ON SKIN	Perfecto		21	24 Feb 96	3
Vocal re-working of Orange (a remix of U2's Lemon).					
DOWN TO EARTH	Perfecto		20	1 Jun 96	2
IF I COULD FLY	Perfecto		29	28 Sep 96	2
HAND IN HAND	Perfecto		38	3 May 97	1
DOWN TO EARTH [RM]	Perfecto		29	26 Jul 97	2
Remixed by Stephen Jones. The first track on the CD format was You're Not Mine, but this was not common to all formats.					
NOT OVER YET 99 [RI]	Code Blue		16	14 Aug 99	4

Edited version of the original release.
Above hit: PLANET PERFECTO featuring GRACE.

GRACE BROTHERS — UK

SINGLES:		HITS 1			WEEKS 1
ARE YOU BEING SERVED?	EMI Premier		51	20 Apr 96	1

Bridgette GRACE - See TRUE FAITH and Bridgette GRACE with FINAL CUT

Janey Lee GRACE - See HYPERSTATE featuring Janey Lee GRACE

Charlie GRACIE — US

SINGLES:		HITS 4			WEEKS 41
BUTTERFLY	Parlophone		12	20 Apr 57	8
FABULOUS	Parlophone		8	15 Jun 57	16
I LOVE YOU SO MUCH IT HURTS / WANDERING EYES	London		14	24 Aug 57	2
From 7 Sep 57, both sides started separate chart runs.					
I LOVE YOU SO MUCH IT HURTS	London		20	7 Sep 57	2
Originally recorded by Jimmy Wakely in 1948.					
WANDERING EYES	London		6	7 Sep 57	12
COOL BABY	London		26	11 Jan 58	1

Eve GRAHAM - See NEW SEEKERS

Jaki GRAHAM — UK

SINGLES:		HITS 12			WEEKS 75
COULD IT BE I'M FALLING IN LOVE	Chrysalis		5	23 Mar 85	11
Originally recorded by Detroit Spinners.					
Above hit: David GRANT and Jaki GRAHAM.					
ROUND AND AROUND	EMI		9	29 Jun 85	11
HEAVEN KNOWS	EMI		59	31 Aug 85	3
Original release reached No. 80 in 1984.					
MATED	EMI		20	16 Nov 85	10
Originally recorded by Utopia.					
Above hit: David GRANT and Jaki GRAHAM.					
SET ME FREE	EMI		7	3 May 86	12
BREAKING AWAY	EMI		16	9 Aug 86	8
STEP RIGHT UP	EMI		15	15 Nov 86	12
NO MORE TEARS	EMI		60	9 Jul 88	2
FROM NOW ON	EMI		73	24 Jun 89	2
AIN'T NOBODY	Pulse 8		44	16 Jul 94	2

YOU CAN COUNT ON ME	*Avex UK*	62	*4 Feb 95*	1
ABSOLUTE E-SENSUAL	*Avex UK*	69	*8 Jul 95*	1
ALBUMS:	**HITS 2**		**WEEKS 10**	
HEAVEN KNOWS	*EMI*	48	*14 Sep 85*	5
BREAKING AWAY	*EMI*	25	*20 Sep 86*	5

Larry GRAHAM US

SINGLES:	**HITS 1**		**WEEKS 4**	
SOONER OR LATER	*Warner Brothers*	54	*3 Jul 82*	4

Ron GRAINER ORCHESTRA UK

SINGLES:	**HITS 1**		**WEEKS 7**	
A TOUCH OF VELVET – A STING OF BRASS	*Casino Classics*	60	*9 Dec 78*	7
EPS:	**HITS 1**		**WEEKS 1**	
THEME MUSIC FROM "INSPECTOR MAIGRET"	*Warner Brothers*	13	*20 Jan 62*	1

GRAM'MA FUNK - See GROOVE ARMADA

GRAND FUNK RAILROAD US

SINGLES:	**HITS 1**		**WEEKS 1**	
INSIDE LOOKING OUT	*Capitol*	40	*6 Feb 71*	1

GRAND PLAZ UK

SINGLES:	**HITS 1**		**WEEKS 4**	
WOW WOW – NA NA	*Urban*	41	*8 Sep 90*	4
Based around Steam's Na Na Hey Hey Kiss Him Goodbye.				

GRAND PRIX UK

SINGLES:	**HITS 1**		**WEEKS 1**	
KEEP ON BELIEVING	*RCA*	75	*27 Feb 82*	1
ALBUMS:	**HITS 1**		**WEEKS 2**	
SAMURAI	*Chrysalis*	65	*18 Jun 83*	2

GRAND PUBA - See INFINITI featuring GRAND PUBA; SHAGGY

GRANDAD ROBERTS and his son ELVIS UK

SINGLES:	**HITS 1**		**WEEKS 1**	
MEAT PIE SAUSAGE ROLL (COME ON ENGLAND GI'S A GOAL)	*WEA*	67	*20 Jun 98*	1
Originally a terrace chant at Oldham Athletic FC.				

GRANDMASTER FLASH and the FURIOUS FIVE US

SINGLES:	**HITS 3**		**WEEKS 56**	
THE MESSAGE	*Sugar Hill*	8	*28 Aug 82*	9
WHITE LINES (DON'T DON'T DO IT)	*Sugar Hill*	60	*19 Nov 83*	3
Above hit: GRAND MASTER and Melle MEL.				
WHITE LINES (DON'T DON'T DO IT) [RE-1ST]	*Sugar Hill*	7	*11 Feb 84*	38
Peak position reached on 28 Jul 84.				
WHITE LINES (DON'T DON'T DO IT) [RE-2ND]	*Sugar Hill*	75	*24 Nov 84*	1
WHITE LINES (DON'T DON'T DO IT) [RE-3RD]	*Sugar Hill*	73	*5 Jan 85*	1
SIGN OF THE TIMES	*Elektra*	72	*16 Feb 85*	1
Above hit: GRANDMASTER FLASH.				
WHITE LINES (DON'T DO IT) [RM]	*WGAF*	59	*8 Jan 94*	3
Remixed by D & S.				
Above hit: GRANDMASTER FLASH and Melle MEL.				
ALBUMS:	**HITS 3**		**WEEKS 20**	
THE MESSAGE	*Sugar Hill*	77	*23 Oct 82*	3
GREATEST MESSAGES	*Sugar Hill*	41	*23 Jun 84*	16
THEY SAID IT COULDN'T BE DONE	*Elektra*	95	*23 Feb 85*	1
Above hit: GRANDMASTER FLASH.				

GRANDMASTER Melle MEL and the FURIOUS FIVE - See Melle MEL

GRANDMIXER D.ST US

SINGLES:	**HITS 1**		**WEEKS 3**	
CRAZY CUTS	*Island*	73	*24 Dec 83*	2
CRAZY CUTS [RE]	*Island*	71	*14 Jan 84*	1

GRANGE HILL CAST (Rap: Mmoloki CHRYSTIE) UK

SINGLES:	**HITS 1**		**WEEKS 6**	
JUST SAY NO	*BBC*	5	*19 Apr 86*	6

Gerri GRANGER
US

SINGLES:		HITS 1		WEEKS 3	
I GO TO PIECES (EVERYTIME)	Casino Classics	50	30 Sep 78	3

Amy GRANT
US

SINGLES:		HITS 8		WEEKS 39	
BABY BABY	A&M	2	11 May 91	13
Written about Grant's six-year-old daughter, Millie.				
EVERY HEARTBEAT	A&M	25	3 Aug 91	7
THAT'S WHAT LOVE IS FOR	A&M	60	2 Nov 91	3
GOOD FOR ME	A&M	60	15 Feb 92	1
LUCKY ONE	A&M	60	13 Aug 94	1
SAY YOU'LL BE MINE	A&M	41	22 Oct 94	2
BIG YELLOW TAXI	A&M	20	24 Jun 95	10
HOUSE OF LOVE	A&M	46	14 Oct 95	2
Above hit: Amy GRANT with Vince GILL.				

ALBUMS:		HITS 1		WEEKS 15	
HEART IN MOTION	A&M	25	22 Jun 91	15

Andrea GRANT featuring DARKMAN
UK

SINGLES:		HITS 1		WEEKS 1	
REPUTATIONS (JUST BE GOOD TO ME)	WEA	75	14 Nov 98	1

Boysie GRANT - See Ezz RECO and the LAUNCHERS with Boysie GRANT

David GRANT
UK

SINGLES:		HITS 8		WEEKS 59	
STOP AND GO	Chrysalis	19	30 Apr 83	9
WATCHING YOU, WATCHING ME	Chrysalis	10	16 Jul 83	13
LOVE WILL FIND A WAY	Chrysalis	24	8 Oct 83	6
ROCK THE MIDNIGHT	Chrysalis	46	26 Nov 83	4
COULD IT BE I'M FALLING IN LOVE	Chrysalis	5	23 Mar 85	11
Originally recorded by Detroit Spinners.				
MATED	EMI	20	16 Nov 85	10
Originally recorded by Utopia.				
Above 2: David GRANT and Jaki GRAHAM.				
CHANGE	Polydor	55	1 Aug 87	4
KEEP IT TOGETHER	Fourth & Broadway	56	12 May 90	2

ALBUMS:		HITS 2		WEEKS 7	
DAVID GRANT	Chrysalis	32	5 Nov 83	6
HOPES AND DREAMS	Chrysalis	96	18 May 85	1

Eddy GRANT
Guyana

SINGLES:		HITS 11		WEEKS 94	
LIVING ON THE FRONT LINE	Ensign	11	2 Jun 79	11
DO YOU FEEL MY LOVE?	Ensign	8	15 Nov 80	11
CAN'T GET ENOUGH OF YOU	Ensign	13	4 Apr 81	10
I LOVE YOU, YES I LOVE YOU	Ensign	37	25 Jul 81	6
I DON'T WANNA DANCE	Ice	1	16 Oct 82	15
ELECTRIC AVENUE	Ice	2	15 Jan 83	9
LIVING ON THE FRONT LINE [RI] / DO YOU FEEL MY LOVE [RI]	Mercury	47	19 Mar 83	4
WAR PARTY	Ice	42	23 Apr 83	4
TILL I CAN'T TAKE LOVE NO MORE	Ice	42	29 Oct 83	7
ROMANCING THE STONE	Ice	52	19 May 84	3
GIMME HOPE JO'ANNA	Ice	7	23 Jan 88	12
WALKING ON SUNSHINE	Blue Wave	63	27 May 89	2

ALBUMS:		HITS 4		WEEKS 47	
CAN'T GET ENOUGH	Ice	39	30 May 81	6
KILLER ON THE RAMPAGE	Ice	7	27 Nov 82	23
ALL THE HITS	K-Tel	23	17 Nov 84	10
WALKING ON SUNSHINE (THE VERY BEST OF EDDY GRANT)	Parlophone	20	1 Jul 89	8

Gogi GRANT
US

SINGLES:		HITS 1		WEEKS 11	
WAYWARD WIND	London	9	30 Jun 56	11

Julie GRANT
UK

SINGLES:		HITS 3		WEEKS 17	
UP ON THE ROOF	Pye	33	5 Jan 63	3
COUNT ON ME	Pye	24	30 Mar 63	9
COME TO ME	Pye	31	26 Sep 64	5

Rudy GRANT
Guyana

SINGLES:	HITS 1			WEEKS 3
LATELY	Ensign	58	14 Feb 81	3

GRANT LEE BUFFALO
US

ALBUMS:	HITS 3			WEEKS 5
FUZZY	Slash	74	10 Jul 93	1
MIGHTY JOE MOON	Slash	24	1 Oct 94	2
COPPEROPOLIS	Slash	34	15 Jun 96	2

GRAPEFRUIT
UK

SINGLES:	HITS 2			WEEKS 19
DEAR DELILAH	RCA Victor	21	17 Feb 68	9
C'MON MARIANNE	RCA Victor	31	17 Aug 68	10

GRASS-SHOW
Sweden

SINGLES:	HITS 2			WEEKS 2
1962	Food	53	22 Mar 97	1
OUT OF THE VOID	Food	75	23 Aug 97	1

Original release reached No. 128 in 1996.

GRATEFUL DEAD
US

(See also Bob Dylan and the Grateful Dead.)

ALBUMS:	HITS 6			WEEKS 9
WORKINGMAN'S DEAD	Warner Brothers	69	19 Sep 70	2
GRATEFUL DEAD FROM THE MARS HOTEL	Warner Brothers	47	3 Aug 74	1
BLUES FOR ALLAH	United Artists	45	1 Nov 75	1
STEAL YOUR FACE	United Artists	42	4 Sep 76	1
Early releases were issued with bonus album titled For Dead Heads Only.				
TERRAPIN STATION	Arista	30	20 Aug 77	1
IN THE DARK	Arista	57	19 Sep 87	3

Jorn GRAUENGAARD and his Orchestra - See NINA and FREDERIK

GRAVEDIGGAZ
US

SINGLES:	HITS 4			WEEKS 6
SIX FEET DEEP [EP]	Gee Street	64	11 Mar 95	1
Lead track: Bang Your Head.				
THE HELL [EP]	Fourth & Broadway	12	5 Aug 95	3
Lead track: Hell Is Around The Corner.				
Above hit: TRICKY vs. the GRAVEDIGGAZ.				
THE NIGHT THE EARTH CRIED	Gee Street	44	24 Jan 98	1
UNEXPLAINED	Gee Street	48	25 Apr 98	1
ALBUMS:	HITS 1			WEEKS 1
THE PICK, THE SICKLE AND THE SHOVEL	Gee Street	24	4 Oct 97	1

Barry GRAY ORCHESTRA
UK

SINGLES:	HITS 2			WEEKS 8
THUNDERBIRDS	PRT	61	11 Jul 81	2
JOE 90 (THEME)('86 DANCE MIX) / CAPTAIN SCARLET THEME	PRT	53	14 Jun 86	6
Above hit: Barry GRAY ORCHESTRA featuring keyboards by Peter BECKETT.				

David GRAY
UK

SINGLES:	HITS 1			WEEKS 1
PLEASE FORGIVE ME	IHT	72	4 Dec 99	1

David GRAY and Tommy TYCHO
UK

ALBUMS:	HITS 1			WEEKS 6
ARMCHAIR MELODIES	K-Tel	21	16 Oct 76	6

Dobie GRAY
UK

SINGLES:	HITS 2			WEEKS 11
THE IN CROWD	London	25	27 Feb 65	7
OUT ON THE FLOOR	Black Magic	42	27 Sep 75	4

Dorian GRAY
UK

SINGLES:	HITS 1			WEEKS 7
I'VE GOT YOU ON MY MIND	Parlophone	36	30 Mar 68	7

Johnnie GRAY and the BAND OF THE DAY - See STARGAZERS

Les GRAY
UK

SINGLES:		HITS 1		WEEKS 5
A GROOVY KIND OF LOVE	Warner Brothers	32	26 Feb 77	5

Macy GRAY
US

SINGLES:		HITS 2		WEEKS 14
DO SOMETHING	Epic	51	3 Jul 99	1
I TRY	Epic	6	9 Oct 99	13
ALBUMS:		HITS 1		WEEKS 25
ON HOW LIFE IS	Epic	3	17 Jul 99	25

Alltrinna GRAYSON – See Wilton FELDER

GREASE – See TRICKY

GREAT WHITE
US

SINGLES:		HITS 3		WEEKS 5
HOUSE OF BROKEN LOVE	Capitol	44	24 Feb 90	2
CONGO SQUARE	Capitol	62	16 Feb 91	1
CALL IT ROCK N' ROLL	Capitol	67	7 Sep 91	2
ALBUMS:		HITS 1		WEEKS 1
HOOKED	Capitol	43	9 Mar 91	1

Buddy GRECO
US

SINGLES:		HITS 1		WEEKS 8
THE LADY IS A TRAMP	Fontana	26	9 Jul 60	8

GREECE 2000
Holland

SINGLES:		HITS 1		WEEKS 5
THREE DRIVES	Hooj Choons	44	27 Jun 98	1
THREE DRIVES [RI]	Hollywood	12	30 Jan 99	4

Original version with vocal by Julie Harrington added.

GREED featuring Ricardo DA FORCE
UK

SINGLES:		HITS 1		WEEKS 2
PUMP UP THE VOLUME	Stress	51	18 Mar 95	2

GREEDIES
UK/Ireland/US

SINGLES:		HITS 1		WEEKS 5
A MERRY JINGLE	Vertigo	28	15 Dec 79	5

Al GREEN
US

SINGLES:		HITS 9		WEEKS 67
TIRED OF BEING ALONE	London	4	9 Oct 71	13
LET'S STAY TOGETHER	London	7	8 Jan 72	12
LOOK WHAT YOU DONE FOR ME	London	44	20 May 72	4
I'M STILL IN LOVE WITH YOU	London	35	19 Aug 72	5
SHA-LA-LA (MAKE ME HAPPY)	London	20	16 Nov 74	10
L.O.V.E. (LOVE)	London	24	15 Mar 75	8
PUT A LITTLE LOVE IN YOUR HEART	A&M	28	3 Dec 88	8

Originally recorded by Jackie de Shannon.
Above hit: Annie LENNOX and Al GREEN.

THE MESSAGE IS LOVE	Breakout	38	21 Oct 89	5

Above hit: Arthur BAKER and the BACKBEAT DISCIPLES featuring Al GREEN.

LOVE IS A BEAUTIFUL THING	Arista	56	2 Oct 93	2
ALBUMS:		HITS 3		WEEKS 25
AL GREEN'S GREATEST HITS	London	18	26 Apr 75	16
HI LIFE - THE BEST OF AL GREEN	K-Tel	34	1 Oct 88	7
AL	Beechwood	41	24 Oct 92	2

Dotty GREEN – See Mark FISHER (featuring Dotty GREEN)

Jesse GREEN
US

SINGLES:		HITS 3		WEEKS 26
NICE AND SLOW	EMI	17	7 Aug 76	12
FLIP	EMI	26	18 Dec 76	8
COME WITH ME	EMI	29	11 Jun 77	6

Peter GREEN
UK

ALBUMS:		HITS 4		WEEKS 19
IN THE SKIES	Creole	32	9 Jun 79	13
LITTLE DREAMER	PUK	34	24 May 80	4

SPLINTER GROUP	Artisan	71	24 May 97	1

Includes live tracks recorded in late 1996.

THE ROBERT JOHNSON SONGBOOK	Artisan	57	30 May 98	1

Above hit: Peter GREEN with Nigel WATSON and the SPLINTER GROUP.

Robson GREEN and Jerome FLYNN – See ROBSON and JEROME

GREEN DAY   US

SINGLES:	HITS 10		WEEKS 34	
BASKET CASE	Reprise	55	20 Aug 94	2
WELCOME TO PARADISE	Reprise	20	29 Oct 94	3
BASKET CASE [RI]	Reprise	7	28 Jan 95	6
LONGVIEW	Reprise	30	18 Mar 95	3
WHEN I COME AROUND	Reprise	27	20 May 95	3
GEEK STINK BREATH	Reprise	16	7 Oct 95	3
STUCK WITH ME	Reprise	24	6 Jan 96	3
BRAIN STEW / JADED [M]	Reprise	28	6 Jul 96	2
HITCHIN' A RIDE	Reprise	25	11 Oct 97	2
TIME OF YOUR LIFE (GOOD RIDDANCE)	Reprise	11	31 Jan 98	5
REDUNDANT	Reprise	27	9 May 98	2
ALBUMS:	**HITS 3**		**WEEKS 64**	
DOOKIE	Reprise	13	5 Nov 94	53

Includes re-entries through to 1999.

INSOMNIAC	Reprise	8	21 Oct 95	5
NIMROD	Reprise	11	25 Oct 97	6

GREEN JELLY   US

SINGLES:	HITS 3		WEEKS 15	
THREE LITTLE PIGS	Zoo	5	5 Jun 93	8
ANARCHY IN THE UK	Zoo	27	14 Aug 93	3
I'M THE LEADER OF THE GANG	Arista	25	25 Dec 93	4

Above hit: Hulk HOGAN with GREEN JELLY and the WRESTLING BOOT TRASH CAN BAND.

ALBUMS:	**HITS 1**		**WEEKS 10**	
CEREAL KILLER SOUNDTRACK	Zoo	18	3 Jul 93	10

GREEN ON RED   US

ALBUMS:	HITS 1		WEEKS 1	
NO FREE LUNCH	Mercury	99	26 Oct 85	1

Norman GREENBAUM   US

SINGLES:	HITS 1		WEEKS 20	
SPIRIT IN THE SKY	Reprise	1	21 Mar 70	20

Lorne GREENE   US

SINGLES:	HITS 1		WEEKS 8	
RINGO	RCA Victor	22	19 Dec 64	8

Dave GREENFIELD and Jean-Jacques BURNEL   UK

(See also Jean-Jacques Burnel.)

ALBUMS:	HITS 1		WEEKS 1	
BURNEL				
FIRE AND WATER	Epic	94	3 Dec 83	1

GREENSLADE   UK

ALBUMS:	HITS 1		WEEKS 3	
SPYGLASS GUEST	Warner Brothers	34	14 Sep 74	3

Lee GREENWOOD   US

SINGLES:	HITS 1		WEEKS 6	
THE WIND BENEATH MY WINGS	MCA	49	19 May 84	6

Christina GREGG   UK

ALBUMS:	HITS 1		WEEKS 1	
MUSIC 'N' MOTION	Warwick	51	27 May 78	1

Iain GREGORY   UK

SINGLES:	HITS 1		WEEKS 2	
CAN'T YOU HEAR THE BEAT OF A BROKEN HEART	Pye	39	06 Jan 62	2

Johnny GREGORY and his Orchestra – See Russ HAMILTON

GREYHOUND

Jamaica

SINGLES:		HITS 3			WEEKS 33
BLACK AND WHITE	Trojan		6	26 Jun 71	13
MOON RIVER	Trojan		12	8 Jan 72	11
I AM WHAT I AM	Trojan		20	25 Mar 72	9

GRID

UK

SINGLES:		HITS 9			WEEKS 47
FLOATATION	East West		60	7 Jul 90	2
A BEAT CALLED LOVE	East West		64	29 Sep 90	4
FIGURE OF EIGHT	Virgin		50	25 Jul 92	3
HEARTBEAT	Virgin		72	3 Oct 92	2
CRYSTAL CLEAR	Virgin		27	13 Mar 93	4
TEXAS COWBOYS	Deconstruction		21	30 Oct 93	3
SWAMP THING	Deconstruction		3	4 Jun 94	17
ROLLERCOASTER	Deconstruction		19	17 Sep 94	4
TEXAS COWBOYS [RI]	Deconstruction		17	3 Dec 94	6
DIABLO	Deconstruction		32	23 Sep 95	2
ALBUMS:		HITS 2			WEEKS 4
EVOLVER	Deconstruction		14	1 Oct 94	3
MUSIC FOR DANCING	Deconstruction		67	14 Oct 95	1

Zaine GRIFF

New Zealand

SINGLES:		HITS 2			WEEKS 6
TONIGHT	Automatic		54	16 Feb 80	3
ASHES AND DIAMONDS	Automatic		68	31 May 80	3

Billy GRIFFIN

US

SINGLES:		HITS 2			WEEKS 12
HOLD ME TIGHTER IN THE RAIN	CBS		17	8 Jan 83	9
SERIOUS	CBS		64	14 Jan 84	3

Clive GRIFFIN

UK

SINGLES:		HITS 2			WEEKS 5
HEAD ABOVE WATER	Mercury		60	24 Jun 89	2
I'LL BE WAITING	Mercury		56	11 May 91	3

Nanci GRIFFITH

US

ALBUMS:		HITS 7			WEEKS 26
LITTLE LOVE AFFAIRS	MCA		78	26 Mar 88	1
STORMS	MCA		38	23 Sep 89	3
LATE NIGHT GRANDE HOTEL	MCA		40	28 Sep 91	5
OTHER VOICES/OTHER ROOMS	MCA		18	20 Mar 93	6
THE BEST OF NANCI GRIFFITH	MCA		27	13 Nov 93	4
FLYER	MCA		20	1 Oct 94	4
BLUE ROSES FROM THE MOONS	Elektra		64	5 Apr 97	3

Features the Crickets.

Roni GRIFFITH

US

SINGLES:		HITS 1			WEEKS 4
(THE BEST PART OF) BREAKIN' UP	Making Waves		63	30 Jun 84	4

Original release reached No. 85 in 1983.

GRIFTERS featuring TALL PAUL and Brandon BLOCK

UK

(See also Blockster; Tall Paul.)

SINGLES:		HITS 1			WEEKS 1
FLASH	Duty Free		63	20 Feb 99	1

Samples Liason D's Future FJP.

GRIMETHORPE COLLIERY BAND

UK

(See also Peter Skellern.)

ALBUMS:		HITS 1			WEEKS 4
BRASSED OFF [OST]	RCA Victor		36	6 Jun 98	4

First released 1996. Charted after the film was aired on Channel 4.

Dave GROHL - See PUFF DADDY

GROOVE ARMADA

UK

SINGLES:		HITS 3			WEEKS 11
IF EVERYBODY LOOKED THE SAME	Pepper		25	8 May 99	2

Samples the Chi-Lites' We Are Neighbors and A Tribe Called Quest's Ince Again (The Twister Mix).

AT THE RIVER	Pepper	19	7 Aug 99	5

Samples Patti Page's Old Cape Cod. Originally released in 1997.

I SEE YOU BABY	Pepper	17	27 Nov 99	4

Above hit: GROOVE ARMADA featuring GRAM'MA FUNK.

ALBUMS:	HITS 1		WEEKS 11	
VERTIGO	Pepper	23	5 Jun 99	11

GROOVE CONNEKTION 2 — UK

SINGLES:	HITS 1		WEEKS 1	
CLUB LONELY	XL Recordings	54	11 Apr 98	1

GROOVE CORPORATION featuring ROMILLIE — UK/Italy

SINGLES:	HITS 1		WEEKS 1	
RAIN	Six6	71	16 Apr 94	1

GROOVE GENERATION featuring Leo SAYER — UK

SINGLES:	HITS 1		WEEKS 3	
YOU MAKE ME FEEL LIKE DANCING	Brothers Organisation	32	8 Aug 98	3

Re-recorded vocals by Leo Sayer.

GROOVE THEORY — UK

(See also Sweetback featuring Amel Larrieux from Groove Theory.)

SINGLES:	HITS 1		WEEKS 3	
TELL ME	Epic	31	18 Nov 95	3

Jay GROOVE - See FANTASY U.F.O.

GROOVERIDER — UK

SINGLES:	HITS 2		WEEKS 3	
RAINBOWS OF COLOUR	Higher Ground	40	26 Sep 98	2

Above hit: GROOVERIDER with Guest Vocalist ROYA ARAB.

WHERE'S JACK THE RIPPER?	Higher Ground	61	19 Jun 99	1
ALBUMS:	HITS 1		WEEKS 1	
MYSTERIES OF FUNK	Higher Ground	50	10 Oct 98	1

Scott GROOVES — US

SINGLES:	HITS 2		WEEKS 3	
EXPANSIONS	Soma Recordings	68	16 May 98	1

Above hit: Scott GROOVES featuring Roy AYERS.

MOTHERSHIP RECONNECTION	Soma Recordings	55	28 Nov 98	1

Samples Parliament-Funkadelic's Mothership Connection Live.
Above hit: Scott GROOVES featuring PARLIAMENT / FUNKADELIC.

MOTHERSHIP RECONNECTION [RM]	Virgin	55	21 Aug 99	1

Remixed by Daft Punk.
Above hit: Scott GROOVES featuring PARLIAMENT-FUNKADELIC.

Henry GROSS — US

SINGLES:	HITS 1		WEEKS 4	
SHANNON	Lifesong	32	28 Aug 76	4

Written about his dog that died.

GROUND LEVEL — Australia

SINGLES:	HITS 1		WEEKS 2	
DREAMS OF HEAVEN	Faze 2	54	30 Jan 93	2

GROUNDHOGS — UK

ALBUMS:	HITS 4		WEEKS 50	
THANK CHRIST FOR THE BOMB	Liberty	9	6 Jun 70	13
SPLIT	Liberty	5	3 Apr 71	27
WHO WILL SAVE THE WORLD	United Artists	8	18 Mar 72	9
SOLID	WWA	31	13 Jul 74	1

GROUP THERAPY — US

SINGLES:	HITS 1		WEEKS 1	
EAST COAST/WEST COAST KILLAS	Interscope	51	30 Nov 96	1

Boring Bob GROVER - See PIRANHAS

Sir Charles GROVES - See ROYAL PHILHARMONIC ORCHESTRA

GUESS WHO — Canada

SINGLES:	HITS 2		WEEKS 14	
HIS GIRL	King	45	18 Feb 67	1

| AMERICAN WOMAN | RCA Victor | 45 | 9 May 70 | 2 |
| AMERICAN WOMAN [RE] | RCA Victor | 19 | 30 May 70 | 11 |

GUILDFORD CATHEDRAL CHOIR conductor: Barry ROSE   UK

ALBUMS:	HITS 1			WEEKS 4
CHRISTMAS CAROLS FROM GUILDFORD CATHEDRAL	Music For Pleasure	24	10 Dec 66	4

GUITAR CORPORATION   UK

ALBUMS:	HITS 1			WEEKS 5
IMAGES	Quality Television	41	15 Feb 92	5

GUN   UK

SINGLES:	HITS 1			WEEKS 11
RACE WITH THE DEVIL	CBS	8	23 Nov 68	11

GUN   UK

SINGLES:	HITS 14			WEEKS 46
BETTER DAYS	A&M	33	1 Jul 89	9
MONEY (EVERYBODY LOVES HER)	A&M	73	16 Sep 89	2
INSIDE OUT	A&M	57	11 Nov 89	2
TAKING ON THE WORLD	A&M	50	10 Feb 90	3
SHAME ON YOU	A&M	33	14 Jul 90	4
STEAL YOUR FIRE	A&M	24	14 Mar 92	4
HIGHER GROUND	A&M	48	2 May 92	2
WELCOME TO THE REAL WORLD	A&M	43	4 Jul 92	2
WORD UP	A&M	8	9 Jul 94	7
DON'T SAY IT'S OVER	A&M	19	24 Sep 94	3
THE ONLY ONE	A&M	29	25 Feb 95	3
SOMETHING WORTHWHILE	A&M	39	15 Apr 95	2
CRAZY YOU	A&M	21	26 Apr 97	2
MY SWEET JANE	A&M	51	12 Jul 97	1

Above 2: G.U.N.

ALBUMS:	HITS 4			WEEKS 23
TAKING ON THE WORLD	A&M	44	22 Jul 89	10
GALLUS	A&M	14	18 Apr 92	4
SWAGGER	A&M	5	13 Aug 94	7
0141 632 6326	A&M	32	24 May 97	2

Title is phone number set up for fans to leave messages.
Above hit: G.U.N.

GUNS N' ROSES   US

SINGLES:	HITS 15			WEEKS 107
WELCOME TO THE JUNGLE	Geffen	67	3 Oct 87	2
SWEET CHILD O' MINE	Geffen	24	20 Aug 88	8

Written about his then girlfriend Erin Everly.

WELCOME TO THE JUNGLE [RI] / NIGHTRAIN	Geffen	24	29 Oct 88	5
PARADISE CITY	Geffen	6	18 Mar 89	9
SWEET CHILD O' MINE [RM]	Geffen	6	3 Jun 89	9

Remixed by Steve Thomson and Michael Barbiero.

PATIENCE	Geffen	10	1 Jul 89	7
NIGHTRAIN [RI]	Geffen	17	2 Sep 89	5
YOU COULD BE MINE	Geffen	3	13 Jul 91	10

From the film 'Terminator 2 Judgement Day'.

DON'T CRY	Geffen	8	21 Sep 91	4
LIVE AND LET DIE	Geffen	5	21 Dec 91	7
NOVEMBER RAIN	Geffen	4	7 Mar 92	5
KNOCKIN' ON HEAVEN'S DOOR	Geffen	2	23 May 92	9

Live recording from Wembley Stadium at the Freddie Mercury Tribute Concert on 20 Apr 92.

YESTERDAYS / NOVEMBER RAIN [RI]	Geffen	8	21 Nov 92	9

November Rain listed from 28 Nov 92.

THE "CIVIL WAR" [EP]	Geffen	11	29 May 93	3

Lead track: Civil War (LP Version).

AIN'T IT FUN	Geffen	9	20 Nov 93	3
SINCE I DON'T HAVE YOU	Geffen	10	4 Jun 94	6

Original by the Skyliners reached No. 12 in the US in 1959.

SYMPATHY FOR THE DEVIL	Geffen	9	14 Jan 95	6

From the film 'Interview With The Vampire'.

ALBUMS:	HITS 6			WEEKS 367
APPETITE FOR DESTRUCTION	Geffen	15	1 Aug 87	20

Chart position reached in 1988.

G N' R THE LIES, THE SEX, THE DRUGS, THE VIOLENCE, THE SHOCKING TRUTH	Geffen	32	17 Dec 89	
APPETITE FOR DESTRUCTION [RE-1ST]	Geffen	5	7 Jan 89	65

Peak position reached on 22 Jul 89.

G N' R THE LIES, THE SEX, THE DRUGS, THE VIOLENCE, THE SHOCKING TRUTH [RE-1ST]	Geffen	22	18 Mar 89	30
APPETITE FOR DESTRUCTION [RE-2ND]	Geffen	31	24 Aug 91	62
Re-released. Chart position reached in 1992. Includes re-entries through to 1999.				
USE YOUR ILLUSION I	Geffen	2	28 Sep 91	83
USE YOUR ILLUSION II	Geffen	1	28 Sep 91	84
G N' R THE LIES, THE SEX, THE DRUGS, THE VIOLENCE, THE SHOCKING TRUTH [RE-2ND]	Geffen	69	23 May 92	2
Re-released.				
THE SPAGHETTI INCIDENT?	Geffen	2	4 Dec 93	10
LIVE – ERA '87–'93	Geffen	45	11 Dec 99	2

GUNSHOT — UK

ALBUMS:	HITS 1			WEEKS 1
PATRIOT GAMES	Vinyl Solution	60	19 Jun 93	1

David GUNSON — UK

ALBUMS:	HITS 1			WEEKS 2
WHAT GOES UP MIGHT COME DOWN	Big Ben	92	25 Dec 82	2

Peter GUNZ – See LORD TARIQ and Peter GUNZ; Shaquille O'NEAL

GURU — US

(See also Various Artists (EPs) 'Help EP'.)

SINGLES:	HITS 5			WEEKS 11
TRUST ME	Cooltempo	34	11 Sep 93	2
Above hit: GURU featuring N'Dea DAVENPORT.				
NO TIME TO PLAY	Cooltempo	25	13 Nov 93	3
Above hit: GURU featuring vocals by D.C. LEE.				
WATCH WHAT YOU SAY	Cooltempo	28	19 Aug 95	3
Sleeve gives title as an EP: Jazzmatazz Vol.2, The New Reality.				
Above hit: GURU featuring Chaka KHAN.				
FEEL THE MUSIC	Cooltempo	34	18 Nov 95	2
Above hit: GURU: JAZZMATAZZ VOL. II THE NEW REALITY.				
LIVIN' IN THE WORLD / LIFESAVER	Cooltempo	61	13 Jul 96	1
Features Donald Byrd on trumpet and vocals by N'Dea Davenport.				
ALBUMS:	HITS 2			WEEKS 11
JAZZAMATAZZ	Cooltempo	58	29 May 93	2
Above hit: GURU featuring VARIOUS ARTISTS.				
JAZZAMATAZZ VOLUME II – THE NEW REALITY	Cooltempo	12	15 Jul 95	9

GURU JOSH — UK

SINGLES:	HITS 2			WEEKS 14
INFINITY (1990'S: TIME FOR THE GURU)	Deconstruction	5	24 Feb 90	10
WHOSE LAW (IS IT ANYWAY?)	Deconstruction	26	16 Jun 90	4
ALBUMS:	HITS 1			WEEKS 2
INFINITY	Deconstruction	41	14 Jul 90	2

Adrian GURVITZ — UK

SINGLES:	HITS 2			WEEKS 16
CLASSIC	RAK	8	30 Jan 82	13
YOUR DREAM	RAK	61	12 Jun 82	3

GUSGUS — Iceland

SINGLES:	HITS 3			WEEKS 3
POLYESTERDAY	4AD	55	21 Feb 98	1
LADYSHAVE	4AD	64	13 Mar 99	1
STARLOVERS	4AD	62	24 Apr 99	1

GUSTO — US

SINGLES:	HITS 2			WEEKS 8
DISCO'S REVENGE	Manifesto	9	2 Mar 96	5
Samples Harvey Mason's 70s disco hit Groovin You.				
LET'S ALL CHANT	Manifesto	21	7 Sep 96	3

Arlo GUTHRIE — US

ALBUMS:	HITS 1			WEEKS 1
ALICE'S RESTAURANT	Reprise	44	7 Mar 70	1

Gwen GUTHRIE — US

SINGLES:	HITS 3			WEEKS 25
AIN'T NOTHIN' GOIN' ON BUT THE RENT	Boiling Point	5	19 Jul 86	12
(THEY LONG TO BE) CLOSE TO YOU	Boiling Point	25	11 Oct 86	7

GOOD TO GO LOVER / OUTSIDE IN THE RAIN	*Boiling Point*	37	*14 Feb 87*	4
AIN'T NOTHIN' GOIN' ON BUT THE RENT [RM]	*Polydor*	42	*4 Sep 93*	2

Remixed by Nigel Wright.

ALBUMS:		**HITS 1**		**WEEKS 14**
GOOD TO GO LOVER	*Boiling Point*	42	*23 Aug 86*	14

GUY   US

(See also Various Artists (EPs) 'New York Undercover 4-Track EP'.)

SINGLES:		**HITS 1**		**WEEKS 4**
HER	*MCA*	58	*4 May 91*	4

Buddy GUY   US

ALBUMS:		**HITS 2**		**WEEKS 9**
DAMM RIGHT, I'VE GOT THE BLUES	*Silvertone*	43	*22 Jun 91*	5
FEELS LIKE RAIN	*Silvertone*	36	*13 Mar 93*	4

A GUY CALLED GERALD   UK

SINGLES:		**HITS 2**		**WEEKS 23**
VOODOO RAY [EP]	*Rham!*	55	*8 Apr 89*	8

Lead track: Voodoo Ray.

VOODOO RAY [EP] [RE]	*Rham!*	12	*24 Jun 89*	10
FX / EYES OF SORROW	*Subscape*	52	*16 Dec 89*	5

ALBUMS:		**HITS 2**		**WEEKS 2**
AUTOMANIKK	*Subscape*	68	*14 Apr 90*	1
BLACK SECRET TECHNOLOGY	*Juice Box*	64	*1 Apr 95*	1

GUYS 'N' DOLLS   UK

SINGLES:		**HITS 5**		**WEEKS 33**
THERE'S A WHOLE LOT OF LOVING	*Magnet*	2	*1 Mar 75*	11
HERE I GO AGAIN	*Magnet*	33	*17 May 75*	5
YOU DON'T HAVE TO SAY YOU LOVE ME	*Magnet*	5	*21 Feb 76*	8
STONEY GROUND	*Magnet*	38	*6 Nov 76*	4
ONLY LOVING DOES IT	*Magnet*	42	*13 May 78*	5

Song used in the Oxo TV commercial.

ALBUMS:		**HITS 1**		**WEEKS 1**
GUYS 'N' DOLLS	*Magnet*	43	*31 May 75*	1

Jonas GWANGWA – See CRY FREEDOM

GWENT CHORALE – See Bryn YEMM

GYRES   UK

SINGLES:		**HITS 2**		**WEEKS 2**
POP COP	*Sugar*	71	*13 Apr 96*	1
ARE YOU READY?	*Sugar*	71	*6 Jul 96*	1

H

H.H.C.   UK

SINGLES:		**HITS 1**		**WEEKS 1**
WE'RE NOT ALONE	*Perfecto*	44	*19 Apr 97*	1

H.W.A. featuring SONIC The HEDGEHOG   UK

SINGLES:		**HITS 1**		**WEEKS 6**
SUPERSONIC	*Internal Affairs*	33	*5 Dec 92*	6

HABIT   UK

SINGLES:		**HITS 1**		**WEEKS 2**
LUCY	*Virgin*	56	*30 Apr 88*	2

Bobby HACKETT – See Tony BENNETT

Steve HACKETT   UK

SINGLES:		**HITS 1**		**WEEKS 2**
CELL 151	*Charisma*	66	*2 Apr 83*	2

ALBUMS:		**HITS 8**		**WEEKS 38**
VOYAGE OF THE ACOLYTE	*Charisma*	26	*1 Nov 75*	4
PLEASE DON'T TOUCH	*Charisma*	38	*6 May 78*	5
SPECTRAL MORNINGS	*Charisma*	22	*26 May 79*	11
DEFECTOR	*Charisma*	9	*21 Jun 80*	7

CURED	*Charisma*	15	*29 Aug 81*	5
HIGHLY STRUNG	*Charisma*	16	*30 Apr 83*	3
BAY OF KINGS	*Lamborghini*	70	*19 Nov 83*	1
TILL WE HAVE FACES	*Lamborghini*	54	*22 Sep 84*	2

HADDAWAY
Trinidad & Tobago

SINGLES:	HITS 6			WEEKS 52
WHAT IS LOVE	*Logic*	2	*5 Jun 93*	15
LIFE	*Logic*	6	*25 Sep 93*	9
I MISS YOU	*Logic*	9	*18 Dec 93*	14
ROCK MY HEART	*Logic*	9	*2 Apr 94*	9
FLY AWAY	*Logic*	20	*24 Jun 95*	3
CATCH A FIRE	*Logic*	39	*23 Sep 95*	2
ALBUMS:	**HITS 1**			**WEEKS 16**
HADDAWAY - THE ALBUM	*Logic*	19	*23 Oct 93*	5
HADDAWAY - THE ALBUM [RE]	*Logic*	9	*29 Jan 94*	11

Repackaged.

Tony HADLEY
UK

SINGLES:	HITS 4			WEEKS 9
LOST IN YOUR LOVE	*EMI*	42	*7 Mar 92*	4
FOR YOUR BLUE EYES ONLY	*EMI*	67	*29 Aug 92*	2
THE GAME OF LOVE	*EMI*	72	*16 Jan 93*	1
DANCE WITH ME	*VC Recordings*	35	*10 May 97*	2

Above hit: TIN TIN OUT featuring Tony HADLEY.

ALBUMS:	**HITS 1**			**WEEKS 3**
TONY HADLEY	*PolyGram TV*	45	*20 Sep 97*	3

Sammy HAGAR
US

(See also Hagar, Schon, Aaronson, Shrieve.)

SINGLES:	HITS 4			WEEKS 15
THIS PLANET'S ON FIRE (BURN IN HELL) / SPACE STATION NO. 5	*Capitol*	52	*15 Dec 79*	5
I'VE DONE EVERYTHING FOR YOU	*Capitol*	36	*16 Feb 80*	5
HEARTBEAT / LOVE OR MONEY	*Capitol*	67	*24 May 80*	2
PIECE OF MY HEART	*Geffen*	67	*16 Jan 82*	1
PIECE OF MY HEART [RE]	*Geffen*	67	*30 Jan 82*	2
ALBUMS:	**HITS 5**			**WEEKS 19**
STREET MACHINE	*Capitol*	38	*29 Sep 79*	4
LOUD AND CLEAR	*Capitol*	12	*22 Mar 80*	8
DANGER ZONE	*Capitol*	25	*7 Jun 80*	3
STANDING HAMPTON	*Geffen*	84	*13 Feb 82*	2
SAMMY HAGAR	*Geffen*	86	*4 Jul 87*	2

HAGAR, SCHON, AARONSON, SHRIEVE
US

(See also Sammy Hagar.)

ALBUMS:	HITS 1			WEEKS 1
THROUGH THE FIRE	*Geffen*	92	*19 May 84*	1

Nina HAGEN - See ADAMSKI

Paul HAIG
UK

SINGLES:	HITS 1			WEEKS 3
HEAVEN SENT	*Island*	74	*28 May 83*	3
ALBUMS:	**HITS 1**			**WEEKS 2**
RHYTHM OF LIFE	*Island*	82	*22 Oct 83*	2

HAIRCUT ONE HUNDRED
UK

SINGLES:	HITS 5			WEEKS 47
FAVOURITE SHIRTS (BOY MEETS GIRL)	*Arista*	4	*24 Oct 81*	14
LOVE PLUS ONE	*Arista*	3	*30 Jan 82*	12
FANTASTIC DAY	*Arista*	9	*10 Apr 82*	9
NOBODY'S FOOL	*Arista*	9	*21 Aug 82*	7
PRIME TIME	*Polydor*	46	*6 Aug 83*	5
ALBUMS:	**HITS 1**			**WEEKS 34**
PELICAN WEST	*Arista*	2	*6 Mar 82*	34

Curtis HAIRSTON
US

SINGLES:	HITS 3			WEEKS 16
I WANT YOU (ALL TONIGHT)	*RCA*	44	*15 Oct 83*	5
I WANT YOUR LOVIN' (JUST A LITTLE BIT)	*London*	13	*27 Apr 85*	7
CHILLIN' OUT	*Atlantic*	57	*6 Dec 86*	4

Gary HAISMAN - See D-MOB

HAL featuring Gillian ANDERSON · UK

SINGLES:	HITS 1			WEEKS 3
EXTREMIS	Virgin	23	24 May 97	3

HALE and PACE and the STONKERS · UK

SINGLES:	HITS 1			WEEKS 7
THE STONK	London	1	9 Mar 91	7

Charity record in aid of Comic Relief's Red Nose Day.

Bill HALEY and his COMETS · US

SINGLES:	HITS 14			WEEKS 199
SHAKE, RATTLE AND ROLL	Brunswick	4	18 Dec 54	14

Originally recorded by Joe Turner. Additional credit reads: featuring Bill Haley and Ensemble.

(WE'RE GONNA) ROCK AROUND THE CLOCK	Brunswick	17	8 Jan 55	2

From the film 'The Blackboard Jungle'. Originally recorded by Sunny Dae and the Knights in 1952.

MAMBO ROCK	Brunswick	14	16 Apr 55	2
(WE'RE GONNA) ROCK AROUND THE CLOCK [RE-1ST]	Brunswick	1	15 Oct 55	17
ROCK-A-BEATIN' BOOGIE	Brunswick	4	31 Dec 55	9

Originally recorded by Esquire Boys in 1953.

SEE YOU LATER, ALLIGATOR	Brunswick	7	10 Mar 56	13

Originally recorded by Bobby Charles.

THE SAINTS ROCK 'N ROLL	Brunswick	5	26 May 56	24
ROCKIN' THROUGH THE RYE	Brunswick	3	18 Aug 56	18
RAZZLE DAZZLE	Brunswick	13	15 Sep 56	8
SEE YOU LATER, ALLIGATOR [RE]	Brunswick	12	22 Sep 56	8
(WE'RE GONNA) ROCK AROUND THE CLOCK [RE-2ND]	Brunswick	5	22 Sep 56	11
ROCK 'N' ROLL STAGE SHOW [LP]	Brunswick	30	10 Nov 56	1

12-track album, first track: Calling All Comets.

RIP IT UP	Brunswick	4	10 Nov 56	18
RUDY'S ROCK	Brunswick	30	24 Nov 56	1
RUDY'S ROCK [RE]	Brunswick	26	15 Dec 56	4
(WE'RE GONNA) ROCK AROUND THE CLOCK [RE-3RD]	MCA	24	15 Dec 56	2
ROCKIN' THROUGH THE RYE [RE]	Brunswick	19	5 Jan 57	5
(WE'RE GONNA) ROCK AROUND THE CLOCK [RE-4TH]	MCA	25	5 Jan 57	2
(WE'RE GONNA) ROCK AROUND THE CLOCK [RE-5TH]	Brunswick	22	26 Jan 57	2
ROCK THE JOINT	London	20	2 Feb 57	4

Originally recorded by the Treniers.

DON'T KNOCK THE ROCK	Brunswick	7	9 Feb 57	8
(WE'RE GONNA) ROCK AROUND THE CLOCK [RI-1ST]	MCA	20	6 Apr 68	11
(WE'RE GONNA) ROCK AROUND THE CLOCK [R1-2ND]	MCA	12	16 Mar 74	10
HALEY'S GOLDEN MEDLEY [M]	MCA	50	25 Apr 81	5

ALBUMS:	HITS 1			WEEKS 5
ROCK AROUND THE CLOCK	Ace Of Hearts	34	18 May 68	5

HALF MAN HALF BISCUIT · UK

ALBUMS:	HITS 2			WEEKS 14
BACK IN THE D.H.S.S.	Probe	60	8 Feb 86	9
BACK AGAIN IN THE D.H.S.S.	Probe	59	21 Feb 87	5

Aaron HALL · US

(See also Various Artists (EPs) 'Dangerous Minds EP'.)

SINGLES:	HITS 2			WEEKS 3
DON'T BE AFRAID	MCA	56	13 Jun 92	2
GET A LITTLE FREAKY WITH ME	MCA	66	23 Oct 93	1

Audrey HALL · Jamaica

SINGLES:	HITS 2			WEEKS 20
ONE DANCE WON'T DO	Germain	20	25 Jan 86	11
SMILE	Germain	14	5 Jul 86	9

Above hit: Audrey HALL featuring Sly DUNBAR and Robert SHAKESPEARE.

Daryl HALL · US

(See also Daryl Hall and John Oates.)

SINGLES:	HITS 6			WEEKS 26
DREAMTIME	RCA	28	2 Aug 86	8
I'M IN A PHILLY MOOD	Epic	59	25 Sep 93	2
STOP LOVING ME, STOP LOVING YOU	Epic	30	8 Jan 94	6

Originally recorded by Marvin Gaye.

I'M IN A PHILLY MOOD [RE]	Epic	52	26 Mar 94	2
HELP ME FIND A WAY TO YOUR HEART	Epic	70	14 May 94	1
GLORYLAND	Mercury	36	2 Jul 94	4

The official theme song of the USA 1994 World Cup.
Above hit: Daryl HALL and SOUNDS OF BLACKNESS.

WHEREVER WOULD I BE	Columbia	44	10 Jun 95	3

Above hit: Dusty SPRINGFIELD and Daryl HALL.

ALBUMS:		HITS 2		WEEKS 9
THREE HEARTS IN THE HAPPY ENDING MACHINE	RCA	26	23 Aug 86	5
SOUL ALONE	Epic	57	23 Oct 93	1
SOUL ALONE [RI]	Columbia	55	12 Feb 94	3

Daryl HALL and John OATES — US

(See also Daryl Hall.)

SINGLES:		HITS 16		WEEKS 84
SHE'S GONE	Atlantic	42	16 Oct 76	4
RUNNING FROM PARADISE	RCA	41	14 Jun 80	6
YOU'VE LOST THAT LOVIN' FEELIN'	RCA	55	20 Sep 80	3
KISS ON MY LIST	RCA	33	15 Nov 80	8
I CAN'T GO FOR THAT (NO CAN DO)	RCA	8	23 Jan 82	10
PRIVATE EYES	RCA	32	10 Apr 82	7
MANEATER	RCA	6	30 Oct 82	11
ONE ON ONE	RCA	63	22 Jan 83	3
FAMILY MAN	RCA	15	30 Apr 83	7
SAY IT ISN'T SO	RCA	69	12 Nov 83	3
ADULT EDUCATION	RCA	63	10 Mar 84	2
OUT OF TOUCH	RCA	48	20 Oct 84	5
METHOD OF MODERN LOVE	RCA	21	9 Feb 85	8
OUT OF TOUCH [RM]	RCA	62	22 Jun 85	3
A NITE AT THE APOLLO LIVE! [M]	RCA	58	21 Sep 85	2

Medley of The Way You Do The Things You Do and My Girl.
Above hit: Daryl HALL and John OATES featuring David RUFFIN and Eddie KENDRICK.

SO CLOSE	Arista	69	29 Sep 90	1
EVERYWHERE I LOOK	Arista	74	26 Jan 91	1

ALBUMS:		HITS 11		WEEKS 150
HALL AND OATES	RCA Victor	56	3 Jul 76	1
BIGGER THAN BOTH OF US	RCA Victor	25	18 Sep 76	7
BEAUTY ON A BACK STREET	RCA Victor	40	15 Oct 77	2
PRIVATE EYES	RCA	8	6 Feb 82	21
H2O	RCA	24	23 Oct 82	35
ROCK 'N' SOUL (PART ONE)	RCA	16	29 Oct 83	45

Compilation.

BIG BAM BOOM	RCA	28	27 Oct 84	13
HALL AND OATES LIVE AT THE APOLLO WITH DAVID RUFFIN AND EDDIE KENDRICK	RCA	32	28 Sep 85	5

Live recordings from the Apollo Theater, Harlem, May 85 to benefit the United Negro College Fund.

OOH YEAH!	RCA	52	18 Jun 88	3
CHANGE OF SEASON	Arista	44	27 Oct 90	2
THE BEST OF DARYL HALL AND JOHN OATES – LOOKING BACK	Arista	9	19 Oct 91	16

Lynden David HALL — UK

SINGLES:		HITS 3		WEEKS 8
SEXY CINDERELLA	Cooltempo	45	25 Oct 97	2

Features Me'shell Ndegeocello on bass guitar.

DO I QUALIFY?	Cooltempo	26	14 Mar 98	2
CRESCENT MOON	Cooltempo	45	4 Jul 98	1
SEXY CINDERELLA [RI]	Cooltempo	17	31 Oct 98	3

ALBUMS:		HITS 1		WEEKS 2
MEDICINE 4 MY PAIN	Cooltempo	43	14 Nov 98	2

Originally released in 1997, charted after being repackaged with additional tracks.

Pam HALL — Jamaica

SINGLES:		HITS 1		WEEKS 4
DEAR BOOPSIE	Bluemountain	54	16 Aug 86	4

Terry HALL — UK

SINGLES:		HITS 5		WEEKS 6
MISSING	Chrysalis	75	11 Nov 89	1

Credit is as per sleeve. Label only lists Terry Hall.
Above hit: TERRY, BLAIR and ANOUCHKA.

FOREVER J	AnXious	67	27 Aug 94	1
SENSE	AnXious	54	12 Nov 94	2
RAINBOWS [EP]	AnXious	62	28 Oct 95	1

Lead track: Chasing A Rainbow (with Damon Albarn).

BALLAD OF A LANDLORD	Southsea Bubble Co	50	14 Jun 97	1

ALBUMS:		HITS 1		WEEKS 1
LAUGH	Southsea Bubble Co	50	18 Oct 97	1

Toni HALLIDAY - See LEFTFIELD

Geri HALLIWELL UK

SINGLES:		HITS 3		WEEKS 35	
LOOK AT ME	EMI		2	22 May 99	12
LOOK AT ME [RE]	EMI		60	28 Aug 99	2
MI CHICO LATINO	EMI		1	28 Aug 99	13
LIFT ME UP	EMI		1	13 Nov 99	8
ALBUMS:		HITS 1		WEEKS 28	
SCHIZOPHONIC	EMI		4	19 Jun 99	28

Jack HALLORAN SINGERS - See Ray CHARLES

HALO JAMES UK

SINGLES:		HITS 4		WEEKS 24	
WANTED	Epic		45	7 Oct 89	5
COULD HAVE TOLD YOU SO	Epic		6	23 Dec 89	12
BABY	Epic		43	17 Mar 90	4
MAGIC HOUR	Epic		59	19 May 90	3
ALBUMS:		HITS 1		WEEKS 4	
WITNESS	Epic		18	14 Apr 90	4

HAMBURG STUDENTS CHOIR Germany

ALBUMS:		HITS 1		WEEKS 6	
HARK THE HERALD ANGELS SING	Pye Golden Guinea		11	17 Dec 60	6

HAMILTON, Joe FRANK and REYNOLDS US

SINGLES:		HITS 1		WEEKS 6	
FALLIN' IN LOVE	Pye International		33	13 Sep 75	6

George HAMILTON IV US

SINGLES:		HITS 2		WEEKS 13	
WHY DON'T THEY UNDERSTAND	His Master's Voice		22	8 Mar 58	9
I KNOW WHERE I'M GOIN'	His Master's Voice		29	19 Jul 58	1
I KNOW WHERE I'M GOIN' [RE]	His Master's Voice		23	9 Aug 58	3
ALBUMS:		HITS 3		WEEKS 11	
CANADIAN PACIFIC	RCA Victor		45	10 Apr 71	1
REFLECTIONS	Lotus		25	10 Feb 79	9
SONGS FOR A WINTER'S NIGHT	Ronco		94	13 Nov 82	1

Lynne HAMILTON UK

SINGLES:		HITS 1		WEEKS 11	
ON THE INSIDE (THEME FROM 'PRISONER CELL BLOCK H')	A.1		3	29 Apr 89	11

Theme from the TV soap.

Mike 'Tone' HAMILTON - See Ian McNABB

Russ HAMILTON UK

SINGLES:		HITS 2		WEEKS 26	
WE WILL MAKE LOVE	Oriole		2	25 May 57	20
WEDDING RING	Oriole		20	28 Sep 57	6

Above hit: Russ HAMILTON with Johnny GREGORY and his Orchestra with the TONETTES.

Marvin HAMLISCH US

SINGLES:		HITS 1		WEEKS 13	
THE ENTERTAINER - MUSIC FROM "THE STING"	MCA		25	30 Mar 74	13

From the film 'The Sting'. Composed by Scott Joplin in 1901.
Above hit: featuring Marvin HAMLISCH on Piano.

ALBUMS:		HITS 1		WEEKS 35	
THE STING [OST]	MCA		7	23 Mar 74	35

HAMMER US

SINGLES:		HITS 12		WEEKS 68	
U CAN'T TOUCH THIS	Capitol		3	9 Jun 90	16

Based around Super Freak by Rick James.

HAVE YOU SEEN HER	Capitol		8	6 Oct 90	7
PRAY	Capitol		8	8 Dec 90	10

Based around Prince's When Doves Cry.

HERE COMES THE HAMMER	Capitol		15	23 Feb 91	5
YO!! SWEETNESS	Capitol		16	1 Jun 91	5
(HAMMER HAMMER) THEY PUT ME IN THE MIX	Capitol		20	20 Jul 91	4

Above 6: M.C. HAMMER.

2 LEGIT 2 QUIT	Capitol	60	26 Oct 91	2
Above hit: HAMMER (Introducing SAJA).				
ADDAMS GROOVE	Capitol	4	21 Dec 91	9
From the film 'The Addams Family'.				
DO NOT PASS ME BY	Capitol	14	21 Mar 92	6
Above hit: HAMMER (featuring Tremaine HAWKINS introducing Trina JOHNSON & VOICES).				
IT'S ALL GOOD	RCA	52	12 Mar 94	2
DON'T STOP	RCA	72	13 Aug 94	1
STRAIGHT TO MY FEET	Priority	57	3 Jun 95	1
From the film 'Street Fighter II'.				
Above hit: HAMMER/Deion SANDERS.				
ALBUMS:	HITS 3		WEEKS 67	
PLEASE HAMMER DON'T HURT 'EM	Capitol	8	28 Jul 90	59
LET'S GET IT STARTED	Capitol	46	6 Apr 91	2
Above 2: M.C. HAMMER.				
TOO LEGIT TO QUIT	Capitol	41	2 Nov 91	6

Jan HAMMER Czechoslovakia

SINGLES:	HITS 3		WEEKS 26	
MIAMI VICE THEME	MCA	5	12 Oct 85	8
CROCKETT'S THEME	MCA	2	19 Sep 87	12
Above 2 from the TV series 'Miami Vice'.				
CROCKETT'S THEME [RI] / CHANCER	MCA	47	1 Jun 91	6
ALBUMS:	HITS 1		WEEKS 12	
ESCAPE FROM TV	MCA	34	14 Nov 87	12

Albert HAMMOND UK

THE SINGLES:	HITS 1		WEEKS 11	
FREE ELECTRIC BAND	Mums	19	30 Jun 73	11

Beres HAMMOND - See Maxi PRIEST

Herbie HANCOCK US

SINGLES:	HITS 6		WEEKS 41	
I THOUGHT IT WAS YOU	CBS	15	26 Aug 78	9
YOU BET YOUR LOVE	CBS	18	3 Feb 79	10
ROCKIT	Epic	8	30 Jul 83	12
AUTODRIVE	CBS	33	8 Oct 83	4
FUTURE SHOCK	CBS	54	21 Jan 84	3
HARDROCK	CBS	65	4 Aug 84	3
ALBUMS:	HITS 3		WEEKS 24	
SUNLIGHT	CBS	27	9 Sep 78	6
FEETS DON'T FAIL ME NOW	CBS	28	24 Feb 79	8
FUTURE SHOCK	CBS	27	27 Aug 83	10

Tony HANCOCK UK

EPS:	HITS 1		WEEKS 39	
LITTLE PIECES OF HANCOCK	Pye	6	12 May 62	39
ALBUMS:	HITS 3		WEEKS 51	
THIS IS HANCOCK	Pye	2	9 Apr 60	22
PIECES OF HANCOCK	Pye	17	12 Nov 60	2
HANCOCK	Pye	12	3 Mar 62	23
THIS IS HANCOCK [RI]	Pye Golden Guinea	16	14 Sep 63	4

HANDBAGGERS UK

SINGLES:	HITS 1		WEEKS 1	
U FOUND OUT	Tidy Trax	55	15 Jun 96	1
Samples Depeche Modes' Just Can't Get Enough.				

Vernon HANDLEY - See Nigel KENNEDY

HANDLEY FAMILY UK

SINGLES:	HITS 1		WEEKS 7	
WAM BAM	GL	30	7 Apr 73	7

HANDS OF DR. TELENY - See Peter STRAKER and the HANDS OF DR. TELENY

Jayn HANNA UK

SINGLES:	HITS 2		WEEKS 2	
LOVELIGHT (RIDE ON A LOVE TRAIN)	VC Recordings	42	13 Apr 96	1
LOST WITHOUT YOU	VC Recordings	44	1 Feb 97	1

HANNAH - See MAN WITH NO NAME

HANNAH and Her SISTERS - See Hannah JONES; PJB Featuring HANNAH and Her SISTERS

Bo HANNSON · Sweden

ALBUMS:	HITS 1			WEEKS 2
LORD OF THE RINGS	Charisma	34	18 Nov 72	2

HANOI ROCKS · UK/Finland

SINGLES:	HITS 1			WEEKS 2
UP AROUND THE BEND	CBS	61	7 Jul 84	2
ALBUMS:	HITS 2			WEEKS 4
BACK TO MYSTERY CITY	Lick	87	11 Jun 83	1
TWO STEPS FROM THE MOVE	CBS	28	20 Oct 84	3

HANSON · US

SINGLES:	HITS 5			WEEKS 43
MMMBOP	Mercury	1	7 Jun 97	13
First debut single to simultaneously top the UK & US single chart.				
WHERE'S THE LOVE	Mercury	4	13 Sep 97	9
I WILL COME TO YOU	Mercury	5	22 Nov 97	9
WEIRD	Mercury	19	28 Mar 98	5
From the film 'The Borrowers'.				
THINKING OF YOU	Mercury	23	4 Jul 98	6
THINKING OF YOU [RE]	Mercury	69	5 Sep 98	1
ALBUMS:	HITS 2			WEEKS 30
MIDDLE OF NOWHERE	Mercury	1	21 Jun 97	29
3 CAR GARAGE - INDIE RECORDINGS 95-96	Mercury	39	13 Jun 98	1
Tracks culled from two earlier US-only releases.				

John HANSON · UK

ALBUMS:	HITS 3			WEEKS 12
THE STUDENT PRINCE	Pye	17	23 Apr 60	1
THE STUDENT PRINCE / THE VAGABOND KING	Pye Golden Guinea	9	2 Sep 61	7
'The Student Prince' was a 1954 film musical featuring the voice of Mario Lanza. 'The Vagabond King' was a musical from 1956.				
JOHN HANSON SINGS 20 SHOWTIME GREATS	K-Tel	16	10 Dec 77	4

HAPPENINGS · US

SINGLES:	HITS 2			WEEKS 14
I GOT RHYTHM	Stateside	28	20 May 67	9
Originally recorded by Red Nichols in 1931.				
MY MAMMY	Pye International	34	19 Aug 67	5
Originally recorded by Paul Whiteman in 1921. From 26 Aug 68 the US B.T Puppy label was credited on the chart.				

HAPPY CLAPPERS · UK

SINGLES:	HITS 4			WEEKS 19
I BELIEVE	Shindig	21	3 Jun 95	3
HOLD ON	Shindig	27	26 Aug 95	2
I BELIEVE [RI]	Shindig	7	18 Nov 95	8
CAN'T HELP IT	Coliseum	18	15 Jun 96	3
NEVER AGAIN	Coliseum	49	21 Dec 96	1
I BELIEVE 97 [RM]	Coalition	28	22 Nov 97	2
Remixed by Sash.				

HAPPY MONDAYS · UK

SINGLES:	HITS 10			WEEKS 53
W.F.L. (WROTE FOR LUCK)	Factory	68	30 Sep 89	2
MADCHESTER RAVE ON [EP]	Factory	19	25 Nov 89	14
Lead track: Hallelujah. From 13 Jan 90 repackaged as a remixed version climbing back up to No. 22.				
STEP ON	Factory	5	7 Apr 90	11
Above hit: HAPPY MONDAYS Guest Vocal: ROWETTA.				
LAZYITIS - ONE ARMED BOXER	Factory	46	9 Jun 90	3
Above hit: HAPPY MONDAYS and Karl DENVER.				
KINKY AFRO	Factory	5	20 Oct 90	7
LOOSE FIT	Factory	17	9 Mar 91	7
JUDGE FUDGE	Factory	24	30 Nov 91	3
STINKIN' THINKIN'	Factory	31	19 Sep 92	3
SUNSHINE AND LOVE	Factory	62	21 Nov 92	1
THE BOYS ARE BACK IN TOWN	London	24	22 May 99	2
ALBUMS:	HITS 6			WEEKS 55
BUMMED	Factory	59	27 Jan 90	14
PILLS 'N' THRILLS AND BELLYACHES	Factory	4	17 Nov 90	29
HAPPY MONDAYS - LIVE	Factory	21	12 Oct 91	3

. . . YES PLEASE!	*Factory*	14	*10 Oct 92*	3
LOADS - THE BEST OF THE HAPPY MONDAYS	*Factory*	41	*18 Nov 95*	2
GREATEST HITS	*London*	11	*5 Jun 99*	4

Paul HARDCASTLE
UK

(See also Direct Drive; First Light; Silent Underdog.)

SINGLES:	HITS 11		WEEKS 66	
YOU'RE THE ONE FOR ME – DAYBREAK – A.M.	*Total Control*	41	*7 Apr 84*	4
Above hit: Paul HARDCASTLE vocals by Kevin HENRY.				
GUILTY	*Total Control*	55	*28 Jul 84*	3
RAIN FOREST	*BlueBird*	41	*22 Sep 84*	5
EAT YOUR HEART OUT	*Cooltempo*	59	*17 Nov 84*	4
Above hit: Paul HARDCASTLE vocals by Kevin HENRY.				
19	*Chrysalis*	1	*4 May 85*	16
19 was the average age of an American soldier in the Vietnam war.				
RAIN FOREST [RI]	*BlueBird*	53	*15 Jun 85*	4
JUST FOR MONEY	*Chrysalis*	19	*9 Nov 85*	5
Features the voices of Laurence Olivier, Bob Hoskins, Ed O'Ross and AlanTalbot.				
DON'T WASTE MY TIME	*Chrysalis*	8	*1 Feb 86*	11
Above hit: Paul HARDCASTLE Lead vocals – Carol KENYON.				
FOOLIN' YOURSELF	*Chrysalis*	51	*21 Jun 86*	3
Above hit: Paul HARDCASTLE introducing Kevin HENRY.				
THE WIZARD	*Chrysalis*	15	*11 Oct 86*	6
Theme to BBC TV's 'Top Of The Pops'.				
WALK IN THE NIGHT	*Chrysalis*	54	*9 Apr 88*	3
40 YEARS	*Chrysalis*	53	*4 Jun 88*	2
ALBUMS:	HITS 1		WEEKS 5	
PAUL HARDCASTLE	*Chrysalis*	53	*30 Nov 85*	5

HARDCORE RHYTHM TEAM
UK

SINGLES:	HITS 1		WEEKS 1	
HARDCORE - THE FINAL CONFLICT	*Furious*	69	*14 Mar 92*	1

Duane HARDEN – See POWERHOUSE featuring Duane HARDEN; Armand VAN HELDEN

HARDFLOOR
Germany

SINGLES:	HITS 2		WEEKS 6	
HARDTRANCE ACPERIENCE [EP]	*Harthouse UK*	56	*26 Dec 92*	4
Various mixes of the track Acperience.				
TRANCESCRIPT	*Harthouse UK*	72	*10 Apr 93*	1
ACPERIENCE [RM]	*Eye-Q*	60	*25 Oct 97*	1
Remixed by Dex and Jonsey.				
ALBUMS:	HITS 1		WEEKS 1	
HOME RUN	*Harthouse*	68	*29 Jun 96*	1

Ronan HARDIMAN
Ireland

ALBUMS:	HITS 1		WEEKS 8	
MICHAEL FLATLEY'S LORD OF THE DANCE	*PolyGram TV*	37	*2 Nov 96*	8

Tim HARDIN
US

SINGLES:	HITS 1		WEEKS 1	
HANG ON A DREAM	*Verve*	50	*7 Jan 67*	1

Carolyn HARDING – See PROSPECT PARK Featuring Carolyn HARDING

Mike HARDING
UK

SINGLES:	HITS 1		WEEKS 8	
ROCHDALE COWBOY	*Rubber*	22	*2 Aug 75*	8
ALBUMS:	HITS 4		WEEKS 24	
MRS 'ARDIN'S KID	*Rubber*	24	*30 Aug 75*	6
ONE MAN SHOW	*Philips*	19	*10 Jul 76*	10
OLD FOUR EYES IS BACK	*Philips*	31	*11 Jun 77*	6
CAPTAIN PARALYTIC AND THE BROWN ALE COWBOY	*Philips*	60	*24 Jun 78*	2

Francoise HARDY
France

SINGLES:	HITS 3		WEEKS 26	
TOUS LES GARCONS ET LES FILLES	*Pye*	36	*27 Jun 64*	7
ET MEME	*Pye*	31	*9 Jan 65*	4
ALL OVER THE WORLD	*Pye*	16	*27 Mar 65*	15
EPS:	HITS 2		WEEKS 23	
C'EST FAB	*Pye*	5	*4 Jul 64*	21
C'EST FRANCOISE	*Pye*	18	*10 Oct 64*	2

Tynetta HARE – See Joey B. ELLIS

Niki HARE – See SNAP!

Morten HARKET   Norway

SINGLES:	HITS 1			WEEKS 1
A KIND OF CHRISTMAS CARD	Warner Brothers	53	19 Aug 95	1

HARLEM COMMUNITY CHOIR – See John LENNON

HARLEQUIN 4'S – See BUNKER KRU/HARLEQUIN 4'S

Steve HARLEY and COCKNEY REBEL   UK

SINGLES:	HITS 9			WEEKS 69
JUDY TEEN	EMI	5	11 May 74	11
MR. SOFT	EMI	8	10 Aug 74	9
Above 2: COCKNEY REBEL.				
MAKE ME SMILE (COME UP AND SEE ME)	EMI	1	8 Feb 75	9
MR. RAFFLES (MAN, IT WAS MEAN)	EMI	13	7 Jun 75	6
HERE COMES THE SUN	EMI	10	31 Jul 76	7
Originally recorded by the Beatles.				
(I BELIEVE) LOVE'S A PRIMA DONNA	EMI	41	6 Nov 76	4
FREEDOM'S PRISONER	EMI	58	20 Oct 79	3
Above hit: Steve HARLEY.				
BALLERINA (PRIMA DONNA)	Stiletto	51	13 Aug 83	5
THE PHANTOM OF THE OPERA	Polydor	7	11 Jan 86	10
From the musical 'The Phantom Of The Opera'.				
Above hit: Sarah BRIGHTMAN and Steve HARLEY.				
MAKE ME SMILE (COME UP AND SEE ME) [RI-1ST]	EMI	46	25 Apr 92	2
MAKE ME SMILE (COME UP AND SEE ME) [R1-2ND]	EMI	33	30 Dec 95	3
Featured in the Carlsberg lager TV commercial.				
ALBUMS:	HITS 5			WEEKS 52
THE PSYCHOMODO	EMI	8	22 Jun 74	20
Above hit: COCKNEY REBEL.				
THE BEST YEARS OF OUR LIVES	EMI	4	22 Mar 75	19
TIMELESS FLIGHT	EMI	18	14 Feb 76	6
LOVE'S A PRIMA DONNA	EMI	28	27 Nov 76	3
FACE TO FACE – A LIVE RECORDING	EMI	40	30 Jul 77	4
Live recordings dating from 1974/75.				

HARLEY QUINNE   UK

SINGLES:	HITS 1			WEEKS 8
NEW ORLEANS	Bell	19	14 Oct 72	8

HARMONIUM   UK

(See also Blowing Free; Hypnosis; In Tune; Raindance; School Of Excellence.)

ALBUMS:	HITS 1			WEEKS 4
SPIRIT OF TRANQUILITY	Global Television	25	21 Mar 98	4

HARMONIX   UK

SINGLES:	HITS 1			WEEKS 2
LANDSLIDE	Deconstruction	28	30 Mar 96	2
Samples U2's Where The Streets Have No Name.				

HARMONY GRASS   UK

SINGLES:	HITS 1			WEEKS 7
MOVE IN A LITTLE CLOSER BABY	RCA Victor	24	1 Feb 69	7

Ben HARPER   US

SINGLES:	HITS 1			WEEKS 1
FADED	Virgin	54	4 Apr 98	1

Charlie HARPER   UK

SINGLES:	HITS 1			WEEKS 1
BARMY LONDON ARMY	Gems	68	19 Jul 80	1

Roy HARPER   UK

ALBUMS:	HITS 4			WEEKS 9
VALENTINE	Harvest	27	9 Mar 74	1
H.Q.	Harvest	31	21 Jun 75	2
BULLINAMINGVASE	Harvest	25	12 Mar 77	2
WHATEVER HAPPENED TO JUGULA?	Beggars Banquet	44	16 Mar 85	4
Above hit: Roy HARPER with Jimmy PAGE.				

HARPERS BIZARRE
US

SINGLES:	HITS 2			WEEKS 13
59TH STREET BRIDGE SONG (FEELIN' GROOVY)	*Warner Brothers*	34	*1 Apr 67*	7
Originally recorded by Simon and Garfunkel.				
ANYTHING GOES	*Warner Brothers*	33	*7 Oct 67*	6
Written by Cole Porter in 1934.				

HARPO
Sweden

SINGLES:	HITS 1			WEEKS 6
MOVIE STAR	*DJM*	24	*17 Apr 76*	6
Features Agnetha and Frida from Abba on backing vocals.				

Anita HARRIS
UK

SINGLES:	HITS 4			WEEKS 50
JUST LOVING YOU	*CBS*	6	*2 Jul 67*	30
THE PLAYGROUND	*CBS*	46	*14 Oct 67*	3
ANNIVERSARY WALTZ	*CBS*	21	*27 Jan 68*	9
DREAM A LITTLE DREAM OF ME	*CBS*	33	*17 Aug 68*	8
ALBUMS:	HITS 1			WEEKS 5
JUST LOVING YOU	*CBS*	29	*27 Jan 68*	5

Emmylou HARRIS
US

(See also Dolly Parton, Linda Ronstadt and Emmylou Harris.)

SINGLES:	HITS 1			WEEKS 6
HERE, THERE & EVERYWHERE	*Reprise*	30	*6 Mar 76*	6
Originally recorded by the Beatles.				
ALBUMS:	HITS 7			WEEKS 31
ELITE HOTEL	*Reprise*	17	*14 Feb 76*	11
LUXURY LINER	*Warner Brothers*	17	*29 Jan 77*	6
QUARTER MOON IN A TEN CENT TOWN	*Warner Brothers*	40	*4 Feb 78*	5
HER BEST SONGS	*K-Tel*	36	*29 Mar 80*	3
EVANGELINE	*Warner Brothers*	53	*14 Feb 81*	4
WRECKING BALL	*Grapevine*	46	*7 Oct 95*	1
SPYBOY	*Grapevine*	57	*29 Aug 98*	1

Jet HARRIS
UK

(See also Jet Harris and Tony Meehan.)

SINGLES:	HITS 2			WEEKS 18
BESAME MUCHO	*Decca*	22	*26 May 62*	7
MAIN TITLE THEME (FROM "THE MAN WITH THE GOLDEN ARM")	*Decca*	12	*18 Aug 62*	11
Theme from the film.				

Jet HARRIS and Tony MEEHAN
UK

(See also Jet Harris; Tony Meehan.)

SINGLES:	HITS 3			WEEKS 39
DIAMONDS	*Decca*	1	*12 Jan 63*	13
SCARLET O'HARA	*Decca*	2	*27 Apr 63*	13
APPLEJACK	*Decca*	4	*7 Sep 63*	13
EPS:	HITS 1			WEEKS 21
JET AND TONY	*Decca*	3	*29 Jun 63*	21

Keith HARRIS and ORVILLE
UK

SINGLES:	HITS 3			WEEKS 20
ORVILLE'S SONG	*BBC*	4	*18 Dec 82*	11
COME TO MY PARTY	*BBC*	44	*24 Dec 83*	4
Above hit: Keith HARRIS and ORVILLE with DIPPY.				
WHITE CHRISTMAS	*Columbia*	40	*14 Dec 85*	5
ALBUMS:	HITS 1			WEEKS 1
AT THE END OF THE RAINBOW	*BBC*	92	*4 Jun 83*	1
Above hit: Keith HARRIS, ORVILLE and CUDDLES.				

Major HARRIS
US

SINGLES:	HITS 2			WEEKS 9
LOVE WON'T LET ME WAIT	*Atlantic*	37	*9 Aug 75*	7
ALL MY LIFE	*London*	61	*5 Nov 83*	2

Max HARRIS with his Group
UK

SINGLES:	HITS 1			WEEKS 10
GURNEY SLADE	*Fontana*	11	*3 Dec 60*	10
From the TV series 'The Strange World Of Gurney Slade'.				

Rahni HARRIS and F.L.O. vocals by T. HARRINGTON and O. RASBURY · US

SINGLES:	HITS 1			WEEKS 7
SIX MILLION STEPS (WEST RUNS SOUTH)	Mercury	43	16 Dec 78	7

Richard HARRIS · Ireland

SINGLES:	HITS 1			WEEKS 18
MACARTHUR PARK	RCA Victor	4	29 Jun 68	12
MACARTHUR PARK [RI]	Probe	38	8 Jul 72	6

Rochelle HARRIS - See ANGELHEART

Rolf HARRIS · Australia

SINGLES:	HITS 8			WEEKS 74
TIE ME KANGAROO DOWN SPORT	Columbia	9	23 Jul 60	13
Above hit: Rolf HARRIS with his Wobble Board and the RHYTHM SPINNERS.				
SUN ARISE	Columbia	3	27 Oct 62	16
JOHNNY DAY	Columbia	44	2 Mar 63	2
BLUER THAN BLUE	Columbia	30	19 Apr 69	8
TWO LITTLE BOYS	Columbia	1	22 Nov 69	24
Originally recorded in 1903 by Harry Lauder about the American Civil War.				
TWO LITTLE BOYS [RE]	Columbia	50	20 Jun 70	1
STAIRWAY TO HEAVEN	Vertigo	7	13 Feb 93	6
BOHEMIAN RHAPSODY	Living Beat	50	1 Jun 96	1
SUN ARISE [RR]	EMI	26	25 Oct 97	3
EPS:	HITS 1			WEEKS 2
ROLF HARRIS AND SHAMUS O'SHEAN THE LEPRACHAUN	Columbia	9	22 Oct 66	2
ALBUMS:	HITS 1			WEEKS 1
CAN YOU TELL WHAT IT IS YET?	EMI	70	1 Nov 97	1

Ronnie HARRIS · UK

SINGLES:	HITS 1			WEEKS 3
THE STORY OF TINA	Columbia	12	25 Sep 54	3

Sam HARRIS · US

SINGLES:	HITS 1			WEEKS 2
HEARTS ON FIRE / OVER THE RAINBOW	Motown	67	9 Feb 85	2
The second white male solo to hit on Motown after R. Dean Taylor.				

Simon HARRIS · UK

(See also Ambassadors Of Funk featuring MC Mario; World Warrior.)

SINGLES:	HITS 5			WEEKS 17
BASS (HOW LOW CAN YOU GO)	ffrr	12	19 Mar 88	6
HERE COMES THAT SOUND	ffrr	38	29 Oct 88	4
(I'VE GOT YOUR) PLEASURE CONTROL	ffrr	60	24 Jun 89	3
Above hit: Simon HARRIS featuring Lonnie GORDON.				
ANOTHER MONSTERJAM	ffrr	65	18 Nov 89	1
Above hit: Simon HARRIS featuring EINSTEIN.				
RAGGA HOUSE (ALL NIGHT LONG)	Living Beat	56	10 Mar 90	3
Above hit: Simon HARRIS Starring DADDY FREDDY.				

George HARRISON · UK

SINGLES:	HITS 10			WEEKS 82
MY SWEET LORD	Apple	1	23 Jan 71	17
Originally recorded by Billy Preston and backing vocals from Phil Spector.				
BANGLA-DESH	Apple	10	14 Aug 71	9
GIVE ME LOVE (GIVE ME PEACE ON EARTH)	Apple	8	2 Jun 73	10
DING DONG	Apple	38	21 Dec 74	5
YOU	Apple	38	11 Oct 75	5
BLOW AWAY	Dark Horse	51	10 Mar 79	5
ALL THOSE YEARS AGO	Dark Horse	13	23 May 81	7
A tribute to John Lennon.				
GOT MY MIND SET ON YOU	Dark Horse	2	24 Oct 87	14
Originally recorded by James Ray.				
WHEN WE WAS FAB	Dark Horse	25	6 Feb 88	7
THIS IS LOVE	Dark Horse	55	25 Jun 88	3
ALBUMS:	HITS 7			WEEKS 76
ALL THINGS MUST PASS	Apple	4	26 Dec 70	24
LIVING IN THE MATERIAL WORLD	Apple	2	7 Jul 73	12
EXTRA TEXTURE (READ ALL ABOUT IT)	Apple	16	18 Oct 75	4
THIRTY THREE AND A THIRD	Dark Horse	35	18 Dec 76	4
GEORGE HARRISON	Dark Horse	39	17 Mar 79	5
SOMEWHERE IN ENGLAND	Dark Horse	13	13 Jun 81	4
CLOUD NINE	Dark Horse	10	14 Nov 87	23

Jane HARRISON

UK

ALBUMS:	HITS 1			WEEKS 1
NEW DAY	Stylus	70	4 Feb 89	1

Noel HARRISON

UK

SINGLES:	HITS 1			WEEKS 14
THE WINDMILLS OF YOUR MIND	Reprise	8	1 Mar 69	14
From the film 'The Thomas Crown Affair'.				

Deborah HARRY

US

SINGLES:	HITS 10			WEEKS 52
BACKFIRED	Chrysalis	32	1 Aug 81	6
FRENCH KISSIN' IN THE USA	Chrysalis	8	15 Nov 86	10
FREE TO FALL	Chrysalis	46	28 Feb 87	4
IN LOVE WITH LOVE	Chrysalis	45	9 May 87	5
Above 4: Debbie HARRY.				
I WANT THAT MAN	Chrysalis	13	7 Oct 89	10
BRITE SIDE	Chrysalis	59	2 Dec 89	4
SWEET AND LOW	Chrysalis	57	31 Mar 90	3
WELL, DID YOU EVAH!	Chrysalis	42	5 Jan 91	4
Above hit: Deborah HARRY and Iggy POP.				
I CAN SEE CLEARLY	Chrysalis	23	3 Jul 93	4
STRIKE ME PINK	Chrysalis	46	18 Sep 93	2
ALBUMS:	HITS 6			WEEKS 53
KOO KOO	Chrysalis	6	8 Aug 81	7
ROCKBIRD	Chrysalis	31	29 Nov 86	11
Above 2 Debbie HARRY.				
ONCE MORE INTO THE BLEACH	Chrysalis	50	17 Dec 88	4
Remix album of Debbie Harry's solo and group material.				
Above hit: Debbie HARRY and BLONDIE.				
DEF DUMB AND BLONDE	Chrysalis	12	28 Oct 89	7
THE COMPLETE PICTURE - THE VERY BEST OF DEBORAH HARRY AND BLONDIE	Chrysalis	3	16 Mar 91	22
Above hit: Deborah HARRY and BLONDIE.				
DEBRAVATION	Chrysalis	24	31 Jul 93	2

HARRY J. ALL STARS

Jamaica

SINGLES:	HITS 1			WEEKS 25
LIQUIDATOR	Harry J	9	25 Oct 69	20
LIQUIDATOR [RI]	Trojan	42	29 Mar 80	5
[AA] listed with Long Shot Kick De Bucket by the Pioneers.				

Keef HARTLEY BAND

UK

ALBUMS:	HITS 1			WEEKS 3
THE TIME IS NEAR	Deram	41	5 Sep 70	3

Richard HARTLEY - See Michael REED ORCHESTRA

Dan HARTMAN

US

SINGLES:	HITS 5			WEEKS 34
INSTANT REPLAY	Blue Sky	8	21 Oct 78	15
THIS IS IT	Blue Sky	17	13 Jan 79	8
SECOND NATURE	MCA	66	18 May 85	2
I CAN DREAM ABOUT YOU	MCA	12	24 Aug 85	8
Original release reached No. 78 in 1984.				
KEEP THE FIRE BURNIN'	Columbia	49	1 Apr 95	1
Above hit: Dan HARTMAN Starring Loleatta HOLLOWAY.				

Alex HARVEY - See SENSATIONAL ALEX HARVEY BAND

PJ HARVEY

UK

(See also John Parish + Polly Jean Harvey; Various Artists (EPs) 'The Help EP'.)

SINGLES:	HITS 10			WEEKS 18
SHEELA-NA-GIG	Too Pure	69	29 Feb 92	1
50 FT QUEENIE	Island	27	1 May 93	2
MAN-SIZE	Island	42	17 Jul 93	2
DOWN BY THE WATER	Island	38	18 Feb 95	2
C'MON BILLY	Island	29	22 Jul 95	2
SEND HIS LOVE TO ME	Island	34	28 Oct 95	2
HENRY LEE	Mute	36	9 Mar 96	1
Based on a traditional folk tale.				
Above hit: Nick CAVE and PJ HARVEY and the BAD SEEDS.				

BROKEN HOMES	Island	25	30 May 98	2

[AA] listed with Money Greedy by Tricky.
Above hit: TRICKY featuring Polly Jean HARVEY.

A PERFECT DAY ELISE	Island	25	26 Sep 98	2
THE WIND	Island	29	23 Jan 99	2
ALBUMS:	**HITS 5**		**WEEKS 19**	
DRY	Too Pure	11	11 Apr 92	5
RID OF ME	Island	3	8 May 93	4
4-TRACK DEMOS	Island	19	30 Oct 93	2

Budget album of demos from the time of Rid Of Me.

TO BRING YOU MY LOVE	Island	12	11 Mar 95	6
IS THIS DESIRE?	Island	17	10 Oct 98	2

Richard HARVEY and FRIENDS — UK

ALBUMS:	**HITS 1**		**WEEKS 1**	
EVENING FALLS	Telstar	72	6 May 89	1

Steve HARVEY — UK

SINGLES:	**HITS 2**		**WEEKS 6**	
SOMETHING SPECIAL	London	46	28 May 83	4
TONIGHT	London	63	29 Oct 83	2

HARVEY DANGER — US

SINGLES:	**HITS 1**		**WEEKS 1**	
FLAGPOLE SITTA	Slash	57	1 Aug 98	1

David HASSELHOFF — US

SINGLES:	**HITS 1**		**WEEKS 2**	
IF I COULD ONLY SAY GOODBYE	Arista	35	13 Nov 93	2

Tony HATCH — UK

(See also Brook Brothers.)

SINGLES:	**HITS 1**		**WEEKS 1**	
OUT OF THIS WORLD	Pye	50	6 Oct 62	1

Linzi HATELEY, David EASTER and Johnny AMOBI - See Jason DONOVAN

Juliana HATFIELD — US

SINGLES:	**HITS 2**		**WEEKS 2**	
MY SISTER	East West	71	11 Sep 93	1

Above hit: Juliana HATFIELD THREE.

UNIVERSAL HEART-BEAT	East West	65	18 Mar 95	1
ALBUMS:	**HITS 2**		**WEEKS 3**	
BECOME WHAT YOU ARE	East West	44	14 Aug 93	2

Above hit: Juliana HATFIELD THREE.

ONLY EVERYTHING	East West	59	8 Apr 95	1

HATFIELD AND THE NORTH — UK

ALBUMS:	**HITS 1**		**WEEKS 1**	
ROTTERS CLUB	Virgin	43	29 Mar 75	1

Donny HATHAWAY - See Roberta FLACK and Donny HATHAWAY

Lalah HATHAWAY — US

SINGLES:	**HITS 3**		**WEEKS 10**	
HEAVEN KNOWS	Virgin America	66	1 Sep 90	2
BABY DON'T CRY	Virgin America	54	2 Feb 91	3
FAMILY AFFAIR	Ten Records	37	27 Jul 91	5

Above hit: B.E.F. featuring Lalah HATHAWAY.

HAVANA — UK

SINGLES:	**HITS 1**		**WEEKS 1**	
ETHNIC PRAYER	Limbo	71	6 Mar 93	1

Nic HAVERSON — UK

SINGLES:	**HITS 1**		**WEEKS 3**	
HEAD OVER HEELS	Telstar	48	30 Jan 93	3

From the Carlton ITV series of the same name.

Chesney HAWKES — UK

SINGLES:	**HITS 4**		**WEEKS 25**	
THE ONE AND ONLY	Chrysalis	1	23 Feb 91	16

Written by Nik Kershaw.

I'M A MAN NOT A BOY	Chrysalis	27	22 Jun 91	5
SECRETS OF THE HEART	Chrysalis	57	28 Sep 91	3
Above 3 from the film 'Buddy's Song'.				
WHAT'S WRONG WITH THIS PICTURE?	Chrysalis	63	29 May 93	1
ALBUMS:	**HITS 1**			**WEEKS 8**
BUDDY'S SONG [OST]	Chrysalis	18	13 Apr 91	8

Edwin HAWKINS SINGERS. Soloist: Dorothy Combs MORRISON   US

SINGLES:	**HITS 1**			**WEEKS 13**
OH HAPPY DAY	Buddah	2	24 May 69	12
Produced by Paul Anka.				
OH HAPPY DAY [RE]	Buddah	43	23 Aug 69	1

Screamin' Jay HAWKINS   US

SINGLES:	**HITS 1**			**WEEKS 3**
HEART ATTACK AND VINE	Columbia	42	3 Apr 93	3
Featured in the Levi's Jeans TV commercial. Originally recorded by Tom Waits from his 1980 album of the same name.				

Sophie B. HAWKINS   US

SINGLES:	**HITS 6**			**WEEKS 37**
DAMN I WISH I WAS YOUR LOVER	Columbia	14	4 Jul 92	9
CALIFORNIA HERE I COME	Columbia	53	12 Sep 92	3
I WANT YOU	Columbia	49	6 Feb 93	2
RIGHT BESIDE YOU	Columbia	13	13 Aug 94	12
DON'T DON'T TELL ME NO	Columbia	36	26 Nov 94	5
AS I LAY ME DOWN	Columbia	24	11 Mar 95	6
ALBUMS:	**HITS 2**			**WEEKS 6**
TONGUES AND TAILS	Columbia	46	1 Aug 92	2
WHALER	Columbia	46	3 Sep 94	4

Ted HAWKINS   US

ALBUMS:	**HITS 1**			**WEEKS 1**
HAPPY HOUR	Windows	82	18 Apr 87	1

Tremaine HAWKINS – See HAMMER

HAWKLORDS – See HAWKWIND

HAWKWIND   UK

SINGLES:	**HITS 3**			**WEEKS 28**
SILVER MACHINE	United Artists	3	1 Jul 72	15
Live recording from the Roundtree, 13 Feb 72.				
URBAN GUERRILLA	United Artists	39	11 Aug 73	3
SILVER MACHINE [RE-1ST]	United Artists	34	21 Oct 78	5
SHOT DOWN IN THE NIGHT	Bronze	59	19 Jul 80	3
SILVER MACHINE [RE-2ND]	United Artists	67	15 Jan 83	2
ALBUMS:	**HITS 22**			**WEEKS 101**
IN SEARCH OF SPACE	United Artists	18	6 Nov 71	19
DOREMI FASOL LATIDO	United Artists	14	23 Dec 72	5
SPACE RITUAL ALIVE	United Artists	9	2 Jun 73	5
From their tour in Dec 73.				
HALL OF THE MOUNTAIN GRILL	United Artists	16	21 Sep 74	5
WARRIOR ON THE EDGE OF TIME	United Artists	13	31 May 75	7
ROAD HAWKS	United Artists	34	24 Apr 76	4
Compilation.				
ASTONISHING SOUNDS, AMAZING MUSIC	Charisma	33	18 Sep 76	5
QUARK STRANGENESS AND CHARM	Charisma	30	9 Jul 77	6
25 YEARS ON	Charisma	48	21 Oct 78	3
Above hit: HAWKLORDS.				
PXR 5	Charisma	59	30 Jun 79	5
LIVE 1979	Bronze	15	9 Aug 80	7
Live recordings from St. Albans, Nov 79.				
LEVITATION	Bronze	21	8 Nov 80	4
SONIC ATTACK	RCA	19	24 Oct 81	5
THE CHURCH OF HAWKWIND	RCA	26	22 May 82	6
CHOOSE YOUR MASQUES	RCA	29	23 Oct 82	5
ZONES	Flicknife	57	5 Nov 83	2
HAWKWIND	Liberty	75	25 Feb 84	1
Re-issue of their debut album from 1970.				
CHRONICLE OF THE BLACK SWORD	Flicknife	65	16 Nov 85	2
THE XENON CODEX	GWR	79	14 May 88	2
SPACE BANDITS	GWR	70	6 Oct 90	1
ELECTRIC TEPEE	Essential	53	23 May 92	1
IT IS THE BUSINESS OF THE FUTURE TO BE DANGEROUS	Essential	75	6 Nov 93	1

Bill HAYES | | | | US

SINGLES:		HITS 1		WEEKS 9
BALLAD OF DAVY CROCKETT	London	2	7 Jan 56	9

From the Walt Disney film 'Davy Crockett'.
Above hit: Bill HAYES with Archie BLEYER'S ORCHESTRA.

Isaac HAYES | | | | US

(See also Chef.)

SINGLES:		HITS 2		WEEKS 21
THEME FROM "SHAFT"	Stax	4	4 Dec 71	12
Theme from the film.				
DISCO CONNECTION	ABC	10	3 Apr 76	9
Above hit: Isaac HAYES MOVEMENT.				
ALBUMS:		HITS 2		WEEKS 14
SHAFT	Polydor	17	18 Dec 71	13
BLACK MOSES	Stax	38	12 Feb 72	1

HAYSI FANTAYZEE | | | | UK

SINGLES:		HITS 4		WEEKS 25
JOHN WAYNE IS BIG LEGGY	Regard	11	24 Jul 82	10
HOLY JOE	Regard	51	13 Nov 82	3
SHINY SHINY	Regard	16	22 Jan 83	10
SISTER FRICTION	Regard	62	25 Jun 83	2
ALBUMS:		HITS 1		WEEKS 5
BATTLE HYMNS FOR CHILDREN SINGING	Regard	53	26 Feb 83	5

Justin HAYWARD | | | | UK

(See also Justin Hayward and John Lodge; Justin Hayward with Mike Batt and the London Philharmonic Orchestra.)

SINGLES:		HITS 1		WEEKS 13
FOREVER AUTUMN	CBS	5	8 Jul 78	13

Originally recorded by Vigrass and Osbourne.
Above hit: From Jeff WAYNE'S "WAR OF THE WORLDS" featuring Justin
* HAYWARD.*

ALBUMS:		HITS 3		WEEKS 10
SONGWRITER	Deram	28	5 Mar 77	5
NIGHT FLIGHT	Decca	41	19 Jul 80	4
MOVING MOUNTAINS	Towerbell	78	19 Oct 85	1

Justin HAYWARD with Mike BATT and the LONDON PHILHARMONIC ORCHESTRA | UK

(See also Mike Batt; Justin Hayward; London Philharmonic Orchestra.)

ALBUMS:		HITS 1		WEEKS 7
CLASSIC BLUE	Trax	47	28 Oct 89	7

Justin HAYWARD and John LODGE | | | | UK

(See also Justin Hayward; John Lodge.)

SINGLES:		HITS 1		WEEKS 7
BLUE GUITAR	Threshold	8	25 Oct 75	7
ALBUMS:		HITS 1		WEEKS 18
BLUE JAYS	Threshold	4	29 Mar 75	18

Leon HAYWOOD | | | | US

SINGLES:		HITS 1		WEEKS 11
DON'T PUSH IT DON'T FORCE IT	20th Century	12	15 Mar 80	11

HAYWOODE | | | | UK

SINGLES:		HITS 4		WEEKS 31
A TIME LIKE THIS	CBS	48	17 Sep 83	7
I CAN'T LET YOU GO	CBS	63	29 Sep 84	4
ROSES	CBS	65	13 Apr 85	3
GETTING CLOSER	CBS	67	5 Oct 85	2
ROSES [RI]	CBS	11	21 Jun 86	11
I CAN'T LET YOU GO [RI]	CBS	50	13 Sep 86	4

Ofra HAZA | | | | Israel

SINGLES:		HITS 2		WEEKS 9
IM NIN'ALU	WEA	15	30 Apr 88	8
BABYLON	warner.esp	65	3 Apr 99	1

Above hit: BLACK DOG featuring Ofra HAZA.

Lee HAZLEWOOD - See Nancy SINATRA and Lee HAZLEWOOD

Murray HEAD
UK

SINGLES:		HITS 2			WEEKS 15	
SUPERSTAR		MCA	47	29 Jan 72		1

From the musical 'Jesus Christ Superstar'. This was a 4-track maxi single, but only Superstar and I Don't Know How To Love Him by Yvonne Elliman/Various Artists were credited.
Above hit: Murray HEAD with the TRINIDAD SINGERS.

ONE NIGHT IN BANGKOK		RCA	12	10 Nov 84		13

From the musical 'Chess'.

ONE NIGHT IN BANGKOK [RE]		RCA	74	16 Feb 85		1

Roy HEAD
US

SINGLES:		HITS 1			WEEKS 5	
TREAT HER RIGHT		Vocalion	30	6 Nov 65		5

HEADBANGERS
UK

SINGLES:		HITS 1			WEEKS 3	
STATUS ROCK [M]		Magnet	60	10 Oct 81		3

Medley of Status Quo hits.

HEADBOYS
UK

SINGLES:		HITS 1			WEEKS 8	
THE SHAPE OF THINGS TO COME		RSO	45	22 Sep 79		8

HEADGIRL - See GIRLSCHOOOL; MOTORHEAD

Max HEADROOM - See ART OF NOISE

HEADS
UK

SINGLES:		HITS 1			WEEKS 4	
AZTEC LIGHTNING - THEME FROM BBC WORLD CUP GRANDSTAND		BBC	45	21 Jun 86		4

HEADS with Shaun RYDER
UK/US

(See also Talking Heads.)

SINGLES:		HITS 1			WEEKS 1	
DON'T TAKE MY KINDNESS FOR WEAKNESS		Radioactive	60	9 Nov 96		1

HEADSWIM
UK

SINGLES:		HITS 3			WEEKS 5	
CRAWL		Epic	64	25 Feb 95		1
TOURNIQUET		Epic	30	14 Feb 98		3
BETTER MADE		Epic	42	16 May 98		1
ALBUMS:		HITS 1			WEEKS 2	
DESPITE YOURSELF		Epic	24	30 May 98		2

Jeff HEALEY BAND
Canada

ALBUMS:		HITS 4			WEEKS 16	
SEE THE LIGHT		Arista	58	14 Jan 89		7
HELL TO PAY		Arista	18	9 Jun 90		6
FEEL THIS		Arista	72	28 Nov 92		1
COVER TO COVER		Arista	50	18 Mar 95		2

Jeremy HEALY and AMOS
UK

(See also Amos.)

SINGLES:		HITS 2			WEEKS 7	
STAMP!		Positiva	11	12 Oct 96		5
ARGENTINA		Positiva	30	31 May 97		2

Both songs were recorded to accompany John Galliano's fashion shows.

Imogen HEAP - See URBAN SPECIES

HEAR 'N AID
UK/US

SINGLES:		HITS 1			WEEKS 6	
STARS		Vertigo	26	19 Apr 86		6

Charity record for famine relief in Africa.

HEART
US

SINGLES:		HITS 12			WEEKS 76	
THESE DREAMS		Capitol	62	29 Mar 86		4
ALONE		Capitol	3	13 Jun 87		16

Originally recorded by I-Ten.

WHO WILL YOU RUN TO		Capitol	30	19 Sep 87		7
THERE'S THE GIRL		Capitol	34	12 Dec 87		7
NEVER / THESE DREAMS [RI]		Capitol	8	5 Mar 88		9

WHAT ABOUT LOVE	Capitol	14	14 May 88	6
NOTHIN' AT ALL	Capitol	38	22 Oct 88	3
Original release reached No. 76 in 1986.				
ALL I WANNA DO IS MAKE LOVE TO YOU	Capitol	8	24 Mar 90	13
I DIDN'T WANT TO NEED YOU	Capitol	47	28 Jul 90	3
STRANDED	Capitol	60	17 Nov 90	2
YOU'RE THE VOICE	Capitol	56	14 Sep 91	2
Live recording.				
WILL YOU BE THERE (IN THE MORNING)	Capitol	19	20 Nov 93	4
ALBUMS:	**HITS 9**			**WEEKS 143**
DREAMBOAT ANNIE	Arista	36	22 Jan 77	8
LITTLE QUEEN	Portrait	34	23 Jul 77	4
PRIVATE AUDITION	Epic	77	19 Jun 82	2
HEART	Capitol	46	26 Oct 85	17
BAD ANIMALS	Capitol	7	6 Jun 87	56
HEART [RE]	Capitol	19	5 Mar 88	26
BRIGADE	Capitol	3	14 Apr 90	20
ROCK THE HOUSE 'LIVE'	Capitol	45	28 Sep 91	2
DESIRE WALKS ON	Capitol	32	11 Dec 93	2
THESE DREAMS – GREATEST HITS	Capitol	33	19 Apr 97	6

HEARTBEAT   UK

SINGLES:	**HITS 2**			**WEEKS 5**
TEARS FROM HEAVEN	Priority	32	24 Oct 87	4
THE WINNER	Priority	70	23 Apr 88	1

HEARTBEAT COUNTRY   UK

SINGLES:	**HITS 1**			**WEEKS 1**
HEARTBEAT	Mmmm	75	31 Dec 94	1

HEARTBREAKERS   US

ALBUMS:	**HITS 1**			**WEEKS 1**
L.A.M.F.	Track	55	5 Nov 77	1

HEARTISTS   Italy

SINGLES:	**HITS 1**			**WEEKS 5**
BELO HORIZONTI	VC Recordings	42	9 Aug 97	3
Samples Celebration Suite by Airto Moreira.				
BELO HORIZONTI [RI]	VC Recordings	40	31 Jan 98	2

Ted HEATH and his Music   UK

SINGLES:	**HITS 9**			**WEEKS 56**
VANESSA	Decca	11	17 Jan 53	1
HOT TODDY	Decca	6	4 Jul 53	11
DRAGNET	Decca	12	24 Oct 53	1
DRAGNET [RE-1ST]	Decca	9	28 Nov 53	1
DRAGNET [RE-2ND]	Decca	11	12 Dec 53	1
DRAGNET [RE-3RD]	Decca	11	16 Jan 54	1
DRAGNET [RE-4TH]	Decca	12	6 Feb 54	1
SKIN DEEP	Decca	9	13 Feb 54	3
THE FAITHFUL HUSSAR	Decca	18	7 Jul 56	9
SWINGIN' SHEPHERD BLUES	Decca	3	15 Mar 58	14
TEQUILA	Decca	21	12 Apr 58	6
TOM HARK	Decca	24	5 Jul 58	2
SUCU SUCU (THEME FROM "TOP SECRET")	Decca	36	7 Oct 61	4
SUCU SUCU (THEME FROM "TOP SECRET") [RE]	Decca	47	11 Nov 61	1
ALBUMS:	**HITS 1**			**WEEKS 5**
BIG BAND PERCUSSION	Decca	17	21 Apr 62	5

HEATWAVE   US/UK

SINGLES:	**HITS 9**			**WEEKS 80**
BOOGIE NIGHTS	GTO	2	22 Jan 77	14
TOO HOT TO HANDLE / SLIP YOUR DISC TO THIS	GTO	15	7 May 77	11
THE GROOVE LINE	GTO	12	14 Jan 78	8
MIND BLOWING DECISIONS	GTO	12	3 Jun 78	11
ALWAYS AND FOREVER / MIND BLOWING DECISIONS [RM]	GTO	9	4 Nov 78	14
Mind Blowing Decisions is a remixed version of the original.				
RAZZLE DAZZLE	GTO	43	26 May 79	5
GANSTERS OF THE GROOVE	GTO	19	17 Jan 81	8
JITTERBUGGIN'	GTO	34	21 Mar 81	7
MIND BLOWING DECISIONS [RR]	Brothers Organisation	65	1 Sep 90	2
Rap by Johnny Daviz.				

ALBUMS:		HITS 4			WEEKS 27	
TOO HOT TO HANDLE		GTO	46	11 Jun 77		2
CENTRAL HEATING		GTO	26	6 May 78		15
CANDLES		GTO	29	14 Feb 81		9
GANGSTERS OF THE GROOVE - THE 90'S MIX		Telstar	56	23 Feb 91		1

HEAVEN 17 — UK

SINGLES:		HITS 12			WEEKS 87	
(WE DON'T NEED THIS) FASCIST GROOVE THANG		Virgin	45	21 Mar 81		5
PLAY TO WIN		Virgin	46	5 Sep 81		7
PENTHOUSE AND PAVEMENT		Virgin	57	14 Nov 81		3
LET ME GO		Virgin	41	30 Oct 82		6
TEMPTATION		Virgin	2	16 Apr 83		13
Female vocal by Carol Kenyon.						
COME LIVE WITH ME		Virgin	5	25 Jun 83		11
CRUSHED BY THE WHEELS OF INDUSTRY		Virgin	17	10 Sep 83		7
SUNSET NOW		Virgin	24	1 Sep 84		6
THIS IS MINE		Virgin	23	27 Oct 84		7
. . . (AND THAT'S NO LIE)		Virgin	52	19 Jan 85		5
TROUBLE		Virgin	51	17 Jan 87		3
TEMPTATION [RM]		Virgin	4	21 Nov 92		11
Female vocal by Carol Kenyon, remixed by Brothers In Rhythm.						
(WE DON'T NEED THIS) FASCIST GROOVE THANG [RR]		Virgin	40	27 Feb 93		2
PENTHOUSE AND PAVEMENT [RM]		Virgin	54	10 Apr 93		1
Remixed by Tommy D.						
ALBUMS:		HITS 6			WEEKS 128	
PENTHOUSE AND PAVEMENT		Virgin	14	26 Sep 81		76
THE LUXURY GAP		Virgin	4	7 May 83		36
HOW MEN ARE		Virgin	12	6 Oct 84		11
ENDLESS		Virgin	70	12 Jul 86		2
First album to chart on Cassette and CD formats only.						
PLEASURE ONE		Virgin	78	29 Nov 86		1
HIGHER AND HIGHER - THE BEST OF HEAVEN 17		Virgin	31	20 Mar 93		2

HEAVY D and the BOYZ — US

SINGLES:		HITS 5			WEEKS 28	
MR. BIG STUFF		MCA	61	6 Dec 86		8
Originally recorded by Jean Knight.						
WE GOT OUR OWN THANG		MCA	69	15 Jul 89		2
Chart for 15 Jul 89 lists an import catalogue number.						
NOW THAT WE'VE FOUND LOVE		MCA	2	6 Jul 91		12
Originally recorded by the O'Jays.						
IS IT GOOD TO YOU		MCA	46	28 Sep 91		3
THIS IS YOUR NIGHT		MCA	30	8 Oct 94		3
Samples Kool and The Gang's Ladies Night and George Benson's Give Me The Night.						
ALBUMS:		HITS 1			WEEKS 3	
PEACEFUL JOURNEY		MCA	40	10 Aug 91		3

HEAVY PETTIN' — UK

SINGLES:		HITS 1			WEEKS 2	
LOVE TIMES LOVE		Polydor	69	17 Mar 84		2
ALBUMS:		HITS 2			WEEKS 4	
LETTIN' LOOSE		Polydor	55	29 Oct 83		2
ROCK AIN'T DEAD		Polydor	81	13 Jul 85		2

HEAVY STEREO — UK

SINGLES:		HITS 4			WEEKS 4	
SLEEP FREAK		Creation	46	22 Jul 95		1
SMILER		Creation	46	28 Oct 95		1
CHINESE BURN		Creation	45	10 Feb 96		1
MOUSE IN A HOLE		Creation	53	24 Aug 96		1

HEAVY WEATHER — US

SINGLES:		HITS 1			WEEKS 1	
LOVE CAN'T TURN AROUND		Pukka	56	29 Jun 96		1

Bobby HEBB — US

SINGLES:		HITS 2			WEEKS 15	
SUNNY		Philips	12	10 Sep 66		9
Written about Hebb's brother, Hal, who was killed in a mugging.						
LOVE LOVE LOVE		Philips	32	19 Aug 72		6
Originally recorded by William Bonney.						

HED BOYS | | | | UK

SINGLES:	HITS 1			WEEKS 6
GIRLS + BOYS	Deconstruction	21	6 Aug 94	4
Samples Girls Out On The Floor by Jessie Veles.				
GIRLS & BOYS [RI]	Deconstruction	36	4 Nov 95	2

HEDGEHOPPERS ANONYMOUS | | | | UK

SINGLES:	HITS 1			WEEKS 12
IT'S GOOD NEWS WEEK	Decca	5	2 Oct 65	12
Written & produced by Jonathan King.				

Neal HEFTI | | | | US

SINGLES:	HITS 1			WEEKS 4
BATMAN THEME	RCA	55	9 Apr 88	4
Original 1966 TV version.				

Den HEGARTY | | | | UK

SINGLES:	HITS 1			WEEKS 2
VOODOO VOODOO	Magnet	73	31 Mar 79	2

Anita HEGERLAND and Barry PALMER - See Mike OLDFIELD

HEINZ | | | | UK

SINGLES:	HITS 5			WEEKS 35
JUST LIKE EDDIE	Decca	5	10 Aug 63	15
COUNTRY BOY	Decca	26	30 Nov 63	9
YOU WERE THERE	Decca	26	29 Feb 64	8
QUESTIONS I CAN'T ANSWER	Columbia	39	17 Oct 64	2
DIGGIN' MY POTATOES	Columbia	49	20 Mar 65	1
Above hit: HEINZ and the WILD BOYS.				

EPS:	HITS 1			WEEKS 9
LIVE IT UP	Decca	12	1 Feb 64	9

HELEN LOVE | | | | UK

SINGLES:	HITS 2			WEEKS 2
DOES YOUR HEART GO BOOM	Che	71	20 Sep 97	1
LONG LIVE THE UK MUSIC SCENE	Che	65	19 Sep 98	1

HELICOPTER | | | | UK

SINGLES:	HITS 1			WEEKS 4
ON YA WAY	Helicopter	32	27 Aug 94	2
Originallly released in 1992.				
ON YA WAY [RM]	Systematic	37	22 Jun 96	2

HELIOCENTRIC WORLD | | | | UK

SINGLES:	HITS 1			WEEKS 2
WHERE'S YOUR LOVE BEEN	Talkin Loud	71	14 Jan 95	2

HELIOTROPIC featuring Verna V. | | | | UK

SINGLES:	HITS 1			WEEKS 2
ALIVE	Multiply	33	16 Oct 99	2

Pete HELLER | | | | UK

(See also Fire Island.)

SINGLES:	HITS 2			WEEKS 14
ULTRA FLAVA	AM:PM	22	24 Feb 96	3
ULTRA FLAVA [RM]	AM:PM	32	28 Dec 96	4
Remixed by Rhythm Masters.				
Above 2: HELLER and FARLEY PROJECT.				
BIG LOVE	Essential Recordings	12	15 May 99	7
Samples Stargard's Wear It Out.				

HELLO | | | | UK

SINGLES:	HITS 2			WEEKS 21
TELL HIM	Bell	6	9 Nov 74	12
Originally recorded by the Exciters.				
NEW YORK GROOVE	Bell	9	18 Oct 75	9

HELLOWEEN | | | | US

SINGLES:	HITS 3			WEEKS 7
DR STEIN	Noise International	57	27 Aug 88	3
I WANT OUT	Noise International	69	12 Nov 88	2

KIDS OF THE CENTURY	EMI	56	2 Mar 91	2

ALBUMS:	**HITS 3**			**WEEKS 9**
KEEPER OF THE SEVEN KEYS PART 2	Noise International	24	17 Sep 88	5
LIVE IN THE UK	EMI	26	15 Apr 89	2
PINK BUBBLES GO APE	EMI	41	23 Mar 91	2

HELMET
US

ALBUMS:	**HITS 1**			**WEEKS 1**
BETTY	Interscope	38	2 Jul 94	1

Bobby HELMS
US

SINGLES:	**HITS 3**			**WEEKS 7**
MY SPECIAL ANGEL	Brunswick	22	30 Nov 57	3
Above hit: Bobby HELMS and Anita KERR SINGERS.				
NO OTHER BABY	Brunswick	30	22 Feb 58	1
Originally recorded by Dickie Bishop and the Sidekicks.				
JACQUELINE	Brunswick	20	2 Aug 58	3
From the film 'The Case Against Brooklyn'.				
Above hit: Bobby HELMS and Anita KERR SINGERS.				

Jimmy HELMS
UK

SINGLES:	**HITS 1**			**WEEKS 10**
GONNA MAKE YOU AN OFFER YOU CAN'T REFUSE	Cube	8	24 Feb 73	10

HELTAH SKELTER and ORIGINOO GUNN CLAPPAZ as the FABULOUS FIVE
US

SINGLES:	**HITS 1**			**WEEKS 1**
BLAH	Priority	60	1 Jun 96	1

Eddie HENDERSON
US

SINGLES:	**HITS 1**			**WEEKS 6**
PRANCE ON	Capitol	44	28 Oct 78	6

Joe "Mr. Piano" HENDERSON
UK

SINGLES:	**HITS 5**			**WEEKS 23**
SING IT WITH JOE [M]	Polygon	14	4 Jun 55	4
SING IT AGAIN WITH JOE [M]	Polygon	18	3 Sep 55	3
Above 2: Joe 'Mr. Piano' HENDERSON and his Friends.				
TRUDIE	Pye Nixa	14	26 Jul 58	12
Above hit: Joe "Mr. Piano" HENDERSON with the Beryl STOTT CHORUS.				
TRUDIE [M]	Pye Nixa	23	25 Oct 58	2
TREBLE CHANCE	Pye	28	24 Oct 59	1
OOH LA LA	Pye	44	26 Mar 60	1

Wayne HENDERSON - See Roy AYERS

Billy HENDRIX
Germany

SINGLES:	**HITS 1**			**WEEKS 2**
THE BODY SHINE [EP]	Hooj Choons	55	12 Sep 98	2
Various mixes of track The Body Shine.				

Jimi HENDRIX
US

SINGLES:	**HITS 10**			**WEEKS 87**
HEY JOE	Polydor	6	7 Jan 67	10
Originally recorded by the Leaves.				
PURPLE HAZE	Track	3	25 Mar 67	14
THE WIND CRIES MARY	Track	6	13 May 67	11
BURNING OF THE MIDNIGHT LAMP	Track	18	2 Sep 67	9
ALL ALONG THE WATCHTOWER	Track	5	26 Oct 68	11
Originally recorded by Bob Dylan.				
CROSSTOWN TRAFFIC	Track	37	19 Apr 69	3
VOODOO CHILE	Track	1	7 Nov 70	13
GYPSY EYES/REMEMBER	Track	35	30 Oct 71	5
Above 8: Jimi HENDRIX EXPERIENCE.				
JOHNNY B. GOODE	Polydor	35	12 Feb 72	5
Originally recorded by Chuck Berry.				
CROSSTOWN TRAFFIC [RI]	Polydor	61	21 Apr 90	3
ALL ALONG THE WATCHTOWER [EP]	Polydor	52	20 Oct 90	3
Lead track: Alll Along The Watchtower. (This and the other tracks are re-issues).				

ALBUMS:	**HITS 26**			**WEEKS 263**
ARE YOU EXPERIENCED	Track	2	27 May 67	33
AXIS: BOLD AS LOVE	Track	5	16 Dec 67	16
SMASH HITS	Track	4	27 Apr 68	25
Above 3: Jimi HENDRIX EXPERIENCE.				

GET THAT FEELING	London	39	18 May 68	2

Above hit: Jimi HENDRIX and Curtis KNIGHT.

ELECTRIC LADYLAND	Track	6	16 Nov 68	12

Above hit: Jimi HENDRIX EXPERIENCE.

BAND OF GYPSIES	Track	6	4 Jul 70	30

Live recordings from Fillmore East, New York, 31 Dec 69.

CRY OF LOVE	Track	2	3 Apr 71	14
EXPERIENCE	Ember	9	28 Aug 71	6
JIMI HENDRIX AT THE ISLE OF WIGHT	Track	17	20 Nov 71	2

Live recordings from the festival, 30 Aug 70.

RAINBOW BRIDGE [OST]	Reprise	16	4 Dec 71	8

Recordings from 1968-70.

HENDRIX IN THE WEST	Polydor	7	5 Feb 72	14
WAR HEROES	Polydor	23	11 Nov 72	3
SOUNDTRACK RECORDINGS FROM THE FILM 'JIMI HENDRIX' [OST]	Warner Brothers	37	21 Jul 73	1
JIMI HENDRIX	Polydor	35	29 Mar 75	4
CRASH LANDING	Polydor	35	30 Aug 75	3
MIDNIGHT LIGHTNING	Polydor	46	29 Nov 75	1
THE JIMI HENDRIX CONCERTS	CBS	16	14 Aug 82	11

Live recordings from 1968-70.

THE SINGLES ALBUM	Polydor	77	19 Feb 83	4
RADIO ONE	Castle Collectors	30	11 Mar 89	6

Recordings made for BBC Radio 1.

CORNERSTONES - JIMI HENDRIX 1967-1970	Polydor	5	3 Nov 90	16
JIMI HENDRIX - THE ULTIMATE EXPERIENCE	PolyGram TV	25	14 Nov 92	26
BLUES	Polydor	10	30 Apr 94	3
WOODSTOCK	Polydor	32	13 Aug 94	3

Live recordings from Woodstock, Aug 69.

FIRST RAYS OF THE NEW RISING SUN	MCA	37	10 May 97	2

Recreation of the album Hendrix was working on at the time of his death.

ELECTRIC LADYLAND [RI]	MCA	47	2 Aug 97	1

Charted after being featured on BBC1 TV's 'Classic Albums' series.
Above hit: Jimi HENDRIX EXPERIENCE.

EXPERIENCE HENDRIX - THE BEST OF JIMI HENDRIX	Telstar TV	18	13 Sep 97	15
BBC SESSIONS	MCA	42	13 Jun 98	2

Collection of BBC Radio and TV performances.
Above hit: Jimi HENDRIX EXPERIENCE.

Nona HENDRYX   US

(See also Bounty Killer (featuring Cocoa Brovaz, Nona Hendryx and Free).)

SINGLES:	HITS 1		WEEKS 2	
WHY SHOULD I CRY?	EMI America	60	16 May 87	2

Don HENLEY   US

SINGLES:	HITS 4		WEEKS 30	
DIRTY LAUNDRY	Asylum	59	12 Feb 83	3

Features guitar solo by Joe Walsh.

THE BOYS OF SUMMER	Geffen	12	9 Feb 85	10
THE END OF THE INNOCENCE	Geffen	48	29 Jul 89	5

Features Bruce Hornsby on piano.

SOMETIMES LOVE JUST AIN'T ENOUGH	MCA	22	3 Oct 92	6

Above hit: Patty SMYTH with Don HENLEY.

THE BOYS OF SUMMER [RI]	Geffen	12	18 Jul 98	6

This re-issue has longer intro than original chart entry.

ALBUMS:	HITS 2		WEEKS 27	
BUILDING THE PERFECT BEAST	Geffen	14	9 Mar 85	11
THE END OF THE INNOCENCE	Geffen	17	8 Jul 89	16

Clarence "Frogman" HENRY   US

SINGLES:	HITS 3		WEEKS 35	
BUT I DO	Pye International	3	6 May 61	19
YOU ALWAYS HURT THE ONE YOU LOVE	Pye International	6	15 Jul 61	12

Originally recorded by the Mills Brothers in 1944.

LONELY STREET / WHY CAN'T YOU	Pye International	42	23 Sep 61	2
(I DON'T KNOW WHY) BUT I DO [RI]	MCA	65	17 Jul 93	2

Featured in the Fiat Cinquecento TV commercial.

Kevin HENRY - See Paul HARDCASTLE; L.A. MIX

Paul HENRY and the Mayson GLEN ORCHESTRA   UK

SINGLES:	HITS 1		WEEKS 2	
BENNY'S THEME	Pye	39	14 Jan 78	2

From the ATV soap 'Crossroads'.

Pauline HENRY
UK

SINGLES:		HITS 8			WEEKS 21
TOO MANY PEOPLE	Sony S2	38	18 Sep 93	2
FEEL LIKE MAKING LOVE	Sony S2	12	6 Nov 93	7
CAN'T TAKE YOUR LOVE	Sony S2	30	29 Jan 94	3
WATCH THE MIRACLE START	Sony S2	54	21 May 94	1
SUGAR FREE	Sony S2	57	30 Sep 95	2
LOVE HANGOVER	Sony S2	37	23 Dec 95	3
NEVER KNEW LOVE LIKE THIS	Sony S2	40	24 Feb 96	2
Above hit: Pauline HENRY featuring Wayne MARSHALL.				
HAPPY	Sony S2	46	1 Jun 96	1
ALBUMS:	**HITS 1**			**WEEKS 1**
PAULINE	Sony S2	45	19 Feb 94	1

Pierre HENRY/Michel COLOMBIER
France

SINGLES:		HITS 1			WEEKS 1
PSYCHE ROCK	Hi-Life	58	4 Oct 97	1

HEPBURN
UK

SINGLES:		HITS 2			WEEKS 12
I QUIT	Columbia	8	29 May 99	7
BUGS	Columbia	14	28 Aug 99	5
ALBUMS:	**HITS 1**			**WEEKS 2**
HEPBURN	Columbia	28	11 Sep 99	2

Band and Chorus Of HER MAJESTY'S GUARDS DIVISION
UK

ALBUMS:		HITS 1			WEEKS 4
30 SMASH HITS OF THE WAR YEARS	Warwick	38	22 Nov 75	4

HERBIE - See 3T

HERD
UK

SINGLES:		HITS 3			WEEKS 35
FROM THE UNDERWORLD	Fontana	6	16 Sep 67	13
PARADISE LOST	Fontana	15	23 Dec 67	9
I DON'T WANT OUR LOVING TO DIE	Fontana	5	13 Apr 68	13
ALBUMS:	**HITS 1**			**WEEKS 1**
PARADISE LOST	Fontana	38	24 Feb 68	1

HERMAN'S HERMITS
UK

SINGLES:		HITS 20			WEEKS 211
I'M INTO SOMETHING GOOD	Columbia	1	22 Aug 64	15
Originally recorded by Earl Jean.				
SHOW ME GIRL	Columbia	19	21 Nov 64	9
SILHOUETTES	Columbia	3	20 Feb 65	12
Original by the Rays reached No. 3 in the US in 1957.				
WONDERFUL WORLD	Columbia	7	1 May 65	9
JUST A LITTLE BIT BETTER	Columbia	15	4 Sep 65	9
A MUST TO AVOID	Columbia	6	25 Dec 65	11
YOU WON'T BE LEAVING	Columbia	20	26 Mar 66	7
THIS DOOR SWINGS BOTH WAYS	Columbia	18	25 Jun 66	7
NO MILK TODAY	Columbia	7	8 Oct 66	11
EAST WEST	Columbia	37	3 Dec 66	7
THERE'S A KIND OF HUSH	Columbia	7	11 Feb 67	11
Originally recorded by New Vaudeville Band.				
I CAN TAKE OR LEAVE YOUR LOVING	Columbia	11	20 Jan 68	9
SLEEPY JOE	Columbia	12	4 May 68	10
SUNSHINE GIRL	Columbia	8	20 Jul 68	14
SOMETHING'S HAPPENING	Columbia	6	21 Dec 68	15
MY SENTIMENTAL FRIEND	Columbia	2	26 Apr 69	12
HERE COMES THE STAR	Columbia	33	8 Nov 69	9
YEARS MAY COME, YEARS MAY GO	Columbia	7	7 Feb 70	11
YEARS MAY COME, YEARS MAY GO [RE]	Columbia	45	2 May 70	1
BET YER LIFE I DO	RAK	22	23 May 70	10
LADY BARBARA	RAK	13	14 Nov 70	12
Above two co-written by Errol Brown from Hot Chocolate.				
Above hit: Peter NOONE and HERMAN'S HERMITS.				
EPS:	**HITS 4**			**WEEKS 42**
HERMANIA	Columbia	19	30 Jan 65	1
MRS. BROWN YOU'VE GOT A LOVELY DAUGHTER	Columbia	3	12 Jun 65	21
HERMAN'S HERMITS HITS	Columbia	10	25 Sep 65	10
MUSIC FROM THE SOUNDTRACK "HOLD ON"	Columbia	4	27 Aug 66	10

ALBUMS:	HITS 3			WEEKS 11
HERMAN'S HERMITS	Columbia	16	18 Sep 65	2
THE MOST OF HERMAN'S HERMITS	Music For Pleasure	14	25 Sep 71	5
GREATEST HITS	Columbia	37	8 Oct 77	4

HERNANDEZ — UK

SINGLES:	HITS 1			WEEKS 3
ALL MY LOVE	Epic	58	15 Apr 89	3

Patrick HERNANDEZ — France

SINGLES:	HITS 1			WEEKS 14
BORN TO BE ALIVE	GEM	10	16 Jun 79	14

HERREY'S — Sweden

SINGLES:	HITS 1			WEEKS 3
DIGGI LOO - DIGGI LEY	Panther	46	26 May 84	3

Eurovision Song Contest winners in 1984.

Kristin HERSH — US

SINGLES:	HITS 2			WEEKS 3
YOUR GHOST	4AD	45	22 Jan 94	2

Features vocals by Michael Stipe (R.E.M.).

| STRINGS [EP] | 4AD | 60 | 16 Apr 94 | 1 |

Lead track: A Loon.

ALBUMS:	HITS 2			WEEKS 5
HIPS AND MAKERS	4AD	7	5 Feb 94	4
STRANGE ANGELS	4AD	64	14 Feb 98	1

Howard HEWETT – See BABYFACE

Nick HEYWARD — UK

SINGLES:	HITS 13			WEEKS 65
WHISTLE DOWN THE WIND	Arista	13	19 Mar 83	8
TAKE THAT SITUATION	Arista	11	4 Jun 83	10
BLUE HAT FOR A BLUE DAY	Arista	14	24 Sep 83	8
ON A SUNDAY	Arista	52	3 Dec 83	5
LOVE ALL DAY	Arista	31	2 Jun 84	6
WARNING SIGN	Arista	25	3 Nov 84	8
WARNING SIGN [RE]	Arista	72	5 Jan 85	1
LAURA	Arista	45	8 Jun 85	4
OVER THE WEEKEND	Arista	43	10 May 86	5
YOU'RE MY WORLD	Warner Brothers	67	10 Sep 88	2
KITE	Epic	44	21 Aug 93	2
HE DOESN'T LOVE YOU LIKE I DO	Epic	58	16 Oct 93	2
THE WORLD	Epic	47	30 Sep 95	2
ROLLERBLADE	Epic	37	13 Jan 96	2
ALBUMS:	HITS 1			WEEKS 13
NORTH OF A MIRACLE	Arista	10	29 Oct 83	13

HI-FIVE — US

SINGLES:	HITS 2			WEEKS 8
I LIKE THE WAY (THE KISSING GAME)	Jive	43	1 Jun 91	6
SHE'S PLAYING HARD TO GET	Jive	55	24 Oct 92	2

HI-GLOSS — US

SINGLES:	HITS 1			WEEKS 13
YOU'LL NEVER KNOW	Epic	12	8 Aug 81	13

HI-JACK — US

ALBUMS:	HITS 1			WEEKS 1
THE HORNS OF JERICO	Warner Brothers	54	19 Oct 91	1

HI-LUX — UK

SINGLES:	HITS 2			WEEKS 3
FEEL IT	Cheeky	41	18 Feb 95	2
NEVER FELT THIS WAY / FEEL IT	Champion	58	2 Sep 95	1

HI POWER — Germany

SINGLES:	HITS 1			WEEKS 1
CULT OF SNAP / SIMBA GROOVE	Rumour	73	1 Sep 90	1

HI TEK 3 featuring YA KID K — Belgium

(See also Technotronic.)

SINGLES:	HITS 1			WEEKS 10
SPIN THAT WHEEL	Brothers Organisation	69	3 Feb 90	3
SPIN THAT WHEEL (TURTLES GET REAL) [RI]	Brothers Organisation	15	29 Sep 90	7
From the film 'Teenage Mutant Ninja Turtles'.				

HI TENSION — US

SINGLES:	HITS 2			WEEKS 23
HI-TENSION	Island	13	6 May 78	12
BRITISH HUSTLE / PEACE ON EARTH	Island	8	12 Aug 78	11
Peace On Earth listed from 2 Sep 78.				
ALBUMS:	HITS 1			WEEKS 4
HI TENSION	Island	74	6 Jan 79	4

John HIATT — US

ALBUMS:	HITS 3			WEEKS 3
STOLEN MOMENTS	A&M	72	7 Jul 90	1
PERFECTLY GOOD GUITAR	A&M	67	11 Sep 93	1
WALK ON	Capitol	74	11 Nov 95	1

Toots HIBBERT – See JAMAICA UNITED

Al HIBBLER — US

SINGLES:	HITS 1			WEEKS 17
UNCHAINED MELODY	Brunswick	2	14 May 55	17
From the film 'Unchained'.				

Hinda HICKS — UK

SINGLES:	HITS 4			WEEKS 14
IF YOU WANT ME	Island	25	7 Mar 98	3
Samples Kool And The Gang's Too Hot.				
YOU THINK YOU OWN ME	Island	19	16 May 98	4
I WANNA BE YOUR LADY	Island	14	15 Aug 98	5
Original release reached No. 109 in 1997. Features backing vocals by Shaznay Lewis of All Saints.				
TRULY	Island	31	24 Oct 98	2
ALBUMS:	HITS 1			WEEKS 4
HINDA	Island	20	29 Aug 98	4

Bertie HIGGINS — US

SINGLES:	HITS 1			WEEKS 4
KEY LARGO	Epic	60	5 Jun 82	4

HIGH — UK

SINGLES:	HITS 4			WEEKS 11
UP AND DOWN	London	53	25 Aug 90	4
TAKE YOUR TIME	London	56	27 Oct 90	2
BOX SET GO	London	28	12 Jan 91	3
Original release reached No. 76 in 1990.				
MORE . . .	London	67	6 Apr 91	1
ALBUMS:	HITS 1			WEEKS 2
SOMEWHERE SOON	London	59	17 Nov 90	2

HIGH FIDELITY — UK

SINGLES:	HITS 1			WEEKS 1
LUV DUP	Plastique	70	25 Jul 98	1

HIGH LLAMAS — UK/Ireland

ALBUMS:	HITS 1			WEEKS 1
HAWAII	Alpaca Park	62	6 Apr 96	1

HIGH NUMBERS — UK

(See also Who.)

SINGLES:	HITS 1			WEEKS 4
I'M THE FACE	Back Door	49	5 Apr 80	4
Originally released in 1964 on the Fontana label.				

HIGH SOCIETY — UK

SINGLES:	HITS 1			WEEKS 4
I NEVER GO OUT IN THE RAIN	Eagle	53	15 Nov 80	4

HIGHLY LIKELY — UK

SINGLES:	HITS 1			WEEKS 4
WHATEVER HAPPENED TO YOU (LIKELY LADS THEME)	BBC	35	21 Apr 73	4

Theme from the BBC1 TV comedy 'Whatever Happened To The Likely Lads'.

HIGHWAYMEN — US

SINGLES:	HITS 2			WEEKS 18
MICHAEL	His Master's Voice	1	9 Sep 61	14
GYPSY ROVER (THE WHISTLING GYPSY)	His Master's Voice	41	9 Dec 61	3
GYPSY ROVER (THE WHISTLING GYPSY) [RE]	His Master's Voice	43	13 Jan 62	1

HIJACK — UK

SINGLES:	HITS 1			WEEKS 3
THE BADMAN IS ROBBIN'	Rhyme Syndicate	56	6 Jan 90	3

Benny HILL — UK

SINGLES:	HITS 4			WEEKS 43
GATHER IN THE MUSHROOMS	Pye	12	18 Feb 61	8
TRANSISTOR RADIO	Pye	24	3 Jun 61	6
THE HARVEST OF LOVE	Pye	20	18 May 63	8

Above hit: Benny HILL with the KESTRELS.

ERNIE (THE FASTEST MILKMAN IN THE WEST)	Columbia	1	13 Nov 71	17
ERNIE (THE FASTEST MILKMAN IN THE WEST) [RI]	EMI	29	30 May 92	4

ALBUMS:	HITS 1			WEEKS 8
WORDS AND MUSIC	Columbia	9	11 Dec 71	8

Chris HILL — UK

SINGLES:	HITS 2			WEEKS 14
RENTA SANTA	Philips	10	6 Dec 75	7
BIONIC SANTA	Philips	10	4 Dec 76	7

Above 2 weave comic storylines around copious samples from other hits.

Dan HILL — Canada

SINGLES:	HITS 1			WEEKS 13
SOMETIMES WHEN WE TOUCH	20th Century	46	18 Feb 78	1
SOMETIMES WHEN WE TOUCH [RE]	20th Century	13	4 Mar 78	12

Faith HILL — US

SINGLES:	HITS 2			WEEKS 12
THIS KISS	Warner Brothers	13	14 Nov 98	11
LET ME LET GO	Warner Brothers	72	17 Apr 99	1

From the film 'Message In A Bottle'.

Lauryn HILL — US

SINGLES:	HITS 6			WEEKS 32
THE SWEETEST THING	Columbia	18	6 Sep 97	4

From the film 'Love Jones'. Male rap by John Forte.
Above hit: REFUGEE CAMP ALLSTARS featuring Lauryn HILL.

ALL MY TIME	One World Entertainment	57	27 Dec 97	1

Above hit: PAID and LIVE featuring Lauryn HILL.

DOO WOP (THAT THING)	Ruffhouse	3	3 Oct 98	7
EX-FACTOR	Ruffhouse	4	27 Feb 99	9

Samples Wu Tang Clan's Can It All Be So Simple (which was itself an interpretation of Gladys Knight's The Way We Were).

EX-FACTOR [RE]	Ruffhouse	67	22 May 99	1
EVERYTHING IS EVERYTHING	Ruffhouse	19	10 Jul 99	6
TURN YOUR LIGHTS DOWN LOW	Columbia	15	11 Dec 99	4

From the film 'The Best Man'.
Above hit: Bob MARLEY featuring Lauryn HILL.

ALBUMS:	HITS 1			WEEKS 62
THE MISEDUCATION OF LAURYN HILL	Ruffhouse	2	10 Oct 98	62

Lonnie HILL — US

SINGLES:	HITS 1			WEEKS 4
GALVESTON BAY	10 Records	51	22 Mar 86	4

Roni HILL — US

SINGLES:	HITS 1			WEEKS 4
YOU KEEP ME HANGING ON / STOP! IN THE NAME OF LOVE [M]	Creole	36	7 May 77	4

Vince HILL
UK

SINGLES:		HITS 11			WEEKS 91
THE RIVER'S RUN DRY	Piccadilly	49	9 Jun 62		1
THE RIVER'S RUN DRY [RE]	Piccadilly	41	30 Jun 62		1
TAKE ME TO YOUR HEART AGAIN (LA VIE EN ROSE)	Columbia	13	8 Jan 66		11
HEARTACHES	Columbia	28	19 Mar 66		5
Above hit: Vince HILL with the Eddie LESTER SINGERS.					
MERCI CHERI	Columbia	36	4 Jun 66		6
EDELWEISS	Columbia	2	11 Feb 67		17
From the film 'The Sound Of Music'.					
ROSE OF PICARDY	Columbia	13	13 May 67		11
LOVE LETTERS IN THE SAND	Columbia	23	30 Sep 67		9
THE IMPORTANCE OF YOUR LOVE (L'IMPORTANT, C'EST LA ROSE)	Columbia	32	29 Jun 68		12
Originally recorded by Gilbert Becaud.					
Above 4: Vince HILL with the Eddie LESTER SINGERS.					
DOESN'T ANYBODY KNOW MY NAME?	Columbia	50	15 Feb 69		1
LITTLE BLUEBIRD	Columbia	42	25 Oct 69		1
LOOK AROUND (AND YOU'LL FIND ME THERE)	Columbia	12	25 Sep 71		16
From the film 'Love Story'.					
ALBUMS:		**HITS 2**			**WEEKS 10**
EDELWEISS	Columbia	23	20 May 67		9
THAT LOVING FEELING	K-Tel	51	29 Apr 78		1

Steve HILLAGE
UK

ALBUMS:		HITS 8			WEEKS 41
FISH RISING	Virgin	33	3 May 75		3
L	Virgin	10	16 Oct 76		12
MOTIVATION RADIO	Virgin	28	22 Oct 77		5
GREEN VIRGIN	Virgin	30	29 Apr 78		8
LIVE HERALD	Virgin	54	17 Feb 79		5
RAINBOW DOME MUSIC	Virgin	52	5 May 79		5
OPEN	Virgin	71	27 Oct 79		1
FOR TO NEXT	Virgin	48	5 Mar 83		2

HILLMAN MINX
UK/France

SINGLES:		HITS 1			WEEKS 1
I'VE HAD ENOUGH	Mercury	72	5 Sep 98		1

HILLTOPPERS
US

SINGLES:		HITS 3			WEEKS 30
ONLY YOU (AND YOU ALONE)	London	3	28 Jan 56		22
ONLY YOU (AND YOU ALONE) [RE]	London	24	11 Aug 56		1
TRYIN'	London	30	15 Sep 56		1
MARIANNE	London	20	6 Apr 57		2
Originally recorded by Terry Gilkyson and the Easyriders.					
Above hit: HILLTOPPERS with Billy VAUGHN'S ORCHESTRA.					
MARIANNE [RE]	London	23	27 Apr 57		4

Ronnie HILTON
UK

SINGLES:		HITS 17			WEEKS 136
I STILL BELIEVE	His Master's Voice	3	27 Nov 54		14
VENI VIDI VICI	His Master's Voice	12	11 Dec 54		8
Above 2 entries were separate sides of the same release, each had its own chart run.					
A BLOSSOM FELL	His Master's Voice	10	12 Mar 55		5
STARS SHINE IN YOUR EYES	His Master's Voice	13	27 Aug 55		7
From the film 'La Strada'.					
THE YELLOW ROSE OF TEXAS	His Master's Voice	15	12 Nov 55		2
YOUNG AND FOOLISH	His Master's Voice	17	11 Feb 56		1
YOUNG AND FOOLISH [RE-1ST]	His Master's Voice	20	25 Feb 56		1
YOUNG AND FOOLISH [RE-2ND]	His Master's Voice	19	10 Mar 56		1
NO OTHER LOVE	His Master's Voice	1	21 Apr 56		14
From the film 'Me And Juliet'.					
WHO ARE WE	His Master's Voice	6	30 Jun 56		12
A WOMAN IN LOVE	His Master's Voice	30	22 Sep 56		1
From the film 'Guys And Dolls'.					
TWO DIFFERENT WORLDS	His Master's Voice	13	10 Nov 56		13
AROUND THE WORLD	His Master's Voice	4	25 May 57		18
From the film 'Around The World In Eighty Days'.					
WONDERFUL, WONDERFUL	His Master's Voice	27	3 Aug 57		2
MAGIC MOMENTS	His Master's Voice	22	22 Feb 58		2
I MAY NEVER PASS THIS WAY AGAIN	His Master's Voice	30	19 Apr 58		1
I MAY NEVER PASS THIS WAY AGAIN [RE-1ST]	His Master's Voice	30	3 May 58		1
I MAY NEVER PASS THIS WAY AGAIN [RE-2ND]	His Master's Voice	27	7 Jun 58		1
THE WORLD OUTSIDE	His Master's Voice	18	10 Jan 59		6
Above 4: Ronnie HILTON with the Michael SAMMES SINGERS.					

THE WONDER OF YOU	His Master's Voice	22	22 Aug 59	3
Above hit: Ronnie HILTON with the RIDDELLE SINGERS.				
DON'T LET THE RAIN COME DOWN (CROOKED LITTLE MAN)	His Master's Voice	21	23 May 64	10
Above hit: Ronnie HILTON with the Michael SAMMES SINGERS.				
A WINDMILL IN OLD AMSTERDAM	His Master's Voice	23	13 Feb 65	13
Above hit: Ronnie HILTON with the Michael SAMMES SINGERS and ORCHESTRA.				

HINDSIGHT
UK

SINGLES:	HITS 1			WEEKS 3
LOWDOWN	Circa	62	5 Sep 87	3

Deni HINES
Australia

SINGLES:	HITS 4			WEEKS 6
IT'S ALRIGHT	Mushroom	35	14 Jun 97	2
I LIKE THE WAY	Mushroom	37	20 Sep 97	2
DELICIOUS	Mushroom	52	28 Feb 98	1
Above hit: Deni HINES featuring DON-E.				
JOY	Mushroom	47	23 May 98	1

Gregory HINES – See Luther VANDROSS

HIPSWAY
UK

SINGLES:	HITS 6			WEEKS 21
THE BROKEN YEARS	Mercury	72	13 Jul 85	3
ASK THE LORD	Mercury	72	14 Sep 85	1
THE HONEYTHIEF	Mercury	17	22 Feb 86	9
ASK THE LORD [RR]	Mercury	50	10 May 86	5
LONG WHITE CAR	Mercury	55	20 Sep 86	2
YOUR LOVE	Mercury	66	1 Apr 89	1
ALBUMS:	HITS 1			WEEKS 23
HIPSWAY	Mercury	42	19 Apr 86	23

David HIRSCHFELDER
Australia

ALBUMS:	HITS 1			WEEKS 9
SHINE [OST]	Philips	46	2 Aug 97	9

HISTORY featuring Q-TEE
UK

SINGLES:	HITS 1			WEEKS 5
AFRIKA	SBK.One	42	21 Apr 90	5

Carol HITCHCOCK
Australia

SINGLES:	HITS 1			WEEKS 5
GET READY	A&M	56	30 May 87	5

HITHOUSE
Holland

SINGLES:	HITS 2			WEEKS 13
JACK TO THE SOUND OF THE UNDERGROUND	Supreme	14	5 Nov 88	12
MOVE YOUR FEET TO THE RHYTHM OF THE BEAT	Supreme	69	19 Aug 89	1

HITMAN HOWIE TEE – See REAL ROXANNE

Chorus of Members of HM FORCES – See Vera LYNN

Helen HOBSON – See Cliff RICHARD

Edmund HOCKRIDGE
Canada

SINGLES:	HITS 3			WEEKS 18
YOUNG AND FOOLISH	Pye Nixa	10	18 Feb 56	7
From the musical 'Plain And Fancy'.				
Above hit: Edmund HOCKRIDGE with Tony OSBORNE and his Orchestra.				
YOUNG AND FOOLISH [RE-1ST]	Pye Nixa	28	14 Apr 56	1
YOUNG AND FOOLISH [RE-2ND]	Pye Nixa	26	5 May 56	1
NO OTHER LOVE	Pye Nixa	24	12 May 56	2
NO OTHER LOVE [RE-1ST]	Pye Nixa	29	2 Jun 56	1
NO OTHER LOVE [RE-2ND]	Pye Nixa	30	16 Jun 56	1
BY THE FOUNTAINS OF ROME	Pye Nixa	17	1 Sep 56	5
Above hit: Edmund HOCKRIDGE with Beryl STOTT CHORUS and Tony OSBORNE ORCHESTRA.				
EPS:	HITS 2			WEEKS 6
MOST HAPPY FELLA	Pye	8	21 May 60	4
THE MUSIC MAN	Pye	20	8 Apr 61	2

Eddie HODGES | US

SINGLES:		HITS 2			WEEKS 10
I'M GONNA KNOCK ON YOUR DOOR	London	37	30 Sep 61	6
Originally recorded by the Isley Brothers.					
(GIRLS GIRLS GIRLS) MADE TO LOVE	London	37	11 Aug 62	4
Written by Phil Everly.					

Roger HODGSON | UK

(See also Supertramp.)

ALBUMS:		HITS 1			WEEKS 4
IN THE EYE OF THE STORM	A&M	70	20 Oct 84	4

Gerard HOFFNUNG | Germany

ALBUMS:		HITS 1			WEEKS 20
AT THE OXFORD UNION	Decca	4	3 Sep 60	20

Susanna HOFFS | US

SINGLES:		HITS 3			WEEKS 8
MY SIDE OF THE BED	Columbia	44	2 Mar 91	4
UNCONDITIONAL LOVE	Columbia	65	11 May 91	2
ALL I WANT	London	32	19 Oct 96	2
ALBUMS:		HITS 1			WEEKS 2
WHEN YOU'RE A BOY	Columbia	56	6 Apr 91	2

Hulk HOGAN with GREEN JELLY and the WRESTLING BOOT TRASH CAN BAND | US

SINGLES:		HITS 1			WEEKS 4
I'M THE LEADER OF THE GANG	Arista	25	25 Dec 93	4

Christopher HOGWOOD - See ACADEMY Of ANCIENT MUSIC conducted by Christopher HOGWOOD

HOLE | US

SINGLES:		HITS 7			WEEKS 15
BEAUTIFUL SON	City Slang	54	17 Apr 93	1
MISS WORLD	City Slang	64	9 Apr 94	1
DOLL PARTS	Geffen	16	15 Apr 95	3
VIOLET	Geffen	17	29 Jul 95	2
CELEBRITY SKIN	Geffen	19	12 Sep 98	4
MALIBU	Geffen	22	30 Jan 99	2
AWFUL	Geffen	42	10 Jul 99	2
ALBUMS:		HITS 3			WEEKS 10
PRETTY ON THE INSIDE	City Slang	59	12 Oct 91	1
LIVE THROUGH THIS	City Slang	13	23 Apr 94	5
CELEBRITY SKIN	Geffen	11	19 Sep 98	4

HOLE IN ONE | Holland

SINGLES:		HITS 1			WEEKS 2
LIFE'S TOO SHORT	Manifesto	36	15 Feb 97	2

Billie HOLIDAY | US

ALBUMS:		HITS 2			WEEKS 11
THE LEGEND OF BILLIE HOLIDAY	MCA	60	16 Nov 85	10
LADY DAY - THE VERY BEST OF BILLIE HOLIDAY	Columbia	63	6 Sep 97	1

Jools HOLLAND and his R&B ORCHESTRA | UK

ALBUMS:		HITS 3			WEEKS 4
WORLD OF HIS OWN	I.R.S.	71	5 May 90	1
Above hit: Jools HOLLAND.					
SEX & JAZZ & ROCK & ROLL	Coliseum	38	26 Oct 96	2
LIFT THE LID	Coalition	50	25 Oct 97	1

HOLLAND-DOZIER featuring Lamont DOZIER | US

SINGLES:		HITS 1			WEEKS 5
WHY CAN'T WE BE LOVERS	Invictus	29	28 Oct 72	5

Jennifer HOLLIDAY | US

SINGLES:		HITS 1			WEEKS 6
AND I'M TELLING YOU I'M NOT GOING	Geffen	32	4 Sep 82	6
From the musical 'Dream Girls'.					

Michael HOLLIDAY — UK

SINGLES:	HITS 10			WEEKS 66
NOTHIN' TO DO	Columbia	20	31 Mar 56	1
Above hit: Michael HOLLIDAY with Norrie PARAMOR and his Orchestra and Chorus.				
NOTHIN' TO DO [RE]	Columbia	23	28 Apr 56	2
THE GAL WITH THE YALLER SHOES	Columbia	13	16 Jun 56	3
From the film 'Viva Las Vegas'.				
HOT DIGGITY (DOG ZIGGITY BOOM)	Columbia	14	23 Jun 56	5
Above 2 entries were separate sides of the same release, each had its own chart run.				
HOT DIGGITY (DOG ZIGGITY BOOM) / THE GAL WITH THE YALLER SHOES [RE]	Columbia	17	4 Aug 56	3
The Gal With The Yaller Shoes only listed on 18 Aug 56 once single had dropped to No. 25.				
Above 3: Michael HOLLIDAY with Norrie PARAMOR and his Orchestra and the FOUR SHEPHERD BOYS.				
TEN THOUSAND MILES	Columbia	24	6 Oct 56	3
Above hit: Michael HOLLIDAY with Norrie PARAMOR and his Orchestra with the Michael SAMMES SINGERS.				
THE STORY OF MY LIFE	Columbia	1	18 Jan 58	15
Original by Marty Robbins reached No. 15 in the US in 1957.				
IN LOVE	Columbia	26	15 Mar 58	3
STAIRWAY OF LOVE	Columbia	3	17 May 58	13
Originally recorded by Marty Robbins.				
I'LL ALWAYS BE IN LOVE WITH YOU	Columbia	27	12 Jul 58	1
Above 2: Michael HOLLIDAY with Norrie PARAMOR and his Orchestra.				
STARRY EYED	Columbia	1	2 Jan 60	13
Originally recorded by Gary Stites.				
Above hit: Michael HOLLIDAY with the Michael SAMMES SINGERS.				
SKYLARK	Columbia	39	16 Apr 60	3
LITTLE BOY LOST	Columbia	50	3 Sep 60	1
Above hit: Michael HOLLIDAY with Norrie PARAMOR and his Orchestra.				

HOLLIES — UK

SINGLES:	HITS 29			WEEKS 318
JUST LIKE ME	Parlophone	25	1 Jun 63	10
SEARCHIN'	Parlophone	12	31 Aug 63	14
Originally recorded by the Coasters.				
STAY	Parlophone	8	23 Nov 63	16
JUST ONE LOOK	Parlophone	2	29 Feb 64	13
Original by Doris Troy reached No. 10 in the US in 1963.				
HERE I GO AGAIN	Parlophone	4	23 May 64	12
WE'RE THROUGH	Parlophone	7	19 Sep 64	11
YES I WILL	Parlophone	9	30 Jan 65	13
I'M ALIVE	Parlophone	1	29 May 65	14
LOOK THROUGH ANY WINDOW	Parlophone	4	4 Sep 65	11
IF I NEEDED SOMEONE	Parlophone	20	11 Dec 65	9
I CAN'T LET GO	Parlophone	2	26 Feb 66	10
Originally recorded by Evie Sands.				
BUS STOP	Parlophone	5	25 Jun 66	9
STOP STOP STOP	Parlophone	2	15 Oct 66	12
ON A CAROUSEL	Parlophone	4	18 Feb 67	11
CARRIE ANNE	Parlophone	3	3 Jun 67	11
KING MIDAS IN REVERSE	Parlophone	18	30 Sep 67	8
JENNIFER ECCLES	Parlophone	7	30 Mar 68	11
LISTEN TO ME	Parlophone	11	5 Oct 68	11
SORRY SUZANNE	Parlophone	3	8 Mar 69	12
HE AIN'T HEAVY . . . HE'S MY BROTHER	Parlophone	3	4 Oct 69	15
Originally recorded by Kelly Gordon.				
I CAN'T TELL THE BOTTOM FROM THE TOP	Parlophone	7	18 Apr 70	10
Above two feature Elton John on Piano.				
GASOLINE ALLEY BRED	Parlophone	14	3 Oct 70	7
HEY WILLY	Parlophone	22	22 May 71	7
THE BABY	Polydor	26	26 Feb 72	6
Originally recorded by Chip Taylor.				
LONG COOL WOMAN IN A BLACK DRESS	Parlophone	32	2 Sep 72	8
THE DAY THAT CURLY BILLY SHOT CRAZY SAM MCGEE	Polydor	24	13 Oct 73	6
THE AIR THAT I BREATHE	Polydor	2	9 Feb 74	13
Originally recorded by Albert Hammond.				
SOLDIER'S SONG	Polydor	58	14 Jun 80	3
HOLLIEDAZE (A MEDLEY) [M]	EMI	28	29 Aug 81	7
Medley of old hits.				
HE AIN'T HEAVY, HE'S MY BROTHER [RI]	EMI	1	3 Sep 88	11
Featured in the Miller Lite lager TV commercial.				
THE AIR THAT I BREATHE [RI]	EMI	60	3 Dec 88	5
THE WOMAN I LOVE	EMI	42	20 Mar 93	2
Released to celebrate their 30th Anniversary.				
EPS:	HITS 4			WEEKS 33
THE HOLLIES	Parlophone	6	6 Jun 64	8

JUST ONE LOOK	Parlophone	10	27 Jun 64	8
I'M ALIVE	Parlophone	5	25 Sep 65	15
I CAN'T LET GO	Parlophone	9	9 Jul 66	2
ALBUMS:	**HITS 13**		**WEEKS 150**	
STAY WITH THE HOLLIES	Parlophone	2	15 Feb 64	25
HOLLIES	Parlophone	8	2 Oct 65	14
WOULD YOU BELIEVE	Parlophone	16	16 Jul 66	8
FOR CERTAIN BECAUSE	Parlophone	23	17 Dec 66	7
EVOLUTION	Parlophone	13	17 Jun 67	10
THE HOLLIES' GREATEST	Parlophone	1	17 Aug 68	27
HOLLIES SING DYLAN	Parlophone	3	17 May 69	7
CONFESSIONS OF THE MIND	Parlophone	30	28 Nov 70	5
HOLLIES	Polydor	38	16 Mar 74	3
Both self titled albums are different.				
HOLLIES LIVE HITS	Polydor	4	19 Mar 77	12
Live recordings from Christchurch, New Zealand, Feb 76.				
20 GOLDEN GREATS	EMI	2	22 Jul 78	15
20 GOLDEN GREATS [RE]	EMI	64	10 Sep 88	5
ALL THE HITS AND MORE	EMI	51	1 Oct 88	5
THE AIR THAT I BREATHE - THE BEST OF THE HOLLIES	EMI	15	3 Apr 93	7

Mark HOLLIS — UK

ALBUMS:	**HITS 1**		**WEEKS 1**	
MARK HOLLIS	Polydor	53	14 Feb 98	1

Laurie HOLLOWAY – See SOUTH BANK ORCHESTRA conducted by Joseph MOROVITZ and Laurie HOLLOWAY

Loleatta HOLLOWAY — US

(See also Cevin Fisher ; Marky Mark and the Funky Bunch.)

SINGLES:	**HITS 4**		**WEEKS 9**	
TAKE ME AWAY	PWL Continental	25	18 Jan 92	5
Above hit: CAPPELLA featuring Loleatta HOLLOWAY.				
STAND UP	Six6	68	26 Mar 94	1
KEEP THE FIRE BURNIN'	Columbia	49	1 Apr 95	1
Above hit: Dan HARTMAN Starring Loleatta HOLLOWAY.				
SHOUT TO THE TOP	JBO	23	11 Apr 98	2
Above hit: FIRE ISLAND featuring Loleatta HOLLOWAY.				

HOLLOWAY and CO. — UK

SINGLES:	**HITS 1**		**WEEKS 1**	
I'LL DO ANYTHING - TO MAKE YOU MINE	INCredible	58	21 Aug 99	1

Buddy HOLLY — US

(See also Crickets.)

SINGLES:	**HITS 19**		**WEEKS 190**	
PEGGY SUE	Vogue Coral	6	7 Dec 57	17
Title originally called Cindy-Lou.				
LISTEN TO ME	Coral	16	15 Mar 58	2
RAVE ON	Coral	5	21 Jun 58	14
Originally recorded by Sonny West.				
EARLY IN THE MORNING	Coral	17	30 Aug 58	4
Originally recorded by Bobby Darin and the Rinky Dinks.				
HEARTBEAT	Coral	30	17 Jan 59	1
IT DOESN'T MATTER ANYMORE	Coral	1	28 Feb 59	21
Originally recorded by Paul Anka.				
MIDNIGHT SHIFT	Brunswick	26	1 Aug 59	3
PEGGY SUE GOT MARRIED	Coral	13	12 Sep 59	10
HEARTBEAT [RI]	Coral	30	30 Apr 60	3
TRUE LOVE WAYS	Coral	25	28 May 60	7
LEARNING THE GAME	Coral	36	22 Oct 60	3
WHAT TO DO	Coral	34	28 Jan 61	6
BABY I DON'T CARE / VALLEY OF TEARS	Coral	12	8 Jul 61	14
Valley of Tears listed from 22 Jul 61. Baby I Don't Care originally recorded by Elvis Presley.				
LISTEN TO ME [RI]	Coral	48	17 Mar 62	1
REMINISCING	Coral	17	15 Sep 62	11
BROWN EYED HANDSOME MAN	Coral	3	16 Mar 63	17
Originally recorded by Chuck Berry in 1956.				
BO DIDDLEY	Coral	4	8 Jun 63	12
Originally recorded by Bo Diddley.				
WISHING	Coral	10	7 Sep 63	11
WHAT TO DO [RR]	Coral	27	21 Dec 63	8
YOU'VE GOT LOVE	Coral	40	16 May 64	6
Above hit: Buddy HOLLY and the CRICKETS.				
LOVE'S MADE A FOOL OF YOU	Coral	39	12 Sep 64	6
PEGGY SUE [RI] / RAVE ON [RI]	MCA	32	6 Apr 68	9
TRUE LOVE WAYS [RI]	MCA	65	10 Dec 88	4

EPS:		HITS 5		WEEKS 90	
THE LATE GREAT BUDDY HOLLY	Coral	4	19 Mar 60	43	
RAVE ON	Coral	9	22 Jul 61	22	
BUDDY HOLLY NO. 1	Brunswick	18	26 Aug 61	2	
HEARTBEAT	Coral	13	2 Sep 61	6	
LISTEN TO ME	Coral	12	17 Mar 62	17	

ALBUMS:		HITS 13		WEEKS 339	
THE BUDDY HOLLY STORY	Coral	2	2 May 59	156	
THE BUDDY HOLLY STORY VOLUME 2	Coral	7	15 Oct 60	14	
THAT'LL BE THE DAY	Ace Of Hearts	5	21 Oct 61	14	
REMINISCING	Coral	2	6 Apr 63	31	
BUDDY HOLLY SHOWCASE	Coral	3	13 Jun 64	16	
HOLLY IN THE HILLS	Coral	13	26 Jun 65	6	
Above 6: Buddy HOLLY and the CRICKETS.					
BUDDY HOLLY'S GREATEST HITS	Ace Of Hearts	10	15 Jul 67	21	
BUDDY HOLLY'S GREATEST HITS [RE]	Ace Of Hearts	9	11 May 68	19	
GIANT	MCA	13	12 Apr 69	1	
Above hit: Buddy HOLLY and the CRICKETS.					
BUDDY HOLLY'S GREATEST HITS [RI-1ST]	Coral	32	21 Aug 71	6	
BUDDY HOLLY'S GREATEST HITS [RI-1ST] [RE]	Coral	42	12 Jul 75	3	
Repackaged with additional tracks.					
20 GOLDEN GREATS	EMI	1	11 Mar 78	20	
Above hit: Buddy HOLLY and the CRICKETS.					
BUDDY HOLLY'S GREATEST HITS [RI-2ND]	MCA	100	8 Sep 84	1	
TRUE LOVE WAYS	Telstar	8	18 Feb 89	11	
WORDS OF LOVE	PolyGram TV/MCA	1	20 Feb 93	9	
Above hit: Buddy HOLLY and the CRICKETS.					
THE VERY BEST OF BUDDY HOLLY	Dino	24	7 Dec 96	8	
THE VERY BEST OF BUDDY HOLLY AND THE CRICKETS	Universal Music TV	25	28 Aug 99	3	
Above hit: Buddy HOLLY and the CRICKETS.					

HOLLY and the IVYS   UK

SINGLES:		HITS 1		WEEKS 4	
CHRISTMAS ON 45 [M]	Decca	40	19 Dec 81	4	

HOLLYWOOD ARGYLES   US

SINGLES:		HITS 1		WEEKS 10	
ALLEY-OOP	London	24	23 Jul 60	10	

HOLLYWOOD BEYOND   UK

SINGLES:		HITS 2		WEEKS 14	
WHAT'S THE COLOUR OF MONEY?	WEA	7	12 Jul 86	10	
Features Mica Paris on backing vocals.					
NO MORE TEARS	WEA	47	20 Sep 86	4	

Eddie HOLMAN   US

SINGLES:		HITS 1		WEEKS 13	
(HEY THERE) LONELY GIRL	ABC	4	19 Oct 74	13	

David HOLMES   UK

SINGLES:		HITS 4		WEEKS 7	
GONE	Go! Discs	75	6 Apr 96	1	
Vocals by Sarah Cracknell of Saint Etienne.					
GRITTY SHAKER	Go.Beat	53	23 Aug 97	1	
DON'T DIE JUST YET	Go.Beat	33	10 Jan 98	3	
MY MATE PAUL	Go.Beat	39	4 Apr 98	2	

ALBUMS:		HITS 2		WEEKS 3	
THIS FILM'S CRAP, LET'S SLASH THE SEATS	Go! Discs	51	22 Jul 95	1	
LET'S GET KILLED	Go.Beat	34	13 Sep 97	2	

Rupert HOLMES   US

SINGLES:		HITS 2		WEEKS 14	
ESCAPE (THE PINA COLADA SONG)	Infinity	23	12 Jan 80	7	
HIM	MCA	31	22 Mar 80	7	

John HOLT   Jamaica

SINGLES:		HITS 1		WEEKS 14	
HELP ME MAKE IT THROUGH THE NIGHT	Trojan	6	14 Dec 74	14	
Originally recorded by Kris Kristofferson.					

ALBUMS:		HITS 1		WEEKS 2	
A THOUSAND VOLTS OF HOLT	Trojan	42	1 Feb 75	2	

HOME
UK

ALBUMS:		HITS 1		WEEKS 1
DREAMER	CBS	41	11 Nov 72	1

A HOMEBOY, A HIPPIE and A FUNKI DREDD
UK

SINGLES:		HITS 3		WEEKS 9
TOTAL CONFUSION	Tam Tam	56	13 Oct 90	3
FREEDOM	Tam Tam	68	29 Dec 90	4
HERE WE GO AGAIN	Polydor	57	8 Jan 94	2

HOMER - See SIMPSONS

HONDY
Italy

SINGLES:		HITS 1		WEEKS 2
HONDY (NO ACCESS)	Manifesto	26	12 Apr 97	2

HONEYBUS
UK

SINGLES:		HITS 1		WEEKS 12
I CAN'T LET MAGGIE GO	Deram	8	23 Mar 68	12

HONEYCOMBS
UK

SINGLES:		HITS 4		WEEKS 39
HAVE I THE RIGHT?	Pye	1	25 Jul 64	15
IS IT BECAUSE?	Pye	38	24 Oct 64	6
SOMETHING BETTER BEGINNING	Pye	39	1 May 65	4
Originally recorded by the Kinks.				
THAT'S THE WAY	Pye	12	7 Aug 65	14

HONEYCRACK
UK

SINGLES:		HITS 4		WEEKS 9
SITTING AT HOME	Epic	42	4 Nov 95	2
GO AWAY	Epic	41	24 Feb 96	2
KING OF MISERY	Epic	32	11 May 96	2
SITTING AT HOME [RI]	Epic	32	20 Jul 96	2
ANYWAY	E'G	67	16 Nov 96	1
ALBUMS:		**HITS 1**		**WEEKS 1**
PROZAIC	Epic	34	1 Jun 96	1

HONEYDRIPPERS
UK/US

SINGLES:		HITS 1		WEEKS 3
SEA OF LOVE	Es Paranza	56	2 Feb 85	3
ALBUMS:		**HITS 1**		**WEEKS 10**
THE HONEYDRIPPERS VOLUME ONE	Es Paranza	56	1 Dec 84	10

HONEYZ
UK/France

SINGLES:		HITS 4		WEEKS 41
FINALLY FOUND	Mercury	4	5 Sep 98	12
END OF THE LINE	Mercury	5	19 Dec 98	12
END OF THE LINE [RE]	Mercury	64	24 Apr 99	2
LOVE OF A LIFETIME	Mercury	9	24 Apr 99	9
NEVER LET YOU DOWN	Mercury	7	23 Oct 99	6
ALBUMS:		**HITS 1**		**WEEKS 20**
WONDER NO.8	Mercury	33	5 Dec 98	19
WONDER NO.8 [RE]	Mercury	46	13 Nov 99	1
Re-released with additional track.				

HONKY
UK

SINGLES:		HITS 1		WEEKS 5
JOIN THE PARTY	Creole	28	28 May 77	5

HONKY
UK

SINGLES:		HITS 4		WEEKS 5
THE HONKY DOODLE DAY [EP]	ZTT	61	30 Oct 93	1
Lead track: K.K.K. (Boom Boom Tra La La La).				
THE WHISTLER	ZTT	41	19 Feb 94	2
HIP HOP DON'T YA DROP	Higher Ground	70	20 Apr 96	1
WHAT'S GOIN DOWN	Higher Ground	49	10 Aug 96	1
Samples Ian Dury's Sex & Drugs & Rock & Roll.				

Frank HOOKER and POSITIVE PEOPLE
US

SINGLES:		HITS 1		WEEKS 4
THIS FEELIN'	DJM	48	5 Jul 80	4

John Lee HOOKER | US

SINGLES:	HITS 6			WEEKS 23
DIMPLES	Stateside	23	13 Jun 64	10
BOOM BOOM	Pointblank	16	24 Oct 92	5
Featured in the Lee Jeans TV commercial. Originally released in 1963.				
BOOGIE AT RUSSIAN HILL	Pointblank	53	16 Jan 93	2
GLORIA	Exile	31	15 May 93	3
Original by Them was the B-side to Baby Please Don't Go in 1964.				
Above hit: Van MORRISON and John Lee HOOKER.				
CHILL OUT (THINGS GONNA CHANGE)	Pointblank	45	11 Feb 95	2
Features Carlos Santana.				
BABY LEE	Silvertone	65	20 Apr 96	1
Featured in the Lee Jeans TV commercial.				
Above hit: John Lee HOOKER with Robert CRAY.				
ALBUMS:	HITS 6			WEEKS 31
HOUSE OF THE BLUES	Marble Arch	34	4 Feb 67	2
THE HEALER	Silvertone	63	11 Nov 89	8
Above hit: John Lee HOOKER and FRIENDS.				
MR. LUCKY	Silvertone	3	21 Sep 91	10
BOOM BOOM	Pointblank	15	7 Nov 92	4
CHILL OUT	Pointblank	23	4 Mar 95	5
DON'T LOOK BACK	Pointblank	63	22 Mar 97	2

HOOTERS | US

SINGLES:	HITS 1			WEEKS 9
SATELLITE	CBS	22	21 Nov 87	9

HOOTIE AND THE BLOWFISH | US

SINGLES:	HITS 4			WEEKS 6
HOLD MY HAND	Atlantic	50	25 Feb 95	3
LET HER CRY	Atlantic	75	27 May 95	1
OLD MAN & ME (WHEN I GET TO HEAVEN)	Atlantic	57	4 May 96	1
I WILL WAIT	Atlantic	57	7 Nov 98	1
ALBUMS:	HITS 3			WEEKS 30
CRACKED REAR VIEW	Atlantic	12	18 Mar 95	11
FAIRWEATHER JOHNSON	Atlantic	9	4 May 96	16
MUSICAL CHAIRS	Atlantic	15	26 Sep 98	3

HOPE A.D. | UK

(See also Mind Of Kane.)

SINGLES:	HITS 1			WEEKS 1
TREE FROG	Sun-Up	73	4 Jun 94	1
Originally released in 1993.				

Mary HOPKIN | UK

(See also Various Artists (EPs) 'The Apple EP'.)

SINGLES:	HITS 7			WEEKS 74
THOSE WERE THE DAYS	Apple	1	7 Sep 68	21
Originally recorded in English by the Limeliters.				
GOODBYE	Apple	2	5 Apr 69	14
Written by Lennon/McCartney.				
TEMMA HARBOUR	Apple	6	31 Jan 70	11
KNOCK, KNOCK WHO'S THERE?	Apple	2	28 Mar 70	14
UK's Eurovision entry in 1970, it came 2nd.				
THINK ABOUT YOUR CHILDREN	Apple	19	31 Oct 70	7
Written by Errol Brown and Tony Wilson of Hot Chocolate.				
THINK ABOUT YOUR CHILDREN [RE]	Apple	46	2 Jan 71	2
LET MY NAME BE SORROW	Apple	46	31 Jul 71	1
IF YOU LOVE ME (I WON'T CARE)	Good Earth	32	20 Mar 76	4
ALBUMS:	HITS 1			WEEKS 9
POSTCARD	Apple	3	1 Mar 69	9

Anthony HOPKINS | UK

SINGLES:	HITS 1			WEEKS 1
DISTANT STAR	Juice	75	27 Dec 86	1

Nick HORNBY - See VARIOUS ARTISTS (EPs) 'Fever Pitch The EP'

James HORNER | US

ALBUMS:	HITS 3			WEEKS 82
BRAVEHEART [OST]	Decca	27	23 Sep 95	9
Above hit: LONDON SYMPHONY ORCHESTRA, conductor James HORNER.				

TITANIC [OST]	Sony Classical	1	31 Jan 98	55
Above hit: Music composed and conducted by James HORNER.				
BACK TO TITANIC	Sony Classical	10	12 Sep 98	18

Bruce HORNSBY and the RANGE
US

SINGLES:	HITS 3			WEEKS 15
THE WAY IT IS	RCA	15	2 Aug 86	10
MANDOLIN RAIN	RCA	70	25 Apr 87	1
THE VALLEY ROAD	RCA	44	28 May 88	4
ALBUMS:	HITS 4			WEEKS 54
THE WAY IT IS	RCA	16	13 Sep 86	26
SCENES FROM THE SOUTHSIDE	RCA	18	14 May 88	18
A NIGHT ON THE TOWN	RCA	23	30 Jun 90	7
HARBOR LIGHTS	RCA	32	8 May 93	3
Above hit: Bruce HORNSBY.				

HORNY UNITED – See BONEY M

HORSE
UK

SINGLES:	HITS 4			WEEKS 10
CAREFUL	Capitol	52	24 Nov 90	3
SHAKE THIS MOUNTAIN	Oxygen	52	21 Aug 93	2
GOD'S HOME MOVIE	Oxygen	56	23 Oct 93	1
CELEBRATE	Oxygen	49	15 Jan 94	2
CAREFUL [RM]	Stress	44	5 Apr 97	2
Remixed by Brothers In Rhythm.				
ALBUMS:	HITS 2			WEEKS 4
THE SAME SKY	Echo Chamber	44	23 Jun 90	2
GOD'S HOME MOVIE	Oxygen	42	13 Nov 93	2

HORSLIPS
Ireland

ALBUMS:	HITS 1			WEEKS 3
THE BOOK OF INVASIONS – A CELTIC SYMPHONY	DJM	39	30 Apr 77	3

Johnny HORTON
US

SINGLES:	HITS 2			WEEKS 15
THE BATTLE OF NEW ORLEANS	Philips	16	27 Jun 59	4
NORTH TO ALASKA	Philips	23	21 Jan 61	11
From the film of the same name.				

Robert HORTON
US

EPS:	HITS 1			WEEKS 8
SUNDAY NIGHT AT THE LONDON PALLADIUM	Pye	7	12 Mar 60	8

HOT BLOOD
France

SINGLES:	HITS 1			WEEKS 5
SOUL DRACULA	Creole	32	9 Oct 76	5

HOT BUTTER
US

SINGLES:	HITS 1			WEEKS 19
POPCORN	Pye International	5	22 Jul 72	16
POPCORN [RE]	Pye International	50	23 Dec 72	3

HOT CHOCOLATE
UK

SINGLES:	HITS 30			WEEKS 283
LOVE IS LIFE	RAK	6	15 Aug 70	12
Accompanied by the Trinidad Singers.				
YOU COULD'VE BEEN A LADY	RAK	22	6 Mar 71	9
I BELIEVE (IN LOVE)	RAK	8	28 Aug 71	11
YOU'LL ALWAYS BE A FRIEND	RAK	23	28 Oct 72	8
BROTHER LOUIE	RAK	7	14 Apr 73	10
RUMOURS	RAK	44	18 Aug 73	3
EMMA	RAK	3	16 Mar 74	10
CHERI BABY	RAK	31	30 Nov 74	9
DISCO QUEEN	RAK	11	24 May 75	7
A CHILD'S PRAYER	RAK	7	9 Aug 75	10
YOU SEXY THING	RAK	2	8 Nov 75	12
DON'T STOP IT NOW	RAK	11	20 Mar 76	8
MAN TO MAN	RAK	14	26 Jun 76	8
HEAVEN IS IN THE BACK SEAT OF MY CADILLAC	RAK	25	21 Aug 76	8
SO YOU WIN AGAIN	RAK	1	18 Jun 77	11
PUT YOUR LOVE IN ME	RAK	10	26 Nov 77	9
EVERY 1'S A WINNER	RAK	12	4 Mar 78	11

I'LL PUT YOU TOGETHER AGAIN (FROM DEAR ANYONE)	*RAK*	13	*2 Dec 78*	11

Originally recorded by Pandora and the Correspondants.

MINDLESS BOOGIE	*RAK*	46	*19 May 79*	5
GOING THROUGH THE MOTIONS	*RAK*	53	*28 Jul 79*	4
NO DOUBT ABOUT IT	*RAK*	2	*3 May 80*	11
ARE YOU GETTING ENOUGH OF WHAT MAKES YOU HAPPY	*RAK*	17	*19 Jul 80*	7
LOVE ME TO SLEEP	*RAK*	50	*13 Dec 80*	5
YOU'LL NEVER BE SO WRONG	*RAK*	52	*30 May 81*	4
GIRL CRAZY	*RAK*	7	*17 Apr 82*	11
IT STARTED WITH A KISS	*RAK*	5	*10 Jul 82*	12
CHANCES	*RAK*	32	*25 Sep 82*	5
WHAT KINDA BOY YOU'RE LOOKIN' FOR (GIRL)	*RAK*	10	*7 May 83*	9
TEARS ON THE TELEPHONE	*RAK*	37	*17 Sep 83*	5
I GAVE YOU MY HEART (DIDN'T I)	*RAK*	13	*4 Feb 84*	10
YOU SEXY THING [RM]	*EMI*	10	*17 Jan 87*	10

Remixed by Ben Liebrand.

EVERY 1'S A WINNER (GROOVE MIX) [RM]	*EMI*	69	*4 Apr 87*	2
IT STARTED WITH A KISS [RI-1ST]	*EMI*	31	*6 Mar 93*	5
YOU SEXY THING [RI]	*EMI*	6	*22 Nov 97*	8

From the film 'The Full Monty'.

IT STARTED WITH A KISS [RI-2ND]	*EMI*	18	*14 Feb 98*	3

Above hit: HOT CHOCOLATE featuring Errol BROWN.

ALBUMS:	**HITS 8**		**WEEKS 152**	
HOT CHOCOLATE	*RAK*	34	*15 Nov 75*	7
MAN TO MAN	*RAK*	32	*7 Aug 76*	7
GREATEST HITS	*RAK*	6	*20 Nov 76*	35
EVERY 1'S A WINNER	*RAK*	30	*8 Apr 78*	8
20 HOTTEST HITS	*RAK*	3	*15 Dec 79*	19
MYSTERY	*RAK*	24	*25 Sep 82*	7
THE VERY BEST OF HOT CHOCOLATE	*RAK*	1	*21 Feb 87*	28
THEIR GREATEST HITS	*EMI*	1	*20 Mar 93*	41

HOT GOSSIP - See Sarah BRIGHTMAN

HOT HOUSE   UK

SINGLES:	**HITS 1**		**WEEKS 3**	
DON'T COME TO STAY	*Deconstruction*	74	*14 Feb 87*	1
DON'T COME TO STAY [RI]	*Deconstruction*	70	*24 Sep 88*	2

HOT 'N' JUICY - See MOUSSE T. Vs HOT 'N' JUICY

HOT STREAK   US

SINGLES:	**HITS 1**		**WEEKS 8**	
BODY WORK	*Polydor*	19	*10 Sep 83*	8

HOTHOUSE FLOWERS   Ireland

SINGLES:	**HITS 10**		**WEEKS 36**	
DON'T GO	*London*	11	*14 May 88*	8
I'M SORRY	*London*	53	*23 Jul 88*	3
GIVE IT UP	*London*	30	*12 May 90*	5
I CAN SEE CLEARLY NOW	*London*	23	*28 Jul 90*	7
MOVIES	*London*	68	*20 Oct 90*	2
AN EMOTIONAL TIME	*London*	38	*13 Feb 93*	4
ONE TONGUE	*London*	45	*8 May 93*	3
ISN'T IT AMAZING	*London*	46	*19 Jun 93*	2
THIS IS IT (YOUR SOUL)	*London*	67	*27 Nov 93*	1
YOU CAN LOVE ME NOW	*London*	65	*16 May 98*	1

ALBUMS:	**HITS 3**		**WEEKS 51**	
PEOPLE	*London*	2	*18 Jun 88*	19
HOME	*London*	5	*16 Jun 90*	21
SONGS FROM THE RAIN	*London*	7	*20 Mar 93*	11

HOTLEGS   UK

SINGLES:	**HITS 1**		**WEEKS 14**	
NEANDERTHAL MAN	*Fontana*	2	*4 Jul 70*	14

HOTSHOTS   UK

SINGLES:	**HITS 1**		**WEEKS 15**	
SNOOPY VERSUS THE RED BARON	*Mooncrest*	4	*2 Jun 73*	15

Steven HOUGHTON   UK

SINGLES:	**HITS 2**		**WEEKS 22**	
WIND BENEATH MY WINGS	*RCA*	3	*29 Nov 97*	15
TRULY	*RCA*	23	*7 Mar 98*	5

Both songs were featured in the ITV series 'London's Burning'.

TRULY [RE]		RCA	72	2 May 98	2
ALBUMS:		**HITS 1**		**WEEKS 7**	
STEVEN HOUGHTON		RCA	21	29 Nov 97	7

HOUND DOG and the MEGAMIXERS
UK

ALBUMS:		**HITS 1**		**WEEKS 9**	
THE GREATEST EVER JUNIOR PARTY MEGAMIX		Pop & Arts	34	1 Dec 90	9

A HOUSE
Ireland

SINGLES:		**HITS 4**		**WEEKS 8**	
ENDLESS ART		Setanta	46	13 Jun 92	3
TAKE IT EASY ON ME		Setanta	55	8 Aug 92	2
WHY ME?		Setanta	52	25 Jun 94	1
HERE COME THE GOOD TIMES		Setanta	37	1 Oct 94	2

HOUSE ENGINEERS
UK

SINGLES:		**HITS 1**		**WEEKS 2**	
GHOST HOUSE		Syncopate	69	5 Dec 87	2

HOUSE MASTER BOYZ and the RUDE BOY OF HOUSE
US

SINGLES:		**HITS 1**		**WEEKS 14**	
HOUSE NATION		Magnetic Dance	48	9 May 87	6
HOUSE NATION [RE]		Magnetic Dance	8	12 Sep 87	8

HOUSE OF LOVE
UK/Germany/New Zealand

SINGLES:		**HITS 8**		**WEEKS 21**	
NEVER		Fontana	41	22 Apr 89	2
I DON'T KNOW WHY I LOVE YOU		Fontana	41	18 Nov 89	3
SHINE ON		Fontana	20	3 Feb 90	4
BEATLES AND THE STONES		Fontana	36	7 Apr 90	4
THE GIRL WITH THE LONELIEST EYES		Fontana	58	26 Oct 91	1
FEEL		Fontana	45	2 May 92	3
YOU DON'T UNDERSTAND		Fontana	46	27 Jun 92	3
CRUSH ME		Fontana	67	5 Dec 92	1
ALBUMS:		**HITS 4**		**WEEKS 14**	
HOUSE OF LOVE		Fontana	8	10 Mar 90	10
THE HOUSE OF LOVE		Fontana	49	10 Nov 90	1
BABE RAINBOW		Fontana	34	18 Jul 92	2
AUDIENCE WITH THE MIND		Fontana	38	3 Jul 93	1

HOUSE OF PAIN
US

SINGLES:		**HITS 7**		**WEEKS 24**	
JUMP AROUND		XL Recordings	32	10 Oct 92	4
JUMP AROUND [RI] / TOP O' THE MORNING TO YA		XL Recordings	8	22 May 93	7
SHAMROCKS AND SHENANIGANS / WHO'S THE MAN		XL Recordings	23	23 Oct 93	4
Shamrocks And Shenanigans originally reached No. 97 in Jan 93. Who's The Man samples David Bowie's Fame.					
ON POINT		XL Recordings	19	16 Jul 94	3
Samples Cannonball Adderley's Inside Straight.					
IT AIN'T A CRIME		XL Recordings	37	12 Nov 94	2
Samples Red Hot Chili Pepper's Under The Bridge.					
OVER THERE (I DON'T CARE)		XL Recordings	20	1 Jul 95	3
FED UP		Tommy Boy	68	5 Oct 96	1
Featured in the Lucozade TV commercial.					
ALBUMS:		**HITS 2**		**WEEKS 7**	
HOUSE OF PAIN		XL Recordings	73	21 Nov 92	1
SAME AS IT EVER WAS		XL Recordings	8	30 Jul 94	6

HOUSE OF VIRGINISM
Sweden

SINGLES:		**HITS 3**		**WEEKS 6**	
I'LL BE THERE FOR YOU (DOYA DODODO DOYA)		ffrr	29	20 Nov 93	3
REACHIN		ffrr	35	30 Jul 94	2
EXCLUSIVE		Logic	67	17 Feb 96	1
Above hit: APOLLO Presents HOUSE OF VIRGINISM.					

HOUSE OF ZEKKARIYAS - See WOMACK and WOMACK

HOUSE TRAFFIC
UK/Italy

SINGLES:		**HITS 1**		**WEEKS 3**	
EVERYDAY OF MY LIFE		Logic	24	4 Oct 97	3
Originally reached No. 101 in 1994.					

406

HOUSEMARTINS UK

SINGLES:	HITS 8			WEEKS 59
SHEEP	Go! Discs	54	8 Mar 86	3
SHEEP [RE]	Go! Discs	71	5 Apr 86	1
HAPPY HOUR	Go! Discs	3	7 Jun 86	13
THINK FOR A MINUTE (NEW VERSION)	Go! Discs	18	4 Oct 86	8
CARAVAN OF LOVE	Go! Discs	1	6 Dec 86	11
Originally recorded by Isley Jasper Isley.				
FIVE GET OVEREXCITED	Go! Discs	11	23 May 87	6
ME AND THE FARMER	Go! Discs	15	5 Sep 87	5
BUILD	Go! Discs	15	21 Nov 87	8
THERE IS ALWAYS SOMETHING THERE TO REMIND ME	Go! Discs	35	23 Apr 88	4
ALBUMS:	**HITS 4**			**WEEKS 71**
LONDON 0 HULL 4	Go! Discs	3	5 Jul 86	41
THE HOUSEMARTINS' CHRISTMAS SINGLES BOX	Go! Discs	84	27 Dec 86	1
4 singles in foldout sleeve.				
THE PEOPLE WHO GRINNED THEMSELVES TO DEATH	Go! Discs	9	3 Oct 87	18
NOW THAT'S WHAT I CALL QUITE GOOD!	Go! Discs	8	21 May 88	11

Thelma HOUSTON US

SINGLES:	HITS 4			WEEKS 22
DON'T LEAVE ME THIS WAY	Motown	13	5 Feb 77	8
IF YOU FEEL IT	RCA	48	27 Jun 81	4
YOU USED TO HOLD ME SO TIGHT	MCA	49	1 Dec 84	8
DON'T LEAVE ME THIS WAY [RR]	Dynamo	35	21 Jan 95	2

Whitney HOUSTON US

SINGLES:	HITS 29			WEEKS 281
(See also Various Artists: Films – Original Soundtracks 'The Bodyguard'; 'Waiting To Exhale'.)				
SAVING ALL MY LOVE FOR YOU	Arista	1	16 Nov 85	16
Originally recorded by Billy Davis Jr & Marilyn McCoo.				
HOLD ME	Asylum	44	25 Jan 86	5
Above hit: Teddy PENDERGRASS with Whitney HOUSTON.				
HOW WILL I KNOW	Arista	5	25 Jan 86	12
Originally written for Janet Jackson, backing vocals by Whitney's mother Cissy.				
GREATEST LOVE OF ALL	Arista	8	12 Apr 86	11
I WANNA DANCE WITH SOMEBODY (WHO LOVES ME)	Arista	1	23 May 87	16
Written by Boy Meets Girl.				
DIDN'T WE ALMOST HAVE IT ALL	Arista	14	22 Aug 87	8
SO EMOTIONAL	Arista	5	14 Nov 87	11
WHERE DO BROKEN HEARTS GO	Arista	14	12 Mar 88	8
LOVE WILL SAVE THE DAY	Arista	10	28 May 88	7
ONE MOMENT IN TIME	Arista	1	24 Sep 88	12
The official theme for the Olympic Games in Seoul, South Korea.				
IT ISN'T, IT WASN'T, IT AIN'T NEVER GONNA BE	Arista	29	9 Sep 89	5
Label only credits Aretha Franklin.				
Above hit: ARETHA and WHITNEY.				
I'M YOUR BABY TONIGHT	Arista	5	20 Oct 90	9
ALL THE MAN THAT I NEED	Arista	13	22 Dec 90	10
Originally recorded by Linda Clifford in 1978, features Kenny G on saxophone.				
I'M YOUR BABY TONIGHT [RE]	Arista	69	29 Dec 90	1
MY NAME IS NOT SUSAN	Arista	29	6 Jul 91	5
I BELONG TO YOU	Arista	54	28 Sep 91	2
I WILL ALWAYS LOVE YOU	Arista	1	14 Nov 92	23
Originally recorded by Dolly Parton in 1974.				
I'M EVERY WOMAN	Arista	4	20 Feb 93	11
Backing vocals by Jeanie Tracy (Weather Girls).				
I HAVE NOTHING	Arista	3	24 Apr 93	10
RUN TO YOU	Arista	15	31 Jul 93	6
QUEEN OF THE NIGHT	Arista	14	6 Nov 93	5
Above 5 from the film 'The Bodyguard'.				
I WILL ALWAYS LOVE YOU [RE]	Arista	25	18 Dec 93	6
SOMETHING IN COMMON	MCA	16	22 Jan 94	5
Above hit: Bobby BROWN (Duet with Whitney HOUSTON).				
EXHALE (SHOOP SHOOP)	Arista	11	18 Nov 95	9
COUNT ON ME	Arista	12	24 Feb 96	6
Above 2 from the film 'Waiting To Exhale'.				
Above hit: Whitney HOUSTON and CeCe WINANS.				
STEP BY STEP	Arista	13	21 Dec 96	13
Backing vocals by Annie Lennox.				
I BELIEVE IN YOU AND ME	Arista	16	29 Mar 97	5
Above 2 from the film 'The Preacher's Wife'.				
WHEN YOU BELIEVE (FROM THE PRINCE OF EGYPT)	Columbia	4	19 Dec 98	11
From the film 'The Prince Of Egypt'.				
Above hit: Mariah CAREY and Whitney HOUSTON.				
IT'S NOT RIGHT BUT IT'S OKAY	Arista	3	6 Mar 99	15

WHEN YOU BELIEVE (FROM THE PRINCE OF EGYPT) [RE]	Columbia	68	27 Mar 99	2
MY LOVE IS YOUR LOVE	Arista	2	3 Jul 99	12
Including backing vocals from the Family Friends Community Choir.				
I LEARNED FROM THE BEST	Arista	19	11 Dec 99	4
ALBUMS:	**HITS 5**		**WEEKS 314**	
WHITNEY HOUSTON	Arista	2	14 Dec 85	119
WHITNEY	Arista	1	13 Jun 87	101
I'M YOUR BABY TONIGHT	Arista	4	17 Nov 90	29
THE PREACHER'S WIFE [OST]	Arista	35	4 Jan 97	7
MY LOVE IS YOUR LOVE	Arista	4	28 Nov 98	58
Peak position reached on 24 Jul 99.				

Adina HOWARD   US

SINGLES:	**HITS 2**		**WEEKS 16**	
FREAK LIKE ME	East West America	67	4 Mar 95	1
FREAK LIKE ME [RE]	East West America	33	6 May 95	3
WHAT'S LOVE GOT TO DO WITH IT	Interscope	2	23 Nov 96	12
Above hit: Warren G featuring Adina HOWARD.				

Billy HOWARD   UK

SINGLES:	**HITS 1**		**WEEKS 12**	
KING OF THE COPS	Penny Farthing	6	13 Dec 75	12
Impersonations of TV cops to the music of King Of The Road.				

Miki HOWARD   US

SINGLES:	**HITS 1**		**WEEKS 2**	
UNTIL YOU COME BACK TO ME (THAT'S WHAT I'M GONNA DO)	Atlantic	67	26 May 90	2

Nick HOWARD   Australia

SINGLES:	**HITS 1**		**WEEKS 1**	
EVERYBODY NEEDS SOMEBODY	Bell	64	21 Jan 95	1

Robert HOWARD and Kym MAZELLE   UK/US

(See also Kym Mazelle.)				
SINGLES:	**HITS 1**		**WEEKS 10**	
WAIT	RCA	7	14 Jan 89	10

Steve HOWE   UK

ALBUMS:	**HITS 2**		**WEEKS 6**	
BEGINNINGS	Atlantic	22	15 Nov 75	4
THE STEVE HOWE ALBUM	Atlantic	68	24 Nov 79	2

HOWLIN' WOLF   US

SINGLES:	**HITS 1**		**WEEKS 5**	
SMOKESTACK LIGHTNIN'	Pye International	42	6 Jun 64	5
EPS:	**HITS 1**		**WEEKS 4**	
TELL ME	Pye International	16	10 Oct 64	4

H2O   UK

SINGLES:	**HITS 2**		**WEEKS 16**	
I DREAM TO SLEEP	RCA	17	21 May 83	10
Title as per sleeve. Label just shows Dream To Sleep.				
JUST OUTSIDE OF HEAVEN	RCA	38	13 Aug 83	6

H2O featuring BILLIE   US/Switzerland

SINGLES:	**HITS 2**		**WEEKS 4**	
NOBODY'S BUSINESS	AM:PM	19	14 Sep 96	3
SATISFIED (TAKE ME HIGHER)	AM:PM	66	30 Aug 97	1
Above hit: H2O.				

HUDDERSFIELD CHORAL SOCIETY   UK

ALBUMS:	**HITS 2**		**WEEKS 14**	
THE HYMNS ALBUM	His Master's Voice	8	15 Mar 86	10
Above hit: HUDDERSFIELD CHORAL SOCIETY conductor Owain Arwel HUGHES.				
THE CAROLS ALBUM	EMI	29	13 Dec 86	4

Al HUDSON   US

SINGLES:	**HITS 4**		**WEEKS 22**	
DANCE, GET DOWN (FEEL THE GROOVE) / HOW DO YOU DO	ABC	57	9 Sep 78	4

YOU CAN DO IT	MCA	15	15 Sep 79	10
Above hit: Al HUDSON and the PARTNERS.				
MUSIC	MCA	56	8 Dec 79	6
Above hit: ONE WAY featuring Al HUDSON.				
LET'S TALK ABOUT SHHHH	MCA	64	29 Jun 85	2
Sleeve reads as Let's Talk (Parts 1 & 2).				
Above hit: ONE WAY.				

Lavine HUDSON   UK

SINGLES:		HITS 1		WEEKS 3
INTERVENTION	Virgin	57	21 May 88	3

HUDSON-FORD   UK

(See also Monks.)

SINGLES:		HITS 3		WEEKS 20
PICK UP THE PIECES	A&M	8	18 Aug 73	9
BURN BABY BURN	A&M	15	16 Feb 74	9
FLOATING IN THE WIND	A&M	35	29 Jun 74	2

HUE and CRY   UK

SINGLES:		HITS 10		WEEKS 59
LABOUR OF LOVE	Circa	6	13 Jun 87	16
STRENGTH TO STRENGTH	Circa	46	19 Sep 87	5
I REFUSE	Circa	47	30 Jan 88	3
Original release reached No. 85 in 1987.				
ORDINARY ANGEL	Circa	42	22 Oct 88	6
LOOKING FOR LINDA	Circa	15	28 Jan 89	9
VIOLENTLY [EP]	Circa	21	6 May 89	6
Lead track: Violently.				
SWEET INVISIBILITY	Circa	55	30 Sep 89	3
MY SALT HEART	Circa	47	25 May 91	3
LONG TERM LOVERS OF PAIN [EP]	Circa	48	3 Aug 91	3
Lead track: Long Term Lovers Of Pain.				
PROFOUNDLY YOURS	Fidelity	74	11 Jul 92	1
LABOUR OF LOVE [RM]	Circa	25	13 Mar 93	4
Remixed by Dave Lee and Doc Livingstone.				
ALBUMS:		HITS 5		WEEKS 74
SEDUCED AND ABANDONED	Circa	22	7 Nov 87	11
REMOTE	Circa	10	10 Dec 88	40
REMOTE / THE BITTER SUITE [RE]	Circa	47	16 Dec 89	8
The Bitter Suite was a remix album listed from 10 Jan 90, sales were combined.				
STARS CRASH DOWN	Circa	10	29 Jun 91	9
TRUTH AND LOVE	Fidelity	33	29 Aug 92	2
LABOURS OF LOVE - THE BEST OF HUE AND CRY	Circa	27	10 Apr 93	4

HUES CORPORATION   US

SINGLES:		HITS 2		WEEKS 16
ROCK THE BOAT	RCA Victor	6	27 Jul 74	10
ROCKIN' SOUL	RCA Victor	24	19 Oct 74	6

HUFF   UK

SINGLES:		HITS 2		WEEKS 8
HELP ME MAKE IT	Skyway	31	2 Nov 96	2
Samples Gladys Knight's live version of Help Me Make It Through The Night.				
HELP ME MAKE IT THROUGH THE NIGHT [RM]	Skyway	37	21 Jun 97	2
Remixed by Rollo and Sister Bliss.				
Above 2: HUFF and PUFF.				
FEELING GOOD	Planet 3	31	6 Dec 97	3
FEELING GOOD 98 [RM]	Planet 3	69	7 Nov 98	1
Remixed by Curtis & Moore.				
Above 2: HUFF and HERB.				

HUGGY BEAR – See Andy G'S STARSKY and HUTCH ALLSTARS

David HUGHES with the Wally STOTT ORCHESTRA   UK

SINGLES:		HITS 1		WEEKS 1
BY THE FOUNTAINS OF ROME	Philips	27	22 Sep 56	1

Owain Arwel HUGHES – See HUDDERSFIELD CHORAL SOCIETY

HUGO and LUIGI their Orchestra and Children's Chorus   US

SINGLES:		HITS 1		WEEKS 2
LA PLUME DE MA TANTE	RCA	29	25 Jul 59	2

Alan HULL | | | | UK

ALBUMS:		HITS 1			WEEKS 3
PIPEDREAM		*Charisma*	29	*28 Jul 73*	3

HUMAN LEAGUE | | | | UK

SINGLES:		HITS 21			WEEKS 155
HOLIDAY 80 [EP]		*Virgin*	56	*3 May 80*	5
Double-pack single, lead track: Being Boiled.					
EMPIRE STATE HUMAN		*Virgin*	62	*21 Jun 80*	2
BOYS AND GIRLS		*Virgin*	48	*28 Feb 81*	4
THE SOUND OF THE CROWD		*Virgin*	12	*2 May 81*	10
LOVE ACTION (I BELIEVE IN LOVE)		*Virgin*	3	*8 Aug 81*	13
Above 2: HUMAN LEAGUE RED.					
OPEN YOUR HEART		*Virgin*	6	*10 Oct 81*	9
Above hit: HUMAN LEAGUE BLUE.					
DON'T YOU WANT ME		*Virgin*	1	*5 Dec 81*	13
First No.1 hit on the Virgin label.					
Above hit: HUMAN LEAGUE 100.					
BEING BOILED		*Fast Product*	6	*9 Jan 82*	9
Originally released in 1978.					
HOLIDAY 80 [EP] [RE]		*Virgin*	46	*6 Feb 82*	5
MIRROR MAN		*Virgin*	2	*20 Nov 82*	10
(KEEP FEELING) FASCINATION		*Virgin*	2	*23 Apr 83*	9
THE LEBANON		*Virgin*	11	*5 May 84*	6
THE LEBANON [RE]		*Virgin*	75	*23 Jun 84*	1
LIFE ON YOUR OWN		*Virgin*	16	*30 Jun 84*	6
LOUISE		*Virgin*	13	*17 Nov 84*	10
HUMAN		*Virgin*	8	*23 Aug 86*	8
I NEED YOUR LOVING		*Virgin*	72	*22 Nov 86*	1
Above hit: HUMAN LEAGUE RED.					
LOVE IS ALL THAT MATTERS		*Virgin*	41	*15 Oct 88*	5
HEART LIKE A WHEEL		*Virgin*	29	*18 Aug 90*	5
TELL ME WHEN		*East West*	6	*7 Jan 95*	9
ONE MAN IN MY HEART		*East West*	13	*18 Mar 95*	8
FILLING UP WITH HEAVEN		*East West*	36	*17 Jun 95*	2
DON'T YOU WANT ME [RM]		*Virgin*	16	*28 Oct 95*	3
Remixed by Red Jerry.					
STAY WITH ME TONIGHT		*East West*	40	*20 Jan 96*	2
ALBUMS:		HITS 9			WEEKS 258
TRAVELOGUE		*Virgin*	16	*31 May 80*	42
REPRODUCTION		*Virgin*	34	*22 Aug 81*	23
First released 1979. This is a mid-price re-issue.					
DARE		*Virgin*	1	*24 Oct 81*	71
LOVE AND DANCING		*Virgin*	3	*17 Jul 82*	52
Mini-album containing dance remixes from Dare.					
Above hit: LEAGUE UNLIMITED ORCHESTRA.					
HYSTERIA		*Virgin*	3	*19 May 84*	18
CRASH		*Virgin*	7	*20 Sep 86*	6
GREATEST HITS		*Virgin*	3	*12 Nov 88*	24
Includes re-entries during 1994/1995.					
ROMANTIC?		*Virgin*	24	*29 Sep 90*	2
OCTOPUS		*East West*	6	*4 Feb 95*	12
GREATEST HITS [RE]		*Virgin*	28	*11 Nov 95*	8
Repackaged with additional tracks.					

HUMAN NATURE | | | | Australia

SINGLES:		HITS 2			WEEKS 2
WISHES		*Epic*	44	*10 May 97*	1
WHISPER YOUR NAME		*Epic*	53	*30 Aug 97*	1

HUMAN RESOURCE | | | | Holland

SINGLES:		HITS 2			WEEKS 14
DOMINATOR		*R&S*	36	*14 Sep 91*	7
THE COMPLETE DOMINATOR [RM]		*R&S*	18	*21 Dec 91*	7
Remixed by Beltram.					

HUMANOID | | | | UK

SINGLES:		HITS 2			WEEKS 13
STAKKER HUMANOID		*Westside*	17	*26 Nov 88*	8
SLAM		*Westside*	54	*22 Apr 89*	2
STAKKER HUMANOID [RI]		*Jumpin' & Pumpin'*	40	*8 Aug 92*	3

HUMATE

				Germany
SINGLES:		**HITS 1**		**WEEKS 4**
LOVE SIMULATION	Deviant	18	30 Jan 99	4

Originally released in 1992.

HUMBLE PIE

				UK
SINGLES:		**HITS 1**		**WEEKS 10**
NATURAL BORN BUGIE	Immediate	4	23 Aug 69	10
ALBUMS:		**HITS 4**		**WEEKS 10**
AS SAFE AS YESTERDAY IS	Immediate	32	6 Sep 69	1
ROCKING AT THE FILLMORE	A&M	32	22 Jan 72	2
SMOKIN'	A&M	28	15 Apr 72	5
EAT IT	A&M	34	7 Apr 73	2

Engelbert HUMPERDINCK

				UK
SINGLES:		**HITS 15**		**WEEKS 238**
RELEASE ME	Decca	1	28 Jan 67	56

Originally recorded by Eddie Miller.

THERE GOES MY EVERYTHING	Decca	2	27 May 67	29

Originally recorded by Jack Greene.

THE LAST WALTZ	Decca	1	26 Aug 67	27
AM I THAT EASY TO FORGET	Decca	3	13 Jan 68	13

Originally recorded by Carl Belew.

A MAN WITHOUT LOVE	Decca	2	27 Apr 68	15
LES BICYCLETTES DE BELSIZE	Decca	5	28 Sep 68	15
THE WAY IT USED TO BE	Decca	3	8 Feb 69	14
I'M A BETTER MAN (FOR HAVING LOVED YOU)	Decca	15	9 Aug 69	13
WINTER WORLD OF LOVE	Decca	7	15 Nov 69	13
MY MARIE	Decca	31	30 May 70	7
SWEETHEART	Decca	22	12 Sep 70	6

Originally recorded by the Bee Gees.

SWEETHEART [RE]	Decca	50	31 Oct 70	1
ANOTHER TIME, ANOTHER PLACE	Decca	13	11 Sep 71	12
TOO BEAUTIFUL TO LAST	Decca	14	4 Mar 72	10

From the film 'Nicholas And Alexandra'.

LOVE IS ALL	Decca	44	20 Oct 73	3
LOVE IS ALL [RE]	Decca	45	17 Nov 73	1
QUANDO QUANDO QUANDO	The Hit Label	40	30 Jan 99	3
ALBUMS:		**HITS 12**		**WEEKS 239**
RELEASE ME	Decca	6	20 May 67	58
THE LAST WALTZ	Decca	3	25 Nov 67	33
A MAN WITHOUT LOVE	Decca	3	3 Aug 68	45
ENGELBERT	Decca	3	1 Mar 69	8
ENGELBERT HUMPERDINCK	Decca	5	6 Dec 69	23
WE MADE IT HAPPEN	Decca	17	11 Jul 70	11
ANOTHER TIME, ANOTHER PLACE	Decca	48	18 Sep 71	1
LIVE AT THE RIVIERA LAS VEGAS	Decca	45	26 Feb 72	1
ENGELBERT HUMPERDINCK – HIS GREATEST HITS	Decca	1	21 Dec 74	34
GETTING SENTIMENTAL	Telstar	35	4 May 85	10
THE ENGELBERT HUMPERDINCK COLLECTION	Telstar	35	4 Apr 87	9
LOVE UNCHAINED	EMI	16	10 Jun 95	6

Peter HUNNINGDALE – See ARSENAL F.C.

Geraldine HUNT

				Canada
SINGLES:		**HITS 1**		**WEEKS 5**
CAN'T FAKE THE FEELING	Champagne	44	25 Oct 80	5

Lisa HUNT – See LOVESTATION

Marsha HUNT

				US
SINGLES:		**HITS 2**		**WEEKS 3**
WALK ON GILDED SPLINTERS	Track	46	24 May 69	2

Originally recorded by Dr John.

KEEP THE CUSTOMER SATISFIED	Track	41	2 May 70	1

Originally recorded by Simon and Garfunkel.

Tommy HUNT

				US
SINGLES:		**HITS 3**		**WEEKS 17**
CRACKIN' UP	Spark	39	11 Oct 75	5
LOVING ON THE LOSING SIDE	Spark	28	21 Aug 76	9
ONE FINE MORNING	Spark	44	4 Dec 76	3

HUNTER featuring Ruby TURNER · UK

(See also Ruby Turner.)

SINGLES:	HITS 1			WEEKS 1
SHAKABOOM!	Telstar	64	9 Dec 95	1

Featured on 'Junior Gladiators' on TV's 'Scratchy And Co.'.

Alfonzo HUNTER · US

SINGLES:	HITS 1			WEEKS 2
JUST THE WAY	Cooltempo	38	22 Feb 97	2

Ian HUNTER · UK

SINGLES:	HITS 1			WEEKS 10
ONCE BITTEN TWICE SHY	CBS	14	3 May 75	10
ALBUMS:	HITS 5			WEEKS 26
IAN HUNTER	CBS	21	12 Apr 75	15
ALL AMERICAN ALIEN BOY	CBS	29	29 May 76	4
YOU'RE NEVER ALONE WITH A SCHIZOPHRENIC	Chrysalis	49	5 May 79	3
WELCOME TO THE CLUB	Chrysalis	61	26 Apr 80	2
SHORT BACK 'N' SIDES	Chrysalis	79	29 Aug 81	2

Tab HUNTER · US

SINGLES:	HITS 2			WEEKS 30
YOUNG LOVE	London	1	9 Feb 57	18

Originally recorded by Ric Cartey.
Above hit: Tab HUNTER with Billy VAUGHN's ORCHESTRA and Chorus.

NINETY-NINE WAYS	London	5	13 Apr 57	11

Originally recorded by Charlie Gracie.
Above hit: Tab HUNTER with Billy VAUGHN's ORCHESTRA.

NINETY-NINE WAYS [RE]	London	29	6 Jul 57	1

Terry HUNTER · US

SINGLES:	HITS 1			WEEKS 1
HARVEST FOR THE WORLD	Delirious	48	26 Jul 97	1

Lead vocals: Curtis Harmon. Additional vocals: Paul Johnson.

HUNTERS - See Dave SAMPSON and the HUNTERS

Steve 'Silk' HURLEY · US

SINGLES:	HITS 1			WEEKS 9
JACK YOUR BODY	London	1	10 Jan 87	9

HURRAH! · UK

ALBUMS:	HITS 1			WEEKS 1
TELL GOD I'M HERE	Kitchenware	71	28 Feb 87	1

HURRICANE G - See PUFF DADDY

HURRICANE #1 · UK

SINGLES:	HITS 6			WEEKS 17
STEP INTO MY WORLD	Creation	29	10 May 97	2
JUST ANOTHER ILLUSION	Creation	35	5 Jul 97	2
CHAIN REACTION	Creation	30	6 Sep 97	2
STEP INTO MY WORLD [RM]	Creation	19	1 Nov 97	3

Remixed by Paul Oakenfold and Steve Osbourne.

ONLY THE STRONGEST SURVIVE	Creation	19	21 Feb 98	6
RISING SIGN	Creation	47	24 Oct 98	1
THE GREATEST HIGH	Creation	43	3 Apr 99	1
ALBUMS:	HITS 2			WEEKS 3
HURRICANE #1	Creation	11	27 Sep 97	2
ONLY THE STRONG SURVIVE	Creation	55	1 May 99	1

Phil HURTT · US

SINGLES:	HITS 1			WEEKS 5
GIVING IT BACK	Fantasy	36	11 Nov 78	5

HUSKER DU · US

ALBUMS:	HITS 1			WEEKS 1
WAREHOUSE: SONGS AND STORIES	Warner Brothers	72	14 Feb 87	1

HUSTLERS CONVENTION featuring Dave LAUDAT and Ondrea DUVERNEY — UK

SINGLES:	HITS 1			WEEKS 1
THE 'DANCE' TO THE MUSIC [EP]	Stress	71	20 May 95	1
Lead track: Dance To The Music.				

Willie HUTCH — US

SINGLES:	HITS 2			WEEKS 8
IN AND OUT	Motown	51	4 Dec 82	7
KEEP ON JAMMIN'	Motown	73	6 Jul 85	1

June HUTTON and Axel STORDAHL with the BOYS NEXT DOOR and the STORDAHL ORCHESTRA — US

SINGLES:	HITS 1			WEEKS 7
SAY YOU'RE MINE AGAIN	Capitol	10	8 Aug 53	3
SAY YOU'RE MINE AGAIN [RE]	Capitol	6	5 Sep 53	4

HYBRID — UK

SINGLES:	HITS 2			WEEKS 2
FINISHED SYMPHONY	Distinct'ive	58	10 Jul 99	1
All orchestral parts performed by the Russian Federal Orchestra.				
IF I SURVIVE	Distinct'ive	52	11 Sep 99	1
Above hit: HYBRID featuring Julee CRUISE.				

ALBUMS:	HITS 1			WEEKS 1
WIDE ANGLE	Distinct'ive	45	25 Sep 99	1

Brian HYLAND — US

SINGLES:	HITS 6			WEEKS 72
ITSY BITSY TEENIE WEENIE YELLOW POLKADOT BIKINI	London	8	9 Jul 60	13
Spoken female voice is Trudy Packer.				
FOUR LITTLE HEELS	London	29	22 Oct 60	6
GINNY COME LATELY	His Master's Voice	5	12 May 62	15
SEALED WITH A KISS	His Master's Voice	3	4 Aug 62	15
WARMED OVER KISSES (LEFT OVER LOVE)	His Master's Voice	28	10 Nov 62	6
GYPSY WOMAN	Uni	45	27 Mar 71	1
GYPSY WOMAN [RE]	Uni	42	10 Apr 71	5
SEALED WITH A KISS [RI]	ABC	7	28 Jun 75	11

Sheila HYLTON — Jamaica

SINGLES:	HITS 2			WEEKS 12
BREAKFAST IN BED	Ballistic	57	15 Sep 79	5
THE BED'S TOO BIG WITHOUT YOU	Island	35	17 Jan 81	7

Unforgettable Sound of the Dick HYMAN TRIO — US

SINGLES:	HITS 1			WEEKS 10
THEME FROM "THE THREEPENNY OPERA"	MGM	9	17 Mar 56	10

Phyllis HYMAN — US

SINGLES:	HITS 2			WEEKS 9
YOU KNOW HOW TO LOVE ME	Arista	47	16 Feb 80	6
YOU SURE LOOK GOOD TO ME	Arista	56	12 Sep 81	3

ALBUMS:	HITS 1			WEEKS 1
LIVING ALL ALONE	Philadelphia International	97	20 Sep 86	1

Chrissie HYNDE - See CHER, Chrissie HYNDE and Neneh CHERRY with Eric CLAPTON; MOODSWINGS features the voice of Chrissie HYNDE; UB40

HYPER GO-GO — UK

SINGLES:	HITS 5			WEEKS 15
HIGH	Deconstruction	30	22 Aug 92	5
NEVER LET GO	Positiva	45	31 Jul 93	3
RAISE	Positiva	36	5 Feb 94	2
IT'S ALRIGHT	Positiva	49	26 Nov 94	1
DO WATCHA DO	Avex UK	54	6 Apr 96	1
Above hit: HYPER GO GO and ADEVA.				
HIGH [RM]	Distinct'ive	32	12 Oct 96	2
Remixed by Rhythm Masters.				
DO WATCHA DO [RM]	Distinct'ive	60	12 Apr 97	1
Remixed by K-Klass.				
Above hit: HYPER GO GO and ADEVA.				

HYPERLOGIC — UK

SINGLES:	HITS 1			WEEKS 3
ONLY ME	Systematic	35	29 Jul 95	2
Samples New Year's Day by U2 and Sleep Talk by Alyson Williams.				

| ONLY ME [RM] | Tidy Trax | 48 | 9 May 98 | 1 |
| *Remixed by Red Vinyl.* | | | | |

HYPERSTATE featuring Janey Lee GRACE   UK

SINGLES:	HITS 1		WEEKS 1	
TIME AFTER TIME	M&G	71	6 Feb 93	1
Janey Lee Grace was only credited on the back of the sleeve and not on the chart.				

HYPNOSIS   UK

(See also Blowing Free; Harmonium; In Tune; Raindance; School Of Excellence.)

ALBUMS:	HITS 2		WEEKS 16	
VOICES OF TRANQUILITY	Dino	16	17 Aug 96	12
VOICES OF TRANQUILITY - VOLUME 2	Dino	32	15 Mar 97	4

HYPNOTIST   UK

SINGLES:	HITS 2		WEEKS 5	
THE HOUSE IS MINE	Rising High	65	28 Sep 91	2
THE HARDCORE [EP]	Rising High	68	21 Dec 91	3
Lead track: Hardcore U Know The Score.				

HYSTERIC EGO   UK

SINGLES:	HITS 3		WEEKS 8	
WANT LOVE	WEA	28	31 Aug 96	4
MINISTRY OF LOVE	WEA	39	21 Jun 97	2
WANT LOVE - THE REMIXES [RM]	WEA	46	28 Feb 98	1
Remixed by the Timewriter.				
TIME TO GET BACK	WEA	50	13 Feb 99	1
Samples N-Joi's Adrenalin.				

HYSTERICS   UK

SINGLES:	HITS 1		WEEKS 5	
JINGLE BELLS LAUGHING ALL THE WAY (OVER THE RAINBOW MUSIC)	Recorded Delivery	44	12 Dec 81	5

HYSTERIX   UK

SINGLES:	HITS 2		WEEKS 4	
MUST BE THE MUSIC	Deconstruction	40	7 May 94	3
EVERYTHING	Deconstruction	65	18 Feb 95	1

I

I-LEVEL   UK

SINGLES:	HITS 2		WEEKS 9	
MINEFIELD	Virgin	52	16 Apr 83	6
TEACHER	Virgin	56	18 Jun 83	3
ALBUMS:	HITS 1		WEEKS 4	
I-LEVEL	Virgin	50	9 Jul 83	4

IAN and the BLOCKHEADS - See Ian DURY and the BLOCKHEADS

Janis IAN   US

SINGLES:	HITS 2		WEEKS 10	
FLY TOO HIGH	CBS	44	17 Nov 79	7
THE OTHER SIDE OF THE SUN	CBS	44	28 Jun 80	3

ICE CUBE   US

(See also Scarface.)

SINGLES:	HITS 9		WEEKS 23	
IT WAS A GOOD DAY	Fourth & Broadway	27	27 Mar 93	4
CHECK YO SELF	Fourth & Broadway	36	7 Aug 93	4
Above hit: ICE CUBE featuring DAS EFX.				
WICKED	Fourth & Broadway	62	11 Sep 93	1
REALLY DOE	Fourth & Broadway	66	18 Dec 93	1
YOU KNOW HOW WE DO IT	Fourth & Broadway	41	26 Mar 94	3
BOP GUN (ONE NATION)	Fourth & Broadway	22	27 Aug 94	3
Samples Funkadelic's One Nation Under A Groove.				
Above hit: ICE CUBE featuring George CLINTON.				
YOU KNOW HOW WE DO IT [RE]	Fourth & Broadway	46	24 Dec 94	2
HAND OF THE DEAD BODY	Virgin	41	11 Mar 95	2
Above hit: SCARFACE (featuring ICE CUBE).				
NATURAL BORN KILLAZ	Death Row	45	15 Apr 95	2
From the film 'Murder Was The Case'.				
Above hit: DR. DRE and ICE CUBE.				

THE WORLD IS MINE	Jive	60	22 Mar 97	1

From the film 'Dangerous Ground'.

ALBUMS:		HITS 4		WEEKS 10
AMERIKKKA'S MOST WANTED	Fourth & Broadway	48	28 Jul 90	5
KILL AT WILL	Fourth & Broadway	66	9 Mar 91	3
THE PREDATOR	Fourth & Broadway	73	5 Dec 92	1
LETHAL INJECTION	Fourth & Broadway	52	18 Dec 93	1

ICE MC   UK

SINGLES:		HITS 2		WEEKS 5
THINK ABOUT THE WAY (BOM DIGI DIGI BOM . . .)	WEA	42	6 Aug 94	2

Features German vocalist Jasmine.

IT'S A RAINY DAY	Eternal	73	8 Apr 95	1
BOM DIGI BOM (THINK ABOUT THE WAY) [RI]	Eternal	38	14 Sep 96	2

From the film 'Trainspotting'.

ICE-T   US

SINGLES:		HITS 9		WEEKS 29
HIGH ROLLERS	Sire	63	18 Mar 89	2
YOU PLAYED YOURSELF	Sire	64	17 Feb 90	2
SUPERFLY 1990	Capitol	48	29 Sep 90	3

Above hit: Curtis MAYFIELD and ICE-T.

I AIN'T NEW TA THIS	Rhyme Syndicate	62	8 May 93	2
THAT'S HOW I'M LIVIN'	Rhyme Syndicate	21	18 Dec 93	6
GOTTA LOTTA LOVE	Rhyme Syndicate	24	9 Apr 94	4

Samples Mike Oldfield's Tubular Bells.

BORN TO RAISE HELL	Fox	47	10 Dec 94	2

From the film 'Airheads'.
Above hit: MOTORHEAD with ICE-T and Whitfield CRANE.

I MUST STAND	Rhyme Syndicate	23	1 Jun 96	3

Samples Portishead's Numb.

THE LANE	Rhyme Syndicate	18	7 Dec 96	5

Samples Jean Jaques Perry's Eva.

ALBUMS:		HITS 4		WEEKS 15
THE ICEBERG/FREEDOM OF SPEECH	Sire	42	21 Oct 89	2
O.G. ORIGINAL GANGSTER	Sire	38	25 May 91	4
HOME INVASION	Rhyme Syndicate	15	3 Apr 93	7
VI: RETURN OF THE REAL	Rhyme Syndicate	26	8 Jun 96	2

ICEHOUSE   New Zealand/Australia/UK

SINGLES:		HITS 5		WEEKS 28
HEY LITTLE GIRL	Chrysalis	17	5 Feb 83	10
STREET CAFE	Chrysalis	62	23 Apr 83	4
NO PROMISES	Chrysalis	72	3 May 86	1
CRAZY	Chrysalis	74	29 Aug 87	1
CRAZY [RE]	Chrysalis	38	13 Feb 88	8
ELECTRIC BLUE	Chrysalis	53	14 May 88	4
ALBUMS:		HITS 2		WEEKS 7
LOVE IN MOTION	Chrysalis	64	5 Mar 83	6
MAN OF COLOURS	Chrysalis	93	2 Apr 88	1

ICICLE WORKS   UK

SINGLES:		HITS 7		WEEKS 28
LOVE IS SUCH A WONDERFUL COLOUR	Beggars Banquet	15	24 Dec 83	8
BIRDS FLY (WHISPER TO A SCREAM) / IN THE CAULDRON OF LOVE	Beggars Banquet	53	10 Mar 84	4

Original release reached No. 90 in 1983.

UNDERSTANDING JANE	Beggars Banquet	52	26 Jul 86	3
WHO DO YOU WANT FOR YOUR LOVE?	Beggars Banquet	54	4 Oct 86	4
EVANGELINE	Beggars Banquet	53	14 Feb 87	4
LITTLE GIRL LOST	Beggars Banquet	59	30 Apr 88	4
MOTORCYCLE RIDER	Epic	73	17 Mar 90	1
ALBUMS:		HITS 6		WEEKS 19
THE ICICLE WORKS	Beggars Banquet	24	31 Mar 84	6
THE SMALL PRICE OF A BICYCLE	Beggars Banquet	55	28 Sep 85	3
SEVEN SINGLES DEEP	Beggars Banquet	52	1 Mar 86	2
IF YOU WANT TO DEFEAT YOUR ENEMY SING HIS SONG	Beggars Banquet	28	21 Mar 87	4
BLIND	Beggars Banquet	40	14 May 88	3
THE BEST OF THE ICICLE WORKS	Beggars Banquet	60	5 Sep 92	1

ICON   UK

SINGLES:		HITS 1		WEEKS 1
TAINTED LOVE	Eternal	51	15 Jun 96	1

IDEAL · UK

SINGLES:	HITS 1			WEEKS 2
HOT	Cleveland City	49	6 Aug 94	2

IDES OF MARCH · US

SINGLES:	HITS 1			WEEKS 9
VEHICLE	Warner Brothers	31	6 Jun 70	9

Eric IDLE featuring Richard WILSON · UK

SINGLES:	HITS 1			WEEKS 3
ONE FOOT IN THE GRAVE	Victa	50	17 Dec 94	3

Dance mix of the theme from the BBC1 TV sitcom of the same name. Originally released in 1990.

IDLEWILD · UK

SINGLES:	HITS 5			WEEKS 7
A FILM FOR THE FUTURE	Food	53	9 May 98	1
EVERYONE SAYS YOU'RE SO FRAGILE	Food	47	25 Jul 98	1
I'M A MESSAGE	Food	41	24 Oct 98	1
WHEN I ARGUE I SEE SHAPES	Food	19	13 Feb 99	2
LITTLE DISCOURAGE	Food	24	2 Oct 99	2
ALBUMS:	HITS 1			WEEKS 1
HOPE IS IMPORTANT	Food	53	7 Nov 98	1

Billy IDOL · UK

SINGLES:	HITS 15			WEEKS 106
HOT IN THE CITY	Chrysalis	58	11 Sep 82	4
REBEL YELL	Chrysalis	62	24 Mar 84	2
EYES WITHOUT A FACE	Chrysalis	18	30 Jun 84	11
FLESH FOR FANTASY	Chrysalis	54	29 Sep 84	3
WHITE WEDDING	Chrysalis	6	13 Jul 85	15
REBEL YELL [RI]	Chrysalis	6	14 Sep 85	12
TO BE A LOVER	Chrysalis	22	4 Oct 86	8

Originally recorded by William Bell as I Forgot To Be Your Lover.

DON'T NEED A GUN	Chrysalis	26	7 Mar 87	5
SWEET SIXTEEN	Chrysalis	17	13 Jun 87	9
MONY MONY (LIVE)	Chrysalis	7	3 Oct 87	10
HOT IN THE CITY (EXTERMINATOR FIX) [RM]	Chrysalis	13	16 Jan 88	9
CATCH MY FALL	Chrysalis	63	13 Aug 88	3
CRADLE OF LOVE	Chrysalis	34	28 Apr 90	4
L.A. WOMAN	Chrysalis	70	11 Aug 90	2
PRODIGAL BLUES	Chrysalis	47	22 Dec 90	4
SHOCK TO THE SYSTEM	Chrysalis	30	26 Jun 93	3
SPEED	Fox	47	10 Sep 94	2

From the film of the same name.

ALBUMS:	HITS 6			WEEKS 100
VITAL IDOL	Chrysalis	7	8 Jun 85	34

Compilation.

REBEL YELL	Chrysalis	36	28 Sep 85	11
WHIPLASH SMILE	Chrysalis	8	1 Nov 86	20
IDOL SONGS: 11 OF THE BEST	Chrysalis	2	2 Jul 88	25
CHARMED LIFE	Chrysalis	15	12 May 90	8
CYBERPUNK	Chrysalis	20	10 Jul 93	2

Frank IFIELD · UK

SINGLES:	HITS 16			WEEKS 163
LUCKY DEVIL	Columbia	22	20 Feb 60	6
LUCKY DEVIL [RE]	Columbia	33	9 Apr 60	2
GOTTA GET A DATE	Columbia	49	1 Oct 60	1
I REMEMBER YOU	Columbia	1	7 Jul 62	28

Song was originally from the 1942 film 'The Fleet's In'. Originally recorded by Jimmy Dorsey in 1942.

LOVESICK BLUES	Columbia	1	27 Oct 62	17

Originally recorded by Elsie Clark in 1922.

THE WAYWARD WIND	Columbia	1	26 Jan 63	13

Above 2: Frank IFIELD with Norrie PARAMOR and his Orchestra.

NOBODY'S DARLIN' BUT MINE	Columbia	4	13 Apr 63	16
CONFESSIN' (THAT I LOVE YOU)	Columbia	1	29 Jun 63	16
MULE TRAIN	Columbia	22	19 Oct 63	6
DON'T BLAME ME	Columbia	8	11 Jan 64	13

Originally recorded by Ethel Waters in 1933.
Above hit: Frank IFIELD with Norrie PARAMOR and his Orchestra.

ANGRY AT THE BIG OAK TREE	Columbia	25	25 Apr 64	8
I SHOULD CARE	Columbia	33	25 Jul 64	3

SUMMER IS OVER	*Columbia*	25	*3 Oct 64*	6
PARADISE	*Columbia*	26	*21 Aug 65*	9
NO ONE WILL EVER KNOW	*Columbia*	25	*25 Jun 66*	4
CALL HER YOUR SWEETHEART	*Columbia*	24	*10 Dec 66*	11
THE YODELING SONG	*EMI*	40	*7 Dec 91*	4

Originally the B-side of Lovesick Blues.
Above hit: Frank IFIELD featuring the BACKROOM BOYS.

EPS:	**HITS 6**			**WEEKS 103**
FRANK IFIELD'S HITS	*Columbia*	1	*8 Dec 62*	59
MORE OF FRANK IFIELD'S HITS	*Columbia*	4	*22 Jun 63*	15
JUST ONE MORE CHANCE	*Columbia*	5	*21 Sep 63*	13
VIVA IFIELD	*Columbia*	11	*12 Oct 63*	11
PLEASE	*Columbia*	18	*25 Jan 64*	3
DON'T BLAME ME	*Columbia*	19	*18 Apr 64*	2

ALBUMS:	**HITS 4**			**WEEKS 83**
I'LL REMEMBER YOU	*Columbia*	3	*16 Feb 63*	36
BORN FREE	*Columbia*	3	*21 Sep 63*	32
BLUE SKIES	*Columbia*	10	*28 Mar 64*	12
GREATEST HITS	*Columbia*	9	*19 Dec 64*	3

IGGY and the STOOGES – See Iggy POP

Enrique IGLESIAS   Spain

SINGLES:	**HITS 2**			**WEEKS 11**
BAILAMOS	*Interscope*	4	*11 Sep 99*	9

From the film 'Wild Wild West'.

RHYTHM DIVINE	*Interscope*	45	*18 Dec 99*	2

Julio IGLESIAS   Spain

SINGLES:	**HITS 9**			**WEEKS 75**
BEGIN THE BEGUINE (VOLVER A EMPEZAR)	*CBS*	1	*24 Oct 81*	14

Written by Cole Porter.

QUIEREME MUCHO (YOURS)	*CBS*	3	*6 Mar 82*	9
AMOR	*CBS*	32	*9 Oct 82*	7
HEY!	*CBS*	31	*9 Apr 83*	7
TO ALL THE GIRLS I'VE LOVED BEFORE	*CBS*	17	*7 Apr 84*	10

Originally recorded by Albert Hammond.
Above hit: Julio IGLESIAS and Willie NELSON.

ALL OF YOU	*CBS*	43	*7 Jul 84*	8

Above hit: Julio IGLESIAS and Diana ROSS.

MY LOVE	*CBS*	5	*6 Aug 88*	11

Above hit: Julio IGLESIAS featuring Stevie WONDER.

CRAZY	*Columbia*	43	*4 Jun 94*	3
CRAZY [RE]	*Columbia*	50	*27 Aug 94*	2
FRAGILE	*Columbia*	53	*26 Nov 94*	2

Backing vocals by Sting.

FRAGILE [RE]	*Columbia*	66	*31 Dec 94*	2

ALBUMS:	**HITS 12**			**WEEKS 171**
DE NINA A MUJER	*CBS*	43	*7 Nov 81*	5
BEGIN THE BEGUINE	*CBS*	5	*28 Nov 81*	28
AMOR	*CBS*	14	*16 Oct 82*	14
JULIO	*CBS*	5	*2 Jul 83*	17
1100 BEL AIR PLACE	*CBS*	14	*1 Sep 84*	14
LIBRA	*CBS*	61	*19 Oct 85*	4
NON STOP	*CBS*	33	*3 Sep 88*	14
STARRY NIGHT	*CBS*	27	*1 Dec 90*	20
CRAZY	*Columbia*	6	*28 May 94*	37
LA CARRETERA	*Columbia*	6	*12 Aug 95*	6
TANGO	*Columbia*	56	*30 Nov 96*	3
MY LIFE: THE GREATEST HITS	*Columbia*	18	*7 Nov 98*	9

IGNORANTS   UK

SINGLES:	**HITS 1**			**WEEKS 3**
PHAT GIRLS	*Spaghetti*	59	*25 Dec 93*	3

ILLEGAL MOTION featuring Simone CHAPMAN   UK

SINGLES:	**HITS 1**			**WEEKS 1**
SATURDAY LOVE	*Arista*	67	*9 Oct 93*	1

IMAANI   UK

SINGLES:	**HITS 1**			**WEEKS 7**
WHERE ARE YOU	*EMI*	15	*9 May 98*	7

UK's Eurovision entry in 1998, it came 2nd.

IMAGINATION

					UK
SINGLES:		**HITS 12**			**WEEKS 105**
BODY TALK	R&B	4	16 May 81	18	
IN AND OUT OF LOVE	R&B	16	5 Sep 81	9	
FLASHBACK	R&B	16	14 Nov 81	13	
JUST AN ILLUSION	R&B	2	6 Mar 82	11	
MUSIC AND LIGHTS	R&B	5	26 Jun 82	9	
IN THE HEAT OF THE NIGHT	R&B	22	25 Sep 82	8	
CHANGES	R&S	31	11 Dec 82	8	
LOOKING AT MIDNIGHT	R&B	29	4 Jun 83	7	
NEW DIMENSION	R&B	56	5 Nov 83	3	
STATE OF LOVE	R&B	67	26 May 84	2	
THANK YOU MY LOVE	R&B	22	24 Nov 84	15	
INSTINCTUAL	RCA	62	16 Jan 88	2	
ALBUMS:		**HITS 5**			**WEEKS 122**
BODY TALK	R&B	20	24 Oct 81	53	
Peak position reached on 10 Apr 82.					
IN THE HEAT OF THE NIGHT	R&B	7	11 Sep 82	29	
NIGHT DUBBING	R&M	9	14 May 83	20	
SCANDALOUS	R&B	25	12 Nov 83	8	
IMAGINATION - ALL THE HITS	Stylus	4	12 Aug 89	12	

IMAGINATIONS - See Mari WILSON

IMAJIN

					US
SINGLES:		**HITS 3**			**WEEKS 6**
SHORTY (YOU KEEP PLAYIN' WITH MY MIND)	Jive	22	27 Jun 98	3	
Above hit: IMAJIN featuring Keith MURRAY.					
NO DOUBT	Jive	42	20 Feb 99	2	
Samples the Spinners It's A Natural Affair.					
BOUNCE, ROCK, SKATE, ROLL	Jive	45	24 Apr 99	1	
Above hit: BABY DC featuring IMAJIN.					

Natalie IMBRUGLIA

					Australia
SINGLES:		**HITS 4**			**WEEKS 39**
TORN	RCA	2	8 Nov 97	17	
Originally recorded by Trena Rayne.					
BIG MISTAKE	RCA	2	14 Mar 98	10	
WISHING I WAS HERE	RCA	19	6 Jun 98	5	
SMOKE	RCA	5	17 Oct 98	7	
ALBUMS:		**HITS 1**			**WEEKS 81**
LEFT OF THE MIDDLE	RCA	5	6 Dec 97	81	

IMMACULATE FOOLS

					UK
SINGLES:		**HITS 1**			**WEEKS 4**
IMMACULATE FOOLS	A&M	51	26 Jan 85	4	
ALBUMS:		**HITS 1**			**WEEKS 2**
HEARTS OF FORTUNE	A&M	65	11 May 85	2	

IMMATURE (featuring SMOOTH)

					US
SINGLES:		**HITS 1**			**WEEKS 2**
WE GOT IT	MCA	26	16 Mar 96	2	

IMPALAS

					US
SINGLES:		**HITS 1**			**WEEKS 1**
SORRY (I RAN ALL THE WAY HOME)	MGM	28	22 Aug 59	1	

IMPEDANCE

					UK
SINGLES:		**HITS 1**			**WEEKS 4**
TAINTED LOVE	Jumpin' & Pumpin'	54	11 Nov 89	4	

Carlo IMPERATO and "the WATERS" - See KIDS FROM "FAME"

IMPERIAL DRAG

					UK
SINGLES:		**HITS 1**			**WEEKS 1**
BOY OR A GIRL	Columbia	54	12 Oct 96	1	

IMPERIAL TEEN

					US
SINGLES:		**HITS 1**			**WEEKS 1**
YOU'RE ONE	Slash	69	7 Sep 96	1	

IMPERIALS - See LITTLE ANTHONY and the IMPERIALS

IMPERIALS QUARTET - See Elvis PRESLEY

IMPOSTER - See Elvis COSTELLO and the ATTRACTIONS

IMPRESSIONS US

SINGLES:	HITS 1			WEEKS 10
FIRST IMPRESSIONS	*Curtom*	16	*22 Nov 75*	10

IN CROWD UK

SINGLES:	HITS 1			WEEKS 1
THAT'S HOW STRONG MY LOVE IS	*Parlophone*	48	*22 May 65*	1

IN FULL ROCK-A-PHONIC SOUND - See COLUMBO presents IN FULL ROCK-A-PHONIC SOUND featuring OOE

IN TUA NUA Ireland

SINGLES:	HITS 1			WEEKS 2
ALL I WANTED	*Virgin*	69	*14 May 88*	2

IN TUNE UK

(See also Blowing Free; Harmonium; Hypnosis; Raindance; School Of Excellence.)

ALBUMS:	HITS 1			WEEKS 3
ACOUSTIC MOODS	*Global Television*	21	*17 Jun 95*	3

INAURA UK

SINGLES:	HITS 1			WEEKS 1
COMA AROMA	*EMI*	57	*18 May 96*	1

INCANTATION UK

SINGLES:	HITS 1			WEEKS 12
CACHARPAYA (ANDES PUMPSA DESI)	*Beggars Banquet*	12	*4 Dec 82*	12
ALBUMS:	**HITS 3**			**WEEKS 52**
CACHARPAYA (PANPIPES OF THE ANDES)	*Beggars Banquet*	9	*11 Dec 82*	26
DANCE OF THE FLAMES	*Beggars Banquet*	61	*17 Dec 83*	7
THE BEST OF INCANTATION: MUSIC FROM THE ANDES	*West Five*	28	*28 Dec 85*	19

INCOGNITO UK

SINGLES:	HITS 13			WEEKS 38
PARISIENNE GIRL	*Ensign*	73	*15 Nov 80*	2
ALWAYS THERE	*Talkin Loud*	6	*29 Jun 91*	9
Originally recorded by Ronnie Laws.				
Above hit: INCOGNITO featuring Jocelyn BROWN.				
CRAZY FOR YOU	*Talkin Loud*	59	*14 Sep 91*	2
Above hit: INCOGNITO featuring CHYNA.				
DON'T YOU WORRY 'BOUT A THING	*Talkin Loud*	19	*6 Jun 92*	6
Originally recorded by Stevie Wonder.				
CHANGE	*Talkin Loud*	52	*15 Aug 92*	2
STILL A FRIEND OF MINE	*Talkin Loud*	47	*21 Aug 93*	2
GIVIN' IT UP	*Talkin Loud*	43	*20 Nov 93*	2
PIECES OF A DREAM	*Talkin Loud*	35	*12 Mar 94*	2
EVERYDAY	*Talkin Loud*	23	*27 May 95*	3
Vocals by Pamela Anderson (cousin of Carleen Anderson).				
I HEAR YOUR NAME	*Talkin Loud*	42	*5 Aug 95*	3
JUMP TO MY LOVE / ALWAYS THERE [RR]	*Talkin Loud*	29	*11 May 96*	3
OUT OF THE STORM	*Talkin Loud*	57	*26 Oct 96*	1
NIGHTS OVER EGYPT	*Talkin Loud*	56	*10 Apr 99*	1
Originally recorded by the Jones Girls in 1981.				
ALBUMS:	**HITS 6**			**WEEKS 19**
JAZZ FUNK	*Ensign*	28	*18 Apr 81*	8
INSIDE LIFE	*Talkin Loud*	44	*27 Jul 91*	2
TRIBES, VIBES AND SCRIBES	*Talkin Loud*	41	*4 Jul 92*	2
POSITIVITY	*Talkin Loud*	55	*6 Nov 93*	2
100 DEGREES AND RISING	*Talkin Loud*	11	*17 Jun 95*	4
REMIXED	*Talkin Loud*	56	*1 Jun 96*	1

INCREDIBLE STRING BAND UK

ALBUMS:	HITS 7			WEEKS 37
5,000 SPIRITS OR THE LAYERS OF THE ONION	*Elektra*	25	*21 Oct 67*	5
THE HANGMAN'S BEAUTIFUL DAUGHTER	*Elektra*	5	*6 Apr 68*	21
THE INCREDIBLE STRING BAND	*Elektra*	34	*20 Jul 68*	3
Originally issued in 1966.				
CHANGING HORSES	*Elektra*	30	*24 Jan 70*	1
I LOOKED UP	*Elektra*	30	*9 May 70*	4
U	*Elektra*	34	*31 Oct 70*	2
LIQUID ACROBAT AS REGARDS THE AIR	*Island*	46	*30 Oct 71*	1

INDEEP | US

SINGLES:	HITS 2		WEEKS 11	
LAST NIGHT A D.J. SAVED MY LIFE	Sound Of New York	13	22 Jan 83	9
WHEN BOYS TALK	Sound Of New York	67	14 May 83	2

INDIA – See MASTERS AT WORK present INDIA; NUYORICAN SOUL; Tito PUENTO Jr. and the LATIN RHYTHM featuring Tito PUENTE, INDIA and Cali ALEMAN; RIVER OCEAN featuring INDIA

INDIAN VIBES | UK

SINGLES:	HITS 1		WEEKS 2	
MATHAR	Virgin	68	24 Sep 94	1
Original version by the Dave Pike Set.				
MATHAR [RI]	VC Recordings	52	2 May 98	1

INDIGO GIRLS | US

ALBUMS:	HITS 2		WEEKS 3	
SWAMP OPHELIA	Epic	66	11 Jun 94	1
4.5 THE BEST OF THE INDIGO GIRLS	Epic	43	15 Jul 95	2

Count INDIGO | UK

SINGLES:	HITS 1		WEEKS 1	
MY UNKNOWN LOVE	Cowboy	59	9 Mar 96	1

Los INDIOS TABAJARAS | Brazil

SINGLES:	HITS 1		WEEKS 17	
MARIA ELENA	RCA Victor	5	2 Nov 63	17

INDO | US

SINGLES:	HITS 1		WEEKS 3	
R U SLEEPING	Satellite	31	18 Apr 98	3
Original release reached No. 130 in 1996.				

INDUSTRY STANDARD | UK

SINGLES:	HITS 1		WEEKS 3	
INDUSTRY STANDARD VOL. 1 (WHAT YOU WANT)	Satellite	34	10 Jan 98	3

INFA RIOT | UK

ALBUMS:	HITS 1		WEEKS 4	
STILL OUT OF ORDER	Secret	42	7 Aug 82	4

INFINITI featuring GRAND PUBA | US

SINGLES:	HITS 1		WEEKS 1	
WILL YOU BE MY BABY?	GHQ	53	30 Mar 96	1

INGRAM | US

SINGLES:	HITS 1		WEEKS 2	
SMOOTHIN' GROOVIN'	Streetwave	56	11 Jun 83	2

James INGRAM | US

(See also Quincy Jones.)

SINGLES:	HITS 4		WEEKS 41	
BABY, COME TO ME	Qwest	11	12 Feb 83	10
Above hit: Patti AUSTIN and James INGRAM.				
YAH MO B THERE	Qwest	44	18 Feb 84	5
YAH MO B THERE [RE]	Qwest	69	7 Apr 84	3
YAH MO B THERE [RM]	Qwest	12	12 Jan 85	8
Remixed by John 'Jellybean' Benitez. This remix had the same catalogue number as the original.				
Above 3: James INGRAM (with Michael McDONALD).				
SOMEWHERE OUT THERE	MCA	8	11 Jul 87	13
From the film 'An American Tail'.				
Above hit: Linda RONSTADT and James INGRAM.				
THE DAY I FALL IN LOVE (LOVE THEME FROM BEETHOVEN'S 2ND)	Columbia	64	16 Apr 94	2
From the film 'Beethoven's 2nd'.				
Above hit: Dolly PARTON and James INGRAM.				
ALBUMS:	HITS 2		WEEKS 19	
IT'S YOUR NIGHT	Warner Brothers	25	31 Mar 84	17
NEVER FELT SO GOOD	Qwest	72	30 Aug 86	2

INK SPOTS | US

SINGLES:	HITS 1		WEEKS 4	
MELODY OF LOVE	Parlophone	10	30 Apr 55	4

John INMAN UK

SINGLES:	HITS 1		WEEKS 6	
ARE YOU BEING SERVED SIR?	*DJM*	39	*25 Oct 75*	6

INMATES UK

SINGLES:	HITS 1		WEEKS 9	
THE WALK	*Radar*	36	*8 Dec 79*	9

Originally recorded by Jimmy McCracklin.

INNER CIRCLE Jamaica

SINGLES:	HITS 5		WEEKS 35	
EVERYTHING IS GREAT	*Island*	37	*24 Feb 79*	8
STOP BREAKING MY HEART	*Island*	50	*12 May 79*	3
SWEAT (A LA LA LA LA LONG)	*Magnet*	43	*31 Oct 92*	5
SWEAT (A LA LA LA LA LA LONG) [RE]	*Magnet*	3	*1 May 93*	14
BAD BOYS	*Magnet*	52	*31 Jul 93*	3
GAMES PEOPLE PLAY	*Magnet*	67	*10 Sep 94*	2
ALBUMS:	HITS 1		WEEKS 2	
BAD TO THE BONE	*Magnet*	44	*29 May 93*	2

INNER CITY US

SINGLES:	HITS 17		WEEKS 81	
BIG FUN (RADIO FUN)	*10 Records*	8	*3 Sep 88*	14
Above hit: INNER CITY (featuring Kevin SAUNDERSON) Vocals by PARIS.				
GOOD LIFE	*10 Records*	4	*10 Dec 88*	12
AIN'T NOBODY BETTER	*10 Records*	10	*22 Apr 89*	7
DO YOU LOVE WHAT YOU FEEL	*10 Records*	16	*29 Jul 89*	7
WHATCHA GONNA DO WITH MY LOVIN'	*10 Records*	12	*18 Nov 89*	9
THAT MAN (HE'S ALL MINE)	*Ten Records*	42	*13 Oct 90*	4
TILL WE MEET AGAIN	*Ten Records*	47	*23 Feb 91*	2
LET IT REIGN	*Ten Records*	51	*7 Dec 91*	2
HALLELUJAH '92	*Ten Records*	22	*4 Apr 92*	4
PENNIES FROM HEAVEN	*Ten Records*	24	*13 Jun 92*	4
Background vocals from Members Of The House, Rachel Choate and Ann Saunderson.				
PRAISE	*Ten Records*	59	*12 Sep 92*	2
TILL WE MEET AGAIN [RM]	*Ten Records*	55	*27 Feb 93*	1
Remixed by Brothers In Rhythm.				
BACK TOGETHER AGAIN	*Six6*	49	*14 Aug 93*	1
DO YA	*Six6*	44	*5 Feb 94*	2
SHARE MY LIFE	*Six6*	62	*9 Jul 94*	1
YOUR LOVE	*Six6*	28	*10 Feb 96*	2
DO ME RIGHT	*Six6*	47	*5 Oct 96*	1
GOOD LIFE (BUENA VIDA) [RR]	*PIAS Recordings*	10	*6 Feb 99*	6
ALBUMS:	HITS 4		WEEKS 39	
PARADISE	*10 Records*	3	*20 May 89*	30
PARADISE REMIXED	*10 Records*	17	*10 Feb 90*	6
PRAISE	*Ten Records*	52	*11 Jul 92*	1
TESTAMENT '93	*Ten Records*	33	*15 May 93*	2

INNER SANCTUM Canada

SINGLES:	HITS 1		WEEKS 1	
HOW SOON IS NOW	*Malarky*	75	*23 May 98*	1

INNERZONE ORCHESTRA US

SINGLES:	HITS 1		WEEKS 1	
BUG IN THE BASSBIN	*Mo Wax*	68	*28 Sep 96*	1

First released in the US in 1992.

INNOCENCE UK

SINGLES:	HITS 8		WEEKS 33	
NATURAL THING	*Cooltempo*	16	*3 Mar 90*	7
SILENT VOICE	*Cooltempo*	37	*21 Jul 90*	5
LET'S PUSH IT	*Cooltempo*	25	*13 Oct 90*	6
A MATTER OF FACT	*Cooltempo*	37	*8 Dec 90*	7
REMEMBER THE DAY	*Cooltempo*	56	*30 Mar 91*	2
I'LL BE THERE	*Cooltempo*	26	*20 Jun 92*	3
ONE LOVE IN MY LIFETIME	*Cooltempo*	40	*3 Oct 92*	2
BUILD	*Cooltempo*	72	*21 Nov 92*	1
ALBUMS:	HITS 2		WEEKS 20	
BELIEF	*Cooltempo*	24	*10 Nov 90*	19
BUILD	*Cooltempo*	66	*31 Oct 92*	1

INSANE CLOWN POSSE

US

SINGLES:	HITS 2			WEEKS 2
HALLS OF ILLUSIONS	Island	56	17 Jan 98	1
HOKUS POKUS	Island	53	6 Jun 98	1

INSPEKTAH DECK A.K.A. ROLLIE FINGERS - See GENIUS/GZA

INSPIRAL CARPETS

UK

SINGLES:	HITS 15			WEEKS 50
MOVE	Cow	49	18 Nov 89	2
THIS IS HOW IT FEELS	Cow	14	17 Mar 90	8
SHE COMES IN THE FALL	Cow	27	30 Jun 90	6
ISLAND HEAD [EP]	Cow	21	17 Nov 90	4
Lead track: Biggest Mountain.				
CARAVAN	Cow	30	30 Mar 91	5
PLEASE BE CRUEL	Cow	50	22 Jun 91	2
DRAGGING ME DOWN	Cow	12	29 Feb 92	5
TWO WORLDS COLLIDE	Cow	32	30 May 92	2
GENERATIONS	Cow	28	19 Sep 92	3
BITCHES BREW	Cow	36	14 Nov 92	2
HOW IT SHOULD BE	Cow	49	5 Jun 93	1
SATURN 5	Cow	20	22 Jan 94	4
I WANT YOU	Cow	18	5 Mar 94	3
Above hit: INSPIRAL CARPETS featuring Mark E. SMITH.				
UNIFORM	Cow	51	7 May 94	1
JOE	Cow	37	16 Sep 95	2
Originally released in 1989.				
ALBUMS:	HITS 5			WEEKS 36
LIFE	Cow	2	5 May 90	21
THE BEAST INSIDE	Cow	5	4 May 91	6
REVENGE OF THE GOLDFISH	Cow	17	17 Oct 92	3
DEVIL HOPPING	Cow	10	19 Mar 94	3
THE SINGLES	Cow	17	30 Sep 95	3

INSPIRATIONAL CHOIR

US

SINGLES:	HITS 1			WEEKS 11
ABIDE WITH ME	Epic	44	22 Dec 84	5
ABIDE WITH ME [RI]	Portrait	36	14 Dec 85	6
The Royal Choral Society not credited on the original issue.				
Above hit: INSPIRATIONAL CHOIR with the ROYAL CHORAL SOCIETY.				
ALBUMS:	HITS 1			WEEKS 4
SWEET INSPIRATION	Portrait	59	18 Jan 86	4

INSPIRATIONS

UK

ALBUMS:	HITS 5			WEEKS 35
PAN PIPE INSPIRATIONS	Pure Music	10	29 Apr 95	10
PAN PIPE DREAMS	Pure Music	10	23 Sep 95	8
PURE EMOTIONS	Pure Music	37	11 Nov 95	4
PAN PIPE IMAGES	Telstar	23	6 Apr 96	6
THE VERY BEST OF THE PAN PIPES	Telstar	37	12 Oct 96	7

INSTANT FUNK

US

SINGLES:	HITS 1			WEEKS 5
GOT MY MIND MADE UP	Salsoul	46	20 Jan 79	5

INTASTELLA

UK

SINGLES:	HITS 4			WEEKS 6
DREAM SOME PARADISE	MCA	69	25 May 91	1
PEOPLE	MCA	74	24 Aug 91	2
CENTURY	MCA	70	16 Nov 91	2
THE NIGHT	Planet 3	60	23 Sep 95	1

INTELLIGENT HOODLUM

US

SINGLES:	HITS 1			WEEKS 3
BACK TO REALITY	A&M	55	6 Oct 90	3

INTERACTIVE

Germany

SINGLES:	HITS 1			WEEKS 4
FOREVER YOUNG	Ffrreedom	28	13 Apr 96	4
Original recording by Alphaville in 1984.				

INTI ILLIMANI-GUAMARY

Chile

ALBUMS:	HITS 1			WEEKS 7
THE FLIGHT OF THE CONDOR [OST-TV]	BBC	62	17 Dec 83	7

INTRUDERS

US

SINGLES:	HITS 3			WEEKS 21
I'LL ALWAYS LOVE MY MAMA	Philadelphia International	32	13 Apr 74	7
WIN, PLACE OR SHOW (SHE'S A WINNER)	Philadelphia International	14	06 Jul 74	9
Features backing vocals by Daryl Hall.				
WHO DO YOU LOVE	Streetwave	65	22 Dec 84	5

INVISIBLE GIRLS - See Pauline MURRAY and the INVISIBLE GIRLS

INVISIBLE MAN

UK

SINGLES:	HITS 1			WEEKS 1
GIVE A LITTLE LOVE	Serious	48	17 Apr 99	1

INXS

Australia

SINGLES:	HITS 23			WEEKS 121
WHAT YOU NEED	Mercury	51	19 Apr 86	6
LISTEN LIKE THIEVES	Mercury	46	28 Jun 86	7
KISS THE DIRT (FALLING DOWN THE MOUNTAIN)	Mercury	54	30 Aug 86	3
NEED YOU TONIGHT	Mercury	58	24 Oct 87	3
NEW SENSATION	Mercury	25	9 Jan 88	6
DEVIL INSIDE	Mercury	47	12 Mar 88	5
NEVER TEAR US APART	Mercury	24	25 Jun 88	7
NEED YOU TONIGHT [RI]	Mercury	2	12 Nov 88	11
MYSTIFY	Mercury	14	8 Apr 89	7
SUICIDE BLONDE	Mercury	11	15 Sep 90	6
DISAPPEAR	Mercury	21	8 Dec 90	8
GOOD TIMES	Atlantic	18	26 Jan 91	8
From the film 'The Lost Boys'.				
Above hit: Jimmy BARNES and INXS.				
BY MY SIDE	Mercury	42	30 Mar 91	4
BITTER TEARS	Mercury	30	13 Jul 91	3
SHINING STAR [EP]	Mercury	27	2 Nov 91	3
Lead track: Shining Star.				
HEAVEN SENT	Mercury	31	18 Jul 92	3
BABY DON'T CRY	Mercury	20	5 Sep 92	5
TASTE IT	Mercury	21	14 Nov 92	4
BEAUTIFUL GIRL	Mercury	23	13 Feb 93	5
THE GIFT	Mercury	11	23 Oct 93	4
PLEASE (YOU GOT THAT . . .)	Mercury	50	11 Dec 93	3
Features vocals by Ray Charles.				
THE STRANGEST PARTY (THESE ARE THE TIMES)	Mercury	15	22 Oct 94	5
ELEGANTLY WASTED	Mercury	20	22 Mar 97	4
EVERYTHING	Mercury	71	7 Jun 97	1
ALBUMS:	HITS 8			WEEKS 237
LISTEN LIKE THIEVES	Mercury	48	8 Feb 86	15
KICK	Mercury	9	28 Nov 87	103
X	Mercury	2	6 Oct 90	50
LIVE BABY LIVE	Mercury	8	16 Nov 91	9
WELCOME TO WHEREVER YOU ARE	Mercury	1	15 Aug 92	33
FULL MOON, DIRTY HEARTS	Mercury	3	13 Nov 93	8
INXS - THE GREATEST HITS	Mercury	3	12 Nov 94	16
ELEGANTLY WASTED	Mercury	16	19 Apr 97	3

Tommy IOMMI - See BLACK SABBATH

IQ

UK

ALBUMS:	HITS 1			WEEKS 1
THE WAKE	Sahara	72	22 Jun 85	1

Sweetie IRIE - See ASWAD; SCRITTI POLITTI

Tippa IRIE

UK

(See also Arsenal FC.)

SINGLES:	HITS 3			WEEKS 11
HELLO DARLING	UK Bubblers	22	22 Mar 86	7
HEARTBEAT	UK Bubblers	59	19 Jul 86	3
STAYING ALIVE 95	Telstar	48	8 Jul 95	1
Above hit: FEVER featuring Tippa IRIE.				

IRON MAIDEN

UK

SINGLES:	HITS 29			WEEKS 147
RUNNING FREE	EMI	34	23 Feb 80	5
SANCTUARY	EMI	29	7 Jun 80	5
WOMEN IN UNIFORM	EMI	35	8 Nov 80	4
TWILIGHT ZONE/WRATH CHILD	EMI	31	14 Mar 81	5
PURGATORY	EMI	52	27 Jun 81	3
MAIDEN JAPAN [EP]	EMI	43	26 Sep 81	4
Lead track: Running Free. Live recordings from their shows in Japan.				
RUN TO THE HILLS	EMI	7	20 Feb 82	10
THE NUMBER OF THE BEAST	EMI	18	15 May 82	8
FLIGHT OF ICARUS	EMI	11	23 Apr 83	6
THE TROOPER	EMI	12	2 Jul 83	7
2 MINUTES TO MIDNIGHT	EMI	11	18 Aug 84	6
ACES HIGH	EMI	20	3 Nov 84	5
RUNNING FREE [RR]	EMI	19	5 Oct 85	5
Live recording.				
RUN TO THE HILLS [RR]	EMI	26	14 Dec 85	6
Live recording from the Long Beach Arena, Mar 85.				
WASTED YEARS	EMI	18	6 Sep 86	4
STRANGER IN A STRANGE LAND	EMI	22	22 Nov 86	4
STRANGER IN A STRANGE LAND [RE]	EMI	71	27 Dec 86	2
CAN I PLAY WITH MADNESS	EMI	3	26 Mar 88	6
THE EVIL THAT MEN DO	EMI	5	13 Aug 88	6
THE CLAIRVOYANT	EMI	6	19 Nov 88	8
INFINITE DREAMS (LIVE)	EMI	6	18 Nov 89	5
Live recording from Birmingham NEC 27/28 Nov 88.				
INFINITE DREAMS (LIVE) [RE]	EMI	74	30 Dec 89	1
HOLY SMOKE	EMI	3	22 Sep 90	4
BRING YOUR DAUGHTER . . . TO THE SLAUGHTER	EMI	1	5 Jan 91	5
BE QUICK OR BE DEAD	EMI	2	25 Apr 92	4
FROM HERE TO ETERNITY	EMI	21	11 Jul 92	4
FEAR OF THE DARK (LIVE)	EMI	8	13 Mar 93	3
Live recording from the Isbhallen, Helsinki, Finland 5 Jun 92.				
HALLOWED BE THY NAME (LIVE)	EMI	9	16 Oct 93	3
Live recording from the Olympic Arena, Moscow 4 Jun 93.				
MAN ON THE EDGE	EMI	10	7 Oct 95	3
VIRUS	EMI	16	21 Sep 96	3
THE ANGEL AND THE GAMBLER	EMI	18	21 Mar 98	3

ALBUMS:	HITS 26			WEEKS 194
IRON MAIDEN	EMI	4	26 Apr 80	15
KILLERS	EMI	12	28 Feb 81	8
THE NUMBER OF THE BEAST	EMI	1	10 Apr 82	31
PIECE OF MIND	EMI	3	28 May 83	18
POWERSLAVE	EMI	2	15 Sep 84	13
IRON MAIDEN [RI]	Fame	71	15 Jun 85	2
Mid-price re-issue.				
LIVE AFTER DEATH	EMI	2	26 Oct 85	14
Live recordings from their World Slavery tour between Apr 84 and Jul 85.				
SOMEWHERE IN TIME	EMI	3	11 Oct 86	11
THE NUMBER OF THE BEAST [RI]	Fame	98	20 Jun 87	1
Mid-price re-issue.				
SEVENTH SON OF A SEVENTH SON	EMI	1	23 Apr 88	18
RUNNING FREE/SANCTUARY	EMI	10	24 Feb 90	4
WOMEN IN UNIFORM/TWILIGHT ZONE	EMI	10	3 Mar 90	3
PURGATORY/MAIDEN JAPAN	EMI	5	10 Mar 90	3
RUN TO THE HILLS/THE NUMBER OF THE BEAST	EMI	3	17 Mar 90	2
FLIGHT OF ICARUS/THE TROOPER	EMI	7	24 Mar 90	2
2 MINUTES TO MIDNIGHT/ACES HIGH	EMI	11	31 Mar 90	2
RUNNING FREE (LIVE)/RUN TO THE HILLS (LIVE)	EMI	9	7 Apr 90	2
WASTED YEARS/STRANGER IN A STRANGE LAND	EMI	9	14 Apr 90	2
CAN I PLAY WITH MADNESS/THE EVIL THAT MEN DO	EMI	10	21 Apr 90	3
THE CLAIRVOYANT/INFINITE DREAMS (LIVE)	EMI	11	28 Apr 90	2
Above 10 are double 12"/CD singles, too long and expensive to be eligible for the singles chart.				
NO PRAYER FOR THE DYING	EMI	2	13 Oct 90	14
FEAR OF THE DARK	EMI	1	23 May 92	5
A REAL LIVE ONE	EMI	3	3 Apr 93	4
A REAL DEAD ONE	EMI	12	30 Oct 93	3
Above 2 are live recordings from their 1992/1993 European tour.				
LIVE AT DONNINGTON	EMI	23	20 Nov 93	1
Limited edition (5,000 copies) bootleg of their appearance at Donnington, issued as a farewell to Bruce Dickinson.				
THE X FACTOR	EMI	8	14 Oct 95	4
THE BEST OF THE BEAST	EMI	16	5 Oct 96	5
VIRTUAL XI	EMI	16	4 Apr 98	2

IRONHORSE
Canada

SINGLES:		HITS 1		WEEKS 3
SWEET LUI-LOUISE	Scotti Brothers	60	5 May 79	3

Big Dee IRWIN
US

SINGLES:		HITS 1		WEEKS 17
SWINGING ON A STAR	Colpix	7	23 Nov 63	17

Although she is not credited, single is a duet with Little Eva. Originally recorded by Bing Crosby in 1944.

Gregory ISAACS
Jamaica

ALBUMS:		HITS 2		WEEKS 6
MORE GREGORY	Pre	93	12 Sep 81	1
NIGHT NURSE	Island	32	4 Sep 82	5

Chris ISAAK
US

SINGLES:		HITS 5		WEEKS 22
WICKED GAME	London	10	24 Nov 90	10
From the film 'Wild At Heart'.				
BLUE HOTEL	Reprise	17	2 Feb 91	7
Original release reached No. 100 in 1987.				
CAN'T DO A THING (TO STOP ME)	Reprise	36	3 Apr 93	3
SAN FRANCISCO DAYS	Reprise	62	10 Jul 93	1
BABY DID A BAD BAD THING	Reprise	44	2 Oct 99	1
From the film 'Eyes Wide Shut'.				

ALBUMS:		HITS 3		WEEKS 38
WICKED GAME	Reprise	3	26 Jan 91	30
SAN FRANCISCO DAYS	Reprise	12	24 Apr 93	5
FOREVER BLUE	Reprise	27	3 Jun 95	3

ISHA-D
UK

SINGLES:		HITS 1		WEEKS 4
STAY (TONIGHT)	Cleveland City Blues	28	22 Jul 95	3
STAY [RM]	Satellite	58	5 Jul 97	1

Remixed by Andy Ling.

Ronald ISLEY - See Warren G; R. KELLY; Rod STEWART

ISLEY BROTHERS
US

SINGLES:		HITS 13		WEEKS 108
TWIST AND SHOUT	Stateside	42	27 Jul 63	1
Originally recorded by the Top Notes in 1961.				
THIS OLD HEART OF MINE (IS WEAK FOR YOU)	Tamla Motown	47	30 Apr 66	1
I GUESS I'LL ALWAYS LOVE YOU	Tamla Motown	45	3 Sep 66	2
THIS OLD HEART OF MINE (IS WEAK FOR YOU) [RE]	Tamla Motown	3	26 Oct 68	16
I GUESS I'LL ALWAYS LOVE YOU [RI]	Tamla Motown	11	18 Jan 69	9
BEHIND A PAINTED SMILE	Tamla Motown	5	19 Apr 69	12
IT'S YOUR THING	Major Minor	30	28 Jun 69	5
PUT YOURSELF IN MY PLACE	Tamla Motown	13	30 Aug 69	11
THAT LADY	Epic	14	22 Sep 73	9
HIGHWAY OF MY LIFE	Epic	25	19 Jan 74	8
SUMMER BREEZE	Epic	16	25 May 74	8
Originally recorded by Seals and Croft.				
HARVEST FOR THE WORLD	Epic	10	10 Jul 76	8
TAKE ME TO THE NEXT PHASE (PARTS 1 & 2)	Epic	50	13 May 78	4
IT'S A DISCO NIGHT (ROCK DON'T STOP)	Epic	14	3 Nov 79	11
BETWEEN THE SHEETS	Epic	52	16 Jul 83	3

ALBUMS:		HITS 5		WEEKS 24
THIS OLD HEART OF MINE	Tamla Motown	23	14 Dec 68	6
HARVEST FOR THE WORLD	Epic	50	14 Aug 76	5
GO FOR YOUR GUNS	Epic	46	14 May 77	2
SHOWDOWN	Epic	50	24 Jun 78	1
GREATEST HITS	Telstar	41	5 Mar 88	10

ISLEY JASPER ISLEY
US

SINGLES:		HITS 1		WEEKS 5
CARAVAN OF LOVE	Epic	52	23 Nov 85	5

ISOTONIK
UK

SINGLES:		HITS 2		WEEKS 9
DIFFERENT STROKES	Ffrreedom	12	11 Jan 92	5
EVERYWHERE I GO / LET'S GET DOWN	Ffrreedom	25	2 May 92	4

Let's Get Down listed from 9 May 92. Sleeve gives title as an EP:The Isotronik E.P.

IT BITES
UK

SINGLES:	HITS 4		WEEKS 21
CALLING ALL THE HEROS	Virgin	6	12 Jul 86	12
WHOLE NEW WORLD	Virgin	54	18 Oct 86	3
THE OLD MAN AND THE ANGEL	Virgin	72	23 May 87	1
STILL TOO YOUNG TO REMEMBER	Virgin	66	13 May 89	3
STILL TOO YOUNG TO REMEMBER [RM]	Virgin	60	24 Feb 90	2
Remixed by Nick Davies.				

ALBUMS:	HITS 4		WEEKS 12
THE BIG LAD IN THE WINDMILL	Virgin	35	6 Sep 86	5
ONCE AROUND THE WORLD	Virgin	43	2 Apr 88	3
EAT ME IN ST. LOUIS	Virgin	40	24 Jun 89	3
THANK YOU AND GOODNIGHT	Virgin	59	31 Aug 91	1

IT'S A BEAUTIFUL DAY
US

ALBUMS:	HITS 2		WEEKS 3
IT'S A BEAUTIFUL DAY	CBS	58	23 May 70	1
MARRYING MAIDEN	CBS	45	18 Jul 70	2

IT'S IMMATERIAL
UK

SINGLES:	HITS 2		WEEKS 10
DRIVING AWAY FROM HOME (JIM'S TUNE)	Siren	18	12 Apr 86	7
ED'S FUNKY DINER (FRIDAY NIGHT, SATURDAY MORNING)	Siren	65	2 Aug 86	3

ALBUMS:	HITS 1		WEEKS 3
LIFE'S HARD AND THEN YOU DIE	Siren	62	27 Sep 86	3

ITTY BITTY BOOZY WOOZY
Holland

(See also Klubbheads.)

SINGLES:	HITS 1		WEEKS 2
TEMPO FIESTA (PARTY TIME)	Systematic	34	25 Nov 95	2

Burl IVES
US

SINGLES:	HITS 2		WEEKS 25
A LITTLE BITTY TEAR	Brunswick	9	27 Jan 62	15
FUNNY WAY OF LAUGHIN'	Brunswick	29	19 May 62	10

IVY LEAGUE
UK

SINGLES:	HITS 4		WEEKS 31
FUNNY HOW LOVE CAN BE	Piccadilly	8	6 Feb 65	9
THAT'S WHY I'M CRYING	Piccadilly	22	8 May 65	8
TOSSING AND TURNING	Piccadilly	3	26 Jun 65	13
WILLOW TREE	Piccadilly	50	16 Jul 66	1

IZIT
UK

SINGLES:	HITS 1		WEEKS 3
STORIES	ffrr	52	2 Dec 89	3

J

J.A.L.N. BAND
UK/Jamaica

SINGLES:	HITS 3		WEEKS 17
DISCO MUSIC/I LIKE IT [M]	Magnet	21	11 Sep 76	9
I GOT TO SING	Magnet	40	27 Aug 77	4
GET UP (AND LET YOURSELF GO)	Magnet	53	1 Jul 78	4

J.B.'S ALL STARS
UK

SINGLES:	HITS 1		WEEKS 4
BACKFIELD IN MOTION	RCA Victor	48	11 Feb 84	4
Original by Mel and Tim reached No. 10 in the US in 1969.				

J.C.
UK

SINGLES:	HITS 1		WEEKS 1
SO HOT	East West Dance	74	7 Feb 98	1

J.J.
UK

SINGLES:	HITS 1		WEEKS 3
IF THIS IS LOVE	Columbia	55	9 Feb 91	3

J.K.D. BAND featuring the voice of Bruce LEE · UK

SINGLES:		HITS 1			WEEKS 4
DRAGON POWER (A TRIBUTE TO BRUCE LEE)	Satril	58	1 Jul 78	4

J.M. SILK US

SINGLES:		HITS 2			WEEKS 6
I CAN'T TURN AROUND	RCA	62	25 Oct 86	3
LET THE MUSIC TAKE CONTROL	RCA	47	7 Mar 87	3

J.M.D. – See TYREE

J.PAC UK

SINGLES:		HITS 1			WEEKS 2
ROCK 'N' ROLL (DOLE)	East West	51	22 Jul 95	2

J.T. and the BIG FAMILY Italy

SINGLES:		HITS 1			WEEKS 8
MOMENTS IN SOUL	Champion	7	3 Mar 90	8

JA RULE – See JAY-Z

JACK 'N' CHILL UK

SINGLES:		HITS 2			WEEKS 21
THE JACK THAT HOUSE BUILT	10 Records	48	6 Jun 87	5
THE JACK THAT HOUSE BUILT [RE]	10 Records	6	9 Jan 88	11
BEATIN' THE HEAT	10 Records	42	9 Jul 88	5

JACK RADICS – See Chaka DEMUS and PLIERS; SUPERCAT

Susan JACKS – See POPPY FAMILY (featuring Susan JACKS)

Terry JACKS Canada

SINGLES:		HITS 2			WEEKS 21
SEASONS IN THE SUN	Bell	1	23 Mar 74	12
IF YOU GO AWAY	Bell	8	29 Jun 74	9

Above 2 originally recorded by Jacques Brel.

Chad JACKSON UK

SINGLES:		HITS 1			WEEKS 10
HEAR THE DRUMMER (GET WICKED)	Big Wave	3	2 Jun 90	10

Dee D. JACKSON UK

SINGLES:		HITS 2			WEEKS 14
AUTOMATIC LOVER	Mercury	4	22 Apr 78	9
METEOR MAN	Mercury	48	2 Sep 78	5

Freddie JACKSON US

SINGLES:		HITS 8			WEEKS 31
YOU ARE MY LADY	Capitol	49	23 Nov 85	4
ROCK ME TONIGHT (FOR OLD TIME'S SAKE)	Capitol	18	22 Feb 86	9
TASTY LOVE	Capitol	73	11 Oct 86	1
HAVE YOU EVER LOVED SOMEBODY	Capitol	33	7 Feb 87	6
NICE AND SLOW	Capitol	56	9 Jul 88	2
CRAZY (FOR ME)	Capitol	41	15 Oct 88	3
ME AND MRS. JONES	Capitol	32	5 Sep 92	5
MAKE LOVE EASY	RCA	70	15 Jan 94	1

ALBUMS:		HITS 4			WEEKS 48
ROCK ME TONIGHT	Capitol	73	18 May 85	6
ROCK ME TONIGHT [RE]	Capitol	27	25 Jan 86	16
JUST LIKE THE FIRST TIME	Capitol	30	8 Nov 86	15
DON'T LET LOVE SLIP AWAY	Capitol	24	30 Jul 88	9
DO ME AGAIN	Capitol	48	17 Nov 90	2

Gisele JACKSON US

SINGLES:		HITS 1			WEEKS 1
LOVE COMMANDMENTS	Manifesto	54	30 Aug 97	1

Janet JACKSON US

SINGLES:		HITS 32			WEEKS 245
WHAT HAVE YOU DONE FOR ME LATELY	A&M	3	22 Mar 86	14
NASTY	A&M	19	31 May 86	9
WHEN I THINK OF YOU	A&M	10	9 Aug 86	10
CONTROL	A&M	42	1 Nov 86	5
LET'S WAIT AWHILE	Breakout	3	21 Mar 87	10

THE PLEASURE PRINCIPLE	Breakout	24	13 Jun 87	5
Label on 7" format reads Pleasure Principle Remix: (The Shep Pettibone Mix).				
FUNNY HOW TIME FLIES (WHEN YOU'RE HAVING FUN)	Breakout	59	14 Nov 87	2
MISS YOU MUCH	Breakout	22	2 Sep 89	7
RHYTHM NATION	Breakout	23	4 Nov 89	5
COME BACK TO ME	Breakout	20	27 Jan 90	7
ESCAPADE	Breakout	17	31 Mar 90	7
ALRIGHT	Breakout	20	7 Jul 90	5
BLACK CAT	A&M	15	8 Sep 90	6
Lead guitar by Vernon Reid of Living Colour.				
LOVE WILL NEVER DO (WITHOUT YOU)	A&M	34	27 Oct 90	4
THE BEST THINGS IN LIFE ARE FREE	Perspective	2	15 Aug 92	13
From the film 'Mo' Money'.				
Above hit: Luther VANDROSS and Janet JACKSON with special guests BBD and Ralph TRESVANT.				
THAT'S THE WAY LOVE GOES	Virgin	2	8 May 93	10
IF	Virgin	14	31 Jul 93	7
AGAIN	Virgin	6	20 Nov 93	11
BECAUSE OF LOVE	Virgin	19	12 Mar 94	4
ANY TIME, ANY PLACE	Virgin	13	18 Jun 94	5
YOU WANT THIS	Virgin	14	26 Nov 94	3
Samples Love Child by Diana Ross and the Supremes.				
WHOOPS NOW / WHAT'LL I DO	Virgin	9	18 Mar 95	8
SCREAM	Epic	3	10 Jun 95	12
Above hit: Michael JACKSON (Duet with Michael JACKSON and Janet JACKSON).				
SCREAM [RM]	Epic	43	24 Jun 95	2
Remixed by David Morales.				
RUNAWAY	A&M	6	23 Sep 95	7
SCREAM [RE]	Epic	72	2 Dec 95	1
THE BEST THINGS IN LIFE ARE FREE [RM]	A&M	7	16 Dec 95	7
Remixed by K-Klass.				
Above hit: Luther VANDROSS and Janet JACKSON.				
TWENTY FOREPLAY	A&M	22	6 Apr 96	4
GOT 'TIL IT'S GONE	Virgin	6	4 Oct 97	9
Above hit: JANET (featuring Q-TIP and Joni MITCHELL).				
TOGETHER AGAIN	Virgin	4	13 Dec 97	19
Above hit: JANET.				
I GET LONELY	Virgin	5	4 Apr 98	7
Above hit: JANET (featuring BLACKSTREET).				
GO DEEP	Virgin	13	27 Jun 98	5
EVERY TIME	Virgin	46	19 Dec 98	1
Above 2: JANET.				
GIRLFRIEND / BOYFRIEND	Interscope	11	17 Apr 99	7
One song. Rap by Ja Rule and Eve.				
Above hit: BLACKSTREET featuring JANET.				
WHAT'S IT GONNA BE?!	Elektra	6	1 May 99	7
Above hit: Busta RHYMES featuring JANET.				

ALBUMS:	HITS 6		WEEKS 250	
CONTROL	A&M	15	5 Apr 86	43
CONTROL [RE]	A&M	8	21 Mar 87	29
CONTROL - THE REMIXES	Breakout	20	14 Nov 87	14
JANET JACKSON'S RHYTHM NATION 1814	A&M	4	30 Sep 89	43
JANET	Virgin	1	29 May 93	49
Repackaged from 12 Feb 94.				
JANET / JANET - REMIXED [RE]	Virgin	15	25 Mar 95	8
Janet – Remixed was a remix album, sales were combined.				
DESIGN OF A DECADE - 1986/1996	A&M	2	14 Oct 95	21
Compilation.				
THE VELVET ROPE	Virgin	6	18 Oct 97	43

Jermaine JACKSON US

SINGLES:	HITS 7		WEEKS 43	
LET'S GET SERIOUS	Motown	8	10 May 80	11
Written, produced and backing vocals by Stevie Wonder.				
BURNIN' HOT	Motown	32	26 Jul 80	6
YOU LIKE ME DON'T YOU	Motown	41	30 May 81	5
SWEETEST SWEETEST	Arista	52	12 May 84	4
WHEN THE RAIN BEGINS TO FALL	Arista	68	27 Oct 84	2
From the film 'Voyage Of The Rock Aliens'.				
Above hit: Jermaine JACKSON and Pia ZADORA.				
DO WHAT YOU DO	Arista	6	16 Feb 85	13
DON'T TAKE IT PERSONAL	Arista	69	21 Oct 89	2

ALBUMS:	HITS 2		WEEKS 12	
LET'S GET SERIOUS	Motown	22	31 May 80	6
DYNAMITE	Arista	57	12 May 84	6

Joe JACKSON

UK

SINGLES:	HITS 8			WEEKS 49
IS SHE REALLY GOING OUT WITH HIM?	A&M	13	4 Aug 79	9
IT'S DIFFERENT FOR GIRLS	A&M	5	12 Jan 80	9
JUMPIN' JIVE	A&M	43	4 Jul 81	5
Above hit: Joe JACKSON'S JUMPIN' JIVE.				
STEPPIN' OUT	A&M	6	8 Jan 83	8
BREAKING US IN TWO	A&M	59	12 Mar 83	4
HAPPY ENDING	A&M	58	28 Apr 84	3
Elaine Caswell was only credited on the back of the sleeve.				
Above hit: Joe JACKSON featuring Elaine CASWELL.				
BE MY NUMBER TWO	A&M	70	7 Jul 84	2
LEFT OF CENTRE	A&M	32	7 Jun 86	9
Sleeve has British spelling; the sleeve the US variant 'Center'.				
Above hit: Suzanne VEGA featuring Joe JACKSON on piano.				
ALBUMS:	HITS 11			WEEKS 106
LOOK SHARP	A&M	40	17 Mar 79	11
I'M THE MAN	A&M	12	13 Oct 79	16
BEAT CRAZY	A&M	42	18 Oct 80	3
JUMPIN' JIVE	A&M	14	4 Jul 81	14
Above hit: Joe JACKSON'S JUMPIN' JIVE.				
NIGHT AND DAY	A&M	44	3 Jul 82	11
NIGHT AND DAY [RE]	A&M	3	22 Jan 83	16
BODY AND SOUL	A&M	14	7 Apr 84	14
BIG WORLD	A&M	41	5 Apr 86	5
LIVE 1980–86	A&M	66	7 May 88	2
BLAZE OF GLORY	A&M	36	29 Apr 89	3
STEPPING OUT – THE VERY BEST OF JOE JACKSON	A&M	7	15 Sep 90	9
LAUGHTER AND LUST	Virgin America	41	11 May 91	2

Michael JACKSON

US

SINGLES:	HITS 49			WEEKS 480
GOT TO BE THERE	Tamla Motown	5	12 Feb 72	11
ROCKIN' ROBIN	Tamla Motown	3	20 May 72	14
AIN'T NO SUNSHINE	Tamla Motown	8	19 Aug 72	11
Originally recorded by Bill Withers in 1972.				
BEN	Tamla Motown	7	25 Nov 72	14
EASE ON DOWN THE ROAD	MCA	45	18 Nov 78	4
Originally recorded by the Consumer Rapport. From the film 'The Wiz'.				
Above hit: Diana ROSS / Michael JACKSON.				
DON'T STOP 'TILL YOU GET ENOUGH	Epic	3	15 Sep 79	12
OFF THE WALL	Epic	7	24 Nov 79	10
ROCK WITH YOU	Epic	7	9 Feb 80	9
SHE'S OUT OF MY LIFE	Epic	3	3 May 80	9
GIRLFRIEND	Epic	41	26 Jul 80	5
ONE DAY IN YOUR LIFE	Tamla Motown	1	23 May 81	14
Originally released in 1975.				
WE'RE ALMOST THERE	Motown	46	1 Aug 81	4
THE GIRL IS MINE	Epic	8	6 Nov 82	9
Above hit: Michael JACKSON and Paul McCARTNEY.				
THE GIRL IS MINE [RE]	Epic	75	15 Jan 83	1
BILLIE JEAN	Epic	1	29 Jan 83	15
BEAT IT	Epic	3	9 Apr 83	12
Features Eddie Van Halen on guitar.				
WANNA BE STARTIN' SOMETHIN'	Epic	8	11 Jun 83	9
HAPPY (LOVE THEME FROM 'LADY SINGS THE BLUES')	Tamla Motown	52	23 Jul 83	3
From the film 'Lady Sings The Blues'.				
SAY SAY SAY	Parlophone	2	15 Oct 83	15
Above hit: Paul McCARTNEY and Michael JACKSON.				
THRILLER	Epic	10	19 Nov 83	18
P.Y.T. (PRETTY YOUNG THING)	Epic	11	31 Mar 84	8
FAREWELL MY SUMMER LOVE	Motown	7	2 Jun 84	12
GIRL YOU'RE SO TOGETHER	Motown	33	11 Aug 84	8
I JUST CAN'T STOP LOVING YOU	Epic	1	8 Aug 87	9
Above hit: Michael JACKSON with Siedah GARRETT.				
BAD	Epic	3	26 Sep 87	11
THE WAY YOU MAKE ME FEEL	Epic	3	5 Dec 87	10
MAN IN THE MIRROR	Epic	21	20 Feb 88	5
Siedah Garrett and the Winans on backing vocals.				
GET IT	Motown	37	28 May 88	4
Above hit: Stevie WONDER and Michael JACKSON.				
DIRTY DIANA	Epic	4	16 Jul 88	8
ANOTHER PART OF ME	Epic	15	10 Sep 88	6
SMOOTH CRIMINAL	Epic	8	26 Nov 88	10
LEAVE ME ALONE	Epic	2	25 Feb 89	9
LIBERIAN GIRL	Epic	13	15 Jul 89	6

429

BLACK OR WHITE *Slash from Guns N' Roses on guitar, rap is by Bill Bottrell.*	Epic	1	23 Nov 91	10
BLACK OR WHITE [RM] *Remixed by Clivilles and Cole.*	Epic	14	18 Jan 92	4
REMEMBER THE TIME / COME TOGETHER *Come Together listed from 7 Mar 92 once single had dropped down to No.10.*	Epic	3	15 Feb 92	8
IN THE CLOSET *Above hit: Michael JACKSON and MYSTERY GIRL: Duet.*	Epic	8	2 May 92	6
WHO IS IT	Epic	10	25 Jul 92	7
JAM *Rap by Heavy D.*	Epic	13	12 Sep 92	5
PRELUDE/HEAL THE WORLD	Epic	2	5 Dec 92	15
GIVE IN TO ME *Above hit: Michael JACKSON featuring special guitar performance by SLASH.*	Epic	2	27 Feb 93	9
WILL YOU BE THERE	Epic	9	10 Jul 93	8
GONE TOO SOON	Epic	33	18 Dec 93	5
SCREAM *Above hit: Michael JACKSON (Duet with Michael JACKSON and Janet JACKSON).*	Epic	3	10 Jun 95	12
SCREAM [RM] *Remixed by David Morales.*	Epic	43	24 Jun 95	2
YOU ARE NOT ALONE *Written and produced by R.Kelly*	Epic	1	2 Sep 95	15
SCREAM [RE]	Epic	72	2 Dec 95	1
EARTH SONG	Epic	1	9 Dec 95	17
THEY DON'T CARE ABOUT US	Epic	4	20 Apr 96	12
THEY DON'T CARE ABOUT US [RE-1ST]	Epic	66	3 Aug 96	1
THEY DON'T CARE ABOUT US [RE-2ND]	Epic	66	17 Aug 96	1
WHY *Above hit: 3T featuring Michael JACKSON.*	Epic	2	24 Aug 96	9
STRANGER IN MOSCOW	Epic	4	16 Nov 96	10
STRANGER IN MOSCOW [RE]	Epic	69	1 Mar 97	1
BLOOD ON THE DANCE FLOOR	Epic	1	3 May 97	9
HISTORY / GHOSTS *Though listed as a double A-side, Ghosts did not appear on the second CD format.*	Epic	5	19 Jul 97	8

ALBUMS:		HITS 21		WEEKS 844
COMPILATION ALBUMS:		**HITS 1**		**WEEKS 2**
GOT TO BE THERE	Tamla Motown	37	3 Jun 72	5
BEN	Tamla Motown	17	13 Jan 73	7
OFF THE WALL *Includes re-entries through to 1987.*	Epic	5	29 Sep 79	160
THE BEST OF MICHAEL JACKSON	Motown	11	4 Jul 81	18
ONE DAY IN YOUR LIFE	Motown	29	18 Jul 81	8
THRILLER	Epic	1	11 Dec 82	173
E.T. – THE EXTRA TERRESTRIAL STORYBOOK	MCA	82	12 Feb 83	2
18 GREATEST HITS *Above hit: Michael JACKSON plus the JACKSON FIVE.*	Telstar	1	9 Jul 83	55
MICHAEL JACKSON 9 SINGLE PACK *This is a package of 9 x 7" singles on red vinyl.*	Epic	66	3 Dec 83	3
FAREWELL MY SUMMER LOVE	Motown	9	9 Jun 84	14
DIANA, MICHAEL, GLADYS. STEVIE – THEIR VERY BEST – BACK TO BACK *Compilation featuring tracks by each act.* *Above hit: Diana ROSS/Michael JACKSON/Gladys KNIGHT/Stevie WONDER.*	Priority V	21	15 Nov 86	10
BAD	Epic	1	12 Sep 87	115
LOVE SONGS *Compilation of each artist's solo recordings. When the compilation chart commenced on 14 Jan 89 it was listed there. See separate entry below.* *Above hit: Michael JACKSON and Diana ROSS.*	Telstar	12	31 Oct 87	24
THE MICHAEL JACKSON MIX	Stylus	27	26 Dec 87	25
THE MICHAEL JACKSON BAD SOUVENIR SINGLES PACK *5 x 7" square-shaped picture discs.*	Epic	91	30 Jul 88	1
OFF THE WALL [RE-1ST] *Re-released at mid-price. Includes re-entries in 1992.*	Epic	36	16 Jul 88	16
18 GREATEST HITS [RI] *Above hit: Michael JACKSON Plus the JACKSON FIVE.*	Motown	85	30 Jul 88	3
LOVE SONGS *Above entry was in the compilation chart.* *Above hit: Michael JACKSON and Diana ROSS.*	Telstar	18	14 Jan 89	2
DANGEROUS	Epic	1	30 Nov 91	96
MOTOWN'S GREATEST HITS: MICHAEL JACKSON	Motown	53	29 Feb 92	2
TOUR SOUVENIR PACK *4-picture CD box set.*	Epic	32	15 Aug 92	3
HISTORY – PAST, PRESENT AND FUTURE, BOOK 1 *Double CD, one of which is a greatest hits compilation.*	Epic	1	24 Jun 95	77
OFF THE WALL [RE-2ND]	Epic	60	23 Sep 95	2
BLOOD ON THE DANCE FLOOR – HISTORY IN THE MIX *Features 5 new songs and mixes from last album.*	Epic	1	24 May 97	16

THE BEST OF MICHAEL JACKSON AND THE JACKSON FIVE	PolyGram TV	5	19 Jul 97	9

Contains both Jackson's solo and group material.
Above hit: Michael JACKSON and the JACKSON FIVE.

Mick JACKSON
UK

SINGLES:	HITS 2		WEEKS 16	
BLAME IT ON THE BOOGIE	Atlantic	15	30 Sep 78	8
WEEKEND	Atlantic	38	3 Feb 79	8

Millie JACKSON
US

SINGLES:	HITS 3		WEEKS 8	
MY MAN A SWEET MAN	Mojo	50	18 Nov 72	1
I FEEL LIKE WALKING IN THE RAIN	Sire	55	10 Mar 84	2
ACT OF WAR	Rocket	32	15 Jun 85	5

Above hit: Elton JOHN and Millie JACKSON.

ALBUMS:	HITS 2		WEEKS 7	
E.S.P.	Sire	59	18 Feb 84	5
LIVE AND UNCENSORED	Important	81	6 Apr 85	2

Originally released in 1980.

Stonewall JACKSON
US

SINGLES:	HITS 1		WEEKS 2	
WATERLOO	Philips	24	18 Jul 59	2

Tony JACKSON and the VIBRATIONS
UK

SINGLES:	HITS 1		WEEKS 3	
BYE BYE BABY	Pye	38	10 Oct 64	3

Originally recorded by Mary Wells.

Tony JACKSON - See Q

Wanda JACKSON
US

SINGLES:	HITS 2		WEEKS 11	
LET'S HAVE A PARTY	Capitol	32	3 Sep 60	8

Backing vocals by Gene Vincent's Blue Caps.

MEAN MEAN MAN	Capitol	46	28 Jan 61	1
MEAN MEAN MAN [RE]	Capitol	40	11 Feb 61	2

JACKSON FIVE - See JACKSONS

JACKSON SISTERS
US

SINGLES:	HITS 1		WEEKS 2	
I BELIEVE IN MIRACLES	Urban	72	20 Jun 87	2

JACKSONS
US

(See also Stevie Wonder.)

SINGLES:	HITS 26		WEEKS 235	
I WANT YOU BACK	Tamla Motown	2	31 Jan 70	13
A B C	Tamla Motown	8	16 May 70	11
THE LOVE YOU SAVE	Tamla Motown	7	1 Aug 70	9
I'LL BE THERE	Tamla Motown	4	21 Nov 70	16
MAMA'S PEARL	Tamla Motown	25	10 Apr 71	7
NEVER CAN SAY GOODBYE	Tamla Motown	33	17 Jul 71	7
LOOKIN' THROUGH THE WINDOWS	Tamla Motown	9	11 Nov 72	11
SANTA CLAUS IS COMIN' TO TOWN	Tamla Motown	43	23 Dec 72	3
DOCTOR MY EYES	Tamla Motown	9	17 Feb 73	10

Originally recorded by Jackson Browne.

HALLELUJAH DAY	Tamla Motown	20	9 Jun 73	9

Above 10: JACKSON 5.

SKYWRITER	Tamla Motown	25	8 Sep 73	8

Above hit: JACKSON FIVE.

ENJOY YOURSELF	Epic	42	9 Apr 77	4

Originally released in 1976.

SHOW YOU THE WAY TO GO	Epic	1	4 Jun 77	10
DREAMER	Epic	22	13 Aug 77	9
GOIN' PLACES	Epic	26	5 Nov 77	7
EVEN THOUGH YOU'VE GONE	Epic	31	11 Feb 78	4
BLAME IT ON THE BOOGIE	Epic	8	23 Sep 78	12
DESTINY	Epic	39	3 Feb 79	6
SHAKE YOUR BODY (DOWN TO THE GROUND)	Epic	4	24 Mar 79	12
LOVELY ONE	Epic	29	25 Oct 80	6
HEARTBREAK HOTEL	Epic	44	13 Dec 80	6
CAN YOU FEEL IT	Epic	6	28 Feb 81	15
WALK RIGHT NOW	Epic	7	4 Jul 81	11

STATE OF SHOCK	Epic	14	7 Jul 84	8
Above hit: JACKSONS lead vocals by Michael JACKSON and Mick JAGGER.				
TORTURE	Epic	26	8 Sep 84	6
I WANT YOU BACK ('88 REMIX) [RM]	Motown	8	16 Apr 88	9
Remixed by Phil Harding.				
Above hit: Michael JACKSON with the JACKSON FIVE.				
NOTHIN (THAT COMPARES 2 U)	Epic	33	13 May 89	6
ALBUMS:	**HITS 13**		**WEEKS 149**	
DIANA ROSS PRESENTS THE JACKSON FIVE	Tamla Motown	16	21 Mar 70	4
ABC	Tamla Motown	22	15 Aug 70	6
GREATEST HITS	Tamla Motown	26	7 Oct 72	14
LOOKIN' THROUGH THE WINDOWS	Tamla Motown	16	18 Nov 72	8
Above 4: JACKSON 5.				
THE JACKSONS	Epic	54	16 Jul 77	1
GOIN' PLACES	Epic	45	3 Dec 77	1
DESTINY	Epic	33	5 May 79	7
TRIUMPH	Epic	13	11 Oct 80	16
THE JACKSONS - LIVE	Epic	53	12 Dec 81	9
18 GREATEST HITS	Telstar	1	9 Jul 83	55
Above hit: Michael JACKSON plus the JACKSON FIVE.				
VICTORY	Epic	3	21 Jul 84	13
18 GREATEST HITS [RI]	Motown	85	30 Jul 88	3
Above hit: Michael JACKSON plus the JACKSON FIVE.				
2300 JACKSON ST	Epic	39	1 Jul 89	3
THE BEST OF MICHAEL JACKSON AND THE JACKSON FIVE	PolyGram TV	5	19 Jul 97	9
Contains both Jackson's solo and group material.				
Above hit: Michael JACKSON and the JACKSON FIVE.				

JACKY - See Jackie LEE

JACQUELINE – MACK VIBE featuring JACQUELINE

JADE

				US
SINGLES:	**HITS 5**		**WEEKS 28**	
DON'T WALK AWAY	Giant	7	20 Mar 93	8
I WANNA LOVE YOU	Giant	13	3 Jul 93	7
ONE WOMAN	Giant	22	18 Sep 93	5
ALL THRU THE NITE	Giant	32	5 Feb 94	3
Above hit: P.O.V. duet with JADE.				
EVERY DAY OF THE WEEK	Giant	19	11 Feb 95	5
ALBUMS:	**HITS 1**		**WEEKS 3**	
JADE TO THE MAX	Giant	43	29 May 93	3

JADE 4 U - See PRAGA KHAN

JAGGED EDGE

				UK
SINGLES:	**HITS 1**		**WEEKS 2**	
YOU DON'T LOVE ME	Polydor	66	15 Sep 90	2

Mick JAGGER

				UK
(See also Jacksons.)				
SINGLES:	**HITS 5**		**WEEKS 34**	
MEMO FROM TURNER	Decca	32	14 Nov 70	5
From the film 'Performance'.				
JUST ANOTHER NIGHT	CBS	32	16 Feb 85	6
DANCING IN THE STREET	EMI America	1	7 Sep 85	12
Charity record with proceeds to Live Aid.				
Above hit: David BOWIE and Mick JAGGER.				
LET'S WORK	CBS	31	12 Sep 87	7
SWEET THING	Atlantic	24	6 Feb 93	4
ALBUMS:	**HITS 3**		**WEEKS 20**	
SHE'S THE BOSS	CBS	6	16 Mar 85	11
PRIMITIVE COOL	CBS	26	26 Sep 87	5
WANDERING SPIRIT	Atlantic	12	20 Feb 93	4

JAGS

				UK
SINGLES:	**HITS 2**		**WEEKS 11**	
BACK OF MY HAND	Island	17	8 Sep 79	10
WOMAN'S WORLD	Island	75	2 Feb 80	1

JAM

				UK
SINGLES:	**HITS 18**		**WEEKS 205**	
IN THE CITY	Polydor	40	7 May 77	6
ALL AROUND THE WORLD	Polydor	13	23 Jul 77	8
THE MODERN WORLD	Polydor	36	5 Nov 77	4
NEWS OF THE WORLD	Polydor	27	11 Mar 78	5

DAVID WATTS / "A" BOMB IN WARDOUR STREET	Polydor	25	26 Aug 78	8
DOWN IN THE TUBE STATION AT MIDNIGHT	Polydor	15	21 Oct 78	7
STRANGE TOWN	Polydor	15	17 Mar 79	9
WHEN YOU'RE YOUNG	Polydor	17	25 Aug 79	7
THE ETON RIFLES	Polydor	3	3 Nov 79	12
GOING UNDERGROUND / THE DREAMS OF CHILDREN	Polydor	1	22 Mar 80	9
ALL AROUND THE WORLD [RE-1ST]	Polydor	43	26 Apr 80	3
DAVID WATTS / "A" BOMB IN WARDOUR STREET [RE]	Polydor	54	26 Apr 80	3
IN THE CITY [RE-1ST]	Polydor	40	26 Apr 80	4
NEWS OF THE WORLD [RE-1ST]	Polydor	53	26 Apr 80	3
STRANGE TOWN [RE-1ST]	Polydor	44	26 Apr 80	4
THE MODERN WORLD [RE-1ST]	Polydor	52	26 Apr 80	3
START	Polydor	1	23 Aug 80	8
THAT'S ENTERTAINMENT	Metronome	21	7 Feb 81	7
Import.				
FUNERAL PYRE	Polydor	4	6 Jun 81	6
ABSOLUTE BEGINNERS	Polydor	4	24 Oct 81	6
TOWN CALLED MALICE / PRECIOUS	Polydor	1	13 Feb 82	8
JUST WHO IS THE 5 O'CLOCK HERO	Polydor	8	3 Jul 82	5
Import.				
THE BITTEREST PILL (I EVER HAD TO SWALLOW)	Polydor	2	18 Sep 82	7
Vocals by Jenny McKeowen of the Belle Stars.				
BEAT SURRENDER	Polydor	1	4 Dec 82	9
ALL AROUND THE WORLD [RE-2ND]	Polydor	38	22 Jan 83	4
DAVID WATTS/"A" BOMB IN WARDOUR STREET [RE-2ND]	Polydor	50	22 Jan 83	4
DOWN IN THE TUBE STATION AT MIDNIGHT [RE]	Polydor	30	22 Jan 83	6
GOING UNDERGROUND / THE DREAMS OF CHILDREN [RE]	Polydor	21	22 Jan 83	6
IN THE CITY [RE-2ND]	Polydor	47	22 Jan 83	4
NEWS OF THE WORLD [RE-2ND]	Polydor	39	22 Jan 83	4
STRANGE TOWN [RE-2ND]	Polydor	42	22 Jan 83	5
THE MODERN WORLD [RE-2ND]	Polydor	51	22 Jan 83	4
WHEN YOU'RE YOUNG [RE]	Polydor	53	22 Jan 83	4
THAT'S ENTERTAINMENT [RI-1ST]	Polydor	60	29 Jan 83	3
START [RE]	Polydor	62	5 Feb 83	2
THE ETON RIFLES [RE]	Polydor	54	5 Feb 83	3
TOWN CALLED MALICE / PRECIOUS [RE]	Polydor	73	5 Feb 83	1
THAT'S ENTERTAINMENT [RE-2ND]	Polydor	57	29 Jun 91	2
THE BITTEREST PILL (I EVER HAD TO SWALLOW) [RI]	Polydor	30	11 Oct 97	2
ALBUMS:	**HITS 14**			**WEEKS 190**
IN THE CITY	Polydor	20	28 May 77	18
THIS IS THE MODERN WORLD	Polydor	22	26 Nov 77	5
ALL MOD CONS	Polydor	6	11 Nov 78	17
SETTING SONS	Polydor	4	24 Nov 79	19
SOUND AFFECTS	Polydor	2	6 Dec 80	19
THE GIFT	Polydor	1	20 Mar 82	24
DIG THE NEW BREED	Polydor	2	18 Dec 82	15
IN THE CITY [RE]	Polydor	100	27 Aug 83	1
Re-released.				
SNAP!	Polydor	2	22 Oct 83	30
GREATEST HITS	Polydor	2	13 Jul 91	21
EXTRAS	Polydor	15	18 Apr 92	4
LIVE JAM	Polydor	28	6 Nov 93	2
THE JAM COLLECTION	Polydor	58	27 Jul 96	1
Collection of B-sides and lesser-known album tracks.				
DIRECTION REACTION CREATION	Polydor	8	7 Jun 97	4
5 CD box set of their 6 studio albums and 22 unreleased tracks.				
THE VERY BEST OF THE JAM	Polydor	9	25 Oct 97	10

JAM MACHINE
US / Italy

SINGLES:	**HITS 1**			**WEEKS 1**
EVERYDAY	Deconstruction	68	23 Dec 89	1

JAM ON THE MUTHA
UK

SINGLES:	**HITS 1**			**WEEKS 2**
HOTEL CALIFORNIA	M&G	62	11 Aug 90	2

JAM and SPOON featuring PLAVKA
Germany

(See also Tokyo Ghetto Pussy.)

SINGLES:	**HITS 5**			**WEEKS 24**
TALES FROM A DANCEOGRAPHIC OCEAN [EP]	R&S	49	2 May 92	1
Lead track: Stella.				
THE COMPLETE STELLA [RM]	Outer Rhythm	66	6 Jun 92	2
Remix of the track Stella from the EP listed above.				
Above 2: JAM and SPOON.				
RIGHT IN THE NIGHT (FALL IN LOVE WITH MUSIC)	Epic	31	26 Feb 94	4
FIND ME (ODYSSEY TO ANYOONA)	Epic	37	24 Sep 94	3

RIGHT IN THE NIGHT (FALL IN LOVE WITH MUSIC) [RI]	Epic	10	10 Jun 95	8
FIND ME (ODYSSEY TO ANYOONA) [RI]	Epic	22	16 Sep 95	3
ANGEL (LADADI O-HEYO)	Epic	26	25 Nov 95	2
KALEIDOSCOPE SKIES	Epic	48	30 Aug 97	1

ALBUMS: HITS 1   WEEKS 1

TRIPOMATIC FAIRYTALES 2001	Epic	71	19 Feb 94	1

Act released two albums simultaneously; the other, Tripomatic Fairytales 2002, charted at No. 119.

JAM TRONIK
US/Germany

SINGLES: HITS 1   WEEKS 7

ANOTHER DAY IN PARADISE	Debut	19	24 Mar 90	7

JAMAICA UNITED starring Ziggy MARLEY, Buju BANTON, Diana KING, SHAGGY, Maxi PRIEST, Ini KAMOZE, Toots HIBBER
Jamaica

SINGLES: HITS 1   WEEKS 1

RISE UP	Columbia	54	4 Jul 98	1

JAMELIA
UK

SINGLES: HITS 1   WEEKS 2

I DO	Parlophone Rhythm Series	36	31 Jul 99	2

JAMES
UK

SINGLES: HITS 19   WEEKS 86

HOW WAS IT FOR YOU?	Fontana	32	12 May 90	3
COME HOME	Fontana	32	7 Jul 90	4

Original release reached No. 84 in 1989.

LOSE CONTROL	Fontana	38	8 Dec 90	5
SIT DOWN	Fontana	2	30 Mar 91	10

Original release reached No. 77 in 1989.

SOUND	Fontana	9	30 Nov 91	7
BORN OF FRUSTRATION	Fontana	13	1 Feb 92	6
RING THE BELLS	Fontana	37	4 Apr 92	2
SEVEN [EP]	Fontana	46	18 Jul 92	2

Lead track: Seven.

SOMETIMES	Fontana	18	11 Sep 93	4
LAID	Fontana	25	13 Nov 93	4
JAM J / SAY SOMETHING	Fontana	24	2 Apr 94	4

Say Something only listed for first two weeks, it was not available on all formats.

SHE'S A STAR	Fontana	9	22 Feb 97	5
TOMORROW	Fontana	12	3 May 97	3
WALTZING ALONE	Fontana	23	5 Jul 97	4
DESTINY CALLING	Fontana	17	21 Mar 98	4
RUNAGROUND	Fontana	29	6 Jun 98	2
SIT DOWN [RM]	Fontana	7	21 Nov 98	7

Remixed by Apollo 440 for the Manchester 2002 Commonwealth Games launch in Oct 98.

I KNOW WHAT I'M HERE FOR	Mercury	22	31 Jul 99	5
JUST LIKE FRED ASTAIRE	Mercury	17	16 Oct 99	3
WE'RE GOING TO MISS YOU	Mercury	48	25 Dec 99	2

ALBUMS: HITS 9   WEEKS 149

STUTTER	Blanco Y Negro	68	2 Aug 86	2
STRIP MINE	Sire	90	8 Oct 88	1
GOLD MOTHER	Fontana	16	16 Jun 90	12
GOLD MOTHER [RE]	Fontana	2	4 May 91	22

Repackaged with additional track.

SEVEN	Fontana	2	29 Feb 92	14
LAID	Fontana	3	9 Oct 93	16
WAH WAH	Fontana	11	24 Sep 94	2

Out-takes and alternate versions from the Laid sessions.
Above hit: JAMES and Brian ENO.

WHIPLASH	Fontana	9	8 Mar 97	19
THE BEST OF JAMES	Fontana	1	4 Apr 98	53
MILLIONAIRES	Mercury	2	23 Oct 99	8

Dick JAMES
UK

SINGLES: HITS 2   WEEKS 13

ROBIN HOOD	Parlophone	14	21 Jan 56	8

Above hit: Dick JAMES with Stephen JAMES and his CHUMS.

ROBIN HOOD [RE] / THE BALLAD OF DAVY CROCKETT	Parlophone	29	19 May 56	1

The Ballad Of Davy Crockett is only credited to Dick James.

THE GARDEN OF EDEN	Parlophone	18	12 Jan 57	4

Above hit: Dick JAMES with Ron GOODWIN and his Orchestra.

Doris JAMES – See SLICK

Etta JAMES — UK

SINGLES:		HITS 1			WEEKS 7
I JUST WANT TO MAKE LOVE TO YOU	MCA	5	10 Feb 96	7
Featured in the Diet Coke TV commercial.				

Freddie JAMES — Canada

SINGLES:		HITS 1			WEEKS 3
GET UP AND BOOGIE	Warner Brothers	54	24 Nov 79	3

Jimmy JAMES and the VAGABONDS — UK

SINGLES:		HITS 3			WEEKS 25
RED RED WINE	Pye	36	14 Sep 68	8
I'LL GO WHERE YOUR MUSIC TAKES ME	Pye	23	24 Apr 76	8
NOW IS THE TIME	Pye	5	17 Jul 76	9

Joni JAMES — US

SINGLES:		HITS 2			WEEKS 2
WHY DON'T YOU BELIEVE ME?	MGM	11	7 Mar 53	1
Above hit: Joni JAMES with Lew DOUGLAS and his Orchestra.				
THERE MUST BE A WAY	MGM	24	31 Jan 59	1
Originally recorded by Johnnie Johnson in 1945.				

Rick JAMES — US

SINGLES:		HITS 6			WEEKS 30
YOU AND I	Motown	46	8 Jul 78	7
I'M A SUCKER FOR YOUR LOVE	Motown	43	7 Jul 79	8
Above hit: Teena MARIE Co-lead vocals: Rick JAMES.				
BIG TIME	Motown	41	6 Sep 80	6
GIVE IT TO ME BABY	Motown	47	4 Jul 81	3
STANDING ON THE TOP (PART 1)	Motown	53	12 Jun 82	3
Above hit: TEMPTATIONS featuring Rick JAMES.				
DANCE WIT' ME	Motown	53	3 Jul 82	3
ALBUMS:		**HITS 1**			**WEEKS 2**
THROWIN' DOWN	Motown	93	24 Jul 82	2

Sonny JAMES — US

SINGLES:		HITS 2			WEEKS 8
THE CAT CAME BACK	Capitol	30	1 Dec 56	1
YOUNG LOVE	Capitol	11	9 Feb 57	7

Stephen JAMES and his CHUMS - See Dick JAMES

Tommy JAMES and the SHONDELLS — US

SINGLES:		HITS 2			WEEKS 25
HANKY PANKY	Roulette	38	23 Jul 66	7
Originally recorded by The Raindrops in 1963.				
MONY MONY	Major Minor	1	8 Jun 68	18

Wendy JAMES — UK

SINGLES:		HITS 2			WEEKS 4
THE NAMELESS ONE	MCA	34	20 Feb 93	3
LONDON'S BRILLIANT	MCA	62	17 Apr 93	1
ALBUMS:		**HITS 1**			**WEEKS 1**
NOW AIN'T THE TIME FOR YOUR TEARS	MCA	43	20 Mar 93	1

JAMES BOYS — UK

SINGLES:		HITS 1			WEEKS 6
OVER AND OVER	Penny Farthing	39	19 May 73	6

JAMESTOWN featuring Jocelyn BROWN — US

(See also Jocelyn Brown.)

SINGLES:		HITS 2			WEEKS 4
SHE GOT SOUL	A&M	57	14 Sep 91	3
I BELIEVE	Playola	62	27 Mar 99	1

JAMIROQUAI — UK

SINGLES:		HITS 16			WEEKS 106
WHEN YOU GONNA LEARN?	Acid Jazz	52	31 Oct 92	2
WHEN YOU GONNA LEARN? [RE]	Acid Jazz	69	20 Feb 93	1
TOO YOUNG TO DIE	Sony S2	10	13 Mar 93	7
BLOW YOUR MIND	Sony S2	12	5 Jun 93	6
EMERGENCY ON PLANET EARTH	Sony S2	32	14 Aug 93	3

WHEN YOU GONNA LEARN? [RI]	Sony S2	28	25 Sep 93	3
SPACE COWBOY	Sony S2	17	8 Oct 94	5
HALF THE MAN	Sony S2	15	19 Nov 94	8
STILLNESS IN TIME	Sony S2	9	1 Jul 95	5
DO U KNOW WHERE YOU'RE COMING FROM	Renk	12	1 Jun 96	5
Above hit: M-BEAT featuring JAMIROQUAI.				
VIRTUAL INSANITY	Sony S2	3	31 Aug 96	11
COSMIC GIRL	Sony S2	6	7 Dec 96	10
ALRIGHT	Sony S2	6	10 May 97	5
HIGH TIMES	Sony S2	20	13 Dec 97	6
DEEPER UNDERGROUND	Sony S2	1	25 Jul 98	11
From the film 'Godzilla'.				
CANNED HEAT	Sony S2	4	5 Jun 99	10
SUPERSONIC	Sony S2	22	25 Sep 99	4
KING FOR A DAY	Sony S2	20	11 Dec 99	4
ALBUMS:	**HITS 4**		**WEEKS 156**	
EMERGENCY ON PLANET EARTH	Sony S2	1	26 Jun 93	32
THE RETURN OF THE SPACE COWBOY	Sony S2	2	29 Oct 94	29
TRAVELLING WITHOUT MOVING	Sony S2	2	21 Sep 96	72
SYNKRONIZED	Sony S2	1	26 Jun 99	23

JAMMERS
US

SINGLES:	HITS 1		WEEKS 2	
BE MINE TONIGHT	Salsoul	65	29 Jan 83	2

JAN and DEAN
US

SINGLES:	HITS 2		WEEKS 18	
HEART AND SOUL	London	24	26 Aug 61	8
Written by Hoagy Carmichael and originally recorded by Larry Clinton in 1938.				
SURF CITY	Liberty	26	17 Aug 63	10
Backing vocals by Brian Wilson of the Beach Boys.				
ALBUMS:	**HITS 1**		**WEEKS 2**	
THE JAN AND DEAN STORY	K-Tel	67	12 Jul 80	2

JAN and KJELD
Denmark

SINGLES:	HITS 1		WEEKS 4	
BANJO BOY	Ember	36	23 Jul 60	4

JANE'S ADDICTION
US

SINGLES:	HITS 2		WEEKS 4	
BEEN CAUGHT STEALING	Warner Brothers	34	23 Mar 91	3
CLASSIC GIRL	Warner Brothers	60	1 Jun 91	1
ALBUMS:	**HITS 1**		**WEEKS 2**	
RITUAL DE LO HABITUAL	Warner Brothers	37	8 Sep 90	2

JANET - See Janet JACKSON

Horst JANKOWSKI his Orchestra and Chorus
Germany

SINGLES:	HITS 1		WEEKS 18	
A WALK IN THE BLACK FOREST (EINE SCHWARZWALDFAHRT)	Mercury	3	31 Jul 65	18

Samantha JANUS
UK

SINGLES:	HITS 1		WEEKS 3	
A MESSAGE TO YOUR HEART	Hollywood	30	11 May 91	3
UK's Eurovision entry in 1991, it came 10th.				

Philip JAP
UK

SINGLES:	HITS 2		WEEKS 8	
SAVE US	A&M	53	31 Jul 82	4
TOTAL ERASURE	A&M	41	25 Sep 82	4

JAPAN
UK

(See also Rain Tree Crow.)

SINGLES:	HITS 12		WEEKS 81	
GENTLEMEN TAKE POLAROIDS	Virgin	60	18 Oct 80	2
THE ART OF PARTIES	Virgin	48	9 May 81	5
QUIET LIFE	Hansa	19	19 Sep 81	9
VISIONS OF CHINA	Virgin	32	7 Nov 81	12
EUROPEAN SON	Hansa	31	23 Jan 82	6
GHOSTS	Virgin	5	20 Mar 82	8
CANTONESE BOY	Virgin	24	22 May 82	6
I SECOND THAT EMOTION	Hansa	9	3 Jul 82	11
LIFE IN TOKYO	Hansa	28	9 Oct 82	6

NIGHTPORTER	*Virgin*	29	*20 Nov 82*	9
ALL TOMORROW'S PARTIES	*Hansa*	38	*12 Mar 83*	4
CANTON (LIVE)	*Virgin*	42	*21 May 83*	3
ALBUMS:	**HITS 6**		**WEEKS 135**	
QUIET LIFE	*Ariola Hansa*	72	*9 Feb 80*	3
GENTLEMEN TAKE POLAROIDS	*Virgin*	45	*15 Nov 80*	10
ASSEMBLAGE	*Hansa*	30	*26 Sep 81*	26
TIN DRUM	*Virgin*	12	*28 Nov 81*	50
QUIET LIFE [RE]	*Ariola Hansa*	53	*30 Jan 82*	5
ASSEMBLAGE [RE]	*Hansa*	26	*24 Jul 82*	20
OIL ON CANVAS	*Virgin*	5	*18 Jun 83*	14
Live recordings from their 1982 tour.				
EXORCISING GHOSTS	*Virgin*	45	*8 Dec 84*	7
Compilation.				

JARK PRONGO
Holland

SINGLES:	**HITS 1**		**WEEKS 1**	
MOVIN' THRU YOUR SYSTEM	*Hollywood*	58	*3 Apr 99*	1

Jeff JARRATT and Don REEDMAN
UK

ALBUMS:	**HITS 1**		**WEEKS 8**	
MASTERWORKS	*K-Tel*	39	*22 Nov 80*	8

Jean Michel JARRE
France

SINGLES:	**HITS 9**		**WEEKS 39**	
OXYGENE (PART 4)	*Polydor*	4	*27 Aug 77*	9
EQUINOXE PART 5	*Polydor*	45	*20 Jan 79*	5
FOURTH RENDEZ-VOUS	*Polydor*	65	*23 Aug 86*	4
REVOLUTIONS	*Polydor*	52	*5 Nov 88*	2
LONDON KID	*Polydor*	52	*7 Jan 89*	3
Above hit: Jean Michel JARRE featuring Hank MARVIN.				
OXYGENE IV (NEW VERSION) [RM]	*Polydor*	65	*7 Oct 89*	2
CHRONOLOGIE PART 4	*Polydor*	55	*26 Jun 93*	2
CHRONOLOGIE PART IV [RM]	*Polydor*	56	*30 Oct 93*	1
OXYGENE 8	*Epic*	17	*22 Mar 97*	3
OXYGENE 10	*Epic*	21	*5 Jul 97*	2
RENDEZ-VOUS 98 [RR]	*Epic*	12	*11 Jul 98*	6
Theme to ITV's sports coverage of the 1988 World Cup.				
Above hit: Jean Michel JARRE and APOLLO FOUR FORTY.				
ALBUMS:	**HITS 16**		**WEEKS 235**	
OXYGENE	*Polydor*	2	*20 Aug 77*	24
EQUINOXE	*Polydor*	11	*16 Dec 78*	26
MAGNETIC FIELDS	*Polydor*	6	*6 Jun 81*	17
THE CONCERTS IN CHINA	*Polydor*	6	*15 May 82*	17
Live recordings from Oct 81.				
THE ESSENTIAL JEAN-MICHEL JARRE	*Polystar*	14	*12 Nov 83*	29
ZOOLOOK	*Polydor*	47	*24 Nov 84*	14
RENDEZ-VOUS	*Polydor*	9	*12 Apr 86*	38
JEAN-MICHEL JARRE IN CONCERT LYON/HOUSTON	*Polydor*	18	*18 Jul 87*	15
Lyon recording from 1985, Houston from Apr 86.				
REVOLUTIONS	*Polydor*	2	*8 Oct 88*	13
JARRE LIVE	*Polydor*	16	*14 Oct 89*	4
WAITING FOR COUSTEAU	*Polydor*	14	*23 Jun 90*	10
IMAGES - THE BEST OF JEAN MICHEL JARRE	*Polydor*	14	*26 Oct 91*	12
CHRONOLOGIE	*Polydor*	11	*5 Jun 93*	8
CHRONOLOGIE PART 6	*Polydor*	60	*28 May 94*	1
6 track CD single.				
OXYGENE 7-13	*Epic*	11	*1 Mar 97*	5
ODYSSEY THROUGH O2	*Epic*	50	*23 May 98*	2
Remixes of Oxygene 7-13.				

Maurice JARRE
France

EPS:	**HITS 1**		**WEEKS 15**	
LAWRENCE OF ARABIA [OST]	*Colpix*	13	*9 May 64*	15
Above hit: Composed and conducted by Maurice JARRE; Performed by the LONDON				
PHILHARMONIC ORCHESTRA.				
ALBUMS:	**HITS 1**		**WEEKS 106**	
DOCTOR ZHIVAGO [OST]	*MGM*	3	*10 Sep 66*	106
Above hit: M.G.M. STUDIO ORCHESTRA Composed and conducted by Maurice Jarre.				

Al JARREAU
US

SINGLES:	**HITS 7**		**WEEKS 30**	
WE'RE IN THIS LOVE TOGETHER / EASY	*Warner Brothers*	55	*26 Sep 81*	4
Easy only listed on 26 Sep 81 at its chart entry position of No. 67.				
MORNIN'	*WEA*	28	*14 May 83*	6

TROUBLE IN PARADISE	*WEA International*	36	*16 Jul 83*	5
BOOGIE DOWN	*WEA*	63	*24 Sep 83*	3
DAY BY DAY	*Polydor*	53	*16 Nov 85*	3
Above hit: SHAKATAK with Al JARREAU.				
THE MUSIC OF GOODBYE (LOVE THEME FROM OUT OF AFRICA)	*MCA*	75	*5 Apr 86*	1
From the film.				
Above hit: MELISSA MANCHESTER and Al JARREAU.				
MOONLIGHTING "THEME"	*WEA*	8	*7 Mar 87*	8
Theme from the TV series.				
ALBUMS:	**HITS 4**			**WEEKS 37**
BREAKING AWAY	*Warner Brothers*	60	*5 Sep 81*	8
JARREAU	*WEA International*	39	*30 Apr 83*	18
HIGH CRIME	*WEA*	81	*17 Nov 84*	1
L IS FOR LOVER	*WEA*	50	*13 Sep 86*	4
L IS FOR LOVER [RE]	*WEA*	45	*4 Apr 87*	6
Repackaged.				

Kenny "Jammin" JASON and "Fast" Eddie SMITH   US
(See also DJ Fast Eddie.)

SINGLES:	**HITS 1**			**WEEKS 4**
CAN U DANCE	*Champion*	71	*11 Apr 87*	2
CAN U DANCE [RE]	*Champion*	67	*14 Nov 87*	2

JAVELLS featuring Nosmo KING   UK

SINGLES:	**HITS 1**			**WEEKS 8**
GOODBYE NOTHIN' TO SAY	*Pye Disco Demand*	26	*9 Nov 74*	8

Peter JAY and the JAYWALKERS   UK

SINGLES:	**HITS 1**			**WEEKS 11**
CAN-CAN '62	*Decca*	31	*10 Nov 62*	11

Simone JAY - See DJ DADO

JAY and the AMERICANS   US

EPS:	**HITS 1**			**WEEKS 1**
LIVING WITH JAY AND THE AMERICANS	*United Artists*	10	*1 Oct 66*	1

JAY-Z   US

SINGLES:	**HITS 14**			**WEEKS 54**
CAN'T KNOCK THE HUSTLE	*Northwestside*	30	*1 Mar 97*	2
Samples Much Too Much by Marcus Miller.				
Above hit: JAY-Z featuring Mary J. BLIGE.				
AIN'T NO PLAYA	*Northwestside*	31	*10 May 97*	2
Above hit: JAY-Z featuring Foxy BROWN.				
I'LL BE	*Def Jam*	9	*21 Jun 97*	5
Samples Rene and Angela's I'll Be Good and Blondie's Rapture.				
Above hit: Foxy BROWN featuring JAY Z.				
WHO YOU WIT	*Qwest*	65	*23 Aug 97*	1
From the film 'Sprung'.				
SUNSHINE	*Northwestside*	25	*25 Oct 97*	2
Above hit: JAY-Z featuring BABYFACE and Foxy BROWN.				
WISHING ON A STAR	*Northwestside*	13	*14 Feb 98*	4
Above hit: JAY-Z featuring Gwen DICKEY.				
TIME AFTER TIME	*Atlantic*	35	*4 Apr 98*	2
Above hit: CHANGING FACES (featuring JAY-Z).				
THE CITY IS MINE	*Northwestside*	38	*27 Jun 98*	2
Above hit: JAY-Z featuring BLACKSTREET.				
HARD KNOCK LIFE (GHETTO ANTHEM)	*Northwestside*	2	*12 Dec 98*	11
Samples It's A Hard Knock Life by the Original Broadway Cast of the show 'Annie'.				
CAN I GET A ...	*Def Jam*	24	*13 Mar 99*	3
Sleeve gives title as an EP: Def Jam's Rush Hour. From the film 'Rush Hour'.				
Above hit: JAY-Z featuring (AMIL of MAJOR COINZ) and JA RULE.				
BE ALONE NO MORE	*Northwestside*	11	*10 Apr 99*	9
Jay-Z was not credited on the original release. Remix by Cutfather & Joe. Charity record in aid of				
* Capital Radio's Help A London Child.*				
Above hit: ANOTHER LEVEL featuring JAY Z.				
LOBSTER & SCRIMP	*Virgin*	48	*19 Jun 99*	1
Above hit: TIMBALAND featuring JAY-Z.				
HEARTBREAKER	*Columbia*	5	*6 Nov 99*	9
Samples Stacy Lattisaw's Attack Of The Name Game.				
Above hit: Mariah CAREY featuring JAY-Z.				
WHAT YOU THINK OF THAT	*Roc-A-Fella*	58	*4 Dec 99*	1
Samples Keith Mansfield's High Velocity.				
Above hit: Memphis BLEEK featuring JAY-Z.				

JAYDEE
Holland

SINGLES:		HITS 1		WEEKS 3
PLASTIC DREAMS	R&S	18	20 Sep 97	3

Original release reached No. 93 in 1993.

Ollie JAYE - See JON THE DENTIST vs Ollie JAYE

JAYHAWKS
US

SINGLES:		HITS 1		WEEKS 1
BAD TIME	American Recordings	70	15 Jul 95	1

Originally recorded by Grand Funk.

ALBUMS:		HITS 2		WEEKS 2
TOMORROW THE GREEN GRASS	American Recordings	41	25 Feb 95	1
SOUND OF LIES	American Recordings	61	3 May 97	1

JAZZ and the BROTHERS GRIMM
UK

SINGLES:		HITS 1		WEEKS 2
(LET'S ALL GO BACK) DISCO NIGHTS	Ensign	57	9 Jul 88	2

JAZZY JEFF and the FRESH PRINCE
US

SINGLES:		HITS 8		WEEKS 49
GIRLS AIN'T NOTHIN BUT TROUBLE	Champion	21	4 Oct 86	8
SUMMERTIME	Jive	8	3 Aug 91	8
RING MY BELL	Jive	53	9 Nov 91	2

Above 3: D.J. JAZZY JEFF and the FRESH PRINCE.

BOOM! SHAKE THE ROOM	Jive	1	11 Sep 93	13
I'M LOOKING FOR THE ONE (TO BE WITH ME)	Jive	24	20 Nov 93	4
CAN'T WAIT TO BE WITH YOU	Jive	29	19 Feb 94	4

Samples Never Too Much by Luther Vandross.

TWINKLE TWINKLE (I'M NOT A STAR)	Jive	62	4 Jun 94	2
SUMMERTIME [RE]	Jive	29	6 Aug 94	4

Above hit: DJ JAZZY JEFF and the FRESH PRINCE.

BOOM! SHAKE THE ROOM [RM]	Jive	40	2 Dec 95	2

Remixed by Hula of the Outhere Brothers.

LOVELY DAZE	Jive	37	11 Jul 98	2

Samples Lovely Day by Bill Withers.
Above hit: DJ JAZZY JEFF and the FRESH PRINCE.

ALBUMS:		HITS 5		WEEKS 15
ROCK THE HOUSE	Champion	97	28 Feb 87	1
HE'S THE DJ, I'M THE RAPPER	Jive	68	21 May 88	2
HOMEBASE	Jive	69	14 Sep 91	1

Above 3: D.J. JAZZY JEFF and the FRESH PRINCE.

CODE RED	Jive	50	11 Dec 93	6
GREATEST HITS	Jive	20	16 May 98	5

Includes Will Smith's Men In Black.
Above hit: DJ JAZZY JEFF and FRESH PRINCE.

JAZZY JOYCE - See REGGAE PHILHARMONIC ORCHESTRA

JC-001
UK

SINGLES:		HITS 2		WEEKS 4
NEVER AGAIN	AnXious	67	24 Apr 93	2
CUPID	AnXious	56	26 Jun 93	2

JD - See DESTINY'S CHILD; SNOOP DOGGY DOG

JDS
UK/Italy

SINGLES:		HITS 2		WEEKS 2
NINE WAYS	ffrr	61	27 Sep 97	1
LONDON TOWN	Pepper	49	23 May 98	1

Wyclef JEAN
US

SINGLES:		HITS 6		WEEKS 32
WE TRYING TO STAY ALIVE	Columbia	13	28 Jun 97	5

Samples the Bee Gees' Staying Alive.

GUANTANAMERA	Columbia	25	27 Sep 97	2

Above 2: Wyclef JEAN featuring REFUGEE ALLSTARS.

NO NO NO	Columbia	5	28 Mar 98	8

Above hit: DESTINY'S CHILD (featuring Wyclef JEAN).

GONE TILL NOVEMBER	Columbia	3	16 May 98	9
ANOTHER ONE BITES THE DUST	Dreamworks	5	14 Nov 98	6

From the film 'Small Soldiers'.
Above hit: QUEEN/Wyclef JEAN featuring PRAS and FREE.

NEW DAY	Columbia	23	23 Oct 99	2

Official Single of the Net Aid concert, 9 Oct 99 at London, New York, Geneva. Charity record in aid of NetAid, Wyclef Jean Foundation and War Child.
Above hit: Wyclef JEAN featuring BONO.

ALBUMS:	HITS 1		WEEKS 6	
THE CARNIVAL	Columbia	40	5 Jul 97	6

Above hit: Wyclef JEAN and the REFUGEE ALLSTARS.

JEFFERSON
UK

SINGLES:	HITS 1		WEEKS 8	
THE COLOUR OF MY LOVE	Pye	22	12 Apr 69	8

Originally recorded by Barry Ryan.

JEFFERSON AIRPLANE - See STARSHIP

JEFFERSON STARSHIP - See STARSHIP

Garland JEFFREYS
US

SINGLES:	HITS 1		WEEKS 1	
HAIL HAIL ROCK 'N' ROLL	RCA	72	8 Feb 92	1

JELLYBEAN
US

SINGLES:	HITS 6		WEEKS 47	
SIDEWALK TALK	EMI America	47	1 Feb 86	4

Written by Madonna.
Above hit: JELLYBEAN featuring Catherine BUCHANAN.

THE REAL THING	Chrysalis	13	26 Sep 87	10

Above hit: JELLYBEAN featuring Steven DANTE.

WHO FOUND WHO	Chrysalis	10	28 Nov 87	10

Above hit: JELLYBEAN featuring Elisa FIORILLO.

JINGO	Chrysalis	12	12 Dec 87	10

Originally recorded by Michael Oluntunji.

JUST A MIRAGE	Chrysalis	13	12 Mar 88	10

Above hit: JELLYBEAN featuring Adele BERTEI.

COMING BACK FOR MORE	Chrysalis	41	20 Aug 88	3

Above hit: JELLYBEAN featuring Richard DARBYSHIRE.

ALBUMS:	HITS 2		WEEKS 35	
JUST VISITING THIS PLANET	Chrysalis	15	31 Oct 87	28
ROCKS THE HOUSE!	Chrysalis	16	3 Sep 88	7

JELLYFISH
US

SINGLES:	HITS 6		WEEKS 20	
THE KING IS HALF UNDRESSED	Charisma	39	26 Jan 91	6
BABY'S COMING BACK	Charisma	51	27 Apr 91	4
THE SCARY-GO-ROUND [EP]	Charisma	49	3 Aug 91	3

Lead track: Now She Knows She's Wrong.

I WANNA STAY HOME	Charisma	59	26 Oct 91	2
THE GHOST AT NUMBER ONE	Charisma	43	1 May 93	3
NEW MISTAKE	Virgin	55	17 Jul 93	2

ALBUMS:	HITS 1		WEEKS 2	
SPILT MILK	Charisma	21	22 May 93	2

Gordon JENKINS and his Chorus and Orchestra - See Danny KAYE with Gordon JENKINS and his Chorus and Orchestra

Karl JENKINS - See ADIEMUS

JERU THE DAMAJA
US

SINGLES:	HITS 1		WEEKS 1	
YA PLAYIN' YASELF	ffrr	67	7 Dec 96	1

JESSICA
Sweden

SINGLES:	HITS 1		WEEKS 1	
HOW WILL I KNOW (WHO YOU ARE)	Jive	47	20 Mar 99	1

JESUS JONES
UK

(See also Various Artists (EPs) 'The Food Christmas EP 1989'.)

SINGLES:	HITS 12		WEEKS 52	
INFO-FREAKO	Food	42	25 Feb 89	3
NEVER ENOUGH	Food	42	8 Jul 89	3
BRING IT ON DOWN	Food	46	23 Sep 89	3
REAL REAL REAL	Food	19	7 Apr 90	8
RIGHT HERE, RIGHT NOW	Food	31	6 Oct 90	4
INTERNATIONAL BRIGHT YOUNG THING	Food	7	12 Jan 91	7
WHO? WHERE? WHY?	Food	21	2 Mar 91	7

RIGHT HERE, RIGHT NOW [RI]	Food	31	20 Jul 91	4
THE DEVIL YOU KNOW	Food	10	9 Jan 93	5
THE RIGHT DECISION	Food	36	10 Apr 93	3
ZEROES AND ONES	Food	30	10 Jul 93	3
THE NEXT BIG THING	Food	49	14 Jun 97	1
CHEMICAL #1	Food	71	16 Aug 97	1
ALBUMS:	**HITS 3**			**WEEKS 31**
LIQUIDIZER	Food	32	14 Oct 89	3
DOUBT	Food	1	9 Feb 91	24
PERVERSE	Food	6	6 Feb 93	4

JESUS LIZARD
US

SINGLES:	**HITS 1**			**WEEKS 2**
PUSS	Touch And Go	12	6 Mar 93	2
[AA] listed with Oh, The Guilt by Nirvana.				
ALBUMS:	**HITS 1**			**WEEKS 1**
DOWN	Touch And Go	64	10 Sep 94	1

JESUS LOVES YOU
UK

(See also Boy George.)

SINGLES:	**HITS 4**			**WEEKS 18**
AFTER THE LOVE	More Protein	68	11 Nov 89	1
BOW DOWN MISTER	More Protein	27	23 Feb 91	8
GENERATIONS OF LOVE	More Protein	35	8 Jun 91	8
Original release reached No. 80 in 1990.				
SWEET TOXIC LOVE	Virgin	65	12 Dec 92	1
ALBUMS:	**HITS 1**			**WEEKS 1**
THE MARTYR MANTRAS	More Protein	60	13 Apr 91	1

JESUS AND MARY CHAIN
UK

SINGLES:	**HITS 20**			**WEEKS 59**
NEVER UNDERSTAND	Blanco Y Negro	47	2 Mar 85	4
YOU TRIP ME UP	Blanco Y Negro	55	8 Jun 85	3
JUST LIKE HONEY	Blanco Y Negro	45	12 Oct 85	3
SOME CANDY TALKING	Blanco Y Negro	13	26 Jul 86	5
APRIL SKIES	Blanco Y Negro	8	2 May 87	6
HAPPY WHEN IT RAINS	Blanco Y Negro	25	15 Aug 87	5
DARKLANDS	Blanco Y Negro	33	7 Nov 87	4
SIDEWALKING	Blanco Y Negro	30	9 Apr 88	3
BLUES FROM A GUN	Blanco Y Negro	32	23 Sep 89	2
HEAD ON	Blanco Y Negro	57	18 Nov 89	2
ROLLERCOASTER [EP]	Blanco Y Negro	46	8 Sep 90	2
Lead track: Rollercoaster.				
REVERENCE	Blanco Y Negro	10	15 Feb 92	4
FAR GONE AND OUT	Blanco Y Negro	23	14 Mar 92	3
ALMOST GOLD	Blanco Y Negro	41	4 Jul 92	2
SOUND OF SPEED [EP]	Blanco Y Negro	30	10 Jul 93	2
Lead track: Snakedriver.				
SOMETIMES ALWAYS	Blanco Y Negro	22	30 Jul 94	3
Vocals by Hope Sandoval of Mazzy Star.				
COME ON	Blanco Y Negro	52	22 Oct 94	2
I HATE ROCK 'N' ROLL	Blanco Y Negro	61	17 Jun 95	1
CRACKING UP	Creation	35	18 Apr 98	2
ILOVEROCKNROLL	Creation	38	30 May 98	1
ALBUMS:	**HITS 8**			**WEEKS 40**
PSYCHOCANDY	Blanco Y Negro	31	30 Nov 85	10
DARKLANDS	Blanco Y Negro	5	12 Sep 87	7
BARBED WIRE KISSES	Blanco Y Negro	9	30 Apr 88	7
AUTOMATIC	Blanco Y Negro	11	21 Oct 89	4
HONEY'S DEAD	Blanco Y Negro	14	4 Apr 92	5
THE SOUND OF SPEED	Blanco Y Negro	15	24 Jul 93	3
STONED AND DETHRONED	Blanco Y Negro	13	27 Aug 94	3
MUNKI	Creation	47	13 Jun 98	1

JETHRO TULL
UK

SINGLES:	**HITS 9**			**WEEKS 68**
LOVE STORY	Island	29	4 Jan 69	8
LIVING IN THE PAST	Island	3	17 May 69	14
SWEET DREAM	Chrysalis	7	1 Nov 69	11
THE WITCH'S PROMISE / TEACHER	Chrysalis	4	24 Jan 70	9
Some copies may only reflect title as Witch's Promise.				
LIFE IS A LONG SONG / UP THE POOL	Chrysalis	11	18 Sep 71	8
RING OUT SOLSTICE BELLS [EP]	Chrysalis	28	11 Dec 76	6
Lead track: Ring Out Solstice Bells.				
LAP OF LUXURY	Chrysalis	70	15 Sep 84	2

441

SAID SHE WAS A DANCER	Chrysalis	55	16 Jan 88	4
ROCKS ON THE ROAD	Chrysalis	47	21 Mar 92	3
LIVING IN THE PAST [RI]	Chrysalis	32	22 May 93	3

The 2nd CD format was titled Living In The (Slightly More Recent Past) and was a live recording from Montreal, Canada in 1992.

ALBUMS:		HITS 26		WEEKS 236
THIS WAS	Island	10	2 Nov 68	22
STAND UP	Island	1	9 Aug 69	29
BENEFIT	Island	3	9 May 70	13
AQUALUNG	Island	4	3 Apr 71	21
THICK AS A BRICK	Chrysalis	5	18 Mar 72	14
LIVING IN THE PAST	Chrysalis	8	15 Jul 72	11

Compilation of unreleased material plus one side recorded live at Carnegie Hall, New York.

A PASSION PLAY	Chrysalis	13	28 Jul 73	8

Originally premiered as a live show.

WAR CHILD	Chrysalis	14	2 Nov 74	4
MINSTREL IN THE GALLERY	Chrysalis	20	27 Sep 75	6
M.U. THE BEST OF JETHRO TULL	Chrysalis	44	31 Jan 76	5
TOO OLD TO ROCK 'N' ROLL: TOO YOUNG TO DIE	Chrysalis	25	15 May 76	10
SONGS FROM THE WOOD	Chrysalis	13	19 Feb 77	12
HEAVY HORSES	Chrysalis	20	29 Apr 78	10
LIVE BURSTING OUT	Chrysalis	17	14 Oct 78	8
STORM WATCH	Chrysalis	27	6 Oct 79	4
A	Chrysalis	25	6 Sep 80	5
BROADSWORD AND THE BEAST	Chrysalis	27	17 Apr 82	19
UNDER WRAPS	Chrysalis	18	15 Sep 84	5
ORIGINAL MASTERS	Chrysalis	63	2 Nov 85	3

Compilation of material up to 1977.

CREST OF A KNAVE	Chrysalis	19	19 Sep 87	10
20 YEARS OF JETHRO TULL	Chrysalis	78	9 Jul 88	1

5-LP box set or 3-CD box set.

ROCK ISLAND	Chrysalis	18	2 Sep 89	6
CATFISH RISING	Chrysalis	27	14 Sep 91	3
A LITTLE LIGHT MUSIC	Chrysalis	34	26 Sep 92	2
ROOTS TO BRANCHES	Chrysalis	20	16 Sep 95	3
AQUALUNG [RI]	Chrysalis	53	29 Jun 96	1

Digitally remastered, featuring 5 extra tracks recorded in the 1960s.

J-TULL DOT COM	Papillon	44	4 Sep 99	1

JETS   UK

SINGLES:		HITS 8		WEEKS 38
SUGAR DOLL	EMI	55	22 Aug 81	3

Originally recorded by Jesse Belvin.

YES TONIGHT JOSEPHINE	EMI	25	31 Oct 81	11
LOVE MAKES THE WORLD GO ROUND	EMI	21	6 Feb 82	9
THE HONEYDRIPPER	EMI	58	24 Apr 82	3
SOMEBODY TO LOVE	EMI	56	9 Oct 82	3

Originally recorded by Bobby Darin.

BLUE SKIES	EMI	53	6 Aug 83	3
ROCKIN' AROUND THE CHRISTMAS TREE	PRT	62	17 Dec 83	4
PARTY DOLL	PRT	72	13 Oct 84	2
ALBUMS:		HITS 1		WEEKS 6
100 PERCENT COTTON	EMI	30	10 Apr 82	6

JETS   US

SINGLES:		HITS 3		WEEKS 19
CRUSH ON YOU	MCA	5	31 Jan 87	13
CURIOSITY	MCA	41	25 Apr 87	4
ROCKET 2 U	MCA	69	28 May 88	2
ALBUMS:		HITS 1		WEEKS 4
CRUSH ON YOU	MCA	57	11 Apr 87	4

Joan JETT and the BLACKHEARTS   US

SINGLES:		HITS 4		WEEKS 21
I LOVE ROCK 'N ROLL	Epic	4	24 Apr 82	10

Originally recorded by the Arrows.

CRIMSON AND CLOVER	Epic	60	10 Jul 82	3
I HATE MYSELF FOR LOVING YOU	London	46	20 Aug 88	6
DIRTY DEEDS	Chrysalis	69	31 Mar 90	1

Above hit: Joan JETT.

I LOVE ROCK AND ROLL [RI]	Reprise	75	19 Feb 94	1
ALBUMS:		HITS 1		WEEKS 7
I LOVE ROCK 'N' ROLL	Epic	25	8 May 82	7

JEWEL | | | | US

SINGLES:	HITS 4			WEEKS 8	
WHO WILL SAVE YOUR SOUL	Atlantic	52	14 Jun 97	1
YOU WERE MEANT FOR ME	Atlantic	53	9 Aug 97	1
YOU WERE MEANT FOR ME [RE]	Atlantic	32	22 Nov 97	2
HANDS	Atlantic	41	21 Nov 98	2
DOWN SO LONG	Atlantic	38	26 Jun 99	2
ALBUMS:	**HITS 1**			**WEEKS 1**
SPIRIT	Atlantic	54	28 Nov 98	1

JEZ and CHOOPIE | | | | UK/Israel

SINGLES:	HITS 1			WEEKS 2	
YIM	Multiply	36	21 Mar 98	2

JHELISA | | | | US

SINGLES:	HITS 1			WEEKS 1	
FRIENDLY PRESSURE	Dorado	75	1 Jul 95	1

JIGSAW | | | | UK

SINGLES:	HITS 2			WEEKS 16	
SKY HIGH	Splash	9	1 Nov 75	11
From the film 'The Man From Hong Kong'.				
IF I HAVE TO GO AWAY	Splash	36	6 Aug 77	5

JILTED JOHN | | | | UK

SINGLES:	HITS 1			WEEKS 12	
JILTED JOHN	EMI International	4	12 Aug 78	12

JIMMY THE HOOVER | | | | UK

SINGLES:	HITS 1			WEEKS 8	
TANTALISE (WO WO EE YEH YEH)	Inner Vision	18	25 Jun 83	8

JINGLE BELLES | | | | UK/US

SINGLES:	HITS 1			WEEKS 4	
CHRISTMAS SPECTRE	Passion	37	17 Dec 83	4

JINNY | | | | US

SINGLES:	HITS 3			WEEKS 16	
KEEP WARM	Virgin	68	29 Jun 91	3
FEEL THE RHYTHM	Logic	74	22 May 93	1
KEEP WARM [RI]	Multiply	11	15 Jul 95	8
WANNA BE WITH YOU	Multiply	30	16 Dec 95	4

JIVE BUNNY and the MASTERMIXERS | | | | UK

(See also Liz Kershaw and Bruno Brookes.)

SINGLES:	HITS 10			WEEKS 68	
SWING THE MOOD [M]	Music Factory Dance	1	15 Jul 89	19
THAT'S WHAT I LIKE [M]	Music Factory Dance	1	14 Oct 89	12
LET'S PARTY [M]	Music Factory Dance	1	16 Dec 89	6
THAT SOUNDS GOOD TO ME [M]	Music Factory Dance	4	17 Mar 90	6
CAN CAN YOU PARTY [M]	Music Factory Dance	8	25 Aug 90	6
LET'S SWING AGAIN [M]	Music Factory Dance	19	17 Nov 90	5
THE CRAZY PARTY MIXES [M]	Music Factory Dance	13	22 Dec 90	5
This is title on the sleeve. The tracks on the 7" format were The Crazy Conga Mix on the A-side and Crazy Party Mix on the B-side.				
OVER TO YOU JOHN (HERE WE GO AGAIN) [M]	Music Factory Dance	28	23 Mar 91	5
Charity record with proceeds to St. John's Ambulance.				
HOT SUMMER SALSA [M]	Music Factory Dance	43	20 Jul 91	2
ROCK 'N' ROLL DANCE PARTY [M]	Music Factory Dance	48	23 Nov 91	2
ALBUMS:	**HITS 2**			**WEEKS 29**
JIVE BUNNY – THE ALBUM	Telstar	2	9 Dec 89	22
IT'S PARTY TIME	Telstar	23	8 Dec 90	7

JO JO GUNNE | | | | US

SINGLES:	HITS 1			WEEKS 12	
RUN RUN RUN	Asylum	6	25 Mar 72	12

JOAN COLLINS' FAN CLUB | | | | UK

SINGLES:	HITS 1			WEEKS 3	
LEADER OF THE PACK	10 Records	60	18 Jun 88	3

John Paul JOANS
UK

SINGLES:		HITS 1			WEEKS 7
THE MAN FROM NAZARETH	RAK		41	19 Dec 70	3
THE MAN FROM NAZARETH [RE]	RAK		25	16 Jan 71	4

JOBOXERS
UK

SINGLES:		HITS 4			WEEKS 33
BOXERBEAT	RCA		3	19 Feb 83	15
JUST GOT LUCKY	RCA		7	21 May 83	9
JOHNNY FRIENDLY	RCA		31	13 Aug 83	8
JEALOUS LOVE	RCA		72	12 Nov 83	1
ALBUMS:		HITS 1			WEEKS 5
LIKE GANGBUSTERS	RCA		18	24 Sep 83	5

JOCASTA
UK

SINGLES:		HITS 2			WEEKS 2
GO	Epic		50	15 Feb 97	1
Originally released in 1996.					
CHANGE ME	Epic		60	3 May 97	1

JOCKMASTER B.A. - See MAD JOCKS featuring JOCKMASTER B.A.

JOCKO
US

SINGLES:		HITS 1			WEEKS 3
RHYTHM TALK	Philadelphia International		56	23 Feb 80	3
Backing music is McFadden and Whitehead's 'Ain't No Stoppin' Us Now.					

JODE featuring YO-HANS
UK

SINGLES:		HITS 1			WEEKS 2
WALK . . . (THE DOG) LIKE AN EGYPTIAN	Logic		48	19 Dec 98	2

JODECI
US

SINGLES:		HITS 6			WEEKS 19
CHERISH	MCA		56	16 Jan 93	2
CRY FOR YOU	MCA		56	11 Dec 93	1
FEENIN'	MCA		18	16 Jul 94	3
CRY FOR YOU [RI]	Uptown		20	28 Jan 95	3
FREEK 'N YOU	Uptown		17	24 Jun 95	5
LOVE U 4 LIFE	Uptown		23	9 Dec 95	3
GET ON UP	MCA		20	25 May 96	2
Samples Velas by Quincy Jones.					
ALBUMS:		HITS 1			WEEKS 8
THE SHOW, THE AFTER-PARTY, THE HOTEL	Uptown		4	29 Jul 95	8

JODIE
Australia

SINGLES:		HITS 1			WEEKS 1
ANYTHING YOU WANT	Mercury		47	25 Feb 95	1

JOE
US

SINGLES:		HITS 9			WEEKS 21
I'M IN LUV	Mercury		22	22 Jan 94	4
THE ONE FOR ME	Mercury		34	25 Jun 94	2
ALL OR NOTHING	Mercury		56	22 Oct 94	1
ALL THE THINGS (YOUR MAN WON'T DO)	Island		34	27 Apr 96	3
From the film 'Don't Be A Menace'.					
DON'T WANNA BE A PLAYER	Jive		16	14 Jun 97	3
From the film 'Booty Call'.					
THE LOVE SCENE	Jive		22	27 Sep 97	2
GOOD GIRLS	Jive		29	10 Jan 98	3
NO ONE ELSE COMES CLOSE	Jive		41	22 Aug 98	2
ALL THAT I AM	Jive		52	31 Oct 98	1
ALBUMS:		HITS 2			WEEKS 5
EVERYTHING	Vertigo		53	12 Feb 94	1
ALL THAT I AM	Jive		26	9 Aug 97	4

JOE PUBLIC
US

SINGLES:		HITS 2			WEEKS 5
LIVE AND LEARN	Columbia		43	11 Jul 92	4
I'VE BEEN WATCHIN'	Columbia		75	28 Nov 92	1

Billy JOEL   US

SINGLES:		HITS 20			WEEKS 146
JUST THE WAY YOU ARE	CBS	19	11 Feb 78	9
Written about his first wife & manager Elizabeth.				
MOVIN' OUT (ANTHONY'S SONG)	CBS	35	24 Jun 78	6
MY LIFE	CBS	12	2 Dec 78	15
Backing vocals by Peter Cetera.				
UNTIL THE NIGHT	CBS	50	28 Apr 79	3
ALL FOR LEYNA	CBS	40	12 Apr 80	4
IT'S STILL ROCK AND ROLL TO ME	CBS	14	9 Aug 80	11
UPTOWN GIRL	CBS	1	15 Oct 83	17
Written about his then girlfriend Christie Brinkley.				
TELL HER ABOUT IT	CBS	4	10 Dec 83	10
AN INNOCENT MAN	CBS	8	18 Feb 84	10
THE LONGEST TIME	CBS	25	28 Apr 84	8
GOODNIGHT SAIGON / LEAVE A TENDER MOMENT ALONE	CBS	29	23 Jun 84	7
Goodnight Saigon listed from 30 Jun 84 and took first credit.				
SHE'S ALWAYS A WOMAN / JUST THE WAY YOU ARE [RI]	CBS	53	22 Feb 86	1
A MATTER OF TRUST	CBS	52	20 Sep 86	4
WE DIDN'T START THE FIRE	CBS	7	30 Sep 89	10
LENINGRAD	CBS	53	16 Dec 89	4
I GO TO EXTREMES	CBS	70	10 Mar 90	2
ALL SHOOK UP	Epic	27	29 Aug 92	4
From the film 'Honeymoon In Vegas'.				
THE RIVER OF DREAMS	Columbia	3	31 Jul 93	14
ALL ABOUT SOUL	Columbia	32	23 Oct 93	4
Backing vocals by Color Me Badd.				
NO MAN'S LAND	Columbia	50	26 Feb 94	3
ALBUMS:		HITS 14			WEEKS 324
THE STRANGER	CBS	25	25 Mar 78	40
52ND STREET	CBS	10	25 Nov 78	43
GLASS HOUSES	CBS	9	22 Mar 80	24
SONGS IN THE ATTIC	CBS	57	10 Oct 81	3
THE NYLON CURTAIN	CBS	27	2 Oct 82	8
AN INNOCENT MAN	CBS	2	10 Sep 83	94
Peak position reached on 23 Jun 84.				
COLD SPRING HARBOUR	CBS	95	4 Feb 84	1
Originally released in 1972.				
PIANO MAN	CBS	98	23 Jun 84	1
Originally released in 1973.				
GREATEST HITS VOLUME I AND VOLUME II	CBS	7	20 Jul 85	39
THE BRIDGE	CBS	38	16 Aug 86	10
KOHYEPT - LIVE IN LENINGRAD	CBS	92	28 Nov 87	1
Live recordings from Apr 87.				
STORM FRONT	CBS	5	4 Nov 89	25
RIVER OF DREAMS	Columbia	3	14 Aug 93	26
AN INNOCENT MAN [RI]	Columbia	66	23 Sep 95	1
GREATEST HITS - VOLUME III	Columbia	23	1 Nov 97	4
GREATEST HITS - VOLUMES I, II & III [RI]	Columbia	33	13 Jun 98	4
Double re-issue of the 2 previous hits packages.				

JOHANN   Germany

SINGLES:		HITS 1			WEEKS 1
NEW KICKS	Perfecto	54	16 Mar 96	1

Angela JOHN - See Jose PADILLA featuring Angela JOHN

Elton JOHN   UK

(See also Dionne Warwick; Various Artists: Films - Original Soundtracks 'The Lion King'.)

SINGLES:		HITS 73			WEEKS 557
YOUR SONG	DJM	7	23 Jan 71	12
ROCKET MAN (I THINK IT'S GOING TO BE A LONG LONG TIME)	DJM	2	22 Apr 72	13
HONKY CAT	DJM	31	9 Sep 72	6
CROCODILE ROCK	DJM	5	4 Nov 72	14
DANIEL	DJM	4	20 Jan 73	10
SATURDAY NIGHT'S ALRIGHT FOR FIGHTING	DJM	7	7 Jul 73	9
GOODBYE YELLOW BRICK ROAD	DJM	6	29 Sep 73	16
STEP INTO CHRISTMAS	DJM	24	8 Dec 73	7
CANDLE IN THE WIND	DJM	11	2 Mar 74	9
DON'T LET THE SUN GO DOWN ON ME	DJM	16	1 Jun 74	8
Backing vocals by Captain and Tennille and Carl Wilson and Bruce Johnston of the Beach Boys.				
THE BITCH IS BACK	DJM	15	14 Sep 74	7
Backing vocals by Dusty Springfield.				
LUCY IN THE SKY WITH DIAMONDS	DJM	10	23 Nov 74	10
Written by Lennon/McCartney.				

PHILADELPHIA FREEDOM	DJM	12	8 Mar 75	9
Tribute to tennis star Billie Jean King.				
Above hit: Elton JOHN BAND.				
SOMEONE SAVED MY LIFE TONIGHT	DJM	22	28 Jun 75	5
Written about Long John Baldry.				
ISLAND GIRL	DJM	14	4 Oct 75	8
PINBALL WIZARD	DJM	7	20 Mar 76	7
From the film 'Tommy'.				
DON'T GO BREAKING MY HEART	Rocket	1	3 Jul 76	14
Above hit: Elton JOHN and Kiki DEE.				
BENNY AND THE JETS	DJM	37	25 Sep 76	5
SORRY SEEMS TO BE THE HARDEST WORD	Rocket	11	13 Nov 76	10
CRAZY WATER	Rocket	27	26 Feb 77	6
BITE YOUR LIP (GET UP AND DANCE)	Rocket	28	11 Jun 77	4
[AA] listed with Chicago by Kiki Dee.				
EGO	Rocket	34	15 Apr 78	6
PART TIME LOVE	Rocket	15	21 Oct 78	13
SONG FOR GUY	Rocket	4	16 Dec 78	10
ARE YOU READY FOR LOVE	Rocket	42	12 May 79	6
LITTLE JEANIE	Rocket	33	24 May 80	7
Sleeve reflects title as Little Jeannie.				
SARTORIAL ELOQUENCE	Rocket	44	23 Aug 80	5
I SAW HER STANDING THERE	DJM	40	21 Mar 81	4
Above hit: Elton JOHN BAND featuring John LENNON and the MUSCLE SHOALS HORNS.				
NOBODY WINS	Rocket	42	23 May 81	5
BLUE EYES	Rocket	8	27 Mar 82	10
EMPTY GARDEN	Rocket	51	12 Jun 82	4
Tribute to John Lennon.				
I GUESS THAT'S WHY THEY CALL IT THE BLUES	Rocket	5	30 Apr 83	15
Features Stevie Wonder on Harmonica.				
I'M STILL STANDING	Rocket	4	30 Jul 83	11
KISS THE BRIDE	Rocket	20	15 Oct 83	7
COLD AS CHRISTMAS (IN THE MIDDLE OF THE YEAR)	Rocket	33	10 Dec 83	6
Even though not listed, this was released as a double A-side with 'Crystal'.				
SAD SONGS (SAY SO MUCH)	Rocket	7	26 May 84	12
PASSENGERS	Rocket	5	11 Aug 84	11
WHO WEARS THESE SHOES?	Rocket	50	20 Oct 84	3
BREAKING HEARTS (AIN'T WHAT IT USED TO BE)	Rocket	59	2 Mar 85	3
ACT OF WAR	Rocket	32	15 Jun 85	5
Above hit: Elton JOHN and Millie JACKSON.				
NIKITA	Rocket	3	12 Oct 85	13
WRAP HER UP	Rocket	12	7 Dec 85	10
Above 2 features backing vocals by George Michael.				
CRY TO HEAVEN	Rocket	47	1 Mar 86	4
HEARTACHE ALL OVER THE WORLD	Rocket	45	4 Oct 86	4
SLOW RIVERS	Rocket	44	29 Nov 86	8
Backing vocals by Kiki Dee.				
Above hit: Elton JOHN and Cliff RICHARD.				
FLAMES OF PARADISE	CBS	59	20 Jun 87	3
Above hit: Jennifer RUSH (duet with Elton JOHN).				
CANDLE IN THE WIND [RR-1ST]	Rocket	5	16 Jan 88	11
With the Melbourne Symphony Orchestra, recorded live in Australia, 1986.				
I DON'T WANNA GO ON WITH YOU LIKE THAT	Rocket	30	4 Jun 88	8
TOWN OF PLENTY	Rocket	74	3 Sep 88	1
THROUGH THE STORM	Arista	41	6 May 89	3
Above hit: Aretha FRANKLIN and Elton JOHN.				
HEALING HANDS	Rocket	45	26 Aug 89	5
SACRIFICE	Rocket	55	4 Nov 89	3
SACRIFICE [RI] / HEALING HANDS [RI]	Rocket	1	9 Jun 90	15
CLUB AT THE END OF THE STREET / WHISPERS	Rocket	47	18 Aug 90	3
YOU GOTTA LOVE SOMEONE	Rocket	33	20 Oct 90	4
EASIER TO WALK AWAY	Rocket	67	15 Dec 90	1
EASIER TO WALK AWAY [RE]	Rocket	63	29 Dec 90	1
DON'T LET THE SUN GO DOWN ON ME	Epic	1	7 Dec 91	10
Live recording in London, Mar 91.				
Above hit: George MICHAEL with Elton JOHN.				
THE ONE	Rocket	10	6 Jun 92	8
RUNAWAY TRAIN	Rocket	31	1 Aug 92	4
Above hit: Elton JOHN and Eric CLAPTON.				
THE LAST SONG	Rocket	21	7 Nov 92	4
SIMPLE LIFE	Rocket	44	22 May 93	2
TRUE LOVE	Rocket	2	20 Nov 93	10
Above hit: Elton JOHN – duet with Kiki DEE.				
DON'T GO BREAKING MY HEART	Rocket	7	26 Feb 94	7
Above hit: Elton JOHN and RUPAUL.				
AIN'T NOTHING LIKE THE REAL THING	London	24	14 May 94	4
Above hit: Marcella DETROIT and Elton JOHN.				
CAN YOU FEEL THE LOVE TONIGHT	Mercury	14	9 Jul 94	9

Backing vocals by Gary Barlow, Kiki Dee and Rick Astley.

CIRCLE OF LIFE	Rocket	11	8 Oct 94	12

Above 2 from the film 'The Lion King'.

BELIEVE	Rocket	15	4 Mar 95	7
MADE IN ENGLAND	Rocket	18	20 May 95	5
PLEASE	Rocket	33	3 Feb 96	3
LIVE LIKE HORSES	Rocket	9	14 Dec 96	6

Above hit: Elton JOHN and Luciano PAVAROTTI.

SOMETHING ABOUT THE WAY YOU LOOK TONIGHT / CANDLE IN THE WIND 1997 [RR-2ND]	Rocket	1	20 Sep 97	24

Biggest Selling single of all time. Lyrics were changed for the funeral of Diana, Princess Of Wales on 6 Sep 97.

RECOVER YOUR SOUL	Rocket	16	14 Feb 98	3
IF THE RIVER CAN BEND	Rocket	32	13 Jun 98	2

Proceeds from the majority of John's later singles were donated to charity.

WRITTEN IN THE STARS	Rocket	10	6 Mar 99	7

From the Walt Disney film 'Aida'.
Above hit: Elton JOHN and LeAnn RIMES.

WRITTEN IN THE STARS [RE]	Rocket	63	22 May 99	1

ALBUMS:		HITS 36		WEEKS 869
ELTON JOHN	DJM	11	23 May 70	14
TUMBLEWEED CONNECTION	DJM	6	16 Jan 71	20
THE ELTON JOHN LIVE ALBUM 17-11-70	DJM	20	1 May 71	2

Live recording of a concert in New York by the W-PLJ FM radio station.

MADMAN ACROSS THE WATER	DJM	41	20 May 72	2
HONKY CHATEAU	DJM	2	3 Jun 72	23
DON'T SHOOT ME I'M ONLY THE PIANO PLAYER	DJM	1	10 Feb 73	42
GOODBYE YELLOW BRICK ROAD	DJM	1	3 Nov 73	84
CARIBOU	DJM	1	13 Jul 74	18
ELTON JOHN'S GREATEST HITS	DJM	1	23 Nov 74	84
CAPTAIN FANTASTIC AND THE BROWN DIRT COWBOY	DJM	2	7 Jun 75	24
ROCK OF THE WESTIES	DJM	5	8 Nov 75	12
HERE AND THERE	DJM	6	15 May 76	9

Live recordings from the Royal Festival Hall and Madison Square Garden, 1974.

BLUE MOVES	Rocket	3	6 Nov 76	15
GREATEST HITS VOLUME 2	DJM	6	15 Oct 77	24
A SINGLE MAN	Rocket	8	4 Nov 78	26
VICTIM OF LOVE	Rocket	41	20 Oct 79	3
LADY SAMANTHA	DJM	56	8 Mar 80	2
21 AT 33	Rocket	12	31 May 80	13
THE VERY BEST OF ELTON JOHN	K-Tel	24	25 Oct 80	13
THE FOX	Rocket	12	30 May 81	12
JUMP UP	Rocket	13	17 Apr 82	12
LOVE SONGS	TV Records	39	6 Nov 82	13
TOO LOW FOR ZERO	Rocket	7	11 Jun 83	73
BREAKING HEARTS	Rocket	2	30 Jun 84	23
ICE ON FIRE	Rocket	3	16 Nov 85	23
LEATHER JACKETS	Rocket	24	15 Nov 86	9
LIVE IN AUSTRALIA	Rocket	70	12 Sep 87	2

Live recordings from his 1986 Australian tour. Melbourne Symphony Orchestra conducted by James Newton Howard. This was based on sales of a box set.
Above hit: Elton JOHN and the MELBOURNE SYMPHONY ORCHESTRA.

LIVE IN AUSTRALIA [RE]	Rocket	43	5 Mar 88	5

Standard package re-release.

REG STRIKES BACK	Rocket	18	16 Jul 88	6
SLEEPING WITH THE PAST	Rocket	6	23 Sep 89	9
SLEEPING WITH THE PAST [RE]	Rocket	1	16 Jun 90	33
THE VERY BEST OF ELTON JOHN	Rocket	1	10 Nov 90	96

Includes re-entries through to 1997.

THE ONE	Rocket	2	27 Jun 92	18
DUETS	Rocket	5	4 Dec 93	18

Above hit: Elton JOHN and VARIOUS ARTISTS.

MADE IN ENGLAND	Rocket	3	1 Apr 95	14
LOVE SONGS	Rocket	4	18 Nov 95	48
THE BIG PICTURE	Rocket	3	11 Oct 97	23
ELTON JOHN AND TIM RICE'S AIDA	Rocket	29	3 Apr 99	2

Above hit: Elton JOHN and FRIENDS.

Robert JOHN
US

SINGLES:		HITS 2		WEEKS 13
IF YOU DON'T WANT MY LOVE	CBS	42	20 Jul 68	5
SAD EYES	EMI America	31	20 Oct 79	8

JOHN and YOKO - See John LENNON

JOHNNA
US

SINGLES:		HITS 2		WEEKS 3
DO WHAT YOU FEEL	PWL International	43	10 Feb 96	2

IN MY DREAMS	PWL	66	11 May 96	1

JOHNNY and CHARLEY — Spain

SINGLES:	HITS 1		WEEKS 1	
LA YENKA	Pye International	49	16 Oct 65	1

JOHNNY HATES JAZZ — UK

SINGLES:	HITS 5		WEEKS 45	
SHATTERED DREAMS	Virgin	5	11 Apr 87	14
I DON'T WANT TO BE A HERO	Virgin	11	29 Aug 87	10
TURN BACK THE CLOCK	Virgin	12	21 Nov 87	11
HEART OF GOLD	Virgin	19	27 Feb 88	7
DON'T SAY IT'S LOVE	Virgin	48	9 Jul 88	3
ALBUMS:	HITS 1		WEEKS 39	
TURN BACK THE CLOCK	Virgin	1	23 Jan 88	39

JOHNNY and the HURRICANES — US

SINGLES:	HITS 7		WEEKS 88	
RED RIVER ROCK	London	3	10 Oct 59	16
REVEILLE ROCK	London	14	26 Dec 59	5
BEATNIK FLY	London	8	19 Mar 60	19
DOWN YONDER	London	8	18 Jun 60	11
Originally recorded by Hare and Jones in 1921.				
ROCKING GOOSE	London	3	1 Oct 60	20
JA-DA	London	14	4 Mar 61	9
Originally recorded by Arthur Fields in 1919.				
OLD SMOKIE / HIGH VOLTAGE	London	24	8 Jul 61	8
ALBUMS:	HITS 2		WEEKS 5	
STORMSVILLE	London	18	3 Dec 60	1
BIG SOUND OF JOHNNY AND THE HURRICANES	London	13	1 Apr 61	4

JOHNSON — UK

SINGLES:	HITS 1		WEEKS 1	
SAY YOU LOVE ME	Higher Ground	56	27 Mar 99	1

Bryan JOHNSON — UK

SINGLES:	HITS 1		WEEKS 11	
LOOKING HIGH, HIGH, HIGH	Decca	20	12 Mar 60	11
UK's Eurovision entry in 1960, it came 2nd.				

Carey JOHNSON — Australia

SINGLES:	HITS 1		WEEKS 8	
REAL FASHION REGGAE STYLE	10 Records	19	25 Apr 87	8

Denise JOHNSON — UK

SINGLES:	HITS 2		WEEKS 4	
DON'T FIGHT IT, FEEL IT	Creation	41	24 Aug 91	2
Above hit: PRIMAL SCREAM featuring Denise JOHNSON.				
RAYS OF THE RISING SUN	Magnet	45	14 May 94	2

Don JOHNSON — US

SINGLES:	HITS 2		WEEKS 12	
HEARTBEAT	Epic	46	18 Oct 86	5
TILL I LOVED YOU (THE LOVE THEME FROM GOYA)	CBS	16	5 Nov 88	7
Above hit: Barbra STREISAND and Don JOHNSON.				

General JOHNSON – See CHAIRMEN OF THE BOARD

Holly JOHNSON — UK

(See also Christians, Holly Johnson, Paul McCartney, Gerry Marsden, Stock Aitken Waterman.)

SINGLES:	HITS 6		WEEKS 31	
LOVE TRAIN	MCA	4	14 Jan 89	11
Features Brian May on guitar.				
AMERICANOS	MCA	4	1 Apr 89	11
ATOMIC CITY	MCA	18	24 Jun 89	4
HEAVEN'S HERE	MCA	62	30 Sep 89	2
WHERE HAS LOVE GONE?	MCA	73	1 Dec 90	1
THE POWER OF LOVE	Pleasuredome	56	25 Dec 99	2
ALBUMS:	HITS 1		WEEKS 17	
BLAST	MCA	1	6 May 89	17

Howard JOHNSON — US

SINGLES:		HITS 1			WEEKS 6
KEEPIN' LOVE NEW / SO FINE	A&M		45	4 Sep 82	6

Keepin' Love New listed only on 4 Sep 82 at its chart entry position of No. 64.

Johnny JOHNSON and the BANDWAGON — US

SINGLES:		HITS 5			WEEKS 50
BREAKIN' DOWN THE WALLS OF HEARTACHE	Direction		4	19 Oct 68	15

Above hit: BANDWAGON.
Some later copies credit Johnny Johnson and the Bandwagon.

YOU	Direction		34	8 Feb 69	4
LET'S HANG ON	Direction		36	31 May 69	6
SWEET INSPIRATION	Bell		10	25 Jul 70	12
SWEET INSPIRATION [RE]	Bell		46	24 Oct 70	1
(BLAME IT) ON THE PONY EXPRESS	Bell		7	28 Nov 70	12

Kevin JOHNSON — Australia

SINGLES:		HITS 1			WEEKS 6
ROCK AND ROLL (I GAVE YOU THE BEST YEARS OF MY LIFE)	UK		23	11 Jan 75	6

L J JOHNSON — US

SINGLES:		HITS 1			WEEKS 6
YOUR MAGIC PUT A SPELL ON ME	Philips		27	7 Feb 76	6

Laurie JOHNSON ORCHESTRA — UK

SINGLES:		HITS 2			WEEKS 14
SUCU SUCU	Pye		9	30 Sep 61	12

Theme from the TV series 'Top Secret'.

THEME FROM THE PROFESSIONALS	Virgin		36	17 May 97	2

Theme from the 1970s ITV series.
Above hit: Laurie JOHNSON'S LONDON BIG BAND.

Linton Kwesi JOHNSON — Jamaica

ALBUMS:		HITS 3			WEEKS 8
FORCE OF VICTORY	Island		66	30 Jun 79	1
BASS CULTURE	Island		46	31 May 80	5
MAKING HISTORY	Island		73	10 Mar 84	2

Lou JOHNSON — US

SINGLES:		HITS 1			WEEKS 2
MESSAGE TO MARTHA (KENTUCKY BLUEBIRD)	London		36	28 Nov 64	2

Marv JOHNSON — US

SINGLES:		HITS 5			WEEKS 40
YOU GOT WHAT IT TAKES	London		7	13 Feb 60	17
I LOVE THE WAY YOU LOVE	London		35	7 May 60	3
AIN'T GONNA BE THAT WAY	London		50	13 Aug 60	1
I'LL PICK A ROSE FOR MY ROSE	Tamla Motown		10	25 Jan 69	11
I MISS YOU BABY (HOW I MISS YOU)	Tamla Motown		25	25 Oct 69	8

Orlando JOHNSON - See SECCHI featuring Orlando JOHNSON

Paul JOHNSON — UK

SINGLES:		HITS 2			WEEKS 7
WHEN LOVE COMES CALLING	CBS		52	21 Feb 87	5
NO MORE TOMORROWS	CBS		67	25 Feb 89	2
ALBUMS:		HITS 2			WEEKS 3
PAUL JOHNSON	CBS		63	4 Jul 87	2
PERSONAL	CBS		70	16 Sep 89	1

Paul JOHNSON — US

SINGLES:		HITS 1			WEEKS 8
GET GET DOWN	Defected		5	25 Sep 99	8

Puff JOHNSON — US

SINGLES:		HITS 2			WEEKS 6
OVER AND OVER	Columbia		20	18 Jan 97	4

From the film 'The First Wives Club'.

FOREVER MORE	Columbia		29	12 Apr 97	2

Teddy JOHNSON and Pearl CARR — UK

SINGLES:	HITS 2			WEEKS 19	
SING LITTLE BIRDIE	Columbia	12	21 Mar 59	8
UK's Eurovision entry in 1959, it came 2nd.					
HOW WONDERFUL TO KNOW	Columbia	23	8 Apr 61	11
Above hit: Teddy JOHNSON and Pearl CARR with Geoff LOVE and his Orchestra.					

Trina JOHNSON and VOICES - See HAMMER

Bruce JOHNSTON — US

SINGLES:	HITS 1			WEEKS 4	
PIPELINE	CBS	33	27 Aug 77	4

James A. JOHNSTON — US

ALBUMS:	HITS 1			WEEKS 8	
WORLD WRESTLING FEDERATION - THE MUSIC - VOLUME 4	Koch International	44	13 Nov 99	8
Volume 4 is the first UK retail release, includes track by German rock group H-Blockx.					

Jan JOHNSTON - See BT; FREEFALL featuring Jan JOHNSTON; SUB.MERGE featuring Jan JOHNSTON.

Sabrina JOHNSTON — US

SINGLES:	HITS 4			WEEKS 19	
PEACE	East West	8	7 Sep 91	10
FRIENDSHIP	East West	58	7 Dec 91	4
I WANNA SING	East West	46	11 Jul 92	2
PEACE [RM]	Epic	35	3 Oct 92	2
[AA] listed with a remix of Gypsy Woman by Crystal Waters. Remixed by David Morales. From the 'Red Hot + Dance' album (to benefit Aids research).					
SATISFY MY LOVE	Champion	62	13 Aug 94	1

JOHNSTON BROTHERS — UK

(See also All Star Hit Parade.)

SINGLES:	HITS 10			WEEKS 33	
OH HAPPY DAY	Decca	4	4 Apr 53	8
WAIT FOR ME, DARLING	Decca	18	6 Nov 54	1
Above hit: Joan REGAN and the JOHNSTON BROTHERS.					
HAPPY DAYS AND LONELY NIGHTS	Decca	14	22 Jan 55	2
Above hit: Suzi MILLER and the JOHNSTON BROTHERS.					
HERNANDO'S HIDEAWAY	Decca	1	8 Oct 55	13
Originally recorded by Carol Haney.					
Above hit: JOHNSTON BROTHERS with Johnny DOUGLAS and his Orchestra (Elsa BRUNELLESCHI-Castanets).					
JOIN IN AND SING AGAIN [M]	Decca	9	31 Dec 55	1
Above hit: JOHNSTON BROTHERS and the George CHISHOLM SOUR-NOTE SIX.					
NO OTHER LOVE	Decca	22	14 Apr 56	1
Above hit: JOHNSTON BROTHERS with Bob SHARPLES and his Music.					
IN THE MIDDLE OF THE HOUSE	Decca	27	1 Dec 56	1
Above hit: JOHNSTON BROTHERS and the KEYNOTES.					
JOIN IN AND SING NO. 3 [M]	Decca	30	8 Dec 56	1
Above hit: JOHNSTON BROTHERS and the George CHISHOLM SOUR-NOTE SIX.					
JOIN IN AND SING NO. 3 [M] [RE]	Decca	24	29 Dec 56	1
GIVE HER MY LOVE	Decca	27	9 Feb 57	1
HEART	Decca	23	20 Apr 57	3
Above hit: JOHNSTON BROTHERS with Roland SHAW and his Orchestra.					

Brian JOHNSTONE — UK

ALBUMS:	HITS 1			WEEKS 3	
AN EVENING WITH JOHNNERS	Listen For Pleasure	46	5 Mar 94	3

James JOLIS - See Barry MANILOW

JOLLY BROTHERS — Jamaica

SINGLES:	HITS 1			WEEKS 7	
CONSCIOUS MAN	United Artists	46	28 Jul 79	7

JOLLY ROGER — UK

SINGLES:	HITS 1			WEEKS 12	
ACID MAN	10 Records	23	10 Sep 88	12

Al JOLSON — US

ALBUMS:	HITS 2			WEEKS 11	
20 GOLDEN GREATS	MCA	18	14 Mar 81	7
THE AL JOLSON COLLECTION	Ronco	67	17 Dec 83	4

JOMALSKI - See WILDCHILD

JOMANDA
US

SINGLES:		HITS 4		WEEKS 10
MAKE MY BODY ROCK (FEEL IT)	RCA	44	22 Apr 89	3
GOT A LOVE FOR YOU	Giant	43	29 Jun 91	4
I LIKE IT	Atlantic	67	11 Sep 93	1
NEVER	Big Beat	40	13 Nov 93	2

JON and VANGELIS
UK/Greece

(See also Jon Anderson; Anderson Bruford Wakeman Howe; Vangelis.)

SINGLES:		HITS 4		WEEKS 28
I HEAR YOU NOW	Polydor	8	5 Jan 80	11
I'LL FIND MY WAY HOME	Polydor	6	12 Dec 81	13
HE IS SAILING	Polydor	61	30 Jul 83	2
STATE OF INDEPENDENCE	Polydor	67	18 Aug 84	2

ALBUMS:		HITS 4		WEEKS 53
SHORT STORIES	Polydor	4	26 Jan 80	11
THE FRIENDS OF MR. CAIRO	Polydor	17	11 Jul 81	8
THE FRIENDS OF MR. CAIRO [RE]	Polydor	6	23 Jan 82	15
Re-released with additional track.				
PRIVATE COLLECTION	Polydor	22	2 Jul 83	10
THE BEST OF JON AND VANGELIS	Polydor	42	11 Aug 84	9

JON OF THE PLEASED WIMMIN
UK

SINGLES:		HITS 2		WEEKS 5
PASSION	Perfecto	27	18 Feb 95	3
GIVE ME STRENGTH	Perfecto	30	6 Apr 96	2

JON THE DENTIST vs Ollie JAYE
UK

SINGLES:		HITS 1		WEEKS 1
IMAGINATION	Tidy Trax	72	24 Jul 99	1

Aled JONES
UK

(See also Mike Oldfield.)

SINGLES:		HITS 3		WEEKS 18
MEMORY: THEME FROM THE MUSICAL 'CATS'	BBC	42	20 Jul 85	4
Above hit: Aled JONES with the LONDON SYMPHONY ORCHESTRA.				
WALKING IN THE AIR	EMI	5	30 Nov 85	11
From 'The Snowman'.				
A WINTER STORY	His Master's Voice	51	20 Dec 86	3
From the S4C/Channel 4 TV film of the same name.				

ALBUMS:		HITS 8		WEEKS 141
VOICES FROM THE HOLY LAND	BBC	6	27 Apr 85	43
Above hit: BBC WELSH CHORUS/Aled JONES (treble) conducted By John Hugh THOMAS.				
ALL THROUGH THE NIGHT	BBC	2	29 Jun 85	44
Above hit: Aled JONES with the BBC WELSH SYMPHONY ORCHESTRA and CHORUS conducted by Robin STAPLETON.				
ALED JONES WITH THE BBC WELSH CHORUS	10 Records	11	23 Nov 85	10
Above hit: Aled JONES with the BBC WELSH CHORUS conducted by John Hugh THOMAS.				
WHERE E'ER YOU WALK	10 Records	36	22 Feb 86	6
PIE JESU	10 Records	25	12 Jul 86	16
AN ALBUM OF HYMNS	Telstar	18	29 Nov 86	11
ALED (MUSIC FROM THE TV SERIES) [OST-TV]	10 Records	52	14 Mar 87	6
Above hit: Aled JONES with the BBC WELSH CHORUS.				
THE BEST OF ALED JONES	10 Records	59	5 Dec 87	5

Barbara JONES
Jamaica

SINGLES:		HITS 1		WEEKS 7
JUST WHEN I NEEDED YOU MOST	Sonet	31	31 Jan 81	7

Catherine Zeta JONES
UK

SINGLES:		HITS 3		WEEKS 9
FOR ALL TIME	Columbia	36	19 Sep 92	5
From the album Jeff Wayne's Musical Version Of 'Spartacus'.				
TRUE LOVE WAYS	PolyGram TV	38	26 Nov 94	3
Above hit: David ESSEX and Catherine Zeta JONES.				
IN THE ARMS OF LOVE	Wow!	72	1 Apr 95	1

Donell JONES
US

SINGLES:		HITS 1		WEEKS 1
KNOCKS ME OFF MY FEET	LaFace	58	15 Feb 97	1
Originally recorded by Stevie Wonder.				

Georgia JONES - See DIVA SURPRISE featuring Georgia JONES; PLUX featuring Georgia JONES.

Glenn JONES US

ALBUMS:	HITS 1			WEEKS 1
GLENN JONES	Jive	62	31 Oct 87	1

Grace JONES US

SINGLES:	HITS 8			WEEKS 45
PRIVATE LIFE	Island	17	26 Jul 80	8
Originally recorded by the Pretenders in 1980.				
PULL UP TO THE BUMPER	Island	53	20 Jun 81	4
THE APPLE STRETCHING / NIPPLE TO THE BOTTLE	Island	50	30 Oct 82	4
MY JAMAICAN GUY	Island	56	9 Apr 83	3
SLAVE TO THE RHYTHM	ZTT	12	12 Oct 85	8
PULL UP TO THE BUMPER [RI] / LA VIE EN ROSE	Island	12	18 Jan 86	9
La Vie En Rose listed from 1 Feb 86 and originally recorded by Edith Piaf. Titles listed in reverse from 8 Feb 86.				
LOVE IS THE DRUG	Island	35	1 Mar 86	4
I'M NOT PERFECT (BUT I'M PERFECT FOR YOU)	Manhattan	56	15 Nov 86	3
SLAVE TO THE RHYTHM [RI]	ZTT	28	7 May 94	2
Re-released to coincide with the ZTT label's 10th anniversary.				
ALBUMS:	HITS 6			WEEKS 80
WARM LEATHERETTE	Island	45	30 Aug 80	2
NIGHTCLUBBING	Island	35	23 May 81	16
LIVING MY LIFE	Island	15	20 Nov 82	22
SLAVE TO THE RHYTHM	Island	12	9 Nov 85	8
ISLAND LIFE	Island	4	14 Dec 85	30
Compilation.				
INSIDE STORY	Manhattan	61	29 Nov 86	2

Hannah JONES US

SINGLES:	HITS 2			WEEKS 9
BRIDGE OVER TROUBLED WATER	Dance Pool	21	14 Sep 91	8
Above hit: PJB featuring HANNAH and her SISTERS.				
KEEP IT ON	TMRC	67	30 Jan 93	1

Howard JONES UK

SINGLES:	HITS 14			WEEKS 103
NEW SONG	WEA	3	17 Sep 83	12
WHAT IS LOVE?	WEA	2	26 Nov 83	15
NEW SONG [RE]	WEA	60	14 Jan 84	3
HIDE AND SEEK	WEA	12	18 Feb 84	9
PEARL IN THE SHELL	WEA	7	26 May 84	10
LIKE TO GET TO KNOW YOU WELL	WEA	4	11 Aug 84	12
THINGS CAN ONLY GET BETTER	WEA	6	9 Feb 85	8
LOOK MAMA	WEA	10	20 Apr 85	6
LIFE IN ONE DAY	WEA	14	29 Jun 85	7
NO ONE IS TO BLAME	WEA	16	15 Mar 86	7
Drums and production by Phil Collins.				
ALL I WANT	WEA	35	4 Oct 86	4
YOU KNOW I LOVE YOU . . . DON'T YOU?	WEA	43	29 Nov 86	3
LITTLE BIT OF SNOW	WEA	70	21 Mar 87	1
EVERLASTING LOVE	WEA	62	4 Mar 89	3
LIFT ME UP	East West	52	11 Apr 92	3
ALBUMS:	HITS 6			WEEKS 122
HUMAN'S LIB	WEA	1	17 Mar 84	57
THE 12" ALBUM	WEA	15	8 Dec 84	33
Mini-album of remixes/extended version of previous singles.				
DREAM INTO ACTION	WEA	2	23 Mar 85	25
ONE TO ONE	WEA	10	25 Oct 86	4
CROSS THAT LINE	WEA	64	1 Apr 89	1
THE BEST OF HOWARD JONES	East West	36	5 Jun 93	2

Jack JONES US

ALBUMS:	HITS 6			WEEKS 70
A SONG FOR YOU	RCA Victor	9	29 Apr 72	6
BREAD WINNERS	RCA Victor	7	3 Jun 72	36
TOGETHER	RCA Victor	8	7 Apr 73	10
HARBOUR	RCA Victor	10	23 Feb 74	5
THE FULL LIFE	RCA Victor	41	19 Feb 77	5
ALL TO YOURSELF	RCA Victor	10	21 May 77	8

Janie JONES UK

SINGLES:	HITS 1			WEEKS 3
WITCHES BREW	His Master's Voice	46	29 Jan 66	3

Jimmy JONES | | | | US

SINGLES:		HITS 5		WEEKS 47
HANDY MAN	MGM	3	19 Mar 60	21
GOOD TIMIN'	MGM	1	18 Jun 60	15
HANDY MAN [RE]	MGM	32	20 Aug 60	3
I JUST GO FOR YOU	MGM	35	10 Sep 60	4
READY FOR LOVE	MGM	46	19 Nov 60	1
I TOLD YOU SO	MGM	33	1 Apr 61	3

FABULOUS Josie JONES - See Pete WYLIE

Juggy JONES | | | | US

SINGLES:		HITS 1		WEEKS 4
INSIDE AMERICA	Contempo	39	7 Feb 76	4

Lavina JONES | | | | South Africa

SINGLES:		HITS 1		WEEKS 2
SING IT TO YOU (DEE - DOOB -DEE -DOO)	Virgin	45	18 Feb 95	2

Mick JONES - See AZTEC CAMERA

Oran "Juice" JONES | | | | US

SINGLES:		HITS 1		WEEKS 14
THE RAIN	Def Jam	4	15 Nov 86	14

Paul JONES | | | | UK

SINGLES:		HITS 4		WEEKS 34
HIGH TIME	His Master's Voice	4	8 Oct 66	15
I'VE BEEN A BAD, BAD BOY	His Master's Voice	5	21 Jan 67	9
From the film 'Privilege'.				
Above hit: Paul JONES with Mike LEANDER and his Orchestra.				
THINKIN' AIN'T FOR ME	His Master's Voice	47	26 Aug 67	1
THINKIN' AIN'T FOR ME [RE]	His Master's Voice	32	16 Sep 67	7
AQUARIUS	Columbia	45	8 Feb 69	2
EPS:		**HITS 1**		**WEEKS 31**
PRIVILEGE	His Master's Voice	1	6 May 67	31

Quincy JONES | | | | US

(See also Frank Sinatra.)

SINGLES:		HITS 8		WEEKS 42
STUFF LIKE THAT	A&M	34	29 Jul 78	9
Vocals by Ashford and Simpson and Chaka Khan.				
AI NO CORRIDA (I-NO-KO-REE-DA)	A&M	14	11 Apr 81	10
Originally recorded by Chas Jankel.				
Above hit: Quincy JONES featuring the vocals of DUNE.				
RAZZAMATAZZ	A&M	11	20 Jun 81	9
Vocals by Patti Austin.				
BETCHA' WOULDN'T HURT ME	A&M	52	5 Sep 81	3
I'LL BE GOOD TO YOU	Qwest	21	13 Jan 90	7
Above hit: Quincy JONES featuring Ray CHARLES and Chaka KHAN.				
THE SECRET GARDEN (SWEET SEDUCTION SUITE)	Qwest	67	31 Mar 90	1
Above hit: Quincy JONES featuring Al B SURE!, James INGRAM, El DEBARGE and Barry WHITE.				
STOMP - THE REMIXES	Qwest	28	14 Sep 96	2
First track on CD remixed by Mousse-T.				
Above hit: Quincy JONES featuring: Melle MEL/COOLIO/YO-YO/Shaquille O'NEAL/LUNIZ.				
SOUL BOSSA NOVA	Manifesto	47	1 Aug 98	1
Original recorded by Jones in 1962, this mix was featured in a Nike TV commercial and the opening scene to the film 'Austin Powers'.				
Above hit: COOL, The FAB and the GROOVY present Quincy JONES.				
ALBUMS:		**HITS 3**		**WEEKS 41**
THE DUDE	A&M	19	18 Apr 81	25
THE BEST OF QUINCY JONES	A&M	41	20 Mar 82	4
BACK ON THE BLOCK	Qwest	26	20 Jan 90	12

Rickie Lee JONES | | | | US

SINGLES:		HITS 1		WEEKS 9
CHUCK E.'S IN LOVE	Warner Brothers	18	23 Jun 79	9
Written about singer/songwriter Chuck E. Weiss.				
ALBUMS:		**HITS 5**		**WEEKS 39**
RICKIE LEE JONES	Warner Brothers	18	16 Jun 79	19
PIRATES	Warner Brothers	37	8 Aug 81	11

GIRL AT HER VOLCANO	Warner Brothers	51	2 Jul 83	3
10" format mini-album.				
THE MAGAZINE	Warner Brothers	40	13 Oct 84	4
FLYING COWBOYS	Geffen	50	7 Oct 89	2

Shirley JONES – See PARTRIDGE FAMILY

Steve JONES – See SEX PISTOLS

Tammy JONES   UK

SINGLES:	HITS 1			WEEKS 10
LET ME TRY AGAIN	Epic	5	26 Apr 75	10
ALBUMS:	HITS 1			WEEKS 5
LET ME TRY AGAIN	Epic	38	12 Jul 75	5

Tom JONES   UK
(See also Various Artists: Studio Cast 'Matador'.)

SINGLES:	HITS 36			WEEKS 366
IT'S NOT UNUSUAL	Decca	1	13 Feb 65	14
Originally written for Sandie Shaw. Lead guitar by Big Jim Sullivan.				
ONCE UPON A TIME	Decca	32	8 May 65	4
WITH THESE HANDS	Decca	13	10 Jul 65	11
Originally recorded by Eddie Fisher in 1953.				
WHAT'S NEW PUSSYCAT?	Decca	11	14 Aug 65	10
From the film of the same name.				
THUNDERBALL	Decca	35	15 Jan 66	4
Theme from the James Bond film of the same name.				
ONCE THERE WAS A TIME / NOT RESPONSIBLE	Decca	18	21 May 66	9
THIS AND THAT	Decca	44	20 Aug 66	3
GREEN, GREEN GRASS OF HOME	Decca	1	12 Nov 66	22
Originally recorded by Johnny Darrell in 1964.				
DETROIT CITY	Decca	8	18 Feb 67	10
Original by Bobby Bare reached No. 16 in the US in 1963.				
FUNNY FAMILIAR FORGOTTEN FEELINGS	Decca	7	15 Apr 67	15
Originally recorded by Mickey Newbury.				
I'LL NEVER FALL IN LOVE AGAIN	Decca	2	29 Jul 67	25
Originally recorded by Lonnie Donegan.				
I'M COMING HOME	Decca	2	25 Nov 67	16
DELILAH	Decca	2	2 Mar 68	17
HELP YOURSELF	Decca	5	20 Jul 68	26
A MINUTE OF YOUR TIME	Decca	14	30 Nov 68	15
LOVE ME TONIGHT	Decca	9	17 May 69	12
WITHOUT LOVE	Decca	10	13 Dec 69	11
Originally recorded by Clyde McPhatter.				
WITHOUT LOVE [RE]	Decca	49	14 Mar 70	1
DAUGHTER OF DARKNESS	Decca	5	18 Apr 70	15
I (WHO HAVE NOTHING)	Decca	16	15 Aug 70	8
I (WHO HAVE NOTHING) [RE]	Decca	47	17 Oct 70	3
SHE'S A LADY	Decca	13	16 Jan 71	9
Written by Paul Anka.				
SHE'S A LADY [RE]	Decca	47	27 Mar 71	1
PUPPET MAN	Decca	49	5 Jun 71	1
Written by Neil Sedaka and Howard Greenfield.				
PUPPET MAN [RE]	Decca	50	19 Jun 71	1
TILL	Decca	2	23 Oct 71	15
Original by Roger Williams reached No. 22 in the US in 1957.				
THE YOUNG NEW MEXICAN PUPPETEER	Decca	6	1 Apr 72	12
LETTER TO LUCILLE	Decca	31	14 Apr 73	8
SOMETHIN' 'BOUT YOU BABY I LIKE	Decca	36	7 Sep 74	5
SAY YOU'LL STAY UNTIL TOMORROW	EMI	40	16 Apr 77	3
A BOY FROM NOWHERE	Epic	2	18 Apr 87	12
From the musical 'Matador'.				
IT'S NOT UNUSUAL [RI]	Decca	17	30 May 87	8
I WAS BORN TO BE ME	Epic	61	2 Jan 88	1
From the musical 'Matador'.				
KISS	China	5	29 Oct 88	7
Above hit: ART OF NOISE featuring Tom JONES.				
MOVE CLOSER	Jive	49	29 Apr 89	3
COULDN'T SAY GOODBYE	Dover	51	26 Jan 91	2
CARRYING A TORCH	Dover	57	16 Mar 91	2
Originally recorded by and features backing vocals by Van Morrison.				
DELILAH [RI]	The Hit Label	68	4 Jul 92	2
ALL YOU NEED IS LOVE	Childline	19	6 Feb 93	4
Charity record for the Childline Appeal. Backing vocals by Kiki Dee.				
Above hit: Tom JONES and Dave STEWART.				
IF I ONLY KNEW	ZTT	11	5 Nov 94	9

BURNING DOWN THE HOUSE	Gut	7	25 Sep 99	7

Originally recorded by Talking Heads on their 1983 album Speaking In Tongues.
Above hit: Tom JONES and the CARDIGANS.

BABY, IT'S COLD OUTSIDE	Gut	17	18 Dec 99	3

Originally recorded by Esther Williams and Ricardo Montalban.
Above hit: Tom JONES and CERYS of CATATONIA.

EPS:	HITS 1		WEEKS 28	
ON STAGE	Decca	3	10 Apr 65	28

ALBUMS:	HITS 26		WEEKS 441	
ALONG CAME JONES	Decca	11	5 Jun 65	5
FROM THE HEART	Decca	23	8 Oct 66	8
GREEN GREEN GRASS OF HOME	Decca	3	8 Apr 67	49
TOM JONES LIVE! AT THE TALK OF THE TOWN	Decca	6	24 Jun 67	90
13 SMASH HITS	Decca	5	30 Dec 67	49
DELILAH	Decca	1	27 Jul 68	29
HELP YOURSELF	Decca	4	21 Dec 68	9
THIS IS TOM JONES	Decca	2	28 Jun 69	20
TOM JONES LIVE IN LAS VEGAS	Decca	2	15 Nov 69	45
TOM	Decca	4	25 Apr 70	18
I WHO HAVE NOTHING	Decca	10	14 Nov 70	10
SHE'S A LADY	Decca	9	29 May 71	7
LIVE AT CAESAR'S PALACE	Decca	27	27 Nov 71	5
CLOSE UP	Decca	17	24 Jun 72	4
THE BODY AND SOUL OF TOM JONES	Decca	31	23 Jun 73	1
GREATEST HITS	Decca	15	5 Jan 74	13
20 GREATEST HITS	Decca	1	22 Mar 75	21
I'M COMING HOME	Lotus	12	7 Oct 78	9
THE GREATEST HITS	Telstar	16	16 May 87	12
AT THIS MOMENT	Jive	34	13 May 89	3
TOM JONES AFTER DARK	Stylus	46	8 Jul 89	4
CARRYING A TORCH	Dover	44	6 Apr 91	4
THE COMPLETE TOM JONES	Fontana	8	27 Jun 92	6
THE LEAD AND HOW TO SWING IT	ZTT	55	26 Nov 94	1
THE ULTIMATE HITS COLLECTION	PolyGram TV	75	14 Nov 98	1
RELOAD	Gut	1	9 Oct 99	13

Duets album.

THE ULTIMATE HITS COLLECTION [RI]	Universal Music TV	26	9 Oct 99	5

Trevor JONES UK

ALBUMS:	HITS 1		WEEKS 2	
LABYRINTH [OST]	EMI America	38	5 Jul 86	2

Original score is by Trevor Jones and features David Bowie (who starred in the film) on certain
*   tracks.*

JONESTOWN US

SINGLES:	HITS 1		WEEKS 1	
SWEET THANG	Universal	49	13 Jun 98	1

Samples Sister Sledge's He's The Greatest Dancer.

Janis JOPLIN US

ALBUMS:	HITS 3		WEEKS 11	
PEARL	CBS	50	17 Apr 71	1
JANIS JOPLIN IN CONCERT	CBS	30	22 Jul 72	6

First side is with Big Brother and the Holding Co., the second with the Full Tilt Boogie Band.

THE ULTIMATE COLLECTION	Columbia	26	29 Aug 98	4

Alison JORDAN UK

SINGLES:	HITS 1		WEEKS 4	
BOY FROM NEW YORK CITY	Arista	23	9 May 92	4

Dick JORDAN UK

SINGLES:	HITS 2		WEEKS 4	
HALLELUJAH I LOVE HER SO	Oriole	47	19 Mar 60	1
LITTLE CHRISTINE	Oriole	39	11 Jun 60	3

Jack JORDAN – Clavioline - See Frank CHACKSFIELD and his Orchestra

Montell JORDAN US

SINGLES:	HITS 4		WEEKS 17	
THIS IS HOW WE DO IT	Def Jam	11	13 May 95	8
SOMETHIN' 4 DA HONEYZ	Def Jam	15	2 Sep 95	4

Samples Summer Madness by Kool and the Gang.

I LIKE	Def Jam	24	19 Oct 96	3

From the film 'The Nutty Professor'. Samples I Get Lifted by KC & the Sunshine Band.
Above hit: Montell JORDAN featuring SLICK RICK.

LET'S RIDE	Def Jam	25	23 May 98	2

Above hit: Montell JORDAN featuring MASTER P and SILKK "THE SHOCKER".

ALBUMS:	HITS 2		WEEKS 3	
THIS IS HOW WE DO IT	RAL	53	24 Jun 95	2
MORE TO TELL	Def Jam	66	14 Sep 96	1

Ronny JORDAN UK

SINGLES:	HITS 4		WEEKS 7	
SO WHAT!	Antilles	32	1 Feb 92	4

Originally recorded by Miles Davis.

UNDER YOUR SPELL	Island	72	25 Sep 93	1

Above hit: Ronny JORDAN with Special Guests Fay SIMPSON and Truth ANTHONY.

TINSEL TOWN	Island	64	15 Jan 94	1
COME WITH ME	Island	63	28 May 94	1

Originally recorded by Tania Marie in 1993.
Above hit: Ronny JORDAN (Guest vocalist Fay SIMPSON).

ALBUMS:	HITS 3		WEEKS 7	
THE ANTIDOTE	Island	52	7 Mar 92	4
THE QUIET REVOLUTION	Island	49	9 Oct 93	2
BAD BROTHERS	Island	58	3 Sep 94	1

Mixes of Jordan's material by DJ Krush.
Above hit: Ronny JORDAN Meets DJ KRUSH.

JORDANAIRES - See Elvis PRESLEY

David JOSEPH UK

SINGLES:	HITS 4		WEEKS 21	
YOU CAN'T HIDE (YOUR LOVE FROM ME)	Island	13	26 Feb 83	9
LET'S LIVE IT UP (NITE PEOPLE)	Island	26	28 May 83	5
JOYS OF LIFE	Island	61	18 Feb 84	2
EXPANSIONS '86 (EXPAND YOUR MIND)	Fourth & Broadway	58	31 May 86	5

Above hit: Chris PAUL featuring the voice of David JOSEPH.

Martyn JOSEPH UK

SINGLES:	HITS 4		WEEKS 10	
DOLPHINS MAKE ME CRY	Epic	34	20 Jun 92	4
WORKING MOTHER	Epic	65	12 Sep 92	1
PLEASE SIR	Epic	45	9 Jan 93	3
TALK ABOUT IT IN THE MORNING	Epic	43	3 Jun 95	2

JOURNEY US

SINGLES:	HITS 2		WEEKS 9	
DON'T STOP BELIEVIN'	CBS	62	27 Feb 82	4
WHO'S CRYING NOW	CBS	46	11 Sep 82	5
ALBUMS:	HITS 4		WEEKS 30	
ESCAPE	CBS	79	20 Mar 82	4
ESCAPE [RE]	CBS	32	21 Aug 82	12
FRONTIERS	CBS	6	19 Feb 83	8
EVOLUTION	CBS	100	6 Aug 83	1

Originally released in 1979.

RAISED ON RADIO	CBS	22	24 May 86	5

JOY - See A VERY GOOD FRIEND OF MINE featuring JOY

Ruth JOY UK

SINGLES:	HITS 3		WEEKS 4	
DON'T PUSH IT	MCA	66	26 Aug 89	2
FEEL	MCA	67	22 Feb 92	1
WALKING ON SUNSHINE	Network	71	14 Nov 92	1

Above hit: KRUSH featuring Ruth JOY.

JOY DIVISION UK

SINGLES:	HITS 2		WEEKS 24	
LOVE WILL TEAR US APART	Factory	13	28 Jun 80	9
LOVE WILL TEAR US APART [RE]	Factory	19	29 Oct 83	7
ATMOSPHERE	Factory	34	18 Jun 88	5
LOVE WILL TEAR US APART [RM]	London	19	17 Jun 95	3

Mixed by Don German.
Above hit: JOY DIVISION 1995.

ALBUMS:	HITS 6		WEEKS 33	
CLOSER	Factory	6	26 Jul 80	8
UNKNOWN PLEASURES	Factory	71	30 Aug 80	1

First released in 1979.

STILL	Factory	5	17 Oct 81	12
1977-1980 SUBSTANCE	Factory	7	23 Jul 88	8

PERMANENT: JOY DIVISION 1995	London	16	1 Jul 95	3

Released to coincide with Ian Curtis's biography, written by his widow.

HEART AND SOUL	London	70	7 Feb 98	1

Re-issued 4CD box set, first released on 8 Dec 97.

JOY STRINGS   UK

SINGLES:	HITS 2		WEEKS 11	
IT'S AN OPEN SECRET	Regal Zonophone	32	29 Feb 64	7
A STARRY NIGHT	Regal Zonophone	35	19 Dec 64	4

Dale JOYNER – See XPANSIONS

JOYRIDER   UK

SINGLES:	HITS 2		WEEKS 4	
RUSH HOUR	Paradox	22	27 Jul 96	3
ALL GONE AWAY	A&M	54	28 Sep 96	1

JT PLAYAZ   UK

SINGLES:	HITS 2		WEEKS 4	
JUST PLAYIN'	Pukka	30	5 Apr 97	3
LET'S GET DOWN	MCA	64	2 May 98	1

Based around Kool And The Gang's Celebration.

JTQ with Noel McKOY – See James TAYLOR QUARTET

JU JU HOUNDS – See Izzy STRADLIN'

JUDAS PRIEST   UK

SINGLES:	HITS 13		WEEKS 51	
TAKE ON THE WORLD	CBS	14	20 Jan 79	10
EVENING STAR	CBS	53	12 May 79	4
LIVING AFTER MIDNIGHT	CBS	12	29 Mar 80	7
BREAKING THE LAW	CBS	12	7 Jun 80	6
UNITED	CBS	26	23 Aug 80	8
DON'T GO	CBS	51	21 Feb 81	3
HOT ROCKIN'	CBS	60	25 Apr 81	3
YOU'VE GOT ANOTHER THING COMIN'	CBS	66	21 Aug 82	2
FREEWHEEL BURNIN'	CBS	42	21 Jan 84	3
JOHNNY B. GOODE	Atlantic	64	23 Apr 88	2
PAIN KILLER	CBS	74	15 Sep 90	1
A TOUCH OF EVIL	Columbia	58	23 Mar 91	1
NIGHT CRAWLER	Columbia	63	24 Apr 93	1
ALBUMS:	HITS 13		WEEKS 78	
SIN AFTER SIN	CBS	23	14 May 77	6
STAINED GLASS	CBS	27	25 Feb 78	5
KILLING MACHINE	CBS	32	11 Nov 78	9
UNLEASHED IN THE EAST	CBS	10	6 Oct 79	8
BRITISH STEEL	CBS	4	19 Apr 80	17
POINT OF ENTRY	CBS	14	7 Mar 81	5
SCREAMING FOR VENGEANCE	CBS	11	17 Jul 82	9
DEFENDERS OF THE FAITH	CBS	19	28 Jan 84	5
TURBO	CBS	33	19 Apr 86	4
PRIEST LIVE	CBS	47	13 Jun 87	2

Live recordings from their 1986 World tour.

RAM IT DOWN	CBS	24	28 May 88	5
PAINKILLER	CBS	26	29 Sep 90	2
METAL WORKS 73 – 93	Columbia	37	8 May 93	1

Retrospective issued to commemorate their 20th anniversary.

JUDGE DREAD   UK

SINGLES:	HITS 11		WEEKS 95	
BIG SIX	Big Shot	11	26 Aug 72	27
BIG SEVEN	Big Shot	8	9 Dec 72	18
BIG EIGHT	Big Shot	14	21 Apr 73	10
JE T'AIME (MOI NON PLUS)	Cactus	9	5 Jul 75	9
BIG 10	Cactus	14	27 Sep 75	7
CHRISTMAS IN DREADLAND / COME OUTSIDE	Cactus	14	6 Dec 75	7
THE WINKLE MAN	Cactus	35	8 May 76	4
Y VIVA SUSPENDERS	Cactus	27	28 Aug 76	4
5TH ANNIVERSARY [EP]	Cactus	31	2 Apr 77	4

Lead track: Jamaica Jerk (Off).

UP WITH THE COCK / BIG PUNK	Cactus	49	14 Jan 78	1
HOKEY COKEY / JINGLE BELLS	EMI	59	16 Dec 78	4
ALBUMS:	HITS 2		WEEKS 14	
BEDTIME STORIES	Cactus	26	6 Dec 75	12
40 BIG ONES	Creole	51	7 Mar 81	2

JUICE
Denmark

SINGLES:		HITS 2			WEEKS 3
BEST DAYS	Chrysalis	28	18 Apr 98	2
I'LL COME RUNNIN'	Chrysalis	48	22 Aug 98	1

JUICY
US

SINGLES:		HITS 1			WEEKS 5
SUGAR FREE	Epic	45	22 Feb 86	5

JUICY LUCY
UK

SINGLES:		HITS 2			WEEKS 17
WHO DO YOU LOVE	Vertigo	14	7 Mar 70	12
PRETTY WOMAN	Vertigo	45	10 Oct 70	2
PRETTY WOMAN [RE]	Vertigo	44	31 Oct 70	3
ALBUMS:		HITS 2			WEEKS 5
JUICY LUCY	Vertigo	41	18 Apr 70	4
LIE BACK AND ENJOY IT	Vertigo	53	21 Nov 70	1

Thomas JULES-STOCK
UK

SINGLES:		HITS 1			WEEKS 1
DIDN'T I TELL YOU TRUE	Mercury	59	15 Aug 98	1

JULIA and COMPANY
US

SINGLES:		HITS 2			WEEKS 10
BREAKIN' DOWN (SUGAR SAMBA)	London	15	3 Mar 84	8
I'M SO HAPPY	London	56	23 Feb 85	2
Above hit: JULIA and CO.				

JULUKA
UK/South Africa

SINGLES:		HITS 1			WEEKS 4
SCATTERLINGS OF AFRICA	Safari	44	12 Feb 83	4
ALBUMS:		HITS 1			WEEKS 3
SCATTERLINGS	Safari	50	23 Jul 83	3

JUMP
UK

SINGLES:		HITS 1			WEEKS 1
FUNKATARIUM	Heat Recordings	56	1 Mar 97	1
Original release reached No. 156 in 1996.				

Wally JUMP JR. and the CRIMINAL ELEMENT
US

SINGLES:		HITS 5			WEEKS 19
TURN ME LOOSE	London	60	28 Feb 87	2
PUT THE NEEDLE TO THE RECORD	Cooltempo	63	5 Sep 87	3
Above hit: CRIMINAL ELEMENT ORCHESTRA.				
TIGHTEN UP/I JUST CAN'T STOP DANCIN'	Breakout	24	12 Dec 87	7
Above hit is one track.				
PRIVATE PARTY	Breakout	57	19 Mar 88	3
EVERYBODY (RAP)	Deconstruction	30	6 Oct 90	4
Above hit: CRIMINAL ELEMENT ORCHESTRA featuring Wendell WILLIAMS.				

Rosemary JUNE
US

SINGLES:		HITS 1			WEEKS 9
"I'LL BE WITH YOU" IN APPLE BLOSSOM TIME	Pye International	14	24 Jan 59	9

JUNGLE BOOK DISNEY CAST
US

SINGLES:		HITS 1			WEEKS 8
THE JUNGLE BOOK GROOVE [M]	Hollywood	14	8 May 93	8

JUNGLE BROTHERS
US

(See also De La Soul.)

SINGLES:		HITS 9			WEEKS 34
I'LL HOUSE YOU	Gee Street	22	22 Oct 88	5
Above hit: Richie RICH Meets JUNGLE BROTHERS.				
BLACK IS BLACK / STRAIGHT OUT OF THE JUNGLE	Gee Street	72	18 Mar 89	1
WHAT "U" WAITIN' "4"?	Eternal	35	31 Mar 90	5
DOIN' OUR OWN DANG	Eternal	33	21 Jul 90	6
Above hit: JUNGLE BROTHERS featuring DE LA SOUL, Monie LOVE, TRIBE CALLED QUEST and QUEEN LATIFAH.				
BRAIN	Gee Street	52	19 Jul 97	1
JUNGLE BROTHER	Gee Street	56	29 Nov 97	1
JUNGLE BROTHER [RE]	Gee Street	18	9 May 98	4

I'LL HOUSE YOU '98 [RM]	ffrr	26	11 Jul 98	5
Remixed by The Hitmen.				
BECAUSE I GOT IT LIKE THAT	Gee Street	32	28 Nov 98	2
V.I.P.	Gee Street	33	10 Jul 99	3
Samples 'I Dream Of Jeanie'.				
GET DOWN	Gee Street	52	6 Nov 99	1
Vocal harmonies by Carol Gardenas. Samples Kool And The Gang's Get Down On It.				
ALBUMS:		**HITS 1**		**WEEKS 3**
DONE BY THE FORCES OF NATURE	Eternal	41	3 Feb 90	3

JUNGLE HIGH with BLUE PEARL — UK/US

(See also Blue Pearl.)

SINGLES:		**HITS 1**		**WEEKS 1**
FIRE OF LOVE	Logic	71	27 Nov 93	1

JUNIOR — UK

SINGLES:		**HITS 11**		**WEEKS 57**
MAMA USED TO SAY	Mercury	7	24 Apr 82	13
Originally released in 1981.				
TOO LATE	Mercury	20	10 Jul 82	9
LET ME KNOW / I CAN'T HELP IT	Mercury	53	25 Sep 82	3
COMMUNICATION BREAKDOWN	Mercury	57	23 Apr 83	3
SOMEBODY	London	64	8 Sep 84	2
DO YOU REALLY (WANT MY LOVE)	London	47	9 Feb 85	4
OH LOUISE	London	74	30 Nov 85	3
ANOTHER STEP (CLOSER TO YOU)	MCA	6	4 Apr 87	11
Above hit: Kim WILDE and JUNIOR.				
STEP OFF	MCA	63	25 Aug 90	3
THEN CAME YOU	MCA	32	15 Aug 92	5
ALL OVER THE WORLD	MCA	74	31 Oct 92	1
Above 3: Junior GISCOMBE.				
ALBUMS:		**HITS 1**		**WEEKS 14**
JI	Mercury	28	5 Jun 82	14

JUNIOR M.A.F.I.A. — US

SINGLES:		**HITS 2**		**WEEKS 2**
I NEED YOU TONIGHT	Big Beat	66	3 Feb 96	1
Above hit: JUNIOR M.A.F.I.A. featuring AALIYAH.				
GETTIN' MONEY (THE GET MONEY REMIX)	Big Beat	63	19 Oct 96	1
Rap by Notorious B.I.G. Sleeve shows title as Get Money (The Gettin' Money Remix).				

JUNO REACTOR — UK/Germany

SINGLES:		**HITS 1**		**WEEKS 1**
JUNGLE HIGH	Perfecto	45	8 Feb 97	1

Eric JUPP and his Orchestra - See Bille ANTHONY; Tony BRENT; Ray BURNS; CORONETS: Norman WISDOM

JURASSIC 5 — US

SINGLES:		**HITS 2**		**WEEKS 4**
JAYOU	Pan	56	25 Jul 98	1
CONCRETE SCHOOLYARD	Pan	35	24 Oct 98	3
ALBUMS:		**HITS 1**		**WEEKS 1**
JURASSIC 5	Pan	70	13 Jun 98	1

Christopher JUST — Austria

SINGLES:		**HITS 1**		**WEEKS 2**
I'M A DISCO DANCER (AND A SWEET ROMANCER)	Slut Trax	72	13 Dec 97	1
I'M A DISCO DANCER (AND A SWEET ROMANCER) [RM]	XL Recordings	69	6 Feb 99	1
This is the original Olav Basoski remix, recorded before the Fat Boy Slim remix charted in 1997.				

JUST LUIS — Australia

SINGLES:		**HITS 1**		**WEEKS 3**
AMERICAN PIE	Pro-activ	31	14 Oct 95	2
AMERICAN PIE [RM]	Pro-activ	70	17 Feb 96	1
Remixed by Almighty Associates.				

Jimmy JUSTICE — UK

SINGLES:		**HITS 3**		**WEEKS 35**
WHEN MY LITTLE GIRL IS SMILING	Pye	9	31 Mar 62	13
AIN'T THAT FUNNY	Pye	8	16 Jun 62	11
SPANISH HARLEM	Pye	20	25 Aug 62	11

JUSTIFIED ANCIENTS OF MU MU
UK
(See also KLF, Timelords, 2K.)

SINGLES:		HITS 1		WEEKS 6	
IT'S GRIM UP NORTH	*KLF Commuications*	10	*9 Nov 91*	5
IT'S GRIM UP NORTH [RE]	*KLF Commuications*	67	*4 Jan 92*	1

JUSTIN
UK

SINGLES:		HITS 3		WEEKS 9	
THIS BOY	*Streamline*	34	*22 Aug 98*	2
OVER YOU	*Streamline*	11	*16 Jan 99*	4
IT'S ALL ABOUT YOU	*Streamline*	34	*17 Jul 99*	3

Bill JUSTIS
US

SINGLES:		HITS 1		WEEKS 8	
RAUNCHY	*London*	24	*11 Jan 58*	2
RAUNCHY [RE]	*London*	11	*1 Feb 58*	6

Patrick JUVET
France

SINGLES:		HITS 2		WEEKS 19	
GOT A FEELING	*Casablanca*	34	*2 Sep 78*	7
I LOVE AMERICA	*Casablanca*	12	*4 Nov 78*	12

JX
UK

SINGLES:		HITS 4		WEEKS 33	
SON OF A GUN	*Internal Dance*	13	*2 Apr 94*	6
YOU BELONG TO ME	*Ffrreedom*	17	*1 Apr 95*	5
SON OF A GUN [RI]	*Ffrreedom*	6	*19 Aug 95*	6
THERE'S NOTHING I WON'T DO	*Ffrreedom*	4	*18 May 96*	13
Vocals by Karlina.				
CLOSE TO YOUR HEART	*Ffrreedom*	18	*8 Mar 97*	3

K

Frank 'K' (featuring Wiston OFFICE)
US/Italy

SINGLES:		HITS 1		WEEKS 1	
EVERYBODY LET'S SOMEBODY LOVE	*Urban*	61	*26 Jan 91*	1

Leila K
Sweden

SINGLES:		HITS 4		WEEKS 22	
GOT TO GET	*Arista*	8	*25 Nov 89*	14
Above hit: ROB 'N' RAZ featuring Leila K.				
ROK THE NATION	*Arista*	41	*17 Mar 90*	3
Above hit: ROB 'N' RAZ with Leila K.				
OPEN SESAME	*Polydor*	23	*23 Jan 93*	4
CA PLANE POUR MOI	*Polydor*	69	*3 Jul 93*	1

K-CI – See Will SMITH

K-CI and JOJO
US

SINGLES:		HITS 5		WEEKS 22	
HOW DO YOU WANT IT	*Death Row*	17	*27 Jul 96*	4
Above hit: 2PAC (featuring KC and JOJO).				
YOU BRING ME UP	*MCA*	21	*23 Aug 97*	2
ALL MY LIFE	*MCA*	8	*18 Apr 98*	11
DON'T RUSH (TAKE LOVE SLOWLY)	*MCA*	16	*19 Sep 98*	3
TELL ME IT'S REAL	*MCA*	40	*2 Oct 99*	2
ALBUMS:		HITS 2		WEEKS 3	
LOVE ALWAYS	*MCA*	64	*28 Jun 97*	1
This entry was based on import sales.				
LOVE ALWAYS [RE]	*MCA*	51	*9 May 98*	1
IT'S REAL	*MCA*	56	*3 Jul 99*	1

K-CREATIVE
UK

SINGLES:		HITS 1		WEEKS 2	
THREE TIMES A MAYBE	*Talkin Loud*	58	*7 Mar 92*	2
[AA] listed with Feed The Feeling by Perception.				

Ernie K-DOE
US

SINGLES:	HITS 1			WEEKS 7
MOTHER-IN-LAW	London	29	13 May 61	7

Guest bass vocal by Benny Spellman.

K.I.D.
Antilles

SINGLES:	HITS 1			WEEKS 4
DON'T STOP	EMI	49	28 Feb 81	4

K-KLASS
UK

SINGLES:	HITS 6			WEEKS 31
RHYTHM IS A MYSTERY	Creed	61	4 May 91	2

Vocals by Bobby Depasois.

RHYTHM IS A MYSTERY [RI]	Deconstruction	3	9 Nov 91	10
SO RIGHT	Deconstruction	20	25 Apr 92	5
DON'T STOP	Deconstruction	32	7 Nov 92	3
LET ME SHOW YOU	Deconstruction	13	27 Nov 93	7
WHAT YOU'RE MISSING	Deconstruction	24	28 May 94	3
BURNIN'	Parlophone	45	1 Aug 98	1

Vocals by Rachel McFarlane.

ALBUMS:	HITS 1			WEEKS 1
UNIVERSAL	Deconstruction	73	4 Jun 94	1

K.P. and ENVYI
US

SINGLES:	HITS 1			WEEKS 4
SWING MY WAY	East West America	14	13 Jun 98	4

K.W.S.
UK

SINGLES:	HITS 7			WEEKS 37
PLEASE DON'T GO / GAME BOY	Network	1	25 Apr 92	16

Game Boy listed from 9 May 92.

ROCK YOUR BABY / TOTAL STATE OF KONFUSION	Network	8	22 Aug 92	7

Total State Of Konfusion only listed for the week of 29 Aug 92.

HOLD BACK THE NIGHT	Network	30	12 Dec 92	6

Above hit: KWS features guest vocals from the TRAMMPS.

CAN'T GET ENOUGH OF YOUR LOVE	Network	71	5 Jun 93	1
IT SEEMS TO HANG ON	X-Clusive	58	9 Apr 94	1

Above 2: KWS.

AIN'T NOBODY (LOVES ME BETTER)	X-Clusive	21	2 Jul 94	4

Sleeve reflects artist credits in reverse.
Above hit: Gwen DICKEY and K.W.S.

THE MORE I GET, THE MORE I WANT	X-Clusive	35	19 Nov 94	2

Originally recorded by Teddy Pendergrass when he was with Harold Melvin and the Blluenotes.
Above hit: KWS featuring Teddy PENDERGRASS.

Joshua KADISON
US

SINGLES:	HITS 3			WEEKS 19
JESSIE	SBK	69	26 Feb 94	2
JESSIE [RE]	SBK	48	1 Oct 94	3
BEAUTIFUL IN MY EYES	SBK	65	12 Nov 94	1
JESSIE [RI]	SBK	15	29 Apr 95	10

Edited version to the original release.

BEAUTIFUL IN MY EYES [RI]	SBK	37	12 Aug 95	3

ALBUMS:	HITS 1			WEEKS 4
PAINTED DESERT SERENADE	SBK	45	27 May 95	4

KADOC
Spain

SINGLES:	HITS 3			WEEKS 11
THE NIGHTRAIN	Positiva	14	6 Apr 96	8

Import reached No. 186 before its UK release. Originally recorded by Jimmy Forest.

YOU GOT TO BE THERE	Positiva	45	17 Aug 96	1
ROCK THE BELLS	Manifesto	34	23 Aug 97	2

Bert KAEMPFERT and his Orchestra
Germany

SINGLES:	HITS 1			WEEKS 10
BYE BYE BLUES	Polydor	24	25 Dec 65	10

Originally recorded by Bert Lown's Orchestra in 1930.

ALBUMS:	HITS 10			WEEKS 104
BYE BYE BLUES	Polydor	4	5 Mar 66	22
BEST OF BERT KAEMPFERT	Polydor	27	16 Apr 66	1
SWINGING SAFARI	Polydor	20	28 May 66	15
STRANGERS IN THE NIGHT	Polydor	13	30 Jul 66	26
RELAXING SOUND OF BERT KAEMPFERT	Polydor	33	4 Feb 67	3

BERT KAEMPFERT – BEST SELLER	Polydor	25	18 Feb 67	18
HOLD ME	Polydor	36	29 Apr 67	5
KAEMPFERT SPECIAL	Polydor	24	26 Aug 67	5
ORANGE COLOURED SKY	Polydor	49	19 Jun 71	1
SOUNDS SENSATIONAL	Polydor	17	5 Jul 80	8

KAJAGOOGOO   UK

SINGLES:	HITS 7		WEEKS 50	
TOO SHY	EMI	1	22 Jan 83	13
Co-produced by Nick Rhodes of Duran Duran.				
OOH TO BE AH	EMI	7	2 Apr 83	8
HANG ON NOW	EMI	13	4 Jun 83	7
BIG APPLE	EMI	8	17 Sep 83	8
THE LION'S MOUTH	EMI	25	3 Mar 84	7
TURN YOUR BACK ON ME	EMI	47	5 May 84	4
SHOULDN'T DO THAT	Parlophone	63	21 Sep 85	3
Above hit: KAJA.				
ALBUMS:	**HITS 2**		**WEEKS 23**	
WHITE FEATHERS	EMI	5	30 Apr 83	20
ISLANDS	EMI	35	2 Jun 84	3

KALEEF   UK

SINGLES:	HITS 5		WEEKS 12	
WALK LIKE A CHAMPION	Payday	23	30 Mar 96	3
Above hit: KALIPHZ featuring PRINCE NASEEM.				
GOLDEN BROWN	Unity	22	7 Dec 96	4
TRIALS OF LIFE	Unity	75	14 Jun 97	1
Samples Brass In Pocket by the Pretenders. Charity record with proceeds donated to Manchester Drug Agency.				
I LIKE THE WAY (THE KISSING GAME)	Unity	58	11 Oct 97	1
SANDS OF TIME	Unity	26	24 Jan 98	3
Samples Clannad's Theme From Harry's Game.				

KALIN TWINS   US

SINGLES:	HITS 1		WEEKS 18	
WHEN	Brunswick	1	19 Jul 58	18
Co-written by Paul Evans.				

KALIPHZ featuring PRINCE NASEEM – See KALEEF

Kitty KALLEN   US

SINGLES:	HITS 1		WEEKS 23	
LITTLE THINGS MEAN A LOT	Brunswick	1	3 Jul 54	23

Gunter KALLMAN CHOIR   Germany

SINGLES:	HITS 1		WEEKS 3	
ELISABETH SERENADE	Polydor	45	26 Dec 64	3

KAMASULTRA featuring Jocelyn BROWN   Italy

(See also Jocelyn Brown.)

SINGLES:	HITS 1		WEEKS 1	
HAPPINESS	S3	45	22 Nov 97	1

Michael KAMEN - See Eric CLAPTON; VARIOUS ARTISTS: FILMS - ORIGINAL SOUNDTRACKS 'Robin Hood: Prince Of Thieves'

Nick KAMEN   UK

SINGLES:	HITS 5		WEEKS 33	
EACH TIME YOU BREAK MY HEART	WEA	5	8 Nov 86	12
Co-written and produced by Madonna.				
LOVING YOU IS SWEETER THAN EVER	WEA	16	28 Feb 87	9
NOBODY ELSE	WEA	47	16 May 87	3
TELL ME	WEA	40	28 May 88	5
I PROMISED MYSELF	WEA	50	28 Apr 90	4
ALBUMS:	**HITS 1**		**WEEKS 7**	
NICK KAMEN	WEA	34	18 Apr 87	7

Ini KAMOZE   Jamaica

(See also Jamaica United.)

SINGLES:	HITS 1		WEEKS 15	
HERE COMES THE HOTSTEPPER	Columbia	4	7 Jan 95	15
From the film 'Pret-A-Porter'.				

KANDIDATE

			UK
SINGLES:	HITS 4		WEEKS 28
DON'T WANNA SAY GOODNIGHT	RAK	47	19 Aug 78	6
I DON'T WANNA LOSE YOU	RAK	11	17 Mar 79	12
GIRLS GIRLS GIRLS	RAK	34	4 Aug 79	7
LET ME ROCK YOU	RAK	58	22 Mar 80	3

KANE – See NALIN and KANE

Eden KANE

			UK
SINGLES:	HITS 5		WEEKS 73
WELL I ASK YOU	Decca	1	3 Jun 61	21
GET LOST	Decca	10	16 Sep 61	11
FORGET ME NOT	Decca	3	20 Jan 62	14
I DON'T KNOW WHY	Decca	7	12 May 62	13
BOYS CRY	Fontana	8	1 Feb 64	14
EPS:	HITS 1		WEEKS 8
HITS	Decca	12	29 Sep 62	8

KANE GANG

			UK
SINGLES:	HITS 6		WEEKS 37
SMALL TOWN CREED	Kitchenware	60	19 May 84	2
CLOSEST THING TO HEAVEN	Kitchenware	12	7 Jul 84	11
RESPECT YOURSELF	Kitchenware	21	10 Nov 84	10
RESPECT YOURSELF [RE]	Kitchenware	75	26 Jan 85	1
GUN LAW	Kitchenware	53	9 Mar 85	4
MOTORTOWN	Kitchenware	45	27 Jun 87	5
DON'T LOOK ANY FURTHER	Kitchenware	52	16 Apr 88	4
ALBUMS:	HITS 2		WEEKS 12
THE BAD AND LOWDOWN WORLD OF THE KANE GANG	Kitchenware	21	23 Feb 85	8
MIRACLE	Kitchenware	41	8 Aug 87	4

KANSAS

			US
SINGLES:	HITS 1		WEEKS 7
CARRY ON WAYWARD SON	Kirshner	51	1 Jul 78	7

Mory KANTE

			Guinea
SINGLES:	HITS 1		WEEKS 14
YE KE YE KE	London	29	23 Jul 88	9
YEKE YEKE [RM-1ST]	Ffrreedom	25	11 Mar 95	3
Remixed by Martin Young.			
YEKE YEKE – 96 REMIXES [RM-2ND]	ffrr	28	30 Nov 96	2
Remixed by Hardfloor.			

KAOMA

			France
SINGLES:	HITS 2		WEEKS 20
LAMBADA	CBS	4	21 Oct 89	18
DANCANDO LAMBADA	CBS	62	27 Jan 90	2

KAOTIC CHEMISTRY

			UK
SINGLES:	HITS 1		WEEKS 1
L.S.D. [EP]	Moving Shadow	68	31 Oct 92	1
Lead track: Space Cakes.			

KARIN – See UNIQUE 3

KARIYA

			US
SINGLES:	HITS 1		WEEKS 9
LET ME LOVE YOU FOR TONIGHT	Sleeping Bag	44	8 Jul 89	6
LET ME LOVE YOU FOR TONIGHT [RE]	Sleeping Bag	57	21 Oct 89	3

Mick KARN

			UK
SINGLES:	HITS 2		WEEKS 6
AFTER A FASHION	Musicfest	39	9 Jul 83	4
Above hit: Midge URE and Mick KARN.			
BUOY	Virgin	63	17 Jan 87	2
Above hit: Mick KARN featuring David SYLVIAN.			
ALBUMS:	HITS 2		WEEKS 4
TITLES	Virgin	74	20 Nov 82	3
DREAMS OF REASON PRODUCE MONSTERS	Virgin	89	28 Feb 87	1

KARTOON KREW
US

SINGLES:	HITS 1			WEEKS 6
INSPECTOR GADGET	Champion	58	7 Dec 85	6

KASENETZ-KATZ SINGING ORCHESTRAL CIRCUS
US

SINGLES:	HITS 1			WEEKS 15
QUICK JOEY SMALL (RUN JOEY RUN)	Buddah	19	23 Nov 68	15
Lead vocals by Joey Levine.				

KATCHA
UK

SINGLES:	HITS 1			WEEKS 1
TOUCHED BY GOD	Hooj Choons	57	21 Aug 99	1

KATRINA and the WAVES
US/UK

SINGLES:	HITS 3			WEEKS 34
WALKING ON SUNSHINE	Capitol	8	4 May 85	12
SUN STREET	Capitol	22	5 Jul 86	9
WALKING ON SUNSHINE [RI]	EMI Premier	53	8 Jun 96	1
Used by GMTV for their Get Up And Give appeal.				
LOVE SHINE A LIGHT	Eternal	3	10 May 97	12
UK's Eurovision entry in 1997. It came 1st.				
ALBUMS:	HITS 2			WEEKS 7
KATRINA AND THE WAVES	Capitol	28	8 Jun 85	6
WAVES	Capitol	70	10 May 86	1

KAVANA
UK

SINGLES:	HITS 8			WEEKS 26
CRAZY CHANCE	Nemesis	35	11 May 96	3
Co-written by Howard Donald of Take That.				
WHERE ARE YOU	Nemesis	26	24 Aug 96	2
I CAN MAKE YOU FEEL GOOD	Nemesis	8	11 Jan 97	5
MFEO	Nemesis	8	19 Apr 97	4
Acronym of Made For Each Other.				
CRAZY CHANCE 97 [RR]	Nemesis	16	13 Sep 97	3
SPECIAL KIND OF SOMETHING	Virgin	13	29 Aug 98	4
FUNKY LOVE	Virgin/Sam	32	12 Dec 98	2
FUNKY LOVE [RE]	Virgin	73	9 Jan 99	1
WILL YOU WAIT FOR ME	Virgin	29	20 Mar 99	2
ALBUMS:	HITS 1			WEEKS 2
KAVANA	Nemesis	29	10 May 97	2

Niamh KAVANAGH
Ireland

SINGLES:	HITS 1			WEEKS 5
IN YOUR EYES	Arista	24	12 Jun 93	5
Eurovision Song Contest winner in 1993.				

Janet KAY
UK

SINGLES:	HITS 2			WEEKS 24
SILLY GAMES	Scope	2	9 Jun 79	14
SILLY GAMES [RR]	Arista	22	11 Aug 90	7
Above hit: Lindy LAYTON featuring Janet KAY.				
SILLY GAMES (THE MUSIC FACTORY REMIX) [RM]	Music Factory Dance	62	11 Aug 90	3

Danny KAYE with Gordon JENKINS and his Chorus and Orchestra
US

(See also Various Artists: Films - Original Soundtracks 'The Five Pennies'.)

SINGLES:	HITS 1			WEEKS 10
WONDERFUL COPENHAGEN	Brunswick	5	28 Feb 53	10
From the film 'Hans Christian Andersen'.				

Gordon KAYE - See RENE and YVETTE featuring Gordon KAYE and Vicki MICHELLE

KAYE SISTERS
UK

SINGLES:	HITS 5			WEEKS 45
IVORY TOWER	His Master's Voice	20	26 May 56	5
Originally recorded by Cathy Carr.				
Above hit: THREE KAYES.				
GOT-TA HAVE SOMETHING IN THE BANK, FRANK	Philips	8	2 Nov 57	11
Originally recorded by Bob Jaxon.				
Above hit: Frankie VAUGHAN and the KAYE SISTERS with Wally STOTT and his Orchestra.				
SHAKE ME I RATTLE / ALONE	Philips	27	4 Jan 58	1
Above hit: KAYE SISTERS with Wally STOTT and his Orchestra.				

COME SOFTLY TO ME	Philips	9	2 May 59	9
Above hit: Frankie VAUGHAN and the KAYE SISTERS with Wally STOTT and his Orchestra.				
PAPER ROSES	Philips	7	9 Jul 60	19

KC and the SUNSHINE BAND — US

SINGLES:	HITS 13			WEEKS 104
QUEEN OF CLUBS	Jay Boy	7	17 Aug 74	12
SOUND YOUR FUNKY HORN	Jay Boy	17	23 Nov 74	9
GET DOWN TONIGHT	Jay Boy	21	29 Mar 75	9
THAT'S THE WAY (I LIKE IT)	Jay Boy	4	2 Aug 75	10
I'M SO CRAZY (BOUT YOU)	Jay Boy	34	22 Nov 75	3
(SHAKE, SHAKE, SHAKE) SHAKE YOUR BOOTY	Jay Boy	22	17 Jul 76	8
KEEP IT COMIN' LOVE	Jay Boy	31	11 Dec 76	8
I'M YOUR BOOGIE MAN	TK	41	30 Apr 77	4
BOOGIE SHOES	TK	34	6 May 78	5
From the film 'Saturday Night Fever'. Originally was the B-side of I'm So Crazy (Bout You).				
IT'S THE SAME OLD SONG	TK	47	22 Jul 78	5
PLEASE DON'T GO	TK	3	8 Dec 79	12
GIVE IT UP	Epic	1	16 Jul 83	14
(YOU SAID) YOU'D GIMME SOME MORE	Epic	41	24 Sep 83	3
THAT'S THE WAY (I LIKE IT) [RM]	Music Factory Dance	59	11 May 91	2
ALBUMS:	HITS 3			WEEKS 17
K.C. AND THE SUNSHINE BAND	Jay Boy	26	30 Aug 75	7
GREATEST HITS	TK	10	1 Mar 80	6
ALL IN A NIGHT'S WORK	Epic	46	27 Aug 83	4

KE — US

SINGLES:	HITS 1			WEEKS 1
STRANGE WORLD	Venture	73	13 Apr 96	1

Johnny KEATING — UK

(See also Adam Faith; Emile Ford and the Checkmates.)

SINGLES:	HITS 1			WEEKS 14
THEME FROM Z-CARS (JOHNNY TODD)	Piccadilly	8	3 Mar 62	14
Theme from the BBC TV series.				

Ronan KEATING — Ireland

SINGLES:	HITS 1			WEEKS 17
WHEN YOU SAY NOTHING AT ALL	Polydor	1	7 Aug 99	15
From the film 'Notting Hill'. Originally recorded by Keith Whitley in 1987.				
WHEN YOU SAY NOTHING AT ALL [RE-1ST]	Polydor	75	27 Nov 99	1
WHEN YOU SAY NOTHING AT ALL [RE-2ND]	Polydor	66	1 Jan 00	1

Kevin KEEGAN — UK

SINGLES:	HITS 1			WEEKS 6
HEAD OVER HEELS IN LOVE	EMI	31	9 Jun 79	6

KEEL — US

ALBUMS:	HITS 1			WEEKS 2
THE FINAL FRONTIER	Vertigo	83	17 May 86	2

Howard KEEL — US

ALBUMS:	HITS 3			WEEKS 36
AND I LOVE YOU SO	Warwick	6	14 Apr 84	19
REMINISCING – THE HOWARD KEEL COLLECTION	Telstar	20	9 Nov 85	12
JUST FOR YOU	Telstar	51	26 Mar 88	5

Yvonne KEELY - See Scott FITZGERALD

Nelson KEENE — UK

SINGLES:	HITS 1			WEEKS 5
IMAGE OF A GIRL	His Master's Voice	37	27 Aug 60	4
IMAGE OF A GIRL [RE]	His Master's Voice	45	1 Oct 60	1

KEITH — US

SINGLES:	HITS 2			WEEKS 8
98.6	Mercury	24	28 Jan 67	7
Backing vocals by the Tokens.				
TELL ME TO MY FACE	Mercury	50	18 Mar 67	1

Jerry KELLER   US

SINGLES:		HITS 1		WEEKS 14	
HERE COMES SUMMER	London	1	29 Aug 59	14	

Frank KELLY   Ireland

SINGLES:		HITS 1		WEEKS 5	
CHRISTMAS COUNTDOWN	Ritz	26	24 Dec 83	4	
CHRISTMAS COUNTDOWN [RE]	Ritz	54	29 Dec 84	1	

Frankie KELLY   US

SINGLES:		HITS 1		WEEKS 2	
AIN'T THAT THE TRUTH	10 Records	65	2 Nov 85	2	

Grace KELLY - See Bing CROSBY; VARIOUS ARTISTS: FILMS - ORIGINAL SOUNDTRACKS 'High Society'.

Janis KELLY - See Barrington PHELOUNG

Keith KELLY   UK

SINGLES:		HITS 2		WEEKS 5	
(MUST YOU ALWAYS) TEASE ME	Parlophone	46	7 May 60	1	
(MUST YOU ALWAYS) TEASE ME [RE]	Parlophone	27	21 May 60	3	
LISTEN LITTLE GIRL	Parlophone	47	20 Aug 60	1	

R. KELLY   US

SINGLES:		HITS 17		WEEKS 116	
SHE'S GOT THAT VIBE	Jive	57	9 May 92	2	
SEX ME	Jive	75	20 Nov 93	1	
Above 2: R. KELLY and PUBLIC ANNOUNCEMENT.					
YOUR BODY'S CALLIN'	Jive	19	14 May 94	4	
SUMMER BUNNIES	Jive	23	3 Sep 94	3	
Samples Outstanding by the Gap Band.					
SHE'S GOT THAT VIBE [RI]	Jive	3	22 Oct 94	13	
BUMP N' GRIND	Jive	8	21 Jan 95	9	
Originally reached No. 79 in 1994.					
THE 4 PLAY [EP]	Jive	23	6 May 95	3	
Lead track: Your Body's Callin'. This is a re-issue.					
YOU REMIND ME OF SOMETHING	Jive	24	11 Nov 95	3	
DOWN LOW (NOBODY HAS TO KNOW) THE MOVIE	Jive	23	2 Mar 96	3	
From the film 'Down Low'.					
Above hit: R. KELLY featuring Ronald ISLEY.					
THANK GOD IT'S FRIDAY	Jive	14	22 Jun 96	4	
I BELIEVE I CAN FLY	Jive	1	29 Mar 97	17	
GOTHAM CITY	Jive	9	19 Jul 97	8	
From the film 'Batman And Robin'.					
BE CAREFUL	Jive	7	18 Jul 98	6	
Above hit: SPARKLE featuring R. KELLY.					
BE CAREFUL [RE]	Jive	75	5 Sep 98	1	
HALF ON A BABY	Jive	16	26 Sep 98	4	
HOME ALONE	Jive	17	14 Nov 98	5	
Above hit: R. KELLY featuring Keith MURRAY.					
I'M YOUR ANGEL	Epic	3	28 Nov 98	13	
Above hit: Celine DION and R. KELLY.					
DID YOU EVER THINK	Jive	20	31 Jul 99	5	
Samples Curtis Mayfield's Right On For The Darkness.					
Above hit: R. KELLY featuring NAS.					
IF I COULD TURN BACK THE HANDS OF TIME	Jive	57	16 Oct 99	2	
Import. Background vocals Sparkle and Bruce Kelly (R. Kelly's brother). Tribute to Kelly's mother.					
IF I COULD TURN BACK THE HANDS OF TIME	Jive	2	30 Oct 99	10	
ALBUMS:		HITS 4		WEEKS 77	
BORN INTO THE 90'S	Jive	67	29 Feb 92	1	
Above hit: R. KELLY and PUBLIC ANNOUNCEMENT.					
12 PLAY	Jive	39	27 Nov 93	26	
Chart position reached in 1994.					
12 PLAY [RE]	Jive	20	14 Jan 95	18	
R. KELLY	Jive	18	25 Nov 95	10	
R.	Jive	27	21 Nov 98	22	

Roberta KELLY   US

SINGLES:		HITS 1		WEEKS 3	
ZODIACS	Oasis	48	21 Jan 78	1	
ZODIACS [RE]	Oasis	44	4 Feb 78	2	

KELLY FAMILY   Ireland

SINGLES:		HITS 1		WEEKS 1	
AN ANGEL	EMI	69	21 Oct 95	1	

Johnny KEMP
Barbados

SINGLES:		HITS 1		WEEKS 1
JUST GOT PAID	CBS	68	27 Aug 88	1

Tara KEMP
US

SINGLES:		HITS 1		WEEKS 2
HOLD YOU TIGHT	Giant	69	20 Apr 91	2

Felicity KENDAL
UK

ALBUMS:		HITS 1		WEEKS 47
SHAPE UP AND DANCE WITH FELICITY KENDAL (VOLUME ONE)	Lifestyle	53	19 Jun 82	14
SHAPE UP AND DANCE WITH FELICITY KENDAL (VOLUME ONE) [RE]	Lifestyle	29	22 Jan 83	33

Graham KENDRICK
UK

SINGLES:		HITS 1		WEEKS 4
LET THE FLAME BURN BRIGHTER	Power	55	9 Sep 89	4

Eddie KENDRICKS
US

SINGLES:		HITS 2		WEEKS 18
KEEP ON TRUCKIN'	Tamla Motown	18	3 Nov 73	14
BOOGIE DOWN	Tamla Motown	39	16 Mar 74	4

KENICKIE
UK

SINGLES:		HITS 6		WEEKS 13
PUNKA	Emidisc	43	14 Sep 96	2
MILLIONAIRE SWEEPER	Emidisc	60	16 Nov 96	1
IN YOUR CAR	Emidisc	24	11 Jan 97	3
NIGHTLIFE	Emidisc	27	3 May 97	2
PUNKA [RI]	Emidisc	38	5 Jul 97	2
I WOULD FIX YOU	EMI	36	6 Jun 98	2
STAY IN THE SUN	EMI	43	22 Aug 98	1
ALBUMS:		**HITS 2**		**WEEKS 5**
AT THE CLUB	Emidisc	9	24 May 97	3
GET IN	EMI	32	12 Sep 98	2

Jane KENNAWAY and STRANGE BEHAVIOUR
UK

SINGLES:		HITS 1		WEEKS 3
I.O.U.	Deram	65	24 Jan 81	3

Brian KENNEDY
UK

SINGLES:		HITS 3		WEEKS 8
A BETTER MAN	RCA	28	22 Jun 96	3
LIFE, LOVE & HAPPINESS	RCA	27	21 Sep 96	3
PUT THE MESSAGE IN THE BOX	RCA	37	5 Apr 97	2
ALBUMS:		**HITS 2**		**WEEKS 4**
THE GREAT WAR OF WORDS	RCA	64	31 Mar 90	1
A BETTER MAN	RCA	19	19 Oct 96	3

Nigel KENNEDY
UK

ALBUMS:		HITS 8		WEEKS 123
ELGAR: VIOLIN CONCERTO	EMI	97	1 Mar 86	1
Above hit: Nigel KENNEDY with the LONDON PHILHARMONIC ORCHESTRA , conducted by Vernon HANDLEY.				
VIVALDI: THE FOUR SEASONS	EMI	3	7 Oct 89	81
Above hit: Nigel KENNEDY with the ENGLISH CHAMBER ORCHESTRA.				
MENDELSSOHN/BRUCH/SCHUBERT	His Master's Voice	28	5 May 90	15
Above hit: Nigel KENNEDY with Jeffrey TATE conducting the ENGLISH CHAMBER ORCHESTRA.				
BRAHMS: VIOLIN CONCERTO	EMI	16	6 Apr 91	12
Above hit: Nigel KENNEDY with the LONDON PHILHARMONIC ORCHESTRA conducted by Klaus TENNSTEDT.				
JUST LISTEN . . .	EMI Classics	56	22 Feb 92	1
Above hit: Nigel KENNEDY with the LONDON PHILHARMONIC ORCHESTRA, conducted by Simon RATTLE.				
BEETHOVEN VIOLIN CONCERTO, CORIOLAN OVERTURE	EMI Classics	40	21 Nov 92	6
Above hit: Nigel KENNEDY with Klaus TENNSTEDT conducting the NORTH GERMAN RADIO SYMPHONY ORCHESTRA.				
KAFKA	EMI	67	29 Jun 96	1
CLASSIC KENNEDY	EMI Classics	51	6 Nov 99	6
Above hit: KENNEDY with the ENGLISH CHAMBER ORCHESTRA.				

KENNY

Ireland

SINGLES:		HITS 2		WEEKS 16	
HEART OF STONE	RAK		11	3 Mar 73	13
GIVE IT TO ME NOW	RAK		38	30 Jun 73	3

KENNY

UK

SINGLES:		HITS 4		WEEKS 39	
THE BUMP	RAK		3	7 Dec 74	15
Originally recorded by the Bay City Rollers.					
FANCY PANTS	RAK		4	8 Mar 75	9
BABY I LOVE YOU, OK!	RAK		12	7 Jun 75	7
JULIE ANNE	RAK		10	16 Aug 75	8
ALBUMS:		HITS 1		WEEKS 1	
THE SOUND OF SUPER K	RAK		56	17 Jan 76	1

Gerard KENNY

US

SINGLES:		HITS 4		WEEKS 21	
NEW YORK, NEW YORK	RCA Victor		43	9 Dec 78	8
FANTASY	RCA		65	21 Jun 80	1
FANTASY [RE]	RCA		34	5 Jul 80	5
THE OTHER WOMAN, THE OTHER MAN	Impression		69	18 Feb 84	4
NO MAN'S LAND	WEA		56	4 May 85	3
Theme from the Thames ITV series 'Widows'.					
ALBUMS:		HITS 1		WEEKS 4	
MADE IT THROUGH THE RAIN	RCA Victor		19	21 Jul 79	4

KENT

Sweden

SINGLES:		HITS 1		WEEKS 1	
747	RCA Victor		61	13 Mar 99	1

Klark KENT

UK

SINGLES:		HITS 1		WEEKS 4	
DON'T CARE	A&M		48	26 Aug 78	4
Stewart Copeland (from the Police) under a pseudonym.					

KENTISH MAN – See CHUBBY CHUNKS

Carol KENYON – See Paul HARDCASTLE; HEAVEN 17; RAPINATION

KERBDOG

Ireland

SINGLES:		HITS 4		WEEKS 5	
DRY RISER	Vertigo		60	12 Mar 94	1
DUMMY CRUSHER	Vertigo		37	6 Aug 94	2
SALLY	Fontana		69	12 Oct 96	1
MEXICAN WAVE	Fontana		49	29 Mar 97	1
ALBUMS:		HITS 1		WEEKS 1	
ON THE TURN	Fontana		64	12 Apr 97	1

Anita KERR SINGERS – See Bobby HELMS

KERRI-ANN

Ireland

SINGLES:		HITS 1		WEEKS 1	
DO YOU LOVE ME BOY?	Raglan Road		58	8 Aug 98	1

KERRI and MICK

Australia

SINGLES:		HITS 1		WEEKS 3	
"SONS AND DAUGHTERS" THEME	A.1		68	28 Apr 84	3
Theme from the Australian TV soap.					

Liz KERSHAW and Bruno BROOKES

UK

SINGLES:		HITS 2		WEEKS 3	
IT TAKES TWO, BABY	Spartan		53	2 Dec 89	2
Above hit: Liz KERSHAW, Bruno BROOKES, JIVE BUNNY and LONDONBEAT.					
LET'S DANCE	Jive		54	1 Dec 90	1
Above 2 were charity records with proceeds to BBC's Children In Need.					
Above hit: BRUNO and LIZ and the RADIO 1 DJ POSSE.					

Nik KERSHAW

UK

SINGLES:		HITS 13		WEEKS 89	
I WON'T LET THE SUN GO DOWN ON ME	MCA		47	19 Nov 83	5
WOULDN'T IT BE GOOD	MCA		4	28 Jan 84	14
DANCING GIRLS	MCA		13	14 Apr 84	9
I WON'T LET THE SUN GO DOWN ON ME [RI]	MCA		2	16 Jun 84	13

HUMAN RACING	MCA	19	15 Sep 84	7
THE RIDDLE	MCA	3	17 Nov 84	11
WIDE BOY	MCA	9	16 Mar 85	8
DON QUIXOTE	MCA	10	3 Aug 85	7
WHEN A HEART BEATS	MCA	27	30 Nov 85	7
NOBODY KNOWS	MCA	44	11 Oct 86	3
RADIO MUSICOLA	MCA	43	13 Dec 86	2
ONE STEP AHEAD	MCA	55	4 Feb 89	1
SOMEBODY LOVES YOU	Eagle	70	27 Feb 99	1
SOMETIMES	Wall Of Sound	56	7 Aug 99	1

Above hit: LES RYTHMES DIGITALES featuring Nik KERSHAW.

ALBUMS:		**HITS 3**		**WEEKS 100**
HUMAN RACING	MCA	5	10 Mar 84	61
THE RIDDLE	MCA	8	1 Dec 84	36
RADIO MUSICOLA	MCA	47	8 Nov 86	3

KEVIN THE GERBIL
UK

SINGLES:		**HITS 1**		**WEEKS 6**
SUMMER HOLIDAY	Rodent	50	4 Aug 84	6

Above hit: Roland RAT SUPERSTAR presents KEVIN THE GERBIL.

KEY WEST featuring ERIK
UK

SINGLES:		**HITS 1**		**WEEKS 2**
LOOKS LIKE I'M IN LOVE AGAIN	PWL Sanctuary	46	10 Apr 93	2

KEYNOTES - See JOHNSTON BROTHERS, Dave KING

Nusrat Fateh Ali KHAN/Michael BROOK
Pakistan/UK

ALBUMS:		**HITS 1**		**WEEKS 1**
NIGHT SONG	Realworld	65	6 Apr 96	1

Chaka KHAN
US

(See also Quincy Jones; Rufus.)

SINGLES:		**HITS 10**		**WEEKS 66**
I'M EVERY WOMAN	Warner Brothers	11	2 Dec 78	13
I FEEL FOR YOU	Warner Brothers	1	20 Oct 84	16

Features rap by Grandmaster Melle Mel and harmonica by Stevie Wonder. Written and originally recorded by Prince.

THIS IS MY NIGHT	Warner Brothers	14	19 Jan 85	6
EYE TO EYE	Warner Brothers	16	20 Apr 85	7
LOVE OF A LIFETIME	Warner Brothers	52	12 Jul 86	4
IT'S MY PARTY	Warner Brothers	71	21 Jan 89	2
I'M EVERY WOMAN [RM]	Warner Brothers	8	6 May 89	8

Remixed by Dancin' Danny Dee.

I FEEL FOR YOU [RM]	Warner Brothers	45	7 Oct 89	2
LOVE YOU ALL MY LIFETIME	Warner Brothers	49	28 Mar 92	3
DON'T LOOK AT ME THAT WAY	Warner Brothers	73	17 Jul 93	1
WATCH WHAT YOU SAY	Cooltempo	28	19 Aug 95	3

Sleeve gives title as an EP: Jazzmatazz Vol.2, The New Reality.
Above hit: GURU featuring Chaka KHAN.

NEVER MISS THE WATER	Reprise	59	1 Mar 97	1

Above hit: Chaka KHAN featuring Me'shell NDEGEOCELLO.

ALBUMS:		**HITS 4**		**WEEKS 40**
I FEEL FOR YOU	Warner Brothers	15	20 Oct 84	22
DESTINY	Warner Brothers	77	9 Aug 86	2
LIFE IS A DANCE - THE REMIX PROJECT	Warner Brothers	14	3 Jun 89	15

Compilation.

BEST OF CHAKA KHAN - I'M EVERY WOMAN	warner.esp	62	4 Sep 99	1

Aram KHATCHATURIAN - See VIENNA PHILHARMONIC ORCHESTRA conducted by Aram KHACHATURIAN

Mary KIANI
UK

SINGLES:		**HITS 5**		**WEEKS 15**
WHEN I CALL YOUR NAME	Mercury	18	12 Aug 95	4
I GIVE IT ALL TO YOU / I IMAGINE	Mercury	35	23 Dec 95	4
LET THE MUSIC PLAY	Mercury	19	27 Apr 96	3
100%	Mercury	23	18 Jan 97	3
WITH OR WITHOUT YOU	Mercury	46	21 Jun 97	1

KICK HORNS - See DODGY

KICK SQUAD
UK/Germany

SINGLES:		**HITS 1**		**WEEKS 2**
SOUND CLASH (CHAMPION SOUND)	Kickin	59	10 Nov 90	2

KICKING BACK with TAXMAN

SINGLES:						UK
		HITS 2			**WEEKS 8**	
DEVOTION		10 Records	47	17 Mar 90	4	
EVERYTHING		10 Records	54	7 Jul 90	4	

Sleeve has artist credit Kicking Back featuring Taxman.

KICKS LIKE A MULE

SINGLES:						UK
		HITS 1			**WEEKS 6**	
THE BOUNCER		Tribal Bass	7	1 Feb 92	6	

KID 'N' PLAY

SINGLES:						US
		HITS 3			**WEEKS 7**	
LAST NIGHT		Cooltempo	71	18 Jul 87	1	
DO THIS MY WAY		Cooltempo	48	26 Mar 88	3	
GITTIN' FUNKY		Cooltempo	55	17 Sep 88	3	

KID ROCK

SINGLES:						US
		HITS 1			**WEEKS 2**	
COWBOY		Atlantic	36	23 Oct 99	2	

KID UNKNOWN

SINGLES:						UK
		HITS 1			**WEEKS 1**	
NIGHTMARE		Warp	64	2 May 92	1	

Carol KIDD featuring Terry WAITE

SINGLES:						UK
		HITS 1			**WEEKS 3**	
WHEN I DREAM		The Hit Label	58	17 Oct 92	3	

Johnny KIDD and the PIRATES

SINGLES:						UK
		HITS 9			**WEEKS 62**	
PLEASE DON'T TOUCH		His Master's Voice	26	13 Jun 59	3	
PLEASE DON'T TOUCH [RE]		His Master's Voice	25	18 Jul 59	2	
YOU GOT WHAT IT TAKES		His Master's Voice	25	13 Feb 60	3	
SHAKIN' ALL OVER		His Master's Voice	1	18 Jun 60	19	
RESTLESS		His Master's Voice	22	8 Oct 60	7	
LINDA LU		His Master's Voice	47	15 Apr 61	1	

Originally recorded by Ray Sharpe in 1959.

A SHOT OF RHYTHM AND BLUES		His Master's Voice	48	12 Jan 63	1	
I'LL NEVER GET OVER YOU		His Master's Voice	4	27 Jul 63	15	
HUNGRY FOR LOVE		His Master's Voice	20	30 Nov 63	10	
ALWAYS AND EVER		His Master's Voice	46	2 May 64	1	

EPS:						
		HITS 1			**WEEKS 7**	
SHAKIN' ALL OVER		His Master's Voice	11	14 Jan 61	7	

KIDS FROM "FAME"

SINGLES:						US
		HITS 4			**WEEKS 36**	
HI-FIDELITY		RCA	5	14 Aug 82	10	

Above hit: KIDS FROM "FAME" featuring Valerie LANDSBURG.

STARMAKER		RCA	3	2 Oct 82	10	

Originally recorded by Bruce Roberts.
Above hit: KIDS FROM "FAME" featuring the KIDS FROM "FAME".

MANNEQUIN		RCA	50	11 Dec 82	6	

Above hit: KIDS FROM "FAME" featuring Gene Anthony RAY.

FRIDAY NIGHT (LIVE VERSION)		RCA	13	9 Apr 83	10	

Above hit: KIDS FROM FAME featuring Carlo IMPERATO and "The WATERS".

ALBUMS:						
		HITS 5			**WEEKS 117**	
THE KIDS FROM FAME		BBC	1	24 Jul 82	45	
THE KIDS FROM FAME AGAIN		RCA	2	16 Oct 82	21	
THE KIDS FROM FAME LIVE		RCA	8	26 Feb 83	28	
THE KIDS FROM FAME SONGS		BBC	14	14 May 83	16	
THE KIDS FROM FAME SING FOR YOU		BBC	28	20 Aug 83	7	

Greg KIHN BAND

SINGLES:						US
		HITS 1			**WEEKS 2**	
JEOPARDY		Beserkley	63	23 Apr 83	2	

KILLAH PRIEST

SINGLES:						US
		HITS 1			**WEEKS 1**	
ONE STEP		Geffen	45	7 Feb 98	1	

Vocals by Tekitha.

KILLING JOKE
UK

SINGLES:	HITS 15			WEEKS 48
FOLLOW THE LEADERS	E'G	55	23 May 81	5
EMPIRE SONG	E'G	43	20 Mar 82	4
BIRDS OF A FEATHER	E'G	64	30 Oct 82	2
LET'S ALL GO (TO THE FIRE DANCES)	E'G	51	25 Jun 83	3
ME OR YOU?	E'G	57	15 Oct 83	1
EIGHTIES	E'G	60	7 Apr 84	5
A NEW DAY	E'G	56	21 Jul 84	2
LOVE LIKE BLOOD	E'G	16	2 Feb 85	9
KINGS AND QUEENS	E'G	58	30 Mar 85	3
ADORATIONS	E'G	42	16 Aug 86	6
SANITY	E'G	70	18 Oct 86	1
MILLENIUM	Butterfly	34	7 May 94	2
THE PANDEMONIUM SINGLE [EP]	Butterfly	28	16 Jul 94	3
EP features Pandemonium and various mixes of the track.				
JANA	Butterfly	54	4 Feb 95	1
DEMOCRACY	Butterfly	39	23 Mar 96	1
ALBUMS:	HITS 10			WEEKS 34
KILLING JOKE	Polydor	39	25 Oct 80	4
WHAT'S THIS FOR	E'G	42	20 Jun 81	4
REVELATIONS	E'G	12	8 May 82	6
"HA" – KILLING JOKE LIVE	E'G	66	27 Nov 82	2
FIRE DANCES	E'G	29	23 Jul 83	3
NIGHT TIME	E'G	11	9 Mar 85	9
BRIGHTER THAN A THOUSAND SUNS	E'G	54	22 Nov 86	1
OUTSIDE THE GATE	E'G	92	9 Jul 88	1
PANDEMONIUM	Butterfly	16	6 Aug 94	3
DEMOCRACY	Butterfly	71	13 Apr 96	1

Andy KIM
Canada

SINGLES:	HITS 1			WEEKS 12
ROCK ME GENTLY	Capitol	2	24 Aug 74	12

KIMERA with the LONDON SYMPHONY ORCHESTRA
Korea

(See also London Symphony Orchestra.)

ALBUMS:	HITS 1			WEEKS 4
HITS ON OPERA	Stylus	38	26 Oct 85	4

KINANE
Ireland

SINGLES:	HITS 4			WEEKS 4
ALL THE LOVER I NEED	Coliseum	59	18 May 96	1
THE WOMAN IN ME	Coliseum	73	21 Sep 96	1
Above 2: Bianca KINANE.				
HEAVEN	Coalition	49	16 May 98	1
SO FINE	Coalition	63	22 Aug 98	1

KING
UK/Ireland

SINGLES:	HITS 5			WEEKS 44
LOVE AND PRIDE	CBS	2	12 Jan 85	14
Original release reached No. 84 in 1984.				
WON'T YOU HOLD MY HAND NOW	CBS	24	23 Mar 85	8
ALONE WITHOUT YOU	CBS	8	17 Aug 85	9
THE TASTE OF YOUR TEARS	CBS	11	19 Oct 85	9
TORTURE	CBS	23	11 Jan 86	4
ALBUMS:	HITS 2			WEEKS 32
STEPS IN TIME	CBS	6	9 Feb 85	21
BITTER SWEET	CBS	16	23 Nov 85	11

Albert KING - See Gary MOORE

B.B. KING
US

SINGLES:	HITS 2			WEEKS 10
WHEN LOVE COMES TO TOWN	Island	6	15 Apr 89	7
Above hit: U2 with B.B. KING.				
SINCE I MET YOU BABY	Virgin	59	18 Jul 92	3
Above hit: Gary MOORE and B.B. KING.				
ALBUMS:	HITS 2			WEEKS 9
TAKE IT HOME	MCA	60	25 Aug 79	5
HIS DEFINITIVE GREATEST HITS	Universal Music TV	24	1 May 99	4
Compilation covering the years 1964–1993.				

Ben E. KING
US

SINGLES:		HITS 4			WEEKS 35
FIRST TASTE OF LOVE	London	27	4 Feb 61	11
STAND BY ME	London	50	24 Jun 61	1
STAND BY ME [RE]	London	27	8 Jul 61	6
AMOR, AMOR	London	38	7 Oct 61	4
STAND BY ME [RI]	Arista	1	14 Feb 87	11
Featured in the Levi's 501 TV commercial.				
SAVE THE LAST DANCE FOR ME	Manhattan	69	4 Jul 87	2
ALBUMS:	HITS 4			WEEKS 30
SPANISH HARLEM	Atlantic	30	1 Jul 67	3
STAND BY ME (THE ULTIMATE COLLECTION)	Atlantic	14	14 Mar 87	8
THE VERY BEST OF BEN E. KING AND THE DRIFTERS	Telstar	15	20 Oct 90	16
THE VERY BEST OF BEN E. KING AND THE DRIFTERS	Warner.esp/Global TV	41	7 Nov 98	3

Above 2 albums are different and include both Ben E. King's solo and group material.
Above 3: KING and the DRIFTERS.

Carole KING
UK

SINGLES:		HITS 2			WEEKS 29
IT MIGHT AS WELL RAIN UNTIL SEPTEMBER	London	3	22 Sep 62	13
She wrote it for Bobby Vee.				
IT'S TOO LATE	A&M	6	7 Aug 71	12
IT MIGHT AS WELL RAIN UNTIL SEPTEMBER [RI]	London	43	28 Oct 72	4
ALBUMS:	HITS 3			WEEKS 103
TAPESTRY	A&M	4	24 Jul 71	90
MUSIC	A&M	18	15 Jan 72	10
RHYMES AND REASONS	Ode	40	2 Dec 72	2
TAPESTRY [RI]	Epic	64	7 Feb 98	1

Dave KING
UK

(See also All Star Hit Parade.)

SINGLES:		HITS 4			WEEKS 29
MEMORIES ARE MADE OF THIS	Decca	5	18 Feb 56	15
YOU CAN'T BE TRUE TO TWO	Decca	11	14 Apr 56	9
Above 2: Dave KING with the Roland SHAW ORCHESTRA and the KEYNOTES.				
CHRISTMAS AND YOU	Decca	23	22 Dec 56	2
THE STORY OF MY LIFE	Decca	20	25 Jan 58	3

Above hit: Dave KING and the Roland SHAW ORCHESTRA.

Denis KING and his Orchestra
UK

SINGLES:		HITS 1			WEEKS 6
THE THEME FROM "WE'LL MEET AGAIN"	Multi-Media Tapes	36	24 Apr 82	6

Theme to the LWT ITV series. [AA] listed with The Song That I Sing by Stutz Bear Cats.

Diana KING
Jamaica

(See also Jamaica United.)

SINGLES:		HITS 3			WEEKS 22
SHY GUY	Columbia	2	8 Jul 95	13
From the film 'Bad Boys'.				
AIN'T NOBODY	Columbia	13	28 Oct 95	5
I SAY A LITTLE PRAYER	Columbia	17	1 Nov 97	4
ALBUMS:	HITS 1			WEEKS 2
TOUGHER THAN LOVE	Columbia	50	12 Aug 95	2

Evelyn 'Champagne' KING
US

SINGLES:		HITS 11			WEEKS 76
SHAME	RCA Victor	39	13 May 78	23
I DON'T KNOW IF IT'S RIGHT	RCA Victor	67	3 Feb 79	2
I'M IN LOVE	RCA	27	27 Jun 81	11
IF YOU WANT MY LOVIN'	RCA	43	26 Sep 81	6
LOVE COME DOWN	RCA	7	28 Aug 82	13
BACK TO LOVE	RCA	40	20 Nov 82	4
GET LOOSE	RCA	45	19 Feb 83	5
Above 5: Evelyn KING.				
YOUR PERSONAL TOUCH	RCA	37	9 Nov 85	5
HIGH HORSE	RCA	55	29 Mar 86	3
HOLD ON TO WHAT YOU'VE GOT	Manhattan	47	23 Jul 88	3
SHAME (HARDCORE MIX) [RM]	Network	74	10 Oct 92	1
Above hit: ALTERN 8 vs Evelyn KING.				
ALBUMS:	HITS 1			WEEKS 9
GET LOOSE	RCA	35	11 Sep 82	9

John KING – See DUST BROTHERS (Michael SIMPSON and John KING) featuring Tyler DURDEN

Jonathan KING
UK

SINGLES:	HITS 17		WEEKS 128	
EVERYONE'S GONE TO THE MOON	Decca	4	31 Jul 65	11
LET IT ALL HANG OUT	Decca	26	10 Jan 70	7
IT'S THE SAME OLD SONG	B&C	19	16 Jan 71	9
Above hit: WEATHERMEN.				
SUGAR SUGAR	RCA Victor	12	3 Apr 71	14
Above hit: SAKKARIN.				
LAZYBONES	Decca	23	29 May 71	8
Originally recorded by the Hombres.				
HOOKED ON A FEELING	Decca	23	20 Nov 71	10
FLIRT!	Decca	22	5 Feb 72	9
LOOP DI LOVE	UK	4	14 Oct 72	13
Originally recorded by J. Bastos.				
Above hit: SHAG.				
(I CAN'T GET NO) SATISFACTION	UK	29	26 Jan 74	5
Above hit: BUBBLEROCK.				
UNA PALOMA BLANCA (WHITE DOVE)	UK	5	6 Sep 75	11
CHICK-A-BOOM (DON'T YA JES LOVE IT)	UK	36	20 Sep 75	4
Originally recorded by Daddy Dewdrop.				
Above hit: 53RD & 3RD featuring the SOUND OF SHAG.				
IN THE MOOD	UK	46	7 Feb 76	3
Above hit: SOUND 9418.				
IT ONLY TAKES A MINUTE	UK	9	26 Jun 76	9
Above hit: ONE HUNDRED TON AND A FEATHER.				
ONE FOR YOU, ONE FOR ME	GTO	29	7 Oct 78	6
LICK A SMURP FOR CHRISTMAS (ALL FALL DOWN)	Petrol/Magnet	58	16 Dec 78	4
Initially issued as a single sided flexi disc on the Petrol label, it was then available on Magnet from 23 Dec 78.				
Above hit: FATHER ABRAPHART and the SMURPS.				
YOU'RE THE GREATEST LOVER	UK International	67	16 Jun 79	2
GLORIA	Ariola	65	3 Nov 79	3

Mark KING
UK

ALBUMS:	HITS 1		WEEKS 2	
INFLUENCES	Polydor	77	21 Jul 84	2

Nosmo KING – See JAVELLS featuring Nosmo KING

Paul KING
UK

SINGLES:	HITS 1		WEEKS 3	
I KNOW	CBS	59	2 May 87	3

Solomon KING
US

SINGLES:	HITS 2		WEEKS 28	
SHE WEARS MY RING	Columbia	3	6 Jan 68	18
Originally recorded by Roy Orbison.				
WHEN WE WERE YOUNG	Columbia	21	4 May 68	10
ALBUMS:	HITS 1		WEEKS 1	
SHE WEARS MY RING	Columbia	40	22 Jun 68	1

Tony KING – See VISION MASTERS and Tony KING featuring Kylie MINOGUE

KING BEE
UK

SINGLES:	HITS 2		WEEKS 6	
MUST BEE THE MUSIC	Torso Dance	44	26 Jan 91	4
Above hit: KING BEE featuring MICHELE.				
BACK BY DOPE DEMAND	1st Bass	61	23 Mar 91	2

KING BROTHERS
UK

SINGLES:	HITS 8		WEEKS 74	
A WHITE SPORT COAT (AND A PINK CARNATION)	Parlophone	6	1 Jun 57	14
Originally recorded by Marty Robbins.				
Above hit: KING BROTHERS with the KING BROTHERS and Geoff LOVE and his Orchestra.				
IN THE MIDDLE OF AN ISLAND	Parlophone	19	10 Aug 57	13
Above hit: KING BROTHERS with Geoff LOVE and his Orchestra and the Rita WILLIAMS SINGERS.				
WAKE UP LITTLE SUSIE	Parlophone	22	7 Dec 57	3
PUT A LIGHT IN THE WINDOW	Parlophone	29	1 Feb 58	1
PUT A LIGHT IN THE WINDOW [RE-1ST]	Parlophone	28	15 Feb 58	1
PUT A LIGHT IN THE WINDOW [RE-2ND]	Parlophone	25	1 Mar 58	2
Above 4: KING BROTHERS with Geoff LOVE and his Orchestra.				
STANDING ON THE CORNER	Parlophone	4	16 Apr 60	11
From the musical 'The Most Happy Fella'.				

MAIS OUI	Parlophone	16	30 Jul 60	10
Above 2: KING BROTHERS and the Rita WILLIAMS SINGERS with Geoff LOVE and his Orchestra.				
DOLL HOUSE	Parlophone	21	14 Jan 61	8
Above hit: KING BROTHERS and the Rita WILLIAMS SINGERS.				
SEVENTY-SIX TROMBONES	Parlophone	19	4 Mar 61	11
Originally recorded by Robert Preston.				
Above hit: KING BROTHERS and the Rita WILLIAMS SINGERS with Geoff LOVE and his Orchestra.				

KING CRIMSON
UK

ALBUMS:	**HITS 11**			**WEEKS 54**
IN THE COURT OF THE CRIMSON KING	Island	5	1 Nov 69	18
IN THE WAKE OF POSEIDON	Island	4	30 May 70	13
LIZARD	Island	30	16 Jan 71	1
ISLANDS	Island	30	8 Jan 72	1
LARKS' TONGUES IN ASPIC	Island	20	7 Apr 73	4
STARLESS AND BIBLE BLACK	Island	28	13 Apr 74	2
RED	Island	45	26 Oct 74	1
DISCIPLINE	E'G	41	10 Oct 81	4
BEAT	E'G	39	26 Jun 82	5
Songs based on work by US beat poet Jack Kerouac.				
THREE OF A PERFECT PAIR	E'G	30	31 Mar 84	4
THRAK	Virgin	58	15 Apr 95	1

KING KURT
UK

SINGLES:	**HITS 5**			**WEEKS 16**
DESTINATION ZULU LAND	Stiff	36	15 Oct 83	6
MACK THE KNIFE	Stiff	55	28 Apr 84	4
BANANA BANANA	Stiff	54	4 Aug 84	4
AMERICA	Polydor	73	15 Nov 86	1
THE LAND OF RING DANG DO	Polydor	67	2 May 87	1
ALBUMS:	**HITS 2**			**WEEKS 5**
OOH WALLAH WALLAH	Stiff	99	10 Dec 83	1
BIG COCK	Stiff	50	8 Mar 86	4

KING SUN-D MOET
US

SINGLES:	**HITS 1**			**WEEKS 3**
HEY LOVE	Flame	66	11 Jul 87	3

KING TRIGGER
UK

SINGLES:	**HITS 1**			**WEEKS 4**
RIVER	Chrysalis	57	14 Aug 82	4

KINGDOM COME
US

SINGLES:	**HITS 2**			**WEEKS 2**
GET IT ON	Polydor	75	16 Apr 88	1
DO YOU LIKE IT	Polydor	73	6 May 89	1
ALBUMS:	**HITS 2**			**WEEKS 10**
KINGDOM COME	Polydor	43	26 Mar 88	6
IN YOUR FACE	Polydor	25	13 May 89	4

KINGMAKER
UK

SINGLES:	**HITS 8**			**WEEKS 22**
IDIOTS AT THE WHEEL [EP]	Chrysalis	30	18 Jan 92	3
Lead track: Really Scrape The Sky.				
EAT YOURSELF WHOLE	Scorch	15	23 May 92	3
Single also gives title as an EP: The Killjoy Was Here.				
ARMCHAIR ANARCHIST	Scorch	47	31 Oct 92	2
10 YEARS ASLEEP	Scorch	15	8 May 93	4
QUEEN JANE	Scorch	29	19 Jun 93	4
SATURDAY'S NOT WHAT IT USED TO BE	Scorch	63	30 Oct 93	1
YOU AND I WILL NEVER SEE THINGS EYE TO EYE	Chrysalis	33	15 Apr 95	3
IN THE BEST POSSIBLE TASTE (PART 2)	Chrysalis	41	3 Jun 95	2
ALBUMS:	**HITS 2**			**WEEKS 10**
EAT YOURSELF WHOLE	Scorch	29	19 Oct 91	3
SLEEPWALKING	Scorch	15	29 May 93	7

Choir Of KING'S COLLEGE, CAMBRIDGE
UK

ALBUMS:	**HITS 1**			**WEEKS 3**
THE WORLD OF CHRISTMAS	Argo	38	11 Dec 71	3

KINGS OF SWING ORCHESTRA — Australia

SINGLES:	HITS 1		WEEKS 5	
SWITCHED ON SWING [M]	*Philips*	48	*1 May 82*	5
ALBUMS:	**HITS 1**		**WEEKS 11**	
SWITCHED ON SWING	*K-Tel*	28	*29 May 82*	11

KING'S X — US

ALBUMS:	HITS 4		WEEKS 4	
GRETCHEN GOES TO NEBRASKA	*Megaforce*	52	*1 Jul 89*	1
FAITH HOPE LOVE	*Megaforce*	70	*10 Nov 90*	1
KING'S X	*Atlantic*	46	*28 Mar 92*	1
DOGMAN	*Atlantic*	49	*12 Feb 94*	1

KINGSMEN — US

SINGLES:	HITS 1		WEEKS 7	
LOUIE LOUIE	*Pye International*	26	*1 Feb 64*	7

Originally recorded by Richard Berry and the Pharoahs in 1957.

KINGSTON TRIO — US

SINGLES:	HITS 2		WEEKS 15	
TOM DOOLEY	*Capitol*	5	*22 Nov 58*	14
Written as Tom Dula in 1958.				
SAN MIGUEL	*Capitol*	29	*5 Dec 59*	1

KINKS — UK

SINGLES:	HITS 23		WEEKS 215	
YOU REALLY GOT ME	*Pye*	1	*15 Aug 64*	12
ALL DAY AND ALL OF THE NIGHT	*Pye*	2	*31 Oct 64*	14
TIRED OF WAITING FOR YOU	*Pye*	1	*23 Jan 65*	10
EVERYBODY'S GONNA BE HAPPY	*Pye*	17	*27 Mar 65*	8
SET ME FREE	*Pye*	9	*29 May 65*	11
SEE MY FRIEND	*Pye*	10	*7 Aug 65*	9
TILL THE END OF THE DAY	*Pye*	8	*4 Dec 65*	12
DEDICATED FOLLOWER OF FASHION	*Pye*	4	*5 Mar 66*	11
SUNNY AFTERNOON	*Pye*	1	*11 Jun 66*	13
DEAD END STREET	*Pye*	5	*26 Nov 66*	11
WATERLOO SUNSET	*Pye*	2	*13 May 67*	11
AUTUMN ALMANAC	*Pye*	3	*21 Oct 67*	11
WONDERBOY	*Pye*	36	*20 Apr 68*	5
DAY'S	*Pye*	12	*20 Jul 68*	10
PLASTIC MAN	*Pye*	31	*19 Apr 69*	4
VICTORIA	*Pye*	33	*10 Jan 70*	4
LOLA	*Pye*	2	*4 Jul 70*	14
APEMAN	*Pye*	5	*12 Dec 70*	14
SUPERSONIC ROCKET SHIP	*RCA Victor*	16	*27 May 72*	8
BETTER THINGS	*Arista*	46	*27 Jun 81*	5
COME DANCING	*Arista*	12	*6 Aug 83*	9
DON'T FORGET TO DANCE	*Arista*	58	*15 Oct 83*	3
YOU REALLY GOT ME [RI]	PRT	47	*15 Oct 83*	4
THE DAYS [EP]	*When!*	35	*18 Jan 97*	2

Lead track: Days. Featured in the Yellow Pages TV commercial. This and the other tracks are all re-issues.

EPS:	HITS 4		WEEKS 79	
KINKSIZE SESSION	*Pye*	1	*12 Dec 64*	22
KINKSIZE HITS	*Pye*	3	*30 Jan 65*	21
KWYET KINKS	*Pye*	1	*25 Sep 65*	32
DEDICATED KINKS	*Pye*	7	*23 Jul 66*	4
ALBUMS:	**HITS 13**		**WEEKS 135**	
KINKS	*Pye*	3	*17 Oct 64*	25
KINDA KINKS	*Pye*	3	*13 Mar 65*	15
KINDA KONTROVERSY	*Pye*	9	*4 Dec 65*	12
WELL RESPECTED KINKS	*Marble Arch*	5	*10 Sep 66*	31
FACE TO FACE	*Pye*	12	*5 Nov 66*	11
SOMETHING ELSE	*Pye*	35	*14 Oct 67*	2
SUNNY AFTERNOON	*Marble Arch*	9	*2 Dec 67*	11
GOLDEN HOUR OF THE KINKS	*Golden Hour*	21	*23 Oct 71*	4
20 GOLDEN GREATS	*Ronco*	19	*14 Oct 78*	6
KINKS GREATEST HITS - DEAD END STREET	PRT	96	*5 Nov 83*	1
THE ULTIMATE COLLECTION	*Castle Communications*	35	*16 Sep 89*	7
THE DEFINITIVE COLLECTION	*PolyGram TV*	18	*18 Sep 93*	7
THE VERY BEST OF THE KINKS	*PolyGram TV*	42	*12 Apr 97*	3

Includes Dave Davies' solo hits.

KINKY
UK

(See also Erasure; E-Z Posse.)

SINGLES:		HITS 1		WEEKS 1	
EVERYBODY	*Feverpitch*		71	*24 Aug 96*	1

KINKY MACHINE
UK

SINGLES:		HITS 4		WEEKS 4	
SUPERNATURAL GIVER	*Lemon*	70	*6 Mar 93*	1
SHOCKAHOLIC	*Oxygen*	70	*29 May 93*	1
GOING OUT WITH GOD	*Oxygen*	74	*14 Aug 93*	1
10 SECOND BIONIC MAN	*Oxygen*	66	*2 Jul 94*	1

Fern KINNEY
US

SINGLES:		HITS 1		WEEKS 11	
TOGETHER WE ARE BEAUTIFUL	*WEA*	1	*16 Feb 80*	11

Originally recorded by Ken Leray.

KINSHASA BAND - See Johnny WAKELIN

Kathy KIRBY
UK

SINGLES:		HITS 5		WEEKS 54	
DANCE ON	*Decca*	11	*17 Aug 63*	13
SECRET LOVE	*Decca*	4	*9 Nov 63*	18
LET ME GO, LOVER	*Decca*	10	*22 Feb 64*	11
YOU'RE THE ONE	*Decca*	17	*9 May 64*	9
I BELONG	*Decca*	36	*6 Mar 65*	3

UK's Eurovision entry in 1965, it came 2nd.

EPS:		HITS 2		WEEKS 10	
KATHY KIRBY VOLUME 2	*Decca*	20	*28 Nov 64*	1
BBC TV'S SONG FOR EUROPE	*Decca*	9	*6 Mar 65*	9

ALBUMS:		HITS 1		WEEKS 8	
16 HITS FROM 'STARS AND GARTERS'	*Decca*	11	*4 Jan 64*	8

From the TV series.

Bo KIRKLAND and Ruth DAVIS
US

SINGLES:		HITS 1		WEEKS 9	
YOU'RE GONNA GET NEXT TO ME	*EMI International*	12	*4 Jun 77*	9

Dominic KIRWAN
Ireland

ALBUMS:		HITS 1		WEEKS 1	
THE MUSIC'S BACK	*Ritz*	54	*1 Nov 97*	1

KISS
US

SINGLES:		HITS 13		WEEKS 57	
I WAS MADE FOR LOVIN' YOU	*Casablanca*	50	*30 Jun 79*	7
A WORLD WITHOUT HEROES	*Casablanca*	55	*20 Feb 82*	3
CREATURES OF THE NIGHT	*Casablanca*	34	*30 Apr 83*	4
LICK IT UP	*Vertigo*	31	*29 Oct 83*	5
HEAVEN'S ON FIRE	*Vertigo*	43	*8 Sep 84*	3
TEARS ARE FALLING	*Vertigo*	57	*9 Nov 85*	2
CRAZY CRAZY NIGHTS	*Vertigo*	4	*3 Oct 87*	9
REASON TO LIVE	*Vertigo*	33	*5 Dec 87*	7
TURN ON THE NIGHT	*Vertigo*	41	*10 Sep 88*	3
HIDE YOUR HEART	*Vertigo*	59	*18 Nov 89*	2
FOREVER	*Vertigo*	65	*31 Mar 90*	2

Co-written by Michael Bolton.

GOD GAVE ROCK AND ROLL TO YOU II	*Interscope*	4	*11 Jan 92*	8

From the film 'Bill And Ted's Bogus Journey'.

UNHOLY	*Vertigo*	26	*9 May 92*	2

ALBUMS:		HITS 19		WEEKS 71	
DESTROYER	*Casablanca*	22	*29 May 76*	5
ALIVE!	*Casablanca*	49	*26 Jun 76*	2

Live recordings from their 1975 tour.

ALIVE	*Casablanca*	60	*17 Dec 77*	1

Titled 'Alive II' in the US. Live recordings from the LA Forum between 25 & 27 Aug 77.

DYNASTY	*Casablanca*	50	*7 Jul 79*	6
UNMASKED	*Mercury*	48	*28 Jun 80*	3
THE ELDER	*Casablanca*	51	*5 Dec 81*	3
KILLERS	*Casablanca*	42	*26 Jun 82*	6
CREATURES OF THE NIGHT	*Casablanca*	22	*6 Nov 82*	4
LICK IT UP	*Casablanca*	7	*8 Oct 83*	7
ANIMALIZE	*Vertigo*	11	*6 Oct 84*	4
ASYLUM	*Vertigo*	12	*5 Oct 85*	3
CRAZY NIGHTS	*Vertigo*	4	*7 Nov 87*	14

SMASHES, THRASHES AND HITS	*Vertigo*	62	*10 Dec 88*	2
HOT IN THE SHADE	*Fontana*	35	*4 Nov 89*	2
REVENGE	*Mercury*	10	*23 May 92*	3
ALIVE III	*Mercury*	24	*29 May 93*	2

Live recordings from their 1992 concerts in Detroit, Cleveland and Indianapolis.

MTV UNPLUGGED	*Mercury*	74	*23 Mar 96*	1

Live recordings for the TV station.

GREATEST HITS	*PolyGram TV*	58	*12 Jul 97*	2
PSYCHO-CIRCUS	*Mercury*	47	*3 Oct 98*	1

KISS AMC
UK

SINGLES: | HITS 2 | | | WEEKS 5

A BIT OF . . .	*Syncopate*	58	*1 Jul 89*	2

Samples U2's Pride (In The Name Of Love). A copyright dispute prevented the U2 credit.
Above hit: <Kiss AMC.>

A BIT OF U2 [RE]	*Syncopate*	58	*19 Aug 89*	2
MY DOCS	*Syncopate*	66	*3 Feb 90*	1

KISSING THE PINK
UK

SINGLES: | HITS 1 | | | WEEKS 14

LAST FILM	*Magnet*	19	*5 Mar 83*	14

Sleeve shows title as 'The Last Film'.

ALBUMS: | HITS 1 | | | WEEKS 5

NAKED	*Magnet*	54	*4 Jun 83*	5

Mac and Katie KISSOON
UK

SINGLES: | HITS 5 | | | WEEKS 33

CHIRPY CHIRPY CHEEP CHEEP	*Young Blood*	41	*19 Jun 71*	1
SUGAR CANDY KISSES	*Polydor*	3	*18 Jan 75*	10
DON'T DO IT BABY	*State*	9	*3 May 75*	8
LIKE A BUTTERFLY	*State*	18	*30 Aug 75*	9
THE TWO OF US	*State*	46	*15 May 76*	5

Kevin KITCHEN
UK

SINGLES: | HITS 1 | | | WEEKS 3

PUT MY ARMS AROUND YOU	*China*	64	*20 Apr 85*	3

KITCHENS OF DISTINCTION
UK

ALBUMS: | HITS 2 | | | WEEKS 2

STRANGE FREE WORLD	*One Little Indian*	45	*30 Mar 91*	1
THE DEATH OF COOL	*One Little Indian*	72	*15 Aug 92*	1

Eartha KITT
US

SINGLES: | HITS 6 | | | WEEKS 34

UNDER THE BRIDGES OF PARIS	*His Master's Voice*	7	*2 Apr 55*	9

Above hit: Eartha KITT with Henri RENE and his Orchestra.

UNDER THE BRIDGES OF PARIS [RE]	*His Master's Voice*	20	*11 Jun 55*	1
WHERE IS MY MAN	*Record Shack*	36	*3 Dec 83*	11
I LOVE MEN	*Record Shack*	50	*7 Jul 84*	3
THIS IS MY LIFE	*Record Shack*	73	*12 Apr 86*	1
CHA CHA HEELS	*Arista*	32	*1 Jul 89*	7

Above hit: Eartha KITT and BRONSKI BEAT.

IF I LOVE YA, THEN I NEED YA, IF I NEED YA, I WANT'CHA AROUND	*RCA*	43	*5 Mar 94*	2

Featured in the Flora margarine TV commercial.

EPS: | HITS 1 | | | WEEKS 1

REVISITED	*London*	18	*1 Dec 62*	1

ALBUMS: | HITS 1 | | | WEEKS 1

REVISITED	*London*	17	*11 Feb 61*	1

KLAXONS
Belgium

SINGLES: | HITS 1 | | | WEEKS 6

CLAP CLAP SOUND	*PRT*	45	*10 Dec 83*	6

Originally recorded by the Pepe's.

KLEEER
US

SINGLES: | HITS 2 | | | WEEKS 10

KEEP YOUR BODY WORKING	*Atlantic*	51	*17 Mar 79*	6
GET TOUGH	*Atlantic*	49	*14 Mar 81*	4

ALBUMS: | HITS 2 | | | WEEKS 3

SEEEKRET	*Atlantic*	96	*6 Jul 85*	1
THE ARTISTS VOLUME III	*Street Sounds*	87	*12 Oct 85*	2

Compilation featuring tracks by each artist.
Above hit: WOMACK and WOMACK/The O'JAYS/KLEEER/The S.O.S. BAND.

KLESHAY
UK

SINGLES:	HITS 2			WEEKS 5
REASONS	*Jerv*	33	*19 Sep 98*	2
RUSH	*Jerv*	19	*20 Feb 99*	3

KLF
UK

(See also Justified Ancients Of Mu Mu; Timelords, 2K.)

SINGLES:	HITS 5			WEEKS 51
WHAT TIME IS LOVE? (LIVE AT TRANCENTRAL)	*KLF Communications*	5	*11 Aug 90*	12
Samples Kick Out The Jams by MC5.				
3 A.M. ETERNAL (LIVE AT THE S.S.L.)	*KLF Communications*	1	*19 Jan 91*	11
Vocals by Maxine Harvey.				
Above 2: KLF featuring the CHILDREN OF THE REVOLUTION.				
LAST TRAIN TO TRANCENTRAL (LIVE FROM THE LOST CONTINENT)	*KLF Communications*	2	*4 May 91*	9
JUSTIFIED AND ANCIENT	*KLF Communications*	2	*7 Dec 91*	12
Above hit: KLF (Lead Vocals: "the First Lady of Country" Miss Tammy WYNETTE).				
AMERICA: WHAT TIME IS LOVE? [RR]	*KLF Communications*	4	*7 Mar 92*	7
ALBUMS:	HITS 1			WEEKS 46
THE WHITE ROOM	*KLF Communications*	3	*16 Mar 91*	46

KLUBBHEADS
Holland

(See also Itty Bitty Boozy Woozy.)

SINGLES:	HITS 3			WEEKS 10
KLUBBHOPPING	*AM:PM*	10	*11 May 96*	6
DISCOHOPPING	*AM:PM*	35	*16 Aug 97*	2
Samples Born To Be Alive by Patrick Hernandez.				
KICKIN' HARD	*Wonderboy*	36	*15 Aug 98*	2

Earl KLUGH - See George BENSON and Earl KLUGH

KNACK
US

SINGLES:	HITS 2			WEEKS 12
MY SHARONA	*Capitol*	6	*30 Jun 79*	10
GOOD GIRLS DON'T	*Capitol*	66	*13 Oct 79*	2
ALBUMS:	HITS 1			WEEKS 2
GET THE KNACK	*Capitol*	65	*4 Aug 79*	2

KNACK - See MOUNT RUSHMORE presents the KNACK

Beverley KNIGHT
UK

SINGLES:	HITS 7			WEEKS 23
FLAVOUR OF THE OLD SCHOOL	*Dome*	50	*8 Apr 95*	2
DOWN FOR THE ONE	*Dome*	55	*2 Sep 95*	1
FLAVOUR OF THE OLD SCHOOL [RI]	*Dome*	33	*21 Oct 95*	2
MOVING ON UP (ON THE RIGHT SIDE)	*Dome*	42	*23 Mar 96*	1
MADE IT BACK	*Parlophone*	21	*30 May 98*	3
Above hit: Beverley KNIGHT featuring REDMAN.				
REWIND (FIND A WAY)	*Parlophone Rhythm Series*	40	*22 Aug 98*	2
MADE IT BACK 99 [RM]	*Parlophone Rhythm Series*	19	*10 Apr 99*	5
Samples Chic's Good Times.				
Above hit: Beverley KNIGHT featuring REDMAN.				
GREATEST DAY	*Parlophone Rhythm Series*	14	*17 Jul 99*	5
SISTA SISTA	*Parlophone Rhythm Series*	31	*4 Dec 99*	2
ALBUMS:	HITS 1			WEEKS 11
PRODIGAL SISTA	*Parlophone Rhythm Series*	54	*5 Sep 98*	2
PRODIGAL SISTA [RE-1ST]	*Parlophone Rhythm Series*	56	*1 May 99*	1
Re-released to include 3 new mixes by Mike Spencer, TNT And Jus Bounce.				
PRODIGAL SISTA [RE-2ND]	*Parlophone Rhythm Series*	42	*8 May 99*	8
2 separate entries for this album, due to the charts reflecting the repackaged album as a new entry on 1 May 99 and the following week, a re-entry of the original version.				

Curtis KNIGHT - See Jimmy HENDRIX

Frederick KNIGHT
US

SINGLES:	HITS 1			WEEKS 10
I'VE BEEN LONELY FOR SO LONG	*Stax*	22	*10 Jun 72*	10

Gladys KNIGHT and the PIPS
US

(See also Dionne Warwick.)

SINGLES:	HITS 23			WEEKS 179
TAKE ME IN YOUR ARMS AND LOVE ME	*Tamla Motown*	13	*10 Jun 67*	15
I HEARD IT THROUGH THE GRAPEVINE	*Tamla Motown*	47	*30 Dec 67*	1
JUST WALK IN MY SHOES	*Tamla Motown*	35	*17 Jun 72*	8
HELP ME MAKE IT THROUGH THE NIGHT	*Tamla Motown*	11	*25 Nov 72*	17

THE LOOK OF LOVE	*Tamla Motown*	21	*3 Mar 73*	9
NEITHER ONE OF US (WANTS TO BE THE FIRST TO SAY GOODNIGHT)	*Tamla Motown*	31	*26 May 73*	7
THE WAY WE WERE/TRY TO REMEMBER [M]	*Buddah*	4	*5 Apr 75*	15
BEST THING THAT EVER HAPPENED TO ME	*Buddah*	7	*2 Aug 75*	10
PART TIME LOVE	*Buddah*	30	*15 Nov 75*	5

Certain copies were released with the title shown as 'Part Time Lover'. Originally recorded by David Gates.

MIDNIGHT TRAIN TO GEORGIA	*Buddah*	10	*8 May 76*	9

Originally recorded by Cissy Houston.

MAKE YOURS A HAPPY HOME	*Buddah*	35	*21 Aug 76*	4
SO SAD THE SONG	*Buddah*	20	*6 Nov 76*	10
NOBODY BUT YOU	*Buddah*	34	*15 Jan 77*	2
BABY DON'T CHANGE YOUR MIND	*Buddah*	4	*28 May 77*	12
HOME IS WHERE THE HEART IS	*Buddah*	35	*24 Sep 77*	4
THE ONE AND ONLY	*Buddah*	32	*8 Apr 78*	4

From the film of the same name.

THE ONE AND ONLY [RE]	*Buddah*	66	*13 May 78*	1
COME BACK AND FINISH WHAT YOU STARTED	*Buddah*	15	*24 Jun 78*	13
IT'S A BETTER THAN GOOD TIME	*Buddah*	59	*30 Sep 78*	4
TASTE OF BITTER LOVE	*CBS*	35	*30 Aug 80*	6
BOURGIE, BOURGIE	*CBS*	32	*8 Nov 80*	6

Originally recorded by Ashford and Simpson.

WHEN A CHILD IS BORN	*CBS*	74	*26 Dec 81*	2

Above hit: Johnny MATHIS and Gladys KNIGHT and the PIPS.

LOVE OVERBOARD	*MCA*	42	*16 Jan 88*	4
LICENCE TO KILL	*MCA*	6	*10 Jun 89*	11

Theme from the James Bond film of the same name.
Above hit: Gladys KNIGHT.

ALBUMS:	**HITS 9**		**WEEKS 117**	
I FEEL A SONG	*Buddah*	20	*31 May 75*	15
THE BEST OF GLADYS KNIGHT & THE PIPS	*Buddah*	6	*28 Feb 76*	43
STILL TOGETHER	*Buddah*	42	*16 Jul 77*	3
30 GREATEST	*K-Tel*	3	*12 Nov 77*	22
A TOUCH OF LOVE	*K-Tel*	16	*4 Oct 80*	6
THE COLLECTION – 20 GREATEST HITS	*Starblend*	43	*4 Feb 84*	5
DIANA . MICHAEL . GLADYS . STEVIE – THEIR VERY BEST – BACK TO BACK	*PrioriTyV*	21	*15 Nov 86*	10

Compilation featuring tracks by each artist.
Above hit: Diana ROSS/Michael JACKSON/Gladys KNIGHT/Stevie WONDER.

ALL OUR LOVE	*MCA*	80	*27 Feb 88*	1
THE SINGLES ALBUM	*PolyGram*	12	*28 Oct 89*	10
THE SINGLES ALBUM [RI]	*PolyGram TV*	69	*29 Mar 97*	2

Repackaged.

Jordan KNIGHT
US

SINGLES:	**HITS 1**		**WEEKS 8**	
GIVE IT TO YOU	*Interscope*	5	*16 Oct 99*	8

Peter KNIGHT ORCHESTRA/SINGERS - See Petula CLARK; Nat 'King' COLE; Emile FORD and the CHECKMATES; Joan REGAN; Marion RYAN with the Peter KNIGHT Orchestra and the Beryl STOTT CHORUS; Frankie VAUGHAN; Malcolm VAUGHN.

Robert KNIGHT
US

SINGLES:	**HITS 2**		**WEEKS 26**	
EVERLASTING LOVE	*Monument*	40	*20 Jan 68*	2
LOVE ON A MOUNTAIN TOP	*Monument*	10	*24 Nov 73*	16
EVERLASTING LOVE [RI]	*Monument*	19	*9 Mar 74*	8

KNIGHTSBRIDGE STRINGS
UK

ALBUMS:	**HITS 1**		**WEEKS 1**	
STRING SWAY	*Top Rank*	20	*25 Jun 60*	1

David KNOPFLER
UK

ALBUMS:	**HITS 1**		**WEEKS 1**	
RELEASE	*Peach River*	82	*19 Nov 83*	1

Mark KNOPFLER
UK

(See also Chet Atkins and Mark Knopfler.)

SINGLES:	**HITS 3**		**WEEKS 7**	
GOING HOME: THEME OF THE LOCAL HERO	*Vertigo*	56	*12 Mar 83*	3

Theme from the film.

DARLING PRETTY	*Vertigo*	33	*16 Mar 96*	2
CANNIBALS	*Vertigo*	42	*25 May 96*	2
ALBUMS:	**HITS 3**		**WEEKS 31**	
LOCAL HERO [OST]	*Vertigo*	14	*16 Apr 83*	11

CAL [OST]	*Vertigo*	65	*20 Oct 84*	3
GOLDEN HEART	*Vertigo*	9	*6 Apr 96*	17

KNOWLEDGE
Italy

SINGLES:	HITS 1			WEEKS 1
AS (UNTIL THE DAY)	*ffrr*	70	*8 Nov 97*	1

Originally recorded by Stevie Wonder for his 1976 album 'Songs In The Key Of Life'.

Buddy KNOX
US

SINGLES:	HITS 2			WEEKS 5
PARTY DOLL	*Columbia*	29	*11 May 57*	3

Above hit: Buddy KNOX with the RHYTHM ORCHIDS.

SHE'S GONE	*Liberty*	45	*18 Aug 62*	2

Above hit: Buddy KNOX with the Johnny MANN SINGERS.

Frankie KNUCKLES
US

SINGLES:	HITS 7			WEEKS 19
TEARS	*ffrr*	50	*17 Jun 89*	3

Above hit: Frankie KNUCKLES presents Satoshi TOMIIE featuring Robert OWENS.

YOUR LOVE	*Trax*	59	*21 Oct 89*	4
THE WHISTLE SONG	*Virgin America*	17	*27 Jul 91*	5
IT'S HARD SOMETIME	*Virgin America*	67	*23 Nov 91*	1

Above hit: Frankie KNUCKLES featuring Shelton BECTON.

RAIN FALLS	*Virgin America*	48	*6 Jun 92*	2

Above hit: Frankie KNUCKLES featuring Lisa MICHAELIS.

TOO MANY FISH	*Virgin*	34	*27 May 95*	2
WHADDA U WANT (FROM ME)	*Virgin*	36	*18 Nov 95*	2

Above 2: Frankie KNUCKLES featuring ADEVA.

ALBUMS:	HITS 1			WEEKS 2
BEYOND THE MIX	*Virgin America*	59	*17 Aug 91*	2

Moe KOFFMAN QUARTETTE
Canada

SINGLES:	HITS 1			WEEKS 2
SWINGIN' SHEPHERD BLUES	*London*	23	*29 Mar 58*	2

KOFI – See SOUL II SOUL

Mike KOGLIN
Germany

SINGLES:	HITS 2			WEEKS 4
THE SILENCE	*Multiply*	20	*28 Nov 98*	2
ON MY WAY	*Multiply*	28	*29 May 99*	2

Above hit: Mike KOGLIN featuring BEATRICE.

Eugene KOHN – See Placido DOMINGO

KOKOMO, his Piano and Orchestra
US

SINGLES:	HITS 1			WEEKS 7
ASIA MINOR	*London*	35	*15 Apr 61*	7

Adapted from Grieg's Piano Concerto.

KOKOMO
UK

SINGLES:	HITS 1			WEEKS 3
A LITTLE BIT FURTHER AWAY	*CBS*	45	*29 May 82*	3

KON KAN
Canada

SINGLES:	HITS 1			WEEKS 13
I BEG YOUR PARDON	*Atlantic*	5	*4 Mar 89*	13

Samples Lynn Anderson's Rose Garden and Disco Nights (Rock Freak) by GQ.

John KONGOS
UK

SINGLES:	HITS 2			WEEKS 25
HE'S GONNA STEP ON YOU AGAIN	*Fly*	4	*22 May 71*	14
TOKOLOSHE MAN	*Fly*	4	*20 Nov 71*	11

ALBUMS:	HITS 1			WEEKS 2
KONGOS	*Fly*	29	*15 Jan 72*	2

KOOL AND THE GANG
US

SINGLES:	HITS 21			WEEKS 207
LADIES NIGHT	*Mercury*	9	*27 Oct 79*	12
TOO HOT	*Mercury*	23	*19 Jan 80*	8
HANGIN' OUT	*De-Lite*	52	*12 Jul 80*	4
CELEBRATION	*De-Lite*	7	*1 Nov 80*	13

*A record 24 years and 6 months elapsed between **Tom Jones'** last two No.1 albums. (Rex Features)*

K *by* **Kula Shaker** *is the shortest title to top the album chart. (LFI)*

The **Johnston Brothers** *were the first set of unrelated brothers to top the chart. (LFI)*

*Only **Ronan Keating** has topped the singles chart as a solo artist and, at the same time, held down the album chart top spot as a member of a group (Boyzone). (LFI)*

*A youthful **Jimmy Page**, Led Zeppelin's guitar maestro. (Harry Goodwin).*

*There was a delay of 28 years and 5 months between **Led Zeppelin**'s first appearance on the album chart and their debut on the singles listings. (Rex Features)*

'Cold' by **Annie Lennox** was the first hit single in the CD age not to be available on vinyl. (LFI)

Johnny Logan *took longer than any act to chart a follow-up to a No.1 hit. (LFI)*

*When 'Kinky Boots' by **Patrick MacNee** and **Honor Blackman** finally charted, the duo's combined age totalled 132. (Rex Features)*

JONES VS JONES / SUMMER MADNESS / FUNKY STUFF / HOLLYWOOD SWINGING	De-Lite	17	21 Feb 81	11

Though all 4 tracks were listed on the chart, the last 2 were only available on the 12" and 7" doublepack formats.

TAKE IT TO THE TOP (CLIMBING)	De-Lite	15	30 May 81	9
STEPPIN' OUT	De-Lite	12	31 Oct 81	13
GET DOWN ON IT	De-Lite	3	19 Dec 81	12
TAKE MY HEART (YOU CAN HAVE IT IF YOU WANT IT)	De-Lite	29	6 Mar 82	7
BIG FUN	De-Lite	14	7 Aug 82	8
OOH LA LA LA (LET'S GO DANCIN')	De-Lite	6	16 Oct 82	9
HI DE HI, HI DE HO	De-Lite	29	4 Dec 82	8
STRAIGHT AHEAD	De-Lite	15	10 Dec 83	10
JOANNA / TONIGHT	De-Lite	2	11 Feb 84	11
(WHEN YOU SAY YOU LOVE SOMEBODY) IN THE HEART	De-Lite	7	14 Apr 84	8
FRESH	De-Lite	11	24 Nov 84	12
MISLED	De-Lite	28	9 Feb 85	5
CHERISH	De-Lite	4	11 May 85	22
EMERGENCY	De-Lite	50	2 Nov 85	3
VICTORY	Club	67	22 Nov 86	2
VICTORY [RE]	Club	30	20 Dec 86	10
STONE LOVE	Club	45	21 Mar 87	4
CELEBRATION [RM]	Club	56	31 Dec 88	5

Remixed by Stock Aitken Waterman.

GET DOWN ON IT [RM]	Mercury	69	6 Jul 91	1

Remixed by Oliver Momm.

ALBUMS:	**HITS 7**		**WEEKS 115**	
SOMETHING SPECIAL	De-Lite	10	21 Nov 81	20
AS ONE	De-Lite	49	2 Oct 82	10
TWICE AS KOOL	Polystar	4	7 May 83	23
IN THE HEART	De-Lite	18	14 Jan 84	23
EMERGENCY	De-Lite	47	15 Dec 84	25
THE SINGLES COLLECTION	De-Lite	28	12 Nov 88	13
KOOL LOVE	Telstar	50	27 Oct 90	1

KOOL ROCK STEADY - See TYREE

KOON + STEPHENSON - See WESTBAM

KORGIS
UK

SINGLES:	**HITS 3**		**WEEKS 27**	
IF I HAD YOU	Rialto	13	23 Jun 79	12
EVERYBODY'S GOT TO LEARN SOMETIME	Rialto	5	24 May 80	12
IF IT'S ALRIGHT WITH YOU BABY	Rialto	56	30 Aug 80	3
ALBUMS:	**HITS 1**		**WEEKS 4**	
DUMB WAITERS	Rialto	40	26 Jul 80	4

KORN
US

SINGLES:	**HITS 5**		**WEEKS 10**	
NO PLACE TO HIDE	Epic	26	19 Oct 96	2
A.D.I.D.A.S.	Epic	22	15 Feb 97	2

Acronym for All Day I Dream About Sex.

GOOD GOD	Epic	25	7 Jun 97	2
GOT THE LIFE	Epic	23	22 Aug 98	2
FREAK ON A LEASH	Epic	24	8 May 99	2
ALBUMS:	**HITS 3**		**WEEKS 7**	
LIFE IS PEACHY	Epic	32	26 Oct 96	2
FOLLOW THE LEADER	Epic	5	29 Aug 98	4
ISSUES	Epic	37	27 Nov 99	1

KRAFTWERK
Germany

SINGLES:	**HITS 8**		**WEEKS 70**	
AUTOBAHN	Vertigo	11	10 May 75	9
NEON LIGHTS	Capitol	53	28 Oct 78	3
POCKET CALCULATOR	EMI	39	9 May 81	6
COMPUTER LOVE / THE MODEL	EMI	36	11 Jul 81	8
THE MODEL / COMPUTER LOVE [RE]	EMI	1	26 Dec 81	13
SHOWROOM DUMMIES	EMI	25	20 Feb 82	5
TOUR DE FRANCE	EMI	22	6 Aug 83	8
TOUR DE FRANCE ('BREAKDANCE' REMIX) [RE]	EMI	24	25 Aug 84	11

Though this had the same catalogue number, it was actually a remix for the film 'Breakdance'.

THE ROBOTS	EMI	20	1 Jun 91	4
RADIOACTIVITY	EMI	43	2 Nov 91	2
TOUR DE FRANCE [RI]	EMI	61	23 Oct 99	1
ALBUMS:	**HITS 6**		**WEEKS 71**	
AUTOBAHN	Vertigo	4	17 May 75	18
THE MAN-MACHINE	Capitol	53	20 May 78	3

COMPUTER WORLD	EMI	15	23 May 81	22
THE MAN-MACHINE [RE]	Capitol	9	23 Jan 82	10
TRANS-EUROPE EXPRESS	Capitol	49	6 Feb 82	7
Originally released in 1977.				
AUTOBAHN [RI]	Parlophone	61	22 Jun 85	3
ELECTRIC CAFE	EMI	58	15 Nov 86	2
THE MIX	EMI	15	22 Jun 91	6

Diana KRALL
Canada

ALBUMS:	HITS 1			WEEKS 1
WHEN I LOOK IN YOUR EYES	Verve	72	12 Jun 99	1

Billy J. KRAMER with the DAKOTAS
UK

SINGLES:	HITS 6			WEEKS 71
DO YOU WANT TO KNOW A SECRET	Parlophone	2	4 May 63	15
BAD TO ME	Parlophone	1	3 Aug 63	14
I'LL KEEP YOU SATISFIED	Parlophone	4	9 Nov 63	13
Above 3 written by Lennon/McCartney.				
LITTLE CHILDREN	Parlophone	1	29 Feb 64	13
FROM A WINDOW	Parlophone	10	25 Jul 64	8
Written by Lennon/ McCartney.				
TRAINS AND BOATS AND PLANES	Parlophone	12	22 May 65	8
EPS:	HITS 1			WEEKS 13
THE BILLY J. KRAMER HITS	Parlophone	8	26 Oct 63	13
ALBUMS:	HITS 1			WEEKS 17
LISTEN TO BILLY J. KRAMER	Parlophone	11	16 Nov 63	17

KRANKIES
UK

SINGLES:	HITS 1			WEEKS 6
FAN' DABI' DOZI	Monarch	71	7 Feb 81	1
FAN' DABI' DOZI [RE]	Monarch	46	7 Mar 81	5

Lenny KRAVITZ
US

SINGLES:	HITS 16			WEEKS 68
MR. CABDRIVER	Virgin America	58	2 Jun 90	2
LET LOVE RULE	Virgin America	39	4 Aug 90	4
ALWAYS ON THE RUN	Virgin America	41	30 Mar 91	3
IT AIN'T OVER 'TIL IT'S OVER	Virgin America	11	15 Jun 91	8
STAND BY MY WOMAN	Virgin America	55	14 Sep 91	3
ARE YOU GONNA GO MY WAY	Virgin America	4	20 Feb 93	11
BELIEVE	Virgin America	30	22 May 93	5
HEAVEN HELP	Virgin	20	28 Aug 93	7
IS THERE ANY LOVE IN YOUR HEART	Virgin	52	4 Dec 93	2
BUDDHA OF SUBURBIA	Arista	35	4 Dec 93	3
Theme from the BBC TV series of the same name.				
Above hit: David BOWIE (featuring Lenny KRAVITZ on Guitar).				
ROCK AND ROLL IS DEAD	Virgin	22	9 Sep 95	3
CIRCUS	Virgin	54	23 Dec 95	2
CAN'T GET YOU OFF MY MIND	Virgin	54	2 Mar 96	2
IF YOU CAN'T SAY NO	Virgin	48	16 May 98	2
I BELONG TO YOU	Virgin	75	10 Oct 98	1
FLY AWAY	Virgin	1	20 Feb 99	10
Featured in the Peugeot 206 TV commercial. Original release reached No. 162 in 1998.				
ALBUMS:	HITS 5			WEEKS 95
LET LOVE RULE	Virgin America	56	26 May 90	4
MAMA SAID	Virgin America	8	13 Apr 91	27
ARE YOU GONNA GO MY WAY	Virgin	1	13 Mar 93	47
CIRCUS	Virgin	5	23 Sep 95	4
5	Virgin	18	23 May 98	13

KRAZE
US

SINGLES:	HITS 2			WEEKS 6
THE PARTY	MCA	29	22 Oct 88	5
LET'S PLAY HOUSE	MCA	71	17 Jun 89	1

KREUZ
UK

SINGLES:	HITS 1			WEEKS 1
PARTY ALL NIGHT	Diesel	75	8 Jul 95	1
ALBUMS:	HITS 1			WEEKS 2
KREUZ KONTROL	Diesel	48	18 Mar 95	2

Chantal KREVIAZUK   Canada

SINGLES:	HITS 1			WEEKS 1
LEAVING ON A JET PLANE	Epic	59	6 Mar 99	1

From the film 'Armageddon'.

KREW-KATS   UK

SINGLES:	HITS 1			WEEKS 10
TRAMBONE	His Master's Voice	33	11 Mar 61	9

Originally recorded by Chet Atkins.

TRAMBONE [RE]	His Master's Voice	49	20 May 61	1

KRIS KROSS   US

SINGLES:	HITS 5			WEEKS 22
JUMP	Columbia	2	30 May 92	8
WARM IT UP	Columbia	16	25 Jul 92	6
I MISSED THE BUS	Columbia	57	17 Oct 92	1
IT'S A SHAME	Columbia	31	19 Dec 92	5
ALRIGHT	Columbia	47	11 Sep 93	2

Features rap by Supercat. Samples Slave's Just A Touch Of Love.

ALBUMS:	HITS 1			WEEKS 8
TOTALLY KROSSED OUT	Columbia	31	27 Jun 92	8

Kris KRISTOFFERSON and Rita COOLIDGE   US

(See also Rita Coolidge; Barbra Streisand.)

ALBUMS:	HITS 1			WEEKS 4
NATURAL ACT	A&M	35	6 May 78	4

KROKUS   Switzerland/Argentina

SINGLES:	HITS 1			WEEKS 2
INDUSTRIAL STRENGTH [EP]	Ariola	62	16 May 81	2

Lead track: Bedside Radio.

ALBUMS:	HITS 3			WEEKS 11
HARDWARE	Ariola	44	21 Feb 81	4
ONE VICE AT A TIME	Arista	28	20 Feb 82	5
HEADHUNTERS	Arista	74	16 Apr 83	2

KRS ONE   US

SINGLES:	HITS 5			WEEKS 8
RAPPAZ R.N. DAINJA	Jive	47	18 May 96	1
WORD PERFECT	Jive	70	8 Feb 97	1
STEP INTO A WORLD (RAPTURE'S DELIGHT)	Jive	24	26 Apr 97	2

Track based on Blondie's 1981 hit Rapture.

HEARTBEAT / A FRIEND	Jive	66	20 Sep 97	1

Above hit: KRS-ONE featuring REDMAN and Angie MARTINEZ.

DIGITAL	ffrr	13	1 Nov 97	3

Above hit: GOLDIE featuring KRS ONE.

ALBUMS:	HITS 1			WEEKS 1
I GOT NEXT	Jive	58	31 May 97	1

KRUSH   UK

SINGLES:	HITS 2			WEEKS 16
HOUSE ARREST	Club	3	5 Dec 87	15
WALKING ON SUNSHINE	Network	71	14 Nov 92	1

Above hit: KRUSH featuring Ruth JOY.

KRUSH PERSPECTIVE   US

SINGLES:	HITS 1			WEEKS 2
LET'S GET TOGETHER (SO GROOVY NOW)	Perspective	61	16 Jan 93	2

KRUST featuring Saul WILLIAMS   UK

SINGLES:	HITS 1			WEEKS 1
CODED LANGUAGE	Talkin Loud	66	23 Oct 99	1

K7   US

SINGLES:	HITS 3			WEEKS 22
COME BABY COME	Big Life	3	11 Dec 93	16
HI DE HO	Big Life	17	2 Apr 94	5
ZUNGA ZENG	Big Life	63	25 Jun 94	1

Above 2: K7 and the SWING KIDS.

ALBUMS:	HITS 1			WEEKS 3
SWING BATTA SWING	Big Life	27	5 Feb 94	3

K3M
Italy

SINGLES:	HITS 1			WEEKS 1	
LISTEN TO THE RHYTHM	*PWL Continental*	71	*21 Mar 92*	1

KULA SHAKER
UK

SINGLES:	HITS 8			WEEKS 48	
GRATEFUL WHEN YOU'RE DEAD/JERRY WAS THERE [M]	*Columbia*	35	*4 May 96*	3
TATTVA	*Columbia*	4	*6 Jul 96*	8
HEY DUDE	*Columbia*	2	*7 Sep 96*	7
GOVINDA	*Columbia*	7	*23 Nov 96*	8
Originally recorded by Radha Krishna Temple.				
HUSH	*Columbia*	2	*8 Mar 97*	8
Originally recorded by Joe South in 1968, though the arrangement for this version was adapted from Deep Purple's version.				
HUSH [RE]	*Columbia*	70	*9 Aug 97*	1
SOUND OF DRUMS	*Columbia*	3	*2 May 98*	6
MYSTICAL MACHINE GUN	*Columbia*	14	*6 Mar 99*	3
SHOWER YOUR LOVE	*Columbia*	14	*15 May 99*	4
ALBUMS:	**HITS 2**			**WEEKS 54**	
K	*Columbia*	1	*28 Sep 96*	44
PEASANTS, PIGS & ASTRONAUTS	*Columbia*	9	*20 Mar 99*	10

KULAY
Philippines

SINGLES:	HITS 1			WEEKS 1	
DELICIOUS	*INCredible*	73	*12 Sep 98*	1

Charlie KUNZ
UK

SINGLES:	HITS 1			WEEKS 4	
CHARLIE KUNZ PIANO MEDLEY NO. 114 [M]	*Decca*	20	*18 Dec 54*	3
Medley of songs from 1954.				
CHARLIE KUNZ PIANO MEDLEY NO. 114 [M] [RE]	*Decca*	16	*15 Jan 55*	1
ALBUMS:	**HITS 1**			**WEEKS 11**	
THE WORLD OF CHARLIE KUNZ	*Decca*	9	*14 Jun 69*	11

KURSAAL FLYERS
UK

SINGLES:	HITS 1			WEEKS 10	
LITTLE DOES SHE KNOW	*CBS*	14	*20 Nov 76*	10

KUT KLOSE
US

SINGLES:	HITS 1			WEEKS 1	
I LIKE	*Elektra*	72	*29 Apr 95*	1

Li KWAN
UK

(See also Joey Negro.)

SINGLES:	HITS 1			WEEKS 2	
I NEED A MAN	*Deconstruction*	51	*17 Dec 94*	2

KY-MANI – See PM DAWN

KYO (aka Carole LEEMING) – See John DIGWEED and Nick MUIR Present BEDROCK

L

Jonny L
UK

SINGLES:	HITS 2			WEEKS 2	
OOH I LIKE IT	*XL Recordings*	73	*28 Aug 93*	1
20 DEGREES	*XL Recordings*	66	*31 Oct 98*	1
Above hit: Jonny L featuring SILVAH BULLET.				

L.A. GUNS
US

SINGLES:	HITS 2			WEEKS 4	
SOME LIE 4 LOVE	*Mercury*	61	*30 Nov 91*	1
THE BALLAD OF JAYNE	*Mercury*	53	*21 Dec 91*	3
ALBUMS:	**HITS 3**			**WEEKS 4**	
L.A. GUNS	*Vertigo*	73	*5 Mar 88*	1
COCKED AND LOADED	*Vertigo*	45	*30 Sep 89*	2
HOLLYWOOD VAMPIRES	*Mercury*	44	*13 Jul 91*	1

L.A. MIX
UK

SINGLES:		HITS 7			WEEKS 25
DON'T STOP (JAMMIN')	Breakout	47	10 Oct 87		4
CHECK THIS OUT	Breakout	6	21 May 88		7
GET LOOSE	Breakout	25	8 Jul 89		6
Above hit: L.A. MIX featuring Jazzi P.					
LOVE TOGETHER	Breakout	66	16 Sep 89		2
Above hit: L.A. MIX featuring Kevin HENRY.					
COMING BACK FOR MORE	A&M	50	15 Sep 90		3
MYSTERIES OF LOVE	A&M	46	19 Jan 91		2
WE SHOULDN'T HOLD HANDS IN THE DARK	A&M	69	23 Mar 91		1

L.R.S. - See D-MOB

L.T.D.
US

SINGLES:		HITS 1			WEEKS 3
HOLDING ON (WHEN LOVE IS GONE)	A&M	70	9 Sep 78		3

L.V.
US

SINGLES:		HITS 3			WEEKS 25
GANGSTA'S PARADISE	Tommy Boy	1	28 Oct 95		20
From the film 'Dangerous Minds'. Samples Stevie Wonder's Pastime Paradise.					
Above hit: COOLIO featuring L.V.					
THROW YOUR HANDS UP / GANGSTA'S PARADISE [RR]	Tommy Boy	24	23 Dec 95		4
I AM L.V.	Tommy Boy	64	4 May 96		1

L.W.S.
Italy

SINGLES:		HITS 1			WEEKS 1
GOSP	Transworld	65	29 Oct 94		1

LA GANZ (EL - E – GANZ)
US

SINGLES:		HITS 1			WEEKS 1
LIKE A PLAYA	Jive	75	9 Nov 96		1

LA NA NEE NEE NOO NOO - See BANANARAMA

Julius LA ROSA with Nick PERITO and his Orchestra
US

SINGLES:		HITS 1			WEEKS 9
TORERO	RCA	15	5 Jul 58		9

Danny LA RUE
UK

SINGLES:		HITS 1			WEEKS 9
ON MOTHER KELLY'S DOORSTEP	Page One	33	21 Dec 68		9

LA'S
UK

(See also Various Artists (EPs) 'Fever Pitch The EP'.)

SINGLES:		HITS 3			WEEKS 19
THERE SHE GOES	Go! Discs	59	14 Jan 89		4
TIMELESS MELODY	Go! Discs	57	15 Sep 90		2
THERE SHE GOES [RI]	Go! Discs	13	3 Nov 90		9
FEELIN'	Go! Discs	43	16 Feb 91		3
THERE SHE GOES [RI-2ND]	Polydor	65	2 Oct 99		1
Released after the success of the cover by Sixpence None The Richer.					

ALBUMS:		HITS 1			WEEKS 20
THE LA'S	Go! Discs	30	13 Oct 90		20

LA TREC - See SASH!

LABELLE
US

SINGLES:		HITS 1			WEEKS 9
LADY MARMALADE (VOULEZ-VOUS COUCHER AVEC MOI CE SOIR?)	Epic	17	22 Mar 75		9
Originally recorded by the Eleventh Hour.					

Patti LABELLE
US

SINGLES:		HITS 3			WEEKS 21
ON MY OWN	MCA	2	3 May 86		13
Above hit: Patti LABELLE and Michael McDONALD.					
OH, PEOPLE	MCA	26	2 Aug 86		6
THE RIGHT KINDA LOVER	MCA	50	3 Sep 94		2
From the film 'Beverly Hill Cop II'.					

ALBUMS:		HITS 1			WEEKS 17
WINNER IN YOU	MCA	30	24 May 86		17

LADIES CHOICE | UK

SINGLES:	HITS 1			WEEKS 4
FUNKY SENSATION	*Sure Delight*	41	*25 Jan 86*	4

LADY J and the SECRETARY OF ENT. - See RAZE

LADY OF RAGE | US

SINGLES:	HITS 1			WEEKS 1
AFRO PUFFS	*Interscope*	72	*8 Oct 94*	1

Features vocals by Dr. Dre and Snoop Doggy Dogg. From the film 'Above The Rim'.

LADYSMITH BLACK MAMBAZO | South Africa

SINGLES:	HITS 5			WEEKS 20
SWING LOW SWEET CHARIOT	*PolyGram TV*	15	*3 Jun 95*	6

The England theme for the Rugby World Cup.
Above hit: LADYSMITH BLACK MAMBAZO featuring CHINA BLACK.

WORLD IN UNION '95	*PolyGram TV*	47	*3 Jun 95*	5

The ITV Rugby World Cup theme.
Above hit: LADYSMITH BLACK MAMBAZO featuring P.J. POWERS.

INKANYEZI NEZAZI (THE STAR AND THE WISEMAN)	*A&M*	33	*15 Nov 97*	3

Featured in the Heinz Beans TV commerical.

INKANYEZI NEZAZI (THE STAR AND THE WISEMAN) [RI]	*AM:PM*	63	*11 Jul 98*	1
AIN'T NO SUNSHINE	*Universal*	42	*16 Oct 99*	2

Originally recorded by Bill Withers reaching No. 3 in the US in 1971.
Above hit: LADYSMITH BLACK MAMBAZO featuring DES'REE.

I SHALL BE THERE	*Glow Worm*	13	*18 Dec 99*	3

*Above hit: B*WITCHED featuring LADYSMITH BLACK MAMBAZO.*

ALBUMS:	HITS 4			WEEKS 66
SHAKA ZULU	*Warner Brothers*	34	*11 Apr 87*	11
HEAVENLY	*A&M*	53	*22 Nov 97*	16
THE BEST OF LADYSMITH BLACK MAMBAZO - THE STAR AND THE WISEMAN	*PolyGram TV*	2	*3 Oct 98*	34

Label changed to Universal Music TV from 13 Mar 99.

IN HARMONY	*Universal Music TV*	15	*16 Oct 99*	5

LAGAUNA | Italy

SINGLES:	HITS 1			WEEKS 2
SPILLER FROM RIO (DO IT EASY)	*Positiva*	40	*1 Nov 97*	2

LAID BACK | Norway

SINGLES:	HITS 1			WEEKS 4
BAKERMAN	*Arista*	44	*5 May 90*	4

Cleo LAINE | UK

(See also Cleo Laine and James Galway; Cleo Laine and John Williams.)

SINGLES:	HITS 2			WEEKS 14
LET'S SLIP AWAY	*Fontana*	42	*31 Dec 60*	1
YOU'LL ANSWER TO ME	*Fontana*	5	*16 Sep 61*	13

Originally recorded by Patti Page.

ALBUMS:	HITS 1			WEEKS 1
CLEO	*Arcade*	68	*2 Dec 78*	1

Cleo LAINE and James GALWAY | UK

(See also James Galway; Cleo Laine.)

ALBUMS:	HITS 1			WEEKS 14
SOMETIMES WHEN WE TOUCH	*RCA*	15	*31 May 80*	14

Cleo LAINE and John WILLIAMS | UK

(See also Cleo Laine; John Williams.)

ALBUMS:	HITS 1			WEEKS 22
BEST OF FRIENDS	*RCA Victor*	18	*7 Jan 78*	22

Frankie LAINE | US

SINGLES:	HITS 27			WEEKS 282
HIGH NOON (DO NOT FORSAKE ME)	*Columbia*	7	*15 Nov 52*	7

From the film 'High Noon'.

SUGAR BUSH	*Columbia*	8	*15 Nov 52*	2

Above hit: Doris DAY and Frankie LAINE with Carl FISCHER'S ORCHESTRA and the
Norman LUBOFF CHOIR.

SUGAR BUSH [RE]	*Columbia*	8	*6 Dec 52*	6
THE GIRL IN THE WOOD	*Columbia*	11	*21 Mar 53*	1

Above hit: Frankie LAINE with Paul WESTON and his Orchestra and the Norman
LUBOFF CHOIR (Carl FISCHER at the Piano).

I BELIEVE	Philips	1	4 Apr 53	36
The single to have spent the longest time at No. 1 (18 weeks).				
Above hit: Frankie LAINE with Paul WESTON and his Orchestra.				
TELL ME A STORY	Philips	5	9 May 53	15
Features accompaniment by Norman Luboff and Carl Fischer on piano.				
Above hit: Jimmy BOYD-Frankie LAINE.				
WHERE THE WINDS BLOW	Philips	2	5 Sep 53	12
Above hit: Frankie LAINE; Carl FISCHER-Piano.				
TELL ME A STORY [RE]	Philips	12	12 Sep 53	1
HEY JOE!	Philips	1	17 Oct 53	8
ANSWER ME	Philips	1	31 Oct 53	17
Above 2: Frankie LAINE with Paul WESTON and his Orchestra and the Norman LUBOFF CHOIR (Carl FISCHER-Piano).				
BLOWING WILD (THE BALLAD OF BLACK GOLD)	Philips	2	9 Jan 54	12
From the film 'Blowing Wild'.				
Above hit: Frankie LAINE (Carl FISCHER: Piano).				
GRANADA	Philips	10	27 Mar 54	1
Above hit: Frankie LAINE with Paul WESTON and his Orchestra (Carl FISCHER: Piano).				
GRANADA [RE]	Philips	9	10 Apr 54	1
THE KID'S LAST FIGHT	Philips	3	17 Apr 54	10
Above hit: Frankie LAINE with Carl FISCHER At the Upright and the Norman LUBOFF CHOIR.				
MY FRIEND	Philips	3	14 Aug 54	15
Above hit: Frankie LAINE with Paul WESTON and his Orchestra and the Norman LUBOFF CHOIR.				
THERE MUST BE A REASON	Philips	9	9 Oct 54	9
Above hit: Frankie LAINE with Paul WESTON and his Orchestra (Carl FISCHER: Piano).				
RAIN, RAIN, RAIN	Philips	8	23 Oct 54	16
Above hit: Frankie LAINE and the FOUR LADS with the Buddy COLE QUARTET				
IN THE BEGINNING	Philips	20	12 Mar 55	1
Above hit: Frankie LAINE with Paul WESTON his Orchestra and the Norman LUBOFF CHOIR.				
COOL WATER	Philips	2	25 Jun 55	22
Originally recorded by Sons Of The Pioneers in 1941.				
Above hit: Frankie LAINE with Paul WESTON and his Orchestra and the MELLOMEN.				
STRANGE LADY IN TOWN	Philips	6	16 Jul 55	13
From the film of the same name.				
Above hit: Frankie LAINE with Mitch MILLER and his Orchestra and Chorus.				
HUMMINGBIRD	Philips	16	12 Nov 55	1
HAWK-EYE	Philips	7	26 Nov 55	8
Above hit: Frankie LAINE with Ray CONIFF and his Orchestra.				
SIXTEEN TONS	Philips	10	21 Jan 56	3
Above hit: Frankie LAINE with the MELLOMEN.				
HELL HATH NO FURY	Philips	28	5 May 56	1
Above hit: Frankie LAINE with Ray CONNIFF and his Orchestra.				
A WOMAN IN LOVE	Philips	1	8 Sep 56	21
Some copies only reflect title as 'Woman In Love'. From the film 'Guys And Dolls'. Originally recorded by Marlon Brando.				
Above hit: Frankie LAINE with Percy FAITH and his Orchestra.				
MOONLIGHT GAMBLER	Philips	13	29 Dec 56	12
Above hit: Frankie LAINE with Ray CONNIFF and his Orchestra.				
MOONLIGHT GAMBLER [RE]	Philips	28	30 Mar 57	1
LOVE IS A GOLDEN RING	Philips	19	27 Apr 57	5
Above hit: Frankie LAINE with the EASY RIDERS.				
UP ABOVE MY HEAD, I HEAR MUSIC IN THE AIR / GOOD EVENING FRIENDS	Philips	25	5 Oct 57	4
Up Above My Head originally recorded by Sister Rosetta Tharpe.				
Above hit: Johnnie RAY – Frankie LAINE with Ray CONNIFF and his Orchestra / Frankie LAINE – Johnnie RAY with Ray CONNIFF and his Orchestra.				
RAWHIDE	Philips	6	14 Nov 59	18
From the TV series of the same name.				
Above hit: Frankie LAINE with Jimmy CARROLL and his Orchestra.				
RAWHIDE [RE]	Philips	41	2 Apr 60	2
GUNSLINGER	Philips	50	13 May 61	1
Main title theme from the CBS-TV Network show of the same name.				

EPS:	**HITS 1**		**WEEKS 12**	
WESTERN FAVOURITES	Philips	7	22 Jul 61	12

ALBUMS:	**HITS 2**		**WEEKS 29**	
HELL BENT FOR LEATHER	Philips	7	24 Jun 61	23
THE VERY BEST OF FRANKIE LAINE	Warwick	7	24 Sep 77	6

Greg LAKE
UK

(See also Emerson, Lake and Palmer; Emerson, Lake and Powell.)

SINGLES:	**HITS 1**		**WEEKS 12**	
I BELIEVE IN FATHER CHRISTMAS	Manticore	2	6 Dec 75	7
I BELIEVE IN FATHER CHRISTMAS [RE-1ST]	Manticore	72	25 Dec 82	3
I BELIEVE IN FATHER CHRISTMAS [RE-2ND]	Manticore	65	24 Dec 83	2

ALBUMS:		HITS 1		WEEKS 3
GREG LAKE	Chrysalis	62	17 Oct 81	3

LAMB
UK

SINGLES:		HITS 3		WEEKS 4
GORECKI	Fontana	30	29 Mar 97	2
Inspired by Polish composer Henri Gorecki's Symphony Of Sorrow Songs.				
B LINE	Fontana	52	3 Apr 99	1
ALL IN YOUR HANDS	Fontana	71	22 May 99	1
ALBUMS:		HITS 1		WEEKS 1
FEAR OF FOURS	Fontana	37	29 May 99	1

Annabel LAMB
UK

SINGLES:		HITS 1		WEEKS 7
RIDERS ON THE STORM	A&M	27	27 Aug 83	7
ALBUMS:		HITS 1		WEEKS 1
THE FLAME	A&M	84	28 Apr 84	1

LAMBRETTAS
UK

SINGLES:		HITS 3		WEEKS 24
POISON IVY	Rocket	7	1 Mar 80	12
D-A-A-ANCE	Rocket	12	24 May 80	8
ANOTHER DAY (ANOTHER GIRL)	Rocket	49	23 Aug 80	4
ALBUMS:		HITS 1		WEEKS 8
BEAT BOYS IN THE JET AGE	Rocket	28	5 Jul 80	8

LANCASTRIANS
UK

SINGLES:		HITS 1		WEEKS 2
WE'LL SING IN THE SUNSHINE	Pye	47	26 Dec 64	2
Originally recorded by Gale Garnett.				

Major LANCE
US

SINGLES:		HITS 1		WEEKS 2
UM UM UM UM UM UM	Columbia	40	15 Feb 64	2

James LANCELOT – See Sarah BRIGHTMAN

LANCERS – See Teresa BREWER

Charlie LANDSBOROUGH
UK

ALBUMS:		HITS 4		WEEKS 13
WITH YOU IN MIND	Ritz	49	12 Oct 96	6
FURTHER DOWN THE ROAD	Ritz	42	8 Nov 97	3
THE VERY BEST OF CHARLIE LANDSBOROUGH	Ritz	41	10 Oct 98	2
STILL CAN'T SAY GOODBYE	Ritz	39	2 Oct 99	2

Valerie LANDSBURG – See KIDS FROM "FAME"

LANDSCAPE
UK

SINGLES:		HITS 2		WEEKS 20
EINSTEIN A GO-GO	RCA	5	28 Feb 81	13
NORMAN BATES	RCA	40	23 May 81	7
ALBUMS:		HITS 1		WEEKS 13
FROM THE TEAROOMS OF MARS TO THE HELLHOLES OF URANUS	RCA	16	21 Mar 81	13

Desmond LANE – See Alma COGAN; Cyril STAPLETON and his Orchestra

Ronnie LANE and the band SLIM CHANCE
UK

(See also Pete Townshend and Ronnie Lane.)

SINGLES:		HITS 2		WEEKS 12
HOW COME?	GM	11	12 Jan 74	8
Above hit: Ronnie LANE Accompanied by the Band "SLIM CHANCE".				
THE POACHER	GM	36	15 Jun 74	4
ALBUMS:		HITS 1		WEEKS 1
ANYMORE FOR ANYMORE	GM	48	17 Aug 74	1

Don LANG
UK

SINGLES:		HITS 4		WEEKS 18
CLOUDBURST	His Master's Voice	16	5 Nov 55	2
Originally recorded by Jon Hendricks.				
Above hit: Don LANG with the MAIRANTS-LANGHORN BIG SIX.				
CLOUDBURST [RE-1ST]	His Master's Voice	18	3 Dec 55	1
CLOUDBURST [RE-2ND]	His Master's Voice	20	14 Jan 56	1

SCHOOL DAY (RING RING GOES THE BELL)	His Master's Voice	26	6 Jul 57	2
WITCH DOCTOR	His Master's Voice	5	24 May 58	11

Above 2: Don LANG and his "FRANTIC FIVE".

SINK THE BISMARCK	His Master's Voice	43	12 Mar 60	1

k.d. lang   Canada

SINGLES:		HITS 7		WEEKS 25
CONSTANT CRAVING	Sire	52	16 May 92	4
CRYING	Virgin America	13	22 Aug 92	6

Above hit: Roy ORBISON (duet with k.d. lang).

CONSTANT CRAVING [RI]	Sire	15	27 Feb 93	8
THE MIND OF LOVE (WHERE IS YOUR HEAD KATHRYN?)	Sire	72	1 May 93	1
MISS CHATELAINE	Sire	68	26 Jun 93	2

Original release reached No. 84 in 1992.

JUST KEEP ME MOVING	Sire	59	11 Dec 93	1

From the film 'Even Cowgirls Get The Blues'.

IF I WERE YOU	Sire	53	30 Sep 95	1
YOU'RE OK	Warner Brothers	44	18 May 96	2
ALBUMS:		HITS 4		WEEKS 62
INGENUE	Sire	28	28 Mar 92	13
INGENUE [RE]	Sire	3	27 Feb 93	39
EVEN COW GIRLS GET THE BLUES [OST]	Sire	36	13 Nov 93	2
ALL YOU CAN EAT	Warner Brothers	7	14 Oct 95	5
DRAG	Warner Brothers	19	12 Jul 97	3

All songs on the album have a reference to smoking.

Thomas LANG   UK

SINGLES:		HITS 1		WEEKS 3
THE HAPPY MAN	Epic	67	30 Jan 88	3
ALBUMS:		HITS 1		WEEKS 1
SCALLYWAG JAZ	Epic	92	20 Feb 88	1

LANGE   UK

SINGLES:		HITS 1		WEEKS 1
I BELIEVE	Additive	68	19 Jun 99	1

Chart also credits Sarah Dyer.

LANTERNS   UK

SINGLES:		HITS 1		WEEKS 1
HIGHRISE TOWN	Columbia	50	6 Feb 99	1

Mario LANZA   US

SINGLES:		HITS 4		WEEKS 32
BECAUSE YOU'RE MINE	His Master's Voice	3	15 Nov 52	24

From the film of the same name.
Above hit: Mario LANZA-Tenor with RCA VICTOR ORCHESTRA and the Jeff ALEXANDER CHOIR Cond. by Constantine CALLINICOS.

DRINKING SONG	His Master's Voice	13	5 Feb 55	1

From the film 'The Student Prince'.

I'LL WALK WITH GOD	His Master's Voice	18	19 Feb 55	1
SERENADE	His Master's Voice	19	23 Apr 55	1

Above entry and Drinking Song were separate sides of the same release, each had its own chart run.

I'LL WALK WITH GOD [RE]	His Master's Voice	20	7 May 55	1
SERENADE [RE]	His Master's Voice	15	7 May 55	2

Above 5 also had Orchestra and Chorus conducted by Constantine Callinicos.

SERENADE	His Master's Voice	25	15 Sep 56	1

Both hits titled Serenade are different songs.

SERENADE [RE]	His Master's Voice	29	13 Oct 56	1
EPS:		HITS 3		WEEKS 30
THE GREAT CARUSO	RCA	16	16 Apr 60	1
THE STUDENT PRINCE	Camden	8	23 Apr 60	27
SINGS CHRISTMAS CAROLS	RCA	10	3 Dec 60	2
ALBUMS:		HITS 6		WEEKS 63
THE STUDENT PRINCE / THE GREAT CARUSO [OST]	RCA	4	6 Dec 58	21
THE GREAT CARUSO	RCA	3	23 Jul 60	15
HIS GREATEST HITS VOLUME 1	RCA Victor	39	9 Jan 71	1
THE LEGEND OF MARIO LANZA	K-Tel	29	5 Sep 81	11
A PORTRAIT OF MARIO LANZA	Stylus	49	14 Nov 87	8
MARIO LANZA – THE ULTIMATE COLLECTION	RCA Victor	13	12 Mar 94	7

LAPTOP   US

SINGLES:		HITS 1		WEEKS 1
NOTHING TO DECLARE	Island	74	12 Jun 99	1

LARD
UK

ALBUMS:	HITS 1			WEEKS 1
THE LAST TEMPTATION OF REID	*Alternative Tentacles*	69	*6 Oct 90*	1

Amel LARRIEUX - See SWEETBACK featuring Amel LARRIEUX from GROOVE THEORY

Denise LASALLE
US

SINGLES:	HITS 1			WEEKS 13
MY TOOT TOOT	*Epic*	6	*15 Jun 85*	13
Originally recorded by Rockin' Sydney.				

James LAST
Germany

(See also Richard Clayderman and James Last.)

SINGLES:	HITS 1			WEEKS 4
THE SEDUCTION (LOVE THEME)	*Polydor*	48	*3 May 80*	4
Written by Giorgio Moroder and from the film 'American Gigolo'.				
Above hit: James LAST BAND.				

ALBUMS:	HITS 60			WEEKS 417
THIS IS JAMES LAST	*Polydor*	6	*15 Apr 67*	48
HAMMOND A-GO-GO	*Polydor*	27	*22 Jul 67*	10
LOVE THIS IS MY SONG	*Polydor*	32	*26 Aug 67*	2
NON-STOP DANCING	*Polydor*	35	*26 Aug 67*	1
JAMES LAST GOES POP	*Polydor*	32	*22 Jun 68*	3
DANCING '68 VOLUME 1	*Polydor*	40	*8 Feb 69*	1
TRUMPET A-GO-GO	*Polydor*	13	*31 May 69*	1
NON-STOP DANCING '69	*Polydor*	26	*9 Aug 69*	1
NON-STOP DANCING '69/2	*Polydor*	27	*24 Jan 70*	3
NON-STOP EVERGREENS	*Polydor*	26	*23 May 70*	1
CLASSICS UP TO DATE	*Polydor*	44	*11 Jul 70*	1
NON-STOP DANCING '70	*Polydor*	67	*11 Jul 70*	1
VERY BEST OF JAMES LAST	*Polydor*	45	*24 Oct 70*	4
NON-STOP DANCING '71	*Polydor*	21	*8 May 71*	4
SUMMER HAPPENING	*Polydor*	38	*26 Jun 71*	1
BEACH PARTY 2	*Polydor*	47	*18 Sep 71*	1
YESTERDAY'S MEMORIES	*Contour*	17	*2 Oct 71*	14
NON-STOP DANCING 12	*Polydor*	30	*16 Oct 71*	3
NON-STOP DANCING 13	*Polydor*	32	*19 Feb 72*	2
POLKA PARTY	*Polydor*	22	*4 Mar 72*	3
JAMES LAST IN CONCERT	*Polydor*	13	*29 Apr 72*	6
VOODOO PARTY	*Polydor*	45	*24 Jun 72*	1
CLASSICS UP TO DATE VOLUME 2	*Polydor*	49	*16 Sep 72*	1
LOVE MUST BE THE REASON	*Polydor*	32	*30 Sep 72*	2
THE MUSIC OF JAMES LAST	*Polydor*	19	*27 Jan 73*	12
JAMES LAST IN RUSSIA	*Polydor*	12	*24 Feb 73*	9
NON-STOP DANCING VOLUME 14	*Polydor*	27	*24 Feb 73*	3
OLE	*Polydor*	24	*28 Jul 73*	5
NON-STOP DANCING VOLUME 15	*Polydor*	34	*1 Sep 73*	2
NON-STOP DANCING VOLUME 16	*Polydor*	43	*20 Apr 74*	2
IN CONCERT VOLUME 2	*Polydor*	49	*29 Jun 74*	1
GOLDEN MEMORIES	*Polydor*	39	*23 Nov 74*	2
TEN YEARS NON-STOP JUBILEE	*Polydor*	5	*26 Jul 75*	16
VIOLINS IN LOVE	*K-Tel*	60	*2 Aug 75*	1
MAKE THE PARTY LAST	*Polydor*	3	*22 Nov 75*	19
CLASSICS UP TO DATE VOLUME 3	*Polydor*	54	*8 May 76*	1
EAST TO WEST	*Polydor*	49	*6 May 78*	4
LAST THE WHOLE NIGHT LONG	*Polydor*	2	*14 Apr 79*	45
THE BEST FROM 150 GOLD RECORDS	*Polydor*	56	*23 Aug 80*	3
CLASSICS FOR DREAMING	*Polydor*	12	*1 Nov 80*	18
ROSES FROM THE SOUTH	*Polydor*	41	*14 Feb 81*	5
HANSIMANIA	*Polydor*	18	*21 Nov 81*	13
LAST FOREVER	*Polydor*	88	*28 Nov 81*	2
BLUEBIRD	*Polydor*	57	*5 Mar 83*	3
NON-STOP DANCING '83 – PARTY POWER	*Polydor*	56	*30 Apr 83*	2
THE BEST OF MY GOLD RECORDS	*Polydor*	42	*30 Apr 83*	5
THE GREATEST SONGS OF THE BEATLES	*Polydor*	52	*3 Dec 83*	8
THE ROSE OF TRALEE AND OTHER IRISH FAVOURITES	*Polydor*	21	*24 Mar 84*	11
PARADISE	*Polydor*	74	*13 Oct 84*	1
JAMES LAST IN SCOTLAND	*Polydor*	68	*8 Dec 84*	9
LEAVE THE BEST TO LAST	*Polydor*	11	*14 Sep 85*	27
BY REQUEST	*Polydor*	22	*18 Apr 87*	11
DANCE DANCE DANCE	*Polydor*	38	*26 Nov 88*	8
CLASSICS BY MOONLIGHT	*Polydor*	12	*14 Apr 90*	12
POP SYMPHONIES	*Polydor*	10	*15 Jun 91*	11
VIVA ESPANA	*PolyGram TV*	23	*12 Sep 92*	5
JAMES LAST PLAYS ANDREW LLOYD WEBBER	*Polydor*	12	*20 Nov 93*	10
THE VERY BEST OF JAMES LAST AND HIS ORCHESTRA	*Polydor*	36	*18 Nov 95*	7

POP SYMPHONIES 2	Polydor	32	28 Mar 98	3
COUNTRY ROADS	Polydor	18	24 Apr 99	5

LAST RHYTHM · Italy

SINGLES:		HITS 1		WEEKS 1
LAST RHYTHM	Stress	62	14 Sep 96	1

Originally recorded in 1991.

LATE SHOW · UK

SINGLES:		HITS 1		WEEKS 6
BRISTOL STOMP	Decca	40	3 Mar 79	6

Originally recorded by the Dovels.

LATIN QUARTER · UK

SINGLES:		HITS 2		WEEKS 10
RADIO AFRICA	Rockin' Horse	19	18 Jan 86	9

Original release reached No. 76 in 1985.

NOMZAMO (ONE PEOPLE ONE CAUSE)	Rockin' Horse	73	18 Apr 87	1

ALBUMS:		HITS 2		WEEKS 3
MODERN TIMES	Rockin' Horse	91	1 Mar 86	2
MICK AND CAROLINE	Rockin' Horse	96	6 Jun 87	1

LATIN RHYTHM – See Tito PUENTE Jr. and the LATIN RHYTHM featuring Tito PUENTE, INDIA and Cali ALEMAN

LATIN THING · Canada/Spain

SINGLES:		HITS 1		WEEKS 1
LATIN THING	Faze 2	41	13 Jul 96	1

Gino LATINO · Italy

SINGLES:		HITS 1		WEEKS 7
WELCOME	ffrr	17	20 Jan 90	7

LATINO RAVE · Italy

SINGLES:		HITS 2		WEEKS 13
DEEP HEAT '89 [M]	Deep Heat	12	25 Nov 89	11
THE SIXTH SENSE [M]	Deep Heat	49	28 Apr 90	2

LATOUR · US

SINGLES:		HITS 1		WEEKS 7
PEOPLE ARE STILL HAVING SEX	Polydor	15	8 Jun 91	7

Stacy LATTISAW · US

SINGLES:		HITS 2		WEEKS 14
JUMP TO THE BEAT	Atlantic	3	14 Jun 80	11
DYNAMITE	Atlantic	51	30 Aug 80	3

Dave LAUDAT – See HUSTLERS CONVENTION featuring Dave LAUDAT and Ondrea DUVERNEY

LAUNCHERS – See Ezz RECO and the LAUNCHERS with Boysie GRANT

Cyndi LAUPER · US

SINGLES:		HITS 17		WEEKS 103
GIRLS JUST WANT TO HAVE FUN	Portrait	2	14 Jan 84	12
TIME AFTER TIME	Portrait	54	24 Mar 84	4
TIME AFTER TIME [RE]	Portrait	3	16 Jun 84	13
SHE BOP	Portrait	46	1 Sep 84	5
ALL THROUGH THE NIGHT	Portrait	64	17 Nov 84	2

Originally recorded by Jules Shear.

TRUE COLORS	Portrait	12	20 Sep 86	11
CHANGE OF HEART	Portrait	74	27 Dec 86	1

Features the Bangles on backing vocals.

CHANGE OF HEART [RE]	Portrait	67	10 Jan 87	1
WHAT'S GOING ON	Portrait	57	28 Mar 87	3
I DROVE ALL NIGHT	Epic	7	20 May 89	12
MY FIRST NIGHT WITH YOU	Epic	53	5 Aug 89	4
HEADING WEST	Epic	68	30 Dec 89	1
THE WORLD IS STONE	Epic	15	6 Jun 92	7
THAT'S WHAT I THINK	Epic	31	13 Nov 93	4
WHO LET IN THE RAIN	Epic	32	8 Jan 94	4
HEY NOW (GIRLS JUST WANT TO HAVE FUN) [RR]	Epic	4	17 Sep 94	13
I'M GONNA BE STRONG	Epic	37	11 Feb 95	2
COME ON HOME	Epic	39	26 Aug 95	2
YOU DON'T KNOW	Epic	27	1 Feb 97	2

ALBUMS:		HITS 6			WEEKS 92
SHE'S SO UNUSUAL	Portrait	16		18 Feb 84	31
TRUE COLORS	Portrait	25		11 Oct 86	12
A NIGHT TO REMEMBER	Epic	9		1 Jul 89	12
SHE'S SO UNUSUAL [RE]	Portrait	71		5 Aug 89	1
Repackaged.					
HAT FULL OF STARS	Epic	56		27 Nov 93	1
TWELVE DEADLY CYNS . . . AND THEN SOME	Epic	2		3 Sep 94	34
Compilation.					
SISTERS OF AVALON	Epic	59		22 Feb 97	1

LAUREL and HARDY
US/UK

SINGLES:		HITS 1			WEEKS 10
THE TRAIL OF THE LONESOME PINE	United Artists	2		22 Nov 75	10

From the 1937 film 'Way Out West'.
Above hit: LAUREL and HARDY with the AVALON BOYS featuring Chill WILLS.

ALBUMS:		HITS 1			WEEKS 4
THE GOLDEN AGE OF HOLLYWOOD COMEDY	United Artists	55		6 Dec 75	4

LAUREL and HARDY
UK

SINGLES:		HITS 1			WEEKS 2
CLUNK CLICK	CBS	65		2 Apr 83	2

LAURNEA
US

SINGLES:		HITS 1			WEEKS 2
DAYS OF YOUTH	Epic	36		12 Jul 97	2

LAW
UK/US

ALBUMS:		HITS 1			WEEKS 1
THE LAW	Atlantic	61		6 Apr 91	1

Joanna LAW
UK

SINGLES:		HITS 2			WEEKS 8
FIRST TIME EVER	Citybeat	67		7 Jul 90	3
THE GIFT	Deconstruction	15		14 Sep 96	5

Samples Joanna Law's First Time Ever.
Above hit: WAY OUT WEST featuring Miss Joanna LAW.

Billy LAWRENCE – See RAMPAGE featuring Billy LAWRENCE

Joey LAWRENCE
US

SINGLES:		HITS 4			WEEKS 15
NOTHIN' MY LOVE CAN'T FIX	EMI	13		26 Jun 93	7
I CAN'T HELP MYSELF	EMI	27		28 Aug 93	4
STAY FOREVER	EMI	41		30 Oct 93	3
NEVER GONNA CHANGE MY MIND	Curb	49		19 Sep 98	1

ALBUMS:		HITS 1			WEEKS 3
JOEY LAWRENCE	EMI	39		31 Jul 93	3

Lee LAWRENCE
UK

SINGLES:		HITS 2			WEEKS 10
CRYING IN THE CHAPEL	Decca	11		21 Nov 53	1
CRYING IN THE CHAPEL [RE]	Decca	7		12 Dec 53	5
SUDDENLY THERE'S A VALLEY	Columbia	19		3 Dec 55	1

Above hit: Lee LAWRENCE with Ray MARTIN and his Orchestra.

SUDDENLY THERE'S A VALLEY [RE]	Columbia	14		17 Dec 55	3

Sophie LAWRENCE
UK

SINGLES:		HITS 1			WEEKS 7
LOVE'S UNKIND	IQ	21		3 Aug 91	7

Steve LAWRENCE
US

SINGLES:		HITS 3			WEEKS 27
FOOTSTEPS	His Master's Voice	4		23 Apr 60	13
GIRLS GIRLS GIRLS	London	49		20 Aug 60	1
I WANT TO STAY HERE	CBS	3		24 Aug 63	13

Above hit: STEVE and EYDIE.

Syd LAWRENCE
UK

ALBUMS:		HITS 4			WEEKS 9
MORE MILLER AND OTHER BIG BAND MAGIC	Philips	14		8 Aug 70	4
MUSIC OF GLENN MILLER IN SUPER STEREO	Philips	43		25 Dec 71	2

SYD LAWRENCE WITH THE GLENN MILLER SOUND	Fontana	31	25 Dec 71	2
SOMETHING OLD, SOMETHING NEW	Philips	34	26 Feb 72	1

Ronnie LAWS — US

ALBUMS:	**HITS 1**		**WEEKS 1**	
SOLID GROUND	Liberty	100	17 Oct 81	1

Lindy LAYTON — UK

SINGLES:	**HITS 6**		**WEEKS 28**	
DUB BE GOOD TO ME	Go.Beat	1	10 Feb 90	13

Above hit: BEATS INTERNATIONAL featuring LINDY.

SILLY GAMES	Arista	22	11 Aug 90	7

Above hit: Lindy LAYTON featuring Janet KAY.

ECHO MY HEART	Arista	42	26 Jan 91	2
WITHOUT YOU (ONE AND ONE)	Arista	71	31 Aug 91	2
WE GOT THE LOVE ('93 REMIX)	PWL International	38	24 Apr 93	3
SHOW ME	PWL International	47	30 Oct 93	1

Doug LAZY — US

SINGLES:	**HITS 2**		**WEEKS 9**	
LET IT ROLL	Atlantic	27	15 Jul 89	5

Chart has the credit as Raze Presents Doug Lazy, though this is not reflected on the single itself.

LET THE RHYTHM PUMP	Atlantic	45	4 Nov 89	3
LET THE RHYTHM PUMP [RM]	Atlantic	63	26 May 90	1

Remixed by Dakeyne and Anderson of DMC UK.

ALBUMS:	**HITS 1**		**WEEKS 1**	
DOUG LAZY GETTIN' CRAZY	Atlantic	65	10 Mar 90	1

LCD — UK

SINGLES:	**HITS 1**		**WEEKS 9**	
ZORBA'S DANCE	Virgin	20	27 Jun 98	5
ZORBA'S DANCE [RI]	Virgin	22	9 Oct 99	4

LE CLICK — US/Sweden

SINGLES:	**HITS 1**		**WEEKS 2**	
CALL ME	Logic	38	30 Aug 97	2

Kele LE ROC — UK

SINGLES:	**HITS 2**		**WEEKS 14**	
LITTLE BIT OF LOVIN'	Wild Card	8	31 Oct 98	7
MY LOVE	Wild Card	8	27 Mar 99	7
ALBUMS:	**HITS 1**		**WEEKS 2**	
EVERYBODY'S SOMEBODY	Wild Card	44	10 Apr 99	2

LEAGUE UNLIMITED ORCHESTRA - See HUMAN LEAGUE

Vicky LEANDROS — Greece

SINGLES:	**HITS 3**		**WEEKS 29**	
COME WHAT May (APRES - TOI)	Philips	2	8 Apr 72	16

Eurovision Song Contest winner for Luxembourg in 1972.

THE LOVE IN YOUR EYES	Philips	48	23 Dec 72	3
THE LOVE IN YOUR EYES [RE-1ST]	Philips	40	20 Jan 73	4
THE LOVE IN YOUR EYES [RE-2ND]	Philips	46	7 Apr 73	1
WHEN BOUZOUKIS PLAYED	Philips	44	7 Jul 73	2
WHEN BOUZOUKIS PLAYED [RE]	Philips	45	28 Jul 73	3

Denis LEARY — US

SINGLES:	**HITS 1**		**WEEKS 2**	
ASSHOLE	A&M	58	13 Jan 96	2

Keith LeBLANC - See Malcolm X, music by Keith LeBLANC

LED ZEPPELIN — UK

SINGLES:	**HITS 1**		**WEEKS 2**	
WHOLE LOTTA LOVE	Atlantic	21	13 Sep 97	2

This is their first official single release in the UK.

ALBUMS:	**HITS 14**		**WEEKS 473**	
LED ZEPPELIN	Atlantic	6	12 Apr 69	79
LED ZEPPELIN 2	Atlantic	1	8 Nov 69	138

Repackaged from March 72.

LED ZEPPELIN 3	Atlantic	1	7 Nov 70	40
FOUR SYMBOLS (LED ZEPPELIN 4)	Atlantic	1	27 Nov 71	58

Repackaged from March 72. Album was untitled, but was commonly referred to as per the two titles above. Includes re-entries through to 1981.

HOUSES OF THE HOLY	*Atlantic*	1	*14 Apr 73*	13
PHYSICAL GRAFFITI	*Swan Song*	1	*15 Mar 75*	27
PRESENCE	*Swan Song*	1	*24 Apr 76*	14
THE SONG REMAINS THE SAME [OST]	*Swan Song*	1	*6 Nov 76*	15
Includes the Madison Square Garden concert from March 73.				
IN THROUGH THE OUT DOOR	*Swan Song*	1	*8 Sep 79*	16
FOUR SYMBOLS (LED ZEPPELIN 4) [RE-1ST]	*Atlantic*	69	*14 Aug 82*	5
Chart position reached in 1991.				
CODA	*Swan Song*	4	*4 Dec 82*	7
REMASTERS	*Atlantic*	10	*27 Oct 90*	45
LED ZEPPELIN (BOX SET)	*Atlantic*	48	*10 Nov 90*	2
LED ZEPPELIN BOXED SET II	*Atlantic*	56	*9 Oct 93*	1
Above 2 are compilations.				
FOUR SYMBOLS (LED ZEPPELIN 4) [RE-2ND]	*Atlantic*	48	*2 Apr 94*	6
Includes re-entry in 1999.				
BBC SESSIONS	*Atlantic*	23	*29 Nov 97*	7

Ann LEE   UK

SINGLES:	HITS 1			WEEKS 14
2 TIMES	*ZYX*	57	*11 Sep 99*	2
German import. Removed from chart when it was discovered the running time broke eligibility rules.				
2 TIMES	*Systematic*	2	*16 Oct 99*	12

Brenda LEE   US

SINGLES:	HITS 22			WEEKS 210
SWEET NUTHIN'S	*Brunswick*	45	*19 Mar 60*	1
SWEET NUTHIN'S [RE]	*Brunswick*	4	*9 Apr 60*	18
I'M SORRY	*Brunswick*	12	*2 Jul 60*	16
Features Floyd Cramer on piano.				
I WANT TO BE WANTED	*Brunswick*	31	*22 Oct 60*	6
LET'S JUMP THE BROOMSTICK	*Brunswick*	12	*21 Jan 61*	15
EMOTIONS	*Brunswick*	45	*8 Apr 61*	1
DUM DUM	*Brunswick*	22	*22 Jul 61*	8
Written by Jackie De Shannon.				
FOOL NUMBER ONE	*Brunswick*	38	*18 Nov 61*	3
Originally recorded by Loretta Lynn.				
BREAK IT TO ME GENTLY	*Brunswick*	46	*10 Feb 62*	2
SPEAK TO ME PRETTY	*Brunswick*	3	*7 Apr 62*	12
From the film 'Two Little Bears'.				
HERE COMES THAT FEELING	*Brunswick*	5	*23 Jun 62*	12
IT STARTED ALL OVER AGAIN	*Brunswick*	15	*15 Sep 62*	11
ROCKIN' AROUND THE CHRISTMAS TREE	*Brunswick*	6	*1 Dec 62*	7
ALL ALONE AM I	*Brunswick*	7	*19 Jan 63*	17
LOSING YOU	*Brunswick*	10	*30 Mar 63*	16
I WONDER	*Brunswick*	14	*20 Jul 63*	9
SWEET IMPOSSIBLE YOU	*Brunswick*	28	*2 Nov 63*	6
AS USUAL	*Brunswick*	5	*11 Jan 64*	15
THINK	*Brunswick*	26	*11 Apr 64*	8
IS IT TRUE	*Brunswick*	17	*12 Sep 64*	8
CHRISTMAS WILL BE JUST ANOTHER LONELY DAY	*Brunswick*	29	*12 Dec 64*	5
THANKS A LOT	*Brunswick*	41	*6 Feb 65*	2
Originally recorded by Ernest Tubb in 1963.				
TOO MANY RIVERS	*Brunswick*	22	*31 Jul 65*	12
EPS:	HITS 2			WEEKS 11
SPEAK TO ME PRETTY	*Brunswick*	18	*10 Nov 62*	3
ALL ALONE AM I	*Brunswick*	8	*3 Aug 63*	8
ALBUMS:	HITS 8			WEEKS 64
ALL THE WAY	*Brunswick*	20	*24 Nov 62*	2
BRENDA - THAT'S ALL	*Brunswick*	13	*16 Feb 63*	13
ALL ALONE AM I	*Brunswick*	8	*13 Apr 63*	20
BYE BYE BLUES	*Brunswick*	21	*16 Jul 66*	2
LITTLE MISS DYNAMITE - BRENDA LEE	*Warwick*	15	*1 Nov 80*	11
25TH ANNIVERSARY	*MCA*	65	*7 Jan 84*	4
THE VERY BEST OF BRENDA LEE	*MCA*	16	*30 Mar 85*	9
THE VERY BEST OF BRENDA LEE . . . WITH LOVE	*Telstar*	20	*15 Oct 94*	7

Byron LEE – See Boris GARDINER

Curtis LEE   US

SINGLES:	HITS 1			WEEKS 2
PRETTY LITTLE ANGEL EYES	*London*	47	*2 Sep 61*	1
Backing vocals by the Halos.				
PRETTY LITTLE ANGEL EYES [RE]	*London*	48	*16 Sep 61*	1

Dee C. LEE | UK

(See also Style Council.)

SINGLES:		HITS 3		WEEKS 20	
SEE THE DAY	CBS		3	9 Nov 85	12
COME HELL OR WATERS HIGH	CBS		46	8 Mar 86	5
Originally recorded by Judie Tzuke.					
NO TIME TO PLAY	Cooltempo		25	13 Nov 93	3
Above hit: GURU featuring vocals by D.C. LEE.					

Garry LEE and SHOWDOWN | Canada

SINGLES:		HITS 1		WEEKS 3	
THE RODEO SONG	Party Dish		44	31 Jul 93	3

Jackie LEE | Ireland

SINGLES:		HITS 2		WEEKS 31	
WHITE HORSES	Philips		10	13 Apr 68	14
Theme from the BBC1 TV children's series of the same name.					
Above hit: JACKY.					
RUPERT	Pye		14	2 Jan 71	17
Theme from the ITV children's series 'Rupert The Bear'.					

Leapy LEE | UK

SINGLES:		HITS 2		WEEKS 28	
LITTLE ARROWS	MCA		2	24 Aug 68	21
GOOD MORNING	MCA		47	20 Dec 69	1
GOOD MORNING [RE]	MCA		29	10 Jan 70	6

Peggy LEE | US

SINGLES:		HITS 3		WEEKS 29	
MR. WONDERFUL	Brunswick		5	25 May 57	13
From the musical of the same name.					
FEVER	Capitol		5	16 Aug 58	11
TILL THERE WAS YOU	Capitol		40	25 Mar 61	1
From the film 'The Music Man'. Originally recorded by Robert Preston and Barbara Cook.					
TILL THERE WAS YOU [RE]	Capitol		30	8 Apr 61	3
Above 3: Peggy LEE with Jack MARSHALL'S MUSIC.					
FEVER [RI]	Capitol		75	22 Aug 92	1
ALBUMS:		**HITS 3**		**WEEKS 17**	
LATIN A LA LEE	Capitol		8	4 Jun 60	15
BEST OF PEGGY LEE VOLUME 2	Brunswick		18	20 May 61	1
BLACK COFFEE	Ace Of Hearts		20	21 Oct 61	1

Peggy LEE and George SHEARING | US

(See also Peggy Lee; George Shearing Quartet.)

ALBUMS:		HITS 1		WEEKS 6	
BEAUTY AND THE BEAT	Capitol		16	11 Jun 60	6

Toney LEE | US

SINGLES:		HITS 1		WEEKS 4	
REACH UP	TMT Productions		64	29 Jan 83	4

Tracey LEE | US

SINGLES:		HITS 1		WEEKS 1	
THE THEME: IT'S PARTY TIME	Universal		51	19 Jul 97	1

Bruce LEE - See J.K.D. BAND featuring the voice of Bruce LEE

LEEDS UNITED FOOTBALL TEAM | UK

SINGLES:		HITS 2		WEEKS 13	
LEEDS UNITED	Chapter 1		10	29 Apr 72	10
LEEDS, LEEDS, LEEDS, (MARCHING ON TOGETHER)	Q Music		61	25 Apr 92	1
Above hit: LEEDS UNITED A.F.C. (1970'S).					
LEEDS, LEEDS, LEEDS, (MARCHING ON TOGETHER) [RE]	Q Music		54	9 May 92	2

Carol LEEMING - BEDROCK; STAXX

Raymond LEFEVRE | France

SINGLES:		HITS 1		WEEKS 2	
SOUL COAXING	Major Minor		46	18 May 68	2
ALBUMS:		**HITS 2**		**WEEKS 9**	
RAYMOND LEFEVRE	Major Minor		10	7 Oct 67	7
RAYMOND LEFEVRE VOLUME 2	Major Minor		37	17 Feb 68	2

LEFT EYE - See LIL' KIM

LEFTFIELD   UK

SINGLES:	HITS 7			WEEKS 22
SONG OF LIFE	*Hard Hands*	59	*12 Dec 92*	1
OPEN UP	*Hard Hands*	13	*13 Nov 93*	5
Above hit: LEFTFIELD LYDON.				
ORIGINAL	*Hard Hands*	18	*25 Mar 95*	3
Above hit: LEFTFIELD HALLIDAY.				
THE AFRO-LEFT [EP]	*Hard Hands*	22	*5 Aug 95*	3
Lead track: Afro Left.				
Above hit: LEFTFIELD featuring DJUM DJUM.				
RELEASE THE PRESSURE	*Hard Hands*	13	*20 Jan 96*	3
AFRIKA SHOX	*Hard Hands*	7	*18 Sep 99*	5
Above hit: LEFTFIELD. BAMBAATAA.				
DUSTED	*Hard Hands*	28	*11 Dec 99*	2
Above hit: LEFTFIELD. ROOTS MANUVA.				
ALBUMS:	HITS 2			WEEKS 83
LEFTISM	*Hard Hands*	3	*11 Feb 95*	69
RHYTHM AND STEALTH	*Hard Hands*	1	*2 Oct 99*	14

LEGEND   US

(See also Raze.)

SINGLES:	HITS 1			WEEKS 1
CAN YOU FEEL IT (CHAMPION MEGAMIX) (M) / CAN YOU FEEL IT (RAZE MEGAMIX) (M)	*Champion*	62	*10 Feb 90*	1
Montage of tracks by Raze.				

LEGEND B   Germany

SINGLES:	HITS 1			WEEKS 1
LOST IN LOVE	*Perfecto*	45	*22 Feb 97*	1

Tom LEHRER   US

ALBUMS:	HITS 2			WEEKS 26
SONGS BY TOM LEHRER	*Decca*	7	*8 Nov 58*	19
AN EVENING WASTED WITH TOM LEHRER	*Decca*	7	*25 Jun 60*	7

LEILANI   UK

SINGLES:	HITS 2			WEEKS 6
MADNESS THING	*ZTT*	19	*6 Feb 99*	4
DO YOU WANT ME?	*ZTT*	40	*12 Jun 99*	2

Paul LEKAKIS   US

SINGLES:	HITS 1			WEEKS 4
BOOM BOOM (LET'S GO BACK TO MY ROOM)	*Champion*	60	*30 May 87*	4

LEMON PIPERS   US

SINGLES:	HITS 2			WEEKS 16
GREEN TAMBOURINE	*Pye International*	7	*10 Feb 68*	11
RICE IS NICE	*Pye International*	41	*4 May 68*	5

LEMON TREES   UK

SINGLES:	HITS 5			WEEKS 9
LOVE IS IN YOUR EYES	*Oxygen*	75	*26 Sep 92*	1
THE WAY I FEEL	*Oxygen*	62	*7 Nov 92*	2
LET IT LOOSE	*Oxygen*	55	*13 Feb 93*	2
CHILD OF LOVE	*Oxygen*	55	*17 Apr 93*	3
I CAN'T FACE THE WORLD	*Oxygen*	52	*3 Jul 93*	1

LEMONHEADS   US/Australia

SINGLES:	HITS 8			WEEKS 26
IT'S A SHAME ABOUT RAY	*Atlantic*	70	*17 Oct 92*	1
MRS. ROBINSON / BEING AROUND	*Atlantic*	19	*5 Dec 92*	9
CONFETTI / MY DRUG BUDDY	*Atlantic*	44	*6 Feb 93*	2
IT'S A SHAME ABOUT RAY [RI]	*Atlantic*	31	*10 Apr 93*	3
INTO YOUR ARMS	*Atlantic*	14	*16 Oct 93*	4
IT'S ABOUT TIME	*Atlantic*	57	*27 Nov 93*	2
BIG GAY HEART	*Atlantic*	55	*14 May 94*	2
IF I COULD TALK I'D TELL YOU	*Atlantic*	39	*28 Sep 96*	2
IT'S ALL TRUE	*Atlantic*	61	*14 Dec 96*	1
ALBUMS:	HITS 3			WEEKS 32
IT'S A SHAME ABOUT RAY	*Atlantic*	69	*1 Aug 92*	1

IT'S A SHAME ABOUT RAY [RE]	Atlantic	33	26 Dec 92	15
Repackaged.				
COME ON FEEL THE LEMONHEADS	Atlantic	5	23 Oct 93	14
CAR BUTTON CLOTH	Atlantic	28	12 Oct 96	2

LEN
Canada

SINGLES:	HITS 1			WEEKS 3
STEAL MY SUNSHINE	Columbia	8	18 Dec 99	3
Samples Andrea True Connection's More More More.				

LENA – See Lena FIAGBE

John LENNON
UK

SINGLES:	HITS 18			WEEKS 186
GIVE PEACE A CHANCE	Apple	2	12 Jul 69	13
Recorded in room 1742 Hotel La Reine Elizabeth, Montreal and features his son Sean.				
COLD TURKEY	Apple	14	1 Nov 69	8
Features Eric Clapton on guitar.				
Above 2: PLASTIC ONO BAND.				
INSTANT KARMA	Apple	5	21 Feb 70	9
Features George Harrison on guitar and Billy Preston on piano.				
Above hit: LENNON/ONO with the PLASTIC ONO BAND.				
POWER TO THE PEOPLE	Apple	7	20 Mar 71	9
Above hit: John LENNON/PLASTIC ONO BAND.				
HAPPY XMAS (WAR IS OVER)	Apple	4	9 Dec 72	8
Above hit: JOHN and YOKO/the PLASTIC ONO BAND with the HARLEM COMMUNITY CHOIR.				
MIND GAMES	Apple	26	24 Nov 73	9
WHATEVER GETS YOU THRU' THE NIGHT	Apple	36	19 Oct 74	4
Features Elton John on backing vocals.				
Above hit: John LENNON with the PLASTIC ONO NUCLEAR BAND.				
HAPPY XMAS (WAR IS OVER) [RE-1ST]	Apple	48	4 Jan 75	1
Above hit: JOHN and YOKO/the PLASTIC ONO BAND with the HARLEM COMMUNITY CHOIR.				
#9 DREAM	Apple	23	8 Feb 75	8
STAND BY ME	Apple	30	3 May 75	7
IMAGINE	Apple	6	1 Nov 75	11
(JUST LIKE) STARTING OVER	Geffen	1	8 Nov 80	15
HAPPY XMAS (WAR IS OVER) [RE-2ND]	Apple	2	20 Dec 80	9
Above hit: JOHN and YOKO and the PLASTIC ONO BAND with the HARLEM COMMUNITY CHOIR.				
IMAGINE [RE]	Apple	1	27 Dec 80	13
WOMAN	Geffen	1	24 Jan 81	11
GIVE PEACE A CHANCE [RE]	Apple	33	24 Jan 81	5
Above hit: PLASTIC ONO BAND.				
I SAW HER STANDING THERE	DJM	40	21 Mar 81	4
Above hit: Elton JOHN BAND featuring John LENNON and the MUSCLE SHOALS HORNS.				
WATCHING THE WHEELS	Geffen	30	4 Apr 81	6
Above hit: John LENNON and Yoko ONO.				
HAPPY XMAS (WAR IS OVER) [RE-3RD]	Apple	28	19 Dec 81	5
Above hit: JOHN and YOKO/the PLASTIC ONO BAND with the HARLEM COMMUNITY CHOIR.				
LOVE	Parlophone	41	20 Nov 82	7
HAPPY XMAS (WAR IS OVER) [RE-4TH]	Apple	56	25 Dec 82	3
Above hit: JOHN and YOKO/the PLASTIC ONO BAND with the HARLEM COMMUNITY CHOIR.				
NOBODY TOLD ME	Polydor	6	21 Jan 84	6
BORROWED TIME	Polydor	32	17 Mar 84	6
JEALOUS GUY	Parlophone	65	30 Nov 85	2
IMAGINE [RI-1ST] / JEALOUS GUY [RI] / HAPPY XMAS (WAR IS OVER) [RI-1ST]	Parlophone	45	10 Dec 88	5
IMAGINE [RI-2ND]	Parlophone	3	25 Dec 99	2
Above hit: John LENNON and the PLASTIC ONO BAND (with the FLUX FIDDLERS).				

ALBUMS:	HITS 14			WEEKS 332
JOHN LENNON AND THE PLASTIC ONO BAND	Apple	11	16 Jan 71	11
Above hit: John LENNON and the PLASTIC ONO BAND.				
IMAGINE	Apple	1	30 Oct 71	85
Above hit: John LENNON and the PLASTIC ONO BAND (with the FLUX FIDDLERS).				
SOMETIME IN NEW YORK CITY	Apple	11	14 Oct 72	6
Above hit: John and Yoko LENNON with the PLASTIC ONO BAND and ELEPHANT'S MEMORY.				
MIND GAMES	Apple	13	8 Dec 73	12
WALLS AND BRIDGES	Apple	6	19 Oct 74	10
ROCK AND ROLL	Apple	6	8 Mar 75	25
Collection of Lennon's favourite rock'n'roll songs.				
SHAVED FISH	Apple	8	8 Nov 75	17
Compilation.				

DOUBLE FANTASY	Geffen	1	22 Nov 80	36
Tracks divided equally between each artist.				
Above hit: John LENNON and Yoko ONO.				
IMAGINE [RI]	Parlophone	5	20 Dec 80	16
Above hit: John LENNON and the PLASTIC ONO BAND (with the FLUX FIDDLERS).				
SHAVED FISH [RI]	Parlophone	11	17 Jan 81	12
ROCK AND ROLL [RI]	Parlophone	64	17 Jan 81	3
THE JOHN LENNON COLLECTION	Parlophone	1	20 Nov 82	42
MILK AND HONEY – A HEART PLAY	Polydor	3	4 Feb 84	13
Recordings from 1980. Tracks divided equally between each artist.				
Above hit: John LENNON and Yoko ONO.				
JOHN LENNON LIVE IN NEW YORK CITY	Parlophone	55	8 Mar 86	3
Live recordings from Madison Square Gardens, 30 Aug 72.				
IMAGINE: JOHN LENNON [OST]	Parlophone	64	22 Oct 88	6
Includes Beatles material.				
THE JOHN LENNON COLLECTION [RE]	Parlophone	73	20 Apr 96	1
LENNON LEGEND - THE VERY BEST OF JOHN LENNON	Parlophone	4	8 Nov 97	33
THE JOHN LENNON ANTHOLOGY	Capitol	62	14 Nov 98	1
4 CD box set titled 'Ascot', 'New York', 'Lost Weekend' and 'Dakota'. A separate condensed version, Wonsaponatime, reached No. 76 the same week.				

Julian LENNON   UK

SINGLES:	HITS 9			WEEKS 47
TOO LATE FOR GOODBYES	Charisma	6	6 Oct 84	11
VALOTTE	Charisma	55	15 Dec 84	6
SAY YOU'RE WRONG	Charisma	75	9 Mar 85	1
BECAUSE	EMI	40	7 Dec 85	7
From the musical 'Time'.				
NOW YOU'RE IN HEAVEN	Virgin	59	11 Mar 89	3
SALTWATER	Virgin	6	24 Aug 91	13
HELP YOURSELF	Virgin	53	30 Nov 91	2
GET A LIFE	Virgin	56	25 Apr 92	3
DAY AFTER DAY	Music From Another	66	23 May 98	1
ALBUMS:	HITS 3			WEEKS 20
VALOTTE	Charisma	20	3 Nov 84	15
THE SECRET VALUE OF DAYDREAMING	Charisma	93	5 Apr 86	1
HELP YOURSELF	Virgin	42	5 Oct 91	4

Annie LENNOX   UK

SINGLES:	HITS 10			WEEKS 68
PUT A LITTLE LOVE IN YOUR HEART	A&M	28	3 Dec 88	8
Above hit: Annie LENNOX and Al GREEN.				
WHY	RCA	5	28 Mar 92	8
PRECIOUS	RCA	23	6 Jun 92	5
WALKING ON BROKEN GLASS	RCA	8	22 Aug 92	8
COLD	RCA	26	31 Oct 92	4
LITTLE BIRD / LOVE SONG FOR A VAMPIRE	RCA	3	13 Feb 93	12
Love Song For A Vampire from the film 'Bram Stoker's Dracula'.				
NO MORE "I LOVE YOU'S"	RCA	2	18 Feb 95	12
A WHITER SHADE OF PALE	RCA	16	10 Jun 95	6
WAITING IN VAIN	RCA	31	30 Sep 95	3
SOMETHING SO RIGHT	RCA	44	9 Dec 95	2
Originally recorded by Paul Simon, from his 1973 album There Goes Rhymin' Simon.				
Above hit: Annie LENNOX featuring Paul SIMON on guitar and vocals.				
ALBUMS:	HITS 2			WEEKS 129
DIVA	RCA	1	18 Apr 92	80
MEDUSA	RCA	1	18 Mar 95	49
Album of cover versions.				

Rula LENSKA - See Julie COVINGTON, Charlotte CORNWELL, Rula LENSKA, Sue JONES-DAVIES

Phillip LEO   UK

SINGLES:	HITS 2			WEEKS 3
SECOND CHANCE	EMI	57	23 Jul 94	2
THINKING ABOUT YOUR LOVE	EMI	64	25 Mar 95	1

Deke LEONARD   UK

ALBUMS:	HITS 1			WEEKS 1
KAMIKAZE	United Artists	50	13 Apr 74	1

Paul LEONI   UK

ALBUMS:	HITS 1			WEEKS 19
FLIGHTS OF FANCY	Nouveau Music	17	24 Sep 83	19
Covers of popular hits.				

LeROYS - See Simon SCOTT and the LeROYS

LES RYTHMES DIGITALES
France

SINGLES:	HITS 3			WEEKS 3
MUSIC MAKES YOU LOSE CONTROL	Wall Of Sound	69	25 Apr 98	1
SOMETIMES	Wall Of Sound	56	7 Aug 99	1
Above hit: LES RYTHMES DIGITALES featuring Nik KERSHAW.				
JAQUES YOUR BODY [MAKE ME SWEAT] '99 MIX	Wall Of Sound	60	30 Oct 99	1
Featured in the Sunny Delight TV commercial.				
ALBUMS:	HITS 1			WEEKS 1
DARKDANCER	Wall Of Sound	53	5 Jun 99	1

LeSHAUN - See LL COOL J

LESTER - See Norman COOK

Eddie LESTER SINGERS - See Vince HILL

Ketty LESTER
US

SINGLES:	HITS 2			WEEKS 16
LOVE LETTERS	London	4	21 Apr 62	12
Originally recorded by Dick Haymes in 1945.				
BUT NOT FOR ME	London	45	21 Jul 62	4

LET LOOSE
UK

SINGLES:	HITS 8			WEEKS 62
CRAZY FOR YOU	Vertigo	44	24 Apr 93	3
SEVENTEEN	Mercury	44	9 Apr 94	2
CRAZY FOR YOU [RI]	Mercury	2	25 Jun 94	20
SEVENTEEN [RM]	Mercury	11	22 Oct 94	6
Remixed by Let Loose and Nick Kershaw.				
CRAZY FOR YOU [RI] [RE]	Mercury	46	24 Dec 94	4
SEVENTEEN [RM] [RE]	Mercury	47	7 Jan 95	3
ONE NIGHT STAND	Mercury	12	28 Jan 95	6
BEST IN ME	Mercury	8	29 Apr 95	5
EVERYBODY SAY EVERYBODY DO	Mercury	29	4 Nov 95	3
EVERYBODY SAY EVERYBODY DO [RE]	Mercury	71	13 Jan 96	1
MAKE IT WITH YOU	Mercury	7	22 Jun 96	6
TAKE IT EASY	Mercury	25	7 Sep 96	2
DARLING BE HOME SOON	Mercury	65	16 Nov 96	1
ALBUMS:	HITS 2			WEEKS 15
LET LOOSE	Mercury	20	19 Nov 94	14
ROLLERCOASTER	Mercury	42	5 Oct 96	1

Gerald LETHAN - See WALL OF SOUND featuring Gerald LETHAN

LETTERMEN
US

SINGLES:	HITS 1			WEEKS 3
THE WAY YOU LOOK TONIGHT	Capitol	36	25 Nov 61	3
Originally recorded by Fred Astaire in 1936.				

LEVEL 42
UK

SINGLES:	HITS 29			WEEKS 177
LOVE MEETING LOVE	Polydor	61	30 Aug 80	4
LOVE GAMES	Polydor	38	18 Apr 81	6
TURN IT ON	Polydor	57	8 Aug 81	6
STARCHILD	Polydor	47	14 Nov 81	4
ARE YOU HEARING (WHAT I HEAR)?	Polydor	49	8 May 82	5
WEAVE YOUR SPELL	Polydor	43	2 Oct 82	4
THE CHINESE WAY	Polydor	24	15 Jan 83	8
OUT OF SIGHT.OUT OF MIND	Polydor	41	16 Apr 83	4
THE SUN GOES DOWN (LIVING IT UP)	Polydor	10	30 Jul 83	12
MICRO-KID	Polydor	37	22 Oct 83	5
HOT WATER	Polydor	18	1 Sep 84	9
THE CHANT HAS BEGUN	Polydor	41	3 Nov 84	5
SOMETHING ABOUT YOU	Polydor	6	21 Sep 85	17
LEAVING ME NOW	Polydor	15	7 Dec 85	11
LESSONS IN LOVE	Polydor	3	26 Apr 86	13
RUNNING IN THE FAMILY	Polydor	6	14 Feb 87	10
TO BE WITH YOU AGAIN	Polydor	10	25 Apr 87	7
IT'S OVER	Polydor	10	12 Sep 87	8
CHILDREN SAY	Polydor	22	12 Dec 87	6
HEAVEN IN MY HANDS	Polydor	12	3 Sep 88	5
TAKE A LOOK	Polydor	32	29 Oct 88	4
TRACIE	Polydor	25	21 Jan 89	5
TAKE CARE OF YOURSELF	Polydor	39	28 Oct 89	3
GUARANTEED	RCA	17	17 Aug 91	4

OVERTIME	RCA	62	19 Oct 91	2
MY FATHER'S SHOES	RCA	55	18 Apr 92	1
FOREVER NOW	RCA	19	26 Feb 94	4
ALL OVER YOU	RCA	26	30 Apr 94	2
LOVE IN A PEACEFUL WORLD	RCA	31	6 Aug 94	3
ALBUMS:	**HITS 13**			**WEEKS 228**
LEVEL 42	Polydor	20	29 Aug 81	18
THE EARLY TAPES JULY-AUGUST 1980	Polydor	46	10 Apr 82	6
THE PURSUIT OF ACCIDENTS	Polydor	17	18 Sep 82	16
STANDING IN THE LIGHT	Polydor	9	3 Sep 83	13
TRUE COLOURS	Polydor	14	13 Oct 84	8
A PHYSICAL PRESENCE	Polydor	28	6 Jul 85	5
Live recordings, mainly from small club tours in the UK.				
WORLD MACHINE	Polydor	3	26 Oct 85	72
RUNNING IN THE FAMILY	Polydor	2	28 Mar 87	54
STARING AT THE SUN	Polydor	2	1 Oct 88	11
LEVEL BEST	Polydor	5	18 Nov 89	15
Compilation.				
GUARANTEED	RCA	3	14 Sep 91	5
FOREVER NOW	RCA	8	26 Mar 94	3
THE VERY BEST OF LEVEL 42	Polydor	41	7 Nov 98	2

LEVELLERS UK

SINGLES:	**HITS 16**			**WEEKS 55**
ONE WAY	China	51	21 Sep 91	2
FAR FROM HOME	China	71	7 Dec 91	1
15 YEARS [EP]	China	11	23 May 92	5
Lead track: 15 years.				
BELARUSE	China	12	10 Jul 93	5
THIS GARDEN	China	12	30 Oct 93	4
THE JULIE [EP]	China	17	14 May 94	3
Lead track: Julie (New Version).				
HOPE ST.	China	12	12 Aug 95	5
FANTASY	China	16	14 Oct 95	3
JUST THE ONE	China	12	23 Dec 95	8
Above hit: LEVELLERS Special guest Joe STRUMMER on piano.				
EXODUS - LIVE	China	24	20 Jul 96	2
WHAT A BEAUTIFUL DAY	China	13	9 Aug 97	5
CELEBRATE	China	28	18 Oct 97	2
Vocals by Eddi Reader.				
DOG TRAIN	China	24	20 Dec 97	5
TOO REAL	China	46	14 Mar 98	1
BOZOS	China	44	24 Oct 98	2
ONE WAY [RR]	China	33	6 Feb 99	2
ALBUMS:	**HITS 6**			**WEEKS 79**
LEVELLING THE LAND	China	14	19 Oct 91	22
LEVELLING THE LAND [RE]	China	40	24 Jul 93	8
Re-released.				
LEVELLERS	China	2	4 Sep 93	14
ZEITGEIST	China	1	9 Sep 95	14
BEST LIVE - HEADLIGHTS WHITE LINES BLACK TAR RIVERS: BEST LIVE	China	13	31 Aug 96	4
Live recordings from their European tour from Sep to Dec 95.				
MOUTH TO MOUTH	China	5	6 Sep 97	6
ONE WAY OF LIFE - THE BEST OF THE LEVELLERS	China	15	7 Nov 98	11

LEVERT US

SINGLES:	**HITS 1**			**WEEKS 10**
CASANOVA	Atlantic	9	22 Aug 87	10
ALBUMS:	**HITS 1**			**WEEKS 1**
THE BIG THROWDOWN	Atlantic	86	29 Aug 87	1

LEVERT SWEAT GILL US

SINGLES:	**HITS 3**			**WEEKS 7**
MY BODY	East West America	21	14 Mar 98	3
CURIOUS	East West America	23	6 Jun 98	2
Above hit: LEVERT SWEAT GILL featuring L.L. COOL J., Busta RHYMES and MC LYTE.				
DOOR #1	East West America	45	12 Sep 98	2

Hank LEVINE US

SINGLES:	**HITS 1**			**WEEKS 4**
IMAGE	His Master's Voice	45	23 Dec 61	4

James LEVINE - See 3 TENORS: Jose CARRERAS, Placido DOMINGO, Luciano PAVAROTTI

LEVITATION
UK

ALBUMS:	HITS 1		WEEKS 1	
NEED FOR NOT	Rough Trade	45	16 May 92	1

LEVITICUS
UK

SINGLES:	HITS 1		WEEKS 1	
BURIAL	ffrr	66	25 Mar 95	1

Song based on Madamoiselle by Foxy.

Barrington LEVY
Jamaica

(See also Rebel MC.)

SINGLES:	HITS 2		WEEKS 5	
HERE I COME	London	41	2 Feb 85	4
WORK	MCA	65	24 Sep 94	1

Jona LEWIE
UK

(See also Terry Dactyl and the Dinosaurs.)

SINGLES:	HITS 2		WEEKS 20	
YOU'LL ALWAYS FIND ME IN THE KITCHEN AT PARTIES	Stiff	16	10 May 80	9
Some copies have title as Kitchen At Parties.				
STOP THE CAVALRY	Stiff	3	29 Nov 80	11

C.J. LEWIS
UK

SINGLES:	HITS 5		WEEKS 32	
SWEETS FOR MY SWEET	Black Market	3	23 Apr 94	13
EVERYTHING IS ALRIGHT (UPTIGHT)	Black Market	10	23 Jul 94	7
BEST OF MY LOVE	Black Market	13	8 Oct 94	6
DOLLARS	Black Market	34	17 Dec 94	4
R TO THE A	Black Market	34	9 Sep 95	2
ALBUMS:	HITS 1		WEEKS 2	
DOLLARS	Black Market	44	3 Sep 94	2

Danny J LEWIS
UK

SINGLES:	HITS 1		WEEKS 2	
SPEND THE NIGHT	Locked On	29	20 Jun 98	2

Darlene LEWIS - See LOVELAND featuring the voice of Rachel McFARLANE

Dee LEWIS
UK

(See also Mondo Kane featuring Dee Lewis and Coral Gordon, guest star Georgie Fame.)

SINGLES:	HITS 1		WEEKS 5	
THE BEST OF MY LOVE	Mercury	47	18 Jun 88	5

Donna LEWIS
UK

SINGLES:	HITS 2		WEEKS 16	
I LOVE YOU ALWAYS FOREVER	Atlantic	5	7 Sep 96	14
Inspired by the H.E. Bates novel 'Love For Lydia'.				
WITHOUT LOVE	Atlantic	39	8 Feb 97	2
ALBUMS:	HITS 1		WEEKS 1	
NOW IN A MINUTE	Atlantic	52	12 Oct 96	1

Gary LEWIS and the PLAYBOYS
US

SINGLES:	HITS 1		WEEKS 7	
MY HEART'S SYMPHONY	United Artists	36	8 Feb 75	7

Originally released in 1966, reaching No. 13 in the US.

Georgia LEWIS - See TECHNICIAN 2 featuring Georgia LEWIS

Huey LEWIS and the NEWS
US

SINGLES:	HITS 8		WEEKS 66	
IF THIS IS IT	Chrysalis	39	27 Oct 84	6
POWER OF LOVE	Chrysalis	11	31 Aug 85	10
From the film 'Back To The Future'.				
THE HEART AND SOUL [EP]	Chrysalis	61	23 Nov 85	4
Lead track: Heart And Soul.				
THE POWER OF LOVE [RE] + [RI] / DO YOU BELIEVE IN LOVE	Chrysalis	9	8 Feb 86	12
Do You Believe In Love listed from 15 Feb 86 on the re-issued release.				
THE HEART OF ROCK AND ROLL	Chrysalis	49	10 May 86	3
Original release reached No. 78 in 1984, it was also a track on The Heart And Soul EP.				
STUCK WITH YOU	Chrysalis	12	23 Aug 86	12
HIP TO BE SQUARE	Chrysalis	41	6 Dec 86	8
SIMPLE AS THAT	Chrysalis	47	21 Mar 87	5

PERFECT WORLD	Chrysalis	48	16 Jul 88	6
ALBUMS:	**HITS 5**		**WEEKS 94**	
SPORTS	Chrysalis	23	14 Sep 85	24
FORE!	Chrysalis	8	20 Sep 86	52
SMALL WORLD	Chrysalis	12	6 Aug 88	8
HARD AT PLAY	Chrysalis	39	18 May 91	2
THE HEART OF ROCK AND ROLL - BEST OF HUEY LEWIS AND THE NEWS	Chrysalis	23	21 Nov 92	8

Jerry LEWIS
US

SINGLES:	**HITS 1**		**WEEKS 8**	
ROCK-A-BYE YOUR BABY WITH A DIXIE MELODY	Brunswick	12	9 Feb 57	7
Originally recorded by Al Jolson in 1918.				
ROCK-A-BYE YOUR BABY WITH A DIXIE MELODY [RE]	Brunswick	22	6 Apr 57	1

Jerry Lee LEWIS
US

SINGLES:	**HITS 10**		**WEEKS 68**	
WHOLE LOTTA SHAKIN' GOIN' ON	London	8	28 Sep 57	10
Originally recorded by Big Maybelle in 1955.				
GREAT BALLS OF FIRE	London	1	21 Dec 57	12
From the film 'Jamboree'.				
WHOLE LOTTA SHAKIN' GOIN' ON [RE]	London	26	28 Dec 57	1
BREATHLESS	London	8	12 Apr 58	7
HIGH SCHOOL CONFIDENTIAL	London	12	24 Jan 59	6
From the film of the same name.				
LOVIN' UP A STORM	London	28	2 May 59	1
BABY BABY BYE BYE	London	47	11 Jun 60	1
WHAT'D I SAY	London	10	6 May 61	12
Originally recorded by Ray Charles.				
WHAT'D I SAY [RE]	London	49	5 Aug 61	2
SWEET LITTLE SIXTEEN	London	38	8 Sep 62	5
GOOD GOLLY MISS MOLLY	London	31	16 Mar 63	6
CHANTILLY LACE	Mercury	33	6 May 72	5
EPS:	**HITS 2**		**WEEKS 11**	
JERRY LEE LEWIS - NO. 4	London	13	6 Oct 62	5
JERRY LEE LEWIS - NO. 5	London	14	27 Oct 62	6
ALBUMS:	**HITS 1**		**WEEKS 6**	
JERRY LEE LEWIS VOLUME 2	London	14	2 Jun 62	6

Linda LEWIS
UK

SINGLES:	**HITS 4**		**WEEKS 30**	
ROCK A DOODLE DOO	Raft	15	2 Jun 73	11
IT'S IN HIS KISS	Arista	6	12 Jul 75	8
BABY I'M YOURS	Arista	33	17 Apr 76	6
I'D BE SURPRISINGLY GOOD FOR YOU	Ariola	40	2 Jun 79	5
ALBUMS:	**HITS 1**		**WEEKS 4**	
NOT A LITTLE GIRL ANYMORE	Arista	40	9 Aug 75	4

Ramsey LEWIS TRIO
US

SINGLES:	**HITS 1**		**WEEKS 8**	
WADE IN THE WATER	Chess	31	15 Apr 72	8
Above hit: Ramsey LEWIS.				
ALBUMS:	**HITS 1**		**WEEKS 4**	
HANG ON RAMSEY	Chess	20	21 May 66	4

Shirley LEWIS - See Arthur BAKER and the BACKBEAT DISCIPLES

John LEYTON
UK

SINGLES:	**HITS 9**		**WEEKS 70**	
JOHNNY REMEMBER ME	Top Rank	1	5 Aug 61	15
Female backing vocals by Lissa Gray.				
WILD WIND	Top Rank	2	7 Oct 61	10
SON THIS IS SHE	His Master's Voice	15	30 Dec 61	10
LONE RIDER	His Master's Voice	40	17 Mar 62	5
Originally recorded by the Flee-Rekkers.				
LONELY CITY	His Master's Voice	14	5 May 62	11
DOWN THE RIVER NILE	His Master's Voice	42	25 Aug 62	3
CUPBOARD LOVE	His Master's Voice	22	23 Feb 63	12
I'LL CUT YOUR TAIL OFF	His Master's Voice	50	20 Jul 63	1
I'LL CUT YOUR TAIL OFF [RE]	His Master's Voice	36	10 Aug 63	2
MAKE LOVE TO ME	His Master's Voice	49	22 Feb 64	1
EPS:	**HITS 1**		**WEEKS 13**	
JOHN LEYTON	Top Rank	11	10 Mar 62	13

LEYTON BUZZARDS
UK

SINGLES:	**HITS 1**		**WEEKS 5**	
SATURDAY NIGHT (BENEATH THE PLASTIC PALM TREES)	*Chrysalis*	53	*3 Mar 79*	5

LFO
UK

SINGLES:	**HITS 3**		**WEEKS 15**	
LFO	*Warp*	12	*14 Jul 90*	10
WE ARE BACK / NURTURE	*Warp*	47	*6 Jul 91*	3
WHAT IS HOUSE [EP]	*Warp*	62	*1 Feb 92*	2
Lead track: Tan Ta Ra.				
ALBUMS:	**HITS 2**		**WEEKS 3**	
FREQUENCIES	*Warp*	42	*3 Aug 91*	2
ADVANCE	*Warp*	44	*10 Feb 96*	1

LIBERACE
US

SINGLES:	**HITS 2**		**WEEKS 2**	
UNCHAINED MELODY	*Philips*	20	*18 Jun 55*	1
From the film 'Unchained'.				
I DON'T CARE AS LONG AS YOU CARE FOR ME	*Columbia*	28	*20 Oct 56*	1

LIBERATION
UK

SINGLES:	**HITS 1**		**WEEKS 3**	
LIBERATION	*ZYX*	28	*24 Oct 92*	3

LIBIDO
Norway

SINGLES:	**HITS 1**		**WEEKS 1**	
OVERTHROWN	*Fire*	53	*31 Jan 98*	1

LIBRA presents TAYLOR
UK

SINGLES:	**HITS 1**		**WEEKS 1**	
ANOMALY – CALLING YOUR NAME	*Platipus*	71	*26 Oct 96*	1
Originally released in 1995.				

LICK THE TINS
UK

SINGLES:	**HITS 1**		**WEEKS 8**	
CAN'T HELP FALLING IN LOVE	*Sedition*	42	*29 Mar 86*	8

Ben LIEBRAND
Holland

SINGLES:	**HITS 1**		**WEEKS 2**	
PULS(T)AR	*Epic*	68	*9 Jun 90*	2

LIEUTENANT PIGEON
UK

SINGLES:	**HITS 2**		**WEEKS 29**	
MOULDY OLD DOUGH	*Decca*	1	*16 Sep 72*	19
DESPERATE DAN	*Decca*	17	*16 Dec 72*	10

LIGHT OF THE WORLD
UK

SINGLES:	**HITS 6**		**WEEKS 25**	
SWINGIN'	*Ensign*	45	*14 Apr 79*	5
MIDNIGHT GROOVIN'	*Ensign*	72	*14 Jul 79*	1
LONDON TOWN	*Ensign*	41	*18 Oct 80*	5
I SHOT THE SHERIFF	*Ensign*	40	*17 Jan 81*	5
I'M SO HAPPY / TIME	*Mercury*	35	*28 Mar 81*	6
RIDE THE LOVE TRAIN	*EMI*	49	*21 Nov 81*	3
ALBUMS:	**HITS 1**		**WEEKS 1**	
ROUND TRIP	*Ensign*	73	*24 Jan 81*	1

LIGHTER SHADE OF BROWN
US

SINGLES:	**HITS 1**		**WEEKS 3**	
HEY D.J.	*Mercury*	33	*9 Jul 94*	3
Samples the World Famous Supreme Team's Hey DJ.				

Gordon LIGHTFOOT
Canada

SINGLES:	**HITS 4**		**WEEKS 26**	
IF YOU COULD READ MY MIND	*Reprise*	30	*19 Jun 71*	9
SUNDOWN	*Reprise*	33	*3 Aug 74*	7
THE WRECK OF THE EDMUND FITZGERALD	*Reprise*	40	*15 Jan 77*	4
DAYLIGHT KATY	*Warner Brothers*	41	*16 Sep 78*	6
ALBUMS:	**HITS 2**		**WEEKS 2**	
DON QUIXOTE	*Reprise*	44	*20 May 72*	1
SUNDOWN	*Reprise*	45	*17 Aug 74*	1

Terry LIGHTFOOT'S NEW ORLEANS JAZZMEN UK

SINGLES:		HITS 3			WEEKS 17
TRUE LOVE	Columbia	33	9 Sep 61		4
KING KONG	Columbia	29	25 Nov 61		12
TAVERN IN THE TOWN	Columbia	49	5 May 62		1
EPS:		HITS 1			WEEKS 1
CLARINET JAMBOREE	Columbia	19	4 Mar 61		1

Above hit: Mr. Acker BILK and Terry LIGHTFOOT.

LIGHTHOUSE FAMILY UK

SINGLES:		HITS 9			WEEKS 76
LIFTED	Wild Card	61	27 May 95		2
OCEAN DRIVE	Wild Card	34	14 Oct 95		3
From the film 'Jack And Sarah'.					
LIFTED [RI]	Wild Card	4	10 Feb 96		10
OCEAN DRIVE [RI]	Wild Card	11	1 Jun 96		8
GOODBYE HEARTBREAK	Wild Card	14	21 Sep 96		6
Backing vocals by Nu Colours.					
LOVING EVERY MINUTE	Wild Card	20	21 Dec 96		7
RAINCLOUD	Wild Card	6	11 Oct 97		7
HIGH	Wild Card	4	10 Jan 98		14
LOST IN SPACE	Wild Card	6	27 Jun 98		8
QUESTION OF FAITH	Wild Card	21	10 Oct 98		5
POSTCARDS FROM HEAVEN	Wild Card	24	9 Jan 99		6
ALBUMS:		HITS 2			WEEKS 225
OCEAN DRIVE	Wild Card	74	18 Nov 95		1
OCEAN DRIVE [RE]	Wild Card	3	16 Mar 96		153
Peak position reached on 8 Mar 97.					
POSTCARDS FROM HEAVEN	Wild Card	2	1 Nov 97		71

LIGHTNING SEEDS UK

SINGLES:		HITS 15			WEEKS 96
PURE	Ghetto	16	22 Jul 89		8
THE LIFE OF RILEY	Virgin	28	14 Mar 92		6
SENSE	Virgin	31	30 May 92		5
LUCKY YOU	Epic	43	20 Aug 94		2
CHANGE	Epic	13	14 Jan 95		6
MARVELLOUS	Epic	24	15 Apr 95		5
PERFECT	Epic	18	22 Jul 95		5
LUCKY YOU [RI]	Epic	15	21 Oct 95		6
READY OR NOT	Epic	20	9 Mar 96		4
THREE LIONS (THE OFFICIAL SONG OF THE ENGLAND FOOTBALL TEAM)	Epic	1	1 Jun 96		15
Official anthem for England's football team in Euro 1996.					
Above hit: BADDIEL and SKINNER and LIGHTNING SEEDS.					
WHAT IF …	Epic	14	2 Nov 96		3
WHAT IF … [RE]	Epic	64	11 Jan 97		1
SUGAR COATED ICEBERG	Epic	12	18 Jan 97		4
Co written by Stephen Jones (Babybird).					
YOU SHOWED ME	Epic	8	26 Apr 97		5
Originally recorded by the Byrds in 1964. The Turtles' version reached No. 6 in the US in 1969.					
WHAT YOU SAY	Epic	41	13 Dec 97		5
3 LIONS '98 [RR]	Epic	1	20 Jun 98		13
Re-recorded for the 1998 World Cup in France.					
Above hit: BADDIEL, SKINNER and the LIGHTNING SEEDS.					
LIFE'S TOO SHORT	Epic	27	27 Nov 99		3
ALBUMS:		HITS 7			WEEKS 139
CLOUDCUCKOOLAND	Ghetto	50	10 Feb 90		2
SENSE	Virgin	53	18 Apr 92		1
JOLLIFICATION	Epic	30	17 Sep 94		7
Chart position reached in 1995.					
JOLLIFICATION [RE]	Epic	12	15 Jul 95		51
PURE LIGHTNING SEEDS	Virgin	27	18 May 96		9
DIZZY HEIGHTS	Epic	11	23 Nov 96		26
LIKE YOU DO … THE BEST OF LIGHTNING SEEDS	Epic	5	22 Nov 97		41
TILT	Epic	46	4 Dec 99		2

LIL' KIM US

(See also Missy "Misdemeanor" Elliott; Puff Daddy.)

SINGLES:		HITS 3			WEEKS 11
NO TIME	Atlantic	45	26 Apr 97		1
Samples Just Take Me As I Am by Lyn Collins.					
Above hit: LIL' KIM featuring PUFF DADDY.					
CRUSH ON YOU	Atlantic	36	5 Jul 97		2
Samples Jeff Lorber's Rain Dance.					

NOT TONIGHT	Atlantic	11	16 Aug 97	5

From the film 'Nothing To Lose'; samples Kool And The Gang's Ladies Night.
Above hit: LIL' KIM featuring DA BRAT, LEFT EYE, Missy "Misdemeanor" ELLIOTT and Angie MARTINEZ.

CRUSH ON YOU [RE]	Atlantic	23	25 Oct 97	3

LIL' LOUIS

US

(See also Black Magic.)

SINGLES:	HITS 3			WEEKS 18
FRENCH KISS	ffrr	2	29 Jul 89	11
I CALLED U	ffrr	16	13 Jan 90	6
SAVED MY LIFE	ffrr	74	26 Sep 92	1

Above 2: LIL' LOUIS and the WORLD.

ALBUMS:	HITS 1			WEEKS 5
FRENCH KISSES	ffrr	35	26 Aug 89	5

LIL' MISS MAX - See BLUE ADONIS featuring LIL' MISS MAX

LIL' MO featuring Missy "Misdemeanor" ELLIOTT

US

(See also Missy "Misdemeanor" Elliott.)

SINGLES:	HITS 1			WEEKS 1
5 MINUTES	East West America	72	21 Nov 98	1

From the film 'Why Do Fools Fall In Love'.

LIL MO' YIN YANG

US

SINGLES:	HITS 1			WEEKS 2
REACH	Multiply	28	9 Mar 96	2

LILY - See MAXIMA featuring LILY

LILYS

US

SINGLES:	HITS 1			WEEKS 4
A NANNY IN MANHATTAN	Che	16	21 Feb 98	4

Featured in the Levi's Jeans TV commercial.

LIMAHL

UK

SINGLES:	HITS 3			WEEKS 25
ONLY FOR LOVE	EMI	16	5 Nov 83	7
ONLY FOR LOVE [RE]	EMI	75	7 Jan 84	1
TOO MUCH TROUBLE	EMI	64	2 Jun 84	3
THE NEVER ENDING STORY	EMI	4	13 Oct 84	14

From the film of the same name. Duet with Beth Anderson.

ALBUMS:	HITS 1			WEEKS 3
DON'T SUPPOSE	EMI	63	1 Dec 84	3

Alison LIMERICK

UK

SINGLES:	HITS 9			WEEKS 39
WHERE LOVE LIVES (COME ON IN)	Arista	27	30 Mar 91	8

Original release reached No. 87 in 1990.

COME BACK (FOR REAL LOVE)	Arista	53	12 Oct 91	2
MAGIC'S BACK (THEME FROM 'THE GHOSTS OF OXFORD STREET')	RCA	42	21 Dec 91	4

Theme from the Channel 4 TV programme.
Above hit: Malcolm McLAREN featuring Alison LIMERICK.

MAKE IT ON MY OWN	Arista	16	29 Feb 92	6
GETTIN' IT RIGHT	Arista	57	18 Jul 92	2
HEAR MY CALL	Arista	73	28 Nov 92	1
TIME OF OUR LIVES	Arista	36	8 Jan 94	4
LOVE COME DOWN	Arista	36	19 Mar 94	2
LOVE WILL KEEP US TOGETHER	Acid Jazz	63	25 Feb 95	1

Above hit: James TAYLOR QUARTET featuring Alison LIMERICK.

WHERE LOVE LIVES [RM]	Arista	9	6 Jul 96	6
MAKE IT ON MY OWN [RM]	Arista	30	14 Sep 96	2

Above 2 remixed by Dancing Divaz.

PUT YOUR FAITH IN ME	MBA	42	23 Aug 97	1

ALBUMS:	HITS 1			WEEKS 2
AND STILL I RISE	Arista	53	4 Apr 92	2

LIMIT

Holland

SINGLES:	HITS 1			WEEKS 8
SAY YEAH	Portrait	17	5 Jan 85	8

LIMMIE and FAMILY COOKIN'
US

SINGLES:		HITS 3		WEEKS 28	
YOU CAN DO MAGIC	Avco	3	21 Jul 73	13
DREAMBOAT	Avco	31	20 Oct 73	5
A WALKIN' MIRACLE	Avco	6	6 Apr 74	10
Original by the Essex reached No. 12 in the US in 1963.					

LIMP BIZKIT
US

ALBUMS:		HITS 1		WEEKS 2	
SIGNIFICANT OTHER	Interscope	26	3 Jul 99	2

Bob LIND
US

SINGLES:		HITS 2		WEEKS 10	
ELUSIVE BUTTERFLY	Fontana	5	12 Mar 66	9
REMEMBER THE RAIN	Fontana	46	28 May 66	1

LINDA and the FUNKY BOYS - See Linda CARR

LINDISFARNE
UK

SINGLES:		HITS 6		WEEKS 55	
MEET ME ON THE CORNER	Charisma	5	26 Feb 72	11
LADY ELEANOR	Charisma	3	13 May 72	11
ALL FALL DOWN	Charisma	34	23 Sep 72	5
RUN FOR HOME	Mercury	10	3 Jun 78	15
JUKE BOX GYPSY	Mercury	56	7 Oct 78	4
FOG ON THE TYNE (REVISITED)	Best	2	10 Nov 90	9
Above hit: GAZZA and LINDISFARNE.					

ALBUMS:		HITS 8		WEEKS 118	
FOG ON THE TYNE	Charisma	1	30 Oct 71	56
NICELY OUT OF TUNE	Charisma	8	15 Jan 72	30
DINGLY DELL	Charisma	95	30 Sep 72	10
LINDISFARNE LIVE	Charisma	25	11 Aug 73	6
FINEST HOUR	Charisma	55	18 Oct 75	1
Compilation.					
BACK AND FOURTH	Mercury	22	24 Jun 78	11
MAGIC IN THE AIR	Mercury	71	9 Dec 78	1
SLEEPLESS NIGHTS	LMP	59	23 Oct 82	3

Mort LINDSEY and his Orchestra - See Pat BOONE

LINER
UK

SINGLES:		HITS 2		WEEKS 6	
KEEP REACHING OUT FOR LOVE	Atlantic	49	10 Mar 79	3
YOU AND ME	Atlantic	44	26 May 79	3

Laurie LINGO and the DIPSTICKS
UK

SINGLES:		HITS 1		WEEKS 7	
CONVOY G.B.	State	4	17 Apr 76	7
Parody of C.W. McCall's Convoy.					

LINK
US

SINGLES:		HITS 1		WEEKS 1	
WHATCHA GONNA DO?	Epic	48	7 Nov 98	1

LINOLEUM
UK

SINGLES:		HITS 1		WEEKS 1	
MARQUIS	Lino Vinyl	73	12 Jul 97	1

LINX
UK

SINGLES:		HITS 6		WEEKS 45	
YOU'RE LYING	Chrysalis	15	20 Sep 80	10
INTUITION	Chrysalis	7	7 Mar 81	11
THROW AWAY THE KEY	Chrysalis	21	13 Jun 81	9
SO THIS IS ROMANCE	Chrysalis	15	5 Sep 81	9
CAN'T HELP MYSELF	Chrysalis	55	21 Nov 81	3
PLAYTHING	Chrysalis	48	10 Jul 82	3

ALBUMS:		HITS 2		WEEKS 23	
INTUITION	Chrysalis	8	28 Mar 81	19
GO AHEAD	Chrysalis	35	31 Oct 81	4

LIONROCK
UK

SINGLES:		HITS 8		WEEKS 14	
LIONROCK	Deconstruction	63	5 Dec 92	1

PACKET OF PEACE	*Deconstruction*	32	*8 May 93*	3
CARNIVAL [EP]	*Arista*	34	*23 Oct 93*	2
Lead track: Are You Willing To Testify?				
TRIPWIRE	*Deconstruction*	44	*27 Aug 94*	1
STRAIGHT AT YER HEAD	*Deconstruction*	33	*6 Apr 96*	2
FIRE UP THE SHOESAW	*Deconstruction*	43	*27 Jul 96*	1
RUDE BOY ROCK	*Concrete*	20	*14 Mar 98*	3
SCATTER & SWING	*Concrete*	54	*30 May 98*	1
ALBUMS:	**HITS 2**		**WEEKS 3**	
AN INSTINCT FOR DETECTION	*Deconstruction*	30	*20 Apr 96*	2
CITY DELIRIOUS	*Concrete*	73	*28 Mar 98*	1

LIPPS INC.   US

SINGLES:	**HITS 1**		**WEEKS 13**	
FUNKYTOWN	*Casablanca*	2	*17 May 80*	13

LIQUID   UK

SINGLES:	**HITS 6**		**WEEKS 19**	
SWEET HARMONY [EP]	*XL Recordings*	15	*21 Mar 92*	6
Lead track: Sweet Harmony.				
THE FUTURE MUSIC [EP]	*XL Recordings*	59	*5 Sep 92*	2
Lead track: Liquid Is Liquid.				
TIME TO GET UP	*XL Recordings*	46	*20 Mar 93*	2
SWEET HARMONY [RM] / ONE LOVE FAMILY	*XL Recordings*	14	*8 Jul 95*	6
Remixed by Liquid.				
CLOSER	*XL Recordings*	47	*21 Oct 95*	2
STRONG	*Higher Ground*	59	*25 Jul 98*	1

LIQUID CHILD   Germany

SINGLES:	**HITS 1**		**WEEKS 2**	
DIVING FACES	*Essential Recordings*	25	*23 Oct 99*	2
Original release on the Reef label reached No. 95 in 1998.				

LIQUID GOLD   UK

SINGLES:	**HITS 6**		**WEEKS 46**	
ANYWAY YOU DO IT	*Creole*	41	*2 Dec 78*	7
DANCE YOURSELF DIZZY	*Polo*	2	*23 Feb 80*	14
SUBSTITUTE	*Polo*	8	*31 May 80*	9
THE NIGHT, THE WINE AND THE ROSES	*Polo*	32	*1 Nov 80*	7
DON'T PANIC	*Polo*	42	*28 Mar 81*	5
WHERE DID WE GO WRONG	*Polo*	56	*21 Aug 82*	4
ALBUMS:	**HITS 1**		**WEEKS 3**	
LIQUID GOLD	*Polo*	34	*16 Aug 80*	3

LIQUID OXYGEN   UK

SINGLES:	**HITS 1**		**WEEKS 2**	
THE PLANET DANCE (MOVE YA BODY)	*Champion*	56	*28 Apr 90*	2

LISA LISA and CULT JAM   US

SINGLES:	**HITS 4**		**WEEKS 32**	
I WONDER IF I TAKE YOU HOME	*CBS*	53	*4 May 85*	6
Above hit: LISA LISA and CULT JAM with FULL FORCE.				
I WONDER IF I TAKE YOU HOME [RE]	*CBS*	12	*3 Aug 85*	11
LOST IN EMOTION	*CBS*	58	*31 Oct 87*	4
LET THE BEAT HIT 'EM	*Columbia*	17	*13 Jul 91*	6
LET THE BEAT HIT 'EM PART 2 [RM]	*Columbia*	49	*24 Aug 91*	2
SKIP TO MY LU	*Chrysalis*	34	*26 Mar 94*	3
Above hit: LISA LISA.				
ALBUMS:	**HITS 1**		**WEEKS 1**	
LISA LISA AND CULT JAM WITH FULL FORCE	*CBS*	96	*21 Sep 85*	1
Above hit: LISA LISA and CULT JAM with FULL FORCE.				

LISA MARIE EXPERIENCE   UK

SINGLES:	**HITS 2**		**WEEKS 15**	
KEEP ON JUMPIN'	*ffrr*	7	*27 Apr 96*	10
Originally recorded by Musique in 1978.				
KEEP ON JUMPIN' [RE]	*ffrr*	61	*20 Jul 96*	3
DO THAT TO ME	*Positiva*	33	*10 Aug 96*	2
Originally released in 1995.				

LIT   US

SINGLES:	**HITS 2**		**WEEKS 5**	
MY OWN WORST ENEMY	*RCA*	16	*26 Jun 99*	4

ZIP-LOCK	RCA	60	25 Sep 99	1
ALBUMS:	**HITS 1**			**WEEKS 1**
A PLACE IN THE SUN	RCA	55	10 Jul 99	1

LITHIUM and Sonya MADAN — US

SINGLES:	**HITS 1**			**WEEKS 2**
RIDE A ROCKET	ffrr	40	1 Mar 97	2

De Etta LITTLE and Nelson PIGFORD — US

SINGLES:	**HITS 1**			**WEEKS 5**
YOU TAKE MY HEART AWAY	United Artists	35	13 Aug 77	5
From the film 'Rocky'.				

LITTLE ANGELS — UK

SINGLES:	**HITS 13**			**WEEKS 41**
BIG BAD [EP]	Polydor	74	4 Mar 89	1
Lead Track: She's A Little Angel.				
KICKING UP DUST	Polydor	46	24 Feb 90	4
RADICAL YOUR LOVER	Polydor	34	12 May 90	4
Above hit: LITTLE ANGELS (featuring the BIG BAD HORNS).				
SHE'S A LITTLE ANGEL	Polydor	21	4 Aug 90	3
BONEYARD	Polydor	33	2 Feb 91	4
Sleeve has title as We're All Going Down To The Boneyard.				
PRODUCT OF THE WORKING CLASS	Polydor	40	30 Mar 91	2
YOUNG GODS	Polydor	34	1 Jun 91	2
I AIN'T GONNA CRY	Polydor	26	20 Jul 91	3
TOO MUCH TOO YOUNG	Polydor	22	7 Nov 92	3
WOMANKIND	Polydor	12	9 Jan 93	5
SOAPBOX	Polydor	33	24 Apr 93	4
SAIL AWAY	Polydor	45	25 Sep 93	3
TEN MILES HIGH	Polydor	18	9 Apr 94	3
ALBUMS:	**HITS 4**			**WEEKS 15**
YOUNG GODS	Polydor	17	2 Mar 91	6
JAM	Polydor	1	6 Feb 93	5
LITTLE OF THE PAST	Polydor	20	23 Apr 94	2
TOO POSH TO MOSH, TOO GOOD TO LAST!	Essential	18	2 Jul 94	2
Remixed/remastered version of their debut album from 1987.				

LITTLE ANTHONY and the IMPERIALS — US

SINGLES:	**HITS 2**			**WEEKS 13**
BETTER USE YOUR HEAD	United Artists	42	31 Jul 76	4
WHO'S GONNA LOVE ME	Power Exchange	17	24 Dec 77	9
Above hit: IMPERIALS.				

LITTLE BENNY and the MASTERS — US

SINGLES:	**HITS 1**			**WEEKS 7**
WHO COMES TO BOOGIE	BlueBird	33	2 Feb 85	7

LITTLE CAESAR — UK

SINGLES:	**HITS 1**			**WEEKS 3**
THE WHOLE OF THE MOON	A.1.	68	9 Jun 90	3

LITTLE EVA — US

(See also Big Dee Irwin.)

SINGLES:	**HITS 3**			**WEEKS 45**
THE LOCO-MOTION	London	2	8 Sep 62	17
Carole King on vocals and the Cookies on backing vocals.				
KEEP YOUR HANDS OFF MY BABY	London	30	5 Jan 63	5
LET'S TURKEY TROT	London	13	9 Mar 63	12
THE LOCO-MOTION [RE]	London	11	29 Jul 72	11

LITTLE FEAT — US

ALBUMS:	**HITS 5**			**WEEKS 19**
THE LAST RECORD ALBUM	Warner Brothers	36	6 Dec 75	3
TIME LOVES A HERO	Warner Brothers	8	21 May 77	11
WAITING FOR COLUMBUS	Warner Brothers	43	11 Mar 78	1
Live recordings.				
DOWN ON THE FARM	Warner Brothers	46	1 Dec 79	3
HOY=HOY!	Warner Brothers	76	8 Aug 81	1
Compilation.				

LITTLE LOUIE – See "Little" Louie VEGA and Marc ANTHONY

LITTLE RICHARD
US

SINGLES:		HITS 16			WEEKS 116
RIP IT UP	London	30	15 Dec 56	1
LONG TALL SALLY	London	3	9 Feb 57	16
TUTTI FRUTTI	London	29	23 Feb 57	1
Above 2 entries were separate sides of the same release, each had its own chart run.				
SHE'S GOT IT	London	15	9 Mar 57	7
THE GIRL CAN'T HELP IT	London	9	16 Mar 57	11
Above 2 entries were separate sides of the same release, each had its own chart run.				
SHE'S GOT IT [RE]	London	28	25 May 57	2
LUCILLE	London	10	29 Jun 57	9
JENNY JENNY	London	11	14 Sep 57	5
Above 7: LITTLE RICHARD and his Band.				
KEEP A KNOCKIN'	London	21	30 Nov 57	7
GOOD GOLLY MISS MOLLY	London	8	1 Mar 58	9
Originally recorded by the Valiants.				
OOH! MY SOUL	London	30	12 Jul 58	1
OOH! MY SOUL [RE]	London	22	26 Jul 58	3
BABY FACE	London	2	3 Jan 59	15
BY THE LIGHT OF THE SILVERY MOON	London	17	4 Apr 59	5
KANSAS CITY	London	26	6 Jun 59	5
Originally recorded by Little Willie Littlefield as 'KC Lovin'.				
HE GOT WHAT HE WANTED (BUT HE LOST WHAT HE HAD)	Mercury	38	13 Oct 62	4
Above hit: LITTLE RICHARD with Roger BLACKWELL and his Orchestra.				
BAMA LAMA BAMA LOO	London	20	6 Jun 64	7
GOOD GOLLY MISS MOLLY! [RR] / RIP IT UP! [RR]	Creole	37	2 Jul 77	4
GREAT GOSH A'MIGHTY (IT'S A MATTER OF TIME)	MCA	62	14 Jun 86	2
From the film 'Down And Out In Beverly Hills'.				
OPERATOR	WEA	67	25 Oct 86	2

LITTLE SHAWN - See VARIOUS ARTISTS (EPs) 'New York Undercover 4-Track EP'

LITTLE STEVEN
US

SINGLES:		HITS 1			WEEKS 3
BITTER FRUIT	Manhattan	66	23 May 87	3
ALBUMS:		HITS 2			WEEKS 4
MEN WITHOUT WOMEN	EMI America	73	6 Nov 82	2
Above hit: LITTLE STEVEN and the DISCIPLES Of SOUL.				
FREEDOM NO COMPROMISE	Manhattan	52	6 Jun 87	2

LITTLE T - See REBEL MC

LITTLE TONY and his BROTHERS
Italy

SINGLES:		HITS 1			WEEKS 3
TOO GOOD	Decca	19	16 Jan 60	3

LITTLE VILLAGE
UK/US

ALBUMS:		HITS 1			WEEKS 4
LITTLE VILLAGE	Reprise	23	29 Feb 92	4

LIVE
US

SINGLES:		HITS 6			WEEKS 12
I ALONE	Radioactive	48	18 Feb 95	4
SELLING THE DRAMA	Radioactive	30	1 Jul 95	2
ALL OVER YOU	Radioactive	48	7 Oct 95	1
LIGHTNING CRASHES	Radioactive	33	13 Jan 96	2
LAKINI'S JUICE	Radioactive	29	15 Mar 97	2
FREAKS	Radioactive	60	12 Jul 97	1
ALBUMS:		HITS 3			WEEKS 9
THROWING COPPER	Radioactive	37	15 Jul 95	6
SECRET SAMADHI	Radioactive	31	29 Mar 97	2
THE DISTANCE TO HERE	Radioactive	56	16 Oct 99	1

LIVE REPORT
UK

SINGLES:		HITS 1			WEEKS 1
WHY DO I ALWAYS GET IT WRONG	Brouhaha	73	20 May 89	1
UK's Eurovision entry in 1989, it came 2nd.				

LIVERPOOL CATHEDRALS' CHOIRS - See Ian TRACEY with the LIVERPOOL CATHEDRALS' CHOIRS

LIVERPOOL EXPRESS
UK

SINGLES:		HITS 4			WEEKS 26
YOU ARE MY LOVE	Warner Brothers	11	26 Jun 76	9
HOLD TIGHT	Warner Brothers	46	16 Oct 76	2

| EVERY MAN MUST HAVE A DREAM | *Warner Brothers* | 17 | *18 Dec 76* | 11 |
| DREAMIN' | *Warner Brothers* | 40 | *4 Jun 77* | 4 |

LIVERPOOL FOOTBALL CLUB   UK

SINGLES:		HITS 5		WEEKS 21
WE CAN DO IT [EP]	*State*	15	*28 May 77*	4
Lead track: We Can Do It.				
Above hit: LIVERPOOL FOOTBALL TEAM 76/77.				
LIVERPOOL (WE'RE NEVER GONNA STOP) / LIVERPOOL (ANTHEM)	*Mean*	54	*23 Apr 83*	4
SITTING ON THE TOP OF THE WORLD	*Columbia*	50	*17 May 86*	2
Above hit: LIVERPOOL FOOTBALL TEAM 1986.				
ANFIELD RAP (RED MACHINE IN FULL EFFECT)	*Virgin*	3	*14 May 88*	6
Above hit: LIVERPOOL F.C.				
PASS & MOVE (IT'S THE LIVERPOOL GROOVE)	*Telstar*	4	*18 May 96*	5
Above hit: LIVERPOOL FC and the BOOT ROOM BOYZ.				

LIVIN' JOY   US/Italy

SINGLES:		HITS 5		WEEKS 44
DREAMER	*Undiscovered*	18	*3 Sep 94*	6
DREAMER [RI]	*Undiscovered*	1	*13 May 95*	11
DON'T STOP MOVIN'	*Undiscovered*	5	*15 Jun 96*	14
FOLLOW THE RULES	*Undiscovered*	9	*2 Nov 96*	5
WHERE CAN I FIND LOVE	*Undiscovered*	12	*5 Apr 97*	4
DEEP IN YOU	*Undiscovered*	17	*23 Aug 97*	4
ALBUMS:		**HITS 1**		**WEEKS 2**
DON'T STOP MOVIN	*Undiscovered*	41	*16 Nov 96*	2

LIVING BASS - See Jay MONDI and the LIVING BASS.

LIVING COLOUR   US

SINGLES:		HITS 6		WEEKS 22
TYPE	*Epic*	75	*27 Oct 90*	1
LOVE REARS ITS UGLY HEAD	*Epic*	12	*2 Feb 91*	11
SOLACE OF YOU	*Epic*	33	*1 Jun 91*	5
CULT OF PERSONALITY	*Epic*	67	*26 Oct 91*	2
LEAVE IT ALONE	*Epic*	34	*20 Feb 93*	2
AUSLANDER	*Epic*	53	*17 Apr 93*	1
ALBUMS:		**HITS 2**		**WEEKS 22**
TIME'S UP	*Epic*	20	*15 Sep 90*	19
STAIN	*Epic*	19	*6 Mar 93*	3

LIVING IN A BOX   UK

SINGLES:		HITS 8		WEEKS 62
LIVING IN A BOX	*Cooltempo*	5	*4 Apr 87*	13
SCALES OF JUSTICE	*Chrysalis*	30	*13 Jun 87*	6
SO THE STORY GOES	*Chrysalis*	34	*26 Sep 87*	8
Uncredited vocals by Bobby Womack.				
LOVE IS THE ART	*Chrysalis*	45	*30 Jan 88*	4
BLOW THE HOUSE DOWN	*Chrysalis*	10	*18 Feb 89*	9
Features Brian May on guitar.				
GATECRASHING	*Chrysalis*	36	*10 Jun 89*	6
ROOM IN YOUR HEART	*Chrysalis*	5	*23 Sep 89*	13
DIFFERENT AIR	*Chrysalis*	64	*30 Dec 89*	1
DIFFERENT AIR [RE]	*Chrysalis*	57	*13 Jan 90*	2
ALBUMS:		**HITS 2**		**WEEKS 35**
LIVING IN A BOX	*Chrysalis*	25	*9 May 87*	19
GATECRASHING	*Chrysalis*	21	*8 Jul 89*	13
GATECRASHING [RE]	*Chrysalis*	59	*13 Jan 90*	3
Re-released.				

Dandy LIVINGSTONE   Jamaica

SINGLES:		HITS 2		WEEKS 19
SUZANNE BEWARE OF THE DEVIL	*Horse*	14	*2 Sep 72*	11
BIG CITY / THINK ABOUT THAT	*Horse*	26	*13 Jan 73*	8

LL COOL J   US

(See also B Real, Busta Rhymes, Coolio, LL Cool J and Method Man; Babyface; Levert Sweat Gill.)

SINGLES:		HITS 15		WEEKS 70
I'M BAD	*Def Jam*	71	*4 Jul 87*	1
I NEED LOVE	*Def Jam*	8	*12 Sep 87*	10
GO CUT CREATOR GO	*Def Jam*	66	*21 Nov 87*	2
GOING BACK TO CALI / JACK THE RIPPER	*Def Jam*	37	*13 Feb 88*	4
Jack The Ripper listed from 20 Feb 88.				
I'M THAT TYPE OF GUY	*Def Jam*	43	*10 Jun 89*	5

AROUND THE WAY GIRL / MAMA SAID KNOCK YOU OUT	*Def Jam*	41	*1 Dec 90*	4
AROUND THE WAY GIRL [RE]	*Def Jam*	36	*9 Mar 91*	4
HOW I'M COMIN'	*Def Jam*	37	*10 Apr 93*	2
Samples Bobby Byrd's Hot Pants – I'm Coming – I'm Coming – I'm Coming.				
HEY LOVER	*Def Jam*	17	*20 Jan 96*	4
Song based on Michael Jackson's 'Lady In My Life' and features Boyz II Men on backing vocals.				
Above hit: LL COOL J featuring BOYZ II MEN.				
DOIN IT	*Def Jam*	15	*1 Jun 96*	3
Guest vocalist is Leshaun and samples My Jamaican Guy by Grace Jones.				
Above hit: LL COOL J (Guest Vocalist LeSHAUN).				
LOUNGIN	*Def Jam*	7	*5 Oct 96*	8
Features Total and samples Al B. Sures' Night And Day.				
AIN'T NOBODY	*Geffen*	1	*8 Feb 97*	9
From the film 'Beavis And Butthead Do America'.				
PHENOMENON	*Def Jam*	9	*1 Nov 97*	5
Samples Bill Withers' Who Is He And What Is He To You.				
FATHER	*Def Jam*	10	*28 Mar 98*	5
Featuring the Kirk Franklin Gospel Choir. Samples George Michael's Father Figure.				
ZOOM	*Interscope*	15	*11 Jul 98*	3
From the film 'Bulworth'.				
Above hit: DR. DRE LL COOL J.				
INCREDIBLE	*Jive*	52	*5 Dec 98*	1
Samples James Brown's Sportin' Life.				
Above hit: Keith MURRAY featuring LL COOL J.				
ALBUMS:	**HITS 7**		**WEEKS 38**	
RADIO	*Def Jam*	71	*15 Feb 86*	1
BIGGER AND DEFFER	*Def Jam*	54	*13 Jun 87*	19
WALKING WITH A PANTHER	*Def Jam*	43	*8 Jul 89*	3
MAMA SAID KNOCK YOU OUT	*Def Jam*	49	*13 Oct 90*	2
14 SHOTS TO THE DOME	*Def Jam*	74	*17 Apr 93*	1
ALL WORLD	*Def Jam*	23	*16 Nov 96*	8
Compilation.				
PHENOMENON	*Def Jam*	37	*25 Oct 97*	4

LLAMA FARMERS   UK

SINGLES:	**HITS 2**		**WEEKS 2**	
BIG WHEELS	*Beggars Banquet*	67	*6 Feb 99*	1
GET THE KEYS AND GO	*Beggars Banquet*	74	*15 May 99*	1

Kelly LLORENNA   UK

SINGLES:	**HITS 3**		**WEEKS 7**	
SET YOU FREE	*All Around The World*	39	*7 May 94*	4
Original release reached No.81 in 1993.				
Above hit: N-TRANCE featuring Kelly LLORENNA.				
BRIGHTER DAY	*Pukka*	43	*24 Feb 96*	2
HEART OF GOLD	*Diverse*	55	*25 Jul 98*	1
Above hit: FORCE and STYLES featuring Kelly LLORENNA.				

Andrew LLOYD WEBBER   UK

ALBUMS:	**HITS 2**		**WEEKS 37**	
VARIATIONS	*MCA*	2	*11 Feb 78*	19
Above hit: Andrew LLOYD WEBBER featuring cellist Julian LLOYD WEBBER.				
ANDREW LLOYD WEBBER: REQUIEM	*His Master's Voice*	4	*23 Mar 85*	18
Above hit: Placido DOMINGO, Sarah BRIGHTMAN, Paul MILES-KINGSTON,				
WINCHESTER CATHEDRAL CHOIR and the ENGLISH CHAMBER				
ORCHESTRA conducted by Lorin MAAZEL.				

Julian LLOYD WEBBER   UK

(See also Andrew Lloyd Webber.)

ALBUMS:	**HITS 3**		**WEEKS 19**	
PIECES	*Polydor*	59	*14 Sep 85*	5
Above hit: Julian LLOYD WEBBER and the LONDON SYMPHONY ORCHESTRA.				
ELGAR CELLO CONCERTO	*Philips*	94	*21 Feb 87*	1
Above hit: Julian LLOYD WEBBER with the ROYAL PHILHARMONIC				
ORCHESTRA conducted by Sir Yehudi MENUHIN.				
LLOYD WEBBER PLAYS LLOYD WEBBER	*Philips*	15	*27 Oct 90*	13
Above hit: Julian LLOYD WEBBER with the ROYAL PHILHARMONIC				
ORCHESTRA.				

Don LLOYDIE - See SOUNDMAN and Don LLOYDIE with Elisabeth TROY

LNR   US

SINGLES:	**HITS 1**		**WEEKS 2**	
WORK IT TO THE BONE	*Kool Kat*	64	*3 Jun 89*	2

LO FIDELITY ALLSTARS
UK

SINGLES:	HITS 3			WEEKS 5
DISCO MACHINE GUN	Skint	50	11 Oct 97	1
VISION INCISION	Skint	30	2 May 98	2
BATTLEFLAG	Skint	36	28 Nov 98	2

Track started out as a remix of a single by Sub Pop act Pigeonhed.
Above hit: LO FIDELITY ALLSTARS featuring PIGEONHED.

ALBUMS:	HITS 1			WEEKS 4
HOW TO OPERATE WITH A BLOWN MIND	Skint	15	6 Jun 98	4

LO-PRO - See X-PRESS 2

LOBO
US

SINGLES:	HITS 2			WEEKS 25
ME AND YOU AND A DOG NAMED BOO	Philips	4	19 Jun 71	14
I'D LOVE YOU TO WANT ME	UK	5	8 Jun 74	11

LOBO
Holland

SINGLES:	HITS 1			WEEKS 11
THE CARIBBEAN DISCO SHOW [M]	Polydor	8	25 Jul 81	11

Medley of Calypso songs.

Tone LOC
US

SINGLES:	HITS 3			WEEKS 19
WILD THING / LOC'ED AFTER DARK	Fourth & Broadway	21	11 Feb 89	8
FUNKY COLD MEDINA / ON FIRE	Fourth & Broadway	13	20 May 89	9
I GOT IT GOIN' ON	Fourth & Broadway	55	5 Aug 89	2

Samples Tom Browne's Funkin' For Jamaica.

ALBUMS:	HITS 1			WEEKS 16
LOC'ED AFTER DARK	Fourth & Broadway	22	25 Mar 89	16

Josef LOCKE
Ireland

ALBUMS:	HITS 3			WEEKS 20
THE WORLD OF JOSEF LOCKE TODAY	Decca	29	28 Jun 69	1
HEAR MY SONG (THE BEST OF JOSEF LOCKE)	EMI	7	21 Mar 92	17
TAKE A PAIR OF SPARKLING EYES	EMI	41	27 Jun 92	2

Hank LOCKLIN
US

SINGLES:	HITS 4			WEEKS 41
PLEASE HELP ME, I'M FALLING	RCA	9	13 Aug 60	19
FROM HERE TO THERE TO YOU	RCA	44	17 Feb 62	3
WE'RE GONNA GO FISHIN'	RCA	18	17 Nov 62	11
I FEEL A CRY COMING ON	RCA Victor	29	7 May 66	8

LOCKSMITH
US

SINGLES:	HITS 1			WEEKS 6
UNLOCK THE FUNK	Arista	42	23 Aug 80	6

Malcolm LOCKYER - See Max BYGRAVES; Petula CLARK; Terry DENE with the Malcolm LOCKYER GROUP

LOCOMOTIVE
UK

SINGLES:	HITS 1			WEEKS 8
RUDI'S IN LOVE	Parlophone	25	19 Oct 68	8

John LODGE
UK

(See also Justin Hayward and John Lodge.)

ALBUMS:	HITS 1			WEEKS 2
NATURAL AVENUE	Decca	38	19 Feb 77	2

LODGER
UK

SINGLES:	HITS 1			WEEKS 2
I'M LEAVING	Island	40	2 May 98	2

Features Supergrass drummer Danny Goffey.

Lisa LOEB and NINE STORIES
US

SINGLES:	HITS 2			WEEKS 17
STAY (I MISSED YOU)	RCA	6	3 Sep 94	15

From the film 'Reality Bites'.

DO YOU SLEEP?	Geffen	45	16 Sep 95	2

ALBUMS:	HITS 1			WEEKS 2
TAILS	Geffen	39	7 Oct 95	2

Nils LOFGREN
US

SINGLES:	HITS 1		WEEKS 3	
SECRETS IN THE STREET	Towerbell	53	8 Jun 85	3
ALBUMS:	**HITS 8**		**WEEKS 30**	
CRY TOUGH	A&M	8	17 Apr 76	11
I CAME TO DANCE	A&M	30	26 Mar 77	4
NIGHT AFTER NIGHT	A&M	38	5 Nov 77	2
NIGHT FADES AWAY	Backstreet/MCA	50	26 Sep 81	3
A RHYTHM ROMANCE	A&M	100	1 May 82	1
Compilation.				
FLIP	Towerbell	36	6 Jul 85	7
CODE OF THE ROAD	Towerbell	86	5 Apr 86	1
SILVER LINING	Essential	61	27 Apr 91	1

Johnny LOGAN
Ireland

SINGLES:	HITS 3		WEEKS 24	
WHAT'S ANOTHER YEAR	Epic	1	3 May 80	8
Eurovision Song Contest winner in 1980.				
HOLD ME NOW	Epic	2	23 May 87	11
Eurovision Song Contest winner in 1987.				
I'M NOT IN LOVE	Epic	51	22 Aug 87	5
ALBUMS:	**HITS 1**		**WEEKS 1**	
HOLD ME NOW	CBS	83	22 Aug 87	1

Kenny LOGGINS
US

SINGLES:	HITS 2		WEEKS 21	
FOOTLOOSE	CBS	6	28 Apr 84	10
From the film of the same name.				
DANGER ZONE	CBS	45	1 Nov 86	11
From the film 'Top Gun'.				

LOLA
US

SINGLES:	HITS 1		WEEKS 1	
WAX THE VAN	Syncopate	65	28 Mar 87	1
Originally recorded by Arthur Russell.				

LOLLY
UK

SINGLES:	HITS 3		WEEKS 24	
VIVA LA RADIO	Polydor	6	10 Jul 99	9
MICKEY	Polydor	4	18 Sep 99	10
BIG BOYS DON'T CRY / ROCKIN' ROBIN	Polydor	10	4 Dec 99	5
ALBUMS:	**HITS 1**		**WEEKS 11**	
MY FIRST ALBUM	Polydor	21	2 Oct 99	11

Jackie LOMAX – See VARIOUS ARTISTS (EPs) 'The Apple EP'

Alain LOMBARD – See Mady MESPLE and Danielle MILLET, PARIS OPERA – COMIQUE ORCHESTRA conducted by Alain LOMBARD.

Julie LONDON
US

SINGLES:	HITS 1		WEEKS 3	
CRY ME A RIVER	London	22	6 Apr 57	3
From the film 'The Girl Can't Help It'.				

Laurie LONDON with Geoff LOVE his Orchestra and Chorus
UK

SINGLES:	HITS 1		WEEKS 12	
HE'S GOT THE WHOLE WORLD IN HIS HANDS	Parlophone	12	9 Nov 57	12

LONDON BOYS
UK

SINGLES:	HITS 6		WEEKS 46	
REQUIEM	WEA	59	10 Dec 88	6
REQUIEM [RE]	WEA	4	1 Apr 89	15
LONDON NIGHTS	WEA	2	1 Jul 89	9
HARLEM DESIRE	WEA	17	16 Sep 89	7
MY LOVE	WEA	46	2 Dec 89	6
CHAPEL OF LOVE	East West	75	16 Jun 90	1
FREEDOM	East West	54	19 Jan 91	2
ALBUMS:	**HITS 1**		**WEEKS 29**	
THE TWELVE COMMANDMENTS OF DANCE	WEA	2	29 Jul 89	29

LONDON COMMUNITY GOSPEL CHOIR – See Sal SOLO

LONDON PHILHARMONIC CHOIR
UK

ALBUMS:		HITS 3			WEEKS 20
THE MESSIAH	Pye Golden Guinea	10	3 Dec 60	7
Above hit: LONDON PHILHARMONIC CHOIR with the LONDON ORCHESTRA conducted by Walter SUSSKIND.				
SOUND OF GLORY	Arcade	10	13 Nov 76	10
PRAISE – 18 CHORAL MASTERPIECES	Pop & Arts	54	13 Apr 91	3
Above 2: LONDON PHILHARMONIC CHOIR with the NATIONAL PHILHARMONIC ORCHESTRA conducted by John ALDISS.				

LONDON PHILHARMONIC ORCHESTRA
UK

(See also Adiemus; Justin Hayward with Mike Batt and the London Philharmonic Orchestra; Maurice Jarre; Nigel Kennedy; Ennio Morricone; Cliff Richard.)

ALBUMS:		HITS 2			WEEKS 5
RAVEL'S BOLERO	London	15	23 Apr 60	4
VICTORY AT SEA	Pye Golden Guinea	12	8 Apr 61	1

LONDON SINFONIETTA – See Dawn UPSHAW (Soprano)/The LONDON SINFONIETTA/David ZINMAN (conductor)

LONDON STRING CHORALE
UK

SINGLES:		HITS 1			WEEKS 13
GALLOPING HOME	Polydor	49	15 Dec 73	3
Theme from the ITV children's series 'The Adventures Of Black Beauty'.				
GALLOPING HOME [RE]	Polydor	31	19 Jan 74	10

LONDON SYMPHONY ORCHESTRA
UK

(See also Shirley Bassey; Sarah Brightman; Michael Crawford; Placido Domingo; Roger Daltrey; James Horner; Aled Jones; Julian Lloyd Webber; Kimera with the London Symphony Orchestra; Spike Milligan: Rick Wakeman; John Williams.)

SINGLES:		HITS 1			WEEKS 5
THEME FROM SUPERMAN (MAIN TITLE)	Warner Brothers	32	6 Jan 79	5
Theme from the film.				
Above hit: Composed and conducted by John WILLIAMS Performed by the LONDON SYMPHONY ORCHESTRA.				

ALBUMS:		HITS 15			WEEKS 173
TOP TV THEMES	Studio Two	13	18 Mar 72	7
THE STRAUSS FAMILY [OST-TV]	Polydor	2	16 Dec 72	21
Above hit: LONDON SYMPHONY ORCHESTRA conducted by Cyril ORNADEL.				
MUSIC FROM 'EDWARD VII' [OST-TV]	Polydor	52	5 Jul 75	1
Above 2 from the ITV drama series.				
CLASSIC ROCK	K-Tel	3	8 Jul 78	39
CLASSIC ROCK – THE SECOND MOVEMENT	K-Tel	26	10 Feb 79	8
RHAPSODY IN BLACK	K-Tel	34	5 Jan 80	5
CLASSIC ROCK – ROCK CLASSICS	K-Tel	5	1 Aug 81	23
Above hit: LONDON SYMPHONY ORCHESTRA with the ROYAL CHORAL SOCIETY.				
THE BEST OF CLASSIC ROCK	K-Tel	35	27 Nov 82	11
CLASSIC ROCK – ROCK SYMPHONIES	K-Tel	40	27 Aug 83	9
THE POWER OF CLASSIC ROCK	Portrait	13	16 Nov 85	15
Above 3: LONDON SYMPHONY ORCHESTRA with the ROYAL CHORAL SOCIETY and the Roger SMITH CHORALE.				
CLASSIC ROCK COUNTDOWN	CBS	32	14 Nov 87	16
CLASSIC ROCK – THE LIVING YEARS	CBS	51	18 Nov 89	6
WIND OF CHANGE – CLASSIC ROCK	Columbia	24	18 Jan 92	8
Above hit: LONDON SYMPHONY ORCHESTRA and the ROYAL CHORAL SOCIETY.				
THE WORKS OF RICE AND LLOYD WEBBER	Vision	55	19 Nov 94	2
PAUL MCCARTNEY'S STANDING STONE	EMI Classics	34	25 Oct 97	2
A 'symphonic poem' commissioned by EMI to mark their centenary.				
Above hit: LONDON SYMPHONY ORCHESTRA conducted by Lawrence FOSTER.				

LONDON WELSH MALE VOICE CHOIR
UK

ALBUMS:		HITS 1			WEEKS 10
SONGS OF THE VALLEYS	K-Tel	61	5 Sep 81	10

LONDONBEAT
UK/US

(See also Liz Kershaw and Bruno Brookes.)

SINGLES:		HITS 9			WEEKS 45
9 A.M. (THE COMFORT ZONE)	AnXious	19	26 Nov 88	10
FALLING IN LOVE AGAIN	AnXious	60	18 Feb 89	2
I'VE BEEN THINKING ABOUT YOU	AnXious	2	1 Sep 90	13
A BETTER LOVE	AnXious	52	24 Nov 90	5
NO WOMAN NO CRY	AnXious	64	2 Mar 91	2
A BETTER LOVE [RI]	AnXious	23	20 Jul 91	6
YOU BRING ON THE SUN	AnXious	32	27 Jun 92	4

THAT'S HOW I FEEL ABOUT YOU	AnXious	69	24 Oct 92	1
I'M JUST YOUR PUPPET ON A . . . (STRING!)	AnXious	55	8 Apr 95	1

One of the contenders for Eurovision's A Song For Europe, it came 6th (out of 8).

COME BACK	AnXious	69	20 May 95	1
ALBUMS:	**HITS 1**		**WEEKS 6**	
IN THE BLOOD	Anxious	34	13 Oct 90	6

LONE JUSTICE — US

SINGLES:	**HITS 1**		**WEEKS 4**	
I FOUND LOVE	Geffen	45	7 Mar 87	4
ALBUMS:	**HITS 2**		**WEEKS 5**	
LONE JUSTICE	Geffen	49	6 Jul 85	2
SHELTER	Geffen	84	8 Nov 86	3

LONE STAR — UK

ALBUMS:	**HITS 2**		**WEEKS 7**	
LONE STAR	Epic	47	2 Oct 76	1
FIRING ON ALL SIX	CBS	36	17 Sep 77	6

Shorty LONG — US

SINGLES:	**HITS 1**		**WEEKS 7**	
HERE COMES THE JUDGE	Tamla Motown	30	20 Jul 68	7

LONG RYDERS — US

SINGLES:	**HITS 1**		**WEEKS 4**	
LOOKING FOR LEWIS AND CLARKE	Island	59	5 Oct 85	4
ALBUMS:	**HITS 1**		**WEEKS 1**	
STATE OF OUR UNION	Island	66	16 Nov 85	1

LONG AND THE SHORT — UK

SINGLES:	**HITS 2**		**WEEKS 8**	
THE LETTER	Decca	35	12 Sep 64	5
CHOC ICE	Decca	49	26 Dec 64	3

LONGPIGS — UK

SINGLES:	**HITS 7**		**WEEKS 17**	
SHE SAID	Mother	67	22 Jul 95	1
JESUS CHRIST	Mother	61	28 Oct 95	1
FAR	Mother	37	17 Feb 96	2
ON AND ON	Mother	16	13 Apr 96	3
SHE SAID [RI]	Mother	16	22 Jun 96	4
LOST MYSELF	Mother	22	5 Oct 96	3
BLUE SKIES	Mother	21	9 Oct 99	2
THE FRANK SONATA	Mother	57	18 Dec 99	1
ALBUMS:	**HITS 2**		**WEEKS 10**	
THE SUN IS OFTEN OUT	Mother	26	11 May 96	9
MOBILE HOME	Mother	33	23 Oct 99	1

Joe LONGTHORNE — UK

SINGLES:	**HITS 2**		**WEEKS 6**	
YOUNG GIRL	EMI	61	30 Apr 94	2
PASSING STRANGERS	EMI	34	10 Dec 94	4

Above hit: Joe LONGTHORNE and Liz DAWN.

ALBUMS:	**HITS 5**		**WEEKS 32**	
THE JOE LONGTHORNE SONGBOOK	Telstar	16	3 Dec 88	12
ESPECIALLY FOR YOU	Telstar	22	29 Jul 89	10
THE JOE LONGTHORNE CHRISTMAS ALBUM	Telstar	44	9 Dec 89	4
I WISH YOU LOVE	EMI	47	13 Nov 93	4
LIVE AT THE ROYAL ALBERT HALL	Premier	57	8 Oct 94	2

LOOK — UK

SINGLES:	**HITS 2**		**WEEKS 15**	
I AM THE BEAT	MCA	6	20 Dec 80	12
FEEDING TIME	MCA	50	29 Aug 81	3

LOOP — UK

ALBUMS:	**HITS 2**		**WEEKS 2**	
FADE OUT	Chapter 22	51	4 Feb 89	1
A GILDED ETERNITY	Situation Two	39	3 Feb 90	1

LOOP DA LOOP
UK

SINGLES:		HITS 2			WEEKS 4
GO WITH THE FLOW	*Manifesto*	47	*7 Jun 97*		1
Features rap from MC Duke.					
HAZEL	*Manifesto*	20	*20 Feb 99*		3
Samples Stetasonic's Sally.					

LOOSE ENDS
UK

SINGLES:		HITS 12			WEEKS 76
TELL ME WHAT YOU WANT	*Virgin*	74	*25 Feb 84*		1
EMERGENCY (DIAL 999)	*Virgin*	41	*28 Apr 84*		6
CHOOSE ME (RESCUE ME)	*Virgin*	59	*21 Jul 84*		3
HANGIN' ON A STRING (CONTEMPLATING)	*Virgin*	13	*23 Feb 85*		13
MAGIC TOUCH	*Virgin*	16	*11 May 85*		7
GOLDEN YEARS	*Virgin*	59	*27 Jul 85*		4
STAY A LITTLE WHILE, CHILD	*Virgin*	52	*14 Jun 86*		5
SLOW DOWN	*Virgin*	27	*20 Sep 86*		7
NIGHTS OF PLEASURE	*Virgin*	42	*29 Nov 86*		7
MR. BACHELOR	*Virgin*	50	*4 Jun 88*		4
DON'T BE A FOOL	*10 Records*	13	*25 Aug 90*		9
LOVE'S GOT ME	*Ten Records*	40	*17 Nov 90*		4
HANGIN' ON A STRING [RM]	*Ten Records*	25	*20 Jun 92*		5
Remixed by Frankie Knuckles.					
MAGIC TOUCH [RM]	*Ten Records*	75	*5 Sep 92*		1
ALBUMS:		HITS 6			WEEKS 41
A LITTLE SPICE	*Virgin*	46	*21 Apr 84*		9
SO WHERE ARE YOU?	*Virgin*	13	*20 Apr 85*		13
ZAGORA	*Virgin*	15	*18 Oct 86*		8
THE REAL CHUCKEEBOO	*Virgin*	52	*2 Jul 88*		4
LOOK HOW LONG	*Ten Records*	19	*29 Sep 90*		5
TIGHTEN UP VOLUME 1	*Ten Records*	40	*19 Sep 92*		2

Jennifer LOPEZ
US

SINGLES:		HITS 2			WEEKS 21
IF YOU HAD MY LOVE	*Columbia*	4	*3 Jul 99*		13
WAITING FOR TONIGHT	*Columbia*	5	*13 Nov 99*		8
ALBUMS:		HITS 1			WEEKS 21
ON THE 6	*Columbia*	14	*17 Jul 99*		21

Trini LOPEZ
US

SINGLES:		HITS 5			WEEKS 37
IF I HAD A HAMMER	*Reprise*	4	*14 Sep 63*		17
Originally recorded by Peter Paul and Mary.					
KANSAS CITY	*Reprise*	35	*14 Dec 63*		5
I'M COMING HOME CINDY	*Reprise*	28	*14 May 66*		5
GONNA GET ALONG WITHOUT YA NOW	*Reprise*	41	*8 Apr 67*		5
TRINI-TRAXS [M]	*RCA*	59	*19 Dec 81*		5
EPS:		HITS 2			WEEKS 11
TRINI LOPEZ AT P.J.'S	*Reprise*	11	*7 Dec 63*		7
AMERICA	*Reprise*	16	*19 Sep 64*		4
ALBUMS:		HITS 2			WEEKS 42
TRINI LOPEZ AT P.J.'S	*Reprise*	7	*26 Oct 63*		25
TRINI LOPEZ IN LONDON	*Reprise*	6	*25 Mar 67*		17
Above 2 are live recordings.					

Jeff LORBER
US

ALBUMS:		HITS 1			WEEKS 2
STEP BY STEP	*Club*	97	*18 May 85*		2

LORD ROCKINGHAM'S XI
UK/South Africa

SINGLES:		HITS 2			WEEKS 21
HOOTS MON	*Decca*	1	*25 Oct 58*		17
WEE TOM	*Decca*	16	*7 Feb 59*		3
Above 2 from the ITV series 'Oh! Boy'.					
Above 2: Jack GOOD presents LORD ROCKINGHAM'S XI.					
HOOTS MON [RI]	*Decca*	60	*25 Sep 93*		1
Featured in the Maynard's Wine Gums TV commercial.					

LORD TANAMO
Trinidad & Tobago

SINGLES:		HITS 1			WEEKS 2
I'M IN THE MOOD FOR LOVE	*Mooncrest*	58	*1 Dec 90*		2
Featured in the Paxo TV commercial. Originally released in 1965.					

LORD TARIQ and Peter GUNZ
US

SINGLES:		HITS 1		WEEKS 3
DEJA VU (UPTOWN BABY)	Columbia	21	2 May 98	3

Based around Steely Dan's Deja Vu.

Jerry LORDAN
UK

SINGLES:		HITS 3		WEEKS 16
I'LL STAY SINGLE	Parlophone	26	9 Jan 60	2
WHO COULD BE BLUER?	Parlophone	16	27 Feb 60	10
I'LL STAY SINGLE [RE]	Parlophone	41	12 Mar 60	1
WHO COULD BE BLUER? [RE]	Parlophone	45	21 May 60	1
SING LIKE AN ANGEL	Parlophone	36	4 Jun 60	2

Traci LORDS
US

SINGLES:		HITS 1		WEEKS 1
FALLEN ANGEL	Radioactive	72	7 Oct 95	1

LORDS OF THE UNDERGROUND
US

ALBUMS:		HITS 1		WEEKS 1
KEEPERS OF THE FUNK	Pendulum	68	12 Nov 94	1

Sophia LOREN – See Peter SELLERS and Sophia LOREN

Trey LORENZ
US

(See also Mariah Carey.)

SINGLES:		HITS 2		WEEKS 5
SOMEONE TO HOLD	Epic	65	21 Nov 92	2
PHOTOGRAPH OF MARY	Epic	38	30 Jan 93	3

LORI and the CHAMELEONS
UK

SINGLES:		HITS 1		WEEKS 1
TOUCH	Sire	70	8 Dec 79	1

LORRAINE – See BOMB THE BASS

LOS DEL CHIPMUNKS – See CHIPMUNKS

LOS DEL MAR featuring Wil. VELOZ
Canada/Cuba

SINGLES:		HITS 1		WEEKS 7
MACARENA	Pulse 8	66	8 Jun 96	2
MACARENA [RE]	Pulse 8	43	6 Jul 96	5

LOS DEL RIO
Spain

SINGLES:		HITS 1		WEEKS 19
MACARENA	RCA	64	1 Jun 96	1
MACARENA [RE]	RCA	2	13 Jul 96	18

LOS LOBOS
US

SINGLES:		HITS 3		WEEKS 24
DON'T WORRY BABY / WILL THE WOLF SURVIVE	Slash	57	6 Apr 85	4
LA BAMBA	Slash	1	18 Jul 87	11
COME ON, LET'S GO	Slash	18	26 Sep 87	9

Above 2 from the film 'La Bamba'.

ALBUMS:		HITS 3		WEEKS 24
HOW WILL THE WOLF SURVIVE?	Slash	77	6 Apr 85	6
BY THE LIGHT OF THE MOON	Slash	77	7 Feb 87	3
LA BAMBA [OST]	London	24	22 Aug 87	15

Majority of the tracks are by Los Lobos.
Above hit: LOS LOBOS / VARIOUS.

LOS UMBRELLOS
Denmark

SINGLES:		HITS 1		WEEKS 2
NO TENGO DINERO	Virgin	33	3 Oct 98	2

Melody is based on the theme from the film 'Never On Sunday'.

Joe LOSS and his Orchestra
UK

(See also George Mitchell Minstrels.)

SINGLES:		HITS 5		WEEKS 53
WHEELS - CHA CHA	His Master's Voice	21	1 Jul 61	21
SUCU SUCU	His Master's Voice	48	21 Oct 61	1
THE MAIGRET THEME	His Master's Voice	20	31 Mar 62	10
MUST BE MADISON	His Master's Voice	20	3 Nov 62	13
MARCH OF THE MODS (FINNJENKA DANCE)	His Master's Voice	35	7 Nov 64	4

MARCH OF THE MODS (FINNJENKA DANCE) [RE]	*His Master's Voice*	31	*26 Dec 64*	4
EPS:	**HITS 2**			**WEEKS 4**
DANCING TIME FOR LATINS	*HMV*	17	*16 Dec 61*	3
LATIN STYLE	*HMV*	19	*27 Jan 62*	1
ALBUMS:	**HITS 1**			**WEEKS 10**
ALL-TIME PARTY HITS	*Music For Pleasure*	24	*30 Oct 71*	10

LOST   UK

SINGLES:	**HITS 1**			**WEEKS 1**
TECHNOFUNK	*Perfecto*	75	*22 Jun 91*	1

LOST BOYZ   US

(See also Various Artists (EPs) 'New York Undercover 4-Track EP'.)

SINGLES:	**HITS 2**			**WEEKS 2**
MUSIC MAKES ME HIGH	*Universal*	42	*2 Nov 96*	1
LOVE, PEACE & NAPPINESS	*Universal*	57	*12 Jul 97*	1
ALBUMS:	**HITS 1**			**WEEKS 1**
LEGAL DRUG MONEY	*MCA*	64	*6 Jul 96*	1

LOST TRIBE   UK

SINGLES:	**HITS 1**			**WEEKS 3**
GAMEMASTER	*Hooj Choons*	24	*11 Sep 99*	3

Originally appeared on their Distant Voice EP, which reached No. 79 in 1997.

LOST WITNESS   UK

SINGLES:	**HITS 2**			**WEEKS 7**
HAPPINESS HAPPENING	*Sound Of Ministry*	18	*29 May 99*	4
RED SUN RISING	*Sound Of Ministry*	22	*18 Sep 99*	3

LOTUS EATERS   UK

SINGLES:	**HITS 2**			**WEEKS 16**
THE FIRST PICTURE OF YOU	*Sylvan*	15	*2 Jul 83*	12
YOU DON'T NEED SOMEONE NEW	*Sylvan*	53	*8 Oct 83*	4
ALBUMS:	**HITS 1**			**WEEKS 1**
NO SENSE OF SIN	*Sylvan*	96	*16 Jun 84*	1

Bonnie LOU   US

SINGLES:	**HITS 1**			**WEEKS 10**
TENNESSEE WIG WALK	*Parlophone*	4	*6 Feb 54*	10

Lippy LOU   UK

SINGLES:	**HITS 1**			**WEEKS 2**
LIBERATION	*More Protein*	57	*22 Apr 95*	2

Louchie LOU and Michie ONE   UK

SINGLES:	**HITS 6**			**WEEKS 36**
SHOUT	*ffrr*	7	*29 May 93*	8
SOMEBODY ELSE'S GUY (ME DID LOVE YOU)	*ffrr*	54	*14 Aug 93*	2
GET DOWN ON IT	*China*	58	*26 Aug 95*	1
CECILIA	*WEA*	4	*13 Apr 96*	17

Above hit: SUGGS featuring Louchie LOU and Michie ONE.

GOOD SWEET LOVIN'	*Indochina*	34	*15 Jun 96*	2
CECILIA [RE-1ST]	*WEA*	65	*24 Aug 96*	1
CECILIA [RE-2ND]	*WEA*	59	*7 Sep 96*	1
NO MORE ALCOHOL	*WEA*	24	*21 Sep 96*	4

Samples the Champs' Tequila.
Above hit: SUGGS featuring Louchie LOU and Michie ONE.

LOUD   UK

SINGLES:	**HITS 1**			**WEEKS 2**
EASY	*China*	67	*28 Mar 92*	2

John D. LOUDERMILK   US

SINGLES:	**HITS 1**			**WEEKS 10**
LANGUAGE OF LOVE	*RCA*	13	*6 Jan 62*	10

Louie LOUIE   US

SINGLES:	**HITS 1**			**WEEKS 5**
THE THOUGHT OF IT	*Hardback*	34	*19 Dec 92*	5

LOUISE
UK

SINGLES:		HITS 8		WEEKS 57	
LIGHT OF MY LIFE	EMI		8	7 Oct 95	8
IN WALKED LOVE	EMI		17	16 Mar 96	6
Originally recorded by Expose.					
NAKED	EMI		5	8 Jun 96	8
UNDIVIDED LOVE	EMI		5	31 Aug 96	6
ONE KISS FROM HEAVEN	EMI		9	30 Nov 96	7
ARMS AROUND THE WORLD	EMI		4	4 Oct 97	7
LET'S GO ROUND AGAIN	EMI		10	29 Nov 97	9
ALL THAT MATTERS	EMI		11	4 Apr 98	5
Backing vocals by Miriam Stockley and Lance Ellington.					
ALL THAT MATTERS [RE]	EMI		73	20 Jun 98	1
ALBUMS:		**HITS 2**		**WEEKS 50**	
NAKED	EMI		7	6 Jul 96	31
WOMAN IN ME	EMI		5	18 Oct 97	19

Jacques LOUSSIER
France

ALBUMS:		HITS 1		WEEKS 3	
JACQUES LOUSSIER – THE BEST OF PLAY BACH	Start		58	30 Mar 85	3

LOVE
US

ALBUMS:		HITS 2		WEEKS 8	
FOREVER CHANGES	Elektra		24	24 Feb 68	6
OUT HERE	Harvest		29	16 May 70	2

Darlene LOVE
US

SINGLES:		HITS 1		WEEKS 5	
ALL ALONE ON CHRISTMAS	Arista		31	19 Dec 92	4
Features Little Steven and the Jersey Allstars. From the film 'Home Alone 2: Lost In New York'.					
ALL ALONE ON CHRISTMAS [RE]	Arista		72	1 Jan 94	1

Geoff LOVE and his Orchestra
UK

(See also Shirley Bassey; Alma Cogan; Russ Conway; Ken Dodd; Teddy Johnson and Pearl Carr; King Brothers; Laurie London with Geoff Love his Orchestra and Chorus; Manuel and the Music Of The Mountains; Rita Pavone; Peter and Gordon; Ann Shelton; Ricky Stevens with the Rita Williams Singers and Geoff Love and his Orchestra ; Frankie Vaughan; Danny Williams.)

ALBUMS:		HITS 3		WEEKS 28	
BIG WAR MOVIE THEMES	Music For Pleasure		11	7 Aug 71	20
BIG WESTERN MOVIE THEMES	Music For Pleasure		38	21 Aug 71	3
BIG LOVE MOVIE THEMES	Music For Pleasure		28	30 Oct 71	5

Monie LOVE
UK

(See also De La Soul; Jungle Brothers.)

SINGLES:		HITS 10		WEEKS 49	
I CAN DO THIS	Cooltempo		37	4 Feb 89	4
Samples the Whispers' And The Beat Goes On.					
GRANDPA'S PARTY	Cooltempo		16	24 Jun 89	9
MONIE IN THE MIDDLE	Cooltempo		46	14 Jul 90	3
IT'S A SHAME (MY SISTER)	Cooltempo		12	22 Sep 90	8
Above hit: Monie LOVE (featuring TRUE IMAGE).					
DOWN TO EARTH	Cooltempo		31	1 Dec 90	6
RING MY BELL	Cooltempo		20	6 Apr 91	5
Above hit: Monie LOVE vs ADEVA.					
FULL TERM LOVE	Cooltempo		34	25 Jul 92	4
From the film 'Class Act'.					
BORN 2 B.R.E.E.D.	Cooltempo		18	13 Mar 93	5
B.R.E.E.D is an acronym for Build Relationships where Education and Enlightenment Dominate.					
IN A WORD OR 2 / THE POWER	Cooltempo		33	12 Jun 93	3
NEVER GIVE UP	Cooltempo		41	21 Aug 93	2
ALBUMS:		**HITS 1**		**WEEKS 3**	
DOWN TO EARTH	Cooltempo		30	20 Oct 90	3

Vikki LOVE – See NUANCE featuring Vikki LOVE

LOVE AFFAIR
UK

SINGLES:		HITS 5		WEEKS 56	
EVERLASTING LOVE	CBS		1	6 Jan 68	12
RAINBOW VALLEY	CBS		5	20 Apr 68	13
Above 2 originally recorded by Robert Knight.					
Above hit: LOVE AFFAIR with the Keith MANSFIELD ORCHESTRA.					
A DAY WITHOUT LOVE	CBS		6	14 Sep 68	12
ONE ROAD	CBS		16	22 Feb 69	9
BRINGING ON BACK THE GOOD TIMES	CBS		9	19 Jul 69	10

LOVE AND MONEY — UK

SINGLES:	HITS 6			WEEKS 23
CANDYBAR EXPRESS	*Mercury*	56	*24 May 86*	4
LOVE AND MONEY	*Mercury*	68	*25 Apr 87*	4
HALLELUIAH MAN	*Fontana*	63	*17 Sep 88*	4
STRANGE KIND OF LOVE	*Fontana*	45	*14 Jan 89*	5
JOCELYN SQUARE	*Fontana*	51	*25 Mar 89*	4
WINTER	*Fontana*	52	*16 Nov 91*	2
ALBUMS:	HITS 2			WEEKS 2
STRANGE KIND OF LOVE	*Fontana*	71	*29 Oct 88*	1
DOGS IN THE TRAFFIC	*Fontana*	41	*3 Aug 91*	1

LOVE CITY GROOVE — UK

SINGLES:	HITS 1			WEEKS 11
LOVE CITY GROOVE	*Planet 3*	7	*8 Apr 95*	11

UK's Eurovision entry in 1995, it came 10th.

LOVE DECADE — UK

SINGLES:	HITS 5			WEEKS 14
DREAM ON (IS THIS A DREAM)	*All Around The World*	52	*6 Jul 91*	2
SO REAL	*All Around The World*	14	*23 Nov 91*	7
I FEEL YOU	*All Around The World*	34	*11 Apr 92*	3
WHEN THE MORNING COMES	*All Around The World*	69	*6 Feb 93*	1
IS THIS A DREAM? [RR]	*All Around The World*	39	*17 Feb 96*	1

LOVE DECREE — UK

SINGLES:	HITS 1			WEEKS 4
SOMETHING SO REAL (THE CHINHEADS THEME)	*Ariola*	61	*16 Sep 89*	4

LOVE/HATE — US

SINGLES:	HITS 2			WEEKS 4
EVIL TWIN	*Columbia*	59	*30 Nov 91*	1
WASTED IN AMERICA	*Columbia*	38	*4 Apr 92*	3
ALBUMS:	HITS 2			WEEKS 5
WASTED IN AMERICA	*Columbia*	20	*7 Mar 92*	4
LET'S RUMBLE	*RCA*	24	*24 Jul 93*	1

LOVE INC featuring M.C. NOISE — UK

SINGLES:	HITS 1			WEEKS 3
LOVE IS THE MESSAGE	*Love*	59	*9 Feb 91*	3

LOVE NELSON – See FIRE ISLAND

LOVE SCULPTURE — UK

SINGLES:	HITS 1			WEEKS 14
SABRE DANCE	*Parlophone*	5	*30 Nov 68*	14

Composed by Khatchaturian.

LOVE SQUAD – See Linda CARR

A LOVE SUPREME — UK

SINGLES:	HITS 1			WEEKS 2
NIALL QUINN'S DISCO PANTS	*Cherry Red*	59	*17 Apr 99*	2

Based on a terrace chant of Sunderland FC supporters.

LOVE TO INFINITY — UK

SINGLES:	HITS 3			WEEKS 4
KEEP LOVE TOGETHER	*Mushroom*	38	*24 Jun 95*	2
SOMEDAY	*Mushroom*	75	*18 Nov 95*	1
PRAY FOR LOVE	*Mushroom*	69	*3 Aug 96*	1

LOVE TRIBE — US

SINGLES:	HITS 1			WEEKS 3
STAND UP	*AM:PM*	23	*29 Jun 96*	3

Song is based around Fire Island's There But For The Grace Of God.

LOVE UNLIMITED — US

SINGLES:	HITS 2			WEEKS 19
WALKIN' IN THE RAIN WITH THE ONE I LOVE	*Uni*	14	*17 Jun 72*	10

Vocals midway through song at the 'telephone break' are by Barry White.

IT MAY BE WINTER OUTSIDE (BUT IN MY HEART IT'S SPRING)	*20th Century*	11	*25 Jan 75*	9

Originally recorded by Felice Taylor.

LOVE UNLIMITED ORCHESTRA | | | | US

SINGLES:	HITS 1			WEEKS 10
LOVE'S THEME	Pye International	10	2 Feb 74	10
ALBUMS:	HITS 1			WEEKS 1
RHAPSODY IN WHITE	Pye International	50	6 Apr 74	1

LOVEBUG STARSKI | | | | US

SINGLES:	HITS 1			WEEKS 9
AMITYVILLE (THE HOUSE ON THE HILL)	Epic	12	31 May 86	9

LOVEDEEJAY AKEMI - See YOSH presents LOVEDEEJAY AKEMI

LOVEHAPPY | | | | UK/US

SINGLES:	HITS 1			WEEKS 3
MESSAGE OF LOVE	MCA	37	18 Feb 95	2
Vocals by Ellie Lawson. Background vocals by Lance Ellington and Miriam Stockley.				
MESSAGE OF LOVE [RM]	MCA	70	20 Jul 96	1
Remixed by K-Klass.				

Bill LOVELADY | | | | UK

SINGLES:	HITS 1			WEEKS 10
REGGAE FOR IT NOW	Charisma	12	18 Aug 79	10

LOVELAND featuring the voice of Rachel McFARLANE | | | | UK

SINGLES:	HITS 5			WEEKS 15
LET THE MUSIC (LIFT YOU UP)	KMS	16	16 Apr 94	4
Darlene Lewis' vocals did not appear on the lead track of this release.				
Above hit: LOVELAND featuring Rachel McFARLANE vs. Darlene LEWIS.				
(KEEP ON) SHINING / HOPE (NEVER GIVE UP)	Eastern Bloc	37	5 Nov 94	2
Above hit: LOVELAND featuring Rachel McFARLANE.				
I NEED SOMEBODY	Eastern Bloc	21	14 Jan 95	3
Cover of a Keicha Jenkins track from 1989. Backing vocals by Yvonne Shelton.				
DON'T MAKE ME WAIT	Eastern Bloc	22	10 Jun 95	3
THE WONDER OF LOVE	Eastern Bloc	53	2 Sep 95	1
I NEED SOMEBODY [RM]	Eastern Bloc	38	11 Nov 95	2
Remixed by Topham/Twigg/Waterman.				

LOVER SPEAKS | | | | UK

SINGLES:	HITS 1			WEEKS 5
NO MORE "I LOVE YOU'S"	A&M	58	16 Aug 86	5

Michael LOVESMITH | | | | US

SINGLES:	HITS 1			WEEKS 1
AIN'T NOTHIN' LIKE IT	Motown	75	5 Oct 85	1

LOVESTATION | | | | UK/US

SINGLES:	HITS 5			WEEKS 17
SHINE ON ME	RCA	71	13 Mar 93	1
Above hit: LOVESTATION featuring Lisa HUNT.				
BEST OF MY LOVE	Fresh	73	13 Nov 93	1
LOVE COME RESCUE ME	Fresh	42	18 Mar 95	2
Originally released in 1992.				
TEARDROPS	Fresh	14	1 Aug 98	6
SENSUALITY	Fresh	16	5 Dec 98	7

Lyle LOVETT | | | | US

ALBUMS:	HITS 2			WEEKS 2
I LOVE EVERYBODY	MCA	54	8 Oct 94	1
THE ROAD TO ENSENADA	MCA	62	29 Jun 96	1

Lene LOVICH | | | | US

SINGLES:	HITS 6			WEEKS 38
LUCKY NUMBER	Stiff	3	17 Feb 79	11
SAY WHEN	Stiff	19	12 May 79	10
BIRD SONG	Stiff	39	20 Oct 79	7
WHAT WILL I DO WITHOUT YOU	Stiff	58	29 Mar 80	3
NEW TOY	Stiff	53	14 Mar 81	5
IT'S YOU, ONLY YOU (MEIN SCHMERZ)	Stiff	68	27 Nov 82	2
ALBUMS:	HITS 2			WEEKS 17
STATELESS	Stiff	35	17 Mar 79	11
FLEX	Stiff	19	2 Feb 80	6

LOVIN' SPOONFUL
US/Canada

SINGLES:		HITS 4		WEEKS 33	
DAYDREAM	Pye International	2	16 Apr 66	13
SUMMER IN THE CITY	Kama Sultra	8	16 Jul 66	11
NASHVILLE CATS	Kama Sultra	26	7 Jan 67	7
DARLING BE HOME SOON	Kama Sultra	44	11 Mar 67	2
From the film 'You're A Big Boy Now'.				
EPS:		HITS 2		WEEKS 13
DID YOU EVER HAVE TO MAKE UP YOUR MIND	Kama Sutra	3	25 Jun 66	11
JUG BAND MUSIC	Kama Sutra	8	27 Aug 66	2
ALBUMS:		HITS 1		WEEKS 11
DAYDREAM	Pye International	8	7 May 66	11

LOVINDEER
Jamaica

SINGLES:		HITS 1		WEEKS 3	
MAN SHORTAGE	TSOJ	69	27 Sep 86	3

Gary LOW
Italy

SINGLES:		HITS 1		WEEKS 3	
I WANT YOU	Savoir	52	8 Oct 83	3

Patti LOW and DOOGIE – See BUG KANN and the PLASTIC JAM

Jim LOWE with the HIGH FIVES
US

SINGLES:		HITS 1		WEEKS 9	
THE GREEN DOOR	London	8	27 Oct 56	9

Nick LOWE
UK

SINGLES:		HITS 4		WEEKS 27	
I LOVE THE SOUND OF BREAKING GLASS	Radar	7	11 Mar 78	8
CRACKING UP	Radar	34	9 Jun 79	5
CRUEL TO BE KIND	Radar	12	25 Aug 79	11
HALF A BOY AND HALF A MAN	F-Beat	53	26 May 84	3
ALBUMS:		HITS 3		WEEKS 17
THE JESUS OF COOL	Radar	22	11 Mar 78	9
LABOUR OF LUST	Radar	43	23 Jun 79	6
NICK THE KNIFE	F-Beat	99	20 Feb 82	2

LOWRELL
US

SINGLES:		HITS 1		WEEKS 9	
MELLOW MELLOW RIGHT ON	AVI	37	24 Nov 79	9

LOX – See PUFF DADDY

L7
US

SINGLES:		HITS 4		WEEKS 18	
PRETEND WE'RE DEAD	Slash	21	4 Apr 92	7
EVERGLADE	Slash	27	30 May 92	3
MONSTER	Slash	33	12 Sep 92	3
PRETEND WE'RE DEAD [RI]	Slash	50	28 Nov 92	3
ANDRES	Slash	34	9 Jul 94	2
ALBUMS:		HITS 2		WEEKS 8
BRICKS ARE HEAVY	Slash	24	2 May 92	6
HUNGRY FOR STINK	Slash	26	23 Jul 94	2

LSG
Germany

SINGLES:		HITS 1		WEEKS 1	
NETHERWORLD	Hooj Choons	63	10 May 97	1

Norman LUBOFF CHOIR – See Doris DAY; Frankie LAINE; Jo STAFFORD

LUCAS
US

SINGLES:		HITS 1		WEEKS 4	
LUCAS WITH THE LID OFF	WEA	37	6 Aug 94	4

Carrie LUCAS
US

SINGLES:		HITS 1		WEEKS 6	
DANCE WITH YOU	Solar	40	16 Jun 79	6

Tammy LUCAS – See Teddy RILEY featuring Tammy LUCAS

LUCIANA
UK

SINGLES:		HITS 3			WEEKS 5
GET IT UP FOR LOVE	Chrysalis	55	23 Apr 94		2
IF YOU WANT	Chrysalis	47	6 Aug 94		2
WHAT GOES AROUND / ONE MORE RIVER	Chrysalis	67	5 Nov 94		1

One More River was featured in the TV detective series 'Anna Lee'.

LUCID
UK

SINGLES:		HITS 3			WEEKS 15
I CAN'T HELP MYSELF	ffrr	7	8 Aug 98		8
CRAZY	ffrr	14	27 Feb 99		5
STAY WITH ME TILL DAWN	ffrr	25	16 Oct 99		2

LUCKY MONKEYS
UK

SINGLES:		HITS 1			WEEKS 1
BJANGO	Hi-Life	50	9 Nov 96		1

Baz LUHRMANN presents
Australia

SINGLES:		HITS 1			WEEKS 16
EVERYBODY'S FREE (TO WEAR SUNSCREEN) THE SUNSCREEN SONG (CLASS OF '99)	EMI	1	12 Jun 99		16

Vocals by Lee Perry. Samples the instrumental from Quindon Tarver's version of Everybody's Free (To Feel Good) from the film 'Romeo And Juliet'. Lyrics are from an article in the Chicago Tribune by Mary Schmich.

Robin LUKE
US

SINGLES:		HITS 1			WEEKS 6
SUSIE DARLIN'	London	24	18 Oct 58		3
SUSIE DARLIN' [RE-1ST]	London	23	22 Nov 58		1
SUSIE DARLIN' [RE-2ND]	London	23	6 Dec 58		2

LUKK featuring Felicia COLLINS
US

SINGLES:		HITS 1			WEEKS 1
ON THE ONE	Important/Towerbell	72	28 Sep 85		1

LULU
UK

SINGLES:		HITS 24			WEEKS 169
SHOUT	Decca	7	16 May 64		13

Originally recorded by the Isley Brothers.
Above hit: LULU and the LUVVERS.

HERE COMES THE NIGHT	Decca	50	14 Nov 64		1
LEAVE A LITTLE LOVE	Decca	8	19 Jun 65		11
TRY TO UNDERSTAND	Decca	25	4 Sep 65		8
THE BOAT THAT I ROW	Columbia	6	15 Apr 67		11

Originally recorded by Neil Diamond.

LET'S PRETEND	Columbia	11	2 Jul 67		11
LOVE LOVES TO LOVE, LOVE	Columbia	32	11 Nov 67		6
ME, THE PEACEFUL HEART	Columbia	9	2 Mar 68		9
BOY	Columbia	15	8 Jun 68		7
I'M A TIGER	Columbia	9	9 Nov 68		13

Written by Marty Wilde.

BOOM BANG-A-BANG	Columbia	2	15 Mar 69		13

UK's Eurovision entry in 1969, it came joint 1st.

OH ME OH MY (I'M A FOOL FOR YOU BABY)	Atco	47	22 Nov 69		2
THE MAN WHO SOLD THE WORLD	Polydor	3	26 Jan 74		9

Originally recorded by David Bowie who also plays saxophone on the track.

TAKE YOUR MAMA FOR A RIDE	Chelsea	37	19 Apr 75		4
I COULD NEVER MISS YOU (MORE THAN I DO)	Alfa	62	12 Dec 81		4
I COULD NEVER MISS YOU (MORE THAN I DO) [RE]	Alfa	63	16 Jan 82		1
SHOUT [RR]	Jive	8	19 Jul 86		10
SHOUT [RI]	Decca	8	26 Jul 86		9

Both versions were listed separately until 2 Aug 86 when sales for each were combined.
Above hit: LULU and the LUVVERS.

INDEPENDENCE	Dome	11	30 Jan 93		5
I'M BACK FOR MORE	Dome	27	3 Apr 93		5

Originally recorded by Al Johnson and Jean Carn.
Above hit: LULU and Bobby WOMACK.

LET ME WAKE UP IN YOUR ARMS	Dome	51	4 Sep 93		2
RELIGHT MY FIRE	RCA	1	9 Oct 93		14

Above hit: TAKE THAT featuring LULU.

HOW 'BOUT US	Dome	46	27 Nov 93		3
GOODBYE BABY AND AMEN	Dome	40	27 Aug 94		2
EVERY WOMAN KNOWS	Dome	44	26 Nov 94		2
HURT ME SO BAD	Rocket	42	29 May 99		2

ALBUMS:		HITS 2		WEEKS 7	
THE MOST OF LULU		*Music For Pleasure*	15	*25 Sep 71*	6
INDEPENDENCE		*Dome*	67	*6 Mar 93*	1

Bob LUMAN
US

SINGLES:		HITS 3		WEEKS 21	
LET'S THINK ABOUT LIVING		*Warner Brothers*	6	*10 Sep 60*	18
WHY WHY BYE BYE		*Warner Brothers*	46	*17 Dec 60*	1
THE GREAT SNOW MAN		*Warner Brothers*	49	*6 May 61*	2
Originally recorded by John D. Loudermilk.					

ALBUMS:		HITS 1		WEEKS 1	
LET'S THINK ABOUT LIVING		*Warner Brothers*	18	*14 Jan 61*	1

LUMINAIRE – See Jonathan PETERS presents LUMINAIRE

LUNIZ
US

(See also Quincy Jones.)

SINGLES:		HITS 2		WEEKS 18	
I GOT 5 ON IT		*Virgin*	3	*17 Feb 96*	13
Samples Timex Social Club's Rumours.					
PLAYA HATA		*Virgin*	20	*11 May 96*	3
Samples Bobby Caldwell's What You Won't Do For Love.					
I GOT 5 ON IT – URBAN TAKEOVER REMIX [RM]		*VC Recordings*	28	*31 Oct 98*	2
Remixed by Mickey Finn and Aphrodite. Featured in Channel 5's advertising campaign.					

ALBUMS:		HITS 1		WEEKS 3	
OPERATION STACKOLA		*Virgin*	41	*16 Mar 96*	3

LURKERS
UK

SINGLES:		HITS 5		WEEKS 11	
AIN'T GOT A CLUE		*Beggars Banquet*	45	*3 Jun 78*	3
I DON'T NEED TO TELL HER		*Beggars Banquet*	49	*5 Aug 78*	4
JUST THIRTEEN		*Beggars Banquet*	66	*3 Feb 79*	2
OUT IN THE DARK / CYANIDE		*Beggars Banquet*	72	*9 Jun 79*	1
NEW GUITAR IN TOWN		*Beggars Banquet*	72	*17 Nov 79*	1

ALBUMS:		HITS 1		WEEKS 1	
FULHAM FALLOUT		*Beggars Banquet*	57	*1 Jul 78*	1

LUSCIOUS JACKSON
US

SINGLES:		HITS 4		WEEKS 5	
DEEP SHAG / CITYSONG		*Grand Royal*	69	*18 Mar 95*	1
HERE		*Grand Royal*	59	*21 Oct 95*	1
From the film 'Clueless'.					
NAKED EYE		*Grand Royal*	25	*12 Apr 97*	2
LADYFINGERS		*Grand Royal*	43	*3 Jul 99*	1

ALBUMS:		HITS 1		WEEKS 1	
FEVER IN FEVER OUT		*Grand Royal*	55	*26 Apr 97*	1

LUSH
UK

SINGLES:		HITS 9		WEEKS 19	
MAD LOVE [EP]		*4AD*	55	*10 Mar 90*	1
Lead track: De-Luxe.					
SWEETNESS AND LIGHT		*4AD*	47	*27 Oct 90*	2
NOTHING NATURAL		*4AD*	43	*19 Oct 91*	2
FOR LOVE [EP]		*4AD*	35	*11 Jan 92*	2
Lead track: For Love.					
DESIRE LINES		*4AD*	60	*11 Jun 94*	1
HYPOCRITE		*4AD*	52	*11 Jun 94*	2
SINGLE GIRL		*4AD*	21	*20 Jan 96*	3
LADYKILLERS		*4AD*	22	*9 Mar 96*	3
500 (SHAKE BABY SHAKE)		*4AD*	21	*27 Jul 96*	3

ALBUMS:		HITS 3		WEEKS 10	
SPOOKY		*4AD*	7	*8 Feb 92*	3
SPLIT		*4AD*	19	*25 Jun 94*	2
LOVELIFE		*4AD*	8	*30 Mar 96*	5

LUSTRAL
UK

SINGLES:		HITS 1		WEEKS 3	
EVERYTIME		*Hooj Choons*	60	*18 Oct 97*	1
Vocals by Tracey Ackerman. Samples Robert Flack's First Time Ever I Saw Your Face.					
EVERYTIME [RM]		*Hooj Choons*	30	*4 Dec 99*	2
Remixed by Way Out West.					

LUVVERS – See LULU

Annabella LWIN — Burma

SINGLES:	HITS 1		WEEKS 1
DO WHAT YOU DO	Sony S2	61	28 Jan 95	1

John LYDON — UK

(See also Time Zone featuring John Lydon and Afrika Bambaataa.)

SINGLES:	HITS 2		WEEKS 6
OPEN UP	Hard Hands	13	13 Nov 93	5
Above hit: LEFTFIELD LYDON.				
SUN	Virgin	42	2 Aug 97	1

Frankie LYMON and the TEENAGERS — US

SINGLES:	HITS 3		WEEKS 38
WHY DO FOOLS FALL IN LOVE	Columbia	1	30 Jun 56	16
Above hit: TEENAGERS featuring Frankie LYMON.				
I'M NOT A JUVENILE DELINQUENT	Columbia	12	30 Mar 57	7
BABY, BABY	Columbia	4	13 Apr 57	12
Above 2 entries were separate sides of the same release, each had its own chart run. Both sides from the film 'Rock, Rock, Rock'.				
GOODY GOODY	Columbia	24	21 Sep 57	3
Originally recorded by Benny Goodman in 1936.				

Read by Des LYNAM performed by the WIMBLEDON CHORAL SOCIETY — UK

(See also Wimbledon Choral Society.)

SINGLES:	HITS 1		WEEKS 3
IF: KIPLING'S POEM WITH THE BBC WORLD CUP '98 THEME – PAVANE	BBC Worldwide Music	45	12 Dec 98	3
Read by Lynam at the end of the BBC's coverage of the 1998 World Cup.				

Kenny LYNCH — UK

SINGLES:	HITS 8		WEEKS 59
MOUNTAIN OF LOVE	His Master's Voice	33	2 Jul 60	3
Originally recorded by Harold Dorman.				
Above hit: Kenny LYNCH with the Michael SAMMES SINGERS.				
PUFF (UP IN SMOKE)	His Master's Voice	33	15 Sep 62	5
PUFF (UP IN SMOKE) [RE]	His Master's Voice	46	27 Oct 62	1
UP ON THE ROOF	His Master's Voice	10	8 Dec 62	12
Originally recorded by Little Eva.				
YOU CAN NEVER STOP ME LOVING YOU	His Master's Voice	10	22 Jun 63	14
STAND BY ME	His Master's Voice	39	18 Apr 64	7
WHAT AM I TO YOU	His Master's Voice	37	29 Aug 64	4
WHAT AM I TO YOU [RE]	His Master's Voice	44	3 Oct 64	2
I'LL STAY BY YOU	His Master's Voice	29	19 Jun 65	7
HALF THE DAY'S GONE AND WE HAVEN'T EARNE'D A PENNY	Satril	50	20 Aug 83	4

Cheryl LYNN — US

SINGLES:	HITS 1		WEEKS 2
ENCORE	Streetwave	68	8 Sep 84	2

Patti LYNN — UK

SINGLES:	HITS 1		WEEKS 5
JOHNNY ANGEL	Fontana	37	12 May 62	5

Tami LYNN — US

SINGLES:	HITS 1		WEEKS 20
I'M GONNA RUN AWAY FROM YOU	Mojo	4	22 May 71	14
I'M GONNA RUN AWAY FROM YOU [RI]	Contempo Raries	36	3 May 75	6

Vera LYNN — UK

SINGLES:	HITS 9		WEEKS 46
FORGET-ME-NOT	Decca	7	15 Nov 52	1
THE HOMING WALTZ	Decca	9	15 Nov 52	3
Above hit: Vera LYNN with SAILORS, SOLDIERS and AIRMEN Of HER MAJESTY'S FORCES.				
AUF WIEDERSEH'N SWEETHEART	Decca	10	15 Nov 52	1
Above hit: Vera LYNN with SOLDIERS and AIRMEN Of HER MAJESTY'S FORCES.				
FORGET-ME-NOT [RE]	Decca	5	29 Nov 52	5
THE WINDSOR WALTZ	Decca	11	6 Jun 53	1
Above hit: Vera LYNN with Chorus of Members of HM FORCES.				
MY SON, MY SON	Decca	1	16 Oct 54	14
Originally recorded by Eddie Calvert.				
Above hit: Vera LYNN and Frank WEIR and his Saxophone, his Chorus and Orchestra.				
WHO ARE WE	Decca	30	9 Jun 56	1
A HOUSE WITH LOVE IN IT	Decca	17	27 Oct 56	13

THE FAITHFUL HUSSAR (DON'T CRY MY LOVE)	*Decca*	29	*16 Mar 57*	2
TRAVELLIN' HOME	*Decca*	20	*22 Jun 57*	5
ALBUMS:	**HITS 2**		**WEEKS 15**	
20 FAMILY FAVOURITES	*EMI*	25	*21 Nov 81*	12
WE'LL MEET AGAIN	*Telstar*	44	*9 Sep 89*	3

Jeff LYNNE   UK

(See also Various Artists: Films – Original Soundtracks 'Robin Hood: Prince Of Thieves'.)

SINGLES:	**HITS 1**		**WEEKS 4**	
EVERY LITTLE THING	*Reprise*	59	*30 Jun 90*	4
ALBUMS:	**HITS 1**		**WEEKS 4**	
ARMCHAIR THEATRE	*Reprise*	24	*4 Aug 90*	4

Philip LYNOTT   Ireland

SINGLES:	**HITS 4**		**WEEKS 36**	
DEAR MISS LONELY HEARTS	*Vertigo*	32	*5 Apr 80*	6
KING'S CALL	*Vertigo*	35	*21 Jun 80*	6
Tribute to Elvis Presley. Features Mark Knopfler.				
YELLOW PEARL	*Vertigo*	56	*21 Mar 81*	3
YELLOW PEARL [RE]	*Vertigo*	14	*26 Dec 81*	9
Re-released after being used as the theme to BBC1 TV's Top Of The Pops.				
OUT IN THE FIELDS	*10 Records*	5	*18 May 85*	10
Above hit: Gary MOORE and Phil LYNOTT.				
KING'S CALL [RM]	*Vertigo*	68	*24 Jan 87*	2
ALBUMS:	**HITS 2**		**WEEKS 16**	
SOLO IN SOHO	*Vertigo*	28	*26 Apr 80*	6
SOLDIER OF FORTUNE – THE BEST OF PHIL LYNOTT AND THIN LIZZY	*Telstar*	55	*14 Nov 87*	10
Features Lynott's solo and group material.				
Above hit: Phil LYNOTT and THIN LIZZY.				

LYNYRD SKYNYRD   US

SINGLES:	**HITS 1**		**WEEKS 21**	
SWEET HOME ALABAMA / DOUBLE TROUBLE	*MCA*	31	*11 Sep 76*	4
Initial chart entry was listed as AA side, though later listed as an EP. Free Bird was the track on the flip side.				
FREE BIRD [EP] [RE-1ST]	*MCA*	43	*22 Dec 79*	8
A tribute to Duane Allman from the Allman Brothers.				
FREE BIRD [EP] [RE-2ND]	*MCA*	21	*19 Jun 82*	9
ALBUMS:	**HITS 6**		**WEEKS 19**	
NUTHIN' FANCY	*MCA*	43	*3 May 75*	1
GIMME BACK MY BULLETS	*MCA*	34	*28 Feb 76*	5
ONE MORE FOR THE ROAD	*MCA*	17	*6 Nov 76*	4
Live recordings from Atlanta.				
STREET SURVIVORS	*MCA*	13	*12 Nov 77*	4
SKYNYRD'S FIRST AND LAST	*MCA*	50	*4 Nov 78*	1
Unreleased recordings from 1970–72.				
GOLD AND PLATINUM	*MCA*	49	*9 Feb 80*	4
Compilation.				

Barbara LYON   US

SINGLES:	**HITS 2**		**WEEKS 12**	
STOWAWAY	*Columbia*	12	*25 Jun 55*	8
Above hit: Barbara LYON with Ray MARTIN and his Orchestra.				
LETTER TO A SOLDIER	*Columbia*	27	*22 Dec 56*	4

LYTE FUNKIE ONES   US

SINGLES:	**HITS 2**		**WEEKS 8**	
CAN'T HAVE YOU	*Logic*	54	*22 May 99*	1
SUMMERGIRLS	*Logic*	16	*18 Sep 99*	7
Based around the melody of Extreme's More Than Words.				

Humphrey LYTTELTON and his Band   UK

SINGLES:	**HITS 1**		**WEEKS 6**	
BAD PENNY BLUES	*Parlophone*	19	*14 Jul 56*	6

M

M   UK

SINGLES:	**HITS 4**		**WEEKS 39**	
POP MUZIK	*MCA*	2	*7 Apr 79*	14

MOONLIGHT AND MUZAK	*MCA*	33	*8 Dec 79*	9
THAT'S THE WAY THE MONEY GOES	*MCA*	45	*15 Mar 80*	5
OFFICIAL SECRETS	*MCA*	64	*22 Nov 80*	2
POP MUZIK (THE 1989 RE-MIX) [RM]	*Freestyle*	15	*10 Jun 89*	9
Remixed by Robin Scott and Simon Rogers.				

Bobby M featuring Jean CARN — US

SINGLES:	**HITS 1**			**WEEKS 3**
LET'S STAY TOGETHER	*Gordy*	53	*29 Jan 83*	3

M.A.N.I.C. — UK

SINGLES:	**HITS 1**			**WEEKS 1**
I'M COMIN' HARDCORE	*Union City*	60	*18 Apr 92*	1

M/A/R/R/S — UK

SINGLES:	**HITS 1**			**WEEKS 14**
PUMP UP THE VOLUME / ANITINA (THE FIRST TIME I SEE SHE DANCE)	*4AD*	1	*5 Sep 87*	14

M-BEAT — UK

SINGLES:	**HITS 3**			**WEEKS 24**
INCREDIBLE	*Renk*	39	*18 Jun 94*	3
INCREDIBLE [RM]	*Renk*	8	*10 Sep 94*	9
Above 2: M-BEAT featuring GENERAL LEVY.				
SWEET LOVE	*Renk*	18	*17 Dec 94*	7
Above hit: M-BEAT featuring NAZLYN.				
DO U KNOW WHERE YOU'RE COMING FROM	*Renk*	12	*1 Jun 96*	5
Above hit: M-BEAT featuring JAMIROQUAI.				

M-D-EMM — UK

SINGLES:	**HITS 2**			**WEEKS 3**
GET DOWN	*Strictly Underground*	55	*22 Feb 92*	2
MOVE YOUR FEET	*Strictly Underground*	67	*30 May 92*	1

M + M — Canada

(See also Martha and the Muffins.)

SINGLES:	**HITS 1**			**WEEKS 4**
BLACK STATIONS/WHITE STATIONS	*RCA*	46	*28 Jul 84*	4
One track (not AA).				

M. and O. BAND — UK

SINGLES:	**HITS 1**			**WEEKS 6**
LET'S DO THE LATIN HUSTLE	*Creole*	16	*28 Feb 76*	6

M PEOPLE — UK

SINGLES:	**HITS 19**			**WEEKS 137**
HOW CAN I LOVE YOU MORE?	*Deconstruction*	29	*26 Oct 91*	9
COLOUR MY LIFE	*Deconstruction*	35	*7 Mar 92*	4
SOMEDAY	*Deconstruction*	38	*18 Apr 92*	3
Above hit: M-PEOPLE with Heather SMALL.				
EXCITED	*Deconstruction*	29	*10 Oct 92*	5
HOW CAN I LOVE YOU MORE? [RM]	*Deconstruction*	8	*6 Feb 93*	8
Remixed by Sasha and Tom Frederikse.				
ONE NIGHT IN HEAVEN	*Deconstruction*	6	*26 Jun 93*	11
MOVING ON UP	*Deconstruction*	2	*25 Sep 93*	11
DON'T LOOK ANY FURTHER	*Deconstruction*	9	*4 Dec 93*	10
RENAISSANCE	*Deconstruction*	5	*12 Mar 94*	7
Theme from BBC2's 'The Living Soap'.				
ELEGANTLY AMERICAN [EP]	*Deconstruction*	31	*17 Sep 94*	2
3 remixes of One Night In Heaven by David Morales and 1 of Moving On Up by MK (Mark Kinchen).				
SIGHT FOR SORE EYES	*Deconstruction*	6	*19 Nov 94*	9
OPEN YOUR HEART	*Deconstruction*	9	*4 Feb 95*	7
SEARCH FOR THE HERO	*Deconstruction*	9	*24 Jun 95*	7
LOVE RENDEZVOUS	*Deconstruction*	32	*14 Oct 95*	4
ITCHYCOO PARK	*Deconstruction*	11	*25 Nov 95*	8
JUST FOR YOU	*M People*	8	*4 Oct 97*	7
FANTASY ISLAND	*M People*	33	*6 Dec 97*	8
Backing vocals by Will Downing.				
FANTASY ISLAND [RE]	*M People*	69	*28 Feb 98*	1
ANGEL ST	*M People*	8	*28 Mar 98*	6
TESTIFY	*M People*	12	*7 Nov 98*	6
DREAMING	*M People*	13	*13 Feb 99*	4
ALBUMS:	**HITS 5**			**WEEKS 270**
NORTHERN SOUL	*Deconstruction*	53	*6 Mar 93*	2

ELEGANT SLUMMING	*Deconstruction*	2	*16 Oct 93*	87
BIZARRE FRUIT	*Deconstruction*	4	*26 Nov 94*	52
NORTHERN SOUL [RE]	*Deconstruction*	26	*16 Sep 95*	3
BIZARRE FRUIT / BIZARRE FRUIT II [RE]	*Deconstruction*	3	*9 Dec 95*	63
Bizzarre Fruit II was a remix album, sales were combined.				
FRESCO	*M People*	2	*25 Oct 97*	40
THE BEST OF M PEOPLE	*M People*	2	*14 Nov 98*	23

Lorin MAAZEL – See Andrew LLOYD WEBBER; PHILHARMONIA ORCHESTRA conducted by Lorin MAAZEL

Keith MAC PROJECT — UK

SINGLES:	HITS 1			WEEKS 1
DE DAH DAH (SPICE OF LIFE)	*Public Demand*	66	*25 Jun 94*	1

Pete MAC Junior — US

SINGLES:	HITS 1			WEEKS 4
THE WATER MARGIN	*BBC*	37	*15 Oct 77*	4

Japanese theme from the BBC1 TV series of the same name. [AA] listed with Godiego's English version.

Scott MAC – See SIGNUM

MAC BAND featuring the McCAMPBELL BROTHERS — US

SINGLES:	HITS 2			WEEKS 17
ROSES ARE RED	*MCA*	8	*18 Jun 88*	13
Chart for 18 Jun 88 reflects 12" only import catalogue number. Originally written for the Whispers who rejected it.				
STALEMATE	*MCA*	40	*10 Sep 88*	4
ALBUMS:	**HITS 1**			**WEEKS 3**
THE MAC BAND	*MCA*	61	*20 Aug 88*	3

David McALMONT — UK

(See also McAlmont and Butler.)

SINGLES:	HITS 3			WEEKS 5
HYMN	*Blanco Y Negro*	65	*27 Apr 96*	1
Above hit: ULTRAMARINE (featuring David McALMONT).				
LOOK AT YOURSELF	*Hut*	40	*9 Aug 97*	2
DIAMONDS ARE FOREVER	*East West*	39	*22 Nov 97*	2
Above hit: David McALMONT/David ARNOLD.				

McALMONT and BUTLER — UK

(See also Bernard Butler; David McAlmont.)

SINGLES:	HITS 2			WEEKS 12
YES	*Hut*	8	*27 May 95*	8
YOU DO	*Hut*	17	*4 Nov 95*	4
ALBUMS:	**HITS 1**			**WEEKS 8**
THE SOUND OF MCALMONT AND BUTLER	*Hut*	33	*9 Dec 95*	8

Neil MacARTHUR — UK

(See also Colin Blunstone.)

SINGLES:	HITS 1			WEEKS 5
SHE'S NOT THERE	*Deram*	34	*8 Feb 69*	5

David MacBETH – Kim DRAKE MUSIC – Beryl STOTT GROUP — UK

SINGLES:	HITS 1			WEEKS 4
MR. BLUE	*Pye*	18	*31 Oct 59*	4

Nicko McBRAIN — UK

SINGLES:	HITS 1			WEEKS 1
RHYTHM OF THE BEAST	*EMI*	72	*13 Jul 91*	1

Frankie McBRIDE — Ireland

SINGLES:	HITS 1			WEEKS 15
FIVE LITTLE FINGERS	*Emerald*	19	*12 Aug 67*	15
ALBUMS:	**HITS 1**			**WEEKS 3**
FRANKIE MCBRIDE	*Emerald*	29	*17 Feb 68*	3

MACC LADS — UK

ALBUMS:	HITS 1			WEEKS 1
FROM BEER TO ETERNITY	*Hectic House*	72	*7 Oct 89*	1

Dan McCAFFERTY | | | | UK

SINGLES:		HITS 1		WEEKS 3
OUT OF TIME	Mountain	41	13 Sep 75	3

C.W. McCALL | | | | US

SINGLES:		HITS 1		WEEKS 10
CONVOY	MGM	2	14 Feb 76	10

The song that brought the CB (Citizen Broadcast) Radio craze and slang to the public's attention in the UK.

David McCALLUM | | | | UK

SINGLES:		HITS 1		WEEKS 4
COMMUNICATION	Capitol	32	16 Apr 66	4

McCAMPBELL BROTHERS - See MAC BAND featuring the McCAMPBELL BROTHERS

Linda McCARTNEY | | | | UK

(See also Paul and Linda McCartney.)

SINGLES:		HITS 2		WEEKS 2
WIDE PRAIRIE	Parlophone	74	21 Nov 98	1
THE LIGHT COMES FROM WITHIN	Parlophone	56	6 Feb 99	1

Paul McCARTNEY | | | | UK

(See also Christians, Holly Johnson, Paul McCartney, Gerry Marsden and Stock Aitken Waterman; Paul and Linda McCartney.)

SINGLES:		HITS 49		WEEKS 396
ANOTHER DAY	Apple	2	27 Feb 71	12
GIVE IRELAND BACK TO THE IRISH	Apple	16	26 Feb 72	8
MARY HAD A LITTLE LAMB	Apple	9	27 May 72	11
HI, HI, HI/C MOON	Apple	5	9 Dec 72	13

Above 3 WINGS.

MY LOVE	Apple	9	7 Apr 73	11

Above hit: Paul McCARTNEY and WINGS.

LIVE AND LET DIE	Apple	9	9 Jun 73	13

From the James Bond film of the same name.
Above hit: WINGS.

LIVE AND LET DIE [RE]	Apple	49	15 Sep 73	1
HELEN WHEELS	Apple	12	3 Nov 73	12
JET	Apple	7	2 Mar 74	9
BAND ON THE RUN	Apple	3	6 Jul 74	11
JUNIOR'S FARM	Apple	16	9 Nov 74	10

Above 4: Paul McCARTNEY and WINGS.

LISTEN TO WHAT THE MAN SAID	Capitol	6	31 May 75	8
LETTING GO	Capitol	41	18 Oct 75	3
SILLY LOVE SONGS	Parlophone	2	15 May 76	11
LET 'EM IN	Parlophone	2	7 Aug 76	10
MAYBE I'M AMAZED	Parlophone	28	19 Feb 77	5
MULL OF KINTYRE / GIRLS' SCHOOL	Capitol	1	19 Nov 77	17

The best selling single of all-time in the UK until replaced by Band Aid's Do They Know It's Christmas in 1984.

WITH A LITTLE LUCK	Parlophone	5	1 Apr 78	9
I'VE HAD ENOUGH	Parlophone	42	1 Jul 78	7
LONDON TOWN	Parlophone	60	9 Sep 78	4
GOODNIGHT TONIGHT	Parlophone	5	7 Apr 79	10
OLD SIAM, SIR	Parlophone	35	16 Jun 79	6
GETTING CLOSER / BABY'S REQUEST	Parlophone	60	1 Sep 79	3

Above 12: WINGS.

WONDERFUL CHRISTMASTIME	Parlophone	6	1 Dec 79	8
COMING UP	Parlophone	2	19 Apr 80	9
WATERFALLS	Parlophone	9	21 Jun 80	8
EBONY AND IVORY	Parlophone	1	10 Apr 82	10

Above hit: Paul McCARTNEY with additional vocals by Stevie WONDER.

TAKE IT AWAY	Parlophone	15	3 Jul 82	10
TUG OF WAR	Parlophone	53	9 Oct 82	3
THE GIRL IS MINE	Epic	8	6 Nov 82	9

Above hit: Michael JACKSON and Paul McCARTNEY.

THE GIRL IS MINE [RE]	Epic	75	15 Jan 83	1
SAY SAY SAY	Parlophone	2	15 Oct 83	15

Above hit: Paul McCARTNEY and Michael JACKSON.

PIPES OF PEACE	Parlophone	1	17 Dec 83	12
NO MORE LONELY NIGHTS (BALLAD)	Parlophone	2	6 Oct 84	15

From the film 'Give My Regards To Broad Street'.

WE ALL STAND TOGETHER	Parlophone	3	24 Nov 84	13

From the animated film 'Rupert And The Frog Song'.
Above hit: Paul McCARTNEY and the FROG CHORUS.

SPIES LIKE US	Parlophone	13	30 Nov 85	10

From the film of the same name.

WE ALL STAND TOGETHER [RE]	*Parlophone*	32	*21 Dec 85*	5
PRESS	*Parlophone*	25	*26 Jul 86*	8
ONLY LOVE REMAINS	*Parlophone*	34	*13 Dec 86*	5
ONCE UPON A LONG AGO	*Parlophone*	10	*28 Nov 87*	7
MY BRAVE FACE	*Parlophone*	18	*20 May 89*	5
Co-written by Elvis Costello.				
THIS ONE	*Parlophone*	18	*29 Jul 89*	6
FIGURE OF EIGHT	*Parlophone*	42	*25 Nov 89*	3
PUT IT THERE	*Parlophone*	32	*17 Feb 90*	2
BIRTHDAY	*Parlophone*	29	*20 Oct 90*	3
ALL MY TRIALS	*Parlophone*	35	*8 Dec 90*	5
HOPE OF DELIVERANCE	*Parlophone*	18	*9 Jan 93*	6
C'MON PEOPLE	*Parlophone*	41	*6 Mar 93*	3
YOUNG BOY	*Parlophone*	19	*10 May 97*	3
THE WORLD TONIGHT	*Parlophone*	23	*19 Jul 97*	2
BEAUTIFUL NIGHT	*Parlophone*	25	*27 Dec 97*	4
Features Ringo Starr on drums, George Martin on backing vocals and Jeff Lynne on guitar.				
NO OTHER BABY / BROWN EYED HANDSOME MAN	*Parlophone*	42	*6 Nov 99*	2
No Other Baby originally recorded by Dickie Bishop and the Sidekicks but based on the Vipers'				
version from 1958. Brown Eyed Handsome Man originally recorded by Chuck Berry in 1956.				

ALBUMS:	**HITS 25**		**WEEKS 525**	
MCCARTNEY	*Apple*	2	*2 May 70*	32
WINGS WILDLIFE	*Apple*	11	*18 Dec 71*	9
Above hit: WINGS.				
RED ROSE SPEEDWAY	*Apple*	5	*19 May 73*	16
BAND ON THE RUN	*Apple*	1	*15 Dec 73*	124
Peak position reached on 27 Jul 74.				
Above 2: Paul McCARTNEY and WINGS.				
VENUS AND MARS	*Apple*	1	*21 Jun 75*	29
WINGS AT THE SPEED OF SOUND	*Apple*	2	*17 Apr 76*	35
WINGS OVER AMERICA	*Parlophone*	8	*15 Jan 77*	22
Live recordings from their 1976 US tour.				
LONDON TOWN	*Parlophone*	4	*15 Apr 78*	23
WINGS GREATEST HITS	*Parlophone*	5	*16 Dec 78*	32
BACK TO THE EGG	*Parlophone*	6	*23 Jun 79*	15
Above 6: WINGS.				
MCCARTNEY II	*Parlophone*	1	*31 May 80*	18
THE MCCARTNEY INTERVIEW	*EMI*	34	*7 Mar 81*	4
Originally a promotional record for US radio stations.				
TUG OF WAR	*Parlophone*	1	*8 May 82*	27
PIPES OF PEACE	*Parlophone*	4	*12 Nov 83*	23
GIVE MY REGARDS TO BROAD STREET [OST]	*Parlophone*	1	*3 Nov 84*	21
PRESS TO PLAY	*Parlophone*	8	*13 Sep 86*	6
ALL THE BEST!	*Parlophone*	2	*14 Nov 87*	21
FLOWERS IN THE DIRT	*Parlophone*	1	*17 Jun 89*	20
TRIPPING THE LIVE FANTASTIC	*Parlophone*	17	*17 Nov 90*	11
UNPLUGGED - THE OFFICIAL BOOTLEG	*Parlophone*	7	*1 Jun 91*	3
CHOBA B CCCP (THE RUSSIAN ALBUM)	*Parlophone*	63	*12 Oct 91*	1
Originally released in Russia,1988.				
OFF THE GROUND	*Parlophone*	5	*13 Feb 93*	4
PAUL IS LIVE	*Parlophone*	34	*20 Nov 93*	2
Live recordings from his 1993 tour.				
FLAMING PIE	*Parlophone*	2	*17 May 97*	15
BAND ON THE RUN [RI]	*Parlophone*	69	*27 Mar 99*	1
25th anniversary edition.				
Above hit: Paul McCARTNEY and WINGS.				
RUN DEVIL RUN	*Parlophone*	12	*16 Oct 99*	11
Collection of rock'n'roll covers.				

Paul and Linda McCARTNEY   UK

(See also Linda McCartney; Paul McCartney.)

SINGLES:	**HITS 1**		**WEEKS 5**	
THE BACK SEAT OF MY CAR	*Apple*	39	*28 Aug 71*	5

ALBUMS:	**HITS 1**		**WEEKS 24**	
RAM	*Apple*	1	*5 Jun 71*	24

William McCLINTOCK BUNBURY – See George BOWYER and William McCLINTOCK BUNBURY

Kirsty MacCOLL   UK

(See also Billy Bragg.)

SINGLES:	**HITS 9**		**WEEKS 63**	
THERE'S A GUY WORKS DOWN THE CHIP SHOP, SWEARS HE'S ELVIS	*Polydor*	14	*13 Jun 81*	9
A NEW ENGLAND	*Stiff*	7	*19 Jan 85*	10
Originally recorded by Billy Bragg.				
FAIRYTALE OF NEW YORK	*Pogue Mahone*	2	*5 Dec 87*	9
Above hit: POGUES featuring Kirsty MacCOLL.				
FREE WORLD	*Virgin*	43	*8 Apr 89*	6

DAYS	Virgin	12	1 Jul 89	9
WALKING DOWN MADISON	Virgin	23	25 May 91	7
MY AFFAIR	Virgin	56	17 Aug 91	2
FAIRYTALE OF NEW YORK [RI]	PM	36	14 Dec 91	5

Above hit: POGUES featuring Kirsty MacCOLL.

| CAROLINE | Virgin | 58 | 4 Mar 95 | 2 |
| PERFECT DAY | Virgin | 75 | 24 Jun 95 | 1 |

Above hit: Kirsty MacCOLL and Evan DANDO.

| DAYS [RI] | Virgin | 42 | 29 Jul 95 | 3 |

Featured in the Sony Handcam Camcorder TV commerical.

ALBUMS:	HITS 4		WEEKS 49	
KITE	Virgin	34	20 May 89	12
ELECTRIC LANDLADY	Virgin	17	6 Jul 91	8
TITANIC DAYS	ZTT	46	12 Mar 94	2
GALORE - THE BEST OF KIRSTY MACCOLL	Virgin	6	18 Mar 95	27

Marilyn McCOO and Billy DAVIS, JR.   US

| SINGLES: | HITS 1 | | WEEKS 9 | |
| YOU DON'T HAVE TO BE A STAR (TO BE IN MY SHOW) | ABC | 7 | 19 Mar 77 | 9 |

Del McCOURY BAND - See Steve EARLE

Van McCOY   US

| SINGLES: | HITS 4 | | WEEKS 36 | |
| THE HUSTLE | Avco | 3 | 31 May 75 | 12 |

Above hit: Van McCOY and the SOUL CITY SYMPHONY.

CHANGE WITH THE TIMES	Avco	36	1 Nov 75	4
SOUL CHA CHA	H&L	34	12 Feb 77	6
THE SHUFFLE	H&L	4	9 Apr 77	14
ALBUMS:	HITS 1		WEEKS 11	
DISCO BABY	Avco	32	5 Jul 75	11

Above hit: Van McCOY and the SOUL CITY SYMPHONY.

McCOYS   US

| SINGLES: | HITS 2 | | WEEKS 18 | |
| HANG ON SLOOPY | Immediate | 5 | 4 Sep 65 | 14 |

Originally recorded by the Vibrations as My Girl Sloopy.

| FEVER | Immediate | 44 | 18 Dec 65 | 4 |

Originally recorded by Little Willie John.

George McCRAE   US

SINGLES:	HITS 8		WEEKS 62	
ROCK YOUR BABY	Jay Boy	1	29 Jun 74	14
I CAN'T LEAVE YOU ALONE	Jay Boy	9	5 Oct 74	9
YOU CAN HAVE IT ALL	Jay Boy	23	14 Dec 74	9
SING A HAPPY SONG	Jay Boy	38	22 Mar 75	4
IT'S BEEN SO LONG	Jay Boy	4	19 Jul 75	11
I AIN'T LYIN'	Jay Boy	12	18 Oct 75	7
HONEY I	Jay Boy	33	24 Jan 76	4
ONE STEP CLOSER (TO LOVE)	President	57	25 Feb 84	4
ALBUMS:	HITS 2		WEEKS 29	
ROCK YOUR BABY	Jay Boy	13	3 Aug 74	28
GEORGE MCCRAE	Jay Boy	54	13 Sep 75	1

Gwen McCRAE   US

SINGLES:	HITS 2		WEEKS 5	
ALL THIS LOVE THAT I'M GIVING	Flame	63	30 Apr 88	2
ALL THIS LOVE I'M GIVING [RR]	KTDA	36	13 Feb 93	3

Above hit: MUSIC and MYSTERY featuring Gwen McCRAE.

McCRARYS   US

| SINGLES: | HITS 1 | | WEEKS 4 | |
| LOVE ON A SUMMER NIGHT | Capitol | 52 | 31 Jul 82 | 4 |

Mindy McCREADY   US

| SINGLES: | HITS 1 | | WEEKS 3 | |
| OH ROMEO | BNA | 41 | 1 Aug 98 | 3 |

Ian McCULLOCH   UK

| SINGLES: | HITS 4 | | WEEKS 14 | |
| SEPTEMBER SONG | Korova | 51 | 15 Dec 84 | 5 |

Originally recorded by Walter Huston.

| PROUD TO FALL | WEA | 51 | 2 Sep 89 | 4 |

CANDLELAND (THE SECOND COMING)	*East West*	75	*12 May 90*	1

Above hit: Ian McCULLOCH featuring Elizabeth FRASER.

LOVER LOVER LOVER	*WEA*	47	*22 Feb 92*	4
ALBUMS:	**HITS 2**			**WEEKS 4**
CANDLELAND	*WEA*	18	*7 Oct 89*	3
MYSTERIO	*East West*	46	*21 Mar 92*	1

Martine McCUTCHEON — UK

SINGLES:	**HITS 4**			**WEEKS 36**
ARE YOU MAN ENOUGH	*Avex UK*	62	*18 Nov 95*	1

Above hit: UNO CLIO featuring Martine McCUTCHEON.

PERFECT MOMENT	*Innocent*	1	*17 Apr 99*	15

Originally recorded by Edyta Gorniak in 1997.

PERFECT MOMENT [RE]	*Innocent*	59	*14 Aug 99*	5
I'VE GOT YOU	*Innocent*	6	*11 Sep 99*	10
TALKING IN YOUR SLEEP / LOVE ME	*Innocent*	6	*4 Dec 99*	5

Charity record in aid of the BBC's Children In Need Appeal.

ALBUMS:	**HITS 1**			**WEEKS 16**
YOU, ME & US	*Innocent*	2	*18 Sep 99*	16

Gene McDANIELS — US

SINGLES:	**HITS 1**			**WEEKS 2**
TOWER OF STRENGTH	*London*	49	*18 Nov 61*	1

Backing vocals by the Johnny Mann Singers.

TOWER OF STRENGTH [RE]	*London*	49	*2 Dec 61*	1

Julie McDERMOTT - See AWESOME 3; THIRD DIMENSION featuring Julie McDERMOTT

Chas McDEVITT SKIFFLE GROUP (featuring Nancy WHISKEY) — UK

SINGLES:	**HITS 2**			**WEEKS 20**
FREIGHT TRAIN	*Oriole*	5	*13 Apr 57*	17
GREENBACK DOLLAR	*Oriole*	28	*15 Jun 57*	1
GREENBACK DOLLAR [RE]	*Oriole*	30	*6 Jul 57*	1
FREIGHT TRAIN [RE]	*Oriole*	27	*21 Sep 57*	1

Jane McDONALD — UK

SINGLES:	**HITS 1**			**WEEKS 7**
CRUISE INTO CHRISTMAS [M]	*Focus Music International*	10	*26 Dec 98*	7
ALBUMS:	**HITS 1**			**WEEKS 27**
JANE MCDONALD	*Focus Music International*	1	*25 Jul 98*	27

First new act to debut at No. 1 without a hit single.

Michael McDONALD — US

(See also Doobie Brothers.)

SINGLES:	**HITS 4**			**WEEKS 45**
YAH MO B THERE	*Qwest*	44	*18 Feb 84*	5
YAH MO B THERE [RE]	*Qwest*	69	*7 Apr 84*	3
YAH MO B THERE [RM]	*Qwest*	12	*12 Jan 85*	8

Remixed by John 'Jellybean' Benitez. The remix had the same catalogue number as the original.
Above 3: James INGRAM (with Michael McDONALD).

ON MY OWN	*MCA*	2	*3 May 86*	13

Above hit: Patti LABELLE and Michael McDONALD.

I KEEP FORGETTIN'	*Warner Brothers*	43	*26 Jul 86*	6

Originally released 1982, reaching No. 4 in the US. Originally recorded by Chuck Jackson.

SWEET FREEDOM	*MCA*	12	*6 Sep 86*	10

From the film 'Running Scared'.

ALBUMS:	**HITS 2**			**WEEKS 39**
SWEET FREEDOM: BEST OF MICHAEL McDONALD	*Warner Brothers*	6	*22 Nov 86*	35
TAKE IT TO HEART	*Reprise*	35	*26 May 90*	4

Carrie McDOWELL — US

SINGLES:	**HITS 1**			**WEEKS 3**
UH UH, NO NO CASUAL SEX	*Motown*	68	*26 Sep 87*	3

John McENROE and Pat CASH with the FULL METAL RACKET — US/Australia

SINGLES:	**HITS 1**			**WEEKS 1**
ROCK AND ROLL	*Music For Nations*	66	*13 Jul 91*	1

Reba McENTIRE — US

SINGLES:	**HITS 1**			**WEEKS 1**
DOES HE LOVE YOU	*MCA Nashville*	62	*19 Jun 99*	1

MACEO and the MACKS — US

SINGLES:	HITS 1			WEEKS 5	
CROSS THE TRACK (WE BETTER GO BACK)	Urban		54	16 May 87	5

McFADDEN and WHITEHEAD — US

SINGLES:	HITS 1			WEEKS 10	
AIN'T NO STOPPIN' US NOW	Philadelphia International		5	19 May 79	10

Rachel McFARLANE — UK

(See also Loveland featuring the Voice Of Rachel McFarlane.)

SINGLES:	HITS 1			WEEKS 2	
LOVER	Multiply		38	1 Aug 98	2

Bobby McFERRIN — US

SINGLES:	HITS 2			WEEKS 15	
DON'T WORRY BE HAPPY	Manhattan		2	24 Sep 88	11
THINKIN' ABOUT YOUR BODY	Manhattan		46	17 Dec 88	4

Featured in the Cadbury's chocolate TV commercial with ammended words.

ALBUMS:	HITS 1			WEEKS 1	
SIMPLE PLEASURES	Manhattan		92	29 Oct 88	1

McGANNS — UK

SINGLES:	HITS 2			WEEKS 4	
JUST MY IMAGINATION	Coalition		59	14 Nov 98	1
A HEARTBEAT AWAY	Coalition		42	6 Feb 99	3

Kate and Anna McGARRIGLE — Canada

ALBUMS:	HITS 1			WEEKS 4	
DANCER WITH BRUISED KNEES	Warner Brothers		35	26 Feb 77	4

Mike McGEAR — UK

SINGLES:	HITS 1			WEEKS 4	
LEAVE IT	Warner Brothers		36	5 Oct 74	4

Maureen McGOVERN — US

SINGLES:	HITS 1			WEEKS 8	
THE CONTINENTAL	20th Century		16	5 Jun 76	8

Shane MacGOWAN — UK

SINGLES:	HITS 5			WEEKS 9	
WHAT A WONDERFUL WORLD	Mute		72	12 Dec 92	1

Above hit: Nick CAVE andShane MacGOWAN.

THE CHURCH OF THE HOLY SPOOK	ZTT		74	3 Sep 94	1
THAT WOMAN'S GOT ME DRINKING	ZTT		34	15 Oct 94	3

Features actor Johnny Depp on guitar.
Above 2: Shane MacGOWAN and the POPES.

HAUNTED	ZTT		30	29 Apr 95	2

Above hit: Shane MacGOWAN and Sinead O'CONNOR.

MY WAY	ZTT		29	20 Apr 96	2

Featured in the Nike Swoosh trainers TV commercial.

ALBUMS:	HITS 2			WEEKS 3	
THE SNAKE	ZTT		37	29 Oct 94	2
THE CROCK OF GOLD	ZTT		59	8 Nov 97	1

Above 2: Shane MacGOWAN and the POPES.

Ewan McGREGOR - See PF PROJECT featuring Ewan McGREGOR

Freddie McGREGOR — Jamaica

SINGLES:	HITS 2			WEEKS 16	
JUST DON'T WANT TO BE LONELY	Germain		9	27 Jun 87	11
THAT GIRL (GROOVY SITUATION)	Polydor		47	19 Sep 87	5

Mary MacGREGOR — US

SINGLES:	HITS 1			WEEKS 10	
TORN BETWEEN TWO LOVERS	Ariola America		4	19 Feb 77	10
ALBUMS:	HITS 1			WEEKS 1	
TORN BETWEEN TWO LOVERS	Ariola America		59	23 Apr 77	1

McGUINNESS FLINT — UK

SINGLES:	HITS 2			WEEKS 26
WHEN I'M DEAD AND GONE	Capitol	2	21 Nov 70	14
Originally recorded by Laura Nyro.				
MALT AND BARLEY BLUES	Capitol	5	1 May 71	12
ALBUMS:	**HITS 1**			**WEEKS 10**
MCGUINNESS FLINT	Capitol	9	23 Jan 71	10

Barry McGUIRE — US

SINGLES:	HITS 1			WEEKS 13
EVE OF DESTRUCTION	RCA Victor	3	11 Sep 65	13
Originally recorded by P.F.Sloan.				

McGUIRE SISTERS — US

SINGLES:	HITS 4			WEEKS 24
NO MORE	Vogue Coral	20	2 Apr 55	1
SINCERELY	Vogue Coral	14	16 Jul 55	4
Above 2 entries were separate sides of the same release, each had its own chart run.				
DELILAH JONES	Vogue Coral	24	2 Jun 56	2
SUGARTIME	Coral	14	15 Feb 58	6
MAY YOU ALWAYS	Coral	15	2 May 59	10
MAY YOU ALWAYS [RE]	Coral	28	18 Jul 59	1

MACHEL — Trinidad

SINGLES:	HITS 1			WEEKS 1
COME DIG IT	London	56	14 Sep 96	1
Featured in the Lilt TV commercial.				

MACHINE HEAD — US

SINGLES:	HITS 3			WEEKS 4
OLD	Roadrunner	43	27 May 95	2
TAKE MY SCARS	Roadrunner	73	6 Dec 97	1
FROM THIS DAY	Roadrunner	74	18 Dec 99	1
ALBUMS:	**HITS 3**			**WEEKS 8**
BURN MY EYES	Roadrunner	25	20 Aug 94	3
THE MORE THINGS CHANGE . . .	Roadrunner	16	5 Apr 97	3
THE BURNING RED	Roadrunner	13	21 Aug 99	2

Hal McINTRYE and his Orchestra - See MILLS BROTHERS with Hal McINTRYE and his Orchestra

Craig MACK — US

(See also Various Artists (EPs) 'Dangerous Minds EP'.)

SINGLES:	HITS 3			WEEKS 5
FLAVA IN YA EAR	Bad Boy	57	12 Nov 94	2
Features rapping by Busta Rhymes.				
GET DOWN	Puff Daddy	54	1 Apr 95	1
SPIRIT	A&M	35	7 Jun 97	2
Above hit: SOUNDS OF BLACKNESS featuring Craig MACK.				

Lizzy MACK — UK

SINGLES:	HITS 2			WEEKS 3
THE POWER OF LOVE	Media	49	5 Nov 94	2
Above hit: FITS OF GLOOM featuring Lizzy MACK.				
DON'T GO	Media	52	4 Nov 95	1

Lonnie MACK — US

SINGLES:	HITS 1			WEEKS 3
MEMPHIS	Lightning	47	14 Apr 79	3
[AA] listed with Let's Dance by Chris Montez. It was originally recorded by Chuck Berry in 1959; Mack's version reached No.5 in the US in 1963.				

MACK VIBE featuring JACQUELINE — US

SINGLES:	HITS 1			WEEKS 1
I CAN'T LET YOU GO	MCA	53	4 Feb 95	1

Duff McKAGAN — US

ALBUMS:	HITS 1			WEEKS 2
BELIEVE IN ME	Geffen	27	9 Oct 93	2

Maria McKEE   US

SINGLES:	HITS 5			WEEKS 23
SHOW ME HEAVEN	Epic	1	15 Sep 90	14
From the film 'Days Of Thunder'.				
BREATHE	Geffen	59	26 Jan 91	1
SWEETEST CHILD	Geffen	45	1 Aug 92	4
I'M GONNA SOOTHE YOU	Geffen	35	22 May 93	3
I CAN'T MAKE IT ALONE	Geffen	74	18 Sep 93	1
ALBUMS:	HITS 2			WEEKS 6
MARIA MCKEE	Geffen	49	24 Jun 89	3
YOU GOTTA SIN TO GET SAVED	Geffen	26	12 Jun 93	3

Kenneth McKELLAR   UK

SINGLES:	HITS 1			WEEKS 4
A MAN WITHOUT LOVE	Decca	30	12 Mar 66	4
UK's Eurovision entry in 1966, it came 9th.				
EPS:	HITS 4			WEEKS 7
KENNETH McKELLAR SINGS HANDEL	Decca	12	26 Mar 60	3
HANDEL'S ARIAS	Decca	9	3 Sep 60	1
KENNETH McKELLAR NO. 2	Decca	13	24 Sep 60	1
ROAD TO THE ISLES	Decca	8	24 Dec 60	2
ALBUMS:	HITS 2			WEEKS 10
THE WORLD OF KENNETH MCKELLAR	Decca	27	28 Jun 69	7
ECCO DI NAPOLI	Decca	45	31 Jan 70	3

Terence McKENNA – See SHAMEN

Billy MacKENZIE   UK

ALBUMS:	HITS 1			WEEKS 1
BEYOND THE SUN	Nude	64	18 Oct 97	1
Charity record with proceeds to the Samaritans/Macmillan Cancer Relief Fund.				

Gisele MacKENZIE   Canada

SINGLES:	HITS 1			WEEKS 6
SEVEN LONELY DAYS	Capitol	12	18 Jul 53	1
SEVEN LONELY DAYS [RE-1ST]	Capitol	11	1 Aug 53	1
SEVEN LONELY DAYS [RE-2ND]	Capitol	6	22 Aug 53	4

Scott McKENZIE   US

SINGLES:	HITS 2			WEEKS 18
SAN FRANCISCO (BE SURE TO WEAR SOME FLOWERS IN YOUR HAIR)	CBS	1	15 Jul 67	17
LIKE AN OLD TIME MOVIE	CBS	50	4 Nov 67	1
Above hit: Voice Of Scott McKENZIE.				

Ken MacKINTOSH, his Saxophone and his Orchestra   UK

SINGLES:	HITS 3			WEEKS 9
THE CREEP	His Master's Voice	12	16 Jan 54	1
THE CREEP [RE]	His Master's Voice	10	30 Jan 54	1
RAUNCHY	His Master's Voice	19	8 Feb 58	6
NO HIDING PLACE	His Master's Voice	45	12 Mar 60	1
Above hit: Ken MACKINTOSH.				

Brian McKNIGHT   US

SINGLES:	HITS 2			WEEKS 4
ANYTIME	Motown	48	6 Jun 98	2
YOU SHOULD BE MINE (DON'T WASTE YOUR TIME)	Motown	36	3 Oct 98	2
Above hit: Brian McKNIGHT featuring MASE.				

Vivienne McKONE   UK

SINGLES:	HITS 2			WEEKS 5
SING	ffrr	47	25 Jul 92	4
BEWARE	ffrr	69	31 Oct 92	1

McKOY   UK

SINGLES:	HITS 1			WEEKS 2
FIGHT	Rightrack	54	6 Mar 93	2

Noel McKOY – See McKoy; James Taylor Quartet

Craig McLACHLAN   Australia
(See also Various Artists: Stage Cast - London 'Grease'.)

SINGLES:		HITS 8		WEEKS 40	
MONA	Epic		2	16 Jun 90	11
Originally recorded by Bo Diddley.					
AMANDA	Epic		19	4 Aug 90	6
I ALMOST FELT LIKE CRYING	Epic		50	10 Nov 90	3
Above 3: Craig McLACHLAN and CHECK 1-2.					
ONE REASON WHY	Epic		29	23 May 92	6
ON MY OWN	Columbia		59	14 Nov 92	2
YOU'RE THE ONE THAT I WANT	Epic		13	24 Jul 93	6
Above hit: Craig McLACHLAN and Debbie GIBSON.					
GREASE	Epic		44	25 Dec 93	4
Above 2 from the show 'Grease'.					
EVERYDAY	MDMC		65	8 Jul 95	2
Above hit: Craig McLACHLAN and the CULPRITS.					
ALBUMS:		HITS 1		WEEKS 11	
CRAIG MCLACHLAN AND CHECK 1-2	Epic		10	21 Jul 90	11
Above hit: Craig McLACHLAN and CHECK 1-2.					

Sarah McLACHLAN   Canada

SINGLES:		HITS 1		WEEKS 5	
ADIA	Arista		18	3 Oct 98	5
ALBUMS:		HITS 1		WEEKS 2	
SURFACING	Arista		47	17 Oct 98	2

Tommy McLAIN   US

SINGLES:		HITS 1		WEEKS 1	
SWEET DREAMS	London		49	10 Sep 66	1
Originally recorded by Don Gibson.					

Malcolm McLAREN   UK

SINGLES:		HITS 11		WEEKS 66	
BUFFALO GALS	Charisma		9	4 Dec 82	12
Above hit: Malcolm McLAREN and the WORLD'S FAMOUS SUPREME TEAM.					
SOWETO	Charisma		32	26 Feb 83	5
Above hit: Malcolm McLAREN with the McLARENETTES.					
DOUBLE DUTCH	Charisma		3	2 Jul 83	13
DUCK FOR THE OYSTER	Charisma		54	17 Dec 83	5
MADAM BUTTERFLY (UN BEL DI VEDREMO)	Charisma		13	1 Sep 84	9
WALTZ DARLING	Epic		31	27 May 89	8
Above hit: Malcolm McLAREN and the BOOTZILLA ORCHESTRA.					
SOMETHING'S JUMPIN' IN YOUR SHIRT	Epic		29	19 Aug 89	7
Sleeve credits Lisa Marie with Malcolm McLaren and the Bootzilla Orchestra.					
Above hit: Malcolm McLAREN and the BOOTZILLA ORCHESTRA.					
HOUSE OF THE BLUE DANUBE	Epic		73	25 Nov 89	1
Above hit: Malcolm McLAREN and the BOOTZILLA ORCHESTRA.					
OPERAA HOUSE	Virgin		75	8 Dec 90	1
Above hit: Malcolm McLAREN presents the WORLD FAMOUS SUPREME TEAM SHOW.					
MAGIC'S BACK (THEME FROM 'THE GHOSTS OF OXFORD STREET')	RCA		42	21 Dec 91	4
Theme from the Channel 4 TV programme.					
Above hit: Malcolm McLAREN featuring Alison LIMERICK.					
BUFFALO GALS STAMPEDE [RR]	Virgin		65	3 Oct 98	1
Roger Sanchez remixed track 1 (as per CD order). Rakim appeared on track 2: Buffalo Gals (Back To Skool).					
Above hit: Malcolm McLAREN and the WORLD FAMOUS SUPREME TEAM versus RAKIM and Roger SANCHEZ.					
ALBUMS:		HITS 5		WEEKS 41	
DUCK ROCK	Charisma		18	4 Jun 83	17
WOULD YA LIKE MORE SCRATCHIN'	Charisma		44	26 May 84	4
Above hit: Malcolm McLAREN and the WORLD'S FAMOUS SUPREME TEAM SHOW.					
FANS	Charisma		47	29 Dec 84	8
WALTZ DARLING	Epic		30	15 Jul 89	11
Above hit: Malcolm McLAREN and the BOOTZILLA ORCHESTRA.					
PARIS	No!		44	20 Aug 94	1

McLARENETTES - See Malcolm McLAREN

Mahavishnu John McLAUGHLIN - See MAHAVISHNU ORCHESTRA; Carlos SANTANA and Mahavishnu John McLAUGHLIN

Bitty McLEAN   UK

SINGLES:		HITS 10		WEEKS 50	
IT KEEPS RAININ' (TEARS FROM MY EYES)	Brilliant		2	31 Jul 93	15

PASS IT ON	Brilliant	35	30 Oct 93	3
Originally recorded by Bob Marley & The Wailers.				
HERE I STAND	Brilliant	10	15 Jan 94	6
Originally recorded by Wade Flemons.				
DEDICATED TO THE ONE I LOVE	Brilliant	6	9 Apr 94	10
WHAT GOES AROUND	Brilliant	36	6 Aug 94	3
OVER THE RIVER	Brilliant	27	8 Apr 95	4
Originally recorded by Justin Hinds.				
WE'VE ONLY JUST BEGUN	Brilliant	23	17 Jun 95	5
NOTHING CAN CHANGE THIS LOVE	Brilliant	55	30 Sep 95	2
Originally recorded by Sam Cooke reached No. 12 in the US in 1962.				
NATURAL HIGH	Brilliant	63	27 Jan 96	1
SHE'S ALRIGHT	Kuff	53	5 Oct 96	1
Originally recorded by Otis Redding in 1968.				
ALBUMS:	**HITS 1**			**WEEKS 11**
JUST TO LET YOU KNOW	Brilliant	19	19 Feb 94	11

Don McLEAN · US

SINGLES:	**HITS 5**			**WEEKS 68**
AMERICAN PIE	United Artists	2	22 Jan 72	16
Dedicated to Buddy Holly.				
VINCENT	United Artists	1	13 May 72	15
Dedicated to Vincent Van Gogh.				
EVERY DAY	United Artists	38	14 Apr 73	5
Originally recorded by Buddy Holly.				
CRYING	EMI	1	10 May 80	14
CASTLES IN THE AIR	EMI	47	17 Apr 82	8
New recording of a song first issued in 1972 as the B-side to Vincent.				
AMERICAN PIE [RI]	Liberty	12	5 Oct 91	10
ALBUMS:	**HITS 5**			**WEEKS 89**
AMERICAN PIE	United Artists	3	11 Mar 72	54
TAPESTRY	United Artists	16	17 Jun 72	12
PLAYIN' FAVORITES	United Artists	42	24 Nov 73	2
CHAIN LIGHTNING	EMI International	19	14 Jun 80	9
THE VERY BEST OF DON MCLEAN	United Artists	4	27 Sep 80	12

Jackie McLEAN · US

SINGLES:	**HITS 1**			**WEEKS 4**
DOCTOR JACKYLL AND MISTER FUNK	RCA Victor	53	7 Jul 79	4

Phil McLEAN · US

SINGLES:	**HITS 1**			**WEEKS 4**
SMALL SAD SAM	Top Rank	34	20 Jan 62	4
A parody of Big Bad John.				

Andy McNAB · UK

ALBUMS:	**HITS 1**			**WEEKS 2**
BRAVO TWO ZERO	PolyGram TV	45	21 May 94	2

Ian McNABB · UK

SINGLES:	**HITS 5**			**WEEKS 6**
IF LOVE WAS LIKE GUITARS	This Way Up	67	23 Jan 93	1
YOU MUST BE PREPARED TO DREAM	This Way Up	54	2 Jul 94	1
Above hit: Ian McNABB featuring Ralph MOLINA and Billy TALBOT of CRAZY				
HORSE with Mike 'Tone' HAMILTON – Rhythm guitar.				
GO INTO THE LIGHT	This Way Up	66	17 Sep 94	2
DON'T PUT YOUR SPELL ON ME	This Way Up	72	27 Apr 96	1
MERSEYBEAST	This Way Up	74	6 Jul 96	1
ALBUMS:	**HITS 3**			**WEEKS 5**
TRUTH AND BEAUTY	This Way Up	51	30 Jan 93	1
HEAD LIKE A ROCK	This Way Up	29	16 Jul 94	2
MERSEYBEAST	This Way Up	30	18 May 96	2

Lutricia McNEAL · US

SINGLES:	**HITS 4**			**WEEKS 43**
AIN'T THAT JUST THE WAY	Wildstar	6	29 Nov 97	18
Originally recorded by 1970s porn star Barby Benton.				
STRANDED	Wildstar	3	23 May 98	12
SOMEONE LOVES YOU HONEY	Wildstar	9	26 Sep 98	7
Originally recorded by Brenda Lee.				
THE GREATEST LOVE YOU'LL NEVER KNOW	Wildstar	17	19 Dec 98	6
ALBUMS:	**HITS 1**			**WEEKS 16**
LUTRICIA MCNEAL	Wildstar	16	25 Jul 98	16

537

Patrick MacNEE and Honor BLACKMAN — UK

SINGLES:		HITS 1			WEEKS 7
KINKY BOOTS	Deram		5	1 Dec 90	7

Originally recorded in 1964; it charted after being championed by Simon Mayo's Radio 1 breakfast show.

Rita MacNEIL — Canada

SINGLES:		HITS 1			WEEKS 10
WORKING MAN	Polydor		11	6 Oct 90	10
ALBUMS:		HITS 1			WEEKS 4
REASON TO BELIEVE	Polydor		32	24 Nov 90	4

Clyde McPHATTER — US

SINGLES:		HITS 1			WEEKS 1
TREASURE OF LOVE	London		27	25 Aug 56	1

Carmen McRAE – See Sammy DAVIS JR

Ian McSHANE — UK

ALBUMS:		HITS 1			WEEKS 7
FROM BOTH SIDES NOW	PolyGram TV		40	21 Nov 92	7

Ralph McTELL — UK

SINGLES:		HITS 2			WEEKS 18
STREETS OF LONDON	Reprise		2	7 Dec 74	12
DREAMS OF YOU	Warner Brothers		36	20 Dec 75	6
ALBUMS:		HITS 3			WEEKS 17
NOT TILL TOMORROW	Reprise		36	18 Nov 72	1
EASY	Reprise		31	2 Mar 74	4
STREETS	Warner Brothers		13	15 Feb 75	12

Christine McVIE — US

ALBUMS:		HITS 1			WEEKS 4
CHRISTINE MCVIE	Warner Brothers		58	11 Feb 84	4

David McWILLIAMS — UK

ALBUMS:		HITS 3			WEEKS 9
DAVID MCWILLIAMS SINGS	Major Minor		38	10 Jun 67	2
DAVID MCWILLIAMS VOLUME 2	Major Minor		23	4 Nov 67	6
DAVID MCWILLIAMS VOLUME 3	Major Minor		39	9 Mar 68	1

MAD COBRA featuring Richie STEPHENS — UK/Jamaica

SINGLES:		HITS 1			WEEKS 1
LEGACY	Columbia		64	15 May 93	1

MAD JOCKS featuring JOCKMASTER B.A. — UK

SINGLES:		HITS 2			WEEKS 9
JOCK MIX 1 [M]	Debut		46	19 Dec 87	5
PARTY FOUR [EP]	SMP		57	18 Dec 93	4

Lead track: No Lager, which was listed on the charts for 18 & 25 Dec 93.

MAD MOSES — US

SINGLES:		HITS 1			WEEKS 1
PANTHER PARTY	Hi-Life		50	16 Aug 97	1

Vocals by Bobby McFerrin.

MAD SEASON — UK

ALBUMS:		HITS 1			WEEKS 1
ABOVE	Columbia		41	25 Mar 95	1

MAD STUNTMAN – See REEL 2 REAL featuring the MAD STUNTMAN

Sonya MADAN – See LITHIUM and Sonya MADAN

Danny MADDEN — US

SINGLES:		HITS 1			WEEKS 2
THE FACTS OF LIFE	Eternal		72	14 Jul 90	2

MADDER ROSE — US

SINGLES:		HITS 2			WEEKS 2
PANIC ON	Atlantic		65	26 Mar 94	1
CAR SONG	Atlantic		68	16 Jul 94	1

ALBUMS:		HITS 1		WEEKS 2
PANIC ON	*Atlantic*	52	*9 Apr 94*	2

MADDOG – See STRETCH and VERN Present "MADDOG"

MADISON AVENUE   Australia

SINGLES:		HITS 1		WEEKS 4
DON'T CALL ME BABY	*VC Recordings*	30	*13 Nov 99*	4

Samples Pino D'Anglo's version of the song.

MADNESS   UK

(See also Various Artists (EPs) 'The 2 Tone EP'.)

SINGLES:		HITS 27		WEEKS 267
THE PRINCE	*2-Tone*	16	*1 Sep 79*	11
ONE STEP BEYOND . . .	*Stiff*	7	*10 Nov 79*	14
Originally recorded by Prince Buster and the All-stars.				
MY GIRL	*Stiff*	3	*5 Jan 80*	10
WORK REST AND PLAY [EP]	*Stiff*	6	*5 Apr 80*	8
Lead track: Night Boat To Cairo.				
BAGGY TROUSERS	*Stiff*	3	*13 Sep 80*	20
EMBARRASSMENT	*Stiff*	4	*22 Nov 80*	12
THE RETURN OF THE LOS PALMAS 7	*Stiff*	7	*24 Jan 81*	11
GREY DAY	*Stiff*	4	*25 Apr 81*	10
SHUT UP	*Stiff*	7	*26 Sep 81*	9
IT MUST BE LOVE	*Stiff*	4	*5 Dec 81*	12
CARDIAC ARREST	*Stiff*	14	*20 Feb 82*	10
HOUSE OF FUN	*Stiff*	1	*22 May 82*	9
DRIVING IN MY CAR	*Stiff*	4	*24 Jul 82*	8
OUR HOUSE	*Stiff*	5	*27 Nov 82*	13
TOMORROW'S (JUST ANOTHER DAY) / MADNESS IS ALL IN THE MIND	*Stiff*	8	*19 Feb 83*	9
WINGS OF A DOVE	*Stiff*	2	*20 Aug 83*	10
THE SUN AND THE RAIN	*Stiff*	5	*5 Nov 83*	10
MICHAEL CAINE	*Stiff*	11	*11 Feb 84*	8
ONE BETTER DAY	*Stiff*	17	*2 Jun 84*	7
YESTERDAY'S MEN	*Zarjazz*	18	*31 Aug 85*	7
UNCLE SAM	*Zarjazz*	21	*26 Oct 85*	11
SWEETEST GIRL	*Zarjazz*	35	*1 Feb 86*	6
(WAITING FOR) THE GHOST TRAIN	*Zarjazz*	18	*8 Nov 86*	7
(WAITING FOR) THE GHOST TRAIN [RE]	*Zarjazz*	74	*3 Jan 87*	1
I PRONOUNCE YOU	*Virgin*	44	*19 Mar 88*	4
Above hit: The MADNESS.				
IT MUST BE LOVE [RI]	*Virgin*	6	*15 Feb 92*	9
HOUSE OF FUN [RI]	*Virgin*	40	*25 Apr 92*	3
MY GIRL [RI]	*Virgin*	27	*8 Aug 92*	4
THE HARDER THEY COME	*Go! Discs*	44	*28 Nov 92*	3
NIGHT BOAT TO CAIRO [RI]	*Virgin*	56	*27 Feb 93*	2
Re-issue of track from the Work Rest And Play EP.				
LOVESTRUCK	*Virgin*	10	*31 Jul 99*	7
JOHNNY THE HORSE	*Virgin*	44	*6 Nov 99*	2
ALBUMS:		HITS 13		WEEKS 409
ONE STEP BEYOND	*Stiff*	2	*3 Nov 79*	78
ABSOLUTELY	*Stiff*	2	*4 Oct 80*	46
MADNESS 7	*Stiff*	5	*10 Oct 81*	29
COMPLETE MADNESS	*Stiff*	1	*1 May 82*	88
Compilation.				
THE RISE AND FALL	*Stiff*	10	*13 Nov 82*	22
KEEP MOVING	*Stiff*	6	*3 Mar 84*	19
MAD NOT MAD	*Zarjazz*	16	*12 Oct 85*	9
UTTER MADNESS	*Zarjazz*	29	*6 Dec 86*	8
Compilation.				
THE MADNESS	*Virgin*	65	*7 May 88*	1
Above hit: The MADNESS.				
DIVINE MADNESS	*Virgin*	1	*7 Mar 92*	93
Compilation.				
MADSTOCK!	*Go! Discs*	22	*14 Nov 92*	9
Live recordings.				
THE HEAVY HEAVY HITS	*Virgin*	19	*13 Jun 98*	5
Repackage of Divine Madness with additional track The Harder They Come.				
WONDERFUL	*Virgin*	17	*13 Nov 99*	2

MADONNA   US

(See also Various Artists: Films - Original Soundtracks 'Who's That Girl'.)

SINGLES:		HITS 49		WEEKS 510
HOLIDAY	*Sire*	6	*14 Jan 84*	11
LUCKY STAR	*Sire*	14	*17 Mar 84*	9
BORDERLINE	*Sire*	56	*2 Jun 84*	4

LIKE A VIRGIN	*Sire*	3	*17 Nov 84*	18
MATERIAL GIRL	*Sire*	3	*2 Mar 85*	10
CRAZY FOR YOU	*Geffen*	2	*8 Jun 85*	15
From the film 'Vision Quest'.				
INTO THE GROOVE	*Sire*	1	*27 Jul 85*	14
From the film 'Desperately Seeking Susan'.				
HOLIDAY [RE]	*Sire*	2	*3 Aug 85*	10
ANGEL	*Sire*	5	*21 Sep 85*	9
GAMBLER	*Geffen*	4	*12 Oct 85*	11
From the film 'Vision Quest'.				
DRESS YOU UP	*Sire*	5	*7 Dec 85*	11
GAMBLER [RE]	*Geffen*	61	*4 Jan 86*	1
BORDERLINE [RE]	*Sire*	2	*25 Jan 86*	9
LIVE TO TELL	*Sire*	2	*26 Apr 86*	12
From the film 'Shanghai Surprise'.				
PAPA DON'T PREACH	*Sire*	1	*28 Jun 86*	14
TRUE BLUE	*Sire*	1	*4 Oct 86*	15
OPEN YOUR HEART	*Sire*	4	*13 Dec 86*	9
LA ISLA BONITA	*Sire*	1	*4 Apr 87*	11
WHO'S THAT GIRL	*Sire*	1	*18 Jul 87*	10
CAUSING A COMMOTION	*Sire*	4	*19 Sep 87*	9
THE LOOK OF LOVE	*Sire*	9	*12 Dec 87*	7
Above 3 from the film 'Who's That Girl'.				
LIKE A PRAYER	*Sire*	1	*18 Mar 89*	12
EXPRESS YOURSELF	*Sire*	5	*3 Jun 89*	10
CHERISH	*Sire*	3	*16 Sep 89*	8
DEAR JESSIE	*Sire*	5	*16 Dec 89*	9
VOGUE	*Sire*	1	*7 Apr 90*	14
HANKY PANKY	*Sire*	2	*21 Jul 90*	9
JUSTIFY MY LOVE	*Sire*	2	*8 Dec 90*	10
Co-written by Lenny Kravitz.				
CRAZY FOR YOU [RM]	*Sire*	2	*2 Mar 91*	8
Mixed by Shep Pettibone and Michael Hutchinson.				
RESCUE ME	*Sire*	3	*13 Apr 91*	8
HOLIDAY [RI]	*Sire*	5	*8 Jun 91*	7
THIS USED TO BE MY PLAYGROUND	*Sire*	3	*25 Jul 92*	9
EROTICA	*Maverick*	3	*17 Oct 92*	8
Samples Jungle Boogie by Kool and the Gang.				
DEEPER AND DEEPER	*Maverick*	6	*12 Dec 92*	9
EROTICA [RE]	*Maverick*	65	*9 Jan 93*	1
BAD GIRL	*Maverick*	10	*6 Mar 93*	7
FEVER	*Maverick*	6	*3 Apr 93*	6
RAIN	*Maverick*	7	*31 Jul 93*	8
I'LL REMEMBER (THEME FROM 'WITH HONOURS')	*Maverick*	7	*2 Apr 94*	8
From the film 'With Honors'.				
SECRET	*Maverick*	5	*8 Oct 94*	9
TAKE A BOW	*Maverick*	16	*17 Dec 94*	9
Backing vocals by Babyface.				
BEDTIME STORY	*Maverick*	4	*25 Feb 95*	8
Samples What You Need by Main Source.				
BEDTIME STORY [RE]	*Maverick*	66	*6 May 95*	1
HUMAN NATURE	*Maverick*	8	*26 Aug 95*	5
YOU'LL SEE	*Maverick*	5	*4 Nov 95*	13
OH FATHER	*Maverick*	16	*6 Jan 96*	6
From the 1989 album Like A Prayer.				
ONE MORE CHANCE	*Maverick*	11	*23 Mar 96*	4
YOU MUST LOVE ME	*Warner Brothers*	10	*2 Nov 96*	4
DON'T CRY FOR ME ARGENTINA	*Warner Brothers*	3	*28 Dec 96*	12
YOU MUST LOVE ME [RE-1ST]	*Warner Brothers*	75	*4 Jan 97*	1
YOU MUST LOVE ME [RE-2ND]	*Warner Brothers*	71	*18 Jan 97*	1
ANOTHER SUITCASE IN ANOTHER HALL	*Warner Brothers*	7	*29 Mar 97*	5
Above 3 hits from the film 'Evita'.				
FROZEN	*Maverick*	1	*7 Mar 98*	13
RAY OF LIGHT	*Maverick*	2	*9 May 98*	9
RAY OF LIGHT [RE]	*Maverick*	75	*18 Jul 98*	1
DROWNDED WORLD / SUBSTITUTE FOR LOVE	*Maverick*	10	*5 Sep 98*	5
THE POWER OF GOOD-BYE / LITTLE STAR	*Maverick*	6	*5 Dec 98*	9
NOTHING REALLY MATTERS	*Maverick*	7	*13 Mar 99*	8
NOTHING REALLY MATTERS [RE]	*Maverick*	75	*5 Jun 99*	1
BEAUTIFUL STRANGER	*Maverick*	2	*19 Jun 99*	16
From the film 'Austin Powers – The Spy Who Shagged Me'.				

ALBUMS:	HITS 12		WEEKS 834	
MADONNA	*Sire*	37	*11 Feb 84*	22
LIKE A VIRGIN	*Sire*	1	*24 Nov 84*	152
Repackaged from 10 Aug 95 with additional track. Peak position reached on 21 Sep 85. Includes re-entries through to 1990.				
MADONNA / THE FIRST ALBUM [RE]	*Sire*	6	*27 Jul 85*	101
Repackaged as The First Album from 14 Sep 85.				

TRUE BLUE	*Sire*	1	*12 Jul 86*	81
YOU CAN DANCE	*Sire*	5	*28 Nov 87*	16
Album of dance remixes.				
LIKE A PRAYER	*Sire*	1	*1 Apr 89*	68
I'M BREATHLESS	*Sire*	2	*2 Jun 90*	20
THE IMMACULATE COLLECTION	*Sire*	1	*24 Nov 90*	152
Includes re-entries through to 1999.				
EROTICA	*Maverick*	2	*24 Oct 92*	38
LIKE A PRAYER [RE]	*Sire*	58	*2 Apr 94*	2
Re-released at mid-price. Chart position reached in 1995.				
TRUE BLUE [RE]	*Sire*	39	*9 Apr 94*	4
Re-released at mid-price. Chart position reached in 1995.				
BEDTIME STORIES	*Maverick*	2	*5 Nov 94*	27
SOMETHING TO REMEMBER	*Maverick*	3	*18 Nov 95*	29
Compilation of ballads plus 3 new songs.				
EVITA [OST]	*Warner Brothers*	1	*9 Nov 96*	36
Madonna sings on 17 of the album's 19 tracks.				
Above hit: MADONNA and VARIOUS ARTISTS.				
RAY OF LIGHT	*Maverick*	1	*14 Mar 98*	86

MAGAZINE UK

SINGLES:	HITS 2			WEEKS 7
SHOT BY BOTH SIDES	*Virgin*	41	*11 Feb 78*	4
SWEET HEART CONTRACT	*Virgin*	54	*26 Jul 80*	3

ALBUMS:	HITS 5			WEEKS 24
REAL LIFE	*Virgin*	29	*24 Jun 78*	8
SECONDHAND DAYLIGHT	*Virgin*	38	*14 Apr 79*	8
CORRECT USE OF SOAP	*Virgin*	28	*10 May 80*	4
PLAY	*Virgin*	69	*13 Dec 80*	1
MAGIC, MURDER AND THE WEATHER	*Virgin*	39	*27 Jun 81*	3

MAGIC AFFAIR US/Germany

SINGLES:	HITS 3			WEEKS 8
OMEN III	*EMI*	17	*4 Jun 94*	4
Vocal by Franco Morgano.				
GIVE ME ALL YOUR LOVE	*EMI*	30	*27 Aug 94*	2
IN THE MIDDLE OF THE NIGHT	*EMI*	38	*5 Nov 94*	2

MAGIC BAND – See CAPTAIN BEEFHEART and his MAGIC BAND

MAGIC LADY US

SINGLES:	HITS 1			WEEKS 3
BETCHA CAN'T LOSE (WITH MY LOVE)	*Motown*	58	*14 May 88*	3

MAGIC LANTERNS UK

SINGLES:	HITS 1			WEEKS 3
EXCUSE ME BABY	*CBS*	46	*9 Jul 66*	1
EXCUSE ME BABY [RE-1ST]	*CBS*	44	*30 Jul 66*	1
EXCUSE ME BABY [RE-2ND]	*CBS*	46	*13 Aug 66*	1

MAGNA CARTA UK

ALBUMS:	HITS 1			WEEKS 2
SEASONS	*Vertigo*	55	*8 Aug 70*	2

MAGNUM UK

SINGLES:	HITS 7			WEEKS 26
MAGNUM LIVE [EP]	*Jet*	47	*22 Mar 80*	6
Double single, lead track: Invasion (Live).				
LONELY NIGHT	*Polydor*	70	*12 Jul 86*	2
DAYS OF NO TRUST	*Polydor*	32	*19 Mar 88*	4
START TALKING LOVE	*Polydor*	22	*7 May 88*	4
IT MUST HAVE BEEN LOVE	*Polydor*	33	*2 Jul 88*	4
ROCKIN' CHAIR	*Polydor*	27	*23 Jun 90*	4
HEARTBROKE AND BUSTED	*Polydor*	49	*25 Aug 90*	2

ALBUMS:	HITS 11			WEEKS 47
KINGDOM OF MADNESS	*Jet*	58	*16 Sep 78*	1
MARAUDER	*Jet*	34	*19 Apr 80*	5
CHASE THE DRAGON	*Jet*	17	*6 Mar 82*	7
THE ELEVENTH HOUR	*Jet*	38	*21 May 83*	4
ON A STORYTELLER'S NIGHT	*FM*	24	*25 May 85*	7
VIGILANTE	*Polydor*	24	*4 Oct 86*	5
WINGS OF HEAVEN	*Polydor*	5	*9 Apr 88*	9
GOODNIGHT L.A.	*Polydor*	9	*21 Jul 90*	5
THE SPIRIT	*Polydor*	50	*14 Sep 91*	1

SLEEPWALKING	Music For Nations	27	24 Oct 92	2
ROCK ART	EMI	57	18 Jun 94	1

MAGOO
UK

SINGLES:	HITS 1			WEEKS 1
BLACK SABBATH	Fierce Panda	60	4 Apr 98	1

[AA] listed with Sweet Leaf by Mogwai.

MAGOO – See Missy "Misdemeanor" ELLIOTT; TIMBALAND

Sean MAGUIRE
UK

SINGLES:	HITS 8			WEEKS 34
SOMEONE TO LOVE	Parlophone	14	20 Aug 94	7
TAKE THIS TIME	Parlophone	27	5 Nov 94	4
TAKE THIS TIME [RE]	Parlophone	74	31 Dec 94	1
SUDDENLY	Parlophone	18	25 Mar 95	5
NOW I'VE FOUND YOU	Parlophone	22	24 Jun 95	3
YOU TO ME ARE EVERYTHING	Parlophone	16	18 Nov 95	3
GOOD DAY	Parlophone	12	25 May 96	4
DON'T PULL YOUR LOVE	Parlophone	14	3 Aug 96	4

Originally recorded by Hamilton, Joe Frank and Reynolds reached No. 4 in the US in 1971.

TODAY'S THE DAY	Parlophone	27	29 Mar 97	3
ALBUMS:	**HITS 2**			**WEEKS 3**
SEAN MAGUIRE	Parlophone	75	26 Nov 94	1
SPIRIT	Parlophone	43	15 Jun 96	2

MAHAVISHNU ORCHESTRA
UK

(See also Carlos Santana and Mahavishnu John McLaughlin.)

ALBUMS:	HITS 1			WEEKS 5
BIRDS OF FIRE	CBS	20	31 Mar 73	5

Siobhan MAHER – See OCEANIC

MAHLATHINI and the MAHOTELLA QUEENS – See ART OF NOISE

MAI TAI
Holland

SINGLES:	HITS 3			WEEKS 30
HISTORY	Hot Melt	8	25 May 85	13
BODY AND SOUL	Hot Melt	9	3 Aug 85	13
FEMALE INTUITION	Hot Melt	54	15 Feb 86	4
ALBUMS:	**HITS 1**			**WEEKS 1**
HISTORY	Hot Melt	91	6 Jul 85	1

MAIN INGREDIENT
US

SINGLES:	HITS 1			WEEKS 7
JUST DON'T WANT TO BE LONELY	RCA Victor	27	29 Jun 74	7

MAIRANTS-LANGHORN BIG SIX – See Don LANG

MAISONETTES
UK

SINGLES:	HITS 1			WEEKS 12
HEARTACHE AVENUE	Ready Steady Go!	7	11 Dec 82	12

Raven MAIZE
UK

SINGLES:	HITS 1			WEEKS 1
FOREVER TOGETHER	Republic	67	5 Aug 89	1

MAJESTICS
UK

ALBUMS:	HITS 1			WEEKS 4
TUTTI FRUTTI	BBC	64	4 Apr 87	4

MAJORITY – See Barry RYAN

MAKADOPOULOS and his GREEK SERENADERS
Greece

SINGLES:	HITS 1			WEEKS 14
NEVER ON SUNDAY (JAMAIS LE DIMANCHE)	Palette	36	22 Oct 60	14

From the film of the same name.

MAKAVELI – See 2PAC

Tommy MAKEM – See CLANCY BROTHERS and Tommy MAKEM

Jack E. MAKOSSA
Kenya

SINGLES:	HITS 1			WEEKS 5
THE OPERA HOUSE	Champion	48	12 Sep 87	5

MALA – See BOWA featuring MALA

MALAIKA

		US		
SINGLES:		HITS 1	WEEKS 1	
GOTTA KNOW (YOUR NAME)	A&M	68	31 Jul 93	1

Carl MALCOLM

		Jamaica		
SINGLES:		HITS 1	WEEKS 8	
FATTIE BUM BUM	UK	8	13 Sep 75	8

Valerie MALCOLM – See CANDY GIRLS

Timmy MALLETT – See BOMBALURINA

Yngwie J. MALMSTEEN

		Sweden		
ALBUMS:		HITS 4	WEEKS 11	
ODYSSEY	Polydor	27	21 May 88	7
TRIAL BY FIRE - LIVE IN LENINGRAD	Polydor	65	4 Nov 89	1
ECLIPSE	Polydor	43	28 Apr 90	2
FIRE AND ICE	Elektra	57	29 Feb 92	1

Artie MALVERN SINGERS – See Pat BOONE

MAMA CASS

US

(See also Mamas and the Papas.)

		HITS 2	WEEKS 27	
SINGLES:				
DREAM A LITTLE DREAM OF ME	RCA Victor	11	17 Aug 68	12
Originally recorded by Wayne King in 1931.				
Above hit: MAMA CASS with the MAMAS and PAPAS.				
IT'S GETTING BETTER	Stateside	8	16 Aug 69	15
Originally recorded by Paul Jones in 1967.				

MAMA'S BOYS

		Ireland		
ALBUMS:		HITS 1	WEEKS 4	
POWER AND PASSION	Jive	55	6 Apr 85	4

MAMAS and the PAPAS

US/Canada

(See also Mama Cass.)

		HITS 6	WEEKS 71	
SINGLES:				
CALIFORNIA DREAMIN'	RCA Victor	23	30 Apr 66	9
MONDAY MONDAY	RCA Victor	3	14 May 66	13
I SAW HERE AGAIN	RCA Victor	11	30 Jul 66	11
WORDS OF LOVE	RCA Victor	47	11 Feb 67	3
DEDICATED TO THE ONE I LOVE	RCA Victor	2	8 Apr 67	17
Originally recorded by the Five Royales.				
CREEQUE ALLEY	RCA Victor	9	29 Jul 67	11
CALIFORNIA DREAMIN [RI]	MCA	9	2 Aug 97	7
Featured in the Carling Premier TV commercial.				
ALBUMS:		HITS 7	WEEKS 71	
IF YOU CAN BELIEVE YOUR EYES AND EARS	RCA Victor	3	25 Jun 66	18
CASS, JOHN, MICHELLE, DENNY	RCA Victor	24	28 Jan 67	6
MAMAS AND PAPAS DELIVER	RCA Victor	4	24 Jun 67	22
HITS OF GOLD	Stateside	7	26 Apr 69	2
THE BEST OF THE MAMAS AND PAPAS	Arcade	6	18 Jun 77	13
CALIFORNIA DREAMIN' - THE VERY BEST OF THE MAMAS AND THE PAPAS	PolyGram TV	14	28 Jan 95	6
CALIFORNIA DREAMIN' - GREATEST HITS OF THE MAMAS AND THE PAPAS	Telstar TV	30	6 Sep 97	4
Repackaged version of the previous hits collection.				

MAMMOTH CAVE – See Stan FREBERG

MAN

		UK		
ALBUMS:		HITS 4	WEEKS 11	
BACK INTO THE FUTURE	United Artists	23	20 Oct 73	3
RHINOS WINOS AND LUNATICS	United Artists	24	25 May 74	4
MAXIMUM DARKNESS	United Artists	25	11 Oct 75	2
WELSH CONNECTION	MCA	40	17 Apr 76	2

A MAN CALLED ADAM

		UK		
SINGLES:		HITS 1	WEEKS 4	
BAREFOOT IN THE HEAD	Big Life	70	29 Sep 90	2
BAREFOOT IN THE HEAD [RE]	Big Life	60	20 Oct 90	2

MAN TO MAN
US

SINGLES:		HITS 2		WEEKS 19	
MALE STRIPPER	Bolts	64	13 Sep 86	3
Above hit: MAN 2 MAN Meet Man PARRISH.				
MALE STRIPPER [RE-1ST]	Bolts	63	3 Jan 87	1
MALE STRIPPER [RE-2ND]	Bolts	4	7 Feb 87	12
I NEED A MAN / ENERGY IS EUROBEAT	Bolts	43	4 Jul 87	3

MAN WITH NO NAME
UK

SINGLES:		HITS 5		WEEKS 6	
FLOOR-ESSENCE	Perfecto	68	30 Sep 95	1
PAINT A PICTURE	Perfecto	42	20 Jan 96	2
Above hit: MAN WITH NO NAME featuring HANNAH.				
TELEPORT / SUGAR RUSH	Perfecto	55	12 Oct 96	1
VAVOOM!	Perfecto	43	2 May 98	1
THE FIRST DAY (HORIZON)	Perfecto Fluoro	72	18 Jul 98	1

Melissa MANCHESTER and Al JARREAU
US

(See also Al Jarreau.)

SINGLES:		HITS 1		WEEKS 1	
THE MUSIC OF GOODBYE (LOVE THEME FROM OUT OF AFRICA)	MCA	75	5 Apr 86	1
From the film.				

MANCHESTER BOYS CHOIR
UK

ALBUMS:		HITS 1		WEEKS 2	
THE NEW SOUND OF CHRISTMAS	K-Tel	80	21 Dec 85	2

MANCHESTER UNITED FOOTBALL SQUAD
UK

SINGLES:		HITS 8		WEEKS 56	
MANCHESTER UNITED	Decca	50	8 May 76	1
GLORY GLORY MAN. UNITED	EMI	13	21 May 83	5
Above 2: MANCHESTER UNITED FOOTBALL CLUB.				
WE ALL FOLLOW MAN. UNITED	Columbia	10	18 May 85	5
Above hit: MANCHESTER UNITED FOOTBALL TEAM.				
UNITED (WE LOVE YOU)	Living Beat	37	19 Jun 93	2
Above hit: MANCHESTER UNITED and the CHAMPIONS.				
COME ON YOU REDS	PolyGram TV	1	30 Apr 94	15
Based on Status Quo's Burning Bridges.				
WE'RE GONNA DO IT AGAIN	PolyGram TV	6	13 May 95	6
Based on Status Quo's Again And Again.				
Above hit: MANCHESTER UNITED 1995 FOOTBALL SQUAD featuring STRYKER.				
MOVE MOVE MOVE (THE RED TRIBE)	Music Collection	6	4 May 96	11
Above hit: 1996 MANCHESTER UNITED F.A. CUP SQUAD.				
MOVE MOVE MOVE (THE RED TRIBE) [RE]	Music Collection	50	3 Aug 96	4
LIFT IT HIGH (ALL ABOUT BELIEF)	Music Collection	11	29 May 99	6
Above hit: 1999 MANCHESTER UNITED SQUAD.				
LIFT IT HIGH (ALL ABOUT BELIEF) [RE]	Music Collection	75	21 Aug 99	1

Henry MANCINI and his Orchestra
US

(See also James Galway and Henry Mancini with the National Philharmonic Orchestra; Johnny Mathis and Henry Mancini; Luciano Pavarotti.)

SINGLES:		HITS 4		WEEKS 23	
MOON RIVER	RCA	46	9 Dec 61	2
MOON RIVER [RE]	RCA	44	30 Dec 61	1
HOW SOON	RCA Victor	10	26 Sep 64	12
Theme from 'The Richard Boone Show'.				
THEME FROM 'CADE'S COUNTY'	RCA Victor	42	25 Mar 72	1
THE THORN BIRDS THEME	Warner Brothers	23	11 Feb 84	7
Theme from the BBC1 TV series.				

EPS:		HITS 1		WEEKS 10	
THE PINK PANTHER	RCA Victor	14	18 Apr 64	10

ALBUMS:		HITS 1		WEEKS 8	
HENRY MANCINI	Arcade	26	16 Oct 76	8

Steve MANDELL – See 'DELIVERANCE' SOUNDTRACK

MANFRED MANN
UK/South Africa

SINGLES:		HITS 22		WEEKS 217	
5-4-3-2-1	His Master's Voice	5	25 Jan 64	13
HUBBLE BUBBLE (TOIL AND TROUBLE)	His Master's Voice	11	18 Apr 64	8
DO WAH DIDDY DIDDY	His Master's Voice	1	18 Jul 64	14
Originally recorded by the Exciters.				

SHA LA LA	His Master's Voice	3	17 Oct 64	12

Originally recorded by the Shirelles.

COME TOMORROW	His Master's Voice	4	16 Jan 65	9

Originally recorded by Marie Knight.
Above hit: MANFRED MANN; Vocal: Paul JONES.

OH NO NOT MY BABY	His Master's Voice	11	17 Apr 65	10

Originally recorded by Maxine Brown.

IF YOU GOTTA GO, GO NOW	His Master's Voice	2	18 Sep 65	12

Originally recorded by Bob Dylan.

PRETTY FLAMINGO	His Master's Voice	1	23 Apr 66	12
YOU GAVE ME SOMEBODY TO LOVE	His Master's Voice	36	9 Jul 66	4
JUST LIKE A WOMAN	Fontana	10	6 Aug 66	10
SEMI-DETACHED, SUBURBAN MR. JAMES	Fontana	2	29 Oct 66	12
HA! HA! SAID THE CLOWN	Fontana	4	1 Apr 67	11

Originally recorded by Tony Hazzard.

SWEET PEA	Fontana	36	27 May 67	4

Originally recorded by Tommy Roe.

MIGHTY QUINN	Fontana	1	27 Jan 68	11

Originally recorded by Bob Dylan.

MY NAME IS JACK	Fontana	8	15 Jun 68	11

Originally recorded by John Simon.

FOX ON THE RUN	Fontana	5	21 Dec 68	12

Originally recorded by Tony Hazzard.

RAGAMUFFIN MAN	Fontana	8	3 May 69	11
JOYBRINGER	Vertigo	9	8 Sep 73	10

Based on Jupiter from Holst's Plant Suite.

BLINDED BY THE LIGHT	Bronze	6	28 Aug 76	10

Originally recorded by Bruce Springsteen.

DAVY'S ON THE ROAD AGAIN	Bronze	6	20 May 78	12

Originally recorded by John Simon.

YOU ANGEL YOU	Bronze	54	17 Mar 79	5

Originally recorded by Bob Dylan.

DON'T KILL IT CAROL	Bronze	45	7 Jul 79	4

Originally recorded by Heron.
Above 5: MANFRED MANN'S EARTH BAND.

EPS:	HITS 6			WEEKS 111
GROOVIN' WITH MANFRED MANN	HMV	3	21 Nov 64	18
THE ONE IN THE MIDDLE	HMV	1	12 Jun 65	38
NO LIVING WITHOUT LOVING	HMV	1	27 Nov 65	24
MACHINES	HMV	1	16 Apr 66	13
INSTRUMENTAL ASYLUM	HMV	3	11 Jun 66	9
AS WAS	HMV	4	15 Oct 66	9

ALBUMS:	HITS 12			WEEKS 101
FIVE FACES OF MANFRED MANN	His Master's Voice	3	19 Sep 64	24
MANN MADE	His Master's Voice	7	23 Oct 65	11
MANN MADE HITS	His Master's Voice	11	17 Sep 66	18
AS IS	Fontana	22	29 Oct 66	4
SOUL OF MANN	His Master's Voice	40	21 Jan 67	1

Compilation of instrumental tracks.

THE ROARING SILENCE	Bronze	10	18 Sep 76	9

Above hit: MANFRED MANN'S EARTH BAND.

WATCH	Bronze	33	17 Jun 78	6

Above hit: MANFRED MANN'S EARTH BAND.

ANGEL STATION	Bronze	30	24 Mar 79	8

Above 3: MANFRED MANN'S EARTH BAND.

SEMI-DETACHED SUBURBAN	EMI	9	15 Sep 79	14
SOMEWHERE IN AFRIKA	Bronze	87	26 Feb 83	1

Above hit: MANFRED MANN'S EARTH BAND.

AGES OF MANN - 22 CLASSIC HITS OF THE 60'S	PolyGram TV	23	23 Jan 93	4
THE VERY BEST OF MANFRED MANN'S EARTH BAND	Arcade	69	10 Sep 94	1

Above hit: MANFRED MANN'S EARTH BAND.

MANHATTAN TRANSFER   US

SINGLES:	HITS 9			WEEKS 72
TUXEDO JUNCTION	Atlantic	24	7 Feb 76	6

Originally recorded by Erskine Hawkins.

CHANSON D'AMOUR	Atlantic	1	5 Feb 77	13

Originally recorded by Art and Dotty Todd.

DON'T LET GO	Atlantic	32	28 May 77	6
WALK IN LOVE	Atlantic	48	18 Feb 78	1

Originally recorded by David Batteau.

WALK IN LOVE [RE]	Atlantic	12	4 Mar 78	11
ON A LITTLE STREET IN SINGAPORE	Atlantic	20	20 May 78	9
WHERE DID OUR LOVE GO/JE VOULAIS (TE DIRE QUE JE T'ATTENDS)	Atlantic	40	16 Sep 78	4
WHO, WHAT, WHEN, WHERE, WHY	Atlantic	49	23 Dec 78	6
a. TWILIGHT ZONE b. TWILIGHT TONE [M]	Atlantic	25	17 May 80	8
SPICE OF LIFE	Atlantic	19	21 Jan 84	8

ALBUMS:		HITS 6			WEEKS 85
COMING OUT	*Atlantic*	12	*12 Mar 77*	20
MANHATTAN TRANSFER	*Atlantic*	49	*19 Mar 77*	7
PASTICHE	*Atlantic*	10	*25 Feb 78*	34
LIVE	*Atlantic*	4	*11 Nov 78*	17
EXTENSIONS	*Atlantic*	63	*17 Nov 79*	3
BODIES AND SOULS	*Atlantic*	53	*18 Feb 84*	4

MANHATTANS   US

SINGLES:		HITS 5			WEEKS 31
KISS AND SAY GOODBYE	*CBS*	4	*19 Jun 76*	11
HURT	*CBS*	4	*2 Oct 76*	11

Originally recorded by Roy Hamilton in 1954; Timi Yuro's version reached No. 4 in the US in 1961.

IT'S YOU	*CBS*	43	*23 Apr 77*	3
SHINING STAR	*CBS*	45	*26 Jul 80*	4
CRAZY	*CBS*	63	*6 Aug 83*	2

ALBUMS:		HITS 1			WEEKS 3
MANHATTANS	*CBS*	37	*14 Aug 76*	3

MANIC MC'S featuring Sara CARLSON   UK

SINGLES:		HITS 1			WEEKS 5
MENTAL	*RCA*	30	*12 Aug 89*	5

MANIC STREET PREACHERS   UK

SINGLES:		HITS 22			WEEKS 121
YOU LOVE US	*Heavenly*	62	*25 May 91*	2
STAY BEAUTIFUL	*Columbia*	40	*10 Aug 91*	3
LOVE'S SWEET EXILE / REPEAT	*Columbia*	26	*9 Nov 91*	3
YOU LOVE US [RI-1ST]	*Columbia*	16	*1 Feb 92*	4
SLASH 'N' BURN	*Columbia*	20	*28 Mar 92*	4
MOTORCYCLE EMPTINESS	*Columbia*	17	*13 Jun 92*	6
THEME FROM M.A.S.H. (SUICIDE IS PAINLESS)	*Columbia*	7	*19 Sep 92*	6

[AA] listed with Everything I Do (I Do It For You) by the Fatima Mansions. Track from the NME 40th Anniversary album Ruby Trax.

LITTLE BABY NOTHING	*Columbia*	29	*21 Nov 92*	3
FROM DESPAIR TO WHERE	*Columbia*	25	*12 Jun 93*	4
LA TRISTESSE DURERA (SCREAM TO A SIGH)	*Columbia*	22	*31 Jul 93*	5
ROSES IN THE HOSPITAL	*Columbia*	15	*2 Oct 93*	3
LIFE BECOMING A LANDSLIDE	*Columbia*	36	*12 Feb 94*	2
FASTER / P.C.P.	*Epic*	16	*11 Jun 94*	3
REVOL	*Epic*	22	*13 Aug 94*	3
SHE IS SUFFERING	*Epic*	25	*15 Oct 94*	3
A DESIGN FOR LIFE	*Epic*	2	*27 Apr 96*	10
A DESIGN FOR LIFE [RE]	*Epic*	71	*27 Jul 96*	1
EVERYTHING MUST GO	*Epic*	5	*3 Aug 96*	6
KEVIN CARTER	*Epic*	9	*12 Oct 96*	4

Kevin Carter was photographer friend of the band who had committed suicide.

AUSTRALIA	*Epic*	7	*14 Dec 96*	7
LITTLE BABY NOTHING [RI]	*Epic*	50	*13 Sep 97*	1
LOVE'S SWEET EXILE [RI]	*Epic*	55	*13 Sep 97*	1
MOTORCYCLE EMPTINESS [RI]	*Epic*	41	*13 Sep 97*	2
SLASH 'N' BURN [RI]	*Epic*	54	*13 Sep 97*	1
STAY BEAUTIFUL [RI]	*Epic*	52	*13 Sep 97*	1
YOU LOVE US [RI-2ND]	*Epic*	49	*13 Sep 97*	1
IF YOU TOLERATE THIS YOUR CHILDREN WILL BE NEXT	*Epic*	1	*5 Sep 98*	10
IF YOU TOLERATE THIS YOUR CHILDREN WILL BE NEXT [RE]	*Epic*	69	*5 Dec 98*	1
THE EVERLASTING	*Epic*	11	*12 Dec 98*	8
YOU STOLE THE SUN FROM MY HEART	*Epic*	5	*20 Mar 99*	8
TSUNAMI	*Epic*	11	*17 Jul 99*	5

ALBUMS:		HITS 5			WEEKS 166
GENERATION TERRORISTS	*Columbia*	13	*22 Feb 92*	10
GOLD AGAINST THE SOUL	*Columbia*	8	*3 Jul 93*	11
THE HOLY BIBLE	*Epic*	6	*10 Sep 94*	4
EVERYTHING MUST GO	*Epic*	2	*1 Jun 96*	81
THIS IS MY TRUTH TELL ME YOURS	*Epic*	1	*26 Sep 98*	53
GENERATION TERRORISTS [RE]	*Columbia*	47	*23 Jan 99*	7

Re-released at mid-price.

Barry MANILOW   UK

SINGLES:		HITS 19			WEEKS 136
MANDY	*Arista*	11	*22 Feb 75*	9

Based on Scott English's Brandy.

CAN'T SMILE WITHOUT YOU	*Arista*	43	*6 May 78*	7

Originally recorded by David Martin.

SOMEWHERE IN THE NIGHT / COPACABANA (AT THE COPA)	*Arista*	42	*29 Jul 78*	10

Copacabana (At The Copa) from the film 'Foul Play'. Somewhere In The Night originally recorded by Richard Kerr.

COULD IT BE MAGIC	*Arista*	25	*23 Dec 78*	10

Originally released in 1975. Inspired by F. Chopin's Prelude in C Minor.

LONELY TOGETHER	*Arista*	21	*8 Nov 80*	13
I MADE IT THROUGH THE RAIN	*Arista*	37	*7 Feb 81*	6
BERMUDA TRIANGLE	*Arista*	15	*11 Apr 81*	9
LET'S HANG ON	*Arista*	12	*26 Sep 81*	11
THE OLD SONGS	*Arista*	48	*12 Dec 81*	8
IF I SHOULD LOVE AGAIN	*Arista*	66	*20 Feb 82*	2
STAY	*Arista*	23	*17 Apr 82*	8

Sales of the live and studio recordings were combined.
Above hit: Barry MANILOW featuring Kevin DESIMONE and James JOLIS.

I WANNA DO IT WITH YOU	*Arista*	8	*16 Oct 82*	8
I'M GONNA SIT RIGHT DOWN AND WRITE MYSELF A LETTER	*Arista*	36	*4 Dec 82*	7

Originally recorded by Fats Waller.

SOME KIND OF FRIEND	*Arista*	48	*25 Jun 83*	2
YOU'RE LOOKIN' HOT TONIGHT	*Arista*	47	*27 Aug 83*	6
READ 'EM AND WEEP	*Arista*	17	*10 Dec 83*	7

Originally recorded by Meatloaf.

PLEASE DON'T BE SCARED	*Arista*	35	*8 Apr 89*	5
COPACABANA (AT THE COPA) - THE 1993 REMIX [RM]	*Arista*	22	*10 Apr 93*	4

Remixed by Dave Ford..

COULD IT BE MAGIC 1993 [RR]	*Arista*	36	*20 Nov 93*	3
LET ME BE YOUR WINGS	*EMI*	73	*6 Aug 94*	1

From the film 'Thumbelina'. Features the Irish Film Orchestra.
Above hit: Barry MANILOW and Debra BYRD.

ALBUMS:	HITS 21		WEEKS 340	
EVEN NOW	*Arista*	12	*23 Sep 78*	28
MANILOW MAGIC - THE BEST OF BARRY MANILOW	*Arista*	3	*3 Mar 79*	151
ONE VOICE	*Arista*	18	*20 Oct 79*	7
BARRY	*Arista*	5	*29 Nov 80*	34
GIFT SET	*Arista*	62	*25 Apr 81*	1
IF I SHOULD LOVE AGAIN	*Arista*	5	*3 Oct 81*	26
BARRY LIVE IN BRITAIN	*Arista*	1	*1 May 82*	23
I WANNA DO IT WITH YOU	*Arista*	7	*27 Nov 82*	9
A TOUCH MORE MAGIC	*Arista*	10	*8 Oct 83*	12
2.00 A.M. PARADISE CAFE	*Arista*	28	*1 Dec 84*	6
MANILOW	*RCA*	40	*16 Nov 85*	6
SWING STREET	*Arista*	81	*20 Feb 88*	1
SONGS TO MAKE THE WHOLE WORLD SING	*Arista*	20	*20 May 89*	4
LIVE ON BROADWAY	*Arista*	19	*17 Mar 90*	3
THE SONGS 1975-1990	*Arista*	13	*30 Jun 90*	7
SHOWSTOPPERS	*Arista*	53	*2 Nov 91*	3
HIDDEN TREASURES	*Arista*	36	*3 Apr 93*	7

Album of remixes, unreleased demos and 3 new tracks.

THE PLATINUM COLLECTION - GREATEST HITS	*Arista*	37	*27 Nov 93*	6
BARRY MANILOW SINGIN' WITH THE BIG BANDS	*Arista*	54	*5 Nov 94*	2

Features the music of Glenn Miller, Benny Goodman and Jimmy Dorsey.

SUMMER OF '78	*Arista*	66	*30 Nov 96*	2
BARRY SINGS SINATRA	*Arista*	72	*21 Nov 98*	2

MANIX | | | | UK |

SINGLES:	HITS 3		WEEKS 6	
MANIC MINDS	*Reinforced*	63	*23 Nov 91*	2
OBLIVION (HEAD IN THE CLOUDS) [EP]	*Reinforced*	43	*7 Mar 92*	3

Lead track: I Can't Stand It. (The title of the EP is the 4th track).

RAINBOW PEOPLE	*Reinforced*	57	*8 Aug 92*	1

MANKEY | | | | UK |

SINGLES:	HITS 1		WEEKS 1	
BELIEVE IN ME	*Frisky*	74	*16 Nov 96*	1

Samples Yazoo's Situation.

MANKIND | | | | UK |

SINGLES:	HITS 1		WEEKS 12	
DR. WHO	*Pinnacle*	25	*25 Nov 78*	12

Aimee MANN | | | | US |

SINGLES:	HITS 2		WEEKS 6	
I SHOULD'VE KNOWN	*Imago*	55	*28 Aug 93*	2
STUPID THING	*Imago*	47	*20 Nov 93*	2
I SHOULD'VE KNOWN [RI]	*Imago*	45	*5 Mar 94*	2

ALBUMS:		HITS 2		WEEKS 2
WHATEVER	Imago	39	18 Sep 93	1
I'M WITH STUPID	Geffen	51	11 Nov 95	1

Johnny MANN SINGERS   US
(See also Walter Brennan; Buddy Knox; Bobby Vee.)

SINGLES:		HITS 1		WEEKS 13
UP-UP AND AWAY	Liberty	6	15 Jul 67	13
Written by Jimmy Webb.				

Roberto MANN   UK

ALBUMS:		HITS 1		WEEKS 9
GREAT WALTZES	Deram	19	9 Dec 67	9

Shelley MANNE   US

ALBUMS:		HITS 1		WEEKS 1
MY FAIR LADY	Vogue	20	18 Jun 60	1

MANOWAR   US

ALBUMS:		HITS 2		WEEKS 3
HAIL TO ENGLAND	Music For Nations	83	18 Feb 84	2
SIGN OF THE HAMMER	10 Records	73	6 Oct 84	1

Keith MANSFIELD STRINGS - See LOVE AFFAIR; TREMELOES

MANSUN   UK

SINGLES:		HITS 11		WEEKS 34
ONE [EP]	Parlophone	37	6 Apr 96	2
Lead track: Egg Shaped Fred.				
TWO [EP]	Parlophone	32	15 Jun 96	2
Lead track: Take It Easy Chicken.				
THREE [EP]	Parlophone	19	21 Sep 96	3
Lead track: Stripper Vicar.				
FOUR [EP]	Parlophone	15	7 Dec 96	4
Lead track: Wide Open Space.				
FIVE [EP]	Parlophone	9	15 Feb 97	5
Lead track: She Makes My Noise Bleed.				
SIX [EP]	Parlophone	15	10 May 97	3
Lead track: Taxloss.				
SEVEN [EP]	Parlophone	10	18 Oct 97	3
Lead track: Closed For Business.				
EIGHT [EP]	Parlophone	7	11 Jul 98	4
Lead track: Legacy.				
NINE [EP]	Parlophone	13	5 Sep 98	3
Lead track: Being A Girl (Part One).				
TEN [EP]	Parlophone	27	7 Nov 98	2
Lead track: Negative.				
ELEVEN [EP]	Parlophone	16	13 Feb 99	3
Lead track: Six.				
Charts only reflected the lead tracks of the EPs Four through to Seven, Ten and Eleven.				

ALBUMS:		HITS 2		WEEKS 23
ATTACK OF THE GREY LANTERN	Parlophone	1	1 Mar 97	19
SIX	Parlophone	6	19 Sep 98	4

MANTOVANI and his Orchestra   UK
(See also David Whitfield.)

SINGLES:		HITS 5		WEEKS 52
WHITE CHRISTMAS	Decca	6	20 Dec 52	3
THE SONG FROM THE MOULIN ROUGE (WHERE IS YOUR HEART)	Decca	1	30 May 53	21
From the film 'Moulin Rouge'.				
SWEDISH RHAPSODY	Decca	2	24 Oct 53	17
From the film 'The Stranger Left No Card'.				
THE SONG FROM THE MOULIN ROUGE (WHERE IS YOUR HEART) [RE-1ST]	Decca	10	14 Nov 53	1
THE SONG FROM THE MOULIN ROUGE (WHERE IS YOUR HEART) [RE-2ND]	Decca	12	5 Dec 53	1
SWEDISH RHAPSODY [RE]	Decca	12	27 Feb 54	1
LONELY BALLERINA	Decca	16	12 Feb 55	3
LONELY BALLERINA [RE]	Decca	18	19 Mar 55	1
AROUND THE WORLD	Decca	20	1 Jun 57	4
From the film 'Around The World In Eighty Days'.				

EPS:		HITS 3		WEEKS 70
MANTOVANI'S BIG FOUR	Decca	6	12 Mar 60	31
DREAMS OF OLWEN	Decca	17	2 Apr 60	4
EXODUS AND OTHER THEMES	Decca	3	1 Apr 61	35

ALBUMS:		HITS 12		WEEKS 151	
CONTINENTAL ENCORES	Decca	4	21 Feb 59	12
CONCERT SPECTACULAR	Decca	16	18 Feb 61	2
MANTOVANI MAGIC	Decca	3	16 Apr 66	15
MR. MUSIC – MANTOVANI	Decca	24	15 Oct 66	3
MANTOVANI'S GOLDEN HITS	Decca	10	14 Jan 67	43
HOLLYWOOD	Decca	37	30 Sep 67	1
THE WORLD OF MANTOVANI	Decca	6	14 Jun 69	31
THE WORLD OF MANTOVANI VOLUME 2	Decca	4	4 Oct 69	19
MANTOVANI TODAY	Decca	16	16 May 70	8
TO LOVERS EVERYWHERE	Decca	44	26 Feb 72	1
20 GOLDEN GREATS	Warwick	9	3 Nov 79	13
MANTOVANI MAGIC	Telstar	52	16 Mar 85	3

Above hit: MANTOVANI ORCHESTRA conducted by Roland SHAW.

MANTRONIK vs EPMD   US

(See also EPMD; Mantronix.)

SINGLES:		HITS 1		WEEKS 1	
STRICTLY BUSINESS	Parlophone	43	15 Aug 98	1

Samples Eric Clapton's I Shot The Sheriff.

MANTRONIX   US/Jamaica

(See also Mantronik vs EPMD.)

SINGLES:		HITS 10		WEEKS 48	
LADIES	10 Records	55	22 Feb 86	4
BASSLINE	10 Records	34	17 May 86	6
WHO IS IT?	10 Records	40	7 Feb 87	6
SCREAM	10 Records	46	4 Jul 87	4
SING A SONG (BREAK IT DOWN)	10 Records	61	30 Jan 88	2
SIMPLE SIMON (YOU GOTTA REGARD)	10 Records	72	12 Mar 88	2
GOT TO HAVE YOUR LOVE	Capitol	4	6 Jan 90	11
TAKE YOUR TIME	Capitol	10	12 May 90	7

Above 2: MANTRONIX featuring WONDRESS.

DON'T GO MESSIN' WITH MY HEART	Capitol	22	2 Mar 91	5
STEP TO ME (DO ME)	Capitol	59	22 Jun 91	1

ALBUMS:		HITS 5		WEEKS 17	
THE ALBUM	10 Records	45	29 Mar 86	3
MUSICAL MADNESS	10 Records	97	13 Dec 86	1
MUSICAL MADNESS [RE]	10 Records	66	8 Aug 87	2
IN FULL EFFECT	10 Records	39	2 Apr 88	3
THIS SHOULD MOVE YA	Capitol	18	17 Feb 90	6
THE INCREDIBLE SOUND MACHINE	Capitol	36	30 Mar 91	2

MANUEL and the MUSIC OF THE MOUNTAINS   UK

(See also Geoff Love and his Orchestra.)

SINGLES:		HITS 4		WEEKS 31	
THE HONEYMOON SONG	Columbia	29	29 Aug 59	2

From the film 'Honeymoon'.

THE HONEYMOON SONG [RE-1ST]	Columbia	22	26 Sep 59	5
THE HONEYMOON SONG [RE-2ND]	Columbia	27	7 Nov 59	2
NEVER ON SUNDAY (JAMAIS LE DIMANCHE)	Columbia	29	15 Oct 60	10

From the film of the same name.

SOMEWHERE MY LOVE	Columbia	42	15 Oct 66	2
RODRIGO'S GUITAR CONCERTO DE ARANJUEZ (THEME FROM 2ND MOVEMENT)	EMI	3	31 Jan 76	10

ALBUMS:		HITS 3		WEEKS 38	
MUSIC OF THE MOUNTAINS	Columbia	17	10 Sep 60	1
THIS IS MANUEL	Studio Two	18	7 Aug 71	19
CARNIVAL	Studio Two	3	31 Jan 76	18

Phil MANZANERA   UK

ALBUMS:		HITS 1		WEEKS 1	
DIAMOND HEAD	Island	40	24 May 75	1

MARATHON   UK/Germany

SINGLES:		HITS 1		WEEKS 3	
MOVIN'	Ten Records	36	25 Jan 92	3

MARAUDERS   UK

SINGLES:		HITS 1		WEEKS 4	
THAT'S WHAT I WANT	Decca	48	10 Aug 63	1
THAT'S WHAT I WANT [RE]	Decca	43	24 Aug 63	3

MARBLES
UK

SINGLES:		HITS 2			WEEKS 18	
ONLY ONE WOMAN		Polydor	5	28 Sep 68	12
Written by the Bee Gees.						
THE WALLS FELL DOWN		Polydor	28	29 Mar 69	6

MARC ET CLAUDE
Germany

SINGLES:		HITS 1			WEEKS 3	
LA		Positiva	28	21 Nov 98	3

MARC and the MAMBAS – See Marc ALMOND

MARCELS
US

SINGLES:		HITS 2			WEEKS 17	
BLUE MOON		Pye International	1	15 Apr 61	13
Originally recorded by Glen Gray Orchestra in 1935.						
SUMMERTIME		Pye International	46	10 Jun 61	4

Little Peggy MARCH
US

SINGLES:		HITS 1			WEEKS 7	
HELLO HEARTACHE GOODBYE LOVE		RCA Victor	29	14 Sep 63	7

MARCY PLAYGROUND
US

SINGLES:		HITS 1			WEEKS 3	
SEX AND CANDY		EMI	29	18 Apr 98	3
ALBUMS:		**HITS 1**			**WEEKS 1**	
MARCY PLAYGROUND		EMI	61	9 May 98	1

MARDI GRAS
US

SINGLES:		HITS 1			WEEKS 9	
TOO BUSY THINKING ABOUT MY BABY		Bell	19	5 Aug 72	9

MARIA – See Maria NAYLER

Kelly MARIE
UK

SINGLES:		HITS 4			WEEKS 36	
FEELS LIKE I'M IN LOVE		Calibre	1	2 Aug 80	16
Originally intended for Elvis Presley and originally recorded by Ray Dorset.						
LOVING JUST FOR FUN		Calibre	21	18 Oct 80	7
HOT LOVE		Calibre	22	7 Feb 81	10
LOVE TRIAL		Calibre	51	30 May 81	3

Lisa MARIE – See Malcolm McLAREN

Rose MARIE
UK

SINGLES:		HITS 1			WEEKS 5	
WHEN I LEAVE THE WORLD BEHIND		A.1	75	19 Nov 83	1
Written by Irving Berlin and originally recorded by Henry Burr.						
WHEN I LEAVE THE WORLD BEHIND [RE-1ST]		A.1	63	3 Dec 83	2
WHEN I LEAVE THE WORLD BEHIND [RE-2ND]		A.1	66	24 Dec 83	2
ALBUMS:		**HITS 5**			**WEEKS 35**	
ROSE MARIE SINGS JUST FOR YOU		A.1	30	13 Apr 85	13
SO LUCKY		A.1	62	24 May 86	3
SENTIMENTALLY YOURS		Telstar	22	14 Nov 87	11
TOGETHER AGAIN		Telstar	52	19 Nov 88	7
MEMORIES OF HOME		Telstar	51	23 Mar 96	1
Collection of traditional Irish songs.						

Teena MARIE
US

(See also Snoop Doggy Dogg.)

SINGLES:		HITS 5			WEEKS 28	
I'M A SUCKER FOR YOUR LOVE		Motown	43	7 Jul 79	8
Above hit: Teena MARIE Co-lead vocals: Rick JAMES.						
BEHIND THE GROOVE		Motown	6	31 May 80	10
I NEED YOUR LOVIN'		Motown	28	11 Oct 80	6
OOO LA LA LA		Epic	74	26 Mar 88	2
SINCE DAY ONE		Epic	69	10 Nov 90	2

MARILLION
UK

SINGLES:		HITS 22			WEEKS 103	
MARKET SQUARE HEROES		EMI	60	20 Nov 82	2
HE KNOWS YOU KNOW		EMI	35	12 Feb 83	4
MARKET SQUARE HEROES [RE]		EMI	53	16 Apr 83	6

GARDEN PARTY - THE GREAT CUCUMBER MASSACRE	EMI	16	18 Jun 83	5
PUNCH AND JUDY	EMI	29	11 Feb 84	4
ASSASSING	EMI	22	12 May 84	5
KAYLEIGH	EMI	2	18 May 85	14
LAVENDER	EMI	5	7 Sep 85	9
HEART OF LOTHIAN	EMI	29	30 Nov 85	6
INCOMMUNICADO	EMI	6	23 May 87	5
SUGAR MICE	EMI	22	25 Jul 87	5
WARM WET CIRCLES	EMI	22	7 Nov 87	4
FREAKS (LIVE)	EMI	24	26 Nov 88	3
HOOKS IN YOU	EMI	30	9 Sep 89	3
UNINVITED GUEST	EMI	53	9 Dec 89	2
EASTER	EMI	34	14 Apr 90	2
COVER MY EYES (PAIN AND HEAVEN)	EMI	34	8 Jun 91	4
NO ONE CAN	EMI	33	3 Aug 91	4
DRY LAND	EMI	34	5 Oct 91	2
SYMPATHY	EMI	17	23 May 92	3
NO ONE CAN [RI]	EMI	26	1 Aug 92	4
THE HOLLOW MAN	EMI	30	26 Mar 94	3
ALONE AGAIN IN THE LAP OF LUXURY	EMI	53	7 May 94	3
BEAUTIFUL	EMI	29	10 Jun 95	2

ALBUMS: — **HITS 16** — **WEEKS 165**

SCRIPT FOR A JESTER'S TEAR	EMI	7	26 Mar 83	31
FUGAZI	EMI	5	24 Mar 84	20
REAL TO REEL	EMI	8	17 Nov 84	22

Budget price album featuring live recordings from Leicester, UK and Montreal, Canada.

MISPLACED CHILDHOOD	EMI	1	29 Jun 85	41
CLUTCHING AT STRAWS	EMI	2	4 Jul 87	15
B SIDES THEMSELVES	EMI	64	23 Jul 88	6
THE THIEVING MAGPIE	EMI	25	10 Dec 88	6
SEASON'S END	EMI	7	7 Oct 89	4
HOLIDAYS IN EDEN	EMI	7	6 Jul 91	7
A SINGLES COLLECTION 1982-1992	EMI	27	20 Jun 92	2
BRAVE	EMI	10	19 Feb 94	4
AFRAID OF SUNLIGHT	EMI	16	8 Jul 95	2
MADE AGAIN	EMI	37	6 Apr 96	1

Live recordings.

THIS STRANGE ENGINE	Raw Power	27	3 May 97	2
RADIATION	Raw Power	35	3 Oct 98	1
MARILLION.COM	Raw Power	53	30 Oct 99	1

MARILYN — UK

SINGLES: — **HITS 4** — **WEEKS 26**

CALLING YOUR NAME	Mercury	4	5 Nov 83	12
CRY AND BE FREE	Love	31	11 Feb 84	6
YOU DON'T LOVE ME	Love	40	21 Apr 84	7
BABY U LEFT ME (IN THE COLD)	Mercury	70	13 Apr 85	1

MARILYN MANSON — US

SINGLES: — **HITS 4** — **WEEKS 10**

THE BEAUTIFUL PEOPLE	Interscope	18	7 Jun 97	3

10" format was titled 'The Horrible People'.

TOURNIQUET	Interscope	28	20 Sep 97	2
THE DOPE SHOW	Interscope	12	21 Nov 98	3
ROCK IS DEAD	Maverick	23	26 Jun 99	2

From the film 'The Matrix'.

ALBUMS: — **HITS 3** — **WEEKS 5**

ANTICHRIST SUPERSTAR	Interscope	73	26 Oct 96	1
MECHANICAL ANIMAL	Interscope	8	26 Sep 98	3
THE LAST TOUR ON EARTH	Interscope	61	27 Nov 99	1

Live recordings from their US Rock Is Dead tour, early 1999.

Marino MARINI and his QUARTET — Italy

SINGLES: — **HITS 2** — **WEEKS 23**

VOLARE (NEL BLU DIPINTO DI BLU)	Durium	13	4 Oct 58	7
COME PRIMA	Durium	2	11 Oct 58	14

Above 2 entries were separate sides of the same release, each had its own chart run.

CIAO CIAO BAMBINA	Durium	25	21 Mar 59	1
CIAO CIAO BAMBINA [RE]	Durium	24	4 Apr 59	1

MARION — UK

SINGLES: — **HITS 5** — **WEEKS 9**

SLEEP	London	53	25 Feb 95	1
TOYS FOR BOYS	London	57	13 May 95	1
LET'S ALL GO TOGETHER	London	37	21 Oct 95	2
TIME	London	29	3 Feb 96	2

| SLEEP [RM] | London | 17 | 30 Mar 96 | 2 |
CD1 is titled The Sleep EP; CD2 is titled The Acoustic EP. Featured in the Peugeot car TV commercial.

| MIYAKO HIDEAWAY | London | 45 | 7 Mar 98 | 1 |
Named after a hotel in Japan.

ALBUMS:	HITS 1			WEEKS 2
THIS WORLD AND BODY	London	10	17 Feb 96	2

MARK' OH   Germany

SINGLES:	HITS 1			WEEKS 3
TEARS DON'T LIE	Systematic	24	6 May 95	3
Based on an Italian folk song and Johnny Mathis' When A Child Is Born.

Pigmeat MARKHAM   US

SINGLES:	HITS 1			WEEKS 8
HERE COMES THE JUDGE	Chess	19	20 Jul 68	8

Biz MARKIE   US

SINGLES:	HITS 1			WEEKS 2
JUST A FRIEND	Cold Chillin'	55	26 May 90	2

Yannis MARKOPOULOS   Greece

SINGLES:	HITS 1			WEEKS 8
WHO PAYS THE FERRYMAN?	BBC	11	17 Dec 77	8
Theme from the BBC TV series of the same name.

ALBUMS:	HITS 1			WEEKS 8
WHO PAYS THE FERRYMAN	BBC	22	26 Aug 78	8

Guy MARKS   US

SINGLES:	HITS 1			WEEKS 8
LOVING YOU HAS MADE ME BANANAS	ABC	25	13 May 78	8

MARKSMEN – See Houston WELLS and the MARKSMEN

MARKY MARK and the FUNKY BUNCH   US

SINGLES:	HITS 3			WEEKS 14
GOOD VIBRATIONS	Interscope	14	31 Aug 91	7
Loletta Holoway's vocals are sampled from Love Sensation.
Above hit: MARKY MARK and the FUNKY BUNCH (featuring Loletta HOLLOWAY).

| WILDSIDE | Interscope | 42 | 2 Nov 91 | 3 |
| YOU GOTTA BELIEVE | Atlantic | 54 | 12 Dec 92 | 4 |

ALBUMS:	HITS 1			WEEKS 1
MUSIC FOR THE PEOPLE	Interscope	61	5 Oct 91	1

Bob MARLEY and the WAILERS   Jamaica

SINGLES:	HITS 17			WEEKS 156
NO WOMAN NO CRY	Island	22	27 Sep 75	7
EXODUS	Island	14	25 Jun 77	9
WAITING IN VAIN	Island	27	10 Sep 77	6
JAMMING / PUNKY REGGAE PARTY	Island	9	10 Dec 77	12
IS THIS LOVE	Island	9	25 Feb 78	9
SATISFY MY SOUL	Island	21	10 Jun 78	10
SO MUCH TROUBLE IN THE WORLD	Island	56	20 Oct 79	4
COULD YOU BE LOVED	Island	5	21 Jun 80	12
THREE LITTLE BIRDS	Island	17	13 Sep 80	9
NO WOMAN NO CRY [RE]	Island	8	13 Jun 81	11
BUFFALO SOLDIER	Island	4	7 May 83	12
ONE LOVE/PEOPLE GET READY [M]	Island	5	21 Apr 84	11
WAITING IN VAIN [RI]	Island	31	23 Jun 84	7
COULD YOU BE LOVED [RI]	Island	71	8 Dec 84	2
ONE LOVE – PEOPLE GET READY [M] [RI]	Tuff Gong	42	18 May 91	3
IRON LION ZION	Tuff Gong	5	19 Sep 92	9
WHY SHOULD I / EXODUS [RR]	Tuff Gong	42	28 Nov 92	3
Exodus was listed from 5 Dec 92, once single had dropped to No. 53.

| WHY SHOULD I / EXODUS [RR] [RE] | Tuff Gong | 75 | 2 Jan 93 | 1 |
| KEEP ON MOVING | Tuff Gong | 17 | 20 May 95 | 4 |
'Re-modelled' from original 1977 recording by Trevor Wyatt and Ingmar Kianh.

| WHAT GOES AROUND COMES AROUND | Anansi | 42 | 8 Jun 96 | 1 |
Above hit: Bob MARLEY.

| SUN IS SHINING | Club Tools | 3 | 25 Sep 99 | 10 |
Marley first recorded the track for the Trojan label in the late 1960s and re-recorded it in 1978 for the Kaya album. This is the Trojan version remixed by Funkstar de Luxe.
Above hit: Bob MARLEY vs. FUNKSTAR DE LUXE REMIX.

TURN YOUR LIGHTS DOWN LOW	Columbia	15	11 Dec 99	4

From the film 'The Best Man'.
Above hit: Bob MARLEY featuring Lauryn HILL.

ALBUMS:	HITS 14		WEEKS 478	
NATTY DREAD	Island	43	4 Oct 75	5
LIVE	Island	38	20 Dec 75	5

Live recordings from the Lyceum Ballroom, London, summer 1975.

RASTAMAN VIBRATION	Island	15	8 May 76	13
EXODUS	Island	8	11 Jun 77	56
KAYA	Island	4	1 Apr 78	24
BABYLON BY BUS	Island	40	16 Dec 78	11

Live recordings.

SURVIVAL	Island	20	13 Oct 79	6
UPRISING	Island	6	28 Jun 80	17
LIVE AT THE LYCEUM [RE]	Island	68	25 Jul 81	6
CONFRONTATION	Island	5	28 May 83	19
LEGEND – THE BEST OF BOB MARLEY AND THE WAILERS	Island	1	19 May 84	106
REBEL MUSIC	Island	54	28 Jun 86	3
LEGEND – THE BEST OF BOB MARLEY AND THE WAILERS [RI]	Tuff Gong	11	18 May 91	191

Digitally remastered version. Includes re-entries through to 1999.

SONGS OF FREEDOM	Tuff Gong	10	3 Oct 92	5

Above hit: Bob MARLEY.

NATURAL MYSTIC	Tuff Gong	5	3 Jun 95	8

Released to celebate 50th anniversary of Marley's birth.

THE SUN IS SHINING	Club Tool	40	4 Sep 99	3

Import single. It was too long and expensive to be eligible for the singles chart. See also entry in the
*   singles section above.*
Above hit: Bob MARLEY vs FUNKSTAR DE LUXE.

Ziggy MARLEY and the MELODY MAKERS — Jamaica

(See also Jamaica United.)

SINGLES:	HITS 2		WEEKS 11	
TOMORROW PEOPLE	Virgin	22	11 Jun 88	10

Features Jerry Harrison (of Talking Heads) on organ.

LOOK WHO'S DANCING	Virgin America	65	23 Sep 89	1

MARLO — UK

SINGLES:	HITS 1		WEEKS 1	
HOW DO I KNOW?	Polydor	56	24 Jul 99	1

MARMALADE — UK

SINGLES:	HITS 11		WEEKS 130	
LOVIN' THINGS	CBS	6	25 May 68	13

Originally recorded by Grassroots.

WAIT FOR ME MARY-ANNE	CBS	30	26 Oct 68	5
OB-LA-DI OB-LA-DA	CBS	1	7 Dec 68	20

Originally recorded by the Beatles.

BABY MAKE IT SOON	CBS	9	14 Jun 69	13
REFLECTIONS OF MY LIFE	Decca	3	20 Dec 69	12
RAINBOW	Decca	3	18 Jul 70	14
MY LITTLE ONE	Decca	15	27 Mar 71	11
COUSIN NORMAN	Decca	6	4 Sep 71	11
BACK ON THE ROAD	Decca	35	27 Nov 71	7
BACK ON THE ROAD [RE]	Decca	50	22 Jan 72	1
RADANCER	Decca	6	1 Apr 72	12
FALLING APART AT THE SEAMS	Target	9	21 Feb 76	11

MARMION — Holland/Spain

SINGLES:	HITS 1		WEEKS 2	
SCHONEBERG	Hooj Choons	53	18 May 96	1

First released in Germany, 1993.

SCHONEBERG [RI]	ffrr	56	14 Feb 98	1

Johnny MARR – See Billy BRAGG

MARRADONA — UK

SINGLES:	HITS 1		WEEKS 5	
OUT OF MY HEAD	Peach	38	26 Feb 94	3
OUT OF MY HEAD 97 [RM]	Soopa	39	26 Jul 97	2

Remixed by Twink.

Neville MARRINER and the ACADEMY OF ST. MARTIN IN THE FIELDS — UK

ALBUMS:	HITS 1		WEEKS 6	
AMADEUS [OST]	London	64	6 Apr 85	6

Bernie MARSDEN — UK

ALBUMS:	HITS 1			WEEKS 2	
LOOK AT ME NOW	Parlophone	71	5 Sep 81	2

Gerry MARSDEN - See CHRISTIANS, Holly JOHNSON, Paul McCARTNEY, Gerry MARSDEN and STOCK AITKEN WATERMAN; GERRY and the PACEMAKERS

Matthew MARSDEN — UK

SINGLES:	HITS 2			WEEKS 10	
THE HEART'S LONE DESIRE	Columbia	13	11 Jul 98	7
SHE'S GONE	Columbia	24	7 Nov 98	3

Above hit: Matthew MARSDEN (featuring DESTINY'S CHILD).

Stevie MARSH — UK

SINGLES:	HITS 1			WEEKS 4	
IF YOU WERE THE ONLY BOY IN THE WORLD	Decca	29	5 Dec 59	2

Originally recorded by Rudy Vallee and his Conneticut Yankees as If You Were The Only Girl In The World.

IF YOU WERE THE ONLY BOY IN THE WORLD [RE]	Decca	24	26 Dec 59	2

MARSHA - See SHAGGY

Amanda MARSHALL — Canada

ALBUMS:	HITS 1			WEEKS 2	
AMANDA MARSHALL	Epic	47	3 Aug 96	2

Jack MARSHALL'S MUSIC - See Peggy LEE

Joy MARSHALL — UK

SINGLES:	HITS 1			WEEKS 2	
THE MORE I SEE YOU	Decca	34	25 Jun 66	2

Keith MARSHALL — UK

SINGLES:	HITS 1			WEEKS 10	
ONLY CRYING	Arrival	12	4 Apr 81	10

Wayne MARSHALL — UK

SINGLES:	HITS 3			WEEKS 7	
OOH AAH (G-SPOT)	Soultown	29	1 Oct 94	3
SPIRIT	Soultown	58	3 Jun 95	1

From the film 'Spirit Of The Pharoah'.

NEVER KNEW LOVE LIKE THIS	Sony S2	40	24 Feb 96	2

Above hit: Pauline HENRY featuring Wayne MARSHALL.

G SPOT [RM]	MBA	50	7 Dec 96	1

Remixed by Roger Benov.

MARSHALL, HAIN — UK

SINGLES:	HITS 2			WEEKS 19	
DANCING IN THE CITY	Harvest	3	3 Jun 78	15
COMING HOME	Harvest	39	14 Oct 78	4

MARTAY featuring ZZ TOP — UK/US

(See also ZZ Top.)

SINGLES:	HITS 1			WEEKS 2	
GIMME ALL YOUR LOVIN' 2000	Riverhorse	28	16 Oct 99	2

Samples ZZ Top's Gimme All Your Lovin.

Lena MARTELL — UK

SINGLES:	HITS 1			WEEKS 18	
ONE DAY AT A TIME	Pye	1	29 Sep 79	18

Written by Kris Kristofferson and originally recorded by Marilyn Sellars reached No.37 in the US in 1974.

ALBUMS:	HITS 6			WEEKS 71	
THAT WONDERFUL SOUND OF LENA MARTELL	Pye	35	25 May 74	2
THE BEST OF LENA MARTELL	Pye	13	8 Jan 77	16
THE LENA MARTELL COLLECTION	Ronco	12	27 May 78	19
LENA'S MUSIC ALBUM	Pye	5	20 Oct 79	18
BY REQUEST	Ronco	9	19 Apr 80	9
BEAUTIFUL SUNDAY	Ronco	23	29 Nov 80	7

MARTHA and the MUFFINS   Canada

(See also M + M.)

SINGLES:	HITS 1			WEEKS 10
ECHO BEACH	Dindisc	10	1 Mar 80	10
ALBUMS:	HITS 1			WEEKS 6
METRO MUSIC	DinDisc	34	15 Mar 80	6

MARTHA and the VANDELLAS - See Martha REEVES and the VANDELLAS

MARTIKA   US

SINGLES:	HITS 7			WEEKS 57
TOY SOLDIERS	CBS	5	29 Jul 89	11
I FEEL THE EARTH MOVE	CBS	7	14 Oct 89	14
Originally recorded by Carole King.				
MORE THAN YOU KNOW	CBS	15	13 Jan 90	7
WATER	CBS	59	17 Mar 90	3
LOVE . . . THY WILL BE DONE	Columbia	9	17 Aug 91	9
MARTIKA'S KITCHEN	Columbia	17	30 Nov 91	10
Above 2 written by Prince.				
COLOURED KISSES	Columbia	41	22 Feb 92	3
ALBUMS:	HITS 2			WEEKS 52
MARTIKA	CBS	11	16 Sep 89	37
MARTIKA'S KITCHEN	Columbia	15	7 Sep 91	15

Billie Ray MARTIN   Germany

SINGLES:	HITS 5			WEEKS 20
YOUR LOVING ARMS	Magnet	38	19 Nov 94	3
YOUR LOVING ARMS [RI]	Magnet	6	20 May 95	10
RUNNING AROUND TOWN	Magnet	29	2 Sep 95	2
IMITATION OF LIFE	Magnet	29	6 Jan 96	3
SPACE OASIS	Magnet	66	6 Apr 96	1
HONEY	React	54	21 Aug 99	1
ALBUMS:	HITS 1			WEEKS 2
DEADLINE FOR MY MEMORIES	Magnet	47	3 Feb 96	2

Dean MARTIN   US

SINGLES:	HITS 16			WEEKS 163
KISS	Capitol	9	19 Sep 53	1
KISS [RE]	Capitol	5	3 Oct 53	7
THAT'S AMORE	Capitol	2	23 Jan 54	11
From the film 'The Caddy'.				
Above hit: Dean MARTIN with Dick STABILE and his Orchestra.				
SWAY	Capitol	6	2 Oct 54	7
HOW DO YOU SPEAK TO AN ANGEL?	Capitol	15	23 Oct 54	2
HOW DO YOU SPEAK TO AN ANGEL? [RE]	Capitol	17	20 Nov 54	4
THE NAUGHTY LADY OF SHADY LANE	Capitol	5	29 Jan 55	10
MAMBO ITALIANO	Capitol	14	5 Feb 55	2
LET ME GO LOVER	Capitol	3	26 Feb 55	9
Above entry and Naughty Lady Of Shady Lane were separate sides of the same release, each had its own chart run.				
UNDER THE BRIDGES OF PARIS	Capitol	6	2 Apr 55	8
MEMORIES ARE MADE OF THIS	Capitol	1	11 Feb 56	16
YOUNG AND FOOLISH	Capitol	20	3 Mar 56	1
INNAMORATA	Capitol	21	28 Apr 56	3
From the film 'Artists And Models'.				
THE MAN WHO PLAYS THE MANDOLINO (GUAGLIONE)	Capitol	21	23 Mar 57	2
From the film 'Ten Thousand Bedrooms'. Certain copies did not reflect (Guaglione) in the title.				
RETURN TO ME	Capitol	2	14 Jun 58	22
Originally recorded by Guy Lombardo.				
VOLARE (NEL BLU DIPINTO DI BLU)	Capitol	2	30 Aug 58	14
EVERYBODY LOVES SOMEBODY	Reprise	11	29 Aug 64	13
Originally recorded by Frank Sinatra in 1948.				
THE DOOR IS STILL OPEN TO MY HEART	Reprise	42	14 Nov 64	4
Originally recorded by the Cardinals in 1955.				
GENTLE ON MY MIND	Reprise	2	8 Feb 69	23
Originally recorded by Glen Campbell in 1967.				
GENTLE ON MY MIND [RE]	Reprise	49	30 Aug 69	1
THAT'S AMORE [RI]	EMI Premier	43	22 Jun 96	2
Featured in the Loyal Supporters TV commercial for the Euro '96 football championships.				
SWAY [RI]	Capitol	66	21 Aug 99	1
Featured in the Eurostar TV commercial.				
ALBUMS:	HITS 9			WEEKS 54
THIS TIME I'M SWINGIN'!	Capitol	18	13 May 61	1
AT EASE WITH DEAN	Reprise	35	25 Feb 67	1
WELCOME TO MY WORLD	Reprise	39	4 Nov 67	1

DEAN MARTIN'S GREATEST HITS VOLUME 1	*Reprise*	40	*12 Oct 68*	1
GENTLE ON MY MIND	*Reprise*	9	*22 Feb 69*	8
THE BEST OF DEAN MARTIN	*Capitol*	9	*22 Feb 69*	1
WHITE CHRISTMAS	*Music For Pleasure*	45	*27 Nov 71*	1

Budget compilation.
Above hit: Nat 'King' COLE and Dean MARTIN.

20 ORIGINAL DEAN MARTIN HITS	*Reprise*	7	*13 Nov 76*	11
THE VERY BEST OF DEAN MARTIN – THE CAPITAL & REPRISE YEARS	*EMI*	5	*5 Jun 99*	29

Originally released in 1998, it charted after a BBC TV 'Omnibus' programme on the artist.

George MARTIN   UK

(See also Beatles.)

ALBUMS:		HITS 1		WEEKS 13
IN MY LIFE	*Echo*	5	*4 Apr 98*	13

Features Celine Dion, Phil Collins, Jim Carrey, Robin Williams.
Above hit: George MARTIN and VARIOUS ARTISTS.

Juan MARTIN with the ROYAL PHILHARMONIC ORCHESTRA conducted by Louis CLARK   Spain

(See also Royal Philharmonic Orchestra.)

SINGLES:		HITS 1		WEEKS 7
LOVE THEME FROM THE THORN BIRDS	*WEA*	10	*28 Jan 84*	7

From the BBC1 TV series.

ALBUMS:		HITS 1		WEEKS 9
SERENADE	*K-Tel*	21	*11 Feb 84*	9

Linda MARTIN   Ireland

SINGLES:		HITS 1		WEEKS 2
WHY ME?	*Columbia*	59	*30 May 92*	2

Eurovision Song Contest winner in 1992.

Marilyn MARTIN – See Phil COLLINS

Mary MARTIN   US

EPS:		HITS 1		WEEKS 2
SOUTH PACIFIC	*Philips*	20	*9 Apr 60*	2

Ray MARTIN and his Concert Orchestra   UK

(See also Lee Lawrence; Barbara Lyon; Jimmy Parkinson; Ruby Murray.)

SINGLES:		HITS 3		WEEKS 11
BLUE TANGO	*Columbia*	8	*15 Nov 52*	1

Originally recorded by Leroy Anderson.

BLUE TANGO [RE]	*Columbia*	10	*29 Nov 52*	3
SWEDISH RHAPSODY	*Columbia*	10	*5 Dec 53*	1
SWEDISH RHAPSODY [RE]	*Columbia*	4	*19 Dec 53*	3
THE CAROUSEL WALTZ	*Columbia*	28	*16 Jun 56*	1
THE CAROUSEL WALTZ [RE]	*Columbia*	24	*4 Aug 56*	2

Ricky MARTIN   Puerto Rico

SINGLES:		HITS 4		WEEKS 33
UN, DOS, TRES) MARIA	*Columbia*	6	*20 Sep 97*	6
THE CUP OF LIFE	*Columbia*	29	*11 Jul 98*	3

Official Song of the World Cup 1998, and performed at the opening ceremony.

LIVIN' LA VIDA LOCA	*Columbia*	1	*17 Jul 99*	17
SHAKE YOUR BON-BON	*Columbia*	12	*20 Nov 99*	7

ALBUMS:		HITS 1		WEEKS 30
RICKY MARTIN	*Columbia*	2	*12 Jun 99*	30

Skip MARTIN and his Orchestra – See DE CASTRO SISTERS with Skip MARTIN and his Orchestra

Tony MARTIN with Hugo WINTERHALTER's Orchestra and Chorus   US

SINGLES:		HITS 2		WEEKS 28
STRANGER IN PARADISE	*His Master's Voice*	6	*23 Apr 55*	13

From the musical 'Kismet'.

WALK HAND IN HAND	*His Master's Voice*	2	*14 Jul 56*	15

Vince MARTIN and the TARRIERS   UK

(See also Tarriers.)

SINGLES:		HITS 1		WEEKS 1
CINDY OH CINDY	*London*	26	*15 Dec 56*	1

Wink MARTINDALE   US

SINGLES:		HITS 1		WEEKS 41	
DECK OF CARDS	London	18	5 Dec 59	5
Originally recorded by Texas T. Tyler.				
DECK OF CARDS [RE-1ST]	London	28	16 Jan 60	2
DECK OF CARDS [RE-2ND]	London	45	2 Apr 60	1
DECK OF CARDS [RE-3RD]	London	5	20 Apr 63	21
DECK OF CARDS [RI]	Dot	22	20 Oct 73	12
EPS:		HITS 1		WEEKS 12
DECK OF CARDS	London	11	13 Jul 63	12

Angie MARTINEZ – See KRS ONE; LIL' KIM

Al MARTINO   US

SINGLES:		HITS 10		WEEKS 87	
HERE IN MY HEART	Capitol	1	15 Nov 52	18
The first No. 1 single.				
TAKE MY HEART	Capitol	9	22 Nov 52	1
NOW	Capitol	3	31 Jan 53	12
RACHEL	Capitol	10	11 Jul 53	4
RACHEL [RE]	Capitol	12	12 Sep 53	1
WANTED	Capitol	12	5 Jun 54	1
WANTED [RE-1ST]	Capitol	4	19 Jun 54	14
THE STORY OF TINA	Capitol	10	2 Oct 54	8
WANTED [RE-2ND]	Capitol	17	2 Oct 54	1
THE MAN FROM LARAMIE	Capitol	19	24 Sep 55	2
THE MAN FROM LARAMIE [RE]	Capitol	20	29 Oct 55	1
SUMMERTIME	Top Rank	49	2 Apr 60	1
I LOVE YOU BECAUSE	Capitol	48	31 Aug 63	1
SPANISH EYES	Capitol	49	22 Aug 70	1
SPANISH EYES [RE]	Capitol	5	14 Jul 73	21

MARTY – See NEW SEEKERS

John MARTYN   UK

ALBUMS:		HITS 9		WEEKS 29	
ONE WORLD	Island	54	4 Feb 78	1
GRACE AND DANGER	Island	54	1 Nov 80	2
GLORIOUS FOOL	Geffen	25	26 Sep 81	7
WELL KEPT SECRET	WEA	20	4 Sep 82	7
SAPPHIRE	Island	57	17 Nov 84	2
PIECE BY PIECE	Island	28	8 Mar 86	4
COULDN'T LOVE YOU MORE	Permanent	65	10 Oct 92	2
AND	Go! Discs	32	10 Aug 96	3
THE CHURCH WITH ONE BELL	Independiente	51	4 Apr 98	1
Album of cover versions.				

MARVELETTES   US

SINGLES:		HITS 1		WEEKS 10	
WHEN YOU'RE YOUNG AND IN LOVE	Tamla Motown	13	17 Jun 67	10

Hank MARVIN   UK

(See also Marvin, Welch and Farrar; Cliff Richard.)

SINGLES:		HITS 5		WEEKS 25	
THROW DOWN A LINE	Columbia	7	13 Sep 69	9
THE JOY OF LIVING	Columbia	25	21 Feb 70	8
Above 2: CLIFF and HANK.				
DON'T TALK	Polydor	49	6 Mar 82	4
LONDON KID	Polydor	52	7 Jan 89	3
Above hit: Jean-Michel JARRE featuring Hank MARVIN.				
WE ARE THE CHAMPIONS	PolyGram TV	66	17 Oct 92	1
Above hit: Hank MARVIN featuring Brian MAY.				
ALBUMS:		HITS 10		WEEKS 61
HANK MARVIN	Columbia	14	22 Nov 69	2
WORDS AND MUSIC	Polydor	66	20 Mar 82	3
INTO THE LIGHT	Polydor	18	31 Oct 92	10
HEARTBEAT	PolyGram TV	17	20 Nov 93	9
THE BEST OF HANK MARVIN AND THE SHADOWS	PolyGram TV	19	22 Oct 94	11
Includes both solo and group material.				
Above hit: Hank MARVIN and the SHADOWS.				
HANK PLAYS CLIFF	PolyGram TV	33	18 Nov 95	7
Includes guest appearance from Cliff Richard.				
HANK PLAYS HOLLY	PolyGram TV	34	23 Nov 96	7
Album of Buddy Holly/Crickets covers.				

HANK PLAYS LIVE	PolyGram TV	71	5 Apr 97	1
Live recordings from Birmingham Symphony Hall, late 1996.				
PLAY ANDREW LLOYD WEBBER AND TIM RICE	PolyGram TV	41	22 Nov 97	6
Songs from their musicals.				
VERY BEST OF HANK MARVIN AND THE SHADOWS – THE FIRST 40 YEARS	PolyGram TV	56	14 Nov 98	5
Above 2 includes both solo and group material.				
Above 2: Hank MARVIN and the SHADOWS.				

Lee MARVIN   US

(See also Various Artists: Films – Original Soundtracks 'Paint Your Wagon'.)

SINGLES:		HITS 1		WEEKS 23
WAND'RIN' STAR	Paramount	1	7 Feb 70	18
[AA] listed with I Talk To The Trees by Clint Eastwood, which was only listed for the first 2				
weeks. From the film 'Paint Your Wagon'.				
WAND'RIN' STAR [RE-1ST]	Paramount	42	20 Jun 70	3
WAND'RIN' STAR [RE-2ND]	Paramount	47	15 Aug 70	2

MARVIN and TAMARA   UK

SINGLES:		HITS 2		WEEKS 7
GROOVE MACHINE	Epic	11	7 Aug 99	5
NORTH, SOUTH, EAST, WEST	Epic	44	25 Dec 99	2
Climbed to No.38 on 8 Jan 00.				

MARVIN, WELCH and FARRAR   UK

(See also Hank Marvin.)

ALBUMS:		HITS 1		WEEKS 4
MARVIN, WELCH AND FARRAR	Regal Zonophone	30	3 Apr 71	4

MARVIN, THE PARANOID ANDROID   UK

SINGLES:		HITS 1		WEEKS 4
MARVIN	Polydor	53	16 May 81	4

Richard MARX   US

SINGLES:		HITS 15		WEEKS 75
SHOULD'VE KNOWN BETTER	Manhattan	50	27 Feb 88	5
ENDLESS SUMMER NIGHTS	Manhattan	50	14 May 88	3
SATISFIED	EMI USA	52	17 Jun 89	4
RIGHT HERE WAITING	EMI USA	2	2 Sep 89	10
ANGELIA	EMI USA	45	11 Nov 89	4
TOO LATE TO SAY GOODBYE	EMI USA	38	24 Mar 90	3
CHILDREN OF THE NIGHT	EMI USA	54	7 Jul 90	2
ENDLESS SUMMER NIGHTS [RI] / HOLD ON TO THE NIGHTS	EMI USA	60	1 Sep 90	2
KEEP COMING BACK	Capitol	55	19 Oct 91	2
HAZARD	Capitol	3	9 May 92	15
TAKE THIS HEART	Capitol	13	29 Aug 92	6
CHAINS AROUND MY HEART	Capitol	29	28 Nov 92	6
NOW AND FOREVER	Capitol	13	29 Jan 94	6
SILENT SCREAM	Capitol	32	30 Apr 94	4
THE WAY SHE LOVES ME	Capitol	38	13 Aug 94	3
ALBUMS:		HITS 5		WEEKS 42
RICHARD MARX	Manhattan	68	9 Apr 88	2
REPEAT OFFENDER	EMI-USA	8	20 May 89	12
RUSH STREET	Capitol	60	16 Nov 91	1
RUSH STREET [RE]	Capitol	7	13 Jun 92	19
PAID VACATION	Capitol	11	19 Feb 94	5
GREATEST HITS	Capitol	34	21 Feb 98	3

MARXMAN   UK/Ireland

SINGLES:		HITS 2		WEEKS 5
ALL ABOUT EVE	Talkin Loud	28	6 Mar 93	4
SHIP AHOY	Talkin Loud	64	1 May 93	1
Vocals by Sinead O'Connor.				
ALBUMS:		HITS 1		WEEKS 1
33 REVOLUTIONS PER MINUTE	Talkin Loud	69	3 Apr 93	1

MARY JANE GIRLS   US

SINGLES:		HITS 3		WEEKS 15
CANDY MAN	Gordy	60	21 May 83	4
ALL NIGHT LONG	Gordy	13	25 Jun 83	9
BOYS	Gordy	74	8 Oct 83	1
ALL NIGHT LONG [RM]	Motown	51	18 Feb 95	1
Remixed by Mike Gray and Jon Pearn.				

ALBUMS:		HITS 1		WEEKS 9	
MARY JANE GIRLS	Gordy	51	28 May 83		9

Carolyne MAS
US

SINGLES:		HITS 1		WEEKS 2	
QUOTE GOODBYE QUOTE	Mercury	71	2 Feb 80		2

MA$E
US

(See also Blackstreet; Notorious B.I.G.; Puff Daddy.)

SINGLES:		HITS 7		WEEKS 36	
CAN'T NOBODY HOLD ME DOWN	Puff Daddy	19	29 Mar 97		4
Samples Grandmaster Flash and the Furious Five's The Message.					
Above hit: PUFF DADDY (featuring MA$E).					
FEEL SO GOOD	Puff Daddy	10	27 Dec 97		8
Samples Kool And The Gang's Hollywood Swinging.					
WHAT YOU WANT	Puff Daddy	15	18 Apr 98		5
Above hit: MA$E featuring TOTAL.					
HORSE & CARRIAGE	Epic	12	19 Sep 98		4
Above hit: CAM'RON featuring MA$E.					
YOU SHOULD BE MINE (DON'T WASTE YOUR TIME)	Motown	36	3 Oct 98		2
Above hit: Brian McKNIGHT featuring MA$E.					
TOP OF THE WORLD	Atlantic	2	10 Oct 98		8
Above hit: BRANDY featuring MA$E.					
TOP OF THE WORLD [RE]	Atlantic	61	9 Jan 99		1
GET READY	Puff Daddy	32	10 Jul 99		4
Samples Shalamar's A Night To Remember.					
Above hit: MA$E (featuring BLACKSTREET).					

ALBUMS:		HITS 2		WEEKS 9	
HARLEM WORLD	Puff Daddy	53	24 Jan 98		7
DOUBLE UP	Puff Daddy	47	24 Jul 99		2

M.A.S.H.
US

SINGLES:		HITS 1		WEEKS 12	
THEME FROM M*A*S*H* (SUICIDE IS PAINLESS)	CBS	1	10 May 80		12
Theme from the TV series. Originally recorded in 1970.					

MASH!
UK/US

SINGLES:		HITS 2		WEEKS 3	
U DON'T HAVE TO SAY U LOVE ME	React	37	21 May 94		2
Features vocals by Taffy.					
LET'S SPEND THE NIGHT TOGETHER	Playa	66	4 Feb 95		1

MASH UP – See Matt DAREY presents MASH UP

MASON – See CHICANE

Barbara MASON
US

SINGLES:		HITS 1		WEEKS 5	
ANOTHER MAN	Streetwave	45	21 Jan 84		5

Glen MASON
UK

SINGLES:		HITS 2		WEEKS 7	
GLENDORA	Parlophone	28	29 Sep 56		2
Above hit: Glen MASON with Ron GOODWIN'S CHORUS and ORCHESTRA.					
THE GREEN DOOR	Parlophone	24	17 Nov 56		5

Mary MASON
UK

SINGLES:		HITS 1		WEEKS 6	
ANGEL OF THE MORNING/ANY WAY THAT YOU WANT ME [M]	Epic	27	8 Oct 77		6

MASQUERADE
UK

SINGLES:		HITS 2		WEEKS 10	
ONE NATION	Streetwave	54	11 Jan 86		6
(SOLUTION TO) THE PROBLEM	Streetwave	65	5 Jul 86		2
(SOLUTION TO) THE PROBLEM [RE]	Streetwave	64	26 Jul 86		2

MASS ORDER
US

SINGLES:		HITS 2		WEEKS 5	
LIFT EVERY VOICE (TAKE ME AWAY)	Columbia	35	14 Mar 92		3
LET'S GET HAPPY	Columbia	45	23 May 92		2

MASS PRODUCTION

US

SINGLES:	HITS 2			WEEKS 7	
WELCOME TO OUR WORLD (OF MERRY MUSIC)	Cotillion	44	12 Mar 77	3
SHANTE	Atlantic	59	17 May 80	4

MASS SYNDICATE featuring Su Su BOBIEN

US

SINGLES:	HITS 1			WEEKS 1	
YOU DON'T KNOW	ffrr	71	24 Oct 98	1

MASSED WELSH CHOIRS

UK

ALBUMS:	HITS 1			WEEKS 7	
CYMANSA GANN	BBC	5	9 Aug 69	7

Zeitia MASSIAH

UK

SINGLES:	HITS 2			WEEKS 2	
I SPECIALIZE IN LOVE	Union	74	12 Mar 94	1
Above hit: ARIZONA featuring ZEITIA.				
THIS IS THE PLACE	Virgin	62	24 Sep 94	1

MASSIEL

Spain

SINGLES:	HITS 1			WEEKS 4	
LA LA LA	Philips	35	27 Apr 68	4
Eurovision Song Contest winner in 1968.				

MASSIVE ATTACK

UK

SINGLES:	HITS 9			WEEKS 42	
UNFINISHED SYMPATHY	Wild Bunch	13	23 Feb 91	9
Group name cut from Massive Attack because of the Gulf War.				
Above hit: MASSIVE.				
SAFE FROM HARM	Wild Bunch	25	8 Jun 91	6
MASSIVE ATTACK [EP]	Wild Bunch	27	22 Feb 92	4
Lead track: Hymn Of The Big Wheel.				
SLY	Wild Bunch	24	29 Oct 94	4
PROTECTION	Wild Bunch	14	21 Jan 95	4
Above hit: MASSIVE ATTACK with Tracey THORN.				
THE KARMACOMA [EP]	Wild Bunch	28	1 Apr 95	4
Various mixes of Karmacoma.				
RISINGSON	Circa	11	19 Jul 97	3
Samples the Velvet Underground's I Found A Reason.				
TEAR DROP	Circa	10	9 May 98	6
Features vocals by Elizabeth Fraser.				
ANGEL	Circa	30	25 Jul 98	2
Features vocals by Horace Andy.				
ALBUMS:	HITS 3			WEEKS 186	
BLUE LINES	Wild Bunch	13	20 Apr 91	67
Includes re-entries through to 1999.				
Above hit: MASSIVE.				
PROTECTION	Wild Bunch	4	8 Oct 94	8
PROTECTION / NO PROTECTION [RE]	Wild Bunch	10	7 Jan 95	61
No Protection was a remix album listed from 4 Mar 95, sales were combined. Remixed by the Mad Professor.				
MEZZANINE	Circa	1	2 May 98	50

MASSIVO featuring TRACY

UK

SINGLES:	HITS 1			WEEKS 11	
LOVING YOU	Debut	25	26 May 90	11

MASTER P and SILKK "THE SHOCKER" – See Montel JORDAN

MASTER SINGERS

UK

SINGLES:	HITS 2			WEEKS 7	
THE HIGHWAY CODE	Parlophone	25	16 Apr 66	6
WEATHER FORECAST	Parlophone	50	19 Nov 66	1

Sammy MASTERS

US

SINGLES:	HITS 1			WEEKS 5	
ROCKIN' RED WING	Warner Brothers	36	11 Jun 60	5

MASTERS AT WORK presents INDIA

US

(See also Nuyorican Soul; River Ocean featuring India.)

SINGLES:	HITS 2			WEEKS 5	
I CAN'T GET NO SLEEP '95	AM:PM	44	5 Aug 95	2

TO BE IN LOVE	*Defected*	23	*31 Jul 99*	3

Above hit: MAW presents INDIA.

MATCH · UK

SINGLES:	HITS 1		WEEKS 3	
BOOGIE MAN	*Flamingo*	48	*16 Jun 79*	3

MATCHBOX · UK

SINGLES:	HITS 8		WEEKS 66	
ROCKABILLY REBEL	*Magnet*	18	*3 Nov 79*	12
BUZZ BUZZ A DIDDLE IT	*Magnet*	22	*19 Jan 80*	8
Originally recorded by Freddie Cannon.				
MIDNITE DYNAMOS	*Magnet*	14	*10 May 80*	12
WHEN YOU ASK ABOUT LOVE	*Magnet*	4	*27 Sep 80*	12
OVER THE RAINBOW/YOU BELONG TO ME [M]	*Magnet*	15	*29 Nov 80*	11
BABES IN THE WOOD	*Magnet*	46	*4 Apr 81*	6
LOVE'S MADE A FOOL OF YOU	*Magnet*	63	*1 Aug 81*	3
ONE MORE SATURDAY NIGHT	*Magnet*	63	*29 May 82*	2

ALBUMS:	HITS 2		WEEKS 14	
MATCHBOX	*Magnet*	44	*2 Feb 80*	5
MIDNITE DYNAMOS	*Magnet*	23	*11 Oct 80*	9

MATCHBOX 20 · US

SINGLES:	HITS 2		WEEKS 3	
PUSH	*Atlantic*	38	*11 Apr 98*	2
3AM	*Atlantic*	64	*4 Jul 98*	1

ALBUMS:	HITS 1		WEEKS 1	
YOURSELF OR SOMEONE LIKE YOU	*Atlantic*	50	*25 Apr 98*	1

MATCHROOM MOB with CHAS and DAVE - See CHAS and DAVE

Mireille MATHIEU · France

SINGLES:	HITS 1		WEEKS 7	
LA DERNIERE VALSE (THE LAST WALTZ)	*Columbia*	26	*16 Dec 67*	7

EPS:	HITS 1		WEEKS 6	
MIRIELLE MATHIEU	*Fontana*	9	*12 Aug 67*	6

ALBUMS:	HITS 1		WEEKS 1	
MIREILLE MATHIEU	*Columbia*	39	*2 Mar 68*	1

Johnny MATHIS · US

(See also Johnny Mathis and Deniece Williams; Johnny Mathis and Henry Mancini; Johnny Mathis and Natalie Cole.)

SINGLES:	HITS 14		WEEKS 118	
TEACHER, TEACHER	*Fontana*	27	*24 May 58*	5
A CERTAIN SMILE	*Fontana*	4	*27 Sep 58*	16
From the film of the same name.				
Above hit: Johnny MATHIS with Ray ELLIS and his Orchestra.				
WINTER WONDERLAND	*Fontana*	17	*20 Dec 58*	3
SOMEONE	*Fontana*	6	*8 Aug 59*	15
Originally recorded by Jesse Belvin.				
Above hit: Johnny MATHIS with Ray ELLIS and his Orchestra.				
THE BEST OF EVERYTHING	*Fontana*	30	*28 Nov 59*	1
MISTY	*Fontana*	12	*30 Jan 60*	10
Originally recorded by Errol Garner.				
YOU ARE BEAUTIFUL	*Fontana*	38	*26 Mar 60*	8
Above hit: Johnny MATHIS with Ray ELLIS and his Orchestra.				
MISTY [RE]	*Fontana*	46	*16 Apr 60*	2
YOU ARE BEAUTIFUL [RE]	*Fontana*	46	*28 May 60*	1
STARBRIGHT	*Fontana*	47	*30 Jul 60*	2
MY LOVE FOR YOU	*Fontana*	9	*8 Oct 60*	18
WHAT WILL MARY SAY	*CBS*	49	*6 Apr 63*	1
I'M STONE IN LOVE WITH YOU	*CBS*	10	*25 Jan 75*	12
Originally recorded by Stylistics.				
WHEN A CHILD IS BORN (SOLEADO)	*CBS*	1	*13 Nov 76*	12
GONE, GONE, GONE	*CBS*	15	*11 Aug 79*	10
Co-written by Leon Haywood.				
WHEN A CHILD IS BORN	*CBS*	74	*26 Dec 81*	2
Originally recorded by the Daniel SentaCruz Ensemble As Soleado.				
Above hit: Johnny MATHIS and Gladys KNIGHT and the PIPS.				

EPS:	HITS 4		WEEKS 4	
MEET MISTER MATHIS	*Fontana*	18	*7 May 60*	1
IT'S LOVE	*Fontana*	20	*15 Apr 61*	1
FOUR HITS	*Fontana*	17	*26 Aug 61*	1
FOUR SHOW HITS	*Fontana*	17	*7 Oct 61*	1

ALBUMS:		HITS 24		WEEKS 193	
WARM	*Fontana*	6	*8 Nov 58*	2	
SWING SOFTLY	*Fontana*	10	*24 Jan 59*	1	
RIDE ON A RAINBOW	*Fontana*	10	*13 Feb 60*	2	
RHYTHMS AND BALLADS OF BROADWAY	*Fontana*	6	*10 Dec 60*	10	
I'LL BUY YOU A STAR	*Fontana*	18	*17 Jun 61*	1	
RAINDROPS KEEP FALLING ON MY HEAD	*CBS*	23	*16 May 70*	10	
LOVE STORY	*CBS*	27	*3 Apr 71*	5	
FIRST TIME EVER I SAW YOUR FACE	*CBS*	40	*9 Sep 72*	3	
MAKE IT EASY ON YOURSELF	*CBS*	49	*16 Dec 72*	1	
I'M COMING HOME	*CBS*	18	*8 Mar 75*	11	
THE HEART OF A WOMAN	*CBS*	39	*5 Apr 75*	2	
WHEN WILL I SEE YOU AGAIN	*CBS*	13	*26 Jul 75*	10	
I ONLY HAVE EYES FOR YOU	*CBS*	14	*3 Jul 76*	12	
GREATEST HITS VOLUME IV	*CBS*	31	*19 Feb 77*	5	
THE JOHNNY MATHIS COLLECTION	*CBS*	1	*18 Jun 77*	40	
SWEET SURRENDER	*CBS*	55	*17 Dec 77*	1	
YOU LIGHT UP MY LIFE	*CBS*	3	*29 Apr 78*	19	
THE BEST DAYS OF MY LIFE	*CBS*	38	*7 Apr 79*	5	
MATHIS MAGIC	*CBS*	59	*3 Nov 79*	4	
TEARS AND LAUGHTER	*CBS*	1	*8 Mar 80*	15	
ALL FOR YOU	*CBS*	20	*12 Jul 80*	8	
CELEBRATION	*CBS*	9	*19 Sep 81*	16	
FRIENDS IN LOVE	*CBS*	34	*15 May 82*	7	
A SPECIAL PART OF ME	*CBS*	45	*15 Sep 84*	3	

Johnny MATHIS and Natalie COLE   US

(See also Natalie Cole; Johnny Mathis.)

ALBUMS:		HITS 1		WEEKS 16	
UNFORGETTABLE: A MUSICAL TRIBUTE TO NAT KING COLE	*CBS*	5	*17 Sep 83*	16	

Johnny MATHIS and Henry MANCINI   US

(See also Henry Mancini and his Orchestra; Johnny Mathis.)

ALBUMS:		HITS 1		WEEKS 8	
THE HOLLYWOOD MUSICALS	*CBS*	46	*13 Dec 86*	8	

Johnny MATHIS and Deniece WILLIAMS   US

(See also Johnny Mathis; Deniece Williams.)

SINGLES:		HITS 2		WEEKS 20	
TOO MUCH, TOO LITTLE, TOO LATE	*CBS*	3	*25 Mar 78*	14	
Above hit: Johnny MATHIS/Deniece WILLIAMS.					
YOU'RE ALL I NEED TO GET BY	*CBS*	45	*29 Jul 78*	6	
ALBUMS:		**HITS 1**		**WEEKS 11**	
THAT'S WHAT FRIENDS ARE FOR	*CBS*	16	*26 Aug 78*	11	

Ivan MATIAS   US

SINGLES:		HITS 1		WEEKS 1	
SO GOOD (TO COME HOME TO) / I'VE HAD ENOUGH	*Arista*	69	*6 Apr 96*	1	

MATT BIANCO   UK

SINGLES:		HITS 10		WEEKS 65	
GET OUT OF YOUR LAZY BED	*WEA*	15	*11 Feb 84*	8	
SNEAKING OUT THE BACK DOOR / MATT'S MOOD	*WEA*	44	*14 Apr 84*	7	
Matt's Mood listed from 5 May 84. Titles were listed on the chart in reverse from 19 May 84.					
HALF A MINUTE	*WEA*	23	*10 Nov 84*	10	
MORE THAN I CAN BEAR	*WEA*	50	*2 Mar 85*	7	
YEH YEH	*WEA*	13	*5 Oct 85*	10	
JUST CAN'T STAND IT	*WEA*	66	*1 Mar 86*	2	
DANCING IN THE STREET	*WEA*	64	*14 Jun 86*	3	
DON'T BLAME IT ON THAT GIRL / WAP-BAM-BOOGIE	*WEA*	11	*4 Jun 88*	13	
Re-packaged from 2 July 88 with Wap-Bam-Boogie as first side.					
GOOD TIMES	*WEA*	55	*27 Aug 88*	3	
NERVOUS (RE-RECORDED VERSION) / WAP BAM BOOGIE (LATIN REMIX) [RM]	*WEA*	59	*4 Feb 89*	2	
Wap Bam Boogie remixed by Mixmaster Phil Harding.					
ALBUMS:		**HITS 4**		**WEEKS 67**	
WHOSE SIDE ARE YOU ON	*WEA*	44	*8 Sep 84*	6	
WHOSE SIDE ARE YOU ON [RE]	*WEA*	35	*10 Nov 84*	33	
Peak position reached on 6 Apr 85.					
MATT BIANCO	*WEA*	26	*22 Mar 86*	13	
INDIGO	*WEA*	23	*9 Jul 88*	13	
THE BEST OF MATT BIANCO	*East West*	49	*3 Nov 90*	2	

Kathy MATTEA | | | | US
ALBUMS:		HITS 2		WEEKS 2
READY FOR THE STORM (FAVOURITE CUTS)	Mercury	61	15 Apr 95	1

Compilation of tracks from her 8 Mercury albums since 1984.

| LOVE TRAVELS | Mercury | 65 | 8 Feb 97 | 1 |

Al MATTHEWS | | | | US
SINGLES:		HITS 1		WEEKS 8
FOOL	CBS	16	23 Aug 75	8

John MATTHEWS - See UNDERCOVER

MATTHEWS' SOUTHERN COMFORT | | | | UK
SINGLES:		HITS 1		WEEKS 18
WOODSTOCK	Uni	1	26 Sep 70	18

Originally recorded by Joni Mitchell.

ALBUMS:		HITS 1		WEEKS 4
SECOND SPRING	Uni	52	25 Jul 70	4

MATUMBI | | | | UK
SINGLES:		HITS 1		WEEKS 7
POINT OF VIEW (SQUEEZE A LITTLE LOVIN)	Matumbi	35	29 Sep 79	7

Susan MAUGHAN | | | | UK
SINGLES:		HITS 3		WEEKS 25
BOBBY'S GIRL	Philips	3	13 Oct 62	19

Originally recorded by Marcie Blaine.
Above hit: Susan MAUGHAN with Wally STOTT and his Orchestra and Chorus.

| HAND A HANDKERCHIEF TO HELEN | Philips | 41 | 16 Feb 63 | 3 |
| SHE'S NEW TO YOU | Philips | 45 | 11 May 63 | 3 |

Above hit: Susan MAUGHAN with Wally STOTT and his Orchestra and Chorus.

MAUREEN | | | | UK
SINGLES:		HITS 3		WEEKS 22
SAY A LITTLE PRAYER	Rhythm King	10	26 Nov 88	10

Above hit: BOMB THE BASS featuring MAUREEN.

| THINKING OF YOU | Urban | 11 | 16 Jun 90 | 9 |

Above hit: Maureen WALSH.

| WHERE HAS ALL THE LOVE GONE | Urban | 51 | 12 Jan 91 | 3 |

Paul MAURIAT and his Orchestra | | | | France
SINGLES:		HITS 1		WEEKS 14
LOVE IS BLUE (L'AMOUR EST BLEU)	Philips	12	24 Feb 68	14

MAVERICKS | | | | US
SINGLES:		HITS 3		WEEKS 23
DANCE THE NIGHT AWAY	MCA	4	2 May 98	18
I'VE GOT THIS FEELING	MCA	27	26 Sep 98	4
SOMEONE SHOULD TELL HER	MCA Nashville	45	5 Jun 99	1
ALBUMS:		HITS 3		WEEKS 54
MUSIC FOR ALL OCCASIONS	MCA	56	11 May 96	1

Originally released in 1995.

| TRAMPOLINE | MCA Nashville | 10 | 14 Mar 98 | 48 |
| THE BEST OF THE MAVERICKS | Mercury | 40 | 4 Dec 99 | 5 |

MAW presents INDIA - See MASTERS AT WORK presents INDIA

MAX Q | | | | Australia
SINGLES:		HITS 1		WEEKS 3
SOMETIMES	Mercury	53	17 Feb 90	3
ALBUMS:		HITS 1		WEEKS 1
MAX Q	Mercury	69	4 Nov 89	1

MAX WEBSTER | | | | Canada
SINGLES:		HITS 1		WEEKS 3
PARADISE SKIES	Capitol	43	19 May 79	3

MAXIMA featuring LILY | | | | UK/Spain
SINGLES:		HITS 1		WEEKS 2
IBIZA	Yo! Yo!	55	14 Aug 93	2

MAXWELL

US

SINGLES:	HITS 3		WEEKS 10	
. . . TIL THE COPS COME KNOCKIN' THE OPUS	Columbia	63	11 May 96	1
ASCENSION NO ONE'S GONNA LOVE YOU, SO DON'T EVER WONDER	Columbia	39	24 Aug 96	3
SUMTHIN' SUMTHIN' THE MANTRA	Columbia	27	1 Mar 97	3
ASCENSION DON'T EVER WONDER THE ENCORE [RI]	Columbia	28	24 May 97	3
ALBUMS:	HITS 3		WEEKS 18	
URBAN HANG SUITE	Columbia	57	13 Apr 96	1
URBAN HANG SUITE [RE]	Columbia	39	1 Mar 97	9
MTV UNPLUGGED [EP]	Columbia	45	26 Jul 97	2
Mini album of live recordings from New York, May 97.				
EMBRYA	Columbia	11	4 Jul 98	6

MAXX

UK/Sweden/Germany

SINGLES:	HITS 4		WEEKS 24	
GET-A-WAY	Pulse 8	4	21 May 94	12
NO MORE (I CAN'T STAND IT)	Pulse 8	8	6 Aug 94	8
YOU CAN GET IT	Pulse 8	21	29 Oct 94	3
I CAN MAKE YOU FEEL LIKE	Pulse 8	56	22 Jul 95	1
ALBUMS:	HITS 1		WEEKS 1	
TO THE MAXXIMUM	Pulse 8	66	23 Jul 94	1

Billy May and his Orchestra

US

(See also Nat 'King' Cole; Frank Sinatra.)

SINGLES:	HITS 1		WEEKS 10	
MAIN TITLE (FROM THE FILM "THE MAN WITH THE GOLDEN ARM")	Capitol	9	28 Apr 56	10

Brian MAY

UK

SINGLES:	HITS 9		WEEKS 33	
STAR FLEET	EMI	65	5 Nov 83	3
Based on the theme of a Japanese children's puppet sci-fi series.				
Above hit: Brian May and FRIENDS.				
DRIVEN BY YOU	Parlophone	6	7 Dec 91	9
TOO MUCH LOVE WILL KILL YOU	Parlophone	5	5 Sep 92	9
WE ARE THE CHAMPIONS	PolyGram TV	66	17 Oct 92	1
Above hit: Hank MARVIN featuring Brian MAY.				
BACK TO THE LIGHT	Parlophone	19	21 Nov 92	4
RESURRECTION	Parlophone	23	19 Jun 93	3
Above hit: Brian May with Cozy POWELL.				
LAST HORIZON	Parlophone	51	18 Dec 93	2
THE BUSINESS (ROCK ON COZY MIX)	Parlophone	51	6 Jun 98	1
A tribute to Cozy Powell, who died in Apr that year.				
WHY DON'T WE TRY AGAIN	Parlophone	44	12 Sep 98	1
ALBUMS:	HITS 4		WEEKS 23	
STAR FLEET PROJECT	EMI	35	12 Nov 83	4
Above hit: Brian May and FRIENDS.				
BACK TO THE LIGHT	Parlophone	6	10 Oct 92	14
LIVE AT BRIXTON ACADEMY	Parlophone	20	19 Feb 94	3
Live recordings from June 93.				
Above hit: Brian May BAND.				
ANOTHER WORLD	Parlophone	23	13 Jun 98	2

Lisa MAY

UK

SINGLES:	HITS 2		WEEKS 2	
WISHING ON A STAR	Urban Gorilla	61	15 Jul 95	1
Above hit: 88.3 featuring Lisa MAY.				
THE CURSE OF VOODOO RAY	Fontana	64	14 Sep 96	1

Mary MAY

UK

SINGLES:	HITS 1		WEEKS 1	
ANYONE WHO HAD A HEART	Fontana	49	29 Feb 64	1

Shernette MAY

UK

SINGLES:	HITS 1		WEEKS 1	
ALL THE MAN THAT I NEED	Virgin	50	6 Jun 98	1

Simon MAY

UK

(See also Anita Dobson; Marti Webb.)

SINGLES:	HITS 3		WEEKS 21	
THE SUMMER OF MY LIFE	Pye	7	9 Oct 76	8
WE'LL GATHER LILACS/ALL MY LOVING [M]	Pye	49	21 May 77	1
WE'LL GATHER LILACS/ALL MY LOVING [M] [RE]	Pye	50	4 Jun 77	1

HOWARDS' WAY (THEME FROM THE BBC TV SERIES)	BBC	21	26 Oct 85	11

Above hit: Simon May ORCHESTRA.

ALBUMS:		HITS 1		WEEKS 7
SIMON'S WAY	BBC	59	27 Sep 86	7

Above hit: Simon May ORCHESTRA.

MAYA - See TAMPERER featuring MAYA

John MAYALL   UK

ALBUMS:		HITS 14		WEEKS 115
BLUES BREAKERS	Decca	6	30 Jul 66	17

Above hit: John MAYALL with Eric CLAPTON.

| A HARD ROAD | Decca | 10 | 4 Mar 67 | 19 |
| CRUSADE | Decca | 8 | 23 Sep 67 | 14 |

Above 2: John MAYALL and his BLUESBREAKERS.

THE BLUES ALONE	Ace Of Clubs	24	25 Nov 67	5
THE DIARY OF A BAND VOLUME 1	Decca	27	16 Mar 68	9
THE DIARY OF A BAND VOLUME 2	Decca	28	16 Mar 68	5

Above 2 are live recordings from 1967.

| BARE WIRES | Decca | 3 | 20 Jul 68 | 17 |

Above 3: John MAYALL'S BLUESBREAKERS.

| BLUES FROM LAUREL CANYON | Decca | 33 | 18 Jan 69 | 3 |
| LOOKING BACK | Decca | 14 | 23 Aug 69 | 7 |

Compilation of tracks recorded during 1964-67.

THE TURNING POINT	Polydor	11	15 Nov 69	7
EMPTY ROOMS	Polydor	9	11 Apr 70	8
U.S.A. UNION	Polydor	50	12 Dec 70	1
BACK TO THE ROOTS	Polydor	31	26 Jun 71	2
WAKE UP CALL	Silvertone	61	17 Apr 93	1

Henry MAYER ORCHESTRA - See Petula CLARK

Curtis MAYFIELD   US

SINGLES:		HITS 4		WEEKS 18
MOVE ON UP	Buddah	12	31 Jul 71	10
NO GOODBYES	Atlantic	65	2 Dec 78	3
(CELEBRATE) THE DAY AFTER YOU	RCA	52	30 May 87	2

Above hit: BLOW MONKEYS with Curtis MAYFIELD.

| SUPERFLY 1990 | Capitol | 48 | 29 Sep 90 | 3 |

Above hit: Curtis MAYFIELD and ICE-T.

ALBUMS:		HITS 2		WEEKS 4
SUPERFLY [OST]	Buddah	26	31 Mar 73	2
NEW WORLD ORDER	Warner Brothers	44	15 Feb 97	2

MAYTALS   Jamaica

SINGLES:		HITS 1		WEEKS 4
MONKEY MAN	Trojan	50	25 Apr 70	1
MONKEY MAN [RE]	Trojan	47	9 May 70	3

MAYTE   US

SINGLES:		HITS 1		WEEKS 1
IF EYE LOVE U 2 NIGHT	NPG	67	18 Nov 95	1

Written by Prince.

MAZE featuring Frankie BEVERLY   US

SINGLES:		HITS 3		WEEKS 14
TOO MANY GAMES	Capitol	36	20 Jul 85	7
I WANNA BE WITH YOU	Capitol	55	23 Aug 86	3
JOY AND PAIN	Capitol	57	27 May 89	4

Above hit: MAZE.

ALBUMS:		HITS 4		WEEKS 25
WE ARE ONE	Capitol	38	7 May 83	6
CAN'T STOP THE LOVE	Capitol	41	9 Mar 85	12
LIVE IN LOS ANGELES	Capitol	70	27 Sep 86	2
SILKY SOUL	Warner Brothers	43	16 Sep 89	5

Kym MAZELLE   UK

SINGLES:		HITS 12		WEEKS 65
USELESS (I DON'T NEED YOU NOW)	Syncopate	53	12 Nov 88	3
WAIT	RCA	7	14 Jan 89	10

Above hit: Robert HOWARD and Kym MAZELLE.

GOT TO GET YOU BACK	Syncopate	29	25 Mar 89	4
LOVE STRAIN	Syncopate	52	7 Oct 89	3
WAS THAT ALL IT WAS	Syncopate	33	20 Jan 90	6

USELESS (I DON'T NEED YOU NOW) [RM]	*Syncopate*	48	*26 May 90*	2
Remixed by Norman Cook.				
MISSING YOU	*Ten Records*	22	*24 Nov 90*	7
Above hit: SOUL II SOUL (Vocals: Kym MAZELLE).				
NO ONE CAN LOVE YOU MORE THAN ME	*Parlophone*	62	*25 May 91*	2
LOVE ME THE RIGHT WAY	*Logic*	22	*26 Dec 92*	10
Above hit: RAPINATION and Kym MAZELLE.				
NO MORE TEARS (ENOUGH IS ENOUGH)	*Bell*	13	*11 Jun 94*	7
Above hit: Kym MAZELLE and Jocelyn BROWN.				
GIMME ALL YOUR LOVIN'	*Bell*	22	*8 Oct 94*	3
Above hit: Jocelyn BROWN and Kym MAZELLE.				
SEARCHING FOR THE GOLDEN EYE	*Eternal*	40	*23 Dec 95*	3
Above hit: MOTIV 8 and Kym MAZELLE.				
LOVE ME THE RIGHT WAY '96 [RM]	*Logic*	55	*28 Sep 96*	1
Remixed by the Rapino Brothers.				
Above hit: RAPINATION and Kym MAZELLE.				
YOUNG HEARTS RUN FREE	*EMI*	20	*16 Aug 97*	4
From the film 'Romeo + Juliet'.				

MAZZY STAR US

SINGLES:	HITS 2			WEEKS 3
FADE INTO YOU	*Capitol*	48	*27 Aug 94*	1
FLOWERS IN DECEMBER	*Capitol*	40	*2 Nov 96*	2
ALBUMS:	**HITS 2**			**WEEKS 2**
SO TONIGHT THAT I MIGHT SEE	*Capitol*	68	*9 Oct 93*	1
AMONG MY SWAN	*Capitol*	57	*16 Nov 96*	1

M.C. DUKE UK

SINGLES:	HITS 1			WEEKS 1
I'M RIFFIN (ENGLISH RASTA)	*Music Of Life*	75	*11 Mar 89*	1

MC ERIC – See TECHNOTRONIC

MC FIXX IT – See ANTICAPPELLA

MC Mikee FREEDOM – See NOMAD

M.C. HAMMER – See HAMMER

MC LETHAL UK

SINGLES:	HITS 1			WEEKS 1
THE RAVE DIGGER	*Network*	66	*14 Nov 92*	1

MC LYTE US

(See also Levert Sweat Gill.)

SINGLES:	HITS 5			WEEKS 14
RUFFNECK	*Atlantic*	67	*15 Jan 94*	1
KEEP ON, KEEPIN' ON	*East West America*	39	*29 Jun 96*	2
From the film 'Sunset Park'. Samples Liberian Girl by Michael Jackson.				
Above hit: MC LYTE featuring XSCAPE.				
COLD ROCK A PARTY (BAD BOY REMIX)	*East West America*	15	*18 Jan 97*	4
Samples Upside Down by Diana Ross.				
KEEP ON KEEPIN' ON [RI]	*East West America*	27	*19 Apr 97*	2
Above hit: MC LYTE featuring XSCAPE.				
I CAN'T MAKE A MISTAKE	*East West America*	46	*5 Sep 98*	1
IT'S ALL YOURS	*East West America*	36	*19 Dec 98*	4
Above hit: MC LYTE (featuring Gina THOMPSON).				

M.C. MARIO – See AMBASSADORS OF FUNK featuring M.C. MARIO

M.C. MIKER 'G' and DEEJAY SVEN Holland

SINGLES:	HITS 1			WEEKS 7
HOLIDAY RAP	*Debut*	6	*6 Sep 86*	7
Rap over Madonna's Holiday.				

MC NEAT – See DJ LUCK and MC NEAT

M.C. NOISE – See LOVE INC featuring M.C. NOISE

MC NUMBER 6 – See F.A.B.

MC PARKER – See F.A.B.

MC SAR and the REAL McCOY – See REAL McCOY

M.C. SKAT KAT and the STRAY MOB US

SINGLES:	HITS 1			WEEKS 2
SKAT STRUT	*Virgin America*	64	*9 Nov 91*	2
Samples Let's Groove by Earth, Wind and Fire.				

MC SOLAAR - See Missy "Misdemeanor" ELLIOTT; URBAN SPECIES

MC SPY-D + FRIENDS
UK

SINGLES:	HITS 1			WEEKS 2
THE AMAZING SPIDER-MAN	Parlophone	37	11 Mar 95	2

From the BBC Radio 1 series on Mark Goodier's show.

MC STYLES - See Scott GARCIA featuring MC STYLES, Scott

MC TUNES
UK

SINGLES:	HITS 3			WEEKS 19
THE ONLY RHYME THAT BITES	ZTT	10	2 Jun 90	10
TUNES SPLITS THE ATOM	ZTT	18	15 Sep 90	7
Above 2: MC TUNES versus 808 STATE.				
PRIMARY RHYMING	ZTT	67	1 Dec 90	1
THE ONLY RHYME THAT BITES 99 [RI]	ZTT	53	6 Mar 99	1
Though billed as a remix, the lead track is a longer version of the original.				
Above hit: MC TUNES vs 808 STATE.				
ALBUMS:	HITS 1			WEEKS 3
THE NORTH AT ITS HEIGHTS	ZTT	26	13 Oct 90	3

MC WILDSKI
UK

SINGLES:	HITS 2			WEEKS 10
BLAME IT ON THE BASSLINE	Go.Beat	29	8 Jul 89	6
Above hit: Norman COOK featuring M.C. WILDSKI.				
WARRIOR	Arista	49	3 Mar 90	4

ME AND YOU featuring 'WE THE PEOPLE BAND'
UK/Jamaica

SINGLES:	HITS 1			WEEKS 9
YOU NEVER KNOW WHAT YOU'VE GOT	Laser	31	28 Jul 79	9

ME ME ME
UK

SINGLES:	HITS 1			WEEKS 4
HANGING AROUND	Indolent	19	17 Aug 96	4

Abigail MEAD and Nigel GOULDING
UK/US

SINGLES:	HITS 1			WEEKS 10
FULL METAL JACKET (I WANNA BE YOUR DRILL INSTRUCTOR)	Warner Brothers	2	26 Sep 87	10

From the film 'Full Metal Jacket'.

Vaughn MEADER
US

ALBUMS:	HITS 1			WEEKS 8
THE FIRST FAMILY	London	12	29 Dec 62	8

Features Naomi Brossart as Jackie Kennedy.

David MEASHAM - See Roger DALTREY

MEAT BEAT MANIFESTO
UK

SINGLES:	HITS 1			WEEKS 1
MINDSTREAM	Play	55	20 Feb 93	1

MEAT LOAF
US

SINGLES:	HITS 19			WEEKS 146
YOU TOOK THE WORDS RIGHT OUT OF MY MOUTH	Epic	33	20 May 78	8
TWO OUT OF THREE AIN'T BAD	Epic	32	19 Aug 78	8
BAT OUT OF HELL	Epic	15	10 Feb 79	7
I'M GONNA LOVE HER FOR BOTH OF US	Epic	62	26 Sep 81	3
DEAD RINGER FOR LOVE	Epic	5	28 Nov 81	17
Uncredited vocals by Cher.				
IF YOU REALLY WANT TO	Epic	59	28 May 83	2
MIDNIGHT AT THE LOST & FOUND	Epic	17	24 Sep 83	8
RAZOR'S EDGE	Epic	41	14 Jan 84	3
Original release reached No. 93 in 1983.				
MODERN GIRL	Arista	17	6 Oct 84	9
NOWHERE FAST	Arista	67	22 Dec 84	4
PIECE OF THE ACTION	Arista	47	23 Mar 85	5
ROCK 'N' ROLL MERCENARIES	Arista	31	30 Aug 86	6
Above hit: MEAT LOAF with John PARR.				
DEAD RINGER FOR LOVE [RI]	Epic	53	22 Jun 91	2
TWO OUT OF THREE AIN'T BAD [RI]	Epic	69	27 Jun 92	1
I'D DO ANYTHING FOR LOVE (BUT I WON'T DO THAT)	Virgin	1	9 Oct 93	19
Vocals by Patti Russo.				
BAT OUT OF HELL [RI]	Epic	8	18 Dec 93	9
ROCK AND ROLL DREAMS COME THROUGH	Virgin	11	19 Feb 94	7

OBJECTS IN THE REAR VIEW MIRROR MAY APPEAR CLOSER THAN THEY ARE	*Virgin*	26	*7 May 94*	4
I'D LIE FOR YOU (AND THAT'S THE TRUTH)	*Virgin*	2	*28 Oct 95*	11
Vocals by Patti Russo.				
NOT A DRY EYE IN THE HOUSE	*Virgin*	7	*27 Jan 96*	6
RUNNIN' FOR THE RED LIGHT (I GOTTA LIFE)	*Virgin*	21	*27 Apr 96*	3
IS NOTHING SACRED	*Virgin*	15	*17 Apr 99*	4
Above hit: MEAT LOAF featuring Patti RUSSO.				

ALBUMS:	**HITS 11**		**WEEKS 763**	

COMPILATION ALBUMS:	**HITS 1**		**WEEKS 16**	
BAT OUT OF HELL	*Epic*	9	*11 Mar 78*	395
Peak position reached on 23 Aug 81. Includes re-entries through to 1987.				
DEAD RINGER	*Epic*	1	*12 Sep 81*	46
MIDNIGHT AT THE LOST AND FOUND	*Epic*	7	*7 May 83*	23
BAD ATTITUDE	*Arista*	8	*10 Nov 84*	16
HITS OUT OF HELL	*Epic*	2	*26 Jan 85*	33
BLIND BEFORE I STOP	*Arista*	28	*11 Oct 86*	6
'LIVE' AT WEMBLEY	*RCA*	60	*7 Nov 87*	2
HITS OUT OF HELL [RE-1ST]	*Epic*	26	*16 Apr 88*	25
Re-released at mid-price. Chart position reached in 1993. Includes re-entries through to 1993.				
HEAVEN AND HELL	*Telstar*	9	*25 Nov 89*	12
Features solo recordings by each artist and was thus an entry in the compilation chart.				
Above hit: MEAT LOAF/Bonnie TYLER.				
BAT OUT OF HELL [RE]	*Epic*	12	*27 Jul 91*	78
Repackaged with additional track. Chart position reached in 1994. Includes re-entries through to 1999.				
BAT OUT OF HELL II – BACK INTO HELL	*Virgin*	1	*18 Sep 93*	59
HITS OUT OF HELL [RE-2ND]	*Epic*	31	*25 Dec 93*	22
Re-released. Chart position reached in 1995.				
ALIVE IN HELL	*Pure Music*	33	*22 Oct 94*	4
Live recordings from 1987.				
HEAVEN AND HELL [RI]	*Columbia*	12	*16 Sep 95*	4
Above hit: MEAT LOAF/Bonnie TYLER.				
WELCOME TO THE NEIGHBOURHOOD	*Virgin*	3	*11 Nov 95*	27
THE VERY BEST OF MEAT LOAF	*Virgin/Sony TV*	14	*14 Nov 98*	27

MECO — US

SINGLES:	**HITS 1**		**WEEKS 9**	
STAR WARS THEME/CANTINA BAND [M]	*RCA Victor*	7	*1 Oct 77*	9

Glenn MEDEIROS — US

SINGLES:	**HITS 3**		**WEEKS 26**	
NOTHING'S GONNA CHANGE MY LOVE FOR YOU	*London*	1	*18 Jun 88*	13
Originally recorded by George Benson.				
LONG AND LASTING LOVE (ONCE IN A LIFETIME)	*London*	42	*3 Sep 88*	4
SHE AIN'T WORTH IT	*London*	12	*30 Jun 90*	9
Above hit: Glenn MEDEIROS (featuring Bobby BROWN).				

ALBUMS:	**HITS 1**		**WEEKS 2**	
NOT ME	*London*	63	*8 Oct 88*	2

Paul MEDFORD – See Letitia DEAN and Paul MEDFORD

MEDIAEVAL BAEBES — International

ALBUMS:	**HITS 2**		**WEEKS 7**	
SALVA NOS	*Virgin*	62	*29 Nov 97*	6
WORLDES BLYSSE	*Venture*	73	*31 Oct 98*	1

MEDICINE HEAD — UK

SINGLES:	**HITS 4**		**WEEKS 37**	
(AND THE) PICTURES IN THE SKY	*Dandelion*	22	*26 Jun 71*	8
ONE & ONE IS ONE	*Polydor*	3	*5 May 73*	13
RISING SUN	*Polydor*	11	*4 Aug 73*	9
SLIP AND SLIDE	*Polydor*	22	*9 Feb 74*	7

MEDICINE SHOW – See DR. HOOK

Bill MEDLEY — US

SINGLES:	**HITS 2**		**WEEKS 29**	
(I'VE HAD) THE TIME OF MY LIFE (LOVE THEME FROM 'DIRTY DANCING')	*RCA*	6	*31 Oct 87*	12
From the film 'Dirty Dancing'.				
Above hit: Bill MEDLEY and Jennifer WARNES.				
HE AIN'T HEAVY, HE'S MY BROTHER	*Scotti Brothers*	25	*27 Aug 88*	6
From the film 'Rambo III'.				
(I'VE HAD) THE TIME OF MY LIFE (LOVE THEME FROM 'DIRTY DANCING') [RE]	*RCA*	8	*15 Dec 90*	11

Michael MEDWIN, Bernard BRESSLAW, Alfie BASS and Leslie FYSON — UK

(See also Bernard Bresslaw.)

SINGLES:	HITS 1			WEEKS 9
THE SIGNATURE TUNE OF THE ARMY GAME	His Master's Voice	5	31 May 58	9

Theme from the ITV comedy series.

MEECHIE — US

SINGLES:	HITS 1			WEEKS 1
YOU BRING ME JOY	Vibe	74	2 Sep 95	1

Tony MEEHAN — UK

(See also Jet Harris and Tony Meehan.)

SINGLES:	HITS 1			WEEKS 4
SONG OF MEXICO	Decca	39	18 Jan 64	4

MEGA CITY FOUR — UK

SINGLES:	HITS 5			WEEKS 7
WORDS THAT SAY	Big Life	66	19 Oct 91	1
STOP [EP]	Big Life	36	8 Feb 92	2
Lead track: Stop.				
SHIVERING SAND	Big Life	35	16 May 92	2
IRON SKY	Big Life	48	1 May 93	1
WALLFLOWER	Big Life	69	17 Jul 93	1

ALBUMS:	HITS 3			WEEKS 3
TRANZOPHOBIA	Decoy	67	17 Jun 89	1
SEBASTAPOL ROAD	Big Life	41	7 Mar 92	1
MAGIC BULLETS	Big Life	57	22 May 93	1

MEGABASS — UK

SINGLES:	HITS 1			WEEKS 9
TIME TO MAKE THE FLOOR BURN [M]	Brothers Organisation	16	10 Nov 90	9

Mix of dance tracks.

MEGADETH — US

SINGLES:	HITS 10			WEEKS 32
WAKE UP DEAD	Capitol	65	19 Dec 87	2
ANARCHY IN THE U.K.	Capitol	45	27 Feb 88	3
MARY JANE	Capitol	46	21 May 88	2
NO MORE MR. NICE GUY	SBK	13	13 Jan 90	6
HOLY WARS . . . THE PUNISHMENT DUE	Capitol	24	29 Sep 90	3
HANGAR 18	Capitol	26	16 Mar 91	4
SYMPHONY OF DESTRUCTION	Capitol	15	27 Jun 92	3
SKIN O' MY TEETH	Capitol	13	24 Oct 92	3
SWEATING BULLETS	Capitol	26	29 May 93	3
TRAIN OF CONSEQUENCES	Capitol	22	7 Jan 95	3

ALBUMS:	HITS 6			WEEKS 25
SO FAR, SO GOOD . . . SO WHAT!	Capitol	18	26 Mar 88	5
RUST IN PEACE	Capitol	8	6 Oct 90	4
COUNTDOWN TO EXTINCTION	Capitol	5	18 Jul 92	8
YOUTHANASIA	Capitol	6	5 Nov 94	4
YOUTHANASIA / HIDDEN TREASURE [RE]	Capitol	28	25 Mar 95	1
Hidden Treasure is the title of the 2nd disc that was repackaged with Youthanasia.				
CRYPTIC WRITINGS	Capitol	38	19 Jul 97	1
RISK	Capitol	29	18 Sep 99	2

Zubin MEHTA - See 3 TENORS: José CARRERAS, Placido DOMINGO, Luciano PAVAROTTI

MEJA — Sweden

SINGLES:	HITS 1			WEEKS 5
ALL 'BOUT THE MONEY	Columbia	12	24 Oct 98	5

Melle MEL — US

(See also Quincy Jones.)

SINGLES:	HITS 6			WEEKS 77
MESSAGE II (SURVIVAL)	Sugar Hill	74	22 Jan 83	2
Above hit: Melle MEL and Duke BOOTEE.				
WHITE LINES (DON'T DON'T DO IT)	Sugar Hill	60	19 Nov 83	3
Above hit: GRAND MASTER and Melle MEL.				
WHITE LINES (DON'T DON'T DO IT) [RE-1ST]	Sugar Hill	7	11 Feb 84	38
Peak position reached on 28 Jul 84.				
BEAT STREET BREAKDOWN	Atlantic / Sugar Hill	42	30 Jun 84	7
Sales combined for 7" on Atlantic and 12" on Sugar Hill. From the film 'Beat Street'.				

WE DON'T WORK FOR FREE	Sugar Hill	45	22 Sep 84	4
Above 2: GRANDMASTER Melle MEL and the FURIOUS FIVE.				
WHITE LINES (DON'T DON'T DO IT) [RE-2ND]	Sugar Hill	75	24 Nov 84	1
Above hit: GRAND MASTER and Melle MEL.				
STEP OFF	Sugar Hill	8	15 Dec 84	12
Above hit: GRANDMASTER Melle MEL and the FURIOUS FIVE.				
WHITE LINES (DON'T DON'T DO IT) [RE-3RD]	Sugar Hill	73	5 Jan 85	1
Above hit: GRAND MASTER and Melle MEL.				
THE MEGA MELLE MIX [M] / PUMP ME UP	Sugar Hill	45	16 Mar 85	6
The Mega Melle mix was only available on the 12" release; it was listed from 6 Apr 85, after dropping to No. 46.				
Above hit: GRANDMASTER Melle MEL and the FURIOUS FIVE.				
WHITE LINES (DON'T DO IT) [RM]	WGAF	59	8 Jan 94	3
Remixed by D & S.				
Above hit: GRANDMASTER FLASH and Melle MEL.				
ALBUMS:	**HITS 1**		**WEEKS 5**	
WORK PARTY	Sugar Hill	45	20 Oct 84	5
Above hit: GRANDMASTER Melle MEL and the FURIOUS FIVE.				

MEL and KIM UK

(See also Kim Appleby.)

SINGLES:	**HITS 4**		**WEEKS 51**	
SHOWING OUT (GET FRESH AT THE WEEKEND)	Supreme	3	20 Sep 86	19
RESPECTABLE	Supreme	1	7 Mar 87	15
F.L.M.	Supreme	7	11 Jul 87	10
THAT'S THE WAY IT IS	Supreme	10	27 Feb 88	7
ALBUMS:	**HITS 1**		**WEEKS 25**	
F.L.M.	Supreme	3	25 Apr 87	25

MEL and KIM - See Mel SMITH; Kim WILDE

MELACHRINO ORCHESTRA conducted by George MELACHRINO UK

SINGLES:	**HITS 1**		**WEEKS 9**	
AUTUMN CONCERTO	His Master's Voice	18	13 Oct 56	9

MELANIE US

SINGLES:	**HITS 4**		**WEEKS 35**	
RUBY TUESDAY	Buddah	9	26 Sep 70	14
RUBY TUESDAY [RE] / WHAT HAVE THEY DONE TO MY SONG MA	Buddah	39	9 Jan 71	2
Ruby Tuesday was only listed on 9 January 71 when it charted at No. 43. The following week What Have They Done To My Song Ma was the side listed.				
BRAND NEW KEY	Buddah	4	1 Jan 72	12
WILL YOU LOVE ME TOMORROW	Neighbourhood	37	16 Feb 74	5
EVERY BREATH OF THE WAY	Neighbourhood	70	24 Sep 83	2
ALBUMS:	**HITS 6**		**WEEKS 69**	
CANDLES IN THE RAIN	Buddah	5	19 Sep 70	27
LEFTOVER WINE	Buddah	22	16 Jan 71	11
Live recordings.				
THE GOOD BOOK	Buddah	9	29 May 71	9
GATHER ME	Buddah	14	8 Jan 72	14
GARDEN IN THE CITY	Buddah	19	1 Apr 72	6
THE FOUR SIDES OF MELANIE	Buddah	23	7 Oct 72	2

MELBOURNE SYMPHONY ORCHESTRA - See Elton JOHN

MELISSA - See TECHNOTRONIC

MELKY SEDECK US

SINGLES:	**HITS 1**		**WEEKS 1**	
RAW	MCA	50	8 May 99	1
Rap performed by Elementary and Mic Masters from Bob Foundation.				

John Cougar MELLENCAMP US

SINGLES:	**HITS 4**		**WEEKS 18**	
JACK AND DIANE	Riva	25	23 Oct 82	8
Above hit: John COUGAR.				
SMALL TOWN	Riva	53	1 Feb 86	4
R.O.C.K. IN THE U.S.A.	Riva	67	10 May 86	3
WILD NIGHT	Mercury	34	3 Sep 94	3
Above hit: John MELLENCAMP with Me'shell NDEGEOCELLO.				
ALBUMS:	**HITS 7**		**WEEKS 31**	
AMERICAN FOOL	Riva	37	6 Nov 82	6
Above hit: John COUGAR.				
UH-HUH	Riva	92	3 Mar 84	1
THE LONESOME JUBILEE	Mercury	31	3 Oct 87	12

BIG DADDY	Mercury	25	27 May 89	4
WHENEVER WE WANTED	Mercury	39	19 Oct 91	2
HUMAN WHEELS	Mercury	37	18 Sep 93	2
THE BEST THAT I COULD DO 1978-1988	Mercury	25	17 Jan 98	4

Above 3: John MELLENCAMP.

MELLOMEN - See Rosemary CLOONEY; Doris DAY; Frankie LAINE; Elvis PRESLEY

Will MELLOR
UK

SINGLES:	HITS 2			WEEKS 9
WHEN I NEED YOU	Unity	5	28 Feb 98	6
NO MATTER WHAT I DO	Jive	23	27 Jun 98	3

MELODIANS
Jamaica

SINGLES:	HITS 1			WEEKS 1
SWEET SENSATION	Trojan	41	10 Jan 70	1

MELODY MAKERS - See Ziggy MARLEY and the MELODY MAKERS

MELTDOWN
UK/US

SINGLES:	HITS 1			WEEKS 1
MY LIFE IS IN YOUR HANDS	Sony	44	27 Apr 96	1

Harold MELVIN and the BLUENOTES
US

SINGLES:	HITS 9			WEEKS 52
IF YOU DON'T KNOW ME BY NOW	CBS	9	13 Jan 73	9
THE LOVE I LOST	Philadelphia International	21	12 Jan 74	8
SATISFACTION GUARANTEED (OR TAKE YOUR LOVE BACK)	Philadelphia International	32	13 Apr 74	6
GET OUT (AND LET ME CRY)	Route	35	31 May 75	5
WAKE UP EVERYBODY	Philadelphia International	23	28 Feb 76	7
Above hit: Harold MELVIN and the BLUE NOTES.				
DON'T LEAVE ME THIS WAY	Philadelphia International	5	22 Jan 77	10
Above hit: Harold MELVIN and the BLUENOTES featuring Theodore PENDERGRASS.				
REACHING FOR THE WORLD	ABC	48	2 Apr 77	1
DON'T GIVE ME UP	Philly World/London	59	28 Apr 84	4
Above 2: Harold MELVIN and the BLUE NOTES.				
TODAY'S YOUR LUCKY DAY	Philly World/London	66	4 Aug 84	2
Above hit: Harold MELVIN and the BLUE NOTES featuring NIKKO.				

MEMBERS
UK

SINGLES:	HITS 2			WEEKS 14
THE SOUND OF THE SUBURBS	Virgin	12	3 Feb 79	9
OFFSHORE BANKING BUSINESS	Virgin	31	7 Apr 79	5
ALBUMS:	**HITS 1**			**WEEKS 5**
AT THE CHELSEA NIGHTCLUB	Virgin	45	28 Apr 79	5

MEMPHIS HORNS - See Robert CRAY BAND

MEN AT WORK
Australia

SINGLES:	HITS 5			WEEKS 39
WHO CAN IT BE NOW	Epic	45	30 Oct 82	5
DOWN UNDER	Epic	1	8 Jan 83	12
OVERKILL	Epic	21	9 Apr 83	10
IT'S A MISTAKE	Epic	33	2 Jul 83	6
DR. HECKYLL AND MR. JIVE	Epic	31	10 Sep 83	6
ALBUMS:	**HITS 2**			**WEEKS 71**
BUSINESS AS USUAL	Epic	1	15 Jan 83	44
CARGO	Epic	8	30 Apr 83	27

MEN OF VIZION
US

SINGLES:	HITS 1			WEEKS 2
DO YOU FEEL ME? (...FREAK YOU)	MJJ	36	27 Mar 99	2

Rap performed by Mr. Cheeks.

MEN THEY COULDN'T HANG
UK

SINGLES:	HITS 1			WEEKS 4
THE COLOURS	Magnet	61	2 Apr 88	4
ALBUMS:	**HITS 5**			**WEEKS 9**
NIGHT OF A THOUSAND CANDLES	Imp	91	27 Jul 85	2
HOW GREEN IS THE VALLEY	MCA	68	8 Nov 86	2
WAITING FOR BONAPARTE	Magnet	41	23 Apr 88	2
SILVER TOWN	Silvertone	39	6 May 89	2
THE DOMINO CLUB	Silvertone	53	1 Sep 90	1

MEN WITHOUT HATS
Canada

SINGLES:		HITS 1			WEEKS 11
THE SAFETY DANCE	Statik	6	8 Oct 83	11
ALBUMS:		HITS 1			WEEKS 1
RHYTHM OF YOUTH	Statik	96	12 Nov 83	1

Sergio MENDES featuring Joe PIZZULO and Leza MILLER
Brazil

SINGLES:		HITS 1			WEEKS 5
NEVER GONNA LET YOU GO	A&M	45	9 Jul 83	5

Andrea MENDEZ
UK

SINGLES:		HITS 1			WEEKS 1
BRING ME LOVE	AM:PM	44	3 Aug 96	1

MENSWEAR
UK

SINGLES:		HITS 6			WEEKS 18
I'LL MANAGE SOMEHOW	Laurel	49	15 Apr 95	1
DAYDREAMER	Laurel	14	1 Jul 95	4
STARDUST	Laurel	16	30 Sep 95	3
Based on the David Essex film of the same name.				
SLEEPING IN	Laurel	24	16 Dec 95	3
BEING BRAVE	Laurel	10	23 Mar 96	4
WE LOVE YOU	Laurel	22	7 Sep 96	3
ALBUMS:		HITS 1			WEEKS 6
NUISANCE	Laurel	11	21 Oct 95	6

MENTAL AS ANYTHING
Australia/New Zealand

SINGLES:		HITS 1			WEEKS 13
LIVE IT UP	Epic	3	7 Feb 87	13
From the film 'Crocodile Dundee'.				

Sir Yehudi MENUHIN – See Julian LLOYD WEBBER

Natalie MERCHANT
US

ALBUMS:		HITS 2			WEEKS 3
TIGERLILY	Elektra	39	1 Jul 95	2
OPHELIA	Elektra	52	13 Jun 98	1

Freddie MERCURY
UK

(See also Freddie Mercury and Montserrat Caballe.)

SINGLES:		HITS 7			WEEKS 62
LOVE KILLS	CBS	10	22 Sep 84	8
From the film 'Metropolis'.				
I WAS BORN TO LOVE YOU	CBS	11	20 Apr 85	10
MADE IN HEAVEN	CBS	57	13 Jul 85	4
LIVING ON MY OWN	CBS	50	21 Sep 85	3
TIME	EMI	32	24 May 86	5
THE GREAT PRETENDER	Parlophone	4	7 Mar 87	9
IN MY DEFENCE	Parlophone	8	12 Dec 92	7
Originally from Dave Clark's musical 'Time'.				
THE GREAT PRETENDER [RI]	Parlophone	29	6 Feb 93	3
From the film 'Night In The City'.				
LIVING ON MY OWN [RM]	Parlophone	1	31 Jul 93	13
Rearranged and recorded by No More Brothers, initially for release only in Belgium.				
ALBUMS:		HITS 2			WEEKS 48
MR BAD GUY	CBS	6	11 May 85	23
THE FREDDIE MERCURY ALBUM	Parlophone	4	28 Nov 92	25

Freddie MERCURY and Montserrat CABALLE
UK/Spain

(See also Placido Domingo, Jose Carreras and Montserrat Caballe; Freddie Mercury.)

SINGLES:		HITS 1			WEEKS 17
BARCELONA	Polydor	8	7 Nov 87	9
BARCELONA [RI]	Polydor	2	8 Aug 92	8
Re-issued to coincide with the 1992 Olympic Games in Barcelona.				
ALBUMS:		HITS 1			WEEKS 8
BARCELONA	Polydor	25	22 Oct 88	4
BARCELONA [RE]	Polydor	15	22 Aug 92	4
Re-entered due to the use of the title track at the 1992 Olympic Games.				

MERCURY REV
US

SINGLES:		HITS 3			WEEKS 7
GODDESS ON A HIWAY	V2	51	14 Nov 98	1

DELTA SUN BOTTLENECK STOMP	*V2*	26	*6 Feb 99*	2
OPUS 40	*V2*	31	*22 May 99*	2
GODDESS ON A HIWAY [RI]	*V2*	26	*28 Aug 99*	2
ALBUMS:	**HITS 2**		**WEEKS 13**	
BOCES	*Beggars Banquet*	43	*12 Jun 93*	1
DESERTER'S SONGS	*V2*	27	*17 Oct 98*	12

MERCY MERCY UK

SINGLES:	**HITS 1**		**WEEKS 2**	
WHAT ARE WE GONNA DO ABOUT IT?	*Ensign*	59	*21 Sep 85*	2

MERLE and ROY UK

ALBUMS:	**HITS 1**		**WEEKS 5**	
REQUESTS	*Myndd Mawr*	74	*26 Sep 87*	4
REQUESTS [RI]	*International*	93	*3 Sep 88*	1

MERLIN – See BEATMASTERS; BOMB THE BASS

Tony MERRICK UK

SINGLES:	**HITS 1**		**WEEKS 1**	
LADY JANE	*Columbia*	49	*4 Jun 66*	1
Written by Jagger and Richards.				

MERSEYBEATS UK

SINGLES:	**HITS 7**		**WEEKS 64**	
IT'S LOVE THAT REALLY COUNTS	*Fontana*	24	*14 Sep 63*	12
I THINK OF YOU	*Fontana*	5	*18 Jan 64*	17
Written by Daniel Boone.				
DON'T TURN AROUND	*Fontana*	13	*18 Apr 64*	11
WISHIN' AND HOPIN'	*Fontana*	13	*11 Jul 64*	10
Originally recorded by Dionne Warwick.				
LAST NIGHT	*Fontana*	40	*7 Nov 64*	3
I LOVE YOU, YES I DO	*Fontana*	22	*16 Oct 65*	8
I STAND ACCUSED	*Fontana*	38	*22 Jan 66*	3
EPS:	**HITS 2**		**WEEKS 37**	
I THINK OF YOU	*Fontana*	8	*21 Mar 64*	12
ON STAGE	*Fontana*	2	*11 Apr 64*	25
ALBUMS:	**HITS 1**		**WEEKS 9**	
THE MERSEYBEATS	*Fontana*	12	*20 Jun 64*	9

MERSEYS UK

SINGLES:	**HITS 1**		**WEEKS 13**	
SORROW	*Fontana*	4	*30 Apr 66*	13
Originally recorded by the McCoys.				

MERTON PARKAS UK

SINGLES:	**HITS 1**		**WEEKS 6**	
YOU NEED WHEELS	*Beggars Banquet*	40	*4 Aug 79*	6

MERZ UK

SINGLES:	**HITS 2**		**WEEKS 2**	
MANY WEATHERS APART	*Epic*	48	*17 Jul 99*	1
LOVELY DAUGHTER	*Epic*	60	*16 Oct 99*	1

MESCALEROS – See Joe STRUMMER

Mady MESPLE and Danielle MILLET, PARIS OPERA – COMIQUE ORCHESTRA conducted by Alain LOMBARD France

SINGLES:	**HITS 1**		**WEEKS 4**	
FLOWER DUET (FROM 'LAKME')	*EMI*	47	*6 Apr 85*	4

MESSIAH UK

SINGLES:	**HITS 3**		**WEEKS 13**	
TEMPLE OF DREAMS	*Kickin*	20	*20 Jun 92*	5
I FEEL LOVE	*Kickin*	19	*26 Sep 92*	5
Above hit: MESSIAH Vocals by Precious WILSON.				
THUNDERDOME	*WEA*	29	*27 Nov 93*	3

METAL GURUS UK

SINGLES:	**HITS 1**		**WEEKS 2**	
MERRY XMAS EVERYBODY	*Mercury*	55	*8 Dec 90*	2

METALHEADS – See GOLDIE

METALLICA　　　　　　　　　　　　　　　　　　　　　US/Denmark

SINGLES:	HITS 15			WEEKS 56
THE $5.98 E.P. – GARAGE DAYS RE-REVISITED [EP]	Vertigo	27	22 Aug 87	4
Lead track: Helpless.				
HARVESTER OF SORROW	Vertigo	20	3 Sep 88	3
ONE	Vertigo	13	22 Apr 89	7
ENTER SANDMAN	Vertigo	5	10 Aug 91	4
THE UNFORGIVEN	Vertigo	15	9 Nov 91	4
NOTHING ELSE MATTERS	Vertigo	6	2 May 92	6
WHEREVER I MAY ROAM	Vertigo	25	31 Oct 92	4
SAD BUT TRUE	Vertigo	20	20 Feb 93	3
UNTIL IT SLEEPS	Vertigo	5	1 Jun 96	4
HERO OF THE DAY	Vertigo	17	28 Sep 96	4
Dedicated to Lemmy of Motorhead.				
MAMA SAID	Vertigo	19	7 Dec 96	2
THE MEMORY REMAINS	Vertigo	13	22 Nov 97	3
Backing vocals by Marinne Faithfull.				
THE UNFORGIVEN II	Vertigo	15	7 Mar 98	4
FUEL	Vertigo	31	4 Jul 98	2
WHISKEY IN THE JAR	Vertigo	29	27 Feb 99	2
ALBUMS:	HITS 11			WEEKS 116
RIDE THE LIGHTNING	Music For Nations	87	11 Aug 84	2
MASTER OF PUPPETS	Music For Nations	41	15 Mar 86	4
. . . AND JUSTICE FOR ALL	Vertigo	4	17 Sep 88	6
THE GOOD THE BAD AND THE LIVE: THE 6½ YEARS ANNIVERSARY COLLECTION	Vertigo	56	19 May 90	1
6 × 12" box set plus 4-track live EP.				
METALLICA	Vertigo	1	24 Aug 91	70
LIVE SHIT – BINGE AND PURGE	Vertigo	54	11 Dec 93	1
Package containing 3 videos/2CDs & a 72 page booklet. Live recordings from Mexico Feb 93.				
LOAD	Vertigo	1	15 Jun 96	18
HERO OF THE DAY	Vertigo	47	5 Oct 96	1
This was a 4th format release of the single. With 5 tracks and retailing at the same as a mid-price LP it was not eligible for the singles chart.				
RELOAD	Vertigo	4	29 Nov 97	9
GARAGE INC.	Vertigo	29	5 Dec 98	2
Tracks from 1987's Gararge Days Revisited EP plus B-sides and newly recorded covers.				
S&M	Vertigo	33	4 Dec 99	2
Re-recorded with the San Francisco Symphony Orchestra, conducted by Michael Kamen.				

METEORS　　　　　　　　　　　　　　　　　　　　　　　　　　　UK

SINGLES:	HITS 1			WEEKS 2
JOHNNY REMEMBER ME	I.D.	66	26 Feb 83	2
ALBUMS:	HITS 1			WEEKS 3
WRECKIN' CREW	I.D.	53	26 Feb 83	3

Pat METHENY GROUP – See David BOWIE

METHOD MAN　　　　　　　　　　　　　　　　　　　　　　　　US

(See also B Real, Busta Rhymes, Coolio, LL Cool J and Method Man; Method Man and Redman.)

SINGLES:	HITS 3			WEEKS 8
RELEASE YO'DELF	Def Jam	46	29 Apr 95	1
I'LL BE THERE FOR YOU/YOU'RE ALL I NEED TO GET BY [M]	Def Jam	10	29 Jul 95	5
Above hit: METHOD MAN featuring Mary J. BLIGE.				
BREAK UPS 2 MAKE UPS	Def Jam	33	22 May 99	2
Above hit: METHOD MAN featuring D'ANGELO.				
ALBUMS:	HITS 1			WEEKS 1
TICAL 2000: JUDGEMENT DAY	Def Jam	49	28 Nov 98	1

METHOD MAN and REDMAN　　　　　　　　　　　　　　　　　　US

(See also Method Man; Redman.)

ALBUMS:	HITS 1			WEEKS 3
BLACK OUT!	Def Jam	45	9 Oct 99	3

David METHREN – See MUNROS featuring David METHREN

MEZZOFORTE　　　　　　　　　　　　　　　　　　　　　　Iceland

SINGLES:	HITS 2			WEEKS 10
GARDEN PARTY	Steinar	17	5 Mar 83	9
ROCKALL	Steinar	75	11 Jun 83	1
ALBUMS:	HITS 2			WEEKS 10
SURPRISE SURPRISE	Steinar	23	5 Mar 83	9
CATCHING UP WITH MEZZOFORTE	Steinar	95	2 Jul 83	1

MFSB

SINGLES:		HITS 3		WEEKS 18	
					US
TSOP (THE SOUND OF PHILADELPHIA)	Philadelphia International	22	27 Apr 74	9
Above hit: MFSB featuring the THREE DEGREES.				
SEXY	Philadelphia International	37	26 Jul 75	5
MYSTERIES OF THE WORLD	The Sound Of Philadelphia	41	31 Jan 81	4

MIAMI SOUND MACHINE - See Gloria ESTEFAN

George MICHAEL

SINGLES:		HITS 26		WEEKS 238	
					UK
CARELESS WHISPER	Epic	1	4 Aug 84	17
A DIFFERENT CORNER	Epic	1	5 Apr 86	10
I KNEW YOU WERE WAITING (FOR ME)	Epic	1	31 Jan 87	9
Above hit: Aretha FRANKLIN and George MICHAEL.				
I WANT YOUR SEX RHYTHM 1 LUST	Epic	3	13 Jun 87	10
FAITH	Epic	2	24 Oct 87	12
FATHER FIGURE	Epic	11	9 Jan 88	6
ONE MORE TRY	Epic	8	23 Apr 88	7
MONKEY	Epic	13	16 Jul 88	6
KISSING A FOOL	Epic	18	3 Dec 88	6
PRAYING FOR TIME	Epic	6	25 Aug 90	7
WAITING FOR THAT DAY	Epic	23	27 Oct 90	5
FREEDOM! 90	Epic	28	15 Dec 90	6
HEAL THE PAIN	Epic	31	16 Feb 91	4
COWBOYS AND ANGELS	Epic	45	30 Mar 91	3
DON'T LET THE SUN GO DOWN ON ME	Epic	1	7 Dec 91	10
Live recording from London, March 91.				
Above hit: George MICHAEL with Elton JOHN.				
TOOFUNKY	Epic	4	13 Jun 92	9
FIVE LIVE [EP]	Parlophone	1	1 May 93	11
Lead track: Somebody To Love, a live recording from the Freddie Mercury Tribute Concert April 92. Lisa Stansfield only sang on These Are The Days Of Our Lives. Proceeds to the Mercury Phoenix Trust.				
Above hit: George MICHAEL and QUEEN with Lisa STANSFIELD.				
FIVE LIVE [EP] [RE]	Parlophone	74	24 Jul 93	1
JESUS TO A CHILD	Virgin	1	20 Jan 96	10
JESUS TO A CHILD [RE-1ST]	Virgin	68	20 Apr 96	1
FASTLOVE	Virgin	1	4 May 96	14
Samples Patrice Rushen's Forget Me Nots.				
JESUS TO A CHILD [RE-2ND]	Virgin	65	4 May 96	2
SPINNING THE WHEEL	Virgin	2	31 Aug 96	12
OLDER / I CAN'T MAKE YOU LOVE ME	Virgin	3	1 Feb 97	8
Also credited as The Older EP, though not listed as such on the chart.				
OLDER / I CAN'T MAKE YOU LOVE ME [RE]	Virgin	70	12 Apr 97	1
STAR PEOPLE '97	Virgin	2	10 May 97	9
WALTZ AWAY DREAMING	Aegean	10	7 Jun 97	4
Dedicated to George Michael's late mother.				
Above hit: Toby BOURKE with George MICHAEL.				
STAR PEOPLE '97 [RE]	Virgin	59	19 Jul 97	4
YOU HAVE BEEN LOVED / THE STRANGEST THING '97	Virgin	2	20 Sep 97	8
The Strangest Thing '97 listed from 27 Sep 97.				
OUTSIDE	Epic	2	31 Oct 98	14
OUTSIDE [RE]	Epic	61	13 Feb 99	2
AS	Epic	4	13 Mar 99	10
Originally recorded by Stevie Wonder for his 1976 album Songs In The Key Of Life.				
Above hit: George MICHAEL – Mary J. BLIGE.				
ALBUMS:		HITS 5		WEEKS 288	
FAITH	Epic	1	14 Nov 87	77
LISTEN WITHOUT PREJUDICE VOLUME 1	Epic	1	15 Sep 90	57
OLDER / OLDER & UPPER	Virgin	1	25 May 96	99
The double-pack, Older & Upper, listed from 13 Dec 97.				
LADIES & GENTLEMEN – THE BEST OF GEORGE MICHAEL	Epic	1	21 Nov 98	52
SONGS FROM THE LAST CENTURY	Virgin	2	18 Dec 99	3

MICHAELA

SINGLES:		HITS 2		WEEKS 6	
					UK
-H-A-P-P-Y- RADIO	ffrr	62	2 Sep 89	4
TAKE GOOD CARE OF MY HEART	London	66	28 Apr 90	2

Lisa MICHAELIS - See Frankie KNUCKLES

Pras MICHEL - See PRAS

MICHELE - See KING BEE

Yvette MICHELE
US

SINGLES:		HITS 1		WEEKS 3
I'M NOT FEELING YOU	Loud	36	5 Apr 97	3

Keith MICHELL
Australia

SINGLES:		HITS 3		WEEKS 25
I'LL GIVE YOU THE EARTH (TOUS LES BATEAUX, TOUS LES OISEAUX)	Spark	43	27 Mar 71	1
I'LL GIVE YOU THE EARTH (TOUS LES BATEAUX, TOUS LES OISEAUX) [RE]	Spark	30	17 Apr 71	10
CAPTAIN BEAKY / WILFRED THE WEASEL	Polydor	5	26 Jan 80	10
Became popular due to airplay on Noel Edmunds BBC Radio 1 Sunday morning show.				
THE TRIAL OF HISSING SID	Polydor	53	29 Mar 80	4
Above 2: Keith MICHELL, CAPTAIN BEAKY and his BAND.				
ALBUMS:		HITS 1		WEEKS 12
CAPTAIN BEAKY AND HIS BAND	Polydor	28	9 Feb 80	12
Above hit: Keith MICHELL and VARIOUS ARTISTS.				

MICHELLE
Trinidad

SINGLES:		HITS 1		WEEKS 1
STANDING HERE ALL ALONE	Positiva	69	8 Jun 96	1

Vicki MICHELLE - See RENE and YVETTE featuring Gordon KAYE and Vicki MICHELLE

Lloyd MICHELS - See MISTURA featuring Lloyd MICHELS (trumpet)

MICK and PAT - See PAT and MICK

MICROBE
UK

SINGLES:		HITS 1		WEEKS 7
GROOVY BABY	CBS	29	17 May 69	7
Features the voice of three-year-old Ian Doody, backing singers are Lesley Duncan, Madeline Bell and Dusty Springfield.				

MICRODISNEY
Ireland

SINGLES:		HITS 1		WEEKS 3
TOWN TO TOWN	Virgin	55	21 Feb 87	3

MIDDLE OF THE ROAD
UK

SINGLES:		HITS 5		WEEKS 76
CHIRPY CHIRPY CHEEP CHEEP	RCA Victor	1	5 Jun 71	34
Originally recorded by Lally Stott.				
TWEEDLE DEE, TWEEDLE DUM	RCA Victor	2	4 Sep 71	17
SOLEY SOLEY	RCA Victor	5	11 Dec 71	12
SACRAMENTO (A WONDERFUL TOWN)	RCA Victor	49	25 Mar 72	1
SACRAMENTO (A WONDERFUL TOWN) [RE]	RCA Victor	23	8 Apr 72	6
SAMSON AND DELILAH	RCA Victor	26	29 Jul 72	6

MIDDLESBOROUGH FC featuring Bob MORTIMER and Chris REA
UK

(See also Chis Rea.)

SINGLES:		HITS 1		WEEKS 1
LET'S DANCE	Magnet	44	24 May 97	1
Re-recorded version of Rea's hit. Charity record with proceeds to NSPCC.				

MIDGET
UK

SINGLES:		HITS 2		WEEKS 2
ALL FALL DOWN	Radarscope	57	31 Jan 98	1
INVISIBLE BALOON	Radarscope	66	18 Apr 98	1

MIDI XPRESS
UK

SINGLES:		HITS 1		WEEKS 1
CHASE	Labello Dance	73	11 May 96	1

Bette MIDLER
US

SINGLES:		HITS 3		WEEKS 27
WIND BENEATH MY WINGS	Atlantic	5	17 Jun 89	12
From the film 'Beaches'. Originally recorded by Sheena Easton in 1982.				
FROM A DISTANCE	Atlantic	45	13 Oct 90	5
Originally recorded by Nanci Griffith.				
FROM A DISTANCE [RE]	Atlantic	6	15 Jun 91	9
MY ONE TRUE FRIEND	Warner Brothers	58	5 Dec 98	1
From the film 'One True Thing'.				
ALBUMS:		HITS 6		WEEKS 41
THE ROSE [OST]	Atlantic	68	8 Mar 80	1
BEACHES [OST]	Atlantic	21	15 Jul 89	9

SOME PEOPLE'S LIVES	*Atlantic*	5	*13 Jul 91*	11
FOR THE BOYS [OST]	*Atlantic*	75	*15 Feb 92*	1
EXPERIENCE THE DIVINE – GREATEST HITS	*Atlantic*	3	*30 Oct 93*	15
BETTE OF ROSES	*Atlantic*	55	*25 Nov 95*	4

MIDNIGHT BLUE (A Project with) Louise TUCKER — UK

SINGLES:	HITS 1			WEEKS 5
MIDNIGHT BLUE	*Ariola*	59	*9 Apr 83*	5

Originally recorded by Melissa Manchester.

MIDNIGHT OIL — Australia

SINGLES:	HITS 6			WEEKS 32
BEDS ARE BURNING	*CBS*	48	*23 Apr 88*	5
THE DEAD HEART	*CBS*	68	*2 Jul 88*	2
BEDS ARE BURNING [RI]	*CBS*	6	*25 Mar 89*	13
THE DEAD HEART [RI]	*CBS*	62	*1 Jul 89*	4
BLUE SKY MINE	*CBS*	66	*10 Feb 90*	2
TRUGANINI	*Columbia*	29	*17 Apr 93*	4

Truganni was was supposedly the last Van Diemen's Land Aborigine, she died in 1876.

MY COUNTRY	*Columbia*	66	*3 Jul 93*	1
IN THE VALLEY	*Columbia*	60	*6 Nov 93*	1
ALBUMS:	HITS 3			WEEKS 21
DIESEL AND DUST	*CBS*	71	*25 Jun 88*	3
DIESEL AND DUST [RE]	*CBS*	19	*13 May 89*	13
BLUE SKY MINING	*CBS*	28	*10 Mar 90*	3
EARTH AND SUN AND MOON	*Columbia*	27	*1 May 93*	2

MIDNIGHT STAR — US

SINGLES:	HITS 5			WEEKS 26
OPERATOR	*Solar*	66	*23 Feb 85*	2
HEADLINES	*Solar*	16	*28 Jun 86*	8
MIDAS TOUCH	*Solar*	8	*4 Oct 86*	10
ENGINE NO. 9	*Solar*	64	*7 Feb 87*	3
WET MY WHISTLE	*Solar*	60	*2 May 87*	3
ALBUMS:	HITS 2			WEEKS 6
PLANETARY INVASION	*Solar*	85	*2 Feb 85*	2
HEADLINES	*Solar*	42	*5 Jul 86*	4

MIGHTY AVENGERS — UK

SINGLES:	HITS 1			WEEKS 2
SO MUCH IN LOVE	*Decca*	46	*28 Nov 64*	2

MIGHTY DUB KATZ — UK

(See also Norman Cook; Fatboy Slim.)

SINGLES:	HITS 2			WEEKS 5
JUST ANOTHER GROOVE	*ffrr*	43	*7 Dec 96*	1
MAGIC CARPET RIDE	*ffrr*	24	*2 Aug 97*	4

MIGHTY LEMON DROPS — UK

SINGLES:	HITS 3			WEEKS 6
THE OTHER SIDE OF YOU	*Blue Guitar*	67	*13 Sep 86*	1
OUT OF HAND	*Blue Guitar*	66	*18 Apr 87*	3
INSIDE OUT	*Blue Guitar*	74	*23 Jan 88*	2
ALBUMS:	HITS 2			WEEKS 5
HAPPY HEAD	*Blue Guitar*	58	*4 Oct 86*	2
THE WORLD WITHOUT END	*Blue Guitar*	34	*27 Feb 88*	3

MIGHTY MIGHTY BOSSTONES — US

SINGLES:	HITS 2			WEEKS 6
THE IMPRESSION THAT I GET	*Mercury*	12	*25 Apr 98*	5
THE RASCAL KING	*Mercury*	63	*27 Jun 98*	1
ALBUMS:	HITS 1			WEEKS 2
LET'S FACE IT	*Mercury*	40	*16 May 98*	2

MIGHTY MORPH'N POWER RANGERS — US

SINGLES:	HITS 1			WEEKS 13
POWER RANGERS	*RCA*	3	*17 Dec 94*	9
POWER RANGERS [RE-1ST]	*RCA*	57	*25 Feb 95*	2
POWER RANGERS [RE-2ND]	*RCA*	65	*25 Mar 95*	1
POWER RANGERS [RE-3RD]	*RCA*	74	*8 Apr 95*	1
ALBUMS:	HITS 1			WEEKS 3
POWER RANGERS – THE ALBUM – A ROCK ADVENTURE	*RCA*	50	*24 Dec 94*	3

MIGHTY WAH! - See WAH!

MIGIL 5

SINGLES:	HITS 2			UK WEEKS 20	
MOCKIN' BIRD HILL	Pye	10	21 Mar 64	13
Originally recorded by the Pinetoppers.				
NEAR YOU	Pye	31	6 Jun 64	7
Originally recorded by Francis Craig.				

MIG29

SINGLES:	HITS 1			Italy WEEKS 2	
MIG29	Champion	62	22 Feb 92	2

MIKAELA - See SUPERCAR

MIKE

SINGLES:	HITS 1			UK WEEKS 2	
TWANGLING THREE FINGERS IN A BOX	Pukka	40	19 Nov 94	2

MIKE and the MECHANICS

(See also Mike Rutherford.)

SINGLES:	HITS 12			UK WEEKS 67	
SILENT RUNNING (ON DANGEROUS GROUND)	WEA	21	15 Feb 86	9
ALL I NEED IS A MIRACLE	WEA	53	31 May 86	4
THE LIVING YEARS	WEA	2	14 Jan 89	11
Co-written by B.A.Robertson.				
WORD OF MOUTH	Virgin	13	16 Mar 91	10
A TIME AND A PLACE	Virgin	58	15 Jun 91	3
EVERYBODY GETS A SECOND CHANCE	Virgin	56	8 Feb 92	4
OVER MY SHOULDER	Virgin	12	25 Feb 95	9
A BEGGAR ON A BEACH OF GOLD	Virgin	33	17 Jun 95	5
ANOTHER CUP OF COFFEE	Virgin	51	2 Sep 95	4
ALL I NEED IS A MIRACLE '96 [RR]	Virgin	27	17 Feb 96	4
SILENT RUNNING [RI]	Virgin	61	1 Jun 96	1
Featured in the Tennents Extra Larger TV commercial.				
NOW THAT YOU'RE GONE	Virgin	35	5 Jun 99	2
WHENEVER I STOP	Virgin	73	28 Aug 99	1
ALBUMS:	HITS 6			WEEKS 99	
MIKE AND THE MECHANICS	WEA	78	15 Mar 86	3
THE LIVING YEARS	WEA	2	26 Nov 88	19
WORD OF MOUTH	Virgin	11	27 Apr 91	7
BEGGAR ON A BEACH OF GOLD	Virgin	9	18 Mar 95	33
THE LIVING YEARS [RI]	WEA International	67	2 Mar 96	2
Re-released at mid-price.				
HITS	Virgin	3	16 Mar 96	31
MIKE AND THE MECHANICS	Virgin	14	12 Jun 99	4
Both eponymous albums are different.				

MIKI and GRIFF

SINGLES:	HITS 4			UK WEEKS 25	
HOLD BACK TOMORROW	Pye	26	3 Oct 59	2
Above hit: Lonnie Donegan Presents MIKI and GRIFF with the Lonnie DONEGAN GROUP.				
ROCKIN' ALONE (IN AN OLD ROCKING CHAIR)	Pye	44	15 Oct 60	3
Above hit: MIKI and GRIFF with the Lonnie DONEGAN GROUP.				
A LITTLE BITTY TEAR	Pye	16	3 Feb 62	13
I WANT TO STAY HERE	Pye	23	24 Aug 63	7
EPS:	HITS 1			WEEKS 22	
THIS IS MIKI AND GRIFF	Pye	2	3 Sep 60	22

Buddy MILES - See Carlos SANTANA and Buddy MILES

John MILES

SINGLES:	HITS 4			UK WEEKS 30	
HIGHFLY	Decca	17	18 Oct 75	6
MUSIC	Decca	3	20 Mar 76	9
REMEMBER YESTERDAY	Decca	32	16 Oct 76	5
SLOW DOWN	Decca	10	18 Jun 77	10
ALBUMS:	HITS 5			WEEKS 25	
REBEL	Decca	9	27 Mar 76	10
STRANGER IN THE CITY	Decca	37	26 Feb 77	3
ZARAGON	Decca	43	1 Apr 78	5
MORE MILES PER HOUR	Decca	46	21 Apr 79	5
MILES HIGH	EMI	96	29 Aug 81	2

Robert MILES — Italy

SINGLES:	HITS 4			WEEKS 48
CHILDREN	Deconstruction	2	24 Feb 96	18
Import reached No. 86 a month prior to release.				
FABLE	Deconstruction	7	8 Jun 96	7
Features vocals by Fiorella Quinn.				
FABLE [RE-1ST]	Deconstruction	71	3 Aug 96	1
FABLE [RE-2ND]	Deconstruction	69	31 Aug 96	1
ONE & ONE	Deconstruction	3	16 Nov 96	17
Above hit: Robert MILES featuring Maria NAYLER.				
FREEDOM	Deconstruction	15	29 Nov 97	4
Above hit: Robert MILES featuring Kathy SLEDGE.				
ALBUMS:	HITS 2			WEEKS 51
DREAMLAND	Deconstruction	7	22 Jun 96	48
23AM	Deconstruction	42	6 Dec 97	3

June MILES-KINGSTON – See Jimmy SOMERVILLE

Paul MILES-KINGSTON – See Sarah BRIGHTMAN; Andrew LLOYD WEBBER

MILK AND HONEY featuring Gali ATARI — Israel

SINGLES:	HITS 1			WEEKS 8
HALLELUJAH	Polydor	5	14 Apr 79	8
Eurovision Song Contest winner in 1979. Some copies did not credit Gali Atari.				

MILK INCORPORATED — Belgium

SINGLES:	HITS 1			WEEKS 3
GOOD ENOUGH (LA VACHE)	Malarky	23	28 Feb 98	3
Vocals by Jade 4 U.				

MILL GIRLS – See Billy COTTON and his BAND

MILLA — US

SINGLES:	HITS 1			WEEKS 1
GENTLEMAN WHO FELL	SBK	65	18 Jun 94	1

Frankie MILLER — UK

SINGLES:	HITS 4			WEEKS 32
BE GOOD TO YOURSELF	Chrysalis	27	4 Jun 77	6
Originally recorded by Andy Fraser.				
DARLIN'	Chrysalis	6	14 Oct 78	15
Originally recorded by Poacher.				
WHEN I'M AWAY FROM YOU	Chrysalis	42	20 Jan 79	5
CALEDONIA	MCS	45	21 Mar 92	6
ALBUMS:	HITS 1			WEEKS 1
FALLING IN LOVE	Chrysalis	54	14 Apr 79	1

Gary MILLER — UK

SINGLES:	HITS 6			WEEKS 35
THE YELLOW ROSE OF TEXAS	Pye Nixa	13	22 Oct 55	5
Above hit: Gary MILLER with Dennis WILSON and his Orchestra and the Beryl STOTT CHORUS.				
ROBIN HOOD	Pye Nixa	10	14 Jan 56	6
GARDEN OF EDEN	Pye Nixa	14	12 Jan 57	6
GARDEN OF EDEN [RE]	Pye Nixa	27	2 Mar 57	1
WONDERFUL, WONDERFUL	Pye Nixa	29	20 Jul 57	1
Above 4: Gary MILLER with the Tony OSBORNE ORCHESTRA and the Beryl STOTT CHORUS.				
THE STORY OF MY LIFE	Pye Nixa	14	18 Jan 58	6
Above hit: Gary MILLER with the Kim DRAKE ORCHESTRA and the Beryl STOTT CHORUS.				
THERE GOES THAT SONG AGAIN / THE NIGHT IS YOUNG (AND YOU'RE SO BEAUTIFUL)	Pye	29	23 Dec 61	9
The Night Is Young had first credit but was no longer listed from 13 Jan 62. As an AA side it peaked at No. 32.				
THERE GOES THAT SONG AGAIN [RE]	Pye	48	3 Mar 62	1

Glenn MILLER and his Orchestra — US

SINGLES:	HITS 2			WEEKS 9
MOONLIGHT SERENADE	His Master's Voice	12	13 Mar 54	1
Originally released in 1946.				
MOONLIGHT SERENADE [RI] / LITTLE BROWN JUG / IN THE MOOD	RCA Victor Maximillion	13	24 Jan 76	8

ALBUMS:		HITS 9			WEEKS 80
GLENN MILLER PLAYS SELECTIONS FROM 'THE GLENN MILLER STORY'					
AND OTHER HITS [OST]	RCA	10	28 Jan 61	18	
Includes re-entries through to 1970.					
THE BEST OF GLENN MILLER	RCA International	5	5 Jul 69	14	
NEARNESS OF YOU	RCA International	30	6 Sep 69	2	
A MEMORIAL 1944-1969	RCA Victor	18	25 Apr 70	17	
THE REAL GLENN MILLER AND HIS ORCHESTRA PLAY THE ORIGINAL MUSIC					
OF THE FILM 'THE GLENN MILLER STORY' AND OTHER HITS [OST] [RI]	RCA International	28	25 Dec 71	2	
A LEGENDARY PERFORMER	RCA Victor	41	14 Feb 76	5	
A LEGENDARY PERFORMER VOLUME 2	RCA Victor	53	14 Feb 76	2	
THE UNFORGETTABLE GLENN MILLER	RCA Victor	4	9 Apr 77	8	
THE ULTIMATE GLENN MILLER	Bluebird	11	20 Mar 93	6	
THE LOST RECORDINGS	Happy Days	22	25 Feb 95	6	
Recorded during Sep & Nov 44.					

Jody MILLER   US

SINGLES:		HITS 1			WEEKS 1
HOME OF THE BRAVE	Capitol	49	23 Oct 65	1	
Originally recorded by Bonnie and the Treasures.					

Leza MILLER – See Sergio MENDES featuring Joe PIZZULO and Leza MILLER

Mitch MILLER with his Orchestra and Chorus   US

(See also Frankie Laine; Guy Mitchell.)

SINGLES:		HITS 1			WEEKS 13
THE YELLOW ROSE OF TEXAS	Philips	2	8 Oct 55	13	

Ned MILLER   US

SINGLES:		HITS 2			WEEKS 22
FROM A JACK TO A KING	London	2	16 Feb 63	21	
DO WHAT YOU DO DO WELL	London	48	20 Feb 65	1	

Roger MILLER   US

SINGLES:		HITS 5			WEEKS 42
KING OF THE ROAD	Philips	1	20 Mar 65	15	
ENGINE ENGINE NO. 9	Philips	33	5 Jun 65	5	
KANSAS CITY STAR	Philips	48	23 Oct 65	1	
ENGLAND SWINGS	Philips	45	18 Dec 65	1	
ENGLAND SWINGS [RE]	Philips	13	8 Jan 66	7	
LITTLE GREEN APPLES	Mercury	19	30 Mar 68	10	
LITTLE GREEN APPLES [RE-1ST]	Mercury	48	5 Apr 69	1	
LITTLE GREEN APPLES [RE-2ND]	Mercury	39	10 May 69	2	

Steve MILLER BAND   US

SINGLES:		HITS 4			WEEKS 36
ROCK 'N' ME	Mercury	11	23 Oct 76	9	
ABRACADABRA	Mercury	2	19 Jun 82	11	
KEEPS ME WONDERING WHY	Mercury	52	4 Sep 82	3	
THE JOKER	Capitol	1	11 Aug 90	13	
Featured in the Levi's 501 Jeans commercial. Originally released in 1974, it reached No. 1 in the US.					

ALBUMS:		HITS 6			WEEKS 51
FLY LIKE AN EAGLE	Mercury	11	12 Jun 76	17	
BOOK OF DREAMS	Mercury	12	4 Jun 77	12	
ABRACADABRA	Mercury	10	19 Jun 82	16	
STEVE MILLER BAND LIVE!	Mercury	79	7 May 83	2	
Live recordings from their 1982 UK tour.					
THE BEST OF 1968-1973	Capitol	34	6 Oct 90	3	
GREATEST HITS	PolyGram TV	58	10 Oct 98	1	

Suzi MILLER and the JOHNSTON BROTHERS   UK

(See also Johnston Brothers.)

SINGLES:		HITS 1			WEEKS 2
HAPPY DAYS AND LONELY NIGHTS	Decca	14	22 Jan 55	2	

Lisa MILLETT – See SHEER BRONZE featuring Lisa MILLETT

MILLI VANILLI   France/Germany

SINGLES:		HITS 5			WEEKS 50
GIRL YOU KNOW IT'S TRUE	Cooltempo	3	1 Oct 88	13	
Reached No. 99 when first released in Jul 1988. Originally recorded by Numarx.					
BABY DON'T FORGET MY NUMBER	Cooltempo	16	17 Dec 88	11	
BLAME IT ON THE RAIN	Cooltempo	53	22 Jul 89	5	

GIRL I'M GONNA MISS YOU	Cooltempo	2	30 Sep 89	15
BLAME IT ON THE RAIN [RE]	Cooltempo	52	2 Dec 89	5
ALL OR NOTHING	Cooltempo	74	10 Mar 90	1
ALBUMS:	**HITS 1**		**WEEKS 25**	
ALL OR NOTHING	Cooltempo	37	21 Jan 89	6
ALL OR NOTHING / 2 X 2 [RE]	Cooltempo	6	28 Oct 89	19

2 X 2 was a remix album listed from 25 Nov 89, sales were combined.

MILLICAN and NESBITT · UK

SINGLES:	**HITS 2**		**WEEKS 14**	
VAYA CON DIOS (MAY GOD BE WITH YOU)	Pye	20	1 Dec 73	11
FOR OLD TIMES SAKE	Pye	38	18 May 74	3
ALBUMS:	**HITS 2**		**WEEKS 24**	
MILLICAN AND NESBITT	Pye	3	23 Mar 74	21
EVERYBODY KNOWS MILLICAN AND NESBITT	Pye	23	4 Jan 75	3

MILLIE · Jamaica

SINGLES:	**HITS 3**		**WEEKS 33**	
MY BOY LOLLIPOP	Fontana	2	14 Mar 64	18
Originally recorded by Barbie Gaye.				
SWEET WILLIAM	Fontana	30	27 Jun 64	9
BLOODSHOT EYES	Fontana	48	13 Nov 65	1
MY BOY LOLLIPOP [RI]	Island	46	25 Jul 87	5

Spike MILLIGAN · UK

(See also Harry Secombe, Peter Sellers and Spike Milligan.)

ALBUMS:	**HITS 2**		**WEEKS 5**	
MILLIGAN PRESERVED	Parlophone	11	25 Nov 61	4
THE SNOW GOOSE	RCA Victor	49	18 Dec 76	1

Above hit: Spike MILLIGAN with the LONDON SYMPHONY ORCHESTRA.

MILLIONAIRE HIPPIES · UK

SINGLES:	**HITS 2**		**WEEKS 4**	
I AM THE MUSIC, HEAR ME!	Deconstruction	52	18 Dec 93	3
C'MON	Deconstruction	59	10 Sep 94	1

Garry MILLS · UK

SINGLES:	**HITS 3**		**WEEKS 31**	
LOOK FOR A STAR	Top Rank	7	9 Jul 60	14
From the film 'Circus Of Horrors'.				
TOP TEEN BABY	Top Rank	24	22 Oct 60	12
I'LL STEP DOWN	Decca	39	24 Jun 61	5

Hayley MILLS · UK

SINGLES:	**HITS 1**		**WEEKS 11**	
LET'S GET TOGETHER	Decca	17	21 Oct 61	11
From the film 'The Parent Trap'.				
EPS:	**HITS 1**		**WEEKS 1**	
IN SEARCH OF THE CASTAWAYS [OST]	Decca	18	9 Feb 63	1

Above hit: Maurice CHEVALIER and Hayley MILLS.

Stephanie MILLS · US

SINGLES:	**HITS 6**		**WEEKS 33**	
NEVER KNEW LOVE LIKE THIS BEFORE	20th Century	4	18 Oct 80	14
TWO HEARTS	20th Century	49	23 May 81	5
Above hit: Stephanie MILLS 'featuring Teddy PENDERGRASS'.				
THE MEDICINE SONG	Club	29	15 Sep 84	9
(YOU'RE PUTTIN') A RUSH ON ME	MCA	62	5 Sep 87	2
NEVER DO YOU WRONG	MCA	57	1 May 93	2
ALL DAY, ALL NIGHT	MCA	68	10 Jul 93	1

Warren MILLS · Zambia

SINGLES:	**HITS 1**		**WEEKS 1**	
SUNSHINE	Jive	74	28 Sep 85	1

MILLS BROTHERS with Hal McINTRYE and his Orchestra · US

SINGLES:	**HITS 1**		**WEEKS 1**	
THE GLOW WORM	Brunswick	10	31 Jan 53	1

MILLTOWN BROTHERS · UK

SINGLES:	**HITS 5**		**WEEKS 16**	
WHICH WAY SHOULD I JUMP?	A&M	38	2 Feb 91	5

HERE I STAND	A&M	41	13 Apr 91	4
APPLE GREEN	A&M	43	6 Jul 91	4
Original release reached No. 82 in 1990.				
TURN OFF	A&M	55	22 May 93	1
IT'S ALL OVER NOW BABY BLUE	A&M	48	17 Jul 93	2
ALBUMS:	**HITS 1**		**WEEKS 5**	
SLINKY	A&M	27	23 Mar 91	5

C.B. MILTON — Holland

SINGLES:	**HITS 2**		**WEEKS 5**	
IT'S A LOVING THING	Logic	49	21 May 94	2
IT'S A LOVING THING [RM]	Logic	34	25 Mar 95	2
Remixed by Phil Wilde.				
HOLD ON - REMIXES	Logic	62	19 Aug 95	1

Garnett MIMMS and TRUCKIN' COMPANY — US

SINGLES:	**HITS 1**		**WEEKS 1**	
WHAT IT IS	Arista	44	25 Jun 77	1

MIND OF KANE — UK

(See also Hope A.D.)

SINGLES:	**HITS 1**		**WEEKS 1**	
STABBED IN THE BACK	Deja Vu	64	27 Jul 91	1

MINDBENDERS — UK

(See also Wayne Fontana and the Mindbenders.)

SINGLES:	**HITS 4**		**WEEKS 34**	
A GROOVY KIND OF LOVE	Fontana	2	15 Jan 66	14
Originally recorded by Patti Labelle and the Bluebells.				
CAN'T LIVE WITH YOU, CAN'T LIVE WITHOUT YOU	Fontana	28	7 May 66	7
ASHES TO ASHES	Fontana	14	27 Aug 66	9
THE LETTER	Fontana	42	23 Sep 67	4
ALBUMS:	**HITS 1**		**WEEKS 4**	
THE MINDBENDERS	Fontana	28	25 Jun 66	4

MINDFUNK — US

ALBUMS:	**HITS 1**		**WEEKS 1**	
DROPPED	Megaforce	60	15 May 93	1

MINDS OF MEN — UK

SINGLES:	**HITS 1**		**WEEKS 1**	
BRAND NEW DAY	Perfecto	41	22 Jun 96	1

Zodiac MINDWARP and the LOVE REACTION — UK/Canada

ALBUMS:	**HITS 1**		**WEEKS 5**	
PRIME MOVER	Mercury	18	9 May 87	6
BACKSEAT EDUCATION	Mercury	49	14 Nov 87	3
PLANET GIRL	Mercury	63	2 Apr 88	2
SINGLES:	**HITS 3**		**WEEKS 11**	
TATTOOED BEAT MESSIAH	Mercury	20	5 Mar 88	5

Sal MINEO — US

SINGLES:	**HITS 1**		**WEEKS 11**	
START MOVIN' (IN MY DIRECTION)	Philips	16	13 Jul 57	11

Marcello MINERBI E LA SUA ORCHESTRA — Italy

SINGLES:	**HITS 1**		**WEEKS 16**	
ZORBA'S DANCE	Durium	6	24 Jul 65	16
From the film 'Zorba The Greek'.				

MINIMAL FUNK 2 — Italy

SINGLES:	**HITS 1**		**WEEKS 1**	
THE GROOVY THANG	Cleveland City	65	18 Jul 98	1

MINIPOPS — UK

SINGLES:	**HITS 1**		**WEEKS 2**	
SONGS FOR CHRISTMAS '87 [EP]	Bright	39	26 Dec 87	2
Lead track: Thanks For Giving Us Christmas.				
ALBUMS:	**HITS 2**		**WEEKS 12**	
MINIPOPS	K-Tel	63	26 Dec 81	7
WE'RE THE MINIPOPS	K-Tel	54	19 Feb 83	5

MINISTRY
US

SINGLES:	HITS 1			WEEKS 3
N.W.O.	*Sire*	49	*8 Aug 92*	1
THE FALL	*Warner Brothers*	53	*6 Jan 96*	2
ALBUMS:	**HITS 2**			**WEEKS 6**
PSALM 69	*Sire*	33	*25 Jul 92*	5
FILTH PIG	*Warner Brothers*	43	*10 Feb 96*	1

MINK DEVILLE
US

SINGLES:	HITS 1			WEEKS 9
SPANISH STROLL	*Capitol*	20	*6 Aug 77*	9

MINKY
UK

SINGLES:	HITS 1			WEEKS 1
THE WEEKEND HAS LANDED	*Offbeat*	70	*30 Oct 99*	1

Liza MINNELLI
US

(See also Various Artists: Films – Original Soundtracks 'Cabaret'.)

SINGLES:	HITS 4			WEEKS 15
LOSING MY MIND	*Epic*	6	*12 Aug 89*	7
Originally recorded by Pet Shop Boys.				
DON'T DROP BOMBS	*Epic*	46	*7 Oct 89*	3
SO SORRY, I SAID	*Epic*	62	*25 Nov 89*	2
LOVE PAINS	*Epic*	41	*3 Mar 90*	3
ALBUMS:	**HITS 4**			**WEEKS 27**
LIZA WITH A 'Z'	*CBS*	9	*7 Apr 73*	15
THE SINGER	*CBS*	45	*16 Jun 73*	1
RESULTS	*Epic*	6	*21 Oct 89*	10
GENTLY	*Angel*	58	*6 Jul 96*	1

Dannii MINOGUE
Australia

SINGLES:	HITS 13			WEEKS 67
LOVE AND KISSES	*MCA*	8	*30 Mar 91*	8
SUCCESS	*MCA*	11	*18 May 91*	7
JUMP TO THE BEAT	*MCA*	8	*27 Jul 91*	6
BABY LOVE	*MCA*	14	*19 Oct 91*	6
I DON'T WANNA TAKE THIS PAIN	*MCA*	40	*14 Dec 91*	5
SHOW YOU THE WAY TO GO	*MCA*	30	*1 Aug 92*	3
From the NME 40th anniversary album, Ruby Traxs.				
LOVE'S ON EVERY CORNER	*MCA*	44	*12 Dec 92*	4
THIS IS IT	*MCA*	10	*17 Jul 93*	8
THIS IS THE WAY	*MCA*	27	*2 Oct 93*	3
GET INTO YOU	*Mushroom*	36	*11 Jun 94*	2
ALL I WANT TO DO	*Eternal*	4	*23 Aug 97*	8
EVERYTHING I WANTED	*Eternal*	15	*1 Nov 97*	4
DISREMEMBRANCE	*Eternal*	21	*28 Mar 98*	3
Above 4: DANNII.				
ALBUMS:	**HITS 3**			**WEEKS 22**
LOVE AND KISSES	*MCA*	8	*15 Jun 91*	14
LOVE AND KISSES / LOVE AND KISSES AND . . . [RE]	*MCA*	51	*7 Dec 91*	6
Love And Kisses And . . . was a remix album listed from 14 Dec 91, sales were combined.				
GET INTO YOU	*MCA*	52	*16 Oct 93*	1
GIRL	*Eternal*	57	*20 Sep 97*	1
Above hit: DANNII.				

Kylie MINOGUE
Australia

(See also Visionmasters and Tony King featuring Kylie Minogue; Various Artists: Films – Original Soundtracks 'The Delinquents'.)

SINGLES:	HITS 27			WEEKS 216
I SHOULD BE SO LUCKY	*PWL*	1	*23 Jan 88*	16
GOT TO BE CERTAIN	*PWL*	2	*14 May 88*	12
THE LOCO-MOTION	*PWL*	2	*6 Aug 88*	11
Spent 7 weeks at No. 1 in Australia.				
JE NE SAIS PAS POURQUOI	*PWL*	2	*22 Oct 88*	13
ESPECIALLY FOR YOU	*PWL*	1	*10 Dec 88*	14
Above hit: Kylie MINOGUE and Jason DONOVAN.				
HAND ON YOUR HEART	*PWL*	1	*6 May 89*	11
WOULDN'T CHANGE A THING	*PWL*	2	*5 Aug 89*	9
NEVER TOO LATE	*PWL*	4	*4 Nov 89*	10
TEARS ON MY PILLOW	*PWL*	1	*20 Jan 90*	8
From the film 'The Delinquents'. Originally recorded by Little Anthony and the Imperials reached No. 4 in the US in 1958.				
BETTER THE DEVIL YOU KNOW	*PWL*	2	*12 May 90*	10
STEP BACK IN TIME	*PWL*	4	*3 Nov 90*	8

WHAT DO I HAVE TO DO	PWL	6	2 Feb 91	8
SHOCKED	PWL	6	1 Jun 91	7
WORD IS OUT	PWL	16	7 Sep 91	5
IF YOU WERE WITH ME NOW	PWL	4	2 Nov 91	7
Above hit: Kylie MINOGUE and Keith WASHINGTON.				
GIVE ME JUST A LITTLE MORE TIME	PWL	2	25 Jan 92	8
FINER FEELINGS	PWL International	11	25 Apr 92	6
WHAT KIND OF FOOL (HEARD ALL THAT BEFORE)	PWL International	14	22 Aug 92	5
CELEBRATION	PWL International	20	28 Nov 92	7
CONFIDE IN ME	Deconstruction	2	10 Sep 94	9
PUT YOURSELF IN MY PLACE	Deconstruction	11	26 Nov 94	9
WHERE IS THE FEELING?	Deconstruction	16	22 Jul 95	3
Originally recorded by Within A Dream in 1992.				
WHERE THE WILD ROSES GROW	Mute	11	14 Oct 95	4
Above hit: Nick CAVE and the BAD SEEDS + Kylie MINOGUE.				
SOME KIND OF BLISS	Deconstruction	22	20 Sep 97	5
DID IT AGAIN	Deconstruction	14	6 Dec 97	6
BREATHE	Deconstruction	14	21 Mar 98	4
GBI: GERMAN BOLD ITALIC	Arthrob	63	31 Oct 98	1
Above hit: Towa TEI featuring Kylie MINOGUE.				
ALBUMS:	**HITS 8**		**WEEKS 164**	
KYLIE – THE ALBUM	PWL	1	16 Jul 88	67
ENJOY YOURSELF	PWL	1	21 Oct 89	33
RHYTHM OF LOVE	PWL	9	24 Nov 90	22
LET'S GO TO IT	PWL	15	26 Oct 91	12
KYLIE GREATEST HITS	PWL International	1	5 Sep 92	10
KYLIE MINOGUE	Deconstruction	4	1 Oct 94	15
KYLIE MINOGUE	Deconstruction	10	4 Apr 98	4
Intended title was The Impossible Princess, but it was changed after the death of Diana, Princess Of Wales. Both eponymous albums are different.				
MIXES	Deconstruction	63	15 Aug 98	1
9 track album of mixes of 3 songs.				

Morris MINOR and the MAJORS — UK

SINGLES:	**HITS 1**		**WEEKS 11**	
STUTTER RAP (NO SLEEP TIL BEDTIME)	10 Records	4	19 Dec 87	11

Sugar MINOTT — Jamaica

SINGLES:	**HITS 2**		**WEEKS 16**	
GOOD THING GOING (WE'VE GOT A GOOD THING GOING)	RCA	4	28 Mar 81	12
Originally recorded by Michael Jackson.				
NEVER MY LOVE	RCA	52	17 Oct 81	4

MINT CONDITION — US

SINGLES:	**HITS 2**		**WEEKS 3**	
WHAT KIND OF MAN WOULD I BE	Wild Card	38	21 Jun 97	2
LET ME BE THE ONE	Wild Card	63	4 Oct 97	1

MINT JULEPS — UK

SINGLES:	**HITS 2**		**WEEKS 7**	
ONLY LOVE CAN BREAK YOUR HEART	Stiff	62	22 Mar 86	2
Originally recorded by Neil Young reached No. 33 in the US in 1970.				
EVERY KINDA PEOPLE	Stiff	58	30 May 87	5

MINTY — Australia

SINGLES:	**HITS 1**		**WEEKS 1**	
I WANNA BE FREE	Virgin	67	23 Jan 99	1
From the children's TV series 'Minty'.				

MIRACLES — US

(See also Smokey Robinson.)

SINGLES:	**HITS 8**		**WEEKS 81**	
GOING TO A GO-GO	Tamla Motown	44	26 Feb 66	5
(COME 'ROUND HERE) I'M THE ONE YOU NEED	Tamla Motown	45	24 Dec 66	2
I SECOND THAT EMOTION	Tamla Motown	27	30 Dec 67	11
IF YOU CAN WANT	Tamla Motown	50	6 Apr 68	1
THE TRACKS OF MY TEARS	Tamla Motown	9	10 May 69	13
THE TEARS OF A CLOWN	Tamla Motown	1	1 Aug 70	14
(COME ROUND HERE) I'M THE ONE YOU NEED [RI]	Tamla Motown	13	30 Jan 71	9
I DON'T BLAME YOU AT ALL	Tamla Motown	11	5 Jun 71	10
Above 6: Smokey ROBINSON and the MIRACLES.				
LOVE MACHINE	Tamla Motown	3	10 Jan 76	10
TEARS OF A CLOWN [RI]	Tamla Motown	34	2 Oct 76	6
Above hit: Smokey ROBINSON and the MIRACLES.				

ALBUMS:		HITS 1		WEEKS 2
THE GREATEST HITS	PolyGram TV	65	14 Nov 92	2

Includes both Robinson's solo and group material.
Above hit: Smokey ROBINSON and the MIRACLES.

MIRAGE   UK

SINGLES:		HITS 7		WEEKS 35
GIVE ME THE NIGHT [M]	Passion	49	14 Jan 84	4

Above hit: MIRAGE featuring Roy GAYLE.

JACK MIX II [M] / JACK MIX III [M]	Debut	4	9 May 87	11

Jack Mix III was a remixed 12" version, listed on the chart from 6 Jun 87.

SERIOUS MIX [M]	Debut	42	25 Jul 87	4
JACK MIX IV [M]	Debut	8	7 Nov 87	10
JACK MIX VII [M]	Debut	50	27 Feb 88	3
PUSH THE BEAT	Debut	67	2 Jul 88	2
LATINO HOUSE [M]	Debut	70	11 Nov 89	1

All above are medleys of current dance hits.

ALBUMS:		HITS 3		WEEKS 33
THE BEST OF MIRAGE: JACK MIX '88	Stylus	7	26 Dec 87	15
JACK MIX IN FULL EFFECT	Stylus	7	25 Jun 88	12
ROYAL MIX '89	Stylus	34	7 Jan 89	6

MIRAGE   UK

ALBUMS:		HITS 1		WEEKS 3
CLASSIC GUITAR MOODS	PolyGram TV	25	23 Sep 95	3

Danny MIRROR   Holland

SINGLES:		HITS 1		WEEKS 9
I REMEMBER ELVIS PRESLEY (THE KING IS DEAD)	Stone	4	17 Sep 77	9

Official Elvis Presley fan club tribute disc.

MIRRORBALL   UK

SINGLES:		HITS 1		WEEKS 4
GIVEN UP	Multiply	12	13 Feb 99	4

Samples the Three Degrees' Givin' Up Givin' In.

MISHKA   Bermuda

SINGLES:		HITS 1		WEEKS 2
(GIVE YOU ALL THE LOVE)	Creation	34	15 May 99	2

MISS JANE   UK

SINGLES:		HITS 1		WEEKS 1
IT'S A FINE DAY	G1 Recordings	62	30 Oct 99	1

Samples Jane's original vocal version, which reached No. 87 in 1983, with a dance backing by
ATB.

MISS JONES   US

SINGLES:		HITS 1		WEEKS 1
2 WAY STREET	Motown	49	10 Oct 98	1

This listed song is track 2 on the CD; track 1 is (#1 Lady).

MISS X   UK

SINGLES:		HITS 1		WEEKS 6
CHRISTINE	Ember	37	3 Aug 63	6

Based on the Christine Keeler scandal of 1963.

MISSA LUBA Les TROUBADOURS DU ROI BAUDOUIN   Zaire

SINGLES:		HITS 1		WEEKS 11
SANCTUS	Philips	28	22 Mar 69	6

From the film 'If . . .'

SANCTUS [RE]	Philips	37	10 May 69	5

ALBUMS:		HITS 1		WEEKS 1
MISSA LUBA	Philips	59	22 May 76	1

Above hit: TROUBADOURS DU ROI BAUDOUIN.

MISSION   UK

SINGLES:		HITS 16		WEEKS 58
SERPENTS KISS	Chapter 22	70	14 Jun 86	3
LIKE A HURRICANE / GARDEN OF DELIGHT	Chapter 22	49	26 Jul 86	4
STAY WITH ME	Mercury	30	18 Oct 86	4
WASTELAND	Mercury	11	17 Jan 87	6
SEVERINA	Mercury	25	14 Mar 87	5
TOWER OF STRENGTH	Mercury	12	13 Feb 88	7

BEYOND THE PALE		Mercury	32	23 Apr 88	4
BUTTERFLY ON A WHEEL		Mercury	12	13 Jan 90	4
DELIVERANCE		Mercury	27	10 Mar 90	4
INTO THE BLUE		Mercury	32	2 Jun 90	3
HANDS ACROSS THE OCEAN		Mercury	28	17 Nov 90	2
NEVER AGAIN		Mercury	34	25 Apr 92	3
LIKE A CHILD AGAIN		Vertigo	30	20 Jun 92	2
SHADES OF GREEN		Vertigo	49	17 Oct 92	2
TOWER OF STRENGTH [RM]		Vertigo	33	8 Jan 94	3
Remixed by Youth.					
AFTERGLOW		Vertigo	53	26 Mar 94	1
SWOON		Neverland	73	4 Feb 95	1
ALBUMS:	**HITS 9**			**WEEKS 48**	
GOD'S OWN MEDICINE		Mercury	14	22 Nov 86	20
THE FIRST CHAPTER		Mercury	35	4 Jul 87	4
CHILDREN		Mercury	2	12 Mar 88	9
CARVED IN SAND		Mercury	7	17 Feb 90	8
GRAINS OF SAND		Mercury	28	3 Nov 90	2
MASQUE		Vertigo	23	4 Jul 92	2
SUM AND SUBSTANCE		Vertigo	49	19 Feb 94	1
Compilation.					
NEVERLAND		Neverland	58	25 Feb 95	1
BLUE		Equator	73	15 Jun 96	1

MRS. MILLS
UK

SINGLES:	**HITS 1**			**WEEKS 5**	
MRS. MILLS MEDLEY [M]		Parlophone	18	16 Dec 61	5
ALBUMS:	**HITS 4**			**WEEKS 13**	
COME TO MY PARTY		Parlophone	17	10 Dec 66	7
MRS. MILLS' PARTY PIECES		Parlophone	32	28 Dec 68	3
LET'S HAVE ANOTHER PARTY		Parlophone	23	13 Dec 69	2
I'M MIGHTY GLAD		Music For Pleasure	49	6 Nov 71	1

MRS WOOD
UK

SINGLES:	**HITS 3**			**WEEKS 6**	
JOANNA		React	40	16 Sep 95	2
HEARTBREAK		React	44	6 Jul 96	1
Reworking of a track by Working Hard (aka Graeme Ripley of Happy Clappers).					
Above hit: MRS WOOD featuring Eve GALLAGHER.					
JOANNA [RM]		React	34	4 Oct 97	2
Samples Alison Price's Feel My Love. Remixed by Sash.					
1234		React	54	15 Aug 98	1

MISTA E featuring the AWAKENING
UK

SINGLES:	**HITS 1**			**WEEKS 5**	
DON'T BELIEVE THE HYPE		Urban	41	10 Dec 88	5

MR AND MRS SMITH
UK

SINGLES:	**HITS 1**			**WEEKS 1**	
GOTTA GET LOOSE		Hooj Choons	70	12 Oct 96	1

MR. BEAN and SMEAR CAMPAIGN (featuring Bruce DICKINSON)
UK

SINGLES:	**HITS 1**			**WEEKS 5**	
(I WANT TO BE) ELECTED		London	9	4 Apr 92	5

MR. BIG
UK

SINGLES:	**HITS 2**			**WEEKS 14**	
ROMEO		EMI	4	12 Feb 77	10
FEEL LIKE CALLING HOME		EMI	35	21 May 77	4

MR. BIG
US

SINGLES:	**HITS 4**			**WEEKS 17**	
TO BE WITH YOU		Atlantic	3	7 Mar 92	11
JUST TAKE MY HEART		Atlantic	26	23 May 92	4
GREEN TINTED SIXTIES MIND		Atlantic	72	8 Aug 92	1
WILD WORLD		Atlantic	59	20 Nov 93	1
ALBUMS:	**HITS 3**			**WEEKS 14**	
MR. BIG		Atlantic	60	22 Jul 89	1
LEAN INTO IT		Atlantic	52	13 Apr 91	2
LEAN INTO IT [RE]		Atlantic	28	11 Apr 92	10
BUMP AHEAD		Atlantic	61	2 Oct 93	1

MR. BLOBBY UK

SINGLES:	HITS 2			WEEKS 16	
MR BLOBBY	Destiny Music	1	4 Dec 93	12
Features the King's College School Choir, Brentwood Cathedral Choir and Shezwae Powell.				
CHRISTMAS IN BLOBBYLAND	Destiny Music	36	16 Dec 95	4

MR. BLOE UK

SINGLES:	HITS 1			WEEKS 18	
GROOVIN' WITH MR. BLOE	DJM	2	9 May 70	18
Originally recorded by Wind (who was Tony Orlando under an assumed name).				

MR. BUNGLE US

ALBUMS:	HITS 1			WEEKS 1	
MR. BUNGLE	London	57	21 Sep 91	1

MR. FINGERS US

SINGLES:	HITS 3			WEEKS 5	
WHAT ABOUT THIS LOVE	ffrr	74	17 Mar 90	1
CLOSER	MCA	50	7 Mar 92	3
ON MY WAY	MCA	71	23 May 92	1

MR. FOOD UK

SINGLES:	HITS 1			WEEKS 3	
. . . AND THAT'S BEFORE ME TEA!	Tangible	62	9 Jun 90	3

MR. HANKEY POO (An Early '50s recording performed by COWBOY TIMMY) US

SINGLES:	HITS 1			WEEKS 2	
MR. HANKEY THE CHRISTMAS POO	Columbia	4	25 Dec 99	2

MR JACK Belgium

SINGLES:	HITS 1			WEEKS 2	
WIGGLY WORLD	Extravaganza	32	25 Jan 97	2

MR. LEE US

SINGLES:	HITS 2			WEEKS 6	
PUMP UP LONDON	Breakout	64	6 Aug 88	2
GET BUSY	Jive	71	11 Nov 89	1
GET BUSY [RE]	Jive	41	24 Feb 90	3

MR. MISTER US

SINGLES:	HITS 2			WEEKS 22	
BROKEN WINGS	RCA	4	21 Dec 85	13
KYRIE	RCA	11	1 Mar 86	9
ALBUMS:	HITS 1			WEEKS 24	
WELCOME TO THE REAL WORLD	RCA	6	15 Feb 86	24

MR. OIZO France

SINGLES:	HITS 1			WEEKS 15	
FLAT BEAT	F Communications	1	3 Apr 99	13
Featured in the Levi's jeans TV commercial.				
FLAT BEAT [RE]	F Communications	60	7 Aug 99	2

MR. PRESIDENT Germany

SINGLES:	HITS 3			WEEKS 13	
COCO JAMBOO	WEA	8	14 Jun 97	11
I GIVE YOU MY HEART	WEA	52	20 Sep 97	1
JOJO ACTION	WEA	73	25 Apr 98	1

MR. ROY UK

SINGLES:	HITS 2			WEEKS 6	
SOMETHING ABOUT YOU	Fresh	74	7 May 94	1
SAVED	Fresh	24	21 Jan 95	4
SOMETHING ABOUT U (CAN'T BE BEAT) [RM]	Fresh	49	16 Dec 95	1
Samples Nikita Warren's I Need You. Remixed by Strike.				

MR. V UK

SINGLES:	HITS 1			WEEKS 2	
GIVE ME LIFE	Cheeky	40	6 Aug 94	2

MR. VEGAS
Jamaica

SINGLES:	HITS 1		WEEKS 7	
HEADS HIGH	Greensleeves	71	22 Aug 98	1
HEADS HIGH [RI]	Greensleeves	16	13 Nov 99	6
Re-issued after he won the 1999 MOBO award for Best Reggae Act.				

MISTURA featuring Lloyd MICHELS (trumpet)
US

SINGLES:	HITS 1		WEEKS 10	
THE FLASHER	Route	23	15 May 76	10

George MITCHELL MINSTRELS
UK

EPS:	HITS 3		WEEKS 66	
CHRISTMAS WITH THE MINSTRELS	HMV	4	9 Dec 61	10
THE BLACK AND WHITE MINSTREL SHOW	HMV	1	23 Jun 62	55
THE BLACK AND WHITE MINSTREL SHOW NO. 2	HMV	20	2 Mar 63	1
ALBUMS:	**HITS 11**		**WEEKS 292**	
THE BLACK AND WHITE MINSTREL SHOW	His Master's Voice	1	26 Nov 60	142
Peak position reached on 29 July 61.				
ANOTHER BLACK AND WHITE MINSTREL SHOW	His Master's Voice	1	21 Oct 61	64
ON STAGE WITH THE GEORGE MITCHELL MINSTRELS	His Master's Voice	1	20 Oct 62	26
ON TOUR WITH THE GEORGE MITCHELL MINSTRELS	His Master's Voice	6	2 Nov 63	18
SPOTLIGHT ON THE GEORGE MITCHELL MINSTRELS	His Master's Voice	6	12 Dec 64	7
MAGIC OF THE MINSTRELS	His Master's Voice	9	4 Dec 65	7
HERE COME THE MINSTRELS	His Master's Voice	11	26 Nov 66	11
SHOWTIME	His Master's Voice	26	16 Dec 67	2
SING THE IRVING BERLIN SONGBOOK	Columbia	33	14 Dec 68	1
THE MAGIC OF CHRISTMAS	Columbia	32	19 Dec 70	4
30 GOLDEN GREATS	EMI	10	19 Nov 77	10
Above hit: George MITCHELL MINSTRELS with the Joe LOSS ORCHESTRA.				

Guy MITCHELL
US

SINGLES:	HITS 14		WEEKS 165	
FEET UP	Columbia	2	15 Nov 52	10
SHE WEARS RED FEATHERS	Columbia	1	14 Feb 53	15
PRETTY LITTLE BLACK-EYED SUSIE	Columbia	2	25 Apr 53	11
SHE WEARS RED FEATHERS [RE]	Columbia	12	13 Jun 53	1
Above 4: Guy MITCHELL with Mitch MILLER and his Orchestra and Chorus.				
LOOK AT THAT GIRL	Philips	1	29 Aug 53	14
CHICKA BOOM	Philips	5	7 Nov 53	9
From the film 'Those Redheads From Seattle'.				
CLOUD LUCKY SEVEN	Philips	2	19 Dec 53	16
CHICKA BOOM [RE]	Philips	4	16 Jan 54	6
THE CUFF OF MY SHIRT	Philips	9	20 Feb 54	1
Above 4: Guy MITCHELL with Mitch MILLER and his Orchestra and Chorus (and re-entries below).				
SIPPIN' SODA	Philips	11	27 Feb 54	1
Above entry and Cloud Lucky Seven were separate sides of the same release, each had its own chart run.				
Above hit: Guy MITCHELL with Orchestra and CHILDREN'S CHORUS conducted by Norman LUBOFF.				
THE CUFF OF MY SHIRT [RE-1ST]	Philips	12	20 Mar 54	1
THE CUFF OF MY SHIRT [RE-2ND]	Philips	11	3 Apr 54	1
A DIME AND A DOLLAR	Philips	8	1 May 54	1
From the film 'Red Garters'.				
A DIME AND A DOLLAR [RE]	Philips	8	15 May 54	4
SINGING THE BLUES	Philips	1	8 Dec 56	22
Originally recorded by Marty Robbins and features whistling by Ray Conniff.				
Above hit: Guy MITCHELL with Ray CONNIFF and his Orchestra.				
KNEE DEEP IN THE BLUES	Philips	3	16 Feb 57	12
Originally recorded by Marty Robbins.				
Above hit: Guy MITCHELL with Ray CONNIFF.				
ROCK-A-BILLY	Philips	1	27 Apr 57	14
IN THE MIDDLE OF A DARK, DARK NIGHT / SWEET STUFF	Philips	27	27 Jul 57	2
IN THE MIDDLE OF A DARK, DARK NIGHT / SWEET STUFF [RE]	Philips	25	24 Aug 57	2
Above 3: Guy MITCHELL with Jimmy CARROLL.				
CALL ROSIE ON THE PHONE	Philips	17	12 Oct 57	6
Above hit: Guy MITCHELL with Jimmy CARROLL and his Orchestra.				
HEARTACHES BY THE NUMBER	Philips	26	28 Nov 59	2
Originally recorded by Ray Price.				
HEARTACHES BY THE NUMBER [RE]	Philips	5	19 Dec 59	14

Joni MITCHELL
Canada

(See also Janet Jackson.)

SINGLES:	HITS 1		WEEKS 15	
BIG YELLOW TAXI	Reprise	11	13 Jun 70	15

ALBUMS:		HITS 15		WEEKS 116
LADIES OF THE CANYON	Reprise	8	6 Jun 70	25
BLUE	Reprise	3	24 Jul 71	18
COURT AND SPARK	Asylum	14	16 Mar 74	11
MILES OF AISLES	Asylum	34	1 Feb 75	4
Live recordings with Tom Scott and the L.A. Express.				
THE HISSING OF SUMMER LAWNS	Asylum	14	27 Dec 75	10
HEJIRA	Asylum	11	11 Dec 76	5
DON JUAN'S RECKLESS DAUGHTER	Asylum	20	21 Jan 78	7
MINGUS	Asylum	24	14 Jul 79	7
A tribute to, and featuring songs by, jazz musician Charles Mingus who died on 5 Jan 79.				
SHADOWS AND LIGHT	Elektra	63	4 Oct 80	3
Live recordings from Santa Barbara Country Bowl in, Sept 79.				
WILD THINGS RUN FAST	Geffen	32	4 Dec 82	8
DOG EAT DOG	Geffen	57	30 Nov 85	3
CHALK MARK IN A RAIN STORM	Geffen	26	2 Apr 88	7
NIGHT RIDE HOME	Geffen	25	9 Mar 91	5
TURBULENT INDIGO	Reprise	53	5 Nov 94	2
TAMING THE TIGER	Reprise	57	10 Oct 98	1

Willie MITCHELL · US

SINGLES:		HITS 2		WEEKS 3
SOUL SERENADE	London	43	27 Apr 68	1
THE CHAMPION	London	47	11 Dec 76	2

MIX FACTORY · UK

SINGLES:		HITS 1		WEEKS 2
TAKE ME AWAY (PARADISE)	All Around The World	51	30 Jan 93	2

MIXMASTER · Italy

SINGLES:		HITS 1		WEEKS 10
GRAND PIANO	BCM	9	4 Nov 89	10

MIXMASTERS – See UK MIXMASTERS

MIXTURES · Australia/UK

SINGLES:		HITS 1		WEEKS 21
THE PUSHBIKE SONG	Polydor	2	16 Jan 71	21
Written by original member Idris Jones in 1966.				

Hank MIZELL · US

SINGLES:		HITS 1		WEEKS 13
JUNGLE ROCK	Charly	3	20 Mar 76	13
Originally recorded in 1957.				

MK · US

SINGLES:		HITS 2		WEEKS 3
ALWAYS	Activ	69	4 Feb 95	1
Above hit: MK featuring ALANA.				
BURNING	Activ	44	27 May 95	2
Chart credits 'featuring Alana Surrender' though she is not credited on the single itself.				

MN8 · UK/Trinidad

SINGLES:		HITS 7		WEEKS 38
I'VE GOT A LITTLE SOMETHING FOR YOU	Columbia	2	4 Feb 95	13
IF YOU ONLY LET ME IN	Columbia	6	29 Apr 95	7
HAPPY	Columbia	8	15 Jul 95	7
BABY IT'S YOU	Columbia	22	4 Nov 95	2
BABY IT'S YOU [RE]	Columbia	59	6 Jan 96	1
PATHWAY TO THE MOON	Columbia	25	24 Feb 96	2
TUFF ACT TO FOLLOW	Columbia	15	31 Aug 96	3
DREAMING	Columbia	21	26 Oct 96	3
ALBUMS:		**HITS 1**		**WEEKS 4**
TO THE NEXT LEVEL	Columbia	13	27 May 95	4

MNO · Belgium

SINGLES:		HITS 1		WEEKS 2
GOD OF ABRAHAM	A&M	66	28 Sep 91	2

MOBB DEEP · US

ALBUMS:		HITS 1		WEEKS 1
HELL ON EARTH	Loud	67	23 Nov 96	1

MOBILES
UK

SINGLES:	HITS 2		WEEKS 14	
DROWNING IN BERLIN	*Rialto*	9	*9 Jan 82*	10
AMOUR AMOUR	*Rialto*	45	*27 Mar 82*	4

MOBO ALLSTARS
UK/US

SINGLES:	HITS 1		WEEKS 3	
AIN'T NO STOPPING US NOW	*PolyGram TV*	47	*26 Dec 98*	3

Charity record with proceeds to The Sickle Cell Society and The Royal Marsden Hospital Charity Leukaemia Research Fund.

MOBY
US

SINGLES:	HITS 13		WEEKS 46	
GO	*Outer Rhythm*	46	*27 Jul 91*	3
GO [RE]	*Outer Rhythm*	10	*19 Oct 91*	7
I FEEL IT / THOUSAND	*Equator*	38	*3 Jul 93*	3
MOVE	*Mute*	21	*11 Sep 93*	5
HYMN	*Mute*	31	*28 May 94*	2
FEELING SO REAL	*Mute*	30	*29 Oct 94*	2
EVERY TIME YOU TOUCH ME	*Mute*	28	*25 Feb 95*	3
INTO THE BLUE	*Mute*	34	*1 Jul 95*	2
Vocals by Mimi Goese.				
THAT'S WHEN I REACH FOR MY REVOLVER	*Mute*	50	*7 Sep 96*	1
JAMES BOND THEME (MOBY'S RE-VERSION)	*Mute*	8	*15 Nov 97*	7
From the James Bond film 'Tomorrow Never Dies'.				
JAMES BOND THEME (MOBY'S RE-VERSION) [RE]	*Mute*	74	*10 Jan 98*	1
HONEY	*Mute*	33	*5 Sep 98*	2
Samples Bessie Jones' Sometimes.				
RUN ON	*Mute*	33	*8 May 99*	2
BODYROCK	*Mute*	38	*24 Jul 99*	2
Samples Spoony G and the Treacherous' Love Rap.				
WHY DOES MY HEART FEEL SO BAD?	*Mute*	16	*23 Oct 99*	4
Vocals by the Shining Light Gospel Choir.				
ALBUMS:	HITS 3		WEEKS 14	
EVERYTHING IS WRONG	*Mute*	21	*25 Mar 95*	4
EVERYTHING IS WRONG / MIXED & REMIXED [RE]	*Mute*	25	*27 Jan 96*	3
Mixed & Remixed was a remix album, sales were combined.				
ANIMAL RIGHTS	*Mute*	38	*5 Oct 96*	1
PLAY	*Mute*	33	*29 May 99*	6

MOCHA - See Missy "Misdemeanor" ELLIOTT; NICOLE

MOCK TURTLES
UK

SINGLES:	HITS 2		WEEKS 15	
CAN YOU DIG IT?	*Siren*	18	*9 Mar 91*	11
AND THEN SHE SMILES	*Siren*	44	*29 Jun 91*	4
ALBUMS:	HITS 2		WEEKS 4	
TURTLE SOUP	*Imaginary*	54	*25 May 91*	1
TWO SIDES	*Siren*	33	*27 Jul 91*	3

MODERN EON
UK

ALBUMS:	HITS 1		WEEKS 1	
FICTION TALES	*DinDisc*	65	*13 Jun 81*	1

MODERN LOVERS - See Jonathan RICHMAN and the MODERN LOVERS

MODERN ROMANCE
UK

SINGLES:	HITS 8		WEEKS 77	
EVERYBODY SALSA	*WEA*	12	*15 Aug 81*	10
AY AY AY AY MOOSEY	*WEA*	10	*7 Nov 81*	12
QUEEN OF THE RAPPING SCENE (NOTHING EVER GOES THE WAY YOU PLAN)	*WEA*	37	*30 Jan 82*	8
CHERRY PINK AND APPLE BLOSSOM WHITE	*WEA*	15	*14 Aug 82*	8
Above hit: MODERN ROMANCE featuring John DU PREZ.				
BEST YEARS OF OUR LIVES	*WEA*	4	*13 Nov 82*	13
A special Xmas edition of the single was also released. Sales for the two were combined.				
HIGH LIFE	*WEA*	8	*26 Feb 83*	8
DON'T STOP THAT CRAZY RHYTHM	*WEA*	14	*7 May 83*	6
WALKING IN THE RAIN	*WEA*	7	*6 Aug 83*	12
ALBUMS:	HITS 2		WEEKS 13	
TRICK OF THE LIGHT	*WEA*	53	*16 Apr 83*	7
PARTY TONIGHT	*Ronco*	45	*3 Dec 83*	6

MODERN TALKING — Germany

SINGLES:	HITS 4			WEEKS 22	
YOU'RE MY HEART, YOU'RE MY SOUL	Elektra	69	15 Jun 85	2
YOU'RE MY HEART, YOU'RE MY SOUL [RE]	Elektra	56	17 Aug 85	5
YOU CAN WIN IF YOU WANT	Magnet	70	12 Oct 85	2
BROTHER LOUIE	RCA	4	16 Aug 86	10
ATLANTIS IS CALLING (S.O.S. FOR LOVE)	RCA	55	4 Oct 86	3
ALBUMS:	HITS 1			WEEKS 3	
READY FOR ROMANCE	RCA	76	11 Oct 86	3

MODETTES — UK

SINGLES:	HITS 2			WEEKS 6	
PAINT IT BLACK	Deram	42	12 Jul 80	5
Above hit: MO-DETTES.				
TONIGHT	Deram	68	18 Jul 81	1

Domenico MODUGNO — Italy

SINGLES:	HITS 2			WEEKS 13	
VOLARE (NEL BLU DIPINTO DI BLU)	Oriole	10	6 Sep 58	12
Italy's entry for Eurovision; it came 3rd.				
Above hit: Domenico MODUGNO with Alberto SEMPRINI and his AZZURO SEXTET.				
CIAO CIAO BAMBINA (PIOVEO)	Oriole	29	28 Mar 59	1

MOFFATTS — Canada

SINGLES:	HITS 3			WEEKS 6	
CRAZY	Chrysalis	16	20 Feb 99	3
UNTIL YOU LOVED ME	Chrysalis	36	26 Jun 99	2
From the film 'Never Been Kissed'.				
MISERY	EMI	47	23 Oct 99	1
ALBUMS:	HITS 1			WEEKS 1	
CHAPTER 1: A NEW BEGINNING	Chrysalis	62	6 Mar 99	1

MOGWAI — UK

SINGLES:	HITS 3			WEEKS 3	
SWEET LEAF	Fierce Panda	60	4 Apr 98	1
[AA] listed with Black Sabbath by Magoo.				
FEAR SATAN – REMIXES	Eye-Q	57	11 Apr 98	1
NO EDUCATION = NO FUTURE (FUCK THE CURFEW) [EP]	Chemikal Underground	68	11 Jul 98	1
Lead track: Xmas Steps. EP title refers to the night curfew imposed on under 16s in Glasgow.				
ALBUMS:	HITS 2			WEEKS 3	
YOUNG TEAM	Chemikal Underground	75	8 Nov 97	1
Album is largely instrumental with just one vocal track.				
COME ON, DIE YOUNG	Chemikal Underground	29	10 Apr 99	2

MOHAWKS — Jamaica

SINGLES:	HITS 1			WEEKS 2	
THE CHAMP	Pama	58	24 Jan 87	2

Frank 'O MOIRAGHI featuring AMNESIA — Italy

SINGLES:	HITS 1			WEEKS 4	
FEEL MY BODY	Multiply	39	1 Jun 96	2
FEEL MY BODY [RM]	Multiply	40	26 Oct 96	2
Remixed by Rollo and Sister Bliss.				

MOIST — Canada

SINGLES:	HITS 3			WEEKS 10	
PUSH	Chrysalis	35	12 Nov 94	3
SILVER	Chrysalis	50	25 Feb 95	2
FREAKY BE BEAUTIFUL	Chrysalis	47	29 Apr 95	2
PUSH [RI]	Chrysalis	20	19 Aug 95	3
ALBUMS:	HITS 1			WEEKS 3	
SILVER	Chrysalis	49	26 Aug 95	3

MOJO — UK

SINGLES:	HITS 1			WEEKS 3	
DANCE ON [M]	Creole	70	22 Aug 81	3
Medley of Shadows hits.				

MOJOS — UK

SINGLES:	HITS 3			WEEKS 26	
EVERYTHING'S AL' RIGHT	Decca	9	28 Mar 64	11

WHY NOT TONIGHT	*Decca*	25	*13 Jun 64*	10
SEVEN DAFFODILS	*Decca*	30	*12 Sep 64*	5

Originally recorded by Lonnie Donegan.

EPS:	HITS 1			WEEKS 3
THE MOJOS	*Decca*	12	*17 Oct 64*	3

MOKENSTEF
US

SINGLES:	HITS 1			WEEKS 1
HE'S MINE	*Def Jam*	70	*23 Sep 95*	1

MOLELLA featuring the OUTHERE BROTHERS
Italy/US

(See also Outhere Brothers.)

SINGLES:	HITS 1			WEEKS 10
IF YOU WANNA PARTY	*Eternal*	9	*16 Dec 95*	10

Ralph MOLINA and Billy TALBOT of CRAZY HORSE with Mike 'Tone' HAMILTON - See Ian McNAB

Sam MOLLISON - See SASHA

MOLLY HALF HEAD
UK

SINGLES:	HITS 1			WEEKS 1
SHINE	*Columbia*	73	*3 Jun 95*	1

MOLLY HATCHET
US

ALBUMS:	HITS 1			WEEKS 1
DOUBLE TROUBLE – LIVE	*Epic*	94	*25 Jan 86*	1

MOLOKO
UK/Ireland

SINGLES:	HITS 4			WEEKS 15
DOMINOID	*Echo*	65	*24 Feb 96*	1
FUN FOR ME	*Echo*	36	*25 May 96*	2
THE FLIPSIDE	*Echo*	53	*20 Jun 98*	1
SING IT BACK	*Echo*	45	*27 Mar 99*	2
SING IT BACK [RM]	*Echo*	4	*4 Sep 99*	9

Remixed by Boris Dlugosch and Michael Lange.

ALBUMS:	HITS 1			WEEKS 1
I AM NOT A DOCTOR	*Echo*	64	*5 Sep 98*	1

MOMBASSA
UK

SINGLES:	HITS 1			WEEKS 1
CRY FREEDOM	*Sound Proof*	63	*8 Mar 97*	1

Originally released in 1992.

MOMENTS
US

SINGLES:	HITS 4			WEEKS 32
GIRLS	*All Platinum*	3	*8 Mar 75*	10

Above hit: MOMENTS and WHATNAUTS.

DOLLY MY LOVE	*All Platinum*	10	*19 Jul 75*	9
LOOK AT ME (I'M IN LOVE)	*All Platinum*	42	*25 Oct 75*	4
JACK IN THE BOX	*All Platinum*	7	*22 Jan 77*	9

Tony MOMRELLE
UK

SINGLES:	HITS 1			WEEKS 1
LET ME SHOW YOU	*Art & Soul*	67	*15 Aug 98*	1

MONACO
UK

SINGLES:	HITS 3			WEEKS 11
WHAT DO YOU WANT FROM ME?	*Polydor*	11	*15 Mar 97*	6
SWEET LIPS	*Polydor*	18	*31 May 97*	4
SHINE (SOMEONE WHO NEEDS ME)	*Polydor*	55	*20 Sep 97*	1

ALBUMS:	HITS 1			WEEKS 3
MUSIC FOR PLEASURE	*Polydor*	11	*21 Jun 97*	3

Jay MONDI and the LIVING BASS
US

SINGLES:	HITS 1			WEEKS 3
ALL NIGHT LONG	*10 Records*	63	*24 Mar 90*	3

MONDO KANE featuring Dee LEWIS and Coral GORDON Guest star Georgie FAME
UK

SINGLES:	HITS 1			WEEKS 3
NEW YORK AFTERNOON	*Lisson*	70	*16 Aug 86*	3

MONE
US

(See also B-Crew featuring Barbara Tucker, Ultra Nate, Dajae, Mone.)

SINGLES:	HITS 2			WEEKS 2
WE CAN MAKE IT	A&M	64	12 Aug 95	1
MOVIN'	AM:PM	48	16 Mar 96	1

Zoot MONEY and the BIG ROLL BAND
UK

SINGLES:	HITS 1			WEEKS 8
BIG TIME OPERATOR	Columbia	25	20 Aug 66	8
ALBUMS:	HITS 1			WEEKS 3
ZOOT	Columbia	23	15 Oct 66	3

MONEY MARK
US

SINGLES:	HITS 2			WEEKS 3
HAND IN YOUR HEAD	Mo Wax	40	28 Feb 98	2
MAYBE I'M DEAD	Mo Wax	45	6 Jun 98	1
ALBUMS:	HITS 2			WEEKS 6
MARK'S KEYBOARD REPAIR	Mo Wax	35	9 Sep 95	2
PUSH THE BUTTON	Mo Wax	17	16 May 98	4

MONICA - See Shabba RANKS

MONICA
US

SINGLES:	HITS 7			WEEKS 37
DON'T TAKE IT PERSONAL (JUST ONE OF DEM DAYS)	Arista	32	29 Jul 95	3
Samples Back Seat (Of My Jeep) by L.L.Cool J.				
LIKE THIS AND LIKE THAT	Arista	33	17 Feb 96	2
Samples Sugarhill Gang's Spoonin' Rap. Rap performed by Malik from the Outhere Brothers.				
BEFORE YOU WALK OUT OF MY LIFE	Arista	22	8 Jun 96	3
Features backing vocals by Tony Rich.				
FOR YOU I WILL	Atlantic	27	24 May 97	2
From the film 'Space Jam'.				
THE BOY IS MINE	Atlantic	2	6 Jun 98	20
Above hit: BRANDY and MONICA.				
THE FIRST NIGHT	Arista	6	17 Oct 98	6
Samples Diana Ross' Love Hangover.				
ANGEL OF MINE	Arista	55	4 Sep 99	1
ALBUMS:	HITS 1			WEEKS 10
THE BOY IS MINE	Arista	52	25 Jul 98	10

MONIFAH
US

(See also Various Artists (EPs) 'New York Undercover 4-Track EP'.)

SINGLES:	HITS 1			WEEKS 2
TOUCH IT	Universal	29	30 Jan 99	2
Samples Laid Back's White Horse.				

MONKEES
UK/US

SINGLES:	HITS 13			WEEKS 101
I'M A BELIEVER	RCA Victor	1	7 Jan 67	17
Originally recorded by Neil Diamond.				
LAST TRAIN TO CLARKSVILLE	RCA Victor	23	28 Jan 67	7
This was their first UK release in 1966.				
A LITTLE BIT ME, A LITTLE BIT YOU	RCA Victor	3	8 Apr 67	12
Written by Neil Diamond.				
ALTERNATE TITLE	RCA Victor	2	24 Jun 67	12
Originally called Randy Scouse Git.				
PLEASANT VALLEY SUNDAY	RCA Victor	11	19 Aug 67	8
DAYDREAM BELIEVER	RCA Victor	5	18 Nov 67	17
Originally recorded by John Stewart.				
VALLERI	RCA Victor	12	30 Mar 68	8
D.W. WASHBURN	RCA Victor	17	29 Jun 68	6
Originally recorded by the Coasters.				
TEAR DROP CITY	RCA Victor	45	29 Mar 69	1
SOMEDAY MAN	RCA Victor	47	28 Jun 69	1
THE MONKEES [EP]	Arista	33	15 Mar 80	9
Lead track: I'm A Believer.				
THAT WAS THEN, THIS IS NOW	Arista	68	18 Oct 86	1
THE MONKEES [EP]	Arista	62	1 Apr 89	2
Lead track: Daydream Believer. Both self-titled EPs are different and consist of re-issues of former releases.				
ALBUMS:	HITS 7			WEEKS 111
THE MONKEES	RCA Victor	1	28 Jan 67	36
MORE OF THE MONKEES	RCA Victor	1	15 Apr 67	25

HEADQUARTERS	*RCA Victor*	2	*8 Jul 67*	19
PISCES, AQUARIUS, CAPRICORN AND JONES LTD.	*RCA Victor*	5	*13 Jan 68*	11
THE MONKEES	*Arista*	99	*28 Nov 81*	1
Both eponymous albums are different.				
HEY HEY IT'S THE MONKEES - GREATEST HITS	*K-Tel*	12	*15 Apr 89*	9
HERE THEY COME: THE GREATEST HITS OF THE MONKEES	*warner.esp/Telstar*	15	*22 Mar 97*	10

MONKEY MAFIA   UK

(See also Junior Cartier.)

SINGLES:	**HITS 3**			**WEEKS 3**
WORK MI BODY	*Heavenly*	75	*10 Aug 96*	1
Above hit: MONKEY MAFIA featuring PATRA.				
15 STEPS [EP]	*Heavenly*	67	*7 Jun 97*	1
Lead track: Lion In The Hall.				
LONG AS I CAN SEE THE LIGHT	*Heavenly*	51	*2 May 98*	1
ALBUMS:	**HITS 1**			**WEEKS 1**
SHOOT THE BOSS	*Heavenly*	69	*16 May 98*	1

MONKS   UK

(See also Hudson-Ford.)

SINGLES:	**HITS 1**			**WEEKS 9**
NICE LEGS SHAME ABOUT HER FACE	*Carrere*	19	*21 Apr 79*	9

MONKS CHORUS SILOS - See CORO DE MUNJES DEL MONASTERIO BENEDICTINO DE SANTO DOMINGO DE SILOS

MONKS OF AMPLEFORTH ABBEY   UK

ALBUMS:	**HITS 1**			**WEEKS 2**
VISION OF PEACE	*Classic FM*	73	*17 Jun 95*	2

MONO   UK

SINGLES:	**HITS 1**			**WEEKS 1**
LIFE IN MONO	*Echo*	60	*2 May 98*	1
First released in 1996.				
ALBUMS:	**HITS 1**			**WEEKS 1**
FORMICA BLUES	*Echo*	71	*8 Aug 98*	1
First released in 1997, repackaged with an album of remixes.				

MONOCHROME SET   UK

ALBUMS:	**HITS 1**			**WEEKS 4**
STRANGE BOUTIQUE	*DinDisc*	62	*3 May 80*	4

Tony MONOPOLY   Australia

ALBUMS:	**HITS 1**			**WEEKS 4**
TONY MONOPOLY	*BUK*	25	*12 Jun 76*	4

Matt MONRO   UK

SINGLES:	**HITS 13**			**WEEKS 127**
PORTRAIT OF MY LOVE	*Parlophone*	3	*17 Dec 60*	16
MY KIND OF GIRL	*Parlophone*	5	*11 Mar 61*	12
WHY NOT NOW / CAN THIS BE LOVE	*Parlophone*	24	*20 May 61*	9
Can This Be Love? not listed on the chart of 10 June 61.				
GONNA BUILD A MOUNTAIN	*Parlophone*	44	*30 Sep 61*	3
From the show 'Stop The World, I Want To Get Off'.				
SOFTLY AS I LEAVE YOU	*Parlophone*	10	*10 Feb 62*	18
WHEN LOVE COMES ALONG	*Parlophone*	46	*16 Jun 62*	3
MY LOVE AND DEVOTION	*Parlophone*	29	*10 Nov 62*	5
FROM RUSSIA WITH LOVE	*Parlophone*	20	*16 Nov 63*	13
From the James Bond film of the same name.				
WALK AWAY (WARUM NUR WARUM)	*Parlophone*	4	*19 Sep 64*	20
Original version by Udo Jurgens was Austria's entry in the 1964 Eurovision Song Contest.				
FOR MAMA	*Parlophone*	36	*26 Dec 64*	4
WITHOUT YOU	*Parlophone*	37	*27 Mar 65*	4
YESTERDAY	*Parlophone*	8	*23 Oct 65*	12
AND YOU SMILED (EYE LEVEL THEME FROM TV SERIES "VAN DER VALK")	*EMI*	28	*24 Nov 73*	8
EPS:	**HITS 2**			**WEEKS 7**
SONG FOR EUROPE	*Parlophone*	16	*29 Feb 64*	6
SOMEWHERE	*Parlophone*	19	*22 May 65*	1
ALBUMS:	**HITS 4**			**WEEKS 15**
I HAVE DREAMED	*Parlophone*	20	*7 Aug 65*	1
THIS IS THE LIFE	*Capitol*	25	*17 Sep 66*	2
INVITATION TO THE MOVIES	*Capitol*	30	*26 Aug 67*	1
HEARTBREAKERS	*EMI*	5	*15 Mar 80*	11

Gerry MONROE — UK

SINGLES:	HITS 6		WEEKS 57	
SALLY	Chapter 1	4	23 May 70	20
Originally recorded by Gracie Fields.				
CRY	Chapter 1	38	19 Sep 70	5
MY PRAYER	Chapter 1	9	14 Nov 70	12
IT'S A SIN TO TELL A LIE	Chapter 1	13	17 Apr 71	12
Above 2 originally recorded by tthe Inkspots.				
LITTLE DROPS OF SILVER	Chapter 1	37	21 Aug 71	6
GIRL OF MY DREAMS	Chapter 1	43	12 Feb 72	2

Hollis P. MONROE — Canada

SINGLES:	HITS 1		WEEKS 1	
I'M LONELY	Citybeat	51	24 Apr 99	1
Samples Terence Trent D'Arby's And I Need To Be With Someone Tonight.				

MONSOON — UK

SINGLES:	HITS 2		WEEKS 12	
EVER SO LONELY	Mobile Suit Corporation	12	3 Apr 82	9
SHAKTI (THE MEANING OF WITHIN)	Mobile Suit Corporation	41	5 Jun 82	3

MONSTER MAGNET — US

SINGLES:	HITS 5		WEEKS 6	
TWIN EARTH	A&M	67	29 May 93	1
NEGASONIC TEENAGE WARHEAD	A&M	49	18 Mar 95	1
DOPES TO INFINITY	A&M	58	6 May 95	1
POWERTRIP	A&M	39	23 Jan 99	2
From the film 'Soldiers'.				
SPACE LORD	A&M	45	6 Mar 99	1
ALBUMS:	HITS 2		WEEKS 2	
DOPES TO INFINITY	A&M	51	1 Apr 95	1
POWERTRIP	A&M	65	13 Jun 98	1

MONTAGE — UK

SINGLES:	HITS 1		WEEKS 1	
THERE AIN'T NOTHIN' LIKE THE LOVE	Wild Card	64	15 Feb 97	1

MONTANA SEXTET — US

SINGLES:	HITS 1		WEEKS 1	
HEAVY VIBES	Virgin	59	15 Jan 83	1

MONTANO vs the TRUMPET MAN — UK

SINGLES:	HITS 1		WEEKS 1	
ITZA TRUMPET THING	Serious	46	18 Sep 99	1

Hugo MONTENEGRO, his Orchestra and Chorus — US

SINGLES:	HITS 2		WEEKS 26	
THE GOOD, THE BAD AND THE UGLY	RCA Victor	1	14 Sep 68	24
Originally recorded by Ennio Morricone.				
HANG 'EM HIGH	RCA Victor	50	11 Jan 69	1
Above 2 both from the films of the same name.				
THE GOOD, THE BAD AND THE UGLY [RE]	RCA Victor	48	22 Mar 69	1

Chris MONTEZ — US

SINGLES:	HITS 4		WEEKS 61	
LET'S DANCE	London	2	6 Oct 62	18
SOME KINDA FUN	London	10	19 Jan 63	9
THE MORE I SEE YOU	Pye International	3	2 Jul 66	13
From the film 'Diamond Horseshoe'. Originally recorded by Dick Haymes in 1945.				
THERE WILL NEVER BE ANOTHER YOU	Pye International	37	24 Sep 66	4
LET'S DANCE [RI-1ST]	London	9	14 Oct 72	14
LET'S DANCE [RI-2ND]	Lightning	47	14 Apr 79	3
[AA] listed with Memphis by Lonnie Mack.				

MONTROSE — US

SINGLES:	HITS 1		WEEKS 2	
SPACE STATION NUMBER 5 / GOOD ROCKIN' TONIGHT	Warner Brothers	71	28 Jun 80	2
ALBUMS:	HITS 1		WEEKS 1	
MONTROSE	Warner Brothers	43	15 Jun 74	1

MONTROSE AVENUE
UK

SINGLES:	HITS 3			WEEKS 4
WHERE DO I STAND?	Columbia	38	28 Mar 98	2
SHINE	Columbia	58	20 Jun 98	1
START AGAIN	Columbia	59	17 Oct 98	1

MONTY PYTHON'S FLYING CIRCUS
UK

SINGLES:	HITS 1			WEEKS 9
ALWAYS LOOK ON THE BRIGHT SIDE OF LIFE	Virgin	3	5 Oct 91	9

From the film 'The Life Of Brian'.
Above hit: MONTY PYTHON.

ALBUMS:	HITS 8			WEEKS 33
ANOTHER MONTY PYTHON RECORD	Charisma	26	30 Oct 71	3
MONTY PYTHON'S PREVIOUS ALBUM	Charisma	39	27 Jan 73	3
THE MONTY PYTHON MATCHING TIE AND HANKERCHIEF	Charisma	49	23 Feb 74	2
MONTY PYTHON LIVE AT DRURY LANE	Charisma	19	27 Jul 74	8
THE ALBUM OF THE SOUNDTRACK OF THE TRAILER OF THE FILM OF MONTY PYTHON AND THE HOLY GRAIL [OST]	Charisma	45	9 Aug 75	4
MONTY PYTHON'S LIFE OF BRIAN [OST]	Warner Brothers	63	24 Nov 79	3
MONTY PYTHON'S CONTRACTUAL OBLIGATION ALBUM	Charisma	13	18 Oct 80	8
MONTY PYTHON SINGS	Virgin	62	16 Nov 91	2

Originally released in 1989.
Above hit: MONTY PYTHON.

MONYAKA
US/Jamaica

SINGLES:	HITS 1			WEEKS 8
GO DEH YAKA (GO TO THE TOP)	Polydor	14	10 Sep 83	8

MOOD
UK

SINGLES:	HITS 3			WEEKS 10
DON'T STOP	RCA	59	6 Feb 82	4
PARIS IS ONE DAY AWAY	RCA	42	22 May 82	5
PASSION IN DARK ROOMS	RCA	74	30 Oct 82	1

MOODSWINGS features the voice of Chrissie HYNDE
UK/US

SINGLES:	HITS 1			WEEKS 4
SPIRITUAL HIGH (STATE OF INDEPENDENCE)	Arista	66	12 Oct 91	2
SPIRITUAL HIGH (STATE OF INDEPENDENCE) [RI]	Arista	47	23 Jan 93	2

From the film 'Single White Female'.

MOODY BLUES
UK

SINGLES:	HITS 12			WEEKS 114
GO NOW!	Decca	1	12 Dec 64	14

Originally recorded by Bessie Banks.

I DON'T WANT TO GO ON WITHOUT YOU	Decca	33	6 Mar 65	9
FROM THE BOTTOM OF MY HEART (I LOVE YOU)	Decca	22	12 Jun 65	9
EVERYDAY	Decca	44	20 Nov 65	2
NIGHTS IN WHITE SATIN	Deram	19	30 Dec 67	11
VOICES IN THE SKY	Deram	27	10 Aug 68	10
RIDE MY SEE-SAW	Deram	42	7 Dec 68	1
QUESTION	Threshold	2	2 May 70	12
ISN'T LIFE STRANGE	Threshold	13	6 May 72	10
NIGHTS IN WHITE SATIN [RE-1ST]	Deram	9	2 Dec 72	11
I'M JUST A SINGER (IN A ROCK AND ROLL BAND)	Threshold	36	10 Feb 73	4
NIGHTS IN WHITE SATIN [RE-2ND]	Deram	14	10 Nov 79	12
BLUE WORLD	Threshold	35	20 Aug 83	5
I KNOW YOU'RE OUT THERE SOMEWHERE	Polydor	52	25 Jun 88	4

EPS:	HITS 1			WEEKS 14
THE MOODY BLUES	Decca	12	12 Jun 65	14

ALBUMS:	HITS 17			WEEKS 325
DAYS OF FUTURE PASSED	Deram	27	27 Jan 68	16

Features the London Festival Orchestra conducted by Peter Knight.

IN SEARCH OF THE LOST CHORD	Deram	5	3 Aug 68	32
ON THE THRESHOLD OF A DREAM	Deram	1	3 May 69	73
TO OUR CHILDREN'S CHILDREN'S CHILDREN	Threshold	2	6 Dec 69	44
A QUESTION OF BALANCE	Threshold	1	15 Aug 70	19
EVERY GOOD BOY DESERVES FAVOUR	Threshold	1	7 Aug 71	21
SEVENTH SOJOURN	Threshold	5	2 Dec 72	18
THIS IS THE MOODY BLUES	Threshold	14	16 Nov 74	18
OCTAVE	Decca	6	24 Jun 78	18
OUT OF THIS WORLD	K-Tel	15	10 Nov 79	10

Compilation.

LONG DISTANCE VOYAGER	Threshold	7	23 May 81	19
THE PRESENT	Threshold	15	10 Sep 83	8

THE OTHER SIDE OF LIFE	*Threshold*	24	*10 May 86*	6
SUR LA MER	*Polydor*	21	*25 Jun 88*	5
GREATEST HITS	*Threshold*	71	*20 Jan 90*	1
KEYS OF THE KINGDOM	*Threshold*	54	*13 Jul 91*	2
THE VERY BEST OF THE MOODY BLUES	*PolyGram TV*	13	*5 Oct 96*	15

Michael MOOG   US

SINGLES:	HITS 1		WEEKS 2	
THAT SOUND	*ffrr*	32	*11 Dec 99*	2

MOONMAN   Holland

SINGLES:	HITS 1		WEEKS 3	
DON'T BE AFRAID	*Heat Recordings*	60	*9 Aug 97*	1
Originally released on the Sci Fi label in 1996. Vocals by Linda.				
DON'T BE AFRAID '99 [RM]	*Heat Recordings*	41	*27 Nov 99*	2
Remixed by Mick Shiney and Steve Hill (Nylon).				

MOONTREKKERS   UK

SINGLES:	HITS 1		WEEKS 1	
NIGHT OF THE VAMPIRE	*Parlophone*	50	*4 Nov 61*	1

Chante MOORE   US

SINGLES:	HITS 2		WEEKS 4	
LOVE'S TAKEN OVER	*MCA*	54	*20 Mar 93*	3
FREE/SAIL ON [M]	*MCA*	69	*4 Mar 95*	1

Christy MOORE   Ireland

ALBUMS:	HITS 4		WEEKS 8	
SMOKE AND STRONG WHISKEY	*Newbury*	49	*4 May 91*	3
THE CHRISTY MOORE COLLECTION 81-91	*East West*	69	*21 Sep 91*	1
KING PUCK	*Equator*	66	*6 Nov 93*	2
GRAFFITI TONGUE	*Grapevine*	35	*14 Sep 96*	2

Dorothy MOORE   US

SINGLES:	HITS 3		WEEKS 24	
MISTY BLUE	*Contempo*	5	*19 Jun 76*	12
Originally recorded by Wilmer Burgess.				
FUNNY HOW TIME SLIPS AWAY	*Contempo*	38	*16 Oct 76*	3
Originally recorded by Willie Nelson.				
I BELIEVE YOU	*Epic*	20	*15 Oct 77*	9
Originally recorded by the Addrissi Brothers.				

Dudley MOORE   UK

(See also Peter Cook and Dudley Moore; Sir George Solti and Dudley Moore.)

ALBUMS:	HITS 2		WEEKS 19	
THE OTHER SIDE OF DUDLEY MOORE	*Decca*	11	*4 Dec 65*	9
GENUINE DUD	*Decca*	13	*11 Jun 66*	10
Above hit: Dudley MOORE TRIO.				

Gary MOORE   UK

SINGLES:	HITS 21		WEEKS 103	
PARISIENNE WALKWAYS	*MCA*	8	*21 Apr 79*	11
Vocals by Phil Lynott.				
HOLD ON TO LOVE	*10 Records*	65	*21 Jan 84*	3
EMPTY ROOMS	*10 Records*	51	*11 Aug 84*	5
OUT IN THE FIELDS	*10 Records*	5	*18 May 85*	10
Above hit: Gary MOORE and Phil LYNOTT.				
EMPTY ROOMS (SUMMER '85 VERSION) [RM]	*10 Records*	23	*27 Jul 85*	8
OVER THE HILLS AND FAR AWAY	*10 Records*	20	*20 Dec 86*	8
WILD FRONTIER	*10 Records*	35	*28 Feb 87*	5
FRIDAY ON MY MIND	*10 Records*	26	*9 May 87*	6
THE LONER	*10 Records*	53	*29 Aug 87*	5
TAKE A LITTLE TIME	*10 Records*	75	*5 Dec 87*	1
Double-pack single.				
AFTER THE WAR	*Virgin*	37	*14 Jan 89*	4
READY FOR LOVE	*Virgin*	56	*18 Mar 89*	2
OH PRETTY WOMAN	*Virgin*	48	*24 Mar 90*	3
Above hit: Gary MOORE featuring Albert KING.				
STILL GOT THE BLUES (FOR YOU)	*Virgin*	31	*12 May 90*	7
WALKING BY MYSELF	*Virgin*	48	*18 Aug 90*	5
TOO TIRED	*Virgin*	71	*15 Dec 90*	1
Above hit: Gary MOORE featuring Albert COLLINS.				
COLD DAY IN HELL	*Virgin*	24	*22 Feb 92*	5
STORY OF THE BLUES	*Virgin*	40	*9 May 92*	4

SINCE I MET YOU BABY	*Virgin*	59	*18 Jul 92*	3
Above hit: Gary MOORE and B.B. KING.				
SEPARATE WAYS	*Virgin*	59	*24 Oct 92*	1
PARISIENNE WALKWAYS '93 [RR]	*Virgin*	32	*8 May 93*	4
Live recording from the Royal Albert Hall, Oct 92.				
NEED YOUR LOVE SO BAD	*Virgin*	48	*17 Jun 95*	2
From the film 'Mad Dogs And Englishmen'.				

ALBUMS:	**HITS 15**			**WEEKS 103**
BACK ON THE STREETS	*MCA*	70	*3 Feb 79*	1
CORRIDORS OF POWER	*Virgin*	30	*16 Oct 82*	6
VICTIMS OF THE FUTURE	*10 Records*	12	*18 Feb 84*	7
WE WANT MOORE!	*10 Records*	32	*13 Oct 84*	3
RUN FOR COVER	*10 Records*	12	*14 Sep 85*	8
ROCKIN' EVERY NIGHT	*10 Records*	99	*12 Jul 86*	1
WILD FRONTIER	*10 Records*	8	*14 Mar 87*	14
AFTER THE WAR	*Virgin*	23	*11 Feb 89*	5
STILL GOT THE BLUES	*Virgin*	13	*7 Apr 90*	26
AFTER HOURS	*Virgin*	4	*21 Mar 92*	13
BLUES ALIVE	*Virgin*	8	*22 May 93*	5
Live recordings from 1992.				
BALLADS AND BLUES 1982-1994	*Virgin*	33	*26 Nov 94*	6
BLUES FOR GREENEY	*Virgin*	14	*10 Jun 95*	5
Interpretations of Peter Green compositions.				
DARK DAYS IN PARADISE	*Virgin*	43	*7 Jun 97*	2
OUT IN THE FIELDS - THE VERY BEST OF GARY MOORE	*Virgin*	54	*31 Oct 98*	1

Jackie MOORE · US

SINGLES:	**HITS 1**			**WEEKS 5**
THIS TIME BABY	*CBS*	49	*15 Sep 79*	5

Mark MOORE - See S-EXPRESS

Melba MOORE · US

SINGLES:	**HITS 5**			**WEEKS 29**
THIS IS IT	*Buddah*	9	*15 May 76*	8
PICK ME UP, I'LL DANCE	*Epic*	48	*26 May 79*	5
LOVE'S COMIN' AT YA	*EMI America*	15	*9 Oct 82*	8
MIND UP TONIGHT	*Capitol*	22	*15 Jan 83*	6
UNDERLOVE	*Capitol*	60	*5 Mar 83*	2

Pete MOORE ORCHESTRA - See Bing CROSBY

Ray MOORE · UK

SINGLES:	**HITS 2**			**WEEKS 9**
O' MY FATHER HAD A RABBIT	*Play*	24	*29 Nov 86*	7
THE BOG-EYED JOG	*Play*	61	*5 Dec 87*	2
Backing by the Carrot Crunchers and the singers from Marlborough school, St Albans. Above 2 are charity records with proceeds to the BBC's Children In Need.				

COMPILATION ALBUMS:	**HITS 1**			**WEEKS 4**
RAY MOORE - A PERSONAL CHOICE	*BBC*	7	*17 Jun 89*	4
As it featured a variety of acts, the album was only eligible for the compilation chart.				
Above hit: Ray MOORE and VARIOUS ARTISTS.				

Sam MOORE and Lou REED · US

(See also Lou Reed; Sam and Dave.)

SINGLES:	**HITS 1**			**WEEKS 10**
SOUL MAN	*A&M*	30	*17 Jan 87*	10
From the film of the same name.				

Steve MOORE - See Jim REEVES

Tina MOORE · US

SINGLES:	**HITS 2**			**WEEKS 18**
NEVER GONNA LET YOU GO	*Delirious*	7	*30 Aug 97*	15
NOBODY BETTER	*Delirious*	20	*25 Apr 98*	3

Lisa MOORISH · UK

SINGLES:	**HITS 4**			**WEEKS 11**
JUST THE WAY IT IS	*Go.Beat*	42	*7 Jan 95*	3
I'M YOUR MAN	*Go.Beat*	24	*19 Aug 95*	3
Backing vocals by George Michael.				
MR FRIDAY NIGHT	*Go.Beat*	24	*3 Feb 96*	3
LOVE FOR LIFE	*Go.Beat*	37	*18 May 96*	2

Angel MORAES   US

SINGLES:	HITS 2		WEEKS 2	
HEAVEN KNOWS – DEEP DEEP DOWN	*ffrr*	72	*16 Nov 96*	1
I LIKE IT	*AM:PM*	70	*17 May 97*	1

David MORALES   US

(See also Boss; Pulse featuring Antoinette Roberson.)

SINGLES:	HITS 4		WEEKS 14	
GIMME LUV (EENIE MEENIE MINY MO)	*Mercury*	37	*10 Jul 93*	3
THE PROGRAM	*Mercury*	66	*20 Nov 93*	1
Above 2: David MORALES and the BAD YARD CLUB.				
IN DE GHETTO	*Manifesto*	35	*24 Aug 96*	2
Additional vocals by Sly Dunbar (of Sly and Robbie).				
Above hit: David MORALES and the BAD YARD CLUB featuring Crystal WATERS and DELTA.				
NEEDIN' U	*Manifesto*	8	*15 Aug 98*	8
Above hit: David MORALES Presents the FACE.				

Mike MORAN - See Lyndey DE PAUL

Patrick MORAZ   Switzerland

ALBUMS:	HITS 2		WEEKS 8	
PATRICK MORAZ	*Charisma*	28	*10 Apr 76*	7
OUT IN THE SUN	*Charisma*	44	*23 Jul 77*	1

MORCHEEBA   UK

SINGLES:	HITS 7		WEEKS 9	
TAPE LOOP	*Indochina*	42	*13 Jul 96*	1
TRIGGER HIPPIE	*Indochina*	40	*5 Oct 96*	2
THE MUSIC THAT WE HEAR (MOOG ISLAND)	*Indochina*	47	*15 Feb 97*	1
SHOULDER HOLSTER	*Indochina*	53	*11 Oct 97*	1
BLINDFOLD	*Indochina*	56	*11 Apr 98*	1
LET ME SEE	*Indochina*	46	*20 Jun 98*	1
PART OF THE PROCESS	*China*	38	*29 Aug 98*	2

ALBUMS:	HITS 2		WEEKS 54	
WHO CAN YOU TRUST?	*Indochina*	70	*12 Apr 97*	1
Originally released in 1996 reaching No. 94.				
BIG CALM	*Indochina*	18	*28 Mar 98*	53

MORDRED   UK

ALBUMS:	HITS 1		WEEKS 1	
IN THIS LIFE	*Noise International*	70	*16 Feb 91*	1

MORE   UK

SINGLES:	HITS 1		WEEKS 2	
WE ARE THE BAND	*Atlantic*	59	*14 Mar 81*	2

George MOREL featuring Heather WILDMAN   US

SINGLES:	HITS 1		WEEKS 2	
LET'S GROOVE	*Positiva*	42	*26 Oct 96*	2

MORGAN   UK

SINGLES:	HITS 1		WEEKS 1	
MISS PARKER	*Source*	74	*27 Nov 99*	1

Derrick MORGAN Music backing the RUDIES   Jamaica

SINGLES:	HITS 1		WEEKS 1	
MOON HOP	*Crab*	49	*17 Jan 70*	1

Jamie J. MORGAN   US

SINGLES:	HITS 1		WEEKS 6	
WALK ON THE WILD SIDE	*Tabu*	27	*10 Feb 90*	6

Jane MORGAN   US

SINGLES:	HITS 3		WEEKS 22	
THE DAY THE RAINS CAME	*London*	1	*6 Dec 58*	16
IF ONLY I COULD LIVE MY LIFE AGAIN	*London*	27	*23 May 59*	1
ROMANTICA	*London*	39	*23 Jul 60*	5

Meli'sa MORGAN
US

SINGLES:		HITS 2			WEEKS 7
FOOL'S PARADISE		Capitol	41	9 Aug 86	5
GOOD LOVE		Capitol	59	25 Jun 88	2

Ray MORGAN
UK

SINGLES:		HITS 1			WEEKS 6
LONG AND WINDING ROAD		B&C	32	25 Jul 70	6
Originally recorded by the Beatles.					

Erick "More" MORILLO Presents R.A.W.
US

SINGLES:		HITS 1			WEEKS 1
HIGHER (FEEL IT)		A&M	74	4 Feb 95	1

Alanis MORISSETTE
Canada

SINGLES:		HITS 9			WEEKS 45
YOU OUGHTA KNOW		Maverick	22	5 Aug 95	7
HAND IN MY POCKET		Maverick	26	28 Oct 95	3
YOU LEARN		Maverick	24	24 Feb 96	4
IRONIC		Maverick	11	20 Apr 96	9
HEAD OVER FEET		Maverick	7	3 Aug 96	7
ALL I REALLY WANT		Maverick	59	7 Dec 96	1
THANK U		Maverick	5	31 Oct 98	10
JOINING YOU		Maverick	28	13 Mar 99	2
SO PURE		Maverick	38	31 Jul 99	2
ALBUMS:		HITS 3			WEEKS 171
JAGGED LITTLE PILL		Maverick	1	26 Aug 95	145
Peak position reached on 4 May 96.					
SUPPOSED FORMER INFACTUATION JUNKIE		Maverick	3	14 Nov 98	21
MTV UNPLUGGED		Maverick	56	4 Dec 99	5

Giorgio MORODER
Italy

(See also Philip Oakey and Giorgio Moroder.)

SINGLES:		HITS 3			WEEKS 17
FROM HERE TO ETERNITY		Oasis	16	24 Sep 77	10
Above hit: GIORGIO.					
CHASE		Casablanca	48	17 Mar 79	6
From the film 'Midnight Express'.					
CARRY ON		Almighty	65	11 Jul 98	1
Above hit: Donna SUMMER and Giorgio MORODER.					

Joseph MOROVITZ – See SOUTH BANK ORCHESTRA conducted by Joseph MOROVITZ and Laurie HOLLOWAY

Ennio MORRICONE
Italy

SINGLES:		HITS 1			WEEKS 12
CHI MAI (THEME FROM THE TV SERIES THE LIFE AND TIMES OF DAVID LLOYD GEORGE)		BBC	2	11 Apr 81	12
Theme from the BBC TV series.					
ALBUMS:		HITS 5			WEEKS 35
THE GOOD, THE BAD AND THE UGLY [OST]		United Artists	2	12 Oct 68	18
MOSES [OST]		Pye	43	5 Mar 77	2
THIS IS ENNIO MORRICONE		EMI	23	2 May 81	5
CHI MAI		BBC	29	9 May 81	6
THE MISSION [OST]		Virgin	73	7 Mar 87	4
Above hit: Ennio MORRICONE with the LONDON PHILHARMONIC ORCHESTRA.					

Sarah Jane MORRIS – See COMMUNARDS

Treana MORRIS – See Roger TAYLOR

Diana MORRISON – See Michael BALL

Dorothy Combs MORRISON – See Edwin HAWKINS SINGERS. Soloist: Dorothy Combs MORRISON

Jim MORRISON – See DOORS

Mark MORRISON
UK

SINGLES:		HITS 8			WEEKS 68
CRAZY		WEA	19	22 Apr 95	4
LET'S GET DOWN		WEA	39	16 Sep 95	2
RETURN OF THE MACK		WEA	1	16 Mar 96	23
CRAZY [RM]		WEA	6	27 Jul 96	8
Mixed by Phil Chill and Clive Black.					
RETURN OF THE MACK [RE]		WEA	60	31 Aug 96	1
CRAZY [RM] [RE]		WEA	71	19 Oct 96	1

Between 1984 and 1994 **Madonna** *racked up a record 31 consecutive Top 10 hits. (LFI)*

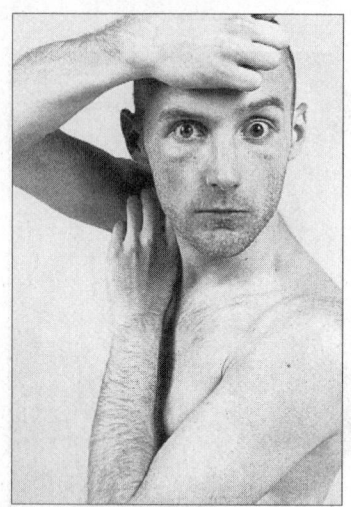

Moby *related to Herman Melville,*
the author of Moby Dick. *(LFI)*

With hits in 1953 and 1999
Dean Martin *has the longest chart*
span of any artist.

'If You Tolerate This Your Children Will Be Next' by the **Manic Street Preachers** *is the joint longest (unbracketed) title for*
a No.1 hit. (LFI)

Oasis *are the only act to have their first three albums enter the chart at No.1. (LFI)*

With a running time of 39 minutes and 58 seconds, the **Orb**'s record-breaking 'Blue Room' single is longer than many albums. (LFI)

Shaquille O'Neill, the 7' 1" basketball player, is the tallest artist in this book. (LFI)

Jimmy Osmond was nine years 251 days old when he became the youngest artist to top the singles chart. (LFI)

The **Pet Shop Boys** have scored more hits than any other duo. (LFI)

*Four ages of **Elvis Presley**.*

***Elvis**'s 'Jailhouse Rock' was the first single to enter the chart at No.1. (LFI)*

The longest word used in a hit title is 'Anotherloverholeinyohead' by **Prince**. *(LFI)*

Queen's 'Bohemian Rhapsody' is the only recording to reach No. 1 on two entirely separate occasions. (LFI)

TRIPPIN'	WEA	8	19 Oct 96	6
HORNY	WEA	5	21 Dec 96	9
MOAN & GROAN	WEA	7	15 Mar 97	6
WHO'S THE MACK!	WEA	13	20 Sep 97	5
BEST FRIEND	WEA	23	4 Sep 99	3

Above hit: Mark MORRISON and Conner REEVES.

ALBUMS:		**HITS 2**		**WEEKS 39**
RETURN OF THE MACK	WEA	4	4 May 96	38
ONLY GOD CAN JUDGE ME	WEA	50	27 Sep 97	1

Includes live recordings from Birmingham NEC and Milan, Italy and excerpts from an interview with Radio 1 DJ Lisa l'Anson.

Van MORRISON   Ireland

(See also Van Morrison and the Chieftains.)

SINGLES:		**HITS 9**		**WEEKS 19**
BRIGHT SIDE OF THE ROAD	Mercury	63	20 Oct 79	3
HAVE I TOLD YOU LATELY	Polydor	74	1 Jul 89	1
WHENEVER GOD SHINES HIS LIGHT	Polydor	20	9 Dec 89	6

Above hit: Van MORRISON with Cliff RICHARD.

GLORIA	Exile	31	15 May 93	3

Originally the B-side of Them's Baby Please Don't Go in 1964.
Above hit: Van MORRISON and John Lee HOOKER.

DAYS LIKE THIS	Exile	65	10 Jun 95	1
NO RELIGION	Exile	54	2 Dec 95	1
THE HEALING GAME	Exile	46	1 Mar 97	1
PRECIOUS TIME	Pointblank	36	6 Mar 99	2
BACK ON TOP	Pointblank	69	22 May 99	1

ALBUMS:		**HITS 24**		**WEEKS 249**
MOONDANCE	Warner Brothers	32	18 Apr 70	2
HARD NOSE THE HIGHWAY	Warner Brothers	22	11 Aug 73	3
VEEDON FLEECE	Warner Brothers	41	16 Nov 74	1
A PERIOD OF TRANSITION	Warner Brothers	23	7 May 77	5
WAVELENGTH	Warner Brothers	27	21 Oct 78	6
INTO THE MUSIC	Vertigo	21	8 Sep 79	9
THE COMMON ONE	Mercury	53	20 Sep 80	3
BEAUTIFUL VISION	Mercury	31	27 Feb 82	14
INARTICULATE SPEECH OF THE HEART	Mercury	14	26 Mar 83	8
LIVE AT THE GRAND OPERA HOUSE BELFAST	Mercury	47	3 Mar 84	4
A SENSE OF WONDER	Mercury	25	9 Feb 85	5
NO GURU, NO METHOD, NO TEACHER	Mercury	27	2 Aug 86	5
POETIC CHAMPIONS COMPOSE	Mercury	26	19 Sep 87	6
AVALON SUNSET	Polydor	13	10 Jun 89	14
THE BEST OF VAN MORRISON	Polydor	4	7 Apr 90	86

Includes re-entries through to 1999.

ENLIGHTENMENT	Polydor	5	20 Oct 90	14
HYMNS TO THE SILENCE	Polydor	5	21 Sep 91	6
THE BEST OF VAN MORRISON VOLUME 2	Polydor	31	27 Feb 93	3
TOO LONG IN EXILE	Exile	4	12 Jun 93	9
A NIGHT IN SAN FRANCISCO	Polydor	8	30 Apr 94	5

Live recordings from Dec 93.

DAYS LIKE THIS	Exile	5	24 Jun 95	15
THE HEALING GAME	Exile	10	15 Mar 97	7
THE PHILOSOPHER'S STONE	Exile	20	27 Jun 98	3

Compilation of rarities and unreleased tracks from 1977–81.

BACK ON TOP	Pontblank	11	20 Mar 99	16

Van MORRISON and the CHIEFTAINS   UK/Ireland

(See also Chieftains; Van Morrison.)

SINGLES:		**HITS 1**		**WEEKS 1**
HAVE I TOLD YOU LATELY THAT I LOVE YOU?	RCA	71	18 Mar 95	1

Above hit: CHIEFTAINS with Van MORRISON.

ALBUMS:		**HITS 1**		**WEEKS 7**
IRISH HEARTBEAT	Mercury	18	2 Jul 88	7

MORRISSEY   UK

SINGLES:		**HITS 24**		**WEEKS 74**
SUEDEHEAD	His Master's Voice	5	27 Feb 88	6
EVERYDAY IS LIKE SUNDAY	His Master's Voice	9	11 Jun 88	6
THE LAST OF THE FAMOUS INTERNATIONAL PLAYBOYS	His Master's Voice	6	11 Feb 89	5
INTERESTING DRUG	His Master's Voice	9	29 Apr 89	4

Features backing vocals by Kirsty MacColl.

OUIJA BOARD, OUIJA BOARD	His Master's Voice	18	25 Nov 89	4
NOVEMBER SPAWNED A MONSTER	His Master's Voice	12	5 May 90	4
PICCADILLY PALARE	His Master's Voice	18	20 Oct 90	2
OUR FRANK	His Master's Voice	26	23 Feb 91	3

SING YOUR LIFE	His Master's Voice	33	13 Apr 91	2
PREGNANT FOR THE LAST TIME	His Master's Voice	25	27 Jul 91	4
MY LOVE LIFE	His Master's Voice	29	12 Oct 91	2
WE HATE IT WHEN OUR FRIENDS BECOME SUCCESSFUL	His Master's Voice	17	9 May 92	3
YOU'RE THE ONE FOR ME, FATTY	His Master's Voice	19	18 Jul 92	3
CERTAIN PEOPLE I KNOW	His Master's Voice	35	19 Dec 92	4
THE MORE YOU IGNORE ME, THE CLOSER I GET	Parlophone	8	12 Mar 94	3
HOLD ON TO YOUR FRIENDS	Parlophone	47	11 Jun 94	2
INTERLUDE	Parlophone	25	20 Aug 94	2

Originally recorded by Timi Yuro.
Above hit: MORRISSEY and SIOUXSIE.

BOXERS	Parlophone	23	28 Jan 95	3
DAGENHAM DAVE	RCA Victor	26	2 Sep 95	2
THE BOY RACER	RCA Victor	36	9 Dec 95	2
SUNNY	Parlophone	42	23 Dec 95	2
ALMA MATTERS	Island	16	2 Aug 97	3
ROY'S KEEN	Island	42	18 Oct 97	1
SATAN REJECTED MY SOUL	Island	39	10 Jan 98	2
ALBUMS:	**HITS 10**		**WEEKS 51**	
VIVA HATE	His Master's Voice	1	26 Mar 88	20
BONA DRAG	His Master's Voice	9	27 Oct 90	4
KILL UNCLE	His Master's Voice	8	16 Mar 91	4
YOUR ARSENAL	His Master's Voice	4	8 Aug 92	5
BEETHOVEN WAS DEAF	His Master's Voice	13	22 May 93	2

Live recordings from Zenih, Paris, 22 Dec 92.

VAUXHALL AND I	Parlophone	1	26 Mar 94	5
WORLD OF MORRISSEY	Parlophone	15	18 Feb 95	2
SOUTHPAW GRAMMAR	RCA Victor	4	9 Sep 95	3
MALADJUSTED	Island	8	23 Aug 97	3
THE BEST OF – SUEDEHEAD	EMI	26	20 Sep 97	3

MORRISSEY MULLEN

UK

ALBUMS:	**HITS 3**		**WEEKS 11**	
BADNESS	Beggars Banquet	43	18 Jul 81	5
LIFE ON THE WIRE	Beggars Banquet	47	3 Apr 82	5
IT'S ABOUT TIME	Beggars Banquet	95	23 Apr 83	1

MORRISTON ORPHEUS MALE VOICE CHOIR - See ALARM

MORRISTOWN ORPHEUS CHOIR - See G.U.S. (FOOTWEAR) BAND and the MORRISTOWN ORPHEUS CHOIR

Buddy MORROW and his Orchestra

US

SINGLES:	**HITS 1**		**WEEKS 1**	
NIGHT TRAIN	His Master's Voice	12	21 Mar 53	1

Originally recorded by Jimmy Forest.

Bob MORTIMER - See MIDDLESBOROUGH FC featuring Bob MORTIMER and Chris REA; Vic REEVES

Mickie MOST

UK

SINGLES:	**HITS 1**		**WEEKS 1**	
MR. PORTER	Decca	45	27 Jul 63	1

MOTELS

UK/US

SINGLES:	**HITS 2**		**WEEKS 7**	
WHOSE PROBLEM?	Capitol	42	11 Oct 80	4
DAYS ARE OK (BUT THE NIGHTS WERE MADE FOR LOVE)	Capitol	41	10 Jan 81	3

Wendy MOTEN

US

SINGLES:	**HITS 2**		**WEEKS 13**	
COME IN OUT OF THE RAIN	EMI USA	8	5 Feb 94	9
SO CLOSE TO LOVE	EMI USA	35	14 May 94	4
ALBUMS:	**HITS 1**		**WEEKS 2**	
WENDY MOTEN	EMI	42	19 Mar 94	2

MOTHER

UK

SINGLES:	**HITS 2**		**WEEKS 4**	
ALL FUNKED UP	Bosting	34	12 Jun 93	2
GET BACK	Six6	73	1 Oct 94	1
ALL FUNKED UP 96 [RM]	Six6	66	31 Aug 96	1

Mixed by Dobs with new vocals by Denise Johnson.

MOTHER EARTH

UK

ALBUMS:	**HITS 1**		**WEEKS**	
THE PEOPLE TREE	Acid Jazz	45	5 Mar 94	2

MOTHERS OF INVENTION

US

ALBUMS:		HITS 3		WEEKS 12
WE'RE ONLY IN IT FOR THE MONEY	Verve	32	29 Jun 68	5
BURNT WEENY SANDWICH	Reprise	17	28 Mar 70	3
WEASELS RIPPED MY FLESH	Reprise	28	3 Oct 70	4

Live recordings previously unreleased and studio material from 1967-70.

MOTHERS PRIDE

UK

SINGLES:		HITS 2		WEEKS 2
FLORIBUNDA	Heat Recordings	42	21 Mar 98	1
LEARNING TO FLY	Devolution	54	6 Nov 99	1

MOTIV 8

UK

SINGLES:		HITS 3		WEEKS 10
ROCKIN' FOR MYSELF	Nuff Respect	67	17 Jul 93	1

Above hit: MOTIV 8 featuring Angie BROWN.

ROCKIN' FOR MYSELF [RM]	WEA	18	7 May 94	4
BREAK THE CHAIN	Eternal	31	21 Oct 95	2
SEARCHING FOR THE GOLDEN EYE	Eternal	40	23 Dec 95	3

Above hit: MOTIV 8 and Kym MAZELLE.

MOTLEY CRUE

US

SINGLES:		HITS 9		WEEKS 28
SMOKIN' IN THE BOYS ROOM	Elektra	71	24 Aug 85	2
SMOKIN' IN THE BOYS ROOM [RI] / HOME SWEET HOME	Elektra	51	8 Feb 86	3
GIRLS, GIRLS, GIRLS	Elektra	26	1 Aug 87	6
YOU'RE ALL I NEED / WILD SIDE	Elektra	23	16 Jan 88	4

Wild Side listed from 30 Jan 88 after single dropped to No. 26.

DR. FEELGOOD	Elektra	50	4 Nov 89	3
WITHOUT YOU	Elektra	39	12 May 90	3
PRIMAL SCREAM	Elektra	32	7 Sep 91	2
HOME SWEET HOME ('91 REMIX) [RM]	Elektra	37	11 Jan 92	2
HOOLIGAN'S HOLIDAY	Elektra	36	5 Mar 94	2
AFRAID	East West America	58	19 Jul 97	1

ALBUMS:		HITS 5		WEEKS 26
THEATRE OF PAIN	Elektra	36	13 Jul 85	3
GIRLS, GIRLS, GIRLS	Elektra	14	30 May 87	11
DR. FEELGOOD	Elektra	4	16 Sep 89	7
DECADE OF DECADENCE '81-'91	Elektra	20	19 Oct 91	3
MOTLEY CRUE	Elektra	17	26 Mar 94	2

MOTORHEAD

UK

SINGLES:		HITS 17		WEEKS 81
LOUIE LOUIE	Bronze	75	16 Sep 78	1

Originally recorded by Richard Berry and the Pharoahs in 1957.

LOUIE LOUIE [RE]	Bronze	68	30 Sep 78	1
OVERKILL	Bronze	39	10 Mar 79	4
OVERKILL [RE]	Bronze	57	14 Apr 79	3
NO CLASS	Bronze	61	30 Jun 79	4
BOMBER	Bronze	34	1 Dec 79	7
THE GOLDEN YEARS LIVE [EP]	Bronze	8	3 May 80	7

Lead track: Leaving Here.

ACE OF SPADES	Bronze	15	1 Nov 80	12
BEER DRINKERS AND HELL RAISERS	Big Beat	43	22 Nov 80	4
ST. VALENTINE'S DAY MASSACRE [EP]	Bronze	5	21 Feb 81	8

Lead track: Please Don't Touch.
Above hit: HEADGIRL (MOTORHEAD and GIRLSCHOOL).

MOTORHEAD	Bronze	6	11 Jul 81	7

Live recording from Hammersmith Odeon, 1980. Originally recorded by Hawkwind.

IRON FIST	Bronze	29	3 Apr 82	5
I GOT MINE	Bronze	46	21 May 83	2
SHINE	Bronze	59	30 Jul 83	2
KILLED BY DEATH	Bronze	51	1 Sep 84	2
DEAF FOREVER	GWR	67	5 Jul 86	1
THE ONE TO SING THE BLUES	Epic	45	5 Jan 91	3
'92 TOUR [EP]	Epic	63	14 Nov 92	1

Lead track: Hellraiser. From the film 'Hellraiser III'.

ACE OF SPADES [RM]	WGAF	23	11 Sep 93	5

Remixed by CCN.

BORN TO RAISE HELL	Fox	47	10 Dec 94	2

From the film 'Airheads'.
Above hit: MOTORHEAD with ICE-T and Whitfield CRANE.

ALBUMS:		HITS 15		WEEKS 102
MOTORHEAD	Chiswick	43	24 Sep 77	1
OVERKILL	Bronze	24	24 Mar 79	11

BOMBER	Bronze	12	27 Oct 79	13
ON PAROLE	United Artists	65	8 Dec 79	2
Originally recorded in 1976.				
ACE OF SPADES	Bronze	4	8 Nov 80	16
NO SLEEP 'TIL HAMMERSMITH	Bronze	1	27 Jun 81	21
Live recordings from London's Hammersmith Odeon, 1980.				
MOTORHEAD [RI]	Ace	76	10 Oct 81	4
IRONFIST	Bronze	6	17 Apr 82	9
WHAT'S WORDS WORTH	Big Beat	71	26 Feb 83	2
Live recordings from London's Roundhouse, 1975.				
ANOTHER PERFECT DAY	Bronze	20	4 Jun 83	4
NO REMORSE	Bronze	14	15 Sep 84	6
ORGASMATRON	GWR	21	9 Aug 86	4
ROCK 'N' ROLL	GWR	34	5 Sep 87	3
NO SLEEP AT ALL	GWR	79	15 Oct 88	1
1916	Epic	24	2 Feb 91	4
MARCH OR DIE	Epic	60	8 Aug 92	1

MOTORS   UK

SINGLES:	HITS 4			WEEKS 29
DANCING THE NIGHT AWAY	Virgin	42	24 Sep 77	4
AIRPORT	Virgin	4	10 Jun 78	13
FORGET ABOUT YOU	Virgin	13	19 Aug 78	9
LOVE AND LONELINESS	Virgin	58	12 Apr 80	3
ALBUMS:	**HITS 2**			**WEEKS 6**
THE MOTORS	Virgin	46	15 Oct 77	5
APPROVED BY THE MOTORS	Virgin	60	3 Jun 78	1

MOTOWN SPINNERS - See DETROIT SPINNERS

MOTT THE HOOPLE   UK

SINGLES:	HITS 7			WEEKS 55
ALL THE YOUNG DUDES	CBS	3	12 Aug 72	11
Written, produced, rhythm guitar and backing vocals by David Bowie.				
HONALOOCHIE BOOGIE	CBS	12	16 Jun 73	9
ALL THE WAY FROM MEMPHIS	CBS	10	8 Sep 73	8
ROLL AWAY THE STONE	CBS	8	24 Nov 73	12
THE GOLDEN AGE OF ROCK 'N' ROLL	CBS	16	30 Mar 74	7
FOXY, FOXY	CBS	33	22 Jun 74	5
SATURDAY GIG	CBS	41	2 Nov 74	3
ALBUMS:	**HITS 8**			**WEEKS 32**
MOTT THE HOOPLE	Island	66	2 May 70	1
MAD SHADOWS	Island	48	17 Oct 70	2
WILD LIFE	Island	44	17 Apr 71	2
ALL THE YOUNG DUDES	CBS	21	23 Sep 72	4
MOTT	CBS	7	11 Aug 73	15
THE HOOPLE	CBS	11	13 Apr 74	5
MOTT THE HOOPLE – LIVE	CBS	32	23 Nov 74	2
Live recordings from London's Hammersmith Odeon (Nov 73) and New York (May 74).				
DRIVE ON	CBS	45	4 Oct 75	1

Bob MOULD   US

ALBUMS:	HITS 2			WEEKS 2
BOB MOULD	Creation	52	11 May 96	1
THE LAST DOG AND PONY SHOW	Creation	58	5 Sep 98	1

MOUNT RUSHMORE presents the KNACK   UK

SINGLES:	HITS 1			WEEKS 1
YOU BETTER	Universal	53	3 Apr 99	1

MOUNTAIN   US/Canada

ALBUMS:	HITS 2			WEEKS 4
NANTUCKET SLEIGHRIDE	Island	43	5 Jun 71	1
THE ROAD GOES EVER ON	Island	21	8 Jul 72	3

Nana MOUSKOURI   Greece

(See also Vladimir Cosma.)

SINGLES:	HITS 1			WEEKS 11
ONLY LOVE	Carrere	2	11 Jan 86	11
Single was released on both the Philips and Carrere record labels. Sales were combined.				
ALBUMS:	**HITS 10**			**WEEKS 208**
OVER AND OVER	Fontana	10	7 Jun 69	105
THE EXQUISITE NANA MOUSKOURI	Fontana	10	4 Apr 70	25
RECITAL '70	Fontana	68	10 Oct 70	1

TURN ON THE SUN	*Fontana*	16	*3 Apr 71*	15
BRITISH CONCERT	*Fontana*	29	*29 Jul 72*	11
SONGS FROM HER TV SERIES	*Fontana*	29	*28 Apr 73*	11
SPOTLIGHT ON NANA MOUSKOURI	*Fontana*	38	*28 Sep 74*	6
PASSPORT	*Philips*	3	*10 Jul 76*	16
ALONE	*Philips*	19	*22 Feb 86*	10
THE MAGIC OF NANA MOUSKOURI	*Philips*	44	*8 Oct 88*	8

MOUSSE T. vs HOT 'N' JUICY   Germany/UK

SINGLES:	HITS 1			WEEKS 17
HORNY	*AM:PM*	2	*6 Jun 98*	17

MOUTH and McNEAL   Holland

SINGLES:	HITS 1			WEEKS 10
I SEE A STAR	*Decca*	8	*4 May 74*	10

The Dutch Eurovision entry for 1974; it came 3rd.

MOVE   UK

SINGLES:	HITS 10			WEEKS 110
NIGHT OF FEAR	*Deram*	2	*7 Jan 67*	10

Based on Tchaikovsky's 1812 Overture.

I CAN HEAR THE GRASS GROW	*Deram*	5	*8 Apr 67*	10
FLOWERS IN THE RAIN	*Regal Zonophone*	2	*9 Sep 67*	13

The first record played on BBC Radio 1 by DJ Tony Blackburn.

FIRE BRIGADE	*Regal Zonophone*	3	*10 Feb 68*	11
BLACKBERRY WAY	*Regal Zonophone*	1	*28 Dec 68*	12
CURLY	*Regal Zonophone*	12	*26 Jul 69*	12
BRONTOSAURUS	*Regal Zonophone*	7	*25 Apr 70*	10
TONIGHT	*Harvest*	11	*3 Jul 71*	10
CHINATOWN	*Harvest*	23	*23 Oct 71*	8
CALIFORNIA MAN	*Harvest*	7	*13 May 72*	14

ALBUMS:	HITS 1			WEEKS 9
MOVE	*Regal Zonophone*	15	*13 Apr 68*	9

MOVEMENT   US

SINGLES:	HITS 1			WEEKS 2
JUMP!	*Arista*	57	*24 Oct 92*	2

MOVEMENT. 98 featuring Carroll THOMPSON   UK

(See also Courtney Pine.)

SINGLES:	HITS 2			WEEKS 8
JOY AND HEARTBREAK	*Circa*	27	*19 May 90*	5
SUNRISE	*Circa*	58	*15 Sep 90*	3

MOVIN' MELODIES   Holland

(See also Artemesia; Ethics; Subliminal Cuts.)

SINGLES:	HITS 3			WEEKS 3
LA LUNA	*Effective*	64	*22 Oct 94*	1

Above hit: MOVIN' MELODIES PRODUCTION.

INDICA	*Hooj Choons*	62	*29 Jun 96*	1
ROLLERBLADE	*Movin' Melodies*	71	*26 Jul 97*	1

Alison MOYET   UK

SINGLES:	HITS 16			WEEKS 107
LOVE RESURRECTION	*CBS*	10	*23 Jun 84*	11
ALL CRIED OUT	*CBS*	8	*13 Oct 84*	11
INVISIBLE	*CBS*	21	*1 Dec 84*	10
THAT OLE DEVIL CALLED LOVE	*CBS*	2	*16 Mar 85*	10

Originally recorded by Billie Holiday.

IS THIS LOVE?	*CBS*	3	*29 Nov 86*	16
WEAK IN THE PRESENCE OF BEAUTY	*CBS*	6	*7 Mar 87*	10

Originally recorded by Floy Joy.

ORDINARY GIRL	*CBS*	43	*30 May 87*	4
LOVE LETTERS	*CBS*	4	*28 Nov 87*	10

Originally recorded by Dick Haymes.

IT WON'T BE LONG	*Columbia*	50	*6 Apr 91*	4
WISHING YOU WERE HERE	*Columbia*	72	*1 Jun 91*	1
THIS HOUSE	*Columbia*	40	*12 Oct 91*	5
FALLING	*Columbia*	42	*16 Oct 93*	3
WHISPERING YOUR NAME	*Columbia*	18	*12 Mar 94*	7

Originally recorded by Jules Shear in 1983.

GETTING INTO SOMETHING	*Columbia*	51	*28 May 94*	2
ODE TO BOY	*Columbia*	59	*22 Oct 94*	1
SOLID WOOD	*Columbia*	44	*26 Aug 95*	2

ALBUMS:		HITS 5			WEEKS 181
ALF	CBS		1	17 Nov 84	84
RAINDANCING	CBS		2	18 Apr 87	52
HOODOO	Columbia		11	4 May 91	6
ESSEX	Columbia		24	2 Apr 94	4
SINGLES	Columbia		1	3 Jun 95	35

Features 3 Yazoo tracks.

MOZAIC UK

SINGLES:		HITS 3			WEEKS 7
SING IT (THE HALLELUJAH SONG)	Perfecto		14	5 Aug 95	4
RAYS OF THE RISING SUN	Perfecto		32	10 Aug 96	2
MOVING UP MOVING ON	Perfecto		62	30 Nov 96	1

MSG – See Michael SCHENKER GROUP

M3 UK

SINGLES:		HITS 1			WEEKS 2
BAILAMOS	Inferno		40	30 Oct 99	2

MTUME US

SINGLES:		HITS 2			WEEKS 12
JUICY FRUIT	Epic		34	14 May 83	9
PRIME TIME	Epic		57	22 Sep 84	3
ALBUMS:		HITS 1			WEEKS 1
YOU, ME AND HE	Epic		85	6 Oct 84	1

MUD UK

SINGLES:		HITS 15			WEEKS 139
CRAZY	RAK		12	10 Mar 73	12
HYPNOSIS	RAK		16	23 Jun 73	13
DYNA-MITE	RAK		4	27 Oct 73	12
TIGER FEET	RAK		1	19 Jan 74	11
THE CAT CREPT IN	RAK		2	13 Apr 74	9
ROCKET	RAK		6	27 Jul 74	9
LONELY THIS CHRISTMAS	RAK		1	30 Nov 74	10
THE SECRETS THAT YOU KEEP	RAK		3	15 Feb 75	9
OH BOY	RAK		1	26 Apr 75	9
MOONSHINE SALLY	RAK		10	21 Jun 75	7
ONE NIGHT	RAK		32	2 Aug 75	4
L'L' LUCY	Private Stock		10	4 Oct 75	6
SHOW ME YOU'RE A WOMAN	Private Stock		8	29 Nov 75	8
SHAKE IT DOWN	Private Stock		12	15 May 76	8
LEAN ON ME	Private Stock		7	27 Nov 76	9
LONELY THIS CHRISTMAS [RI]	EMI		61	21 Dec 85	3
ALBUMS:		HITS 4			WEEKS 58
MUD ROCK	RAK		8	28 Sep 74	35
MUD ROCK VOLUME 2	RAK		6	26 Jul 75	12
MUD'S GREATEST HITS	RAK		25	1 Nov 75	6
USE YOUR IMAGINATION	Private Stock		33	27 Dec 75	5

MUDHONEY US

SINGLES:		HITS 2			WEEKS 2
LET IT SLIDE	Sub-Pop		60	17 Aug 91	1
SUCK YOU DRY	Reprise		65	24 Oct 92	1
ALBUMS:		HITS 3			WEEKS 5
EVERY GOOD BOY DESERVES FUDGE	Sub-Pop		34	31 Aug 91	2
PIECE OF CAKE	Reprise		39	17 Oct 92	2
MY BROTHER THE COW	Reprise		70	8 Apr 95	1

MUDLARKS UK

SINGLES:		HITS 3			WEEKS 19
LOLLIPOP	Columbia		2	3 May 58	9

Original by Ronald and Ruby reached No. 20 in the US the same year.

BOOK OF LOVE	Columbia		8	7 Jun 58	9

Originally recorded by the Monotones.
Above hit: MUDLARKS with the Ken JONES JIVE GROUP.

THE LOVE GAME	Columbia		30	28 Feb 59	1

Above hit: MUDLARKS with the Ken JONES GROUP.

Idris MUHAMMAD US

SINGLES:		HITS 1			WEEKS 3
COULD HEAVEN EVER BE LIKE THIS	Kudu		42	17 Sep 77	3

Nick MUIR – BEDROCK

MUKKAA
		UK		
SINGLES:	HITS 1		WEEKS 1	
BURUCHACCA	Limbo	74	27 Feb 93	1

Maria MULDAUR
		US		
SINGLES:	HITS 1		WEEKS 8	
MIDNIGHT AT THE OASIS	Reprise	21	29 Jun 74	8

Arthur MULLARD – See Hylda BAKER and Arthur MULLARD

Larry MULLEN – See Adam CLAYTON and Larry MULLEN

Werner MULLER and the RIAS DANCE ORCHESTRA – See Caterina VALENTE – Werner MULLER and the RIAS DANCE ORCHESTRA

Gerry MULLIGAN and Ben WEBSTER
		US		
ALBUMS:	HITS 1		WEEKS 1	
GERRY MULLIGAN MEETS BEN WEBSTER	His Master's Voice	15	24 Sep 60	1

Shawn MULLINS
		US		
SINGLES:	HITS 2		WEEKS 11	
LULLABY	Columbia	9	6 Mar 99	10
Song is a tale about growing up privileged but spiritually empty in Hollywood.				
WHAT IS LIFE	Columbia	62	2 Oct 99	1
From the film 'Big Daddy'. Originally recorded by George Harrison as the B-side to My Sweet Lord.				
ALBUMS:	HITS 1		WEEKS 1	
SOUL'S CORE	Columbia	60	20 Mar 99	1

MULU
		UK		
SINGLES:	HITS 1		WEEKS 1	
PUSSYCAT	Dedicated	50	2 Aug 97	1

Coati MUNDI – See Kid CREOLE and the COCONUTS

MUNDY
		Ireland		
SINGLES:	HITS 2		WEEKS 2	
TO YOU I BESTOW	Epic	60	3 Aug 96	1
LIFE'S A CINCH	Epic	75	5 Oct 96	1

MUNGO JERRY
		UK		
SINGLES:	HITS 9		WEEKS 88	
IN THE SUMMERTIME	Dawn	1	6 Jun 70	20
BABY JUMP	Dawn	32	6 Feb 71	1
BABY JUMP [RE]	Dawn	1	20 Feb 71	12
LADY ROSE	Dawn	5	29 May 71	12
YOU DON'T HAVE TO BE IN THE ARMY TO FIGHT IN THE WAR	Dawn	13	18 Sep 71	8
OPEN UP	Dawn	21	22 Apr 72	8
ALRIGHT, ALRIGHT, ALRIGHT	Dawn	3	7 Jul 73	12
Originally recorded by Jacques DuTronc at Et Moi Et Moi Et Moi.				
WILD LOVE	Dawn	32	10 Nov 73	5
LONG LEGGED WOMAN DRESSED IN BLACK	Dawn	13	6 Apr 74	9
SUPPORT THE TOON - IT'S YOUR DUTY [EP]	Saraja	57	29 May 99	1
Lead track: The Blaydon Races ('99). Supporters single of Newcastle FC, who reached the FA Cup Final that year.				
Above hit: MUNGO JERRY and the TOON TRAVELLERS.				
ALBUMS:	HITS 2		WEEKS 14	
MUNGO JERRY	Dawn	13	8 Aug 70	6
ELECTRONICALLY TESTED	Dawn	14	10 Apr 71	8

MUNICH MACHINE
		Germany		
SINGLES:	HITS 2		WEEKS 9	
GET ON THE FUNK TRAIN	Oasis	41	10 Dec 77	5
A WHITER SHADE OF PALE	Oasis	42	4 Nov 78	4
Above hit: MUNICH MACHINE Introducing Chris BENNETT.				

MUNICH PHILHARMONIC ORCHESTRA – See Michael NYMAN

MUNROS featuring David METHREN
		UK		
ALBUMS:	HITS 1		WEEKS 3	
THE LONE PIPER	Virgin	46	27 Jun 98	3
Compilation of traditional Scottish melodies.				

David MUNROW – See EARLY MUSIC CONSORT, directed by David MUNROW

MUPPETS
US

SINGLES:		HITS 2		WEEKS 15
HALFWAY DOWN THE STAIRS	Pye	7	28 May 77	8
Above hit: MUPPETS Sung by Kermit's Nephew ROBIN.				
The voice of Robin was Jerry Nelson.				
THE MUPPET SHOW MUSIC HALL [EP]	Pye	19	17 Dec 77	7
Lead track: Don't Dilly Dally On The Way. (Though some weeks it was listed as an AA with Waiting At The Church).				

ALBUMS:		HITS 2		WEEKS 45
THE MUPPET SHOW	Pye	1	11 Jun 77	35
THE MUPPET SHOW VOLUME 2	Pye	16	25 Feb 78	10

Lydia MURDOCK
US

SINGLES:		HITS 1		WEEKS 9
SUPERSTAR	Korova	14	24 Sep 83	9
Based on Michael Jackson's Billie Jean.				

Shirley MURDOCK
US

SINGLES:		HITS 1		WEEKS 2
TRUTH OR DARE	Elektra	60	12 Apr 86	2

Eddie MURPHY featuring Shabba RANKS
US/Jamaica

(See also Shabba Ranks.)

SINGLES:		HITS 1		WEEKS 1
I WAS A KING	Motown	64	6 Mar 93	1

Noel MURPHY
Ireland

SINGLES:		HITS 1		WEEKS 4
MURPHY AND THE BRICKS	Murphy's	57	27 Jun 87	4

Peter MURPHY
UK

ALBUMS:		HITS 1		WEEKS 1
SHOULD THE WORLD FAIL TO FALL APART	Beggars Banquet	82	26 Jul 86	1

Walter MURPHY and the BIG APPLE BAND
US

SINGLES:		HITS 1		WEEKS 9
A FIFTH OF BEETHOVEN	Private Stock	28	10 Jul 76	9

Anne MURRAY
Canada

SINGLES:		HITS 5		WEEKS 40
SNOWBIRD	Capitol	23	24 Oct 70	17
DESTINY	Capitol	41	21 Oct 72	4
YOU NEEDED ME	Capitol	22	9 Dec 78	14
I JUST FALL IN LOVE AGAIN	Capitol	58	21 Apr 79	2
DAYDREAM BELIEVER	Capitol	61	19 Apr 80	3

ALBUMS:		HITS 1		WEEKS 10
THE VERY BEST OF ANNE MURRAY	Capitol	14	3 Oct 81	10

Keith MURRAY
US

SINGLES:		HITS 4		WEEKS 10
THE RHYME	Jive	59	2 Nov 96	1
SHORTY (YOU KEEP PLAYIN' WITH MY MIND)	Jive	22	27 Jun 98	3
Above hit: IMAJIN featuring Keith MURRAY.				
HOME ALONE	Jive	17	14 Nov 98	5
Above hit: R. KELLY featuring Keith MURRAY.				
INCREDIBLE	Jive	52	5 Dec 98	1
Samples James Brown's Sportin' Life.				
Above hit: Keith MURRAY featuring LL COOL J.				

Pauline MURRAY and the INVISIBLE GIRLS
UK

SINGLES:		HITS 1		WEEKS 2
DREAM SEQUENCE (ONE)	Illusive	67	2 Aug 80	2

ALBUMS:		HITS 1		WEEKS 4
PAULINE MURRAY AND THE INVISIBLE GIRLS	Elusive	25	11 Oct 80	4

Ruby MURRAY
UK

SINGLES:		HITS 9		WEEKS 114
HEARTBEAT	Columbia	3	4 Dec 54	16
SOFTLY SOFTLY	Columbia	1	29 Jan 55	22
HAPPY DAYS AND LONELY NIGHTS	Columbia	6	5 Feb 55	8

LET ME GO LOVER	Columbia	5	5 Mar 55	7

Above 2 entries were separate sides of the same release, each had its own chart run.
Above 4: Ruby MURRAY with Ray MARTIN and his Orchestra.

IF ANYONE FINDS THIS, I LOVE YOU	Columbia	4	19 Mar 55	11

Above hit: Ruby MURRAY and Anne WARREN with Ray MARTIN and his Orchestra.

EVERMORE	Columbia	3	2 Jul 55	17
SOFTLY SOFTLY [RE]	Columbia	20	9 Jul 55	1
I'LL COME WHEN YOU CALL	Columbia	6	15 Oct 55	7
YOU ARE MY FIRST LOVE	Columbia	16	1 Sep 56	4

From the film 'It's Great To Be Young'.

YOU ARE MY FIRST LOVE [RE]	Columbia	21	6 Oct 56	1

Above 5: Ruby MURRAY with Ray MARTIN and his Orchestra.

REAL LOVE	Columbia	18	13 Dec 58	6
GOODBYE JIMMY, GOODBYE	Columbia	10	6 Jun 59	13

Above 2: Ruby MURRAY with Norrie PARAMOR and his Orchestra and Chorus.

GOODBYE JIMMY, GOODBYE [RE]	Columbia	26	10 Oct 59	1

Junior MURVIN
Jamaica

SINGLES:	HITS 1			WEEKS 9
POLICE AND THIEVES	Island	23	3 May 80	9

MUSCLE SHOALS HORNS - See Elton JOHN

MUSE
UK

SINGLES:	HITS 3			WEEKS 4
UNO	Mushroom	73	26 Jun 99	1
CAVE	Mushroom	52	18 Sep 99	1
MUSCLE MUSEUM	Mushroom	43	4 Dec 99	2
ALBUMS:	HITS 1			WEEKS 1
SHOWBIZ	Mushroom	69	16 Oct 99	1

MUSIC and MYSTERY featuring Gwen McCRAE
UK/US

(See also Gwen McCrae.)

SINGLES:	HITS 1			WEEKS 3
ALL THIS LOVE I'M GIVING	KTDA	36	13 Feb 93	3

MUSIC RELIEF '94
UK

SINGLES:	HITS 1			WEEKS 1
WHAT'S GOING ON	Jive	70	5 Nov 94	1

Originally recorded by Marvin Gaye.
Charity record with proceeds to aid Rwanda.

MUSIC STUDENTS - See Ian DURY and the BLOCKHEADS

MUSICAL YOUTH
UK

(See also Donna Summer.)

SINGLES:	HITS 7			WEEKS 55
PASS THE DUTCHIE	MCA	1	25 Sep 82	12

Originally recorded by the Mighty Diamonds as Pass The Kutchie.

YOUTH OF TODAY	MCA	13	20 Nov 82	9
PASS THE DUTCHIE [RE]	MCA	65	8 Jan 83	1
NEVER GONNA GIVE YOU UP	MCA	6	12 Feb 83	10
HEARTBREAKER	MCA	44	16 Apr 83	3
TELL ME WHY	MCA	33	9 Jul 83	6
007	MCA	26	22 Oct 83	6
SIXTEEN	MCA	23	14 Jan 84	8
ALBUMS:	HITS 1			WEEKS 22
THE YOUTH OF TODAY	MCA	24	4 Dec 82	22

MUSIQUE
US

SINGLES:	HITS 1			WEEKS 12
IN THE BUSH	CBS	16	18 Nov 78	12

MUTANT DISCO - See PHATS and SMALL

MUTTON BIRDS
New Zealand

ALBUMS:	HITS 1			WEEKS 1
ENVY OF ANGELS	Virgin	64	12 Jul 97	1

MXM
Italy

SINGLES:	HITS 1			WEEKS 1
NOTHING COMPARES 2 U	London	68	2 Jun 90	1

MY BLOODY VALENTINE
UK

SINGLES:	HITS 2			WEEKS 5
SOON	Creation	41	5 May 90	3
TO HERE KNOWS WHEN	Creation	29	16 Feb 91	2
ALBUMS:	HITS 1			WEEKS 2
LOVELESS	Creation	24	23 Nov 91	2

MY LIFE STORY
UK

(See also Marc Almond; PJ Proby.)

SINGLES:	HITS 7			WEEKS 11
12 REASONS WHY I LOVE HER	Parlophone	32	17 Aug 96	2
SPARKLE	Parlophone	34	9 Nov 96	2
THE KING OF KISSINGDOM	Parlophone	35	1 Mar 97	1
STRUMPET	Parlophone	27	17 May 97	2
DUCHESS	Parlophone	39	23 Aug 97	1
IT'S A GIRL THING	It Records	37	19 Jun 99	2
EMPIRE LINE	It Records	58	30 Oct 99	1
ALBUMS:	HITS 1			WEEKS 1
THE GOLDEN MILE	Parlophone	36	22 Mar 97	1

MYA – See BLACKSTREET; PRAS

Tim MYCROFT – See SOUNDS NICE featuring Tim MYCROFT On Organ

Alicia MYERS
US

SINGLES:	HITS 1			WEEKS 3
YOU GET THE BEST FROM ME (SAY, SAY, SAY)	MCA	58	1 Sep 84	3

Billie MYERS
UK

SINGLES:	HITS 2			WEEKS 12
KISS THE RAIN	Universal	4	11 Apr 98	9
TELL ME	Universal	28	25 Jul 98	3
ALBUMS:	HITS 1			WEEKS 9
GROWING, PAINS	Universal	19	2 May 98	9

Richard MYHILL
UK

SINGLES:	HITS 1			WEEKS 9
IT TAKES TWO TO TANGO	Mercury	17	1 Apr 78	9

Alannah MYLES
Canada

SINGLES:	HITS 2			WEEKS 17
BLACK VELVET	Atlantic	2	17 Mar 90	15
LOVE IS	Atlantic	61	16 Jun 90	2
ALBUMS:	HITS 1			WEEKS 21
ALANNAH MYLES	Atlantic	3	28 Apr 90	21

Marie MYRIAM
France

SINGLES:	HITS 1			WEEKS 4
L'OUISEAU ET L'ENFANT	Polydor	42	28 May 77	4

Eurovision Song Contest winner in 1977.

MYRON
US

SINGLES:	HITS 1			WEEKS 1
WE CAN GET DOWN	Island Black Music	74	22 Nov 97	1

MYSTERY GIRL – See Michael JACKSON

MYSTI – see CAMOUFLAGE featuring 'MYSTI'

MYSTIC MERLIN
US

SINGLES:	HITS 1			WEEKS 9
JUST CAN'T GIVE YOU UP	Capitol	20	26 Apr 80	9

MYSTICA
Israel

SINGLES:	HITS 2			WEEKS 2
EVER REST	Perfecto Fluoro	62	24 Jan 98	1
AFRICAN HORIZON	Perfecto Fluoro	59	9 May 98	1

MYTOWN
Ireland

SINGLES:	HITS 1			WEEKS 2
PARTY ALL NIGHT	Universal	22	13 Mar 99	2

N

N-JOI
UK

SINGLES:	HITS 6			WEEKS 28
ANTHEM	Deconstruction	45	27 Oct 90	5
ADRENALIN [EP]	Deconstruction	23	2 Mar 91	5
Lead track: Adrenalin.				
ANTHEM [RI]	Deconstruction	8	6 Apr 91	8
LIVE IN MANCHESTER	Deconstruction	12	22 Feb 92	5
This was the track title which consisted of 2 parts.				
THE DRUMSTRUCK [EP]	Deconstruction	33	24 Jul 93	3
Lead track: The Void.				
PAPILLON	Deconstruction	70	17 Dec 94	1
BAD THINGS	Deconstruction	57	8 Jul 95	1
Above hit: NJOI.				

N.T. GANG
Germany

SINGLES:	HITS 1			WEEKS 1
WAM BAM	Cooltempo	71	2 Apr 88	1

N-TRANCE
UK

SINGLES:	HITS 9			WEEKS 61
SET YOU FREE	All Around The World	39	7 May 94	4
Original release reached No.81 in 1993. Features rap by T-1K.				
Above hit: N-TRANCE featuring Kelly LLORENNA.				
TURN UP THE POWER	All Around The World	23	22 Oct 94	3
Features vocals by Rachel McFarlane.				
SET YOU FREE [RM]	All Around The World	2	14 Jan 95	15
This was the original version although it was not the first track on the 1994 chart entry. Features uncredited vocals by Kelly Llorenna.				
STAYIN' ALIVE	All Around The World	2	16 Sep 95	11
Above hit: N-TRANCE featuring Ricardo DA FORCE.				
ELECTRONIC PLEASURE	All Around The World	11	24 Feb 96	4
Rap by Ricardo Da Force. Vocals by Gillian Wisdom.				
D.I.S.C.O.	All Around The World	11	5 Apr 97	6
THE MIND OF THE MACHINE	All Around The World	15	23 Aug 97	4
Features a vocal from actor/director Steven Berkoff.				
DA YA THINK I'M SEXY?	All Around The World	7	1 Nov 97	10
Rod Stewart's vocals are sampled from his hit of the same name.				
Above hit: N-TRANCE featuring Rod STEWART.				
PARADISE CITY	All Around The World	28	12 Sep 98	3
TEARS IN THE RAIN	All Around The World	53	19 Dec 98	1

N-TYCE
UK

SINGLES:	HITS 4			WEEKS 15
HEY DJ! (PLAY THAT SONG)	Telstar	20	5 Jul 97	2
WE COME TO PARTY	Telstar	12	13 Sep 97	4
TELEFUNKIN'	Telstar	16	28 Feb 98	5
BOOM BOOM	Telstar	18	6 Jun 98	4
Rap is by Dionne Warwick's son Damon Elliott.				
ALBUMS:	**HITS 1**			**WEEKS 1**
ALL DAY EVERY DAY	Telstar	44	20 Jun 98	1

N.W.A.
US

SINGLES:	HITS 4			WEEKS 15
EXPRESS YOURSELF	Fourth & Broadway	50	9 Sep 89	4
Originally recorded by Charles Wright and the Watts 103rd Street Band.				
EXPRESS YOURSELF [RE]	Fourth & Broadway	26	26 May 90	5
GANGSTA, GANGSTA	Fourth & Broadway	70	1 Sep 90	1
100 MILES AND RUNNIN'	Fourth & Broadway	38	10 Nov 90	3
ALWAYZ INTO SOMETHIN'	Fourth & Broadway	60	23 Nov 91	2
ALBUMS:	**HITS 3**			**WEEKS 7**
STRAIGHT OUTTA COMPTON	Fourth & Broadway	41	30 Sep 89	4
EFIL4ZAGGIN	Fourth & Broadway	25	15 Jun 91	2
GREATEST HITS	Priority	56	31 Aug 96	1

N.Y.C.C.
Germany

SINGLES:	HITS 2			WEEKS 6
FIGHT FOR YOUR RIGHT (TO PARTY)	Control	14	30 May 98	5
CAN YOU FEEL IT (ROCK DA HOUSE)	Control	68	19 Sep 98	1

Jimmy NAIL | | | | UK

SINGLES:		HITS 10			WEEKS 73
LOVE DON'T LIVE HERE ANYMORE	Virgin	3	27 Apr 85	11
Produced by Queen's Roger Taylor.				
AIN'T NO DOUBT	East West	1	11 Jul 92	12
Co-written by Charlie Dore.				
LAURA	East West	58	3 Oct 92	2
CROCODILE SHOES	East West	4	26 Nov 94	13
COWBOY DREAMS	East West	13	11 Feb 95	7
CROCODILE SHOES [RE-1ST]	East West	68	11 Mar 95	3
CROCODILE SHOES [RE-2ND]	East West	56	8 Apr 95	4
CALLING OUT YOUR NAME	East West	65	6 May 95	1
Above 3 featured in the BBC1 TV series 'Crocodile Shoes'.				
BIG RIVER	East West	18	28 Oct 95	5
Features Mark Knopfler from Dire Straits on guitar.				
LOVE	East West	33	23 Dec 95	4
BIG RIVER '96 [RM]	East West	72	3 Feb 96	2
Remixed by Jon Kelly.				
COUNTRY BOY	East West	25	16 Nov 96	8
From the BBC1 TV series 'Crocodile Shoes II'.				
THE FLAME STILL BURNS	London	47	21 Nov 98	1
From the film 'Still Crazy'.				
Above hit: Jimmy NAIL with STRANGE FRUIT.				
ALBUMS:		HITS 5			WEEKS 85
GROWING UP IN PUBLIC	East West	2	8 Aug 92	12
CROCODILE SHOES	East West	2	3 Dec 94	31
Music from the BBC1 TV series.				
BIG RIVER	East West	8	18 Nov 95	15
CROCODILE SHOES II	East West	10	30 Nov 96	13
Music from the BBC1 TV series.				
THE NAIL FILE – THE BEST OF JIMMY NAIL	East West	8	18 Oct 97	14

NAILBOMB | | | | US/Brazil

ALBUMS:		HITS 1			WEEKS 1
POINT BLANK	Roadrunner	62	2 Apr 94	1

NAKATOMI | | | | UK

SINGLES:		HITS 1			WEEKS 2
CHILDREN OF THE NIGHT (QFT REMIXES)	Peach	47	7 Feb 98	2
Original release reached No. 149 in 1996.				

NAKED EYES | | | | UK

SINGLES:		HITS 1			WEEKS 3
ALWAYS SOMETHING THERE TO REMIND ME	EMI	59	23 Jul 83	3

NALIN and KANE | | | | Germany

SINGLES:		HITS 2			WEEKS 7
BEACHBALL	ffrr	48	1 Nov 97	1
Vocals by Shondell Mims and Andrea Kanta.				
PLANET VIOLET	Logic	51	28 Mar 98	1
Above hit: NALIN I.N.C.				
BEACHBALL [RM]	ffrr	17	3 Oct 98	5
Remixed by Tall Paul.				

NAPALM DEATH | | | | UK

ALBUMS:		HITS 3			WEEKS 3
HARMONY OF CORRUPTION	Earache	67	15 Sep 90	1
UTOPIA BANISHED	Earache	58	30 May 92	1
DIATRIBES	Earache	74	3 Feb 96	1

NAPOLEON XIV | | | | US

SINGLES:		HITS 1			WEEKS 10
THEY'RE COMING TO TAKE ME AWAY, HA-HAAA!	Warner Brothers	4	6 Aug 66	10

NARADA – See Narada Michael WALDEN

NAS | | | | US

(See also Nas Escobar, Foxy Brown, Az and Nature present the Firm featuring Dawn Robinson.)

SINGLES:		HITS 6			WEEKS 26
IT AIN'T HARD TO TELL	Columbia	64	28 May 94	1
Samples Michael Jackson;'s Human Nature and N.T by Kool and the Gang.				
IF I RULED THE WORLD	Columbia	12	17 Aug 96	7
Features vocals from Lauryn Hill.				

STREET DREAMS	Columbia	12	25 Jan 97	4
Samples Sweet Dreams by the Eurythmics.				
HEAD OVER HEELS	Epic	18	14 Jun 97	3
Samples MC Shan's The Bridge.				
Above hit: ALLURE featuring NAS.				
HATE ME NOW	Columbia	14	29 May 99	6
Above hit: NAS (featuring PUFF DADDY).				
DID YOU EVER THINK	Jive	20	31 Jul 99	5
Samples Curtis Mayfield's Right On For The Darkness.				
Above hit: R. KELLY featuring NAS.				
ALBUMS:	**HITS 2**		**WEEKS 10**	
IT WAS WRITTEN	Columbia	38	13 Jul 96	6
I AM . . .	Columbia	31	17 Apr 99	4

Graham NASH   UK

(See also Crosby, Stills, Nash and Young; Graham Nash and David Crosby.)

ALBUMS:	**HITS 1**		**WEEKS 8**	
SONGS FOR BEGINNERS	Atlantic	13	26 Jun 71	8

Graham NASH and David CROSBY   UK

(See also David Crosby; Crosby, Stills, Nash and Young; Graham Nash.)

ALBUMS:	**HITS 1**		**WEEKS 5**	
GRAHAM NASH AND DAVID CROSBY	Atlantic	13	13 May 72	5

Johnny NASH   US

SINGLES:	**HITS 10**		**WEEKS 106**	
HOLD ME TIGHT	Regal Zonophone	5	10 Aug 68	16
YOU GOT SOUL	Major Minor	6	11 Jan 69	12
Originally recorded by Bill Johnson.				
CUPID	Major Minor	6	5 Apr 69	11
CUPID [RE]	Major Minor	50	28 Jun 69	1
STIR IT UP	CBS	13	1 Apr 72	12
Originally recorded by Bob Marley & the Wailers.				
I CAN SEE CLEARLY NOW	CBS	5	24 Jun 72	15
Backing vocals by Dawn Penn and the Wailers.				
THERE ARE MORE QUESTIONS THAN ANSWERS	CBS	9	7 Oct 72	9
TEARS ON MY PILLOW (I CAN'T TAKE IT)	CBS	1	14 Jun 75	11
LET'S BE FRIENDS	CBS	42	11 Oct 75	3
(WHAT A) WONDERFUL WORLD	Epic	25	12 Jun 76	7
ROCK ME BABY	2000 AD	47	9 Nov 85	4
I CAN SEE CLEARLY NOW [RM]	Epic	54	15 Apr 89	5
ALBUMS:	**HITS 2**		**WEEKS 17**	
I CAN SEE CLEARLY NOW	CBS	39	5 Aug 72	6
JOHNNY NASH COLLECTION	Epic	18	10 Dec 77	11

NASH THE SLASH   Canada

ALBUMS:	**HITS 1**		**WEEKS 1**	
CHILDREN OF THE NIGHT	DinDisc	61	21 Feb 81	1

NASHVILLE TEENS   UK

SINGLES:	**HITS 5**		**WEEKS 37**	
TOBACCO ROAD	Decca	6	11 Jul 64	13
GOOGLE EYE	Decca	10	24 Oct 64	11
Above 2 originally recorded by John D. Loudermilk.				
FIND MY WAY BACK HOME	Decca	34	6 Mar 65	6
THIS LITTLE BIRD	Decca	38	22 May 65	4
Originally recorded by John D.Loudermilk.				
THE HARD WAY	Decca	45	5 Feb 66	2
THE HARD WAY [RE]	Decca	48	26 Feb 66	1

NATASHA   UK

SINGLES:	**HITS 2**		**WEEKS 16**	
IKO IKO	Towerbell	10	5 Jun 82	11
THE BOOM BOOM ROOM	Towerbell	44	4 Sep 82	5
ALBUMS:	**HITS 1**		**WEEKS 3**	
CAPTURED	Towerbell	53	9 Oct 82	3

Ultra NATE   US

(See also B-Crew featuring Barbara Tucker, Ultra Nate, Dajae, Mone; Stars On 54: Ultra Nate, Amber, Jocelyn Enriquez; System 7.)

SINGLES:	**HITS 6**		**WEEKS 36**	
IT'S OVER NOW	Eternal	62	9 Dec 89	3
IS IT LOVE?	Eternal	71	23 Feb 91	1
Above hit: BASEMENT BOYS present Ultra NATE.				

SHOW ME	Warner Brothers	62	29 Jan 94	1
FREE	AM:PM	4	14 Jun 97	17
FREE [RI]	AM:PM	33	24 Jan 98	2

CD credits Free (The Mixes), although the first track is the original radio edit.

FOUND A CURE	AM:PM	6	18 Apr 98	7
NEW KIND OF MEDICINE	AM:PM	14	25 Jul 98	5

ALBUMS:	HITS 1			WEEKS 4
SITUATION:CRITICAL	AM:PM	17	9 May 98	4

NATIONAL BRASS BAND
UK

ALBUMS:	HITS 1			WEEKS 10
GOLDEN MEMORIES	K-Tel	15	10 May 80	10

NATIONAL PHILHARMONIC ORCHESTRA - See James GALWAY; James GALWAY and Henry MANCINI with the NATIONAL PHILHARMONIC ORCHESTRA; LONDON PHILHARMONIC CHOIR; Henri MANCINI and his Orchestra

NATURAL BORN CHILLERS
UK

SINGLES:	HITS 1			WEEKS 3
ROCK THE FUNKY BEATS	East West Dance	30	1 Nov 97	3

NATURAL BORN GROOVES
Belgium

SINGLES:	HITS 2			WEEKS 3
FORERUNNER	XL Recordings	64	2 Nov 96	1
GROOVEBIRD	Positiva	21	19 Apr 97	2

NATURAL LIFE
UK

SINGLES:	HITS 1			WEEKS 3
NATURAL LIFE	Tribe	47	7 Mar 92	3

NATURAL SELECTION
US

SINGLES:	HITS 1			WEEKS 2
DO ANYTHING	East West America	69	9 Nov 91	2

NATURALS
UK

SINGLES:	HITS 1			WEEKS 9
I SHOULD HAVE KNOWN BETTER	Parlophone	24	22 Aug 64	9

From the film 'A Hard Day's Night'. Originally recorded by the Beatles.

NATURE - See Nas ESCOBAR, Foxy BROWN, AZ and NATURE Present The FIRM featuring Dawn ROBINSON

David NAUGHTON
US

SINGLES:	HITS 1			WEEKS 6
MAKIN' IT	RSO	44	25 Aug 79	6

From the TV series of the same name.

NAUGHTY BY NATURE
US

SINGLES:	HITS 5			WEEKS 17
O.P.P.	Big Life	73	9 Nov 91	1

Samples Jackson Five's ABC.

O.P.P. [RI]	Big Life	35	20 Jun 92	3
HIP HOP HOORAY	Big Life	22	30 Jan 93	3
IT'S ON	Big Life	48	19 Jun 93	2
HIP HOP HOORAY [RI]	Big Life	20	27 Nov 93	4

Sleeve gives title as an EP: The Essential EP.

FEEL ME FLOW	Big Life	23	29 Apr 95	3
JAMBOREE	Arista	51	11 Sep 99	1

Samples Benny Golson's I'm Always Dancin' To The Music.
Above hit: NAUGHTY BY NATURE (featuring ZHANE).

ALBUMS:	HITS 2			WEEKS 5
19 NAUGHTY III	Big Life	40	6 Mar 93	2
POVERTY'S PARADISE	Big Life	20	27 May 95	3

NAVIGATOR - See FREESTYLERS

Maria NAYLER
UK

SINGLES:	HITS 4			WEEKS 25
BE AS ONE	Deconstruction	17	9 Mar 96	4

Above hit: SASHA and MARIA.

ONE & ONE	Deconstruction	3	16 Nov 96	17

Above hit: Robert MILES featuring Maria NAYLER.

NAKED AND SACRED	Deconstruction	32	7 Mar 98	3
WILL YOU BE WITH ME / LOVE IS THE GOD	Deconstruction	65	5 Sep 98	1

NAZARETH
UK

SINGLES:		HITS 11			WEEKS 75
BROKEN DOWN ANGEL	*Mooncrest*		9	*5 May 73*	11
BAD BAD BOY	*Mooncrest*		10	*21 Jul 73*	9
THIS FLIGHT TONIGHT	*Mooncrest*		11	*13 Oct 73*	13
Originally recorded by Joni Mitchell.					
SHANGHAI'D IN SHANGHAI	*Mooncrest*		41	*23 Mar 74*	4
MY WHITE BICYCLE	*Mooncrest*		14	*14 Jun 75*	8
Originally recorded by Tomorrow.					
HOLY ROLLER	*Mountain*		36	*15 Nov 75*	4
HOT TRACKS [EP]	*Mountain*		15	*24 Sep 77*	11
Lead track: Love Hurts.					
GONE DEAD TRAIN	*Mountain*		49	*18 Feb 78*	2
PLACE IN YOUR HEART	*Mountain*		70	*13 May 78*	1
PLACE IN YOUR HEART [RE]	*Mountain*		74	*27 May 78*	1
MAY THE SUNSHINE	*Mountain*		22	*27 Jan 79*	8
STAR	*Mountain*		54	*28 Jul 79*	3
ALBUMS:		**HITS 7**			**WEEKS 51**
RAZAMANAZ	*Mooncrest*		11	*26 May 73*	25
LOUD 'N' PROUD	*Mooncrest*		10	*24 Nov 73*	7
RAMPANT	*Mooncrest*		13	*18 May 74*	3
GREATEST HITS	*Mountain*		54	*13 Dec 75*	1
NO MEAN CITY	*Mountain*		34	*3 Feb 79*	9
THE FOOL CIRCLE	*NEMS*		60	*28 Feb 81*	3
NAZARETH LIVE	*NEMS*		78	*3 Oct 81*	3

NAZLYN – See ADVENTURES OF STEVIE V; M-BEAT

Me'shell NDEGEOCELLO
US

SINGLES:		HITS 3			WEEKS 5
IF THAT'S YOUR BOYFRIEND (HE WASN'T LAST NIGHT)	*Maverick*		74	*12 Feb 94*	1
WILD NIGHT	*Mercury*		34	*3 Sep 94*	3
Above hit: John MELLENCAMP with Me'shell NDEGEOCELLO.					
NEVER MISS THE WATER	*Reprise*		59	*1 Mar 97*	1
Above hit: Chaka KHAN featuring Me'shell NDEGEOCELLO.					

Youssou N'DOUR
Senegal

SINGLES:		HITS 4			WEEKS 35
SHAKIN' THE TREE	*Virgin*		61	*3 Jun 89*	3
Above hit: Youssou N'DOUR and Peter GABRIEL.					
SHAKING THE TREE [RI]	*Virgin*		57	*22 Dec 90*	4
[AA] listed with re-issue of Solisbury Hill by Peter Gabriel.					
Above hit: Peter GABRIEL and Youssou N'DOUR.					
7 SECONDS	*Columbia*		3	*25 Jun 94*	21
Above hit: Youssou N'DOUR (featuring Neneh CHERRY).					
7 SECONDS [RE]	*Columbia*		54	*24 Dec 94*	4
UNDECIDED	*Columbia*		53	*14 Jan 95*	2
HOW COME	*Interscope*		52	*10 Oct 98*	1
From the film 'Bulworth'.					
Above hit: Youssou N'DOUR and CANIBUS.					

NEARLY GOD
UK

SINGLES:		HITS 1			WEEKS 2
POEMS	*Durban Poison*		28	*20 Apr 96*	2
ALBUMS:		**HITS 1**			**WEEKS 4**
NEARLY GOD – POEMS	*Durban Poison*		10	*4 May 96*	4

Martin NEARY – See Sarah BRIGHTMAN; WESTMINSTER ABBEY CHOIR/conductor: Martin NEARY

Terry NEASON
UK

SINGLES:		HITS 1			WEEKS 1
LIFEBOAT (THEME FROM THE BBC TV SERIES 'THE LIFEBOAT')	*WEA*		72	*25 Jun 94*	1

NEBULA II
UK

SINGLES:		HITS 2			WEEKS 3
SEANCE / ATHEAMA	*Reinforced*		55	*1 Feb 92*	2
FLATLINERS	*J4M*		54	*16 May 92*	1

NED'S ATOMIC DUSTBIN
UK

SINGLES:		HITS 8			WEEKS 24
KILL YOUR TELEVISION	*Chapter 22*		53	*14 Jul 90*	2
UNTIL YOU FIND OUT	*Chapter 22*		51	*27 Oct 90*	2
HAPPY	*Furtive*		16	*9 Mar 91*	4
TRUST	*Furtive*		21	*21 Sep 91*	4
NOT SLEEPING AROUND	*Furtive*		19	*10 Oct 92*	3

INTACT	*Furtive*	36	*5 Dec 92*	6
ALL I ASK OF MYSELF IS THAT I HOLD TOGETHER	*Sony S2*	33	*25 Mar 95*	2
STUCK	*Furtive*	64	*15 Jul 95*	1
ALBUMS:	**HITS 3**			**WEEKS 8**
BITE	*Rough Trade*	72	*9 Feb 91*	1
German import.				
GOD FODDER	*Furtive*	4	*13 Apr 91*	5
ARE YOU NORMAL?	*Furtive*	13	*31 Oct 92*	2

Joey NEGRO   UK

(See also Li Kwan.)

SINGLES:	**HITS 4**			**WEEKS 10**
REACHIN'	*Republic*	70	*18 Mar 89*	1
Above hit: PHASE II.				
DO WHAT YOU FEEL	*Ten Records*	36	*16 Nov 91*	3
Above hit: Joey NEGRO – voice of Debbie FRENCH.				
REACHIN' [RM]	*Republic*	70	*21 Dec 91*	1
Remixed by Dave Lee.				
Above hit: Joey NEGRO presents PHASE II.				
ENTER YOUR FANTASY [EP]	*Ten Records*	35	*18 Jul 92*	3
Lead track: Love Fantasy (with credit: vocals by: Jannette Saul and Debbie French).				
WHAT HAPPENED TO THE MUSIC	*Virgin*	51	*25 Sep 93*	2

neil   UK

SINGLES:	**HITS 1**			**WEEKS 10**
HOLE IN MY SHOE	*WEA*	2	*14 Jul 84*	10

Vince NEIL   US

SINGLES:	**HITS 1**			**WEEKS 1**
YOU'RE INVITED (BUT YOUR FRIEND CAN'T COME)	*Hollywood*	63	*3 Oct 92*	1
ALBUMS:	**HITS 1**			**WEEKS 1**
EXPOSED	*Warner Brothers*	44	*8 May 93*	1

NEJA   Italy

SINGLES:	**HITS 1**			**WEEKS 1**
RESTLESS (I KNOW YOU KNOW)	*Panorama*	47	*26 Sep 98*	1

NEK   Italy

SINGLES:	**HITS 1**			**WEEKS 1**
LAURA	*Coalition*	59	*29 Aug 98*	1

NELSON   US

SINGLES:	**HITS 1**			**WEEKS 3**
(I CAN'T LIVE WITHOUT YOUR) LOVE & AFFECTION	*DGC*	54	*27 Oct 90*	3

Bill NELSON   UK

SINGLES:	**HITS 4**			**WEEKS 12**
FURNITURE MUSIC	*Harvest*	59	*24 Feb 79*	3
REVOLT INTO STYLE	*Harvest*	69	*5 May 79*	2
Above 2: Bill NELSON'S RED NOISE.				
DO YOU DREAM IN COLOUR?	*Cocteau*	52	*5 Jul 80*	4
YOUTH OF NATION ON FIRE	*Mercury*	73	*13 Jun 81*	3
ALBUMS:	**HITS 5**			**WEEKS 21**
SOUND ON SOUND	*Harvest*	33	*24 Feb 79*	5
Above hit: Bill NELSON'S RED NOISE.				
QUIT DREAMING AND GET ON THE BEAM	*Mercury*	7	*23 May 81*	6
THE LOVE THAT WHIRLS (DIARY OF A THINKING HEART)	*Mercury*	28	*3 Jul 82*	4
CHIMERA	*Mercury*	30	*14 May 83*	5
GETTING THE HOLY GHOST ACROSS	*Portrait*	91	*3 May 86*	1

Pete NELSON – See WHITE PLAINS

Phyllis NELSON   US

SINGLES:	**HITS 1**			**WEEKS 24**
MOVE CLOSER	*Carrere*	1	*23 Feb 85*	21
MOVE CLOSER [RI]	*EMI*	34	*21 May 94*	3
Featured in the Soft and Gentle anti-perspirant TV commercial.				
ALBUMS:	**HITS 1**			**WEEKS 10**
MOVE CLOSER	*Carrere*	29	*20 Apr 85*	10

Ricky NELSON
US

SINGLES:		HITS 15		WEEKS 150
STOOD UP	London	27	22 Feb 58	1
STOOD UP [RE]	London	29	8 Mar 58	1
POOR LITTLE FOOL	London	4	23 Aug 58	13
SOMEDAY	London	9	8 Nov 58	13
Originally recorded by the Mills Brothers.				
I GOT A FEELING	London	27	22 Nov 58	1
Above 2 entries were separate sides of the same release, each had its own chart run.				
POOR LITTLE FOOL [RE]	London	28	29 Nov 58	1
IT'S LATE	London	3	18 Apr 59	20
Originally recorded by Dorsey Burnette.				
NEVER BE ANYONE ELSE BUT YOU	London	19	16 May 59	1
Above 2 entries were separate sides of the same release, each had its own chart run.				
NEVER BE ANYONE ELSE BUT YOU [RE]	London	14	6 Jun 59	9
SWEETER THAN YOU	London	19	5 Sep 59	3
JUST A LITTLE TOO MUCH	London	11	12 Sep 59	8
Above 2 entries were separate sides of the same release, each had its own chart run.				
I WANNA BE LOVED	London	30	16 Jan 60	1
YOUNG EMOTIONS	London	48	9 Jul 60	1
HELLO MARYLOU GOODBYE HEART / TRAVELIN' MAN	London	2	3 Jun 61	18
Travelin' Man only listed for the week of 3 June 61 when it entered at No. 32 and had first credit.				
Hello Marylou Goodbye Heart originally recorded by Gene Pitney.				
EVERLOVIN'	London	23	18 Nov 61	5
YOUNG WORLD	London	19	31 Mar 62	13
TEEN AGE IDOL	London	39	1 Sep 62	4
IT'S UP TO YOU	London	22	19 Jan 63	9
FOOLS RUSH IN	Brunswick	12	19 Oct 63	9
Originally recorded by Glenn Miller in 1940.				
FOR YOU	Brunswick	14	1 Feb 64	10
Originally recorded by Glenn Gray in 1933.				
GARDEN PARTY	MCA	41	21 Oct 72	4
Features the Stone Canyon Band on backing vocals.				
Above 3: Rick NELSON.				
HELLO MARY LOU (GOODBYE HEART) [RI]	Liberty	45	24 Aug 91	5

Sandy NELSON
US

SINGLES:		HITS 4		WEEKS 42
TEEN BEAT	Top Rank	9	7 Nov 59	11
Features Bruce Johnston (Beach Boys) on piano.				
TEEN BEAT [RE]	Top Rank	25	6 Feb 60	1
LET THERE BE DRUMS	Top Rank	3	16 Dec 61	16
Features Scott Walker on bass.				
DRUMS ARE MY BEAT	London	30	24 Mar 62	6
DRUMMIN' UP A STORM	London	39	9 Jun 62	8

Shara NELSON
UK

SINGLES:		HITS 7		WEEKS 23
DOWN THAT ROAD	Cooltempo	19	24 Jul 93	6
ONE GOODBYE IN TEN	Cooltempo	21	18 Sep 93	5
UPTIGHT	Cooltempo	19	12 Feb 94	5
NOBODY	Cooltempo	49	4 Jun 94	1
INSIDE OUT / DOWN THAT ROAD [RM]	Cooltempo	34	10 Sep 94	3
Down That Road remixed by David Morales.				
ROUGH WITH THE SMOOTH	Cooltempo	30	16 Sep 95	2
SENSE OF DANGER	Pagan	61	5 Dec 98	1
Above hit: PRESENCE featuring Shara NELSON.				

ALBUMS:		HITS 2		WEEKS 11
WHAT SILENCE KNOWS	Cooltempo	22	2 Oct 93	9
FRIENDLY FIRE	Cooltempo	44	7 Oct 95	2

Shelley NELSON – See TIN TIN OUT

Willie NELSON
US

SINGLES:		HITS 2		WEEKS 13
ALWAYS ON MY MIND	CBS	49	31 Jul 82	3
TO ALL THE GIRLS I'VE LOVED BEFORE	CBS	17	7 Apr 84	10
Originally recorded by Albert Hammond.				
Above hit: Julio IGLESIAS and Willie NELSON.				

NENA
Germany

SINGLES:		HITS 2		WEEKS 14
99 RED BALLOONS	Epic	1	4 Feb 84	12
JUST A DREAM	Epic	70	5 May 84	2

ALBUMS:		HITS 1			WEEKS 5
NENA		Epic	31	24 Mar 84	5

NERIO'S DUBWORK – See Darryl PANDY

Frances NERO
US

SINGLES:		HITS 1			WEEKS 9
FOOTSTEPS FOLLOWING ME		Debut	17	13 Apr 91	9

NERO and the GLADIATORS
US

SINGLES:		HITS 2			WEEKS 6
ENTRY OF THE GLADIATORS		Decca	50	25 Mar 61	1
ENTRY OF THE GLADIATORS [RE]		Decca	37	8 Apr 61	4
IN THE HALL OF THE MOUNTAIN KING		Decca	48	29 Jul 61	1

Ann NESBY
US

SINGLES:		HITS 2			WEEKS 3
WITNESS [EP]		AM:PM	42	21 Dec 96	2
Lead track: Can I Get A Witness.					
HOLD ON [EP]		AM:PM	75	17 May 97	1
Lead track: Hold On.					

Michael NESMITH
US

SINGLES:		HITS 1			WEEKS 6
RIO		Island	28	26 Mar 77	6

NETWORK
UK

SINGLES:		HITS 1			WEEKS 4
BROKEN WINGS		Chrysalis	46	12 Dec 92	4

NEVADA
UK

SINGLES:		HITS 1			WEEKS 1
IN THE BLEAK MIDWINTER		Polydor	71	8 Jan 83	1

Robbie NEVIL
US

SINGLES:		HITS 3			WEEKS 24
C'EST LA VIE		Manhattan	3	20 Dec 86	11
Originally recorded by Beau Williams.					
DOMINOES		Manhattan	26	2 May 87	6
WOT'S IT TO YA		Manhattan	43	11 Jul 87	7
ALBUMS:		HITS 1			WEEKS 1
C'EST LA VIE		Manhattan	93	13 Jun 87	1

Aaron NEVILLE – See NEVILLE BROTHERS; Linda RONSTADT

NEVILLE BROTHERS
US

SINGLES:		HITS 2			WEEKS 7
WITH GOD ON OUR SIDE		A&M	47	25 Nov 89	6
BIRD ON A WIRE		A&M	72	7 Jul 90	1
ALBUMS:		HITS 1			WEEKS 3
BROTHER'S KEEPER		A&M	35	18 Aug 90	3

Jason NEVINS
US

SINGLES:		HITS 3			WEEKS 24
IT'S LIKE THAT		Columbia	63	21 Feb 98	3
German import.					
IT'S LIKE THAT		Sm:)e Communications	65	14 Mar 98	1
US import.					
IT'S LIKE THAT		Sm:)e Communications	1	21 Mar 98	16
(IT'S) TRICKY		Epidrome	74	18 Apr 98	1
German import. Remixed by Jason Nevins.					
Above 4: RUN-D.M.C. vs Jason NEVINS.					
INSANE IN THE BRAIN		INCredible	19	26 Jun 99	3
Above hit: Jason NEVINS vs. CYPRESS HILL.					

NEW ATLANTIC
UK

SINGLES:		HITS 4			WEEKS 15
I KNOW		3 Beat	12	29 Feb 92	7
INTO THE FUTURE		3 Beat	70	3 Oct 92	1
Above hit: NEW ATLANTIC featuring Linda WRIGHT.					
TAKE OFF SOME TIME		3 Beat	64	13 Feb 93	1

THE SUNSHINE AFTER THE RAIN | *Ffrreedom* | | 26 | *26 Nov 94* | 6
Re-Issued in 1995, credited solely to Berri.
Above hit: NEW ATLANTIC/U4EA featuring BERRI.

NEW BOHEMIANS - See Edie BRICKELL and NEW BOHEMIANS

NEW CHRISTY MINSTRELS
					US
EPS:	**HITS 1**			**WEEKS**	**10**
THREE WHEELS ON MY WAGON	*CBS*		5	*19 Mar 66*	10

NEW EDITION - See Mike BATT (with the NEW EDITION)

NEW EDITION
					US
SINGLES:	**HITS 6**			**WEEKS**	**36**
CANDY GIRL	*London*		1	*16 Apr 83*	13
POPCORN LOVE	*London*		43	*13 Aug 83*	5
MR. TELEPHONE MAN	*MCA*		19	*23 Feb 85*	9
Written and produced by Ray Parker Jr.					
CRUCIAL	*MCA*		70	*15 Apr 89*	1
HIT ME OFF	*MCA*		20	*10 Aug 96*	4
Samples I Got Cha Opin by Black Moon.					
SOMETHING ABOUT YOU	*MCA*		16	*7 Jun 97*	4
Samples Edie Brickell's What I Am.					
ALBUMS:	**HITS 1**			**WEEKS**	**3**
HOME AGAIN	*MCA*		22	*14 Sep 96*	3

NEW FAST AUTOMATIC DAFFODILS
					UK
ALBUMS:	**HITS 2**			**WEEKS**	**2**
PIGEON HOLE	*Play It*		49	*17 Nov 90*	1
BODY EXIT MIND	*Play It*		57	*24 Oct 92*	1

NEW GENERATION
					UK
SINGLES:	**HITS 1**			**WEEKS**	**5**
SMOKEY BLUE'S AWAY	*Spark*		38	*29 Jun 68*	5

NEW KIDS ON THE BLOCK
					US
SINGLES:	**HITS 13**			**WEEKS**	**90**
HANGIN' TOUGH	*CBS*		52	*16 Sep 89*	4
YOU GOT IT (THE RIGHT STUFF)	*CBS*		1	*11 Nov 89*	13
HANGIN' TOUGH [RI]	*CBS*		1	*6 Jan 90*	9
I'LL BE LOVING YOU (FOREVER)	*CBS*		5	*17 Mar 90*	8
COVER GIRL	*CBS*		4	*12 May 90*	8
STEP BY STEP	*CBS*		2	*16 Jun 90*	7
TONIGHT	*CBS*		3	*4 Aug 90*	10
LET'S TRY IT AGAIN / DIDN'T I (BLOW YOUR MIND)	*CBS*		8	*13 Oct 90*	5
THIS ONE'S FOR THE CHILDREN	*CBS*		9	*8 Dec 90*	7
Charity record with proceeds to United Cerebral Palsy.					
GAMES	*Columbia*		14	*9 Feb 91*	4
CALL IT WHAT YOU WANT	*Columbia*		12	*18 May 91*	5
Above 2: Sleeve shows group name as NKTOB.					
IF YOU GO AWAY	*Columbia*		9	*14 Dec 91*	5
DIRTY DAWG	*Columbia*		27	*19 Feb 94*	3
NEVER LET YOU GO	*Columbia*		42	*26 Mar 94*	2
Above 2: NKTOB.					
ALBUMS:	**HITS 7**			**WEEKS**	**106**
HANGIN' TOUGH	*CBS*		2	*9 Dec 89*	41
STEP BY STEP	*CBS*		1	*30 Jun 90*	31
NEW KIDS ON THE BLOCK	*CBS*		6	*3 Nov 90*	13
MERRY, MERRY CHRISTMAS	*CBS*		13	*15 Dec 90*	5
NO MORE GAMES/THE REMIX ALBUM	*Columbia*		15	*2 Mar 91*	11
H.I.T.S.	*Columbia*		50	*21 Dec 91*	4
FACE THE MUSIC	*Columbia*		36	*12 Mar 94*	1
Above hit: NKOTB.					

NEW MODEL ARMY
					UK
SINGLES:	**HITS 14**			**WEEKS**	**33**
NO REST	*EMI*		28	*27 Apr 85*	5
BETTER THAN THEM / NO SENSE	*EMI*		49	*3 Aug 85*	2
Sleeve gives title as an EP:The Acoustic EP.					
BRAVE NEW WORLD	*EMI*		57	*30 Nov 85*	1
FIFTY-FIRST STATE	*EMI*		71	*8 Nov 86*	2
POISON STREET	*EMI*		64	*28 Feb 87*	1
WHITECOATS [EP]	*EMI*		50	*26 Sep 87*	3
Lead track: Whitecoats.					
STUPID QUESTIONS	*EMI*		31	*21 Jan 89*	3

VAGABONDS	EMI	37	11 Mar 89	3
GREEN AND GREY	EMI	37	10 Jun 89	3
GET ME OUT	EMI	34	8 Sep 90	3
PURITY	EMI	61	3 Nov 90	2
SPACE	EMI	39	8 Jun 91	2
HERE COMES THE WAR	Epic	25	20 Feb 93	2
LIVING IN THE ROSE (THE BALLADS EP) [EP]	Epic	51	24 Jul 93	1

Lead track: Living In The Rose.

ALBUMS:	HITS 8			WEEKS 21
VENGENCE	Abstract	73	12 May 84	5
NO REST FOR THE WICKED	EMI	22	25 May 85	3
THE GHOST OF CAIN	EMI	45	11 Oct 86	3
THUNDER AND CONSOLATION	EMI	20	18 Feb 89	3
IMPURITY	EMI	23	6 Oct 90	2
RAW MELODY MEN	EMI	43	22 Jun 91	2
THE LOVE OF HOPELESS CAUSES	Epic	22	10 Apr 93	2
STRANGE BROTHERHOOD	Eagle	72	25 Apr 98	1

NEW MUSIK
UK

SINGLES:	HITS 4			WEEKS 27
STRAIGHT LINES	GTO	53	6 Oct 79	5
LIVING BY NUMBERS	GTO	13	19 Jan 80	8
THIS WORLD OF WATER	GTO	31	26 Apr 80	7
SANCTUARY	GTO	31	12 Jul 80	7
ALBUMS:	HITS 2			WEEKS 11
FROM A TO B	GTO	35	17 May 80	9
ANYWHERE	GTO	68	14 Mar 81	2

NEW ORDER
UK

SINGLES:	HITS 23			WEEKS 179
CEREMONY	Factory	34	14 Mar 81	5
PROCESSION / EVERYTHING'S GONE GREEN	Factory	38	3 Oct 81	5
TEMPTATION	Factory	29	22 May 82	7
BLUE MONDAY	Factory	12	19 Mar 83	17
BLUE MONDAY [RE-1ST]	Factory	9	13 Aug 83	17
CONFUSION	Factory	12	3 Sep 83	7
BLUE MONDAY [RE-2ND]	Factory	52	7 Jan 84	4
THIEVES LIKE US	Factory	18	28 Apr 84	5
THE PERFECT KISS	Factory	46	25 May 85	4
SUB-CULTURE	Factory	63	9 Nov 85	4
SHELLSHOCK	Factory	28	29 Mar 86	5
STATE OF THE NATION	Factory	30	27 Sep 86	3
THE PEEL SESSIONS (1ST June1982) [EP]	Strange Fruit	54	27 Sep 86	1

Lead track: Turn The Heater On. Recordings for DJ John Peel's evening show on BBC Radio 1.

BIZARRE LOVE TRIANGLE	Factory	56	15 Nov 86	2
TRUE FAITH	Factory	4	1 Aug 87	10
TOUCHED BY THE HAND OF GOD	Factory	20	19 Dec 87	7
BLUE MONDAY 1988 [RM-1ST]	Factory	3	7 May 88	11

Issued on 7" for first time. Remixed by John Potoker.

FINE TIME	Factory	11	10 Dec 88	8
ROUND & ROUND	Factory	21	11 Mar 89	7
RUN 2	Factory	49	9 Sep 89	2
WORLD IN MOTION . . .	Factory	1	2 Jun 90	12

The 1990 England World Cup team's official song.
Above hit: ENGLANDNEWORDER.

REGRET	Centredate Co.	4	17 Apr 93	7
RUINED IN A DAY	Centredate Co.	22	3 Jul 93	4
WORLD (THE PRICE OF LOVE)	Centredate Co.	13	4 Sep 93	5
SPOOKY	Centredate Co.	22	18 Dec 93	2
TRUE FAITH – 94 [RM]	London	9	19 Nov 94	8

Remixed by Stephen Hague and Mike 'Spike' Drake.

NINETEEN63	London	21	21 Jan 95	4

Originally was the B-side of the 1987 release of True Faith.

BLUE MONDAY-95 [RM-2ND]	London	17	5 Aug 95	4

Remixed by Hardfloor.

ALBUMS:	HITS 9			WEEKS 145
MOVEMENT	Factory	30	28 Nov 81	10
POWER, CORRUPTION AND LIES	Factory	4	14 May 83	29
LOW-LIFE	Factory	7	25 May 85	10
BROTHERHOOD	Factory	9	11 Oct 86	5
SUBSTANCE	Factory	3	29 Aug 87	37
TECHNIQUE	Factory	1	11 Feb 89	14
BBC RADIO 1 LIVE IN CONCERT	Windsong International	33	22 Feb 92	2
REPUBLIC	Centredate Co	1	15 May 93	19
SUBSTANCE 1987 [RI]	London	32	17 Jul 93	2
? (THE BEST OF NEW ORDER)	London	4	3 Dec 94	13

? (THE BEST OF NEW ORDER) / ? (THE REST OF NEW ORDER) [RE]	London	5	2 Sep 95	4

? (The Rest Of New Order) was a remix album, sales were combined.

NEW POWER GENERATION | | | | US

(See also Prince.)

SINGLES:	HITS 3			WEEKS 13
GET WILD	NPG	19	1 Apr 95	4

Above hit: NPG.

THE GOOD LIFE	NPG	29	19 Aug 95	3
THE GOOD LIFE [RE]	NPG	15	5 Jul 97	5
COME ON	RCA	65	21 Nov 98	1

Backing vocals by Chaka Khan.

ALBUMS:	HITS 2			WEEKS 5
EXODUS	NPG	11	8 Apr 95	3
NEWPOWER SOUL	NPG	38	11 Jul 98	2

NEW RADICALS | | | | US

SINGLES:	HITS 2			WEEKS 18
YOU GET WHAT YOU GIVE	MCA	5	3 Apr 99	17
SOMEDAY WE'LL KNOW	MCA	48	25 Sep 99	1

ALBUMS:	HITS 1			WEEKS 12
MAYBE YOU'VE BEEN BRAINWASHED TOO	MCA	10	17 Apr 99	12

NEW SEEKERS | | | | UK

SINGLES:	HITS 14			WEEKS 143
WHAT HAVE THEY DONE TO MY SONG MA	Philips	48	17 Oct 70	1

Above hit: NEW SEEKERS featuring Eve GRAHAM.

| WHAT HAVE THEY DONE TO MY SONG MA [RE] | Philips | 44 | 31 Oct 70 | 1 |
| NEVER ENDING SONG OF LOVE | Philips | 2 | 10 Jul 71 | 19 |

Originally recorded by Delaney and Bonnie.and Friends.

| I'D LIKE TO TEACH THE WORLD TO SING (IN PERFECT HARMONY) | Polydor | 1 | 18 Dec 71 | 21 |

Featured in the Coca-Cola TV commercial.

| BEG, STEAL OR BORROW | Polydor | 2 | 4 Mar 72 | 13 |

UK Eurovision entry in 1972, it came 2nd.

| CIRCLES | Polydor | 4 | 10 Jun 72 | 16 |

Originally recorded by Harry Chapin.

| COME SOFTLY TO ME | Polydor | 20 | 2 Dec 72 | 11 |

Above hit: NEW SEEKERS featuring MARTY.

| PINBALL WIZARD/SEE ME, FEEL ME [M] | Polydor | 16 | 24 Feb 73 | 8 |
| NEVERTHELESS (I'M IN LOVE WITH YOU) | Polydor | 34 | 7 Apr 73 | 5 |

Above hit: Eve GRAHAM and the NEW SEEKERS.

| GOODBYE IS JUST ANOTHER WORD | Polydor | 36 | 16 Jun 73 | 5 |
| YOU WON'T FIND ANOTHER FOOL LIKE ME | Polydor | 1 | 24 Nov 73 | 16 |

Above hit: NEW SEEKERS featuring Lyn PAUL.

I GET A LITTLE SENTIMENTAL OVER YOU	Polydor	5	9 Mar 74	9
IT'S SO NICE (TO HAVE YOU HOME)	CBS	44	14 Aug 76	4
I WANNA GO BACK	CBS	25	29 Jan 77	4
ANTHEM (ONE DAY IN EVERY WEEK)	CBS	21	15 Jul 78	10

ALBUMS:	HITS 6			WEEKS 49
NEW COLOURS	Polydor	40	5 Feb 72	4
WE'D LIKE TO TEACH THE WORLD TO SING	Polydor	2	1 Apr 72	25
NEVER ENDING SONG OF LOVE	Polydor	35	12 Aug 72	4
CIRCLES	Polydor	23	14 Oct 72	5
NOW	Polydor	47	21 Apr 73	2
TOGETHER	Polydor	12	30 Mar 74	9

NEW VAUDEVILLE BAND (featuring TRISTAM VII) | | | | UK

SINGLES:	HITS 4			WEEKS 43
WINCHESTER CATHEDRAL	Fontana	4	10 Sep 66	19

Above hit: NEW VAUDEVILLE BAND.

PEEK-A-BOO	Fontana	7	28 Jan 67	11
FINCHLEY CENTRAL	Fontana	11	13 May 67	9
GREEN STREET GREEN	Fontana	37	5 Aug 67	4

NEW WORLD | | | | Australia

SINGLES:	HITS 5			WEEKS 53
ROSE GARDEN	RAK	15	27 Feb 71	11
TOM-TOM TURNAROUND	RAK	6	3 Jul 71	15

Originally recorded by Sweet.

KARA, KARA	RAK	17	4 Dec 71	13
SISTER JANE	RAK	9	13 May 72	13
ROOFTOP SINGING	RAK	50	12 May 73	1

NEW WORLD THEATRE ORCHESTRA — UK

ALBUMS:		HITS 1		WEEKS 1
LET'S DANCE TO THE HITS OF THE 30'S AND 40'S	Pye Golden Guinea	20	24 Dec 60	1

NEW YORK CITY — US

SINGLES:		HITS 1		WEEKS 11
I'M DOIN' FINE NOW	RCA Victor	20	21 Jul 73	11

NEW YORK SKYY — US

SINGLES:		HITS 1		WEEKS 2
LET'S CELEBRATE	Epic	71	16 Jan 82	1
LET'S CELEBRATE [RE]	Epic	67	30 Jan 82	1

NEWBEATS — US

SINGLES:		HITS 2		WEEKS 22
BREAD AND BUTTER	Hickory	15	12 Sep 64	9
RUN, BABY, RUN (BACK INTO MY ARMS) / AM I NOT MY BROTHERS KEEPER	London	10	23 Oct 71	13

Booker NEWBURY III — US

SINGLES:		HITS 2		WEEKS 11
LOVE TOWN	Polydor	6	28 May 83	8
TEDDY BEAR	Polydor	44	8 Oct 83	3

Mickey NEWBURY — US

SINGLES:		HITS 1		WEEKS 5
AMERICAN TRILOGY	Elektra	42	1 Jul 72	5

NEWCLEUS — US

SINGLES:		HITS 1		WEEKS 6
JAM ON REVENGE (THE WIKKI-WIKKI SONG)	Becket	44	3 Sep 83	6
ALBUMS:		HITS 1		WEEKS 2
JAM ON REVENGE	Sunnyview	84	25 Aug 84	2

Bob NEWHART — US

EPS:		HITS 2		WEEKS 65
THE BUTTON-DOWN MIND OF BOB NEWHART VOLUME 1	Warner Brothers	2	10 Jun 61	64
THE BUTTON-DOWN MOON STRIKES BACK	Warner Brothers	20	20 Oct 62	1
ALBUMS:		HITS 1		WEEKS 37
BUTTON-DOWN MIND OF BOB NEWHART	Warner Brothers	2	1 Oct 60	37

Anthony NEWLEY — UK

(See also Anthony Newley, Peter Sellers, Joan Collins; Various Artists: Stage Cast – London 'Stop The World – I Want To Get Off'.)

SINGLES:		HITS 12		WEEKS 130
I'VE WAITED SO LONG	Decca	3	2 May 59	15
IDLE ON PARADE [EP]	Decca	13	9 May 59	4
Lead track: I've Waited So Long. Above 2 from the film 'Idle On Parade'.				
PERSONALITY	Decca	6	13 Jun 59	12
WHY	Decca	1	16 Jan 60	18
DO YOU MIND	Decca	1	26 Mar 60	15
IF SHE SHOULD COME TO YOU (LA MONTANA)	Decca	4	16 Jul 60	15
STRAWBERRY FAIR	Decca	3	26 Nov 60	11
AND THE HEAVENS CRIED	Decca	6	18 Mar 61	12
Originally recorded by Ronnie Savoy.				
POP GOES THE WEASEL / BEE BOM	Decca	12	17 Jun 61	9
Bee Bom no longer listed from 1 July 61. As an AA side it had reached No. 15.				
WHAT KIND OF FOOL AM I	Decca	36	5 Aug 61	8
From the film 'Stop The World, I Want To Get Off'.				
D-DARLING	Decca	25	27 Jan 62	6
THAT NOISE	Decca	34	28 Jul 62	5
EPS:		HITS 1		WEEKS 9
TONY'S HITS	Decca	6	16 Apr 60	9
ALBUMS:		HITS 2		WEEKS 14
LOVE IS A NOW AND THEN THING	Decca	19	14 May 60	2
TONY	Decca	5	8 Jul 61	12

Anthony NEWLEY, Peter SELLERS, Joan COLLINS — UK

(See also Anthony Newley; Peter Sellers.)

ALBUMS:		HITS 1		WEEKS 10
FOOL BRITANNIA	Ember	10	28 Sep 63	10

Tara NEWLEY – See E-ZEE POSSEE

Brad NEWMAN | UK

SINGLES:	HITS 1			WEEKS 1
SOMEBODY TO LOVE	Fontana	47	24 Feb 62	1

Dave NEWMAN | UK

SINGLES:	HITS 1			WEEKS 6
THE LION SLEEPS TONIGHT (WIMOWEH)	Pye	48	15 Apr 72	1
THE LION SLEEPS TONIGHT (WIMOWEH) [RE]	Pye	34	29 Apr 72	5

NEWS | UK

SINGLES:	HITS 1			WEEKS 3
AUDIO VIDEO	George	52	29 Aug 81	3

NEWTON | UK

SINGLES:	HITS 3			WEEKS 6
SKY HIGH	Bags Of Fun	56	15 Jul 95	2
Originally reached No. 83 in 1994.				
SOMETIMES WHEN WE TOUCH	Dominion	32	15 Feb 97	3
DON'T WORRY	Dominion	61	16 Aug 97	1

Juice NEWTON | US

SINGLES:	HITS 1			WEEKS 6
ANGEL OF THE MORNING	Capitol	43	2 May 81	6

Olivia NEWTON-JOHN | UK

(See also Various Artists: Films – Original Soundtracks 'Grease'.)

SINGLES:	HITS 24			WEEKS 234
IF NOT FOR YOU	Pye International	7	20 Mar 71	11
Originally recorded by Bob Dylan.				
BANKS OF THE OHIO	Pye International	6	23 Oct 71	17
Originally recorded by Blue Sky Boys in 1936.				
WHAT IS LIFE	Pye International	16	11 Mar 72	8
Originally recorded by George Harrison.				
TAKE ME HOME COUNTRY ROADS	Pye International	15	13 Jan 73	13
LONG LIVE LOVE	Pye International	11	16 Mar 74	8
UK's Eurovision entry in 1974, it came 4th.				
I HONESTLY LOVE YOU	EMI	22	12 Oct 74	6
SAM	EMI	6	11 Jun 77	11
YOU'RE THE ONE THAT I WANT	RSO	1	20 May 78	26
Above hit: John TRAVOLTA and Olivia NEWTON-JOHN.				
SUMMER NIGHTS	RSO	1	16 Sep 78	19
Above hit: John TRAVOLTA, Olivia NEWTON-JOHN and CAST.				
HOPELESSLY DEVOTED TO YOU	RSO	2	4 Nov 78	11
Above 3 from the film 'Grease'.				
A LITTLE MORE LOVE	EMI	4	16 Dec 78	12
DEEPER THAN THE NIGHT	EMI	64	30 Jun 79	3
XANADU	Jet	1	21 Jun 80	11
Above hit: Olivia NEWTON-JOHN/ELECTRIC LIGHT ORCHESTRA.				
MAGIC	Jet	32	23 Aug 80	7
SUDDENLY	Jet	15	25 Oct 80	7
Above 3 from the film 'Xanadu'.				
Above hit: Olivia NEWTON-JOHN with Cliff RICHARD.				
PHYSICAL	EMI	7	10 Oct 81	16
LANDSLIDE	EMI	18	16 Jan 82	9
MAKE A MOVE ON ME	EMI	43	17 Apr 82	3
Sleeve credits just Olivia.				
HEART ATTACK	EMI	46	23 Oct 82	4
I HONESTLY LOVE YOU [RI]	EMI	52	15 Jan 83	4
TWIST OF FATE	EMI	57	12 Nov 83	2
From the film 'Two Of A Kind'.				
THE GREASE MEGAMIX [M]	Polydor	3	22 Dec 90	10
Above hit: John TRAVOLTA and Olivia NEWTON-JOHN.				
GREASE – THE DREAM MIX [M]	Polydor	47	23 Mar 91	2
Above 2 are medleys of songs from the film 'Grease'.				
Above hit: Frankie VALLI, John TRAVOLTA and Olivia NEWTON-JOHN.				
I NEED LOVE	Mercury	75	4 Jul 92	1
HAD TO BE	EMI	22	9 Dec 95	4
Above hit: Cliff RICHARD with Olivia NEWTON-JOHN.				
YOU'RE THE ONE THAT I WANT [RI]	Polydor	4	25 Jul 98	9
20th anniversary re-issue.				
Above hit: John TRAVOLTA Olivia NEWTON-JOHN.				
ALBUMS:	**HITS 13**			**WEEKS 120**
MUSIC MAKES MY DAY	Pye	37	2 Mar 74	3
LONG LIVE LOVE	EMI	40	29 Jun 74	2

HAVE YOU NEVER BEEN MELLOW	EMI	37	26 Apr 75	2
COME ON OVER	EMI	49	29 May 76	4
MAKING A GOOD THING BETTER	EMI	60	27 Aug 77	1
GREATEST HITS	EMI	19	21 Jan 78	9
TOTALLY HOT	EMI	30	9 Dec 78	9
XANADU [OST]	Jet	2	19 Jul 80	17

Album divided with one side by each artist.
Above hit: Olivia NEWTON-JOHN/ELECTRIC LIGHT ORCHESTRA.

PHYSICAL	EMI	11	31 Oct 81	22

The biggest selling single in the US in the 80s.

GREATEST HITS	EMI	8	23 Oct 82	38

Both Greatest Hits albums are different.

SOUL KISS	Mercury	66	8 Mar 86	3
BACK TO BASICS – THE ESSENTIAL COLLECTION 1971-1992	Mercury	12	25 Jul 92	6
GAIA (ONE WOMAN'S JOURNEY)	D-Sharp	33	4 Feb 95	4

NEXT   US

SINGLES:	HITS 1			WEEKS 3
TOO CLOSE	Arista	24	6 Jun 98	3

NEXT OF KIN   UK

SINGLES:	HITS 2			WEEKS 6
24 HOURS FROM YOU	Universal	13	20 Feb 99	4
MORE LOVE	Universal	33	19 Jun 99	2

NIAGRA   UK

SINGLES:	HITS 1			WEEKS 1
CLOUDBURST	Freeflow	65	27 Sep 97	1

NICE   UK

SINGLES:	HITS 1			WEEKS 15
AMERICA	Immediate	21	13 Jul 68	15

From the film/show 'West Side Story'.

ALBUMS:	HITS 3			WEEKS 38
NICE	Immediate	3	13 Sep 69	6
FIVE BRIDGES	Charisma	2	27 Jun 70	21
ELEGY	Charisma	5	17 Apr 71	11

Paul NICHOLAS   UK

(See also Various Artists: Stage Cast – London 'Hair'.)

SINGLES:	HITS 4			WEEKS 31
REGGAE LIKE IT USED TO BE	RSO	17	17 Apr 76	8
DANCING WITH THE CAPTAIN	RSO	8	9 Oct 76	9
GRANDMA'S PARTY	RSO	9	4 Dec 76	11
HEAVEN ON THE 7TH FLOOR	RSO	40	9 Jul 77	3
ALBUMS:	HITS 1			WEEKS 8
JUST GOOD FRIENDS	K-Tel	30	29 Nov 86	8

Sue NICHOLLS   UK

SINGLES:	HITS 1			WEEKS 8
WHERE WILL YOU BE	Pye	17	6 Jul 68	8

Stevie NICKS   US

SINGLES:	HITS 8			WEEKS 30
STOP DRAGGIN' MY HEART AROUND	WEA	50	15 Aug 81	4

Above hit: Stevie NICKS (with Tom PETTY and the HEARTBREAKERS).

I CAN'T WAIT	Parlophone	54	25 Jan 86	4
TALK TO ME	Parlophone	68	29 Mar 86	2
ROOMS ON FIRE	EMI	16	6 May 89	7
LONG WAY TO GO	EMI	60	12 Aug 89	2
WHOLE LOTTA TROUBLE	EMI	62	11 Nov 89	2
SOMETIMES IT'S A BITCH	EMI	40	24 Aug 91	4

Written by and features Jon Bon Jovi on guitar.

I CAN'T WAIT [RI]	EMI	47	9 Nov 91	2
MAYBE LOVE	EMI	42	2 Jul 94	3
ALBUMS:	HITS 6			WEEKS 80
BELLA DONNA	WEA	11	8 Aug 81	15
THE WILD HEART	WEA International	28	2 Jul 83	19
ROCK A LITTLE	Modern	30	14 Dec 85	22
BELLA DONNA [RI]	Warner Brothers	72	28 Feb 87	1

Re-released with different catalogue number.

THE OTHER SIDE OF THE MIRROR	EMI	3	10 Jun 89	14

| TIMESPACE – THE BEST OF STEVIE NICKS | EMI | 15 | 14 Sep 91 | 6 |
| STREET ANGEL | EMI | 16 | 4 Jun 94 | 3 |

Hector NICOL · UK

ALBUMS:	HITS 1		WEEKS 1	
BRAVO JULIET!	Klub	92	28 Apr 84	1

NICOLE · Germany

SINGLES:	HITS 2		WEEKS 10	
A LITTLE PEACE	CBS	1	8 May 82	9
Eurovision Song Contest winner in 1982. Also the 500th number one single in the UK.				
GIVE ME MORE TIME	CBS	75	21 Aug 82	1
ALBUMS:	HITS 1		WEEKS 2	
A LITTLE PEACE	CBS	85	2 Oct 82	2

NICOLE · US

SINGLES:	HITS 3		WEEKS 9	
NEW YORK EYES	Portrait	41	28 Dec 85	7
Above hit: NICOLE with Timmy THOMAS.				
ROCK THE HOUSE	Truelove	63	26 Dec 92	1
Above hit: SOURCE vocals by NICOLE.				
RUNNIN' AWAY	Ore	69	6 Jul 96	1

NICOLE · US

SINGLES:	HITS 2		WEEKS 5	
MAKE IT HOT	East West America	22	22 Aug 98	4
Above hit: NICOLE featuring Missy "Misdemeanor" ELLIOTT and MOCHA.				
I CAN'T SEE	East West America	55	5 Dec 98	1
Above hit: Nicole RAY (featuring MOCHA).				

NICOLETTE · UK

SINGLES:	HITS 1		WEEKS 1	
NO GOVERNMENT	Talkin Loud	67	23 Dec 95	1
ALBUMS:	HITS 1		WEEKS 2	
LET NO ONE LIVE RENT FREE IN YOUR HEAD	Talkin Loud	36	10 Aug 96	2

NIGHTCRAWLERS featuring John REID · UK

SINGLES:	HITS 7		WEEKS 36	
PUSH THE FEELING ON	ffrr	22	15 Oct 94	5
Originally released in 1992.				
PUSH THE FEELING ON [RM]	ffrr	3	4 Mar 95	11
Remixed by MK (Marc Kinchen).				
Above 2: NIGHTCRAWLERS.				
SURRENDER YOUR LOVE	Final Vinyl	7	27 May 95	7
DON'T LET THE FEELING GO	Final Vinyl	13	9 Sep 95	4
LET'S PUSH IT	Final Vinyl	23	20 Jan 96	4
SHOULD I EVER (FALL IN LOVE)	Arista	34	20 Apr 96	2
KEEP ON PUSHING OUR LOVE	Arista	30	27 Jul 96	2
Above hit: NIGHTCRAWLERS featuring John REID and Alysha WARREN.				
NEVER KNEW LOVE	Riverhorse	59	3 Jul 99	1
Above hit: NIGHTCRAWLERS.				
ALBUMS:	HITS 1		WEEKS 5	
LET'S PUSH IT	Final Vinyl	14	30 Sep 95	5

Maxine NIGHTINGALE · UK

SINGLES:	HITS 2		WEEKS 16	
RIGHT BACK WHERE WE STARTED FROM	United Artists	8	1 Nov 75	8
LOVE HIT ME	United Artists	11	12 Mar 77	8
Above 2 originally recorded by J. Vincent Edwards.				

NIGHTMARES ON WAX · UK

SINGLES:	HITS 2		WEEKS 6	
AFTERMATH / I'M FOR REAL	Warp	38	27 Oct 90	5
I'm For Real only listed until 17 Nov 90.				
FINER	Warp	63	26 Jun 99	1
Vocals by Sara Winton.				
ALBUMS:	HITS 1		WEEKS 2	
CAR BOOT SOUL	Warp	71	24 Apr 99	2

NIGHTWRITERS · US

SINGLES:	HITS 1		WEEKS 2	
LET THE MUSIC USE YOU	Ffrreedom	51	23 May 92	2

NIKKE? NICOLE!   US

SINGLES:		HITS 1			WEEKS 1
NIKKE DOES IT BETTER	Love		73	1 Jun 91	1

Features scratching by DJ Rhythm.

NIKKO - See Harold MELVIN and the BLUENOTES

NILSSON   US

SINGLES:		HITS 4			WEEKS 55
EVERYBODY'S TALKIN'	RCA Victor		50	27 Sep 69	1
Originally recorded by Fred Neil.					
EVERYBODY'S TALKIN' [RE-1ST]	RCA Victor		23	11 Oct 69	9
EVERYBODY'S TALKIN' [RE-2ND]	RCA Victor		39	14 Mar 70	5
WITHOUT YOU	RCA Victor		1	5 Feb 72	20
Originally recorded by Bad Finger.					
COCONUT	RCA Victor		42	3 Jun 72	5
WITHOUT YOU [RI-1ST]	RCA Victor Maximillion		22	16 Oct 76	8
ALL I THINK ABOUT IS YOU	RCA Victor		43	20 Aug 77	3
Above hit: Harry NILSSON.					
WITHOUT YOU [RI-2ND]	RCA		47	19 Feb 94	4
ALBUMS:		HITS 4			WEEKS 43
THE POINT [OST-TV]	RCA Victor		46	29 Jan 72	1
Originally released 1971. From an animated children's TV programme.					
NILSSON SCHMILSSON	RCA Victor		4	5 Feb 72	22
SON OF SCHMILSSON	RCA Victor		41	19 Aug 72	1
A LITTLE TOUCH OF SCHMILSSON IN THE NIGHT	RCA Victor		20	28 Jul 73	1

Charlotte NILSSON   Sweden

SINGLES:		HITS 1			WEEKS 4
TAKE ME TO YOUR HEAVEN	Arista		20	3 Jul 99	4

Eurovision Song Contest winner in 1999.

NINA and FREDERIK   Denmark

SINGLES:		HITS 5			WEEKS 29
MARY'S BOY CHILD	Columbia		26	19 Dec 59	1
LISTEN TO THE OCEAN	Columbia		47	12 Mar 60	1
Above hit: NINA and FREDERIK; Jorn GRAUENGAARD and his Orchestra.					
LISTEN TO THE OCEAN [RE]	Columbia		46	9 Apr 60	1
LITTLE DONKEY	Columbia		3	19 Nov 60	10
Above hit: NINA and FREDERIK with the Jorn GRAUENGAARD QUINTET.					
LONGTIME BOY	Columbia		43	30 Sep 61	3
SUCU – SUCU	Columbia		23	7 Oct 61	13
EPS:		HITS 7			WEEKS 169
NINA AND FREDERIK VOLUME 1	Columbia		2	12 Mar 60	115
NINA AND FREDERIK NO. 1	Pye Nixa		13	2 Apr 60	2
NINA AND FREDERIK NO. 2	Pye Nixa		8	23 Apr 60	7
NINA AND FREDERIK VOLUME 2	Columbia		3	11 Jun 60	26
NINA AND FREDERIK VOLUME 3	Columbia		8	26 Nov 60	7
CHRISTMAS AT HOME WITH NINA AND FREDERICK	Columbia		2	18 Nov 61	9
WHITE CHRISTMAS	Columbia		11	15 Dec 62	3
ALBUMS:		HITS 2			WEEKS 6
NINA AND FREDERIK	Pye		9	13 Feb 60	2
NINA AND FREDERIK	Columbia		11	29 Apr 61	4

Both self titled albums are different.

9 BELOW ZERO   UK

ALBUMS:		HITS 2			WEEKS 12
DON'T POINT YOUR FINGER	A&M		56	14 Mar 81	6
THIRD DEGREE	A&M		38	20 Mar 82	6

NINE INCH NAILS   US

SINGLES:		HITS 6			WEEKS 15
HEAD LIKE A HOLE	Island		45	14 Sep 91	4
SIN	Island		35	16 Nov 91	2
MARCH OF THE PIGS	Island		45	9 Apr 94	3
CLOSER	Island		25	18 Jun 94	3
THE PERFECT DRUG	Interscope		43	13 Sep 97	1
From the film 'The Lost Highway'.					
WE'RE IN THIS TOGETHER	Nothing		39	18 Dec 99	2
ALBUMS:		HITS 4			WEEKS 12
PRETTY HATE MACHINE	TVT		67	12 Oct 91	1
BROKEN	Interscope		18	17 Oct 92	3
THE DOWNWARD SPIRAL	Island		9	19 Mar 94	4
THE FRAGILE	Island		10	9 Oct 99	4

999
UK

SINGLES:		HITS 5		WEEKS 13	
HOMICIDE	United Artists	40	25 Nov 78	3
FOUND OUT TOO LATE	Radar	69	27 Oct 79	2
OBSESSED	Albion	71	16 May 81	1
LIL RED RIDING HOOD	Albion	59	18 Jul 81	3
INDIAN RESERVATION	Albion	51	14 Nov 81	4
ALBUMS:		**HITS 1**		**WEEKS 1**
999	United Artists	53	25 Mar 78	1

911
UK

SINGLES:		HITS 13		WEEKS 94	
NIGHT TO REMEMBER	Ginga	38	11 May 96	2
LOVE SENSATION	Ginga	21	10 Aug 96	4
DON'T MAKE ME WAIT	Virgin	10	9 Nov 96	6
DON'T MAKE ME WAIT [RE]	Virgin	63	4 Jan 97	2
THE DAY WE FIND LOVE	Virgin	4	22 Feb 97	8
BODYSHAKIN'	Virgin	3	3 May 97	7
THE JOURNEY	Virgin	3	12 Jul 97	7
PARTY PEOPLE . . . FRIDAY NIGHT	Virgin	5	1 Nov 97	7
PARTY PEOPLE . . . FRIDAY NIGHT [RE]	Virgin	60	3 Jan 98	3
ALL I WANT IS YOU	Virgin	4	4 Apr 98	6
ALL I WANT IS YOU [RE]	Virgin	64	20 Jun 98	1
HOW DO YOU WANT ME TO LOVE YOU?	Virgin	10	4 Jul 98	7
HOW DO YOU WANT ME TO LOVE YOU? [RE]	Virgin	57	29 Aug 98	2
MORE THAN A WOMAN	Virgin	2	24 Oct 98	9
MORE THAN A WOMAN [RE]	Virgin	64	2 Jan 99	4
A LITTLE BIT MORE	Virgin	1	23 Jan 99	9
PRIVATE NUMBER	Virgin	3	15 May 99	7
WONDERLAND	Virgin	13	23 Oct 99	3
ALBUMS:		**HITS 4**		**WEEKS 26**
THE JOURNEY	Virgin	13	8 Mar 97	17
MOVING ON	Virgin	10	18 Jul 98	4
THERE IT IS	Virgin	8	6 Feb 99	4
THE GREATEST HITS AND A LITTLE MORE . . .	Virgin	40	6 Nov 99	1

9.9
US

SINGLES:		HITS 1		WEEKS 3	
ALL OF ME FOR ALL OF YOU	RCA	53	6 Jul 85	3

NINE YARDS
UK

SINGLES:		HITS 3		WEEKS 3	
LONELINESS IS GONE	Virgin	70	21 Nov 98	1
MATTER OF TIME	Virgin	59	10 Apr 99	1
ALWAYS FIND A WAY	Virgin	50	28 Aug 99	1

1910 FRUITGUM CO.
US

SINGLES:		HITS 1		WEEKS 16	
SIMON SAYS	Pye International	2	23 Mar 68	16

1927
Australia

SINGLES:		HITS 1		WEEKS 6	
THAT'S WHEN I THINK OF YOU	WEA	46	22 Apr 89	6

1999 MANCHESTER UNITED SQUAD - See MANCHESTER UNITED FOOTBALL SQUAD

98°
US

SINGLES:		HITS 3		WEEKS 4	
INVISIBLE MAN	Motown	66	29 Nov 97	1
TRUE TO YOUR HEART	Motown	51	31 Oct 98	1

From the Walt Disney film 'Mulan'.
Above hit: 98° (featuring Stevie WONDER).

| BECAUSE OF YOU | Motown | 36 | 13 Mar 99 | 2 |

99TH FLOOR ELEVATORS featuring Tony DE VIT
UK

(See also Tony De Vit.)

SINGLES:		HITS 2		WEEKS 4	
HOOKED	Labello Dance	28	12 Aug 95	2
I'LL BE THERE	Labello Dance	37	30 Mar 96	2

Vocals by Lorraine.

Los NINOS
UK

ALBUMS:	HITS 1			WEEKS 1
FRAGILE - MYSTICAL SOUNDS OF THE PANPIPES	Pearls	74	22 Jul 95	1

NIRVANA
US

SINGLES:	HITS 1			WEEKS 6
RAINBOW CHASER	Island	34	18 May 68	6

NIRVANA
US

SINGLES:	HITS 7			WEEKS 36
SMELLS LIKE TEEN SPIRIT	DGC	7	30 Nov 91	6
COME AS YOU ARE	DGC	9	14 Mar 92	5
LITHIUM	DGC	11	25 Jul 92	6
IN BLOOM	Geffen	28	12 Dec 92	7
OH, THE GUILT	Touch And Go	12	6 Mar 93	2
[AA] listed with Puss by Jesus Lizard.				
HEART-SHAPED BOX	Geffen	5	11 Sep 93	5
ALL APOLOGIES / RAPE ME	Geffen	32	18 Dec 93	5

ALBUMS:	HITS 6			WEEKS 289
NEVERMIND	DGC	7	5 Oct 91	184
Includes re-entries through to 1999. Label change to Geffen from 12 Feb 94.				
BLEACH	Tupelo	33	7 Mar 92	7
Originally released in the US on the Sub Pop label in 1989.				
INCESTICIDE	Geffen	14	26 Dec 92	11
B-sides, demos and Radio 1 sessions.				
IN UTERO	Geffen	1	25 Sep 93	41
UNPLUGGED IN NEW YORK	Geffen	1	12 Nov 94	40
Live recordings broadcast on MTV, 18 Nov 93.				
FROM THE MUDDY BANKS OF THE WISHKAH	Geffen	4	12 Oct 96	6
Live recordings between 1989-94.				

NITRO DELUXE
US

SINGLES:	HITS 1			WEEKS 16
THIS BRUTAL HOUSE	Cooltempo	47	14 Feb 87	7
THIS BRUTAL HOUSE [RE]	Cooltempo	62	13 Jun 87	4
LET'S GET BRUTAL (ROK DA RADIO) [RM]	Cooltempo	24	6 Feb 88	5
Re-mix of This Brutal House. Not all copies had (Rok Da Radio) listed.				

NITZER EBB
UK

SINGLES:	HITS 3			WEEKS 3
GODHEAD	Mute	56	11 Jan 92	1
ASCEND	Mute	52	11 Apr 92	1
KICK IT	Mute	75	4 Mar 95	1

NKOTB - See NEW KIDS ON THE BLOCK

NO AUTHORITY
US

SINGLES:	HITS 1			WEEKS 1
DON'T STOP	Epic	54	14 Mar 98	1
Contains sample of Teddy Riley's Don't Stop.				

NO DICE
UK

SINGLES:	HITS 1			WEEKS 2
COME DANCING	EMI	65	5 May 79	2

NO DOUBT
US/UK

SINGLES:	HITS 5			WEEKS 35
JUST A GIRL	Interscope	38	26 Oct 96	2
DON'T SPEAK	Interscope	1	22 Feb 97	18
Produced by Matthew Wilder.				
JUST A GIRL [RI]	Interscope	3	5 Jul 97	7
SPIDERWEBS	Interscope	16	4 Oct 97	3
SUNDAY MORNING	Interscope	50	20 Dec 97	3
NEW	Higher Ground	30	12 Jun 99	2
From the film 'Go'.				

ALBUMS:	HITS 1			WEEKS 44
TRAGIC KINGDOM	Interscope	3	18 Jan 97	44

NO MERCY
US/Cuba

SINGLES:	HITS 3			WEEKS 26
WHERE DO YOU GO	Arista	2	18 Jan 97	15
Originally recorded by La Bouche in 1995.				
PLEASE DON'T GO	Arista	4	24 May 97	7

KISS YOU ALL OVER	*Arista*	16	*6 Sep 97*	4
ALBUMS:	**HITS 1**		**WEEKS 4**	
MY PROMISE	*Arista*	17	*7 Jun 97*	4

NO SWEAT   Ireland

SINGLES:	**HITS 2**		**WEEKS 5**	
HEART AND SOUL	*London*	64	*13 Oct 90*	4
TEAR DOWN THE WALLS	*London*	61	*2 Feb 91*	1
Original release reached No. 84 in 1990.

NO WAY JOSE   US

SINGLES:	**HITS 1**		**WEEKS 6**	
TEQUILA	*Fourth & Broadway*	47	*3 Aug 85*	6

NO WAY SIS   UK

SINGLES:	**HITS 1**		**WEEKS 4**	
I'D LIKE TO TEACH THE WORLD TO SING	*EMI*	27	*21 Dec 96*	4

NOFX   US

ALBUMS:	**HITS 1**		**WEEKS 1**	
HEAVY PETTING ZOO	*Epitaph*	60	*10 Feb 96*	1

NOISE FACTORY - See VARIOUS ARTISTS (EPs) 'Fourplay Volume 1 EP'

NOLANS   Ireland

SINGLES:	**HITS 9**		**WEEKS 90**	
SPIRIT, BODY AND SOUL	*Epic*	34	*6 Oct 79*	6
Above hit: NOLAN SISTERS.				
I'M IN THE MOOD FOR DANCING	*Epic*	3	*22 Dec 79*	15
DON'T MAKE WAVES	*Epic*	12	*12 Apr 80*	11
GOTTA PULL MYSELF TOGETHER	*Epic*	9	*13 Sep 80*	13
WHO'S GONNA ROCK YOU	*Epic*	12	*6 Dec 80*	11
Originally recorded by Billy Ocean.				
ATTENTION TO ME	*Epic*	9	*14 Mar 81*	13
CHEMISTRY	*Epic*	15	*15 Aug 81*	8
DON'T LOVE ME TOO HARD	*Epic*	14	*20 Feb 82*	12
I'M IN THE MOOD FOR DANCING [RR]	*Living Beat*	51	*1 Apr 95*	1
ALBUMS:	**HITS 6**		**WEEKS 84**	
20 GIANT HITS	*Target*	3	*29 Jul 78*	12
Above hit: NOLAN SISTERS.				
NOLANS	*Epic*	15	*19 Jan 80*	13
MAKING WAVES	*Epic*	11	*25 Oct 80*	33
PORTRAIT	*Epic*	7	*27 Mar 82*	10
ALTOGETHER	*Epic*	52	*20 Nov 82*	8
GIRLS JUST WANNA HAVE FUN	*Towerbell*	39	*17 Nov 84*	8

NOMAD   UK

SINGLES:	**HITS 5**		**WEEKS 22**	
(I WANNA GIVE YOU) DEVOTION	*Rumour*	2	*2 Feb 91*	10
Above hit: NOMAD featuring MC Mikee FREEDOM.				
JUST A GROOVE	*Rumour*	16	*4 May 91*	6
SOMETHING SPECIAL	*Rumour*	73	*28 Sep 91*	1
YOUR LOVE IS LIFTING ME	*Rumour*	60	*25 Apr 92*	2
24 HOURS A DAY	*Rumour*	61	*7 Nov 92*	1
(I WANNA GIVE YOU) DEVOTION [RM]	*Rumour*	42	*25 Nov 95*	2
ALBUMS:	**HITS 1**		**WEEKS 2**	
CHANGING CABINS	*Rumour*	48	*22 Jun 91*	2

NONCHALANT   US

SINGLES:	**HITS 1**		**WEEKS 1**	
5 O'CLOCK	*MCA*	44	*29 Jun 96*	1

Peter NOONE   UK

(See also Herman's Hermits.)

SINGLES:	**HITS 1**		**WEEKS 9**	
OH YOU PRETTY THING	*RAK*	12	*22 May 71*	9
Originally recorded by David Bowie.				

NOOTROPIC   UK

SINGLES:	**HITS 1**		**WEEKS 1**	
I SEE ONLY YOU	*Hi-Life*	42	*16 Mar 96*	1

Narration by Ken NORDENE - See Billy VAUGHN and his Orchestra

NOREAGA   US

ALBUMS:	HITS 1			WEEKS 1
N.O.R.E.	Penalty Recordings	72	25 Jul 98	1

Chris NORMAN - See Suzi QUATRO

NORTH GERMAN RADIO SYMPHONY ORCHESTRA - See Nigel KENNEDY

NORTH AND SOUTH   UK

SINGLES:	HITS 4			WEEKS 16
I'M A MAN NOT A BOY	RCA	7	17 May 97	5
TARANTINO'S NEW STAR	RCA	18	9 Aug 97	5
BREATHING	RCA	27	8 Nov 97	2
NO SWEAT '98	RCA	29	4 Apr 98	4

NORTHERN LINE   UK/South Africa

SINGLES:	HITS 1			WEEKS 4
RUN FOR YOUR LIFE	Global Talent	18	9 Oct 99	4

NORTHERN UPROAR   UK

SINGLES:	HITS 6			WEEKS 11
ROLLERCOASTER / ROUGH BOYS	Heavenly	41	21 Oct 95	2
FROM A WINDOW / THIS MORNING	Heavenly	17	3 Feb 96	3
LIVIN' IT UP	Heavenly	24	20 Apr 96	2
Backing vocals by James Dean Bradfield of the Manic Street Preachers.				
TOWN	Heavenly	48	22 Jun 96	1
ANY WAY YOU LOOK	Heavenly	36	7 Jun 97	2
A GIRL I ONCE KNEW	Heavenly	63	23 Aug 97	1
ALBUMS:	HITS 1			WEEKS 2
NORTHERN UPROAR	Heavenly	22	11 May 96	2

NORTHSIDE   UK

SINGLES:	HITS 3			WEEKS 12
SHALL WE TAKE A TRIP / MOODY PLACES	Factory	50	9 Jun 90	5
MY RISING STAR	Factory	32	3 Nov 90	3
TAKE 5	Factory	40	1 Jun 91	4
ALBUMS:	HITS 1			WEEKS 3
CHICKEN RHYTHMS	Factory	19	29 Jun 91	3

NOT THE NINE O'CLOCK NEWS CAST   UK/New Zealand

ALBUMS:	HITS 3			WEEKS 51
NOT THE NINE O'CLOCK NEWS	BBC	5	8 Nov 80	23
NOT THE NINE O'CLOCK NEWS – HEDGEHOG SANDWICH	BBC	5	17 Oct 81	24
THE MEMORY KINDA LINGERS	BBC	63	23 Oct 82	4

Freddie NOTES and the RUDIES   Jamaica

SINGLES:	HITS 1			WEEKS 2
MONTEGO BAY	Trojan	45	10 Oct 70	2

NOTORIOUS B.I.G.   US

(See also Puff Daddy.)

SINGLES:	HITS 8			WEEKS 25
JUICY	Bad Boy	72	29 Oct 94	1
BIG POPPA	Puff Daddy	63	1 Apr 95	1
Samples Between The Sheets by the Isley Brothers.				
CAN'T YOU SEE	Tommy Boy	43	15 Jul 95	2
From the film 'New Jersey Drive'.				
Above hit: TOTAL featuring the NOTORIOUS B.I.G.				
ONE MORE CHANCE/STAY WITH ME [M]	Puff Daddy	34	19 Aug 95	2
HYPNOTIZE	Puff Daddy	10	3 May 97	4
MO MONEY MO PROBLEMS	Puff Daddy	6	9 Aug 97	10
Samples Diana Ross's I'm Coming Out.				
Above hit: NOTORIOUS B.I.G. featuring PUFF DADDY and MASE.				
SKY'S THE LIMIT	Puff Daddy	35	14 Feb 98	2
Above hit: NOTORIOUS B.I.G. featuring 112.				
RUNNIN'	Black Jam	15	18 Jul 98	3
Above hit: 2PAC and NOTORIOUS B.I.G.				
ALBUMS:	HITS 2			WEEKS 17
LIFE AFTER DEATH	Puff Daddy	23	5 Apr 97	16
BORN AGAIN	Puff Daddy	70	18 Dec 99	1
Compilation.				

NOTTING HILLBILLIES

UK

ALBUMS:		HITS 1		WEEKS 14	
MISSING . . . PRESUMED HAVING A GOOD TIME	Vertigo	2	17 Mar 90	14

NOTTINGHAM FOREST with PAPER LACE

UK

(See also Paper Lace.)

SINGLES:		HITS 1		WEEKS 6	
WE GOT THE WHOLE WORLD IN OUR HANDS	Warner Brothers	24	4 Mar 78	6

Heather NOVA

US

SINGLES:		HITS 1		WEEKS 1	
WALK THIS WORLD	Butterfly	69	25 Feb 95	1
ALBUMS:		**HITS 2**		**WEEKS 2**	
OYSTER	Butterfly	72	8 Apr 95	1
SIREN	V2	55	20 Jun 98	1

Nancy NOVA

UK

SINGLES:		HITS 1		WEEKS 2	
NO, NO, NO	EMI	63	4 Sep 82	2

NOVY vs. ENIAC

Germany

SINGLES:		HITS 1		WEEKS 3	
SUPERSTAR	D:disco	32	2 May 98	3

NRG

UK

SINGLES:		HITS 1		WEEKS 2	
NEVER LOST HIS HARDCORE	Top Banana	71	29 Mar 97	1
NEVER LOST HIS HARDCORE '98 [RM]	Banana Recordings	61	12 Dec 98	1
Remixed by Floorplay.				

*NSYNC

US

SINGLES:		HITS 2		WEEKS 23	
TEARIN' UP MY HEART	Arista	40	13 Sep 97	2
I WANT YOU BACK	Arista	62	22 Nov 97	1
Above 2: 'N SYNC.				
I WANT YOU BACK [RI]	Northwestside	5	27 Feb 99	8
I WANT YOU BACK [RI] [RE]	Northwestside	62	8 May 99	2
TEARIN* UP MY HEART [RI]	Northwestside	9	26 Jun 99	8
TEARIN* UP MY HEART [RI] [RE]	Northwestside	73	11 Sep 99	2
ALBUMS:		**HITS 1**		**WEEKS 2**	
*NSYNC	Northwestside	30	17 Jul 99	2

NU-BIRTH

UK

SINGLES:		HITS 1		WEEKS 2	
ANYTIME	XL Recordings	48	6 Sep 97	1
Single started out as a remix of Richard Darbyshire's Wherever Love Is Found.				
ANYTIME [RI]	Locked On	41	6 Jun 98	1

NU COLOURS

UK

SINGLES:		HITS 5		WEEKS 11	
TEARS	Wild Card	55	6 Jun 92	2
POWER	Wild Card	64	10 Oct 92	1
WHAT IN THE WORLD	Wild Card	57	5 Jun 93	2
POWER (THE E SMOOVE REMIXES) [RM]	Wild Card	40	27 Nov 93	2
Remixed by Eric "E-Smoove" Miller.				
DESIRE	Wild Card	31	25 May 96	2
SPECIAL KIND OF LOVER	Wild Card	38	24 Aug 96	2

NU-MATIC

UK

SINGLES:		HITS 1		WEEKS 1	
SPRING IN MY STEP	XL Recordings	58	8 Aug 92	1

NU SHOOZ

US

SINGLES:		HITS 2		WEEKS 17	
I CAN'T WAIT	Atlantic	2	24 May 86	14
POINT OF NO RETURN	Atlantic	48	26 Jul 86	3
ALBUMS:		**HITS 1**		**WEEKS 8**	
POOLSIDE	Atlantic	32	14 Jun 86	8

NU SOUL featuring Kelli RICH
US

SINGLES:	HITS 1			WEEKS 2
HIDE-A-WAY	*ffrr*	27	13 Jan 96	2

NUANCE featuring Vikki LOVE
US

SINGLES:	HITS 1			WEEKS 3
LOVERIDE	*Fourth & Broadway*	59	19 Jan 85	3

NUBIAN PRINZ – See POWERCUT featuring NUBIAN PRINZ

NUCLEAR ASSAULT
US

ALBUMS:	HITS 1			WEEKS 1
HANDLE WITH CARE	*Under One Flag*	60	7 Oct 89	1

NUCLEUS
UK

ALBUMS:	HITS 1			WEEKS 1
ELASTIC ROCK	*Vertigo*	46	11 Jul 70	1

NUFF JUICE – See D-MOB

Ted NUGENT
US

ALBUMS:	HITS 6			WEEKS 14
TED NUGENT	*Epic*	56	4 Sep 76	1
FREE FOR ALL	*Epic*	33	30 Oct 76	2
CAT SCRATCH FEVER	*Epic*	28	2 Jul 77	5
DOUBLE LIVE GONZO!	*Epic*	47	11 Mar 78	2
SCREAM DREAM	*Epic*	37	14 Jun 80	3
IN 10 CITIES	*Epic*	75	25 Apr 81	1

Gary NUMAN
UK

(See also Sharpe and Numan.)

SINGLES:	HITS 29			WEEKS 148
ARE 'FRIENDS' ELECTRIC?	*Beggars Banquet*	1	19 May 79	16
Above hit: TUBEWAY ARMY.				
CARS	*Beggars Banquet*	1	1 Sep 79	11
COMPLEX	*Beggars Banquet*	6	24 Nov 79	9
WE ARE GLASS	*Beggars Banquet*	5	24 May 80	7
I DIE: YOU DIE	*Beggars Banquet*	6	30 Aug 80	7
THIS WRECKAGE	*Beggars Banquet*	20	20 Dec 80	7
SHE'S GOT CLAWS	*Beggars Banquet*	6	29 Aug 81	6
Features Roger Taylor from Queen on drums.				
LOVE NEEDS NO DISGUISE	*Beggars Banquet*	33	5 Dec 81	7
Above hit: Gary NUMAN and DRAMATIS.				
MUSIC FOR CHAMELEONS	*Beggars Banquet*	19	6 Mar 82	7
WE TAKE MYSTERY (TO BED)	*Beggars Banquet*	9	19 Jun 82	4
WHITE BOYS AND HEROES	*Beggars Banquet*	20	28 Aug 82	4
WARRIORS	*Beggars Banquet*	20	3 Sep 83	5
SISTER SURPRISE	*Beggars Banquet*	32	22 Oct 83	3
BERSERKER	*Numa*	32	3 Nov 84	5
MY DYING MACHINE	*Numa*	66	22 Dec 84	1
GARY NUMAN – THE LIVE [EP]	*Numa*	27	25 May 85	4
Lead track: Are "Friends" Electric?. Live recordings from Hammersmith Odeon, London, Dec 84.				
YOUR FASCINATION	*Numa*	46	10 Aug 85	5
CALL OUT THE DOGS	*Numa*	49	21 Sep 85	2
MIRACLES	*Numa*	49	16 Nov 85	3
THIS IS LOVE	*Numa*	28	19 Apr 86	3
I CAN'T STOP	*Numa*	27	28 Jun 86	4
I STILL REMEMBER	*Numa*	74	6 Dec 86	1
Charity record with proceeds to the R..S.P.C.A.				
RADIO HEART	*GFM*	35	28 Mar 87	6
LONDON TIMES	*GFM*	48	13 Jun 87	2
Above 2: RADIO HEART featuring Gary NUMAN.				
CARS ('E' REG MODEL) [RM-1ST] / ARE 'FRIENDS' ELECTRIC [RM]	*Beggars Banquet*	16	19 Sep 87	7
NEW ANGER	*Illegal*	46	1 Oct 88	1
AMERICA	*Illegal*	49	3 Dec 88	1
HEART	*I.R.S.*	43	16 Mar 91	2
THE SKIN GAME	*Numa*	68	21 Mar 92	1
MACHINE + SOUL	*Numa*	72	1 Aug 92	1
CARS [RM-2ND]	*Beggars Banquet*	53	4 Sep 93	1
Remixed by Charles Pierre and Francis Usmar of Native Soul.				
CARS (PREMIER MIX) [RM-1ST] [RI]	*PolyGram TV*	17	16 Mar 96	4
Featured in the Carling Premier Lager TV commercial.				
ALBUMS:	**HITS 24**			**WEEKS 142**
REPLICAS	*Beggars Banquet*	1	9 Jun 79	31

TUBEWAY ARMY	*Beggars Banquet*	14	*25 Aug 79*	10

Originally released in 1978.
Above 2: TUBEWAY ARMY.

THE PLEASURE PRINCIPLE	*Beggars Banquet*	1	*22 Sep 79*	21
TELEKON	*Beggars Banquet*	1	*13 Sep 80*	11
LIVING ORNAMENTS 1979–1980	*Beggars Banquet*	2	*2 May 81*	4

Double boxed set of the 2 separate Living Ornaments albums.

LIVING ORNAMENTS 1980	*Beggars Banquet*	39	*2 May 81*	3
LIVING ORNAMENTS 1979	*Beggars Banquet*	47	*2 May 81*	3
DANCE	*Beggars Banquet*	3	*12 Sep 81*	8
I, ASSASSIN	*Beggars Banquet*	8	*18 Sep 82*	6
NEW MAN NUMAN – THE BEST OF GARY NUMAN	*TV Records*	45	*27 Nov 82*	7
WARRIORS	*Beggars Banquet*	12	*24 Sep 83*	6
THE PLAN 1978	*Beggars Banquet*	29	*6 Oct 84*	4

Above hit: TUBEWAY ARMY and Gary NUMAN.

BERSERKER	*Numa*	45	*24 Nov 84*	3
WHITE NOISE – LIVE	*Numa*	29	*13 Apr 85*	5

Live recordings from 1984.

THE FURY	*Numa*	24	*28 Sep 85*	5
STRANGE CHARM	*Numa*	59	*8 Nov 86*	2
EXHIBITION	*Beggars Banquet*	43	*3 Oct 87*	3

Compilation.

METAL RHYTHM	*Illegal*	48	*8 Oct 88*	2
SKIN MECHANIC	*I.R.S.*	55	*28 Oct 89*	1
OUTLAND	*I.R.S.*	39	*30 Mar 91*	1
MACHINE + SOUL	*Numa*	42	*22 Aug 92*	1
BEST OF GARY NUMAN 1978-83	*Beggars Banquet*	70	*2 Oct 93*	1
THE PREMIER HITS	*PolyGram TV*	21	*30 Mar 96*	3

Above hit: Gary NUMAN/TUBEWAY ARMY.

EXILE	*Eagle*	48	*1 Nov 97*	1

NUMBER ONE CUP — US

SINGLES:	HITS 1			WEEKS 1
DIVEBOMB	*Blue Rose*	61	*2 Mar 96*	1

From the film 'Learning Curves'.

Jose NUNEZ featuring OCTAHVIA — US

SINGLES:	HITS 2			WEEKS 2
IN MY LIFE	*Ministry Of Sound*	56	*5 Sep 98*	1
HOLD ON	*Sound Of Ministry*	44	*5 Jun 99*	1

Bobby NUNN — US

SINGLES:	HITS 1			WEEKS 3
DON'T KNOCK IT (UNTIL YOU TRY IT)	*Motown*	65	*4 Feb 84*	3

NUSH — UK

(See also Congress.)

SINGLES:	HITS 2			WEEKS 7
U GIRLS	*Blunted Vinyl*	58	*23 Jul 94*	1
MOVE THAT BODY	*Blunted Vinyl*	46	*22 Apr 95*	2
U GIRLS (LOOK SO SEXY) [RM]	*Blunted Vinyl*	15	*16 Sep 95*	4

This is the original Nush mix that was released before the 1994 entry above.

NUT — UK

SINGLES:	HITS 3			WEEKS 4
BRAINS	*Epic*	64	*8 Jun 96*	1
CRAZY	*Epic*	56	*21 Sep 96*	1
SCREAM	*Epic*	43	*11 Jan 97*	2

Originally released in 1996.

NUTTIN' NYCE — US

SINGLES:	HITS 2			WEEKS 2
DOWN 4 WHATEVA	*Jive*	62	*10 Jun 95*	1

From the film 'A Low Down Dirty Shame'. Samples Back To Life by Soul II Soul.

FROGGY STYLE	*Jive*	68	*12 Aug 95*	1

NUYORICAN SOUL — US

(See also Masters At Work present India; River Ocean featuring India.)

SINGLES:	HITS 3			WEEKS 8
RUNAWAY	*Talkin Loud*	24	*8 Feb 97*	4

*Features backing vocals from Vincent Montana of Montana Sextet. Originaly recorded by Loleatta
    Holloway in the early 1980s.*
Above hit: NUYORICAN SOUL featuring INDIA.

IT'S ALRIGHT, I FEEL IT!	*Talkin Loud*	26	*10 May 97*	2

I AM THE BLACK GOLD OF THE SUN	Talkin Loud	31	25 Oct 97	2

Originally recorded by Minnie Riperton's band The Rotary Connection.
Above 2: NUYORICAN SOUL featuring Jocelyn BROWN.

ALBUMS:		HITS 1		WEEKS 2
NUYORICAN SOUL	Talkin Loud	25	1 Mar 97	2

Joe NYE - See DNA

NYLON MOON
Italy

SINGLES:		HITS 1		WEEKS 2
SKY PLUS	Positiva	43	13 Apr 96	2

Michael NYMAN
UK

SINGLES:		HITS 1		WEEKS 2
(THE PIANO SINGLE) THE HEART ASKS PLEASURE FIRST/THE PROMISE [M]	Virgin	60	19 Mar 94	2

From the film 'The Piano'. Features the Munich Philharmonic Orchestra.

ALBUMS:		HITS 1		WEEKS 15
NYMAN: THE PIANO [OST]	Venture	31	12 Feb 94	15

Above hit: Michael NYMAN with the MUNICH PHILHARMONIC ORCHESTRA.

O

O.R.G.A.N.
Spain

SINGLES:		HITS 1		WEEKS 2
TO THE WORLD	Multiply	33	16 May 98	2

O.R.N.
UK

SINGLES:		HITS 1		WEEKS 1
SNOW	Deconstruction	61	1 Mar 97	1

O.T. QUARTET - See OUR TRIBE/ONE TRIBE/O.T. QUARTET

Philip OAKEY and Giorgio MORODER
UK/Italy

(See also Giorgio Moroder.)

SINGLES:		HITS 2		WEEKS 18
TOGETHER IN ELECTRIC DREAMS	Virgin	3	22 Sep 84	13

From the film 'Electric Dreams'.
Above hit: Giorgio MORODER with Philip OAKEY.

GOOD-BYE BAD TIMES	Virgin	44	29 Jun 85	5

ALBUMS:		HITS 1		WEEKS 5
PHILIP OAKEY AND GIORGIO MORODER	Virgin	52	10 Aug 85	5

OASIS
UK

ALBUMS:		HITS 1		WEEKS 14
OASIS	WEA	23	28 Apr 84	14

OASIS
UK

SINGLES:		HITS 13		WEEKS 283
SUPERSONIC	Creation	31	23 Apr 94	3
SHAKERMAKER	Creation	11	2 Jul 94	5
LIVE FOREVER	Creation	10	20 Aug 94	5
CIGARETTES AND ALCOHOL	Creation	7	22 Oct 94	6
CIGARETTES AND ALCOHOL [RE-1ST]	Creation	69	31 Dec 94	1
WHATEVER	Creation	3	31 Dec 94	10
SOME MIGHT SAY	Creation	1	6 May 95	14
SOME MIGHT SAY	Creation	71	13 May 95	1

Sales from 12" format which, as there were already 3 formats available was listed separately.

SUPERSONIC [RE-1ST]	Creation	44	24 Jun 95	3
WHATEVER [RE-1ST]	Creation	48	24 Jun 95	3
LIVE FOREVER [RE-1ST]	Creation	50	24 Jun 95	3
SHAKERMAKER [RE-1ST]	Creation	52	24 Jun 95	3
CIGARETTES AND ALCOHOL [RE-2ND]	Creation	53	24 Jun 95	3
ROLL WITH IT	Creation	2	26 Aug 95	11

The 12" format reached No. 92.

SOME MIGHT SAY [RE-1ST]	Creation	73	26 Aug 95	1
WONDERWALL	Creation	2	11 Nov 95	20
WIBBLING RIVALRY: A LOT OF SWEARING AND CUSSING / EVEN MORE SWEARING AND CUSSING	Fierce Panda	52	25 Nov 95	2

2 tracks of an argument between Liam and Noel Gallagher recorded after they had finished an interview for Radio One.
Above hit: OAS*S.

WHATEVER [RE-2ND]	Creation	75	9 Dec 95	1

SUPERSONIC [RE-2ND]	*Creation*	54	*30 Dec 95*	4
WHATEVER [RE-3RD]	*Creation*	55	*30 Dec 95*	3
CIGARETTES AND ALCOHOL [RE-3RD]	*Creation*	58	*30 Dec 95*	7
SOME MIGHT SAY [RE-2ND]	*Creation*	59	*6 Jan 96*	3
SHAKERMAKER [RE-2ND]	*Creation*	61	*6 Jan 96*	2
LIVE FOREVER [RE-2ND]	*Creation*	64	*6 Jan 96*	1
ROLL WITH IT [RE-1ST]	*Creation*	65	*6 Jan 96*	3
LIVE FOREVER [RE-3RD]	*Creation*	71	*20 Jan 96*	2
WHATEVER [RE-4TH]	*Creation*	61	*27 Jan 96*	3
WHATEVER [RE-5TH]	*Creation*	55	*24 Feb 96*	15
DON'T LOOK BACK IN ANGER	*Creation*	1	*2 Mar 96*	16
CIGARETTES AND ALCOHOL [RE-4TH]	*Creation*	62	*2 Mar 96*	4
SUPERSONIC [RE-3RD]	*Creation*	71	*2 Mar 96*	1
LIVE FOREVER [RE-4TH]	*Creation*	74	*2 Mar 96*	2
SHAKERMAKER [RE-3RD]	*Creation*	74	*2 Mar 96*	1
SOME MIGHT SAY [RE-3RD]	*Creation*	75	*16 Mar 96*	1
CIGARETTES AND ALCOHOL [RE-5TH]	*Creation*	74	*13 Apr 96*	2
CIGARETTES AND ALCOHOL [RE-6TH]	*Creation*	72	*11 May 96*	3
WHATEVER [RE-6TH]	*Creation*	62	*17 Aug 96*	4
WONDERWALL [RE-1ST]	*Creation*	60	*24 Aug 96*	5
SOME MIGHT SAY [RE-8TH]	*Creation*	70	*24 Aug 96*	1
CIGARETTES AND ALCOHOL [RE-7TH]	*Creation*	72	*24 Aug 96*	1
WHATEVER [RE-7TH]	*Creation*	66	*21 Sep 96*	1
WHATEVER [RE-8TH]	*Creation*	34	*16 Nov 96*	10
WONDERWALL [RE-2ND]	*Creation*	36	*16 Nov 96*	9
CIGARETTES AND ALCOHOL [RE-8TH]	*Creation*	38	*16 Nov 96*	5
SOME MIGHT SAY [RE-5TH]	*Creation*	40	*16 Nov 96*	4
LIVE FOREVER [RE-5TH]	*Creation*	42	*16 Nov 96*	2
SUPERSONIC [RE-4TH]	*Creation*	47	*16 Nov 96*	2
SHAKERMAKER [RE-4TH]	*Creation*	48	*16 Nov 96*	2
DON'T LOOK BACK IN ANGER [RE-1ST]	*Creation*	53	*16 Nov 96*	5
ROLL WITH IT [RE-2ND]	*Creation*	55	*16 Nov 96*	2
All the above singles re-entered on 16 Nov 96 after a promotion offering 3 singles for £10.				
DON'T LOOK BACK IN ANGER [RE-2ND]	*Creation*	53	*28 Dec 96*	3
CIGARETTES AND ALCOHOL [RE-9TH]	*Creation*	56	*28 Dec 96*	3
SOME MIGHT SAY [RE-6TH]	*Creation*	58	*28 Dec 96*	3
LIVE FOREVER [RE-6TH]	*Creation*	59	*28 Dec 96*	3
SHAKERMAKER [RE-5TH]	*Creation*	61	*4 Jan 97*	2
ROLL WITH IT [RE-3RD]	*Creation*	62	*4 Jan 97*	2
SUPERSONIC [RE-5TH]	*Creation*	63	*4 Jan 97*	1
D'YOU KNOW WHAT I MEAN?	*Creation*	1	*19 Jul 97*	18
STAND BY ME	*Creation*	2	*4 Oct 97*	18
ALL AROUND THE WORLD	*Creation*	1	*24 Jan 98*	7
Longest single to reach No.1 at 9 minutes 38 seconds.				
ALL AROUND THE WORLD [RE]	*Creation*	68	*11 Apr 98*	2
ALBUMS:	**HITS 6**		**WEEKS 383**	
DEFINITELY MAYBE	*Creation*	1	*10 Sep 94*	174
Includes re-entries through to 1999.				
(WHAT'S THE STORY) MORNING GLORY?	*Creation*	1	*14 Oct 95*	145
The 2nd best selling album in the UK.				
(WHAT'S THE STORY) MORNING GLORY? SINGLES BOX – GOLD	*Creation*	24	*16 Nov 96*	3
DEFINITELY MAYBE SINGLES BOX – SILVER	*Creation*	23	*16 Nov 96*	3
BE HERE NOW	*Creation*	1	*30 Aug 97*	36
THE MASTERPLAN	*Creation*	2	*14 Nov 98*	22

John OATES – See Daryl HALL and John OATES

OBERNKIRCHEN CHILDREN'S CHOIR
			Germany	
SINGLES:	**HITS 1**		**WEEKS 26**	
THE HAPPY WANDERER (DER FROHLICHE WANDERER)	*Parlophone*	2	*23 Jan 54*	23
THE HAPPY WANDERER (DER FROHLICHE WANDERER) [RE]	*Parlophone*	8	*10 Jul 54*	3

OBITUARY
			US	
ALBUMS:	**HITS 2**		**WEEKS 2**	
THE END COMPLETE	*Roadrunner*	52	*18 Apr 92*	1
WORLD DEMISE	*Roadrunner*	65	*17 Sep 94*	1

Dermot O'BRIEN and his CLUBMEN
			Ireland	
SINGLES:	**HITS 1**		**WEEKS 2**	
THE MERRY PLOUGHBOY (OFF TO DUBLIN IN THE GREEN)	*Envoy*	46	*22 Oct 66*	1
THE MERRY PLOUGHBOY (OFF TO DUBLIN IN THE GREEN) [RE]	*Envoy*	50	*5 Nov 66*	1

Billy OCEAN
			UK	
SINGLES:	**HITS 19**		**WEEKS 153**	
LOVE REALLY HURTS WITHOUT YOU	*GTO*	2	*21 Feb 76*	10
L.O.D. (LOVE ON DELIVERY)	*GTO*	19	*10 Jul 76*	8

STOP ME (IF YOU'VE HEARD IT ALL BEFORE)	GTO	12	13 Nov 76	11
RED LIGHT SPELLS DANGER	GTO	2	19 Mar 77	10
Some copies have title as Red Light.				
AMERICAN HEARTS	GTO	54	1 Sep 79	5
ARE YOU READY	GTO	42	19 Jan 80	7
CARIBBEAN QUEEN (NO MORE LOVE ON THE RUN)	Jive	6	13 Oct 84	14
Originally released as European Queen, reaching No. 82 in June 84.				
LOVERBOY	Jive	15	19 Jan 85	10
SUDDENLY	Jive	4	11 May 85	14
MYSTERY LADY	Jive	49	17 Aug 85	4
WHEN THE GOING GETS TOUGH, THE TOUGH GET GOING	Jive	1	25 Jan 86	13
From the film 'The Jewel Of The Nile'.				
THERE'LL BE SAD SONGS (TO MAKE YOU CRY)	Jive	12	12 Apr 86	13
LOVE ZONE	Jive	49	9 Aug 86	3
BITTERSWEET	Jive	44	11 Oct 86	4
LOVE IS FOREVER	Jive	34	10 Jan 87	7
GET OUTTA MY DREAMS, GET INTO MY CAR	Jive	3	6 Feb 88	11
CALYPSO CRAZY	Jive	35	7 May 88	4
THE COLOUR OF LOVE	Jive	65	6 Aug 88	3
PRESSURE	Jive	55	6 Feb 93	2
ALBUMS:	**HITS 4**			**WEEKS 142**
SUDDENLY	Jive	46	24 Nov 84	13
SUDDENLY [RE]	Jive	9	11 May 85	46
LOVE ZONE	Jive	2	17 May 86	32
TEAR DOWN THESE WALLS	Jive	3	19 Mar 88	13
GREATEST HITS	Jive	4	28 Oct 89	17
LOVE IS FOR EVER	Jive	7	16 Aug 97	21
Expanded version of the Greatest Hits album including 1993 material.				

OCEAN COLOUR SCENE　　　　　　　　　　　　　　　　　　　　UK

(See also England United.)

SINGLES:	**HITS 11**			**WEEKS 55**
YESTERDAY TODAY	!Phffft	49	23 Mar 91	1
THE RIVERBOAT SONG	MCA	15	17 Feb 96	5
Features Paul Weller on organ.				
YOU'VE GOT IT BAD	MCA	7	6 Apr 96	4
THE DAY WE CAUGHT THE TRAIN	MCA	4	15 Jun 96	11
THE CIRCLE	MCA	6	28 Sep 96	6
HUNDRED MILE HIGH CITY	MCA	4	28 Jun 97	7
TRAVELLERS TUNE	MCA	5	6 Sep 97	5
BETTER DAY	MCA	9	22 Nov 97	5
IT'S A BEAUTIFUL THING	MCA	12	28 Feb 98	4
Above hit: OCEAN COLOUR SCENE with PP ARNOLD.				
PROFIT IN PEACE	Island	13	4 Sep 99	5
SO LOW	Island	34	27 Nov 99	2
ALBUMS:	**HITS 5**			**WEEKS 137**
MOSELEY SHOALS	MCA	2	20 Apr 96	73
OCEAN COLOUR SCENE	Fontana	54	21 Sep 96	2
Originally released in 1992.				
B-SIDES, SEASIDES & FREERIDES	MCA	4	15 Mar 97	14
MARCHIN' ALREADY	MCA	1	27 Sep 97	37
ONE FROM THE MODERN	Island	4	25 Sep 99	11

OCEANIA　　　　　　　　　　　　　　　　　　　　　　　　Australia

ALBUMS:	**HITS 1**			**WEEKS 1**
OCEANIA	Point Music	70	23 Oct 99	1
Album of aboriginal chants.				

OCEANIC　　　　　　　　　　　　　　　　　　　　　　　　　UK

SINGLES:	**HITS 4**			**WEEKS 26**
INSANITY	Dead Dead Good	3	24 Aug 91	15
WICKED LOVE	Dead Dead Good	25	30 Nov 91	3
WICKED LOVE [RE]	Dead Dead Good	65	28 Dec 91	2
CONTROLLING ME	Dead Dead Good	14	13 Jun 92	5
IGNORANCE	Dead Dead Good	72	14 Nov 92	1
Above hit: OCEANIC featuring Siobhan MAHER.				
ALBUMS:	**HITS 1**			**WEEKS 2**
THAT ALBUM BY OCEANIC	Dead Dead Good	49	4 Jul 92	2

Des O'CONNOR　　　　　　　　　　　　　　　　　　　　　　UK

SINGLES:	**HITS 8**			**WEEKS 117**
CARELESS HANDS	Columbia	6	4 Nov 67	17
Originally recorded by Mel Torme.				
Above hit: Des O'CONNOR with the Mike SAMMES SINGERS and Alyn				
AINSWORTH and his Orchestra.				

I PRETEND	Columbia	1	11 May 68	36
ONE, TWO, THREE O'LEARY	Columbia	4	23 Nov 68	11
DICK-A-DUM-DUM (KING'S ROAD)	Columbia	14	10 May 69	10
Co-written by actor Jim Dale.				
LONELINESS (NON SONO MADDALENA)	Columbia	18	29 Nov 69	11
I'LL GO ON HOPING	Columbia	30	14 Mar 70	7
THE TIP OF MY FINGERS	Columbia	15	26 Sep 70	15
Originally recorded by Bill Anderson.				
Above 5: Des O'CONNOR with Alyn AINSWORTH and his Orchestra.				
THE SKYE BOAT SONG	Tembo	10	8 Nov 86	10
Above hit: Roger WHITTAKER and Des O'CONNOR.				
ALBUMS:	**HITS 6**			**WEEKS 45**
I PRETEND	Columbia	8	7 Dec 68	10
WITH LOVE	Columbia	40	5 Dec 70	4
SING A FAVOURITE SONG	Pye	25	2 Dec 72	6
JUST FOR YOU	Warwick	17	2 Feb 80	7
DES O'CONNOR NOW	Telstar	24	13 Oct 84	14
PORTRAIT	Columbia	63	5 Dec 92	4

Hazel O'CONNOR   UK

SINGLES:	**HITS 7**			**WEEKS 46**
EIGHTH DAY	A&M	5	16 Aug 80	11
GIVE ME AN INCH	A&M	41	25 Oct 80	4
Above 2 from the film 'Breaking Glass'.				
D-DAYS	Albion	10	21 Mar 81	9
WILL YOU?	A&M	8	23 May 81	10
From the film 'Breaking Glass'. Saxophone solo by Wesley McGoogan.				
(COVER PLUS) WE'RE ALL GROWN UP	Albion	41	1 Aug 81	6
HANGING AROUND	Albion	45	3 Oct 81	3
CALLS THE TUNE	A&M	60	23 Jan 82	3
From the film 'Breaking Glass'.				
ALBUMS:	**HITS 2**			**WEEKS 45**
BREAKING GLASS [OST]	A&M	5	9 Aug 80	38
COVER PLUS	Albion	32	12 Sep 81	7

Sinead O'CONNOR   Ireland

SINGLES:	**HITS 14**			**WEEKS 64**
MANDINKA	Ensign	17	16 Jan 88	9
NOTHING COMPARES 2 U	Ensign	1	20 Jan 90	14
Written by Prince and originally recorded by The Family.				
THE EMPEROR'S NEW CLOTHES	Ensign	31	21 Jul 90	5
THREE BABIES	Ensign	42	20 Oct 90	4
MY SPECIAL CHILD	Ensign	42	8 Jun 91	3
SILENT NIGHT	Ensign	60	14 Dec 91	4
SUCCESS HAS MADE A FAILURE OF OUR HOME	Ensign	18	12 Sep 92	4
DON'T CRY FOR ME ARGENTINA	Ensign	53	12 Dec 92	4
YOU MADE ME THE THIEF OF YOUR HEART	Island	42	19 Feb 94	3
From the film 'The Name Of The Father'.				
THANK YOU FOR HEARING ME	Ensign	13	26 Nov 94	7
HAUNTED	ZTT	30	29 Apr 95	2
Above hit: Shane MacGOWAN and Sinead O'CONNOR.				
FAMINE	Chrysalis	51	26 Aug 95	1
GOSPEL OAK [EP]	Chrysalis	28	17 May 97	3
Lead track: This Is To Mother You. Features vocals by Jah Wobble.				
THIS IS A REBEL SONG	Columbia	60	6 Dec 97	1
ALBUMS:	**HITS 5**			**WEEKS 88**
THE LION AND THE COBRA	Ensign	27	23 Jan 88	20
I DO NOT WANT WHAT I HAVEN'T GOT	Ensign	1	24 Mar 90	51
AM I NOT YOUR GIRL?	Ensign	6	26 Sep 92	6
UNIVERSAL MOTHER	Ensign	19	24 Sep 94	8
SO FAR . . . THE BEST OF SINEAD O'CONNOR	Chrysalis	28	22 Nov 97	3

OCTAHVIA - See Jose NUNEZ featuring OCTAHVIA

OCTOPUS   UK/France

SINGLES:	**HITS 3**			**WEEKS 5**
YOUR SMILE	Food	42	22 Jun 96	2
SAVED	Food	40	14 Sep 96	2
JEALOUSY	Food	59	23 Nov 96	1

Alan O'DAY   US

SINGLES:	**HITS 1**			**WEEKS 3**
UNDERCOVER ANGEL	Atlantic	43	2 Jul 77	3

ODB - See OMAR; PRAS

ODETTA - See Harry BELAFONTE

Daniel O'DONNELL　　　　　　　　　　　　　　　　　　　　　Ireland

SINGLES:		HITS 15		WEEKS 55	
I JUST WANT TO DANCE WITH YOU	Ritz	20	12 Sep 92	7
THE THREE BELLS	Ritz	71	2 Jan 93	1
THE LOVE IN YOUR EYES	Ritz	47	8 May 93	3
WHAT EVER HAPPENED TO OLD FASHIONED LOVE	Ritz	21	7 Aug 93	5
Originally recorded by B.J. Thomas.				
SINGING THE BLUES	Ritz	23	16 Apr 94	3
THE GIFT	Ritz	46	26 Nov 94	3
SECRET LOVE	Ritz	28	10 Jun 95	3
TIMELESS	Ritz	32	9 Mar 96	3
Above 2: Daniel O'DONNELL and Mary DUFF.				
FOOTSTEPS	Ritz	25	28 Sep 96	5
THE LOVE SONGS [EP]	Ritz	27	7 Jun 97	4
Lead track: Save The Last Dance For Me.				
GIVE A LITTLE LOVE	Ritz	7	11 Apr 98	5
Charity single with proceeds to The Romanian Challenge Appeal.				
THE MAGIC IS THERE	Ritz	16	17 Oct 98	4
THE WAY DREAMS ARE	Ritz	18	20 Mar 99	3
UNO MAS	Ritz	25	24 Jul 99	3
A CHRISTMAS KISS	Ritz	20	18 Dec 99	3
ALBUMS:		**HITS 16**		**WEEKS 143**
FROM THE HEART	Telstar	56	15 Oct 88	12
THOUGHTS OF HOME	Telstar	43	28 Oct 89	10
FAVOURITES	Ritz	75	21 Apr 90	1
THE LAST WALTZ	Ritz	53	17 Nov 90	5
THE VERY BEST OF DANIEL O'DONNELL	Ritz	34	9 Nov 91	14
FOLLOW YOUR DREAM	Ritz	17	21 Nov 92	9
A DATE WITH DANIEL - LIVE	Ritz	21	6 Nov 93	10
Live recordings from The Point in Dublin.				
THE LAST WALTZ [RE]	Ritz	46	30 Jul 94	2
FAVOURITES [RE]	Ritz	61	30 Jul 94	2
ESPECIALLY FOR YOU	Ritz	14	22 Oct 94	11
CHRISTMAS WITH DANIEL	Ritz	34	3 Dec 94	5
THE CLASSIC COLLECTION	Ritz	34	11 Nov 95	9
Collection of his most popular recordings plus 7 new tracks.				
TIMELESS	Ritz	13	6 Apr 96	5
Above hit: Daniel O'DONNELL and Mary DUFF.				
THE DANIEL O'DONNELL IRISH COLLECTION	Ritz	35	20 Jul 96	3
Album of his most requested Irish songs.				
SONGS OF INSPIRATION	Ritz	11	26 Oct 96	16
Traditional ballads with a religious theme.				
I BELIEVE	Ritz	11	8 Nov 97	11
LOVE SONGS	Ritz	9	31 Oct 98	10
GREATEST HITS	Ritz	10	2 Oct 99	8

ODYSSEY　　　　　　　　　　　　　　　　　　　　　　　　　　　US

SINGLES:		HITS 9		WEEKS 82	
NATIVE NEW YORKER	RCA Victor	5	24 Dec 77	11
Originally recorded by Frankie Valli.				
USE IT UP AND WEAR IT OUT	RCA	1	21 Jun 80	12
IF YOU'RE LOOKIN' FOR A WAY OUT	RCA	6	13 Sep 80	15
HANG TOGETHER	RCA	36	17 Jan 81	7
GOING BACK TO MY ROOTS	RCA	4	30 May 81	12
Originally recorded by Lamont Dozier.				
IT WILL BE ALRIGHT	RCA	43	19 Sep 81	5
INSIDE OUT	RCA	3	12 Jun 82	11
MAGIC TOUCH	RCA	41	11 Sep 82	5
(JOY) I KNOW IT	Mirror	51	17 Aug 85	4
ALBUMS:		**HITS 5**		**WEEKS 32**
HANG TOGETHER	RCA	38	16 Aug 80	3
I'VE GOT THE MELODY	RCA	29	4 Jul 81	7
HAPPY TOGETHER	RCA	21	3 Jul 82	9
THE MAGIC TOUCH OF ODYSSEY	Telstar	69	20 Nov 82	5
THE GREATEST HITS	Stylus	26	26 Sep 87	8

OEDIPUS WRECKS - See Pete WYLIE

Esther and Abi OFARIM　　　　　　　　　　　　　　　　　　　　Israel

SINGLES:		HITS 2		WEEKS 22	
CINDERELLA ROCKAFELLA	Philips	1	17 Feb 68	13
Originally recorded by Mason Williams.				
ONE MORE DANCE	Philips	13	22 Jun 68	9

ALBUMS:		HITS 2		WEEKS 24	
2 IN 3		*Philips*	6	*24 Feb 68*	20
OFARIM CONCERT - LIVE '69		*Philips*	29	*12 Jul 69*	4

OFF-SHORE
UK/Germany

SINGLES:		HITS 2		WEEKS 12	
I CAN'T TAKE THE POWER		*CBS*	7	*22 Dec 90*	11
I GOT A LITTLE SONG		*Dance Pool*	64	*17 Aug 91*	1

Wiston OFFICE – See Frank 'K' (featuring Wiston OFFICE)

OFFICIAL RUGBY TEAM SONG featuring Russell WATSON
UK

SINGLES:		HITS 1		WEEKS 2	
SWING LOW '99		*Decca*	38	*30 Oct 99*	2

Official song of the 1999 England World Cup team.

OFFICIAL SCOTLAND WORLD CUP SQUAD and FRIENDS – See SCOTTISH WORLD CUP SQUAD

OFFSPRING
US

SINGLES:		HITS 8		WEEKS 35	
SELF ESTEEM		*Epitaph*	37	*25 Feb 95*	3
GOTTA GET AWAY		*Out Of Step*	43	*19 Aug 95*	2
ALL I WANT		*Epitaph*	31	*1 Feb 97*	2
GONE AWAY		*Epitaph*	42	*26 Apr 97*	1
PRETTY FLY (FOR A WHITE GUY)		*Columbia*	1	*30 Jan 99*	11
Samples Def Leppard's Rock Of Ages.					
WHY DON'T YOU GET A JOB?		*Columbia*	2	*8 May 99*	8
THE KIDS AREN'T ALRIGHT		*Columbia*	11	*11 Sep 99*	6
SHE'S GOT ISSUES		*Columbia*	41	*4 Dec 99*	2
ALBUMS:		HITS 3		WEEKS 80	
SMASH		*Epitaph*	21	*4 Mar 95*	34
IXNAY ON THE HOMBRE		*Epitaph*	17	*15 Feb 97*	3
AMERICANA		*Columbia*	10	*28 Nov 98*	43

OH WELL
Germany

SINGLES:		HITS 2		WEEKS 7	
OH WELL		*Parlophone*	28	*14 Oct 89*	6
RADAR LOVE		*Parlophone*	65	*3 Mar 90*	1

Mary O'HARA
UK

ALBUMS:		HITS 2		WEEKS 12	
MARY O'HARA AT THE ROYAL FESTIVAL HALL		*Chrysalis*	37	*8 Apr 78*	3
TRANQUILLITY		*Warwick*	12	*1 Dec 79*	9

OHIO EXPRESS
US

SINGLES:		HITS 1		WEEKS 15	
YUMMY YUMMY YUMMY		*Pye International*	5	*8 Jun 68*	15

OHIO PLAYERS
US

SINGLES:		HITS 1		WEEKS 4	
WHO'D SHE COO?		*Mercury*	43	*10 Jul 76*	4

David OISTRAKH – See Herbert VON KARAJAN conducting the BERLIN PHILHARMONIC ORCHESTRA

O'JAYS
US

(See also Philadelphia International All-Stars: Lou Rawls, Billy Paul, Archie Bell, Teddy Pendergrass, O'Jays, Dee Dee Sharp, Gamble.)

SINGLES:		HITS 8		WEEKS 72	
BACK STABBERS		*CBS*	14	*23 Sep 72*	9
LOVE TRAIN		*CBS*	9	*3 Mar 73*	13
I LOVE MUSIC		*Philadelphia International*	13	*31 Jan 76*	9
DARLIN' DARLIN' BABY (SWEET, TENDER, LOVE)		*Philadelphia International*	24	*12 Feb 77*	6
I LOVE MUSIC [RI]		*Philadelphia International*	36	*8 Apr 78*	3
USED TA BE MY GIRL		*Philadelphia International*	12	*17 Jun 78*	12
BRANDY		*Philadelphia International*	21	*30 Sep 78*	9
SING A HAPPY SONG		*Philadelphia International*	39	*29 Sep 79*	6
PUT OUR HEADS TOGETHER		*Philadelphia International*	45	*30 Jul 83*	5
ALBUMS:		HITS 1		WEEKS 2	
THE ARTISTS VOLUME III		*Street Sounds*	87	*12 Oct 85*	2

Compilation album with tracks by each artist.
Above hit: WOMACK and WOMACK/O'JAYS/KLEEER/S.O.S. BAND.

John O'KANE
UK

SINGLES:		HITS 1		WEEKS 4	
STAY WITH ME		*Circa*	41	*9 May 92*	4

OL' DIRTY BASTARD - See OMAR; PRAS

OLD SCHOOL JUNKIES PT. 2 - See Armand VAN HELDEN

OLD SKOOL ORCHESTRA
UK

SINGLES:		HITS 1		WEEKS 1
B-BOY HUMP	East West	55	23 Jan 99	1

Samples Engelbert Humperdinck's Can't Take My Eyes Off You.

Mike OLDFIELD
UK

SINGLES:		HITS 19		WEEKS 113
MIKE OLDFIELD'S SINGLE (THEME FROM MIKE OLDFIELD'S ALBUM 'TUBULAR BELLS')	Virgin	31	13 Jul 74	6
IN DULCI JUBILO / ON HORSEBACK	Virgin	4	20 Dec 75	10

On Horseback credited to Mike Oldfield.
Above hit: Mike OLDFIELD; recorder: Leslie PENNING.

PORTSMOUTH	Virgin	3	27 Nov 76	12
TAKE 4 [EP]	Virgin	72	23 Dec 78	3

Lead track: Portsmouth, which is a re-issue.

GUILTY	Virgin	22	21 Apr 79	8
BLUE PETER	Virgin	19	8 Dec 79	9

Charity record with proceeds to the BBC TV's 'Blue Peter Cambodia Appeal'.

FIVE MILES OUT	Virgin	43	20 Mar 82	5
FAMILY MAN	Virgin	45	12 Jun 82	6
MOONLIGHT SHADOW	Virgin	4	28 May 83	17

Tribute to John Lennon.

CRIME OF PASSION	Virgin	61	14 Jan 84	3

Above 3 feature vocals by Maggie Reilly, though she does not have a credit on the label or front of the sleeve.

TO FRANCE	Virgin	48	30 Jun 84	7

Above hit: Mike OLDFIELD vocals by Maggie Reilly.

PICTURES IN THE DARK	Virgin	50	14 Dec 85	6

Above hit: Mike OLDFIELD featuring Aled JONES, Anita HEGERLAND and Barry PALMER.

SENTINEL (SINGLE RESTRUCTURE) TUBULAR BELLS II	WEA	10	3 Oct 92	6
TATTOO	WEA	33	19 Dec 92	5
THE BELL (MC VIV STANSHALL)	WEA	50	17 Apr 93	2
MOONLIGHT SHADOW [RI]	Virgin	52	9 Oct 93	2
HIBERNACULUM	WEA	47	17 Dec 94	3
LET THERE BE LIGHT	WEA	51	2 Sep 95	1
WOMEN OF IRELAND	WEA	70	22 Nov 97	1
FAR ABOVE THE CLOUDS	WEA	53	24 Apr 99	1

ALBUMS:		HITS 23		WEEKS 545
TUBULAR BELLS	Virgin	1	14 Jul 73	264

Peak position reached on 5 Oct 74. Includes re-entries through to 1983.

HERGEST RIDGE	Virgin	1	14 Sep 74	17
THE ORCHESTRAL TUBULAR BELLS	Virgin	17	8 Feb 75	7

Above hit: Mike OLDFIELD with the ROYAL PHILHARMONIC ORCHESTRA.

OMMADAWN	Virgin	4	15 Nov 75	23
BOXED	Virgin	22	20 Nov 76	13

4 album boxed set includes remixed versions of his three hit albums to date and a compilation of singles.

INCANTATIONS	Virgin	14	9 Dec 78	17
EXPOSED	Virgin	16	11 Aug 79	9

Live recordings from his 1979 tour.

PLATINUM	Virgin	24	8 Dec 79	9

Compilation.

QE 2	Virgin	27	8 Nov 80	12
FIVE MILES OUT	Virgin	7	27 Mar 82	27
CRISES	Virgin	6	4 Jun 83	29
DISCOVERY	Virgin	15	7 Jul 84	16
THE KILLING FIELDS [OST]	Virgin	97	15 Dec 84	1
THE COMPLETE MIKE OLDFIELD	Virgin	36	2 Nov 85	17
ISLANDS	Virgin	29	10 Oct 87	5
EARTH MOVING	Virgin	30	22 Jul 89	5
AMAROK	Virgin	49	9 Jun 90	2
TUBULAR BELLS II	WEA	1	12 Sep 92	30
TUBULAR BELLS [RE-1ST]	Virgin	43	12 Sep 92	10

Chart position reached in 1996.

ELEMENTS - THE BEST OF MIKE OLDFIELD	Virgin	5	25 Sep 93	10
THE SONGS OF DISTANT EARTH	WEA	24	3 Dec 94	6

Inspired by the book of the same name written by Arthur C. Clarke.

VOYAGER	WEA	12	7 Sep 96	5
TUBULAR BELLS [RE-2ND]	Virgin	43	6 Jun 98	2

Digitally remastered 25th Anniversary edition.

TUBULAR BELLS III	WEA	4	12 Sep 98	7
GUITARS	WEA	40	5 Jun 99	2

Sally OLDFIELD — UK

SINGLES:	HITS 1			WEEKS 13
MIRRORS	Bronze	19	9 Dec 78	13

Misty OLDLAND — UK

SINGLES:	HITS 3			WEEKS 7
GOT ME A FEELING	Columbia	59	16 Oct 93	2
A FAIR AFFAIR (JE T'AIME)	Columbia	49	12 Mar 94	4
I WROTE YOU A SONG	Columbia	73	9 Jul 94	1

OLGA — Italy

SINGLES:	HITS 1			WEEKS 1
I'M A BITCH	UMM	68	1 Oct 94	1

A reworking of an old club track by A Bitch Called Joanna.

OLIVE — UK

SINGLES:	HITS 3			WEEKS 24
YOU'RE NOT ALONE	RCA	42	7 Sep 96	4
MIRACLE	RCA	41	15 Mar 97	2

Original release reached No. 118 in 1996.

YOU'RE NOT ALONE [RI]	RCA	1	17 May 97	13
OUTLAW	RCA	14	16 Aug 97	4
MIRACLE [RI]	RCA	41	8 Nov 97	1
ALBUMS:	HITS 1			WEEKS 3
EXTRA VIRGIN	RCA	15	31 May 97	3

OLIVER — US

SINGLES:	HITS 1			WEEKS 18
GOOD MORNING STARSHINE	CBS	6	9 Aug 69	16

From the musical 'Hair'.

GOOD MORNING STARSHINE [RE]	CBS	39	27 Dec 69	2

Frankie OLIVER — UK

SINGLES:	HITS 1			WEEKS 1
GIVE HER WHAT SHE WANTS	Island Jamaica	58	7 Jun 97	1

OLLIE and JERRY — US

SINGLES:	HITS 2			WEEKS 14
BREAKIN' . . . THERE'S NO STOPPING US	Polydor	5	23 Jun 84	11

From the film 'Breakdance'.

ELECTRIC BOOGALOO	Polydor	57	9 Mar 85	3

OLYMPIC ORCHESTRA — UK

SINGLES:	HITS 1			WEEKS 15
REILLY	Red Bus	26	1 Oct 83	15

Theme from the Thames ITV series 'Reilly, Ace Of Spies'.

OLYMPIC RUNNERS — UK

SINGLES:	HITS 4			WEEKS 21
WHATEVER IT TAKES	RCA Victor	61	13 May 78	2

Above hit: OLYMPIC RUNNERS with George CHANDLER.

GET IT WHILE YOU CAN	Polydor	35	14 Oct 78	6
SIR DANCEALOT	Polydor	35	20 Jan 79	6
THE BITCH	Polydor	37	28 Jul 79	7

From the film of the same name.

OLYMPICS — US

SINGLES:	HITS 2			WEEKS 9
WESTERN MOVIES	His Master's Voice	12	4 Oct 58	8
I WISH I COULD SHIMMY LIKE MY SISTER KATE	Vogue	40	21 Jan 61	1

OMAR — UK

SINGLES:	HITS 7			WEEKS 18
THERE'S NOTHING LIKE THIS	Talkin Loud	14	22 Jun 91	7

Original release reached No. 78 in 1990.

YOUR LOSS MY GAIN	Talkin Loud	47	23 May 92	2
MUSIC	Talkin Loud	53	26 Sep 92	2
OUTSIDE / SATURDAY	RCA	43	23 Jul 94	2

Outside features vocal by Nu Colours.

KEEP STEPPIN'	RCA	57	15 Oct 94	1

SAY NOTHIN'	RCA	29	2 Aug 97	2
Above hit: OMAR featuring OL' DIRTY BASTARD Of WU-TANG CLAN.				
GOLDEN BROWN	RCA	37	18 Oct 97	2
ALBUMS:	**HITS 4**		**WEEKS 14**	
THERE'S NOTHING LIKE THIS	Kongo Dance	54	14 Jul 90	4
THERE'S NOTHING LIKE THIS [RI]	Talkin Loud	19	27 Jul 91	6
MUSIC	Talkin Loud	37	24 Oct 92	2
FOR PLEASURE	RCA	50	2 Jul 94	1
THIS IS NOT A LOVE SONG	RCA	50	16 Aug 97	1

OMC
New Zealand

SINGLES:	HITS 2		WEEKS 17	
HOW BIZARRE	Polydor	5	20 Jul 96	16
ON THE RUN	Polydor	56	18 Jan 97	1

OMD – See ORCHESTRAL MANOEUVRES IN THE DARK

OMNI TRIO
UK

ALBUMS:	HITS 2		WEEKS 2	
THE DEEPEST CUT – VOLUME 1	Moving Shadow	60	11 Feb 95	1
THE HAUNTED SCIENCE	Moving Shadow	43	24 Aug 96	1

ON-U-SOUND – See Gary CLAIL ON-U SOUND SYSTEM; PRIMAL SCREAM

ONE
UK

SINGLES:	HITS 1		WEEKS 2	
ONE MORE CHANCE	Mercury	31	11 Jan 97	2

Michie ONE – See Louchie LOU and Michie ONE

Phoebe ONE
UK

SINGLES:	HITS 2		WEEKS 3	
DOIN' OUR THING / ONE MAN'S BITCH	Mecca Recordings	59	12 Dec 98	1
Above hit: Phoebe ONE featuring RED RAT, GOOFY and BUCCANEER (MAIN STREET CREW).				
GET ON IT	Mecca Recordings	38	15 May 99	2
Samples Rod Stewart's Baby Jane.				

ONE DOVE
UK

SINGLES:	HITS 3		WEEKS 9	
WHITE LOVE	Boys Own Productions	43	7 Aug 93	3
BREAKDOWN	London	24	16 Oct 93	3
WHY DON'T YOU TAKE ME?	Boys Own Productions	30	15 Jan 94	3
ALBUMS:	**HITS 1**		**WEEKS 2**	
MORNING DOVE WHITE	London	30	25 Sep 93	2

ONE HUNDRED TON AND A FEATHER – See Jonathan KING

101 STRINGS
Germany

ALBUMS:	HITS 5		WEEKS 35	
GYPSY CAMPFIRES	Pye Golden Guinea	9	26 Sep 59	7
THE SOUL OF SPAIN	Pye Golden Guinea	17	26 Mar 60	1
GRAND CANYON SUITE	Pye Golden Guinea	10	16 Apr 60	1
DOWN DRURY LANE TO MEMORY LANE	Pye Golden Guinea	1	27 Aug 60	21
The first double album set to reach No. 1.				
MORNING NOON AND NIGHT	Ronco	32	15 Oct 83	5

112 – See ALLURE; Faith EVANS; NOTORIOUS B.I.G.; PUFF DADDY

187 LOCKDOWN
UK

SINGLES:	HITS 4		WEEKS 16	
GUNMAN	East West Dance	16	15 Nov 97	4
Samples Ennio Morricone's Sixty Seconds To What.				
KUNG-FU	East West Dance	9	25 Apr 98	5
GUNMAN [RI]	East West	17	25 Jul 98	4
THE DON	East West	29	3 Oct 98	2
ALL 'N' ALL	East West	43	13 Feb 99	1
Above hit: 187 LOCKDOWN (featuring D'EMPRESS).				

ONE THE JUGGLER
UK

SINGLES:	HITS 1		WEEKS 1	
PASSION KILLER	Regard	71	19 Feb 83	1

1000 CLOWNS US

SINGLES:		HITS 1		WEEKS 4
(NOT THE) GREATEST RAPPER	Elektra	23	22 May 99	4

ONE TRIBE - See OUR TRIBE/ONE TRIBE/O.T. QUARTET

ONE 2 MANY Norway

SINGLES:		HITS 1		WEEKS 11
DOWNTOWN	A&M	65	12 Nov 88	4
DOWNTOWN [RE]	A&M	43	3 Jun 89	7

ONE WAY - See Al HUDSON

ONE WORLD UK

ALBUMS:		HITS 1		WEEKS 3
ONE WORLD ONE VOICE	Virgin	27	9 Jun 90	3

Alexander O'NEAL US

SINGLES:		HITS 22		WEEKS 107
SATURDAY LOVE	Tabu	6	28 Dec 85	11

Above hit: CHERRELLE with Alexander O'NEAL.

IF YOU WERE HERE TONIGHT	Tabu	13	15 Feb 86	10
A BROKEN HEART CAN MEND	Tabu	53	5 Apr 86	4

Original release reached No. 96 in 1985.

FAKE	Tabu	33	6 Jun 87	6
CRITICIZE	Tabu	4	31 Oct 87	14
NEVER KNEW LOVE LIKE THIS	Tabu	26	6 Feb 88	7

Above hit: Alexander O'NEAL featuring CHERRELLE.

THE LOVERS	Tabu	28	28 May 88	4
(WHAT CAN I SAY) TO MAKE YOU LOVE ME	Tabu	27	23 Jul 88	5
FAKE 88 [RM]	Tabu	16	24 Sep 88	7

Remixed by Keith Cohen and Steve Beltran.

THE CHRISTMAS SONG (CHESTNUTS ROASTING ON AN OPEN FIRE) / THANK YOU FOR A GOOD YEAR	Tabu	30	10 Dec 88	5
HEARSAY 89	Tabu	56	25 Feb 89	2
SUNSHINE	Tabu	72	2 Sep 89	1
HITMIX (THE OFFICIAL BOOTLEG MEGA-MIX) [M]	Tabu	19	9 Dec 89	7

Medley of 4 tracks from his Hearsay album.

SATURDAY LOVE (FEELIN' LUV MIX) [RM]	Tabu	55	24 Mar 90	2

Remixed by Olimar and D.J. Shapps.
Above hit: CHERRELLE with Alexander O'NEAL.

ALL TRUE MAN	Tabu	18	12 Jan 91	6
WHAT IS THIS THING CALLED LOVE?	Tabu	53	23 Mar 91	2
SHAME ON ME	Tabu	71	11 May 91	1
SENTIMENTAL	Epic	53	9 May 92	2
LOVE MAKES NO SENSE	Tabu	26	30 Jan 93	3
IN THE MIDDLE	Tabu	32	3 Jul 93	3
ALL THAT MATTERS TO ME	A&M	67	25 Sep 93	1
LET'S GET TOGETHER	EMI Premier	38	2 Nov 96	2
BABY COME TO ME	One World Entertainment	56	2 Aug 97	1

Above hit: Alexander O'NEAL and CHERRELLE.

CRITICIZE '98 MIX [RR]	One World Entertainment	51	12 Dec 98	1

ALBUMS:		HITS 6		WEEKS 162
ALEXANDER O'NEAL	Tabu	53	1 Jun 85	6
ALEXANDER O'NEAL [RE]	Tabu	19	15 Mar 86	12
HEARSAY	Tabu	4	8 Aug 87	96

Peak position reached on 26 March 88.

MY GIFT TO YOU	Tabu	53	17 Dec 88	3
HEARSAY / ALL MIXED UP [RE]	Tabu	60	15 Jul 89	7

All Mixed Up was a remix album, sales were combined.

ALL TRUE MAN	Tabu	2	2 Feb 91	16
THIS THING CALLED LOVE - THE GREATEST HITS OF ALEXANDER O'NEAL	Tabu	4	30 May 92	18
LOVE MAKES NO SENSE	Tabu	14	20 Feb 93	4

Shaquille O'NEAL US

(See also Quincy Jones.)

SINGLES:		HITS 3		WEEKS 4
I'M OUTSTANDING	Jive	70	26 Mar 94	1

Samples Outstanding by the Gap Band, Don't Stop The Music by Yarbrough & Peoples and Funkin' For Jamaica by Tom Browne.

YOU CAN'T STOP THE REIGN	Interscope	40	1 Feb 97	2

Features Biggie Smalls (Notorious B.I.G.).

THE WAY IT'S GOIN' DOWN (T.W.ISM. FOR LIFE)	A&M	62	17 Oct 98	1

Above hit: Shaquille O'NEAL featuring Peter GUNZ.

ONEPHATDEEVA - See A.T.F.C. presents ONEPHATDEEVA

ONLY ONES — UK

SINGLES:	HITS 1			WEEKS 2	
ANOTHER GIRL – ANOTHER PLANET	Columbia	57	1 Feb 92		2
Originally released in 1978.					

ALBUMS:	HITS 3			WEEKS 8	
THE ONLY ONES	CBS	56	3 Jun 78		1
EVEN SERPENTS SHINE	CBS	42	31 Mar 79		2
BABY'S GOT A GUN	CBS	37	3 May 80		5

Yoko ONO — Japan

(See also John Lennon.)

SINGLES:	HITS 2			WEEKS 11	
WATCHING THE WHEELS	Geffen	30	4 Apr 81		6
Above hit: John LENNON and Yoko ONO.					
WALKING ON THIN ICE	Geffen	35	28 Feb 81		5
A tribute to her husband John Lennon.					

ALBUMS:	HITS 3			WEEKS 51	
DOUBLE FANTASY	Geffen	1	22 Nov 80		36
Tracks divided equally between each artist.					
Above hit: John LENNON and Yoko ONO.					
SEASON OF GLASS	Geffen	47	20 Jun 81		2
MILK AND HONEY – A HEART PLAY	Polydor	3	4 Feb 84		13
Recordings from 1980. Tracks divided equally between each artist.					
Above hit: John LENNON and Yoko ONO.					

ONSLAUGHT — UK

SINGLES:	HITS 1			WEEKS 3	
LET THERE BE ROCK	London	50	6 May 89		3

ALBUMS:	HITS 1			WEEKS 2	
IN SEARCH OF SANITY	London	46	20 May 89		2

ONYX — US

SINGLES:	HITS 3			WEEKS 8	
SLAM	Columbia	31	28 Aug 93		4
THROW YA GUNZ	Columbia	34	27 Nov 93		3
ROC-IN-IT	Independiente	59	20 Feb 99		1
Above hit: DEEJAY PUNK-ROC vs ONYX.					

ALBUMS:	HITS 1			WEEKS 3	
BACDAFUCUP	Columbia	59	4 Sep 93		3

OO LA LA — UK

SINGLES:	HITS 1			WEEKS 2	
OO . . . AH . . . CANTONA	North Speed	64	5 Sep 92		2

OOBERMAN — UK

SINGLES:	HITS 3			WEEKS 4	
BLOSSOMS FALLING	Independiente	39	8 May 99		2
MILLION SUNS	Independiente	43	17 Jul 99		1
TEARS FROM A WILLOW	Independiente	63	23 Oct 99		1

OOE – See COLUMBO presents IN FULL ROCK-A-PHONIC SOUND featuring OOE

OPEN ARMS featuring ROWETTA — UK

SINGLES:	HITS 1			WEEKS 1	
HEY MR DJ	All Around The World	62	15 Jun 96		1

OPTIMYSTIC — UK

SINGLES:	HITS 3			WEEKS 6	
CAUGHT UP IN MY HEART	WEA	49	17 Sep 94		3
NOTHING BUT LOVE	WEA	37	10 Dec 94		2
BEST THING IN THE WORLD	WEA	70	13 May 95		1

OPUS — Austria

SINGLES:	HITS 1			WEEKS 15	
LIVE IS LIFE	Polydor	6	15 Jun 85		15

OPUS III — UK

SINGLES:	HITS 3			WEEKS 10	
IT'S A FINE DAY	PWL International	5	22 Feb 92		8
Originally recorded by Jane reaching No. 87 in 1985.					

I TALK TO THE WIND	PWL International	52	27 Jun 92	1
Originally recorded by King Crimson.				
WHEN YOU MADE THE MOUNTAIN	PWL	71	11 Jun 94	1

ORANGE
UK

SINGLES:	HITS 1		WEEKS 1	
JUDY OVER THE RAINBOW	Chrysalis	73	8 Oct 94	1

ORANGE JUICE
UK

SINGLES:	HITS 9		WEEKS 34	
L.O.V.E . . . LOVE	Polydor	65	7 Nov 81	2
FELICITY	Polydor	63	30 Jan 82	3
TWO HEARTS TOGETHER / HOKOYO	Polydor	60	21 Aug 82	2
I CAN'T HELP MYSELF	Polydor	42	23 Oct 82	3
RIP IT UP	Polydor	8	19 Feb 83	11
FLESH OF MY FLESH	Polydor	41	4 Jun 83	6
BRIDGE	Polydor	67	25 Feb 84	2
WHAT PRESENCE?!	Polydor	47	12 May 84	4
LEAN PERIOD	Polydor	74	27 Oct 84	1
ALBUMS:	**HITS 3**		**WEEKS 18**	
YOU CAN'T HIDE YOUR LOVE FOREVER	Polydor	21	6 Mar 82	6
RIP IT UP	Polydor	39	20 Nov 82	8
TEXAS FEVER	Polydor	34	10 Mar 84	4
Mini album.				

ORB
UK

SINGLES:	HITS 7		WEEKS 30	
PERPETUAL DAWN	Big Life	61	15 Jun 91	1
BLUE ROOM	Big Life	8	20 Jun 92	6
ASSASSIN	Big Life	12	17 Oct 92	5
LITTLE FLUFFY CLOUDS	Big Life	10	13 Nov 93	5
Original release reached No. 95 in 1991.				
PERPETUAL DAWN [RI]	Big Life	18	5 Feb 94	5
Though the CD is a re-issue, the cassette and 12" formats have the same catalogue numbers as the original entry.				
OXBOW LAKES	Island	38	27 May 95	2
TOXYGENE	Island	4	8 Feb 97	4
ASYLUM	Island	20	24 May 97	2
ALBUMS:	**HITS 7**		**WEEKS 28**	
THE ORB'S ADVENTURES BEYOND THE ULTRAWORLD	Big Life	29	27 Apr 91	4
THE ORB'S ADVENTURES BEYOND THE ULTRAWORLD / AUBREY MIXES [RE]	Big Life	44	14 Dec 91	1
Aubrey Mixes was a remix album, sales were combined.				
U.F. ORB	Big Life	1	18 Jul 92	9
LIVE 93	Island	23	4 Dec 93	2
Live recordings from Glastonbury, Tokyo and Copenhagen between June and September 1993.				
POMME FRITZ	Inter-Modo	6	25 Jun 94	4
ORBVS TERRARVM	Island	20	1 Apr 95	3
OBLIVION	Island	19	8 Mar 97	3
U.F.OFF – THE BEST OF THE ORB	Island	38	17 Oct 98	2

Roy ORBISON
US

SINGLES:	HITS 33		WEEKS 345	
ONLY THE LONELY (KNOW HOW I FEEL)	London	36	30 Jul 60	1
Roy originally wrote the song for Elvis Presley.				
ONLY THE LONELY (KNOW HOW I FEEL) [RE]	London	1	13 Aug 60	23
BLUE ANGEL	London	11	29 Oct 60	16
RUNNIN' SCARED	London	9	27 May 61	15
CRYIN'	London	25	23 Sep 61	9
DREAM BABY	London	2	10 Mar 62	14
THE CROWD	London	40	30 Jun 62	4
WORKIN' FOR THE MAN	London	50	10 Nov 62	1
IN DREAMS	London	6	2 Mar 63	23
FALLING	London	9	1 Jun 63	11
BLUE BAYOU / MEAN WOMAN BLUES	London	3	21 Sep 63	19
Mean Woman Blues originally recorded by Elvis Presley.				
BORNE ON THE WIND	London	15	22 Feb 64	10
IT'S OVER	London	1	2 May 64	18
OH, PRETTY WOMAN	London	1	12 Sep 64	18
PRETTY PAPER	London	6	21 Nov 64	11
Originally recorded by Willie Nelson.				
GOODNIGHT	London	14	13 Feb 65	9
(SAY) YOU'RE MY GIRL	London	23	24 Jul 65	8
RIDE AWAY	London	34	11 Sep 65	6
CRAWLING BACK	London	19	6 Nov 65	9
BREAKIN' UP IS BREAKIN' MY HEART	London	22	29 Jan 66	6
TWINKLE TOES	London	29	9 Apr 66	5

LANA	*London*	15	*18 Jun 66*	9
Originally recorded by the Velvets.				
TOO SOON TO KNOW	*London*	3	*20 Aug 66*	17
Originally recorded by Don Gibson.				
THERE WON'T BE MANY COMING HOME	*London*	18	*3 Dec 66*	9
SO GOOD	*London*	32	*25 Feb 67*	6
WALK ON	*London*	39	*27 Jul 68*	10
HEARTACHE	*London*	44	*28 Sep 68*	4
MY FRIEND	*London*	35	*3 May 69*	4
PENNY ARCADE	*London*	40	*13 Sep 69*	3
PENNY ARCADE [RE]	*London*	27	*11 Oct 69*	11
YOU GOT IT	*Virgin*	3	*14 Jan 89*	10
SHE'S A MYSTERY TO ME	*Virgin*	27	*1 Apr 89*	5
Written by Bono and the Edge.				
I DROVE ALL NIGHT	*MCA*	7	*4 Jul 92*	10
CRYING [RR]	*Virgin America*	13	*22 Aug 92*	6
Originally the B-side of She's A Mystery To Me.				
Above hit: Roy ORBISON (duet with k.d Lang).				
HEARTBREAK RADIO	*Virgin America*	36	*7 Nov 92*	3
I DROVE ALL NIGHT [RI]	*Virgin*	47	*13 Nov 93*	2
EPS:	**HITS 5**		**WEEKS 101**	
ONLY THE LONELY	*London*	15	*1 Jun 63*	11
IN DREAMS	*London*	6	*10 Aug 63*	44
IT'S OVER	*London*	3	*29 Aug 64*	23
OH PRETTY WOMAN	*London*	9	*9 Jan 65*	15
ROY ORBISON'S STAGE SHOW HITS	*London*	10	*27 Mar 65*	8
ALBUMS:	**HITS 20**		**WEEKS 234**	
LONELY AND BLUE	*London*	15	*8 Jun 63*	8
CRYING	*London*	17	*29 Jun 63*	3
IN DREAMS	*London*	6	*30 Nov 63*	58
THE EXCITING SOUNDS OF ROY ORBISON	*Ember*	17	*25 Jul 64*	2
Compilation of early Sun recordings.				
OH PRETTY WOMAN	*London*	4	*5 Dec 64*	16
Compilation.				
THERE IS ONLY ONE ROY ORBISON	*London*	10	*25 Sep 65*	12
THE ORBISON WAY	*London*	11	*26 Feb 66*	10
THE CLASSIC ROY ORBISON	*London*	12	*24 Sep 66*	8
ORBISONGS	*Monument*	40	*22 Jul 67*	1
ROY ORBISON'S GREATEST HITS	*Monument*	40	*30 Sep 67*	1
ALL-TIME GREATEST HITS	*Monument*	39	*27 Jan 73*	3
THE BEST OF ROY ORBISON	*Arcade*	1	*29 Nov 75*	20
GOLDEN DAYS	*Monument*	63	*18 Jul 81*	1
IN DREAMS: THE GREATEST HITS	*Virgin*	86	*4 Jul 87*	2
THE LEGENDARY ROY ORBISON	*Telstar*	1	*29 Oct 88*	38
MYSTERY GIRL	*Virgin*	2	*11 Feb 89*	23
A BLACK AND WHITE NIGHT	*Virgin*	51	*25 Nov 89*	3
BALLADS – 22 CLASSIC LOVE SONGS	*Telstar*	38	*3 Nov 90*	10
KING OF HEARTS	*Virgin America*	23	*28 Nov 92*	4
THE VERY BEST OF ROY ORBISON	*Virgin*	18	*16 Nov 96*	11

William ORBIT UK

SINGLES:	**HITS 2**		**WEEKS 4**	
WATER FROM A VINE LEAF	*Virgin*	59	*26 Jun 93*	1
BARBER'S ADAGIO FOR STRINGS	*WEA*	4	*18 Dec 99*	3

ORBITAL UK

SINGLES:	**HITS 13**		**WEEKS 47**	
CHIME	*ffrr*	17	*24 Mar 90*	7
OMEN	*ffrr*	46	*22 Sep 90*	3
SATAN	*ffrr*	31	*19 Jan 91*	4
MUTATIONS [EP]	*ffrr*	24	*15 Feb 92*	3
Lead track: Chime Chime.				
RADICCIO [EP]	*Internal*	37	*26 Sep 92*	2
Lead track: Halcyon.				
LUSH 3	*Internal*	43	*21 Aug 93*	2
ARE WE HERE?	*Internal*	33	*24 Sep 94*	2
BELFAST/WASTED	*Volume*	53	*27 May 95*	1
[AA] listed with Innocent X by Therapy?				
THE BOX	*Internal*	11	*27 Apr 96*	4
Vocals by writer Grant Fulton.				
SATAN [RR]	*Internal*	3	*11 Jan 97*	6
Released on 3 CD formats. CD1 contained live recording from the Irvine Plaza, New York. CD3 was the studio recording.				
THE SAINT	*ffrr*	3	*19 Apr 97*	7
From the film of the same name. Original theme was written in 1963.				
STYLE	*ffrr*	13	*20 Mar 99*	4
Samples Suzi Quatro's Devil Gate Drive and Dollar's Mirror Mirror.				

NOTHING LEFT	*ffrr*	32	*17 Jul 99*	2
Vocals by Alison Goldfrapp.				

ALBUMS:	HITS 7		WEEKS 29	
ORBITAL	*ffrr*	71	*12 Oct 91*	1
ORBITAL	*Internal*	28	*5 Jun 93*	2
Above 2 self-titled albums are different.				
PEEL SESSIONS	*Internal*	32	*19 Mar 94*	2
4-track album recorded Sept 93 for John Peel's BBC Radio 1 show.				
SNIVILISATION	*Internal Dance*	4	*20 Aug 94*	4
IN SIDES	*Internal*	5	*11 May 96*	12
SATAN	*Internal*	48	*25 Jan 97*	1
Double-pack 12" single ineligible for the singles chart.				
THE MIDDLE OF NOWHERE	*ffrr*	4	*17 Apr 99*	7

ORCHESTRA e coro DELL'ACCADEMIA NAZIONALE di SANTA CECILIA conducted by Myung-Whun CHUNG – See Andrea BOCELLI

ORCHESTRA ON THE HALF SHELL   US

SINGLES:	HITS 1		WEEKS 6	
TURTLE RHAPSODY	*SBK*	36	*15 Dec 90*	6
From the film 'Teenage Mutant Ninja Turtles'.				

ORCHESTRAL MANOEUVRES IN THE DARK / OMD   UK

SINGLES:	HITS 30		WEEKS 201	
RED FRAME/WHITE LIGHT	*Dindisc*	67	*9 Feb 80*	2
MESSAGES	*Dindisc*	13	*10 May 80*	11
ENOLA GAY	*Dindisc*	8	*4 Oct 80*	15
Enola Gay is the name of the aeroplane that dropped the atomic bomb on Hiroshima.				
SOUVENIR	*Dindisc*	3	*29 Aug 81*	12
JOAN OF ARC	*Dindisc*	5	*24 Oct 81*	14
MAID OF ORLEANS (THE WALTZ JOAN OF ARC)	*Dindisc*	4	*23 Jan 82*	10
GENETIC ENGINEERING	*Virgin*	20	*19 Feb 83*	8
TELEGRAPH	*Virgin*	42	*9 Apr 83*	4
LOCOMOTION	*Virgin*	5	*14 Apr 84*	11
TALKING LOUD AND CLEAR	*Virgin*	11	*16 Jun 84*	10
TESLA GIRLS	*Virgin*	21	*8 Sep 84*	8
NEVER TURN AWAY	*Virgin*	70	*10 Nov 84*	2
SO IN LOVE	*Virgin*	27	*25 May 85*	7
SECRET	*Virgin*	34	*20 Jul 85*	7
LE FEMME ACCIDENT	*Virgin*	42	*26 Oct 85*	4
IF YOU LEAVE	*Virgin*	48	*3 May 86*	4
(FOREVER) LIVE AND DIE	*Virgin*	11	*6 Sep 86*	10
WE LOVE YOU	*Virgin*	54	*15 Nov 86*	5
SHAME (RE-RECORDED VERSION)	*Virgin*	52	*2 May 87*	3
DREAMING	*Virgin*	50	*6 Feb 88*	3
DREAMING [RE]	*Virgin*	60	*2 Jul 88*	3
SAILING ON THE SEVEN SEAS	*Virgin*	3	*30 Mar 91*	13
PANDORA'S BOX	*Virgin*	7	*6 Jul 91*	10
THEN YOU TURN AWAY	*Virgin*	50	*14 Sep 91*	4
CALL MY NAME	*Virgin*	50	*7 Dec 91*	2
STAND ABOVE ME	*Virgin*	21	*15 May 93*	4
DREAM OF ME (BASED ON LOVE'S THEME)	*Virgin*	24	*17 Jul 93*	5
EVERYDAY	*Virgin*	59	*18 Sep 93*	2
WALKING ON THE MILKY WAY	*Virgin*	17	*17 Aug 96*	5
UNIVERSAL	*Virgin*	55	*2 Nov 96*	1
THE OMD REMIXES [EP]	*Virgin*	35	*26 Sep 98*	2
Lead track: Enola Gay (remixed backing track by Sash! with re-recorded vocals).				

ALBUMS:	HITS 12		WEEKS 226	
ORCHESTRAL MANOEUVRES IN THE DARK	*DinDisc*	27	*1 Mar 80*	29
ORGANISATION	*DinDisc*	6	*1 Nov 80*	25
ARCHITECTURE AND MORALITY	*DinDisc*	3	*14 Nov 81*	39
DAZZLE SHIPS	*Virgin*	5	*12 Mar 83*	13
JUNK CULTURE	*Virgin*	9	*12 May 84*	27
CRUSH	*Virgin*	13	*29 Jun 85*	12
THE PACIFIC AGE	*Virgin*	15	*11 Oct 86*	7
THE BEST OF O.M.D.	*Virgin*	2	*12 Mar 88*	33
SUGAR TAX	*Virgin*	3	*18 May 91*	29
LIBERATOR	*Virgin*	14	*26 Jun 93*	6
UNIVERSAL	*Virgin*	24	*14 Sep 96*	2
THE OMD SINGLES	*Virgin*	16	*10 Oct 98*	4
Includes re-recorded versions and remixes.				

ORCHESTRE DE CHAMBRE Jean-Francois PAILLARD   France

SINGLES:	HITS 1		WEEKS 3	
THEME FROM TV'S "VIETNAM" - CANON IN D MAJOR (PACHELBEL)	*Debut*	61	*20 Aug 88*	3

L'ORCHESTRE ELECTRONIQUE
UK

ALBUMS:	HITS 1			WEEKS 1
SOUND WAVES	Nouveau Music	75	29 Oct 83	1

ORCHESTRE NATIONAL DE LA RADIO DIFFUSION FRANCAISE, conducted by Sir Thomas BEECHAM
France/UK

ALBUMS:	HITS 1			WEEKS 2
CARMEN	His Master's Voice	18	26 Mar 60	2

Raul ORELLANA
Italy

SINGLES:	HITS 1			WEEKS 8
THE REAL WILD HOUSE	BCM	29	30 Sep 89	8

ORIGIN UNKNOWN
UK

SINGLES:	HITS 1			WEEKS 1
VALLEY OF THE SHADOWS	Ram	60	13 Jul 96	1

ORIGINAL
US

SINGLES:	HITS 2			WEEKS 14
I LUV U BABY	Ore	31	14 Jan 95	3
I LUV U BABY [RM]	Ore	2	19 Aug 95	9

Remixed by Dancing Divaz. Extra vocals by Everett Bradley.

B 2 GETHER	Ore	29	11 Nov 95	2

ORIGINAL MOTION PICTURE SOUNDTRACK
US

SINGLES:	HITS 1			WEEKS 4
MIDNIGHT COWBOY	United Artists	47	8 Nov 80	4

From the film of the same name.

ORIGINAL ODC. MC. – See TZANT

ORIGINOO GUNN CLAPPAZ – See HELTAH SKELTER and ORIGINOO GUNN CLAPPAZ as the FABULOUS FIVE

ORLANDO – See VARIOUS ARTISTS (EPs) 'Fever Pitch The EP'

Tony ORLANDO
US

(See also Dawn.)

SINGLES:	HITS 1			WEEKS 11
BLESS YOU	Fontana	5	7 Oct 61	11

ORLONS
US

SINGLES:	HITS 1			WEEKS 3
DON'T HANG UP	Cameo-Parkway	50	29 Dec 62	1
DON'T HANG UP [RE]	Cameo-Parkway	39	12 Jan 63	2

Cyril ORNADEL – See LONDON SYMPHONY ORCHESTRA

Beth ORTON
UK

SINGLES:	HITS 6			WEEKS 11
TOUCH ME WITH YOUR LOVE	Heavenly	60	1 Feb 97	1
SOMEONE'S DAUGHTER	Heavenly	49	5 Apr 97	1
SHE CRIES YOUR NAME	Heavenly	40	14 Jun 97	2

Original release reached No. 96 in 1996.

BEST BIT [EP]	Heavenly	36	13 Dec 97	3

Lead track: Best Bit. Though credited on the chart, Terry Callier only featured on 2 of the EP's tracks.
Above hit: Beth ORTON featuring Terry CALLIER.

STOLEN CAR	Heavenly	34	13 Mar 99	2
CENTRAL RESERVATION	Heavenly	37	25 Sep 99	2
ALBUMS:	HITS 2			WEEKS 10
TRAILER PARK	Heavenly	68	26 Oct 96	3
CENTRAL RESERVATION	Heavenly	17	27 Mar 99	7

ORVILLE – See Keith HARRIS and ORVILLE

Jeffrey OSBORNE
US

SINGLES:	HITS 6			WEEKS 38
DON'T YOU GET SO MAD	A&M	54	17 Sep 83	2
STAY WITH ME TONIGHT	A&M	18	14 Apr 84	11

Features Queen's Roger Taylor on drums.

ON THE WINGS OF LOVE	A&M	11	23 Jun 84	14
DON'T STOP	A&M	61	20 Oct 84	2
SOWETO	A&M	44	26 Jul 86	5
SOWETO [RE]	A&M	75	6 Sep 86	1

LOVE POWER	Arista	63	15 Aug 87	3

Above hit: Dionne WARWICK and Jeffrey OSBORNE.

ALBUMS:		**HITS 2**	**WEEKS 10**	
STAY WITH ME TONIGHT	A&M	56	5 May 84	7
DON'T STOP	A&M	59	13 Oct 84	3

Joan OSBORNE   US

SINGLES:		**HITS 2**	**WEEKS 13**	
ONE OF US	Blue Gorilla	6	10 Feb 96	10
ST TERESA	Blue Gorilla	33	8 Jun 96	3
ALBUMS:		**HITS 1**	**WEEKS 18**	
RELISH	Blue Gorilla	5	9 Mar 96	18

Tony OSBORNE SOUND featuring Joanne BROWN   UK

(See also Petula Clark; Russ Conway; Gracie Fields; Edmund Hockridge; Gary Miller; Dorothy Squires; Jimmy Young.)

SINGLES:		**HITS 2**	**WEEKS 3**	
THE MAN FROM MADRID	His Master's Voice	50	25 Feb 61	1
THE SHEPHERD'S SONG	Philips	46	3 Feb 73	2

Ozzy OSBOURNE   UK

SINGLES:		**HITS 11**	**WEEKS 42**	
CRAZY TRAIN	Jet	49	13 Sep 80	4
MR. CROWLEY	Jet	46	15 Nov 80	3

Above 2: Ozzy OSBOURNE BLIZZARD OF OZ.

BARK AT THE MOON	Epic	21	26 Nov 83	8
SO TIRED	Epic	20	2 Jun 84	9
SHOT IN THE DARK	Epic	20	1 Feb 86	6
THE ULTIMATE SIN / LIGHTNING STRIKES	Epic	72	9 Aug 86	1
CLOSE MY EYES FOREVER	Dreamland	47	20 May 89	3

Above hit: Lita FORD (Duet with Ozzy OSBOURNE).

NO MORE TEARS	Epic	32	28 Sep 91	3
MAMA I'M COMING HOME	Epic	46	30 Nov 91	2
PERRY MASON	Epic	23	25 Nov 95	2
I JUST WANT YOU	Epic	43	31 Aug 96	1

Features Michael Borden of Faith No More on drums.

ALBUMS:		**HITS 11**	**WEEKS 61**	
OZZY OSBOURNE'S BLIZZARD OF OZ	Jet	7	20 Sep 80	8

Above hit: Ozzy OSBOURNE'S BLIZZARD OF OZ.

DIARY OF A MADMAN	Jet	14	7 Nov 81	12

Also the title of his autobiography.

TALK OF THE DEVIL	Jet	21	27 Nov 82	6
BARK AT THE MOON	Epic	24	10 Dec 83	7
THE ULTIMATE SIN	Epic	8	22 Feb 86	10
TRIBUTE	Epic	13	23 May 87	6

Live recordings from 1981. A tribute to guitarist Randy Rhoads who performs on the album.

NO REST FOR THE WICKED	Epic	23	22 Oct 88	4
JUST SAY OZZY (LIVE)	Epic	69	17 Mar 90	1
NO MORE TEARS	Epic	17	19 Oct 91	3
OZZMOSIS	Epic	22	4 Nov 95	3
THE OZZMAN COMETH – THE BEST OF OZZY OSBOURNE	Epic	68	15 Nov 97	1

OSIBISA   Ghana/Nigeria

SINGLES:		**HITS 2**	**WEEKS 12**	
SUNSHINE DAY	Bronze	17	17 Jan 76	6
DANCE THE BODY MUSIC	Bronze	31	5 Jun 76	6
ALBUMS:		**HITS 2**	**WEEKS 17**	
OSIBISA	MCA	11	22 May 71	10
WOYAYA	MCA	11	5 Feb 72	7

Donny OSMOND   US

(See also Donny and Marie Osmond; Osmonds.)

SINGLES:		**HITS 11**	**WEEKS 118**	
PUPPY LOVE	MGM	1	17 Jun 72	17
TOO YOUNG	MGM	5	16 Sep 72	12

Originally recorded by Nat King Cole in 1951.

PUPPY LOVE [RE-1ST]	MGM	45	21 Oct 72	2
WHY	MGM	3	11 Nov 72	20
PUPPY LOVE [RE-2ND]	MGM	46	23 Dec 72	3
TOO YOUNG [RE]	MGM	47	23 Dec 72	3
PUPPY LOVE [RE-3RD]	MGM	48	27 Jan 73	1
THE TWELFTH OF NEVER	MGM	1	10 Mar 73	14
YOUNG LOVE	MGM	1	18 Aug 73	10
WHEN I FALL IN LOVE	MGM	4	10 Nov 73	13
WHERE DID ALL THE GOOD TIMES GO	MGM	18	9 Nov 74	10

I'M IN IT FOR LOVE	*Virgin*	70	*26 Sep 87*	1
SOLDIER OF LOVE	*Virgin*	29	*6 Aug 88*	8
IF IT'S LOVE THAT YOU WANT	*Virgin*	70	*12 Nov 88*	2
MY LOVE IS A FIRE	*Capitol*	64	*9 Feb 91*	2
ALBUMS:	**HITS 6**			**WEEKS 104**
PORTRAIT OF DONNY	*MGM*	5	*23 Sep 72*	43
TOO YOUNG	*MGM*	7	*16 Dec 72*	24
ALONE TOGETHER	*MGM*	6	*26 May 73*	19
A TIME FOR US	*MGM*	4	*15 Dec 73*	13
DONNY	*MGM*	16	*8 Feb 75*	4
DISCOTRAIN	*Polydor*	59	*2 Oct 76*	1

Donny and Marie OSMOND   US

(See also Donny Osmond; Marie Osmond; Osmonds.)

SINGLES:	**HITS 4**			**WEEKS 37**
I'M LEAVING IT (ALL) UP TO YOU	*MGM*	2	*3 Aug 74*	12
Originally recorded by Don & Dewey in 1957.				
MORNING SIDE OF THE MOUNTAIN	*MGM*	5	*14 Dec 74*	12
Originally recorded by Tommy Edwards.				
MAKE THE WORLD GO AWAY	*MGM*	18	*21 Jun 75*	6
DEEP PURPLE	*MGM*	25	*17 Jan 76*	7
Originally recorded by the Larry Clinton Orchestra in 1939.				
ALBUMS:	**HITS 3**			**WEEKS 19**
I'M LEAVING IT ALL UP TO YOU	*MGM*	13	*2 Nov 74*	15
MAKE THE WORLD GO AWAY	*MGM*	30	*26 Jul 75*	3
DEEP PURPLE	*Polydor*	48	*5 Jun 76*	1

Little Jimmy OSMOND   US

SINGLES:	**HITS 3**			**WEEKS 50**
LONG HAIRED LOVER FROM LIVERPOOL	*MGM*	1	*25 Nov 72*	24
Originally recorded by the Mike Curb Congregation.				
Above hit: Little Jimmy OSMOND with the Mike CURB CONGREGATION.				
TWEEDLEE DEE	*MGM*	4	*31 Mar 73*	13
Originally recorded by Laverne Baker in 1955.				
LONG HAIRED LOVER FROM LIVERPOOL [RE]	*MGM*	41	*19 May 73*	3
I'M GONNA KNOCK ON YOUR DOOR	*MGM*	11	*23 Mar 74*	10
Originally recorded by the Isley Brothers.				
Above hit: Jimmy OSMOND.				
ALBUMS:	**HITS 1**			**WEEKS 12**
KILLER JOE	*MGM*	20	*17 Feb 73*	12

Marie OSMOND   US

(See also Donny and Marie Osmond.)

SINGLES:	**HITS 1**			**WEEKS 15**
PAPER ROSES	*MGM*	2	*17 Nov 73*	15
Originally recorded by Lola Dee.				
ALBUMS:	**HITS 1**			**WEEKS 1**
PAPER ROSES	*MGM*	46	*9 Feb 74*	1

OSMOND BOYS   US

SINGLES:	**HITS 2**			**WEEKS 6**
BOYS WILL BE BOYS	*Curb*	65	*9 Nov 91*	2
SHOW ME THE WAY	*Curb*	60	*11 Jan 92*	4

OSMONDS   US

SINGLES:	**HITS 10**			**WEEKS 94**
DOWN BY THE LAZY RIVER	*MGM*	40	*25 Mar 72*	5
CRAZY HORSES	*MGM*	2	*11 Nov 72*	18
GOIN' HOME	*MGM*	4	*14 Jul 73*	10
LET ME IN	*MGM*	2	*27 Oct 73*	14
I CAN'T STOP	*MCA*	12	*20 Apr 74*	10
LOVE ME FOR A REASON	*MGM*	1	*24 Aug 74*	9
Originally recorded by Johnny Bristol.				
HAVING A PARTY	*MGM*	28	*1 Mar 75*	8
Originally recorded by H.B.Barnum.				
THE PROUD ONE	*MGM*	5	*24 May 75*	8
Originally recorded by the Four Seasons.				
I'M STILL GONNA NEED YOU	*MGM*	32	*15 Nov 75*	4
I CAN'T LIVE A DREAM	*Polydor*	37	*30 Oct 76*	5
CRAZY HORSES [RM]	*Polydor*	50	*23 Sep 95*	1
Remixed by the Utah Saints.				
CRAZY HORSES [RI]	*Polydor*	34	*12 Jun 99*	2
Featured in the Virgin Atlantic TV commercial.				

ALBUMS:		HITS 8		WEEKS 108	
OSMONDS LIVE	MGM	13	18 Nov 72	22	
CRAZY HORSES	MGM	9	16 Dec 72	19	
THE PLAN	MGM	6	25 Aug 73	25	
OUR BEST TO YOU	MGM	5	17 Aug 74	20	
LOVE ME FOR A REASON	MGM	13	7 Dec 74	9	
I'M STILL GONNA NEED YOU	MGM	19	14 Jun 75	7	
AROUND THE WORLD – LIVE IN CONCERT	MGM	41	10 Jan 76	1	
THE VERY BEST OF THE OSMONDS	Polydor	17	20 Apr 96	5	

Includes solo hits from Donny, Marie, Donny and Marie and Jimmy.

Glenn OSSER and his Orchestra – See Georgia GIBBS

Gilbert O'SULLIVAN
Ireland

SINGLES:		HITS 16		WEEKS 145	
NOTHING RHYMED	MAM	8	28 Nov 70	11	
UNDERNEATH THE BLANKET GO	MAM	40	3 Apr 71	1	
UNDERNEATH THE BLANKET GO [RE]	MAM	42	17 Apr 71	3	
WE WILL	MAM	16	24 Jul 71	11	
NO MATTER HOW I TRY	MAM	5	27 Nov 71	15	
ALONE AGAIN (NATURALLY)	MAM	3	4 Mar 72	12	
OOH-WAKKA-DOO-WAKKA-DAY	MAM	8	17 Jun 72	11	
CLAIR	MAM	1	21 Oct 72	14	
GET DOWN	MAM	1	17 Mar 73	13	
OOH BABY	MAM	18	15 Sep 73	7	
WHY, OH WHY, OH WHY	MAM	6	10 Nov 73	14	
HAPPINESS IS ME AND YOU	MAM	19	9 Feb 74	7	
A WOMAN'S PLACE	MAM	42	24 Aug 74	3	
CHRISTMAS SONG	MAM	12	14 Dec 74	6	
I DON'T LOVE YOU BUT I THINK I LIKE YOU	MAM	14	14 Jun 75	6	
WHAT'S IN A KISS	CBS	19	27 Sep 80	9	
SO WHAT	Dover	70	24 Feb 90	2	
ALBUMS:		HITS 7		WEEKS 195	
GILBERT O'SULLIVAN HIMSELF	MAM	5	25 Sep 71	82	
BACK TO FRONT	MAM	1	18 Nov 72	64	
I'M A WRITER NOT A FIGHTER	MAM	2	6 Oct 73	25	
STRANGER IN MY OWN BACK YARD	MAM	9	26 Oct 74	8	
GREATEST HITS	MAM	13	18 Dec 76	11	
20 GOLDEN GREATS	K-Tel	98	12 Sep 81	1	
NOTHING BUT THE BEST	Castle Communication	50	11 May 91	4	

OTHER TWO
UK

SINGLES:		HITS 2		WEEKS 5	
TASTY FISH	Factory	41	9 Nov 91	3	
SELFISH	London	46	6 Nov 93	2	

Johnny OTIS SHOW with Marie ADAMS
US

SINGLES:		HITS 2		WEEKS 22	
MA (HE'S MAKIN' EYES AT ME)	Capitol	2	23 Nov 57	15	

Originally recorded by Dick Robertson in 1940.
Above hit: Johnny OTIS SHOW; Johnny OTIS and his Orchestra with Marie ADAMS and the THREE TONS OF JOY.

BYE BYE BABY	Capitol	20	11 Jan 58	7	

Above hit: Johnny OTIS SHOW, vocals by Marie ADAMS and Johnny OTIS.

OTT
Ireland

SINGLES:		HITS 4		WEEKS 18	
LET ME IN	Epic	12	15 Feb 97	5	
FOREVER GIRL	Epic	24	17 May 97	3	
ALL OUT OF LOVE	Epic	11	23 Aug 97	4	
THE STORY OF LOVE	Epic	11	24 Jan 98	6	

OTTAWAN
France

SINGLES:		HITS 4		WEEKS 45	
D.I.S.C.O.	Carrere	2	13 Sep 80	18	
YOU'RE O.K.	Carrere	56	13 Dec 80	5	
HANDS UP (GIVE ME YOUR HEART)	Carrere	3	29 Aug 81	15	
HELP, GET ME SOME HELP!	Carrere	49	5 Dec 81	6	

Originally recorded by the Love Affair.

John OTWAY and Wild Willy BARRETT
UK

SINGLES:		HITS 2		WEEKS 12	
REALLY FREE	Polydor	27	3 Dec 77	8	
DK 50-80	Polydor	45	5 Jul 80	4	

Above hit: OTWAY and BARRETT.

ALBUMS:	HITS 1			WEEKS 1	
DEEP AND MEANINGLESS	Polydor	44	1 Jul 78		1

OUI 3
US/UK/Switzerland

SINGLES:	HITS 6			WEEKS 21	
FOR WHAT IT'S WORTH	MCA	28	20 Feb 93		6
Originally recorded by Buffalo Springfield reaching No. 7 in the US in 1967.					
ARMS OF SOLITUDE	MCA	54	24 Apr 93		2
BREAK FROM THE OLD ROUTINE	MCA	17	17 Jul 93		6
FOR WHAT IT'S WORTH [RM]	MCA	26	23 Oct 93		3
Remixed by Soulshock and Karlin.					
FACTS OF LIFE	MCA	38	29 Jan 94		2
THE JOY OF LIVING	MCA	55	27 May 95		2
ALBUMS:	HITS 1			WEEKS 3	
OUI LOVE YOU	MCA	39	7 Aug 93		3

OUR DAUGHTER'S WEDDING
US

SINGLES:	HITS 1			WEEKS 6	
LAWNCHAIRS	EMI America	49	1 Aug 81		6

OUR HOUSE
Australia

SINGLES:	HITS 1			WEEKS 1	
FLOOR SPACE	Perfecto	52	31 Aug 96		1

OUR KID
UK

SINGLES:	HITS 1			WEEKS 11	
YOU JUST MIGHT SEE ME CRY	Polydor	2	29 May 76		11

OUR TRIBE/ONE TRIBE/O.T. QUARTET
UK/US

SINGLES:	HITS 5			WEEKS 12	
WHAT HAVE YOU DONE (IS THIS ALL)	Inner Rhythm	52	20 Jun 92		2
Above hit: ONE TRIBE featuring GEM.					
I BELIEVE IN YOU	Ffrreedom	42	27 Mar 93		2
Above hit: OUR TRIBE.					
HOLD THAT SUCKER DOWN	Cheeky	24	30 Apr 94		3
Above hit: O.T. QUARTET.					
LOVE COME HOME	Triangle	73	21 May 94		1
Above hit: OUR TRIBE with Franke PHAROAH and Kristine W.					
HIGH AS A KITE	ffrr	55	13 May 95		1
Above hit: ONE TRIBE featuring ROGER.					
HOLD THAT SUCKER DOWN [RI]	Cheeky	26	30 Sep 95		3
Above hit: O.T. QUARTET.					

OUT OF MY HAIR
UK

SINGLES:	HITS 1			WEEKS 1	
MISTER JONES	RCA	73	1 Jul 95		1

OUTHERE BROTHERS
US

SINGLES:	HITS 5			WEEKS 50	
DON'T STOP (WIGGLE WIGGLE)	Eternal	1	18 Mar 95		15
BOOM BOOM BOOM	Eternal	1	17 Jun 95		15
LA LA LA HEY HEY	Eternal	7	23 Sep 95		7
IF YOU WANNA PARTY	Eternal	9	16 Dec 95		10
Above hit: MOLELLA featuring the OUTHERE BROTHERS.					
LET ME HEAR YOU SAY "OLE OLE"	Eternal	18	25 Jan 97		3
ALBUMS:	HITS 2			WEEKS 9	
1 POLISH 2 BISCUITS AND A FISH SANDWICH	Eternal	56	27 May 95		5
PARTY ALBUM	Eternal	41	30 Dec 95		4
Alternate version of their first album, without the offensive language.					

OUTLANDER
Belgium

SINGLES:	HITS 1			WEEKS 3	
VAMP	R&S	51	31 Aug 91		2
THE VAMP (REVAMPED) [RI]	R&S	62	7 Feb 98		1
Despite the 'revamped' credit, CD1 track 1 is a straight re-issue.					

OUTLAWS
UK

(See also Mike Berry.)

SINGLES:	HITS 2			WEEKS 4	
SWINGIN' LOW	His Master's Voice	46	15 Apr 61		2
AMBUSH	His Master's Voice	43	10 Jun 61		2

OUTRAGE
US

SINGLES:	HITS 1		WEEKS 2	
TALL 'N' HANDSOME	Effective	57	11 Mar 95	1
TALL N HANDSOME [RM]	Positiva	51	23 Nov 96	1

Remixed by Nush.

OVERLANDERS
UK

SINGLES:	HITS 1		WEEKS 10	
MICHELLE	Pye	1	15 Jan 66	10

OVERLORD X
UK

ALBUMS:	HITS 1		WEEKS 1	
WEAPON IS MY LYRIC	Mango Street	68	4 Feb 89	1

OVERWEIGHT POOCH featuring Ce Ce PENISTON
US

(See also Ce Ce Peniston.)

SINGLES:	HITS 1		WEEKS 2	
I LIKE IT	A&M	58	18 Jan 92	2

Mark OWEN
UK

SINGLES:	HITS 3		WEEKS 24	
CHILD	RCA	3	30 Nov 96	11
CLEMENTINE	RCA	3	15 Feb 97	6
CHILD [RE]	RCA	45	22 Feb 97	4
I AM WHAT I AM	RCA	29	23 Aug 97	3
ALBUMS:	HITS 1		WEEKS 11	
GREEN MAN	RCA	33	14 Dec 96	11

Reg OWEN and his Orchestra
UK

SINGLES:	HITS 2		WEEKS 10	
MANHATTAN SPIRITUAL	Pye International	20	28 Feb 59	8
OBSESSION	Palette	43	29 Oct 60	2

Sid OWEN and Patsy PALMER
UK

SINGLES:	HITS 1		WEEKS 1	
BETTER BELIEVE IT (CHILDREN IN NEED)	Trinity	60	16 Dec 95	1

Charity record with proceeds to BBC TV's Children In Need appeal.

Robert OWENS
US

(See also Frankie Knuckles.)

SINGLES:	HITS 1		WEEKS 4	
I'LL BE YOUR FRIEND	Perfecto	75	7 Dec 91	2
I'LL BE YOUR FRIEND [RM]	Perfecto	25	26 Apr 97	2

Remixed by David Morales.

OZOMATLI
US

SINGLES:	HITS 2		WEEKS 2	
CUT CHEMIST SUITE	Almo Sounds	58	20 Mar 99	1
Samples Jurassic 5's Unified Rebelution.				
SUPER BOWL SUNDAE	Almo Sounds	68	22 May 99	1

OZRIC TENTACLES
UK

ALBUMS:	HITS 3		WEEKS 7	
STRANGEITUDE	Dovetail	70	31 Aug 91	1
JURASSIC SHIFT	Dovetail	11	1 May 93	4
ARBORESCENCE	Dovetail	18	9 Jul 94	2

P

Jazzi P
UK

(See also DNA.)

SINGLES:	HITS 3		WEEKS 12	
GET LOOSE	Breakout	25	8 Jul 89	6
Above hit: L.A. MIX featuring Jazzi P.				
FEEL THE RHYTHM	A&M USA	51	9 Jun 90	2
REBEL WOMAN	DNA	42	3 Aug 91	4

Samples David Bowie's Rebel Rebel.
Above hit: DNA rap performed by Jazzi P.

P.H.D | | | | UK

SINGLES:	HITS 1			WEEKS 14
I WON'T LET YOU DOWN	WEA	3	3 Apr 82	14
ALBUMS:	**HITS 1**			**WEEKS 8**
PH.D	WEA	33	1 May 82	8

P.I.L. - See PUBLIC IMAGE LTD.

P.J. - See PJ

P.O.V. duet with JADE | | | | US

(See also Jade.)

SINGLES:	HITS 1			WEEKS 3
ALL THRU THE NITE	Giant	32	5 Feb 94	3

Thom PACE | | | | US

SINGLES:	HITS 1			WEEKS 15
MAYBE	RSO	14	19 May 79	15

Theme from the film 'The Life And Times Of Grizzly Adams'.

PACIFICA | | | | UK

SINGLES:	HITS 1			WEEKS 1
LOST IN THE TRANSLATION (HEART OF GLASS)	Wildstar	54	31 Jul 99	1

Samples Blondie's Heart Of Glass.

PACK featuring Nigel BENN | | | | UK

SINGLES:	HITS 1			WEEKS 2
STAND AND FIGHT	IQ	61	8 Dec 90	2

PACKABEATS | | | | UK

SINGLES:	HITS 1			WEEKS 1
GYPSY BEAT	Parlophone	49	25 Feb 61	1

Jose PADILLA featuring Angela JOHN | | | | Spain

SINGLES:	HITS 1			WEEKS 1
WHO DO YOU LOVE	Manifesto	59	8 Aug 98	1

PAGANINI TRAXX | | | | Italy

SINGLES:	HITS 1			WEEKS 1
ZOE	Sony	47	1 Feb 97	1

Jimmy PAGE | | | | UK

(See also Jimmy Page and Robert Plant.)

SINGLES:	HITS 1			WEEKS 11
COME WITH ME	Epic	75	1 Aug 98	1

US Import. Based on guitar riff from Led Zeppelin's 'Kashmir' from 1975. From the film 'Godzilla'.

COME WITH ME	Epic	2	8 Aug 98	10

Above 2: PUFF DADDY featuring Jimmy PAGE.

ALBUMS:	**HITS 3**			**WEEKS 14**
DEATHWISH II [OST]	Swan Song	40	27 Feb 82	4
WHATEVER HAPPENED TO JUGULA?	Beggars Banquet	44	16 Mar 85	4

Above hit: Roy HARPER with Jimmy PAGE.

OUTRIDER	Geffen	27	2 Jul 88	6

Jimmy PAGE and Robert PLANT | | | | UK

(See also Jimmy Page; Robert Plant.)

SINGLES:	HITS 2			WEEKS 5
GALLOWS POLE	Fontana	35	17 Dec 94	3

This version recorded for their MTV Unledded performance.

MOST HIGH	Mercury	26	11 Apr 98	2
ALBUMS:	**HITS 2**			**WEEKS 19**
NO QUARTER - JIMMY PAGE AND ROBERT PLANT UNLEDDED	Fontana	7	19 Nov 94	13

Live recordings for MTV.

WALKING INTO CLARKSDALE	Mercury	3	2 May 98	6

Patti PAGE | | | | US

SINGLES:	HITS 1			WEEKS 5
(HOW MUCH IS) THAT DOGGIE IN THE WINDOW	Oriole	9	28 Mar 53	5

Tommy PAGE
US

SINGLES:		HITS 1		WEEKS 3
I'LL BE YOUR EVERYTHING	Sire	53	26 May 90	3

Backing vocals by New Kids On The Block

Wendy PAGE - See TIN TIN OUT

PAGLIARO
Canada

SINGLES:		HITS 1		WEEKS 6
LOVIN' YOU AIN'T EASY	Pye	31	19 Feb 72	6

PAID and LIVE featuring Lauryn HILL
US

(See also Lauryn Hill.)

SINGLES:		HITS 1		WEEKS 1
ALL MY TIME	One World Entertainment	57	27 Dec 97	1

Elaine PAIGE
UK

SINGLES:		HITS 7		WEEKS 41
DON'T WALK AWAY TILL I TOUCH YOU	EMI	46	21 Oct 78	5
MEMORY	Polydor	6	6 Jun 81	12

From the Andrew Lloyd Webber musical 'Cats'.

MEMORY [RE]	Polydor	67	30 Jan 82	3
SOMETIMES (THEME FROM 'CHAMPIONS')	Island	72	14 Apr 84	1
I KNOW HIM SO WELL	RCA	1	5 Jan 85	16

From the musical 'Chess'.
Above hit: Elaine PAIGE and Barbara DICKSON.

THE SECOND TIME (THEME FROM "BILITIS")	WEA	69	21 Nov 87	1
HYMNE A L'AMOUR (IF YOU LOVE ME)	WEA	68	21 Jan 95	1
MEMORY [RR]	WEA	36	24 Oct 98	2

Taken from the Soundtrack of 'Cats – The Video'. Re-recorded with a 70-piece orchestra.

ALBUMS:		HITS 13		WEEKS 155
ELAINE PAIGE	WEA	56	1 May 82	6
STAGES	K-Tel	2	5 Nov 83	48
CINEMA	K-Tel	12	20 Oct 84	25
LOVE HURTS	WEA	8	16 Nov 85	20
CHRISTMAS	WEA	27	29 Nov 86	6
MEMORIES – THE BEST OF ELAINE PAIGE	Telstar	14	5 Dec 87	15
THE QUEEN ALBUM	Siren	51	19 Nov 88	8

Songs written by Queen.

LOVE CAN DO THAT	RCA	36	27 Apr 91	4
THE BEST OF ELAINE PAIGE AND BARBARA DICKSON	Telstar	22	28 Nov 92	9

Features their duet as well as solo recordings.
Above hit: Elaine PAIGE and Barbara DICKSON.

ROMANCE AND THE STAGE	RCA	71	10 Apr 93	1
PIAF	WEA	46	19 Nov 94	3

Songs from the show 'Piaf' who Paige portrayed on stage during 1993/94.

ENCORE	WEA	20	1 Jul 95	6
ON REFLECTION – THE VERY BEST OF ELAINE PAIGE	Telstar TV/WEA	60	28 Nov 98	4

Hal PAIGE and the WHALERS
US

SINGLES:		HITS 1		WEEKS 1
GOING BACK TO MY HOME TOWN	Melodisc	50	27 Aug 60	1

Jennifer PAIGE
US

SINGLES:		HITS 2		WEEKS 13
CRUSH	E.A.R.	4	12 Sep 98	12
SOBER	E.A.R.	68	20 Mar 99	1
ALBUMS:		HITS 1		WEEKS 1
JENNIFER PAIGE	E.A.R.	67	31 Oct 98	1

Jean-Francois PAILLARD - See ORCHESTRE DE CHAMBRE Jean-Francois PAILLARD

PALE
France

SINGLES:		HITS 1		WEEKS 2
DOGS WITH NO TAILS	A&M	51	13 Jun 92	2

PALE FOUNTAINS
UK

SINGLES:		HITS 1		WEEKS 6
THANK YOU	Virgin	48	27 Nov 82	6
ALBUMS:		HITS 2		WEEKS 3
PACIFIC STREET	Virgin	85	10 Mar 84	2
FROM ACROSS THE KITCHEN TABLE	Virgin	94	16 Feb 85	1

PALE SAINTS
Australia

SINGLES:	HITS 1			WEEKS 1
KINKY LOVE	4AD	72	6 Jul 91	1
ALBUMS:	**HITS 2**			**WEEKS 3**
THE COMFORTS OF MADNESS	4AD	40	24 Feb 90	2
IN RIBBONS	4AD	61	4 Apr 92	1

PALLAS
UK

ALBUMS:	HITS 2			WEEKS 4
SENTINEL	Harvest	41	25 Feb 84	3
THE WEDGE	Harvest	70	22 Feb 86	1

Barry PALMER - See Mike OLDFIELD

Patsy PALMER - See Sid OWEN and Patsy PALMER

Robert PALMER
UK

SINGLES:	HITS 23			WEEKS 128
EVERY KINDA PEOPLE	Island	53	20 May 78	4
BAD CASE OF LOVIN' YOU (DOCTOR DOCTOR)	Island	61	7 Jul 79	2
Originally recorded by Moon Martin.				
JOHNNY AND MARY	Island	44	6 Sep 80	8
LOOKING FOR CLUES	Island	33	22 Nov 80	9
SOME GUYS HAVE ALL THE LUCK	Island	16	13 Feb 82	8
Originally recorded by the Persuaders.				
YOU ARE IN MY SYSTEM	Island	53	2 Apr 83	4
Originally recorded by the System.				
YOU CAN HAVE IT (TAKE MY HEART)	Island	66	18 Jun 83	2
ADDICTED TO LOVE	Island	5	10 May 86	15
I DIDN'T MEAN TO TURN YOU ON	Island	9	19 Jul 86	9
Originally recorded by Cherrelle.				
DISCIPLINE OF LOVE	Island	68	1 Nov 86	1
Original release reached No. 95 in 1985.				
SWEET LIES	Island	58	26 Mar 88	3
SIMPLY IRRESISTIBLE	EMI	44	11 Jun 88	4
SHE MAKES MY DAY	EMI	6	15 Oct 88	12
CHANGE HIS WAYS	EMI	28	13 May 89	7
IT COULD HAPPEN TO YOU	EMI	71	26 Aug 89	1
I'LL BE YOUR BABY TONIGHT	EMI	6	3 Nov 90	10
Originally recorded by Bob Dylan.				
Above hit: Robert PALMER and UB40.				
MERCY MERCY ME/I WANT YOU [M]	EMI	9	5 Jan 91	9
Both originally recorded by Marvin Gaye.				
DREAMS TO REMEMBER	EMI	68	15 Jun 91	1
EVERY KINDA PEOPLE [RI]	Island	43	7 Mar 92	3
WITCHCRAFT	EMI	50	17 Oct 92	3
GIRL U WANT	EMI	57	9 Jul 94	2
Features Nuno Bettencourt from Extreme on guitar.				
KNOW BY NOW	EMI	25	3 Sep 94	5
YOU BLOW ME AWAY	EMI	38	24 Dec 94	4
RESPECT YOURSELF	EMI	45	14 Oct 95	2
Originally recorded by the Staple Singers.				
ALBUMS:	**HITS 13**			**WEEKS 162**
SOME PEOPLE CAN DO WHAT THEY LIKE	Island	46	6 Nov 76	1
SECRETS	Island	54	14 Jul 79	4
CLUES	Island	31	6 Sep 80	8
MAYBE IT'S LIVE	Island	32	3 Apr 82	6
Include both studio and live recordings from his concert at London's Dominion Theatre, Nov 80.				
PRIDE	Island	37	23 Apr 83	9
RIPTIDE	Island	69	16 Nov 85	2
RIPTIDE [RE]	Island	5	24 May 86	35
HEAVY NOVA	EMI	17	9 Jul 88	25
ADDICTIONS VOLUME 1	Island	7	11 Nov 89	17
DON'T EXPLAIN	EMI	9	17 Nov 90	20
ADDICTIONS VOLUME 2	Island	12	4 Apr 92	7
RIDIN' HIGH	EMI	32	31 Oct 92	3
HONEY	EMI	25	24 Sep 94	4
THE VERY BEST OF ROBERT PALMER	EMI	4	28 Oct 95	21

Suzanne PALMER - See ABSOLUTE; CLUB 69

PAN POSITION
Italy/Venezuela

SINGLES:	HITS 1			WEEKS 1
ELEPHANT PAW (GET DOWN TO THE FUNK)	Positiva	55	18 Jun 94	1

PANDORA'S BOX US

SINGLES:	HITS 1			WEEKS 3
IT'S ALL COMING BACK TO ME NOW	Virgin	51	21 Oct 89	3

Darryl PANDY US

SINGLES:	HITS 3			WEEKS 5
LOVE CAN'T TURN AROUND	4 Liberty	40	14 Dec 96	2

This was a remix. Darryl Pandy was not credited on the original 1986 release.
Above hit: Farley 'Jackmaster' FUNK featuring Darryl PANDY.

RAISE YOUR HANDS	VC Recordings	40	20 Feb 99	2

Above hit: BIG ROOM GIRL featuring Darryl PANDY.

SUNSHINE & HAPPINESS	Azuli	68	2 Oct 99	1

Above hit: Darryl PANDY meets NERIO'S DUBWORK.

Johnny PANIC and the BIBLE OF DREAMS UK

SINGLES:	HITS 1			WEEKS 2
JOHNNY PANIC AND THE BIBLE OF DREAMS	Fontana	70	2 Feb 91	2

PANTERA US

SINGLES:	HITS 4			WEEKS 8
MOUTH FOR WAR	Atco	73	10 Oct 92	1
WALK	Atco	35	27 Feb 93	2
I'M BROKEN	East West America	19	19 Mar 94	2
PLANET CARAVAN	East West America	26	22 Oct 94	3

Originally recorded by Black Sabbath.

ALBUMS:	HITS 4			WEEKS 9
VULGAR DISPLAY OF POWER	Atco	64	7 Mar 92	1
FAR BEYOND DRIVEN	Atco	3	2 Apr 94	4
THE GREAT SOUTHERN TRENDKILL	East West	17	18 May 96	3
OFFICIAL LIVE - 101 PROOF	East West	54	30 Aug 97	1

Live recordings plus 2 studio tracks.

PAPER DOLLS UK

SINGLES:	HITS 1			WEEKS 13
SOMETHING HERE IN MY HEART (KEEPS A TELLIN' ME NO)	Pye	11	16 Mar 68	13

PAPER LACE UK

SINGLES:	HITS 4			WEEKS 41
BILLY-DON'T BE A HERO	Bus Stop	1	23 Feb 74	14
THE NIGHT CHICAGO DIED	Bus Stop	3	4 May 74	11
THE BLACK-EYED BOYS	Bus Stop	11	24 Aug 74	10
WE GOT THE WHOLE WORLD IN OUR HANDS	Warner Brothers	24	04 Mar 78	6

Above hit: NOTTINGHAM FOREST with PAPER LACE.

PAPERDOLLS UK

SINGLES:	HITS 1			WEEKS 1
GONNA MAKE YOU BLUSH	MCA	65	12 Sep 98	1

PAPPA BEAR featuring Van DER TOORN Germany

SINGLES:	HITS 1			WEEKS 1
CHERISH	Universal	47	16 May 98	1

Vanessa PARADIS France

SINGLES:	HITS 4			WEEKS 30
JOE LE TAXI	FA	3	13 Feb 88	10
BE MY BABY	Polydor	6	10 Oct 92	15
SUNDAY MONDAYS	Polydor	49	27 Feb 93	4
JUST AS LONG AS YOU ARE THERE	Polydor	57	24 Jul 93	1

ALBUMS:	HITS 1			WEEKS 2
VANESSA PARADIS	Remark	45	7 Nov 92	2

PARADISE UK

SINGLES:	HITS 1			WEEKS 4
ONE MIND TWO HEARTS	Priority	42	10 Sep 83	4

PARADISE LOST UK

SINGLES:	HITS 3			WEEKS 3
THE LAST TIME	Music For Nations	60	20 May 95	1
FOREVER FAILURE	Music For Nations	66	7 Oct 95	1
SAY JUST WORDS	Music For Nations	53	28 Jun 97	1

ALBUMS:		HITS 3			WEEKS 6	
DRACONIAN TIMES		Music For Nations	16	24 Jun 95	3	
ONE SECOND		Music For Nations	31	26 Jul 97	2	
HOST		EMI	61	19 Jun 99	1	

PARADISE ORGANISATION
UK

SINGLES:		HITS 1			WEEKS 1	
PRAYER TOWER		Cowboy	70	23 Jan 93	1	

PARADOX
UK

SINGLES:		HITS 1			WEEKS 2	
JAILBREAK		Ronin	66	24 Feb 90	2	

Norrie PARAMOR ORCHESTRA
UK

(See also Tony Brent; Eddie Calvert (The Man with the Golden Trumpet); Michael Holliday; Frank Ifield; Ruby Murray; Cliff Richard; Shadows; Helen Shapiro; Norman Wisdom.)

SINGLES:		HITS 2			WEEKS 8	
THEME FROM 'SUMMER PLACE'		Columbia	36	19 Mar 60	2	
Theme from the film of the same name.						
Above hit: Norrie PARAMOR and his Orchestra.						
THEME FROM Z-CARS (JOHNNY TODD)		Columbia	33	24 Mar 62	6	
Theme from the BBC-TV series.						

PARAMOUNT JAZZ BAND - See Mr. Acker BILK

PARAMOUNTS
UK

SINGLES:		HITS 1			WEEKS 7	
POISON IVY		Parlophone	35	18 Jan 64	7	

PARCHMENT
UK

SINGLES:		HITS 1			WEEKS 5	
LIGHT UP THE FIRE		Pye	31	16 Sep 72	5	

PARIS - See INNER CITY

PARIS
UK

SINGLES:		HITS 1			WEEKS 4	
NO GETTING OVER YOU		RCA	49	19 Jun 82	4	

PARIS
US

SINGLES:		HITS 1			WEEKS 2	
GUERRILLA FUNK		Virgin	38	21 Jan 95	2	

Mica PARIS
UK

SINGLES:		HITS 15			WEEKS 63	
MY ONE TEMPTATION		Fourth & Broadway	7	7 May 88	11	
LIKE DREAMERS DO		Fourth & Broadway	26	30 Jul 88	5	
Above hit: Mica PARIS featuring Courtney PINE.						
BREATHE LIFE INTO ME		Fourth & Broadway	26	22 Oct 88	10	
WHERE IS THE LOVE		Fourth & Broadway	19	21 Jan 89	7	
Above hit: Mica PARIS and Will DOWNING.						
CONTRIBUTION		Fourth & Broadway	33	6 Oct 90	4	
Above hit: Mica PARIS featuring RAKIM.						
SOUTH OF THE RIVER		Fourth & Broadway	50	1 Dec 90	2	
IF I LOVE U 2 NITE		Fourth & Broadway	43	23 Feb 91	3	
Written by Prince.						
YOUNG SOUL REBELS		Big Life	61	31 Aug 91	3	
I NEVER FELT LIKE THIS BEFORE		Fourth & Broadway	15	3 Apr 93	5	
I WANNA HOLD ON TO YOU		Fourth & Broadway	27	5 Jun 93	3	
TWO IN A MILLION		Fourth & Broadway	51	7 Aug 93	2	
WHISPER A PRAYER		Fourth & Broadway	65	4 Dec 93	1	
ONE		Cooltempo	29	8 Apr 95	4	
STAY		Cooltempo	40	16 May 98	2	
BLACK ANGEL		Cooltempo	72	14 Nov 98	1	
ALBUMS:		HITS 4			WEEKS 40	
SO GOOD		Fourth & Broadway	6	3 Sep 88	32	
CONTRIBUTION		Fourth & Broadway	26	27 Oct 90	3	
WHISPER A PRAYER		Fourth & Broadway	20	26 Jun 93	4	
BLACK ANGEL		Cooltempo	59	22 Aug 98	1	

Ryan PARIS
Italy

SINGLES:		HITS 1			WEEKS 10	
DOLCE VITA		Carrere	5	3 Sep 83	10	

PARIS ANGELS — UK

SINGLES:		HITS 3		WEEKS 5	
SCOPE	Sheer Joy	75	3 Nov 90	1
PERFUME	Virgin	55	20 Jul 91	3
Original release reached No. 91 in 1990.				
FADE	Virgin	70	21 Sep 91	1
ALBUMS:		**HITS 1**		**WEEKS 2**
SUNDEW	Virgin	37	17 Aug 91	2

PARIS OPERA – COMIQUE ORCHESTRA – See Mady MESPLE and Danielle MILLET, PARIS OPERA – COMIQUE ORCHESTRA conducted by Alain LOMBARD

PARIS RED — US/Germany

SINGLES:		HITS 2		WEEKS 2	
GOOD FRIEND	Columbia	61	29 Feb 92	1
PROMISES	Columbia	59	15 May 93	1

John PARISH + Polly Jean HARVEY — US

(See also PJ Harvey.)

SINGLES:		HITS 1		WEEKS 1	
THAT WAS MY VEIL	Island	75	23 Nov 96	1
ALBUMS:		**HITS 1**		**WEEKS 1**
DANCE HALL AT LOUSE POINT	Island	46	5 Oct 96	1

Simon PARK ORCHESTRA — UK

SINGLES:		HITS 1		WEEKS 24	
EYE LEVEL (THEME FROM THE THAMES T.V. SERIES "VAN DER VALK")	Columbia	41	25 Nov 72	2
EYE LEVEL (THEME FROM THE THAMES T.V. SERIES "VAN DER VALK") [RE]	Columbia	1	15 Sep 73	22

Graham PARKER and the RUMOUR — UK

SINGLES:		HITS 3		WEEKS 16	
THE PINK PARKER [EP]	Vertigo	24	19 Mar 77	5
Lead track: Hold Back The Night.				
HEY LORD, DON'T ASK ME QUESTIONS	Vertigo	32	22 Apr 78	7
TEMPORARY BEAUTY	RCA	50	20 Mar 82	4
Above hit: Graham PARKER.				
ALBUMS:		**HITS 6**		**WEEKS 35**
HEAT TREATMENT	Vertigo	52	27 Nov 76	2
STICK TO ME	Vertigo	19	12 Nov 77	4
PARKERILLA	Vertigo	14	27 May 78	5
Live recordings.				
SQUEEZING OUT SPARKS	Vertigo	18	7 Apr 79	8
THE UP ESCALATOR	Stiff	11	7 Jun 80	10
ANOTHER GREY AREA	RCA	40	27 Mar 82	6
Above hit: Graham PARKER.				

Ray PARKER JR. — US

SINGLES:		HITS 4		WEEKS 47	
GHOSTBUSTERS	Arista	2	25 Aug 84	31
Theme from the film of the same name.				
GIRLS ARE MORE FUN	Arista	46	18 Jan 86	4
I DON'T THINK THAT MAN SHOULD SLEEP ALONE	Geffen	13	3 Oct 87	10
OVER YOU	Geffen	65	30 Jan 88	2
ALBUMS:		**HITS 1**		**WEEKS 7**
AFTER DARK	WEA	40	10 Oct 87	7

Robert PARKER — US

SINGLES:		HITS 1		WEEKS 8	
BAREFOOTIN'	Island	24	6 Aug 66	8

Sara PARKER — US

SINGLES:		HITS 1		WEEKS 2	
MY LOVE IS DEEP	Manifesto	22	12 Apr 97	2

Jimmy PARKINSON — Australia

SINGLES:		HITS 3		WEEKS 19	
THE GREAT PRETENDER	Columbia	9	3 Mar 56	13
Above hit: Jimmy PARKINSON with Ray MARTIN and his Orchestra.				
WALK HAND IN HAND	Columbia	30	18 Aug 56	1
Above hit: Jimmy PARKINSON with the Bill SHEPHERD CHORUS.				
WALK HAND IN HAND [RE]	Columbia	26	6 Oct 56	1

IN THE MIDDLE OF THE HOUSE	Columbia	26	10 Nov 56	2
Above hit: Jimmy PARKINSON with Ray MARTIN and his Orchestra.				
IN THE MIDDLE OF THE HOUSE [RE]	Columbia	20	1 Dec 56	2

PARLIAMENT – See Scott GROOVES

John PARR   US

SINGLES:	HITS 3		WEEKS 22	
ST. ELMO'S FIRE (MAN IN MOTION)	London	6	14 Sep 85	13
From the film 'St. Elmo's Fire'.				
NAUGHTY NAUGHTY	London	58	18 Jan 86	3
ROCK 'N' ROLL MERCENARIES	Arista	31	30 Aug 86	6
Above hit: MEAT LOAF with John PARR.				
ALBUMS:	**HITS 1**		**WEEKS 2**	
JOHN PARR	London	60	2 Nov 85	2

Dean PARRISH   US

SINGLES:	HITS 1		WEEKS 5	
I'M ON MY WAY	UK USA	38	8 Feb 75	5

Man PARRISH   US

SINGLES:	HITS 3		WEEKS 26	
HIP HOP, BE BOP (DON'T STOP)	Polydor	41	26 Mar 83	6
BOOGIE DOWN (BRONX)	Boiling Point	56	23 Mar 85	4
MALE STRIPPER	Bolts	64	13 Sep 86	3
Above hit: MAN 2 MAN meet Man PARRISH.				
MALE STRIPPER [RE-1ST]	Bolts	63	3 Jan 87	1
MALE STRIPPER [RE-2ND]	Bolts	4	7 Feb 87	12

Alan PARSONS PROJECT   UK

SINGLES:	HITS 2		WEEKS 4	
OLD AND WISE	Arista	74	15 Jan 83	1
Above hit: Alan PARSONS PROJECT lead vocals by Colin BLUNSTONE.				
DON'T ANSWER ME	Arista	58	10 Mar 84	3
ALBUMS:	**HITS 10**		**WEEKS 38**	
TALES OF MYSTERY AND IMAGINATION	Charisma	56	28 Aug 76	1
Inspired by the work of Edgar Allan Poe.				
I ROBOT	Arista	30	13 Aug 77	1
Title comes from writer Isaac Asimov's science fiction book.				
PYRAMID	Arista	49	10 Jun 78	4
EVE	Arista	74	29 Sep 79	1
THE TURN OF A FRIENDLY CARD	Arista	38	15 Nov 80	4
EYE IN THE SKY	Arista	27	29 May 82	11
Title taken from a novel by Philip K. Dick.				
THE BEST OF THE ALAN PARSONS PROJECT	Arista	99	26 Nov 83	1
AMMONIA AVENUE	Arista	24	3 Mar 84	8
VULTURE CULTURE	Arista	40	23 Feb 85	5
GAUDI	Arista	66	14 Feb 87	2
Gaudi was a Spanish painter; the album is based on his life.				

Bill PARSONS   US

SINGLES:	HITS 1		WEEKS 2	
THE ALL-AMERICAN BOY	London	22	11 Apr 59	2
The actual vocalist is Bobby Bare. Parson's name is on label in error.				

PARTISANS   UK

ALBUMS:	HITS 1		WEEKS 1	
THE PARTISANS	No Future	94	19 Feb 83	1

PARTIZAN   UK

SINGLES:	HITS 2		WEEKS 3	
DRIVE ME CRAZY	Multiply	36	8 Feb 97	2
KEEP YOUR LOVE	Multiply	53	6 Dec 97	1
Above hit: PARTIZAN featuring Natalie ROBB.				

PARTNERS – See Al HUDSON

PARTNERS IN KRYME   US

SINGLES:	HITS 1		WEEKS 10	
TURTLE POWER	SBK	1	21 Jul 90	10
From the film 'Teenage Mutant Ninja Turtles'.				

David PARTON
UK

SINGLES:		HITS 1		WEEKS 9
ISN'T SHE LOVELY	Pye	4	15 Jan 77	9

Original comes from Stevie Wonder's 1976 album Songs In The Key Of Life.

Dolly PARTON
US

(See also Dolly Parton, Linda Ronstadt and Emmylou Harris.)

SINGLES:		HITS 5		WEEKS 33
JOLENE	RCA Victor	7	15 May 76	10
9 TO 5	RCA	47	21 Feb 81	5
ISLANDS IN THE STREAM	RCA	7	12 Nov 83	15

Written by the Bee Gees.
Above hit: Kenny ROGERS Duet with Dolly PARTON.

HERE YOU COME AGAIN	RCA	75	7 Apr 84	1
THE DAY I FALL IN LOVE (LOVE THEME FROM BEETHOVEN'S 2ND)	Columbia	64	16 Apr 94	2

From the film 'Beethoven's 2nd'.
Above hit: Dolly PARTON and James INGRAM.

ALBUMS:		HITS 5		WEEKS 21
DOLLY PARTON/BOTH SIDES	Lotus	24	25 Nov 78	12

Compilation.

GREATEST HITS	RCA	74	7 Sep 85	1
THE GREATEST HITS	Telstar	65	22 Oct 94	2
A LIFE IN MUSIC - ULTIMATE COLLECTION	RCA	38	8 Nov 97	3
HUNGRY AGAIN	MCA Nashville	41	26 Sep 98	3

Dolly PARTON, Linda RONSTADT and Emmylou HARRIS
US

(See also Emmylou Harris; Dolly Parton; Linda Ronstadt.)

ALBUMS:		HITS 1		WEEKS 4
TRIO	Warner Brothers	60	14 Mar 87	4

Stella PARTON
US

SINGLES:		HITS 1		WEEKS 4
THE DANGER OF A STRANGER	Elektra	35	22 Oct 77	4

Alan PARTRIDGE
UK

ALBUMS:		HITS 1		WEEKS 3
KNOWING ME, KNOWING YOU 3	BBC	41	18 Mar 95	3

Taken from the BBC Radio 4 show 'On The Hour' (later became 'Day To Day').

Don PARTRIDGE
UK

SINGLES:		HITS 3		WEEKS 32
ROSIE	Columbia	4	10 Feb 68	12
BLUE EYES	Columbia	3	1 Jun 68	13
BREAKFAST ON PLUTO	Columbia	26	22 Feb 69	7

PARTRIDGE FAMILY
US

SINGLES:		HITS 5		WEEKS 53
I THINK I LOVE YOU	Bell	18	13 Feb 71	9
IT'S ONE OF THOSE NIGHTS (YES LOVE)	Bell	11	26 Feb 72	11
BREAKING UP IS HARD TO DO	Bell	3	8 Jul 72	13

Above 3: PARTRIDGE FAMILY starring Shirley JONES– featuring David CASSIDY.

LOOKING THRU THE EYES OF LOVE	Bell	9	3 Feb 73	9
WALKING IN THE RAIN	Bell	10	19 May 73	11

Originally recorded by the Ronettes.
Above 2: PARTRIDGE FAMILY starring David CASSIDY.

ALBUMS:		HITS 4		WEEKS 13
UP TO DATE	Bell	46	8 Jan 72	2
THE PARTRIDGE FAMILY SOUND MAGAZINE	Bell	14	22 Apr 72	7
SHOPPING BAG	Bell	28	30 Sep 72	3
CHRISTMAS CARD	Bell	45	9 Dec 72	1

PARTY ANIMALS
Holland

SINGLES:		HITS 2		WEEKS 3
HAVE YOU EVER BEEN MELLOW?	Mokum	56	1 Jun 96	1
HAVE YOU EVER BEEN MELLOW? [EP]	Mokum	43	19 Oct 96	2

Lead track: Have You Ever Been Mellow?, which is a re-issue.

PARTY FAITHFUL
UK

SINGLES:		HITS 1		WEEKS 1
BRASS: LET THERE BE HOUSE	Ore	54	22 Jul 95	1

PASADENAS

US

SINGLES:		HITS 10			WEEKS 57	
TRIBUTE (RIGHT ON)		CBS	5	28 May 88	14
RIDING ON A TRAIN		CBS	13	17 Sep 88	9
ENCHANTED LADY		CBS	31	26 Nov 88	6
LOVE THING		CBS	22	12 May 90	5
REELING		CBS	75	14 Jul 90	1
I'M DOING FINE NOW		Columbia	4	1 Feb 92	10
No refs here????					
MAKE IT WITH YOU		Columbia	20	4 Apr 92	4
I BELIEVE IN MIRACLES		Columbia	34	6 Jun 92	3
MOVING IN THE RIGHT DIRECTION		Columbia	49	29 Aug 92	2
LET'S STAY TOGETHER		Columbia	22	21 Nov 92	3
ALBUMS:		**HITS 2**			**WEEKS 32**	
TO WHOM IT MAY CONCERN		CBS	3	22 Oct 88	21
YOURS SINCERELY		Columbia	6	7 Mar 92	11

PASSENGERS

UK/Ireland/Italy

SINGLES:		HITS 1			WEEKS 9	
MISS SARAJEVO		Island	6	2 Dec 95	9
Inspired by the TV documentary that reported on a beauty pageant in the besieged Bosnian capital.					
ALBUMS:		**HITS 1**			**WEEKS 5**	
ORIGINAL SOUNDTRACKS 1		Island	12	18 Nov 95	5

PASSION

UK

SINGLES:		HITS 1			WEEKS 1	
SHARE YOUR LOVE (DIGGITY REMIXES)		Charm	62	25 Jan 97	1
Based on Blackstreet's No Diggity.					

PASSIONS

UK

SINGLES:		HITS 1			WEEKS 8	
I'M IN LOVE WITH A GERMAN FILM STAR		Polydor	25	31 Jan 81	8
ALBUMS:		**HITS 1**			**WEEKS 1**	
THIRTY THOUSAND FEET OVER CHINA		Polydor	92	3 Oct 81	1

PAT and MICK

UK

SINGLES:		HITS 5			WEEKS 27	
LET'S ALL CHANT / ON THE NIGHT		PWL	11	9 Apr 88	9
On The Night listed for the week of 4 Jun 88 once single had dropped to No. 70.					
Above hit: MICK and PAT.					
I HAVEN'T STOPPED DANCING YET		PWL	9	25 Mar 89	8
USE IT UP AND WEAR IT OUT		PWL	22	14 Apr 90	6
GIMME SOME		PWL	53	23 Mar 91	2
HOT HOT HOT		PWL International	47	15 May 93	2
All singles above were to support London's Capital Radio 'Help A London Child' appeal.					

PATIENCE and PRUDENCE

US

SINGLES:		HITS 2			WEEKS 8	
TONIGHT YOU BELONG TO ME		London	28	3 Nov 56	3
Originally recorded by Gene Austin in 1927.					
GONNA GET ALONG WITHOUT YA NOW		London	22	2 Mar 57	4
Originally recorded by Teresa Brewer in 1952.					
GONNA GET ALONG WITHOUT YA NOW [RE]		London	24	13 Apr 57	1

PATRA

Jamaica

(See also Shabba Ranks.)

SINGLES:		HITS 2			WEEKS 3	
PULL UP TO THE BUMPER		Epic	50	30 Sep 95	2
WORK MI BODY		Heavenly	75	10 Aug 96	1
Above hit: MONKEY MAFIA featuring PATRA.					

PATRIC

UK

SINGLES:		HITS 1			WEEKS 2	
LOVE ME		Bell	54	9 Jul 94	2

Dee PATTEN

UK

SINGLES:		HITS 1			WEEKS 1	
WHO'S THE BAD MAN?		Higher Ground	42	30 Jan 99	1
Originally released on the Hard Hand's label in 1992.					

Kellee PATTERSON   US

SINGLES:	HITS 1		WEEKS 7	
IF IT DON'T FIT DON'T FORCE IT	EMI International	44	18 Feb 78	7

Rahsaan PATTERSON   US

SINGLES:	HITS 2		WEEKS 2	
STOP BY	MCA	50	26 Jul 97	1
WHERE YOU ARE	MCA	55	21 Mar 98	1

Billy PAUL   US

(See also Philadelphia International All Stars: Lou Rawls, Billy Paul, Archie Bell, Teddy Pendergrass, O'Jays, Dee Dee Sharp, Gamble.)

SINGLES:	HITS 7		WEEKS 45	
ME & MRS JONES	Epic	12	13 Jan 73	9
THANKS FOR SAVING MY LIFE	Philadelphia International	33	12 Jan 74	6
LET'S MAKE A BABY	Philadelphia International	30	22 May 76	5
LET 'EM IN	Philadelphia International	26	30 Apr 77	5
YOUR SONG	Philadelphia International	37	16 Jul 77	7
ONLY THE STRONG SURVIVE	Philadelphia International	33	19 Nov 77	8
Originally recorded by Jerry Butler.				
BRING THE FAMILY BACK	Philadelphia International	51	14 Jul 79	5

Chris PAUL   UK

SINGLES:	HITS 3		WEEKS 8	
EXPANSIONS '86 (EXPAND YOUR MIND)	Fourth & Broadway	58	31 May 86	5
Above hit: Chris PAUL featuring the voice of David JOSEPH.				
BACK IN MY ARMS	Syncopate	74	21 Nov 87	2
TURN THE MUSIC UP	Syncopate	73	13 Aug 88	1

Frankie PAUL – See APACHIE INDIAN

Les PAUL and Mary FORD   US

SINGLES:	HITS 1		WEEKS 4	
VAYA CON DIOS (MAY GOD BE WITH YOU)	Capitol	7	21 Nov 53	4

Lyn PAUL   UK

(See also New Seekers.)

SINGLES:	HITS 1		WEEKS 6	
IT OUGHTA SELL A MILLION	Polydor	37	28 Jun 75	6
Featured in the Coca-Cola TV commercial.				

Owen PAUL   UK

SINGLES:	HITS 1		WEEKS 14	
MY FAVOURITE WASTE OF TIME	Epic	3	31 May 86	14
Originally recorded by Marshall Crenshaw.				

PAUL and PAULA   US

SINGLES:	HITS 2		WEEKS 31	
HEY PAULA	Philips	8	16 Feb 63	12
YOUNG LOVERS	Philips	9	20 Apr 63	14
HEY PAULA [RE]	Philips	37	18 May 63	5

Luciano PAVAROTTI   Italy

(See also Passengers; 3 Tenors: José Carreras, Placido Domingo, Luciano Pavarotti.)

SINGLES:	HITS 3		WEEKS 22	
NESSUN DORMA	Decca	2	16 Jun 90	11
The Official BBC TV Grandstand World Cup Theme for 1990.				
MISERERE	London	15	24 Oct 92	5
Above hit: ZUCCHERO with Luciano PAVAROTTI.				
LIVE LIKE HORSES	Rocket	9	14 Dec 96	6
Above hit: Elton JOHN and Luciano PAVAROTTI.				

ALBUMS:	HITS 13		WEEKS 180	
PAVAROTTI'S GREATEST HITS	Decca	95	15 May 82	1
MAMMA	Decca	96	30 Jun 84	1
Above hit: Luciano PAVAROTTI with the Henry MANCINI ORCHESTRA.				
THE PAVAROTTI COLLECTION	Stylus	12	9 Aug 86	34
THE NEW PAVAROTTI COLLECTION LIVE!	Stylus	63	16 Jul 88	8
THE ESSENTIAL PAVAROTTI	Decca	1	17 Mar 90	72
ESSENTIAL PAVAROTTI II	Decca	1	20 Jul 91	28
PAVAROTTI IN HYDE PARK	Decca	19	15 Feb 92	7
Live recordings.				
TI AMO - PUCCINI'S GREATEST LOVE SONGS	Decca	23	4 Sep 93	4
Compilation of recordings from 1972–79.				

MY HEART'S DELIGHT	Decca	44	12 Feb 94	4
Live recordings from his home town of Modena.				
Above hit: Luciano PAVAROTTI with the ROYAL PHILHARMONIC ORCHESTRA.				
TOGETHER FOR THE CHILDREN OF BOSNIA	Decca	11	30 Mar 96	6
Live recordings from the Concert in his home town of Modena, Sep 95. Features Brian Eno, Bono,				
The Edge, Dolores O'Riordan, Meat Loaf, Simon Le Bon, Michael Bolton, Chieftains,				
Zucchero, Jovanotti, Michael Kamen.				
PAVAROTTI AND FRIENDS FOR WAR CHILD	Decca	45	14 Dec 96	4
Features Elton John, Liza Minnelli, Sheryl Crow & Joan Osborne.				
Above 2: PAVAROTTI and FRIENDS.				
THE ULTIMATE COLLECTION	Decca	39	25 Oct 97	5
LOVE SONGS	Decca	26	19 Jun 99	6

PAVEMENT
US

SINGLES:	HITS 5		WEEKS 6	
WATERY, DOMESTIC [EP]	Big Cat	58	28 Nov 92	1
Lead track: Brick Wall.				
CUT YOUR HAIR	Big Cat	52	12 Feb 94	1
STEREO	Domino	48	8 Feb 97	1
SHADY LANE (KROSSFADER)	Domino	40	3 May 97	1
CARROT ROPE	Domino	27	22 May 99	1
ALBUMS:	HITS 6		WEEKS 13	
SLANTED AND ENCHANTED	Big Cat	72	25 Apr 92	1
WESTING (BY MUSKET AND SEXTANT)	Big Cat	30	3 Apr 93	2
CROOKED RAIN CROOKED RAIN	Big Cat	15	26 Feb 94	3
WOWEE ZOWEE	Big Cat	18	22 Apr 95	2
BRIGHTEN THE CORNERS	Domino	27	22 Feb 97	2
TERROR TWILIGHT	Domino	19	19 Jun 99	3

Rita PAVONE
Italy

SINGLES:	HITS 2		WEEKS 19	
HEART	RCA Victor	27	3 Dec 66	12
Above hit: Rita PAVONE with Charles BLACKWELL and his Orchestra.				
YOU ONLY YOU	RCA Victor	21	21 Jan 67	7
Above hit: Rita PAVONE with Geoff LOVE and his Orchestra.				

George PAXTON Orchestra and Chorus – See Adam WADE with the George PAXTON Orchestra and Chorus

Tom PAXTON
US

ALBUMS:	HITS 3		WEEKS 10	
NO. 6	Elektra	23	13 Jun 70	5
THE COMPLEAT TOM PAXTON	Elektra	18	3 Apr 71	4
PEACE WILL COME	Reprise	47	1 Jul 72	1

Freda PAYNE
US

SINGLES:	HITS 3		WEEKS 30	
BAND OF GOLD	Invictus	1	5 Sep 70	19
Features Ray Parker Jr on piano.				
DEEPER AND DEEPER	Invictus	33	21 Nov 70	9
CHERISH WHAT IS DEAR TO YOU (WHILE IT'S NEAR TO YOU)	Invictus	46	27 Mar 71	2

Tammy PAYNE
UK

SINGLES:	HITS 1		WEEKS 2	
TAKE ME NOW	Talkin Loud	55	20 Jul 91	2

PEACE BY PIECE
UK

SINGLES:	HITS 2		WEEKS 2	
SWEET SISTER	Blanco Y Negro	46	21 Sep 96	1
NOBODY'S BUSINESS	Blanco Y Negro	50	25 Apr 98	1

PEACH
UK/Belgium

SINGLES:	HITS 1		WEEKS 1	
ON MY OWN	Mute	69	17 Jan 98	1

PEACHES and HERB
US

SINGLES:	HITS 2		WEEKS 23	
SHAKE YOUR GROOVE THING	Polydor	26	20 Jan 79	10
REUNITED	Polydor	4	21 Apr 79	13

Mary PEARCE – See UP YER RONSON featuring Mary PEARCE

Natasha PEARL – See TASTE XPERIENCE featuring Natasha PEARL

PEARL JAM · US

SINGLES:		HITS 12		WEEKS 38	
ALIVE	Epic	16	15 Feb 92	6
EVEN FLOW	Epic	27	18 Apr 92	3
JEREMY	Epic	15	26 Sep 92	4
DAUGHTER	Epic	18	1 Jan 94	5
DISSIDENT	Epic	14	28 May 94	4
SPIN THE BLACK CIRCLE	Epic	10	26 Nov 94	3
NOT FOR YOU	Epic	34	25 Feb 95	2
MERKINBALL: I GOT ID / LONG ROAD	Epic	25	16 Dec 95	3

Chart only reflected title as Merkinball which was the sleeve title.

WHO YOU ARE	Epic	18	17 Aug 96	2
GIVEN TO FLY	Epic	12	31 Jan 98	3
WISHLIST	Epic	30	23 May 98	2
LAST KISS	Epic	42	14 Aug 99	1

Original by J. Frank Wilson and the Cavaliers reached No. 2 in the US in 1964. This was first released as a free Xmas single to their fan club.

ALBUMS:		HITS 6		WEEKS 113	
TEN	Epic	18	7 Mar 92	65
VS	Epic	2	23 Oct 93	24
VITALOGY	Epic	4	3 Dec 94	11

Entered at No. 54 with first week sales only on vinyl.

NO CODE	Epic	3	7 Sep 96	5
YIELD	Epic	7	14 Feb 98	7
LIVE – ON TWO LEGS	Epic	68	5 Dec 98	1

PEARLS · UK

SINGLES:		HITS 4		WEEKS 24	
THIRD FINGER, LEFT HAND	Bell	31	27 May 72	6
YOU CAME, YOU SAW, YOU CONQUERED	Bell	32	23 Sep 72	5
YOU ARE EVERYTHING	Bell	41	24 Mar 73	3
GUILTY	Bell	10	1 Jun 74	10

Johnny PEARSON ORCHESTRA · UK

SINGLES:		HITS 1		WEEKS 15	
SLEEPY SHORES	Penny Farthing	8	18 Dec 71	15

Theme from the BBC1 TV series 'Owen M.D.'.

David PEASTON · UK

ALBUMS:		HITS 1		WEEKS 1	
INTRODUCING . . . DAVID PEASTON	Geffen	66	26 Aug 89	1

PEBBLES · US

SINGLES:		HITS 3		WEEKS 17	
GIRLFRIEND	MCA	8	19 Mar 88	11
MERCEDES BOY	MCA	42	28 May 88	4
GIVING YOU THE BENEFIT	MCA	73	27 Oct 90	2
ALBUMS:		**HITS 1**		**WEEKS 4**	
PEBBLES	MCA	56	14 May 88	4

PEDDLERS · UK

SINGLES:		HITS 3		WEEKS 14	
LET THE SUN SHINE IN	Philips	50	9 Jan 65	1
BIRTH	CBS	17	23 Aug 69	9
GIRLIE	CBS	34	31 Jan 70	4
ALBUMS:		**HITS 2**		**WEEKS 16**	
FREE WHEELERS	CBS	27	16 Mar 68	13
BIRTHDAY	CBS	16	7 Feb 70	3

PEE BEE SQUAD · UK

SINGLES:		HITS 1		WEEKS 3	
RUGGED AND MEAN, BUTCH AND ON SCREEN	Project	52	5 Oct 85	3

DJ Paul Burnett with a spoof take off of Rambo.

Ann PEEBLES · US

SINGLES:		HITS 1		WEEKS 3	
I CAN'T STAND THE RAIN	London	50	20 Apr 74	1
I CAN'T STAND THE RAIN [RE]	London	41	4 May 74	2

PEECH BOYS · US

SINGLES:		HITS 1		WEEKS 3	
DON'T MAKE ME WAIT	TMT Productions	49	30 Oct 82	3

Kevin PEEK — UK

(See also Kevin Peek and Rick Wakeman featuring Jeff Wayne narration Patrick Allen.)

ALBUMS:	HITS 1			WEEKS 2
AWAKENING	Ariola	52	21 Mar 81	2

Kevin PEEK and Rick WAKEMAN featuring Jeff WAYNE narration Patrick ALLEN — UK

(See also Kevin PEEK; Rick WAKEMAN; Jeff WAYNE.)

ALBUMS:	HITS 1			WEEKS 6
BEYOND THE PLANETS	Telstar	64	13 Oct 84	6

Donald PEERS — UK

SINGLES:	HITS 2			WEEKS 27
PLEASE DON'T GO	Columbia	3	21 Dec 68	18
PLEASE DON'T GO [RE]	Columbia	38	3 May 69	3
GIVE ME ONE MORE CHANCE	Decca	36	24 Jun 72	6

Above hit: Donald PEERS; The Les REED ORCHESTRA and CHORUS.

PELE — UK

SINGLES:	HITS 3			WEEKS 3
MEGALOMANIA	M&G	73	15 Feb 92	1
FAIR BLOWS THE WIND FOR FRANCE	M&G	62	13 Jun 92	1
FAT BLACK HEART	M&G	75	31 Jul 93	1

Debbie PENDER — US

SINGLES:	HITS 1			WEEKS 2
MOVIN' ON	AM:PM	41	30 May 98	2

Teddy PENDERGRASS — US

(See also Harold Melvin And The Bluenotes; Philadelphia International All Stars: Lou Rawls, Billy Paul, Archie Bell, Teddy Pendergrass, O'Jays, Dee Dee Sharp, Gamble.)

SINGLES:	HITS 6			WEEKS 24
THE WHOLE TOWN'S LAUGHING AT ME	Philadelphia International	44	21 May 77	3
ONLY YOU / CLOSE THE DOOR	Philadelphia International	41	28 Oct 78	6
TWO HEARTS	20th Century	49	23 May 81	5

Above hit: Stephanie MILLS 'featuring Teddy PENDERGRASS'.

HOLD ME	Asylum	44	25 Jan 86	5

Above hit: Teddy PENDERGRASS with Whitney HOUSTON.

JOY	Elektra	58	28 May 88	3
THE MORE I GET, THE MORE I WANT	X-Clusive	35	19 Nov 94	2

He originally recorded it with Harold Melvin and the Bluenotes.
Above hit: KWS featuring Teddy PENDERGRASS.

ALBUMS:	HITS 2			WEEKS 12
THE ARTISTS VOLUME 2	Street Sounds	45	13 Jul 85	4

Compilation album with tracks by each artist.
Above hit: Luther VANDROSS/Teddy PENDERGRASS/CHANGE/ATLANTIC STARR.

JOY	Elektra	45	21 May 88	8

PENETRATION — UK

ALBUMS:	HITS 2			WEEKS 8
MOVING TARGETS	Virgin	22	28 Oct 78	4
COMING UP FOR AIR	Virgin	36	6 Oct 79	4

PENGUIN CAFE ORCHESTRA — UK

ALBUMS:	HITS 1			WEEKS 5
SIGNS OF LIFE	EG	49	4 Apr 87	5

Ce Ce PENISTON — US

SINGLES:	HITS 10			WEEKS 53
FINALLY	A&M	29	12 Oct 91	7

Rap by MC Lethal.

WE GOT A LOVE THANG	A&M	6	11 Jan 92	8

Backing vocals by Kym Sims.

I LIKE IT	A&M	58	18 Jan 92	2

Above hit: OVERWEIGHT POOCH featuring Ce Ce PENISTON.

FINALLY [RI]	A&M	2	21 Mar 92	8
KEEP ON WALKIN'	A&M	10	23 May 92	6
CRAZY LOVE	A&M	44	5 Sep 92	3
INSIDE THAT I CRIED	A&M	42	12 Dec 92	2
I'M IN THE MOOD	A&M	16	15 Jan 94	4
KEEP GIVIN' ME YOUR LOVE	A&M	36	2 Apr 94	2
HIT BY LOVE	A&M	33	6 Aug 94	2

FINALLY [RM]	AM:PM	26	13 Sep 97	5
Remixed by Eric Kupper.				
SOMEBODY ELSE'S GUY	AM:PM	13	7 Feb 98	4
ALBUMS:	**HITS 2**		**WEEKS 21**	
FINALLY	A&M	10	8 Feb 92	19
THOUGHT 'YA KNEW	A&M	31	5 Feb 94	2

Dawn PENN   Jamaica

SINGLES:	HITS 1		WEEKS 12	
YOU DON'T LOVE ME (NO, NO, NO)	Big Beat	3	11 Jun 94	12
She wrote this song back in 1969, originally recorded by Sonny and Cher.				
ALBUMS:	**HITS 1**		**WEEKS 2**	
NO, NO, NO	Big Beat	51	9 Jul 94	2

Leslie PENNING - See Mike OLDFIELD

Barbara PENNINGTON   US

SINGLES:	HITS 2		WEEKS 8	
FAN THE FLAME	Record Shack	62	27 Apr 85	3
ON A CROWDED STREET	Record Shack	57	27 Jul 85	5

Tricia PENROSE   UK

SINGLES:	HITS 1		WEEKS 1	
WHERE DID OUR LOVE GO	RCA	71	7 Dec 96	1

PENTANGLE   UK

SINGLES:	HITS 2		WEEKS 4	
ONCE I HAD A SWEETHEART	Big T	46	31 May 69	1
LIGHT FLIGHT (THEME FROM TAKE THREE GIRLS)	Big T	43	14 Feb 70	1
Certain copies has the title as Take Three Girls (Light Flight).				
LIGHT FLIGHT (THEME FROM TAKE THREE GIRLS) [RE]	Big T	45	28 Feb 70	2
ALBUMS:	**HITS 3**		**WEEKS 39**	
THE PENTANGLE	Transatlantic	21	15 Jun 68	9
BASKET OF LIGHT	Transatlantic	5	1 Nov 69	28
CRUEL SISTER	Transatlantic	51	12 Dec 70	2

PENTHOUSE 4   UK

SINGLES:	HITS 1		WEEKS 3	
BUST THIS HOUSE DOWN	Syncopate	56	23 Apr 88	3

PEOPLES CHOICE   US

SINGLES:	HITS 2		WEEKS 9	
DO IT ANY WAY YOU WANNA	Philadelphia International	36	20 Sep 75	5
JAM, JAM, JAM (ALL NIGHT LONG)	Philadelphia International	40	21 Jan 78	4
Above hit: PEOPLE'S CHOICE.				

Danny PEPPERMINT and the JUMPING JACKS   US

SINGLES:	HITS 1		WEEKS 8	
THE PEPPERMINT TWIST	London	26	20 Jan 62	8

PEPPERS   France

SINGLES:	HITS 1		WEEKS 12	
PEPPER BOX	Spark	6	26 Oct 74	12

PEPSI and SHIRLIE   UK

SINGLES:	HITS 4		WEEKS 24	
HEARTACHE	Polydor	2	17 Jan 87	12
GOODBYE STRANGER	Polydor	9	30 May 87	7
CAN'T GIVE ME LOVE	Polydor	58	26 Sep 87	3
ALL RIGHT NOW	Polydor	50	12 Dec 87	2
ALBUMS:	**HITS 1**		**WEEKS 2**	
ALL RIGHT NOW	Polydor	69	7 Nov 87	2

PERCEPTION   UK

SINGLES:	HITS 1		WEEKS 2	
FEED THE FEELING	Talkin Loud	58	7 Mar 92	2
[AA] listed with Three Times A Maybe by K-Creative.				

Lance PERCIVAL   UK

SINGLES:	HITS 1		WEEKS 3	
SHAME AND SCANDAL IN THE FAMILY	Parlophone	37	30 Oct 65	3
Originally recorded by Shawn Elliot.				

Hugo PERETTI and his Orchestra - See Valerie CARR with Hugo PERETTI and his Orchestra; Jimmy RODGERS

PERFECT - See PUFF DADDY

PERFECT DAY UK

SINGLES:	HITS 2			WEEKS 4
LIBERTY TOWN	London	58	21 Jan 89	3
JANE	London	68	1 Apr 89	1

PERFECT PHASE Holland

SINGLES:	HITS 1			WEEKS 2
HORNY HORNS	Positiva	21	25 Dec 99	2

Samples 49ers featuring Anne Marie Smith's Move Your Feet.

PERFECTLY ORDINARY PEOPLE UK

SINGLES:	HITS 1			WEEKS 3
"THEME FROM P.O.P."	Urban	61	22 Oct 88	3

PERFECTO ALLSTARZ UK

(See also Planet Perfecto.)

SINGLES:	HITS 1			WEEKS 11
REACH UP (PAPA'S GOT A BRAND NEW PIG BAG)	Perfecto	6	4 Feb 95	11

PERFUME UK

SINGLES:	HITS 1			WEEKS 1
HAVEN'T SEEN YOU	Aromasound	71	10 Feb 96	1

Emilio PERICOLI Italy

SINGLES:	HITS 1			WEEKS 14
AL DI LA (THEME FROM LOVERS MUST LEARN)	Warner Brothers	30	30 Jun 62	14

Nick PERITO and his Orchestra - See Julius LA ROSA with Nick PERITO and his Orchestra

Carl PERKINS US

SINGLES:	HITS 1			WEEKS 8
BLUE SUEDE SHOES	London	10	19 May 56	8
ALBUMS:	HITS 1			WEEKS 3
OL' BLUE SUEDES IS BACK	Jet	38	15 Apr 78	3

PERPETUAL MOTION UK

SINGLES:	HITS 1			WEEKS 5
KEEP ON DANCIN' (LET'S GO)	Positiva	12	2 May 98	5

Samples D.O.P.s Here I Go.

Nigel PERRIN - See Cliff RICHARD

Lee 'Scratch' PERRY Jamaica

ALBUMS:	HITS 1			WEEKS 1
ARKOLOGY	Island Jamaica	49	26 Jul 97	1

51 track, 4-CD boxed set of Perry-produced tracks.

Steve PERRY UK

SINGLES:	HITS 1			WEEKS 1
STEP BY STEP	His Master's Voice	41	6 Aug 60	1
ALBUMS:	HITS 2			WEEKS 3
STREET TALK	CBS	59	14 Jul 84	2
FOR THE LOVE OF STRANGE MEDICINE	Columbia	64	27 Aug 94	1

Jon PERTWEE UK

SINGLES:	HITS 1			WEEKS 7
WORZEL'S SONG	Decca	33	1 Mar 80	7

Worzel Gummage is the character he played in the Children's ITV series

PESHAY UK

SINGLES:	HITS 2			WEEKS 2
MILES FROM HOME	Mo Wax	75	9 May 98	1
SWITCH	Island Blue	59	17 Jul 99	1
ALBUMS:	HITS 1			WEEKS 1
MILES FROM HOME	Island Blue	63	31 Jul 99	1

PESTALOZZI CHILDREN'S CHOIR — International

ALBUMS:		HITS 1		WEEKS 2
SONGS OF JOY	K-Tel	65	26 Dec 81	2

PET SHOP BOYS — UK

SINGLES:		HITS 32		WEEKS 223
WEST END GIRLS	Parlophone	1	23 Nov 85	15
Originally release reached No. 121 in 1984.				
LOVE COMES QUICKLY	Parlophone	19	8 Mar 86	9
OPPORTUNITIES (LET'S MAKE LOTS OF MONEY)	Parlophone	11	31 May 86	8
SUBURBIA	Parlophone	8	4 Oct 86	9
IT'S A SIN	Parlophone	1	27 Jun 87	11
WHAT HAVE I DONE TO DESERVE THIS?	Parlophone	2	22 Aug 87	9
Above hit: PET SHOP BOYS and Dusty SPRINGFIELD.				
RENT	Parlophone	8	24 Oct 87	7
ALWAYS ON MY MIND	Parlophone	1	12 Dec 87	11
Originally recorded by Brenda Lee in 1971.				
HEART	Parlophone	1	2 Apr 88	10
DOMINO DANCING	Parlophone	7	24 Sep 88	8
LEFT TO MY OWN DEVICES	Parlophone	4	26 Nov 88	8
IT'S ALRIGHT	Parlophone	5	8 Jul 89	8
Originally recorded by Sterling Void.				
SO HARD	Parlophone	4	6 Oct 90	6
BEING BORING	Parlophone	20	24 Nov 90	8
WHERE THE STREETS HAVE NO NAME (CAN'T TAKE ME EYES OF YOU) [M] / HOW CAN YOU EXPECT TO BE TAKEN SERIOUSLY	Parlophone	4	23 Mar 91	8
JEALOUSY	Parlophone	12	8 Jun 91	5
DJ CULTURE	Parlophone	13	26 Oct 91	3
DJ CULTURE MIX [RM]	Parlophone	40	23 Nov 91	2
WAS IT WORTH IT?	Parlophone	24	21 Dec 91	4
CAN YOU FORGIVE HER?	Parlophone	7	12 Jun 93	7
GO WEST	Parlophone	2	18 Sep 93	9
I WOULDN'T NORMALLY DO THIS KIND OF THING	Parlophone	13	11 Dec 93	7
LIBERATION	Parlophone	14	16 Apr 94	5
ABSOLUTELY FABULOUS	Parlophone	6	11 Jun 94	7
Charity record to support Comic Relief. Featuring extracts by Jennifer Saunders and Joanne Lumley from the BBC1TV sitcom of the same name.				
Above hit: ABSOLUTELY FABULOUS.				
YESTERDAY, WHEN I WAS MAD	Parlophone	13	10 Sep 94	4
PANINARO '95	Parlophone	15	5 Aug 95	4
This was originally the B side to Suburbia.				
BEFORE	Parlophone	7	4 May 96	5
SE A VIDA E (THAT'S THE WAY LIFE IS)	Parlophone	8	24 Aug 96	8
SINGLE-BILINGUAL	Parlophone	14	23 Nov 96	3
Above 2 feature the Scottish female drumming troupe Sheboom.				
A RED LETTER DAY	Parlophone	9	29 Mar 97	3
Features the Choral Academy Of Moscow.				
SOMEWHERE	Parlophone	9	5 Jul 97	5
I DON'T KNOW WHAT YOU WANT BUT I CAN'T GIVE IT ANY MORE	Parlophone	15	31 Jul 99	3
NEW YORK CITY BOY	Parlophone	14	9 Oct 99	4

ALBUMS:		HITS 11		WEEKS 336
PLEASE	Parlophone	3	5 Apr 86	82
DISCO	EMI	15	29 Nov 86	72
Features 6 12" mixes of hit singles originally on the Please album.				
PET SHOP BOYS, ACTUALLY	Parlophone	2	19 Sep 87	59
INTROSPECTIVE	Parlophone	2	22 Oct 88	39
BEHAVIOUR	Parlophone	2	3 Nov 90	14
DISCOGRAPHY	Parlophone	3	16 Nov 91	28
Includes re-entries through to 1999.				
VERY	Parlophone	1	9 Oct 93	22
DISCO 2	Parlophone	6	24 Sep 94	4
Megamix of current hits remixed by Rollo, Beatmasters, Farley and Heller, Jam and Spoon, David Morales and Brothers In Rhythm.				
ALTERNATIVE	Parlophone	2	19 Aug 95	5
Compilation featuring all their B-sides.				
BILINGUAL	Parlophone	4	14 Sep 96	8
NIGHTLIFE	Parlophone	7	23 Oct 99	3

PETER and GORDON — UK

SINGLES:		HITS 7		WEEKS 77
A WORLD WITHOUT LOVE	Columbia	1	14 Mar 64	14
NOBODY I KNOW	Columbia	10	6 Jun 64	11
Above 2 written by Lennon/McCartney.				
TRUE LOVE WAYS	Columbia	2	10 Apr 65	15
TO KNOW YOU IS TO LOVE YOU	Columbia	5	26 Jun 65	10
BABY I'M YOURS	Columbia	19	23 Oct 65	9

WOMAN	Columbia	28	26 Feb 66	7
Written by Paul McCartney under the name J.Webb.				
LADY GODIVA	Columbia	16	24 Sep 66	11
Above hit: PETER and GORDON with Geoff LOVE and his Orchestra.				
EPS:	**HITS 1**			**WEEKS 1**
JUST FOR YOU	Columbia	20	22 Aug 64	1
ALBUMS:	**HITS 1**			**WEEKS 1**
PETER AND GORDON	Columbia	18	20 Jun 64	1

PETER, PAUL and MARY   US

SINGLES:	**HITS 4**			**WEEKS 38**
BLOWING IN THE WIND	Warner Brothers	13	12 Oct 63	16
Originally recorded by Bob Dylan.				
TELL IT ON THE MOUNTAIN	Warner Brothers	33	18 Apr 64	4
THE TIMES THEY ARE A-CHANGIN'	Warner Brothers	44	17 Oct 64	2
LEAVING ON A JET PLANE	Warner Brothers	2	17 Jan 70	16
Originally recorded by John Denver.				
EPS:	**HITS 4**			**WEEKS 99**
PETER, PAUL AND MARY	Warner Brothers	3	30 Nov 63	79
MOVING	Warner Brothers	16	18 Apr 64	2
BLOWIN' IN THE WIND	Warner Brothers	13	28 Nov 64	12
IN THE WIND VOLUME 1	Warner Brothers	12	8 May 65	6
ALBUMS:	**HITS 4**			**WEEKS 26**
PETER PAUL AND MARY	Warner Brothers	18	4 Jan 64	1
IN THE WIND	Warner Brothers	11	21 Mar 64	19
IN CONCERT VOLUME 1	Warner Brothers	20	13 Feb 65	2
TEN YEARS TOGETHER	Warner Brothers	60	5 Sep 70	4

Jonathan PETERS presents LUMINAIRE   US

SINGLES:	**HITS 1**			**WEEKS 1**
FLOWER DUET	Pelican	75	24 Jul 99	1
Samples the version by Choeurs et Orchestre de Theatre National de L'Opera Comique, conducted by Georges Pretre, mezzo-soprano: Jane Berbie. seprano: Glanna d' Angelo. From the opera 'Lakme'.				

PETERS and LEE   UK

SINGLES:	**HITS 5**			**WEEKS 57**
WELCOME HOME	Philips	1	26 May 73	24
BY YOUR SIDE	Philips	39	3 Nov 73	9
DON'T STAY AWAY TOO LONG	Philips	3	20 Apr 74	15
RAINBOW	Philips	17	17 Aug 74	7
HEY, MR. MUSIC MAN	Philips	16	6 Mar 76	7
ALBUMS:	**HITS 5**			**WEEKS 166**
WE CAN MAKE IT	Philips	1	30 Jun 73	55
BY YOUR SIDE	Philips	9	22 Dec 73	48
RAINBOW	Philips	6	21 Sep 74	27
FAVOURITES	Philips	2	4 Oct 75	32
INVITATION	Philips	44	18 Dec 76	4

Ray PETERSON   US

SINGLES:	**HITS 3**			**WEEKS 9**
THE WONDER OF YOU	RCA	23	5 Sep 59	1
ANSWER ME	RCA	47	26 Mar 60	1
CORRINE, CORRINA	London	48	21 Jan 61	1
Originally recorded by Bo Carter.				
CORRINE, CORRINA [RE]	London	41	4 Feb 61	6

Tom PETTY and the HEARTBREAKERS   US

SINGLES:	**HITS 11**			**WEEKS 43**
ANYTHING THAT'S ROCK 'N' ROLL	Shelter	36	25 Jun 77	3
AMERICAN GIRL	Shelter	40	13 Aug 77	5
STOP DRAGGIN' MY HEART AROUND	WEA	50	15 Aug 81	4
Above hit: Stevie NICKS (with Tom PETTY and the HEARTBREAKERS).				
DON'T COME AROUND HERE NO MORE	MCA	50	13 Apr 85	4
I WON'T BACK DOWN	MCA	28	13 May 89	10
RUNNIN' DOWN A DREAM	MCA	55	12 Aug 89	4
FREE FALLIN'	MCA	64	25 Nov 89	2
Above 3: Tom PETTY.				
LEARNING TO FLY	MCA	46	29 Jun 91	4
TOO GOOD TO BE TRUE	MCA	34	4 Apr 92	3
SOMETHING IN THE AIR	MCA	53	30 Oct 93	2
Above hit: Tom PETTY.				
MARY JANE'S LAST DANCE	MCA	52	12 Mar 94	2

ALBUMS:		HITS 13		WEEKS 98
TOM PETTY AND THE HEARTBREAKERS	Shelter	24	4 Jun 77	12
YOU'RE GONNA GET IT	Island	34	1 Jul 78	5
DAMN THE TORPEDOES	MCA	57	17 Nov 79	4
HARD PROMISES	MCA	32	23 May 81	5
LONG AFTER DARK	MCA	45	20 Nov 82	4
SOUTHERN ACCENTS	MCA	23	20 Apr 85	6
LET ME UP (I'VE HAD ENOUGH)	MCA	59	2 May 87	2
FULL MOON FEVER	MCA	8	8 Jul 89	16
Above hit: Tom PETTY.				
INTO THE GREAT WIDE OPEN	MCA	3	20 Jul 91	18
GREATEST HITS	MCA	10	13 Nov 93	20
WILDFLOWERS	Warner Brothers	36	12 Nov 94	2
Above hit: Tom PETTY.				
SHE'S THE ONE [OST]	Warner Brothers	37	24 Aug 96	2
ECHO	Warner Brothers	43	1 May 99	2

PF PROJECT featuring Ewan McGREGOR — UK

SINGLES:		HITS 1		WEEKS 11
CHOOSE LIFE	Positiva	6	15 Nov 97	11

From the film 'Trainspotting'. Samples McGregor's opening monologue.

PHANTOMS - See Johnny BRANDON with the PHANTOMS

PHARAO — Germany

SINGLES:		HITS 1		WEEKS 2
THERE IS A STAR	Epic	43	4 Mar 95	2

PHARAOHS - See SAM THE SHAM and the PHARAOHS

PHARCYDE — US

SINGLES:		HITS 3		WEEKS 6
PASSIN' ME BY	Atlantic	55	31 Jul 93	3
Samples Summer In The City by Quincy Jones.				
RUNNIN'	Delicious Vinyl/ Go. Beat	36	6 Apr 96	2
Samples Bob Marley's Running Away.				
SHE SAID	Delicious Vinyl/ Go. Beat	51	10 Aug 96	1
ALBUMS:		HITS 2		WEEKS 2
BIZARRE RIDE II THE PHARCYDE	Atlantic	58	21 Aug 93	1
LABCABINCALIFORNIA	Delicious Vinyl/ Go. Beat	46	13 Apr 96	1

Franke PHAROAH - See FRANKE; OUR TRIBE/ONE TRIBE/O.T. QUARTET

PHASE II - See Joey NEGRO

PHAT 'N' PHUNKY — UK

SINGLES:		HITS 1		WEEKS 1
LET'S GROOVE	Chase	61	14 Jun 97	1

PHATS and SMALL — UK

SINGLES:		HITS 3		WEEKS 29
TURN AROUND	Multiply	2	10 Apr 99	16
Originally released on Bush Records in 1998. Samples Toney Lee's Reach Up.				
Above hit: PHATS and SMALL presents MUTANT DISCO.				
FEEL GOOD	Multiply	7	14 Aug 99	8
TONITE	Multiply	11	4 Dec 99	5
Samples Delgations Heartache No. 9.				

Barrington PHELOUNG — Australia

SINGLES:		HITS 1		WEEKS 2
INSPECTOR MORSE THEME	Virgin	61	13 Mar 93	2
Single and album releases below are all from the Central ITV series.				
ALBUMS:		HITS 3		WEEKS 53
INSPECTOR MORSE - ORIGINAL MUSIC FROM THE ITV SERIES	Virgin	4	2 Mar 91	30
INSPECTOR MORSE VOLUME 2 - MUSIC FROM THE TV SERIES	Virgin Television	18	7 Mar 92	12
INSPECTOR MORSE VOLUME 3	Virgin	20	16 Jan 93	11
Above hit: Barrington PHELOUNG and Janis KELLY.				

PHENOMENA — UK

ALBUMS:		HITS 1		WEEKS 2
PHENOMENA	Bronze	63	6 Jul 85	2

PHILADELPHIA INTERNATIONAL ALL STARS: Lou RAWLS, Billy PAUL, Archie BELL, Teddy PENDERGRASS, O'JAYS, Dee Dee SHARP, GAMBLE

US

(See also Archie Bell and the Drells; O'Jays; Billy Paul; Teddy Pendergrass; Lou Rawls; Dee Dee Sharp.)

SINGLES:	HITS 1			WEEKS 8
LET'S CLEAN UP THE GHETTO	Philadelphia International	34	13 Aug 77	8

PHILHARMONIA ORCHESTRA conducted by Lorin MAAZEL

UK

SINGLES:	HITS 1			WEEKS 7
THEME MUSIC FROM THE FILM "2001"A SPACE ODYSSEY THUS SPAKE ZARATHUSTRA	Columbia	33	2 Aug 69	7

Arlene PHILLIPS

UK

ALBUMS:	HITS 2			WEEKS 25
KEEP IN SHAPE SYSTEM WITH ARLENE PHILLIPS	Supershape	41	28 Aug 82	24
Includes music by Funk Federation.				
KEEP IN SHAPE SYSTEM VOLUME 2	Supershape	100	18 Feb 84	1

Chynna PHILLIPS

US

(See also Wilson Phillips.)

SINGLES:	HITS 1			WEEKS 1
NAKED AND SACRED	EMI	62	3 Feb 96	1

Esther PHILLIPS

US

SINGLES:	HITS 1			WEEKS 8
WHAT A DIFFERENCE A DAY MADE	Kudu	6	4 Oct 75	8
Originally recorded by the Dorsey Brothers in 1934.				

Shola PHILLIPS – See ASTRO TRAX TEAM featuring Shola PHILLIPS

Sid PHILLIPS and his Orchestra – See DEEP RIVER BOYS with Sid PHILLIPS and his Orchestra

Paul PHOENIX (treble) with instrumental ensemble – James WATSON (trumpet), John SCOTT (organ), conducted by Barry ROSE

UK

SINGLES:	HITS 1			WEEKS 4
NUNC DIMITTIS (THEME FROM TINKER, TAILOR, SOLDIER, SPY)	Different	56	3 Nov 79	4
From the BBC TV series.				

PHOTEK

UK

SINGLES:	HITS 2			WEEKS 3
NI – TEN – ICHI – RYU (TWO SWORDS TECHNIQUE)	Science	37	22 Mar 97	2
MODUS OPERANDI	Science	66	28 Feb 98	1

ALBUMS:	HITS 3			WEEKS 4
THE HIDDEN CAMERA	Science	39	15 Jun 96	1
This is an EP which due to the timing of all tracks is not eligible for the singles chart.				
MODUS OPERANDI	Science	30	27 Sep 97	2
FORM & FUNCTION	Science	61	26 Sep 98	1
Predominantly made up of tracks that appeared on his Photek 1–6 series of singles released between 1994–96.				

PHOTOS

UK

SINGLES:	HITS 1			WEEKS 4
IRENE	Epic	56	17 May 80	4

ALBUMS:	HITS 1			WEEKS 9
THE PHOTOS	CBS	4	21 Jun 80	9

PHUNKY PHANTOM

UK

SINGLES:	HITS 1			WEEKS 3
GET UP STAND UP	Distinct'ive	27	16 May 98	3

PHUTURE ASSASSINS

UK

SINGLES:	HITS 1			WEEKS 1
FUTURE SOUND [EP]	Suburban Base	64	6 Jun 92	1
Lead track: Future Sound.				

PIA – See Pia ZADORA

Edith PIAF

France

SINGLES:	HITS 1			WEEKS 15
MILORD	Columbia	41	14 May 60	4
MILORD [RE]	Columbia	24	5 Nov 60	11

ALBUMS:		HITS 1			WEEKS 5
HEART AND SOUL	*Stylus*		58	*26 Sep 87*	5

PIANOHEADZ — US

SINGLES:		HITS 1			WEEKS 2
IT'S OVER (DISTORTION)	*INCredible*		39	*11 Jul 98*	2

PIANOMAN — UK

(See also Bass Boyz.)

SINGLES:		HITS 2			WEEKS 8
BLURRED	*3 Beat*		6	*15 Jun 96*	7

Samples Blur's Girls And Boys.

PARTY PEOPLE (LIVE YOUR LIFE BE FREE)	*3 Beat*		43	*26 Apr 97*	1

Track based on Belinda Carlisle's 1991 hit.

Bobby (Boris) PICKETT and the CRYPT-KICKERS — US

SINGLES:		HITS 1			WEEKS 13
MONSTER MASH	*London*		3	*1 Sep 73*	13

Originally released in the US in 1962 reaching No. 1.

Wilson PICKETT — US

SINGLES:		HITS 9			WEEKS 61
IN THE MIDNIGHT HOUR	*Atlantic*		12	*25 Sep 65*	11
DON'T FIGHT IT	*Atlantic*		29	*27 Nov 65*	8
634-5789	*Atlantic*		36	*12 Mar 66*	5
LAND OF 1000 DANCES	*Atlantic*		22	*3 Sep 66*	9

Originally written and recorded by Chris Kenner in 1965.

MUSTANG SALLY	*Atlantic*		28	*17 Dec 66*	7
FUNKY BROADWAY	*Atlantic*		43	*30 Sep 67*	3

Originally recorded by Dyke and the Blazers.

I'M A MIDNIGHT MOVER	*Atlantic*		38	*14 Sep 68*	6
HEY JUDE	*Atlantic*		16	*11 Jan 69*	9
IN THE MIDNIGHT HOUR (MIDNIGHT MIX – 1987 –) [RR]	*Motown*		62	*21 Nov 87*	3

PICKETTYWITCH — UK

SINGLES:		HITS 3			WEEKS 34
THAT SAME OLD FEELING	*Pye*		5	*28 Feb 70*	14
(IT'S LIKE A) SAD OLD KINDA' MOVIE	*Pye*		16	*4 Jul 70*	10
BABY I WON'T LET YOU DOWN	*Pye*		27	*7 Nov 70*	10

Mauro PICOTTO — Italy

(See also R.A.F.)

SINGLES:		HITS 1			WEEKS 5
LIZARD (GONNA GET YOU)	*VC Recordings*		27	*12 Jun 99*	3
LIZARD GONNA GET YA (REMIXES MAURO PICOTTO) [RM]	*VC Recordings*		33	*20 Nov 99*	2

Remixed by Mauro Picotto.

PICOTTO and Gigi D'AGOSTINO - see R.A.F.

PIGBAG — UK

SINGLES:		HITS 4			WEEKS 20
SUNNY DAY	*Y Records*		53	*7 Nov 81*	3
GETTING UP	*Y Records*		61	*27 Feb 82*	3
PAPA'S GOT A BRAND NEW PIGBAG	*Y Records*		3	*3 Apr 82*	11

Originally released 1981, constantly selling to keep appearing in the bubbling under section of the chart until its entry.

THE BIG BEAN	*Y Records*		40	*10 Jul 82*	3
ALBUMS:		HITS 1			WEEKS 14
DR. HECKLE AND MR. JIVE	*Y Records*		18	*13 Mar 82*	14

PIGEONHED - See LO FIDELITY ALLSTARS

Nelson PIGFORD - See De Etta LITTLE and Nelson PIGFORD

PIGLETS — UK

SINGLES:		HITS 1			WEEKS 12
JOHNNY REGGAE	*Bell*		3	*6 Nov 71*	12

Dick PIKE - See Ruby WRIGHT

PIL - See PUBLIC IMAGE LTD.

PILOT — UK

SINGLES:		HITS 4			WEEKS 29
MAGIC	*EMI*		11	*2 Nov 74*	11

JANUARY	EMI	1	18 Jan 75	10
CALL ME ROUND	EMI	34	19 Apr 75	4
JUST A SMILE	EMI	31	27 Sep 75	4
ALBUMS:	**HITS 1**			**WEEKS 1**
SECOND FLIGHT	EMI	48	31 May 75	1

PILTDOWN MEN — US

SINGLES:	**HITS 3**			**WEEKS 36**
MCDONALD'S CAVE	Capitol	14	10 Sep 60	18
PILTDOWN RIDES AGAIN	Capitol	14	14 Jan 61	10
GOODNIGHT MRS. FLINTSTONE	Capitol	18	11 Mar 61	8

Courtney PINE — UK

SINGLES:	**HITS 2**			**WEEKS 6**
LIKE DREAMERS DO	Fourth & Broadway	26	30 Jul 88	5
Above hit: Mica PARIS featuring Courtney PINE.				
I'M STILL WAITING	Mango	66	7 Jul 90	1
Above hit: Courtney PINE featuring Carroll THOMPSON.				
ALBUMS:	**HITS 2**			**WEEKS 13**
JOURNEY TO THE URGE WITHIN	Island	39	25 Oct 86	11
DESTINY'S SONGS	Antilles	54	6 Feb 88	2

PING PING and Al VERLANE — Unknown

SINGLES:	**HITS 1**			**WEEKS 4**
SUCU SUCU	Oriole	41	30 Sep 61	4

PINK FAIRIES — UK

ALBUMS:	**HITS 1**			**WEEKS 1**
WHAT A BUNCH OF SWEETIES	Polydor	48	29 Jul 72	1

PINK FLOYD — UK

SINGLES:	**HITS 9**			**WEEKS 55**
ARNOLD LAYNE	Columbia	20	1 Apr 67	8
SEE EMILY PLAY	Columbia	6	24 Jun 67	12
Above two hits: The PINK FLOYD.				
ANOTHER BRICK IN THE WALL PART II	Harvest	1	1 Dec 79	12
WHEN THE TIGERS BROKE FREE	Harvest	39	7 Aug 82	5
From the film 'The Wall'.				
NOT NOW, JOHN	Harvest	30	7 May 83	4
ON THE TURNING AWAY	EMI	55	19 Dec 87	4
ONE SLIP	EMI	50	25 Jun 88	3
TAKE IT BACK	EMI	23	4 Jun 94	4
HIGH HOPES / KEEP TALKING	EMI	26	29 Oct 94	3
ALBUMS:	**HITS 18**			**WEEKS 877**
THE PIPER AT THE GATES OF DAWN	EMI	6	19 Aug 67	14
SAUCERFUL OF SECRETS	Columbia	9	13 Jul 68	11
MORE [OST]	Columbia	9	28 Jun 69	5
UMMAGUMMA	Harvest	5	15 Nov 69	21
Contains one record of live recordings and the other being solo tracks by each member of group.				
ATOM HEART MOTHER	Harvest	1	24 Oct 70	23
RELICS	Starline	32	7 Aug 71	6
Compilation.				
MEDDLE	Harvest	3	20 Nov 71	82
OBSCURED BY CLOUDS [OST]	Harvest	6	17 Jun 72	14
THE DARK SIDE OF THE MOON	Harvest	2	31 Mar 73	292
Includes re-entries through to 1982.				
A NICE PAIR [RI]	Harvest	21	19 Jan 74	20
Double re-issue of Piper At The Gates Of Dawn and Saucerful Of Secrets.				
WISH YOU WERE HERE	Harvest	1	27 Sept 75	83
ANIMALS	Harvest	2	19 Feb 77	33
THE WALL	Harvest	3	8 Dec 79	46
Includes re-entry in 1982.				
A COLLECTION OF GREAT DANCE SONGS	Harvest	37	5 Dec 81	10
THE FINAL CUT	Harvest	1	2 Apr 83	25
THE DARK SIDE OF THE MOON [RE-1ST]	Harvest	69	1 Oct 83	9
Chart position reached in 1990. Includes re-entries through to 1991.				
A MOMENTARY LAPSE OF REASON	EMI	3	19 Sep 87	34
WISH YOU WERE HERE [RE]	Harvest	97	20 Aug 88	1
DELICATE SOUND OF THUNDER	EMI	11	3 Dec 88	12
THE WALL [RE]	Harvest	52	4 Aug 90	5
THE DARK SIDE OF THE MOON [RE-2ND]	Harvest	4	20 Mar 93	9
Digitally remastered 20th Anniversary edition.				
THE DIVISION BELL	EMI	1	9 Apr 94	51
THE DARK SIDE OF THE MOON [RI]	EMI	38	6 Aug 94	41
Chart position reached in 1995.				

WISH YOU WERE HERE [RI]	EMI	52	6 Aug 94	5
Mid-price re-issue.				
PULSE	EMI	1	10 Jun 95	21
Live recordings from over 20 European shows.				
RELICS [RI]	EMI	48	9 Mar 96	2
First appearance on CD with new cover.				
THE PIPER AT THE GATES OF DAWN [RI]	EMI	44	16 Aug 97	2
30th Anniversary edition. The vinyl format is a remastered edition of the mono version.				

PINKEES   UK

SINGLES:	HITS 1		WEEKS 9	
DANGER GAMES	Creole	8	18 Sep 82	9

PINKERTON'S 'ASSORT'. COLOURS   UK

SINGLES:	HITS 2		WEEKS 12	
MIRROR, MIRROR	Decca	9	15 Jan 66	11
DON'T STOP LOVING ME BABY	Decca	50	23 Apr 66	1

PINKY and PERKY   UK

SINGLES:	HITS 1		WEEKS 3	
REET PETITE	Telstar	47	29 May 93	3
Featured in the HTV Childrens' series 'The Pig Attraction'. Even though not listed, this was *released as an [AA] with It Only Takes A Minute Girl.*				
EPS:	HITS 1		WEEKS 4	
CHRISTMAS WITH PINKY AND PERKY	Columbia	16	23 Dec 61	4
COMPILATION ALBUMS:	HITS 1		WEEKS 2	
THE PIG ATTRACTION FEATURING PINKY AND PERKY	Telstar	19	12 Jun 93	2
Childrens series shown on ITV. Listed on the Compilation chart as certain tracks are by other *artists.*				

PIONEERS   Jamaica

SINGLES:	HITS 3		WEEKS 34	
LONG SHOT KICK THE BUCKET	Trojan	21	18 Oct 69	10
LONG SHOT KICK THE BUCKET [RE]	Trojan	40	10 Jan 70	1
LET YOUR YEAH BE YEAH	Trojan	5	31 Jul 71	12
Originally recorded by Jimmy Cliff.				
GIVE AND TAKE	Trojan	35	15 Jan 72	6
LONG SHOT KICK DE BUCKET [RI]	Trojan	42	29 Mar 80	5
[AA] listed with Liquidator by Harry J. All Stars.				

PIPKINS   UK

SINGLES:	HITS 1		WEEKS 10	
GIMME DAT DING	Columbia	6	28 Mar 70	10

PIPS - See Gladys KNIGHT and the PIPS

PIRANHAS   UK

SINGLES:	HITS 2		WEEKS 21	
TOM HARK	Sire	6	2 Aug 80	12
ZAMBEZI	Dakota	17	16 Oct 82	9
Above hit: PIRANHAS featuring Boring Bob GROVER – The Man with the Golden *Trumpet.*				
ALBUMS:	HITS 1		WEEKS 3	
PIRANHAS	Sire	69	20 Sep 80	3

PIRATES   UK

(See also Johnny Kidd and the Pirates.)

ALBUMS:	HITS 1		WEEKS 3	
OUT OF THEIR SKULLS	Warner Brothers	57	19 Nov 77	3

PITCH SHIFTER   UK

SINGLES:	HITS 2		WEEKS 2	
GENIUS	Geffen	71	28 Feb 98	1
MICROWAVED	Geffen	54	26 Sep 98	1

Gene PITNEY   US

SINGLES:	HITS 22		WEEKS 212	
(I WANNA) LOVE MY LIFE AWAY	London	26	25 Mar 61	11
TOWN WITHOUT PITY	His Master's Voice	32	10 Mar 62	6
From the film of the same name.				
TWENTY FOUR HOURS FROM TULSA	United Artists	5	7 Dec 63	19
THAT GIRL BELONGS TO YESTERDAY	United Artists	7	7 Mar 64	12
Written by Jagger/Richards.				

IT HURTS TO BE IN LOVE	*United Artists*	36	*17 Oct 64*	4
I'M GONNA BE STRONG	*Stateside*	2	*14 Nov 64*	14
Originally recorded by Frankie Laine.				
I MUST BE SEEING THINGS	*Stateside*	6	*20 Feb 65*	10
LOOKING THRU THE EYES OF LOVE	*Stateside*	3	*12 Jun 65*	12
PRINCESS IN RAGS	*Stateside*	9	*6 Nov 65*	12
Originally recorded by Tony Bennett.				
BACKSTAGE	*Stateside*	4	*19 Feb 66*	10
NOBODY NEEDS YOUR LOVE	*Stateside*	2	*11 Jun 66*	13
JUST ONE SMILE	*Stateside*	8	*12 Nov 66*	12
Above 2 originally recorded by Randy Newman.				
(IN THE) COLD LIGHT OF DAY	*Stateside*	38	*25 Feb 67*	6
SOMETHING'S GOTTEN HOLD OF MY HEART	*Stateside*	5	*18 Nov 67*	13
SOMEWHERE IN THE COUNTRY	*Stateside*	19	*6 Apr 68*	9
YOURS UNTIL TOMORROW	*Stateside*	34	*30 Nov 68*	7
MARIA ELENA	*Stateside*	25	*8 Mar 69*	6
A STREET CALLED HOPE	*Stateside*	37	*14 Mar 70*	5
SHADY LADY	*Stateside*	29	*3 Oct 70*	8
24 SYCAMORE	*Pye International*	34	*28 Apr 73*	7
Originally recorded by Wayne Fontana.				
BLUE ANGEL	*Bronze*	49	*2 Nov 74*	1
BLUE ANGEL [RE]	*Bronze*	39	*16 Nov 74*	3
SOMETHING'S GOTTEN HOLD OF MY HEART	*Parlophone*	1	*14 Jan 89*	12
Above hit: Marc ALMOND featuring special guest star Gene PITNEY.				

EPS:		**HITS 3**		**WEEKS 26**
TWENTY FOUR HOURS FROM TULSA	*United Artists*	7	*29 Feb 64*	16
THAT GIRL BELONGS TO YESTERDAY	*Stateside*	13	*27 Feb 65*	7
BACKSTAGE	*Stateside*	6	*9 Jul 66*	3

ALBUMS:		**HITS 9**		**WEEKS 73**
BLUE GENE	*United Artists*	7	*11 Apr 64*	11
GENE PITNEY'S BIG SIXTEEN	*Stateside*	12	*6 Feb 65*	6
I'M GONNA BE STRONG	*Stateside*	15	*20 Mar 65*	2
LOOKIN' THRU THE EYES OF LOVE	*Stateside*	15	*20 Nov 65*	5
NOBODY NEEDS YOUR LOVE	*Stateside*	13	*17 Sep 66*	17
YOUNG WARM AND WONDERFUL	*Stateside*	39	*4 Mar 67*	1
GENE PITNEY'S BIG SIXTEEN [RE]	*Stateside*	40	*22 Apr 67*	1
Re-released.				
BEST OF GENE PITNEY	*Stateside*	8	*20 Sep 69*	9
HIS 20 GREATEST HITS	*Arcade*	6	*2 Oct 76*	14
BACKSTAGE – THE GREATEST HITS AND MORE	*Polydor*	17	*20 Oct 90*	7

Mario PIU
Italy

SINGLES:		**HITS 1**		**WEEKS 4**
COMMUNICATION (SOMEBODY ANSWER THE PHONE)	*Incentive*	5	*11 Dec 99*	4

PIXIES
US

SINGLES:		**HITS 6**		**WEEKS 13**
MONKEY GONE TO HEAVEN	*4AD*	60	*1 Apr 89*	3
HERE COMES YOUR MAN	*4AD*	54	*1 Jul 89*	1
VELOURIA	*4AD*	28	*28 Jul 90*	3
DIG FOR FIRE	*4AD*	62	*10 Nov 90*	1
PLANET OF SOUND	*4AD*	27	*8 Jun 91*	3
DEBASER	*4AD*	23	*4 Oct 97*	2
Originally released on the album Doolittle in 1989.				

ALBUMS:		**HITS 6**		**WEEKS 28**
DOOLITTLE	*4AD*	8	*29 Apr 89*	9
BOSSANOVA	*4AD*	3	*25 Aug 90*	8
TROMPE LE MONDE	*4AD*	7	*5 Oct 91*	5
DEATH TO THE PIXIES	*4AD*	28	*18 Oct 97*	3
DEATH TO THE PIXIES – DELUXE EDITION	*4AD*	20	*18 Oct 97*	2
Same album as above plus CD of live tracks. This bonus CD therefore makes the release count as a new entry due to chart rules.				
PIXIES AT THE BBC	*4AD*	45	*18 Jul 98*	1
Material recorded for both John Peel and Mark Goodier's BBC Radio1 shows.				

PIZZAMAN
UK

SINGLES:		**HITS 4**		**WEEKS 18**
TRIPPIN ON SUNSHINE	*Loaded*	33	*27 Aug 94*	2
Takes its chorus from Rocker's Revenge's Walking On Sunshine.				
SEX ON THE STREETS	*Loaded*	24	*10 Jun 95*	4
HAPPINESS	*Loaded*	19	*18 Nov 95*	4
SEX ON THE STREETS [RE]	*Loaded*	23	*6 Jan 96*	4
TRIPPIN' ON SUNSHINE [RI]	*Loaded*	18	*1 Jun 96*	3
HELLO HONKY TONKS (ROCK YOUR BODY)	*Loaded*	41	*14 Sep 96*	1

PIZZICATO FIVE — Japan

SINGLES:		HITS 1		WEEKS 1
MON AMOUR TOKYO	Matador	72	1 Nov 97	1

Joe PIZZULO - See Sergio MENDES featuring Joe PIZZULO and Leza MILLER

PJ — Canada

SINGLES:		HITS 1		WEEKS 2
HAPPY DAYS	Deconstruction	72	20 Sep 97	1

First released in Canada 1996.
Above hit: P.J.

HAPPY DAYS [RM]	Defected	57	04 Sept 99	1

Remixed by Phats and Small. Samples Northend featuring Michelle Wallace's Tee's Happy.

PJ and DUNCAN - See ANT and DEC

PJ HARVEY - See PJ HARVEY

PJB featuring HANNAH and her SISTERS — US

(See also Hannah Jones.)

SINGLES:		HITS 1		WEEKS 8
BRIDGE OVER TROUBLED WATER	Dance Pool	21	14 Sep 91	8

PKA — UK

SINGLES:		HITS 2		WEEKS 2
TEMPERATURE RISING	Stress	68	20 Apr 91	1
POWERGEN (ONLY YOUR LOVE)	Stress	70	7 Mar 92	1

Above hit: P.K.A.

PLACEBO — US/Sweden

SINGLES:		HITS 6		WEEKS 28
TEENAGE ANGST	Elevator Music	30	28 Sep 96	3
NANCY BOY	Elevator Music	4	1 Feb 97	6
BRUISE PRISTINE	Elevator Music	14	24 May 97	3
PURE MORNING	Hut	4	15 Aug 98	6
YOU DON'T CARE ABOUT US	Hut	5	10 Oct 98	5
EVERY YOU EVERY ME	Hut	11	6 Feb 99	5

ALBUMS:		HITS 2		WEEKS 30
PLACEBO	Elevator Music	40	29 Jun 96	1
PLACEBO [RE]	Elevator Music	5	15 Feb 97	12
WITHOUT YOU I'M NOTHING	Hut	7	24 Oct 98	17

PLANET PATROL — US

SINGLES:		HITS 1		WEEKS 3
CHEAP THRILLS	Polydor	64	17 Sep 83	3

PLANET PERFECTO — UK

(See also Perfecto Allstarz.)

SINGLES:		HITS 2		WEEKS 8
NOT OVER YET 99	Code Blue	16	14 Aug 99	4

Edited version of the original 1995 release which was only credited to Grace.
Above hit: PLANET PERFECTO featuring GRACE.

BULLET IN THE GUN	Perfecto	15	13 Nov 99	4

PLANETS — UK

SINGLES:		HITS 2		WEEKS 8
LINES	Rialto	36	18 Aug 79	6
DON'T LOOK DOWN	Rialto	66	25 Oct 80	2

Robert PLANT — UK

(See also Jimmy Page and Robert Plant.)

SINGLES:		HITS 7		WEEKS 28
BURNING DOWN ONE SIDE	Swan Song	73	9 Oct 82	1
BIG LOG	WEA	11	16 Jul 83	10
HEAVEN KNOWS	Es Paranza	33	30 Jan 88	5
HURTING KIND (I'VE GOT MY EYES ON YOU)	Es Paranza	45	28 Apr 90	3
29 PALMS	Es Paranza	21	8 May 93	5
I BELIEVE	Es Paranza	64	3 Jul 93	2
IF I WERE A CARPENTER	Fontana	63	25 Dec 93	2

ALBUMS:		HITS 6		WEEKS 57
PICTURES AT ELEVEN	Swan Song	2	10 Jul 82	15
THE PRINCIPLE OF MOMENTS	Atlantic	7	23 Jul 83	14
SHAKEN 'N' STIRRED	Es Paranza	19	1 Jun 85	4

NOW AND ZEN	Es Paranza	10	12 Mar 88	7
MANIC NIRVANA	Es Paranza	15	31 Mar 90	9
FATE OF NATIONS	Es	6	5 Jun 93	8

PLASMATICS

US

SINGLES:	HITS 1		WEEKS 4	
BUTCHER BABY	Stiff	55	26 Jul 80	4
ALBUMS:	HITS 1		WEEKS 3	
NEW HOPE FOR THE WRETCHED	Stiff	55	11 Oct 80	3

PLASTIC BERTRAND

Belgium

SINGLES:	HITS 2		WEEKS 17	
CA PLANE POUR MOI	Sire	8	13 May 78	12
SHA LA LA LA LEE	Vertigo	39	5 Aug 78	5

PLASTIC JAM – See BUG KANN and the PLASTIC JAM

PLASTIC ONO BAND – See John LENNON

PLASTIC PENNY

UK

| SINGLES: | HITS 1 | | WEEKS 10 | |
| EVERYTHING I AM | Page One | 6 | 6 Jan 68 | 10 |

Originally recorded by the Box Tops.

PLASTIC POPULATION – See YAZZ

PLASTIK MAN

Canada

(See also Fuse.)

| ALBUMS: | HITS 1 | | WEEKS 1 | |
| MUSIK | Novamute | 58 | 19 Nov 94 | 1 |

PLATINUM HOOK

US

| SINGLES: | HITS 1 | | WEEKS 1 | |
| STANDING ON THE VERGE (OF GETTING IT ON) | Motown | 72 | 2 Sep 78 | 1 |

PLATTERS

US

SINGLES:	HITS 8		WEEKS 92	
THE GREAT PRETENDER / ONLY YOU (AND YOU ALONE)	Mercury	5	8 Sep 56	12
From the film 'Rock Around The Clock'.				
MY PRAYER	Mercury	4	3 Nov 56	10
Originally recorded by Glenn Miller in 1939.				
THE GREAT PRETENDER / ONLY YOU (AND YOU ALONE) [RE-1ST]	Mercury	21	8 Dec 56	1
MY PRAYER [RE-1ST]	Mercury	28	19 Jan 57	2
YOU'LL NEVER, NEVER KNOW / IT ISN'T RIGHT	Mercury	23	26 Jan 57	1
YOU'LL NEVER, NEVER KNOW / IT ISN'T RIGHT [RE-1ST]	Mercury	29	9 Feb 57	1
MY PRAYER [RE-2ND]	Mercury	22	30 Mar 57	1
ONLY YOU (AND YOU ALONE) [RE-2ND]	Mercury	18	30 Mar 57	3
YOU'LL NEVER, NEVER KNOW / IT ISN'T RIGHT [RE-2ND]	Mercury	29	13 Apr 57	1
I'M SORRY	Mercury	18	18 May 57	6
Originally recorded by Bobby Wayne in 1952.				
I'M SORRY [RE-1ST]	Mercury	23	6 Jul 57	1
I'M SORRY [RE-2ND]	Mercury	22	20 Jul 57	1
TWILIGHT TIME	Mercury	3	17 May 58	18
Originally recorded by the Three Suns.				
SMOKE GETS IN YOUR EYES	Mercury	1	17 Jan 59	20
Original recorded by Paul Whiteman in 1933.				
REMEMBER WHEN	Mercury	25	29 Aug 59	2
Above hit: PLATTERS solo vocal by Tony WILLIAMS.				
HARBOUR LIGHTS	Mercury	11	30 Jan 60	12
Originally recorded by Frances Langford in 1937.				
ALBUMS:	HITS 1		WEEKS 13	
20 CLASSIC HITS	Mercury	8	8 Apr 78	13

PLAVKA – See JAM and SPOON featuring PLAVKA

PLAYBOYS – See Dorothy PROVINE

PLAYBOYS – See Gary LEWIS and the PLAYBOYS

PLAYER

UK/US

| SINGLES: | HITS 1 | | WEEKS 7 | |
| BABY COME BACK | RSO | 32 | 25 Feb 78 | 7 |

PLAYERS ASSOCIATION

US

| SINGLES: | HITS 3 | | WEEKS 17 | |
| TURN THE MUSIC UP! | Vanguard | 8 | 10 Mar 79 | 9 |

RIDE THE GROOVE		*Vanguard*	42	*5 May 79*	5
WE GOT THE GROOVE		*Vanguard*	61	*9 Feb 80*	3
ALBUMS:	**HITS 1**			**WEEKS 4**	
TURN THE MUSIC UP		*Vanguard*	54	*17 Mar 79*	4

PLAYN JAYN — UK

| **ALBUMS:** | **HITS 1** | | | **WEEKS 1** | |
| FRIDAY THE 13TH (LIVE AT THE MARQUEE) | | *A&M* | 93 | *1 Sep 84* | 1 |

PLUS ONE featuring SIRRON — UK

| **SINGLES:** | **HITS 1** | | | **WEEKS 4** | |
| IT'S HAPPENIN' | | *MCA* | 40 | *19 May 90* | 4 |

PLUTO - See Pluto SHERVINGTON

PLUX featuring Georgia JONES — US

| **SINGLES:** | **HITS 1** | | | **WEEKS 2** | |
| OVER & OVER | | *ffrr* | 33 | *4 May 96* | 2 |

Samples Rufus and Chaka Khan's Ain't Nobody, Bucketheads' The Bomb and Patrick Juvet's Got A Feeling.

PM DAWN — US

SINGLES:	**HITS 10**			**WEEKS 39**	
A WATCHER'S POINT OF VIEW (DON'T CHA THINK)		*Gee Street*	36	*8 Jun 91*	5
SET ADRIFT ON MEMORY BLISS		*Gee Street*	3	*17 Aug 91*	8
Samples Spandau Ballet's True.					
PAPER DOLL		*Gee Street*	49	*19 Oct 91*	3
REALITY USED TO BE A FRIEND OF MINE		*Gee Street*	29	*22 Feb 92*	4
I'D DIE WITHOUT YOU		*Gee Street*	30	*7 Nov 92*	5
LOOKING THROUGH PATIENT EYES		*Gee Street*	11	*13 Mar 93*	7
Samples Father Figure by George Michael and features backing vocals by Cathy Dennis.					
MORE THAN LIKELY		*Gee Street*	40	*12 Jun 93*	3
Above hit: PM DAWN featuring BOY GEORGE.					
DOWNTOWN VENUS		*Gee Street*	58	*30 Sep 95*	2
Samples Deep Purple's Hush.					
Above hit: P.M. DAWN.					
SOMETIMES I MISS YOU SO MUCH (DEDICATED TO THE CHRIST CONSCIOUSNESS)		*Gee Street*	58	*6 Apr 96*	1
GOTTA BE . . . MOVIN' ON UP		*Gee Street*	68	*31 Oct 98*	1
Samples Imagination's Just An Illusion.					
Above hit: P.M. DAWN featuring KY-MANI.					
ALBUMS:	**HITS 2**			**WEEKS 17**	
OF THE HEART, OF THE SOUL AND OF THE CROSS – THE UTOPIAN EXPERIENCE		*Gee Street*	8	*14 Sept 91*	8
OF THE HEART, OF THE SOUL AND OF THE CROSS – THE UTOPIAN EXPERIENCE [RE]		*Gee Street*	44	*14 Mar 92*	4
Repackaged with additional tracks.					
THE BLISS ALBUM . . . ? (VIBRATIONS OF LOVE AND ANGER AND THE PONDERANCE OF LIFE AND EXISTENCE)		*Gee Street*	9	*3 Apr 93*	5

POB featuring DJ Patrick REID — UK

| **SINGLES:** | **HITS 1** | | | **WEEKS 1** | |
| BLUEBOTTLE / FLY | | *Platipus* | 74 | *11 Dec 99* | 1 |

POETS — UK

| **SINGLES:** | **HITS 1** | | | **WEEKS 5** | |
| NOW WE'RE THRU' | | *Decca* | 31 | *31 Oct 64* | 5 |

POGUES — Ireland/UK

SINGLES:	**HITS 17**			**WEEKS 70**	
A PAIR OF BROWN EYES		*Stiff*	72	*6 Apr 85*	2
SALLY MACLENNANE		*Stiff*	51	*22 Jun 85*	4
DIRTY OLD TOWN		*Stiff*	62	*14 Sep 85*	3
POGUETRY IN MOTION [EP]		*Stiff*	29	*8 Mar 86*	6
Lead track: London Girl.					
HAUNTED (FROM THE MOTION PICTURE SOUNDTRACK SID AND NANCY)		*MCA*	42	*30 Aug 86*	4
THE IRISH ROVER		*Stiff*	8	*28 Mar 87*	8
Above hit: POGUES and the DUBLINERS.					
FAIRYTALE OF NEW YORK		*Pogue Mahone*	2	*5 Dec 87*	9
Above hit: POGUES featuring Kirsty MacCOLL.					
IF I SHOULD FALL FROM GRACE WITH GOD		*Pogue Mahone*	58	*5 Mar 88*	3
FIESTA		*Pogue Mahone*	24	*16 Jul 88*	5
YEAH, YEAH, YEAH, YEAH, YEAH		*Pogue Mahone*	43	*17 Dec 88*	4
MISTY MORNING, ALBERT BRIDGE		*Pogue Mahone*	41	*8 Jul 89*	3

JACK'S HEROES / WHISKEY IN THE JAR	*Pogue Mahone*	63	*16 Jun 90*	2
Above hit: POGUES and the DUBLINERS.				
SUMMER IN SIAM	*Pogue Mahone*	64	*15 Sep 90*	2
A RAINY NIGHT IN SOHO	*PM*	67	*21 Sep 91*	1
Re-Issue of track from the Poguety In Motion EP.				
FAIRYTALE OF NEW YORK [RI]	*PM*	36	*14 Dec 91*	5
Above hit: POGUES featuring Kirsty MacCOLL.				
HONKY TONK WOMEN	*PM*	56	*30 May 92*	2
TUESDAY MORNING	*PM*	18	*21 Aug 93*	5
ONCE UPON A TIME	*PM*	66	*22 Jan 94*	2
ALBUMS:	**HITS 7**			**WEEKS 64**
RED ROSES FOR ME	*Stiff*	89	*3 Nov 84*	1
RUM, SODOMY AND THE LASH	*Stiff*	13	*17 Aug 85*	14
IF I SHOULD FALL FROM GRACE WITH GOD	*Stiff*	3	*30 Jan 88*	16
PEACE AND LOVE	*Pogue Mahone*	5	*29 Jul 89*	8
HELL'S DITCH	*Pogue Mahone*	12	*13 Oct 90*	5
THE BEST OF THE POGUES	*PM*	11	*12 Oct 91*	17
WAITING FOR HERB	*PM*	20	*11 Sep 93*	3

POINT BREAK   UK

SINGLES:	**HITS 1**			**WEEKS 2**
DO WE ROCK	*Eternal*	29	*9 Oct 99*	2

POINTER SISTERS   US

SINGLES:	**HITS 10**			**WEEKS 87**
EVERYBODY IS A STAR	*Planet*	61	*3 Feb 79*	3
Original by Sly and the Family Stone reached No. 1 in the US in 1970.				
FIRE	*Planet*	34	*17 Mar 79*	8
Originally recorded by Bruce Springsteen.				
SLOW HAND	*Planet*	10	*22 Aug 81*	11
SHOULD I DO IT?	*Reprise*	50	*5 Dec 81*	5
AUTOMATIC	*Planet*	2	*14 Apr 84*	15
JUMP (FOR MY LOVE)	*Planet*	6	*23 Jun 84*	10
I NEED YOU	*Planet*	25	*11 Aug 84*	9
I'M SO EXCITED	*Planet*	11	*27 Oct 84*	11
NEUTRON DANCE	*Planet*	31	*12 Jan 85*	7
From the film 'Beverley Hills Cop'.				
DARE ME	*Planet*	17	*20 Jul 85*	8
ALBUMS:	**HITS 4**			**WEEKS 88**
BLACK AND WHITE	*Planet*	21	*29 Aug 81*	13
BREAK OUT	*Planet*	9	*5 May 84*	58
CONTACT	*Planet*	34	*27 Jul 85*	7
JUMP – THE BEST OF THE POINTER SISTERS	*RCA*	11	*29 Jul 89*	10

POISON   US

SINGLES:	**HITS 10**			**WEEKS 43**
TALK DIRTY TO ME	*Music For Nations*	67	*23 May 87*	1
NOTHIN' BUT A GOOD TIME	*Capitol*	35	*7 May 88*	3
FALLEN ANGEL	*Capitol*	59	*5 Nov 88*	1
EVERY ROSE HAS ITS THORN	*Capitol*	13	*11 Feb 89*	9
YOUR MAMA DON'T DANCE	*Capitol*	13	*29 Apr 89*	7
Original by Loggins and Messina reached No. 4 in the US in 1972.				
NOTHIN' BUT A GOOD TIME [RI]	*Capitol*	48	*23 Sep 89*	3
UNSKINNY BOP	*Capitol*	15	*30 Jun 90*	7
Single (as per 7" format) starts with a 1min 26sec track called Swampjuice (Soul-O) before going into Unskinny Bop.				
SOMETHING TO BELIEVE IN	*Capitol*	35	*27 Oct 90*	4
SO TELL ME WHY	*Capitol*	25	*23 Nov 91*	2
STAND	*Capitol*	25	*13 Feb 93*	3
UNTIL YOU SUFFER SOME (FIRE AND ICE)	*Capitol*	32	*24 Apr 93*	3
ALBUMS:	**HITS 4**			**WEEKS 37**
OPEN UP AND SAY . . . AAH!	*Capitol*	18	*21 May 88*	21
FLESH AND BLOOD	*Capitol*	3	*21 Jul 90*	11
SWALLOW THIS LIVE	*Capitol*	52	*14 Dec 91*	2
NATIVE TONGUE	*Capitol*	20	*6 Mar 93*	3

POLECATS   UK

SINGLES:	**HITS 3**			**WEEKS 18**
JOHN I'M ONLY DANCING / BIG GREEN CAR	*Mercury*	35	*7 Mar 81*	8
ROCKABILLY GUY	*Mercury*	35	*16 May 81*	6
JEEPSTER / MARIE CELESTE	*Mercury*	53	*22 Aug 81*	4
ALBUMS:	**HITS 1**			**WEEKS 2**
POLECATS	*Vertigo*	28	*4 Jul 81*	2

POLICE
UK

SINGLES:		HITS 18			WEEKS 150
CAN'T STAND LOSING YOU	A&M		42	7 Oct 78	5
ROXANNE	A&M		12	28 Apr 79	9
Originally released in 1978.					
CAN'T STAND LOSING YOU [RE]	A&M		2	7 Jul 79	11
MESSAGE IN A BOTTLE	A&M		1	22 Sep 79	11
FALL OUT	Illegal		47	17 Nov 79	4
Originally released in 1977.					
WALKING ON THE MOON	A&M		1	1 Dec 79	10
SO LONELY	A&M		6	16 Feb 80	10
SIX PACK [EP]	A&M		17	14 Jun 80	4
Lead track: The Bed's Too Big Without You. The package includes the previous 5 A&M releases to make up a 6x7" blue vinyl set.					
DON'T STAND SO CLOSE TO ME	A&M		1	27 Sep 80	10
DE DO DO DO, DE DA DA DA	A&M		5	13 Dec 80	8
INVISIBLE SUN	A&M		2	26 Sep 81	8
EVERY LITTLE THING SHE DOES IS MAGIC	A&M		1	24 Oct 81	13
SPIRITS IN THE MATERIAL WORLD	A&M		12	12 Dec 81	8
EVERY BREATH YOU TAKE	A&M		1	28 May 83	11
WRAPPED AROUND YOUR FINGER	A&M		7	23 Jul 83	7
SYNCHRONICITY II	A&M		17	5 Nov 83	4
KING OF PAIN	A&M		17	14 Jan 84	5
DON'T STAND SO CLOSE TO ME '86 [RR]	A&M		24	11 Oct 86	4
CAN'T STAND LOSING YOU (LIVE) [RR]	A&M		27	13 May 95	2
Live recording from the Orpheus, Boston, 1979.					
ROXANNE '97 [RM]	A&M		17	20 Dec 97	6
Remixed by Puff Daddy. Samples U.T.F.O.'s Roxanne Roxanne and Kool And The Gang's Kool's Back Again.					
Above hit: STING and the POLICE.					

ALBUMS:		HITS 9			WEEKS 381
OUTLANDOS D'AMOUR	A&M		6	21 Apr 79	96
REGGATTA DE BLANC	A&M		1	13 Oct 79	74
ZENYATTA MONDATTA	A&M		1	11 Oct 80	31
GHOST IN THE MACHINE	A&M		1	10 Oct 81	27
SYNCHRONICITY	A&M		1	25 Jun 83	48
EVERY BREATH YOU TAKE – THE SINGLES	A&M		1	8 Nov 86	55
GREATEST HITS	A&M		10	10 Oct 92	21
LIVE!	A&M		25	10 Jun 95	3
Live recordings of 2 complete shows from their US tours in 1979 and 1983.					
THE VERY BEST OF STING AND THE POLICE	A&M		11	22 Nov 97	26
Features both Sting's solo and group material.					
Above hit: STING/The POLICE.					

Su POLLARD
UK

SINGLES:		HITS 2			WEEKS 11
COME TO ME (I AM WOMAN)	Rainbow		71	5 Oct 85	1
STARTING TOGETHER	Rainbow		2	1 Feb 86	10
Theme from the BBC TV series 'The Marriage'.					

ALBUMS:		HITS 1			WEEKS 3
SU	K-Tel		86	22 Nov 86	3

Jimi POLO
US

SINGLES:		HITS 2			WEEKS 5
NEVER GOIN' DOWN (INCORPORATING FUTURE FREAK)	MCA		51	9 Nov 91	2
[AA] listed with Born To Be Alive! by Adamski + Soho.					
Above hit: ADAMSKI + Jimi POLO.					
EXPRESS YOURSELF	Perfecto		59	1 Aug 92	2
EXPRESS YOURSELF [RM]	Perfecto Red		62	9 Aug 97	1
Remixed by Mousse T.					

Marco POLO
Italy

SINGLES:		HITS 1			WEEKS 1
A PRAYER TO THE MUSIC	Hi-Life		65	8 Apr 95	1

POLTERGEIST
UK

SINGLES:		HITS 1			WEEKS 2
VICIOUS CIRCLES	Manifesto		32	6 Jul 96	2
Originally released in 1993.					

Peter POLYCARPOU
UK

SINGLES:		HITS 1			WEEKS 4
LOVE HURTS	Soundtrack Music		26	20 Feb 93	4
Theme from the BBC TV series of the same name.					

POLYGON WINDOW | UK

(See also Aphex Twin.)

SINGLES:		HITS 1		WEEKS 1
QUOTH	*Warp*	49	*3 Apr 93*	1

PONI-TAILS | US

SINGLES:		HITS 2		WEEKS 14
BORN TOO LATE	*His Master's Voice*	5	*20 Sep 58*	11
Certain releases reflected the artist credit as Pony-Tails.				
EARLY TO BED	*His Master's Voice*	26	*11 Apr 59*	3

Maurice PONKE and his Orchestre Fromage – See GOONS

Brian POOLE and the TREMELOES | UK

(See also Tremeloes.)

SINGLES:		HITS 8		WEEKS 90
TWIST AND SHOUT	*Decca*	4	*6 Jul 63*	14
Originally recorded by the Top Notes.				
DO YOU LOVE ME	*Decca*	1	*14 Sep 63*	14
Original by the Contours reached No. 3 in the US in 1962.				
I CAN DANCE	*Decca*	31	*30 Nov 63*	8
CANDY MAN	*Decca*	6	*1 Feb 64*	13
Originally recorded by Roy Orbison.				
SOMEONE, SOMEONE	*Decca*	2	*9 May 64*	17
Originally recorded by the Crickets.				
TWELVE STEPS TO LOVE	*Decca*	32	*22 Aug 64*	7
THREE BELLS	*Decca*	17	*9 Jan 65*	9
I WANT CANDY	*Decca*	25	*24 Jul 65*	8
Original by the Strangeloves reached No. 11 in the US in 1965.				

Glyn POOLE | UK

SINGLES:		HITS 1		WEEKS 8
MILLY MOLLY MANDY	*York*	35	*20 Oct 73*	8
He sang this on the Yorkshire ITV children's series 'Junior Showtime'.				

Iggy POP | US

SINGLES:		HITS 8		WEEKS 28
REAL WILD CHILD (WILD ONE)	*A&M*	10	*13 Dec 86*	11
Originally recorded by Johnny O'Keefe.				
LIVIN' ON THE EDGE OF THE NIGHT	*Virgin America*	51	*10 Feb 90*	4
CANDY	*Virgin America*	67	*13 Oct 90*	1
WELL, DID YOU EVAH!	*Chrysalis*	42	*5 Jan 91*	4
Above hit: Deborah HARRY and Iggy POP.				
THE WILD AMERICA [EP]	*Virgin*	63	*4 Sep 93*	1
Lead track: Wild America. Features Henry Rollins.				
BESIDE YOU	*Virgin*	47	*21 May 94*	2
LUST FOR LIFE	*Virgin*	26	*23 Nov 96*	2
THE PASSENGER	*Virgin*	22	*7 Mar 98*	3
Originally released in 1977. Featured in the Toyota Avensis car TV commercial.				
ALBUMS:		HITS 9		WEEKS 27
THE IDIOT	*RCA Victor*	30	*9 Apr 77*	3
RAW POWER	*Embassy*	44	*4 Jun 77*	2
Originally released in 1973.				
Above hit: IGGY and the STOOGES.				
LUST FOR LIFE	*RCA Victor*	28	*1 Oct 77*	5
NEW VALUES	*Arista*	60	*19 May 79*	4
SOLDIER	*Arista*	62	*16 Feb 80*	2
BLAH-BLAH-BLAH	*A&M*	43	*11 Oct 86*	7
INSTINCT	*A&M*	61	*2 Jul 88*	1
BRICK BY BRICK	*Virgin America*	50	*21 Jul 90*	2
AMERICAN CAESAR	*Virgin*	43	*25 Sep 93*	1

Los POP-TOPS | Spain

SINGLES:		HITS 1		WEEKS 6
MAMY BLUE	*A&M*	35	*9 Oct 71*	6

POP WILL EAT ITSELF | UK

SINGLES:		HITS 15		WEEKS 43
THERE IS NO LOVE BETWEEN US ANYMORE	*Chapter 22*	66	*30 Jan 88*	1
DEF. CON ONE	*Chapter 22*	63	*23 Jul 88*	4
CAN U DIG IT?	*RCA*	38	*11 Feb 89*	4
WISE UP! SUCKER	*RCA*	41	*22 Apr 89*	3

682

VERY METAL NOISE POLLUTION [EP]	RCA	45	2 Sep 89	3

Lead track: Def Con. 1989 Including The Twilight Zone.

TOUCHED BY THE HAND OF CICCIOLINA	RCA	28	9 Jun 90	4

Above hit: PWEI.

DANCE OF THE MAD	RCA	32	13 Oct 90	2
X, Y AND ZEE	RCA	15	12 Jan 91	4
92 DEGREES F	RCA	23	1 Jun 91	3
KARMADROME / EAT ME DRINK ME LOVE ME KILL ME	RCA	17	6 Jun 92	2
BULLETPROOF!	RCA	24	29 Aug 92	3
GET THE GIRL! KILL THE BADDIES	RCA	9	16 Jan 93	4
R.S.V.P. / FAMILIUS HORRIBILUS	Infectious	27	16 Oct 93	2
ICH BIN EIN AUSLANDER	Infectious	28	12 Mar 94	2
EVERYTHING'S COOL?	Infectious	23	10 Sep 94	2
ALBUMS:	**HITS 7**			**WEEKS 14**
THIS IS THE DAY . . . THIS IS THE HOUR . . . THIS IS THIS!	RCA	24	13 May 89	2
CURE FOR SANITY	RCA	33	3 Nov 90	2
THE POP WILL EAT ITSELF CURE FOR SANITY [RE]	RCA	58	6 Jul 91	1

Repackaged.

THE LOOKS OR THE LIFESTYLE	RCA	15	19 Sep 92	3
WEIRD'S BAR AND GRILLS	RCA	44	6 Mar 93	1
16 DIFFERENT FLAVOURS OF HELL	RCA	73	6 Nov 93	1

Compilation.

DOS DEDOS MIS AMIGOS	Infectious	11	1 Oct 94	2
TWO FINGERS MY FRIENDS!	Infectious	25	18 Mar 95	2

Remixed album of their previous chart entry.

POPE JOHN PAUL II
Poland

ALBUMS:	**HITS 2**			**WEEKS 8**
JOHN PAUL II – THE PILGRIM POPE	BBC	71	3 Jul 82	4
THE ROSARY	Pure Music	50	10 Dec 94	4

The Rosary is a prayer recreating the 15 mysteries of the Virgin Mary and Christ's life. Pope John Paul recites in Latin while Father Colm Kilcoyne's is in English.
Above hit: POPE JOHN PAUL II / FATHER Colm KILCOYNE.

POPES – See Shane MacGOWAN

POPPERS present AURA
UK

SINGLES:	**HITS 1**			**WEEKS 1**
EVERY LITTLE TIME	VC Recordings	44	25 Oct 97	1

POPPY FAMILY (featuring Susan JACKS)
Canada

SINGLES:	**HITS 1**			**WEEKS 14**
WHICH WAY YOU GOIN' BILLY?	Decca	7	15 Aug 70	14

PORN KINGS
UK

SINGLES:	**HITS 3**			**WEEKS 9**
UP TO NO GOOD	All Around The World	28	28 Sep 96	2
AMOUR (C'MON)	All Around The World	17	21 Jun 97	3
UP TO THE WILDSTYLE	All Around The World	10	16 Jan 99	4

Above hit: PORN KINGS v's DJ SUPREME.

PORNO FOR PYROS
US

SINGLES:	**HITS 1**			**WEEKS 2**
PETS	Warner Brothers	53	5 Jun 93	2
ALBUMS:	**HITS 2**			**WEEKS 5**
PORNO FOR PYROS	Warner Brothers	13	8 May 93	3
GOOD GOD'S URGE	Warner Brothers	40	8 Jun 96	2

PORTISHEAD
UK

SINGLES:	**HITS 5**			**WEEKS 20**
SOUR TIMES	Go.Beat	57	13 Aug 94	1
GLORY BOX	Go.Beat	13	14 Jan 95	7
SOUR TIMES [RE]	Go.Beat	13	22 Apr 95	4
ALL MINE	Go.Beat	8	20 Sep 97	4
OVER	Go.Beat	25	22 Nov 97	2
ONLY YOU	Go.Beat	35	14 Mar 98	2
ALBUMS:	**HITS 3**			**WEEKS 95**
DUMMY	Go.Beat	32	03 Sept 94	5
DUMMY [RE]	Go.Beat	2	24 Dec 94	66

Peak position reached on 6 May 95.

PORTISHEAD	Go.Beat	2	11 Oct 97	22
PNYC	Go.Beat	40	14 Nov 98	2

Live recordings from the Roseland Ballroom in New York, Jul 97.

Nick PORTLOCK – See ROYAL PHILHARMONIC ORCHESTRA

Gary PORTNOY
US

SINGLES:		HITS 1		WEEKS 3
THEME FROM CHEERS (WHERE EVERYBODY KNOWS YOUR NAME)	Starblend	58	25 Feb 84	3

Theme from the TV series.

PORTRAIT
US

SINGLES:		HITS 3		WEEKS 6
HERE WE GO AGAIN!	Capitol	37	27 Mar 93	3
I CAN CALL YOU	Capitol	61	8 Apr 95	1
HOW DEEP IS YOUR LOVE	Capitol	41	8 Jul 95	2

PORTSMOUTH SINFONIA
UK

SINGLES:		HITS 1		WEEKS 4
CLASSICAL MUDDLY [M]	Springtime	38	12 Sep 81	4

Spoof take-off on the Royal Philharmonic Orchestra's version. Instruments are played out of tune.

Sandy POSEY
US

SINGLES:		HITS 3		WEEKS 32
BORN A WOMAN	MGM	24	17 Sep 66	11
SINGLE GIRL	MGM	15	7 Jan 67	13
WHAT A WOMAN IN LOVE WON'T DO	MGM	48	15 Apr 67	3
THE SINGLE GIRL [RI]	MGM	35	6 Sep 75	5
ALBUMS:		HITS 1		WEEKS 1
BORN A WOMAN	MGM	39	11 Mar 67	1

POSIES
US

SINGLES:		HITS 1		WEEKS 1
DEFINITE DOOR	Geffen	67	19 Mar 94	1

POSITIVE FORCE
UK

SINGLES:		HITS 1		WEEKS 9
WE GOT THE FUNK	Sugar Hill	18	22 Dec 79	9

POSITIVE GANG
UK

SINGLES:		HITS 2		WEEKS 5
SWEET FREEDOM	PWL Continental	34	17 Apr 93	4
SWEET FREEDOM PART II - (THE RETURN)	PWL Continental	67	31 Jul 93	1

POSITIVE K
US

SINGLES:		HITS 1		WEEKS 2
I GOT A MAN	Fourth & Broadway	43	15 May 93	2

Mike POST
US

SINGLES:		HITS 3		WEEKS 18
AFTERNOON OF THE RHINO	Warner Brothers	48	9 Aug 75	1
Above hit: Mike POST COALITION.				
AFTERNOON OF THE RHINO [RE]	Warner Brothers	47	23 Aug 75	1
THE THEME FROM HILL STREET BLUES	Elektron	25	16 Jan 82	11
Above hit: Mike POST featuring Larry CARLTON.				
THE A TEAM	RCA	45	29 Sep 84	5

Above 2 are themes from the TV series.

POTTERS
UK

SINGLES:		HITS 1		WEEKS 2
WE'LL BE WITH YOU	Pye	34	1 Apr 72	2

Frank POURCEL
France

ALBUMS:		HITS 1		WEEKS 7
THIS IS POURCEL	Studio Two	8	20 Nov 71	7

POWDER
UK

SINGLES:		HITS 1		WEEKS 1
AFRODISIAC	Parkway	72	24 Jun 95	1

Bryan POWELL
UK

SINGLES:		HITS 3		WEEKS 3
IT'S ALRIGHT	Talkin Loud	73	13 Mar 93	1
I THINK OF YOU	Talkin Loud	61	15 May 93	1
NATURAL	Talkin Loud	73	7 Aug 93	1

Cozy POWELL — UK

(See also Emerson, Lake and Powell.)

SINGLES:	HITS 5			WEEKS 38	
DANCE WITH THE DEVIL	RAK	3	8 Dec 73	15
THE MAN IN BLACK	RAK	18	25 May 74	8
NA NA NA	RAK	10	10 Aug 74	10
THEME ONE	Ariola	62	10 Nov 79	2
Originally recorded by George Martin.				
RESURRECTION	Parlophone	23	19 Jun 93	3
Above hit: Brian MAY with Cozy POWELL.				
ALBUMS:	HITS 3			WEEKS 8
OVER THE TOP	Ariola	34	26 Jan 80	3
TILT	Polydor	58	19 Sep 81	4
OCTOPUSS	Polydor	86	28 May 83	1

Kobie POWELL and RAHSAAN – See US3

Peter POWELL — UK

ALBUMS:	HITS 1			WEEKS 13
KEEP FIT AND DANCE	K-Tel	9	20 Mar 82	13

POWER CIRCLE – See CHICANE

POWER OF DREAMS — Ireland

SINGLES:	HITS 2			WEEKS 2
AMERICAN DREAM	Polydor	74	19 Jan 91	1
THERE I GO AGAIN	Polydor	65	11 Apr 92	1

POWER-PILL — UK

SINGLES:	HITS 1			WEEKS 3
PAC-MAN	Ffrreedom	43	6 Jun 92	3

POWER STATION — UK

SINGLES:	HITS 4			WEEKS 17
SOME LIKE IT HOT	Parlophone	14	16 Mar 85	8
GET IT ON	Parlophone	22	11 May 85	7
COMMUNICATION	Parlophone	75	9 Nov 85	1
SHE CAN ROCK IT	Chrysalis	63	12 Oct 96	1
ALBUMS:	HITS 1			WEEKS 23
THE POWER STATION	Parlophone	12	6 Apr 85	23

POWERCUT featuring NUBIAN PRINZ — US

SINGLES:	HITS 1			WEEKS 4
GIRLS	Eternal	50	22 Jun 91	4

POWERHOUSE — UK

SINGLES:	HITS 1			WEEKS 4
RHYTHM OF THE NIGHT	Satellite	38	20 Dec 97	4
Samples DeBarge's song of the same title.				

POWERHOUSE featuring Duane HARDEN — US

SINGLES:	HITS 1			WEEKS 5
WHAT YOU NEED	Defected	13	22 May 99	5

P.J. POWERS – See LADYSMITH BLACK MAMBAZO

Will POWERS — US

SINGLES:	HITS 1			WEEKS 9
KISSING WITH CONFIDENCE	Island	17	1 Oct 83	9
Backing vocals by Carly Simon.				

Perez "Prez" PRADO and his Orchestra — Cuba

SINGLES:	HITS 3			WEEKS 55
CHERRY PINK AND APPLE BLOSSOM WHITE	His Master's Voice	1	26 Mar 55	17
Trumpet solo by Billy Regis. From the film 'Under Water'.				
Above hit: Perez "Prez" PRADO and his Orchestra (The KING OF THE MAMBO).				
PATRICIA	His Master's Voice	8	26 Jul 58	16
Above hit: Perez PRADO and his Orchestra.				
GUAGLIONE	RCA	41	10 Dec 94	4
Featured in the Guinness TV commercial.				
GUAGLIONE [RE-1ST]	RCA	58	8 Apr 95	2
GUAGLIONE [RE-2ND]	RCA	2	6 May 95	16

PRAGA KHAN
			Belgium
SINGLES:	**HITS 2**		**WEEKS 8**

INJECTED WITH A POISON / FREE YOUR BODY	*Profile*	16	*4 Apr 92*	6
Titles were listed in reverse on 4 Apr 92.				
Above hit: Praga KHAN featuring JADE 4 U.				
RAVE ALERT!	*Profile*	39	*11 Jul 92*	2

PRAISE
			UK/South Africa
SINGLES:	**HITS 1**		**WEEKS 7**

ONLY YOU	*Epic*	4	*2 Feb 91*	7
Featured in the Fiat Tempra car TV commercial.				

PRAS
(See also Wyclef Jean; Queen.)

			US
SINGLES:	**HITS 2**		**WEEKS 27**

GHETTO SUPASTAR (THAT IS WHAT YOU ARE)	*Interscope*	2	*27 Jun 98*	17
From the film 'Bulworth'. Interpolation of Kenny Rogers and Dolly Parton's Islands In The Stream.				
Above hit: Pras MICHEL featuring ODB and introducing MYA.				
BLUE ANGELS	*Columbia*	6	*7 Nov 98*	10
Based around the song Grease. Features Lenny Kravitz on guitar.				

ALBUMS:	**HITS 1**		**WEEKS 3**	
GHETTO SUPASTAR	*Columbia*	44	*14 Nov 98*	3

PRATT and McLAIN with BROTHERLOVE
			US
SINGLES:	**HITS 1**		**WEEKS 6**

HAPPY DAYS	*Reprise*	31	*1 Oct 77*	6
Theme from the TV series of the same name.				

PRAXIS featuring Kathy BROWN
			UK
SINGLES:	**HITS 1**		**WEEKS 5**

TURN ME OUT	*Stress*	44	*25 Nov 95*	2
Original release reached No. 86 in 1994.				
TURN ME OUT (TURN TO SUGAR) [RM]	*ffrr*	35	*20 Sep 97*	3
Remixed by The Sol Brothers.				

PRAYING MANTIS
			UK
SINGLES:	**HITS 1**		**WEEKS 2**

CHEATED	*Arista*	69	*31 Jan 81*	2

ALBUMS:	**HITS 1**		**WEEKS 2**	
TIME TELLS NO LIES	*Arista*	60	*11 Apr 81*	2

PRECIOUS
			UK
SINGLES:	**HITS 1**		**WEEKS 11**

SAY IT AGAIN	*EMI*	6	*29 May 99*	9
UK's Eurovision entry in 1999, it came 12th.				
SAY IT AGAIN [RE]	*EMI*	53	*28 Aug 99*	2

PREFAB SPROUT
			UK
SINGLES:	**HITS 16**		**WEEKS 60**

DON'T SING	*Kitchenware*	62	*28 Jan 84*	2
FARON YOUNG	*Kitchenware*	74	*20 Jul 85*	1
WHEN LOVE BREAKS DOWN	*Kitchenware*	25	*9 Nov 85*	10
Original release reached No. 89 in 1984.				
JOHNNY JOHNNY	*Kitchenware*	64	*8 Feb 86*	2
CARS AND GIRLS	*Kitchenware*	44	*13 Feb 88*	5
THE KING OF ROCK 'N' ROLL	*Kitchenware*	7	*30 Apr 88*	10
HEY MANHATTAN!	*Kitchenware*	72	*23 Jul 88*	2
LOOKING FOR ATLANTIS	*Kitchenware*	51	*18 Aug 90*	3
WE LET THE STARS GO	*Kitchenware*	50	*20 Oct 90*	3
JORDAN: THE EP [EP]	*Kitchenware*	35	*5 Jan 91*	4
Lead track: One Of The Broken, though another track Carnival 2000 received more airplay.				
THE SOUND OF CRYING	*Kitchenware*	23	*13 Jun 92*	5
IF YOU DON'T LOVE ME	*Kitchenware*	33	*8 Aug 92*	4
ALL THE WORLD LOVES LOVERS	*Kitchenware*	61	*3 Oct 92*	2
LIFE OF SURPRISES	*Kitchenware*	24	*9 Jan 93*	4
A PRISONER OF THE PAST	*Kitchenware*	30	*10 May 97*	2
ELECTRIC GUITARS	*Kitchenware*	53	*2 Aug 97*	1

ALBUMS:	**HITS 7**		**WEEKS 105**	
SWOON	*Kitchenware*	22	*17 Mar 84*	7
STEVE MCQUEEN	*Kitchenware*	21	*22 Jun 85*	35
FROM LANGLEY PARK TO MEMPHIS	*Kitchenware*	5	*26 Mar 88*	24
PROTEST SONGS	*Kitchenware*	18	*1 Jul 89*	4

JORDAN: THE COMEBACK	*Kitchenware*	7	*8 Sep 90*	17
A LIFE OF SURPRISES – THE BEST OF PREFAB SPROUT	*Kitchenware*	3	*11 Jul 92*	13
ANDROMEDA HEIGHTS	*Kitchenware*	7	*17 May 97*	5

PRELUDE — UK

SINGLES:	HITS 4			WEEKS 26
AFTER THE GOLDRUSH	*Dawn*	21	*26 Jan 74*	9
Original by Neil Young reached No. 1 in the US in 1972.				
PLATINUM BLONDE	*EMI*	45	*26 Apr 80*	7
AFTER THE GOLDRUSH [RR]	*After Hours*	28	*22 May 82*	7
ONLY THE LONELY (KNOW THE WAY I FEEL)	*After Hours*	55	*31 Jul 82*	3

PRESENCE — UK

SINGLES:	HITS 2			WEEKS 2
SENSE OF DANGER	*Pagan*	61	*5 Dec 98*	1
Above hit: PRESENCE featuring Shara NELSON.				
FUTURE LOVE	*Pagan*	66	*19 Jun 99*	1

PRESIDENT BROWN – See SABRE featuring PRESIDENT BROWN

PRESIDENTS OF THE UNITED STATES OF AMERICA — US

SINGLES:	HITS 5			WEEKS 21
LUMP	*Columbia*	15	*6 Jan 96*	7
PEACHES	*Columbia*	8	*20 Apr 96*	7
DUNE BUGGY	*Columbia*	15	*20 Jul 96*	4
MACH 5	*Columbia*	29	*2 Nov 96*	2
VIDEO KILLED THE RADIO STAR	*Maverick*	52	*1 Aug 98*	1
From the film 'The Wedding Singer'.				

ALBUMS:	HITS 2			WEEKS 31
THE PRESIDENTS OF THE UNITED STATES OF AMERICA	*Columbia*	14	*13 Jan 96*	29
II	*Columbia*	36	*16 Nov 96*	2

Elvis PRESLEY — US

SINGLES:	HITS 111			WEEKS 1168
HEARTBREAK HOTEL	*His Master's Voice*	2	*12 May 56*	21
BLUE SUEDE SHOES	*His Master's Voice*	9	*26 May 56*	8
I WANT YOU I NEED YOU I LOVE YOU	*His Master's Voice*	25	*14 Jul 56*	2
I WANT YOU I NEED YOU I LOVE YOU [RE]	*His Master's Voice*	14	*4 Aug 56*	9
BLUE SUEDE SHOES [RE]	*His Master's Voice*	26	*18 Aug 56*	2
HOUND DOG	*His Master's Voice*	2	*22 Sep 56*	23
Originally recorded by Big Mama Thornton.				
HEARTBREAK HOTEL [RE]	*His Master's Voice*	23	*27 Oct 56*	1
BLUE MOON	*His Master's Voice*	9	*17 Nov 56*	11
I DON'T CARE IF THE SUN DON'T SHINE	*His Master's Voice*	29	*24 Nov 56*	1
Above 2 entries were separate sides of the same release, each had its own chart run. Originally recorded by Patti Page in 1950.				
LOVE ME TENDER	*His Master's Voice*	11	*8 Dec 56*	9
From the film of the same name.				
I DON'T CARE IF THE SUN DON'T SHINE [RE]	*His Master's Voice*	23	*22 Dec 56*	3
MYSTERY TRAIN	*His Master's Voice*	25	*16 Feb 57*	5
Originally recorded by Junior Parker. First release in the UK. This was his final Sun single in the US.				
RIP IT UP	*His Master's Voice*	27	*9 Mar 57*	1
TOO MUCH	*His Master's Voice*	6	*11 May 57*	8
Originally recorded by Bernard Hardison.				
ALL SHOOK UP	*His Master's Voice*	24	*15 Jun 57*	1
Only No.1 that Elvis gets a writing credit.				
ALL SHOOK UP [RE]	*His Master's Voice*	1	*29 Jun 57*	20
TOO MUCH [RE]	*His Master's Voice*	26	*13 Jul 57*	1
(LET ME BE YOUR) TEDDY BEAR	*RCA*	3	*13 Jul 57*	19
From the film 'Loving You'.				
Above 5 (including re-entries) Elvis PRESLEY with the JORDANAIRES.				
PARALYSED	*His Master's Voice*	8	*31 Aug 57*	10
PARTY	*RCA*	2	*5 Oct 57*	15
GOT A LOT O' LIVIN' TO DO	*RCA*	17	*19 Oct 57*	4
Above 2 entries were separate sides of the same release, each had its own chart run.				
Above 2: Elvis PRESLEY with the JORDANAIRES.				
TRYING TO GET TO YOU	*His Master's Voice*	16	*2 Nov 57*	4
LOVING YOU	*RCA*	24	*2 Nov 57*	2
Above entry and (Let Me Be Your) Teddy Bear were separate sides of the same release, each had its own chart run.				
Above 3 from the film 'Loving You'.				
Above hit: Elvis PRESLEY with the JORDANAIRES.				
LAWDY MISS CLAWDY	*His Master's Voice*	15	*9 Nov 57*	5
Above entry and Trying To Get To You were separate sides of the same release, each had its own chart run.				
SANTA BRING MY BABY BACK TO ME	*RCA*	7	*16 Nov 57*	8

I'M LEFT, YOU'RE RIGHT, SHE'S GONE	*His Master's Voice*	21	*18 Jan 58*	2
JAILHOUSE ROCK	RCA	1	*25 Jan 58*	14
JAILHOUSE ROCK [EP]	RCA	18	*1 Feb 58*	5

Lead track: Jailhouse Rock. Above 2 from the film of the same name.
Above hit: Elvis PRESLEY with the JORDANAIRES.

I'M LEFT, YOU'RE RIGHT, SHE'S GONE [RE]	*His Master's Voice*	29	*8 Feb 58*	1
DON'T	RCA	2	*1 Mar 58*	11
WEAR MY RING AROUND YOUR NECK	RCA	3	*3 May 58*	10
HARD HEADED WOMAN	RCA	2	*26 Jul 58*	11
KING CREOLE	RCA	2	*4 Oct 58*	15

Above 2 from the film 'King Creole'.
Above 4: Elvis PRESLEY with the JORDANAIRES.

ONE NIGHT / I GOT STUNG	RCA	1	*24 Jan 59*	12

One Night originally recorded by Smiley Lewis.

A FOOL SUCH AS I / I NEED YOUR LOVE TONIGHT	RCA	1	*25 Apr 59*	15

A Fool Such As I originally recorded by Hank Snow.

A BIG HUNK O' LOVE	RCA	4	*25 Jul 59*	9

Above 2: Elvis PRESLEY with the JORDANAIRES.

STRICTLY ELVIS [EP]	RCA	26	*13 Feb 60*	1

Lead track: Old Shep.

STUCK ON YOU	RCA	3	*9 Apr 60*	14
A MESS OF BLUES	RCA	2	*30 Jul 60*	18

The B-side The Girl Of My Best Friend was also popular though it was not listed on the chart.

IT'S NOW OR NEVER (O SOLE MIO)	RCA	1	*5 Nov 60*	19

Originally written in 1901.

ARE YOU LONESOME TONIGHT?	RCA	1	*21 Jan 61*	15

Originally recorded by Vaughn Deleath in 1927.
Above 4: Elvis PRESLEY with the JORDANAIRES.

WOODEN HEART	RCA	1	*11 Mar 61*	27

From the film 'G.I. Blues'.

SURRENDER (TORNA A SURRIENTO)	RCA	1	*27 May 61*	15
WILD IN THE COUNTRY / I FEEL SO BAD	RCA	4	*9 Sep 61*	12

I Feel So Bad originally recorded by Chuck Willis. Wild In The Country from the film of the same name. I Feel So Bad was not listed from 7 Oct 61. The Jordanaires only credited on Wild In The Country.
Above 2: Elvis PRESLEY with the JORDANAIRES.

(MARIE'S THE NAME) HIS LATEST FLAME / LITTLE SISTER	RCA	1	*4 Nov 61*	13

Little Sister only listed for the week of 4 Nov 61 when it entered at No. 4 and had first credit. (Marie's The Name) Of His Latest Flame originally recorded by Del Shannon.

ROCK-A-HULA-BABY ("TWIST SPECIAL") / CAN'T HELP FALLING IN LOVE	RCA	1	*3 Feb 62*	20

Can't Help Falling In Love listed from 3 Mar 62 and has first credit. From the film 'Blue Hawaii'.

GOOD LUCK CHARM	RCA	1	*12 May 62*	17

Above 2: Elvis PRESLEY with the JORDANAIRES.

FOLLOW THAT DREAM [EP]	RCA	34	*23 Jun 62*	2

Lead track: Follow That Dream. Removed from the chart due to problems with assessing returns. See also EP section. From the film of the same name.

SHE'S NOT YOU	RCA	1	*1 Sep 62*	14
RETURN TO SENDER	RCA	1	*1 Dec 62*	14

From the film 'Girls, Girls, Girls'.
Above 2: Elvis PRESLEY with the JORDANAIRES.

ONE BROKEN HEART FOR SALE	RCA Victor	12	*2 Mar 63*	9

From the film 'It Happened At The World's Fair'.
Above hit: Elvis PRESLEY with the MELLO MEN.

(YOU'RE THE) DEVIL IN DISGUISE	RCA Victor	1	*6 Jul 63*	12
BOSSA NOVA BABY	RCA Victor	13	*26 Oct 63*	8

From the film 'Fun In Acapulco'. Originally recorded by Tippie and the Clovers.

KISS ME QUICK	RCA Victor	14	*21 Dec 63*	10
VIVA LAS VEGAS	RCA Victor	17	*14 Mar 64*	12

From the film 'Love In Las Vegas'.

KISSIN' COUSINS	RCA Victor	10	*27 Jun 64*	11

From the film of the same name.

SUCH A NIGHT	RCA Victor	13	*22 Aug 64*	10

Above 6: Elvis PRESLEY with the JORDANAIRES.

AIN'T THAT LOVING YOU BABY	RCA Victor	15	*31 Oct 64*	8

Originally recorded by Jimmy Reed.

BLUE CHRISTMAS	RCA Victor	11	*5 Dec 64*	7
DO THE CLAM	RCA Victor	19	*13 Mar 65*	8

From the film 'Girl Happy'.

CRYING IN THE CHAPEL	RCA Victor	1	*29 May 65*	15

Originally recorded by Sonny Til and the Orioles.

TELL ME WHY	RCA Victor	15	*13 Nov 65*	10

Originally recorded in 1957.
Above 4: Elvis PRESLEY with the JORDANAIRES.

BLUE RIVER	RCA Victor	22	*26 Feb 66*	7
FRANKIE AND JOHNNY	RCA Victor	21	*9 Apr 66*	9

From the film of the same name.

LOVE LETTERS	RCA Victor	6	*9 Jul 66*	10

Originally recorded by Dick Haymes in 1945.

ALL THAT I AM	RCA Victor	18	15 Oct 66	8
From the film 'Spinout'.				
Above hit: Elvis PRESLEY with the JORDANAIRES.				
IF EVERY DAY WAS LIKE CHRISTMAS	RCA Victor	13	3 Dec 66	7
INDESCRIBABLY BLUE	RCA Victor	21	11 Feb 67	5
Above 2: Elvis PRESLEY with the JORDANAIRES and the IMPERIALS QUARTET.				
YOU GOTTA STOP / THE LOVE MACHINE	RCA Victor	38	13 May 67	5
From the film 'Easy Come, Easy Go'.				
LONG LEGGED GIRL (WITH THE SHORT DRESS ON)	RCA Victor	49	19 Aug 67	2
From the film 'Double Trouble'.				
Above hit: Elvis PRESLEY with the JORDANAIRES.				
GUITAR MAN	RCA Victor	19	24 Feb 68	9
U.S. MALE	RCA Victor	15	18 May 68	8
Above 2 originally recorded by Jerry Reed.				
YOUR TIME HASN'T COME YET BABY	RCA Victor	22	20 Jul 68	11
From the film 'Speedway'.				
YOU'LL NEVER WALK ALONE	RCA Victor	44	19 Oct 68	3
Above 3: Elvis PRESLEY with the JORDANAIRES.				
IF I CAN DREAM	RCA Victor	11	1 Mar 69	10
IN THE GHETTO	RCA Victor	2	14 Jun 69	16
Originally recorded by Mac Davis.				
CLEAN UP YOUR OWN BACK YARD	RCA Victor	21	6 Sep 69	7
From the film 'The Trouble With Girls (And How To Get Into It)'.				
IN THE GHETTO [RE]	RCA Victor	50	18 Oct 69	1
SUSPICIOUS MINDS	RCA Victor	2	29 Nov 69	14
Originally recorded by Mark James.				
DON'T CRY DADDY	RCA Victor	8	28 Feb 70	11
Originally recorded by Mac Davis.				
KENTUCKY RAIN	RCA Victor	21	16 May 70	11
Originally recorded by Eddie Rabbitt.				
THE WONDER OF YOU	RCA Victor	1	11 Jul 70	20
Live recording from the International Hotel, Las Vegas, Feb 70.				
KENTUCKY RAIN [RE]	RCA Victor	46	8 Aug 70	1
I'VE LOST YOU	RCA Victor	9	14 Nov 70	12
YOU DON'T HAVE TO SAY YOU LOVE ME	RCA Victor	9	9 Jan 71	7
Live recording.				
THE WONDER OF YOU [RE]	RCA Victor	47	23 Jan 71	1
YOU DON'T HAVE TO SAY YOU LOVE ME [RE]	RCA Victor	35	6 Mar 71	3
THERE GOES MY EVERYTHING	RCA Victor	6	20 Mar 71	11
Originally recorded by Jack Greene.				
RAGS TO RICHES	RCA Victor	9	15 May 71	11
Originally recorded by Tony Bennett.				
HEARTBREAK HOTEL [RI-1ST] /HOUND DOG [RI]	RCA Victor Maximillion	10	17 Jul 71	12
I'M LEAVIN'	RCA Victor	23	2 Oct 71	9
I JUST CAN'T HELP BELIEVING	RCA Victor	6	4 Dec 71	16
From the film 'Elvis: That's The Way It Is'. Originally recorded by B.J.Thomas.				
JAILHOUSE ROCK [RI-1ST]	RCA Victor Maximillion	42	11 Dec 71	5
UNTIL IT'S TIME FOR YOU TO GO	RCA Victor	5	1 Apr 72	9
Originally recorded by Buffy Saint Marie. Excluding the 2 re-issues, above 4 have vocal				
accompaniment by The Imperials Quartet.				
AN AMERICAN TRILOGY	RCA Victor	8	17 Jun 72	11
Live recording.				
BURNING LOVE	RCA Victor	7	30 Sep 72	9
Originally recorded by Dennis Linde.				
ALWAYS ON MY MIND	RCA Victor	9	16 Dec 72	13
Originally recorded by Brenda Lee.				
POLK SALAD ANNIE	RCA Victor	23	26 May 73	7
Live recording. Originally recorded by Tony Joe White.				
FOOL	RCA Victor	15	11 Aug 73	10
Excluding Polk Salad Annie, above 3 have vocal backing by J.D Summer and the Stamps.				
RAISED ON ROCK	RCA Victor	36	24 Nov 73	7
Originally recorded by Mark James.				
I'VE GOT A THING ABOUT YOU BABY	RCA Victor	33	16 Mar 74	5
Originally recorded by Tony Joe White.				
IF YOU TALK IN YOUR SLEEP	RCA Victor	40	13 Jul 74	3
MY BOY	RCA Victor	5	16 Nov 74	13
Originally recorded by Richard Harris.				
PROMISED LAND	RCA Victor	9	18 Jan 75	8
T.R.O.U.B.L.E.	RCA Victor	31	24 May 75	4
GREEN GREEN GRASS OF HOME	RCA Victor	29	29 Nov 75	7
HURT	RCA Victor	37	1 May 76	5
Originally recorded by Roy Hamilton in 1954.				
THE GIRL OF MY BEST FRIEND	RCA Victor	9	4 Sep 76	12
Originally the B-side of A Mess Of Blues.				
Above hit: Elvis PRESLEY with the JORDANAIRES.				
SUSPICION	RCA Victor	9	25 Dec 76	12
Originally recorded in 1962.				
MOODY BLUE	RCA Victor	6	5 Mar 77	9
Originally recorded by Mark James.				

WAY DOWN	RCA Victor	1	13 Aug 77	13
Originally recorded by Layne Martine.				
IT'S NOW OR NEVER [RI]	RCA Victor	39	3 Sep 77	2
ALL SHOOK UP [RI]	RCA Victor	41	3 Sep 77	2
RETURN TO SENDER [RI]	RCA Victor	42	3 Sep 77	3
CRYING IN THE CHAPEL [RI]	RCA Victor	43	3 Sep 77	2
Above 4: Elvis PRESLEY with the JORDANAIRES.				
JAILHOUSE ROCK [RI-2ND]	RCA Victor	44	3 Sep 77	2
ARE YOU LONESOME TONIGHT [RI]	RCA Victor	46	3 Sep 77	1
Above hit: Elvis PRESLEY with the JORDANAIRES.				
THE WONDER OF YOU [RI]	RCA Victor	48	3 Sep 77	1
WOODEN HEART [RI]	RCA Victor	49	3 Sep 77	1
MY WAY	RCA Victor	9	10 Dec 77	8
Live recording from earlier in the year.				
DON'T BE CRUEL (TO A HEART THAT'S TRUE)	RCA Victor	24	24 Jun 78	12
Originally the B-side to Hound Dog in 1956.				
IT WON'T SEEM LIKE CHRISTMAS (WITHOUT YOU)	RCA	13	15 Dec 79	6
IT'S ONLY LOVE / BEYOND THE REEF	RCA	3	30 Aug 80	10
Beyond The Reef no longer listed from 20 Sep 80. As an AA side it peaked at No. 7.				
SANTA CLAUS IS BACK IN TOWN	RCA	41	6 Dec 80	6
Recording from 1957.				
GUITAR MAN [RR]	RCA	43	14 Feb 81	4
LOVING ARMS	RCA	47	18 Apr 81	6
ARE YOU LONESOME TONIGHT (LAUGHING VERSION) [RR]	RCA	25	13 Mar 82	7
Live recording from the International Hotel, Las Vegas, Aug 69.				
THE SOUND OF YOUR CRY	RCA	59	26 Jun 82	2
Above hit: Elvis PRESLEY with the IMPERIALS QUARTET.				
JAILHOUSE ROCK [RE]	RCA	27	5 Feb 83	6
This is a 25th Anniversary re-issue with the original catalogue number.				
BABY I DON'T CARE	RCA	61	7 May 83	3
From the film 'Jailhouse Rock'. Originally appeared on the Jailhouse Rock EP.				
I CAN HELP	RCA	30	3 Dec 83	9
THE LAST FAREWELL	RCA	48	10 Nov 84	6
THE ELVIS MEDLEY [M]	RCA	51	19 Jan 85	3
Above hit: Elvis PRESLEY with the JORDANAIRES.				
ALWAYS ON MY MIND [RR]	RCA	59	10 Aug 85	4
From the film documentary 'This Is Elvis'.				
AIN'T THAT LOVIN' YOU BABY [RR] / BOSSA NOVA BABY [RR]	RCA	47	11 Apr 87	5
Above hit: Elvis PRESLEY / Elvis PRESLEY with the JORDANAIRES and the AMIGOS.				
LOVE ME TENDER [RI] / IF I CAN DREAM [RI]	RCA Victor	56	22 Aug 87	3
Re-issue to mark the 10th Anniversary of his death.				
STUCK ON YOU [RI]	RCA	58	16 Jan 88	2
Featured in a glue TV commercial.				
Above hit: Elvis PRESLEY with the JORDANAIRES.				
ARE YOU LONESOME TONIGHT (THE FAMOUS "LAUGHING VERSION") [RI]	RCA	68	17 Aug 91	2
Above hit: Elvis PRESLEY LIVE IN LAS VEGAS.				
DON'T BE CRUEL [RI]	RCA	42	29 Aug 92	2
THE TWELFTH OF NEVER	RCA	21	11 Nov 95	3
Previously unrealised track from a cassette deck recording, 16 Aug 74.				
HEARTBREAK HOTEL [RI-2ND] / I WAS THE ONE	RCA Victor	45	18 May 96	1
40th anniversary commemorative edition. I Was The One was the original B-side of Heartbreak Hotel.				
ALWAYS ON MY MIND [RI]	RCA	13	24 May 97	6
Featured in the BT TV commercial.				
Above hit: ELVIS.				
EPS:	**HITS 15**			**WEEKS 366**
STRICTLY ELVIS	RCA	1	12 Mar 60	64
A TOUCH OF GOLD	RCA	8	19 Mar 60	11
A TOUCH OF GOLD VOLUME 2	RCA	10	9 Apr 60	13
SUCH A NIGHT	RCA	4	5 Nov 60	62
ELVIS SINGS CHRISTMAS SONGS	RCA	16	26 Nov 60	5
JAILHOUSE ROCK [OST]	RCA	14	26 Aug 61	7
PEACE IN THE VALLEY	RCA	12	16 Sep 61	10
FOLLOW THAT DREAM [OST]	RCA	1	9 Jun 62	51
KID GALAHAD [OST]	RCA	1	3 Nov 62	44
LOVE IN LAS VEGAS [OST]	RCA Victor	3	18 Apr 64	25
ELVIS FOR YOU VOLUME 1	RCA Victor	11	23 May 64	6
ELVIS FOR YOU VOLUME 2	RCA Victor	18	20 Jun 64	1
TICKLE ME [OST]	RCA Victor	3	10 Jul 65	26
TICKLE ME VOLUME 2 [OST]	RCA Victor	8	4 Sep 65	18
EASY COME, EASY GO [OST]	RCA Victor	1	1 Jul 67	23
ALBUMS:	**HITS 98**			**WEEKS 1121**
ELVIS' GOLDEN RECORDS	RCA	3	8 Nov 58	44
Includes re-entries through to 1964.				
KING CREOLE [OST]	RCA	4	8 Nov 58	14
ELVIS (ROCK 'N' ROLL NO. 1)	His Master's Voice	4	4 Apr 59	9
Compilation.				

A DATE WITH ELVIS	RCA	4	8 Aug 59	15
ELVIS' GOLDEN RECORDS VOLUME 2	RCA	4	18 Jun 60	20
ELVIS IS BACK!	RCA	1	23 Jul 60	27
G.I. BLUES [OST]	RCA	1	10 Dec 60	55
HIS HAND IN MINE	RCA	3	20 May 61	25
Gospel Album.				
SOMETHING FOR EVERYBODY	RCA	2	4 Nov 61	18
BLUE HAWAII [OST]	RCA	1	9 Dec 61	65
POT LUCK	RCA	1	7 Jul 62	25
ROCK 'N' ROLL NUMBER 2	RCA Victor	3	8 Dec 62	17
Originally released in 1957.				
GIRLS! GIRLS! GIRLS! [OST]	RCA Victor	2	26 Jan 63	21
IT HAPPENED AT THE WORLD'S FAIR [OST]	RCA Victor	4	11 May 63	21
FUN IN ACAPULCO [OST]	RCA Victor	9	28 Dec 63	14
ELVIS' GOLDEN RECORDS VOLUME 3	RCA Victor	6	11 Apr 64	13
KISSIN' COUSINS [OST]	RCA Victor	5	4 Jul 64	17
ROUSTABOUT [OST]	RCA Victor	12	9 Jan 65	4
GIRL HAPPY [OST]	RCA Victor	8	1 May 65	18
FLAMING STAR AND SUMMER KISSES	RCA Victor	11	25 Sep 65	4
Compilation of tracks from the album Loving You and the EP Elvis By Request.				
ELVIS FOR EVERYONE	RCA Victor	8	4 Dec 65	8
Compilation of unissued studio and film recordings.				
HAREM HOLIDAY [OST]	RCA Victor	11	15 Jan 66	5
FRANKIE AND JOHNNY [OST]	RCA Victor	11	30 Apr 66	5
PARADISE HAWAIIAN STYLE [OST]	RCA Victor	7	6 Aug 66	9
CALIFORNIA HOLIDAY [OST]	RCA Victor	17	26 Nov 66	6
HOW GREAT THOU ART	RCA Victor	11	8 Apr 67	14
Religious recordings.				
DOUBLE TROUBLE [OST]	RCA Victor	34	2 Sep 67	1
CLAMBAKE [OST]	RCA Victor	39	20 Apr 68	1
ELVIS – NBC TV SPECIAL [OST-TV]	RCA Victor	2	3 May 69	26
Transmitted on NBC TV in the US, Dec 68.				
ELVIS SINGS FLAMING STAR	RCA International	2	5 Jul 69	14
Budget Compilation.				
FROM ELVIS IN MEMPHIS	RCA Victor	1	23 Aug 69	13
PORTRAIT IN MUSIC	RCA Victor	36	28 Feb 70	1
Import.				
FROM MEMPHIS TO VEGAS – FROM VEGAS TO MEMPHIS	RCA Victor	3	14 Mar 70	16
Features live recordings from the International Hotel, Las Vegas as well as studio recordings in Memphis.				
ON STAGE, FEBRUARY 1970	RCA Victor	2	1 Aug 70	18
Live recordings from the International Hotel, Las Vegas.				
ELVIS' GOLDEN RECORDS VOLUME 1 [RI]	RCA	21	5 Dec 70	11
Original release was titled Elvis' Golden Records.				
WORLDWIDE 50 GOLD AWARD HITS VOLUME 1 – A TOUCH OF GOLD	RCA Victor	49	12 Dec 70	2
4 album box set anthologizing most of his hits.				
THAT'S THE WAY IT IS [OST]	RCA Victor	12	30 Jan 71	41
Features live recordings.				
I'M 10,000 YEARS OLD – ELVIS COUNTRY	RCA Victor	6	10 Apr 71	9
LOVE LETTERS FROM ELVIS	RCA Victor	7	24 Jul 71	5
C'MON EVERYBODY	RCA International	5	7 Aug 71	21
Budget Compilation featuring tracks from film EPs.				
YOU'LL NEVER WALK ALONE	RCA Camden	20	7 Aug 71	4
ALMOST IN LOVE	RCA International	38	25 Sep 71	2
Above 2 are budget compilations.				
ELVIS' CHRISTMAS ALBUM	RCA International	7	4 Dec 71	5
Original released in 1957. This is a budget album release.				
I GOT LUCKY	RCA International	26	18 Dec 71	3
Budget compilation featuring tracks from film EPs.				
ELVIS NOW	RCA Victor	12	27 May 72	8
ROCK AND ROLL [RI]	RCA Victor	34	3 Jun 72	4
Re-Issue of the 1959 entry Elvis (Rock 'N' Roll No. 1).				
ELVIS FOR EVERYONE	RCA Victor	48	3 Jun 72	1
This edition also has US disc. Originally released in 1965.				
ELVIS AS RECORDED AT MADISON SQUARE GARDEN	RCA Victor	3	15 Jul 72	20
Live recordings, 10 Jun 72.				
HE TOUCHED ME	RCA Victor	38	12 Aug 72	3
ALOHA FROM HAWAII VIA SATELLITE [OST-TV]	RCA Victor	11	24 Feb 73	10
Live recordings from the TV show at the Honolulu International Center on, 14 Jan 73. Benefit concert for the Kuiokalakani Lee Cancer Fund.				
ELVIS	RCA Victor	16	15 Sep 73	4
ELVIS – A LEGENDARY PERFORMER VOLUME 1	RCA Victor	20	2 Mar 74	3
Compilation including unreleased material.				
GOOD TIMES	RCA Victor	42	25 May 74	1
ELVIS AS RECORDED ON STAGE IN MEMPHIS	RCA Victor	44	7 Sep 74	1
Live recordings.				
PROMISED LAND	RCA Victor	21	22 Feb 75	4
TODAY	RCA Victor	48	14 Jun 75	3

ELVIS'S 40 GREATEST HITS	Arcade	25	5 Jul 75	2
THE ELVIS PRESLEY SUN COLLECTION	RCA Starcall	16	6 Sep 75	13
Recordings made for the Sun record label in the 1950s.				
FROM ELVIS PRESLEY BOULEVARD, MEMPHIS, TENNESSEE	RCA Victor	29	19 Jun 76	5
ELVIS IN DEMAND	RCA Victor	12	19 Feb 77	11
Compiled by the UK fan club of hard to find recordings.				
MOODY BLUE	RCA Victor	3	27 Aug 77	15
Includes both live and studio recordings dating back to 1964.				
ELVIS'S 40 GREATEST HITS [RE]	Arcade	1	3 Sep 77	36
WELCOME TO MY WORLD	RCA Victor	7	3 Sep 77	9
G.I. BLUES [OST][RE]	RCA	14	03 Sept 77	10
Includes re-entry in 1980.				
BLUE HAWAII [OST] [RE]	RCA	26	10 Sept 77	6
Re-released.				
ELVIS' GOLDEN RECORDS VOLUME 2 [RE]	RCA	27	10 Sept 77	4
Re-released.				
HITS OF THE 70'S	RCA Victor	30	10 Sep 77	4
ELVIS' GOLDEN RECORDS VOLUME 3 [RI]	RCA	49	10 Sept 77	2
PICTURES OF ELVIS	RCA Starcall	52	10 Sep 77	1
THE SUN YEARS	Charly	31	8 Oct 77	2
Early recordings from his time at the Sun label.				
LOVING YOU	RCA Victor	24	15 Oct 77	3
ELVIS IN CONCERT [OST-TV]	RCA Victor	13	19 Nov 77	11
Features both TV and live recordings from his last tour, Jun 77.				
HE WALKS BESIDE ME	RCA Victor	37	22 Apr 78	1
Gospel album.				
THE '56 SESSIONS VOLUME 1	RCA Victor	47	3 Jun 78	4
Compilation of early tracks.				
TV SPECIAL	RCA Victor	50	2 Sep 78	2
ELVIS'S 40 GREATEST HITS [RI]	RCA Victor	40	11 Nov 78	14
A LEGENDARY PERFORMER VOLUME 3	RCA Victor	43	3 Feb 79	3
OUR MEMORIES OF ELVIS	RCA Victor	72	5 May 79	1
LOVE SONGS	K-Tel	4	24 Nov 79	13
ELVIS PRESLEY SINGS LIEBER AND STOLLER	RCA International	32	21 Jun 80	5
Compilation.				
ELVIS ARON PRESLEY	RCA	21	23 Aug 80	4
8 LP box set including unheard material.				
PARADISE HAWAIIAN STYLE [OST] [RI]	RCA International	53	23 Aug 80	2
INSPIRATION	K-Tel	6	29 Nov 80	8
Gospel compilation.				
GUITAR MAN	RCA	33	14 Mar 81	5
THIS IS ELVIS PRESLEY [OST]	RCA	47	9 May 81	4
THE ULTIMATE PERFORMANCE	K-Tel	45	28 Nov 81	6
THE SOUND OF YOUR CRY	RCA	31	13 Feb 82	12
Compilation featuring rare recordings.				
ELVIS PRESLEY EP PACK	RCA	97	6 Mar 82	1
Box set of re-issued EPs with booklet.				
ROMANTIC ELVIS – 20 LOVE SONGS / ROCKIN' ELVIS – THE SIXTIES				
20 GREAT TRACKS	RCA	62	21 Aug 82	5
IT WON'T SEEM LIKE CHRISTMAS WITHOUT YOU	RCA International	80	18 Dec 82	1
JAILHOUSE ROCK/LOVE IN LAS VEGAS	RCA	40	30 Apr 83	2
Songs from the films.				
I WAS THE ONE	RCA	83	20 Aug 83	1
A LEGENDARY PERFORMER VOLUME 4	RCA	91	3 Dec 83	1
I CAN HELP	RCA	71	7 Apr 84	3
THE FIRST LIVE RECORDINGS	RCA International	69	21 Jul 84	2
Early 1950s recordings from 'The Louisiana Hayride'.				
20 GREATEST HITS VOLUME 2	RCA International	98	26 Jan 85	1
RECONSIDER BABY	RCA	92	25 May 85	1
Blues recordings.				
ELVIS PRESLEY – BALLADS: 18 CLASSIC LOVE SONGS	Telstar	23	12 Oct 85	17
PRESLEY – THE ALL TIME GREATEST HITS	RCA	4	29 Aug 87	32
STEREO '57 (ESSENTIAL ELVIS VOLUME 2)	RCA	60	28 Jan 89	2
HITS LIKE NEVER BEFORE (ESSENTIAL ELVIS VOLUME 3)	RCA	71	21 Jul 90	1
THE GREAT PERFORMANCES	RCA	62	1 Sep 90	1
COLLECTORS GOLD	RCA	57	24 Aug 91	1
FROM THE HEART – HIS GREATEST LOVE SONGS	RCA	4	22 Feb 92	18
THE ESSENTIAL COLLECTION	RCA	6	10 Sep 94	25
ELVIS 56	RCA	42	11 May 96	3
Released to celebrate the 40th anniversary of his first hit single.				
ALWAYS ON MY MIND – ULTIMATE LOVE SONGS	RCA	3	7 Jun 97	33
Compilation commemorating the 20th anniversary of his death.				
BLUE SUEDE SHOES	RCA	39	28 Feb 98	4
Compilation of his early hits.				

PRESSURE DROP featuring Constantine WEIR and Martin FISHLEY UK

SINGLES:	HITS 1			WEEKS 1
SILENTLY BAD MINDED	Higher Ground	53	21 Mar 98	1

Billy PRESTON   US

(See also Various Artists (EPs) 'The Apple EP'.)

SINGLES:		HITS 5			WEEKS 51.
GET BACK	Apple	1	26 Apr 69	17
Above hit: BEATLES with Billy PRESTON.				
THAT'S THE WAY GOD PLANNED IT	Apple	11	5 Jul 69	10
Produced by George Harrison.				
OUTA SPACE	A&M	44	16 Sep 72	3
GET BACK [RE-1ST]	Apple	28	3 Apr 76	5
Above hit: BEATLES with Billy PRESTON.				
WITH YOU I'M BORN AGAIN	Motown	2	15 Dec 79	11
Written by Carol Connors of the Teddy Bears.				
IT WILL COME IN TIME	Motown	47	8 Mar 80	4
Above 2: Billy PRESTON and SYREETA.				
GET BACK [RE-2ND]	Apple	74	22 Apr 89	1
Above hit: BEATLES with Billy PRESTON.				

Johnny PRESTON   US

SINGLES:		HITS 5			WEEKS 46
RUNNING BEAR	Mercury	1	13 Feb 60	15
Features backing vocals by the Big Bopper (who also wrote the song) and country star George Jones.				
CRADLE OF LOVE	Mercury	2	23 Apr 60	16
RUNNING BEAR [RE]	Mercury	41	4 Jun 60	1
I'M STARTING TO GO STEADY	Mercury	49	30 Jul 60	1
FEEL SO FINE	Mercury	18	13 Aug 60	10
Above 2 entries were separate sides of the same release, each had its own chart run. Originally recorded by Shirley and Lee as Feels So Good.				
CHARMING BILLY	Mercury	34	10 Dec 60	1
CHARMING BILLY [RE]	Mercury	42	24 Dec 60	2

Mike PRESTON   UK

SINGLES:		HITS 4			WEEKS 33
MR. BLUE	Decca	12	31 Oct 59	8
I'D DO ANYTHING	Decca	23	27 Aug 60	10
From the musical 'Oliver!'.				
TOGETHERNESS	Decca	41	24 Dec 60	5
MARRY ME	Decca	14	11 Mar 61	10

PRETENDERS   US

(See also John Barry.)

SINGLES:		HITS 18			WEEKS 131
STOP YOUR SOBBING	Real	34	10 Feb 79	9
Originally recorded by the Kinks.				
KID	Real	33	14 Jul 79	7
BRASS IN POCKET	Real	1	17 Nov 79	17
TALK OF THE TOWN	Real	8	5 Apr 80	8
MESSAGE OF LOVE	Real	11	14 Feb 81	7
DAY AFTER DAY	Real	45	12 Sep 81	4
I GO TO SLEEP	Real	7	14 Nov 81	10
Written by Ray Davies.				
BACK ON THE CHAIN GANG	Real	17	2 Oct 82	9
2000 MILES	Real	15	26 Nov 83	9
THIN LINE BETWEEN LOVE AND HATE	Real	49	9 Jun 84	3
Originally recorded by the Persuaders and features Paul Carrack on piano and backing vocals.				
DON'T GET ME WRONG	Realworld	10	11 Oct 86	9
HYMN TO HER	Real	8	13 Dec 86	12
IF THERE WAS A MAN	Real	49	15 Aug 87	6
From the James Bond film 'The Living Daylights'.				
Above hit: PRETENDERS FOR 007.				
I'LL STAND BY YOU	WEA	10	23 Apr 94	10
NIGHT IN MY VEINS	WEA	25	2 Jul 94	5
977	WEA	66	15 Oct 94	2
KID [RR]	WEA	73	14 Oct 95	1
Acoustic version.				
HUMAN	WEA	33	15 May 99	3
ALBUMS:		**HITS 9**			**WEEKS 162**
PRETENDERS	Real	1	19 Jan 80	35
PRETENDERS II	Real	7	15 Aug 81	27
LEARNING TO CRAWL	Real	11	21 Jan 84	16
GET CLOSE	Real	6	1 Nov 86	28
THE SINGLES	Real	6	7 Nov 87	25
PACKED!	WEA	19	26 May 90	5
LAST OF THE INDEPENDENTS	WEA	8	21 May 94	13
THE ISLE OF VIEW	WEA	23	28 Oct 95	4

THE SINGLES [RI]	*WEA*	47	*31 Jan 98*	7
Mid-price reissue.				
VIVA EL AMOR	*WEA*	32	*29 May 99*	2

PRETTY BOY FLOYD
US

SINGLES:	HITS 1		WEEKS 1	
ROCK AND ROLL (IS GONNA SET THE NIGHT ON FIRE)	*MCA*	75	*10 Mar 90*	1

PRETTY THINGS
UK

SINGLES:	HITS 7		WEEKS 41	
ROSALYN	*Fontana*	41	*20 Jun 64*	5
DON'T BRING ME DOWN	*Fontana*	10	*24 Oct 64*	11
HONEY I NEED	*Fontana*	13	*27 Feb 65*	10
CRY TO ME	*Fontana*	28	*17 Jul 65*	7
MIDNIGHT TO SIX MAN	*Fontana*	46	*22 Jan 66*	1
COME SEE ME	*Fontana*	43	*7 May 66*	5
A HOUSE IN THE COUNTRY	*Fontana*	50	*23 Jul 66*	1
A HOUSE IN THE COUNTRY [RE]	*Fontana*	50	*6 Aug 66*	1
EPS:	**HITS 2**		**WEEKS 37**	
THE PRETTY THINGS	*Fontana*	6	*12 Dec 64*	28
RAININ' IN MY HEART	*Fontana*	12	*23 Oct 65*	9
ALBUMS:	**HITS 2**		**WEEKS 13**	
PRETTY THINGS	*Fontana*	6	*27 Mar 65*	10
PARACHUTE	*Harvest*	43	*27 Jun 70*	3

Alan PRICE
UK

SINGLES:	HITS 11		WEEKS 87	
I PUT A SPELL ON YOU	*Decca*	9	*2 Apr 66*	10
Originally recorded by Screaming Jay Hawkins.				
HI-LILI, HI-LO	*Decca*	11	*16 Jul 66*	12
SIMON SMITH AND THE AMAZING DANCING BEAR	*Decca*	4	*4 Mar 67*	12
Originally recorded by Randy Newman.				
THE HOUSE THAT JACK BUILT	*Decca*	4	*5 Aug 67*	10
SHAME	*Decca*	45	*18 Nov 67*	2
DON'T STOP THE CARNIVAL	*Decca*	13	*3 Feb 68*	8
Originally recorded by Sonny Rollins.				
Above 6: Alan PRICE SET.				
ROSETTA	*CBS*	11	*10 Apr 71*	10
Above hit: FAME and PRICE, PRICE and FAME TOGETHER.				
JARROW SONG	*Warner Brothers*	6	*25 May 74*	9
JUST FOR YOU	*Jet*	43	*29 Apr 78*	7
BABY OF MINE / JUST FOR YOU [RI]	*Jet*	32	*17 Feb 79*	3
CHANGES	*Ariola*	54	*30 Apr 88*	4
ALBUMS:	**HITS 1**		**WEEKS 10**	
BETWEEN TODAY AND YESTERDAY	*Warner Brothers*	9	*8 Jun 74*	10

Kelly PRICE
US

SINGLES:	HITS 2		WEEKS 5	
FRIEND OF MINE	*Island Black Music*	25	*7 Nov 98*	3
SECRET LOVE	*Island Black Music*	26	*8 May 99*	2

Lloyd PRICE
US

SINGLES:	HITS 5		WEEKS 36	
STAGGER LEE	*His Master's Voice*	7	*14 Feb 59*	14
Above hit: Lloyd PRICE with Don COSTA ORCHESTRA.				
WHERE WERE YOU (ON OUR WEDDING DAY)	*His Master's Voice*	15	*16 May 59*	6
PERSONALITY	*His Master's Voice*	9	*13 Jun 59*	8
Above hit: Lloyd PRICE and his Orchestra.				
PERSONALITY [RE]	*His Master's Voice*	25	*15 Aug 59*	2
I'M GONNA GET MARRIED	*His Master's Voice*	23	*12 Sep 59*	5
LADY LUCK	*His Master's Voice*	45	*23 Apr 60*	1
Above hit: Lloyd PRICE and his Orchestra.				

PRICKLY HEAT
UK

SINGLES:	HITS 1		WEEKS 1	
OOOIE, OOOIE, OOOIE	*Virgin*	57	*26 Dec 98*	1
Theme to the Sky TV series 'Prickly Heat'.				

Charley PRIDE
US

ALBUMS:	HITS 4		WEEKS 17	
CHARLEY PRIDE SPECIAL	*RCA Victor*	29	*10 Apr 71*	1
SHE'S JUST AN OLD LOVE TURNED MEMORY	*RCA Victor*	34	*28 May 77*	2
SOMEONE LOVES YOU HONEY	*RCA Victor*	48	*3 Jun 78*	2
GOLDEN COLLECTION	*K-Tel*	6	*26 Jan 80*	12

Dickie PRIDE · UK

SINGLES:	HITS 1			WEEKS 1
PRIMROSE LANE	Columbia	28	31 Oct 59	1

Maxi PRIEST · UK

(See also Jamaica United.)

SINGLES:	HITS 19			WEEKS 106
STROLLIN' ON	10 Records	32	29 Mar 86	9
IN THE SPRINGTIME (THE SUMMERTIME REMIX)	10 Records	54	12 Jul 86	3
CRAZY LOVE	10 Records	67	8 Nov 86	5
LET ME KNOW	10 Records	49	4 Apr 87	4
SOME GUYS HAVE ALL THE LUCK	10 Records	12	24 Oct 87	12
HOW CAN WE EASE THE PAIN	10 Records	41	20 Feb 88	6
Above hit: Maxi PRIEST featuring Beres HAMMOND.				
WILD WORLD	10 Records	5	4 Jun 88	9
Originally recorded by Cat Stevens.				
GOODBYE TO LOVE AGAIN	10 Records	57	27 Aug 88	3
CLOSE TO YOU	10 Records	7	9 Jun 90	10
PEACE THROUGHOUT THE WORLD	10 Records	41	1 Sep 90	4
Above hit: Maxi PRIEST (featuring Jazzie B.).				
HUMAN WORK OF ART	Ten Records	75	1 Dec 90	1
HUMAN WORK OF ART [RE]	Ten Records	71	15 Dec 90	3
HOUSECALL	Epic	31	24 Aug 91	7
Above hit: Shabba RANKS featuring Maxi PRIEST.				
THE MAXI PRIEST [EP]	Ten Records	62	5 Oct 91	3
Lead track: Just A Little Bit Longer.				
GROOVIN' IN THE MIDNIGHT	Ten Records	50	26 Sep 92	2
JUST WANNA KNOW / FE REAL	Ten Records	33	28 Nov 92	3
Above hit: Maxi PRIEST / Maxi PRIEST and APACHE INDIAN.				
ONE MORE CHANCE	Ten Records	40	20 Mar 93	3
HOUSECALL [RI]	Epic	8	8 May 93	8
Above hit: Shabba RANKS featuring Maxi PRIEST.				
WAITING IN VAIN	GRP	65	31 Jul 93	2
Above hit: Lee RITENOUR with Maxi PRIEST.				
THAT GIRL	Virgin	15	22 Jun 96	7
Samples Booker T. And The M.G.s Green Onions.				
Above hit: Maxi PRIEST featuring SHAGGY.				
WATCHING THE WORLD GO BY	Virgin	36	21 Sep 96	2
ALBUMS:	HITS 5			WEEKS 35
INTENTIONS	10 Records	96	6 Dec 86	1
MAXI	10 Records	48	5 Dec 87	9
MAXI [RE]	10 Records	25	9 Jul 88	6
BONAFIDE	10 Records	11	14 Jul 90	13
THE BEST OF ME	Ten Records	23	9 Nov 91	5
FE REAL	Ten Records	60	14 Nov 92	1

Louis PRIMA · US

SINGLES:	HITS 1			WEEKS 1
BUONA SERA	Capitol	25	22 Feb 58	1
Above hit: Louis PRIMA with Sam BUTERA and the WITNESSES.				
EPS:	HITS 1			WEEKS 2
STRICTLY PRIMA	Capitol	12	25 Jun 60	2

PRIMA DONNA · UK

SINGLES:	HITS 1			WEEKS 4
LOVE ENOUGH FOR TWO	Ariola	48	26 Apr 80	4
UK's Eurovision Entry in 1980, it came 3rd.				

PRIMAL SCREAM · UK

SINGLES:	HITS 13			WEEKS 46
LOADED	Creation	16	3 Mar 90	9
COME TOGETHER	Creation	26	18 Aug 90	6
HIGHER THAN THE SUN	Creation	40	22 Jun 91	2
DON'T FIGHT IT, FEEL IT	Creation	41	24 Aug 91	2
Above hit: PRIMAL SCREAM featuring Denise JOHNSON.				
DIXIE-NARCO [EP]	Creation	11	8 Feb 92	6
Lead track: Movin' On Up.				
ROCKS / FUNKY JAM	Creation	7	12 Mar 94	5
JAILBIRD	Creation	29	18 Jun 94	2
(I'M GONNA) CRY MYSELF BLIND	Creation	49	10 Dec 94	2
THE BIG MAN AND THE SCREAM TEAM MEET THE BARMY ARMY UPTOWN	Creation	17	15 Jun 96	2
Above hit: PRIMAL SCREAM, Irvine WELSH and ON-U-SOUND present . . .				
KOWALSKI	Creation	8	17 May 97	3
Kowalski was the protagonist in the 70s movie 'Vanishing Point'.				
STAR	Creation	16	28 Jun 97	3

BURNING WHEEL	*Creation*	17	*25 Oct 97*	2
SWASTIKA EYES	*Creation*	22	*20 Nov 99*	2
ALBUMS:	**HITS 5**		**WEEKS 57**	
SONIC FLOWER GROOVE	*Elevation*	62	*17 Oct 87*	1
SCREAMADELICA	*Creation*	8	*5 Oct 91*	27

Winner of the 1992 Mercury Music Prize. Includes re-entries through to 1999.

GIVE OUT, BUT DON'T GIVE UP	*Creation*	2	*9 Apr 94*	18
VANISHING POINT	*Creation*	2	*19 Jul 97*	10

Title taken from the cult 1970s road film.

ECHO DEK	*Creation*	43	*8 Nov 97*	1

Dub version of 'Vanishing Point' reworked by Adrian Sherwood.

PRIME MOVERS   US

SINGLES:	**HITS 1**		**WEEKS 1**	
ON THE TRAIL	*Island*	74	*8 Feb 86*	1

PRIMITIVE RADIO GODS   US

SINGLES:	**HITS 1**		**WEEKS 1**	
STANDING OUTSIDE A BROKEN PHONE BOOTH WITH MONEY IN MY HAND	*Columbia*	74	*30 Mar 96*	1

PRIMITIVES   UK/Australia

SINGLES:	**HITS 6**		**WEEKS 27**	
CRASH	*Lazy*	5	*27 Feb 88*	10
OUT OF REACH	*Lazy*	25	*30 Apr 88*	4
WAY BEHIND ME	*Lazy*	36	*3 Sep 88*	4
SICK OF IT	*Lazy*	24	*29 Jul 89*	4
SECRETS	*Lazy*	49	*30 Sep 89*	3
YOU ARE THE WAY	*RCA*	58	*3 Aug 91*	2
ALBUMS:	**HITS 3**		**WEEKS 13**	
LOVELY	*Lazy*	6	*9 Apr 88*	10
LAZY 86-88	*Lazy*	73	*2 Sep 89*	1
PURE	*RCA*	33	*28 Oct 89*	2

PRIMUS   US

ALBUMS:	**HITS 1**		**WEEKS 1**	
PORK SODA	*Interscope*	56	*8 May 93*	1

PRINCE   US

SINGLES:	**HITS 45**		**WEEKS 302**	
I WANNA BE YOUR LOVER	*Warner Brothers*	41	*19 Jan 80*	3
1999	*Warner Brothers*	25	*29 Jan 83*	7
LITTLE RED CORVETTE	*Warner Brothers*	54	*30 Apr 83*	6
LITTLE RED CORVETTE [RI-1ST]	*Warner Brothers*	66	*26 Nov 83*	2
WHEN DOVES CRY	*Warner Brothers*	4	*30 Jun 84*	15
PURPLE RAIN	*Warner Brothers*	8	*22 Sep 84*	9
I WOULD DIE 4 U	*Warner Brothers*	58	*8 Dec 84*	6

Above 3 from the film 'Purple Rain'.
Above 2: PRINCE and the REVOLUTION.

1999 [RI-1ST] / LITTLE RED CORVETTE [RI-2ND]	*Warner Brothers*	2	*19 Jan 85*	10
LET'S GO CRAZY / TAKE ME WITH YOU	*Warner Brothers*	7	*23 Feb 85*	9
PAISLEY PARK	*Paisley Park*	18	*25 May 85*	10
RASPBERRY BERET	*Paisley Park*	25	*27 Jul 85*	8
POP LIFE	*Paisley Park*	60	*26 Oct 85*	2
KISS	*Paisley Park*	6	*8 Mar 86*	9
MOUNTAINS	*Paisley Park*	45	*14 Jun 86*	4
GIRLS & BOYS	*Paisley Park*	11	*16 Aug 86*	8
ANOTHERLOVERHOLENYOHEAD	*Paisley Park*	36	*1 Nov 86*	3

Above 8: PRINCE and the REVOLUTION.

SIGN 'O' THE TIMES	*Paisley Park*	10	*14 Mar 87*	9
IF I WAS YOUR GIRLFRIEND	*Paisley Park*	20	*20 Jun 87*	6
U GOT THE LOOK	*Paisley Park*	11	*15 Aug 87*	9

Features vocals by Sheena Easton.

I COULD NEVER TAKE THE PLACE OF YOUR MAN	*Paisley Park*	29	*28 Nov 87*	6
ALPHABET ST.	*Paisley Park*	9	*7 May 88*	6
GLAM SLAM	*Paisley Park*	29	*23 Jul 88*	4
I WISH U HEAVEN	*Paisley Park*	24	*5 Nov 88*	5
BATDANCE	*Warner Brothers*	2	*24 Jun 89*	12
PARTYMAN	*Warner Brothers*	14	*9 Sep 89*	6
THE ARMS OF ORION	*Warner Brothers*	27	*18 Nov 89*	5

Above 3 from the film 'Batman'.
Above hit: PRINCE with Sheena EASTON.

THIEVES IN THE TEMPLE	*Paisley Park*	7	*4 Aug 90*	6
NEW POWER GENERATION	*Paisley Park*	26	*10 Nov 90*	4

Tevin Campbell and Mavis Staples on backing vocals.

GETT OFF	Paisley Park	4	31 Aug 91	8
CREAM	Paisley Park	15	21 Sep 91	7
DIAMONDS & PEARLS	Paisley Park	25	7 Dec 91	6
MONEY DON'T MATTER 2 NIGHT	Paisley Park	19	28 Mar 92	5
THUNDER	Paisley Park	28	27 Jun 92	3
SEXY MF/STROLLIN'	Paisley Park	4	18 Jul 92	7
MY NAME IS PRINCE	Paisley Park	7	10 Oct 92	5
MY NAME IS PRINCE [RM]	Paisley Park	51	14 Nov 92	1
7	Paisley Park	27	5 Dec 92	6
Samples Tramp by Lowell Fulsom.				
THE MORNING PAPERS	Paisley Park	52	13 Mar 93	3
Above 10: PRINCE and the NEW POWER GENERATION.				
PEACH	Paisley Park	14	16 Oct 93	5
CONTROVERSY	Paisley Park	5	11 Dec 93	5
THE MOST BEAUTIFUL GIRL IN THE WORLD	NPG	1	9 Apr 94	12
THE BEAUTIFUL EXPERIENCE [RM]	NPG	18	4 Jun 94	3
Consists of 7 mixes of The Most Beautiful Girl In The World.				
Above 2: SYMBOL.				
LETITGO	Warner Brothers	30	10 Sep 94	4
PURPLE MEDLEY [M]	Warner Brothers	33	18 Mar 95	2
EYE HATE U	Warner Brothers	20	23 Sep 95	3
GOLD	Warner Brothers	10	9 Dec 95	9
DINNER WITH DELORES	Warner Brothers	36	3 Aug 96	2
Above 3: SYMBOL.				
BETCHA BY GOLLY WOW!	NPG	11	14 Dec 96	7
THE HOLY RIVER	NPG	19	8 Mar 97	3
Above 2: ARTIST.				
1999 [RI-2ND]	Warner Brothers	10	9 Jan 99	4
1999 [RI-2ND] [RE]	Warner Brothers	49	18 Dec 99	3
ALBUMS:	**HITS 20**			**WEEKS 420**
PURPLE RAIN [OST]	Warner Brothers	7	21 Jul 84	86
Peak position reached on 16 Mar 85. Includes re-entries through to 1992.				
Above hit: PRINCE and the REVOLUTION.				
1999	Warner Brothers	30	8 Sep 84	21
Originally released in 1983.				
AROUND THE WORLD IN A DAY	Warner Brothers	5	4 May 85	20
PARADE - MUSIC FROM "UNDER THE CHERRY MOON" [OST]	Warner Brothers	4	12 Apr 86	26
Above 2: PRINCE and the REVOLUTION.				
SIGN 'O' THE TIMES	Paisley Park	4	11 Apr 87	32
LOVESEXY	Paisley Park	1	21 May 88	32
BATMAN [OST]	Warner Brothers	1	1 Jul 89	20
GRAFFITI BRIDGE	Paisley Park	1	01 Sept 90	8
GETT OFF	Paisley Park	33	24 Aug 91	3
US Import single. Total timing was too long to be eligible for the singles chart.				
DIAMONDS AND PEARLS	Paisley Park	2	12 Oct 91	57
SYMBOL	Paisley Park	1	17 Oct 92	21
Above 3: PRINCE and the NEW POWER GENERATION.				
THE HITS 1	Paisley Park	5	25 Sep 93	27
THE HITS 2	Paisley Park	5	25 Sep 93	28
THE HITS/THE B-SIDES	Paisley Park	4	25 Sep 93	7
COME	Warner Brothers	1	27 Aug 94	8
THE BLACK ALBUM	Warner Brothers	36	3 Dec 94	3
Originally withdrawn prior to release in 1987, though widely bootlegged.				
PURPLE RAIN [OST] [RI]	Paisley Park	18	18 Feb 95	5
Mid-price reissue.				
Above hit: PRINCE and the REVOLUTION.				
THE GOLD EXPERIENCE	Warner Brothers	4	7 Oct 95	5
CHAOS AND DISORDER	Warner Brothers	14	20 Jul 96	4
Above 2: ♀				
EMANCIPATION	NPG	18	30 Nov 96	6
Above hit: ARTIST.				
THE VAULT . . . OLD FRIENDS 4 SALE	Warner Brothers	47	4 Sept 99	1
Previously unreleased records spanning 1985–94.				

PRINCE BUSTER and ALL STARS — Jamaica

SINGLES:	**HITS 2**			**WEEKS 16**
AL CAPONE	Blue Beat	18	25 Feb 67	13
Originally released in 1965.				
WHINE AND GRINE	Island	21	4 Apr 98	3
Featured from the Levi's Jeans TV commercial. His original recording made in 1968.				
Above hit: PRINCE BUSTER.				

PRINCE CHARLES and the CITY BEAT BAND — US

SINGLES:	**HITS 1**			**WEEKS 2**
WE CAN MAKE IT HAPPEN	PRT	56	22 Feb 86	2
ALBUMS:	**HITS 1**			**WEEKS 1**
STONE KILLERS	Virgin	84	30 Apr 83	1

PRINCE NASEEM - See KALEEF

PRINCESS | | | | | UK

SINGLES:		HITS 6			WEEKS 44
SAY I'M YOUR NUMBER ONE	Supreme	7	3 Aug 85	12
AFTER THE LOVE HAS GONE	Supreme	28	9 Nov 85	13
I'LL KEEP ON LOVING YOU	Supreme	16	19 Apr 86	8
TELL ME TOMORROW	Supreme	34	5 Jul 86	5
From the film 'Knights And Emeralds'.				
IN THE HEAT OF A PASSIONATE MOMENT	Supreme	74	25 Oct 86	1
RED HOT	Polydor	58	13 Jun 87	5
ALBUMS:	**HITS 1**			**WEEKS 14**
PRINCESS	Supreme	15	17 May 86	14

PRINCESS IVORI | | | | | US

SINGLES:		HITS 1			WEEKS 2
WANTED	Supreme	69	17 Mar 90	2

Patrick PRINZ – See ARTEMESIA; ETHICS; MOVIN' MELODIES; SUBLIMINAL CUTS

Maddy PRIOR from STEELEYE SPAN - See STATUS QUO; STEELEYE SPAN

PRIVATE LIVES | | | | | UK

SINGLES:		HITS 1			WEEKS 4
LIVING IN A WORLD (TURNED UPSIDE DOWN)	EMI	53	11 Feb 84	4

PRIZNA featuring the DEMOLITION MAN | | | | | UK

SINGLES:		HITS 1			WEEKS 2
FIRE	Labello Blanco	33	29 Apr 95	2

P.J. PROBY | | | | | US

SINGLES:		HITS 12			WEEKS 91
HOLD ME	Decca	3	30 May 64	15
Originally recorded by Art Hickman in 1919.				
TOGETHER	Decca	8	5 Sep 64	11
Originally recorded by Paul Whiteman Orchestra in 1928.				
SOMEWHERE	Liberty	6	12 Dec 64	12
From the show/film 'West Side Story'.				
I APOLOGISE	Liberty	11	27 Feb 65	8
Originally recorded by Billy Eckstein.				
LET THE WATER RUN DOWN	Liberty	19	10 Jul 65	8
Originally recorded by Ben E.King.				
THAT MEANS A LOT	Liberty	30	2 Oct 65	6
MARIA	Liberty	8	27 Nov 65	9
From the show/film 'West Side Story'.				
YOU'VE COME BACK	Liberty	25	12 Feb 66	7
TO MAKE A BIG MAN CRY	Liberty	34	18 Jun 66	3
I CAN'T MAKE IT ALONE	Liberty	37	29 Oct 66	5
IT'S YOUR DAY TODAY	Liberty	32	9 Mar 68	5
YESTERDAY HAS GONE	EMI Premier	58	28 Dec 96	1
Originally recorded by Little Anthony & The Imperials.				
Above hit: P.J. PROBY; Marc ALMOND featuring the MY LIFE STORY				
ORCHESTRA.				
YESTERDAY HAS GONE [RE]	EMI Premier	69	11 Jan 97	1
EPS:	**HITS 2**			**WEEKS 11**
P. J. PROBY	Liberty	13	9 Jan 65	6
SOMEWHERE	Liberty	19	9 Oct 65	5
ALBUMS:	**HITS 1**			**WEEKS 3**
I'M P.J. PROBY	Liberty	16	27 Feb 65	3

PROCLAIMERS | | | | | UK

SINGLES:		HITS 9			WEEKS 50
LETTER FROM AMERICA	Chrysalis	3	14 Nov 87	10
Produced by Gerry Rafferty.				
MAKE MY HEART FLY	Chrysalis	63	5 Mar 88	3
I'M GONNA BE (500 MILES)	Chrysalis	11	27 Aug 88	11
SUNSHINE ON LEITH	Chrysalis	41	12 Nov 88	5
I'M ON MY WAY	Chrysalis	43	11 Feb 89	4
KING OF THE ROAD [EP]	Chrysalis	9	24 Nov 90	8
Lead track: King Of The Road.				
LET'S GET MARRIED	Chrysalis	21	19 Feb 94	4
WHAT MAKES YOU CRY	Chrysalis	38	16 Apr 94	3
THESE ARMS OF MINE	Chrysalis	51	22 Oct 94	2
ALBUMS:	**HITS 3**			**WEEKS 54**
THIS IS THE STORY	Chrysalis	52	9 May 87	6

THIS IS THE STORY [RE]	Chrysalis	43	21 Nov 87	15
SUNSHINE ON LEITH	Chrysalis	6	24 Sep 88	27
HIT THE HIGHWAY	Chrysalis	8	19 Mar 94	6

PROCOL HARUM   UK

SINGLES:	HITS 6		WEEKS 56	
A WHITER SHADE OF PALE	Deram	1	27 May 67	15
Based on Bach's Cantata No.3 in D.				
HOMBURG	Regal Zonophone	6	7 Oct 67	10
QUITE RIGHTLY SO	Regal Zonophone	50	27 Apr 68	1
A SALTY DOG	Regal Zonophone	44	21 Jun 69	1
A SALTY DOG [RE-1ST]	Regal Zonophone	44	5 Jul 69	1
A SALTY DOG [RE-2ND]	Regal Zonophone	44	19 Jul 69	1
A WHITER SHADE OF PALE [RI]	Fly	13	22 Apr 72	13
CONQUISTADOR	Chrysalis	22	5 Aug 72	7
PANDORA'S BOX	Chrysalis	16	23 Aug 75	7
ALBUMS:	HITS 6		WEEKS 11	
A SALTY DOG	Regal Zonophone	27	19 Jul 69	2
HOME	Regal Zonophone	49	27 Jun 70	1
BROKEN BARRICADES	Chrysalis	42	3 Jul 71	1
A WHITER SHADE OF PALE/A SALTY DOG	Fly Double Back	26	6 May 72	4
Double re-issue although A Whiter Shade Of Pale never charted previously.				
PROCOL HARUM LIVE IN CONCERT WITH THE EDMONTON SYMPHONY ORCHESTRA	Chrysalis	48	6 May 72	1
Live recordings from 6 Aug 71.				
PROCOL'S NINTH	Chrysalis	41	30 Aug 75	2

Michael PROCTER - See URBAN BLUES PROJECT present Michael PROCTER

PRODIGY   UK

SINGLES:	HITS 12		WEEKS 139	
CHARLY	XL Recordings	3	24 Aug 91	10
EVERYBODY IN THE PLACE [EP]	XL Recordings	2	4 Jan 92	9
Lead track: Everybody In The Place.				
FIRE / JERICHO	XL Recordings	11	26 Sep 92	4
OUT OF SPACE / RUFF IN THE JUNGLE BIZNESS	XL Recordings	5	21 Nov 92	12
Ruff In The Jungle Bizness no longer listed from 5 Dec 92. As an AA side it peaked at No. 6.				
WIND IT UP (REWOUND)	XL Recordings	11	17 Apr 93	7
ONE LOVE	XL Recordings	8	16 Oct 93	6
NO GOOD (START THE DANCE)	XL Recordings	4	28 May 94	12
VOODOO PEOPLE	XL Recordings	13	24 Sep 94	5
POISON	XL Recordings	15	18 Mar 95	6
FIRESTARTER	XL Recordings	1	30 Mar 96	19
First single to feature vocals by Keith Flint. Samples Art Of Noise's Close To The Edit.				
OUT OF SPACE / RUFF IN THE JUNGLE BIZNESS [RE]	XL Recordings	52	20 Apr 96	2
NO GOOD (START THE DANCE) [RE]	XL Recordings	57	20 Apr 96	2
POISON [RE]	XL Recordings	62	20 Apr 96	1
FIRE / JERICHO [RE]	XL Recordings	63	20 Apr 96	1
CHARLY [RE]	XL Recordings	66	20 Apr 96	1
WIND IT UP (REWOUND) [RE]	XL Recordings	71	20 Apr 96	1
VOODOO PEOPLE [RE]	XL Recordings	75	20 Apr 96	1
EVERYBODY IN THE PLACE [RE]	XL Recordings	69	27 Apr 96	1
All re-entries were due to promotional offer of purchasing 3 of the singles for £10.				
BREATHE	XL Recordings	1	23 Nov 96	17
FIRESTARTER [RE-1ST]	XL Recordings	54	14 Dec 96	4
FIRESTARTER [RE-2ND]	XL Recordings	53	25 Jan 97	7
BREATHE [RE]	XL Recordings	71	5 Apr 97	1
SMACK MY BITCH UP	XL Recordings	8	29 Nov 97	10
Additional vocals by Shakim Bador.				
ALBUMS:	HITS 3		WEEKS 189	
EXPERIENCE	XL Recordings	12	10 Oct 92	31
MUSIC FOR THE JILTED GENERATION	XL Recordings	1	16 Jul 94	98
THE FAT OF THE LAND	XL Recordings	1	12 Jul 97	60

PROFESSIONALS   UK

SINGLES:	HITS 1		WEEKS 4	
1-2-3	Virgin	43	11 Oct 80	4

PROFESSOR - See DJ PROFESSOR

PROFESSOR T - See SHUT UP AND DANCE

PROGRAM 2 BELTRAM - See BELTRAM

PROGRESS presents the BOY WUNDA | | | UK

SINGLES:	HITS 1		WEEKS 3
EVERYBODY	Manifesto	7	18 Dec 99 3

Samples the string section from Madonna's Papa Don't Preach.

PROGRESS FUNK | | | Italy

SINGLES:	HITS 1		WEEKS 1
AROUND MY BRAIN	Deconstruction	73	11 Oct 97 1

PROJECT featuring GERIDEAU | | | US

(See also Gerideau.)

SINGLES:	HITS 1		WEEKS 1
BRING IT BACK 2 LUV	Fruittree	65	27 Aug 94 1

PROJECT D | | | UK

ALBUMS:	HITS 2		WEEKS 18
THE SYNTHESIZER ALBUM	Telstar	13	17 Feb 90 11
SYNTHESIZER 2	Telstar	25	29 Sep 90 7

PROJECT ONE | | | UK

SINGLES:	HITS 2		WEEKS 3
ROUGH NECK [EP]	Rising High	49	16 May 92 2
Lead track: Come My Selector.			
DON CARGON COMIN'	Rising High	64	29 Aug 92 1

PRONG | | | US

SINGLES:	HITS 1		WEEKS 1
WHOSE FIST IS THIS ANYWAY [EP]	Epic	58	25 Apr 92 1
Lead track: Prove You Wrong.			
ALBUMS:	**HITS 1**		**WEEKS 1**
CLEANSING	Epic	71	12 Feb 94 1

PROPAGANDA | | | Germany

SINGLES:	HITS 5		WEEKS 35
DR MABUSE	ZTT	27	17 Mar 84 9
DUEL	ZTT	21	4 May 85 12
P:MACHINERY	ZTT	50	10 Aug 85 5
HEAVEN GIVE ME WORDS	Virgin	36	28 Apr 90 5
ONLY ONE WORD	Virgin	71	8 Sep 90 4
ALBUMS:	**HITS 3**		**WEEKS 16**
SECRET WISH	ZTT	16	13 Jul 85 12
WISHFUL THINKING	ZTT	82	23 Nov 85 2
1234	Virgin	46	9 Jun 90 2

PROPELLERHEADS | | | UK

(See also 808 State.)

SINGLES:	HITS 5		WEEKS 15
TAKE CALIFORNIA	Wall Of Sound	69	7 Dec 96 1
SPYBREAK!	Wall Of Sound	40	17 May 97 1
From the film 'Playing God'.			
ON HER MAJESTY'S SECRET SERVICE	East West	7	18 Oct 97 5
Above hit: PROPELLERHEADS/David ARNOLD.			
HISTORY REPEATING	Wall Of Sound	19	20 Dec 97 7
Above hit: PROPELLERHEADS featuring Miss Shirley BASSEY.			
BANG ON!	Wall Of Sound	53	27 Jun 98 1
ALBUMS:	**HITS 1**		**WEEKS 13**
DECKSANDRUMSANDROCKANDROLL	Wall Of Sound	6	7 Feb 98 13

PROPHETS OF SOUND | | | UK

SINGLES:	HITS 1		WEEKS 1
HIGH	Distinct'ive	73	14 Nov 98 1

PROSPECT PARK featuring Carolyn HARDING | | | UK

SINGLES:	HITS 1		WEEKS 1
MOVIN' ON	AM:PM	55	8 Aug 98 1

Originally a club hit for Roach Motel in 1991.

Shaila PROSPERE – See RIMES featuring Shaila PROSPERE

Brian PROTHEROE   UK

SINGLES:	HITS 1			WEEKS 6
PINBALL	*Chrysalis*	22	*7 Sep 74*	6

Dorothy PROVINE   US

SINGLES:	HITS 2			WEEKS 15
DON'T BRING LULU	*Warner Brothers*	17	*9 Dec 61*	12
CRAZY WORDS CRAZY TUNES (VO-DO-DE-O)	*Warner Brothers*	45	*30 Jun 62*	3

Above 2 from the TV show 'The Roaring 20s'.
Above hit: Dorothy PROVINE and the CHORUS GIRLS with the PLAYBOYS.

ALBUMS:	HITS 2			WEEKS 49
THE ROARING TWENTIES – SONGS FROM THE TV SERIES	*Warner Brothers*	3	*2 Dec 61*	42
VAMP OF THE ROARING TWENTIES	*Warner Brothers*	9	*10 Feb 62*	7

Above 2 feature medley of songs from the 1920s

PSEUDO ECHO   Australia

SINGLES:	HITS 1			WEEKS 12
FUNKY TOWN	*RCA*	8	*18 Jul 87*	12

PSYCHEDELIC FURS   UK

SINGLES:	HITS 7			WEEKS 31
DUMB WAITERS	*CBS*	59	*2 May 81*	2
PRETTY IN PINK	*CBS*	43	*27 Jun 81*	5
LOVE MY WAY	*CBS*	42	*31 Jul 82*	6
HEAVEN	*CBS*	29	*31 Mar 84*	6
THE GHOST IN YOU	*CBS*	68	*16 Jun 84*	2
PRETTY IN PINK [RR]	*CBS*	18	*23 Aug 86*	9

From the film of the same name.

ALL THAT MONEY WANTS	*CBS*	75	*9 Jul 88*	1

ALBUMS:	HITS 8			WEEKS 39
PSYCHEDELIC FURS	*CBS*	18	*15 Mar 80*	6
TALK TALK TALK	*CBS*	30	*23 May 81*	9
FOREVER NOW	*CBS*	20	*2 Oct 82*	6
MIRROR MOVES	*CBS*	15	*19 May 84*	9
MIDNIGHT TO MIDNIGHT	*CBS*	12	*14 Feb 87*	5
ALL OF THIS AND NOTHING	*CBS*	67	*13 Aug 88*	2
BOOK OF DAYS	*CBS*	74	*18 Nov 89*	1
WORLD OUTSIDE	*East West*	68	*13 Jul 91*	1

PSYCHIC TV   UK

SINGLES:	HITS 2			WEEKS 4
GODSTAR	*Temple*	67	*26 Apr 86*	2

Above hit: PSYCHIC TV and the ANGELS OF LIGHT.

GOOD VIBRATIONS / ROMAN P	*Temple*	65	*20 Sep 86*	2

PSYCHOTROPIC - See FREEFALL featuring PSYCHOTROPIC

PUBLIC ANNOUNCEMENT   US

(See also R. Kelly.)

SINGLES:	HITS 1			WEEKS 2
BODY BUMPIN' YIPPIE-YI-YO	*A&M*	38	*4 Jul 98*	2

PUBLIC DEMAND   UK

SINGLES:	HITS 1			WEEKS 2
INVISIBLE	*ZTT*	41	*15 Feb 97*	2

PUBLIC ENEMY   US

SINGLES:	HITS 16			WEEKS 53
REBEL WITHOUT A PAUSE	*Def Jam*	37	*21 Nov 87*	5
REBEL WITHOUT A PAUSE [RE]	*Def Jam*	71	*2 Jan 88*	2
BRING THE NOISE	*Def Jam*	32	*9 Jan 88*	5
DON'T BELIEVE THE HYPE	*Def Jam*	18	*2 Jul 88*	5
NIGHT OF THE LIVING BASEHEADS	*Def Jam*	63	*15 Oct 88*	2
FIGHT THE POWER	*Motown*	29	*24 Jun 89*	5
WELCOME TO THE TERROR DOME	*Def Jam*	18	*20 Jan 90*	4
911 IS A JOKE	*Def Jam*	41	*7 Apr 90*	3
BROTHERS GONNA WORK IT OUT	*Def Jam*	46	*23 Jun 90*	2
CAN'T DO NUTTIN' FOR YA MAN	*Def Jam*	53	*3 Nov 90*	2
CAN'T TRUSS IT	*Def Jam*	22	*12 Oct 91*	4
SHUT 'EM DOWN	*Def Jam*	21	*25 Jan 92*	3
NIGHTTRAIN	*Def Jam*	55	*11 Apr 92*	2
GIVE IT UP	*Def Jam*	18	*13 Aug 94*	3
SO WHATCHA GONNA DO NOW?	*Def Jam*	50	*29 Jul 95*	1

HE GOT GAME	*Def Jam*	16	*6 Jun 98*	4

From the film 'He Got Game'. Samples Buffalo Springfield's For What It's Worth and features Stephen Stills on guitar and vocals.

DO YOU WANNA GO OUR WAY???	*PIAS Recordings*	66	*25 Sept 99*	1
ALBUMS:	**HITS 7**		**WEEKS 37**	
IT TAKES A NATION OF MILLIONS TO HOLD US BACK	*Def Jam*	8	*30 Jul 88*	9
FEAR OF A BLACK PLANET	*Def Jam*	4	*28 Apr 90*	10
APOCALYPSE 91 . . . THE ENEMY STRIKES BLACK	*Def Jam*	8	*19 Oct 91*	7
GREATEST MISSES	*Def Jam*	14	*3 Oct 92*	3
MUSE SICK-N-HOUR MESS AGE	*Def Jam*	12	*3 Sep 94*	3
HE GOT GAME [OST]	*Def Jam*	50	*16 May 98*	4
THERE'S A POISON GOIN ON . . .	*PIAS Recordings*	55	*31 Jul 99*	1

Previously only available from the internet US label Atomic Pop.

PUBLIC IMAGE LTD   UK

(Certain releases below were credited with just PIL or P.I.L.)

SINGLES:	**HITS 12**		**WEEKS 61**	
PUBLIC IMAGE	*Virgin*	9	*21 Oct 78*	8
DEATH DISCO	*Virgin*	20	*7 Jul 79*	7
MEMORIES	*Virgin*	60	*20 Oct 79*	2
FLOWERS OF ROMANCE	*Virgin*	24	*4 Apr 81*	7
THIS IS NOT A LOVE SONG	*Virgin*	5	*17 Sep 83*	10
BAD LIFE	*Virgin*	71	*19 May 84*	2
RISE	*Virgin*	11	*1 Feb 86*	8
HOME	*Virgin*	75	*3 May 86*	1
SEATTLE	*Virgin*	47	*22 Aug 87*	4
DISAPPOINTED	*Virgin*	38	*6 May 89*	5
DON'T ASK ME	*Virgin*	22	*20 Oct 90*	5
CRUEL	*Virgin*	49	*22 Feb 92*	2
ALBUMS:	**HITS 12**		**WEEKS 51**	
PUBLIC IMAGE	*Virgin*	22	*23 Dec 78*	11
METAL BOX	*Virgin*	18	*8 Dec 79*	8

Title is due to format being available in a metal container with three 12" singles inside.

SECOND EDITION OF PIL	*Virgin*	46	*8 Mar 80*	2

Repackage of Metal Box.

PARIS AU PRINTEMPS (PARIS IN THE SPRING)	*Virgin*	61	*22 Nov 80*	2

Live recordings from Paris concert, Mar 80.

FLOWERS OF ROMANCE	*Virgin*	11	*18 Apr 81*	5
PIL LIVE IN TOKYO	*Virgin*	28	*8 Oct 83*	6
THIS IS WHAT YOU WANT . . . THIS IS WHAT YOU GET	*Virgin*	56	*21 Jul 84*	2
ALBUM / CASSETTE	*Virgin*	14	*15 Feb 86*	6

Vinyl format is titled Album while the Cassette form is called the latter.

HAPPY?	*Virgin*	40	*26 Sep 87*	2
9	*Virgin*	36	*10 Jun 89*	2
THE GREATEST HITS, SO FAR	*Virgin*	20	*10 Nov 90*	3
THAT WHAT IS NOT	*Virgin*	46	*7 Mar 92*	2

Gary PUCKETT and the UNION GAP   UK/Canada

SINGLES:	**HITS 3**		**WEEKS 47**	
YOUNG GIRL	*CBS*	1	*20 Apr 68*	17

Above hit: UNION GAP featuring Gary PUCKETT.

LADY WILLPOWER	*CBS*	5	*10 Aug 68*	16
WOMAN, WOMAN	*CBS*	48	*31 Aug 68*	1

Originally recorded by Jimmy Payne.
Above hit: UNION GAP featuring Gary PUCKETT.

YOUNG GIRL [RI]	*CBS*	6	*15 Jun 74*	13
ALBUMS:	**HITS 1**		**WEEKS 4**	
UNION GAP	*CBS*	24	*29 Jun 68*	4

Tito PUENTE – See Tito PUENTO Jr. and the LATIN RHYTHM featuring Tito PUENTE, INDIA and Cali ALEMAN

Tito PUENTE Jr. and the LATIN RHYTHM featuring Tito PUENTE, INDIA and Cali ALEMAN   US

SINGLES:	**HITS 1**		**WEEKS 3**	
OYE COMO VA	*Media*	36	*16 Mar 96*	2

Originally recorded by Tito Puente in 1962 on his album El Rey Brava. Also a No. 13 hit in the US for Santana in 1971.

OYE COMO VA [RM]	*Nukleus*	56	*19 Jul 97*	1

Remixed by Joey Musaphia.

PUFF DADDY   US

(See also Notorious B.I.G.)

SINGLES:	**HITS 11**		**WEEKS 65**	
CAN'T NOBODY HOLD ME DOWN	*Puff Daddy*	19	*29 Mar 97*	4

Samples Grandmaster Flash and the Furious Five's The Message.
Above hit: PUFF DADDY (featuring MASE).

NO TIME	Atlantic	45	26 Apr 97	1
Above hit: LIL' KIM featuring PUFF DADDY.				
I'LL BE MISSING YOU	Puff Daddy	1	28 Jun 97	21
Samples The Police's Every Breath You Take. Sleeve gives title as an EP: Tribute To The Notorious B.I.G.				
Above hit: PUFF DADDY and Faith EVANS (featuring 112).				
SOMEONE	RCA	34	13 Sep 97	2
Above hit: SWV featuring PUFF DADDY.				
BEEN AROUND THE WORLD	Puff Daddy	20	1 Nov 97	4
Samples the bass line from David Bowie's Let's Dance with lyrics from Lisa Stansfield's All Around The World.				
Above hit: PUFF DADDY and the FAMILY featuring the NOTORIOUS B.I.G. and MASE.				
BEEN AROUND THE WORLD [RE]	Puff Daddy	56	3 Jan 98	2
IT'S ALL ABOUT THE BENJAMINS	Puff Daddy	18	7 Feb 98	3
Above hit: PUFF DADDY and the FAMILY (featuring the NOTORIOUS B.I.G., LIL' KIM, the LOX, Dave GROHL, PERFECT, FUZZBUBBLE and Rob ZOMBIE).				
COME WITH ME	Epic	75	1 Aug 98	1
US import. Based on guitar riff from Led Zeppelin's Kashmir from 1975. From the film 'Godzilla'.				
COME WITH ME	Epic	2	8 Aug 98	10
Above 2: PUFF DADDY featuring Jimmy PAGE.				
ALL NIGHT LONG	Puff Daddy	23	1 May 99	3
Samples Unlimited Touch's I Hear Music In The Street.				
Above hit: Faith EVANS (featuring PUFF DADDY).				
HATE ME NOW	Columbia	14	29 May 99	6
Above hit: NAS (featuring PUFF DADDY).				
P.E. 2000	Puff Daddy	13	21 Aug 99	4
Samples Public Enemy's Public Enemy No. 1.				
Above hit: PUFF DADDY [featuring HURRICANE G].				
BEST FRIEND	Puff Daddy	24	20 Nov 99	4
Samples Christopher Cross' Sailing.				
Above hit: PUFF DADDY (featuring Mario WINANS).				
ALBUMS:	**HITS 2**		**WEEKS 19**	
NO WAY OUT	Puff Daddy	8	2 Aug 97	13
Above hit: PUFF DADDY and the FAMILY.				
FOREVER	Puff Daddy	9	04 Sept 99	6

PULP　　　　　　　　　　　　　　　　　　　　　　　　　　　　UK

SINGLES:	**HITS 11**		**WEEKS 70**	
LIP GLOSS	Island	50	27 Nov 93	2
DO YOU REMEMBER THE FIRST TIME?	Island	33	2 Apr 94	4
THE SISTERS [EP]	Island	19	4 Jun 94	4
Lead track: Babies. This track was originally released in 1992.				
COMMON PEOPLE	Island	2	3 Jun 95	13
MIS-SHAPES / SORTED FOR E'S & WIZZ	Island	2	7 Oct 95	8
DISCO 2000	Island	7	9 Dec 95	11
MIS-SHAPES / SORTED FOR E'S & WIZZ [RE]	Island	62	30 Dec 95	3
SOMETHING CHANGED	Island	10	6 Apr 96	5
SOMETHING CHANGED [RE-1ST]	Island	62	8 Jun 96	1
SOMETHING CHANGED [RE-2ND]	Island	61	22 Jun 96	1
DO YOU REMEMBER THE FIRST TIME? [RE]	Island	73	7 Sep 96	1
HELP THE AGED	Island	8	22 Nov 97	7
HELP THE AGED [RE]	Island	68	24 Jan 98	2
THIS IS HARDCORE	Island	12	28 Mar 98	4
A LITTLE SOUL	Island	22	20 Jun 98	2
PARTY HARD	Island	29	19 Sep 98	2
ALBUMS:	**HITS 4**		**WEEKS 132**	
HIS 'N' HERS	Island	9	30 Apr 94	43
DIFFERENT CLASS	Island	1	11 Nov 95	62
COUNTDOWN 1992-1983	Nectar Masters	10	23 Mar 96	6
Compilation of tracks from their 4 non charted albums If from 1983, Masters Of The Universe from 1986, Freaks in 1987 and Separations from 1992.				
THIS IS HARDCORE	Island	1	11 Apr 98	21

PULSE featuring Antoinette ROBERSON　　　　　　　　　　　　　US

(See also David Morales.)

SINGLES:	**HITS 1**		**WEEKS 3**	
THE LOVER THAT YOU ARE	ffrr	22	25 May 96	3

PURE SUGAR vocals by Jennifer STARR　　　　　　　　　　　　UK

SINGLES:	**HITS 1**		**WEEKS 1**	
DELICIOUS	Geffen	70	24 Oct 98	1

PURESSENCE
UK

SINGLES:	HITS 3			WEEKS 5
THIS FEELING	Island	33	23 May 98	2
IT DOESN'T MATTER ANYMORE	Island	47	8 Aug 98	1
ALL I WANT	Island	39	21 Nov 98	2
ALBUMS:	**HITS 1**			**WEEKS 2**
ONLY FOREVER	Island	36	29 Aug 98	2

James and Bobby PURIFY
US

SINGLES:	HITS 2			WEEKS 16
I'M YOUR PUPPET	Mercury	12	24 Apr 76	10
Originally recorded by Dan Penn.				
MORNING GLORY	Mercury	27	7 Aug 76	6
Originally recorded by Mac Gayden.				

PURPLE HEARTS
UK

SINGLES:	HITS 2			WEEKS 5
MILLIONS LIKE US	Fiction	57	22 Sep 79	3
JIMMY	Fiction	60	8 Mar 80	2

PURPLE KINGS
UK

SINGLES:	HITS 1			WEEKS 3
THAT'S THE WAY YOU DO IT	Positiva	26	15 Oct 94	3
Based around the guitar riff from Dire Strait's Money For Nothing.				

PUSH
Belgium

SINGLES:	HITS 1			WEEKS 4
UNIVERSAL NATION	Inferno	36	15 May 99	2
UNIVERSAL NATION '99 [RI]	Inferno	35	9 Oct 99	2
Though billed as a remix, the lead track is just a re-issue.				

PUSSYCAT
Holland

SINGLES:	HITS 2			WEEKS 30
MISSISSIPPI	Sonet	1	28 Aug 76	22
SMILE	Sonet	24	25 Dec 76	8

PWEI - See POP WILL EAT ITSELF

PYRAMIDS
Jamaica

SINGLES:	HITS 1			WEEKS 4
TRAIN TOUR TO RAINBOW CITY	President	35	25 Nov 67	4

PYTHON LEE JACKSON
Australia

SINGLES:	HITS 1			WEEKS 12
IN A BROKEN DREAM	Young Blood	3	30 Sep 72	12
Features lead vocals by Rod Stewart. Recorded in 1970.				

Q

Q
UK

SINGLES:	HITS 2			WEEKS 6
GET HERE	Arista	37	5 Jun 93	4
Above hit: Q-featuring Tracy ACKERMAN.				
(EVERYTHING I DO) I DO IT FOR YOU	Bell	47	12 Mar 94	2
Above hit: Q featuring Tony JACKSON.				

Q-BASS
UK

(See also Various Artists (EPs) 'Subplates Volume 1 EP'.)

SINGLES:	HITS 1			WEEKS 1
HARDCORE WILL NEVER DIE	Suburban Base	64	8 Feb 92	1

Q-CLUB
Italy

SINGLES:	HITS 1			WEEKS 3
TELL IT TO MY HEART	Manifesto	28	6 Jan 96	3

Q TEE
UK

SINGLES:	HITS 2			WEEKS 7
AFRIKA	SBK.One	42	21 Apr 90	5
Above hit: HISTORY featuring Q-TEE.				
GIMME THAT BODY	Heavenly	40	10 Feb 96	2

Q-TEX

UK

SINGLES:	HITS 4			WEEKS 7
THE POWER OF LOVE	Stoatin'	65	9 Apr 94	1
BELIEVE	23rd Precinct	41	26 Nov 94	2
LET THE LOVE	23rd Precinct	30	15 Jun 96	2
DO YOU WANT ME	23rd Precinct	48	30 Nov 96	1
POWER OF LOVE 97 [RM]	23rd Precinct	49	28 Jun 97	1
Remixed by Scott Brown and Stuart Crichton.				

Q-TIP - See DE LA SOUL; Janet JACKSON; Raphael SAADIQ and Q-TIP

Q-TIPS

UK

ALBUMS:	HITS 1			WEEKS 1
Q-TIPS	Chrysalis	50	30 Aug 80	1

Q UNIQUE - See C&C MUSIC FACTORY

QATTARA

UK

(See also Alex Whitcombe and Big C.)

SINGLES:	HITS 1			WEEKS 2
COME WITH ME	Positiva	31	15 Mar 97	2

QFX

UK

SINGLES:	HITS 5			WEEKS 16
FREEDOM [EP]	Epidemic	41	6 May 95	3
Lead track: Freedom. Vocals by Moira Rankin.				
EVERY TIME YOU TOUCH ME	Epidemic	22	3 Feb 96	4
YOU GOT THE POWER	Epidemic	33	3 Aug 96	3
FREEDOM 2	Epidemic	21	18 Jan 97	4
This is a re-recording of the track from the Freedom EP. Vocals by Kerry McGregor.				
SAY YOU'LL BE MINE	Quality Recordings	34	20 Mar 99	2
Above hit: Q.F.X.				

ALBUMS:	HITS 1			WEEKS 1
ALIEN CHILD	Epidemic	62	8 Mar 97	1

QUAD CITY DJ'S

US

SINGLES:	HITS 1			WEEKS 1
SPACE JAM	Atlantic	57	15 Nov 97	1
From the film of the same name.				

QUADROPHONIA

Belgium

SINGLES:	HITS 3			WEEKS 15
QUADROPHONIA	ARS	14	13 Apr 91	9
THE WAVE OF THE FUTURE	ARS	40	6 Jul 91	3
FIND THE TIME (PART 1)	ARS	41	21 Dec 91	3

QUADS

UK

SINGLES:	HITS 1			WEEKS 2
THERE MUST BE THOUSANDS	Big Bear	66	22 Sep 79	2

QUAKE featuring Marcia RAE

UK

SINGLES:	HITS 1			WEEKS 1
THE DAY WILL COME	ffrr	53	29 Aug 98	1

QUANTUM JUMP

UK

SINGLES:	HITS 1			WEEKS 10
THE LONE RANGER	Electric	5	2 Jun 79	10

QUARTERFLASH

US

SINGLES:	HITS 1			WEEKS 5
HARDEN MY HEART	Geffen	49	27 Feb 82	5

QUARTZ

UK

SINGLES:	HITS 3			WEEKS 19
WE'RE COMIN' AT YA	Mercury	65	17 Mar 90	2
Above hit: QUARTZ featuring STEPZ.				
IT'S TOO LATE	Mercury	8	2 Feb 91	14
Above hit: QUARTZ introducing Dina CARROLL.				
NAKED LOVE (JUST SAY YOU WANT ME)	Mercury	39	15 Jun 91	3
Above hit: QUARTZ and Dina CARROLL.				

Jakie QUARTZ
France

SINGLES:		HITS 1			WEEKS 3
A LA VIE, A L'AMOUR		*PWL Continental*	55	*11 Mar 89*	3

QUARTZ LOCK featuring Lonnie GORDON
UK

(See also Lonnie Gordon.)

SINGLES:		HITS 1			WEEKS 2
LOVE EVICTION		*Xplode*	32	*7 Oct 95*	2

Suzi QUATRO
US

SINGLES:		HITS 16			WEEKS 122
CAN THE CAN		*RAK*	1	*19 May 73*	14
48 CRASH		*RAK*	3	*28 Jul 73*	9
DAYTONA DEMON		*RAK*	14	*27 Oct 73*	13
DEVIL GATE DRIVE		*RAK*	1	*9 Feb 74*	11
TOO BIG		*RAK*	14	*29 Jun 74*	6
THE WILD ONE		*RAK*	7	*9 Nov 74*	10
YOUR MAMMA WON'T LIKE ME		*RAK*	31	*8 Feb 75*	5
TEAR ME APART		*RAK*	27	*5 Mar 77*	6
IF YOU CAN'T GIVE ME LOVE		*RAK*	4	*18 Mar 78*	13
THE RACE IS ON		*RAK*	43	*22 Jul 78*	5
STUMBLIN' IN		*RAK*	41	*11 Nov 78*	8
Above hit: Suzi QUATRO and Chris NORMAN.					
SHE'S IN LOVE WITH YOU		*RAK*	11	*20 Oct 79*	9
MAMA'S BOY		*RAK*	34	*19 Jan 80*	5
I'VE NEVER BEEN IN LOVE		*RAK*	56	*5 Apr 80*	3
ROCK HARD		*Dreamland*	68	*25 Oct 80*	2
HEART OF STONE		*Polydor*	60	*13 Nov 82*	3
ALBUMS:		HITS 2			WEEKS 13
SUZI QUATRO		*RAK*	32	*13 Oct 73*	4
SUZI QUATRO'S GREATEST HITS		*RAK*	4	*26 Apr 80*	9

Finley QUAYE
UK

SINGLES:		HITS 5			WEEKS 20
SUNDAY SHINING		*Epic*	16	*21 Jun 97*	6
EVEN AFTER ALL		*Epic*	10	*13 Sep 97*	5
IT'S GREAT WHEN WE'RE TOGETHER		*Epic*	29	*29 Nov 97*	3
YOUR LOVE GETS SWEETER		*Epic*	16	*7 Mar 98*	5
ULTRA STIMULATION		*Epic*	51	*15 Aug 98*	1
ALBUMS:		HITS 1			WEEKS 56
MAVERICK A STRIKE		*Epic*	3	*4 Oct 97*	56

QUEDO BRASS - See CHAQUITO ORCHESTRA

QUEEN
UK

SINGLES:		HITS 48			WEEKS 403
SEVEN SEAS OF RHYE		*EMI*	10	*9 Mar 74*	10
KILLER QUEEN		*EMI*	2	*26 Oct 74*	12
NOW I'M HERE		*EMI*	11	*25 Jan 75*	7
BOHEMIAN RHAPSODY		*EMI*	1	*8 Nov 75*	17
Video to the song is established as the first to be used as a promotional tool to sell the single.					
YOU'RE MY BEST FRIEND		*EMI*	7	*3 Jul 76*	8
SOMEBODY TO LOVE		*EMI*	2	*27 Nov 76*	9
TIE YOUR MOTHER DOWN		*EMI*	31	*19 Mar 77*	4
QUEEN'S FIRST EP [EP]		*EMI*	17	*4 Jun 77*	10
Lead track: Good Old Fashioned Lover Boy. On certain weeks, the chart listed only the lead track.					
WE ARE THE CHAMPIONS		*EMI*	2	*22 Oct 77*	12
SPREAD YOUR WINGS		*EMI*	34	*25 Feb 78*	4
BICYCLE RACE / FAT BOTTOMED GIRLS		*EMI*	11	*28 Oct 78*	12
DON'T STOP ME NOW		*EMI*	9	*10 Feb 79*	12
LOVE OF MY LIFE		*EMI*	63	*14 Jul 79*	2
Live recording.					
CRAZY LITTLE THING CALLED LOVE		*EMI*	2	*20 Oct 79*	14
SAVE ME		*EMI*	11	*2 Feb 80*	6
PLAY THE GAME		*EMI*	14	*14 Jun 80*	8
ANOTHER ONE BITES THE DUST		*EMI*	7	*6 Sep 80*	9
FLASH		*EMI*	10	*6 Dec 80*	13
From the film 'Flash Gordon'.					
UNDER PRESSURE		*EMI*	1	*14 Nov 81*	11
Above hit: QUEEN and David BOWIE.					
BODY LANGUAGE		*EMI*	25	*1 May 82*	6
LAS PALABRAS DE AMOR		*EMI*	17	*12 Jun 82*	8
BACK CHAT		*EMI*	40	*21 Aug 82*	4
RADIO GA GA		*EMI*	2	*4 Feb 84*	9

I WANT TO BREAK FREE	EMI	3	14 Apr 84	15
IT'S A HARD LIFE	EMI	6	28 Jul 84	9
HAMMER TO FALL	EMI	13	22 Sep 84	7
THANK GOD IT'S CHRISTMAS	EMI	21	8 Dec 84	6
ONE VISION	EMI	7	16 Nov 85	10
A KIND OF MAGIC	EMI	3	29 Mar 86	11

From the film 'Highlander'.

FRIENDS WILL BE FRIENDS	EMI	14	21 Jun 86	8
WHO WANTS TO LIVE FOREVER?	EMI	24	27 Sep 86	5
I WANT IT ALL	Parlophone	3	13 May 89	7
BREAKTHRU'	Parlophone	7	1 Jul 89	7
THE INVISIBLE MAN	Parlophone	12	19 Aug 89	6
SCANDAL	Parlophone	25	21 Oct 89	4
THE MIRACLE	Parlophone	21	9 Dec 89	5
INNUENDO	Parlophone	1	26 Jan 91	6
I'M GOING SLIGHTLY MAD	Parlophone	22	16 Mar 91	5
HEADLONG	Parlophone	14	25 May 91	4
THE SHOW MUST GO ON	Parlophone	16	26 Oct 91	5
THE SHOW MUST GO ON [RE]	Parlophone	27	7 Dec 91	5
BOHEMIAN RHAPSODY [RI] / THESE ARE THE DAYS OF OUR LIVES	Parlophone	1	21 Dec 91	14

Only time that the same recording has reached No. 1 on a separate issue.

FIVE LIVE [EP]	Parlophone	1	1 May 93	11

Lead track: Somebody To Love, a live recording from the Freddie Mercury Tribute Concert, Apr 92. Lisa Stansfield only sang on These Are The Days Of Our Lives. Proceeds to the Mercury Phoenix Trust.
Above hit: George MICHAEL and QUEEN with Lisa STANSFIELD.

FIVE LIVE [EP] [RE]	Parlophone	74	24 Jul 93	1
HEAVEN FOR EVERYONE	Parlophone	2	4 Nov 95	12

Originally recorded in 1988 by Taylor's group the Cross for their Shove It album.

A WINTER'S TALE	Parlophone	6	23 Dec 95	6
TOO MUCH LOVE WILL KILL YOU	Parlophone	15	9 Mar 96	6
LET ME LIVE	Parlophone	9	29 Jun 96	4
YOU DON'T FOOL ME - THE REMIXES	Parlophone	17	30 Nov 96	4

Lead track is the album version. The remixes are by Dancing Divaz, Jam and Spoon and David Richards.

NO-ONE BUT YOU (ONLY THE GOOD DIE YOUNG) / TIE YOUR MOTHER DOWN [RI]	Parlophone	13	17 Jan 98	4
ANOTHER ONE BITES THE DUST [RR]	Dreamwords	5	14 Nov 98	6

From the film 'Small Soldiers'. Remix of original with additional rap.
Above hit: QUEEN/Wyclef JEAN featuring PRAS and FREE.

UNDER PRESSURE [RM]	Parlophone	14	18 Dec 99	3

Remixed by Queen, Joshua J. Macrae and Justin Shirley-Smith.
Above hit: QUEEN + David BOWIE.

ALBUMS:	HITS 23		WEEKS 1177	
QUEEN 2	EMI	5	23 Mar 74	29
QUEEN	EMI	24	30 Mar 74	18

Originally released in 1973.

SHEER HEART ATTACK	EMI	2	23 Nov 74	42
A NIGHT AT THE OPERA	EMI	1	13 Dec 75	50
A DAY AT THE RACES	EMI	1	25 Dec 76	24
NEWS OF THE WORLD	EMI	4	12 Nov 77	20
JAZZ	EMI	2	25 Nov 78	27
LIVE KILLERS	EMI	3	7 Jul 79	27

Live recordings from their UK tour.

THE GAME	EMI	1	12 Jul 80	18
FLASH GORDON [OST]	EMI	10	20 Dec 80	15
QUEEN GREATEST HITS	EMI	1	7 Nov 81	331

Includes re-entries through to 1991. From 12 Dec 87, label changed to Parlophone.

HOT SPACE	EMI	4	15 May 82	19
THE WORKS	EMI	2	10 Mar 84	93
A KIND OF MAGIC	EMI	1	14 Jun 86	62
LIVE MAGIC	EMI	3	13 Dec 86	40
THE MIRACLE	Parlophone	1	3 Jun 89	32
QUEEN AT THE BEEB	Band Of Joy	67	16 Dec 89	1

Recordings made for BBC radio shows.

INNUENDO	Parlophone	1	16 Feb 91	37
GREATEST HITS II	Parlophone	1	9 Nov 91	104

Includes re-entries through to 1999.

QUEEN GREATEST HITS [RE]	Parlophone	6	9 Nov 91	115

Includes re-entries through to 1999. Chart position reached in 1992.

LIVE MAGIC [RI]	Parlophone	51	7 Dec 91	3
A KIND OF MAGIC [RI]	Parlophone	66	7 Dec 91	1
LIVE AT WEMBLEY '86	Parlophone	2	6 Jun 92	15

Live recordings from their show, Jul 86.

GREATEST HITS I AND II [RI]	EMI	37	19 Nov 94	7

Double re-issue of both their previous Greatest Hits albums.

MADE IN HEAVEN	Parlophone	1	18 Nov 95	28

May, Taylor and Deacon spent 4 years working on the music to accompany Mercury's final vocal performances.

QUEEN ROCKS *Compilation with one new track with vocals by May and Taylor.*	*Parlophone*	7	*15 Nov 97*	12
GREATEST HITS III *Includes solo recordings by Brian May and Freddie Mercury.*	*Parlophone*	5	*20 Nov 99*	7

QUEEN LATIFAH   US
(See also De La Soul; Jungle Brothers.)

SINGLES:	HITS 6			WEEKS 17
MAMMA GAVE BIRTH TO THE SOUL CHILDREN *Above hit: QUEEN LATIFAH + DE LA SOUL.*	*Gee Street*	14	*24 Mar 90*	7
FIND A WAY *Above hit: COLDCUT featuring QUEEN LATIFAH.*	*Ahead Of Our Time*	52	*26 May 90*	2
FLY GIRL	*Gee Street*	67	*31 Aug 91*	1
WHAT'CHA GONNA DO? *Above hit: Shabba RANKS featuring QUEEN LATIFAH.*	*Epic*	21	*26 Jun 93*	4
U.N.I.T.Y. *Samples Message From The Inner City by the Crusaders.*	*Motown*	74	*26 Mar 94*	1
MR. BIG STUFF *Original by Jean Knight reached No. 2 in the US in 1971. From the film 'Te Associate'.* *Above hit: QUEEN LATIFAH, SHADES and FREE.*	*Motown*	31	*12 Apr 97*	2

QUEEN PEN   US

SINGLES:	HITS 3			WEEKS 10
MAN BEHIND THE MUSIC *Features vocals by Teddy Riley of Blackstreet.*	*Interscope*	38	*7 Mar 98*	2
ALL MY LOVE *Samples Luther Vandross' Never Too Much.* *Above hit: QUEEN PEN featuring Eric WILLIAMS of BLACKSTREET.*	*Interscope*	11	*9 May 98*	5
IT'S TRUE *Samples Spandau Ballet's True.*	*Interscope*	24	*5 Sep 98*	3

QUEENSRYCHE   US

SINGLES:	HITS 7			WEEKS 21
EYES OF A STRANGER	*EMI USA*	59	*13 May 89*	1
EMPIRE	*EMI USA*	61	*10 Nov 90*	1
SILENT LUCIDITY	*EMI USA*	34	*20 Apr 91*	5
BEST I CAN	*EMI USA*	36	*6 Jul 91*	3
JET CITY WOMAN	*EMI USA*	39	*7 Sep 91*	2
SILENT LUCIDITY [RI]	*EMI USA*	18	*8 Aug 92*	4
I AM I	*EMI*	40	*28 Jan 95*	2
BRIDGE	*EMI*	40	*25 Mar 95*	3
ALBUMS:	**HITS 6**			**WEEKS 12**
THE WARNING	*EMI America*	100	*29 Sep 84*	1
RAGE FOR ORDER	*EMI America*	66	*26 Jul 86*	1
OPERATION MINDCRIME	*EMI Manhattan*	58	*4 Jun 88*	3
EMPIRE	*EMI USA*	13	*22 Sep 90*	3
PROMISED LAND	*EMI*	13	*22 Oct 94*	3
HEAR IN THE NOW FRONTIER	*EMI*	46	*29 Mar 97*	1

QUENCH   Australia

SINGLES:	HITS 1			WEEKS 1
DREAMS	*Infectious*	75	*17 Feb 96*	1

QUENTIN and ASH   UK

SINGLES:	HITS 1			WEEKS 3
TELL HIM	*East West*	25	*6 Jul 96*	3

? and the MYSTERIANS   US

SINGLES:	HITS 1			WEEKS 4
96 TEARS	*Cameo-Parkway*	37	*19 Nov 66*	4

QUESTIONS   UK

SINGLES:	HITS 3			WEEKS 8
THE PRICE YOU PAY	*Respond*	56	*23 Apr 83*	3
TEAR SOUP	*Respond*	66	*17 Sep 83*	1
TUESDAY SUNSHINE	*Respond*	46	*10 Mar 84*	4

QUICK   UK

SINGLES:	HITS 1			WEEKS 7
THE RHYTHM OF THE JUNGLE	*Epic*	41	*15 May 82*	7

Tommy QUICKLY and the REMO 4 — UK

SINGLES:	HITS 1			WEEKS 8
WILD SIDE OF LIFE	Pye	33	24 Oct 64	8

QUIET FIVE — UK

SINGLES:	HITS 2			WEEKS 3
WHEN THE MORNING SUN DRIES THE DEW	Parlophone	45	15 May 65	1
HOMEWARD BOUND	Parlophone	44	23 Apr 66	2

QUIET RIOT — US

SINGLES:	HITS 1			WEEKS 5
METAL HEALTH / CUM ON FEEL THE NOIZE	Epic	45	3 Dec 83	5

Cum On Feel The Noize listed from 10 Dec 83.

ALBUMS:	HITS 1			WEEKS 1
CONDITION CRITICAL	Epic	71	4 Aug 84	1

Eimear QUINN — Ireland

SINGLES:	HITS 1			WEEKS 2
THE VOICE	Polydor	40	15 Jun 96	2

Eurovision Song Contest winner in 1996.

Paul QUINN and Edwyn COLLINS — UK

SINGLES:	HITS 1			WEEKS 2
PALE BLUE EYES	Swamplands	72	11 Aug 84	2

QUINTESSENCE — UK/Australia

ALBUMS:	HITS 3			WEEKS 6
QUINTESSENCE	Island	22	27 Jun 70	4
DIVE DEEP	Island	43	3 Apr 71	1
SELF	RCA Victor	50	27 May 72	1

QUIREBOYS — UK

SINGLES:	HITS 6			WEEKS 27
7 O'CLOCK	Parlophone	36	4 Nov 89	4
HEY YOU	Parlophone	14	6 Jan 90	7
I DON'T LOVE YOU ANYMORE	Parlophone	24	7 Apr 90	6
THERE SHE GOES AGAIN/MISLED	Parlophone	37	8 Sep 90	4

Original release reached No. 87 in 1988.

TRAMPS AND THIEVES	Parlophone	41	10 Oct 92	3
BROTHER LOUIE	Parlophone	31	20 Feb 93	3

ALBUMS:	HITS 2			WEEKS 17
A BIT OF WHAT YOU FANCY	Parlophone	2	10 Feb 90	15
BITTER SWEET AND TWISTED	Parlophone	31	27 Mar 93	2

QUIVER – See SUTHERLAND BROTHERS and QUIVER

QUIVVER — UK

SINGLES:	HITS 2			WEEKS 3
SAXY LADY	A&M	56	5 Mar 94	2
BELIEVE IN ME	Perfecto	56	18 Nov 95	1

QWENT CHORALE – See Bryn YEMM

QWILO and FELIX DA HOUSECAT featuring Lynn CROUCH — US

SINGLES:	HITS 1			WEEKS 1
DIRTY MOTHA	Manifesto	66	6 Sep 97	1

R

R.A.F. — Italy

(See also Mauro Picotto.)

SINGLES:	HITS 3			WEEKS 6
WE'VE GOT TO LIVE TOGETHER	PWL Continental	34	14 Mar 92	3
TAKE ME HIGHER	Media	71	5 Mar 94	1
TAKE ME HIGHER [RM]	Media	59	23 Mar 96	1

Remixed by Primax.

ANGEL'S SYMPHONY	Media	73	27 Jul 96	1

Above hit: R.A.F. by PICOTTO and Gigi D'AGOSTINO.

R.A.W. – See Erick "More" MORILLO presents R.A.W.

R.E.M.

US

SINGLES:	HITS 26			WEEKS 141
THE ONE I LOVE	I.R.S.	51	28 Nov 87	8
FINEST WORKSONG	I.R.S.	50	30 Apr 88	2
STAND	Warner Brothers	51	4 Feb 89	3
ORANGE CRUSH	Warner Brothers	28	3 Jun 89	5
STAND [RI]	Warner Brothers	48	12 Aug 89	2
LOSING MY RELIGION	Warner Brothers	19	9 Mar 91	9
SHINY HAPPY PEOPLE	Warner Brothers	6	18 May 91	11
Features backing vocals by Kate Pierson of the B-52's.				
NEAR WILD HEAVEN	Warner Brothers	27	17 Aug 91	4
THE ONE I LOVE [RI]	I.R.S.	16	21 Sep 91	6
RADIO SONG	Warner Brothers	28	16 Nov 91	3
IT'S THE END OF THE WORLD AS WE KNOW IT (AND I FEEL FINE)	I.R.S.	39	14 Dec 91	4
Original release reached No. 87 in 1987.				
DRIVE	Warner Brothers	11	3 Oct 92	5
MAN ON THE MOON	Warner Brothers	18	28 Nov 92	8
Tribute to comedian Andy Kaufman.				
THE SIDEWINDER SLEEPS TONITE	Warner Brothers	17	20 Feb 93	6
EVERYBODY HURTS	Warner Brothers	7	17 Apr 93	12
NIGHTSWIMMING	Warner Brothers	27	24 Jul 93	5
FIND THE RIVER	Warner Brothers	54	11 Dec 93	1
WHAT'S THE FREQUENCY, KENNETH?	Warner Brothers	9	17 Sep 94	7
BANG AND BLAME	Warner Brothers	15	12 Nov 94	4
CRUSH WITH EYELINER	Warner Brothers	23	4 Feb 95	3
STRANGE CURRENCIES	Warner Brothers	9	15 Apr 95	4
TONGUE	Warner Brothers	13	29 Jul 95	5
E - BOW THE LETTER	Warner Brothers	4	31 Aug 96	5
Backing vocals by Patti Smith.				
BITTERSWEET ME	Warner Brothers	19	2 Nov 96	2
ELECTROLITE	Warner Brothers	29	14 Dec 96	2
DAYSLEEPER	Warner Brothers	6	24 Oct 98	6
LOTUS	Warner Brothers	26	19 Dec 98	5
AT MY MOST BEAUTIFUL	Warner Brothers	10	20 Mar 99	4
ALBUMS:	HITS 13			WEEKS 469
RECKONING	I.R.S.	91	28 Apr 84	2
FABLES OF THE RECONSTRUCTION	I.R.S.	35	29 Jun 85	3
LIFES RICH PAGEANT	I.R.S.	43	6 Sep 86	4
DEAD LETTER OFFICE	I.R.S.	60	16 May 87	2
DOCUMENT	I.R.S.	28	26 Sept 87	3
EPONYMOUS	I.R.S.	69	29 Oct 88	3
GREEN	Warner Brothers	27	19 Nov 88	20
OUT OF TIME	Warner Brothers	1	23 Mar 91	153
THE BEST OF R.E.M.	I.R.S.	7	12 Oct 91	28
Includes re-entries through to 1995.				
AUTOMATIC FOR THE PEOPLE	Warner Brothers	1	10 Oct 92	141
Includes re-entries through to 1999.				
MONSTER	Warner Brothers	1	8 Oct 94	56
DOCUMENT [RE]	I.R.S.	49	4 Mar 95	2
Re-released at mid-price.				
FABLES OF THE RECONSTRUCTION [RE]	I.R.S.	58	11 Mar 95	1
Re-released at mid-price.				
NEW ADVENTURES IN HI-FI	Warner Brothers	1	21 Sep 96	20
GREEN [RE]	Warner Brothers	58	31 Jan 98	2
Re-released at mid-price.				
UP	Warner Brothers	2	7 Nov 98	29

R.H.C.

Belgium

SINGLES:	HITS 1			WEEKS 1
FEVER CALLED LOVE	R&S	65	11 Jan 92	1

R.I.P. PRODUCTIONS

UK

(See also Double 99.)

SINGLES:	HITS 2			WEEKS 2
THE CHANT (WE R) / R.I.P. PRODUCTIONS	Satellite	58	29 Nov 97	1
The Chant (We R) samples Lennie De-Ice's We Are I E.				
ALL OF THE GIRLS (ALL AI-DI GIRL DEM)	Pepper	51	12 Sep 98	1
Track recorded specifically for the Notting Hill Carnival.				
Above hit: CARNIVAL featuring R.I.P. vs. RED RAT.				

Eddie RABBITT

US

SINGLES:	HITS 2			WEEKS 14
EVERY WHICH WAY BUT LOOSE	Elektra	41	27 Jan 79	9
From the film of the same name.				
I LOVE A RAINY NIGHT	Elektra	53	28 Feb 81	5

Harry RABINOVITZ – See ROYAL PHILHARMONIC ORCHESTRA

Steve RACE and his Group | | | UK

SINGLES:	HITS 1			WEEKS 9
THE PIED PIPER (THE BEEJE)	Parlophone	29	2 Mar 63	9

RACEY | | | UK

SINGLES:	HITS 4			WEEKS 44
LAY YOUR LOVE ON ME	RAK	3	25 Nov 78	14
SOME GIRLS	RAK	2	31 Mar 79	11
BOY OH BOY	RAK	22	18 Aug 79	9
RUNAROUND SUE	RAK	13	20 Dec 80	10

RACING CARS | | | UK

SINGLES:	HITS 1			WEEKS 7
THEY SHOOT HORSES DON'T THEY?	Chrysalis	14	12 Feb 77	7
ALBUMS:	HITS 1			WEEKS 6
DOWNTOWN TONIGHT	Chrysalis	39	19 Feb 77	6

Jimmy RADCLIFFE | | | US

SINGLES:	HITS 1			WEEKS 2
LONG AFTER TONIGHT IS OVER	Stateside	40	6 Feb 65	2

RADHA KRISHNA TEMPLE (LONDON) | | | UK

SINGLES:	HITS 2			WEEKS 17
HARE KRISHNA MANTRA	Apple	12	13 Sep 69	9
GOVINDA	Apple	23	28 Mar 70	8

Above hit: RADHA KRISHNA TEMPLE.

RADICAL ROB | | | UK

SINGLES:	HITS 1			WEEKS 1
MONKEY WAH	R&S	67	11 Jan 92	1

RADIO HEART featuring Gary NUMAN | | | UK

(See also Gary Numan.)

SINGLES:	HITS 2			WEEKS 8
RADIO HEART	GFM	35	28 Mar 87	6
LONDON TIMES	GFM	48	13 Jun 87	2

RADIO 1 POSSEE – See Liz KERSHAW and Bruno BROOKES

RADIO STARS | | | UK

SINGLES:	HITS 1			WEEKS 3
NERVOUS WRECK	Chiswick	39	4 Feb 78	3

RADIOHEAD | | | UK

(See also Various Artists (EPs) 'The Help EP'.)

SINGLES:	HITS 11			WEEKS 43
ANYONE CAN PLAY GUITAR	Parlophone	32	13 Feb 93	2
POP IS DEAD	Parlophone	42	22 May 93	2
CREEP	Parlophone	7	18 Sep 93	6
Original release reached No. 78 in 1992.				
MY IRON LUNG [EP]	Parlophone	24	8 Oct 94	2
Lead track: My Iron Lung.				
HIGH AND DRY / PLANET TELEX	Parlophone	17	11 Mar 95	4
FAKE PLASTIC TREES	Parlophone	20	27 May 95	4
JUST	Parlophone	19	2 Sep 95	3
STREET SPIRIT (FADE OUT)	Parlophone	5	3 Feb 96	4
PARANOID ANDROID	Parlophone	3	7 Jun 97	5
KARMA POLICE	Parlophone	8	6 Sep 97	4
NO SURPRISES	Parlophone	4	24 Jan 98	6
NO SURPRISES [RE]	Parlophone	74	4 Apr 98	1
ALBUMS:	HITS 3			WEEKS 315
PABLO HONEY	Parlophone	25	6 Mar 93	65
THE BENDS	Parlophone	6	25 Mar 95	35
THE BENDS [RE]	Parlophone	4	30 Dec 95	125
OK COMPUTER	Parlophone	1	28 Jun 97	73
PABLO HONEY [RE]	Parlophone	22	31 Jan 98	17

RADISH

				US
SINGLES:	HITS 2			**WEEKS 3**
LITTLE PINK STARS	*Mercury*	32	*30 Aug 97*	2
SIMPLE SINCERITY	*Mercury*	50	*15 Nov 97*	1

Fonda RAE

				US
SINGLES:	HITS 1			**WEEKS 4**
TUCH ME	*Streetwave*	49	*6 Oct 84*	4

Jesse RAE

				UK
SINGLES:	HITS 1			**WEEKS 2**
OVER THE SEA	*Scotland Video*	65	*11 May 85*	2

Marcia RAE – See QUAKE featuring Marcia RAE

RAE and CHRISTIAN featuring VEBA

				UK
SINGLES:	HITS 1			**WEEKS 1**
ALL I ASK	*Grand Central*	67	*6 Mar 99*	1

Samples Brian and Brenda Russell's World Called Love.

RAELETS – See Ray CHARLES

Gerry RAFFERTY

				UK
SINGLES:	HITS 5			**WEEKS 47**
BAKER STREET	*United Artists*	3	*18 Feb 78*	15
Sax solo by Raphael Ravenscroft.				
NIGHT OWL	*United Artists*	5	*26 May 79*	13
GET IT RIGHT NEXT TIME	*United Artists*	30	*18 Aug 79*	9
BRING IT ALL HOME	*United Artists*	54	*22 Mar 80*	4
ROYAL MILE	*United Artists*	67	*21 Jun 80*	2
BAKER STREET [RM]	*EMI*	53	*10 Mar 90*	4
ALBUMS:	HITS 7			**WEEKS 99**
CITY TO CITY	*United Artists*	6	*25 Feb 78*	37
NIGHT OWL	*United Artists*	9	*2 Jun 79*	24
SNAKES AND LADDERS	*United Artists*	15	*26 Apr 80*	9
SLEEPWALKING	*Liberty*	39	*25 Sep 82*	4
NORTH AND SOUTH	*London*	43	*21 May 88*	4
ON A WING AND A PRAYER	*A&M*	73	*13 Feb 93*	1
ONE MORE DREAM – THE VERY BEST OF GERRY RAFFERTY	*PolyGram TV*	17	*28 Oct 95*	20

RAGE

				UK
SINGLES:	HITS 3			**WEEKS 15**
RUN TO YOU	*Pulse 8*	3	*31 Oct 92*	11
WHY DON'T YOU	*Pulse 8*	44	*27 Feb 93*	2
HOUSE OF THE RISING SUN	*Pulse 8*	41	*15 May 93*	2

RAGE AGAINST THE MACHINE

				US
SINGLES:	HITS 6			**WEEKS 17**
KILLING IN THE NAME	*Epic*	25	*27 Feb 93*	4
BULLET IN THE HEAD	*Epic*	16	*8 May 93*	4
BOMBTRACK	*Epic*	37	*4 Sep 93*	2
BULLS ON PARADE	*Epic*	8	*13 Apr 96*	3
PEOPLE OF THE SUN	*Epic*	26	*7 Sep 96*	2
GUERRILLA RADIO	*Epic*	32	*6 Nov 99*	2
ALBUMS:	HITS 3			**WEEKS 51**
RAGE AGAINST THE MACHINE	*Epic*	17	*13 Feb 93*	42
EVIL EMPIRE	*Epic*	4	*27 Apr 96*	7
THE BATTLE OF LOS ANGELES	*Epic*	23	*13 Nov 99*	2

RAGGA TWINS

				UK
SINGLES:	HITS 6			**WEEKS 12**
LAMBORGHINI	*Shut Up And Dance*	55	*28 Jul 90*	2
Above hit: SHUT UP AND DANCE featuring the RAGGA TWINS.				
ILLEGAL GUNSHOT / SPLIFFHEAD	*Shut Up And Dance*	51	*10 Nov 90*	2
WIPE THE NEEDLE / JUGGLING	*Shut Up And Dance*	71	*6 Apr 91*	2
HOOLIGAN 69	*Shut Up And Dance*	56	*6 Jul 91*	2
MIXED TRUTH / BRING UP THE MIC SOME MORE	*Shut Up And Dance*	65	*7 Mar 92*	2
SHINE EYE	*Shut Up And Dance*	63	*11 Jul 92*	2
Above hit: RAGGA TWINS featuring Junior REID.				
ALBUMS:	HITS 1			**WEEKS 5**
REGGAE OWES ME MONEY	*Shut Up And Dance*	26	*1 Jun 91*	5

RAGTIMERS
UK

SINGLES:	HITS 1			WEEKS 8
THE STING	Pye	46	16 Mar 74	1
Based on The Entertainer theme from the film 'The Sting'.				
THE STING [RE]	Pye	31	30 Mar 74	7

RAH BAND
UK

SINGLES:	HITS 7			WEEKS 50
THE CRUNCH	Good Earth	6	9 Jul 77	12
FALCON	DJM	35	1 Nov 80	7
SLIDE	DJM	50	7 Feb 81	7
PERFUMED GARDEN	KR	45	1 May 82	7
MESSAGES FROM THE STARS	TMT Productions	42	9 Jul 83	5
ARE YOU SATISFIED? (FUNKY NOVA)	RCA	70	19 Jan 85	2
CLOUDS ACROSS THE MOON	RCA	6	30 Mar 85	10
ALBUMS:	**HITS 1**			**WEEKS 6**
MYSTERY	RCA	60	6 Apr 85	6

RAHSAAN PATTERSON – See US3

RAILWAY CHILDREN
UK

SINGLES:	HITS 4			WEEKS 13
EVERY BEAT OF THE HEART	Virgin	68	24 Mar 90	2
MUSIC STOP	Virgin	66	2 Jun 90	2
SO RIGHT	Virgin	68	20 Oct 90	1
EVERY BEAT OF THE HEART [RE]	Virgin	24	2 Feb 91	6
SOMETHING SO GOOD	Virgin	57	20 Apr 91	2
ALBUMS:	**HITS 2**			**WEEKS 3**
RECURRENCE	Virgin	96	21 May 88	1
NATIVE PLACE	Virgin	59	16 Mar 91	2

RAIN – See Stephanie DE SYKES

RAIN PARADE
US

ALBUMS:	HITS 1			WEEKS 1
BEYOND THE SUNSET	Island	78	29 Jun 85	1

RAIN TREE CROW
UK

(See also Japan.)

SINGLES:	HITS 1			WEEKS 1
BLACKWATER	Virgin	62	30 Mar 91	1
ALBUMS:	**HITS 1**			**WEEKS 3**
RAIN TREE CROW	Virgin	24	20 Apr 91	3

RAINBOW
UK

SINGLES:	HITS 10			WEEKS 62
KILL THE KING	Polydor	44	17 Sep 77	3
Live recording.				
LONG LIVE ROCK 'N' ROLL	Polydor	33	8 Apr 78	3
L.A. CONNECTION	Polydor	40	30 Sep 78	4
SINCE YOU BEEN GONE	Polydor	6	15 Sep 79	10
Originally recorded by Russ Ballard.				
ALL NIGHT LONG	Polydor	5	16 Feb 80	11
I SURRENDER	Polydor	3	31 Jan 81	10
Originally recorded by Russ Ballard.				
CAN'T HAPPEN HERE	Polydor	20	20 Jun 81	8
KILL THE KING [RE]	Polydor	41	11 Jul 81	4
STONE COLD	Polydor	34	3 Apr 82	4
STREET OF DREAMS	Polydor	52	27 Aug 83	3
CAN'T LET YOU GO	Polydor	43	5 Nov 83	2
ALBUMS:	**HITS 10**			**WEEKS 163**
RITCHIE BLACKMORE'S RAINBOW	Oyster	11	13 Sep 75	6
RAINBOW RISING	Polydor	11	5 Jun 76	33
Above 2: Ritchie BLACKMORE'S RAINBOW.				
ON STAGE	Polydor	7	30 Jul 77	10
Live recordings from their 1976 tour.				
LONG LIVE ROCK 'N' ROLL	Polydor	7	6 May 78	12
DOWN TO EARTH	Polydor	6	18 Aug 79	37
DIFFICULT TO CURE	Polydor	3	21 Feb 81	22
RITCHIE BLACKMORE'S RAINBOW [RI]	Polydor	91	8 Aug 81	2
Above hit: Ritchie BLACKMORE'S RAINBOW.				
THE BEST OF RAINBOW	Polydor	14	21 Nov 81	17
STRAIGHT BETWEEN THE EYES	Polydor	5	24 Apr 82	14
BENT OUT OF SHAPE	Polydor	11	17 Sep 83	6

| FINYL VINYL | Polydor | 31 | 8 Mar 86 | 4 |

Compilation including live recordings and tracks only previously available as B-sides.

RAINBOW COTTAGE
UK

| SINGLES: | HITS 1 | | | WEEKS 4 |
| SEAGULL | Penny Farthing | 33 | 6 Mar 76 | 4 |

RAINDANCE
UK

(See also Blowing Free; Hypnosis; In Tune; School Of Excellence.)

| ALBUMS: | HITS 1 | | | WEEKS 7 |
| RAINDANCE | PolyGram TV | 15 | 27 Apr 96 | 7 |

RAINMAKERS
US

| SINGLES: | HITS 1 | | | WEEKS 11 |
| LET MY PEOPLE GO-GO | Mercury | 18 | 7 Mar 87 | 11 |

Marvin RAINWATER
US

SINGLES:	HITS 2			WEEKS 22
WHOLE LOTTA WOMAN	MGM	1	8 Mar 58	15
I DIG YOU BABY	MGM	19	7 Jun 58	7

Bonnie RAITT
US

SINGLES:	HITS 4			WEEKS 9
I CAN'T MAKE YOU LOVE ME	Capitol	50	14 Dec 91	4
LOVE SNEAKIN' UP ON YOU	Capitol	69	9 Apr 94	1
YOU	Capitol	31	18 Jun 94	2
ROCK STEADY	Capitol	50	11 Nov 95	2

Above hit: Bonnie RAITT and Bryan ADAMS.

ALBUMS:	HITS 5			WEEKS 15
NICK OF TIME	Capitol	51	28 Apr 90	5
LUCK OF THE DRAW	Capitol	38	6 Jul 91	3
LONGING IN THEIR HEARTS	Capitol	26	16 Apr 94	5
ROAD TESTED	Capitol	69	25 Nov 95	1

Live recordings from her 1995 world tour.

| FUNDAMENTAL | Capitol | 52 | 18 Apr 98 | 1 |

RAJA NEE
US

| SINGLES: | HITS 1 | | | WEEKS 2 |
| TURN IT UP | Perspective | 42 | 4 Mar 95 | 2 |

From the film 'Low Down Dirty Shame'.

RAKIM
US

(See also Eric B. and Rakim.)

| SINGLES: | HITS 5 | | | WEEKS 10 |
| CONTRIBUTION | Fourth & Broadway | 33 | 6 Oct 90 | 4 |

Above hit: Mica PARIS featuring RAKIM.

| GUESS WHO'S BACK | Universal | 32 | 27 Dec 97 | 3 |
| STAY A WHILE | Universal | 53 | 22 Aug 98 | 1 |

Samples Loose End's Stay A Little While Child.

| BUFFALO GALS STAMPEDE | Virgin | 65 | 3 Oct 98 | 1 |

Roger Sanchez remixed track 1 (as per CD order). Rakim appeared on track 2: Buffalo Gals (Back To Skool).
Above hit: Malcolm McLAREN and the WORLD FAMOUS SUPREME TEAM versus RAKIM and Roger SANCHEZ.

| METAFORCE | ZTT | 53 | 26 Jun 99 | 1 |

Homage to the French poet Charles Baudelaire. Includes narration by John Hurt.
Above hit: ART OF NOISE your forecaster: RAKIM.

| ALBUMS: | HITS 1 | | | WEEKS 1 |
| 18TH LETTER | Universal | 72 | 22 Nov 97 | 1 |

Big Sound of Don RALKE — See Ed BYRNES; Connie STEVENS

Tony RALLO and the MIDNITE BAND
US/France

| SINGLES: | HITS 1 | | | WEEKS 8 |
| HOLDIN' ON | Calibre | 34 | 23 Feb 80 | 8 |

Sheryl Lee RALPH
US

| SINGLES: | HITS 1 | | | WEEKS 2 |
| IN THE EVENING | Arista | 64 | 26 Jan 85 | 2 |

RAM JAM   US

SINGLES:		HITS 1			WEEKS 20	
BLACK BETTY		Epic	7	10 Sep 77	12
Originally recorded by Ledbelly.						
BLACK BETTY (ROUGH 'N READY REMIX) [RM]		Epic	13	17 Feb 90	8
Remixed by Ben Liebrand.						

RAM JAM BAND – See Geno WASHINGTON and the RAM JAM BAND

RAMBLERS – See Perry COMO

RAMBLERS (from the ABBEY HEY JUNIOR SCHOOL)   UK

SINGLES:		HITS 1			WEEKS 15	
THE SPARROW		Decca	11	13 Oct 79	15

Karen RAMIREZ   UK

SINGLES:		HITS 3			WEEKS 15	
TROUBLED GIRL		Manifesto	50	28 Mar 98	1
LOOKING FOR LOVE		Manifesto	8	27 Jun 98	11
IF WE TRY		Manifesto	23	21 Nov 98	3
ALBUMS:		HITS 1			WEEKS 2	
DISTANT DREAMS		Manifesto	45	1 Aug 98	2

RAMONES   US

SINGLES:		HITS 8			WEEKS 32	
SHEENA IS A PUNK ROCKER		Sire	22	21 May 77	7
SWALLOW MY PRIDE		Sire	36	6 Aug 77	3
DON'T COME CLOSE		Sire	39	30 Sep 78	5
ROCK 'N' ROLL HIGH SCHOOL		Sire	67	8 Sep 79	2
From the film of the same name.						
BABY, I LOVE YOU		Sire	8	26 Jan 80	9
DO YOU REMEMBER ROCK 'N' ROLL RADIO?		Sire	54	19 Apr 80	3
Sleeve credit: Rock N' Roll Radio.						
SOMETHING TO BELIEVE IN / SOMEBODY PUT SOMETHING IN MY DRINK		Beggars Banquet	69	10 May 86	1
POISON HEART		Chrysalis	69	19 Dec 92	2
ALBUMS:		HITS 10			WEEKS 29	
LEAVE HOME		Philips	45	23 Apr 77	1
ROCKET TO RUSSIA		Sire	60	24 Dec 77	2
ROAD TO RUIN		Sire	32	7 Oct 78	2
IT'S ALIVE		Sire	27	16 Jun 79	8
Live recordings from London's Rainbow Theatre.						
END OF THE CENTURY		Sire	14	19 Jan 80	8
TOO TOUGH TO DIE		Beggars Banquet	63	26 Jan 85	3
ANIMAL BOY		Beggars Banquet	38	31 May 86	2
HALFWAY TO SANITY		Beggars Banquet	78	10 Oct 87	1
BRAIN DRAIN		Chrysalis	75	19 Aug 89	1
!ADIOS AMIGOS!		Chrysalis	62	8 Jul 95	1

RAMP   UK

SINGLES:		HITS 1			WEEKS 1	
ROCK THE DISCOTEK '96		Loaded	49	8 Jun 96	1

RAMPAGE   UK

SINGLES:		HITS 1			WEEKS 1	
THE MONKEES		Almo	51	25 Nov 95	1
Jungle version of 'The Monkees' TV theme.						

RAMPAGE featuring Billy LAWRENCE   US

SINGLES:		HITS 1			WEEKS 1	
TAKE IT TO THE STREETS		Elektra	58	18 Oct 97	1

RAMRODS   US

SINGLES:		HITS 1			WEEKS 12	
RIDERS IN THE SKY		London	8	25 Feb 61	12
Originally recorded by Stan Jones.						

RANCID   US

SINGLES:		HITS 1			WEEKS 1	
TIME BOMB		Out Of Step	56	7 Oct 95	1
ALBUMS:		HITS 2			WEEKS 3	
... AND OUT COME THE WOLVES		Epitaph	55	2 Sep 95	1
LIFE WON'T WAIT		Epitaph	32	4 Jul 98	2

RANGE – See Bruce HORNSBY and the RANGE

RANKING ANN – See SCRITTI POLITTI

RANKING ROGER – See Pato BANTON

Cutty RANKS – See BLESSING

Shabba RANKS
Jamaica

SINGLES:		HITS 10			WEEKS 67
SHE'S A WOMAN					
Above hit: SCRITTI POLITTI (featuring Shabba RANKS).	Virgin	20	16 Mar 91	7
TRAILOR LOAD A GIRLS	Epic	63	18 May 91	2
HOUSECALL	Epic	31	24 Aug 91	7
Above hit: Shabba RANKS featuring Maxi PRIEST.				
MR. LOVERMAN	Epic	23	8 Aug 92	7
Features co-vocalist Chevelle Franklin.				
SLOW AND SEXY	Epic	17	28 Nov 92	7
Above hit: Shabba RANKS (featuring Johnny GILL).				
I WAS A KING	Motown	64	6 Mar 93	1
Above hit: Eddie MURPHY featuring Shabba RANKS.				
MR. LOVERMAN [RI]	Epic	3	13 Mar 93	11
From the film 'Deep Cover'.				
HOUSECALL [RI]	Epic	8	8 May 93	8
Above hit: Shabba RANKS featuring Maxi PRIEST.				
WHAT'CHA GONNA DO?	Epic	21	26 Jun 93	4
Above hit: Shabba RANKS featuring QUEEN LATIFAH.				
FAMILY AFFAIR	Polydor	18	25 Dec 93	8
From the film 'Addams Family Values'.				
Above hit: Shabba RANKS featuring PATRA and TERRI and MONICA.				
LET'S GET IT ON	Epic	22	29 Apr 95	3
SHINE EYE GAL	Epic	46	5 Aug 95	2
Above hit: Shabba RANKS (featuring Mykal ROSE).				
ALBUMS:		**HITS 3**		**WEEKS 10**
AS RAW AS EVER	Epic	51	22 Jun 91	2
ROUGH AND READY VOLUME 1	Epic	71	22 Aug 92	2
X-TRA NAKED	Epic	38	24 Apr 93	6

RAPINATION
Italy

SINGLES:		HITS 2			WEEKS 12
LOVE ME THE RIGHT WAY	Logic	22	26 Dec 92	10
Above hit: RAPINATION and Kym MAZELLE.				
HERE'S MY A	Logic	69	10 Jul 93	1
Above hit: RAPINATION featuring Carol KENYON.				
LOVE ME THE RIGHT WAY '96 [RM]	Logic	55	28 Sep 96	1
Remixed by the Rapino Brothers.				
Above hit: RAPINATION and Kym MAZELLE.				

RAPPIN' 4-TAY
US

SINGLES:		HITS 2			WEEKS 5
I'LL BE AROUND	Cooltempo	30	24 Jun 95	4
The (Detroit) Spinners vocals are sampled from their recording of the song.				
Above hit: RAPPIN' 4-TAY featuring the SPINNERS.				
PLAYAZ CLUB	Cooltempo	63	30 Sep 95	1

RAPSODY – See Warren G; SISSEL

RARE
UK

SINGLES:		HITS 1			WEEKS 1
SOMETHING WILD	Equator	57	17 Feb 96	1

RARE BIRD
UK

SINGLES:		HITS 1			WEEKS 8
SYMPATHY	Charisma	27	14 Feb 70	8

O. RASBURY – See Rahni HARRIS and F.L.O. vocals by T. HARRINGTON and ' O.' RASBURY

Roland RAT SUPERSTAR
UK

SINGLES:		HITS 4			WEEKS 26
RAT RAPPING (BRILLIANT ISN'T IT)	Rodent	14	19 Nov 83	12
LOVE ME TENDER	Rodent	32	28 Apr 84	7
SUMMER HOLIDAY	Rodent	50	4 Aug 84	6
Above hit: Roland RAT SUPERSTAR presents KEVIN THE GERBIL.				
NO. 1 RAT FAN	Rodent	72	2 Mar 85	1
ALBUMS:		**HITS 1**		**WEEKS 3**
THE CASSETTE OF THE ALBUM	Rodent	67	15 Dec 84	3

RATPACK
UK

SINGLES:	HITS 1			WEEKS 3
SEARCHIN' FOR MY RIZLA	Big Giant	58	6 Jun 92	3

RATT
US

ALBUMS:	HITS 4			WEEKS 5
INVASION OF YOUR PRIVACY	Atlantic	50	13 Jul 85	2
DANCING UNDERCOVER	Atlantic	51	25 Oct 86	1
REACH FOR THE SKY	Atlantic	82	12 Nov 88	1
DETONATOR	Atlantic	55	8 Sep 90	1

Simon RATTLE – See Nigel KENNEDY

RATTLES
Germany

SINGLES:	HITS 1			WEEKS 15
THE WITCH	Decca	8	3 Oct 70	15

Mark RATTRAY
UK

(See also Marti Webb and Mark Rattray.)

ALBUMS:	HITS 1			WEEKS 7
MARK RATTRAY PERFORMS THE SONGS OF THE MUSICALS	Telstar	46	8 Dec 90	7

Nick RAUCHEN conducting the BALL'S POND ROAD near "The One-in-Harmony" – See GOONS

RAVEN
UK

ALBUMS:	HITS 1			WEEKS 3
ROCK UNTIL YOU DROP	Neat	63	17 Oct 81	3

Thurl RAVENSCROFT – See Rosemary CLOONEY

RAVESIGNAL III
UK

(See also C.J. Bolland.)

SINGLES:	HITS 1			WEEKS 2
HORSEPOWER	R&S	61	14 Dec 91	2

RAW SILK
US

SINGLES:	HITS 2			WEEKS 12
DO IT TO THE MUSIC	KR	18	16 Oct 82	9
JUST IN TIME	West End	49	10 Sep 83	3

RAW STYLUS
UK

SINGLES:	HITS 1			WEEKS 1
BELIEVE IN ME	Wired	66	26 Oct 96	1

Lou RAWLS
US

(See also Philadelphia International All Stars: Lou Rawls, Billy Paul, Archie Bell, Teddy Pendergrass, O'Jays, Dee Dee Sharp, Gamble.)

SINGLES:	HITS 1			WEEKS 10
YOU'LL NEVER FIND ANOTHER LOVE LIKE MINE	Philadelphia International	10	31 Jul 76	10

Gene Anthony RAY – See KIDS FROM "FAME"

Jimmy RAY
UK

SINGLES:	HITS 2			WEEKS 6
ARE YOU JIMMY RAY?	Sony S2	13	25 Oct 97	5
GOIN' TO VEGAS	Sony S2	49	14 Feb 98	1

Johnnie RAY
US

SINGLES:	HITS 18			WEEKS 166
WALKIN' MY BABY BACK HOME	Columbia	12	15 Nov 52	1
Above hit: Johnnie RAY with the Buddy COLE QUARTET.				
FAITH CAN MOVE MOUNTAINS	Columbia	7	20 Dec 52	2
Above hit: Johnnie RAY and the FOUR LADS.				
FAITH CAN MOVE MOUNTAINS [RE]	Columbia	9	10 Jan 53	1
MA SAYS PA SAYS	Columbia	12	4 Apr 53	1
Above hit: Doris DAY and Johnnie RAY.				
SOMEBODY STOLE MY GAL	Philips	6	11 Apr 53	1
Above hit: Johnnie RAY with the Buddy COLE QUARTET.				
FULL TIME JOB	Columbia	11	18 Apr 53	1
Above entry and Ma Says Pa Says were separate sides of the same release, each had its own chart run.				
Above hit: Doris DAY and Johnnie RAY.				
SOMEBODY STOLE MY GAL [RE-1ST]	Philips	6	25 Apr 53	4

717

SOMEBODY STOLE MY GAL [RE-2ND]	*Philips*	12	*30 May 53*	1
LET'S WALK THAT-A-WAY	*Philips*	4	*25 Jul 53*	14
Above hit: Doris DAY and Johnnie RAY with Paul WESTON and his Orchestra.				
SOMEBODY STOLE MY GAL [RE-3RD]	*Philips*	11	*8 Aug 53*	1
SUCH A NIGHT	*Philips*	1	*10 Apr 54*	18
IF YOU BELIEVE	*Philips*	15	*9 Apr 55*	1
From the film 'There's No Business Like Show Business'.				
Above hit: Johnnie RAY with Percy FAITH and his Orchestra.				
IF YOU BELIEVE [RE]	*Philips*	7	*14 May 55*	10
PATHS OF PARADISE	*Philips*	20	*21 May 55*	1
Above hit: Johnnie RAY with Joe REISMAN and his Orchestra.				
HERNANDO'S HIDEAWAY	*Philips*	11	*8 Oct 55*	5
HEY THERE	*Philips*	5	*15 Oct 55*	9
Above 2 entries were separate sides of the same release, each had its own chart run.				
Above 2 from the film 'The Pajama Game'.				
SONG OF THE DREAMER	*Philips*	10	*29 Oct 55*	5
Above hit: Johnnie RAY with George SIRAVO and his Orchestra.				
WHO'S SORRY NOW	*Philips*	17	*18 Feb 56*	2
Above hit: Johnnie RAY with Paul WESTON and his Orchestra.				
AIN'T MISBEHAVIN'	*Philips*	17	*21 Apr 56*	6
AIN'T MISBEHAVIN' [RE]	*Philips*	24	*9 Jun 56*	1
JUST WALKING IN THE RAIN	*Philips*	1	*13 Oct 56*	19
Originally recorded by the Prisonaires.				
Above 3: Johnnie RAY with Ray CONNIFF and his Orchestra and Chorus.				
YOU DON'T OWE ME A THING/LOOK HOMEWARD, ANGEL	*Philips*	15	*19 Jan 57*	5
You Don't Owe Me A Thing originally recorded by Marty Robbins. Look Homeward Angel listed from 9 Feb 57. From 23 Feb 57 both sides had their own separate chart runs as listed below.				
LOOK HOMEWARD, ANGEL	*Philips*	7	*23 Feb 57*	14
YOU DON'T OWE ME A THING	*Philips*	12	*23 Feb 57*	10
YES TONIGHT, JOSEPHINE	*Philips*	1	*11 May 57*	16
BUILD YOUR LOVE (ON A STRONG FOUNDATION)	*Philips*	17	*7 Sep 57*	7
Above 5: Johnnie RAY with Ray CONNIFF.				
UP ABOVE MY HEAD, I HEAR MUSIC IN THE AIR / GOOD EVENING FRIENDS	*Philips*	25	*5 Oct 57*	4
Above hit: Johnnie RAY- Frankie LAINE with Ray CONNIFF and his Orchestra / Frankie LAINE- Johnnie RAY with Ray CONNIFF and his Orchestra.				
I'LL NEVER FALL IN LOVE AGAIN	*Philips*	26	*5 Dec 59*	4
I'LL NEVER FALL IN LOVE AGAIN [RE-1ST]	*Philips*	26	*9 Jan 60*	1
I'LL NEVER FALL IN LOVE AGAIN [RE-2ND]	*Philips*	28	*6 Feb 60*	1

Nicole RAY – See NICOLE

RAY-J
US

SINGLES:		HITS 1		WEEKS 1
THAT'S WHY I LIE	*Atlantic*	71	*17 Oct 98*	1
From the film 'Dr. Dolittle'.				

RAYDIO
US

SINGLES:		HITS 2		WEEKS 21
JACK AND JILL	*Arista*	11	*8 Apr 78*	12
IS THIS A LOVE THING	*Arista*	27	*8 Jul 78*	9

Simon RAYMOND – See Harold BUDD, Elizabeth FRASER, Robin GUTHRIE and Simon RAYMONDE

RAYVON – See SHAGGY

RAZE
US

(See also Doug Lazy; Legend.)

SINGLES:		HITS 4		WEEKS 41
JACK THE GROOVE	*Champion*	57	*1 Nov 86*	7
JACK THE GROOVE [RE]	*Champion*	20	*3 Jan 87*	8
LET THE MUSIC MOVE U	*Champion*	57	*28 Feb 87*	3
BREAK 4 LOVE	*Champion*	28	*31 Dec 88*	11
Originally released earlier in the year reaching No. 85.				
BREAK 4 LOVE [RE]	*Champion*	59	*2 Sep 89*	5
ALL FOR LOVE (BREAK FOR LOVE 1990) [RR]	*Champion*	30	*27 Jan 90*	5
Above hit: RAZE featuring LADY J and the SECRETARY OF ENT.				
BREAK 4 LOVE [RM]	*Champion*	44	*24 Sep 94*	2

RCA VICTOR ORCHESTRA – See Mario LANZA

RE-FLEX
UK

SINGLES:		HITS 1		WEEKS 9
THE POLITICS OF DANCING	*EMI*	28	*28 Jan 84*	9

Chris REA   UK

(See also Middlesborough FC featuring Bob Mortimer and Chris Rea.)

SINGLES:		HITS 30		WEEKS 119
FOOL (IF YOU THINK IT'S OVER)	Magnet	30	7 Oct 78	7
DIAMONDS	Magnet	44	21 Apr 79	3
LOVING YOU	Magnet	65	27 Mar 82	3
I CAN HEAR YOUR HEARTBEAT	Magnet	60	1 Oct 83	2
I DON'T KNOW WHAT IT IS BUT I LOVE IT	Magnet	65	17 Mar 84	2
STAINSBY GIRLS	Magnet	26	30 Mar 85	10
JOSEPHINE	Magnet	67	29 Jun 85	2
IT'S ALL GONE	Magnet	69	29 Mar 86	1
ON THE BEACH (SPECIAL REMIX)	Magnet	57	31 May 86	3
ON THE BEACH (SPECIAL REMIX) [RE-1ST]	Magnet	75	28 Jun 86	1
ON THE BEACH (SPECIAL REMIX) [RE-2ND]	Magnet	66	12 Jul 86	4
LET'S DANCE	Magnet	12	6 Jun 87	10
LOVING YOU AGAIN	Magnet	47	29 Aug 87	4
JOYS OF CHRISTMAS	Magnet	67	5 Dec 87	1
QUE SERA (RERECORDED '88)	Magnet	73	13 Feb 88	2
ON THE BEACH SUMMER '88 [RR]	WEA	12	13 Aug 88	6
I CAN HEAR YOUR HEARTBEAT [RR]	WEA	74	22 Oct 88	2
THE CHRISTMAS [EP]	WEA	53	17 Dec 88	3
Lead track: Driving Home For Christmas.				
WORKING ON IT	WEA	53	18 Feb 89	3
THE ROAD TO HELL (PARTS 1 & 2)	WEA	10	14 Oct 89	9
One track.				
TELL ME THERE'S A HEAVEN	East West	24	10 Feb 90	6
TEXAS	East West	69	5 May 90	1
AUBERGE	East West	16	16 Feb 91	6
HEAVEN	East West	57	6 Apr 91	2
LOOKING FOR THE SUMMER	East West	49	29 Jun 91	3
WINTER SONG	East West	27	9 Nov 91	4
NOTHING TO FEAR	East West	16	24 Oct 92	4
GOD'S GREAT BANANA SKIN	East West	31	28 Nov 92	3
SOFT TOP, HARD SHOULDER	East West	53	30 Jan 93	2
From the film of the same name.				
JULIA	Magnet	18	23 Oct 93	5
YOU CAN GO YOUR OWN WAY	East West	28	12 Nov 94	3
Adapted from the version featured in the Ford Probe car TV commercial.				
TELL ME THERE'S A HEAVEN [RI]	East West	70	24 Dec 94	1
'DISCO' LA PASSIONE	East West	41	16 Nov 96	1
From the film 'La Passione'.				
Above hit: Chris REA/Shirley BASSEY.				

ALBUMS:		HITS 17		WEEKS 343
DELTICS	Magnet	54	28 Apr 79	3
TENNIS	Magnet	60	12 Apr 80	1
CHRIS REA	Magnet	52	3 Apr 82	4
WATER SIGN	Magnet	64	18 Jun 83	2
WIRED TO THE MOON	Magnet	35	21 Apr 84	7
SHAMROCK DIARIES	Magnet	15	25 May 85	14
ON THE BEACH	Magnet	11	26 Apr 86	37
DANCING WITH STRANGERS	Magnet	2	26 Sep 87	46
ON THE BEACH [RI]	WEA	37	13 Aug 88	10
THE BEST OF CHIS REA – NEW LIGHT THROUGH OLD WINDOWS	WEA	5	29 Oct 88	49
Label change to East West from 24 Feb 90.				
THE ROAD TO HELL	WEA	1	11 Nov 89	69
Label change to East West from 17 Feb 90.				
AUBERGE	East West	1	9 Mar 91	37
GOD'S GREAT BANANA SKIN	East West	4	14 Nov 92	15
ESPRESSO LOGIC	East West	8	13 Nov 93	10
THE BEST OF CHIS REA – NEW LIGHT THROUGH OLD WINDOWS [RI]	East West	68	7 May 94	2
Re-released at mid-price.				
THE BEST OF CHRIS REA	East West	3	5 Nov 94	18
THE ROAD TO HELL [RI]	East West	23	18 Feb 95	7
Re-released at mid-price.				
LA PASSIONE [OST]	East West	43	23 Nov 96	4
THE BLUE CAFE	East West	10	31 Jan 98	7
THE ROAD TO HELL – PART 2	East West	54	20 Nov 99	1

REACT 2 RHYTHM   UK

SINGLES:		HITS 1		WEEKS 1
INTOXICATION	Jackpot	73	28 Jun 97	1
Originally released in 1991 with a remix in 1992.				

Eddi READER   UK

SINGLES:		HITS 5		WEEKS 14
PATIENCE OF ANGELS	Blanco Y Negro	33	4 Jun 94	5

JOKE (I'M LAUGHING)	Blanco Y Negro	42	13 Aug 94	3
DEAR JOHN	Blanco Y Negro	48	5 Nov 94	2
TOWN WITHOUT PITY	Blanco Y Negro	26	22 Jun 96	3
FRAGILE THING	Track Record	69	21 Aug 99	1

Above hit: BIG COUNTRY (featuring Eddi READER).

ALBUMS:	**HITS 4**		**WEEKS 21**	
MIRMAMA	RCA	34	7 Mar 92	2
EDDI READER	Blanco Y Negro	4	2 Jul 94	12
CANDYFLOSS AND MEDICINE	Blanco Y Negro	24	20 Jul 96	5
ANGELS & ELECTRICITY	Blanco Y Negro	49	23 May 98	2

READING CHOIR – See SLADE

READY FOR THE WORLD   US

SINGLES:	**HITS 2**		**WEEKS 8**	
OH SHEILA	MCA	50	26 Oct 85	5
LOVE YOU DOWN	MCA	60	14 Mar 87	3

REAL EMOTION   UK

SINGLES:	**HITS 1**		**WEEKS 1**	
BACK FOR GOOD	Living Beat	67	1 Jul 95	1

REAL McCOY   US/Germany

SINGLES:	**HITS 5**		**WEEKS 36**	
ANOTHER NIGHT	Logic	61	6 Nov 93	1
ANOTHER NIGHT [RM]	Logic	2	5 Nov 94	12

Remixed by the Berman Brothers.

| RUN AWAY | Logic | 6 | 28 Jan 95 | 10 |

Above 3: (MC SAR and) the REAL McCOY.

| LOVE & DEVOTION | Logic | 11 | 22 Apr 95 | 8 |
| COME AND GET YOUR LOVE | Logic | 19 | 26 Aug 95 | 4 |

Originally by Redbone reached No. 5 in the US in 1974.

| AUTOMATIC LOVER (CALL FOR LOVE) | Logic | 58 | 11 Nov 95 | 1 |

ALBUMS:	**HITS 1**		**WEEKS 5**	
ANOTHER NIGHT - U.S. ALBUM	Logic	6	20 May 95	5

REAL PEOPLE   UK

SINGLES:	**HITS 4**		**WEEKS 8**	
OPEN UP YOUR MIND (LET ME IN)	Columbia	70	16 Feb 91	1
THE TRUTH	Columbia	73	20 Apr 91	1
WINDOW PANE [EP]	Columbia	60	6 Jul 91	1

Lead track: Window Pane.

| THE TRUTH [RI] | Columbia | 41 | 11 Jan 92 | 3 |
| BELIEVER | Columbia | 38 | 23 May 92 | 2 |

ALBUMS:	**HITS 1**		**WEEKS 1**	
THE REAL PEOPLE	Columbia	59	18 May 91	1

REAL ROXANNE   US

SINGLES:	**HITS 2**		**WEEKS 10**	
(BANG ZOOM) LET'S GO GO	Cooltempo	11	28 Jun 86	9

Above hit: REAL ROXANNE with HITMAN HOWIE TEE.

| RESPECT | Cooltempo | 71 | 12 Nov 88 | 1 |

Features vocals by Dee Dee Scott.

REAL THING   UK

SINGLES:	**HITS 11**		**WEEKS 114**	
YOU TO ME ARE EVERYTHING	Pye International	1	5 Jun 76	11
CAN'T GET BY WITHOUT YOU	Pye	2	4 Sep 76	10

Originally recorded by Carl Lewis.

YOU'LL NEVER KNOW WHAT YOU'RE MISSING	Pye	16	12 Feb 77	9
LOVE'S SUCH A WONDERFUL THING	Pye	33	30 Jul 77	5
WHENEVER YOU WANT MY LOVE	Pye	18	4 Mar 78	9
LET'S GO DISCO	Pye	39	3 Jun 78	7

From the film 'The Stud'.

RAININ' THROUGH MY SUNSHINE	Pye	40	12 Aug 78	8
CAN YOU FEEL THE FORCE?	Pye	5	17 Feb 79	11
BOOGIE DOWN (GET FUNKY NOW)	Pye	33	21 Jul 79	6
SHE'S A GROOVY FREAK	Calibre	52	22 Nov 80	4
YOU TO ME ARE EVERYTHING (THE DECADE REMIX '76-'86) [RM]	PRT	5	8 Mar 86	12

Remixed by Froggy, Simon Harris and KC.

CAN'T GET BY WITHOUT YOU (THE SECOND DECADE REMIX) [RM]	PRT	6	24 May 86	13
YOU TO ME ARE EVERYTHING (THE DECADE REMIX '76-'86) [RM] [RE]	PRT	72	7 Jun 86	1
CAN YOU FEEL THE FORCE? ('86 MIX) [RM]	PRT	24	2 Aug 86	6

Above 2 remixed by Bob Mallett.

| STRAIGHT TO THE HEART | Jive | 71 | 25 Oct 86 | 2 |

Cliff Richard *is the only artist to have No.1 hits in five decades. (Harry Goodwin)*

Run DMC *were the first band to wait more than 10 years between their first hit and their first chart topper. (LFI)*

Del Shannon*'s cover of 'From Me To You' was the first Lennon/McCartney composition to chart in the US. (LFI)*

Sixpence None The Richer *took their name from a passage in* Mere Christianity, *a book by C.S. Lewis. (LFI)*

Sandie Shaw *was the first Eurovision winner to top the UK chart. (Harry Goodwin)*

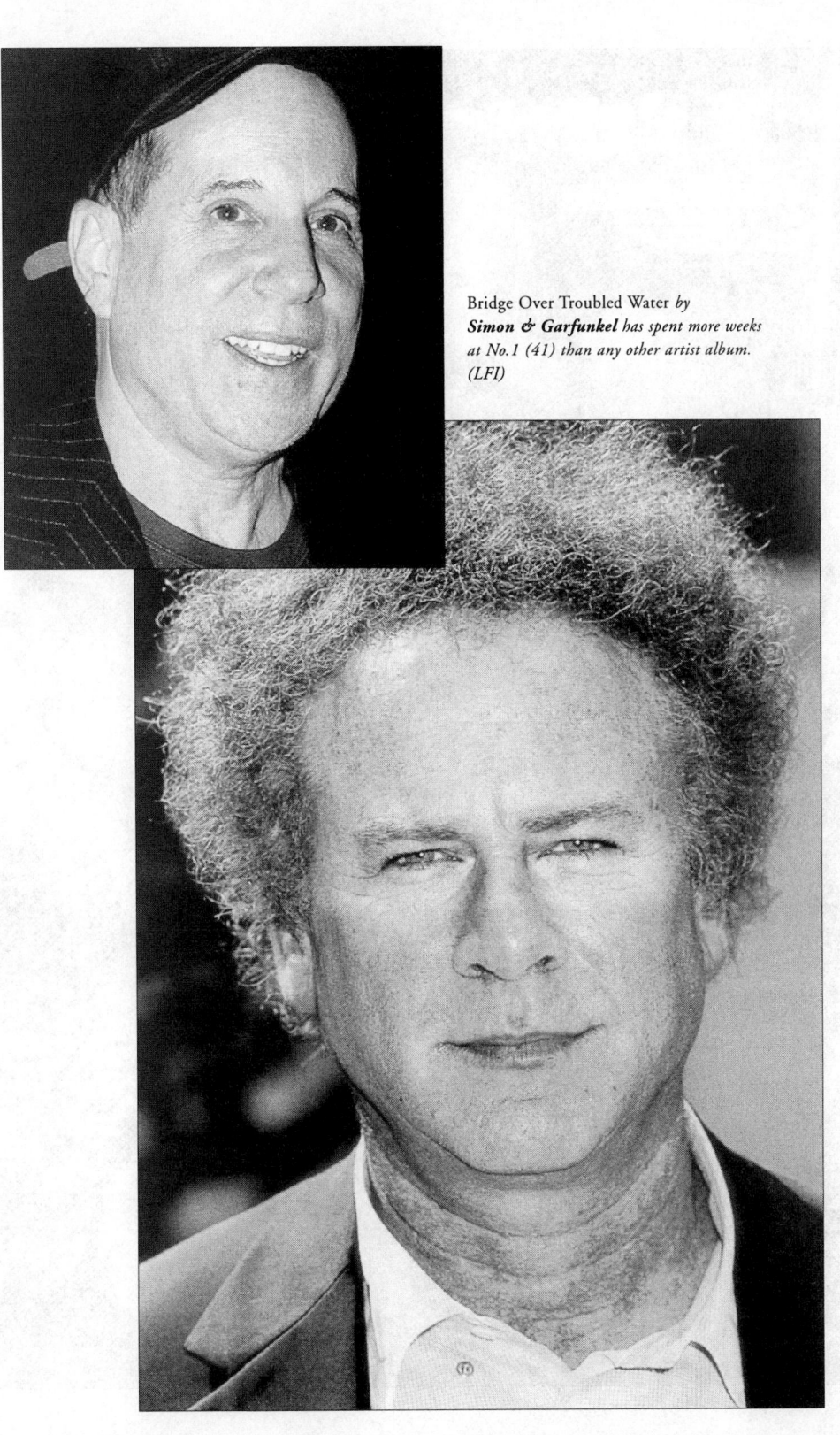

Bridge Over Troubled Water *by*
Simon & Garfunkel *has spent more weeks
at No.1 (41) than any other artist album.
(LFI)*

The Spice Girls were the first act since The Beatles to have three consecutive Christmas No. 1s. (LFI)

'Baby One More Time' by **Britney Spears** sold 463,722 copies in its first week on sale, the fastest selling single by a new act. (LFI)

ALBUMS:		HITS 4		WEEKS 17	
REAL THING	Pye	34	6 Nov 76	3
CAN YOU FEEL THE FORCE	Pye	73	7 Apr 79	1
20 GREATEST HITS	K-Tel	56	10 May 80	2
THE BEST OF THE REAL THING	West Five	24	12 Jul 86	11

REAL TO REEL   US

SINGLES:		HITS 1		WEEKS 2	
LOVE ME LIKE THIS	Arista	68	21 Apr 84	2

REBEL MC   UK

SINGLES:		HITS 9		WEEKS 52	
JUST KEEP ROCKIN'	Desire	11	27 May 89	12
Above hit: DOUBLE TROUBLE and the REBEL MC.				
STREET TUFF	Desire	3	7 Oct 89	14
Above hit: REBEL MC DOUBLE TROUBLE.				
BETTER WORLD	Desire	20	31 Mar 90	6
REBEL MUSIC	Desire	53	2 Jun 90	2
THE WICKEDEST SOUND	Desire	43	6 Apr 91	6
Above hit: REBEL MC (featuring TENOR FLY).				
TRIBAL BASE	Desire	20	15 Jun 91	6
Above hit: REBEL M.C. featuring TENOR FLY and Barrington LEVY.				
BLACK MEANING GOOD	Desire	73	31 Aug 91	1
RICH AH GETTING RICHER	Big Life	48	21 Mar 92	4
Above hit: REBEL M.C. introducing LITTLE T.				
HUMANITY	Big Life	62	8 Aug 92	1
Above hit: REBEL M.C. featuring Prince Lincoln THOMPSON.				
ALBUMS:		HITS 2		WEEKS 11	
REBEL MUSIC	Desire	18	28 Apr 90	7
BLACK MEANING GOOD	Desire	23	13 Jul 91	4

REBEL ROUSERS – See Cliff BENNETT and the REBEL ROUSERS

REBELETTES – See Duane EDDY

REBELS – See Duane EDDY

Ivan REBROFF   Russia

ALBUMS:		HITS 1		WEEKS 4	
THE VERY BEST OF IVAN REBROFF	BBC	57	16 Jun 90	4

Ezz RECO and the LAUNCHERS with Boysie GRANT   Jamaica

SINGLES:		HITS 1		WEEKS 4	
KING OF KINGS	Columbia	44	7 Mar 64	4
Originally recorded by Jimmy Cliff.				

RECOIL   UK

SINGLES:		HITS 1		WEEKS 1	
FAITH HEALER	Mute	60	21 Mar 92	1

RED BOX   UK

SINGLES:		HITS 3		WEEKS 28	
LEAN ON ME (AH-LI-AYO)	Sire	3	24 Aug 85	14
FOR AMERICA	Sire	10	25 Oct 86	12
HEART OF THE SUN	Sire	71	31 Jan 87	2
ALBUMS:		HITS 1		WEEKS 4	
THE CIRCLE AND THE SQUARE	Sire	73	6 Dec 86	4

RED CAR AND THE BLUE CAR   UK

SINGLES:		HITS 1		WEEKS 4	
HOME FOR CHRISTMAS DAY	Virgin	44	14 Dec 91	4

RED DRAGON with Brian and Tony GOLD   Jamaica

SINGLES:		HITS 1		WEEKS 15	
COMPLIMENTS ON YOUR KISS	Mango	2	30 Jul 94	13
COMPLIMENTS ON YOUR KISS [RE]	Mango	49	31 Dec 94	2

RED EYE   UK

SINGLES:		HITS 1		WEEKS 1	
KUT IT	Champion	62	3 Dec 94	1

RED 5
Germany

SINGLES:	HITS 2			WEEKS 10
I LOVE YOU . . . STOP!	*Multiply*	11	*10 May 97*	5
Vocals by Maxine Harvey.				
LIFT ME UP	*Multiply*	26	*20 Dec 97*	5

RED HILL CHILDREN
UK

SINGLES:	HITS 1			WEEKS 2
WHEN CHILDREN RULE THE WORLD	*Really Useful*	40	*30 Nov 96*	2
From the Andrew Lloyd Webber musical 'Whistle Down The Wind'. Also used as the theme tune for the BBC's Children In Need appeal.				

RED HOT CHILI PEPPERS
US

SINGLES:	HITS 11			WEEKS 49
HIGHER GROUND	*EMI USA*	55	*10 Feb 90*	3
TASTE THE PAIN	*EMI USA*	29	*23 Jun 90*	3
HIGHER GROUND [RI]	*EMI USA*	54	*8 Sep 90*	3
UNDER THE BRIDGE	*Warner Brothers*	26	*14 Mar 92*	4
BREAKING THE GIRL	*Warner Brothers*	41	*15 Aug 92*	3
GIVE IT AWAY	*Warner Brothers*	9	*5 Feb 94*	4
UNDER THE BRIDGE [RI]	*Warner Brothers*	13	*30 Apr 94*	6
WARPED	*Warner Brothers*	31	*2 Sep 95*	2
MY FRIENDS	*Warner Brothers*	29	*21 Oct 95*	2
AEROPLANE	*Warner Brothers*	11	*17 Feb 96*	3
Child vocal from Flea's daughter Clara.				
LOVE ROLLERCOASTER	*Geffen*	7	*14 Jun 97*	8
Original by the Ohio Players reached No. 1 in the US in 1976. From the film 'Beavis And Butt-Head Do America'.				
SCAR TISSUE	*Warner Brothers*	15	*12 Jun 99*	6
AROUND THE WORLD	*Warner Brothers*	35	*4 Sept 99*	2
ALBUMS:	HITS 5			WEEKS 114
BLOOD SUGAR SEX MAGIK	*Warner Brothers*	25	*12 Oct 91*	72
Includes re-entries through to 1999.				
WHAT HITS!?	*EMI USA*	23	*17 Oct 92*	6
OUT IN LA	*EMI*	61	*19 Nov 94*	1
Demos, remixes, live recordings and previously unreleased tracks.				
ONE HOT MINUTE	*Warner Brothers*	2	*23 Sep 95*	11
CALIFORNICATION	*Warner Brothers*	5	*19 Jun 99*	24

RED HOUSE PAINTERS
US

ALBUMS:	HITS 2			WEEKS 2
RED HOUSE PAINTERS	*4AD*	63	*5 Jun 93*	1
RED HOUSE PAINTERS	*4AD*	68	*30 Oct 93*	1
Both albums are different.				

RED JERRY – See WESTBAM

RED NOISE – See Bill NELSON

RED NOSED BURGLARS – See Ivor BIGGUN

RED RAT – See Phoebe ONE featuring RED RAT, GOOFY and BUCCANEER (MAIN STREET CREW); R.I.P. PRODUCTIONS

RED RAW featuring 007
UK

SINGLES:	HITS 1			WEEKS 1
OOH LA LA LA	*Media*	59	*28 Oct 95*	1

RED SNAPPER
UK

SINGLES:	HITS 1			WEEKS 1
IMAGE OF YOU	*Warp*	60	*21 Nov 98*	1
ALBUMS:	HITS 2			WEEKS 2
PRINCE BLIMEY	*Warp*	60	*21 Sep 96*	1
MAKING BONES	*Warp*	59	*10 Oct 98*	1

RED VENOM – See BIG BOSS STYLUS presents RED VENOM

REDBONE
US

SINGLES:	HITS 1			WEEKS 12
THE WITCH QUEEN OF NEW ORLEANS	*Epic*	2	*25 Sep 71*	12

Sharon REDD
US

SINGLES:	HITS 5			WEEKS 32
CAN YOU HANDLE IT	*Epic*	31	*28 Feb 81*	8
NEVER GIVE YOU UP / BEAT THE STREET	*Prelude*	20	*2 Oct 82*	9

IN THE NAME OF LOVE	Prelude	31	15 Jan 83	5
LOVE HOW YOU FEEL	Prelude	39	22 Oct 83	5
CAN YOU HANDLE IT	EMI	17	1 Feb 92	5

Above hit: DNA featuring Sharon REDD.

ALBUMS:	HITS 1			WEEKS 5
REDD HOTT	Prelude	59	23 Oct 82	5

REDD KROSS | US

SINGLES:	HITS 3			WEEKS 4
VISIONARY	This Way Up	75	5 Feb 94	1
YESTERDAY ONCE MORE	A&M	45	10 Sep 94	2

[AA] listed with Superstar by Sonic Youth. From the 25th Anniversary tribute album to the Carpenters, If I Were A Carpenter.

GET OUT OF MYSELF	This Way Up	63	1 Feb 97	1

Otis REDDING | US

(See also Otis Redding and Carla Thomas.)

SINGLES:	HITS 13			WEEKS 108
MY GIRL	Atlantic	11	27 Nov 65	16
(I CAN'T GET NO) SATISFACTION	Atlantic	33	9 Apr 66	4
MY LOVER'S PRAYER	Atlantic	37	16 Jul 66	6
I CAN'T TURN YOU LOOSE	Atlantic	29	27 Aug 66	8
FA FA FA FA FA (SAD SONGS)	Atlantic	23	26 Nov 66	9
TRY A LITTLE TENDERNESS	Atlantic	46	28 Jan 67	4

Originally recorded by Ted Lewis in 1933.

DAY TRIPPER	Stax	43	25 Mar 67	6
LET ME COME ON HOME	Stax	48	6 May 67	1
SHAKE	Stax	28	17 Jun 67	10
MY GIRL [RI]	Atlantic	36	17 Feb 68	9
(SITTIN' ON) THE DOCK OF THE BAY	Stax	3	24 Feb 68	15
THE HAPPY SONG (DUM-DUM)	Stax	24	1 Jun 68	5
HARD TO HANDLE	Atlantic	15	3 Aug 68	12
LOVE MAN	Atco	43	12 Jul 69	3

ALBUMS:	HITS 9			WEEKS 208
OTIS BLUE: OTIS REDDING SINGS SOUL	Atlantic	6	19 Feb 66	21
OTIS BLUE: OTIS REDDING SINGS SOUL [RE]	Atlantic	7	21 Jan 67	54

Re-released with a new catalogue number. Peak position reached in 1968.

THE GREAT OTIS REDDING SINGS SOUL BALLADS	Atlantic	30	23 Apr 66	1

Originally released in 1965.

THE SOUL ALBUM	Atlantic	22	23 Jul 66	9
COMPLETE AND UNBELIEVABLE . . . THE OTIS REDDING DICTIONARY OF SOUL	Atlantic	23	21 Jan 67	16
PAIN IN MY HEART	Atlantic	28	29 Apr 67	9
THE HISTORY OF OTIS REDDING	Stax	2	10 Feb 68	43
OTIS REDDING IN EUROPE	Stax	14	30 Mar 68	16

Live recordings.

DOCK OF THE BAY	Stax	1	1 Jun 68	15

Compilation.

IMMORTAL OTIS REDDING	Atlantic	19	12 Oct 68	8
DOCK OF THE BAY - THE DEFINITIVE COLLECTION[RI]	Atlantic	50	11 Sept 93	16

Remastered CD re-issue of Dock Of The Bay, which was originally released in 1992. Its first chart appearance was after 'The Atlantic Story' was broadcast on Channel 4. Includes re-entries through to 1998.

Otis REDDING and Carla THOMAS | US

(See also Otis Redding.)

SINGLES:	HITS 2			WEEKS 16
TRAMP	Stax	18	22 Jul 67	11

Originally recorded by Lowell Fulsom.

KNOCK ON WOOD	Stax	35	14 Oct 67	5

ALBUMS:	HITS 1			WEEKS 17
KING AND QUEEN	Atlantic	18	1 Jul 67	17

Helen REDDY | Australia

SINGLES:	HITS 2			WEEKS 18
ANGIE BABY	Capitol	5	18 Jan 75	10

Originally recorded by Alan O'Day.

I CAN'T SAY GOODBYE TO YOU	MCA	43	28 Nov 81	8

ALBUMS:	HITS 2			WEEKS 27
FREE AND EASY	Capitol	17	8 Feb 75	9
THE BEST OF HELEN REDDY	Capitol	6	14 Feb 76	18

REDHEAD KINGPIN and the F.B.I.   US

SINGLES:	HITS 2			WEEKS 11	
DO THE RIGHT THING	10 Records	13	22 Jul 89	10
SUPERBAD SUPERSLICK	10 Records	68	2 Dec 89	1
ALBUMS:	HITS 1			WEEKS 3	
A SHADE OF RED	10 Records	35	9 Sep 89	3

REDMAN   US

(See also KRS One; Method Man and Redman.)

SINGLES:	HITS 4			WEEKS 18	
RAP SCHOLAR	East West America	42	25 Apr 98	1
Above hit: DAS EFX featuring REDMAN.				
HOW DEEP IS YOUR LOVE	Island Black Music	9	24 Oct 98	7
Above hit: DRU HILL (featuring REDMAN).				
HOW DEEP IS YOUR LOVE [RE]	Island Black Music	75	16 Jan 99	1
MADE IT BACK 99 [RM]	Parlophone Rhythm Series	19	10 Apr 99	5
Samples Chic's Good Times.				
Above hit: Beverley KNIGHT featuring REDMAN.				
DA GOODNESS	Def Jam	52	12 Jun 99	1
Samples Duke Ellington's Caravan.				

REDNEX   Sweden

SINGLES:	HITS 3			WEEKS 23	
COTTON EYE JOE	Internal Affairs	1	17 Dec 94	16
Originally recorded by Bob Wills and his Texas Playboys.				
OLD POP IN AN OAK	Internal Affairs	12	25 Mar 95	6
WILD 'N FREE	Internal Affairs	55	21 Oct 95	1

REDS UNITED   UK

SINGLES:	HITS 2			WEEKS 13	
SING UP FOR THE CHAMPIONS!	Music Collection International	12	6 Dec 97	9
The Official 1997 Manchester United supporters' single.				
UNITED CALYPSO '98	Music Collection International	33	9 May 98	4
The Official 1998 Manchester United supporters' single. First recorded in 1954.				

REDSKINS   UK

SINGLES:	HITS 3			WEEKS 12	
KEEP ON KEEPIN' ON!	Decca	43	10 Nov 84	5
(BURN IT UP) BRING IT DOWN! (THIS INSANE THING)	Decca	33	22 Jun 85	5
THE POWER IS YOURS	Decca	59	22 Feb 86	2
ALBUMS:	HITS 1			WEEKS 4	
NEITHER WASHINGTON NOR MOSCOW ...	Decca	31	22 Mar 86	4

Alex REECE   UK

SINGLES:	HITS 3			WEEKS 7	
FEEL THE SUNSHINE	Blunted Vinyl	69	16 Dec 95	1
Vocals by Deborah Anderson.				
FEEL THE SUNSHINE – REMIXES [RI]	Fourth & Broadway	26	11 May 96	3
Though listed as a remix, the first track on CD1 is the original version.				
CANDLES	Fourth & Broadway	33	27 Jul 96	2
ACID LAB	Fourth & Broadway	64	16 Nov 96	1
ALBUMS:	HITS 1			WEEKS 5	
SO FAR	Fourth & Broadway	19	17 Aug 96	5

Dan REED NETWORK   US

SINGLES:	HITS 6			WEEKS 16	
COME BACK BABY	Mercury	51	20 Jan 90	3
RAINBOW CHILD	Mercury	60	17 Mar 90	3
STARDATE 1990 / RAINBOW CHILD [RI]	Mercury	39	21 Jul 90	4
From 4 Aug 90 titles were listed in reverse.				
LOVER/MONEY	Mercury	45	8 Sep 90	3
MIX IT UP	Mercury	49	13 Jul 91	2
BABY NOW I	Mercury	65	21 Sep 91	1
ALBUMS:	HITS 2			WEEKS 6	
SLAM	Mercury	66	4 Nov 89	2
THE HEAT	Mercury	15	27 Jul 91	4

Eileen REED – See CADETS with Eileen REED lead vocal

Jimmy REED   US

SINGLES:	HITS 1			WEEKS 2	
SHAME SHAME SHAME	Stateside	45	12 Sep 64	2

Les REED ORCHESTRA and CHORUS – See Donald PEERS

Lou REED   US

SINGLES:	HITS 2			WEEKS 19	
WALK ON THE WILD SIDE	RCA Victor	10	12 May 73	9
SOUL MAN	A&M	30	17 Jan 87	10
From the film of the same name.
Above hit: Sam MOORE and Lou REED.

ALBUMS:	HITS 12			WEEKS 85	
TRANSFORMER	RCA Victor	13	21 Apr 73	25
BERLIN	RCA Victor	7	20 Oct 73	5
ROCK 'N' ROLL ANIMAL	RCA Victor	26	16 Mar 74	1
Live recordings from New York's Academy of Music.
CONEY ISLAND BABY	RCA Victor	52	14 Feb 76	1
TRANSFORMER [RI-1ST]	RCA International	91	3 Jul 82	2
NEW SENSATIONS	RCA	92	9 Jun 84	1
MISTRIAL	RCA	69	24 May 86	1
NEW YORK	Sire	14	28 Jan 89	22
RETRO	RCA	29	7 Oct 89	5
SONGS FOR DRELLA	Sire	22	5 May 90	5
Above hit: Lou REED and John CALE.
| MAGIC AND LOSS | Sire | 6 | 25 Jan 92 | 6 |
| THE BEST OF LOU REED AND THE VELVET UNDERGROUND | Global Television | 56 | 28 Oct 95 | 4 |
Features both Lou Reed's solo and group material.
Above hit: Lou REED and the VELVET UNDERGROUND.
| SET THE TWILIGHT REELING | Warner Brothers | 26 | 2 Mar 96 | 2 |
| TRANSFORMER [RI-2ND] | RCA | 32 | 7 Feb 98 | 8 |
Peak position reached in 1999.

Michael REED ORCHESTRA   UK

SINGLES:	HITS 1			WEEKS 10	
THE MUSIC OF TORVILL AND DEAN [EP]	Safari	9	25 Feb 84	10
Lead track: Bolero. Although uncredited, the first two tracks on the EP are, in fact, by Richard Hartley.

Don REEDMAN – See Jeff JARRATT and Don REEDMAN

REEF   UK

SINGLES:	HITS 10			WEEKS 39	
GOOD FEELING	Sony S2	24	15 Apr 95	4
NAKED	Sony S2	11	3 Jun 95	5
WEIRD	Sony S2	19	5 Aug 95	3
PLACE YOUR HANDS	Sony S2	6	2 Nov 96	7
COME BACK BRIGHTER	Sony S2	8	25 Jan 97	5
CONSIDERATION	Sony S2	13	5 Apr 97	4
YER OLD	Sony S2	21	2 Aug 97	3
I'VE GOT SOMETHING TO SAY	Sony S2	15	10 Apr 99	6
SWEETY	Sony S2	46	5 Jun 99	1
NEW BIRD	Sony S2	73	11 Sept 99	1

ALBUMS:	HITS 3			WEEKS 50	
REPLENISH	Sony S2	9	1 Jul 95	11
GLOW	Sony S2	1	8 Feb 97	32
RIDES	Sony S2	3	1 May 99	7

REEL 2 REAL featuring the MAD STUNTMAN   US

SINGLES:	HITS 7			WEEKS 53	
I LIKE TO MOVE IT	Positiva	5	12 Feb 94	20
GO ON MOVE	Positiva	7	2 Jul 94	9
CAN YOU FEEL IT?	Positiva	13	1 Oct 94	5
Duet with Althea McQueen.
RAISE YOUR HANDS	Positiva	14	3 Dec 94	6
CONWAY	Positiva	27	1 Apr 95	4
JAZZ IT UP	Positiva	7	6 Jul 96	7
ARE YOU READY FOR SOME MORE?	Positiva	24	5 Oct 96	2
Above 2: REEL 2 REAL.

ALBUMS:	HITS 1			WEEKS 8	
MOVE IT!	Positiva	8	22 Oct 94	8

Maureen REES   UK

SINGLES:	HITS 1			WEEKS 4	
DRIVING IN MY CAR	Eagle	49	20 Dec 97	4

Tony REES and the COTTAGERS | UK

SINGLES:		HITS 1		WEEKS 1
VIVA EL FULHAM (BASED ON Y VIVA ESPANA)	*Sonet*	46	*10 May 75*	1

REESE PROJECT | US

SINGLES:		HITS 4		WEEKS 7
THE COLOUR OF LOVE	*Network*	52	*8 Aug 92*	2
I BELIEVE	*Network*	74	*12 Dec 92*	1
Featured vocals from Terrence FM.				
SO DEEP	*Network*	54	*13 Mar 93*	2
THE COLOUR OF LOVE [RM]	*Network*	55	*24 Sep 94*	1
Remixed by the Playboys (Tim Jeffrey and J. Creid).				
DIRECT-ME	*Network*	44	*6 May 95*	1
Originally recorded in 1991. Vocals by Rachel Kapp.				

Conner REEVES | UK

SINGLES:		HITS 5		WEEKS 18
MY FATHER'S SON	*Wildstar*	12	*30 Aug 97*	5
EARTHBOUND	*Wildstar*	14	*22 Nov 97*	4
READ MY MIND	*Wildstar*	19	*11 Apr 98*	4
SEARCHING FOR A SOUL	*Wildstar*	28	*3 Oct 98*	2
BEST FRIEND	*WEA*	23	*04 Sept 99*	3
Above hit: Mark MORRISON and Conner REEVES.				
ALBUMS:		HITS 1		WEEKS 8
EARTHBOUND	*Wildstar*	25	*6 Dec 97*	8

Jim REEVES | US

SINGLES:		HITS 26		WEEKS 322
HE'LL HAVE TO GO	*RCA*	36	*26 Mar 60*	1
Originally recorded by Billy Brown.				
HE'LL HAVE TO GO [RE]	*RCA*	12	*9 Apr 60*	30
WHISPERING HOPE	*RCA*	50	*18 Mar 61*	1
YOU'RE THE ONLY GOOD THING (THAT HAPPENED TO ME)	*RCA*	17	*25 Nov 61*	19
ADIOS AMIGO	*RCA*	23	*30 Jun 62*	21
I'M GONNA CHANGE EVERYTHING	*RCA*	42	*24 Nov 62*	2
WELCOME TO MY WORLD	*RCA Victor*	6	*15 Jun 63*	15
GUILTY	*RCA Victor*	29	*19 Oct 63*	7
I LOVE YOU BECAUSE	*RCA Victor*	5	*22 Feb 64*	39
Originally recorded by Leon Payne in 1950.				
I WON'T FORGET YOU	*RCA Victor*	3	*20 Jun 64*	25
THERE'S A HEARTACHE FOLLOWING ME	*RCA Victor*	6	*7 Nov 64*	13
I WON'T FORGET YOU [RE]	*RCA Victor*	47	*9 Jan 65*	1
IT HURTS SO MUCH (TO SEE YOU GO)	*RCA Victor*	8	*6 Feb 65*	10
NOT UNTIL THE NEXT TIME	*RCA Victor*	13	*17 Apr 65*	12
HOW LONG HAS IT BEEN	*RCA Victor*	45	*8 May 65*	5
THIS WORLD IS NOT MY HOME	*RCA Victor*	22	*17 Jul 65*	9
Recorded in 1962.				
IS IT REALLY OVER	*RCA Victor*	17	*13 Nov 65*	9
DISTANT DRUMS	*RCA Victor*	1	*20 Aug 66*	25
First UK No.1 written solely by a female, Cindy Walker. Originally recorded by Roy Orbison.				
I WON'T COME IN WHILE HE'S THERE	*RCA Victor*	12	*4 Feb 67*	11
TRYING TO FORGET	*RCA Victor*	33	*29 Jul 67*	5
I HEARD A HEART BREAK LAST NIGHT	*RCA Victor*	38	*25 Nov 67*	6
PRETTY BROWN EYES	*RCA Victor*	33	*30 Mar 68*	5
WHEN TWO WORLDS COLLIDE	*RCA Victor*	17	*28 Jun 69*	17
BUT YOU LOVE ME DADDY	*RCA Victor*	15	*6 Dec 69*	16
Above hit: Jim REEVES with Steve MOORE.				
NOBODY'S FOOL	*RCA Victor*	32	*21 Mar 70*	5
ANGELS DON'T LIE	*RCA Victor*	44	*12 Sep 70*	1
ANGELS DON'T LIE [RE]	*RCA Victor*	32	*26 Sep 70*	2
I LOVE YOU BECAUSE [RI] / HE'LL HAVE TO GO [RI] / MOONLIGHT AND ROSES (BRING BACK MEMORIES OF YOU)	*RCA Victor Maximillion*	34	*26 Jun 71*	8
YOU'RE FREE TO GO	*RCA Victor*	48	*19 Feb 72*	2
EPS:		HITS 6		WEEKS 79
SONGS TO WARM THE HEART	*RCA*	12	*1 Dec 62*	12
WELCOME TO MY WORLD	*RCA Victor*	6	*4 Apr 64*	25
FROM THE HEART	*RCA Victor*	4	*15 Aug 64*	26
SONGS TO WARM THE HEART VOLUME 2	*RCA Victor*	9	*12 Sep 64*	10
FROM THE HEART VOLUME 2	*RCA Victor*	14	*26 Sep 64*	1
CHRISTMAS CARD FROM JIM REEVES	*RCA Victor*	3	*3 Dec 66*	5
ALBUMS:		HITS 28		WEEKS 399
GOOD 'N' COUNTRY	*RCA Camden*	10	*28 Mar 64*	35
GENTLEMAN JIM	*RCA Victor*	3	*9 May 64*	23
A TOUCH OF VELVET	*RCA Victor*	8	*15 Aug 64*	9

INTERNATIONAL JIM REEVES	*RCA Victor*	11	*15 Aug 64*	17
HE'LL HAVE TO GO	*RCA Victor*	16	*22 Aug 64*	4
GOD BE WITH YOU	*RCA Victor*	10	*29 Aug 64*	10
THE INTIMATE JIM REEVES	*RCA Victor*	12	*29 Aug 64*	4
MOONLIGHT AND ROSES	*RCA Victor*	2	*5 Sep 64*	52
COUNTRY SIDE OF JIM REEVES	*RCA Camden*	12	*19 Sep 64*	5
WE THANK THEE	*RCA Victor*	17	*26 Sep 64*	3
TWELVE SONGS OF CHRISTMAS	*RCA Victor*	4	*28 Nov 64*	17
Includes re-entries through to 1970.				
THE BEST OF JIM REEVES	*RCA Victor*	3	*30 Jan 65*	47
HAVE I TOLD YOU LATELY THAT I LOVE YOU	*RCA Camden*	12	*10 Apr 65*	5
THE JIM REEVES WAY	*RCA Victor*	16	*22 May 65*	4
DISTANT DRUMS	*RCA Victor*	2	*5 Nov 66*	34
Compilation.				
A TOUCH OF SADNESS	*RCA Victor*	15	*18 Jan 69*	5
ACCORDING TO MY HEART	*RCA International*	1	*5 Jul 69*	14
JIM REEVES AND SOME FRIENDS	*RCA Victor*	24	*23 Aug 69*	4
ON STAGE	*RCA Victor*	13	*29 Nov 69*	4
MY CATHEDRAL	*RCA Victor*	48	*26 Dec 70*	2
JIM REEVES WRITES YOU A RECORD	*RCA Victor*	47	*3 Jul 71*	2
JIM REEVES' GOLDEN RECORDS	*RCA International*	9	*7 Aug 71*	21
THE INTIMATE JIM REEVES [RI]	*RCA International*	8	*14 Aug 71*	15
GIRLS I HAVE KNOWN	*RCA International*	35	*21 Aug 71*	5
TWELVE SONGS OF CHRISTMAS [RI]	*RCA International*	3	*27 Nov 71*	6
A TOUCH OF VELVET [RI]	*RCA International*	49	*27 Nov 71*	2
MY FRIEND	*RCA Victor*	32	*15 Apr 72*	5
40 GOLDEN GREATS	*Arcade*	1	*20 Sep 75*	25
COUNTRY GENTLEMAN	*K-Tel*	53	*6 Sep 80*	4
THE DEFINITIVE JIM REEVES	*Arcade*	9	*8 Aug 92*	10
THE ULTIMATE COLLECTION	*RCA Victor*	17	*28 Sep 96*	6

Martha REEVES and the VANDELLAS | US

SINGLES:	HITS 7		WEEKS 85	
DANCING IN THE STREET	*Stateside*	28	*31 Oct 64*	8
NOWHERE TO RUN	*Tamla Motown*	26	*3 Apr 65*	8
I'M READY FOR LOVE	*Tamla Motown*	29	*3 Dec 66*	8
JIMMY MACK	*Tamla Motown*	21	*1 Apr 67*	9
Above 4: MARTHA and the VANDELLAS.				
HONEY CHILE	*Tamla Motown*	30	*20 Jan 68*	9
DANCING IN THE STREET [RI]	*Tamla Motown*	4	*18 Jan 69*	12
NOWHERE TO RUN [RI-1ST]	*Tamla Motown*	42	*19 Apr 69*	3
JIMMY MACK [RE]	*Tamla Motown*	21	*29 Aug 70*	12
Above hit: MARTHA and the VANDELLAS.				
FORGET ME NOT	*Tamla Motown*	11	*13 Feb 71*	8
BLESS YOU	*Tamla Motown*	33	*8 Jan 72*	5
NOWHERE TO RUN [RI-2ND]	*A&M*	52	*23 Jul 88*	3
[AA] listed with I Got You (I Feel Good) by James Brown.				

Vic REEVES | UK.

SINGLES:	HITS 4		WEEKS 29	
BORN FREE	*Sense*	6	*27 Apr 91*	6
Above hit: Vic REEVES and the ROMAN NUMERALS.				
DIZZY	*Sense*	1	*26 Oct 91*	12
Above hit: Vic REEVES and the WONDER STUFF.				
ABIDE WITH ME	*Sense*	47	*14 Dec 91*	3
I'M A BELIEVER	*Parlophone*	3	*8 Jul 95*	8
Above hit: EMF and REEVES and MORTIMER.				
ALBUMS:	HITS 1		WEEKS 9	
I WILL CURE YOU	*Sense*	16	*16 Nov 91*	9

REFUGEE ALLSTARS – See FUGEES (REFUGEE CAMP); Wyclef JEAN

REFUGEE CAMP ALLSTARS featuring Lauryn HILL – See FUGEES (REFUGEE CAMP); Lauryn HILL

Joan REGAN | UK

(See also All Star Hit Parade.)

SINGLES:	HITS 11		WEEKS 62	
RICHOCHET	*Decca*	8	*12 Dec 53*	1
Originally recorded by Teresa Brewer.				
Above hit: Joan REGAN with the SQUADRONAIRES directed by Ronnie ALDRICH.				
RICHOCHET [RE]	*Decca*	9	*9 Jan 54*	4
SOMEONE ELSE'S ROSES	*Decca*	5	*15 May 54*	8
IF I GIVE MY HEART TO YOU	*Decca*	20	*2 Oct 54*	1
IF I GIVE MY HEART TO YOU [RE]	*Decca*	3	*30 Oct 54*	10
WAIT FOR ME, DARLING	*Decca*	18	*6 Nov 54*	1
Above hit: Joan REGAN and the JOHNSTON BROTHERS.				

PRIZE OF GOLD		Decca	6	26 Mar 55	8

From the film of the same name.
Above hit: Joan REGAN with Johnny DOUGLAS and his Orchestra.

OPEN UP YOUR HEART		Decca	19	7 May 55	1
MAY YOU ALWAYS		His Master's Voice	9	2 May 59	16
HAPPY ANNIVERSARY		Pye	29	6 Feb 60	1
HAPPY ANNIVERSARY [RE]		Pye	29	20 Feb 60	1
PAPA LOVES MAMA		Pye	29	30 Jul 60	8
ONE OF THE LUCKY ONES		Pye	47	26 Nov 60	1
MUST BE SANTA		Pye	42	7 Jan 61	1

Above hit: Joan REGAN and DR. BARNARDO'S CHILDREN with the Peter KNIGHT ORCHESTRA.

REGENTS
UK

SINGLES:	HITS 2			WEEKS 14
7 TEEN	Rialto	11	22 Dec 79	12
SEE YOU LATER	Arista	55	7 Jun 80	2

REGGAE BOYZ
Jamaica

SINGLES:	HITS 1			WEEKS 1
KICK IT	Universal	59	27 Jun 98	1

Features reggae rhythm section of Sly and Robbie.

REGGAE PHILHARMONIC ORCHESTRA
UK

SINGLES:	HITS 2			WEEKS 11
MINNIE THE MOOCHER	Mango	35	19 Nov 88	9
LOVELY THING	Mango	71	28 Jul 90	2

Above hit: REGGAE PHILHARMONIC ORCHESTRA featuring JAZZY JOYCE.

REGGAE REVOLUTION – See Pato BANTON

REGGIE – See TECHNOTRONIC

REGINA
US

SINGLES:	HITS 1			WEEKS 3
BABY LOVE	Funkin' Marvellous	50	1 Feb 86	3

Features backing vocals by Siedah Garrett and sax solo by David Sanborn.

REID
UK

SINGLES:	HITS 4			WEEKS 12
ONE WAY OUT	Syncopate	66	8 Oct 88	2
REAL EMOTION	Syncopate	65	11 Feb 89	2
GOOD TIMES	Syncopate	55	15 Apr 89	6
LOVIN' ON THE SIDE	Syncopate	71	21 Oct 89	2

Ellen REID – See CRASH TEST DUMMIES

John REID – See NIGHTCRAWLERS featuring John REID

Junior REID – See COLDCUT; RAGGA TWINS; SOUP DRAGONS

Mike REID
UK

SINGLES:	HITS 2			WEEKS 10
THE UGLY DUCKLING	Pye	10	22 Mar 75	8
THE MORE I SEE YOU	Telstar TV	46	24 Apr 99	2

Above hit: Barbara WINDSOR and Mike REID.

Neil REID
UK

SINGLES:	HITS 2			WEEKS 26
MOTHER OF MINE	Decca	2	1 Jan 72	20
THAT'S WHAT I WANT TO BE	Decca	49	8 Apr 72	1
THAT'S WHAT I WANT TO BE [RE]	Decca	45	22 Apr 72	5
ALBUMS:	HITS 2			WEEKS 18
NEIL REID	Decca	1	5 Feb 72	16
SMILE	Decca	47	2 Sep 72	2

DJ Patrick REID – See POB featuring DJ Patrick REID

Maggie REILLY – See Mike OLDFIELD

Joe REISMAN and his Orchestra – See Johnnie RAY; Sarah VAUGHAN

Keith RELF
UK

SINGLES:	HITS 1			WEEKS 1
MR. ZERO	Columbia	50	28 May 66	1

Original written and recorded by Bob Lind.

REMBRANDTS

SINGLES:		HITS 2			US WEEKS 28
I'LL BE THERE FOR YOU (THEME FROM "FRIENDS")	East West America		3	2 Sep 95	12
Theme from the TV series screened on Channel 4.					
THIS HOUSE IS NOT A HOME	East West America		58	20 Jan 96	1
I'LL BE THERE FOR YOU (THEME FROM "FRIENDS") [RE]	East West America		5	24 May 97	15
ALBUMS:		HITS 1			WEEKS 5
LP	East West America		14	23 Sep 95	5

REMO 4 – See Tommy QUICKLY and the REMO 4

RENAISSANCE

SINGLES:		HITS 1			UK WEEKS 11
NORTHERN LIGHTS	Warner Brothers		10	15 Jul 78	11
ALBUMS:		HITS 3			WEEKS 10
RENAISSANCE	Island		60	21 Feb 70	1
A SONG FOR ALL SEASONS	Warner Brothers		35	19 Aug 78	8
AZUR D'OR	Warner Brothers		73	2 Jun 79	1

RENATO – See RENEE and RENATO

RENE and ANGELA

SINGLES:		HITS 3			US WEEKS 15
SAVE YOUR LOVE (FOR # 1)	Club		66	15 Jun 85	2
Above hit: RENE and ANGELA with Kurtis BLOW.					
I'LL BE GOOD	Club		22	7 Sep 85	10
SECRET RENDEZVOUS	Champion		54	2 Nov 85	3

RENE and YVETTE featuring Gordon KAYE and Vicki MICHELLE

SINGLES:		HITS 1			UK WEEKS 4
JE T'AIME (ALLO ALLO) / RENE D.M.C. (DEVASTATING MACHO CHARISMA)	Sedition		57	22 Nov 86	4

Nicole RENEE

SINGLES:		HITS 1			US WEEKS 1
STRAWBERRY	Atlantic		55	12 Dec 98	1
Samples Grover Washington Jr's Paradise.					

RENEE and RENATO

SINGLES:		HITS 2			UK/Italy WEEKS 22
SAVE YOUR LOVE	Hollywood		1	30 Oct 82	16
JUST ONE MORE KISS	Hollywood		48	12 Feb 83	6
ALBUMS:		HITS 1			WEEKS 14
SAVE YOUR LOVE	Lifestyle		26	25 Dec 82	14
Above hit: RENATO.					

RENEGADE SOUNDWAVE

SINGLES:		HITS 2			UK WEEKS 7
PROBABLY A ROBBERY	Mute		38	3 Feb 90	6
RENEGADE SOUNDWAVE	Mute		64	5 Feb 94	1
ALBUMS:		HITS 1			WEEKS 1
SOUNDCLASH	Mute		74	24 Mar 90	1

REO SPEEDWAGON

SINGLES:		HITS 3			US WEEKS 38
KEEP ON LOVING YOU	Epic		7	11 Apr 81	14
TAKE IT ON THE RUN	Epic		19	27 Jun 81	14
CAN'T FIGHT THIS FEELING	Epic		16	16 Mar 85	10
ALBUMS:		HITS 2			WEEKS 36
HI INFIDELITY	Epic		6	25 Apr 81	29
GOOD TROUBLE	Epic		29	17 Jul 82	7

REPARATA and the DELRONS

SINGLES:		HITS 2			US WEEKS 12
CAPTAIN OF YOUR SHIP	Bell		13	23 Mar 68	10
SHOES	Dart		43	18 Oct 75	2
Originally recorded by the New Settlers.					
Above hit: REPARATA.					

REPLAYS – See Rocky SHARPE and the REPLAYS

REPRAZENT/Roni SIZE – See Roni SIZE REPRAZENT

REPUBLICA

				UK
SINGLES:		**HITS 3**		**WEEKS 18**
READY TO GO	*Deconstruction*	43	*27 Apr 96*	2
READY TO GO [RI]	*Deconstruction*	13	*1 Mar 97*	6
DROP DEAD GORGEOUS	*Deconstruction*	7	*3 May 97*	7
From the film 'Scream'.				
FROM RUSH HOUR WITH LOVE	*Deconstruction*	20	*3 Oct 98*	3
ALBUMS:		**HITS 2**		**WEEKS 38**
REPUBLICA	*Deconstruction*	4	*15 Mar 97*	36
SPEED BALLADS	*Deconstruction*	37	*17 Oct 98*	2

REST ASSURED

				UK
SINGLES:		**HITS 1**		**WEEKS 7**
TREAT INFAMY	*ffrr*	14	*28 Feb 98*	7
Taken from the string line of Verve's Bitter Sweet Symphony, which originally comes from an orchestral version of The Rolling Stones' The Last Time by Andrew Loog Oldham.				

REUNION

				US
SINGLES:		**HITS 1**		**WEEKS 4**
LIFE IS A ROCK (BUT THE RADIO ROLLED ME)	*RCA Victor*	33	*21 Sep 74*	4

REVILLOS – See REZILLOS

REVIVAL 3000

				UK
SINGLES:		**HITS 1**		**WEEKS 1**
THE MIGHTY HIGH	*Hi-Life*	47	*1 Nov 97*	1

REVOLTING COCKS

				US
SINGLES:		**HITS 1**		**WEEKS 1**
DO YA THINK I'M SEXY?	*Devotion*	61	*18 Sep 93*	1
ALBUMS:		**HITS 1**		**WEEKS 1**
LINGER FICKEN' GOOD	*Devotion*	39	*2 Oct 93*	1

REVOLUTION – See PRINCE

Debbie REYNOLDS

				US
SINGLES:		**HITS 1**		**WEEKS 17**
TAMMY	*Vogue Coral*	2	*31 Aug 57*	17
From the film 'Tammy And The Bachelor'.				

Jody REYNOLDS

				US
SINGLES:		**HITS 1**		**WEEKS 1**
ENDLESS SLEEP	*Lightning*	66	*14 Apr 79*	1
[AA] listed with To Know Him Is To Love Him by the Teddy Bears. Reached No. 5 in the US in 1958.				

L.J. REYNOLDS

				US
SINGLES:		**HITS 1**		**WEEKS 3**
DON'T LET NOBODY HOLD YOU DOWN	*Club*	53	*30 Jun 84*	3

REYNOLDS GIRLS

				UK
SINGLES:		**HITS 1**		**WEEKS 12**
I'D RATHER JACK	*PWL*	8	*25 Feb 89*	12

REZILLOS

				UK
SINGLES:		**HITS 4**		**WEEKS 21**
TOP OF THE POPS	*Sire*	17	*12 Aug 78*	9
DESTINATION VENUS	*Sire*	43	*25 Nov 78*	4
I WANNA BE YOUR MAN / I CAN'T STAND MY BABY	*Sensible*	71	*18 Aug 79*	1
I WANNA BE YOUR MAN / I CAN'T STAND MY BABY [RE]	*Sensible*	75	*1 Sep 79*	1
MOTORBIKE BEAT	*Dindisc*	45	*26 Jan 80*	6
Above hit: REVILLOS.				
ALBUMS:		**HITS 2**		**WEEKS 15**
CAN'T STAND THE REZILLOS	*Sire*	16	*5 Aug 78*	10
MISSION ACCOMPLISHED BUT THE BEAT GOES ON	*Sire*	30	*28 Apr 79*	5

RHODA with the SPECIAL A.K.A. – See SPECIALS

Busta RHYMES   US

(See also B Real, Busta Rhymes, Coolio, LL Cool J and Method Man; Flipmode Squad (starring Busta Rhymes, Baby Sham, Rah Digga and Spliff Star; Fugees (Refugee Camp); Levert Sweat Gill.)

SINGLES:		HITS 9		WEEKS 43
WOO-HAH!! GOT YOU ALL IN CHECK	Elektra	8	11 May 96	7
IT'S A PARTY	Elektra	23	21 Sep 96	2
Above hit: Busta RHYMES featuring ZHANE.				
DO MY THING	Elektra	39	3 May 97	1
PUT YOUR HANDS WHERE MY EYES COULD SEE	Elektra	16	18 Oct 97	3
DANGEROUS	Elektra	32	20 Dec 97	4
TURN IT UP (REMIX)/FIRE IT UP [M]	Elektra	2	18 Apr 98	10
ONE	Elektra	23	11 Jul 98	3
Above hit: Busta RHYMES (featuring Erykah BADU).				
GIMME SOME MORE	Elektra	5	30 Jan 99	6
WHAT'S IT GONNA BE?!	Elektra	6	1 May 99	7
Above hit: Busta RHYMES featuring JANET.				
ALBUMS:		HITS 3		WEEKS 16
THE COMING	Elektra	48	30 Mar 96	4
WHEN DISASTER STRIKES	Elektra	34	4 Oct 97	5
EXTINCTION LEVEL EVENT/FINAL WORLD FRONT	Elektra	54	16 Jan 99	7

RHYTHIM IS RHYTHIM   US

SINGLES:		HITS 1		WEEKS 1
STRINGS OF LIFE '89	Kool Kat	74	11 Nov 89	1

RHYTHM ETERNITY   UK

SINGLES:		HITS 1		WEEKS 1
PINK CHAMPAGNE	Dead Dead Good	72	23 May 92	1

RHYTHM FACTOR   US

SINGLES:		HITS 1		WEEKS 2
YOU BRING ME JOY	Multiply	53	29 Apr 95	2

RHYTHM MASTERS   UK

SINGLES:		HITS 2		WEEKS 2
COME ON Y'ALL	Faze 2	49	16 Aug 97	1
Samples Todd Terry and Aretha Franklin.				
ENTER THE SCENE	Distinct'ive	49	6 Dec 97	1
Above hit: DJ SUPREME vs the RHYTHM MASTERS.				

RHYTHM-N-BASS   UK

SINGLES:		HITS 2		WEEKS 4
ROSES	Epic	56	19 Sep 92	2
CAN'T STOP THIS FEELING	Epic	59	3 Jul 93	2

RHYTHM ON THE LOOSE   UK

SINGLES:		HITS 1		WEEKS 2
BREAK OF DAWN	Six6	36	19 Aug 95	2

RHYTHM QUEST   UK

SINGLES:		HITS 1		WEEKS 2
DREAMS [EP]	Network	45	20 Jun 92	2
Lead track: Closer To All Your Dreams. The EP title was not listed for the chart of 27 Jun 92.				

RHYTHM SECTION   UK

SINGLES:		HITS 1		WEEKS 1
MIDSUMMER MADNESS [EP]	Rhythm Section	66	18 Jul 92	1
Lead track: Dreamworld.				

RHYTHM SOURCE   UK

SINGLES:		HITS 1		WEEKS 1
LOVE SHINE	A&M	74	17 Jun 95	1

RHYTHMATIC   UK

SINGLES:		HITS 2		WEEKS 3
TAKE ME BACK	Network	74	12 May 90	1
TAKE ME BACK [RE]	Network	71	26 May 90	1
FREQUENCY	Network	62	3 Nov 90	1

RHYTHMATIC JUNKIES | | | | | UK

SINGLES:	HITS 1				WEEKS 1
THE FEELIN' (CLAP YOUR HANDS)	Ride Recordings		67	15 May 99	1

RIALTO | | | | | UK

SINGLES:	HITS 4				WEEKS 8
MONDAY MORNING 5:19	East West		37	8 Nov 97	2
UNTOUCHABLE	East West		20	17 Jan 98	3
DREAM ANOTHER DREAM	East West		39	28 Mar 98	2
SUMMER'S OVER	China		60	17 Oct 98	1
ALBUMS:	**HITS 1**				**WEEKS 3**
RIALTO	China		21	25 Jul 98	3

RIAS DANCE ORCHESTRA – See Caterina VALENTE

Reva RICE and Greg ELLIS | | | | | UK

SINGLES:	HITS 1				WEEKS 2
NEXT TIME YOU FALL IN LOVE	Really Useful		59	27 Mar 93	2
From the musical 'The New Starlight Express'.					

Charlie RICH | | | | | US

SINGLES:	HITS 3				WEEKS 29
THE MOST BEAUTIFUL GIRL	Epic		2	16 Feb 74	14
Originally recorded by Norro Wilson.					
BEHIND CLOSED DOORS	Epic		16	13 Apr 74	10
Originally recorded by Kenny O'Dell.					
WE LOVE EACH OTHER	Epic		37	1 Feb 75	5
ALBUMS:	**HITS 2**				**WEEKS 28**
BEHIND CLOSED DOORS	Epic		4	23 Mar 74	26
VERY SPECIAL LOVE SONGS	Epic		34	13 Jul 74	2

Kelli RICH – See NU SOUL featuring Kelli RICH

Richie RICH | | | | | UK

SINGLES:	HITS 6				WEEKS 16
TURN IT UP	Club		48	16 Jul 88	3
I'LL HOUSE YOU	Gee Street		22	22 Oct 88	5
Above hit: Richie RICH meets JUNGLE BROTHERS.					
MY DJ (PUMP IT UP SOME)	Gee Street		74	10 Dec 88	1
SALSA HOUSE	ffrr		50	2 Sep 89	3
YOU USED TO SALSA	ffrr		52	9 Mar 91	3
Above hit: Richie RICH'S SALSA HOUSE (featuring Ralphi ROSARIO).					
STAY WITH ME	Castle Communications		58	29 Mar 97	1
Above hit: Richie RICH and Esera TUAOLO.					
ALBUMS:	**HITS 1**				**WEEKS 1**
I CAN MAKE YOU DANCE	Gee Street		65	22 Jul 89	1

Tony RICH PROJECT | | | | | US

SINGLES:	HITS 3				WEEKS 22
NOBODY KNOWS	LaFace		4	4 May 96	17
LIKE A WOMAN	LaFace		27	31 Aug 96	4
LEAVIN'	LaFace		52	14 Dec 96	1
ALBUMS:	**HITS 1**				**WEEKS 10**
WORDS	LaFace		27	25 May 96	10

RICH IN PARADISE – See F.P.I. PROJECT

RICH KIDS | | | | | UK

SINGLES:	HITS 1				WEEKS 5
RICH KIDS	EMI		24	28 Jan 78	5
ALBUMS:	**HITS 1**				**WEEKS 1**
GHOST OF PRINCES IN TOWERS	EMI		51	7 Oct 78	1

Cliff RICHARD | | | | | UK

(See also Shadows; Various Artists: Stage Cast - London 'Heathcliff Live (The Show)'.)

SINGLES:	HITS 122				WEEKS 1134
MOVE IT!	Columbia		2	13 Sep 58	17
The flip side Schoolboy Crush was originally to be the A-side.					
HIGH CLASS BABY	Columbia		7	22 Nov 58	10
Label reflects 'with' instead of 'and' The Drifters.					
LIVIN' LOVIN' DOLL	Columbia		20	31 Jan 59	6
MEAN STREAK	Columbia		10	9 May 59	9

NEVER MIND	Columbia	21	16 May 59	2

Above 2 entries were separate sides of the same release, each had its own chart run.

LIVING DOLL	Columbia	1	11 Jul 59	21

From the film 'Serious Charge'.
Above 6: Cliff RICHARD and the DRIFTERS.

TRAVELLIN' LIGHT	Columbia	1	10 Oct 59	17
DYNAMITE	Columbia	16	10 Oct 59	2

Above 2 entries were separate sides of the same release, each had its own chart run.

DYNAMITE [RE]	Columbia	21	31 Oct 59	2

Above 3: Cliff RICHARD and the SHADOWS.

LIVING DOLL [RE-1ST]	Columbia	26	12 Dec 59	1
LIVING DOLL [RE-2ND]	Columbia	28	2 Jan 60	1

Above 2: Cliff RICHARD and the DRIFTERS.

EXPRESSO BONGO [EP]	Columbia	14	16 Jan 60	7

Lead track: Love. This charted at No. 1 on the EP chart when it began on 12 Mar 60. See EP section.

A VOICE IN THE WILDERNESS	Columbia	2	23 Jan 60	14

Above 2 from the film 'Expresso Bongo'. This track is also on the Expresso Bongo EP.

FALL IN LOVE WITH YOU	Columbia	2	26 Mar 60	15
A VOICE IN THE WILDERNESS [RE]	Columbia	36	7 May 60	2
PLEASE DON'T TEASE	Columbia	1	2 Jul 60	18

Song was chosen by members of his fan club from tracks just recorded as the best bet for a hit single.

NINE TIMES OUT OF TEN	Columbia	3	24 Sep 60	12

The fans' third choice.

I LOVE YOU	Columbia	1	3 Dec 60	16
THEME FOR A DREAM	Columbia	3	4 Mar 61	14
GEE WHIZ IT'S YOU	Columbia	4	1 Apr 61	14

Export single which sold enough in the UK to chart.

A GIRL LIKE YOU	Columbia	3	24 Jun 61	14

Above 10: Cliff RICHARD and the SHADOWS.

WHEN THE GIRL IN YOUR ARMS IS THE GIRL IN YOUR HEART	Columbia	3	21 Oct 61	15

Above hit: Cliff RICHARD with Norrie PARAMOR and his Orchestra.

THE YOUNG ONES	Columbia	1	13 Jan 62	21

Above 2 from the film 'The Young Ones'.
Above hit: Cliff RICHARD and the SHADOWS.

I'M LOOKIN' OUT THE WINDOW / DO YOU WANT TO DANCE	Columbia	2	12 May 62	17

I'm Looking Out The Window originally recorded by Peggy Lee; Do You Want To Dance originally recorded by Bobby Freeman, it reached No. 5 in the US in 1958.
Above hit: Cliff RICHARD with the Norrie PARAMOR ORCHESTRA / Cliff RICHARD and the SHADOWS.

IT'LL BE ME	Columbia	2	8 Sep 62	12

Originally recorded by Jerry Lee Lewis.
Above hit: Cliff RICHARD and the SHADOWS.

THE NEXT TIME / BACHELOR BOY	Columbia	1	8 Dec 62	18

Bachelor Boy listed from 12 Jan 63 and only credited to Cliff Richard and the Shadows.
Above hit: Cliff RICHARD, the SHADOWS and the Norrie PARAMOR STRINGS.

SUMMER HOLIDAY	Columbia	1	23 Feb 63	18

Above 2 from the film 'Summer Holiday'.
Above hit: Cliff RICHARD and the SHADOWS and the Norrie PARAMOR STRINGS.

LUCKY LIPS	Columbia	4	11 May 63	15

Original by Ruth Brown reached No. 25 in the US in 1957.
Above hit: Cliff RICHARD and the SHADOWS.

IT'S ALL IN THE GAME	Columbia:	2	24 Aug 63	13
DON'T TALK TO HIM	Columbia	2	9 Nov 63	13
I'M THE LONELY ONE	Columbia	8	8 Feb 64	10
DON'T TALK TO HIM [RE]	Columbia	50	15 Feb 64	1

Above 3: Cliff RICHARD and the SHADOWS.

CONSTANTLY (L'EDERA)	Columbia	4	2 May 64	13
ON THE BEACH	Columbia	7	4 Jul 64	13

From the film 'Wonderful Life'.
Above hit: Cliff RICHARD and the SHADOWS.

THE TWELFTH OF NEVER	Columbia	8	10 Oct 64	11

Original by Johnny Mathis reached No. 9 in the US in 1957.

I COULD EASILY FALL (IN LOVE WITH YOU)	Columbia	9	12 Dec 64	11

From the Pantomime 'Aladdin'.
Above hit: Cliff RICHARD and the SHADOWS.

THE MINUTE YOU'RE GONE	Columbia	1	13 Mar 65	14

Originally recorded by Sonny James.

ON MY WORD	Columbia	12	12 Jun 65	10
THE TIME IN BETWEEN	Columbia	22	21 Aug 65	8
WIND ME UP (LET ME GO)	Columbia	2	6 Nov 65	16
BLUE TURNS TO GREY	Columbia	15	26 Mar 66	9

Written By Jagger/Richards.
Above 3: Cliff RICHARD and the SHADOWS

VISIONS	Columbia	7	23 Jul 66	12

Used as the closing theme to his BBC TV series.

TIME DRAGS BY	Columbia	10	15 Oct 66	12

From the film 'Finders Keepers'.

IN THE COUNTRY	Columbia	6	17 Dec 66	10

From the Pantomime 'Cinderella'.
Above 2: Cliff RICHARD and the SHADOWS.

IT'S ALL OVER	Columbia	9	18 Mar 67	10

Originally recorded by the Everly Brothers.
Above hit: Cliff RICHARD with Bernard EBBINGHOUSE and his Orchestra.

I'LL COME RUNNIN'	Columbia	26	10 Jun 67	8

Originally recorded by Neil Diamond.

THE DAY I MET MARIE	Columbia	10	19 Aug 67	14
ALL MY LOVE	Columbia	6	18 Nov 67	12

Above hit: Cliff RICHARD with Bernard EBBINGHOUSE and his Orchestra.

CONGRATULATIONS	Columbia	1	23 Mar 68	13

UK's Eurovision entry in 1968, It came 2nd.

I'LL LOVE YOU FOREVER TODAY	Columbia	27	29 Jun 68	6

From the film 'Two A Penny'.

MARIANNE	Columbia	22	28 Sep 68	8

Written by actor Bill Owen.

DON'T FORGET TO CATCH ME	Columbia	21	30 Nov 68	10

Above hit: Cliff RICHARD and the SHADOWS.

GOOD TIMES	Columbia	12	1 Mar 69	11
BIG SHIP	Columbia	8	31 May 69	10
THROW DOWN A LINE	Columbia	7	13 Sep 69	9

Above hit: CLIFF and HANK.

WITH THE EYES OF A CHILD	Columbia	20	6 Dec 69	11
THE JOY OF LIVING	Columbia	25	21 Feb 70	8

Theme from the TV series of the same name.
Above hit: CLIFF and HANK.

GOODBYE SAM, HELLO SAMANTHA	Columbia	6	6 Jun 70	15
I AIN'T GOT TIME ANYMORE	Columbia	21	5 Sep 70	7
SUNNY HONEY GIRL	Columbia	19	23 Jan 71	8
SILVERY RAIN	Columbia	27	10 Apr 71	6
FLYING MACHINE	Columbia	37	17 Jul 71	7
SING A SONG OF FREEDOM	Columbia	13	13 Nov 71	12
JESUS	Columbia	35	11 Mar 72	3
LIVING IN HARMONY	Columbia	12	26 Aug 72	10
POWER TO ALL OUR FRIENDS	EMI	4	17 Mar 73	12

UK's Eurovision entry in 1973, It came 4th.

HELP IT ALONG / TOMORROW RISING	EMI	29	12 May 73	6

These were the only listed tracks on a 4 track EP of Eurovision entry songs for
*   1973.*

TAKE ME HIGH	EMI	27	1 Dec 73	12

Theme from the film of the same name.

(YOU KEEP ME) HANGIN' ON	EMI	13	18 May 74	8
MISS YOU NIGHTS	EMI	15	7 Feb 76	10
DEVIL WOMAN	EMI	9	8 May 76	8

Originally recorded by Kristine.

I CAN'T ASK FOR ANYMORE THAN YOU	EMI	17	21 Aug 76	8

Originally recorded by Ian Sinclair.

HEY MR. DREAM MAKER	EMI	31	4 Dec 76	6
MY KINDA LIFE	EMI	15	5 Mar 77	8
WHEN TWO WORLDS DRIFT APART	EMI	46	16 Jul 77	3
GREEN LIGHT	EMI	57	31 Mar 79	3
WE DON'T TALK ANYMORE	EMI	1	21 Jul 79	14
HOT SHOT	EMI	46	3 Nov 79	5
CARRIE	EMI	4	2 Feb 80	10
DREAMIN'	EMI	8	16 Aug 80	10

Co-written by Leo Sayer.

SUDDENLY	Jet	15	25 Oct 80	7

From the film 'Xanadu'.
Above hit: Olivia NEWTON-JOHN with Cliff RICHARD.

A LITTLE IN LOVE	EMI	15	24 Jan 81	8
WIRED FOR SOUND	EMI	4	29 Aug 81	9
DADDY'S HOME	EMI	2	21 Nov 81	12

Original by Shep and the Limelites reached No. 2 in the US in 1961. It was an answer
*   song to the Heartbeats' A Thousand Miles Away.*

THE ONLY WAY OUT	EMI	10	17 Jul 82	9
WHERE DO WE GO FROM HERE	EMI	60	25 Sep 82	3
LITTLE TOWN	EMI	11	4 Dec 82	7

Update of the Christmas carol O Little Town Of Bethlehem.
Above hit: Cliff RICHARD featuring Tony RIVERS and Nigel PERRIN.

SHE MEANS NOTHING TO ME	Capitol	9	19 Feb 83	9

Above hit: Phil EVERLY / Cliff RICHARD.

TRUE LOVE WAYS	EMI	8	16 Apr 83	8

Live recording.
Above hit: Cliff RICHARD with the LONDON PHILHARMONIC ORCHESTRA.

DRIFTING	DJM	64	4 Jun 83	2

Above hit: Sheila WALSH and Cliff RICHARD.

NEVER SAY DIE (GIVE A LITTLE BIT MORE)	EMI	15	3 Sep 83	7
PLEASE DON'T FALL IN LOVE	EMI	7	26 Nov 83	9

BABY YOU'RE DYNAMITE / OCEAN DEEP	EMI	27	31 Mar 84	6

Ocean Deep listed from 28 Apr 84 once it had dropped to No. 41.

OCEAN DEEP / BABY YOU'RE DYNAMITE [RE]	EMI	72	19 May 84	1
SHOOTING FROM THE HEART	EMI	51	3 Nov 84	4
HEART USER	EMI	46	9 Feb 85	3
SHE'S SO BEAUTIFUL	EMI	17	14 Sep 85	9

All instruments played by Stevie Wonder.

IT'S IN EVERY ONE OF US	EMI	45	7 Dec 85	6

Above 2 from Dave Clarke's musical 'Time'.

LIVING DOLL	WEA	1	22 Mar 86	11

Charity record to support projects in Africa and Britain.
Above hit: COMIC RELIEF presents Cliff RICHARD and the YOUNG ONES featuring Hank MARVIN.

ALL I ASK OF YOU	Polydor	3	4 Oct 86	16

From the Andrew Lloyd Webber musical 'The Phantom Of The Opera'.
Above hit: Cliff RICHARD and Sarah BRIGHTMAN with the ROYAL PHILHARMONIC ORCHESTRA conducted by David CADDICK.

SLOW RIVERS	Rocket	44	29 Nov 86	8

Above hit: Elton JOHN and Cliff RICHARD.

MY PRETTY ONE	EMI	6	20 Jun 87	10

Originally recorded by Jamie Rae.

SOME PEOPLE	EMI	3	29 Aug 87	10
REMEMBER ME	EMI	35	31 Oct 87	4
TWO HEARTS	EMI	34	13 Feb 88	3
MISTLETOE AND WINE	EMI	1	3 Dec 88	8

Originally recorded by Twiggy.

THE BEST OF ME	EMI	2	10 Jun 89	7

Cliff's 100th single. Written by Richard Marx and originally recorded by David Foster and Olivia Newton-John.

I JUST DON'T HAVE THE HEART	EMI	3	26 Aug 89	8

Written and produced by Stock, Aitken and Waterman

LEAN ON YOU	EMI	17	14 Oct 89	6
WHENEVER GOD SHINES HIS LIGHT	Polydor	20	9 Dec 89	6

Above hit: Van MORRISON with Cliff RICHARD.

STRONGER THAN THAT	EMI	14	24 Feb 90	5
SILHOUETTES	EMI	10	25 Aug 90	7
FROM A DISTANCE	EMI	11	13 Oct 90	6

Above 2 are live recordings from Wembley Stadium earlier in the year.

SAVIOURS DAY	EMI	1	8 Dec 90	7
MORE TO LIFE	EMI	23	14 Sep 91	5

Theme from the BBC1 TV series 'Trainer'.

WE SHOULD BE TOGETHER	EMI	10	7 Dec 91	6
THIS NEW YEAR	EMI	30	11 Jan 92	2
I STILL BELIEVE IN YOU	EMI	7	5 Dec 92	6
PEACE IN OUR TIME	EMI	8	27 Mar 93	5
HUMAN WORK OF ART	EMI	24	12 Jun 93	4
NEVER LET GO	EMI	32	2 Oct 93	3
HEALING LOVE	EMI	19	18 Dec 93	5
ALL I HAVE TO DO IS DREAM / MISS YOU NIGHTS [RI]	EMI	14	10 Dec 94	6

Above hit: Cliff RICHARD (with Phil EVERLY) / Cliff RICHARD.

ALL I HAVE TO DO IS DREAM / MISS YOU NIGHTS [RI] [RE]	EMI	58	25 Feb 95	3
MISUNDERSTOOD MAN	EMI	19	21 Oct 95	3
HAD TO BE	EMI	22	9 Dec 95	4

Above hit: Cliff RICHARD with Olivia NEWTON-JOHN.

THE WEDDING	EMI	40	30 Mar 96	1

Above hit: Cliff RICHARD with Helen HOBSON.

BE WITH ME ALWAYS	EMI	52	25 Jan 97	1

Above 4 from the musical 'Heathcliff'.

CAN'T KEEP THIS FEELING IN	EMI	10	24 Oct 98	4
THE MIRACLE	EMI	23	7 Aug 99	2

Features backing vocals by James Ingram and Siedah Garrett.

THE MILLENNIUM PRAYER	Papillon	1	27 Nov 99	6

Combines together The Lord's Prayer with the tune of Auld Lang Syne. Charity record in aid of Children's Promise, The Millennium Final Hour Appeal.

EPS:		**HITS 22**		**WEEKS 432**
CLIFF SINGS NO. 1	Columbia	4	12 Mar 60	18
EXPRESSO BONGO [OST]	Columbia	1	12 Mar 60	28
CLIFF SINGS NO. 2	Columbia	3	19 Mar 60	36

Above 3: Cliff RICHARD and the SHADOWS.

CLIFF SINGS NO. 3	Columbia	2	4 Jun 60	15
CLIFF'S SILVER DISCS	Columbia	1	10 Dec 60	57
ME AND MY SHADOWS NO. 1	Columbia	5	11 Feb 61	23
ME AND MY SHADOWS NO. 2	Columbia	8	29 Apr 61	4
ME AND MY SHADOWS NO. 3	Columbia	6	29 Apr 61	11
LISTEN TO CLIFF NO. 1	Columbia	17	4 Nov 61	2
DREAM	Columbia	3	18 Nov 61	51
CLIFF'S HIT PARADE	Columbia	4	10 Feb 62	42
HITS FROM 'THE YOUNG ONES'	Columbia	1	14 Apr 62	40

CLIFF RICHARD NO. 2	*Columbia*	19	*23 Jun 62*	2
HOLIDAY CARNIVAL	*Columbia*	1	*18 May 63*	22
HITS FROM 'SUMMER HOLIDAY'	*Columbia*	4	*15 Jun 63*	21
CLIFF'S LUCKY LIPS	*Columbia*	17	*19 Oct 63*	5

Above 12: Cliff RICHARD and the SHADOWS.

LOVE SONGS	*Columbia*	4	*16 Nov 63*	15
CLIFF SINGS 'DON'T TALK TO HIM'	*Columbia*	15	*30 May 64*	1
WONDERFUL LIFE	*Columbia*	3	*15 Aug 64*	21
CLIFF'S HITS FROM 'ALADDIN AND HIS WONDERFUL LAMP'	*Columbia*	20	*22 May 65*	1

Songs from the 1964 Pantomime.
Above 3: Cliff RICHARD and the SHADOWS.

LOOK IN MY EYES, MARIA	*Columbia*	15	*24 Jul 65*	1
TAKE FOUR	*Columbia*	4	*2 Oct 65*	16

Above hit: Cliff RICHARD and the SHADOWS.

ALBUMS:	**HITS 53**			**WEEKS 779**
CLIFF	*Columbia*	4	*18 Apr 59*	31

Above hit: Cliff RICHARD and the DRIFTERS.

CLIFF SINGS	*Columbia*	2	*14 Nov 59*	36
ME AND MY SHADOWS	*Columbia*	2	*15 Oct 60*	33
LISTEN TO CLIFF	*Columbia*	2	*22 Apr 61*	28
I'M 21 TODAY	*Columbia*	1	*21 Oct 61*	16
THE YOUNG ONES [OST]	*Columbia*	1	*23 Dec 61*	42
32 MINUTES AND 17 SECONDS	*Columbia*	3	*29 Sep 62*	21
SUMMER HOLIDAY [OST]	*Columbia*	1	*26 Jan 63*	36
CLIFF'S HIT ALBUM	*Columbia*	2	*13 Jul 63*	19
WHEN IN SPAIN	*Columbia*	8	*28 Sep 63*	10

Songs recorded in Spanish at studios located in Barcelona.

WONDERFUL LIFE [OST]	*Columbia*	2	*11 Jul 64*	23
ALADDIN AND HIS WONDERFUL LAMP	*Columbia*	13	*9 Jan 65*	5

From the pantomime that opened at the London Palladium, Dec 63. Cast included Arthur Askey
and Una Stubbs.
Above 11: Cliff RICHARD and the SHADOWS.

CLIFF RICHARD	*Columbia*	9	*17 Apr 65*	5
MORE HITS BY CLIFF	*Columbia*	20	*14 Aug 65*	1
LOVE IS FOREVER	*Columbia*	19	*8 Jan 66*	1

Collection of romantic ballads.
Above 2: Cliff RICHARD and the SHADOWS.

KINDA LATIN	*Columbia*	9	*21 May 66*	12
FINDERS KEEPERS [OST]	*Columbia*	6	*17 Dec 66*	18
CINDERELLA	*Columbia*	30	*7 Jan 67*	6

From the pantomime that opened at the London Palladium, Dec 66.
Above 2: Cliff RICHARD and the SHADOWS.

DON'T STOP ME NOW . . .	*Columbia*	23	*15 Apr 67*	9
GOOD NEWS	*Columbia*	37	*11 Nov 67*	1

Gospel album.

CLIFF IN JAPAN	*Columbia*	29	*1 Jun 68*	2

Live recordings from the Sankei Hall, Tokyo.

ESTABLISHED 1958	*Columbia*	30	*16 Nov 68*	4

Album divided between tracks recorded by Cliff and The Shadows. Released to celebrate their 10th
Anniversary.

THE BEST OF CLIFF	*Columbia*	5	*12 Jul 69*	17

Above 2: Cliff RICHARD and the SHADOWS.

SINCERELY	*Columbia*	24	*27 Sep 69*	3
TRACKS 'N' GROOVES	*Columbia*	37	*12 Dec 70*	2
THE BEST OF CLIFF VOLUME 2	*Columbia*	49	*23 Dec 72*	2

Above hit: Cliff RICHARD and the SHADOWS.

TAKE ME HIGH [OST]	*EMI*	41	*19 Jan 74*	4
I'M NEARLY FAMOUS	*EMI*	5	*29 May 76*	21
EVERY FACE TELLS A STORY	*EMI*	8	*26 Mar 77*	10
40 GOLDEN GREATS	*EMI*	1	*22 Oct 77*	19

Above hit: Cliff RICHARD and the SHADOWS.

SMALL CORNERS	*EMI*	33	*4 Mar 78*	1

Gospel album.

GREEN LIGHT	*EMI*	25	*21 Oct 78*	3
THANK YOU VERY MUCH – REUNION CONCERT AT THE LONDON PALLADIUM	*EMI*	5	*17 Feb 79*	12

Live recordings from their concerts, Feb 78.
Above hit: Cliff RICHARD and the SHADOWS.

ROCK 'N' ROLL JUVENILE	*EMI*	3	*15 Sep 79*	22
I'M NO HERO	*EMI*	4	*13 Sep 80*	12
LOVE SONGS	*EMI*	1	*4 Jul 81*	43

The Shadows appear on some of the tracks.

WIRED FOR SOUND	*EMI*	4	*26 Sep 81*	25
NOW YOU SEE ME . . . NOW YOU DON'T	*EMI*	4	*4 Sep 82*	14
DRESSED FOR THE OCCASION	*EMI*	7	*21 May 83*	17

Live recordings.
Above hit: Cliff RICHARD and the LONDON PHILHARMONIC
ORCHESTRA.

SILVER	EMI	7	15 Oct 83	18

Released as a boxed-set.

SILVER [RE]	EMI	28	7 Apr 84	6

Re-released with standard packaging.

20 ORIGINAL GREATS	EMI	43	14 Jul 84	6

The Shadows appear on some of the tracks.

THE ROCK CONNECTION	EMI	43	1 Dec 84	5
ALWAYS GUARANTEED	EMI	5	26 Sep 87	25
PRIVATE COLLECTION 1979 - 1988	EMI	1	19 Nov 88	26

Compilation of his favourite tracks.

STRONGER	EMI	7	11 Nov 89	21
FROM A DISTANCE . . . . .THE EVENT	EMI	3	17 Nov 90	15

Live recordings from Wembley Stadium earlier in the year. The first disc of the album is a collaboration with the Oh! Boy team which includes the Dallas Boys, Kalin Twins and the Vernon Girls.

TOGETHER WITH CLIFF RICHARD	EMI	10	30 Nov 91	7
CLIFF RICHARD - THE ALBUM	EMI	1	1 May 93	15
THE HIT LIST	EMI	3	15 Oct 94	21

Compilation to celebrate his 35th Anniversary in the music business.

SONGS FROM "HEATHCLIFF"	EMI	15	11 Nov 95	9

Musical project based on the novel by Emily Bronte.

CLIFF AT THE MOVIES - 1959-1974	EMI	17	24 Aug 96	3

Tracks from his movies.

THE ROCK 'N' ROLL YEARS	EMI	32	2 Aug 97	3

Features rarities and unreleased live versions.

REAL AS I WANNA BE	EMI	10	31 Oct 98	9

Wendy RICHARD – See Mike SARNE

Keith RICHARDS UK

ALBUMS:	HITS 2			WEEKS 4
TALK IS CHEAP	Virgin	37	15 Oct 88	3
MAIN OFFENDER	Virgin America	45	31 Oct 92	1

Neil RICHARDSON ORCHESTRA – See Iris WILLIAMS

Lionel RICHIE US

SINGLES:	HITS 20			WEEKS 167
ENDLESS LOVE	Motown	7	12 Sep 81	12

From the film of the same name.
Above hit: Diana ROSS and Lionel RICHIE.

TRULY	Motown	6	20 Nov 82	11
YOU ARE	Motown	43	29 Jan 83	7
MY LOVE	Motown	70	7 May 83	3
ALL NIGHT LONG (ALL NIGHT)	Motown	2	1 Oct 83	16
RUNNING WITH THE NIGHT	Motown	9	3 Dec 83	12
HELLO	Motown	1	10 Mar 84	15

Above 2 feature backing vocals by Richard Marx.

STUCK ON YOU	Motown	12	23 Jun 84	12
PENNY LOVER	Motown	18	20 Oct 84	7
SAY YOU, SAY ME (TITLE SONG FROM "WHITE NIGHTS")	Motown	8	16 Nov 85	11

From the film.

DANCING ON THE CEILING	Motown	7	26 Jul 86	11
LOVE WILL CONQUER ALL	Motown	45	11 Oct 86	5
BALLERINA GIRL / DEEP RIVER WOMAN	Motown	17	20 Dec 86	8

Deep River Woman listed from 17 Jan 87.
Above hit: Lionel RICHIE / Lionel RICHIE Background vocals: ALABAMA.

SELA	Motown	43	28 Mar 87	6
DO IT TO ME	Motown	33	9 May 92	6
MY DESTINY	Motown	7	22 Aug 92	13
LOVE, OH LOVE	Motown	52	28 Nov 92	3
LOVE, OH LOVE [RE]	Motown	73	26 Dec 92	1
DON'T WANNA LOSE YOU	Mercury	17	6 Apr 96	5
STILL IN LOVE	Mercury	66	23 Nov 96	1
CLOSEST THING TO HEAVEN	Mercury	26	27 Jun 98	2
ALBUMS:	HITS 7			WEEKS 396
LIONEL RICHIE	Motown	9	27 Nov 82	86
CAN'T SLOW DOWN	Motown	1	29 Oct 83	154
DANCING ON THE CEILING	Motown	2	23 Aug 86	53
BACK TO FRONT	Motown	1	6 Jun 92	74

Includes re-entries through to 1997.

LOUDER THAN WORDS	Mercury	11	20 Apr 96	5
TRULY - THE LOVE SONGS	Motown	5	31 Jan 98	21

Includes his recordings with the Commodores and Diana Ross.

TIME	Mercury	31	11 Jul 98	3

Jonathan RICHMAN and the MODERN LOVERS — US

SINGLES:	HITS 3			WEEKS 27
ROADRUNNER	Beserkley	11	16 Jul 77	9
A-side by Jonathan Richman. B-side by the Modern Lovers.				
EGYPTIAN REGGAE	Beserkley	5	29 Oct 77	14
THE MORNING OF OUR LIVES	Beserkley	29	21 Jan 78	4
Live recording. Sleeve only credits the Modern Lovers.				
ALBUMS:	HITS 1			WEEKS 3
ROCK 'N' ROLL WITH THE MODERN LOVERS	Beserkeley	50	27 Aug 77	3

RICHMOND STRINGS with the Mike SAMMES SINGERS — UK

(See also Mike Sammes Singers.)

ALBUMS:	HITS 1			WEEKS 7
MUSIC OF AMERICA	Ronco	18	17 Jan 76	7

Svatoslav RICHTER – See Herbert VON KARAJAN conducting the BERLIN PHILHARMONIC ORCHESTRA

Adam RICKITT — UK

SINGLES:	HITS 2			WEEKS 16
I BREATHE AGAIN	Polydor	5	26 Jun 99	10
EVERYTHING MY HEART DESIRES	Polydor	15	16 Oct 99	6
ALBUMS:	HITS 1			WEEKS 1
GOOD TIMES	Polydor	41	30 Oct 99	1

RICO – See SPECIALS

Frank RICOTTI ALL STARS — UK

ALBUMS:	HITS 1			WEEKS 3
COMPILATION ALBUMS:	HITS 1			WEEKS 5
THE BEIDERBECKE COLLECTION	Dormouse	89	24 Dec 88	2
THE BEIDERBECKE COLLECTION	Dormouse	14	14 Jan 89	5
Incorrectly included in the Compilation chart.				
THE BEIDERBECKE COLLECTION [RE]	Dormouse	73	26 Jun 93	1

RIDDELLE SINGERS – See Ronnie HILTON

Nelson RIDDLE and his Orchestra – See Shirley BASSEY; Nat 'King' COLE; FOUR KNIGHTS; Linda RONSTADT; Frank SINATRA; Kiri TE KANAWA

RIDE — UK

SINGLES:	HITS 10			WEEKS 22
RIDE [EP]	Creation	71	27 Jan 90	2
Lead track: Chelsea Girl.				
PLAY [EP]	Creation	32	14 Apr 90	3
Lead track: Like A Daydream.				
FALL [EP]	Creation	34	29 Sep 90	3
Lead track: Dreams Burn Down.				
TODAY FOREVER [EP]	Creation	14	16 Mar 91	4
Lead track: Today Forever.				
LEAVE THEM ALL BEHIND	Creation	9	15 Feb 92	3
TWISTERELLA	Creation	36	25 Apr 92	2
BIRDMAN	Creation	38	30 Apr 94	2
HOW DOES IT FEEL TO FEEL?	Creation	58	25 Jun 94	1
Originally recorded by the Creation in 1968.				
I DON'T KNOW WHERE IT COMES FROM	Creation	46	8 Oct 94	1
Features the Christchurch Cathedral Choir.				
BLACK NITE CRASH	Creation	67	24 Feb 96	1
ALBUMS:	HITS 4			WEEKS 16
NOWHERE	Creation	11	27 Oct 90	5
GOING BLANK AGAIN	Creation	5	21 Mar 92	5
CARNIVAL OF LIGHT	Creation	5	2 Jul 94	4
TARANTULA	Creation	21	23 Mar 96	2

Andrew RIDGELEY — UK

SINGLES:	HITS 1			WEEKS 3
SHAKE	Epic	58	31 Mar 90	3

Stan RIDGWAY — US

SINGLES:	HITS 1			WEEKS 12
CAMOUFLAGE	I.R.S.	4	5 Jul 86	12

RIGHEIRA
Italy

SINGLES:		HITS 1		WEEKS 3	
VAMOS A LA PLAYA	A&M		53	24 Sep 83	3

RIGHT SAID FRED
UK

SINGLES:		HITS 8		WEEKS 61	
I'M TOO SEXY	Tug		2	27 Jul 91	16
DON'T TALK JUST KISS	Tug		3	7 Dec 91	11

Above hit: RIGHT SAID FRED guest vocal Jocelyn BROWN.

DEEPLY DIPPY	Tug		1	21 Mar 92	14
THOSE SIMPLE THINGS / (WHAT A DAY FOR A) DAYDREAM	Tug		29	1 Aug 92	5
STICK IT OUT	Tug		4	27 Feb 93	7

Charity Record for Comic Relief's Red Nose day (12 Mar 93). Friends are Hugh Laurie, Peter Cook, Alan Freeman, Jools Holland, Steve Coogan, Clive Anderson, Linda Robson, Pauline Quirke, Sir Basil Brush and Bernard Cribbins.
Above hit: RIGHT SAID FRED and FRIENDS.

BUMPED	Tug		32	23 Oct 93	4
HANDS UP (4 LOVERS)	Tug		60	18 Dec 93	3
WONDERMAN	Tug		55	19 Mar 94	1

Featured in the Sega Sonic 3 TV commercial.

ALBUMS:		HITS 2		WEEKS 53	
UP	Tug		1	28 Mar 92	49
SEX AND TRAVEL	Tug		35	13 Nov 93	4

RIGHTEOUS BROTHERS
US

SINGLES:		HITS 7		WEEKS 86	
YOU'VE LOST THAT LOVIN' FEELIN'	London		1	16 Jan 65	10
UNCHAINED MELODY	London		14	14 Aug 65	12

Originally recorded by Alex North as an instrumental.

EBB TIDE	London		48	15 Jan 66	2

Originally recorded by Robert Maxwell.

(YOU'RE MY) SOUL AND INSPIRATION	Verve		15	16 Apr 66	10
THE WHITE CLIFFS OF DOVER	London		21	12 Nov 66	9
ISLAND IN THE SUN	Verve		36	24 Dec 66	5
YOU'VE LOST THAT LOVIN' FEELIN' [RI-1ST]	London		10	15 Feb 69	11
YOU'VE LOST THAT LOVIN' FEELIN' [RI-2ND]	Phil Spector International		42	19 Nov 77	4
UNCHAINED MELODY [RI]	Verve		1	27 Oct 90	14

From the film 'Ghosts'.

YOU'VE LOST THAT LOVIN' FEELING [RI-3RD] / EBB TIDE [RI]	Verve		3	15 Dec 90	9

Ebb Tide listed from 22 Dec 90.

ALBUMS:		HITS 1		WEEKS 17	
THE VERY BEST OF THE RIGHTEOUS BROTHERS: UNCHAINED MELODY	Verve		11	1 Dec 90	17

Cheryl Pepsi RILEY
US

SINGLES:		HITS 1		WEEKS 1	
THANKS FOR MY CHILD	CBS		75	28 Jan 89	1

Jeannie C. RILEY
US

SINGLES:		HITS 1		WEEKS 15	
HARPER VALLEY P. T. A.	Polydor		12	19 Oct 68	15

Originally recorded by Alice Joy.

Teddy RILEY featuring Tammy LUCAS
US

(See also Blackstreet.)

SINGLES:		HITS 1		WEEKS 2	
IS IT GOOD TO YOU	MCA		53	21 Mar 92	2

RIMES featuring Shaila PROSPERE
UK

SINGLES:		HITS 1		WEEKS 1	
IT'S OVER	Universal		51	22 May 99	1

Original by Oddyssey was the B-side of Use It Up And Wear It Out.

LeAnn RIMES
US

SINGLES:		HITS 5		WEEKS 53	
HOW DO I LIVE	Curb		7	7 Mar 98	33
LOOKING THROUGH YOUR EYES / COMMITMENT	Curb		38	12 Sep 98	2

From the film 'The Magic Sword: Quest For Camelot'.

HOW DO I LIVE [RE]	Curb		72	31 Oct 98	1
BLUE	Curb		23	12 Dec 98	6

Written for Patsy Cline who died before she could record it

WRITTEN IN THE STARS	*Rocket*	10	*6 Mar 99*	7

From the Walt Disney film 'Aida'.
Above hit: Elton JOHN and LeAnn RIMES.

WRITTEN IN THE STARS [RE]	*Rocket*	63	*22 May 99*	1
CRAZY	*Curb*	36	*18 Dec 99*	3
ALBUMS:	**HITS 1**		**WEEKS 22**	
SITTIN' ON TOP OF THE WORLD	*Curb*	11	*6 Jun 98*	22

RIMSHOTS US

SINGLES:	**HITS 1**		**WEEKS 5**	
7-6-5-4-3-2-1 (BLOW YOUR WHISTLE)	*All Platinum*	26	*19 Jul 75*	5

Originally recorded by Blue Mink.

RIO and MARS UK/France

SINGLES:	**HITS 1**		**WEEKS 3**	
BOY I GOTTA HAVE YOU	*Dome*	43	*28 Jan 95*	2
BOY I GOTTA HAVE YOU [RI]	*Feverpitch*	46	*13 Apr 96*	1

Miguel RIOS Spain

SINGLES:	**HITS 1**		**WEEKS 12**	
SONG OF JOY	*A&M*	16	*11 Jul 70*	12

Adapted from the last movement of Beethoven's Ninth Symphony. Conducted by Waldo de los Rios
and his Orchestra.

RIP RIG AND PANIC UK/US

ALBUMS:	**HITS 1**		**WEEKS 3**	
I AM COLD	*Virgin*	67	*26 Jun 82*	3

Minnie RIPERTON US

SINGLES:	**HITS 1**		**WEEKS 10**	
LOVIN' YOU	*Epic*	2	*12 Apr 75*	10
ALBUMS:	**HITS 1**		**WEEKS 3**	
PERFECT ANGEL	*Epic*	33	*17 May 75*	3

Angela RIPPON UK

ALBUMS:	**HITS 1**		**WEEKS 26**	
SHAPE UP AND DANCE FEATURING ANGELA RIPPON (VOLUME II)	*Lifestyle*	8	*17 Apr 82*	26

RISE UK

SINGLES:	**HITS 1**		**WEEKS 1**	
THE SINGLE	*East West*	70	*3 Sep 94*	1

Features rappers Hawkeye and Anita from Yo Yo Honey.

RITCHIE FAMILY US

SINGLES:	**HITS 3**		**WEEKS 19**	
BRAZIL	*Polydor*	41	*23 Aug 75*	4
THE BEST DISCO IN TOWN	*Polydor*	10	*18 Sep 76*	9
AMERICAN GENERATION	*Mercury*	49	*17 Feb 79*	6

Lee RITENOUR with Maxi PRIEST US/UK

(See also Maxi Priest.)

SINGLES:	**HITS 1**		**WEEKS 2**	
WAITING IN VAIN	*GRP*	65	*31 Jul 93*	2

Tex RITTER US

SINGLES:	**HITS 1**		**WEEKS 14**	
THE WAYWARD WIND	*Capitol*	8	*23 Jun 56*	14
EPS:	**HITS 1**		**WEEKS 1**	
DECK OF CARDS	*Capitol*	19	*8 Dec 62*	1

Paco RIVAZ – See GAMBAFREAKS featuring Paco RIVAZ

RIVER CITY PEOPLE UK

SINGLES:	**HITS 6**		**WEEKS 27**	
(WHAT'S WRONG WITH) DREAMING?	*EMI*	70	*12 Aug 89*	3
WALKING ON ICE	*EMI*	62	*3 Mar 90*	2
CARRY THE BLAME / CALIFORNIA DREAMIN'	*EMI*	13	*30 Jun 90*	10

From 4 Aug 90 titles were listed in reverse.

(WHAT'S WRONG WITH) DREAMING? [RI]	*EMI*	40	*22 Sep 90*	3
WHEN I WAS YOUNG	*EMI*	62	*2 Mar 91*	2
SPECIAL WAY	*EMI*	44	*28 Sep 91*	3
STANDING IN THE NEED OF LOVE	*EMI*	36	*22 Feb 92*	4

ALBUMS:	HITS 2			WEEKS 10
SAY SOMETHING GOOD	EMI	23	25 Aug 90	9
THIS IS THE WORLD	EMI	56	2 Nov 91	1

RIVER DETECTIVES — UK

SINGLES:	HITS 1			WEEKS 4
CHAINS	WEA	51	29 Jul 89	4
ALBUMS:	HITS 1			WEEKS 1
SATURDAY NIGHT SUNDAY MORNING	WEA	51	23 Sep 89	1

RIVER OCEAN featuring INDIA — UK

(See also Masters At Work present India; Nuyorican Soul.)

SINGLES:	HITS 1			WEEKS 2
LOVE AND HAPPINESS (YEMAYA Y OCHUN)	Cooltempo	50	26 Feb 94	2

Danny RIVERS — UK

SINGLES:	HITS 1			WEEKS 3
CAN'T YOU HEAR MY HEART	Decca	36	14 Jan 61	3

Tony RIVERS and Nigel PERRIN – See Cliff RICHARD

RM PROJECT — UK

SINGLES:	HITS 1			WEEKS 1
GET IT UP	Inferno	49	3 Jul 99	1

Vocals by Triple A.

David ROACH — UK

ALBUMS:	HITS 1			WEEKS 1
I LOVE SAX	Nouveau Music	73	14 Apr 84	1

ROACH MOTEL — UK

SINGLES:	HITS 2			WEEKS 2
AFRO SLEEZE / TRANSATLANTIC	Junior Boy's Own	73	21 Aug 93	1
HAPPY BIZZNESS / WILD LUV	Junior Boy's Own	75	10 Dec 94	1

ROACHFORD — UK

SINGLES:	HITS 12			WEEKS 61
CUDDLY TOY	CBS	61	18 Jun 88	4
CUDDLY TOY [RI]	CBS	4	14 Jan 89	9
FAMILY MAN	CBS	25	18 Mar 89	6
KATHLEEN	CBS	43	1 Jul 89	5
GET READY!	Columbia	22	13 Apr 91	8
ONLY TO BE WITH YOU	Columbia	21	19 Mar 94	7
LAY YOUR LOVE ON ME	Columbia	36	18 Jun 94	5
THIS GENERATION	Columbia	38	20 Aug 94	4
CRY FOR ME	Columbia	46	3 Dec 94	2
I KNOW YOU DON'T LOVE ME	Columbia	42	1 Apr 95	2
THE WAY I FEEL	Columbia	20	11 Oct 97	4
HOW COULD I? (INSECURITY)	Columbia	34	14 Feb 98	3
NAKED WITHOUT YOU	Columbia	53	11 Jul 98	2
ALBUMS:	HITS 4			WEEKS 56
ROACHFORD	CBS	69	23 Jul 88	3
ROACHFORD [RE]	CBS	11	11 Feb 89	24
GET READY!	Columbia	20	18 May 91	5
PERMANENT SHADE OF BLUE	Columbia	25	16 Apr 94	21
FEEL	Columbia	19	25 Oct 97	3

ROB 'N' RAZ — Sweden

SINGLES:	HITS 2			WEEKS 17
GOT TO GET	Arista	8	25 Nov 89	14

Above hit: ROB 'N' RAZ featuring Leila K.

ROK THE NATION	Arista	41	17 Mar 90	3

Above hit: ROB 'N' RAZ with Leila K.

Natalie ROBB – See PARTIZAN

Kate ROBBINS and BEYOND — UK

SINGLES:	HITS 1			WEEKS 10
MORE THAN IN LOVE	RCA	2	30 May 81	10

Featured in the ATV soap 'Crossroads'.

Marty ROBBINS
US

SINGLES:		HITS 4		WEEKS 33	
EL PASO	*Fontana*	19	*30 Jan 60*	8
EL PASO [RE]	*Fontana*	44	*9 Apr 60*	1
BIG IRON	*Fontana*	48	*28 May 60*	1
DEVIL WOMAN	*CBS*	5	*29 Sep 62*	17
RUBY ANN	*CBS*	24	*19 Jan 63*	6
ALBUMS:		**HITS 2**		**WEEKS 15**
GUNFIGHTER BALLADS AND TRAIL SONGS	*Fontana*	20	*13 Aug 60*	1
MARTY ROBBINS COLLECTION	*Lotus*	5	*10 Feb 79*	14

Antoinette ROBERSON – See PULSE featuring Antoinette ROBERSON

Austin ROBERTS
US

SINGLES:		HITS 1		WEEKS 7	
ROCKY	*Private Stock*	22	*25 Oct 75*	7

Joe ROBERTS
UK

SINGLES:		HITS 5		WEEKS 17	
BACK IN MY LIFE	*London*	59	*28 Aug 93*	1
LOVER	*ffrr*	22	*29 Jan 94*	5
BACK IN MY LIFE [RI]	*ffrr*	39	*14 May 94*	3
ADORE	*ffrr*	45	*6 Aug 94*	3
Prince's original version appeared on his 1987 album Sign 'O' The Times.				
YOU ARE EVERYTHING	*Columbia*	28	*18 Feb 95*	4
Original by the Stylistics reached No. 9 in the US in 1971.				
Above hit: Melanie WILLIAMS and Joe ROBERTS.				
HAPPY DAYS	*Grass Green*	63	*24 Feb 96*	1
Above hit: SWEET MERCY featuring Joe ROBERTS.				

Juliet ROBERTS
UK

SINGLES:		HITS 5		WEEKS 29	
CAUGHT IN THE MIDDLE	*Cooltempo*	24	*31 Jul 93*	6
FREE LOVE	*Cooltempo*	25	*6 Nov 93*	3
Original release reached No. 83 in 1992.				
AGAIN / I WANT YOU	*Cooltempo*	33	*19 Mar 94*	3
CAUGHT IN THE MIDDLE (MY HEART BEATS LIKE A DRUM) [RM]	*Cooltempo*	14	*2 Jul 94*	5
Remixed by David Morales and Peter 'Ski' Schwartz.				
I WANT YOU [RI]	*Cooltempo*	28	*15 Oct 94*	3
SO GOOD / FREE LOVE 98 [RM]	*Delirious*	15	*31 Jan 98*	4
Free Love remixed by Bumpy Sunday.				
BAD GIRLS / I LIKE	*Delirious*	17	*23 Jan 99*	5
ALBUMS:		**HITS 1**		**WEEKS 1**
NATURAL THING	*Cooltempo*	65	*2 Apr 94*	1

Malcolm ROBERTS
UK

SINGLES:		HITS 3		WEEKS 29	
TIME ALONE WILL TELL	*RCA Victor*	45	*13 May 67*	2
MAY I HAVE THE NEXT DREAM WITH YOU	*Major Minor*	8	*2 Nov 68*	14
MAY I HAVE THE NEXT DREAM WITH YOU [RE]	*Major Minor*	45	*15 Feb 69*	1
LOVE IS ALL	*Major Minor*	12	*22 Nov 69*	12

Paddy ROBERTS
South Africa

EPS:		HITS 2		WEEKS 90	
STRICTLY FOR GROWN UPS	*Decca*	1	*12 Mar 60*	66
PADDY ROBERTS STRIKES AGAIN	*Decca*	1	*30 Jul 60*	24
ALBUMS:		**HITS 2**		**WEEKS 6**
STRICTLY FOR GROWN-UPS	*Decca*	8	*26 Sep 59*	5
PADDY ROBERTS TRIES AGAIN	*Decca*	16	*17 Sep 60*	1

B.A. ROBERTSON
UK

SINGLES:		HITS 6		WEEKS 60	
BANG BANG	*Asylum*	2	*28 Jul 79*	12
KNOCKED IT OFF	*Asylum*	8	*27 Oct 79*	12
KOOL IN THE KAFTAN	*Asylum*	17	*1 Mar 80*	12
TO BE OR NOT TO BE	*Asylum*	9	*31 May 80*	11
HOLD ME	*Swan Song*	11	*17 Oct 81*	8
Above hit: B.A. ROBERTSON and Maggie BELL.				
TIME	*Epic*	45	*17 Dec 83*	5
Above hit: FRIDA and B.A. ROBERTSON.				
ALBUMS:		**HITS 2**		**WEEKS 10**
INITIAL SUCCESS	*Asylum*	32	*29 Mar 80*	8
BULLY FOR YOU	*Asylum*	61	*4 Apr 81*	2

Don ROBERTSON
US

SINGLES:		HITS 1			WEEKS 9
THE HAPPY WHISTLER	Capitol		8	12 May 56	9

Robbie ROBERTSON
Canada

SINGLES:		HITS 2			WEEKS 11
SOMEWHERE DOWN THE CRAZY RIVER	Geffen		15	23 Jul 88	10
TAKE YOUR PARTNER BY THE HAND	Polydor		74	11 Apr 98	1
Above hit: Howie B featuring Robbie ROBERTSON.					
ALBUMS:		HITS 2			WEEKS 16
ROBBIE ROBERTSON	Geffen		52	14 Nov 87	3
ROBBIE ROBERTSON [RE]	Geffen		23	13 Aug 88	11
STORYVILLE	Geffen		30	12 Oct 91	2

Ivo ROBIC und die SING-MASTERS
Yugoslavia

SINGLES:		HITS 1			WEEKS 1
MORGEN (ONE MORE SUNRISE) SLOW-FOX	Polydor		23	7 Nov 59	1

ROBIN – See MUPPETS

Dawn ROBINSON – See Nas ESCOBAR, Foxy BROWN, AZ and NATURE present the FIRM featuring Dawn ROBINSON

Floyd ROBINSON
US

SINGLES:		HITS 1			WEEKS 9
MAKIN' LOVE	RCA		9	17 Oct 59	9

Smokey ROBINSON
US

(See also Miracles; Diana Ross, Marvin Gaye, Smokey Robinson and Stevie Wonder.)

SINGLES:		HITS 5			WEEKS 40
JUST MY SOUL RESPONDING	Tamla Motown		35	23 Feb 74	6
BEING WITH YOU	Motown		1	9 May 81	13
TELL ME TOMORROW	Motown		51	13 Mar 82	4
JUST TO SEE HER	Motown		52	28 Mar 87	6
INDESTRUCTIBLE [RM]	Arista		55	17 Sep 88	4
Remixed by Phil Harding and Ian Curnow.					
INDESTRUCTIBLE	Arista		30	25 Feb 89	7
This was actually the original US recording, it charted after the UK mix. Smokey Robinson was only credited on the back of the sleeves of both releases.					
Above 2: FOUR TOPS featuring Smokey ROBINSON.					
ALBUMS:		HITS 3			WEEKS 21
BEING WITH YOU	Motown		17	20 Jun 81	10
LOVE SONGS	Telstar		69	12 Nov 88	9
Compilation divided between the two artists.					
Above hit: Marvin GAYE and Smokey ROBINSON.					
THE GREATEST HITS	PolyGram TV		65	14 Nov 92	2
Includes both Smokey Robinson's solo and group material.					
Above hit: Smokey ROBINSON and the MIRACLES.					

Tom ROBINSON BAND
UK

SINGLES:		HITS 7			WEEKS 41
2. 4. 6. 8. MOTORWAY	EMI		5	22 Oct 77	9
RISING FREE [EP]	EMI		18	18 Feb 78	6
Lead track: Don't Take No For An Answer. This track was listed on the chart of 18 Feb 78, EP title listed on 25 Feb 78 and the track Sing If You're Glad To Be Gay on 4 Mar 78.					
UP AGAINST THE WALL	EMI		33	13 May 78	6
BULLY FOR YOU	EMI		68	17 Mar 79	2
WAR BABY	Panic		6	25 Jun 83	9
LISTEN TO THE RADIO: ATMOSPHERICS	Panic		39	12 Nov 83	6
RIKKI DON'T LOSE THAT NUMBER	Castaway		58	15 Sep 84	3
Above 3: Tom ROBINSON.					
ALBUMS:		HITS 3			WEEKS 23
POWER IN THE DARKNESS	EMI		4	3 Jun 78	12
TRB2	EMI		18	24 Mar 79	6
HOPE AND GLORY	Castaway		21	29 Sep 84	5
Above hit: Tom ROBINSON.					

Vicki Sue ROBINSON
US

SINGLES:		HITS 1			WEEKS 1
HOUSE OF JOY	Logic		48	27 Sep 97	1

ROBSON and JEROME   UK

SINGLES:	HITS 3			WEEKS 45
UNCHAINED MELODY / (THERE'LL BE BLUEBIRDS OVER) THE WHITE CLIFFS OF DOVER	RCA	1	20 May 95	17
Unchained Melody originally recorded by Alex North as an instrumental.				
Above hit: Robson GREEN and Jerome FLYNN.				
I BELIEVE / UP ON THE ROOF	RCA	1	11 Nov 95	14
WHAT BECOMES OF THE BROKEN HEARTED / SATURDAY NIGHT AT THE MOVIES / YOU'LL NEVER WALK ALONE	RCA	1	9 Nov 96	14
ALBUMS:	HITS 3			WEEKS 53
ROBSON & JEROME	RCA	1	25 Nov 95	31
TAKE TWO	RCA	1	23 Nov 96	16
HAPPY DAYS - THE BEST OF ROBSON AND JEROME	RCA	20	29 Nov 97	6

ROBYN   Sweden

SINGLES:	HITS 4			WEEKS 14
YOU'VE GOT THAT SOMETHIN'	RCA	54	20 Jul 96	1
DO YOU KNOW (WHAT IT TAKES)	RCA	26	16 Aug 97	3
SHOW ME LOVE	RCA	8	7 Mar 98	6
DO YOU REALLY WANT ME	RCA	20	30 May 98	4

John ROCCA – See FREEEZ

ROCHELLE   US

SINGLES:	HITS 1			WEEKS 6
MY MAGIC MAN	Warner Brothers	27	1 Feb 86	6

Chubb ROCK   US

SINGLES:	HITS 1			WEEKS 1
TREAT 'EM RIGHT	Champion	67	19 Jan 91	1

Pete ROCK and C.L. SMOOTH   US

ALBUMS:	HITS 1			WEEKS 1
THE MAIN INGREDIENT	Elektra	69	19 Nov 94	1

ROCK AID ARMEMIA   UK

SINGLES:	HITS 1			WEEKS 5
SMOKE ON THE WATER	Life Aid Armenia	39	16 Dec 89	5

ROCK CANDY   UK

SINGLES:	HITS 1			WEEKS 6
REMEMBER	MCA	32	11 Sep 71	6

ROCK GODDESS   UK

SINGLES:	HITS 2			WEEKS 5
MY ANGEL	A&M	64	5 Mar 83	2
I DIDN'T KNOW I LOVED YOU (TILL I SAW YOU ROCK 'N' ROLL)	A&M	57	24 Mar 84	3
ALBUMS:	HITS 2			WEEKS 3
ROCK GODDESS	A&M	65	12 Mar 83	2
HELL HATH NO FURY	A&M	84	29 Oct 83	1

Roland ROCKCAKE and his WHOLLY ROLLERS – See GOONS

ROCKERS REVENGE featuring Donnie CALVIN   US

SINGLES:	HITS 2			WEEKS 20
WALKING ON SUNSHINE	London	4	14 Aug 82	13
Originally recorded by Eddy Grant.				
THE HARDER THEY COME	London	30	29 Jan 83	7

ROCKET FROM THE CRYPT   US

SINGLES:	HITS 4			WEEKS 7
BORN IN '69	Elemental	68	27 Jan 96	1
YOUNG LIVERS	Elemental	67	13 Apr 96	1
ON A ROPE	Elemental	12	14 Sep 96	4
LIPSTICK	Elemental	64	29 Aug 98	1
ALBUMS:	HITS 2			WEEKS 4
SCREAM, DRACULA, SCREAM!	Elemental	41	3 Feb 96	3
RFTC	Elemental	63	18 Jul 98	1

ROCKETS – See Tony CROMBIE and his ROCKETS

ROCKFORD FILES
UK

SINGLES:	HITS 1			WEEKS 4	
YOU SEXY DANCER	Escapade	34	11 Mar 95		3
YOU SEXY DANCER [RI]	Escapade	59	6 Apr 96		1

ROCKIN' BERRIES
UK

SINGLES:	HITS 6			WEEKS 41	
I DIDN'T MEAN TO HURT YOU	Piccadilly	43	3 Oct 64		1
HE'S IN TOWN	Piccadilly	3	17 Oct 64		13
Originally recorded by the Tokens.					
WHAT IN THE WORLD'S COME OVER YOU	Piccadilly	23	23 Jan 65		7
POOR MAN'S SON	Piccadilly	5	15 May 65		11
Originally recorded by the Reflections.					
YOU'RE MY GIRL	Piccadilly	40	28 Aug 65		7
THE WATER IS OVER MY HEAD	Piccadilly	43	8 Jan 66		1
THE WATER IS OVER MY HEAD [RE]	Piccadilly	50	22 Jan 66		1
ALBUMS:	HITS 1			WEEKS 1	
IN TOWN	Pye	15	19 Jun 65		1

ROCKINGBIRDS – See VARIOUS ARTISTS (EPs) 'The Fred EP'

ROCKNEY – See CHAS and DAVE

ROCKPILE
UK

(See also Dave Edmunds.)

ALBUMS:	HITS 1			WEEKS 5	
SECONDS OF PLEASURE	F-Beat	34	18 Oct 80		5

ROCKSTEADY CREW
US

SINGLES:	HITS 2			WEEKS 16	
(HEY YOU) THE ROCKSTEADY CREW	Charisma	6	1 Oct 83		12
UPROCK	Charisma	64	5 May 84		4
ALBUMS:	HITS 1			WEEKS 1	
READY FOR BATTLE	Charisma	73	16 Jun 84		1

ROCKWELL
US

SINGLES:	HITS 1			WEEKS 11	
SOMEBODY'S WATCHING ME	Motown	6	4 Feb 84		11
Vocals by Michael Jackson.					
ALBUMS:	HITS 1			WEEKS 5	
SOMEBODY'S WATCHING ME	Motown	52	25 Feb 84		5

"ROCKY V" featuring Joey B. ELLIS and Tynetta HARE – See Joey B. ELLIS

ROCOCO
UK/Italy

SINGLES:	HITS 1			WEEKS 5	
ITALO HOUSE MIX [M]	Mercury	54	16 Dec 89		5

RODEO JONES
UK/Granada

SINGLES:	HITS 2			WEEKS 2	
NATURAL WORLD	A&M	75	30 Jan 93		1
SHADES OF SUMMER	A&M	59	3 Apr 93		1

Clodagh RODGERS
Ireland

SINGLES:	HITS 6			WEEKS 59	
COME BACK AND SHAKE ME	RCA Victor	3	29 Mar 69		14
GOODNIGHT MIDNIGHT	RCA Victor	4	12 Jul 69		11
GOODNIGHT MIDNIGHT [RE]	RCA Victor	48	4 Oct 69		1
BILJO	RCA Victor	22	8 Nov 69		9
EVERYBODY GO HOME THE PARTY'S OVER	RCA Victor	47	4 Apr 70		2
JACK IN THE BOX	RCA Victor	4	20 Mar 71		10
UK's Eurovision entry in 1971, it came 4th.					
LADY LOVE BUG	RCA Victor	28	9 Oct 71		12
ALBUMS:	HITS 1			WEEKS 1	
CLODAGH RODGERS	RCA Victor	27	13 Sep 69		1

Eric RODGERS and his ORCHESTRA – See Max BYGRAVES

Jimmy RODGERS
US

SINGLES:	HITS 5			WEEKS 37	
HONEY COMB	Columbia	30	2 Nov 57		1
Originally recorded by Georgie Shaw.					

KISSES SWEETER THAN WINE	Columbia	7	21 Dec 57	11

Originally recorded by the Weavers.
Above 2: Jimmy RODGERS with Hugo PERETTI and his Orchestra.

OH-OH, I'M FALLING IN LOVE AGAIN	Columbia	18	29 Mar 58	6
WOMAN FROM LIBERIA	Columbia	18	20 Dec 58	6
ENGLISH COUNTRY GARDEN	Columbia	5	16 Jun 62	13

Paul RODGERS — UK

SINGLES:	HITS 1			WEEKS 2
MUDDY WATER BLUES	Victory	45	12 Feb 94	2
ALBUMS:	HITS 2			WEEKS 11
MUDDY WATER BLUES	Victory	9	3 Jul 93	7

Tribute to blues guitarist Muddy Waters.

NOW	SPV Recordings	30	15 Feb 97	4

RODRIGUEZ – See SASH!

RODS – See EDDIE and the HOT RODS

RODS — US

ALBUMS:	HITS 1			WEEKS 4
WILD DOGS	Arista	75	24 Jul 82	4

Tommy ROE — US

SINGLES:	HITS 6			WEEKS 74
SHEILA	His Master's Voice	3	8 Sep 62	14
SUSIE DARLIN'	His Master's Voice	37	8 Dec 62	5
THE FOLK SINGER	His Master's Voice	4	23 Mar 63	13
EVERYBODY	His Master's Voice	9	28 Sep 63	11
EVERYBODY [RE]	His Master's Voice	49	21 Dec 63	3
DIZZY	Stateside	1	19 Apr 69	19
HEATHER HONEY	Stateside	24	26 Jul 69	9

ROFO — UK

SINGLES:	HITS 1			WEEKS 3
ROFO'S THEME	PWL Continental	44	1 Aug 92	3

ROGER — US

SINGLES:	HITS 3			WEEKS 8
I WANT TO BE YOUR MAN	Reprise	61	17 Oct 87	4
BOOM! THERE SHE WAS	Virgin	55	12 Nov 88	3

Above hit: SCRITTI POLITTI featuring ROGER.

HIGH AS A KITE	ffrr	55	13 May 95	1

Above hit: ONE TRIBE featuring ROGER.

Julie ROGERS — UK

SINGLES:	HITS 3			WEEKS 38
THE WEDDING (LA NOVIA)	Mercury	3	15 Aug 64	23

Originally recorded by Anita Bryant.
Above hit: Julie ROGERS with Johnny ARTHEY and his Orchestra and Chorus.

LIKE A CHILD	Mercury	21	12 Dec 64	9
HAWAIIAN WEDDING SONG	Mercury	31	27 Mar 65	6

Kenny ROGERS — US

SINGLES:	HITS 10			WEEKS 109
RUBY, DON'T TAKE YOUR LOVE TO TOWN	Reprise	2	18 Oct 69	23

Originally recorded by Johnny Darrell.

SOMETHING'S BURNING	Reprise	8	7 Feb 70	14

Originally recorded by Mac David.
Above 2: Kenny ROGERS and the FIRST EDITION.

LUCILLE	United Artists	1	30 Apr 77	14

Originally recorded by Johnny Darrell.

DAYTIME FRIENDS	United Artists	39	17 Sep 77	4
SHE BELIEVES IN ME	United Artists	42	2 Jun 79	7

Originally recorded by Steve Gibb.

COWARD OF THE COUNTY	United Artists	1	26 Jan 80	12
LADY	United Artists	12	15 Nov 80	12

Written by Lionel Richie.

WE'VE GOT TONIGHT	Liberty	28	12 Feb 83	7

Above hit: Kenny ROGERS and Sheena EASTON.

EYES THAT SEE IN THE DARK	RCA	61	22 Oct 83	1
ISLANDS IN THE STREAM	RCA	7	12 Nov 83	15

Written by the Bee Gees.
Above hit: Kenny ROGERS duet with Dolly PARTON.

ALBUMS:		HITS 10		WEEKS 111	
KENNY ROGERS	United Artists	14	18 Jun 77	7
THE KENNY ROGERS SINGLES ALBUM	United Artists	12	6 Oct 79	22
KENNY	United Artists	7	9 Feb 80	10
LADY	Liberty	40	31 Jan 81	5
EYES THAT SEE IN THE DARK	RCA	53	1 Oct 83	19
WHAT ABOUT ME?	RCA	97	27 Oct 84	1
THE KENNY ROGERS STORY	Liberty	4	27 Jul 85	29
DAYTIME FRIENDS – THE VERY BEST OF KENNY ROGERS	EMI	16	25 Sep 93	5
LOVE SONGS	Virgin	27	22 Nov 97	7
ALL THE HITS & ALL NEW LOVE SONGS	EMI	14	29 May 99	6

ROKOTTO   UK

SINGLES:		HITS 2		WEEKS 10	
BOOGIE ON UP	State	40	22 Oct 77	4
FUNK THEORY	State	49	10 Jun 78	6

ROLLING STONES   UK

SINGLES:		HITS 46		WEEKS 366	
COME ON	Decca	21	27 Jul 63	14
Originally recorded by Chuck Berry.				
I WANNA BE YOUR MAN	Decca	12	16 Nov 63	16
Originally recorded by the Beatles.				
NOT FADE AWAY	Decca	3	29 Feb 64	15
IT'S ALL OVER NOW	Decca	1	4 Jul 64	15
Originally recorded by the Valentinos.				
LITTLE RED ROOSTER	Decca	1	21 Nov 64	12
Originally recorded by Willie Dixon.				
THE LAST TIME	Decca	1	6 Mar 65	13
(I CAN'T GET NO) SATISFACTION	Decca	1	28 Aug 65	12
GET OFF OF MY CLOUD	Decca	1	30 Oct 65	12
19TH NERVOUS BREAKDOWN	Decca	2	12 Feb 66	8
PAINT IT, BLACK	Decca	1	21 May 66	10
HAVE YOU SEEN YOUR MOTHER BABY, STANDING IN THE SHADOW?	Decca	5	1 Oct 66	8
LET'S SPEND THE NIGHT TOGETHER / RUBY TUESDAY	Decca	3	21 Jan 67	10
WE LOVE YOU / DANDELION	Decca	8	26 Aug 67	8
Backing vocals by John Lennon and Paul McCartney.				
JUMPIN' JACK FLASH	Decca	1	1 Jun 68	11
HONKY TONK WOMEN	Decca	1	12 Jul 69	17
BROWN SUGAR / BITCH/LET IT ROCK	Rolling Stones	2	24 Apr 71	13
STREET FIGHTING MAN	Decca	21	3 Jul 71	8
TUMBLING DICE	Rolling Stones	5	29 Apr 72	8
ANGIE	Rolling Stones	5	1 Sep 73	10
Written about Angie Bowie.				
IT'S ONLY ROCK 'N ROLL	Rolling Stones	10	3 Aug 74	7
OUT OF TIME	Decca	45	20 Sep 75	2
FOOL TO CRY	Rolling Stones	6	1 May 76	10
MISS YOU / FARAWAY EYES	Rolling Stones	3	3 Jun 78	13
Faraway Eyes listed from 15 Jul 78 once single had dropped to No. 10.				
RESPECTABLE	Rolling Stones	23	30 Sep 78	9
EMOTIONAL RESCUE	Rolling Stones	9	5 Jul 80	8
SHE'S SO COLD	Rolling Stones	33	4 Oct 80	6
START ME UP	Rolling Stones	7	29 Aug 81	9
WAITING ON A FRIEND	Rolling Stones	50	12 Dec 81	6
GOING TO A GO GO (LIVE)	Rolling Stones	26	12 Jun 82	6
TIME IS ON MY SIDE (LIVE)	Rolling Stones	62	2 Oct 82	2
Above 2 are live recordings from the American Concerts in 1981.				
UNDERCOVER OF THE NIGHT	Rolling Stones	11	12 Nov 83	9
SHE WAS HOT	Rolling Stones	42	11 Feb 84	4
BROWN SUGAR [RI]	Rolling Stones	58	21 Jul 84	2
HARLEM SHUFFLE	Rolling Stones	13	15 Mar 86	7
MIXED EMOTIONS	Rolling Stones	36	2 Sep 89	5
ROCK AND A HARD PLACE	Rolling Stones	63	2 Dec 89	1
PAINT IT BLACK [RI]	London	61	23 Jun 90	3
ALMOST HEAR YOU SIGH	Rolling Stones	31	30 Jun 90	5
HIGHWIRE	Rolling Stones	29	30 Mar 91	4
RUBY TUESDAY (LIVE) [RR]	Rolling Stones	59	1 Jun 91	2
LOVE IS STRONG	Virgin	14	16 Jul 94	5
YOU GOT ME ROCKING	Virgin	23	8 Oct 94	3
OUT OF TEARS	Virgin	36	10 Dec 94	4
I GO WILD	Virgin	29	15 Jul 95	3
LIKE A ROLLING STONE	Virgin	12	11 Nov 95	5
ANYBODY SEEN MY BABY?	Virgin	22	4 Oct 97	3
SAINT OF ME	Virgin	26	7 Feb 98	2
OUT OF CONTROL	Virgin	51	22 Aug 98	1

EPS:	HITS 3		WEEKS 154	
THE ROLLING STONES	Decca	1	18 Jan 64	58
FIVE BY FIVE	Decca	1	22 Aug 64	54
GOT LIVE IF YOU WANT IT!	Decca	1	19 Jun 65	42
ALBUMS:	**HITS 42**		**WEEKS 761**	
COMPILATION ALBUMS:	**HITS 1**		**WEEKS 1**	
THE ROLLING STONES	Decca	1	25 Apr 64	51
ROLLING STONES NUMBER 2	Decca	1	23 Jan 65	37
OUT OF OUR HEADS	Decca	2	2 Oct 65	24
AFTERMATH	Decca	1	23 Apr 66	28
BIG HITS (HIGH TIDE AND GREEN GRASS)	Decca	4	12 Nov 66	43
BETWEEN THE BUTTONS	Decca	3	28 Jan 67	22
THEIR SATANIC MAJESTIES REQUEST	Decca	3	23 Dec 67	13
BEGGARS BANQUET	Decca	3	21 Dec 68	12
THROUGH THE PAST DARKLY (BIG HITS VOLUME 2)	Decca	2	27 Sep 69	37
LET IT BLEED	Decca	1	20 Dec 69	29
'GET YER YA-YA'S OUT!' - THE ROLLING STONES IN CONCERT	Decca	1	19 Sept 70	15
Live recordings from Madison Square Garden, New York on 27&28 Nov 69.				
STONE AGE	Decca	4	3 Apr 71	7
STICKY FINGERS	Rolling Stones	1	8 May 71	25
GIMME SHELTER	Decca	19	18 Sep 71	5
MILESTONES	Decca	14	11 Mar 72	8
EXILE ON MAIN STREET	Rolling Stones	1	10 Jun 72	16
ROCK 'N' ROLLING STONES	Decca	41	11 Nov 72	1
GOAT'S HEAD SOUP	Rolling Stones	1	22 Sep 73	14
IT'S ONLY ROCK 'N' ROLL	Rolling Stones	2	2 Nov 74	9
MADE IN THE SHADE	Rolling Stones	14	28 Jun 75	12
Compilation.				
METAMORPHOSIS	Decca	45	28 Jun 75	1
Collection of mainly Jagger/Richard songs from the 1960s which were demoed for other artists. All Decca albums above from Stone Age are re-packagings of old material.				
ROLLED GOLD - THE VERY BEST OF THE ROLLING STONES	Decca	7	29 Nov 75	50
BLACK AND BLUE	Rolling Stones	2	8 May 76	14
LOVE YOU LIVE	Rolling Stones	3	8 Oct 77	8
Live recordings from early 1977.				
GET STONED	Arcade	8	5 Nov 77	15
SOME GIRLS	Rolling Stones	2	24 Jun 78	25
EMOTIONAL RESCUE	Rolling Stones	1	5 Jul 80	18
TATTOO YOU	Rolling Stones	2	12 Sep 81	29
STILL LIFE (AMERICAN CONCERTS 1981)	Rolling Stones	4	12 Jun 82	18
Live recordings from the 1981 US tour.				
IN CONCERT	Decca	94	31 Jul 82	3
Dutch import.				
STORY OF THE STONES	K-Tel	24	11 Dec 82	12
UNDERCOVER	Rolling Stones	3	19 Nov 83	18
REWIND 1971-1984 (THE BEST OF THE ROLLING STONES)	Rolling Stones	23	7 Jul 84	13
DIRTY WORK	Rolling Stones	4	5 Apr 86	10
Dedicated to Ian Stewart who died from a heart-attack 12 Dec 85.				
STEEL WHEELS	Rolling Stones	2	23 Sep 89	18
HOT ROCKS - THE GREATEST HITS 1964-1971	London	3	7 Jul 90	18
REWIND 1971-1984 (THE BEST OF THE ROLLING STONES) [RE]	Rolling Stones	45	7 Jul 90	5
Re-released with a new catalogue number.				
FLASHPOINT	Rolling Stones	6	20 Apr 91	7
JUMP BACK - THE BEST OF THE ROLLING STONES 1971-93	Virgin	16	4 Dec 93	22
Includes re-entries through to 1999.				
STICKY FINGERS [RI]	Virgin	74	2 Jul 94	1
Issued for the first time on CD.				
VOODOO LOUNGE	Virgin	1	23 Jul 94	24
HOT ROCKS - THE GREATEST HITS 1964-1971 [RE]	London	41	22 Jul 95	6
Re-released with a new catalogue number. Includes re-entry in 1999.				
STRIPPED	Virgin	9	25 Nov 95	11
Live recordings from Olympia Theatre in Paris, the Paradise Club in Amsterdam and a rehearsal at the Toshiba-EMI studios in Tokyo.				
THE ROLLING STONES ROCK AND ROLL CIRCUS	Abkco	12	26 Oct 96	1
Recordings from the TV show filmed on 10 Dec 68 featuring the Who, Eric Clapton and John Lennon. This was an entry in the Compilation Chart.				
Above hit: ROLLING STONES and VARIOUS ARTISTS.				
BRIDGES TO BABYLON	Virgin	6	11 Oct 97	6
NO SECURITY	Virgin	67	14 Nov 98	1
Live recordings from shows during the Bridges To Babylon tour.				

ROLLINS BAND

US

SINGLES:	HITS 2		WEEKS 4	
TEARING	Imago	54	12 Sep 92	2
LIAR/DISCONNECT	Imago	27	10 Sep 94	2
ALBUMS:	**HITS 1**		**WEEKS 2**	
WEIGHT	Imago	22	23 Apr 94	2

ROLLO GOES . . . UK

SINGLES:	HITS 3		WEEKS 8	
GET OFF YOUR HIGH HORSE	Cheeky	43	29 Jan 94	2
Above hit: ROLLO GOES CAMPING.				
GET OFF YOUR HIGH HORSE [RE]	Cheeky	47	1 Oct 94	2
Above hit: ROLLO GOES CAMPING.				
LOVE, LOVE, LOVE - HERE I COME	Cheeky	32	10 Jun 95	2
Features vocals by Pauline Taylor of Gloworm.				
Above hit: ROLLO GOES MYSTIC.				
LET THIS BE A PRAYER	Cheeky	26	8 Jun 96	2
Above hit: ROLLO GOES SPIRITUAL with Pauline TAYLOR.				

ROMAN HOLLIDAY UK

SINGLES:	HITS 3		WEEKS 19	
STAND BY	Jive	61	2 Apr 83	3
DON'T TRY TO STOP IT	Jive	14	2 Jul 83	9
MOTORMANIA	Jive	40	24 Sep 83	7
ALBUMS:	**HITS 1**		**WEEKS 3**	
COOKIN' ON THE ROOF	Jive	31	22 Oct 83	3

ROMAN NUMERALS – See Vic REEVES

ROMANTICS – See RUBY and the ROMANTICS

Max ROMEO Jamaica

SINGLES:	HITS 1		WEEKS 25	
WET DREAM	Unity	10	31 May 69	24
WET DREAM [RE]	Unity	50	29 Nov 69	1

Harry 'Choo Choo' ROMERO presents Inaya DAY US

SINGLES:	HITS 1		WEEKS 2	
JUST CAN'T GET ENOUGH	Almo Sounds	39	22 May 99	2

RONALDO'S REVENGE UK

SINGLES:	HITS 1		WEEKS 2	
MAS QUE MANCADA	AM:PM	37	1 Aug 98	2

RONDO VENEZIANO Italy

SINGLES:	HITS 1		WEEKS 3	
LA SERENISSIMA - THEME FROM VENICE IN PERIL	Ferroway	58	22 Oct 83	3
ALBUMS:	**HITS 2**		**WEEKS 33**	
VENICE IN PERIL	Ferroway	59	5 Nov 83	3
VENICE IN PERIL [RE]	Ferroway	39	31 Mar 84	10
THE GENIUS OF VENICE	Ferroway	60	10 Nov 84	13
VENICE IN PERIL [RI]	Fanfare	34	9 Jul 88	7

RONETTES US

SINGLES:	HITS 4		WEEKS 34	
BE MY BABY	London	4	19 Oct 63	13
Features Cher on backing vocals.				
BABY, I LOVE YOU	London	11	11 Jan 64	14
(THE BEST PART OF) BREAKIN' UP	London	43	29 Aug 64	3
DO I LOVE YOU	London	35	10 Oct 64	4

RONNETTE – See FIDELFATTI featuring RONNETTE

Mick RONSON UK

SINGLES:	HITS 1		WEEKS 1	
DON'T LOOK DOWN	Epic	55	7 May 94	1
Above hit: Mick RONSON with Joe ELLIOTT.				
ALBUMS:	**HITS 2**		**WEEKS 10**	
SLAUGHTER ON TENTH AVENUE	RCA Victor	9	16 Mar 74	7
PLAY DON'T WORRY	RCA Victor	29	8 Mar 75	3

Linda RONSTADT US

(See also Dolly Parton, Linda Ronstadt and Emmylou Harris.)

SINGLES:	HITS 5		WEEKS 34	
TRACKS OF MY TEARS	Asylum	42	8 May 76	3
BLUE BAYOU	Asylum	35	28 Jan 78	4
ALISON	Asylum	66	26 May 79	2
SOMEWHERE OUT THERE	MCA	8	11 Jul 87	13
From the film 'An American Tail'.				
Above hit: Linda RONSTADT and James INGRAM.				

DON'T KNOW MUCH	Elektra	2	11 Nov 89	12

Originally recorded by Bill Medley.
Above hit: Linda RONSTADT featuring Aaron NEVILLE.

ALBUMS:	HITS 8		WEEKS 39	
HASTEN DOWN THE WIND	Asylum	32	4 Sep 76	8
GREATEST HITS	Asylum	37	25 Dec 76	9
SIMPLE DREAMS	Asylum	15	1 Oct 77	5
LIVING IN THE USA	Asylum	39	14 Oct 78	2
MAD LOVE	Asylum	65	8 Mar 80	1

Featuring the Cretones as backing group.

WHAT'S NEW	Asylum	31	28 Jan 84	5
LUSH LIFE	Asylum	100	19 Jan 85	1

Above 2: Linda RONSTADT with the Nelson RIDDLE ORCHESTRA.

CRY LIKE A RAINSTORM - HOWL LIKE THE WIND	Elektra	43	11 Nov 89	8

Above hit: Linda RONSTADT featuring Aaron NEVILLE.

ROOFTOP SINGERS
US

SINGLES:	HITS 1		WEEKS 12	
WALK RIGHT IN	Fontana	10	2 Feb 63	12

Originally recorded by Gus Cannon and the Jugstompers.

ROOTJOOSE
UK

SINGLES:	HITS 3		WEEKS 3	
CAN'T KEEP LIVING THIS WAY	Rage	73	17 May 97	1
MR. FIXIT	Rage	54	2 Aug 97	1
LONG WAY	Rage	68	4 Oct 97	1
ALBUMS:	HITS 1		WEEKS 1	
RHUBARB	Rage	58	18 Oct 97	1

ROOTS
US

SINGLES:	HITS 2		WEEKS 3	
WHAT THEY DO	Geffen	49	3 May 97	1
YOU GOT ME	MCA	31	6 Mar 99	2

Above hit: ROOTS featuring Erykah BADU.

ROOTS MANUVA – See LEFTFIELD

Ralphi ROSARIO – See Richie RICH

Barry ROSE – see GUILDFORD CATHEDRAL CHOIR conductor: Barry ROSE; Paul PHOENIX (treble) with Instrumental Ensemble – James WATSON (trumpet), John SCOTT (organ), conducted by Barry ROSE

David ROSE – See Connie FRANCIS

Mykal ROSE – See Shabba RANKS

ROSE OF ROMANCE ORCHESTRA
UK

SINGLES:	HITS 1		WEEKS 1	
TARA'S THEME FROM 'GONE WITH THE WIND'	BBC	71	9 Jan 82	1

ROSE ROYCE
US

SINGLES:	HITS 14		WEEKS 113	
CAR WASH	MCA	9	25 Dec 76	12
PUT YOUR MONEY WHERE YOUR MOUTH IS	MCA	44	22 Jan 77	5

The group's first UK release in 1976.

I WANNA GET NEXT TO YOU	MCA	14	2 Apr 77	8

Above 3 from the film 'Car Wash'. Originally recorded by Rhythm Aces.

DO YOUR DANCE	Whitfield	30	24 Sep 77	6
WISHING ON A STAR	Whitfield	3	14 Jan 78	14
IT MAKES YOU FEEL LIKE DANCIN'	Whitfield	16	6 May 78	10
LOVE DON'T LIVE HERE ANYMORE	Whitfield	2	16 Sep 78	10
I'M IN LOVE (AND I LOVE THE FEELING)	Whitfield	51	3 Feb 79	4
IS IT LOVE YOU'RE AFTER	Whitfield	13	17 Nov 79	13
OOH BOY	Whitfield	46	8 Mar 80	7
R.R. EXPRESS	Warner Brothers	52	21 Nov 81	3
MAGIC TOUCH	Streetwave	43	1 Sep 84	8
LOVE ME RIGHT NOW	Streetwave	60	6 Apr 85	3
CAR WASH [RI] / IS IT LOVE YOU'RE AFTER [RI]	MCA	20	11 Jun 88	7
CAR WASH [RR]	MCA	18	31 Oct 98	3

Sub titled: 1998 – The Monday Night Club Mixes.
Above hit: ROSE ROYCE featuring Gwen DICKEY.

ALBUMS:	HITS 6		WEEKS 66	
COMPILATION ALBUMS:	**HITS 1**		**WEEKS 6**	
IN FULL BLOOM	Whitfield	18	22 Oct 77	13
STRIKES AGAIN	Whitfield	7	30 Sep 78	11
RAINBOW CONNECTION IV	Atlantic	72	22 Sep 79	2

ROSE ROYCE GREATEST HITS	*Whitfield*	1	*1 Mar 80*	34
MUSIC MAGIC	*Streetwave*	69	*13 Oct 84*	2
THE ARTISTS VOLUME 1	*Street Sounds*	65	*9 Mar 85*	4

Compilation album with tracks by each artist.
Above hit: EARTH WIND AND FIRE/Jean CARN/ROSE ROYCE.

CHIC AND ROSE ROYCE – THEIR GREATEST HITS – SIDE BY SIDE	*Dino*	8	*27 Jul 91*	6

Album contained tracks by two different recording acts and was thus ineligible for the main album chart.
Above hit: ROSE ROYCE and CHIC.

ROSE TATTOO — Australia

SINGLES:	HITS 1			WEEKS 4
ROCK 'N' ROLL OUTLAW	*Carrere*	60	*11 Jul 81*	4
ALBUMS:	**HITS 1**			**WEEKS 4**
ASSAULT AND BATTERY	*Carrere*	40	*26 Sep 81*	4

Jimmy ROSELLI — US

SINGLES:	HITS 1			WEEKS 8
WHEN YOUR OLD WEDDING RING WAS NEW	*A.1.*	51	*5 Mar 83*	5
WHEN YOUR OLD WEDDING RING WAS NEW [RI]	*First Night*	52	*20 Jun 87*	3

Diana ROSS — US

(See also Placido Domingo, Diana Ross and Jose Carreras; Diana Ross and Marvin Gaye; Diana Ross and the Supremes and the Temptations; Diana Ross, Marvin Gaye, Smokey Robinson and Stevie Wonder; Supremes.)

SINGLES:	HITS 56			WEEKS 412
REACH OUT AND TOUCH	*Tamla Motown*	33	*18 Jul 70*	5
AIN'T NO MOUNTAIN HIGH ENOUGH	*Tamla Motown*	6	*12 Sep 70*	12

Original by Marvin Gaye and Tammy Terrell reached No. 9 in the US in 1967.

REMEMBER ME	*Tamla Motown*	7	*3 Apr 71*	12
I'M STILL WAITING	*Tamla Motown*	1	*31 Jul 71*	14
SURRENDER	*Tamla Motown*	10	*30 Oct 71*	11
DOOBEDOOD'NDOOBE, DOOBEDOOD'NDOOBE, DOOBEDOOD'NDOO	*Tamla Motown*	12	*13 May 72*	9
TOUCH ME IN THE MORNING	*Tamla Motown*	9	*14 Jul 73*	12
TOUCH ME IN THE MORNING [RE]	*Tamla Motown*	50	*13 Oct 73*	1
ALL OF MY LIFE	*Tamla Motown*	9	*5 Jan 74*	13
LAST TIME I SAW HIM	*Tamla Motown*	35	*4 May 74*	4
LOVE ME	*Tamla Motown*	38	*28 Sep 74*	5
SORRY DOESN'T ALWAYS MAKE IT RIGHT	*Tamla Motown*	23	*29 Mar 75*	9
THEME FROM MAHOGANY "DO YOU KNOW WHERE YOU'RE GOING TO"	*Tamla Motown*	5	*3 Apr 76*	8

From the film 'Mahogany'.

LOVE HANGOVER	*Tamla Motown*	10	*24 Apr 76*	10
I THOUGHT IT TOOK A LITTLE TIME (BUT TODAY I FELL IN LOVE)	*Tamla Motown*	32	*10 Jul 76*	5
I'M STILL WAITING [RI]	*Tamla Motown*	41	*16 Oct 76*	4
GETTIN' READY FOR LOVE	*Motown*	23	*19 Nov 77*	8
LOVIN', LIVIN' AND GIVIN'	*Motown*	54	*22 Jul 78*	6

From the film 'Thank God It's Friday'.

EASE ON DOWN THE ROAD	*MCA*	45	*18 Nov 78*	4

From the film 'The Wiz'. Originally recorded by Consumer Rapport.
Above hit: Diana ROSS / Michael JACKSON.

THE BOSS	*Motown*	40	*21 Jul 79*	7
NO ONE GETS THE PRIZE	*Motown*	59	*6 Oct 79*	3
IT'S MY HOUSE	*Motown*	32	*24 Nov 79*	10
UPSIDE DOWN	*Motown*	2	*19 Jul 80*	12
MY OLD PIANO	*Motown*	5	*20 Sep 80*	9
I'M COMING OUT	*Motown*	13	*15 Nov 80*	10
IT'S MY TURN	*Motown*	16	*17 Jan 81*	8

From the film of the same name.

ONE MORE CHANCE	*Motown*	49	*28 Mar 81*	5
CRYIN' MY HEART OUT FOR YOU	*Motown*	58	*13 Jun 81*	3
ENDLESS LOVE	*Motown*	7	*12 Sep 81*	12

From the film of the same name.
Above hit: Diana ROSS and Lionel RICHIE.

WHY DO FOOLS FALL IN LOVE	*Capitol*	4	*7 Nov 81*	12
TENDERNESS	*Motown*	73	*23 Jan 82*	1

Originally recorded in 1980.

MIRROR MIRROR	*Capitol*	36	*30 Jan 82*	5
TENDERNESS [RE]	*Motown*	75	*6 Feb 82*	1
WORK THAT BODY	*Capitol*	7	*29 May 82*	11
IT'S NEVER TOO LATE	*Capitol*	41	*7 Aug 82*	4

Above 2 written by Dan Hartman.

MUSCLES	*Capitol*	15	*23 Oct 82*	9

Written, produced and backing vocals by Michael Jackson.

SO CLOSE	*Capitol*	43	*15 Jan 83*	4
PIECES OF ICE	*Capitol*	46	*23 Jul 83*	3
ALL OF YOU	*CBS*	43	*7 Jul 84*	8

Above hit: Julio IGLESIAS and Diana ROSS.

TOUCH BY TOUCH	*Capitol*	47	*15 Sep 84*	6
EATEN ALIVE	*Capitol*	71	*28 Sep 85*	1
Co-written, produced and backing vocals by Michael Jackson.				
CHAIN REACTION	*Capitol*	1	*25 Jan 86*	17
EXPERIENCE	*Capitol*	47	*3 May 86*	3
Above 2 written by the Bee Gees.				
DIRTY LOOKS	*EMI*	49	*13 Jun 87*	3
MR. LEE	*EMI*	58	*8 Oct 88*	2
LOVE HANGOVER [RM]	*RCA*	75	*26 Nov 88*	1
Remixed at PWL.				
WORKIN' OVERTIME	*EMI*	32	*6 May 89*	5
PARADISE	*EMI*	61	*29 Jul 89*	2
Above 2: DIANA.				
I'M STILL WAITING [RM]	*Motown*	21	*7 Jul 90*	6
Remixed by Phil Chill.				
WHEN YOU TELL ME THAT YOU LOVE ME	*EMI*	2	*30 Nov 91*	11
THE FORCE BEHIND THE POWER	*EMI*	27	*15 Feb 92*	3
Written by Stevie Wonder.				
ONE SHINING MOMENT	*EMI*	10	*20 Jun 92*	8
IF WE HOLD ON TOGETHER	*EMI*	11	*28 Nov 92*	10
HEART (DON'T CHANGE MY MIND)	*EMI*	31	*13 Mar 93*	3
CHAIN REACTION [RI]	*EMI*	20	*9 Oct 93*	5
YOUR LOVE	*EMI*	14	*11 Dec 93*	8
THE BEST YEARS OF MY LIFE	*EMI*	28	*2 Apr 94*	4
WHY DO FOOLS FALL IN LOVE [RI] /I'M COMING OUT				
(JOEY NEGRO 1994 REMIX) [RM]	*EMI*	36	*9 Jul 94*	4
TAKE ME HIGHER	*EMI*	32	*2 Sep 95*	4
I'M GONE	*EMI*	36	*25 Nov 95*	3
I WILL SURVIVE	*EMI*	14	*17 Feb 96*	4
Above hit: DIANA.				
IN THE ONES YOU LOVE	*EMI*	34	*21 Dec 96*	4
NOT OVER YOU YET	*EMI*	9	*6 Nov 99*	6
ALBUMS:	**HITS 40**			**WEEKS 535**
COMPILATION ALBUMS:	**HITS 1**			**WEEKS 2**
DIANA ROSS	*Tamla Motown*	14	*24 Oct 70*	5
EVERTHING IS EVERYTHING	*Tamla Motown*	31	*19 Jun 71*	3
DIANA [OST-TV]	*Tamla Motown*	43	*9 Oct 71*	1
Features Bill Cosby, Danny Thomas and the Jackson 5.				
I'M STILL WAITING	*Tamla Motown*	10	*9 Oct 71*	11
GREATEST HITS	*Tamla Motown*	34	*11 Nov 72*	10
TOUCH ME IN THE MORNING	*Tamla Motown*	7	*1 Sep 73*	35
LADY SINGS THE BLUES [OST]	*Tamla Motown*	50	*27 Oct 73*	1
Ross played the role of Billie Holiday.				
LAST TIME I SAW HIM	*Tamla Motown*	41	*2 Mar 74*	1
DIANA ROSS LIVE AT CAESAR'S PALACE	*Tamla Motown*	21	*8 Jun 74*	8
Live recordings from her show in Las Vegas.				
DIANA ROSS	*Tamla Motown*	4	*27 Mar 76*	26
This self-titled album is different from the earlier chart entry.				
GREATEST HITS 2	*Tamla Motown*	2	*7 Aug 76*	29
AN EVENING WITH DIANA ROSS	*Motown*	52	*19 Mar 77*	1
Live recordings from the Ahmanson Theater, Los Angeles, 1976.				
THE BOSS	*Motown*	52	*4 Aug 79*	2
20 GOLDEN GREATS	*Motown*	2	*17 Nov 79*	29
DIANA	*Motown*	12	*21 Jun 80*	32
This self-titled album is different from the earlier chart entry.				
TO LOVE AGAIN	*Motown*	26	*28 Mar 81*	10
WHY DO FOOLS FALL IN LOVE	*Capital*	17	*7 Nov 81*	24
ALL THE GREAT HITS	*Motown*	21	*21 Nov 81*	31
DIANA'S DUETS	*Motown*	43	*13 Feb 82*	6
SILK ELECTRIC	*Capitol*	33	*23 Oct 82*	12
LOVE SONGS	*K-Tel*	5	*4 Dec 82*	17
ROSS	*Capitol*	44	*16 Jul 83*	5
PORTRAIT	*Telstar*	8	*24 Dec 83*	31
Compilation.				
SWEPT AWAY	*Capitol*	40	*6 Oct 84*	5
EATEN ALIVE	*Capitol*	11	*28 Sep 85*	19
DIANA . MICHAEL . GLADYS . STEVIE – THEIR VERY BEST – BACK TO BACK	*PrioriTyV*	21	*15 Nov 86*	10
Compilation featuring tracks by each act.				
Above hit: Diana ROSS/Michael JACKSON/Gladys KNIGHT/Stevie WONDER.				
RED HOT RHYTHM 'N' BLUES	*EMI*	47	*30 May 87*	4
Her versions of R&B classics.				
LOVE SONGS	*Telstar*	12	*31 Oct 87*	24
Compilation of each artist's solo recordings. When the compilation chart commenced on 14 Jan 89 it				
was listed there. See separate entry below.				
Above hit: Michael JACKSON and Diana ROSS.				
LOVE SONGS	*Telstar*	18	*14 Jan 89*	2
Above entry was in the compilation chart.				
Above hit: Michael JACKSON and Diana ROSS.				

WORKIN' OVERTIME	EMI	23	27 May 89	4
GREATEST HITS LIVE	EMI	34	25 Nov 89	6
THE FORCE BEHIND THE POWER	EMI	11	14 Dec 91	31
MOTOWN'S GREATEST HITS	Motown	20	29 Feb 92	11
LIVE, STOLEN MOMENTS - THE LADY SINGS THE BLUES	EMI	45	24 Apr 93	2

Live recordings from New York's Ritz club, Dec 92. Released to mark her 30th anniversary in Showbiz.

ONE WOMAN - THE ULTIMATE COLLECTION	EMI	1	30 Oct 93	67
DIANA EXTENDED - THE REMIXES	EMI	58	23 Apr 94	1
A VERY SPECIAL SEASON	EMI	37	26 Nov 94	6

Christmas songs.

TAKE ME HIGHER	EMI	10	16 Sep 95	3
VOICE OF LOVE	EMI	42	23 Nov 96	7
40 GOLDEN MOTOWN GREATS	Motown	35	31 Oct 98	4

Features both her solo and group recordings.
Above hit: Diana ROSS and the SUPREMES.

EVERY DAY IS A NEW DAY	EMI	71	20 Nov 99	1

Includes tracks recorded for the TV film 'Double Platinum'.

Diana ROSS and Marvin GAYE   US

(See also Marvin Gaye; Diana Ross.)

SINGLES:	HITS 2		WEEKS 20	
YOU ARE EVERYTHING	Tamla Motown	5	23 Mar 74	12

Original by the Stylistics reached No. 9 in the US in 1971.

STOP, LOOK, LISTEN (TO YOUR HEART)	Tamla Motown	25	20 Jul 74	8

ALBUMS:	HITS 1		WEEKS 45	
DIANA AND MARVIN	Tamla Motown	6	19 Jan 74	43
DIANA AND MARVIN [RI]	Motown	78	29 Aug 81	2

Diana ROSS, Marvin GAYE, Smokey ROBINSON and Stevie WONDER   US

(See also Marvin Gaye; Smokey Robinson; Diana Ross; Stevie Wonder.)

SINGLES:	HITS 1		WEEKS 5	
POPS, WE LOVE YOU	Motown	66	24 Feb 79	5

Recorded to honour Berry Gordy's father's 90th birthday.

Diana ROSS and the SUPREMES and the TEMPTATIONS   US

(See also Diana Ross; Supremes; Temptations.)

SINGLES:	HITS 3		WEEKS 27	
I'M GONNA MAKE YOU LOVE ME	Tamla Motown	3	1 Feb 69	11

Originally recorded by Dee Dee Warwick.

I'M GONNA MAKE YOU LOVE ME [RE]	Tamla Motown	49	26 Apr 69	1
I SECOND THAT EMOTION	Tamla Motown	18	20 Sep 69	8
WHY (MUST WE FALL IN LOVE)	Tamla Motown	31	21 Mar 70	7

ALBUMS:	HITS 3		WEEKS 31	
DIANA ROSS AND THE SUPREMES JOIN THE TEMPTATIONS	Tamla Motown	1	25 Jan 69	15
THE ORIGINAL SOUNDTRACK FROM TCB [OST-TV]	Tamla Motown	11	28 Jun 69	12

From the TV special featuring both groups, transmitted in the US, Feb 69.

TOGETHER	Tamla Motown	28	14 Feb 70	4

Ricky ROSS   UK

SINGLES:	HITS 2		WEEKS 3	
RADIO ON	Epic	35	18 May 96	2
GOOD EVENING PHILADELPHIA	Epic	58	10 Aug 96	1

ALBUMS:	HITS 1		WEEKS 1	
WHAT YOU ARE	Epic	36	15 Jun 96	1

Francis ROSSI   UK

(See also Status Quo.)

SINGLES:	HITS 2		WEEKS 6	
MODERN ROMANCE (I WANT TO FALL IN LOVE AGAIN)	Vertigo	54	11 May 85	4

Above hit: Francis ROSSI and Bernard FROST.

GIVE MYSELF TO LOVE	Virgin	42	3 Aug 96	2

Above hit: Francis ROSSI of STATUS QUO.

Nini ROSSO   Italy

SINGLES:	HITS 1		WEEKS 14	
IL SILENZIO	Durium	8	28 Aug 65	14

ROSTAL and SCHAEFER   UK

ALBUMS:	HITS 1		WEEKS 2	
BEATLES CONCERTO	Parlophone	61	14 Jul 79	2

Mstilav ROSTROPOVICH – See Herbert VON KARAJAN conducting the BERLIN PHILHARMONIC ORCHESTRA

David Lee ROTH   US

SINGLES:	HITS 6			WEEKS 15
CALIFORNIA GIRLS	Warner Brothers	68	23 Feb 85	2
Features backing vocals by Carl Wilson from the Beach Boys.				
JUST LIKE PARADISE	Warner Brothers	27	5 Mar 88	7
DAMN GOOD / STAND UP	Warner Brothers	72	3 Sep 88	1
A LIL' AIN'T ENOUGH	Warner Brothers	32	12 Jan 91	3
SHE'S MY MACHINE	Reprise	64	19 Feb 94	1
NIGHT LIFE	Reprise	72	28 May 94	1
Originally recorded by Willie Nelson.				
ALBUMS:	HITS 5			WEEKS 32
CRAZY FROM THE HEAT	Warner Brothers	91	2 Mar 85	2
EAT 'EM AND SMILE	Warner Brothers	28	19 Jul 86	9
SKYSCRAPER	Warner Brothers	11	6 Feb 88	12
A LITTLE AIN'T ENOUGH	Warner Brothers	4	26 Jan 91	7
YOUR FILTHY LITTLE MOUTH	Reprise	28	19 Mar 94	2

Uli Jon ROTH and ELECTRIC SUN   Germany

ALBUMS:	HITS 1			WEEKS 2
BEYOND THE ASTRAL SKIES	EMI	64	23 Feb 85	2

ROTTERDAM TERMINATION SOURCE   Holland

SINGLES:	HITS 2			WEEKS 6
POING	Sep	27	7 Nov 92	4
MERRY X-MESS	React	73	25 Dec 93	2

ROULA – See 20 FINGERS

ROULETTES – See Adam FAITH

Thomas ROUND – See Jun BRONHILL and Thomas ROUND

Demis ROUSSOS   Greece

SINGLES:	HITS 6			WEEKS 44
HAPPY TO BE ON AN ISLAND IN THE SUN	Philips	5	22 Nov 75	10
CAN'T SAY HOW MUCH I LOVE YOU	Philips	35	28 Feb 76	5
EXCEPTS FROM THE ROUSSOS PHENOMENON [EP]	Philips	1	26 Jun 76	12
Lead track: Forever And Ever. A collection of old recordings.				
WHEN FOREVER HAS GONE	Philips	2	2 Oct 76	10
BECAUSE	Philips	39	19 Mar 77	4
KYRILA [EP]	Philips	33	18 Jun 77	3
Lead track: Kyrila				
ALBUMS:	HITS 6			WEEKS 143
FOREVER AND EVER	Philips	2	22 Jun 74	68
Reached its peak position after re-entering on 26 Jun 76.				
SOUVENIRS	Philips	25	19 Apr 75	18
HAPPY TO BE	Philips	4	24 Apr 76	34
MY ONLY FASCINATION	Philips	39	3 Jul 76	6
THE MAGIC OF DEMIS ROUSSOS	Philips	29	16 Apr 77	6
LIFE AND LOVE	Philips	36	28 Oct 78	11

ROUTERS   US

SINGLES:	HITS 1			WEEKS 7
LET'S GO (PONY}	Warner Brothers	32	29 Dec 62	7
Bass and hand claps by Scott Walker.				

Maria ROWE   UK

SINGLES:	HITS 1			WEEKS 2
SEXUAL	ffrr	67	20 May 95	2

ROWETTA – See HAPPY MONDAYS; OPEN ARMS featuring ROWETTA; VARIOUS ARTISTS (EPs) 'The Further Adventures Of North – More Underground Dance EP'

Kevin ROWLAND – See DEXY'S MIDNIGHT RUNNERS

John ROWLES   New Zealand

SINGLES:	HITS 2			WEEKS 28
IF I ONLY HAD TIME	MCA	3	16 Mar 68	18
HUSH . . . NOT A WORD TO MARY	MCA	12	22 Jun 68	10

ROXETTE   Sweden

SINGLES:	HITS 22			WEEKS 143
THE LOOK	EMI	7	22 Apr 89	10

DRESSED FOR SUCCESS	*EMI*	48	*15 Jul 89*	5
LISTEN TO YOUR HEART	*EMI*	62	*28 Oct 89*	3
IT MUST HAVE BEEN LOVE	*EMI*	3	*2 Jun 90*	14
From the film 'Pretty Woman'.				
LISTEN TO YOUR HEART [RI] /DANGEROUS	*EMI*	6	*11 Aug 90*	9
DRESSED FOR SUCCESS [RI]	*EMI*	18	*27 Oct 90*	7
JOYRIDE	*EMI*	4	*9 Mar 91*	10
FADING LIKE A FLOWER (EVERY TIME YOU LEAVE)	*EMI*	12	*11 May 91*	6
THE BIG L	*EMI*	21	*7 Sep 91*	6
SPENDING MY TIME	*EMI*	22	*23 Nov 91*	4
CHURCH OF YOUR HEART	*EMI*	21	*28 Mar 92*	4
HOW DO YOU DO!	*EMI*	13	*1 Aug 92*	7
QUEEN OF RAIN	*EMI*	28	*7 Nov 92*	4
ALMOST UNREAL	*EMI*	7	*24 Jul 93*	9
From the film 'Super Mario Bros'.				
IT MUST HAVE BEEN LOVE [RI]	*EMI*	10	*18 Sep 93*	8
Re-issued due to first TV transmission of the film 'Pretty Woman'.				
SLEEPING IN MY CAR	*EMI*	14	*26 Mar 94*	6
CRASH! BOOM! BANG!	*EMI*	26	*4 Jun 94*	5
FIREWORKS	*EMI*	30	*17 Sep 94*	4
RUN TO YOU	*EMI*	27	*3 Dec 94*	6
VULNERABLE	*EMI*	44	*8 Apr 95*	2
THE LOOK '95 [RM]	*EMI*	28	*25 Nov 95*	3
Remixed by Chaps.				
YOU DON'T UNDERSTAND ME	*EMI*	42	*30 Mar 96*	2
JUNE AFTERNOON	*EMI*	52	*20 Jul 96*	1
WISH I COULD FLY	*EMI*	11	*20 Mar 99*	7
STARS	*EMI*	56	*9 Oct 99*	1
ALBUMS:	**HITS 6**			**WEEKS 157**
LOOK SHARP!	*EMI*	45	*17 Jun 89*	2
LOOK SHARP! [RE]	*EMI*	4	*30 Jun 90*	51
JOYRIDE	*EMI*	2	*13 Apr 91*	48
TOURISM	*EMI*	2	*12 Sep 92*	17
CRASH BOOM BANG	*EMI*	3	*23 Apr 94*	16
DON'T BORE US, GET TO THE CHORUS! – GREATEST HITS	*EMI*	5	*4 Nov 95*	20
HAVE A NICE DAY	*EMI*	28	*10 Apr 99*	3

ROXY MUSIC
UK

SINGLES:	**HITS 16**			**WEEKS 155**
VIRGINIA PLAIN	*Island*	4	*19 Aug 72*	12
PYJAMARAMA	*Island*	10	*10 Mar 73*	12
STREET LIFE	*Island*	9	*17 Nov 73*	12
ALL I WANT IS YOU	*Island*	12	*12 Oct 74*	8
LOVE IS THE DRUG	*Island*	2	*11 Oct 75*	10
BOTH ENDS BURNING	*Island*	25	*27 Dec 75*	7
VIRGINIA PLAIN [RI]	*Polydor*	11	*22 Oct 77*	6
TRASH	*Polydor*	40	*3 Mar 79*	6
DANCE AWAY	*Polydor*	2	*28 Apr 79*	14
ANGEL EYES	*Polydor*	4	*11 Aug 79*	11
OVER YOU	*Polydor*	5	*17 May 80*	9
OH YEAH (ON THE RADIO)	*Polydor*	5	*2 Aug 80*	8
THE SAME OLD SCENE	*E'G*	12	*8 Nov 80*	7
JEALOUS GUY	*E'G*	1	*21 Feb 81*	11
Tribute to John Lennon.				
MORE THAN THIS	*E'G*	6	*3 Apr 82*	8
AVALON	*E'G*	13	*19 Jun 82*	6
TAKE A CHANCE WITH ME	*E'G*	26	*25 Sep 82*	6
LOVE IS THE DRUG [RM]	*E'G*	33	*27 Apr 96*	2
Remixed by Rollo and Sister Bliss.				
ALBUMS:	**HITS 15**			**WEEKS 420**
ROXY MUSIC	*Island*	10	*29 Jul 72*	16
FOR YOUR PLEASURE	*Island*	4	*7 Apr 73*	27
STRANDED	*Island*	1	*1 Dec 73*	17
COUNTRY LIFE	*Island*	3	*30 Nov 74*	10
SIREN	*Island*	4	*8 Nov 75*	17
VIVA! ROXY MUSIC	*Island*	6	*31 Jul 76*	12
Live recordings from 1972–75.				
GREATEST HITS	*Polydor*	20	*19 Nov 77*	11
MANIFESTO	*Polydor*	7	*24 Mar 79*	34
FLESH AND BLOOD	*Polydor*	1	*31 May 80*	60
AVALON	*E'G*	1	*5 Jun 82*	57
MUSIQUE/THE HIGH ROAD	*E'G*	26	*19 Mar 83*	7
Imported mini-album. Live recordings from Glasgow's Apollo Theatre.				
ROXY MUSIC – THE ATLANTIC YEARS (1973 - 1980)	*E'G*	23	*12 Nov 83*	25
STREET LIFE - 20 GREAT HITS	*E'G*	1	*26 Apr 86*	77
Above hit: Bryan FERRY ROXY MUSIC.				
THE ULTIMATE COLLECTION	*E'G*	6	*19 Nov 88*	27

THE ULTIMATE COLLECTION [RI]	*Virgin*	26	*17 Sept 94*	8
MORE THAN THIS – THE BEST OF BRYAN FERRY AND ROXY MUSIC	*Virgin*	15	*4 Nov 95*	15

Above 2: Bryan FERRY and ROXY MUSIC.

ROYA ARAB – See GROOVERIDER

Billy Joe ROYAL   US

SINGLES:	HITS 1			WEEKS 4
DOWN IN THE BOONDOCKS	*CBS*	38	*9 Oct 65*	4

Originally recorded by Joe South.

Central Band of the ROYAL AIR FORCE
(by permission of the Air Council) cond: Wing Comdr. A.E. SIMS O.B.E. (Organising Director of Music)   UK

SINGLES:	HITS 1			WEEKS 1
THE DAM BUSTERS – MARCH	*His Master's Voice*	18	*22 Oct 55*	1

From the film of the same name.

ROYAL CHORAL SOCIETY – See LONDON SYMPHONY ORCHESTRA

ROYAL GUARD HORNS – See Elvis COSTELLO and the ATTRACTIONS

ROYAL GUARDSMEN   US

SINGLES:	HITS 2			WEEKS 17
SNOOPY VS. THE RED BARON	*Stateside*	8	*21 Jan 67*	13
THE RETURN OF THE RED BARON	*Stateside*	37	*8 Apr 67*	4

ROYAL HOUSE   US

SINGLES:	HITS 2			WEEKS 18
CAN YOU PARTY	*Champion*	14	*10 Sep 88*	14
YEAH BUDDY	*Champion*	35	*7 Jan 89*	4

ROYAL LIVERPOOL PHILHARMONIC ORCHESTRA and CHOIR – See Carl DAVIS and the ROYAL LIVERPOOL PHILHARMONIC ORCHESTRA and CHOIR

ROYAL PHILHARMONIC ORCHESTRA   UK

(See also Sarah Brightman; Elkie Brooks; Richard Clayderman; Elvis Costello and the Attractions; Michael Crawford; Julian Lloyd-Webber; Juan Martin with the Royal Philharmonic Orchestra conducted by Louis Clark; Mike Oldfield; Cliff Richard; Andy Williams; Various Artists: Studio Cast 'Leonard Bernstein's West Side Story'.)

SINGLES:	HITS 4			WEEKS 19
HOOKED ON CLASSICS [M]	*RCA*	2	*25 Jul 81*	11
Though not credited, conductor is Louis Clark.				
HOOKED ON A CAN CAN [M]	*RCA*	47	*24 Oct 81*	3
Above 2 are segued tracks of classical songs.				
Above hit: Louis CLARK conducting the ROYAL PHILHARMONIC ORCHESTRA.				
BBC WORLD CUP GRANDSTAND	*BBC*	61	*10 Jul 82*	3
Theme from BBC sports TV coverage of the 1982 World Cup in Spain.				
IF YOU KNEW SOUSA (AND FRIENDS) [M]	*RCA*	71	*7 Aug 82*	2
Above hit: Louis CLARK conducting the ROYAL PHILHARMONIC ORCHESTRA.				

ALBUMS:	HITS 12			WEEKS 131
CLASSICAL GOLD	*Ronco*	24	*8 Jan 77*	13
CLASSIC GOLD VOLUME 2	*Ronco*	31	*23 Dec 78*	4
HOOKED ON CLASSICS	*K-Tel*	4	*19 Sep 81*	43
CAN'T STOP THE CLASSICS – HOOKED ON CLASSICS 2	*K-Tel*	13	*31 Jul 82*	26
JOURNEY THROUGH THE CLASSICS – HOOKED ON CLASSICS 3	*K-Tel*	19	*9 Apr 83*	15
Above 3: Louis CLARK conducting the ROYAL PHILHARMONIC ORCHESTRA.				
LOVE CLASSICS	*Nouveau Music*	30	*8 Oct 83*	9
Above hit: ROYAL PHILHARMONIC ORCHESTRA conducted by Nick PORTLOCK.				
THE BEST OF HOOKED ON CLASSICS	*K-Tel*	51	*10 Dec 83*	6
Above hit: ROYAL PHILHARMONIC ORCHESTRA conducted by Louis CLARK.				
AS TIME GOES BY	*Telstar*	95	*26 May 84*	2
Above hit: ROYAL PHILHARMONIC ORCHESTRA conducted by Harry RABINOVITZ.				
RHYTHM AND CLASSICS	*Telstar*	96	*26 Nov 88*	1
Above hit: Louis CLARK conducting the ROYAL PHILHARMONIC ORCHESTRA.				
MUSIC FOR THE LAST NIGHT OF THE PROMS	*Cirrus*	39	*29 Sep 90*	4
Above hit: Sir. Charles GROVES conducting the ROYAL PHILHARMONIC ORCHESTRA and CHORUS with Sarah WALKER (soprano).				
SERIOUSLY ORCHESTRAL	*Virgin*	31	*5 Oct 91*	6
Above hit: Louis CLARK conducting the ROYAL PHILHARMONIC ORCHESTRA.				
BIG SCREEN CLASSICS	*Quality Television*	49	*30 Jul 94*	2
Conducted by Richard Homes.				

Pipes and Drums and Military Band of the ROYAL SCOTS DRAGOON GUARDS · UK

SINGLES:		HITS 3		WEEKS 43	
AMAZING GRACE		RCA Victor	1	1 Apr 72	24

Above hit: Pipes and Drums and Military Band of the ROYAL SCOTS DRAGOON GUARDS (CARABINIERS & GREYS) Bandmaster W.O.I.C.I. HERBERT, Pipe Major W.O.I.I.J. PRYDE.

HEYKEN'S SERENADE (STANDCHEN) / THE DAY IS ENDED (THE DAY THOU GAVE US LORD, IS ENDED)	RCA Victor	30	19 Aug 72	7

Above hit: Pipes and Drums and Military Band of the ROYAL SCOTS DRAGOON GUARDS Bandmaster W.O.I.C.I. HERBERT Pipe Major A. CREASE.

LITTLE DRUMMER BOY	RCA Victor	13	2 Dec 72	9

Above hit: Pipes and Drums and Military Band of the ROYAL SCOTS DRAGOON GUARDS (CARABINIERS & GREYS) Bandmaster: WOI P.STANDING, Pipe Major A.J. CREASE.

AMAZING GRACE [RE]	RCA Victor	42	23 Dec 72	3

Above hit: Pipes and Drums and Military Band of the ROYAL SCOTS DRAGOON GUARDS (CARABINIERS & GREYS) Bandmaster W.O.I.C.I. HERBERT, Pipe Major W.O.I.I.J. PRYDE.

ROYALLE DELITE · US

SINGLES:	HITS 1		WEEKS 6	
(I'LL BE A) FREAK FOR YOU	Streetwave	45	14 Sep 85	6

Lita ROZA · UK

(See also All Star Hit Parade.)

SINGLES:	HITS 3		WEEKS 18	
(HOW MUCH IS) THAT DOGGIE IN THE WINDOW	Decca	1	14 Mar 53	11

Originally recorded by Patti Page.

HEY THERE	Decca	17	8 Oct 55	2
JIMMY UNKNOWN	Decca	15	24 Mar 56	5

Originally recorded by Doris Day.
Above 2: Lita ROZA with Bob SHARPLES and his Orchestra.

ROZALLA · Zimbabwe

SINGLES:	HITS 10		WEEKS 48	
FAITH (IN THE POWER OF LOVE)	Pulse 8	65	27 Apr 91	2
EVERYBODY'S FREE (TO FEEL GOOD)	Pulse 8	6	7 Sep 91	11
FAITH (IN THE POWER OF LOVE) [RI]	Pulse 8	11	16 Nov 91	6
ARE YOU READY TO FLY	Pulse 8	14	22 Feb 92	6
LOVE BREAKDOWN	Pulse 8	65	9 May 92	2
IN 4 CHOONS LATER [M]	Pulse 8	50	15 Aug 92	2
DON'T PLAY WITH ME	Pulse 8	50	30 Oct 93	1
I LOVE MUSIC	Epic	18	5 Feb 94	5

From the film 'Carlito's Way'.

THIS TIME I FOUND LOVE	Epic	33	6 Aug 94	3
YOU NEVER LOVE THE SAME WAY TWICE	Epic	16	29 Oct 94	5
BABY	Epic	26	4 Mar 95	3
EVERYBODY'S FREE [RM]	Pulse 8	30	31 Aug 96	2

Remixed by Ca$ino (Paul Gotel and Aron Friedman).

ALBUMS:	HITS 1		WEEKS 4	
EVERYBODY'S FREE	Pulse 8	20	4 Apr 92	4

RTE CONCERT ORCHESTRA – See Bill WHELAN

RUBBADUBB · UK

SINGLES:	HITS 1		WEEKS 1	
TRIBUTE TO OUR ANCESTORS	Perfecto	56	18 Jul 98	1

RUBETTES · UK

SINGLES:	HITS 9		WEEKS 68	
SUGAR BABY LOVE	Polydor	1	4 May 74	10
TONIGHT	Polydor	12	13 Jul 74	9
JUKE BOX JIVE	Polydor	3	16 Nov 74	12
I CAN DO IT	State	7	8 Mar 75	9
FOE-DEE-O-DEE	State	15	21 Jun 75	6
LITTLE DARLING	State	30	22 Nov 75	5
YOU'RE THE REASON WHY	State	28	1 May 76	4
UNDER ONE ROOF	State	40	25 Sep 76	3
BABY I KNOW	State	10	12 Feb 77	10

ALBUMS:	HITS 1		WEEKS 1	
WE CAN DO IT	State	41	10 May 75	1

RUBY and the ROMANTICS — US

SINGLES:		HITS 1		WEEKS 6	
OUR DAY WILL COME	London	38	30 Mar 63	6

RUDIES – See Derrick MORGAN Music backing the RUDIES; Freddie NOTES and the RUDIES

RUFF DRIVERZ — UK

SINGLES:		HITS 6		WEEKS 21	
DON'T STOP	Inferno	30	7 Feb 98	2
DEEPER LOVE	Inferno	19	23 May 98	3
SHAME	Inferno	51	24 Oct 98	2
DREAMING	Inferno	10	28 Nov 98	8
LA MUSICA	Inferno	14	24 Apr 99	4
Above 2: RUFF DRIVERZ presents ARROLA.				
WAITING FOR THE SUN	Inferno	37	2 Oct 99	2

Frances RUFFELLE — UK

SINGLES:		HITS 1		WEEKS 6	
LONELY SYMPHONY (WE WILL BE FREE)	Virgin	25	16 Apr 94	6
UK's Eurovision entry in 1994, it came 10th.				

Bruce RUFFIN — Jamaica

SINGLES:		HITS 2		WEEKS 23	
RAIN	Trojan	19	1 May 71	11
Originally recorded by José Feliciano.				
MAD ABOUT YOU	Rhino	9	24 Jun 72	12

David RUFFIN — US

(See also Daryl Hall and John Oates.)

SINGLES:		HITS 1		WEEKS 8	
WALK AWAY FROM LOVE	Tamla Motown	10	17 Jan 76	8

Jimmy RUFFIN — US

SINGLES:		HITS 9		WEEKS 106	
WHAT BECOMES OF THE BROKENHEARTED	Tamla Motown	10	29 Oct 66	15
I'VE PASSED THIS WAY BEFORE	Tamla Motown	29	11 Feb 67	7
GONNA GIVE HER ALL THE LOVE I'VE GOT	Tamla Motown	26	22 Apr 67	6
I'VE PASSED THIS WAY BEFORE [RI]	Tamla Motown	33	9 Aug 69	6
FAREWELL IS A LONELY SOUND	Tamla Motown	8	28 Feb 70	16
I'LL SAY FOREVER MY LOVE	Tamla Motown	7	4 Jul 70	12
Originally released in 1968.				
IT'S WONDERFUL (TO BE LOVED BY YOU)	Tamla Motown	6	17 Oct 70	14
WHAT BECOMES OF THE BROKEN HEARTED [RI]	Tamla Motown	4	27 Jul 74	12
FAREWELL IS A LONELY SOUND [RI]	Tamla Motown	30	2 Nov 74	5
TELL ME WHAT YOU WANT	Polydor	39	16 Nov 74	4
HOLD ON TO MY LOVE	RSO	7	3 May 80	8
Co-written by Robin Gibb.				
THERE WILL NEVER BE ANOTHER YOU	EMI	68	26 Jan 85	1
Backing vocals by Junior Giscombe.				
ALBUMS:		HITS 2		WEEKS 10	
THE JIMMY RUFFIN WAY	Tamla Motown	32	13 May 67	6
GREATEST HITS	Tamla Motown	41	1 Jun 74	4

Kim RUFFIN – See CHUBBY CHUNKS

RUFFNECK featuring YAVAHN — US

SINGLES:		HITS 2		WEEKS 5	
EVERYBODY BE SOMEBODY	Positiva	13	11 Nov 95	4
Samples Yello's Bostich.				
MOVE YOUR BODY	Positiva	60	7 Sep 96	1

RUFUS — US

SINGLES:		HITS 1		WEEKS 21	
AIN'T NOBODY	Warner Brothers	8	31 Mar 84	12
Live recording from the New York Savoy Theater, Feb 82.				
AIN'T NOBODY [RM]	Warner Brothers	6	8 Jul 89	9
Remixed by Frankie Knuckles.				
Above 2: RUFUS and Chaka KHAN.				
ALBUMS:		HITS 2		WEEKS 7	
RUFUSIZED	ABC	48	12 Apr 75	2
STOMPIN' AT THE SAVOY	Warner Brothers	64	21 Apr 84	5
Live recordings from the New York Savoy Theater, Feb 82.				
Above hit: RUFUS and Chaka KHAN.				

RUKMANI – See SNAP!

RUMOUR – See Graham PARKER and the RUMOUR

RUMPLE-STILTS-SKIN

US

SINGLES:	HITS 1			WEEKS 4
I THINK I WANT TO DANCE WITH YOU	Polydor	51	24 Sep 83	4

RUN D.M.C.

US

SINGLES:	HITS 10			WEEKS 59
MY ADIDAS / PETER PIPER	London	62	19 Jul 86	2
WALK THIS WAY	London	8	6 Sep 86	10
Features Aerosmith's Steve Tyler and Joe Perry. Aerosmith's original reached No. 10 in the US in 1976.				
YOU BE ILLIN'	London	42	7 Feb 87	4
IT'S TRICKY	London	16	30 May 87	7
CHRISTMAS IN HOLLIS	London	56	12 Dec 87	4
RUN'S HOUSE	London	37	21 May 88	4
GHOSTBUSTERS	MCA	65	2 Sep 89	2
WHAT'S IT ALL ABOUT	Profile	48	1 Dec 90	3
DOWN WITH THE KING	Profile	69	27 Mar 93	2
IT'S LIKE THAT	Columbia	63	21 Feb 98	3
German import.				
IT'S LIKE THAT	Sm:)e Communications	65	14 Mar 98	1
US import.				
IT'S LIKE THAT	Sm:)e Communications	1	21 Mar 98	16
(IT'S) TRICKY [RM]	Epidrome	74	18 Apr 98	1
German import. Remixed by Jason Nevins.				
Above 4: RUN-D.M.C. vs Jason NEVINS.				

ALBUMS:	HITS 4			WEEKS 36
RAISING HELL	Profile	41	26 Jul 86	26
TOUGHER THAN LEATHER	Profile	13	4 Jun 88	5
DOWN WITH THE KING	Profile	44	15 May 93	2
TOGETHER FOREVER - GREATEST HITS 1983–1998	Profile	31	6 Jun 98	3

RUN TINGS

UK

(See also Various Artists (EPs) 'Subplates Volume 1 EP'.)

SINGLES:	HITS 1			WEEKS 1
FIRES BURNING	Suburban Base	58	16 May 92	1

Todd RUNDGREN

US

SINGLES:	HITS 2			WEEKS 8
I SAW THE LIGHT	Bearsville	36	30 Jun 73	6
Originally released in 1972.				
LOVING YOU'S A DIRTY JOB BUT SOMEBODY'S GOTTA DO IT	CBS	73	14 Dec 85	2
Above hit: Bonnie TYLER, guest vocalist Todd RUNDGREN.				

ALBUMS:	HITS 1			WEEKS 3
HERMIT OF MINK HOLLOW	Bearsville	42	6 May 78	3

RUNRIG

UK

SINGLES:	HITS 9			WEEKS 28
CAPTURE THE HEART [EP]	Chrysalis	49	29 Sep 90	2
Lead track: Stepping Down The Glory Road.				
HEARTHAMMER [EP]	Chrysalis	25	7 Sep 91	4
Lead track: Hearthammer. Not listed as an EP on the chart of 7 Sep 91.				
FLOWER OF THE WEST	Chrysalis	43	9 Nov 91	2
WONDERFUL	Chrysalis	29	6 Mar 93	3
THE GREATEST FLAME	Chrysalis	36	15 May 93	3
THIS TIME OF YEAR	Chrysalis	38	7 Jan 95	2
Live recording from an outdoor concert in Scotland, Summer '94.				
AN UBHAL AS AIRDE (THE HIGHEST APPLE)	Chrysalis	18	6 May 95	5
Featured in the Carlsberg lager TV commercial.				
THINGS THAT ARE	Chrysalis	40	4 Nov 95	2
RHYTHM OF MY HEART	Chrysalis	24	12 Oct 96	2
Recorded for the film 'Loch Ness', but it was never used.				
THE GREATEST FLAME [RM]	Chrysalis	30	11 Jan 97	3
Remixed by Pete Woodroffe.				

ALBUMS:	HITS 10			WEEKS 49
ONCE IN A LIFETIME	Chrysalis	61	26 Nov 88	2
SEARCHLIGHT	Chrysalis	11	7 Oct 89	4
THE BIG WHEEL	Chrysalis	4	22 Jun 91	15
AMAZING THINGS	Chrysalis	2	27 Mar 93	6
TRANSMITTING LIVE	Chrysalis	41	26 Nov 94	3
Live recordings from concerts in Scotland and Germany during the summer of 1994.				

THE CUTTER AND THE CLAN	Chrysalis	45	20 May 95	2
Originally released in 1988.				
MARA	Chrysalis	24	18 Nov 95	4
Mara is Gaelic for the sea. Features the Scottish National Orchestra and the Hebridean Gaelic Choir.				
LONG DISTANCE – THE BEST OF RUNRIG	Chrysalis	13	19 Oct 96	10
THE GAELIC COLLECTION 1973-1995	Ridge	71	23 May 98	1
Compilation of the band's Gaelic songs.				
IN SEARCH OF ANGELS	Ridge	29	13 Mar 99	2

RUPAUL · US

SINGLES:	HITS 5		WEEKS 19	
SUPERMODEL (YOU BETTER WORK)	Union	39	26 Jun 93	4
HOUSE OF LOVE / BACK TO MY ROOTS	Union	40	18 Sep 93	2
SUPERMODEL [RI] / LITTLE DRUMMER BOY	Union	61	22 Jan 94	2
DON'T GO BREAKING MY HEART	Rocket	7	26 Feb 94	7
Charity record with royalties to the Elton John AIDS Foundation.				
Above hit: Elton JOHN and RUPAUL.				
HOUSE OF LOVE [RM]	Virgin	68	21 May 94	1
Remixed by T-Empo.				
IT'S RAINING MEN . . . THE SEQUEL	Logic	21	28 Feb 98	3
Above hit: Martha WASH featuring RUPAUL.				

RUSH · Canada

SINGLES:	HITS 12		WEEKS 43	
CLOSER TO THE HEART	Mercury	36	11 Feb 78	3
THE SPIRIT OF RADIO	Mercury	13	15 Mar 80	7
VITAL SIGNS / A PASSAGE TO BANGKOK / IN THE MOOD	Mercury	41	28 Mar 81	4
In The Mood, though listed was only available on the 12" format.				
TOM SAWYER (LIVE)	Exit	25	31 Oct 81	6
Sleeve gives title as an EP: Rush Live.				
NEW WORLD MAN	Mercury	42	4 Sep 82	3
SUBDIVISIONS	Mercury	53	30 Oct 82	2
COUNTDOWN / NEW WORLD MAN [RI]	Vertigo	36	7 May 83	5
THE BODY ELECTRIC	Vertigo	56	26 May 84	3
THE BIG MONEY	Vertigo	46	12 Oct 85	3
TIME STAND STILL	Vertigo	42	31 Oct 87	3
Vocals by Aimee Mann.				
PRIME MOVER	Vertigo	43	23 Apr 88	3
ROLL THE BONES	Atlantic	49	7 Mar 92	1
ALBUMS:	HITS 15		WEEKS 98	
FAREWELL TO KINGS	Mercury	22	8 Oct 77	4
HEMISPHERES	Mercury	14	25 Nov 78	6
PERMANENT WAVES	Mercury	3	26 Jan 80	16
MOVING PICTURES	Mercury	3	21 Feb 81	11
EXIT STAGE LEFT	Mercury	6	7 Nov 81	14
Live recordings.				
SIGNALS	Mercury	3	18 Sep 82	9
GRACE UNDER PRESSURE	Vertigo	5	28 Apr 84	12
POWER WINDOWS	Vertigo	9	9 Nov 85	4
HOLD YOUR FIRE	Vertigo	10	21 Nov 87	4
A SHOW OF HANDS	Vertigo	12	28 Jan 89	4
PRESTO	Atlantic	27	9 Dec 89	2
CHRONICLES	Vertigo	42	13 Oct 90	2
ROLL THE BONES	Atlantic	10	14 Sep 91	4
COUNTERPARTS	Atlantic	14	30 Oct 93	3
TEST FOR ECHO	Atlantic	25	21 Sep 96	3

Donell RUSH · US

SINGLES:	HITS 1		WEEKS 1	
SYMPHONY	ID	66	5 Dec 92	1

Jennifer RUSH · US

SINGLES:	HITS 5		WEEKS 58	
THE POWER OF LOVE	CBS	1	29 Jun 85	32
Peak position reached on 12 Oct 85.				
RING OF ICE	CBS	14	14 Dec 85	10
THE POWER OF LOVE [RE]	CBS	55	20 Dec 86	4
FLAMES OF PARADISE	CBS	59	20 Jun 87	3
Above hit: Jennifer RUSH (duet with Elton JOHN).				
TILL I LOVED YOU	CBS	24	27 May 89	9
Above hit: Placido DOMINGO and Jennifer RUSH.				
ALBUMS:	HITS 3		WEEKS 43	
JENNIFER RUSH	CBS	7	16 Nov 85	35
MOVIN'	CBS	32	3 May 86	5
HEART OVER MIND	CBS	48	18 Apr 87	3

Patrice RUSHEN — US

SINGLES:	HITS 5			WEEKS 25
HAVEN'T YOU HEARD	Elektra	62	1 Mar 80	3
NEVER GONNA GIVE YOU UP (WON'T LET YOU BE)	Elektra	66	24 Jan 81	3
FORGET ME NOTS	Elektra	8	24 Apr 82	11
I WAS TIRED OF BEING ALONE	Elektra	39	10 Jul 82	5
FEELS SO REAL (WON'T LET GO)	Elektra	51	9 Jun 84	3
ALBUMS:	HITS 2			WEEKS 17
STRAIGHT FROM THE HEART	Elektra	24	1 May 82	14
NOW	Elektra	73	16 Jun 84	3

Brenda RUSSELL — US

SINGLES:	HITS 2			WEEKS 17
SO GOOD, SO RIGHT / IN THE THICK OF IT	A&M	51	19 Apr 80	5
PIANO IN THE DARK	Breakout	23	12 Mar 88	12
ALBUMS:	HITS 1			WEEKS 4
GET HERE	A&M	77	23 Apr 88	4

Leon RUSSELL — US

ALBUMS:	HITS 1			WEEKS 1
LEON RUSSELL AND THE SHELTER PEOPLE	A&M	29	3 Jul 71	1

Patti RUSSO – See MEAT LOAF

RUTH — UK

SINGLES:	HITS 1			WEEKS 1
I DON'T KNOW	Arc	66	12 Apr 97	1

Mike RUTHERFORD — UK

(See also Mike and the Mechanics.)

ALBUMS:	HITS 2			WEEKS 11
SMALLCREEP'S DAY	Charisma	13	23 Feb 80	7
ACTING VERY STRANGE	WEA	23	18 Sep 82	4

Paul RUTHERFORD — UK

SINGLES:	HITS 2			WEEKS 6
GET REAL	Fourth & Broadway	47	8 Oct 88	3
OH WORLD	Fourth & Broadway	61	19 Aug 89	3

RUTHLESS RAP ASSASSINS — UK

SINGLES:	HITS 2			WEEKS 2
JUST MELLOW	Syncopate	75	9 Jun 90	1
AND IT WASN'T A DREAM	Syncopate	75	1 Sep 90	1

Above hit: RUTHLESS RAP ASSASSINS featured vocalist – Tracey CARMEN.

RUTLES — UK

SINGLES:	HITS 2			WEEKS 5
I MUST BE IN LOVE	Warner Brothers	39	15 Apr 78	3
I MUST BE IN LOVE [RE]	Warner Brothers	64	13 May 78	1
SHANGRI-LA	Virgin	68	16 Nov 96	1
ALBUMS:	HITS 1			WEEKS 11
THE RUTLES	Warner Brothers	12	15 Apr 78	11

RUTS — UK

SINGLES:	HITS 4			WEEKS 28
BABYLON'S BURNING	Virgin	7	16 Jun 79	11
SOMETHING THAT I SAID	Virgin	29	8 Sep 79	5
STARING AT THE RUDE BOYS	Virgin	22	19 Apr 80	8
WEST ONE (SHINE ON ME)	Virgin	43	30 Aug 80	4
ALBUMS:	HITS 2			WEEKS 10
THE CRACK	Virgin	16	13 Oct 79	6
GRIN AND BEAR IT	Virgin	28	18 Oct 80	4

Above hit: RUTS D.C.

Barry RYAN — UK

(See also Paul and Barry Ryan.)

SINGLES:	HITS 6			WEEKS 33
ELOISE	MGM	2	26 Oct 68	12
LOVE IS LOVE	MGM	25	22 Feb 69	4

Above 2: Barry RYAN with the MAJORITY.

THE HUNT	Polydor	34	4 Oct 69	5

MAGICAL SPIEL	Polydor	49	21 Feb 70	1
KITSCH	Polydor	37	16 May 70	6
Above hit: Barry RYAN with the Paul RYAN ORCHESTRA.				
CAN'T LET YOU GO	Polydor	32	15 Jan 72	5

Marion RYAN with the Peter KNIGHT ORCHESTRA and the Beryl STOTT CHORUS   UK

SINGLES:	HITS 1		WEEKS 11	
LOVE ME FOREVER	Pye Nixa	5	25 Jan 58	11

Paul and Barry RYAN   UK

(See also Barry Ryan.)

SINGLES:	HITS 8		WEEKS 43	
DON'T BRING ME YOUR HEARTACHES	Decca	13	13 Nov 65	9
HAVE PITY ON THE BOY	Decca	18	5 Feb 66	6
I LOVE HER	Decca	17	14 May 66	8
I LOVE HOW YOU LOVE ME	Decca	21	16 Jul 66	7
HAVE YOU EVER LOVED SOMEBODY	Decca	49	1 Oct 66	1
Originally recorded by the Hollies.				
MISSY, MISSY	Decca	43	10 Dec 66	4
KEEP IT OUT OF SIGHT	Decca	30	4 Mar 67	6
CLAIRE	Decca	47	2 Jul 67	2

Rebekah RYAN   UK

SINGLES:	HITS 3		WEEKS 5	
YOU LIFT ME UP	MCA	26	18 May 96	3
Backing vocals by Carol Kenyon, Lance Ellington and Miriam Stockley.				
JUST A LITTLE BIT OF LOVE	MCA	51	7 Sep 96	1
WOMAN IN LOVE	MCA	64	17 May 97	1

Bobby RYDELL   US

SINGLES:	HITS 8		WEEKS 60	
WILD ONE	Columbia	7	12 Mar 60	14
WILD ONE [RE]	Columbia	47	25 Jun 60	1
SWINGIN' SCHOOL	Columbia	44	2 Jul 60	1
From the film 'Because They're Young'.				
VOLARE	Columbia	46	3 Sep 60	1
VOLARE [RE]	Columbia	22	17 Sep 60	5
SWAY	Columbia	12	17 Dec 60	13
GOOD TIME BABY	Columbia	42	25 Mar 61	7
TEACH ME TO TWIST	Columbia	45	21 Apr 62	1
Above hit: Cubby CHECKER; Bobby RYDELL.				
JINGLE BELL ROCK	Cameo-Parkway	40	22 Dec 62	3
Above hit: Bobby RYDELL and Chubby CHECKER.				
FORGET HIM	Cameo-Parkway	13	25 May 63	14

Mitch RYDER and the DETROIT WHEELS   US

SINGLES:	HITS 1		WEEKS 5	
JENNY TAKE A RIDE! [M]	Stateside	44	12 Feb 66	1
JENNY TAKE A RIDE! [M] [RE]	Stateside	33	26 Feb 66	4
This is in fact a medley of Chuck Willis' See See Rider and Little Richard's Jenny Jenny, though label does not list it as such.				

Shaun RYDER – See HEADS with Shaun RYDER

RYTHM SYNDICATE   US

SINGLES:	HITS 1		WEEKS 5	
P.A.S.S.I.O.N.	Impact American	58	27 Jul 91	5

RZA   US

ALBUMS:	HITS 1		WEEKS 1	
BOBBY DIGITAL IN STEREO	Gee Street	70	28 Nov 98	1
Album is an extension of the film 'Bobby Digital' in which he starred.				

S

Robin S   US

SINGLES:	HITS 7		WEEKS 37	
SHOW ME LOVE	Champion	59	16 Jan 93	4
SHOW ME LOVE [RE]	Champion	6	13 Mar 93	13
LUV 4 LUV	Champion	11	31 Jul 93	7
WHAT I DO BEST	Champion	43	4 Dec 93	2
I WANT TO THANK YOU	Champion	48	19 Mar 94	1
BACK IT UP	Champion	43	5 Nov 94	2

SHOW ME LOVE [RM]	Champion	9	8 Mar 97	5
Remixed by Lisa Marie.				
IT MUST BE LOVE	Atlantic	37	12 Jul 97	2
YOU GOT THE LOVE	Champion	62	4 Oct 97	1
Above hit: T2 featuring Robin S.				

ALBUMS:	**HITS 1**		**WEEKS 3**	
SHOW ME LOVE	Champion	34	4 Sep 93	3

S CLUB 7 — UK

SINGLES:	**HITS 3**		**WEEKS 29**	
BRING IT ALL BACK	Polydor	1	19 Jun 99	15
S CLUB PARTY	Polydor	2	2 Oct 99	12
TWO IN A MILLION / YOU'RE MY NUMBER ONE	Polydor	5	25 Dec 99	2

ALBUMS:	**HITS 1**		**WEEKS 12**	
S CLUB	Polydor	2	16 Oct 99	12

S-EXPRESS — UK

SINGLES:	**HITS 6**		**WEEKS 50**	
THEME FROM S-EXPRESS	Rhythm King	1	16 Apr 88	13
Samples Rose Royce's Is It Love You're After.				
SUPERFLY GUY	Rhythm King	5	23 Jul 88	9
HEY MUSIC LOVER	Rhythm King	6	18 Feb 89	10
Chart also credits featuring Eric and Billy, they are Eric Robinson and Billy Ray Martin.				
MANTRA FOR A STATE OF MIND	Rhythm King	21	16 Sep 89	8
NOTHING TO LOSE	Rhythm King	32	15 Sep 90	4
FIND 'EM, FOOL 'EM, FORGET 'EM	Rhythm King	43	30 May 92	2
Originally recorded by Dobie Gray.				
THEME FROM S.EXPRESS: THE RETURN TRIP [RM]	Rhythm King	14	11 May 96	4
Remixed by Tony De Vit and Simon Parkes.				
Above hit: Mark MOORE presents S.EXPRESS.				

ALBUMS:	**HITS 1**		**WEEKS 9**	
ORIGINAL SOUNDTRACK	Rhythm King	5	1 Apr 89	9

S.F.X. — UK

SINGLES:	**HITS 1**		**WEEKS 3**	
LEMMINGS	Parlophone	51	15 May 93	3
Inspired by the Computer game 'Lemmings 2 – The Tribes'. Each format of this release included a different map and level solution to the game.				

S-J — UK

SINGLES:	**HITS 3**		**WEEKS 4**	
FEVER	React	46	11 Jan 97	1
I FEEL DIVINE	React	30	24 Jan 98	2
SHIVER	React	59	7 Nov 98	1

S*M*A*S*H — UK

SINGLES:	**HITS 1**		**WEEKS 1**	
(I WANT TO) KILL SOMEBODY	Hi-Rise Recordings	26	6 Aug 94	1

ALBUMS:	**HITS 2**		**WEEKS 4**	
S*M*A*S*H	Hi-Rise Recordings	28	2 Apr 94	3
Mini-album comprising their first two singles and B-sides.				
SELF ABUSED	Hi-Rise Recordings	59	17 Sep 94	1

S.O.A.P. — Denmark

SINGLES:	**HITS 1**		**WEEKS 2**	
THIS IS HOW WE PARTY	Columbia	36	25 Jul 98	2

S.O.S. BAND — US

SINGLES:	**HITS 8**		**WEEKS 46**	
TAKE YOUR TIME (DO IT RIGHT)	Tabu	51	19 Jul 80	4
GROOVIN' (THAT'S WHAT WE'RE DOIN')	Tabu	72	26 Feb 83	1
JUST BE GOOD TO ME	Tabu	13	7 Apr 84	11
JUST THE WAY YOU LIKE IT	Tabu	32	4 Aug 84	7
WEEKEND GIRL	Tabu	51	13 Oct 84	5
THE FINEST	Tabu	17	29 Mar 86	10
BORROWED TIME	Tabu	50	5 Jul 86	5
NO LIES	Tabu	64	2 May 87	3

ALBUMS:	**HITS 3**		**WEEKS 21**	
JUST THE WAY YOU LIKE IT	Tabu	29	1 Sep 84	10
THE ARTISTS VOLUME III	Street Sounds	87	12 Oct 85	2
Compilation album with tracks by each artist.				
Above hit: WOMACK and WOMACK/O'JAYS/KLEEER/S.O.S. BAND.				
SANDS OF TIME	Tabu	15	17 May 86	9

S.O.U.L. S.Y.S.T.E.M. introducing Michelle VISAGE
US

SINGLES:		HITS 1		WEEKS 5
IT'S GONNA BE A LOVELY DAY	Arista	17	16 Jan 93	5

From the film 'The Bodyguard'. Based around Bill Withers' Lovely Day.

Raphael SAADIQ and Q-TIP
US

(See also A Tribe Called Quest.)

SINGLES:		HITS 1		WEEKS 2
GET INVOLVED	Hollywood	36	19 Jun 99	2

From the animated TV series 'The P.J.'s'. Samples the Intruders' I'll Always Love My Mama.

SABRE featuring PRESIDENT BROWN
Jamaica

SINGLES:		HITS 1		WEEKS 1
WRONG OR RIGHT	Greensleeves	71	19 Aug 95	1

SABRES – See Denny SEYTON and the SABRES

SABRES OF PARADISE
UK

SINGLES:		HITS 3		WEEKS 8
SMOKEBELCH II	Sabres Of Paradise	55	2 Oct 93	3
THEME	Sabres Of Paradise	56	9 Apr 94	3
WILMOT	Warp	36	17 Sep 94	2

Samples a 1929 calypso record by Wilmot Houdini and the Night Owls.

ALBUMS:		HITS 2		WEEKS 3
SABRESONIC	Warp	29	23 Oct 93	2
HAUNTED DANCEHALL	Warp	57	10 Dec 94	1

SABRINA
Italy

SINGLES:		HITS 3		WEEKS 22
BOYS (SUMMERTIME LOVE)	Ibiza	60	6 Feb 88	3
BOYS (SUMMERTIME LOVE) [RE]	Ibiza	3	11 Jun 88	11
ALL OF ME	PWL	25	1 Oct 88	7
LIKE A YO-YO	Videogram	72	1 Jul 89	1

SACRED SPIRIT
Europe

(See also Divine Works.)

SINGLES:		HITS 2		WEEKS 5
YEHA-NOHA (WISHES OF HAPPINESS AND PROSPERITY)	Virgin	71	15 Apr 95	1

Featured in the Survival For Tribal People cinema advert.

WISHES OF HAPPINESS & PROSPERITY (YEHA-NOHA) [RI]	Virgin	37	18 Nov 95	2
WINTER CEREMONY (TOR-CHENEY-NAHANA)	Virgin	45	16 Mar 96	2

Theme from the Channel 4 TV series 'Tribal Cops'.

ALBUMS:		HITS 2		WEEKS 30
CHANTS AND DANCES OF THE NATIVE AMERICAN INDIAN	Virgin	62	1 Apr 95	3
CHANTS AND DANCES OF THE NATIVE AMERICAN INDIAN [RE]	Virgin	9	28 Oct 95	24
VOLUME 2 – CULTURE CLASH	Virgin	24	26 Apr 97	3

Fuses blues with classical music.

SAD CAFE
UK

SINGLES:		HITS 6		WEEKS 44
EVERY DAY HURTS	RCA	3	22 Sep 79	12

Produced by Eric Stewart of 10cc.

STRANGE LITTLE GIRL	RCA	32	19 Jan 80	5
MY OH MY	RCA	14	15 Mar 80	11
NOTHING LEFT TOULOUSE	RCA	62	21 Jun 80	4
LA-DI-DA	RCA	41	27 Sep 80	6
I'M IN LOVE AGAIN	RCA	40	20 Dec 80	6

ALBUMS:		HITS 6		WEEKS 36
FANX TA RA	RCA Victor	56	1 Oct 77	1
MISPLACED IDEALS	RCA Victor	50	29 Apr 78	1
FACADES	RCA	8	29 Sep 79	23

Title is an anagram of the group's name.

SAD CAFE	RCA	46	25 Oct 80	5
LIVE	RCA	37	21 Mar 81	4
OLE	Polydor	72	24 Oct 81	2

SADE
UK

SINGLES:		HITS 11		WEEKS 63
YOUR LOVE IS KING	Epic	6	25 Feb 84	11
YOUR LOVE IS KING [RE]	Epic	75	19 May 84	1
WHEN AM I GONNA MAKE A LIVING	Epic	36	26 May 84	5
SMOOTH OPERATOR	Epic	19	15 Sep 84	10
THE SWEETEST TABOO	Epic	31	12 Oct 85	5

IS IT A CRIME	Epic	49	11 Jan 86	3
LOVE IS STRONGER THAN PRIDE	Epic	44	2 Apr 88	3
PARADISE	Epic	29	4 Jun 88	7
NO ORDINARY LOVE	Epic	26	10 Oct 92	3
FEEL NO PAIN	Epic	56	28 Nov 92	2
KISS OF LIFE	Epic	44	8 May 93	3
NO ORDINARY LOVE [RE]	Epic	14	5 Jun 93	8

Re-entered after being featured in the film 'Indecent Proposal'.

CHERISH THE DAY	Epic	53	31 Jul 93	2
ALBUMS:	**HITS 5**			**WEEKS 190**
DIAMOND LIFE	Epic	2	28 Jul 84	99
PROMISE	Epic	1	16 Nov 85	31
STRONGER THAN PRIDE	Epic	3	14 May 88	17
LOVE DELUXE	Epic	10	7 Nov 92	27
THE BEST OF SADE	Epic	6	12 Nov 94	16

Staff Sergeant Barry SADLER — US

| **SINGLES:** | **HITS 1** | | | **WEEKS 8** |
| THE BALLAD OF THE GREEN BERETS | RCA Victor | 24 | 26 Mar 66 | 8 |

A tribute to the Special Forces Unit of the US army.

SAFFRON — UK

| **SINGLES:** | **HITS 1** | | | **WEEKS 2** |
| CIRCLES | WEA | 60 | 16 Jan 93 | 2 |

SAGAT — US

SINGLES:	**HITS 2**			**WEEKS 6**
FUNK DAT	ffrr	25	4 Dec 93	5
LUVSTUFF	ffrr	71	3 Dec 94	1

Carole Bayer SAGER — US

| **SINGLES:** | **HITS 1** | | | **WEEKS 9** |
| YOU'RE MOVING OUT TODAY | Elektra | 6 | 28 May 77 | 9 |

Originally recorded by Bette Midler.

Mike SAGER and CRESTERS — UK

| **SINGLES:** | **HITS 1** | | | **WEEKS 5** |
| DEEP FEELING | His Master's Voice | 44 | 10 Dec 60 | 5 |

Bally SAGOO — UK

| **SINGLES:** | **HITS 4** | | | **WEEKS 8** |
| CHURA LIYA | Columbia | 64 | 3 Sep 94 | 1 |

First chart hit to be sung predominantly in Hindi.

| CHOLI KE PEECHE | Columbia | 45 | 22 Apr 95 | 1 |

Roughly translated in English as What's Behind Your Blouse?

| DIL CHEEZ (MY HEART ...) | Higher Ground | 12 | 19 Oct 96 | 3 |

Features vocals from Shabnam Majid, Kash Rex and K.C.

TUM BIN JIYA	Higher Ground	21	1 Feb 97	3
ALBUMS:	**HITS 1**			**WEEKS 1**
RISING FROM THE EAST	Higher Ground	63	9 Nov 96	1

SAILOR — UK

SINGLES:	**HITS 3**			**WEEKS 24**
A GLASS OF CHAMPAGNE	Epic	2	6 Dec 75	12
GIRLS, GIRLS, GIRLS	Epic	7	27 Mar 76	8
ONE DRINK TOO MANY	Epic	35	19 Feb 77	4
ALBUMS:	**HITS 1**			**WEEKS 8**
TROUBLE	Epic	45	7 Feb 76	8

SAILORS, SOLDIERS and AIRMEN of HER MAJESTY'S FORCES – See Vera LYNN

ST. ANDREWS CHORALE — UK

| **SINGLES:** | **HITS 1** | | | **WEEKS 5** |
| CLOUD 99 (SOLEADO) | Decca | 31 | 14 Feb 76 | 5 |

ST. CECELIA — UK

| **SINGLES:** | **HITS 1** | | | **WEEKS 17** |
| LEAP UP AND DOWN | Polydor | 12 | 19 Jun 71 | 17 |

Some copies had title as Leap Up And Down (Wave Your Knickers In The Air).

SAINT ETIENNE — UK

(See also Various Artists (EPs) 'The Fred EP'.)

SINGLES:	HITS 13			WEEKS 44	
NOTHING CAN STOP US / SPEEDWELL	Heavenly	54	18 May 91		3
ONLY LOVE CAN BREAK YOUR HEART / FILTHY	Heavenly	39	7 Sep 91		4
Only Love Can Break Your Heart originally recorded and written by Neil Young. His version reached No. 33 in the US in 1970.					
JOIN OUR CLUB / PEOPLE GET REAL	Heavenly	21	16 May 92		3
AVENUE	Heavenly	40	17 Oct 92		2
YOU'RE IN A BAD WAY	Heavenly	12	13 Feb 93		5
HOBART PAVING / WHO DO YOU THINK YOU ARE	Heavenly	23	22 May 93		5
XMAS 93: I WAS BORN ON CHRISTMAS DAY	Heavenly	37	18 Dec 93		5
Vocals by Tim Burgess of the Charlatans.					
PALE MOVIE	Heavenly	28	19 Feb 94		3
LIKE A MOTORWAY	Heavenly	47	28 May 94		2
HUG MY SOUL	Heavenly	32	1 Oct 94		2
Based upon a refrain from Andrea True Connection's More More More.					
HE'S ON THE PHONE	Heavenly	11	11 Nov 95		5
Above hit: SAINT ETIENNE featuring Etienne DAHO.					
SYLVIE	Creation	12	7 Feb 98		3
THE BAD PHOTOGRAPHER	Creation	27	2 May 98		2
ALBUMS:	HITS 7			WEEKS 29	
FOXBASE ALPHA	Heavenly	34	26 Oct 91		3
SO TOUGH	Heavenly	7	6 Mar 93		7
TIGER BAY	Heavenly	8	12 Mar 94		4
TOO YOUNG TO DIE – THE SINGLES	Heavenly	17	25 Nov 95		9
RESERECTION	Virgin	50	27 Jan 96		1
Above hit: SAINT ETIENNE DAHO.					
CASINO CLASSICS	Heavenly	34	19 Oct 96		2
Remixes.					
GOOD HUMOR	Creation	18	16 May 98		3

ST GERMAIN — France

SINGLES:	HITS 1			WEEKS 1	
ALABAMA BLUES REVISITED	F. Communications	50	31 Aug 96		1
First appeared on the French Motherlane EP in 1993.					

Barry ST. JOHN — UK

SINGLES:	HITS 1			WEEKS 1	
COME AWAY MELINDA	Columbia	47	11 Dec 65		1

ST. JOHN'S COLLEGE SCHOOL CHOIR and the Band of the GRENADIER GUARDS — UK

SINGLES:	HITS 1			WEEKS 3	
THE QUEEN'S BIRTHDAY SONG	Columbia	40	3 May 86		3
To commemorate Queen Elizabeth II's 60th Birthday.					

ST. LOUIS UNION — UK

SINGLES:	HITS 1			WEEKS 10	
GIRL	Decca	11	15 Jan 66		10
Originally recorded by the Beatles.					

ST. PAUL'S BOYS' CHOIR — UK

ALBUMS:	HITS 1			WEEKS 8	
REJOICE	K-Tel	36	29 Nov 80		8

Crispian ST. PETERS — UK

SINGLES:	HITS 3			WEEKS 31	
YOU WERE ON MY MIND	Decca	2	8 Jan 66		14
THE PIED PIPER	Decca	5	2 Apr 66		13
CHANGES	Decca	49	17 Sep 66		1
CHANGES [RE]	Decca	47	1 Oct 66		3

ST. PHILIPS CHOIR — UK

SINGLES:	HITS 1			WEEKS 4	
SING FOR EVER	BBC	49	12 Dec 87		4

ST. THOMAS MORE SCHOOL CHOIR – See Scott FITZGERALD

ST. WINIFRED'S SCHOOL CHOIR — UK

SINGLES:	HITS 1			WEEKS 11	
THERE'S NO ONE QUITE LIKE GRANDMA	Music For Pleasure	1	22 Nov 80		11
Label only shows title as No One Quite Like Grandma.					

Buffy SAINTE-MARIE — Canada

SINGLES:		HITS 4			WEEKS 29
SOLDIER BLUE	RCA Victor		7	17 Jul 71	18
From the film of the same name.					
I'M GONNA BE A COUNTRY GIRL AGAIN	Vanguard		34	18 Mar 72	5
THE BIG ONES GET AWAY	Ensign		39	8 Feb 92	5
FALLEN ANGELS	Ensign		57	4 Jul 92	1
ALBUMS:		**HITS 1**			**WEEKS 2**
COINCIDENCE (AND LIKELY STORIES)	Ensign		39	21 Mar 92	2

SAINTS — Australia

SINGLES:		HITS 1			WEEKS 4
THIS PERFECT DAY	Harvest		34	16 Jul 77	4

SAJA – See HAMMER

Kyu SAKAMOTO — Japan

SINGLES:		HITS 1			WEEKS 13
SUKIYAKI (UE O MUITE ARUKO)	His Master's Voice		6	29 Jun 63	13
English translation: I Look Up When I Walk.					

Riuichi SAKAMOTO — Japan

SINGLES:		HITS 3			WEEKS 15
BAMBOO HOUSES / BAMBOO MUSIC	Virgin		30	7 Aug 82	4
Above hit: SYLVIAN SAKAMOTO.					
FORBIDDEN COLOURS	Virgin		16	2 Jul 83	8
Vocal version of the theme from the film 'Merry Christmas Mr. Lawrence'.					
Above hit: David SLVIAN and Riuichi SAKAMOTO.					
HEARTBEAT (TAINAI KAIKI II) RETURNING TO THE WOMB	Virgin America		58	13 Jun 92	3
Above hit: David SYLVIAN and Riuichi SAKAMOTO featuring Ingrid CHAVEZ.					
ALBUMS:		**HITS 1**			**WEEKS 9**
MERRY CHRISTMAS MR LAWRENCE [OST]	Virgin		36	3 Sep 83	9

SAKKARIN – See Jonathan KING

SALAD — UK/Holland

SINGLES:		HITS 5			WEEKS 5
DRINK THE ELIXIR	Island Red		66	11 Mar 95	1
MOTORBIKE TO HEAVEN	Island Red		42	13 May 95	1
GRANITE STATUE	Island Red		50	16 Sep 95	1
I WANT YOU	Island		60	26 Oct 96	1
CARDBOY KING	Island		65	17 May 97	1
ALBUMS:		**HITS 1**			**WEEKS 2**
DRINK ME	Island Red		16	27 May 95	2

SALFORD JETS — UK

SINGLES:		HITS 1			WEEKS 2
WHO YOU LOOKING AT?	RCA		72	31 May 80	2

SALSOUL ORCHESTRA – See CHARO and the SALSOUL ORCHESTRA

SALT-N-PEPA — US

SINGLES:		HITS 15			WEEKS 123
PUSH IT / I AM DOWN	ffrr		41	26 Mar 88	6
I Am Down listed from 2 Apr 88.					
PUSH IT / TRAMP	Champion & ffrr		2	25 Jun 88	13
Sales were combined with the ffrr release whch had also been repackaged to include Tramp. The Champion label had the original mix of Push It with a remixed version of Tramp by Bayside Studios, while the ffrr label had the remix of Push It by Hurby 'Lovebug' Azor with the original version of Tramp. Tramp originally recorded by Lowell Fulsom.					
SHAKE YOUR THANG (IT'S YOUR THING)	ffrr		22	3 Sep 88	8
Above hit: SALT N PEPA – featuring E.U.					
TWIST AND SHOUT	ffrr		4	12 Nov 88	9
Originally recorded by the Top Notes.					
EXPRESSION	ffrr		40	14 Apr 90	6
Sleeve subtitled The Brixton Bass Mix.					
DO YOU WANT ME	ffrr		5	25 May 91	12
Male vocalist is Herbie Luv Bug.					
LET'S TALK ABOUT SEX	ffrr		2	31 Aug 91	13
YOU SHOWED ME	ffrr		15	30 Nov 91	9
Originally recorded by the Byrds.					
EXPRESSION [RM]	ffrr		23	28 Mar 92	6
Remixed by Ben Liebrand.					
START ME UP	ffrr		39	3 Oct 92	3
SHOOP	ffrr		29	9 Oct 93	3

WHATTA MAN	ffrr	7	19 Mar 94	10

Originally recorded by Linda Lyndell.
Above hit: SALT 'N' PEPA with EN VOGUE.

SHOOP [RM]	ffrr	13	28 May 94	8

Remixed by Cheryl "Salt" James.

NONE OF YOUR BUSINESS	ffrr	19	12 Nov 94	4
NONE OF YOUR BUSINESS [RE]	ffrr	64	7 Jan 95	1
CHAMPAGNE	MCA	23	21 Dec 96	6

From the film 'Bulletproof'.

R U READY	ffrr	24	29 Nov 97	2
THE BRICK TRACK VERSUS GITTY UP	ffrr	22	11 Dec 99	4

Samples Pink Floyd's Another Brick In The Wall.

ALBUMS:		HITS 6		WEEKS 57
A SALT WITH A DEADLY PEPA	London	19	6 Aug 88	27
BLACKS' MAGIC	ffrr	70	12 May 90	1
A BLITZ OF SALT-N-PEPA HITS (THE HITS REMIXED)	ffrr	70	6 Jul 91	2
THE GREATEST HITS	ffrr	6	19 Oct 91	20
RAPPED IN REMIXES	ffrr	37	25 Apr 92	2
VERY NECESSARY	ffrr	36	23 Apr 94	5

SALT TANK　　　　　　　　　　　　　　　　　　　　UK

SINGLES:		HITS 2		WEEKS 3
EUGINA	Internal	40	11 May 96	2
DIMENSION	Hooj Choons	52	3 Jul 99	1

SALVATION ARMY　　　　　　　　　　　　　　　　　UK

ALBUMS:		HITS 1		WEEKS 5
BY REQUEST	Warwick	16	24 Dec 77	5

SAM and DAVE　　　　　　　　　　　　　　　　　　US

(See also Lou Reed.)

SINGLES:		HITS 4		WEEKS 39
SOOTHE ME	Stax	48	18 Mar 67	2

Originally recorded by Sam Cooke.

SOOTHE ME [RE]	Stax	35	15 Apr 67	6
SOUL MAN	Stax	24	4 Nov 67	14
I THANK YOU	Stax	34	16 Mar 68	9
SOUL SISTER BROWN SUGAR	Atlantic	15	1 Feb 69	8

ALBUMS:		HITS 3		WEEKS 20
HOLD ON I'M A COMIN'	Atlantic	35	21 Jan 67	7
DOUBLE DYNAMITE	Stax	28	22 Apr 67	5
SOUL MEN	Stax	32	23 Mar 68	8

SAM THE SHAM and the PHARAOHS　　　　　　　　US

SINGLES:		HITS 2		WEEKS 18
WOOLY BULLY	MGM	11	26 Jun 65	15
LIL' RED RIDING HOOD	MGM	48	6 Aug 66	1
LIL' RED RIDING HOOD [RE]	MGM	46	20 Aug 66	2

Richie SAMBORA　　　　　　　　　　　　　　　　　US

SINGLES:		HITS 3		WEEKS 4
BALLAD OF YOUTH	Mercury	59	7 Sep 91	1
HARD TIMES COME EASY	Mercury	37	7 Mar 98	2
IN IT FOR LOVE	Mercury	58	1 Aug 98	1

ALBUMS:		HITS 2		WEEKS 5
STRANGER IN THIS TOWN	Mercury	20	14 Sep 91	3
UNDISCOVERED SOUL	Mercury	24	14 Mar 98	2

Mike SAMMES SINGERS　　　　　　　　　　　　　　UK

(See also Alma Cogan; Carol Deene; Michael Flanders with the Michael Sammes Singers; Ronnie Hilton; Des O'Connor; Andy Stewart; Malcolm Vaughan; Michael Ward; Jimmy Young.)

SINGLES:		HITS 1		WEEKS 38
SOMEWHERE MY LOVE	His Master's Voice	22	17 Sep 66	19

Lara's Theme from the film 'Dr. Zhivago'.

SOMEWHERE MY LOVE [RE]	His Master's Voice	14	15 Jul 67	19

Dave SAMPSON and the HUNTERS　　　　　　　　UK

SINGLES:		HITS 1		WEEKS 6
SWEET DREAMS	Columbia	48	21 May 60	1
SWEET DREAMS [RE]	Columbia	29	4 Jun 60	5

SAMSON — UK

SINGLES:	HITS 3			WEEKS 6
RIDING WITH THE ANGELS	RCA	55	4 Jul 81	3
LOSING MY GRIP	Polydor	63	24 Jul 82	2
RED SKIES	Polydor	65	5 Mar 83	1
ALBUMS:	HITS 1			WEEKS 6
HEAD ON	Gem	34	26 Jul 80	6

SAN JOSE featuring Rodriguez ARGENTINA — UK

(See also Argent; Silsoe.)

SINGLES:	HITS 1			WEEKS 8
ARGENTINE MELODY (CANCION DE ARGENTINA)	MCA	14	17 Jun 78	8

The BBC theme to their coverage of the 1978 World Cup.

SAN REMO STRINGS — US

SINGLES:	HITS 1			WEEKS 8
FESTIVAL TIME	Tamla Motown	39	18 Dec 71	8

David SANBORN — US

ALBUMS:	HITS 1			WEEKS 1
A CHANGE OF HEART	Warner Brothers	86	14 Mar 87	1

Junior SANCHEZ featuring DAJAE — US

SINGLES:	HITS 1			WEEKS 2
B WITH U	Manifesto	31	16 Oct 99	2

Roger SANCHEZ — US

SINGLES:	HITS 3			WEEKS 4
RELEASE YO SELF	Deconstruction	43	22 Mar 97	1

Above hit: Roger SANCHEZ presents TRANSATLANTIC SOUL.

BUFFALO GALS STAMPEDE	Virgin	65	3 Oct 98	1

Roger Sanchez remixed track 1 (as per CD order). Rakim only appeared on track 2 titled 'Buffalo Gals (Back To Skool)'.
Above hit: Malcolm McLAREN and the WORLD FAMOUS SUPREME TEAM versus RAKIM and Roger SANCHEZ.

I WANT YOUR LOVE	Perpetual	31	20 Feb 99	2

Above hit: Roger SANCHEZ presents TWILIGHT.

Deion SANDERS – See HAMMER

Chris SANDFORD — UK

SINGLES:	HITS 1			WEEKS 9
NOT TOO LITTLE - NOT TOO MUCH	Decca	17	14 Dec 63	9

SANDPIPERS — US

SINGLES:	HITS 4			WEEKS 33
GUANTANAMERA	Pye International	7	17 Sep 66	17

Adapted to music by folk singer Pete Seeger, from a poem by Jose Marti.

QUANDO M'INNAMORO (A MAN WITHOUT LOVE)	A&M	33	8 Jun 68	6
KUMBAYA	A&M	38	29 Mar 69	1
KUMBAYA [RE]	A&M	49	12 Apr 69	1
HANG ON SLOOPY	Satril	32	27 Nov 76	8

SANDRA — Germany

SINGLES:	HITS 1			WEEKS 8
EVERLASTING LOVE	Siren	45	17 Dec 88	8

Original release reached No. 88 in 1987.

Jodie SANDS — US

SINGLES:	HITS 1			WEEKS 10
SOMEDAY (YOU'LL WANT ME TO WANT YOU)	His Master's Voice	14	18 Oct 58	10

Originally recorded by Mills Brothers in 1949.

Tommy SANDS — US

SINGLES:	HITS 1			WEEKS 7
THE OLD OAKEN BUCKET	Capitol	25	6 Aug 60	7

Samantha SANG — Australia

SINGLES:	HITS 1			WEEKS 13
EMOTIONS	Private Stock	11	4 Feb 78	13

Written and backing vocals by Robin and Barry Gibb.

SANTA CLAUS and the CHRISTMAS TREES
UK

SINGLES:	HITS 2			WEEKS 10
SINGALONG-A-SANTA [M]	Polydor	19	11 Dec 82	5
SINGALONG-A-SANTA AGAIN [M]	Polydor	39	10 Dec 83	5

Above 2 are medleys of Christmas songs.

SANTA ESMERALDA and Leroy GOMEZ
US/France

SINGLES:	HITS 1			WEEKS 5
DON'T LET ME BE MISUNDERSTOOD	Philips	41	12 Nov 77	5

SANTANA
US

(See also Carlos Santana and Alice Coltrane; Carlos Santana and Buddy Miles; Carlos Santana and Mahavishnu John McLaughlin.)

SINGLES:	HITS 5			WEEKS 27
SAMBA PA TI	CBS	27	28 Sep 74	7
SHE'S NOT THERE	CBS	11	15 Oct 77	13
WELL ALL RIGHT	CBS	53	25 Nov 78	3

Originally recorded by Buddy Holly.

ALL I EVER WANTED	CBS	57	22 Mar 80	3
SMOOTH	Arista	75	23 Oct 99	1

Above hit: SANTANA featuring Rob THOMAS.

ALBUMS:	HITS 22			WEEKS 214
SANTANA	CBS	26	2 May 70	11
ABRAXAS	CBS	7	28 Nov 70	52
SANTANA III	CBS	6	13 Nov 71	14
CARAVANSERAI	CBS	6	25 Nov 72	11
WELCOME	CBS	8	8 Dec 73	6
GREATEST HITS	CBS	14	21 Sep 74	15
BARBOLETTA	CBS	18	30 Nov 74	5
AMIGOS	CBS	21	10 Apr 76	9
FESTIVAL	CBS	27	8 Jan 77	3
MOONFLOWER	CBS	7	5 Nov 77	27

Live recordings.

INNER SECRETS	CBS	17	11 Nov 78	16
ONENESS – SILVER DREAMS GOLDEN REALITY	CBS	55	24 Mar 79	4

Album divided between studio and live recordings from Osaska, Japan.
Above hit: Carlos SANTANA.

MARATHON	CBS	28	27 Oct 79	5
THE SWING OF DELIGHT	CBS	65	20 Sep 80	2

Above hit: Carlos SANTANA.

ZEBOP!	CBS	33	18 Apr 81	4
SHANGO	CBS	35	14 Aug 82	7
HAVANA MOON	CBS	84	30 Apr 83	3

Above hit: Carlos SANTANA.

BEYOND APPEARANCES	CBS	58	23 Mar 85	3
VIVA! SANTANA – THE VERY BEST	K-Tel	50	15 Nov 86	8
SPIRITS DANCING IN THE FLESH	CBS	68	14 Jul 90	1
THE ULTIMATE COLLECTION	Columbia	23	15 Aug 98	6

Compilation released to mark his 30th anniversary.

SUPERNATURAL	Arista	33	04 Sept 99	2

Carlos SANTANA and Alice COLTRANE
US

(See also Santana.)

ALBUMS:	HITS 1			WEEKS 1
ILLUMINATIONS	CBS	40	2 Nov 74	1

Carlos SANTANA and Mahavishnu John McLAUGHLIN
US

(See also Mahavishnu Orchestra; Santana.)

ALBUMS:	HITS 1			WEEKS 9
LOVE, DEVOTION, SURRENDER	CBS	7	28 Jul 73	9

Carlos SANTANA and Buddy MILES
US

(See also Santana.)

ALBUMS:	HITS 1			WEEKS 4
CARLOS SANTANA AND BUDDY MILES LIVE	CBS	29	26 Aug 72	4

Live recordingss from Hawaii's Diamond Head volcano, Sep 72.

SANTO and JOHNNY
US

SINGLES:	HITS 2			WEEKS 5
SLEEP WALK	Pye International	22	17 Oct 59	4
TEARDROP	Parlophone	50	2 Apr 60	1

Mike SARNE | | | | UK

SINGLES:		HITS 4		WEEKS 43
COME OUTSIDE	Parlophone	1	12 May 62	19
Above hit: Mike SARNE featuring Wendy RICHARD.				
WILL I WHAT	Parlophone	18	1 Sep 62	10
Above hit: Mike SARNE featuring Billie DAVIS with the Charles BLACKWELL ORCHESTRA.				
JUST FOR KICKS	Parlophone	22	12 Jan 63	7
CODE OF LOVE	Parlophone	29	30 Mar 63	7

Joy SARNEY | | | | UK

SINGLES:		HITS 1		WEEKS 6
NAUGHTY NAUGHTY NAUGHTY	Alaska	26	7 May 77	6

D.C. SAROME – See D-MOB

SARR BAND | | | | UK/Italy/France

SINGLES:		HITS 1		WEEKS 1
MAGIC MANDRAKE	Calender	68	16 Sep 78	1

Peter SARSTEDT | | | | UK

SINGLES:		HITS 2		WEEKS 25
WHERE DO YOU GO TO (MY LOVELY)	United Artists	1	8 Feb 69	16
FROZEN ORANGE JUICE	United Artists	10	7 Jun 69	9
ALBUMS:		HITS 1		WEEKS 4
PETER SARSTEDT	United Artists	8	15 Mar 69	4

Robin SARSTEDT | | | | UK

SINGLES:		HITS 1		WEEKS 9
MY RESISTANCE IS LOW	Decca	3	8 May 76	9
Originally recorded by Hoagy Carmichael.				

SARTORELLO | | | | Italy

SINGLES:		HITS 1		WEEKS 1
MOVE BABY MOVE	Multiply	56	10 Aug 96	1

SASH! | | | | Germany

SINGLES:		HITS 7		WEEKS 81
ENCORE UNE FOIS	Multiply	2	1 Mar 97	15
ECUADOR	Multiply	2	5 Jul 97	12
Above hit: SASH! featuring RODRIGUEZ.				
STAY	Multiply	2	18 Oct 97	14
Above hit: SASH! featuring LA TREC.				
LA PRIMAVERA	Multiply	3	4 Apr 98	12
MYSTERIOUS TIMES	Multiply	2	15 Aug 98	12
Above hit: SASH! featuring Tina COUSINS.				
MOVE MANIA	Multiply	8	28 Nov 98	10
Above hit: SASH! featuring SHANNON.				
COLOUR THE WORLD	Multiply	15	3 Apr 99	6
Vocals by Finnish singer Inka and Doctor Alban.				
ALBUMS:		HITS 2		WEEKS 57
IT'S MY LIFE – THE ALBUM	Multiply	6	19 Jul 97	38
LIFE GOES ON	Multiply	5	05 Sept 98	19

SASHA | | | | UK

SINGLES:		HITS 4		WEEKS 12
TOGETHER	ffrr	57	31 Jul 93	1
Above hit: Danny CAMPBELL and SASHA.				
HIGHER GROUND	Deconstruction	19	19 Feb 94	3
Vocals by Sam Mollison.				
MAGIC	Deconstruction	32	27 Aug 94	4
Above hit: SASHA with vocals by Sam MOLLISON.				
BE AS ONE	Deconstruction	17	9 Mar 96	4
Above hit: SASHA and MARIA.				
ALBUMS:		HITS 2		WEEKS 5
THE QAT COLLECTION	Deconstruction	55	12 Mar 94	2
EXPANDER [EP]	Deconstruction	18	17 Jul 99	3
This EP was too long to be eligible for the singles chart.				

Joe SATRIANI | | | | US

SINGLES:		HITS 1		WEEKS 1
THE SATCH [EP]	Epic	53	13 Feb 93	1
Lead track: The Extremist.				

ALBUMS:		HITS 4			WEEKS 13
THE EXTREMEIST	Epic	13	15 Aug 92	6
TIME MACHINE	Epic	32	6 Nov 93	2
JOE SATRIANI	Epic	21	14 Oct 95	3
CRYSTAL PLANET	Epic	32	14 Mar 98	2

SATURDAY NIGHT BAND
US

SINGLES:		HITS 1			WEEKS 9
COME ON DANCE, DANCE	CBS	16	1 Jul 78	9

Jannette SAUL – See Joey NEGRO

Jessie SAUNDERS – See Farley "Jackmaster" FUNK

Kevin SAUNDERSON – See INNER CITY

Chantay SAVAGE
US

SINGLES:		HITS 2			WEEKS 9
I WILL SURVIVE	RCA	12	4 May 96	8
REMINDING ME (OF SEF)	Epic	59	8 Nov 97	1
Above hit: COMMON featuring Chantay SAVAGE.				
ALBUMS:	HITS 1			WEEKS 1
I WILL SURVIVE (DOIN' IT MY WAY)	RCA	66	25 May 96	1

Edna SAVAGE with CHORUS of SERVICE MEN from the NUFFIELD CENTRE, LONDON
UK

SINGLES:		HITS 1			WEEKS 1
ARRIVEDERCI DARLING	Parlophone	19	14 Jan 56	1
Originally recorded by Renato Rascel.				

SAVAGE GARDEN
Australia

SINGLES:		HITS 5			WEEKS 71
I WANT YOU	Columbia	11	21 Jun 97	7
TO THE MOON AND BACK	Columbia	55	27 Sep 97	1
TRULY MADLY DEEPLY	Columbia	4	28 Feb 98	23
TO THE MOON AND BACK [RI]	Columbia	3	22 Aug 98	16
I WANT YOU '98 [RM]	Columbia	12	12 Dec 98	10
Remix by Dave Bascombe.				
THE ANIMAL SONG	Columbia	16	10 Jul 99	6
I KNEW I LOVED YOU	Columbia	10	13 Nov 99	8
ALBUMS:	HITS 2			WEEKS 73
SAVAGE GARDEN	Columbia	2	14 Mar 98	66
Peak position reached on 19 Sep 98.				
AFFIRMATION	Columbia	12	20 Nov 99	7

Telly SAVALAS
US

SINGLES:		HITS 2			WEEKS 12
IF	MCA	1	22 Feb 75	9
Original by Bread reached No. 4 in the US in 1971.				
YOU'VE LOST THAT LOVIN' FEELIN'	MCA	47	31 May 75	3
ALBUMS:	HITS 1			WEEKS 10
TELLY	MCA	12	22 Mar 75	10

SAVANNA
UK

SINGLES:		HITS 1			WEEKS 4
I CAN'T TURN AWAY	R&B	61	10 Oct 81	4

SAVOY BROWN
UK

ALBUMS:		HITS 1			WEEKS 1
LOOKIN' IN	Decca	50	28 Nov 70	1

SAVUKA – See Johnny CLEGG and SAVUKA

SAW DOCTORS
Ireland

SINGLES:		HITS 4			WEEKS 9
SMALL BIT OF LOVE	Shamtown	24	12 Nov 94	3
WORLD OF GOOD	Shamtown	15	27 Jan 96	3
TO WIN JUST ONCE	Shamtown	14	13 Jul 96	2
Inspired by former keyboardist Tony Lambert winning £1m on Irish Lottery.				
SIMPLE THINGS	Shamtown	56	6 Dec 97	1
Compilation.				
ALBUMS:	HITS 4			WEEKS 11
IF THIS IS ROCK AND ROLL, I WANT MY OLD JOB BACK	Solid	69	8 Jun 91	2
ALL THE WAY FROM TUAM	Solid	33	31 Oct 92	2

SAME OUL' TOWN	*Shamtown*	6	24 Feb 96	5
SONGS FROM SUN STREET	*Shamtown*	24	24 Oct 98	2

Nitin SAWHNEY   UK

ALBUMS:	HITS 1		WEEKS 2	
BEYOND SKIN	*Outcaste*	44	25 Sept 99	2

SAXON   UK

SINGLES:	HITS 15		WEEKS 61	
WHEELS OF STEEL	*Carrere*	20	22 Mar 80	11
747 (STRANGERS IN THE NIGHT)	*Carrere*	13	21 Jun 80	9
BACKS TO THE WALL	*Carrere*	64	28 Jun 80	2
BIG TEASER / RAINBOW THEME/FROZEN RAINBOW [M]	*Carrere*	66	28 Jun 80	2
Big Teaser originally released in 1979. Medley is only the last two tracks.				
STRONG ARM OF THE LAW	*Carrere*	63	29 Nov 80	3
AND THE BANDS PLAYED ON	*Carrere*	12	11 Apr 81	8
NEVER SURRENDER	*Carrere*	18	18 Jul 81	6
PRINCESS OF THE NIGHT	*Carrere*	57	31 Oct 81	3
POWER AND THE GLORY	*Carrere*	32	23 Apr 83	5
NIGHTMARE	*Carrere*	50	30 Jul 83	3
BACK ON THE STREETS	*Parlophone*	75	31 Aug 85	1
ROCK 'N' ROLL GYPSY	*Parlophone*	71	29 Mar 86	1
WAITING FOR THE NIGHT	*EMI*	66	30 Aug 86	2
RIDE LIKE THE WIND	*EMI*	52	5 Mar 88	4
I CAN'T WAIT ANYMORE	*EMI*	71	30 Apr 88	1
ALBUMS:	HITS 9		WEEKS 97	
WHEELS OF STEEL	*Carrere*	5	12 Apr 80	29
STRONG ARM OF THE LAW	*Carrere*	11	15 Nov 80	13
DENIM AND LEATHER	*Carrere*	9	3 Oct 81	11
THE EAGLE HAS LANDED	*Carrere*	5	22 May 82	19
POWER AND THE GLORY	*Carrere*	15	26 Mar 83	9
CRUSADER	*Carrere*	18	11 Feb 84	7
INNOCENCE IS NO EXCUSE	*Parlophone*	36	14 Sep 85	4
ROCK THE NATIONS	*EMI*	34	27 Sep 86	3
DESTINY	*EMI*	49	9 Apr 88	2

Al SAXON   UK

SINGLES:	HITS 4		WEEKS 10	
YOU'RE THE TOP-CHA	*Fontana*	17	17 Jan 59	4
ONLY SIXTEEN	*Fontana*	24	29 Aug 59	3
BLUE-EYED BOY	*Fontana*	39	24 Dec 60	2
THERE I'VE SAID IT AGAIN	*Piccadilly*	48	9 Sep 61	1
Above hit: Al SAXON and his Orchestra.				

Leo SAYER   UK

SINGLES:	HITS 17		WEEKS 151	
THE SHOW MUST GO ON	*Chrysalis*	2	15 Dec 73	13
ONE MAN BAND	*Chrysalis*	6	15 Jun 74	9
LONG TALL GLASSES	*Chrysalis*	4	14 Sep 74	9
MOONLIGHTING	*Chrysalis*	2	30 Aug 75	8
YOU MAKE ME FEEL LIKE DANCING	*Chrysalis*	2	30 Oct 76	12
WHEN I NEED YOU	*Chrysalis*	1	29 Jan 77	13
Originally recorded by Albert Hammond.				
HOW MUCH LOVE	*Chrysalis*	10	9 Apr 77	8
THUNDER IN MY HEART	*Chrysalis*	22	10 Sep 77	8
I CAN'T STOP LOVING YOU (THOUGH I TRY)	*Chrysalis*	6	16 Sep 78	11
RAINING IN MY HEART	*Chrysalis*	21	25 Nov 78	10
MORE THAN I CAN SAY	*Chrysalis*	2	5 Jul 80	11
HAVE YOU EVER BEEN IN LOVE	*Chrysalis*	10	13 Mar 82	9
Originally recorded by Paris.				
HEART (STOP BEATING IN TIME)	*Chrysalis*	22	19 Jun 82	10
ORCHARD ROAD	*Chrysalis*	16	12 Mar 83	8
UNTIL YOU COME BACK TO ME	*Chrysalis*	51	15 Oct 83	3
Sleeve reflects title as Til You Come Back To Me.				
UNCHAINED MELODY	*Chrysalis*	54	8 Feb 86	4
WHEN I NEED YOU [RI]	*Chrysalis*	65	13 Feb 93	2
YOU MAKE ME FEEL LIKE DANCING [RR]	*Brothers Organisation*	32	8 Aug 98	3
Above hit: GROOVE GENERATION featuring Leo SAYER.				
ALBUMS:	HITS 13		WEEKS 238	
SILVER BIRD	*Chrysalis*	2	5 Jan 74	22
JUST A BOY	*Chrysalis*	4	26 Oct 74	14
Line from Roger Daltrey's Giving It All Away.				
ANOTHER YEAR	*Chrysalis*	8	20 Sep 75	9
ENDLESS FLIGHT	*Chrysalis*	4	27 Nov 76	66
THUNDER IN MY HEART	*Chrysalis*	8	22 Oct 77	16
LEO SAYER	*Chrysalis*	15	2 Sep 78	25

THE VERY BEST OF LEO SAYER	*Chrysalis*	1	*31 Mar 79*	37
HERE	*Chrysalis*	44	*13 Oct 79*	4
LIVING IN A FANTASY	*Chrysalis*	15	*23 Aug 80*	9
WORLD RADIO	*Chrysalis*	30	*8 May 82*	12
HAVE YOU EVER BEEN IN LOVE	*Chrysalis*	15	*12 Nov 83*	18
ALL THE BEST	*Chrysalis*	26	*6 Mar 93*	4
THE DEFINITIVE HITS COLLECTION	*PolyGram TV*	35	*20 Feb 99*	2

Alexei SAYLE — UK

SINGLES:	**HITS 1**		**WEEKS 8**	
'ULLO JOHN! GOTTA NEW MOTOR?	*Island*	15	*25 Feb 84*	8
ALBUMS:	**HITS 1**		**WEEKS 5**	
THE FISH PEOPLE TAPES	*Island*	62	*17 Mar 84*	5

SCAFFOLD — UK

SINGLES:	**HITS 5**		**WEEKS 62**	
THANK U VERY MUCH	*Parlophone*	4	*25 Nov 67*	12
DO YOU REMEMBER?	*Parlophone*	34	*30 Mar 68*	5
LILY THE PINK	*Parlophone*	1	*9 Nov 68*	24
GIN GAN GOOLIE	*Parlophone*	38	*1 Nov 69*	11
GIN GAN GOOLIE [RE]	*Parlophone*	50	*24 Jan 70*	1
LIVERPOOL LOU	*Warner Brothers*	7	*1 Jun 74*	9

Originally recorded by Dominic Behan.

Boz SCAGGS — US

SINGLES:	**HITS 4**		**WEEKS 31**	
LOWDOWN	*CBS*	28	*30 Oct 76*	4
WHAT CAN I SAY	*CBS*	10	*22 Jan 77*	10
LIDO SHUFFLE	*CBS*	13	*14 May 77*	9
HOLLYWOOD	*CBS*	33	*10 Dec 77*	8
ALBUMS:	**HITS 3**		**WEEKS 29**	
SILK DEGREES	*CBS*	37	*12 Mar 77*	24
DOWN TWO, THEN LEFT	*CBS*	55	*17 Dec 77*	1
MIDDLE MAN	*CBS*	52	*3 May 80*	4

SCARFACE — US

SINGLES:	**HITS 3**		**WEEKS 6**	
HAND OF THE DEAD BODY	*Virgin*	41	*11 Mar 95*	2

Above hit: SCARFACE (featuring ICE CUBE).

I SEEN A MAN DIE	*Virgin*	55	*5 Aug 95*	2
GAME OVER	*Virgin*	34	*5 Jul 97*	2

Samples Indeep's Last Night A DJ Saved My Life.
Above hit: SCARFACE featuring DR. DRE, ICE CUBE, TOO SHORT.

SCARFO — UK

SINGLES:	**HITS 2**		**WEEKS 2**	
ALKALINE	*Deceptive*	61	*19 Jul 97*	1
COSMONAUT NO.7	*Deceptive*	67	*18 Oct 97*	1

SCARLET — UK

SINGLES:	**HITS 4**		**WEEKS 18**	
INDEPENDENT LOVE SONG	*WEA*	12	*21 Jan 95*	12
I WANNA BE FREE (TO BE WITH HIM)	*WEA*	21	*29 Apr 95*	4
LOVE HANGOVER	*WEA*	54	*5 Aug 95*	1
BAD GIRL	*WEA*	54	*6 Jul 96*	1
ALBUMS:	**HITS 1**		**WEEKS 2**	
NAKED	*WEA*	59	*11 Mar 95*	2

SCARLET FANTASTIC — UK

SINGLES:	**HITS 2**		**WEEKS 12**	
NO MEMORY	*Arista*	24	*3 Oct 87*	10
PLUG ME IN (TO THE CENTRAL LOVE LINE)	*Arista*	67	*23 Jan 88*	2

SCARLET PARTY — UK

SINGLES:	**HITS 1**		**WEEKS 5**	
101-DAM-NATIONS	*Parlophone*	44	*16 Oct 82*	5

SCARS — UK

ALBUMS:	**HITS 1**		**WEEKS 3**	
AUTHOR! AUTHOR!	*Pre*	67	*18 Apr 81*	3

SCATMAN JOHN · US

SINGLES:	HITS 2			WEEKS 19
SCATMAN (SKI-BA-BOP-BA-DOP-BOP)	RCA	3	13 May 95	12
SCATMAN'S WORLD	RCA	10	2 Sep 95	7

SCHAEFER – See ROSTAL and SCHAEFER

Michael SCHENKER GROUP · UK/Germany

SINGLES:	HITS 3			WEEKS 9
ARMED AND READY	Chrysalis	53	13 Sep 80	3
CRY FOR THE NATIONS	Chrysalis	56	8 Nov 80	3
DANCER	Chrysalis	52	11 Sep 82	3
ALBUMS:	HITS 7			WEEKS 44
MICHAEL SCHENKER GROUP	Chrysalis	8	6 Sep 80	8
MSG	Chrysalis	14	19 Sep 81	8
ONE NIGHT AT BUDOKAN	Chrysalis	5	13 Mar 82	11
Live recordings from Japan, 12 Aug 81.				
ASSAULT ATTACK	Chrysalis	19	23 Oct 82	5
BUILT TO DESTROY	Chrysalis	23	10 Sep 83	5
ROCK WILL NEVER DIE	Chrysalis	24	23 Jun 84	5
Live recordings.				
PERFECT TIMING	EMI	65	24 Oct 87	2

Abbreviated their name to MSG after Rob McCauley had taken the place of Michael Schenker.
Above hit: MSG.

Lalo SCHIFRIN · US

SINGLES:	HITS 2			WEEKS 11
JAWS	CTI	14	9 Oct 76	9
Theme from the film of the same name.				
BULLITT	warner.esp	36	25 Oct 97	2
Theme from the film of the same name. Featured in the Ford Puma car TV commercial.				

Peter SCHILLING · Germany

SINGLES:	HITS 1			WEEKS 6
MAJOR TOM (COMING HOME)	PSP	42	5 May 84	5
MAJOR TOM (COMING HOME) [RE]	PSP	73	16 Jun 84	1

Phillip SCHOFIELD · UK

SINGLES:	HITS 1			WEEKS 6
CLOSE EVERY DOOR	Really Useful	27	5 Dec 92	6
From the musical 'Joseph And The Amazing Technicolor Dreamcoat'.				

SCHON – See HAGAR, SCHON, AARONSON, SHRIEVE

SCHOOL OF EXCELLENCE · UK

(See also Blowing Free; Harmonium; Hypnosis; In Tune; Raindance.)

ALBUMS:	HITS 1			WEEKS 2
PIANO MOODS	Dino	47	28 Oct 95	2

SCIENTIST · UK

SINGLES:	HITS 3			WEEKS 13
THE EXORCIST	Kickin	62	6 Oct 90	3
THE EXORCIST [RE] + [RM]	Kickin	46	1 Dec 90	3
From 8 Dec 90 the remixed format was listed on the chart.				
THE BEE	Kickin	52	15 Dec 90	3
THE BEE [RE]	Kickin	47	26 Jan 91	3
Re-entry was mainly due to a remixed 12" format being made available. This was listed on the chart from 2 Feb 91.				
SPIRAL SYMPHONY	Kickin	74	11 May 91	1

SCOOCH · UK

SINGLES:	HITS 1			WEEKS 4
WHEN MY BABY	Accolade	29	6 Nov 99	4

SCOOTER · UK/Germany

SINGLES:	HITS 5			WEEKS 14
THE MOVE YOUR ASS [EP]	Club Tools	23	21 Oct 95	4
Lead track: Move Your Ass.				
BACK IN THE U.K.	Club Tools	18	17 Feb 96	3
REBEL YELL	Club Tools	30	25 May 96	2
I'M RAVING	Club Tools	33	19 Oct 96	3
FIRE	Club Tools	45	17 May 97	2
ALBUMS:	HITS 1			WEEKS 5
OUR HAPPY HARDCORE	Club Tools	24	13 Apr 96	5

SCORPIONS
Germany

SINGLES:		HITS 10			WEEKS 35
IS THERE ANYBODY THERE? / ANOTHER PIECE OF MEAT	Harvest	39	26 May 79	4
LOVEDRIVE	Harvest	69	25 Aug 79	2
MAKE IT REAL	Harvest	72	31 May 80	2
THE ZOO	Harvest	75	20 Sep 80	1
NO ONE LIKE YOU	Harvest	65	3 Apr 82	3
NO ONE LIKE YOU [RE]	Harvest	64	1 May 82	1
CAN'T LIVE WITHOUT YOU	Harvest	63	17 Jul 82	2
RHYTHM OF LOVE	Harvest	59	4 Jun 88	2
PASSION RULES THE GAME	Harvest	74	18 Feb 89	1
WIND OF CHANGE	Vertigo	53	1 Jun 91	3
WIND OF CHANGE [RI]	Vertigo	2	28 Sep 91	9
SEND ME AN ANGEL	Vertigo	27	30 Nov 91	3
SEND ME AN ANGEL [RE]	Vertigo	68	28 Dec 91	2
ALBUMS:		HITS 8			WEEKS 56
LOVE DRIVE	Harvest	36	21 Apr 79	11
ANIMAL MAGNETISM	Harvest	23	3 May 80	6
BLACKOUT	Harvest	11	10 Apr 82	11
LOVE AT FIRST STING	Harvest	17	24 Mar 84	6
WORLD WIDE LIVE	Harvest	18	29 Jun 85	8
SAVAGE AMUSEMENT	Harvest	18	14 May 88	6
CRAZY WORLD	Vertigo	51	17 Nov 90	1
CRAZY WORLD [RE]	Vertigo	27	2 Nov 91	6
FACE THE HEAT	Mercury	51	25 Sep 93	1

SCOT PROJECT
Germany

SINGLES:		HITS 1			WEEKS 1
U (I GOT A FEELING)	Positiva	66	27 Jul 96	1

SCOTLAND FOOTBALL WORLD CUP SQUAD – See SCOTTISH WORLD CUP SQUAD

Band of the SCOTS GUARDS
UK

ALBUMS:		HITS 1			WEEKS 2
BAND OF THE SCOTS GUARDS	Fontana	25	28 Jun 69	2

Jack SCOTT
Canada

SINGLES:		HITS 4			WEEKS 28
MY TRUE LOVE	London	9	11 Oct 58	10
THE WAY I WALK	London	30	26 Sep 59	1
WHAT IN THE WORLD'S COME OVER YOU	Top Rank	11	12 Mar 60	15
BURNING BRIDGES	Top Rank	32	4 Jun 60	2
ALBUMS:		HITS 2			WEEKS 12
I REMEMBER HANK WILLIAMS	Top Rank	7	7 May 60	11
WHAT IN THE WORLD'S COME OVER YOU	Top Rank	11	3 Sep 60	1

John SCOTT – See Paul PHOENIX

Johnny SCOTT and his Orchestra – See Graham BONNEY with Johnny SCOTT and his Orchestra

Linda SCOTT
US

SINGLES:		HITS 2			WEEKS 14
I'VE TOLD EVERY LITTLE STAR	Columbia	7	20 May 61	13
Originally recorded by Jack Denny.				
DON'T BET MONEY HONEY	Columbia	50	16 Sep 61	1
Above hit: Linda SCOTT with the Hutch DAVIE ORCHESTRA.				

Mike SCOTT
UK

SINGLES:		HITS 4			WEEKS 4
BRING 'EM ALL IN	Chrysalis	56	16 Sep 95	1
BUILDING THE CITY OF LIGHT	Chrysalis	60	11 Nov 95	1
LOVE ANYWAY	Chrysalis	50	27 Sep 97	1
RARE, PRECIOUS AND GONE	Chrysalis	74	14 Feb 98	1
ALBUMS:		HITS 2			WEEKS 4
BRING 'EM ALL IN	Chrysalis	23	30 Sep 95	2
STILL BURNING	Chrysalis	34	11 Oct 97	2

Millie SCOTT
US

SINGLES:		HITS 3			WEEKS 11
PRISONER OF LOVE	Fourth & Broadway	52	12 Apr 86	4
AUTOMATIC	Fourth & Broadway	56	23 Aug 86	3
EV'RY LITTLE BIT	Fourth & Broadway	63	21 Feb 87	4

Simon SCOTT and the LeROYS — UK

SINGLES:	HITS 1			WEEKS 8
MOVE IT BABY	Parlophone	37	15 Aug 64	8

Tony SCOTT — Holland

SINGLES:	HITS 2			WEEKS 6
THAT'S HOW I'M LIVING / THE CHIEF	Champion	48	15 Apr 89	4
The Chief listed from 22 Apr 89.				
Above hit: Toni SCOTT. Name incorrectly spelt on label and sleeve.				
GET INTO IT / THAT'S HOW I'M LIVING [RI]	Champion	63	10 Feb 90	2

SCOTTISH EURO '96 SQUAD – See SCOTTISH WORLD CUP SQUAD

SCOTTISH RUGBY TEAM with Ronnie BROWNE — UK

SINGLES:	HITS 1			WEEKS 1
FLOWER OF SCOTLAND	Greentrax	73	2 Jun 90	1

SCOTTISH WORLD CUP SQUAD — UK

SINGLES:	HITS 5			WEEKS 27
EASY EASY	Polydor	20	22 Jun 74	4
Above hit: SCOTLAND WORLD CUP SQUAD.				
OLE OLA (MUHLER BRASILEIRA)	Riva	4	27 May 78	6
Above hit: Rod STEWART and the SCOTTISH WORLD CUP SQUAD '78.				
WE HAVE A DREAM	WEA	5	1 May 82	9
Also features vocals by John Gordon Sinclair, B.A. Robertson, Willy Carson, Christian, Miss Scotland, Georgina Kearney and the Pipes and Drums of British Caledonian Airways.				
SAY IT WITH PRIDE	RCA	45	9 Jun 90	3
Friends are Fish, James Grant, Donnie Munro and Jimmy O'Neil.				
Above hit: OFFICIAL SCOTTISH WORLD CUP SQUAD and FRIENDS.				
PURPLE HEATHER	Warner Brothers	16	15 Jun 96	5
Official Anthem for the Scottish Football Team in Euro '96.				
Above hit: Rod STEWART with the SCOTTISH EURO '96 SQUAD.				
ALBUMS:	HITS 1			WEEKS 9
EASY EASY	Polydor	3	25 May 74	9
Above hit: SCOTLAND FOOTBALL WORLD CUP SQUAD 1974.				

SCREAMING BLUE MESSIAHS — UK

SINGLES:	HITS 1			WEEKS 6
I WANNA BE A FLINTSTONE	WEA	28	16 Jan 88	6
ALBUMS:	HITS 1			WEEKS 1
GUN-SHY	WEA	90	17 May 86	1

SCREAMING TREES — US

SINGLES:	HITS 2			WEEKS 2
NEARLY LOST YOU	Epic	50	6 Mar 93	1
DOLLAR BILL	Epic	52	1 May 93	1
ALBUMS:	HITS 1			WEEKS 4
DUST	Epic	32	20 Jul 96	4

SCREEN II — UK

ALBUMS:	HITS 1			WEEKS 1
LET THE RECORD SPIN	Cleveland City	36	9 Apr 94	1
12" doublepack single not eligible for the singles chart.				

SCRITTI POLITTI — UK/US

SINGLES:	HITS 14			WEEKS 78
THE SWEETEST GIRL	Rough Trade	64	21 Nov 81	3
FAITHLESS	Rough Trade	56	22 May 82	4
ASYLUMS IN JERUSALEM / JACQUES DERRIDA	Rough Trade	43	7 Aug 82	5
Features Robert Wyatt on keyboards.				
WOOD BEEZ (PRAY LIKE ARETHA FRANKLIN)	Virgin	10	10 Mar 84	12
ABSOLUTE	Virgin	17	9 Jun 84	9
HYPNOTIZE	Virgin	68	17 Nov 84	2
THE WORD GIRL	Virgin	6	11 May 85	12
Above hit: SCRITTI POLITTI featuring RANKING ANN.				
PERFECT WAY	Virgin	48	7 Sep 85	5
OH PATTI (DON'T FEEL SORRY FOR LOVERBOY)	Virgin	13	7 May 88	9
FIRST BOY IN THIS TOWN (LOVE SICK)	Virgin	63	27 Aug 88	3
BOOM! THERE SHE WAS	Virgin	55	12 Nov 88	3
Above hit: SCRITTI POLITTI featuring ROGER.				
SHE'S A WOMAN	Virgin	20	16 Mar 91	7
Above hit: SCRITTI POLITTI (featuring Shabba RANKS).				

TAKE ME IN YOUR ARMS AND LOVE ME	*Virgin*	47	*3 Aug 91*	3
Above hit: SCRITTI POLITTI and Sweetie IRIE.				
TINSELTOWN TO THE BOOGIEDOWN	*Virgin*	46	*31 Jul 99*	1
ALBUMS:	**HITS 4**		**WEEKS 39**	
SONGS TO REMEMBER	*Rough Trade*	12	*11 Sep 82*	7
CUPID AND PSYCHE 85	*Virgin*	5	*22 Jun 85*	19
PROVISION	*Virgin*	8	*18 Jun 88*	11
ANOMIE & BONHOMIE	*Virgin*	33	*7 Aug 99*	2

Earl SCRUGGS – See Lester FLATT and Earl SCRUGGS

SEA FRUIT
UK

SINGLES:	**HITS 1**		**WEEKS 1**	
HELLO WORLD	*Electric Canyon*	59	*24 Jul 99*	1

SEA LEVEL
US

SINGLES:	**HITS 1**		**WEEKS 4**	
FIFTY-FOUR	*Capricorn*	63	*17 Feb 79*	4

SEAGULLS – BRIGHTON AND HOVE ALBION FOOTBALL CLUB
UK

SINGLES:	**HITS 1**		**WEEKS 2**	
THE BOYS IN THE OLD BRIGHTON BLUE	*Energy*	65	*28 May 83*	2

SEAHORSES
UK

SINGLES:	**HITS 4**		**WEEKS 26**	
LOVE IS THE LAW	*Geffen*	3	*10 May 97*	7
BLINDED BY THE SUN	*Geffen*	7	*26 Jul 97*	7
LOVE ME AND LEAVE ME	*Geffen*	16	*11 Oct 97*	4
YOU CAN TALK TO ME	*Geffen*	15	*13 Dec 97*	8
ALBUMS:	**HITS 1**		**WEEKS 38**	
DO IT YOURSELF	*Geffen*	2	*7 Jun 97*	38

SEAL
UK

SINGLES:	**HITS 12**		**WEEKS 70**	
CRAZY	*ZTT*	2	*8 Dec 90*	15
FUTURE LOVE [EP]	*ZTT*	12	*4 May 91*	6
Lead track: Future Love Paradise.				
THE BEGINNING	*ZTT*	24	*20 Jul 91*	6
KILLER ... ON THE LOOSE [EP]	*ZTT*	8	*16 Nov 91*	8
Lead track: Killer. 12" format is titled Killer Dance EP.				
VIOLET	*ZTT*	39	*29 Feb 92*	2
Re-recording of a track from the Future Love EP.				
PRAYER FOR THE DYING	*ZTT*	14	*21 May 94*	5
KISS FROM A ROSE	*ZTT*	20	*30 Jul 94*	5
NEWBORN FRIEND	*ZTT*	45	*5 Nov 94*	2
KISS FROM A ROSE [RI] / I'M ALIVE	*ZTT*	4	*15 Jul 95*	13
I'm Alive from the film 'Batman Forever'.				
DON'T CRY / PRAYER FOR THE DYING [RI]	*ZTT*	51	*9 Dec 95*	2
FLY LIKE AN EAGLE	*ZTT*	13	*29 Mar 97*	5
From the film 'Space Jam'.				
HUMAN BEINGS	*Warner Brothers*	50	*14 Nov 98*	1
ALBUMS:	**HITS 3**		**WEEKS 131**	
SEAL	*ZTT*	1	*1 Jun 91*	65
SEAL	*ZTT*	1	*4 Jun 94*	64
Both self titled albums are different.				
HUMAN BEING	*Warner Brothers*	44	*28 Nov 98*	2

SEARCHERS
UK

SINGLES:	**HITS 14**		**WEEKS 128**	
SWEETS FOR MY SWEET	*Pye*	1	*29 Jun 63*	16
Original by the Drifters reached No. 16 in the US in 1961.				
SWEET NOTHIN'S	*Philips*	48	*12 Oct 63*	2
Live recording from the Star Club, Hamburg, Sep 62.				
SUGAR AND SPICE	*Pye*	2	*26 Oct 63*	13
NEEDLES AND PINS	*Pye*	1	*18 Jan 64*	15
Originally recorded by Jackie De Shannon, co-written by Sonny Bono.				
DON'T THROW YOUR LOVE AWAY	*Pye*	1	*18 Apr 64*	11
Originally recorded by the Orlons.				
SOMEDAY WE'RE GONNA LOVE AGAIN	*Pye*	11	*18 Jul 64*	8
WHEN YOU WALK IN THE ROOM	*Pye*	3	*19 Sep 64*	12
Originally recorded by Jackie De Shannon.				
WHAT HAVE THEY DONE TO THE RAIN	*Pye*	13	*5 Dec 64*	11
An anti-nuclear protest song. Originally recorded by Malvina Reynolds.				
GOODBYE MY LOVE	*Pye*	4	*6 Mar 65*	11
Originally recorded by Jimmy Hughes as Goodbye My Lover Goodbye.				

HE'S GOT NO LOVE	*Pye*	12	*10 Jul 65*	10
WHEN I GET HOME	*Pye*	35	*16 Oct 65*	3
TAKE ME FOR WHAT I'M WORTH	*Pye*	20	*18 Dec 65*	8
Originally recorded by P.F. Sloan.				
TAKE IT OR LEAVE IT	*Pye*	31	*23 Apr 66*	6
Originally recorded by Rolling Stones.				
HAVE YOU EVER LOVED SOMEBODY	*Pye*	48	*15 Oct 66*	2
Originally recorded by the Hollies.				
EPS:	**HITS 7**			**WEEKS 106**
AIN'T GONNA KISS YOU	*Pye*	1	*21 Sep 63*	24
SWEETS FOR MY SWEET	*Pye*	5	*14 Dec 63*	18
HUNGRY FOR LOVE	*Pye*	4	*29 Feb 64*	19
SEARCHERS PLAY THE SYSTEM	*Pye*	4	*12 Dec 64*	18
WHEN YOU WALK IN THE ROOM	*Pye*	12	*27 Mar 65*	2
BUMBLE BEE	*Pye*	1	*8 May 65*	17
SEARCHERS '65	*Pye*	15	*25 Sep 65*	8
ALBUMS:	**HITS 4**			**WEEKS 87**
MEET THE SEARCHERS	*Pye*	2	*10 Aug 63*	44
SUGAR AND SPICE	*Pye*	5	*16 Nov 63*	21
IT'S THE SEARCHERS	*Pye*	4	*30 May 64*	17
SOUNDS LIKE THE SEARCHERS	*Pye*	8	*27 Mar 65*	5

SEASHELLS
UK

SINGLES:	**HITS 1**			**WEEKS 5**
MAYBE I KNOW	*CBS*	32	*9 Sep 72*	5
Originally recorded by Leslie Gore.				

SEB
UK

SINGLES:	**HITS 1**			**WEEKS 1**
SUGAR SHACK	*React*	61	*18 Feb 95*	1

SEBADOH
US

SINGLES:	**HITS 2**			**WEEKS 4**
BEAUTY OF THE RIDE	*Domino*	74	*27 Jul 96*	1
FLAME	*Domino*	30	*30 Jan 99*	3
ALBUMS:	**HITS 4**			**WEEKS 5**
BUBBLE AND SCRAPE	*Domino*	63	*8 May 93*	1
BAKESALE	*Domino*	40	*3 Sep 94*	2
HARMACY	*Domino*	38	*31 Aug 96*	1
THE SEBADOH	*Domino*	45	*6 Mar 99*	1

Jon SECADA
US

SINGLES:	**HITS 9**			**WEEKS 42**
JUST ANOTHER DAY	*SBK*	5	*18 Jul 92*	15
Backing vocals by Gloria Estefan.				
DO YOU BELIEVE IN US	*SBK*	30	*31 Oct 92*	4
ANGEL	*SBK*	23	*6 Feb 93*	5
DO YOU REALLY WANT ME	*SBK*	30	*17 Jul 93*	4
I'M FREE	*SBK*	50	*16 Oct 93*	2
IF YOU GO	*SBK*	39	*14 May 94*	4
IF YOU GO [RE]	*SBK*	71	*2 Jul 94*	1
MENTAL PICTURE	*SBK*	44	*4 Feb 95*	2
From the film 'The Specialist'.				
IF I NEVER KNEW YOU (LOVE THEME FROM POCAHONTAS)	*Walt Disney*	51	*16 Dec 95*	4
From the Walt Disney film 'Pocahontas'.				
Above hit: Jon SECADA and SHANICE.				
TOO LATE, TOO SOON	*SBK*	43	*14 Jun 97*	1
ALBUMS:	**HITS 2**			**WEEKS 16**
JON SECADA	*SBK*	20	*5 Sep 92*	11
HEART, SOUL AND VOICE	*SBK*	17	*4 Jun 94*	5

SECCHI featuring Orlando JOHNSON
US/Italy

SINGLES:	**HITS 1**			**WEEKS 3**
I SAY YEAH	*Epic*	46	*4 May 91*	3

Harry SECOMBE
UK

(See also Harry Secombe and Moira Anderson; Harry Secombe, Peter Sellers and Spike Milligan; Various Artists: Films - Original Soundtracks 'Oliver!'.)

SINGLES:	**HITS 3**			**WEEKS 35**
ON WITH THE MOTLEY (VESTI LA GIUBBA)	*Philips*	16	*10 Dec 55*	3
Originally recorded by Enrico Caruso.				
IF I RULED THE WORLD	*Philips*	44	*5 Oct 63*	2
From the show 'Pickwick'.				
Above hit: Harry SECOMBE with Wally STOTT and his Orchestra and Chorus.				

IF I RULED THE WORLD [RE]	*Philips*	18	*23 Nov 63*	15
THIS IS MY SONG	*Philips*	2	*25 Feb 67*	15

From the film 'A Countess From Hong Kong'. Written by Charlie Chaplin

EPS:	**HITS 6**			**WEEKS 68**
SACRED SONGS	*Philips*	9	*2 Apr 60*	38
LAND OF MY FATHERS	*Philips*	8	*14 May 60*	22
AT YOUR REQUEST VOLUME 2	*Philips*	17	*30 Jul 60*	1
SACRED SONGS VOLUME 2	*Philips*	15	*24 Dec 60*	4
TAUBER FAVOURITES	*Philips*	18	*5 May 62*	1
SHOW SOUVENIRS	*Philips*	18	*28 Jul 62*	2

ALBUMS:	**HITS 6**			**WEEKS 56**
SACRED SONGS	*Philips*	16	*31 Mar 62*	1
SECOMBE'S PERSONAL CHOICE	*Philips*	6	*22 Apr 67*	13
IF I RULED THE WORLD	*Contour*	17	*7 Aug 71*	20
20 SONGS OF JOY	*Warwick*	8	*16 Dec 78*	12
HIGHWAY OF LIFE	*Telstar*	45	*13 Dec 86*	5
YOURS SINCERELY	*Philips*	46	*30 Nov 91*	5

Harry SECOMBE and Moira ANDERSON   UK

(See also Moira Anderson; Harry Secombe.)

ALBUMS:	**HITS 1**			**WEEKS 5**
GOLDEN MEMORIES	*Warwick*	46	*5 Dec 81*	5

Harry SECOMBE, Peter SELLERS and Spike MILLIGAN   UK

(See also Goons; Spike Milligan; Harry Secombe, Peter Sellers.)

ALBUMS:	**HITS 1**			**WEEKS 1**
HOW TO WIN AN ELECTION	*Philips*	20	*18 Apr 64*	1

SECOND CITY SOUND   UK

SINGLES:	**HITS 2**			**WEEKS 8**
TCHAIKOVSKY ONE	*Decca*	22	*22 Jan 66*	7
DREAM OF OLWEN	*Major Minor*	43	*5 Apr 69*	1

SECOND IMAGE   UK

SINGLES:	**HITS 5**			**WEEKS 11**
STAR	*Polydor*	60	*24 Jul 82*	2
BETTER TAKE TIME	*Polydor*	67	*2 Apr 83*	2
DON'T YOU	*MCA*	68	*26 Nov 83*	2
SING AND SHOUT	*MCA*	53	*11 Aug 84*	3
STARTING AGAIN	*MCA*	65	*2 Feb 85*	2

ALBUMS:	**HITS 1**			**WEEKS 1**
STRANGE REFLECTIONS	*MCA*	100	*30 Mar 85*	1

SECOND PHASE   US

SINGLES:	**HITS 1**			**WEEKS 2**
MENTASM	*R&S*	48	*21 Sep 91*	2

SECRET AFFAIR   UK

SINGLES:	**HITS 5**			**WEEKS 34**
TIME FOR ACTION	*I-Spy*	13	*1 Sep 79*	10
LET YOUR HEART DANCE	*I-Spy*	32	*10 Nov 79*	6
MY WORLD	*I-Spy*	16	*8 Mar 80*	9
SOUND OF CONFUSION	*I-Spy*	45	*23 Aug 80*	5
DO YOU KNOW	*I-Spy*	57	*17 Oct 81*	4

ALBUMS:	**HITS 3**			**WEEKS 15**
GLORY BOYS	*I-Spy*	41	*1 Dec 79*	8
BEHIND CLOSED DOORS	*I-Spy*	48	*20 Sep 80*	4
BUSINESS AS USUAL	*I-Spy*	84	*13 Mar 82*	3

SECRET KNOWLEDGE   UK/US

SINGLES:	**HITS 2**			**WEEKS 2**
LOVE ME NOW	*Deconstruction*	66	*27 Apr 96*	1
SUGAR DADDY	*Deconstruction*	75	*24 Aug 96*	1

SECRET LIFE   UK

SINGLES:	**HITS 4**			**WEEKS 10**
AS ALWAYS	*Cowboy*	45	*12 Dec 92*	4

Originally recorded by Stevie Wonder.

LOVE SO STRONG	*Cowboy*	38	*7 Aug 93*	2
SHE HOLDS THE KEY	*Pulse 8*	63	*7 May 94*	1
I WANT YOU	*Pulse 8*	70	*29 Oct 94*	1

LOVE SO STRONG [RM]	Pulse 8	37	28 Jan 95	2

Remixed by Brothers In Rhythm. Backing vocals by Clive Griffin, Lance Ellington and Kate Kissoon

SECRETARY OF ENT. – See RAZE

SECTION-X
France

SINGLES:	HITS 1		WEEKS 1	
ATLANTIS	Perfecto	42	8 Mar 97	1

Neil SEDAKA
US

SINGLES:	HITS 18		WEEKS 190	
I GO APE	RCA	9	25 Apr 59	13
OH! CAROL	RCA	3	14 Nov 59	17

Song written about his high school girlfriend Carol Klein (later to become Carole King).

STAIRWAY TO HEAVEN	RCA	8	16 Apr 60	15
YOU MEAN EVERYTHING TO ME	RCA	45	3 Sep 60	3
CALENDAR GIRL	RCA	8	4 Feb 61	14
LITTLE DEVIL	RCA	9	20 May 61	12

Above 3: Neil SEDAKA with Stan APPLEBAUM and his Orchestra.

HAPPY BIRTHDAY, SWEET SIXTEEN	RCA	3	23 Dec 61	18
KING OF CLOWNS	RCA	23	21 Apr 62	11
BREAKING UP IS HARD TO DO	RCA	7	21 Jul 62	16

Backing vocals by the Cookies.

NEXT DOOR TO AN ANGEL	RCA	29	24 Nov 62	4
LET'S GO STEADY AGAIN	RCA Victor	42	1 Jun 63	1
LET'S GO STEADY AGAIN [RE]	RCA Victor	43	15 Jun 63	2
OH CAROL [RI] / BREAKING UP IS HARD TO DO[RI] / LITTLE DEVIL [RI]	RCA Victor Maximillion	19	7 Oct 72	14

Breaking Up Is Hard To Do and Little Devil have additional credit with Stan Applebaum and his Orchestra.

BEAUTIFUL YOU	RCA Victor	43	4 Nov 72	3
THAT'S WHEN THE MUSIC TAKES ME	RCA Victor	18	24 Feb 73	10
STANDING ON THE INSIDE	MGM	26	2 Jun 73	9
OUR LAST SONG TOGETHER	MGM	31	25 Aug 73	8

Tribute to his songwriting partner Howard Greenfield.

A LITTLE LOVIN'	Polydor	34	9 Feb 74	6
LAUGHTER IN THE RAIN	Polydor	15	22 Jun 74	9
THE QUEEN OF 1964	Polydor	35	22 Mar 75	5

ALBUMS:	HITS 8		WEEKS 80	
THE TRA-LA DAYS ARE OVER	MGM	13	1 Sep 73	10
LAUGHTER IN THE RAIN	Polydor	17	22 Jun 74	10
LIVE AT THE ROYAL FESTIVAL HALL	Polydor	48	23 Nov 74	1

Live recordings with the Royal Philharmonic Orchestra.

OVERNIGHT SUCCESS	Polydor	31	1 Mar 75	6
LAUGHTER AND TEARS – THE BEST OF NEIL SEDAKA TODAY	Polydor	2	10 Jul 76	25
TIMELESS - THE VERY BEST OF NEIL SEDAKA	Polydor	10	2 Nov 91	16
CLASSICALLY SEDAKA	Vision	23	4 Nov 95	9

Sedaka's original lyrics matched to well known classical pieces.

THE VERY BEST OF NEIL SEDAKA	Universal Music TV	33	19 Jun 99	3

SEDUCTION
US

SINGLES:	HITS 1		WEEKS 1	
HEARTBEAT	Breakout	75	21 Apr 90	1

Pete SEEGER
US

EPS:	HITS 1		WEEKS 1	
IN CONCERT	CBS	18	3 Oct 64	1

SEEKERS
Australia/Sri Lanka

SINGLES:	HITS 9		WEEKS 120	
I'LL NEVER FIND ANOTHER YOU	Columbia	1	9 Jan 65	23
A WORLD OF OUR OWN	Columbia	3	17 Apr 65	18
THE CARNIVAL IS OVER	Columbia	1	30 Oct 65	17
SOMEDAY, ONE DAY	Columbia	11	26 Mar 66	11
WALK WITH ME	Columbia	10	10 Sep 66	12
MORNINGTOWN RIDE	Columbia	2	26 Nov 66	15
GEORGY GIRL	Columbia	3	25 Feb 67	11

From the film of the same name. Co-written by actor Jim Dale.

WHEN WILL THE GOOD APPLES FALL	Columbia	11	23 Sep 67	12
EMERALD CITY	Columbia	50	16 Dec 67	1

EPS:	HITS 3		WEEKS 166	
THE SEEKERS	Columbia	1	24 Jul 65	50
HITS FROM THE SEEKERS	Columbia	1	16 Jul 66	73
MORNINGTOWN RIDE	Columbia	1	11 Feb 67	43

ALBUMS:	HITS 7			WEEKS 281
A WORLD OF OUR OWN	Columbia	5	3 Jul 65	36
THE SEEKERS	Decca	16	3 Jul 65	1
COME THE DAY	Columbia	3	19 Nov 66	67
SEEKERS – SEEN IN GREEN	Columbia	15	25 Nov 67	10
LIVE AT THE TALK OF THE TOWN	Columbia	2	14 Sep 68	30
THE BEST OF THE SEEKERS	Columbia	1	16 Nov 68	125
CARNIVAL OF HITS	EMI	7	23 Apr 94	12

Includes both solo and group material.
Above hit: Judith DURHAM and the SEEKERS.

Bob SEGER and the SILVER BULLET BAND   US

SINGLES:	HITS 7			WEEKS 30
HOLLYWOOD NIGHTS	Capitol	42	30 Sep 78	6
WE'VE GOT TONITE	Capitol	41	3 Feb 79	6

Above 2: Bob SEGER.

HOLLYWOOD NIGHTS [RR]	Capitol	49	24 Oct 81	3
WE'VE GOT TONITE [RR]	Capitol	60	6 Feb 82	4

Above 2 are live recordings.

EVEN NOW	Capitol	73	9 Apr 83	2
WE'VE GOT TONIGHT [RI]	Capitol	22	28 Jan 95	5
NIGHT MOVES	Capitol	45	29 Apr 95	2

Reached No. 4 in the US when first released in 1977.

HOLLYWOOD NIGHTS [RI]	Capitol	52	29 Jul 95	1
LOCK AND LOAD	Parlophone	57	10 Feb 96	1
ALBUMS:	HITS 7			WEEKS 52
STRANGER IN TOWN	Capitol	31	3 Jun 78	6
AGAINST THE WIND	Capitol	26	15 Mar 80	6
NINE TONIGHT	Capitol	24	26 Sep 81	10

Live recordings from Boston and Detroit.

THE DISTANCE	Capitol	45	8 Jan 83	10
LIKE A ROCK	Capitol	35	26 Apr 86	6
THE FIRE INSIDE	Capitol	54	21 Sep 91	2
GREATEST HITS	Capitol	6	18 Feb 95	12

SEIKO and Donnie WAHLBERG   Japan/US

SINGLES:	HITS 1			WEEKS 5
THE RIGHT COMBINATION	Epic	44	18 Aug 90	5

SELECTER   UK

(See also Various Artists (EPs) 'The 2 Tone EP'.)

SINGLES:	HITS 4			WEEKS 28
ON MY RADIO	2-Tone	8	13 Oct 79	9
THREE MINUTE HERO	2-Tone	16	2 Feb 80	6
MISSING WORDS	2-Tone	23	29 Mar 80	8

Some labels showed title as Nissing Words.

THE WHISPER	Chrysalis	36	23 Aug 80	5
ALBUMS:	HITS 2			WEEKS 17
TOO MUCH PRESSURE	2-Tone	5	23 Feb 80	13
CELEBRATE THE BULLET	Chrysalis	41	7 Mar 81	4

Peter SELLERS   UK

(See also Peter Sellers and Sophia Loren; Harry Secombe, Peter Sellers and Spike Milligan.)

SINGLES:	HITS 3			WEEKS 20
ANY OLD IRON	Parlophone	21	3 Aug 57	3

Above hit: Peter SELLERS presents MATE'S SPOFFLE GROUP featuring Fred
* SPOONS, E.P.N.S.*

ANY OLD IRON [RE]	Parlophone	17	7 Sep 57	8
A HARD DAY'S NIGHT	Parlophone	14	25 Dec 65	7
A HARD DAY'S NIGHT [EP]	EMI	52	27 Nov 93	2

Lead track: A Hard Day's Night, this itself is a re-issue.

EPS:	HITS 2			WEEKS 4
THE BEST OF SELLERS	Parlophone	15	28 May 60	2
THE BEST OF SELLERS NO. 2	Parlophone	8	27 Aug 60	2
ALBUMS:	HITS 2			WEEKS 84
THE BEST OF SELLERS	Parlophone	3	14 Feb 59	47
SONGS FOR SWINGING SELLERS	Parlophone	3	12 Dec 59	37

Peter SELLERS and Sophia LOREN   UK/Italy

(See also Peter Sellers.)

SINGLES:	HITS 2			WEEKS 19
GOODNESS GRACIOUS ME!	Parlophone	4	12 Nov 60	14
BANGERS AND MASH	Parlophone	22	14 Jan 61	5

782

ALBUMS:		HITS 1			WEEKS 18
PETER AND SOPHIA	*Parlophone*		5	*3 Dec 60*	18

Michael SEMBELLO
US

SINGLES:		HITS 1			WEEKS 6
MANIAC	*Casablanca*		43	*20 Aug 83*	6

From the film 'Flashdance'.

SEMISONIC
US

SINGLES:		HITS 2			WEEKS 16
SECRET SMILE	*MCA*		13	*10 Jul 99*	11
CLOSING TIME	*MCA*		25	*6 Nov 99*	5
ALBUMS:		HITS 1			WEEKS 20
FEELING STRANGELY FINE	*MCA*		16	*24 Jul 99*	20

SEMPRINI
UK

(See also Domenico Modugno.)

SINGLES:		HITS 1			WEEKS 8
EXODUS – MAIN THEME	*His Master's Voice*		25	*18 Mar 61*	8

Theme from the film.

SENSATIONAL ALEX HARVEY BAND
UK

SINGLES:		HITS 3			WEEKS 25
DELILAH	*Vertigo*		7	*26 Jul 75*	7
GAMBLIN' BAR ROOM BLUES	*Vertigo*		38	*22 Nov 75*	8
BOSTON TEA PARTY	*Mountain*		13	*19 Jun 76*	10
ALBUMS:		HITS 6			WEEKS 42
THE IMPOSSIBLE DREAM	*Vertigo*		16	*26 Oct 74*	4
TOMORROW BELONGS TO ME	*Vertigo*		9	*10 May 75*	10
NEXT	*Vertigo*		37	*23 Aug 75*	5
SENSATIONAL ALEX HARVEY BAND LIVE	*Vertigo*		14	*27 Sep 75*	7
PENTHOUSE TAPES	*Vertigo*		14	*10 Apr 76*	7
SAHB STORIES	*Mountain*		11	*31 Jul 76*	9

SENSELESS THINGS
UK

SINGLES:		HITS 9			WEEKS 19
EVERYBODY'S GONE	*Epic*		73	*22 Jun 91*	1
GOT IT AT THE DELMAR	*Epic*		50	*28 Sep 91*	3
EASY TO SMILE	*Epic*		18	*11 Jan 92*	4
HOLD IT DOWN	*Epic*		19	*11 Apr 92*	4
HOMOPHOBIC ASSHOLE	*Epic*		52	*5 Dec 92*	2
PRIMARY INSTINCT	*Epic*		41	*13 Feb 93*	2
TOO MUCH KISSING	*Epic*		69	*12 Jun 93*	1
CHRISTINE KEELER	*Epic*		56	*5 Nov 94*	1
SOMETHING TO MISS	*Epic*		57	*28 Jan 95*	1
ALBUMS:		HITS 2			WEEKS 2
THE FIRST OF TOO MANY	*Epic*		66	*26 Oct 91*	1
EMPIRE OF THE SENSELESS	*Epic*		37	*13 Mar 93*	1

SENSER
UK

SINGLES:		HITS 4			WEEKS 5
THE KEY / NO COMPLY	*Ultimate*		47	*25 Sep 93*	1
SWITCH	*Ultimate*		39	*19 Mar 94*	2
AGE OF PANIC	*Ultimate*		52	*23 Jul 94*	1
CHARMING DEMONS	*Ultimate*		42	*17 Aug 96*	1
ALBUMS:		HITS 2			WEEKS 6
STACKED UP	*Ultimate*		4	*7 May 94*	5
ASYLUM	*Ultimate*		73	*2 May 98*	1

SEPULTURA
Brazil

SINGLES:		HITS 6			WEEKS 12
TERRITORY	*Roadrunner*		66	*2 Oct 93*	2
REFUSE/RESIST	*Roadrunner*		51	*26 Feb 94*	2

This is just one song title.

SLAVE NEW WORLD	*Roadrunner*		46	*4 Jun 94*	2
ROOTS BLOODY ROOTS	*Roadrunner*		19	*24 Feb 96*	2
RATAMAHATTA	*Roadrunner*		23	*17 Aug 96*	2
ATTITUDE	*Roadrunner*		46	*14 Dec 96*	2

Dedicated to Dana Wels, the son of band manager Gloria and stepson of singer Max Cavalera.

ALBUMS:		HITS 4			WEEKS 12
ARISE	*Roadracer*		40	*6 Apr 91*	2
CHAOS A.D.	*Roadrunner*		11	*23 Oct 93*	3

CHAOS A.D. [RE]	Roadrunner	53	19 Mar 94	1
CD repackaged in tin box..				
ROOTS	Roadrunner	4	9 Mar 96	5
AGAINST	Roadrunner	40	17 Oct 98	1

SERIAL DIVA · UK

(See also Three 'N One.)

SINGLES:	HITS 1		WEEKS 1	
KEEP HOPE ALIVE	*Sound Of Ministry*	57	18 Jan 97	1

SERIOUS DANGER · UK

SINGLES:	HITS 2		WEEKS 4	
DEEPER	*Fresh*	40	20 Dec 97	3
HIGH NOON	*Fresh*	54	2 May 98	1

SERIOUS INTENTION · US

SINGLES:	HITS 2		WEEKS 6	
YOU DON'T KNOW (OH-OH-OH)	*Important/Towerbell*	75	16 Nov 85	1
SERIOUS	*Pow Wow*	51	5 Apr 86	5

SERIOUS ROPE · UK

SINGLES:	HITS 2		WEEKS 3	
HAPPINESS (Medley) a) HAPPINESS b) HAPPINESS IS JUST AROUND THE BEND [M]	*Rumour*	54	22 May 93	2
Original by Main Ingredient reached No. 35 in the US in 1974.				
Above hit: SERIOUS ROPE presents Sharon Dee CLARKE.				
HAPPINESS/YOU MAKE ME HAPPY [M] [RR]	*Mercury*	70	1 Oct 94	1

Eric SERRA · France

ALBUMS:	HITS 1		WEEKS 2	
THE FIFTH ELEMENT [OST]	*Virgin*	58	28 Jun 97	2

SET THE TONE · UK

SINGLES:	HITS 2		WEEKS 4	
DANCE SUCKER	*Island*	62	22 Jan 83	2
RAP YOUR LOVE	*Island*	67	26 Mar 83	2

SETTLERS · UK

SINGLES:	HITS 1		WEEKS 5	
THE LIGHTNING TREE	*York*	36	16 Oct 71	5
Theme from the Yorkshire ITV childrens series 'Follyfoot'.				

Brian SETZER ORCHESTRA · US

SINGLES:	HITS 1		WEEKS 3	
JUMP JIVE AN' WAIL	*Interscope*	34	3 Apr 99	3

Taja SEVELLE · US

SINGLES:	HITS 2		WEEKS 13	
LOVE IS CONTAGIOUS	*Paisley Park*	7	20 Feb 88	9
WOULDN'T YOU LOVE TO LOVE ME?	*Paisley Park*	59	14 May 88	4
ALBUMS:	**HITS 1**		**WEEKS 4**	
TAJA SEVELLE	*Paisley Park*	48	26 Mar 88	4

702 · US

(See also Missy "Misdemeanor" Elliott.)

SINGLES:	HITS 4		WEEKS 10	
STEELO	*Motown*	41	14 Dec 96	2
NO DOUBT	*Motown*	59	29 Nov 97	1
WHERE MY GIRLS AT?	*Motown*	22	7 Aug 99	4
YOU DON'T KNOW	*Motown*	36	27 Nov 99	3

740 BOYZ · US

SINGLES:	HITS 1		WEEKS 1	
SHIMMY SHAKE	*MCA*	54	4 Nov 95	1

SEVEN GRAND HOUSING AUTHORITY · UK

SINGLES:	HITS 1		WEEKS 1	
THE QUESTION	*Olympic*	70	23 Oct 93	1

7669

		US		
SINGLES:		HITS 1		WEEKS 1
JOY	Motown	60	18 Jun 94	1

7TH HEAVEN

		UK		
SINGLES:		HITS 1		WEEKS 5
HOT FUN	Mercury	47	14 Sep 85	5

SEVERINE

		France		
SINGLES:		HITS 1		WEEKS 11
UN BANC, UN ARBRE, UNE RUE	Philips	9	24 Apr 71	11

Eurovision Song Contest winner for Monaco in 1971.

David SEVILLE

		US		
(See also Alfi and Harry; Chipmunks.)				
SINGLES:		HITS 2		WEEKS 14
WITCH DOCTOR	London	11	24 May 58	6

Above hit: David SEVILLE with Orchestra and vocal accompaniment effects by the CHIPMUNKS.

RAGTIME COWBOY JOE	London	11	25 Jul 59	8

Above hit: David SEVILLE and the CHIPMUNKS.

Janette SEWELL – See DOUBLE TROUBLE

SEX CLUB

		US		
SINGLES:		HITS 1		WEEKS 1
BIG (BIG) DICK MAN	Club Tools	67	28 Jan 95	1

Features vocals by Brown Sugar. Reply record to 20 Fingers' Short Dick Man.

SEX-O-SONIQUE

		UK		
SINGLES:		HITS 1		WEEKS 3
I THOUGHT IT WAS YOU	ffrr	32	6 Dec 97	3

SEX PISTOLS

		UK		
SINGLES:		HITS 11		WEEKS 89
ANARCHY IN THE U.K.	EMI	38	11 Dec 76	5

May have climbed higher if EMI had not withdrawn the single.

GOD SAVE THE QUEEN	Virgin	2	4 Jun 77	9

Released on A&M in Mar but quickly withdrawn when label terminated their contract. It was claimed that for the week 11 Jun 77 when it peaked at No. 2, it had sold more than Rod Stewart's I Don't Want To Talk About It / First Cut Is The Deepest.

PRETTY VACANT	Virgin	6	9 Jul 77	8
HOLIDAYS IN THE SUN	Virgin	8	22 Oct 77	6
NO ONE IS INNOCENT (A PUNK PRAYER BY RONALD BIGGS) / MY WAY	Virgin	7	8 Jul 78	10

No One Is Innocent recorded with Great Train Robber Ronald Biggs in Rio de Janeiro. Virgin refused to release single with the title Cosh The Driver.

SOMETHING ELSE / FRIGGIN' IN THE RIGGIN'	Virgin	3	3 Mar 79	12

Above hit: SEX PISTOLS vocals: Sid VICIOUS / SEX PISTOLS vocals: Steve JONES.

SILLY THING	Virgin	6	7 Apr 79	8

[AA] listed with Who Killed Bambi by Ten Pole Tudor.

C'MON EVERYBODY	Virgin	3	30 Jun 79	9

Above hit: SEX PISTOLS vocals: Sid VICIOUS.

THE GREAT ROCK 'N' ROLL SWINDLE	Virgin	21	13 Oct 79	6

[AA] listed with Rock Around The Clock by Tenpole Tudor. Above 5 from the film 'The Great Rock 'N' Roll Swindle'.

(I'M NOT YOUR) STEPPING STONE	Virgin	21	14 Jun 80	8

Originally recorded by Paul Revere and the Raiders.

ANARCHY IN THE UK [RI]	Virgin	33	3 Oct 92	3
PRETTY VACANT [RI]	Virgin	56	5 Dec 92	2
PRETTY VACANT LIVE [RR]	Virgin	18	27 Jul 96	3

Live recording from Finsbury Park, London, 23 Jun 96.

ALBUMS:		HITS 7		WEEKS 117
NEVER MIND THE BOLLOCKS, HERE'S THE SEX PISTOLS	Virgin	1	12 Nov 77	48
THE GREAT ROCK 'N' ROLL SWINDLE [OST]	Virgin	7	10 Mar 79	33

Double album featuring out-takes and several songs from the film.

SOME PRODUCT – CARRI ON SEX PISTOLS	Virgin	6	11 Aug 79	10

Non music release with commercials and the interview with Bill Grundy from the Thames ITV 'Today' programme, transmitted 1 Dec 76.

FLOGGING A DEAD HORSE	Virgin	23	16 Feb 80	6
THE GREAT ROCK 'N' ROLL SWINDLE [OST]	Virgin	16	7 Jun 80	11

Single album including 2 tracks by Ten Pole Tudor.

KISS THIS	Virgin	10	17 Oct 92	4
NEVER MIND THE BOLLOCKS, HERE'S THE SEX PISTOLS [RE]	Virgin	45	8 Jun 96	3

Re-packaged as a doublepack with Spunk, a live album.

FILTHY LUCRE LIVE	*Virgin*	26	*10 Aug 96*	2
Live recordings from Finsbury Park, London, 23 Jun 96.				

Denny SEYTON and the SABRES — UK

SINGLES:	HITS 1		WEEKS 1	
THE WAY YOU LOOK TONIGHT	*Mercury*	48	*19 Sep 64*	1

SHABOOM — UK

SINGLES:	HITS 1		WEEKS 1	
SWEET SENSATION	*WEA*	64	*31 Jul 99*	1
Vocals by Chaka Khan's younger sister Taka Boom.				

SHACK — UK

SINGLES:	HITS 2		WEEKS 2	
COMEDY	*London*	44	*26 Jun 99*	1
NATALIE'S PARTY	*London*	63	*14 Aug 99*	1
ALBUMS:	HITS 1		WEEKS 2	
H.M.S. FABLE	*London*	25	*3 Jul 99*	2

SHADES — US

SINGLES:	HITS 2		WEEKS 3	
MR. BIG STUFF	*Motown*	31	*12 Apr 97*	2
Original by Jean Knight reached No. 2 in the US in 1971. From the film of the same name.				
Above hit: QUEEN LATIFAH, SHADES and FREE.				
SERENADE	*Motown*	75	*20 Sep 97*	1

SHADES OF LOVE (Junior VASQUEZ meets Johnny VICIOUS) — US

SINGLES:	HITS 1		WEEKS 1	
KEEP IN TOUCH (BODY TO BODY)	*Vicious-Muzik*	64	*22 Apr 95*	1

SHADES OF RHYTHM — UK

SINGLES:	HITS 7		WEEKS 25	
HOMICIDE / EXORCIST	*ZTT*	53	*2 Feb 91*	3
SWEET SENSATION	*ZTT*	54	*13 Apr 91*	4
THE SOUND OF EDEN (EVERY TIME I SEE HER)	*ZTT*	35	*20 Jul 91*	5
EXTACY	*ZTT*	16	*30 Nov 91*	7
SWEET REVIVAL (KEEP IT COMIN)	*ZTT*	61	*20 Feb 93*	1
SOUND OF EDEN [RI]	*ZTT*	37	*11 Sep 93*	3
THE WANDERING DRAGON [EP]	*Public Demand*	55	*5 Nov 94*	1
Lead track: My Love.				
PSYCHO BASE	*Coalition*	57	*21 Jun 97*	1
ALBUMS:	HITS 1		WEEKS 3	
SHADES	*ZTT*	51	*17 Aug 91*	3

SHADOW – See Edwin STARR

SHADOWS — UK

(See also Cliff Richard.)

SINGLES:	HITS 31		WEEKS 359	
APACHE	*Columbia*	1	*23 Jul 60*	21
Originally recorded by Bert Weedon and features Cliff Richard on bongos.				
MAN OF MYSTERY / THE STRANGER	*Columbia*	5	*12 Nov 60*	15
Man Of Mystery is the theme music of the Edgar Wallace film series. The Stranger was not listed				
from 11 Feb 61.				
F.B.I.	*Columbia*	6	*11 Feb 61*	19
THE FRIGHTENED CITY	*Columbia*	3	*13 May 61*	20
From the film of the same name.				
KON - TIKI	*Columbia*	1	*9 Sep 61*	10
THE SAVAGE	*Columbia*	10	*18 Nov 61*	8
From the film 'The Young Ones'.				
KON - TIKI [RE]	*Columbia*	37	*25 Nov 61*	2
WONDERFUL LAND	*Columbia*	1	*3 Mar 62*	19
GUITAR TANGO	*Columbia*	4	*4 Aug 62*	15
DANCE ON!	*Columbia*	1	*15 Dec 62*	15
FOOT TAPPER	*Columbia*	1	*9 Mar 63*	16
From the film 'Summer Holiday'.				
ATLANTIS	*Columbia*	2	*8 Jun 63*	17
Above hit: SHADOWS and the Norrie PARAMOR STRINGS.				
SHINDIG	*Columbia*	6	*21 Sep 63*	12
GERONIMO	*Columbia*	11	*7 Dec 63*	12
Above hit: SHADOWS with the Norrie PARAMOR STRINGS.				
THEME FOR YOUNG LOVERS	*Columbia*	12	*7 Mar 64*	10
From the film 'Wonderful Life'.				

THE RISE AND FALL OF FLINGEL BUNT	Columbia	5	9 May 64	14
RHYTHM AND GREENS	Columbia	22	5 Sep 64	7

Title track from the short musical comedy film.

GENIE WITH THE LIGHT BROWN LAMP	Columbia	17	5 Dec 64	10

From the pantomine 'Aladdin'.

MARY ANNE	Columbia	17	13 Feb 65	10
STINGRAY	Columbia	19	12 Jun 65	7
DON'T MAKE MY BABY BLUE	Columbia	10	7 Aug 65	10

Original by Frankie Laine in 1963.

THE WAR LORD	Columbia	18	27 Nov 65	9

Theme from the film of the same name.

I MET A GIRL	Columvia	22	19 Mar 66	5
A PLACE IN THE SUN	Columbia	24	9 Jul 66	6
THE DREAMS I DREAM	Columbia	42	5 Nov 66	6
MAROC 7	Columbia	24	15 Apr 67	8

Theme from the film of the same name.

LET ME BE THE ONE	EMI	12	8 Mar 75	9

UK's Eurovision entry in 1975, it came 2nd.

DON'T CRY FOR ME ARGENTINA	EMI	5	16 Dec 78	14

From the Tim Rice/Andrew Lloyd Webber musical 'Evita'.

THEME FROM THE DEER HUNTER (CAVATINA)	EMI	9	28 Apr 79	14
RIDERS IN THE SKY	EMI	12	26 Jan 80	12
EQUINOXE (PART V)	Polydor	50	23 Aug 80	3
THE THIRD MAN	Polydor	44	2 May 81	4

Originally recorded by Anton Karas. Theme from the film of the same name.

EPS:	**HITS 19**			**WEEKS 461**
THE SHADOWS	Columbia	1	21 Jan 61	86
THE SHADOWS TO THE FORE	Columbia	1	10 Jun 61	116
SPOTLIGHT ON THE SHADOWS	Columbia	1	10 Feb 62	59
THE SHADOWS NO. 2	Columbia	12	9 Jun 62	16
THE SHADOWS NO. 3	Columbia	13	11 Aug 62	4
THE WONDERFUL LAND OF THE SHADOWS	Columbia	6	22 Sep 62	34
THE BOYS	Columbia	1	13 Oct 62	46

Songs from the film of the same name.

OUT OF THE SHADOWS	Columbia	3	23 Feb 63	21
DANCE ON WITH THE SHADOWS	Columbia	16	9 Mar 63	5
OUT OF THE SHADOWS NO. 2	Columbia	20	22 Jun 63	1
LOS SHADOS	Columbia	4	21 Sep 63	18

Features Spanish tunes recorded in Barcelona.

FOOT TAPPING WITH THE SHADOWS	Columbia	7	12 Oct 63	10
SHINDIG WITH THE SHADOWS	Columbia	9	14 Dec 63	4
THOSE BRILLIANT SHADOWS	Columbia	6	20 Jun 64	14
RHYTHM AND GREENS [OST]	Columbia	8	24 Oct 64	14
THEMES FROM "ALADDIN AND HIS WONDERFUL LAMP"	Columbia	14	27 Mar 65	2

From the pantomine 'Aladdin'.

DANCE WITH THE SHADOWS NO. 3	Columbia	16	5 Jun 65	2
THOSE TALENTED SHADOWS	Columbia	9	1 Oct 66	2
THUNDERBIRDS ARE GO [OST]	Columbia	6	19 Nov 66	7

From the Gerry Anderson film (where The Shadows feature as puppets). One track is by Cliff Richard.

ALBUMS:	**HITS 28**			**WEEKS 472**
THE SHADOWS	Columbia	1	16 Sep 61	57
OUT OF THE SHADOWS	Columbia	1	13 Oct 62	38
THE SHADOWS' GREATEST HITS	Columbia	2	22 Jun 63	49
DANCE WITH THE SHADOWS	Columbia	2	9 May 64	27
THE SOUND OF THE SHADOWS	Columbia	4	17 Jul 65	17
SHADOW MUSIC	Columbia	5	21 May 66	17
JIGSAW	Columbia	8	15 Jul 67	16
SHADES OF ROCK	Columbia	30	24 Oct 70	4
ROCKIN' WITH CURLY LEADS	EMI	45	13 Apr 74	1
THE SHADOWS' GREATEST HITS [RE]	Columbia	48	11 May 74	6

Re-released with a new catalogue number.

SPECS APPEAL	EMI	30	29 Mar 75	5

As well as new material, it includes the 6 songs picked for Eurovision that year.

SHADOWS 20 GOLDEN GREATS	EMI	1	12 Feb 77	43
STRING OF HITS	EMI	1	15 Sep 79	43
ANOTHER STRING OF HITS	EMI	16	26 Jul 80	8
CHANGE OF ADDRESS	Polydor	17	13 Sep 80	6
HITS RIGHT UP YOUR STREET	Polydor	15	19 Sep 81	16
LIFE IN THE JUNGLE/LIVE AT ABBEY ROAD	Polydor	24	25 Sep 82	6

Live At Abbey Road recorded in front of a studio audience.

XXV	Polydor	34	22 Oct 83	6

Released to celebrate their 25th anniversary.

GUARDIAN ANGEL	Polydor	98	17 Nov 84	1
MOONLIGHT SHADOWS	Polydor	6	24 May 86	19
SIMPLY SHADOWS	Polydor	11	24 Oct 87	17
STEPPIN' TO THE SHADOWS	Polydor	11	20 May 89	9
AT THEIR VERY BEST	Polydor	12	16 Dec 89	9

REFLECTION	*Polydor*		5	*13 Oct 90*	15
THEMES AND DREAMS	*Polydor*		21	*16 Nov 91*	11
SHADOWS IN THE NIGHT - 16 CLASSIC TRACKS	*PolyGram TV*		22	*15 May 93*	4
Compilation of cover versions.					
THE BEST OF HANK MARVIN AND THE SHADOWS	*PolyGram TV*		19	*22 Oct 94*	11
PLAY ANDREW LLOYD WEBBER AND TIM RICE	*PolyGram TV*		41	*22 Nov 97*	6
VERY BEST OF HANK MARVIN AND THE SHADOWS - THE FIRST 40 YEARS	*PolyGram TV*		56	*14 Nov 98*	5
Above 3 includes both solo and group material.					
Above 3:Hank MARVIN and the SHADOWS.					

SHAFT · UK

SINGLES:	**HITS 2**				**WEEKS 9**
ROOBARB AND CUSTARD	*Ffrreedom*		7	*21 Dec 91*	8
Roobarb and Custard are characters from the BBC TV children's show.					
MONKEY	*Ffrreedom*		61	*25 Jul 92*	1

SHAFT · UK

SINGLES:	**HITS 1**				**WEEKS 12**
(MUCHO MAMBO) SWAY	*Wonderboy*		2	*04 Sept 99*	12
Shaft first recorded the track using samples from Rosemary Clooney's version. Permission to use the sample was withheld and so the vocals were recreated by Claire Vaughan.					

SHAG – See Jonathan KING

SHAGGY · Jamaica

(See also Jamaica United.)

SINGLES:	**HITS 8**				**WEEKS 66**
OH CAROLINA	*Greensleeves*		1	*6 Feb 93*	19
Originally recorded by the Folkes Brothers.					
SOON BE DONE	*Greensleeves*		46	*10 Jul 93*	3
IN THE SUMMERTIME	*Virgin*		5	*8 Jul 95*	9
Above hit: SHAGGY featuring RAYVON.					
BOOMBASTIC	*Virgin*		1	*23 Sep 95*	12
Featured in the Levi's Jeans TV commercial. Samples Baby Let Me Kiss You by King Floyd.					
WHY YOU TREAT ME SO BAD	*Virgin*		11	*13 Jan 96*	5
Samples Bob Marley's Mr. Brown.					
Above hit: SHAGGY featuring GRAND PUBA.					
SOMETHING DIFFERENT / THE TRAIN IS COMING	*Virgin*		21	*23 Mar 96*	5
Something Different features vocals by Ken Booth. From the film 'Money Train'.					
Above hit: SHAGGY featuring Wayne WONDER / SHAGGY.					
THAT GIRL	*Virgin*		15	*22 Jun 96*	7
Samples Booker T. and The M.G.s Green Onions.					
Above hit: Maxi PRIEST featuring SHAGGY.					
PIECE OF MY HEART	*Virgin*		7	*19 Jul 97*	6
Samples Erma Franklin's version.					
Above hit: SHAGGY (featuring MARSHA).					
ALBUMS:	**HITS 2**				**WEEKS 7**
PURE PLEASURE	*Greensleeves*		67	*24 Jul 93*	1
BOOMBASTIC	*Virgin*		37	*14 Oct 95*	6

SHAH · UK

SINGLES:	**HITS 1**				**WEEKS 1**
SECRET LOVE	*Evocative*		69	*6 Jun 98*	1

SHAI · US

SINGLES:	**HITS 1**				**WEEKS 6**
IF I EVER FALL IN LOVE	*MCA*		36	*19 Dec 92*	6

SHAKATAK · UK

SINGLES:	**HITS 14**				**WEEKS 85**
FEELS LIKE THE RIGHT TIME	*Polydor*		41	*8 Nov 80*	5
LIVING IN THE U.K.	*Polydor*		52	*7 Mar 81*	4
BRAZILIAN DAWN	*Polydor*		48	*25 Jul 81*	3
EASIER SAID THAN DONE	*Polydor*		12	*21 Nov 81*	17
NIGHT BIRDS	*Polydor*		9	*3 Apr 82*	8
STREETWALKIN'	*Polydor*		38	*19 Jun 82*	6
INVITATIONS	*Polydor*		24	*4 Sep 82*	7
STRANGER	*Polydor*		43	*6 Nov 82*	3
DARK IS THE NIGHT	*Polydor*		15	*4 Jun 83*	8
IF YOU COULD SEE ME NOW	*Polydor*		49	*27 Aug 83*	4
DOWN ON THE STREET	*Polydor*		9	*7 Jul 84*	11
DON'T BLAME IT ON LOVE	*Polydor*		55	*15 Sep 84*	3
DAY BY DAY	*Polydor*		53	*16 Nov 85*	3
Above hit: SHAKATAK with Al JARREAU.					

MR. MANIC AND SISTER COOL	Polydor	56	24 Oct 87	3
ALBUMS:	HITS 7		WEEKS 73	
DRIVIN' HARD	Polydor	35	30 Jan 82	17
NIGHT BIRDS	Polydor	4	15 May 82	28
INVITATIONS	Polydor	30	27 Nov 82	11
OUT OF THIS WORLD	Polydor	30	22 Oct 83	4
DOWN ON THE STREET	Polydor	17	25 Aug 84	9
LIVE!	Polydor	82	23 Feb 85	3
THE COOLEST CUTS	K-Tel	73	22 Oct 88	1

Compilation.

Johnny SHAKER – See THREE 'N ONE

SHAKESPEARS SISTER
UK/US

SINGLES:	HITS 9		WEEKS 52	
YOU'RE HISTORY	ffrr	7	29 Jul 89	9
RUN SILENT	ffrr	54	14 Oct 89	3
DIRTY MIND	ffrr	71	10 Mar 90	1
GOODBYE CRUEL WORLD	London	59	12 Oct 91	2

The sleeves of the above 4 credited Shakespear's Sister'.

STAY	London	1	25 Jan 92	16
I DON'T CARE	London	7	16 May 92	7
GOODBYE CRUEL WORLD [RI]	London	32	18 Jul 92	4
HELLO (TURN YOUR RADIO ON)	London	14	7 Nov 92	6
MY 16TH APOLOGY [EP]	London	61	27 Feb 93	1

*Lead track: My 16th Apology. Other 3 are live tracks recorded by the BBC and broadcast
16 Apr 92.*

I CAN DRIVE	London	30	22 Jun 96	3
ALBUMS:	HITS 2		WEEKS 63	
SACRED HEART	London	9	2 Sep 89	8
HORMONALLY YOURS	London	3	29 Feb 92	55

SHAKIN' PYRAMIDS
UK

ALBUMS:	HITS 1		WEEKS 4	
SKIN 'EM UP	Cuba Libra	48	4 Apr 81	4

SHAKY – See Shakin' STEVENS

SHAKY and BONNIE – See Shakin' STEVENS; Bonnie TYLER

SHALAMAR
US

SINGLES:	HITS 17		WEEKS 134	
UPTOWN FESTIVAL [M]	Soul Train	30	14 May 77	5

Medley of Motown songs.

TAKE THAT TO THE BANK	RCA Victor	20	9 Dec 78	12
THE SECOND TIME AROUND	Solar	45	24 Nov 79	9
RIGHT IN THE SOCKET	Solar	44	9 Feb 80	6
I OWE YOU ONE	Solar	13	30 Aug 80	10
MAKE THAT MOVE	Solar	30	28 Mar 81	10
I CAN MAKE YOU FEEL GOOD	Solar	7	27 Mar 82	11
A NIGHT TO REMEMBER	Solar	5	12 Jun 82	12
THERE IT IS	Solar	5	4 Sep 82	10
FRIENDS	Solar	12	27 Nov 82	10
DEAD GIVEAWAY	Solar	8	11 Jun 83	10
DISAPPEARING ACT	Solar	18	13 Aug 83	8
OVER AND OVER	Solar	23	15 Oct 83	6
DANCING IN THE SHEETS	CBS	41	24 Mar 84	3

From the film 'Footloose'.

| DEADLINE U.S.A. | MCA | 52 | 31 Mar 84 | 3 |

From the film 'Street Fleet'.

AMNESIA	Solar	61	24 Nov 84	2
MY GIRL LOVES ME	Solar	45	2 Feb 85	3
A NIGHT TO REMEMBER (THE M AND M MIX) [RM]	Solar	52	26 Apr 86	4
ALBUMS:	HITS 4		WEEKS 121	
FRIENDS	Solar	6	27 Mar 82	72

Peak position reached on 15 Jan 83.

GREATEST HITS	Solar	71	11 Sep 82	5
THE LOOK	Solar	7	30 Jul 83	20
THE GREATEST HITS	Stylus	5	12 Apr 86	24

SHAM ROCK
Ireland

SINGLES:	HITS 1		WEEKS 11	
TELL ME MA	Jive	13	7 Nov 98	11

SHAM 69 · UK

SINGLES:		HITS 7			WEEKS 53
ANGELS WITH DIRTY FACES	Polydor	19	13 May 78		10
IF THE KIDS ARE UNITED	Polydor	9	29 Jul 78		9
HURRY UP HARRY	Polydor	10	14 Oct 78		8
QUESTIONS AND ANSWERS	Polydor	18	24 Mar 79		9
HERSHAM BOYS	Polydor	6	4 Aug 79		9
YOU'RE A BETTER MAN THAN I	Polydor	49	27 Oct 79		5
TELL THE CHILDREN	Polydor	45	12 Apr 80		3
ALBUMS:		HITS 3			WEEKS 27
TELL US THE TRUTH	Polydor	25	11 Mar 78		8
THAT'S LIFE	Polydor	27	2 Dec 78		11
THE ADVENTURES OF THE HERSHAM BOYS	Polydor	8	29 Sep 79		8

SHAMEN · UK

SINGLES:		HITS 12			WEEKS 77
PRO-GEN	One Little Indian	55	7 Apr 90		4
MAKE IT MINE	One Little Indian	42	22 Sep 90		5
HYPERREAL	One Little Indian	29	6 Apr 91		5
MOVE ANY MOUNTAIN – PROGEN 91 [RM-1ST]	One Little Indian	4	27 Jul 91		10
Remixed by the Beatmasters.					
L.S.I.	One Little Indian	6	18 Jul 92		8
EBENEEZER GOODE	One Little Indian	1	5 Sep 92		10
BOSS DRUM	One Little Indian	4	7 Nov 92		7
BOSS DRUM [RM]	One Little Indian	58	7 Nov 92		1
5th format (a 12" remix) which, due to chart rules, had its own chart run.					
PHOREVER PEOPLE	One Little Indian	5	19 Dec 92		10
RE:EVOLUTION	One Little Indian	18	6 Mar 93		2
Terence McKenna is a new age author whose books have influenced the band.					
Above hit: SHAMEN with Terence McKENNA.					
THE SHAMEN S.O.S. [EP]	One Little Indian	14	6 Nov 93		4
Lead track: Comin' On.					
DESTINATION ESCHATON	One Little Indian	15	19 Aug 95		4
TRANSAMAZONIA	One Little Indian	28	21 Oct 95		2
Above 2 feature former Soul II Soul vocalist Victoria Wilson James.					
HEAL (THE SEPARATION)	One Little Indian	31	10 Feb 96		2
MOVE ANY MOUNTAIN '96 [RM-2ND]	One Little Indian	35	21 Dec 96		3
Remixed by the Beatmasters.					
ALBUMS:		HITS 6			WEEKS 54
EN-TACT	One Little Indian	31	3 Nov 90		10
PROGNEY	One Little Indian	23	28 Sep 91		2
BOSS DRUM	One Little Indian	3	26 Sept 92		30
ON AIR – BBC SESSIONS	Band Of Joy	61	20 Nov 93		1
Compilation of their In Session recordings for BBC Radio 1.					
BOSS DRUM / DIFFERENT DRUM [RE]	One Little Indian	51	18 Dec 93		5
Different Drum was a remix album, sales were combined.					
AXIS MUTATIS	One Little Indian	27	4 Nov 95		2
THE SHAMEN COLLECTION	One Little Indian	26	2 May 98		4
2 album set. First features their radio edit hits while the second includes remixes by Mr. C.					

SHAMPOO · UK

SINGLES:		HITS 5			WEEKS 28
TROUBLE	Food	11	30 Jul 94		12
VIVA LA MEGABABES	Food	27	15 Oct 94		4
DELICIOUS	Food	21	18 Feb 95		4
TROUBLE [RI]	Food	36	5 Aug 95		3
From the film 'Mighty Morphin Power Rangers: The Movie'.					
GIRL POWER	Food	25	13 Jul 96		4
I KNOW WHAT BOYS LIKE	Food	42	21 Sep 96		1
Originally recorded by The Waitresses.					
ALBUMS:		HITS 1			WEEKS 2
WE ARE SHAMPOO	Food	45	5 Nov 94		2

Jimmy SHAND and his Band · UK

SINGLES:		HITS 1			WEEKS 2
BLUEBELL POLKA	Parlophone	20	24 Dec 55		2
Sub titled: Scottish Country Dance In Strict Tempo.					
EPS:		HITS 1			WEEKS 3
DANCE WITH JIMMY SHAND NO. 2	Parlophone	15	6 Jan 62		3
ALBUMS:		HITS 1			WEEKS 2
FIFTY YEARS ON WITH JIMMY SHAND	Ross	97	24 Dec 83		2
Above hit: Jimmy SHAND, his Band and Guests.					

Paul SHANE and the YELLOWCOATS | | | | UK

SINGLES:	HITS 1			WEEKS 5
HI-DE-HI (HOLIDAY ROCK)	EMI	36	16 May 81	5

Theme from the BBC1 TV sitcom 'Hi-Di-Hi'.

SHANGRI-LAS | | | | US

SINGLES:	HITS 2			WEEKS 48
REMEMBER (WALKIN' IN THE SAND)	Red Bird	14	10 Oct 64	13
LEADER OF THE PACK	Red Bird	11	16 Jan 65	9

Features Billy Joel on piano.

LEADER OF THE PACK [RI-1ST]	Kama Sultra	3	14 Oct 72	14
LEADER OF THE PACK [RI-2ND]	Charly	7	5 Jun 76	11
LEADER OF THE PACK [RI-3RD]	Contempo	7	12 Jun 76	10

On 12 Jun 76 there were 2 separate entries on the chart. (Charly issue at No. 43, Contempo at No. 47). From 19 Jun 76 sales were combined.

SHANICE | | | | US

SINGLES:	HITS 5			WEEKS 24
I LOVE YOUR SMILE	Motown	55	23 Nov 91	4
I LOVE YOUR SMILE [RM]	Motown	2	22 Feb 92	10

Remixed by Driza Bone.

LOVIN' YOU	Motown	54	14 Nov 92	1
SAVING FOREVER FOR YOU	Giant	42	16 Jan 93	3

From the film 'Beverley Hills 90210'.

I LIKE	Motown	49	13 Aug 94	2
IF I NEVER KNEW YOU (LOVE THEME FROM POCAHONTAS)	Walt Disney	51	16 Dec 95	4

From the Walt Disney film 'Pocahontas'.
Above hit: Jon SECADA and SHANICE.

ALBUMS:	HITS 1			WEEKS 4
INNER CHILD	Motown	21	21 Mar 92	4

SHANKS and BIGFOOT | | | | UK

(See also Doolally.)

SINGLES:	HITS 1			WEEKS 16
SWEET LIKE CHOCOLATE	Pepper	1	29 May 99	15

Vocals by Sharon Woolf.

SWEET LIKE CHOCOLATE [RE]	Pepper	66	2 Oct 99	1

SHANNON | | | | US

SINGLES:	HITS 6			WEEKS 54
LET THE MUSIC PLAY	Club	51	19 Nov 83	3
LET THE MUSIC PLAY [RE]	Club	14	28 Jan 84	12
GIVE ME TONIGHT	Club	24	7 Apr 84	7
SWEET SOMEBODY	Club	25	30 Jun 84	8
STRONGER TOGETHER	Club	46	20 Jul 85	6
IT'S OVER LOVE	Manifesto	16	6 Dec 97	8

Above hit: Todd TERRY presents SHANNON.

MOVE MANIA	Multiply	8	28 Nov 98	10

Above hit: SASH! featuring SHANNON.

ALBUMS:	HITS 1			WEEKS 12
LET THE MUSIC PLAY	Club	52	10 Mar 84	12

Del SHANNON | | | | US

SINGLES:	HITS 14			WEEKS 147
RUNAWAY	London	1	29 Apr 61	22

Musitron (electric organ) solo by Max Crook.

HATS OFF TO LARRY	London	6	16 Sep 61	12
SO LONG BABY	London	10	9 Dec 61	11
HEY! LITTLE GIRL	London	2	17 Mar 62	15
CRY MYSELF TO SLEEP	London	29	8 Sep 62	6
THE SWISS MAID	London	2	13 Oct 62	17

Originally recorded by Roger Miller.

LITTLE TOWN FLIRT	London	4	19 Jan 63	13
TWO KINDS OF TEARDROPS	London	5	27 Apr 63	13
TWO SILHOUETTES	London	23	24 Aug 63	8
SUE'S GONNA BE MINE	London	21	26 Oct 63	8
MARY JANE	Stateside	35	14 Mar 64	5
HANDY MAN	Stateside	36	1 Aug 64	4
KEEP SEARCHIN' (WE'LL FOLLOW THE SUN)	Stateside	3	16 Jan 65	11
STRANGER IN TOWN	Stateside	40	20 Mar 65	2

EPS:	HITS 2			WEEKS 21
DEL SHANNON	London	14	27 Jan 62	2
DEL SHANNON NO. 2	London	9	11 May 63	19

ALBUMS:		HITS 2		WEEKS 23	
HATS OFF TO DEL SHANNON	London		9	11 May 63	17
Compilation.					
LITTLE TOWN FLIRT	London		15	2 Nov 63	6

Roxanne SHANTE
US

SINGLES:		HITS 3		WEEKS 10	
HAVE A NICE DAY	Cold Chillin'		58	1 Aug 87	3
GO ON GIRL	Breakout		55	4 Jun 88	3
SHARP AS A KNIFE	Club		45	29 Oct 88	3
Above hit: Brandon COOKE featuring Roxanne SHANTE.					
GO ON GIRL (THE HIP HOP MIX) [RM]	Breakout		74	14 Apr 90	1
Remixed by C.J. MacKintosh.					

Helen SHAPIRO
UK

SINGLES:		HITS 11		WEEKS 119	
DON'T TREAT ME LIKE A CHILD	Columbia		3	25 Mar 61	20
YOU DON'T KNOW	Columbia		1	1 Jul 61	23
WALKIN' BACK TO HAPPINESS	Columbia		1	30 Sep 61	19
TELL ME WHAT HE SAID	Columbia		2	17 Feb 62	15
Above hit: Helen SHAPIRO with the Martin SLAVIN ORCHESTRA.					
LET'S TALK ABOUT LOVE	Columbia		23	5 May 62	7
From the film 'It's Trad Dad'.					
Above hit: Helen SHAPIRO with Norrie PARAMOR and his Orchestra.					
LITTLE MISS LONELY	Columbia		8	14 Jul 62	11
Above hit: Helen SHAPIRO with Martin SLAVIN and his Orchestra.					
KEEP AWAY FROM OTHER GIRLS	Columbia		40	20 Oct 62	6
Originally recorded by Babs Tino.					
QUEEN FOR TONIGHT	Columbia		33	9 Feb 63	5
Above hit: Helen SHAPIRO with Martin SLAVIN and his Orchestra.					
WOE IS ME	Columbia		35	27 Apr 63	6
LOOK WHO IT IS	Columbia		47	26 Oct 63	3
FEVER	Columbia		38	25 Jan 64	4
EPS:		HITS 3		WEEKS 92	
HELEN	Columbia		1	25 Nov 61	43
HELEN'S HIT PARADE	Columbia		1	10 Feb 62	41
MORE HITS FROM HELEN	Columbia		12	6 Oct 62	8
ALBUMS:		HITS 1		WEEKS 25	
TOPS WITH ME	Columbia		2	10 Mar 62	25
Collection of her own personal favourites.					

SHARADA HOUSE GANG
Italy

SINGLES:		HITS 3		WEEKS 4	
KEEP IT UP	Media		36	12 Aug 95	2
LET THE RHYTHM MOVE YOU	Media		50	11 May 96	1
Original release reached No. 90 in 1993.					
GYPSY BOY, GYPSY GIRL	Gut		52	18 Oct 97	1

SHARKEY
UK

SINGLES:		HITS 1		WEEKS 1	
REVOLUTIONS [EP]	React		53	8 Mar 97	1
EP consists of various mixes of one song: Revolution.					

Feargal SHARKEY
UK

(See also Undertones.)

SINGLES:		HITS 7		WEEKS 58	
LISTEN TO YOUR FATHER	Zarjazz		23	13 Oct 84	7
LOVING YOU	Virgin		26	29 Jun 85	10
Features Roger Taylor who also co-produced the single.					
A GOOD HEART	Virgin		1	12 Oct 85	16
Written by Maria McKee.					
YOU LITTLE THIEF	Virgin		5	4 Jan 86	9
Written by Tom Petty's drummer Benmont Tench about Maria McKee.					
SOMEBODY TO SOMEBODY	Virgin		64	5 Apr 86	3
MORE LOVE	Virgin		44	16 Jan 88	5
I'VE GOT NEWS FOR YOU	Virgin		12	16 Mar 91	8
ALBUMS:		HITS 2		WEEKS 24	
FEARGAL SHARKEY	Virgin		12	23 Nov 85	20
SONGS FROM THE MARDI GRAS	Virgin		27	20 Apr 91	4

SHARONETTES
US

SINGLES:		HITS 2		WEEKS 8	
PAPA OOM MOW MOW	Black Magic		26	26 Apr 75	5
Originally recorded by the Rivingtons in 1962.					
GOING TO A GO-GO	Black Magic		46	12 Jul 75	3

Debbie SHARP – See DREAM FREQUENCY

Dee Dee SHARP   US

(See also Philadelphia International All Stars: Lou Rawls, Billy Paul, Archie Bell, Teddy Pendergrass, O'Jays, Dee Dee Sharp, Gamble.)

SINGLES:	HITS 1			WEEKS 2
DO THE BIRD	Cameo-Parkway	46	27 Apr 63	2

Barrie K. SHARPE – See Diana BROWN and Barrie K. SHARPE

Rocky SHARPE and the REPLAYS   UK

SINGLES:	HITS 7			WEEKS 41
RAMA LAMA DING DONG	Chiswick	17	16 Dec 78	10
Originally recorded by the Edsels.				
IMAGINATION	Chiswick	39	24 Mar 79	6
Originally recorded by Harry Reser's Orchestra.				
LOVE WILL MAKE YOU FAIL IN SCHOOL	Chiswick	60	25 Aug 79	4
Originally recorded by Mickey and Sylvia.				
MARTIAN HOP	Chiswick	55	9 Feb 80	4
Originally recorded by the Randells.				
Above 2: Rocky SHARPE and the REPLAYS featuring the TOP LINERS.				
SHOUT! SHOUT! (KNOCK YOURSELF OUT)	Chiswick	19	17 Apr 82	9
Original by Ernie Maresca reached No. 6 in the US in 1962.				
CLAP YOUR HANDS	RAK	54	7 Aug 82	3
IF YOU WANNA BE HAPPY	Polydor	46	26 Feb 83	5

SHARPE and NUMAN   UK

(See also Gary Numan; Radio Heart featuring Gary Numan.)

SINGLES:	HITS 4			WEEKS 16
CHANGE YOUR MIND	Polydor	17	9 Feb 85	8
NEW THING FROM LONDON TOWN	Numa	52	4 Oct 86	3
NO MORE LIES	Polydor	34	30 Jan 88	3
I'M ON AUTOMATIC	Polydor	44	3 Jun 89	2
ALBUMS:	HITS 1			WEEKS 1
AUTOMATIC	Polydor	59	8 Jul 89	1

Bob SHARPLES and his Orchestra – See JOHNSTON BROTHERS, Lita ROZA; Jimmy YOUNG

Mark SHAW   UK

SINGLES:	HITS 1			WEEKS 1
LOVE SO BRIGHT	EMI	54	17 Nov 90	1

Roland SHAW ORCHESTRA – See BEVERLEY SISTERS; Don CORNELL; JOHNSTON BROTHERS; Dave KING; MANTOVANI and his Orchestra; Al MARTINO; David WHITFIELD

Sandie SHAW   UK

SINGLES:	HITS 20			WEEKS 165
(THERE'S) ALWAYS SOMETHING THERE TO REMIND ME	Pye	1	10 Oct 64	11
Originally recorded by Lou Johnson.				
GIRL DON'T COME	Pye	3	12 Dec 64	12
I'LL STOP AT NOTHING	Pye	4	20 Feb 65	11
Originally written for Adam Faith.				
LONG LIVE LOVE	Pye	1	15 May 65	14
MESSAGE UNDERSTOOD	Pye	6	25 Sep 65	10
HOW CAN YOU TELL	Pye	21	20 Nov 65	9
TOMORROW	Pye	9	29 Jan 66	9
NOTHING COMES EASY	Pye	14	21 May 66	9
RUN	Pye	32	10 Sep 66	5
THINK SOMETIMES ABOUT ME	Pye	32	26 Nov 66	4
I DON'T NEED ANYTHING	Pye	50	21 Jan 67	1
PUPPET ON A STRING	Pye	1	18 Mar 67	18
UK's Eurovision entry in 1967, it came 1st.				
TONIGHT IN TOKYO	Pye	21	15 Jul 67	6
YOU'VE NOT CHANGED	Pye	18	7 Oct 67	12
TODAY	Pye	27	10 Feb 68	7
MONSIEUR DUPONT	Pye	6	15 Feb 69	15
THINK IT ALL OVER	Pye	42	17 May 69	4
HAND IN GLOVE	Rough Trade	27	21 Apr 84	5
Collaboration with the Smiths.				
ARE YOU READY TO BE HEARTBROKEN?	Polydor	68	14 Jun 86	1
NOTHING LESS THAN BRILLIANT	Virgin	66	12 Nov 94	2
EPS:	HITS 2			WEEKS 26
(THERE'S) ALWAYS SOMETHING THERE TO REMIND ME	Pye	9	30 Jan 65	12
TELL THE BOYS	Pye	4	22 Apr 67	14

ALBUMS:		HITS 2			WEEKS 14
SANDIE	Pye		3	6 Mar 65	13
NOTHING LESS THAN BRILLIANT	Virgin		64	19 Nov 94	1
Compilation to celebrate 30th anniversary of her first No. 1 single.					

Tracy SHAW   UK

SINGLES:		HITS 1			WEEKS 1
HAPPENIN' ALL OVER AGAIN	Recognition		46	4 Jul 98	1
She first performed the song on the Coronation Street special 'Viva Las Vegas'.					

Winifred SHAW   US

SINGLES:		HITS 1			WEEKS 4
LULLABY OF BROADWAY	United Artists		42	14 Aug 76	4
From the film 'Gold Diggers Of 1935'.					

SHE – See URBAN DISCHARGE featuring SHE

SHE ROCKERS   UK

SINGLES:		HITS 1			WEEKS 2
JAM IT JAM	Jive		58	13 Jan 90	2

George SHEARING QUINTET with strings   UK

(See also Nat King Cole/The George Shearing Quintet; Peggy Lee and George Shearing.)

SINGLES:		HITS 1			WEEKS 1
BAUBLES, BANGLES AND BEADS	Capitol		49	6 Oct 62	1

Gary SHEARSTON   Australia

SINGLES:		HITS 1			WEEKS 8
I GET A KICK OUT OF YOU	Charisma		7	5 Oct 74	8
Written by Cole Porter.					

SHED SEVEN   UK

SINGLES:		HITS 13			WEEKS 46
DOLPHIN	Polydor		28	25 Jun 94	4
SPEAKEASY	Polydor		24	27 Aug 94	3
OCEAN PIE	Polydor		33	12 Nov 94	2
WHERE HAVE YOU BEEN TONIGHT?	Polydor		23	13 May 95	2
GETTING BETTER	Polydor		14	27 Jan 96	3
GOING FOR GOLD	Polydor		8	23 Mar 96	5
BULLY BOY	Polydor		22	18 May 96	3
ON STANDBY	Polydor		12	31 Aug 96	4
CHASING RAINBOWS	Polydor		17	23 Nov 96	5
SHE LEFT ME ON FRIDAY	Polydor		11	14 Mar 98	4
THE HEROES	Polydor		18	23 May 98	3
DEVIL IN YOUR SHOES (WALKING ALL OVER)	Polydor		37	22 Aug 98	2
DISCO DOWN	Polydor		13	5 Jun 99	6
Above hit: SHED 7.					
ALBUMS:		HITS 4			WEEKS 44
CHANGE GIVER	Polydor		16	17 Sep 94	2
A MAXIMUM HIGH	Polydor		8	13 Apr 96	26
LET IT RIDE	Polydor		9	13 Jun 98	7
GOING FOR GOLD – THE GREATEST HITS	Polydor		7	12 Jun 99	9

SHEEP ON DRUGS   UK

SINGLES:		HITS 3			WEEKS 5
15 MINUTES OF FAME	Island		44	27 Mar 93	2
FROM A TO H AND BACK AGAIN	Island		40	30 Oct 93	2
LET THE GOOD TIMES ROLL	Island		56	14 May 94	1
ALBUMS:		HITS 1			WEEKS 1
GREATEST HITS	Island		55	10 Apr 93	1

SHEER BRONZE featuring Lisa MILLETT   UK

SINGLES:		HITS 1			WEEKS 1
WALKIN' ON	Go.Beat		63	3 Sep 94	1

SHEER ELEGANCE   UK

SINGLES:		HITS 3			WEEKS 23
MILKY WAY	Pye International		18	20 Dec 75	10
LIFE IS TOO SHORT GIRL	Pye International		9	3 Apr 76	9
IT'S TEMPTATION	Pye International		41	24 Jul 76	4

SHEILA B. DEVOTION
France

SINGLES:	HITS 3			WEEKS 33
SINGIN' IN THE RAIN	Carrere	11	11 Mar 78	13
YOU LIGHT MY FIRE	Carrere	44	22 Jul 78	6
SPACER	Carrere	18	24 Nov 79	14

Above hit: SHEILA and B. DEVOTION.

Doug SHELDON
UK

SINGLES:	HITS 3			WEEKS 15
RUN AROUND SUE	Decca	36	11 Nov 61	3
YOUR MA SAID YOU CRIED IN YOUR SLEEP LAST NIGHT	Decca	29	6 Jan 62	6
I SAW LINDA YESTERDAY	Decca	36	9 Feb 63	6

Originally recorded by Dickey Lee.

Pete SHELLEY
UK

SINGLES:	HITS 1			WEEKS 1
TELEPHONE OPERATOR	Genetic	66	12 Mar 83	1
ALBUMS:	HITS 1			WEEKS 4
XL - 1	Genetic	42	2 Jul 83	4

Peter SHELLEY
UK

SINGLES:	HITS 2			WEEKS 20
GEE BABY	Magnet	4	14 Sep 74	10
LOVE ME LOVE MY DOG	Magnet	3	22 Mar 75	10

Anne SHELTON
UK

SINGLES:	HITS 5			WEEKS 31
ARRIVEDERCI DARLING	His Master's Voice	17	17 Dec 55	4

Originally recorded by Renato Rascel.
Above hit: Anne SHELTON with Geoff LOVE and his Orchestra.

SEVEN DAYS	Philips	20	14 Apr 56	4
LAY DOWN YOUR ARMS	Philips	1	25 Aug 56	14
THE VILLAGE OF ST. BERNADETTE	Philips	27	21 Nov 59	1
SAILOR	Philips	10	28 Jan 61	8

Above 4: Anne SHELTON with Wally STOTT and his Orchestra and Chorus.

SHENA
UK

SINGLES:	HITS 1			WEEKS 2
LET THE BEAT HIT 'EM	VC Recordings	28	2 Aug 97	2

Vikki SHEPARD – See SLEAZESISTERS

Vonda SHEPARD
US

SINGLES:	HITS 1			WEEKS 9
SEARCHIN' MY SOUL	Epic	10	5 Dec 98	9

Theme from the TV series 'Ally McBeal'.

ALBUMS:	HITS 3			WEEKS 43
SONGS FROM 'ALLY MCBEAL' [OST-TV]	Epic	3	17 Oct 98	34
BY 7.30	Epic	39	12 Jun 99	2
HEART & SOUL - NEW SONGS FROM ALLY MCBEAL [OST-TV]	Epic	9	20 Nov 99	7

Bill SHEPHERD CHORUS – See Jimmy PARKINSON

SHEPHERD SINGERS
US

SINGLES:	HITS 1			WEEKS 6
ALONE (WHY MUST I BE ALONE)	His Master's Voice	14	16 Nov 57	5
ALONE (WHY MUST I BE ALONE) [RE]	His Master's Voice	22	4 Jan 58	1

SHERBET
Australia

SINGLES:	HITS 1			WEEKS 10
HOWZAT	Epic	4	25 Sep 76	10

Tony SHERIDAN and the BEATLES
UK

(See also Beatles.)

SINGLES:	HITS 1			WEEKS 1
MY BONNIE	Polydor	48	8 Jun 63	1

Originally released in 1962.

Allan SHERMAN
US

SINGLES:	HITS 1			WEEKS 10
HELLO MUDDAH! HELLO FADDUH! (A LETTER FROM CAMP)	Warner Brothers	14	14 Sep 63	10

Novelty song with music addapted from Ponchielli's Dance Of The Hours.

Bim SHERMAN – See Gary CLAIL ON-U SOUND SYSTEM

Bobby SHERMAN
US

SINGLES:	HITS 1			WEEKS 4
JULIE, DO YA LOVE ME	CBS	28	31 Oct 70	4

SHERRICK
US

SINGLES:	HITS 2			WEEKS 10
JUST CALL	Warner Brothers	23	1 Aug 87	8
LET'S BE LOVERS TONIGHT	Warner Brothers	63	21 Nov 87	2
ALBUMS:	HITS 1			WEEKS 6
SHERRICK	Warner Brothers	27	29 Aug 87	6

Pluto SHERVINGTON
Jamaica

SINGLES:	HITS 3			WEEKS 20
DAT	Opal	6	7 Feb 76	8
RAM GOAT RIVER	Trojan	43	10 Apr 76	4
YOUR HONOUR	KR	19	6 Mar 82	8
Above hit: PLUTO.				

Holly SHERWOOD
US

SINGLES:	HITS 1			WEEKS 7
DAY BY DAY (INCORPORATING "PREPARE YE THE WAY OF THE LORD")	Bell	29	5 Feb 72	7
From the musical 'Godspell'.				

Tony SHEVETON
UK

SINGLES:	HITS 1			WEEKS 1
MILLION DRUMS	Orole	49	15 Feb 64	1

SHIMMON and WOOLFSON
UK

(See also Sundance.)

SINGLES:	HITS 1			WEEKS 1
WELCOME TO THE FUTURE	React	69	10 Jan 98	1

Brendan SHINE
Ireland

ALBUMS:	HITS 4			WEEKS 29
THE BRENDAN SHINE COLLECTION	Play	51	12 Nov 83	12
WITH LOVE	Play	74	3 Nov 84	4
MEMORIES	Play	81	16 Nov 85	7
MAGIC MOMENTS	Stylus	62	18 Nov 89	6

SHINEHEAD
Jamaica

SINGLES:	HITS 2			WEEKS 6
JAMAICAN IN NEW YORK	Elektra	30	3 Apr 93	5
Based on Sting's An Englishman In New York.				
LET 'EM IN	Elektra	70	26 Jun 93	1

SHIREHORSES
UK

ALBUMS:	HITS 1			WEEKS 4
THE WORST ALBUM IN THE WORLD EVER . . . EVER!	East West	22	15 Nov 97	4
Features the Shirehorses' group incarnations (Charley Twins, Baby Bloke, Creeper, Doofergrass, Po-Fasis).				

SHIRELLES
US

SINGLES:	HITS 3			WEEKS 29
WILL YOU LOVE ME TOMORROW	Top Rank	4	11 Feb 61	15
SOLDIER BOY	His Master's Voice	23	2 Jun 62	9
FOOLISH LIITLE GIRL	Stateside	38	25 May 63	5

SHIRLEY and COMPANY
US

SINGLES:	HITS 1			WEEKS 9
SHAME, SHAME, SHAME	All Platinum	6	8 Feb 75	9
Male vocal by Jesus Alvarez.				

SHIRLEY and LEE
US

EPS:	HITS 1			WEEKS 5
SHIRLEY AND LEE	Vogue	16	25 Jun 60	5

SHIVA
UK

SINGLES:		HITS 2			WEEKS 5
WORK IT OUT	*ffrr*		36	*13 May 95*	2
FREEDOM	*ffrr*		18	*19 Aug 95*	3

SHO NUFF
US

SINGLES:		HITS 1			WEEKS 4
IT'S ALRIGHT	*Ensign*		53	*24 May 80*	4

Michelle SHOCKED
US

SINGLES:		HITS 3			WEEKS 10
ANCHORAGE	*Cooking Vinyl*		60	*8 Oct 88*	4
IF LOVE WAS A TRAIN	*Cooking Vinyl*		63	*14 Jan 89*	3
WHEN I GROW UP	*Cooking Vinyl*		67	*11 Mar 89*	3
ALBUMS:		HITS 3			WEEKS 24
SHORT SHARP SHOCKED	*Cooking Vinyl*		33	*10 Sep 88*	19
CAPTAIN SWING	*Cooking Vinyl*		31	*18 Nov 89*	3
ARKANSAS TRAVELER	*London*		46	*11 Apr 92*	2

SHOCKING BLUE
Holland

SINGLES:		HITS 2			WEEKS 14
VENUS	*Penny Farthing*		8	*17 Jan 70*	11
MIGHTY JOE	*Penny Farthing*		43	*25 Apr 70*	3

SHOCKING PINKS – See Neil YOUNG

Troy SHONDELL
US

SINGLES:		HITS 1			WEEKS 11
THIS TIME	*London*		22	*4 Nov 61*	11

Originally recorded by Thomas Wayne.

SHONDELLS – See Tommy JAMES and the SHONDELLS

SHOOTING PARTY
UK

SINGLES:		HITS 1			WEEKS 2
LET'S HANG ON	*Lisson*		66	*31 Mar 90*	2

SHOP ASSISTANTS
UK

ALBUMS:		HITS 1			WEEKS 1
SHOP ASSISTANTS	*Blue Guitar*		100	*29 Nov 86*	1

SHOWADDYWADDY
UK

SINGLES:		HITS 23			WEEKS 209
HEY ROCK AND ROLL	*Bell*		2	*18 May 74*	14
ROCK 'N' ROLL LADY	*Bell*		15	*17 Aug 74*	9
HEY MISTER CHRISTMAS	*Bell*		13	*30 Nov 74*	8
Accompanied by the National Childrens Home Harpenden Choir.					
SWEET MUSIC	*Bell*		14	*22 Feb 75*	9
THREE STEPS TO HEAVEN	*Bell*		2	*17 May 75*	11
HEARTBEAT	*Bell*		7	*6 Sep 75*	7
HEAVENLY	*Bell*		34	*15 Nov 75*	6
TROCADERO	*Bell*		32	*29 May 76*	3
UNDER THE MOON OF LOVE	*Bell*		1	*6 Nov 76*	15
Originally recorded by Curtis Lee.					
WHEN	*Arista*		3	*5 Mar 77*	11
YOU GOT WHAT IT TAKES	*Arista*		2	*23 Jul 77*	10
DANCIN' PARTY	*Arista*		4	*5 Nov 77*	11
I WONDER WHY	*Arista*		2	*25 Mar 78*	11
A LITTLE BIT OF SOAP	*Arista*		5	*24 Jun 78*	12
Original by the Jarmels reached No. 12 in the US in 1961.					
PRETTY LITTLE ANGEL EYES	*Arista*		5	*4 Nov 78*	12
Originally recorded by Curtis Lee.					
REMEMBER THEN	*Arista*		17	*31 Mar 79*	8
Original by the Earls reached No. 24 in the US in 1963.					
SWEET LITTLE ROCK 'N' ROLLER	*Arista*		15	*28 Jul 79*	9
A NIGHT AT DADDY GEES	*Arista*		39	*10 Nov 79*	5
Originally recorded by Curtis Lee in 1962.					
WHY DO LOVERS BREAK EACH OTHERS' HEARTS	*Arista*		22	*27 Sep 80*	10
BLUE MOON	*Arista*		32	*29 Nov 80*	9
MULTIPLICATION	*Arista*		39	*13 Jun 81*	4
FOOTSTEPS	*Bell*		31	*28 Nov 81*	9
WHO PUT THE BOMP (IN THE BOMP-A-BOMP-A-BOMP)	*RCA*		37	*28 Aug 82*	6
ALBUMS:		HITS 10			WEEKS 126
SHOWADDYWADDY	*Bell*		9	*7 Dec 74*	19

797

STEP TWO	*Bell*	7	*12 Jul 75*	17
TROCADERO	*Bell*	41	*29 May 76*	3
GREATEST HITS	*Arista*	4	*25 Dec 76*	26
RED STAR	*Arista*	20	*3 Dec 77*	10
GREATEST HITS (1976–1978)	*Arista*	1	*9 Dec 78*	17
CREPES AND DRAPES	*Arista*	8	*10 Nov 79*	14
BRIGHT LIGHTS	*Arista*	33	*20 Dec 80*	8
THE VERY BEST OF SHOWADDYWADDY	*Arista*	33	*7 Nov 81*	11
THE BEST STEPS TO HEAVEN	*Tiger*	90	*5 Dec 87*	1

SHOWDOWN
US

SINGLES:		**HITS 1**		**WEEKS 4**
KEEP DOIN' IT	*State*	41	*17 Dec 77*	4

SHOWDOWN – See Garry LEE and SHOWDOWN

SHOWSTOPPERS
US

SINGLES:		**HITS 2**		**WEEKS 25**
AIN'T NOTHING BUT A HOUSEPARTY	*Beacon*	11	*16 Mar 68*	15
EENY MEENY	*MGM*	33	*16 Nov 68*	7
AIN'T NOTHING BUT A HOUSEPARTY [RI]	*Beacon*	43	*30 Jan 71*	1
AIN'T NOTHING BUT A HOUSEPARTY [RI] [RE-1ST]	*Beacon*	33	*13 Feb 71*	1
AIN'T NOTHING BUT A HOUSEPARTY [RI] [RE-2ND]	*Beacon*	36	*27 Feb 71*	1

SHRIEKBACK
UK

SINGLES:		**HITS 1**		**WEEKS 4**
HAND ON MY HEART	*Arista*	52	*28 Jul 84*	4
ALBUMS:		**HITS 1**		**WEEKS 1**
JAM SCIENCE	*Arista*	85	*11 Aug 84*	1

SHRIEVE – See HAGAR, SCHON, AARONSON, SHRIEVE

SHRINK
Holland

SINGLES:		**HITS 1**		**WEEKS 2**
(NERVOUS.(.BREAKDOWN)	*VC Recordings*	42	*10 Oct 98*	2

SHUT UP AND DANCE
UK

SINGLES:		**HITS 7**		**WEEKS 14**
£20 TO GET IN	*Shut Up And Dance*	56	*21 Apr 90*	3

This track was actually the second track on this 12" only release. Track 1 was called Raps My Occupation.

LAMBORGHINI	*Shut Up And Dance*	55	*28 Jul 90*	2

Above hit: SHUT UP AND DANCE featuring the RAGGA TWINS.

AUTOBIOGRAPHY OF A CRACKHEAD / THE GREEN MAN	*Shut Up And Dance*	43	*8 Feb 92*	2
RAVING I'M RAVING	*Shut Up And Dance*	2	*30 May 92*	2

Samples Marc Cohn's Walking In Memphis. As copyright clearance was not given it was deleted, with an order that proceeds from the sales of those released be given to charity.
Above hit: SHUT UP AND DANCE featuring Peter BOUNCER.

THE ART OF MOVING BUTTS	*Shut Up And Dance*	69	*15 Aug 92*	1

Above hit: SHUT UP AND DANCE featuring ERIN.

SAVE IT 'TIL THE MOURNING AFTER	*Pulse 8*	25	*1 Apr 95*	3

Samples Duran Duran's Save A Prayer.

I LOVE U	*Pulse 8*	68	*8 Jul 95*	1

Samples Perez Prado's Guaglione.
Above hit: SHUT UP AND DANCE featuring Richie DAVIS and PROFESSOR T.

ALBUMS:		**HITS 1**		**WEEKS 2**
DEATH IS NOT THE END	*Shut Up And Dance*	38	*27 Jun 92*	2

SHY
UK

SINGLES:		**HITS 1**		**WEEKS 3**
GIRL (IT'S ALL I HAVE)	*Gallery*	60	*19 Apr 80*	3
ALBUMS:		**HITS 1**		**WEEKS 2**
EXCESS ALL AREAS	*RCA*	74	*11 Apr 87*	2

SHY FX
UK

(See UK Apachi with Shy FX.)

SINGLES:		**HITS 2**		**WEEKS 4**
ORIGINAL NUTTAH	*Sound Of Underground*	39	*1 Oct 94*	3

Samples Cypress Hill's I Ain't Going Out Like That and vocal introduction from the film 'Goodfellas'.
Above hit: UK APACHI with SHY FX.

BAMBAATA 2012	*Ebony*	60	*20 Mar 99*	1

Original release reached No. 120 in 1998.

SHYHEIM | US

SINGLES:	HITS 1			WEEKS 1
THIS IZ REAL	*Noo Trybe*	61	*8 Jun 96*	1

Labi SIFFRE | UK

SINGLES:	HITS 5			WEEKS 44
IT MUST BE LOVE	*Pye International*	14	*27 Nov 71*	12
CRYING, LAUGHING, LOVING, LYING	*Pye International*	11	*25 Mar 72*	9
WATCH ME	*Pye International*	29	*29 Jul 72*	6
(SOMETHING INSIDE) SO STRONG	*China*	4	*4 Apr 87*	13
A protest song against apartheid in South Africa.				
NOTHING'S GONNA CHANGE	*China*	52	*21 Nov 87*	4
ALBUMS:	**HITS 2**			**WEEKS 2**
SINGER AND THE SONG	*Pye*	47	*24 Jul 71*	1
CRYING, LAUGHING, LOVING, LYING	*Pye*	46	*14 Oct 72*	1

SIGNUM | Holland

SINGLES:	HITS 2			WEEKS 2
WHAT YA GOT 4 ME	*Tidy Trax*	70	*28 Nov 98*	1
COMING ON STRONG	*Tidy Trax*	66	*31 Jul 99*	1
Above hit: SIGNUM featuring Scott MAC.				

SIGUE SIGUE SPUTNIK | UK

SINGLES:	HITS 5			WEEKS 20
LOVE MISSILE F1-11	*Parlophone*	3	*1 Mar 86*	9
21ST CENTURY BOY	*Parlophone*	20	*7 Jun 86*	5
SUCCESS	*Parlophone*	31	*19 Nov 88*	3
DANCERAMA	*Parlophone*	50	*1 Apr 89*	2
ALBINONI VS STAR WARS	*Parlophone*	75	*20 May 89*	1
ALBUMS:	**HITS 2**			**WEEKS 7**
FLAUNT IT	*Parlophone*	10	*9 Aug 86*	6
DRESS FOR EXCESS	*Parlophone*	53	*15 Apr 89*	1

SIL | Holland

SINGLES:	HITS 1			WEEKS 1
WINDOWS '98	*Hooj Choons*	58	*11 Apr 98*	1
Originally released in Holland in 1992.				

SILENCERS | UK

SINGLES:	HITS 3			WEEKS 7
PAINTED MOON	*RCA*	57	*25 Jun 88*	4
SCOTTISH RAIN	*RCA*	71	*27 May 89*	2
I CAN FEEL IT	*RCA*	62	*15 May 93*	1
ALBUMS:	**HITS 2**			**WEEKS 3**
DANCE TO THE HOLY MAN	*RCA*	39	*23 Mar 91*	2
SECONDS OF PLEASURE	*RCA*	52	*5 Jun 93*	1

SILENT UNDERDOG | UK

(See also Paul Hardcastle.)

SINGLES:	HITS 1			WEEKS 1
PAPA'S GOT A BRAND NEW PIGBAG	*Kaz*	73	*16 Feb 85*	1

SILJE | Norway

SINGLES:	HITS 1			WEEKS 6
TELL ME WHERE YOU'RE GOING	*EMI*	55	*15 Dec 90*	6
Original release reached No. 85 earlier in the year.				

SILK | US

SINGLES:	HITS 3			WEEKS 10
FREAK ME	*Elektra*	46	*24 Apr 93*	5
GIRL U FOR ME	*Elektra*	67	*5 Jun 93*	2
BABY IT'S YOU	*Elektra*	44	*9 Oct 93*	2
FREAK ME [RE]	*Elektra*	72	*26 Feb 94*	1

SILKIE | UK

SINGLES:	HITS 1			WEEKS 6
YOU'VE GOT TO HIDE YOUR LOVE AWAY	*Fontana*	28	*25 Sep 65*	6

SILSOE
UK

(See also Argent; San Jose featuring Rodriguez Argentina.)

SINGLES:		HITS 1		WEEKS 4
AZTEC GOLD – THE OFFICIAL ITV THEME FOR THE WORLD CUP	CBS	48	21 Jun 86	4

SILVAH BULLET – See Jonny L

SILVER BULLET
UK

SINGLES:		HITS 3		WEEKS 20
BRING FORTH THE GUILLOTINE	Tam Tam	70	2 Sep 89	1
20 SECONDS TO COMPLY	Tam Tam	11	9 Dec 89	10
BRING FORTH THE GUILLOTINE [RE]	Tam Tam	45	3 Mar 90	5
UNDERCOVER ANARCHIST	Parlophone	33	13 Apr 91	4
ALBUMS:		HITS 1		WEEKS 2
BRING DOWN THE WALLS NO LIMIT SQUAD RETURNS	Parlophone	38	4 May 91	2

SILVER BULLET BAND – See Bob SEGER and the SILVER BULLET BAND

SILVER CITY
UK

SINGLES:		HITS 1		WEEKS 1
LOVE INFINITY	Silver City	62	30 Oct 93	1

SILVER CONVENTION
US/Germany

SINGLES:		HITS 5		WEEKS 35
SAVE ME	Magnet	30	5 Apr 75	7
FLY ROBIN FLY	Magnet	28	15 Nov 75	8
GET UP AND BOOGIE	Magnet	7	3 Apr 76	11
TIGER BABY / NO, NO JOE	Magnet	41	19 Jun 76	4
EVERYBODY'S TALKING 'BOUT LOVE	Magnet	25	29 Jan 77	5
ALBUMS:		HITS 1		WEEKS 3
SILVER CONVENTION: GREATEST HITS	Magnet	34	25 Jun 77	3

SILVER SUN
UK

SINGLES:		HITS 6		WEEKS 13
LAVA	Polydor	54	2 Nov 96	1
LAST DAY	Polydor	48	22 Feb 97	1
GOLDEN SKIN	Polydor	32	3 May 97	2
JULIA	Polydor	51	5 Jul 97	1
LAVA [RI]	Polydor	35	18 Oct 97	2
TOO MUCH, TOO LITTLE, TOO LATE	Polydor	20	20 Jun 98	4
I'LL SEE YOU AROUND	Polydor	26	26 Sep 98	2
ALBUMS:		HITS 2		WEEKS 2
SILVER SUN	Polydor	30	24 May 97	1
NEO WAVE	Polydor	74	17 Oct 98	1

SILVERCHAIR
Australia

SINGLES:		HITS 5		WEEKS 8
PURE MASSACRE	Murmur	71	29 Jul 95	1
TOMORROW	Murmur	59	9 Sep 95	2
FREAK	Murmur	34	5 Apr 97	2
ABUSE ME	Murmur	40	19 Jul 97	2
ANA'S SONG (OPEN FIRE)	Murmur	45	15 May 99	1
ALBUMS:		HITS 3		WEEKS 5
FROGSTOMP	Murmur	49	23 Sep 95	1
FREAK SHOW	Murmur	38	15 Feb 97	2
NEON BALLROOM	Murmur	29	27 Mar 99	2

SILVERFISH
US

ALBUMS:		HITS 1		WEEKS 1
ORGAN FAN	Creation	65	27 Jun 92	1

Dooley SILVERSPOON
US

SINGLES:		HITS 1		WEEKS 3
LET ME BE THE NO. 1 (LOVE OF YOUR LIFE)	Seville	44	31 Jan 76	3

Harry SIMEONE CHORALE
US

SINGLES:		HITS 2		WEEKS 14
THE LITTLE DRUMMER BOY	Top Rank	13	14 Feb 59	7
ONWARD CHRISTIAN SOLDIERS	Ember	35	24 Dec 60	1
ONWARD CHRISTIAN SOLDIERS [RE-1ST]	Ember	38	7 Jan 61	1
ONWARD CHRISTIAN SOLDIERS [RE-2ND]	Ember	36	23 Dec 61	1
ONWARD CHRISTIAN SOLDIERS [RI]	Ember	38	22 Dec 62	2

EPS:		HITS 1		WEEKS 7
GOLDEN HITS OF THE HARRY SIMEONE CHORALE	*Ember*	8	*9 Dec 61*	7

Gene SIMMONS US

SINGLES:		HITS 1		WEEKS 4
RADIOACTIVE	*Casablanca*	41	*27 Jan 79*	4

Carly SIMON US

(See also Will Powers.)

SINGLES:		HITS 6		WEEKS 76
YOU'RE SO VAIN	*Elektra*	3	*16 Dec 72*	15
Backing vocals by Mick Jagger.				
THE RIGHT THING TO DO	*Elektra*	17	*31 Mar 73*	9
MOCKINGBIRD	*Elektra*	34	*16 Mar 74*	5
Duet with James Taylor.				
NOBODY DOES IT BETTER	*Elektra*	7	*6 Aug 77*	12
From the James Bond film 'The Spy Who Loved Me'.				
WHY	*WEA*	10	*21 Aug 82*	13
From the film 'Soup For One'.				
COMING AROUND AGAIN	*Arista*	10	*24 Jan 87*	12
From the film 'Heartburn'.				
WHY [RI]	*WEA*	56	*10 Jun 89*	5
YOU'RE SO VAIN [RI]	*Elektra*	41	*20 Apr 91*	5
ALBUMS:		**HITS 5**		**WEEKS 67**
NO SECRETS	*Elektra*	3	*20 Jan 73*	26
HOT CAKES	*Elektra*	19	*16 Mar 74*	9
COMING AROUND AGAIN	*Arista*	25	*9 May 87*	20
GREATEST HITS LIVE	*Arista*	49	*3 Sep 88*	6
Live recordings from the Gay Head harbour in Massachusetts.				
NOBODY DOES IT BETTER – THE VERY BEST OF CARLY SIMON	*warner.esp/Global TV*	22	*20 Mar 99*	6

Joe SIMON US

SINGLES:		HITS 1		WEEKS 10
STEP BY STEP	*Mojo*	14	*16 Jun 73*	10

Paul SIMON US

(See also Simon and Garfunkel.)

SINGLES:		HITS 11		WEEKS 86
MOTHER AND CHILD REUNION	*CBS*	5	*19 Feb 72*	12
Written after eating egg fried rice and chicken in a chinese restaurant.				
ME AND JULIO DOWN BY THE SCHOOLYARD	*CBS*	15	*29 Apr 72*	9
TAKE ME TO THE MARDI GRAS	*CBS*	7	*16 Jun 73*	11
LOVE ME LIKE A ROCK	*CBS*	39	*22 Sep 73*	5
Above hit: Paul SIMON with the DIXIE HUMMINGBIRDS.				
50 WAYS TO LEAVE YOUR LOVER	*CBS*	23	*10 Jan 76*	6
Backing vocals by Patti Austin, Phoebe Snow and Valerie Simpson.				
SLIP SLIDIN' AWAY	*CBS*	36	*3 Dec 77*	6
Oak Ridge Boys on backing vocals.				
LATE IN THE EVENING	*Warner Brothers*	58	*6 Sep 80*	4
From the film 'One-Trick Pony'.				
YOU CAN CALL ME AL	*Warner Brothers*	4	*13 Sep 86*	13
THE BOY IN THE BUBBLE	*Warner Brothers*	26	*13 Dec 86*	8
THE OBVIOUS CHILD	*Warner Brothers*	15	*6 Oct 90*	10
SOMETHING SO RIGHT	*RCA*	44	*9 Dec 95*	2
Originally appeared on Simon's 1973 album There Goes Rhymin' Simon.				
Above hit: Annie LENNOX featuring Paul SIMON on guitar and vocals.				
ALBUMS:		**HITS 10**		**WEEKS 275**
PAUL SIMON	*CBS*	1	*26 Feb 72*	26
THERE GOES RHYMIN' SIMON	*CBS*	4	*2 Jun 73*	22
STILL CRAZY AFTER ALL THESE YEARS	*CBS*	6	*1 Nov 75*	31
GREATEST HITS, ETC.	*CBS*	6	*3 Dec 77*	15
ONE-TRICK PONY [OST]	*Warner Brothers*	17	*30 Aug 80*	12
HEARTS AND BONES	*Warner Brothers*	34	*12 Nov 83*	8
GRACELAND	*Warner Brothers*	1	*13 Sept 86*	101
Includes re-entries through to 1993.				
GREATEST HITS, ETC. [RE]	*CBS*	73	*24 Jan 87*	2
Re-released at mid-price.				
NEGOTIATIONS AND LOVE SONGS 1971-1986	*Warner Brothers*	17	*05 Nov 88*	15
THE RHYTHM OF THE SAINTS	*Warner Brothers*	1	*27 Oct 90*	28
PAUL SIMON'S CONCERT IN THE PARK – AUGUST 15TH, 1991	*Warner Brothers*	60	*23 Nov 91*	1
GRACELAND [RE]	*Warner Brothers*	27	*9 Aug 97*	14
Re-released at mid-price. Charted after being featured on BBC TV's 'Classic Albums' series.				

Ronni SIMON
UK

SINGLES:		HITS 2		WEEKS 2	
B GOOD 2 ME	Network		73	13 Aug 94	1
TAKE YOU THERE	Network		58	10 Jun 95	1

Tito SIMON
Jamaica

SINGLES:		HITS 1		WEEKS 4	
THIS MONDAY MORNING FEELING	Horse		45	8 Feb 75	4

SIMON and GARFUNKEL
US

(See also Art Garfunkel; Paul Simon.)

SINGLES:		HITS 8		WEEKS 87	
HOMEWARD BOUND	CBS		9	26 Mar 66	12
Written on Widnes railway station.					
I AM A ROCK	CBS		17	18 Jun 66	10
Originally a solo Paul Simon recording from 1964.					
MRS. ROBINSON	CBS		4	13 Jul 68	12
From the film 'The Graduate'.					
MRS. ROBINSON [EP]	CBS		9	11 Jan 69	5
Lead track: Mrs. Robinson, which is a re-issue. Its chart life of 5 weeks would have been longer but for a decision not to allow EPs in the singles chart.					
THE BOXER	CBS		6	3 May 69	14
BRIDGE OVER TROUBLED WATER	CBS		1	21 Feb 70	19
Piano by Larry Knetchel.					
BRIDGE OVER TROUBLED WATER [RE]	CBS		45	15 Aug 70	1
AMERICA	CBS		25	7 Oct 72	7
SEVEN O'CLOCK NEWS/SILENT NIGHT [M] / A HAZY SHADE OF WINTER	Columbia		30	7 Dec 91	6
A Hazy Shade Of Winter listed from 28 Dec 91 and had first credit on the chart.					
THE BOXER [RI]	Columbia		75	15 Feb 92	1
EPS:		**HITS 1**		**WEEKS 11**	
I AM A ROCK	CBS		4	18 Jun 66	11
ALBUMS:		**HITS 10**		**WEEKS 1095**	
SOUNDS OF SILENCE	CBS		13	16 Apr 66	104
Includes re-entries through to 1971.					
BOOKENDS	CBS		1	3 Aug 68	77
PARSLEY, SAGE, ROSEMARY AND THYME	CBS		15	31 Aug 68	24
THE GRADUATE [OST]	CBS		3	26 Oct 68	71
WEDNESDAY MORNING 3 A.M.	CBS		24	9 Nov 68	6
Their debut album, originally released in 1964.					
PARSLEY, SAGE, ROSEMARY AND THYME [RE]	CBS		13	1 Mar 69	42
BRIDGE OVER TROUBLED WATER	CBS		1	21 Feb 70	303
SIMON AND GARFUNKEL'S GREATEST HITS	CBS		2	22 Jul 72	280
Includes re-entries through to 1981.					
THE SIMON AND GARFUNKEL COLLECTION – 17 OF THEIR ALL-TIME GREATEST RECORDINGS	CBS		4	21 Nov 81	80
THE CONCERT IN CENTRAL PARK	Geffen		6	20 Mar 82	43
Live recordings from 19 Sep 81.					
SOUNDS OF SILENCE [RE]	CBS		68	4 Apr 81	1
Re-released with a new catalogue number.					
SIMON AND GARFUNKEL'S GREATEST HITS [RE]	CBS		78	24 Jul 82	3
Peak position reached in 1984.					
THE DEFINITIVE SIMON AND GARFUNKEL	Columbia		8	30 Nov 91	27
THE DEFINITIVE SIMON AND GARFUNKEL [RE]	Columbia		12	30 Apr 94	30
Re-released. Peak position reached in 1997.					
BRIDGE OVER TROUBLED WATER [RI]	Columbia		56	23 Sept 95	4
Peak position reached in 1996.					

SIMONE
US

SINGLES:		HITS 1		WEEKS 1	
MY FAMILY DEPENDS ON ME	Strictly Rhythm		75	23 Nov 91	1

Nina SIMONE
US

SINGLES:		HITS 5		WEEKS 46	
I PUT A SPELL ON YOU	Philips		49	7 Aug 65	1
AIN'T GOT NO-I GOT LIFE / DO WHAT YOU GOTTA DO	RCA Victor		2	19 Oct 68	18
Do What You Gotta Do no longer listed from 14 Dec 68. As an AA side it peaked at No. 7.					
I PUT A SPELL ON YOU [RI]	Philips		28	18 Jan 69	4
TO LOVE SOMEBODY	RCA Victor		5	18 Jan 69	9
MY BABY JUST CARES FOR ME	Charly		5	31 Oct 87	11
Original release reached No. 82 in 1985. Originally recorded by Lesley Serony.					
FEELING GOOD	Mercury		40	9 Jul 94	3
Featured in the VW car TV commercial.					
ALBUMS:		**HITS 5**		**WEEKS 30**	
I PUT A SPELL ON YOU	Philips		18	24 Jul 65	3

'NUFF SAID	RCA Victor	11	15 Feb 69	1
MY BABY JUST CARES FOR ME	Charly	56	14 Nov 87	8
FEELING GOOD – THE VERY BEST OF NINA SIMONE	PolyGram TV	9	16 Jul 94	8
BLUE FOR YOU – THE VERY BEST OF NINA SIMONE	Global Television	12	7 Feb 98	10

Victor SIMONELLI presents SOLUTION   US

SINGLES:	HITS 1			WEEKS 1
FEELS SO RIGHT	MCA	63	2 Nov 96	1

SIMPLE MINDS   UK

SINGLES:	HITS 28			WEEKS 187
LIFE IN A DAY	Zoom	62	12 May 79	2
THE AMERICAN	Virgin	59	23 May 81	3
LOVE SONG	Virgin	47	15 Aug 81	4
SWEAT IN BULLET	Virgin	52	7 Nov 81	3
PROMISED YOU A MIRACLE	Virgin	13	10 Apr 82	11
GLITTERING PRIZE	Virgin	16	28 Aug 82	11
SOMEONE SOMEWHERE (IN SUMMERTIME)	Virgin	36	13 Nov 82	5
WATERFRONT	Virgin	13	26 Nov 83	10
SPEED YOUR LOVE TO ME	Virgin	20	28 Jan 84	4
UP ON THE CATWALK	Virgin	27	24 Mar 84	5
DON'T YOU (FORGET ABOUT ME)	Virgin	7	20 Apr 85	11
From the film 'The Breakfast Club'. Originally written for Roxy Music who turned it down.				
DON'T YOU (FORGET ABOUT ME) [RE-1ST]	Virgin	61	17 Aug 85	8
ALIVE AND KICKING	Virgin	7	12 Oct 85	9
DON'T YOU (FORGET ABOUT ME) [RE-2ND]	Virgin	74	28 Dec 85	1
ALIVE AND KICKING [RE]	Virgin	60	4 Jan 86	2
SANCTIFY YOURSELF	Virgin	10	1 Feb 86	7
DON'T YOU (FORGET ABOUT ME) [RE-3RD]	Virgin	62	15 Feb 86	3
DON'T YOU (FORGET ABOUT ME) [RE-4TH]	Virgin	68	15 Mar 86	1
ALL THE THINGS SHE SAID	Virgin	9	12 Apr 86	8
ALL THE THINGS SHE SAID [RE]	Virgin	73	14 Jun 86	1
GHOSTDANCING	Virgin	13	15 Nov 86	6
Live recording.				
GHOSTDANCING [RE]	Virgin	68	3 Jan 87	2
PROMISED YOU A MIRACLE [RR]	Virgin	19	20 Jun 87	7
Live recording from Le Zenith, Paris, France, Aug 86.				
Above hit: SIMPLE MINDS LIVE				
BELFAST CHILD	Virgin	1	18 Feb 89	11
Sleeve gives title as an EP: Ballad Of The Streets, though the 7" format only had 2 tracks.				
THIS IS YOUR LAND	Virgin	13	22 Apr 89	4
KICK IT IN	Virgin	15	29 Jul 89	5
THE AMSTERDAM [EP]	Virgin	18	9 Dec 89	6
Lead track: Sign O' The Times.				
LET THERE BE LOVE	Virgin	6	23 Mar 91	7
SEE THE LIGHTS	Virgin	20	25 May 91	4
STAND BY LOVE	Virgin	13	31 Aug 91	4
REAL LIFE	Virgin	34	26 Oct 91	3
LOVE SONG [RM] / ALIVE AND KICKING [RI]	Virgin	6	10 Oct 92	6
Love Song remixed by Greg Jackman.				
SHE'S A RIVER	Virgin	9	28 Jan 95	5
HYPNOTISED	Virgin	18	8 Apr 95	5
GLITTERBALL	Chrysalis	18	14 Mar 98	2
WAR BABIES	Chrysalis	43	30 May 98	1
ALBUMS:	HITS 13			WEEKS 350
A LIFE IN THE DAY	Zoom	30	5 May 79	6
EMPIRES AND DANCE	Arista	41	27 Sep 80	3
SONS AND FASCINATIONS / SISTERS FEELINGS CALL	Virgin	11	12 Sep 81	7
Double package of 2 earlier album releases.				
CELEBRATION	Arista	45	27 Feb 82	7
Compilation of early recordings.				
NEW GOLD DREAM (81,82,83,84)	Virgin	3	25 Sep 82	52
SPARKLE IN THE RAIN	Virgin	1	18 Feb 84	57
ONCE UPON A TIME	Virgin	1	2 Nov 85	83
LIVE IN THE CITY OF LIGHT	Virgin	1	6 Jun 87	23
Live recordings from Le Zenith, Paris, France, Aug 86 (apart from 1 track which is from the Sydney Entertainment Centre, Australia).				
STREET FIGHTING YEARS	Virgin	1	13 May 89	28
LIVE IN THE CITY OF LIGHT [RE]	Virgin	66	5 Aug 89	3
Re-released at mid-price.				
REAL LIFE	Virgin	2	20 Apr 91	25
GLITTERING PRIZE 81/92	Virgin	1	24 Oct 92	39
GOOD NEWS FROM THE NEXT WORLD	Virgin	2	11 Feb 95	14
NEAPOLIS	Chrysalis	19	28 Mar 98	3

SIMPLICIOUS US

(See also Eugene Wilde.)

SINGLES:		HITS 1		WEEKS 3
LET HER FEEL IT	*Fourth & Broadway*	65	*29 Sep 84*	3

SIMPLY RED UK

SINGLES:		HITS 29		WEEKS 212
MONEY'S TOO TIGHT (TO MENTION)	*Elektra*	13	*15 Jun 85*	12
Originally recorded by the Valentine Brothers.				
COME TO MY AID	*Elektra*	66	*21 Sep 85*	2
HOLDING BACK THE YEARS	*Elektra*	51	*16 Nov 85*	4
Originally recorded by Mick Hucknell's previous group the Frantic Elevators.				
JERICHO	*WEA*	53	*8 Mar 86*	3
HOLDING BACK THE YEARS [RI]	*WEA*	2	*17 May 86*	13
OPEN UP THE RED BOX	*WEA*	61	*9 Aug 86*	4
THE RIGHT THING	*WEA*	11	*14 Feb 87*	10
INFIDELITY	*WEA*	31	*23 May 87*	5
EV'RY TIME WE SAY GOODBYE	*WEA*	11	*28 Nov 87*	9
I WON'T FEEL BAD	*WEA*	68	*12 Mar 88*	3
IT'S ONLY LOVE	*WEA*	13	*28 Jan 89*	8
IF YOU DON'T KNOW ME BY NOW	*WEA*	2	*8 Apr 89*	10
A NEW FLAME	*WEA*	17	*8 Jul 89*	8
YOU'VE GOT IT	*WEA*	46	*28 Oct 89*	3
SOMETHING GOT ME STARTED	*East West*	11	*21 Sep 91*	8
STARS	*East West*	8	*30 Nov 91*	10
FOR YOUR BABIES	*East West*	9	*8 Feb 92*	8
THRILL ME	*East West*	33	*2 May 92*	5
YOUR MIRROR	*East West*	17	*25 Jul 92*	4
MONTREUX [EP]	*East West*	11	*21 Nov 92*	10
Live recordings from the 26th Montreux Jazz Festival, 8 Jul 92. Lead track: Love For Sale, written by Cole Porter, though the track Lady Godiva's Room also received airplay.				
FAIRGROUND	*East West*	1	*30 Sep 95*	14
REMEMBERING THE FIRST TIME	*East West*	22	*16 Dec 95*	6
NEVER NEVER LOVE	*East West*	18	*24 Feb 96*	4
WE'RE IN THIS TOGETHER	*East West*	11	*22 Jun 96*	6
Official theme song for football's Euro '96.				
ANGEL	*East West*	4	*9 Nov 96*	13
NIGHT NURSE	*East West*	13	*20 Sep 97*	8
Originally recorded by Gregory Isaacs in 1982.				
Above hit: SLY and ROBBIE featuring SIMPLY RED.				
SAY YOU LOVE ME	*East West*	7	*16 May 98*	7
Features the Pro Arte Orchestra Of London conducted by David Sinclair Whitaker.				
THE AIR THAT I BREATHE	*East West*	6	*22 Aug 98*	7
GHETTO GIRL	*East West*	34	*12 Dec 98*	2
AIN'T THAT A LOT OF LOVE	*East West*	14	*30 Oct 99*	6
Orginally recorded by Homer Banks in 1966.				
ALBUMS:		**HITS 8**		**WEEKS 542**
PICTURE BOOK	*Elektra*	33	*26 Oct 85*	13
PICTURE BOOK [RE]	*Elektra*	2	*8 Mar 86*	109
Includes re-entries through to 1992.				
MEN AND WOMEN	*WEA*	2	*21 Mar 87*	56
A NEW FLAME	*WEA*	1	*25 Feb 89*	84
STARS	*East West*	1	*12 Oct 91*	132
PICTURE BOOK [RI]	*East West*	33	*21 Mar 92*	13
Digitally remastered. Peak position reached in 1996.				
MEN AND WOMEN [RI]	*East West*	20	*4 Mar 95*	7
Re-released at mid-price.				
LIFE	*East West*	1	*21 Oct 95*	47
A NEW FLAME [RI]	*East West*	28	*24 Feb 96*	6
Re-released at mid-price.				
GREATEST HITS	*East West*	1	*19 Oct 96*	41
BLUE	*East West*	1	*30 May 98*	26
LOVE AND THE RUSSIAN WINTER	*East West*	6	*13 Nov 99*	8

SIMPLY RED AND WHITE UK

SINGLES:		HITS 1		WEEKS 4
DAYDREAM BELIEVER (CHEER UP PETER REID)	*Ropery*	41	*6 Apr 96*	3
Peter Reid is Sunderland FC's manager.				
DAYDREAM BELIEVER (CHEER UP PETER REID) [RE]	*Ropery*	74	*4 May 96*	1

SIMPLY SMOOTH US

SINGLES:		HITS 1		WEEKS 1
LADY (YOU BRING ME UP)	*Big Bang*	70	*17 Oct 98*	1

Michael SIMPSON and John KING — See DUST BROTHERS (Michael SIMPSON and John KING) featuring Tyler DURDEN

Paul SIMPSON featuring ADEVA   US

(See also Adeva.)

SINGLES:		HITS 1		WEEKS 8
MUSICAL FREEDOM (MOVING ON UP)	Cooltempo	22	25 Mar 89	8

Fay SIMPSON – See Ronny JORDAN

Vida SIMPSON   US

SINGLES:		HITS 1		WEEKS 1
OOHHH BABY	Hi-Life	70	18 Feb 95	1

SIMPSONS   US

SINGLES:		HITS 2		WEEKS 19
DO THE BARTMAN	Geffen	1	26 Jan 91	12
DEEP, DEEP TROUBLE	Geffen	7	6 Apr 91	7

Above hit: SIMPSONS featuring BART and HOMER.

ALBUMS:		HITS 1		WEEKS 30
COMPILATION ALBUMS:		HITS 1		WEEKS 2
THE SIMPSONS SING THE BLUES	Geffen	6	2 Feb 91	30
THE SIMPSONS - SONGS IN THE KEY OF SPRINGFIELD	Rhino	18	12 Sep 98	2

Above entry was in the compilation chart.

A.E. SIMS – see Central Band of the ROYAL AIR FORCE (by permission of the Air Council) cond: Wing Comdr. A.E. SIMS
O.B.E. (Organising director of music)

Joyce SIMS   US

SINGLES:		HITS 6		WEEKS 36
ALL AND ALL	London	16	19 Apr 86	10
LIFETIME LOVE	London	34	13 Jun 87	6
COME INTO MY LIFE	London	7	9 Jan 88	9
WALK AWAY	London	24	23 Apr 88	6
LOOKING FOR A LOVE	ffrr	39	17 Jun 89	4

Title as per sleeve and chart. Label only has Looking For Love.

COME INTO MY LIFE [RR]	Club Tools	72	27 May 95	1
ALBUMS:		HITS 2		WEEKS 25
COME INTO MY LIFE	London	5	9 Jan 88	24
ALL ABOUT LOVE	ffrr	64	16 Sep 89	1

Kym SIMS   US

SINGLES:		HITS 4		WEEKS 23
TOO BLIND TO SEE IT	Atco	5	7 Dec 91	12
TAKE MY ADVICE	Atco	13	28 Mar 92	7
A LITTLE BIT MORE	Atco	30	27 Jun 92	3
WE GOTTA LOVE	Pulse 8	58	8 Jun 96	1
ALBUMS:		HITS 1		WEEKS 2
TOO BLIND TO SEE IT	Atco	39	18 Apr 92	2

SIN WITH SEBASTIAN   Germany

SINGLES:		HITS 1		WEEKS 2
SHUT UP (AND SLEEP WITH ME)	Sing Sing	44	16 Sep 95	1
SHUT UP (AND SLEEP WITH ME) [RM]	Sing Sing	46	27 Jan 96	1

Remixed by George Morel.

Frank SINATRA   US

(See also Frank Sinatra and Count Basie and his Orchestra; Various Artists: Films - Original Soundtracks 'Can Can', 'Pal Joey', 'High Society'.)

SINGLES:		HITS 35		WEEKS 433
YOUNG-AT-HEART	Capitol	12	10 Jul 54	1

From the film of the same name.

THREE COINS IN THE FOUNTAIN	Capitol	1	17 Jul 54	19

From the film of the same name.

YOU MY LOVE	Capitol	13	11 Jun 55	3

From the film 'Young At Heart'.

YOU MY LOVE [RE-1ST]	Capitol	17	23 Jul 55	2
LEARNIN' THE BLUES	Capitol	2	6 Aug 55	13

Above hit: Frank SINATRA with Nelson RIDDLE and his Orchestra.

YOU MY LOVE [RE-2ND]	Capitol	17	13 Aug 55	2
NOT AS A STRANGER	Capitol	18	3 Sep 55	1
LOVE AND MARRIAGE ("OUR TOWN")	Capitol	3	14 Jan 56	8

From the American TV series 'Our Town'.

(LOVE IS) THE TENDER TRAP	Capitol	2	21 Jan 56	9

From the film 'The Tender Trap'.

SONGS FOR SWINGIN' LOVERS [LP]	Capitol	12	16 Jun 56	8

15 track LP, first track: You Make Me Feel So Young. In 1958 it entered the album chart. See album section below.

ALL THE WAY / CHICAGO	Capitol	3	23 Nov 57	20

All The Way was listed on 23 Nov 57 at No. 29, the following week Chicago was listed at No. 25, and on 7 Dec 57 both sides were listed together at No. 21. From 14 Dec 57 All The Way was the only side listed.

WITCHCRAFT	Capitol	12	8 Feb 58	8
MR. SUCCESS	Capitol	29	15 Nov 58	1
MR. SUCCESS [RE-1ST]	Capitol	25	13 Dec 58	2
MR. SUCCESS [RE-2ND]	Capitol	26	3 Jan 59	1
FRENCH FOREIGN LEGION	Capitol	18	11 Apr 59	5
COME DANCE WITH ME! [LP]	Capitol	30	16 May 59	1

12 track LP, first track: Come Dance With Me. This also entered the album chart the same week. See album section below.

Above hit: Frank SINATRA with Billy MAY and his Orchestra.

HIGH HOPES	Capitol	28	29 Aug 59	1

From the film 'A Hole In The Head'. Backing vocals and hand claps by Eddie Hodges.

HIGH HOPES [RE-1ST]	Capitol	6	12 Sep 59	13
HIGH HOPES [RE-2ND]	Capitol	42	12 Mar 60	1
IT'S NICE TO GO TRAV'LING	Capitol	48	9 Apr 60	2
RIVER STAY 'WAY FROM MY DOOR	Capitol	18	18 Jun 60	9

Originally recorded by Kate Smith and Guy Lombardo.

NICE 'N' EASY	Capitol	15	10 Sep 60	12
OL' MAC DONALD	Capitol	11	26 Nov 60	8
MY BLUE HEAVEN	Capitol	33	22 Apr 61	7

The majority of the singles listed above had backing orchestra conducted by Nelson Riddle.

GRANADA	Reprise	15	30 Sep 61	8

Originally recorded by Frankie Laine.

Above hit: Frank SINATRA with Billy MAY and his Orchestra.

THE COFFEE SONG	Reprise	39	25 Nov 61	3
EVERYBODY'S TWISTIN'	Reprise	22	7 Apr 62	12
ME AND MY SHADOW	Reprise	20	15 Dec 62	7

Originally recorded by Whispering Jack Smith in 1927.

Above hit: Frank SINATRA and Sammy DAVIS Jnr.

ME AND MY SHADOW [RE]	Reprise	47	9 Feb 63	2
STRANGERS IN THE NIGHT	Reprise	1	14 May 66	20

From the film 'A Man Could Get Killed'.

SUMMER WIND	Reprise	36	1 Oct 66	5
THAT'S LIFE	Reprise	46	17 Dec 66	5

Originally recorded by O.C.Smith.

SOMETHIN' STUPID	Reprise	1	25 Mar 67	18

Above hit: Nancy SINATRA and Frank SINATRA.

THE WORLD WE KNEW (OVER AND OVER)	Reprise	33	26 Aug 67	11
MY WAY	Reprise	5	5 Apr 69	42

The single with most weeks on the singles chart, 124 weeks in total. Originally recorded by Claude Francois with English lyric by Paul Anka.

LOVE'S BEEN GOOD TO ME	Reprise	8	4 Oct 69	18

Originally recorded by Rod McKuen.

MY WAY [RE-1ST]	Reprise	49	31 Jan 70	1
MY WAY [RE-2ND]	Reprise	30	28 Feb 70	5
MY WAY [RE-3RD]	Reprise	33	11 Apr 70	9
MY WAY [RE-4TH]	Reprise	28	27 Jun 70	21
MY WAY [RE-5TH]	Reprise	18	28 Nov 70	16
I WILL DRINK THE WINE	Reprise	16	6 Mar 71	12
MY WAY [RE-6TH]	Reprise	22	27 Mar 71	19
MY WAY [RE-7TH]	Reprise	39	4 Sep 71	8
MY WAY [RE-8TH]	Reprise	50	1 Jan 72	1
I BELIEVE I'M GONNA LOVE YOU	Reprise	34	20 Dec 75	7
THEME FROM NEW YORK, NEW YORK	Reprise	59	9 Aug 80	4
THEME FROM NEW YORK, NEW YORK [RE]	Reprise	4	22 Feb 86	10
I'VE GOT YOU UNDER MY SKIN	Island	4	4 Dec 93	9

[AA] listed with Stay (Faraway, So Close) by U2. It was not available on the 2nd CD format.

Above hit: Frank SINATRA with BONO.

MY WAY [RI]	Reprise	45	16 Apr 94	2

Featured in the Dulux Paint TV commercial.

THEY ALL LAUGHED	Reprise	41	30 Jan 99	1

Featured in the Carlsberg lager TV commercial. Originally recorded by Fred Astaire and Ginger Rogers in 1937, Sinatra's recording is from 1980.

EPS:	HITS 7			WEEKS 49
COME DANCE WITH ME NO. 1	Capitol	11	26 Mar 60	2
THE SONG IS YOU	Fontana	19	2 Apr 60	1
SONGS FOR SWINGIN' LOVERS NO. 1	Capitol	20	16 Apr 60	1
THE LADY IS A TRAMP	Capitol	7	23 Apr 60	19
I'VE GOT A CRUSH ON YOU	Fontana	14	9 Jul 60	1
COME DANCE WITH ME NO. 2	Capitol	13	26 Nov 60	10
ALL THE WAY	Capitol	6	14 Jan 61	15

ALBUMS:		HITS 52		WEEKS 684	
COME FLY WITH ME	Capitol	2	8 Nov 58	18
SONGS FOR SWINGING LOVERS	Capitol	8	15 Nov 58	8
First entered the singles chart in 1956. See singles section above.				
FRANK SINATRA STORY	Fontana	8	29 Nov 58	1
FRANK SINATRA SINGS FOR ONLY THE LONELY	Capitol	5	13 Dec 58	13
COME DANCE WITH ME!	Capitol	2	16 May 59	30
Also entered the singles chart the same week. See singles section above.				
Above hit: Frank SINATRA with Billy MAY and his Orchestra.				
LOOK TO YOUR HEART	Capitol	5	22 Aug 59	8
COME BACK TO SORRENTO	Fontana	6	11 Jun 60	9
SWING EASY	Capitol	5	29 Oct 60	17
NICE 'N EASY	Capitol	4	21 Jan 61	28
SINATRA SOUVENIR	Fontana	18	15 Jul 61	1
WHEN YOUR LOVER HAS GONE	Encore	6	19 Aug 61	10
SINATRA'S SWINGING SESSION!!!	Capitol	6	23 Sep 61	8
SINATRA SWINGS	Reprise	8	28 Oct 61	8
SINATRA PLUS	Fontana	7	25 Nov 61	9
RING-A-DING-DING	Reprise	8	16 Dec 61	9
COME SWING WITH ME	Capitol	13	17 Feb 62	4
I REMEMBER TOMMY . . .	Reprise	10	7 Apr 62	12
Songs first performed by Tommy Dorsey.				
SINATRA AND STRINGS	Reprise	6	9 Jun 62	20
GREAT SONGS FROM GREAT BRITAIN	Reprise	12	27 Oct 62	9
SINATRA WITH SWINGING BRASS	Reprise	14	29 Dec 62	11
CONCERT SINATRA	Reprise	8	27 Jul 63	18
SINATRA'S SINATRA	Reprise	9	5 Oct 63	24
SOFTLY AS I LEAVE YOU	Reprise	20	20 Mar 65	1
A MAN AND HIS MUSIC	Reprise	9	22 Jan 66	19
Compilation with narration by Sinatra.				
MOONLIGHT SINATRA	Reprise	18	21 May 66	8
STRANGERS IN THE NIGHT	Reprise	4	2 Jul 66	18
IN CONCERT: SINATRA AT 'THE SANDS'	Reprise	7	1 Oct 66	18
Live recordings featuring backing by Count Basie and his Orchestra.				
FRANK SINATRA SINGS SONGS FOR PLEASURE	Music For Pleasure	26	3 Dec 66	2
THAT'S LIFE	Reprise	22	25 Feb 67	12
FRANK SINATRA	Reprise	28	7 Oct 67	5
GREATEST HITS	Reprise	8	19 Oct 68	38
BEST OF FRANK SINATRA	Capitol	17	7 Dec 68	10
MY WAY	Reprise	2	7 Jun 69	59
A MAN ALONE – THE WORDS AND MUSIC OF ROD MCKUEN	Reprise	18	4 Oct 69	7
WATERTOWN	Reprise	14	9 May 70	9
GREATEST HITS VOLUME 2	Reprise	6	12 Dec 70	40
SINATRA AND COMPANY	Reprise	9	5 Jun 71	9
FRANK SINATRA SINGS RODGERS AND HART	Starline	35	27 Nov 71	1
GREATEST HITS VOLUME 2 [RE]	Reprise	29	8 Jan 72	3
Re-released with new catalogue number.				
MY WAY [RE]	Reprise	35	8 Jan 72	1
Re-released with new catalogue number.				
OL' BLUE EYES IS BACK	Warner Brothers	12	1 Dec 73	13
SOME NICE THINGS I'VE MISSED	Reprise	35	17 Aug 74	3
SINATRA – THE MAIN EVENT LIVE [OST-TV]	Reprise	30	15 Feb 75	2
Live recordings from Madison Square Garden. Featured backing from Woody Herman and the Young Thundering Herd.				
THE BEST OF OL' BLUE EYES	Reprise	30	14 Jun 75	3
PORTRAIT OF SINATRA	Reprise	1	19 Mar 77	18
Compilation.				
20 GOLDEN GREATS	Capitol	4	13 May 78	11
L.A. IS MY LADY	Qwest	41	18 Aug 84	8
Above hit: Frank SINATRA with the Quincy JONES ORCHESTRA.				
NEW YORK, NEW YORK (GREATEST HITS)	Warner Brothers	13	22 Mar 86	12
THE FRANK SINATRA COLLECTION	Capitol	40	4 Oct 86	5
DUETS	Capitol	5	6 Nov 93	14
DUETS II	Capitol	29	26 Nov 94	6
Above 2, as the titles suggest are collaborations with various artists.				
THIS IS FRANK SINATRA 1953 – 1957	Music For Pleasure	56	11 Mar 95	1
SINATRA 80TH – ALL THE BEST	Capitol	49	2 Dec 95	5
MY WAY – THE BEST OF FRANK SINATRA	Reprise	13	16 Aug 97	14
Sales combined of either a single 20 track album or a double 46 track.				
MY WAY – THE BEST OF FRANK SINATRA [RE]	Reprise	7	23 May 98	33
SONGS FOR SWINGING LOVERS [RE]	Capitol	63	30 May 98	1
Re-released with new catalogue number.				

Frank SINATRA and Count BASIE and his Orchestra   US

(See also Count Basie and his Orchestra; Frank Sinatra.)

SINGLES:		HITS 2		WEEKS 7	
MY KIND OF GIRL	Reprise	35	9 Mar 63	6

HELLO DOLLY	Reprise	47	26 Sep 64	1
From the musical of the same name.				
ALBUMS:	**HITS 2**		**WEEKS 27**	
SINATRA - BASIE	Reprise	2	23 Feb 63	23
IT MIGHT AS WELL BE SWING	Reprise	17	19 Sep 64	4

Nancy SINATRA   US

(See also Nancy Sinatra and Lee Hazlewood.)

SINGLES:	**HITS 6**		**WEEKS 79**	
THESE BOOTS ARE MADE FOR WALKIN'	Reprise	1	29 Jan 66	14
HOW DOES THAT GRAB YOU, DARLIN'?	Reprise	19	30 Apr 66	8
SUGAR TOWN	Reprise	8	21 Jan 67	10
SOMETHIN' STUPID	Reprise	1	25 Mar 67	18
Above hit: Nancy SINATRA and Frank SINATRA.				
YOU ONLY LIVE TWICE	Reprise	11	8 Jul 67	19
From the James Bond film of the same name. [AA] listed with Jackson by Nancy Sinatra and Lee Hazlewood.				
THE HIGHWAY SONG	Reprise	21	29 Nov 69	10
ALBUMS:	**HITS 3**		**WEEKS 15**	
BOOTS	Reprise	12	16 Apr 66	9
HOW DOES THAT GRAB YOU	Reprise	17	18 Jun 66	3
NANCY'S GREATEST HITS	Reprise	39	10 Oct 70	3

Nancy SINATRA and Lee HAZLEWOOD   US

(See also Nancy Sinatra.)

SINGLES:	**HITS 3**		**WEEKS 38**	
JACKSON	Reprise	11	15 Jul 67	18
[AA] listed with You Only Live Twice by Nancy Sinatra.				
LADY BIRD	Reprise	47	11 Nov 67	1
DID YOU EVER	Reprise	2	21 Aug 71	19
Originally recorded by Charles Louvin and Melba Mongomery.				
ALBUMS:	**HITS 2**		**WEEKS 17**	
NANCY AND LEE	Reprise	17	29 Jun 68	12
NANCY AND LEE [RE]	Reprise	42	25 Sept 71	1
Re-released with new catalogue number.				
DID YOU EVER	RCA Victor	31	29 Jan 72	4

SINCLAIR   UK

SINGLES:	**HITS 3**		**WEEKS 8**	
AIN'T NO CASANOVA	Dome	28	21 Aug 93	5
(I WANNA KNOW) WHY	Dome	58	26 Feb 94	2
DON'T LIE	Dome	70	6 Aug 94	1

Bob SINCLAR featuring Lee A. GENESIS   France

SINGLES:	**HITS 1**		**WEEKS 1**	
MY ONLY LOVE	East West	56	20 Mar 99	1

SINDY   UK

SINGLES:	**HITS 1**		**WEEKS 1**	
SATURDAY NIGHT	Love This	70	5 Oct 96	1

SINE   US

SINGLES:	**HITS 1**		**WEEKS 9**	
JUST LET ME DO MY THING	CBS	33	10 Jun 78	9

SINFONIA OF LONDON – Howard BLAKE conducting the SINFONIA OF LONDON; SNOWMAN

Talvin SINGH   UK

SINGLES:	**HITS 1**		**WEEKS 4**	
KISS THEM FOR ME	Wonderland	32	25 May 91	4
Above hit: SIOUXSIE and the BANSHEES featuring Talvin SINGH.				
ALBUMS:	**HITS 1**		**WEEKS 4**	
OK	Island	41	18 Sept 99	4
Originally released in 1998, charted after winning the 1999 Mercury Music Prize.				

SINGING CORNER meets DONOVAN   UK

SINGLES:	**HITS 1**		**WEEKS 1**	
JENNIFER JUNIPER	Fontana	68	1 Dec 90	1

SINGING DOGS – See Don CHARLES presents the SINGING DOGS

SINGING NUN (SOEUR SOURIRE) — Belgium

SINGLES:		HITS 1			WEEKS 14
DOMINIQUE (SOEUR SOURIRE)	Philips		7	7 Dec 63	14

SINGING SHEEP — Denmark

SINGLES:		HITS 1			WEEKS 5
BAA BAA BLACK SHEEP	Sheep		42	18 Dec 82	5

Maxine SINGLETON — US

SINGLES:		HITS 1			WEEKS 3
YOU CAN'T RUN FROM LOVE	Creole		57	2 Apr 83	3

SINITTA — US

SINGLES:		HITS 12			WEEKS 104
SO MACHO / CRUISING	Fanfare		47	8 Mar 86	11
SO MACHO / CRUISING [RE]	Fanfare		2	28 Jun 86	17
FEELS LIKE THE FIRST TIME	Fanfare		45	11 Oct 86	5
TOY BOY	Fanfare		4	25 Jul 87	14
G.T.O.	Fanfare		15	12 Dec 87	9
CROSS MY BROKEN HEART	Fanfare		6	19 Mar 88	9
I DON'T BELIEVE IN MIRACLES	Fanfare		22	24 Sep 88	8
RIGHT BACK WHERE WE STARTED FROM	Fanfare		4	3 Jun 89	10
Originally recorded by J.Vincent Edwards.					
LOVE ON A MOUNTAIN TOP	Fanfare		20	7 Oct 89	6
HITCHIN' A RIDE	Fanfare		24	21 Apr 90	6
LOVE AND AFFECTION	Fanfare		62	22 Sep 90	3
SHAME, SHAME, SHAME	Arista		28	4 Jul 92	4
THE SUPREME [EP]	Arista		49	17 Apr 93	2
Lead track: Where Did Our Love Go?					

ALBUMS:		HITS 2			WEEKS 23
SINITTA!	Fanfare		34	26 Dec 87	19
WICKED!	Fanfare		52	9 Dec 89	4

SINNAMON — US

SINGLES:		HITS 1			WEEKS 1
I NEED YOU NOW	Worx		70	28 Sep 96	1

SIOUXSIE and the BANSHEES — UK

SINGLES:		HITS 30			WEEKS 150
HONG KONG GARDEN	Polydor		7	26 Aug 78	10
THE STAIRCASE (MYSTERY)	Polydor		24	31 Mar 79	8
PLAYGROUND TWIST	Polydor		28	7 Jul 79	6
MITTAGEISEN (METAL POSTCARD)	Polydor		47	29 Sep 79	3
HAPPY HOUSE	Polydor		17	15 Mar 80	8
CHRISTINE	Polydor		22	7 Jun 80	8
ISRAEL	Polydor		41	6 Dec 80	8
SPELLBOUND	Polydor		22	30 May 81	8
ARABIAN KNIGHTS	Polydor		32	1 Aug 81	7
FIRE WORKS	Polydor		22	29 May 82	6
SLOWDIVE	Polydor		41	9 Oct 82	4
MELT / IL EST NE LE DIVIN ENFANT	Polydor		49	4 Dec 82	5
Il Est Ne Le Divin Enfant is a French Christmas song.					
DEAR PRUDENCE	Wonderland		3	1 Oct 83	8
Originally recorded by the Beatles, written about Mia Farrow's sister.					
SWIMMING HORSES	Wonderland		28	24 Mar 84	4
DAZZLE	Wonderland		33	2 Jun 84	3
THE THORN [EP]	Wonderland		47	27 Oct 84	3
Lead track: Overground, features the Chandos Players.					
CITIES IN DUST	Wonderland		21	26 Oct 85	6
CANDYMAN	Wonderland		34	8 Mar 86	5
THIS WHEEL'S ON FIRE	Wonderland		14	17 Jan 87	6
THE PASSENGER	Wonderland		41	28 Mar 87	6
Originally recorded by Iggy Pop.					
SONG FROM THE EDGE OF THE WORLD	Wonderland		59	25 Jul 87	3
PEEK A BOO	Wonderland		16	30 Jul 88	6
THE KILLING JAR	Wonderland		41	8 Oct 88	3
THE LAST BEAT OF MY HEART	Wonderland		44	3 Dec 88	1
KISS THEM FOR ME	Wonderland		32	25 May 91	4
Above hit: SIOUXSIE and the BANSHEES featuring Talvin SINGH.					
SHADOWTIME	Wonderland		57	13 Jul 91	1
FACE TO FACE	Wonderland		21	25 Jul 92	4
INTERLUDE	Parlophone		25	20 Aug 94	2
Originally recorded by Timi Yuro in 1968.					
Above hit: MORRISSEY and SIOUXSIE.					

O BABY	*Wonderland*	34	7 Jan 95	3
STARGAZER	*Wonderland*	64	18 Feb 95	1
ALBUMS:	**HITS 14**		**WEEKS 119**	
THE SCREAM	*Polydor*	12	2 Dec 78	11
JOIN HANDS	*Polydor*	13	22 Sep 79	5
KALEIDOSCOPE	*Polydor*	5	16 Aug 80	6
JU JU	*Polydor*	7	27 Jun 81	17
ONCE UPON A TIME – THE SINGLES	*Polydor*	21	12 Dec 81	26
A KISS IN THE DREAMHOUSE	*Polydor*	11	13 Nov 82	11
NOCTURNE	*Wonderland*	29	3 Dec 83	10
Live recordings.				
HYENA	*Wonderland*	15	16 Jun 84	6
TINDERBOX	*Wonderland*	13	26 Apr 86	6
THROUGH THE LOOKING GLASS	*Wonderland*	15	14 Mar 87	8
Album of covers.				
PEEPSHOW	*Wonderland*	20	17 Sep 88	5
SUPERSTITION	*Wonderland*	25	22 Jun 91	4
TWICE UPON A TIME – THE SINGLES	*Wonderland*	26	17 Oct 92	2
THE RAPTURE	*Wonderland*	33	28 Jan 95	2

SIR DOUGLAS QUINTET US

SINGLES:	**HITS 1**		**WEEKS 10**	
SHE'S ABOUT A MOVER	*London*	15	19 Jun 65	10

SIR MIX-A-LOT US

SINGLES:	**HITS 1**		**WEEKS 2**	
BABY GOT BACK	*Def American*	56	8 Aug 92	2

George SIRAVO and his Orchestra – See Johnnie RAY

SIRRON – See PLUS ONE featuring SIRRON

SISSEL US/Norway

SINGLES:	**HITS 1**		**WEEKS 7**	
PRINCE IGOR	*Def Jam*	15	10 Jan 98	7
Based on music composed by Borodin.				
Above hit: RAPSODY: Warren G and SISSEL.				
ALBUMS:	**HITS 1**		**WEEKS 1**	
DEEP WITHIN MY SOUL	*Mercury*	58	20 May 95	1
Nordic electronic folk songs.				

SISTA featuring Craig MACK – See VARIOUS ARTISTS (EPs) 'Dangerous Minds EP'

SISTER BLISS with COLETTE UK

SINGLES:	**HITS 3**		**WEEKS 7**	
CANTGETAMAN, CANTGETAJOB (LIFE'S A BITCH!)	*Go.Beat*	31	15 Oct 94	4
OH! WHAT A WORLD	*Go.Beat*	40	15 Jul 95	2
Colette, though the vocalist, is not credited on this release.				
Above hit: SISTER BLISS.				
BAD MAN	*Junk Dog*	51	29 Jun 96	1
Above hit: SISTER BLISS.				

SISTER SLEDGE US

(See also Kathy Sledge.)

SINGLES:	**HITS 9**		**WEEKS 111**	
MAMA NEVER TOLD ME	*Atlantic*	20	21 Jun 75	6
HE'S THE GREATEST DANCER	*Atlantic*	6	17 Mar 79	11
WE ARE FAMILY	*Atlantic*	8	26 May 79	10
Backing vocals by Luther Vandross.				
LOST IN MUSIC	*Atlantic*	17	11 Aug 79	10
GOT TO LOVE SOMEBODY	*Atlantic*	34	19 Jan 80	4
ALL AMERICAN GIRLS	*Atlantic*	41	28 Feb 81	5
THINKING OF YOU	*Atlantic*	11	26 May 84	13
Originally recorded in 1979.				
LOST IN MUSIC [RI]	*Atlantic*	4	8 Sep 84	12
WE ARE FAMILY [RM-1ST]	*Atlantic*	33	17 Nov 84	4
FRANKIE	*Atlantic*	1	1 Jun 85	16
DANCING ON THE JAGGED EDGE	*Atlantic*	50	31 Aug 85	3
WE ARE FAMILY ('93 MIXES) [RM-2ND]	*Atlantic*	5	23 Jan 93	8
LOST IN MUSIC (SURE IS PURE REMIXES) [RM]	*Atlantic*	14	13 Mar 93	5
Above 2 remixed by Sure Is Pure.				
THINKING OF YOU ('93 REMIXES) [RM]	*Atlantic*	17	12 Jun 93	4
Remixed by Ramp.				
ALBUMS:	**HITS 4**		**WEEKS 58**	
WE ARE FAMILY	*Atlantic*	15	12 May 79	23
WE ARE FAMILY [RE]	*Atlantic*	7	29 Sept 84	16

WHEN THE BOYS MEET THE GIRLS	*Atlantic*	19	*22 Jun 85*	11
FREAK OUT	*Telstar*	72	*5 Dec 87*	3
Compilation of hits by both groups.				
Above hit: CHIC and SISTER SLEDGE.				
THE VERY BEST OF SISTER SLEDGE 1973 - 1993	*Atlantic*	19	*20 Feb 93*	5
Includes originals and remixes.				

SISTERHOOD — UK

ALBUMS:		HITS 1		WEEKS 1
GIFT	*Merciful Release*	90	*26 Jul 86*	1

SISTERS OF MERCY — UK

SINGLES:		HITS 10		WEEKS 40
BODY AND SOUL / TRAIN	*Merciful Release*	46	*16 Jun 84*	3
WALK AWAY	*Merciful Release*	45	*20 Oct 84*	3
NO TIME TO CRY	*Merciful Release*	63	*9 Mar 85*	2
THIS CORROSION	*Merciful Release*	7	*3 Oct 87*	6
DOMINION	*Merciful Release*	13	*27 Feb 88*	6
LUCRETIA MY REFLECTION	*Merciful Release*	20	*18 Jun 88*	4
MORE	*Merciful Release*	14	*13 Oct 90*	4
DOCTOR JEEP	*Merciful Release*	37	*22 Dec 90*	4
TEMPLE OF LOVE (1992) TOUCHED BY THE HAND OF OFRA HAZA	*Merciful Release*	3	*2 May 92*	5
Original recording was released in 1983.				
UNDER THE GUN	*Merciful Release*	19	*28 Aug 93*	3
Vocals provided by Terri Nunn of Berlin.				
ALBUMS:		HITS 5		WEEKS 42
FIRST AND LAST AND ALWAYS	*Merciful Release*	14	*23 Mar 85*	8
FLOODLAND	*Merciful Release*	9	*28 Nov 87*	20
VISION THING	*Merciful Release*	11	*3 Nov 90*	4
SOME GIRLS WANDER BY MISTAKE	*Merciful Release*	5	*9 May 92*	5
GREATEST HITS VOLUME 1	*Merciful Release*	14	*4 Sep 93*	5

SISTERS OF SOUL – See Steve WRIGHT

SIVUCA — Brazil

SINGLES:		HITS 1		WEEKS 3
AIN'T NO SUNSHINE	*London*	56	*28 Jul 84*	3

SIX BY SEVEN — UK

SINGLES:		HITS 1		WEEKS 1
CANDLELIGHT	*Mantra*	70	*9 May 98*	1

6 BY SIX — UK

SINGLES:		HITS 1		WEEKS 1
INTO YOUR HEART	*Six6*	51	*4 May 96*	1
A re-mix of the 1995 club hit by Rozzo.				

666 — Germany

SINGLES:		HITS 1		WEEKS 1
ALARMA	*Danceteria*	58	*3 Oct 98*	1

SIXPENCE NONE THE RICHER — US

SINGLES:		HITS 2		WEEKS 17
KISS ME	*Elektra*	4	*29 May 99*	12
THERE SHE GOES	*Elektra*	14	*18 Sept 99*	5
ALBUMS:		HITS 1		WEEKS 3
SIXPENCE NONE THE RICHER	*Elektra*	27	*26 Jun 99*	3

60FT DOLLS — UK

SINGLES:		HITS 4		WEEKS 4
STAY	*Indolent*	48	*3 Feb 96*	1
TALK TO ME	*Indolent*	37	*11 May 96*	1
HAPPY SHOPPER	*Indolent*	38	*20 Jul 96*	1
ALISON'S ROOM	*Indolent*	61	*9 May 98*	1
ALBUMS:		HITS 1		WEEKS 2
THE BIG 3	*Indolent*	36	*8 Jun 96*	2

Roni SIZE REPRAZENT — UK

SINGLES:		HITS 4		WEEKS 9
SHARE THE FALL	*Talkin Loud*	37	*14 Jun 97*	2
Above hit: REPRAZENT/Roni SIZE.				
HEROES	*Talkin Loud*	31	*13 Sep 97*	2
BROWN PAPER BAG	*Talkin Loud UK*	20	*15 Nov 97*	3

WATCHING WINDOWS	*Talkin Loud UK*	28	*14 Mar 98*	2
ALBUMS:	**HITS 1**			**WEEKS 34**
NEW FORMS	*Talkin Loud*	8	*5 Jul 97*	34
Climbed to its peak position after winning the 1997 Mercury Music Prize.				

SIZE 9   US

(See also Josh Wink.)

SINGLES:	**HITS 1**			**WEEKS 4**
I'M READY	*Virgin*	52	*17 Jun 95*	1
Samples B-Beat Girls' For The Same Man and Raw Silk's Do It To The Music.				
I'M READY [RI]	*VC Recordings*	30	*11 Nov 95*	3
Lead track on the CD is a radio edit of the original chart entry. The lead track of that entry was the full version of 11 minutes 54 seconds.				
Above hit: Josh WINK'S SIZE 9.				

SIZLA   Jamaica

SINGLES:	**HITS 1**			**WEEKS 2**
RAIN SHOWERS	*Xterminator*	51	*17 Apr 99*	2

SKATALITES   Jamaica

SINGLES:	**HITS 1**			**WEEKS 6**
GUNS OF NAVARONE	*Island*	36	*22 Apr 67*	6
Originally recorded by Joe Reisman.				

SKEE-LO   US

SINGLES:	**HITS 2**			**WEEKS 10**
I WISH	*Wild Card*	15	*9 Dec 95*	8
TOP OF THE STAIRS	*Wild Card*	38	*27 Apr 96*	2
From the film 'Money Train'.				

Beverli SKEETE – See DE-CODE featuring Beverli SKEETE

Peter SKELLERN   UK

SINGLES:	**HITS 3**			**WEEKS 24**
YOU'RE A LADY	*Decca*	3	*23 Sep 72*	11
HOLD ON TO LOVE	*Decca*	14	*29 Mar 75*	9
LOVE IS THE SWEETEST THING	*Mercury*	60	*28 Oct 78*	4
Above hit: Peter SKELLERN featuring the GRIMETHORPE COLLIERY BAND.				
ALBUMS:	**HITS 4**			**WEEKS 31**
SKELLERN	*Mercury*	48	*9 Sep 78*	3
ASTAIRE	*Mercury*	23	*8 Dec 79*	20
A STRING OF PEARLS	*Mercury*	67	*4 Dec 82*	5
STARDUST MEMORIES	*WEA*	50	*1 Apr 95*	3
Tribute album to the Ink Spots and Hoagy Carmichael.				

SKID ROW   UK

ALBUMS:	**HITS 1**			**WEEKS 3**
SKID	*CBS*	30	*17 Oct 70*	3

SKID ROW   US

SINGLES:	**HITS 8**			**WEEKS 27**
YOUTH GONE WILD	*Atlantic*	42	*18 Nov 89*	3
18 AND LIFE	*Atlantic*	12	*3 Feb 90*	6
I REMEMBER YOU	*Atlantic*	36	*31 Mar 90*	4
MONKEY BUSINESS	*Atlantic*	19	*15 Jun 91*	3
SLAVE TO THE GRIND	*Atlantic*	43	*14 Sep 91*	2
WASTED TIME	*Atlantic*	20	*23 Nov 91*	3
YOUTH GONE WILD [RI] / DELIVERING THE GOODS	*Atlantic*	22	*29 Aug 92*	4
Delivering The Goods is a live recording from Phoenix, Arizona, 17 Mar 92 featuring Rob Halford of Judas Priest.				
BREAKIN' DOWN	*Atlantic*	48	*18 Nov 95*	2
From the film 'The Phrophecy'.				
ALBUMS:	**HITS 3**			**WEEKS 28**
SKID ROW	*Atlantic*	30	*2 Sep 89*	16
SLAVE TO THE GRIND	*Atlantic*	5	*22 Jun 91*	9
SUBHUMAN RACE	*Atlantic*	8	*8 Apr 95*	3

SKIDS   UK

SINGLES:	**HITS 10**			**WEEKS 60**
SWEET SUBURBIA	*Virgin*	70	*23 Sep 78*	1
SWEET SUBURBIA [RE]	*Virgin*	71	*7 Oct 78*	2
THE SAINTS ARE COMING	*Virgin*	48	*4 Nov 78*	3
INTO THE VALLEY	*Virgin*	10	*17 Feb 79*	11
MASQUERADE	*Virgin*	14	*26 May 79*	9

CHARADE	Virgin	31	29 Sep 79	6
WORKING FOR THE YANKEE DOLLAR	Virgin	20	24 Nov 79	11
ANIMATION	Virgin	56	1 Mar 80	3
CIRCUS GAMES	Virgin	32	16 Aug 80	7
GOODBYE CIVILIAN	Virgin	52	18 Oct 80	4
WOMEN IN WINTER	Virgin	49	6 Dec 80	3
ALBUMS:	**HITS 3**			**WEEKS 20**
SCARED TO DANCE	Virgin	19	17 Mar 79	10
DAYS IN EUROPA	Virgin	32	27 Oct 79	5
THE ABSOLUTE GAME	Virgin	9	27 Sep 80	5

SKIN
UK/Germany

SINGLES:	**HITS 9**			**WEEKS 19**
THE SKIN UP [EP]	Parlophone	67	25 Dec 93	2
Lead track: Look But Don't Touch.				
HOUSE OF LOVE	Parlophone	45	12 Mar 94	2
THE MONEY EP [EP]	Parlophone	18	30 Apr 94	3
Lead track: Money.				
TOWER OF STRENGTH	Parlophone	19	23 Jul 94	3
LOOK BUT DON'T TOUCH [EP]	Parlophone	33	15 Oct 94	3
Lead track: Look But Don't Touch. A re-issue from The Skin Up EP.				
TAKE ME DOWN THE RIVER	Parlophone	26	20 May 95	2
HOW LUCKY YOU ARE	Parlophone	32	23 Mar 96	2
PERFECT DAY	Parlophone	33	18 May 96	2
ALBUMS:	**HITS 3**			**WEEKS 5**
SKIN	Parlophone	9	14 May 94	3
LUCKY	Parlophone	38	6 Apr 96	1
EXPERIENCE ELECTRIC	Recall	72	13 Sep 97	1
Originally released in Japan in 1996 with the title Big Fat Slice Of Life.				

SKIN UP
UK

SINGLES:	**HITS 3**			**WEEKS 9**
IVORY	Love	48	7 Sep 91	3
A JUICY RED APPLE	Love	32	14 Mar 92	4
ACCELERATE	Love	45	18 Jul 92	2

SKINNY
UK

| **SINGLES:** | **HITS 1** | | | **WEEKS 2** |
| FAILURE | Cheeky | 31 | 11 Apr 98 | 2 |

SKIPWORTH and TURNER
US

SINGLES:	**HITS 2**			**WEEKS 12**
THINKING ABOUT YOUR LOVE	Fourth & Broadway	24	27 Apr 85	10
MAKE IT LAST	Fourth & Broadway	60	21 Jan 89	2

Nick SKITZ – See FUNKY CHOAD featuring Nick SKITZ

SKUNK ANANSIE
UK

SINGLES:	**HITS 11**			**WEEKS 41**
SELLING JESUS	One Little Indian	46	25 Mar 95	1
I CAN DREAM	One Little Indian	41	17 Jun 95	2
CHARITY	One Little Indian	40	2 Sep 95	2
WEAK	One Little Indian	20	27 Jan 96	5
CHARITY [RI]	One Little Indian	20	27 Apr 96	3
ALL I WANT	One Little Indian	14	28 Sep 96	4
TWISTED (EVERYDAY HURTS)	One Little Indian	26	30 Nov 96	4
HEDONISM (JUST BECAUSE YOU FEEL GOOD)	One Little Indian	13	1 Feb 97	6
BRAZEN 'WEEP'	One Little Indian	11	14 Jun 97	5
CHARLIE BIG POTATO	Virgin	17	13 Mar 99	3
SECRETLY	Virgin	16	22 May 99	4
LATELY	Virgin	33	7 Aug 99	2
ALBUMS:	**HITS 3**			**WEEKS 101**
PARANOID & SUNBURNT	One Little Indian	8	30 Sep 95	32
STOOSH	One Little Indian	9	19 Oct 96	55
Stoosh is Jamaican slang for street posh.				
POST ORGASMIC CHILL	Virgin	16	3 Apr 99	14

SKY
UK/Australia

SINGLES:	**HITS 1**			**WEEKS 11**
TOCCATA	Ariola	5	5 Apr 80	11
Written by J.S. Bach.				
ALBUMS:	**HITS 8**			**WEEKS 202**
SKY	Ariola	9	2 Jun 79	56
SKY 2	Ariola Hansa	1	26 Apr 80	53

SKY 3	*Arista*	3	*28 Mar 81*	23
SKY 4 – FORTHCOMING	*Ariola*	7	*3 Apr 82*	22
SKY FIVE LIVE	*Ariola*	14	*22 Jan 83*	14
CADMIUM	*Ariola*	44	*3 Dec 83*	10
MASTERPIECES – THE VERY BEST OF SKY	*Telstar*	15	*12 May 84*	18
THE GREAT BALLOON RACE	*Epic*	63	*13 Apr 85*	6

SKYHOOKS
Australia

SINGLES:	HITS 1			WEEKS 1
WOMEN IN UNIFORM	*United Artists*	73	*9 Jun 79*	1

SKYY
US

ALBUMS:	HITS 1			WEEKS 1
FROM THE LEFT SIDE	*Capitol*	85	*21 Jun 86*	1

SLACKER
UK

SINGLES:	HITS 2			WEEKS 4
SCARED	*XL Recordings*	36	*26 Apr 97*	2
YOUR FACE	*XL Recordings*	33	*30 Aug 97*	2

Samples Roberta Flack's First Time Ever I Saw Your Face.

SLADE
UK

SINGLES:	HITS 35			WEEKS 279
GET DOWN AND GET WITH IT	*Polydor*	16	*19 Jun 71*	14

Originally recorded by Bobby Marchan.

COZ I LUV YOU	*Polydor*	1	*30 Oct 71*	15
LOOK WOT YOU DUN	*Polydor*	4	*5 Feb 72*	10
TAKE ME BAK 'OME	*Polydor*	1	*3 Jun 72*	13
MAMA WEER ALL CRAZEE NOW	*Polydor*	1	*2 Sep 72*	10
GUDBUY T'JANE	*Polydor*	2	*25 Nov 72*	13
CUM ON FEEL THE NOIZE	*Polydor*	1	*3 Mar 73*	12
SKWEEZE ME, PLEEZE ME	*Polydor*	1	*30 Jun 73*	10
MY FRIEND STAN	*Polydor*	2	*6 Oct 73*	8
MERRY XMAS EVERYBODY	*Polydor*	1	*15 Dec 73*	9
EVERYDAY	*Polydor*	3	*6 Apr 74*	7
THE BANGIN MAN	*Polydor*	3	*6 Jul 74*	7
FAR FAR AWAY	*Polydor*	2	*19 Oct 74*	6
HOW DOES IT FEEL?	*Polydor*	15	*15 Feb 75*	7

Above 2 from the film 'Slade In Flame'.

THANKS FOR THE MEMORY (WHAM BAM THANK YOU MAM)	*Polydor*	7	*17 May 75*	7
IN FOR A PENNY	*Polydor*	11	*22 Nov 75*	8
LET'S CALL IT QUITS	*Polydor*	11	*7 Feb 76*	7
GYPSY ROADHOG	*Barn*	48	*5 Feb 77*	2
MY BABY LEFT ME/THAT'S ALL RIGHT [M]	*Barn*	32	*29 Oct 77*	4
SLADE – ALIVE AT READING '80 [EP]	*Cheapskate*	44	*18 Oct 80*	5

Lead track: When I'm Dancin' I Ain't Fightin'.

MERRY XMAS EVERYBODY [RR]	*Cheapskate*	70	*27 Dec 80*	2

Above 2 are live recordings from the Reading Rock Festival, Aug 80.
Above hit: SLADE and the READING CHOIR.

WE'LL BRING THE HOUSE DOWN	*Cheapskate*	10	*31 Jan 81*	9
WHEELS AIN'T COMING DOWN	*Cheapskate*	60	*4 Apr 81*	3
LOCK UP YOUR DAUGHTERS	*RCA*	29	*19 Sep 81*	8
MERRY XMAS EVERYBODY [RE-1ST]	*Polydor*	32	*19 Dec 81*	4
RUBY RED	*RCA*	51	*27 Mar 82*	3
(AND NOW – THE WALTZ) C'EST LA VIE	*RCA*	50	*27 Nov 82*	6
MERRY XMAS EVERYBODY [RE-2ND]	*Polydor*	67	*25 Dec 82*	3
MY OH MY	*RCA*	2	*19 Nov 83*	11
MERRY XMAS EVERYBODY [RE-3RD]	*Polydor*	20	*10 Dec 83*	5
RUN RUNAWAY	*RCA*	7	*4 Feb 84*	10
ALL JOIN HANDS	*RCA*	15	*17 Nov 84*	9
MERRY XMAS EVERYBODY [RE-4TH]	*Polydor*	47	*15 Dec 84*	4
7 YEAR BITCH	*RCA*	60	*26 Jan 85*	3
MYZSTERIOUS MIZSTER JONES	*RCA*	50	*23 Mar 85*	5
DO YOU BELIEVE IN MIRACLES	*RCA*	54	*30 Nov 85*	6
MERRY XMAS EVERYBODY [RI]	*Polydor*	48	*21 Dec 85*	3
MERRY XMAS EVERYBODY [RI] [RE]	*Polydor*	71	*27 Dec 86*	1
STILL THE SAME	*RCA*	73	*21 Feb 87*	2
RADIO WALL OF SOUND	*Polydor*	21	*19 Oct 91*	5

Backing DJ vocals from Mike Read.

MERRY XMAS EVERYBODY '98 [RM]	*Polydor*	30	*26 Dec 98*	3

Though labelled as a remix by Stefan Runqvist and Sven Oslen (aka Flush), the only vocals come
from the chorus of the original.
Above hit: SLADE vs. FLUSH.

ALBUMS:	HITS 17			WEEKS 212
SLADE ALIVE!	*Polydor*	2	*8 Apr 72*	58

Live recordings from the Command Theatre Studio.

| SLAYED? | Polydor | 1 | 9 Dec 72 | 34 |
| SLADEST | Polydor | 1 | 6 Oct 73 | 24 |

Compilation.

OLD NEW BORROWED AND BLUE	Polydor	1	23 Feb 74	16
SLADE IN FLAME [OST]	Polydor	6	14 Dec 74	18
NOBODY'S FOOL	Polydor	14	27 Mar 76	4
SLADE SMASHES	Polydor	21	22 Nov 80	15
WE'LL BRING THE HOUSE DOWN	Cheapskate	25	21 Mar 81	4
TILL DEAF US DO PART	RCA	68	28 Nov 81	2
SLADE ON STAGE	RCA	58	18 Dec 82	3

Live recordings.

THE AMAZING KAMIKAZE SYNDROME	RCA	49	24 Dec 83	13
SLADE'S GREATZ	Polydor	89	9 Jun 84	1
ROGUES GALLERY	RCA	60	6 Apr 85	2
"CRACKERS" - THE SLADE CHRISTMAS PARTY ALBUM	Telstar	34	30 Nov 85	7
YOU BOYZ MAKE BIG NOIZE	RCA	98	9 May 87	1

Named after a comment made by the tea lady at the recording studio.

| WALL OF HITS | Polydor | 34 | 23 Nov 91 | 5 |
| GREATEST HITS - FEEL THE NOIZE | Polydor | 19 | 25 Jan 97 | 5 |

SLAMM   UK

SINGLES:	HITS 4			WEEKS 6
ENERGIZE	PWL International	57	17 Jul 93	2
VIRGINIA PLAIN	PWL International	60	23 Oct 93	1
THAT'S WHERE MY MIND GOES	PWL International	68	22 Oct 94	1
CAN'T GET BY	PWL International	47	4 Feb 95	2

SLARTA JOHN – See BASEMENT JAXX

SLASH'S SNAKEPIT   US

(See also Michael Jackson.)

ALBUMS:	HITS 1			WEEKS 4
IT'S FIVE O'CLOCK SOMEWHERE	Geffen	15	25 Feb 95	4

SLAUGHTER   US

SINGLES:	HITS 2			WEEKS 2
UP ALL NIGHT	Chrysalis	62	29 Sep 90	1
FLY TO THE ANGELS	Chrysalis	55	2 Feb 91	1
ALBUMS:	**HITS 1**			**WEEKS 1**
THE WILD LIFE	Chrysalis	64	23 May 92	1

SLAVE   US

SINGLES:	HITS 1			WEEKS 3
JUST A TOUCH OF LOVE	Atlantic	64	8 Mar 80	3

Martin SLAVIN ORCHESTRA – See Helen SHAPIRO

SLAYER   US

SINGLES:	HITS 3			WEEKS 3
CRIMINALLY INSANE	London	64	13 Jun 87	1
SEASONS IN THE ABYSS	Def American	51	26 Oct 91	1
SERENITY IN MURDER	American Recordings	50	9 Sep 95	1
ALBUMS:	**HITS 7**			**WEEKS 20**
REIGN IN BLOOD	London	47	2 May 87	3
SOUTH OF HEAVEN	London	25	23 Jul 88	4
SEASONS IN THE ABYSS	Def American	18	6 Oct 90	3
DECADE OF AGGRESSION - LIVE	Def American	29	2 Nov 91	2
DIVINE INTERVENTION	American Recordings	15	15 Oct 94	4
UNDISPUTED ATTITUDE	American Recordings	31	1 Jun 96	2

Consists mainly of punk rock covers.

| DIABOLUS IN MUSICA | American Recordings | 27 | 20 Jun 98 | 2 |

SLEAZESISTERS   UK

SINGLES:	HITS 3			WEEKS 3
SEX	Pulse 8	53	29 Jul 95	1

Vocals by Jeanie Tracy.

| LET'S WHIP IT UP (YOU GO GIRL) | Pulse 8 | 46 | 30 Mar 96 | 1 |

Above 2: SLEAZESISTERS with Vikki SHEPARD.

| WORK IT UP | Logic | 74 | 26 Sep 98 | 1 |

Kathy SLEDGE   US

(See also Sister Sledge.)

SINGLES:	HITS 3			WEEKS 7
TAKE ME BACK TO LOVE AGAIN	Epic	62	16 May 92	2

ANOTHER STAR	NRC	54	18 Feb 95	1
FREEDOM	Deconstruction	15	29 Nov 97	4
Above hit: Robert MILES featuring Kathy SLEDGE.				

Percy SLEDGE · US

SINGLES:	HITS 2		WEEKS 34	
WHEN A MAN LOVES A WOMAN	Atlantic	4	14 May 66	17
WARM AND TENDER LOVE	Atlantic	34	6 Aug 66	7
WHEN A MAN LOVES A WOMAN [RI]	Atlantic	2	14 Feb 87	10
Featured in the Levi's 501 Jeans commercial.				
ALBUMS:	**HITS 1**		**WEEKS 4**	
WHEN A MAN LOVES A WOMAN (THE ULTIMATE COLLECTION)	Atlantic	36	14 Mar 87	4

SLEEPER · UK

SINGLES:	HITS 9		WEEKS 29	
DELICIOUS	Indolent	75	21 May 94	1
INBETWEENER	Indolent	16	21 Jan 95	4
VEGAS	Indolent	33	8 Apr 95	3
WHAT DO I DO NOW?	Indolent	14	7 Oct 95	4
SALE OF THE CENTURY	Indolent	10	4 May 96	5
NICE GUY EDDIE	Indolent	10	13 Jul 96	5
STATUESQUE	Indolent	17	5 Oct 96	3
SHE'S A GOOD GIRL	Indolent	28	4 Oct 97	2
ROMEO ME	Indolent	39	6 Dec 97	2
ALBUMS:	**HITS 3**		**WEEKS 48**	
SMART	Indolent	5	25 Feb 95	11
THE IT GIRL	Indolent	5	18 May 96	34
PLEASED TO MEET YOU	Indolent	7	25 Oct 97	3

SLEIGHRIDERS · UK

ALBUMS:	HITS 1		WEEKS 1	
A VERY MERRY DISCO	Warwick	100	17 Dec 83	1

SLICK · US

SINGLES:	HITS 2		WEEKS 15	
SPACE BASS	Fantasy	16	16 Jun 79	10
SEXY CREAM	Fantasy	47	15 Sep 79	5
Above hit: SLICK (featuring Doris JAMES).				

Grace SLICK · US

SINGLES:	HITS 1		WEEKS 4	
DREAMS	RCA	50	24 May 80	4
ALBUMS:	**HITS 1**		**WEEKS 6**	
DREAMS	RCA	28	31 May 80	6

SLICK RICK – See Montell JORDAN; Al B SURE!

SLIK · UK

SINGLES:	HITS 2		WEEKS 18	
FOREVER AND EVER	Bell	1	17 Jan 76	9
Originally recorded by Kenny.				
REQUIEM	Bell	24	8 May 76	9
ALBUMS:	**HITS 1**		**WEEKS 1**	
SLIK	Bell	58	12 Jun 76	1

SLIM CHANCE – See Ronnie LANE and the Band SLIM CHANCE

SLIPKNOT · US

ALBUMS:	HITS 1		WEEKS 1	
SLIPKNOT	Roadrunner	37	10 Jul 99	1

SLIPSTREEM · UK

SINGLES:	HITS 1		WEEKS 7	
WE ARE RAVING - THE ANTHEM	Boogie Food	18	19 Dec 92	7
Based on Rod Stewart's Sailing.				

SLITS · UK

SINGLES:	HITS 1		WEEKS 3	
TYPICAL GIRLS /I HEARD IT THROUGH THE GRAPEVINE	Island	60	13 Oct 79	3
ALBUMS:	**HITS 1**		**WEEKS 5**	
CUT	Island	30	22 Sep 79	5

SLO MOSHUN | | | | UK

SINGLES:		HITS 2			WEEKS 4	
BELLS OF NY	Six6		29	5 Feb 94		3
HELP MY FRIEND	Six6		52	30 Jul 94		1

P.F. SLOAN | | | | US

SINGLES:		HITS 1			WEEKS 3	
SINS OF THE FAMILY	RCA Victor		38	6 Nov 65		3

SLOWDIVE | | | | UK

SINGLES:		HITS 2			WEEKS 2	
CATCH THE BREEZE / SHINE	Creation		52	15 Jun 91		1
OUTSIDE YOUR ROOM [EP]	Creation		69	29 May 93		1

Lead track: Outside Your Room.

ALBUMS:		HITS 2			WEEKS 3	
JUST FOR A DAY	Creation		32	14 Sep 91		2
SOUVLAKI	Creation		51	12 Jun 93		1

SL2 | | | | UK

SINGLES:		HITS 3			WEEKS 25	
DJS TAKE CONTROL / WAY IN MY BRAIN	XL Recordings		11	2 Nov 91		5
DJS TAKE CONTROL / WAY IN MY BRAIN [RE]	XL Recordings		71	4 Jan 92		1
ON A RAGGA TIP	XL Recordings		2	18 Apr 92		11
WAY IN MY BRAIN [RM] / DRUMBEATS	XL Recordings		26	19 Dec 92		6
ON A RAGGA TIP '97 [RM]	XL Recordings		31	15 Feb 97		2

Remixed by Goodfello's.

SLY and the FAMILY STONE | | | | US

SINGLES:		HITS 5			WEEKS 42	
DANCE TO THE MUSIC	Direction		7	13 Jul 68		14
M'LADY	Direction		32	5 Oct 68		7
EVERYDAY PEOPLE	Direction		36	22 Mar 69		1
EVERYDAY PEOPLE [RE]	Direction		37	12 Apr 69		4
FAMILY AFFAIR	Epic		15	8 Jan 72		8
RUNNIN' AWAY	Epic		17	15 Apr 72		8

ALBUMS:		HITS 1			WEEKS 2	
THERE'S A RIOT GOIN' ON	Epic		31	5 Feb 72		2

SLY FOX | | | | US

SINGLES:		HITS 1			WEEKS 16	
LET'S GO ALL THE WAY	Capitol		3	31 May 86		16

SLY and ROBBIE | | | | Jamaica

SINGLES:		HITS 4			WEEKS 32	
SMILE	Germain		14	5 Jul 86		9

Above hit: Audrey HALL featuring Sly DUNBAR and Robert SHAKESPEARE.

BOOPS (HERE TO GO)	Fourth & Broadway		12	4 Apr 87		11
FIRE	Fourth & Broadway		60	25 Jul 87		4
NIGHT NURSE	East West		13	20 Sep 97		8

Originally recorded by Gregory Isaacs in 1982.
Above hit: SLY and ROBBIE featuring SIMPLY RED.

ALBUMS:		HITS 1			WEEKS 5	
RHYTHM KILLERS	Fourth & Broadway		35	9 May 87		5

Heather SMALL – See M PEOPLE

SMALL ADS | | | | UK

SINGLES:		HITS 1			WEEKS 3	
SMALL ADS	Bronze		63	18 Apr 81		3

SMALL FACES | | | | UK

SINGLES:		HITS 12			WEEKS 137	
WHATCHA GONNA DO ABOUT IT?	Decca		14	4 Sep 65		12
SHA-LA-LA-LA-LEE	Decca		3	12 Feb 66		11

Co-written by Kenny Lynch.

HEY GIRL	Decca		10	14 May 66		9
ALL OR NOTHING	Decca		1	13 Aug 66		12
MY MIND'S EYE	Decca		4	19 Nov 66		11

Part of its melody is from the Christmas carol Angels From The Realms Of Glory.

I CAN'T MAKE IT	Decca		26	11 Mar 67		7
HERE COMES THE NICE	Immediate		12	10 Jun 67		10
ITCHYCOO PARK	Immediate		3	12 Aug 67		14
TIN SOLDIER	Immediate		9	9 Dec 67		12

LAZY SUNDAY	*Immediate*	2	*20 Apr 68*	11
THE UNIVERSAL	*Immediate*	16	*13 Jul 68*	11
AFTERGLOW OF YOUR LOVE	*Immediate*	36	*22 Mar 69*	1
ITCHYCOO PARK [RI]	*Immediate*	9	*13 Dec 75*	11
LAZY SUNDAY [RI]	*Immediate*	39	*20 Mar 76*	5
ALBUMS:	**HITS 5**		**WEEKS 67**	
SMALL FACES	*Decca*	3	*14 May 66*	25
FROM THE BEGINNING	*Decca*	17	*17 Jun 67*	5
Compilation.				
SMALL FACES	*Immediate*	21	*1 Jul 67*	17
Both self titled albums are different.				
OGDEN'S NUT GONE FLAKE	*Immediate*	1	*15 Jun 68*	19
Features comedian Stanley Unwin speaking between tracks on one side of the album.				
THE DECCA ANTHOLOGY 1965–1967	*Deram*	66	*11 May 96*	1

SMALLER
UK

SINGLES:	**HITS 2**		**WEEKS 2**	
WASTED	*Better*	72	*28 Sep 96*	1
IS	*Better*	55	*29 Mar 97*	1
Noel Gallagher on guitar.				

SMART E'S
UK

SINGLES:	**HITS 1**		**WEEKS 9**	
SESAME'S TREET	*Suburban Base*	2	*11 Jul 92*	9
Based on the theme from the Children's TV series 'Sesame Street'.				

SMASH MOUTH
US

SINGLES:	**HITS 2**		**WEEKS 9**	
WALKIN' ON THE SUN	*Interscope*	19	*25 Oct 97*	4
ALL STAR	*Interscope*	24	*31 Jul 99*	5
From the film 'Mystery Man'.				

SMASHING PUMPKINS
US

SINGLES:	**HITS 11**		**WEEKS 33**	
I AM ONE	*Hut*	73	*5 Sep 92*	1
CHERUB ROCK	*Hut*	31	*3 Jul 93*	2
TODAY	*Hut*	44	*25 Sep 93*	2
DISARM	*Hut*	11	*5 Mar 94*	3
BULLET WITH BUTTERFLY WINGS	*Virgin*	20	*28 Oct 95*	3
1979	*Hut*	16	*10 Feb 96*	3
TONIGHT, TONIGHT	*Virgin*	7	*18 May 96*	6
THIRTY THREE	*Virgin*	21	*23 Nov 96*	2
THE END IS THE BEGINNING IS THE END	*Warner Brothers*	10	*14 Jun 97*	4
From the film 'Batman And Robin'.				
THE END IS THE BEGINNING IS THE END [RM]	*Warner Brothers*	72	*23 Aug 97*	1
Remixed by Fluke.				
AVA ADORE	*Hut*	11	*30 May 98*	4
PERFECT	*Hut*	24	*19 Sep 98*	2
ALBUMS:	**HITS 3**		**WEEKS 64**	
SIAMESE DREAM	*Hut*	4	*31 Jul 93*	15
MELLON COLLIE AND THE INFINITE SADNESS	*Virgin*	4	*4 Nov 95*	37
Double album, the first is titled Dawn To Dust and the second From Starlight To Twilight.				
ADORE	*Hut*	5	*13 Jun 98*	12

SMELLS LIKE HEAVEN
Italy

SINGLES:	**HITS 1**		**WEEKS 1**	
LONDRES STRUTT	*Deconstruction*	57	*10 Jul 93*	1
Originally an underground dance hit in 1991.				

Allan SMETHURST
UK

EPS:	**HITS 2**		**WEEKS 12**	
THE SINGING POSTMAN	*Ralph*	20	*5 Jun 65*	2
FIRST DELIVERY	*Parlophone*	7	*10 Dec 66*	10

Ann-Marie SMITH
UK

SINGLES:	**HITS 3**		**WEEKS 5**	
MUSIC	*Synthetic*	34	*23 Jan 93*	2
Above hit: FARGETTA and Anne-Marie SMITH.				
ROCKIN' MY BODY	*Media*	31	*18 Mar 95*	2
Above hit: 49ERS featuring Ann-Marie SMITH.				
(YOU'RE MY ONE AND ONLY) TRUE LOVE	*Media*	46	*15 Jul 95*	1

Brian SMITH and his HAPPY PIANO — UK

ALBUMS:		HITS 1		WEEKS 1
PLAY IT AGAIN	Deram	97	19 Sep 81	1

"Fast" Eddie SMITH – See DJ FAST EDDIE; Kenny "Jammin" JASON and "Fast" Eddie SMITH

Elliott SMITH — US

SINGLES:		HITS 2		WEEKS 2
WALTZ #2 (XO)	Dreamworks	52	19 Dec 98	1
BABY BRITAIN	Dreamworks	55	1 May 99	1

Hurricane SMITH — UK

SINGLES:		HITS 3		WEEKS 35
DON'T LET IT DIE	Columbia	2	12 Jun 71	12
OH BABE, WHAT WOULD YOU SAY	Columbia	4	29 Apr 72	16
WHO WAS IT	Columbia	23	2 Sep 72	7

Originally recorded by Gilbert O'Sullivan.

Whistling Jack SMITH — UK

SINGLES:		HITS 1		WEEKS 12
I WAS KAISER BILL'S BATMAN	Deram	5	4 Mar 67	12

Jimmy SMITH — US

SINGLES:		HITS 1		WEEKS 3
GOT MY MOJO WORKING	Verve	48	30 Apr 66	2
GOT MY MOJO WORKING [RE]	Verve	48	21 May 66	1
EPS:		HITS 1		WEEKS 3
SWINGING WITH THE INCREDIBLE JIMMY SMITH	Verve	10	23 Jul 66	1
ALBUMS:		HITS 1		WEEKS 1
GOT MY MOJO WORKING	Verve	19	18 Jun 66	3

Keely SMITH — US

SINGLES:		HITS 1		WEEKS 10
YOU'RE BREAKING MY HEART	Reprise	14	20 Mar 65	10
ALBUMS:		HITS 1		WEEKS 9
LENNON-McCARTNEY SONGBOOK	Reprise	12	16 Jan 65	9

Mandy SMITH — UK

SINGLES:		HITS 1		WEEKS 2
DON'T YOU WANT ME BABY	PWL	59	20 May 89	2

Mark E. SMITH – See D.O.S.E. featuring Mark E. SMITH; INSPIRAL CARPETS

Mel SMITH — UK

(See also Smith and Jones.)

SINGLES:		HITS 2		WEEKS 10
ROCKIN' AROUND THE CHRISTMAS TREE	10 Records	3	5 Dec 87	7

To support Comic Relief Red Nose Day, 5 Feb 88.
Above hit: COMIC RELIEF presents MEL and KIM performed by Kim WILDE and Mel SMITH.

| ANOTHER BLOOMING CHRISTMAS | Epic | 59 | 21 Dec 91 | 3 |

From the animated film 'Father Christmas'.

Muriel SMITH with Wally STOTT and his Orchestra — UK

SINGLES:		HITS 1		WEEKS 17
HOLD ME, THRILL ME, KISS ME	Philips	3	16 May 53	17

O. C. SMITH — US

SINGLES:		HITS 2		WEEKS 23
THE SON OF HICKORY HOLLER'S TRAMP	CBS	2	1 Jun 68	15

Originally recorded by Johnny Darrell.

TOGETHER	Caribou	25	26 Mar 77	8
ALBUMS:		HITS 1		WEEKS 1
HICKORY HOLLER REVISITED	CBS	40	17 Aug 68	1

Patti SMITH GROUP — US

SINGLES:		HITS 3		WEEKS 16
BECAUSE THE NIGHT	Arista	5	29 Apr 78	12

Co-written by Bruce Springsteen.

| PRIVILEGE (SET ME FREE) | Arista | 72 | 19 Aug 78 | 1 |
| FREDERICK | Arista | 63 | 2 Jun 79 | 3 |

ALBUMS:		HITS 4		WEEKS 23	
EASTER	Arista	16	1 Apr 78	14
WAVE	Arista	41	19 May 79	6
DREAM OF LIFE	Arista	70	16 Jul 88	1
GONE AGAIN	Arista	44	13 Jul 96	2

Above 2: Patti SMITH.

Rex SMITH and Rachel SWEET — US

(See also Rachel Sweet.)

SINGLES:		HITS 1		WEEKS 7	
EVERLASTING LOVE	CBS	35	22 Aug 81	7

Richard Jon SMITH — South Africa

SINGLES:		HITS 1		WEEKS 2	
SHE'S THE MASTER (OF THE GAME)	Jive	63	16 Jul 83	2

Roger SMITH CHORALE – See LONDON SYMPHONY ORCHESTRA

Rose SMITH – See DELAKOTA

Steven SMITH and FATHER — UK

ALBUMS:		HITS 1		WEEKS 3	
STEVEN SMITH AND FATHER AND 16 GREAT SONGS	Decca	17	13 May 72	3

Will SMITH — US

SINGLES:		HITS 8		WEEKS 88	
MEN IN BLACK	Columbia	1	16 Aug 97	16
From the film of the same name. Samples Patrice Rushen's Forget Me Nots.				
JUST CRUISIN'	Columbia	23	13 Dec 97	6
Samples Al Johnson's I'm Back For More.				
GETTIN' JIGGY WIT IT	Columbia	3	7 Feb 98	10
Samples Sister Sledge's He's The Greatest Dancer.				
JUST THE TWO OF US	Columbia	2	1 Aug 98	10
Dedicated to his son Tre.				
MIAMI	Columbia	3	5 Dec 98	14
Samples The Whispers' And The Beat Goes On.				
BOY YOU KNOCK ME OUT	MJJ	3	13 Feb 99	8
Samples Bobby Caldwell's What You Won't Do For Love.				
Above hit: Tatyana ALI featuring Will SMITH.				
BOY YOU KNOCK ME OUT [RE]	MJJ	69	15 May 99	1
WILD WILD WEST	Columbia	2	10 Jul 99	16
Samples Stevie Wonder's I Wish. From the film of the same name.				
Above hit: Will SMITH (featuring DRU HILL).				
WILL 2K	Columbia	2	20 Nov 99	7
Based on the Clash's Rock The Casbah.				
Above hit: Will SMITH (featuring K-CI).				

ALBUMS:		HITS 2		WEEKS 76	
BIG WILLIE STYLE	Columbia	11	6 Dec 97	39
BIG WILLIE STYLE [RE]	Columbia	9	5 Dec 98	31
WILLENNIUM	Columbia	10	27 Nov 99	6

SMITH and JONES — UK

(See also Mel Smith.)

ALBUMS:		HITS 1		WEEKS 8	
SCRATCH AND SNIFF	10 Records	62	15 Nov 86	8

SMITHS — UK

SINGLES:		HITS 17		WEEKS 105	
THIS CHARMING MAN	Rough Trade	25	12 Nov 83	12
WHAT DIFFERENCE DOES IT MAKE?	Rough Trade	12	28 Jan 84	9
HEAVEN KNOWS I'M MISERABLE NOW	Rough Trade	10	2 Jun 84	8
WILLIAM, IT WAS REALLY NOTHING	Rough Trade	17	1 Sep 84	6
HOW SOON IS NOW?	Rough Trade	24	9 Feb 85	6
SHAKESPEARE'S SISTER	Rough Trade	26	30 Mar 85	4
THAT JOKE ISN'T FUNNY ANYMORE	Rough Trade	49	13 Jul 85	3
THE BOY WITH THE THORN IN HIS SIDE	Rough Trade	23	5 Oct 85	5
BIG MOUTH STRIKES AGAIN	Rough Trade	26	31 May 86	4
PANIC	Rough Trade	11	2 Aug 86	8
ASK	Rough Trade	14	1 Nov 86	5
SHOPLIFTERS OF THE WORLD UNITE	Rough Trade	12	7 Feb 87	4
SHEILA TAKE A BOW	Rough Trade	10	25 Apr 87	5
GIRLFRIEND IN A COMA	Rough Trade	13	22 Aug 87	5
I STARTED SOMETHING I COULDN'T FINISH	Rough Trade	23	14 Nov 87	4
LAST NIGHT I DREAMT THAT SOMEBODY LOVED ME	Rough Trade	30	19 Dec 87	4
THIS CHARMING MAN [RI]	WEA	8	15 Aug 92	5

HOW SOON IS NOW? [RI]	*WEA*	16	*12 Sep 92*	4
THERE IS A LIGHT THAT NEVER GOES OUT	*WEA*	25	*24 Oct 92*	3

Originally from their 1986 album, The Queen Is Dead.

ASK [RI]	*WEA*	62	*18 Feb 95*	1
ALBUMS:	**HITS 11**			**WEEKS 199**
THE SMITHS	*Rough Trade*	2	*3 Mar 84*	33
HATFUL OF HOLLOW	*Rough Trade*	7	*24 Nov 84*	46

BBC radio sessions and B-sides.

MEAT IS MURDER	*Rough Trade*	1	*23 Feb 85*	13
THE QUEEN IS DEAD	*Rough Trade*	2	*28 Jun 86*	22
THE WORLD WON'T LISTEN	*Rough Trade*	2	*7 Mar 87*	15

Compilation.

LOUDER THAN BOMBS	*Rough Trade*	38	*30 May 87*	5

Import compilation.

STRANGEWAYS, HERE WE COME	*Rough Trade*	2	*10 Oct 87*	17
RANK	*Rough Trade*	2	*17 Sep 88*	7

Live recordings from the National Ballroom, Kilburn, London, Oct 86.

BEST . . . I	*WEA*	1	*29 Aug 92*	9
BEST . . . II	*WEA*	29	*14 Nov 92*	5
SINGLES	*WEA*	5	*4 Mar 95*	8
HATFUL OF HOLLOW [RI]	*WEA*	26	*4 Mar 95*	3
THE QUEEN IS DEAD [RI]	*WEA*	30	*4 Mar 95*	4
STRANGEWAYS, HERE WE COME [RI]	*WEA*	38	*4 Mar 95*	4
MEAT IS MURDER [RI]	*WEA*	39	*4 Mar 95*	2
THE SMITHS [RI]	*WEA*	42	*4 Mar 95*	4
THE WORLD WON'T LISTEN [RI]	*WEA*	52	*4 Mar 95*	2

Above 5 were re-issued at mid-price.

SMOKE — UK

SINGLES:	**HITS 1**			**WEEKS 3**
MY FRIEND JACK	*Columbia*	45	*11 Mar 67*	3

SMOKE CITY — UK/Brazil

SINGLES:	**HITS 1**			**WEEKS 5**
UNDERWATER LOVE	*Jive*	4	*12 Apr 97*	5

Featured in the Levi's Jeans TV commercial.

SMOKIE — UK

SINGLES:	**HITS 13**			**WEEKS 125**
IF YOU THINK YOU KNOW HOW TO LOVE ME	*RAK*	3	*19 Jul 75*	9
DON'T PLAY YOUR ROCK 'N' ROLL TO ME	*RAK*	8	*4 Oct 75*	7

Above 2: SMOKEY.

SOMETHING'S BEEN MAKING ME BLUE	*RAK*	17	*31 Jan 76*	8
I'LL MEET YOU AT MIDNIGHT	*RAK*	11	*25 Sep 76*	9
LIVING NEXT DOOR TO ALICE	*RAK*	5	*4 Dec 76*	11

Originally recorded by New World.

LAY BACK IN THE ARMS OF SOMEONE	*RAK*	12	*19 Mar 77*	9
IT'S YOUR LIFE	*RAK*	5	*16 Jul 77*	9
NEEDLES AND PINS	*RAK*	10	*15 Oct 77*	9
FOR A FEW DOLLARS MORE	*RAK*	17	*28 Jan 78*	6
OH CAROL	*RAK*	5	*20 May 78*	13
MEXICAN GIRL	*RAK*	19	*23 Sep 78*	9
TAKE GOOD CARE OF MY BABY	*RAK*	34	*19 Apr 80*	7
LIVING NEXT DOOR TO ALICE (WHO THE F**K IS ALICE?) [RR]	*N.O.W.*	64	*13 May 95*	2

Altered lyrics to the original. Proceeds to the family of Alan Barton who was lead singer at the time of his death in Mar of that year.
Above hit: SMOKIE featuring Roy Chubby BROWN.

LIVING NEXT DOOR TO ALICE (WHO THE F**K IS ALICE?) [RR] [RE]	*N.O.W.*	3	*26 Aug 95*	17
ALBUMS:	**HITS 4**			**WEEKS 42**
SMOKIE/CHANGING ALL THE TIME	*RAK*	18	*1 Nov 75*	5
GREATEST HITS	*RAK*	6	*30 Apr 77*	22
THE MONTREUX ALBUM	*RAK*	52	*4 Nov 78*	2
SMOKIE'S HITS	*RAK*	23	*11 Oct 80*	13

SMOKIN BEATS featuring Lyn EDEN — UK

SINGLES:	**HITS 1**			**WEEKS 3**
DREAMS	*AM:PM*	23	*17 Jan 98*	3

SMOKIN' MOJO FILTERS — UK/US

SINGLES:	**HITS 1**			**WEEKS 5**
COME TOGETHER (WAR CHILD)	*Go! Discs*	19	*23 Dec 95*	5

Charity record to support aid for the children of Bosnia.

SMOOTH | | | | US

SINGLES:		HITS 5			WEEKS 7
MIND BLOWIN'	Jive		36	22 Jul 95	2
IT'S SUMMERTIME (LET IT GET INTO YOU)	Jive		46	7 Oct 95	1
LOVE GROOVE (GROOVE WITH YOU)	Jive		46	16 Mar 96	1
WE GOT IT	MCA		26	16 Mar 96	2
Above hit: IMMATURE (featuring SMOOTH).					
UNDERCOVER LOVER	Jive		41	6 Jul 96	1

C.L. SMOOTH – See Pete ROCK and C.L. SMOOTH

Joe SMOOTH | | | | US

SINGLES:		HITS 1			WEEKS 4
PROMISED LAND	DJ International		56	4 Feb 89	4

SMOOTH TOUCH | | | | US

SINGLES:		HITS 1			WEEKS 1
HOUSE OF LOVE (IN MY HOUSE)	Six6		58	2 Apr 94	1

SMURFS | | | | Holland

SINGLES:		HITS 5			WEEKS 52
THE SMURF SONG	Decca		2	3 Jun 78	17
DIPPETY DAY	Decca		13	30 Sep 78	12
Above 2: FATHER ABRAHAM.					
CHRISTMAS IN SMURFLAND	Decca		19	2 Dec 78	7
Above hit: FATHER ABRAHAM and the SMURFS.					
I'VE GOT A LITTLE PUPPY	EMI TV		4	7 Sep 96	10
Based on Techohead's I Want To Be A Hippy.					
YOUR CHRISTMAS WISH	EMI TV		8	21 Dec 96	6
ALBUMS:		HITS 6			WEEKS 77
FATHER ABRAHAM IN SMURFLAND	Decca		19	25 Nov 78	11
Above hit: FATHER ABRAHAM and the SMURFS.					
THE SMURFS GO POP!	EMI TV		2	6 Jul 96	33
SMURF'S CHRISTMAS PARTY	EMI TV		8	16 Nov 96	9
Alternative versions of Xmas classics.					
THE SMURFS HITS '97 – VOLUME 1	EMI TV		2	22 Feb 97	11
GO POP! AGAIN	EMI		15	6 Sep 97	7
GREATEST HITS	EMI		28	18 Apr 98	6

Patty SMYTH with Don HENLEY | | | | US

(See also Don Henley.)

SINGLES:		HITS 1			WEEKS 6
SOMETIMES LOVE JUST AIN'T ENOUGH	MCA		22	3 Oct 92	6

SNAKEBITE | | | | Italy

SINGLES:		HITS 1			WEEKS 2
THE BIT GOES ON	Multiply		25	9 Aug 97	2

SNAP! | | | | US/Germany

SINGLES:		HITS 14			WEEKS 115
THE POWER	Arista		1	24 Mar 90	15
Samples Loleatta Holloway's Love's Gonna Get You.					
OOOPS UP	Arista		5	16 Jun 90	12
CULT OF SNAP	Arista		8	22 Sep 90	7
MARY HAD A LITTLE BOY	Arista		8	8 Dec 90	10
SNAP MEGAMIX [M]	Arista		10	30 Mar 91	6
COLOUR OF LOVE	Arista		54	21 Dec 91	3
RHYTHM IS A DANCER	Logic		1	4 Jul 92	19
Features vocals by Thea Austin.					
EXTERMINATE!	Logic		2	9 Jan 93	11
DO YOU SEE THE LIGHT (LOOKING FOR)	Logic		10	12 Jun 93	8
Above 2: SNAP! featuring Niki HARIS.					
WELCOME TO TOMORROW (ARE YOU READY?)	Arista		6	17 Sep 94	13
WELCOME TO TOMORROW (ARE YOU READY?) [RE]	Arista		75	14 Jan 95	1
THE FIRST THE LAST ETERNITY (TIL THE END)	Arista		15	1 Apr 95	7
THE WORLD IN MY HANDS	Arista		44	28 Oct 95	1
Above 4: SNAP! featuring SUMMER.					
RAME	Arista		50	13 Apr 96	1
Above hit: SNAP! featuring 'RUKMANI'.					
THE POWER 96 [RR]	Arista		42	24 Aug 96	1
Above hit: SNAP! featuring EINSTEIN.					
ALBUMS:		HITS 4			WEEKS 56
WORLD POWER	Arista		21	26 May 90	23
WORLD POWER [RE]	Arista		10	22 Dec 90	16

THE MADMAN'S RETURN	Logic	20	8 Aug 92	8
THE MADMAN'S RETURN [RE]	Logic	8	13 Feb 93	7
Repackaged from 20 Feb 93.				
WELCOME TO TOMORROW	Ariola	69	15 Oct 94	1
SNAP! ATTACK - THE BEST OF SNAP! / SNAP! ATTACK - THE REMIXES	Ariola	47	7 Sep 96	1
Available as either a single album or double album including the remixes.				

SNEAKER PIMPS

UK

SINGLES:	HITS 5		WEEKS 19	
6 UNDERGROUND	Clean Up	15	19 Oct 96	4
SPIN SPIN SUGAR	Clean Up	21	15 Mar 97	3
SIX UNDERGROUND [RI]	Clean Up	9	7 Jun 97	4
From the film 'The Saint'.				
POST MODERN SLEAZE	Clean Up	22	30 Aug 97	3
SPIN SPIN SUGAR [RM]	Clean Up	46	7 Feb 98	2
Remixed by Armand Van Helden.				
LOW FIVE	Clean Up	39	21 Aug 99	2
TEN TO TWENTY	Clean Up	56	30 Oct 99	1
ALBUMS:	HITS 1		WEEKS 7	
BECOMING X	Clean Up	72	31 Aug 96	1
BECOMING X [RE]	Clean Up	27	21 Jun 97	6

SNIFF N' THE TEARS

UK

SINGLES:	HITS 1		WEEKS 5	
DRIVER'S SEAT	Chiswick	42	23 Jun 79	5

SNIFFLE GROUP – See Stan FREBERG

Miss SNOBB and CLASS 3C – See WIZZARD

SNOOP DOGGY DOGG

US

SINGLES:	HITS 9		WEEKS 31	
WHAT'S MY NAME?	Death Row	20	4 Dec 93	8
GIN AND JUICE	Death Row	39	12 Feb 94	3
Samples Watching You by Slave.				
DOGGY DOGG WORLD	Death Row	32	20 Aug 94	3
Features backing vocals by the Dramatics.				
SNOOP'S UPSIDE YA HEAD	Interscope	12	14 Dec 96	7
Above hit: SNOOP DOGGY DOGG featuring Charlie WILSON.				
WANTED DEAD OR ALIVE	Def Jam	16	26 Apr 97	3
From the film 'Gridlock'd'.				
Above hit: 2 PAC and SNOOP DOGGY DOGG.				
VAPORS	Interscope	18	3 May 97	2
Original was by rapper Biz Markie.				
Above hit: SNOOP DOGGY DOGG featuring Charlie WILSON and Teena MARIE.				
WE JUST WANNA PARTY WITH YOU	Columbia	21	20 Sep 97	2
From the film 'Men In Black'.				
Above hit: SNOOP DOGGY DOGG featuring JD.				
THA DOGGFATHER	Interscope	36	24 Jan 98	2
Above hit: SNOOP DOGGY DOGG.				
COME AND GET WITH ME	Elektra	58	12 Dec 98	1
Above hit: Keith SWEAT featuring SNOOP DOGG.				
ALBUMS:	HITS 4		WEEKS 42	
DOGGYSTYLE	Death Row	38	11 Dec 93	27
THA DOGGFATHER	Interscope	15	23 Nov 96	11
DA GAMES IS TO BE SOLD, NOT TO BE TOLD	Priority	28	15 Aug 98	3
TOP DOGG	Priority	48	5 Jun 99	1
Above 2: SNOOP DOGG.				

Sid SNOTT – See Kenny EVERETT

SNOW

Canada

SINGLES:	HITS 3		WEEKS 18	
INFORMER	East West America	2	13 Mar 93	15
GIRL, I'VE BEEN HURT	East West America	48	5 Jun 93	2
UHH IN YOU	Atlantic	67	4 Sep 93	1
ALBUMS:	HITS 1		WEEKS 4	
12 INCHES OF SNOW	East West America	41	17 Apr 93	4

Mark SNOW

UK

SINGLES:	HITS 1		WEEKS 15	
THE X FILES	Warner Brothers	2	30 Mar 96	15
Theme from the TV series of the same name.				
ALBUMS:	HITS 1		WEEKS 2	
TRUTH AND THE LIGHT: MUSIC FROM THE X-FILES	Warner Brothers	42	12 Oct 96	2
Includes themes used in the X-Files interspersed with dialogue.				

Phoebe SNOW US

SINGLES:		HITS 1			WEEKS 7
EVERY NIGHT	CBS		37	6 Jan 79	7

Originally recorded by Paul McCartney.

SNOWMAN UK

(See also Howard Blake conducting the Sinfonia Of London, narration: Bernard Cribbins; Digital Dream Baby.)

SINGLES:		HITS 1			WEEKS 9
WALKING IN THE AIR	Stiff		42	14 Dec 85	5

Original release reached No. 99 in 1984.
Above hit: SNOWMAN featuring Peter AUTY.

WALKING IN THE AIR (FROM THE SNOWMAN) [RI]	CBS		37	19 Dec 87	4

Peter Auty is not credited on this issue.

SNOWMEN UK

SINGLES:		HITS 2			WEEKS 12
HOKEY COKEY	Slack		18	12 Dec 81	8
XMAS PARTY [M]	Solid		44	18 Dec 82	4

SNUG UK

SINGLES:		HITS 1			WEEKS 1
BEATNIK GIRL	WEA		55	18 Apr 98	1

SO UK

SINGLES:		HITS 1			WEEKS 3
ARE YOU SURE	Parlophone		62	13 Feb 88	3

SOAPY UK

SINGLES:		HITS 1			WEEKS 2
HORNY AS FUNK	WEA		35	14 Sep 96	2

Gino SOCCIO Canada

SINGLES:		HITS 1			WEEKS 5
DANCER	Warner Brothers		46	28 Apr 79	5

SOEUR SOURIRE – See SINGING NUN (SOEUR SOURIRE)

SOFT CELL UK

SINGLES:		HITS 10			WEEKS 107
TAINTED LOVE	Some Bizzare		1	1 Aug 81	16

Originally recorded by Gloria Jones in 1964.

BEDSITTER	Some Bizzare		4	14 Nov 81	12
TAINTED LOVE [RE-1ST]	Some Bizzare		43	9 Jan 82	10
SAY HELLO WAVE GOODBYE	Some Bizzare		3	6 Feb 82	9
TORCH	Some Bizzare		2	29 May 82	9
TAINTED LOVE [RE-2ND]	Some Bizzare		50	24 Jul 82	4
WHAT	Some Bizzare		3	21 Aug 82	8

Originally recorded by Judy Street in 1978.

WHERE THE HEART IS	Some Bizzare		21	4 Dec 82	7
NUMBERS / BARRIERS	Some Bizzare		25	5 Mar 83	4
SOUL INSIDE	Some Bizzare		16	24 Sep 83	5
DOWN IN THE SUBWAY	Some Bizzare		24	25 Feb 84	6

Originally recorded by Jack Hammer.

TAINTED LOVE [RE-3RD]	Some Bizzare		43	9 Feb 85	6
SAY HELLO WAVE GOODBYE '91 [RR]	Mercury		38	23 Mar 91	3
TAINTED LOVE [RI]	Mercury		5	18 May 91	8

Above 2: SOFT CELL Marc ALMOND.

ALBUMS:		HITS 6			WEEKS 101
NON-STOP EROTIC CABARET	Some Bizzare		5	12 Dec 81	46
NON-STOP ECSTATIC DANCING	Some Bizzare		6	26 Jun 82	18

Dance remixes of tracks from their previous album.

THE ART OF FALLING APART	Some Bizzare		5	22 Jan 83	10
THIS LAST NIGHT IN SODOM	Some Bizzare		12	31 Mar 84	5
THE SINGLES ALBUM	Some Bizzare		58	20 Dec 86	9
MEMORABILIA – THE SINGLES	Mercury		8	1 Jun 91	13

Includes both Almond's solo and group material.
Above hit: SOFT CELL Marc ALMOND.

SOFT MACHINE UK

ALBUMS:		HITS 2			WEEKS 8
THIRD	CBS		18	4 Jul 70	6
FOURTH	CBS		32	3 Apr 71	2

824

SOHO

		UK		
SINGLES:	HITS 2		WEEKS 11	
HIPPYCHICK	S&M	67	5 May 90	1
Samples How Soon is Now by the Smiths.				
HIPPYCHICK [RE]	S&M	8	19 Jan 91	8
BORN TO BE ALIVE!	MCA	51	9 Nov 91	2
[AA] listed with Never Goin' Down (Incorporating Future Freak) by Adamski + Jimi Polo.				
Above hit: ADAMSKI + SOHO.				

SOLAR STONE

		UK		
SINGLES:	HITS 2		WEEKS 3	
THE IMPRESSIONS [EP]	Hooj Choons	75	21 Feb 98	1
Lead track: The Calling.				
SEVEN CITIES	Hooj Choons	39	6 Nov 99	2

SOLID GOLD CHARTBUSTERS

		UK		
SINGLES:	HITS 1		WEEKS 1	
I WANNA 1-2-1 WITH YOU	Virgin	62	25 Dec 99	1
Based around the Grand Valse mobile phone ringing tone.				

SOLID HARMONIE

		UK/US		
SINGLES:	HITS 4		WEEKS 11	
I'LL BE THERE FOR YOU	Jive	18	31 Jan 98	3
I WANT YOU TO WANT ME	Jive	16	18 Apr 98	3
I WANNA LOVE YOU	Jive	20	15 Aug 98	4
TO LOVE ONCE AGAIN	Jive	55	21 Nov 98	1

SOLID SENDERS

		UK		
ALBUMS:	HITS 1		WEEKS 3	
SOLID SENDERS	Virgin	42	23 Sep 78	3

SOLO

		UK		
SINGLES:	HITS 2		WEEKS 4	
RAINBOW (SAMPLE-FREE)	Reverb	59	20 Jul 91	2
Based on the theme of the Children's ITV programme.				
COME ON!	Reverb	75	18 Jan 92	1
COME ON! [RM]	Stoatin'	63	11 Sep 93	1
Remix has replaced the vocals of Jasmine Rennie with Mary Kiani's.				

SOLO (US)

		US		
SINGLES:	HITS 2		WEEKS 3	
HEAVEN	Perspective	35	3 Feb 96	2
Samples Isley Brothers' Between The Sheets.				
WHERE DO U WANT ME TO PUT IT	Perspective	45	30 Mar 96	1
Above hit: SOLO U.S.				

Sal SOLO

		UK		
SINGLES:	HITS 2		WEEKS 13	
SAN DAMIANO (HEART AND SOUL)	MCA	15	15 Dec 84	10
MUSIC AND YOU	MCA	52	6 Apr 85	3
Above hit: Sal SOLO with the LONDON COMMUNITY GOSPEL CHOIR.				

Diane SOLOMON

		UK		
ALBUMS:	HITS 1		WEEKS 6	
TAKE TWO	Philips	26	9 Aug 75	6

Sir Georg SOLTI and Dudley MOORE

(See also Dudley Moore.)

		UK		
ALBUMS:	HITS 1		WEEKS 5	
ORCHESTRA!	Decca	38	26 Jan 91	5

SOLUTION – See Victor SIMONELLI presents SOLUTION

Belouis SOME

		UK		
SINGLES:	HITS 3		WEEKS 26	
IMAGINATION	Parlophone	50	27 Apr 85	7
IMAGINATION [RI]	Parlophone	17	18 Jan 86	10
SOME PEOPLE	Parlophone	33	12 Apr 86	7
Original release reached No. 83 in 1985.				
LET IT BE WITH YOU	Parlophone	53	16 May 87	2

Glen SOMERS and his Orchestra – See Eve BOSWELL with Glenn SOMERS and his Orchestra

Jimmy SOMERVILLE
UK

(See also Bronski Beat.)

SINGLES:		HITS 9			WEEKS 49
COMMENT TE DIRE ADIEU	London		14	11 Nov 89	9
Originally recorded by Francois Hardy.					
Above hit: Jimmy SOMERVILLE featuring June MILES KINGSTON.					
YOU MAKE ME FEEL (MIGHTY REAL)	London		5	13 Jan 90	8
READ MY LIPS (ENOUGH IS ENOUGH)	London		26	17 Mar 90	6
TO LOVE SOMEBODY	London		8	3 Nov 90	11
RUN FROM LOVE	London		52	10 Aug 91	2
HEARTBEAT	London		24	28 Jan 95	4
HURT SO GOOD	London		15	27 May 95	6
BY YOUR SIDE	London		41	28 Oct 95	2
DARK SKY	Gut		66	13 Sep 97	1
ALBUMS:		**HITS 3**			**WEEKS 42**
READ MY LIPS	London		29	9 Dec 89	14
THE SINGLES COLLECTION 1984/1990	London		4	24 Nov 90	26
Includes his recordings with Bronski Beat and the Communards as well as his own solo material.					
DARE TO LOVE	London		38	24 Jun 95	2

SOMETHIN' FOR THE PEOPLE featuring TRINA and TAMARA
US

(See also Trina and Tamara.)

SINGLES:		HITS 1			WEEKS 1
MY LOVE IS THE SHHH!	Warner Brothers		64	7 Feb 98	1

SOMORE featuring Damon TRUEITT
US

SINGLES:		HITS 1			WEEKS 2
I REFUSE (WHAT YOU WANT)	XL Recordings		21	24 Jan 98	2

SON'Z OF A LOOP DA LOOP ERA
UK

(See also Various Artists (EPs) 'Subplates Volume 1 EP'.)

SINGLES:		HITS 2			WEEKS 4
FAR OUT	Suburban Base		36	15 Feb 92	3
PEACE + LOVEISM	Suburban Base		60	17 Oct 92	1

SONGSTRESS
US

SINGLES:		HITS 1			WEEKS 1
SEE LINE WOMAN '99	Locked On		64	27 Feb 99	1
Samples Nina Simone's See Line Woman.					

SONIA
UK

SINGLES:		HITS 12			WEEKS 78
YOU'LL NEVER STOP ME LOVING YOU	Chrysalis		1	24 Jun 89	13
CAN'T FORGET YOU	Chrysalis		17	7 Oct 89	6
LISTEN TO YOUR HEART	Chrysalis		10	9 Dec 89	10
COUNTING EVERY MINUTE	Chrysalis		16	7 Apr 90	7
YOU'VE GOT A FRIEND	Jive		14	23 Jun 90	6
Charity record in aid of Childline.					
Above hit: BIG FUN and SONIA featuring Gary BARNACLE on saxophone.					
END OF THE WORLD	Chrysalis		18	25 Aug 90	7
ONLY FOOLS (NEVER FALL IN LOVE)	IQ		10	1 Jun 91	8
BE YOUNG, BE FOOLISH, BE HAPPY	IQ		22	31 Aug 91	5
YOU TO ME ARE EVERYTHING	IQ		13	16 Nov 91	5
BOOGIE NIGHTS	Arista		30	12 Sep 92	3
BETTER THE DEVIL YOU KNOW	Arista		15	1 May 93	7
UK's Eurovision entry in 1993, it came 2nd.					
HOPELESSLY DEVOTED TO YOU	Cockney		61	30 Jul 94	1
From the musical 'Grease'.					
ALBUMS:		**HITS 3**			**WEEKS 14**
EVERYBODY KNOWS	Chrysalis		7	5 May 90	10
SONIA	IQ		33	19 Oct 91	2
BETTER THE DEVIL YOU KNOW	Arista		32	29 May 93	2

SONIC BOOM
UK

ALBUMS:		HITS 1			WEEKS 1
SPECTRUM	Silvertone		65	17 Mar 90	1

SONIC The HEDGEHOG – See H.W.A. featuring SONIC The HEDGEHOG

SONIC SOLUTION
UK

SINGLES:		HITS 1			WEEKS 1
BEATSTIME	R&S		59	4 Apr 92	1

826

SONIC SURFERS
Holland

SINGLES:		HITS 2		WEEKS 2	
TAKE ME UP	A&M	61	20 Mar 93	1
Above hit: SONIC SURFERS featuring Jocelyn BROWN.				
DON'T GIVE IT UP	Brilliant	54	30 Jul 94	1

SONIC YOUTH
US

SINGLES:		HITS 6		WEEKS 14	
100%	DGC	28	11 Jul 92	4
YOUTH AGAINST FASCISM	Geffen	52	7 Nov 92	2
SUGAR KANE	Geffen	26	3 Apr 93	3
BULL IN THE HEATHER	Geffen	24	7 May 94	2
SUPERSTAR	A&M	45	10 Sep 94	2
[AA] listed with Yesterday Once More by Redd Kross. From the Various Artists 25th anniversary tribute album to the Carpenters, If I Were A Carpenter.				
SUNDAY	Geffen	72	11 Jul 98	1
ALBUMS:		HITS 8		WEEKS 14	
DAYDREAM NATION	Blast First	99	29 Oct 88	1
THE WHITEY ALBUM	Blast First	63	4 Feb 89	1
Above hit: CICCONE YOUTH.				
"GOO"	DGC	32	7 Jul 90	2
THE DIRTY BOOTS EP - PLUS 5 LIVE TRACKS	DGC	69	4 May 91	1
DIRTY	DGC	6	1 Aug 92	5
EXPERIMENTAL JET SET, TRASH AND NO STAR	Geffen	10	21 May 94	2
WASHING MACHINE	Geffen	39	14 Oct 95	1
A THOUSAND LEAVES	Geffen	38	23 May 98	1

SONIQUE
UK

SINGLES:		HITS 2		WEEKS 5	
I PUT A SPELL ON YOU	Serious	36	13 Jun 98	2
IT FEELS SO GOOD	Serious	24	5 Dec 98	3

SONNY
US

(See also Sonny and Cher.)

SINGLES:		HITS 1		WEEKS 11	
LAUGH AT ME	Atlantic	9	21 Aug 65	11

SONNY and CHER
US

(See Cher; Sonny.)

SINGLES:		HITS 9		WEEKS 78	
I GOT YOU BABE	Atlantic	1	14 Aug 65	12
BABY DON'T GO	Reprise	11	18 Sep 65	9
Originally released earlier in the year.				
BUT YOU'RE MINE	Atlantic	17	23 Oct 65	8
WHAT NOW MY LOVE	Atlantic	13	19 Feb 66	11
HAVE I STAYED TOO LONG	Atlantic	42	2 Jul 66	3
LITTLE MAN	Atlantic	4	10 Sep 66	10
LIVING FOR YOU	Atlantic	44	19 Nov 66	4
THE BEAT GOES ON	Atlantic	29	4 Feb 67	8
ALL I EVER NEED IS YOU	MCA	8	15 Jan 72	12
Originally recorded by Ray Sanders.				
I GOT YOU BABE [RI]	Epic	66	22 May 93	1
From the film 'Groundhog Day'.				
ALBUMS:		HITS 2		WEEKS 20	
LOOK AT US	Atlantic	7	16 Oct 65	13
THE WONDEROUS WORLD OF SONNY AND CHER	Atlantic	15	14 May 66	7

SORROWS
UK

SINGLES:		HITS 1		WEEKS 8	
TAKE A HEART	Piccadilly	21	18 Sep 65	8

David SOUL
US

SINGLES:		HITS 5		WEEKS 56	
DON'T GIVE UP ON US	Private Stock	1	18 Dec 76	16
GOING IN WITH MY EYES OPEN	Private Stock	2	26 Mar 77	8
SILVER LADY	Private Stock	1	27 Aug 77	14
LET'S HAVE A QUIET NIGHT IN	Private Stock	8	17 Dec 77	9
IT SURE BRINGS OUT THE LOVE IN YOUR EYES	Private Stock	12	27 May 78	9
ALBUMS:		HITS 2		WEEKS 51	
DAVID SOUL	Private Stock	2	27 Nov 76	28
PLAYING TO AN AUDIENCE OF ONE	Private Stock	8	17 Sep 77	23

Jimmy SOUL — US

SINGLES:	HITS 1		WEEKS 5	
IF YOU WANNA BE HAPPY	Stateside	39	13 Jul 63	2
IF YOU WANNA BE HAPPY [RI]	Epic	68	15 Jun 91	3

SOUL ASYLUM — US

SINGLES:	HITS 5		WEEKS 33	
RUNAWAY TRAIN	Columbia	37	19 Jun 93	8
SOMEBODY TO SHOVE	Columbia	34	4 Sep 93	3
RUNAWAY TRAIN [RE]	Columbia	7	13 Nov 93	11
BLACK GOLD	Columbia	26	22 Jan 94	4
SOMEBODY TO SHOVE [RI]	Columbia	32	26 Mar 94	3
MISERY	Columbia	30	15 Jul 95	3
JUST LIKE ANYONE	Columbia	52	2 Dec 95	1
ALBUMS:	HITS 2		WEEKS 29	
GRAVE DANCERS UNION	Columbia	27	31 Jul 93	25
LET YOUR DIM LIGHT SHINE	Columbia	22	1 Jul 95	4

SOUL BROTHERS — UK

SINGLES:	HITS 1		WEEKS 3	
I KEEP RINGING MY BABY	Decca	43	24 Apr 65	3

SOUL CITY ORCHESTRA — UK

SINGLES:	HITS 1		WEEKS 1	
IT'S JURASSIC (VERSION OF THE THEME TO JURASSIC PARK)	London	70	11 Dec 93	1

SOUL CITY SYMPHONY – See Van McCOY

SOUL FAMILY SENSATION — UK/US

SINGLES:	HITS 1		WEEKS 4	
I DON'T EVEN KNOW IF I SHOULD CALL YOU BABY	One Little Indian	49	11 May 91	4

SOUL FOR REAL — US

SINGLES:	HITS 2		WEEKS 4	
CANDY RAIN	Uptown	23	8 Jul 95	2
EVERY LITTLE THING I DO	Uptown	31	23 Mar 96	2

SOUL SONIC FORCE – See Afrika BAMBAATAA

SOUL II SOUL — UK

SINGLES:	HITS 15		WEEKS 89	
FAIRPLAY	10 Records	63	21 May 88	3
Above hit: SOUL II SOUL featuring Rose WINDROSS.				
FEEL FREE	10 Records	64	17 Sep 88	2
Above hit: SOUL II SOUL featuring DO'REEN.				
KEEP ON MOVIN'	10 Records	5	18 Mar 89	12
Features the Reggae Philharmonic Orchestra.				
BACK TO LIFE (HOWEVER DO YOU WANT ME)	10 Records	1	10 Jun 89	14
Certain copies did not credit Caron Wheeler on either the sleeve or the label.				
Above 2: SOUL II SOUL featuring Caron WHEELER.				
GET A LIFE	10 Records	3	9 Dec 89	13
The B-side was called Jazzie's Groove, which was also popular.				
A DREAMS A DREAM	10 Records	6	5 May 90	6
Vocals by Victoria Wilson James.				
MISSING YOU	Ten Records	22	24 Nov 90	7
Above hit: SOUL II SOUL (vocals: Kym MAZELLE).				
JOY	Ten Records	4	4 Apr 92	7
Richie Stephens on lead vocals.				
MOVE ME NO MOUNTAIN	Ten Records	31	13 Jun 92	4
Above hit: SOUL II SOUL, Lead vocals by KOFI.				
JUST RIGHT	Ten Records	38	26 Sep 92	2
WISH	Virgin	24	6 Nov 93	4
LOVE ENUFF	Virgin	12	22 Jul 95	6
Vocals by Penny Ford.				
I CARE (SOUL II SOUL)	Virgin	17	21 Oct 95	4
KEEP ON MOVIN' [RI]	Virgin	31	19 Oct 96	2
Featured in the Renault Clio car TV commercial.				
REPRESENT	Island	39	30 Aug 97	2
Vocals by Paul Johnson.				
PLEASURE DOME	Island	51	8 Nov 97	1
ALBUMS:	HITS 5		WEEKS 108	
CLUB CLASSICS VOLUME ONE	10 Records	1	22 Apr 89	60
VOLUME II (1990 A NEW DECADE)	10 Records	1	2 Jun 90	20
VOLUME III JUST RIGHT	Ten Records	3	25 Apr 92	11

| VOLUME IV THE CLASSICS SINGLES 88-93 | Virgin | 10 | 27 Nov 93 | 13 |
| VOLUME V - BELIEVE | Virgin | 13 | 12 Aug 95 | 4 |

SOULED OUT
UK/US/Italy

SINGLES:	HITS 1		WEEKS 1
IN MY LIFE	Columbia	75	9 May 92	1

SOULFLY
US/Brazil

ALBUMS:	HITS 1		WEEKS 2
SOULFLY	Roadrunner	16	2 May 98	2

SOULSEARCHER
US

SINGLES:	HITS 1		WEEKS 7
CAN'T GET ENOUGH	Defected	8	13 Feb 99	7

Vocals by Thea Austin. Samples Gary's Gang's Let Love Dance Tonight.

SOUND FACTORY
Sweden

SINGLES:	HITS 1		WEEKS 1
2 THE RHYTHM	Logic	72	5 Jun 93	1

SOUND 5
UK

SINGLES:	HITS 1		WEEKS 1
ALA KABOO	Gut	69	24 Apr 99	1

SOUND 9418 – See Jonathan KING

SOUND OF ONE featuring GLADEZZ
US

SINGLES:	HITS 1		WEEKS 1
AS I AM	Cooltempo	65	20 Nov 93	1

SOUNDGARDEN
US

SINGLES:	HITS 10		WEEKS 24
JESUS CHRIST POSE	A&M	30	11 Apr 92	3
RUSTY CAGE	A&M	41	20 Jun 92	1
OUTSHINED	A&M	50	21 Nov 92	1
SPOONMAN	A&M	20	26 Feb 94	3

Written about a Seattle resident who has written books on the philosophy of spoon-playing.

THE DAY I TRIED TO LIVE	A&M	42	30 Apr 94	2
BLACK HOLE SUN	A&M	12	20 Aug 94	5
FELL ON BLACK DAYS	A&M	24	28 Jan 95	2
PRETTY NOOSE	A&M	14	18 May 96	3
BURDEN IN MY HAND	A&M	33	28 Sep 96	2
BLOW UP THE OUTSIDE WORLD	A&M	40	28 Dec 96	2
ALBUMS:	**HITS 3**		**WEEKS 32**	
BADMOTORFINGER	A&M	39	25 Apr 92	2
SUPERUNKNOWN	A&M	4	19 Mar 94	24
DOWN ON THE UPSIDE	A&M	7	1 Jun 96	6

SOUNDMAN and Don LLOYDIE with Elisabeth TROY
UK

SINGLES:	HITS 1		WEEKS 2
GREATER LOVE	Sound Of Underground	49	25 Feb 95	2

SOUNDS INCORPORATED
UK

(See also Gene Vincent.)

SINGLES:	HITS 2		WEEKS 11
THE SPARTANS	Columbia	30	25 Apr 64	6
SPANISH HARLEM	Columbia	35	1 Aug 64	5

SOUNDS NICE featuring Tim MYCROFT on organ
UK

SINGLES:	HITS 1		WEEKS 11
LOVE AT FIRST SIGHT (JE T'AIME . . . MOI NON PLUS)	Parlophone	18	6 Sep 69	11

SOUNDS OF BLACKNESS
US

SINGLES:	HITS 7		WEEKS 32
OPTIMISTIC	Perspective	45	22 Jun 91	4
THE PRESSURE PART 1	Perspective	71	28 Sep 91	1
OPTIMISTIC [RI]	Perspective	28	15 Feb 92	4
THE PRESSURE PART 1 [RM-1ST]	Perspective	49	25 Apr 92	2

Remixed by C.J. Macintosh.

I'M GOING ALL THE WAY	Perspective	27	8 May 93	3
I BELIEVE	A&M	17	26 Mar 94	4

GLORYLAND	Mercury	36	2 Jul 94	4

Offical theme song of the 1994 World Cup in the US and used by ITV Sport for their coverage of the games.
Above hit: Daryl HALL and SOUNDS OF BLACKNESS.

EVERYTHING IS GONNA BE ALRIGHT	A&M	29	20 Aug 94	3

Samples Isaac Hayes' Walk On By.

I'M GOING ALL THE WAY [RI]	A&M	14	14 Jan 95	4
SPIRIT	A&M	35	7 Jun 97	2

Above hit: SOUNDS OF BLACKNESS featuring Craig MACK.

THE PRESSURE [RM-2ND]	AM:PM	46	14 Feb 98	1

Remixed by Marc Pomeroy and Brian Tappert.

ALBUMS:	HITS 1		WEEKS 6	
AFRICA TO AMERICA: THE JOURNEY OF THE DRUM	A&M	28	30 Apr 94	6

SOUNDS ORCHESTRAL   UK

SINGLES:	HITS 2		WEEKS 18	
CAST YOUR FATE TO THE WIND	Piccadilly	5	5 Dec 64	16

Original by Vince Guaraldi Trio in 1962, reached No. 22 in the US the following year.

MOONGLOW (INTRODUCING THEME FROM PICNIC)	Piccadilly	43	10 Jul 65	2

ALBUMS:	HITS 1		WEEKS 1	
CAST YOUR FATE TO THE WIND	Piccadilly	17	12 Jun 65	1

SOUNDSATION   UK

SINGLES:	HITS 1		WEEKS 1	
PEACE AND JOY	Ffrreedom	48	14 Jan 95	1

Originally featured a guitar sample from Lenny Kravitz's Are You Gonna Go My Way but clearance was denied.

SOUNDSCAPE   UK

SINGLES:	HITS 1		WEEKS 1	
DUBPLATE CULTURE	Satellite	61	14 Feb 98	1

SOUNDSOURCE   UK/Sweden

SINGLES:	HITS 1		WEEKS 1	
TAKE ME UP	ffrr	62	11 Jan 92	1

SOUP DRAGONS   UK

SINGLES:	HITS 5		WEEKS 23	
CAN'T TAKE NO MORE	Raw TV Products	65	20 Jun 87	1
SOFT AS YOUR FACE	Raw TV Products	66	5 Sep 87	2
I'M FREE	Raw TV Products	5	14 Jul 90	12

Originally recorded by the Rolling Stones.
Above hit: SOUP DRAGONS featuring Junior REID.

MOTHER UNIVERSE	Big Life	26	20 Oct 90	5

Original release reached No. 94 earlier in the year.

DIVINE THING	Big Life	53	11 Apr 92	3

ALBUMS:	HITS 3		WEEKS 17	
THIS IS OUR ART	Siren	60	7 May 88	1
LOVEGOD	Raw TV Products	60	5 May 90	1
LOVEGOD [RE]	Raw TV Products	7	18 Aug 90	14

Re-released with additional track.

HOTWIRED	Big Life	74	16 May 92	1

SOURCE   UK

SINGLES:	HITS 3		WEEKS 22	
YOU GOT THE LOVE	Truelove	4	2 Feb 91	11

Original release reached No. 95 in 1986. Original vocal version of the song was by Jamie Principal and was called Your Love.
Above hit: SOURCE featuring Candi STATON.

ROCK THE HOUSE	Truelove	63	26 Dec 92	1

Above hit: SOURCE vocals by NICOLE.

YOU GOT THE LOVE [RM]	React	3	1 Mar 97	8

Remixed by Now Voyager (AKA John Truelove).
Above hit: SOURCE featuring Candi STATON.

CLOUDS	XL Recordings	38	23 Aug 97	2

Original recording was by Chaka Khan in 1980.

Joe SOUTH   US

SINGLES:	HITS 1		WEEKS 11	
GAMES PEOPLE PLAY	Capitol	6	8 Mar 69	11

SOUTH BANK ORCHESTRA conducted by Joseph MOROVITZ and Laurie HOLLOWAY — UK

ALBUMS:	HITS 1			WEEKS 6
LILLIE [OST-TV]	Sounds	47	2 Dec 78	6

Jeri SOUTHERN — US

SINGLES:	HITS 1			WEEKS 3
FIRE DOWN BELOW	Brunswick	22	22 Jun 57	3

SOUTHERN DEATH CULT – See CULT

SOUTHLANDERS — UK

SINGLES:	HITS 1			WEEKS 10
ALONE	Decca	17	23 Nov 57	10

SOUVLAKI — UK

(See also Mark Summers.)

SINGLES:	HITS 2			WEEKS 4
INFERNO	Wonderboy	24	15 Feb 97	3
MY TIME	Wonderboy	63	8 Aug 98	1

SOVEREIGN COLLECTION — UK

SINGLES:	HITS 1			WEEKS 6
MOZART 40	Capitol	27	3 Apr 71	6

Red SOVINE — US

SINGLES:	HITS 1			WEEKS 8
TEDDY BEAR	Starday	4	13 Jun 81	8

Originally reached No. 40 in the US in 1976.

SOX — UK

SINGLES:	HITS 1			WEEKS 1
GO FOR THE HEART	Living Beat	47	15 Apr 95	1

One of the contenders for Eurovision's A Song For Europe, it came 4th (out of 8).

Bob B SOXX and the BLUE JEANS — US

SINGLES:	HITS 1			WEEKS 2
ZIP-A-DEE-DOO-DAH	London	45	2 Feb 63	2

Originally recorded by Johnny Mercer.

SPACE — France

SINGLES:	HITS 1			WEEKS 12
MAGIC FLY	Pye International	2	13 Aug 77	12
ALBUMS:	**HITS 1**			**WEEKS 9**
MAGIC FLY	Pye International	11	17 Sep 77	9

SPACE — UK

(See also England United.)

SINGLES:	HITS 8			WEEKS 50
NEIGHBOURHOOD	Gut	56	6 Apr 96	1
FEMALE OF THE SPECIES	Gut	14	8 Jun 96	10
ME AND YOU VERSUS THE WORLD	Gut	9	7 Sep 96	6
NEIGHBOURHOOD [RI]	Gut	11	2 Nov 96	6
DARK CLOUDS	Gut	14	22 Feb 97	4
AVENGING ANGELS	Gut	6	10 Jan 98	8
THE BALLAD OF TOM JONES	Gut	4	7 Mar 98	8

Above hit: SPACE with CERYS of CATATONIA.

BEGIN AGAIN	Gut	21	4 Jul 98	4
THE BAD DAYS [EP]	Gut	20	5 Dec 98	3

Lead track: Bad Days. The track on CD1, We Gotta Get Out Of This Place was featured in the Honda Accord car TV commercial.

ALBUMS:	HITS 2			WEEKS 67
SPIDERS	Gut	5	28 Sep 96	42
TIN PLANET	Gut	3	21 Mar 98	25

SPACE BROTHERS — UK

SINGLES:	HITS 4			WEEKS 15
SHINE	Manifesto	23	17 May 97	3
FORGIVEN (I FEEL YOU LOVE)	Manifesto	27	13 Dec 97	7
LEGACY [SHOW ME LOVE]	Manifesto	31	10 Jul 99	3
HEAVEN WILL COME	Manifesto	25	9 Oct 99	2

Vocals by Kate Cameron.

SPACE KITTENS — UK

SINGLES:		HITS 1		WEEKS 1
STORM	Hooj Choons	58	13 Apr 96	1

SPACE MONKEY — UK

SINGLES:		HITS 1		WEEKS 4
CAN'T STOP RUNNING	Inner Vision	53	8 Oct 83	4

SPACE RAIDERS — UK

SINGLES:		HITS 1		WEEKS 1
GLAM RAID	Skint	68	28 Mar 98	1

Samples Kenny's The Bump.

SPACE 2000 — UK

SINGLES:		HITS 1		WEEKS 1
DO U WANNA FUNK?	Wired	50	12 Aug 95	1

SPACEBABY — UK

SINGLES:		HITS 1		WEEKS 1
FREE YOUR MIND	Hooj Choons	55	8 Jul 95	1

SPACEDUST — UK

SINGLES:		HITS 2		WEEKS 12
GYM AND TONIC	East West Dance	1	24 Oct 98	8

Originally recorded by Bob Sinclar. Contains sample from Jane Fonda's Workout record.

GYM AND TONIC [RE]	East West	55	9 Jan 99	2
LET'S GET DOWN	East West	20	27 Mar 99	2

Samples Chic's I Want Your Love. Vocals by Lisa Millet.

SPACEHOG — UK

SINGLES:		HITS 2		WEEKS 8
IN THE MEANTIME	Sire	70	11 May 96	1
IN THE MEANTIME [RE]	Sire	29	28 Dec 96	6
CARRY ON	Sire	43	7 Feb 98	1
ALBUMS:		**HITS 1**		**WEEKS 2**
RESIDENT ALIEN	Sire	40	15 Feb 97	2

SPACEMAID — UK

SINGLES:		HITS 1		WEEKS 1
BABY COME ON	Big Star	70	5 Apr 97	1

SPACEMEN 3 — UK

ALBUMS:		HITS 1		WEEKS 1
RECURRING	Fire	46	9 Mar 91	1

SPAGHETTI SURFERS — UK

SINGLES:		HITS 1		WEEKS 1
MISIRLOU (THEME TO THE MOTION PICTURE 'PULP FICTION')	Tempo	55	22 Jul 95	1

SPAGNA — Italy

SINGLES:		HITS 3		WEEKS 23
CALL ME	CBS	2	25 Jul 87	12
EASY LADY	CBS	62	17 Oct 87	3
EVERY GIRL AND BOY	CBS	23	20 Aug 88	8

SPANDAU BALLET — UK

SINGLES:		HITS 20		WEEKS 159
TO CUT A LONG STORY SHORT	Reformation	5	15 Nov 80	11
THE FREEZE	Reformation	17	24 Jan 81	8
MUSCLE BOUND / GLOW	Reformation	10	4 Apr 81	10
CHANT NO.1 (I DON'T NEED THIS PRESSURE ON)	Reformation	3	18 Jul 81	10

Features backing from Beggar And Co.

PAINT ME DOWN	Reformation	30	14 Nov 81	5
SHE LOVED LIKE DIAMOND	Reformation	49	30 Jan 82	4
INSTINCTION	Reformation	10	10 Apr 82	11
LIFELINE	Reformation	7	2 Oct 82	9
COMMUNICATION	Reformation	12	12 Feb 83	10
TRUE	Reformation	1	23 Apr 83	12
GOLD	Reformation	2	13 Aug 83	9
ONLY WHEN YOU LEAVE	Reformation	3	9 Jun 84	9
ONLY WHEN YOU LEAVE [RE]	Reformation	74	18 Aug 84	1
I'LL FLY FOR YOU	Reformation	9	25 Aug 84	9

HIGHLY STRUNG	Reformation	15	20 Oct 84	5
ROUND AND ROUND	Reformation	18	8 Dec 84	8
FIGHT FOR OURSELVES	Reformation	15	26 Jul 86	7
THROUGH THE BARRICADES	Reformation	6	8 Nov 86	10
HOW MANY LIES?	Reformation	34	14 Feb 87	4
RAW	CBS	47	3 Sep 88	3
BE FREE WITH YOUR LOVE	CBS	42	26 Aug 89	4
ALBUMS:	**HITS 8**		**WEEKS 251**	
JOURNEY TO GLORY	Reformation	5	14 Mar 81	29
DIAMOND	Reformation	15	20 Mar 82	18
TRUE	Reformation	1	12 Mar 83	90
PARADE	Reformation	2	7 Jul 84	39
THE SINGLES COLLECTION	Chrysalis	3	16 Nov 85	50
THROUGH THE BARRICADES	Reformation	7	29 Nov 86	19
HEART LIKE A SKY	CBS	31	30 Sep 89	3
THE BEST OF SPANDAU BALLET	Chrysalis	44	28 Sep 91	3

SPARKLE   US

SINGLES:	**HITS 3**		**WEEKS 10**	
BE CAREFUL	Jive	7	18 Jul 98	6
Above hit: SPARKLE featuring R. KELLY.				
BE CAREFUL [RE]	Jive	75	5 Sep 98	1
TIME TO MOVE ON	Jive	40	7 Nov 98	2
LOVIN' YOU	Jive	65	28 Aug 99	1
Even though not listed, this was released as an [AA] with What About.				
ALBUMS:	**HITS 1**		**WEEKS 1**	
SPARKLE	Jive	57	1 Aug 98	1

SPARKLEHORSE   US

SINGLES:	**HITS 2**		**WEEKS 2**	
RAINMAKER	Capitol	61	31 Aug 96	1
SICK OF GOODBYES	Parlophone	57	17 Oct 98	1
ALBUMS:	**HITS 2**		**WEEKS 3**	
VIVADIXIESUBMARINETRANSMISSIONPLOT	Capitol	58	18 May 96	1
GOOD MORNING SPIDER	Parlophone	30	1 Aug 98	2

SPARKS   US

SINGLES:	**HITS 14**		**WEEKS 81**	
THIS TOWN AIN'T BIG ENOUGH FOR BOTH OF US	Island	2	4 May 74	10
AMATEUR HOUR	Island	7	20 Jul 74	9
NEVER TURN YOUR BACK ON MOTHER EARTH	Island	13	19 Oct 74	7
SOMETHING FOR THE GIRL WITH EVERYTHING	Island	17	18 Jan 75	7
GET IN THE SWING	Island	27	19 Jul 75	7
LOOKS, LOOKS, LOOKS	Island	26	4 Oct 75	4
THE NUMBER ONE SONG IN HEAVEN	Virgin	14	21 Apr 79	12
BEAT THE CLOCK	Virgin	10	21 Jul 79	9
TRYOUTS FOR THE HUMAN RACE	Virgin	45	27 Oct 79	5
WHEN DO I GET TO SING "MY WAY"	Logic	38	29 Oct 94	3
WHEN I KISS YOU (I HEAR CHARLIE PARKER PLAYING)	Logic	36	11 Mar 95	2
WHEN DO I GET TO SING "MY WAY" [RI]	Logic	32	20 May 95	2
NOW THAT I OWN THE BBC	Logic	60	9 Mar 96	1
THE NUMBER ONE SONG IN HEAVEN [RR]	Roadrunner	70	25 Oct 97	1
THIS TOWN AIN'T BIG ENOUGH FOR BOTH OF US [RR]	Roadrunner	40	13 Dec 97	2
Above hit: SPARKS vs. FAITH NO MORE.				
ALBUMS:	**HITS 4**		**WEEKS 42**	
KIMONO MY HOUSE	Island	4	1 Jun 74	24
PROPAGANDA	Island	9	23 Nov 74	13
INDISCREET	Island	18	18 Oct 75	4
NUMBER ONE IN HEAVEN	Virgin	73	8 Sep 79	1

SPEAR OF DESTINY   UK

SINGLES:	**HITS 10**		**WEEKS 43**	
THE WHEEL	Epic	59	21 May 83	5
PRISONER OF LOVE	Epic	59	21 Jan 84	3
LIBERATOR	Epic	67	14 Apr 84	2
ALL MY LOVE (ASK NOTHING)	Epic	61	15 Jun 85	3
COME BACK	Epic	55	10 Aug 85	3
STRANGERS IN OUR TOWN	10 Records	49	7 Feb 87	4
NEVER TAKE ME ALIVE	10 Records	14	4 Apr 87	11
WAS THAT YOU?	10 Records	55	25 Jul 87	4
THE TRAVELLER	10 Records	44	3 Oct 87	3
SO IN LOVE WITH YOU	Virgin	36	24 Sep 88	5
ALBUMS:	**HITS 6**		**WEEKS 35**	
GRAPES OF WRATH	Epic	62	23 Apr 83	2

ONE EYED JACKS	Epic	22	28 Apr 84	7
WORLD SERVICE	Epic	11	7 Sep 85	7
OUTLAND	10 Records	16	2 May 87	13
S.O.D. THE EPIC YEARS	Epic	53	16 May 87	3
Compilation.				
THE PRICE YOU PAY	Virgin	37	22 Oct 88	3

SPEARHEAD US

SINGLES:	HITS 4			WEEKS 5
OF COURSE YOU CAN	Capitol	74	17 Dec 94	1
HOLE IN THE BUCKET	Capitol	55	22 Apr 95	1
PEOPLE IN THA MIDDLE	Capitol	49	15 Jul 95	2
WHY OH WHY	Capitol	45	15 Mar 97	1
ALBUMS:	HITS 1			WEEKS 1
CHOCOLATE SUPA HIGHWAY	Capitol	68	29 Mar 97	1

Billie Jo SPEARS US

SINGLES:	HITS 4			WEEKS 40
BLANKET ON THE GROUND	United Artists	6	12 Jul 75	13
WHAT I'VE GOT IN MIND	United Artists	4	17 Jul 76	13
SING ME AN OLD FASHIONED SONG	United Artists	34	11 Dec 76	9
I WILL SURVIVE	United Artists	47	21 Jul 79	5
ALBUMS:	HITS 3			WEEKS 28
WHAT I'VE GOT IN MIND	United Artists	47	11 Sep 76	2
THE BILLIE JO SPEARS SINGLES ALBUM	United Artists	7	19 May 79	17
COUNTRY GIRL	Warwick	17	21 Nov 81	9

Britney SPEARS US

SINGLES:	HITS 3			WEEKS 49
. . . BABY ONE MORE TIME	Jive	1	27 Feb 99	22
SOMETIMES	Jive	3	26 Jun 99	16
(YOU DRIVE ME) CRAZY (THE STOP REMIX!)	Jive	5	2 Oct 99	11
From the film of the same name.				
ALBUMS:	HITS 1			WEEKS 42
. . . BABY ONE MORE TIME	Jive	4	20 Mar 99	42

SPECIALS UK

(See also Various Artists (EPs) 'The 2 Tone EP'.)

SINGLES:	HITS 12			WEEKS 101
GANGSTERS	2-Tone	6	28 Jul 79	12
Tribute to the Prince Buster's 1965 ska recording Al Capone.				
Above hit: SPECIAL A.K.A.				
A MESSAGE TO YOU RUDY / NITE KLUB	2-Tone	10	27 Oct 79	14
A Message To You Rudy originally recorded by Dandy Livingstone.				
Above hit: SPECIALS featuring RICO +.				
THE SPECIAL A.K.A. LIVE! [EP]	2-Tone	1	26 Jan 80	10
Live recordings from the Lyceum, London on side 1 and Tiffany's, Coventry on side 2. Lead track: Too Much Too Young. Other tracks are covers of ska and reggae songs.				
Above hit: SPECIALS featuring RICO.				
RAT RACE / RUDE BUOYS OUTA JAIL'	2-Tone	5	24 May 80	9
STEREOTYPE / INTERNATIONAL JET SET	2-Tone	6	20 Sep 80	8
DO NOTHING / MAGGIE'S FARM	2-Tone	4	13 Dec 80	11
Maggie's Farm listed from 10 Jan 81.				
Above hit: SPECIALS featuring RICO with the ICE RINK STRING SOUNDS / SPECIALS				
GHOST TOWN	2-Tone	1	20 Jun 81	14
THE BOILER	2-Tone	35	23 Jan 82	5
Above hit: RHODA with the SPECIAL A.K.A.				
RACIST FRIEND / BRIGHT LIGHT	2-Tone	60	3 Sep 83	3
NELSON MANDELA	2-Tone	9	17 Mar 84	10
Nelson Mandela was imprisoned for treason in 1964. This song demanded his release.				
WHAT I LIKE MOST ABOUT YOU IS YOUR GIRLFRIEND	2-Tone	51	8 Sep 84	4
Above 3: SPECIAL AKA				
HYPOCRITE	Kuff	66	10 Feb 96	1
Originally recorded by Bob Marley in 1967.				
ALBUMS:	HITS 4			WEEKS 79
SPECIALS	2-Tone	4	3 Nov 79	45
MORE SPECIALS	2-Tone	5	4 Oct 80	19
IN THE STUDIO	2-Tone	34	23 Jun 84	6
Above hit: SPECIAL AKA.				
THE SPECIALS SINGLES	2-Tone	10	7 Sep 91	9

Phil SPECTOR

US

ALBUMS:	HITS 3			WEEKS 29	
PHIL SPECTOR'S CHRISTMAS ALBUM	Apple	21	23 Dec 72	3
PHIL SPECTOR'S ECHOES OF THE 60'S	Phil Spector International	21	15 Oct 77	10
PHIL SPECTOR'S CHRISTMAS ALBUM [RI-1ST]	Phil Spector International	96	25 Dec 82	2
PHIL SPECTOR'S GREATEST HITS / PHIL SPECTOR'S CHRISTMAS ALBUM [RI-2ND]	Impression	19	10 Dec 83	8
THE PHIL SPECTOR CHRISTMAS ALBUM [RI-3RD]	Chrysalis	69	12 Dec 87	6

Phil Spector is only the producer, all the above compilations are by various artists.

SPECTRUM

UK

SINGLES:	HITS 1			WEEKS 1	
TRUE LOVE WILL FIND YOU IN THE END	Silvertone	70	26 Sep 92	1

Chris SPEDDING

UK

SINGLES:	HITS 1			WEEKS 8	
MOTOR BIKIN'	RAK	14	23 Aug 75	8

SPEECH

US

SINGLES:	HITS 1			WEEKS 2	
LIKE MARVIN GAYE SAID (WHAT'S GOING ON)	Cooltempo	35	17 Feb 96	2

SPEEDY

UK

SINGLES:	HITS 1			WEEKS 1	
BOY WONDER	Boiler House!	56	9 Nov 96	1

SPEEDY J

Holland

ALBUMS:	HITS 1			WEEKS 1	
GINGER	Warp	68	10 Jul 93	1

SPELLBOUND

India

SINGLES:	HITS 1			WEEKS 1	
HEAVEN ON EARTH	East West	73	31 May 97	1

Johnny SPENCE and his Orchestra

UK

SINGLES:	HITS 1			WEEKS 15	
THE DR. KILDARE THEME	Parlophone	15	3 Mar 62	15

Theme from the TV series.

Don SPENCER

UK

SINGLES:	HITS 1			WEEKS 12	
FIREBALL	His Master's Voice	32	23 Mar 63	11

Theme from the Gerry Anderson children's animated TV series 'Fireball XL5'.

| FIREBALL [RE] | His Master's Voice | 49 | 15 Jun 63 | 1 |

Jon SPENCER BLUES EXPLOSION

US

SINGLES:	HITS 1			WEEKS 1	
WAIL	Mute	66	10 May 97	1
ALBUMS:	HITS 2			WEEKS 2	
NOW I GOT WORRY	Mute	50	12 Oct 96	1
ACME	Mute	72	31 Oct 98	1

Tracie SPENCER

US

SINGLES:	HITS 2			WEEKS 3	
THIS HOUSE	Capitol	65	4 May 91	2
IT'S ALL ABOUT YOU (NOT ABOUT ME)	Parlophone Rhythm Series	65	6 Nov 99	1

SPHINX

UK/US

SINGLES:	HITS 1			WEEKS 2	
WHAT HOPE HAVE I	Champion	43	25 Mar 95	2

SPICE GIRLS

UK

(See also England United.)

SINGLES:	HITS 9			WEEKS 162	
WANNABE	Virgin	1	20 Jul 96	26
SAY YOU'LL BE THERE	Virgin	1	26 Oct 96	17
2 BECOME 1	Virgin	1	28 Dec 96	19
MAMA / WHO DO YOU THINK YOU ARE	Virgin	1	15 Mar 97	15

Charity record for Comic Relief's Red Nose day, 14 Mar 97.

2 BECOME 1 [RE]	Virgin	54	17 May 97	4
SPICE UP YOUR LIFE	Virgin	1	25 Oct 97	15
TOO MUCH	Virgin	1	27 Dec 97	15
First act to have their first six releases top the chart.				
STOP	Virgin	2	21 Mar 98	15
STOP [RE]	Virgin	52	11 Jul 98	2
VIVA FOREVER	Virgin	1	1 Aug 98	13
GOODBYE	Virgin	1	26 Dec 98	21
ALBUMS:	**HITS 2**			**WEEKS 127**
SPICE	Virgin	1	16 Nov 96	72
SPICEWORLD	Virgin	1	15 Nov 97	55

SPIDER
UK

SINGLES:	**HITS 2**			**WEEKS 5**
WHY D'YA LIE TO ME	RCA	65	5 Mar 83	2
HERE WE GO ROCK 'N' ROLL	A&M	57	10 Mar 84	3
ALBUMS:	**HITS 2**			**WEEKS 2**
ROCK 'N' ROLL GYPSIES	RCA	75	23 Oct 82	1
ROUGH JUSTICE	A&M	96	7 Apr 84	1

SPIKEY TEE – See BOMB THE BASS

SPIN DOCTORS
US

SINGLES:	**HITS 8**			**WEEKS 28**
TWO PRINCES	Epic	3	15 May 93	15
LITTLE MISS CAN'T BE WRONG	Epic	23	14 Aug 93	5
Original release reached No. 80 earlier that year.				
JIMMY OLSEN'S BLUES	Epic	40	9 Oct 93	2
Jimmy Olsen was the photographer at the Daily Planet in 'Superman'.				
WHAT TIME IS IT?	Epic	56	4 Dec 93	1
CLEOPATRA'S CAT	Epic	29	25 Jun 94	2
YOU LET YOUR HEART GO TOO FAST	Epic	66	30 Jul 94	1
MARY JANE	Epic	55	29 Oct 94	1
SHE USED TO BE MINE	Epic	55	8 Jun 96	1
ALBUMS:	**HITS 2**			**WEEKS 57**
POCKET FULL OF KRYPTONITE	Epic	2	20 Mar 93	48
Re-released from 12 Sept 94 with additional track.				
TURN IT UPSIDE DOWN	Epic	3	9 Jul 94	9

SPINAL TAP
UK/US

SINGLES:	**HITS 2**			**WEEKS 3**
BITCH SCHOOL	MCA	35	28 Mar 92	2
THE MAJESTY OF ROCK	MCA	61	2 May 92	1
ALBUMS:	**HITS 1**			**WEEKS 2**
BREAK LIKE THE WIND	MCA	51	11 Apr 92	2

SPINNERS
UK

ALBUMS:	**HITS 4**			**WEEKS 24**
THE SPINNERS ARE IN TOWN	Fontana	40	5 Sep 70	5
SPINNERS LIVE PERFORMANCE	Contour	14	7 Aug 71	12
THE SWINGING CITY	Philips	20	13 Nov 71	3
LOVE IS TEASING	Columbia	33	8 Apr 72	4

SPINNERS – See DETROIT SPINNERS; RAPPIN' 4-TAY

SPIRAL TRIBE
UK

SINGLES:	**HITS 2**			**WEEKS 2**
BREACH THE PEACE	Butterfly	66	29 Aug 92	1
FORWARD THE REVOLUTION	Butterfly	70	21 Nov 92	1

SPIRIT
US

ALBUMS:	**HITS 1**			**WEEKS 2**
POTATO LAND	Beggars Banquet	40	18 Apr 81	2
Originally recorded in the early 1970s.				

SPIRITS
UK

SINGLES:	**HITS 2**			**WEEKS 5**
DON'T BRING ME DOWN	MCA	31	19 Nov 94	3
SPIRIT INSIDE	MCA	39	8 Apr 95	2

SPIRITUAL COWBOYS – See David A. STEWART

SPIRITUALIZED | UK

SINGLES:		HITS 8		WEEKS 12	
ANYWAY THAT YOU WANT ME / STEP INTO THE BREEZE	Dedicated	75	30 Jun 90	1
RUN	Dedicated	59	17 Aug 91	1
MEDICATION	Dedicated	55	25 Jul 92	1
ELECTRIC MAINLINE [EP]	Dedicated	49	23 Oct 93	1
Lead track: Good Times.				
LET IT FLOW	Dedicated	30	4 Feb 95	2
Above hit: SPIRITUALIZED ELECTRIC MAINLINE.				
ELECTRICITY	Dedicated	32	9 Aug 97	2
I THINK I'M IN LOVE	Dedicated	27	14 Feb 98	2
THE ABBEY ROAD [EP]	Deconstruction	39	6 Jun 98	2
Lead track: Come Together.				

ALBUMS:		HITS 4		WEEKS 20	
LAZER GUIDED MELODIES	Dedicated	27	11 Apr 92	2
PURE PHASE	Dedicated	20	18 Feb 95	2
Features contributions from Michael Nyman's string section, the Balanescu Quartet.				
Above hit: SPIRITUALIZED ELECTRIC MAINLINE.				
LADIES & GENTLEMEN WE ARE FLOATING IN SPACE	Dedicated	4	28 Jun 97	15
CD comes foil wrapped in a pill box. A second CD format contains 12 × 3" CDs, one for each track.				
LIVE AT THE ROYAL ALBERT HALL	Deconstruction	38	7 Nov 98	1
Live recordings from London's Royal Albert Hall, 10 Oct 97.				

SPIRO and WIX | UK

SINGLES:		HITS 1		WEEKS 2	
TARA'S THEME	EMI Premier	29	10 Aug 96	2
Theme from the BBC's coverage of the 1996 Olympic Games.				

SPITTING IMAGE | UK

SINGLES:		HITS 2		WEEKS 18	
THE CHICKEN SONG	Virgin	1	10 May 86	10
THE CHICKEN SONG [RE]	Virgin	67	26 Jul 86	1
SANTA CLAUS IS ON THE DOLE / 1ST ATHEIST TABERNACLE CHOIR	Virgin	22	6 Dec 86	7

ALBUMS:		HITS 1		WEEKS 3	
SPIT IN YOUR EAR	Virgin	55	18 Oct 86	3

SPLINTER | UK

SINGLES:		HITS 1		WEEKS 10	
COSTAFINE TOWN	Dark Horse	17	2 Nov 74	10
Features George Harrison on bass guitar.				

SPLIT ENZ | UK/New Zealand

SINGLES:		HITS 2		WEEKS 15	
I GOT YOU	A&M	12	16 Aug 80	11
HISTORY NEVER REPEATS	A&M	63	23 May 81	4

ALBUMS:		HITS 2		WEEKS 9	
TRUE COLOURS	A&M	42	30 Aug 80	8
TIME AND TIDE	A&M	71	8 May 82	1

A SPLIT SECOND | Italy/Belgium

SINGLES:		HITS 1		WEEKS 1	
FLESH	ffrr	68	14 Dec 91	1

SPLODGENESSABOUNDS | UK

SINGLES:		HITS 3		WEEKS 17	
SIMON TEMPLER / TWO PINTS OF LAGER AND A PACKET OF CRISPS PLEASE	Deram	7	14 Jun 80	8
TWO LITTLE BOYS / HORSE	Deram	26	6 Sep 80	7
Two Little Boys originally written in 1903 about the American Civil War.				
COWPUNK MEDLUM	Deram	69	13 Jun 81	2

SPONGE | US

SINGLES:		HITS 1		WEEKS 1	
PLOWED	Columbia	74	19 Aug 95	1

SPOOKY | UK

SINGLES:		HITS 1		WEEKS 1	
SCHMOO	Guerilla	72	13 Mar 93	1
Backing vocals by Heather Sian Wildman.				

Fred SPOONS, E.P.N.S – See Peter SELLERS

SPORTY THIEVZ
US

SINGLES:		HITS 1		WEEKS 6
NO PIGEONS	Columbia	21	10 Jul 99	6

Answer record to TLC's No Scrubs. Samples Sporty Thievz's Cheapskate and TLC's No Scrubs.

SPOTNICKS
Sweden

SINGLES:		HITS 4		WEEKS 37
ORANGE BLOSSOM SPECIAL	Oriole	29	16 Jun 62	10
THE ROCKET MAN	Oriole	38	8 Sep 62	9
HAVA NAGILA	Oriole	13	2 Feb 63	12
JUST LISTEN TO MY HEART	Oriole	36	27 Apr 63	6
EPS:		HITS 1		WEEKS 27
ON THE AIR	Oriole	2	30 Mar 63	27
ALBUMS:		HITS 1		WEEKS 1
OUT-A-SPACE	Oriole	20	9 Feb 63	1

Dusty SPRINGFIELD
UK

(See also Springfields.)

SINGLES:		HITS 26		WEEKS 211
I ONLY WANT TO BE WITH YOU	Philips	4	23 Nov 63	18
The first song played on BBC TV's 'Top Of The Pops', 1 Jan 64.				
STAY AWHILE	Philips	13	22 Feb 64	10
I JUST DON'T KNOW WHAT TO DO WITH MYSELF	Philips	3	4 Jul 64	12
Originally recorded by Tommy Hunt.				
LOSING YOU	Philips	9	24 Oct 64	13
YOUR HURTIN' KINDA LOVE	Philips	37	20 Feb 65	4
IN THE MIDDLE OF NOWHERE	Philips	8	3 Jul 65	10
SOME OF YOUR LOVIN'	Philips	8	18 Sep 65	12
Backing vocals by Madeleine Bell and Doris Troy.				
LITTLE BY LITTLE	Philips	17	29 Jan 66	9
YOU DON'T HAVE TO SAY YOU LOVE ME (IO CHE NO VIVO SENZA TE)	Philips	1	2 Apr 66	13
GOIN' BACK	Philips	10	9 Jul 66	10
ALL I SEE IS YOU	Philips	9	17 Sep 66	12
I'LL TRY ANYTHING	Philips	13	25 Feb 67	9
GIVE ME TIME	Philips	24	27 May 67	6
I CLOSE MY EYES AND COUNT TO TEN	Philips	4	13 Jul 68	12
SON-OF-A PREACHER MAN	Philips	9	7 Dec 68	9
AM I THE SAME GIRL	Philips	43	20 Sep 69	3
Originally recorded by Barbara Acklin.				
AM I THE SAME GIRL [RE]	Philips	46	18 Oct 69	1
HOW CAN I BE SURE	Philips	36	19 Sep 70	4
BABY BLUE	Mercury	61	20 Oct 79	5
WHAT HAVE I DONE TO DESERVE THIS?	Parlophone	2	22 Aug 87	9
Above hit: PET SHOP BOYS and Dusty SPRINGFIELD.				
NOTHING HAS BEEN PROVED	Parlophone	16	25 Feb 89	7
From the film 'Scandal'.				
IN PRIVATE	Parlophone	14	2 Dec 89	10
REPUTATION	Parlophone	38	26 May 90	6
Originally recorded by Brian Spence.				
ARRESTED BY YOU	Parlophone	70	24 Nov 90	2
HEART AND SOUL	Columbia	75	30 Oct 93	1
Above hit: Cilla BLACK and Dusty SPRINGFIELD.				
WHEREVER WOULD I BE	Columbia	44	10 Jun 95	3
Above hit: Dusty SPRINGFIELD and Daryl HALL.				
ROLL AWAY	Columbia	68	4 Nov 95	1
EPS:		HITS 4		WEEKS 51
I ONLY WANT TO BE WITH YOU	Philips	8	28 Mar 64	19
DUSTY	Philips	3	19 Sep 64	20
DUSTY IN NEW YORK	Philips	13	8 May 65	9
MADEMOISELLE DUSTY	Philips	17	7 Aug 65	3
ALBUMS:		HITS 12		WEEKS 134
A GIRL CALLED DUSTY	Philips	6	25 Apr 64	23
EVERYTHING'S COMING UP DUSTY	Philips	6	23 Oct 65	12
GOLDEN HITS	Philips	2	22 Oct 66	36
WHERE AM I GOING?	Philips	40	11 Nov 67	1
DUSTY . . . DEFINITELY	Philips	30	21 Dec 68	6
FROM DUSTY . . . WITH LOVE	Philips	35	2 May 70	2
IT BEGINS AGAIN	Mercury	41	4 Mar 78	2
DUSTY - THE SILVER COLLECTION	Phonogram	14	30 Jan 88	10
REPUTATION	Parlophone	18	7 Jul 90	6
GOIN' BACK - THE VERY BEST OF DUSTY SPRINGFIELD 1962-1994	Philips	5	14 May 94	11

This compilation includes her recordings with the Springfields and the Pet Shop Boys as well as her own solo material.

A VERY FINE LOVE	*Columbia*	43	*8 Jul 95*	1
THE BEST OF DUSTY SPRINGFIELD	*Mercury/PolyGram TV*	19	*7 Nov 98*	24

From 27 Mar 99 label changed to Mercury/Universal Music TV.

Rick SPRINGFIELD   US

SINGLES:	HITS 2		WEEKS 13	
HUMAN TOUCH / SOULS	*RCA*	23	*14 Jan 84*	7

Souls listed from 11 Feb 84 once single had dropped to No. 24.

JESSIE'S GIRL	*RCA*	43	*24 Mar 84*	6

Originally released in 1981 reaching No. 1 in the US.

ALBUMS:	HITS 3		WEEKS 8	
LIVING IN OZ	*RCA*	41	*11 Feb 84*	4
TAO	*RCA*	68	*25 May 85*	3
ROCK OF LIFE	*RCA*	80	*26 Mar 88*	1

SPRINGFIELDS   UK

(See also Dusty Springfield.)

SINGLES:	HITS 5		WEEKS 66	
BREAKAWAY	*Philips*	31	*2 Sep 61*	8
BAMBINO	*Philips*	16	*18 Nov 61*	11
ISLAND OF DREAMS	*Philips*	5	*15 Dec 62*	26
SAY I WON'T BE THERE	*Philips*	5	*30 Mar 63*	15
COME ON HOME	*Philips*	31	*27 Jul 63*	6

Bruce SPRINGSTEEN   US

SINGLES:	HITS 23		WEEKS 147	
HUNGRY HEART	*CBS*	44	*22 Nov 80*	4

Howard Kaylan and Mark Volman of the Turtles on backing vocals.

THE RIVER	*CBS*	35	*13 Jun 81*	6
JOLE BLON	*EMI America*	51	*22 Aug 81*	3

Above hit: Gary U.S. BONDS with Bruce SPRINGSTEEN.

DANCING IN THE DARK	*CBS*	28	*26 May 84*	7
COVER ME	*CBS*	38	*6 Oct 84*	5
DANCING IN THE DARK [RE]	*CBS*	4	*12 Jan 85*	16
COVER ME [RE]	*CBS*	16	*23 Mar 85*	8
I'M ON FIRE / BORN IN THE U.S.A.	*CBS*	5	*15 Jun 85*	12
GLORY DAYS	*CBS*	17	*3 Aug 85*	6
SANTA CLAUS IS COMIN' TO TOWN / MY HOMETOWN	*CBS*	9	*14 Dec 85*	5

Santa Claus Is Comin' To Town is a live recording from C.W. Post College, Greenvale, New York, 12 Dec 85, and was originally recorded by George Hall in 1934.

WAR	*CBS*	18	*29 Nov 86*	7
FIRE	*CBS*	54	*7 Feb 87*	2

Above 2: Bruce SPRINGSTEEN and the E STREET BAND.

BORN TO RUN (LIVE)	*CBS*	16	*23 May 87*	4
BRILLIANT DISGUISE	*CBS*	20	*3 Oct 87*	5
TUNNEL OF LOVE	*CBS*	45	*12 Dec 87*	4
TOUGHER THAN THE REST	*CBS*	13	*18 Jun 88*	8
SPARE PARTS	*CBS*	32	*24 Sep 88*	3
HUMAN TOUCH	*Columbia*	11	*21 Mar 92*	5
BETTER DAYS	*Columbia*	34	*23 May 92*	3
57 CHANNELS (AND NOTHIN' ON)	*Columbia*	32	*25 Jul 92*	4
LEAP OF FAITH	*Columbia*	46	*24 Oct 92*	3
LUCKY TOWN (LIVE)	*Columbia*	48	*10 Apr 93*	3

Live recording for TV channel MTV.

STREETS OF PHILADELPHIA	*Columbia*	2	*19 Mar 94*	12

From the film 'Philadelphia'.

SECRET GARDEN	*Columbia*	44	*22 Apr 95*	3
HUNGRY HEART [RI]	*Columbia*	28	*11 Nov 95*	3
THE GHOST OF TOM JOAD	*Columbia*	26	*4 May 96*	2

Tom Joad is a character in the novel 'The Grapes Of Wrath' by John Steinbeck.

SECRET GARDEN [RI]	*Columbia*	17	*19 Apr 97*	4

From the film 'Jerry Maguire'.

ALBUMS:	HITS 16		WEEKS 479	
BORN TO RUN	*CBS*	36	*1 Nov 75*	29

Includes re-entries through to 1985.

DARKNESS ON THE EDGE OF TOWN	*CBS*	16	*17 Jun 78*	12
THE RIVER	*CBS*	2	*25 Oct 80*	88
NEBRASKA	*CBS*	3	*2 Oct 82*	19
BORN IN THE U.S.A.	*CBS*	1	*16 Jun 84*	126

Peak position reached on 16 Feb 85.

DARKNESS ON THE EDGE OF TOWN [RE]	*CBS*	24	*26 Jan 85*	28

Re-released with a new catalogue number.

BORN TO RUN [RE]	*CBS*	17	*27 Apr 85*	21
GREETING FROM ASBURY PARK, N.J.	*CBS*	41	*15 Jun 85*	10

Originally released in 1973.

THE WILD, THE INNOCENT AND THE E. STREET SHUFFLE	*CBS*	33	*15 Jun 85*	12
Originally released in 1973.				
LIVE/1975-1985	*CBS*	4	*22 Nov 86*	9
Boxed set of live recordings.				
Above hit: Bruce SPRINGSTEEN and the E STREET BAND.				
TUNNEL OF LOVE	*CBS*	1	*17 Oct 87*	33
HUMAN TOUCH	*Columbia*	1	*4 Apr 92*	17
LUCKY TOWN	*Columbia*	2	*4 Apr 92*	11
BORN IN THE U.S.A. [RI]	*Columbia*	41	*11 Jul 92*	2
IN CONCERT – MTV PLUGGED	*Columbia*	4	*24 Apr 93*	7
Live recordings for TV channel MTV.				
GREATEST HITS	*Columbia*	1	*11 Mar 95*	33
THE GHOST OF TOM JOAD	*Columbia*	16	*25 Nov 95*	14
TRACKS	*Columbia*	50	*21 Nov 98*	1
4CD set.				
18 TRACKS	*Columbia*	23	*24 Apr 99*	7
Highlights from the 1998 boxed set Tracks.				

SPRINGWATER UK

SINGLES:	HITS 1		WEEKS 12	
I WILL RETURN	*Polydor*	5	*23 Oct 71*	12

SPRINKLER UK/US

SINGLES:	HITS 1		WEEKS 2	
LEAVE 'EM SOMETHING TO DESIRE	*Island*	45	*11 Jul 98*	2

SPYRO GYRA US

SINGLES:	HITS 1		WEEKS 10	
MORNING DANCE	*Infinity*	17	*21 Jul 79*	10
ALBUMS:	**HITS 2**		**WEEKS 22**	
MORNING DANCE	*Infinity*	11	*14 Jul 79*	16
CATCHING THE SUN	*MCA*	31	*23 Feb 80*	6

SQUADRONAIRES directed by Ronnie ALDRICH – See Joan REGAN

SQUEEZE UK

SINGLES:	HITS 21		WEEKS 123	
TAKE ME I'M YOURS	*A&M*	19	*8 Apr 78*	9
Was originally to be released on the BTM label in 1977 but it was withdrawn.				
BANG BANG	*A&M*	49	*10 Jun 78*	5
GOODBYE GIRL	*A&M*	63	*18 Nov 78*	2
COOL FOR CATS	*A&M*	2	*24 Mar 79*	11
UP THE JUNCTION	*A&M*	2	*2 Jun 79*	11
SLAP & TICKLE	*A&M*	24	*8 Sep 79*	8
ANOTHER NAIL IN MY HEART	*A&M*	17	*1 Mar 80*	9
PULLING MUSSELS (FROM THE SHELL)	*A&M*	44	*10 May 80*	6
IS THAT LOVE	*A&M*	35	*16 May 81*	8
TEMPTED	*A&M*	41	*25 Jul 81*	5
Lead vocals by Paul Carrack.				
LABELLED WITH LOVE	*A&M*	4	*10 Oct 81*	10
BLACK COFFEE IN BED	*A&M*	51	*24 Apr 82*	4
Features backing vocals from Elvis Costello and Paul Young.				
ANNIE GET YOUR GUN	*A&M*	43	*23 Oct 82*	4
LAST TIME FOREVER	*A&M*	45	*15 Jun 85*	5
HOURGLASS	*A&M*	16	*8 Aug 87*	10
TRUST ME TO OPEN MY MOUTH	*A&M*	72	*17 Oct 87*	1
COOL FOR CATS [RI]	*A&M*	62	*25 Apr 92*	2
Featured in the milk TV commercial.				
THIRD RAIL	*A&M*	39	*24 Jul 93*	3
SOME FANTASTIC PLACE	*A&M*	73	*11 Sep 93*	1
THIS SUMMER	*A&M*	36	*9 Sep 95*	3
ELECTRIC TRAINS	*A&M*	44	*18 Nov 95*	2
HEAVEN KNOWS	*A&M*	27	*15 Jun 96*	2
From the film 'Hackers'.				
THIS SUMMER [RM]	*A&M*	32	*24 Aug 96*	2
Remixed by Mark Stent.				
ALBUMS:	**HITS 13**		**WEEKS 124**	
COOL FOR CATS	*A&M*	45	*28 Apr 79*	11
ARGY BARGY	*A&M*	32	*16 Feb 80*	15
EAST SIDE STORY	*A&M*	19	*23 May 81*	26
SWEETS FROM A STRANGER	*A&M*	20	*15 May 82*	7
SINGLES – 45'S AND UNDER	*A&M*	3	*6 Nov 82*	29
COSI FAN TUTTI FRUTTI	*A&M*	31	*7 Sep 85*	7
BABYLON AND ON	*A&M*	14	*19 Sep 87*	8
FRANK	*A&M*	58	*23 Sep 89*	1

Every Picture Tells A Story *by **Rod Stewart** was the first album to lead the British and American albums charts simultaneously. (LFI)*

The **Stock, Aitken & Waterman** production trio have written 55 Top 20 hits. (LFI)

Andy Stewart's 'A Scottish Soldier' spent 40 weeks on the chart without climbing higher than No.19. (LFI)

The Supremes were the first female group to top the chart. (Harry Goodwin)

In 1967, the year they won the FA Cup for the fifth time, **Tottenham Hotspur FC** became the first football team to reach the EP charts. (Popperfoto)

The Tornados were the first British group to top the US chart. (Decca Records)

Veruca Salt *were named after a character in Roald Dahl's Charlie & The Chocolate Factory. (LFI)*

The longest album title to hit No.1 is by **T.Rex**. *(LFI)*

No other Top 10 hit has spent fewer weeks in the chart than 'Come Play With Me' by **The Wedding Present**. *(LFI)*

White Zombie *were named after a 1932 Bela Lugosi film. (LFI)*

Whigfield *was the first new artist to debut at No.1 on the singles chart. (LFI)*

Jimmy Young's *'Unchained Melody' was the first of seven versions of the song to chart. (LFI)*

Lena Zavaroni *was the youngest female singer to have a Top 10 single and album. (Rex Features)*

A ROUND AND A BOUT	*I.R.S.*	50	*7 Apr 90*	1
PLAY	*Reprise*	41	*7 Sep 91*	1
GREATEST HITS	*A&M*	6	*23 May 92*	13
SOME FANTASTIC PLACE	*A&M*	26	*25 Sep 93*	4
RIDICULOUS	*A&M*	50	*25 Nov 95*	1

Billy SQUIER — US

SINGLES:		HITS 1		WEEKS 3
THE STROKE	*Capitol*	52	*3 Oct 81*	3

Chris SQUIRE — UK

ALBUMS:		HITS 1		WEEKS 7
FISH OUT OF WATER	*Atlantic*	25	*6 Dec 75*	7

Dorothy SQUIRES — UK

SINGLES:		HITS 5		WEEKS 56
I'M WALKING BEHIND YOU	*Polygon*	12	*6 Jun 53*	1
SAY IT WITH FLOWERS	*Columbia*	23	*26 Aug 61*	10
Above hit: Dorothy SQUIRES/Russ CONWAY with Tony OSBORNE and his Orchestra.				
FOR ONCE IN MY LIFE	*President*	24	*20 Sep 69*	10
FOR ONCE IN MY LIFE [RE]	*President*	48	*20 Dec 69*	1
TILL	*President*	25	*21 Feb 70*	10
TILL [RE]	*President*	48	*9 May 70*	1
MY WAY (COMME D'HABITUDE)	*President*	40	*8 Aug 70*	5
MY WAY (COMME D'HABITUDE) [RE-1ST]	*President*	34	*19 Sep 70*	8
MY WAY (COMME D'HABITUDE) [RE-2ND]	*President*	25	*28 Nov 70*	10

STABBS — US/Finland/Cameroon

SINGLES:		HITS 1		WEEKS 1
JOY AND HAPPINESS	*Hi-Life*	65	*24 Dec 94*	1

STACCATO — UK/Holland

SINGLES:		HITS 1		WEEKS 1
I WANNA KNOW	*Multiply*	65	*20 Jul 96*	1

Jim STAFFORD — US

SINGLES:		HITS 2		WEEKS 16
SPIDERS & SNAKES	*MGM*	14	*27 Apr 74*	8
Originally recorded by the Bellamy Brothers.				
MY GIRL BILL	*MGM*	20	*6 Jul 74*	8

Jo STAFFORD — US

SINGLES:		HITS 4		WEEKS 28
YOU BELONG TO ME	*Columbia*	1	*15 Nov 52*	19
Above hit: Jo STAFFORD with Paul WESTON and his Orchestra				
JAMBALAYA (ON THE BAYOU)	*Columbia*	11	*20 Dec 52*	2
Originally recorded by Hank Williams.				
Above hit: Jo STAFFORD with Paul WESTON and his Orchestra and the Norman LUBOFF CHOIR.				
MAKE LOVE TO ME!	*Philips*	8	*8 May 54*	1
Above hit: Jo STAFFORD with Paul WESTON and his Orchestra.				
SUDDENLY THERE'S A VALLEY	*Philips*	12	*10 Dec 55*	5
Above hit: Jo STAFFORD with the Norman LUBOFF CHOIR.				
SUDDENLY THERE'S A VALLEY [RE]	*Philips*	19	*4 Feb 56*	1

Terry STAFFORD — US

SINGLES:		HITS 1		WEEKS 9
SUSPICION	*London*	31	*9 May 64*	9
Originally recorded by Elvis Presley in 1962.				

STAIFFI et Ses MUSTAFA'S — France

SINGLES:		HITS 1		WEEKS 1
MUSTAFA - CHA CHA ORIENTAL	*Pye International*	43	*30 Jul 60*	1

STAKKA BO — Sweden

SINGLES:		HITS 2		WEEKS 12
HERE WE GO	*Polydor*	13	*25 Sep 93*	8
DOWN THE DRAIN	*Polydor*	64	*18 Dec 93*	4

Frank STALLONE
US

(See also Various Artists: Films – Original Soundtracks 'Rocky III'.)

SINGLES:	HITS 1			WEEKS 2
FAR FROM OVER	RSO	68	22 Oct 83	2
From the film 'Staying Alive'.				

STAMFORD BRIDGE
UK

SINGLES:	HITS 1			WEEKS 1
CHELSEA	Penny Farthing	47	16 May 70	1

STAN
UK

SINGLES:	HITS 1			WEEKS 3
SUNTAN	Hug	40	31 Jul 93	3

Chuck STANLEY – See Alyson WILLIAMS

Lisa STANSFIELD
UK

(See also George Michael; Queen.)

SINGLES:	HITS 17			WEEKS 114
PEOPLE HOLD ON	Ahead Of Our Time	11	25 Mar 89	9
Above hit: COLDCUT featuring Lisa STANSFIELD.				
THIS IS THE RIGHT TIME	Arista	13	12 Aug 89	8
ALL AROUND THE WORLD	Arista	1	28 Oct 89	14
LIVE TOGETHER	Arista	10	10 Feb 90	6
WHAT DID I DO TO YOU? [EP]	Arista	25	12 May 90	4
Lead track: What Did I Do To You?				
CHANGE	Arista	10	19 Oct 91	7
ALL WOMAN	Arista	20	21 Dec 91	8
TIME TO MAKE YOU MINE	Arista	14	14 Mar 92	8
SET YOUR LOVING FREE	Arista	28	6 Jun 92	4
SOMEDAY (I'M COMING BACK)	Arista	10	19 Dec 92	9
From the film 'The Bodyguard'.				
IN ALL THE RIGHT PLACES	MCA	8	5 Jun 93	11
From the film 'Indecent Proposal'.				
SO NATURAL	Arista	15	23 Oct 93	5
LITTLE BIT OF HEAVEN	Arista	32	11 Dec 93	4
PEOPLE HOLD ON (THE BOOTLEG MIXES) [RR]	Arista	4	18 Jan 97	6
Features same baseline as Armand Van Helden's mix of Tori Amos' Professional Widow.				
Above hit: Lisa STANSFIELD vs the DIRTY ROTTEN SCOUNDRELS.				
THE REAL THING	Arista	9	22 Mar 97	7
NEVER, NEVER GONNA GIVE YOU UP	Arista	25	21 Jun 97	3
THE LINE	Arista	64	4 Oct 97	1
ALBUMS:	HITS 4			WEEKS 114
AFFECTION	Arista	2	2 Dec 89	31
REAL LOVE	Arista	3	23 Nov 91	51
SO NATURAL	Arista	6	20 Nov 93	14
LISA STANSFIELD	Arista	2	5 Apr 97	18

STAPLE SINGERS
US

SINGLES:	HITS 2			WEEKS 14
I'LL TAKE YOU THERE	Stax	30	10 Jun 72	8
IF YOU'RE READY (COME GO WITH ME)	Stax	34	8 Jun 74	6

Cyril STAPLETON and his Orchestra
UK

(See also David Whitfield.)

SINGLES:	HITS 5			WEEKS 27
ELEPHANT TANGO	Decca	20	28 May 55	2
ELEPHANT TANGO [RE-1ST]	Decca	20	2 Jul 55	1
ELEPHANT TANGO [RE-2ND]	Decca	19	23 Jul 55	1
BLUE STAR (THE "MEDIC" THEME)	Decca	2	24 Sep 55	12
Above hit: Cyril STAPLETON and his Orchestra featuring Julie DAWN.				
THE ITALIAN THEME	Decca	18	7 Apr 56	2
THE HAPPY WHISTLER	Decca	22	2 Jun 56	4
Above hit: Cyril STAPLETON and his Orchestra featuring Desmond LANE – The penny-whistle boy.				
FORGOTTEN DREAMS	Decca	27	20 Jul 57	5

Robin STAPLETON – See Aled JONES

STAR SOUND
Holland

SINGLES:	HITS 4			WEEKS 37
STARS ON 45 [M]	CBS	2	18 Apr 81	14
Consists mainly of Beatles songs.				

STARS ON 45 VOLUME 2 [M]	CBS	2	4 Jul 81	10
Consists mainly of Abba songs.				
STARS ON 45 VOLUME 3 [M]	CBS	17	19 Sep 81	6
Consists of instrumental intros.				
STARS ON STEVIE [M]	CBS	14	27 Feb 82	7
Consists of Stevie Wonder songs.				
ALBUMS:	**HITS 3**		**WEEKS 28**	
STARS ON 45	CBS	1	16 May 81	21
STARS ON 45 VOLUME 2	CBS	18	19 Sep 81	6
STARS MEDLEY	CBS	94	3 Apr 82	1

STARDUST — Sweden

SINGLES:	**HITS 1**		**WEEKS 3**	
ARIANA	Satril	42	8 Oct 77	3

STARDUST — France

SINGLES:	**HITS 1**		**WEEKS 26**	
MUSIC SOUNDS BETTER WITH YOU	Roule	55	1 Aug 98	3
French import on 12" vinyl only.				
MUSIC SOUNDS BETTER WITH YOU	Virgin	2	22 Aug 98	23
Samples Chaka Khan's Fate.				

Alvin STARDUST — UK

(See also Shane Fenton and the Fentones.)

SINGLES:	**HITS 13**		**WEEKS 119**	
MY COO CA CHOO	Magnet	2	3 Nov 73	21
Vocals by Peter Shelley.				
JEALOUS MIND	Magnet	1	16 Feb 74	11
RED DRESS	Magnet	7	4 May 74	8
YOU YOU YOU	Magnet	6	31 Aug 74	10
TELL ME WHY	Magnet	16	30 Nov 74	8
GOOD LOVE CAN NEVER DIE	Magnet	11	1 Feb 75	9
SWEET CHEATIN' RITA	Magnet	37	12 Jul 75	4
PRETEND	Stiff	4	5 Sep 81	10
A WONDERFUL TIME UP THERE	Stiff	56	21 Nov 81	8
I FEEL LIKE BUDDY HOLLY	Chrysalis	7	5 May 84	11
I WON'T RUN AWAY	Chrysalis	7	27 Oct 84	13
SO NEAR TO CHRISTMAS	Chrysalis	29	15 Dec 84	4
GOT A LITTLE HEARTACHE	Chrysalis	55	23 Mar 85	2
ALBUMS:	**HITS 3**		**WEEKS 17**	
THE UNTOUCHABLE	Magnet	4	16 Mar 74	12
ALVIN STARDUST	Magnet	37	21 Dec 74	3
ROCK WITH ALVIN	Magnet	52	4 Oct 75	2

STARGARD — US

SINGLES:	**HITS 3**		**WEEKS 14**	
THEME SONG FROM "WHICH WAY IS UP"	MCA	19	28 Jan 78	7
Theme from the film.				
LOVE IS SO EASY	MCA	45	15 Apr 78	1
WHAT YOU WAITIN' FOR	MCA	39	9 Sep 78	6

STARGAZERS — UK

SINGLES:	**HITS 9**		**WEEKS 68**	
BROKEN WINGS	Decca	11	14 Feb 53	1
Originally recorded by Art and Dotty Todd.				
BROKEN WINGS [RE]	Decca	1	28 Feb 53	11
I SEE THE MOON	Decca	1	20 Feb 54	15
Above hit: STARGAZERS with Syd DEAN and his Orchestra.				
THE HAPPY WANDERER	Decca	12	10 Apr 54	1
Above hit: STARGAZERS with Syd DEAN and his Band.				
THE FINGER OF SUSPICION	Decca	1	18 Dec 54	15
Above hit: Dickie VALENTINE with the STARGAZERS.				
SOMEBODY	Decca	20	5 Mar 55	1
Above hit: STARGAZERS with Sonny FARRAR and his Banjo Band.				
THE CRAZY OTTO RAG	Decca	18	4 Jun 55	3
CLOSE THE DOOR	Decca	6	10 Sep 55	9
Above hit: STARGAZERS with Johnnie GRAY and the Band of the Day.				
TWENTY TINY FINGERS	Decca	4	12 Nov 55	11
Above hit: STARGAZERS with Syd DEAN and his Band.				
HOT DIGGITY (DOG ZIGGITY BOOM)	Decca	28	23 Jun 56	1
Above hit: STARGAZERS with Johnnie GRAY and his Band of the Day.				

STARGAZERS
UK

SINGLES:		HITS 1		WEEKS 3
GROOVE BABY GROOVE [EP]	Epic	56	6 Feb 82	3

Lead track: Groove Baby Groove.

Ed STARINK
US

ALBUMS:		HITS 2		WEEKS 11
SYNTHESIZER GREATEST	Arcade	22	27 Oct 90	5
SYNTHESIZER GOLD	Arcada	29	9 Jan 93	6

STARJETS
UK

SINGLES:		HITS 1		WEEKS 5
WAR STORIES	Epic	51	8 Sep 79	5

STARLAND VOCAL BAND
US

SINGLES:		HITS 1		WEEKS 10
AFTERNOON DELIGHT	RCA Victor	18	7 Aug 76	10

STARLIGHT
Italy

SINGLES:		HITS 1		WEEKS 11
NUMERO UNO	Citybeat	9	19 Aug 89	11

STARLITERS – See Joey DEE and the STARLITERS

Edwin STARR
US

SINGLES:		HITS 9		WEEKS 70
STOP HER ON SIGHT (SOS)	Polydor	35	14 May 66	8
HEADLINE NEWS	Polydor	39	20 Aug 66	3
STOP HER ON SIGHT (SOS) [RI] / HEADLINE NEWS [RI]	Polydor	11	14 Dec 68	11

Headline News no longer listed from 25 Jan 69. As an AA side it peaked at No. 16.

25 MILES	Tamla Motown	36	13 Sep 69	6
WAR	Tamla Motown	3	24 Oct 70	12

Originally recorded by the Temptations.

STOP THE WAR NOW	Tamla Motown	33	20 Feb 71	1
CONTACT	20th Century	6	27 Jan 79	12
H.A.P.P.Y. RADIO	20th Century	9	26 May 79	11
IT AIN'T FAIR	Hippodrome	56	1 Jun 85	4
WAR [RR]	Weekend	69	30 Oct 93	2

The instrumental version is used to accompany the ITV series 'Gladiators'. [AA] listed with Wild
*   Thing by The Troggs and Wolf.*
Above hit: Edwin STARR and SHADOW.

Freddie STARR
UK

SINGLES:		HITS 2		WEEKS 14
IT'S YOU	Tiffany	9	23 Feb 74	10
WHITE CHRISTMAS	Thunderbird	41	20 Dec 75	4

Recorded as an impressionist of people from his TV show.

ALBUMS:		HITS 2		WEEKS 16
AFTER THE LAUGHTER	Dover	10	18 Nov 89	9
THE WANDERER	Dover	33	17 Nov 90	7

Jennifer STARR – See PURE SUGAR vocals by Jennifer STARR

Kay STARR
US

SINGLES:		HITS 5		WEEKS 58
COMES A-LONG A-LOVE	Capitol	1	6 Dec 52	16
SIDE BY SIDE	Capitol	7	25 Apr 53	4
CHANGING PARTNERS	Capitol	4	20 Mar 54	14
AM I A TOY OR TREASURE	Capitol	17	16 Oct 54	3
AM I A TOY OR TREASURE [RE]	Capitol	20	13 Nov 54	1
ROCK AND ROLL WALTZ	His Master's Voice	1	18 Feb 56	20

Above hit: Kay STARR with Hugo WINTERHALTER'S ORCHESTRA and CHORUS.

ALBUMS:		HITS 1		WEEKS 1
MOVIN'	Capitol	16	26 Mar 60	1

Ringo STARR
UK

SINGLES:		HITS 6		WEEKS 56
IT DON'T COME EASY	Apple	4	17 Apr 71	11

Features both George Harrison and Stephen Stills on guitar and Badfinger on backing vocals.

BACK OFF BOOGALOO	Apple	2	1 Apr 72	10
PHOTOGRAPH	Apple	8	27 Oct 73	13

Features George Harrison on backing vocal and guitar.

YOU'RE SIXTEEN	Apple	4	23 Feb 74	10

Features backing vocals from Harry Nilsson and Paul McCartney.

ONLY YOU	Apple	28	30 Nov 74	11
WEIGHT OF THE WORLD	Private Music	74	6 Jun 92	1
ALBUMS:	**HITS 3**			**WEEKS 28**
SENTIMENTAL JOURNEY	Apple	7	18 Apr 70	6
RINGO	Apple	7	8 Dec 73	20
GOODNIGHT VIENNA	Apple	30	7 Dec 74	2

STARS ON 54: Ultra NATE, AMBER, Jocelyn ENRIQUEZ — US

SINGLES:	**HITS 1**			**WEEKS 3**
IF YOU COULD READ MY MIND	Tommy Boy	23	28 Nov 98	3

STARSHIP — US

SINGLES:	**HITS 4**			**WEEKS 41**
JANE	Grunt	21	26 Jan 80	9
Above hit: JEFFERSON STARSHIP.				
WE BUILT THIS CITY	RCA	12	16 Nov 85	12
SARA	RCA	66	8 Feb 86	3
NOTHING'S GONNA STOP US NOW	Grunt	1	11 Apr 87	17
From the film 'Mannequin'.				
ALBUMS:	**HITS 7**			**WEEKS 28**
BLESS ITS POINTED LITTLE HEAD	RCA Victor	38	28 Jun 69	1
Live recordings.				
VOLUNTEERS	RCA Victor	34	7 Mar 70	7
BARK	Grunt	42	2 Oct 71	1
LONG JOHN SILVER	Grunt	30	2 Sep 72	1
Above 4: JEFFERSON AIRPLANE.				
SPITFIRE	Grunt	30	31 Jul 76	2
FREEDOM AT POINT ZERO	Grunt	22	9 Feb 80	11
Above 2: JEFFERSON STARSHIP.				
NO PROTECTION	Grunt	26	18 Jul 87	5

STARSHIP TROOPERS – See Sarah BRIGHTMAN

STARTRAX — UK

SINGLES:	**HITS 1**			**WEEKS 8**
STARTRAX CLUB DISCO [M]	Picksy	18	1 Aug 81	8
Consists of Bee Gees' songs.				
ALBUMS:	**HITS 1**			**WEEKS 7**
STARTRAX CLUB DISCO	Picksy	26	1 Aug 81	7

STARTURN ON 45 (PINTS) — UK

SINGLES:	**HITS 2**			**WEEKS 9**
STARTURN ON 45 (PINTS) [M]	V Tone	45	24 Oct 81	4
Parody of the influx of medleys charting during 1981.				
PUMP UP THE BITTER (BRUTAL MIX)	Pacific	12	30 Apr 88	5
Parody of M/A/R/R/S' Pump Up The Volume and Bomb The Bass' Beat Dis.				

STARVATION/TAM-TAM POUR L'ETHIOPIE — Multi-National

SINGLES:	**HITS 1**			**WEEKS 6**
STARVATION / TAM-TAM POUR L'ETHIOPIE	Zarjazz	33	9 Mar 85	6
Charity record in aid of African famine charities: Oxfam, War On Want and Medecins Sans Frontieres.				

STARVING SOULS — UK

SINGLES:	**HITS 1**			**WEEKS 1**
I BE THE PROPHET [EP]	Durban Poison	66	21 Oct 95	1
Lead track: I Be The Prophet, which features vocals by Terry Hall.				

STATE OF MIND — UK

SINGLES:	**HITS 2**			**WEEKS 3**
THIS IS IT	Sound Of Ministry	30	18 Apr 98	2
TAKE CONTROL	Sound Of Ministry	46	25 Jul 98	1

STATE OF THE HEART — UK

ALBUMS:	**HITS 2**			**WEEKS 9**
PURE SAX	Virgin	18	16 Mar 96	7
SAX AT THE MOVIES	Virgin	62	12 Oct 96	2

STATLER BROTHERS — US

SINGLES:	**HITS 1**			**WEEKS 4**
FLOWERS ON THE WALL	CBS	38	26 Feb 66	4

Candi STATON US

SINGLES:	HITS 8		WEEKS 71
YOUNG HEARTS RUN FREE	*Warner Brothers*	2	29 May 76	13
DESTINY	*Warner Brothers*	41	18 Sep 76	3
NIGHTS ON BROADWAY	*Warner Brothers*	6	23 Jul 77	12
Original by the Bee Gees reached No. 7 in the US in 1975.				
HONESTLY I DO LOVE YOU	*Warner Brothers*	48	3 Jun 78	5
SUSPICIOUS MINDS	*Sugar Hill*	31	24 Apr 82	9
YOUNG HEARTS RUN FREE [RI]	*Warner Brothers*	47	31 May 86	5
YOU GOT THE LOVE	*Truelove*	4	2 Feb 91	11
Original release reached No. 95 in 1986. Original vocal version of the song was by Jamie Principal and was called Your Love.				
YOU GOT THE LOVE [RM]	*React*	3	1 Mar 97	8
Remixed by Now Voyager (AKA John Truelove).				
Above 2: SOURCE featuring Candi STATON.				
LOVE ON LOVE	*React*	27	17 Apr 99	3
YOUNG HEARTS RUN FREE [RR]	*React*	29	7 Aug 99	2
ALBUMS:	**HITS 1**		**WEEKS 3**
YOUNG HEARTS RUN FREE	*Warner Brothers*	34	24 Jul 76	3

STATUS IV US

SINGLES:	HITS 1		WEEKS 3
YOU AIN'T REALLY DOWN	*TMT Productions*	56	9 Jul 83	3

STATUS QUO UK

(See also Francis Rossi.)

SINGLES:	HITS 55		WEEKS 412
PICTURES OF MATCHSTICK MEN	*Pye*	7	27 Jan 68	12
ICE IN THE SUN	*Pye*	8	24 Aug 68	12
Written by Marty Wilde.				
ARE YOU GROWING TIRED OF MY LOVE	*Pye*	46	31 May 69	2
Originally recorded by Nancy Sinatra.				
ARE YOU GROWING TIRED OF MY LOVE [RE]	*Pye*	50	21 Jun 69	1
DOWN THE DUSTPIPE	*Pye*	12	2 May 70	17
IN MY CHAIR	*Pye*	21	7 Nov 70	14
PAPER PLANE	*Vertigo*	8	13 Jan 73	11
MEAN GIRL	*Pye*	20	14 Apr 73	11
CAROLINE	*Vertigo*	5	8 Sep 73	13
Originally written in 1970.				
BREAK THE RULES	*Vertigo*	8	4 May 74	8
DOWN DOWN	*Vertigo*	1	7 Dec 74	11
ROLL OVER LAY DOWN	*Vertigo*	9	17 May 75	8
RAIN	*Vertigo*	7	14 Feb 76	7
MYSTERY SONG	*Vertigo*	11	10 Jul 76	9
WILD SIDE OF LIFE	*Vertigo*	9	11 Dec 76	12
Originally recorded by Hank Thompson.				
ROCKIN' ALL OVER THE WORLD	*Vertigo*	3	8 Oct 77	16
Original by John Fogerty reached No. 27 in the US in 1975.				
AGAIN AND AGAIN	*Vertigo*	13	2 Sep 78	9
ACCIDENT PRONE	*Vertigo*	36	25 Nov 78	8
WHATEVER YOU WANT	*Vertigo*	4	22 Sep 79	9
LIVING ON AN ISLAND	*Vertigo*	16	24 Nov 79	10
WHAT YOU'RE PROPOSING	*Vertigo*	2	11 Oct 80	11
LIES / DON'T DRIVE MY CAR	*Vertigo*	11	6 Dec 80	10
Don't Drive My Car listed from 20 Dec 80.				
SOMETHING 'BOUT YOU BABY I LIKE	*Vertigo*	9	28 Feb 81	7
ROCK N' ROLL	*Vertigo*	8	28 Nov 81	11
DEAR JOHN	*Vertigo*	10	27 Mar 82	8
SHE DON'T FOOL ME	*Vertigo*	36	12 Jun 82	5
CAROLINE (LIVE AT THE N.E.C.) [RR]	*Vertigo*	13	30 Oct 82	7
OL' RAG BLUES	*Vertigo*	9	10 Sep 83	8
A MESS OF BLUES	*Vertigo*	15	5 Nov 83	6
MARGUERITA TIME	*Vertigo*	3	10 Dec 83	11
GOING DOWN TOWN TONIGHT	*Vertigo*	20	19 May 84	6
THE WANDERER	*Vertigo*	7	27 Oct 84	11
ROLLIN' HOME	*Vertigo*	9	17 May 86	6
RED SKY	*Vertigo*	19	26 Jul 86	8
Originally recorded by Bolland and Bolland.				
IN THE ARMY NOW	*Vertigo*	2	4 Oct 86	14
DREAMIN'	*Vertigo*	15	6 Dec 86	6
AIN'T COMPLAINING	*Vertigo*	19	26 Mar 88	6
WHO GETS THE LOVE?	*Vertigo*	34	21 May 88	4
RUNNING ALL OVER THE WORLD [RR]	*Vertigo*	17	20 Aug 88	6
Alternative wording to support the Sport Aid '88 charity. The worldwide run took place 11 Sep 88.				
BURNING BRIDGES (ON AND OFF AND ON AGAIN)	*Vertigo*	5	3 Dec 88	10
NOT AT ALL	*Vertigo*	50	28 Oct 89	2

THE ANNIVERSARY WALTZ – PART ONE [M]	Vertigo	2	29 Sep 90	9
THE ANNIVERSARY WALTZ (PART TWO) [M]	Vertigo	16	15 Dec 90	7
Above 2 medleys of rock 'n' roll classics were live recordings from Bray.				
CAN'T GIVE YOU MORE	Vertigo	37	7 Sep 91	3
ROCK 'TIL YOU DROP	Vertigo	38	18 Jan 92	3
ROADHOUSE MEDLEY (ANNIVERSARY WALTZ PART 25) [M]	Polydor	21	10 Oct 92	4
I DIDN'T MEAN IT	Polydor	21	6 Aug 94	4
SHERRI DON'T FAIL ME NOW!	Polydor	38	22 Oct 94	2
RESTLESS	Polydor	39	3 Dec 94	2
Originally recorded by Jennifer Warnes.				
WHEN YOU WALK IN THE ROOM	PolyGram TV	34	4 Nov 95	2
FUN FUN FUN	PolyGram TV	24	2 Mar 96	4
Above hit: STATUS QUO with the BEACH BOYS.				
DON'T STOP	PolyGram TV	35	13 Apr 96	2
ALL AROUND MY HAT	PolyGram TV	47	9 Nov 96	1
Above hit: STATUS QUO with Maddy PRIOR from STEELEYE SPAN.				
THE WAY IT GOES	Eagle	39	20 Mar 99	2
LITTLE WHITE LIES	Eagle	47	12 Jun 99	1
TWENTY WILD HORSES	Eagle	53	2 Oct 99	1
ALBUMS:	**HITS 30**			**WEEKS 454**
PILEDRIVER	Vertigo	5	20 Jan 73	37
THE BEST OF STATUS QUO	Pye	32	9 Jun 73	7
HELLO	Vertigo	1	6 Oct 73	28
QUO	Vertigo	2	18 May 74	16
ON THE LEVEL	Vertigo	1	1 Mar 75	27
DOWN THE DUSTPIPE	Golden Hour	20	8 Mar 75	6
Material recorded for Pye records during 1970/71.				
BLUE FOR YOU	Vertigo	1	20 Mar 76	30
STATUS QUO - LIVE	Vertigo	3	12 Mar 77	14
ROCKIN' ALL OVER THE WORLD	Vertigo	5	26 Nov 77	15
IF YOU CAN'T STAND THE HEAT	Vertigo	3	11 Nov 78	14
WHATEVER YOU WANT	Vertigo	3	20 Oct 79	14
12 GOLD BARS	Vertigo	3	22 Mar 80	48
Compilation.				
JUST SUPPOSIN'	Vertigo	4	25 Oct 80	18
NEVER TOO LATE	Vertigo	2	28 Mar 81	13
FRESH QUOTA	PRT	74	10 Oct 81	1
Compilation of rarities from late 1960s/early 1970s.				
1982	Vertigo	1	24 Apr 82	20
"FROM THE MAKERS OF . . ."	Vertigo	4	13 Nov 82	18
Compilation which includes album of live recordings from the Birmingham N.E.C.				
BACK TO BACK	Vertigo	9	3 Dec 83	22
STATUS QUO LIVE AT THE N.E.C.	Vertigo	83	4 Aug 84	3
Dutch import.				
12 GOLD BARS VOLUME TWO - (AND ONE)	Vertigo	12	1 Dec 84	18
New compilation including the 1980 package.				
IN THE ARMY NOW	Vertigo	7	6 Sep 86	23
AIN'T COMPLAINING	Vertigo	12	18 Jun 88	5
PERFECT REMEDY	Vertigo	49	2 Dec 89	2
ROCKING ALL OVER THE YEARS	Vertigo	2	20 Oct 90	25
Compilation.				
ROCK 'TIL YOU DROP	Vertigo	10	5 Oct 91	7
LIVE ALIVE QUO	Polydor	37	14 Nov 92	1
THIRSTY WORK	Polydor	13	3 Sep 94	3
DON'T STOP - THE 30TH ANNIVERSARY ALBUM	PolyGram TV	2	17 Feb 96	11
Cover versions.				
WHATEVER YOU WANT - THE VERY BEST OF STATUS QUO	Mercury TV	13	25 Oct 97	6
UNDER THE INFLUENCE	Eagle	26	10 Apr 99	2

STAXX				**UK**
SINGLES:	**HITS 2**			**WEEKS 11**
JOY	Champion	25	2 Oct 93	6
YOU	Champion	50	20 May 95	1
JOY [RM]	Champion	14	13 Sep 97	4
Remixed by Mondo.				

STEALERS WHEEL				**UK**
SINGLES:	**HITS 3**			**WEEKS 22**
STUCK IN THE MIDDLE	A&M	8	26 May 73	10
Some copies have title in full as Stuck In The Middle With You.				
EVERYTHING'L TURN OUT FINE	A&M	33	1 Sep 73	6
STAR	A&M	25	26 Jan 74	6

STEAM				**US**
SINGLES:	**HITS 1**			**WEEKS 14**
NA NA HEY HEY KISS HIM GOODBYE	Fontana	9	31 Jan 70	14

STEEL – See UNITONE ROCKERS featuring STEEL

Anthony STEEL with the RADIO REVELLERS and Jackie BROWN and his Music UK

SINGLES:		HITS 1		WEEKS 6	
WEST OF ZANZIBAR	*Polygon*		11	*11 Sep 54*	6

STEEL HORSES – See TRUMAN and WOLFF featuring STEEL HORSES

STEEL PULSE UK

SINGLES:		HITS 3		WEEKS 12	
KU KLUX KLAN	*Island*		41	*1 Apr 78*	4
PRODIGAL SON	*Island*		35	*8 Jul 78*	6
SOUND SYSTEM	*Island*		71	*23 Jun 79*	2
ALBUMS:		**HITS 2**		**WEEKS 18**	
HANDSWORTH REVOLUTION	*Island*		9	*5 Aug 78*	12
TRIBUTE TO MARTYRS	*Island*		42	*14 Jul 79*	6

Tommy STEELE and the STEELMEN UK

(See also All Star Hit Parade.)

SINGLES:		HITS 17		WEEKS 147	
ROCK WITH THE CAVEMAN	*Decca*		13	*27 Oct 56*	4
ROCK WITH THE CAVEMAN [RE]	*Decca*		23	*1 Dec 56*	1
SINGING THE BLUES	*Decca*		1	*15 Dec 56*	13
KNEE DEEP IN THE BLUES	*Decca*		15	*16 Feb 57*	9
SINGING THE BLUES [RE-1ST]	*Decca*		24	*20 Apr 57*	1
BUTTERFINGERS	*Decca*		25	*4 May 57*	1
From the film 'The Tommy Steele Story'.					
BUTTERFINGERS [RE]	*Decca*		8	*18 May 57*	17
SINGING THE BLUES [RE-2ND]	*Decca*		29	*18 May 57*	1
WATER, WATER / A HANDFUL OF SONGS	*Decca*		5	*17 Aug 57*	16
A Handful Of Songs listed from 24 Aug 57. From the film 'The Tommy Steele Story'. A Handful Of Songs was also used as the theme to his TV show.					
SHIRALEE	*Decca*		11	*31 Aug 57*	4
From the film of the same name.					
HEY, YOU!	*Decca*		28	*23 Nov 57*	1
A HANDFUL OF SONGS / WATER, WATER [RE]	*Decca*		28	*14 Dec 57*	1
NAIROBI	*Decca*		3	*8 Mar 58*	11
Originally recorded by Bob Merrill.					
HAPPY GUITAR	*Decca*		20	*26 Apr 58*	5
From the film 'The Duke Wore Jeans'.					
THE ONLY MAN ON THE ISLAND	*Decca*		16	*19 Jul 58*	8
COME ON, LET'S GO	*Decca*		10	*15 Nov 58*	13
Original by Richie Valens reached No. 42 in the US.					
TALLAHASSEE LASSIE	*Decca*		16	*15 Aug 59*	4
GIVE! GIVE! GIVE!	*Decca*		28	*29 Aug 59*	2
Above 2 entries were separate sides of the same release, each had its own chart run.					
TALLAHASSEE LASSIE [RE]	*Decca*		25	*26 Sep 59*	1
LITTLE WHITE BULL	*Decca*		6	*5 Dec 59*	12
From the film 'Tommy The Toreador'.					
LITTLE WHITE BULL [RE]	*Decca*		30	*12 Mar 60*	5
WHAT A MOUTH (WHAT A NORTH AND SOUTH)	*Decca*		5	*25 Jun 60*	11
MUST BE SANTA	*Decca*		40	*31 Dec 60*	1
THE WRITING ON THE WALL	*Decca*		30	*19 Aug 61*	5
Original by Adam Wade reached No. 5 in the US in 1961.					
Above 9: Tommy STEELE.					
EPS:		**HITS 1**		**WEEKS 14**	
TOMMY THE TOREADOR [OST]	*Decca*		4	*12 Mar 60*	14
Above hit: Tommy STEELE.					

STEELEYE SPAN UK

SINGLES:		HITS 2		WEEKS 18	
GAUDETE	*Chrysalis*		14	*8 Dec 73*	9
Originally released in 1972.					
ALL AROUND MY HAT	*Chrysalis*		5	*15 Nov 75*	9
ALBUMS:		**HITS 7**		**WEEKS 48**	
PLEASE TO SEE THE KING	*B&C*		45	*10 Apr 71*	2
BELOW THE SALT	*Chrysalis*		43	*14 Oct 72*	1
PARCEL OF ROGUES	*Chrysalis*		26	*28 Apr 73*	5
NOW WE ARE SIX	*Chrysalis*		13	*23 Mar 74*	13
COMMONER'S CROWN	*Chrysalis*		21	*15 Feb 75*	4
ALL AROUND MY HAT	*Chrysalis*		7	*25 Oct 75*	20
ROCKET COTTAGE	*Chrysalis*		41	*16 Oct 76*	3

STEELY DAN | | | | US

SINGLES:		HITS 4			WEEKS 21
DO IT AGAIN	ABC		39	30 Aug 75	4
HAITIAN DIVORCE	ABC		17	11 Dec 76	9
FM (NO STATIC AT ALL)	MCA		49	29 Jul 78	4
From the film 'FM'.					
FM (NO STATIC AT ALL) [RE]	MCA		75	2 Sep 78	1
RIKKI DON'T LOSE THAT NUMBER	ABC		58	10 Mar 79	3
ALBUMS:		HITS 12			WEEKS 83
PRETZEL LOGIC	Probe		37	30 Mar 74	2
KATY LIED	ABC		13	3 May 75	6
CAN'T BUY A THRILL	ABC		38	20 Sep 75	1
Originally released in 1973.					
ROYAL SCAM	ABC		11	22 May 76	13
AJA	ABC		5	8 Oct 77	10
GREATEST HITS	ABC		41	2 Dec 78	18
GAUCHO	MCA		27	29 Nov 80	12
GOLD	MCA		44	3 Jul 82	6
Compilation.					
REELIN' IN THE YEARS - VERY BEST OF STEELY DAN	MCA		43	26 Oct 85	5
DO IT AGAIN - THE VERY BEST OF STEELY DAN	Telstar		64	10 Oct 87	4
REMASTERED - THE BEST OF STEELY DAN	MCA		42	20 Nov 93	5
ALIVE IN AMERICA	Giant		62	28 Oct 95	1
Live recordings from their 1993/94 tour.					

Wout STEENHUIS | | | | Holland

ALBUMS:		HITS 1			WEEKS 7
HAWAIIAN PARADISE/CHRISTMAS	Warwick		28	21 Nov 81	7

Jim STEINMAN | | | | US

SINGLES:		HITS 2			WEEKS 9
ROCK AND ROLL DREAMS COME THROUGH	Epic		52	4 Jul 81	7
Features vocals by Rory Dodd.					
TONIGHT IS WHAT IT MEANS TO BE YOUNG	MCA		67	23 Jun 84	2
Above hit: Jim STEINMAN and FIRE INC.					
ALBUMS:		HITS 1			WEEKS 25
BAD FOR GOOD	Epic		7	9 May 81	25

STEINSKI and MASS MEDIA | | | | US

SINGLES:		HITS 1			WEEKS 2
WE'LL BE RIGHT BACK	Fourth & Broadway		63	31 Jan 87	2

Doreen STEPHENS – See Billy COTTON and his BAND

Richie STEPHENS featuring GENERAL DEGREE | | | | Jamaica

SINGLES:		HITS 2			WEEKS 2
LEGACY	Columbia		64	15 May 93	1
Above hit: MAD COBRA featuring Richie STEPHENS.					
COME GIVE ME YOUR LOVE	Delirious		61	9 Aug 97	1
Features Sly and Robbie's Taxi Gang.					

Martin STEPHENSON and the DAINTEES | | | | UK

SINGLES:		HITS 3			WEEKS 7
BOAT TO BOLIVIA	Kitchenware		70	8 Nov 86	2
TROUBLE TOWN	Kitchenware		58	17 Jan 87	3
Above hit: DAINTEES.					
BIG SKY NEW LIGHT	Kitchenware		71	27 Jun 92	2
ALBUMS:		HITS 4			WEEKS 11
BOAT TO BOLIVIA	Kitchenware		85	17 May 86	3
GLADSOME, HUMOUR AND BLUE	Kitchenware		39	16 Apr 88	4
SALUTATION ROAD	Kitchenware		35	19 May 90	3
THE BOY'S HEART	Kitchenware		68	25 Jul 92	1

STEPPENWOLF | | | | US/Canada

SINGLES:		HITS 1			WEEKS 14
BORN TO BE WILD	Stateside		30	14 Jun 69	7
Originally released in 1968. From the film 'Easy Rider'.					
BORN TO BE WILD [RE]	Stateside		50	9 Aug 69	2
BORN TO BE WILD [RI]	Universal		18	27 Feb 99	5
Featured in the Ford Cougar TV commercial.					
ALBUMS:		HITS 3			WEEKS 20
MONSTER	Stateside		43	28 Feb 70	4

STEPPENWOLF	*Stateside*	59	*25 Apr 70*	2
Originally released in 1968.				
STEPPENWOLF LIVE	*Stateside*	16	*4 Jul 70*	14

STEPS UK

(See also Steps Tina Cousins Cleopatra B*Witched Billie.)

SINGLES:	HITS 8		WEEKS 113	
5,6,7,8	*Jive*	14	*22 Nov 97*	17
LAST THING ON MY MIND	*Jive*	6	*2 May 98*	14
Originally recorded by Bananarama.				
ONE FOR SORROW	*Jive*	2	*5 Sep 98*	11
HEARTBEAT / TRAGEDY	*Jive*	1	*21 Nov 98*	30
BETTER BEST FORGOTTEN	*Jive*	2	*20 Mar 99*	15
BETTER BEST FORGOTTEN [RE]	*Jive*	49	*10 Jul 99*	2
LOVE'S GOT A HOLD ON MY HEART	*Jive*	2	*24 Jul 99*	11
AFTER THE LOVE HAS GONE	*Jive*	5	*23 Oct 99*	9
LOVE'S GOT A HOLD ON MY HEART [RE]	*Jive*	73	*23 Oct 99*	1
SAY YOU'LL BE MINE / BETTER THE DEVIL YOU KNOW	*Jive*	7	*25 Dec 99*	2
AFTER THE LOVE HAS GONE [RE]	*Jive*	70	*1 Jan 00*	1
ALBUMS:	HITS 2		WEEKS 71	
STEP ONE	*Jive*	2	*26 Sept 98*	62
STEPTACULAR	*Jive*	1	*6 Nov 99*	9

STEPS Tina COUSINS CLEOPATRA B*WITCHED BILLIE UK/Ireland

(See also B*Witched; Billie; Cleopatra; Tina Cousins; Steps.)

SINGLES:	HITS 1		WEEKS 13	
THANK ABBA FOR THE MUSIC [M]	*Epic*	4	*10 Apr 99*	13
Charity record in aid of the BRIT trust.				

STEPZ – See QUARTZ

STEREO MC'S UK

SINGLES:	HITS 6		WEEKS 31	
ELEVATE MY MIND	*Fourth & Broadway*	74	*29 Sep 90*	1
LOST IN MUSIC	*Fourth & Broadway*	46	*9 Mar 91*	3
CONNECTED	*Fourth & Broadway*	18	*26 Sep 92*	6
Samples Jimmy "Bo" Horne's Let Me (Let Me Be Your Lover). Featured in the Carphone warehouse Radio commercials.				
STEP IT UP	*Fourth & Broadway*	12	*5 Dec 92*	12
GROUND LEVEL	*Fourth & Broadway*	19	*20 Feb 93*	5
CREATION	*Fourth & Broadway*	19	*29 May 93*	4
ALBUMS:	HITS 1		WEEKS 52	
CONNECTED	*Fourth & Broadway*	2	*17 Oct 92*	52

STEREO NATION UK

SINGLES:	HITS 1		WEEKS 1	
I'VE BEEN WAITING	*EMI Premier*	53	*17 Aug 96*	1

STEREOLAB UK/France

SINGLES:	HITS 5		WEEKS 6	
JENNY ONDIOLINE / FRENCH DISKO	*Duophonic Ultra High Frequency*	75	*8 Jan 94*	1
Originally released in 1993.				
PING PONG	*Duophonic Ultra High Frequency*	45	*30 Jul 94*	2
WOW AND FLUTTER	*Duophonic Ultra High Frequency*	70	*12 Nov 94*	1
CYBELE'S REVERIE	*Duophonic Ultra High Frequency*	62	*2 Mar 96*	1
MISS MODULAR	*Duophonic Ultra High Frequency*	60	*13 Sep 97*	1
ALBUMS:	HITS 6		WEEKS 11	
TRANSIENT RANDOM NOISE BURSTS	*Duophonic Ultra High Frequency*	62	*18 Sep 93*	1
MARS AUDIAC QUINTET	*Duophonic Ultra High Frequency*	16	*20 Aug 94*	3
MUSIC FOR AMORPHOUS BODY STUDY CENTRE	*Duophonic Ultra High Frequency*	59	*29 Apr 95*	1
Music set to accompany sculptor Charle's Long's exhibition in New York.				
REFRIED ECTOPLASM (SWITCHED ON - VOLUME 2)	*Duophonic Ultra High Frequency*	30	*16 Sep 95*	2
Collection of early limited edition singles.				
EMPEROR TOMATO KETCHUP	*Duophonic Ultra High Frequency*	27	*30 Mar 96*	2
DOTS AND LOOPS	*Duophonic Ultra High Frequency*	19	*4 Oct 97*	2

STEREOPHONICS UK

SINGLES:	HITS 9		WEEKS 56	
LOCAL BOY IN THE PHOTOGRAPH	*V2*	51	*29 Mar 97*	1
MORE LIFE IN A TRAMPS VEST	*V2*	33	*31 May 97*	2
A THOUSAND TREES	*V2*	22	*23 Aug 97*	3
TRAFFIC	*V2*	20	*8 Nov 97*	3
LOCAL BOY IN THE PHOTOGRAPH [RI]	*V2*	14	*21 Feb 98*	4
THE BARTENDER AND THE THIEF	*V2*	3	*21 Nov 98*	12

JUST LOOKING	V2	4	6 Mar 99	8
PICK A PART THAT'S NEW	V2	4	15 May 99	9
JUST LOOKING [RE]	V2	73	29 May 99	1
I WOULDN'T BELIEVE YOUR RADIO	V2	11	4 Sept 99	6
I WOULDN'T BELIEVE YOUR RADIO [RE]	V2	71	30 Oct 99	1
HURRY UP AND WAIT	V2	11	20 Nov 99	5
HURRY UP AND WAIT [RE]	V2	75	1 Jan 00	1
ALBUMS:	**HITS 2**		**WEEKS 123**	
WORD GETS AROUND	V2	6	6 Sept 97	81
PERFORMANCE AND COCKTAILS	V2	1	20 Mar 99	42

STETSASONIC   US

SINGLES:	**HITS 1**		**WEEKS 3**	
TALKIN' ALL THAT JAZZ	Breakout	73	24 Sep 88	2
Samples a Donald Byrd trumpet solo.				
TALKIN ALL THAT JAZZ [RM]	Tommy Boy	54	7 Nov 98	1
Remixed by Dimiti From Paris.				

STEVE and EYDIE – See Eydie GORME; Steve LAWRENCE

April STEVENS – See Nino TEMPO and April STEVENS

Cat STEVENS   UK

SINGLES:	**HITS 11**		**WEEKS 96**	
I LOVE MY DOG	Deram	28	22 Oct 66	7
MATTHEW AND SON	Deram	2	14 Jan 67	10
I'M GONNA GET ME A GUN	Deram	6	1 Apr 67	10
A BAD NIGHT	Deram	20	5 Aug 67	8
KITTY	Deram	47	23 Dec 67	1
LADY D'ARBANVILLE	Island	8	27 Jun 70	13
Dedicated to his ex-girlfriend Patti D'Arbanville. Flute by Peter Gabriel.				
MOON SHADOW	Island	22	28 Aug 71	11
MORNING HAS BROKEN	Island	9	1 Jan 72	13
His version of Eleanor Fareon's children's hymn featuring Rick Wakeman on piano.				
CAN'T KEEP IT IN	Island	13	9 Dec 72	12
ANOTHER SATURDAY NIGHT	Island	19	24 Aug 74	8
(REMEMBER THE DAYS OF THE) OLD SCHOOL YARD	Island	44	2 Jul 77	3
Features vocal by Elkie Brooks.				
ALBUMS:	**HITS 11**		**WEEKS 265**	
MATTHEW AND SON	Deram	7	25 Mar 67	16
MONA BONE JAKON	Island	63	11 Jul 70	4
TEA FOR THE TILLERMAN	Island	20	28 Nov 70	39
TEASER AND THE FIRECAT	Island	3	2 Oct 71	93
CATCH BULL AT FOUR	Island	2	7 Oct 72	27
FOREIGNER	Island	3	21 Jul 73	10
BUDDAH AND THE CHOCOLATE BOX	Island	3	6 Apr 74	15
GREATEST HITS	Island	2	19 Jul 75	24
IZITSO	Island	18	14 May 77	15
THE VERY BEST OF CAT STEVENS	Island	4	3 Feb 90	16
REMEMBER CAT STEVENS - THE ULTIMATE COLLECTION	Island	31	27 Nov 99	6

Connie STEVENS   US

SINGLES:	**HITS 2**		**WEEKS 20**	
SIXTEEN REASONS	Warner Brothers	9	7 May 60	11
Above hit: Connie STEVENS with the Big Sound of Don RALKE.				
KOOKIE, KOOKIE (LEND ME YOUR COMB)	Warner Brothers	27	7 May 60	8
From the TV series '77 Sunset Strip'.				
Above hit: Edward BYRNES and Connie STEVENS with the Big Sound of				
Don RALKE.				
SIXTEEN REASONS [RE]	Warner Brothers	45	6 Aug 60	1

Ray STEVENS   US

SINGLES:	**HITS 7**		**WEEKS 64**	
EVERYTHING IS BEAUTIFUL	CBS	6	16 May 70	16
Children on the intro are Susie and Timmy Ragsdale (Ray Stevens' children) and Julie Shacklett				
(Brenda Lee's daughter).				
BRIDGET THE MIDGET (THE QUEEN OF THE BLUES)	CBS	2	13 Mar 71	14
TURN YOUR RADIO ON	CBS	33	25 Mar 72	4
THE STREAK	Janus	1	25 May 74	12
MISTY	Janus	2	21 Jun 75	10
INDIAN LOVE CALL	Janus	34	27 Sep 75	4
Originally recorded by Paul Whiteman Orchestra.				
IN THE MOOD	Warner Brothers	31	5 Mar 77	4
Billed in the US as Henhouse Five Plus Too.				

ALBUMS:		HITS 2			WEEKS 8
EVERYTHING IS BEAUTIFUL	CBS		62	26 Sep 70	1
MISTY	Janus		23	13 Sep 75	7

Ricky STEVENS with the Rita WILLIAMS SINGERS and Geoff LOVE and his Orchestra — UK

SINGLES:		HITS 1			WEEKS 7
I CRIED FOR YOU	Columbia		34	16 Dec 61	7

Shakin' STEVENS — UK

SINGLES:		HITS 37			WEEKS 277
HOT DOG	Epic		24	16 Feb 80	9
Originally recorded by Buck Owens.					
MARIE MARIE	Epic		19	16 Aug 80	10
Originally recorded by the Blasters.					
THIS OLE HOUSE	Epic		1	28 Feb 81	17
Originally recorded by Stuart Hamblen. Features Matchbox on backing vocals.					
YOU DRIVE ME CRAZY	Epic		2	2 May 81	12
GREEN DOOR	Epic		1	25 Jul 81	12
IT'S RAINING	Epic		10	10 Oct 81	9
Originally recorded by Irma Thomas.					
OH JULIE	Epic		1	16 Jan 82	10
SHIRLEY	Epic		6	24 Apr 82	6
Originally recorded by John Fred and his Playboy Band in 1968.					
GIVE ME YOUR HEART TONIGHT	Epic		11	21 Aug 82	10
I'LL BE SATISFIED	Epic		10	16 Oct 82	8
Original by Jackie Wilson reached No. 20 in the US in 1959.					
THE SHAKIN' STEVENS [EP]	Epic		2	11 Dec 82	7
Lead track: Blue Christmas.					
IT'S LATE	Epic		11	23 Jul 83	7
CRY JUST A LITTLE BIT	Epic		3	5 Nov 83	12
A ROCKIN' GOOD WAY	Epic		5	7 Jan 84	9
Originally recorded by Priscilla Bowman.					
Above hit: SHAKY and BONNIE.					
A LOVE WORTH WAITING FOR	Epic		2	24 Mar 84	10
A LETTER TO YOU	Epic		10	15 Sep 84	8
Originally recorded by Dennis Linde.					
TEARDROPS	Epic		5	24 Nov 84	9
BREAKING UP MY HEART	Epic		14	2 Mar 85	7
LIPSTICK POWDER AND PAINT	Epic		11	12 Oct 85	9
Originally recorded by Joe Turner in 1957.					
MERRY CHRISTMAS EVERYONE	Epic		1	7 Dec 85	8
TURNING AWAY	Epic		15	8 Feb 86	7
BECAUSE I LOVE YOU	Epic		14	1 Nov 86	10
MERRY CHRISTMAS EVERYONE [RE]	Epic		58	20 Dec 86	3
A LITTLE BOOGIE WOOGIE (IN THE BACK OF MY MIND)	Epic		12	27 Jun 87	10
COME SEE ABOUT ME	Epic		24	19 Sep 87	6
WHAT DO YOU WANT TO MAKE THOSE EYES AT ME FOR	Epic		5	28 Nov 87	8
FEEL THE NEED IN ME	Epic		26	23 Jul 88	5
HOW MANY TEARS CAN YOU HIDE	Epic		47	15 Oct 88	4
TRUE LOVE	Epic		23	10 Dec 88	6
JEZEBEL	Epic		58	18 Feb 89	2
LOVE ATTACK	Epic		28	13 May 89	4
I MIGHT	Epic		18	24 Feb 90	6
YES I DO	Epic		60	12 May 90	2
PINK CHAMPAGNE	Epic		59	18 Aug 90	2
MY CUTIE CUTIE	Epic		75	13 Oct 90	1
THE BEST CHRISTMAS OF THEM ALL	Epic		19	15 Dec 90	4
I'LL BE HOME THIS CHRISTMAS	Epic		34	7 Dec 91	5
RADIO	Epic		37	10 Oct 92	3
Above hit: SHAKY featuring Roger TAYLOR.					

ALBUMS:		HITS 12			WEEKS 158
TAKE ONE!	Epic		62	15 Mar 80	2
THIS OLE HOUSE	Epic		2	4 Apr 81	28
SHAKIN' STEVENS	Hallmark		34	8 Aug 81	5
Mid-price release of early material from the 1970s.					
SHAKY	Epic		1	19 Sep 81	28
GIVE ME YOUR HEART TONIGHT	Epic		3	9 Oct 82	18
THE BOP WON'T STOP	Epic		21	26 Nov 83	27
SHAKIN' STEVENS GREATEST HITS	Epic		8	17 Nov 84	22
LIPSTICK POWDER AND PAINT	Epic		37	16 Nov 85	9
LET'S BOOGIE	Epic		59	31 Oct 87	7
A WHOLE LOTTA SHAKY	Epic		42	19 Nov 88	8
THERE'S TWO KINDS OF MUSIC: ROCK 'N' ROLL!	Telstar		65	20 Oct 90	2
THE EPIC YEARS	Epic		57	31 Oct 92	2
Above hit: SHAKY.					

STEVENSON'S ROCKET — UK

SINGLES: | HITS 1 | | WEEKS 5

ALRIGHT BABY	Magnet	37	29 Nov 75	2
ALRIGHT BABY [RE]	Magnet	45	20 Dec 75	3

Al STEWART — UK

SINGLES: | HITS 1 | | WEEKS 6

YEAR OF THE CAT	RCA Victor	31	29 Jan 77	6

Written about comedian Tony Hancock.

ALBUMS: | HITS 5 | | WEEKS 20

ZERO SHE FLIES	CBS	40	11 Apr 70	4
YEAR OF THE CAT	RCA Victor	38	5 Feb 77	7
TIME PASSAGES	RCA Victor	39	21 Oct 78	1
24 CARAT	RCA	55	6 Sep 80	6
RUSSIANS AND AMERICANS	RCA	83	9 Jun 84	2

Amii STEWART — US

SINGLES: | HITS 7 | | WEEKS 61

KNOCK ON WOOD	Atlantic	6	7 Apr 79	12
LIGHT MY FIRE/137 DISCO HEAVEN [M]	Atlantic	5	16 Jun 79	11
JEALOUSY	Atlantic	58	3 Nov 79	3
PARADISE BIRD / THE LETTER	Atlantic	39	19 Jan 80	4
MY GUY - MY GIRL [M]	Atlantic	39	19 Jul 80	5

Above hit: Amii STEWART and Johnny BRISTOL.

FRIENDS	RCA	12	29 Dec 84	11
KNOCK ON WOOD [RM] / LIGHT MY FIRE/137 DISCO HEAVEN [M] [RM]	Sedition	7	17 Aug 85	12

Remixed by Barry Leng and Alan Coulthard.

MY GUY, MY GIRL [M] [RR]	Sedition	63	25 Jan 86	3

Above hit: Amii STEWART and Dion ESTUS.

Andy STEWART — UK

SINGLES: | HITS 4 | | WEEKS 67

DONALD WHERE'S YOUR TROOSERS	Top Rank	37	17 Dec 60	1
A SCOTTISH SOLDIER (GREEN HILLS OF TYROL)	Top Rank	19	14 Jan 61	38
THE BATTLE'S O'ER	Top Rank	28	3 Jun 61	13
A SCOTTISH SOLDIER (GREEN HILLS OF TYROL) [RE]	Top Rank	43	14 Oct 61	2

Above 3: Andy STEWART with the Michael SAMMES SINGERS.

DR. FINLAY	His Master's Voice	50	14 Aug 65	1
DR. FINLAY [RE]	His Master's Voice	43	28 Aug 65	4
DONALD WHERE'S YOUR TROOSERS? [RI]	Stone	4	9 Dec 89	8

Made popular again due to constant airplay on Simon Mayo's BBC Radio 1 breakfast show.

EPS: | HITS 2 | | WEEKS 54

ANDY SINGS	Top Rank	3	17 Jun 61	48
ANDY STEWART SINGS	Top Rank	12	27 Jan 62	6

ALBUMS: | HITS 1 | | WEEKS 2

ANDY STEWART	Top Rank	13	3 Feb 62	2

Billy STEWART — US

SINGLES: | HITS 1 | | WEEKS 2

SUMMERTIME	Chess	39	10 Sep 66	2

From the film 'Porgy And Bess'. Originally recorded by Billie Holiday in 1936.

Dave STEWART — UK

SINGLES: | HITS 4 | | WEEKS 30

WHAT BECOMES OF THE BROKEN HEARTED?	Stiff	13	14 Mar 81	10

Above hit: Dave STEWART Guest vocals Colin BLUNSTONE.

IT'S MY PARTY	Stiff	1	19 Sep 81	13

Above hit: Dave STEWART with Barbara GASKIN.

BUSY DOING NOTHING	Broken	49	13 Aug 83	4
THE LOCOMOTION	Broken	70	14 Jun 86	3

Above 2: Dave STEWART and Barbara GASKIN.

David A. STEWART — UK

SINGLES: | HITS 4 | | WEEKS 23

LILY WAS HERE	AnXious	6	24 Feb 90	12

From the film of the same name.
Above hit: David A. STEWART featuring Candy DULFER.

JACK TALKING	RCA	69	18 Aug 90	2

Above hit: Dave STEWART and the SPIRITUAL COWBOYS.

ALL YOU NEED IS LOVE	Childline	19	6 Feb 93	4

Charity record for the Childline Appeal. Backing vocals by Kiki Dee.
Above hit: Tom JONES and Dave STEWART.

HEART OF STONE	East West	36	3 Sep 94	5

Above hit: Dave STEWART.

ALBUMS:	HITS 2			WEEKS 7
LILY WAS HERE [OST]	Anxious	35	7 Apr 90	5

Features Candy Dulfer and Various Artists.

DAVE STEWART AND THE SPIRITUAL COWBOYS	RCA	38	15 Sep 90	2

Above hit: Dave STEWART and the SPIRITUAL COWBOYS.

Jermaine STEWART   US

SINGLES:	HITS 5			WEEKS 42
WE DON'T HAVE TO . . .	10 Records	2	9 Aug 86	14
JODY	10 Records	50	1 Nov 86	4
SAY IT AGAIN	10 Records	7	16 Jan 88	12
GET LUCKY	Siren	13	2 Apr 88	9
DON'T TALK DIRTY TO ME	Siren	61	24 Sep 88	3

ALBUMS:	HITS 2			WEEKS 12
FRANTIC ROMANTIC	10 Records	49	4 Oct 86	4
SAY IT AGAIN	Siren	32	5 Mar 88	8

John STEWART   US

SINGLES:	HITS 1			WEEKS 6
GOLD	RSO	43	30 Jun 79	6

Patrick STEWART – See Rick WAKEMAN

Rod STEWART   UK

(See also Jeff Beck; Faces; Glass Tiger; N-Trance; Python Lee Jackson.)

SINGLES:	HITS 56			WEEKS 450
MAGGIE MAY / REASON TO BELIEVE	Mercury	1	4 Sep 71	21

Reason To Believe was listed for 4 Sep 71 and 11 Sep 71 reaching No. 19. From 18 Sep 71,
*   Maggie May was listed, and became the official A-side. Reason To Believe originally recorded by*
*   Tim Hardin. Maggie May features Ron Wood on guitar and Pete Sears of Jefferson Airplane on*
*   piano.*

YOU WEAR IT WELL	Mercury	1	12 Aug 72	12
ANGEL / WHAT MADE MILWAUKEE FAMOUS (HAS MADE A LOSER OUT OF ME)	Mercury	4	18 Nov 72	11

Angel originally recorded by Jimi Hendrix. What Made Milwaukee Famous originally recorded by
*   Jerry Lee Lewis in 1968.*

OH! NO NOT MY BABY	Mercury	6	8 Sep 73	9

Original by Maxine Brown reached No. 24 in the US in 1964.

FAREWELL / BRING IT ON HOME TO ME / YOU SEND ME	Mercury	7	5 Oct 74	7
SAILING	Warner Brothers	1	16 Aug 75	11

Originally recorded by the Sutherland Brothers.

THIS OLD HEART OF MINE	Riva	4	15 Nov 75	9
TONIGHT'S THE NIGHT	Riva	5	5 Jun 76	9

Whispers by Britt Eckland.

THE KILLING OF GEORGIE PARTS 1 & 2	Riva	2	21 Aug 76	10
SAILING [RE-1ST]	Warner Brothers	3	4 Sep 76	20

Re-entered after being used by BBC TV as the theme to their documentary 'Sailor'.

GET BACK	Riva	11	20 Nov 76	9

From the film 'All This And World War II'.

MAGGIE MAY [RI]	Mercury	31	4 Dec 76	7
I DON'T WANT TO TALK ABOUT IT / FIRST CUT IS THE DEEPEST	Riva	1	23 Apr 77	13

I Don't Want To Talk About It originally recorded by Crazy Horse, First Cut Is
*   The Deepest originally recorded by Cat Stevens.*

YOU'RE IN MY HEART	Riva	3	15 Oct 77	10
HOT LEGS / I WAS ONLY JOKING	Riva	5	28 Jan 78	8
OLE OLA (MUHLER BRASILEIRA)	Riva	4	27 May 78	6

Above hit: Rod STEWART and the SCOTTISH WORLD CUP
*   SQUAD '78.*

DO 'YA' THINK I'M SEXY?	Riva	1	18 Nov 78	13

Royalties from the song donated to the United Nations' UNICEF children's charity.

AIN'T LOVE A BITCH	Riva	11	3 Feb 79	8
BLONDES (HAVE MORE FUN)	Riva	63	5 May 79	3
IF LOVING YOU IS WRONG (I DON'T WANT TO BE RIGHT)	Riva	23	31 May 80	9

Originally recorded by Luther Ingram.

PASSION	Riva	17	8 Nov 80	10
MY GIRL	Riva	32	20 Dec 80	7
TONIGHT I'M YOURS (DON'T HURT ME)	Riva	8	17 Oct 81	13
YOUNG TURKS	Riva	11	12 Dec 81	9
HOW LONG	Riva	41	27 Feb 82	4
BABY JANE	Warner Brothers	1	4 Jun 83	14
WHAT AM I GONNA DO (I'M SO IN LOVE WITH YOU)	Warner Brothers	3	27 Aug 83	8
SWEET SURRENDER	Warner Brothers	23	10 Dec 83	9
INFATUATION	Warner Brothers	27	26 May 84	7

Features guitar by Jeff Beck.

SOME GUYS HAVE ALL THE LUCK	Warner Brothers	15	28 Jul 84	10
Original by the Persuaders reached No. 39 in the US in 1973.				
LOVE TOUCH (FROM THE MOTION PICTURE 'LEGAL EAGLES')	Warner Brothers	27	24 May 86	5
LOVE TOUCH (FROM THE MOTION PICTURE 'LEGAL EAGLES') [RE]	Warner Brothers	69	5 Jul 86	3
EVERY BEAT OF MY HEART	Warner Brothers	2	12 Jul 86	9
ANOTHER HEARTACHE	Warner Brothers	54	20 Sep 86	2
Co-written by Bryan Adams.				
SAILING [RE-2ND]	Warner Brothers	41	28 Mar 87	3
Proceeds from this entry went to the Zeebrugge Channel Ferry Disaster Fund.				
LOST IN YOU	Warner Brothers	21	28 May 88	6
FOREVER YOUNG	Warner Brothers	57	13 Aug 88	3
Above 2 feature Duran Duran's Andy Taylor on guitar.				
MY HEART CAN'T TELL YOU NO	Warner Brothers	49	6 May 89	4
THIS OLD HEART OF MINE [RR]	Warner Brothers	51	11 Nov 89	3
Above hit: Rod STEWART featuring Ronald ISLEY.				
DOWNTOWN TRAIN	Warner Brothers	10	13 Jan 90	12
Originally recorded by Tom Waits on his 1983 album Rain Dogs.				
IT TAKES TWO	Warner Brothers	5	24 Nov 90	8
Above hit: Rod STEWART and Tina TURNER.				
RHYTHM OF MY HEART	Warner Brothers	3	16 Mar 91	11
THE MOTOWN SONG	Warner Brothers	10	15 Jun 91	8
Above hit: Rod STEWART (with the TEMPTATIONS).				
BROKEN ARROW	Warner Brothers	54	7 Sep 91	3
Originally recorded by Robbie Robertson.				
PEOPLE GET READY	Epic	49	7 Mar 92	3
Above hit: Jeff BECK and Rod STEWART.				
YOUR SONG / BROKEN ARROW [RI]	Warner Brothers	41	18 Apr 92	4
Rod's version of Your Song was a tribute to Freddie Mercury.				
TOM TRAUBERT'S BLUES (WALTZING MATILDA)	Warner Brothers	6	5 Dec 92	9
Originally recorded by Tom Waits.				
RUBY TUESDAY	Warner Brothers	11	20 Feb 93	6
SHOTGUN WEDDING	Warner Brothers	21	17 Apr 93	4
HAVE I TOLD YOU LATELY	Warner Brothers	5	26 Jun 93	9
Originally recorded by Van Morrison.				
REASON TO BELIEVE (LIVE VERSION) [RR]	Warner Brothers	51	21 Aug 93	3
Above hit: Rod STEWART with special guest Ronnie WOOD.				
PEOPLE GET READY (LIVE VERSION) [RR]	Warner Brothers	45	18 Dec 93	4
This also features Ronnie Wood, though credit is only reflected in the small print on the label. Above 2 are live recordings from Los Angeles, 5 Feb 93.				
ALL FOR LOVE	A&M	2	15 Jan 94	13
From the film 'The Three Musketeers'.				
Above hit: Bryan ADAMS, Rod STEWART and STING.				
YOU'RE THE STAR	Warner Brothers	19	20 May 95	5
LADY LUCK	Warner Brothers	56	19 Aug 95	1
PURPLE HEATHER	Warner Brothers	16	15 Jun 96	5
Offical anthem for the Scottish Football Team in Euro '96.				
Above hit: Rod STEWART with the SCOTTISH EURO '96 SQUAD.				
IF WE FALL IN LOVE TONIGHT	Warner Brothers	58	14 Dec 96	1
OOH LA LA	Warner Brothers	16	30 May 98	5
Original was the title track of the Faces 1973 album with vocals by Ronnie Lane. This release was dedicated to him after he died in 1996 of multiple sclerosis.				
ROCKS	Warner Brothers	55	5 Sep 98	1
FAITH OF THE HEART	Universal	60	17 Apr 99	1
From the film 'Patch Adams'.				

ALBUMS:	HITS 26			WEEKS 791
GASOLINE ALLEY	Vertigo	62	3 Oct 70	1
EVERY PICTURE TELLS A STORY	Mercury	1	24 Jul 71	81
NEVER A DULL MOMENT	Philips	1	5 Aug 72	36
SING IT AGAIN ROD	Mercury	1	25 Aug 73	30
Compilation.				
SMILER	Mercury	1	19 Oct 74	20
ATLANTIC CROSSING	Warner Brothers	1	30 Aug 75	88
A NIGHT ON THE TOWN	Riva	1	3 Jul 76	47
THE BEST OF ROD STEWART	Mercury	18	16 Jul 77	22
FOOT LOOSE AND FANCY FEEE	Riva	3	19 Nov 77	26
ATLANTIC CROSSING [RI]	Riva	60	21 Jan 78	1
BLONDES HAVE MORE FUN	Riva	3	9 Dec 78	31
ROD STEWART – GREATEST HITS VOL. 1	Riva	1	10 Nov 79	47
FOOLISH BEHAVIOUR	Riva	4	22 Nov 80	13
TONIGHT I'M YOURS	Riva	8	14 Nov 81	21
ABSOLUTELY LIVE	Riva	35	13 Nov 82	5
BODY WISHES	Warner Brothers	5	18 Jun 83	27
ROD STEWART – GREATEST HITS VOL. 1 [RE]	Riva	62	21 Jan 84	27
Re-released. Charts credited label as Warner Brothers from 2 Jun 84 until 9 Feb 85. Peak position reached in 1987.				
CAMOUFLAGE	Warner Brothers	8	23 Jun 84	17
EVERY BEAT OF MY HEART	Warner Brothers	5	5 Jul 86	17
OUT OF ORDER	Warner Brothers	11	4 Jun 88	8

THE BEST OF ROD STEWART	*Warner Brothers*	3	*25 Nov 89*	74
VAGABOND HEART	*Warner Brothers*	2	*6 Apr 91*	27
THE BEST OF ROD STEWART AND THE FACES 1971-1975	*Mercury*	58	*7 Nov 92*	1
Features both Rod Stewart's solo and group material.				
Above hit: Rod STEWART and the FACES.				
THE BEST OF ROD STEWART [RE]	*Warner Brothers*	22	*27 Feb 93*	46
Re-released at mid-price. Peak position reached in 1994. Includes re-entries through to 1999.				
ROD STEWART, LEAD VOCALIST	*Warner Brothers*	3	*6 Mar 93*	9
Features old tracks with Faces, Jeff Beck Group as well as new cover versions.				
UNPLUGGED . . . AND SEATED	*Warner Brothers*	2	*5 Jun 93*	27
Acoustic set recorded in Los Angeles, 5 Feb 95.				
A SPANNER IN THE WORKS	*Warner Brothers*	4	*10 Jun 95*	12
IF WE FALL IN LOVE TONIGHT	*Warner Brothers*	8	*16 Nov 96*	19
Compilation of hit ballads spanning 1975–93.				
WHEN WE WERE THE NEW BOYS	*Atlantic*	2	*13 Jun 98*	11

STEX · UK

SINGLES:	HITS 1		WEEKS 2	
STILL FEEL THE RAIN	*Some Bizzare*	63	*19 Jan 91*	2

STIFF LITTLE FINGERS · UK

SINGLES:	HITS 8		WEEKS 39	
STRAW DOGS	*Chrysalis*	44	*29 Sep 79*	4
AT THE EDGE	*Chrysalis*	15	*16 Feb 80*	9
NOBODY'S HERO / TIN SOLDIERS	*Chrysalis*	36	*24 May 80*	5
BACK TO FRONT	*Chrysalis*	49	*2 Aug 80*	4
JUST FADE AWAY	*Chrysalis*	47	*28 Mar 81*	6
SILVER LINING	*Chrysalis*	68	*30 May 81*	3
LISTEN [EP]	*Chrysalis*	33	*23 Jan 82*	6
Lead track: Listen.				
BITS OF KIDS	*Chrysalis*	73	*18 Sep 82*	2
ALBUMS:	**HITS 6**		**WEEKS 57**	
INFLAMMABLE MATERIAL	*Rough Trade*	14	*3 Mar 79*	19
NOBODY'S HEROES	*Chrysalis*	8	*15 Mar 80*	10
HANX	*Chrysalis*	9	*20 Sep 80*	5
GO FOR IT	*Chrysalis*	14	*25 Apr 81*	8
NOW THEN . . .	*Chrysalis*	24	*2 Oct 82*	6
ALL THE BEST	*Chrysalis*	19	*12 Feb 83*	9

Curtis STIGERS · US

SINGLES:	HITS 6		WEEKS 34	
I WONDER WHY	*Arista*	5	*18 Jan 92*	10
YOU'RE ALL THAT MATTERS TO ME	*Arista*	6	*28 Mar 92*	12
SLEEPING WITH THE LIGHTS ON	*Arista*	53	*11 Jul 92*	4
NEVER SAW A MIRACLE	*Arista*	34	*17 Oct 92*	4
THIS TIME	*Arista*	28	*3 Jun 95*	3
KEEP ME FROM THE COLD	*Arista*	57	*2 Dec 95*	1
ALBUMS:	**HITS 2**		**WEEKS 52**	
CURTIS STIGERS	*Arista*	7	*29 Feb 92*	50
TIME WAS	*Arista*	34	*1 Jul 95*	2

Stephen STILLS · US

(See also Crosby, Stills, Nash and Young; Stephen Stills' Manassas; Stills-Young Band.)

SINGLES:	HITS 1		WEEKS 4	
LOVE THE ONE YOU'RE WITH	*Atlantic*	37	*13 Mar 71*	4
Backing vocals by John Sebastian, Rita Coolidge, David Crosby and Graham Nash.				
ALBUMS:	**HITS 4**		**WEEKS 7**	
STEPHEN STILLS	*Atlantic*	30	*19 Dec 70*	1
STEPHEN STILLS 2	*Atlantic*	22	*14 Aug 71*	3
STILLS	*CBS*	31	*26 Jul 75*	1
ILLEGAL STILLS	*CBS*	54	*29 May 76*	2

Stephen STILLS' MANASSAS · US

(See also Stephen Stills.)

ALBUMS:	HITS 2		WEEKS 7	
MANASSAS	*Atlantic*	30	*20 May 72*	5
DOWN THE ROAD	*Atlantic*	33	*19 May 73*	2

STILLS-YOUNG BAND · US

(See also Crosby, Stills, Nash and Young; Stephen Stills; Neil Young.)

ALBUMS:	HITS 1		WEEKS 5	
LONG MAY YOU RUN	*Reprise*	12	*9 Oct 76*	5

STILTSKIN

UK

SINGLES:	HITS 2			WEEKS 15
INSIDE	White Water	1	7 May 94	13
Featured in the Levi's 501 Jeans TV commercial.				
FOOTSTEPS	White Water	34	24 Sep 94	2
ALBUMS:	**HITS 1**			**WEEKS 4**
THE MIND'S EYE	White Water	17	29 Oct 94	4

STING

UK

(See also Police; Various Artists: Films – Original Soundtracks 'Brimstone And Treacle'.)

SINGLES:	HITS 29			WEEKS 136
SPREAD A LITTLE HAPPINESS	A&M	16	14 Aug 82	8
From the film 'Brimstone And Treacle'. Originally recorded by Binnie Hale.				
IF YOU LOVE SOMEBODY SET THEM FREE	A&M	26	8 Jun 85	7
LOVE IS THE SEVENTH WAVE (NEW MIX)	A&M	41	24 Aug 85	5
FORTRESS AROUND YOUR HEART	A&M	49	19 Oct 85	3
RUSSIANS	A&M	12	7 Dec 85	11
MOON OVER BOURBIN STREET	A&M	44	15 Feb 86	4
RUSSIANS [RE]	A&M	71	1 Mar 86	1
WE'LL BE TOGETHER	A&M	41	7 Nov 87	4
ENGLISHMAN IN NEW YORK	A&M	51	20 Feb 88	3
Written about Quentin Crisp.				
FRAGILE	A&M	70	9 Apr 88	2
AN ENGLISHMAN IN NEW YORK [RM]	A&M	15	11 Aug 90	7
Remixed by Ben Liebrand.				
ALL THIS TIME	A&M	22	12 Jan 91	4
MAD ABOUT YOU	A&M	56	9 Mar 91	2
THE SOUL CAGES	A&M	57	4 May 91	1
IT'S PROBABLY ME	A&M	30	29 Aug 92	5
From the film 'Lethal Weapon 3'.				
Above hit: STING with Eric CLAPTON.				
IF I EVER LOSE MY FAITH IN YOU	A&M	14	13 Feb 93	6
SEVEN DAYS	A&M	25	24 Apr 93	4
FIELDS OF GOLD	A&M	16	19 Jun 93	6
SHAPE OF MY HEART	A&M	57	4 Sep 93	1
DEMOLITION MAN	A&M	21	20 Nov 93	4
From the film of the same name.				
ALL FOR LOVE	A&M	2	15 Jan 94	13
From the film 'The Three Musketeers'.				
Above hit: Bryan ADAMS, Rod STEWART and STING.				
NOTHING 'BOUT ME	A&M	32	26 Feb 94	3
WHEN WE DANCE	A&M	9	29 Oct 94	7
THIS COWBOY SONG	A&M	15	11 Feb 95	6
Jimmy Nail on backing vocals.				
Above hit: STING (featuring Pato BANTON).				
SPIRITS IN THE MATERIAL WORLD	MCA	36	20 Jan 96	2
From the film 'Ace Ventura When Nature Calls'.				
Above hit: Pato BANTON with STING.				
LET YOUR SOUL BE YOUR PILOT	A&M	15	2 Mar 96	4
YOU STILL TOUCH ME	A&M	27	11 May 96	3
LIVE AT T.F.I. FRIDAY [EP]	A&M	53	22 Jun 96	2
Lead track: You Still Touch Me. Live recordings from Chris Evans' Channel 4 TV show.				
I WAS BROUGHT TO MY SENSES	A&M	31	14 Sep 96	2
I'M SO HAPPY I CAN'T STOP CRYING	A&M	54	30 Nov 96	1
BRAND NEW DAY	A&M	13	25 Sept 99	5
ALBUMS:	**HITS 9**			**WEEKS 301**
THE DREAM OF THE BLUE TURTLES	A&M	3	29 Jun 85	64
BRING ON THE NIGHT	A&M	16	28 Jun 86	12
Live recordings from the documentary film of his 1985 tour in Paris, France.				
NOTHING LIKE THE SUN	A&M	1	24 Oct 87	47
THE SOUL CAGES	A&M	1	2 Feb 91	16
TEN SUMMONER'S TALES	A&M	2	13 Mar 93	60
FIELDS OF GOLD – THE BEST OF STING 1984-1994	A&M	2	19 Nov 94	41
MERCURY FALLING	A&M	4	16 Mar 96	27
THE VERY BEST OF STING AND THE POLICE	A&M	11	22 Nov 97	26
Features both Sting's solo and group material.				
Above hit: STING/the POLICE.				
BRAND NEW DAY	A&M	5	9 Oct 99	8

Byron STINGILY

US

SINGLES:	HITS 4			WEEKS 12
GET UP (EVERYBODY)	Manifesto	14	25 Jan 97	5
Based around Sylvester's Dance (Disco Heat).				
SING A SONG	Manifesto	38	1 Nov 97	2
YOU MAKE ME FEEL (MIGHTY REAL)	Manifesto	13	31 Jan 98	4
TESTIFY	Manifesto	48	13 Jun 98	1

STIX 'N' STONED — UK

SINGLES:	HITS 1			WEEKS 2
OUTRAGEOUS	Positiva	39	20 Jul 96	2

Catherine STOCK — UK

SINGLES:	HITS 1			WEEKS 6
TO HAVE AND TO HOLD (THEME SONG FROM THE LWT SERIES)	Sierra	17	18 Oct 86	6

STOCK AITKEN WATERMAN — UK

(See also Christians, Holly Johnson, Paul McCartney, Gerry Marsden and Stock Aitken Waterman.)

SINGLES:	HITS 4			WEEKS 19
ROADBLOCK	Breakout	13	25 Jul 87	9
PACKJAMMED (WITH THE PARTY POSSE)	Breakout	41	12 Dec 87	6
Features samples from tracks they had produced.				
ALL THE WAY	MCA	64	21 May 88	2
Above hit: ENGLAND FOOTBALL TEAM with the 'sound' of STOCK, AITKEN and WATERMAN.				
S.S. PAPARAZZI	PWL	68	3 Dec 88	2

STOCKLAND GREEN BILATERAL SCHOOL FIRST YEAR CHOIR – See WIZZARD

Miriam STOCKLEY – See ADIEMUS

Rhet STOLLER — UK

SINGLES:	HITS 1			WEEKS 8
CHARIOT	Decca	26	14 Jan 61	8

Morris STOLOFF conducting the COLUMBIA PICTURES ORCHESTRA — US

SINGLES:	HITS 1			WEEKS 11
MOONGLOW/THEME FROM "PICNIC" [M]	Brunswick	7	2 Jun 56	11

R and J STONE — UK/US

SINGLES:	HITS 1			WEEKS 9
WE DO IT	RCA Victor	5	10 Jan 76	9

STONE FREE — UK

SINGLES:	HITS 1			WEEKS 1
CAN'T SAY 'BYE	Ensign	73	23 May 87	1

STONE ROSES — UK

SINGLES:	HITS 12			WEEKS 77
SHE BANGS THE DRUMS	Silvertone	36	29 Jul 89	3
FOOLS GOLD / WHAT THE WORLD IS WAITING FOR	Silvertone	8	25 Nov 89	14
The chart for 25 Nov 89 had titles listed in reverse.				
SALLY CINNAMON	Black/FM-Revolver	75	6 Jan 90	1
Originally released in 1987.				
SALLY CINNAMON [RE]	Black/FM-Revolver	46	20 Jan 90	4
ELEPHANT STONE	Silvertone	8	3 Mar 90	6
Originally released in 1988.				
MADE OF STONE	Silvertone	20	17 Mar 90	4
Original release reached No. 90 in 1989.				
SHE BANGS THE DRUMS [RE]	Silvertone	34	31 Mar 90	3
ONE LOVE	Silvertone	4	14 Jul 90	7
FOOLS GOLD / WHAT THE WORLD IS WAITING FOR [RE-1ST]	Silvertone	22	15 Sep 90	5
I WANNA BE ADORED	Silvertone	20	14 Sep 91	3
WATERFALL	Silvertone	27	11 Jan 92	4
I AM THE RESURRECTION	Silvertone	33	11 Apr 92	2
FOOLS GOLD [RE-2ND]	Silvertone	73	30 May 92	1
12" and CD releases have the 9.53 extended version.				
LOVE SPREADS	Geffen	2	3 Dec 94	8
TEN STORY LOVE SONG	Geffen	11	11 Mar 95	3
FOOLS GOLD '95 [RI]	Silvertone	25	29 Apr 95	3
Though listed as Fool's Gold '95, the first track of the CD was the original version.				
BEGGING YOU	Geffen	15	11 Nov 95	3
FOOLS GOLD [RM]	Jive Electro	25	6 Mar 99	3
Remixed by the Grooverider.				
ALBUMS:	HITS 6			WEEKS 144
THE STONE ROSES	Silvertone	32	13 May 89	17
THE STONE ROSES [RE-1ST]	Silvertone	19	2 Dec 89	50
TURNS INTO STONE	Silvertone	32	1 Aug 92	3
SECOND COMING	Geffen	4	17 Dec 94	28
Includes re-entries through to 1999.				
THE STONE ROSES [RE-2ND]	Silvertone	23	29 Apr 95	19
Re-released with additional tracks. Peak position reached in 1998.				

THE COMPLETE STONE ROSES	Silvertone	4	27 May 95	23
GARAGE FLOWER	Silvertone	58	7 Dec 96	1

Contains previously unreleased songs and early B-sides.

STONE ROSES - 10TH ANNIVERSARY EDITION	Silvertone	26	16 Oct 99	3

Reissue of their first album plus a second enhanced CD.

STONE TEMPLE PILOTS   US

SINGLES:	HITS 4			WEEKS 11
SEX TYPE THING	Atlantic	60	27 Mar 93	2
PLUSH	Atlantic	23	4 Sep 93	4
SEX TYPE THING [RI]	Atlantic	55	27 Nov 93	2
VASOLINE	Atlantic	48	20 Aug 94	2
INTERSTATE LOVE SONG	Atlantic	53	10 Dec 94	1
ALBUMS:	**HITS 3**			**WEEKS 19**
CORE	Atlantic	27	4 Sep 93	8

Originally released in 1992.

PURPLE	Atlantic	10	18 Jun 94	9
TINY MUSIC . . . SONGS FROM THE VATICAN GIFT SHOP	Atlantic	31	6 Apr 96	2

STONE THE CROWS   UK

ALBUMS:	HITS 1			WEEKS 3
CONTINUOUS PERFORMANCE	Polydor	33	7 Oct 72	3

STONEBRIDGE McGUINNESS   UK

SINGLES:	HITS 1			WEEKS 2
OO-EEH BABY	RCA Victor	54	14 Jul 79	2

STONEPROOF°   UK

SINGLES:	HITS 1			WEEKS 1
EVERYTHING'S NOT YOU	VC Recordings	68	15 May 99	1

STONKERS – See HALE and PACE and the STONKERS

STOOGES – See Iggy POP

STOP THE VIOLENCE MOVEMENT   US

SINGLES:	HITS 1			WEEKS 1
SELF-DESTRUCTION	Jive	75	18 Feb 89	1

Axel STORDAHL – See June HUTTON and Axel STORDAHL with the BOYS NEXT DOOR

STORM   UK

SINGLES:	HITS 1			WEEKS 10
IT'S MY HOUSE	Scope	36	17 Nov 79	10

STORM   Germany

SINGLES:	HITS 1			WEEKS 2
STORM	Positiva	32	29 Aug 98	2

Danny STORM   UK

SINGLES:	HITS 1			WEEKS 4
HONEST I DO	Piccadilly	42	14 Apr 62	4

Rebecca STORM   UK

SINGLES:	HITS 1			WEEKS 13
THE SHOW (THEME FROM CONNIE)	Towerbell	22	13 Jul 85	13

Theme from the Central region ITV series.

STORYVILLE JAZZMEN – See Bob WALLIS and his STORYVILLE JAZZMEN

Beryl STOTT CHORUS – See Petula CLARK; Joe "Mr. Piano" HENDERSON; Edmund HOCKRIDGE; George FORMBY with the Beryl STOTT CHORUS; David MacBETH – Kim DRAKE MUSIC – Beryl STOTT GROUP; Gary MILLER; Marion RYAN with the Peter KNIGHT ORCHESTRA and the Beryl STOTT CHORUS

Wally STOTT and his Orchestra – see Winifred ATWELL; Shirley BASSEY; Ronnie CARROLL; Roy CASTLE; Lonnie DONEGAN; Robert EARL; David HUGHES with the Wally STOTT ORCHESTRA; KAYE SISTERS; Susan MAUGHAN; Harry SECOMBE; Anne SHELTON; Muriel SMITH with Wally STOTT and his Orchestra; Dickie VALENTINE; Frankie VAUGHAN

Izzy STRADLIN'   US

SINGLES:		HITS 1		WEEKS 2
PRESSURE DROP	Geffen	45	26 Sep 92	2
ALBUMS:		**HITS 1**		**WEEKS 1**
IZZY STRADLIN' AND THE JU JU HOUNDS	Geffen	52	24 Oct 92	1

Above hit: Izzy STRADLIN' and the JU JU HOUNDS.

Nick STRAKER BAND   UK

SINGLES:		HITS 2		WEEKS 15
A WALK IN THE PARK	CBS	20	2 Aug 80	12
LEAVING ON THE MIDNIGHT TRAIN	CBS	61	15 Nov 80	3

Peter STRAKER – The HANDS OF DOCTOR TELENY   UK

SINGLES:		HITS 1		WEEKS 4
THE SPIRIT IS WILLING	RCA Victor	40	19 Feb 72	4

STRANGE BEHAVIOUR – See Jane KENNAWAY and STRANGE BEHAVIOUR

STRANGE FRUIT – See Jimmy NAIL

STRANGELOVE   UK

SINGLES:		HITS 6		WEEKS 8
LIVING WITH THE HUMAN MACHINES	Food	53	20 Apr 96	1
BEAUTIFUL ALONE	Food	35	15 Jun 96	2
SWAY	Food	47	19 Oct 96	1
THE GREATEST SHOW ON EARTH	Food	36	26 Jul 97	1
FREAK	Food	43	11 Oct 97	2
ANOTHER NIGHT IN	Food	46	21 Feb 98	1
ALBUMS:		**HITS 3**		**WEEKS 3**
TIME FOR THE REST OF YOUR LIFE	Food	69	13 Aug 94	1
LOVE AND OTHER DEMONS	Food	44	29 Jun 96	1
STRANGELOVE	Food	67	18 Oct 97	1

STRANGLERS   UK

SINGLES:		HITS 31		WEEKS 194
(GET A) GRIP (ON YOURSELF)	United Artists	44	19 Feb 77	4
PEACHES / GO BUDDY GO	United Artists	8	21 May 77	14
Go Buddy Go listed from 11 Jun 77.				
SOMETHING BETTER CHANGE / STRAIGHTEN OUT	United Artists	9	30 Jul 77	8
Straighten Out listed from 13 Aug 77.				
NO MORE HEROES	United Artists	8	24 Sep 77	9
5 MINUTES	United Artists	11	4 Feb 78	9
NICE 'N' SLEAZY	United Artists	18	6 May 78	8
WALK ON BY	United Artists	21	12 Aug 78	8
DUCHESS	United Artists	14	18 Aug 79	9
NUCLEAR DEVICE (THE WIZARD OF AUS)	United Artists	36	20 Oct 79	4
DON'T BRING HARRY [EP]	United Artists	41	1 Dec 79	3
Lead track: Don't Bring Harry.				
BEAR CAGE	United Artists	36	22 Mar 80	5
WHO WANTS THE WORLD	United Artists	39	7 Jun 80	4
THROWN AWAY	Liberty	42	31 Jan 81	4
LET ME INTRODUCE YOU TO THE FAMILY	United Artists	42	14 Nov 81	3
GOLDEN BROWN	Liberty	2	9 Jan 82	12
LA FOLIE	Liberty	47	24 Apr 82	3
STRANGE LITTLE GIRL	Liberty	7	24 Jul 82	9
EUROPEAN FEMALE	Epic	9	8 Jan 83	6
MIDNIGHT SUMMER DREAM	Epic	35	26 Feb 83	4
PARADISE	Epic	48	6 Aug 83	3
SKIN DEEP	Epic	15	6 Oct 84	7
NO MERCY	Epic	37	1 Dec 84	7
LET ME DOWN EASY	Epic	48	16 Feb 85	4
NICE IN NICE	Epic	30	23 Aug 86	5
ALWAYS THE SUN	Epic	30	18 Oct 86	5
BIG IN AMERICA	Epic	48	13 Dec 86	6
SHAKIN' LIKE A LEAF	Epic	58	7 Mar 87	4
ALL DAY AND ALL OF THE NIGHT	Epic	7	9 Jan 88	7
GRIP '89 (GET A) GRIP (ON YOURSELF) [RM]	EMI	33	28 Jan 89	3
Remixed by Taff B. Dylan and Barry Cooder.				
96 TEARS	Epic	17	17 Feb 90	6
SWEET SMELL OF SUCCESS	Epic	65	21 Apr 90	2
ALWAYS THE SUN [RM]	Epic	29	5 Jan 91	5
GOLDEN BROWN [RM]	Epic	68	30 Mar 91	2
HEAVEN OR HELL	Psycho	46	22 Aug 92	2
ALBUMS:		**HITS 19**		**WEEKS 219**
STRANGLERS IV (RATTUS NORVEGICUS)	United Artists	4	30 Apr 77	34

NO MORE HEROES	United Artists	2	8 Oct 77	19
BLACK AND WHITE	United Artists	2	3 Jun 78	18
LIVE (X CERT)	United Artists	7	10 Mar 79	10
THE RAVEN	United Artists	4	6 Oct 79	8
THEMENINBLACK	Liberty	8	21 Feb 81	5
LA FOLIE	Liberty	11	21 Nov 81	18
THE COLLECTION 1977 – 1982	Liberty	12	25 Sep 82	16
FELINE	Epic	4	22 Jan 83	11
AURAL SCULPTURE	Epic	14	17 Nov 84	10
OFF THE BEATEN TRACK	Liberty	80	20 Sep 86	2
Compilation of early recordings.				
DREAMTIME	Epic	16	8 Nov 86	6
ALL LIVE AND ALL OF THE NIGHT	Epic	12	20 Feb 88	6
Consists mainly of live recordings from 1987.				
THE SINGLES - THE UA YEARS	EMI	57	18 Feb 89	2
10	Epic	15	17 Mar 90	4
GREATEST HITS 1977-1990	Epic	47	1 Dec 90	3
GREATEST HITS 1977-1990 [RE]	Epic	4	12 Jan 91	44
Peak position reached on 6 Jul 91.				
STRANGLERS IN THE NIGHT	Psycho	33	19 Sep 92	1
ABOUT TIME	When!	31	27 May 95	1
Album of demos recorded in 1975.				
WRITTEN IN RED	When!	52	8 Feb 97	1

STRAW
UK

SINGLES:	HITS 2			WEEKS 3
THE AEROPLANE SONG	WEA	37	6 Feb 99	2
MOVING TO CALIFORNIA	WEA	50	24 Apr 99	1

STRAWBERRY SWITCHBLADE
UK

SINGLES:	HITS 3			WEEKS 26
SINCE YESTERDAY	Korova	5	17 Nov 84	17
LET HER GO	Korova	59	23 Mar 85	5
JOLENE	Korova	53	21 Sep 85	3
ALBUMS:	**HITS 1**			**WEEKS 4**
STRAWBERRY SWITCHBLADE	Korova	25	13 Apr 85	4

STRAWBS
UK

SINGLES:	HITS 3			WEEKS 27
LAY DOWN	A&M	12	28 Oct 72	13
PART OF THE UNION	A&M	2	27 Jan 73	11
SHINE ON SILVER SUN	A&M	34	6 Oct 73	3
ALBUMS:	**HITS 5**			**WEEKS 31**
JUST A COLLECTION OF ANTIQUES AND CURIOS	A&M	27	21 Nov 70	2
FROM THE WITCHWOOD	A&M	39	17 Jul 71	2
GRAVE NEW WORLD	A&M	11	26 Feb 72	12
BUSTING AT THE SEAMS	A&M	2	24 Feb 73	12
HERO AND HEROINE	A&M	35	27 Apr 74	3

STRAY CATS
US

SINGLES:	HITS 7			WEEKS 49
RUNAWAY BOYS	Arista	9	29 Nov 80	10
ROCK THIS TOWN	Arista	9	7 Feb 81	8
STRAY CAT STRUT	Arista	11	25 Apr 81	10
THE RACE IS ON	Swan Song	34	20 Jun 81	6
Above hit: Dave EDMUNDS and the STRAY CATS.				
YOU DON'T BELIEVE ME	Arista	57	7 Nov 81	3
(SHE'S) SEXY AND 17	Arista	29	6 Aug 83	9
BRING IT BACK AGAIN	EMI USA	64	4 Mar 89	3
ALBUMS:	**HITS 4**			**WEEKS 32**
STRAY CATS	Arista	6	28 Feb 81	22
GONNA BALL	Arista	48	21 Nov 81	4
RANT 'N' RAVE WITH THE STRAY CATS	Arista	51	3 Sep 83	5
BLAST OFF	EMI	58	8 Apr 89	1

STREETBAND
UK

SINGLES:	HITS 1			WEEKS 6
TOAST / HOLD ON	Logo	18	4 Nov 78	6

STREETWALKERS
UK

ALBUMS:	HITS 1			WEEKS 6
RED CARD	Vertigo	16	12 Jun 76	6

Barbra STREISAND

SINGLES:	HITS 18			WEEKS 155	
SECOND HAND ROSE	CBS	14	22 Jan 66	13
STONEY END	CBS	46	30 Jan 71	1
Originally recorded by Laura Nyro.				
STONEY END [RE]	CBS	27	13 Feb 71	10
THE WAY WE WERE	CBS	31	30 Mar 74	6
From the film of the same name.				
LOVE THEME FROM "A STAR IS BORN" (EVERGREEN)	CBS	3	9 Apr 77	19
Theme from the film.				
YOU DON'T BRING ME FLOWERS	CBS	5	25 Nov 78	12
Above hit: BARBRA and NEIL.				
NO MORE TEARS (ENOUGH IS ENOUGH)	CBS & Casablanca	3	3 Nov 79	13
Sales combined for the 7" on Casablanca and the 12" on CBS.				
Above hit: Donna SUMMER/Barbra STREISAND.				
WOMAN IN LOVE	CBS	1	4 Oct 80	16
Written by Barry Gibb.				
GUILTY	CBS	34	6 Dec 80	10
Above hit: Barbra STREISAND and Barry GIBB.				
COMIN' IN AND OUT OF YOUR LIFE	CBS	66	30 Jan 82	3
MEMORY	CBS	34	20 Mar 82	6
From the Andrew Lloyd Webber musical 'Cats'.				
TILL I LOVED YOU (THE LOVE THEME FROM GOYA)	CBS	16	5 Nov 88	7
From the film 'Goya'.				
Above hit: Barbra STREISAND and Don JOHNSON.				
PLACES THAT BELONG TO YOU	Columbia	17	7 Mar 92	5
From the film 'The Prince Of Tides'.				
WITH ONE LOOK	Columbia	30	5 Jun 93	3
From the musical 'Sunset Boulevard'.				
THE MUSIC OF THE NIGHT	Columbia	54	15 Jan 94	3
From the Andrew Lloyd Webber musical 'The Phantom Of The Opera'.				
Above hit: Barbra STREISAND (duet with Michael CRAWFORD).				
AS IF WE NEVER SAID GOODBYE (FROM SUNSET BOULEVARD)	Columbia	20	30 Apr 94	3
From the musical.				
I FINALLY FOUND SOMEONE	A&M	10	8 Feb 97	7
From the film 'The Mirror Has Two Faces'.				
Above hit: Barbra STREISAND and Bryan ADAMS.				
TELL HIM	Columbia	3	15 Nov 97	15
Above hit: Barbra STREISAND/Celine DION.				
IF YOU EVER LEAVE ME	Columbia	26	30 Oct 99	3
Above hit: Barbra STREISAND / Vince GILL.				
EPS:	**HITS 2**			**WEEKS 14**	
MY MAN	CBS	8	15 Jan 66	13
EN FRANCAIS	CBS	10	11 Jun 66	1
ALBUMS:	**HITS 24**			**WEEKS 517**	
MY NAME IS BARBRA, TWO	CBS	6	22 Jan 66	22
FUNNY GIRL	Capitol	19	30 Apr 66	3
London cast recording.				
FUNNY GIRL [OST]	CBS	11	10 May 69	22
Includes track by Mae Questal and Kay Medford.				
HELLO DOLLY! [OST]	EMI Stateside	45	14 Mar 70	2
Includes tracks by Michael Crawford, Marianne McAndrew and Walter Matthau.				
BARBRA STREISAND'S GREATEST HITS	CBS	44	4 Apr 70	2
STONEY END	CBS	28	17 Apr 71	2
THE WAY WE WERE	CBS	49	15 Jun 74	1
A STAR IS BORN [OST]	CBS	1	9 Apr 77	54
Features Kris Kristofferson on 5 tracks.				
STREISAND SUPERMAN	CBS	32	23 Jul 77	9
SONGBIRD	CBS	50	15 Jul 78	1
BARBRA STREISAND GREATEST HITS VOLUME 2	CBS	1	17 Mar 79	30
WET	CBS	25	17 Nov 79	13
GUILTY	CBS	1	11 Oct 80	82
LOVE SONGS	CBS	1	16 Jan 82	129
YENTL [OST]	CBS	21	19 Nov 83	35
EMOTION	CBS	15	27 Oct 84	12
THE BROADWAY ALBUM	CBS	3	18 Jan 86	16
Songs from the musicals.				
ONE VOICE	CBS	27	30 May 87	7
Live recordings in front of 500 invited guests at her home in Malibu.				
TILL I LOVED YOU	CBS	29	3 Dec 88	13
A COLLECTION - GREATEST HITS ... AND MORE	CBS	22	25 Nov 89	20
BACK TO BROADWAY	Columbia	4	10 Jul 93	17
Sequel to the 1986 album.				
A COLLECTION - GREATEST HITS ... AND MORE [RI]	Columbia	37	30 Apr 94	3
BARBRA - THE CONCERT	Columbia	63	29 Oct 94	1
Live recordings of her New York Madison Square Garden concert.				

HIGHER GROUND	Columbia	12	22 Nov 97	12
A LOVE LIKE OURS	Columbia	12	2 Oct 99	9

STRESS   UK

SINGLES:	HITS 1		WEEKS 1	
BEAUTIFUL PEOPLE	Eternal	74	13 Oct 90	1

STRETCH   UK

SINGLES:	HITS 1		WEEKS 9	
WHY DID YOU DO IT	Anchor	16	8 Nov 75	9

STRETCH and VERN present "MADDOG"   UK

SINGLES:	HITS 2		WEEKS 14	
I'M ALIVE	ffrr	6	14 Sep 96	9
Samples Earth, Wind And Fire and the Emotions' Boogie Wonderland.				
GET UP! GO INSANE!	ffrr	17	9 Aug 97	5
Samples House Of Pain's Jump Around.				
Above hit: STRETCH 'N' VERN present "MADDOG".				

STRICT INSTRUCTOR   Russia

SINGLES:	HITS 1		WEEKS 1	
STEP-TWO-THREE-FOUR	All Around The World	49	24 Oct 98	1
Based around Bob Sinclair's Jane Fonda work-out inspired disc Gymtonic.				

STRIKE   UK/Australia

SINGLES:	HITS 5		WEEKS 24	
U SURE DO	Fresh	31	24 Dec 94	5
Vocals by Australian singer Vicky Newton from the group Eden.				
U SURE DO [RE]	Fresh	4	1 Apr 95	9
THE MORNING AFTER (FREE AT LAST)	Fresh	38	23 Sep 95	1
INSPIRATION	Fresh	27	29 Jun 96	2
MY LOVE IS FOR REAL	Fresh	35	16 Nov 96	2
I HAVE PEACE	Fresh	17	31 May 97	4
Features rapper K-Gee.				
U SURE DO '99 [RM]	Fresh	53	25 Sept 99	1
Remixed by Jono Grant.				

STRIKERS   US

SINGLES:	HITS 1		WEEKS 5	
BODY MUSIC	Epic	45	6 Jun 81	5

STRING-A-LONGS   US

SINGLES:	HITS 1		WEEKS 16	
WHEELS	London	8	25 Feb 61	16

STRINGS FOR PLEASURE   UK

ALBUMS:	HITS 1		WEEKS 1	
THE BEST OF BACHARACH	Music For Pleasure	49	4 Dec 71	1

STRINGS OF LOVE   Italy

SINGLES:	HITS 1		WEEKS 2	
NOTHING HAS BEEN PROVED	Breakout	59	3 Mar 90	2

Joe STRUMMER   UK

(See also Black Grape.)

SINGLES:	HITS 2		WEEKS 9	
LOVE KILLS	CBS	69	2 Aug 86	1
JUST THE ONE	China	12	23 Dec 95	8
Above hit: LEVELLERS Special guest Joe STRUMMER on piano.				

ALBUMS:	HITS 2		WEEKS 2	
EARTHQUAKE WEATHER	Epic	58	14 Oct 89	1
ROCK ART AND THE X-RAY STYLE	Mercury	71	30 Oct 99	1
Above hit: Joe STRUMMER and the MESCALEROS.				

STRYKER – See MANCHESTER UNITED FOOTBALL SQUAD

Chad STUART and Jeremy CLYDE   UK

SINGLES:	HITS 1		WEEKS 7	
YESTERDAY'S GONE	Ember	37	30 Nov 63	7
Originally recorded by Little Anthony and the Imperials.				

STUDIO 45   Germany

SINGLES:		HITS 1			WEEKS 2
FREAK IT!	*Azuli*	36	*20 Feb 99*		2

STUDIO 2   Jamaica

SINGLES:		HITS 1			WEEKS 1
TRAVELLING MAN	*Multiply*	40	*27 Jun 98*		1

STUMP   UK

SINGLES:		HITS 1			WEEKS 1
CHARLTON HESTON	*Ensign*	72	*13 Aug 88*		1

Cupid STUNT – See Kenny EVERETT

STUTZ BEAR CATS   UK

SINGLES:		HITS 1			WEEKS 6
THE SONG THAT I SING	*Multi-Media Tapes*	36	*24 Apr 82*		6

Vocal version of the theme to the LWT ITV series 'We'll Meet Again'. [AA] listed with The Theme From "We'll Meet Again" by Denis King and his Orchestra.

STYLE COUNCIL   UK

SINGLES:		HITS 17			WEEKS 103
SPEAK LIKE A CHILD	*Polydor*	4	*19 Mar 83*		8
MONEY GO ROUND (PART 1)	*Polydor*	11	*28 May 83*		6
LONG HOT SUMMER / THE PARIS MATCH	*Polydor*	3	*13 Aug 83*		9

The Paris Match listed from 3 Sep 83 once single had dropped to No 7. Sleeve gives title as an EP: A Paris.

MONEY GO ROUND (PART 1) [RE]	*Polydor*	74	*20 Aug 83*		1
A SOLID BOND IN YOUR HEART	*Polydor*	11	*19 Nov 83*		8

Was planned as the Jam's last single.

MY EVER CHANGING MOODS	*Polydor*	5	*18 Feb 84*		7
GROOVIN' (YOU'RE THE BEST THING) / GROOVIN' (THE BIG BOSS GROOVE)	*Polydor*	5	*26 May 84*		8
SHOUT TO THE TOP	*Polydor*	7	*13 Oct 84*		8
WALLS COME TUMBLING DOWN!	*Polydor*	6	*11 May 85*		7
COME TO MILTON KEYNES	*Polydor*	23	*6 Jul 85*		5
THE LODGERS	*Polydor*	13	*28 Sep 85*		6

Above hit: STYLE COUNCIL featuring Dee C. LEE.

HAVE YOU EVER HAD IT BLUE	*Polydor*	14	*5 Apr 86*		6

From the film 'Absolute Beginners'.

IT DIDN'T MATTER	*Polydor*	9	*17 Jan 87*		5
WAITING	*Polydor*	52	*14 Mar 87*		3
WANTED	*Polydor*	20	*31 Oct 87*		4
LIFE AT A TOP PEOPLES HEALTH FARM	*Polydor*	28	*28 May 88*		3
HOW SHE THREW IT ALL AWAY	*Polydor*	41	*23 Jul 88*		2
PROMISED LAND	*Polydor*	27	*18 Feb 89*		5
LONG HOT SUMMER '89 [RM]	*Polydor*	48	*27 May 89*		2

ALBUMS:		HITS 8			WEEKS 95
CAFE BLEU	*Polydor*	2	*24 Mar 84*		38
OUR FAVOURITE SHOP	*Polydor*	1	*8 Jun 85*		22
HOME AND ABROAD	*Polydor*	8	*17 May 86*		8
THE COST OF LOVING	*Polydor*	2	*14 Feb 87*		7
CONFESSIONS OF A POP GROUP	*Polydor*	15	*2 Jul 88*		3
THE SINGULAR ADVENTURES OF THE STYLE COUNCIL GREATEST HITS VOLUME 1	*Polydor*	3	*18 Mar 89*		15
HERE'S SOME THAT GOT AWAY	*Polydor*	39	*10 Jul 93*		1

Compilation of B-sides, demos, cover versions and previously unavailable tracks.

THE STYLE COUNCIL COLLECTION	*Polydor*	60	*2 Mar 96*		1

STYLISTICS   US

SINGLES:		HITS 16			WEEKS 143
BETCHA BY GOLLY, WOW	*Avco*	13	*24 Jun 72*		12

Above hit: STYLISTICS featuring Russell THOMPKINS, JR.

I'M STONE IN LOVE WITH YOU	*Avco*	9	*4 Nov 72*		10
BREAK UP TO MAKE UP	*Avco*	34	*17 Mar 73*		5
PEEK-A-BOO	*Avco*	35	*30 Jun 73*		6
ROCKIN' ROLL BABY	*Avco*	6	*19 Jan 74*		9
YOU MAKE ME FEEL BRAND NEW	*Avco*	2	*13 Jul 74*		14

Above hit: STYLISTICS (featuring Airrion LOVE and Russell THOMPKINS, Jr.).

LET'S PUT IT ALL TOGETHER	*Avco*	9	*19 Oct 74*		9
STAR ON A TV SHOW	*Avco*	12	*25 Jan 75*		8
SING BABY SING	*Avco*	3	*10 May 75*		10
CAN'T GIVE YOU ANYTHING (BUT MY LOVE)	*Avco*	1	*26 Jul 75*		11
NA-NA IS THE SADDEST WORD	*Avco*	5	*15 Nov 75*		10
FUNKY WEEKEND	*Avco*	10	*14 Feb 76*		7
CAN'T HELP FALLING IN LOVE	*H&L*	4	*24 Apr 76*		7

SIXTEEN BARS	*H&L*	7	*7 Aug 76*	9
YOU'LL NEVER GET TO HEAVEN [EP]	*H&L*	24	*27 Nov 76*	9
Lead track: You''ll Never Get To Heaven (If You Break My Heart).				
$7000 AND YOU	*H&L*	24	*26 Mar 77*	7
ALBUMS:	**HITS 9**			**WEEKS 142**
ROCKIN' ROLL BABY	*Avco*	42	*24 Aug 74*	3
LET'S PUT IT ALL TOGETHER	*Avco*	26	*21 Sep 74*	14
FROM THE MOUNTAIN	*Avco*	36	*1 Mar 75*	1
Title was 'Heavy' in the US.				
THE BEST OF THE STYLISTICS	*Avco*	1	*5 Apr 75*	63
THANK YOU BABY	*Avco*	5	*5 Jul 75*	23
YOU ARE BEAUTIFUL	*Avco*	26	*6 Dec 75*	9
FABULOUS	*H&L*	21	*12 Jun 76*	5
BEST OF THE STYLISTICS VOLUME 2	*H&L*	1	*18 Sep 76*	21
THE GREATEST HITS OF THE STYLISTICS	*Mercury*	34	*17 Oct 92*	3

STYX   US

SINGLES:	**HITS 3**			**WEEKS 18**
BABE	*A&M*	6	*5 Jan 80*	10
THE BEST OF TIMES	*A&M*	42	*24 Jan 81*	5
Labelled as the world's first laser-etched single.				
DON'T LET IT END	*A&M*	56	*18 Jun 83*	3
ALBUMS:	**HITS 4**			**WEEKS 24**
CORNERSTONE	*A&M*	36	*3 Nov 79*	8
PARADISE THEATER	*A&M*	8	*24 Jan 81*	8
KILROY WAS HERE	*A&M*	67	*12 Mar 83*	6
CAUGHT IN THE ACT	*A&M*	44	*5 May 84*	2
Live recordings.				

SUB.MERGE featuring Jan JOHNSTON   US

SINGLES:	**HITS 1**			**WEEKS 2**
TAKE ME BY THE HAND	*AM:PM*	28	*8 Feb 97*	2

SUB SUB   UK

SINGLES:	**HITS 2**			**WEEKS 12**
AIN'T NO LOVE (AIN'T NO USE)	*Rob's Records*	3	*10 Apr 93*	11
Above hit: SUB SUB featuring Melanie WILLIAMS.				
RESPECT	*Rob's Records*	49	*19 Feb 94*	1
Samples the Fatback Band's Double Dutch.				

SUBCIRCUS   UK/Denmark

SINGLES:	**HITS 2**			**WEEKS 2**
YOU LOVE YOU	*Echo*	61	*26 Apr 97*	1
86'D	*Echo*	56	*12 Jul 97*	1
Original release reached No. 88 earlier in the year.				

SUBLIME   US

SINGLES:	**HITS 1**			**WEEKS 1**
WHAT I GOT	*MCA*	71	*5 Jul 97*	1

SUBLIMINAL CUTS   Holland

(See also Artemesia; Ethics; Movin' Melodies.)

SINGLES:	**HITS 1**			**WEEKS 3**
LE VOIE LE SOLEIL	*XL Recordings*	69	*15 Oct 94*	1
LE VOIE LE SOLEIL [RM]	*XL Recordings*	23	*20 Jul 96*	2
Remixed by Way Out West.				

SUBSONIC 2   UK

SINGLES:	**HITS 1**			**WEEKS 3**
UNSUNG HEROES OF HIP HOP	*Unity*	63	*13 Jul 91*	3

SUBTERRANIA featuring Ann CONSUELO   Sweden

SINGLES:	**HITS 1**			**WEEKS 1**
DO IT FOR LOVE	*Champion*	68	*5 Jun 93*	1

SUEDE   UK

SINGLES:	**HITS 17**			**WEEKS 68**
THE DROWNERS / TO THE BIRDS	*Nude*	49	*23 May 92*	2
METAL MICKEY	*Nude*	17	*26 Sep 92*	3
ANIMAL NITRATE	*Nude*	7	*6 Mar 93*	7
SO YOUNG	*Nude*	22	*29 May 93*	3
STAY TOGETHER	*Nude*	3	*26 Feb 94*	6

WE ARE THE PIGS	Nude	18	24 Sep 94	3
Brass accompaniment by The Kick Horns.				
THE WILD ONES	Nude	18	19 Nov 94	4
NEW GENERATION	Nude	21	11 Feb 95	3
NEW GENERATION [RE]	Nude	75	11 Mar 95	1
TRASH	Nude	3	10 Aug 96	6
BEAUTIFUL ONES	Nude	8	26 Oct 96	5
SATURDAY NIGHT	Nude	6	25 Jan 97	4
LAZY	Nude	9	19 Apr 97	3
FILMSTAR	Nude	9	23 Aug 97	4
ELECTRICITY	Nude	5	24 Apr 99	5
SHE'S IN FASHION	Nude	13	3 Jul 99	5
EVERYTHING WILL FLOW	Nude	24	18 Sept 99	2
CAN'T GET ENOUGH	Nude	23	20 Nov 99	2
ALBUMS:	**HITS 5**			**WEEKS 101**
SUEDE	Nude	1	10 Apr 93	22
DOG MAN STAR	Nude	3	22 Oct 94	16
COMING UP	Nude	1	14 Sep 96	44
SCI-FI LULLABIES	Nude	9	18 Oct 97	3
Compilation containing all the B-sides of their singles to date.				
HEAD MUSIC	Nude	1	15 May 99	16

SUEDETTES – See WIZZARD

SUENO LATINO featuring Carolina DAMAS   Italy

SINGLES:	**HITS 1**			**WEEKS 5**
SUENO LATINO	BCM	47	23 Sep 89	5

SUGAR   US

SINGLES:	**HITS 5**			**WEEKS 7**
A GOOD IDEA	Creation	65	31 Oct 92	1
IF I CAN'T CHANGE YOUR MIND	Creation	30	30 Jan 93	2
TILTED	Creation	48	21 Aug 93	1
YOUR FAVORITE THING	Creation	40	3 Sep 94	2
BELIEVE WHAT YOU'RE SAYING	Creation	73	29 Oct 94	1
ALBUMS:	**HITS 3**			**WEEKS 19**
COPPER BLUE	Creation	10	19 Sep 92	11
BEASTER	Creation	3	17 Apr 93	5
FILE UNDER EASY LISTENING	Creation	7	17 Sep 94	3

SUGAR CANE   US

SINGLES:	**HITS 1**			**WEEKS 5**
MONTEGO BAY	Ariola Hansa	54	30 Sep 78	5

SUGAR RAY   US

SINGLES:	**HITS 2**			**WEEKS 10**
FLY	Atlantic	58	31 Jan 98	1
Above hit: SUGAR RAY (featuring SUPER CAT).				
EVERY MORNING	Atlantic	10	29 May 99	9
ALBUMS:	**HITS 1**			**WEEKS 1**
14:59	Atlantic	60	19 Jun 99	1

SUGARCUBES   Iceland

SINGLES:	**HITS 6**			**WEEKS 22**
BIRTHDAY	One Little Indian	65	14 Nov 87	3
COLD SWEAT	One Little Indian	56	30 Jan 88	4
DEUS	One Little Indian	51	16 Apr 88	3
BIRTHDAY [RR]	One Little Indian	65	3 Sep 88	3
REGINA	One Little Indian	55	16 Sep 89	2
HIT	One Little Indian	17	11 Jan 92	6
BIRTHDAY [RM]	One Little Indian	64	3 Oct 92	1
Remixed by Justin Robertson.				
ALBUMS:	**HITS 4**			**WEEKS 14**
LIFE'S TOO GOOD	One Little Indian	14	7 May 88	6
HERE TODAY, TOMORROW, NEXT WEEK	One Little Indian	15	14 Oct 89	3
STICK AROUND FOR JOY	One Little Indian	16	22 Feb 92	4
IT'S IT	One Little Indian	47	17 Oct 92	1

SUGARHILL GANG   US

SINGLES:	**HITS 2**			**WEEKS 16**
RAPPER'S DELIGHT	Sugar Hill	3	1 Dec 79	11
The first rap record to chart. Based around Chic's Good Times.				
THE LOVER IN YOU	Sugar Hill	54	11 Sep 82	3
RAPPERS DELIGHT '89 [RM]	Sugar Hill	58	25 Nov 89	2

SUGGS | UK

SINGLES:		HITS 7		WEEKS 46	
I'M ONLY SLEEPING / OFF ON HOLIDAY	WEA	7	12 Aug 95	6
I'm Only Sleeping originally recorded by the Beatles on their 1966 album Revolver.					
CAMDEN TOWN	WEA	14	14 Oct 95	6
THE TUNE	WEA	33	16 Dec 95	3
Sleeve gives title as an EP: The Christmas EP.					
CECILIA	WEA	4	13 Apr 96	17
Originally recorded by Simon and Garfunkel from their 1970 album Bridge Over Troubled Water.					
CECILIA [RE-1ST]	WEA	65	24 Aug 96	1
CECILIA [RE-2ND]	WEA	59	7 Sep 96	1
NO MORE ALCOHOL	WEA	24	21 Sep 96	4
Samples the Champs' Tequila.					
Above 4: SUGGS featuring Louchie LOU and Michie ONE.					
BLUE DAY	WEA	22	17 May 97	5
Above hit: SUGGS and CO. featuring the CHELSEA TEAM.					
I AM	WEA	38	5 Sep 98	3
From the film 'The Avengers'.					
ALBUMS:		HITS 1		WEEKS 5	
THE LONE RANGER	WEA	14	28 Oct 95	5

SUICIDAL TENDENCIES | UK

ALBUMS:		HITS 2		WEEKS 2	
JOIN THE ARMY	Virgin	81	9 May 87	1
LIGHTS . . . CAMERA . . . REVOLUTION	Epic	59	21 Jul 90	1

SULTANA | Italy

SINGLES:		HITS 1		WEEKS 1	
TE AMO	Union	57	26 Mar 94	1

SULTANS OF PING | Ireland

SINGLES:		HITS 7		WEEKS 12	
WHERE'S ME JUMPER?	Divine	67	8 Feb 92	2
STUPID KID	Divine	67	9 May 92	1
VERONICA	Divine	69	10 Oct 92	1
YOU TALK TOO MUCH	Rhythm King	26	9 Jan 93	3
Above 4: SULTANS OF PING F.C.					
TEENAGE PUNKS	Epic	49	11 Sep 93	2
MICHIKO	Epic	43	30 Oct 93	2
WAKE UP AND SCRATCH ME	Epic	50	19 Feb 94	1
ALBUMS:		HITS 2		WEEKS 3	
CASUAL SEX IN THE CINEPLEX	Rhythm King	26	13 Feb 93	2
Above hit: SULTANS OF PING F.C.					
TEENAGE DRUG	Epic	57	5 Mar 94	1

SUMMER – See SNAP!

Donna SUMMER | US

SINGLES:		HITS 39		WEEKS 299	
LOVE TO LOVE YOU BABY	GTO	4	17 Jan 76	9
COULD IT BE MAGIC	GTO	40	29 May 76	7
WINTER MELODY	GTO	27	25 Dec 76	6
I FEEL LOVE	GTO	1	9 Jul 77	11
DOWN DEEP INSIDE (THEME FROM THE DEEP)	Casablanca	5	20 Aug 77	10
From the film 'The Deep'.					
I REMEMBER YESTERDAY	GTO	14	24 Sep 77	7
LOVE'S UNKIND	GTO	3	3 Dec 77	13
I LOVE YOU	Casablanca	10	10 Dec 77	9
RUMOUR HAS IT	Casablanca	19	25 Feb 78	8
BACK IN LOVE AGAIN	GTO	29	22 Apr 78	7
LAST DANCE	Casablanca	70	10 Jun 78	1
From the film 'Thank God It's Friday'.					
LAST DANCE [RE]	Casablanca	51	24 Jun 78	8
MACARTHUR PARK	Casablanca	5	14 Oct 78	10
HEAVEN KNOWS	Casablanca	34	17 Feb 79	8
Features Brooklyn Dreams.					
HOT STUFF	Casablanca	11	12 May 79	10
BAD GIRLS	Casablanca	14	7 Jul 79	10
DIM ALL THE LIGHTS	Casablanca	29	1 Sep 79	9
NO MORE TEARS (ENOUGH IS ENOUGH)	Casablanca & CBS	3	3 Nov 79	13
Sales combined for the 7" on Casablanca & the 12" on CBS.					
Above hit: Donna SUMMER/Barbra STREISAND.					
ON THE RADIO	Casablanca	32	16 Feb 80	6
SUNSET PEOPLE	Casablanca	46	21 Jun 80	5
THE WANDERER	Geffen	48	27 Sep 80	6

COLD LOVE	Geffen	44	17 Jan 81	3
LOVE IS IN CONTROL (FINGER ON THE TRIGGER)	Warner Brothers	18	10 Jul 82	11
STATE OF INDEPENDENCE	Warner Brothers	14	6 Nov 82	11

Features an All-Star Chorus (see later remix entry for details when they got a full artist credit on the sleeve).

I FEEL LOVE [RM]	Casablanca	21	4 Dec 82	10

Remixed by Patrick Cowley.

THE WOMAN IN ME	Warner Brothers	62	5 Mar 83	2
SHE WORKS HARD FOR THE MONEY	Mercury	25	18 Jun 83	8
UNCONDITIONAL LOVE	Mercury	14	24 Sep 83	12

Featuring backing vocals by Musical Youth.

STOP, LOOK AND LISTEN	Mercury	57	21 Jan 84	2
DINNER WITH GERSHWIN	Warner Brothers	13	24 Oct 87	11

Originally recorded by Brenda Russell.

ALL SYSTEMS GO	Warner Brothers	54	23 Jan 88	3
THIS TIME I KNOW IT'S FOR REAL	Warner Brothers	3	25 Feb 89	14
I DON'T WANNA GET HURT	Warner Brothers	7	27 May 89	9
LOVE'S ABOUT TO CHANGE MY HEART	Warner Brothers	20	26 Aug 89	6
WHEN LOVE TAKES OVER YOU	Warner Brothers	72	25 Nov 89	1
STATE OF INDEPENDENCE [RI]	Warner Brothers	45	17 Nov 90	3
BREAKAWAY	Warner Brothers	49	12 Jan 91	4
WORK THAT MAGIC	Warner Brothers	74	30 Nov 91	1
MELODY OF LOVE (WANNA BE LOVED)	Mercury	21	12 Nov 94	3
I FEEL LOVE [RR]	Manifesto	8	9 Sep 95	5

Re-recorded as the record label lost the original multi-track.

STATE OF INDEPENDENCE [RM]	Manifesto	13	6 Apr 96	5

Remix programmed by Phil Ramacon and edited by Bruno Morelli.
Above hit: Donna SUMMER; ALL STAR CHOIR featuring Dara BERNARD, Dylan CANNON, Christopher CROSS, James INGRAM, Michael JACKSON, Peggy Lipton JONES, Quincy JONES, Kenny LOGGINS, Michael McDONALD, Lionel RICHIE, Brenda RUSSELL, Donna SUMMER, Dionne WARWICK and Stevie WONDER.

CARRY ON	Almighty	65	11 Jul 98	1

Above hit: Donna SUMMER and Giorgio MORODER.

I WILL GO WITH YOU (CON TE PARTIRO)	Epic	44	30 Oct 99	1

ALBUMS:	HITS 15			WEEKS 198
LOVE TO LOVE YOU BABY	GTO	16	31 Jan 76	9
A LOVE TRILOGY	GTO	41	22 May 76	10
I REMEMBER YESTERDAY	GTO	3	25 Jun 77	23
ONCE UPON A TIME	Casablanca	24	26 Nov 77	13
GREATEST HITS	GTO	4	7 Jan 78	18
LIVE AND MORE	Casablanca	16	21 Oct 78	16

Three sides are live recordings.

BAD GIRLS	Casablanca	23	2 Jun 79	23
ON THE RADIO - GREATEST HITS VOLUMES 1 & 2	Casablanca	24	10 Nov 79	22
THE WANDERER	Geffen	55	1 Nov 80	2
DONNA SUMMER	Warner Brothers	13	31 Jul 82	16
SHE WORKS HARD FOR THE MONEY	Mercury	28	16 Jul 83	5
CATS WITHOUT CLAWS	Warner Brothers	69	15 Sep 84	2
ANOTHER PLACE AND TIME	Warner Brothers	17	25 Mar 89	28
THE BEST OF DONNA SUMMER	Warner Brothers	24	24 Nov 90	9
ENDLESS SUMMER - GREATEST HITS	Mercury	37	26 Nov 94	2

SUMMER DAZE
UK

SINGLES:	HITS 1			WEEKS 1
SAMBA MAGIC	VC Recordings	61	26 Oct 96	1

Originaly released in 1995.

Mark SUMMERS
UK

(See also Souvlaki.)

SINGLES:	HITS 1			WEEKS 6
SUMMERS MAGIC	Fourth & Broadway	27	26 Jan 91	6

Samples the theme from BBC1 children's programme 'The Magic Roundabout'.

SUNDANCE – See DJ FAST EDDIE

SUNDANCE
UK

(See also Shimmon and Woolfson.)

SINGLES:	HITS 2			WEEKS 5
SUNDANCE	React	33	8 Nov 97	2

Uses composer Lamont Booker's piano line from Smokebelch.

SUNDANCE '98 [RM]	React	37	3 Oct 98	2

Remixed by Shimmon and Woolfson.

THE LIVING DREAM	React	56	27 Feb 99	1

SUNDAYS
UK

SINGLES:	HITS 4			WEEKS 12
CAN'T BE SURE	Rough Trade	45	11 Feb 89	5
GOODBYE	Parlophone	27	3 Oct 92	2
SUMMERTIME	Parlophone	15	20 Sep 97	4
CRY	Parlophone	43	22 Nov 97	1
ALBUMS:	HITS 3			WEEKS 15
READING WRITING AND ARITHMETIC	Rough Trade	4	27 Jan 90	8
BLIND	Parlophone	15	31 Oct 92	3
STATIC & SILENCE	Parlophone	10	4 Oct 97	4

SUNDRAGON
UK

SINGLES:	HITS 1			WEEKS 1
GREEN TAMBOURINE	MGM	50	24 Feb 68	1

SUNFIRE
US

SINGLES:	HITS 1			WEEKS 11
YOUNG, FREE AND SINGLE	Warner Brothers	20	12 Mar 83	11

SUNKIDS featuring CHANCE
US

SINGLES:	HITS 1			WEEKS 2
RESCUE ME	A&M	50	13 Nov 99	2

SUNNY
UK

SINGLES:	HITS 1			WEEKS 10
DOCTOR'S ORDERS	CBS	7	30 Mar 74	10

SUNSCREEM
UK

SINGLES:	HITS 9			WEEKS 33
PRESSURE	Sony S2	60	29 Feb 92	2
LOVE U MORE	Sony S2	23	18 Jul 92	6
PERFECT MOTION	Sony S2	18	17 Oct 92	5
BROKEN ENGLISH	Sony S2	13	9 Jan 93	5
Originally recorded by Marianne Faithfull in 1979.				
PRESSURE US [RM]	Sony S2	19	27 Mar 93	5
WHEN	Sony S2	47	2 Sep 95	2
EXODUS	Sony S2	40	18 Nov 95	2
WHITE SKIES	Sony S2	25	20 Jan 96	3
SECRETS	Sony S2	36	23 Mar 96	2
CATCH	Pulse 8	55	6 Sep 97	1
ALBUMS:	HITS 2			WEEKS 6
O3	Sony S2	33	13 Feb 93	5
CHANGE OR DIE	Sony S2	53	30 Mar 96	1

Monty SUNSHINE – See Chris BARBER'S JAZZ BAND

SUPER FURRY ANIMALS
UK

SINGLES:	HITS 12			WEEKS 28
HOMETOWN UNICORN	Creation	47	9 Mar 96	1
GOD! SHOW ME MAGIC	Creation	33	11 May 96	2
SOMETHING 4 THE WEEKEND	Creation	18	13 Jul 96	3
IF YOU DON'T WANT ME TO DESTROY YOU	Creation	18	12 Oct 96	2
THE MAN DON'T GIVE A FUCK	Creation	22	14 Dec 96	2
HERMANN LOVES PAULINE	Creation	26	24 May 97	2
Hermann and Pauline were the parents of Albert Einstein.				
THE INTERNATIONAL LANGUAGE OF SCREAMING	Creation	24	26 Jul 97	2
PLAY IT COOL	Creation	27	4 Oct 97	2
DEMONS	Creation	27	6 Dec 97	2
ICE HOCKEY HAIR	Creation	12	6 Jun 98	3
NORTHERN LITES	Creation	11	22 May 99	4
FIRE IN MY HEART	Creation	25	21 Aug 99	3
ALBUMS:	HITS 4			WEEKS 19
FUZZY LOGIC	Creation	23	1 Jun 96	6
RADIATOR	Creation	8	6 Sep 97	3
OUT SPACED	Creation	44	5 Dec 98	1
Includes early singles recorded for the Ankst label, B-sides and BBC sessions.				
GUERRILLA	Creation	10	26 Jun 99	9

SUPERCAR
Italy

SINGLES:	HITS 2			WEEKS 6
TONITE	Pepper	15	13 Feb 99	5
COMPUTER LOVE	Pepper	67	21 Aug 99	1
Above hit: SUPERCAR featuring MIKAELA.				

SUPERCAT
Jamaica

SINGLES:	HITS 3			WEEKS 6
IT FE DONE	Columbia	66	1 Aug 92	1
MY GIRL JOSEPHINE	Columbia	22	6 May 95	4
From the film 'Pret-A-Porter'.				
Above hit: SUPER CAT featuring JACK RADICS.				
FLY	Atlantic	58	31 Jan 98	1
Above hit: SUGAR RAY (featuring SUPER CAT).				

SUPERGRASS
UK

SINGLES:	HITS 12			WEEKS 53
CAUGHT BY THE FUZZ	Parlophone	43	29 Oct 94	2
MANSIZE ROOSTER	Parlophone	20	18 Feb 95	3
LOSE IT	Sub-Pop	75	25 Mar 95	1
LENNY	Parlophone	10	13 May 95	3
ALRIGHT / TIME	Parlophone	2	15 Jul 95	10
GOING OUT	Parlophone	5	9 Mar 96	6
RICHARD III	Parlophone	2	12 Apr 97	5
SUN HITS THE SKY	Parlophone	10	21 Jun 97	4
LATE IN THE DAY	Parlophone	18	18 Oct 97	4
PUMPING ON YOUR STEREO	Parlophone	11	5 Jun 99	6
PUMPING ON YOUR STEREO [RE]	Parlophone	74	21 Aug 99	1
MOVING	Parlophone	9	18 Sept 99	5
MARY	Parlophone	36	4 Dec 99	3
ALBUMS:	HITS 3			WEEKS 75
I SHOULD COCO	Parlophone	1	27 May 95	36
IN IT FOR THE MONEY	Parlophone	2	3 May 97	25
SUPERGRASS	Parlophone	3	2 Oct 99	14

SUPERNATURALS
UK

SINGLES:	HITS 8			WEEKS 15
LAZY LOVER	Food	34	26 Oct 96	2
THE DAY BEFORE YESTERDAY'S MAN	Food	25	8 Feb 97	3
SMILE	Food	23	26 Apr 97	2
LOVE HAS PASSED AWAY	Food	38	12 Jul 97	2
PREPARE TO LAND	Food	48	25 Oct 97	1
I WASN'T BUILT TO GET UP	Food	25	1 Aug 98	3
SHEFFIELD SONG (I LOVE HER MORE THAN I LOVE YOU)	Food	45	24 Oct 98	1
EVEREST	Food	52	13 Mar 99	1
ALBUMS:	HITS 2			WEEKS 7
IT DOESN'T MATTER ANYMORE	Food	9	17 May 97	4
A TUNE A DAY	Food	21	22 Aug 98	3

SUPERNOVA
UK

SINGLES:	HITS 1			WEEKS 1
SOME MIGHT SAY	Sing Sing	55	11 May 96	1

SUPERSTAR
UK

SINGLES:	HITS 2			WEEKS 2
EVERY DAY I FALL APART	Camp Fabulous	66	7 Feb 98	1
SUPERSTAR	Camp Fabulous	49	25 Apr 98	1

SUPERTRAMP
UK

SINGLES:	HITS 6			WEEKS 52
DREAMER	A&M	13	15 Feb 75	10
GIVE A LITTLE BIT	A&M	29	25 Jun 77	7
THE LOGICAL SONG	A&M	7	31 Mar 79	11
BREAKFAST IN AMERICA	A&M	9	30 Jun 79	10
GOODBYE STRANGER	A&M	57	27 Oct 79	3
IT'S RAINING AGAIN	A&M	26	30 Oct 82	11
Above hit: SUPERTRAMP featuring vocals by Roger HODGSON.				
ALBUMS:	HITS 11			WEEKS 181
CRIME OF THE CENTURY	A&M	4	23 Nov 74	22
CRISIS? WHAT CRISIS?	A&M	20	6 Dec 75	15
EVEN IN THE QUIETEST MOMENTS . . .	A&M	12	23 Apr 77	22
BREAKFAST IN AMERICA	A&M	3	31 Mar 79	53
PARIS	A&M	7	4 Oct 80	17
Live recordings from the Paris Pavilion, 29 Nov 79.				
" . . . FAMOUS LAST WORDS . . . "	A&M	6	6 Nov 82	16
BROTHER WHERE YOU BOUND	A&M	20	25 May 85	5
THE AUTOBIOGRAPHY OF SUPERTRAMP	A&M	9	18 Oct 86	19
FREE AS A BIRD	A&M	93	31 Oct 87	1
THE VERY BEST OF SUPERTRAMP	A&M	24	15 Aug 92	4

SOME THINGS NEVER CHANGE	Chrysalis	74	3 May 97	1
THE VERY BEST OF SUPERTRAMP [RI]	PolyGram TV	8	27 Sep 97	6

SUPREMES   US

(See also Diana Ross and the Supremes and the Temptations; Supremes and Four Tops.)

SINGLES:	HITS 24		WEEKS 259	
WHERE DID OUR LOVE GO	Stateside	3	5 Sep 64	14
Song was originally written for the Marvelettes, but they rejected it.				
BABY LOVE	Stateside	1	24 Oct 64	15
COME SEE ABOUT ME	Stateside	27	23 Jan 65	6
STOP! IN THE NAME OF LOVE	Tamla Motown	7	27 Mar 65	12
BACK IN MY ARMS AGAIN	Tamla Motown	40	12 Jun 65	5
I HEAR A SYMPHONY	Tamla Motown	50	11 Dec 65	1
I HEAR A SYMPHONY [RE]	Tamla Motown	39	25 Dec 65	4
YOU CAN'T HURRY LOVE	Tamla Motown	3	10 Sep 66	12
YOU KEEP ME HANGIN' ON	Tamla Motown	8	3 Dec 66	10
LOVE IS HERE AND NOW YOU'RE GONE	Tamla Motown	17	4 Mar 67	10
THE HAPPENING	Tamla Motown	6	13 May 67	12
From the film of the same name.				
REFLECTIONS	Tamla Motown	5	2 Sep 67	14
IN AND OUT OF LOVE	Tamla Motown	13	2 Dec 67	13
FOREVER CAME TODAY	Tamla Motown	28	13 Apr 68	8
SOME THINGS YOU NEVER GET USED TO	Tamla Motown	34	6 Jul 68	6
LOVE CHILD	Tamla Motown	15	23 Nov 68	14
Co-written by R. Dean Taylor.				
I'M LIVIN' IN SHAME	Tamla Motown	14	26 Apr 69	9
I'M LIVIN' IN SHAME [RE]	Tamla Motown	50	5 Jul 69	1
NO MATTER WHAT SIGN YOU ARE	Tamla Motown	37	19 Jul 69	7
SOMEDAY WE'LL BE TOGETHER	Tamla Motown	13	13 Dec 69	13
Originally recorded by Johnny Bristol.				
Above 9: Diana ROSS and the SUPREMES.				
UP THE LADDER TO THE ROOF	Tamla Motown	6	2 May 70	15
STONED LOVE	Tamla Motown	3	16 Jan 71	13
NATHAN JONES	Tamla Motown	5	21 Aug 71	11
FLOY JOY	Tamla Motown	9	4 Mar 72	10
Written and produced by Smokey Robinson.				
AUTOMATICALLY SUNSHINE	Tamla Motown	10	15 Jul 72	9
BAD WEATHER	Tamla Motown	37	21 Apr 73	4
Written and produced by Stevie Wonder.				
BABY LOVE [RI]	Tamla Motown	12	24 Aug 74	10
STOP! IN THE NAME OF LOVE [RI]	Motown	62	18 Feb 89	1
Above 2: Diana ROSS and the SUPREMES.				

EPS:	HITS 1		WEEKS 12	
THE SUPREMES	Tamla Motown	6	1 May 65	12

ALBUMS:	HITS 12		WEEKS 184	
MEET THE SUPREMES	Stateside	8	5 Dec 64	6
SUPREMES A GO-GO	Tamla Motown	15	17 Dec 66	21
THE SUPREMES SING MOTOWN	Tamla Motown	15	13 May 67	16
THE SUPREMES SING RODGERS AND HART	Tamla Motown	25	30 Sep 67	7
DIANA ROSS AND THE SUPREMES GREATEST HITS	Tamla Motown	1	20 Jan 68	60
'LIVE' AT LONDON'S TALK OF THE TOWN	Tamla Motown	6	30 Mar 68	18
REFLECTIONS	Tamla Motown	30	20 Jul 68	2
LOVE CHILD	Tamla Motown	8	1 Feb 69	6
Above 4: Diana ROSS and the SUPREMES.				
TOUCH	Tamla Motown	40	25 Sep 71	1
DIANA ROSS AND THE SUPREMES' 20 GOLDEN GREATS	Motown	1	17 Sep 77	34
LOVE SUPREME	Motown	10	21 Jan 89	9
40 GOLDEN MOTOWN GREATS	Motown	35	31 Oct 98	4
Features both her solo and group recordings.				
Above 3: Diana ROSS and the SUPREMES.				

SUPREMES and FOUR TOPS   US

(See also Four Tops; Supremes.)

SINGLES:	HITS 2		WEEKS 20	
RIVER DEEP - MOUNTAIN HIGH	Tamla Motown	11	26 Jun 71	10
YOU GOTTA HAVE LOVE IN YOUR HEART	Tamla Motown	25	20 Nov 71	10

ALBUMS:	HITS 1		WEEKS 11	
THE MAGNIFICENT SEVEN	Tamla Motown	6	29 May 71	11

AI B. SURE!   US

(See also Quincy Jones.)

SINGLES:	HITS 4		WEEKS 12	
NITE AND DAY	Uptown	44	16 Apr 88	5
OFF ON YOUR OWN (GIRL)	Uptown	70	30 Jul 88	2

IF I'M NOT YOUR LOVER	*Uptown*		54	*10 Jun 89*	3
Above hit: Al B. SURE! featuring SLICK RICK.					
BLACK TIE WHITE NOISE	*Arista*		36	*12 Jun 93*	2
Above hit: David BOWIE featuring Al B. SURE!					

SURFACE   US

SINGLES:	HITS 4			WEEKS 14	
FALLING IN LOVE	*Salsoul*	67	*23 Jul 83*		3
WHEN YOUR 'EX' WANTS YOU BACK	*Salsoul*	52	*23 Jun 84*		4
HAPPY	*CBS*	56	*28 Feb 87*		5
THE FIRST TIME	*Columbia*	60	*12 Jan 91*		2

SURFACE NOISE   UK

SINGLES:	HITS 2			WEEKS 11	
THE SCRATCH	*WEA*	26	*31 May 80*		8
DANCIN' ON A WIRE	*Groove*	59	*30 Aug 80*		3

SURFARIS   US

SINGLES:	HITS 1			WEEKS 14	
WIPE OUT	*London*	5	*27 Jul 63*		14
The laugh at the start is by their manager Dale Smallin.					

SURPRISE SISTERS   UK

SINGLES:	HITS 1			WEEKS 3	
LA BOOGA ROOGA	*Good Earth*	38	*13 Mar 76*		3

SURVIVOR   US

(See also Various Artists: Films – Original Soundtracks 'Rocky III', 'Rocky IV'.)

SINGLES:	HITS 2			WEEKS 26	
EYE OF THE TIGER	*Scotti Brothers*	1	*31 Jul 82*		15
From the film 'Rocky III'.					
BURNING HEART	*Scotti Brothers*	5	*1 Feb 86*		11
From the film 'Rocky IV'. While this was still in the Top 40 in March, it was also released as an [AA] with I Can't Hold Back which reached No. 80.					
ALBUMS:	HITS 1			WEEKS 10	
EYE OF THE TIGER	*Scotti Brothers*	12	*21 Aug 82*		10

Peter SUSSKIND – See LONDON PHILHARMONIC CHOIR

SUTHERLAND BROTHERS and QUIVER   UK

SINGLES:	HITS 3			WEEKS 20	
ARMS OF MARY	*CBS*	5	*3 Apr 76*		12
SECRETS	*CBS*	35	*20 Nov 76*		4
EASY COME, EASY GO	*CBS*	50	*2 Jun 79*		4
Above hit: SUTHERLAND BROTHERS.					
ALBUMS:	HITS 2			WEEKS 11	
REACH FOR THE SKY	*CBS*	26	*15 May 76*		8
SLIPSTREAM	*CBS*	49	*9 Oct 76*		3

Pat SUZUKI   US

SINGLES:	HITS 1			WEEKS 1	
I ENJOY BEING A GIRL	*RCA*	49	*16 Apr 60*		1

Billy SWAN   US

SINGLES:	HITS 2			WEEKS 13	
I CAN HELP	*Monument*	6	*14 Dec 74*		9
DON'T BE CRUEL	*Monument*	42	*24 May 75*		4

SWAN LAKE   US

SINGLES:	HITS 1			WEEKS 4	
IN THE NAME OF LOVE	*Champion*	53	*17 Sep 88*		4

SWANS WAY   UK

SINGLES:	HITS 2			WEEKS 12	
SOUL TRAIN	*Exit*	20	*4 Feb 84*		7
ILLUMINATIONS	*Balgier*	57	*26 May 84*		5
ALBUMS:	HITS 1			WEEKS 1	
THE FUGITIVE KIND	*Balgier*	88	*3 Nov 84*		1

Patrick SWAYZE featuring Wendy FRASER | | | | US |

SINGLES:	HITS 1			WEEKS 11
SHE'S LIKE THE WIND	RCA	17	26 Mar 88	11

From the film 'Dirty Dancing'.

Keith SWEAT | | | | US |

SINGLES:	HITS 8			WEEKS 23
I WANT HER	Elektra	26	20 Feb 88	10
SOMETHING JUST AIN'T RIGHT	Elektra	55	14 May 88	3
HOW DO YOU LIKE IT?	Elektra	71	14 May 94	1

Features rap by Lisa Lopes of TLC.

TWISTED	Elektra	39	22 Jun 96	2

Features vocals by Kut Klose.

JUST A TOUCH	Elektra	35	23 Nov 96	2
NOBODY	Elektra	30	3 May 97	2

Above hit: Keith SWEAT featuring Athena CAGE.

I WANT HER [RM]	Elektra	44	6 Dec 97	1

Remixed by Femi Fem.

COME AND GET WITH ME	Elektra	58	12 Dec 98	1

Above hit: Keith SWEAT featuring SNOOP DOGG.

I'M NOT READY	Elektra	53	27 Mar 99	1
ALBUMS:	HITS 5			WEEKS 32
MAKE IT LAST FOREVER	Elektra	41	16 Jan 88	21
I'LL GIVE ALL MY LOVE TO YOU	Elektra	47	23 Jun 90	4
GET UP ON IT	Elektra	20	9 Jul 94	4
KEITH SWEAT	Elektra	36	29 Jun 96	2
STILL IN THE GAME	Elektra	62	3 Oct 98	1

Michelle SWEENEY | | | | US |

SINGLES:	HITS 1			WEEKS 1
THIS TIME	Big Beat	57	29 Oct 94	1

SWEET | | | | UK |

SINGLES:	HITS 17			WEEKS 159
FUNNY, FUNNY	RCA Victor	13	13 Mar 71	14
CO-CO	RCA Victor	2	12 Jun 71	15
ALEXANDER GRAHAM BELL	RCA Victor	33	16 Oct 71	5
POPPA JOE	RCA Victor	11	5 Feb 72	12
LITTLE WILLY	RCA Victor	4	10 Jun 72	14
WIG-WAM BAM	RCA Victor	4	9 Sep 72	13
BLOCK BUSTER!	RCA Victor	1	13 Jan 73	15
HELL RAISER	RCA Victor	2	5 May 73	11
THE BALLROOM BLITZ	RCA Victor	2	22 Sep 73	9
TEENAGE RAMPAGE	RCA Victor	2	19 Jan 74	8
THE SIX TEENS	RCA Victor	9	13 Jul 74	7
TURN IT DOWN	RCA Victor	41	9 Nov 74	2
FOX ON THE RUN	RCA Victor	2	15 Mar 75	10
ACTION	RCA Victor	15	12 Jul 75	6
THE LIES IN YOUR EYES	RCA Victor	35	24 Jan 76	4
LOVE IS LIKE OXYGEN	Polydor	9	28 Jan 78	9

From the film 'The Bitch'.

IT'S IT'S THE SWEET MIX [M]	Anagram	45	26 Jan 85	5

Mixed together by Sanny X.

ALBUMS:	HITS 3			WEEKS 14
SWEET FANNY ADAMS	RCA Victor	27	18 May 74	2
SWEET SIXTEEN – IT'S IT'S . . . SWEET'S HITS	Anagram	49	22 Sep 84	6
BALLROOM HITZ – THE VERY BEST OF SWEET	PolyGram TV	15	20 Jan 96	6

Rachel SWEET | | | | US |

SINGLES:	HITS 2			WEEKS 15
B-A-B-Y	Stiff	35	9 Dec 78	8

Original by Carla Thomas reached No. 14 in the US in 1966.

EVERLASTING LOVE	CBS	35	22 Aug 81	7

Above hit: Rex SMITH and Rachel SWEET.

SWEET DREAMS | | | | UK |

SINGLES:	HITS 1			WEEKS 12
HONEY HONEY	Bradley's	10	20 Jul 74	12

Originally recorded by Abba.

SWEET DREAMS | | | | UK |

SINGLES:	HITS 1			WEEKS 7
I'M NEVER GIVING UP	Ariola	21	9 Apr 83	7

UK's Eurovision in 1983, it came 6th.

SWEET MERCY featuring Joe ROBERTS — UK

SINGLES:	HITS 1			WEEKS 1
HAPPY DAYS	*Grass Green*	63	*24 Feb 96*	1

SWEET PEOPLE — France

SINGLES:	HITS 1			WEEKS 10
AND THE BIRDS WERE SINGING (ET LES OISEAUX CHANTAIENT)	*Polydor*	4	*4 Oct 80*	8
AND THE BIRDS WERE SINGING (ET LES OISEAUX CHANTAIENT) [RE]	*Polydor*	73	*29 Aug 87*	2

SWEET PUSSY PAULINE – See CANDY GIRLS

SWEET SENSATION — UK

SINGLES:	HITS 2			WEEKS 17
SAD SWEET DREAMER	*Pye*	1	*14 Sep 74*	10
Written by David Parton under the name Des Parton.				
PURELY BY COINCIDENCE	*Pye*	11	*18 Jan 75*	7

SWEET TEE — US

(See also Tin Tin Out.)

SINGLES:	HITS 1			WEEKS 6
I GOT DA FEELIN' / IT'S LIKE THAT Y'ALL	*Cooltempo*	31	*16 Jan 88*	6

SWEETBACK featuring Amel LARRIEUX from GROOVE THEORY — UK

SINGLES:	HITS 1			WEEKS 1
YOU WILL RISE	*Epic*	64	*29 Mar 97*	1

SWEETBOX — US/Germany

SINGLES:	HITS 1			WEEKS 12
EVERYTHING'S GONNA BE ALRIGHT	*RCA*	5	*22 Aug 98*	12
Based around Bach's Air On A 'G' String. Featured in the Lancome Oui! fragrance TV commercial.				

Sally SWEETLAND – See Eddie FISHER

SWERVEDRIVER — UK

SINGLES:	HITS 3			WEEKS 3
SANDBLASTED [EP]	*Creation*	67	*10 Aug 91*	1
Lead track: Sandblaster.				
NEVER LOSE THAT FEELING	*Creation*	62	*30 May 92*	1
DUEL	*Creation*	60	*14 Aug 93*	1
ALBUMS:	**HITS 2**			**WEEKS 2**
RAISE	*Creation*	44	*12 Oct 91*	1
MEZCAL HEAD	*Creation*	55	*9 Oct 93*	1

SWIMMING WITH SHARKS — Germany

SINGLES:	HITS 1			WEEKS 3
CARELESS LOVE	*WEA*	63	*7 May 88*	3

SWING featuring DR. ALBAN — US/Nigeria

(See also Dr. Alban.)

SINGLES:	HITS 1			WEEKS 1
SWEET DREAMS	*Logic*	59	*29 Apr 95*	1

SWING 52 — US

SINGLES:	HITS 1			WEEKS 1
COLOR OF MY SKIN	*ffrr*	60	*25 Feb 95*	1

SWING KIDS – See K7

SWING OUT SISTER — UK

SINGLES:	HITS 9			WEEKS 55
BREAKOUT	*Mercury*	4	*25 Oct 86*	14
SURRENDER	*Mercury*	7	*10 Jan 87*	8
TWILIGHT WORLD	*Mercury*	32	*18 Apr 87*	6
FOOLED BY A SMILE	*Mercury*	43	*11 Jul 87*	4
YOU ON MY MIND	*Fontana*	28	*8 Apr 89*	9
WHERE IN THE WORLD	*Fontana*	47	*8 Jul 89*	4
AM I THE SAME GIRL	*Fontana*	21	*11 Apr 92*	6
Originally recorded by Barbara Acklin.				
NOTGONNACHANGE	*Fontana*	49	*20 Jun 92*	2
LA LA (MEANS I LOVE YOU)	*Fontana*	37	*27 Aug 94*	2
From the film 'Four Weddings And A Funeral'.				

ALBUMS:		HITS 3		WEEKS 36	
IT'S BETTER TO TRAVEL	Mercury	1	23 May 87	21
KALEIDOSCOPE WORLD	Fontana	9	20 May 89	11
GET IN TOUCH WITH YOURSELF	Fontana	27	16 May 92	4

SWINGING BLUE JEANS   UK

SINGLES:		HITS 5		WEEKS 57	
IT'S TOO LATE NOW	His Master's Voice	30	22 Jun 63	6
IT'S TOO LATE NOW [RE]	His Master's Voice	46	10 Aug 63	3
HIPPY HIPPY SHAKE	His Master's Voice	2	14 Dec 63	17
Originally recorded by Chan Romero in 1959.				
GOOD GOLLY MISS MOLLY	His Master's Voice	11	21 Mar 64	10
YOU'RE NO GOOD	His Master's Voice	3	6 Jun 64	13
Originally recorded by Betty Everett the same year.				
DON'T MAKE ME OVER	His Master's Voice	31	22 Jan 66	8
Original by Dionne Warwick reached No. 21 in the US in 1963.				

EPS:		HITS 1		WEEKS 8	
SHAKE WITH THE SWINGING BLUE JEANS	His Master's Voice	13	18 Apr 64	8

SWINGLE SINGERS   US/France

EPS:		HITS 1		WEEKS 18	
JAZZ SEBASTIAN BACH	Philips	11	16 May 64	14

ALBUMS:		HITS 1		WEEKS 14	
JAZZ SEBASTIAN BACH	Philips	13	1 Feb 64	18

SWIRL 360   US

SINGLES:		HITS 1		WEEKS 1	
HEY NOW NOW	Mercury	61	14 Nov 98	1

SWITCH   US

SINGLES:		HITS 1		WEEKS 3	
KEEPING SECRETS	Total Experience	61	10 Nov 84	3

SWV   US

SINGLES:		HITS 9		WEEKS 43	
I'M SO INTO YOU	RCA	17	1 May 93	6
WEAK	RCA	33	26 Jun 93	3
RIGHT HERE	RCA	3	28 Aug 93	12
Samples Michael Jackson's Human Nature from his 1982 album Thriller.				
DOWNTOWN	RCA	19	26 Feb 94	5
ANYTHING	RCA	24	11 Jun 94	3
From the film 'Above The Rim'.				
YOU'RE THE ONE	RCA	13	25 May 96	3
IT'S ALL ABOUT U	RCA	36	21 Dec 96	5
CAN WE	Jive	18	12 Apr 97	4
From the film 'Booty Call'.				
SOMEONE	RCA	34	13 Sep 97	2
Above hit: SWV featuring PUFF DADDY.				

ALBUMS:		HITS 3		WEEKS 27	
IT'S ABOUT TIME	RCA	17	17 Jul 93	17
NEW BEGINNING	RCA	26	4 May 96	5
RELEASE SOME TENSION	RCA	19	16 Aug 97	5

SYBIL   US

SINGLES:		HITS 12		WEEKS 69	
FALLING IN LOVE	Champion	68	1 Nov 86	3
LET YOURSELF GO	Champion	32	25 Apr 87	6
MY LOVE IS GUARANTEED	Champion	42	29 Aug 87	5
DON'T MAKE ME OVER	Champion	59	22 Jul 89	5
Original by Dionne Warwick reached No. 21 in the US in 1963.				
DON'T MAKE ME OVER [RE]	Champion	19	14 Oct 89	6
WALK ON BY	PWL	6	27 Jan 90	9
CRAZY FOR YOU	PWL	71	21 Apr 90	1
THE LOVE I LOST	PWL Sanctuary	3	16 Jan 93	13
Above hit: WEST END featuring SYBIL.				
WHEN I'M GOOD AND READY	PWL International	5	20 Mar 93	13
BEYOND YOUR WILDEST DREAMS	PWL International	41	26 Jun 93	2
STRONGER TOGETHER	PWL International	41	11 Sep 93	2
MY LOVE IS GUARANTEED [RM]	PWL International	48	11 Dec 93	1
Remixed by Tony King.				
SO TIRED OF BEING ALONE	PWL International	53	9 Mar 96	1
WHEN I'M GOOD AND READY [RM]	Next Plateau	66	8 Mar 97	1
Remixed by Love To Infinity.				
STILL A THRILL	Coalition	55	26 Jul 97	1

ALBUMS:	HITS 3			WEEKS 12
LET YOURSELF GO	Champion	92	5 Sep 87	1
WALK ON BY	PWL	21	24 Feb 90	5
GOOD 'N' READY	PWL International	13	12 Jun 93	6

SYLK 130   US

SINGLES:	HITS 1			WEEKS 2
LAST NIGHT A DJ SAVED MY LIFE	Sony S2	33	25 Apr 98	2

SYLVESTER   US

SINGLES:	HITS 6			WEEKS 45
YOU MAKE ME FEEL (MIGHTY REAL)	Fantasy	8	19 Aug 78	15
DANCE (DISCO HEAT)	Fantasy	29	18 Nov 78	12
I (WHO HAVE NOTHING)	Fantasy	46	31 Mar 79	5
STARS	Fantasy	47	7 Jul 79	3
DO YA WANNA FUNK	London	32	11 Sep 82	8
Above hit: SYLVESTER with Patrick COWLEY.				
BAND OF GOLD	London	67	3 Sep 83	2
ALBUMS:	HITS 1			WEEKS 3
MIGHTY REAL	Fantasy	62	23 Jun 79	3

SYLVIA   US

SINGLES:	HITS 1			WEEKS 11
PILLOW TALK	London	14	23 Jun 73	11
She wrote it for Al Green but he rejected it.				

SYLVIA (VRETHAMMAR)   Sweden

SINGLES:	HITS 2			WEEKS 33
Y VIVA ESPANA	Sonet	4	10 Aug 74	19
Appeared in the breakers section under the chart from February of that year before finally charting.				
Y VIVA ESPANA [RE]	Sonet	35	4 Jan 75	9
HASTA LA VISTA	Sonet	38	26 Apr 75	5
Above hit: SYLVIA.				

David SYLVIAN   UK

(See also David Sylvian and Robert Fripp.)

SINGLES:	HITS 11			WEEKS 34
BAMBOO HOUSES / BAMBOO MUSIC	Virgin	30	7 Aug 82	4
Above hit: SYLVIAN SAKAMOTO.				
FORBIDDEN COLOURS	Virgin	16	2 Jul 83	8
Vocal version of the theme from the film 'Mr. Christmas Mr. Lawrence'.				
Above hit: David SYLVIAN and Riuichi SAKAMOTO.				
RED GUITAR	Virgin	17	2 Jun 84	5
THE INK IN THE WELL	Virgin	36	18 Aug 84	3
PULLING PUNCHES	Virgin	56	3 Nov 84	2
WORDS WITH THE SHAMAN	Virgin	72	14 Dec 85	1
TAKING THE VEIL	Virgin	53	9 Aug 86	3
Sleeve has title as A Little Girl Dreams Of Taking The Veil.				
BUOY	Virgin	63	17 Jan 87	2
Above hit: Mick KARN featuring David SYLVIAN.				
LET THE HAPPINESS IN	Virgin	66	10 Oct 87	1
HEARTBEAT (TAINAI KAIKI II) RETURNING TO THE WOMB	Virgin America	58	13 Jun 92	3
Above hit: David SYLVIAN and Riuichi SAKAMOTO featuring Ingrid CHAVEZ.				
I SURRENDER	Virgin	40	27 Mar 99	2
ALBUMS:	HITS 5			WEEKS 24
BRILLIANT TREES	Virgin	4	7 Jul 84	14
GONE TO EARTH	Virgin	24	13 Sep 86	5
SECRETS OF THE BEEHIVE	Virgin	37	7 Nov 87	2
PLIGHT AND PREMONITION	Virgin	71	2 Apr 88	1
Above hit: David SYLVIAN and Holgar CZUKAY.				
DEAD BEES ON A CAKE	Virgin	31	10 Apr 99	2

David SYLVIAN and Robert FRIPP   UK

(See also Robert Fripp; David Sylvian.)

SINGLES:	HITS 1			WEEKS 2
JEAN THE BIRDMAN	Virgin	68	28 Aug 93	2
ALBUMS:	HITS 1			WEEKS 2
THE FIRST DAY	Virgin	21	17 Jul 93	2

SYMARIP   UK

SINGLES:	HITS 1			WEEKS 3
SKINHEAD MOONSTOMP	Trojan	54	2 Feb 80	3

SYMBOLS | | | | UK

SINGLES:	HITS 2			WEEKS 15
BYE BYE BABY	*President*	44	*5 Aug 67*	3
(THE BEST PART OF) BREAKING UP	*President*	25	*6 Jan 68*	12

Terri SYMON | | | | UK

SINGLES:	HITS 1			WEEKS 1
I WANT TO KNOW WHAT LOVE IS	*A&M*	54	*10 Jun 95*	1

SYMPHONIQUE | | | | UK

ALBUMS:	HITS 1			WEEKS 4
MOODS SYMPHONIQUE 95	*Vision*	21	*1 Apr 95*	4

SYMPOSIUM | | | | UK

SINGLES:	HITS 6			WEEKS 10
FAREWELL TO TWILIGHT	*Infectious*	25	*22 Mar 97*	2
THE ANSWER TO WHY I HATE YOU	*Infectious*	32	*31 May 97*	2
FAIRWEATHER FRIEND	*Infectious*	25	*30 Aug 97*	3
AVERAGE MAN	*Infectious*	45	*14 Mar 98*	1
BURY YOU	*Infectious*	41	*16 May 98*	1
BLUE	*Infectious*	48	*18 Jul 98*	1
ALBUMS:	HITS 2			WEEKS 3
ONE DAY AT A TIME	*Infectious*	29	*8 Nov 97*	2
ON THE OUTSIDE	*Infectious*	32	*30 May 98*	1

SYNTHPHONIC VARIATIONS | | | | UK

ALBUMS:	HITS 1			WEEKS 1
SEASONS	*CBS*	84	*1 Nov 86*	1

SYREETA | | | | US

SINGLES:	HITS 5			WEEKS 30
SPINNIN' AND SPINNIN'	*Tamla Motown*	49	*21 Sep 74*	3
YOUR KISS IS SWEET	*Tamla Motown*	12	*1 Feb 75*	8
Written by Stevie Wonder.				
HARMOUR LOVE	*Tamla Motown*	32	*12 Jul 75*	4
WITH YOU I'M BORN AGAIN	*Motown*	2	*15 Dec 79*	11
IT WILL COME IN TIME	*Motown*	47	*8 Mar 80*	4
Above 2: Billy PRESTON and SYREETA.				

Stanislas SYREWICZ – See Anthony WAY

SYSTEM | | | | US

SINGLES:	HITS 1			WEEKS 2
I WANNA MAKE YOU FEEL GOOD	*Polydor*	73	*9 Jun 84*	2

SYSTEM F | | | | Holland

SINGLES:	HITS 1			WEEKS 6
OUT OF THE BLUE	*Essential Recordings*	14	*3 Apr 99*	6

SYSTEM 7 | | | | UK/France

SINGLES:	HITS 2			WEEKS 2
7:7 EXPANSION	*Big Life*	39	*13 Feb 93*	1
SINBAD / QUEST	*Big Life*	74	*17 Jul 93*	1
ALBUMS:	HITS 2			WEEKS 3
ALTITUDE	*Ten Records*	75	*20 Jun 92*	1
Above hit: SYSTEM 7 featuring Ultra NATE.				
777	*WAU*	30	*20 Mar 93*	2

T

T.A.F.K.A.P. – See PRINCE

T-BOZ | | | | US

SINGLES:	HITS 1			WEEKS 1
TOUCH MYSELF	*LaFace*	48	*23 Nov 96*	1
From the film 'Fled'.				

T-CONNECTION | | | | US

SINGLES:	HITS 5			WEEKS 27
DO WHAT YOU WANNA DO	*TK*	11	*18 Jun 77*	8

ON FIRE	TK	16	*14 Jan 78*	5
LET YOURSELF GO	TK	52	*10 Jun 78*	3
AT MIDNIGHT	TK	53	*24 Feb 79*	5
SATURDAY NIGHT	TK	41	*5 May 79*	6

T-COY – See VARIOUS ARTISTS (EPs) 'The Further Adventures Of North – More Underground Dance EP'

T-EMPO   UK

SINGLES:		HITS 2		WEEKS 4
SATURDAY NIGHT, SUNDAY MORNING	*ffrr*	19	*7 May 94*	3
Original by Thelma Houston reached No. 34 in the US in 1979.				
THE LOOK OF LOVE / THE BLUE ROOM	*ffrr*	71	*9 Nov 96*	1
The Look Of Love samples New Order's Blue Monday.				
Above hit: T-EMPO featuring FEEBI / T-EMPO featuring Doreen EDWARDS.				

T.H.S. – THE HORNE SECTION   US

SINGLES:		HITS 1		WEEKS 3
LADY SHINE (SHINE ON)	*Fourth & Broadway*	54	*18 Aug 84*	3

T'PAU   UK

SINGLES:		HITS 10		WEEKS 77
HEART AND SOUL	*Siren*	4	*8 Aug 87*	13
CHINA IN YOUR HAND	*Siren*	1	*24 Oct 87*	15
VALENTINE	*Siren*	9	*30 Jan 88*	8
SEX TALK (LIVE)	*Siren*	23	*2 Apr 88*	7
Live recording from the Scottish Exhibition Centre, 29 Oct 87. Originally titled Intimate Strangers				
when studio version was first released in 1987.				
I WILL BE WITH YOU	*Siren*	14	*25 Jun 88*	6
SECRET GARDEN	*Siren*	18	*1 Oct 88*	7
ROAD TO OUR DREAM	*Siren*	42	*3 Dec 88*	6
ONLY THE LONELY	*Siren*	28	*25 Mar 89*	6
WHENEVER YOU NEED ME	*Siren*	16	*18 May 91*	6
WALK ON AIR	*Siren*	62	*27 Jul 91*	2
VALENTINE [RI]	*Virgin*	53	*20 Feb 93*	1
ALBUMS:		**HITS 4**		**WEEKS 85**
BRIDGE OF SPIES	*Siren*	1	*26 Sep 87*	59
RAGE	*Siren*	4	*5 Nov 88*	17
THE PROMISE	*Siren*	10	*22 Jun 91*	7
HEART AND SOUL – THE VERY BEST OF T'PAU	*Virgin*	35	*27 Feb 93*	2

T.POWER   UK

SINGLES:		HITS 1		WEEKS 1
POLICE STATE	*Sour*	63	*13 Apr 96*	1
Comment on the Criminal Justice Bill.				

T. REX   UK

SINGLES:		HITS 25		WEEKS 235
DEBORA	*Regal Zonophone*	34	*11 May 68*	7
ONE INCH ROCK	*Regal Zonophone*	28	*7 Sep 68*	7
KING OF THE RUMBLING SPIRES	*Regal Zonophone*	44	*9 Aug 69*	1
Above 3: TYRANNOSAURUS REX.				
RIDE A WHITE SWAN	*Fly*	2	*24 Oct 70*	20
HOT LOVE	*Fly*	1	*27 Feb 71*	17
GET IT ON	*Fly*	1	*10 Jul 71*	13
Howard Kaylan and Mark Volman of the Turtles on backing vocals.				
JEEPSTER	*Fly*	2	*13 Nov 71*	15
TELEGRAM SAM	*T.Rex*	1	*29 Jan 72*	12
DEBORA [RI] / ONE INCH ROCK [RI]	*Magnifly*	7	*1 Apr 72*	10
Above hit: TYRANNOSAURUS REX.				
METAL GURU	*EMI*	1	*13 May 72*	14
CHILDREN OF THE REVOLUTION	*EMI*	2	*16 Sep 72*	10
SOLID GOLD EASY ACTION	*EMI*	2	*9 Dec 72*	11
20TH CENTURY BOY	*EMI*	3	*10 Mar 73*	9
THE GROOVER	*EMI*	4	*16 Jun 73*	9
TRUCK ON (TYKE)	*EMI*	12	*24 Nov 73*	11
TEENAGE DREAM	*EMI*	13	*9 Feb 74*	5
Above hit: Marc BOLAN and T. REX.				
LIGHT OF LOVE	*EMI*	22	*13 Jul 74*	5
ZIP GUN BOOGIE	*EMI*	41	*16 Nov 74*	3
Above hit: Marc BOLAN/T.REX.				
NEW YORK CITY	*EMI*	15	*12 Jul 75*	8
DREAMY LADY	*EMI*	30	*11 Oct 75*	5
Above hit: T. REX DISCO PARTY.				
LONDON BOYS	*EMI*	40	*6 Mar 76*	3
I LOVE TO BOOGIE	*EMI*	13	*19 Jun 76*	9
Based on Teenage Boogie by Webb Pierce.				

LASER LOVE	*EMI*	41	*2 Oct 76*	4
THE SOUL OF MY SUIT	*EMI*	42	*2 Apr 77*	3
RETURN OF THE ELECTRIC WARRIOR [EP]	*Rarn*	50	*9 May 81*	4
Lead track: Sing Me A Song.				
YOU SCARE ME TO DEATH	*Cherry Red*	51	*19 Sep 81*	4
Above 2: Marc BOLAN.				
TELEGRAM SAM [RI]	*EMI*	69	*27 Mar 82*	2
MEGAREX [M]	*Marc On Wax*	72	*18 May 85*	2
Mixed by Sanny X of Disco Mix Club (UK).				
GET IT ON [RM]	*Marc On Wax*	54	*9 May 87*	4
20TH CENTURY BOY [RI]	*Marc On Wax*	13	*24 Aug 91*	8
Featured in the Levi's 501 Jeans TV commercial.				
Above hit: Marc BOLAN and T-REX.				

ALBUMS:	**HITS 21**		**WEEKS 219**	
MY PEOPLE WERE FAIR AND HAD SKY IN THEIR HAIR BUT NOW THEY'RE CONTENT TO WEAR STARS ON THEIR BROWS	*Regal Zonophone*	15	*13 Jul 68*	9
UNICORN	*Regal Zonophone*	12	*7 Jun 69*	3
A BEARD OF STARS	*Regal Zonophone*	21	*14 Mar 70*	6
Above 3: TYRANNOSAURUS REX.				
T. REX	*Fly*	13	*16 Jan 71*	24
THE BEST OF T. REX	*Flyback*	21	*7 Aug 71*	7
Consists mainly of material from when they were Tyrannosaurus Rex.				
ELECTRIC WARRIOR	*Fly*	1	*9 Oct 71*	44
PROPHETS, SEERS AND SAGES THE ANGELS OF THE AGES / MY PEOPLE WERE FAIR AND HAD SKY IN THEIR HAIR BUT NOW THEY'RE CONTENT TO WEAR STARS ON THEIR BROWS [RI]	*Fly Double Back*	1	*29 Apr 72*	12
Prophets, Seers And Sages was originally released in 1968.				
Above hit: TYRANNOSAURUS REX.				
BOLAN BOOGIE	*Fly*	1	*20 May 72*	19
Compilation.				
THE SLIDER	*EMI*	4	*5 Aug 72*	18
A BEARD OF STARS / UNICORN [RI]	*Cube*	44	*9 Dec 72*	2
Above hit: TYRANNOSAURUS REX.				
TANX	*EMI*	4	*31 Mar 73*	12
GREAT HITS	*EMI*	32	*10 Nov 73*	3
ZINC ALLOY AND THE HIDDEN RIDERS OF TOMORROW	*EMI*	12	*16 Mar 74*	3
Above hit: Marc BOLAN and T. REX.				
FUTURISTIC DRAGON	*EMI*	50	*21 Feb 76*	1
DANDY IN THE UNDERWORLD	*EMI*	26	*9 Apr 77*	3
SOLID GOLD	*EMI*	51	*30 Jun 79*	3
T. REX IN CONCERT	*Marc*	35	*12 Sep 81*	6
Live recordings.				
YOU SCARE ME TO DEATH	*Cherry Red*	88	*7 Nov 81*	1
DANCE IN THE MIDNIGHT	*Marc On Wax*	83	*24 Sep 83*	3
Above 2: Marc BOLAN.				
BEST OF THE 20TH CENTURY BOY	*K-Tel*	5	*4 May 85*	21
THE ULTIMATE COLLECTION	*Telstar*	4	*28 Sep 91*	16
THE ESSENTIAL COLLECTION	*PolyGram TV*	24	*7 Oct 95*	3
Released to coincide with the 18th anniversary of his death.				
Above 3: Marc BOLAN and T. REX.				

T.S. MONK
US

SINGLES:	**HITS 2**		**WEEKS 6**	
BON BON VIE	*Mirage*	63	*7 Mar 81*	2
CANDIDATE FOR LOVE	*Mirage*	58	*25 Apr 81*	4

T-SHIRT
UK

SINGLES:	**HITS 1**		**WEEKS 1**	
YOU SEXY THING	*Eternal*	63	*13 Sep 97*	1

T-SPOON
Holland

SINGLES:	**HITS 2**		**WEEKS 15**	
SEX ON THE BEACH	*Control*	2	*19 Sep 98*	13
TOM'S PARTY	*Control*	27	*23 Jan 99*	2
Adapted around 10CC's Dreadlock Holiday and Suzanne Vega's Tom's Diner.				

TABERNACLE
UK

SINGLES:	**HITS 1**		**WEEKS 2**	
I KNOW THE LORD	*Good Groove*	62	*4 Mar 95*	1
Track rearranged around Bessie Griffin's recording of the song from the 1940s.				
I KNOW THE LORD [RM]	*Good Groove*	55	*3 Feb 96*	1
Remixed by Tabernacle.				

TACK HEAD

US

SINGLES:		HITS 1		WEEKS 3
DANGEROUS SEX	SBK.One	48	30 Jun 90	3

Features Mark E. Smith of the Fall.

TAFFY

UK

SINGLES:		HITS 2		WEEKS 14
I LOVE MY RADIO [MIDNIGHT RADIO]	Transglobal	6	10 Jan 87	10
STEP BY STEP	Transglobal	59	18 Jul 87	4

A 7" remix was sub credited [Dee Jay's Radio] instead.

TAG TEAM

US

SINGLES:		HITS 2		WEEKS 8
WHOOMP! (THERE IT IS)	Club Tools	34	8 Jan 94	5
ADDAMS FAMILY (WHOOMP!) [RR]	Atlas	53	29 Jan 94	1
WHOOMP! (THERE IT IS) [RM]	Club Tools	48	10 Sep 94	2

Samples I'm Ready by Kano. (under WHOOMP! first)

From the film 'Addams Family Values'. This is an alternative recording of Whoomp! (There It Is).

Sales of the remix were combined with sales of the 3 original formats released earlier in the year.

TAK TIX

US

SINGLES:		HITS 1		WEEKS 2
FEEL LIKE SINGING	A&M	33	20 Jan 96	2

TAKE 5

US

SINGLES:		HITS 2		WEEKS 4
I GIVE	Edel	70	7 Nov 98	1
NEVER HAD IT SO GOOD	Edel	34	27 Mar 99	3

TAKE THAT

UK

SINGLES:		HITS 16		WEEKS 158
PROMISES	RCA	38	23 Nov 91	2
ONCE YOU'VE TASTED LOVE	RCA	47	8 Feb 92	3
IT ONLY TAKES A MINUTE	RCA	7	6 Jun 92	8
I FOUND HEAVEN	RCA	15	15 Aug 92	6
A MILLION LOVE SONGS - THE LOVE SONGS [EP]	RCA	7	10 Oct 92	9
COULD IT BE MAGIC	RCA	3	12 Dec 92	12
WHY CAN'T I WAKE UP WITH YOU?	RCA	2	20 Feb 93	10
PRAY	RCA	1	17 Jul 93	11
RELIGHT MY FIRE	RCA	1	9 Oct 93	14
BABE	RCA	1	18 Dec 93	10
EVERYTHING CHANGES	RCA	1	9 Apr 94	10
LOVE AIN'T HERE ANYMORE	RCA	3	9 Jul 94	10
LOVE AIN'T HERE ANYMORE [RE]	RCA	55	15 Oct 94	2
SURE	RCA	1	15 Oct 94	15
BACK FOR GOOD	RCA	1	8 Apr 95	13
NEVER FORGET	RCA	1	5 Aug 95	9
HOW DEEP IS YOUR LOVE	RCA	1	9 Mar 96	13
HOW DEEP IS YOUR LOVE [RE]	RCA	74	15 Jun 96	1

Lead track: A Million Love Songs. (under A MILLION LOVE SONGS)

Inspired by Prelude in C Minor by F. Chopin. (under COULD IT BE MAGIC)

Originally recorded by Dan Hartman.
Above hit: TAKE THAT featuring LULU. (under RELIGHT MY FIRE)

Charity record in aid of the Nordoff Robbins Music Therapy charity. (under NEVER FORGET)

ALBUMS:		HITS 5		WEEKS 224
TAKE THAT AND PARTY	RCA	2	5 Sep 92	73
EVERYTHING CHANGES	RCA	1	23 Oct 93	78
NOBODY ELSE	RCA	1	13 May 95	33
NOBODY ELSE (US VERSION)	Arista	26	26 Aug 95	4
GREATEST HITS	RCA	1	6 Apr 96	36

US import version with different track listing to the UK release. (under NOBODY ELSE (US VERSION))

Billy TALBOT – See Ian McNABB

TALK TALK

UK

SINGLES:		HITS 9		WEEKS 73
TALK TALK	EMI	52	24 Apr 82	4
TODAY	EMI	14	24 Jul 82	13
TALK TALK [RI]	EMI	23	13 Nov 82	10
MY FOOLISH FRIEND	EMI	57	19 Mar 83	3
IT'S MY LIFE	EMI	46	14 Jan 84	5
SUCH A SHAME	EMI	49	7 Apr 84	6
DUM DUM GIRL	EMI	74	11 Aug 84	1

LIFE'S WHAT YOU MAKE IT	EMI	16	*18 Jan 86*	9
LIVING IN ANOTHER WORLD	EMI	48	*15 Mar 86*	4
GIVE IT UP	*Parlophone*	59	*17 May 86*	3
IT'S MY LIFE [RI]	*Parlophone*	13	*19 May 90*	9
LIFE'S WHAT YOU MAKE IT [RI]	*Parlophone*	23	*1 Sep 90*	6
ALBUMS:	**HITS 8**			**WEEKS 86**
THE PARTY'S OVER	EMI	21	*24 Jul 82*	25
IT'S MY LIFE	EMI	35	*25 Feb 84*	8
THE COLOUR OF SPRING	EMI	8	*1 Mar 86*	21
SPIRIT OF EDEN	*Parlophone*	19	*24 Sep 88*	5
THE VERY BEST OF TALK TALK - NATURAL HISTORY	*Parlophone*	3	*9 Jun 90*	21
HISTORY REVISITED - THE REMIXES	*Parlophone*	35	*6 Apr 91*	2
LAUGHING STOCK	*Verve*	26	*28 Sep 91*	2
THE VERY BEST OF TALK TALK	EMI	54	*8 Feb 97*	2

TALKING HEADS
UK/US

(See also Heads with Shaun Ryder.)

SINGLES:	**HITS 10**			**WEEKS 54**
ONCE IN A LIFETIME	*Sire*	14	*7 Feb 81*	10
HOUSES IN MOTION	*Sire*	50	*9 May 81*	3
THIS MUST BE THE PLACE (NAIVE MELODY)	*Sire*	51	*21 Jan 84*	3
SLIPPERY PEOPLE (LIVE VERSION)	EMI	68	*3 Nov 84*	2
Live recording from the Pantages Theatre, Hollywood, Dec 83.				
ROAD TO NOWHERE	EMI	6	*12 Oct 85*	16
AND SHE WAS	EMI	17	*8 Feb 86*	8
WILD WILD LIFE	EMI	43	*6 Sep 86*	4
RADIO HEAD (LP VERSION)	EMI	52	*16 May 87*	2
BLIND	EMI	59	*13 Aug 88*	3
LIFETIME PILING UP	EMI	50	*10 Oct 92*	3
ALBUMS:	**HITS 11**			**WEEKS 230**
TALKING HEADS '77	*Sire*	60	*25 Feb 78*	1
MORE SONGS ABOUT BUILDINGS AND FOOD	*Sire*	21	*29 Jul 78*	3
FEAR OF MUSIC	*Sire*	33	*15 Sep 79*	5
REMAIN IN LIGHT	*Sire*	21	*1 Nov 80*	17
THE NAME OF THIS BAND IS TALKING HEADS	*Sire*	22	*10 Apr 82*	5
Live recordings and out-takes.				
SPEAKING IN TONGUES	*Sire*	21	*18 Jun 83*	12
STOP MAKING SENSE	EMI	37	*27 Oct 84*	81
Live recordings from the Pantages Theatre, Hollywood, Dec 83.				
LITTLE CREATURES	EMI	10	*29 Jun 85*	65
TRUE STORIES	EMI	7	*27 Sep 86*	9
NAKED	EMI	3	*26 Mar 88*	15
ONCE IN A LIFETIME - THE BEST OF TALKING HEADS/ SAND IN THE VASELINE	EMI	7	*24 Oct 92*	16
Both albums sold separately, but sales combined.				
STOP MAKING SENSE [RE]	EMI	74	*18 Sept 99*	1
Re-released to celebrate the reissue of Jonathan Demme's live concert film. It has been remixed/remastered and includes extra tracks.				

TALL PAUL
UK

(See also Grifters featuring Tall Paul and Brandon Block.)

SINGLES:	**HITS 2**			**WEEKS 5**
ROCK DA HOUSE	*VC Recordings*	12	*29 Mar 97*	4
BE THERE	*Duty Free*	45	*29 May 99*	1

TAM-TAM POUR L'ETHIOPIE – See STARVATION / TAM-TAM POUR L'ETHIOPIE

TAMARA – See TRINA and TAMARA

TAMARA – See MARVIN and TAMARA

TAMBA TRIO
Argentina

SINGLES:	**HITS 1**			**WEEKS 2**
MAS QUE NADA	*Talkin Loud*	34	*18 Jul 98*	2
Featured in the Nike TV commercial.				

TAMPERER featuring MAYA
US/Italy

SINGLES:	**HITS 2**			**WEEKS 31**
FEEL IT	*Pepper*	1	*25 Apr 98*	17
Samples the Jacksons' Can You Feel It.				
IF YOU BUY THIS RECORD YOUR LIFE WILL BE BETTER	*Pepper*	3	*14 Nov 98*	14
Samples Madonna's Material Girl.				

TAMS
US

SINGLES:	**HITS 3**			**WEEKS 31**
BE YOUNG BE FOOLISH, BE HAPPY	*Stateside*	32	*14 Feb 70*	7

HEY GIRL DON'T BOTHER ME	*Probe*	1	*31 Jul 71*	17
THERE AIN'T NOTHING LIKE SHAGGIN'	*Virgin*	21	*21 Nov 87*	7

Norma TANEGA
US

SINGLES:		HITS 1		WEEKS 8
WALKIN' MY CAT NAMED DOG	*Stateside*	22	*9 Apr 66*	8

TANGERINE DREAM
Germany

ALBUMS:		HITS 16		WEEKS 77
PHAEDRA	*Virgin*	15	*20 Apr 74*	15
RUBYCON	*Virgin*	12	*5 Apr 75*	14
RICOCHET	*Virgin*	40	*20 Dec 75*	2
STRATOSFEAR	*Virgin*	39	*13 Nov 76*	4
SORCERER [OST]	*MCA*	25	*23 Jul 77*	7
ENCORE	*Virgin*	55	*19 Nov 77*	1
CYCLONE	*Virgin*	37	*1 Apr 78*	4
FORCE MAJEURE	*Virgin*	26	*17 Feb 79*	7
TANGRAM	*Virgin*	36	*7 Jun 80*	5
THIEF [OST]	*Virgin*	43	*18 Apr 81*	3
EXIT	*Virgin*	43	*19 Sep 81*	5
WHITE EAGLE	*Virgin*	57	*10 Apr 82*	5
HYPERBOREA	*Virgin*	45	*5 Nov 83*	2
POLAND	*Jive Electro*	90	*10 Nov 84*	1
UNDERWATER SUNLIGHT	*Jive Electro*	97	*26 Jul 86*	1
TYGER	*Jive*	88	*27 Jun 87*	1

TANK
UK

ALBUMS:		HITS 1		WEEKS 5
FILTH HOUNDS OF HADES	*Kamaflage*	33	*13 Mar 82*	5

Children of TANSLEY SCHOOL
UK

SINGLES:		HITS 1		WEEKS 4
MY MUM IS ONE IN A MILLION	*EMI*	27	*28 Mar 81*	4

Jimmy TARBUCK
UK

SINGLES:		HITS 1		WEEKS 2
AGAIN	*Safari*	74	*16 Nov 85*	1
AGAIN [RE]	*Safari*	68	*30 Nov 85*	1

Bill TARMEY
UK

SINGLES:		HITS 3		WEEKS 9
ONE VOICE	*Arista*	16	*3 Apr 93*	4
Featuring backing vocals by St. Winifred's School Choir.				
THE WIND BENEATH MY WINGS	*EMI*	40	*19 Feb 94*	3
I.O.U.	*EMI*	55	*19 Nov 94*	2
ALBUMS:		HITS 3		WEEKS 25
A GIFT OF LOVE	*EMI*	15	*27 Nov 93*	14
TIME FOR LOVE	*EMI*	28	*5 Nov 94*	9
AFTER HOURS	*EMI Premier*	61	*18 May 96*	2

TARRIERS
US

SINGLES:		HITS 2		WEEKS 6
CINDY OH CINDY	*London*	26	*15 Dec 56*	1
Above hit: Vince MARTIN and the TARRIERS.				
THE BANANA BOAT SONG	*Columbia*	15	*2 Mar 57*	5

TARTAN ARMY featuring the WEE'IST PIPE BAND IN THE WORLD
UK

SINGLES:		HITS 1		WEEKS 4
SCOTLAND BE GOOD (JOCK & ROLL)	*Precious Organisation*	54	*6 Jun 98*	4

TASTE
Ireland

ALBUMS:		HITS 2		WEEKS 12
ON THE BOARDS	*Polydor*	18	*7 Feb 70*	11
TASTE – LIVE AT THE ISLE OF WIGHT	*Polydor*	41	*9 Sep 72*	1

A TASTE OF HONEY
US

SINGLES:		HITS 1		WEEKS 19
BOOGIE OOGIE OOGIE	*Capitol*	3	*17 Jun 78*	16
BOOGIE OOGIE OOGIE [RM]	*Capitol*	59	*18 May 85*	3
Remixed by John Luongo.				

TASTE XPERIENCE featuring Natasha PEARL
UK

SINGLES:	HITS 1			WEEKS 1
SUMMERSAULT	Manifesto	66	6 Nov 99	1

Jeffrey TATE – See Nigel KENNEDY

TATJANA
Croatia

SINGLES:	HITS 1			WEEKS 2
SANTA MARIA	Love This	40	21 Sep 96	2

Original release reached No. 102 in 1995.

TAVARES
US

SINGLES:	HITS 9			WEEKS 77
HEAVEN MUST BE MISSING AN ANGEL	Capitol Soul	4	10 Jul 76	11
DON'T TAKE AWAY THE MUSIC	Capitol Soul	4	9 Oct 76	10
THE MIGHTY POWER OF LOVE	Capitol	25	5 Feb 77	6
WHODUNIT	Capitol	5	9 Apr 77	10
ONE STEP AWAY	Capitol	16	2 Jul 77	7
THE GHOST OF LOVE	Capitol	29	18 Mar 78	6
MORE THAN A WOMAN	Capitol	7	6 May 78	11

From the film 'Saturday Night Fever'. Originally recorded by the Bee Gees.

SLOW TRAIN TO PARADISE	Capitol	62	12 Aug 78	3
HEAVEN MUST BE MISSING AN ANGEL [RM]	Capitol	12	22 Feb 86	9

Remixed by Ben Liebrand.

IT ONLY TAKES A MINUTE	Capitol	46	3 May 86	4

Original release reached No. 10 in the US in 1975.

ALBUMS:	HITS 2			WEEKS 15
SKY HIGH	Capitol Soul	22	21 Aug 76	13
THE BEST OF TAVARES	Capitol	39	1 Apr 78	2

TAXI GANG – See BEENIE MAN; Chaka DEMUS and PLIERS

TAXMAN – See KICKING BACK with TAXMAN

TAYLOR – See LIBRA presents TAYLOR

Andy TAYLOR
UK

SINGLES:	HITS 1			WEEKS 2
LOLA	A&M	60	20 Oct 90	2
ALBUMS:	HITS 1			WEEKS 1
THUNDER	MCA	61	30 May 87	1

Felice TAYLOR
US

SINGLES:	HITS 1			WEEKS 13
I FEEL LOVE COMIN' ON	President	11	28 Oct 67	13

James TAYLOR
US

(See also Carly Simon.)

SINGLES:	HITS 2			WEEKS 18
FIRE AND RAIN	Warner Brothers	42	21 Nov 70	3
YOU'VE GOT A FRIEND	Warner Brothers	4	28 Aug 71	15

Originally recorded by Carole King from her 1971 album Tapestry.

ALBUMS:	HITS 5			WEEKS 112
SWEET BABY JAMES	Warner Brothers	7	21 Nov 70	53
MUD SLIDE SLIM AND THE BLUE HORIZON	Warner Brothers	4	29 May 71	41
SWEET BABY JAMES [RE]	Warner Brothers	34	8 Jan 72	6
MUD SLIDE SLIM AND THE BLUE HORIZON [RE]	Warner Brothers	49	18 Mar 72	1

Above 2 were re-released with new catalogue numbers.

ONE MAN DOG	Warner Brothers	27	9 Dec 72	5
CLASSIC SONGS	CBS/WEA	53	4 Apr 87	5
HOURGLASS	Columbia	46	21 Jun 97	1

James TAYLOR QUARTET
UK

SINGLES:	HITS 3			WEEKS 6
LOVE THE LIFE	Big Life	34	3 Apr 93	3
SEE A BRIGHTER DAY	Big Life	49	3 Jul 93	2

Above 2: JTQ with Noel McKOY.

LOVE WILL KEEP US TOGETHER	Acid Jazz	63	25 Feb 95	1

Above hit: James TAYLOR QUARTET featuring Alison LIMERICK.

ALBUMS:	HITS 3			WEEKS 5
SUPERNATURAL FEELING	Big Life	36	1 May 93	3

Above hit: JTQ with Noel McKOY.

EXTENDED PLAY	Acid Jazz	70	29 Oct 94	1
IN THE HAND OF THE INEVITABLE	Acid Jazz	63	11 Mar 95	1

John TAYLOR
UK

SINGLES:		HITS 1		WEEKS 4	
I DO WHAT I DO (THEME FOR 9½ WEEKS)	Parlophone	42	15 Mar 86	4
Theme from the film.					

Johnnie TAYLOR
US

SINGLES:		HITS 1		WEEKS 7	
DISCO LADY	CBS	25	24 Apr 76	7

J.T. TAYLOR
US

SINGLES:		HITS 3		WEEKS 5	
LONG HOT SUMMER NIGHT	MCA	63	24 Aug 91	2
FEEL THE NEED	MCA	57	30 Nov 91	1
FOLLOW ME	MCA	59	18 Apr 92	2

Pauline TAYLOR
UK

SINGLES:		HITS 2		WEEKS 3	
LET THIS BE A PRAYER	Cheeky	26	8 Jun 96	2
Above hit: ROLLO GOES SPIRITUAL with Pauline TAYLOR.					
CONSTANTLY WAITING	Cheeky	51	9 Nov 96	1

R. Dean TAYLOR
Canada

SINGLES:		HITS 4		WEEKS 48	
GOTTA SEE JANE	Tamla Motown	17	22 Jun 68	12
INDIANA WANTS ME	Tamla Motown	2	3 Apr 71	15
THERE'S A GHOST IN MY HOUSE	Tamla Motown	3	11 May 74	12
WINDOW SHOPPING	Polydor	36	31 Aug 74	5
GOTTA SEE JANE [RI]	Tamla Motown	41	21 Sep 74	4

Roger TAYLOR
UK

SINGLES:		HITS 8		WEEKS 18	
FUTURE MANAGEMENT	EMI	49	18 Apr 81	4
MAN ON FIRE	EMI	66	16 Jun 84	2
RADIO	Epic	37	10 Oct 92	3
Above hit: SHAKY featuring Roger TAYLOR.					
NAZIS 1994	Parlophone	22	14 May 94	2
FOREIGN SAND	Parlophone	26	1 Oct 94	2
Above hit: Roger TAYLOR and YOSHIKI.					
HAPPINESS	Parlophone	32	26 Nov 94	2
PRESSURE ON	Parlophone	45	10 Oct 98	1
SURRENDER	Parlophone	38	10 Apr 99	2
Above hit: Roger TAYLOR featuring Treana MORRIS.					
ALBUMS:		HITS 4		WEEKS 11	
FUN IN SPACE	EMI	18	18 Apr 81	5
STRANGE FRONTIER	EMI	30	7 Jul 84	4
HAPPINESS?	Parlophone	22	17 Sep 94	1
ELECTRIC FIRE	Parlophone	53	10 Oct 98	1

TC
Italy

SINGLES:		HITS 3		WEEKS 5	
BERRY (THE REMIXES)	Union City	73	14 Mar 92	1
Above hit: TC 1991.					
FUNKY GUITAR	Union City	40	21 Nov 92	2
Above hit: TC 1992.					
HARMONY	Union	51	10 Jul 93	2
Samples the Temptations' Undisputed Truth.					
Above hit: TC 1993.					

Kiri TE KANAWA
New Zealand

(See also Various Artists: Studio Cast 'West Side Story', 'South Pacific', 'My Fair Lady'.)

SINGLES:		HITS 1		WEEKS 11	
WORLD IN UNION	Columbia	4	28 Sep 91	11
Theme from the ITV Rugby World Cup broadcasts. Based around Gustav Holst's Planet Suite.					
ALBUMS:		HITS 7		WEEKS 52	
CHANTS D'AUVERGNE VOLUME 1	Decca	57	2 Apr 83	1
Above hit: Kiri TE KANAWA with the ENGLISH CHAMBER ORCHESTRA.					
BLUE SKIES	London	41	26 Oct 85	18
Above hit: Kiri TE KANAWA with Nelson RIDDLE and his ORCHESTRA.					
BLUE SKIES [RE]	London	40	17 May 86	11
CHRISTMAS WITH KIRI	Decca	47	13 Dec 86	4
KIRI	K-Tel	70	17 Dec 88	3
THE ESSENTIAL KIRI	Decca	23	29 Feb 92	10
KIRI SIDETRACKS – THE JAZZ ALBUM	Philips	73	23 May 92	1

KIRI!	PolyGram TV	16	9 Apr 94	4

Live recordings from the Royal Albert Hall, 10 Mar 94 to celebrate her 50th birthday.

TEACH-IN
Holland

SINGLES:	HITS 1		WEEKS 7	
DING-A-DONG	Polydor	13	12 Apr 75	7

Eurovision Song Contest winner in 1975.

TEAM
UK

SINGLES:	HITS 1		WEEKS 5	
WICKI WACKY HOUSE PARTY	EMI	55	1 Jun 85	5

TEAM DEEP
Belgium

SINGLES:	HITS 1		WEEKS 1	
MORNINGLIGHT	Multiply	42	17 May 97	1

TEARDROP EXPLODES
UK

SINGLES:	HITS 7		WEEKS 50	
WHEN I DREAM	Mercury	47	27 Sep 80	6
REWARD	Mercury	6	31 Jan 81	13

Trumpet played by "Hurricane" Smith.

TREASON (IT'S JUST A STORY)	Mercury	18	2 May 81	8

Originally released in 1980.

PASSIONATE FRIEND	Zoo/Mercury	25	29 Aug 81	10
COLOURS FLY AWAY	Mercury	54	21 Nov 81	3
TINY CHILDREN	Mercury	44	19 Jun 82	7
YOU DISAPPEAR FROM VIEW	Mercury	41	19 Mar 83	3
ALBUMS:	HITS 4		WEEKS 45	
KILIMANJARO	Mercury	35	18 Oct 80	4
KILIMANJARO [RE]	Mercury	24	14 Mar 81	31
WILDER	Mercury	29	5 Dec 81	6
EVERYBODY WANTS TO SHAG . . . THE TEARDROP EXPLODES	Fontana	72	14 Apr 90	1
FLOORED GENIUS – THE BEST OF JULIAN COPE AND THE TEARDROP EXPLODES	Island	22	15 Aug 92	3

Features both Julian Cope's solo and group material.
Above hit: Julian COPE and the TEARDROP EXPLODES.

TEARS FOR FEARS
UK

SINGLES:	HITS 19		WEEKS 143	
MAD WORLD	Mercury	3	2 Oct 82	16
CHANGE	Mercury	4	5 Feb 83	9
PALE SHELTER	Mercury	5	30 Apr 83	8

Originally released in 1982.

THE WAY YOU ARE	Mercury	24	3 Dec 83	8
MOTHERS TALK	Mercury	14	18 Aug 84	8
SHOUT	Mercury	4	1 Dec 84	16
EVERYBODY WANTS TO RULE THE WORLD	Mercury	2	30 Mar 85	14
HEAD OVER HEELS	Mercury	12	22 Jun 85	9
SUFFER THE CHILDREN	Mercury	52	31 Aug 85	4

This was their first single release in 1981.

PALE SHELTER [RI]	Mercury	73	7 Sep 85	2
I BELIEVE (A SOULFUL RE-RECORDING)	Mercury	23	12 Oct 85	4
EVERYBODY WANTS TO RULE THE WORLD [RE]	Mercury	73	22 Feb 86	1
EVERYBODY WANTS TO RUN THE WORLD [RR]	Mercury	5	31 May 86	6

Re-written version to support Sport Aid's Race Against Time on 15 May 86.

EVERYBODY WANTS TO RUN THE WORLD [RR] [RE]	Mercury	73	19 Jul 86	1
SOWING THE SEEDS OF LOVE	Fontana	5	2 Sep 89	9
WOMAN IN CHAINS	Fontana	26	18 Nov 89	8

Vocals by Oleta Adams and Phil Collins on drums.

ADVICE FOR THE YOUNG AT HEART	Fontana	36	3 Mar 90	4
LAID SO LOW (TEARS ROLL DOWN)	Fontana	17	22 Feb 92	5
WOMAN IN CHAINS [RI]	Fontana	57	25 Apr 92	1

Above hit: TEARS FOR FEARS featuring Oleta ADAMS.

BREAK IT DOWN AGAIN	Mercury	20	29 May 93	5
COLD	Mercury	72	31 Jul 93	1
RAOUL AND THE KINGS OF SPAIN	Epic	31	7 Oct 95	3
GOD'S MISTAKE	Epic	61	29 Jun 96	1
ALBUMS:	HITS 6		WEEKS 211	
THE HURTING	Mercury	1	19 Mar 83	65
SONGS FROM THE BIG CHAIR	Mercury	2	9 Mar 85	81
THE SEEDS OF LOVE	Fontana	1	7 Oct 89	30
TEARS ROLL DOWN (GREATEST HITS 1982–1992)	Fontana	2	14 Mar 92	27
ELEMENTAL	Mercury	5	19 Jun 93	7
RAOUL AND THE KINGS OF SPAIN	Epic	41	28 Oct 95	1

A tribute to Roland Orzabal's Spanish father.

TECHNICIAN 2 featuring Georgia LEWIS | | | UK

SINGLES:	HITS 1			WEEKS 1
PLAYING WITH THE BOY	MCA	70	14 Nov 92	1

TECHNIQUE | | | UK

SINGLES:	HITS 2			WEEKS 2
SUN IS SHINING	Creation	64	10 Apr 99	1
YOU + ME	Creation	56	28 Aug 99	1

TECHNO TWINS | | | UK

SINGLES:	HITS 1			WEEKS 2
FALLING IN LOVE AGAIN	PRT	75	16 Jan 82	1
FALLING IN LOVE AGAIN [RE]	PRT	70	30 Jan 82	1

TECHNOCAT featuring Tom WILSON – See Tom WILSON

TECHNOHEAD | | | UK

(See also G.T.O.; Tricky Disco.)

SINGLES:	HITS 3			WEEKS 20
I WANNA BE A HIPPY	Mokum	6	3 Feb 96	14
HAPPY BIRTHDAY	Mokum	18	27 Apr 96	5
BANANA-NA-NA (DUMB DIDDY DUMB)	Mokum	64	12 Oct 96	1

Vocals by Dutch ragga artist Whoops.

TECHNOTRONIC | | | UK/Belgium

SINGLES:	HITS 8			WEEKS 66
PUMP UP THE JAM	Swanyard	2	2 Sep 89	15
Though single credits Felly, vocals are actually by Ya Kid K.				
Above hit: TECHNOTRONIC featuring FELLY.				
GET UP (BEFORE THE NIGHT IS OVER)	Swanyard	2	3 Feb 90	10
Above hit: TECHNOTRONIC featuring YA KID K.				
THIS BEAT IS TECHNOTRONIC	Swanyard	14	7 Apr 90	7
Above hit: TECHNOTRONIC featuring MC ERIC.				
ROCKIN' OVER THE BEAT	Swanyard	9	14 Jul 90	9
Above hit: TECHNOTRONIC featuring YA KID K.				
MEGAMIX [M]	Swanyard	6	6 Oct 90	8
Mix of their previous hits.				
TURN IT UP	Swanyard	42	15 Dec 90	4
Above hit: TECHNOTRONIC featuring MELISSA and EINSTEIN.				
MOVE THAT BODY	ARS	12	25 May 91	7
Above hit: TECHNOTRONIC featuring REGGIE.				
WORK	ARS	40	3 Aug 91	4
Above 2: TECHNOTRONIC featuring REGGIE.				
PUMP UP THE JAM '96 [RM]	Worx	36	14 Dec 96	2
Remixed by Tin Tin Out.				
ALBUMS:	HITS 3			WEEKS 62
PUMP UP THE JAM	Swanyard	2	6 Jan 90	44
TRIP ON THIS – REMIXES	Telstar	7	3 Nov 90	14
Above hit: TECHNOTRONIC and HI TEK 3.				
BODY TO BODY	ARS	27	15 Jun 91	4

TEDDY BEARS | | | US

SINGLES:	HITS 1			WEEKS 17
TO KNOW HIM, IS TO LOVE HIM	London	2	20 Dec 58	16
Inspired by the epitaph on Phil Spector's father's tombstone. Features Sandy Nelson on drums.				
TO KNOW HIM IS TO LOVE HIM [RI]	Lightning	66	14 Apr 79	1
[AA] listed with Endless Sleep by Jody Reynolds.				

TEENAGE FANCLUB | | | UK

SINGLES:	HITS 13			WEEKS 20
STAR SIGN	Creation	44	24 Aug 91	2
THE CONCEPT	Creation	51	2 Nov 91	1
WHAT YOU DO TO ME [EP]	Creation	31	8 Feb 92	2
Lead track: What You Do To Me.				
RADIO	Creation	31	26 Jun 93	2
NORMAN 3	Creation	50	2 Oct 93	1
FALLIN'	Epic	59	2 Apr 94	1
From the film 'Judgement Night'. Samples Tom Petty's Free Fallin.				
Above hit: TEENAGE FANCLUB and DE LA SOUL.				
MELLOW DOUBT	Creation	34	8 Apr 95	2
SPARKY'S DREAM	Creation	40	27 May 95	2
NEIL JUNG	Creation	62	2 Sep 95	1
HAVE LOST IT [EP]	Creation	53	16 Dec 95	1
Lead track: Don't Look Back.				

AIN'T THAT ENOUGH	*Creation*	17	*12 Jul 97*	3
I DON'T WANT CONTROL OF YOU	*Creation*	43	*30 Aug 97*	1
START AGAIN	*Creation*	54	*29 Nov 97*	1
ALBUMS:	**HITS 5**		**WEEKS 21**	
THE KING	*Creation*	53	*7 Sep 91*	2
BANDWAGONESQUE	*Creation*	22	*16 Nov 91*	7
THIRTEEN	*Creation*	14	*16 Oct 93*	3
Title refers to the number of tracks on the album.				
GRAND PRIX	*Creation*	7	*10 Jun 95*	4
SONGS FROM NORTHERN BRITAIN	*Creation*	3	*2 Aug 97*	5

TEENAGERS – See Frankie LYMON and the TEENAGERS

Towa TEI featuring Kylie MINOGUE   Japan/Australia

(See also Kylie Minogue.)

SINGLES:	**HITS 1**		**WEEKS 1**	
GBI: GERMAN BOLD ITALIC	*Arthrob*	63	*31 Oct 98*	1

TEKNO TOO   UK

SINGLES:	**HITS 1**		**WEEKS 2**	
JET-STAR	*D-Zone*	56	*13 Jul 91*	2

TELETUBBIES   UK

SINGLES:	**HITS 1**		**WEEKS 32**	
TELETUBBIES SAY "EH-OH!"	*BBC Worldwide Music*	1	*13 Dec 97*	29
TELETUBBIES SAY "EH-OH!" [RE-1ST]	*BBC Worldwide Music*	66	*18 Jul 98*	2
TELETUBBIES SAY "EH-OH!" [RE-2ND]	*BBC Worldwide Music*	72	*15 Aug 98*	1
ALBUMS:	**HITS 1**		**WEEKS 4**	
THE ALBUM	*BBC Worldwide Music*	31	*4 Apr 98*	4

TELEVISION   US

SINGLES:	**HITS 3**		**WEEKS 10**	
MARQUEE MOON	*Elektra*	30	*16 Apr 77*	4
PROVE IT	*Elektra*	25	*30 Jul 77*	4
FOXHOLE	*Elektra*	36	*22 Apr 78*	2
ALBUMS:	**HITS 2**		**WEEKS 17**	
MARQUEE MOON	*Elektra*	28	*26 Mar 77*	13
ADVENTURE	*Elektra*	7	*29 Apr 78*	4

TELEX   Belgium

SINGLES:	**HITS 1**		**WEEKS 7**	
ROCK AROUND THE CLOCK	*Sire*	34	*21 Jul 79*	7

Sylvia TELLA – See BLOW MONKEYS

TEMPERANCE SEVEN vocal refrain by Mr. Paul MACDOWELL   UK

SINGLES:	**HITS 4**		**WEEKS 45**	
YOU'RE DRIVING ME CRAZY	*Parlophone*	1	*1 Apr 61*	16
George Martin's first No.1 as a producer. Originally recorded by Guy Lombardo in 1930.				
PASADENA	*Parlophone*	4	*17 Jun 61*	17
Originally recorded by Murray and Smalle in 1924.				
HARD HEARTED HANNAH / CHILI BOM BOM	*Parlophone*	28	*30 Sep 61*	4
Chili Bom Bom listed from 12 Oct 61.				
THE CHARLESTON	*Parlophone*	22	*9 Dec 61*	8
EPS:	**HITS 2**		**WEEKS 57**	
THE MUSICK	*Argo*	2	*13 May 61*	21
TEMPERANCE SEVEN	*Parlophone*	3	*23 Sep 61*	36
ALBUMS:	**HITS 2**		**WEEKS 10**	
TEMPERANCE SEVEN PLUS ONE	Argo	19	*13 May 61*	1
TEMPERANCE SEVEN 1961	*Parlophone*	8	*25 Nov 61*	9

TEMPLE CHURCH CHOIR   UK

ALBUMS:	**HITS 1**		**WEEKS 3**	
CHRISTMAS CAROLS	*His Master's Voice*	8	*16 Dec 61*	3

TEMPLE OF THE DOG   US

SINGLES:	**HITS 1**		**WEEKS 2**	
HUNGER STRIKE	*A&M*	51	*24 Oct 92*	2

Nino TEMPO and April STEVENS
US

SINGLES:	HITS 2			WEEKS 19
DEEP PURPLE	London	17	9 Nov 63	11
Originally recorded by Larry Clinton Orchestra in 1939.				
WHISPERING	London	20	18 Jan 64	8
Originally recorded by Paul Whiteman Orchestra in 1920.				

TEMPTATIONS
US

(See also Diana Ross and the Supremes and the Temptations; Bruce Willis.)

SINGLES:	HITS 24			WEEKS 184
MY GIRL	Stateside	43	20 Mar 65	1
IT'S GROWING	Tamla Motown	49	3 Apr 65	1
IT'S GROWING [RE]	Tamla Motown	45	17 Apr 65	1
AIN'T TOO PROUD TO BEG	Tamla Motown	21	16 Jul 66	11
BEAUTY IS ONLY SKIN DEEP	Tamla Motown	18	8 Oct 66	10
(I KNOW) I'M LOSING YOU	Tamla Motown	19	17 Dec 66	9
YOU'RE MY EVERYTHING	Tamla Motown	26	9 Sep 67	15
I WISH IT WOULD RAIN	Tamla Motown	45	9 Mar 68	1
I COULD NEVER LOVE ANOTHER (AFTER LOVING YOU)	Tamla Motown	47	15 Jun 68	1
GET READY	Tamla Motown	10	8 Mar 69	9
Original release reached No. 29 in the US in 1966.				
CLOUD NINE	Tamla Motown	15	23 Aug 69	10
I CAN'T GET NEXT TO YOU	Tamla Motown	13	17 Jan 70	9
PSYCHEDELIC SHACK	Tamla Motown	33	13 Jun 70	7
BALL OF CONFUSION (THAT'S WHAT THE WORLD IS TODAY)	Tamla Motown	7	19 Sep 70	12
BALL OF CONFUSION (THAT'S WHAT THE WORLD IS TODAY) [RE]	Tamla Motown	48	19 Dec 70	3
JUST MY IMAGINATION (RUNNING AWAY WITH ME)	Tamla Motown	8	22 May 71	16
SUPERSTAR (REMEMBER HOW YOU GOT WHERE YOU ARE)	Tamla Motown	32	5 Feb 72	5
TAKE A LOOK AROUND	Tamla Motown	13	15 Apr 72	10
PAPA WAS A ROLLIN' STONE	Tamla Motown	14	13 Jan 73	8
LAW OF THE LAND	Tamla Motown	41	29 Sep 73	4
Above 2 originally recorded by Undisputed Truth.				
STANDING ON THE TOP (PART 1)	Motown	53	12 Jun 82	3
Above hit: TEMPTATIONS featuring Rick JAMES.				
TREAT HER LIKE A LADY	Motown	12	17 Nov 84	10
PAPA WAS A ROLLIN' STONE [RM]	Motown	31	15 Aug 87	6
Remixed by Freddy Bastone.				
LOOK WHAT YOU STARTED	Motown	63	6 Feb 88	2
ALL I WANT FROM YOU	Motown	71	21 Oct 89	1
THE MOTOWN SONG	Warner Brothers	10	15 Jun 91	8
Above hit: Rod STEWART (with the TEMPTATIONS).				
MY GIRL [RI]	Epic	2	15 Feb 92	10
From the film of the same name.				
THE JONES'	Motown	69	22 Feb 92	1
EPS:	HITS 2			WEEKS 3
THE TEMPTATIONS	Tamla Motown	18	3 Apr 65	1
IT'S THE TEMPTATIONS	Tamla Motown	8	18 Feb 67	2
ALBUMS:	HITS 13			WEEKS 108
GETTING READY	Tamla Motown	40	24 Dec 66	2
TEMPTATIONS GREATEST HITS	Tamla Motown	26	11 Feb 67	17
THE TEMPTATIONS LIVE!	Tamla Motown	20	22 Jul 67	4
TEMPTATIONS GREATEST HITS [RE]	Tamla Motown	17	20 Jan 68	23
WITH A LOT O'SOUL	Tamla Motown	19	18 Nov 67	18
CLOUD NINE	Tamla Motown	32	20 Sep 69	1
PUZZLE PEOPLE	Tamla Motown	20	14 Feb 70	4
PSYCHEDELIC SHACK	Tamla Motown	56	11 Jul 70	1
GREATEST HITS VOLUME 2	Tamla Motown	35	26 Dec 70	12
SOLID ROCK	Tamla Motown	34	29 Apr 72	2
ALL DIRECTIONS	Tamla Motown	19	20 Jan 73	7
MASTERPIECE	Tamla Motown	28	7 Jul 73	3
TRULY FOR YOU	Motown	75	8 Dec 84	5
MOTOWN'S GREATEST HITS	Motown	8	11 Apr 92	9

10 C.C.
UK

SINGLES:	HITS 14			WEEKS 133
DONNA	UK	2	23 Sep 72	13
RUBBER BULLETS	UK	1	19 May 73	15
THE DEAN AND I	UK	10	25 Aug 73	8
THE WALL STREET SHUFFLE	UK	10	15 Jun 74	10
SILLY LOVE	UK	24	14 Sep 74	7
LIFE IS A MINESTRONE	Mercury	7	5 Apr 75	8
I'M NOT IN LOVE	Mercury	1	31 May 75	11
ART FOR ARTS SAKE	Mercury	5	29 Nov 75	10
I'M MANDY FLY ME	Mercury	6	20 Mar 76	9
THE THINGS WE DO FOR LOVE	Mercury	6	11 Dec 76	11
GOOD MORNING JUDGE	Mercury	5	16 Apr 77	12

DREADLOCK HOLIDAY	Mercury	1	12 Aug 78	13

Song written about the experiences of Justin Hayward's Caribbean holiday.

RUN AWAY	Mercury	50	7 Aug 82	4
I'M NOT IN LOVE (ACOUSTIC SESSION '95) [RR]	Avex UK	29	18 Mar 95	2
ALBUMS:	**HITS 13**		**WEEKS 219**	
10 C.C.	UK	36	1 Sep 73	5
SHEET MUSIC	UK	9	15 Jun 74	24
THE ORIGINAL SOUNDTRACK	Mercury	4	22 Mar 75	40
GREATEST HITS OF 10 C.C.	Decca	9	7 Jun 75	18
HOW DARE YOU?	Mercury	5	31 Jan 76	31
DECEPTIVE BENDS	Mercury	3	14 May 77	21
LIVE AND LET LIVE	Mercury	14	10 Dec 77	15

Live recordings from their UK tour, May 77.

BLOODY TOURISTS	Mercury	3	23 Sep 78	15
GREATEST HITS 1972-1978	Mercury	5	6 Oct 79	21
LOOK HEAR?	Mercury	35	5 Apr 80	5
WINDOW IN THE JUNGLE	Mercury	70	15 Oct 83	2
CHANGING FACES - THE VERY BEST OF 10CC AND GODLEY AND CREME	ProTV	4	29 Aug 87	18

Features both Godley and Creme's material as a duo and with 10CC.
Above hit: 10 CC and GODLEY and CRÈME.

THE VERY BEST OF 10CC	Mercury TV	37	5 Apr 97	4

Also includes 3 hits from Godley and Creme.

TEN CITY   US

SINGLES:	**HITS 6**		**WEEKS 21**	
THAT'S THE WAY LOVE IS	Atlantic	8	21 Jan 89	10
DEVOTION	Atlantic	29	8 Apr 89	4
WHERE DO WE GO?	Atlantic	60	22 Jul 89	1
WHATEVER MAKES YOU HAPPY	Atlantic	60	27 Oct 90	2
ONLY TIME WILL TELL / MY PEACE OF HEAVEN	East West America	63	15 Aug 92	2
FANTASY	Columbia	45	11 Sep 93	2
ALBUMS:	**HITS 1**		**WEEKS 12**	
FOUNDATION	Atlantic	22	18 Feb 89	12

TEN SHARP   Holland

SINGLES:	**HITS 2**		**WEEKS 15**	
YOU	Columbia	10	21 Mar 92	13
AIN'T MY BEATING HEART	Columbia	63	20 Jun 92	2
ALBUMS:	**HITS 1**		**WEEKS 2**	
UNDER THE WATER-LINE	Columbia	46	9 May 92	2

10,000 MANIACS   US

SINGLES:	**HITS 3**		**WEEKS 7**	
THESE ARE DAYS	Elektra	58	12 Sep 92	3
CANDY EVERYBODY WANTS	Elektra	47	10 Apr 93	3
BECAUSE THE NIGHT	Elektra	65	23 Oct 93	1
ALBUMS:	**HITS 3**		**WEEKS 12**	
BLIND MAN'S ZOO	Elektra	18	27 May 89	8
OUR TIME IN EDEN	Elektra	33	10 Oct 92	2
UNPLUGGED	Elektra	40	6 Nov 93	2

Live recordings for the MTV channel.

TEN YEARS AFTER   UK

SINGLES:	**HITS 1**		**WEEKS 18**	
LOVE LIKE A MAN	Deram	10	6 Jun 70	18
ALBUMS:	**HITS 8**		**WEEKS 73**	
UNDEAD	Deram	26	21 Sep 68	7
STONEDHENGE	Deram	6	22 Feb 69	5
SSSSH	Deram	4	4 Oct 69	18
CRICKLEWOOD GREEN	Deram	4	2 May 70	27
WATT	Deram	5	9 Jan 71	12
A SPACE IN TIME	Chrysalis	36	13 Nov 71	1
ROCK & ROLL MUSIC TO THE WORLD	Chrysalis	27	7 Oct 72	1
RECORDED LIVE	Chrysalis	36	28 Jul 73	2

Danny TENAGLIA   US

SINGLES:	**HITS 2**		**WEEKS 5**	
MUSIC IS THE ANSWER (DANCIN' AND PRANCIN')	Twisted UK	36	5 Sep 98	3

Above hit: Danny TENAGLIA + CELEDA.

TURN ME ON	Twisted UK	53	10 Apr 99	1

Above hit: Danny TENAGLIA featuring Liz TORRES.

MUSIC IS THE ANSWER '99 (DANCIN' AND PRANCIN') [RM]	Twisted UK	50	23 Oct 99	1

Remixed by Future Shock.
Above hit: Danny TENAGLIA + CELEDA.

TENNESSEE THREE – See Johnny CASH

Klaus TENNSTEDT – See Nigel KENNEDY

TENOR FLY

UK

(See also Rebel MC.)

SINGLES:		HITS 3			WEEKS 11
THE WICKEDEST SOUND	Desire	43	6 Apr 91		6
Above hit: REBEL MC (featuring TENOR FLY).					
BRIGHT SIDE OF LIFE	Mango	51	7 Jan 95		2
Samples Nina Simone's My Baby Just Cares For Me.					
B-BOY STANCE	Freskanova	23	7 Feb 98		3
Above hit: FREESTYLERS featuring TENOR FLY.					

TENPOLE TUDOR

UK

SINGLES:		HITS 5			WEEKS 40
WHO KILLED BAMBI	Virgin	6	7 Apr 79		8
[AA] listed with Silly Thing by the Sex Pistols.					
Above hit: TEN POLE TUDOR.					
ROCK AROUND THE CLOCK	Virgin	21	13 Oct 79		6
[AA] listed with The Great Rock 'N' Roll Swindle by the Sex Pistols. Above 2 from the film 'The Great Rock 'N' Roll Swindle'.					
SWORDS OF A THOUSAND MEN	Stiff	6	25 Apr 81		12
WUNDERBAR	Stiff	16	1 Aug 81		9
THROWING MY BABY OUT WITH THE BATH WATER	Stiff	49	14 Nov 81		5
ALBUMS:		HITS 1			WEEKS 8
EDDIE, OLD BOB, DICK & GARRY	Stiff	44	9 May 81		8

Bryn TERFEL

UK

SINGLES:		HITS 1			WEEKS 3
WORLD IN UNION	Decca	35	23 Oct 99		3
Official ITV theme to the 1999 Rugby World Cup. Features The Morriston Rugby Club Choir and the City of Prague Philharmonic Orchestra.					
Above hit: Shirley BASSEY, Bryn TERFEL and the BLACK MOUNTAIN MALE CHORUS.					
ALBUMS:		HITS 1			WEEKS 1
SOMETHING WONDERFUL	Deutsche Grammophon	72	16 Nov 96		1
Interpretations of Rodgers and Hammerstein songs.					

Max TERR CHOIR – See Bing CROSBY

TERRA FERMA

Italy

SINGLES:		HITS 1			WEEKS 1
FLOATING	Platipus	64	18 May 96		1

TERRAPLANE

UK

ALBUMS:		HITS 1			WEEKS 1
BLACK AND WHITE	Epic	74	25 Jan 86		1

Tammi TERRELL – See Marvin GAYE and Tammi TERRELL

TERRI and MONICA – See Shabba RANKS

TERRORIZE

UK

SINGLES:		HITS 2			WEEKS 6
IT'S JUST A FEELING	Hamster	52	2 May 92		3
FEEL THE RHYTHM	Hamster	69	22 Aug 92		1
IT'S JUST A FEELING [RI]	Hamster	47	14 Nov 92		2

TERRORVISION

UK

SINGLES:		HITS 15			WEEKS 53
AMERICAN T.V.	Total Vegas	63	19 Jun 93		1
NEW POLICY ONE	Total Vegas	42	30 Oct 93		2
MY HOUSE	Total Vegas	29	8 Jan 94		4
OBLIVION	Total Vegas	21	9 Apr 94		5
MIDDLEMAN	Total Vegas	25	25 Jun 94		4
PRETEND BEST FRIEND	Total Vegas	25	3 Sep 94		3
ALICE WHAT'S THE MATTER?	Total Vegas	24	29 Oct 94		4
SOME PEOPLE SAY	Total Vegas	22	18 Mar 95		3
PERSEVERANCE	Total Vegas	5	2 Mar 96		4
CELEBRITY HIT LIST	Total Vegas	20	4 May 96		3
BAD ACTRESS	Total Vegas	10	20 Jul 96		3
EASY	Total Vegas	12	11 Jan 97		4
JOSEPHINE	Total Vegas	23	3 Oct 98		2
TEQUILA	Total Vegas	2	30 Jan 99		10
III WISHES	Total Vegas	42	15 May 99		1

ALBUMS:		HITS 4			WEEKS 40
FORMALDEHYDE	Total Vegas	75	15 May 93	1
HOW TO MAKE FRIENDS AND INFLUENCE PEOPLE	Total Vegas	18	30 Apr 94	25
REGULAR URBAN SURVIVORS	Total Vegas	8	23 Mar 96	12
SHAVING PEACHES	Total Vegas	34	17 Oct 98	2

Helen TERRY   UK

SINGLES:		HITS 1			WEEKS 6
LOVE LIES LOST	Virgin	34	12 May 84	6

Todd TERRY   US

SINGLES:		HITS 6			WEEKS 33
WEEKEND	Sleeping Bag	56	12 Nov 88	3
WEEKEND [RM]	Ore	28	14 Oct 95	3

Remixed by Mike Gray and Jon Pearn for DMC (UK).
Above 2: Todd TERRY PROJECT.

KEEP ON JUMPIN'	Manifesto	8	13 Jul 96	6
SOMETHING GOIN' ON	Manifesto	5	12 Jul 97	10

Originally recorded by Musique as the B-side to the US release of In The Bush.
Above 2: Todd TERRY featuring Martha WASH and Jocelyn BROWN.

IT'S OVER LOVE	Manifesto	16	6 Dec 97	8

Above hit: Todd TERRY presents SHANNON.

READY FOR A NEW DAY	Manifesto	20	11 Apr 98	2

Above hit: Todd TERRY features Martha WASH.

LET IT RIDE	Arrested	58	3 Jul 99	1

Above 2 with vocals by Antoinette Robertson.

ALBUMS:		HITS 1			WEEKS 1
THE MINISTRY OF SOUNDS PRESENTS A DAY IN THE LIFE OF TODD TERRY	Sound Of Ministry	73	5 Aug 95	1

Tony TERRY   US

SINGLES:		HITS 1			WEEKS 6
LOVEY DOVEY	Epic	44	27 Feb 88	6

TERRY, BLAIR and ANOUCHKA – See Terry HALL

TESLA   US

SINGLES:		HITS 1			WEEKS 1
SIGNS	Geffen	70	27 Apr 91	1
ALBUMS:		HITS 4			WEEKS 6
THE GREAT RADIO CONTROVERSY	Geffen	34	11 Feb 89	2
FIVE MAN ACOUSTICAL JAM	Geffen	59	2 Mar 91	1
PSYCHOTIC SUPPER	Geffen	44	21 Sep 91	2
BUST A NUT	Geffen	51	3 Sep 94	1

TESTAMENT   US

ALBUMS:		HITS 4			WEEKS 6
THE NEW ORDER	Megaforce	81	28 May 88	1
PRACTICE WHAT YOU PREACH	Atlantic	40	19 Aug 89	2
SOULS OF BLACK	Megaforce	35	6 Oct 90	2
THE RITUAL	Atlantic	48	30 May 92	1

Joe TEX   US

SINGLES:		HITS 1			WEEKS 11
AIN'T GONNA BUMP NO MORE (WITH NO BIG FAT WOMAN)	Epic	2	23 Apr 77	11

TEXAS   UK

SINGLES:		HITS 19			WEEKS 102
I DON'T WANT A LOVER	Mercury	8	4 Feb 89	11
THRILL HAS GONE	Mercury	60	6 May 89	3
EVERYDAY NOW	Mercury	44	5 Aug 89	5
PRAYER FOR YOU	Mercury	73	2 Dec 89	1
WHY BELIEVE IN YOU	Mercury	66	7 Sep 91	1
IN MY HEART	Mercury	74	26 Oct 91	1
ALONE WITH YOU	Mercury	32	8 Feb 92	4
TIRED OF BEING ALONE	Mercury	19	25 Apr 92	6
SO CALLED FRIEND	Vertigo	30	11 Sep 93	3
YOU OWE IT ALL TO ME	Vertigo	39	30 Oct 93	3
SO IN LOVE WITH YOU	Vertigo	28	12 Feb 94	2
SAY WHAT YOU WANT	Mercury	3	18 Jan 97	10
HALO	Mercury	10	19 Apr 97	7
BLACK EYED BOY	Mercury	5	9 Aug 97	6
PUT YOUR ARMS AROUND ME	Mercury	10	15 Nov 97	5
PUT YOUR ARMS AROUND ME [RE-1ST]	Mercury	75	3 Jan 98	1

PUT YOUR ARMS AROUND ME [RE-2ND]	Mercury	64	17 Jan 98	2
SAY WHAT YOU WANT (ALL DAY EVERY DAY) [RR] / INSANE	Mercury	4	21 Mar 98	7

They first sang this together at the 1998 Brit Awards on 9 Feb 98. Insane is only credited to
  Texas.
Above hit: TEXAS featuring the WU TANG CLAN.

IN OUR LIFETIME	Mercury	4	1 May 99	9
SUMMER SON	Mercury	5	28 Aug 99	9
WHEN WE ARE TOGETHER	Mercury	12	27 Nov 99	6
ALBUMS:	**HITS 5**		**WEEKS 167**	
SOUTHSIDE	Mercury	3	25 Mar 89	29

Includes re-entry in 1997.

MOTHERS HEAVEN	Mercury	32	5 Oct 91	4
RICKS ROAD	Vertigo	18	13 Nov 93	2
WHITE ON BLONDE	Mercury	1	15 Feb 97	98
THE HUSH	Mercury	1	22 May 99	33
SOUTHSIDE [RE]	Mercury	45	22 May 99	1

THA DOGG POUND   US

ALBUMS:	**HITS 1**		**WEEKS 2**	
DOGG FOOD	Death Row	66	11 Nov 95	2

THAT KID CHRIS   US

SINGLES:	**HITS 1**		**WEEKS 1**	
FEEL THA VIBE	Manifesto	52	22 Feb 97	1

THAT PETROL EMOTION   UK

SINGLES:	**HITS 7**		**WEEKS 24**	
BIG DECISION	Polydor	43	11 Apr 87	7
DANCE	Polydor	64	11 Jul 87	2
GENIUS MOVE	Virgin	65	17 Oct 87	2
ABANDON	Virgin	73	31 Mar 90	1
HEY VENUS	Virgin	49	1 Sep 90	4
TINGLE	Virgin	49	9 Feb 91	4
SENSITIZE	Virgin	55	27 Apr 91	4

Original release reached No. 99 in 1990.

ALBUMS:	**HITS 4**		**WEEKS 8**	
MANIC POP THRILL	Demon	84	10 May 86	2
BABBLE	Polydor	30	23 May 87	3
END OF MILLENNIUM PSYCHOSIS BLUES	Virgin	53	24 Sep 88	2
CHEMICRAZY	Virgin	62	21 Apr 90	1

THE   UK

SINGLES:	**HITS 15**		**WEEKS 52**	
UNCERTAIN SMILE	Epic	68	4 Dec 82	3
THIS IS THE DAY	Epic	71	17 Sep 83	3
HEARTLAND	Some Bizzare	29	9 Aug 86	10
INFECTED	Some Bizzare	48	25 Oct 86	5
SLOW TRAIN TO DAWN	Some Bizzare	64	24 Jan 87	2
SWEET BIRD OF TRUTH	Epic	55	23 May 87	2
THE BEAT(EN) GENERATION	Epic	18	1 Apr 89	5
GRAVITATE TO ME	Epic	63	22 Jul 89	3
ARMAGEDDON DAYS ARE HERE (AGAIN)	Epic	70	7 Oct 89	2
SHADES OF BLUE [EP]	Epic	54	2 Mar 91	1

Lead track: Jealous Of Youth.

DOGS OF LUST	Epic	25	16 Jan 93	4
SLOW MOTION REPLAY	Epic	35	17 Apr 93	3
LOVE IS STRONGER THAN DEATH	Epic	39	19 Jun 93	3
DIS-INFECTED [EP]	Epic	17	15 Jan 94	4

Lead track: That Was The Day, which is a re-recording of This Is The Day.

I SAW THE LIGHT	Epic	31	4 Feb 95	2

Originally recorded by Hank Williams in 1953.

ALBUMS:	**HITS 6**		**WEEKS 51**	
SOUL MINING	Epic	27	29 Oct 83	5
INFECTED	Some Bizzare	14	29 Nov 86	30
MIND BOMB	Epic	4	27 May 89	9
DUSK	Epic	2	6 Feb 93	4
BURNING BLUE SOUL	4AD	65	19 Jun 93	1

Originally released in 1981 credited to Matt Johnson.

HANKY PANKY	Epic	28	25 Feb 95	2

Tribute to Hank Willams.

THEATRE OF HATE   UK

SINGLES:	**HITS 2**		**WEEKS 9**	
DO YOU BELIEVE IN THE WESTWORLD	Burning Rome	40	23 Jan 82	7
THE HOP	Burning Rome	70	29 May 82	2

ALBUMS:	HITS 2			WEEKS 9	
WESTWORLD	Burning Rome	17	13 Mar 82	6
REVOLUTION	Burning Rome	67	18 Aug 84	3

THEAUDIENCE · UK

SINGLES:	HITS 3			WEEKS 5	
IF YOU CAN'T DO IT WHEN YOU'RE YOUNG; WHEN CAN YOU DO IT?	ElleFre	48	7 Mar 98	1
A PESSIMIST IS NEVER DISAPPOINTED	ElleFre	27	23 May 98	2
I KNOW ENOUGH (I DON'T GET ENOUGH)	ElleFre	25	8 Aug 98	2

ALBUMS:	HITS 1			WEEKS 2	
THEAUDIENCE	ElleFre	22	29 Aug 98	2

THEM · UK

SINGLES:	HITS 2			WEEKS 23	
BABY PLEASE DON'T GO	Decca	10	9 Jan 65	9
Originally recorded by Big Joe Williams.				
HERE COMES THE NIGHT	Decca	2	27 Mar 65	12
Originally recorded by Lulu.				
BABY PLEASE DON'T GO [RI]	London	65	9 Feb 91	2
From the film 'Wild At Heart'. Featured in the Peugeot 205 TV commercial.				

EPS:	HITS 1			WEEKS 18	
THEM	Decca	5	20 Mar 65	18

THEN JERICO · UK

SINGLES:	HITS 6			WEEKS 36	
LET HER FALL	London	65	31 Jan 87	3
THE MOTIVE	London	18	25 Jul 87	12
MUSCLE DEEP	London	48	24 Oct 87	4
Original release reached No. 85 in 1986.				
BIG AREA	London	13	28 Jan 89	7
WHAT DOES IT TAKE?	London	33	8 Apr 89	4
SUGAR BOX	London	22	12 Aug 89	6

ALBUMS:	HITS 2			WEEKS 24	
FIRST (THE SOUND OF MUSIC)	London	35	3 Oct 87	7
THE BIG AREA	London	4	4 Mar 89	17

THERAPY? · UK

SINGLES:	HITS 13			WEEKS 33	
TEETHGRINDER	A&M	30	31 Oct 92	2
SHORTSHARPSHOCK [EP]	A&M	9	20 Mar 93	4
Lead track: Screamager.				
FACE THE STRANGE [EP]	A&M	18	12 Jun 93	3
Lead track: Turn.				
OPAL MANTRA	A&M	13	28 Aug 93	3
NOWHERE	A&M	18	29 Jan 94	4
TRIGGER INSIDE	A&M	22	12 Mar 94	3
DIE LAUGHING	A&M	29	11 Jun 94	2
INNOCENT X	Volume	53	27 May 95	1
[AA] listed with Belfast/Wasted by Orbital.				
STORIES	A&M	14	3 Jun 95	3
LOOSE	A&M	25	29 Jul 95	3
DIANE	A&M	26	18 Nov 95	2
Originally recorded by Husker Du.				
CHURCH OF MOISE	A&M	29	14 Mar 98	2
LONELY, CRYIN', ONLY	A&M	32	30 May 98	1

ALBUMS:	HITS 6			WEEKS 24	
PLEASURE DEATH	Wiiija	52	8 Feb 92	1
NURSE	A&M	38	14 Nov 92	3
TROUBLEGUM	A&M	5	19 Feb 94	11
INFERNAL LOVE	A&M	9	24 Jun 95	7
SEMI-DETACHED	A&M	21	11 Apr 98	1
SUICIDE PACT – YOU FIRST	Ark 21	61	30 Oct 99	1

THESE ANIMAL MEN · UK

SINGLES:	HITS 3			WEEKS 3	
THIS IS THE SOUND OF YOUTH	Hi-Rise Recordings	72	24 Sep 94	1
Originally appeared on the Fierce Panda label release Shagging In The Streets EP.				
LIFE SUPPORT MACHINE	Hut	62	8 Feb 97	1
LIGHT EMITTING ELECTRICAL WAVE	Hut	72	12 Apr 97	1

ALBUMS:	HITS 3			WEEKS 4	
TOO SUSSED?	Hi-Rise Recordings	39	2 Jul 94	2
(COME ON, JOIN) THE HIGH SOCIETY	Hi-Rise Recordings	62	8 Oct 94	1
TAXI FOR THESE ANIMAL MEN	Hi-Rise Recordings	64	25 Mar 95	1
6-track mini album.				

THEY MIGHT BE GIANTS

US

SINGLES:		HITS 2		WEEKS 13	
BIRDHOUSE IN YOUR SOUL	Elektra	6	3 Mar 90	11
ISTANBUL (NOT CONSTANTINOPLE)	Elektra	61	2 Jun 90	2
ALBUMS:		HITS 1		WEEKS 12	
FLOOD	Elektra	14	7 Apr 90	12

THIN LIZZY

UK/Ireland

SINGLES:		HITS 18		WEEKS 128	
WHISKY IN THE JAR	Decca	6	20 Jan 73	12
THE BOYS ARE BACK IN TOWN	Vertigo	8	29 May 76	10
JAILBREAK	Vertigo	31	14 Aug 76	4
DON'T BELIEVE A WORD	Vertigo	12	15 Jan 77	7
DANCING IN THE MOONLIGHT (IT'S CAUGHT ME IN IT'S SPOTLIGHT)	Vertigo	14	13 Aug 77	8
ROSALIE/ (COWGIRLS' SONG) [M]	Vertigo	20	13 May 78	13
Live recording from the Hammersmith Odeon, London, 14 Nov 76. Originally recorded by Bob Seger.				
WAITING FOR AN ALIBI	Vertigo	9	3 Mar 79	8
DO ANYTHING YOU WANT TO	Vertigo	14	16 Jun 79	9
SARAH	Vertigo	24	20 Oct 79	13
CHINATOWN	Vertigo	21	24 May 80	9
KILLER ON THE LOOSE	Vertigo	10	27 Sep 80	7
KILLERS LIVE [EP]	Vertigo	19	2 May 81	7
Lead track: Are You Ready.				
TROUBLE BOYS	Vertigo	53	8 Aug 81	4
HOLLYWOOD (DOWN ON YOUR LUCK)	Vertigo	53	6 Mar 82	3
COLD SWEAT	Vertigo	27	12 Feb 83	5
THUNDER AND LIGHTNING	Vertigo	39	7 May 83	2
THE SUN GOES DOWN	Vertigo	52	6 Aug 83	3
DEDICATION	Vertigo	35	26 Jan 91	3
THE BOYS ARE BACK IN TOWN [RI]	Vertigo	63	23 Mar 91	1
ALBUMS:		HITS 14		WEEKS 250	
FIGHTING	Vertigo	60	27 Sep 75	1
JAILBREAK	Vertigo	10	10 Apr 76	50
JOHNNY THE FOX	Vertigo	11	6 Nov 76	24
BAD REPUTATION	Vertigo	4	1 Oct 77	9
LIVE AND DANGEROUS	Vertigo	2	17 Jun 78	62
Live recordings from the Hammersmith Odeon, London, 14 Nov 76 and the Seneca College Fieldhouse, Toronto, 28 Oct 77.				
BLACK ROSE (A ROCK LEGEND)	Vertigo	2	5 May 79	21
CHINATOWN	Vertigo	7	18 Oct 80	7
THE ADVENTURES OF THIN LIZZY	Vertigo	6	11 Apr 81	13
RENEGADE	Vertigo	38	5 Dec 81	8
THUNDER AND LIGHTNING	Vertigo	4	12 Mar 83	11
LIFE - LIVE	Vertigo	29	26 Nov 83	6
SOLDIER OF FORTUNE - THE BEST OF PHIL LYNOTT AND THIN LIZZY	Telstar	55	14 Nov 87	10
Features Lynott's solo and group material.				
Above hit: Phil LYNOTT and THIN LIZZY.				
DEDICATION - THE VERY BEST OF THIN LIZZY	Vertigo	8	16 Feb 91	17
WILD ONE - THE VERY BEST OF THIN LIZZY	Vertigo	18	13 Jan 96	11

3RD BASS

US

SINGLES:		HITS 3		WEEKS 5	
THE GAS FACE	Def Jam	71	10 Feb 90	1
BROOKLYN-QUEENS	Def Jam	61	7 Apr 90	2
POP GOES THE WEASEL	Def Jam	64	22 Jun 91	2
Samples Sledgehammer by Peter Gabriel and You Haven't Done Nothin' by Stevie Wonder.				
ALBUMS:		HITS 1		WEEKS 1	
DERELICTS OF DIALECT	Def Jam	46	20 Jul 91	1

THIRD DIMENSION featuring Julie McDERMOTT

UK

SINGLES:		HITS 1		WEEKS 2	
DON'T GO	Sound Proof	34	12 Oct 96	2

THIRD EAR BAND

UK

ALBUMS:		HITS 1		WEEKS 2	
AIR, EARTH, FIRE, WATER	Harvest	49	27 Jun 70	2

THIRD EYE BLIND

US

SINGLES:		HITS 2		WEEKS 6	
SEMI-CHARMED LIFE	Elektra	33	27 Sep 97	5
HOW'S IT GOING TO BE	Elektra	51	21 Mar 98	1

3RD STOREE
US

SINGLES:		HITS 1		WEEKS 1
IF EVER	Elektra	53	5 Jun 99	1

Samples Unlimited Touch's I Hear Music In The Street.

THIRD WORLD
Jamaica

SINGLES:		HITS 5		WEEKS 53
NOW THAT WE'VE FOUND LOVE	Island	10	23 Sep 78	9

Originally recorded by the O'Jays.

COOL MEDITATION	Island	17	6 Jan 79	10
TALK TO ME	Island	56	16 Jun 79	5
DANCING ON THE FLOOR (HOOKED ON LOVE)	CBS	10	6 Jun 81	15
TRY JAH LOVE	CBS	47	17 Apr 82	6

Written by Stevie Wonder.

NOW THAT WE'VE FOUND LOVE [RI]	Island	22	9 Mar 85	8
ALBUMS:		**HITS 3**		**WEEKS 18**
JOURNEY TO ADDIS	Island	30	21 Oct 78	6
ROCKS THE WORLD	CBS	37	11 Jul 81	9
YOU'VE GOT THE POWER	CBS	87	15 May 82	3

THIRST
UK

SINGLES:		HITS 1		WEEKS 2
THE ENEMY WITHIN	Ten Records	61	6 Jul 91	2

1300 DRUMS featuring the UNJUSTIFIED ANCIENTS OF MU
UK

SINGLES:		HITS 1		WEEKS 4
OOH! AAH! CANTONA	Dynamo	11	18 May 96	4

THIS ISLAND EARTH
UK

SINGLES:		HITS 1		WEEKS 5
SEE THAT GLOW	Magnet	47	5 Jan 85	5

THIS MORTAL COIL
UK

SINGLES:		HITS 1		WEEKS 3
SONG TO THE SIREN	4AD	66	22 Oct 83	2

When it appeared in the Breakers section 2 weeks before charting, the flip side 16 Days was listed instead. Originally recorded by Tim Buckley.

SONG TO THE SIREN [RE]	4AD	75	12 Nov 83	1
ALBUMS:		**HITS 3**		**WEEKS 10**
IT'LL END IN TEARS	4AD	38	20 Oct 84	4
FILIGREE AND SHADOW	4AD	53	11 Oct 86	3
BLOOD	4AD	28	4 May 91	3

THIS WAY UP
UK

SINGLES:		HITS 1		WEEKS 2
TELL ME WHY	Virgin	72	22 Aug 87	2

THIS YEAR'S BLONDE
UK

SINGLES:		HITS 2		WEEKS 8
PLATINUM POP [M]	Creole	46	10 Oct 81	5

Medley covering hits of Blondie.

WHO'S THAT MIX [M]	Debut	62	14 Nov 87	3

Medley covering hits of Madonna.

B. J. THOMAS
US

SINGLES:		HITS 1		WEEKS 4
RAINDROPS KEEP FALLIN' ON MY HEAD	Wand	38	21 Feb 70	3

From the film 'Butch Cassidy And The Sundance Kid'.

RAINDROPS KEEP FALLIN' ON MY HEAD [RE]	Wand	49	2 May 70	1

Carla THOMAS – See Otis REDDING and Carla THOMAS

Evelyn THOMAS
US

SINGLES:		HITS 4		WEEKS 29
WEAK SPOT	20th Century	26	24 Jan 76	7
DOOMSDAY	20th Century	41	17 Apr 76	1
DOOMSDAY [RE]	20th Century	45	1 May 76	1
HIGH ENERGY	Record Shack	5	21 Apr 84	17
MASQUERADE	Record Shack	60	25 Aug 84	3

Jamo THOMAS and his PARTY BROTHERS ORCHESTRA — US

SINGLES:	HITS 1			WEEKS 3	
I SPY (FOR THE FBI)	Polydor	48	1 Mar 69	1	
I SPY (FOR THE FBI) [RE-1ST]	Polydor	44	15 Mar 69	1	
I SPY (FOR THE FBI) [RE-2ND]	Polydor	50	29 Mar 69	1	

John Hugh THOMAS – See Aled JONES

Kenny THOMAS — UK

SINGLES:	HITS 9			WEEKS 54	
OUTSTANDING	Cooltempo	12	26 Jan 91	10	
Original release reached No. 79 in 1990.					
THINKING ABOUT YOUR LOVE	Cooltempo	4	1 Jun 91	13	
BEST OF YOU	Cooltempo	11	5 Oct 91	7	
Originally recorded by Booker T Jones.					
TENDER LOVE	Cooltempo	26	30 Nov 91	6	
STAY	Cooltempo	22	10 Jul 93	6	
Originally recorded by the Controllers.					
TRIPPIN' ON YOUR LOVE	Cooltempo	17	4 Sep 93	5	
Originally recorded by the Staple Singers.					
PIECE BY PIECE	Cooltempo	36	6 Nov 93	3	
DESTINY	Cooltempo	59	14 May 94	1	
WHEN I THINK OF YOU	Cooltempo	27	2 Sep 95	3	
ALBUMS:	HITS 2			WEEKS 28	
VOICES	Cooltempo	3	26 Oct 91	23	
WAIT FOR ME	Cooltempo	10	25 Sep 93	5	

Lillo THOMAS — US

SINGLES:	HITS 3			WEEKS 10	
SETTLE DOWN	Capitol	66	27 Apr 85	2	
SEXY GIRL	Capitol	23	21 Mar 87	5	
I'M IN LOVE	Capitol	54	30 May 87	3	
ALBUMS:	HITS 1			WEEKS 7	
LILLO	Capitol	43	2 May 87	7	

Millard THOMAS – See Harry BELAFONTE

Nicky THOMAS — Jamaica

SINGLES:	HITS 1			WEEKS 14	
LOVE OF THE COMMON PEOPLE	Trojan	9	13 Jun 70	14	
Originally recorded by the Four Preps.					

Ray THOMAS — UK

ALBUMS:	HITS 1			WEEKS 3	
FROM MIGHTY OAKS	Threshold	23	26 Jul 75	3	

Rob THOMAS – See SANTANA

Rufus THOMAS — US

SINGLES:	HITS 1			WEEKS 12	
DO THE FUNKY CHICKEN	Stax	18	11 Apr 70	12	

Steve THOMAS – See VARIOUS ARTISTS (EPs) 'Trade EP 2'

Tasha THOMAS — US

SINGLES:	HITS 1			WEEKS 3	
SHOOT ME (WITH YOUR LOVE)	Atlantic	59	20 Jan 79	3	

Timmy THOMAS — US

SINGLES:	HITS 2			WEEKS 20	
WHY CAN'T WE LIVE TOGETHER	Mojo	12	24 Feb 73	11	
NEW YORK EYES	Portrait	41	28 Dec 85	7	
Above hit: NICOLE with Timmy THOMAS.					
WHY CAN'T WE LIVE TOGETHER (1990 REMIX) [RM]	T.K.	54	14 Jul 90	2	
Remixed by Pluto.					

THOMAS and TAYLOR — US

SINGLES:	HITS 1			WEEKS 5	
YOU CAN'T BLAME LOVE	Cooltempo	53	17 May 86	5	

Russell THOMPKINS, JR – See STYLISTICS

Amanda THOMPSON – Lesley GARRETT

Carroll THOMPSON – See MOVEMENT. 98 featuring Carroll THOMPSON; Courtney PINE

Chris THOMPSON | | | | UK

SINGLES:		HITS 1		WEEKS 5
IF YOU REMEMBER ME	Planet	42	27 Oct 79	5
From the film 'The Champ'.				

Danny THOMPSON – See Richard THOMPSON

Gina THOMPSON – See MC LYTE

Prince Lincoln THOMPSON – See REBEL MC

Richard THOMPSON | | | | UK

ALBUMS:		HITS 8		WEEKS 15
ACROSS A CROWDED ROOM	Polydor	80	27 Apr 85	2
DARING ADVENTURES	Polydor	92	18 Oct 86	1
AMNESIA	Capitol	89	29 Oct 88	1
RUMOR AND SIGH	Capital	32	25 May 91	3
MIRROR BLUE	Capitol	23	29 Jan 94	3
Title taken from the poem by Tennyson 'The Lady Of Shalott'.				
YOU? ME? US?	Capitol	32	20 Apr 96	2
INDUSTRY	Parlophone	69	24 May 97	1
Above hit: Richard and Danny THOMPSON.				
MOCK TUDOR	Capitol	28	4 Sept 99	2

Sue THOMPSON | | | | US

SINGLES:		HITS 2		WEEKS 9
SAD MOVIES	Polydor	46	4 Nov 61	1
SAD MOVIES [RE]	Polydor	48	18 Nov 61	1
PAPER TIGER	Hickory	50	23 Jan 65	1
Both hits written by John D. Loudermilk.				
PAPER TIGER [RE]	Hickory	30	13 Feb 65	6

THOMPSON TWINS | | | | UK/New Zealand

SINGLES:		HITS 16		WEEKS 110
LIES	Arista	67	6 Nov 82	3
LOVE ON YOUR SIDE	Arista	9	29 Jan 83	12
WE ARE DETECTIVE	Arista	7	16 Apr 83	9
WATCHING	Arista	33	16 Jul 83	6
HOLD ME NOW	Arista	4	19 Nov 83	15
DOCTOR DOCTOR	Arista	3	4 Feb 84	10
YOU TAKE ME UP	Arista	2	31 Mar 84	9
SISTER OF MERCY	Arista	11	7 Jul 84	8
SISTER OF MERCY [RE]	Arista	66	8 Sep 84	1
LAY YOUR HANDS ON ME	Arista	13	8 Dec 84	9
DON'T MESS WITH DOCTOR DREAM	Arista	15	31 Aug 85	6
KING FOR A DAY	Arista	22	19 Oct 85	6
REVOLUTION	Arista	56	7 Dec 85	3
Originally recorded by the Beatles on the B-side of Hey Jude.				
REVOLUTION [RE]	Arista	75	4 Jan 86	1
GET THAT LOVE	Arista	68	21 Mar 87	2
GET THAT LOVE [RE]	Arista	66	11 Apr 87	1
IN THE NAME OF LOVE '88	Arista	46	15 Oct 88	3
Original release in 1982 appeared in the Bubbling Under section of the chart.				
COME INSIDE	Warner Brothers	56	28 Sep 91	4
THE SAINT	Warner Brothers	53	25 Jan 92	2
ALBUMS:		HITS 6		WEEKS 128
SET	Tee	48	13 Mar 82	3
QUICK STEP & SIDE KICK	Arista	2	26 Feb 83	56
INTO THE GAP	Arista	1	25 Feb 84	51
HERE'S TO FUTURE DAYS	Arista	5	28 Sep 85	9
CLOSE TO THE BONE	Arista	90	2 May 87	1
THOMPSON TWINS - THE GREATEST HITS	Stylus	23	10 Mar 90	8

Tracey THORN – See MASSIVE ATTACK

David THORNE with Richard WOLFF and his Orchestra | | | | US

SINGLES:		HITS 1		WEEKS 8
THE ALLEY CAT SONG	Stateside	21	26 Jan 63	8

Ken THORNE and his Orchestra; trumpet solo: Ray DAVIES | | | | UK

SINGLES:		HITS 1		WEEKS 15
THEME FROM FILM "THE LEGION'S LAST PATROL" (CONCERTO DISPERATO)	His Master's Voice	4	20 Jul 63	15

897

George THOROGOOD and the DESTROYERS
US

ALBUMS:	HITS 1			WEEKS 1
GEORGE THOROGOOD AND THE DESTROYERS	Sonet	67	2 Dec 78	1

THOSE 2 GIRLS
UK

SINGLES:	HITS 2			WEEKS 4
WANNA MAKE YOU GO . . . UUH!	Final Vinyl	74	5 Nov 94	1
ALL I WANT	Final Vinyl	36	4 Mar 95	3

THOUSAND YARD STARE
UK

SINGLES:	HITS 4			WEEKS 5
SEASONSTREAM [EP]	Stifled Aardvark	65	26 Oct 91	1
Lead track: O-O-AET.				
COMEUPPANCE [EP]	Stifled Aardvark	37	8 Feb 92	2
Lead track: Comeuppance.				
SPINDRIFT [EP]	Stifled Aardvark	58	11 Jul 92	1
Lead track: Wideshire Two.				
VERSION OF ME	Polydor	57	8 May 93	1
ALBUMS:	HITS 1			WEEKS 2
HANDS ON	Polydor	38	7 Mar 92	2

THRASHING DOVES
UK

SINGLES:	HITS 1			WEEKS 3
BEAUTIFUL IMBALANCE	A&M	50	24 Jan 87	3

THREE AMIGOS
UK

SINGLES:	HITS 1			WEEKS 6
LOUIE LOUIE	Inferno	15	3 Jul 99	6
From the film 'American Pie'.				

3 COLOURS RED
UK

SINGLES:	HITS 7			WEEKS 17
NUCLEAR HOLIDAY	Creation	22	18 Jan 97	2
SIXTY MILE SMILE	Creation	20	15 Mar 97	3
PURE	Creation	28	10 May 97	1
COPPER GIRL	Creation	30	12 Jul 97	2
THIS IS MY HOLLYWOOD	Creation	48	8 Nov 97	1
Original release reached No. 162 in 1996.				
BEAUTIFUL DAY	Creation	11	23 Jan 99	6
THIS IS MY TIME	Creation	36	29 May 99	2
ALBUMS:	HITS 2			WEEKS 4
PURE	Creation	16	24 May 97	2
REVOLT	Creation	17	20 Feb 99	2

THREE DEGREES
US

SINGLES:	HITS 15			WEEKS 113
YEAR OF DECISION	Philadelphia International	13	13 Apr 74	10
TSOP (THE SOUND OF PHILADELPHIA)	Philadelphia International	22	27 Apr 74	9
Above hit: MFSB featuring the THREE DEGREES.				
WHEN WILL I SEE YOU AGAIN	Philadelphia International	1	13 Jul 74	16
GET YOUR LOVE BACK	Philadelphia International	34	2 Nov 74	4
TAKE GOOD CARE OF YOURSELF	Philadelphia International	9	12 Apr 75	9
LONG LOST LOVER	Philadelphia International	40	5 Jul 75	4
TOAST OF LOVE	Epic	36	1 May 76	4
GIVING UP, GIVING IN	Ariola	12	7 Oct 78	10
WOMAN IN LOVE	Ariola	3	13 Jan 79	11
THE RUNNER	Ariola	10	24 Mar 79	10
THE GOLDEN LADY	Ariola	56	23 Jun 79	3
From the film of the same name.				
JUMP THE GUN	Ariola	48	29 Sep 79	5
MY SIMPLE HEART	Ariola	9	24 Nov 79	11
Originally recorded by the Dukes.				
THE HEAVEN I NEED	Supreme	42	5 Oct 85	5
LAST CHRISTMAS	Wildstar	54	26 Dec 98	2
Above hit: ALIEN VOICES featuring the THREE DEGREES.				
ALBUMS:	HITS 6			WEEKS 91
THREE DEGREES	Philadelphia International	12	10 Aug 74	22
TAKE GOOD CARE OF YOURSELF	Philadelphia International	6	17 May 75	16
NEW DIMENSIONS	Ariola	34	24 Feb 79	13
A COLLECTION OF THEIR 20 GREATEST HITS	Epic	8	3 Mar 79	18
3D	Ariola	61	15 Dec 79	7
GOLD	Ariola	9	27 Sep 80	15

THREE DOG NIGHT US

SINGLES:		HITS 2		WEEKS 23
MAMA TOLD ME NOT TO COME	Stateside	3	8 Aug 70	14
Written and originally recorded by Randy Newman.				
JOY TO THE WORLD	Probe	24	29 May 71	9

THREE GOOD REASONS UK

SINGLES:		HITS 1		WEEKS 3
NOWHERE MAN	Mercury	47	12 Mar 66	3
Originally recorded by the Beatles.				

3 JAYS UK

SINGLES:		HITS 1		WEEKS 5
FEELING IT TOO	Multiply	17	31 Jul 99	5

THREE KAYES – See KAYE SISTERS

THREE 'N ONE Germany

SINGLES:		HITS 2		WEEKS 3
REFLECT	ffrr	66	7 Jun 97	1
PEARL RIVER	Low Sense	32	15 May 99	2
Originally released as an instrumental in 1997.				
Above hit: THREE 'N ONE presents Johnny SHAKER [featuring SERIAL DIVA].				

3T US

SINGLES:		HITS 5		WEEKS 45
ANYTHING	Epic	2	27 Jan 96	14
24/7	Epic	11	4 May 96	7
WHY	Epic	2	24 Aug 96	9
Above hit: 3T featuring Michael JACKSON.				
I NEED YOU	Epic	3	7 Dec 96	10
Backing vocals by Michael Jackson.				
GOTTA BE YOU	Epic	10	5 Apr 97	5
Above hit: 3T (featuring HERBIE).				
ALBUMS:		**HITS 1**		**WEEKS 15**
BROTHERHOOD	Epic	11	24 Feb 96	15

3 TENORS: José CARRERAS, Placido DOMINGO, Luciano PAVAROTTI Spain/Italy

(See also José Carreras; Placido Domingo; Luciano Pavarotti.)

SINGLES:		HITS 2		WEEKS 8
LIBIAMO, NE' LIETI CALICI FROM VERDI LA TRAVIATA / LA DONNA E MOBILE FROM VERDI RIGOLETTO	Teldec	21	30 Jul 94	4
Live recording from Monte Carlo, 9 Jun 94.				
Above hit: THREE TENORS IN CONCERT 1994 – CARRERAS DOMINGO PAVAROTTI with MEHTA.				
YOU'LL NEVER WALK ALONE	Decca	35	25 Jul 98	4
Above hit: Tibor RUDAS presents the 3 TENORS PARIS 1988: Jose CARRERAS, Placido DOMINGO, Luciano PAVAROTTI.				
ALBUMS:		**HITS 3**		**WEEKS 110**
IN CONCERT	Decca	1	1 Sep 90	78
Live recordings before the 1990 World Cup Final at Terme di Caracalla, Roma, 7 Jul 90.				
Above hit: CARRERAS DOMINGO PAVAROTTI Orchestra del Maggio Musicale Fiorentino Orchestra del Teatro dell'Opera di Roma Zubin MEHTA.				
THE 3 TENORS IN CONCERT 1994	Teldec	1	10 Sep 94	26
Live recordings before the 1994 World Cup Final at Los Angeles' Dodger Stadium, 16 Jul 94.				
Above hit: CARRERAS DOMINGO PAVAROTTI with Orchestra conducted by Zubin MEHTA.				
THE 3 TENORS PARIS 1998	Decca	14	29 Aug 98	6
Live recordings at the Effiel Tower, Paris, France, 10 Jul 98.				
Above hit: CARRERAS DOMINGO PAVAROTTI with James LEVINE.				

THREE TONS OF JOY – See Johnny OTIS SHOW with Marie ADAMS

THROWING MUSES US

SINGLES:		HITS 4		WEEKS 6
COUNTING BACKWARDS	4AD	70	9 Feb 91	2
FIREPILE [EP]	4AD	46	1 Aug 92	1
Lead track: Firepile.				
BRIGHT YELLOW GUN	4AD	51	24 Dec 94	2
SHARK	4AD	53	10 Aug 96	1
ALBUMS:		**HITS 6**		**WEEKS 13**
HUNKPAPA	4AD	59	4 Feb 89	1
THE REAL RAMONA	4AD	26	2 Mar 91	4
RED HEAVEN	4AD	13	22 Aug 92	3

THE CURSE	4AD	74	28 Nov 92	1
UNIVERSITY	4AD	10	28 Jan 95	3
LIMBO	4AD	36	31 Aug 96	1

Harry THUMANN   Germany

SINGLES:		HITS 1		WEEKS 6
UNDERWATER	Decca	41	21 Feb 81	6

THUNDER   UK

SINGLES:		HITS 18		WEEKS 52
DIRTY LOVE	EMI	32	17 Feb 90	4
BACKSTREET SYMPHONY	EMI	25	12 May 90	4
GIMME SOME LOVIN'	EMI	36	14 Jul 90	3
SHE'S SO FINE	EMI	34	29 Sep 90	3
LOVE WALKED IN	EMI	21	23 Feb 91	4
LOW LIFE IN HIGH PLACES	EMI	22	15 Aug 92	5
EVERYBODY WANTS HER	EMI	36	10 Oct 92	4
A BETTER MAN	EMI	18	13 Feb 93	4
LIKE A SATELLITE [EP]	EMI	28	19 Jun 93	2
Lead track: Like A Satellite.				
STAND UP	EMI	23	7 Jan 95	4
RIVER OF PAIN	EMI	31	25 Feb 95	2
CASTLES IN THE SAND	EMI	30	6 May 95	3
IN A BROKEN DREAM	EMI	26	23 Sep 95	2
DON'T WAIT UP	Raw Power	27	25 Jan 97	2
LOVE WORTH DYING FOR	Raw Power	60	5 Apr 97	1
THE ONLY ONE	Eagle	31	7 Feb 98	2
PLAY THAT FUNKY MUSIC	Eagle	39	27 Jun 98	2
YOU WANNA KNOW	Eagle	49	20 Mar 99	1
ALBUMS:		HITS 7		WEEKS 39
BACK STREET SYMPHONY	EMI	21	17 Mar 90	16
LAUGHING ON JUDGEMENT DAY	EMI	2	5 Sep 92	10
BEHIND CLOSED DOORS	EMI	5	4 Feb 95	5
BEST OF THUNDER - THEIR FINEST HOUR (AND A BIT)	EMI	22	7 Oct 95	3
THE THRILL OF IT ALL	Raw Power	14	15 Feb 97	3
LIVE	Eagle	35	28 Feb 98	1
Live recordings from their 1997 UK tour.				
GIVING THE GAME AWAY	Eagle	49	27 Mar 99	1

THUNDERBUGS   UK/France/Germany

SINGLES:		HITS 2		WEEKS 13
FRIENDS FOREVER	Epic	5	18 Sept 99	9
FRIENDS FOREVER [RE]	Epic	71	11 Dec 99	1
IT'S ABOUT TIME YOU WERE MINE	Epic	43	18 Dec 99	3

THUNDERCLAP NEWMAN   UK

SINGLES:		HITS 2		WEEKS 13
SOMETHING IN THE AIR	Track	1	14 Jun 69	12
ACCIDENTS	Track	46	27 Jun 70	1

THUNDERTHIGHS   UK

SINGLES:		HITS 1		WEEKS 5
CENTRAL PARK ARREST	Philips	30	22 Jun 74	5
Originally recorded by Lynsey De Paul for the B-side to No Honestly.				

Bobby THURSTON   US

SINGLES:		HITS 1		WEEKS 10
CHECK OUT THE GROOVE	Epic	10	29 Mar 80	10

TIFFANY   US

SINGLES:		HITS 6		WEEKS 45
I THINK WE'RE ALONE NOW	MCA	1	16 Jan 88	13
Original by Tommy James and the Shondells reached No. 4 in the US in 1967.				
COULD'VE BEEN	MCA	4	19 Mar 88	9
I SAW HIM STANDING THERE	MCA	8	4 Jun 88	7
Female version of the Beatles' I Saw Her Standing There				
FEELINGS OF FOREVER	MCA	52	6 Aug 88	2
RADIO ROMANCE	MCA	13	12 Nov 88	11
ALL THIS TIME	MCA	47	11 Feb 89	3
ALBUMS:		HITS 2		WEEKS 27
TIFFANY	MCA	5	27 Feb 88	21
HOLD AN OLD FRIEND'S HAND	MCA	56	17 Dec 88	6

TIGER
UK/Ireland

SINGLES:	HITS 4			WEEKS 5
RACE	Trade 2	37	31 Aug 96	2
MY PUPPET PAL	Trade 2	62	16 Nov 96	1
ON THE ROSE	Trade 2	57	22 Feb 97	1
FRIENDS	Trade 2	72	22 Aug 98	1

TIGERTAILZ
US

SINGLES:	HITS 2			WEEKS 2
LOVE BOMB BABY	Music For Nations	75	24 Jun 89	1
HEAVEN	Music For Nations	71	16 Feb 91	1
ALBUMS:	HITS 1			WEEKS 2
BEZERK	Music For Nations	36	7 Apr 90	2

TIGHT FIT
UK

SINGLES:	HITS 5			WEEKS 49
BACK TO THE 60'S [M]	Jive	4	18 Jul 81	11
BACK TO THE 60'S (PART II) [M]	Jive	33	26 Sep 81	5
Above 2 are medleys of 1960s hits.				
THE LION SLEEPS TONIGHT	Jive	1	23 Jan 82	15
Originally recorded by Solomon Linda and the Evening Birds as Mbube in 1939.				
FANTASY ISLAND	Jive	5	1 May 82	12
SECRET HEART	Jive	41	31 Jul 82	6
ALBUMS:	HITS 2			WEEKS 6
BACK TO THE SIXTIES	Jive	38	26 Sep 81	4
TIGHT FIT	Jive	87	4 Sep 82	2

TIJUANA BRASS – See Herb ALPERT and the TIJUANA BRASS

TIK and TOK
UK

SINGLES:	HITS 1			WEEKS 2
COOL RUNNING	Survival	69	8 Oct 83	2
ALBUMS:	HITS 1			WEEKS 2
INTOLERANCE	Survival	89	4 Aug 84	2

Tanita TIKARAM
UK

SINGLES:	HITS 9			WEEKS 31
GOOD TRADITION	WEA	10	30 Jul 88	10
TWIST IN MY SOBRIETY	WEA	22	22 Oct 88	8
CATHEDRAL SONG	WEA	48	14 Jan 89	3
WORLD OUTSIDE YOUR WINDOW	WEA	58	18 Mar 89	2
WE ALMOST GOT IT TOGETHER	WEA	52	13 Jan 90	3
ONLY THE ONES WE LOVE	East West	69	9 Feb 91	1
I MIGHT BE CRYING	East West	64	4 Feb 95	2
STOP LISTENING	Mother	67	6 Jun 98	1
I DON'T WANNA LOSE AT LOVE	Mother	73	29 Aug 98	1
ALBUMS:	HITS 5			WEEKS 62
ANCIENT HEART	WEA	3	24 Sep 88	49
THE SWEET KEEPER	East West	3	10 Feb 90	7
EVERYBODY'S ANGEL	East West	19	16 Feb 91	4
LOVERS IN THE CITY	East West	75	25 Feb 95	1
THE CAPPUCCINO SONGS	Mother	69	19 Sep 98	1

Johnny TILLOTSON
US

SINGLES:	HITS 6			WEEKS 50
POETRY IN MOTION	London	1	3 Dec 60	15
JIMMY'S GIRL	London	50	4 Feb 61	1
JIMMY'S GIRL [RE]	London	43	18 Feb 61	1
IT KEEPS RIGHT ON A-HURTIN'	London	31	14 Jul 62	10
SEND ME THE PILLOW YOU DREAM ON	London	21	6 Oct 62	10
Originally recorded by Hank Locklin.				
I CAN'T HELP IT	London	42	29 Dec 62	1
Originally recorded by Hank Williams in 1952.				
I CAN'T HELP IT [RE-1ST]	London	47	12 Jan 63	1
I CAN'T HELP IT [RE-2ND]	London	41	26 Jan 63	4
OUT OF MY MIND	London	34	11 May 63	5
POETRY IN MOTION [RI] / PRINCESS PRINCESS	Lightning	67	14 Apr 79	2
Princess Princess was the original B-side of Poetry in Motion in 1960.				

TILT
UK

SINGLES:	HITS 6			WEEKS 7
I DREAM	Perfecto	69	2 Dec 95	1
MY SPIRIT	Perfecto	61	10 May 97	1

PLACES	Perfecto	64	13 Sep 97	1
BUTTERFLY	Perfecto Mainline	41	7 Feb 98	1
Above hit: TILT featuring ZEE.				
CHILDREN	Deconstruction	51	27 Mar 99	1
INVISIBLE	Hollywood	20	8 May 99	2

TIMBALAND   US

SINGLES:	HITS 3			WEEKS 7
GET ON THE BUS	East West	15	23 Jan 99	5
From the film 'Why Do Fools Fall In Love'.				
Above hit: DESTINY'S CHILD (featuring TIMBALAND).				
HERE WE COME	Virgin	43	13 Mar 99	1
Samples the melody from the Spiderman cartoon series.				
Above hit: TIMBALAND featuring Missy "Misdemeanor" ELLIOTT and MAGOO.				
LOBSTER & SCRIMP	Virgin	48	19 Jun 99	1
Above hit: TIMBALAND featuring JAY-Z.				

TIMBUK 3   US

SINGLES:	HITS 1			WEEKS 7
THE FUTURE'S SO BRIGHT I GOTTA WEAR SHADES	I.R.S.	21	31 Jan 87	7
ALBUMS:	**HITS 1**			**WEEKS 4**
GREETINGS FROM TIMBUK 3	I.R.S.	51	14 Feb 87	4

TIME   US

ALBUMS:	HITS 1			WEEKS 1
PANDEMONIUM	Paisley Park	66	28 Jul 90	1

TIME FREQUENCY   UK

SINGLES:	HITS 6			WEEKS 33
REAL LOVE	Jive	60	6 Jun 92	1
NEW EMOTION [EP]	Internal Affairs	36	9 Jan 93	6
Lead track: New Emotion.				
THE POWER ZONE [EP]	Internal Affairs	17	12 Jun 93	11
Lead track: The Ultimate High.				
REAL LOVE '93 [RM]	Internal Affairs	8	6 Nov 93	6
Remixed by the Time Frenquency.				
REAL LOVE '93 [RM] [RE]	Internal Affairs	71	1 Jan 94	2
SUCH A PHANTASY [EP]	Internal Affairs	25	28 May 94	4
Lead track: Such A Fantasy.				
DREAMSCAPE '94	Internal Affairs	32	8 Oct 94	3
ALBUMS:	**HITS 1**			**WEEKS 4**
DOMINATOR	Internal Affairs	23	18 Jun 94	4

TIME OF THE MUMPH   UK

SINGLES:	HITS 1			WEEKS 1
CONTROL	Fresh	69	11 Feb 95	1

TIME UK   UK

SINGLES:	HITS 1			WEEKS 3
THE CABARET	Red Bus	63	8 Oct 83	3

TIME ZONE featuring John LYDON and Afrika BAMBAATAA   UK/US

(See also Afrika Bambaataa, John Lydon.)

SINGLES:	HITS 1			WEEKS 9
WORLD DESTRUCTION	Virgin	44	19 Jan 85	9

TIMEBOX   UK

SINGLES:	HITS 1			WEEKS 4
BEGGIN'	Deram	38	27 Jul 68	4
Original by the Four Seasons reached No. 16 in the US in 1967.				

TIMELORDS   UK

(See also Justified Ancients Of Mu Mu; KLF; 2K.)

SINGLES:	HITS 1			WEEKS 9
DOCTORIN' THE TARDIS	KLF Commuications	1	4 Jun 88	9
Based around Gary Glitter's Rock And Roll and the theme to Dr. Who.				

TIMEX SOCIAL CLUB   US

SINGLES:	HITS 1			WEEKS 9
RUMORS	Cooltempo	13	13 Sep 86	9

TIN MACHINE

		UK/US		
SINGLES:	HITS 4		WEEKS 10	
UNDER THE GOD	EMI U.S.A	51	1 Jul 89	2
TIN MACHINE / MAGGIE'S FARM (LIVE)	EMI U.S.A	48	9 Sep 89	2
Maggie's Farm (Live) only listed on the chart for 16 Sep 89.				
YOU BELONG IN ROCK N' ROLL	London	33	24 Aug 91	3
BABY UNIVERSAL	London	48	2 Nov 91	3
ALBUMS:	HITS 2		WEEKS 12	
TIN MACHINE	EMI U.S.A	3	3 Jun 89	9
TIN MACHINE II	London	23	14 Sep 91	3

TIN TIN – See Stephen 'Tin Tin' DUFFY

TIN TIN OUT

		UK		
SINGLES:	HITS 9		WEEKS 38	
THE FEELING	Deep Distraxion	32	13 Aug 94	2
Sweet Tee's vocals are sampled from her 1988 single I Got Da Feelin.				
Above hit: TIN TIN OUT featuring SWEET TEE.				
ALWAYS SOMETHING THERE TO REMIND ME	WEA	14	25 Mar 95	5
Started out as a solo Espiritu track in 1994 but was never released.				
Above hit: TIN TIN OUT featuring ESPIRITU.				
ALL I WANNA DO	VC Recordings	31	8 Feb 97	2
DANCE WITH ME	VC Recordings	35	10 May 97	2
Above hit: TIN TIN OUT featuring Tony HADLEY.				
STRINGS FOR YASMIN	VC Recordings	31	20 Sep 97	3
HERE'S WHERE THE STORY ENDS	VC Recordings	7	28 Mar 98	10
Originally recorded by the Sundays on their 1990 album Reading, Writing And Arithmetic.				
Above hit: TIN TIN OUT featuring Shelley NELSON.				
SOMETIMES	VC Recordings	20	12 Sep 98	4
Above hit: TIN TIN OUT with Shelley NELSON.				
ELEVEN TO FLY	VC Recordings	26	11 Sept 99	2
Above hit: TINTINOUT featuring Wendy PAGE.				
WHAT I AM	VC Recordings	2	13 Nov 99	8
Above hit: TIN TIN OUT featuring Emma BUNTON.				
ALBUMS:	HITS 1		WEEKS 1	
ADVENTURES IN TIN TIN OUT LAND	VC Recordings	65	5 Oct 96	1
12" double-pack single.				

TINA – See Tina TURNER

TINDERSTICKS

		UK		
SINGLES:	HITS 6		WEEKS 6	
KATHLEEN [EP]	This Way Up	61	5 Feb 94	1
Lead track: Kathleen, originally recorded by Townes Van Zandt.				
NO MORE AFFAIRS	This Way Up	58	18 Mar 95	1
TRAVELLING LIGHT	This Way Up	51	12 Aug 95	1
BATHTIME	This Way Up	38	7 Jun 97	1
RENTED ROOMS	This Way Up	56	1 Nov 97	1
CAN WE START AGAIN?	Island	54	4 Sept 99	1
ALBUMS:	HITS 5		WEEKS 8	
TINDERSTICKS	This Way Up	56	23 Oct 93	1
THE SECOND TINDERSTICKS ALBUM	This Way Up	13	15 Apr 95	3
LIVE AT THE BLOOMSBURY THEATRE 12.3.95	This Way Up	32	28 Oct 95	1
Live recordings with backing Orchestra.				
CURTAINS	This Way Up	37	21 Jun 97	2
SIMPLE PLEASURE	Island	36	18 Sept 99	1

TINGO TANGO

		UK		
SINGLES:	HITS 1		WEEKS 2	
IT IS JAZZ	Champion	68	21 Jul 90	2

TINMAN

(See also James Brown.)

		UK		
SINGLES:	HITS 2		WEEKS 9	
EIGHTEEN STRINGS	ffrr	9	20 Aug 94	8
Recorded earlier in the year with a sample from Nirvana's Smells Like Teen Spirit. Clearance was refused so Tinman sampled the Monkees' (I'm Not Your) Steppin' Stone.				
GUDVIBE	ffrr	49	3 Jun 95	1
Samples Yello's The Race.				

TINY TIM

		US		
SINGLES:	HITS 1		WEEKS 1	
GREAT BALLS OF FIRE	Reprise	45	8 Feb 69	1

TITANIC
UK/Norway

SINGLES:		HITS 1		WEEKS 12	
SULTANA	CBS		5	25 Sep 71	12

TITIYO
Sweden

SINGLES:		HITS 3		WEEKS 6	
AFTER THE RAIN	Arista		60	3 Mar 90	3
FLOWERS	Arista		71	6 Oct 90	1
TELL ME (I'M NOT DREAMING)	Arista		45	5 Feb 94	2

Cara TIVEY – See Billy BRAGG

TJR featuring XAVIER
UK

SINGLES:		HITS 1		WEEKS 2	
JUST GETS BETTER	Multiply		28	27 Sep 97	2

TLC
US

SINGLES:		HITS 10		WEEKS 77	
AIN'T 2 PROUD 2 BEG	LaFace		13	20 Jun 92	5
Samples James Brown's Escapeism, Kool and the Gang's Jungle Boogie, Average White Band's School Boy Crush and Silver Convention's Fly Robin Fly.					
BABY-BABY-BABY	LaFace		55	22 Aug 92	3
WHAT ABOUT YOUR FRIENDS	LaFace		59	24 Oct 92	2
CREEP	LaFace		22	21 Jan 95	4
Samples Hey Young World by Slick Rick.					
RED LIGHT SPECIAL	LaFace		18	22 Apr 95	4
WATERFALLS	LaFace		4	5 Aug 95	14
DIGGIN' ON YOU	LaFace		18	4 Nov 95	5
CREEP 96 [RI]	LaFace		6	13 Jan 96	7
Though issued as a remix, the first track of the CD is the original.					
NO SCRUBS	LaFace		3	3 Apr 99	19
UNPRETTY	LaFace		6	28 Aug 99	11
DEAR LIE	LaFace		32	18 Dec 99	3
ALBUMS:		**HITS 2**		**WEEKS 83**	
CRAZYSEXYCOOL	LaFace		4	20 May 95	39
FANMAIL	LaFace		7	6 Mar 99	44

T99
Belgium

SINGLES:		HITS 2		WEEKS 10	
ANASTHASIA	XL Recordings		14	11 May 91	6
NOCTURINE	Emphasis		33	19 Oct 91	4

TOADS – See Stan FREBERG

Art and Dotty TODD
US

SINGLES:		HITS 1		WEEKS 7	
BROKEN WINGS	His Master's Voice		6	14 Feb 53	7

TOGETHER
UK

SINGLES:		HITS 1		WEEKS 8	
HARDCORE UPROAR	ffrr		12	4 Aug 90	8

TOKENS
US

SINGLES:		HITS 1		WEEKS 12	
THE LION SLEEPS TONIGHT (WIMOWEH)	RCA		11	23 Dec 61	12

TOKYO GHETTO PUSSY
Germany

(See also Jam and Spoon featuring Plavka.)

SINGLES:		HITS 2		WEEKS 4	
EVERYBODY ON THE FLOOR (PUMP IT)	Epic		26	16 Sep 95	2
Vocals by Joan Faulkner.					
I KISS YOUR LIPS	Epic		55	16 Mar 96	2

TOL and TOL
Holland

SINGLES:		HITS 1		WEEKS 2	
ELENI	Dover		73	14 Apr 90	2

TOM TOM CLUB
US

SINGLES:		HITS 3		WEEKS 20	
WORDY RAPPINGHOOD	Island		7	20 Jun 81	9
GENIUS OF LOVE	Island		65	10 Oct 81	2
UNDER THE BOARDWALK	Island		22	7 Aug 82	9

ALBUMS:		HITS 1		WEEKS 1
TOM TOM CLUB	Island	78	24 Oct 81	1

Satoshi TOMIIE – See Frankie KNUCKLES

TOMITA   Japan

ALBUMS:		HITS 4		WEEKS 33
SNOWFLAKES ARE DANCING	RCA Red Seal	17	7 Jun 75	20
PICTURES AT AN EXHIBITION	RCA Red Seal	42	16 Aug 75	5
HOLST: THE PLANETS	RCA Red Seal	41	7 May 77	6
TOMITA'S GREATEST HITS	RCA Red Seal	66	9 Feb 80	2

TOMSKI   UK

SINGLES:		HITS 1		WEEKS 1
14 HOURS TO SAVE THE EARTH	Xtravaganza	42	18 Apr 98	1

Includes sample from the 1980 film 'Flash Gordon'.

TONETTES – See Russ HAMILTON

TONGUE 'N' CHEEK   UK

SINGLES:		HITS 5		WEEKS 28
NOBODY (CAN LOVE ME)	Criminal	59	27 Feb 88	6

Above hit: TONGUE IN CHEEK.

ENCORE	Syncopate	41	25 Nov 89	4
TOMORROW	Syncopate	20	14 Apr 90	7
NOBODY	Syncopate	37	4 Aug 90	5
FORGET ME NOTS	Syncopate	26	19 Jan 91	6
ALBUMS:		HITS 1		WEEKS 3
THIS IS TONGUE 'N' CHEEK	Syncopate	45	22 Sep 90	3

TONIGHT   UK

SINGLES:		HITS 2		WEEKS 10
DRUMMER MAN	TDS Records	14	28 Jan 78	8
MONEY THAT'S YOUR PROBLEM	TDS Records	66	20 May 78	2

TONY! TONI! TONE!   US

SINGLES:		HITS 4		WEEKS 12
OAKLAND STROKE	Wing	50	30 Jun 90	5
IT NEVER RAINS (IN SOUTHERN CALIFORNIA)	Wing	69	9 Mar 91	2

Original by Albert Hammond reached No. 5 in the US in 1972.

IF I HAD NO LOOT	Polydor	44	4 Sep 93	3

Above hit: TONY TONI TONE.

LET'S GET DOWN	Mercury	33	3 May 97	2

Above hit: TONY TONI TONE featuring DJ QUIK.

ALBUMS:		HITS 1		WEEKS 1
SONS OF SOUL	Polydor	66	2 Oct 93	1

TOO SHORT – See SCARFACE

TOO TOUGH TEE – See DYNAMIX II featuring: TOO TOUGH TEE

TOON TRAVELLERS – See MUNGO JERRY

TOP   UK

SINGLES:		HITS 1		WEEKS 2
NUMBER ONE DOMINATOR	Island	67	20 Jul 91	2

TOP CAT – See DOUBLE 99

TOP LINERS – See Rocky SHARPE and the REPLAYS

TOPLOADER   UK

SINGLES:		HITS 2		WEEKS 2
ACHILLES HEEL	Sony S2	64	22 May 99	1
LET THE PEOPLE KNOW	Sony S2	52	7 Aug 99	1

TOPOL   Israel

(See also Various Artists: Films – Original Soundtracks 'Fiddler On The Roof'; Stage Cast - London 'Fiddler On The Roof'.)

SINGLES:		HITS 1		WEEKS 20
IF I WERE A RICH MAN	CBS	9	22 Apr 67	20

From the musical 'Fiddler On The Roof'. Originally recorded by Zero Mostel.

ALBUMS:		HITS 1		WEEKS 1
TOPOL'S ISRAEL	BBC	80	11 May 85	1

905

Bernie TORME
UK

ALBUMS:		HITS 1		WEEKS 3	
TURN OUT THE LIGHTS	Kamaflage	50	3 Jul 82	3

Mel TORME
US

SINGLES:		HITS 2		WEEKS 32	
MOUNTAIN GREENERY	Vogue Coral	15	28 Apr 56	11
Originally recorded by Frank Crumit in 1929.				
MOUNTAIN GREENERY [RE]	Vogue Coral	4	28 Jul 56	13
COMIN' HOME BABY	London	13	5 Jan 63	8

TORNADOS
UK

(See also Various Artists: Films – Original Soundtracks 'Just For Fun').

SINGLES:		HITS 5		WEEKS 59	
TELSTAR	Decca	1	1 Sep 62	25
Title was the name of the world's first communications satellite, launched on 10 Jul 62.				
GLOBETROTTER	Decca	5	12 Jan 63	11
ROBOT	Decca	17	23 Mar 63	12
THE ICE CREAM MAN	Decca	18	8 Jun 63	9
From the film 'Farewell Performance'.				
DRAGONFLY	Decca	41	12 Oct 63	2

EPS:		HITS 5		WEEKS 88	
THE SOUND OF THE TORNADOS	Decca	2	15 Dec 62	26
TELSTAR	Decca	4	2 Feb 63	22
MORE SOUNDS FROM THE TORNADOS	Decca	8	13 Apr 63	11
BILLY FURY AND THE TORNADOS	Decca	2	25 May 63	16
Above hit: Billy FURY and the TORNADOS.				
TORNADO ROCK	Decca	7	17 Aug 63	13

Mitchell TOROK
US

SINGLES:		HITS 2		WEEKS 19	
WHEN MEXICO GAVE UP THE RHUMBA	Brunswick	6	29 Sep 56	17
RED LIGHT, GREEN LIGHT	Brunswick	29	12 Jan 57	1
Above hit: Mitchell TOROK and the TULANE SISTERS.				
WHEN MEXICO GAVE UP THE RHUMBA [RE]	Brunswick	30	2 Feb 57	1

Liz TORRES – See Danny TENAGLIA

Peter TOSH
US

SINGLES:		HITS 2		WEEKS 12	
(YOU GOTTA WALK) DON'T LOOK BACK	Rolling Stones	43	21 Oct 78	7
Mick Jagger on backing vocals.				
JOHNNY B. GOODE	Radic	48	2 Apr 83	5
Original by Chuck Berry reached No. 8 in the US in 1958.				

ALBUMS:		HITS 1		WEEKS 1	
LEGALIZE IT	Virgin	54	25 Sep 76	1

TOTAL
US

SINGLES:		HITS 4		WEEKS 10	
CAN'T YOU SEE	Tommy Boy	43	15 Jul 95	2
From the film 'New Jersey Drive'.				
Above hit: TOTAL featuring the NOTORIOUS B.I.G.				
KISSIN' YOU	Puff Daddy	29	14 Sep 96	2
DO YOU THINK ABOUT US	Puff Daddy	49	15 Feb 97	1
WHAT YOU WANT	Puff Daddy	15	18 Apr 98	5
Above hit: MASE featuring TOTAL.				

TOTAL CONTRAST
UK

SINGLES:		HITS 4		WEEKS 22	
TAKES A LITTLE TIME	London	17	3 Aug 85	10
HIT AND RUN	London	41	19 Oct 85	5
THE RIVER	London	44	1 Mar 86	3
WHAT YOU GONNA DO ABOUT IT	London	63	10 May 86	4

ALBUMS:		HITS 1		WEEKS 3	
TOTAL CONTRAST	London	66	8 Mar 86	3

TOTO
US

SINGLES:		HITS 5		WEEKS 35	
HOLD THE LINE	CBS	14	10 Feb 79	11
AFRICA	CBS	3	5 Feb 83	10
ROSANNA	CBS	12	9 Apr 83	8
Originally released in 1982. Written about actress Rosanna Arquette who at the time was dating keyboard player Steve Porcaro.				

I WON'T HOLD YOU BACK	*CBS*	37	*18 Jun 83*	5
I WILL REMEMBER	*Columbia*	64	*18 Nov 95*	1
ALBUMS:	**HITS 5**			**WEEKS 39**
TOTO	*CBS*	37	*31 Mar 79*	5
TOTO IV	*CBS*	4	*26 Feb 83*	30
ISOLATION	*CBS*	67	*17 Nov 84*	2
FAHRENHEIT	*CBS*	99	*20 Sep 86*	1
THE SEVENTH ONE	*CBS*	73	*9 Apr 88*	1

TOTO COELO — UK

SINGLES:	**HITS 2**			**WEEKS 14**
I EAT CANNIBALS (PART ONE)	*Radialchoice*	8	*7 Aug 82*	10
DRACULA'S TANGO (SUCKER FOR YOUR LOVE) / MUCHO MACHO	*Radialchoice*	54	*13 Nov 82*	4

TOTTENHAM HOTSPUR F.A. CUP FINAL SQUAD — UK

SINGLES:	**HITS 4**			**WEEKS 23**
OSSIE'S DREAM . . . (SPURS ARE ON THEIR WAY TO WEMBLEY)	*Shelf*	5	*9 May 81*	8
Above hit: TOTTENHAM HOTSPUR F.A. CUP FINAL SQUAD SEASON 1980/81.				
TOTTENHAM, TOTTENHAM	*Shelf*	19	*1 May 82*	7
Above hit: TOTTENHAM HOTSPUR F.A. CUP FINAL SQUAD 1981/82 SEASON.				
HOT SHOT TOTTENHAM!	*Rainbow*	18	*9 May 87*	5
Above hit: TOTTENHAM HOTSPUR F.A. CUP FINAL SQUAD 1986/87 SEASON with CHAS and DAVE.				
WHEN THE YEAR ENDS IN 1	*A.1.*	44	*11 May 91*	3
New lyrics composed by Chas 'N' Dave to the music of their 1983 hit London Girls.				
Above hit: TOTTENHAM HOTSPUR with CHAS 'N' DAVE.				
EPS:	**HITS 1**			**WEEKS 3**
SPURS GO MARCHING ON	*Columbia*	6	*10 Jun 67*	3
Above hit: TOTTENHAM HOTSPUR F.A. CUP SQUAD.				

TOUCH AND GO — UK/Japan

SINGLES:	**HITS 1**			**WEEKS 12**
WOULD YOU . . . ?	*V2*	3	*7 Nov 98*	12

TOUCH OF SOUL — UK

SINGLES:	**HITS 1**			**WEEKS 3**
WE GOT THE LOVE	*Cooltempo*	46	*19 May 90*	3

TOUR DE FORCE — UK

SINGLES:	**HITS 1**			**WEEKS 1**
CATALAN	*East West Dance*	71	*16 May 98*	1

Ali Farka TOURE and Ry COODER — Mali/US

(See also Ry Cooder.)

ALBUMS:	**HITS 1**			**WEEKS 3**
TALKING TIMBUKTU	*World Circuit*	44	*9 Apr 94*	3

TOURISTS — UK

SINGLES:	**HITS 5**			**WEEKS 40**
BLIND AMONG THE FLOWERS	*Logo*	52	*9 Jun 79*	5
THE LONELIEST MAN IN THE WORLD	*Logo*	32	*8 Sep 79*	7
I ONLY WANT TO BE WITH YOU	*Logo*	4	*10 Nov 79*	14
SO GOOD TO BE BACK HOME AGAIN	*Logo*	8	*9 Feb 80*	9
DON'T SAY I TOLD YOU SO	*RCA*	40	*18 Oct 80*	5
ALBUMS:	**HITS 3**			**WEEKS 18**
THE TOURISTS	*Logo*	72	*14 Jul 79*	1
REALITY EFFECT	*Logo*	23	*3 Nov 79*	16
LUMINOUS BASEMENT	*RCA*	75	*22 Nov 80*	1

TOUTES LES FILLES — UK

SINGLES:	**HITS 1**			**WEEKS 1**
THAT'S WHAT LOVE CAN DO	*London*	44	*4 Sept 99*	1
Original by Boy Krazy reached No. 18 in the US in 1993.				

Carol Lynn TOWNES — US

SINGLES:	**HITS 2**			**WEEKS 7**
99½	*Polydor*	47	*4 Aug 84*	4
BELIEVE IN THE BEAT	*Polydor*	56	*19 Jan 85*	3

Fuzz TOWNSHEND   UK

SINGLES:		HITS 1		WEEKS 1
HELLO DARLIN	Echo	51	6 Sep 97	1

Originally released in Jul on the Fidelity Lo label reaching No. 131.

Pete TOWNSHEND   UK

(See also Pete Townshend and Ronnie Lane.)

SINGLES:		HITS 3		WEEKS 17
ROUGH BOYS	Atco	39	5 Apr 80	6
LET MY LOVE OPEN THE DOOR	Atco	46	21 Jun 80	6
UNIFORMS (CORPS D'ESPRIT)	Atco	48	21 Aug 82	5
ALBUMS:		**HITS 4**		**WEEKS 25**
WHO CAME FIRST	Track	30	21 Oct 72	2
EMPTY GLASS	Atco	11	3 May 80	14
ALL THE BEST COWBOYS HAVE CHINESE EYES	Acto	32	3 Jul 82	8
WHITE CITY	Atco	70	30 Nov 85	1

Pete TOWNSHEND and Ronnie LANE   UK

(See also Ronnie Lane and the Band Slim Chance; Pete Townshend.)

ALBUMS:		HITS 1		WEEKS 3
ROUGH MIX	Polydor	44	15 Oct 77	3

TOXIC TWO   US

SINGLES:		HITS 1		WEEKS 6
RAVE GENERATOR	PWL International	13	7 Mar 92	6

TOY-BOX   Denmark

SINGLES:		HITS 1		WEEKS 2
BEST FRIEND	Edel	41	18 Sept 99	2

TOY DOLLS   UK

SINGLES:		HITS 1		WEEKS 12
NELLIE THE ELEPHANT	Volume	4	1 Dec 84	12

Originally recorded by Mandy Miller.

ALBUMS:		HITS 1		WEEKS 1
A FAR OUT DISC	Volume	71	25 May 85	1

TOYAH   UK

SINGLES:		HITS 12		WEEKS 87
FOUR FROM TOYAH [EP]	Safari	4	14 Feb 81	14

Lead track: It's A Mystery.

I WANT TO BE FREE	Safari	8	16 May 81	11
THUNDER IN THE MOUNTAINS	Safari	4	3 Oct 81	9
FOUR MORE FROM TOYAH [EP]	Safari	14	28 Nov 81	9

Lead track: Good Morning Universe.

BRAVE NEW WORLD	Safari	21	22 May 82	8
IEYA	Safari	48	17 Jul 82	5

Originally released in 1981.

BE PROUD BE LOUD (BE HEARD)	Safari	30	9 Oct 82	7
REBEL RUN	Safari	24	24 Sep 83	5
THE VOW	Safari	50	19 Nov 83	5
DON'T FALL IN LOVE (I SAID)	Portrait	22	27 Apr 85	6
SOUL PASSING THROUGH SOUL	Portrait	57	29 Jun 85	3
ECHO BEACH	E'G	54	25 Apr 87	5
ALBUMS:		**HITS 8**		**WEEKS 97**
THE BLUE MEANING	Safari	40	14 Jun 80	4
TOYAH! TOYAH! TOYAH!	Safari	22	17 Jan 81	14
ANTHEM	Safari	2	30 May 81	46
THE CHANGELING	Safari	6	19 Jun 82	12
WARRIOR ROCK – TOYAH ON TOUR	Safari	20	13 Nov 82	6

Live recordings.

LOVE IS THE LAW	Safari	28	5 Nov 83	7
TOYAH! TOYAH! TOYAH!	K-Tel	43	25 Feb 84	4

Compilation. This is a different album to the 1981 entry.

MINX	Portrait	24	3 Aug 85	4

TOYS   US

SINGLES:		HITS 2		WEEKS 17
A LOVER'S CONCERTO	Stateside	5	6 Nov 65	13

Adapted from Bach's Minuet In G.

ATTACK	Stateside	36	29 Jan 66	4

TQ
US

SINGLES:		HITS 4			WEEKS 25
WESTSIDE	Epic		4	30 Jan 99	9
Dedicated to Tupac Shakur and NWA's Easy-E.					
BYE BYE BABY	Epic		7	1 May 99	7
BETTER DAYS	Epic		32	21 Aug 99	2
SUMMERTIME	Northwestside		7	04 Sept 99	7
Above hit: ANOTHER LEVEL featuring TQ.					

ALBUMS:		HITS 1			WEEKS 7
THEY NEVER SAW ME COMING	Epic		27	8 May 99	7
Originally released in 1998.					

Ian TRACEY with the LIVERPOOL CATHEDRALS' CHOIRS
UK

ALBUMS:		HITS 1			WEEKS 3
YOUR FAVOURITE HYMNS	Virgin Classics		62	21 Mar 92	3

TRACIE
UK

SINGLES:		HITS 5			WEEKS 24
THE HOUSE THAT JACK BUILT	Respond		9	26 Mar 83	8
GIVE IT SOME EMOTION	Respond		24	16 Jul 83	9
SOUL'S ON FIRE	Respond		73	14 Apr 84	2
(I LOVE YOU) WHEN YOU SLEEP	Respond		59	9 Jun 84	3
I CAN'T LEAVE YOU ALONE	Respond		60	17 Aug 85	2
Above hit: Tracie YOUNG.					

ALBUMS:		HITS 1			WEEKS 2
FAR FROM THE HURTING KIND	Respond		64	30 Jun 84	2

TRACY – See MASSIVO featuring TRACY

Jeanie TRACY
US

SINGLES:		HITS 3			WEEKS 3
IF THIS IS LOVE	Pulse 8		73	11 Jun 94	1
DO YOU BELIEVE IN THE WONDER	Pulse 8		57	5 Nov 94	1
IT'S A MAN'S MAN'S MAN'S WORLD	Pulse 8		73	13 May 95	1
Above hit: Jeanie TRACY and Bobby WOMACK.					

TRAFFIC
UK

SINGLES:		HITS 4			WEEKS 40
PAPER SUN	Island		5	3 Jun 67	10
HOLE IN MY SHOE	Island		2	9 Sep 67	14
HERE WE GO ROUND THE MULBERRY BUSH	Island		8	2 Dec 67	12
From the film of the same name.					
NO FACE, NO NAME, NO NUMBER	Island		40	9 Mar 68	4

ALBUMS:		HITS 6			WEEKS 41
MR. FANTASY	Island		8	30 Dec 67	16
TRAFFIC	Island		9	26 Oct 68	8
JOHN BARLEYCORN MUST DIE	Island		11	8 Aug 70	9
TRAFFIC - ON THE ROAD	Island		40	24 Nov 73	3
Live recordings from their 1973 World Tour.					
WHEN THE EAGLE FLIES	Island		31	28 Sep 74	1
FAR FROM HOME	Virgin		29	21 May 94	4

TRAMAINE
US

SINGLES:		HITS 1			WEEKS 2
FALL DOWN (SPIRIT OF LOVE)	A&M		60	5 Oct 85	2

TRAMMPS
US

SINGLES:		HITS 7			WEEKS 56
ZING WENT THE STRINGS OF MY HEART	Buddah		29	23 Nov 74	10
Originally recorded by Judy Garland in 1943.					
SIXTY MINUTE MAN	Buddah		40	1 Feb 75	4
Originally recorded by Billy Ward and the Dominoes in 1951.					
HOLD BACK THE NIGHT	Buddah		5	11 Oct 75	8
THAT'S WHERE THE HAPPY PEOPLE GO	Atlantic		35	13 Mar 76	8
SOUL SEARCHING TIME	Atlantic		42	24 Jul 76	3
DISCO INFERNO	Atlantic		16	14 May 77	7
DISCO INFERNO [RI]	Atlantic		47	24 Jun 78	10
From the film 'Saturday Night Fever'.					
HOLD BACK THE NIGHT [RR]	Network		30	12 Dec 92	6
Above hit: KWS features guest vocals from the TRAMMPS.					

TRANS-X | | | Canada

SINGLES:	HITS 1			WEEKS 9	
LIVING ON VIDEO ('85 RE-MIX)	Boiling Point	9	13 Jul 85	9
Original release reached No. 77 in 1984.				

TRANSA | | | UK

SINGLES:	HITS 2			WEEKS 2	
PROPHASE	Perfecto Fluoro	65	30 Aug 97	1
ENERVATE	Perfecto Fluoro	42	21 Feb 98	1

TRANSATLANTIC SOUL – See Roger SANCHEZ

TRANSFORMER 2 | | | Holland/Belgium

SINGLES:	HITS 1			WEEKS 1	
JUST CAN'T GET ENOUGH	Positiva	45	24 Feb 96	1

TRANSGLOBAL UNDERGROUND | | | UK

ALBUMS:	HITS 3			WEEKS 3	
DREAM OF 100 NATIONS	Nation	45	30 Oct 93	1
INTERNATIONAL TIMES	Nation	40	29 Oct 94	1
PSYCHIC KARAOKE	Nation	62	25 May 96	1

TRANSISTOR | | | UK/US

SINGLES:	HITS 1			WEEKS 1	
LOOK WHO'S PERFECT NOW	Virgin	56	28 Mar 98	1

TRANSVISION VAMP | | | UK

SINGLES:	HITS 10			WEEKS 59	
TELL THAT GIRL TO SHUT UP	MCA	45	16 Apr 88	3
Originally recorded by Holly and the Italians.				
I WANT YOUR LOVE	MCA	5	25 Jun 88	13
REVOLUTION BABY	MCA	30	17 Sep 88	5
Original release reached No. 77 in 1987.				
SISTER MOON	MCA	41	19 Nov 88	5
BABY I DON'T CARE	MCA	3	1 Apr 89	11
THE ONLY ONE	MCA	15	10 Jun 89	6
LANDSLIDE OF LOVE	MCA	14	5 Aug 89	5
BORN TO BE SOLD	MCA	22	4 Nov 89	4
(I JUST WANNA) B WITH U	MCA	30	13 Apr 91	4
IF LOOKS COULD KILL	MCA	41	22 Jun 91	3
ALBUMS:	**HITS 2**			**WEEKS 58**	
POP ART	MCA	4	15 Oct 88	32
VELVETEEN	MCA	1	8 Jul 89	26

TRASH | | | UK

SINGLES:	HITS 1			WEEKS 3	
GOLDEN SLUMBERS/CARRY THAT WEIGHT [M]	Apple	35	25 Oct 69	3
Originally recorded by the Beatles.				

TRASH CAN SINATRAS | | | UK

SINGLES:	HITS 1			WEEKS 1	
HAYFEVER	Go! Discs	61	24 Apr 93	1
ALBUMS:	**HITS 2**			**WEEKS 2**	
CAKE	Go! Discs	74	7 Jul 90	1
I'VE SEEN EVERYTHING	Go! Discs	50	15 May 93	1

TRAVEL | | | France

SINGLES:	HITS 1			WEEKS 2	
BULGARIAN	Tidy Trax	67	24 Apr 99	2

TRAVELING WILBURYS | | | UK/US

SINGLES:	HITS 3			WEEKS 19	
HANDLE WITH CARE	Wilbury	21	29 Oct 88	13
END OF THE LINE	Wilbury	52	11 Mar 89	4
NOBODY'S CHILD	Wilbury	44	30 Jun 90	2
ALBUMS:	**HITS 2**			**WEEKS 44**	
THE TRAVELING WILBURYS VOLUME 1	Wilbury	16	5 Nov 88	35
THE TRAVELING WILBURYS VOLUME 3	Wilbury	14	10 Nov 90	9

Pat TRAVERS | | | US

ALBUMS:	HITS 1			WEEKS 3	
MAKIN' MAGIC	Polydor	40	2 Apr 77	3

TRAVIS   UK

SINGLES:	HITS 9			WEEKS 36
U16 GIRLS	Independiente	40	12 Apr 97	2
ALL I WANT TO DO IS ROCK	Independiente	39	28 Jun 97	2
First issued in 1996 as a 500 copy limited edition 10" on the Red Telephone Box Records label.				
TIED TO THE 90'S	Independiente	30	23 Aug 97	2
HAPPY	Independiente	38	25 Oct 97	2
MORE THAN US [EP]	Independiente	16	11 Apr 98	3
Lead track: More Than Us, with Anne Dudley.				
WRITING TO REACH YOU	Independiente	14	20 Mar 99	5
DRIFTWOOD	Independiente	13	29 May 99	5
WHY DOES IT ALWAYS RAIN ON ME?	Independiente	10	14 Aug 99	8
TURN	Independiente	8	20 Nov 99	7
ALBUMS:	HITS 2			WEEKS 35
GOOD FEELING	Independiente	9	20 Sept 97	4
THE MAN WHO	Independiente	1	5 Jun 99	31

Randy TRAVIS   US

SINGLES:	HITS 1			WEEKS 6
FOREVER AND EVER, AMEN	Warner Brothers	55	21 May 88	6
ALBUMS:	HITS 1			WEEKS 2
OLD 8 X 10	Warner Brothers	64	6 Aug 88	2

John TRAVOLTA   US

(See also Various Artists: Films - Original Soundtracks 'Grease'.)

SINGLES:	HITS 6			WEEKS 90
YOU'RE THE ONE THAT I WANT	RSO	1	20 May 78	26
Above hit: John TRAVOLTA and Olivia NEWTON-JOHN.				
SUMMER NIGHTS	RSO	1	16 Sep 78	19
Above hit: John TRAVOLTA, Olivia NEWTON-JOHN and CAST.				
SANDY	Midsong	2	7 Oct 78	15
GREASED LIGHTNING	Midsong/Polydor	11	2 Dec 78	9
Above 4 from the film 'Grease'.				
THE GREASE MEGAMIX [M]	Polydor	3	22 Dec 90	10
Above hit: John TRAVOLTA and Olivia NEWTON-JOHN.				
GREASE – THE DREAM MIX [M]	Polydor	47	23 Mar 91	2
Above 2 are medleys of songs from the film 'Grease'.				
Above hit: Frankie VALLI, John TRAVOLTA and Olivia NEWTON-JOHN.				
YOU'RE THE ONE THAT I WANT [RI]	Polydor	4	25 Jul 98	9
20th anniversary re-issue.				
Above hit: John TRAVOLTA Olivia NEWTON-JOHN.				
ALBUMS:	HITS 1			WEEKS 6
SANDY	Midsong	40	23 Dec 78	6
Apart from the title track, all others are earlier recordings from 1976/77.				

TREMELOES   UK

(See also Brian Poole and the Tremeloes.)

SINGLES:	HITS 13			WEEKS 131
HERE COMES MY BABY	CBS	4	4 Feb 67	11
Originally recorded by Cat Stevens.				
SILENCE IS GOLDEN	CBS	1	29 Apr 67	15
Originally recorded by the Four Seaons for the B-side of Rag Doll.				
EVEN THE BAD TIMES ARE GOOD	CBS	4	5 Aug 67	13
BE MINE (MI SEGUIRAI)	CBS	39	11 Nov 67	2
SUDDENLY YOU LOVE ME	CBS	6	20 Jan 68	11
HELULE HELULE	CBS	14	11 May 68	9
MY LITTLE LADY	CBS	6	21 Sep 68	12
I SHALL BE RELEASED	CBS	29	14 Dec 68	5
Above hit: TREMELOES with the Keith MANSFIELD STRINGS.				
HELLO WORLD	CBS	14	22 Mar 69	8
(CALL ME) NUMBER ONE	CBS	2	1 Nov 69	14
BY THE WAY	CBS	35	21 Mar 70	6
ME AND MY LIFE	CBS	4	12 Sep 70	18
HELLO BUDDY	CBS	32	10 Jul 71	7
ALBUMS:	HITS 1			WEEKS 7
HERE COMES THE TREMELOES	CBS	15	3 Jun 67	7

Jackie TRENT   UK

SINGLES:	HITS 3			WEEKS 17
WHERE ARE YOU NOW	Pye	1	24 Apr 65	11
WHEN SUMMERTIME IS OVER	Pye	39	3 Jul 65	2
I'LL BE THERE	Pye	38	5 Apr 69	4

Ralph TRESVANT US

(See also Janet Jackson; Luther Vandross.)

SINGLES:		HITS 1		WEEKS 8
SENSITIVITY	MCA	18	12 Jan 91	8
ALBUMS:		**HITS 1**		**WEEKS 3**
RALPH TRESVANT	MCA	37	23 Feb 91	3

TRI UK

SINGLES:		HITS 1		WEEKS 1
WE GOT THE LOVE	Epic	61	2 Sep 95	1

TRIBAL HOUSE US

SINGLES:		HITS 1		WEEKS 2
MOTHERLAND -A-FRI-CA-	Cooltempo	57	3 Feb 90	2

Tony TRIBE Jamaica

SINGLES:		HITS 1		WEEKS 2
RED, RED WINE	Downtown	50	19 Jul 69	1
RED, RED WINE [RE]	Downtown	46	9 Aug 69	1

A TRIBE CALLED QUEST US

(See also Fugees (Refugee Camp); Jungle Brothers.)

SINGLES:		HITS 7		WEEKS 18
BONITA APPLEBUM	Jive	47	18 Aug 90	3
CAN I KICK IT?	Jive	15	19 Jan 91	7
Samples Lou Reed's Walk On The Wild Side.				
OH MY GOD	Jive	68	11 Jun 94	1
1NCE AGAIN	Jive	34	13 Jul 96	2
Vocals by Tammy Lucas.				
STRESSED OUT	Jive	33	23 Nov 96	2
Above hit: A TRIBE CALLED QUEST featuring Faith EVANS and Raphael SAADIQ.				
THE JAM [EP]	Jive	61	23 Aug 97	1
Lead track: Jam. 2 other tracks on the EP, Mardi Fras At Midnight and Same Ol' Thing, are from the film 'Men In Black'.				
FIND A WAY	Jive	41	29 Aug 98	2
Samples Towa Tei's Dubnova (Parts 1 & 2).				
ALBUMS:		**HITS 5**		**WEEKS 9**
PEOPLE'S INSTINCTIVE TRAVELS . . .	Jive	54	19 May 90	1
THE LOW END THEORY	Jive	58	12 Oct 91	1
MIDNIGHT MARAUDERS	Jive	70	27 Nov 93	1
BEATS, RHYMES AND LIFE	Jive	28	10 Aug 96	4
THE LOVE MOVEMENT	Jive	38	10 Oct 98	1

A TRIBE OF TOFFS UK

SINGLES:		HITS 1		WEEKS 5
JOHN KETTLEY (IS A WEATHERMAN)	Completely Different	21	24 Dec 88	5

TRICKBABY UK

SINGLES:		HITS 1		WEEKS 2
INDIE-YARN	Logic	47	12 Oct 96	2

TRICKSTER (CMV'S) UK

SINGLES:		HITS 1		WEEKS 3
MOVE ON UP	AM:PM	19	4 Apr 98	3

TRICKY UK

SINGLES:		HITS 11		WEEKS 29
AFTERMATH	Fourth & Broadway	69	5 Feb 94	1
OVERCOME	Fourth & Broadway	34	28 Jan 95	3
BLACK STEEL	Fourth & Broadway	28	15 Apr 95	3
Originally recorded by Public Enemy from their 1988 album It Takes A Nation Of Millions To Hold Us Back.				
THE HELL [EP]	Fourth & Broadway	12	5 Aug 95	3
Lead track: Hell Is Around The Corner. The Gravediggaz appear on the EP's other tracks.				
Above hit: TRICKY vs. the GRAVEDIGGAZ.				
PUMPKIN	Fourth & Broadway	26	11 Nov 95	2
Vocals by Alison Goldfrapp.				
CHRISTIANSANDS	Fourth & Broadway	36	9 Nov 96	2
Vocals by Martina.				

MILK	*Mushroom*	10	*23 Nov 96*	7
Though credited on the chart, Tricky's contribution was only as a remixer of a secondary track of the CD.				
Above hit: GARBAGE featuring TRICKY.				
TRICKY KID	*Fourth & Broadway*	28	*11 Jan 97*	2
Samples the Commodores' The Zoo (The Human Zoo).				
MILK [RE]	*Mushroom*	74	*18 Jan 97*	1
MAKES ME WANNA DIE	*Fourth & Broadway*	29	*3 May 97*	2
Vocals by Martina. Samples Eric B and Rakim's To The Listeners.				
MONEY GREEDY / BROKEN HOMES	*Island*	25	*30 May 98*	2
Above hit: TRICKY / TRICKY featuring Polly Jean HARVEY.				
FOR REAL	*Island*	45	*21 Aug 99*	1
Vocals by Kioka Williams and Mad Dog.				
ALBUMS:	**HITS 4**		**WEEKS 41**	
MAXINQUAYE	*Fourth & Broadway*	3	*4 Mar 95*	35
PRE-MILLENNIUM TENSION	*Fourth & Broadway*	30	*23 Nov 96*	2
ANGELS WITH DIRTY FACES	*Island*	23	*6 Jun 98*	2
JUXTAPOSE	*Island*	22	*28 Aug 99*	2
Above hit: TRICKY with DJ MUGGS and GREASE.				

TRICKY DISCO   UK

(See also G.T.O.; Technohead.)

SINGLES:	**HITS 2**		**WEEKS 10**	
TRICKY DISCO	*Warp*	14	*28 Jul 90*	8
HOUSE FLY	*Warp*	55	*20 Apr 91*	2

TRIFFIDS   New Zealand

SINGLES:	**HITS 1**		**WEEKS 1**	
A TRICK OF THE LIGHT	*Island*	73	*6 Feb 88*	1
ALBUMS:	**HITS 1**		**WEEKS 1**	
THE BLACK SWAN	*Island*	63	*22 Apr 89*	1

TRILOGY – See C&C MUSIC FACTORY

TRINA and TAMARA   US

SINGLES:	**HITS 2**		**WEEKS 3**	
MY LOVE IS THE SHHH!	*Warner Brothers*	64	*7 Feb 98*	1
Above hit: SOMETHIN' FOR THE PEOPLE featuring TRINA and TAMARA.				
WHAT'D YOU COME HERE FOR?	*Columbia*	46	*12 Jun 99*	2

TRINIDAD OIL COMPANY   Trinidad

SINGLES:	**HITS 1**		**WEEKS 5**	
THE CALENDAR SONG (JANUARY, FEBRUARY, MARCH, APRIL, MAY)	*Harvest*	34	*21 May 77*	5

TRINIDAD SINGERS – See Murray HEAD

TRINITY – See Julie DRISCOLL, Brian AUGER and the TRINITY

TRIO   Germany

SINGLES:	**HITS 1**		**WEEKS 10**	
DA DA DA	*Mobile Suit Corporation*	2	*3 Jul 82*	10

TRIPLE X   Italy

SINGLES:	**HITS 1**		**WEEKS 2**	
FEEL THE SAME	*Sound Of Ministry*	32	*30 Oct 99*	2
Samples Delegations' You & I.				

TRIPPING DAISY   US

SINGLES:	**HITS 1**		**WEEKS 1**	
PIRANHA	*Island*	72	*30 Mar 96*	1

TRISTRAM VII – See NEW VAUDEVILLE BAND

TRIUMPH   Canada

SINGLES:	**HITS 1**		**WEEKS 2**	
I LIVE FOR THE WEEKEND	*RCA*	59	*22 Nov 80*	2
ALBUMS:	**HITS 2**		**WEEKS 8**	
PROGRESSIONS OF POWER	*RCA*	61	*10 May 80*	5
ALLIED FORCES	*RCA*	64	*3 Oct 81*	3

TROGGS   UK

SINGLES:	**HITS 10**		**WEEKS 87**	
WILD THING	*Fontana*	2	*7 May 66*	12
Originally recorded by Jordan Christopher and the Wild Ones.				

TRONIKHOUSE - TRUE

WITH A GIRL LIKE YOU	*Fontana*	1	*16 Jul 66*	12
I CAN'T CONTROL MYSELF	*Page One*	2	*1 Oct 66*	14
ANY WAY THAT YOU WANT ME	*Page One*	8	*17 Dec 66*	10
GIVE IT TO ME	*Page One*	12	*18 Feb 67*	10
NIGHT OF THE LONG GRASS	*Page One*	17	*3 Jun 67*	6
HI HI HAZEL	*Page One*	42	*29 Jul 67*	3
LOVE IS ALL AROUND	*Page One*	5	*21 Oct 67*	14
LITTLE GIRL	*Page One*	37	*2 Mar 68*	4
WILD THING [RR]	*Weekend*	69	*30 Oct 93*	2

Instrumental version used to accompany the ITV series 'Gladiators'. [AA] listed with War by Edwin Starr and Shadow.
Above hit: TROGGS and WOLF.

EPS:		**HITS 1**		**WEEKS 4**	
TROGGS TOPS	*Page One*	8	*25 Mar 67*	4

ALBUMS:		**HITS 4**		**WEEKS 35**	
FROM NOWHERE ... THE TROGGS	*Fontana*	6	*30 Jul 66*	16
TROGGLODYNAMITE	*Page One*	10	*25 Feb 67*	11
THE BEST OF THE TROGGS	*Page One*	24	*5 Aug 67*	5
GREATEST HITS	*PolyGram TV*	27	*16 Jul 94*	3

TRONIKHOUSE   US

SINGLES:		**HITS 1**		**WEEKS 1**	
UP TEMPO	*KMS UK*	68	*14 Mar 92*	1

John Scott TROTTER and his Orchestra – See Bing CROSBY

TROUBLE FUNK   US

SINGLES:		**HITS 1**		**WEEKS 3**	
WOMAN OF PRINCIPLE	*Fourth & Broadway*	65	*27 Jun 87*	3

ALBUMS:		**HITS 2**		**WEEKS 4**	
SAY WHAT!	*Fourth & Broadway*	75	*8 Nov 86*	2
TROUBLE OVER HERE, TROUBLE OVER THERE	*Fourth & Broadway*	54	*5 Sep 87*	2

Robin TROWER   UK

ALBUMS:		**HITS 5**		**WEEKS 16**	
FOR EARTH BELOW	*Chrysalis*	26	*1 Mar 75*	4
ROBIN TROWER LIVE	*Chrysalis*	15	*13 Mar 76*	6
LONG MISTY DAYS	*Chrysalis*	31	*30 Oct 76*	1
IN CITY DREAMS	*Chrysalis*	58	*29 Oct 77*	1
VICTIMS OF THE FURY	*Chrysalis*	61	*16 Feb 80*	4

Doris TROY   US

SINGLES:		**HITS 1**		**WEEKS 12**	
WHAT'CHA GONNA DO ABOUT IT?	*Atlantic*	37	*21 Nov 64*	7
WHAT'CHA GONNA DO ABOUT IT? [RE]	*Atlantic*	38	*23 Jan 65*	5

Elisabeth TROY – See SOUNDMAN and Don LLOYDIE with Elisabeth TROY; Y TRIBE featuring Elisabeth TROY

TRUBBLE   UK

SINGLES:		**HITS 1**		**WEEKS 5**	
DANCING BABY (OOGA - CHAKA)	*Yum! Yum! Boogie Food*	21	*26 Dec 98*	5

As seen on the TV series 'Ally McBeal'. Samples Blue Swede's Hooked On A Feeling.

TRUCE   UK

SINGLES:		**HITS 4**		**WEEKS 6**	
THE FINEST	*Big Life*	54	*2 Sep 95*	1
CELEBRATION OF LIFE	*Big Life*	51	*30 Mar 96*	1
NOTHIN' BUT A PARTY	*Big Life*	71	*29 Nov 97*	1
EYES DON'T LIE	*Big Life*	20	*5 Sep 98*	3

Andrea TRUE CONNECTION   US

SINGLES:		**HITS 2**		**WEEKS 16**	
MORE, MORE, MORE	*Buddah*	5	*17 Apr 76*	10
WHAT'S YOUR NAME, WHAT'S YOUR NUMBER	*Buddah*	34	*4 Mar 78*	6

TRUE FAITH and Bridgette GRACE with FINAL CUT   US

SINGLES:		**HITS 1**		**WEEKS 4**	
TAKE ME AWAY	*Network*	51	*2 Mar 91*	4

TRUE IMAGE – See Monie LOVE

Damon TRUEITT – See SOMORE featuring Damon TRUEITT

TRUMAN and WOLFF featuring STEEL HORSES
UK

SINGLES:	HITS 1			WEEKS 1
COME AGAIN	Multiply	57	22 Aug 98	1

TRUMPET MAN – See MONTANO vs the TRUMPET MAN

TRUSSEL
US

SINGLES:	HITS 1			WEEKS 4
LOVE INJECTION	Elektra	43	8 Mar 80	4

TRUTH
UK

SINGLES:	HITS 1			WEEKS 6
GIRL	Pye	27	5 Feb 66	6

Originally recorded by the Beatles.

TRUTH
UK

SINGLES:	HITS 3			WEEKS 16
CONFUSION (HITS US EVERYTIME)	Formation	22	11 Jun 83	7
A STEP IN THE RIGHT DIRECTION	Formation	32	27 Aug 83	7
NO STONE UNTURNED	Formation	66	4 Feb 84	2

TSD
UK

SINGLES:	HITS 2			WEEKS 2
HEART & SOUL	Avex UK	69	17 Feb 96	1
BABY I LOVE YOU	Avex UK	64	30 Mar 96	1

T2 featuring Robin S
US

(See also Robin S.)

SINGLES:	HITS 1			WEEKS 1
YOU GOT THE LOVE	Champion	62	4 Oct 97	1

Esera TUAOLO – See Richie RICH

TUBES
US

SINGLES:	HITS 3			WEEKS 18
WHITE PUNKS ON DOPE	A&M	28	19 Nov 77	4
PRIME TIME	A&M	34	28 Apr 79	10
DON'T WANT TO WAIT ANYMORE	Capitol	60	12 Sep 81	4
ALBUMS:	HITS 3			WEEKS 7
WHAT DO YOU WANT FROM LIFE	A&M	38	4 Mar 78	1

Live recordings.

REMOTE CONTROL	A&M	40	2 Jun 79	5
OUTSIDE INSIDE	Capitol	77	4 Jun 83	1

TUBEWAY ARMY – See Gary NUMAN

Barbara TUCKER
US

(See also B-Crew featuring Barbara Tucker, Ultra Nate, Dajae, Mone.)

SINGLES:	HITS 4			WEEKS 8
BEAUTIFUL PEOPLE	Positiva	23	5 Mar 94	3

Backing vocals from Byron Stingley of Ten City, Michael Watford and India.

I GET LIFTED	Positiva	33	26 Nov 94	2
STAY TOGETHER	Positiva	46	23 Sep 95	1
EVERYBODY DANCE (THE HORN SONG)	Positiva	28	8 Aug 98	2

Junior TUCKER
UK

SINGLES:	HITS 1			WEEKS 2
DON'T TEST	10 Records	54	2 Jun 90	2

Louise TUCKER – See MIDNIGHT BLUE (A project with) Louise TUCKER

Tommy TUCKER
US

SINGLES:	HITS 1			WEEKS 10
HI-HEEL SNEEKERS	Pye	23	28 Mar 64	10

TUFF JAM
UK

SINGLES:	HITS 1			WEEKS 1
NEED GOOD LOVE	Locked On	44	10 Oct 98	1

TULANE SISTERS – See Mitchell TOROK

Ike and Tina TURNER   US

(See also Tina Turner.)

SINGLES:	HITS 4			WEEKS 44	
RIVER DEEP - MOUNTAIN HIGH	London	3	11 Jun 66	13
TELL HER I'M NOT HOME	Warner Brothers	48	30 Jul 66	1
A LOVE LIKE YOURS	London	16	29 Oct 66	10
Originally recorded by Martha Reeves and the Vandellas.				
RIVER DEEP MOUNTAIN HIGH [RI]	London	33	15 Feb 69	7
NUTBUSH CITY LIMITS	United Artists	4	8 Sep 73	13
ALBUMS:	**HITS 1**			**WEEKS 1**
RIVER DEEP - MOUNTAIN HIGH	London	27	1 Oct 66	1

Ruby TURNER   UK

SINGLES:	HITS 7			WEEKS 31	
IF YOU'RE READY (COME GO WITH ME)	Jive	30	25 Jan 86	7
Above hit: Ruby TURNER featuring Jonathan BUTLER.				
I'M IN LOVE	Jive	61	29 Mar 86	4
BYE BABY	Jive	52	13 Sep 86	3
I'D RATHER GO BLIND	Jive	24	14 Mar 87	8
Originally recorded by Etta James.				
I'M IN LOVE [RI]	Jive	57	16 May 87	2
IT'S GONNA BE ALRIGHT	Jive	57	13 Jan 90	3
STAY WITH ME BABY	M&G	39	5 Feb 94	3
Theme from the Channel 4 TV series 'Comics'. Originally recorded by Lorraine Ellison in 1966.				
SHAKABOOM!	Telstar	64	9 Dec 95	1
Featured on 'Junior Gladiators' from TV's 'Scratchy And Co.'.				
Above hit: HUNTER featuring Ruby TURNER.				
ALBUMS:	**HITS 3**			**WEEKS 19**
WOMEN HOLD UP HALF THE SKY	Jive	47	18 Oct 86	11
THE MOTOWN SONG BOOK	Jive	22	8 Oct 88	6
PARADISE	Jive	74	17 Feb 90	2

Sammy TURNER   US

SINGLES:	HITS 1			WEEKS 2	
ALWAYS	London	26	14 Nov 59	2

Tina TURNER   US

(See also Ike and Tina Turner.)

SINGLES:	HITS 35			WEEKS 221	
LET'S STAY TOGETHER	Capitol	6	19 Nov 83	13
HELP	Capitol	40	25 Feb 84	6
WHAT'S LOVE GOT TO DO WITH IT	Capitol	3	16 Jun 84	16
BETTER BE GOOD TO ME	Capitol	45	15 Sep 84	5
PRIVATE DANCER	Capitol	26	17 Nov 84	9
Written by Mark Knopfler and features Jeff Beck on guitar.				
I CAN'T STAND THE RAIN	Capitol	57	2 Mar 85	3
Original by Ann Peebles reached No. 38 in the US in 1973.				
WE DON'T NEED ANOTHER HERO (THUNDERDOME)	Capitol	3	20 Jul 85	12
From the film 'Mad Max: Beyond Thunderdome'.				
ONE OF THE LIVING	Capitol	55	12 Oct 85	2
IT'S ONLY LOVE	A&M	29	2 Nov 85	6
Above hit: Bryan ADAMS and Tina TURNER.				
TYPICAL MALE	Capitol	33	23 Aug 86	6
TWO PEOPLE	Capitol	43	8 Nov 86	4
WHAT YOU GET IS WHAT YOU SEE	Capitol	30	14 Mar 87	7
BREAK EVERY RULE	Capitol	43	13 Jun 87	3
TEARING US APART	Duck	56	20 Jun 87	3
Above hit: Eric CLAPTON and Tina TURNER.				
ADDICTED TO LOVE (LIVE)	Capitol	71	19 Mar 88	2
THE BEST	Capitol	5	2 Sep 89	12
Edgar Winter on sax, originally recorded by Bonnie Tyler.				
I DON'T WANNA LOSE YOU	Capitol	8	18 Nov 89	11
STEAMY WINDOWS	Capitol	13	17 Feb 90	6
Originally recorded by Tony Joe White.				
LOOK ME IN THE HEART	Capitol	31	11 Aug 90	6
BE TENDER WITH ME BABY	Capitol	28	13 Oct 90	4
IT TAKES TWO	Warner Brothers	5	24 Nov 90	8
Above hit: Rod STEWART and Tina TURNER.				
NUTBUSH CITY LIMITS (THE 90'S VERSION)	Capitol	23	21 Sep 91	5
WAY OF THE WORLD	Capitol	13	23 Nov 91	7
LOVE THING	Capitol	29	15 Feb 92	4
I WANT YOU NEAR ME	Capitol	22	6 Jun 92	4
I DON'T WANNA FIGHT	Parlophone	7	22 May 93	9
Originally recorded by Lulu.				
DISCO INFERNO	Parlophone	12	28 Aug 93	6

WHY MUST WE WAIT UNTIL TONIGHT	*Parlophone*	16	*30 Oct 93*	4
Above 3 from the film 'What's Love Got To Do With It'.				
GOLDENEYE	*Parlophone*	10	*18 Nov 95*	9
From the James Bond film of the same name.				
WHATEVER YOU WANT	*Parlophone*	23	*23 Mar 96*	6
ON SILENT WINGS	*Parlophone*	13	*8 Jun 96*	6
Features backing vocals by Sting.				
MISSING YOU	*Parlophone*	12	*27 Jul 96*	5
SOMETHING BEAUTIFUL REMAINS	*Parlophone*	27	*19 Oct 96*	2
IN YOUR WILDEST DREAMS	*Parlophone*	32	*21 Dec 96*	3
Above hit: Tina TURNER featuring Barry WHITE.				
WHEN THE HEARTACHE IS OVER	*Parlophone*	10	*30 Oct 99*	7
Above hit: TINA.				
ALBUMS:	**HITS 8**			**WEEKS 510**
PRIVATE DANCER	*Capitol*	2	*30 Jun 84*	147
BREAK EVERY RULE	*Capitol*	2	*20 Sep 86*	49
LIVE IN EUROPE	*Capitol*	8	*2 Apr 88*	13
Live recordings from the European leg of her world tour, 1987.				
FOREIGN AFFAIR	*Capitol*	1	*30 Sep 89*	78
SIMPLY THE BEST	*Capitol*	2	*12 Oct 91*	141
Compilation.				
WHAT'S LOVE GOT TO DO WITH IT [OST]	*Parlophone*	1	*19 Jun 93*	33
WILDEST DREAMS	*Parlophone*	4	*13 Apr 96*	41
TWENTY FOUR SEVEN	*Parlophone*	9	*13 Nov 99*	8

TURNTABLE ORCHESTRA
US

SINGLES:	**HITS 1**			**WEEKS 4**
YOU'RE GONNA MISS ME	*Republic*	52	*21 Jan 89*	4

TURTLES
US

SINGLES:	**HITS 3**			**WEEKS 39**
HAPPY TOGETHER	*London*	12	*25 Mar 67*	12
SHE'D RATHER BE WITH ME	*London*	4	*17 Jun 67*	15
ELENORE	*London*	7	*2 Nov 68*	12
ALBUMS:	**HITS 1**			**WEEKS 9**
HAPPY TOGETHER	*London*	18	*22 Jul 67*	9

TWA
UK

SINGLES:	**HITS 1**			**WEEKS 1**
NASTY GIRLS	*Mercury*	51	*16 Sep 95*	1

Shania TWAIN
Canada

SINGLES:	**HITS 5**			**WEEKS 57**
YOU'RE STILL THE ONE	*Mercury*	10	*28 Feb 98*	10
WHEN	*Mercury*	18	*13 Jun 98*	4
FROM THIS MOMENT ON	*Mercury*	9	*28 Nov 98*	8
Features the Brooklyn Philharmonic Orchestra.				
THAT DON'T IMPRESS ME MUCH	*Mercury*	3	*22 May 99*	21
MAN! I FEEL LIKE A WOMAN!	*Mercury*	3	*2 Oct 99*	14
ALBUMS:	**HITS 1**			**WEEKS 74**
COME ON OVER	*Mercury*	15	*21 Mar 98*	36
COME ON OVER [RE]	*Mercury*	1	*17 Apr 99*	38
From 5 Jun 99 re-released with additional track. Peak position reached on 11 Sep 99.				

TWEETS
UK

SINGLES:	**HITS 2**			**WEEKS 34**
BIRDIE SONG (BIRDIE DANCE)	*PRT*	2	*12 Sep 81*	23
Originally recorded by Cash And Carry. Certain copies were released with title reflecting only Birdie Song.				
LET'S ALL SING LIKE THE BIRDIES SING	*PRT*	44	*5 Dec 81*	6
BIRDIE SONG (BIRDIE DANCE) [RE]	*PRT*	46	*18 Dec 82*	5

TWELFTH NIGHT
UK

ALBUMS:	**HITS 1**			**WEEKS 2**
ART AND ILLUSION	*Music For Nations*	83	*27 Oct 84*	2

20 FINGERS
US

SINGLES:	**HITS 2**			**WEEKS 14**
SHORT DICK MAN	*Multiply*	21	*26 Nov 94*	4
SHORT SHORT MAN [RM]	*Multiply*	11	*30 Sep 95*	7
Remixed by Strike.				
Above 2: 20 FINGERS featuring GILLETTE.				
LICK IT	*ZYX*	48	*30 Sep 95*	3
Above hit: 20 FINGERS featuring ROULA.				

21ST CENTURY GIRLS
UK

SINGLES:		HITS 1			WEEKS 4
21ST CENTURY GIRLS	*19 Recordings*	16	*12 Jun 99*	4

TWENTY 4 SEVEN featuring CAPTAIN HOLLYWOOD
Germany/US

(See also Captain Hollywood Project.)

SINGLES:		HITS 2			WEEKS 20
I CAN'T STAND IT	*BCM*	7	*22 Sep 90*	10
ARE YOU DREAMING?	*BCM*	17	*24 Nov 90*	10

ALBUMS:		HITS 1			WEEKS 2
STREET MOVES	*BCM*	69	*19 Jan 91*	2

TWICE AS MUCH
UK

SINGLES:		HITS 1			WEEKS 9
SITTIN' ON A FENCE	*Immediate*	25	*18 Jun 66*	9

TWIGGY
UK

SINGLES:		HITS 1			WEEKS 10
HERE I GO AGAIN	*Mercury*	17	*14 Aug 76*	10

ALBUMS:		HITS 2			WEEKS 11
TWIGGY	*Mercury*	33	*21 Aug 76*	8
PLEASE GET MY NAME RIGHT	*Mercury*	35	*30 Apr 77*	3

TWILIGHT – See Roger SANCHEZ

TWIN HYPE
US

SINGLES:		HITS 1			WEEKS 2
DO IT TO THE CROWD	*Profile*	65	*15 Jul 89*	2

TWINKLE
UK

SINGLES:		HITS 2			WEEKS 20
TERRY	*Decca*	4	*28 Nov 64*	15
GOLDEN LIGHTS	*Decca*	21	*27 Feb 65*	5

TWISTED SISTER
US

SINGLES:		HITS 5			WEEKS 28
I AM (I'M ME)	*Atlantic*	18	*26 Mar 83*	9
THE KIDS ARE BACK	*Atlantic*	32	*28 May 83*	6
YOU CAN'T STOP ROCK 'N' ROLL	*Atlantic*	43	*20 Aug 83*	4
WE'RE NOT GONNA TAKE IT	*Atlantic*	58	*2 Jun 84*	6
LEADER OF THE PACK	*Atlantic*	47	*18 Jan 86*	3

ALBUMS:		HITS 5			WEEKS 20
UNDER THE BLADE	*Secret*	70	*25 Sep 82*	3
YOU CAN'T STOP ROCK 'N' ROLL	*Atlantic*	14	*7 May 83*	9
STAY HUNGRY	*Atlantic*	34	*16 Jun 84*	5
COME OUT AND PLAY	*Atlantic*	95	*14 Dec 85*	1
LOVE IS FOR SUCKERS	*Atlantic*	57	*25 Jul 87*	2

Conway TWITTY
US

SINGLES:		HITS 5			WEEKS 36
IT'S ONLY MAKE BELIEVE	*MGM*	1	*15 Nov 58*	15
THE STORY OF MY LOVE	*MGM*	30	*28 Mar 59*	1
MONA LISA	*MGM*	5	*22 Aug 59*	14
IS A BLUE BIRD BLUE	*MGM*	43	*23 Jul 60*	3
C'EST SI BON (IT'S SO GOOD)	*MGM*	40	*25 Feb 61*	3

Originally recorded by Danny Kaye in 1950.

2 BAD MICE
UK

SINGLES:		HITS 2			WEEKS 4
HOLD IT DOWN	*Moving Shadow*	70	*15 Feb 92*	1
HOLD IT DOWN [RE]	*Moving Shadow*	48	*8 Aug 92*	2
BOMBSCARE	*Arista*	46	*7 Sep 96*	1

Vocals by Lady Mouse Brucella.

TWO COWBOYS
Italy

SINGLES:		HITS 1			WEEKS 11
EVERYBODY GONFI GON	*3 Beat*	7	*9 Jul 94*	11

2 EIVISSA
Germany

SINGLES:		HITS 1		WEEKS 6	
OH LA LA LA	Club Tools	13	4 Oct 97	6
Samples Crystal Waters' Gypsy Woman.				

2 FOR JOY
UK

SINGLES:		HITS 2		WEEKS 3	
IN A STATE	Mercury	61	1 Dec 90	1
Above hit: 2 FOR JOY featuring Addell BENJAMIN.				
LET THE BASS KICK	All Around The World	67	9 Nov 91	2

2-4 FAMILY
UK/US/Korea

SINGLES:		HITS 1		WEEKS 1	
LEAN ON ME (WITH THE FAMILY)	Epic	69	29 May 99	1

2 FUNKY 2 featuring Kathryn DION
UK

SINGLES:		HITS 1		WEEKS 4	
BROTHERS AND SISTERS	Logic	56	6 Nov 93	2
Above hit: 2 FUNKY 2 starring Kathryn DION.				
BROTHERS AND SISTERS [RM]	All Around The World	36	30 Nov 96	2
Remixed by the Porn Kings.				

2 HOUSE
US

SINGLES:		HITS 1		WEEKS 1	
GO TECHNO	Atlantic	65	21 Mar 92	1

2 IN A ROOM
US

SINGLES:		HITS 6		WEEKS 15	
SOMEBODY IN THE HOUSE SAY YEAH!	Big Life	66	18 Nov 89	1
WIGGLE IT	SBK	3	26 Jan 91	8
SHE'S GOT ME GOING CRAZY	SBK	54	6 Apr 91	2
EL TRAGO (THE DRINK)	Positiva	34	22 Oct 94	2
AHORA ES (NOW IS THE TIME)	Positiva	43	8 Apr 95	1
GIDDY-UP	Encore	74	17 Aug 96	1
ALBUMS:		HITS 1		WEEKS 1	
WIGGLE IT	SBK	73	2 Mar 91	1

2 IN A TENT
UK

SINGLES:		HITS 2		WEEKS 7	
WHEN I'M CLEANING WINDOWS (TURNED OUT NICE AGAIN)	Silly Money	25	17 Dec 94	5
Samples George Formby's 1936 recording of the song.				
BOOGIE WOOGIE BUGLE BOY (DON'T STOP)	Bald Cat	48	13 May 95	1
Marrying together recordings from the Andrew Sisters with the Outhere Brothers.				
Above hit: 2 IN A TANK.				
WHEN I'M CLEANING WINDOWS (TURNED OUT NICE AGAIN) [RE]	Silly Money	62	6 Jan 96	1

2 MAD
UK

SINGLES:		HITS 1		WEEKS 4	
THINKIN' ABOUT YOUR BODY	Big Life	43	9 Feb 91	4

TWO MAN SOUND
Belgium

SINGLES:		HITS 1		WEEKS 7	
QUE TAL AMERICA	Miracle/Gull	46	20 Jan 79	7

TWO MEN, A DRUM MACHINE AND A TRUMPET
UK

SINGLES:		HITS 2		WEEKS 17	
I'M TIRED OF GETTING PUSHED AROUND	London	18	9 Jan 88	8
The label credits act as Two Guys, while the sleeve credits Two Men.				
HEAT IT UP	Jive	21	25 Jun 88	9
Above hit: WEE PAPA GIRL RAPPERS featuring TWO MEN AND A DRUM MACHINE.				

TWO NATIONS
UK

SINGLES:		HITS 1		WEEKS 1	
THAT'S THE WAY IT FEELS	10 Records	74	20 Jun 87	1

TWO PEOPLE
UK

SINGLES:		HITS 1		WEEKS 2	
HEAVEN	Polydor	63	31 Jan 87	2

2WO THIRD3
UK

SINGLES:		HITS 4			WEEKS 15
HEAR ME CALLING	Epic	48	19 Feb 94	3
EASE THE PRESSURE	Epic	45	11 Jun 94	2
I WANT THE WORLD	Epic	20	8 Oct 94	5
Backing vocals by Helen Terry.				
I WANT TO BE ALONE	Epic	29	17 Dec 94	5

2 UNLIMITED
Holland

SINGLES:		HITS 14			WEEKS 112
GET READY FOR THIS	PWL Continental	2	5 Oct 91	15
TWILIGHT ZONE	PWL Continental	2	25 Jan 92	10
WORKAHOLIC	PWL Continental	4	2 May 92	7
THE MAGIC FRIEND	PWL Continental	11	15 Aug 92	7
NO LIMIT	PWL Continental	1	30 Jan 93	16
TRIBAL DANCE	PWL Continental	4	8 May 93	11
FACES	PWL Continental	8	4 Sep 93	7
MAXIMUM OVERDRIVE	PWL Continental	15	20 Nov 93	8
LET THE BEAT CONTROL YOUR BODY	PWL Continental	6	19 Feb 94	9
THE REAL THING	PWL Continental	6	21 May 94	7
NO ONE	PWL Continental	17	1 Oct 94	6
HERE I GO	PWL Continental	22	25 Mar 95	3
DO WHAT'S GOOD FOR ME	PWL Continental	16	21 Oct 95	4
WANNA GET UP	Big Life	38	11 Jul 98	2
ALBUMS:		HITS 4			WEEKS 38
GET READY	PWL Continental	37	7 Mar 92	3
NO LIMITS	PWL Continental	1	22 May 93	21
REAL THINGS	PWL Continental	1	18 Jun 94	9
HITS UNLIMITED	PWL International	27	11 Nov 95	5

2K
UK

(See also Justified Ancients Of Mu Mu; KLF; Timelords.)

SINGLES:		HITS 1			WEEKS 2
***K THE MILLENNIUM	Blast First	28	25 Oct 97	2
Samples The KLF's Kick Out The Jams and Isaac Hayes' Theme From Shaft.				

2PAC
US

SINGLES:		HITS 13			WEEKS 60
CALIFORNIA LOVE	Death Row	6	13 Apr 96	8
Samples Roger's So Ruff So Tuff and Joe Cocker's Woman To Woman.				
Above hit: 2PAC featuring DR DRE.				
HOW DO YOU WANT IT	Death Row	17	27 Jul 96	4
Samples Body Heat by Quincy Jones.				
Above hit: 2PAC (featuring KC and JOJO).				
I AIN'T MAD AT CHA	Death Row	13	30 Nov 96	9
TO LIVE & DIE IN LA	Interscope	10	12 Apr 97	4
Above hit: MAKAVELI (2 PAC is MAKAVELI).				
WANTED DEAD OR ALIVE	Def Jam	16	26 Apr 97	3
From the film 'Gridlock'd'.				
Above hit: 2 PAC and SNOOP DOGGY DOGG.				
TOSS IT UP	Interscope	15	9 Aug 97	3
Above hit: MAKAVELI.				
I WONDER IF HEAVEN GOT A GHETTO	Jive	21	10 Jan 98	4
Vocals by Charmayne Maxee of Brownstone. Samples Cameo's The Two Of Us.				
HAIL MARY	Interscope	43	14 Feb 98	1
Above hit: MAKAVELI.				
DO FOR LOVE	Jive	12	13 Jun 98	4
Samples Bobby Caldwell's What You Can't Do For Love.				
Above hit: 2PAC featuring Eric WILLIAMS of BLACKSTREET.				
RUNNIN'	Black Jam	15	18 Jul 98	3
Originally recorded in 1995.				
Above hit: 2PAC and NOTORIOUS B.I.G.				
HAPPY HOME	Eagle	17	28 Nov 98	2
CHANGES	Jive	3	20 Feb 99	12
Samples Bruce Hornsby And The Range's The Way It Is.				
DEAR MAMA	Jive	27	3 Jul 99	3
Tribute to his mother Afeni Shakur.				
ALBUMS:		HITS 5			WEEKS 37
ALL EYEZ ON ME	Death Row	32	9 Mar 96	5
THE DON KILLUMINATI – THE SEVEN DAY THEORY	Death Row	53	16 Nov 96	1
Above hit: MAKAVELI.				
R U STILL DOWN? (REMEMBER ME)	Jive	44	6 Dec 97	1
Album of previously unreleased songs.				

IN HIS OWN WORDS	Eagle	65	8 Aug 98	1
Consists of studio interviews at KMEL Radio.				
GREATEST HITS	Jive	17	12 Dec 98	29
Compilation includes 4 unreleased tracks.				

Tommy TYCHO – See David GRAY and Tommy TYCHO

TYGERS OF PAN TANG   UK

SINGLES:	HITS 4		WEEKS 15	
HELLBOUND	MCA	48	14 Feb 81	3
LOVE POTION NO. 9	MCA	45	27 Mar 82	6
Original by the Clovers reached No. 23 in the US in 1959.				
RENDEZVOUS	MCA	49	10 Jul 82	4
PARIS BY AIR	MCA	63	11 Sep 82	2
ALBUMS:	**HITS 4**		**WEEKS 20**	
WILD CAT	MCA	18	30 Aug 80	5
SPELLBOUND	MCA	33	18 Apr 81	4
CRAZY NIGHTS	MCA	51	21 Nov 81	3
THE CAGE	MCA	13	28 Aug 82	8

Bonnie TYLER   UK

SINGLES:	HITS 11		WEEKS 82	
LOST IN FRANCE	RCA Victor	9	30 Oct 76	11
MORE THAN A LOVER	RCA Victor	27	19 Mar 77	6
IT'S A HEARTACHE	RCA Victor	4	3 Dec 77	12
Features Mike Gibbins from Badfinger on drums.				
Above hit: Bonnie TYLER and the Bonnie TYLER BAND.				
MARRIED MEN	RCA Victor	35	30 Jun 79	6
From the film 'The World Is Full Of Married Men'.				
TOTAL ECLIPSE OF THE HEART	CBS	1	19 Feb 83	12
Male vocalist is Rory Dodd.				
FASTER THAN THE SPEED OF LIGHT	CBS	43	7 May 83	4
HAVE YOU EVER SEEN THE RAIN	CBS	47	25 Jun 83	3
A ROCKIN' GOOD WAY	Epic	5	7 Jan 84	9
Originally recorded by Priscilla Bowman.				
Above hit: SHAKY and BONNIE.				
HOLDING OUT FOR A HERO	CBS	2	31 Aug 85	13
From the film 'Footloose'. Original release reached No. 96 in 1984.				
LOVING YOU'S A DIRTY JOB BUT SOMEBODY'S GOTTA DO IT	CBS	73	14 Dec 85	2
Above hit: Bonnie TYLER, guest vocalist Todd RUNDGREN.				
HOLDING OUT FOR A HERO [RI]	Total	69	28 Dec 91	2
MAKING LOVE (OUT OF NOTHING AT ALL)	East West	45	27 Jan 96	2
Original by Air Supply reached No. 2 in the US in 1983.				
ALBUMS:	**HITS 4**		**WEEKS 75**	
COMPILATION ALBUMS:	**HITS 1**		**WEEKS 16**	
FASTER THAN THE SPEED OF NIGHT	CBS	1	16 Apr 83	45
SECRET DREAMS AND FORBIDDEN FIRE	CBS	24	17 May 86	12
THE GREATEST HITS	Telstar	24	29 Nov 86	17
HIDE YOUR HEART	CBS	78	21 May 88	1
HEAVEN AND HELL	Telstar	9	25 Nov 89	12
Features solo recordings by each artist and was thus an entry in the compilation chart.				
Above hit: MEAT LOAF/Bonnie TYLER.				
HEAVEN AND HELL [RI]	Columbia	12	16 Sep 95	4

TYMES   US

SINGLES:	HITS 5		WEEKS 41	
SO MUCH IN LOVE	Cameo-Parkway	21	27 Jul 63	8
PEOPLE	Direction	16	18 Jan 69	10
From the film 'Funny Girl'.				
YOU LITTLE TRUSTMAKER	RCA Victor	18	21 Sep 74	9
M/S GRACE	RCA Victor	1	21 Dec 74	11
GOD'S GONNA PUNISH YOU	RCA Victor	41	17 Jan 76	3

TYPE O NEGATIVE   US

ALBUMS:	HITS 2		WEEKS 2	
OCTOBER RUST	Roadrunner	26	14 Sep 96	1
WORLD COMING DOWN	Roadrunner	49	2 Oct 99	1

TYPICALLY TROPICAL   UK

SINGLES:	HITS 1		WEEKS 11	
BARBADOS	Gull	1	5 Jul 75	11

TYRANNOSAURUS REX – See T. REX

TYREE

<table>
<tr><td colspan="5" align="right">US</td></tr>
<tr><td>SINGLES:</td><td>HITS 3</td><td></td><td colspan="2" align="right">WEEKS 10</td></tr>
<tr><td>TURN UP THE BASS</td><td>ffrr</td><td>12</td><td>25 Feb 89</td><td>7</td></tr>
<tr><td colspan="5">Above hit: TYREE Rap by KOOL ROCK STEADY.</td></tr>
<tr><td>HARDCORE HIP HOUSE</td><td>DJ International</td><td>70</td><td>6 May 89</td><td>2</td></tr>
<tr><td>MOVE YOUR BODY</td><td>DJ International</td><td>72</td><td>2 Dec 89</td><td>1</td></tr>
<tr><td colspan="5">Above hit: TYREE featuring J.M.D.</td></tr>
</table>

TYRESE

<table>
<tr><td colspan="5" align="right">US</td></tr>
<tr><td>SINGLES:</td><td>HITS 2</td><td></td><td colspan="2" align="right">WEEKS 2</td></tr>
<tr><td>NOBODY ELSE</td><td>RCA</td><td>59</td><td>31 Jul 99</td><td>1</td></tr>
<tr><td>SWEET LADY</td><td>RCA</td><td>55</td><td>25 Sept 99</td><td>1</td></tr>
</table>

TYRREL CORPORATION

<table>
<tr><td colspan="5" align="right">UK</td></tr>
<tr><td>SINGLES:</td><td>HITS 5</td><td></td><td colspan="2" align="right">WEEKS 9</td></tr>
<tr><td>THE BOTTLE</td><td>Volante</td><td>71</td><td>14 Mar 92</td><td>1</td></tr>
<tr><td>GOING HOME</td><td>Volante</td><td>58</td><td>15 Aug 92</td><td>2</td></tr>
<tr><td>WAKING WITH A STRANGER / ONE DAY</td><td>Volante</td><td>59</td><td>10 Oct 92</td><td>1</td></tr>
<tr><td>YOU'RE NOT HERE</td><td>Cooltempo</td><td>42</td><td>24 Sep 94</td><td>2</td></tr>
<tr><td colspan="5">Backing vocals by Juliet Roberts.</td></tr>
<tr><td>BETTER DAYS AHEAD</td><td>Cooltempo</td><td>29</td><td>14 Jan 95</td><td>3</td></tr>
</table>

TZANT

<table>
<tr><td colspan="5" align="right">UK</td></tr>
<tr><td>SINGLES:</td><td>HITS 3</td><td></td><td colspan="2" align="right">WEEKS 10</td></tr>
<tr><td>HOT & WET (BELIEVE IT)</td><td>Logic</td><td>36</td><td>7 Sep 96</td><td>2</td></tr>
<tr><td>SOUNDS OF WICKEDNESS</td><td>Logic</td><td>11</td><td>25 Apr 98</td><td>6</td></tr>
<tr><td colspan="5">Above hit: TZANT featuring the ORIGINAL ODC. MC.</td></tr>
<tr><td>BOUNCE WITH THE MASSIVE</td><td>Logic</td><td>39</td><td>22 Aug 98</td><td>2</td></tr>
</table>

Judie TZUKE

<table>
<tr><td colspan="5" align="right">UK</td></tr>
<tr><td>SINGLES:</td><td>HITS 1</td><td></td><td colspan="2" align="right">WEEKS 10</td></tr>
<tr><td>STAY WITH ME TILL DAWN</td><td>Rocket</td><td>16</td><td>14 Jul 79</td><td>10</td></tr>
<tr><td>ALBUMS:</td><td>HITS 8</td><td></td><td colspan="2" align="right">WEEKS 61</td></tr>
<tr><td>WELCOME TO THE CRUISE</td><td>Rocket</td><td>14</td><td>4 Aug 79</td><td>17</td></tr>
<tr><td>SPORTS CAR</td><td>Rocket</td><td>7</td><td>10 May 80</td><td>11</td></tr>
<tr><td>I AM PHOENIX</td><td>Rocket</td><td>17</td><td>16 May 81</td><td>10</td></tr>
<tr><td>SHOOT THE MOON</td><td>Chrysalis</td><td>19</td><td>17 Apr 82</td><td>10</td></tr>
<tr><td>ROAD NOISE – THE OFFICIAL BOOTLEG</td><td>Chrysalis</td><td>39</td><td>30 Oct 82</td><td>4</td></tr>
<tr><td>RITMO</td><td>Chrysalis</td><td>26</td><td>1 Oct 83</td><td>5</td></tr>
<tr><td>THE CAT IS OUT</td><td>Legacy</td><td>35</td><td>15 Jun 85</td><td>3</td></tr>
<tr><td>TURNING STONES</td><td>Polydor</td><td>57</td><td>29 Apr 89</td><td>1</td></tr>
</table>

U

U.C.C. – See URBAN COOKIE COLLECTIVE

U.F.O.

<table>
<tr><td colspan="5" align="right">UK/Germany</td></tr>
<tr><td>SINGLES:</td><td>HITS 7</td><td></td><td colspan="2" align="right">WEEKS 31</td></tr>
<tr><td>ONLY YOU CAN ROCK ME</td><td>Chrysalis</td><td>50</td><td>5 Aug 78</td><td>4</td></tr>
<tr><td>DOCTOR DOCTOR</td><td>Chrysalis</td><td>35</td><td>27 Jan 79</td><td>6</td></tr>
<tr><td>SHOOT, SHOOT</td><td>Chrysalis</td><td>48</td><td>31 Mar 79</td><td>5</td></tr>
<tr><td colspan="5">Above 2 are live recordings. The studio recording of Doctor Doctor was originally released in 1974.</td></tr>
<tr><td>YOUNG BLOOD</td><td>Chrysalis</td><td>36</td><td>12 Jan 80</td><td>5</td></tr>
<tr><td colspan="5">Produced by George Martin.</td></tr>
<tr><td>LONELY HEART</td><td>Chrysalis</td><td>41</td><td>17 Jan 81</td><td>5</td></tr>
<tr><td>LET IT RAIN</td><td>Chrysalis</td><td>62</td><td>30 Jan 82</td><td>3</td></tr>
<tr><td>WHEN IT'S TIME TO ROCK</td><td>Chrysalis</td><td>70</td><td>19 Mar 83</td><td>3</td></tr>
<tr><td>ALBUMS:</td><td>HITS 9</td><td></td><td colspan="2" align="right">WEEKS 48</td></tr>
<tr><td>LIGHTS OUT</td><td>Chrysalis</td><td>54</td><td>4 Jun 77</td><td>2</td></tr>
<tr><td>OBSESSION</td><td>Chrysalis</td><td>26</td><td>15 Jul 78</td><td>7</td></tr>
<tr><td>STRANGERS IN THE NIGHT</td><td>Chrysalis</td><td>8</td><td>10 Feb 79</td><td>11</td></tr>
<tr><td colspan="5">Live recordings.</td></tr>
<tr><td>NO PLACE TO RUN</td><td>Chrysalis</td><td>11</td><td>19 Jan 80</td><td>7</td></tr>
<tr><td>THE WILD THE WILLING AND THE INNOCENT</td><td>Chrysalis</td><td>19</td><td>24 Jan 81</td><td>5</td></tr>
<tr><td>MECHANIX</td><td>Chrysalis</td><td>8</td><td>20 Feb 82</td><td>6</td></tr>
<tr><td>MAKING CONTACT</td><td>Chrysalis</td><td>32</td><td>12 Feb 83</td><td>4</td></tr>
<tr><td>HEADSTONE – THE BEST OF UFO</td><td>Chrysalis</td><td>39</td><td>3 Sep 83</td><td>4</td></tr>
<tr><td>MISDEMEANOR</td><td>Chrysalis</td><td>74</td><td>16 Nov 85</td><td>2</td></tr>
</table>

U.H.F.

<table>
<tr><td colspan="5" align="right">US</td></tr>
<tr><td>SINGLES:</td><td>HITS 1</td><td></td><td colspan="2" align="right">WEEKS 4</td></tr>
<tr><td>U.H.F. / EVERYTHING</td><td>XL Recordings</td><td>46</td><td>14 Dec 91</td><td>4</td></tr>
</table>

U.K. | | | | UK

SINGLES:	HITS 1			WEEKS 2
NOTHING TO LOSE	Polydor	67	30 Jun 79	2
ALBUMS:	**HITS 1**			**WEEKS 3**
U.K.	Polydor	43	27 May 78	3

U.K. SUBS | | | | UK

SINGLES:	HITS 7			WEEKS 39
STRANGLEHOLD	Gems	26	23 Jun 79	8
TOMORROW'S GIRLS	Gems	28	8 Sep 79	6
SHE'S NOT THERE/KICKS [EP]	Gems	36	1 Dec 79	7
Lead track: She's Not There.				
WARHEAD	Gems	30	8 Mar 80	4
TEENAGE	Gems	32	17 May 80	5
PARTY IN PARIS	Gems	37	25 Oct 80	4
KEEP ON RUNNING (TILL YOU BURN)	Gems	41	18 Apr 81	5
ALBUMS:	**HITS 4**			**WEEKS 26**
ANOTHER KIND OF BLUES	Gem	21	13 Oct 79	6
BRAND NEW AGE	Gem	18	19 Apr 80	9
CRASH COURSE	Gem	8	27 Sep 80	6
DIMINISHED RESPONSIBILITY	Gem	18	21 Feb 81	5

U.S.U.R.A. – See USURA

U.T.F.O. | | | | US

ALBUMS:	HITS 1			WEEKS 1
ROXANNE ROXANNE (6 TRACK VERSION)	Streetwave	72	16 Mar 85	1
12" single ineligible for the singles chart.				

UB40 | | | | UK

SINGLES:	HITS 45			WEEKS 327
KING / FOOD FOR THOUGHT	Graduate	4	8 Mar 80	13
King is dedicated to Martin Luther King.				
MY WAY OF THINKING / I THINK IT'S GOING TO RAIN TODAY	Graduate	6	14 Jun 80	10
I Think I'ts Going To Rain Today was originally recorded by Randy Newman in 1968.				
Above 2: U.B.40.				
THE EARTH DIES SCREAMING / DREAM A LIE	Graduate	10	1 Nov 80	12
DON'T LET IT PASS YOU BY / DON'T SLOW DOWN	DEP International	16	23 May 81	9
ONE IN TEN	DEP International	7	8 Aug 81	10
Written about the unemployment situation in the UK at the time.				
I WON'T CLOSE MY EYES	DEP International	32	13 Feb 82	6
LOVE IS ALL IS ALRIGHT	DEP International	29	15 May 82	7
SO HERE I AM	DEP International	25	28 Aug 82	9
I'VE GOT MINE	DEP International	45	5 Feb 83	4
RED RED WINE	DEP International	1	20 Aug 83	14
Originally recorded by Neil Diamond in 1968.				
PLEASE DON'T MAKE ME CRY	DEP International	10	15 Oct 83	8
Originally recorded by Winston Groovy.				
MANY RIVERS TO CROSS	DEP International	16	10 Dec 83	8
Originally recorded by Jimmy Cliff.				
CHERRY OH BABY	DEP International	12	17 Mar 84	8
Originally recorded by Eric Donaldson.				
IF IT HAPPENS AGAIN	DEP International	9	22 Sep 84	8
RIDDLE ME	DEP International	59	1 Dec 84	2
I GOT YOU BABE	DEP International	1	3 Aug 85	13
Above hit: UB40 Guest vocals by Chrissie HYNDE.				
DON'T BREAK MY HEART	DEP International	3	26 Oct 85	13
SING OUR OWN SONG	DEP International	5	12 Jul 86	9
Released to support black activists in South Africa.				
ALL I WANT TO DO	DEP International	41	27 Sep 86	4
RAT IN MI KITCHEN	DEP International	12	17 Jan 87	7
WATCHDOGS	DEP International	39	9 May 87	4
MAYBE TOMORROW	DEP International	14	10 Oct 87	8
RECKLESS	EMI	17	27 Feb 88	8
Above hit: Afrika BAMBAATAA and FAMILY featuring UB40.				
BREAKFAST IN BED	DEP International	6	18 Jun 88	11
Originally recorded by Dusty Springfield.				
Above hit: UB40 with Chrissie HYNDE.				
WHERE DID I GO WRONG	DEP International	26	20 Aug 88	6
I WOULD DO FOR YOU	DEP International	45	17 Jun 89	4
HOMELY GIRL	DEP International	6	18 Nov 89	10
HERE I AM (COME AND TAKE ME)	DEP International	46	27 Jan 90	3
Original by Al Green reached No. 10 in the US in 1973.				
KINGSTON TOWN	DEP International	4	31 Mar 90	12
Originally recorded by Lord Creator.				

WEAR YOU TO THE BALL	DEP International	35	28 Jul 90	6
I'LL BE YOUR BABY TONIGHT	EMI	6	3 Nov 90	10
Above hit: UB40 PALMER and UB40.				
IMPOSSIBLE LOVE	DEP International	47	1 Dec 90	2
THE WAY YOU DO THE THINGS YOU DO	DEP International	49	2 Feb 91	3
ONE IN TEN [RM]	ZTT	17	12 Dec 92	8
Though classed as a remix by 808 State, they have only utilised the chorus and the saxophone intro.				
Above hit: 808 STATE UB40.				
(I CAN'T HELP) FALLING IN LOVE WITH YOU	DEP International	1	22 May 93	16
From the film 'Sliver'.				
HIGHER GROUND	DEP International	8	21 Aug 93	9
BRING ME YOUR CUP	DEP International	24	11 Dec 93	6
C'EST LA VIE	DEP International	37	2 Apr 94	3
REGGAE MUSIC	DEP International	28	27 Aug 94	2
UNTIL MY DYING DAY	DEP International	15	4 Nov 95	6
TELL ME IS IT TRUE	DEP International	14	30 Aug 97	4
From the film 'Speed 2'.				
ALWAYS THERE	DEP International	53	15 Nov 97	1
COME BACK DARLING	DEP International	10	10 Oct 98	6
Originally recorded by Johnny Osborne in 1969.				
HOLLY HOLY	DEP International	31	19 Dec 98	3
Original by Neil Diamond reached No. 6 in the US in 1969.				
THE TRAIN IS COMING	DEP International	30	1 May 99	2
Originally recorded by Ken Boothe in 1973.				
ALBUMS:	**HITS 17**		**WEEKS 567**	
SIGNING OFF	Graduate	2	6 Sep 80	71
PRESENT ARMS	DEP International	2	6 Jun 81	38
PRESENT ARMS IN DUB	DEP International	38	10 Oct 81	7
Reworking of tracks from the last studio album.				
THE SINGLES ALBUM	Graduate	17	28 Aug 82	8
UB 44	DEP International	4	9 Oct 82	8
UB40 LIVE	DEP International	44	26 Feb 83	5
LABOUR OF LOVE	DEP International	1	24 Sep 83	76
This album plus the later editions consist of cover versions.				
GEFFERY MORGAN . . .	DEP International	3	20 Oct 84	14
BAGGARIDDIM	DEP International	14	14 Sep 85	23
Dub versions from the last 2 studio albums.				
RAT IN THE KITCHEN	DEP International	8	9 Aug 86	20
THE BEST OF UB40 - VOLUME ONE	DEP International	3	7 Nov 87	132
Includes re-entries through to 1996.				
UB40	DEP International	12	23 Jul 88	12
LABOUR OF LOVE II	DEP International	3	9 Dec 89	69
PROMISES AND LIES	DEP International	1	24 Jul 93	37
LABOUR OF LOVE - VOLUMES I AND II [RI]	DEP International	5	12 Nov 94	15
Combined repackage of both previous Labour Of Love albums.				
THE BEST OF UB40 - VOLUME TWO	DEP International	12	11 Nov 95	11
GUNS IN THE GHETTO	DEP International	7	12 Jul 97	9
LABOUR OF LOVE III	DEP International	8	24 Oct 98	12

UBM
Germany

SINGLES:	**HITS 1**		**WEEKS 1**	
LOVIN' YOU	Logic	46	23 May 98	1

U4EA featuring BERRI – See NEW ATLANTIC

UGLY KID JOE
US

SINGLES:	**HITS 6**		**WEEKS 28**	
EVERYTHING ABOUT YOU	Mercury	3	16 May 92	9
From the film 'Wayne's World'.				
NEIGHBOR	Mercury	28	22 Aug 92	4
SO DAMN COOL	Mercury	44	31 Oct 92	2
CATS IN THE CRADLE	Mercury	7	13 Mar 93	9
Original by Harry Chapin reached No. 1 in the US in 1974. From the film 'Wayne's World'.				
BUSY BEE	Mercury	39	19 Jun 93	2
MILKMAN'S SON	Mercury	39	8 Jul 95	2
ALBUMS:	**HITS 3**		**WEEKS 42**	
AS UGLY AS THEY WANNA BE	Mercury	9	13 Jun 92	13
AMERICA'S LEAST WANTED	Vertigo	11	12 Sep 92	24
MENACE TO SOBRIETY	Mercury	25	17 Jun 95	5

UK
Canada/Spain

SINGLES:	**HITS 1**		**WEEKS 1**	
SMALL TOWN BOY	Media	74	3 Aug 96	1

UK APACHI with SHY FX — UK

(See also Shy FX.)

SINGLES:		HITS 1		WEEKS 3	
ORIGINAL NUTTAH	Sound Of Underground	39	1 Oct 94	3	

Samples Cypress Hill's I Ain't Going Out Like That and vocal introduction from the film 'Goodfellas'.

UK MIXMASTERS — UK

SINGLES:		HITS 3		WEEKS 15	
THE NIGHT FEVER MEGAMIX [M]	IQ	23	2 Feb 91	5	

Songs from Saturday Night Fever.
Above hit: MIXMASTERS.

THE LUCKY 7 MEGAMIX [M]	IQ	43	27 Jul 91	3

Songs that were hits for Kylie Minogue.

THE BARE NECESSITIES MEGAMIX [M]	Connect	14	7 Dec 91	7

Features the songs from The Jungle Book– I Wanna Be Like You and Bare Necessities.

UK PLAYERS — UK

SINGLES:		HITS 1		WEEKS 3	
LOVE'S GONNA GET YOU	RCA	52	14 May 83	3	

Tracey ULLMAN — UK

SINGLES:		HITS 6		WEEKS 49	
BREAKAWAY	Stiff	4	19 Mar 83	11	

Originally recorded by Jackie De Shannon.

THEY DON'T KNOW	Stiff	2	24 Sep 83	11

Originally recorded by Kirsty MacColl in 1979.

MOVE OVER DARLING	Stiff	8	3 Dec 83	9
MY GUY'S MAD AT ME	Stiff	23	3 Mar 84	6

Cover of Madness' My Girl.

SUNGLASSES	Stiff	18	28 Jul 84	9

Originally recorded by John D. Loudermilk.

HELPLESS	Stiff	61	27 Oct 84	3
ALBUMS:		HITS 2		WEEKS 22	
YOU BREAK MY HEART IN 17 PLACES	Stiff	14	3 Dec 83	20
YOU CAUGHT ME OUT	Stiff	92	8 Dec 84	2

ULTIMATE KAOS — UK

SINGLES:		HITS 6		WEEKS 28	
SOME GIRLS	Wild Card	9	22 Oct 94	8	
SOME GIRLS [RE]	Wild Card	67	7 Jan 95	1	
HOOCHIE BOOTY	Wild Card	17	21 Jan 95	4	
SHOW A LITTLE LOVE	Wild Card	23	1 Apr 95	5	
RIGHT HERE	Wild Card	18	1 Jul 95	4	
CASANOVA	Polydor	24	8 Mar 97	3	
CASANOVA [RI]	Mercury	29	18 Jul 98	2	
ANYTHING YOU WANT (I'VE GOT IT)	Mercury	52	5 Jun 99	1	
ALBUMS:		HITS 1		WEEKS 1	
ULTIMATE KAOS	Wild Card	51	29 Apr 95	1	

ULTRA — UK

SINGLES:		HITS 4		WEEKS 22	
SAY YOU DO	East West	11	18 Apr 98	7	
SAY IT ONCE	East West	16	4 Jul 98	6	
THE RIGHT TIME	East West	28	10 Oct 98	2	
THE RIGHT TIME [RE]	East West	74	31 Oct 98	1	
RESCUE ME	East West	8	16 Jan 99	6	
ALBUMS:		HITS 1		WEEKS 1	
ULTRA	East West	37	6 Feb 99	2	

ULTRA HIGH — UK

SINGLES:		HITS 2		WEEKS 3	
STAY WITH ME	MCA	36	2 Dec 95	2	
ARE YOU READY FOR LOVE	MCA	45	20 Jul 96	1	

ULTRA-SONIC — UK

SINGLES:		HITS 2		WEEKS 2	
OBSESSION	Clubscene	75	3 Sep 94	1	
DO YOU BELIEVE IN LOVE	Clubscene	47	21 Sep 96	1	
ALBUMS:		HITS 1		WEEKS 1	
GLOBALTEKNO	Clubscene	58	11 Nov 95	1	

ULTRA VIVID SCENE
US

ALBUMS:	HITS 1			WEEKS 1
JOY 1967–1990	4AD	58	19 May 90	1

ULTRACYNIC
UK

SINGLES:	HITS 1			WEEKS 3
NOTHING IS FOREVER	380 PEW	50	29 Aug 92	2
NOTHING IS FOREVER [RM]	All Around The World	47	19 Apr 97	1
Remixed by Ultracynic.				

ULTRAMARINE
UK

SINGLES:	HITS 3			WEEKS 4
KINGDOM	Blanco Y Negro	46	24 Jul 93	2
BAREFOOT [EP]	Blanco Y Negro	61	29 Jan 94	1
Lead track: Happy Land, this track and the previous hit feature vocals by Robert Wyatt.				
HYMN	Blanco Y Negro	65	27 Apr 96	1
Above hit: ULTRAMARINE (featuring David McALMONT).				

ALBUMS:	HITS 1			WEEKS 1
UNITED KINGDOMS	Blanco Y Negro	49	4 Sep 93	1

ULTRASOUND
UK

SINGLES:	HITS 3			WEEKS 5
BEST WISHES	Nude	68	7 Mar 98	1
STAY YOUNG	Nude	30	13 Jun 98	2
FLOODLIT WORLD	Nude	39	10 Apr 99	2

ALBUMS:	HITS 1			WEEKS 1
EVERYTHING PICTURE	Nude	23	1 May 99	1

ULTRAVOX
UK/Canada

(See also Midge Ure.)

SINGLES:	HITS 17			WEEKS 142
SLEEPWALK	Chrysalis	29	5 Jul 80	11
PASSING STRANGERS	Chrysalis	57	18 Oct 80	4
VIENNA	Chrysalis	2	17 Jan 81	14
SLOW MOTION	Island	33	28 Mar 81	4
Originally released in 1978.				
ALL STOOD STILL	Chrysalis	8	6 Jun 81	10
THE THIN WALL	Chrysalis	14	22 Aug 81	8
THE VOICE	Chrysalis	16	7 Nov 81	12
REAP THE WILD WIND	Chrysalis	12	25 Sep 82	9
HYMN	Chrysalis	11	27 Nov 82	11
VISIONS IN BLUE	Chrysalis	15	19 Mar 83	6
WE CAME TO DANCE	Chrysalis	18	4 Jun 83	7
Above 4 produced by George Martin.				
ONE SMALL DAY	Chrysalis	27	11 Feb 84	6
DANCING WITH TEARS IN MY EYES	Chrysalis	3	19 May 84	10
LAMENT	Chrysalis	22	7 Jul 84	6
DANCING WITH TEARS IN MY EYES [RE]	Chrysalis	74	4 Aug 84	1
LAMENT [RE]	Chrysalis	73	25 Aug 84	1
LOVE'S GREAT ADVENTURE	Chrysalis	12	20 Oct 84	9
SAME OLD STORY	Chrysalis	31	27 Sep 86	4
ALL FALL DOWN	Chrysalis	30	22 Nov 86	5
VIENNA [RI]	Chrysalis	13	6 Feb 93	4

ALBUMS:	HITS 8			WEEKS 231
VIENNA	Chrysalis	14	19 Jul 80	12
VIENNA [RE]	Chrysalis	3	24 Jan 81	60
RAGE IN EDEN	Chrysalis	4	19 Sep 81	23
QUARTET	Chrysalis	6	23 Oct 82	30
MONUMENT – THE SOUNDTRACK	Chrysalis	9	22 Oct 83	15
LAMENT	Chrysalis	8	14 Apr 84	26
THE COLLECTION	Chrysalis	2	10 Nov 84	53
U-VOX	Chrysalis	9	25 Oct 86	6
IF I WAS: THE VERY BEST OF MIDGE URE AND ULTRAVOX	Chrysalis	10	6 Mar 93	6
Includes tracks with Band Aid, Visage, Phil Lynott and Mick Karn.				
Above hit: Midge URE/ULTRAVOX.				

UMBOZA
UK

SINGLES:	HITS 2			WEEKS 9
CRY INDIA	Positiva	19	23 Sep 95	4
Samples Lionel Ritchie's All Night Long.				
SUNSHINE	Positiva	14	20 Jul 96	5
Samples the Gipsy Kings' Bomboleo.				

Piero UMILIANI — Italy

SINGLES:	HITS 1			WEEKS 8
MAH-NA, MAH-NA	EMI International	8	30 Apr 77	8

Originally released in the US in 1969.

UNATION — UK

SINGLES:	HITS 2			WEEKS 3
HIGHER AND HIGHER	MCA	42	5 Jun 93	2

Features 16-piece string section arranged by Barrington Pheloung.

DO YOU BELIEVE IN LOVE?	MCA	75	7 Aug 93	1

UNBELIEVABLE TRUTH — UK

SINGLES:	HITS 3			WEEKS 5
HIGHER THAN REASON	Virgin	38	14 Feb 98	2
SOLVED	Virgin	39	9 May 98	2
SETTLE DOWN / DUNE SEA	Virgin	46	18 Jul 98	1
ALBUMS:	HITS 1			WEEKS 2
ALMOST HERE	Virgin	21	23 May 98	2

UNCANNY ALLIANCE — US

SINGLES:	HITS 1			WEEKS 5
I GOT MY EDUCATION	A&M	39	19 Dec 92	5

UNCLE SAM — US

SINGLES:	HITS 1			WEEKS 2
I DON'T EVER WANT TO SEE YOU AGAIN	Epic	30	16 May 98	2

UNDERCOVER — UK

SINGLES:	HITS 4			WEEKS 29
BAKER STREET	PWL International	2	15 Aug 92	14
NEVER LET HER SLIP AWAY	PWL International	5	14 Nov 92	11
I WANNA STAY WITH YOU	PWL International	28	6 Feb 93	3
LOVESICK	PWL International	62	14 Aug 93	1

Above hit: UNDERCOVER featuring John MATTHEWS.

ALBUMS:	HITS 1			WEEKS 9
CHECK OUT THE GROOVE	PWL International	26	5 Dec 92	9

UNDERTAKERS — UK

SINGLES:	HITS 1			WEEKS 1
JUST A LITTLE BIT	Pye	49	11 Apr 64	1

UNDERTONES — UK

SINGLES:	HITS 10			WEEKS 67
TEENAGE KICKS	Sire	31	21 Oct 78	6

Originally released on the Good Vibrations record label earlier in the year.

GET OVER YOU	Sire	57	3 Feb 79	4
JIMMY JIMMY	Sire	16	28 Apr 79	10
HERE COMES THE SUMMER	Sire	34	21 Jul 79	6
YOU'VE GOT MY NUMBER (WHY DON'T YOU USE IT!)	Sire	32	20 Oct 79	6
MY PERFECT COUSIN	Sire	9	5 Apr 80	10
WEDNESDAY WEEK	Sire	11	5 Jul 80	9
IT'S GOING TO HAPPEN!	Ardeck	18	2 May 81	9
JULIE OCEAN	Ardeck	41	25 Jul 81	5
TEENAGE KICKS [EP]	Ardeck	60	9 Jul 83	2

Lead track: Teenage Kicks, which itself is a re-issue.

ALBUMS:	HITS 7			WEEKS 50
THE UNDERTONES	Sire	13	19 May 79	21
HYPNOTISED	Sire	6	26 Apr 80	10
POSITIVE TOUCH	Ardeck	17	16 May 81	6
THE SIN OF PRIDE	Ardeck	43	19 Mar 83	5
ALL WRAPPED UP	Ardeck	67	10 Dec 83	4

Compilation.

CHER O'BOWLIES - PICK OF THE UNDERTONES	Ardeck	96	14 Jun 86	1

Above hit: UNDERTONES featuring Feargal SHARKEY.

THE BEST OF THE UNDERTONES - TEENAGE KICKS	Castle Communications	45	25 Sep 93	3

Released to celebrate 15th anniversary of the release of Teenage Kicks.

UNDERWORLD — UK

SINGLES:	HITS 7			WEEKS 39
SPIKEE / DOGMAN GO WOOF	Junior Boy's Own	63	18 Dec 93	1
DARK AND LONG	Junior Boy's Own	57	25 Jun 94	1
BORN SLIPPY	Junior Boy's Own	52	13 May 95	2

PEARL'S GIRL	*Junior Boy's Own*	24	*18 May 96*	2
BORN SLIPPY [RM]	*Junior Boy's Own*	2	*13 Jul 96*	16

From the film 'Trainspotting'. This remix was actually the 2nd track on the original CD release.

PEARL'S GIRL [RI]	*Junior Boy's Own*	22	*9 Nov 96*	3
BORN SLIPPY [RM] [RE]	*Junior Boy's Own*	58	*28 Dec 96*	5
PUSH UPSTAIRS	*JBO*	12	*27 Mar 99*	4
JUMBO	*JBO*	21	*5 Jun 99*	2
KING OF SNAKE	*JBO*	17	*28 Aug 99*	3

Based around Donna Summer's I Feel Love.

ALBUMS:	**HITS 3**		**WEEKS 42**	
DUB NO BASS WITH MY HEAD MAN	*Junior Boy's Own*	12	*5 Feb 94*	4
SECOND TOUGHEST IN THE INFANTS	*Junior Boy's Own*	9	*23 Mar 96*	28
BEAUCOUP FISH	*JBO*	3	*13 Mar 99*	10

UNDISPUTED TRUTH   US

SINGLES:	**HITS 1**		**WEEKS 4**	
YOU + ME = LOVE	*Warner Brothers*	43	*22 Jan 77*	4

U96   Germany

SINGLES:	**HITS 3**		**WEEKS 7**	
DAS BOOT	*M&G*	18	*29 Aug 92*	5
INSIDE YOUR DREAMS	*Logic*	44	*4 Jun 94*	1
CLUB BIZARRE	*Urban*	70	*29 Jun 96*	1

UNION   UK/Holland

SINGLES:	**HITS 1**		**WEEKS 7**	
SWING LOW (RUN WITH THE BALL)	*Columbia*	16	*12 Oct 91*	7

Above hit: UNION featuring the ENGLAND RUGBY WORLD CUP SQUAD.

ALBUMS:	**HITS 1**		**WEEKS 6**	
WORLD IN UNION	*Columbia*	17	*26 Oct 91*	6

Features Various Artists.

UNION GAP – See Gary PUCKETT and the UNION GAP

UNIQUE   US

SINGLES:	**HITS 1**		**WEEKS 7**	
WHAT I GOT IS WHAT YOU NEED	*Prelude*	27	*10 Sep 83*	7

UNIQUE 3   UK

SINGLES:	**HITS 4**		**WEEKS 12**	
THE THEME	*10 Records*	61	*4 Nov 89*	3
MUSICAL MELODY / WEIGHT FOR THE BASS	*10 Records*	29	*14 Apr 90*	5
RHYTHM TAKES CONTROL	*Ten Records*	41	*10 Nov 90*	3

Above hit: UNIQUE 3 (featuring KARIN).

NO MORE	*Ten Records*	74	*16 Nov 91*	1

UNIT FOUR PLUS TWO   UK

SINGLES:	**HITS 4**		**WEEKS 29**	
GREEN FIELDS	*Decca*	48	*15 Feb 64*	2
CONCRETE AND CLAY	*Decca*	1	*27 Feb 65*	15
(YOU'VE) NEVER BEEN IN LOVE LIKE THIS BEFORE	*Decca*	14	*15 May 65*	11
BABY NEVER SAY GOODBYE	*Decca*	49	*19 Mar 66*	1

EPS:	**HITS 1**		**WEEKS 5**	
UNIT FOUR PLUS TWO	*Decca*	11	*5 Jun 65*	5

UNITED CITIZEN FEDERATION featuring Sarah BRIGHTMAN   UK

(See also Sarah Brightman.)

SINGLES:	**HITS 1**		**WEEKS 1**	
STARSHIP TROOPERS	*Coalition*	58	*14 Feb 98*	1

UNITED KINGDOM SYMPHONY ORCHESTRA conducted by Donald GOULD   UK

SINGLES:	**HITS 1**		**WEEKS 4**	
SHADES (THEME FROM THE CROWN PAINT TELEVISION COMMERCIAL)	*Food For Thought*	68	*27 Jul 85*	4

UNITONE – See Laurel AITKEN and the UNITONE

UNITONE ROCKERS featuring STEEL   UK

SINGLES:	**HITS 1**		**WEEKS 1**	
CHILDREN OF THE REVOLUTION	*The Hit Label*	60	*26 Jun 93*	1

UNITY   UK

SINGLES:	**HITS 1**		**WEEKS 2**	
UNITY	*Cardiac*	64	*31 Aug 91*	2

UNIVERSAL | | | Australia

SINGLES:		HITS 2		WEEKS 6
ROCK ME GOOD	London	19	2 Aug 97	4
MAKE IT WITH YOU	London	33	18 Oct 97	2

UNJUSTIFIED ANCIENTS OF M U – See 1300 DRUMS featuring the UNJUSTIFIED ANCIENTS OF M U

UNKLE | | | UK

SINGLES:		HITS 1		WEEKS 6
BE THERE	Mo Wax	8	20 Feb 99	6

Above hit: UNKLE featuring Ian BROWN.

ALBUMS:		HITS 2		WEEKS 10
THE TIME HAS COME [EP]	Mo Wax	73	21 Jan 95	1

12" double-pack of remixes.
Above hit: U.N.K.L.E.

PSYENCE FICTION	Mo Wax	4	5 Sept 98	9

UNO CLIO featuring Martine McCUTCHEON | | | UK

(See also Martine McCutcheon.)

SINGLES:		HITS 1		WEEKS 1
ARE YOU MAN ENOUGH	Avex UK	62	18 Nov 95	1

UNTOUCHABLES | | | US

SINGLES:		HITS 2		WEEKS 16
FREE YOURSELF	Stiff	26	6 Apr 85	11
(I SPY FOR THE) FBI	Stiff	59	27 Jul 85	5
ALBUMS:		HITS 1		WEEKS 7
WILD CHILD	Stiff	51	13 Jul 85	7

UP YER RONSON featuring Mary PEARCE | | | UK

SINGLES:		HITS 3		WEEKS 7
LOST IN LOVE	Hi-Life	27	5 Aug 95	3
ARE YOU GONNA BE THERE?	Hi-Life	27	30 Mar 96	2

Originally recorded by Shay Jones in 1991.

I WILL BE RELEASED	Hi-Life	32	19 Apr 97	2

Phil UPCHURCH COMBO | | | US

SINGLES:		HITS 1		WEEKS 2
YOU CAN'T SIT DOWN	Sue	39	7 May 66	2

UPSETTERS | | | Jamaica

SINGLES:		HITS 1		WEEKS 15
RETURN OF DJANGO / DOLLAR IN THE TEETH	Upsetter	5	4 Oct 69	15

Dawn UPSHAW (soprano)/The LONDON SINFONIETTA/David ZINMAN (conductor) | | | US/UK/US

ALBUMS:		HITS 1		WEEKS 18
GORECKI: SYMPHONY NO. 3	Elektra Nonsuch	6	23 Jan 93	18

First released in 1992, charted after extensive airplay on radio station Classic FM.

UPSIDE DOWN | | | UK

SINGLES:		HITS 4		WEEKS 16
CHANGE YOUR MIND	World	11	20 Jan 96	7

Originally recorded by Bad Boys Inc.

EVERY TIME I FALL IN LOVE	World	18	13 Apr 96	3
EVERY TIME I FALL IN LOVE [RE]	World	71	8 Jun 96	1
NEVER FOUND A LOVE LIKE THIS BEFORE	World	19	29 Jun 96	3
IF YOU LEAVE ME NOW	World	27	23 Nov 96	2

URBAN ALL STARS | | | UK/US

SINGLES:		HITS 1		WEEKS 2
IT BEGAN IN AFRICA FEATURING I BELIEVE IN MIRACLES & CROSS THE TRACK [M]	Urban	64	27 Aug 88	2

URBAN BLUES PROJECT present Michael PROCTER | | | US

SINGLES:		HITS 1		WEEKS 1
LOVE DON'T LIVE	AM:PM	55	10 Aug 96	1

URBAN COOKIE COLLECTIVE | | | UK

SINGLES:		HITS 8		WEEKS 37
THE KEY: THE SECRET	Pulse 8	2	10 Jul 93	16
FEELS LIKE HEAVEN	Pulse 8	5	13 Nov 93	9

SAIL AWAY	*Pulse 8*	18	*19 Feb 94*	4
HIGH ON A HAPPY VIBE	*Pulse 8*	31	*23 Apr 94*	3
BRING IT ON HOME	*Pulse 8*	56	*15 Oct 94*	1
SPEND THE DAY	*Pulse 8*	59	*27 May 95*	1
REST OF MY LOVE	*Pulse 8*	67	*9 Sep 95*	1
SO BEAUTIFUL	*Pulse 8*	68	*16 Dec 95*	1
THE KEY, THE SECRET [RM]	*Pulse 8*	52	*24 Aug 96*	1

Remixed by Dancing Divaz.
Above hit: U.C.C.

ALBUMS:		HITS 1		WEEKS 2
HIGH ON A HAPPY VIBE	*Pulse 8*	28	*26 Mar 94*	2

URBAN DISCHARGE featuring SHE   US

SINGLES:		HITS 1		WEEKS 1
WANNA DROP A HOUSE (ON THAT BITCH)	*MCA*	51	*27 Jan 96*	1

URBAN HYPE   UK

SINGLES:		HITS 3		WEEKS 12
A TRIP TO TRUMPTON	*Faze 2*	6	*11 Jul 92*	8

Samples from the BBC Children's TV show 'Trumpton'.

THE FEELING	*Faze 2*	67	*17 Oct 92*	1
LIVING IN A FANTASY	*Faze 2*	57	*9 Jan 93*	3

URBAN SHAKEDOWN featuring Micky FINN   UK/Italy

SINGLES:		HITS 3		WEEKS 8
SOME JUSTICE	*Urban Shakedown*	23	*27 Jun 92*	5

Samples vocals of Ce Ce Rogers.

BASS SHAKE	*Urban Shakedown*	59	*12 Sep 92*	2
SOME JUSTICE '95 [RR]	*Urban Shakedown*	49	*10 Jun 95*	1

Above hit: URBAN SHAKEDOWN featuring D.BO GENERAL.

URBAN SOUL   UK

SINGLES:		HITS 3		WEEKS 11
ALRIGHT	*Cooltempo*	60	*30 Mar 91*	4
ALRIGHT (THE SASHA MIXES) [RM]	*Cooltempo*	43	*21 Sep 91*	1

Remixed by Sasha.

ALWAYS	*Cooltempo*	41	*28 Mar 92*	3
LOVE IS SO NICE	*VC Recordings*	75	*13 Jun 98*	1

URBAN SPECIES   UK

SINGLES:		HITS 4		WEEKS 10
SPIRITUAL LOVE	*Talkin Loud*	35	*12 Feb 94*	4
BROTHER	*Talkin Loud*	40	*16 Apr 94*	3
LISTEN	*Talkin Loud*	47	*20 Aug 94*	2

Original release reached No. 79 in 1993.
Above hit: URBAN SPECIES featuring MC SOLAAR.

BLANKET	*Talkin Loud*	56	*6 Mar 99*	1

Above hit: URBAN SPECIES featuring Imogen HEAP.

ALBUMS:		HITS 1		WEEKS 2
LISTEN	*Talkin Loud*	43	*7 May 94*	2

Midge URE   UK

SINGLES:		HITS 10		WEEKS 56
NO REGRETS	*Chrysalis*	9	*12 Jun 82*	10

Originally recorded by Tom Rush.

AFTER A FASHION	*Musicfest*	39	*9 Jul 83*	4

Above hit: Midge URE and Mick KARN.

IF I WAS	*Chrysalis*	1	*14 Sep 85*	11
THAT CERTAIN SMILE	*Chrysalis*	28	*16 Nov 85*	4
WASTELANDS	*Chrysalis*	46	*8 Feb 86*	3
CALL OF THE WILD	*Chrysalis*	27	*7 Jun 86*	8
ANSWERS TO NOTHING	*Chrysalis*	49	*20 Aug 88*	4
DEAR GOD	*Chrysalis*	55	*19 Nov 88*	4
COLD, COLD HEART	*Arista*	17	*17 Aug 91*	7
BREATHE	*Arista*	70	*25 May 96*	1

ALBUMS:		HITS 4		WEEKS 26
THE GIFT	*Chrysalis*	2	*19 Oct 85*	15
ANSWERS TO NOTHING	*Chrysalis*	30	*10 Sep 88*	3
PURE	*Arista*	36	*28 Sep 91*	2
IF I WAS: THE VERY BEST OF MIDGE URE AND ULTRAVOX	*Chrysalis*	10	*6 Mar 93*	6

Includes tracks with Band Aid, Visage, Phil Lynott and Mick Karn.
Above hit: Midge URE/ULTRAVOX.

URGE OVERKILL US

SINGLES:	HITS 3			WEEKS 6
SISTER HAVANA	Geffen	67	21 Aug 93	1
POSITIVE BLEEDING	Geffen	61	16 Oct 93	1
GIRL, YOU'LL BE A WOMAN SOON	MCA	37	19 Nov 94	4

From the film 'Pulp Fiction'. Original by Neil Diamond reached No. 10 in the US in 1967.

URIAH HEEP UK

ALBUMS:	HITS 12			WEEKS 51
LOOK AT YOURSELF	Island	39	13 Nov 71	1
DEMONS AND WIZARDS	Bronze	20	10 Jun 72	11
THE MAGICIAN'S BIRTHDAY	Bronze	28	2 Dec 72	3
URIAH HEEP LIVE	Island	23	19 May 73	8
SWEET FREEDOM	Island	18	29 Sep 73	3
WONDERWORLD	Bronze	23	29 Jun 74	3
RETURN TO FANTASY	Bronze	7	5 Jul 75	6
HIGH AND MIGHTY	Island	55	12 Jun 76	1
CONQUEST	Bronze	37	22 Mar 80	3
ABOMINOG	Bronze	34	17 Apr 82	6
HEAD FIRST	Bronze	46	18 Jun 83	4
EQUATOR	Portrait	79	6 Apr 85	2

URUSEI YATSURA UK

SINGLES:	HITS 4			WEEKS 4
STATEGIC HAMLETS	Che	64	22 Feb 97	1
FAKE FUR	Che	58	28 Jun 97	1
HELLO TIGER	Che	40	21 Feb 98	1
SLAIN BY ELF	Che	63	6 Jun 98	1
ALBUMS:	**HITS 1**			**WEEKS 1**
SLAIN BY	Che	64	14 Mar 98	1

USA FOR AFRICA US

SINGLES:	HITS 1			WEEKS 9
WE ARE THE WORLD	CBS	1	13 Apr 85	9

Charity record in aid of famine relief in Africa. 5,000 radio stations globally aired the song on 5 Apr 95 at 3.50pm GMT.

ALBUMS:	**HITS 1**			**WEEKS 5**
WE ARE THE WORLD	CBS	31	25 May 85	5

Contains previously unreleased tracks from Bruce Springsteen, Prince, Huey Lewis and the News, Chicago, Tina Turner, Pointer Sisters, Kenny Rodgers, Steve Perry plus the Canadian charity ensemble Northern Lights.

USHER US

SINGLES:	HITS 3			WEEKS 19
THINK OF YOU	LaFace	70	18 Mar 95	1

Rap by Biz Markie, backing vocals by Faith Evans and samples Tidal Wave by Ronnie Laws.

YOU MAKE ME WANNA ...	LaFace	1	31 Jan 98	12
NICE & SLOW	LaFace	24	2 May 98	5
YOU MAKE ME WANNA ... [RE]	LaFace	72	2 May 98	1
ALBUMS:	**HITS 1**			**WEEKS 18**
MY WAY	LaFace	16	17 Jan 98	18

US3 UK

SINGLES:	HITS 4			WEEKS 15
RIDDIM	Blue Note	34	10 Jul 93	6

Above hit: US3 featuring Tukka YOOT.

CANTALOOP (FLIP FANTASIA)	Blue Note	23	25 Sep 93	5

Samples Cantaloupe Island by Herbie Hancock.
Above hit: US3 featuring RAHSAAN.

I GOT IT GOIN' ON	Blue Note	52	28 May 94	2

Above hit: US3 featuring Kobie POWELL and RAHSAAN.

COME ON EVERYBODY (GET DOWN)	Blue Note	38	1 Mar 97	2
ALBUMS:	**HITS 1**			**WEEKS 6**
HAND ON THE TORCH	Blue Note	40	31 Jul 93	5
HAND ON THE TORCH / JAZZ MIXES [RE]	Blue Note	54	11 Jun 94	1

Jazz Mixes was a remix album, sales were combined.

USURA Italy

SINGLES:	HITS 2			WEEKS 15
OPEN YOUR MIND	Deconstruction	7	23 Jan 93	9
SWEAT	Deconstruction	29	10 Jul 93	3

OPEN YOUR MIND '97 [RM]	*Malarky*	21	*6 Dec 97*	3

Remixed by DJ Quicksilver.
Above hit: U.S.U.R.A.

UTAH SAINTS   UK

SINGLES:	HITS 6			WEEKS 35
WHAT CAN YOU DO FOR ME	*ffrr*	10	*24 Aug 91*	11

Samples Eurythmics' There Must Be An Angel (Playing With My Heart) and Gwen Guthrie's
Ain't Nothing Goin' On But The Rent.

SOMETHING GOOD	*ffrr*	4	*6 Jun 92*	9

Samples Kate Bush's Cloudbusting.

BELIEVE IN ME	*ffrr*	8	*8 May 93*	6

Samples Crown Heights Affair's You Gave Me Love and the Human League's Love Action (I
Believe In Love).

I WANT YOU	*ffrr*	25	*17 Jul 93*	5

Samples Slayer's War Ensemble.

I STILL THINK OF YOU	*ffrr*	32	*25 Jun 94*	2

A re-working of an album track Too Much To Swallow. From the film 'Shopping'.

OHIO	*ffrr*	42	*2 Sep 95*	2

Samples Jocelyn Brown's Somebody Else's Guy.

ALBUMS:	HITS 1			WEEKS 15
UTAH SAINTS	*ffrr*	10	*5 Jun 93*	15

UTOPIA   UK

ALBUMS:	HITS 3			WEEKS 9
RA	*Bearsville*	27	*29 Jan 77*	6
OOPS! SORRY WRONG PLANET	*Bearsville*	59	*1 Oct 77*	1
ADVENTURES IN UTOPIA	*Island*	57	*16 Feb 80*	2

U2   Ireland

SINGLES:	HITS 28			WEEKS 212
FIRE	*Island*	35	*8 Aug 81*	6
GLORIA	*Island*	55	*17 Oct 81*	4
A CELEBRATION	*Island*	47	*3 Apr 82*	4
NEW YEAR'S DAY	*Island*	10	*22 Jan 83*	8
TWO HEARTS BEAT AS ONE	*Island*	18	*2 Apr 83*	5
PRIDE (IN THE NAME OF LOVE)	*Island*	3	*15 Sep 84*	11

Dedicated to Martin Luther King Jr.

THE UNFORGETTABLE FIRE	*Island*	6	*4 May 85*	6
WITH OR WITHOUT YOU	*Island*	4	*28 Mar 87*	11
I STILL HAVEN'T FOUND WHAT I'M LOOKING FOR	*Island*	6	*6 Jun 87*	11
WHERE THE STREETS HAVE NO NAME	*Island*	4	*12 Sep 87*	6
IN GOD'S COUNTRY	*Island*	48	*26 Dec 87*	4

Import.

DESIRE	*Island*	1	*1 Oct 88*	8
ANGEL OF HARLEM	*Island*	9	*17 Dec 88*	6

Tribute to Billie Holiday.

WHEN LOVE COMES TO TOWN	*Island*	6	*15 Apr 89*	7

Above hit: U2 with B.B. KING.

ALL I WANT IS YOU	*Island*	4	*24 Jun 89*	6
THE FLY	*Island*	1	*2 Nov 91*	5
MYSTERIOUS WAYS	*Island*	13	*14 Dec 91*	7
THE FLY [RE]	*Island*	62	*4 Jan 92*	1
ONE	*Island*	7	*7 Mar 92*	6
EVEN BETTER THAN THE REAL THING	*Island*	12	*20 jJun 92*	7
EVEN BETTER THAN THE REAL THING (THE PERFECTO MIX) [RM]	*Island*	8	*11 Jul 92*	7

Remixed by Paul Oakenfold and Steve Osborne.

WHO'S GONNA RIDE YOUR WILD HORSES	*Island*	14	*5 Dec 92*	8
STAY (FARAWAY, SO CLOSE!)	*Island*	4	*4 Dec 93*	9

[AA] listed with I've Got You Under My Skin by Frank Sinatra with Bono, although that track
was not available on the 2nd CD format.

HOLD ME, THRILL ME, KISS ME, KILL ME	*Atlantic*	2	*17 Jun 95*	14

From the film 'Batman Forever'.

DISCOTHEQUE	*Island*	1	*15 Feb 97*	9
STARING AT THE SUN	*Island*	3	*26 Apr 97*	6
DISCOTHEQUE [RE]	*Island*	72	*17 May 97*	2
LAST NIGHT ON EARTH	*Island*	10	*2 Aug 97*	4
LAST NIGHT ON EARTH [RE]	*Island*	68	*6 Sep 97*	1
PLEASE	*Island*	7	*4 Oct 97*	4
IF GOD WILL SEND HIS ANGELS	*Island*	12	*20 Dec 97*	6

Second CD format has Mofo as the lead track.

SWEETEST THING	*Island*	3	*31 Oct 98*	13

ALBUMS:	HITS 14			WEEKS 958
BOY	*Island*	52	*29 Aug 81*	31

Originally released in 1980.

OCTOBER	*Island*	11	*24 Oct 81*	41

WAR	Island	1	12 Mar 83	145

Includes re-entries through to 1992.

U2 LIVE "UNDER A BLOOD RED SKY"	Island	2	3 Dec 83	203

Includes re-entries through to 1992. Live recordings from Boston in Massachusetts, Red Rocks festival in Colorado and West Germany.

THE UNFORGETTABLE FIRE	Island	1	13 Oct 84	130
WIDE AWAKE IN AMERICA	Island	11	27 Jul 85	16

US import EP.

THE JOSHUA TREE	Island	1	21 Mar 87	130

Includes re-entries through to 1996.

THE JOSHUA TREE SINGLES	Island	100	20 Feb 88	1

Release is 4 x 7" singles set.

RATTLE AND HUM	Island	1	22 Oct 88	54

Live recordings between 1986–88 and rare studio tracks.

ACHTUNG BABY	Island	2	30 Nov 91	80
OCTOBER [RE]	Island	72	13 Jun 92	1
ZOOROPA	Island	1	17 Jul 93	31
WAR [RE]	Island	38	21 Aug 93	2
POP	Island	1	15 Mar 97	35
THE JOSHUA TREE [RE]	Island	46	26 Jul 97	8
THE BEST OF 1980-1990 & B-SIDES	Island	1	14 Nov 98	9
THE BEST OF 1980-1990	Island	4	21 Nov 98	41

Both compilations listed above had separate chart entries due to chart rules. The first entry had additional CD of B-sides.

V

Verna V. – See HELIOTROPIC featuring Verna V.

V.D.C. – See BLAST featuring V.D.C.

V.I.M. — UK

SINGLES:	HITS 1		WEEKS 1	
MAGGIE'S LAST PARTY	Boz	68	26 Jan 91	1

V.I.P.'S — UK

SINGLES:	HITS 1		WEEKS 4	
THE QUARTER MOON	Gems	55	6 Sep 80	4

VAGABONDS – See Jimmy JAMES and the VAGABONDS

Steve VAI — US

ALBUMS:	HITS 4		WEEKS 20	
PASSION AND WARFARE	Food	8	2 Jun 90	10
SEX AND RELIGION	Relativity	17	7 Aug 93	6

Above hit: VAI.

ALIEN LOVE SECRETS	Relativity	39	15 Apr 95	2
FIRE GARDEN	Epic	41	28 Sep 96	2

Ricky VALANCE — UK

SINGLES:	HITS 1		WEEKS 16	
TELL LAURA I LOVE HER	Columbia	1	27 Aug 60	16

Original by Ray Peterson reached No. 7 in the US in 1960.

Ritchie VALENS — US

SINGLES:	HITS 2		WEEKS 5	
DONNA	London	29	7 Mar 59	1
LA BAMBA	RCA	49	1 Aug 87	4

Originally the B-side of Donna in 1959. Re-issued after the release of the biopic of the same name.

Caterina VALENTE – Werner MULLER and the RIAS DANCE ORCHESTRA — France

SINGLES:	HITS 1		WEEKS 14	
THE BREEZE AND I (ANDALUCIA)	Polydor	5	20 Aug 55	14

Originally recorded by Jimmy Dorsey in 1940.

Dickie VALENTINE — UK

(See also All Star Hit Parade.)

SINGLES:	HITS 14		WEEKS 92	
BROKEN WINGS	Decca	12	21 Feb 53	1
ALL THE TIME AND EV'RYWHERE	Decca	9	14 Mar 53	3
IN A GOLDEN COACH (THERE'S A HEART OF GOLD)	Decca	7	6 Jun 53	1
ENDLESS	Decca	19	6 Nov 54	1

MISTER SANDMAN	Decca	5	18 Dec 54	12

Above hit: Dickie VALENTINE with Johnny DOUGLAS and his Orchestra.

THE FINGER OF SUSPICION	Decca	1	18 Dec 54	15

Above hit: Dickie VALENTINE with the STARGAZERS.

A BLOSSOM FELL	Decca	9	19 Feb 55	9
A BLOSSOM FELL [RE]	Decca	18	30 Apr 55	1
I WONDER	Decca	4	4 Jun 55	15
CHRISTMAS ALPHABET	Decca	1	26 Nov 55	7

Above 4: Dickie VALENTINE with Johnny DOUGLAS and his Orchestra.

THE OLD PI-ANNA RAG	Decca	15	17 Dec 55	5
CHRISTMAS ISLAND	Decca	8	8 Dec 56	5

Above hit: Dickie VALENTINE with Johnny DOUGLAS and his Orchestra.

SNOWBOUND FOR CHRISTMAS	Decca	28	28 Dec 57	1
VENUS	Pye Nixa	28	14 Mar 59	1
VENUS [RE-1ST]	Pye Nixa	25	4 Apr 59	1
VENUS [RE-2ND]	Pye Nixa	20	18 Apr 59	4
VENUS [RE-3RD]	Pye Nixa	25	23 May 59	1
VENUS [RE-4TH]	Pye Nixa	28	20 Jun 59	1
ONE MORE SUNRISE (MORGEN)	Pye Nixa	14	24 Oct 59	8

Above hit: Dickie VALENTINE; Wally STOTT ORCHESTRA and Chorus.

VALENTINE BROTHERS — US

SINGLES:	HITS 1		WEEKS 1	
MONEY'S TOO TIGHT (TO MENTION)	Energy	73	23 Apr 83	1

Joe VALINO — US

SINGLES:	HITS 1		WEEKS 2	
THE GARDEN OF EDEN	His Master's Voice	23	19 Jan 57	2

Frankie VALLI — US

(See also Four Seasons.)

SINGLES:	HITS 6		WEEKS 52	
YOU'RE READY NOW	Philips	11	12 Dec 70	13

Originally released in 1966.

MY EYES ADORED YOU	Private Stock	5	1 Feb 75	11
SWEARIN' TO GOD	Private Stock	31	21 Jun 75	5
FALLEN ANGEL	Private Stock	11	17 Apr 76	7

Originally recorded by Rogue.

GREASE	RSO	3	26 Aug 78	14

From the film of the same name. Written by Barry Gibb.

GREASE - THE DREAM MIX [M]	Polydor	47	23 Mar 91	2

Medley of songs from the film 'Grease'.
Above hit: Frankie VALLI, John TRAVOLTA and Olivia NEWTON-JOHN.

ALBUMS:	HITS 2		WEEKS 24	
THE COLLECTION – THE 20 GREATEST HITS	Telstar	38	21 May 88	9

CD format is titled The 22 Greatest Hits.

THE VERY BEST OF FRANKIE VALLI AND THE FOUR SEASONS	PolyGram TV	7	7 Mar 92	15

Above 2 contain Frankie Valli's solo and group material.
Above 2: Frankie VALLI and the FOUR SEASONS.

Mark VAN DALE with ENRICO — Belgium

SINGLES:	HITS 1		WEEKS 1	
WATER WAVE	Club Tools	71	3 Oct 98	1

Raved-up version of the Verve's Bittersweet Symphony.

David VAN DAY — UK

SINGLES:	HITS 1		WEEKS 3	
YOUNG AMERICANS TALKING	WEA	43	14 May 83	3

VAN DE GRAAFF GENERATOR — UK

ALBUMS:	HITS 1		WEEKS 2	
THE LEAST WE CAN DO IS WAVE TO EACH OTHER	Charisma	47	25 Apr 70	2

George VAN DUSEN — UK

SINGLES:	HITS 1		WEEKS 4	
IT'S PARTY TIME AGAIN	Bri-Tone	43	17 Dec 88	4

Paul VAN DYK — Germany

SINGLES:	HITS 4		WEEKS 11	
FORBIDDEN FRUIT	Deviant	69	17 May 97	1
WORDS	Deviant	54	15 Nov 97	1

Above hit: Paul VAN DYK featuring Toni HALLIDAY.

FOR AN ANGEL	Deviant	28	5 Sep 98	4
ANOTHER WAY / AVENUE	Deviant	13	20 Nov 99	5

Leroy VAN DYKE

US

SINGLES:		HITS 2			WEEKS 20
WALK ON BY	Mercury	5	6 Jan 62	17
BIG MAN IN A BIG HOUSE	Mercury	34	28 Apr 62	3

Niels VAN GOGH

Germany

SINGLES:		HITS 1			WEEKS 1
PULVERTURM	Kosmo	75	10 Apr 99	1

VAN HALEN

US

SINGLES:		HITS 12			WEEKS 51
RUNNIN' WITH THE DEVIL	Warner Brothers	52	28 Jun 80	3
JUMP	Warner Brothers	7	4 Feb 84	13
PANAMA	Warner Brothers	61	19 May 84	2
WHY CAN'T THIS BE LOVE	Warner Brothers	8	5 Apr 86	14
DREAMS	Warner Brothers	62	12 Jul 86	2
WHEN IT'S LOVE	Warner Brothers	28	6 Aug 88	7
FEELS SO GOOD	Warner Brothers	63	1 Apr 89	1
POUNDCAKE	Warner Brothers	74	22 Jun 91	1
TOP OF THE WORLD	Warner Brothers	63	19 Oct 91	1
JUMP (LIVE VERSION) [RR]	Warner Brothers	26	27 Mar 93	3
DON'T TELL ME	Warner Brothers	27	21 Jan 95	2
CAN'T STOP LOVIN' YOU	Warner Brothers	33	1 Apr 95	2

ALBUMS:		HITS 13			WEEKS 102
VAN HALEN	Warner Brothers	34	27 May 78	11
VAN HALEN II	Warner Brothers	23	14 Apr 79	7
WOMEN AND CHILDREN FIRST	Warner Brothers	15	5 Apr 80	7
FAIR WARNING	Warner Brothers	49	23 May 81	4
DIVER DOWN	Warner Brothers	36	1 May 82	5
1984	Warner Brothers	15	4 Feb 84	23
5150	Warner Brothers	16	5 Apr 86	18
OU812	Warner Brothers	16	4 Jun 88	12
FOR UNLAWFUL CARNAL KNOWLEDGE	Warner Brothers	12	29 Jun 91	5
LIVE: RIGHT HERE, RIGHT NOW	Warner Brothers	24	6 Mar 93	4
BALANCE	Warner Brothers	8	4 Feb 95	3
1984 [RE]	Warner Brothers	75	11 Mar 95	1
Re-released at mid-price.				
THE BEST OF VAN HALEN – VOLUME 1	Warner Brothers	45	9 Nov 96	1
VAN HALEN 3	Warner Brothers	43	28 Mar 98	1

Armand VAN HELDEN

US

(See also Deep Creed 94.)

SINGLES:		HITS 4			WEEKS 20
THE FUNK PHENOMENA	ZYX	38	8 Mar 97	2
Above hit: Armand VAN HELDEN presents OLD SCHOOL JUNKIES PT. 2.				
ULTRAFUNKULA	ffrr	46	8 Nov 97	1
YOU DON'T KNOW ME	ffrr	1	6 Feb 99	11
Originally appeared on the 2 Future 4U EP which reached No. 92 on the album charts in 1998.				
Above hit: Armand VAN HELDEN featuring Duane HARDEN.				
FLOWERS	ffrr	18	1 May 99	5
Above hit: Armand VAN HELDEN featuring Roland CLARK.				
YOU DON'T KNOW ME [RE]	ffrr	72	15 May 99	1

ALBUMS:		HITS 1			WEEKS 6
2 FUTURE 4 U	ffrr	22	10 Apr 99	6

Paul VAN KEMPEN

Holland

EPS:		HITS 1			WEEKS 20
1812 OVERTURE	Philips	11	19 Mar 60	20

VAN TWIST

Belgium/Zaire

SINGLES:		HITS 1			WEEKS 2
SHAFT	Polydor	57	16 Feb 85	2

VANDELLAS – See Martha REEVES and the VANDELLAS

Luther VANDROSS

US

SINGLES:		HITS 25			WEEKS 147
NEVER TOO MUCH	Epic	44	19 Feb 83	6
Originally released in 1981 reaching No. 19 in the US.				
GIVE ME THE REASON	Epic	60	26 Jul 86	3
From the film 'Ruthless People'.				
GIVE ME THE REASON [RI-1ST]	Epic	71	21 Feb 87	2
SEE ME	Epic	60	28 Mar 87	4

Title	Label	Pos	Date	Wks
I REALLY DIDN'T MEAN IT	Epic	16	11 Jul 87	10
STOP TO LOVE	Epic	24	5 Sep 87	7
SO AMAZING	Epic	33	7 Nov 87	6
GIVE ME THE REASON [RI-2ND]	Epic	26	23 Jan 88	6
I GAVE IT UP (WHEN I FELL IN LOVE)	Epic	28	16 Apr 88	5
THERE'S NOTHING BETTER THAN LOVE	Epic	72	9 Jul 88	1

Above hit: Luther VANDROSS (duet with Gregory HINES).

Title	Label	Pos	Date	Wks
ANY LOVE	Epic	31	8 Oct 88	4
SHE WON'T TALK TO ME	Epic	34	4 Feb 89	4
COME BACK	Epic	53	22 Apr 89	3
NEVER TOO MUCH – REMIX '89 [RM]	Epic	13	28 Oct 89	7

Remixed by Justin Strauss.

Title	Label	Pos	Date	Wks
HERE AND NOW	Epic	43	6 Jan 90	3
POWER OF LOVE/LOVE POWER [M]	Epic	46	27 Apr 91	5

Backing vocals by Darlene Love and Cissy Houston.

Title	Label	Pos	Date	Wks
THE RUSH	Epic	53	18 Jan 92	3
THE BEST THINGS IN LIFE ARE FREE	Perspective	2	15 Aug 92	13

From the film 'Mo'Money'.
Above hit: Luther VANDROSS and Janet JACKSON with special guests BBD and Ralph TRESVANT.

Title	Label	Pos	Date	Wks
LITTLE MIRACLES (HAPPEN EVERY DAY)	Epic	28	22 May 93	3
HEAVEN KNOWS	Epic	34	18 Sep 93	3
LOVE IS ON THE WAY (REAL LOVE)	Epic	38	4 Dec 93	2
ENDLESS LOVE	Epic	3	17 Sep 94	10

Above hit: Luther VANDROSS and Mariah CAREY.

Title	Label	Pos	Date	Wks
LOVE THE ONE YOU'RE WITH	Epic	31	26 Nov 94	4
ENDLESS LOVE [RE-1ST]	Epic	70	7 Jan 95	2
ALWAYS AND FOREVER	Epic	20	4 Feb 95	5
ENDLESS LOVE [RE-2ND]	Epic	55	4 Feb 95	4
AIN'T NO STOPPIN' US NOW	Epic	22	15 Apr 95	3
POWER OF LOVE/LOVE POWER [M] [RM]	Epic	31	11 Nov 95	3

Remixed by Frankie Knuckles.

Title	Label	Pos	Date	Wks
THE BEST THINGS IN LIFE ARE FREE [RM]	A&M	7	16 Dec 95	7

Remixed by K-Klass.
Above hit: Luther VANDROSS and Janet JACKSON.

Title	Label	Pos	Date	Wks
EVERY YEAR, EVERY CHRISTMAS	Epic	43	23 Dec 95	2
YOUR SECRET LOVE	Epic	14	12 Oct 96	5
I CAN MAKE IT BETTER	Epic	44	28 Dec 96	2
ALBUMS:	**HITS 15**			**WEEKS 269**
BUSY BODY	Epic	42	21 Jan 84	8
THE NIGHT I FELL IN LOVE	Epic	19	6 Apr 85	10
THE ARTISTS VOLUME 2	Street Sounds	45	13 Jul 85	4

Compilation album with tracks by each artist.
Above hit: Luther VANDROSS/Teddy PENDERGRASS/CHANGE/ATLANTIC STARR.

Title	Label	Pos	Date	Wks
GIVE ME THE REASON	Epic	13	1 Nov 86	10
GIVE ME THE REASON [RE]	Epic	3	31 Jan 87	89

Peak position reached on 5 Mar 88.

Title	Label	Pos	Date	Wks
NEVER TOO MUCH	Epic	41	21 Feb 87	30

Originally released in 1981.

Title	Label	Pos	Date	Wks
FOREVER, FOR ALWAYS, FOR LOVE	Epic	23	4 Jul 87	16
BUSY BODY [RE]	Epic	78	16 Apr 88	4

Re-released with a new catalogue number.

Title	Label	Pos	Date	Wks
ANY LOVE	Epic	3	29 Oct 88	22
BEST OF LUTHER VANDROSS – BEST OF LOVE	Epic	14	11 Nov 89	13
POWER OF LOVE	Epic	9	25 May 91	9
NEVER LET ME GO	Epic	11	12 Jun 93	5
SONGS	Epic	1	1 Oct 94	28
GREATEST HITS 1981–1995	Epic	12	28 Oct 95	14
YOUR SECRET LOVE	Epic	14	19 Oct 96	4
ONE NIGHT WITH YOU – THE BEST OF LOVE	Epic	56	11 Oct 97	2

Compilation of love songs.

Title	Label	Pos	Date	Wks
I KNOW	EMI	42	22 Aug 98	1

VANESSA-MAE

UK

SINGLES:	HITS 7			WEEKS 20
TOCCATA AND FUGUE IN D MINOR	EMI Classics	16	28 Jan 95	10
RED HOT	EMI	37	20 May 95	2

She performed the song in front of Queen Elizabeth II at the V.E. Day anniversary celebrations, 8 May 95.

Title	Label	Pos	Date	Wks
CLASSICAL GAS	EMI	41	18 Nov 95	2
I'M A DOUN FOR LACK O'JOHNNIE' (A LITTLE SCOTTISH FANTASY)	EMI	28	26 Oct 96	2

Modern arrangement of an old Scottish folk song.

Title	Label	Pos	Date	Wks
STORM	EMI	54	25 Oct 97	1
I FEEL LOVE	EMI	41	20 Dec 97	2
DEVIL'S TRILL / REFLECTION	EMI	53	5 Dec 98	1

Devil's Trill featured in the Siemens "Be Inspired" TV commercial. Reflection is from the Walt Disney film 'Mulan'.

ALBUMS:		HITS 4			WEEKS 31
THE VIOLIN PLAYER	EMI	11	25 Feb 95	21
CLASSICAL ALBUM 1	EMI Premier	47	2 Nov 96	2
Features Russian conductor Viktor Fadov and the London Symphony Orchestra.				
STORM	EMI	27	8 Nov 97	5
CHINA GIRL – THE CLASSICAL ALBUM 2	EMI Classics	56	7 Feb 98	3
Features the London Philharmonic Orchestra and the Orchestra of the Royal Opera House.				

VANGELIS — Greece

(See also Jon and Vangelis.)

SINGLES:		HITS 3			WEEKS 25
CHARIOTS OF FIRE - TITLES	Polydor	12	9 May 81	10
Theme from the film.				
HEAVEN AND HELL 3RD MOVEMENT (THEME FROM THE TV SERIES COSMOS)	BBC	48	11 Jul 81	6
Theme from Carl Sagan's BBC TV series.				
CHARIOTS OF FIRE - TITLES [RE]	Polydor	41	24 Apr 82	7
CONQUEST OF PARADISE	East West	60	31 Oct 92	2
From the film '1492 – Conquest Of Paradise'.				

ALBUMS:		HITS 10			WEEKS 157
HEAVEN AND HELL	RCA Victor	31	10 Jan 76	7
ALBEDO 0.39	RCA Victor	18	9 Oct 76	6
CHARIOTS OF FIRE [OST]	Polydor	5	18 Apr 81	97
CHARIOTS OF FIRE [OST] [RE]	Polydor	39	5 May 84	9
Re-released with a new catalogue number.				
SOIL FESTIVITIES	Polydor	55	13 Oct 84	4
MASK	Polydor	69	30 Mar 85	2
THEMES	Polydor	11	22 Jul 89	13
1492 - THE CONQUEST OF PARADISE [OST]	East West	33	24 Oct 92	6
BLADERUNNER [OST]	East West	20	18 Jun 94	6
Film was originally released in 1982.				
VOICES	East West	58	2 Mar 96	1
PORTRAIT (SO LONG AGO, SO CLEAR)	Polydor	14	20 Apr 96	6
Compilation featuring 5 tracks with Jon Anderson.				

VANILLA — UK

SINGLES:		HITS 2			WEEKS 10
NO WAY NO WAY	EMI	75	22 Nov 97	1
NO WAY NO WAY [RE]	EMI	14	27 Dec 97	7
TRUE TO US	EMI	36	23 May 98	2

VANILLA FUDGE — US

SINGLES:		HITS 1			WEEKS 11
YOU KEEP ME HANGING ON	Atlantic	18	12 Aug 67	11

ALBUMS:		HITS 1			WEEKS 3
VANILLA FUDGE	Atlantic	31	4 Nov 67	3

VANILLA ICE — US

SINGLES:		HITS 5			WEEKS 32
ICE ICE BABY	SBK	1	24 Nov 90	13
Samples Queen and David Bowie's Under Pressure.				
PLAY THAT FUNKY MUSIC	SBK	10	2 Feb 91	6
I LOVE YOU	SBK	45	30 Mar 91	5
ROLLIN' IN MY 5.0	SBK	27	29 Jun 91	4
SATISFACTION	SBK	22	10 Aug 91	4

ALBUMS:		HITS 2			WEEKS 23
TO THE EXTREME	SBK	4	15 Dec 90	20
EXTREMELY LIVE	SBK	35	6 Jul 91	3

VANITY FARE — UK

SINGLES:		HITS 3			WEEKS 34
I LIVE FOR THE SUN	Page One	20	31 Aug 68	9
EARLY IN THE MORNING	Page One	8	26 Jul 69	12
HITCHIN' A RIDE	Page One	16	27 Dec 69	13

Joe T. VANNELLI PROJECT — Italy

SINGLES:		HITS 1			WEEKS 2
SWEETEST DAY OF MAY	Positiva	45	17 Jun 95	2
Features the Harambee Gospel Choir from New Jersey.				

Randy VANWARMER
US

SINGLES:	HITS 1			WEEKS 11
JUST WHEN I NEEDED YOU MOST	*Bearsville*	8	*4 Aug 79*	11

VAPORS
UK

SINGLES:	HITS 3			WEEKS 23
TURNING JAPANESE	*United Artists*	3	*9 Feb 80*	13
NEWS AT TEN	*United Artists*	44	*5 Jul 80*	4
JIMMIE JONES	*Liberty*	44	*11 Jul 81*	6
ALBUMS:	HITS 1			WEEKS 6
NEW CLEAR DAYS	*United Artists*	44	*7 Jun 80*	6

VARDIS
UK

SINGLES:	HITS 1			WEEKS 4
LET'S GO	*Logo*	59	*27 Sep 80*	4
ALBUMS:	HITS 1			WEEKS 1
100 MPH	*Logo*	52	*1 Nov 80*	1

VARIOUS ARTISTS
Multi-National

SINGLES:	HITS 2			WEEKS 28
THE BRITS 1990 (DANCE MEDLEY) [M]	*RCA*	2	*3 Mar 90*	7
Mix of 8 dance hits by British acts chosen by Jonathan King. It was performed at the Brit Awards, Feb 90.				
PERFECT DAY	*Chrysalis*	1	*29 Nov 97*	19
Charity record with proceeds to BBC Children In Need. Originally recorded by Lou Reed and appeared on the B-side of his 1973 hit Walk On The Wild Side.				
PERFECT DAY [RE]	*Chrysalis*	68	*18 Apr 98*	2

VARIOUS ARTISTS (EPs)

SINGLES:	HITS 13			WEEKS 23
THE FOOD CHRISTMAS EP 1989 [EP]	*Food*	63	*9 Dec 89*	1
Tracks: Like Princes Do (Crazyhead)/ I Don't Want That Kind Of Love (Jesus Jones)/ Info Freako (Diesel Park West).				
THE FURTHER ADVENTURES OF NORTH - MORE UNDERGROUND DANCE [EP]	*Deconstruction*	64	*20 Jan 90*	2
Tracks: Dream 17 (Annette)/ Carino 90 (T-Coy)/ The Way I Feel (Frequency 9)/ Stop This Thing (Dynasty Of Two featuring Rowetta).				
THE APPLE [EP]	*Apple*	60	*2 Nov 91*	1
Tracks: Those Were The Days (Mary Hopkin)/ That's The Way God Planned It (Billy Preston)/ Sour Milk Tea (Jackie Lomax)/ Come And Get It (Badfinger).				
FOURPLAY VOLUME 1 [EP]	*XL Recordings*	45	*11 Jul 92*	2
Tracks: DJ's Unite (DJ's Unite)/ Alright (Glide)/ Be Free (Noise Factory)/ True Devotion (EQ).				
THE FRED [EP]	*Heavenly*	26	*7 Nov 92*	3
Charity Record with Proceeds to The Terrence Higgins Trust (for AIDS research). Tracks: Deeply Dippy (Rockingbirds)/ Don't Talk Just Kiss (Flowered Up)/ I'm Too Sexy (St Etienne).				
GIMME SHELTER [EP]	*Food*	23	*24 Apr 93*	4
Charity release for the 'Putting Our House In Order' project to support the homeless. Only common track available on all formats: Gimme Shelter – Interview. All other tracks on the 4 formats available were by various acts recording their versions of the Rolling Stone song Gimme Shelter.				
SUBPLATES VOLUME 1 [EP]	*Suburban Base*	69	*5 Jun 93*	1
Tracks: Style Warz (Son'z Of A Loop Da Loop Era) / Funky Dope Bass (Q Bass)/ The Chopper (DJ Hype)/ Look No Further (Run Tings).				
THE 2 TONE [EP]	*2-Tone*	30	*9 Oct 93*	3
Tracks: Gangsters (Special A.K.A.)/ The Prince (Madness) / On My Radio (Selecter) / Tears Of A Clown (Beat).				
HELP [EP]	*Go! Discs*	51	*4 Nov 95*	2
Charity Record with Proceeds to 'War Child' (to help Bosnian refugee children). Tracks: Lucky (Radiohead)/ 50ft Queenie (Live) (PJ Harvey)/ Momentum (Guru's Jazzmatazz) (Guru)/ Untitled (no artist credit). The last track was used as incidental music for the Help TV documentary.				
NEW YORK UNDERCOVER 4-TRACK EP [EP]	*Uptown*	39	*16 Mar 96*	1
From the film of the same name. Tracks: Tell Me What You Like (Guy)/ Dom Perignon (Little Shawn) / I Miss You (Monifah)/ Jeeps, Lex Coups, Bimaz & Benz (Lost Boyz).				
DANGEROUS MINDS [EP]	*MCA*	35	*30 Mar 96*	1
From the film of the same name. Tracks: Curiosity (Aaron Hall)/ Gin & Juice (De Vante)/ It's Alright (Sista featuring Craig Mack).				
FEVER PITCH THE EP [EP]	*Blanco Y Negro*	65	*10 May 97*	1
From the film of the same name. Tracks: Goin' Back (Pretenders)/ There She Goes (La's)/ How Can We Hang On To A Dream (Orlando)/ Football (Nick Hornby).				
TRADE EP 2 [EP]	*Tidy Trax*	75	*26 Sep 98*	1
Tracks: Put Your House In Order (Steve Thomas)/ The Dawn (Tony De Vit). This was sales of a 12" only. The CD format had 6 tracks, including the two above, and was not eligible for the charts. The other 4 tracks were available on two other 12" singles. Trade EP 1 charted at No. 103, and Trade EP 3 at No. 96.				

VARIOUS ARTISTS FOR CHILDREN'S PROMISE — UK/US

SINGLES:		HITS 1		WEEKS 2
IT'S ONLY ROCK 'N' ROLL	Universal Music TV	19	25 Dec 99	2

Charity record in aid of The Children's Promise (The Millennium Final Hour Appeal).

Junior VASQUEZ — US

(See also Shades Of Love (Junior Vasquez meets Johnny Vicious).)

SINGLES:		HITS 2		WEEKS 5
GET YOUR HANDS OFF MY MAN!	Positiva	22	15 Jul 95	3
IF MADONNA CALLS	Multiply	24	31 Aug 96	2

Madonna's voice from a phone message left on his answering machine.

Elaine VASSELL – See BEATMASTERS; DEFINITION OF SOUND

Sven VATH — Germany

SINGLES:		HITS 3		WEEKS 5
L'ESPERANZA	Eye-Q	63	24 Jul 93	2
AN ACCIDENT IN PARADISE (REMIXES)	Eye-Q	57	6 Nov 93	2
HARLEQUIN - THE BEAUTY AND THE BEAST	Eye-Q	72	22 Oct 94	1

Frankie VAUGHAN — UK

SINGLES:		HITS 31		WEEKS 232
ISTANBUL (NOT CONSTANTINOPLE)	His Master's Voice	11	30 Jan 54	1
HAPPY DAYS AND LONELY NIGHTS	His Master's Voice	12	29 Jan 55	3
TWEEDLE DEE	Philips	17	23 Apr 55	1
SEVENTEEN	Philips	18	3 Dec 55	3
MY BOY FLAT TOP	Philips	20	4 Feb 56	2
THE GREEN DOOR	Philips	2	10 Nov 56	15
THE GARDEN OF EDEN	Philips	1	12 Jan 57	13
MAN ON FIRE / WANDERIN' EYES	Philips	6	5 Oct 57	12
GOT-TA HAVE SOMETHING IN THE BANK, FRANK	Philips	8	2 Nov 57	11
KISSES SWEETER THAN WINE	Philips	8	21 Dec 57	11
CAN'T GET ALONG WITHOUT YOU / WE ARE NOT ALONE	Philips	11	8 Mar 58	6
KEWPIE DOLL	Philips	10	10 May 58	12
WONDERFUL THINGS	Philips	22	2 Aug 58	3
WONDERFUL THINGS [RE]	Philips	27	13 Sep 58	3
AM I WASTING MY TIME ON YOU	Philips	25	11 Oct 58	2
AM I WASTING MY TIME ON YOU [RE]	Philips	27	10 Jan 59	2
THAT'S MY DOLL	Philips	28	31 Jan 59	2
COME SOFTLY TO ME	Philips	9	2 May 59	9
THE HEART OF A MAN	Philips	5	25 Jul 59	14
WALKIN' TALL	Philips	28	19 Sep 59	1
WALKIN' TALL [RE]	Philips	29	3 Oct 59	1
WHAT MORE DO YOU WANT	Philips	25	30 Jan 60	2
KOOKIE LITTLE PARADISE	Philips	31	24 Sep 60	5
MILORD	Philips	34	29 Oct 60	6
TOWER OF STRENGTH	Philips	1	11 Nov 61	13
DON'T STOP - TWIST!	Philips	22	3 Feb 62	7
HERCULES	Philips	42	29 Sep 62	4
LOOP DE LOOP	Philips	5	26 Jan 63	12

Above hit: Frankie VAUGHAN with the Peter KNIGHT SINGERS.
(under ISTANBUL)

Above hit: Frankie VAUGHAN with Geoff LOVE and his Orchestra.
(under HAPPY DAYS AND LONELY NIGHTS)

Above hit: Frankie VAUGHAN with Wally STOTT and his Orchestra and Chorus.
(under TWEEDLE DEE)

Above hit: Frankie VAUGHAN with Wally STOTT and his Orchestra.
(under SEVENTEEN)

Original by Boyd Bennett reached No. 39 in the US in 1955.
(under MY BOY FLAT TOP)

Man On Fire from the film of the same name and originally recorded by Bing Crosby.
Above 4: Frankie VAUGHAN with Wally STOTT and his Orchestra and Chorus.
(under MAN ON FIRE / WANDERIN' EYES)

Originally recorded by Bob Jaxon.
Above hit: Frankie VAUGHAN and the KAYE SISTERS with Wally STOTT and his Orchestra.
(under GOT-TA HAVE SOMETHING IN THE BANK, FRANK)

Originally recorded by The Weavers in 1951.
Above hit: Frankie VAUGHAN with Wally STOTT and his Orchestra and Chorus.
(under KISSES SWEETER THAN WINE)

Certain pressings had title as We're Not Alone.
Above hit: Frankie VAUGHAN with Ray ELLIS and his Orchestra and Chorus.
(under CAN'T GET ALONG WITHOUT YOU)

Above hit: Frankie VAUGHAN with Wally STOTT and his Orchestra and Chorus.
(under KEWPIE DOLL)

From the film of the same name.
Above hit: Frankie VAUGHAN with Wally STOTT and his Orchestra.
(under WONDERFUL THINGS)

Above hit: Frankie VAUGHAN with Ray ELLIS and his Orchestra.
(under AM I WASTING MY TIME ON YOU)

From the film 'The Lady Is A Square'.
Above hit: Frankie VAUGHAN with Wally STOTT and his Orchestra.
(under THAT'S MY DOLL)

Above hit: Frankie VAUGHAN and the KAYE SISTERS with Wally STOTT and his Orchestra.
(under COME SOFTLY TO ME)

From the film of the same name.
Above hit: Frankie VAUGHAN with Wally STOTT and his Orchestra and Chorus.
(under THE HEART OF A MAN)

Above hit: Frankie VAUGHAN with Wally STOTT and his Orchestra and Chorus.
(under MILORD)

Originally recorded by Gene McDaniels.
(under TOWER OF STRENGTH)

Original by Johnny Thunder reached No. 4 in the US in 1963.
(under LOOP DE LOOP)

HEY MAMA	*Philips*	21	*22 Jun 63*	9
HELLO DOLLY	*Philips*	18	*6 Jun 64*	11
From the musical of the same name.				
SOMEONE MUST HAVE HURT YOU A LOT	*Philips*	46	*13 Mar 65*	1
THERE MUST BE A WAY	*Columbia*	7	*26 Aug 67*	19
SO TIRED	*Columbia*	21	*18 Nov 67*	9
THERE MUST BE A WAY	*Columbia*	30	*6 Jan 68*	2
NEVERTHELESS	*Columbia*	29	*2 Mar 68*	5
Above 3: Frankie VAUGHAN with Alyn AINSWORTH and his Orchestra.				

ALBUMS:	**HITS 4**		**WEEKS 20**	
FRANKIE VAUGHAN AT THE LONDON PALLADIUM	*Philips*	6	*5 Sep 59*	2
FRANKIE VAUGHAN SONGBOOK	*Philips*	40	*4 Nov 67*	1
THERE MUST BE A WAY	*Columbia*	22	*25 Nov 67*	8
100 GOLDEN GREATS	*Ronco*	24	*12 Nov 77*	9

Malcolm VAUGHAN
UK

SINGLES:	**HITS 9**		**WEEKS 106**	
EV'RY DAY OF MY LIFE	*His Master's Voice*	5	*2 Jul 55*	16
WITH YOUR LOVE	*His Master's Voice*	20	*28 Jan 56*	1
Above hit: Malcolm VAUGHAN with the Peter KNIGHT SINGERS.				
WITH YOUR LOVE [RE-1ST]	*His Master's Voice*	18	*11 Feb 56*	1
WITH YOUR LOVE [RE-2ND]	*His Master's Voice*	20	*3 Mar 56*	1
ST. THERESE OF THE ROSES	*His Master's Voice*	27	*27 Oct 56*	1
ST. THERESE OF THE ROSES [RE]	*His Master's Voice*	3	*17 Nov 56*	19
THE WORLD IS MINE	*His Master's Voice*	30	*13 Apr 57*	1
THE WORLD IS MINE [RE-1ST]	*His Master's Voice*	29	*4 May 57*	2
CHAPEL OF THE ROSES	*His Master's Voice*	13	*11 May 57*	8
THE WORLD IS MINE [RE-2ND]	*His Master's Voice*	26	*1 Jun 57*	1
MY SPECIAL ANGEL	*His Master's Voice*	3	*30 Nov 57*	14
TO BE LOVED	*His Master's Voice*	14	*22 Mar 58*	12
MORE THAN EVER (COME PRIMA)	*His Master's Voice*	5	*18 Oct 58*	14
Above 2: Malcolm VAUGHAN with the Michael SAMMES SINGERS.				
WAIT FOR ME (TI DIRO) / WILLINGLY (MELODIE PERDUE)	*His Master's Voice*	28	*28 Feb 59*	1
WAIT FOR ME (TI DIRO) [RE]	*His Master's Voice*	13	*14 Mar 59*	14
Majority of hits listed above had Orchestra conducted by Frank Cordell.				

Norman VAUGHAN with the "CORONA SCHOOL CHILDREN"
UK

SINGLES:	**HITS 1**		**WEEKS 5**	
SWINGING IN THE RAIN (SINGIN' IN THE RAIN)	*Pye*	34	*19 May 62*	5
Originally recorded by Cliff Edwards.				

Sarah VAUGHAN
US

(See also Various Artists: Studio Cast 'South Pacific'.)

SINGLES:	**HITS 3**		**WEEKS 34**	
PASSING STRANGERS	*Mercury*	22	*28 Sep 57*	2
Above hit: Sarah VAUGHAN and Billy ECKSTINE.				
BROKEN-HEARTED MELODY	*Mercury*	7	*12 Sep 59*	13
LET'S / SERENATA	*Columbia*	37	*31 Dec 60*	3
Serenata does not credit the Chorus. Serenata originally recorded as an instrumental by Leroy Anderson.				
Above hit: Sarah VAUGHAN with Joe REISMAN'S ORCHESTRA and Chorus.				
SERENATA [RE]	*Columbia*	47	*4 Feb 61*	1
PASSING STRANGERS [RI]	*Mercury*	20	*15 Mar 69*	15
Above hit: Sarah VAUGHAN and Billy ECKSTINE.				

EPS:	**HITS 1**		**WEEKS 2**	
SMOOTH SARAH	*Mercury*	11	*26 Mar 60*	2

ALBUMS:	**HITS 1**		**WEEKS 1**	
NO COUNT - SARAH	*Mercury*	19	*26 Mar 60*	1

Stevie Ray VAUGHAN and DOUBLE TROUBLE
US

ALBUMS:	**HITS 1**		**WEEKS 1**	
IN STEP	*Epic*	63	*15 Jul 89*	1

VAUGHAN BROTHERS
US

ALBUMS:	**HITS 1**		**WEEKS 1**	
FAMILY STYLE	*Epic*	63	*20 Oct 90*	1

Billy VAUGHN and his Orchestra
US

(See also Pat Boone; Tab Hunter; Hilltoppers.)

SINGLES:	**HITS 2**		**WEEKS 8**	
THE SHIFTING WHISPERING SANDS	*London*	20	*28 Jan 56*	1
Above hit: Billy VAUGHN and his Orchestra and Chorus, narration by Ken NORDENE.				
A THEME FROM THE 'THREEPENNY OPERA' (MACK THE KNIFE)	*London*	12	*24 Mar 56*	7

VEBA – See RAE and CHRISTIAN featuring VEBA

Bobby VEE
US

(See also Bobby Vee and the Crickets.)

SINGLES:		HITS 10		WEEKS 134	
RUBBER BALL	London	4	21 Jan 61	11
Written by Gene Pitney.				
MORE THAN I CAN SAY / STAYIN' IN	London	4	15 Apr 61	16
Stayin' In no longer listed from 13 May 61. As an AA side it peaked at No. 13.				
HOW MANY TEARS	London	10	5 Aug 61	13
TAKE GOOD CARE OF MY BABY	London	3	28 Oct 61	16
Originally recorded by Dion.				
RUN TO HIM	London	6	23 Dec 61	15
PLEASE DON'T ASK ABOUT BARBARA	Liberty	29	10 Mar 62	9
SHARING YOU	Liberty	10	9 Jun 62	13
Above hit: Bobby VEE with the Johnny MANN SINGERS.				
A FOREVER KIND OF LOVE	Liberty	13	29 Sep 62	19
THE NIGHT HAS A THOUSAND EYES	Liberty	3	9 Feb 63	12
From the film 'Just For Fun'.				
BOBBY TOMORROW	Liberty	21	22 Jun 63	10
The B-side Charms was the official A-side in the US.				
Above hit: Bobby VEE with the Johnny MANN SINGERS.				

EPS:		HITS 4		WEEKS 31	
BOBBY VEE NO. 1	London	19	26 Aug 61	1
SINCERELY	Liberty	8	22 Dec 62	24
A FOREVER KIND OF LOVE	Liberty	14	29 Jun 63	4
BOBBY VEE'S BIGGEST HITS	Stateside	16	5 Oct 63	2

ALBUMS:		HITS 6		WEEKS 46	
TAKE GOOD CARE OF MY BABY	London	7	24 Feb 62	8
HITS OF THE ROCKIN' 50'S	London	20	31 Mar 62	1
A BOBBY VEE RECORDING SESSION	Liberty	10	12 Jan 63	11
BOBBY VEE'S GOLDEN GREATS	Liberty	10	20 Apr 63	14
THE NIGHT HAS A THOUSAND EYES	Liberty	15	5 Oct 63	2
THE BOBBY VEE SINGLES ALBUM	United Artists	5	19 Apr 80	10

Bobby VEE and the CRICKETS
US

(See also Crickets; Bobby Vee.)

EPS:		HITS 1		WEEKS 16	
JUST FOR FUN	Liberty	1	20 Apr 63	16
ALBUMS:		**HITS 1**		**WEEKS 27**	
BOBBY VEE MEETS THE CRICKETS	Liberty	2	27 Oct 62	27

Little Louie VEGA and Marc ANTHONY
US

SINGLES:		HITS 1		WEEKS 4	
RIDE ON THE RHYTHM	Atlantic	71	5 Oct 91	1
RIDE ON THE RHYTHM [RI]	Atlantic	70	23 May 92	1
Above hit: Louie VEGA and Marc ANTHONY.				
RIDE ON THE RHYTHM [RM]	Perfecto Red	36	31 Jan 98	2
Remixed by Mr. Roy.				
Above hit: "Little" LOUIE and Marc ANTHONY.				

Suzanne VEGA
US

SINGLES:		HITS 11		WEEKS 52	
SMALL BLUE THING	A&M	65	18 Jan 86	3
MARLENE ON THE WALL	A&M	21	22 Mar 86	9
Original release reached No. 83 in 1985. Written about Marlene Dietrich.				
LEFT OF CENTRE	A&M	32	7 Jun 86	9
Label has British spelling; the sleeve the US variant 'Center'. From the film 'Pretty In Pink'.				
Above hit: Suzanne VEGA featuring Joe JACKSON on piano.				
LUKA	A&M	23	23 May 87	8
TOM'S DINER	A&M	58	18 Jul 87	3
BOOK OF DREAMS	A&M	66	19 May 90	1
TOM'S DINER [RM]	A&M	2	28 Jul 90	10
Though this credits her as a featuring artist, this is actually a remix by DNA of her earlier hit.				
Above hit: DNA featuring Suzanne VEGA.				
IN LIVERPOOL	A&M	52	22 Aug 92	2
99.9° F	A&M	46	24 Oct 92	2
BLOOD MAKES NOISE	A&M	60	19 Dec 92	3
WHEN HEROES GO DOWN	A&M	58	6 Mar 93	1
NO CHEAP THRILL	A&M	40	22 Feb 97	1

ALBUMS:		HITS 6		WEEKS 127	
SUZANNE VEGA	A&M	55	19 Oct 85	14
SUZANNE VEGA [RE]	A&M	11	12 Apr 86	57
SOLITUDE STANDING	A&M	2	9 May 87	39
DAYS OF OPEN HAND	A&M	7	28 Apr 90	7

99.9° F	A&M	20	19 Sep 92	4
NINE OBJECTS OF DESIRE	A&M	43	8 Mar 97	3
TRIED AND TRUE – THE BEST OF SUZANNE VEGA	A&M	46	31 Oct 98	3

Tata VEGA   US

SINGLES:	HITS 1			WEEKS 4
GET IT UP FOR LOVE / I JUST KEEP THINKING ABOUT YOU BABY	Motown	52	26 May 79	4

VEGAS   UK

SINGLES:	HITS 3			WEEKS 10
POSSESSED	RCA	32	19 Sep 92	4
SHE	RCA	43	28 Nov 92	4
WALK INTO THE WIND	RCA	65	3 Apr 93	2

Features vocals by Siobhan Fahey of Shakespears Sister.

Rosie VELA   US

SINGLES:	HITS 1			WEEKS 7
MAGIC SMILE	A&M	27	17 Jan 87	7
ALBUMS:	HITS 1			WEEKS 11
ZAZU	A&M	20	31 Jan 87	11

Wil. VELOZ – See LOS DEL MAR featuring Wil. VELOZ

VELVELETTES   US

SINGLES:	HITS 1			WEEKS 7
THESE THINGS WILL KEEP ME LOVING YOU	Tamla Motown	34	31 Jul 71	7

VELVET UNDERGROUND   UK/US

SINGLES:	HITS 1			WEEKS 1
VENUS IN FURS (LIVE)	Sire	71	12 Mar 94	1

Featured in the Dunlop Tyres TV commercial. Live recording from the Olympia in Paris, Jun 93.

ALBUMS:	HITS 3			WEEKS 9
V.U.	Polydor	47	23 Feb 85	4

Remix album of previously unreleased material.

LIVE MCMXCIII	Sire	70	13 Nov 93	1

Live recordings from the Olympia in Paris, Jun 93.

THE BEST OF LOU REED AND THE VELVET UNDERGROUND	Global Television	56	28 Oct 95	4

Features both Lou Reed's solo and group material.
Above hit: Lou REED and the VELVET UNDERGROUND.

VELVETS   US

SINGLES:	HITS 2			WEEKS 2
THAT LUCKY OLD SUN	London	46	13 May 61	1
TONIGHT (COULD BE THE NIGHT)	London	50	19 Aug 61	1

VENGABOYS   Holland/Hungary/Brazil/Spain/Trinidad

SINGLES:	HITS 5			WEEKS 60
UP AND DOWN	Positiva	4	28 Nov 98	15
WE LIKE TO PARTY! (THE VENGABUS)	Positiva	3	13 Mar 99	14
BOOM, BOOM, BOOM, BOOM!!	Positiva	1	26 Jun 99	15
WE'RE GOING TO IBIZA!	Jive	69	11 Sept 99	1

Import. Based around Typically Tropical's Barbados.
Above hit: DANSKI and DJ DELMUNDO present VENGABOYS.

WE'RE GOING TO IBIZA!	Positiva	1	18 Sept 99	12
KISS (WHEN THE SUN DON'T SHINE)	Positiva	3	18 Dec 99	3
ALBUMS:	HITS 1			WEEKS 40
THE PARTY ALBUM!	Positiva	6	3 Apr 99	40

VENOM   UK

ALBUMS:	HITS 2			WEEKS 2
AT WAR WITH SATAN	Neat	64	21 Apr 84	1
POSSESSED	Neat	99	13 Apr 85	1

VENT 414   UK

SINGLES:	HITS 1			WEEKS 1
FIXER	Polydor	71	28 Sep 96	1

Anthony VENTURA ORCHESTRA   Switzerland

ALBUMS:	HITS 1			WEEKS 4
DREAM LOVER	Lotus	44	20 Jan 79	4

VENTURES | | | | US

SINGLES:		HITS 4			WEEKS 31
WALK DON'T RUN	Top Rank		8	10 Sep 60	13
Originally recorded by Johnny Smith.					
PERFIDIA	London		4	3 Dec 60	13
Originally recorded by Xavier Cugat in 1941.					
RAM-BUNK-SHUSH	London		45	11 Mar 61	1
Originally recorded by Bill Doggett in 1957.					
LULLABY OF THE LEAVES	London		43	13 May 61	4
Originally recorded by George Olsen in 1932.					
EPS:		HITS 1			WEEKS 1
THE VENTURES	London		20	13 May 61	1

VERACOCHA | | | | Holland

SINGLES:		HITS 1			WEEKS 4
CARTE BLANCHE	Positiva		22	15 May 99	4

Tom VERLAINE | | | | US

ALBUMS:		HITS 1			WEEKS 1
FLASH LIGHT	Fontana		99	14 Mar 87	1

Al VERLANE – See PING PING and Al VERLANE

VERNONS GIRLS | | | | UK

SINGLES:		HITS 4			WEEKS 31
LOVER PLEASE	Decca		16	19 May 62	9
LOVER PLEASE [RE] / YOU KNOW WHAT I MEAN	Decca		39	25 Aug 62	7
You Know What I Mean listed from 1 Sep 62.					
THE LOCO-MOTION	Decca		47	8 Sep 62	1
YOU KNOW WHAT I MEAN [RE-1ST]	Decca		37	20 Oct 62	3
YOU KNOW WHAT I MEAN [RE-2ND]	Decca		50	17 Nov 62	1
FUNNY ALL OVER	Decca		31	5 Jan 63	8
DO THE BIRD	Decca		50	20 Apr 63	1
DO THE BIRD [RE]	Decca		44	4 May 63	1

VERNONS WONDERLAND | | | | Germany

SINGLES:		HITS 1			WEEKS 1
VERNONS WONDERLAND	Eye-Q Classics		59	25 May 96	1
First released in Germany, 1993. Used on the TV series 'Baywatch' as incidental music.					

VERUCA SALT | | | | US

SINGLES:		HITS 4			WEEKS 5
SEETHER	Scared Hitless		61	2 Jul 94	1
SEETHER [RI]	Hi-Rise Recordings		73	3 Dec 94	1
NUMBER ONE BLIND	Hi-Rise Recordings		68	4 Feb 95	1
VOLCANO GIRLS	Outpost Recordings		56	22 Feb 97	1
BENJAMIN	Outpost Recordings		75	30 Aug 97	1
ALBUMS:		HITS 1			WEEKS 2
AMERICAN THIGHS	Hi-Rise Recordings		47	15 Oct 94	2
Named after a line in AC/DC's You Shook Me All Night Long.					

VERVE | | | | UK

SINGLES:		HITS 9			WEEKS 50
SHE'S A SUPERSTAR	Hut		66	4 Jul 92	1
BLUE	Hut		69	22 May 93	1
THIS IS MUSIC	Hut		35	13 May 95	3
ON YOUR OWN	Hut		28	24 Jun 95	2
HISTORY	Hut		24	30 Sep 95	3
BITTER SWEET SYMPHONY	Hut		2	28 Jun 97	11
Samples an orchestral version of the Rolling Stones' The Last Time by Andrew Loog Oldham.					
THE DRUGS DON'T WORK	Hut		1	13 Sep 97	12
LUCKY MAN	Hut		7	6 Dec 97	13
BITTER SWEET SYMPHONY [RE]	Hut		70	3 Jan 98	2
THE DRUGS DON'T WORK [RE]	Hut		66	3 Jan 98	1
SONNET	Hut		74	30 May 98	1
Import.					
ALBUMS:		HITS 3			WEEKS 90
A STORM IN HEAVEN	Hut		27	3 Jul 93	2
A NORTHERN SOUL	Hut		13	15 Jul 95	11
URBAN HYMNS	Hut		1	11 Oct 97	77

A VERY GOOD FRIEND OF MINE featuring JOY — Italy

SINGLES:	HITS 1				WEEKS 1
JUST ROUND	Positiva	55	3 Jul	99	1

Samples Stevie Wonder's Uptight.

VIBRATIONS – See Tony JACKSON and the VIBRATIONS

VIBRATORS — UK

SINGLES:	HITS 2				WEEKS 8
AUTOMATIC LOVER	Epic	35	18 Mar 78		5
JUDY SAYS (KNOCK YOU IN THE HEAD)	Epic	70	17 Jun 78		3
ALBUMS:	HITS 2				WEEKS 7
PURE MANIA	Epic	49	25 Jun 77		5
V2	Epic	33	29 Apr 78		2

VICE SQUAD — UK

SINGLES:	HITS 1				WEEKS 1
OUT OF REACH	Riot City	68	13 Feb 82		1
ALBUMS:	HITS 2				WEEKS 10
NO CAUSE FOR CONCERN	Zonophone	32	24 Oct 81		5
STAND STRONG STAND PROUD	Riot City	47	22 May 82		5

Johnny VICIOUS – See SHADES OF LOVE (Junior VASQUEZ meets Johnny VICIOUS)

Sid VICIOUS — UK

(See also Sex Pistols.)

ALBUMS:	HITS 1				WEEKS 8
SID SINGS	Virgin	30	15 Dec 79		8

VICIOUS PINK — UK

SINGLES:	HITS 1				WEEKS 4
CCCAN'T YOU SEE...	Parlophone	67	15 Sep 84		4

Mike VICKERS – See Kenny EVERETT

Original Motion Picture Soundtrack "Body Rock" vocal: Maria VIDAL — US

SINGLES:	HITS 1				WEEKS 13
BODY ROCK	EMI America	11	24 Aug 85		13

From the film of the same name.

VIDEO KIDS — Holland

SINGLES:	HITS 1				WEEKS 1
WOODPECKERS FROM SPACE	Epic	72	5 Oct 85		1

Original release reached No. 89 earlier that year.

VIDEO SYMPHONIC — UK

SINGLES:	HITS 1				WEEKS 3
THE FLAME TREES OF THIKA	EMI	42	24 Oct 81		3

Theme from the Thames ITV series of the same name.

VIENNA PHILHARMONIC ORCHESTRA conducted by Aram KHACHATURIAN — Austria

SINGLES:	HITS 1				WEEKS 14
THE 'ONEDIN LINE' THEME	Decca	15	18 Dec 71		14

Music from Spartacus, adapted for the theme of the BBC1 TV series.

ALBUMS:	HITS 1				WEEKS 15
SPARTACUS	Decca	16	22 Jan 72		15

VIENNA SYMPHONY ORCHESTRA — Austria

ALBUMS:	HITS 1				WEEKS 4
SYMPHONIC ROCK WITH THE VIENNA SYMPHONY ORCHESTRA	Stylus	43	4 Apr 87		4

VIEW FROM THE HILL — UK

SINGLES:	HITS 2				WEEKS 6
NO CONVERSATION	EMI	58	19 Jul 86		3
I'M NO REBEL	EMI	59	21 Feb 87		3

VIKKI — UK

SINGLES:	HITS 1				WEEKS 3
LOVE IS . . .	PRT	49	4 May 85		3

UKs Eurovision entry in 1983, it came 4th.

VILLAGE PEOPLE · US

SINGLES:		HITS 6			WEEKS 67
SAN FRANCISCO (YOU'VE GOT ME)	DJM		45	3 Dec 77	6
Y.M.C.A.	Mercury		1	25 Nov 78	16
IN THE NAVY	Mercury		2	17 Mar 79	9
GO WEST	Mercury		15	16 Jun 79	8
CAN'T STOP THE MUSIC	Mercury		11	9 Aug 80	11
From the film of the same name.					
SEX OVER THE PHONE	Record Shack		59	9 Feb 85	5
Y.M.C.A. '93 REMIX [RM-1ST]			12	4 Dec 93	7
Remixed by Dave Ford.					
IN THE NAVY - 1994 REMIXES [RM]	Bell		36	28 May 94	2
Remixed by Mr. Hyder and Mr. Kalif.					
YMCA MILLENNIUM MIX [RM-2ND]	Wrasse		35	27 Nov 99	3
Remixed by Almighty.					
ALBUMS:		HITS 4			WEEKS 37
CRUISIN'	Mercury		24	27 Jan 79	9
GO WEST	Mercury		14	12 May 79	19
CAN'T STOP THE MUSIC [OST]	Mercury		9	16 Aug 80	8
Includes tracks by Ritchie Family and David London.					
THE BEST OF THE VILLAGE PEOPLE	Bell		72	18 Dec 93	1

Gene VINCENT · US

SINGLES:		HITS 8			WEEKS 51
BE BOP A LULA	Capitol		30	14 Jul 56	2
From the film 'The Girl Can't Help It'.					
BE BOP A LULA [RE-1ST]	Capitol		16	25 Aug 56	3
BE BOP A LULA [RE-2ND]	Capitol		23	29 Sep 56	2
RACE WITH THE DEVIL	Capitol		28	13 Oct 56	1
Above 4: Gene VINCENT and the BLUE CAPS.					
BLUE JEAN BOP	Capitol		16	20 Oct 56	5
WILD CAT	Capitol		21	9 Jan 60	3
MY HEART	Capitol		16	12 Mar 60	6
Above hit: Gene VINCENT and the BLUE CAPS.					
WILD CAT [RE]	Capitol		39	12 Mar 60	3
MY HEART [RE-1ST]	Capitol		47	30 Apr 60	1
MY HEART [RE-2ND]	Capitol		36	21 May 60	1
PISTOL PACKIN' MAMA	Capitol		15	18 Jun 60	9
Originally recorded by Al Dexter.					
Above hit: Gene VINCENT with the BEAT BOYS.					
SHE SHE LITTLE SHEILA	Capitol		22	3 Jun 61	10
Recording from 1959.					
SHE SHE LITTLE SHEILA [RE]	Capitol		44	19 Aug 61	1
I'M GOING HOME (TO SEE MY BABY)	Capitol		36	2 Sep 61	4
Above hit: Gene VINCENT with SOUNDS INCORPORATED.					
EPS:		HITS 1			WEEKS 1
RACE WITH THE DEVIL	Capitol		19	6 Oct 62	1
ALBUMS:		HITS 1			WEEKS 2
CRAZY TIMES	Capitol		12	16 Jul 60	2

Vinnie VINCENT · US

ALBUMS:		HITS 1			WEEKS 2
ALL SYSTEMS GO	Chrysalis		51	28 May 88	2

VINDALOO SUMMER SPECIAL · UK

SINGLES:		HITS 1			WEEKS 3
ROCKIN' WITH RITA (HEAD TO TOE)	Vindaloo		56	19 Jul 86	3

Bobby VINTON · US

SINGLES:		HITS 3			WEEKS 29
ROSES ARE RED (MY LOVE)	Columbia		15	4 Aug 62	8
Originally recorded by Darrell and the Oxfords.					
THERE! I'VE SAID IT AGAIN	Columbia		34	21 Dec 63	10
Originally recorded by the Benny Carter Orchestra in 1941.					
BLUE VELVET	Epic		2	29 Sep 90	10
Featured in the Nivea Lotion TV commercial. Originally recorded by Tony Bennett in 1951.					
ROSES ARE RED (MY LOVE) [RI]	Epic		71	17 Nov 90	1
ALBUMS:		HITS 1			WEEKS 2
BLUE VELVET	Epic		67	17 Nov 90	2
Compilation.					

VIOLENT FEMMES · US

ALBUMS:		HITS 1			WEEKS 1
THE BLIND LEADING THE NAKED	Slash		81	1 Mar 86	1

VIOLINSKI — UK

SINGLES:	HITS 1		WEEKS 9
CLOG DANCE	*Jet*	17	*17 Feb 79* 9
ALBUMS:	HITS 1		WEEKS 1
NO CAUSE FOR ALARM	*Jet*	49	*26 May 79* 1

VIPER — Belgium

SINGLES:	HITS 1		WEEKS 1
THE TWISTER	*Hooj Choons*	55	*7 Feb 98* 1
Samples Nina Simone's Feeling Good.			

VIPERS SKIFFLE GROUP — UK

SINGLES:	HITS 3		WEEKS 18
DON'T YOU ROCK ME DADDY-O	*Parlophone*	10	*26 Jan 57* 9
THE CUMBERLAND GAP	*Parlophone*	10	*23 Mar 57* 6
STREAMLINE TRAIN	*Parlophone*	23	*1 Jun 57* 3

VIRUS — UK

SINGLES:	HITS 2		WEEKS 3
SUN	*Perfecto*	62	*26 Aug 95* 1
MOON	*Perfecto*	36	*25 Jan 97* 2
Based on U2's Lemon.			

VISAGE — UK

(See also Midge Ure.)

SINGLES:	HITS 7		WEEKS 56
FADE TO GREY	*Polydor*	8	*20 Dec 80* 15
MIND OF A TOY	*Polydor*	13	*14 Mar 81* 8
VISAGE	*Polydor*	21	*11 Jul 81* 7
THE DAMNED DON'T CRY	*Polydor*	11	*13 Mar 82* 8
NIGHT TRAIN	*Polydor*	12	*26 Jun 82* 10
PLEASURE BOYS	*Polydor*	44	*13 Nov 82* 3
LOVE GLOVE	*Polydor*	54	*1 Sep 84* 3
FADE TO GREY [RM]	*Polydor*	39	*28 Aug 93* 2
Remixed by Bassheads and Andy Stevenson.			
ALBUMS:	HITS 4		WEEKS 58
VISAGE	*Polydor*	13	*24 Jan 81* 29
THE ANVIL	*Polydor*	6	*3 Apr 82* 16
FADE TO GREY – THE SINGLES COLLECTION	*Polydor*	38	*19 Nov 83* 11
BEAT BOY	*Polydor*	79	*3 Nov 84* 2

Michelle VISAGE – See S.O.U.L. S.Y.S.T.E.M. introducing Michelle VISAGE

VISCOUNTS — UK

SINGLES:	HITS 2		WEEKS 18
SHORT'NIN' BREAD	*Pye*	16	*15 Oct 60* 8
WHO PUT THE BOMP	*Pye*	21	*16 Sep 61* 10

VISION — UK

SINGLES:	HITS 1		WEEKS 1
LOVE DANCE	*MVM*	74	*9 Jul 83* 1

VISION MASTERS and Tony KING featuring Kylie MINOGUE — UK/Australia

(See also Kylie Minogue.)

SINGLES:	HITS 1		WEEKS 1
KEEP ON PUMPIN' IT	*PWL*	49	*30 Nov 91* 1

VIXEN — US

SINGLES:	HITS 6		WEEKS 21
EDGE OF A BROKEN HEART	*Manhattan*	51	*3 Sep 88* 4
Written and produced by Richard Marx.			
CRYIN'	*EMI Manhattan*	27	*4 Mar 89* 4
LOVE MADE ME	*EMI USA*	36	*3 Jun 89* 4
EDGE OF A BROKEN HEART [RI]	*EMI USA*	59	*2 Sep 89* 2
HOW MUCH LOVE	*EMI USA*	35	*28 Jul 90* 3
LOVE IS A KILLER	*EMI USA*	41	*20 Oct 90* 2
NOT A MINUTE TOO SOON	*EMI USA*	37	*16 Mar 91* 2
ALBUMS:	HITS 2		WEEKS 5
VIXEN	*Manhattan*	66	*8 Oct 88* 1
REV IT UP	*EMI USA*	20	*18 Aug 90* 4

VOGGUE
Canada

SINGLES:	HITS 1			WEEKS 6
DANCIN' THE NIGHT AWAY	Mercury	39	18 Jul 81	6

VOICE OF LIFE
US

SINGLES:	HITS 1			WEEKS 2
THE WORD IS LOVE (SAY THE WORD)	AM:PM	26	21 Mar 98	2

VOICE OF THE BEEHIVE
UK/US

SINGLES:	HITS 6			WEEKS 51
I SAY NOTHING	London	45	14 Nov 87	5
I WALK THE EARTH	London	42	5 Mar 88	4
DON'T CALL ME BABY	London	15	14 May 88	10
I SAY NOTHING [RI]	London	22	23 Jul 88	6
I WALK THE EARTH [RI]	London	46	22 Oct 88	4
MONSTERS AND ANGELS	London	17	13 Jul 91	10
I THINK I LOVE YOU	London	25	28 Sep 91	6
PERFECT PLACE	London	37	11 Jan 92	6
ALBUMS:	HITS 2			WEEKS 26
LET IT BEE	London	13	2 Jul 88	13
HONEY LINGERS	London	17	24 Aug 91	13

Sterling VOID
UK

SINGLES:	HITS 1			WEEKS 3
RUNAWAY GIRL / IT'S ALL RIGHT	ffrr	53	4 Feb 89	3

VOLCANO
UK/Norway

SINGLES:	HITS 2			WEEKS 4
MORE TO LOVE	Deconstruction	32	23 Jul 94	3
THAT'S THE WAY LOVE IS	Exp	72	18 Nov 95	1

Above hit: VOLCANO with Sam CARTWRIGHT.

Herbert VON KARAJAN conducting the BERLIN PHILHARMONIC ORCHESTRA
Austria/Germany

ALBUMS:	HITS 5			WEEKS 18
BEETHOVEN TRIPLE CONCERTO	His Master's Voice	51	26 Sep 70	2

Above hit: BERLIN PHILHARMONIC ORCHESTRA conducted by Herbert VON KARAJAN – Soloist: David OISTRAKH (violin), Mstislav ROSTROPOVICH (cello), Sviatoslau RICHTER (piano).

THE ESSENTIAL KARAJAN	Deutsche Grammophon	51	16 Apr 88	5

Above hit: Herbert VON KARAJAN.

HOLST: THE PLANETS	Deutsche Grammophon	52	3 Aug 91	2
KARAJAN: ADAGIO	Deutsche Grammophon	30	7 Oct 95	8
ADAGIO 2	Deutsche Grammophon	63	13 Apr 96	1

Compilation of material from 1964-1986.

VOW WOW
US/Japan

ALBUMS:	HITS 1			WEEKS 1
HELTER SKELTER	Arista	75	18 Mar 89	1

VOYAGE
UK/France

SINGLES:	HITS 3			WEEKS 27
FROM EAST TO WEST / SCOTS MACHINE	GTO	13	17 Jun 78	13

Scots Machine listed from 24 Jun 78.

SOUVENIRS	GTO	56	25 Nov 78	7
LET'S FLY AWAY	GTO	38	24 Mar 79	7
ALBUMS:	HITS 1			WEEKS 1
VOYAGE	GTO	59	9 Sep 78	1

VOYAGER
UK

SINGLES:	HITS 1			WEEKS 8
HALFWAY HOTEL	Mountain	33	26 May 79	8

VYBE
US

SINGLES:	HITS 1			WEEKS 1
WARM SUMMER DAZE	Fourth & Broadway	60	7 Oct 95	1

Samples William Bell and Judy Clay's Private Number.

W

Kristine W
US

(See also Our Tribe/One Tribe/O.T. Quartet.)

SINGLES:		HITS 3		WEEKS 7	
FEEL WHAT YOU WANT	Champion	33	25 Jun 94	3
ONE MORE TRY	Champion	41	25 May 96	1
LAND OF THE LIVING	Champion	57	21 Dec 96	1
FEEL WHAT YOU WANT [RM]	Champion	40	5 Jul 97	2
Remixed by Peter Ries.				

W.A.S.P.
US

SINGLES:		HITS 12		WEEKS 38	
WILD CHILD	Capitol	71	31 May 86	2
95 – NASTY	Capitol	70	11 Oct 86	1
SCREAM UNTIL YOU LIKE IT (THEME FROM 'GHOULIES II')	Capitol	32	29 Aug 87	5
Theme from the film.				
I DON'T NEED NO DOCTOR	Capitol	31	31 Oct 87	5
Live recording from Long Beach Arena, California.				
ANIMAL (F**K LIKE A BEAST)	Music For Nations	61	20 Feb 88	3
Original release reached No. 83 in 1984.				
MEAN MAN	Capitol	21	4 Mar 89	5
THE REAL ME	Capitol	23	27 May 89	5
FOREVER FREE	Capitol	25	9 Sep 89	5
CHAINSAW CHARLIE (MURDERS IN THE NEW MORGUE)	Parlophone	17	4 Apr 92	2
THE IDOL	Parlophone	41	6 Jun 92	2
I AM ONE	Parlophone	56	31 Oct 92	1
SUNSET AND BABYLON	Capitol	38	23 Oct 93	2
ALBUMS:		HITS 8		WEEKS 24	
W.A.S.P.	Capitol	51	8 Sep 84	2
THE LAST COMMAND	Capitol	48	9 Nov 85	1
INSIDE THE ELECTRIC CIRCUS	Capitol	53	8 Nov 86	3
LIVE . . . IN THE RAW	Capitol	23	26 Sep 87	4
THE HEADLESS CHILDREN	Capitol	8	15 Apr 89	10
THE CRIMSON IDOL	Parlophone	21	20 Jun 92	2
FIRST BLOOD . . . LAST CUTS	Capitol	69	6 Nov 93	1
Compilation.				
STILL NOT BLACK ENOUGH	Raw Power	52	1 Jul 95	1

Bill WADDINGTON – See CORONATION STREET CAST

Adam WADE with the George PAXTON Orchestra and Chorus
US

SINGLES:		HITS 1		WEEKS 6	
TAKE GOOD CARE OF HER	His Master's Voice	38	10 Jun 61	1
TAKE GOOD CARE OF HER [RE]	His Master's Voice	38	24 Jun 61	5

WAG YA TAIL
UK

SINGLES:		HITS 1		WEEKS 1	
XPAND YA MIND (EXPANSIONS)	PWL Sanctuary	49	3 Oct 92	1

WAH!
UK

SINGLES:		HITS 3		WEEKS 26	
THE STORY OF THE BLUES	Eternal	3	25 Dec 82	12
HOPE (I WISH YOU'D BELIEVE ME)	WEA	37	19 Mar 83	5
COME BACK	Beggars Banquet	20	30 Jun 84	9
Above hit: MIGHTY WAH!				
ALBUMS:		HITS 2		WEEKS 11	
NAH=POO-THE ART OF BLUFF	Eternal	33	18 Jul 81	5
A WORD TO THE WISE GUY	Beggars Banquet	28	4 Aug 84	6
Above hit: MIGHTY WAH!				

Donny WAHLBERG – See SEIKO and Donnie WAHLBERG

WAIKIKIS
Belgium

SINGLES:		HITS 1		WEEKS 2	
HAWAII TATTOO	Pye International	41	13 Mar 65	2

WAILERS – See Bob MARLEY and the WAILERS

John WAITE
UK

SINGLES:		HITS 1		WEEKS 13	
MISSING YOU	EMI America	9	29 Sep 84	11
MISSING YOU [RI]	Chrysalis	56	13 Feb 93	2

ALBUMS:		HITS 1		WEEKS 3
NO BRAKES	EMI America	64	10 Nov 84	3

Terry WAITE – See Carol KIDD featuring Terry WAITE

WAITRESSES
UK

SINGLES:		HITS 1		WEEKS 4
CHRISTMAS WRAPPING	Ze	45	18 Dec 82	4

Originally released 1981 appearing in the Bubbling Under section of the chart.

Tom WAITS
US

ALBUMS:		HITS 8		WEEKS 25
SWORDFISHTROMBONES	Island	62	8 Oct 83	3
RAIN DOGS	Island	29	19 Oct 85	5
FRANKS WILD YEARS	Island	20	5 Sep 87	5

Contains songs from his musical of the same name that was staged in Chicago and New York
during 1986.

BIG TIME	Island	84	8 Oct 88	1
BONE MACHINE	Island	26	19 Sep 92	3
THE BLACK RIDER	Island	47	20 Nov 93	2
BEAUTIFUL MALADIES 1983-1993: THE ISLAND YEARS	Island	63	27 Jun 98	1
MULE VARIATIONS	Epitaph	9	1 May 99	5

Johnny WAKELIN
UK

SINGLES:		HITS 2		WEEKS 20
BLACK SUPERMAN (MUHAMMAD ALI)	Pye	7	18 Jan 75	10

Above hit: Johnny WAKELIN and the KINSHASA BAND.

IN ZAIRE	Pye	4	24 Jul 76	10

Above 2 are tribute songs to Boxing champion Muhammad Ali. Zaire is where he regained his
world heavyweight title on 29 Oct 74, knocking out George Foreman.

Rick WAKEMAN
UK

(See also Anderson Bruford Wakeman Howe; Kevin Peek and Rick Wakeman featuring Jeff Wayne narration Patrick Allen.)

ALBUMS:		HITS 10		WEEKS 125
THE SIX WIVES OF HENRY VIII	A&M	7	24 Feb 73	22
JOURNEY TO THE CENTRE OF THE EARTH	A&M	1	18 May 74	30

Live recordings.
Above hit: Rick WAKEMAN with the LONDON SYMPHONY ORCHESTRA.

THE MYTHS AND LEGENDS OF KING ARTHUR & THE KNIGHTS OF THE ROUND TABLE	A&M	2	12 Apr 75	28

Above hit: Rick WAKEMAN with the ENGLISH CHAMBER CHOIR and
ORCHESTRA.

NO EARTHLY CONNECTION	A&M	9	24 Apr 76	9
WHITE ROCK [OST]	A&M	14	12 Feb 77	9
RICK WAKEMAN'S CRIMINAL RECORD	A&M	25	3 Dec 77	5
RHAPSODIES	A&M	25	2 Jun 79	10
1984	Charisma	24	27 Jun 81	9
THE GOSPELS	Stylus	94	16 May 87	1
RETURN TO THE CENTRE OF THE EARTH	EMI Classics	34	27 Mar 99	2

Features Katrina Leskanich of Katrina and the Waves, Ozzy Osbourne, Justin Hayward and
Bonnie Tyler.
Above hit: Rick WAKEMAN; LONDON SYMPHONY ORCHESTRA; ENGLISH
CHAMBER CHOIR; narrated by Patrick STEWART.

Narada Michael WALDEN
US

SINGLES:		HITS 3		WEEKS 28
TONIGHT I'M ALRIGHT	Atlantic	34	23 Feb 80	9
I SHOULDA LOVED YA	Atlantic	8	26 Apr 80	9
DIVINE EMOTIONS	Reprise	8	23 Apr 88	10

Above hit: NARADA.

ALBUMS:		HITS 1		WEEKS 5
DIVINE EMOTION	Reprise	60	14 May 88	5

Above hit: NARADA.

Gary WALKER
US

(See also Walker Brothers.)

SINGLES:		HITS 2		WEEKS 12
YOU DON'T LOVE ME	CBS	26	26 Feb 66	6

Originally recorded by Sonny and Cher.

TWINKIE-LEE	CBS	26	28 May 66	6

John WALKER
US

(See also Walker Brothers.)

SINGLES:	HITS 1			WEEKS 6
ANNABELLA	Philips	48	8 Jul 67	1
ANNABELLA [RE]	Philips	24	22 Jul 67	5

Jr. WALKER and the ALL STARS
US

SINGLES:	HITS 6			WEEKS 59
HOW SWEET IT IS (TO BE LOVED BY YOU)	Tamla Motown	22	20 Aug 66	10
ROAD RUNNER	Tamla Motown	12	5 Apr 69	12
WHAT DOES IT TAKE (TO WIN YOUR LOVE)	Tamla Motown	13	18 Oct 69	12
WALK IN THE NIGHT	Tamla Motown	16	26 Aug 72	11
TAKE ME GIRL, I'M READY	Tamla Motown	16	27 Jan 73	9
WAY BACK HOME	Tamla Motown	35	30 Jun 73	5

Originally recorded by the Jazz Crusaders. Above 2 were released in the US in 1971 reaching No. 50 and No. 52 respectively.

Sarah WALKER – See ROYAL PHILHARMONIC ORCHESTRA

Scott WALKER
US

(See also Walker Brothers.)

SINGLES:	HITS 3			WEEKS 30
JACKIE	Philips	22	9 Dec 67	9
Originally recorded by Jacques Brel.				
JOANNA	Philips	7	4 May 68	11
Originally recorded by Tony Hatch and Jackie Trent.				
LIGHTS OF CINCINNATI	Philips	13	14 Jun 69	10

ALBUMS:	HITS 7			WEEKS 57
SCOTT	Philips	3	16 Sep 67	17
SCOTT 2	Philips	1	20 Apr 68	18
SCOTT 3	Philips	3	5 Apr 69	4
SCOTT WALKER SINGS SONGS FROM HIS TV SERIES	Philips	7	5 Jul 69	3
CLIMATE OF HUNTER	Virgin	60	31 Mar 84	2
NO REGRETS - THE BEST OF SCOTT WALKER AND THE WALKER BROTHERS 1965-1976	Fontana	4	25 Jan 92	12

Contains both Scott Walker's solo and group material.
Above hit: Scott WALKER and the WALKER BROTHERS.

TILT	Fontana	27	20 May 95	1

Tracks were written between 1991/92.

WALKER BROTHERS
US

(See also Gary Walker; John Walker; Scott Walker.)

SINGLES:	HITS 10			WEEKS 93
LOVE HER	Philips	20	1 May 65	13
Originally by The Everly Brothers on the B-side of their 1963 hit The Girl Sang The Blues.				
MAKE IT EASY ON YOURSELF	Philips	1	21 Aug 65	14
Original by Jerry Butler reached No. 20 in the US in 1962.				
MY SHIP IS COMING IN	Philips	3	4 Dec 65	12
Originally recorded by Jimmy Radcliffe in 1964.				
THE SUN AIN'T GONNA SHINE ANYMORE	Philips	1	5 Mar 66	11
Originally recorded by Frankie Valli.				
(BABY) YOU DON'T HAVE TO TELL ME	Philips	13	16 Jul 66	8
ANOTHER TEAR FALLS	Philips	12	24 Sep 66	8
Originally recorded by Gene McDaniels in 1962 as the B-side to his single Chip Chip.				
DEADLIER THAN THE MALE	Philips	34	17 Dec 66	6
From the film of the same name.				
STAY WITH ME BABY	Philips	26	11 Feb 67	6
Originally recorded by Lorraine Ellison in 1966.				
WALKING IN THE RAIN	Philips	26	20 May 67	6
Original by the Ronettes reached No. 23 in the US in 1964.				
NO REGRETS	GTO	7	17 Jan 76	9
Originally recorded by Tom Rush in 1968.				

EPS:	HITS 2			WEEKS 32
I NEED YOU	Philips	1	18 Jun 66	25
SOLO JOHN - SOLO SCOTT	Philips	4	10 Dec 66	7

ALBUMS:	HITS 6			WEEKS 108
TAKE IT EASY WITH THE WALKER BROTHERS	Philips	3	18 Dec 65	36
PORTRAIT	Philips	3	3 Sep 66	23
IMAGES	Philips	6	18 Mar 67	15
THE WALKER BROTHERS' STORY	Philips	9	16 Sep 67	19
NO REGRETS	GTO	49	21 Feb 76	3
NO REGRETS - THE BEST OF SCOTT WALKER AND THE WALKER BROTHERS 1965-1976	Fontana	4	25 Jan 92	12

Contains both Scott Walker's solo and group material.
Above hit: Scott WALKER and the WALKER BROTHERS.

WALL OF SOUND featuring Gerald LETHAN   US

SINGLES:		HITS 1			WEEKS 1
CRITICAL (IF YOU ONLY KNEW)	Positiva		73	31 Jul 93	1

WALL OF VOODOO   US

SINGLES:		HITS 1			WEEKS 3
MEXICAN RADIO	Illegal		64	19 Mar 83	3

Jerry WALLACE   US

SINGLES:		HITS 1			WEEKS 1
YOU'RE SINGING OUR LOVE SONG TO SOMEBODY ELSE	London		46	25 Jun 60	1

Fats WALLER   US

EPS:		HITS 1			WEEKS 2
FATS WALLER	RCA		14	3 Sep 60	2

WALLFLOWERS   US

SINGLES:		HITS 1			WEEKS 1
ONE HEADLIGHT	Interscope		54	12 Jul 97	1
ALBUMS:		HITS 1			WEEKS 2
BRINGING DOWN THE HORSE	Interscope		58	21 Jun 97	2

Bob WALLIS and his STORYVILLE JAZZMEN   UK

SINGLES:		HITS 2			WEEKS 7
I'M SHY MARY ELLEN I'M SHY	Pye Jazz Today		44	8 Jul 61	2
COME ALONG PLEASE	Pye Jazz Today		33	6 Jan 62	5
ALBUMS:		HITS 1			WEEKS 1
EVERYBODY LOVES SATURDAY NIGHT	Top Rank		20	11 Jun 60	1

Joe WALSH   US

SINGLES:		HITS 2			WEEKS 15
ROCKY MOUNTAIN WAY [EP]	ABC		39	16 Jul 77	4
Lead track: Rocky Mountain Way.					
LIFE'S BEEN GOOD	Asylum		14	8 Jul 78	11
ALBUMS:		HITS 2			WEEKS 20
YOU CAN'T ARGUE WITH A SICK MIND	Anchor		28	17 Apr 76	3
Live recordings.					
BUT SERIOUSLY FOLKS ...	Asylum		16	10 Jun 78	17

Maureen WALSH – See MAUREEN

Sheila WALSH and Cliff RICHARD   UK

(See also Cliff Richard.)

SINGLES:		HITS 1			WEEKS 2
DRIFTING	DJM		64	4 Jun 83	2

Steve WALSH   UK

SINGLES:		HITS 3			WEEKS 18
I FOUND LOVIN'	A.1		74	18 Jul 87	1
I FOUND LOVIN' [RE]	A.1		9	29 Aug 87	12
LET'S GET TOGETHER TONITE	A.1		74	12 Dec 87	1
AIN'T NO STOPPIN' US NOW (PARTY FOR THE WORLD)	A.1		44	30 Jul 88	4

Trevor WALTERS   UK

SINGLES:		HITS 3			WEEKS 22
LOVE ME TONIGHT	Magnet		27	24 Oct 81	8
STUCK ON YOU	I&S		9	21 Jul 84	12
NEVER LET HER SLIP AWAY	Polydor		73	1 Dec 84	2

WAMDUE PROJECT   US

SINGLES:		HITS 1			WEEKS 7
KING OF MY CASTLE	Orange		61	20 Nov 99	1
Import.					
KING OF MY CASTLE	AM:PM		1	27 Nov 99	6

WANG CHUNG   UK

SINGLES:		HITS 1			WEEKS 12
DANCE HALL DAYS	Geffen		21	28 Jan 84	12
ALBUMS:		HITS 1			WEEKS 5
POINTS ON THE CURVE	Geffen		34	21 Apr 84	5

WANNADIES | | | | Sweden

SINGLES:	HITS 6			WEEKS 11	
MIGHT BE STARS	Indolent	51	18 Nov 95	2	
HOW DOES IT FEEL?	Indolent	53	24 Feb 96	1	
YOU & ME SONG	Indolent	18	20 Apr 96	3	
Originally released 1995 reaching No. 119.					
SOMEONE SOMEWHERE	Indolent	38	7 Sep 96	1	
HIT	Indolent	20	26 Apr 97	2	
Originally released in 1996.					
SHORTY	Indolent	41	5 Jul 97	2	
ALBUMS:	HITS 1			WEEKS 3	
BAGSY ME	Indolent	37	17 May 97	3	

Dexter WANSELL | | | | US

SINGLES:	HITS 1			WEEKS 3	
ALL NIGHT LONG	Philadelphia International	59	20 May 78	3	

WAR | | | | US

(See also Eric Burdon and War.)

SINGLES:	HITS 6			WEEKS 32	
LOW RIDER	Island	12	24 Jan 76	7	
ME AND BABY BROTHER	Island	21	26 Jun 76	7	
Original release reached No. 15 in the US in 1973.					
GALAXY	MCA	14	14 Jan 78	7	
HEY SENORITA	MCA	40	15 Apr 78	2	
YOU GOT THE POWER	RCA	58	10 Apr 82	4	
GROOVIN'	BlueBird	43	6 Apr 85	5	

Anita WARD | | | | US

SINGLES:	HITS 1			WEEKS 11	
RING MY BELL	TK	1	2 Jun 79	11	
Originally recorded by Frederick Knight who also plays all instruments on Anita's version.					

Billy WARD and the DOMINOES | | | | US

SINGLES:	HITS 2			WEEKS 13	
STARDUST	London	13	14 Sep 57	11	
Originally recorded by Isham Jones in 1931.					
DEEP PURPLE	London	30	30 Nov 57	1	
Above hit: Billy WARD and his DOMINOES.					
STARDUST [RE]	London	26	4 Jan 58	1	

Chrissy WARD | | | | US

SINGLES:	HITS 1			WEEKS 2	
RIGHT AND EXACT	Ore	62	24 Jun 95	1	
RIGHT AND EXACT [RM]	Ore	59	8 Feb 97	1	
Remixed by Stonebridge and Nick Nice.					

Clifford T. WARD | | | | UK

SINGLES:	HITS 2			WEEKS 16	
GAYE	Charisma	8	30 Jun 73	11	
SCULLERY	Charisma	37	26 Jan 74	5	
ALBUMS:	HITS 2			WEEKS 5	
HOME THOUGHTS	Charisma	40	21 Jul 73	3	
MANTLE PIECES	Charisma	42	16 Feb 74	2	

Michael WARD | | | | UK

SINGLES:	HITS 1			WEEKS 13	
LET THERE BE PEACE ON EARTH (LET IT BEGIN WITH ME)	Philips	15	29 Sep 73	10	
Above hit: Michael WARD with the Mike SAMMES SINGERS.					
LET THERE BE PEACE ON EARTH (LET IT BEGIN WITH ME) [RE]	Philips	50	15 Dec 73	3	
ALBUMS:	HITS 1			WEEKS 3	
INTRODUCING MICHAEL WARD	Philips	26	5 Jan 74	3	

WARD BROTHERS | | | | UK

SINGLES:	HITS 1			WEEKS 8	
CROSS THAT BRIDGE	Siren	32	10 Jan 87	8	

Justin WARFIELD – See BOMB THE BASS

WARLOCK | | | | Germany

ALBUMS:	HITS 1			WEEKS 2	
TRIUMPH AND AGONY	Vertigo	54	14 Nov 87	2	

WARM JETS

UK/Canada

SINGLES:	HITS 2			WEEKS 4	
NEVER NEVER	*This Way Up*	37	*14 Feb 98*	2
Original release reached No. 97 in 1997.				
HURRICANE	*Island*	34	*25 Apr 98*	2
Original release reached No. 79 in 1997.				
ALBUMS:	HITS 1			WEEKS 1	
FUTURE SIGNS	*Island*	40	*7 Mar 98*	1

WARM SOUNDS

UK

SINGLES:	HITS 1			WEEKS 6	
BIRDS AND BEES	*Deram*	27	*6 May 67*	6

Toni WARNE

UK

SINGLES:	HITS 1			WEEKS 4	
BEN	*Mint*	50	*25 Apr 87*	4

Jennifer WARNES

US

SINGLES:	HITS 3			WEEKS 37	
UP WHERE WE BELONG	*Island*	7	*15 Jan 83*	13
From the film 'An Officer And A Gentleman'.				
Above hit: Joe COCKER and Jennifer WARNES.				
FIRST WE TAKE MANHATTAN	*RCA*	74	*25 Jul 87*	1
Originally recorded by Leonard Cohen.				
(I'VE HAD) THE TIME OF MY LIFE (LOVE THEME FROM 'DIRTY DANCING')	*RCA*	6	*31 Oct 87*	12
From the film 'Dirty Dancing'.				
Above hit: Bill MEDLEY and Jennifer WARNES.				
(I'VE HAD) THE TIME OF MY LIFE (LOVE THEME FROM 'DIRTY DANCING') [RE]	*RCA*	8	*15 Dec 90*	11
ALBUMS:	HITS 1			WEEKS 12	
FAMOUS BLUE RAINCOAT	*RCA*	33	*18 Jul 87*	12
Covers consists of Leonard Cohen songs.				

WARRANT

US

SINGLES:	HITS 1			WEEKS 7	
CHERRY PIE	*CBS*	59	*17 Nov 90*	2
CHERRY PIE [RI]	*Columbia*	35	*9 Mar 91*	5
ALBUMS:	HITS 1			WEEKS 1	
DOG EAT DOG	*Columbia*	74	*19 Sep 92*	1

Alysha WARREN

UK

SINGLES:	HITS 3			WEEKS 4	
I'M SO IN LOVE	*Wild Card*	61	*24 Sep 94*	1
I THOUGHT I MEANT THE WORLD TO YOU	*Wild Card*	40	*25 Mar 95*	1
KEEP ON PUSHING OUR LOVE	*Arista*	30	*27 Jul 96*	2
Above hit: NIGHTCRAWLERS featuring John REID and Alysha WARREN.				

Anne WARREN – See Ruby MURRAY

Nikita WARREN

Italy

SINGLES:	HITS 1			WEEKS 1	
I NEED YOU	*VC Recordings*	48	*13 Jul 96*	1
Originally released in 1991.				

WARSAW PHILHARMONIA – See Anthony WAY

Dionne WARWICK

US

(See also Dionne Warwick Placido Domingo; Stevie Wonder.)

SINGLES:	HITS 14			WEEKS 101	
ANYONE WHO HAD A HEART	*Pye International*	42	*15 Feb 64*	3
WALK ON BY	*Pye International*	9	*18 Apr 64*	14
YOU'LL NEVER GET TO HEAVEN (IF YOU BREAK MY HEART)	*Pye International*	20	*1 Aug 64*	8
REACH OUT FOR ME	*Pye International*	23	*10 Oct 64*	7
YOU CAN HAVE HIM	*Pye International*	37	*3 Apr 65*	5
(THEME FROM) VALLEY OF THE DOLLS	*Pye International*	28	*16 Mar 68*	8
Theme from the film.				
DO YOU KNOW THE WAY TO SAN JOSE	*Pye International*	8	*18 May 68*	10
THEN CAME YOU	*Atlantic*	29	*19 Oct 74*	6
Above hit: Dionne WARWICKE and the DETROIT SPINNERS.				
HEARTBREAKER	*Arista*	2	*23 Oct 82*	13
Features backing vocals by Barry Gibb.				
ALL THE LOVE IN THE WORLD	*Arista*	10	*11 Dec 82*	10
Above 2 written by the Bee Gees.				
YOURS	*Arista*	66	*26 Feb 83*	2

I'LL NEVER LOVE THIS WAY AGAIN	Arista	62	28 May 83	3
Produced by Barry Manilow. Reached No. 5 in the US when first released in 1979.				
THAT'S WHAT FRIENDS ARE FOR	Arista	16	9 Nov 85	9
Charity record with proceeds donated to the American Foundation for AIDS research. Originally recorded by Rod Stewart.				
Above hit: DIONNE and FRIENDS featuring Elton JOHN, Gladys KNIGHT and Stevie WONDER.				
LOVE POWER	Arista	63	15 Aug 87	3
Above hit: Dionne WARWICK and Jeffrey OSBORNE.				

EPS:	HITS 2			WEEKS 10
IT'S LOVE THAT REALLY COUNTS	Pye International	18	15 Aug 64	1
DON'T MAKE ME OVER	Pye International	13	3 Oct 64	9

ALBUMS:	HITS 12			WEEKS 148
PRESENTING DIONNE WARWICK	Pye International	14	23 May 64	10
BEST OF DIONNE WARWICK	Pye International	8	7 May 66	11
HERE WHERE THERE IS LOVE	Pye International	39	4 Feb 67	2
VALLEY OF THE DOLLS	Pye International	10	18 May 68	13
GREATEST HITS VOLUME 1	Wand	31	23 May 70	26
GREATEST HITS VOLUME 2	Wand	28	6 Jun 70	14
HEARTBREAKER	Arista	3	30 Oct 82	33
THE DIONNE WARWICK COLLECTION	Starblend	11	21 May 83	17
SO AMAZING	Arista	60	29 Oct 83	3
WITHOUT YOUR LOVE	Arista	86	23 Feb 85	2
LOVE SONGS	Arista	6	6 Jan 90	13
THE ESSENTIAL COLLECTION	Global Television	58	14 Dec 96	4

Dionne WARWICK   Placido DOMINGO   US/Spain

(See also Placido Domingo; Dionne Warwick.)

ALBUMS:	HITS 1			WEEKS 2
CHRISTMAS IN VIENNA II	Sony Classical	60	10 Dec 94	2
Live recordings from the Hofburg, Vienna, 21 Dec 93.				

WAS (NOT WAS)   US

SINGLES:	HITS 10			WEEKS 58
OUT COME THE FREAKS	Ze	41	3 Mar 84	5
SPY IN THE HOUSE OF LOVE	Fontana	51	18 Jul 87	7
WALK THE DINOSAUR	Fontana	10	3 Oct 87	10
SPY IN THE HOUSE OF LOVE [RE]	Fontana	21	6 Feb 88	8
OUT COME THE FREAKS (AGAIN) [RR]	Fontana	44	7 May 88	3
ANYTHING CAN HAPPEN	Fontana	67	16 Jul 88	3
PAPA WAS A ROLLING STONE	Fontana	12	26 May 90	7
HOW THE HEART BEHAVES	Fontana	53	11 Aug 90	3
LISTEN LIKE THIEVES	Fontana	58	23 May 92	2
SHAKE YOUR HEAD	Fontana	4	11 Jul 92	9
Features vocals by Ozzy Osbourne and Kim Basinger.				
SOMEWHERE IN AMERICA (THERE'S A STREET NAMED AFTER MY DAD)	Fontana	57	26 Sep 92	1

ALBUMS:	HITS 3			WEEKS 15
WHAT UP DOG?	Fontana	47	9 Apr 88	6
ARE YOU OKAY?	Fontana	35	21 Jul 90	6
HELLO DAD . . . I'M IN JAIL	Fontana	61	13 Jun 92	3

Martha WASH   US

(See also Todd Terry.)

SINGLES:	HITS 7			WEEKS 15
CARRY ON	RCA	74	28 Nov 92	1
GIVE IT TO YOU	RCA	37	6 Mar 93	4
RUNAROUND / CARRY ON [RM-1ST]	RCA	49	10 Jul 93	2
CARRY ON [RM-2ND]	Delirious	49	25 Oct 97	1
Remixed by Full Intention.				
IT'S RAINING MEN . . . THE SEQUEL	Logic	21	28 Feb 98	3
Above hit: Martha WASH featuring RUPAUL.				
READY FOR A NEW DAY	Manifesto	20	11 Apr 98	2
Background vocals by Antoinette Robertson.				
Above hit: Todd TERRY features Martha WASH.				
CATCH THE LIGHT	Logic	45	15 Aug 98	1
COME	Logic	64	3 Jul 99	1

Dinah WASHINGTON   US

SINGLES:	HITS 2			WEEKS 8
SEPTEMBER IN THE RAIN	Mercury	35	2 Dec 61	3
Originally recorded by James Melton.				
SEPTEMBER IN THE RAIN [RE]	Mercury	49	20 Jan 62	1
MAD ABOUT THE BOY	Mercury	41	4 Apr 92	4
Featured in the Levi's 501 Jeans TV commercial.				

Geno WASHINGTON and the RAM JAM BAND — US

SINGLES:	HITS 4			WEEKS 20	
WATER	Piccadilly	39	21 May 66	8
HI HI HAZEL	Piccadilly	45	23 Jul 66	3
HI HI HAZEL [RE]	Piccadilly	48	27 Aug 66	1
QUE SERA SERA	Piccadilly	43	8 Oct 66	3
MICHAEL	Piccadilly	39	4 Feb 67	5

EPS:	HITS 1			WEEKS 3	
HI!	Pye	7	4 Feb 67	3

ALBUMS:	HITS 2			WEEKS 51	
HAND CLAPPIN' – FOOT STOMPIN' – FUNKY BUTT – LIVE!	Piccadilly	5	10 Dec 66	38
HIPSTERS, FLIPSTERS, AND FINGER POPPIN' DADDIES	Piccadilly	8	23 Sep 67	13

Grover WASHINGTON JR. — US

SINGLES:	HITS 1			WEEKS 7	
JUST THE TWO OF US	Elektra	34	16 May 81	7

Vocals by Bill Withers.

ALBUMS:	HITS 2			WEEKS 10	
WINELIGHT	Elektra	34	9 May 81	9
COME MORNING	Elektra	98	19 Dec 81	1

Keith WASHINGTON – See Kylie MINOGUE

Sarah WASHINGTON — UK

SINGLES:	HITS 4			WEEKS 13	
I WILL ALWAYS LOVE YOU	Almighty	12	14 Aug 93	7
CARELESS WHISPER	Almighty	45	27 Nov 93	2
HEAVEN	AM:PM	28	25 May 96	2
EVERYTHING	AM:PM	30	12 Oct 96	2

WATERBOYS — UK

SINGLES:	HITS 5			WEEKS 33	
THE WHOLE OF THE MOON	Ensign	26	2 Nov 85	7
FISHERMAN'S BLUES	Ensign	32	14 Jan 89	6
AND A BANG ON THE EAR	Ensign	51	1 Jul 89	4
THE WHOLE OF THE MOON [RI]	Ensign	3	6 Apr 91	9
FISHERMAN'S BLUES [RI]	Ensign	75	8 Jun 91	1
THE RETURN OF PAN	Geffen	24	15 May 93	3
GLASTONBURY SONG	Geffen	29	24 Jul 93	3

Released to celebrate the festival which has been staged by Michael and Jean Eavis at Worthy Farm,
Glastonbury almost every summer since 1970.

ALBUMS:	HITS 6			WEEKS 69	
A PAGAN PLACE	Ensign	100	16 Jun 84	1
THIS IS THE SEA	Ensign	37	28 Sep 85	12
THIS IS THE SEA [RE]	Ensign	73	23 Aug 86	5

Re-released with a new catalogue number.

FISHERMAN'S BLUES	Ensign	13	29 Oct 88	19
ROOM TO ROAM	Ensign	5	29 Sep 90	6
THE BEST OF THE WATERBOYS '81-'90	Ensign	2	11 May 91	16
DREAM HARDER	Geffen	5	5 Jun 93	10

WATERFRONT — UK

SINGLES:	HITS 3			WEEKS 19	
BROKEN ARROW	Polydor	63	15 Apr 89	2
CRY	Polydor	17	27 May 89	13
NATURE OF LOVE	Polydor	63	9 Sep 89	4

Original release reached No. 78 earlier in the year.

ALBUMS:	HITS 1			WEEKS 3	
WATERFRONT	Polydor	45	12 Aug 89	3

Dennis WATERMAN — UK

SINGLES:	HITS 2			WEEKS 17	
I COULD BE SO GOOD FOR YOU	EMI	3	25 Oct 80	12

Theme from the Thames ITV series 'Minder'. Originally recorded by Gerard Kenny.
Above hit: Dennis WATERMAN with the Dennis WATERMAN BAND.

WHAT ARE WE GONNA GET 'ER INDOORS? (INTERPOL. IN THE BLEAK MID-WINTER)	EMI	21	17 Dec 83	5

Sung in the role of their characters in 'Minder', Terry McCann and Arthur Daley.
Above hit: Dennis WATERMAN and George COLE.

Crystal WATERS
US

(See also David Morales.)

SINGLES:		HITS 7			WEEKS 33
GYPSY WOMAN (LA DA DEE)	A&M	2	18 May 91	10
MAKIN' HAPPY	A&M	18	7 Sep 91	6
MEGAMIX [M]	A&M	39	11 Jan 92	3
GYPSY WOMAN [RM]	Epic	35	3 Oct 92	2

[AA] listed with remix of Peace by Sabrina Johnston. Remixed by Joey Negro. From the
Red Hot & Dance album (to benefit AIDS research and relief).

100% PURE LOVE	A&M	15	23 Apr 94	7
GHETTO DAY / WHAT I NEED	A&M	40	2 Jul 94	2
RELAX	Manifesto	37	25 Nov 95	2
SAY . . . IF YOU FEEL ALRIGHT	Mercury	45	19 Apr 97	1

Based around Earth, Wind And Fire's September.

Latanza WATERS – See E-SMOOVE featuring Latanza WATERS

Muddy WATERS
US

SINGLES:		HITS 1			WEEKS 6
MANNISH BOY	Epic	51	16 Jul 88	6

Featured in the Levi's 501 Jeans TV commercial. Originally recorded in 1955.

Roger WATERS
UK

SINGLES:		HITS 3			WEEKS 8
RADIO WAVES	Harvest	74	30 May 87	1
THE TIDE IS TURNING (AFTER LIVE AID)	EMI	54	26 Dec 87	4
WHAT GOD WANTS GOD GETS (PART 1)	Columbia	35	5 Sep 92	3
ALBUMS:		HITS 4			WEEKS 25
THE PROS AND CONS OF HITCH-HIKING	Harvest	13	12 May 84	11
RADIO K.A.O.S.	EMI	25	27 Jun 87	7
THE WALL – LIVE IN BERLIN	Mercury	27	29 Sep 90	3

Live recordings, 21 Jul 90. Songs from Pink Floyd's 1979 album The Wall performed with 12
other acts.
Proceeds to the Memorial Fund for Disaster Relief.
Above hit: Roger WATERS and VARIOUS ARTISTS.

AMUSED TO DEATH	Columbia	8	19 Sep 92	4

Michael WATFORD
US

SINGLES:		HITS 1			WEEKS 2
SO INTO YOU	East West America	53	26 Feb 94	2

Jody WATLEY
US

(See also Babyface.)

SINGLES:		HITS 8			WEEKS 35
LOOKING FOR A NEW LOVE	MCA	13	9 May 87	11
DON'T YOU WANT ME	MCA	55	17 Oct 87	3
REAL LOVE	MCA	31	8 Apr 89	7
FRIENDS	MCA	21	12 Aug 89	6

Above hit: Jody WATLEY with Eric B. and RAKIM.

EVERYTHING	MCA	74	10 Feb 90	2
I'M THE ONE YOU NEED (DRIZA BONE MIX)	MCA	50	11 Apr 92	3
WHEN A MAN LOVES A WOMAN	MCA	33	21 May 94	2
OFF THE HOOK	Atlantic	51	25 Apr 98	1
ALBUMS:		HITS 2			WEEKS 4
JODY WATLEY	MCA	62	5 Sep 87	2
LARGER THAN LIFE	MCA	39	27 May 89	2

James WATSON – See Paul PHOENIX

Johnny Guitar WATSON
US

SINGLES:		HITS 2			WEEKS 8
I NEED IT	DJM	35	28 Aug 76	5
A REAL MOTHER FOR YA	DJM	44	23 Apr 77	3

Nigel WATSON and the SPLINTER GROUP – See Peter GREEN

Russell WATSON – See OFFICIAL RUGBY TEAM SONG featuring Russell WATSON

WAVELENGTH
UK

SINGLES:		HITS 1			WEEKS 12
HURRY HOME	Ariola	17	10 Jul 82	12

WAVES – See KATRINA and the WAVES

WAX
UK/US

SINGLES:		HITS 2		WEEKS 16	
RIGHT BETWEEN THE EYES	RCA		60	12 Apr 86	5
BRIDGE TO YOUR HEART	RCA		12	1 Aug 87	11
ALBUMS:		HITS 1		WEEKS 3	
AMERICAN ENGLISH	RCA		59	12 Sep 87	3

Anthony WAY
UK

SINGLES:		HITS 1		WEEKS 2	
PANIS ANGELICUS	Decca		55	15 Apr 95	2

From the BBC1 TV series 'The Choir'.
Above hit: Anthony WAY and the WARSAW PHILHARMONIA.

ALBUMS:		HITS 4		WEEKS 19	
THE CHOIR - MUSIC FROM THE BBC TV SERIES	Decca		3	8 Apr 95	12

Features the Choir of Gloucester Cathedral.
Above hit: Anthony WAY and Stanislas SYREWICZ.

THE CHOIRBOY	Permanent		61	9 Dec 95	3
THE CHOIRBOY'S CHRISTMAS	Decca		59	14 Dec 96	3
WINGS OF A DOVE	Decca		69	15 Mar 97	1

Recorded with his friends and teachers at his school in Uppingham.

A WAY OF LIFE
US

SINGLES:		HITS 1		WEEKS 3	
TRIPPIN' ON YOUR LOVE	Eternal		55	21 Apr 90	3

WAY OF THE WEST
UK

SINGLES:		HITS 1		WEEKS 5	
DON'T SAY THAT'S JUST FOR WHITE BOYS	Mercury		54	25 Apr 81	5

WAY OUT WEST
UK

SINGLES:		HITS 4		WEEKS 12	
AJARE	Deconstruction		52	3 Dec 94	1
DOMINATION	Deconstruction		38	2 Mar 96	2
THE GIFT	Deconstruction		15	14 Sep 96	5

Samples Joanna Law's First Time Ever.
Above hit: WAY OUT WEST featuring Miss Joanna LAW.

BLUE	Deconstruction		41	30 Aug 97	2

Samples the pianos and chords from the film soundtrack of 'Withnail & I'.

AJARE [RI]	Deconstruction		36	29 Nov 97	2
ALBUMS:		HITS 1		WEEKS 1	
WAY OUT WEST	Deconstruction		42	13 Sep 97	1

Bruce WAYNE
Germany

SINGLES:		HITS 2		WEEKS 2	
READY	Logic		44	13 Dec 97	1

Originally released earlier in the year.

NO GOOD FOR ME	Logic		70	4 Jul 98	1

Jeff WAYNE
US

(See also Kevin Peek and Rick Wakeman featuring Jeff Wayne narration Patrick Allen.)

SINGLES:		HITS 4		WEEKS 37	
FOREVER AUTUMN	CBS		5	8 Jul 78	13

Originally recorded by Vigrass and Osborne.
Above hit: From Jeff WAYNE'S "WAR OF THE WORLDS" featuring Justin
* HAYWARD.*

THE EVE OF THE WAR	CBS		36	9 Sep 78	8

Above hit: Jeff WAYNE'S "THE WAR OF THE WORLDS".

BRAVE NEW WORLD	CBS		55	21 Oct 78	3

Above hit: featuring the vocal performance of David ESSEX from Jeff WAYNE'S "The WAR
* OF THE WORLDS'.*

MATADOR	CBS		57	10 Jul 82	3

ITV theme for their 1982 World Cup coverage in Spain.

THE EVE OF THE WAR (BEN LIEBRAND REMIX) [RM]	CBS		3	25 Nov 89	10

This remix by Ben Liebrand features narration by Richard Burton.

ALBUMS:		HITS 3		WEEKS 260	
JEFF WAYNE'S MUSICAL VERSION OF THE WAR OF THE WORLDS	CBS		5	1 Jul 78	226

Includes re-entries through to 1984. Features Richard Burton, Julie Covington, David Essex,
* Justin Hayward, Phil Lynott, Jo Partridge and Chris Thompson.*

JEFF WAYNE'S MUSICAL VERSION OF THE WAR OF THE WORLDS [RE]	CBS		54	9 Dec 89	6
JEFF WAYNE'S MUSICAL VERSION OF SPARTACUS	Columbia		36	3 Oct 92	2

Features Fish, Bill Fredericks, Jimmy Helms, Anthony Hopkins, Incantation, Catherine Zeta
* Jones, Alan King, Ladysmith Black Mambazo, Jo Partridge and Chris Thompson.*

HIGHLIGHTS FROM JEFF WAYNE'S MUSICAL VERSION OF THE WAR OF THE WORLDS	Columbia	64	19 Oct 96	2

This highlighted edition was originally released in 1981, it charted after being made available at mid-price.

JEFF WAYNE'S MUSICAL VERSION OF THE WAR OF THE WORLDS [RI]	Columbia	23	2 Sep 95	24

Digitally remastered with new remixes. Peak position reached in 1997.
Above 5: Jeff WAYNE'S MUSICAL VERSION.

WAYSTED — UK

ALBUMS:	HITS 2			WEEKS 5
VICES	Chrysalis	78	8 Oct 83	3
WAYSTED	Music For Nations	73	22 Sep 84	2

WE THE PEOPLE BAND – See ME AND YOU featuring "WE THE PEOPLE BAND"

WEATHER GIRLS — US

SINGLES:	HITS 1			WEEKS 14
IT'S RAINING MEN	CBS	73	27 Aug 83	3
IT'S RAINING MEN [RE]	CBS	2	3 Mar 84	11

WEATHER PROPHETS — UK

SINGLES:	HITS 1			WEEKS 2
SHE COMES FROM THE RAIN	Elevation	62	28 Mar 87	2
ALBUMS:	**HITS 1**			**WEEKS 2**
MAYFLOWER	Elevation	67	9 May 87	2

WEATHER REPORT — US

ALBUMS:	HITS 4			WEEKS 12
HEAVY WEATHER	CBS	43	23 Apr 77	6
MR. GONE	CBS	47	11 Nov 78	3
WEATHER REPORT	CBS	88	27 Feb 82	2
DOMINO THEORY	CBS	54	24 Mar 84	1

WEATHERMEN – See Jonathan KING

Geoffrey WEBB — UK

EPS:	HITS 1			WEEKS 1
FOLLOW THAT GIRL	Oriole	19	4 Jun 60	1

Marti WEBB — UK

(See also Marti Webb and Mark Rattray.)

SINGLES:	HITS 6			WEEKS 42
TAKE THAT LOOK OFF YOUR FACE	Polydor	3	9 Feb 80	12
TELL ME ON A SUNDAY	Polydor	67	19 Apr 80	2
YOUR EARS SHOULD BE BURNING NOW	Polydor	61	20 Sep 80	4

Above 3 from the Andrew Lloyd Webber show 'Tell Me On A Sunday'.

BEN	Starblend	5	8 Jun 85	11

Charity record with proceeds to the Ben Hardwick Memorial Fund.

ALWAYS THERE	BBC	13	20 Sep 86	12

Theme from the BBC1 TV series 'Howard's Way'.
Above hit: Marti WEBB with the Simon May ORCHESTRA.

I CAN'T LET GO	Rainbow	65	6 Jun 87	1
ALBUMS:	**HITS 3**			**WEEKS 32**
TELL ME ON A SUNDAY	Polydor	2	16 Feb 80	23

Songs from the show.

ENCORE	Starblend	55	28 Sep 85	4
ALWAYS THERE	BBC	65	6 Dec 86	5

Marti WEBB and Mark RATTRAY — UK

(See also Mark Rattray; Marti Webb.)

ALBUMS:	HITS 1			WEEKS 1
THE MAGIC OF THE MUSICALS	Quality Television	55	10 Oct 92	1

Joan WEBER — US

SINGLES:	HITS 1			WEEKS 1
LET ME GO LOVER	Philips	16	19 Feb 55	1

Originally recorded by Georgie Shaw as Let Me Go Devil.

Bert WEBSTER – See Gerry MULLIGAN and Ben WEBSTER

WEDDING PRESENT — UK

SINGLES:	HITS 23			WEEKS 38
NOBODY'S TWISTING YOUR ARM	Reception	46	5 Mar 88	2
WHY ARE YOU BEING SO REASONABLE NOW?	Reception	42	1 Oct 88	2

KENNEDY	RCA	33	7 Oct 89	3
BRASSNECK	RCA	24	17 Feb 90	3
3 SONGS [EP]	RCA	25	29 Sep 90	4
Lead track: Corduroy, though the track Make Me Smile (Come Up And See Me) received more airplay.				
DALLIANCE	RCA	29	11 May 91	3
LOVENEST	RCA	58	27 Jul 91	1
BLUE EYES	RCA	26	18 Jan 92	2
GO-GO DANCER	RCA	20	15 Feb 92	1
THREE	RCA	14	14 Mar 92	2
SILVER SHORTS	RCA	14	18 Apr 92	1
COME PLAY WITH ME	RCA	10	16 May 92	2
CALIFORNIA	RCA	16	13 Jun 92	1
FLYING SAUCER	RCA	22	18 Jul 92	1
BOING!	RCA	19	15 Aug 92	1
LOVE SLAVE	RCA	17	19 Sep 92	1
STICKY	RCA	17	17 Oct 92	1
THE QUEEN OF OUTER SPACE	RCA	23	14 Nov 92	1
NO CHRISTMAS	RCA	25	19 Dec 92	1
All above 12 hits were limited edition 7" formats only.				
YEAH YEAH YEAH YEAH YEAH	Island	51	10 Sep 94	2
IT'S A GAS	Island	71	26 Nov 94	1
2, 3, GO	Cooking Vinyl	67	31 Aug 96	1
MONTREAL	Cooking Vinyl	40	25 Jan 97	1
ALBUMS:	**HITS 10**			**WEEKS 21**
GEORGE BEST	Reception	47	24 Oct 87	2
TOMMY	Reception	42	23 Jul 88	3
UKRAINSKI VISTUIP V JOHNA PEELA	RCA	22	29 Apr 89	3
BIZZARO	RCA	22	4 Nov 89	3
SEA MONSTERS	RCA	13	8 Jun 91	3
HIT PARADE 1	RCA	22	20 Jun 92	2
HIT PARADE 2	RCA	19	16 Jan 93	2
Above 2 consist of the A and B-side of their 12 singles that charted during 1992. Hit Parade 1, from January–June and Hit Parade 2, from July–December.				
WATUSI	Island	47	24 Sep 94	1
MINI	Cooking Vinyl	40	3 Feb 96	1
Not listed in the chart published in Music Week as incorrectly logged as a budget release. Chart was amended the following week.				
SATURNALIA	Cooking Vinyl	36	21 Sep 96	1

Fred WEDLOCK
UK

SINGLES:	**HITS 1**			**WEEKS 10**
OLDEST SWINGER IN TOWN	Rocket	6	31 Jan 81	10
Became popular due to airplay on the Noel Edmunds BBC Radio 1 Sunday morning show.				

WEE PAPA GIRL RAPPERS
UK

SINGLES:	**HITS 5**			**WEEKS 27**
FAITH	Jive	60	12 Mar 88	4
HEAT IT UP	Jive	21	25 Jun 88	9
Above hit: WEE PAPA GIRL RAPPERS featuring TWO MEN AND A DRUM MACHINE.				
WEE RULE	Jive	6	1 Oct 88	9
SOULMATE	Jive	45	24 Dec 88	4
BLOW THE HOUSE DOWN	Jive	65	25 Mar 89	1
ALBUMS:	**HITS 1**			**WEEKS 3**
THE BEAT, THE RHYME, THE NOISE	Jive	39	5 Nov 88	3

Bert WEEDON
UK

SINGLES:	**HITS 8**			**WEEKS 38**
GUITAR BOOGIE SHUFFLE	Top Rank	10	16 May 59	9
Originally recorded by Arthur Smith as Guitar Boogie in 1945.				
NASHVILLE BOOGIE	Top Rank	29	21 Nov 59	2
BIG BEAT BOOGIE	Top Rank	37	12 Mar 60	3
BIG BEAT BOOGIE [RE]	Top Rank	49	9 Apr 60	1
TWELFTH STREET RAG	Top Rank	47	11 Jun 60	2
Above hit: Bert WEEDON and his "Honky Tonk" Guitar.				
APACHE	Top Rank	44	30 Jul 60	1
APACHE [RE]	Top Rank	24	13 Aug 60	3
SORRY ROBBIE	Top Rank	28	29 Oct 60	11
GINCHY	Top Rank	35	4 Feb 61	5
MR. GUITAR	Top Rank	47	6 May 61	1
ALBUMS:	**HITS 2**			**WEEKS 26**
KING SIZE GUITAR	Top Rank	18	16 Jul 60	1
22 GOLDEN GUITAR GREATS	Warwick	1	23 Oct 76	25

WEE'IST PIPE BAND IN THE WORLD – See TARTAN ARMY featuring the WEE'IST PIPE BAND IN THE WORLD

WEEKEND   Multi-National

SINGLES:	HITS 1			WEEKS 5	
CHRISTMAS MEDLEY (SHORT VERSION) [M] / AULD LANG SYNE	*Lifestyle*	47	*14 Dec 85*		5

Michelle WEEKS   US

SINGLES:	HITS 3			WEEKS 6	
MOMENT OF MY LIFE	*Ministry Of Sound*	23	*2 Aug 97*		3
Originally recorded by Inner Life featuring Jocelyn Brown in 1982.					
Above hit: Bobby D'AMBROSIO featuring Michelle WEEKS.					
DON'T GIVE UP	*Ministry Of Sound*	28	*8 Nov 97*		2
GIVE ME LOVE	*VC Recordings*	59	*11 Jul 98*		1
Above hit: DJ DADO vs Michelle WEEKS.					

WEEN   US

SINGLES:	HITS 1			WEEKS 3	
BEACON LIGHT	*Elektra*	20	*29 Aug 98*		3
[AA] listed with Walking After You by the Foo Fighters. From the film 'The X Files'.					

WEEZER   US

SINGLES:	HITS 4			WEEKS 12	
UNDONE – THE SWEATER SONG	*Geffen*	35	*11 Feb 95*		2
BUDDY HOLLY	*Geffen*	12	*6 May 95*		7
SAY IT AIN'T SO	*Geffen*	37	*22 Jul 95*		2
EL SCORCHO	*Geffen*	50	*5 Oct 96*		1
ALBUMS:	HITS 2			WEEKS 12	
WEEZER	*Geffen*	23	*4 Mar 95*		11
PINKERTON	*Geffen*	43	*12 Oct 96*		1

Constantine WEIR – See PRESSURE DROP featuring Constantine WEIR and Martin FISHLEY

Frank WEIR and his Orchestra   UK

(See also Vera Lynn.)

SINGLES:	HITS 1			WEEKS 4	
CARIBBEAN HONEYMOON	*Oriole*	42	*17 Sep 60*		4

Eric WEISSBERG – See 'DELIVERANCE' SOUNDTRACK

WELCH – See MARVIN, WELCH and FARRAR

Denise WELCH   UK

SINGLES:	HITS 1			WEEKS 3	
YOU DON'T HAVE TO SAY YOU LOVE ME / CRY ME A RIVER	*Virgin*	23	*4 Nov 95*		3
From the Central ITV series 'Soldier, Soldier'.					

Paul WELLER   UK

SINGLES:	HITS 17			WEEKS 61	
INTO TOMORROW	*Freedom High*	36	*18 May 91*		3
Above hit: Paul WELLER MOVEMENT.					
UH HUH OH YEH	*Go! Discs*	18	*15 Aug 92*		5
ABOVE THE CLOUDS	*Go! Discs*	47	*10 Oct 92*		2
SUNFLOWER	*Go! Discs*	16	*17 Jul 93*		5
WILD WOOD	*Go! Discs*	14	*4 Sep 93*		3
THE WEAVER [EP]	*Go! Discs*	18	*13 Nov 93*		3
Lead track: The Weaver.					
HUNG UP	*Go! Discs*	11	*9 Apr 94*		3
OUT OF THE SINKING	*Go! Discs*	20	*5 Nov 94*		3
THE CHANGINGMAN	*Go! Discs*	7	*6 May 95*		4
Backing vocals by Carleen Anderson.					
YOU DO SOMETHING TO ME	*Go! Discs*	9	*22 Jul 95*		6
BROKEN STONES	*Go! Discs*	20	*30 Sep 95*		4
OUT OF THE SINKING [RR]	*Go! Discs*	16	*9 Mar 96*		2
Backing vocals by Carleen Anderson.					
PEACOCK SUIT	*Go! Discs*	5	*17 Aug 96*		5
BRUSHED	*Island*	14	*9 Aug 97*		3
FRIDAY STREET	*Island*	21	*11 Oct 97*		2
Above 2 had sleeves giving title as an EP:A Heavy Soul.					
MERMAIDS	*Island*	30	*6 Dec 97*		2
BRAND NEW START	*Island*	16	*14 Nov 98*		3
WILD WOOD [RI]	*Island*	22	*9 Jan 99*		3
ALBUMS:	HITS 6			WEEKS 182	
PAUL WELLER	*Go! Discs*	8	*12 Sep 92*		7
WILD WOOD	*Go! Discs*	2	*18 Sep 93*		51
LIVE WOOD	*Go! Discs*	13	*24 Sep 94*		5
Live recordings from his UK and European tours, 1993/94.					
STANLEY ROAD	*Go! Discs*	1	*27 May 95*		87

HEAVY SOUL	*Island*	2	*5 Jul 97*	13
MODERN CLASSICS – THE GREATEST HITS	*Island*	7	*21 Nov 98*	19

Brandi WELLS US

SINGLES:	HITS 1			WEEKS 1
WATCH OUT	*WMOT*	74	*20 Feb 82*	1

Houston WELLS and the MARKSMEN UK

SINGLES:	HITS 1			WEEKS 10
ONLY THE HEARTACHES	*Parlophone*	22	*3 Aug 63*	10

Mary WELLS US

SINGLES:	HITS 2			WEEKS 25
MY GUY	*Stateside*	5	*23 May 64*	14
ONCE UPON A TIME	*Stateside*	50	*1 Aug 64*	1
Above bit: Marvin GAYE and Mary WELLS.				
MY GUY [RI]	*Tamla Motown*	14	*8 Jul 72*	10

Terri WELLS US

SINGLES:	HITS 2			WEEKS 9
YOU MAKE IT HEAVEN	*Philly World*	53	*2 Jul 83*	2
I'LL BE AROUND	*Philly World/London*	17	*5 May 84*	7
Original by the Detroit Spinners reached No. 3 in the US in 1972.				

Alex WELSH UK

SINGLES:	HITS 1			WEEKS 4
TANSY	*Columbia*	45	*12 Aug 61*	4

Irvine WELSH and ON-U-SOUND presents . . . – See PRIMAL SCREAM

WENDY and LISA US

SINGLES:	HITS 7			WEEKS 31
WATERFALL	*Virgin*	66	*5 Sep 87*	4
SIDESHOW	*Virgin*	49	*16 Jan 88*	5
ARE YOU MY BABY?	*Virgin*	70	*18 Feb 89*	3
LOLLY LOLLY (ACCORDING TO PRINCE)	*Virgin*	64	*29 Apr 89*	3
SATISFACTION	*Virgin*	27	*8 Jul 89*	8
WATERFALL '89 [RM]	*Virgin*	69	*18 Nov 89*	2
Remixed by Wendy and Lisa.				
STRUNG OUT	*Virgin*	44	*30 Jun 90*	5
RAINBOW LAKE	*Virgin*	70	*10 Nov 90*	1
ALBUMS:	**HITS 3**			**WEEKS 7**
WENDY AND LISA	*Virgin*	84	*10 Oct 87*	2
FRUIT AT THE BOTTOM	*Virgin*	45	*18 Mar 89*	2
EROICA	*Virgin*	33	*4 Aug 90*	3

WES Cameroon

SINGLES:	HITS 2			WEEKS 7
ALANE	*Epic*	11	*14 Feb 98*	6
I LOVE FOOTBALL	*Epic*	75	*27 Jun 98*	1
Official song for the Cameroon 1998 World Cup Squad.				

Dodie WEST UK

SINGLES:	HITS 1			WEEKS 4
GOIN' OUT OF MY HEAD	*Decca*	39	*16 Jan 65*	4

Keith WEST UK

SINGLES:	HITS 2			WEEKS 18
EXCERPT FROM "A TEENAGE OPERA"	*Parlophone*	2	*12 Aug 67*	15
SAM	*Parlophone*	38	*25 Nov 67*	3

Kit WEST – See DEGREES OF MOTION featuring BITI

WEST END featuring SYBIL UK

(See also Sybil.)

SINGLES:	HITS 1			WEEKS 13
THE LOVE I LOST	*PWL Sanctuary*	3	*16 Jan 93*	13

WEST END UK

SINGLES:	HITS 1			WEEKS 2
LOVE RULES	*RCA*	44	*19 Aug 95*	2

WEST HAM UNITED CUP SQUAD

UK

SINGLES:	HITS 1			WEEKS 2	
I'M FOREVER BLOWING BUBBLES	Pye	31	10 May 75	2	

WEST STREET MOB

US

SINGLES:	HITS 1			WEEKS 3	
BREAK DANCIN' – ELECTRIC BOOGIE	Sugar Hill	71	8 Oct 83	1	
BREAK DANCIN' – ELECTRIC BOOGIE [RE]	Sugar Hill	64	22 Oct 83	2	

WESTBAM

Germany

SINGLES:	HITS 5			WEEKS 9	
CELEBRATION GENERATION	Urban	48	9 Jul 94	2	
BAM BAM BAM	Urban	57	19 Nov 94	1	
WIZARDS OF THE SONIC	Urban	32	3 Jun 95	2	
ALWAYS MUSIC	Low Spirit	51	23 Mar 96	1	
Above hit: WESTBAM/KOON + STEPHENSON.					
WIZARDS OF THE SONIC [RM]	Wonderboy	43	13 Jun 98	2	
Mixed by Matt Darey.					
Above hit: WESTBAM vs. RED JERRY.					
ROOF IS ON FIRE	Logic	58	28 Nov 98	1	
Above hit: WESTBAM'S.					

WESTLIFE

Ireland

SINGLES:	HITS 4			WEEKS 36	
SWEAR IT AGAIN	RCA	1	1 May 99	12	
SWEAR IT AGAIN [RE]	RCA	71	14 Aug 99	1	
IF I LET YOU GO	RCA	1	21 Aug 99	11	
FLYING WITHOUT WINGS	RCA	1	30 Oct 99	10	
I HAVE A DREAM / SEASONS IN THE SUN	RCA	1	25 Dec 99	2	
ALBUMS:	HITS 1			WEEKS 8	
WESTLIFE	RCA	2	13 Nov 99	8	

WESTMINSTER ABBEY CHOIR/ conductor: Martin NEARY

UK

ALBUMS:	HITS 2			WEEKS 7	
JOHN TAVENER: INNOCENCE	Sony Classical	34	20 Sep 97	4	
PERFECT PEACE	Sony Classical	58	12 Sep 98	3	
Features songs performed at the funeral service of Diana, Princess Of Wales on 6 Sep 97.					

Kim WESTON – See Marvin GAYE

Paul WESTON and his Orchestra – See Doris DAY; Frankie LAINE; Johnnie RAY, Jo STAFFORD

WESTWORLD

UK/US

SINGLES:	HITS 5			WEEKS 23	
SONIC BOOM BOY	RCA	11	21 Feb 87	7	
BA-NA-NA-BAM-BOO	RCA	37	2 May 87	5	
WHERE THE ACTION IS	RCA	54	25 Jul 87	4	
SILVERMAC	RCA	42	17 Oct 87	5	
EVERYTHING GOOD IS BAD	RCA	72	15 Oct 88	2	
ALBUMS:	HITS 1			WEEKS 2	
WHERE THE ACTION IS	RCA	49	5 Sep 87	2	

WET WET WET

UK

SINGLES:	HITS 26			WEEKS 209	
WISHING I WAS LUCKY	Precious Organisation	6	11 Apr 87	14	
A 12" double pack reached No. 96 on 13 Jun 87.					
SWEET LITTLE MYSTERY	Precious Organisation	5	25 Jul 87	12	
ANGEL EYES (HOME AND AWAY)	Precious Organisation	5	5 Dec 87	12	
TEMPTATION	Precious Organisation	12	19 Mar 88	8	
WITH A LITTLE HELP FROM MY FRIENDS	Childline	1	14 May 88	11	
Charity record in aid of Childline. [AA] listed with She's Leaving Home by Billy Bragg with Cara Tivey.					
SWEET SURRENDER	Precious Organisation	6	30 Sep 89	8	
BROKE AWAY	Precious Organisation	19	9 Dec 89	7	
HOLD BACK THE RIVER	Precious Organisation	31	10 Mar 90	4	
STAY WITH ME HEARTACHE / I FEEL FINE	Precious Organisation	30	11 Aug 90	4	
MAKE IT TONIGHT	Precious Organisation	37	14 Sep 91	3	
PUT THE LIGHT ON	Precious Organisation	56	2 Nov 91	2	
GOODNIGHT GIRL	Precious Organisation	1	4 Jan 92	11	
MORE THAN LOVE	Precious Organisation	19	21 Mar 92	5	
THE LIP SERVICE [EP]	Precious Organisation	15	11 Jul 92	5	
Lead track: Lip Service. Chart only listed as an EP from 1 Aug 92.					
BLUE FOR YOU / THIS TIME (LIVE)	Precious Organisation	38	8 May 93		
Charity record with proceeds to Nordoff Robbins Music Therapy. Live recordings from the Royal Albert Hall, London, 3 Nov 92.					

SHED A TEAR	*Precious Organisation*	22	*6 Nov 93*	5
COLD COLD HEART	*Precious Organisation*	20	*8 Jan 94*	4
LOVE IS ALL AROUND	*Precious Organisation*	1	*21 May 94*	37
From the film 'Four Weddings And A Funeral'.				
JULIA SAYS	*Precious Organisation*	3	*25 Mar 95*	9
DON'T WANT TO FORGIVE ME NOW	*Precious Organisation*	7	*17 Jun 95*	8
SOMEWHERE SOMEHOW	*Precious Organisation*	7	*30 Sep 95*	7
SHE'S ALL ON MY MIND	*Precious Organisation*	17	*2 Dec 95*	7
MORNING	*Precious Organisation*	16	*30 Mar 96*	4
IF I NEVER SEE YOU AGAIN	*Precious Organisation*	3	*22 Mar 97*	8
STRANGE	*Precious Organisation*	13	*14 Jun 97*	4
IF I NEVER SEE YOU AGAIN [RE]	*Precious Organisation*	72	*21 Jun 97*	1
STRANGE [RE]	*Precious Organisation*	74	*19 Jul 97*	1
YESTERDAY	*Precious Organisation*	4	*16 Aug 97*	6
ALBUMS:	**HITS 8**		**WEEKS 278**	
POPPED IN SOULED OUT	*Precious Organisation*	1	*3 Oct 87*	72
Includes re-entry in 1997.				
THE MEMPHIS SESSIONS	*Precious Organisation*	3	*19 Nov 88*	13
HOLDING BACK THE RIVER	*Precious Organisation*	2	*11 Nov 89*	26
HIGH ON THE HAPPY SIDE	*Precious Organisation*	1	*8 Feb 92*	25
LIVE AT THE ROYAL ALBERT HALL	*Precious Organisation*	10	*29 May 93*	4
Live recordings from 3 Nov 92 in aid of Nordoff Robbins Music Therapy.				
Above hit: WET WET WET with the WREN ORCHESTRA.				
END OF PART ONE (THEIR GREATEST HITS)	*Precious Organisation*	4	*20 Nov 93*	17
END OF PART ONE (THEIR GREATEST HITS) [RE]	*Precious Organisation*	1	*30 Apr 94*	50
PICTURE THIS	*Precious Organisation*	1	*22 Apr 95*	45
10	*Precious Organisation*	2	*12 Apr 97*	26

WE'VE GOT A FUZZBOX AND WE'RE GONNA USE IT   UK

SINGLES:	**HITS 6**		**WEEKS 39**	
RULES AND REGULATIONS [EP]	*Vindaloo*	41	*26 Apr 86*	7
Lead track: X X Sex. The chart for 26 Apr 86 only listed entry as an [AA] with Rules And				
Regulations.				
LOVE IS THE SLUG	*Vindaloo*	31	*15 Nov 86*	4
WHAT'S THE POINT	*Vindaloo*	51	*7 Feb 87*	2
Above hit: FUZZBOX.				
INTERNATIONAL RESCUE	*WEA*	11	*25 Feb 89*	10
PINK SUNSHINE	*WEA*	14	*20 May 89*	10
SELF!	*WEA*	24	*5 Aug 89*	6
Above hit: FUZZBOX.				
ALBUMS:	**HITS 1**		**WEEKS 6**	
BIG BANG	*WEA*	5	*26 Aug 89*	6

WHALE   Sweden

SINGLES:	**HITS 3**		**WEEKS 8**	
HOBO HUMPIN SLOBO BABE	*East West*	46	*19 Mar 94*	2
I'LL DO YA	*Hut*	53	*15 Jul 95*	1
HOBO HUMPIN' SLOBO BABE [RI]	*Hut*	15	*25 Nov 95*	4
FOUR BIG SPEAKERS	*Hut*	69	*4 Jul 98*	1
Above hit: WHALE featuring BUS75.				
ALBUMS:	**HITS 1**		**WEEKS 2**	
WE CARE	*Hut*	42	*12 Aug 95*	2

WHALERS – See Hal PAGE and the WHALERS

WHAM!   UK

SINGLES:	**HITS 10**		**WEEKS 137**	
YOUNG GUNS (GO FOR IT)	*Inner Vision*	3	*16 Oct 82*	17
WHAM RAP! (ENJOY WHAT YOU DO)	*Inner Vision*	8	*15 Jan 83*	11
Originally released in 1982 appearing in the Bubbling Under section of the chart.				
BAD BOYS	*Inner Vision*	2	*14 May 83*	14
CLUB TROPICANA	*Inner Vision*	4	*30 Jul 83*	11
CLUB FANTASTIC MEGAMIX [M]	*Inner Vision*	15	*3 Dec 83*	8
Mix of tracks from their album 'Fantastic'.				
WAKE ME UP BEFORE YOU GO GO	*Epic*	1	*26 May 84*	16
FREEDOM	*Epic*	1	*13 Oct 84*	14
LAST CHRISTMAS / EVERYTHING SHE WANTS	*Epic*	2	*15 Dec 84*	13
A repackaged edition was listed from 5 Jan 85 with a remixed version of Everything She Wants as				
the first track.				
Charity record with proceeds to Famine relief in Ethiopia.				
I'M YOUR MAN	*Epic*	1	*23 Nov 85*	12
LAST CHRISTMAS [RI-1ST]	*Epic*	6	*14 Dec 85*	7
THE EDGE OF HEAVEN / WHERE DID YOUR HEART GO?	*Epic*	1	*21 Jun 86*	10
Where Did Your Heart Go? listed from 2 Aug 86 once single had dropped to No. 28. The Edge				
Of Heaven features Elton John on piano.				
LAST CHRISTMAS [RI-2ND]	*Epic*	45	*20 Dec 86*	4

ALBUMS:		HITS 4			WEEKS 259
FANTASTIC	Inner	1	9 Jul 83	116
MAKE IT BIG	Epic	1	17 Nov 84	72
THE FINAL	Epic	2	19 Jul 86	45
Compilation.				
THE BEST OF WHAM! . . . IF YOU WERE THERE	Epic	4	6 Dec 97	24
THE FINAL [RE]	Epic	27	10 Jul 99	2

WHATNAUTS – See MOMENTS

Caron WHEELER   UK

SINGLES:		HITS 7			WEEKS 42
KEEP ON MOVIN'	10 Records	5	18 Mar 89	12
Above hit: SOUL II SOUL (featuring Caron WHEELER).				
BACK TO LIFE (HOWEVER DO YOU WANT ME)	10 Records	1	10 Jun 89	14
Certain copies did not credit Caron Wheeler on either the sleeve or the label.				
Above hit: SOUL II SOUL featuring Caron WHEELER.				
LIVIN' IN THE LIGHT	RCA	14	8 Sep 90	6
UK BLAK	RCA	40	10 Nov 90	4
DON'T QUIT	RCA	53	9 Feb 91	3
I ADORE YOU	A&M	59	7 Nov 92	2
From the film 'Mo'Money'.				
BEACH OF THE WAR GODDESS	EMI	75	11 Sep 93	1
ALBUMS:		**HITS 1**		**WEEKS 5**
UK BLAK	RCA	14	13 Oct 90	5

Bill WHELAN   Ireland

SINGLES:		HITS 1			WEEKS 16
RIVERDANCE	Son	9	17 Dec 94	16
Originally reached No. 95 in June 94. Charted after being performed at the Royal Command				
Performance which was screened on BBC1 TV.				
Above hit: Bill WHELAN featuring ANUNA and the RTE CONCERT ORCHESTRA.				
ALBUMS:		**HITS 1**		**WEEKS 38**
MUSIC FROM RIVERDANCE - THE SHOW	Atlantic	31	25 Mar 95	38
Label changed to Celtic Heartbeat from 17 Jun 95.				

WHEN IN ROME   UK

SINGLES:		HITS 1			WEEKS 3
THE PROMISE	10 Records	58	28 Jan 89	3

WHIGFIELD   Denmark

SINGLES:		HITS 6			WEEKS 52
SATURDAY NIGHT	Systematic	1	17 Sep 94	18
First artist to debut at No. 1. Originally released in Italy, 1993.				
ANOTHER DAY	Systematic	7	10 Dec 94	10
THINK OF YOU	Systematic	7	10 Jun 95	11
CLOSE TO YOU	Systematic	13	9 Sep 95	7
LAST CHRISTMAS / BIG TIME	Systematic	21	16 Dec 95	5
SEXY EYES - REMIXES	ZYX	68	10 Oct 98	1
ALBUMS:		**HITS 1**		**WEEKS 7**
WHIGFIELD	Systematic	13	1 Jul 95	7

WHIPPING BOY   Ireland

SINGLES:		HITS 3			WEEKS 4
WE DON'T NEED NOBODY ELSE	Columbia	51	14 Oct 95	1
WHEN WE WERE YOUNG	Columbia	46	3 Feb 96	2
TWINKLE	Columbia	55	25 May 96	1
Original release reached No. 83 in 1995.				

Nancy WHISKEY – See Chas McDEVITT SKIFFLE GROUP (featuring Nancy WHISKEY)

WHISPERS   US

SINGLES:		HITS 8			WEEKS 52
AND THE BEAT GOES ON	Solar	2	2 Feb 80	12
LADY	Solar	55	10 May 80	3
MY GIRL	Solar	26	12 Jul 80	6
IT'S A LOVE THING	Solar	9	14 Mar 81	11
I CAN MAKE IT BETTER	Solar	44	13 Jun 81	5
CONTAGIOUS	Solar	56	19 Jan 85	3
AND THE BEAT GOES ON [RI]	Solar	45	28 Mar 87	4
ROCK STEADY	Solar	38	23 May 87	6
SPECIAL F./X	Solar	69	15 Aug 87	2
ALBUMS:		**HITS 2**		**WEEKS 9**
IMAGINATION	Solar	42	14 Mar 81	5
JUST GETS BETTER WITH TIME	Solar	63	6 Jun 87	4

WHISTLE
US

SINGLES:		HITS 1		WEEKS 8
(NOTHING SERIOUS) JUST BUGGIN'	Champion	7	1 Mar 86	8

Alex WHITCOMBE and BIG C
UK

(See also Qattara.)

SINGLES:		HITS 1		WEEKS 1
ICE RAIN	Xtravaganza	44	23 May 98	1

Original release reached No. 188 in 1996. Vocals by Luciana.

Alan WHITE
UK

ALBUMS:		HITS 1		WEEKS 4
RAMSHACKLED	Atlantic	41	13 Mar 76	4

Barry WHITE
US

(See also Quincy Jones.)

SINGLES:		HITS 18		WEEKS 136
I'M GONNA LOVE YOU JUST A LITTLE BIT MORE BABY	Pye International	23	9 Jun 73	7
NEVER, NEVER GONNA GIVE YA UP	Pye International	14	26 Jan 74	11
CAN'T GET ENOUGH OF YOUR LOVE, BABE	Pye International	8	17 Aug 74	12
YOU'RE THE FIRST, THE LAST, MY EVERYTHING	20th Century	1	2 Nov 74	14
WHAT AM I GONNA DO WITH YOU?	20th Century	5	8 Mar 75	8
I'LL DO ANYTHING YOU WANT ME TO	20th Century	20	24 May 75	6
LET THE MUSIC PLAY	20th Century	9	27 Dec 75	8
YOU SEE THE TROUBLE WITH ME	20th Century	2	6 Mar 76	10
BABY, WE BETTER TRY TO GET IT TOGETHER	20th Century	15	21 Aug 76	7
DON'T MAKE ME WAIT TOO LONG	20th Century	17	13 Nov 76	9
I'M QUALIFIED TO SATISFY YOU	20th Century	37	5 Mar 77	5
IT'S ECSTASY WHEN YOU LAY DOWN NEXT TO ME	20th Century	40	15 Oct 77	3
JUST THE WAY YOU ARE	20th Century	12	16 Dec 78	12
SHA LA LA MEANS I LOVE YOU	20th Century	55	24 Mar 79	6
SHO' YOU RIGHT	Breakout	14	7 Nov 87	7
NEVER NEVER GONNA GIVE YA UP [RM]	Club	63	16 Jan 88	2
PRACTICE WHAT YOU PREACH / LOVE IS THE ICON	A&M	20	21 Jan 95	4
I ONLY WANT TO BE WITH YOU	A&M	36	8 Apr 95	2
IN YOUR WILDEST DREAMS	Parlophone	32	21 Dec 96	3

Above hit: Tina TURNER featuring Barry WHITE.

ALBUMS:		HITS 11		WEEKS 160
STONE GON'	Pye	18	9 Mar 74	17
CAN'T GET ENOUGH	20th Century	4	2 Nov 74	34
JUST ANOTHER WAY TO SAY I LOVE YOU	20th Century	12	26 Apr 75	15
GREATEST HITS	20th Century	18	22 Nov 75	12
LET THE MUSIC PLAY	20th Century	22	21 Feb 76	14
BARRY WHITE'S GREATEST HITS VOLUME 2	20th Century	17	9 Apr 77	7
THE MAN	20th Century	46	10 Feb 79	4
HEART AND SOUL	K-Tel	34	21 Dec 85	10
Compilation.				
THE RIGHT NIGHT AND BARRY WHITE	Breakout	74	17 Oct 87	6
THE COLLECTION	Mercury	5	2 Jul 88	29
THE BARRY WHITE COLLECTION [RI-1ST]	PolyGram TV	36	19 Feb 94	5
Re-issue of The Collection.				
THE ICON IS LOVE	A&M	44	11 Feb 95	3
Originally released in 1994.				
THE COLLECTION [RI-2ND]	Universal Music TV	22	11 Dec 99	4

Chris WHITE
UK

SINGLES:		HITS 1		WEEKS 4
SPANISH WINE	Charisma	37	20 Mar 76	4

Jesse WHITE – See Stan FREBERG

Karyn WHITE
US

SINGLES:		HITS 6		WEEKS 38
THE WAY YOU LOVE ME	Warner Brothers	42	5 Nov 88	5
SECRET RENDEZVOUS	Warner Brothers	52	18 Feb 89	3
SUPERWOMAN	Warner Brothers	11	10 Jun 89	13
SECRET RENDEZVOUS [RI]	Warner Brothers	22	9 Sep 89	9
ROMANTIC	Warner Brothers	23	17 Aug 91	5
THE WAY I FEEL ABOUT YOU	Warner Brothers	65	18 Jan 92	2
HUNGAH	Warner Brothers	69	24 Sep 94	1
ALBUMS:		HITS 2		WEEKS 30
KARYN WHITE	Warner Brothers	20	11 Mar 89	27
RITUAL OF LOVE	Warner Brothers	31	21 Sep 91	3

Snowy WHITE — UK

SINGLES:	HITS 2			WEEKS 12
BIRD OF PARADISE	*Towerbell*	6	*24 Dec 83*	10
FOR YOU	*R4*	65	*28 Dec 85*	1
FOR YOU [RE]	*R4*	72	*18 Jan 86*	1
ALBUMS:	HITS 2			WEEKS 5
WHITE FLAMES	*Towerbell*	21	*11 Feb 84*	4
SNOWY WHITE	*Towerbell*	88	*9 Feb 85*	1

Tam WHITE — UK

SINGLES:	HITS 1			WEEKS 4
WHAT IN THE WORLD'S COME OVER YOU	*RAK*	36	*15 Mar 75*	4

Tony Joe WHITE — US

SINGLES:	HITS 1			WEEKS 10
GROUPY GIRL	*Monument*	22	*6 Jun 70*	10
ALBUMS:	HITS 1			WEEKS 1
TONY JOE	*CBS*	63	*26 Sep 70*	1

WHITE and TORCH — UK

SINGLES:	HITS 1			WEEKS 4
PARADE	*Chrysalis*	54	*2 Oct 82*	4

WHITE LION — US

ALBUMS:	HITS 2			WEEKS 3
BIG GAME	*Atlantic*	47	*1 Jul 89*	1
MANE ATTRACTION	*Atlantic*	31	*20 Apr 91*	2

WHITE PLAINS — UK

SINGLES:	HITS 5			WEEKS 56
MY BABY LOVES LOVIN'	*Deram*	9	*7 Feb 70*	11
I'VE GOT YOU ON MY MIND	*Deram*	17	*18 Apr 70*	11
JULIE DO YA LOVE ME	*Deram*	8	*24 Oct 70*	14
Above hit: WHITE PLAINS with Pete NELSON.				
WHEN YOU ARE A KING	*Deram*	13	*12 Jun 71*	11
STEP INTO A DREAM	*Deram*	21	*17 Feb 73*	9
Above hit: WHITE PLAINS with Gerry BUTLER STRINGS.				

WHITE TOWN — UK

SINGLES:	HITS 2			WEEKS 10
YOUR WOMAN	*Chrysalis*	1	*25 Jan 97*	9
Based on Al Bowlly's My Woman from 1932.				
UNDRESSED	*Chrysalis*	57	*24 May 97*	1

WHITE ZOMBIE — US

SINGLES:	HITS 2			WEEKS 4
MORE HUMAN THAN HUMAN	*Geffen*	51	*20 May 95*	2
ELECTRIC HEAD PT.2 (THE ECSTASY)	*Geffen*	31	*18 May 96*	2
ALBUMS:	HITS 1			WEEKS 6
ASTRO CREEP 2000	*Geffen*	25	*27 May 95*	3
ASTRO CREEP 2000 / SUPERSEXY SWINGIN' SOUNDS [RE]	*Geffen*	32	*31 Aug 96*	3
Supersexy Swingin' Sounds' is a remix album. Sales were combined.				

WHITEHEAD BROS. — US

SINGLES:	HITS 2			WEEKS 5
YOUR LOVE IS A 187	*Motown*	32	*14 Jan 95*	3
FORGET I WAS A G	*Motown*	40	*13 May 95*	2

WHITEHOUSE — UK/US

SINGLES:	HITS 1			WEEKS 1
AIN'T NO MOUNTAIN HIGH ENOUGH	*Beautiful Noise*	60	*15 Aug 98*	1

WHITEOUT — UK

SINGLES:	HITS 2			WEEKS 2
DETROIT	*Silvertone*	73	*24 Sep 94*	1
JACKIE'S RACING	*Silvertone*	72	*18 Feb 95*	1
ALBUMS:	HITS 1			WEEKS 1
BITE IT	*Silvertone*	71	*1 Jul 95*	1

WHITESNAKE

UK

SINGLES:	HITS 21			WEEKS 112
SNAKE BITE [EP]	EMI International	61	24 Jun 78	3
Lead track: Bloody Mary.				
Above hit: David COVERDALE'S WHITESNAKE.				
LONG WAY FROM HOME	United Artists	55	10 Nov 79	2
FOOL FOR YOUR LOVING	United Artists	13	26 Apr 80	9
READY AN' WILLING (SWEET SATISFACTION)	United Artists	43	12 Jul 80	4
AIN'T NO LOVE IN THE HEART OF THE CITY	Liberty	51	22 Nov 80	4
Live recording from the Hammersmith Odeon, London, Jun 80. A studio version originally appeared on the Snake Bite E.P. Originally recorded by Bobby Bland in 1974.				
DON'T BREAK MY HEART AGAIN	Liberty	17	11 Apr 81	9
WOULD I LIE TO YOU	Liberty	37	6 Jun 81	6
HERE I GO AGAIN / BLOODY LUXURY	Liberty	34	6 Nov 82	10
GUILTY OF LOVE	Liberty	31	13 Aug 83	5
GIVE ME MORE TIME	Liberty	29	14 Jan 84	4
STANDING IN THE SHADOW	Liberty	62	28 Apr 84	2
LOVE AIN'T NO STRANGER	Liberty	44	9 Feb 85	4
STILL OF THE NIGHT	EMI	16	28 Mar 87	8
IS THIS LOVE	EMI	9	6 Jun 87	11
HERE I GO AGAIN (USA REMIX) [RR]	EMI	9	31 Oct 87	11
GIVE ME ALL YOUR LOVE	EMI	18	6 Feb 88	6
FOOL FOR YOUR LOVING [RR]	EMI	43	2 Dec 89	2
THE DEEPER THE LOVE	EMI	35	10 Mar 90	3
NOW YOU'RE GONE	EMI	31	25 Aug 90	4
IS THIS LOVE [RI] / SWEET LADY LUCK	EMI	25	6 Aug 94	4
TOO MANY TEARS	EMI	46	7 Jun 97	1
Above hit: David COVERDALE and WHITESNAKE.				

ALBUMS:	HITS 11			WEEKS 159
TROUBLE	EMI International	50	18 Nov 78	2
LOVE HUNTER	United Artists	29	13 Oct 79	7
READY AND WILLING	United Artists	6	7 Jun 80	15
LIVE IN THE HEART OF THE CITY	United Artists	5	8 Nov 80	15
Live recordings from the 1978 and 1980 Hammersmith Odeon shows in London.				
COME AND GET IT	Liberty	2	18 Apr 81	23
SAINTS 'N' SINNERS	Liberty	9	27 Nov 82	9
SLIDE IT IN	Liberty	9	11 Feb 84	7
WHITESNAKE 1987	EMI	8	11 Apr 87	57
SLIP OF THE TONGUE	EMI	10	25 Nov 89	10
WHITESNAKE'S GREATEST HITS	EMI	4	16 Jul 94	12
RESTLESS HEART	EMI	34	21 Jun 97	2
Above hit: David COVERDALE and WHITESNAKE.				

David WHITFIELD

UK

(See also All Star Hit Parade.)

SINGLES:	HITS 17			WEEKS 190
THE BRIDGE OF SIGHS	Decca	9	3 Oct 53	1
ANSWER ME	Decca	1	17 Oct 53	13
RAGS TO RICHES	Decca	12	12 Dec 53	1
Above 2: David WHITFIELD with Stanley BLACK and his Orchestra.				
RAGS TO RICHES [RE]	Decca	3	9 Jan 54	10
ANSWER ME [RE]	Decca	12	30 Jan 54	1
THE BOOK	Decca	5	20 Feb 54	12
Above hit: David WHITFIELD with Stanley BLACK and his Orchestra with Chorus.				
THE BOOK [RE]	Decca	10	29 May 54	3
CARA MIA	Decca	1	19 Jun 54	25
Above hit: David WHITFIELD with MANTOVANI and his Orchestra and Chorus.				
SANTO NATALE (MERRY CHRISTMAS)	Decca	2	13 Nov 54	10
Above hit: David WHITFIELD with Stanley BLACK and his Orchestra.				
BEYOND THE STARS	Decca	8	12 Feb 55	9
Above hit: David WHITFIELD with MANTOVANI and his Orchestra.				
MAMA	Decca	20	28 May 55	1
MAMA [RE-1ST]	Decca	19	25 Jun 55	2
EV'RYWHERE	Decca	3	9 Jul 55	20
Above 2 entries were separate sides of the same release, each had its own chart run.				
MAMA [RE-2ND]	Decca	12	30 Jul 55	8
Above 4: David WHITFIELD with the Roland SHAW ORCHESTRA.				
WHEN YOU LOSE THE ONE YOU LOVE	Decca	7	26 Nov 55	11
Above hit: David WHITFIELD with MANTOVANI and his Orchestra and Chorus.				
MY SEPTEMBER LOVE	Decca	19	3 Mar 56	2
MY SEPTEMBER LOVE [RE-1ST]	Decca	18	24 Mar 56	1
MY SEPTEMBER LOVE [RE-2ND]	Decca	3	7 Apr 56	20
MY SON JOHN	Decca	22	25 Aug 56	4
MY UNFINISHED SYMPHONY	Decca	29	1 Sep 56	1
Above 2 entries were separate sides of the same release, each had its own chart run.				
MY SEPTEMBER LOVE [RE-3RD]	Decca	25	8 Sep 56	1

THE ADORATION WALTZ	Decca		9	26 Jan 57	11
I'LL FIND YOU	Decca		28	6 Apr 57	2
From the film 'Sea Wife'.					
I'LL FIND YOU [RE]	Decca		27	8 Jun 57	2
Above 9: David WHITFIELD with the Roland SHAW ORCHESTRA.					
CRY MY HEART	Decca		22	15 Feb 58	3
Above hit: David WHITFIELD with MANTOVANI and his Orchestra and Chorus.					
ON THE STREET WHERE YOU LIVE	Decca		16	17 May 58	14
From the show 'My Fair Lady'.					
Above hit: David WHITFIELD with Cyril STAPLETON and his Orchestra.					
THE RIGHT TO LOVE	Decca		30	9 Aug 58	1
I BELIEVE	Decca		49	26 Nov 60	1
EPS:	HITS 2			WEEKS 3	
ROSE MARIE (SELECTION)	Decca		15	24 Jun 61	2
EXCERPTS FROM THE DESERT SONG	Decca		16	28 Apr 62	1

Slim WHITMAN
US

SINGLES:	HITS 7			WEEKS 77	
ROSE MARIE	London		1	16 Jul 55	19
Originally recorded by Nelson Eddy and Jeanette MacDonald.					
INDIAN LOVE CALL	London		7	30 Jul 55	12
Above 2 from the film 'Rose Marie' and originally written in 1924.					
CHINA DOLL	London		15	24 Sep 55	2
Above 2 entries were separate sides of the same release, each had its own chart run.					
TUMBLING TUMBLEWEEDS	London		19	10 Mar 56	2
I'M A FOOL	London		16	14 Apr 56	3
I'M A FOOL [RE]	London		29	12 May 56	1
SERENADE	London		24	23 Jun 56	3
From the film of the same name.					
SERENADE [RE]	London		8	28 Jul 56	12
I'LL TAKE YOU HOME AGAIN KATHLEEN	London		7	13 Apr 57	13
HAPPY ANNIVERSARY	United Artists		14	5 Oct 74	10
ALBUMS:	HITS 7			WEEKS 61	
HAPPY ANNIVERSARY	United Artists		44	14 Dec 74	2
THE VERY BEST OF SLIM WHITMAN	United Artists		1	31 Jan 76	17
RED RIVER VALLEY	United Artists		1	15 Jan 77	14
HOME ON THE RANGE	United Artists		2	15 Oct 77	13
GHOST RIDERS IN THE SKY	United Artists		27	13 Jan 79	6
SLIM WHITMAN'S 20 GREATEST LOVE SONGS	United Artists		18	22 Dec 79	7
THE VERY BEST OF SLIM WHITMAN - 50TH ANNIVERSARY COLLECTION	EMI		54	27 Sep 97	2

Roger WHITTAKER
UK

SINGLES:	HITS 7			WEEKS 85	
DURHAM TOWN (THE LEAVIN')	Columbia		12	8 Nov 69	18
I DON'T BELIEVE IN IF ANY MORE	Columbia		8	11 Apr 70	18
NEW WORLD IN THE MORNING	Columbia		17	10 Oct 70	14
WHY	Columbia		47	3 Apr 71	1
MAMY BLUE	Columbia		31	2 Oct 71	10
THE LAST FAREWELL	EMI		2	26 Jul 75	14
THE SKYE BOAT SONG	Tembo		10	8 Nov 86	10
Above hit: Roger WHITTAKER and Des O'CONNOR.					
ALBUMS:	HITS 11			WEEKS 111	
I DON'T BELIEVE IN IF ANYMORE	Columbia		23	27 Jun 70	1
NEW WORLD IN THE MORNING	Columbia		45	3 Apr 71	2
THE VERY BEST OF ROGER WHITTAKER	Columbia		5	6 Sep 75	42
THE SECOND ALBUM OF THE VERY BEST OF ROGER WHITTAKER	EMI		27	15 May 76	7
ROGER WHITTAKER SINGS THE HITS	Columbia		52	9 Dec 78	5
20 ALL TIME GREATS	Polydor		24	4 Aug 79	9
THE ROGER WHITTAKER ALBUM	K-Tel		18	7 Feb 81	14
SKYE BOAT SONG AND OTHER GREAT SONGS	Tembo		89	27 Dec 86	1
HIS FINEST COLLECTION	Tembo		15	23 May 87	19
HOME LOVIN' MAN	Tembo		20	23 Sep 89	10
A PERFECT DAY - HIS GREATEST HITS & MORE	RCA		74	11 May 96	1
Collection of old hits, songs from stage and screen plus new songs.					

WHO
UK

(See also High Numbers; Various Artists: Films – Original Soundtracks 'Tommy'.)

SINGLES:	HITS 28			WEEKS 247	
I CAN'T EXPLAIN	Brunswick		8	20 Feb 65	13
Backing vocals by the Ivy League and Jimmy Page on guitar.					
ANYWAY ANYHOW ANYWHERE	Brunswick		10	29 May 65	12
Theme to the ITV programme 'Ready Steady Go'.					
MY GENERATION	Brunswick		2	6 Nov 65	13

SUBSTITUTE	Reaction	5	12 Mar 66	13
A LEGAL MATTER	Brunswick	32	26 Mar 66	6
I'M A BOY	Reaction	2	3 Sep 66	13
THE KIDS ARE ALRIGHT	Brunswick	41	3 Sep 66	2
THE KIDS ARE ALRIGHT [RE]	Brunswick	48	24 Sep 66	1
HAPPY JACK	Reaction	3	17 Dec 66	11
PICTURES OF LILY	Track	4	29 Apr 67	10
THE LAST TIME / UNDER MY THUMB	Track	44	29 Jul 67	3

Under My Thumb originally recorded by the Rolling Stones.

I CAN SEE FOR MILES	Track	10	21 Oct 67	12
DOGS	Track	25	22 Jun 68	5
MAGIC BUS	Track	26	26 Oct 68	6
PINBALL WIZARD	Track	4	22 Mar 69	13
THE SEEKER	Track	19	4 Apr 70	11
SUMMERTIME BLUES	Track	38	8 Aug 70	4

Live recording from Leeds University, 14 Feb 70.

WON'T GET FOOLED AGAIN	Track	9	10 Jul 71	12
LET'S SEE ACTION	Track	16	23 Oct 71	12
JOIN TOGETHER	Track	9	24 Jun 72	9
RELAY	Track	21	13 Jan 73	5
5:15	Track	20	13 Oct 73	6
SQUEEZE BOX	Polydor	10	24 Jan 76	9
SUBSTITUTE [RI]	Polydor	7	30 Oct 76	7
WHO ARE YOU	Polydor	18	22 Jul 78	12
LONG LIVE ROCK	Polydor	48	28 Apr 79	5
YOU BETTER YOU BET	Polydor	9	7 Mar 81	8
DON'T LET GO THE COAT	Polydor	47	9 May 81	4
ATHENA	Polydor	40	2 Oct 82	4
READY STEADY WHO [EP]	Polydor	58	26 Nov 83	2

Lead track: Disguises. Originally charted in the EP chart. See EP section below.

MY GENERATION [RI-1ST]	Polydor	68	20 Feb 88	2
MY GENERATION [RI-2ND]	Polydor	31	27 Jul 96	2

Featured in the Calippo TV Commercial.

EPS:	**HITS 1**			**WEEKS 20**
READY STEADY WHO	Reaction	1	26 Nov 66	20

Re-recordings of their performance on 'Ready Steady Who', Oct 66.

ALBUMS:	**HITS 24**			**WEEKS 229**
MY GENERATION	Brunswick	5	25 Dec 65	11
A QUICK ONE	Reaction	4	17 Dec 66	17
THE WHO SELL-OUT	Track	13	13 Jan 68	11
TOMMY	Track	2	7 Jun 69	9
LIVE AT LEEDS	Track	3	6 Jun 70	21

Live recordings from Leeds University, 14 Feb 70.

WHO'S NEXT	Track	1	11 Sep 71	13
MEATY, BEATY, BIG AND BOUNCY	Track	9	18 Dec 71	8

Compilation.

QUADROPHENIA	Track	2	17 Nov 73	13
ODDS AND SODS	Track	10	26 Oct 74	4

Collection of unreleased material from 1964–72.

TOMMY [OST]	Track	30	23 Aug 75	2
THE WHO BY NUMBERS	Polydor	7	18 Oct 75	6
THE STORY OF THE WHO	Polydor	2	9 Oct 76	18
WHO ARE YOU	Polydor	6	9 Sep 78	9
THE KIDS ARE ALRIGHT [OST]	Polydor	26	30 Jun 79	13

Compilation of live recordings and interviews from their career.

QUADROPHENIA [OST]	Polydor	23	6 Oct 79	16

Selected remixed tracks from the original 1973 studio album plus various 1960s tracks from other artists.

MY GENERATION [RI]	Virgin	20	25 Oct 80	7
FACE DANCES	Polydor	2	28 Mar 81	9
IT'S HARD	Polydor	11	11 Sep 82	6
WHO'S LAST	MCA	48	17 Nov 84	4

Live recordings from their concert at Maple Leaf Gardens, Toronto, Canada, 17 Dec 82.

THE WHO COLLECTION	Impression	44	12 Oct 85	6
WHO'S BETTER, WHO'S BEST	Polydor	10	19 Mar 88	11
THE WHO COLLECTION	Stylus	71	19 Nov 88	4

This album is different to the earlier entry.

JOIN TOGETHER	Virgin	59	24 Mar 90	1

Live recordings from their Las Vegas tour of 1989.

30 YEARS OF MAXIMUM R&B	Polydor	48	16 Jul 94	1

4CD boxed set containing unreleased tracks, live cuts, rarities, commercials and studio dialogue.

LIVE AT LEEDS [RI]	Polydor	59	4 Mar 95	1

Includes bonus tracks.

QUADROPHENIA [RI]	Polydor	47	6 Jul 96	2

Digitally remastered.

MY GENERATION – THE VERY BEST OF THE WHO	Polydor	11	24 Aug 96	6

Same track listing as 1988's Who's Better, Who's Best plus 2 other tracks.

WHODINI
US

SINGLES:		HITS 2		WEEKS 10	
MAGIC'S WAND	Jive		47	25 Dec 82	6
MAGIC'S WAND (THE WHODINI ELECTRIC EP) [EP]	Jive		63	17 Mar 84	4
Lead track: Jive Magic Wand.					

WHOOLIGANZ
US

SINGLES:		HITS 1		WEEKS 2	
PUT YOUR HANDZ UP	Positiva		53	13 Aug 94	2

WHOOSH
UK

SINGLES:		HITS 1		WEEKS 1	
WHOOSH	Wonderboy		72	13 Sep 97	1

WHYCLIFFE
UK

SINGLES:		HITS 2		WEEKS 2	
HEAVEN	MCA		56	20 Nov 93	1
ONE MORE TIME	MCA		72	2 Apr 94	1

Jane WIEDLIN
US

SINGLES:		HITS 2		WEEKS 14	
RUSH HOUR	Manhattan		12	6 Aug 88	11
INSIDE A DREAM	Manhattan		64	29 Oct 88	3
ALBUMS:		HITS 1		WEEKS 3	
FUR	Manhattan		48	24 Sep 88	3

WIGAN'S CHOSEN FEW
Canada

SINGLES:		HITS 1		WEEKS 11	
FOOTSEE (INSTRUMENTAL)	Pye Disco Demand		9	18 Jan 75	11

WIGAN'S OVATION
UK

SINGLES:		HITS 3		WEEKS 19	
SKIING IN THE SNOW	Spark		12	15 Mar 75	10
Originally recorded by the Invitations.					
PER-SO-NAL-LY	Spark		38	28 Jun 75	6
Originally recorded by Bobby Paris.					
SUPER LOVE	Spark		41	29 Nov 75	3
Originally recorded by David and the Giants.					

WILCO
US

(See also Billy Bragg and Wilco.)

SINGLES:		HITS 1		WEEKS 1	
CAN'T STAND IT	Reprise		67	17 Apr 99	1
ALBUMS:		HITS 1		WEEKS 2	
SUMMERTEETH	Reprise		38	20 Mar 99	2

Jack WILD
UK

SINGLES:		HITS 1		WEEKS 2	
SOME BEAUTIFUL	Capitol		46	2 May 70	2

WILD BOYS – See HEINZ

WILD CHERRY
US

SINGLES:		HITS 1		WEEKS 11	
PLAY THAT FUNKY MUSIC	Epic		7	9 Oct 76	11

WILD COLOUR
UK

SINGLES:		HITS 1		WEEKS 2	
DREAMS	Perfecto		25	14 Oct 95	2

WILD HORSES
UK

ALBUMS:		HITS 1		WEEKS 4	
WILD HORSES	EMI		38	26 Apr 80	4

WILD PAIR – See Paula ABDUL

WILD WEEKEND | | | | UK

SINGLES:	HITS 2			WEEKS 2
BREAKIN' UP BREAKIN' DOWN	*Parlophone*	74	*29 Apr 89*	1
WHO'S AFRAID OF THE BIG BAD LOVE?	*Parlophone*	70	*5 May 90*	1

WILDCATS – See KREW-KATS, Marty WILDE

WILDCHILD | | | | UK

SINGLES:	HITS 3			WEEKS 20
LEGENDS OF THE DARK BLACK - PT 2	*Hi-Life*	34	*22 Apr 95*	3
RENEGADE MASTER [RI]	*Hi-Life*	11	*21 Oct 95*	4
A re-issue of the the first chart hit with a different title.				
JUMP TO MY BEAT	*Hi-Life*	30	*23 Nov 96*	2
Samples Mark Ryder's Get Down, Aretha Franklin's Jump To It and Lisa Lisa's Let The Beat Hit 'Em.				
RENEGADE MASTER 98 [RM]	*Hi-Life*	3	*17 Jan 98*	10
Remixed by Fatboy Slim.				
BAD BOY	*Polydor*	38	*25 Apr 98*	1
Above hit: WILDCHILD featuring JOMALSKI.				

Eugene WILDE | | | | US

SINGLES:	HITS 2			WEEKS 15
GOTTA GET YOU HOME TONIGHT	*Fourth & Broadway*	18	*13 Oct 84*	9
PERSONALITY / LET HER FEEL IT	*Fourth & Broadway*	34	*2 Feb 85*	6
Though Let Her Feel It is credited to Eugene Wilde, it is actually by Simplicious.				

ALBUMS:	HITS 1			WEEKS 4
EUGENE WILDE	*Fourth & Broadway*	67	*8 Dec 84*	4

Kim WILDE | | | | UK

SINGLES:	HITS 30			WEEKS 194
KIDS IN AMERICA	*RAK*	2	*21 Feb 81*	13
CHEQUERED LOVE	*RAK*	4	*9 May 81*	9
WATER ON GLASS / BOYS	*RAK*	11	*1 Aug 81*	8
CAMBODIA	*RAK*	12	*14 Nov 81*	12
VIEW FROM A BRIDGE	*RAK*	16	*17 Apr 82*	7
CHILD COME AWAY	*RAK*	43	*16 Oct 82*	4
LOVE BLONDE	*RAK*	23	*30 Jul 83*	8
DANCING IN THE DARK	*RAK*	67	*12 Nov 83*	2
THE SECOND TIME	*MCA*	29	*13 Oct 84*	6
THE TOUCH	*MCA*	56	*8 Dec 84*	3
RAGE TO LOVE	*MCA*	19	*27 Apr 85*	8
YOU KEEP ME HANGIN' ON	*MCA*	2	*25 Oct 86*	14
ANOTHER STEP (CLOSER TO YOU)	*MCA*	6	*4 Apr 87*	11
Above hit: Kim WILDE and JUNIOR.				
SAY YOU REALLY WANT ME	*MCA*	29	*8 Aug 87*	5
ROCKIN' AROUND THE CHRISTMAS TREE	*10 Records*	3	*5 Dec 87*	7
To support Comic Relief Red Nose Day (5 Feb 88).				
Above hit: COMIC RELIEF presents MEL and KIM performed by Kim WILDE and Mel SMITH.				
HEY MISTER HEARTACHE	*MCA*	31	*14 May 88*	5
YOU CAME	*MCA*	3	*16 Jul 88*	11
NEVER TRUST A STRANGER	*MCA*	7	*1 Oct 88*	9
FOUR LETTER WORD	*MCA*	6	*3 Dec 88*	12
LOVE IN THE NATURAL WAY	*MCA*	32	*4 Mar 89*	6
IT'S HERE	*MCA*	42	*14 Apr 90*	4
TIME	*MCA*	71	*16 Jun 90*	3
I CAN'T SAY GOODBYE	*MCA*	51	*15 Dec 90*	3
LOVE IS HOLY	*MCA*	16	*2 May 92*	6
HEART OVER MIND	*MCA*	34	*27 Jun 92*	3
WHO DO YOU THINK YOU ARE?	*MCA*	49	*12 Sep 92*	3
IF I CAN'T HAVE YOU	*MCA*	12	*10 Jul 93*	8
IN MY LIFE	*MCA*	54	*13 Nov 93*	1
BREAKIN' AWAY	*MCA*	43	*14 Oct 95*	2
THIS I SWEAR	*MCA*	46	*10 Feb 96*	1

ALBUMS:	HITS 10			WEEKS 88
KIM WILDE	*RAK*	3	*11 Jul 81*	14
SELECT	*RAK*	19	*22 May 82*	11
CATCH AS CATCH CAN	*RAK*	90	*26 Nov 83*	1
TEASES AND DARES	*MCA*	66	*17 Nov 84*	2
THE VERY BEST OF KIM WILDE	*RAK*	78	*18 May 85*	4
ANOTHER STEP	*MCA*	88	*15 Nov 86*	3
ANOTHER STEP [RI]	*MCA*	73	*26 Sep 87*	2
Re-released with bonus disc.				
CLOSE	*MCA*	44	*25 Jun 88*	19
CLOSE [RE]	*MCA*	8	*24 Dec 88*	19
LOVE MOVES	*MCA*	37	*26 May 90*	3

LOVE IS	MCA	21	30 May 92	3
THE SINGLES COLLECTION 1981–1993	MCA	11	25 Sep 93	7

Marty WILDE — UK

SINGLES:	HITS 13		WEEKS 117	
ENDLESS SLEEP	Philips	4	12 Jul 58	14
Original by Jody Reynolds reached No. 5 in the US in 1958.				
Above hit: Marty WILDE and his WILDCATS.				
DONNA	Philips	3	7 Mar 59	16
A TEENAGER IN LOVE	Philips	2	6 Jun 59	17
DONNA [RE]	Philips	25	4 Jul 59	2
SEA OF LOVE	Philips	3	26 Sep 59	12
Original by Phil Phillips reached No. 2 in the US In 1958.				
BAD BOY	Philips	7	12 Dec 59	8
JOHNNY ROCCO	Philips	30	12 Mar 60	4
THE FIGHT	Philips	47	21 May 60	1
LITTLE GIRL	Philips	16	24 Dec 60	9
RUBBER BALL	Philips	9	28 Jan 61	9
Written by Gene Pitney.				
HIDE AND SEEK	Philips	47	29 Jul 61	2
TOMORROW'S CLOWN	Philips	33	11 Nov 61	5
JEZEBEL	Philips	19	26 May 62	11
Originally recorded by Frankie Laine in 1951.				
EVER SINCE YOU SAID GOODBYE	Philips	31	27 Oct 62	7

Matthew WILDER — US

SINGLES:	HITS 1		WEEKS 11	
BREAK MY STRIDE	Epic	4	21 Jan 84	11

WILDHEARTS — UK

SINGLES:	HITS 10		WEEKS 24	
TV TAN	Bronze	53	20 Nov 93	2
CAFFEINE BOMB	Bronze	31	19 Feb 94	3
SUCKERPUNCH	Bronze	38	9 Jul 94	2
IF LIFE IS LIKE A LOVE BANK, I WANT AN OVERDRAFT / GEORDIE IN WONDERLAND	Bronze	31	28 Jan 95	3
I WANNA GO WHERE THE PEOPLE GO	Bronze	16	6 May 95	3
JUST IN LUST	Bronze	28	29 Jul 95	2
SICK OF DRUGS	Round	14	20 Apr 96	3
RED LIGHT – GREEN LIGHT [EP]	Round	30	29 Jun 96	2
Lead track: Red Light – Green Light.				
ANTHEM	Mushroom	21	16 Aug 97	2
URGE	Mushroom	26	18 Oct 97	2
ALBUMS:	HITS 4		WEEKS 8	
EARTH VS THE WILDHEARTS	East West	46	11 Sep 93	1
P.H.U.Q.	East West	6	3 Jun 95	4
FISHING FOR LUCKIES	East West	16	1 Jun 96	2
Originally released in 1994 to the fan club only.				
ENDLESS, NAMELESS	Mushroom	41	8 Nov 97	1

Heather WILDMAN – See George MOREL featuring Heather WILDMAN

Arthur WILKINSON ORCHESTRA — UK

EPS:	HITS 1		WEEKS 14	
BEATLE CRACKER MUSIC	His Master's Voice	7	8 Jan 66	14

Colm WILKINSON — Ireland

ALBUMS:	HITS 1		WEEKS 6	
STAGE HEROES	RCA	27	10 Jun 89	6

Sue WILKINSON — UK

SINGLES:	HITS 1		WEEKS 8	
YOU GOTTA BE A HUSTLER IF YOU WANNA GET ON	Cheapskate	25	2 Aug 80	8

WILL TO POWER — US

SINGLES:	HITS 2		WEEKS 18	
BABY I LOVE YOUR WAY / FREE BIRD [M]	Epic	6	7 Jan 89	9
I'M NOT IN LOVE	Epic	29	22 Dec 90	9

Alyson WILLIAMS — US

SINGLES:	HITS 4		WEEKS 28	
SLEEP TALK	Def Jam	17	4 Mar 89	9
MY LOVE IS SO RAW	Def Jam	34	6 May 89	5
Above hit: Alyson WILLIAMS featuring NIKKI-D.				

I NEED YOUR LOVIN'	*Def Jam*	8	*19 Aug 89*	11
I SECOND THAT EMOTION	*Def Jam*	44	*18 Nov 89*	3

Above hit: Alyson WILLIAMS featuring Chuck STANLEY.

ALBUMS:	**HITS 1**		**WEEKS 21**	
RAW	*Def Jam*	29	*25 Mar 89*	21

Andy WILLIAMS US

SINGLES:	**HITS 21**		**WEEKS 234**	
BUTTERFLY	*London*	1	*20 Apr 57*	15
I LIKE YOUR KIND OF LOVE	*London*	16	*22 Jun 57*	10

Vocals by Peggy Powers. Originally recorded by Melvin Endsley in 1957.

BUTTERFLY [RE]	*London*	29	*31 Aug 57*	1
STRANGER ON THE SHORE	*CBS*	30	*16 Jun 62*	10
CAN'T GET USED TO LOSING YOU	*CBS*	2	*23 Mar 63*	18
A FOOL NEVER LEARNS	*CBS*	40	*29 Feb 64*	4
ALMOST THERE	*CBS*	2	*18 Sep 65*	17
MAY EACH DAY	*CBS*	19	*26 Feb 66*	8
IN THE ARMS OF LOVE	*CBS*	33	*24 Sep 66*	7

From the film 'What Did You Do In The War Daddy?'.

MUSIC TO WATCH GIRLS BY	*CBS*	33	*6 May 67*	6

Original instrumental version by Bob Crew was featured in a US TV commercial for Diet Pepsi and reached No. 15 over there.

MORE AND MORE	*CBS*	45	*5 Aug 67*	1
CAN'T TAKE MY EYES OFF YOU	*CBS*	5	*16 Mar 68*	18
HAPPY HEART	*CBS*	47	*10 May 69*	1
HAPPY HEART [RE]	*CBS*	19	*24 May 69*	9
CAN'T HELP FALLING IN LOVE	*CBS*	3	*14 Mar 70*	17
IT'S SO EASY	*CBS*	13	*1 Aug 70*	13
IT'S SO EASY [RE]	*CBS*	49	*7 Nov 70*	1
HOME LOVIN' MAN	*CBS*	7	*21 Nov 70*	12
(WHERE DO I BEGIN) LOVE STORY	*CBS*	4	*20 Mar 71*	17

From the film 'Love Story'.

(WHERE DO I BEGIN) LOVE STORY [RE]	*CBS*	49	*24 Jul 71*	1
LOVE THEME FROM "THE GODFATHER" (SPEAK SOFTLY LOVE)	*CBS*	50	*5 Aug 72*	1

From the film.

LOVE THEME FROM "THE GODFATHER" (SPEAK SOFTLY LOVE) [RE-1ST]	*CBS*	44	*2 Sep 72*	3
LOVE THEME FROM "THE GODFATHER" (SPEAK SOFTLY LOVE) [RE-2ND]	*CBS*	42	*30 Sep 72*	5
SOLITAIRE	*CBS*	4	*8 Dec 73*	18

Originally recorded by Neil Sedaka.

GETTING OVER YOU	*CBS*	35	*18 May 74*	5
YOU LAY SO EASY ON MY MIND	*CBS*	32	*31 May 75*	7
THE OTHER SIDE OF ME	*CBS*	42	*6 Mar 76*	3
MUSIC TO WATCH GIRLS BY [RI]	*Columbia*	9	*27 Mar 99*	6

Featured in the Fiat Punto car TV commercial.

EPS:	**HITS 3**		**WEEKS 55**	
ANDY WILLIAMS FAVOURITES	*CBS*	3	*7 Aug 65*	38
ANDY WILLIAMS FAVOURITES VOLUME 2	*CBS*	17	*4 Dec 65*	2
ANDY'S NEWEST HITS	*CBS*	6	*14 Jan 67*	15

ALBUMS:	**HITS 26**		**WEEKS 445**	
ALMOST THERE	*CBS*	4	*26 Jun 65*	46
CAN'T GET USED TO LOSING YOU	*CBS*	16	*7 Aug 65*	1
MAY EACH DAY	*CBS*	11	*19 Mar 66*	6
GREAT SONGS FROM MY FAIR LADY	*CBS*	30	*30 Apr 66*	1
SHADOW OF YOUR SMILE	*CBS*	24	*23 Jul 66*	4
BORN FREE	*CBS*	22	*29 Jul 67*	11
LOVE ANDY	*CBS*	1	*11 May 68*	22
HONEY	*CBS*	4	*6 Jul 68*	17
HAPPY HEART	*CBS*	22	*26 Jul 69*	9
GET TOGETHER WITH ANDY WILLIAMS	*CBS*	13	*27 Dec 69*	12

Includes 3 tracks with the Osmonds.

ANDY WILLIAMS' SOUND OF MUSIC	*CBS*	22	*24 Jan 70*	10
ANDY WILLIAMS' GREATEST HITS	*CBS*	1	*11 Apr 70*	116

Peak position reached on 5 Dec 70.

CAN'T HELP FALLING IN LOVE	*CBS*	7	*20 Jun 70*	48
ANDY WILLIAMS SHOW	*CBS*	10	*5 Dec 70*	6
HOME LOVING MAN	*CBS*	1	*3 Apr 71*	25
LOVE STORY	*CBS*	11	*31 Jul 71*	11
THE IMPOSSIBLE DREAM	*CBS*	26	*29 Apr 72*	3
LOVE THEME FROM 'THE GODFATHER'	*CBS*	11	*29 Jul 72*	16
GREATEST HITS VOLUME 2	*CBS*	23	*16 Dec 72*	10
SOLITAIRE	*CBS*	3	*22 Dec 73*	26
THE WAY WE WERE	*CBS*	7	*15 Jun 74*	11
THE OTHER SIDE OF ME	*CBS*	60	*11 Oct 75*	1
REFLECTIONS	*CBS*	2	*28 Jan 78*	17
GREATEST LOVE CLASSICS	*EMI*	22	*27 Oct 84*	10

Above hit: Andy WILLIAMS and the ROYAL PHILHARMONIC ORCHESTRA.

THE BEST OF ANDY WILLIAMS	*Dino*	51	*7 Nov 92*	3

IN THE LOUNGE WITH . . . ANDY WILLIAMS	*Columbia*	39	*10 Apr 99*	3

Compilation originally released in 1996.

Andy and David WILLIAMS   US

SINGLES:	HITS 1			WEEKS 5
I DON'T KNOW WHY (I JUST DO)	*MCA*	37	*24 Mar 73*	5

Billy WILLIAMS   US

SINGLES:	HITS 1			WEEKS 9
I'M GONNA SIT RIGHT DOWN AND WRITE MYSELF A LETTER	*Vogue Coral*	22	*3 Aug 57*	8
I'M GONNA SIT RIGHT DOWN AND WRITE MYSELF A LETTER [RE]	*Vogue Coral*	28	*19 Oct 57*	1

Danny WILLIAMS   US

SINGLES:	HITS 8			WEEKS 74
WE WILL NEVER BE AS YOUNG AS THIS AGAIN	*His Master's Voice*	44	*27 May 61*	3

Above hit: Danny WILLIAMS with the Rita WILLIAMS SINGERS and Geoff LOVE and his Orchestra.

THE MIRACLE OF YOU	*His Master's Voice*	41	*8 Jul 61*	8
MOON RIVER	*His Master's Voice*	1	*4 Nov 61*	19

From the film 'Breakfast At Tiffany's'.
Above hit: Danny WILLIAMS with Geoff LOVE and his Orchestra and the Rita WILLIAMS SINGERS.

JEANNIE	*His Master's Voice*	14	*20 Jan 62*	14

Above hit: Danny WILLIAMS with the Rita WILLIAMS SINGERS and Geoff LOVE and his Orchestra.

THE WONDERFUL WORLD OF THE YOUNG	*His Master's Voice*	8	*14 Apr 62*	13
TEARS	*His Master's Voice*	22	*7 Jul 62*	7

Above 2: Danny WILLIAMS with Geoff LOVE and his Orchestra.

MY OWN TRUE LOVE	*His Master's Voice*	45	*2 Mar 63*	3
DANCIN' EASY	*Ensign*	30	*30 Jul 77*	7

Tune was featured in the Martini TV commercial.

Deniece WILLIAMS   US

(See also Johnny Mathis and Deniece Williams.)

SINGLES:	HITS 4			WEEKS 39
FREE	*CBS*	1	*2 Apr 77*	10
THAT'S WHAT FRIENDS ARE FOR	*CBS*	8	*30 Jul 77*	11
BABY, BABY MY LOVE'S ALL FOR YOU	*CBS*	32	*12 Nov 77*	5
LET'S HEAR IT FOR THE BOY	*CBS*	2	*5 May 84*	12

From the film 'Footloose'.

LET'S HEAR IT FOR THE BOY [RE]	*CBS*	75	*4 Aug 84*	1
ALBUMS:	**HITS 1**			**WEEKS 12**
THIS IS NIECEY	*CBS*	31	*21 May 77*	12

Diana WILLIAMS   US

SINGLES:	HITS 1			WEEKS 3
TEDDY BEAR'S LAST RIDE	*Capitol*	54	*25 Jul 81*	3

Answer song to Red Sovine's Teddy Bear.

Don WILLIAMS   US

SINGLES:	HITS 2			WEEKS 16
I RECALL A GYPSY WOMAN	*ABC*	13	*19 Jun 76*	10
YOU'RE MY BEST FRIEND	*ABC*	35	*23 Oct 76*	6
ALBUMS:	**HITS 14**			**WEEKS 136**
GREATEST HITS VOLUME 1	*ABC*	29	*10 Jul 76*	15
VISIONS	*ABC*	13	*19 Feb 77*	20
COUNTRY BOY	*ABC*	27	*15 Oct 77*	5
IMAGES	*K-Tel*	2	*5 Aug 78*	38
YOU'RE MY BEST THING	*ABC*	58	*5 Aug 78*	1
EXPRESSIONS	*ABC*	28	*4 Nov 78*	8
NEW HORIZONS	*K-Tel*	29	*22 Sep 79*	12
PORTRAIT	*MCA*	58	*15 Dec 79*	4
I BELIEVE IN YOU	*MCA*	36	*6 Sep 80*	5
ESPECIALLY FOR YOU	*MCA*	33	*18 Jul 81*	7
LISTEN TO THE RADIO	*MCA*	69	*17 Apr 82*	3
YELLOW MOON	*MCA*	52	*23 Apr 83*	1
LOVE STORIES	*K-Tel*	22	*15 Oct 83*	13
CAFE CAROLINA	*MCA*	65	*26 May 84*	4

Eric WILLIAMS of BLACKSTREET – See BLACKSTREET; QUEEN PEN; 2PAC

Freedom WILLIAMS   US

SINGLES:	HITS 4			WEEKS 31
GONNA MAKE YOU SWEAT (EVERYBODY DANCE NOW)	*CBS*	3	*15 Dec 90*	12

HERE WE GO	Columbia	20	30 Mar 91	7
THINGS THAT MAKE YOU GO HMMM . . .	Columbia	4	6 Jul 91	11

Above 3: C&C MUSIC FACTORY (featuring Freedom WILLIAMS).

VOICE OF FREEDOM	Columbia	62	5 Jun 93	1

Samples George Michael's Freedom.

Geoffrey WILLIAMS — UK

SINGLES:		HITS 4		WEEKS 8
IT'S NOT A LOVE THING	EMI	63	11 Apr 92	2
SUMMER BREEZE	EMI	56	22 Aug 92	3
DRIVE	Hands On	52	18 Jan 97	2
SEX LIFE	Hands On	71	19 Apr 97	1

Original release reached No. 96 in 1995.

Iris WILLIAMS — UK

SINGLES:		HITS 1		WEEKS 8
HE WAS BEAUTIFUL (CAVATINA) THE THEME FROM 'DEER HUNTER'	Columbia	18	27 Oct 79	8

From the film.
Above hit: Iris WILLIAMS with the Neil RICHARDSON ORCHESTRA.

ALBUMS:		HITS 1		WEEKS 4
HE WAS BEAUTIFUL	Columbia	69	22 Dec 79	4

John WILLIAMS — Australia

(See also Cleo Laine and John Williams.)

SINGLES:		HITS 1		WEEKS 11
CAVATINA	Cube	13	19 May 79	11

Theme from the film 'The Deerhunter'.

ALBUMS:		HITS 6		WEEKS 43
PLAYS SPANISH MUSIC	CBS	46	3 Oct 70	1
RODRIGO: CONCERTO DE ARANJUEZ	CBS	20	7 Feb 76	9

Above hit: John WILLIAMS with the ENGLISH CHAMBER ORCHESTRA conducted by Daniel BARENBOIM.

TRAVELLING	Cube	23	17 Jun 78	5
BRIDGES	Lotus	5	30 Jun 79	22
CAVATINA	Cube	64	4 Aug 79	3
JOHN WILLIAMS PLAYS THE MOVIES	Sony Classical	54	26 Oct 96	3

Released to mark a century of Cinema. Double album consists of 1 disc classical and the other pop.

John WILLIAMS — US

SINGLES:		HITS 3		WEEKS 17
THEME FROM SUPERMAN (MAIN TITLE)	Warner Brothers	32	6 Jan 79	5

Above hit: Composed and conducted by John WILLIAMS performed by the LONDON SYMPHONY ORCHESTRA.

THEME FROM E.T. (THE EXTRA-TERRESTRIAL)	MCA	17	18 Dec 82	10
THEME FROM JURASSIC PARK	MCA	45	14 Aug 93	2

Above 2 are from the films of the respective titles.

ALBUMS:		HITS 8		WEEKS 58
JAWS [OST]	MCA	55	31 Jan 76	1

Above hit: Composed and conducted by John WILLIAMS.

STAR WARS [OST]	20th Century	21	21 Jan 78	12

Above hit: Composed and conducted by John WILLIAMS; performed by the LONDON SYMPHONY ORCHESTRA.

CLOSE ENCOUNTERS OF THE THIRD KIND [OST]	Arista	40	29 Apr 78	6

Above hit: Composed and conducted by John WILLIAMS.

E.T. – THE EXTRATERRESTRIAL [OST]	MCA	47	25 Dec 82	10
RETURN OF THE JEDI [OST]	RSO	85	25 Jun 83	5

Above hit: Composed and conducted by John WILLIAMS; performed by the LONDON SYMPHONY ORCHESTRA.

JURASSIC PARK [OST]	MCA	42	31 Jul 93	5
SCHINDLER'S LIST [OST]	MCA	59	2 Apr 94	2
STAR WARS – THE PHANTOM MENACE [OST]	Sony Classical	8	15 May 99	17

Above hit: Composed and conducted by John WILLIAMS; performed by the LONDON SYMPHONY ORCHESTRA.

Kenny WILLIAMS — US

SINGLES:		HITS 1		WEEKS 8
(YOU'RE) FABULOUS BABE	Decca	35	19 Nov 77	8

Larry WILLIAMS — US

SINGLES:		HITS 2		WEEKS 18
SHORT FAT FANNIE	London	21	21 Sep 57	8
BONY MORONIE	London	11	18 Jan 58	10

Lenny WILLIAMS | | | | US

SINGLES:	HITS 2			WEEKS 7
SHOO DOO FU FU OOH!	ABC	38	5 Nov 77	4
YOU GOT ME RUNNING	ABC	67	16 Sep 78	3

Mark WILLIAMS – See Karen BODDINGTON and Mark WILLIAMS

Mason WILLIAMS | | | | US

SINGLES:	HITS 1			WEEKS 13
CLASSICAL GAS	Warner Brothers	9	31 Aug 68	13

Maurice WILLIAMS and the ZODIACS | | | | US

SINGLES:	HITS 1			WEEKS 9
STAY	Top Rank	14	7 Jan 61	9

Melanie WILLIAMS | | | | UK

SINGLES:	HITS 5			WEEKS 21
AIN'T NO LOVE (AIN'T NO USE)	Rob's Records	3	10 Apr 93	11
Above hit: SUB SUB featuring Melanie WILLIAMS.				
ALL CRIED OUT	Columbia	60	9 Apr 94	2
EVERYDAY THANG	Columbia	38	11 Jun 94	3
NOT ENOUGH?	Columbia	65	17 Sep 94	1
YOU ARE EVERYTHING	Columbia	28	18 Feb 95	4
Original version by the Stylistics reached No. 9 in the US in 1971.				
Above hit: Melanie WILLIAMS and Joe ROBERTS.				

Rita WILLIAMS SINGERS – See Shirley BASSEY; Alma COGAN; Russ CONWAY; Gracie FIELDS; KING BROTHERS; Ricky STEVENS with the Rita WILLIAMS SINGERS and Geoff LOVE and his Orchestra; Danny WILLIAMS

Robbie WILLIAMS | | | | UK

SINGLES:	HITS 10			WEEKS 122
FREEDOM	Chrysalis	2	10 Aug 96	10
FREEDOM [RE]	Chrysalis	56	26 Oct 96	4
OLD BEFORE I DIE	Chrysalis	2	26 Apr 97	9
OLD BEFORE I DIE [RE-1ST]	Chrysalis	72	5 Jul 97	1
OLD BEFORE I DIE [RE-2ND]	Chrysalis	69	19 Jul 97	1
LAZY DAYS	Chrysalis	8	26 Jul 97	5
SOUTH OF THE BORDER	Chrysalis	14	27 Sep 97	4
ANGELS	Chrysalis	4	13 Dec 97	20
LET ME ENTERTAIN YOU	Chrysalis	3	28 Mar 98	12
MILLENNIUM	Chrysalis	1	19 Sep 98	20
Samples theme from the James Bond film 'You Only Live Twice'.				
NO REGRETS	Chrysalis	4	12 Dec 98	13
Features vocals by Neil Tennant (Pet Shop Boys) and Neil Hannon (Divine Comedy). Though issued as an [AA], Antmusic was not listed.				
ANGELS [RE-1ST]	Chrysalis	57	2 Jan 99	4
ANGELS [RE-2ND]	Chrysalis	75	27 Feb 99	1
ANGELS [RE-3RD]	Chrysalis	75	20 Mar 99	1
STRONG	Chrysalis	4	27 Mar 99	9
SHE'S THE ONE / IT'S ONLY US	Chrysalis	1	20 Nov 99	7
She's The One originally recorded by World Party on their 1997 album Egyptology.				
ANGELS [RE-4TH]	Chrysalis	71	1 Jan 00	1
ALBUMS:	**HITS 2**			**WEEKS 173**
LIFE THRU A LENS	Chrysalis	11	11 Oct 97	4
LIFE THRU A LENS [RE]	Chrysalis	1	13 Dec 97	108
Peak position reached on 18 Apr 98.				
I'VE BEEN EXPECTING YOU	Chrysalis	1	7 Nov 98	61

Saul WILLIAMS – See KRUST featuring Saul WILLIAMS

Vanessa WILLIAMS | | | | US

SINGLES:	HITS 6			WEEKS 24
THE RIGHT STUFF	Wing	71	20 Aug 88	1
DREAMIN'	Wing	74	25 Mar 89	2
THE RIGHT STUFF [RM]	Wing	62	19 Aug 89	2
Remixed by Norman Cook.				
SAVE THE BEST FOR LAST	Polydor	3	21 Mar 92	11
THE SWEETEST DAYS	Mercury	41	8 Apr 95	2
THE WAY THAT YOU LOVE	Mercury	52	8 Jul 95	1
COLOURS OF THE WIND	Walt Disney	21	16 Sep 95	5
From the film 'Pocahontas'.				
ALBUMS:	**HITS 1**			**WEEKS 4**
THE COMFORT ZONE	Polydor	24	25 Apr 92	4

Vesta WILLIAMS | | | | US

SINGLES:	HITS 1			WEEKS 13
ONCE BITTEN TWICE SHY	A&M	14	20 Dec 86	13

Wendell WILLIAMS | | | | US

SINGLES:	HITS 2			WEEKS 6
EVERYBODY (RAP)	Deconstruction	30	6 Oct 90	4
Above hit: CRIMINAL ELEMENT ORCHESTRA featuring Wendell WILLIAMS.				
SO GROOVY	Deconstruction	74	18 May 91	2

Wendy O. WILLIAMS | | | | US

ALBUMS:	HITS 1			WEEKS 1
W.O.W.	Music For Nations	100	30 Jun 84	1

Ann WILLIAMSON | | | | UK

ALBUMS:	HITS 2			WEEKS 13
PRECIOUS MEMORIES	Emerald	16	15 Feb 86	9
COUNT YOUR BLESSINGS	Emerald Gem	58	6 Feb 88	4

Sonny Boy WILLIAMSON | | | | US

ALBUMS:	HITS 1			WEEKS 1
DOWN AND OUT BLUES	Pye	20	20 Jun 64	1

WILLING SINNERS – See Marc ALMOND

Bruce WILLIS | | | | US

SINGLES:	HITS 4			WEEKS 30
RESPECT YOURSELF	Motown	7	7 Mar 87	10
UNDER THE BOARDWALK	Motown	2	30 May 87	15
Backing vocals by the Temptations.				
SECRET AGENT MAN/JAMES BOND IS BACK [M]	Motown	43	12 Sep 87	4
COMIN' RIGHT UP	Motown	73	23 Jan 88	1
ALBUMS:	HITS 1			WEEKS 28
THE RETURN OF BRUNO	Motown	4	18 Apr 87	28

Chill WILLS – See LAUREL and HARDY

Viola WILLS | | | | US

SINGLES:	HITS 2			WEEKS 16
GONNA GET ALONG WITHOUT YOU NOW	Ariola Hansa	8	6 Oct 79	10
Originally recorded by Teresa Brewer.				
DARE TO DREAM / BOTH SIDES NOW	Streetwave	35	15 Mar 86	6

WILSATIONS – See Mari WILSON

Al WILSON | | | | US

SINGLES:	HITS 1			WEEKS 5
THE SNAKE	Bell	41	23 Aug 75	5

Brian WILSON | | | | US

ALBUMS:	HITS 2			WEEKS 3
I JUST WASN'T MADE FOR THESE TIMES	MCA	59	16 Sep 95	1
Wilson's compositions re-recorded for Don Was' TV documentary about him.				
IMAGINATION	Giant	30	27 Jun 98	2

Charlie WILSON – See SNOOP DOGGY DOGG

Dennis WILSON and his Orchestra – See Gary MILLER

Dooley WILSON with the voices of Humphrey BOGART and Ingrid BERGMAN | | | | US

SINGLES:	HITS 1			WEEKS 9
AS TIME GOES BY	United Artists	15	3 Dec 77	9
From the 1943 film 'Casablanca'.				

Jackie WILSON | | | | US

SINGLES:	HITS 6			WEEKS 97
REET PETITE	Coral	6	16 Nov 57	14
From the film 'The Sweetest Girl In Town'.				
TO BE LOVED	Coral	27	15 Mar 58	1
TO BE LOVED [RE-1ST]	Coral	23	29 Mar 58	6
TO BE LOVED [RE-2ND]	Coral	23	17 May 58	1
(YOU WERE MADE FOR) ALL MY LOVE	Coral	33	17 Sep 60	6
(YOU WERE MADE FOR) ALL MY LOVE [RE]	Coral	47	5 Nov 60	1

ALONE AT LAST	Coral	50	24 Dec 60	1
Based on Tchaikovsky's Piano Concerto in B flat.				
(YOUR LOVE KEEPS LIFTING ME) HIGHER AND HIGHER	MCA	11	17 May 69	11
I GET THE SWEETEST FEELING	MCA	9	29 Jul 72	13
Originally released in the US in 1968 reaching No. 34.				
I GET THE SWEETEST FEELING [RI-1ST] / (YOUR LOVE KEEPS LIFTING ME)				
HIGHER AND HIGHER [RI 1ST]	Brunswick	25	3 May 75	8
(Your Love Keeps Lifting Me (Higher And Higher) listed from 17 May 75.				
REET PETITE (THE SWEETEST GIRL IN TOWN) [RI]	SMP	1	29 Nov 86	17
I GET THE SWEETEST FEELING [RI-2ND]	SMP	3	28 Feb 87	11
This re-issue originally reached No. 98 in 1983.				
(YOUR LOVE KEEPS LIFTING ME) HIGHER AND HIGHER [RI-2ND]	SMP	15	4 Jul 87	7

Mari WILSON   UK

SINGLES:	HITS 6			WEEKS 34
BEAT THE BEAT	Compact Organisation	59	6 Mar 82	3
Above hit: Mari WILSON and the IMAGINATIONS.				
BABY IT'S TRUE (I CAN'T STOP MYSELF)	Compact Organisation	42	8 May 82	6
JUST WHAT I ALWAYS WANTED	Compact Organisation	8	11 Sep 82	10
(BEWARE) BOYFRIEND	Compact Organisation	51	13 Nov 82	4
CRY ME A RIVER	Compact Organisation	27	19 Mar 83	7
WONDERFUL	Compact Organisation	47	11 Jun 83	4
Above hit: Mari WILSON with the WILSATIONS.				
ALBUMS:	HITS 1			WEEKS 9
SHOW PEOPLE	Compact Organisation	24	26 Feb 83	9
Above hit: Mari WILSON with the WILSATIONS.				

Meri WILSON   US

SINGLES:	HITS 1			WEEKS 10
TELEPHONE MAN	Pye International	6	27 Aug 77	10

Mike 'Hitman' WILSON featuring Shawn CHRISTOPHER   US

(See also Shawn Christopher.)

SINGLES:	HITS 1			WEEKS 1
ANOTHER SLEEPLESS NIGHT	Arista	74	22 Sep 90	1
This single was re-issued in 1991 crediting just Shawn Christopher.				

Precious WILSON – See ERUPTION; MESSIAH

Richard WILSON – See Eric IDLE featuring Richard WILSON

Tom WILSON   UK

SINGLES:	HITS 2			WEEKS 4
TECHNOCAT	Pukka	33	2 Dec 95	3
Above hit: TECHNOCAT featuring Tom WILSON.				
LET YOUR BODY GO	Clubscene	60	16 Mar 96	1

Victoria WILSON JAMES   US

SINGLES:	HITS 1			WEEKS 1
REACH 4 THE MELODY	Sony	72	9 Aug 97	1

WILSON PHILLIPS   US

SINGLES:	HITS 6			WEEKS 33
HOLD ON	SBK	6	26 May 90	12
RELEASE ME	SBK	36	18 Aug 90	5
IMPULSIVE	SBK	42	10 Nov 90	5
YOU'RE IN LOVE	SBK	29	11 May 91	5
YOU WON'T SEE ME CRY	SBK	18	23 May 92	5
GIVE IT UP	SBK	36	22 Aug 92	3
ALBUMS:	HITS 2			WEEKS 38
WILSON PHILLIPS	SBK	7	30 Jun 90	32
SHADOWS AND LIGHT	SBK	6	13 Jun 92	6

Chris WILTSHIRE – See CLASS ACTION featuring Chris WILTSHIRE

WIMBLEDON CHORAL SOCIETY   UK

(See also Read by Des Lynam performed by the Wimbledon Choral Society.)

SINGLES:	HITS 1			WEEKS 5
WORLD CUP '98 – PAVANE BY FAURE	Telstar	20	4 Jul 98	5
BBC TV's theme for the coverage of the 1998 World Cup in France. Originally written in the 19th				
century.				

WIN
		UK		
SINGLES:	HITS 1		WEEKS 3	
SUPER POPOID GROOVE	Swamplands	63	4 Apr 87	3
ALBUMS:	HITS 1		WEEKS 1	
UH! TEARS BABY	London	51	25 Apr 87	1

WINANS
		US		
SINGLES:	HITS 1		WEEKS 1	
LET MY PEOPLE GO	Qwest	71	30 Nov 85	1

BeBe WINANS – See ETERNAL

CeCe WINANS – See Whitney HOUSTON

Mario WINANS – See PUFF DADDY

WINCHESTER CATHEDRAL CHOIR – See Andrew LLOYD WEBBER

WINDJAMMER
		US		
SINGLES:	HITS 1		WEEKS 12	
TOSSING AND TURNING	MCA	18	30 Jun 84	12
ALBUMS:	HITS 1		WEEKS 1	
WINDJAMMER II	MCA	82	25 Aug 84	1

Rose WINDROSS – See SOUL II SOUL

Barbara WINDSOR
		UK		
SINGLES:	HITS 1		WEEKS 2	
THE MORE I SEE YOU	Telstar TV	46	24 Apr 99	2
Above hit: Barbara WINDSOR and Mike REID.				
ALBUMS:	HITS 1		WEEKS 2	
YOU'VE GOT A FRIEND	Telstar TV	45	3 Apr 99	2

WING AND A PRAYER FIFE AND DRUM CORPS
		US		
SINGLES:	HITS 1		WEEKS 7	
BABY FACE	Atlantic	12	24 Jan 76	7
Originally recorded by Jan Garber in 1926.				

WINGER
		US		
SINGLES:	HITS 1		WEEKS 3	
MILES AWAY	Atlantic	56	19 Jan 91	3

Pete WINGFIELD
		UK		
SINGLES:	HITS 1		WEEKS 7	
EIGHTEEN WITH A BULLET	Island	7	28 Jun 75	7

WINGS – See Paul McCARTNEY

Josh WINK
(See also Size 9.)
		US		
SINGLES:	HITS 3		WEEKS 26	
DON'T LAUGH	XL Recordings	38	6 May 95	2
Above hit: WINX.				
HIGHER STATE OF CONSCIOUSNESS	Manifesto	8	21 Oct 95	8
HIGHER STATE OF CONSCIOUSNESS [RE]	Manifesto	60	30 Dec 95	4
HYPNOTIZIN'	XL Recordings	35	2 Mar 96	2
Originally released in the US in 1990.				
Above hit: WINX.				
HIGHER STATE OF CONSCIOUSNESS '96 REMIXES [RM]	Manifesto	7	27 Jul 96	10
Remixed by Dex and Jonesey. Other remixes are by Mr. Spring and Itty Bitty Boozy Woozy.				
Above hit: WINK.				
ALBUMS:	HITS 1		WEEKS 1	
LEFT ABOVE THE CLOUDS	XL Recordings	43	21 Sep 96	1
Above hit: WINX.				

Edgar WINTER GROUP
		US		
SINGLES:	HITS 1		WEEKS 9	
FRANKENSTEIN	Epic	18	26 May 73	9

Johnny WINTER
		US		
ALBUMS:	HITS 3		WEEKS 12	
SECOND WINTER	CBS	59	16 May 70	2

JOHNNY WINTER AND . . .	*CBS*	29	*31 Oct 70*	4
Features the McCoys as backing group.				
JOHNNY WINTER AND . . . LIVE	*CBS*	20	*15 May 71*	6

Hugo WINTERHALTER and his Orchestra – See AMES BROTHERS with Hugo WINTERHALTER and his Orchestra; Perry COMO; Eddie FISHER; Tony MARTIN with Hugo WINTERHALTER's Orchestra and Chorus; Kay STARR

Ruby WINTERS   US

SINGLES:	HITS 4			WEEKS 35
I WILL!	*Creole*	4	*5 Nov 77*	13
Originally recorded by Vic Dana.				
COME TO ME!	*Creole*	11	*29 Apr 78*	12
I WON'T MENTION IT AGAIN	*Creole*	45	*26 Aug 78*	5
BABY LAY DOWN	*Creole*	43	*16 Jun 79*	5
ALBUMS:	HITS 2			WEEKS 16
RUBY WINTERS	*Creole*	27	*10 Jun 78*	7
SONGBIRD	*K-Tel*	31	*23 Jun 79*	9

Steve WINWOOD   UK

SINGLES:	HITS 6			WEEKS 33
WHILE YOU SEE A CHANCE	*Island*	45	*17 Jan 81*	5
VALERIE	*Island*	51	*9 Oct 82*	4
HIGHER LOVE	*Island*	13	*28 Jun 86*	9
Backing vocals by Chaka Khan.				
FREEDOM OVERSPILL	*Island*	69	*13 Sep 86*	1
Features Joe Walsh on guitar.				
BACK IN THE HIGH LIFE AGAIN	*Island*	53	*24 Jan 87*	2
James Taylor on backing vocals.				
VALERIE [RM]	*Island*	19	*19 Sep 87*	8
Remixed by Tom Lord Alge.				
ROLL WITH IT	*Virgin*	53	*11 Jun 88*	4
ALBUMS:	HITS 8			WEEKS 122
STEVE WINWOOD	*Island*	12	*9 Jul 77*	9
ARC OF A DIVER	*Island*	13	*10 Jan 81*	20
TALKING BACK TO THE NIGHT	*Island*	6	*14 Aug 82*	13
BACK IN THE HIGH LIFE	*Island*	8	*12 Jul 86*	42
CHRONICLES	*Island*	12	*7 Nov 87*	17
Compilation.				
ROLL WITH IT	*Virgin*	4	*2 Jul 88*	16
REFUGEES OF THE HEART	*Virgin*	26	*17 Nov 90*	3
JUNCTION SEVEN	*Virgin*	32	*14 Jun 97*	2

WINX – See Josh WINK

WIRE   UK

SINGLES:	HITS 2			WEEKS 4
OUTDOOR MINER	*Harvest*	51	*27 Jan 79*	3
EARDRUM BUZZ	*Mute*	68	*13 May 89*	1
ALBUMS:	HITS 3			WEEKS 3
CHAIRS MISSING	*Harvest*	48	*7 Oct 78*	1
154	*Harvest*	39	*13 Oct 79*	1
THE IDEAL COPY	*Mute*	87	*9 May 87*	1

WIRED   Holland/Finland

SINGLES:	HITS 1			WEEKS 1
TRANSONIC	*Future Groove*	73	*20 Feb 99*	1
Samples Yazoo's Don't Go.				

WIRELESS   UK

SINGLES:	HITS 2			WEEKS 2
I NEED YOU	*Chrysalis*	68	*28 Jun 97*	1
IN LOVE WITH THE FAMILIAR	*Chrysalis*	69	*7 Feb 98*	1

Norman WISDOM   UK

SINGLES:	HITS 2			WEEKS 20
DON'T LAUGH AT ME ('CAUSE I'M A FOOL)	*Columbia*	3	*20 Feb 54*	15
Above hit: Norman WISDOM with Norrie PARAMOR and his Orchestra.				
THE WISDOM OF A FOOL	*Columbia*	13	*16 Mar 57*	5
Above hit: Norman WISDOM with Eric JUPP and his Orchestra.				

WISEGUYS   UK

SINGLES:	HITS 2			WEEKS 13
OOH LA LA	*Wall Of Sound*	55	*6 Jun 98*	1
START THE COMMOTION	*Wall Of Sound*	66	*12 Sep 98*	1

OOH LA LA [RI]	Wall Of Sound	2	5 Jun 99	10

Featured in the Budweiser TV commercial.

START THE COMMOTION [RI]	Wall Of Sound	47	11 Sep 99	1

Samples The Ventures' Wild Child.

WISHBONE ASH — UK

ALBUMS:	HITS 13			WEEKS 75
WISHBONE ASH	MCA	34	23 Jan 71	2
PILGRIMAGE	MCA	14	9 Oct 71	9
ARGUS	MCA	3	20 May 72	20
WISHBONE FOUR	MCA	12	26 May 73	10
THERE'S THE RUB	MCA	16	30 Nov 74	5
LOCKED IN	MCA	36	3 Apr 76	2
NEW ENGLAND	MCA	22	27 Nov 76	3
FRONT PAGE NEWS	MCA	31	29 Oct 77	4
NO SMOKE WITHOUT FIRE	MCA	43	28 Oct 78	3
JUST TESTING	MCA	41	2 Feb 80	4
LIVE DATES II	MCA	40	1 Nov 80	3

Live recordings between 1976–80.

NUMBER THE BRAVE	MCA	61	25 Apr 81	5
TWIN BARRELS BURNING	AVM	22	16 Oct 82	5

Bill WITHERS — US

SINGLES:	HITS 3			WEEKS 29
LEAN ON ME	A&M	18	12 Aug 72	9
LOVELY DAY	CBS	7	14 Jan 78	8
OH YEAH!	CBS	60	25 May 85	3
LOVELY DAY (SUNSHINE MIX) [RM]	CBS	4	10 Sep 88	9

Remixed by Ben Liebrand.

ALBUMS:	HITS 3			WEEKS 10
MENAGERIE	CBS	27	11 Feb 78	5
WATCHING YOU, WATCHING ME	CBS	60	15 Jun 85	1
GREATEST HITS	CBS	90	17 Sep 88	4

WITNESS — UK

SINGLES:	HITS 2			WEEKS 2
SCARS	Island	71	13 Mar 99	1
AUDITION	Island	71	19 Jun 99	1
ALBUMS:	HITS 1			WEEKS 1
BEFORE THE CALM	Island	59	24 Jul 99	1

WITNESSES – See Louis PRIMA

WIX – See SPIRO and WIX

WIZZARD — UK

SINGLES:	HITS 7			WEEKS 77
BALL PARK INCIDENT	Harvest	6	9 Dec 72	12
SEE MY BABY JIVE	Harvest	1	21 Apr 73	17

Above hit: WIZZARD vocal backing – the SUEDETTES.

ANGEL FINGERS (A TEEN BALLAD)	Harvest	1	1 Sep 73	10

Above hit: WIZZARD vocal backing – the SUEDETTES and the BLEACH BOYS.

I WISH IT COULD BE CHRISTMAS EVERYDAY	Harvest	4	8 Dec 73	9

Above hit: WIZZARD vocal backing by the SUEDETTES, plus the STOCKLAND GREEN BILATERAL SCHOOL FIRST CHOIR additional noises MISS SNOB and CLASS 3C.

ROCK N' ROLL WINTER (LOONY'S TUNE)	Warner Brothers	6	27 Apr 74	7
THIS IS THE STORY OF MY LOVE (BABY)	Warner Brothers	34	10 Aug 74	4
ARE YOU READY TO ROCK	Warner Brothers	8	21 Dec 74	10
I WISH IT COULD BE CHRISTMAS EVERYDAY [RI]	Harvest	41	19 Dec 81	4
I WISH IT COULD BE CHRISTMAS EVERYDAY [RI] [RE]	Harvest	23	15 Dec 84	4

Above 2: WIZZARD vocal backing by the SUEDETTES, plus the STOCKLAND GREEN BILATERAL SCHOOL FIRST CHOIR additional noises MISS SNOB and CLASS 3C.

ALBUMS:				WEEKS 11
	HITS 2			
WIZZARD BREW	Harvest	29	19 May 73	7
INTRODUCING EDDY AND THE FALCONS	Warner Brothers	19	17 Aug 74	4

Jah WOBBLE'S INVADERS OF THE HEART — UK

(See also Brian Eno and Jah Wobble.)

SINGLES:	HITS 3			WEEKS 10
VISIONS OF YOU	Oval	35	1 Feb 92	5

Features vocals by Sinead O'Connor.

BECOMING MORE LIKE GOD	Island	36	30 Apr 94	2

Vocals by Anneli M. Decker.

THE SUN DOES RISE	Island	41	25 Jun 94	3

Above hit: Jah WOBBLE'S INVADERS OF THE HEART featuring DOLORES from the CRANBERRIES.

ALBUMS:	HITS 1			WEEKS 5
TAKE ME TO GOD	Island	13	28 May 94	5

Terry WOGAN   Ireland

SINGLES:	HITS 1			WEEKS 5
THE FLORAL DANCE	Philips	21	7 Jan 78	5

WOLF – See TROGGS

Richard WOLFF and his Orchestra – See David THORNE with Richard WOLFF and his Orchestra

WOLFGANG PRESS   UK

ALBUMS:	HITS 1			WEEKS 1
FUNKY LITTLE DEMONS	4AD	75	4 Feb 95	1

WOLFSBANE   US

SINGLES:	HITS 1			WEEKS 1
EZY	Def American	68	5 Oct 91	1
ALBUMS:	HITS 3			WEEKS 3
LIVE FAST, DIE FAST	Def American	48	5 Aug 89	1
ALL HELL'S BREAKING LOOSE . . .	Def American	48	20 Oct 90	1
DOWN FALL THE GOOD GUYS	Def American	53	19 Oct 91	1

Bobby WOMACK   US

(See also Wilton Felder; Living In A Box.)

SINGLES:	HITS 5			WEEKS 13
TELL ME WHY	Motown	60	16 Jun 84	3
I WISH HE DIDN'T TRUST ME SO MUCH	MCA	64	5 Oct 85	2
LIVING IN A BOX	MCA	70	7 Nov 87	2
I'M BACK FOR MORE	Dome	27	3 Apr 93	5

Originally recorded by Al Johnson and Jean Carn.
Above hit: LULU and Bobby WOMACK.

IT'S A MAN'S MAN'S MAN'S WORLD	Pulse 8	73	13 May 95	1

Above hit: Jeanie TRACY and Bobby WOMACK.

ALBUMS:	HITS 2			WEEKS 15
THE POET II	Motown	31	28 Apr 84	8
SO MANY RIVERS	MCA	28	28 Sep 85	7

WOMACK and WOMACK   US

SINGLES:	HITS 7			WEEKS 51
LOVE WARS	Elektra	14	28 Apr 84	10
BABY I'M SCARED OF YOU	Elektra	72	30 Jun 84	2
SOUL LOVE / SOUL MAN [M]	Manhattan	58	6 Dec 86	6
TEARDROPS	Fourth & Broadway	3	6 Aug 88	17
LIFE'S JUST A BALLGAME	Fourth & Broadway	32	12 Nov 88	5
CELEBRATE THE WORLD	Fourth & Broadway	19	25 Feb 89	8
SECRET STAR	Warner Brothers	46	5 Feb 94	3

Above hit: HOUSE OF ZEKKARIYAS Aka WOMACK and WOMACK.

ALBUMS:	HITS 4			WEEKS 54
LOVE WARS	Elektra	45	21 Apr 84	13
RADIO M.U.S.C. MAN	Elektra	56	22 Jun 85	2
THE ARTISTS VOLUME III	Street Sounds	87	12 Oct 85	2

Compilation album with tracks by each artist.
Above hit: WOMACK and WOMACK/O'JAYS/KLEEER/S.O.S. BAND.

CONSCIENCE	Fourth & Broadway	4	27 Aug 88	37

WOMBLES   UK

SINGLES:	HITS 8			WEEKS 95
THE WOMBLING SONG	CBS	4	26 Jan 74	23

Theme from the BBC1 children's TV series 'The Wombles'.

REMEMBER YOU'RE A WOMBLE	CBS	3	6 Apr 74	16
BANANA ROCK	CBS	9	22 Jun 74	13
MINUETTO ALLEGRETTO	CBS	16	12 Oct 74	9
WOMBLING MERRY CHRISTMAS	CBS	2	7 Dec 74	8
WOMBLING WHITE TIE AND TAILS (FOX TROT)	CBS	22	10 May 75	7
SUPER WOMBLE	CBS	20	9 Aug 75	6
LET'S WOMBLE TO THE PARTY TONIGHT	CBS	34	13 Dec 75	5
REMEMBER YOU'RE A WOMBLE [RI]	Columbia	13	21 Mar 98	5
THE WOMBLING SONG (UNDERGROUND OVERGROUND) [RI]	Columbia	27	13 Jun 98	3
ALBUMS:	HITS 5			WEEKS 58
WOMBLING SONGS	CBS	19	2 Mar 74	17

REMEMBER YOU'RE A WOMBLE	*CBS*	18	*13 Jul 74*	31
KEEP ON WOMBLING	*CBS*	17	*21 Dec 74*	6
20 WOMBLING GREATS	*Warwick*	29	*8 Jan 77*	1
THE BEST WOMBLES ALBUM SO FAR – VOLUME 1	*Columbia*	26	*18 Apr 98*	3

Stevie WONDER   US

(See also Diana Ross, Marvin Gaye, Smokey Robinson and Stevie Wonder; Dionne Warwick.)

SINGLES:	HITS 51		WEEKS 401	
UPTIGHT (EVERYTHING'S ALRIGHT)	*Tamla Motown*	14	*5 Feb 66*	10
BLOWIN' IN THE WIND	*Tamla Motown*	36	*20 Aug 66*	5
Featuring vocals by Henry Cosby.				
A PLACE IN THE SUN	*Tamla Motown*	20	*7 Jan 67*	5
I WAS MADE TO LOVE HER	*Tamla Motown*	5	*29 Jul 67*	15
I'M WONDERING	*Tamla Motown*	22	*28 Oct 67*	8
SHOO BE DOO BE DOO DA DAY	*Tamla Motown*	46	*11 May 68*	4
FOR ONCE IN MY LIFE	*Tamla Motown*	3	*21 Dec 68*	13
Originally recorded by Tony Bennett.				
DON'T KNOW WHY I LOVE YOU	*Tamla Motown*	14	*22 Mar 69*	10
DON'T KNOW WHY I LOVE YOU [RE] / MY CHERIE AMOUR	*Tamla Motown*	4	*12 Jul 69*	16
Don't Know Why I Love You only listed for the week of 12 Jul 69 at No.43. From 19 Jul 69, My Cherie Amour was listed instead.				
YESTER-ME, YESTER-YOU, YESTERDAY	*Tamla Motown*	2	*15 Nov 69*	13
Co-written and produced by Johnny Bristol.				
NEVER HAD A DREAM COME TRUE	*Tamla Motown*	6	*28 Mar 70*	12
SIGNED SEALED DELIVERED I'M YOURS	*Tamla Motown*	15	*18 Jul 70*	9
SIGNED SEALED DELIVERED I'M YOURS [RE]	*Tamla Motown*	49	*26 Sep 70*	1
HEAVEN HELP US ALL	*Tamla Motown*	29	*21 Nov 70*	11
WE CAN WORK IT OUT	*Tamla Motown*	27	*15 May 71*	7
IF YOU REALLY LOVE ME	*Tamla Motown*	20	*22 Jan 72*	7
SUPERSTITION	*Tamla Motown*	11	*3 Feb 73*	9
YOU ARE THE SUNSHINE OF MY LIFE	*Tamla Motown*	7	*19 May 73*	11
Introduction vocals are by Jim Gilstrap and Gloria Barley.				
HIGHER GROUND	*Tamla Motown*	29	*13 Oct 73*	5
LIVING FOR THE CITY	*Tamla Motown*	15	*12 Jan 74*	9
HE'S MISSTRA KNOW IT ALL	*Tamla Motown*	10	*13 Apr 74*	9
YOU HAVEN'T DONE NOTHIN'	*Tamla Motown*	30	*19 Oct 74*	5
Above hit: Stevie WONDER doo doo wopsssss by the JACKSON FIVE.				
BOOGIE ON REGGAE WOMAN	*Tamla Motown*	12	*11 Jan 75*	8
I WISH	*Motown*	5	*18 Dec 76*	10
SIR DUKE	*Motown*	2	*9 Apr 77*	9
Tribute to Duke Ellington.				
ANOTHER STAR	*Motown*	29	*10 Sep 77*	5
SEND ONE YOUR LOVE	*Motown*	52	*24 Nov 79*	3
BLACK ORCHID	*Motown*	63	*26 Jan 80*	3
OUTSIDE MY WINDOW	*Motown*	52	*29 Mar 80*	4
MASTERBLASTER (JAMMIN')	*Motown*	2	*13 Sep 80*	10
Inspired by Bob Marley's hit Jamming.				
I AIN'T GONNA STAND FOR IT	*Motown*	10	*27 Dec 80*	10
LATELY	*Motown*	3	*7 Mar 81*	13
HAPPY BIRTHDAY	*Motown*	2	*25 Jul 81*	11
Song was part of Wonder's campaign to have Martin Luther King's birthday (15th January) marked as a US holiday.				
THAT GIRL	*Motown*	39	*23 Jan 82*	6
EBONY AND IVORY	*Parlophone*	1	*10 Apr 82*	10
Above hit: Paul McCARTNEY with additional vocals by Stevie WONDER.				
DO I DO	*Motown*	10	*5 Jun 82*	7
Features Dizzy Gillespie on trumpet.				
RIBBON IN THE SKY	*Motown*	45	*25 Sep 82*	4
I JUST CALLED TO SAY I LOVE YOU	*Motown*	1	*25 Aug 84*	24
LOVE LIGHT IN FLIGHT	*Motown*	44	*1 Dec 84*	5
Above 2 from the film 'The Woman In Red'.				
DON'T DRIVE DRUNK	*Motown*	71	*29 Dec 84*	1
DON'T DRIVE DRUNK [RE]	*Motown*	62	*12 Jan 85*	2
PART-TIME LOVER	*Motown*	3	*7 Sep 85*	12
GO HOME	*Motown*	67	*23 Nov 85*	2
I JUST CALLED TO SAY I LOVE YOU [RE]	*Motown*	64	*28 Dec 85*	2
OVERJOYED	*Motown*	17	*8 Mar 86*	8
STRANGER ON THE SHORE OF LOVE	*Motown*	55	*17 Jan 87*	3
SKELETONS	*Motown*	59	*31 Oct 87*	3
GET IT	*Motown*	37	*28 May 88*	4
Above hit: Stevie WONDER and Michael JACKSON.				
MY LOVE	*CBS*	5	*6 Aug 88*	11
Above hit: Julio IGLESIAS featuring Stevie WONDER.				
FREE	*Motown*	49	*20 May 89*	5
FUN DAY	*Motown*	63	*12 Oct 91*	1
From the film 'Jungle Fever'.				
FOR YOUR LOVE	*Motown*	23	*25 Feb 95*	4
TOMORROW ROBINS WILL SING	*Motown*	71	*22 Jul 95*	1

HOW COME, HOW LONG	Epic	10	19 Jul 97	5
Above hit: BABYFACE featuring Stevie WONDER.				
TRUE TO YOUR HEART	Motown	51	31 Oct 98	1
From the Walt Disney film 'Mulan'.				
Above hit: 98° (featuring Stevie WONDER).				

ALBUMS:	HITS 18		WEEKS 353	
STEVIE WONDER'S GREATEST HITS	Tamla Motown	25	7 Sep 68	10
MY CHERIE AMOUR	Tamla Motown	17	13 Dec 69	2
GREATEST HITS VOLUME 2	Tamla Motown	30	12 Feb 72	4
TALKING BOOK	Tamla Motown	16	3 Feb 73	48
INNERVISIONS	Tamla Motown	8	1 Sep 73	55
FULFILLINGNESS' FIRST FINALE	Tamla Motown	5	17 Aug 74	16
SONGS IN THE KEY OF LIFE	Tamla Motown	2	16 Oct 76	54
JOURNEY THROUGH THE SECRET LIFE OF PLANTS	Motown	8	10 Nov 79	15
HOTTER THAN JULY	Motown	2	8 Nov 80	55
Dedicated to Martin Luther King Jr.				
ORIGINAL MUSIQUARIUM 1	Motown	8	22 May 82	17
Compilation plus some new tracks.				
WOMAN IN RED [OST]	Motown	2	22 Sep 84	19
Above hit: Stevie WONDER and featuring Dionne WARWICK.				
LOVE SONGS – 16 CLASSIC HITS	Telstar	20	24 Nov 84	10
IN SQUARE CIRCLE	Motown	5	28 Sep 85	16
DIANA . MICHAEL . GLADYS . STEVIE – THEIR VERY BEST – BACK TO BACK	PrioriTyV	21	15 Nov 86	10
Compilation featuring hits by each artist.				
Above hit: Diana ROSS/Michael JACKSON/Gladys KNIGHT/Stevie WONDER.				
CHARACTERS	RCA	33	28 Nov 87	4
JUNGLE FEVER [OST]	Motown	56	8 Jun 91	1
CONVERSATION PEACE	Motown	8	25 Mar 95	4
SONG REVIEW – A GREATEST HITS COLLECTION	Motown	19	23 Nov 96	12
SONGS IN THE KEY OF LIFE [RI]	Motown	66	23 Aug 97	1
Charted after being featured on BBC1's 'Classic Albums' series.				

Wayne WONDER – See SHAGGY

WONDER DOG   UK

SINGLES:	HITS 1		WEEKS 7	
RUFF MIX	Flip	31	21 Aug 82	7

WONDER STUFF   UK

SINGLES:	HITS 16		WEEKS 66	
GIVE GIVE GIVE ME MORE MORE MORE	Polydor	72	30 Apr 88	2
A WISH AWAY	Polydor	43	16 Jul 88	5
IT'S YER MONEY I'M AFTER BABY	Polydor	40	24 Sep 88	3
WHO WANTS TO BE THE DISCO KING?	Polydor	28	11 Mar 89	3
DON'T LET ME DOWN GENTLY	Polydor	19	23 Sep 89	4
GOLDEN GREEN / GET TOGETHER	Polydor	33	11 Nov 89	3
CIRCLESQUARE	Polydor	20	12 May 90	4
THE SIZE OF A COW	Polydor	5	13 Apr 91	7
CAUGHT IN MY SHADOW	Polydor	18	25 May 91	3
SLEEP ALONE	Polydor	43	7 Sep 91	2
DIZZY	Sense	1	26 Oct 91	12
Above hit: Vic REEVES and the WONDER STUFF.				
WELCOME TO THE CHEAP SEATS – THE ORIGINAL SOUNDTRACK [EP]	Polydor	8	25 Jan 92	5
Lead track: Welcome To The Cheap Seats.				
ON THE ROPES [EP]	Polydor	10	25 Sep 93	4
Lead track: On The Ropes.				
FULL OF LIFE (HAPPY NOW)	Polydor	28	27 Nov 93	3
HOT LOVE NOW! [EP]	Polydor	19	26 Mar 94	3
Lead track: Hot Love Now!				
UNBEARABLE	Polydor	16	10 Sep 94	3
Originally released in 1987 on the Far Out label.				

ALBUMS:	HITS 6		WEEKS 48	
THE EIGHT LEGGED GROOVE MACHINE	Polydor	18	27 Aug 88	7
HUP	Polydor	5	14 Oct 89	8
NEVER LOVED ELVIS	Polydor	3	8 Jun 91	23
CONSTRUCTION FOR THE MODERN IDIOT	Polydor	4	16 Oct 93	5
IF THE BEATLES HAD READ HUNTER . . . THE SINGLES	Polydor	8	8 Oct 94	4
Compilation.				
LIVE IN MANCHESTER	Windsong	74	29 Jul 95	1
Live recordings from the G-Mex, Manchester, Nov 91.				

WONDERS   US

SINGLES:	HITS 1		WEEKS 3	
THAT THING YOU DO!	Play-Tone	22	22 Feb 97	3
From the film of the same name.				

WONDRESS – See MANTRONIX

Brenton WOOD · UK

SINGLES:		HITS 1			WEEKS 14
GIMME LITTLE SIGN	*Liberty*		8	*30 Dec 67*	14

Ronnie WOOD – See Rod STEWART

Roy WOOD · UK

(See also Doctor and the Medics.)

SINGLES:		HITS 5			WEEKS 37
DEAR ELAINE	*Harvest*		18	*11 Aug 73*	8
FOREVER	*Harvest*		8	*1 Dec 73*	13
GOIN' DOWN THE ROAD (A SCOTTISH REGGAE SONG)	*Harvest*		13	*15 Jun 74*	7
OH WHAT A SHAME	*Jet*		13	*31 May 75*	7
I WISH IT COULD BE CHRISTMAS EVERYDAY	*Woody*		59	*23 Dec 95*	2

Live recording.
Above hit: Roy WOOD BIG BAND LIVE.

ALBUMS:		HITS 2			WEEKS 14
BOULDERS	*Harvest*		15	*18 Aug 73*	8
THE SINGLES	*Speed*		37	*24 Jul 82*	6

WOODENTOPS · UK

SINGLES:		HITS 1			WEEKS 1
LOVE AFFAIR WITH EVERYDAY LIVING	*Rough Trade*		72	*11 Oct 86*	1

ALBUMS:		HITS 2			WEEKS 6
GIANT	*Rough Trade*		35	*12 Jul 86*	4
WOODEN FOOT COPS ON THE HIGHWAY	*Rough Trade*		48	*5 Mar 88*	2

Edward WOODWARD · UK

SINGLES:		HITS 1			WEEKS 2
THE WAY YOU LOOK TONIGHT	*DJM*		50	*16 Jan 71*	1
THE WAY YOU LOOK TONIGHT [RE]	*DJM*		42	*30 Jan 71*	1

ALBUMS:		HITS 2			WEEKS 12
THIS MAN ALONE	*DJM*		53	*6 Jun 70*	2
THE EDWARD WOODWARD ALBUM	*Jam*		20	*19 Aug 72*	10

Sheb WOOLEY · UK

SINGLES:		HITS 1			WEEKS 8
THE PURPLE PEOPLE EATER	*MGM*		12	*21 Jun 58*	8

WOOLFSON – See SHIMMON and WOOLFSON

WOOLPACKERS · UK

SINGLES:		HITS 2			WEEKS 24
HILLBILLY ROCK HILLBILLY ROLL	*RCA*		5	*16 Nov 96*	14
LINE DANCE PARTY	*RCA*		25	*29 Nov 97*	10

Above 2 were featured in the Yorkshire ITV soap 'Emmerdale'.

ALBUMS:		HITS 2			WEEKS 13
EMMERDANCE	*RCA*		26	*14 Dec 96*	10
THE GREATEST LINE DANCING PARTY ALBUM	*RCA*		48	*29 Nov 97*	3

WORKING WEEK · UK

SINGLES:		HITS 1			WEEKS 2
VENCEREMOS - WE WILL WIN	*Virgin*		64	*9 Jun 84*	2

ALBUMS:		HITS 2			WEEKS 10
WORKING NIGHTS	*Virgin*		23	*6 Apr 85*	9
COMPANEROS	*Virgin*		72	*27 Sep 86*	1

WORLD – See LIL' LOUIS

WORLD OF TWIST · UK

SINGLES:		HITS 4			WEEKS 12
THE STORM	*Circa*		42	*24 Nov 90*	3
THE STORM [RE]	*Circa*		74	*5 Jan 91*	2
SONS OF THE STAGE	*Circa*		47	*23 Mar 91*	3
SWEETS	*Circa*		58	*12 Oct 91*	2
SHE'S A RAINBOW	*Circa*		62	*22 Feb 92*	2

ALBUMS:		HITS 1			WEEKS 1
QUALITY STREET	*Circa*		50	*9 Nov 91*	1

WORLD PARTY · UK/Ireland

SINGLES:		HITS 8			WEEKS 29
SHIP OF FOOLS	*Ensign*		42	*14 Feb 87*	6

MESSAGE IN THE BOX	*Ensign*	39	*16 Jun 90*	6
WAY DOWN NOW	*Ensign*	66	*15 Sep 90*	2
THANK YOU WORLD	*Ensign*	68	*18 May 91*	1
IS IT LIKE TODAY?	*Ensign*	19	*10 Apr 93*	6
GIVE IT ALL AWAY	*Ensign*	43	*10 Jul 93*	3
ALL I GAVE	*Ensign*	37	*2 Oct 93*	3
BEAUTIFUL DREAM	*Chrysalis*	31	*7 Jun 97*	2
ALBUMS:	**HITS 4**		**WEEKS 24**	
PRIVATE REVOLUTION	*Chrysalis*	56	*21 Mar 87*	4
GOODBYE JUMBO	*Ensign*	36	*19 May 90*	10
BANG!	*Ensign*	2	*8 May 93*	8
EGYPTOLOGY	*Chrysalis*	34	*28 Jun 97*	2

WORLD PREMIERE · UK

SINGLES:	**HITS 1**		**WEEKS 4**	
SHARE THE NIGHT	*Epic*	64	*28 Jan 84*	4

WORLD WARRIOR · UK

(See also Simon Harris.)

SINGLES:	**HITS 1**		**WEEKS 1**	
STREET FIGHTER II	*Living Beat*	70	*16 Apr 94*	1

Tie-in release with the computer game of the same name.

WORLDS APART · UK/France/Cuba/Jamaica/Bangladesh

SINGLES:	**HITS 5**		**WEEKS 17**	
HEAVEN MUST BE MISSING AN ANGEL	*Arista*	29	*27 Mar 93*	3
WONDERFUL WORLD	*Arista*	51	*3 Jul 93*	1
EVERLASTING LOVE	*Bell*	20	*25 Sep 93*	4
COULD IT BE I'M FALLING IN LOVE	*Bell*	15	*26 Mar 94*	6
BEGGIN' TO BE WRITTEN	*Bell*	29	*4 Jun 94*	3

WORLD'S FAMOUS SUPREME TEAM · US

(See also Malcolm McLaren.)

SINGLES:	**HITS 2**		**WEEKS 6**	
HEY DJ	*Charisma*	52	*25 Feb 84*	5
OPERAA HOUSE	*Virgin*	75	*8 Dec 90*	1

*Above hit: Malcolm McLAREN presents the WORLD FAMOUS SUPREME TEAM
SHOW.*

WRECKLESS ERIC · UK

ALBUMS:	**HITS 2**		**WEEKS 5**	
WRECKLESS ERIC	*Stiff*	46	*1 Apr 78*	1
BIG SMASH	*Stiff*	30	*8 Mar 80*	4

WRECKX-N-EFFECT · US

SINGLES:	**HITS 3**		**WEEKS 18**	
JUICY	*Motown*	29	*13 Jan 90*	7

Above hit: WRECKS-N-EFFECT.

RUMP SHAKER	*MCA*	24	*5 Dec 92*	7

Samples Back To The Hotel by N2Deep.

WRECKX SHOP	*MCA*	26	*7 May 94*	2

Above hit: WRECKX 'N' EFFECT (featuring APACHE INDIAN).

RUMP SHAKER [RI]	*MCA*	40	*13 Aug 94*	2

WREN ORCHESTRA – See WET WET WET

Betty WRIGHT · US

(See also Peter Brown.)

SINGLES:	**HITS 4**		**WEEKS 23**	
SHOO-RAH! SHOO-RAH!	*RCA Victor*	27	*25 Jan 75*	7
WHERE IS THE LOVE	*RCA Victor*	25	*19 Apr 75*	7
PAIN	*Cooltempo*	42	*8 Feb 86*	6
KEEP LOVE NEW	*Sure Delight*	71	*9 Sep 89*	3

Ian WRIGHT · UK

SINGLES:	**HITS 1**		**WEEKS 2**	
DO THE RIGHT THING	*M&G*	43	*28 Aug 93*	2

Originally titled Keep The Peace by DTRT when promoed to DJ's.

Linda WRIGHT – See NEW ATLANTIC

Rick WRIGHT — UK

ALBUMS:		HITS 1		WEEKS 1
BROKEN CHINA	EMI	61	19 Oct 96	1

Ruby WRIGHT — US

SINGLES:		HITS 2		WEEKS 15
BIMBO	Parlophone	7	17 Apr 54	4
BIMBO [RE]	Parlophone	12	22 May 54	1
THREE STARS	Parlophone	19	23 May 59	10

Tribute to Buddy Holly, the Big Bopper and Ritchie Valens who were killed in a plane crash 3 Feb 59. Original by Tommy Dee reached No. 11 in the US in 1959.
Above hit: Ruby WRIGHT (narration by Dick PIKE).

Steve WRIGHT — UK

SINGLES:		HITS 3		WEEKS 10
I'M ALRIGHT	RCA	40	27 Nov 82	6
Above hit: YOUNG STEVE and the AFTERNOON BOYS.				
GET SOME THERAPY	RCA	75	15 Oct 83	1
Above hit: Steve WRIGHT and the SISTERS Of SOUL.				
THE GAY CAVALIEROS (THE STORY SO FAR . . .)	MCA	61	1 Dec 84	3

WU-TANG CLAN — US

SINGLES:		HITS 2		WEEKS 8
TRIUMPH	Loud	46	16 Aug 97	1
Above hit: WU-TANG CLAN (featuring CAPPADONNA).				
SAY WHAT YOU WANT (ALL DAY EVERY DAY)	Mercury	4	21 Mar 98	7
[AA] listed with Insane by Texas.				
Above hit: TEXAS featuring the WU TANG CLAN.				

ALBUMS:		HITS 1		WEEKS 10
WU-TANG FOREVER	Loud	1	14 Jun 97	10

WUBBLE-U — UK

SINGLES:		HITS 1		WEEKS 1
PETAL	Indolent	55	7 Mar 98	1

Klaus WUNDERLICH — Germany

ALBUMS:		HITS 4		WEEKS 19
THE HIT WORLD OF KLAUS WUNDERLICH	Decca	27	30 Aug 75	8
THE UNIQUE KLAUS WUNDERLICH SOUND	Decca	28	20 May 78	4
THE FANTASTIC SOUND OF KLAUS WUNDERLICH	Lotus	43	26 May 79	5
ON THE SUNNY SIDE OF THE STREET	Polydor	81	17 Mar 84	2

WURZELS — UK

SINGLES:		HITS 4		WEEKS 28
DRINK UP THY ZIDER	Columbia	45	4 Feb 67	1
Above hit: Adge CUTLER and the WURZELS.				
THE COMBINE HARVESTER (BRAND NEW KEY)	EMI	1	15 May 76	13
I AM A CIDER DRINKER (PALOMA BLANCA)	EMI	3	11 Sep 76	9
FARMER BILL'S COWMAN (I WAS KAISER BILL'S BATMAN)	EMI	32	25 Jun 77	5
Above 3 are paradies of the respective songs in brackets.				

ALBUMS:		HITS 3		WEEKS 29
ADGE CUTLER AND THE WURZELS	Columbia	38	11 Mar 67	4
Above hit: Adge CUTLER and the WURZELS.				
COMBINE HARVESTER	One Up	15	3 Jul 76	20
GOLDEN DELICIOUS	EMI	32	2 Apr 77	5

WWF SUPERSTARS — UK/US

SINGLES:		HITS 3		WEEKS 15
SLAM JAM	Arista	4	12 Dec 92	8
SLAM JAM [RE]	Arista	75	13 Feb 93	1
WRESTLEMANIA	Arista	14	3 Apr 93	5
U.S.A.	Arista	71	10 Jul 93	1
Above hit: WWF SUPERSTARS featuring HACKSAW Jim DUGGAN.				

ALBUMS:		HITS 1		WEEKS 5
WRESTLEMANIA - THE ALBUM	Arista	10	17 Apr 93	5

Robert WYATT — UK

SINGLES:		HITS 2		WEEKS 11
I'M A BELIEVER	Virgin	29	28 Sep 74	5
SHIPBUILDING	Rough Trade	35	7 May 83	6

Written by Elvis Costello as a protest against the Falklands War.

Michael WYCOFF
US

SINGLES:	HITS 1		WEEKS 2	
(DO YOU REALLY LOVE ME) TELL ME LOVE	RCA	60	23 Jul 83	2

Pete WYLIE
UK

SINGLES:	HITS 3		WEEKS 18	
SINFUL	Eternal	13	3 May 86	10
Above hit: Pete WYLIE and the OEDIPUS WRECKS.				
DIAMOND GIRL	Eternal	57	13 Sep 86	3
Above hit: Pete WYLIE featuring the FABULOUS Josie JONES.				
SINFUL! (SCARY JIGGIN' WITH DOCTOR LOVE)	Siren	28	13 Apr 91	5
Above hit: Pete WYLIE (and the FARM).				

Bill WYMAN
UK

SINGLES:	HITS 2		WEEKS 13	
(SI SI) JE SUIS UN ROCK STAR	A&M	14	25 Jul 81	9
A NEW FASHION	A&M	37	20 Mar 82	4
ALBUMS:	HITS 2		WEEKS 7	
MONKEY GRIP	Rolling Stones	39	8 Jun 74	1
BILL WYMAN	A&M	55	10 Apr 82	6

Jane WYMAN – See Bing CROSBY

Tammy WYNETTE
US

SINGLES:	HITS 4		WEEKS 35	
STAND BY YOUR MAN	Epic	1	26 Apr 75	12
Reached No. 19 in the US in 1968.				
D.I.V.O.R.C.E.	Epic	12	28 Jun 75	7
I DON'T WANNA PLAY HOUSE	Epic	37	12 Jun 76	4
Above 3 originally recorded and released in the U.S. in 1968.				
JUSTIFIED AND ANCIENT	KLF Commuications	2	7 Dec 91	12
Above hit: KLF (lead vocals: "The First Lady of Country" Miss Tammy WYNETTE).				
ALBUMS:	HITS 5		WEEKS 49	
THE BEST OF TAMMY WYNETTE	Epic	4	17 May 75	23
STAND BY YOUR MAN	Epic	13	21 Jun 75	7
20 COUNTRY CLASSICS	CBS	3	17 Dec 77	11
COUNTRY GIRL MEETS COUNTRY BOY	Warwick	43	4 Feb 78	3
ANNIVERSARY – 20 YEARS OF HITS	Epic	45	6 Jun 87	5

Mark WYNTER
UK

SINGLES:	HITS 9		WEEKS 80	
IMAGE OF A GIRL	Decca	11	27 Aug 60	10
KICKIN' UP THE LEAVES	Decca	24	12 Nov 60	10
DREAM GIRL	Decca	27	11 Mar 61	5
EXCLUSIVELY YOURS	Decca	32	10 Jun 61	7
VENUS IN BLUE JEANS	Pye	4	6 Oct 62	15
Original by Jimmy Clanton reached No. 7 in the US in 1962.				
GO AWAY, LITTLE GIRL	Pye	6	15 Dec 62	11
SHY GIRL	Pye	28	8 Jun 63	6
IT'S ALMOST TOMORROW	Decca	12	16 Nov 63	12
ONLY YOU (AND YOU ALONE)	Pye	38	11 Apr 64	4

X

Malcolm X, music by Keith LeBLANC
US

SINGLES:	HITS 1		WEEKS 4	
NO SELL OUT	Tommy Boy	60	7 Apr 84	4
Malcolm X's voice is taken from various speeches during the early 1960s.				

X MAL DEUTSCHLAND
UK/Germany

ALBUMS:	HITS 1		WEEKS 1	
TOCSIN	4AD	86	7 Jul 84	1

X-PRESS 2
UK

SINGLES:	HITS 5		WEEKS 7	
LONDON X-PRESS	Junior Boy's Own	59	5 Jun 93	1
SAY WHAT!	Junior Boy's Own	32	16 Oct 93	2
ROCK 2 HOUSE / HIP HOUSIN'	Junior Boy's Own	55	30 Jul 94	2
Above hit: X-PRESS 2 featuring LO-PRO.				

| THE SOUND | Junior Boy's Own | 38 | 9 Mar 96 | 1 |
| TRANZ EURO XPRESS | Junior Boy's Own | 45 | 12 Oct 96 | 1 |

X-RAY SPEX UK

SINGLES:	HITS 4		WEEKS 33	
THE DAY THE WORLD TURNED DAYGLO	EMI International	23	29 Apr 78	8
IDENTITY	EMI International	24	22 Jul 78	10
GERM FREE ADOLESCENCE	EMI International	19	4 Nov 78	11
HIGHLY INFLAMMABLE	EMI International	45	21 Apr 79	4
ALBUMS:	**HITS 1**		**WEEKS 14**	
GERM FREE ADOLESCENTS	EMI International	30	9 Dec 78	14

X-STATIC Italy

SINGLES:	HITS 1		WEEKS 2	
I'M STANDING (HIGHER)	Positiva	41	4 Feb 95	2

XAVIER featuring George CLINTON and Bootsy COLLINS US
(See also George Clinton.)

SINGLES:	HITS 1		WEEKS 3	
WORK THAT SUCKER TO DEATH / LOVE IS ON THE ONE	Liberty	53	20 Mar 82	3

XAVIER – See TJR featuring XAVIER

XPANSIONS UK

SINGLES:	HITS 2		WEEKS 20	
ELEVATION	Optimism	49	6 Oct 90	5
MOVE YOUR BODY (ELEVATION) [RE]	Optimism	7	23 Feb 91	9
The label was pressed with a different song title on this re-entry, though the sleeve was the original packaging.				
WHAT YOU WANT	Arista	55	15 Jun 91	2
Above hit: XPANSIONS featuring Dale JOYNER.				
MOVE YOUR BODY [RM]	Arista	14	26 Aug 95	4
Remixed by Tony De Vit and Simon Parkes.				
Above hit: XPANSIONS 95.				

XSCAPE US

SINGLES:	HITS 5		WEEKS 15	
JUST KICKIN' IT	Columbia	49	20 Nov 93	2
JUST KICKIN' IT [RI]	Columbia	54	5 Nov 94	2
FEELS SO GOOD	Columbia	34	7 Oct 95	2
WHO CAN I RUN TO	Columbia	31	27 Jan 96	3
Originally recorded by the Jones Girls in 1979. Samples Teddy Pendergrass' Love TKO.				
KEEP ON, KEEPIN' ON	East West America	39	29 Jun 96	2
From the film 'Sunset Park'. Samples Michael Jackson's Liberian Girl.				
KEEP ON KEEPIN' ON [RI]	East West America	27	19 Apr 97	2
Above 2: MC LYTE featuring XSCAPE.				
THE ARMS OF THE ONE WHO LOVES YOU	Columbia	46	22 Aug 98	2

XTC UK

SINGLES:	HITS 12		WEEKS 70	
LIFE BEGINS AT THE HOP	Virgin	54	12 May 79	4
MAKING PLANS FOR NIGEL	Virgin	17	22 Sep 79	11
GENERALS AND MAJORS / DON'T LOSE YOUR TEMPER	Virgin	32	6 Sep 80	8
TOWERS OF LONDON	Virgin	31	18 Oct 80	5
SGT. ROCK (IS GOING TO HELP ME)	Virgin	16	24 Jan 81	9
SENSES WORKING OVERTIME	Virgin	10	23 Jan 82	9
BALL AND CHAIN	Virgin	58	27 Mar 82	4
LOVE ON A FARMBOY'S WAGES	Virgin	50	15 Oct 83	4
ALL YOU PRETTY GIRLS	Virgin	55	29 Sep 84	5
MAYOR OF SIMPLETON	Virgin	46	28 Jan 89	5
THE DISAPPOINTED	Virgin	33	4 Apr 92	5
THE BALLAD OF PETER PUMPKINHEAD	Virgin	71	13 Jun 92	1
ALBUMS:	**HITS 13**		**WEEKS 50**	
WHITE MUSIC	Virgin	38	11 Feb 78	4
GO 2	Virgin	21	28 Oct 78	3
DRUMS AND WIRES	Virgin	34	1 Sep 79	7
BLACK SEA	Virgin	16	20 Sep 80	7
ENGLISH SETTLEMENT	Virgin	5	20 Feb 82	11
WAXWORKS - SOME SINGLES (1977-1982)	Virgin	54	13 Nov 82	3
MUMMER	Virgin	51	10 Sep 83	4
THE BIG EXPRESS	Virgin	38	27 Oct 84	2
SKYLARKING	Virgin	90	8 Nov 86	1

ORANGES AND LEMONS	*Virgin*	28	*11 Mar 89*	3
NONSUCH	*Virgin*	28	*9 May 92*	2
FOSSIL FUEL – THE XTC SINGLES COLLECTION 1977-1992	*Virgin*	33	*28 Sep 96*	2
APPLE VENUS – VOLUME 1	*Cooking Vinyl*	42	*6 Mar 99*	1

Y

Y & T
US

SINGLES:	HITS 1		WEEKS 4	
MEAN STREAK	*A&M*	41	*13 Aug 83*	4
ALBUMS:	**HITS 3**		**WEEKS 15**	
BLACK TIGER	*A&M*	53	*11 Sep 82*	8
MEAN STREAK	*A&M*	35	*10 Sep 83*	4
IN ROCK WE TRUST	*A&M*	33	*18 Aug 84*	3

Y?N-VEE
US

SINGLES:	HITS 1		WEEKS 1	
CHOCOLATE	*RAL*	65	*17 Dec 94*	1

Y-TRAXX
Belgium

SINGLES:	HITS 1		WEEKS 1	
MYSTERY LAND [EP]	*ffrr*	63	*24 May 97*	1

Lead track: Mystery Land.

Y TRIBE featuring Elisabeth TROY
UK

SINGLES:	HITS 1		WEEKS 2	
ENOUGH IS ENOUGH	*Northwest 10*	49	*18 Dec 99*	2

Originally released in 1998 as an instrumental titled 10th Night. Samples the guitar from a recording of Shakespeare's Twelfth Night.

YA KID K – See HI TEK 3 featuring YA KID K; TECHNOTRONIC

"Weird Al" YANKOVIC
US

SINGLES:	HITS 2		WEEKS 8	
EAT IT	*Scotti Brothers*	36	*7 Apr 84*	7

Parody of Michael Jackson's Beat It.

SMELLS LIKE NIRVANA	*Scotti Brothers*	58	*4 Jul 92*	1

Parody of Nirvana's Smells Like Teen Spirit.

YANNI
Greece

ALBUMS:	HITS 1		WEEKS 2	
TRIBUTE	*Virgin*	40	*4 Apr 98*	2

YARBROUGH and PEOPLES
US

SINGLES:	HITS 4		WEEKS 20	
DON'T STOP THE MUSIC	*Mercury*	7	*27 Dec 80*	12
DON'T WASTE YOUR TIME	*Total Experience*	60	*5 May 84*	3
GUILTY	*Total Experience*	53	*11 Jan 86*	3
I WOULDN'T LIE	*Total Experience*	61	*5 Jul 86*	2

YARDBIRDS
UK

SINGLES:	HITS 7		WEEKS 62	
GOOD MORNING LITTLE SCHOOLGIRL	*Columbia*	44	*14 Nov 64*	4
FOR YOUR LOVE	*Columbia*	3	*20 Mar 65*	12
HEART FULL OF SOUL	*Columbia*	2	*19 Jun 65*	13

Above 2 written by Graham Gouldman of 10cc.

EVIL HEARTED YOU / STILL I'M SAD	*Columbia*	3	*16 Oct 65*	10
SHAPES OF THINGS	*Columbia*	3	*5 Mar 66*	9
OVER UNDER SIDEWAYS DOWN	*Columbia*	10	*4 Jun 66*	9
HAPPENINGS TEN YEARS TIME AGO	*Columbia*	43	*29 Oct 66*	5
EPS:	**HITS 1**		**WEEKS 33**	
FIVE YARDBIRDS	*Columbia*	5	*28 Aug 65*	33
ALBUMS:	**HITS 1**		**WEEKS 8**	
YARDBIRDS	*Columbia*	20	*23 Jul 66*	8

YAVAHN – See RUFFNECK featuring YAVAHN

YAZOO | | | | UK
(See also Alison Moyet.)

SINGLES:		HITS 5		WEEKS 55
ONLY YOU	Mute	2	17 Apr 82	14
DON'T GO	Mute	3	17 Jul 82	11
THE OTHER SIDE OF LOVE	Mute	13	20 Nov 82	9
NOBODY'S DIARY	Mute	3	21 May 83	11
SITUATION	Mute	14	8 Dec 90	8
Originally the B-side of Don't Go, remixed by Francois Kevorkian.				
ONLY YOU – 1999 MIX [RM]	Mute	38	4 Sep 99	2
Remixed by Richard Stannard and Julian Gallagher.				

ALBUMS:		HITS 3		WEEKS 86
UPSTAIRS AT ERIC'S	Mute	2	4 Sep 82	63
YOU AND ME BOTH	Mute	1	16 Jul 83	20
ONLY YAZOO – THE BEST OF YAZOO	Mute	22	18 Sep 99	3

YAZZ | | | | UK

SINGLES:		HITS 12		WEEKS 69
DOCTORIN' THE HOUSE	Ahead Our Our Time	6	20 Feb 88	9
Above hit: COLDCUT featuring YAZZ and the PLASTIC POPULATION.				
THE ONLY WAY IS UP	Big Life	1	23 Jul 88	15
Originally recorded by Otis Clay.				
Above hit: YAZZ and the PLASTIC POPULATION.				
STAND UP FOR YOUR LOVE RIGHTS	Big Life	2	29 Oct 88	12
FINE TIME	Big Life	9	4 Feb 89	8
WHERE HAS ALL THE LOVE GONE	Big Life	16	29 Apr 89	6
TREAT ME GOOD	Big Life	20	23 Jun 90	5
ONE TRUE WOMAN	Polydor	60	28 Mar 92	2
HOW LONG	Polydor	31	31 Jul 93	5
Above hit: YAZZ and ASWAD.				
HAVE MERCY	Polydor	42	2 Apr 94	3
EVERYBODY'S GOT TO LEARN SOMETIME	Polydor	56	9 Jul 94	2
GOOD THING GOING	East West	53	28 Sep 96	1
Features Sugar Minott.				
NEVER CAN SAY GOODBYE	East West	61	22 Mar 97	1

ALBUMS:		HITS 1		WEEKS 32
WANTED	Big Life	3	26 Nov 88	30
WANTED / WANTED – THE REMIXES [RE]	Big Life	53	25 Nov 89	2
Wanted – The Remixes was a remix album, sales were combined.				

Trisha YEARWOOD | | | | US

SINGLES:		HITS 1		WEEKS 1
HOW DO I LIVE	MCA	66	9 Aug 97	1
From the film 'Con Air'.				

ALBUMS:		HITS 1		WEEKS 2
WHERE YOUR ROAD LEADS	MCA Nashville	36	25 Jul 98	2

YELL! | | | | UK

SINGLES:		HITS 1		WEEKS 8
INSTANT REPLAY	Fanfare	10	20 Jan 90	8

YELLO | | | | Switzerland

SINGLES:		HITS 12		WEEKS 42
I LOVE YOU	Stiff	41	25 Jun 83	4
LOST AGAIN	Stiff	73	26 Nov 83	1
GOLDRUSH	Mercury	54	9 Aug 86	3
THE RHYTHM DIVINE	Mercury	54	22 Aug 87	2
Above 2: Backing vocals by Billy MacKenzie of the Associates.				
Above hit: YELLO featuring Shirley BASSEY.				
THE RACE	Mercury	7	27 Aug 88	11
TIED UP	Mercury	60	17 Dec 88	5
OF COURSE I'M LYING	Mercury	23	25 Mar 89	8
Features vocals by Billy MacKenzie.				
BLAZING SADDLES	Mercury	47	22 Jul 89	2
RUBBERBANDMAN	Mercury	58	8 Jun 91	2
Features vocals by Billy MacKenzie.				
JUNGLE BILL	Mercury	61	5 Sep 92	2
THE RACE [RI] / BOSTICH	Mercury	55	7 Nov 92	1
HOW HOW	Mercury	59	15 Oct 94	1

ALBUMS:		HITS 5		WEEKS 15
YOU GOTTA SAY YES TO ANOTHER EXCESS	Stiff	65	21 May 83	2
STELLA	Elektra	92	6 Apr 85	1

ONE SECOND		Mercury	48	4 Jul 87	3
FLAG		Mercury	56	10 Dec 88	7
BABY		Mercury	37	29 Jun 91	2

YELLOW DOG   UK/US

SINGLES:	HITS 2			WEEKS 13	
JUST ONE MORE NIGHT		Virgin	8	4 Feb 78	9
WAIT UNTIL MIDNIGHT		Virgin	54	22 Jul 78	4

YELLOW MAGIC ORCHESTRA   Japan

SINGLES:	HITS 1			WEEKS 11	
COMPUTER GAME (THEME FROM THE INVADERS) / FIRECRACKER / TECHNOPOLIS		A&M	17	14 Jun 80	11

Adapted from the computer game 'Space Invaders'. Computer Game was only a 22 second intro before the track Firecracker.

YELLOWCOATS – See Paul SHANE and the YELLOWCOATS

Bryn YEMM   UK

ALBUMS:	HITS 4			WEEKS 14	
HOW DO I LOVE THEE		Lifestyle	57	9 Jun 84	2
HOW GREAT THOU ART		Lifestyle	67	7 Jul 84	8
THE BRYN YEMM CHRISTMAS COLLECTION		Bay	95	22 Dec 84	2
MY TRIBUTE - BRYN YEMM INSPIRATIONAL ALBUM		Word	85	26 Oct 85	2

Above hit: Bryn YEMM and the GWENT CHORALE.

YES   UK

SINGLES:	HITS 6			WEEKS 31	
WONDEROUS STORIES		Atlantic	7	17 Sep 77	9
GOING FOR THE ONE		Atlantic	24	26 Nov 77	4
DON'T KILL THE WHALE		Atlantic	36	9 Sep 78	4
OWNER OF A LONELY HEART		Atco	28	12 Nov 83	9
LEAVE IT		Atco	56	31 Mar 84	4
LOVE WILL FIND A WAY		Atco	73	3 Oct 87	1
ALBUMS:	**HITS 20**			**WEEKS 213**	
TIME AND A WORD		Atlantic	45	1 Aug 70	3
THE YES ALBUM		Atlantic	7	3 Apr 71	29
FRAGILE		Atlantic	7	4 Dec 71	17
CLOSE TO THE EDGE		Atlantic	4	23 Sep 72	13
YESSONGS		Atlantic	7	26 May 73	13

Live recordings from 1972.

TALES FROM TOPOGRAPHIC OCEANS		Atlantic	1	22 Dec 73	15

Inspired by the Shastric scriptures.

RELAYER		Atlantic	4	21 Dec 74	11
YESTERDAYS		Atlantic	27	29 Mar 75	7

Compilation including tracks from their early album releases Yes (from 1969) and Time And A Word.

GOING FOR THE ONE		Atlantic	1	30 Jul 77	28
TORMATO		Atlantic	8	7 Oct 78	11
DRAMA		Atlantic	2	30 Aug 80	8
YESSHOWS		Atlantic	22	10 Jan 81	9

Live recordings from 1976–78.

90125		Atco	16	26 Nov 83	28

Title is the assigned international catalogue number.

9012 LIVE: THE SOLOS		Atco	44	29 Mar 86	3

Mini album of live recordings.

BIG GENERATOR		Atco	17	10 Oct 87	5
UNION		Arista	7	11 May 91	6
TALK		London	20	2 Apr 94	4
KEYS TO ASCENSION		Essential	48	9 Nov 96	1

Live recordings from March 96.

KEYS TO ASCENSION 2		Essential!	62	15 Nov 97	1

Documents the 3 day concert they played at California in 1996.

THE LADDER		Eagle	36	2 Oct 99	1

Melissa YIANNAKOU – See DESIYA featuring Melissa YIANNAKOU

YIN and YAN   UK

SINGLES:	HITS 1			WEEKS 5	
IF		EMI	25	29 Mar 75	5

Spoof take-off based around Telly Savalas' version of the song.

YO-HANS – See JODE featuring YO-HANS

YO-YO – See Quincy JONES

Dwight YOAKAM — US

SINGLES:		HITS 1		WEEKS 2
CRAZY LITTLE THING CALLED LOVE	Reprise	43	10 Jul 99	2

Featured in the Gap clothing TV commercial.

ALBUMS:		HITS 2		WEEKS 4
HILLBILLY DELUXE	Reprise	51	9 May 87	3
BUENAS NOCHES FROM A LONELY ROOM	Reprise	87	13 Aug 88	1

YOMANDA — UK

SINGLES:		HITS 1		WEEKS 10
SYNTH & STRINGS	Manifesto	8	24 Jul 99	10

Samples Liquid Gold's Dance Yourself Dizzy.

Tukka YOOT – See US3

YORK — Germany

SINGLES:		HITS 1		WEEKS 5
THE AWAKENING	Manifesto	11	9 Oct 99	5

YOSH presents LOVEDEEJAY AKEMI — Holland

SINGLES:		HITS 2		WEEKS 5
IT'S WHAT UPFRONT THAT COUNTS	Limbo	69	29 Jul 95	1

Vocals by Loletta Holloway.

IT'S WHAT UPFRONT THAT COUNTS [RM]	Limbo	31	2 Dec 95	2

Remixed by Umboza (Stuart Crichton and Michael Kilkie).

THE SCREAMER	Limbo	38	20 Apr 96	2

YOSHIKI – See Roger TAYLOR

YOTHU YINDI — Australia

SINGLES:		HITS 1		WEEKS 1
TREATY	Hollywood	72	15 Feb 92	1

Faron YOUNG — US

SINGLES:		HITS 1		WEEKS 23
IT'S FOUR IN THE MORNING	Mercury	3	15 Jul 72	23

Vocal accompaniment by the Nashville Edition.

ALBUMS:		HITS 1		WEEKS 5
IT'S FOUR IN THE MORNING	Mercury	27	28 Oct 72	5

Jimmy YOUNG — UK

(See also All Star Hit Parade.)

SINGLES:		HITS 11		WEEKS 88
FAITH CAN MOVE MOUNTAINS	Decca	11	10 Jan 53	1
ETERNALLY (THE THEME FROM "LIMELIGHT")	Decca	8	22 Aug 53	9

From the film.

UNCHAINED MELODY	Decca	1	7 May 55	19

From the film 'Unchained'. Originally recorded by Alex North as an instrumental.

THE MAN FROM LARAMIE	Decca	1	17 Sep 55	12

From the film of the same name.

SOMEONE ON YOUR MIND	Decca	13	24 Dec 55	5
CHAIN GANG	Decca	9	17 Mar 56	6

Original by Bobby Scott reached No. 13 in the US in 1956.

THE WAYWARD WIND	Decca	27	9 Jun 56	1
RICH MAN, POOR MAN	Decca	25	23 Jun 56	1

Above 2 entries were separate sides of the same release, each had its own chart run.

MORE	Decca	4	29 Sep 56	17

Above 7: Jimmy YOUNG with Bob SHARPLES and his Music.

ROUND AND ROUND	Decca	30	4 May 57	1

Above hit: Jimmy YOUNG with the Michael SAMMES SINGERS.

MISS YOU	Columbia	15	12 Oct 63	13

Above hit: Jimmy YOUNG with Tony OSBORNE and his Orchestra.

UNCHAINED MELODY [RR]	Columbia	43	28 Mar 64	3

Above hit: Jimmy YOUNG with the Mike SAMMES SINGERS.

John Paul YOUNG — UK

SINGLES:		HITS 1		WEEKS 16
LOVE IS IN THE AIR	Ariola	5	29 Apr 78	13
LOVE IS IN THE AIR (BALLROOM MIX) [RM]	Columbia	49	14 Nov 92	3

From the film 'Strictly Ballroom'.

Karen YOUNG | | | UK

SINGLES:	HITS 1			WEEKS 21
NOBODY'S CHILD	*Major Minor*	6	*6 Sep 69*	21

Karen YOUNG | | | US

SINGLES:	HITS 1			WEEKS 9
HOT SHOT	*Atlantic*	34	*19 Aug 78*	7
HOT SHOT [RI]	*Atlantic*	75	*24 Feb 79*	1
HOT SHOT '97 [RM]	*Distinct'ive*	68	*15 Nov 97*	1
Remixed by Rollercoaster.				

Leon YOUNG STRING CHORALE – See Mr. Acker BILK

Neil YOUNG | | | Canada

(See also Crosby, Stills, Nash and Young; Stills-Young Band.)

SINGLES:	HITS 6			WEEKS 22
HEART OF GOLD	*Reprise*	10	*11 Mar 72*	11
Backing vocals by Linda Rondstadt and James Taylor.				
FOUR STRONG WINDS	*Reprise*	57	*6 Jan 79*	4
Features vocals by Nicolette Larson. Originally recorded by Ian and Sylvia.				
HARVEST MOON	*Reprise*	36	*27 Feb 93*	3
THE NEEDLE AND THE DAMAGE DONE	*Reprise*	75	*17 Jul 93*	1
Recording made for MTV's Unplugged series. Originally appeared on his 1972 album Harvest.				
LONG MAY YOU RUN (LIVE)	*Reprise*	71	*30 Oct 93*	1
Acoustic version originally recorded with Stephen Stills in 1976.				
PHILADELPHIA	*Reprise*	62	*9 Apr 94*	2
From the film of the same name.				

ALBUMS:	HITS 29			WEEKS 231
AFTER THE GOLDRUSH	*Reprise*	7	*31 Oct 70*	68
HARVEST	*Reprise*	1	*4 Mar 72*	33
TIME FADES AWAY	*Warner Brothers*	20	*27 Oct 73*	2
Features David Crosby and Graham Nash.				
ON THE BEACH	*Reprise*	42	*10 Aug 74*	2
TONIGHT'S THE NIGHT	*Reprise*	48	*5 Jul 75*	1
Dedicated to Cray Horse member Danny Whitten who died from a heroin overdose on 18 Nov 72.				
ZUMA	*Reprise*	44	*27 Dec 75*	2
AMERICAN STARS 'N' BARS	*Reprise*	17	*9 Jul 77*	8
Features unissued studio tracks from previous 3 years.				
DECADE	*Reprise*	46	*17 Dec 77*	4
Compilation including both solo and group material with Buffalo Springfield and Crosby, Stills, Nash and Young.				
COMES A TIME	*Reprise*	42	*28 Oct 78*	3
RUST NEVER SLEEPS	*Reprise*	13	*14 Jul 79*	13
Identically titled film documentary of their 1978 tour was released simultaneously.				
RUST	*Reprise*	55	*1 Dec 79*	3
Live recordings from his 1978 tour.				
Above 2: Neil YOUNG and CRAZY HORSE.				
HAWKS AND DOVES	*Reprise*	34	*15 Nov 80*	3
RE-AC-TOR	*Reprise*	69	*14 Nov 81*	3
Above hit: Neil YOUNG and CRAZY HORSE.				
TRANS	*Geffen*	29	*5 Feb 83*	5
EVERYBODY'S ROCKIN'	*Geffen*	50	*3 Sep 83*	3
Above hit: Neil YOUNG and the SHOCKING PINKS.				
OLD WAYS	*Geffen*	39	*14 Sep 85*	3
LANDING ON WATER	*Geffen*	52	*2 Aug 86*	2
LIFE	*Geffen*	71	*4 Jul 87*	1
Above hit: Neil YOUNG and CRAZY HORSE.				
THIS NOTE'S FOR YOU	*WEA*	56	*30 Apr 88*	3
Above hit: Neil YOUNG and the BLUE NOTES.				
FREEDOM	*Reprise*	17	*21 Oct 89*	5
RAGGED GLORY	*Reprise*	15	*22 Sep 90*	5
WELD	*Reprise*	20	*2 Nov 91*	3
Live recordings.				
Above 2: Neil YOUNG and CRAZY HORSE.				
HARVEST MOON	*Reprise*	9	*14 Nov 92*	18
LUCKY THIRTEEN	*Geffen*	69	*23 Jan 93*	1
Live recordings and unreleased material from 1982–88.				
UNPLUGGED	*Reprise*	4	*26 Jun 93*	13
Live recordings made for MTV, Feb 93.				
HARVEST [RE]	*Reprise*	41	*9 Apr 94*	1
Re-released with a new catalogue number.				
SLEEPS WITH ANGELS	*Reprise*	2	*27 Aug 94*	7
Above hit: Neil YOUNG and CRAZY HORSE.				
MIRROR BALL	*Reprise*	4	*8 Jul 95*	9
Features Pearl Jam as his backing band.				
BROKEN ARROW	*Reprise*	17	*6 Jul 96*	5

YEAR OF THE HORSE *Reprise* 36 *28 Jun 97* 2
Live recordings from Young's back catalogue.
Above 2: Neil YOUNG and CRAZY HORSE.

Paul YOUNG — UK

SINGLES:	HITS 21			WEEKS 134
WHEREVER I LAY MY HAT (THAT'S MY HOME)	CBS	1	18 Jun 83	15

Originally recorded by Marvin Gaye in 1963 and was the B-side to his single 'Too Busy Thinking About My Baby' in 1969.

COME BACK AND STAY	CBS	4	10 Sep 83	9

Originally recorded by Jack Lee.

LOVE OF THE COMMON PEOPLE	CBS	2	19 Nov 83	13

Originally recorded by the Four Preps.

I'M GONNA TEAR YOUR PLAYHOUSE DOWN	CBS	9	13 Oct 84	7

Originally recorded by Ann Peebles in 1973.

EVERYTHING MUST CHANGE	CBS	9	8 Dec 84	11
EVERY TIME YOU GO AWAY	CBS	4	9 Mar 85	11

Originally recorded by Hall and Oates.

TOMB OF MEMORIES	CBS	16	22 Jun 85	7
TOMB OF MEMORIES [RE]	CBS	74	17 Aug 85	1
WONDERLAND	CBS	24	4 Oct 86	5

Originally recorded by Betsy Cook.

SOME PEOPLE	CBS	56	29 Nov 86	3
WHY DOES A MAN HAVE TO BE STRONG?	CBS	63	7 Feb 87	2
SOFTLY WHISPERING I LOVE YOU	CBS	21	12 May 90	6

Originally recorded by David and Jonathan.

OH GIRL	CBS	25	7 Jul 90	6
HEAVEN CAN WAIT	CBS	71	6 Oct 90	2
CALLING YOU	Columbia	57	12 Jan 91	2
SENZA UNA DONNA (WITHOUT A WOMAN)	London	4	30 Mar 91	12

Originally recorded by Zucchero.
Above hit: ZUCCHERO featuring Paul YOUNG.

BOTH SIDES NOW	MCA	74	10 Aug 91	1

Above hit: CLANNAD and Paul YOUNG.

DON'T DREAM IT'S OVER	Columbia	20	26 Oct 91	5
NOW I KNOW WHAT MADE OTIS BLUE	Columbia	14	25 Sep 93	7
HOPE IN A HOPELESS WORLD	Columbia	42	27 Nov 93	3
IT WILL BE YOU	Columbia	34	23 Apr 94	4
I WISH YOU LOVE	East West	33	17 May 97	2
ALBUMS:	**HITS 8**			**WEEKS 229**
NO PARLEZ	CBS	1	30 Jul 83	119
THE SECRET OF ASSOCIATION	CBS	1	6 Apr 85	49
BETWEEN TWO FIRES	CBS	4	1 Nov 86	17
OTHER VOICES	CBS	4	16 Jun 90	11
FROM TIME TO TIME – THE SINGLES COLLECTION	Columbia	1	14 Sep 91	27
THE CROSSING	Columbia	27	23 Oct 93	2
REFLECTIONS	Vision	64	26 Nov 94	2
PAUL YOUNG	East West	39	31 May 97	2

Retta YOUNG — US

SINGLES:	HITS 1			WEEKS 7
(SENDING OUT AN) S.O.S.	All Platinum	28	24 May 75	7

Tracie YOUNG – See TRACIE

Victor YOUNG and his Orchestra and Chorus – See Charlie APPLEWHITE

YOUNG AND MOODY BAND — UK

SINGLES:	HITS 1			WEEKS 4
DON'T DO THAT	Bronze	63	10 Oct 81	4

YOUNG BLACK TEENAGERS — US

SINGLES:	HITS 1			WEEKS 3
TAP THE BOTTLE	MCA	39	9 Apr 94	3

YOUNG and COMPANY — US

SINGLES:	HITS 1			WEEKS 12
I LIKE (WHAT YOU'RE DOING TO ME)	Excaliber	20	1 Nov 80	12

YOUNG DISCIPLES — UK

SINGLES:	HITS 3			WEEKS 17
GET YOURSELF TOGETHER	Talkin Loud	68	13 Oct 90	1
APPARENTLY NOTHIN'	Talkin Loud	46	23 Feb 91	4
APPARENTLY NOTHIN' [RE]	Talkin Loud	13	3 Aug 91	7
GET YOURSELF TOGETHER [RI]	Talkin Loud	65	5 Oct 91	2

YOUNG DISCIPLES [EP] *Lead track: Move On.*	*Talkin Loud*		48	*5 Sep 92*	3
ALBUMS:	**HITS 1**			**WEEKS 5**	
ROAD TO FREEDOM	*Talkin Loud*		21	*31 Aug 91*	5

YOUNG GODS — Switzerland

ALBUMS:	**HITS 1**			**WEEKS 1**	
T.V. SKY	*Play It*		54	*15 Feb 92*	1

YOUNG IDEA — UK

SINGLES:	**HITS 1**			**WEEKS 6**	
WITH A LITTLE HELP FROM MY FRIENDS	*Columbia*		10	*2 Jul 67*	6

YOUNG M.C. — US

SINGLES:	**HITS 3**			**WEEKS 7**	
BUST A MOVE	*Delicious Vinyl / Fourth & Broadway*		73	*15 Jul 89*	2
PRINCIPAL'S OFFICE	*Delicious Vinyl / Fourth & Broadway*		54	*17 Feb 90*	3
THAT'S THE WAY LOVE GOES	*Capitol*		65	*17 Aug 91*	2

YOUNG OFFENDERS — Ireland

SINGLES:	**HITS 1**			**WEEKS 1**	
THAT'S WHY WE LOSE CONTROL	*Columbia*		60	*7 Mar 98*	1

YOUNG ONES – See Cliff RICHARD

YOUNG RASCALS — US/Canada

SINGLES:	**HITS 2**			**WEEKS 17**	
GROOVIN'	*Atlantic*		8	*27 May 67*	13
A GIRL LIKE YOU	*Atlantic*		37	*19 Aug 67*	4

YOUNG STEVE and the AFTERNOON BOYS – See Steve WRIGHT

Sydney YOUNGBLOOD — US

SINGLES:	**HITS 5**			**WEEKS 31**	
IF ONLY I COULD	*Circa*		3	*26 Aug 89*	14
SIT AND WAIT	*Circa*		16	*9 Dec 89*	8
I'D RATHER GO BLIND	*Circa*		44	*31 Mar 90*	5
HOOKED ON YOU	*Circa*		72	*29 Jun 91*	2
ANYTHING	*RCA*		48	*20 Mar 93*	2
ALBUMS:	**HITS 1**			**WEEKS 17**	
FEELING FREE	*Circa*		23	*28 Oct 89*	17

YOUNGER YOUNGER 28'S — UK

SINGLES:	**HITS 1**			**WEEKS 1**	
WE'RE GOING OUT	*V2*		61	*5 Jun 99*	1

Z

Z FACTOR — UK

SINGLES:	**HITS 1**			**WEEKS 1**	
GOTTA KEEP PUSHIN'	*ffrr*		47	*21 Feb 98*	1

Helmut ZACHARIAS and his ORCHESTRA — Germany

SINGLES:	**HITS 1**			**WEEKS 11**	
TOKYO MELODY *Theme to the 1964 Olympic Games held in Tokyo.*	*Polydor*		9	*31 Oct 64*	11

Pia ZADORA — US

SINGLES:	**HITS 2**			**WEEKS 6**	
WHEN THE RAIN BEGINS TO FALL *From the film 'Voyage Of The Rock Aliens'.* *Above hit: Jermaine JACKSON and Pia ZADORA.*	*Arista*		68	*27 Oct 84*	2
DANCE OUT OF MY HEAD *Above hit: PIA.*	*Epic*		65	*12 Nov 88*	4

Michael ZAGER BAND — US

SINGLES:	**HITS 1**			**WEEKS 12**	
LET'S ALL CHANT	*Private Stock*		8	*1 Apr 78*	12

ZAGER and EVANS
US

SINGLES:		HITS 1		WEEKS 13
IN THE YEAR 2525 (EXORDIUM AND TERMINUS)	RCA Victor	1	9 Aug 69	13

Written by Rick Evans in 1964 while in a band called the Eccentrics.

Gheorghe ZAMFIR
Romania

SINGLES:		HITS 1		WEEKS 9
THE LIGHT OF EXPERIENCE 'DOINA DE JALE'	Epic	4	21 Aug 76	9

Theme from the BBC TV series.

Tommy ZANG
US

SINGLES:		HITS 1		WEEKS 1
HEY GOOD LOOKING	Polydor	45	18 Feb 61	1

Originally recorded by Hank Williams.

ZAPP
US

SINGLES:		HITS 2		WEEKS 6
IT DOESN'T REALLY MATTER	Warner Brothers	57	25 Jan 86	3
COMPUTER LOVE (PART 1)	Warner Brothers	64	24 May 86	3

Frank ZAPPA
US

ALBUMS:		HITS 13		WEEKS 57
HOT RATS	Reprise	9	28 Feb 70	27
CHUNGA'S REVENGE	Reprise	43	19 Dec 70	1
ZAPPA IN NEW YORK	Discreet	55	6 May 78	1

Live recordings.

SHEIK YERBOUTI	CBS	32	10 Mar 79	7
JOE'S GARAGE ACT I	CBS	62	13 Oct 79	3
JOE'S GARAGE ACTS II & III	CBS	75	19 Jan 80	1
TINSEL TOWN REBELLION	CBS	55	16 May 81	4
YOU ARE WHAT YOU IS	CBS	51	24 Oct 81	2

Above 2 are live recordings.

SHIP ARRIVING TOO LATE TO SAVE A DROWNING WITCH	CBS	61	19 Jun 82	4
THE MAN FROM UTOPIA	CBS	87	18 Jun 83	1
THEM OR US	EMI	53	27 Oct 84	2
GUITAR	Zappa	82	30 Apr 88	2
STRICTLY COMMERCIAL - THE BEST OF FRANK ZAPPA	Rykodisc	45	2 Sep 95	2

Francesco ZAPPALA
Italy

SINGLES:		HITS 2		WEEKS 3
WE GOTTA DO IT	Fourth & Broadway	57	10 Aug 91	2

Above hit: D.J. PROFESSOR and Francesco ZAPPALA.

NO WAY OUT	PWL Continental	69	2 May 92	1

Lena ZAVARONI
UK

SINGLES:		HITS 2		WEEKS 14
MA! (HE'S MAKING EYES AT ME)	Philips	10	9 Feb 74	11

Originally recorded by Eddie Cantor in 1921.

(YOU'VE GOT) PERSONALITY	Philips	33	1 Jun 74	3
ALBUMS:		HITS 1		WEEKS 5
MA	Philips	8	23 Mar 74	5

ZEE
UK

SINGLES:		HITS 3		WEEKS 4
DREAMTIME	Perfecto	31	6 Jul 96	2
SAY MY NAME	Perfecto	36	22 Mar 97	1
BUTTERFLY	Perfecto Mainline	41	7 Feb 98	1

Above hit: TILT featuring ZEE.

ZEITIA – See ARIZONA featuring ZEITIA; Zeitia MASSIAH

ZEPHYRS
UK

SINGLES:		HITS 1		WEEKS 1
SHE'S LOST YOU	Columbia	48	20 Mar 65	1

ZERO B
UK

SINGLES:		HITS 3		WEEKS 6
THE E.P. (BRAND NEW MIXES) [EP]	Ffrreedom	32	22 Feb 92	4

Lead track: Lock Up.

RECONNECTION [EP]	Internal	54	24 Jul 93	2

Lead track: Lock-Up. This is a remix of the track on the previous EP.

ZERO VU featuring Lorna B UK

SINGLES:		HITS 1			WEEKS 1
FEELS SO GOOD	*Avex UK*	69	*15 Mar 97*		1

ZERO ZERO UK

SINGLES:		HITS 1			WEEKS 1
ZEROXED	*Kickin*	71	*10 Aug 91*		1

ZHANE US

SINGLES:		HITS 9			WEEKS 18
HEY MR. D.J.	*Epic*	26	*11 Sep 93*		3
Samples Looking Up To You by Michael Wycoff.					
HEY MR. D.J. [RE]	*Epic*	50	*4 Dec 93*		2
GROOVE THANG	*Motown*	34	*19 Mar 94*		3
VIBE	*Motown*	67	*20 Aug 94*		1
SHAME	*Jive*	66	*25 Feb 95*		1
From the film 'A Low Down Dirty Shame'.					
IT'S A PARTY	*Elektra*	23	*21 Sep 96*		2
Features vocals by SWV.					
Above hit: Busta RHYMES featuring ZHANE.					
4 MORE	*Tommy Boy*	52	*8 Mar 97*		1
Recreates Sharon Redd's Never Give You Up.					
Above hit: DE LA SOUL featuring ZHANE.					
REQUEST LINE	*Motown*	22	*26 Apr 97*		3
CRUSH	*Motown*	44	*30 Aug 97*		1
JAMBOREE	*Arista*	51	*11 Sep 99*		1
Samples Benny Golson's I'm Always Dancin' To The Music.					
Above hit: NAUGHTY BY NATURE (featuring ZHANE).					
ALBUMS:		**HITS 1**			**WEEKS 1**
SATURDAY NIGHT	*Motown*	52	*10 May 97*		1
Previously released in 1994 with the title Zhane Pronounced Jah-Nay, peaked at No. 89.					

ZIG and ZAG Ireland

SINGLES:		HITS 2			WEEKS 12
THEM GIRLS/THEM GIRLS	*RCA*	5	*24 Dec 94*		9
HANDS UP! HANDS UP!	*RCA*	21	*1 Jul 95*		3

David ZINMAN – See Dawn UPSHAW (soprano)/the LONDON SINFONIETTA/David ZINMAN (conductor)

ZION TRAIN UK

SINGLES:		HITS 1			WEEKS 1
RISE	*China*	61	*27 Jul 96*		1
Track created using Soundpool – an on-line bank of royalty-free samples.					
ALBUMS:		**HITS 1**			**WEEKS 1**
GROW TOGETHER	*China*	56	*13 Jul 96*		1

ZODIACS – See Maurice WILLIAMS and the ZODIACS

ZOE UK

SINGLES:		HITS 3			WEEKS 22
SUNSHINE ON A RAINY DAY	*M&G*	53	*10 Nov 90*		5
SUNSHINE ON A RAINY DAY [RM]	*M&G*	4	*24 Aug 91*		11
Remixed by Youth and Mark Stent.					
LIGHTNING	*M&G*	37	*2 Nov 91*		4
HOLY DAYS	*M&G*	72	*29 Feb 92*		2
ALBUMS:		**HITS 1**			**WEEKS 1**
SCARLET, RED AND BLUE	*M&G*	67	*7 Dec 91*		1

Rob ZOMBIE US

(See also Puff Daddy.)

SINGLES:		HITS 1			WEEKS 2
DRAGULA	*Geffen*	44	*26 Dec 98*		2
ALBUMS:		**HITS 1**			**WEEKS 2**
HELLBILLY DELUXE	*Geffen*	37	*5 Sep 98*		2

ZOMBIES UK

SINGLES:		HITS 2			WEEKS 16
SHE'S NOT THERE	*Decca*	12	*15 Aug 64*		11
TELL HER NO	*Decca*	42	*13 Feb 65*		5

ZOO EXPERIENCE – featuring DESTRY — UK/US

SINGLES:	HITS 1			WEEKS 1
LOVE'S GOT A HOLD ON ME	Cooltempo	66	22 Aug 92	1

ZUCCHERO — Italy

SINGLES:	HITS 3			WEEKS 24
SENZA UNA DONNA (WITHOUT A WOMAN)	London	4	30 Mar 91	12
Originally recorded by Zucchero.				
Above hit: ZUCCHERO featuring Paul YOUNG.				
DIAMANTE	London	44	18 Jan 92	7
Above hit: ZUCCHERO with Randy CRAWFORD.				
MISERERE	London	15	24 Oct 92	5
Above hit: ZUCCHERO with Luciano PAVAROTTI.				

ALBUMS:	HITS 1			WEEKS 4
ZUCCHERO	London	29	18 May 91	4

ZZ TOP — US

(See also Martay featuring ZZ Top.)

SINGLES:	HITS 15			WEEKS 92
GIMME ALL YOUR LOVIN'	Warner Brothers	61	3 Sep 83	3
SHARP DRESSED MAN	Warner Brothers	53	26 Nov 83	3
TV DINNERS	Warner Brothers	67	31 Mar 84	3
GIMME ALL YOUR LOVIN' [RE]	Warner Brothers	10	6 Oct 84	15
SHARP DRESSED MAN [RE]	Warner Brothers	22	15 Dec 84	10
LEGS (SPECIAL US REMIX)	Warner Brothers	16	23 Feb 85	7
THE ZZ TOP SUMMER HOLIDAY [EP]	Warner Brothers	51	13 Jul 85	5
Lead track: Tush. EP of old tracks. Tush was originally released in 1975 and reached No. 20 in the US.				
SLEEPING BAG	Warner Brothers	27	19 Oct 85	5
STAGES	Warner Brothers	43	15 Feb 86	3
ROUGH BOY	Warner Brothers	23	19 Apr 86	9
VELCRO FLY ('86 REMIX)	Warner Brothers	54	4 Oct 86	3
DOUBLEBACK	Warner Brothers	29	21 Jul 90	6
From the film 'Back To The Future III'.				
MY HEAD'S IN MISSISSIPPI	Warner Brothers	37	13 Apr 91	5
VIVA LAS VEGAS	Warner Brothers	10	11 Apr 92	7
ROUGH BOY [RI]	Warner Brothers	49	20 Jun 92	3
PINCUSHION	RCA	15	29 Jan 94	3
BREAKAWAY	RCA	60	7 May 94	1
WHATS UP WITH THAT	RCA	58	29 Jun 96	1

ALBUMS:	HITS 8			WEEKS 209
FANDANGO!	London	60	12 Jul 75	1
One side live, the other has studio recordings.				
EL LOCO	Warner Brothers	88	8 Aug 81	2
ELIMINATOR	Warner Brothers	43	30 Apr 83	24
Peak position reached in 1984.				
ELIMINATOR [RE]	Warner Brothers	3	7 Jul 84	111
Peak position reached on 26 Jan 85.				
AFTERBURNER	Warner Brothers	2	9 Nov 85	40
RECYCLER	Warner Brothers	8	27 Oct 90	7
GREATEST HITS	Warner Brothers	5	25 Apr 92	17
ANTENNA	RCA	3	5 Feb 94	5
Tribute to the Mexican border rock'n'roll radio stations of the 1950s/60s.				
RHYTHMEEN	RCA	32	21 Sep 96	2

THE NUMBER ONE SINGLES & ALBUMS

Singles and albums that reached the No. 1 position in the respective charts. Figure in brackets indicates number of weeks spent at number 1.

*Denotes straight in at No. 1.

1952

SINGLES

15 Nov	*Here In My Heart, Al Martino (9)
	Best seller of the year including pre-chart: 'Auf Wiederseh'n Sweetheart', Vera Lynn with Soldiers & Airmen of her Majesty's Forces.

1953

SINGLES

17 Jan	You Belong To Me, Jo Stafford with Paul Weston & His Orchestra (1)
24 Jan	Comes A-Long A-Love, Kay Starr (1)
31 Jan	Outside Of Heaven, Eddie Fisher with Hugo Winterhalter's Orchestra and Chorus (1)
7 Feb	Don't Let The Stars Get In Your Eyes, Perry Como with The Ramblers (5)
14 March	She Wears Red Feathers, Guy Mitchell with Mitch Miller & His Orchestra and Chorus (4)
11 April	Broken Wings, Stargazers (1)
18 April	(How Much Is) That Doggie In The Window, Lita Roza (1)
25 April	I Believe, Frankie Laine with Paul Weston & His Orchestra (9, 3 July for 6, 22 Aug for 3; best seller of the year)
27 June	I'm Walking Behind You, Eddie Fisher with Hugo Winterhalter and His Orchestra & Sally Sweetland (1)
15 Aug	The Song From The Moulin Rouge (Where Is Your Heart), Mantovani & His Orchestra (1)
12 Sept	Look At That Girl, Guy Mitchell (6)
24 Oct	Hey Joe!, Frankie Laine with Paul Weston & His Orchestra and The Norman Luboff Choir (Carl Fischer: piano) (2)
7 Nov	Answer Me, David Whitfield with Stanley Black & His Orchestra (1, 12 Dec for 1)
14 Nov	Answer Me, Frankie Laine with Paul Weston & His Orchestra and The Norman Luboff Choir (Carl Fischer: piano) (8)
12 Dec	Above two were joint at No. 1.

1954

SINGLES

9 Jan	Oh, Mein Papa, Eddie Calvert (The Man With The Golden Trumpet) with Norrie Paramor & His Orchestra (9)
13 March	I See The Moon, Stargazers with Syd Dean & His Orchestra (5, 24 April for 1)
17 April	Secret Love, Doris Day (1, 8 May for 8; best seller of the year)
1 May	Such A Night, Johnnie Ray (1)
3 July	Cara Mia, David Whitfield with Mantovani & His Orchestra and Chorus (10)
11 Sept	Little Things Mean A Lot, Kitty Kallen (1)
18 Sept	Three Coins In The Fountain, Frank Sinatra (3)
9 Oct	Hold My Hand, Don Cornell (4, 20 Nov for 2)
6 Nov	My Son My Son, Vera Lynn and Frank Weir & His Saxophone, His Chorus and Orchestra (2)
27 Nov	This Ole House, Rosemary Clooney with Buddy Cole & His Orchestra (1)
4 Dec	Let's Have Another Party [M], Winifred Atwell & Her "Other" Piano (5)

1955

SINGLES

8 Jan	The Finger Of Suspicion, Dickie Valentine with The Stargazers (1, 22 Jan for 2)

15 Jan	Mambo Italiano, Rosemary Clooney & The Mellomen (1, 5 Feb for 2)
19 Feb	Softly Softly, Ruby Murray and Ray Martin & His Orchestra (3)
12 March	Give Me Your Word, "Tennessee" Ernie Ford (7)
30 April	Cherry Pink And Apple Blossom White, Perez 'Prez' Prado & His Orchestra, (The King of the Mambo) (2)
14 May	Stranger In Paradise, Tony Bennett with Percy Faith & His Orchestra and Chorus (2)
28 May	Cherry Pink (And Apple Blossom White), Eddie Calvert (The Man with the Golden Trumpet) (4)
25 June	Unchained Melody, Jimmy Young with Bob Sharples & His Music (3)
16 July	Dreamboat, Alma Cogan (2)
30 July	Rose Marie, Slim Whitman (11; best seller of the year)
15 Oct	The Man From Laramie, Jimmy Young with Bob Sharples & His Music (4)
12 Nov	Hernando's Hideaway, Johnston Brothers (2)
26 Nov	(We're Gonna) Rock Around The Clock, Bill Haley & His Comets (2)
17 Dec	Christmas Alphabet, Dickie Valentine with Johnny Douglas & His Orchestra (3)

1956

SINGLES

7 Jan	(We're Gonna) Rock Around The Clock, Bill Haley & His Comets (2)
21 Jan	Sixteen Tons, "Tennessee" Ernie Ford (4)
18 Feb	Memories Are Made Of This, Dean Martin (4)
17 March	It's Almost Tomorrow, Dream Weavers (2, 7 April for 1)
31 March	Rock And Roll Waltz, Kay Starr with Hugo Winterhalter's Orchestra & Chorus (1)
14 April	The Poor People Of Paris, Winifred Atwell & Her "Other" Piano (3)
5 May	No Other Love, Ronnie Hilton (6)
16 June	I'll Be Home, Pat Boone (5; best seller of the year)
21 July	Why Do Fools Fall In Love, Teenagers featuring Frankie Lymon (3)
11 Aug	Whatever Will Be Will Be (Que Sera Sera), Doris Day with Frank De Vol & His Orchestra (6)
22 Sept	Lay Down Your Arms, Anne Shelton with Wally Stott & His Orchestra & Chorus (4)
20 Oct	A Woman In Love, Frankie Laine with Percy Faith & His Orchestra (4)
17 Nov	Just Walking In The Rain, Johnnie Ray with Ray Conniff & His Orchestra (7)

1957

SINGLES

5 Jan	Singing The Blues, Guy Mitchell with Ray Conniff & His Orchestra (1, 18 Jan for 1, 2 Feb for 1)
12 Jan	Singing The Blues, Tommy Steele & The Steelmen (1)
26 Jan	The Garden Of Eden, Frankie Vaughan with Wally Stott & His Orchestra & Chorus (3)
2 Feb	The Garden Of Eden and Singing The Blues (by Guy Mitchell) joint No. 1.
23 Feb	Young Love, Tab Hunter with Billy Vaughn's Orchestra & Chorus (7)
13 April	Cumberland Gap, Lonnie Donegan & His Skiffle Group (5)
18 May	Rock-A-Billy, Guy Mitchell with Jimmy Carroll (1)
25 May	Butterfly, Andy Williams (2)
8 June	Yes Tonight, Josephine, Johnnie Ray with Ray Conniff (3)

29 June	Putting' On The Style/Gamblin' Man, Lonnie Donegan & His Skiffle Group (2)
13 July	All Shook Up, Elvis Presley with The Jordanaires (7)
31 Aug	Diana, Paul Anka (9; best seller of the year)
2 Nov	That'll Be The Day, Crickets (3)
23 Nov	Mary's Boy Child, Harry Belafonte (7)

1958

SINGLES

11 Jan	Great Balls Of Fire, Lewis, Jerry Lee (2)
25 Jan	*Jailhouse Rock, Elvis Presley (3; best seller of the year)
15 Feb	The Story Of My Life, Michael Holliday (2)
1 March	Magic Moments, Perry Como with Mitchell Ayres' Orchestra & The Ray Charles Singers (8)
26 April	Whole Lotta Woman, Marvin Rainwater (3)
17 May	Who's Sorry Now, Connie Francis (4)
28 June	On The Street Where You Live, Vic Damone with Percy Faith & His Orchestra & Chorus (2)
5 July	All I Have To Do Is Dream/Claudette, Everly Brothers (Joint number 1 with above) (7)
23 Aug	When, Kalin Twins (5)
27 Sept	Stupid Cupid/Carolina Moon, Connie Francis (6)
8 Nov	It's All In The Game, Tommy Edwards (6)
29 Nov	Hoots Mon, Jack Good presents Lord Rockingham's XI (3)
20 Dec	It's Only Make Believe, Conway Twitty (5)

ALBUMS

8 Nov	*South Pacific, Original Soundtrack (70; best seller of the year)

1959

SINGLES

24 Jan	The Day The Rains Came, Jane Morgan (1)
31 Jan	One Night/I Got Stung, Elvis Presley (3)
21 Feb	As I Love You, Shirley Bassey with Wally Stott & His Orchestra (4)
21 March	Smoke Gets In Your Eyes, Platters (1)
28 March	Side Saddle, Russ Conway (4)
25 April	It Doesn't Matter Anymore, Buddy Holly (3)
16 May	A Fool Such As I/I Need Your Love Tonight, Elvis Presley with The Jordanaires (5)
20 June	Roulette, Russ Conway (2)
4 July	Dream Lover, Bobby Darin (4)
1 Aug	Living Doll, Cliff Richard & The Drifters (6; best seller of the year)
12 Sept	Only Sixteen, Craig Douglas (4)
10 Oct	Here Comes Summer, Jerry Keller (1)
17 Oct	Mack The Knife, Bobby Darin (2)
31 Oct	Travellin' Light, Cliff Richard & The Shadows (5)
5 Dec	What Do You Want?, Adam Faith (3)
19 Dec	What Do You Want To Make Those Eyes At Me For?, Emile Ford & The Checkmates (Joint number 1 with above) (6)

ALBUMS

No new No. 1's during the year. Best seller of the year: South Pacific, Original Soundtrack.

1960

SINGLES

30 Jan	Starry Eyed, Michael Holliday with the Michael Sammes Singers (1)
6 Feb	Why, Anthony Newley (4)
6 March	Poor Me, Adam Faith (2)
19 March	Running Bear, Johnny Preston (2)
2 April	My Old Man's A Dustman (Ballad Of A Refuse Disposal Officer), Lonnie Donegan & His Group (4)
30 April	Do You Mind, Anthony Newley (1; the 100th No. 1)
7 May	Cathy's Clown, Everly Brothers (7)
5 June	Three Steps To Heaven, Eddie Cochran (2)
9 July	Good Timin', Jimmy Jones (3)
30 July	Please Don't Tease, Cliff Richard & The Shadows (1, *13 Aug* for 1)
6 Aug	Shakin' All Over, Johnny Kidd & The Pirates (1)
27 Aug	Apache, Shadows (5)
1 Oct	Tell Laura I Love Her, Ricky Valance (3)

22 Oct	Only The Lonely (Know How I Feel), Roy Orbison (2)
5 Nov	*It's Now Or Never (O Sole Mio), Elvis Presley with The Jordanaires (8; best seller of the year)
31 Dec	I Love You, Cliff Richard & The Shadows (2)

EPS

12 March	*Expresso Bongo [OST], Cliff Richard & the Shadows (1, *23 April* for 1)
19 March	Strictly Elvis, Elvis Presley (5)
30 April	Strictly For Grown Ups, Paddy Roberts (1, *14 May* for 1, *4 June* for 12, *10 Sept* for 1, *24 Sept* for 3, *5 Nov* for 1)
7 May	Emile, Emile Ford & The Checkmates (1, *21 May* for 2)
27 Aug	Paddy Roberts Strikes Again, Paddy Roberts (2)
17 Sept	South Pacific No. 1, Original Soundtrack (1, *15 Oct* for 3, *12 Nov* for 5, *31 Dec* for 1)
17 Dec	Adam's Hit Parade, Adam Faith (1)
24 Dec	Cliff's Silver Discs, Cliff Richard & The Shadows (1)

ALBUMS

12 March	The Explosive Freddy Cannon, Freddy Cannon (1)
19 March	South Pacific, Original Soundtrack (19, *6 Aug* for 5, *15 Oct* for 13; best seller of the year)
30 July	Elvis Is Back, Elvis Presley (1)
10 Sept	Down Drury Lane To Memory Lane, One Hundred and One Strings (5)

1961

SINGLES

14 Jan	Poetry In Motion, Johnny Tillotson (2)
28 Jan	Are You Lonesome Tonight?, Elvis Presley with The Jordanaires (4; best seller of the year)
25 Feb	Sailor, Petula Clark, Peter Knight Orchestra & Chorus (1)
4 March	Walk Right Back/Ebony Eyes, Everly Brothers (3)
25 March	Wooden Heart, Elvis Presley (6)
6 May	Blue Moon, Marcels (2)
20 May	On The Rebound, Floyd Cramer (1)
27 May	You're Driving Me Crazy, Temperance Seven, vocal refrain by Mr. Paul MacDowall (1)
3 June	Surrender (Torna A Surriento), Elvis Presley with the Jordanaires (4)
1 July	Runaway, Del Shannon (3)
22 July	Temptation, Everly Brothers (2)
5 Aug	Well I Ask You, Eden Kane (1)
12 Aug	You Don't Know, Helen Shapiro (3)
2 Sept	Johnny Remember Me, John Leyton (3, *30 Sept* for 1)
23 Sept	Reach For The Stars/Climb Ev'ry Mountain, Shirley Bassey with Geoff Love & His Orchestra (1)
7 Oct	Kon-Tiki, Shadows (1)
14 Oct	Michael, Highwaymen (1)
21 Oct	Walkin' Back To Happiness, Helen Shapiro (3)
11 Nov	(Marie's The Name) His Latest Flame, Elvis Presley (4)
9 Dec	Tower Of Strength, Frankie Vaughan (3)
30 Dec	Moon River, Danny Williams with Geoff Love & His Orchestra (2)

EPS

7 Jan	Cliff's Silver Discs, Cliff Richard & The Shadows (2)
21 Jan	Adam's Hit Parade, Adam Faith (1, *27 May* for 1)
28 Jan	The Shadows, Shadows (17, *3 June* for 3)
24 June	The Shadows To The Fore, Shadows (23)
2 Dec	Helen, Helen Shapiro (9)

ALBUMS

14 Jan	G.I. Blues [OST], Elvis Presley (7, *11 March* for 3, *8 April* for 12; best seller of the year)
4 March	South Pacific, Original Soundtrack (1, *1 April* for 1, *1 July* for 4, *26 Aug* for 1, *9 Sept* for 1)
29 July	The Black And White Minstrel Show, George Mitchell Minstrels (4, *2 Sept* for 1, *16 Sept* for 1, *21 Oct* for 1)
23 Sept	The Shadows, Shadows (4, *28 Oct* for 1)
4 Nov	I'm 21 Today, Cliff Richard & The Shadows (1)
11 Nov	Another Black And White Minstrel Show, George Mitchell Minstrels (8)

1962

SINGLES

13 Jan	*The Young Ones, Cliff Richard & The Shadows (6)
24 Feb	Rock-A-Hula Baby ("Twist Special")/Can't Help Falling In Love, Elvis Presley with The Jordanaires (4)

24 March	Wonderful Land, Shadows (8)
19 May	Nut Rocker, B. Bumble & The Stingers (1)
26 May	Good Luck Charm, Elvis Presley with The Jordanaires (5)
30 June	Come Outside, Mike Sarne featuring Wendy Richard (2)
14 July	I Can't Stop Loving You, Ray Charles (2)
28 July	I Remember You, Frank Ifield (7; best seller of the year)
15 Sept	She's Not You, Elvis Presley with The Jordanaires (3)
6 Oct	Telstar, Tornados (5)
10 Nov	Lovesick Blues, Frank Ifield with Norrie Paramor & His Orchestra (5)
15 Dec	Return To Sender, Elvis Presley with The Jordanaires (3)

EPS

3 Feb	The Shadows To The Fore, Shadows (4, 19 May for 1)
3 March	Spotlight On The Shadows, Shadows (3, 14 April for 5)
24 March	Helen's Hit Parade, Helen Shapiro (3, 26 May for 1)
2 June	Hits From 'The Young Ones', Cliff Richard & The Shadows (2)
16 June	Follow That Dream [OST], Elvis Presley (20)
3 Nov	The Boys, Shadows (3)
24 Nov	Kid Galahad [OST], Elvis Presley (5)
29 Dec	The Black And White Minstrel Show, George Mitchell Minstrels (1)

ALBUMS

6 Jan	Blue Hawaii [OST], Elvis Presley (1, 24 Feb for 17)
13 Jan	The Young Ones [OST], Cliff Richard & The Shadows (6)
23 June	West Side Story, Original Soundtracks (5, 1 Sept for 1, 15 Sept for 1, 29 Sept for 3, 17 Nov for 1, 15 Dec for 1; best seller of the year)
28 July	Pot Luck, Elvis Presley (5, 8 Sept for 1)
22 Sept	The Best Of Ball, Barber And Bilk, Kenny Ball, Chris Barber & Acker Bilk (1, 20 Oct for 1)
27 Oct	Out Of The Shadows, Shadows (3, 24 Nov for 1, 22 Dec for 1)
1 Dec	On Stage With The George Mitchell Minstrels, George Mitchell Minstrels (2)
29 Dec	The Black And White Minstrel Show, George Mitchell Minstrels (2)

1963

SINGLES

5 Jan	The Next Time/Bachelor Boy, Cliff Richard, The Shadows & The Norrie Paramor Strings (3)
26 Jan	Dance On!, Shadows (1)
2 Feb	Diamonds, Jet Harris & Tony Meehan (3)
23 Feb	The Wayward Wind, Frank Ifield with Norrie Paramor & His Orchestra (3)
16 March	Summer Holiday, Cliff Richard, The Shadows & The Norrie Paramor Strings (2, 6 April for 1)
30 March	Foot Tapper, Shadows (1)
13 April	How Do You Do It?, Gerry & The Pacemakers (3)
4 May	From Me To You, Beatles (7)
22 June	I Like It, Gerry & The Pacemakers (4)
20 July	Confessin' (That I Love You), Frank Ifield (2)
3 Aug	(You're The) Devil In Disguise, Elvis Presley with The Jordanaires (1)
10 Aug	Sweets For My Sweet, Searchers (2)
24 Aug	Bad To Me, Billy J. Kramer & The Dakotas (3)
14 Sept	She Loves You, Beatles (4, 30 Nov for 2; best seller of the year)
12 Oct	Do You Love Me, Brian Poole & The Tremeloes (3)
2 Nov	You'll Never Walk Alone, Gerry & The Pacemakers (4)
14 Dec	I Want To Hold Your Hand, Beatles (5)

EPS

5 Jan	Kid Galahad [OST], Elvis Presley (13)
6 April	Frank Ifield's Hits, Frank Ifield (8, 15 June for 2, 6 July for 2)
1 June	Just For Fun, Bobby Vee & The Crickets (1)
8 June	Holiday Carnival, Cliff Richard & The Shadows (1, 29 June for 1, 20 July for 1)
27 July	Twist And Shout, Beatles (10, 23 Nov for 11)
5 Oct	Ain't Gonna Kiss You, Searchers (4)
2 Nov	The Beatles' Hits, Beatles (3)

ALBUMS

12 Jan	West Side Story, Original Soundtrack (1)
19 Jan	Out Of The Shadows, Shadows (2)

2 Feb	Summer Holiday [OST],Cliff Richard & The Shadows (14)
11 May	Please Please Me, Beatles (30)
7 Dec	With The Beatles, Beatles (21; best seller of the year)

1964

SINGLES

18 Jan	Glad All Over, Dave Clark Five (2)
1 Feb	Needles And Pins, Searchers (3)
22 Feb	Diane, Bachelors (1)
29 Feb	Anyone Who Had A Heart, Cilla Black (3)
21 March	Little Children, Billy J. Kramer & The Dakotas (2)
4 April	Can't Buy Me Love, Beatles (3; best seller of the year)
25 April	A World Without Love, Peter & Gordon (2)
9 May	Don't Throw Your Love Away, Searchers (2)
23 May	Juliet, Four Pennies (1)
30 May	You're My World (Il Mio Mondo), Cilla Black (4)
27 June	It's Over, Roy Orbison (2)
11 July	The House Of The Rising Sun, Animals (1)
18 July	It's All Over Now, Rolling Stones (1)
25 July	A Hard Day's Night, Beatles (3)
15 Aug	Do Wah Diddy Diddy, Manfred Mann (2)
29 Aug	Have I The Right?, Honeycombs (2)
12 Sept	You Really Got Me, Kinks (2)
26 Sept	I'm Into Something Good, Herman's Hermits (2)
10 Oct	Oh, Pretty Woman, Roy Orbison (2, 14 Nov for 1)
24 Oct	(There's) Always Something There To Remind Me, Sandie Shaw (3)
21 Nov	Baby Love, Supremes (2)
5 Dec	Little Red Rooster, Rolling Stones (1)
12 Dec	I Feel Fine, Beatles (5)

EPS

8 Feb	The Rolling Stones, Rolling Stones (3, 25 April for 11)
29 Feb	All My Loving, Beatles (8)
11 July	Long Tall Sally, Beatles (7)
29 Aug	Five By Five, Rolling Stones (15)
12 Dec	A Hard Day's Night, Beatles (2)
26 Dec	Bachelors' Hits, Bachelors (1)

ALBUMS

2 May	Rolling Stones, Rolling Stones (12)
25 July	A Hard Day's Night, Beatles (21)
19 Dec	Beatles For Sale, Beatles (7; best seller of the year)

1965

SINGLES

16 Jan	Yeh, Yeh, Georgie Fame & The Blue Flames (2)
30 Jan	Go Now!, Moody Blues (1)
6 Feb	You've Lost That Lovin' Feelin', Righteous Brothers (2)
20 Feb	Tired Of Waiting For You, Kinks (1)
27 Feb	I'll Never Find Another You, Seekers (2)
13 March	It's Not Unusual, Tom Jones (1)
20 March	The Last Time,Rolling Stones (3)
10 April	Concrete And Clay, Unit Four Plus Two (1)
17 April	The Minute You're Gone, Cliff Richard (1)
24 April	Ticket To Ride, Beatles (3)
15 May	King Of The Road, Roger Miller (1)
22 May	Where Are You Now, Jackie Trent (1)
29 May	Long Live Love, Sandie Shaw (3)
19 June	Crying In The Chapel, Elvis Presley with The Jordanaires (1, 3 July for 1)
26 June	I'm Alive, Hollies (1, 10 July for 2)
24 July	Mr. Tambourine Man, Byrds (2)
7 Aug	Help!, Beatles (3; the 200th No. 1)
28 Aug	I Got You Babe, Sonny & Cher (2)
11 Sept	(I Can't Get No) Satisfaction, Rolling Stones (2)
25 Sept	Make It Easy On Yourself, Walker Bros. (1)
2 Oct	Tears, Ken Dodd with Geoff Love & His Orchestra (5; best seller of the year)
6 Nov	Get Off Of My Cloud, Rolling Stones (3)
27 Nov	The Carnival Is Over, Seekers (3)
18 Dec	Day Tripper/We Can Work It Out, Beatles (5)

EPS

9 Jan	A Hard Day's Night, Beatles (3, 6 Feb for 1)
30 Jan	Five By Five, Rolling Stones (1, 13 Feb for 1, 27 Feb for 1, 27 March for 3)
20 Feb	Kinksize Session, Kinks (1)

6 March Green Shades Of Val Doonican, Val Doonican (3, *17 April* for 1)
24 April Beatles For Sale, Beatles (5, *12 June* for 1)
29 May Bumble Bee, Searchers (2)
19 June The One In The Middle, Manfred Mann (1, *3 July* for 4, *7 Aug* for 4)
26 June Got Live If You Want It!, Rolling Stones (1, *31 July* for 1)
4 Sept The Universal Soldier, DoNovan (8)
30 Oct Kwyet Kinks, Kinks (7)
18 Dec No Living Without Loving, Manfred Mann (7)

ALBUMS

6 Feb Rolling Stones No. 2, Rolling Stones (3, *6 March* for 6, *24 April* for 1)
27 Feb Beatles For Sale, Beatles (1, *1 May* for 3)
17 April The Freewheelin' Bob Dylan, Bob Dylan (1, *22 May* for 1)
29 May Bringing It All Back Home, Bob Dylan (1)
5 June The Sound Of Music, Original Soundtrack (10, *16 Oct* for 10; best seller of the year)
14 Aug *Help, Beatles (9)
25 Dec Rubber Soul, Beatles (8)

1966

SINGLES

22 Jan Keep On Running, Spencer Davis Group (1)
29 Jan Michelle, Overlanders (3)
19 Feb These Boots Are Made For Walkin', Nancy Sinatra (4)
19 March The Sun Ain't Gonna Shine Anymore, Walker Brothers (4)
16 April Somebody Help Me, Spencer Davis Group (2)
30 April You Don't Have To Say You Love Me (Io Che No Vivo Senza Te), Dusty Springfield (1)
7 May Pretty Flamingo, Manfred Mann (3)
28 May Paint It, Black, Rolling Stones (1)
4 June Strangers In The Night, Frank Sinatra (3)
25 June Paperback Writer, Beatles (2)
9 July Sunny Afternoon, Kinks (2)
23 July Get Away, Georgie Fame & The Blue Flames (1)
30 July Out Of Time, Chris Farlowe (1)
6 Aug With A Girl Like You, Troggs (2)
20 Aug Yellow Submarine/Eleanor Rigby, Beatles (4)
17 Sept All Or Nothing, Small Faces (1)
24 Sept Distant Drums, Jim Reeves (5)
29 Oct Reach Out I'll Be There, Four Tops (3)
19 Nov Good Vibrations, Beach Boys (2)
3 Dec Green, Green Grass Of Home, Tom Jones (7; best seller of the year)

EPS

5 Feb The Beatles' Million Sellers, Beatles (2, *12 March* for 2)
19 Feb The Seekers, Seekers (3)
26 March Yesterday, Beatles (8)
21 May With God On Our Side, Joan Baez (1)
28 May Machines, Manfred Mann (1)
4 June The Beach Boy Hits, Beach Boys (4, *10 Sept* for 4, *29 Oct* for 7)
2 July I Need You, Walker Brothers (10, *8 Oct* for 3)
17 Dec Ready Steady Who, Who (5)

ALBUMS

19 Feb The Sound Of Music, Original Soundtrack (10, *25 June* for 7, *1 Oct* for 18; best seller of the year)
30 April Aftermath, Rolling Stones (8)
13 Aug *Revolver, Beatles (7)

1967

SINGLES

21 Jan I'm A Believer, Monkees (4)
18 Feb This Is My Song, Petula Clark (2)
4 March Release Me, Engelbert Humperdinck (6; best seller of the year)
15 April Somethin' Stupid, Nancy Sinatra & Frank Sinatra (2)
29 April Puppet On A String, Sandie Shaw (3)
20 May Silence Is Golden, Tremeloes (3)
10 June A Whiter Shade Of Pale, Procol Harum (6)
22 July All You Need Is Love, Beatles (3)
12 Aug San Francisco (Be Sure To Wear Flowers In Your Hair), Scott McKenzie (4)
9 Sept The Last Waltz, Engelbert Humperdinck (5)

14 Oct Massachusetts (The Lights Went Out In), Bee Gees (4)
11 Nov Baby, Now That I've Found You, Foundations (2)
25 Nov Let The Heartaches Begin, Long John Baldry (2)
9 Dec Hello Goodbye, Beatles (7)

EPS

21 Jan The Beach Boy Hits, Beach Boys (7, *12 Aug* for 6, *30 Sept* for 1, *14 Oct* for 1, *30 Sept* for 1, *25 Nov* for 2)
11 March Morningtown Ride, Seekers (1)
18 March Four Tops Hits, Four Tops (10, *17 June* for 5, *23 Sept* for 1, *7 Oct* for 1, *21 Oct* for 5)
27 May Privilege, Paul Jones (3)
22 July Easy Come, Easy Go [OST], Elvis Presley (3)
The final EP chart was published on Dec 2, 1967.

ALBUMS

4 Feb The Monkees, Monkees (7)
25 March The Sound Of Music, Original Soundtrack (7, *20 May* for 1, *3 June* for 1, *18 Nov* for 1, *2 Dec* for 3)
13 May More Of The Monkees, Monkees (1, *27 May* for 1)
10 June Sergeant Pepper's Lonely Hearts Club Band, Beatles (23, *25 Nov* for 1, *23 Dec* for 2; best seller of the year)

1968

SINGLES

27 Jan The Ballad Of Bonnie And Clyde, Georgie Fame (1)
3 Feb Everlasting Love, Love Affair (2)
17 Feb Mighty Quinn, Manfred Mann (2)
2 March Cinderella Rockafella, Esther & Abi Ofarim (3)
23 March The Legend Of Xanadu, Dave Dee, Dozy, Beaky, Mick & Tich (1)
30 March Lady Madonna, Beatles (2)
13 April Congratulations, Cliff Richard (2)
27 April What A Wonderful World/Cabaret, Louis Armstrong Orchestra & Chorus/Louis Armstrong & His All Stars (4)
25 May Young Girl, Union Gap Featuring Gary Puckett (4)
22 June Jumpin' Jack Flash, Rolling Stones (2)
6 July Baby Come Back, Equals (3)
27 July I Pretend, Des O'Connor (1)
3 Aug Mony, Mony, Tommy James & The Shondells (2, *24 Aug* for 1)
17 Aug Fire!, Crazy World Of Arthur Brown (1)
31 Aug Do It Again, Beach Boys (1)
7 Sept I've Gotta Get A Message To You, Bee Gees (1)
14 Sept Hey Jude, Beatles (2; best seller of the year)
28 Sept Those Were The Days, Mary Hopkin (6)
9 Nov With A Little Help From My Friends, Joe Cocker (1)
16 Nov The Good, The Bad And The Ugly, Hugo Montenegro, His Orchestra & Chorus (4)
14 Dec Lily The Pink, Scaffold (3)

ALBUMS

6 Jan Val Doonican Rocks But Gently, Val Doonican (3)
27 Jan The Sound Of Music, Original Soundtrack (1, *23 Nov* for 1; best seller of the year)
3 Feb Sergeant Pepper's Lonely Hearts Club Band, Beatles (1)
10 Feb Four Tops Greatest Hits, Four Tops (1)
17 Feb Diana Ross & The Supremes Greatest Hits, Diana Ross & The Supremes (3)
9 March John Wesley Harding, Bob Dylan (10, *25 May* for 3)
18 May Scott 2, Scott Walker (1)
15 June Love Andy, Andy Williams (1)
22 June Dock Of The Bay, Otis Redding (1)
29 June Ogden's Nut Gone Flake, Small Faces (6)
10 Aug Delilah, Tom Jones (1, *21 Sept* for 1)
17 Aug Bookends, Simon & Garfunkel (5, *28 Sept* for 2)
12 Oct The Hollies' Greatest, Hollies (6, *30 Nov* for 1)
7 Dec *The Beatles (The White Album), Beatles (7)

1969

SINGLES

4 Jan Ob-La-Di Ob-La-Da, Marmalade (1, *18 Jan* for 1)
11 Jan Lily The Pink, Scaffold (1)
1 Feb Albatross, Fleetwood Mac (1)
8 Feb Blackberry Way, Move (1)
15 Feb (If Paradise Is) Half As Nice, Amen Corner (2)
1 March Where Do You Go To (My Lovely), Peter Sarstedt (4)
29 March I Heard It Through The Grapevine, Marvin Gaye (3)

19 April	Israelites, Desmond Dekker & The Aces (1)
26 April	*Get Back, Beatles with Billy Preston (6)
7 June	Dizzy, Tommy Roe (1)
14 June	The Ballad Of John And Yoko, Beatles (3)
5 July	Something In The Air, Thunderclap Newman (3)
26 July	Honky Tonk Women, Rolling Stones (5)
30 Aug	In The Year 2525 (Exordium And Terminus), Zager & Evans (3)
20 Sept	Bad Moon Rising, Creedence Clearwater Revival (3)
11 Oct	Je T'aime . . . Moi Non Plus, Jane Birkin & Serge Gainsbourg (1)
18 Oct	I'll Never Fall In Love Again, Bobbie Gentry (1)
25 Oct	Sugar, Sugar, Archies (8; best seller of the year)
20 Dec	Two Little Boys, Rolf Harris (6)

ALBUMS

25 Jan	Best Of The Seekers, Seekers (1, *8 Feb* for 1, *29 March* for 2, *19 April* for 1, *3 May* for 1)
1 Feb	The Beatles (The White Album), Beatles (1)
15 Feb	Diana Ross & The Supremes Join The Temptations, Diana Ross & The Supremes with The Temptations (4)
15 March	*Goodbye, Cream (2, *12 April* for 1, *26 April* for 1)
10 May	On The Threshold Of A Dream, Moody Blues (2)
24 May	Nashville Skyline, Bob Dylan (4)
21 June	*His Orchestra, His Chorus, His Singers, His Sound, Ray Conniff (3)
12 July	According To My Heart, Jim Reeves (4)
9 Aug	*Stand Up, Jethro Tull (3, *6 Sept* for 2)
30 Aug	From Elvis In Memphis, Elvis Presley (1)
20 Sept	Blind Faith, Blind Faith (2)
4 Oct	*Abbey Road, Beatles (11, *27 Dec* for 6; best seller of the year)
20 Dec	*Let It Bleed, Rolling Stones (1)

1970

SINGLES

31 Jan	Love Grows (Where My Rosemary Goes), Edison Lighthouse (5)
7 March	Wand'rin Star, Lee Marvin (3)
28 March	Bridge Over Troubled Water, Simon & Garfunkel (3)
18 April	All Kinds Of Everything, Dana (2)
2 May	Spirit In The Sky, Norman Greenbaum (2)
16 May	Back Home, England Football World Cup Squad "70" (3)
6 June	Yellow River, Christie (1)
13 June	In The Summertime, Mungo Jerry (7)
1 Aug	The Wonder Of You, Elvis Presley (6; best seller of the year)
12 Sept	The Tears Of A Clown, Smokey Robinson & The Miracles (1)
19 Sept	Band Of Gold, Freda Payne (6)
31 Oct	Woodstock, Matthews Southern Comfort (3)
21 Nov	Voodoo Chile, Jimi Hendrix Experience (1)
28 Nov	I Hear You Knocking, Dave Edmunds Rockpile (6)

ALBUMS

7 Feb	Led Zeppelin II, Led Zeppelin (1)
14 Feb	Motown Chartbusters Volume 3, Tamla Motown Compilation (1)
21 Feb	*Bridge Over Troubled Water, Simon & Garfunkel (13, *13 June* for 4, *18 July* for 5, *3 Oct* for 1, *17 Oct* for 1; best seller of the year)
23 May	*Let It Be, Beatles (3)
11 July	*Self Portrait, Bob Dylan (1)
22 Aug	A Question Of Balance, Moody Blues (3)
12 Sept	*Cosmo's Factory, Creedence Clearwater Revival (1)
19 Sept	*Get Yer Ya-Ya's Out – The Rolling Stones In Concert, Rolling Stones (2)
10 Oct	Paranoid, Black Sabbath (1)
24 Oct	*Atom Heart Mother, Pink Floyd (1)
31 Oct	Motown Chartbusters Volume 4, Tamla Motown Compilation (1)
7 Nov	*Led Zeppelin 3, Led Zeppelin (3, *12 Dec* for 1)
28 Nov	*New Morning, Bob Dylan (1)
5 Dec	Andy Williams Greatest Hits, Andy Williams (1, *19 Dec* for 4)

1971

SINGLES

9 Jan	Grandad, Clive Dunn (3)
30 Jan	My Sweet Lord, George Harrison (5; best seller of the year)

6 March	Baby Jump, Mungo Jerry (2)
20 March	Hot Love, T. Rex (6)
1 May	Double Barrel, Dave & Ansil Collins (2)
15 May	Knock Three Times, Dawn (5; the 300th No. 1)
19 June	Chirpy Chirpy Cheep Cheep, Middle Of The Road (5)
24 July	Get It On, T. Rex (4)
21 Aug	I'm Still Waiting, Diana Ross (4)
18 Sept	Hey Girl Don't Bother Me, Tams (3)
9 Oct	Maggie May, Rod Stewart (5)
13 Nov	Coz I Luv You, Slade (4)
11 Dec	Ernie (The Fastest Milkman In The West), Benny Hill (4)

ALBUMS

16 Jan	Bridge Over Troubled Water, Simon & Garfunkel (11, *3 July* for 5, 11 *Sept* for 1; best seller of the year)
3 April	*Home Loving Man, Andy Williams (2)
17 April	*Motown Chartbusters Volume 5, Tamla Motown Compilation (3)
8 May	*Sticky Fingers, Rolling Stones (4, *19 June* for 1)
5 June	*Ram, Paul & Linda McCartney (2)
26 June	Tarkus, Emerson, Lake & Palmer (1)
7 Aug	*Hot Hits 6, Anonymous (1)
14 Aug	Every Good Boy Deserves Favour, Moody Blues (1)
21 Aug	Top Of The Pops Volume 18, Anonymous (3)
18 Sept	Who's Next, Who (1)
25 Sept	Fireball, Deep Purple (1)
2 Oct	Every Picture Tells A Story, Rod Stewart (4, *13 Nov* for 2)
30 Oct	*Imagine, John Lennon & The Plastic Ono Band with The Flux Fiddlers (2)
27 Nov	Top Of The Pops Volume 20, Anonymous (1)
4 Dec	Four Symbols, Led Zeppelin (2)
18 Dec	Electric Warrior, T. Rex (6)

1972

SINGLES

8 Jan	I'd Like To Teach The World To Sing (In Perfect Harmony), New Seekers (4; best seller of the year)
5 Feb	Telegram Sam, T. Rex (2)
19 Feb	Son Of My Father, Chicory Tip (3)
11 March	Without You, Nilsson (5)
15 April	Amazing Grace, Pipes & Drums & Military Band of The Royal Scots Dragoon Guards (Carabiniers & Greys) Bandmaster W.O.I.C.I. Herbert, Pipe Major W.O.I.I.J. Pryde (5)
20 May	Metal Guru, T. Rex (4)
17 June	Vincent, Don McLean (2)
1 July	Take Me Bak 'Ome, Slade (1)
8 July	Puppy Love, Donny Osmond (5)
12 Aug	School's Out, Alice Cooper (3)
2 Sept	You Wear It Well, Rod Stewart (1)
9 Sept	Mama Weer All Crazee Now, Slade (3)
30 Sept	How Can I Be Sure, David Cassidy (2)
14 Oct	Mouldy Old Dough, Lieutenant Pigeon (4)
11 Nov	Clair, Gilvert O'Sullivan (2)
25 Nov	My Ding-A-Ling, Chuck Berry (4)
23 Dec	Long Haired Lover From Liverpool, Little Jimmy Osmond with The Mike Curb Congregation (5)

ALBUMS

29 Jan	Concert For Bangladesh (Recorded Live), George Harrison & Friends (1)
5 Feb	Electric Warrior, T. Rex (2)
19 Feb	Neil Reid, Neil Reid (3)
11 March	Harvest, Neil Young (1)
18 March	Paul Simon, Paul Simon (1)
25 March	Fog On The Tyne, Lindisfarne (4)
22 April	Machine Head, Deep Purple (2, *13 May* for 1)
6 May	Prophets, Seers And Sages The Angels Of The Ages / My People Were Fair And Had Sky In Their Hair But Now They're Content To Wear Stars On Their Brows, Tyrannosaurus Rex (1)
20 May	*Bolan Boogie, T. Rex (3)
10 June	*Exile On Main Street, Rolling Stones (1)
17 June	20 Dynamic Hits, K-Tel Compilation (8; best seller of the year)
12 Aug	20 Fantastic Hits, Arcade Compilation (5)
16 Sept	Never A Dull Moment, Rod Stewart (2)
30 Sept	20 Fantastic Hits, Arcade Compilation (1)

7 Oct	*20 All Time Hits Of The 50's, K-Tel Compilation (8, 23 Dec for 3)
2 Dec	*25 Rockin' And Rollin' Greats, K-Tel Compilation (3; the 100th No. 1 album)

1973

SINGLES

27 Jan	Block Buster!, Sweet (5)
3 March	*Cum On Feel The Noize, Slade (4)
31 March	The Twelfth Of Never, Donny Osmond (1)
7 April	Get Down, Gilbert O'Sullivan (2)
21 April	Tie A Yellow Ribbon Round The Ole Oak Tree, Dawn featuring Tony Orlando (4)
19 May	See My Baby Jive, Wizzard, vocal backing – The Suedettes (4)
16 June	Can The Can, Suzi Quatro (1)
23 June	Rubber Bullets, 10cc (1)
30 June	*Skweeze Me, Pleeze Me, Slade (3)
21 July	Welcome Home, Peters & Lee (1)
28 July	I'm The Leader Of The Gang (I Am), Gary Glitter (4)
25 Aug	Young Love, Donny Osmond (4)
22 Sept	Angel Fingers (A Teen Ballad), Wizzard, vocal backing – The Suedettes & The Bleach Boys (1)
29 Sept	Eye Level (Theme From The Thames T.V. Series "Van Der Valk"), Simon Park Orchestra (4)
27 Oct	Daydreamer/The Puppy Song, David Cassidy (3)
17 Nov	*I Love You Love Me Love, Gary Glitter (4; best seller of the year)
15 Dec	*Merry Xmas Everybody, Slade (5)

ALBUMS

13 Jan	Slayed?, Slade (1, 27 Jan for 2)
20 Jan	Back To Front, Gilbert O'Sullivan (1)
10 Feb	*Don't Shoot Me I'm Only The Piano Player, Elton John (6; best seller of the year)
24 March	*Billion Dollar Babies, Alice Cooper (1)
31 March	*20 Flashback Greats Of The Sixties, K-Tel Compilation (2)
14 April	*Houses Of The Holy, Led Zeppelin (2)
28 April	Ooh-La-La, Faces (1)
5 May	*Aladdin Sane, David Bowie (5)
9 June	Pure Gold, EMI Compilation (3)
30 June	That'll Be The Day, Original Soundtrack (7)
18 Aug	We Can Make It, Peters & Lee (2)
1 Sept	Sing It Again Rod, Rod Stewart (3)
22 Sept	*Goat's Head Soup, Rolling Stones (2)
6 Oct	*Sladest, Slade (3)
27 Oct	Hello, Status Quo (1)
3 Nov	*Pin-Ups, David Bowie (5)
8 Dec	Stranded, Roxy Music (1)
15 Dec	Dreams Are Nuthin' More Than Wishes, David Cassidy (1)
22 Dec	Goodbye Yellow Brick Road, Elton John (2)

1974

SINGLES

19 Jan	You Won't Find Another Fool Like Me, New Seekers featuring Lyn Paul (1; best seller of the year)
26 Jan	Tiger Feet, Mud (4)
23 Feb	Devil Gate Drive, Suzi Quatro (2)
9 March	Jealous Mind, Alvin Stardust (1)
16 March	Billy - Don't Be A Hero, Paper Lace (3)
6 April	Seasons In The Sun, Terry Jacks (4)
4 May	Waterloo, Abba (Bjorn, Benny, Anna & Frida) (2)
18 May	Sugar Baby Love, Rubettes (4)
15 June	The Streak, Ray Stevens (1)
22 June	Always Yours, Gary Glitter (1)
29 June	She, Charles Aznavour (4)
27 July	Rock Your Baby, George McCrae (3)
17 Aug	When Will I See You Again, Three Degrees (2)
31 Aug	Love Me For A Reason, Osmonds (3)
21 Sept	Kung Fu Fighting, Carl Douglas (3)
12 Oct	Annie's Song, John Denver (1)
19 Oct	Sad Sweet Dreamer, Sweet Sensation (1)
26 Oct	Everything I Own, Ken Boothe (3)
16 Nov	Gonna Make You A Star, David Essex (3)
7 Dec	You're The First, The Last, My Everything, Barry White (2)
21 Dec	Lonely This Christmas, Mud (4)

ALBUMS

5 Jan	Tales From Topographic Oceans, Yes (2)
19 Jan	Sladest, Slade (1)
26 Jan	And I Love You So, Perry Como (1)
2 Feb	The Singles 1969-1973, Carpenters (4, 9 March for 11, 1 June for 1, 6 July for 1; best seller of the year)
2 March	Old New Borrowed And Blue, Slade (1)
25 May	Journey To The Centre Of The Earth, Rick Wakeman (1)
8 June	*Diamond Dogs, David Bowie (4)
13 July	*Caribou, Elton John (2)
27 July	Band On The Run, Paul McCartney & Wings (7)
14 Sept	*Hergest Ridge, Mike Oldfield (3)
5 Oct	Tubular Bells, Mike Oldfield (1)
12 Oct	*Rollin', Bay City Rollers (1, 26 Oct for 1, 9 Nov for 2)
19 Oct	*Smiler, Rod Stewart (1, 2 Nov for 1)
23 Nov	*Elton John's Greatest Hits, Elton John (11)

1975

SINGLES

18 Jan	Down Down, Status Quo (1)
25 Jan	M/s Grace, Tymes (1)
1 Feb	January, Pilot (3)
22 Feb	Make Me Smile (Come Up And See Me), Steve Harley & Cockney Rebel (2)
8 March	If, Telly Savalas (2)
22 March	Bye Bye Baby, Bay City Rollers (6)
3 May	Oh Boy, Mud (2)
17 May	Stand By Your Man, Tammy Wynette (3)
7 June	Whispering Grass, Windsor Davis as B.S.M. Williams & Don Estelle as Gunner Sugden (Lofty) (3)
28 June	I'm Not In Love, 10cc (2)
12 July	Tears On My Pillow (I Can't Take It), Johnny Nash (1)
19 July	Give A Little Love, Bay City Rollers (3)
9 Aug	Barbados, Typically Tropical (1)
16 Aug	Can't Give You Anything (But My Love), Stylistics (3)
6 Sept	Sailing, Rod Stewart (4)
4 Oct	Hold Me Close, David Essex (3)
25 Oct	I Only Have Eyes For You, Art Garfunkel (2)
8 Nov	Space Oddity, David Bowie (2)
22 Nov	D.I.V.O.R.C.E., Billy Connolly (1)
29 Nov	Bohemian Rhapsody, Queen (9; best seller of the year)

ALBUMS

8 Feb	Engelbert Humperdinck – His Greatest Hits, Engelbert Humperdinck (3)
1 March	*On The Level, Status Quo (2)
15 March	*Physical Graffiti, Led Zeppelin (1)
22 March	*20 Greatest Hits, Tom Jones (3)
19 April	The Best Of The Stylistics, Stylistics (2, 24 May for 5, 16 Aug for 2; best seller of the year)
3 May	*Once Upon A Star, Bay City Rollers (3)
28 June	Venus And Mars, Wings (1, 19 July for 1)
5 July	Horizon, Carpenters (2, 26 July for 3)
30 Aug	*Atlantic Crossing, Rod Stewart (5, 11 Oct for 2)
4 Oct	Wish You Were Here, Pink Floyd (1)
25 Oct	40 Golden Greats, Jim Reeves (3)
15 Nov	We All Had Doctors' Papers, Max Boyce (1)
22 Nov	40 Greatest Hits, Perry Como (5)
27 Dec	A Night At The Opera, Queen (2)

1976

SINGLES

31 Jan	Mamma Mia, Abba (2)
14 Feb	Forever And Ever, Slik (1)
21 Feb	December, 1963 (Oh, What A Night), Four Seasons (2)
6 March	I Love To Love (But My Baby Loves To Dance), Tina Charles (3)
27 March	Save Your Kisses For Me, Brotherhood Of Man (6; best seller of the year)
8 May	Fernando, Abba (4)
5 June	No Charge, J.J. Barrie (1)
12 June	The Combine Harvester (Brand New Key), Wurzels (2)
26 June	You To Me Are Everything, Real Thing (3)
17 July	Excerpts From The Roussos Phenomenon [EP], Demis Roussos (1)

24 July	Don't Go Breaking My Heart, Elton John & Kiki Dee (6)
4 Sept	Dancing Queen, Abba (6)
16 Oct	Mississippi, Pussycat (4)
13 Nov	If You Leave Me Now, Chicago (3)
4 Dec	Under The Moon Of Love, Showaddywaddy (3)
25 Dec	When A Child Is Born (Soleado), Johnny Mathis (3)

ALBUMS

10 Jan	40 Greatest Hits, Perry Como (1)
17 Jan	A Night At The Opera, Queen (2)
31 Jan	The Best Of Roy Orbison, Roy Orbison (1)
7 Feb	The Very Best Of Slim Whitman, Slim Whitman (6)
20 March	*Blue For You, Status Quo (3)
10 April	*Rock Follies, TV Soundtrack (2, *1 May* for 1)
24 April	*Presence, Led Zeppelin (1)
8 May	Greatest Hits, Abba (9, *16 Oct* for 2; best seller of the year)
10 July	A Night On The Town, Rod Stewart (2)
24 July	*20 Golden Greats, Beach Boys (10)
2 Oct	Best Of The Stylistics Volume 2, Stylistics (1)
9 Oct	Stupidity, Dr. Feelgood (1)
30 Oct	Soul Motion, K-Tel Compilation (2)
13 Nov	The Song Remains The Same, Led Zeppelin (1)
20 Nov	22 Golden Guitar Greats, Bert Weedon (1)
27 Nov	20 Golden Greats, Glen Campbell (6)

1977

SINGLES

15 Jan	Don't Give Up On Us. David Soul (4)
12 Feb	Don't Cry For Me Argentina, Julie Covington (1; the 400th No. 1)
19 Feb	When I Need You, Leo Sayer (3)
12 March	Chanson D'Amour, Manhattan Transfer (3)
2 April	Knowing Me, Knowing You, Abba (5)
7 May	Free, Deniece Williams (2)
21 May	I Don't Want To Talk About It/First Cut Is The Deepest, Rod Stewart (4)
18 June	Lucille, Kenny Rogers (1)
25 June	Show You The Way To Go, Jacksons (1)
2 July	So You Win Again, Hot Chocolate (3)
23 July	I Feel Love, Donna Summer (4)
20 Aug	Angelo, Brotherhood Of Man (1)
27 Aug	Float On, Floaters (1)
3 Sept	Way Down, Elvis Presley (5)
8 Oct	Silver Lady, David Soul (3)
29 Oct	Yes Sir, I Can Boogie, Baccara (1)
5 Nov	The Name Of The Game, Abba (4)
3 Dec	Mull Of Kintyre/Girls' School, Wings (9; best seller of the year)

ALBUMS

8 Jan	A Day At The Races, Queen (1)
15 Jan	Arrival, Abba (1, *16 April* for 9; best seller of the year)
22 Jan	Red River Valley, Slim Whitman (4)
19 Feb	20 Golden Greats, Shadows (4)
2 April	Portrait Of Sinatra, Frank Sinatra (2)
18 June	The Beatles Live At The Hollywood Bowl, Beatles (1)
25 June	The Muppet Show, Muppets (1)
2 July	A Star Is Born [OST], Barbra Streisand (2)
16 July	The Johnny Mathis Collection, Johnny Mathis (4)
13 Aug	Going For The One, Yes (2)
27 Aug	20 All Time Greats, Connie Francis (2)
10 Sept	Elvis Presley's 40 Greatest Hits, Elvis Presley (1)
17 Sept	*20 Golden Greats, Diana Ross & The Supremes (7)
5 Nov	40 Golden Greats, Cliff Richard & The Shadows (1)
12 Nov	*Never Mind The Bollocks Here's The Sex Pistols, Sex Pistols (2)
26 Nov	The Sound Of Bread, Bread (2)
10 Dec	Disco Fever, K-Tel Compilation (6)

1978

SINGLES

4 Feb	Up Town Top Ranking, Althia & Donna (1)
11 Feb	Figaro, Brotherhood Of Man (1)
18 Feb	Take A Chance On Me, Abba (3)
11 March	Wuthering Heights, Kate Bush (4)
8 April	Matchstalk Men And Matchstalk Cats And Dogs (Lowry's Song), Brian & Michael (Burke & Jerk) (3)

29 April	Night Fever, Bee Gees (2)
13 May	Rivers Of Babylon, Boney M (5; best seller of the year)
17 June	You're The One That I Want, John Travolta & Olivia Newton-John (9)
19 Aug	Three Times A Lady, Commodores (5)
23 Sept	Dreadlock Holiday, 10cc (1)
30 Sept	Summer Nights, John Travolta, Olivia Newton-John & Cast (7)
18 Nov	Rat Trap, Boomtown Rats (2)
2 Dec	Do 'Ya' Think I'm Sexy?, Rod Stewart, Rod (1)
9 Dec	Mary's Boy Child/Oh My Lord [M], Boney M (4)

ALBUMS

21 Jan	The Sound Of Bread, Bread (1)
28 Jan	Rumours, Fleetwood Mac (1)
4 Feb	*The Album, Abba (7)
25 March	20 Golden Greats, Buddy Holly & The Crickets (3)
15 April	20 Golden Greats, Nat 'King' Cole (3)
6 May	Saturday Night Fever, Original Soundtrack (18; best seller of the year)
9 Sept	Night Flight To Venus, Boney M (4)
7 Oct	Grease, Original Soundtrack (13)

1979

SINGLES

6 Jan	Y.M.C.A., Village People (3; best seller of the year)
27 Jan	Hit Me With Your Rhythm Stick, Ian & The Blockheads (1)
3 Feb	Heart Of Glass, Blondie (4)
3 March	Tragedy, Bee Gees (2)
17 March	I Will Survive, Gloria Gaynor (4)
14 April	Bright Eyes, Art Garfunkel (6)
26 May	Sunday Girl, Blondie (3)
16 June	Ring My Bell, Anita Ward (2)
30 June	Are 'Friends' Electric?, Tubeway Army (4)
28 July	I Don't Like Mondays, Boomtown Rats (4)
25 Aug	We Don't Talk Anymore, Cliff Richard (4)
22 Sept	Cars, Gary Numan (1)
29 Sept	Message In A Bottle, Police (3)
20 Oct	Video Killed The Radio Star, Buggles (1)
27 Oct	One Day At A Time, Lena Martell (3)
17 Nov	When You're In Love With A Beautiful Woman, Dr. Hook (3)
8 Dec	Walking On The Moon, Police (1)
15 Dec	Another Brick In The Wall Part II, Pink Floyd (5)

ALBUMS

6 Jan	Greatest Hits, Showaddywaddy (2)
20 Jan	Don't Walk – Boogie, EMI Compilation (3)
10 Feb	Action Replay, K-Tel Compilation (1)
17 Feb	Parallel Lines, Blondie (4; best seller of the year)
17 March	Spirits Having Flown, Bee Gees (2)
31 March	Barbra Streisand's Greatest Hits Volume 2, Barbra Streisand (4)
28 April	The Very Best Of Leo Sayer, Leo Sayer (3)
19 May	*Voulez-Vous, Abba (4)
16 June	*Discovery, Electric Light Orchestra (5)
21 July	Replicas, Tubeway Army (1)
28 July	The Best Disco Album In The World, WEA Compilation (6)
8 Sept	*In Through The Out Door, Led Zeppelin (2)
22 Sept	*The Pleasure Principle, Gary Numan (1, *6 Oct* for 1)
29 Sept	*Oceans Of Fantasy, Boney M (1)
13 Oct	*Eat To The Beat, Blondie (1)
13 Oct	*Reggatta De Blanc, Police, The (4; the 200th No. 1.)
	[Two album charts were published for the week of 13 Oct.]
10 Nov	Tusk, Fleetwood Mac (1)
17 Nov	Greatest Hits Volume 2, Abba (3)
8 Dec	Rod Stewart – Greatest Hits Vol. 1, Rod Stewart (5)

1980

SINGLES

19 Jan	Brass In Pocket, Pretenders (2)
2 Feb	The Special A.K.A. Live! [EP], Specials featuring Rico (2)
16 Feb	Coward Of The County, Kenny Rogers (2)
1 March	Atomic, Blondie (2)
15 March	Together We Are Beautiful, Fern Kinney (1)
22 March	*Going Underground/The Dreams Of Children, Jam (3)
12 April	Working My Way Back To You, Detroit Spinners, The (2)

26 April   Call Me, Blondie (1)
3 May   Geno, Dexy's Midnight Runners (2)
17 May   What's Another Year, Johnny Logan (2)
31 May   Theme From M*A*S*H*(Suicide Is Painless), Mash (3)
21 June   Crying, Don McLean (1)
12 July   Xanadu, Olivia Newton-John/Electric Light Orchestra (2)
26 July   Use It Up And Wear It Out, Odyssey (2)
9 Aug   The Winner Takes It All, Abba (2)
23 Aug   Ashes To Ashes, David Bowie (2)
6 Sept   Start, Jam (1)
13 Sept   Feels Like I'm In Love, Kelly Marie (2)
27 Sept   *Don't Stand So Close To Me, Police (4; best seller of the year)
25 Oct   Woman In Love, Barbra Streisand (3)
15 Nov   The Tide Is High, Blondie (2)
29 Nov   Super Trouper, Abba (3)
20 Dec   (Just Like) Starting Over, John Lennon (1)
27 Dec   There's No One Quite Like Grandma, St. Winifred's School Choir (2)

ALBUMS

12 Jan   Greatest Hits Volume 2, Abba (1)
19 Jan   *Pretenders, Pretenders (4)
16 Feb   The Last Dance, Motown Compilation (2)
1 March   String Of Hits, Shadows (3)
22 March   Tears And Laughter, Johnny Mathis (2)
5 April   *Duke, Genesis (2)
19 April   Greatest Hits, Rose Royce (2)
3 May   Sky 2, Sky (2)
17 May   The Magic Of Boney M, Boney M (2)
31 May   *McCartney II, Paul McCartney (2)
14 June   Peter Gabriel, Peter Gabriel (2)
28 June   Flesh And Blood, Roxy Music (1, 23 Aug for 3)
5 July   *Emotional Rescue, Rolling Stones (2)
19 July   The Game, Queen (2)
2 Aug   Deepest Purple, Deep Purple (1)
9 Aug   *Back In Black, AC/DC (2)
13 Sept   *Telekon, Gary Numan (1)
20 Sept   *Never For Ever, Kate Bush (1)
27 Sept   *Scary Monsters And Super Creeps, David Bowie (2)
11 Oct   *Zenyatta Mondatta, Police (4)
8 Nov   Guilty, Barbra Streisand (2)
22 Nov   *Super Trouper, Abba (9; best seller of the year)

1981
SINGLES

10 Jan   Imagine, John Lennon (4)
7 Feb   Woman, John Lennon (2)
21 Feb   Shaddap You Face, Joe Dolce Music Theatre (3)
14 March   Jealous Guy, Roxy Music (2)
28 March   This Ole House, Shakin' Stevens (3)
18 April   Making Your Mind Up, Bucks Fizz (3)
9 May   *Stand And Deliver, Adam & The Ants (5)
13 June   Being With You, Smokey Robinson (2)
27 June   One Day In Your Life, Michael Jackson (2)
11 July   Ghost Town, Specials (3)
1 Aug   Green Door, Stevens, Shakin' (4)
29 Aug   Japanese Boy, Aneka (1)
5 Sept   Tainted Love, Soft Cell (2)
19 Sept   Prince Charming, Adam & The Ants (4)
17 Oct   It's My Party, Dave Stewart with Barbara Gaskin (4)
14 Nov   Every Little Thing She Does Is Magic, Police (1)
21 Nov   Under Pressure, Queen & David Bowie (2)
5 Dec   Begin The Beguine (Volver A Empezar), Julio Iglesias (1)
12 Dec   Don't You Want Me, Human League 100 (5; best seller of the year)

ALBUMS

24 Jan   Kings Of The Wild Frontier, Adam & The Ants (2, 14 March for 10; best seller of the year)
7 Feb   Double Fantasy, John Lennon & Yoko Ono (2)
21 Feb   *Face Value, Phil Collins (3)
23 May   Stars On 45, Star Sound (5)
27 June   *No Sleep Till Hammersmith, Motorhead (1)
4 July   Disco Daze And Disco Nites, Ronco Compilation (1)
11 July   Love Songs, Cliff Richard (5)
15 Aug   The Official BBC Album Of The Royal Wedding, Royalty (2)
29 Aug   Time, Electric Light Orchestra (2)

12 Sept   *Dead Ringer, Meat Loaf (2)
26 Sept   *Abacab, Genesis (2)
10 Oct   *Ghost In The Machine, Police (2)
31 Oct   Dare, Human League (1)
7 Nov   Shaky, Shakin' Stevens (1)
14 Nov   Qeen's Greatest Hits, Queen (4)
12 Dec   Chart Hits '81, K-Tel Compilation (1)
19 Dec   *The Visitors, Abba (3)

1982
SINGLES

16 Jan   The Land Of Make Believe, Bucks Fizz (2)
30 Jan   Oh Julie, Shakin' Stevens (1)
6 Feb   The Model/Computer Love, Kraftwerk (1)
13 Feb   *Town Called Malice/Precious, Jam (3)
6 March   The Lion Sleeps Tonight, Tight Fit (3)
27 March   Seven Tears, Goombay Dance Band (3)
17 April   My Camera Never Lies, Bucks Fizz (1)
24 April   Ebony And Ivory, Paul McCartney with additional vocals by Stevie Wonder (3)
15 May   A Little Peace, Nicole (2; the 500th No. 1)
29 May   House Of Fun, Madness (2)
12 June   Goody Two Shoes, Adam Ant (2)
26 June   I've Never Been To Me, Charlene (1)
3 July   Happy Talk, Captain Sensible (2)
17 July   Fame, Irene Cara (3)
7 Aug   Come On Eileen, Dexys Midnight Runners & The Emerald Express (4; best seller of the year)
4 Sept   Eye Of The Tiger, Survivor (4)
2 Oct   Pass The Dutchie, Musical Youth (3)
23 Oct   Do You Really Want To Hurt Me, Culture Club (3)
13 Nov   I Don't Wanna Dance, Eddy Grant (3)
4 Dec   *Beat Surrender, Jam (2)
18 Dec   Save Your Love, Renee & Renato (4)

ALBUMS

9 Jan   Dare, Human League (3)
30 Jan   Love Songs, Barbra Streisand (7, 27 March for 2; best seller of the year)
20 March   *The Gift, Jam (1)
10 April   *The Number Of The Beast, Iron Maiden (2)
24 April   *1982, Status Quo (1)
1 May   *Barry Live In Britain, Barry Manilow (1)
8 May   *Tug Of War, Paul McCartney (2)
22 May   Complete Madness, Madness (2, 12 June for 1)
5 June   *Avalon, Roxy Music (1, 19 June for 2)
3 July   *The Lexicon Of Love, ABC (4)
24 July   Fame, Original Soundtrack (1)
            For 24 July, above two were joint at No. 1.
7 Aug   The Kids From Fame, Kids From "Fame" (8, 30 Oct for 4)
2 Oct   *Love Over Gold, Dire Straits (4)
27 Nov   The Singles – The First Ten Years, Abba (1)
4 Dec   The John Lennon Collection, John Lennon (6)

1983
SINGLES

15 Jan   You Can't Hurry Love, Phil Collins (2)
29 Jan   Down Under, Men At Work (3)
19 Feb   Too Shy, Kajagoogoo (2)
5 March   Billie Jean, Michael Jackson (1)
12 March   Total Eclipse Of The Heart, Bonnie Tyler (2)
26 March   *Is There Something I Should Know?, Duran Duran (2)
9 April   Let's Dance, David Bowie (3)
30 April   True, Spandau Ballet (4)
28 May   Candy Girl, New Edition (1)
4 June   Every Breath You Take, Police (4)
2 July   Baby Jane, Rod Stewart (3)
23 July   Wherever I Lay My Hat (That's My Home), Paul Young (3)
13 Aug   Give It Up, KC & The Sunshine Band (3)
3 Sept   Red Red Wine, UB40 (3)
24 Sept   Karma Chameleon, Culture Club (6; best seller of the year)
5 Nov   Uptown Girl, Billy Joel (5)
10 Dec   Only You, Flying Pickets (5)

ALBUMS

15 Jan   Raiders Of The Pop Charts, Ronco Compilation (2)
29 Jan   Business As Usual, Men At Work (5)

5 March	Thriller, Michael Jackson (1, 19 March for 1, 21 May for 5; best seller of the year)
12 March	*War, U2 (1)
26 March	The Hurting, Tears For Fears (1)
2 April	*The Final Cut, Pink Floyd (2)
16 April	*Faster Than The Speed Of Night, Bonnie Tyler (1)
23 April	*Let's Dance, David Bowie (3)
14 May	True, Spandau Ballet (1)
25 June	*Synchronicity, Police (2)
9 July	*Fantastic!, Wham! (2)
23 July	You And Me Both, Yazoo (2)
6 Aug	The Very Best Of The Beach Boys, Beach Boys (2, 10 Sept for 1)
20 Aug	18 Greatest Hits, Michael Jackson plus the Jackson Five (3)
17 Sept	No Parlez, Paul Young (1, 1 Oct for 2, 10 Dec for 1)
24 Sept	*Labour Of Love, UB40 (1)
15 Oct	*Genesis, Genesis (1)
22 Oct	*Colour By Numbers, Culture Club (3, 19 Nov for 2)
12 Nov	Can't Slow Down, Lionel Richie (1)
3 Dec	*Seven And The Ragged Tiger, Duran Duran (1)
17 Dec	Now, That's What I Call Music, Compilation Series (4)

1984

SINGLES

14 Jan	Pipes Of Peace, Paul McCartney (2)
28 Jan	Relax, Frankie Goes To Hollywood (5)
3 March	99 Red Balloons, Nena (3)
24 March	Hello, Lionel Richie (6)
5 May	The Reflex, Duran Duran (4)
2 June	Wake Me Up Before You Go Go, Wham! (2)
16 June	*Two Tribes, Frankie Goes To Hollywood (9)
18 Aug	Careless Whisper, George Michael (3)
8 Sept	I Just Called To Say I Love You, Stevie Wonder (6)
20 Oct	Freedom, Wham! (3)
10 Nov	I Feel For You, Chaka Khan (3)
1 Dec	I Should Have Known Better, Jim Diamond (1)
8 Dec	The Power Of Love, Frankie Goes To Hollywood (1)
15 Dec	*Do They Know It's Christmas?, Band Aid (5; best seller of the year)

ALBUMS

14 Jan	No Parlez, Paul Young (1)
21 Jan	Now, That's What I Call Music, Compilation Series (1)
28 Jan	Thriller, Michael Jackson (1)
4 Feb	Touch, Eurythmics (2)
18 Feb	*Sparkle In The Rain, Simple Minds (1)
25 Feb	*Into The Gap, Thompson Twins (3)
17 March	*Human's Lib, Howard Jones (2)
31 March	Can't Slow Down, Lionel Richie (2; best seller of the year)
14 April	Now, That's What I Call Music II, Compilation Series (5)
19 May	*Legend – The Best Of Bob Marley & The Wailers, Bob Marley & The Wailers (12)
11 Aug	*Now, That's What I Call Music III, Compilations Series (8)
6 Oct	*Tonight, David Bowie (1)
13 Oct	*The Unforgettable Fire, U2 (2)
27 Oct	*Steeltown, Big Country (1)
3 Nov	*Give My Regards To Broad Street [OST], Paul McCartney (1)
10 Nov	*Welcome To The Pleasuredome, Frankie Goes To Hollywood (1)
17 Nov	*Make It Big, Wham! (2)
1 Dec	*The Hits Album/The Hits Tape – 32 Original Hits, Compilation Series (7)

1985

SINGLES

19 Jan	I Want To Know What Love Is, Foreigner (3)
9 Feb	I Know Him So Well, Elaine Paige & Barbara Dickson (4)
9 March	You Spin Me Round (Like A Record), Dead Or Alive (2)
23 March	Easy Lover, Philip Bailey (duet with Phil Collins) (4)
20 April	We Are The World, USA For Africa (2)
4 May	Move Closer, Phyllis Nelson (1)
11 May	19, Paul Hardcastle (5)
15 June	You'll Never Walk Alone, Crowd (2)
29 June	Frankie, Sister Sledge (4)

27 July	There Must Be An Angel (Playing With My Heart), Eurythmics (1)
3 Aug	Into The Groove, Madonna (4)
31 Aug	I Got You Babe, UB40 Guest vocals by Chrissie Hynde (1)
7 Sept	*Dancing In The Street, David Bowie & Mick Jagger (4)
5 Oct	If I Was, Midge Ure (1)
12 Oct	The Power Of Love, Jennifer Rush (5; best seller of the year)
16 Nov	A Good Heart, Feargal Sharkey (2)
30 Nov	I'm Your Man, Wham! (2)
14 Dec	Saving All My Love For You, Whitney Houston (2)
28 Dec	Merry Christmas Everyone, Shakin' Stevens (2)

ALBUMS

19 Jan	Alf, Alison Moyet (1)
26 Jan	Agent Provocateur, Foreigner (3)
16 Feb	Born In The U.S.A., Bruce Springsteen (1, 6 July for 4)
23 Feb	*Meat Is Murder, Smiths (1)
2 March	*No Jacket Required, Phil Collins (5)
6 April	*The Secret Of Association, Paul Young (1)
13 April	*The Hits Album 2/The Hits Tape 2, Compilation Series (6)
25 May	*Brothers In Arms, Dire Straits (2, 3 Aug for 2; best seller of the year)
8 June	*Our Favourite Shop, Style Council (1)
15 June	*Boys And Girls, Bryan Ferry (2; the 300th No. 1)
29 June	*Misplaced Childhood, Marillion (1)
17 Aug	*Now, That's What I Call Music 5, Compilation Series (5)
21 Sept	Like A Virgin, Madonna (1, 12 Oct for 1)
28 Sept	*Hounds Of Love, Kate Bush (2, 19 Oct for 1)
26 Oct	The Love Songs, George Benson (1, 9 Nov for 1)
2 Nov	*Once Upon A Time, Simple Minds (1)
16 Nov	*Promise, Sade (2)
30 Nov	The Greatest Hits Of 1985, Compilation Series (1)
7 Dec	*Now, That's What I Call Music 6, Compilation Series (2)
21 Dec	Now – The Christmas Album, Compilation Series (2)

1986

SINGLES

11 Jan	West End Girls, Pet Shop Boys (2)
25 Jan	The Sun Always Shines On T.V., A-Ha (2)
8 Feb	When The Going Gets Tough, The Tough Get Going, Billy Ocean (4)
8 March	Chain Reaction, Diana Ross (3)
29 March	Living Doll, Comic Relief present Cliff Richard & The Young Ones featuring Hank Marvin (3)
19 April	A Different Corner, Michael, George (3)
10 May	Rock Me Amadeus, Falco (1)
17 May	The Chicken Song, Spitting Image (3)
7 June	Spirit In The Sky, Doctor & The Medics (3)
28 June	The Edge Of Heaven, Wham! (2)
12 July	Papa Don't Preach, Madonna (3)
2 Aug	The Lady In Red, Chris De Burgh (3)
23 Aug	I Wanna Wake Up With You, Boris Gardiner (3)
13 Sept	Don't Leave Me This Way, Communards with Sarah Jane Morris (4)
11 Oct	True Blue, Madonna (1)
18 Oct	Every Loser Wins, Nick Berry (3; best seller of the year)
8 Nov	Take My Breath Away (Love Theme From "Top Gun"), Berlin (4)
6 Dec	The Final Countdown, Europe (2)
20 Dec	Caravan Of Love, Housemartins (1)
27 Dec	Reet Petite (The Sweetest Girl In Town), Jackie Wilson (4)

ALBUMS

4 Jan	Now, That's What I Call Music 6, Compilation Series (2)
18 Jan	Brothers In Arms, Dire Straits (10)
29 March	*Hits 4, Compilation Series (4)
26 April	*Street Life – 20 Great Hits, Bryan Ferry & Roxy Music (5)
31 May	*So, Peter Gabriel (1)
14 June	*A Kind Of Magic, Queen (1)
21 June	*Invisible Touch, Genesis (3)
12 July	*True Blue, Madonna (6; best seller of the year)
23 Aug	*Now, That's What I Call Music 7, Compilation Series (5)
27 Sept	Silk And Steel, Five Star (1)
4 Oct	Graceland, Paul Simon (5)
8 Nov	*Every Breath You Take – The Singles, Police (2)
22 Nov	*Hits 5, Compilation Series (2)
6 Dec	*Now, That's What I Call Music 8, Compilation Series (6)

1987

SINGLES

24 Jan	Jack Your Body, Steve 'Silk' Hurley (2)
7 Feb	I Knew You Were Waiting (For Me), Aretha Franklin & George Michael (2)
21 Feb	Stand By Me, Ben E. King (3)
14 March	Everything I Own, Boy George (2)
28 March	Respectable, Mel & Kim (1)
4 April	*Let It Be, Ferry Aid (3)
25 April	La Isla Bonita, Madonna (2)
9 May	Nothing's Gonna Stop Us Now, Starship (4)
6 June	I Wanna Dance With Somebody (Who Loves Me), Whitney Houston (2)
20 June	Star Trekkin', Firm (2)
4 July	It's A Sin, Pet Shop Boys (3)
25 July	Who's That Girl, Madonna (1)
1 Aug	La Bamba, Los Lobos (2)
15 Aug	I Just Can't Stop Loving You, Michael Jackson with Siedah Garrett (2)
29 Aug	Never Gonna Give You Up, Rick Astley (5; best seller of the year)
3 Oct	Pump Up The Volume/Anitina (The First Time I See She Dance), M/A/R/R/S (2)
17 Oct	You Win Again, Bee Gees (4)
14 Nov	China In Your Hand, T'Pau (5; the 600th No. 1)
19 Dec	Always On My Mind, Pet Shop Boys (4)

ALBUMS

17 Jan	The Whole Story, Kate Bush (2)
31 Jan	Graceland, Paul Simon (3)
21 Feb	*The Phantom Of The Opera, London Stage Cast (3)
14 March	The Very Best Of Hot Chocolate, Hot Chocolate (1)
21 March	*The Joshua Tree, U2 (2)
4 April	*Now, That's What I Call Music 9, Compilation Series (5)
9 May	*Keep Your Distance, Curiosity Killed The Cat (2)
23 May	*It's Better To Travel, Swing Out Sister (2)
6 June	*Live In The City Of Light, Simple Minds (1)
13 June	*Whitney, Whitney Houston (6)
25 July	*Introducing The Hardline According To Terence Trent D'Arby, Terence Trent D'Arby (1)
1 Aug	Hits 6, Compilation Series (4, 5 Sept for 1)
29 Aug	*Hysteria, Def Leppard (1)
12 Sept	*Bad, Michael Jackson (5; best seller of the year)
17 Oct	*Tunnel Of Love, Bruce Springsteen (1)
24 Oct	*Nothing Like The Sun, Sting (1)
31 Oct	Tango In The Night, Fleetwood Mac (2)
14 Nov	*Faith, George Michael (1)
21 Nov	Bridge Of Spies, T'Pau (1)
28 Nov	*Whenever You Need Somebody, Rick Astley (1)
5 Dec	*Now That's What I Call Music 10, Compilation Series (6)

1988

SINGLES

16 Jan	Heaven Is A Place On Earth, Belinda Carlisle (2)
30 Jan	I Think We're Alone Now, Tiffany (3)
20 Feb	I Should Be So Lucky, Kylie Minogue (5)
26 March	Don't Turn Around, Aswad (1)
9 April	Heart, Pet Shop Boys (3)
30 April	Theme From S-Express, S-Express (2)
14 May	Perfect, Fairground Attraction (1)
21 May	With A Little Help From My Friends/She's Leaving Home, Wet Wet Wet/ Billy Bragg with Cara Tivey (4)
18 June	Doctorin' The Tardis, Timelords (1)
25 June	I Owe You Nothing, Bros (2)
9 July	Nothing's Gonna Change My Love For You, Glenn Medeiros (4)
6 Aug	The Only Way Is Up, Yazz & The Plastic Population (5)
10 Sept	A Groovy Kind Of Love, Phil Collins (2)
24 Sept	He Ain't Heavy, He's My Brother, Hollies (2)
8 Oct	Desire, U2 (1)
15 Oct	One Moment In Time, Whitney Houston (2)
29 Oct	Orinoco Flow (Sail Away), Enya (3)
19 Nov	The First Time, Robin Beck (3)
10 Dec	Mistletoe And Wine, Cliff Richard (4; best seller of the year)

ALBUMS

16 Jan	Popped In Souled Out, Wet Wet Wet (1)
23 Jan	*Turn Back The Clock, Johnny Hates Jazz (1)

30 Jan	Introducing The Hardline According To Terence Trent D'Arby, Terence Trent D'Arby (8)
26 March	*Viva Hate, Morrissey (1)
2 April	*Now That's What I Call Music 11, Compilation Series (3)
23 April	*Seventh Son Of A Seventh Son, Iron Maiden (1)
30 April	*The Innocents, Erasure (1)
7 May	Tango In The Night, Fleetwood Mac (2, 28 May for 1)
21 May	*Lovesexy, Prince (1)
4 June	Nite Flite, CBS Compilation (1)
2 July	Tracy Chapman, Tracy Chapman (3)
23 July	*Now That's What I Call Music 12, Compilation Series (5)
27 Aug	Kylie – The Album, Kylie Minogue (4, 19 Nov for 2; best seller of the year)
24 Sept	Hot City Nights, Vertigo Compilation (1)
1 Oct	*New Jersey, Bon Jovi (2)
15 Oct	*Flying Colours, Chris De Burgh (1)
22 Oct	*Rattle And Hum, U2 (1)
29 Oct	*Money For Nothing, Dire Straits (3)
3 Dec	*Now That's What I Call Music 13, Compilation Series (3)
24 Dec	Private Collection 1979–1988, Cliff Richard (2)

1989

SINGLES

7 Jan	Especially For You, Kylie Minogue & Jason DoNovan (3)
28 Jan	Something's Gotten Hold Of My Heart, Marc Almond featuring special guest star Gene Pitney (4)
25 Feb	Belfast Child, Simple Minds (2)
11 March	Too Many Broken Hearts, Jason DoNovan (2)
25 March	Like A Prayer, Madonna (3)
15 April	Eternal Flame, Bangles (4)
13 May	Hand On Your Heart, Kylie Minogue (1)
20 May	*Ferry 'Cross The Mersey, Christians, Holly Johnson, Paul McCartney, Gerry Marsden & Stock Atken Waterman (3)
10 June	*Sealed With A Kiss, Jason DoNovan (2)
24 June	Back To Life (However Do You Want Me), Soul II Soul featuring Caron Wheeler (4)
22 July	You'll Never Stop Me Loving You, Sonia (2)
5 Aug	Swing The Mood, Jive Bunny & The Mastermixers (5)
9 Sept	Ride On Time, Black Box (6; best seller of the year)
21 Oct	That's What I Like, Jive Bunny & The Mastermixers (3)
11 Nov	All Around The World, Lisa Stansfield (2)
25 Nov	You Got It (The Right Stuff), New Kids On The Block (3)
16 Dec	*Let's Party, Jive Bunny & The Mastermixers (1)
23 Dec	*Do They Know It's Christmas?, Band Aid II (3)

ALBUMS

7 Jan	Now That's What I Call Music 13, Compilation Series (1)
	[From 14 Jan, 1989, the compilation chart was instituted, eliminating all various artist albums from the main chart.]
14 Jan	The Innocents, Erasure (1)
21 Jan	The Legendary Roy Orbison, Roy Orbison (3)
11 Feb	*Technique, New Order (1)
18 Feb	*The Raw And The Cooked, Fine Young Cannibals (1)
25 Feb	*A New Flame, Simply Red (4, 29 April for 1, 22 July for 2)
25 March	Anything For You, Gloria Estefan & Miami Sound Machine (1)
1 April	*Like A Prayer, Madonna (2)
15 April	*When The World Knows Your Name, Deacon Blue (2)
6 May	*Blast!, Holly Johnson (1)
13 May	*Street Fighting Years, Simple Minds (1)
20 May	Ten Good Reasons, Jason Donovan (2, 10 June for 2; best seller of the year)
3 June	*The Miracle, Queen (1)
24 June	Flowers In The Dirt, Paul McCartney (1)
1 July	*Batman [OST], Prince (1)
8 July	*Velveteen, Tranvision Vamp (1)
15 July	Club Classics Volume One, Soul II Soul (1)
5 Aug	*Cuts Both Ways, Gloria Estefan (6)
16 Sept	*Aspects Of Love, London Stage Cast (1)
23 Sept	*We Too Are One, Eurythmics (1)
30 Sept	*Foreign Affair, Tina Turner (2)
7 Oct	*The Seeds Of Love, Tears For Fears (1)
14 Oct	*Crossroads, Tracy Chapman (1)
21 Oct	*Enjoy Yourself, Kylie Minogue (1)
28 Oct	Wild!, Erasure (2)
11 Nov	*The Road To Hell, Chris Rea (3)
2 Dec	*. . . But Seriously, Phil Collins (8)

1990

SINGLES

13 Jan	Hangin' Tough, New Kids On The Block (2)
27 Jan	Tears On My Pillow, Kylie Minogue (1)
3 Feb	Nothing Compares 2 U, Sinead O'Connor (4)
3 March	Dub Be Good To Me, Beats International featuring Lindy (4)
31 March	The Power, Snap! (2)
14 April	Vogue, Madonna (4)
12 May	Killer, Adamski (4)
9 June	World In Motion . . ., Englandneworder (2)
23 June	Sacrifice/Healing Hands, Elton John (5)
28 July	Turtle Power, Partners In Kryme (4)
25 Aug	Itsy Bitsy Teeny Weeny Yellow Polka Dot Bikini, Bombalurina (3)
15 Sept	The Joker, Steve Miller Band (2)
29 Sept	Show Me Heaven, Maria McKee (4)
27 Oct	A Little Time, Beautiful South (1)
3 Nov	Unchained Melody, Righteous Brothers (4; best seller of the year)
1 Dec	Ice Ice Baby, Vanilla Ice (4)
29 Dec	Saviours Day, Cliff Richard (1)

ALBUMS

27 Jan	*Colour, Christians (1)
3 Feb	. . . But Seriously, Phil Collins (7; best seller of the year)
24 March	*I Do Not Want What I Haven't Got, Sinead O'Connor (1)
31 March	Changesbowie, David Bowie (1)
7 April	Only Yesterday – Richard & Karen Carpenter's Greatest Hits, Carpenters (2; 28 April for 5)
21 April	*Behind The Mask, Fleetwood Mac (1)
2 June	*Volume II (1990 A New Decade), Soul II Soul (3)
23 June	The Essential Pavarotti, Luciano Pavarotti (1, 7 July for 3)
30 June	*Step By Step, New Kids On The Block (1)
28 July	Sleeping With The Past, Elton John (5)
1 Sept	*Grafitti Bridge, Prince (1)
8 Sept	In Concert, Carreras Domingo Pavarotti Orchestra del Maggio Musical Fiorentino Orchestra del Teatro dell'opera di Roma Zubin Mehta (1, 22 Sept for 4)
15 Sept	*Listen Without Prejudice Volume 1, George Michael (1)
20 Oct	*Some Friendly, Charlatans (1)
27 Oct	*The Rhythm Of The Saints, Paul Simon (2)
10 Nov	*The Very Best Of Elton John, Elton John (2; the 400th No. 1)
24 Nov	*The Immaculate Collection, Madonna (9)

1991

SINGLES

5 Jan	*Bring Your Daughter . . . To The Slaughter, Iron Maiden (2)
19 Jan	Sadness Part 1, Enigma (1)
26 Jan	*Innuendo, Queen (1)
2 Feb	3 A.M. Eternal (Live At The S.S.I.), KLF featuring the Children of the Revolution (2)
16 Feb	Do The Bartman, Simpsons (3)
9 March	Should I Stay Or Should I Go, Clash (2)
23 March	The Stonk, Hale and Pace & The Stonkers (1)
30 March	The One And Only, Chesney Hawkes (5)
4 May	The Shoop Shoop Song (It's In His Kiss), Cher (5)
8 June	I Wanna Sex You Up, Color Me Badd (3)
29 June	Any Dream Will Do, Jason Donovan (2)
13 July	(Everything I Do) I Do It For You, Bryan Adams (16; best seller of the year)
2 Nov	*The Fly, U2 (1)
9 Nov	Dizzy, Vic Reeves & The Wonder Stuff (2)
23 Nov	*Black Or White, Micael Jackson (2)
7 Dec	*Don't Let The Sun Go Down On Me, George Michael with Elton John (2)
21 Dec	*Bohemian Rhapsody/These Are The Days Of Our Lives, Queen (5)

ALBUMS

26 Jan	MCMCX A.D., Enigma (1)
2 Feb	*The Soul Cages, Sting (1)
9 Feb	*Doubt, Jesus Jones (1)
16 Feb	*Innuendo, Queen (2)
2 March	Circle Of One Adems, Oleta (1)
9 March	*Auberge, Chris Rea (1)
16 March	*Spartacus, Farm (1)
23 March	*Out Of Time, R.E.M. (1)

30 March	*Greatest Hits, Eurythmics (9, 22 June for 1)
1 June	*Seal, Seal (3)
29 June	*Love Hurts, Cher (6)
10 Aug	Essential Pavarotti II, Luciano Pavarotti (2)
24 Aug	*Metallica, Metallica (1)
31 Aug	*Joseph And The Amazing Technicolor Dreamcoat, London Stage Cast (2)
14 Sept	*From Time To Time – The Singles Collection, Paul Young (1)
21 Sept	*On Every Street, Dire Straits (1)
28 Sept	*Use Your Illusion II, Guns N' Roses (1)
5 Oct	*Waking Up The Neighbours, Bryan Adams (1)
12 Oct	*Stars, Simply Red (2, 2 Nov for 1; best seller of the year)
26 Oct	*Chorus, Erasure (1)
9 Nov	*Greatest Hits II, Queen (1, 7 Dec for 4)
16 Nov	*Shepherd Moons, Enya (1)
23 Nov	*We Can't Dance, Genesis (1)
30 Nov	*Dangerous, Michael Jackson (1)

1992

SINGLES

25 Jan	Goodnight Girl, Wet Wet Wet (4)
22 Feb	Stay, Shakespears Sister (8)
18 April	Deeply Dippy, Right Said Fred (3)
9 May	Please Don't Go/Game Boy, K.W.S. (5)
13 June	*Abba-Esque [EP], Erasure (5)
18 July	Ain't No Doubt, Jimmy Nail (3)
8 Aug	Rhythm Is A Dancer, Snap! (6)
19 Sept	Ebeneezer Goode, Shamen (4)
17 Oct	Sleeping Satellite, Tasmin Archer (2)
31 Oct	End Of The Road, Boyz II Men (3)
21 Nov	Would I Lie To You, Charles & Eddie (2)
5 Dec	I Will Always Love You, Whitney Houston (10; best seller of the year)

ALBUMS

4 Jan	Stars, Simply Red (5, 22 Feb for 3, 9 May for 1; best seller of the year)
8 Feb	*High On The Happy Side, Wet Wet Wet (2)
14 March	Divine Madness, Madness (3)
4 April	*Human Touch, Bruce Springsteen (1)
11 April	*Adrenalize, Def Leppard (1)
18 April	*Diva, Annie Lennox (1)
25 April	Up, Right Said Fred (1)
2 May	*Wish, Cure (1)
16 May	*1992 – The Love Album, Carter – The Unstoppable Sex Machine (1)
23 May	*Fear Of The Dark, Iron Maiden (1)
30 May	*Michael Ball, Michael Ball (1)
6 June	*Back To Front, Lionel Richie (6)
18 July	*U.F. Orb, Orb (1)
25 July	The Greatest Hits 1966–1992, Neil Diamond (3)
15 Aug	*Welcome To Wherever You Are, INXS (1)
22 Aug	We Can't Dance, Genesis (1)
29 Aug	*Best . . . I, Smiths (1)
5 Sept	*Kylie Greatest Hits, Kylie Minogue (1)
12 Sept	*Tubular Bells II, Mike Oldfield (2)
26 Sept	The Best Of Belinda Volume 1, Belinda Carlisle (1)
3 Oct	*Gold – Greatest Hits, Abba (1)
10 Oct	*Automatic For The People, R.E.M. (1)
17 Oct	*Symbol, Prince & The New Power Generation (1)
24 Oct	*Glittering Prize 81/92, Simple Minds (3)
14 Nov	*Keep The Faith, Bon Jovi (1)
21 Nov	*Cher's Greatest Hits: 1965–1992, Cher (1, 12 Dec for 6)
28 Nov	*Pop! – The First 20 Hits, Erasure (2)

1993

SINGLES

13 Feb	No Limit, 2 Unlimited (5)
20 March	Oh Carolina, Shaggy (2)
3 April	Young At Heart, Bluebells (4)
1 May	*Five Live [EP], George Michael & Queen with Lisa Stansfield (3)
22 May	All That She Wants, Ace Of Base (3)
12 June	(I Can't Help) Falling In Love With You, UB40 (2)
26 June	Dreams, Gabrielle (3)
17 July	*Pray, Take That (4)

14 Aug	Living On My Own, Freddie Mercury (2)
28 Aug	Mr. Vain, Culture Beat (4)
25 Sept	Boom! Shake The Room, Jazzy Jeff & The Fresh Prince (2)
9 Oct	*Relight My Fire, Take That featuring Lulu (2)
23 Oct	I'd Do Anything For Love (But I Won't Do That), Meat Loaf (7; best seller of the year)
11 Dec	Mr Blobby, Mr Blobby (1, 25 Dec for 2)
18 Dec	*Babe, Take That (1)

ALBUMS

23 Jan	*Live – The Way We Walk Volume 2: The Longs, Genesis (2)
6 Feb	*Jam, Little Angels (1)
13 Feb	*Pure, Cult (1)
20 Feb	*Words Of Love, Buddy Holly & The Crickets (1)
27 Feb	*Walthamstow, East 17 (1)
6 March	Diva, Annie Lennox (1)
13 March	*Are You Gonna Go My Way, Lenny Kravitz (2)
27 March	Their Greatest Hits, Hot Chocolate (1)
3 April	*Songs Of Faith And Devotion, Depeche Mode (1)
10 April	*Suede, Suede (1)
17 April	*Black Tie White Noise, David Bowie (1)
24 April	Automatic For The People, R.E.M. (1, 8 May for 1, 22 May for 1)
1 May	*Cliff Richard – The Album, Cliff Richard (1)
15 May	*Republic, New Order (1)
29 May	*Janet, Janet Jackson (2)
12 June	No Limits, Two Unlimited (1)
19 June	*What's Love Got To Do With It [OST], Tina Turner (1)
26 June	*Emergency On Planet Earth, Jamiroquai (3)
17 July	*Zooropa, U2 (1)
24 July	*Promises And Lies, UB40 (7)
11 Sept	*Music Box, Mariah Carey (1)
18 Sept	*Bat Out Of Hell II – Back Into Hell, Meat Loaf (1, 2 Oct for 1, 16 Oct for 1, 30 Oct for 3, 27 Nov for 5; best seller of the year)
25 Sept	*In Utero, Nirvana (1)
9 Oct	*Very, Pet Shop Boys (1)
23 Oct	*Everything Changes, Take That (1)
20 Nov	*Both Sides, Phil Collinsl (1)

1994

SINGLES

8 Jan	Twist And Shout, Chaka Demus & Pliers with Jack Radics & Taxi Gang (2; the 700th No. 1)
22 Jan	Things Can Only Get Better, D:Ream (4)
19 Feb	*Without You, Mariah Carey (4)
19 March	Doop, Doop (3)
9 April	*Everything Changes, Take That (2)
23 April	The Most Beautiful Girl In The World, Symbol (2)
7 May	The Real Thing, Tony Di Bart (1)
14 May	Inside, Stiltskin (1)
21 May	Come On You Reds, Manchester United Football Squad (2)
4 June	Love Is All Around, Wet Wet Wet (15; best seller of the year)
17 Sept	*Saturday Night, Whigfield (4)
15 Oct	*Sure, Take That (2)
29 Oct	Baby Come Back, Pato Banton featuring Ali & Robin Campbell of UB40 (4)
26 Nov	Let Me Be Your Fantasy, Baby D (2)
10 Dec	Stay Another Day, East 17 (5)

ALBUMS

1 Jan	One Woman - The Ultimate Collection, Diana Ross (1, 22 Jan for 1)
8 Jan	Everything Changes, Take That (1)
15 Jan	So Far So Good, Bryan Adams (1)
29 Jan	Tease Me, Chaka Demus & Pliers (2)
12 Feb	*Under The Pink, Tori Amos (1)
19 Feb	*The Cross Of Changes, Enigma (1)
26 Feb	Music Box, Mariah Carey (4, 2 April for 1)
26 March	*Vauxhall And I, Morrissey (1)
9 April	*The Division Bell, Pink Floyd (4)
7 May	*Parklife, Blur (1)
14 May	Our Town - The Greatest Hits Of Deacon Blue, Deacon Blue (2)
28 May	*I Say I Say I Say, Erasure (1)
4 June	*Seal, Seal (2)

18 June	*Real Things, Two Unlimited (1)
25 June	Everybody Else Is Doing It, So Why Can't We?, Cranberries (1)
2 July	*Happy Nation, Ace Of Base (2)
16 July	*Music For The Jilted Generation, Prodigy (1)
23 July	*Voodoo Lounge, Rolling Stones (1)
30 July	End Of Part One (Their Greatest Hits), Wet Wet Wet (4, 3 Sept for 1)
27 Aug	*Come, Prince (1)
10 Sept	*Definitely Maybe, Oasis (1)
17 Sept	The Three Tenors In Concert 1994, Carreras Domingo Pavarotti with Orchestra conducted by Zubin Mehta (1)
24 Sept	*From The Cradle, Eric Clapton (1)
1 Oct	*Songs, Luther Vandross (1)
8 Oct	*Monster, R.E.M. (2)
22 Oct	*Cross Road - The Best Of Bon Jovi, Bon Jovi (3, 19 Nov for 2; best seller of the year)
12 Nov	*Unplugged In New York, Nirvana (1)
3 Dec	Carry On Up The Charts - The Best Of The Beautiful South, Beautiful South (1, 17 Dec for 6; the 500th No. 1)
10 Dec	*Live At The BBC, Beatles (1)

1995

SINGLES

14 Jan	Cotton Eye Joe, Rednex (3)
4 Feb	Think Twice, Celine Dion (7)
25 March	Love Can Build A Bridge, Cher, Chrissie Hynde & Neneh Cherry with Eric Clapton (1)
1 April	Don't Stop (Wiggle Wiggle), Outhere Brothers (1)
8 April	*Back For Good, Take That (4)
6 May	*Some Might Say, Oasis (1)
13 May	*Dreamer, Livin' Joy (1)
20 May	*Unchained Melody/(There'll Be Bluebirds Over) The White Cliffs Of Dover, Robson Green & Jerome Flynn (7; best seller of the year)
8 July	Boom Boom Boom, Outhere Brothers (4)
5 Aug	*Never Forget, Take That (3)
26 Aug	*Country House, Blur's (2)
9 Sept	You Are Not Alone, Michael Jackson (2)
23 Sept	*Boombastic, Shaggy (1)
30 Sept	*Fairground, Simply Red (4)
28 Oct	*Gangsta's Paradise, Coolio featuring L.V. (2)
11 Nov	*I Believe/Up On The Roof, Robson & Jerome (4)
9 Dec	*Earth Song, Michael Jackson (6)

ALBUMS

28 Jan	The Colour Of My Love, Celine Dion (6, 1 April for 1)
11 March	*Greatest Hits, Bruce Springsteen (1, 15 April for 1)
18 March	*Medusa, Annie Lennox (1)
25 March	*Elastica, Elastica (1)
8 April	*Wake Up!, Boo Radleys (1)
22 April	*Picture This, Wet Wet Wet (3)
13 May	*Nobody Else, Take That (2)
27 May	*Stanley Road, Paul Weller (1)
3 June	*Singles, Alison Moyet (1)
10 June	*Pulse, Pink Floyd (2)
24 June	*History - Past, Present And Future, Book 1, Michael Jackson (1)
1 July	*These Days, Bon Jovi (4)
29 July	I Should Coco, Supergrass (3)
19 Aug	*It's Great When You're Straight . . . Yeah, Black Grape (2)
2 Sept	*Said And Done, Boyzone (1)
9 Sept	*The Charlatans, Charlatans (1)
16 Sept	Zeitgeist, Levellers (1)
23 Sept	*The Great Escape, Blur (2)
7 Oct	*Daydream, Mariah Carey (1)
14 Oct	*(What's The Story) Morning Glory?, Oasis (1)
21 Oct	*Life, Simply Red (3)
11 Nov	*Different Class, Pulp (3)
18 Nov	*Made In Heaven, Queen (1)
25 Nov	*Robson & Jerome, Robson & Jerome (7; best seller of the year)

1996

SINGLES

20 Jan	*Jesus To A Child, George Michael (1)
27 Jan	*Spaceman, Babylon Zoo (5)

2 March	*Don't Look Back In Anger, Oasis (1)
9 March	*How Deep Is Your Love, Take That (3)
30 March	*Firestarter, Prodigy (2)
20 April	Return Of The Mack, Mark Morrison (2)
4 May	*Fastlove, George Michael (3)
25 May	Ooh Aah . . . Just A Little Bit, Gina G (1)
1 June	*Three Lions (The Official Song Of The England Football Team), Baddiel & Skinner & Lightning Seeds (1, 6 July for 1)
8 June	*Killing Me Softly, Fugees (Refugee Camp) (4, 13 July for 1; best seller of the year)
20 July	*Forever Love, Gary Barlow (1)
27 July	Wannabe, Spice Girls (7)
14 Sept	*Flava, Peter Andre (1)
21 Sept	Ready Or Not, Fugees (Refugee Camp) (2)
5 Oct	Breakfast At Tiffany's, Deep Blue Something (1)
12 Oct	*Setting Sun, Chemical Brothers (1)
19 Oct	*Words, Boyzone (1)
26 Oct	*Say You'll Be There, Spice Girls (2)
9 Nov	*What Becomes Of The Broken Hearted / Saturday Night At The Movies/ You'll Never Walk Alone, Robson & Jerome (1)
23 Nov	*Breathe, Prodigy (2)
7 Dec	*I Feel You, Peter Andre (1)
‹ 14 Dec	*A Different Beat, Boyzone (1)
21 Dec	*Knockin' On Heaven's Door/Throw These Guns Away, Dunblane (1)
28 Dec	*2 Become 1, Spice Girls (3)

ALBUMS

13 Jan	(What's The Story) Morning Glory?, Oasis (6, 2 March for 3)
24 Feb	*Expecting To Fly, Bluetones (1)
23 March	*Falling Into You, Celine Dion (1)
30 March	*Anthology 2, Beatles (1)
6 April	*Greatest Hits, Take That (4)
4 May	Jagged Little Pill, Alanis Morissette (2, 29 June for 1, 20 July for 8; best seller of the year)
18 May	*1977, Ash (1)
25 May	*Older, George Michael (3)
15 June	*Load, Metallica (1)
22 June	*18 Til I Die, Bryan Adams (1)
6 July	*Recurring Dream – The Very Best Of Crowded House, Crowded House (2)
14 Sept	*Coming Up, Suede (1)
21 Sept	*New Adventures In Hi-Fi, R.E.M. (1)
28 Sept	*K, Kula Shaker (1)
12 Oct	*Natural, Peter Andre (1)
19 Oct	*Greatest Hits, Simply Red (2)
2 Nov	*Blue Is The Colour, Beautiful South (1)
9 Nov	*A Different Beat, Boyzone (1)
16 Nov	*Spice, Spice Girls (1, 7 Dec for 8)
23 Nov	*Take Two, Robson & Jerome (2)

1997

SINGLES

18 Jan	Professional Widow (It's Got To Be Big), Tori Amos (1)
25 Jan	*Your Woman, White Town (1)
1 Feb	*Beetlebum, Blur (1)
8 Feb	*Ain't Nobody, LL Cool J (1)
15 Feb	*Discotheque, U2 (1)
22 Feb	*Don't Speak, No Doubt (3)
15 March	*Mama / Who Do You Think You Are, Spice Girls (3)
5 April	*Block Rockin' Beats, Chemical Brothers (1)
12 April	I Believe I Can Fly, R. Kelly (3)
3 May	*Blood On The Dance Floor, Michael Jackson (1)
10 May	*Love Won't Wait, Gary Barlow (1)
17 May	*You're Not Alone, Olive (1)
31 May	*I Wanna Be The Only One, Eternal featuring Bebe Winans (1)
7 June	*Mmmbop, Hanson (3)
28 June	*I'll Be Missing You, Puff Daddy & Faith Evans (featuring 112) (3, 26 July for 3)
19 July	*D'you Know What I Mean?, Oasis (1)
16 Aug	*Men In Black, Will Smith (4)
13 Sept	*The Drugs Don't Work, Verve (1)
20 Sept	*Something About The Way You Look Tonight/Candle In The Wind 1997, John, Elton (5; best seller of the year)
25 Oct	*Spice Up Your Life, Spice Girls (1)
1 Nov	Barbie Girl, Aqua (4)

29 Nov	*Perfect Day, Various Artists (2)
13 Dec	*Teletubbies Say "Eh-Oh!", Teletubbies (2)
27 Dec	*Too Much, Spice Girls (2)

ALBUMS

1 Feb	Evita [OST], Madonna & Various Artists (1)
8 Feb	*Glow, Reef (1)
15 Feb	*White On Blonde, Texas (1, 23 Aug for 1)
22 Feb	*Blur, Blur (1)
1 March	*Attack Of The Grey Lantern, Mansun (1)
8 March	Spice, Spice Girls (1, 22 March for 4, 17 May for 1)
15 March	*Pop, U2 (1)
19 April	*Dig Your Own Hole, Chemical Brothers (1)
26 April	*Ultra, Depeche Mode (1)
3 May	*Tellin' Stories, Charlatans (2)
24 May	*Blood On The Dance Floor – History In The Mix, Michael Jackson (2)
7 June	*Open Road, Gary Barlow (1)
14 June	*Wu-Tang Forever, Wu-Tang Clan (1)
21 June	*Middle Of Nowhere, Hanson (1)
28 June	*OK Computer, Radiohead (2)
12 July	*The Fat Of The Land, Prodigy (6)
30 Aug	*Be Here Now, Oasis (4, 4 Oct for (1; best seller of the year)
27 Sept	*Marchin' Already, Ocean Colour Scene (1)
11 Oct	*Urban Hymns, Verve (5)
15 Nov	*Spiceworld, Spice Girls (2, 13 Dec for 1)
29 Nov	*Let's Talk About Love, Celine Dion (2, 20 Dec for 2)

1998

SINGLES

10 Jan	Perfect Day, Various Artists (1)
17 Jan	Never Ever, All Saints (1)
24 Jan	*All Around The World, Oasis (1)
31 Jan	*You Make Me Wanna . . ., Usher (1)
7 Feb	*Doctor Jones, Aqua (2)
21 Feb	*My Heart Will Go On, Dion, Celine (1, 14 March for 1)
28 Feb	*Brimful Of Asha, Cornershop (1)
7 March	*Frozen, Madonna (1)
21 March	*It's Like That, Run-DMC vs Jason Nevins (6)
2 May	*All That I Need, Boyzone (1)
9 May	*Under The Bridge / Lady Marmalade, All Saints (1, 23 May for 1)
16 May	*Turn Back Time, Aqua (1)
30 May	Feel It, Tamperer featuring Maya (1)
6 June	*C'est La Vie, B*Witched (2)
20 June	*3 Lions '98, Baddiel & Skinner & The Lightning Seeds (3)
11 July	*Because We Want To, Billie (1)
18 July	*Freak Me, Another Level (1)
25 July	*Deeper Underground, Jamiriquai (1)
1 Aug	*Viva Forever, Spice Girls (2)
15 Aug	*No Matter What, Boyzone (3)
5 Sept	*If You Tolerate This Your Children Will Be Next, Manic Street Preachers (1)
12 Sept	*Bootie Call, All Saints (1; the 800th No. 1)
19 Sept	*Millennium, Robbie Williams (1)
26 Sept	*I Want You Back, Melanie B Featuring Missy "Misdemeanor" Elliott (1)
3 Oct	*Rollercoaster, B*Witched (2)
17 Oct	*Girlfriend, Billie (1)
24 Oct	*Gym And Tonic, Spacedust (1)
31 Oct	*Believe, Cher (7; best seller of the year)
19 Dec	*To You I Belong, B*Witched (1)
26 Dec	*Goodbye, Spice Girls (1)

ALBUMS

3 Jan	Urban Hymns, Verve (6, 21 Feb for 1)
14 Feb	Titanic [OST], Music composed and conducted by James Horner (1, 28 Feb for 2)
14 March	*Ray Of Light, Madonna (2)
28 March	Let's Talk About Love, Celine Dion (1)
4 April	*The Best Of James, James (1)
11 April	*This Is Hardcore, Pulp (1)
18 April	Life Thru A Lens, Robbie Williams (2)
2 May	*Mezzanine, Massive Attack (2)
16 May	International Velvet, Catatonia (1)
23 May	*Version 2.0, Garbage (1)
30 May	*Blue, Simply Red (1, 13 June for 1)
6 June	*Where We Belong, Boyzone (1, 5 Sept for 2)

20 June	*The Good Will Out, Embrace (1)
27 June	Talk On Corners, Corrs (1, 11 July for 1, 15 Aug for 3, 19 Sept for 1; best seller of the year)
4 July	Five, Five (1)
18 July	*Hello Nasty, Beastie Boys (1)
25 July	*Jane McDonald, Jane McDonald (3)
26 Sept	*This Is My Truth Tell Me Yours, Manic Street Preachers (3)
17 Oct	*Hits, Phil Collins (1)
24 Oct	*Quench, Beautiful South (2)
7 Nov	*I've Been Expecting You, Robbie Williams (1)
14 Nov	*The Best Of 1980–1990 & B-Sides, U2 (1)
21 Nov	*Ladies & Gentlemen – The Best Of George Michael, George Michael (8)

1999

SINGLES

2 Jan	Chocolate Salty Balls (P.S. I Love), Chef (1)
9 Jan	Heartbeat/Tragedy, Steps (1)
16 Jan	*Praise You, Fatboy Slim (1)
23 Jan	*A Little Bit More, 911 (1)
30 Jan	*Pretty Fly (For A White Guy), Offspring (1)
6 Feb	*You Don't Know Me, Armand Van Helden featuring Duane Harden (1)
13 Feb	*Maria, Blondie (1)
20 Feb	*Fly Away, Lenny Kravitz (1)
27 Feb	*. . . Baby One More Time Spears, Britney (2; best seller of the year)
13 March	*When The Going Gets Tough, Boyzone (2)
27 March	*Blame It On The Weatherman, B*Witched (1)
3 April	*Flat Beat, Mr. Oizo (2)
17 April	*Perfect Moment, Martine McCutcheon (2)
1 May	*Swear It Again, Westlife (2)
15 May	*I Want It That Way, Backstreet Boys (1)
22 May	*You Needed Me, Boyzone (1)
29 May	*Sweet Like Chocolate, Shanks & Bigfoot (1)
12 June	*Everybody's Free (To Wear Sunscreen) The Sunscreen Song (Class Of '99), Baz Luhrmann Presents (1)

19 June	*Bring It All Back, S Club 7 (1)
26 June	*Boom, Boom, Boom, Boom!!, Vengaboys (1)
3 July	*9PM (Till I Come), ATB (2)
17 July	*Livin' La Vida Loca, Ricky Martin (3)
7 Aug	*When You Say Nothing At All, Ronan Keating (2)
21 Aug	*If I Let You Go, Westlife (1)
28 Aug	*Mi Chico Latino, Geri Halliwell (1)
4 Sept	*Mambo No. 5 (A Little Bit Of . . .), Lou Bega (2)
18 Sept	*We're Going To Ibiza! Vengaboys (1)
25 Sept	*Blue [Da Ba Dee], Eiffel 65 (3)
16 Oct	*Genie In A Bottle, Christina Aguilera (2)
30 Oct	*Flying Without Wings, Westlife (1)
6 Nov	*Keep On Movin', Five (1)
13 Nov	*Lift Me Up, Geri Halliwell (1)
20 Nov	*She's The One / It's Only Us, Robbie Williams (1)
27 Nov	*King Of My Castle, Wamdue Project (1)
4 Dec	The Millennium Prayer, Cliff Richard (3)
25 Dec	*I Have A Dream/Seasons In The Sun, Westlife (2)

ALBUMS

16 Jan	I've Been Expecting You, Robbie Williams (1, 20 Feb for 1)
23 Jan	You've Come A Long Way, Baby, Fatboy Slim (4)
27 Feb	Talk On Corners, Corrs (3, 10 April for 1)
20 March	*Peformance And Cocktails, Stereophonics (1)
27 March	*13, Blur (2)
17 April	Gold – Greatest Hits, Abba (1, 1 May for 2, 29 May for 2)
24 April	*Equally Cursed And Blessed, Catatonia (1)
15 May	*Head Music, Suede (1)
22 May	*Hush, Texas (1)
12 June	*By Request, Boyzone (2, 10 July for 7)
26 June	*Synkronized, Jamiroquai (1)
3 July	*Surrender, Chemical Brothers (1)
28 Aug	The Man Who, Travis (2)
11 Sept	Come On Over, Shania Twain (3, 16 Oct for 3, 11 Dec for 4; best seller of the year)
2 Oct	*Rhythm And Stealth, Leftfield (1)
9 Oct	*Reload, Tom Jones (1)
6 Nov	*Steptacular, Steps (3, 4 Dec for 1)
27 Nov	*All The Way . . . A Decade Of Songs, Celine Dion (1; the 600th No. 1)

VARIOUS ARTISTS

This section lists all entries which do not constitute an entry under a respective individual artist. This includes compilations, soundtracks and cast recordings. From 14 Jan 89 a Top 20 Compilation chart was established, removing all albums with tracks by more than one artist form the main chart. Totals have been segregated between the two charts.

ANONYMOUS

Album Chart entries in this section during 1971 were all budget releases. They only charted between 7 Aug 71 through to 1 Jan 72 when the Budget chart was combined with the Full Price album chart.

Aral

EPS:	HITS 4			WEEKS 12
TOP TEN RECORD	Aral	15	27 Apr 63	6
TOP TEN RECORD	Aral	16	23 Nov 63	3
TOP TEN RECORD	Aral	17	15 Feb 64	2
The above 3 albums are different.				
TOP TEN RECORD CLUB	Aral	17	21 Mar 64	1

Hallmark

ALBUMS:	HITS 4			WEEKS 32
TOP OF THE POPS VOLUME 18	Hallmark	1	7 Aug 71	12
TOP OF THE POPS VOLUME 17	Hallmark	16	7 Aug 71	3
TOP OF THE POPS VOLUME 19	Hallmark	3	2 Oct 71	9
TOP OF THE POPS VOLUME 20	Hallmark	1	13 Nov 71	8

K-Tel

ALBUMS:	HITS 1			WEEKS 7
40 SINGALONG PUB SONGS	K-Tel	21	27 Sep 75	7

Music For Pleasure

ALBUMS:	HITS 8			WEEKS 30
HOT HITS 6	Music For Pleasure	1	7 Aug 71	7
MILLION SELLER HITS	Music For Pleasure	46	7 Aug 71	2
HOT HITS 5	Music For Pleasure	48	7 Aug 71	1
SMASH HIT SUPREMES STYLE	Music For Pleasure	36	21 Aug 71	3
HOT HITS 7	Music For Pleasure	3	23 Oct 71	9
SMASH HITS COUNTRY STYLE	Music For Pleasure	38	6 Nov 71	1
SMASH HITS '71	Music For Pleasure	21	4 Dec 71	3
HOT HITS 8	Music For Pleasure	2	11 Dec 71	4

Plexium

ALBUMS:	HITS 1			WEEKS 2
NON STOP 20 VOLUME 4	Plexium	35	27 Nov 71	2

Ronco

ALBUMS:	HITS 1			WEEKS 6
FORTY MANIA	Ronco	21	6 Nov 76	6

Top Six

EPS:	HITS 3			WEEKS 10
TOP SIX	Top Six	10	22 Feb 64	4
TOP SIX VOLUME 2	Top Six	10	21 Mar 64	4
TOP SIX VOLUME 3	Top Six	16	11 Apr 64	2
ALBUMS:	HITS 1			WEEKS 2
BEATLEMANIA	Top Six	19	29 Feb 64	2

CHRISTMAS

ALBUMS:	HITS 6			WEEKS 18
A CHRISTMAS GIFT	Ronco	39	13 Dec 75	5
THE CHRISTMAS CAROL COLLECTION	Fame	75	8 Dec 84	3
MERRY CHRISTMAS TO YOU	Warner Brothers	64	22 Dec 84	2
CHRISTMAS AT THE COUNTRY STORE	Country Store/Starblend	94	21 Dec 85	1
SPECIAL OLYMPICS - A VERY SPECIAL CHRISTMAS	A&M	40	5 Dec 87	5
NOEL - CHRISTMAS SONGS AND CAROLS	Trax	89	17 Dec 88	2
COMPILATION ALBUMS:	HITS 8			WEEKS 56
SPECIAL OLYMPICS - A VERY SPECIAL CHRISTMAS	A&M	19	23 Dec 89	1
Benefit album with proceeds to the Special Olympics charity.				
IT'S CHRISTMAS	EMI	3	9 Dec 89	5

IT'S CHRISTMAS [RE]	*EMI*	2	*8 Dec 90*	11
CHRISTMAS GREATEST HITS	*Legends In*	16	*22 Dec 90*	1
A CLASSIC CHRISTMAS	*EMI*	14	*30 Nov 91*	7
CHRISTMAS LOVE SONGS	*Arcade*	11	*14 Dec 91*	6
IT'S CHRISTMAS TIME	*EMI*	3	*21 Nov 92*	15
THAT'S CHRISTMAS	*EMI*	10	*10 Dec 94*	4
THAT'S CHRISTMAS [RI]	*EMI TV*	15	*16 Dec 95*	2
Re-released.				
THE CHRISTMAS ALBUM	*warner.esp/Global TV/Sony TV*	13	*12 Dec 98*	4

COMPILATIONS

From 18 Aug 73, the BPI had requested that TV advertised Compilations were to be removed from the main Full Price chart and placed in the Mid-Price chart. As such, entries in the latter are not listed. They did not appear in the main chart again until 1 Nov 75.

A&M

COMPILATION ALBUMS:		HITS 4		WEEKS 31
SLAMMIN'	*A&M*	1	*29 Sep 90*	6
RAGE – MAKE SOME NOISE VOLUME 1	*A&M*	12	*20 Apr 91*	3
WINGS OF LOVE	*A&M*	1	*29 Jun 91*	21
THE HACIENDA COLLECTION – PLAY BY 01/96	*A&M*	18	*4 Nov 95*	1

Abstract

ALBUMS:		HITS 1		WEEKS 8
PUNK AND DISORDERLY	*Abstract*	48	*27 Mar 82*	8

Ace Of Hearts

ALBUMS:		HITS 1		WEEKS 1
OUT CAME THE BLUES	*Ace Of Hearts*	19	*16 May 64*	1

Acid Jazz

COMPILATION ALBUMS:		HITS 1		WEEKS 1
BEST OF ACID JAZZ VOLUME 2	*Acid Jazz*	16	*29 May 93*	1

Alternative Tentacles

COMPILATION ALBUMS:		HITS 1		WEEKS 1
VIRUS 100 – ALTERNATIVE TENTACLES	*Alternative Tentacles*	15	*9 May 92*	1

Anagram

ALBUMS:		HITS 1		WEEKS 2
PUNK AND DISORDERLY (FURTHER CHARGES)	*Anagram*	91	*4 Sep 82*	2

Arcade

ALBUMS:		HITS 8		WEEKS 85
20 FANTASTIC HITS	*Arcade*	1	*29 Jul 72*	24
20 FANTASTIC HITS VOLUME 2	*Arcade*	2	*25 Nov 72*	14
40 FANTASTIC HITS FROM THE 50'S AND 60'S	*Arcade*	2	*7 Apr 73*	15
20 FANTASTIC HITS VOLUME 3	*Arcade*	3	*26 May 73*	8
DISCO HITS '75	*Arcade*	5	*15 Nov 75*	11
ROCK ON	*Arcade*	16	*26 Mar 77*	10
RULE BRITANNIA	*Arcade*	56	*2 Jul 77*	1
FIRST LOVE	*Arcade*	58	*23 Feb 80*	2
COMPILATION ALBUMS:		**HITS 14**		**WEEKS 73**
POP CLASSICS – 28 CLASSIC TRACKS	*Arcade*	19	*12 Jan 91*	1
SOFT METAL BALLADS	*Arcade*	5	*30 Mar 91*	10
IT STARTED WITH A KISS	*Arcade*	9	*8 Jun 91*	8
THE HEAT IS ON!	*Arcade*	4	*13 Jul 91*	9
DANCE CLASSICS VOLUME 2	*Arcade*	7	*31 Aug 91*	5
DANCE CLASSICS VOLUME 1	*Arcade*	8	*31 Aug 91*	4
GROOVY GHETTO	*Arcade*	1	*21 Sep 91*	6
GROOVY GHETTO – ALL THE RAGE	*Arcade*	15	*2 Nov 91*	2
GROOVY GHETTO 2	*Arcade*	8	*29 Feb 92*	4
THE ESSENTIAL CHILL	*Arcade*	16	*4 Apr 92*	2
ONE LOVE – THE VERY BEST OF REGGAE	*Arcade*	7	*18 Jul 92*	6
ROCK ROMANCE – 18 MOMENTS OF PURE LOVE	*Arcade*	9	*13 Feb 93*	5
WOW! – LET THE MUSIC LIFT YOU UP	*Arcade*	13	*7 May 94*	3
COMMITTED TO SOUL	*Arcade*	11	*13 Aug 94*	7

Ariola

ALBUMS:		HITS 1		WEEKS 5
BROTHERS IN RHYTHM	*Ariola*	35	*8 Oct 88*	5

Arista

ALBUMS:		HITS 1		WEEKS 1
MODS MAYDAY 79	*Arista*	75	*3 Nov 79*	1

Atlantic

ALBUMS:	HITS 9			WEEKS 107
SOLID GOLD SOUL	Atlantic	12	2 Apr 66	27
MIDNIGHT SOUL	Atlantic	22	5 Nov 66	19
THIS IS SOUL	Atlantic	16	14 Jun 69	15
THE NEW AGE OF ATLANTIC	Atlantic	25	25 Mar 72	1
ATLANTIC BLACK GOLD	Atlantic	23	22 Jun 74	7
BY INVITATION ONLY	Atlantic	17	3 Apr 76	6
THIS IS SOUL	Atlantic/ Starblend	78	2 Feb 85	7
ATLANTIC SOUL CLASSICS – 16 HITS	Atlantic	9	6 Jun 87	23
ATLANTIC SOUL BALLADS	Atlantic	84	18 Jun 88	2

Beechwood Music

COMPILATION ALBUMS:	HITS 11			WEEKS 19
THE BEST OF INDIE TOP 20	Beechwood Music	10	11 May 91	3
THIS IS . . . SWING	Beechwood Music	20	9 Mar 96	1
THIS IS . . . HOUSE	Beechwood Music	18	13 Jul 96	1
THIS IS . . . CLUB NATION	Beechwood Music	19	12 Jul 97	1
THIS IS . . . IBIZA	Beechwood Music	13	11 Oct 97	3
THIS IS . . . SPEED GARAGE	Beechwood Music	10	31 Jan 98	3
THIS IS . . . CLUB NATION 2	Beechwood Music	19	21 Mar 98	1
THIS IS . . . IBIZA 98	Beechwood Music	16	26 Sep 98	2
THIS IS . . . R&B	Beechwood Music	14	30 Jan 99	2
THIS IS . . . IBIZA 2000	Beechwood Music	17	5 Jun 99	1
THIS IS . . . TRANCE	Beechwood Music	19	17 Jul 99	1

Beggars Banquet

ALBUMS:	HITS 3			WEEKS 8
SLIP STREAM (BEST BRITISH JAZZ FUNK)	Beggars Banquet	72	21 Nov 81	3
SEX, SWEAT AND BLOOD	Beggars Banquet	88	15 May 82	1
THE BEST OF BRITISH JAZZ FUNK VOLUME TWO	Beggars Banquet	44	11 Sep 82	4

Beyond

COMPILATION ALBUMS:	HITS 1			WEEKS 1
AMBIENT DUB VOLUME 2 – EARTH JUICE	Beyond	20	6 Mar 93	1

Big Beat

ALBUMS:	HITS 1			WEEKS 3
ROCKABILLY PSYCHOS AND THE GARAGE DISEASE	Big Beat	88	21 Jul 84	3

Break Down

COMPILATION ALBUMS:	HITS 2			WEEKS 6
DRUM AND BASS SELECTION 2	Break Down	14	17 Sep 94	3
MAX POWER – MAX BASS	Break Down	13	13 Jul 96	3

Breakout

ALBUMS:	HITS 1			WEEKS 2
HOUSE HALLUCINATIONS (PUMP UP LONDON VOLUME 1)	Breakout	90	3 Sep 88	2

Business

COMPILATION ALBUMS:	HITS 1			WEEKS 1
LOVERS FOR LOVERS VOLUME 3	Business	18	16 Jun 90	1

Cactus

ALBUMS:	HITS 1			WEEKS 1
REGGAE CHARTBUSTERS 75	Cactus	53	31 Jan 76	1

Capitol

COMPILATION ALBUMS:	HITS 1			WEEKS 2
CAPITOL CLASSICS VOLUME 1	Capitol	16	18 Feb 89	2

Castle Communications

COMPILATION ALBUMS:	HITS 7			WEEKS 41
THE ULTIMATE 60'S COLLECTION	Castle Communications	4	7 Jul 90	11
THE ULTIMATE BLUES COLLECTION	Castle Communications	14	12 Jan 91	6
JAZZ ON A SUMMER'S DAY	Castle Classics	4	8 Aug 92	8
BLOCKBUSTER! – THE SENSATIONAL 70'S	Castle Communications	6	10 Oct 92	6
ONE ORIGINAL STEP BEYOND - STORY . . .	Castle Communications	7	5 Jun 93	5
MONSTER HITS OF DANCE	Castle Communications	13	3 Jul 93	3
GOING UNDERGROUND	Castle Communications	18	30 Oct 93	2

CBS

ALBUMS:	HITS 15			WEEKS 258
THRILL TO THE SENSATIONAL SOUNDS OF SUPER STEREO	CBS	20	20 May 67	30
ROCK MACHINE I LOVE YOU	CBS	15	28 Jun 69	5
THE ROCK MACHINE TURNS YOU ON	CBS	18	28 Jun 69	7
THE MUSIC PEOPLE	CBS	10	20 May 72	9
SATIN CITY	CBS	10	21 Oct 78	11

THIS IS IT	CBS	6	2 Jun 79	12
FIRST LADIES OF COUNTRY	CBS	37	19 Apr 80	6
KILLER WATTS	CBS	27	21 Jun 80	6
BITTER SUITE	CBS	55	4 Apr 81	3
REFLECTIONS	CBS	4	16 Oct 82	92
IMAGINATIONS	CBS	15	22 Oct 83	21
CLUB CLASSICS VOLUME 2	CBS	90	20 Apr 85	2
MOVE CLOSER	CBS	4	14 Mar 87	19
THE HOLIDAY ALBUM	CBS	13	27 Jun 87	9
NITE FLITE	CBS	1	30 Apr 88	26
COMPILATION ALBUMS:	**HITS 4**			**WEEKS 75**
CHEEK TO CHEEK	CBS	2	4 Mar 89	32
NITE FLITE 2	CBS	1	13 May 89	26
LAMBADA	CBS	15	30 Dec 89	6
NITE FLITE 3 – BEING WITH YOU	CBS	3	9 Jun 90	11

Champagne

ALBUMS:	**HITS 1**			**WEEKS 5**
RE-MIXTURE	Champagne	32	4 Apr 81	5

Champion

ALBUMS:	**HITS 3**			**WEEKS 6**
ULTIMATE TRAX – VOLUME 1	Champion	66	8 Nov 86	2
ULTIMATE TRAX – VOLUME 2 – BATTLE OF THE D.J.'S	Champion	50	7 Mar 87	2
ULTIMATE TRAX 3 – BATTLE OF THE DJ'S	Champion	69	18 Jul 87	2

Charm

COMPILATION ALBUMS:	**HITS 8**			**WEEKS 16**
PURE LOVERS VOLUME 1	Charm	14	21 Apr 90	4
PURE LOVERS VOLUME 2	Charm	12	22 Sep 90	3
PURE LOVERS VOLUME 3	Charm	16	6 Apr 91	2
PURE LOVERS VOLUME 4	Charm	19	2 Nov 91	1
JUST RAGGA	Charm	17	25 Jul 92	1
PURE LOVERS VOLUME 5	Charm	13	29 Aug 92	3
JUST RAGGA VOLUME III	Charm	19	27 Feb 93	1
PURE LOVERS VOLUME 6	Charm	17	1 May 93	1

Chrysalis

COMPILATION ALBUMS:	**HITS 1**			**WEEKS 3**
RED, HOT AND BLUE	Chrysalis	6	3 Nov 90	3

Benefit album with proceeds to AIDS research. Tracks recorded are also a tribute to Carl Porter.

Club

ALBUMS:	**HITS 1**			**WEEKS 2**
COME WITH CLUB (CLUB TRACKS VOLUME 2)	Club	55	3 Sep 83	2

Columbia

COMPILATION ALBUMS:	**HITS 37**			**WEEKS 278**
THINKING OF YOU . . .	Columbia	1	2 Feb 91	23
THE FISH AND THE TREE AND THE BIRD AND THE BELL	Columbia	9	2 Feb 91	3
EVERYBODY DANCE NOW	Columbia	12	30 Mar 91	3
FREE SPIRIT – 17 CLASSIC ROCK BALLADS	Columbia	4	20 Apr 91	23
YOU'RE THE INSPIRATION – 16 ROMATIC LOVE SONGS	Columbia	10	20 Apr 91	5
SIMPLY. LOVE	Columbia	3	10 Aug 91	10
THE SOUND OF THE SUBURBS	Columbia	1	17 Aug 91	25
THE SOUND OF THE CITY	Columbia	11	29 Feb 92	5
HARD FAX	Columbia	3	27 Jun 92	6
THE BOYS ARE BACK IN TOWN	Columbia	11	4 Jul 92	6
SOMETHING IN THE AIR	Columbia	10	3 Oct 92	5
THE ULTIMATE COUNTRY COLLECTION	Columbia	1	31 Oct 92	23
HARD FAX 2 – TWICE THE VICE!	Columbia	6	21 Nov 92	2
ORIGINALS	Columbia	1	29 May 93	23
AFTER DARK	Columbia	8	21 Aug 93	4
TRUE LOVE WAYS	Columbia	14	15 Jan 94	2
SECRET LOVERS	Columbia	8	12 Feb 94	4
ORIGINALS 2	Columbia	4	19 Mar 94	10
SOUL SEARCHING	Columbia	6	23 Jul 94	5
MUNDO LATINO	Columbia	3	1 Jul 95	5
PURE ATTRACTION	Columbia	5	8 Jul 95	3
RAP FLAVAS	Columbia	6	15 Jun 96	3
TAKE A BREAK	Columbia	10	2 Nov 96	2
WHAT A FEELING!	Columbia	4	17 May 97	12
BOYS	Columbia	15	31 May 97	2
IT'S A SIXTIES PARTY	Columbia	12	18 Oct 97	3
OH! WHAT A NIGHT	Columbia	4	21 Mar 98	9
PERFECT DAY	Columbia	7	28 Mar 98	6
ALLEZ! OLA! OLE!	Columbia	8	27 Jun 98	3
SUMMER DANCE '98	Columbia	12	25 Jul 98	3

ANOTHER PERFECT DAY	*Columbia*	13	*8 Aug 98*	2
THIS IS NOIZE	*Columbia*	17	*27 Feb 99*	1
ESPECIALLY FOR YOU	*Columbia*	1	*20 Mar 99*	2
THE NEW SOUL ALBUM	*Columbia*	9	*8 May 99*	4
MUSIC TO WATCH GIRLS BY	*Columbia*	2	*5 Jun 99*	23
VIVA! LATINO	*Columbia*	11	*4 Sep 99*	4
MORE MUSIC TO WATCH GIRLS BY	*Columbia*	10	*20 Nov 99*	4

Concept
COMPILATION ALBUMS:	HITS 1			WEEKS 7
RAP ATTACK	*Concept*	9	*12 Mar 94*	7

Concrete
COMPILATION ALBUMS:	HITS 1			WEEKS 1
BRIT HOP AND AMYL HOUSE	*Concrete*	16	*10 Feb 96*	1

Conifer Classics
COMPILATION ALBUMS:	HITS 1			WEEKS 1
ONLY CLASSICAL ALBUM YOU'LL EVER NEED	*Conifer Classics*	17	*21 Nov 98*	1

Cookie Jar
COMPILATION ALBUMS:	HITS 10			WEEKS 66
STEAMIN! – HARDCORE '92	*Cookie Jar*	3	*14 Dec 91*	8
TECHNOSTATE – 20 SERIOUS TECHNO AND GARAGE RAVES	*Cookie Jar*	2	*21 Mar 92*	9
THE RAVE GENER8TOR	*Cookie Jar*	1	*23 May 92*	8
THE RAVE GENER8TOR 2	*Cookie Jar*	2	*5 Sep 92*	7
RAVE 92	*Cookie Jar*	3	*28 Nov 92*	11
UNDERGROUND VOLUME 1	*Cookie Jar*	6	*27 Mar 93*	5
JAMMIN'	*Cookie Jar*	7	*7 Aug 93*	5
FULL ON DANCE	*Cookie Jar*	12	*11 Sep 93*	2
SOUL BEAT	*Cookie Jar*	8	*6 Nov 93*	2
FULL ON DANCE '93	*Cookie Jar*	3	*27 Nov 93*	9

Cooltempo
ALBUMS:	HITS 1			WEEKS 6
FIERCE	*Cooltempo*	37	*1 Aug 87*	6
COMPILATION ALBUMS:	HITS 1			WEEKS 2
THIS IS GARAGE	*Cooltempo*	18	*1 Jul 89*	2

Cowboy
COMPILATION ALBUMS:	HITS 1			WEEKS 1
COWBOY COMPILATION – THE ALBUM VOLUME 1	*Cowboy*	18	*8 May 93*	1

Creole
ALBUMS:	HITS 1			WEEKS 6
20 HOLIDAY HITS	*Creole*	48	*24 Aug 85*	6

Dance Pool
COMPILATION ALBUMS:	HITS 1			WEEKS 2
IBIZA: THE CLOSING PARTY	*Dance Pool*	19	*25 Sep 99*	2

Debut
COMPILATION ALBUMS:	HITS 1			WEEKS 1
JUNGLE TEKNO VOLUME 1	*Debut*	18	*27 Jun 92*	1

Decca
ALBUMS:	HITS 1			WEEKS 17
FORMULA 30	*Decca*	6	*26 Nov 83*	17
COMPILATION ALBUMS:	HITS 5			WEEKS 61
THE ESSENTIAL MOZART	*Decca*	1	*1 Jun 91*	23
ESSENTIAL OPERA	*Decca*	2	*16 Nov 91*	28
ESSENTIAL BALLET	*Decca*	9	*26 Sep 92*	4
ESSENTIAL OPERA 2	*Decca*	17	*6 Nov 93*	2
THE GREATEST CLASSICAL STARS ON EARTH	*Decca*	13	*6 Jun 98*	4

Deconstruction
COMPILATION ALBUMS:	HITS 3			WEEKS 9
ITALIA - DANCE MUSIC FROM ITALY	*Deconstruction*	4	*14 Oct 89*	6
FULL ON – A YEAR IN THE LIFE OF HOUSE	*Deconstruction*	18	*27 Feb 93*	2
DECONSTRUCTION CLASSICS – A HISTORY OF DANCE MUSIC	*Deconstruction*	17	*26 Aug 95*	1

Def Jam
ALBUMS:	HITS 1			WEEKS 7
KICK IT - THE DEF JAM SAMPLER VOLUME 1	*Def Jam*	19	*8 Aug 87*	7

Deram/Oi
ALBUMS:	HITS 1			WEEKS 5
STRENGTH THROUGH OI!	*Deram*	51	*30 May 81*	5

Deutsche Grammophon

COMPILATION ALBUMS:	HITS 2			WEEKS 14
ESSENTIAL CLASSICS	*Deutsche Grammophon*	6	*13 Oct 90*	9
LIVING CLASSICS	*Deutsche Grammophon*	7	*28 Mar 92*	5

Dino

COMPILATION ALBUMS:	HITS 70			WEEKS 518
LEATHER AND LACE. THE MEN AND WOMEN OF ROCK	*Dino*	3	*23 Jun 90*	8
THE SUMMER OF LOVE	*Dino*	9	*11 Aug 90*	9
LEATHER AND LACE – THE SECOND CHAPTER	*Dino*	14	*10 Nov 90*	4
ROCK 'N' ROLL LOVE SONGS	*Dino*	4	*24 Nov 90*	29
BACHARACH AND DAVID – THEY WRITE THE SONGS	*Dino*	16	*29 Dec 90*	3
THE TRACKS OF MY TEARS – THE BEST OF SMOKEY ROBINSON: WRITER AND PERFORMER	*Dino*	6	*9 Feb 91*	8
HARDCORE UPROAR	*Dino*	2	*30 Mar 91*	9
LOVE SUPREME	*Dino*	4	*1 Jun 91*	5
THE RHYTHM DIVINE	*Dino*	1	*15 Jun 91*	15
HARDCOAR DANCEFLOOR	*Dino*	2	*13 Jul 91*	10
L.A. FREEWAY	*Dino*	6	*3 Aug 91*	7
WE WILL ROCK YOU	*Dino*	3	*12 Oct 91*	6
HARDCORE ECSTASY	*Dino*	1	*2 Nov 91*	16
RHYTHM DIVINE 2	*Dino*	6	*2 Nov 91*	5
MORE ROCK 'N' ROLL LOVE SONGS	*Dino*	6	*23 Nov 91*	23
PARTY MIX	*Dino*	8	*7 Dec 91*	9
ESSENTIAL HARDCORE	*Dino*	1	*28 Dec 91*	10
HEAVENLY HARDCORE	*Dino*	2	*14 Mar 92*	9
BREAKING HEARTS	*Dino*	3	*28 Mar 92*	10
COLD SWEAT	*Dino*	2	*18 Apr 92*	7
HEARTLANDS	*Dino*	4	*2 May 92*	11
LET'S TALK ABOUT LOVE	*Dino*	3	*20 Jun 92*	4
PRECIOUS	*Dino*	11	*11 Jul 92*	2
MIDNIGHT CRUISING	*Dino*	10	*18 Jul 92*	6
UNDER SPANISH SKIES	*Dino*	5	*1 Aug 92*	7
THE ORIGINALS!	*Dino*	8	*22 Aug 92*	6
TRANCE DANCE	*Dino*	7	*29 Aug 92*	5
SIXTIES BEAT	*Dino*	1	*19 Sep 92*	13
THE GREATEST VOICES	*Dino*	5	*24 Oct 92*	6
SWING HITS	*Dino*	19	*14 Nov 92*	1
ROCK 'N' ROLL IS HERE TO STAY	*Dino*	16	*28 Nov 92*	2
STOMPIN' PARTY	*Dino*	10	*5 Dec 92*	7
MEMORIES . . . ARE MADE OF THIS	*Dino*	8	*12 Dec 92*	12
BLUES BROTHER SOUL SISTER	*Dino*	1	*13 Feb 93*	38
ROCK 'N' ROLL IS HERE TO STAY [RE]	*Dino*	14	*3 Jul 93*	3
HEART FULL OF SOUL	*Dino*	9	*10 Jul 93*	8
BLUES BROTHER SOUL SISTER VOLUME 2	*Dino*	8	*17 Jul 93*	8
RAVE GENERATION	*Dino*	2	*18 Sep 93*	7
MORE THAN UNPLUGGED	*Dino*	11	*25 Sep 93*	3
PLANET ROCK	*Dino*	8	*16 Oct 93*	2
FUTURESHOCK – 20 FURIOUS DANCE TUNES	*Dino*	4	*23 Oct 93*	4
COUNTRY WOMEN	*Dino*	11	*23 Oct 93*	3
AS TIME GOES BY	*Dino*	14	*27 Nov 93*	5
KEEP ON DANCING	*Dino*	14	*4 Dec 93*	6
LOVE IN THE SIXTIES	*Dino*	11	*25 Dec 93*	9
RAVE GENERATION 2	*Dino*	5	*29 Jan 94*	3
SOUL MATE	*Dino*	6	*19 Feb 94*	3
IT'S ELECTRIC	*Dino*	2	*9 Apr 94*	12
BLUES BROTHER SOUL SISTER VOLUME 3	*Dino*	5	*7 May 94*	12
WONDERFUL WORLD	*Dino*	8	*4 Jun 94*	6
THE BEST OF ROCK 'N' ROLL LOVE SONGS	*Dino*	9	*23 Jul 94*	5
START – THE BEST OF BRITISH	*Dino*	13	*30 Jul 94*	3
DANCE MASSIVE	*Dino*	3	*3 Sep 94*	8
WHEN A MAN LOVES A WOMAN	*Dino*	7	*17 Sep 94*	6
ROCK ANTHEMS	*Dino*	3	*10 Dec 94*	17
DANCE MASSIVE 2	*Dino*	8	*17 Dec 94*	6
THE ULTIMATE JUNGLE COLLECTION	*Dino*	17	*7 Jan 95*	2
SKA MANIA	*Dino*	4	*27 May 95*	5
DANCE MASSIVE '95	*Dino*	2	*10 Jun 95*	5
REGGAE MASSIVE	*Dino*	19	*24 Jun 95*	1
RAVE ANTHEMS	*Dino*	7	*15 Jul 95*	5
THE AMERICAN DINER	*Dino*	7	*19 Aug 95*	5
THE GREATEST DANCE ALBUM OF ALL TIME	*Dino*	7	*21 Oct 95*	4
SPIRITUALLY IBIZA	*Dino*	17	*28 Oct 95*	1
VERY BEST OF BLUES BROTHER SOUL SISTER	*Dino*	11	*25 Nov 95*	7
THE GREATEST SOUL ALBUM OF ALL TIME	*Dino*	16	*9 Dec 95*	4
EIGHTIES SOUL WEEKENDER	*Dino*	7	*30 Mar 96*	7
ROCK ANTHEMS – VOLUME 2	*Dino*	10	*11 May 96*	4
PURE JAZZ MOODS – COOL JAZZ FOR A SUMMERS DAY	*Dino*	9	*22 Jun 96*	3

THE VERY BEST OF CAJUN - 40 HOT CAJUN CLASSICS	*Dino*	16	*7 Sep 96*	3
THE VERY BEST OF BRASS	*Dino*	18	*17 May 97*	1

Disco Diamond

ALBUMS:	HITS 1			WEEKS 1
SOLID SOUL SENSATIONS	*Disco Diamond*	30	*15 Mar 75*	1

DJ International

ALBUMS:	HITS 4			WEEKS 26
THE "HOUSE" SOUND OF CHICAGO	*DJ International*	52	*20 Sep 86*	12
THE "HOUSE" SOUND OF CHICAGO - VOL II	*Trax*	38	*18 Apr 87*	7

Label shows as Trax, though this was one of DJ International's releases.

JACKMASTER VOLUME 1	*DJ International*	36	*31 Oct 87*	4
JACKMASTER VOLUME 2	*DJ International*	38	*13 Feb 88*	3

Dover

COMPILATION ALBUMS:	HITS 7			WEEKS 58
AND ALL BECAUSE THE LADY LOVES . . .	*Dover*	2	*4 Mar 89*	10

Issued in conjuction with Cadbury's Milk Tray chocolate.

ALL BY MYSELF	*Dover*	2	*10 Feb 90*	15
A TON OF HITS - THE BEST OF STOCK AITKEN WATERMAN	*Dover*	7	*24 Nov 90*	8
RED HOT METAL - 18 ROCK CLASSICS	*Dover*	4	*20 Apr 91*	6
ALL BY MYSELF VOLUME 2	*Dover*	13	*8 Jun 91*	5
MOMENTS IN SOUL	*Dover*	2	*14 Sep 91*	7
THE GREATEST MOMENTS IN SOUL	*Dover*	4	*16 May 92*	7

Dreamscape

COMPILATION ALBUMS:	HITS 1			WEEKS 1
RADIO DREAMSCAPE - VOLUME 1	*Dreamscape*	20	*17 Jun 95*	1

Earth

COMPILATION ALBUMS:	HITS 1			WEEKS 1
LTJ BUKEM PRESENTS EARTH - VOLUME ONE	*Earth*	19	*16 Nov 96*	1

East West

COMPILATION ALBUMS:	HITS 2			WEEKS 3
I'M YOUR FAN - THE SONGS OF LEONARD COHEN	*East West*	16	*12 Oct 91*	2
DISCO INFERNO	*East West*	17	*26 Jun 93*	1

Elevate

COMPILATION ALBUMS:	HITS 3			WEEKS 8
RAVE 2 - STRICTLY HARDCORE!	*Elevate*	11	*11 Apr 92*	3
RAVING MAD	*Elevate*	17	*8 Aug 92*	2
THE WIND DOWN ZONE	*Elevate*	17	*27 Feb 93*	3

ELF

COMPILATION ALBUMS:	HITS 1			WEEKS 6
EARTHRISE - THE RAINFOREST ALBUM	*ELF*	1	*13 Jun 92*	6

EMI

ALBUMS:	HITS 12			WEEKS 133
IMPACT	*EMI*	15	*21 Jun 69*	14
PURE GOLD	*EMI*	1	*2 Jun 73*	11
DON'T WALK - BOOGIE	*EMI*	1	*18 Nov 78*	23
COUNTRY LIFE	*EMI*	2	*21 Apr 79*	14
KNUCKLE SANDWICH	*EMI International*	19	*2 Jun 79*	6
ALL ABOARD	*EMI*	13	*15 Dec 79*	8
METAL FOR MUTHAS	*EMI*	16	*23 Feb 80*	7
METAL FOR MUTHAS VOLUME 2	*EMI*	58	*14 Jun 80*	1
20 WITH A BULLET	*EMI*	11	*13 Mar 82*	8
THEN CAME ROCK 'N' ROLL	*EMI*	5	*26 May 84*	15
UNFORGETTABLE	*EMI*	5	*5 Mar 88*	21
HELLO CHILDREN . . . EVERYWHERE	*EMI*	59	*3 Dec 88*	5

COMPILATION ALBUMS:	HITS 46			WEEKS 246
UNFORGETTABLE	*EMI*	18	*28 Jan 89*	1
UNFORGETTABLE 2	*EMI*	1	*18 Mar 89*	15
IS THIS LOVE	*EMI*	2	*30 Sep 89*	10
THE 80'S - THE ALBUM OF THE DECADE	*EMI*	1	*18 Nov 89*	12
THE WILD ONE	*EMI*	8	*4 Aug 90*	7
MISSING YOU - AN ALBUM OF LOVE	*EMI*	1	*20 Oct 90*	18
TRULY UNFORGETTABLE	*EMI*	6	*17 Nov 90*	9
MISSING YOU 2 - AN ALBUM OF LOVE	*EMI*	2	*16 Feb 91*	11
SEXUAL HEALING	*EMI*	7	*26 Oct 91*	6
TENDER LOVE - 17 ROMANTIC LOVE SONGS	*EMI*	2	*22 Feb 92*	11
THE CLASSIC ROMANCE	*EMI*	5	*22 Feb 92*	7
MAXIMUM RAVE	*EMI*	2	*22 Aug 92*	9
WICKED!!	*EMI*	2	*17 Oct 92*	5
SMASHIE AND NICEY PRESENT LET'S ROCK!	*EMI*	8	*31 Oct 92*	4

FOREVER	*EMI*	17	*5 Dec 92*	2
SOUL MOODS	*EMI*	4	*20 Feb 93*	8
INNA DANCEHALL STYLE	*EMI*	11	*3 Jul 93*	4
BACK TO THE 70'S	*EMI*	8	*18 Sep 93*	6
LET'S GO DISCO	*EMI*	12	*6 Nov 93*	3
IT TAKES TWO – LOVE'S GREATEST DUETS	*EMI*	17	*27 Nov 93*	1
TRANQUILITY	*EMI*	14	*25 Jun 94*	5
CLUB TOGETHER	*React/EMI*	10	*8 Oct 94*	4
Joint label with EMI catalogue prefix.				
MISSING YOU	*EMI*	8	*29 Oct 94*	5
THE BEST COUNTRY ALBUM IN THE WORLD . . . EVER!	*EMI*	4	*26 Nov 94*	12
UNLACED	*EMI*	8	*11 Mar 95*	4
CLUB TOGETHER 2	*React/EMI*	9	*29 Apr 95*	4
Joint label with EMI catalogue prefix.				
THE BEST CLASSICAL ALBUM IN THE WORLD . . . EVER!	*EMI*	6	*15 Jul 95*	6
MOST EXCELLENT DANCE	EDI	8	*22 Jul 95*	4
DEDICATED TO PLEASURE	*EMI*	18	*29 Jul 95*	3
TECHNO NIGHTS AMBIENT DAWN	*EMI*	16	*23 Sep 95*	3
THAT'S ROCK 'N' ROLL	*EMI*	12	*28 Oct 95*	2
THAT'S COUNTRY	*EMI*	11	*4 Nov 95*	6
THE GREATEST PARTY ALBUM UNDER THE SUN!	*EMI TV*	1	*11 Nov 95*	7
THE GREATEST DANCE ALBUM UNDER THE SUN!	*EMI TV*	8	*2 Mar 96*	4
THE BEST OF THE NINETIES . . . SO FAR	*EMI TV*	9	*9 Mar 96*	5
BABY LOVE	*EMI TV*	11	*16 Mar 96*	2
MIX'O'MATIC	*EMI TV*	8	*11 May 96*	3
LOST PROPERTY	*EMI TV*	12	*18 May 96*	2
COMMON GROUND	*EMI Premier*	17	*1 Jun 96*	2
CLUB TOGETHER 3	*EMI TV*	7	*8 Jun 96*	2
LOVERMAN	*EMI TV*	17	*15 Jun 96*	2
EASY MOODS	*EMI TV*	15	*9 Nov 96*	1
GREATEST NON-STOP PARTY UNDER THE SUN	*EMI TV*	13	*30 Nov 96*	4
THE DOG'S . . . !	*EMI TV*	20	*28 Dec 96*	2
TWENTIETH CENTURY BLUES	*EMI*	14	*25 Apr 98*	1
A SONG FOR EUROTRASH	*EMI*	19	*16 May 98*	1

EMI/Virgin/Polygram

COMPILATION ALBUMS:	HITS 5			WEEKS 43
THE ULTIMATE RAVE	*EMI/Virgin/PolyGram*	1	*25 Jan 92*	15
THE MEGA RAVE	*EMI/Virgin/PolyGram*	2	*30 Jan 93*	8
MEGA DANCE – THE POWER ZONE	*EMI/Virgin/PolyGram*	2	*13 Mar 93*	8
LOADED	*EMI/Virgin/PolyGram*	6	*10 Apr 93*	6
MEGA DANCE 2 – THE ENERGY ZONE	*EMI/Virgin/PolyGram*	3	*17 Apr 93*	6

Epic

ALBUMS:	HITS 3			WEEKS 37
ELECTRO SHOCK VOLTAGE ONE	*Epic*	73	*3 Mar 84*	1
AMERICAN HEARTBEAT	*Epic*	4	*16 Jun 84*	22
HITS FOR LOVERS – 16 OF TODAY'S GREAT LOVE SONGS	*Epic*	2	*8 Mar 86*	14
COMPILATION ALBUMS:	HITS 6			WEEKS 60
JUST THE TWO OF US	*Epic*	1	*24 Mar 90*	37
MELLOW MADNESS	*Epic*	14	*9 Nov 91*	2
RED HOT + DANCE	*Epic*	6	*18 Jul 92*	5
Benefit album with proceeds to AIDS research. Consists of remixed dance tracks.				
ROMANCING THE SCREEN	*Epic*	5	*29 Aug 92*	11
MIX HEAVEN '97	*Epic*	19	*6 Sep 97*	1
DIVAS LIVE	*Epic*	3	*17 Oct 98*	4
Tracks by Maria Carey, Celine Dion, Aretha Franklin, Gloria Estefan and Shania Twain.				

Erato

COMPILATION ALBUMS:	HITS 1			WEEKS 5
THE ULTIMATE OPERA COLLECTION	*Erato*	14	*11 Jul 92*	5

Expansion

COMPILATION ALBUMS:	HITS 1			WEEKS 1
WINNER'S CIRCLE	*Expansion*	20	*24 Apr 93*	1

Fanfare/PWL

ALBUMS:	HITS 2			WEEKS 9
THE HIT FACTORY VOLUME 2	*Fanfare/PWL*	16	*12 Nov 88*	9
COMPILATION ALBUMS:	HITS 2			WEEKS 13
THE HIT FACTORY VOLUME 2	*Fanfare/PWL*	13	*14 Jan 89*	3
THE HIT FACTORY VOLUME 3	*Fanfare/PWL*	3	*15 Jul 89*	10

Fantazia

COMPILATION ALBUMS:	HITS 12			WEEKS 71
FANTAZIA – THE FIRST TASTE	*Fantazia*	13	*5 Dec 92*	5
FANTAZIA – TWICE AS NICE	*Fantazia*	17	*24 Jul 93*	5
FANTAZIA III – MADE IN HEAVEN	*Fantazia*	16	*25 Jun 94*	2

THE HOUSE COLLECTION – VOLUME 2	*Fantazia*	6	*29 Apr 95*	6
THE HOUSE COLLECTION – VOLUME 3	*Fantazia*	4	*30 Sep 95*	7
THE HOUSE COLLECTION – CLUB CLASSICS	*Fantazia*	3	*17 Feb 96*	10
FANTAZIA PRESENT THE HOUSE COLLECTION 4	*Fantazia*	2	*29 Jun 96*	9
THE HOUSE COLLECTION CLUB CLASSICS – 2	*Fantazia*	4	*14 Sep 96*	8
THE HOUSE COLLECTION – VOLUME 5	*Fantazia*	3	*8 Mar 97*	7
CLUB CLASSICS – VOLUME 3	*Fantazia*	4	*7 Jun 97*	6
THE HOUSE COLLECTION 6 – PAUL OKENFOLD/PAUL COSFORD	*Fantazia*	10	*27 Sep 97*	3
FANTAZIA – BRITISH ANTHEMS	*Fantazia*	2	*21 Feb 98*	5

Feverpitch

COMPILATION ALBUMS:	HITS 4			WEEKS 8
TRADE	*Feverpitch*	14	*16 Sep 95*	2
TRADE – VOLUME TWO	*Feverpitch*	11	*20 Apr 96*	3
TRADE – VOLUME THREE	*Feverpitch*	19	*9 Nov 96*	1
TRADE – VOLUME FOUR	*Feverpitch*	15	*12 Apr 97*	2

Ffrr

ALBUMS:	HITS 3			WEEKS 13
THE HOUSE SOUND OF CHICAGO VOLUME 3	*ffrr*	40	*30 Jan 88*	4
THE HOUSE SOUND OF LONDON VOLUME 4	*ffrr*	70	*27 Aug 88*	7
BALEARIC BEATS VOLUME 1	*ffrr*	58	*1 Oct 88*	2
COMPILATION ALBUMS:	HITS 7			WEEKS 19
ESSENTIAL MIX – TONG COX SASHA OAKENFOLD	*ffrr*	12	*20 Jan 96*	3
LTJ BUKEM PRESENTS LOGICAL PROGRESSION	*ffrr*	14	*20 Apr 96*	1
ESSENTIAL MIX 2 – TONG, MACKINTOSH …	*ffrr*	6	*11 May 96*	3
METALHEADZ – PLATINUM BREAKZ	*ffrr*	12	*10 Aug 96*	2
ESSENTIAL MIX 3 – TONG, SEAMAN, JULES ETC	*ffrr*	12	*7 Sep 96*	3
CARL COX – NON STOP 98/01	*ffrr*	8	*8 Aug 98*	5
CARL COX – NON STOP 2000	*ffrr*	13	*30 Oct 99*	2

Firm

COMPILATION ALBUMS:	HITS 1			WEEKS 4
WORLD DANCE – THE DRUM + BASS EXPERIENCE	*Firm*	10	*11 Jan 97*	4

Four Beat

COMPILATION ALBUMS:	HITS 4			WEEKS 7
UNITED DANCE – VOLUME 3	*Fourbeat*	11	*20 Jan 96*	2
UNITED DANCE – VOLUME FOUR	*4 Beat*	17	*25 May 96*	1
UNITED DANCE – VOLUME 5	*4 Beat*	20	*9 Nov 96*	1
UNITED DANCE – VOLUME 6	*Fourbeat*	10	*26 Apr 97*	3

4AD

ALBUMS:	HITS 1			WEEKS 2
LONELY IS AN EYESORE	*4AD*	53	*11 Jul 87*	2

Fourth & Broadway

COMPILATION ALBUMS:	HITS 2			WEEKS 6
THE REBIRTH OF COOL, TOO	*Fourth & Broadway*	13	*7 Mar 92*	2
THE REBIRTH OF COOL III	*Fourth & Broadway*	9	*15 May 93*	4

Freestyle

COMPILATION ALBUMS:	HITS 1			WEEKS 3
BROTHER'S GONNA WORK IT OUT	*Freestyle*	7	*3 Oct 98*	3

Remix album by the Chemical Brothers, includes 1 disc of their own material.

Fresh

COMPILATION ALBUMS:	HITS 1			WEEKS 1
FRESHEN UP VOLUME 1	*Fresh*	20	*3 Jun 95*	1

Global Television

COMPILATION ALBUMS:	HITS 77			WEEKS 361
SOUNDS OF THE SEVENTIES	*Global Television*	11	*17 Dec 94*	5
HITS, HITS AND MORE DANCE HITS	*Global Television*	13	*17 Dec 94*	4
SOFT REGGAE	*Global Television*	2	*21 Jan 95*	7
NEW SOUL REBELS	*Global Television*	6	*18 Feb 95*	6
ON A DANCE TIP	*Global Television*	1	*25 Feb 95*	9
GIRLS AND GUITARS	*Global Television*	8	*4 Mar 95*	4
FIFTY NUMBER ONES OF THE '60S	*Global Television*	8	*15 Apr 95*	4
CLUB CLASS	*Global Television*	4	*22 Apr 95*	5
INTO THE EIGHTIES	*Global Television*	5	*22 Apr 95*	5
ON A DANCE TIP 2	*Global Television*	1	*20 May 95*	7
DANCE BUZZ	*Global Television*	3	*17 Jun 95*	4
CHARTBUSTERS	*Global Television*	2	*1 Jul 95*	6
GREAT SEX	*Global Television*	13	*1 Jul 95*	2
THEMES AND DREAMS	*Global Television*	11	*15 Jul 95*	2
NATURAL WOMAN	*Global Television*	7	*29 Jul 95*	8
SUMMER DANCE PARTY	*Global Television*	2	*12 Aug 95*	5

HITZ BLITZ	Global Television	2	26 Aug 95	5
DANCE TIP 3	Global Television	2	23 Sep 95	6
DRIVING ROCK	Global Television	9	30 Sep 95	6
NIGHTFEVER	Global Television	7	28 Oct 95	5
DANCE TIP '95	Global Television	3	18 Nov 95	12
VYBIN' – YOUNG SOUL REBELS	Global Television	9	17 Feb 96	4
COUNTRY GOLD	Global Television	12	6 Apr 96	3
UNTITLED	Global Television	6	27 Apr 96	4
VYBIN' 3 – NEW SOUL REBELS	Global Television	2	4 May 96	5
DANCE MIX UK	Global Television	6	11 May 96	4
NATURAL WOMAN – VOLUME 2	Global Television	10	25 May 96	3
THE BEST OF ACID JAZZ	Global Television	5	15 Jun 96	5
NO GREATER LOVE	Global Television	4	13 Jul 96	6
SHADES OF SOUL	Global Television	15	20 Jul 96	1
VYBIN' 4	Global Television	7	27 Jul 96	5
UNTITLED 2	Global Television	6	3 Aug 96	6
THE ULTIMATE LINE DANCING ALBUM	Global Television	9	17 Aug 96	6
DANCE MIX UK 2	Global Television	10	14 Sep 96	4
UNTITLED 3	Global Television	20	16 Nov 96	1
THE ULTIMATE PARTY ANIMAL	Global Television	4	30 Nov 96	10
THE ULTIMATE LINE DANCING ALBUM	Global Television	7	8 Feb 97	8
This Album is different from previous chart entry.				
BEST OF ACID JAZZ – VOLUME 2	Global TV / PolyGram TV	13	15 Feb 97	4
GIRL POWER	Global Television	9	15 Mar 97	5
THE OLD SKOOL	PolyGram TV / Global TV	6	5 Apr 97	7
KLUBHOPPIN'	Global Television	6	19 Apr 97	4
CHARTBUSTERS	Global Television	4	24 May 97	6
This Album is different from previous chart entry.				
MODROPHENIA	Global Television	14	31 May 97	3
THE ULTIMATE SUMMER PARTY ANIMAL	Global Television	2	28 Jun 97	8
THE OLD SKOOL REUNION	PolyGram TV / Global TV	12	26 Jul 97	2
DRIVE ON	Global Television	10	30 Aug 97	3
THE BEST DANCE ALBUM OF THE YEAR	Global Television	6	6 Sep 97	5
PURE REGGAE	Global Television	12	20 Sep 97	3
SPEED GARAGE ANTHEMS	Global Television	5	18 Oct 97	4
FUNKY DIVAS	Global Television	3	27 Dec 97	13
THE EIGHTIES MIX	Global TV / PolyGram TV	1	17 Jan 98	7
SHADES OF SOUL	Global Television	9	17 Jan 98	3
This Album is different from previous chart entry.				
ONE WORLD	Global Television	8	31 Jan 98	3
DROP DEAD GORGEOUS	Global Television	4	21 Feb 98	7
SPEED GARAGE ANTHEMS – VOLUME 2	Global Television	5	21 Feb 98	8
CLUB CULTURE EXPOSED!!	Global Television	5	4 Apr 98	4
URBAN RHYMES	Global TV / PolyGram TV	5	18 Apr 98	5
THE BEST DANCE ALBUM OF THE YEAR	Global Television	13	23 May 98	3
This Album is different from previous chart entry.				
DROP DEAD GORGEOUS 2	Global Television	10	30 May 98	3
SPEED GARAGE ANTHEMS IN IBIZA	Global Television	7	1 Aug 98	4
FUNKY DIVAS 2	Global Television	16	5 Dec 98	8
THE GREATEST ROCK 'N' ROLL LOVE SONGS	Global Television	6	13 Feb 99	4
DISCO HOUSE	Global Television	7	6 Mar 99	3
THE VERY BEST OF LATIN JAZZ – 2	Global Television	15	15 May 99	3
FAT DANCE HITS	Global Television	5	12 Jun 99	5
MIDSUMMER CLASSICS	Global Television	20	26 Jun 99	2
UNDER LATIN SKIES	Global Television	14	17 Jul 99	2
IBIZA 99 – THE YEAR OF TRANCE	Global Television	2	24 Jul 99	5
SALSA FEVER!	Global Television	12	31 Jul 99	4
IBIZA DEL MAR	Global Television	11	28 Aug 99	2
SPEED GARAGE ANTHEMS 99	Global Television	13	11 Sep 99	3
FAT POP HITS	Global Television	6	2 Oct 99	5
IBIZA 99 – THE YEAR OF TRANCE – VOLUME TWO	Global Television	11	9 Oct 99	4
ROCK THE WORLD	Global Television	9	9 Oct 99	4
AYIA NAPA – CLUBBERS PARADISE	Global Television	14	23 Oct 99	2
FUNK SOUL BROTHER – THE BEST OF DANCE SOUL & SWING	Global Television	19	20 Nov 99	1
THE BIGGEST CLUB ALBUM OF THE YEAR	Global Television	20	20 Nov 99	1

Global Underground

COMPILATION ALBUMS:	HITS 6			WEEKS 9
JOHN DIGWEED SYDNEY	Global Underground	16	25 Apr 98	1
PAUL OAKENFOLD – NEW YORK	Global Underground	12	6 Jun 98	3
SASHA – SAN FRANCISCO	Global Underground	18	21 Nov 98	1
DANNY TENAGLIA LIVE IN ATHENS	Global Underground	16	27 Feb 99	1
NICK WARREN – BUDAPEST	Global Underground	20	19 Jun 99	1
SASHA – IBIZA	Global Underground	12	2 Oct 99	2

Go! Discs

COMPILATION ALBUMS:	HITS 1			WEEKS 7
HELP – WAR CHILD	Go! Discs	1	16 Sep 95	7
Charity album in aid of children caught up in the Bosnian war.				

Good Looking

COMPILATION ALBUMS:	HITS 3			WEEKS 4
BLAME PRESENT LOGICAL PROGRESSION LEVEL 2	*Good Looking*	12	*10 May 97*	2
LTJ BUKEM PRESENTS EARTH – VOLUME TWO	*Good Looking*	18	*11 Oct 97*	1
INTENSE PRESENTS LOGICAL PROGRESSION LEVEL 3	*Good Looking*	18	*16 May 98*	1

GTO

ALBUMS:	HITS 1			WEEKS 5
NEVER TOO YOUNG TO ROCK	*GTO*	30	*16 Aug 75*	5

Guerilla

COMPILATION ALBUMS:	HITS 1			WEEKS 1
DUB HOUSE DISCO 2000	*Guerilla*	18	*17 Apr 93*	1

Happy Days

COMPILATION ALBUMS:	HITS 1			WEEKS 1
YOU MUST REMEMBER THIS …	*Happy Days*	16	*13 May 95*	1

Harvest

ALBUMS:	HITS 1			WEEKS 12
A MONUMENT TO BRITISH ROCK	*Harvest*	13	*26 May 79*	12

Heart And Soul

COMPILATION ALBUMS:	HITS 4			WEEKS 47
HEART AND SOUL – 18 CLASSIC SOUL CUTS	*Heart & Soul*	2	*19 Aug 89*	12
BODY AND SOUL – HEART AND SOUL II	*Heart & Soul*	2	*17 Feb 90*	14
HEART AND SOUL III – HEART FULL OF SOUL	*Heart & Soul*	4	*4 Aug 90*	9
SOUL REFLECTION	*Heart & Soul*	2	*16 Feb 91*	12

Heaven Music

COMPILATION ALBUMS:	HITS 5			WEEKS 13
HARDCORE HEAVEN – VOLUME ONE	*Heaven Music*	12	*5 Apr 97*	4
HARDCORE HEAVEN – VOLUME 2	*Heaven Music*	13	*9 Aug 97*	2
HARDCORE HEAVEN – VOLUME 3	*Heaven Music*	12	*14 Feb 98*	2
HARDCORE HEAVEN – VOLUME 4	*Heaven Music*	17	*8 Aug 98*	1
HARDCORE HEAVEN – VOLUME 5	*Heaven Music*	17	*13 Feb 99*	4

Heavenly

COMPILATION ALBUMS:	HITS 1			WEEKS 1
LIVE AT THE SOCIAL – VOLUME 1	*Heavenly*	19	*25 May 96*	1

Hi-Life/Polydor

COMPILATION ALBUMS:	HITS 1			WEEKS 1
THE SUMMER OF NINETY SIX – UP YER RONSON	*Hi-Life/Polydor*	17	*2 Nov 96*	1

Higher Ground

COMPILATION ALBUMS:	HITS 1			WEEKS 1
GROOVERIDER PRESENTS THE PROTOTYPE YEARS	*Higher Ground*	19	*12 Apr 97*	1

The Hit Label

COMPILATION ALBUMS:	HITS 11			WEEKS 43
BIG! DANCE HITS OF 92	*The Hit Label*	11	*28 Nov 92*	7
REMEMBER WHEN SINGERS COULD SING	*The Hit Label*	16	*5 Dec 92*	2
THE LEGENDARY JOE BLOGGS DANCE ALBUM	*The Hit Label*	3	*8 May 93*	8
GET IT ON – GREATEST HITS OF THE 70'S	*The Hit Label*	12	*31 Jul 93*	5
THE LEGENDARY JOE BLOGGS ALBUM 2	*The Hit Label*	15	*30 Oct 93*	2
IT MUST BE LOVE	*The Hit Label*	11	*13 Nov 93*	4
THE BOYZ WHO SOULED THE WORLD	*The Hit Label*	9	*5 Mar 94*	4
THE ULTIMATE GOLD COLLECTION	*The Hit Label*	12	*27 Aug 94*	4
ULTIMATE LOVE	*The Hit Label*	13	*4 Feb 95*	4
FEEL LIKE MAKING LOVE	*The Hit Label*	17	*18 Feb 95*	2
REGGAE GROOVE	*The Hit Label*	12	*8 Jul 95*	1

Ignition

COMPILATION ALBUMS:	HITS 1			WEEKS 1
FIRE & SKILL – THE SONGS OF THE JAM	*Ignition*	12	*13 Nov 99*	1

Tribute album to the Jam.

Immediate

ALBUMS:	HITS 1			WEEKS 1
BLUES ANYTIME	*Immediate*	40	*11 May 68*	1

IMP Classics & Pickwick

Both labels sales were combined.

COMPILATION ALBUMS:	HITS 2			WEEKS 6
DISCOVER THE CLASSICS VOLUME 2	*IMP Classics / Pickwick*	12	*11 Apr 92*	3
DISCOVER THE CLASSICS VOLUME 1	*IMP Classics / Pickwick*	15	*11 Apr 92*	3

Impression

ALBUMS:	HITS 7			WEEKS 51
BEST FRIENDS	Impression	28	16 Oct 82	21
SUNNY AFTERNOON	Impression	13	3 Sep 83	8
PRECIOUS MOMENTS	Impression	77	26 Nov 83	5
ALWAYS AND FOREVER – THE COLLECTION	Impression	24	7 Apr 84	12
WIPEOUT – 20 INSTRUMENTAL GREATS	Impression	37	21 Jul 84	3
SUNNY AFTERNOON VOLUME TWO	Impression	90	28 Jul 84	1
FRIENDS AGAIN	Impression	91	22 Dec 84	1

INCredible

COMPILATION ALBUMS:	HITS 7			WEEKS 26
GATECRASHER	INCredible	7	31 Oct 98	2
NORTHERN EXPOSURE – SASHA + JON DIGWEED	INCredible	6	6 Mar 99	2
Sales of vinyl format had its own entry reaching No. 37.				
INCREDIBLE SOUND OF TREVOR NELSON	INCredible	14	20 Mar 99	3
GATECRASHER RED	INCredible	4	10 Apr 99	8
INCREDIBLE SOUND OF DRUM'N'BASS: MIXED BY GOLDIE	INCredible	16	8 May 99	2
GATECRASHER.WET	INCredible	3	7 Aug 99	6
GATECRASHER DISCO-TECH	INCredible	6	20 Nov 99	3

Island

ALBUMS:	HITS 5			WEEKS 51
CLUB SKA '67	Island	37	26 Aug 67	19
YOU CAN ALL JOIN IN	Island	18	14 Jun 69	10
CLUB SKA '67 [RE]	Island	53	29 Mar 80	6
Re-released with a new catalogue number.				
CREW CUTS	Island	71	16 Jun 84	4
CREW CUTS – LESSON 2	Island	95	27 Oct 84	2
THE ISLAND STORY	Island	9	18 Jul 87	10

COMPILATION ALBUMS:	HITS 4			WEEKS 17
HAPPY DAZE . . . VOLUME 1	Island	7	3 Nov 90	4
HAPPY DAZE VOLUME 2	Island	17	6 Apr 91	2
REGGAE 93	PolyGram TV	5	30 Oct 93	6
PURE REGGAE – VOLUME 1	Island	10	27 Aug 94	5

Jack Trax

ALBUMS:	HITS 3			WEEKS 8
JACK TRAX – THE FIRST ALBUM	Jack Trax	83	18 Jul 87	2
JACK TRAX – THE SECOND ALBUM	Jack Trax	61	3 Oct 87	2
JACK TRAX – THE FOURTH ALBUM	Jack Trax	49	5 Mar 88	4

JDJ

COMPILATION ALBUMS:	HITS 1			WEEKS 2
DANCE WARS – JUDGE JULES VS. JOHN KELLY	JDJ	11	30 Mar 96	2

Jetstar

ALBUMS:	HITS 4			WEEKS 21
REGGAE HITS VOLUME ONE	Jetstar	32	30 Mar 85	11
REGGAE HITS VOLUME 2	Jetstar	86	26 Oct 85	2
REGGAE HITS VOLUME 4	JetStar	56	4 Jun 88	7
REGGAE HITS VOLUME 5	JetStar	96	17 Dec 88	1

COMPILATION ALBUMS:	HITS 7			WEEKS 39
REGGAE HITS VOLUME 6	JetStar	13	5 Aug 89	6
REGGAE HITS VOLUME 7	Jetstar	13	23 Dec 89	6
REGGAE HITS VOLUME 8	Jetstar	7	30 Jun 90	5
REGGAE HITS VOLUME 10	Jetstar	6	20 Jul 91	7
REGGAE HITS VOLUME 12	Jetstar	5	18 Apr 92	6
REGGAE HITS VOLUME 14	Jetstar	13	28 Aug 93	1
JUNGLE HITS VOLUME 1	Jetstar	9	3 Sep 94	8

Jive

ALBUMS:	HITS 1			WEEKS 2
THE WORD VOLUME 2	Jive	70	26 Mar 88	2

Jumpin' And Pumpin'

COMPILATION ALBUMS:	HITS 2			WEEKS 4
NOISE	Jumpin' & Pumpin'	20	18 Jan 92	1
NOISE 2	Jumpin' & Pumpin'	11	16 May 92	3

Junior Boy's Own

COMPILATION ALBUMS:	HITS 1			WEEKS 1
JUNIOR BOY'S OWN COLLECTION	Junior Boy's Own	20	13 Aug 94	1

Kasino

ALBUMS:	HITS 1			WEEKS 3
STARGAZERS	Kasino	69	16 Feb 85	3

Knight

COMPILATION ALBUMS:	HITS 1		WEEKS 2	
SOUTHERN NIGHTS	*Knight*	13	*18 May 91*	2

K-Tel

ALBUMS:	HITS 113		WEEKS 1147	
20 DYNAMIC HITS	*K-Tel*	1	*10 Jun 72*	28
20 ALL TIME GREATS OF THE 50'S	*K-Tel*	1	*7 Oct 72*	22
25 DYNAMIC HITS VOLUME 2	*K-Tel*	2	*25 Nov 72*	12
25 ROCKIN' AND ROLLIN' GREATS	*K-Tel*	1	*2 Dec 72*	18
20 FLASHBACK GREATS OF THE SIXTIES	*K-Tel*	1	*31 Mar 73*	11
BELIEVE IN MUSIC	*K-Tel*	2	*21 Apr 73*	8
40 SUPER GREATS	*K-Tel*	9	*13 Dec 75*	8
MUSIC EXPRESS	*K-Tel*	3	*31 Jan 76*	10
JUKE BOX JIVE	*K-Tel*	3	*10 Apr 76*	13
GREAT ITALIAN LOVE SONGS	*K-Tel*	17	*17 Apr 76*	14
HIT MACHINE	*K-Tel*	4	*15 May 76*	10
SUMMER CRUISING	*K-Tel*	30	*2 Oct 76*	1
SOUL MOTION	*K-Tel*	1	*16 Oct 76*	14
COUNTRY COMFORT	*K-Tel*	8	*16 Oct 76*	12
DISCO ROCKET	*K-Tel*	3	*4 Dec 76*	14
44 SUPERSTARS	*K-Tel*	14	*11 Dec 76*	10
HEARTBREAKERS	*K-Tel*	2	*12 Feb 77*	18
DANCE TO THE MUSIC	*K-Tel*	5	*19 Feb 77*	9
HIT ACTION	*K-Tel*	15	*7 May 77*	9
SOUL CITY	*K-Tel*	12	*29 Oct 77*	7
FEELINGS	*K-Tel*	3	*12 Nov 77*	24
DISCO FEVER	*K-Tel*	1	*26 Nov 77*	20
40 NUMBER ONE HITS	*K-Tel*	15	*21 Jan 78*	7
DISCO STARS	*K-Tel*	6	*4 Mar 78*	8
DISCO DOUBLE	*K-Tel*	10	*10 Jun 78*	6
ROCK RULES	*K-Tel*	12	*8 Jul 78*	11
THE WORLD'S WORST RECORD SHOW	*Yuk/K-Tel*	47	*8 Jul 78*	2
Release was collaboration with Kenny Everett.				
STAR PARTY	*K-Tel*	4	*19 Aug 78*	9
EMOTIONS	*K-Tel*	2	*4 Nov 78*	17
MIDNIGHT HUSTLE	*K-Tel*	2	*25 Nov 78*	13
ACTION REPLAY	*K-Tel*	1	*20 Jan 79*	14
DISCO INFERNO	*K-Tel*	11	*7 Apr 79*	9
HI ENERGY	*K-Tel*	17	*5 May 79*	7
HOT TRACKS	*K-Tel*	31	*22 Sep 79*	8
NIGHT MOVES	*K-Tel*	10	*24 Nov 79*	10
TOGETHER	*K-Tel*	35	*24 Nov 79*	8
VIDEO STARS	*K-Tel*	5	*12 Jan 80*	10
THE SUMMIT	*K-Tel*	17	*26 Jan 80*	5
STAR TRACKS	*K-Tel*	6	*29 Mar 80*	8
GOOD MORNING AMERICA	*K-Tel*	15	*26 Apr 80*	12
MAGIC REGGAE	*K-Tel*	9	*17 May 80*	17
HAPPY DAYS	*K-Tel*	32	*17 May 80*	1
HOT WAX	*K-Tel*	3	*14 Jun 80*	10
MOUNTING EXCITEMENT	*K-Tel*	2	*27 Sep 80*	8
THE LOVE ALBUM	*K-Tel*	6	*11 Oct 80*	16
AXE ATTACK	*K-Tel*	15	*25 Oct 80*	14
CHART EXPLOSION	*K-Tel*	6	*15 Nov 80*	17
NIGHTLIFE	*K-Tel*	25	*27 Dec 80*	10
HIT MACHINE	*K-Tel*	17	*14 Feb 81*	6
This album is different from previous chart entry.				
RHYTHM 'N' REGGAE	*K-Tel*	42	*21 Mar 81*	4
CHART BLASTERS 81	*K-Tel*	3	*25 Apr 81*	9
AXE ATTACK 2	*K-Tel*	31	*2 May 81*	6
THEMES	*K-Tel*	6	*23 May 81*	15
CALIFORNIA DREAMING	*K-Tel*	27	*29 Aug 81*	11
DANCE DANCE DANCE	*K-Tel*	29	*19 Sep 81*	5
THE PLATINUM ALBUM	*K-Tel*	32	*3 Oct 81*	11
LOVE IS . . .	*K-Tel*	10	*10 Oct 81*	15
CHART HITS '81	*K-Tel*	1	*21 Nov 81*	17
MODERN DANCE	*K-Tel*	6	*9 Jan 82*	10
DREAMING	*K-Tel*	2	*6 Feb 82*	12
ACTION TRAX	*K-Tel*	2	*6 Mar 82*	12
MIDNIGHT HOUR	*K-Tel*	98	*1 May 82*	1
TURBO TRAX	*K-Tel*	17	*3 Jul 82*	7
THE NO. 1 SOUNDS OF THE SEVENTIES	*K-Tel*	83	*4 Sep 82*	1
CHARTBEAT/CHARTHEAT	*K-Tel*	2	*11 Sep 82*	14
THE LOVE SONGS ALBUM	*K-Tel*	28	*30 Oct 82*	8
CHART HITS '82	*K-Tel*	11	*6 Nov 82*	17
DISCO DANCER	*K-Tel*	26	*6 Nov 82*	8
STREETSCENE	*K-Tel*	42	*18 Dec 82*	6
VISIONS	*K-Tel*	5	*15 Jan 83*	21

HEAVY	*K-Tel*	46	*12 Feb 83*	12
HOTLINE	*K-Tel*	3	*5 Mar 83*	9
CHART STARS	*K-Tel*	7	*11 Jun 83*	9
COOL HEAT	*K-Tel*	79	*20 Aug 83*	3
HEADLINE HITS	*K-Tel*	5	*10 Sep 83*	6
THE TWO OF US	*K-Tel*	3	*8 Oct 83*	16
IMAGES	*K-Tel*	33	*8 Oct 83*	6
CHART HITS '83 VOLUMES 1 AND 2	*K-Tel*	6	*12 Nov 83*	11
NIGHT MOVES	*K-Tel*	90	*24 Mar 84*	1
This album is different from previous chart entry.				
HUNGRY FOR HITS	*K-Tel*	4	*26 May 84*	11
THE THEMES ALBUM	*K-Tel*	43	*23 Jun 84*	3
BREAKDANCE, YOU CAN DO IT!	*K-Tel*	18	*28 Jul 84*	12
NIGHT MOVES [RE]	*K-Tel*	15	*15 Sep 84*	10
ALL BY MYSELF	*K-Tel*	7	*22 Sep 84*	16
HOOKED ON NUMBER ONES – 100 NON-STOP HITS	*K-Tel*	25	*1 Dec 84*	15
FOUR STAR COUNTRY	*K-Tel*	52	*2 Feb 85*	6
MODERN LOVE – 24 LOVE SONGS FOR TODAY	*K-Tel*	13	*2 Mar 85*	7
EXPRESSIONS – 24 BEAUTIFUL BALLADS	*K-Tel*	11	*5 Oct 85*	8
ROCK ANTHEMS	*K-Tel*	10	*9 Nov 85*	11
THE BEST OF ANDREW LLOYD WEBBER – OVATION	*K-Tel*	34	*9 Nov 85*	12
Features tracks by Barbara Dickson, Paul Nicholas and Rebecca Storm.				
MASTERS OF METAL	*K-Tel*	38	*22 Mar 86*	4
HEART TO HEART – 24 LOVE SONG DUETS	*K-Tel*	8	*12 Apr 86*	15
ROCK ANTHEMS – VOLUME 2	*K-Tel*	43	*19 Apr 86*	9
RAP IT UP – RAP'S GREATEST HITS	*K-Tel*	50	*5 Jul 86*	4
DRIVE TIME USA – 22 SUMMER CRUISING GREATS	*K-Tel*	20	*19 Jul 86*	8
DANCE HITS '86	*K-Tel*	35	*18 Oct 86*	7
TOGETHER	*K-Tel*	20	*1 Nov 86*	10
This album is different from previous chart entry.				
IMPRESSIONS – 15 INSTRUMENTAL IMAGES	*K-Tel*	15	*7 Feb 87*	14
RHYTHM OF THE NIGHT	*K-Tel*	36	*21 Mar 87*	7
HITS REVIVAL	*K-Tel (Holland)*	63	*21 Mar 87*	1
Holland import.				
FRIENDS AND LOVERS	*K-Tel*	10	*13 Jun 87*	10
HITS REVIVAL	*K-Tel*	10	*27 Jun 87*	9
TRUE LOVE	*K-Tel*	38	*17 Oct 87*	5
FROM MOTOWN WITH LOVE	*K-Tel*	9	*31 Oct 87*	21
ALWAYS	*K-Tel*	65	*14 Nov 87*	4
WOW WHAT A PARTY	*K-Tel*	97	*19 Dec 87*	2
HORIZONS	*K-Tel*	13	*5 Mar 88*	10
HITS REVIVAL 2: REPLAY	*K-Tel*	45	*30 Apr 88*	3
TSOP – THE SOUND OF PHILADELPHIA	*K-Tel*	26	*14 May 88*	9
THE HITS OF HOUSE ARE HERE	*K-Tel*	12	*11 Jun 88*	12
MOTOWN IN MOTION	*K-Tel*	28	*15 Oct 88*	13
THE RETURN OF SUPERBAD	*K-Tel*	83	*15 Oct 88*	4
THE LOVERS	*K-Tel*	50	*5 Nov 88*	5
RAPPIN' UP THE HOUSE	*K-Tel*	43	*26 Nov 88*	7
COMPILATION ALBUMS:	**HITS 10**			**WEEKS 61**
FROM MOTOWN WITH LOVE	*K-Tel*	6	*4 Feb 89*	7
RAPPIN' UP THE HOUSE	*K-Tel*	19	*14 Jan 89*	1
HIP HOUSE – THE DEEPEST BEATS IN TOWN	*K-Tel*	10	*25 Mar 89*	5
GLAM SLAM	*K-Tel*	5	*29 Jul 89*	8
LOVE HOUSE	*K-Tel*	5	*23 Sep 89*	7
ETERNAL LOVE	*K-Tel*	5	*30 Sep 89*	7
RAP ATTACK	*K-Tel*	6	*21 Oct 89*	7
SEDUCTION	*K-Tel*	15	*25 Nov 89*	4
CAN U FEEL IT? – THE CHAMPION LEGEND	*K-Tel*	12	*10 Mar 90*	3
HOOKED ON COUNTRY	*K-Tel*	6	*21 Apr 90*	12

Life Aid Armenia

COMPILATION ALBUMS:	**HITS 1**			**WEEKS 10**
THE EARTHQUAKE ALBUM . . . ROCK AID ARMENIA	*Life Aid Armenia*	3	*21 Apr 90*	10
Charity album to support victims of the Armenian Earthquake.				

Limbo

COMPILATION ALBUMS:	**HITS 1**			**WEEKS 1**
THE TUNNEL MIXES	*Limbo*	17	*18 May 96*	1

London

COMPILATION ALBUMS:	**HITS 6**			**WEEKS 24**
FFRR – SILVER ON BLACK	*London*	8	*10 Jun 89*	5
DANCE DECADE – DANCE HITS OF THE 80'S	*London*	8	*11 Nov 89*	7
THE NORTHERN BEAT	*London*	4	*16 Jun 90*	8
MASSIVE 4	*London*	20	*7 Jul 90*	2
ONLY FOR THE HEADSTRONG	*London*	10	*8 Feb 92*	1
ONLY FOR THE HEADSTRONG II	*London*	18	*20 Jun 92*	1

Loose End
ALBUMS:	HITS 1			WEEKS 5
CHUNKS OF FUNK	Loose Ends	46	11 Aug 84	5

Lotus
ALBUMS:	HITS 1			WEEKS 6
ECSTACY	Lotus	24	28 Oct 78	6

Mango
COMPILATION ALBUMS:	HITS 1			WEEKS 9
ON A REGGAE TIP	Mango	3	3 Jul 93	9

Marble Arch
ALBUMS:	HITS 1			WEEKS 3
STARS OF '68	Marble Arch	23	10 Feb 68	3

Marquee
COMPILATION ALBUMS:	HITS 1			WEEKS 6
MARQUEE METAL	Marquee	5	4 May 91	6

Massive Music
COMPILATION ALBUMS:	HITS 2			WEEKS 7
101% SPEED GARAGE VOLUME 2	Massive Music	16	25 Apr 98	2
101% SPEED GARAGE ANTHEMS	Massive Music	14	17 Apr 99	5

Mastercuts
COMPILATION ALBUMS:	HITS 12			WEEKS 27
CLASSIC MELLOW MASTERCUTS VOLUME 1	Mastercuts	18	28 Sep 91	2
NEW JACK SWING MASTERCUTS VOLUME 1	Mastercuts	8	21 Mar 92	5
CLASSIC FUNK MASTERCUTS VOLUME 1	Mastercuts	14	16 May 92	3
CLASSIC JAZZ-FUNK MASTERCUTS VOLUME 3	Mastercuts	18	4 Jul 92	1
CLASSIC MELLOW MASTERCUTS VOLUME 2	Mastercuts	12	15 Aug 92	3
CLASSIC SALSOUL MASTERCUTS VOLUME 1	Mastercuts	16	6 Mar 93	3
CLASSIC RARE GROOVE MASTERCUTS VOLUME 1	Mastercuts	14	24 Apr 93	3
CLASSIC P-FUNK MASTERCUTS VOLUME 1	Mastercuts	16	22 May 93	1
CLASSIC JAZZ FUNK MASTERCUTS VOLUME 4	Mastercuts	19	22 Jan 94	2
NEW JACK SWING VOLUME 3	Mastercuts	18	26 Mar 94	1
CLASSIC ELECTRO MASTERCUTS VOLUME 1	Mastercuts	18	14 May 94	1
CLASSIC HOUSE MASTERCUTS VOLUME 1	Mastercuts	11	18 Jun 94	2

Mastersound
ALBUMS:	HITS 1			WEEKS 1
HEAT OF SOUL VOLUME 1	Mastersound	96	28 Mar 87	1

Masterworks
COMPILATION ALBUMS:	HITS 1			WEEKS 3
TAKE 2: OPERA FAVOURITES/ORCHESTRAL CLASSICS	Masterworks	18	5 Dec 92	3

Mawson And Wareham
COMPILATION ALBUMS:	HITS 1			WEEKS 3
PETER HETHERINGTON: SONGS FROM THE HEART	Mawson And Wareham	10	16 Mar 91	3

Had 3 chart runs of 1 week each at the same period of time for 3 consecutive years.

MCA
ALBUMS:	HITS 1			WEEKS 2
PRECIOUS METAL	MCA	60	24 May 80	2

COMPILATION ALBUMS:	HITS 3			WEEKS 6
RHYTHM COUNTRY AND BLUES	MCA	19	23 Apr 94	2
MORE BUMP N' GRIND	MCA	9	27 May 95	3
THE TARANTTINO COLLECTION	MCA	18	2 Nov 96	1

MCI Music
COMPILATION ALBUMS:	HITS 1			WEEKS 1
BORN TO BE WILD	MCI Music	20	4 Mar 95	1

Mercury
ALBUMS:	HITS 3			WEEKS 9
WIRED FOR CLUBS (CLUB TRACKS VOLUME 1)	Mercury	58	2 Jul 83	4
BEAT RUNS WILD	Mercury	70	14 Jun 86	2
FORMULA THIRTY - 2	Mercury	80	1 Nov 86	3

COMPILATION ALBUMS:	HITS 1			WEEKS 21
TWO ROOMS - CELEBRATING THE SONGS OF ELTON JOHN AND BERNIE TAUPIN	Mercury	1	26 Oct 91	21

Metropole Music
COMPILATION ALBUMS:	HITS 3			WEEKS 7
DANNY RAMPLING - LOVE GROOVE DANCE PARTY	Metropole Music	10	25 May 96	3

DANNY RAMPLING – LOVE GROOVE DANCE PARTY	Metropole Music	17	8 Feb 97	2
This album is different from previous chart entry.				
DANNY RAMPLING/LOVE GROOVE PARTY 5 & 6	Metropole Music	12	7 Jun 97	2

Ministry Of Sound
Ministry Of Sound is an established nightclub in South London.

COMPILATION ALBUMS:	HITS 24		WEEKS 118	
MINISTRY OF SOUND: THE SESSIONS VOLUME 1	Ministry Of Sound	16	11 Sep 93	2
MINISTRY OF SOUND – THE SESSIONS VOLUME 2	Ministry Of Sound	6	30 Apr 94	5
MINISTRY OF SOUND – THE SESSIONS VOLUME 3	Ministry Of Sound	8	22 Oct 94	3
THE FUTURE SOUND OF NEW YORK	Sound Of Ministry	19	1 Apr 95	1
MINISTRY OF SOUND – THE SESSIONS 4	Sound Of Ministry	9	6 May 95	5
MINISTRY OF SOUND SESSIONS – VOLUME 5	Ministry Of Sound	15	30 Sep 95	5
MINISTRY OF SOUND SESSION SIX – FRANKIE KNUCKLES	Ministry Of Sound	8	16 Mar 96	4
ONE HALF OF A WHOLE DECADE – 5 YEARS . . .	Ministry Of Sound	9	21 Sep 96	6
NORTHERN EXPOSURE – SASHA & JOHN DIGWEED	Ministry Of Sound	7	12 Oct 96	4
SESSIONS SEVEN	Ministry Of Sound	4	1 Mar 97	4
MINISTRY OF SOUND CLASSICS MIXED BY JUDGE JULES	Ministry Of Sound	12	21 Jun 97	3
SESSIONS EIGHT – TODD TERRY	Ministry Of Sound	11	26 Jul 97	3
NORTHERN EXPOSURE 2 – SASHA & DIGWEED	Ministry Of Sound	15	27 Sep 97	2
SESSIONS NINE – ERICK MORILLO	Ministry Of Sound	17	14 Mar 98	1
CLUBBER'S GUIDE TO . . . IBIZA – JULES/TONG	Ministry Of Sound	2	4 Jul 98	9
THE IBIZA ANNUAL	Ministry Of Sound	1	5 Sep 98	9
CLUBBER'S GUIDE TO . . . NINETY NINE	Ministry Of Sound	1	30 Jan 99	7
GALAXY WEEKEND: MIXED BY BOY GEORGE & ALLISTER WHITEHEAD	Ministry Of Sound	6	15 May 99	4
TRANCE NATION: MIXED BY SYSTEM F	Ministry Of Sound	1	29 May 99	9
CLUBBERS GUIDE TO IBIZA – SUMMER '99	Ministry Of Sound	1	19 Jun 99	10
CLUBBER'S GUIDE TO . . . TRANCE: MIXED BY ATB	Ministry Of Sound	4	7 Aug 99	5
THE IBIZA ANNUAL: MIXED BY JUDGE JULES + TALL PAUL	Ministry Of Sound	1	28 Aug 99	8
TRANCE NATION 2: MIXED BY FERRY CORSTEN	Ministry Of Sound	1	9 Oct 99	6
GALAXY MIX – BOY GEORGE	Ministry Of Sound	8	30 Oct 99	3

Miracle

COMPILATION ALBUMS:	HITS 1		WEEKS 4	
LOVE ETERNAL	Miracle	5	4 Feb 95	4

Miss Moneypenny's

COMPILATION ALBUMS:	HITS 1		WEEKS 1	
GLAMOROUS ONE	Miss Moneypeny's	12	22 Mar 97	1

More Protein

COMPILATION ALBUMS:	HITS 1		WEEKS 1	
CLOSET CLASSICS VOLUME 1 – MORE PROTEIN SAMPLER	More Protein	20	1 Feb 92	1

Motown

ALBUMS:	HITS 14		WEEKS 175	
A COLLECTION OF TAMLA MOTOWN HITS	Tamla Motown	16	3 Apr 65	4
16 ORIGINAL BIG HITS – VOLUME 4	Tamla Motown	33	4 Mar 67	3
TAMLA MOTOWN HITS VOLUME 5	Tamla Motown	11	17 Jun 67	40
MOTOWN MEMORIES	Tamla Motown	21	10 Feb 68	13
TAMLA MOTOWN HITS VOLUME 6	Tamla Motown	32	24 Aug 68	4
COLLECTION OF BIG HITS VOLUME 8	Tamla Motown	56	21 Feb 70	1
MOTOWN MEMORIES	Tamla Motown	22	26 Feb 72	4
This album is different from previous chart entry.				
MOTOWN STORY	Tamla Motown	21	18 Mar 72	8
MOTOWN GOLD	Tamla Motown	8	1 Nov 75	35
MOTOWN GOLD VOLUME 2	Motown	28	5 Nov 77	4
BIG WHEELS OF MOTOWN	Motown	2	7 Oct 78	18
THE LAST DANCE	Motown	1	2 Feb 80	23
THE 20TH ANNIVERSARY ALBUM	Motown	53	2 Aug 80	2
MOTOWN DANCE PARTY	Motown	3	21 May 88	18
COMPILATION ALBUMS:	HITS 6		WEEKS 38	
MOTOWN DANCE PARTY 2	Motown	10	19 May 90	7
SOUL DECADE; THE SIXTIES	Motown/Atlantic	3	6 Oct 90	10
MOTOWN'S GREATEST LOVE SONGS	Motown	5	24 Oct 92	5
MOTOWN – THE ULTIMATE HITS COLLECTION	Motown	6	12 Nov 94	13
MOTOWN – THE HITS COLLECTION – VOLUME 2	Motown	19	4 Nov 95	1
MOTOWN 40 FOREVER	Motown	15	12 Sep 98	2

Mountain

ALBUMS:	HITS 1		WEEKS 2	
GOLDEN FIDDLE AWARDS 1976	Mountain	45	3 Jul 76	2

Music For Pleasure

ALBUMS:	HITS 1		WEEKS 1	
BREAKTHROUGH	Music For Pleasure	49	4 Dec 71	1

Music Unites
COMPILATION ALBUMS: HITS 1   WEEKS 1

JOURNEYS BY DJ VOLUME 4	Music Unites	19	12 Mar 94	1

Needle
ALBUMS: HITS 3   WEEKS 14

DANCE MANIA VOLUME 1	Needle	46	4 Jul 87	4
MAD ON HOUSE VOLUME 1	Needle	81	20 Feb 88	2
HOUSE HITS	Needle	25	14 May 88	8

Nems
ALBUMS: HITS 1   WEEKS 2

LIVE AND HEAVY	NEMS	100	12 Dec 81	2

Network
COMPILATION ALBUMS: HITS 2   WEEKS 3

RENAISSANCE - MIX COLLECTION - PART 2	Network	16	20 Jan 96	2
BACK TO BASICS - CUT THE CRAP	Network	20	13 Apr 96	1

Nice
COMPILATION ALBUMS: HITS 1   WEEKS 1

TRIBUTE TO THE SMALL FACES - LONG AGOS/WORLDS APART	Nice	20	14 Sep 96	1

Nouveau Music
ALBUMS: HITS 3   WEEKS 4

CLASSIC THEMES	Nouveau Music	61	24 Sep 83	2
ESSENTIAL DISCO AND DANCE	Nouveau Music	96	2 Jun 84	1
DREAM MELODIES	Nouveau Music	91	30 Mar 85	1

NPG
COMPILATION ALBUMS: HITS 1   WEEKS 1

1-800 NEW FUNK	NPG	15	20 Aug 94	1

Numa
ALBUMS: HITS 1   WEEKS 1

NUMA RECORDS YEAR 1	Numa	94	22 Mar 86	1

Old Gold
COMPILATION ALBUMS: HITS 1   WEEKS 1

LET'S DANCE - SOUND OF THE SIXTIES PART 1	Old Gold	18	7 Apr 90	1

Oriole
ALBUMS: HITS 1   WEEKS 5

THE MERSEY BEAT VOLUME 1	Oriole	17	24 Aug 63	5

Parkfield
COMPILATION ALBUMS: HITS 1   WEEKS 2

NOTHING COMPARES TO THIS	Parkfield	13	28 Jul 90	2

Parlophone
COMPILATION ALBUMS: HITS 2   WEEKS 12

IT'S COOL	Parlophone	3	22 Jun 91	7
60'S SOUL 90'S SOUL	Parlophone	6	3 Sep 94	5

Perfecto
COMPILATION ALBUMS: HITS 2   WEEKS 5

HARDCORE DJS . . . TAKE CONTROL	Perfecto	15	1 Aug 92	4
PERFECTO FLUORO: OAKENFOLD	Perfecto	18	9 Nov 96	1

Philips
ALBUMS: HITS 3   WEEKS 24

20 ORIGINAL CHART HITS	Philips	9	2 Jun 73	11
NICE 'N' EASY	Philips	36	2 Jun 73	1
NEW WAVE	Philips	11	6 Aug 77	12

Polydor
ALBUMS: HITS 4   WEEKS 14

STEREO MUSICALE SHOWCASE	Polydor	26	10 Dec 66	2
THE A-Z OF EASY LISTENING	Polydor	24	9 Oct 71	4
20 OF ANOTHER KIND	Polydor	45	24 Feb 79	3
MONSTERS OF ROCK	Polydor	16	18 Oct 80	5

COMPILATION ALBUMS: HITS 2   WEEKS 26

THE MARQUEE - 30 LEGENDARY YEARS	Polydor	1	4 Feb 89	21
ABSOLUTION - ROCK THE ALTERNATIVE WAY	Polydor	6	5 Oct 91	5

Polydor/EMI
COMPILATION ALBUMS: HITS 1   WEEKS 13

PURPLE RAINBOWS	Polydor/EMI	1	13 Jul 91	13

Polydor/Universal Music TV

COMPILATION ALBUMS:	HITS 1			WEEKS 7
ABBAMANIA	*Polydor/Universal Music TV*	2	*20 Nov 99*	7
Tribute album to Abba.				

PolyGram TV

After Seagram's merger of PolyGram with Universal, charts from 13 March 99 reflected change of label to Universal Music TV on all entries.

COMPILATION ALBUMS:	HITS 97			WEEKS 488
SOUL EMOTION	*PolyGram TV*	1	*21 Mar 92*	10
COUNTRY MOODS	*PolyGram TV*	2	*2 May 92*	10
BEATS RHYMES AND BASSLINES – THE BEST OF RAP	*PolyGram TV*	7	*30 May 92*	3
POWER CUTS – ROCK'S GREATEST HITS	*PolyGram TV*	5	*6 Jun 92*	9
MODERN LOVE	*PolyGram TV*	1	*20 Jun 92*	20
DANCING ON SUNSHINE	*PolyGram TV/Virgin*	4	*18 Jul 92*	11
BLAME IT ON THE BOOGIE	*PolyGram TV*	5	*1 Aug 92*	8
READING – THE INDIE ALBUM	*PolyGram TV*	5	*5 Sep 92*	5
COUNTRY ROADS	*PolyGram TV*	3	*27 Mar 93*	10
MEGA-LO-MANIA	*PolyGram TV*	8	*17 Apr 93*	6
UNDER THE COVERS	*PolyGram TV*	11	*24 Apr 93*	5
MIDNIGHT MOODS – THE LIGHTER SIDE OF JAZZ	*Verve/PolyGram TV*	3	*8 May 93*	8
WOMAN TO WOMAN	*PolyGram TV*	5	*5 Jun 93*	10
THE GIFT OF SONG	*PolyGram TV*	7	*19 Jun 93*	4
SOUL INSPIRATION	*PolyGram TV*	4	*26 Jun 93*	7
THE BLUES EXPERIENCE	*PolyGram TV*	7	*3 Jul 93*	6
TEMPTED	*PolyGram TV*	10	*24 Jul 93*	4
LEADERS OF THE PACK	*PolyGram TV*	9	*14 Aug 93*	9
ALL NIGHT LONG	*PolyGram TV*	15	*14 Aug 93*	3
PROGRESSION	*PolyGram TV*	9	*4 Sep 93*	3
'ROUND MIDNIGHT	*Verve/PolyGram TV*	16	*2 Oct 93*	2
DISCO DIVAS	*PolyGram TV*	4	*9 Oct 93*	5
DANCE DIVAS	*PolyGram TV*	11	*19 Feb 94*	3
FACE THE MUSIC – TORVILL AND DEAN	*PolyGram TV*	8	*5 Mar 94*	3
SOUL DEVOTION	*PolyGram TV*	1	*12 Mar 94*	14
I KNOW THEM SO WELL – TIM RICE	*PolyGram TV*	2	*19 Mar 94*	7
WOMAN 2 WOMAN TWO	*PolyGram TV*	9	*9 Apr 94*	4
ACOUSTIC MOODS	*PolyGram TV*	4	*23 Apr 94*	8
REMEMBER THEN – 30 DOO-WOP GREATS	*PolyGram TV*	10	*21 May 94*	3
ROCK THERAPY	*PolyGram TV*	9	*2 Jul 94*	6
POWER AND SOUL	*PolyGram TV*	5	*23 Jul 94*	10
GROOVIN'	*PolyGram TV*	2	*27 Aug 94*	7
SATIN AND STEEL – WOMEN IN ROCK	*PolyGram TV*	3	*10 Sep 94*	7
SOUL NIGHTS	*PolyGram TV*	3	*17 Sep 94*	6
SENSES	*PolyGram TV*	5	*1 Oct 94*	5
AFTER MIDNIGHT	*PolyGram TV*	17	*15 Oct 94*	1
ENDLESS LOVE	*PolyGram TV*	3	*11 Feb 95*	6
ELECTRIC DREAMS	*PolyGram TV*	3	*25 Feb 95*	8
THE ESSENTIAL GROOVE	*PolyGram TV*	11	*11 Mar 95*	3
EMERALD ROCK	*PolyGram TV*	14	*25 Mar 95*	3
TOGETHER	*PolyGram TV*	2	*1 Apr 95*	5
EVERY SONG TELLS A STORY	*PolyGram TV*	17	*8 Apr 95*	1
ROCKS OFF	*PolyGram TV*	4	*15 Apr 95*	5
LET'S HEAR IT FOR THE GIRLS	*PolyGram TV*	8	*6 May 95*	5
SILK AND STEEL	*PolyGram TV*	3	*20 May 95*	6
TEENAGE KICKS	*PolyGram TV*	8	*3 Jun 95*	3
WORLD IN UNION – ANTHEMS	*PolyGram TV*	8	*10 Jun 95*	4
SUNNY AFTERNOONS	*PolyGram TV*	6	*1 Jul 95*	3
ACOUSTIC FREEWAY	*PolyGram TV*	7	*19 Aug 95*	4
SUMMERTIME SOUL	*PolyGram TV*	5	*26 Aug 95*	4
ACOUSTIC ROCK	*PolyGram TV*	7	*23 Sep 95*	5
SOFT ROCK	*PolyGram TV*	3	*10 Feb 96*	6
PASS THE VIBES	*PolyGram TV*	4	*10 Feb 96*	7
THE LOOK OF LOVE	*PolyGram TV*	6	*10 Feb 96*	7
CLASSIC MOODS	*PolyGram TV*	7	*10 Feb 96*	8
FREEWAY	*PolyGram TV*	17	*2 Mar 96*	1
AMBIENT MOODS	*PolyGram TV*	7	*9 Mar 96*	5
THE BEST OF WOMAN TO WOMAN	*PolyGram TV*	3	*23 Mar 96*	5
GO WITH THE FLOW – ESSENTIAL ACID JAZZ	*PolyGram TV*	9	*27 Apr 96*	2
BOYZ OF SWING	*PolyGram TV*	1	*11 May 96*	4
LADYKILLERS	*PolyGram TV*	3	*1 Jun 96*	4
FUNKMASTER MIX	*PolyGram TV*	16	*8 Jun 96*	2
TRUEBRIT	*PolyGram TV*	7	*15 Jun 96*	4
MIX ZONE	*PolyGram TV*	2	*22 Jun 96*	5
SUMMER VYBES	*PolyGram TV*	8	*29 Jun 96*	3
HORIZONS – 12 DREAMHOUSE ANTHEMS	*PolyGram TV*	17	*6 Jul 96*	1
PURE DANCE '96	*PolyGram TV*	5	*7 Sep 96*	4
THE SAX ALBUM	*PolyGram TV*	6	*7 Sep 96*	4
BOYZ OF SWING II	*PolyGram TV*	6	*14 Sep 96*	5

HITS ZONE '97	PolyGram TV	11	14 Dec 96	5
WIRED	PolyGram TV	2	1 Feb 97	6
CRUSH	PolyGram TV	5	8 Feb 97	5
DRUM & BASS MIX 97	PolyGram TV	11	22 Mar 97	2
FUSED	PolyGram TV	14	17 May 97	2
TRACKSPOTTING	PolyGram TV	12	24 May 97	4
LADYKILLERS 2	PolyGram TV	15	7 Jun 97	2
MIXED EMOTIONS	PolyGram TV	6	21 Jun 97	5
SUGAR HITS!	PolyGram TV	9	12 Jul 97	3
HITS ZONE SUMMER '97	PolyGram TV	8	30 Aug 97	4
DANGER ZONE	PolyGram TV	15	30 Aug 97	2
PURE DANCE 97	PolyGram TV	9	18 Oct 97	3
HEART & SOUL	PolyGram TV	17	8 Nov 97	1
HITS ZONE - THE BEST OF '97	PolyGram TV	18	15 Nov 97	1
LOVE - 39 ALL-TIME LOVE CLASSICS	PolyGram TV	1	14 Feb 98	4
PURE ROCK BALLADS	PolyGram TV	10	21 Feb 98	4
INTO THE BLUE	PolyGram TV	10	28 Mar 98	3
UNDISPUTED	PolyGram TV	6	11 Apr 98	3
FRIDAY NIGHT FEVER	PolyGram TV	6	25 Apr 98	4
CONNECTED	PolyGram TV	18	2 May 98	1
MIXED EMOTIONS II	PolyGram TV	3	4 Jul 98	8
COOL GROOVES	PolyGram TV	12	5 Sep 98	3
POWER & SOUL	PolyGram TV	5	12 Sep 98	5
MOBO 1998 - MUSIC OF BLACK ORIGIN	PolyGram TV	13	24 Oct 98	2
THE BEST OF DRIVE TIME	PolyGram TV	12	31 Oct 98	1
SOUL	PolyGram TV	10	7 Nov 98	3
MUSIC OF THE NIGHT	PolyGram TV	5	12 Dec 98	20
PARTY	PolyGram TV	19	9 Jan 99	1

PolyGram TV/Sony TV

COMPILATION ALBUMS:	**HITS 4**			**WEEKS 26**
MUNDO AFRIKA	Sony TV / PolyGram TV	17	13 Jul 96	1
THE FIRST SUMMER OF LOVE	Sony TV / PolyGram TV	6	2 Aug 97	7
THE SUMMER OF LOVE GOES ON - SIXTIES	Sony TV / PolyGram TV	16	1 Aug 98	1
WOMAN	PolyGram TV / Sony TV	5	21 Nov 98	17

PolyGram TV/Warner.esp

COMPILATION ALBUMS:	**HITS 2**			**WEEKS 16**
ALL MY LOVE	warner.esp / PolyGram TV	7	1 Nov 97	4
LOVE SONGS	PolyGram TV / warner.esp	1	13 Feb 99	12

Polystar

ALBUMS:	**HITS 7**			**WEEKS 72**
BOOGIE BUS	Polystar	23	19 May 79	11
CHAMPAGNE AND ROSES	Polystar	7	3 May 80	14
I AM WOMAN	Polystar	11	30 Aug 80	13
COUNTRY ROUND UP	Polystar	64	11 Oct 80	3
THE HITMAKERS	Polystar	45	6 Dec 80	10
ROLL ON	Polystar	3	4 Apr 81	13
MONSTER TRACKS	Polystar	20	17 Oct 81	8

Portrait

ALBUMS:	**HITS 2**			**WEEKS 18**
THE HEAT IS ON - 16 TRACKS	Portrait	9	16 Aug 86	12
SUMMER DAYS, BOOGIE NIGHTS - 16 TRACKS	Portrait	40	16 Aug 86	6

Positiva

COMPILATION ALBUMS:	**HITS 2**			**WEEKS 4**
PHASE ONE	Positiva	15	2 Apr 94	1
ACCESS ALL AREAS	Positiva	11	26 Apr 97	3

Proto

ALBUMS:	**HITS 1**			**WEEKS 1**
TWELVE INCHES OF PLEASURE	Proto	100	26 Nov 83	1

Prototype

COMPILATION ALBUMS:	**HITS 1**			**WEEKS 2**
SEB FONTAINE - PROTOTYPE	Prototype	14	8 May 99	2

Pump

COMPILATION ALBUMS:	**HITS 4**			**WEEKS 12**
EIGHTIES SOUL WEEKENDER 2	Pump	11	20 Jul 96	4
THE VERY BEST OF PURE SWING	Pump	17	7 Dec 96	3
SLOW JAMS	Pump	10	8 Feb 97	3
EIGHTIES SOUL WEEKENDER 3	Pump	15	10 May 97	2

Pure Music

COMPILATION ALBUMS:	**HITS 7**			**WEEKS 50**
THE LADY SINGS THE BLUES	Pure Music	9	22 Oct 94	4

THE GREATEST NUMBER ONES OF THE EIGHTIES	*Pure Music*	11	*5 Nov 94*	4
DANCE MANIA 95 – VOLUME 1	*Pure Music*	1	*11 Feb 95*	11
DANCE MANIA 95 – VOLUME 2	*Pure Music*	1	*8 Apr 95*	9
DANCE MANIA 95 – VOLUME 3	*Pure Music*	1	*15 Jul 95*	7
DANCE MANIA 95 – VOLUME 4	*Pure Music*	7	*30 Sep 95*	4
THE BEST OF DANCE MANIA 95	*Pure Music*	5	*11 Nov 95*	11

Pure Silk

COMPILATION ALBUMS:	HITS 1			WEEKS 2
PURE SILK – A NEW DIMENSION	*Pure Silk*	15	*6 Nov 99*	2

Pye

ALBUMS:	HITS 9			WEEKS 39
CURTAIN UP	*Pye Nixa*	4	*9 May 59*	13
HONEY HIT PARADE	*Pye Golden Guinea*	13	*23 Jun 62*	7
ALL THE HITS BY ALL THE STARS	*Pye Golden Guinea*	19	*1 Dec 62*	2
HITSVILLE	*Pye Golden Guinea*	11	*7 Sep 63*	6
HITSVILLE VOLUME 2	*Pye Golden Guinea*	20	*23 Nov 63*	1
THE BLUES VOLUME 1	*Pye*	15	*4 Jan 64*	3
THE BLUES VOLUME 2	*Pye*	16	*30 May 64*	3
PYE CHARTBUSTERS	*Pye*	36	*16 Oct 71*	1
PYE CHARTBUSTERS VOLUME 2	*Pye*	29	*18 Dec 71*	3

Quality Price Music

COMPILATION ALBUMS:	HITS 2			WEEKS 3
CLUB IBIZA	*Quality Price Music*	15	*4 Nov 95*	1
CLUB IBIZA SILVER EDITION [RE]	*Quality Price Music*	19	*30 Mar 96*	1
Special repackaged edition.				
CLUB IBIZA – VOLUME 2	*Quality Price Music*	19	*19 Oct 96*	1

Quality Television

COMPILATION ALBUMS:	HITS 13			WEEKS 79
HIT THE DECKS VOLUME 1 – BATTLE OF THE DJS	*Quality Television*	3	*15 Feb 92*	7
TEMPTATION	*Quality Television*	3	*2 May 92*	8
THE SOUND OF SKA	*Quality Television*	4	*6 Jun 92*	6
TO HAVE AND TO HOLD – THE WEDDING ALBUM	*Quality Television*	7	*20 Jun 92*	4
HIT THE DECKS VOLUME 2 – BATTLE OF THE DJS	*Quality Television*	3	*4 Jul 92*	6
CELEBRATION – THE BEST OF REGGAE – 25 YEARS OF TROJAN	*Quality Television*	5	*11 Jul 92*	8
DANGER ZONE VOLUME 1	*Quality Television*	16	*18 Jul 92*	3
THREE STEPS TO HEAVEN – ROCK 'N' ROLL LEGENDS	*Quality Television*	6	*12 Sep 92*	5
HIT THE DECKS VOLUME III	*Quality Television*	3	*7 Nov 92*	4
THE POWER OF LOVE	*Quality Television*	4	*7 Nov 92*	7
RARE GROOVE – DYNAMIC DISCO HITS	*Quality Television*	7	*21 Nov 92*	14
THE NASHVILLE DREAM	*Quality Television*	10	*30 Jan 93*	3
GLAM MANIA	*Quality Television*	10	*8 May 93*	4

R&S

COMPILATION ALBUMS:	HITS 2			WEEKS 2
R & S RECORDS – ORDER TO DANCE	*R&S*	18	*16 Nov 91*	1
IN ORDER TO DANCE 5	*R&S*	16	*24 Sep 94*	1

RCA

ALBUMS:	HITS 1			WEEKS 5
GET ON UP	*RCA*	35	*28 May 83*	5

COMPILATION ALBUMS:	HITS 5			WEEKS 31
RAINBOW WARRIORS	*RCA*	2	*24 Jun 89*	10
Benefit album to support Greenpeace.				
CELTIC HEART	*RCA*	6	*13 Feb 93*	10
PRIDE – THE VERY BEST OF SCOTLAND	*RCA*	13	*1 Jul 95*	4
THE BEAUTIFUL GAME – EUFA EURO '96	*RCA*	10	*1 Jun 96*	6
EVERY WOMAN	*RCA*	19	*11 Apr 98*	1

Reachin'

COMPILATION ALBUMS:	HITS 1			WEEKS 2
RAVE	*Reachin'*	18	*9 Nov 91*	2

React

COMPILATION ALBUMS:	HITS 4			WEEKS 6
FRESKA!	*React*	20	*4 Jun 94*	1
HOUSE NATION 1	*React*	20	*24 Sep 94*	1
LAURENT GARNIER – LABORATOIRE MIX	*React*	16	*2 Nov 96*	1
TWICE AS NICE IN AYIA NAPA – DJ SPOONY	*React*	18	*16 Oct 99*	3

Really Useful/Polydor

ALBUMS:	HITS 1			WEEKS 9
ANDREW LLOYD WEBBER – THE PREMIERE COLLECTION	*Really Useful/Polydor*	3	*12 Nov 88*	9

COMPILATION ALBUMS:	HITS 5			WEEKS 96
ANDREW LLOYD WEBBER – THE PREMIERE COLLECTION	*Really Useful/Polydor*	1	*14 Jan 89*	55

SKINBEAT - THE FIRST TOUCH	Really Useful/Polydor	6	31 Mar 90	8
THE PREMIERE COLLECTION - ENCORE (ANDREW LLOYD WEBBER)	Really Useful/Polydor	2	28 Nov 92	11
THE VERY BEST OF ANDREW LLOYD WEBBER	Really Useful/Polydor	3	5 Nov 94	18
SONGS FROM WHISTLE DOWN THE WIND	Really Useful/Polydor	3	31 Oct 98	4

Re-recording of songs from the Stage Show.

Record Shack
ALBUMS:		HITS 1		WEEKS 4
RECORD SHACK PRESENTS - VOLUME ONE	Record Shack	41	8 Sep 84	4

Reinforced
COMPILATION ALBUMS:		HITS 1		WEEKS 1
INFORCERS 3	Reinforced	18	29 May 93	1

Renaissance Music
COMPILATION ALBUMS:		HITS 1		WEEKS 2
RENAISSANCE WORLDWIDE LONDON	Renaissance	16	18 Oct 97	2

Respond
ALBUMS:		HITS 1		WEEKS 3
RESPOND PACKAGE - LOVE THE REASON	Respond	50	15 Oct 83	3

Rhythm King
ALBUMS:		HITS 1		WEEKS 2
CHICAGO JACKBEAT VOLUME 2	Rhythm King	67	6 Jun 87	2

Ritz
ALBUMS:		HITS 1		WEEKS 6
TEARDROPS	Ritz	37	18 Jun 83	6

Ronco
ALBUMS:		HITS 44		WEEKS 408
20 STAR TRACKS	Ronco	2	21 Oct 72	13
BLAZING BULLETS	Ronco	17	8 Nov 75	8
STAR TRACKIN' 76	Ronco	9	24 Jan 76	5
SUPERGROUPS	Ronco	57	16 Jul 77	1
BLACK JOY	Ronco	26	26 Nov 77	13
BOOGIE NIGHTS	Ronco	5	18 Mar 78	7
BOOGIE FEVER	Ronco	15	18 Nov 78	11
ROCK LEGENDS	Ronco	54	9 Jun 79	3
ROCK 'N' ROLLER DISCO	Ronco	3	3 Nov 79	11
PEACE IN THE VALLEY	Ronco	6	8 Dec 79	18
MILITARY GOLD	Ronco	62	22 Dec 79	3
STREET LEVEL	Ronco	29	25 Oct 80	5
COUNTRY LEGENDS	Ronco	9	8 Nov 80	12
RADIOACTIVE	Ronco	13	15 Nov 80	9
SPACE INVADERS	Ronco	47	29 Nov 80	3
THE LEGENDARY BIG BANDS	Ronco	24	6 Dec 80	6
DISCO DAZE AND DISCO NITES	Ronco	1	9 May 81	23
SUPER HITS 1 & 2	Ronco	2	19 Sep 81	17
COUNTRY SUNRISE/COUNTRY SUNSET	Ronco	27	24 Oct 81	11
ROCK HOUSE	Ronco	44	14 Nov 81	9
MISTY MORNINGS	Ronco	44	12 Dec 81	5
MEMORIES ARE MADE OF THIS	Ronco	84	12 Dec 81	4
HITS, HITS, HITS	Ronco	2	26 Dec 81	10
DISCO UK AND DISCO USA	Ronco	7	24 Apr 82	10
CHARTBUSTERS	Ronco	3	15 May 82	10
OVERLOAD	Ronco	10	3 Jul 82	8
SOUL DAZE/SOUL NITES	Ronco	25	28 Aug 82	10
BREAKOUT	Ronco	4	11 Sep 82	8
MUSIC FOR THE SEASONS	Ronco	41	30 Oct 82	10
CHART WARS	Ronco	30	27 Nov 82	7
THE GREAT COUNTRY MUSIC SHOW	Ronco	38	27 Nov 82	7
THE BEST OF THE COMPOSERS: BEETHOVEN/STRAUSS/TCHAIKOWSKY/ MOZART	Ronco	49	18 Dec 82	10
RAIDERS OF THE POP CHARTS	Ronco	1	25 Dec 82	17
CHART RUNNERS	Ronco	4	19 Mar 83	13
CHART ENCOUNTERS OF THE HIT KIND	Ronco	5	21 May 83	10
LOVERS ONLY	Ronco	12	18 Jun 83	13
HITS ON FIRE	Ronco	11	16 Jul 83	10
THE HIT SQUAD - CHART TRACKING	Ronco	4	17 Sep 83	9
THE HIT SQUAD - NIGHT CLUBBING	Ronco	28	17 Sep 83	7
THE HIT SQUAD - HITS OF '83	Ronco	12	12 Nov 83	11
CHART TREK VOLUMES 1 AND 2	Ronco	20	7 Jan 84	9
SOMETIMES WHEN WE TOUCH	Ronco	8	21 Jan 84	14
BABY LOVE	Ronco	47	24 Mar 84	6
DREAMS AND THEMES	Ronco	75	7 Apr 84	2

Ronco & Telstar

ALBUMS:		HITS 1			WEEKS 27
GREEN VELVET	Ronco	6	17 Dec 83	17
GREEN VELVET [RI]	Telstar	10	15 Dec 84	10

Ronco/Charisma

ALBUMS:		HITS 1			WEEKS 9
WE ARE MOST AMUSED (THE BEST OF BRITISH COMEDY)	Ronco/Charisma	30	19 Dec 81	9

Rough Trade

ALBUMS:		HITS 1			WEEKS 3
SOWETO	Rough Trade	66	14 Aug 82	3

Rumour

COMPILATION ALBUMS:		HITS 5			WEEKS 6
BREAKS, BASS AND BLEEPS 2	Rumour	20	20 Jul 91	1
BREAKS, BASS AND BLEEPS 4	Rumour	20	18 Apr 92	1
MOVIN' ON	Rumour	20	27 Jun 92	1
TRANCE	Rumour	18	26 Sep 92	1
MOVIN' ON 2	Rumour	15	24 Oct 92	2

Satellite

COMPILATION ALBUMS:		HITS 2			WEEKS 3
TUFF JAM PRESENTS UNDERGROUND FREQUENCIES – 1	Satellite	20	19 Jul 97	1
TUFF JAM PRESENTS UNDERGROUND FREQUENCIES – 2	Satellite	14	23 May 98	2

Save The Children Fund

ALBUMS:		HITS 1			WEEKS 16
STARS CHARITY FANTASIA SAVE THE CHILDREN FUND	SCF	6	10 Sep 66	16

Secret

ALBUMS:		HITS 2			WEEKS 8
CARRY ON OI!	Secret	60	31 Oct 81	4
OI! OI! THAT'S YER LOT	Secret	54	25 Sep 82	4

Serious

ALBUMS:		HITS 10			WEEKS 41
SERIOUS HIP-HOP 2	Serious	95	28 Mar 87	1
THE BEST OF HOUSE VOLUME 1	Serious	55	4 Jul 87	12
BEST OF HOUSE VOLUME 2	Serious	30	12 Sep 87	7
HIP-HOP '87	Serious	81	17 Oct 87	1
BEST OF HOUSE VOLUME 3	Serious	61	14 Nov 87	3
BEST OF HOUSE MEGAMIX	Serious	77	12 Dec 87	4
DANCE MANIA VOLUME 2	Serious	59	20 Feb 88	2
BEST OF HOUSE VOLUME 4	Serious	27	12 Mar 88	8
BEST OF HOUSE MEXAMIX VOLUME 2	Serious	73	14 May 88	2
ACID TRAX MEGAMIX VOLUME 1	Serious	93	29 Oct 88	1

Shut Up And Dance

COMPILATION ALBUMS:		HITS 1			WEEKS 1
SHUT UP AND DANCE/FUCK OFF AND DIE	Shut Up And Dance	20	22 Feb 92	1

Six6

COMPILATION ALBUMS:		HITS 2			WEEKS 8
RENAISSANCE	Six6	9	1 Oct 94	5
RENAISSANCE THE MIX COLLECTION – PART 3	Six6	12	6 Jul 96	3

Solar

ALBUMS:		HITS 1			WEEKS 1
THE SOLAR SYSTEM	Solar	70	30 May 87	1

Solid State

COMPILATION ALBUMS:		HITS 2			WEEKS 3
HIP HOP DON'T STOP – 20 CLASSIC HIP HOP SUPERJAMS	Solid State	16	8 Feb 97	1
HOUSE OF HANDBAG – NUOVO DISCO COLLECTION	Solid State	17	29 Mar 97	2

Some Bizarre

ALBUMS:		HITS 1			WEEKS 1
THE SOME BIZZARRE ALBUM	Some Bizzare	58	14 Mar 81	1

Sony TV

COMPILATION ALBUMS:		HITS 1			WEEKS 5
ABSOLUTE GOLD	Sony TV	3	1 Feb 97	5

Sony TV/Global TV

COMPILATION ALBUMS:		HITS 4			WEEKS 26
THIS YEAR'S LOVE IS FOREVER	Sony TV/Global TV	4	25 Nov 95	11
IT TAKES TWO	Sony TV/Global TV	6	13 Apr 96	6

THE BEST OF VYBIN'	Sony TV / Global TV	12	16 Nov 96	2
THIS YEAR'S LOVE (WILL LAST FOREVER) XXX	Sony TV / Global TV	12	30 Nov 96	7

Sony TV/MCI

COMPILATION ALBUMS:	HITS 1		WEEKS 1	
LOVE TRAIN - THE SOUND OF PHILADELPHIA	Sony TV / MCI	18	18 Apr 98	1

Sony Music TV/Universal Music TV

COMPILATION ALBUMS:	HITS 1		WEEKS 8	
COUNTRY	Sony Music TV / Universal Music TV	8	17 Jul 99	8

Sony TV/warner.Esp

COMPILATION ALBUMS:	HITS 1		WEEKS 3	
LIVE 4 EVER	Sony TV / warner.esp	11	11 Jul 98	3

Sound Dimension

COMPILATION ALBUMS:	HITS 7		WEEKS 28	
A RETROSPECTIVE OF HOUSE '91–'95 – VOLUME 1	Sound Dimension	10	5 Aug 95	10
A RETROSPECTIVE OF HOUSE '91–'95 – VOLUME 2	Sound Dimension	15	13 Jan 96	3
A RETROSPECTIVE OF HOUSE '91–'96 – VOLUME 3: JAY/KELLY/ANDERSON	Sound Dimension	9	1 Jun 96	2
A RETROSPECTIVE OF HOUSE '91–'96 – VOLUME 4	Sound Dimension	7	7 Sep 96	5
AN INTROSPECTIVE OF HOUSE: 1ST DIMENSION	Sound Dimension	18	1 Feb 97	2
AN INTROSPECTIVE OF HOUSE: 2ND DIMENSION	Sound Dimension	9	14 Jun 97	4
AN INTROSPECTIVE OF HOUSE: 3RD DIMENSION	Sound Dimension	14	13 Sep 97	2

Starblend

ALBUMS:	HITS 7		WEEKS 31	
IN TOUCH	Starblend	89	12 Nov 83	2
BROKEN DREAMS	Starblend	48	23 Jun 84	7
12 X 12 MEGA MIXES	Starblend	77	27 Apr 85	2
AMERICAN DREAMS	Starblend	43	3 Aug 85	8
DISCOVER COUNTRY/DISCOVER NEW COUNTRY	Starblend	60	12 Jul 86	3
HEARTBREAKERS – 18 CLASSIC LOVE HITS	Starblend	38	16 Aug 86	8
ABSOLUTE ROCK 'N' ROLL	Starblend	88	20 Sep 86	1

Start

COMPILATION ALBUMS:	HITS 1		WEEKS 5	
THE SONGS OF BOB DYLAN	Start	13	15 Apr 89	5

Stax

ALBUMS:	HITS 1		WEEKS 16	
HIT THE ROAD STAX	Stax	10	8 Apr 67	16

Stiff

ALBUMS:	HITS 1		WEEKS 7	
STIFF'S LIVE STIFFS	Stiff	28	11 Mar 78	7

Stoic

ALBUMS:	HITS 1		WEEKS 14	
EMERALD CLASSICS	Stoic	35	16 Jun 84	14

Street Sounds

ALBUMS:	HITS 54		WEEKS 259	
STREET SOUNDS EDITION 2	Street Sounds	35	19 Feb 83	6
STREET SOUNDS EDITION 3	Street Sounds	21	23 Apr 83	5
STREET SOUNDS EDITION 4	Street Sounds	14	25 Jun 83	8
STREET SOUNDS EDITION 5	Street Sounds	16	13 Aug 83	8
STREET SOUNDS EDITION 6	Street Sounds	23	8 Oct 83	5
STREET SOUNDS ELECTRO 1	Street Sounds	18	22 Oct 83	8
STREET SOUNDS EDITION 7	Street Sounds	48	17 Dec 83	4
STREET SOUNDS ELECTRO 2	Street Sounds	49	7 Jan 84	7
STREET SOUNDS HI-ENERGY NO 1	Street Sounds	71	3 Mar 84	1
STREET SOUNDS EDITION 8	Street Sounds	22	10 Mar 84	7
STREET SOUNDS CRUCIAL ELECTRO	Street Sounds	24	10 Mar 84	10
STREET SOUNDS ELECTRO 3	Street Sounds	25	7 Apr 84	9
STREET SOUNDS EDITION 9	Street Sounds	22	12 May 84	5
STREET SOUNDS ELECTRO 4	Street Sounds	25	9 Jun 84	9
STREET SOUNDS UK ELECTRO	Street Sounds	60	30 Jun 84	4
LET THE MUSIC SCRATCH	Street Sounds	91	21 Jul 84	3
STREET SOUNDS CRUCIAL ELECTRO 2	Street Sounds	35	11 Aug 84	6
STREET SOUNDS EDITION 10	Street Sounds	24	18 Aug 84	6
STREET SOUNDS ELECTRO 5	Street Sounds	17	6 Oct 84	6
STREET SOUNDS EDITION 11	Street Sounds	48	10 Nov 84	4
STREET SOUNDS ELECTRO 6	Street Sounds	24	9 Mar 85	10
STREET SOUNDS ELECTRO 7	Street Sounds	12	18 May 85	7
STREET SOUNDS EDITION 12	Street Sounds	23	18 May 85	4
STREET SOUNDS ELECTRO 8	Street Sounds	23	13 Jul 85	5
STREET SOUNDS EDITION 13	Street Sounds	19	17 Aug 85	9

STREET SOUNDS N.Y. VS. L.A. BEATS	Street Sounds	65	17 Aug 85	4
STREET SOUNDS ELECTRO 9	Street Sounds	18	5 Oct 85	6
STREET SOUNDS EDITION 14	Street Sounds	43	16 Nov 85	3
STREET SOUNDS EDITION 15	Street Sounds	58	21 Dec 85	8
STREET SOUNDS ELECTRO 10	Street Sounds	72	21 Dec 85	6
STREET SOUNDS HIP-HOP ELECTRO 11	Street Sounds	19	29 Mar 86	5
STREET SOUNDS EDITION 16	Street Sounds	17	5 Apr 86	7
JAZZ JUICE 2	Street Sounds	96	21 Jun 86	1
STREET SOUNDS HIP-HOP ELECTRO 12	Street Sounds	28	28 Jun 86	4
STREET SOUNDS EDITION 17	Street Sounds	35	19 Jul 86	5
STREET SOUNDS HIP-HOP ELECTRO 13	Street Sounds	23	6 Sep 86	5
STREET SOUNDS EDITION 18	Street Sounds	20	11 Oct 86	5
STREET SOUNDS HIP HOP ELECTRO 14	Street Sounds	40	11 Oct 86	3
JAZZ JUICE 3	Street Sounds	88	11 Oct 86	1
STREET SOUNDS HIP-HOP ELECTRO 15	Street Sounds	46	15 Nov 86	2
STREET SOUNDS EDITION 19	Street Sounds	61	6 Dec 86	3
STREET SOUNDS CRUCIAL ELECTRO - 3	Street Sounds	41	24 Jan 87	3
STREET SOUNDS ANTHEMS - VOLUME 1	Street Sounds	61	7 Feb 87	3
STREET SOUNDS EDITION 20	Street Sounds	25	14 Feb 87	4
STREET SOUNDS HIP-HOP ELECTRO 16	Street Sounds	40	13 Jun 87	3
STREET SOUNDS DANCE MUSIC '87	Street Sounds	40	4 Jul 87	5
STREET SOUNDS HIP-HOP 17	Street Sounds	38	15 Aug 87	3
JAZZ JUICE 5	Street Sounds	97	15 Aug 87	1
STREET SOUNDS 87 VOLUME 2	Street Sounds	47	12 Sep 87	3
BEST OF WEST COAST HIP HOP	Street Sounds	80	12 Sep 87	2
STREET SOUNDS HIP HOP 18	Street Sounds	67	24 Oct 87	1
STREET SOUNDS HIP HOP 20	Street Sounds	39	19 Mar 88	4
STREET SOUNDS 88-1	Street Sounds	73	19 Mar 88	2
STREET SOUNDS HIP HOP 21	Street Sounds	87	4 Jun 88	1

Streetwave

ALBUMS:		HITS 1		WEEKS 4
STREETNOISE VOLUME 1	Streetwave	51	23 Oct 82	4

Strictly Underground

COMPILATION ALBUMS:		HITS 1		WEEKS 1
ILLEGAL RAVE	Strictly Underground	20	19 Sep 92	1

Studio Two

ALBUMS:		HITS 3		WEEKS 27
BREAKTHROUGH	Studio Two	2	21 Oct 67	19
TOTAL SOUND	Studio Two	39	4 Sep 71	4
STUDIO TWO CLASSICS	Studio Two	16	30 Oct 71	4

Stylus

ALBUMS:		HITS 25		WEEKS 267
THE MAGIC OF TORVILL AND DEAN	Stylus	35	3 Aug 85	9
NIGHT BEAT	Stylus	15	17 Aug 85	8
DISCO BEACH PARTY	Stylus	29	24 Aug 85	10
VELVET WATERS	Stylus	54	14 Dec 85	4
CHOICES OF THE HEART	Stylus	87	28 Dec 85	2
NIGHT BEAT II	Stylus	7	8 Mar 86	9
LET'S HEAR IT FOR THE GIRLS	Stylus	17	17 May 86	10
BLACK MAGIC	Stylus	26	1 Nov 86	9
HIT MIX '86	Stylus	10	8 Nov 86	14
CLASSICS BY CANDLELIGHT	Stylus	74	22 Nov 86	4
BANDS OF GOLD - THE SWINGING SIXTIES	Stylus	48	14 Mar 87	6
BANDS OF GOLD - THE SENSATIONAL SEVENTIES	Stylus	75	21 Mar 87	4
BANDS OF GOLD - THE ELECTRIC EIGHTIES	Stylus	82	28 Mar 87	1
SIXTIES MIX - 60 SEQUENCED HITS FROM THE SIXTIES	Stylus	3	11 Jul 87	44
THE HIT FACTORY: THE BEST OF STOCK AITKEN WATERMAN	Stylus	18	24 Oct 87	17
HIT MIX - HITS OF THE YEAR	Stylus	29	21 Nov 87	11
HIP HOP AND RAPPING IN THE HOUSE	Stylus	5	2 Apr 88	13
SIXTIES MIX 2	Stylus	14	7 May 88	20
BACK ON THE ROAD	Stylus	29	4 Jun 88	11
THE GREATEST EVER ROCK 'N' ROLL MIX	Stylus	8	30 Jul 88	15
RAP TRAX	Stylus	3	3 Sep 88	13
RARE GROOVE MIX - 70 SMASH HITS OF THE 70'S	Stylus	20	1 Oct 88	10
SOFT METAL	Stylus	7	22 Oct 88	12
HIT MIX '88	Stylus	48	26 Nov 88	7
THE GREATEST HITS OF HOUSE	Stylus	26	17 Dec 88	4
COMPILATION ALBUMS:		HITS 21		WEEKS 222
SOFT METAL	Stylus	7	14 Jan 89	27
HIT MIX '88	Stylus	15	14 Jan 89	2
THE GREATEST HITS OF HOUSE	Stylus	5	14 Jan 89	9
BEAT THIS - 20 HITS OF RHYTHM KING	Stylus	9	18 Feb 89	8
NEW ROOTS	Stylus	18	11 Mar 89	8
HIP HOUSE	Stylus	3	25 Mar 89	8

THE SINGER AND THE SONG	*Stylus*	5	*22 Apr 89*	11
PRECIOUS METAL	*Stylus*	2	*27 May 89*	29
DON'T STOP THE MUSIC	*Stylus*	7	*24 Jun 89*	6
HOT SUMMER NIGHTS	*Stylus*	4	*15 Jul 89*	11
SUNSHINE MIX	*Stylus*	9	*19 Aug 89*	7
THE GREATEST EVER ROCK 'N' ROLL MIX	*Stylus*	5	*26 Aug 89*	9
MIDNIGHT LOVE	*Stylus*	7	*2 Sep 89*	6
LEGENDS AND HEROES	*Stylus*	6	*16 Sep 89*	10
THE RIGHT STUFF – REMIX '89	*Stylus*	2	*21 Oct 89*	11
JUKE BOX JIVE MIX – ROCK 'N' ROLL GREATS	*Stylus*	13	*25 Nov 89*	8
WARE'S THE HOUSE?	*Stylus*	2	*30 Dec 89*	10
PURE SOFT METAL	*Stylus*	1	*13 Jan 90*	23
THE RIGHT STUFF 2 – NOTHING BUT A HOUSE PARTY	*Stylus*	2	*10 Mar 90*	15
SIXTIES MIX 3	*Stylus*	4	*26 May 90*	9
MOMENTS IN SOUL	*Stylus*	9	*20 Oct 90*	2

Supreme Underground

COMPILATION ALBUMS:	HITS 1			WEEKS 1
HARDCORE EXPLOSION '97	*Supreme Underground*	20	*8 Mar 97*	1

Talkin Loud

COMPILATION ALBUMS:	HITS 1			WEEKS 3
TALKIN LOUD TWO	*Talkin Loud*	6	*30 Jan 93*	3

Teldec

COMPILATION ALBUMS:	HITS 1			WEEKS 2
SENSUAL CLASSICS	*Teldec*	19	*21 Nov 92*	2

Telstar

ALBUMS:	HITS 36			WEEKS 327
CHART ATTACK	*Telstar*	7	*16 Oct 82*	6
MIDNIGHT IN MOTOWN	*Telstar*	34	*6 Nov 82*	16
DIRECT HITS	*Telstar*	89	*18 Dec 82*	1
DANCIN' – 20 ORIGINAL MOTOWN MOVERS	*Telstar*	97	*8 Jan 83*	1
INSTRUMENTAL MAGIC	*Telstar*	68	*5 Feb 83*	5
20 GREAT ITALIAN LOVE SONGS	*Telstar*	28	*30 Apr 83*	6
IN THE GROOVE – THE 12 INCH DISCO PARTY	*Telstar*	20	*4 Jun 83*	12
ROOTS REGGAE 'N' REGGAE ROCK	*Telstar*	34	*12 Nov 83*	6
SUPERCHART '83	*Telstar*	22	*19 Nov 83*	9
THE VERY BEST OF MOTOWN LOVE SONGS	*Telstar*	10	*4 Feb 84*	22
DON'T STOP DANCING	*Telstar*	11	*26 May 84*	12
HITS, HITS, HITS – 18 SMASH ORIGINALS	*Telstar*	6	*13 Oct 84*	9
LOVE SONGS – 16 CLASSIC LOVE SONGS	*Telstar*	20	*8 Dec 84*	12
OPEN TOP CARS AND GIRLS IN T'SHIRTS	*Telstar*	13	*7 Sep 85*	9
THE LOVE ALBUM – 16 CLASSIC LOVE SONGS	*Telstar*	7	*16 Nov 85*	18
PERFORMANCE – THE VERY BEST OF TIM RICE AND ANDREW LLOYD WEBBER	*Telstar*	33	*7 Dec 85*	7
Includes tracks by David Essex abd Elaine Paige.				
MORE GREEN VELVET	*Telstar*	42	*7 Dec 85*	5
THE CHART	*Telstar*	6	*18 Oct 86*	12
ROCK LEGENDS	*Telstar*	54	*1 Nov 86*	7
LOVERS	*Telstar*	14	*8 Nov 86*	16
SIXTIES MANIA	*Telstar*	19	*22 Nov 86*	22
MOTOWN CHARTBUSTERS	*Telstar*	25	*6 Dec 86*	12
THE DANCE CHART	*Telstar*	23	*28 Mar 87*	8
TRACKS OF MY TEARS	*Telstar*	27	*3 Oct 87*	7
DANCE MIX '87	*Telstar*	39	*28 Nov 87*	10
ALWAYS AND FOREVER THE LOVE ALBUM	*Telstar*	41	*28 Nov 87*	10
SIXTIES PARTY MEGAMIX ALBUM	*Telstar*	46	*28 Nov 87*	7
LIFE IN THE FAST LANE	*Telstar*	10	*26 Dec 87*	12
. . . AND THE BEAT GOES ON	*Telstar*	12	*1 Oct 88*	8
THE HEART AND SOUL OF ROCK AND ROLL	*Telstar*	60	*5 Nov 88*	6
THE LOVE ALBUM '88	*Telstar*	51	*12 Nov 88*	9
BEST OF HOUSE '88	*Telstar*	33	*19 Nov 88*	8
INSTRUMENTAL GREATS	*Telstar*	79	*19 Nov 88*	5
BACK TO THE SIXTIES	*Telstar*	47	*3 Dec 88*	6
HYPERACTIVE	*Telstar*	78	*3 Dec 88*	4
MORNING HAS BROKEN	*Telstar*	88	*17 Dec 88*	2
COMPILATION ALBUMS:	**HITS 142**			**WEEKS 847**
BEST OF HOUSE '88	*Telstar*	11	*14 Jan 89*	5
BACK TO THE SIXTIES	*Telstar*	14	*14 Jan 89*	4
PROTECT THE INNOCENT	*Telstar*	9	*15 Jul 89*	9
RHYTHM OF THE SUN	*Telstar*	12	*15 Jul 89*	4
THIS IS SKA	*Telstar*	6	*22 Jul 89*	10
MOTOWN HEARTBREAKERS	*Telstar*	4	*14 Oct 89*	10
NUMBER ONES OF THE EIGHTIES	*Telstar*	2	*18 Nov 89*	19
SOFT ROCK	*Telstar*	15	*9 Dec 89*	5
NEW TRADITIONS	*Telstar*	13	*3 Feb 90*	4

1039

MILESTONES - 20 ROCK OPERAS	*Telstar*	6	*10 Feb 90*	11
PRODUCT 2378	*Telstar*	16	*17 Mar 90*	3
GET ON THIS! - 30 DANCE HITS VOLUME 1	*Telstar*	2	*12 May 90*	12
A NIGHT AT THE OPERA	*Telstar*	2	*19 May 90*	12
MEGABASS	*Telstar*	1	*18 Aug 90*	12
GET ON THIS!!! 2	*Telstar*	3	*25 Aug 90*	9
MOLTEN METAL	*Telstar*	13	*25 Aug 90*	5
COUNTRY'S GREATEST HITS	*Telstar*	9	*15 Sep 90*	7
THE FINAL COUNTDOWN - THE VERY BEST OF SOFT METAL	*Telstar*	9	*27 Oct 90*	6
RAVE	*Telstar*	10	*3 Nov 90*	4
THE MOTOWN COLLECTION	*Telstar*	8	*24 Nov 90*	12
60 NUMBER ONES OF THE SIXTIES	*Telstar*	7	*1 Dec 90*	11
MEGABASS 2	*Telstar*	6	*8 Dec 90*	8
UNCHAINED MELODIES	*Telstar*	1	*23 Feb 91*	20
DON'T STOP . . . DOOWOP!	*Telstar*	15	*23 Mar 91*	4
THIN ICE - THE FIRST STEP	*Telstar*	2	*30 Mar 91*	9
AFTER THE DANCE	*Telstar*	16	*13 Apr 91*	3
MASSIVE HITS	*Telstar*	2	*11 May 91*	6
UNCHAINED MELODIES - II	*Telstar*	3	*18 May 91*	8
MEGABASS 3	*Telstar*	3	*8 Jun 91*	8
THIN ICE 2 - THE SECOND SHIVER	*Telstar*	1	*3 Aug 91*	9
MAKE YOU SWEAT	*Telstar*	4	*28 Sep 91*	6
BORN TO BE WILD	*Telstar*	8	*12 Oct 91*	5
BURNING HEARTS	*Telstar*	7	*2 Nov 91*	10
PUNK AND DISORDERLY - NEW WAVE 1976-1981	*Telstar*	18	*23 Nov 91*	2
CLASSICAL MASTERS	*Telstar*	13	*30 Nov 91*	15
LEGENDS OF SOUL - A WHOLE STACK OF SOUL	*Telstar*	15	*7 Dec 91*	10
KAOS THEORY	*Telstar*	2	*15 Feb 92*	7
ALL THE BEST - LOVE DUETS VOLUME 1	*Telstar*	5	*15 Feb 92*	6
GOLD - 18 EPIC SPORTING ANTHEMS	*Telstar*	15	*29 Feb 92*	3
THE ULTIMATE HARDCORE	*Telstar*	1	*7 Mar 92*	10
CLUB FOR HEROES	*Telstar*	3	*11 Apr 92*	10
KAOS THEORY 2	*Telstar*	2	*2 May 92*	8
INDIE HITS	*Telstar*	13	*2 May 92*	3
FLIGHT OF THE CONDOR	*Telstar*	11	*9 May 92*	6
GARAGE CITY	*Telstar*	8	*23 May 92*	5
RAVING WE'RE RAVING	*Telstar*	2	*6 Jun 92*	6
KT3 - KAOS THEORY 3	*Telstar*	1	*18 Jul 92*	8
THE DIVAS OF DANCE	*Telstar*	9	*1 Aug 92*	4
RAVE ALERT	*Telstar*	2	*8 Aug 92*	10
BLUE EYED SOUL	*Telstar*	4	*19 Sep 92*	6
KAOS THEORY 4	*Telstar*	2	*10 Oct 92*	5
RAVE NATION	*Telstar*	2	*17 Oct 92*	6
MORE THAN LOVE	*Telstar*	4	*17 Oct 92*	9
CLASSIC LOVE	*Telstar*	4	*14 Nov 92*	15
ROCK N ROLL HEARTBEATS	*Telstar*	13	*21 Nov 92*	1
MY GENERATION	*Telstar*	16	*21 Nov 92*	1
SONIC SYSTEM	*Telstar*	17	*19 Dec 92*	3
COUNTRY LOVE	*Telstar*	5	*27 Feb 93*	15
RAGGA HEAT REGGAE BEAT	*Telstar*	4	*3 Jul 93*	14
FRESH DANCE 93	*Telstar*	4	*17 Jul 93*	7
DANCE ADRENALIN	*Telstar*	1	*18 Sep 93*	7
LOVE IS RHYTHM	*Telstar*	5	*9 Oct 93*	5
COUNTRY LOVE 2	*Telstar*	11	*9 Oct 93*	4
THE ALL TIME GREATEST HITS OF DANCE	*Telstar*	11	*20 Nov 93*	7
A HEART OF GOLD	*Telstar*	9	*18 Dec 93*	3
NO 1'S OF DANCE	*Telstar*	16	*8 Jan 94*	2
DANCE HITS 94 - VOLUME 1	*Telstar*	1	*19 Feb 94*	10
LOVE OVER GOLD	*Telstar*	2	*19 Feb 94*	6
LOVE ON FILM	*Telstar*	17	*9 Apr 94*	2
AWESOME DANCE	*Telstar*	2	*7 May 94*	7
DANCE HITS '94 VOLUME 2	*Telstar*	1	*11 Jun 94*	8
JAZZ MOODS	*Telstar*	3	*2 Jul 94*	4
IT'S THE ULTIMATE DANCE ALBUM	*Telstar*	1	*23 Jul 94*	11
JUNGLE MANIA 94	*Telstar*	7	*29 Oct 94*	6
ULTIMATE REGGAE PARTY ALBUM!	*Telstar*	14	*29 Oct 94*	2
JAZZ MOODS 2	*Telstar*	18	*29 Oct 94*	1
JUNGLE MANIA 2	*Telstar*	5	*24 Dec 94*	8
JUNGLE MANIA 3	*Telstar*	5	*25 Mar 95*	6
WARNING! DANCE BOOM	*Telstar*	2	*6 May 95*	6
CLUB ZONE	*Telstar*	4	*5 Aug 95*	5
WARNING! DANCE BOOM 2	*Telstar*	7	*2 Sep 95*	4
CLUB ZONE 2	*Telstar*	10	*7 Oct 95*	3
BEST SWING '95	*Telstar*	10	*4 Nov 95*	3
BEST SWING 96	*Telstar*	2	*6 Jan 96*	7
OUR FRIENDS ELECTRIC	*Telstar*	8	*17 Feb 96*	5
THE GREATEST 90S DANCE HITS	*Telstar*	16	*24 Feb 96*	2
BEST SWING 96 - VOLUME 2	*Telstar*	6	*9 Mar 96*	5
LOVE OVER GOLD 2	*Telstar*	19	*13 Apr 96*	1

Title	Label			
TECHNOHEDZ – 20 FIRESTARTIN' TECHO ANTHEMS	Telstar	12	20 Apr 96	3
LOVE II SWING	Telstar	10	27 Apr 96	3
SWING MIX 96	Telstar	3	25 May 96	6
CAFE LATINO	Telstar	18	29 Jun 96	1
BEST SWING '96 – VOLUME 3	Telstar	20	13 Jul 96	1
F1 ROCK	Telstar	20	20 Jul 96	1
MAD FOR IT	Telstar	12	28 Sep 96	3
THE MOTHER OF ALL SWING ALBUMS	Telstar	9	9 Nov 96	4
THE GREATEST CLASSICAL MOVIE ALBUM	Telstar	15	18 Jan 97	3
THE MOTHER OF ALL SWING MIX ALBUMS	Telstar	7	22 Feb 97	5
ONCE IN A LIFETIME	Telstar	13	8 Mar 97	3
SOUL SURVIVORS – 40 NORTHERN SOUL ANTHEMS	Telstar	10	10 May 97	7
CLUB CUTS 97	Telstar	5	17 May 97	7
CLUBLAND	Telstar TV	3	14 Jun 97	7
SIXTIES SUMMER MIX	Telstar TV	5	21 Jun 97	10
A DECADE OF IBIZA – 1987-1997	Telstar TV	5	5 Jul 97	10
CLUB CUTS 97 – VOLUME 2	Telstar TV	2	19 Jul 97	7
THE MOTHER OF ALL SWING II	Telstar TV	11	2 Aug 97	5
PURE HITS '97	Telstar TV	13	16 Aug 97	2
THE GREATEST DANCE ALBUM EVER MADE	Telstar TV	5	30 Aug 97	5
MOONDANCE – THE ALBUM	Telstar TV	16	20 Sep 97	4
CLUBLAND – VOLUME 2	Telstar TV	6	27 Sep 97	4
CLUB CUTS 97 – VOLUME 3	Telstar TV	5	11 Oct 97	4
CLUBLIFE	Telstar TV	3	7 Mar 98	5
NON-STOP DANCE ANTHEMS	Telstar TV	5	4 Apr 98	6
CLUB HITS 98	Telstar TV	2	2 May 98	7
FANTAZIA – BRITISH ANTHEMS – SUMMERTIME	Telstar TV	3	23 May 98	6
SMILE JAMAICA	Telstar TV	20	20 Jun 98	2
NON STOP HITS	Telstar TV	4	4 Jul 98	5
IBIZA ANTHEMS	Telstar TV	5	11 Jul 98	7
SIXTIES SUMMER MIX 2	Telstar TV	19	15 Aug 98	1
CLUBLIFE 2	Telstar TV	13	22 Aug 98	2
ULTIMATE COUNTRY: 40 COUNTRY GREATS	Telstar TV	8	29 Aug 98	9
NON STOP HITS – VOLUME 2	Telstar TV	19	5 Sep 98	1
SOUL SURVIVORS 2	Telstar TV	17	19 Sep 98	2
SUNDANCE – CHAPTER ONE	Telstar TV	9	10 Oct 98	3
CARWASH	Telstar TV	15	31 Oct 98	1
CHRIS TARRANT PRESENTS ULTIMATE PARTY MEGAMIX	Telstar TV	17	5 Dec 98	1
EUPHORIA	Telstar TV	1	6 Feb 99	17
BORN TO BE WILD	Telstar TV	15	13 Mar 99	1
THE CHILLOUT ALBUM	Telstar TV	4	3 Apr 99	10
BEST DANCE 99	Telstar TV	10	10 Apr 99	5
FUNKY HOUSE	Telstar TV	9	24 Apr 99	3
DEEPER – EUPHORIA II: MIXED BY RED JERRY	Telstar TV	2	29 May 99	6
NATIONAL ANTHEMS 99: MIXED BY RUFF DRIVERZ	Telstar TV	3	5 Jun 99	5
IBIZA ANTHEMS 2	Telstar TV	7	3 Jul 99	4
CHRIS TARRANT'S ULTIMATE SUMMER PARTY	Telstar TV	15	10 Jul 99	2
ADRENALIN	Telstar TV	10	24 Jul 99	3
THE CHILL OUT ALBUM – 2	Telstar TV	14	31 Jul 99	4
SUMMER DANCE ANTHEMS 99	Telstar TV	10	14 Aug 99	3
NATIONAL ANTHEMS 99 – VOLUME 2	Telstar TV	11	4 Sep 99	2
IBIZA EUPHORIA	Telstar TV	5	11 Sep 99	5
CLUB HITS 99	Telstar TV	16	9 Oct 99	1
EUPHORIA – LEVEL 3	Telstar TV	18	25 Dec 99	2

Telstar TV/PolyGram TV

COMPILATION ALBUMS:	HITS 1		WEEKS 3	
STREET JAMS	Telstar TV / PolyGram TV	14	23 May 98	3

Telstar/warner.esp

COMPILATION ALBUMS:	HITS 1		WEEKS 4	
POWER OF A WOMAN	Telstar/warner.esp	13	7 Mar 98	4

Tommy Boy/Island

ALBUMS:	HITS 1		WEEKS 6	
TOMMY BOY GREATEST BEATS	Tommy Boy	44	6 Apr 85	6

Topaz

ALBUMS:	HITS 2		WEEKS 8	
A TOUCH OF COUNTRY	Topaz	7	22 May 76	7
A TOUCH OF CLASS	Topaz	57	3 Jul 76	1

Touchdown

COMPILATION ALBUMS:	HITS 1		WEEKS 4	
D-FROST – 20 GLOBAL DANCE WARNINGS	Touchdown	8	13 Mar 93	4

Towerbell

ALBUMS:	HITS 6		WEEKS 45	
THE DANCE HITS ALBUM	Towerbell	10	8 Feb 86	11

SISTERS ARE DOIN' IT	*Towerbell*	27	*17 May 86*	9
TWO'S COMPANY	*Towerbell*	51	*7 Jun 86*	5
DANCE HITS II	*Towerbell*	25	*28 Jun 86*	8
THE ORIGINALS: 32 ALL-TIME CLASSIC GREATS	*Towerbell*	15	*2 Aug 86*	9
YOU'VE GOT TO LAUGH	*Towerbell*	51	*9 Aug 86*	3

Trax

COMPILATION ALBUMS:	**HITS 5**			**WEEKS 25**
DREAMS OF IRELAND	*Trax*	19	*22 Jul 89*	1
ROCK OF AMERICA	*Trax*	7	*17 Feb 90*	6
FREEDOM TO PARTY - FIRST LEGAL RAVE	*Trax*	4	*19 May 90*	10
SUMMER CHART PARTY	*Trax*	9	*28 Jul 90*	6
FREEDOM 2 - THE ULTIMATE RAVE	*Trax*	16	*3 Nov 90*	2

Trojan

ALBUMS:	**HITS 3**			**WEEKS 12**
TIGHTEN UP VOLUME 4	*Trojan*	20	*7 Aug 71*	7
CLUB REGGAE	*Trojan*	25	*21 Aug 71*	4
20 REGGAE CLASSICS	*Trojan*	89	*16 Jun 84*	1

TV Records

ALBUMS:	**HITS 4**			**WEEKS 25**
MODERN HEROES	*TV Records*	24	*2 Oct 82*	7
ENDLESS LOVE	*TV Records*	26	*9 Oct 82*	8
FLASH TRACKS	*TV Records*	19	*6 Nov 82*	7
PARTY FEVER/DISCO MANIA	*TV Records*	71	*25 Dec 82*	3

TVD Entertainment/Life On Mars

COMPILATION ALBUMS:	**HITS 1**			**WEEKS 3**
OFF YER NUT!!	*TVD Entertainment/Life On Mars*	12	*9 May 98*	3

2 Tone

ALBUMS:	**HITS 1**			**WEEKS 9**
THIS ARE TWO TONE	*2-Tone*	51	*26 Nov 83*	9
COMPILATION ALBUMS:	**HITS 2**			**WEEKS 9**
THE 2 TONE STORY	*2-Tone*	16	*5 Aug 89*	5
THE BEST OF 2 TONE	*Chrysalis*	10	*23 Oct 93*	4

Ultrasound

COMPILATION ALBUMS:	**HITS 2**			**WEEKS 5**
THE HOUSE OF HANDBAG	*Ultrasound*	13	*15 Jul 95*	3
THE HOUSE OF HANDBAG - AUTUMN/WINTER COLLECTION	*Ultrasound*	16	*4 Nov 95*	2

United Dance

COMPILATION ALBUMS:	**HITS 2**			**WEEKS 5**
THE ANTHEMS '92-'97	*United Dance*	8	*18 Jan 97*	3
UNITED DANCE PRESENTS ANTHEMS 2 - '88-'92	*United Dance*	17	*12 Jul 97*	2

Universe

COMPILATION ALBUMS:	**HITS 3**			**WEEKS 5**
UNIVERSE - WORLD TECHNO TRIBE	*Universe*	13	*15 May 93*	2
UNIVERSE PRESENTS THE TRIBAL GATHERING	*Universe*	19	*10 Jun 95*	1
TRIBAL GATHERING '96	*Universe*	15	*19 Oct 96*	2

Universal Music TV

COMPILATION ALBUMS:	**HITS 10**			**WEEKS 32**
THE LOVE SONGS OF BURT BACHARACH	*Universal Music TV*	5	*20 Mar 99*	3
BLUES BROTHER SOUL SISTER CLASSICS	*Universal Music TV*	8	*27 Mar 99*	3
DANCING IN THE STREET - 43 MOTOWN DANCE CLASSICS	*Universal Music TV*	13	*29 May 99*	2
THE SOUND OF MAGIC	*Universal Music TV*	10	*12 Jun 99*	5
SIXTIES SUMMER LOVE	*Universal Music TV*	16	*19 Jun 99*	3
AFRODISIAC	*Universal Music TV*	14	*31 Jul 99*	3
THE SOUND OF MAGIC LOVE	*Universal Music TV*	5	*2 Oct 99*	5
MOBO 1999	*Universal Music TV*	10	*16 Oct 99*	2
Based around the award show that took place on 7 Oct 99.				
LAND OF MY FATHERS	*Decca/Universal Music TV*	1	*16 Oct 99*	6
Official album of the Rugby World Cup 1999.				
THE 90'S	*Universal Music TV*	20	*6 Nov 99*	1

Universal Music TV/Sony TV/Global TV

COMPILATION ALBUMS:	**HITS 1**			**WEEKS 8**
WOMAN II	*Universal Music/Sony TV/ Global TV*	4	*13 Nov 99*	8

Urban

ALBUMS:	**HITS 3**			**WEEKS 12**
URBAN CLASSICS	*Urban*	96	*14 Nov 87*	1

URBAN ACID	Urban	51	24 Sep 88	8
ACID JAZZ AND OTHER ILLICIT GROOVES	Urban	86	8 Oct 88	3

Vertigo

ALBUMS:	HITS 2			WEEKS 16
HEAR 'N' AID	Vertigo	50	21 Jun 86	2
HOT CITY NIGHTS	Vertigo	1	27 Aug 88	14

COMPILATION ALBUMS:	HITS 2			WEEKS 23
ROCK CITY NIGHTS	Vertigo	3	4 Nov 89	14
THE POWER AND THE GLORY	Vertigo	2	28 Sep 91	9

Virgin

ALBUMS:	HITS 3			WEEKS 10
CASH COWS	Virgin	49	22 Nov 80	1
Deleted from chart as it was below retailer price required.				
MUSIC OF QUALITY AND DISTINCTION (VOLUME 1)	Virgin	25	17 Apr 82	6
MASSIVE - AN ALBUM OF REGGAE HITS	Virgin	61	1 Jun 85	3

COMPILATION ALBUMS:	HITS 33			WEEKS 218
MOODS	Virgin Television	2	19 Oct 91	22
THREE MINUTE HEROES	Virgin Television	4	29 Feb 92	10
MOODS 2	Virgin Television	3	16 May 92	8
THE GREATEST DANCE ALBUM IN THE WORLD!	Virgin	2	25 Jul 92	12
NEW ROMANTIC CLASSICS	Virgin	7	31 Oct 92	5
THE SINGER AND THE SONG	Virgin	5	23 Oct 93	6
SWEET SOUL HARMONIES	Virgin	1	29 Jan 94	9
DANCE TO THE MAX	Virgin	2	26 Feb 94	10
RAP TO THE MAX	Virgin	10	12 Mar 94	4
IN THE AIR TONIGHT	Virgin	8	30 Apr 94	10
Released to celebrate 21 years of Virgin records.				
PURE MOODS	Virgin	1	7 May 94	31
DANCE TO THE MAX 2	Virgin	4	28 May 94	8
SUPERFUNK	Virgin	8	9 Jul 94	5
SWEET SOUL HARMONIES 2	Virgin	10	20 Aug 94	2
DANCE TO THE MAX 3	Virgin	12	3 Sep 94	3
DANCE '95	Virgin	8	18 Feb 95	5
CELTIC MOODS	Virgin	8	25 Mar 95	2
STREET SOUL	Virgin	2	6 May 95	9
DANCE HEAT '95	Virgin	8	10 Jun 95	3
CELTIC MOODS 2	Virgin	6	17 Jun 95	5
THE BLUES ALBUM	Virgin	8	15 Jul 95	3
SUMMER SWING	Virgin	18	29 Jul 95	1
SERVE CHILLED	Virgin	16	19 Aug 95	1
THIS IS CULT FICTION	Virgin	9	2 Sep 95	4
INSTRUMENTAL MOODS	Virgin	14	18 Nov 95	5
SHARPE - OVER THE HILLS & FAR AWAY	Virgin	14	18 May 96	3
SPIRITS OF NATURE	Virgin	5	15 Jun 96	5
THE BIG HIT MIX	Virgin	16	29 Jun 96	2
THIS IS THE RETURN OF CULT FICTION	Virgin	15	21 Sep 96	3
THE BEST OF MASTERCUTS	Virgin	11	28 Sep 96	3
WIPEOUT 2097: THE SOUNDTRACK	Virgin	16	12 Oct 96	1
THE SOUL ALBUM	Virgin	1	15 Feb 97	11
GORGEOUS	Virgin	2	29 Mar 97	7

Virgin/EMI

COMPILATION ALBUMS:	HITS 22			WEEKS 87
ELECTRONICA (FULL-ON BIG BEATS)	Virgin/EMI	11	24 May 97	3
CAFE MAMBO	Virgin/EMI	17	30 Aug 97	2
MORE! GIRLS' NIGHT OUT	Virgin/EMI	10	6 Sep 97	3
CLUB HITS 97/98: SOUNDTRACK TO A SEASON	Virgin/EMI	5	20 Sep 97	7
NEW PURE MOODS	Virgin/EMI	16	22 Nov 97	3
MAXIMUM SPEED	Virgin/EMI	3	10 Jan 98	6
THE SOUL ALBUM II	Virgin/EMI	3	7 Feb 98	8
CARIBBEAN UNCOVERED	Virgin/EMI	10	7 Mar 98	5
SUPERWOMAN	Virgin/EMI	2	21 Mar 98	7
CLUB NATION	Virgin/EMI	3	4 Apr 98	6
R.I.P. PRESENTS THE REAL SOUND OF UNDERGROUND	Virgin/EMI	18	2 May 98	2
WORLD MOODS	Virgin/EMI	17	5 Sep 98	2
CLUB NATION 2	Virgin/EMI	8	7 Nov 98	2
DISCO:1999	Virgin/EMI	13	6 Mar 99	2
MAXIMUM SPEED 99	Virgin/EMI	13	10 Apr 99	4
TRANCEFORMER	Virgin/EMI	3	15 May 99	5
21ST CENTURY ROCK	Virgin/EMI	9	29 May 99	3
NEW WOMAN	Virgin/EMI	14	28 Aug 99	4
CLUB ANTHEMS 99	Virgin/EMI	4	4 Sep 99	4
TRANCEMIX 99 - A SPIRITUAL JOURNEY THROUGH TIME AND SPACE	Virgin/EMI	8	25 Sep 99	3
THE CHILLOUT MIX	Virgin/EMI	7	16 Oct 99	4
THE SIXTIES	Virgin/EMI	16	27 Nov 99	2

Vision

COMPILATION ALBUMS:	HITS 4			WEEKS 18
FLARED HITS AND PLATFORM SOUL	Vision	13	4 Mar 95	5
DANCE NATION '95	Vision	6	13 May 95	5
LOVE WITH A REGGAE RHYTHM	Vision	18	10 Jun 95	2
THE BEST DANCE ALBUM OF THE YEAR!	Vision	5	9 Sep 95	6

Vital Sounds

COMPILATION ALBUMS:	HITS 3			WEEKS 6
RED HOT AND WHITE LABELS	Vital Sounds	17	4 Jul 92	2
RED HOT AND WHITE 2	Vital Sounds	13	26 Sep 92	2
STRICTLY RAGGA	Vital Sounds	12	29 May 93	2

Volume

COMPILATION ALBUMS:	HITS 3			WEEKS 6
VOLUME SIX	Volume	19	1 May 93	1
TRANCE EUROPE EXPRESS	Volume	14	2 Oct 93	3
TRANCE EUROPE EXPRESS 2	Volume	17	11 Jun 94	2

V2

COMPILATION ALBUMS:	HITS 2			WEEKS 2
LOADED LOCK IN	V2	20	24 May 97	1
YOU'LL NEVER WALK ALONE	V2	18	14 Jun 97	1

Warner Brothers

COMPILATION ALBUMS:	HITS 3			WEEKS 9
NOBODY'S CHILD - ROMANIAN ANGEL APPEAL	Warner Brothers	18	4 Aug 90	3
Benefit album with proceeds to orphans in Romania.				
BARCELONA GOLD	Warner Brothers	15	15 Aug 92	2
SONGS IN THE KEY OF X	Warner Brothers	8	6 Apr 96	4

warner.esp

COMPILATION ALBUMS:	HITS 9			WEEKS 28
DISCO MIX 96	warner.esp	7	2 Nov 96	4
SUMMER GROOVE	warner.esp	14	7 Jun 97	2
CLUBBIN'	warner.esp	6	16 May 98	5
CLUB CLASS	warner.esp	9	15 Aug 98	2
MUSIC FOR LIFE	warner.esp	17	19 Jun 99	1
CLUB IBIZA	warner.esp	4	10 Jul 99	5
DANCEMIX.UK.V1	warner.esp	13	4 Sep 99	3
THIS YEAR IN IBIZA	warner.esp	5	25 Sep 99	5
THE DEFINITIVE SOUND OF ATLANTIC SOUL	warner.esp	18	2 Oct 99	1

warner.esp/Columbia

COMPILATION ALBUMS:	HITS 1			WEEKS 3
THE CELTIC COLLECTION	warner.esp/Columbia	14	26 Jun 99	3

warner.esp/Global TV

COMPILATION ALBUMS:	HITS 12			WEEKS 62
DANCE TIP 4	warner.esp TV/Global TV	7	2 Mar 96	3
TWELVE	warner.esp TV/Global TV	10	6 Apr 96	5
VIVA! EUROPOP	warner.esp TV/Global TV	4	8 Jun 96	5
DANCE TIP 2000	warner.esp/Global TV	7	21 Dec 96	7
A PERFECT LOVE	warner.esp/Global TV	4	22 Nov 97	15
A LITTLE BLUES IN YOUR SOUL	warner.esp/Global TV	5	7 Mar 98	4
HEART FULL OF SOUL	warner.esp/Global TV	8	8 Aug 98	3
THE FEMALE TOUCH	warner.esp/Global TV	2	24 Oct 98	5
A PERFECT LOVE II	warner.esp/Global TV	9	21 Nov 98	3
THE FEMALE TOUCH 2	warner.esp/Global TV	9	10 Apr 99	7
HEART FULL OF SOUL - 2	warner.esp/Global TV	12	1 May 99	4
CRAZY LITTLE THING CALLED LOVE	warner.esp/Global TV	17	25 Sep 99	1

warner.esp/Global TV/Sony Music TV

COMPILATION ALBUMS:	HITS 5			WEEKS 24
TOTALLY WICKED	warner.esp/Global TV/Sony Music TV	4	22 Aug 98	6
STREET VIBES	warner.esp/Global TV/Sony Music TV	6	22 Aug 98	7
STREET VIBES 2	warner.esp/Global TV/Sony Music TV	5	16 Jan 99	4
TOTALLY WICKED TOO!	warner.esp/Global TV/Sony Music TV	7	6 Feb 99	2
STREET VIBES 3	warner.esp/Global TV/Sony Music TV	6	12 Jun 99	5

Warner Music

COMPILATION ALBUMS:	HITS 3			WEEKS 12
THE ULTIMATE SOUL COLLECTION - 45 SOUL CLASSICS	Warner Music	4	18 Feb 95	9
DISCO INFERNO	Warner Music UK	16	5 Aug 95	1
THE ULTIMATE SOUL COLLECTION - VOLUME 2	Warner Music	11	28 Oct 95	2

Warp
COMPILATION ALBUMS:	HITS 1			WEEKS 2
ARTIFICIAL INTELLIGENCE II	*Warp*	16	*11 Jun 94*	2

Warwick
ALBUMS:	HITS 11			WEEKS 83
ALL-TIME PARTY HITS	*Warner Brothers*	21	*29 Nov 75*	8
INSTRUMENTAL GOLD	*Warner Brothers*	3	*17 Apr 76*	24
SONGS OF PRAISE	*Warner Brothers*	31	*8 Jan 77*	2
HIT SCENE	*Warner Brothers*	19	*29 Jan 77*	5
LOVE SONGS	*Warner Brothers*	47	*25 Nov 78*	7
BLACK VELVET	*Warner Brothers*	72	*2 Dec 78*	3
COUNTRY PORTRAITS	*Warner Brothers*	14	*7 Apr 79*	10
COUNTRY GUITAR	*Warner Brothers*	46	*16 Feb 80*	8
DISCO EROTICA	*Warner Brothers*	35	*14 Nov 81*	8
PS I LOVE YOU	*Warner Brothers*	68	*10 Apr 82*	3
HITS OF THE SCREAMING 60'S	*Warner Brothers*	24	*6 Nov 82*	10

WEA
ALBUMS:	HITS 2			WEEKS 33
THE BEST DISCO ALBUM IN THE WORLD	*WEA*	1	*21 Jul 79*	17
THE LAUGHTER AND TEARS COLLECTION	*WEA*	19	*14 May 83*	16

West Five
ALBUMS:	HITS 1			WEEKS 7
THE POWER OF LOVE	*West Five*	33	*18 Oct 86*	7

Westmoor
COMPILATION ALBUMS:	HITS 1			WEEKS 2
EMERALD CLASSICS VOLUMES I AND II	*Westmoor*	14	*24 Mar 90*	2

Westway Dance
COMPILATION ALBUMS:	HITS 1			WEEKS 3
ELEMENTS – SEB FONTAINE/TONY DE VIT	*Westway Dance*	15	*18 Jul 98*	3

Worlds End
COMPILATION ALBUMS:	HITS 1			WEEKS 1
VOLUME FOUR	*Worlds End*	17	*26 Sep 92*	1

Worldwide Ultimatumn
COMPILATION ALBUMS:	HITS 1			WEEKS 2
CARL COX – FACT 2	*Worldwide Ultimation*	13	*15 Mar 97*	2

XL Recordings
COMPILATION ALBUMS:	HITS 3			WEEKS 20
XL – RECORDINGS – THE SECOND CHAPTER	*XL Recordings*	5	*14 Sep 91*	9
THE THIRD CHAPTER	*XL Recordings*	6	*25 Apr 92*	8
PRODIGY PRESENTS THE DIRTCHAMBER SESSIONS 1	*XL Recordings*	3	*6 Mar 99*	3

Zomba
ALBUMS:	HITS 1			WEEKS 1
THE WORD	*Zomba*	86	*24 Oct 87*	1

ZTT/Island
ALBUMS:	HITS 1			WEEKS 3
IQ 6: ZANG TUMB TUM SAMPLED	*ZTT/Island*	40	*19 Oct 85*	3

CONCERTS AND FESTIVALS

ALBUMS:	HITS 13			WEEKS 91
ALL STAR FESTIVAL	*Philips*	4	*9 Mar 63*	19
FOLK FESTIVAL OF THE BLUES (LIVE RECORDING)	*Pye*	16	*22 Feb 64*	4
WOODSTOCK [OST]	*Atlantic*	35	*18 Jul 70*	19
Music that appeared in the film of the festival during 15+17 Aug 69.				
CONCERT FOR BANGLADESH (RECORDED LIVE)	*Apple*	1	*22 Jan 72*	13
Live recordings from Madison Square Garden, New York, 1 Aug 71 featuring Bob Dylan, Eric Clapton, George Harrison and Ringo Starr. Proceeds to aid victims of the war.				
THE ROXY LONDON WC2 (JAN-APR 77)	*Harvest*	24	*16 Jul 77*	5
HOPE AND ANCHOR FRONT ROW FESTIVAL	*Warner Brothers*	28	*25 Mar 78*	3
THE SECRET POLICEMAN'S BALL	*Island*	33	*5 Jan 80*	6
CONCERTS FOR THE PEOPLE OF KAMPUCHEA	*Atlantic*	39	*11 Apr 81*	2
Live recordings from Hammersmith Odeon, London, over 4 days in Dec 79. Features the Who, Wings, Queen, Clash, Specials, Elvis Costello.				
THE SECRET POLICEMAN'S OTHER BALL	*Springtime*	69	*12 Dec 81*	4
THE SECRET POLICEMAN'S OTHER BALL (THE MUSIC)	*Springtime*	29	*20 Mar 82*	5
Live recordings from the Amnesty International Benefit Concert, London, May 81. Features Jeff Beck, Eric Clapton, Phil Collins, Donovan, Bob Geldof, Sting.				
THE PRINCE'S TRUST COLLECTION	*Telstar*	64	*30 Nov 85*	5

THE PRINCE'S TRUST TENTH ANNIVERSARY BIRTHDAY PARTY	A&M	76	2 May 87	3

Live recordings from Wembley Arena, London, 20 June 86.

THE PRINCE'S TRUST CONCERT 1987	A&M	44	22 Aug 87	3

COMPILATION ALBUMS:	**HITS 1**			**WEEKS 10**
KNEBWORTH – THE ALBUM	Polydor	1	18 Aug 90	10

Live recordings 30 Jun 90 with proceeds to Nordoff-Robbins Music Therapy and the Brit School for the Performing Arts. Featuring Genesis, Paul McCartney, Pink Floyd, Robert Plant, Cliff Richard and the Shadows, Status Quo, Tears For Fears.

EDINBURGH TATTOO

ALBUMS:	**HITS 2**			**WEEKS 5**
EDINBURGH MILITARY TATTOO 1970	Warner Brothers	34	12 Sep 70	4
EDINBURGH MILITARY TATTOO 1971	Warner Brothers	44	18 Sep 71	1

FILMS

(See also Soundtracks under following artists: AC/DC; David Arnold; Burt Bacharach his Orchestra and chorus; Backbeat Band; Band; John Barry Orchestra; Beatles; Blues Brothers; Jon Bon Jovi; Roy Budd; Commitments; Roger Daltrey; Neil Diamond; Doors; Bob Dylan; Electric Light Orchestra; Adam Faith; Brad Fiedel; Grimthorpe Colliery Band; Marvin Hamlisch; Chesney Hawkes; Jimi Hendrix; David Hirschfelder; James Horner; Whitney Houston; Maurice Jarre; Trevor Jones; Mark Knopfler; kd lang; Mario Lanza; Los Lobos; Madonna; Neville Marriner and the Academy of St. Martin In The Fields; Paul McCartney; Bette Midler; Monty Python's Flying Circus; Ennio Morricone; Olivia Newton-John; Michael Nyman; Hazel O'Connor; Mike Oldfield; Jimmy Page; Tom Petty and the Heartbreakers; Pink Floyd; Elvis Presley; Prince; Public Enemy; Queen; Chris Rea; Cliff Richard; Riuichi Sakamoto; Eric Serra; Sex Pistols; Simon And Garfunkel; Frank Sinatra; Barbra Streisand; Tangerine Dream; Tina Turner; Vangelis; Village People; Rick Wakeman; Who; John Williams; Stevie Wonder.)

Original Soundtracks

SINGLES:	**HITS 1**			**WEEKS 2**
CAROUSEL [LP]	Capitol	27	16 Jun 56	1

Features Gordon MacRae, Shirley Jones, Cameron Mitchell. This album appeared in the singles chart as there was no album chart at that period of time. See 1958 entry in album section below.

CAROUSEL [LP] [RE]	Capitol	26	7 Jul 56	1

EPS:	**HITS 7**			**WEEKS 150**
CAROUSEL NO. 1	Capitol	12	14 May 60	11
SOUTH PACIFIC NO. 1	RCA	1	6 Aug 60	86
SEVEN BRIDES FOR SEVEN BROTHERS	MGM	9	6 Aug 60	15
THE KING AND I	Capitol	12	1 Oct 60	5
NEVER ON SUNDAY	London	8	17 Jun 61	11
SEVEN BRIDES FOR SEVEN BROTHERS VOLUME 2	MGM	18	1 Jul 61	1
SOME PEOPLE	Pye	2	25 Aug 62	21

ALBUMS:	**HITS 89**			**WEEKS 2725**
SOUTH PACIFIC	RCA	1	8 Nov 58	286

Features Rossano Brazzi, Mitzi Gaynor, John Kerr. The first Number One Album. Includes re-entries through to 1965.

THE KING AND I	Capitol	4	8 Nov 58	103

Features Deborrah Kerr, Yul Brynner, Rita Moreno.

OKLAHOMA!	Capitol	4	8 Nov 58	90

Features Gordon MacRae, Gloria Grahame, Gene Nelson, Charlotte Greenwood, James Whitmore, Shirley Jones.

CAROUSEL	Capitol	8	6 Dec 58	15

See also singles section above.

GIGI	MGM	2	31 Jan 59	88

Features Leslie Caron, Maurice Chevalier, Louis Jourdan.

PORGY AND BESS	Philips	7	10 Oct 59	5

Features Sidney Poitier, Dorothy Dandrige.

THE FIVE PENNIES	London	2	23 Jan 60	15

Features Danny Kaye, Louis Armstrong, Barbara Bel Geddes.

CAN CAN	Capitol	2	7 May 60	31

Features Frank Sinatra, Shirley MacLaine.

PAL JOEY	Capitol	20	28 May 60	1

Features Frank Sinatra.

HIGH SOCIETY	Capitol	16	23 Jul 60	1

Features Bing Crosby, Grace Kelly, Frank Sinatra. Originally released in 1956. Based around the play 'Philadelphia Story'.

BEN-HUR	MGM	15	5 Nov 60	3
NEVER ON SUNDAY	London	17	21 Jan 61	1

Composed and conducted by Manos Hadjildakis.

SONG WITHOUT END	Pye Golden Guinea	9	18 Feb 61	10
SEVEN BRIDES FOR SEVEN BROTHERS	MGM	6	29 Apr 61	22
EXODUS	RCA	17	3 Jun 61	1

Composed and conducted by Ernest Gold.

GLENN MILLER STORY	Ace Of Hearts	12	11 Nov 61	7
WEST SIDE STORY	Philips	1	24 Mar 62	175

Features Natalie Wood, Richard Beymer, Russ Tamblyn, Rita Moreno, George Chakiris. Re-issued on the CBS label during its chart run.

IT'S TRAD DAD	Columbia	3	28 Apr 62	21
THE MUSIC MAN	Warner Brothers	14	22 Sep 62	9
Features Robert Preston, Shirley Jones, Buddy Hackett.				
PORGY AND BESS	CBS	14	3 Nov 62	7
JUST FOR FUN	Decca	20	15 Jun 63	2
Features the Tornados.				
MY FAIR LADY	CBS	12	31 Oct 64	14
Features Audrey Hepburn, Rex Harrison, Stanley Holloway.				
MARY POPPINS	His Master's Voice	2	16 Jan 65	82
Features Julie Andrews, Dick Van Dyke, David Tomlinson, Glynis Johns, Ed Wynn.				
MY FAIR LADY [RE]	CBS	9	3 Apr 65	37
THE SOUND OF MUSIC	RCA Victor	1	10 Apr 65	381
Features Julie Andrews, Christopher Plummer. Includes re-entries through to 1972.				
A MAN AND A WOMAN	United Artists	35	29 Jul 67	3
THOROUGHLY MODERN MILLIE	Brunswick	9	28 Oct 67	19
Features Julie Andrews.				
THE JUNGLE BOOK	Disney	5	9 Mar 68	51
A MAN AND A WOMAN [RE]	United Artists	31	17 Aug 68	8
STAR!	Stateside	36	21 Sep 68	1
Features Julie Andrews, Richard Crenna, Michael Craig.				
OLIVER!	RCA Victor	7	23 Nov 68	9
Features Ron Moody, Harry Secombe, Shani Wallis, Mark Lester.				
CAMELOT	Warner Brothers	37	23 Nov 68	1
Features Richard Harris, Vanessa Redgrave.				
CHITTY CHITTY BANG BANG	United Artists	10	8 Feb 69	4
Features Dick Van Dyke, Sally Ann Howes, Lionel Jeffries, Gert Frobe.				
OLIVER! [RE]	RCA Victor	4	12 Apr 69	98
2001 – A SPACE ODYSSEY	MGM	3	14 Jun 69	67
EASY RIDER	Stateside	2	20 Dec 69	67
THE JUNGLE BOOK [RE]	Disney	25	24 Jan 70	26
Re-released.				
PAINT YOUR WAGON	Paramount	2	7 Feb 70	102
Features Lee Marvin, Clint Eastwood, Jean Seberg, Harve Presnell.				
LOVE STORY	Paramount	10	24 Apr 71	33
Composed and conducted by Francis Lai.				
CLOCKWORK ORANGE	Warner Brothers	4	12 Feb 72	46
Composed and conducted by Walter Carlos.				
FIDDLER ON THE ROOF	United Artists	26	8 Apr 72	2
Features Topol, Norma Crane.				
2001 – A SPACE ODYSSEY [RE]	MGM	20	13 May 72	2
Re-released.				
SOUTH PACIFIC [RI]	RCA Victor	25	25 Nov 72	2
CABARET	Probe	13	31 Mar 73	22
Features Liza Minnelli.				
LOST HORIZON	Bell	36	14 Apr 73	3
THAT'LL BE THE DAY	Ronco	1	23 Jun 73	7
JESUS CHRIST SUPERSTAR	MCA	23	22 Sep 73	18
Features Ted Neely, Yvonne Elliman, Carl Anderson. Barry Dennen.				
AMERICAN GRAFFITI	MCA	37	27 Apr 74	1
A TOUCH OF CLASS	Philips	32	8 Jun 74	1
SUNSHINE	MCA	47	5 Oct 74	3
TOMMY	Polydor	21	5 Apr 75	9
Features the Who.				
ALL THIS AND WORLD WAR II	Riva	23	27 Nov 76	7
Covers of Beatles songs.				
SATURDAY NIGHT FEVER	RSO	1	11 Mar 78	65
Features the Bee Gees.				
THE STUD	Ronco	2	22 Apr 78	19
THANK GOD IT'S FRIDAY	Casablanca	40	20 May 78	5
FM	MCA	37	27 May 78	7
GREASE	RSO	1	8 Jul 78	47
Features Olivia Newton-John, John Travolta.				
SGT. PEPPER'S LONELY HEARTS CLUB BAND	A&M	38	12 Aug 78	2
Based around the Beatles classic album from 1967. Features Bee Gees, Earth, Wind And Fire, Peter Frampton.				
CONVOY	Capitol	52	7 Oct 78	1
LEMON POPSICLE	Warner Brothers	42	31 Mar 79	6
THAT SUMMER	Arista	36	9 Jun 79	8
THE WORLD IS FULL OF MARRIED MEN	Ronco	25	30 Jun 79	9
THE WARRIORS	A&M	53	14 Jul 79	7
SUNBURN	Warner Brothers	45	9 Feb 80	7
GOING STEADY	Warner Brothers	25	16 Feb 80	10
THE WANDERERS	Gem	48	8 Mar 80	7
FAME	RSO	21	6 Sep 80	7
DANCE CRAZE	2-Tone	5	14 Feb 81	15
FAME [RE]	RSO	1	3 Jul 82	18
Recharted after the showing of the TV series on BBC TV.				
THE SOUND OF MUSIC [RI]	RCA International	98	17 Jul 82	1

ROCKY III	Liberty	42	4 Sep 82	7
Composed and conducted by Bill Conti, features Frank Stallone, Survivor.				
ANNIE	CBS	83	4 Sep 82	2
BRIMSTONE AND TREACLE	A&M	67	11 Sep 82	3
Features Sting.				
AN OFFICER AND A GENTLEMAN	Island	40	12 Feb 83	14
FLASHDANCE	Casablanca	9	2 Jul 83	30
STAYING ALIVE	RSO	14	1 Oct 83	8
Majority of the tracks are by the Bee Gees.				
FOOTLOOSE	CBS	7	21 Apr 84	25
AGAINST ALL ODDS	Virgin	29	21 Apr 84	10
BREAKDANCE	Polydor	6	16 Jun 84	29
BEAT STREET	Atlantic	30	7 Jul 84	13
ELECTRIC DREAMS	Virgin	46	18 Aug 84	7
GHOSTBUSTERS	Arista	24	29 Sep 84	25
BREAKDANCE 2 – ELECTRIC BOOGALOO	Polydor	34	12 Jan 85	20
BEVERLY HILLS COP	MCA	24	16 Feb 85	32
BACK TO THE FUTURE	MCA	66	11 Jan 86	8
ROCKY IV	Scotti Brothers	3	1 Feb 86	22
Features Survivor.				
ABSOLUTE BEGINNERS	Virgin	19	5 Apr 86	9
TOP GUN	CBS	4	11 Oct 86	46
PLATOON	WEA	90	2 May 87	2
BEVERLY HILLS COP II	MCA	71	18 Jul 87	5
WHO'S THAT GIRL	Sire	4	1 Aug 87	25
Features tracks by Madonna.				
FULL METAL JACKET	Warner Brothers	60	3 Oct 87	4
DIRTY DANCING	RCA	4	31 Oct 87	63
Peak position reached on 7 May 88.				
FLASHDANCE [RI]	Mercury	93	16 Jan 88	2
Re-issued at mid-price.				
CRY FREEDOM	MCA	73	20 Feb 88	2
MORE DIRTY DANCING	RCA	3	14 May 88	27
BUSTER	Virgin	6	24 Sep 88	16
Features Phil Collins.				
GOOD MORNING VIETNAM	A&M	50	22 Oct 88	9
COMPILATION ALBUMS:	**HITS 73**			**WEEKS 1075**
DIRTY DANCING	RCA	3	14 Jan 89	96
BUSTER	Virgin	2	14 Jan 89	36
GOOD MORNING VIETNAM	A&M	7	21 Jan 89	28
Peak position reached on 8 Jul 89.				
THE LOST BOYS	Atlantic	13	28 Jan 89	15
COCKTAIL	Elektra	2	4 Feb 89	15
MORE DIRTY DANCING	RCA	14	4 Feb 89	17
SCANDAL	Parlophone	13	18 Mar 89	3
TOP GUN	CBS	12	22 Apr 89	17
LICENCE TO KILL	MCA	17	15 Jul 89	2
GHOSTBUSTERS II	MCA	15	22 Jul 89	4
THE DELIQUENTS	PWL	16	10 Mar 90	1
Features Kylie Minogue.				
PRETTY WOMAN	EMI USA	2	26 May 90	72
TEENAGE MUTANT NINJA TURTLES	SBK	6	23 Jun 90	18
DAYS OF THUNDER	Epic	4	11 Aug 90	15
TOP GUN [RE]	CBS	4	13 Oct 90	17
GHOST	Milan	15	27 Oct 90	4
DIRTY DANCING [RE]	RCA	1	5 Jan 91	52
THE LOST BOYS [RE-1ST]	Atlantic	1	12 Jan 91	44
Above 2 re-charted after they were first transmitted on British TV.				
ROCKY V	Capitol	9	2 Feb 91	9
GREASE	Polydor	8	2 Mar 91	11
THE GODFATHER PART III	Columbia	19	23 Mar 91	1
Composed and conducted by Carmine Coppola and Nina Rota, features Al Martino.				
NEW JACK CITY	Giant	16	27 Apr 91	5
MERMAIDS	Epic	6	1 Jun 91	15
Features Cher.				
ROBIN HOOD: PRINCE OF THIEVES	Polydor	3	27 Jul 91	14
Composed and conducted by Michael Kamen, features Brian Adams, Jeff Lynne.				
BILL AND TED'S BOGUS JOURNEY	Interscope	3	18 Jan 92	8
MY GIRL	Epic	13	29 Feb 92	7
WAYNE'S WORLD	Reprise	5	30 May 92	11
MO' MONEY	Perspective	16	19 Sep 92	1
BOOMERANG	LaFace	17	14 Nov 92	2
THE BODYGUARD	Arista	1	28 Nov 92	78
Features Whitney Houston.				
SISTER ACT	Hollywood	14	30 Jan 93	4
BRAM STOKER'S DRACULA	Columbia	10	13 Feb 93	6
RESERVOIR DOGS	MCA	16	20 Mar 93	3
GOOD MORNING VIETNAM [RE]	A&M	19	8 May 93	1
Re-released at mid-price.				

INDECENT PROPOSAL	MCA	13	5 Jun 93	3
THE LAST ACTION HERO	Columbia	16	24 Jul 93	6
SLIVER	Virgin	20	18 Sep 93	1
SLEEPLESS IN SEATTLE	Epic	10	16 Oct 93	6
JUDGEMENT NIGHT	Epic	16	16 Oct 93	3
ALADDIN	Pickwick	11	8 Jan 94	5
WAYNE'S WORLD 2	Pinnacle	17	5 Mar 94	1
PHILADELPHIA	Epic	5	12 Mar 94	14
THE LOST BOYS [RE-2ND]	Atlantic	17	2 Apr 94	2
Re-released at mid-price.				
ABOVE THE RIM	Interscope	18	7 May 94	1
FOUR WEDDINGS AND A FUNERAL	Vertigo	5	28 May 94	21
THE CROW	Atlantic	13	25 Jun 94	5
THE FLINTSTONES	MCA	18	6 Aug 94	1
THE LION KING	Mercury	4	22 Oct 94	20
Features tracks by Elton John.				
FORREST GUMP	Epic	5	22 Oct 94	13
PULP FICTION	MCA	5	5 Nov 94	56
NATURAL BORN KILLERS	Interscope	10	11 Mar 95	6
BAD BOYS	Work	19	8 Jul 95	1
BATMAN FOREVER	Atlantic	11	29 Jul 95	4
WAITING TO EXHALE	Arista	8	3 Feb 96	5
Features Whitney Houston.				
DANGEROUS MINDS	MCA	13	3 Feb 96	2
TRAINSPOTTING	EMI Premier	2	2 Mar 96	66
MISSION: IMPOSSIBLE	Mother	18	20 Jul 96	1
THE NUTTY PROFESSOR	Def Jam	20	19 Oct 96	1
SPACE JAM	Atlantic	5	29 Mar 97	10
ROMEO + JULIET	Premier Soundtracks	3	5 Apr 97	24
THE SAINT	Virgin	15	3 May 97	1
MEN IN BLACK – THE ALBUM	Columbia	5	2 Aug 97	13
SPRAWN – THE ALBUM	Epic	18	9 Aug 97	1
THE FULL MONTY	RCA Victor	1	13 Sep 97	43
TRAINSPOTTING #2	Premier Soundtracks	11	27 Sep 97	5
BOOGIE NIGHTS	Premier Soundtracks	19	31 Jan 98	1
JACKIE BROWN	Maverick	11	18 Apr 98	7
An import cataloge number was listed on the first 2 weeks charts.				
THE WEDDING SINGER	Maverick	15	27 Jun 98	4
CITY OF ANGELS	Reprise	18	4 Jul 98	3
GREASE [RE]	Polydor	2	18 Jul 98	15
20th Anniversary re-release including CD-ROM with 3 videos.				
GODZILLA – THE ALBUM	Epic	13	25 Jul 98	4
LOCK, STOCK & TWO SMOKING BARRELS	Island	7	12 Sep 98	23
ARMAGEDDON	Columbia	19	26 Sep 98	2
NOTTING HILL	Island	4	5 Jun 99	19
HUMAN TRAFFIC	London	14	19 Jun 99	3
THE MATRIX	Maverick	16	26 Jun 99	4
AUSTIN POWERS – THE SPY WHO SHAGGED ME	Maverick	6	17 Jul 99	11
SOUTH PARK: BIGGER, LONGER & UNCUT	Atlantic	9	11 Sep 99	5
MANUMISSION – THE MOVIE	Telstar TV	17	2 Oct 99	1

Related Compilations

ALBUMS:	HITS 5		WEEKS 29	
GREAT MOTION PICTURE THEMES	His Master's Voice	19	10 Mar 62	1
THE BEST OF CAR WASH	MCA	59	2 Jul 77	1
20 SMASH DISCO HITS (THE BITCH)	Warner Brothers	42	10 Nov 79	5
JAMES BOND'S GREATEST HITS	Liberty	4	27 Mar 82	13
THE CINEMA HITS ALBUM	Towerbell	44	15 Mar 86	9

COMPILATION ALBUMS:	HITS 12		WEEKS 79	
DIRTY DANCING – LIVE IN CONCERT	RCA	19	13 May 89	2
THE BEST FROM THE M.G.M. MUSICALS	EMI	12	1 Dec 90	4
LOVE AT THE MOVIES	Telstar	6	23 Nov 91	14
THE BEST OF JAMES BOND – 30TH ANNIVERSARY COLLECTION	EMI	2	12 Sep 92	11
MOVIE HITS	Telstar	19	23 Jan 93	2
THE MOVIES' GREATEST LOVE SONGS	PolyGram TV	4	19 Feb 94	6
THE LION KING SING-ALONG	Pickwick/Disney	16	5 Nov 94	3
MOVIE KILLERS	Telstar	4	29 Jun 96	16
LOVE AT THE MOVIES … THE ALBUM	EMI TV/Sony TV	16	7 Dec 96	3
MOVIE LOVERS	Telstar	17	21 Feb 98	1
ESSENTIAL SOUNDTRACKS	Telstar TV	4	10 Apr 99	10
THE BEST OF BOND … JAMES BOND	Capitol	6	13 Nov 99	7

KARAOKE

COMPILATION ALBUMS:	HITS 2		WEEKS 10	
KARAOKE PARTY	Trax	20	17 Nov 90	1
KARAOKE PARTY II	Trax	7	16 Mar 91	9

MAGAZINE RELATED

ALBUMS:	HITS 2			WEEKS 10
KERRANG! KOMPILATION – 24 ROCK MONSTERS	EMI/Virgin	84	13 Jul 85	2
Kerrang is a Rock Magazine.				
SERGEANT PEPPER KNEW MY FATHER	NME/Island	37	9 Apr 88	8
Charity album to support Childline. Issued in conunction with the music paper New Musical Express.				
COMPILATION ALBUMS:	**HITS 8**			**WEEKS 39**
JUST SEVENTEEN – HEARTBEATS	Fanfare	3	23 Sep 89	6
JUST SEVENTEEN – GET KICKIN'	Dover	2	22 Sep 90	6
FAST FORWARD	Telstar	4	22 Jun 91	8
Just Seventeen and Fast Forward are teen magazines.				
Q – THE ALBUM VOLUME 1	Telstar	10	14 Sep 91	4
Q THE BLUES	The Hit Label	6	27 Jun 92	5
Q RHYTHM AND BLUES	The Hit Label	14	10 Apr 93	4
Q COUNTRY	The Hit Label	20	21 May 94	1
KERRANG! THE ALBUM	The Hit Label	12	18 Jun 94	5

MISCELLANEOUS

ALBUMS:	HITS 2			WEEKS 2
ELECTRONIC ORGANS TODAY	Ad-Rhythm	48	11 Dec 71	1
STRINGS OF SCOTLAND	Philips	50	27 Dec 75	1
COMPILATION ALBUMS:	**HITS 1**			**WEEKS 1**
TRIVIAL PURSUIT – THE MUSIC MASTER GAME	Telstar	20	28 Dec 91	1

RADIO

Related Compilations

ALBUMS:	HITS 9			WEEKS 66
THE BEST OF RADIO LUXEMBOURG	Pye Golden Guinea	14	14 Sep 63	2
THE WORLD OF YOUR 100 BEST TUNES	Decca	10	7 Aug 71	22
100 Best Tunes was a programme on BBC Radio 2.				
THE WORLD OF YOUR 100 BEST TUNES VOLUME 2	Decca	9	9 Oct 71	13
THE WORLD OF YOUR 100 BEST TUNES VOLUME 10	Decca	41	27 Sep 75	4
THE TOP 25 FROM YOUR 100 BEST TUNES	Decca	21	13 Dec 75	5
HAMILTON'S HOT SHOTS	Warner Brothers	15	29 May 76	5
David Hamiltion was a DJ on BBC Radio 1 and 2.				
10 YEARS OF HITS – RADIO ONE	Super Beeb	39	22 Oct 77	3
SIMON BATES – OUR TUNE	Polydor	58	1 Nov 86	5
BBC Radio 1 Morning DJ with 'Our Tune' being a daily feature.				
ONES ON 1	BBC	10	8 Oct 88	7
Released to coincide with Radio One's 21st anniversary.				
COMPILATION ALBUMS:	**HITS 15**			**WEEKS 57**
32 ONES ON ONE – RADIO 1'S 25TH BIRTHDAY	Connoisseur Collection	8	25 Jul 92	10
BEST OF CAPITAL GOLD – 24 CARAT CLASSIC HITS	The Hit Label	20	17 Oct 92	1
Capitol Gold is a London basis Oldies Radio station.				
ROAD SHOW HITS (21 YEARS OF RADIO 1 FM ROAD SHOW)	Connoisseur Collection	18	3 Jul 93	2
HALL OF FAME	Classic FM	13	20 Apr 96	4
EVENING SESSION – PRIORITY TUNES	Virgin	11	17 Aug 96	4
DAVE PEARCE PRESENTS DANCE ANTHEMS	PolyGram TV	4	30 May 98	7
Dave Pearce is a Dance DJ who's 'Dance Anthems' show was on BBC Radio1.				
ROCK THE DANCEFLOOR	All Around The World	9	22 Aug 98	2
Based around Preston's Rock RM radio station.				
DAVE PEARCE PRESENTS DANCE ANTHEMS VOLUME 2	PolyGram TV	5	17 Oct 98	3
THE HEART OF THE 80S & 90S	Universal	9	17 Oct 98	3
In conjunction with Heart FM radio.				
ROCK THE DANCEFLOOR 2	All Around The World	7	3 Apr 99	1
CLUBZONE – DANCING IN THE CITY	warner.esp/Radio City/3 Beat	20	10 Apr 99	1
DAVE PEARCE PRESENTS 40 CLASSIC DANCE ANTHEMS	Universal Music TV	5	24 Jul 99	6
RELAX . . .	Classic FM	11	16 Oct 99	7
Issued in conjunction with the radio station.				
DAVE PEARCE PRESENTS 40 CLASSIC DANCE ANTHEMS 2	Universal Music TV	7	23 Oct 99	3
RADIO 2 – SONGS OF THE CENTURY	Global TV	9	18 Dec 99	3

Soundtracks

ALBUMS:	HITS 3			WEEKS 4
VICTORY IN EUROPE – BROADCASTS AND REPORTS FROM BBC CORRESPONDENTS	BBC	61	18 May 85	1
World War II news broadcasts.				
DOCTOR WHO – THE PARADISE OF DEATH	BBC	48	18 Sep 93	1
30th Anniversary recording for radio starring Jon Pertwee and Elizabeth Sladen.				
INDEPENDENCE DAY UK	Speaking Volume	66	17 Aug 96	2
BBC Radio 1 broadcast on 4 Aug 96. An amended script based around the film 'Independence Day'. Features Nicky Campbell, Patrick Moore, Toyah Wilcox, Colin Baker and Mark Goodier.				

ROYALTY

ALBUMS:	HITS 4			WEEKS 19	
MUSIC FOR A ROYAL WEDDING	*BBC*	7	*8 Dec 73*	6
Music from the wedding of Princess Anne to Mark Philips, 14 Nov 73.					
THE OFFICAL BBC ALBUM OF THE ROYAL WEDDING	*BBC*	1	*8 Aug 81*	11
Music from the wedding of Prince Charles to Diana Spencer, 29 Jul 81.					
ROYAL ROMANCE	*Windsor*	84	*8 Aug 81*	1
ROYAL WEDDING	*BBC*	55	*9 Aug 86*	1
Music from the wedding of Prince Andrew to Sarah Ferguson, 23 Jul 86.					
COMPILATION ALBUMS:	**HITS 2**			**WEEKS 15**
DIANA PRINCESS OF WALES 1961–1997 – FUNERAL SERVICE	*BBC Worldwide Classics*	3	*27 Sep 97*	5
Music from the service at Westminster Abbey, 6 Sep 97.					
DIANA PRINCESS OF WALES – TRIBUTE	*Diana Memorial Fund*	1	*13 Dec 97*	10

SELECTED SERIES

All Time Greatest

COMPILATION ALBUMS:	HITS 9			WEEKS 76	
THE ALL TIME GREATEST LOVE SONGS . . .	*Columbia*	4	*2 Nov 96*	17
THE ALL TIME GREATEST COUNTRY SONGS	*Columbia*	5	*29 Mar 97*	6
THE ALL TIME GREATEST LOVE SONGS – VOLUME II	*Columbia*	4	*1 Nov 97*	14
THE ALL TIME GREATEST ROCK SONGS	*Sony TV / warner.esp*	7	*8 Nov 97*	4
THE ALL TIME GREATEST MOVIE SONGS	*Sony TV / PolyGram TV*	3	*7 Nov 98*	8
THE ALL TIME GREATEST LOVE SONGS OF THE 60'S, 70'S, 80'S & 90'S VOLUME III	*Columbia*	6	*28 Nov 98*	14
THE ALL TIME GREATEST POP ALBUM	*Columbia*	12	*10 Jul 99*	3
ALL TIME GREATEST MOVIE SONGS – VOLUME TWO	*Sony TV / Universal Music TV*	7	*13 Nov 99*	4
THE ALL TIME GREATEST LOVE SONGS	*Sony TV / Universal Music TV*	9	*27 Nov 99*	6

All Woman

COMPILATION ALBUMS:	HITS 6			WEEKS 51	
ALL WOMAN	*Quality Television*	1	*4 Apr 92*	15
ALL WOMAN 2	*Quality Television*	1	*10 Oct 92*	7
ALL WOMAN – THE COMPLETE WOMAN	*Quality Television*	19	*16 Jan 93*	1
ALL WOMAN 3	*Quality Television*	2	*19 Mar 94*	11
ALL WOMAN 4	*Quality Television*	18	*3 Dec 94*	4
THE BEST OF ALL WOMAN	*Quality Television*	6	*7 Oct 95*	13

The Annual

COMPILATION ALBUMS:	HITS 5			WEEKS 68	
THE ANNUAL	*Ministry Of Sound*	13	*25 Nov 95*	6
THE ANNUAL II – PETE TONG & BOY GEORGE	*Ministry Of Sound*	1	*23 Nov 96*	24
THE ANNUAL III – PETE TONG & BOY GEORGE	*Ministry Of Sound*	1	*15 Nov 97*	15
THE ANNUAL IV – JUDGE JULES & BOY GEORGE	*Ministry Of Sound*	1	*14 Nov 98*	15
THE ANNUAL – MILLENNIUM EDITION – MIXED BY JUDGE JULES & TALL PAUL	*Ministry Of Sound*	2	*13 Nov 99*	8

Awesome

COMPILATION ALBUMS:	HITS 2			WEEKS 23	
AWESOME!! – 20 MASSIVE HITS	*EMI*	1	*23 Feb 91*	12
AWESOME 2	*EMI / Virgin / PolyGram*	2	*2 Nov 91*	11

Best . . . Ever!

COMPILATION ALBUMS:	HITS 81			WEEKS 657	
THE BEST DANCE ALBUM IN THE WORLD . . . EVER!	*Virgin*	1	*17 Jul 93*	19
THE BEST DANCE ALBUM IN THE WORLD . . . EVER! 2	*Virgin*	3	*20 Nov 93*	12
THE BEST CHRISTMAS ALBUM IN THE WORLD . . . EVER!	*Virgin*	2	*4 Dec 93*	9
THE BEST REGGAE ALBUM IN THE WORLD . . . EVER!	*Virgin*	4	*4 Jun 94*	10
THE BEST DANCE ALBUM IN THE WORLD . . . EVER! 3	*Virgin*	2	*30 Jul 94*	11
THE BEST ROCK ALBUM IN THE WORLD . . . EVER!	*Virgin*	1	*3 Sep 94*	24
THE BEST ROCK 'N' ROLL ALBUM IN THE WORLD . . . EVER!	*Virgin*	2	*29 Oct 94*	10
THE BEST DANCE ALBUM IN THE WORLD . . . EVER! 4	*Virgin*	5	*19 Nov 94*	4
THE BEST PUNK ALBUM IN THE WORLD . . . EVER!	*Virgin*	1	*4 Feb 95*	13
THE BEST FUNK ALBUM IN THE WORLD . . . EVER!	*Virgin*	11	*4 Mar 95*	3
THE BEST ROCK ALBUM IN THE WORLD . . . EVER! II	*Virgin*	3	*15 Apr 95*	8
THE BEST DANCE ALBUM IN THE WORLD . . . EVER! 5	*Virgin*	4	*15 Jul 95*	7
THE BEST SUMMER ALBUM IN THE WORLD . . . EVER!	*Virgin*	1	*22 Jul 95*	11
THE BEST ROCK BALLADS ALBUM IN THE WORLD . . . EVER!	*Virgin*	2	*2 Sep 95*	23
THE BEST . . . ALBUM IN THE WORLD . . . EVER!	*Virgin*	2	*16 Sep 95*	8
THE BEST DANCE ALBUM IN THE WORLD . . . 95!	*Virgin*	3	*21 Oct 95*	4
THE BEST 80'S ALBUM IN THE WORLD . . . EVER!	*Virgin*	7	*11 Nov 95*	4
THE BEST PARTY . . . EVER!	*Virgin*	5	*25 Nov 95*	8
THE BEST SIXTIES ALBUM IN THE WORLD . . . EVER!	*Virgin*	2	*2 Dec 95*	17
THE BEST . . . ALBUM IN THE WORLD . . . EVER! 2	*Virgin*	1	*10 Feb 96*	12
THE BEST RAP ALBUM IN THE WORLD . . . EVER!	*Virgin*	2	*23 Mar 96*	10
THE BEST PUNK ALBUM IN THE WORLD . . . EVER! 2	*Virgin*	16	*13 Apr 96*	2
THE BEST . . . ALBUM IN THE WORLD . . . EVER! 3	*Virgin*	2	*27 Apr 96*	7
THE BEST ROCK ANTHEMS ALBUM IN THE WORLD . . . EVER!	*Virgin*	8	*1 Jun 96*	4

THE BEST SWING ALBUM IN THE WORLD . . . EVER!	*Virgin*	3	*15 Jun 96*	10
THE BEST FOOTIE ANTHEMS IN THE WORLD . . . EVER!	*Virgin*	5	*29 Jun 96*	5
THE BEST DANCE ALBUM IN THE WORLD . . . EVER! 6	*Virgin*	1	*17 Aug 96*	13
THE BEST JAZZ ALBUM IN THE WORLD . . . EVER!	*Virgin*	8	*17 Aug 96*	5
THE BEST . . . ALBUM IN THE WORLD . . . EVER! 4	*Virgin*	2	*26 Oct 96*	6
THE BEST OPERA ALBUM IN THE WORLD . . . EVER!	*Virgin*	10	*9 Nov 96*	10
THE BEST IRISH ALBUM IN THE WORLD . . . EVER!	*Virgin*	11	*9 Nov 96*	9
THE BEST SIXTIES ALBUM IN THE WORLD . . . EVER! II	*Virgin*	2	*23 Nov 96*	15
THE BEST MIX ALBUM IN THE WORLD . . . EVER!	*Virgin*	9	*23 Nov 96*	3
THE BEST CHRISTMAS ALBUM IN THE WORLD . . . EVER!	*Virgin*	2	*30 Nov 96*	19
Same tracks that appeared on the 1993 issue plus additional tracks.				
THE BEST . . . ALBUM IN THE WORLD . . . EVER! 5	*Virgin/EMI*	1	*22 Mar 97*	7
SPICE GIRLS PRESENT THE BEST GIRL POWER ALBUM IN THE WORLD . . . EVER!	*Virgin/EMI*	2	*17 May 97*	9
THE BEST CLUB ANTHEMS IN THE WORLD . . . EVER!	*Virgin/EMI*	1	*14 Jun 97*	9
THE BEST SCOTTISH ALBUM IN THE WORLD . . . EVER!	*Virgin/EMI*	9	*21 Jun 97*	6
THE BEST SUMMER ALBUM IN THE WORLD . . . EVER!	*Virgin/EMI*	3	*5 Jul 97*	9
THE BEST DISCO ALBUM IN THE WORLD . . . EVER!	*Virgin/EMI*	1	*12 Jul 97*	15
THE BEST . . . ALBUM IN THE WORLD . . . EVER! 6	*Virgin/EMI*	8	*19 Jul 97*	4
THE BEST DANCE ALBUM IN THE WORLD . . . EVER! 7	*Virgin/EMI*	2	*16 Aug 97*	11
THE BEST LATINO CARNIVAL IN THE WORLD . . . EVER!	*Virgin/EMI*	5	*16 Aug 97*	6
THE BEST . . . ANTHEMS . . . EVER!	*Virgin/EMI*	1	*25 Oct 97*	10
THE MOST RELAXING CLASSICAL ALBUM IN THE WORLD . . . EVER!	*Virgin/EMI*	10	*8 Nov 97*	16
THE BEST SIXTIES ALBUM IN THE WORLD . . . EVER! III	*Virgin/EMI*	3	*22 Nov 97*	12
THE BEST SEVENTIES ALBUM IN THE WORLD . . . EVER!	*Virgin/EMI*	13	*22 Nov 97*	9
THE BEST ROCK BALLADS ALBUM IN THE WORLD . . . EVER! II	*Virgin/EMI*	7	*29 Nov 97*	11
THE BEST CLUB ANTHEMS IN THE WORLD . . . EVER! 2	*Virgin/EMI*	6	*6 Dec 97*	11
THE BEST PARTY IN THE WORLD . . . EVER! 2	*Virgin/EMI*	7	*6 Dec 97*	6
THE BEST . . . ANTHEMS . . . EVER! 2	*Virgin/EMI*	3	*18 Apr 98*	10
THE BEST HIP HOP ANTHEMZ IN THE WORLD . . . EVER!	*Virgin/EMI*	6	*25 Apr 98*	5
THE BEST CLUB ANTHEMS IN THE WORLD . . . EVER! III	*Virgin/EMI*	3	*16 May 98*	6
THE BEST DISCO ALBUM IN THE WORLD . . . EVER! 2	*Virgin/EMI*	7	*30 May 98*	5
THE BEST SIXTIES SUMMER ALBUM IN THE WORLD . . . EVER!	*Virgin/EMI*	2	*27 Jun 98*	11
ALL NEW – THE BEST FOOTIE ANTHEMS IN THE WORLD . . . EVER!	*Virgin/EMI*	6	*27 Jun 98*	3
THE BEST SUMMER PARTY ALBUM IN THE WORLD . . . EVER!	*Virgin/EMI*	6	*11 Jul 98*	6
THE BEST ALBUM . . . IN THE WORLD . . . EVER! 7	*Virgin/EMI*	11	*18 Jul 98*	3
THE BEST DANCE ALBUM IN THE WORLD . . . EVER! 8	*Virgin/EMI*	2	*25 Jul 98*	9
THE BEST RAVE ANTHEMS IN THE WORLD . . . EVER!	*Virgin/EMI*	11	*15 Aug 98*	3
THE BEST CHART HITS ALBUM IN THE WORLD . . . EVER!	*Virgin/EMI*	1	*31 Oct 98*	5
THE MOST RELAXING CLASSICAL ALBUM IN THE WORLD . . . EVER! II	*Virgin/EMI*	12	*7 Nov 98*	9
THE BEST COUNTRY BALLADS IN THE WORLD . . . EVER!	*Virgin/EMI*	14	*14 Nov 98*	3
THE BEST . . . ANTHEMS . . . EVER! 3	*Virgin/EMI*	19	*14 Nov 98*	1
THE BEST ROCK ANTHEMS . . . EVER!	*Virgin/EMI*	10	*21 Nov 98*	2
THE BEST SIXTIES ALBUM IN THE WORLD . . . EVER! IV	*Virgin/EMI*	11	*21 Nov 98*	7
BIGGEST 80'S HITS IN THE WORLD . . . EVER!	*Virgin/EMI*	16	*28 Nov 98*	2
THE BEST CLUB ANTHEMS 99 IN THE WORLD . . . EVER!	*Virgin/EMI*	1	*23 Jan 99*	11
THE BEST SIXTIES LOVE ALBUM . . . EVER!	*Virgin/EMI*	2	*13 Feb 99*	6
THE BEST CHART HITS IN THE WORLD . . . EVER! 99	*Virgin/EMI*	5	*27 Feb 99*	4
THE BEST HOUSE ANTHEMS . . . EVER!	*Virgin/EMI*	5	*8 May 99*	4
THE BEST TRANCE ANTHEMS . . . EVER!	*Virgin/EMI*	7	*10 Jul 99*	4
THE BEST DANCE ALBUM IN THE WORLD . . . EVER! 9	*Virgin/EMI*	1	*24 Jul 99*	9
THE BEST IBIZA ANTHEMS . . . EVER!	*Virgin/EMI*	2	*7 Aug 99*	11
THE BEST PEPSI CHART ALBUM IN THE WORLD . . . EVER!	*Virgin/EMI*	2	*23 Oct 99*	4
THE BEST CLASSICAL ALBUM OF THE MILLENNIUM . . . EVER!	*Virgin/EMI*	10	*6 Nov 99*	3
THE BEST LOVESONGS . . . EVER!	*Virgin/EMI*	11	*20 Nov 99*	7
THE BEST . . . AND FRIENDS ALBUM IN THE WORLD . . . EVER!	*Virgin/EMI*	8	*4 Dec 99*	5
THE BEST MILLENNIUM PARTY . . . EVER!	*Virgin/EMI*	11	*4 Dec 99*	5
THE BEST CLUB ANTHEMS 2000 . . . EVER!	*Virgin/EMI*	10	*11 Dec 99*	4
THE BEST MUSICALS ALBUM IN THE WORLD . . . EVER!	*Virgin/EMI*	12	*11 Dec 99*	4

Best Of Dance

COMPILATION ALBUMS:	HITS 7		WEEKS 60	
THE BEST OF DANCE '91	*Telstar*	2	*9 Nov 91*	15
THE BEST OF DANCE '92 – 32 PUMPIN' CLUB HITS	*Telstar*	1	*7 Nov 92*	17
THE BEST OF DANCE '93	*Telstar*	1	*6 Nov 93*	14
THE BEST OF DANCE 94	*Telstar*	10	*5 Nov 94*	5
THE BEST OF DANCE 96	*Telstar*	13	*9 Nov 96*	3
THE BEST OF DANCE 97	*Telstar TV*	6	*8 Nov 97*	4
THE BEST OF DANCE 98	*Telstar TV*	9	*7 Nov 98*	2

Big Mix

COMPILATION ALBUMS:	HITS 4		WEEKS 24	
BIG MIX 96	*EMI TV/warner.esp*	1	*20 Jul 96*	8
BIG MIX '96 – VOLUME 2	*EMI TV/warner.esp*	7	*28 Sep 96*	4
BIG MIX '97	*Warner/Virgin/EMI*	1	*24 May 97*	7
BIG MIX '97 – VOLUME 2	*Virgin/EMI/warner.esp*	1	*11 Oct 97*	5

Bonkers

COMPILATION ALBUMS:	HITS 6			WEEKS 17	
BONKERS 2	React	10	10 May 97		3
BONKERS 3 - JOURNEY INTO MADNESS	React	9	1 Nov 97		3
BONKERS 4 - WORLD FRENZY	React	8	30 May 98		4
BONKERS 5 - ANARCHY IN THE UNIVERSE	React	12	7 Nov 98		2
BONKERS 6 (WHEEL CRAZY)	React	10	1 May 99		4
BONKERS 7 - MILLENNIUM MADNESS	React	18	16 Oct 99		1

The Box
The Box is a cable TV station which plays music videos selected by viewers.

COMPILATION ALBUMS:	HITS 6			WEEKS 28	
THE BOX HITS 98	Telstar TV	2	21 Mar 98		5
THE BOX HITS 98 - VOLUME 2	Telstar TV	1	13 Jun 98		6
BOX HITS 98 - VOLUME 3	Telstar TV	2	17 Oct 98		4
THE BOX R&B HITS ALBUM	Telstar TV	6	9 Jan 99		6
THE BOX - DANCE HITS	Universal Music TV	2	10 Jul 99		4
THE BOX DANCE HITS - VOLUME 2	Universal Music TV	5	13 Nov 99		3

Brit Awards
The Brits are the Music Industry's Award Presentations in the U.K.

COMPILATION ALBUMS:	HITS 11			WEEKS 67	
THE BRITS - THE AWARDS 1989	Telstar	1	25 Feb 89		8
THE AWARDS 1990	Telstar	3	24 Feb 90		10
THE BRITS 1991 - THE MAGIC OF BRITISH MUSIC	Telstar	7	16 Feb 91		6
THE AWARDS 1992	PolyGram TV	1	22 Feb 92		9
THE AWARDS 1993	PolyGram TV	3	20 Feb 93		7
THE BRIT AWARDS	EMI	6	26 Feb 94		3
THE AWARDS 1995	Columbia	10	4 Mar 95		2
BRIT AWARDS '96	Columbia	6	17 Feb 96		4
THE '97 BRIT AWARDS	Columbia	2	22 Feb 97		6
THE BRIT AWARDS 1998	Columbia	11	7 Feb 98		5
THE 1999 BRIT AWARDS	Columbia	3	13 Feb 99		7

Café Del Mar

COMPILATION ALBUMS:	HITS 5			WEEKS 7	
CAFE DEL MAR IBIZA - VOLUMEN DOS	React	17	12 Aug 95		1
CAFE DEL MAR IBIZA - VOLUMEN TRES	React	16	10 Aug 96		1
CAFE DEL MAR - VOLUMEN CUATRO	Manifesto	18	23 Aug 97		1
CAFE DEL MAR - VOLUMEN CINCO	Manifesto	16	25 Jul 98		2
CAFE DEL MAR - VOLUMEN SEIS	Manifesto	15	21 Aug 99		2

Classic Experience

ALBUMS:	HITS 1			WEEKS 12	
THE CLASSIC EXPERIENCE	EMI	27	22 Oct 88		12

COMPILATION ALBUMS:	HITS 5			WEEKS 111	
THE CLASSIC EXPERIENCE	EMI	12	14 Jan 89		14
THE CLASSIC EXPERIENCE [RE]	EMI	8	11 Nov 89		44
CLASSIC EXPERIENCE II	EMI	1	26 May 90		32
CLASSIC EXPERIENCE III	EMI	3	11 May 91		14
CLASSIC EXPERIENCE IV	EMI	9	27 Mar 93		6
THE VERY BEST OF CLASSICAL EXPERIENCE	Virgin/EMI	18	18 Sep 99		1

Club Mix

COMPILATION ALBUMS:	HITS 9			WEEKS 54	
CLUB MIX 96	PolyGram TV	2	6 Apr 96		7
CLUB MIX 96 - VOLUME 2	PolyGram TV	2	3 Aug 96		8
CLUB MIX 97	PolyGram TV	7	21 Dec 96		8
CLUB MIX 97 - VOLUME 2	PolyGram TV	1	1 Mar 97		6
CLUB MIX 97 - VOLUME 3	PolyGram TV	4	28 Jun 97		5
ULTIMATE CLUB MIX	PolyGram TV	1	7 Feb 98		7
ULTIMATE CLUB MIX 2	PolyGram TV	5	15 Aug 98		5
ULTIMATE CLUB MIX - 98	PolyGram TV	13	7 Nov 98		1
CLUB MIX 99	Universal Music TV	3	21 Aug 99		7

Cream
Cream is a major nightclub in Liverpool.

COMPILATION ALBUMS:	HITS 10			WEEKS 50	
CREAM LIVE	Deconstruction	3	6 May 95		17
CREAM ANTHEMS	Deconstruction	2	11 Nov 95		3
CREAM LIVE - TWO	Deconstruction	3	6 Jul 96		5
CREAM SEPARATES - THE COLLECTION	Deconstruction	16	29 Mar 97		1
CREAM ANTHEMS '97	Deconstruction	11	15 Nov 97		2
CREAM ANTHEMS MIXED BY TALL PAUL AND SEB FONTAINE	Virgin/EMI	15	28 Nov 98		1
RESIDENT - 2 YEARS OF OAKENFOLD AT CREAM	Virgin/EMI	2	27 Mar 99		6
CREAM IBIZA - ARRIVALS	Virgin/EMI	2	12 Jun 99		7
CREAM IBIZA - DEPARTURES	Virgin/EMI	13	18 Sep 99		2
CREAM ANTHEMS 2000	Virgin/EMI	7	27 Nov 99		6

Dance Energy

COMPILATION ALBUMS:		HITS 4			WEEKS 17
DANCE ENERGY	*Virgin Television*	20	*19 Jan 91*	2
DANCE ENERGY 2	*Virgin Television*	6	*1 Jun 91*	5
DANCE ENERGY 3	*Virgin Television*	10	*30 Nov 91*	6
DANCE ENERGY 4 – FEEL THE RHYTHM	*Parlophone*	6	*4 Jul 92*	4

Dance Mix

ALBUMS:		HITS 4			WEEKS 7
DANCE MIX – DANCE HITS VOLUME 1	*Epic*	85	*2 Jul 83*	2
DANCE MIX – DANCE HITS VOLUME 2	*Epic*	51	*24 Sep 83*	3
DANCE MIX – DANCE HITS VOLUME 3	*Epic*	70	*3 Mar 84*	1
DANCE MIX – DANCE HITS VOLUME 4	*Epic*	99	*16 Jun 84*	1

Dance Nation

COMPILATION ALBUMS:		HITS 6			WEEKS 52
DANCE NATION	*Ministry Of Sound*	5	*13 Apr 96*	6
MINISTRY OF SOUND – DANCE NATION PART 2	*Ministry Of Sound*	4	*20 Jul 96*	8
DANCE NATION 3 – PETE TONG & JUDGE JULES	*Ministry Of Sound*	1	*29 Mar 97*	10
DANCE NATION 4 – PETE TONG/BOY GEORGE	*Ministry Of Sound*	2	*13 Sep 97*	8
PETE TONG/BOY GEORGE – DANCE NATION 5	*Ministry Of Sound*	2	*28 Mar 98*	9
DANCE NATION SIX – TALL PAUL & BRANDON BLOCK	*Ministry Of Sound*	1	*27 Mar 99*	11

Dance Zone

COMPILATION ALBUMS:		HITS 11			WEEKS 75
DANCE ZONE – LEVEL ONE	*PolyGram TV*	1	*7 May 94*	8
DANCE ZONE – LEVEL TWO	*PolyGram TV*	1	*16 Jul 94*	6
DANCE ZONE – LEVEL THREE	*PolyGram TV*	1	*8 Oct 94*	6
DANCE ZONE '94	*PolyGram TV*	2	*12 Nov 94*	12
DANCE ZONE – LEVEL FOUR	*PolyGram TV*	1	*25 Mar 95*	8
DANCE ZONE – LEVEL FIVE	*PolyGram TV*	1	*24 Jun 95*	10
DANCE ZONE – LEVEL SIX	*PolyGram TV*	1	*2 Sep 95*	7
DANCE ZONE '95	*PolyGram TV*	8	*11 Nov 95*	4
DANCE ZONE – LEVEL SEVEN	*PolyGram TV*	1	*4 May 96*	5
DANCE ZONE – LEVEL EIGHT	*PolyGram TV*	4	*21 Sep 96*	6
DANCE ZONE – LEVEL NINE	*PolyGram TV*	7	*31 May 97*	3

Deep Heat

COMPILATION ALBUMS:		HITS 14			WEEKS 149
DEEP HEAT – 26 HOTTEST HOUSE HITS	*Telstar*	1	*4 Mar 89*	15
DEEP HEAT – THE SECOND BURN	*Telstar*	2	*22 Apr 89*	13
DEEP HEAT 3 – THE THIRD DEGREE	*Telstar*	2	*22 Jul 89*	13
DEEP HEAT 4 – PLAY WITH FIRE	*Telstar*	1	*23 Sep 89*	11
DEEP HEAT 1989 – FIGHT THE FLAME	*Telstar*	4	*25 Nov 89*	17
DEEP HEAT 5 – FEED THE FEVER – 32 HOTTEST CLUB HITS	*Telstar*	1	*3 Feb 90*	11
DEEP HEAT 6 – THE SIXTH SENSE	*Telstar*	1	*31 Mar 90*	14
DEEP HEAT 7 – SEVENTH HEAVEN	*Telstar*	1	*7 Jul 90*	9
DEEP HEAT 8 – THE HAND OF FATE	*Telstar*	3	*27 Oct 90*	5
DEEP HEAT 90	*Telstar*	3	*24 Nov 90*	12
DEEP HEAT 9 – NINTH LIFE – KISS THE BLISS	*Telstar*	1	*26 Jan 91*	7
DEEP HEAT 10 – THE AWAKENING	*Telstar*	2	*1 Jun 91*	7
DEEP HEAT 11 – SPIRIT OF ECSTASY	*Telstar*	3	*21 Dec 91*	8
DEEP HEAT 93 VOLUME 1	*Telstar*	2	*10 Apr 93*	7

Disney

ALBUMS:		HITS 2			WEEKS 19
GOOFY GREATS	*K-Tel*	19	*8 Nov 75*	7
GREATEST HITS OF WALT DISNEY	*Ronco*	11	*6 Dec 75*	12

COMPILATION ALBUMS:		HITS 4			WEEKS 24
THE VERY BEST OF DISNEY	*Pickwick*	4	*20 Nov 93*	12
THE VERY BEST OF DISNEY 2	*Pickwick/Disney*	9	*19 Nov 94*	4
DISNEY'S HIT SINGLES & MORE!	*Walt Disney*	9	*22 Nov 97*	4
THE DISNEY EXPERIENCE	*Walt Disney*	12	*28 Nov 98*	4

Drive Time

COMPILATION ALBUMS:		HITS 4			WEEKS 24
DRIVE TIME – 36 OF THE GREATEST RADIO ANTHEMS ...	*Dino*	5	*8 Apr 95*	8
DRIVE TIME 2	*Dino*	4	*22 Jul 95*	7
DRIVETIME 3	*Dino*	4	*6 Jan 96*	6
DRIVE TIME 4	*Dino*	8	*31 Aug 96*	3

Energy Rush

COMPILATION ALBUMS:		HITS 14			WEEKS 99
ENERGY RUSH	*Dino*	1	*17 Oct 92*	6
ENERGY RUSH II	*Dino*	7	*12 Dec 92*	7
ENERGY RUSH LEVEL 3	*Dino*	3	*30 Jan 93*	6
ENERGY RUSH PRESENTS DANCE HITS 93	*Dino*	1	*10 Apr 93*	12
ENERGY RUSH PHASE 4	*Dino*	2	*5 Jun 93*	6

ENERGY RUSH DANCE HITS 93 (2ND DIMENSION)	Dino	2	24 Jul 93	8
ENERGY RUSH FACTOR 5	Dino	3	11 Sep 93	5
ENERGY RUSH PRESENTS DANCE HITS OF THE YEAR	Dino	3	16 Oct 93	13
ENERGY RUSH – SAFE SIX	Dino	5	4 Dec 93	7
ENERGY RUSH – EURO DANCE HITS 94	Dino	5	12 Mar 94	4
ENERGY RUSH 7	Dino	2	2 Apr 94	5
ENERGY RUSH – XTERMIN8	Dino	1	28 May 94	8
ENERGY RUSH DANCE HITS 94	Dino	3	6 Aug 94	8
ENERGY RUSH K9	Dino	3	11 Feb 95	4

Essential Selection

COMPILATION ALBUMS:	HITS 12		WEEKS 61	
PETE TONG ESSENTIAL SELECTION – SUMMER 97	PolyGram TV	4	23 Aug 97	5

Pete Tong is a DJ who has the show 'Essential Selection' on BBC Radio 1.

PETE TONG ESSENTIAL SELECTION – WINTER 97	ffrr	10	15 Nov 97	2
PETE TONG ESSENTIAL SELECTION	ffrr	4	18 Apr 98	7
PETE TONG ESSENTIAL SELECTION – SUMMER 1998 (3CD issue)	ffrr	2	29 Aug 98	7
PETE TONG ESSENTIAL SELECTION – SUMMER 1998	ffrr	4	29 Aug 98	9
ESSENTIAL SELECTION '98 – PETE TONG/PAUL OAKENFOLD (3CD issue)	ffrr	11	5 Dec 98	6
ESSENTIAL SELECTION '98 – PETE TONG/PAUL OAKENFOLD	ffrr	13	9 Jan 99	5
PETE TONG – ESSENTIAL SECTION – SPRING 1999 (3CD issue)	ffrr	3	20 Mar 99	6
PETE TONG – ESSENTIAL SECTION – SPRING 1999	ffrr	13	20 Mar 99	3
PETE TONG ESSENTIAL SELECTION – IBIZA 99	ffrr	11	31 Jul 99	5
PETE TONG ESSENTIAL SELECTION – IBIZA 99 (3CD issue)	ffrr	7	31 Jul 99	3

Due to chart rules, sales of the 3CD issues listed above could not be combined with the standard packages.

ESSENTIAL MILLENNIUM – PETE TONG FATBOY SLIM PAUL OAKENFOLD	ffrr	10	13 Nov 99	3

Fantastic

COMPILATION ALBUMS:	HITS 5		WEEKS 27	
FANTASTIC 80'S!	Columbia	1	7 Mar 98	12
FANTASTIC 80'S! – 2	Columbia	4	23 May 98	7
FANTASTIC DANCE!	Columbia	14	29 Aug 98	2
FANTASTIC 70'S!	Columbia	8	3 Oct 98	4
FANTASTIC 80'S! – 3	Columbia	11	14 Nov 98	2

Greatest Hits Of

ALBUMS:	HITS 4		WEEKS 49	
THE GREATEST HITS OF 1985	Telstar	1	16 Nov 85	17
THE GREATEST HITS OF 1986	Telstar	8	8 Nov 86	13
THE GREATEST HITS OF 1987	Telstar	12	21 Nov 87	11
THE GREATEST HITS OF 1988	Telstar	11	19 Nov 88	8
COMPILATION ALBUMS:	HITS 15		WEEKS 139	
THE GREATEST HITS OF 1988	Telstar	8	14 Jan 89	8
THE GREATEST HITS OF 1989	Telstar	4	18 Nov 89	11
THE GREATEST HITS OF 1990	Telstar	4	17 Nov 90	14
THE GREATEST HITS OF 1991	Telstar	4	16 Nov 91	13
THE GREATEST HITS OF 1992	Telstar	4	14 Nov 92	16
THE GREATEST HITS OF DANCE	Telstar	5	28 Nov 92	11
THE GREATEST HITS OF 1993	Telstar	4	13 Nov 93	13
THE GREATEST HITS OF 1994	Telstar	9	12 Nov 94	5
THE GREATEST HITS OF THE 90'S – PART 1	Telstar	19	28 Jan 95	2
THE GREATEST HITS OF 1995	Telstar	8	18 Nov 95	9
THE GREATEST HITS OF 1996 – THE STORY OF THE YEAR	Telstar	4	16 Nov 96	9
THE GREATEST HITS OF 1997	Telstar TV	2	15 Nov 97	12
THE GREATEST HITS OF 1998	Telstar TV	3	14 Nov 98	12
THE GREATEST HITS OF THE NINETIES	Telstar TV	19	6 Nov 99	1
THE GREATEST HITS OF 1999 – THE STORY SO FAR	Telstar TV	8	13 Nov 99	3

Greatest Love

ALBUMS:	HITS 2		WEEKS 42	
THE GREATEST LOVE	Telstar	11	26 Dec 87	40
THE GREATEST LOVE 2	Telstar	37	31 Dec 88	2
COMPILATION ALBUMS:	HITS 9		WEEKS 134	
THE GREATEST LOVE	Telstar	7	14 Jan 89	31
THE GREATEST LOVE 2	Telstar	3	14 Jan 89	23
THE GREATEST LOVE 3	Telstar	4	11 Nov 89	18
THE GREATEST LOVE 4	Telstar	4	27 Oct 90	19
THE VERY BEST OF GREATEST LOVE	Telstar	5	8 Dec 90	17
IN LOVE – GREATEST LOVE 5	Telstar	5	19 Oct 91	11
THE GREATEST LOVE VI – WITH LOVE FROM THE STARS	Telstar	16	20 Nov 93	8
THE GREATEST LOVE EVER	Telstar	6	7 Jan 95	5
THE GREATEST LOVE	Telstar TV	14	30 Jan 99	2

Heartbeat

Heartbeat was a TV series by Yorkshire Television set in the 1960's.

COMPILATION ALBUMS:	HITS 6		WEEKS 84	
HEARTBEAT (MUSIC FROM THE TV SERIES)	Columbia	1	27 Jun 92	14

THE BEST OF HEARTBEAT	*Columbia*	1	*28 Jan 95*	16
HEARTBEAT - FOREVER YOURS	*Columbia*	1	*30 Sep 95*	17
HEARTBEAT - NUMBER 1 LOVE SONGS OF THE '60S	*RCA/Global TV*	2	*19 Oct 96*	21
HEARTBEAT - LOVE ME TENDER	*RCA/Global TV*	6	*1 Nov 97*	5
HEARTBEAT - THE 60'S GOLD COLLECTION	*RCA/Global TV*	7	*28 Nov 98*	11

Hits

ALBUMS:	HITS 9			WEEKS 177
THE HITS ALBUM/THE HITS TAPE - 32 ORIGINAL HITS	*CBS/WEA*	1	*1 Dec 84*	36
THE HITS ALBUM 2/THE HITS TAPE 2	*CBS/WEA*	1	*13 Apr 85*	21
HITS 3	*CBS/WEA*	2	*7 Dec 85*	21
HITS 4	*CBS/WEA/RCA/Ariola*	1	*29 Mar 86*	21
HITS 5	*CBS/RCA/Ariola/WEA*	1	*22 Nov 86*	25
HITS 6	*CBS/WEA/BMG*	1	*25 Jul 87*	19
HITS 7	*CBS/WEA/RCA/Arista*	2	*5 Dec 87*	17
HITS 8	*CBS/WEA/BMG*	2	*30 Jul 88*	13
THE HITS ALBUM	*CBS/WEA/BMG*	5	*17 Dec 88*	4

COMPILATION ALBUMS:	HITS 33			WEEKS 327
THE HITS ALBUM	*CBS/WEA/BMG*	4	*14 Jan 89*	7
THE HITS ALBUM 10	*CBS/WEA/BMG*	1	*3 Jun 89*	13
MONSTER HITS	*CBS/WEA/BMG*	2	*2 Dec 89*	14
SNAP! IT UP - MONSTER HITS 2	*CBS/WEA/BMG*	2	*11 Aug 90*	10
THE HIT PACK: THE BEST OF CHART MUSIC	*CBS/WEA/BMG*	2	*29 Dec 90*	8
From 12 Jan 91 tha labels changed to Sony/WEA/BMG.				
THE HITS ALBUM	*Sony/BMG*	1	*10 Aug 91*	9
This album is different to an earlier chart entry.				
HITS 93 VOLUME 1	*Telstar/BMG*	1	*20 Feb 93*	15
HITS 93 VOLUME 2	*Telstar*	2	*29 May 93*	8
HITS 93 VOLUME 3	*Telstar*	2	*14 Aug 93*	9
HITS 93 VOLUME 4	*Telstar*	2	*20 Nov 93*	9
HITS 94 VOLUME 1	*Telstar/BMG*	3	*19 Mar 94*	7
THE ULTIMATE HITS ALBUM	*Telstar/BMG*	11	*15 Oct 94*	2
HITS 96	*Global TV/Warner TV*	1	*23 Dec 95*	14
NEW HITS 96	*warner.esp/Global TV/Sony TV*	1	*18 May 96*	16
FRESH HITS 96	*warner.esp/Global TV/Sony TV*	2	*31 Aug 96*	10
HUGE HITS 1996	*warner.esp/Global TV/Sony TV*	1	*9 Nov 96*	12
HITS 97	*warner.esp/Global TV/Sony TV*	2	*21 Dec 96*	13
THE HITS ALBUM 1997	*Telstar*	4	*15 Mar 97*	3
NEW HITS 1997	*warner.esp/Global TV/Sony TV*	1	*26 Apr 97*	11
FRESH HITS 1997	*warner.esp/Global TV/Sony TV*	1	*16 Aug 97*	12
HUGE HITS 1997	*warner.esp/Global TV/Sony TV*	1	*1 Nov 97*	7
BIG HITS	*warner.esp/Global TV/Sony TV*	4	*20 Dec 97*	7
NEW HITS 98	*warner.esp/Global TV/Sony TV*	1	*4 Apr 98*	12
FRESH HITS 98	*warner.esp/Global TV/Sony TV*	1	*4 Jul 98*	17
BIG HITS 98	*warner.esp/Global TV/Sony TV*	1	*19 Sep 98*	9
HUGE HITS 1998	*warner.esp/Global TV/Sony TV*	1	*7 Nov 98*	11
HITS 99	*warner.esp/Global TV/Sony TV*	2	*19 Dec 98*	14
NEW HITS 99	*warner.esp/Global TV/Sony TV*	1	*3 Apr 99*	12
FRESH HITS 99	*warner.esp/Global Music TV/Sony Music TV*	1	*3 Jul 99*	9
BIG HITS 99	*warner.esp/Global TV/Sony TV*	1	*4 Sep 99*	11
HUGE HITS 99	*warner.esp/Global TV/Sony TV*	1	*6 Nov 99*	9
MASSIVE DANCE HITS 2000	*warner.esp/Global TV/Universal Music TV*	11	*11 Dec 99*	4
HITS 2000	*warner.esp/Global TV/Sony TV*	2	*18 Dec 99*	3

In The Mix

COMPILATION ALBUMS:	HITS 11			WEEKS 81
IN THE MIX 96	*Virgin*	1	*24 Feb 96*	12
IN THE MIX 96 - 2	*Virgin*	2	*25 May 96*	14
IN THE MIX - 90'S HITS	*Virgin*	3	*27 Jul 96*	6
IN THE MIX 96 - 3	*Virgin*	1	*12 Oct 96*	6
IN THE MIX 97	*Virgin*	1	*8 Feb 97*	11
IN THE MIX 97 - 2	*Virgin/EMI*	2	*26 Apr 97*	7
IN THE MIX 97 - 3	*Virgin/EMI*	2	*2 Aug 97*	6
IN THE MIX 98	*Virgin/EMI*	1	*14 Feb 98*	7
IN THE MIX 98	*Virgin/EMI*	6	*4 Jul 98*	4
IN THE MIX IBIZA	*Virgin/EMI*	1	*24 Oct 98*	4
IN THE MIX 2000	*Virgin/EMI*	3	*13 Mar 99*	4

Kiss

Kiss FM is a London based Radio station.

COMPILATION ALBUMS:	HITS 20			WEEKS 128
THE SOUND OF KISS 100FM	*PolyGram TV*	1	*22 Jan 94*	4
KISS IN IBIZA '95	*PolyGram TV*	3	*14 Oct 95*	5
KISSMIX '96	*PolyGram TV*	5	*13 Jul 96*	3
KISS IN IBIZA '96	*PolyGram TV*	1	*19 Oct 96*	8
KISS ANTHEMS	*PolyGram TV*	2	*19 Apr 97*	7
KISS 100FM - SMOOTH GROOVES	*PolyGram TV*	3	*5 Jul 97*	8
KISS MIX '97	*PolyGram TV*	3	*9 Aug 97*	6

KISS IN IBIZA '97	*PolyGram TV*	1	*27 Sep 97*	7
KISS ANTHEMS '97	*PolyGram TV*	6	*29 Nov 97*	7
KISS SMOOTH GROOVES '98	*PolyGram TV*	2	*28 Feb 98*	7
KISS GARAGE	*PolyGram TV*	3	*9 May 98*	7
KISS MIX '98	*PolyGram TV*	4	*25 Jul 98*	4
KISS IN IBIZA '98	*PolyGram TV*	2	*19 Sep 98*	7
KISS ANTHEMS '98	*PolyGram TV*	8	*28 Nov 98*	9
KISS SMOOTH GROOVES '99	*PolyGram TV*	3	*6 Feb 99*	6
KISS HOUSE NATION	*PolyGram TV*	1	*27 Feb 99*	9
Above 2: Label changed to Universal Music TV from 13 Mar 99.				
KISS CLUBLIFE	*Universal Music TV*	2	*8 May 99*	7
KISS SMOOTH GROOVES – SUMMER '99	*Universal Music TV*	7	*26 Jun 99*	4
KISS IBIZA '99	*Universal Music TV*	1	*18 Sep 99*	8
KISS CLUBLIFE 2000	*Universal Music TV*	6	*27 Nov 99*	5

Love Album

COMPILATION ALBUMS:	HITS 6			WEEKS 83
THE LOVE ALBUM	*Virgin*	1	*19 Nov 94*	23
THE LOVE ALBUM II	*Virgin*	2	*18 Nov 95*	16
THE LOVE ALBUM III	*Virgin*	2	*16 Nov 96*	13
THE LOVE ALBUM IV	*Virgin/EMI*	11	*15 Nov 97*	9
THE VERY BEST OF THE LOVE ALBUM	*Virgin/EMI*	3	*14 Nov 98*	18
THE '80S LOVE ALBUM	*Virgin/EMI*	6	*13 Mar 99*	4

Massive Dance

COMPILATION ALBUMS:	HITS 5			WEEKS 33
MASSIVE DANCE MIX 96	*Telstar*	9	*8 Jun 96*	4
MASSIVE DANCE: 98	*warner.esp/PolyGram TV/Global TV*	8	*13 Dec 97*	9
MASSIVE DANCE: 98 – VOLUME 2	*PolyGram TV/warner.esp/Global TV*	2	*13 Jun 98*	6
MASSIVE DANCE: 99	*warner.esp/PolyGram TV/Global TV*	5	*12 Dec 98*	9
MASSIVE DANCE 99 – VOLUME 2	*warner.esp/Universal Music TV/Global TV*	3	*3 Apr 99*	5

Motown Chartbusters

ALBUMS:	HITS 9			WEEKS 316
BRITISH MOTOWN CHARTBUSTERS	*Tamla Motown*	2	*21 Oct 67*	54
BRITISH MOTOWN CHARTBUSTERS VOLUME 2	*Tamla Motown*	8	*30 Nov 68*	11
MOTOWN CHARTBUSTERS VOLUME 3	*Tamla Motown*	1	*25 Oct 69*	93
MOTOWN CHARTBUSTERS VOLUME 4	*Tamla Motown*	1	*24 Oct 70*	40
MOTOWN CHARTBUSTERS VOLUME 5	*Tamla Motown*	1	*17 Apr 71*	36
MOTOWN CHARTBUSTERS VOLUME 6	*Tamla Motown*	2	*23 Oct 71*	36
MOTOWN CHARTBUSTERS VOLUME 7	*Tamla Motown*	9	*25 Nov 72*	16
MOTOWN CHARTBUSTERS VOLUME 8	*Tamla Motown*	9	*3 Nov 73*	15
MOTOWN CHARTBUSTERS VOLUME 9	*Tamla Motown*	14	*26 Oct 74*	15

Now!

The longest running Compilation series.

ALBUMS:	HITS 19			WEEKS 425
NOW, THAT'S WHAT I CALL MUSIC	*EMI/Virgin*	1	*10 Dec 83*	50
NOW THAT'S WHAT I CALL MUSIC II	*Virgin/EMI*	1	*7 Apr 84*	38
NOW, THAT'S WHAT I CALL MUSIC III	*Virgin/EMI*	1	*11 Aug 84*	30
NOW, THAT'S WHAT I CALL MUSIC 4 – 32 CHART HITS	*Virgin/EMI*	2	*8 Dec 84*	43
NOW DANCE – THE 12" MIXES	*EMI/Virgin*	3	*1 Jun 85*	14
NOW, THAT'S WHAT I CALL MUSIC 5	*Virgin/EMI*	1	*17 Aug 85*	21
NOW – THE CHRISTMAS ALBUM	*Virgin/EMI*	1	*30 Nov 85*	22
NOW, THAT'S WHAT I CALL MUSIC 6	*Virgin/EMI*	1	*7 Dec 85*	40
NOW – THE SUMMER ALBUM – 30 SUMMER HITS	*EMI/Virgin*	7	*19 Jul 86*	9
NOW, THAT'S WHAT I CALL MUSIC 7	*Virgin/EMI*	1	*23 Aug 86*	21
NOW DANCE '86	*EMI/Virgin*	2	*8 Nov 86*	13
NOW, THAT'S WHAT I CALL MUSIC '86	*Virgin/EMI*	65	*29 Nov 86*	4
The first CD only compilation album to chart.				
NOW, THAT'S WHAT I CALL MUSIC 8	*EMI/Virgin/PolyGram*	1	*6 Dec 86*	23
NOW, THAT'S WHAT I CALL MUSIC 9	*Virgin/EMI/PolyGram*	1	*4 Apr 87*	26
NOW! SMASH HITS	*EMI/Virgin/PolyGram*	5	*3 Oct 87*	10
Issued in conjunction with the teen magazine 'Smash Hits'.				
NOW THAT'S WHAT I CALL MUSIC 10	*EMI/Virgin/PolyGram*	1	*5 Dec 87*	21
NOW THAT'S WHAT I CALL MUSIC 11	*EMI/Virgin/PolyGram*	1	*2 Apr 88*	17
NOW THAT'S WHAT I CALL MUSIC 12	*EMI/Virgin/PolyGram*	1	*23 Jul 88*	17
NOW THAT'S WHAT I CALL MUSIC 13	*EMI/Virgin/PolyGram*	1	*3 Dec 88*	6
COMPILATION ALBUMS:	**HITS 60**			**WEEKS 662**
NOW THAT'S WHAT I CALL MUSIC 13	*EMI/Virgin/PolyGram*	1	*14 Jan 89*	15
NOW THAT'S WHAT I CALL MUSIC 14	*EMI/Virgin/PolyGram*	1	*1 Apr 89*	18
NOW DANCE '89 – THE 12" MIXES	*EMI/Virgin*	1	*15 Jul 89*	14
NOW THAT'S WHAT I CALL MUSIC 15	*EMI/Virgin/PolyGram*	1	*26 Aug 89*	13
NOW THAT'S WHAT I CALL MUSIC 16	*EMI/Virgin/PolyGram*	1	*2 Dec 89*	15
NOW DANCE 901 – 20 SMASH DANCE HITS – THE 12" MIXES	*EMI/Virgin/PolyGram*	1	*10 Mar 90*	14
NOW THAT'S WHAT I CALL MUSIC 17	*EMI/Virgin/PolyGram*	1	*5 May 90*	15
NOW DANCE 902	*EMI/Virgin/PolyGram*	1	*28 Jul 90*	13
NOW DANCE 903 – THE 12" MIXES	*EMI/Virgin/PolyGram*	1	*10 Nov 90*	9

NOW! THAT'S WHAT I CALL MUSIC 18	EMI/Virgin/PolyGram	1	1 Dec 90	18
NOW! THAT'S WHAT I CALL MUSIC 19	EMI/Virgin/PolyGram	1	6 Apr 91	16
NOW DANCE 91	EMI/Virgin/PolyGram	1	5 Oct 91	9
NOW THAT'S WHAT I CALL MUSIC! 20	EMI/Virgin/PolyGram	1	30 Nov 91	18
NOW THAT'S WHAT I CALL MUSIC! 21	EMI/Virgin/PolyGram	1	25 Apr 92	13
NOW THAT'S WHAT I CALL MUSIC! 22	EMI/Virgin/PolyGram	1	8 Aug 92	14
NOW DANCE 92	EMI/Virgin/PolyGram	3	14 Nov 92	11
NOW THAT'S WHAT I CALL MUSIC! 23	EMI/Virgin/PolyGram	1	28 Nov 92	18
NOW DANCE 93	EMI/Virgin/PolyGram	1	8 May 93	13
NOW THAT'S WHAT I CALL MUSIC! 24	EMI/Virgin/PolyGram	1	26 Jun 93	9
NOW THAT'S WHAT I CALL MUSIC! 25	EMI/Virgin/PolyGram	1	14 Aug 93	10
NOW THAT'S WHAT I CALL MUSIC! 1983	EMI/Virgin/PolyGram	10	4 Sep 93	5
NOW THAT'S WHAT I CALL MUSIC! 1984	EMI/Virgin/PolyGram	13	4 Sep 93	4
NOW THAT'S WHAT I CALL MUSIC! 1985	EMI/Virgin/PolyGram	15	4 Sep 93	4
NOW THAT'S WHAT I CALL MUSIC! 1986	EMI/Virgin/PolyGram	16	4 Sep 93	2
NOW THAT'S WHAT I CALL MUSIC! 1987	EMI/Virgin/PolyGram	17	4 Sep 93	2
NOW THAT'S WHAT I CALL MUSIC! 1992	EMI/Virgin/PolyGram	14	25 Sep 93	2
NOW THAT'S WHAT I CALL MUSIC! 1988	EMI/Virgin/PolyGram	20	25 Sep 93	1
NOW THAT'S WHAT I CALL MUSIC! 1993	EMI/Virgin/PolyGram	1	9 Oct 93	8
NOW DANCE – THE BEST OF '93	EMI/Virgin/PolyGram	1	30 Oct 93	6
NOW THAT'S WHAT I CALL MUSIC! 26	EMI/Virgin/PolyGram	1	27 Nov 93	15
NOW DANCE 94 VOLUME 1	EMI/Virgin/PolyGram	1	29 Jan 94	7
NOW! THAT'S WHAT I CALL LOVE	EMI/Virgin/PolyGram	6	19 Mar 94	6
NOW! DANCE 94 VOLUME 2	EMI/Virgin/PolyGram	8	19 Mar 94	5
NOW THAT'S WHAT I CALL MUSIC! 27	EMI/Virgin/PolyGram	1	9 Apr 94	15
NOW DANCE – SUMMER 94	EMI/Virgin	1	2 Jul 94	8
NOW THAT'S WHAT I CALL MUSIC! 28	EMI/Virgin/PolyGram	1	13 Aug 94	13
NOW THAT'S WHAT I CALL MUSIC! 1994	EMI/Virgin/PolyGram	1	15 Oct 94	8
NOW THAT'S WHAT I CALL MUSIC! 29	EMI/Virgin/PolyGram	1	26 Nov 94	13
NOW DANCE – THE BEST OF '94	EMI/Virgin	4	10 Dec 94	9
NOW DANCE 95	EMI/Virgin	3	1 Apr 95	6
NOW THAT'S WHAT I CALL MUSIC! 30	EMI/Virgin/PolyGram	1	22 Apr 95	12
NOW DANCE SUMMER 95	EMI/Virgin/PolyGram	3	29 Jul 95	5
NOW THAT'S WHAT I CALL MUSIC! 31	EMI/Virgin/PolyGram	1	12 Aug 95	12
NOW THAT'S WHAT I CALL MUSIC! 1995	EMI/Virgin/PolyGram	2	14 Oct 95	6
NOW THAT'S WHAT I CALL MUSIC! 32	EMI/Virgin/PolyGram	1	25 Nov 95	15
NOW THAT'S WHAT I CALL MUSIC! 33	EMI/Virgin/PolyGram	1	30 Mar 96	13
NOW THAT'S WHAT I CALL MUSIC! 34	EMI/Virgin/PolyGram	1	24 Aug 96	15
NOW THAT'S WHAT I CALL MUSIC! 35	EMI/Virgin/PolyGram	1	30 Nov 96	18
NOW THAT'S WHAT I CALL MUSIC! 36	EMI/Virgin/PolyGram	1	5 Apr 97	16
NOW THAT'S WHAT I CALL MUSIC! 37	EMI/Virgin/PolyGram	1	26 Jul 97	16
NOW DANCE 97	Virgin/EMI	1	1 Nov 97	6
NOW THAT'S WHAT I CALL MUSIC! 38	EMI/Virgin/PolyGram	1	29 Nov 97	17
NOW THAT'S WHAT I CALL MUSIC! 39	EMI/Virgin/PolyGram	1	18 Apr 98	17
NOW DANCE 98	Virgin/EMI	3	7 Nov 98	5
NOW THAT'S WHAT I CALL MUSIC! 40	EMI/Virgin/PolyGram	1	15 Aug 98	14
NOW THAT'S WHAT I CALL MUSIC! 41	EMI/Virgin/PolyGram	1	5 Dec 98	18
NOW THAT'S WHAT I CALL MUSIC! 42	EMI/Virgin/Universal Music TV	1	10 Apr 99	16
NOW THAT'S WHAT I CALL MUSIC! 43	EMI/Virgin/Universal Music TV	1	31 Jul 99	15
NOW DANCE 2000	Virgin/EMI	1	30 Oct 99	7
NOW THAT'S WHAT I CALL MUSIC! 44	EMI/Virgin/Universal Music TV	1	4 Dec 99	5

The Number One

COMPILATION ALBUMS:	HITS 22			WEEKS 96
THE NUMBER ONE CLASSIC SOUL ALBUM	PolyGram TV	5	15 Jul 95	7
THE NUMBER ONE REGGAE ALBUM	PolyGram TV	14	22 Jul 95	2
THE NUMBER ONE '70S ROCK ALBUM	PolyGram TV	3	26 Aug 95	5
THE NUMBER ONE MOVIES ALBUM	PolyGram TV	2	4 Nov 95	12
THE NUMBER ONE ALL TIME ROCK ALBUM	PolyGram TV	16	11 Nov 95	2
THE NUMBER ONE CHRISTMAS ALBUM	PolyGram TV	4	9 Dec 95	9
THE NUMBER ONE LOVE ALBUM	PolyGram TV	1	17 Feb 96	6
THE NUMBER ONE EIGHTIES ALBUM	PolyGram TV	10	27 Jul 96	4
THE NUMBER ONE SUMMER ALBUM	PolyGram TV	12	27 Jul 96	3
THE NUMBER ONE COUNTRY ALBUM	PolyGram TV	16	17 Aug 96	2
THE NUMBER ONE ACOUSTIC ROCK ALBUM	PolyGram TV	6	12 Oct 96	4
THE NUMBER ONE RAP ALBUM	PolyGram TV	12	2 Nov 96	1
THE NUMBER ONE ROCK BALLADS ALBUM	PolyGram TV	18	16 Nov 96	2
THE NUMBER ONE MOTOWN ALBUM	PolyGram TV	2	18 Jan 97	10
THE NUMBER ONE SCIFI ALBUM	PolyGram TV	13	29 Mar 97	4
THE NUMBER ONE SKA ALBUM	PolyGram TV	9	5 Apr 97	5
THE NUMBER ONE DRIVE ALBUM	PolyGram TV	14	6 Sep 97	2
THE NUMBER ONE JAZZ ALBUM	PolyGram TV	13	20 Sep 97	3
THE NUMBER ONE LINE DANCING ALBUM	PolyGram TV	10	4 Oct 97	4
THE NUMBER ONE ROCK 'N' ROLL ALBUM	PolyGram TV	20	11 Oct 97	1
THE NUMBER ONE SEVENTIES ALBUM	PolyGram TV	13	1 Nov 97	2
THE NUMBER ONE CHRISTMAS ALBUM [RE]	PolyGram TV	7	13 Dec 97	4

Re-released with a new catalogue number.

THE NUMBER ONE DANCE PARTY ALBUM	Universal Music TV	17	20 Nov 99	2

100%
COMPILATION ALBUMS:		HITS 29		WEEKS 195	
100% DANCE	Telstar	1	26 Jun 93	15
100% DANCE VOLUME 2	Telstar	1	2 Oct 93	9
100% REGGAE	Telstar	2	11 Dec 93	17
100% DANCE VOLUME 3	Telstar	7	11 Dec 93	9
100% RAP	Telstar	3	12 Mar 94	10
100% DANCE VOLUME 4	Telstar	2	23 Apr 94	7
100% REGGAE VOLUME 2	Telstar	4	30 Apr 94	14
100% SUMMER	Telstar	4	23 Jul 94	7
100% REGGAE VOLUME 3	Telstar	6	6 Aug 94	7
100% HITS	Telstar	2	24 Sep 94	8
100% ACID JAZZ	Telstar	5	8 Oct 94	14
100% PURE LOVE	Telstar	7	5 Nov 94	7
100% CHRISTMAS	Telstar	9	10 Dec 94	6
THE BEST OF 100% DANCE	Telstar	11	7 Jan 95	3
100% CLASSICS	Telstar	8	14 Jan 95	6
100% HOUSE CLASSICS – VOLUME 1	Telstar	16	18 Feb 95	4
100% ACID JAZZ – VOLUME 2	Telstar	14	17 Jun 95	4
100% SUMMER '95	Telstar	7	8 Jul 95	2
100% SUMMER JAZZ	Telstar	11	5 Aug 95	4
100% CARNIVAL!	Telstar	16	2 Sep 95	2
100% CLASSICS – VOLUME 2	Telstar	20	20 Jan 96	1
100% PURE GROOVE	Telstar	4	23 Mar 96	8
100% PURE GROOVE 2	Telstar	12	8 Jun 96	3
100% SUMMER MIX 96	Telstar	7	6 Jul 96	9
100% DANCE HITS 96	Telstar	11	21 Sep 96	3
100% DRUM & BASS	Telstar	11	5 Oct 96	4
100% SUMMER MIX 97	Telstar TV	8	26 Jul 97	6
BEST OF 100% PURE GROOVES	Telstar TV	13	27 Jun 98	2
100% SUMMER MIX 98	Telstar TV	13	18 Jul 98	4

Out Now!
ALBUMS:		HITS 2		WEEKS 28	
OUT NOW! 28 HOT HITS	Chrysalis/MCA	2	25 May 85	16
OUT NOW!! 2 – 28 HOT HITS	Chrysalis/MCA	3	26 Oct 85	12

Pure Swing
COMPILATION ALBUMS:		HITS 6		WEEKS 39	
PURE SWING	Dino	2	11 Mar 95	9
PURE SWING TWO	Dino	4	10 Jun 95	5
PURE SWING III	Dino	3	2 Sep 95	8
PURE SWING IV	Dino	1	18 Nov 95	9
PURE SWING 5	Dino	6	6 Jan 96	5
PURE SWING 96	Dino	9	13 Apr 96	3

Rare
ALBUMS:		HITS 2		WEEKS 2	
RARE	RCA	80	5 Sep 87	1
RARE 2	RCA	88	23 Apr 88	1
COMPILATION ALBUMS:		HITS 1		WEEKS 2	
RARE 3	Ariola	15	11 Feb 89	2

Reactivate
COMPILATION ALBUMS:		HITS 7		WEEKS 16	
REACTIVATE VOLUME 1 – THE BELGIAN TECHNO ANTHEMS	React	13	22 Jun 91	4
REACTIVATE VOLUME 2 – PHASERS ON FULL	React	9	5 Oct 91	4
REACTIVATE VOLUME 4 – TECHNOVATION	React	16	16 May 92	2
REACTIVATE VOLUME 5 – PURE TRANCE AND TECHNO	React	18	5 Sep 92	2
REACTIVATE 10	React	14	3 Jun 95	1
REACTIVATE 11 – STINGER BEAT AND TECHNO RAYS	React	14	26 Oct 96	1
REACTIVATE 12	React	17	21 Jun 97	2

Shine
COMPILATION ALBUMS:		HITS 11		WEEKS 56	
SHINE: 20 BRILLIANT INDIE HITS	PolyGram TV	4	13 May 95	5
SHINE TOO	PolyGram TV	4	2 Sep 95	5
SHINE 3	PolyGram TV	13	18 Nov 95	6
SHINE FOUR	PolyGram TV	3	9 Mar 96	6
SHINE 5	PolyGram TV	2	20 Jul 96	9
SHINE 6	PolyGram TV	2	5 Oct 96	5
SHINE 7	PolyGram TV	13	7 Dec 96	7
SHINE 8	PolyGram TV	6	3 May 97	5
SHINE 9	PolyGram TV	7	13 Sep 97	4
SHINE – BEST OF 97	PolyGram TV	20	17 Jan 98	1
SHINE 10	PolyGram TV	10	29 Aug 98	3

Simply The Best

COMPILATION ALBUMS:		HITS 6		WEEKS 25
SIMPLY THE BEST LOVE SONGS	*warner.esp*	2	*15 Feb 97*	6
SIMPLY THE BEST – CLASSIC SOUL	*warner.esp*	7	*5 Apr 97*	6
SIMPLY THE BEST LOVE SONGS 2	*warner.esp*	2	*14 Feb 98*	6
SIMPLY THE BEST DISCO	*warner.esp*	9	*28 Mar 98*	3
SIMPLY THE BEST CLASSICAL ANTHEMS	*warner.esp*	14	*31 Oct 98*	2
SIMPLY THE BEST RADIO HITS	*warner.esp*	17	*14 Nov 98*	2

Sisters Of Swing

COMPILATION ALBUMS:		HITS 5		WEEKS 25
SISTERS OF SWING	*PolyGram TV*	1	*3 Feb 96*	10
SISTERS OF SWING 2	*PolyGram TV*	4	*1 Jun 96*	3
SISTERS OF SWING III	*PolyGram TV/Global TV*	7	*10 May 97*	4
SISTERS OF SWING 98	*PolyGram TV*	5	*11 Jul 98*	5
SISTERS OF SWING 99	*Universal Music TV*	9	*4 Sep 99*	3

Smash Hits

Smash Hits is a Teen Magazine. From 1988 they held an Awards show each autumn which was broadcast on BBC1 TV.

ALBUMS:		HITS 1		WEEKS 11
SMASH HITS PARTY '88	*Dover*	6	*29 Oct 88*	11

COMPILATION ALBUMS:		HITS 19		WEEKS 149
SMASH HITS PARTY '88	*Dover*	12	*14 Jan 89*	5
SMASH HITS PARTY '89 – 30 SMASH HITS	*Dover*	1	*28 Oct 89*	14
SMASH HITS – RAVE!	*Dover*	1	*14 Jul 90*	10
SMASH HITS 1990	*Dover*	2	*3 Nov 90*	14
SMASH HITS – MASSIVE!	*Dover*	1	*25 May 91*	9
SMASH HITS 1991	*Dover*	3	*26 Oct 91*	16
SMASH HITS – PARTY ON!	*The Hit Label*	9	*22 Aug 92*	5
SMASH HITS '92 – 40 BIG HITS! SORTED!	*Chrysalis*	5	*12 Dec 92*	8
SMASH HITS '93 – 40 TOP CHARTIN' GROOVES	*Chrysalis*	4	*13 Nov 93*	10
SMASH HITS '94	*Telstar*	9	*3 Dec 94*	7
SMASH HITS '95 – VOLUME 1	*Telstar*	1	*18 Mar 95*	7
SMASH HITS '95 – VOLUME 2	*Telstar*	4	*24 Jun 95*	5
SMASH HITS MIX '97	*Virgin*	8	*14 Dec 96*	7
SMASH HITS – SUMMER '97	*Virgin/EMI*	1	*7 Jun 97*	8
SMASH HITS '98	*Virgin/EMI*	9	*13 Dec 97*	7
SMASH HITS – SUMMER '98	*Virgin/EMI*	2	*30 May 98*	6
SMASH HITS '99!	*Virgin/EMI*	10	*26 Dec 98*	4
SMASH HITS – SUMMER '99	*Virgin/EMI*	3	*5 Jun 99*	5
SMASH HITS 2000	*Virgin/EMI*	15	*25 Dec 99*	2

That Loving Feeling

COMPILATION ALBUMS:		HITS 8		WEEKS 140
THAT LOVING FEELING	*Dino*	11	*2 Dec 89*	11
THAT LOVING FEELING VOLUME 2	*Dino*	5	*3 Mar 90*	26
THAT LOVING FEELING VOLUME 3	*Dino*	1	*6 Oct 90*	31
THAT LOVING FEELING VOLUME IV	*Dino*	3	*6 Apr 91*	14
THAT LOVING FEELING VOLUME V	*Dino*	2	*19 Oct 91*	15
THAT LOVING FEELING VOLUME VI	*Dino*	3	*4 Sep 93*	12
THE VERY BEST OF THAT LOVING FEELING	*Dino*	2	*4 Dec 93*	21
THAT LOVING FEELING VOLUME VII	*Dino*	4	*13 Aug 94*	10

Top Of The Pops

BBC TV's 'Top Of The Pops' is the longest running pop music programme. First transmitted 1 Jan 64.

ALBUMS:		HITS 1		WEEKS 5
BBC TV'S BEST OF TOP OF THE POPS	*Super Beeb*	21	*4 Jan 75*	5

COMPILATION ALBUMS:		HITS 8		WEEKS 45
TOP OF THE POPS 1	*Columbia*	1	*10 Jun 95*	6
TOP OF THE POPS 2	*Columbia*	14	*2 Dec 95*	7
TOP OF THE POPS – THE CUTTING EDGE	*Columbia*	10	*28 Sep 96*	3
TOP OF THE POPS 1998 – VOLUME 1	*PolyGram TV*	2	*16 May 98*	7
TOP OF THE POPS 1998 – VOLUME 2	*PolyGram TV/BBC Music*	3	*26 Sep 98*	6
TOP OF THE POPS – BEST OF 1998	*PolyGram TV*	11	*28 Nov 98*	2
TOP OF THE POPS '99 – VOLUME ONE	*BBC/Universal Music TV*	2	*22 May 99*	6
TOP OF THE POPS '99 – VOLUME TWO	*Universal Music TV*	1	*25 Sep 99*	8

Ultimate

COMPILATION ALBUMS:		HITS 8		WEEKS 43
THE ULTIMATE EIGHTIES	*PolyGram TV*	2	*25 Jun 94*	9
THE ULTIMATE 80'S BALLADS	*PolyGram TV*	5	*29 Oct 94*	3
AMOUR – THE ULTIMATE LOVE COLLECTION	*PolyGram TV*	3	*15 Feb 97*	5
ULTIMATE DISCO MIX	*PolyGram TV*	15	*4 Apr 98*	2
THE ULTIMATE SUMMER PARTY ALBUM	*PolyGram TV*	7	*27 Jun 98*	3
RELAX! THE ULTIMATE 80'S MIX	*PolyGram TV*	4	*8 Aug 98*	11

THE ULTIMATE CHRISTMAS COLLECTION	PolyGram TV	11	12 Dec 98	4
RELAX: - THE ULTIMATE 80'S MIX - VOLUME 2	PolyGram TV	8	6 Feb 99	3
THE ULTIMATE CHRISTMAS COLLECTION [RI]	Universal Music TV	15	4 Dec 99	3

Upfront

ALBUMS:	HITS 10			WEEKS 54
UPFRONT 1 - 14 DANCE TRACKS	Serious	17	7 Jun 86	10
UPFRONT 2 - 14 DANCE TRACKS	Serious	27	23 Aug 86	6
UPFRONT 3	Serious	37	1 Nov 86	5
UPFRONT 4	Serious	21	31 Jan 87	5
UPFRONT 5	Serious	21	28 Mar 87	6
UPFRONT 6	Serious	22	23 May 87	6
UPFRONT 7	Serious	31	15 Aug 87	4
UPFRONT 8	Serious	22	17 Oct 87	6
UPFRONT 9	Serious	92	19 Dec 87	1
UPFRONT 10	Serious	45	9 Apr 88	5

COMPILATION ALBUMS:	HITS 1			WEEKS 1
UPFRONT 89	Serious	15	18 Feb 89	1

Warehouse Raves

COMPILATION ALBUMS:	HITS 6			WEEKS 16
WAREHOUSE RAVES	Rumour	15	16 Sep 89	4
WAREHOUSE RAVES 3	Rumour	12	31 Mar 90	5
WAREHOUSE RAVES 4	Rumour	13	29 Sep 90	3
WAREHOUSE RAVES 5	Rumour	18	11 May 91	1
WAREHOUSE RAVES 6	Rumour	16	21 Mar 92	2
WAREHOUSE RAVES 7	Rumour	20	29 Aug 92	1

The World Of

ALBUMS:	HITS 5			WEEKS 26
THE WORLD OF BLUES POWER	Decca	24	28 Jun 69	6
THE WORLD OF BRASS BANDS	Decca	13	5 Jul 69	11
THE WORLD OF HITS VOLUME 2	Decca	7	6 Sep 69	5
THE WORLD OF PROGRESSIVE MUSIC (WOWIE ZOWIE)	Decca	17	20 Sep 69	2
THE WORLD OF PHASE 4 STEREO	Decca	29	20 Sep 69	2

STAGE CAST

(See also Barbra Streisand.)

Broadway

EPS:	HITS 4			WEEKS 37
MY FAIR LADY NO. 4	Philips	20	10 Sep 60	2
THE SOUND OF MUSIC	Philips	13	14 Oct 61	4
WEST SIDE STORY	Philips	5	19 May 62	26
WEST SIDE STORY	CBS	15	26 Jan 63	5

Above 2 entries are different casts to the show.

ALBUMS:	HITS 10			WEEKS 239
MY FAIR LADY	Philips	2	8 Nov 58	129

Features Rex Harrison, Julie Andrews, Stanley Holloway, Robert Coote. Adapted from Bernard Shaw's 'Pygmalion'.

WEST SIDE STORY	Philips	3	24 Jan 59	27
FLOWER DRUM SONG	Philips	2	2 Apr 60	27
MOST HAPPY FELLA	Philips	6	21 May 60	13
WEST SIDE STORY	Philips	14	30 Jul 60	1

This is a different cast recording than the original.

THE SOUND OF MUSIC	Philips	4	24 Jun 61	19
MY FAIR LADY	CBS	19	4 Jan 64	1

This is a different cast recording than the original.

CAMELOT	CBS	10	3 Oct 64	12
HAIR	RCA	29	6 Sep 69	3
MACK AND MABEL	MCA	38	6 Nov 82	7

London

EPS:	HITS 3			WEEKS 23
SALAD DAYS	Oriole	19	21 May 60	1
OLIVER	Decca	5	18 Nov 61	21
THE SOUND OF MUSIC	HMV	19	21 Apr 62	1

ALBUMS:	HITS 39			WEEKS 752
FINGS AIN'T WOT THEY USED TO BE	Decca	5	26 Mar 60	11
AT THE DROP OF A HAT	Parlophone	9	26 Mar 60	1
FOLLOW THAT GIRL	His Master's Voice	5	7 May 60	9
MAKE ME AN OFFER	His Master's Voice	18	21 May 60	1
FLOWER DRUM SONG	His Master's Voice	10	28 May 60	3
MOST HAPPY FELLA	His Master's Voice	19	9 Jul 60	1
OLIVER!	Decca	6	10 Sep 60	31

Features Ron Moody, Georgia Brown, Paul Whitsun-Jones.

MUSIC MAN	His Master's Voice	8	6 May 61	13

OLIVER! [RE]	*Decca*	4	*13 May 61*	60
BEYOND THE FRINGE	*Parlophone*	13	*22 Jul 61*	17
BYE BYE BIRDIE	*Philips*	17	*22 Jul 61*	3
THE SOUND OF MUSIC	*His Master's Voice*	4	*29 Jul 61*	68
STOP THE WORLD – I WANT TO GET OFF	*Decca*	8	*9 Sep 61*	14
Features Anthony Newley.				
BLITZ	*His Master's Voice*	7	*14 Jul 62*	21
HALF A SIXPENCE	*Decca*	20	*18 May 63*	2
PICKWICK	*Philips*	12	*3 Aug 63*	10
AT THE DROP OF ANOTHER HAT	*Parlophone*	12	*22 Feb 64*	11
CAMELOT	*His Master's Voice*	19	*16 Jan 65*	1
FIDDLER ON THE ROOF	*CBS*	4	*11 Mar 67*	50
Features Topol.				
HAIR	*Polydor*	3	*28 Dec 68*	94
Features Paul Nicholas, Vince Edward, Oliver Tobias, Michael Feast.				
THE WORLD OF OLIVER [RI]	*Decca*	23	*30 Aug 69*	4
Re-release of the 1960 cast recording.				
GODSPELL	*Arista*	25	*19 Feb 72*	17
EVITA	*MCA*	24	*18 Nov 78*	18
Features Julie Covington.				
CATS	*Polydor*	6	*1 Aug 81*	26
STARLIGHT EXPRESS	*Starlight*	21	*4 Aug 84*	9
LES MISERABLES	*First Night*	72	*15 Feb 86*	4
THE PHANTOM OF THE OPERA	*Really Useful*	1	*21 Feb 87*	141
Features Sarah Brightman, Michael Crawford.				
ASPECTS OF LOVE	*Really Useful/ Polydor*	1	*16 Sep 89*	29
Features Michael Ball.				
MISS SAIGON	*Geffen*	4	*24 Feb 90*	11
FIVE GUYS NAMED MOE	*First Night*	59	*29 Jun 91*	1
JOSEPH AND THE AMAZING TECHNICOLOR DREAMCOAT	*Really Useful/ Polydor*	1	*31 Aug 91*	38
Features Jason Donovan.				
THE NEW STARLIGHT EXPRESS	*Really Useful/ Polydor*	42	*10 Apr 93*	2
SUNSET BOULEVARD	*Really Useful/ Polydor*	11	*11 Sep 93*	4
GREASE	*Epic*	20	*2 Oct 93*	3
Features Debbie Gibson, Craig McLachlan.				
OLIVER! (1994 LONDON CAST)	*First Night*	36	*1 Apr 95*	3
LES MISERABLES – 10TH ANNIVERSARY CONCERT	*First Night*	32	*11 May 96*	7
Live recordings from the Royal Albert Hall, 8 Oct 95 with the Royal Philharmonic Orchestra.				
MARTIN GUERRE	*First Night*	58	*16 Nov 96*	1
HEATHCLIFF LIVE (THE SHOW)	*EMI*	41	*14 Dec 96*	4
Features Cliff Richard.				
CHICAGO – THE MUSICAL	*RCA Victor*	61	*27 Jun 98*	1
SATURDAY NIGHT FEVER	*Polydor*	17	*22 Aug 98*	6
MAMMA MIA!	*Polydor*	56	*13 Nov 99*	2
Features Siobhan McCarthy, Hilton McCrae, Lisa Stokke, Andrew Langtree, Jenny Galloway, Louise Plowright.				

South Africa

ALBUMS:	HITS 1			WEEKS 8
KING KONG	*Decca*	12	*11 Mar 61*	8

STUDIO CAST

ALBUMS:	HITS 14			WEEKS 170
SHOWBOAT	*His Master's Voice*	12	*25 Jun 60*	1
JESUS CHRIST SUPERSTAR	*MCA*	6	*8 Jan 72*	20
EVITA	*MCA*	4	*22 Jan 77*	35
WHITE MANSIONS	*A&M*	51	*17 Jun 78*	3
CHESS	*RCA*	10	*10 Nov 84*	16
WEST SIDE STORY	*Deutsche Grammophon*	11	*18 May 85*	32
Features Leonard Bernstein, Kiri Te Kanawa, Jose Carreras, Tatiana Troyanos.				
CHESS PIECES	*Telstar*	87	*2 Nov 85*	3
HIGHLIGHTS FROM WEST SIDE STORY	*Deutsche Grammophon*	72	*10 May 86*	6
DAVE CLARK'S TIME THE ALBUM	*EMI*	21	*17 May 86*	6
SOUTH PACIFIC	*CBS*	5	*11 Oct 86*	24
Features Kiri Te Kanawa, Jose Carreras, Sarah Vaughan.				
MATADOR	*Epic*	26	*13 Jun 87*	5
Features Tom Jones.				
MY FAIR LADY	*Decca*	41	*21 Nov 87*	12
Features Kiri Te Kanawa and Jeremy Irons.				
THE KING AND I	*Philips*	57	*10 Oct 92*	2
Features John Mauceri, Julie Andrews, Ben Kingsley, The Hollywood Bowl Orchestra.				
LEONARD BERNSTEIN'S WEST SIDE STORY	*IMG*	33	*10 Apr 93*	5
Features Michael Ball, Barbra Bonny, Barry Wordsworth, Royal Philharmonic Orchestra.				

TELEVISION

(See also Television Soundtracks or related compilations under the following artists: John Barry; Geoffrey Burgon; Clannad; Eric Clapton; Enya; Gladiators; Inti Illimani-Guamary; Elvis Presley; Vonda Shepherd; Simpsons.)

Related Compilations

ALBUMS:	HITS 20			WEEKS 121
JACK GOOD'S 'OH BOY!'	Parlophone	9	13 Dec 58	14
READY STEADY GO	Decca	20	8 Feb 64	1
Above 2 were music programmes on ITV.				
STARS FROM STARS AND GARTERS	Pye Golden Guinea	17	28 Mar 64	2
SUPERSONIC	Stallion	21	6 Dec 75	6
Music programme on ITV.				
FONZIE'S FAVOURITES	Warner Brothers	8	11 Mar 78	16
Fonzie is character in the American sitcom 'Happy Day's' set in the 1950's.				
STARS ON SUNDAY BY REQUEST	Curzon Sounds	65	9 Dec 78	3
Religious programme on ITV.				
THE TUBE	K-Tel	30	18 Feb 84	6
Music programme on Channel 4.				
THE TV HITS ALBUM	Towerbell	26	28 Sep 85	13
THE EASTENDERS SING-ALONG ALBUM	BBC	33	16 Nov 85	10
BBC1 TV soap, album features the Original BBC TV cast.				
TELLYHITS - 16 TOP TV THEMES	Stylus/BBC	34	23 Nov 85	6
JONATHAN KING'S ENTERTAINMENT FROM THE U.S.A.	Stylus	6	15 Feb 86	11
BBC programme reflecting the news and music in the US.				
THE T.V. HITS ALBUM TWO - 16 ORIGINAL HIT-TV THEMES	Towerbell	19	12 Apr 86	7
TELLYHITS 2 - 16 TOP TV THEMES	Stylus/BBC	68	5 Jul 86	2
THE VERY BEST OF ENTERTAINMENT FROM THE USA VOLUME 2	PrioriTyV	44	18 Oct 86	4
THE ROCK 'N' ROLL YEARS 1964-1967	BBC	71	27 Jun 87	2
BBC TV series that each edition reflects a particular years news and music.				
THE ROCK 'N' ROLL YEARS 1968-1971	BBC	77	27 Jun 87	1
THE ROCK 'N' ROLL YEARS 1956-1959	BBC	80	27 Jun 87	2
THE ROCK 'N' ROLL YEARS 1960-1963	BBC	84	27 Jun 87	1
THE CHART SHOW - DANCE HITS 1987	Chrysalis	39	28 Nov 87	6
Music video show, first transmitted on Channel 4 in 1986 before moving to ITV.				
THE CHART SHOW ROCK THE NATION	Dover	16	26 Mar 88	8
COMPILATION ALBUMS:	**HITS 32**			**WEEKS 147**
THE CHART SHOW - ROCK THE NATION 2	Dover	8	20 May 89	4
THE CHART SHOW - DANCE MASTERS	Dover	4	3 Jun 89	7
TV TUNES	K-Tel	17	23 Sep 89	3
THE OLD GREY WHISTLE TEST - BEST OF THE TEST	Windsong International	13	21 Sep 91	3
BBC2 music programme from the 1970s.				
THE BEST OF THE CLASSICAL BITS	Philips	7	30 Jan 93	10
Classical music featured in TV commercials.				
THE CHART SHOW - THE ULTIMATE ROCK ALBUM	The Hit Label	4	17 Apr 93	11
CLASSIC COMMERCIALS	Decca	8	12 Jun 93	6
THE BIG BREAKFAST ALBUM	Arcade	8	7 Aug 93	5
Breakfast show on Channel 4.				
THE CHART SHOW: ULTIMATE ROCK 2	The Hit Label	10	2 Oct 93	3
TALES FROM THE CITY	PolyGram TV	17	23 Oct 93	2
RETURN OF THE GLADIATORS	PolyGram TV	20	20 Nov 93	1
TOP GEAR	Epic	3	4 Jun 94	13
BBC2 TV programme on cars.				
CHART SHOW - ULTIMATE BLUES ALBUM	The Hit Label	13	16 Jul 94	3
DR. HILARY JONES' CLASSIC RELAXATION	PolyGram TV	13	22 Oct 94	2
THE CHART SHOW PRESENTS THE CHART MACHINE	PolyGram TV	18	20 May 95	2
TOP GEAR 2	Columbia	4	27 May 95	6
TOP GEAR CLASSICS - TURBO CLASSICS	Deutsche Grammophon	17	24 Jun 95	1
THE CHART SHOW DANCE ALBUM	PolyGram TV	6	5 Aug 95	3
THE CORONATION STREET ALBUM	EMI Premier	20	18 Nov 95	1
Granada ITV region soap, album features the Original cast.				
TOP GEAR 3	Columbia	11	9 Mar 96	4
TOP GEAR - ON THE ROAD AGAIN	EMI TV	12	9 Nov 96	3
AFTER THE BREAK	Columbia	17	2 Aug 97	1
IBIZA UNCOVERED	Virgin/EMI	1	13 Sep 97	10
Based around the Sky TV holiday documentary.				
READY STEADY GO! - NUMBER ONE SIXTIES ALBUM	PolyGram TV	10	8 Nov 97	2
READY STEADY GO! - SIXTIES MOTOWN SOUND	PolyGram TV	5	21 Mar 98	5
IBIZA UNCOVERED 2	Virgin/EMI	2	22 Aug 98	9
TOP GEAR ANTHEMS	Virgin/EMI	6	26 Sep 98	6
STARSKY AND HUTCH PRESENTS	Virgin/EMI	13	3 Oct 98	2
TV cop series from the 1970's.				
LIVE & KICKING - VIEWERS CHOICE PART 1	Virgin/EMI	12	3 Apr 99	3
MTV IBIZA 99	Columbia	10	28 Aug 99	3
IBIZA UNCOVERED - THE RETURN	Virgin/EMI	2	2 Oct 99	7
MUSIC OF THE MILLENNIUM	Universal/Virgin/EMI	2	27 Nov 99	6
Based around the Channel 4 programme of the same name.				

Soundtracks

ALBUMS:	HITS 20		WEEKS 159	
HUCKLEBERRY HOUND	Pye Golden Guinea	10	4 Mar 61	12
Animated character.				
THAT WAS THE WEEK THAT WAS	Parlophone	11	2 Mar 63	9
ROCK FOLLIES	Island	1	10 Apr 76	15
ITV musical drama series Julie Covington, Charlotte Cornwell and Rula Lenska.				
PENNIES FROM HEAVEN	World Records	10	8 Apr 78	17
ITV musical drama series.				
MORE PENNIES FROM HEAVEN	World Records	31	1 Jul 78	4
FAWLTY TOWERS	BBC	25	15 Dec 79	10
FAWLTY TOWERS VOLUME 2 (TV ORIGINAL CAST)	BBC	26	7 Feb 81	7
Above 2 are from the BBC sitcom starring John Cleese, Prunella Scales, Andrew Sachs and Connie Booth.				
THE HITCHHIKERS GUIDE TO THE GALAXY VOLUME 2	Original	47	14 Feb 81	4
BBC comedy series.				
THE MUSIC OF THE COSMOS	RCA	43	1 Aug 81	10
Carl Sagan's TV series broadcast on BBC1.				
REILLY ACE OF THEMES	Red Bus	54	26 Nov 83	6
ORIGINAL MUSIC FROM AUF WIEDERSEHEN PET	Towerbell	21	4 Feb 84	6
Above 2 are ITV drama series'.				
SONG AND DANCE	RCA	46	8 Sep 84	4
BBC series featuring Sarah Brightman and Wayne Sleep.				
MUSIC FROM THE TELEVISION SERIES 'MIAMI VICE'	BBC	11	26 Oct 85	8
MUSIC FROM THE TELEVISION SERIES 'MIAMI VICE' [RI]	MCA	94	26 Jul 86	1
MUSIC FROM THE BBC-TV SERIES 'THE SINGING DETECTIVE'	BBC	10	6 Dec 86	24
MOONLIGHTING "THE TV SOUNDTRACK ALBUM"	MCA	50	3 Oct 87	6
MIAMI VICE 2	MCA	71	17 Oct 87	4
MOONLIGHTING 2	WEA	5	1 Oct 88	9
MIAMI VICE III	MCA	95	1 Oct 88	1
DOCTOR WHO – THE EVIL OF THE DALEKS	BBC	72	18 Jul 92	1
Featuring Tom Baker.				
DOCTOR WHO – THE POWER OF THE DALEKS	BBC	71	14 Aug 93	1
Featuring Patrick Troughton.				
COMPILATION ALBUMS:	HITS 8		WEEKS 72	
PENNIES FROM HEAVEN	BBC	8	17 Feb 90	13
This is a different album to the previous 1989 chart entry.				
HEAD OVER HEELS	Telstar	3	13 Feb 93	9
LIPSTICK ON YOUR COLLAR - 28 ORIGINAL HITS OF THE 50S	PolyGram TV	2	13 Mar 93	13
Above 2 are ITV musical drama series'.				
CHEF AID - THE SOUTH PARK ALBUM	Columbia	2	5 Dec 98	14
South Park is an adult animated series broadcast by Channel 4.				
QUEER AS FOLK - THE WHOLE THING. SORTED	Almighty	2	17 Apr 99	9
SONGS FROM DAWSON'S CREEK	Columbia	3	12 Jun 99	11
Above 2 are Channel 4 drama series'.				
SEX, CHIPS & ROCK N' ROLL	Virgin/EMI	12	23 Oct 99	1
BBC drama series.				
BUFFY THE VAMPIRE SLAYER - THE ALBUM	Columbia	7	20 Nov 99	2
Songs from the series broadcast on Sky One and the BBC.				

TELEVISION AND RADIO COMBINED

ALBUMS:	HITS 2		WEEKS 10	
THE BBC 1922-1972 (TV AND RADIO EXTRACTS)	BBC	16	4 Nov 72	7
ON THE AIR - 60 YEARS OF BBC THEME MUSIC	BBC	85	23 Oct 82	3

TITLE INDEX OF CHART ENTRIES

The index has been divided into three sections: Singles, EPs and Albums.

The title is reflected first, followed by the artist credit as they appears on the release. This is followed by the year of chart entry and then the highest chart position attained.

Within the singles section, separate entries are reflected where the chart had listed an [AA] release. For EPs within this chart, the title is listed, and also the lead track. The latter will also reflect the title of the EP it came from, or whether it is the same title of the EP. Where there is more than one recording of the same song, the title is listed once with artists below in chronological order. There are certain instances where the actual title on the release is not the same as listed. These are reflected with an asterisk after the artist. The actual song title can also be located elsewhere within the index (unless there is such a slight difference that it does not merit a separate entry). Where a single has charted again as a re-issue or re-mix, a separate year and position is shown.

The EP section refers only to entries in the charts of the Sixties.

The album section also includes entries in the Compilation Charts.

SINGLES INDEX

A B C, Jackson 5, 70-8
A.B.C. (FALLING IN LOVE'S NOT EASY), Direct Drive, 85-75
A-BA-NI-BI, Izhar Cohen and the 'Alpha-Beta', 78-20
"A" BOMB IN WARDOUR STREET, Jam, 78-25, 80-54, 83-50
A.D.I.D.A.S., Korn, 97-22
A LA VIE, A L'AMOUR, Jackie Quartz, 89-55
THE A TEAM, Mike Post, 84-45
AAAH D YAAA, Goats, 93-53
ABACAB, Genesis, 81-9
ABACUS (WHEN I FALL IN LOVE), Axus, 98-62
ABANDON, Dare, 89-71
ABANDON, That Petrol Emotion, 90-73
ABANDON SHIP, Blaggers ITA, 94-48
ABBA-ESQUE [EP], Erasure, 92-1
THE ABBEY ROAD [EP], Spiritualized, 98-39
ABC AND D . . ., Blue Bamboo, 94-23
ABIDE WITH ME:
Inspirational Choir, 84-44, 85-35
Vic Reeves, 91-47
ABOUT 3AM, Dark Star, 99-50
ABOVE THE CLOUDS, Paul Weller, 92-47
ABRACADABRA, Steve Miller Band, 82-2
ABRAHAM, MARTIN AND JOHN, Marvin Gaye, 70-9
ABSOLUT(E), Claudia Brucken, 90-71
ABSOLUTE, Scritti Politti, 84-17
ABSOLUTE BEGINNERS, Jam, 81-4
ABSOLUTE BEGINNERS, David Bowie, 86-2
ABSOLUTE E-SENSUAL, Jaki Graham, 95-69
ABSOLUTE REALITY, Alarm, 85-35
ABSOLUTELY FABULOUS, Absolutely Fabulous, 94-6
ABSTAIN, Five Thirty, 90-75
ABSURD, Fluke, 97-25
ABUSE ME, Silverchair, 97-40
ACAPULCO 1922, Kenny Ball and his Jazzmen, 63-27
ACCELERATE, Skin Up, 92-45
ACCESS, DJ Misjah and DJ Tim, 96-16
AN ACCIDENT IN PARADISE (REMIXES), Sven Vath, 93-57

ACCIDENT OF BIRTH, Bruce Dickinson, 97-54
ACCIDENT PRONE, Status Quo, 78-36
ACCIDENT WAITING TO HAPPEN [EP] + lead track title, Billy Bragg, 92-33
ACCIDENTS, Thunderclap Newman, 70-46
ACCIDENTS WILL HAPPEN, Elvis Costello and the Attractions, 79-28
ACE OF SPADES, Motorhead, 80-15, 93-23
ACES HIGH, Iron Maiden, 84-20
ACHILLES HEEL, Toploader, 99-64
ACHY BREAKY HEART:
Billy Ray Cyrus, 92-3
Alvin and the Chipmunks (with special guest Billy Ray Cyrus), 92-53
ACID LAB, Alex Reece, 96-64
ACID MAN, Jolly Roger, 88-23
ACKEE 1-2-3, Beat, 83-54
ACPERIENCE (from HARDTRANCE ACPERIENCE [EP]), Hardfloor, 92-56, 97-60
ACT OF WAR, Elton John and Millie Jackson, 85-32
ACTION:
Sweet, 75-15
Def Leppard, 94-14
ACTION AND DRAMA, Bis, 99-50
ACTIV 8 (COME WITH ME), Altern 8, 91-3
ACTIVATED, Gerald Alston, 89-73
ADDAMS FAMILY (WHOOMP!) [RR], Tag Team, 94-53
ADDAMS GROOVE, Hammer, 91-4
ADDICTED TO LOVE:
Robert Palmer, 86-5
Tina Turner, 88-71
ADDICTION, Almighty, 93-38
ADIA, Sarah McLachlan, 98-18
ADIDAS WORLD, Edwyn Collins, 97-71
ADIEMUS, Adiemus, 95-48
ADIOS AMIGO, Jim Reeves, 62-23
THE ADORATION WALTZ, David Whitfield with the Roland Shaw Orchestra, 57-9
ADORATIONS, Killing Joke, 86-42
ADORE, Joe Roberts, 94-45
ADORED AND EXPLORED, Marc Almond, 95-25
ADRENALIN [EP] + lead track title, N-Joi, 91-23

ADULT EDUCATION, Daryl Hall and John Oates, 84-63
THE ADVENTURES OF THE LOVE CRUSADER, Sarah Brightman and the Starship Troopers, 79-53
ADVICE FOR THE YOUNG AT HEART, Tears For Fears, 90-36
AEROPLANE, Red Hot Chili Peppers, 96-11
THE AEROPLANE SONG, Straw, 99-37
AFFAIR, Cherrelle, 89-67
AN AFFAIR TO REMEMBER (OUR LOVE AFFAIR), Vic Damone, 57-29
AFRAID, Motley Crue, 97-58
AFRICA, Toto, 83-3
AFRICAN AND WHITE, China Crisis, 82-45
AFRICAN DREAM, Wasis Diop featuring Lena Fiagbe, 96-44
AFRICAN HORIZON, Mystica, 98-59
AFRICAN REIGN, Deep C, 91-75
AFRICAN WALTZ, Johnny Dankworth and his Orchestra, 61-9
AFRIKA, History featuring Q-Tee, 90-42
AFRIKA SHOX, Leftfield. Bambaataa, 99-7
AFRO DIZZI ACT, Cry Sisco!, 89-42, 90-70
AFRO KING, EMF, 95-51
THE AFRO-LEFT [EP] + lead track title, Leftfield featuring Djum Djum, 95-22
AFRO PUFFS, Lady Of Rage, 94-72
AFRO SLEEZE, Roach Motel, 93-73
AFRODISIAC, Powder, 95-72
AFTER A FASHION, Midge Ure and Mick Karn, 83-39
AFTER ALL, Frank And Walters, 93-11
AFTER ALL THESE YEARS, Foster and Allen, 86-43
AFTER THE FIRE, Roger Daltrey, 85-50
AFTER THE GOLDRUSH:
Prelude, 74-21
Prelude, 82-28
AFTER THE LOVE, Jesus Loves You, 89-68
AFTER THE LOVE HAS GONE, Earth, Wind And Fire, 79-4
AFTER THE LOVE HAS GONE, Princess, 85-28
AFTER THE LOVE HAS GONE, Steps, 99-5

AFTER THE RAIN, Titiyo, 90-60
AFTER THE WAR, Gary Moore, 89-37
AFTER THE WATERSHED (EARLY LEARNING THE HARD WAY), Carter – The Unstoppable Sex Machine, 91-11
AFTER YOU'VE GONE, Alice Babs, 63-43
AFTERGLOW, Mission, 94-53
AFTERGLOW OF YOUR LOVE, Small Faces, 69-36
AFTERMATH, Nightmares On Wax, 90-38
AFTERMATH, Tricky, 94-69
AFTERNOON DELIGHT, Starland Vocal Band, 76-18
AFTERNOON OF THE RHINO, Mike Post Coalition, 75-47
(AFTERNOON) SOAPS, Arab Strap, 98-74
AFTERNOONS AND COFFEESPOONS, Crash Test Dummies, 94-23
AGADOO:
Black Lace, 84-2
Black Lace, 98-64
AGAIN, Jimmy Tarbuck, 85-68
AGAIN, Janet Jackson, 93-6
AGAIN, Juliet Roberts, 94-33
AGAIN AND AGAIN, Status Quo, 78-13
AGAINST ALL ODDS (TAKE A LOOK AT ME NOW), Phil Collins, 84-2
AGAINST THE WIND, Maire Brennan, 92-64
AGE AIN'T NOTHING BUT A NUMBER, Aaliyah (Ah-Lee-Yah), 95-32
AGE OF LONELINESS, Enigma, 94-21
THE AGE OF LOVE, Age Of Love, 97-17, 98-38
AGE OF PANIC, Senser, 94-52
AGENT DAN, Agent Provocateur, 97-49
AHORA ES (NOW IS THE TIME), 2 In A Room, 95-43
AI NO CORRIDA (I-NO-KO-REE-DA), Quincy Jones featuring the vocals of Dune, 81-14
AIKEA-GUINEA, Cocteau Twins, 85-41
AIN'T COMPLAINING, Status Quo, 88-19
AIN'T DOIN' NOTHIN', Jet Bronx and the Forbidden, 77-49

DON'T GO BREAKING MY HEART:
Elton John and Kiki Dee, 76-1
Elton John and Rupaul, 94-7
DON'T GO MESSIN' WITH MY HEART, Mantronix, 91-22
DON'T HANG UP, Orlons, 62-39
DON'T HOLD BACK, Chanson, 79-33
DON'T IT MAKE MY BROWN EYES BLUE, Crystal Gayle, 77-5
DON'T IT MAKE YOU FEEL GOOD, Stefan Dennis, 89-16
DON'T JUMP OFF THE ROOF DAD, Tommy Cooper, 61-40
DON'T KILL IT CAROL, Manfred Mann's Earth Band, 79-45
DON'T KILL THE WHALE, Yes, 78-36
DON'T KNOCK IT (UNTIL YOU TRY IT), Bobby Nunn, 84-65
DON'T KNOCK THE ROCK, Bill Haley and his Comets, 57-7
DON'T KNOW MUCH, Linda Ronstadt featuring Aaron Neville, 89-2
DON'T KNOW WHAT YOU GOT (TIL IT'S GONE), Cinderella, 89-54
DON'T KNOW WHY I LOVE YOU, Stevie Wonder, 69-14
DON'T LAUGH, Winx, 95-38
DON'T LAUGH AT ME ('CAUSE I'M A FOOL), Norman Wisdom with Norrie Paramor and his Orchestra, 54-3
DON'T LEAVE, Faithless, 96-34, 97-21
DON'T LEAVE ME, Blackstreet, 97-6
DON'T LEAVE ME, Malandra Burrows, 98-54
DON'T LEAVE ME BEHIND, Everything But The Girl, 86-72
DON'T LEAVE ME THIS WAY:
Harold Melvin and the Bluenotes featuring Theodore Pendergrass, 77-5
Thelma Houston, 77-13
Communards with Sarah Jane Morris, 86-1
Thelma Houston, 95-35
DON'T LET 'EM GRIND YOU DOWN EP (EXTRACTS FROM THE EDINBURGH LIVE NITE, Exploited/Anti-Pasti, 81-70
DON'T LET GO, Manhattan Transfer, 77-32
DON'T LET GO (LOVE), En Vogue, 97-5
DON'T LET GO THE COAT, Who, 81-47
DON'T LET HIM STEAL YOUR HEART AWAY, Phil Collins with the Martyn Ford Orchestra, 83-45
DON'T LET HIM TOUCH YOU, Angelettes, 72-35
DON'T LET IT DIE, Hurricane Smith, 71-2
DON'T LET IT END, Styx, 83-56
DON'T LET IT FADE AWAY, Darts, 78-18
DON'T LET IT GET YOU DOWN, Echo and the Bunnymen, 97-50
DON'T LET IT GO TO YOUR HEAD, Brand New Heavies featuring N'dea Davenport, 92-24
DON'T LET IT PASS YOU BY, UB40, 81-16
DON'T LET IT SHOW ON YOUR FACE, Adeva, 92-34
DON'T LET LOVE GET YOU DOWN, Archie Bell and the Drells, 86-49
DON'T LET ME BE MISUNDERSTOOD:
Animals, 65-3
Santa Esmeralda and Leroy Gomez, 77-41
Costello Music featuring The Confederates, 86-33
Joe Cocker, 96-53

DON'T LET ME DOWN, Farm, 91-36
DON'T LET ME DOWN GENTLY, Wonder Stuff, 89-19
DON'T LET NOBODY HOLD YOU DOWN, L.J. Reynolds, 84-53
DON'T LET THE FEELING GO, Nightcrawlers featuring John Reid, 95-31
DON'T LET THE RAIN COME DOWN (CROOKED LITTLE MAN), Ronnie Hilton with the Michael Sammes Singers, 64-21
DON'T LET THE STARS GET IN YOUR EYES, Perry Como with the Ramblers, 53-1
DON'T LET THE SUN CATCH YOU CRYING, Gerry and the Pacemakers, 64-6
DON'T LET THE SUN GO DOWN ON ME:
Elton John, 74-16
Oleta Adams, 91-33
George Michael with Elton John, 91-1
DON'T LET THIS MOMENT END, Gloria!, 99-28
DON'T LIE, Sinclair, 94-70
DON'T LOOK ANY FURTHER:
Dennis Edwards featuring Siedah Garrett, 84-45, 87-55
Kane Gang, 88-52
M People, 93-9
DON'T LOOK AT ME THAT WAY, Chaka Khan, 93-73
DON'T LOOK BACK, Boston, 78-43
DON'T LOOK BACK, Fine Young Cannibals, 89-34
DON'T LOOK BACK, Lloyd Cole, 90-59
DON'T LOOK BACK (from HAVE LOST IT [EP]), Teenage Fanclub, 95-53
DON'T LOOK BACK IN ANGER, Oasis, 96-1
DON'T LOOK DOWN, Planets, 80-66
DON'T LOOK DOWN, Mick Ronson with Joe Elliott, 94-55
DON'T LOOK DOWN – THE SEQUEL, Go West, 85-13
DON'T LOSE THE MAGIC, Shawn Christopher, 92-30
DON'T LOSE YOUR TEMPER, XTC, 80-32
DON'T LOVE ME TOO HARD, Nolans, 82-14
DON'T MAKE ME (FALL IN LOVE WITH YOU), Babbity Blue, 65-48
DON'T MAKE ME OVER:
Swinging Blue Jeans, 66-31
Sybil, 89-19
DON'T MAKE ME WAIT, Peech Boys, 82-49
DON'T MAKE ME WAIT, Bomb The Bass featuring Lorraine, 88-6
DON'T MAKE ME WAIT, Loveland featuring the voice of Rachel McFarlane, 95-22
DON'T MAKE ME WAIT, 911, 96-10
DON'T MAKE ME WAIT TOO LONG:
Barry White, 76-17
Roberta Flack, 80-44
DON'T MAKE MY BABY BLUE, Shadows, 65-10
DON'T MAKE WAVES, Nolans, 80-12
DON'T MARRY HER, Beautiful South, 96-8
DON'T MESS WITH DOCTOR DREAM, Thompson Twins, 85-15
DON'T MISS THE PARTYLINE, Bizz Nizz, 90-7
DON'T NEED A GUN, Billy Idol, 87-26
DON'T PANIC, Liquid Gold, 81-42
DON'T PAY THE FERRYMAN, Chris De Burgh, 82-48
DON'T PLAY THAT SONG, Aretha Franklin, 70-13

DON'T PLAY WITH ME, Rozalla, 93-50
DON'T PLAY YOUR ROCK 'N' ROLL TO ME, Smokey, 75-8
DON'T PULL YOUR LOVE, Sean Maguire, 96-14
DON'T PUSH IT, Ruth Joy, 89-66
DON'T PUSH IT DON'T FORCE IT, Leon Haywood, 80-12
DON'T PUT YOUR SPELL ON ME, Ian McNabb, 96-72
DON'T QUIT, Caron Wheeler, 91-53
DON'T RUSH (TAKE LOVE SLOWLY), K-Ci and Jojo, 98-16
DON'T SAY I TOLD YOU SO, Tourists, 80-40
DON'T SAY IT'S LOVE, Johnny Hates Jazz, 88-48
DON'T SAY IT'S OVER, Gun, 94-19
DON'T SAY THAT'S JUST FOR WHITE BOYS, Way Of The West, 81-54
DON'T SAY YOUR LOVE IS KILLING ME, Erasure, 97-23
DON'T SET ME FREE, Ray Charles, 63-37
DON'T SHED A TEAR, Paul Carrack, 89-60
DON'T SING, Prefab Sprout, 84-62
DON'T SLEEP IN THE SUBWAY, Petula Clark, 67-12
DON'T SLOW DOWN, UB40, 81-16
DON'T SPEAK:
No Doubt, 97-1
Clueless, 97-61
DON'T STAND SO CLOSE TO ME:
Police, 80-1
Police, 86-24
DON'T STAY AWAY TOO LONG, Peters and Lee, 74-3
DON'T STOP:
Fleetwood Mac, 77-32
Status Quo, 96-35
DON'T STOP, K.I.D., 81-49
DON'T STOP, Mood, 81-59
DON'T STOP, Jeffrey Osborne, 84-61
DON'T STOP, K-Klass, 92-32
DON'T STOP, Hammer, 94-72
DON'T STOP, Ruff Driverz, 98-15
DON'T STOP, No Authority, 98-54
DON'T STOP, ATB, 99-61, 99-3
DON'T STOP BELIEVIN', Journey, 82-62
DON'T STOP IT NOW, Hot Chocolate, 76-11
DON'T STOP (JAMMIN'), L.A. Mix, 87-47
DON'T STOP LOVING ME BABY, Pinkerton's 'Assort'. Colours, 66-50
DON'T STOP ME NOW, Queen, 79-9
DON'T STOP MOVIN', Livin' Joy, 96-5
DON'T STOP NOW, Gene Farrow with the G.F. Band, 78-71
DON'T STOP THAT CRAZY RHYTHM, Modern Romance, 83-14
DON'T STOP THE CARNIVAL, Alan Price Set, 68-13
DON'T STOP THE DANCE, Bryan Ferry, 85-21
DON'T STOP THE FEELING, Roy Ayers, 80-56
DON'T STOP THE MUSIC, Yarbrough and Peoples, 80-7
DON'T STOP TIL YOU GET ENOUGH (MICHAEL JACKSON MEDLEY) [M], Ashaye, 83-45
DON'T STOP 'TILL YOU GET ENOUGH, Michael Jackson, 79-3
DON'T STOP – TWIST!, Frankie Vaughan, 62-22
DON'T STOP (WIGGLE WIGGLE), Outhere Brothers, 95-1
DON'T TAKE AWAY THE MUSIC, Tavares, 76-4

DON'T TAKE IT LYIN' DOWN, Dooleys, 78-60
DON'T TAKE IT PERSONAL, Jermaine Jackson, 89-69
DON'T TAKE IT PERSONAL (JUST ONE OF DEM DAYS), Monica, 95-32
DON'T TAKE MY KINDNESS FOR WEAKNESS, Heads with Shaun Ryder, 96-60
DON'T TAKE ME ON A TRIP, Boy George, 89-68
DON'T TAKE NO FOR AN ANSWER (from RISING FREE [EP]), Tom Robinson Band, 78-18
DON'T TALK, Hank Marvin, 82-49
DON'T TALK ABOUT LOVE, Bad Boys Inc, 93-19
DON'T TALK DIRTY TO ME, Jermaine Stewart, 88-61
DON'T TALK JUST KISS, Right Said Fred Guest vocal Jocelyn Brown, 91-3
DON'T TALK TO HIM, Cliff Richard and the Shadows, 63-2
DON'T TALK TO ME ABOUT LOVE, Altered Images, 83-7
DON'T TELL ME, Central Line, 82-55
DON'T TELL ME, Blancmange, 84-8
DON'T TELL ME, Van Halen, 95-27
DON'T TELL ME LIES, Breathe, 89-45
DON'T TEST, Junior Tucker, 90-54
DON'T THAT BEAT ALL, Adam Faith with Johnny Keating and his Orchestra, 62-8
DON'T THROW AWAY ALL THOSE TEARDROPS, Frankie Avalon, 60-37
DON'T THROW IT ALL AWAY, Gary Benson, 75-20
DON'T THROW YOUR LOVE AWAY, Searchers, 64-1
DON'T TREAT ME BAD, Firehouse, 91-71
DON'T TREAT ME LIKE A CHILD, Helen Shapiro, 61-3
DON'T TRY TO CHANGE ME, Crickets, 63-37
DON'T TRY TO STOP IT, Roman Holliday, 83-14
DON'T TURN AROUND, Merseybeats, 64-13
DON'T TURN AROUND:
Aswad, 88-1
Ace Of Base, 94-5
DON'T TURN IT UP, Thunder, 97-27
DON'T WALK AWAY, Big Supreme, 86-58
DON'T WALK AWAY, Electric Light Orchestra, 80-21
DON'T WALK AWAY, Four Tops, 81-16
DON'T WALK AWAY, Pat Benatar, 88-42
DON'T WALK AWAY, Toni Childs, 89-53
DON'T WALK AWAY, Jade, 93-7
DON'T WALK AWAY TILL I TOUCH YOU, Elaine Paige, 78-46
DON'T WANNA BE A PLAYER, Joe, 97-16
DON'T WANNA FALL IN LOVE, Jane Child, 90-22
DON'T WANNA LOSE YOU, Gloria Estefan, 89-6
DON'T WANNA LOSE YOU, Lionel Richie, 96-17
DON'T WANNA SAY GOODNIGHT, Kandidate, 78-47
DON'T WANT TO FORGIVE ME NOW, Wet Wet Wet, 95-7
DON'T WANT TO WAIT ANYMORE, Tubes, 81-60
DON'T WASTE MY TIME, Paul Hardcastle Lead vocals – Carol Kenyon, 86-8
DON'T WASTE YOUR TIME, Yarbrough and Peoples, 84-60
DON'T WORRY, Johnny Brandon, 55-18

FIGARO, Brotherhood Of Man, 78-1
THE FIGHT, Marty Wilde, 60-47
FIGHT, McKoy, 93-54
FIGHT FOR OURSELVES,
Spandau Ballet, 86-15
FIGHT FOR YOUR RIGHT (TO
PARTY), N.Y.C.C., 98-14
FIGHT THE POWER, Public
Enemy, 89-29
FIGHT THE POWER 95 (from
MAXIMUM [EP]), Dreadzone,
95-56
FIGHT THE YOUTH, Fishbone,
92-60
FIGHTING FIT, Gene, 96-22
FIGURE OF EIGHT, Paul
McCartney, 89-42
FIGURE OF EIGHT, Grid, 92-50
FILL HER UP, Gene, 99-36
FILLING UP WITH HEAVEN,
Human League, 95-36
A FILM FOR THE FUTURE,
Idlewild, 98-53
FILMSTAR, Suede, 97-9
FILTHY, St. Etienne, 91-39
THE FINAL COUNTDOWN:
Europe, 86-1
Europe, 99-39
FINALLY, Ce Ce Peniston, 91-29,
92-2, 97-26
FINALLY FOUND, Honeyz, 98-4
FINCHLEY CENTRAL, New
Vaudeville Band (featuring
Tristam Vii), 67-11
FIND A WAY, Coldcut featuring
Queen Latifah, 90-52
FIND A WAY, A Tribe Called Quest,
98-41
FIND 'EM, FOOL 'EM, FORGET
'EM, S'Express, 92-43
FIND ME (ODYSSEY TO
ANYOONA), Jam and Spoon
featuring Plavka, 94-37, 95-22
FIND MY LOVE, Fairground
Attraction, 88-7
FIND MY WAY BACK HOME,
Nashville Teens, 65-34
FIND THE ANSWER WITHIN,
Boo Radleys, 95-37
FIND THE RIVER, R.E.M., 93-54
FIND THE TIME, Five Star, 86-7
FIND THE TIME (PART 1),
Quadrophonia, 91-41
FINDERS KEEPERS, Chairmen
Of The Board, 73-21
FINE TIME, New Order, 88-11
FINE TIME, Yazz, 89-9
FINER, Nightmares On Wax, 99-63
FINER FEELINGS, Kylie
Minogue, 92-11
THE FINEST:
S.O.S. Band, 86-17
Truce, 95-54
FINEST WORKSONG, R.E.M.,
88-50
FINETIME, Cast, 95-17
THE FINGER OF SUSPICION,
Dickie Valentine with the
Stargazers, 54-1
FINGERS & THUMBS (COLD
SUMMER'S DAY), Erasure,
95-20
FINGERS OF LOVE, Crowded
House, 94-25
FINGS AIN'T WOT THEY USED
T'BE:
Max Bygraves with chorus from the
Gang Show, 60-5
Russ Conway, 60-47
FINISHED SYMPHONY, Hybrid,
99-58
FIRE!, Crazy World Of Arthur
Brown, 68-1
FIRE:
Pointer Sisters, 79-34
Bruce Springsteen and the E Street
Band, 87-54
FIRE, U2, 81-35
FIRE, Sly and Robbie, 87-60
FIRE, Prodigy, 92-11, 96-63
FIRE, Prizna featuring the
Demolition Man, 95-33
FIRE, Scooter, 97-45
FIRE AND RAIN, James Taylor,
70-42
FIRE BRIGADE, Move, 68-3

FIRE DOWN BELOW:
Jeri Southern, 57-22
Shirley Bassey with Wally Stott and
his Orchestra, 57-30
FIRE IN MY HEART, Super Furry
Animals, 99-25
FIRE ISLAND, Fire Island, 92-66
FIRE OF LOVE, Jungle High with
Blue Pearl, 93-71
FIRE UP THE SHOESAW,
Lionrock, 96-43
FIRE WOMAN, Cult, 89-15
FIRE WORKS, Siouxsie and the
Banshees, 82-22
FIREBALL, Don Spencer, 63-32
FIREBALL, Deep Purple, 71-15
FIRED UP, Elevatorman, 95-44
FIRED UP!, Funky Green Dogs,
97-17
FIREPILE [(EP] + lead track title,
Throwing Muses, 92-46
FIRES BURNING, Run Tings,
92-58
FIRESTARTER, Prodigy, 96-1,
97-53
FIREWORKS, Roxette, 94-30
FIREWORKS [EP], Embrace, 97-34
FIRM BIZ, Nas Escobar, Foxy
Brown, Az and Nature present
the Firm featuring Dawn
Robinson, 97-18
1ST ATHEIST TABERNACLE
CHOIR, Spitting Image, 86-22
FIRST BOY IN THIS TOWN
(LOVE SICK), Scritti Politti,
88-63
THE FIRST CUT IS THE
DEEPEST:
P. P. Arnold, 67-18
Rod Stewart, 77-1
THE FIRST DAY (HORIZON),
Man with No Name, 98-72
FIRST IMPRESSIONS,
Impressions, 75-16
1ST MAN IN SPACE, All Seeing I,
99-28
THE FIRST MAN YOU
REMEMBER, Michael Ball and
Diana Morrison, 89-68
THE FIRST NIGHT, Monica, 98-6
FIRST OF MAY, Bee Gees, 69-6
1ST OF THA MONTH, Bone
Thugs-N-Harmony, 95-32, 96-1
THE FIRST PICTURE OF YOU,
Lotus Eaters, 83-15
FIRST TASTE OF LOVE, Ben E.
King, 61-27
THE FIRST THE LAST
ETERNITY (TIL THE
END), Snap! featuring Summer,
95-15
FIRST THING IN THE
MORNING, Kiki Dee, 77-32
THE FIRST TIME, Adam Faith
with the Roulettes, 63-5
FIRST TIME, Robin Beck, 88-1
THE FIRST TIME, Surface, 91-60
THE FIRST TIME EVER I SAW
YOUR FACE:
Roberta Flack, 72-14
Joanna Law *, 90-67
1ST TRANSMISSION (from
BLOOD MUSIC [EP]),
Earthling, 96-69
FIRST WE TAKE MANHATTAN,
Jennifer Warnes, 88-74
FISHERMAN'S BLUES,
Waterboys, 89-32, 91-75
FIVE [EP], Mansun, 97-9
THE $5.98 E.P.-GARAGE DAYS
RE-REVISITED [EP],
Metallica, 87-27
FIVE FATHOMS, Everything But
The Girl, 99-27
5:15, Who, 73-20
555, Delakota, 99-42
5-4-3-2-1, Manfred Mann, 64-5
FIVE GET OVER EXCITED,
Housemartins, 87-11
500 (SHAKE BABY SHAKE), Lush,
96-21
FIVE LITTLE FINGERS, Frankie
McBride, 67-19
FIVE LIVE [EP], George Michael
and Queen with Lisa Stansfield,
93-1

FIVE MILES OUT, Mike Oldfield:
Maggie Reilly – vocals, 82-43
5 MILES TO EMPTY, Brownstone,
97-12
5 MINUTES, Stranglers, 78-11
5 MINUTES, Lil' Mo featuring Missy
"Misdemeanor" Elliott, 98-72
5 O'CLOCK, Nonchalant, 96-44
5 O'CLOCK WORLD, Julian Cope,
89-42
5.7.0.5., City Boy, 78-8
5,6,7,8, Steps, 97-14
5 STEPS, Dru Hill, 97-22
FIX, Blackstreet, 97-7
FIXER, Vent 414, 96-71
FLAGPOLE SITTA, Harvey
Danger, 98-57
THE FLAME, Arcadia, 86-58
THE FLAME, Fine Young
Cannibals, 96-17
FLAME, Sebadoh, 99-30
THE FLAME STILL BURNS,
Jimmy Nail with Strange Fruit,
98-47
THE FLAME TREES OF THIKA,
Video Symphonic, 81-42
FLAMES OF PARADISE, Jennifer
Rush (Duet with Elton John),
87-59
FLAMING JUNE, BT, 97-19, 98-28
FLAMING SWORD, Care, 83-48
FLASH, Queen, 80-10
FLASH, B.B.E., 97-5
FLASH, Grifters featuring Tall Paul
and Brandon Block, 99-63
FLASHBACK, Imagination, 81-16
FLASHBACK JACK, Adamski,
90-46
FLASHDANCE . . . WHAT A
FEELING:
Irene Cara, 83-2
Bjorn Again, 93-65
THE FLASHER, Mistura featuring
Lloyd Michels (trumpet), 76-23
FLAT BEAT, Mr. Oizo, 99-1
FLATLINERS, Nebula II, 92-54
FLAVA, Peter Andre, 96-1
FLAVA IN YA EAR, Craig Mack,
94-57
FLAVOUR OF THE OLD
SCHOOL, Beverley Knight,
95-50, 95-33
FLESH, A Split Second, 91-68
FLESH FOR FANTASY, Billy Idol,
84-54
FLESH OF MY FLESH, Orange
Juice, 83-41
"FLETCH" THEME, Harold
Faltermeyer, 85-74
FLIGHT OF ICARUS, Iron
Maiden, 83-11
FLIP, Jesse Green, 76-26
THE FLIPSIDE, Moloko, 98-53
FLIRT!, Jonathan King, 72-22
FLIRTATION WALTZ, Winifred
Atwell and her piano, 53-10
FLOAT ON, Floaters, 77-1
FLOATATION, Grid, 90-60
FLOATING, Terra Ferma, 96-64
FLOATING IN THE WIND,
Hudson-Ford, 74-35
FLOODLIT WORLD, Ultrasound,
99-39
THE FLOOR, Johnny Gill, 93-53
FLOOR-ESSENCE, Man With No
Name, 95-68
FLOOR SPACE, Our House, 96-52
THE FLORAL DANCE:
Brighouse and Rastrick Brass Band,
77-2
Terry Wogan, 78-21
FLORIBUNDA, Mothers Pride,
98-42
FLOWER DUET (FROM
'LAKME'):
Mady Mesple and Danielle Millet,
Paris Opera – Comique
Orchestra conducted by Alain
Lombard, 85-74
Jonathan Peters presents Luminaire,
99-75
FLOWER OF SCOTLAND,
Scottish Rugby Team with
Ronnie Browne, 90-73
FLOWER OF THE WEST, Runrig,
91-43

FLOWERS, Titiyo, 90-71
FLOWERS, Armand Van Helden
featuring Roland Clark, 99-18
FLOWERS IN DECEMBER,
Mazzy Star, 96-40
FLOWERS IN THE RAIN, Move,
67-2
FLOWERS OF ROMANCE, Public
Image Ltd., 81-24
FLOWERS ON THE WALL,
Statler Brothers, 66-38
FLOWTATION, Vincent De Moor,
97-54
FLOY JOY, Supremes, 72-9
THE FLY, U2, 91-1
FLY, Sugar Ray (featuring Super Cat),
98-58
FLY, Pob featuring DJ Patrick Reid,
99-74
FLY AWAY, Haddaway, 95-20
FLY AWAY, Lenny Kravitz, 99-1
FLY AWAY (BYE BYE), Eyes
Cream, 99-53
FLY GIRL, Queen Latifah, 91-67
FLY LIFE, Basement Jaxx, 97-19
FLY LIKE AN EAGLE, Seal,
97-13
FLY ROBIN FLY, Silver
Convention, 75-28
FLY TO THE ANGELS, Slaughter,
91-55
FLY TOO HIGH, Janis Ian, 79-44
FLYING, Cast, 96-4
FLYING HIGH, Commodores,
78-37
FLYING HIGH, Freeez, 81-35
FLYING HIGH, Captain Hollywood
Project, 95-58
FLYING MACHINE, Cliff Richard,
71-37
FLYING SAUCER, Wedding
Present, 92-22
FLYING WITHOUT WINGS,
Westlife, 99-1
FM (NO STATIC AT ALL), Steely
Dan, 78-49
FOE-DEE-O-DEE, Rubettes, 75-15
FOG ON THE TYNE
(REVISITED), Gazza and
Lindisfarne, 90-2
FOGGY MOUNTAIN
BREAKDOWN, Lester Flatt
and Earl Scruggs, 67-39
FOGHORN, A, 98-63
THE FOLK SINGER, Tommy Roe,
63-4
FOLLOW ME, J.T. Taylor, 92-59
FOLLOW ME, Aly-Us, 92-43
FOLLOW THAT DREAM [EP] +
lead track title, Elvis Presley,
62-34
FOLLOW THE LEADER, Eric B.
and Rakim, 88-24
FOLLOW THE LEADERS, Killing
Joke, 81-55
FOLLOW THE RULES, Livin' Joy,
96-9
FOLLOW YOU DOWN, Gin
Blossoms, 96-30
FOLLOW YOU FOLLOW ME,
Genesis, 78-7
FOLLOWING, Bangles, 87-55
THE FOOD CHRISTMAS EP
1989 [EP], Various Artists (EPs),
89-63
FOOD FOR THOUGHT, U.B.40,
80-4
FOOD FOR THOUGHT [M],
Barron Knights, 79-46
FOOL, Elvis Presley, 73-15
FOOL, Al Matthews, 75-16
A FOOL AM I (DIMMELO
PARLAMI), Cilla Black, 66-13
FOOL FOR YOUR LOVING:
Whitesnake, 80-13
Whitesnake, 89-43
FOOL (IF YOU THINK IT'S
OVER):
Chris Rea, 78-30
Elkie Brooks, 82-17
A FOOL NEVER LEARNS, Andy
Williams, 64-40
FOOL NUMBER ONE, Brenda
Lee, 61-38
THE FOOL ON THE HILL,
Shirley Bassey, 71-48

A FOOL SUCH AS I, Elvis Presley with the Jordanaires, 59-1
FOOL TO CRY, Rolling Stones, 76-6
FOOLED AROUND AND FELL IN LOVE, Elvin Bishop, 76-34
FOOLED BY A SMILE, Swing Out Sister, 87-43
FOOLIN' YOURSELF, Paul Hardcastle introducing Kevin Henry, 86-51
FOOLISH BEAT, Debbie Gibson, 88-9
FOOLISH LITTLE GIRL, Shirelles, 63-38
FOOLS GOLD, Stone Roses, 89-8, 90-22. 92-73, 95-25, 99-25
FOOL'S PARADISE, Meli'sa Morgan, 86-41
FOOLS RUSH IN:
Rick Nelson *, 63-12
Brook Benton, 61-50
FOOT STOMPIN' MUSIC, Hamilton Bohannon, 75-23
FOOT TAPPER, Shadows, 63-1
FOOTLOOSE, Kenny Loggins, 84-6
FOOTPRINT, Disco Citizens, 97-34
FOOTPRINTS IN THE SNOW, Johnny Duncan and the Blue Grass Boys, 57-27
FOOTSEE (INSTRUMENTAL), Wigan's Chosen Few, 75-9
FOOTSTEPS:
Ronnie Carroll with Wally Stott and his Orchestra and Chorus, 60-36
Steve Lawrence, 60-4
Showaddywaddy, 81-31
FOOTSTEPS, Stiltskin, 94-34
FOOTSTEPS, Daniel O'Donnell, 96-25
FOOTSTEPS FOLLOWING ME, Frances Nero, 91-17
FOR A FEW DOLLARS MORE, Smokie, 78-17
FOR A FRIEND, Communards, 88-28
FOR A PENNY, Pat Boone, 59-19
FOR ALL THAT YOU WANT, Gary Barlow, 99-24
FOR ALL THE COWS, Foo Fighters, 95-28
FOR ALL TIME, Catherine Zeta Jones, 92-36
FOR ALL WE KNOW:
Shirley Bassey, 71-6
Carpenters, 71-18
Nicki French, 95-42
FOR AMERICA, Red Box, 86-10
FOR AN ANGEL, Paul Van Dyk, 98-28
FOR BRITAIN ONLY, Alice Cooper, 82-66
(FOR GOD'S SAKE) GIVE MORE POWER TO THE PEOPLE, Chi-Lites, 71-32
FOR HER LIGHT, Fields Of The Nephilim, 90-54
FOR LOVE (EP) + lead track title, Lush, 92-35
FOR MAMA, Matt Monro, 64-36
FOR OLD TIME'S SAKE, Millican and Nesbitt, 74-38
FOR ONCE IN MY LIFE:
Stevie Wonder, 68-3
Dorothy Squires, 69-24
FOR REAL, Tricky, 99-45
FOR SPACIOUS LIES, Norman Cook featuring Lester, 89-48
FOR THE DEAD, Gene, 96-14
FOR THE GOOD TIMES, Perry Como, 73-7
FOR THOSE ABOUT TO ROCK (WE SALUTE YOU), AC/DC, 82-15
FOR TOMORROW, Blur, 93-28
FOR WHAT IT'S WORTH, Oui 3, 93-28, 93-26
FOR WHAT YOU DREAM OF, John Digweed and Nick Muir present Bedrock featuring Kyo (Aka Carole Leeming) 96-25
FOR WHOM THE BELL TOLLS, Simon Dupree and the Big Sound, 68-43
FOR WHOM THE BELLS TOLLS, Bee Gees, 93-4

FOR YOU, Rick Nelson, 64-14
FOR YOU, Farmer's Boys, 83-66
FOR YOU, Snowy White, 85-65
FOR YOU, Electronic, 96-16
FOR YOU FOR LOVE, Average White Band, 80-46
FOR YOU I WILL, Monica, 97-27
FOR YOUR BABIES, Simply Red, 92-9
FOR YOUR BLUE EYES ONLY, Tony Hadley, 92-67
FOR YOUR EYES ONLY, Sheena Easton, 81-8
FOR YOUR LOVE, Yardbirds, 65-3
FOR YOUR LOVE, Stevie Wonder, 95-23
FORBIDDEN CITY, Electronic, 96-14
FORBIDDEN COLOURS, David Sylvian and Riuichi Sakamoto, 83-16
FORBIDDEN FRUIT, Paul Van Dyk, 97-69
FORBIDDEN ZONE, John Digweed and Nick Muir present Bedrock, 97-71
THE FORCE BEHIND THE POWER, Diana Ross, 92-70
FOREIGN SAND, Roger Taylor and Yoshiki, 94-26
FORERUNNER, Natural Born Grooves, 96-64
A FOREST, Cure, 80-31
FOREST FIRE, Lloyd Cole and the Commotions, 84-41
FOREVER, Roy Wood, 73-8
FOREVER, Kiss, 90-65
FOREVER, Damage, 96-6
FOREVER, Tina Cousins, 99-45
FOREVER, Charlatans, 99-12
FOREVER AND A DAY, Brothers In Rhythm present Charvoni, 94-51
FOREVER AND EVER, Slik, 76-1
FOREVER AND EVER (from THE ROUSSOS PHENOMENON [EP]), Demis Roussos, 76-1
FOREVER AND EVER, AMEN, Randy Travis, 88-55
FOREVER AUTUMN, From Jeff Wayne's "War Of The Worlds" featuring Justin Hayward, 78-5
FOREVER CAME TODAY, Diana Ross and the Supremes, 68-28
FOREVER FAILURE, Paradise Lost, 95-66
FOREVER FREE, W.A.S.P., 89-25
FOREVER GIRL, Ott, 97-24
FOREVER IN BLUE JEANS, Neil Diamond, 79-16
FOREVER IN LOVE, Kenny G, 93-47
FOREVER J, Terry Hall, 94-67
A FOREVER KIND OF LOVE, Bobby Vee, 62-13
(FOREVER) LIVE AND DIE, Orchestral Manoeuvres In The Dark, 86-11
FOREVER LOVE, Gary Barlow, 96-1
FOREVER MAN, Eric Clapton, 85-51
FOREVER MORE, Puff Johnson, 97-29
FOREVER NOW, Level 42, 94-19
FOREVER TOGETHER, Raven Maize, 89-67
FOREVER YOUNG, Rod Stewart, 88-57
FOREVER YOUNG, Interactive, 96-28
FOREVER YOUR GIRL, Paula Abdul, 89-24
FOREVERGREEN, Finitribe, 92-51
FORGET ABOUT THE WORLD, Gabrielle, 96-23
FORGET ABOUT YOU, Motors, 78-13
FORGET HIM:
Bobby Rydell, 63-13
Billy Fury, 83-59
FORGET I WAS A G, Whitehead Bros., 95-40
FORGET-ME-NOT, Vera Lynn, 52-5

FORGET ME NOT, Eden Kane, 62-3
FORGET ME NOT, Martha Reeves and the Vandellas, 71-11
FORGET ME NOTS:
Patrice Rushen, 82-8
Tongue 'N' Cheek, 91-26
FORGIVEN (I FEEL YOU LOVE), Space Brothers, 97-27
FORGOTTEN DREAMS:
Leroy Anderson and his Pops Concert Orchestra, 57-24
Stapleton and his Orchestra, 57-27
FORGOTTEN TOWN, Christians, 87-22
FORT WORTH JAIL, Lonnie Donegan, 59-14
FORTRESS AROUND YOUR HEART, Sting, 85-49
FORTUNES OF WAR, Fish, 94-67
40 MILES, Congress, 91-26
FORTY MILES OF BAD ROAD, Duane Eddy, 59-11
40 YEARS, Paul Hardcastle, 88-53
48 CRASH, Suzi Quatro, 73-3
FORWARD THE REVOLUTION, Spiral Tribe, 92-70
FOUND A CURE, Ultra Nate, 98-6
FOUND LOVE, Double Dee (featuring Dany), 90-63, 95-33
FOUND OUT ABOUT YOU, Gin Blossoms, 94-40
FOUND OUT TOO LATE, 999, 79-69
FOUND YOU, Dodgy, 97-19
FOUNDATION, Beenie Man and the Taxi Gang, 98-69
FOUNTAIN O' YOUTH, Candyland, 91-72
FOUR [EP], Mansun, 96-15
FOUR BACHARACH AND DAVID SONGS [EP], Deacon Blue, 90-2
FOUR BIG SPEAKERS, Whale featuring Bus75, 98-69
FOUR FROM BLACKFOOT [EP], Blackfoot, 82-43
FOUR FROM TOYAH [EP], Toyah, 81-4
FOUR LETTER WORD, Kim Wilde, 88-6
FOUR LITTLE HEELS:
Brian Hyland, 60-29
Avons, 60-45
4 MORE, De La Soul featuring Zhane, 97-52
FOUR MORE FROM TOYAH [EP], Toyah, 81-14
4 PAGE LETTER, Aaliyah, 97-24
THE 4 PLAY [EP], R. Kelly, 95-23
FOUR SEASONS IN ONE DAY, Crowded House, 92-28
4 SEASONS OF LONELINESS, Boyz II Men, 97-10
FOUR STRONG WINDS, Neil Young, 79-57
FOURPLAY VOLUME 1 [EP], Various Artists (EPs), 92-45
14 HOURS TO SAVE THE EARTH, Tomski, 98-42
FOURTH RENDEZ-VOUS:
Jean-Michel Jarre, 86-65
Jean Michel Jarre and Apollo Four Forty, 98-12
FOX FORCE FIVE, Chris and James, 95-71
FOX ON THE RUN, Manfred Mann, 68-5
FOX ON THE RUN, Sweet, 75-2
FOXHOLE, Television, 78-36
FOXY, FOXY, Mott The Hoople, 74-33
FRAGGLE ROCK THEME, Fraggles, 84-33
FRAGILE:
Sting, 88-70
Julio Iglesias, 94-53
FRAGILE THING, Big Country (featuring Eddi Reader), 99-69
THE FRANK SONATA, Longpigs, 99-57
FRANKENSTEIN, Edgar Winter Group, 73-18
FRANKIE, Sister Sledge, 85-1

FRANKIE AND JOHNNY:
Mr. Acker Bilk and his Paramount Jazz Band (vocal: Mr. Acker Bilk), 62-42
Sam Cooke, 63-30
Elvis Presley, 66-21
FREAK, Bruce Foxton, 83-23
FREAK, Silverchair, 97-34
FREAK, Strangelove, 97-43
FREAK IT!, Studio 45, 99-36
FREAK LIKE ME, Adina Howard, 95-33
FREAK ME:
Silk, 93-46, 94-72
Another Level, 98-1
FREAK ON A LEASH, Korn, 99-24
FREAKS, Live, 97-65
THE FREAKS COME OUT, Cevin Fisher's Big Break, 98-34
FREAKS (LIVE), Marillion, 88-24
FREAKY BE BEAUTIFUL, Moist, 95-47
THE FRED [EP], Various Artists (EPs), 92-26
FREDERICK, Patti Smith Group, 79-63
FREE:
Deniece Williams, 77-1
Will Downing, 88-58
FREE, Curiosity Killed The Cat, 87-56
FREE, Stevie Wonder, 89-49
FREE, Ultra Nate, 97-4, 98-33
FREE, DJ Quicksilver, 97-7
FREE (EP), Free, 78-11, 82-57
FREE AS A BIRD, Beatles, 95-2
FREE BIRD [EP], Lynyrd Skynyrd, 76-31, 79-43, 82-21
FREE (C'MON), Catch, 90-70
THE FREE ELECTRIC BAND, Albert Hammond, 73-19
FREE FALLIN', Tom Petty, 89-64
FREE GAY AND HAPPY, Coming Out Crew, 95-50
FREE HUEY, Boo Radleys, 98-54
FREE LOVE, Juliet Roberts, 93-25, 98-15
FREE ME, Roger Daltrey, 80-39
FREE ME, Cast, 97-7
FREE 'N' EASY, Almighty, 91-35
FREE RANGE, Fall, 92-40
FREE/SAIL ON [M], Chante Moore, 95-69
FREE SATPAL RAM, Asian Dub Foundation, 98-56
FREE SPIRIT, Kim Appleby, 94-51
THE FREE STYLE MEGA-MIX [M], Bobby Brown, 90-14
FREE TO DECIDE, Cranberries, 96-33
FREE TO FALL, Debbie Harry, 87-46
FREE TO LOVE AGAIN, Suzette Charles, 93-58
FREE WORLD, Kirsty MacColl, 89-43
FREE YOUR BODY
Praga Khan featuring Jade 4 U, 92-16
FREE YOUR MIND, En Vogue, 92-16
FREE YOUR MIND, Spacebaby, 95-55
FREE YOURSELF, Untouchables, 85-26
FREED FROM DESIRE, Gala, 97-2
FREEDOM, Wham!, 84-1
FREEDOM, Alice Cooper, 88-50
FREEDOM, A Homeboy, A Hippie and A Funki Dredd, 90-68
FREEDOM, London Boys, 91-54
FREEDOM:
QFX (from Freedom [EP]), 95-41
QFX, 97-21
FREEDOM, Michelle Gayle, 95-16
FREEDOM, Shiva, 95-18
FREEDOM, Robert Miles featuring Kathy Sledge, 97-15
FREEDOM COME, FREEDOM GO, Fortunes, 71-6
FREEDOM [EP] + lead track title, Qfx, 95-41
FREEDOM GOT AN A.K., Da Lench Mob, 93-51

GOODBYE NOTHIN' TO SAY, Javells featuring Nosmo King, 74-26

GOODBYE SAM, HELLO SAMANTHA, Cliff Richard, 70-6

GOODBYE STRANGER, Supertramp, 79-57

GOODBYE STRANGER, Pepsi and Shirlie, 87-9

GOODBYE SWEET PRINCE, Mr. Acker Bilk and his Paramount Jazz Band, 60-50

GOODBYE TO LOVE, Carpenters, 72-9

GOODBYE TO LOVE AGAIN, Maxi Priest, 88-57

GOODBYE YELLOW BRICK ROAD, Elton John, 73-6

GOODBYEEE, Peter Cook and Dudley Moore with the Dudley Moore Trio, 65-18

GOODGROOVE, Derek B, 88-16

GOODNESS GRACIOUS ME!, Peter Sellers and Sophia Loren, 60-4

GOODNIGHT, Roy Orbison, 65-14

GOODNIGHT, Babybird, 96-28

GOODNIGHT GIRL, Wet Wet Wet, 92-1

GOODNIGHT MIDNIGHT, Clodagh Rodgers, 69-4

GOODNIGHT MRS. FLINTSTONE, Piltdown Men, 61-18

GOODNIGHT SAIGON, Billy Joel, 84-29

GOODNIGHT TONIGHT, Wings, 79-5

GOODWILL CITY, Goodbye Mr. MacKenzie, 89-49

GOODY GOODY, Frankie Lymon and the Teenagers, 57-24

GOODY TWO SHOES, Adam Ant, 82-1

GOOGLE EYE, Nashville Teens, 64-10

GORECKI, Lamb, 97-30

GORGEOUS, Gene Loves Jezebel, 87-68

GOSP, L.W.S., 94-65

GOSPEL OAK [EP], Sinead O'Connor, 97-28

GOSSIP CALYPSO, Bernard Cribbins, 62-25

GOT A FEELING, Patrick Juvet, 78-34

GOT A GIRL, Four Preps, 60-28

GOT A LITTLE HEARTACHE, Alvin Stardust, 85-55

GOT A LOT O' LIVIN' TO DO, Elvis Presley with the Jordanaires, 57-17

GOT A LOVE FOR YOU, Jomanda, 91-43

GOT A MATCH, Russ Conway, 58-30

GOT FUNK, Funk Junkeez, 98-57

GOT IT AT THE DIMBAR, Senseless Things, 91-50

GOT ME A FEELING, Misty Oldland, 93-59

GOT MY MIND MADE UP, Instant Funk, 79-46

GOT MY MIND SET ON YOU, George Harrison, 87-2

GOT MY MOJO WORKING, Jimmy Smith, 66-48

GOT MYSELF TOGETHER, Kenny "Dope" presents The Bucketheads, 96-12

GOT NO BRAINS, Bad Manners, 82-44

GOT THE FEELIN', 5, 98-3

GOT THE LIFE, Korn, 98-23

GOT THE TIME, Anthrax, 91-16

GOT 'TIL IT'S GONE, Janet (featuring Q-Tip and Joni Mitchell), 97-6

GOT TO BE CERTAIN, Kylie Minogue, 88-2

GOT TO BE FREE, 49ers, 92-46

GOT TO BE REAL, Erik, 94-42

GOT TO BE THERE, Michael Jackson, 72-5

GOT TO GET, Rob 'N' Raz featuring Leila K, 89-8

GOT TO GET IT, Culture Beat, 93-4

GOT TO GET UP [RM], Afrika Bambaataa vs. Carpe Diem, 98-22

GOT TO GET YOU BACK, Kym Mazelle, 89-29

GOT TO GET YOU INTO MY LIFE:
Cliff Bennett and the Rebel Rousers, 66-6
Earth, Wind And Fire, 78-33

GOT TO GIVE IT UP:
Marvin Gaye, 77-7
Aaliyah, 96-37

GOT TO GIVE ME LOVE, Dana Dawson, 95-27

GOT TO HAVE YOUR LOVE, Mantronix featuring Wondress, 90-4

GOT TO KEEP ON, Cookie Crew, 89-17

GOT TO LOVE SOMEBODY, Sister Sledge, 80-34

GOT YOU ON MY MIND, Tony Brent, 53-12

GOTHAM CITY, R. Kelly, 97-9

GOTTA BE A SIN, Adam Ant, 95-48

GOTTA BE . . . MOVIN' ON UP, P.M. Dawn featuring Ky-Mani, 98-68

GOTTA BE YOU, 3T (featuring Herbie), 97-10

GOTTA GET A DATE, Frank Ifield, 60-49

GOTTA GET AWAY, Offspring, 95-43

GOTTA GET IT RIGHT, Lena Fiagbe, 93-20

GOTTA GET LOOSE, Mr And Mrs Smith, 96-70

GOTTA GET YOU HOME TONIGHT, Eugene Wilde, 84-18

GOTTA GO HOME, Boney M, 79-12

GOTTA HAVE HOPE, Blackout, 99-46

GOTTA HAVE RAIN, Max Bygraves, 58-28

GOT-TA HAVE SOMETHING IN THE BANK, FRANK, Frankie Vaughan and the Kaye Sisters with Wally Stott and his Orchestra, 57-8

GOTTA KEEP PUSHIN', Z Factor, 98-47

GOTTA KNOW (YOUR NAME), Malaika, 93-68

GOTTA LOTTA LOVE, Ice-T, 94-24

GOTTA PULL MYSELF TOGETHER, Nolans, 80-9

GOTTA SEE BABY TONIGHT, Mr. Acker Bilk and his Paramount Jazz Band (vocal by Mr. Acker Bilk), 62-24

GOTTA SEE JANE, R. Dean Taylor, 68-17, 74-41

GOURYELLA, Gouryella, 99-15

GOVINDA, Radha Krishna Temple, 70-23

GOVINDA, Kula Shaker, 96-7

GRACE, A.K.A., 82-41

GRACELAND, Bible, 89-51

GRANADA:
Frankie Laine with Paul Weston and his Orchestra (Carl Fischer: piano), 54-9
Frank Sinatra with Billy May and his Orchestra, 61-15

THE GRAND COOLIE DAM, Lonnie Donegan and his Skiffle Group, 58-6

GRAND PIANO, Mixmaster, 89-9

GRANDAD, Clive Dunn, 70-1

GRANDMA'S PARTY, Paul Nicholas, 76-9

GRANDPA'S PARTY, Monie Love, 89-16

GRANITE STATUE, Salad, 95-50

GRAPEVINE, Brownstone, 95-16

GRATEFUL WHEN YOU'RE DEAD/JERRY WAS THERE [M], Kula Shaker, 96-35

THE GRAVE AND THE CONSTANT, Fun Lovin' Criminals, 96-72

GRAVITATE TO ME, The, 89-63

GRAVITY, James Brown, 86-65

GREASE:
Frankie Valli, 78-3
Craig McLachlan, 93-44

GREASE – THE DREAM MIX [M], Frankie Valli, John Travolta and Olivia Newton-John, 91-47

THE GREASE MEGAMIX [M], John Travolta and Olivia Newton-John, 90-3

GREASED LIGHTNING, John Travolta, 78-11

GREAT BALLS OF FIRE:
Jerry Lee Lewis, 57-1
Tiny Tim, 69-45

THE GREAT ESCAPE, England Supporters Band, 98-46

GREAT GOSH A'MIGHTY (IT'S A MATTER OF TIME), Little Richard, 86-62

GREAT INDIFFERENCE (from RAGING [EP]), Beyond, 91-68

THE GREAT PRETENDER:
Jimmy Parkinson with Ray Martin and his Orchestra, 56-9
Platters, 56-5
Freddie Mercury, 87-4, 93-29

THE GREAT ROCK 'N' ROLL SWINDLE, Sex Pistols, 79-21

THE GREAT SNOW MAN, Bob Luman, 61-49

THE GREAT SONG OF INDIFFERENCE, Bob Geldof, 90-15

GREAT SPANGLED FRITILLARY (from ECHOES IN A SHALLOW BAY [EP]), Cocteau Twins, 85-65

GREAT THINGS, Echobelly, 95-13

THE GREAT TRAIN ROBBERY, Black Uhuru, 86-62

GREATER LOVE, Soundman and Don Lloydie with Elisabeth Troy, 95-49

THE GREATEST COCKNEY RIP- OFF, Cockney Rejects, 80-21

GREATEST DAY, Beverley Knight, 99-14

THE GREATEST FLAME, Runrig, 93-36, 97-30

THE GREATEST HIGH, Hurricane #1, 99-43

THE GREATEST LOVE OF ALL:
George Benson, 77-27
Whitney Houston, 86-8

THE GREATEST LOVE YOU'LL NEVER KNOW, Lutricia McNeal, 98-17

THE GREATEST SHOW ON EARTH, Strangelove, 97-36

THE GREATNESS AND PERFECTION OF LOVE, Julian Cope, 84-52

GREEDY FLY, Bush, 97-22

GREEN AND GREY, New Model Army, 89-37

THE GREEN DOOR:
Jim Lowe with the High Fives, 56-8
Frankie Vaughan with Wally Stott and his Orchestra and Chorus, 56-2
Glen Mason, 56-24
Shakin' Stevens, 81-1

GREEN FIELDS:
Beverley Sisters, 60-29
Brothers Four *, 60-40

GREEN FIELDS, Unit Four Plus Two, 64-48

GREEN, GREEN GRASS OF HOME:
Tom Jones, 66-1
Elvis Presley, 75-29

GREEN JEANS, Fabulous Flee-Rakkers, 60-23

THE GREEN LEAVES OF SUMMER, Kenny Ball and his Jazzmen, 62-7

GREEN LIGHT, Cliff Richard, 79-57

THE GREEN MAN, Shut Up And Dance, 92-43

THE GREEN MANALISHI (WITH THE TWO PRONG CROWN), Fleetwood Mac, 70-10

GREEN ONIONS, Booker T. and the MGs, 79-7

GREEN RIVER, Creedence Clearwater Revival, 69-19

GREEN SHIRT, Elvis Costello and the Attractions, 85-68

GREEN STREET GREEN, New Vaudeville Band (featuring Tristam Vii), 67-37

GREEN TAMBOURINE:
Lemon Pipers, 68-7
Sundragon, 68-50

GREEN TINTED SIXTIES MIND, Mr. Big, 92-72

GREENBACK DOLLAR, Chas McDevitt Skiffle Group (featuring Nancy Whiskey), 57-28

GREENBACK DRIVE, Christians, 90-63

GREENFIELDS, Brothers Four, 60-40

GREETINGS TO THE NEW BRUNETTE, Billy Bragg with Johnny Marr and Kirsty MacColl, 86-58

GREY DAY, Madness, 81-4

GRIMLY FIENDISH, Damned, 85-21

GRIND, Alice In Chains, 95-23

GRIP '89 (GET A) GRIP (ON YOURSELF) [RM], Stranglers, 89-33

GRITTY SHAKER, David Holmes, 97-53

THE GROOVE, Rodney Franklin, 80-7

GROOVE BABY GROOVE [EP] + lead track title, Stargazers, 82-56

GROOVE IS IN THE HEART, Deee-Lite, 90-2, 91-52

THE GROOVE LINE:
Heatwave, 78-12
Blockster *, 99-18

GROOVE MACHINE, Marvin and Tamara, 99-11

GROOVE OF LOVE, E.V.E., 94-30

GROOVE THANG, Zhane, 94-34

GROOVE TO MOVE, Channel X, 91-67

GROOVEBIRD, Natural Born Grooves, 97-21

GROOVELINE, Blockster, 99-18

THE GROOVER, T.Rex, 73-4

GROOVIN':
Young Rascals, 67-8
War, 85-43
Pato Banton and the Reggae Revolution, 96-14

GROOVIN' (THE BIG BOSS GROOVE), Style Council, 84-5

GROOVIN' IN THE MIDNIGHT, Maxi Priest, 92-50

GROOVIN' (THAT'S WHAT WE'RE DOIN'), S.O.S. Band, 83-72

GROOVIN' WITH MR. BLOE, Mr. Bloe, 70-2

GROOVIN' (YOU'RE THE BEST THING), Style Council, 84-5

GROOVY BABY, Microbe, 69-29

GROOVY BEAT, D.O.P., 96-54

GROOVY FEELING, Fluke, 93-45

A GROOVY KIND OF LOVE:
Mindbenders, 66-2
Les Gray, 77-32
Phil Collins, 88-1

THE GROOVY THANG, Minimal Funk 2, 98-65

GROOVY TRAIN, Farm, 90-6

GROUND LEVEL, Stereo MC's, 93-19

GROUPY GIRL, Tony Joe White, 70-22

GUAGLIONE:
Dean Martin *, 57-21
Perez 'Prez' Prado and his Orchestra, 94-41, 95-2

I'LL PUT YOU TOGETHER AGAIN (FROM DEAR ANYONE), Hot Chocolate, 78-13

I'LL REMEMBER (THEME FROM 'WITH HONOURS'), Madonna, 94-7

I'LL REMEMBER TONIGHT, Pat Boone, 59-18

I'LL SAIL THIS SHIP ALONE, Beautiful South, 89-31

I'LL SAY FOREVER MY LOVE, Jimmy Ruffin, 70-7

I'LL SEE YOU ALONG THE WAY, Rick Clarke, 88-63

I'LL SEE YOU AROUND, Silver Sun, 98-26

I'LL SEE YOU IN MY DREAMS, Pat Boone, 62-27

I'LL SET YOU FREE, Bangles, 89-74

I'LL SLEEP WHEN I'M DEAD, Bon Jovi, 93-17

I'LL STAND BY YOU, Pretenders, 94-10

I'LL STAY BY YOU, Kenny Lynch, 65-29

I'LL STAY SINGLE, Jerry Lordan, 60-26

I'LL STEP DOWN, Garry Mills, 61-39

I'LL STICK AROUND, Foo Fighters, 95-18

I'LL STOP AT NOTHING, Sandie Shaw, 65-4

I'LL TAKE YOU HOME:
Drifters, 63-37
Cliff Bennett and the Rebel Rousers, 65-42

I'LL TAKE YOU HOME AGAIN KATHLEEN, Slim Whitman, 57-7

I'LL TAKE YOU THERE:
Staple Singers, 72-30
General Public, 94-73

I'LL TRY ANYTHING, Dusty Springfield, 67-13

I'LL WAIT, Taylor Dayne, 94-29

I'LL WALK WITH GOD, Mario Lanza, 55-18

I'M A BELIEVER:
Monkees, 67-1, 80-33
Robert Wyatt, 74-29
EMF and Reeves and Mortimer, 95-3

I'M A BETTER MAN (FOR HAVING LOVED YOU), Engelbert Humperdinck, 69-15

I'M A BITCH, Olga, 94-68

I'M A BOY, Who, 66-2

I'M A DISCO DANCER (AND A SWEET ROMANCER), Christopher Just, 97-72, 99-69

I'M A DOUN FOR LACK O'JOHNNIE' (A LITTLE SCOTTISH FANTASY), Vanessa-Mae, 96-28

I'M A FOOL, Slim Whitman, 56-16

I'M A FOOL TO CARE, Joe Barry, 61-49

I'M A MAN:
Spencer Davis Group, 67-9
Chicago, 70-8

I'M A MAN NOT A BOY, Chesney Hawkes, 91-27

I'M A MAN NOT A BOY, North And South, 97-7

I'M A MAN/YE KE KE YE KE [M], Clubhouse, 89-69

I'M A MESSAGE, Idlewild, 98-41

I'M A MIDNIGHT MOVER, Wilson Pickett, 68-38

I'M A MOODY GUY, Shane Fenton and the Fentones, 61-22

I'M A SUCKER FOR YOUR LOVE, Teena Marie Co-lead vocals: Rick James, 79-43

I'M A TIGER, Lulu, 68-9

(I'M A) TV SAVAGE, Bow Wow Wow, 82-45

I'M A WONDERFUL THING, BABY, Kid Creole and the Coconuts, 82-4, 93-60

I'M ALIVE, Hollies, 65-1

I'M ALIVE, Electric Light Orchestra, 80-20

I'M ALIVE, Seal, 95-4

I'M ALIVE, Cut 'N' Move, 95-49

I'M ALIVE, Stretch and Vern present "Maddog", 96-6

I'M ALL YOU NEED, Samantha Fox, 86-41

I'M ALRIGHT, Young Steve and the Afternoon Boys, 82-40

I'M ALRIGHT, Katherine E, 91-41

(I'M ALWAYS HEARING) WEDDING BELLS, Eddie Fisher with Hugo Winterhalter's Orchestra and Chorus, 55-5

(I'M ALWAYS TOUCHED BY YOUR) PRESENCE DEAR, Blondie, 78-10

I'M AN UPSTART, Angelic Upstarts, 79-31

I'M BACK FOR MORE, Lulu and Bobby Womack, 93-27

I'M BAD, L.L. Cool J, 87-71

I'M BORN AGAIN, Boney M, 79-35

I'M BROKEN, Pantera, 94-19

I'M CHILLIN', Kurtis Blow, 86-64

I'M COMIN' HARDCORE, M.A.N.I.C., 92-60

I'M COMING HOME, Tom Jones, 67-2

I'M COMING HOME CINDY, Trini Lopez, 66-28

I'M COMING OUT, Diana Ross, 80-13, 94-36

I'M COUNTING ON YOU, Petula Clark, 62-41

I'M CRYING, Animals, 64-8

I'M DOIN' FINE, Day One, 99-68

I'M DOIN' FINE NOW:
New York City, 73-20
Pasadenas, 92-4

I'M DOING FINE, Jason Donovan, 90-22

I'M EASY, Faith No More, 93-3

I'M EVERY WOMAN:
Chaka Khan, 78-11, 89-8
Whitney Houston, 93-4

I'M FALLING, Bluebells, 84-11

I'M FOR REAL, Nightmares On Wax, 90-38

I'M FREE BLOWING BUBBLES:
West Ham United Cup Squad, 75-31
Cockney Rejects, 80-35

I'M FREE, Roger Daltrey with London Symphony Orchestra and English Chamber Choir, 73-13

I'M FREE, Soup Dragons featuring Junior Reid, 90-5

I'M FREE, Jon Secada, 93-50

I'M GOIN' DOWN, Mary J. Blige, 95-12

I'M GOING ALL THE WAY, Sounds Of Blackness, 93-27, 95-14

I'M GOING HOME (TO SEE MY BABY), Gene Vincent with Sounds Incorporated, 61-36

I'M GOING SLIGHTLY MAD, Queen, 91-22

I'M GONE, Diana Ross, 95-36

I'M GONNA BE A COUNTRY GIRL AGAIN, Buffy Sainte-Marie, 72-34

I'M GONNA BE (500 MILES), Proclaimers, 88-11

I'M GONNA BE STRONG:
Gene Pitney, 64-2
Cyndi Lauper, 95-37

I'M GONNA BE WARM THIS WINTER, Connie Francis, 62-48

I'M GONNA CHANGE EVERYTHING, Jim Reeves, 62-42

(I'M GONNA) CRY MYSELF BLIND, Primal Scream, 94-49

I'M GONNA GET MARRIED, Lloyd Price, 59-23

I'M GONNA GET ME A GUN, Cat Stevens, 67-6

I'M GONNA GET THERE SOMEHOW, Val Doonican, 65-25

I'M GONNA GET YA BABY, Black Connection, 98-62

I'M GONNA GET YOU, Bizarre Inc featuring Angie Brown, 92-3

I'M GONNA GIT YOU SUCKA, Gap Band, 89-63

I'M GONNA KNOCK ON YOUR DOOR:
Eddie Hodges, 61-37
Jimmy Osmond, 74-11

I'M GONNA LOVE HER FOR BOTH OF US, Meat Loaf, 81-62

I'M GONNA LOVE YOU FOREVER, Crown Heights Affair, 78-47

I'M GONNA LOVE YOU JUST A LITTLE BIT MORE BABY, Barry White, 73-23

I'M GONNA MAKE YOU LOVE ME, Diana Ross and the Supremes and the Temptations, 69-3

I'M GONNA MAKE YOU MINE, Lou Christie, 69-2

I'M GONNA MAKE YOU MINE, Tanya Blount, 94-69

I'M GONNA MISS YOU FOREVER, Aaron Carter, 98-24

I'M GONNA RUN AWAY FROM YOU, Tami Lynn, 71-4, 75-36

I'M GONNA SIT RIGHT DOWN AND WRITE MYSELF A LETTER:
Billy Williams, 57-22
Barry Manilow, 82-36

I'M GONNA SOOTHE YOU, Maria McKee, 93-35

I'M GONNA TEAR YOUR PLAYHOUSE DOWN, Paul Young, 84-9

I'M IN A DIFFERENT WORLD, Four Tops, 68-27

I'M IN A PHILLY MOOD, Daryl Hall, 93-59, 94-52

I'M IN FAVOUR OF FRIENDSHIP, Five Smith Brothers, 55-20

I'M IN IT FOR LOVE, Donny Osmond, 87-70

I'M IN LOVE, Fourmost, 63-17

I'M IN LOVE, Evelyn King, 81-27

I'M IN LOVE, Ruby Turner, 86-61, 87-57

I'M IN LOVE, Lillo Thomas, 87-54

I'M IN LOVE AGAIN, Fats Domino, 56-12

I'M IN LOVE AGAIN, Sad Cafe, 80-40

I'M IN LOVE (AND I LOVE THE FEELING), Rose Royce, 79-51

I'M IN LOVE WITH A GERMAN FILM STAR, Passions, 81-25

I'M IN LOVE WITH THE GIRL ON A CERTAIN MANCHESTER MEGASTORE CHECKOUT DESK, Freshies, 81-54

I'M IN LUV, Joe, 94-22

I'M IN THE MOOD, Ce Ce Peniston, 94-16

I'M IN THE MOOD FOR DANCING:
Nolans, 79-3
Nolans, 95-51

I'M IN THE MOOD FOR LOVE, Lord Tanamo, 90-58

I'M IN TROUBLE, Chas and Dave with Rockney, 78-52

I'M IN YOU, Peter Frampton, 77-41

I'M INTO SOMETHING GOOD, Herman's Hermits, 64-1

I'M JUST A BABY, Louise Cordet, 62-13

I'M JUST A SINGER (IN A ROCK AND ROLL BAND), Moody Blues, 73-36

I'M JUST YOUR PUPPET ON A ... (STRING!), Londonbeat, 95-55

I'M LEAVIN', Elvis Presley, 71-23

I'M LEAVING, Lodger, 98-40

I'M LEAVING IT UP TO YOU:
Dale and Grace, 64-42
Donny and Marie Osmond *, 74-2

I'M LEFT, YOU'RE RIGHT, SHE'S GONE, Elvis Presley, 58-21

I'M LIVIN' IN SHAME, Diana Ross and the Supremes, 69-14

I'M LONELY, Hollis P. Monroe, 99-51

I'M LOOKIN' OUT THE WINDOW, Cliff Richard with the Norrie Paramor Orchestra, 62-2

I'M LOOKING FOR THE ONE (TO BE WITH ME), Jazzy Jeff and the Fresh Prince, 93-24

I'M LOST WITHOUT YOU, Billy Fury, 65-16

I'M LUCKY, Joan Armatrading, 81-46

I'M MANDY FLY ME, 10cc, 76-6

I'M NEVER GIVING UP, Sweet Dreams, 83-21

IM NIN'ALU, Ofra Haza, 88-15

I'M NO ANGEL, Marcella Detroit, 94-33

I'M NO REBEL, View From The Hill, 87-59

I'M NOT A FOOL, Cockney Rejects, 79-65

I'M NOT A JUVENILE DELINQUENT, Frankie Lymon and the Teenagers, 57-12

I'M NOT ASHAMED, Big Country, 95-69

I'M NOT FEELING YOU, Yvette Michele, 97-36

I'M NOT GIVING YOU UP, Gloria Estefan, 96-28

I'M NOT GONNA LET YOU, Colonel Abrams, 86-24

I'M NOT IN LOVE:
10 CC, 75-1
Johnny Logan, 87-51
Will To Power, 90-29
10 CC, 95-29
Fun Lovin' Criminals, 97-12

I'M NOT PERFECT (BUT I'M PERFECT FOR YOU), Grace Jones, 86-56

I'M NOT READY, Keith Sweat, 99-53

I'M NOT SATISFIED, Fine Young Cannibals, 90-46

I'M NOT SCARED, Eighth Wonder, 88-7

I'M NOT THE MAN I USED TO BE, Fine Young Cannibals, 89-20

I'M NOT TO BLAME, Alibi, 97-51

(I'M NOT YOUR) STEPPING STONE:
Sex Pistols, 80-21
Farm *, 90-58
PJ and Duncan *, 96-11

I'M ON AUTOMATIC, Sharpe and Numan, 89-44

I'M ON FIRE, 5000 Volts, 75-4

I'M ON FIRE, Bruce Springsteen, 85-5

I'M ON MY WAY, Dean Parrish, 75-38

I'M ON MY WAY, Proclaimers, 89-43

I'M ON MY WAY, Betty Boo, 92-44

I'M ON MY WAY TO A BETTER PLACE, Chairmen Of The Board, 72-30

I'M ONLY SLEEPING, Suggs, 95-7

I'M OUT OF YOUR LIFE, Arnie's Love, 83-67

I'M OUTSTANDING, Shaquille O'Neal, 94-70

I'M QUALIFIED TO SATISFY YOU, Barry White, 77-37

I'M RAVING, Scooter, 96-33

I'M READY, Caveman, 91-65

I'M READY, Size 9, 95-52, 95-30

I'M READY, Bryan Adams, 98-20

I'M READY FOR LOVE, Martha and the Vandellas, 66-29

I'M REAL, James Brown with Full Force, 88-31

I'M RIFFIN (ENGLISH RASTA), M.C. Duke, 89-75

I'M RUSHING, Bump, 92-40, 95-45

LEAN ON YOU, Cliff Richard, 89-17

LEAN PERIOD, Orange Juice, 84-74

LEAP OF FAITH, Bruce Springsteen, 92-46

LEAP UP AND DOWN, St. Cecelia, 71-12

LEARN TO FLY, Foo Fighters, 99-21

LEARNIN' THE BLUES, Frank Sinatra with Nelson Riddle and his Orchestra, 55-2

LEARNING THE GAME, Buddy Holly, 60-36

LEARNING TO FLY, Tom Petty and the Heartbreakers, 91-46

LEARNING TO FLY, Mother's Pride, 99-54

LEAVE A LIGHT ON, Belinda Carlisle, 89-4

LEAVE A LITTLE LOVE, Lulu, 65-8

LEAVE A TENDER MOMENT ALONE, Billy Joel, 84-29

LEAVE 'EM SOMETHING TO DESIRE, Sprinkler, 98-45

LEAVE HOME, Chemical Brothers, 95-17

LEAVE IN SILENCE, Depeche Mode, 82-18

LEAVE IT, Mike McGear, 74-36

LEAVE IT, Yes, 84-56

LEAVE IT ALONE, Living Colour, 93-34

LEAVE ME ALONE, Michael Jackson, 89-2

LEAVE THEM ALL BEHIND, Ride, 92-9

LEAVIN', Tony Rich Project, 96-52

LEAVING HERE:
Birds, 65-45
Motorhead (from The Golden Years Live [EP]), 80-8

LEAVING LAS VEGAS, Sheryl Crow, 94-66

LEAVING ME NOW, Level 42, 85-15

LEAVING ON A JET PLANE:
Peter, Paul and Mary, 70-2
Chantal Kreviazuk, 99-59

LEAVING ON THE MIDNIGHT TRAIN, Nick Straker Band, 80-61

THE LEBANON, Human League, 84-11

LEEDS, LEEDS, LEEDS, (MARCHING ON TOGETHER), Leeds United A.F.C. (1970's), 92-54

LEEDS UNITED, Leeds United Football Team, 72-10

THE LEFT BANK (C'EST A HAMBOURG), Winifred Atwell, 56-14

LEFT OF CENTRE, Suzanne Vega featuring Joe Jackson On Piano, 86-32

LEFT TO MY OWN DEVICES, Pet Shop Boys, 88-4

LEGACY, Mad Cobra featuring Richie Stephens, 93-64

LEGACY (from EIGHT [EP]), Mansun, 98-7

LEGACY [SHOW ME LOVE], Space Brothers, 99-31

A LEGAL MATTER, Who, 66-32

LEGEND OF A COWGIRL, Imani Coppola, 98-32

LEGEND OF THE GOLDEN SNAKE, Depth Charge, 95-75

THE LEGEND OF XANADU, Dave Dee, Dozy, Beaky, Mick and Tich, 68-1

LEGENDS OF THE DARK BLACK – PT 2, Wildchild, 95-34, 95-11, 98-3

LEGO SKANGA, Rupie Edwards, 75-32

LEGS (SPECIAL US REMIX), ZZ Top, 85-16

LEGS, Art Of Noise, 85-69

LEMMINGS, S.F.X., 93-51

LEMON TREE, Fool's Garden, 96-61, 96-26

LENINGRAD, Billy Joel, 89-53

LENNY, Supergrass, 95-10

LENNY AND TERENCE, Carter – The Unstoppable Sex Machine, 93-40

LENNY VALENTINO, Auteurs, 93-41

LEONARD NIMOY, Freaky Realistic, 93-71

LES BICYCLETTES DE BELSIZE, Engelbert Humperdinck, 68-5

L'ESPERANZA, Sven Vath, 93-63

LESSON ONE, Russ Conway, 62-21

LESSONS IN LOVE, Allisons, 62-30

LESSONS IN LOVE, Level 42, 86-3

LET A BOY CRY, Gala, 97-11

LET 'EM IN:
Wings, 76-2
Billy Paul, 77-26
Shinehead, 93-70

LET FOREVER BE, Chemical Brothers, 99-9

LET HER CRY, Hootie and the Blowfish, 95-75

LET HER DOWN EASY, Terence Trent D'Arby, 93-18

LET HER FALL, Then Jerico, 87-65

LET HER FEEL IT:
Simplicious, 84-65
Eugene Wilde, 85-34

LET HER GO, Strawberry Switchblade, 85-59

LET IT ALL BLOW, Dazz Band, 84-12

LET IT ALL HANG OUT, Jonathan King, 70-26

LET IT BE:
Beatles, 70-2
Ferry Aid, 87-1

LET IT BE ME, Everly Brothers, 60-13

LET IT BE WITH YOU, Belouis Some, 87-53

LET IT FLOW, Spiritualized Electric Mainline, 95-30

LET IT LAST, Carleen Anderson, 95-16

LET IT LOOSE, Lemon Trees, 93-55

LET IT RAIN, U.F.O., 82-62

LET IT RAIN, East 17, 95-10

LET IT REIGN, Inner City, 91-51

LET IT RIDE, Todd Terry, 99-58

LET IT ROCK:
Chuck Berry, 63-6
Rolling Stones, 71-2

LET IT ROLL, Doug Lazy, 89-27

LET IT SLIDE, Mudhoney, 91-60

LET IT SLIDE, Ariel, 93-57

LET IT SWING, Bobbysocks, 85-44

LET LOVE BE THE LEADER, FM, 87-71

LET LOVE RULE, Lenny Kravitz, 90-39

LET LOVE SHINE, Amos, 95-31

LET LOVE SPEAK UP ITSELF, Beautiful South, 91-51

LET ME BE, Black Diamond, 94-56

LET ME BE THE NO. 1 (LOVE OF YOUR LIFE), Dooley Silverspoon, 76-44

LET ME BE THE ONE, Shadows, 75-12

LET ME BE THE ONE, Five Star, 85-18

LET ME BE THE ONE, Blessid Union Of Souls, 96-74

LET ME BE THE ONE, Mint Condition, 97-63

LET ME BE YOUR FANTASY, Baby D, 94-1

(LET ME BE YOUR) TEDDY BEAR, Elvis Presley with the Jordanaires, 57-3

LET ME BE YOUR UNDERWEAR, Club 69, 92-33

LET ME BE YOUR WINGS, Barry Manilow and Debra Byrd, 94-73

LET ME BE YOURS, Five Star, 88-51

LET ME CLEAR MY THROAT, DJ Kool, 97-8

LET ME COME ON HOME, Otis Redding, 67-48

LET ME CRY ON YOUR SHOULDER, Ken Dodd with Geoff Love and his Orchestra, 67-11

LET ME DOWN EASY, Stranglers, 85-48

LET ME ENTERTAIN YOU, Robbie Williams, 98-3

LET ME GO, Heaven 17, 82-41

LET ME GO LOVER:
Teresa Brewer with the Lancers, 55-9
Joan Weber, 55-16
Dean Martin, 55-3
Ruby Murray with Ray Martin and his Orchestra, 55-5
Kathy Kirby, 64-10

LET ME HEAR YOU SAY "OLE OLE", Outhere Brothers, 97-18

LET ME IN:
Osmonds, 73-2
OTT, 97-12

LET ME INTRODUCE YOU TO THE FAMILY, Stranglers, 81-42

LET ME KNOW, Junior, 82-53

LET ME KNOW, Maxi Priest, 87-49

LET ME KNOW (I HAVE A RIGHT), Gloria Gaynor, 79-32

LET ME LET GO, Faith Hill, 99-72

LET ME LIVE, Queen, 96-9

LET ME LOVE YOU FOR TONIGHT, Kariya, 89-44

LET ME RIDE, Dr. Dre, 94-31

LET ME ROCK YOU, Kandidate, 80-58

LET ME SEE, Morcheeba, 98-46

LET ME SHOW YOU, K-Klass, 93-13

LET ME SHOW YOU, Camisra, 98-5

LET ME SHOW YOU, Tony Momrelle, 98-67

LET ME TAKE YOU THERE, Betty Boo, 92-12

LET ME TALK, Earth, Wind And Fire, 80-29

LET ME TRY AGAIN, Tammy Jones, 75-5

LET ME WAKE UP IN YOUR ARMS, Lulu, 93-51

LET MY LOVE OPEN THE DOOR, Pete Townshend, 80-46

LET MY NAME BE SORROW, Mary Hopkin, 71-46

LET MY PEOPLE GO, Winans, 85-71

LET MY PEOPLE GO-GO, Rainmakers, 87-18

LET SOMEBODY LOVE YOU, Keni Burke, 81-59

LET THE BASS KICK, 2 For Joy, 91-67

LET THE BEAT CONTROL YOUR BODY, 2 Unlimited, 94-6

LET THE BEAT HIT 'EM:
Lisa Lisa and Cult Jam, 91-17, 91-49
Shena, 97-28

LET THE BEAT HIT 'EM PART 2 [RM], Lisa Lisa and Cult Jam, 91-49

LET THE DAY BEGIN, Call, 89-42

LET THE FLAME BURN BRIGHTER, Graham Kendrick, 89-55

LET THE GOOD TIMES ROLL, Sheep On Drugs, 94-56

LET THE HAPPINESS IN, David Sylvian, 87-66

LET THE HEALING BEGIN, Joe Cocker, 94-32

LET THE HEARTACHES BEGIN, Long John Baldry, 67-1

LET THE LITTLE GIRL DANCE, Billy Bland, 60-15

LET THE LOVE, Q Tex, 96-30

LET THE MUSIC HEAL YOUR SOUL, Bravo All Stars, 98-36

LET THE MUSIC (LIFT YOU UP), Loveland featuring Rachel McFarlane vs. Darlene Lewis, 94-16

LET THE MUSIC MOVE U, Raze, 87-57

LET THE MUSIC PLAY, Barry White, 75-9

LET THE MUSIC PLAY, Charles Earland, 78-46

LET THE MUSIC PLAY:
Shannon, 83-51, 84-14
BBG featuring Erin, 96-46
Mary Kiani, 96-19

LET THE MUSIC TAKE CONTROL, J.M. Silk, 87-47

LET THE MUSIC USE YOU, Nightwriters, 92-51

LET THE PEOPLE KNOW, Toploader, 99-52

LET THE RHYTHM MOVE YOU, Sharada House Gang, 96-50

LET THE RHYTHM PUMP, Doug Lazy, 89-45, 90-63

LET THE SUN SHINE IN, Peddlers, 65-50

LET THE WATER RUN DOWN, P.J. Proby, 65-19

LET THEM ALL TALK, Elvis Costello and the Attractions, 83-59

LET THERE BE DRUMS, Sandy Nelson, 61-3

LET THERE BE HOUSE, Deskee, 90-52

LET THERE BE LIGHT, Mike Oldfield, 95-51

LET THERE BE LOVE, Nat King Cole/The George Shearing Quintet, 62-11

LET THERE BE LOVE, Simple Minds, 91-6

LET THERE BE PEACE ON EARTH (LET IT BEGIN WITH ME), Michael Ward with the Mike Sammes Singers, 73-15

LET THERE BE ROCK, Onslaught, 89-50

LET THIS BE A PRAYER, Rollo Goes Spiritual with Pauline Taylor, 96-26

LET THIS FEELING, Simone Angel, 93-60

LET TRUE LOVE BEGIN, Nat King Cole, 61-29

LET YOUR BODY GO, Tom Wilson, 96-60

LET YOUR BODY GO DOWNTOWN, Martyn Ford Orchestra, 77-38

LET YOUR HEART DANCE, Secret Affair, 79-32

LET YOUR LOVE FLOW, Bellamy Brothers, 76-7

LET YOUR SOUL BE YOUR PILOT, Sting, 96-15

LET YOUR YEAH BE YEAH:
Pioneers, 71-5
Ali Campbell, 95-25

LET YOURSELF GO, T-Connection, 78-52

LET YOURSELF GO, Sybil, 87-32

LET'S, Sarah Vaughan with Joe Reisman's Orchestra and Chorus, 60-37

LET'S ALL CHANT:
Michael Zager Band, 78-8
Mick and Pat, 88-11
Gusto, 96-21

(LET'S ALL GO BACK) DISCO NIGHTS, Jazz and the Brothers Grimm, 88-57

LET'S ALL GO (TO THE FIRE DANCES), Killing Joke, 83-51

LET'S ALL GO TOGETHER, Marion, 95-37

LET'S ALL SING LIKE THE BIRDIES SING, Tweets, 81-44

LET'S BE FRIENDS, Johnny Nash, 75-42

LET'S BE LOVERS TONIGHT, Sherrick, 87-63

LET'S CALL IT QUITS, Slade, 76-11

LET'S CELEBRATE, New York Skyy, 82-67

LET'S CLEAN UP THE GHETTO, Philadelphia International All Stars: Lou Rawls, Billy Paul, Archie Bell, Teddy Pendergrass, O'Jays, Dee Dee Sharp, Gamble, 77-34

LOVE SPREADS, Stone Roses, 94-2
LOVE STORY, Jethro Tull, 69-29
LOVE STRAIN, Kym Mazelle, 89-52
A LOVE SUPREME, Will Downing, 88-14
LOVE TAKE OVER, Five Star, 85-25
LOVE TAKES TIME, Mariah Carey, 90-37
LOVE THE LIFE, JTQ with Noel McKoy, 93-34
LOVE THE ONE YOU'RE WITH:
 Stephen Stills, 71-37
 Bucks Fizz, 86-47
 Luther Vandross, 94-31
LOVE THEME FROM "A STAR IS BORN" (EVERGREEN):
 Barbra Streisand, 77-3
 Hazell Dean *, 84-63
LOVE THEME FROM SPARTACUS, Terry Callier, 98-57
LOVE THEME FROM "THE GODFATHER" (SPEAK SOFTLY LOVE), Andy Williams, 72-42
LOVE THEME FROM THE THORN BIRDS, Juan Martin with the Royal Philharmonic Orchestra conducted by Louis Clark, 84-10
LOVE THING, Pasadenas, 90-22
LOVE THING, Tina Turner, 92-29
LOVE THING, Evolution, 93-32
LOVE . . . THY WILL BE DONE, Martika, 91-9
LOVE X LOVE, George Benson, 80-10
LOVE TIMES LOVE, Heavy Pettin', 84-69
LOVE TO HATE YOU, Erasure, 91-4
LOVE TO LOVE YOU, Corrs, 97-62
LOVE TO LOVE YOU BABY, Donna Summer, 76-4
LOVE TO STAY, Altered Images, 83-46
LOVE TOGETHER, L.A. Mix featuring Kevin Henry, 89-66
LOVE TOUCH (FROM THE MOTION PICTURE 'LEGAL EAGLES'), Rod Stewart, 86-27
LOVE TOWN, Booker Newbury III, 83-6
LOVE TRAIN, O'Jays, 73-9
LOVE TRAIN, Holly Johnson, 89-4
LOVE TRIAL, Kelly Marie, 81-51
LOVE, TRUTH AND HONESTLY, Bananarama, 88-23
LOVE II LOVE, Damage, 96-12
LOVE U 4 LIFE, Jodeci, 95-23
LOVE U MORE, Sunscreem, 92-23
LOVE UNLIMITED, Fun Lovin' Criminals, 98-18
LOVE WALKED IN, Thunder, 91-21
LOVE WARS, Womack and Womack, 84-14
LOVE WILL CONQUER ALL, Lionel Richie, 86-45
LOVE WILL FIND A WAY, David Grant, 83-24
LOVE WILL FIND A WAY, Yes, 87-73
LOVE WILL KEEP US ALIVE, Eagles, 96-52
LOVE WILL KEEP US TOGETHER, Captain and Tennille, 75-32
LOVE WILL KEEP US TOGETHER, James Taylor Quartet featuring Alison Limerick, 95-63
LOVE WILL LEAD YOU BACK, Taylor Dayne, 90-69
LOVE WILL MAKE YOU FAIL IN SCHOOL, Rocky Sharpe and the Replays featuring The Top Liners, 79-60
LOVE WILL NEVER DO (WITHOUT YOU), Janet Jackson, 90-34

LOVE WILL SAVE THE DAY, Whitney Houston, 88-10
LOVE WILL TEAR US APART, Joy Division, 80-13, 83-19, 95-19
LOVE WON'T LET ME WAIT, Major Harris, 75-37
LOVE WON'T WAIT, Gary Barlow, 97-1
LOVE WORTH DYING FOR, Thunder, 97-60
A LOVE WORTH WAITING FOR, Shakin' Stevens, 84-2
LOVE YOU ALL MY LIFETIME, Chaka Khan, 92-49
LOVE YOU DOWN, Ready For The World, 87-60
LOVE YOU INSIDE OUT, Bee Gees, 79-13
LOVE YOU MORE, Buzzcocks, 78-34
THE LOVE YOU SAVE, Jackson 5, 70-7
LOVE YOUR MONEY, Daisy Chainsaw, 92-26
LOVE YOUR SEXY . . . !!, Byker Grooove!, 94-48
LOVE'S A LOADED GUN, Alice Cooper, 91-38
LOVE'S ABOUT TO CHANGE MY HEART, Donna Summer, 89-20
LOVE'S BEEN GOOD TO ME, Frank Sinatra, 69-8
LOVE'S COMIN' AT YA, Melba Moore, 82-15
LOVE'S CRASHING WAVES, Difford and Tilbrook, 84-57
LOVE'S EASY TEARS, Cocteau Twins, 86-53
LOVE'S GONNA GET YOU, UK Players, 83-52
LOVE'S GONNA GET YOU, Jocelyn Brown, 86-70
LOVE'S GOT A HOLD ON ME, Zoo Experience – featuring Destry, 92-66
LOVE'S GOT A HOLD ON MY HEART, Steps, 99-2
LOVE'S GOT ME, Loose Ends, 90-40
LOVE'S GOT ME ON A TRIP SO HIGH, Loni Clark, 94-59
LOVE'S GOTTA HOLD ON ME, Dollar, 79-4
LOVE'S GREAT ADVENTURE, Ultravox, 84-12
LOVE'S JUST A BROKEN HEART, Cilla Black, 66-5
LOVE'S MADE A FOOL OF YOU:
 Crickets, 59-26
 Buddy Holly, 64-39
 Matchbox, 81-63
LOVE'S ON EVERY CORNER, Dannii Minogue, 92-44
LOVE'S SUCH A WONDERFUL THING, Real Thing, 77-33
LOVE'S SWEET EXILE, Manic Street Preachers, 91-26, 97-55
LOVE'S TAKEN OVER, Chante Moore, 93-54
LOVE'S THEME, Love Unlimited Orchestra, 74-10
LOVE'S UNKIND:
 Donna Summer, 77-3
 Sophie Lawrence, 91-21
LOVE ZONE, Billy Ocean, 86-49
LOVEBIRDS, Dodgy, 93-65
LOVEDRIVE, Scorpions, 79-69
LOVEFOOL, Cardigans, 96-21, 97-2
LOVELIGHT (RIDE ON A LOVE TRAIN), Jayn Hanna, 96-42
LOVELY DAUGHTER, Merz, 99-60
LOVELY DAY:
 Bill Withers, 78-7, 88-4
 S.O.U.L. S.Y.S.T.E.M. introducing Michelle Visage *, 93-17
 Jazzy Jeff and Fresh Prince *, 98-37
LOVELY DAZE, Jazzy Jeff and Fresh Prince, 98-37
LOVELY MONEY, Damned, 82-42
LOVELY ONE, Jacksons, 80-29
LOVELY THING, Reggae Philharmonic Orchestra featuring Jazzy Joyce, 90-71

LOVENEST, Wedding Present, 91-58
LOVER, Dan Reed Network, 90-45
LOVER, Joe Roberts, 94-22
LOVER, Rachel McFarlane, 98-38
LOVER BOY, Chairmen Of The Board featuring General Johnson, 86-56
LOVER COME BACK TO ME, Dead Or Alive, 85-11
THE LOVER IN ME, Sheena Easton, 89-15
THE LOVER IN YOU, Sugarhill Gang, 82-54
LOVER LOVER LOVER, Ian McCulloch, 92-47
LOVER PLEASE, Vernons Girls, 62-16
A LOVER SPURNED, Marc Almond, 90-29
THE LOVER THAT YOU ARE, Pulse featuring Antoinette Roberson, 96-22
A LOVER'S CONCERTO, Toys, 65-5
A LOVER'S HOLIDAY, Change, 80-14
LOVER'S LANE, Georgio, 88-54
LOVERBOY, Billy Ocean, 85-15
LOVERIDE, Nuance featuring Vikki Love, 85-59
THE LOVERS, Alexander O'Neal, 88-28
LOVERS OF THE WORLD UNITE, David and Jonathan, 66-7
THE LOVERS WE WERE, Michael Ball, 94-63
LOVESICK, Gang Starr, 91-50
LOVESICK, Undercover featuring John Matthews, 93-62
LOVESICK BLUES, Frank Ifield with Norrie Paramor and his Orchestra, 62-1
LOVESONG, Cure, 89-18
LOVESTRUCK, Madness, 99-10
LOVETOWN, Peter Gabriel, 94-49
LOVEY DOVEY, Tony Terry, 88-44
LOVIN' (LET ME LOVE YOU), Apache Indian, 97-53
LOVIN' ON THE SIDE, Reid, 89-71
LOVIN' THINGS, Marmalade, 68-6
LOVIN' UP A STORM, Jerry Lee Lewis, 59-28
LOVIN' YOU:
 Minnie Riperton, 75-2
 Massivo featuring Tracy, 90-25
 Shanice, 92-54
 UBM, 98-46
 Sparkle, 99-65
LOVIN' YOU AIN'T EASY, Pagliaro, 72-31
LOVIN', LIVIN' AND GIVIN', Diana Ross, 78-54
LOVING AND FREE, Kiki Dee, 76-13
LOVING ARMS, Elvis Presley, 81-47
LOVING EVERY MINUTE, Lighthouse Family, 96-20
LOVING JUST FOR FUN, Kelly Marie, 80-21
LOVING ON THE LOSING SIDE, Tommy Hunt, 76-28
LOVING THE ALIEN, David Bowie, 85-19
LOVING YOU, Elvis Presley with the Jordanaires, 57-24
LOVING YOU, Donald Byrd, 81-41
LOVING YOU, Chris Rea, 82-65
LOVING YOU, Feargal Sharkey, 85-26
LOVING YOU AGAIN, Chris Rea, 87-47
LOVING YOU HAS MADE ME BANANAS, Guy Marks, 78-25
LOVING YOU IS SWEETER THAN EVER:
 Four Tops, 66-21
 Nick Kamen, 87-16
LOVING YOU MORE, B.T. featuring Vincent Covello, 95-28, 96-14

LOVING YOU'S A DIRTY JOB BUT SOMEBODY'S GOTTA DO IT, Bonnie Tyler, Guest vocalist Todd Rundgren, 85-73
LOW, Cracker, 94-43
LOW FIVE, Sneaker Pimps, 99-39
LOW LIFE IN HIGH PLACES, Thunder, 92-22
LOW RIDER, War, 76-12
LOWDOWN:
 Boz Scaggs, 76-28
 Hindsight, 87-62
LOWDOWN, Electrafixion, 95-54
THE LOYALISER, Fatima Mansions, 94-58
LUCAS WITH THE LID OFF, Lucas, 94-37
LUCHINI AKA (THIS IS IT), Camp Lo, 97-74
LUCILLE:
 Little Richard and his Band, 57-10
 Everly Brothers, 60-4
LUCILLE, Kenny Rogers, 77-1
LUCKY (from HELP [EP]), Radiohead – See Various Artists (EPs), 95-51
LUCKY DEVIL:
 Frank Ifield, 60-22
 Carl Dobkins Jr., 60-44
LUCKY FIVE, Russ Conway, 60-14
LUCKY LIPS, Cliff Richard and the Shadows, 63-4
LUCKY LOVE, Ace Of Base, 95-20
LUCKY LUCKY ME, Marvin Gaye, 94-67
LUCKY MAN, Verve, 97-7
LUCKY NUMBER, Lene Lovich, 79-3
THE LUCKY ONE, Laura Branigan, 84-56
LUCKY ONE, Amy Grant, 94-60
THE LUCKY 7 MEGAMIX [M], UK Mixmasters, 91-43
LUCKY STAR, Madonna, 84-14
LUCKY STARS, Dean Friedman, 78-3
LUCKY TOWN (LIVE), Bruce Springsteen, 93-48
LUCKY YOU, Lightning Seeds, 94-43, 95-15
LUCRETIA MY REFLECTION, Sisters of Mercy, 88-20
LUCY, Habit, 88-56
LUCY IN THE SKY WITH DIAMONDS, Elton John, 74-10
LUDI, Dream Warriors, 91-39
LUKA, Suzanne Vega, 87-23
LULLABY, Cure, 89-5
LULLABY, Shawn Mullins, 99-9
LULLABY NO. 2 LOVE ON BOARD (from THE FRIENDS AGAIN [EP]), Friends Again, 84-59
LULLABY OF BROADWAY, Winifred Shaw, 76-42
LULLABY OF THE LEAVES, Ventures, 61-43
LUMBERED, Lonnie Donegan and his Group, 61-6
LUMP, Presidents Of The United States Of America, 96-15
THE LUNATICS (HAVE TAKEN OVER THE ASYLUM), Fun Boy Three, 81-20
LUSH 3, Orbital, 93-43
LUST FOR LIFE, Iggy Pop, 96-26
LUTON AIRPORT, Cats U.K., 79-22
LUV DUP, High Fidelity, 98-70
LUV 4 LUV, Robin S, 93-11
LUV'D UP, Crush, 96-45
LUVSTUFF, Sagat, 94-71
LYDIA, Dean Friedman, 78-31
LYIN' EYES, Eagles, 75-23
M'LADY, Sly and the Family Stone, 68-32
M.O.R., Blur, 97-15
MA BAKER, Boney M, 77-2
MA BAKER / SOMEBODY SCREAM [M], Boney M vs Horny United, 99-22
MA (HE'S MAKIN' EYES AT ME):
 Johnny Otis Show; Johnny Otis his Orchestra with Marie Adams and the Three Tons of Joy, 57-2
 Lena Zavaroni, 74-10

MR FRIDAY NIGHT, Lisa Moorish, 96-24
MR. GUDER, Carpenters, 74-12
MR. GUITAR, Bert Weedon, 61-47
MR. HANKEY THE CHRISTMAS POO, Mr. Hankey Poo (an early '50s recording performed by Cowboy Timmy), 99-4
MR. JONES, Counting Crows, 94-28
MISTER JONES, Out Of My Hair, 95-73
MISTER KIRK'S NIGHTMARE (from COMBAT DANCING [EP]), 4 Hero, 90-73
MR LEE, Diana Ross, 88-58
MR. LOVERMAN, Shabba Ranks, 92-23, 93-3
MR. MANIC AND SISTER COOL, Shakatak, 87-56
MR. PHARMACIST, Fall, 86-75
MR. PORTER, Mickie Most, 63-45
MR. PRESIDENT, D. B. M. and T., 70-33
MR. RAFFLES (MAN, IT WAS MEAN), Steve Harley and Cockney Rebel, 75-13
MISTER SANDMAN:
Dickie Valentine with Johnny Douglas and his Orchestra, 54-5
Four Aces featuring Al Alberts, 55-9
Max Bygraves, 55-16
MR. SANDMAN, Chordettes, 54-11
MR. SECOND CLASS, Spencer Davis Group, 68-35
MR. SLEAZE, Bananarama, 87-3
MR. SOFT, Cockney Rebel, 74-8
MR. SOLITAIRE, Animal Nightlife, 84-25
MR. SUCCESS, Frank Sinatra, 58-25
MR. TAMBOURINE MAN, Byrds, 65-1
MR. TELEPHONE MAN, New Edition, 85-19
MR. VAIN, Culture Beat, 93-1
MR. WENDAL, Arrested Development, 93-4
MR. WONDERFUL, Peggy Lee, 57-5
MR. ZERO, Keith Relf, 66-50
MISTLETOE AND WINE, Cliff Richard, 88-1
MISTY:
Johnny Mathis, 60-12
Ray Stevens, 75-2
MISTY BLUE, Dorothy Moore, 76-5
MISTY MORNING, ALBERT BRIDGE, Pogues, 89-41
MISUNDERSTANDING, Genesis, 80-42
MISUNDERSTOOD MAN, Cliff Richard, 95-19
MITTAGEISEN (METAL POSTCARD), Siouxsie and the Banshees, 79-47
MIX IT UP, Dan Reed Network, 91-49
MIXED EMOTIONS, Rolling Stones, 89-36
MIXED TRUTH, Ragga Twins, 92-65
MIYAKO HIDEAWAY, Marion, 98-45
MMM MMM MMM MMM, Crash Test Dummies, 94-2
MMMBOP, Hanson, 97-1
MO MONEY MO PROBLEMS, Notorious B.I.G. featuring Puff Daddy and Mase, 97-6
MOAN & GROAN, Mark Morrison, 97-7
MOANIN', Chris Farlowe, 67-46
MOB RULES, Black Sabbath, 81-46
MOBILE, Ray Burns with Eric Jupp and his Orchestra, 55-4
MOCKIN' BIRD HILL, Migil 5, 64-10
MOCKINGBIRD:
Inez and Charlie Foxx, 69-33
Carly Simon, 74-34
Belle Stars, 82-51
THE MODEL, Kraftwerk, 81-36, 81-1

MODERN GIRL, Sheena Easton, 80-56, 80-8
MODERN GIRL, Meat Loaf, 84-17
MODERN LOVE, David Bowie, 83-2
MODERN ROMANCE (I WANT TO FALL IN LOVE AGAIN), Francis Rossi and Bernard Frost, 85-54
THE MODERN WORLD, Jam, 77-36, 80-52, 83-51
MODUS OPERANDI, Photek, 98-66
MOIRA JANE'S CAFE, Definition Of Sound, 92-34
MOLLIE'S SONG, Beverley Craven, 93-61
MOLLY, Carrie, 98-56
MOMENT OF MY LIFE, Bobby D'Ambrosio featuring Michelle Weeks, 97-23
MOMENTS IN LOVE, Art Of Noise, 85-51
MOMENTS IN SOUL, J.T. and the Big Family, 90-7
MOMENTS OF PLEASURE, Kate Bush, 93-26
MON AMOUR TOKYO, Pizzicato Five, 97-72
MONA, Craig McLachlan and Check 1-2, 90-2
MONA LISA, Conway Twitty, 59-5
MONDAY MONDAY, Mama's and the Papa's, 66-3
MONDAY MORNING, Candyskins, 97-34
MONDAY MORNING 5:19, Rialto, 97-37
MONEY:
Bern Elliott and the Fenmen, 63-14
Flying Lizards, 79-5
Backbeat Band, 94-48
MONEY, Dan Reed Network, 90-45
MONEY, Charli Baltimore, 98-12
(MONEY CAN'T) BUY ME LOVE, Blackstreet, 97-18
MONEY DON'T MATTER 2 NIGHT, Prince and the New Power Generation, 92-19
THE MONEY EP [EP], Skin, 94-18
MONEY (EVERYBODY LOVES HER), Gun, 89-73
MONEY FOR NOTHING, Dire Straits, 85-4
MONEY GO ROUND, Style Council, 83-11
MONEY GREEDY, Tricky, 98-25
MONEY HONEY, Bay City Rollers, 75-3
MONEY IN MY POCKET, Dennis Brown, 79-14
MONEY LOVE, Neneh Cherry, 92-23
MONEY, MONEY, MONEY, Abba, 76-3
MONEY THAT'S YOUR PROBLEM, Tonight, 78-66
MONEY'S TOO TIGHT (TO MENTION):
Valentine Brothers, 83-73
Simply Red, 85-13
MONEYTALKS, AC/DC, 90-36
MONIE IN THE MIDDLE, Monie Love, 90-46
THE MONKEES, Rampage, 95-51
THE MONKEES [EP], Monkees, 80-33
THE MONKEES [EP], Monkees, 89-62
MONKEY, George Michael, 88-13
MONKEY, Shaft, 92-61
MONKEY BUSINESS, Skid Row, 91-19
MONKEY BUSINESS, Danger Danger, 92-42
MONKEY CHOP, Dan-I, 79-30
MONKEY GONE TO HEAVEN, Pixies, 89-60
MONKEY MAN:
Maytals, 70-47
General Levy, 93-75
MONKEY SPANNER, Dave and Ansil Collins, 71-7
MONKEY WAH, Radical Rob, 92-67

MONKEY WRENCH, Foo Fighters, 97-12
MONSIEUR DUPONT, Sandie Shaw, 69-6
MONSTER, L7, 92-33
MONSTER MASH, Bobby (Boris) Pickett and the Crypt-Kickers, 73-3
MONSTERS AND ANGELS, Voice Of The Beehive, 91-17
MONTEGO BAY:
Bobby Bloom, 70-3
Freddie Notes and the Rudies, 70-45
Sugar Cane, 78-54
Amazulu, 86-16
MONTREAL, Wedding Present, 97-40
MONTREUX [EP], Simply Red, 92-11
MONTUNO, Gloria Estefan, 93-55
MONY MONY:
Tommy James and the Shondells, 68-1
Billy Idol, 87-7
Amazulu, 87-38
THE MOOD CLUB, Firstborn, 99-69
MOODY BLUE, Elvis Presley, 77-6
MOODY PLACES, Northside, 90-50
MOODY RIVER, Pat Boone, 61-18
MOOG ERUPTION, Digital Orgasm, 92-62
MOON, Virus, 97-36
MOON HOP, Derrick Morgan Music backing the Rudies, 70-49
MOON OVER BOURBON STREET, Sting, 86-44
MOON RIVER:
Danny Williams with Geoff Love and his Orchestra and the Rita Williams Singers, 61-1
Henry Mancini and his Orchestra, 61-44
Greyhound, 72-12
MOON SHADOW, Cat Stevens, 71-22
MOON TALK, Perry Como with Mitchell Ayres' Orchestra and the Ray Charles Singers, 58-17
MOONCHILD, Fields Of The Nephilim, 88-28
MOONGLOW/THEME FROM "PICNIC" [M]:
Morris Stoloff conducting the Columbia Pictures Orchestra, 56-7
Sounds Orchestral, 65-43
MOONLIGHT AND MUZAK, M, 79-33
MOONLIGHT AND ROSES (BRING BACK MEMORIES OF YOU), Jim Reeves, 71-34
MOONLIGHT GAMBLER, Frankie Laine with Ray Conniff and his Orchestra, 56-13
MOONLIGHT SERENADE, Glenn Miller and his Orchestra, 54-12, 76-13
MOONLIGHT SHADOW, Mike Oldfield, 83-4, 93-52
MOONLIGHTING, Leo Sayer, 75-2
MOONLIGHTING "THEME", Al Jarreau, 87-8
MOONSHINE SALLY, Mud, 75-10
MORE:
Perry Como and the Ray Charles Singers with Mitchell Ayres and his Orchestra, 56-10
Jimmy Young with Bob Sharples and his Music, 56-4
MORE, Sisters Of Mercy, 90-14
MORE . . . , High, 91-67
MORE AND MORE, Andy Williams, 67-45
MORE AND MORE, Captain Hollywood Project, 93-23
MORE AND MORE PARTY POPS [M], Russ Conway, 59-5
MORE BEATS + PIECES, Coldcut, 97-37
MORE GOOD OLD ROCK 'N ROLL [M], Dave Clark Five, 70-34

MORE HUMAN THAN HUMAN, White Zombie, 95-51
THE MORE I GET, THE MORE I WANT, HWS featuring Teddy Pendergrass, 94-35
THE MORE I SEE (THE LESS I BELIEVE), Fun Boy Three, 83-68
THE MORE I SEE YOU:
Joy Marshall, 66-34
Chris Montez, 66-3
Barbara Windsor and Mike Reid, 99-46
MORE LIFE IN A TRAMPS VEST, Stereophonics, 97-33
MORE LIKE THE MOVIES, Dr. Hook, 78-14
MORE LOVE, Feargal Sharkey, 88-44
MORE LOVE, Next Of Kin, 99-33
MORE MONEY FOR YOU AND ME [M], Four Preps, 61-39
MORE, MORE, MORE:
Andrea True Connection, 76-5
Bananarama, 93-24
MORE, MORE, MORE, Carmel, 84-23
MORE PARTY POPS [M], Russ Conway, 58-10
MORE THAN A FEELING, Boston, 77-22
MORE THAN A LOVER, Bonnie Tyler, 77-27
MORE THAN A WOMAN:
Tavares, 78-7
911, 98-2
MORE THAN EVER (COME PRIMA):
Malcolm Vaughan with the Michael Sammes Singers, 58-5
Robert Earl with Wally Stott and his Orchestra and Chorus, 58-26
MORE THAN I CAN BEAR, Matt Bianco, 85-50
MORE THAN I CAN SAY:
Crickets, 60-42
Bobby Vee, 61-4
Leo Sayer, 80-2
MORE THAN IN LOVE, Kate Robbins and Beyond, 81-2
MORE THAN LIKELY, PM Dawn featuring Boy George, 93-40
MORE THAN LOVE, Ken Dodd with Johnny Pearson and his Orchestra, 66-14
MORE THAN LOVE, Wet Wet Wet, 92-19
MORE THAN ONE KIND OF LOVE, Joan Armatrading, 90-75
MORE THAN PHYSICAL, Bananarama, 86-41
MORE THAN THIS:
Roxy Music, 82-6
Emmie, 99-5
MORE THAN US [EP] + lead track title, Travis, 98-16
MORE THAN WORDS, Extreme, 91-2
MORE THAN YOU KNOW, Martika, 90-15
THE MORE THEY KNOCK THE MORE I LOVE YOU, Gloria D. Brown, 85-57
MORE TO LIFE, Cliff Richard, 91-23
MORE TO LOVE, Volcano, 94-32
MORE TO THIS WORLD, Bad Boys Inc., 94-8
THE MORE YOU IGNORE ME, THE CLOSER I GET, Morrissey, 94-8
THE MORE YOU LIVE, THE MORE YOU LOVE, A Flock Of Seagulls, 84-26
MORGEN (ONE MORE SUNRISE) SLOW-FOX, Ivo Robic und die Sing-Masters, 59-23
MORNIN', Al Jarreau, 83-28
MORNING, Val Doonican, 71-12
MORNING, Wet Wet Wet, 96-16
THE MORNING AFTER (FREE AT LAST), Strike, 95-38
MORNING AFTERGLOW, Electrasy, 98-19

ONLY ONE, Peter Andre, 96-16
THE ONLY ONE, Thunder, 98-31
THE ONLY ONE I KNOW, Charlatans, 90-9
ONLY ONE ROAD, Celine Dion, 95-8
ONLY ONE WOMAN, Marbles, 68-5
ONLY ONE WORD, Propaganda, 90-71
THE ONLY RHYME THAT BITES, MC Tunes versus 808 State, 90-10, 99-53
ONLY SAW TODAY/INSTANT KARMA [M], Amos, 94-48
ONLY SIXTEEN:
  Craig Douglas, 59-1
  Sam Cooke, 59-23
  Al Saxon, 59-24
ONLY TENDER LOVE, Deacon Blue, 93-22
ONLY THE HEARTACHES, Houston Wells and the Marksmen, 63-22
ONLY THE LONELY, T'Pau, 89-28
ONLY THE LONELY (KNOW HOW I FEEL):
  Roy Orbison, 60-1
  Prelude *, 82-55
ONLY THE MOMENT, Marc Almond, 89-45
ONLY THE ONES WE LOVE, Tanita Tikaram, 91-69
ONLY THE STRONG SURVIVE, Billy Paul, 77-33
ONLY THE STRONG SURVIVE, DJ Krush, 96-71
ONLY THE STRONGEST SURVIVE, Hurricane #1, 98-19
THE ONLY THING THAT LOOKS GOOD ON ME IS YOU, Bryan Adams, 96-6
ONLY TIME WILL TELL, Asia, 82-54
ONLY TIME WILL TELL, Ten City, 92-63
ONLY TO BE WITH YOU, Roachford, 94-21
THE ONLY WAY IS UP, Yazz and the Plastic Population, 88-1
THE ONLY WAY OUT, Cliff Richard, 82-10
ONLY WHEN I LOSE MYSELF, Depeche Mode, 98-17
ONLY WHEN I SLEEP, Corrs, 97-58
ONLY WHEN YOU LEAVE, Spandau Ballet, 84-3
ONLY WITH YOU, Captain Hollywood Project, 93-67, 94-61
ONLY WOMEN BLEED, Julie Covington, 77-12
ONLY YESTERDAY, Carpenters, 75-7
ONLY YOU, Teddy Pendergrass, 78-41
ONLY YOU:
  Yazoo, 82-2, 99-38
  Flying Pickets, 83-1
ONLY YOU, Praise, 91-5
ONLY YOU, Portishead, 98-35
ONLY YOU, Casino, 99-72
ONLY YOU (AND YOU ALONE):
  Hilltoppers, 56-3
  Platters, 56-5, 57-18
  Mark Wynter, 64-38
  Jeff Collins *, 72-40
  Ringo Starr *, 74-28
  Child, 79-33
  John Alford *, 96-9
ONLY YOU CAN, Fox, 75-3
ONLY YOU CAN ROCK ME, U.F.O., 78-50
ONLY YOUR LOVE, Bananarama, 90-27
ONWARD CHRISTIAN SOLDIERS, Harry Simeone Chorale, 60-35, 61-36, 62-38
OO . . . AH . . . CANTONA, Oo La La, 92-64
OO-EEH BABY, Stonebridge McGuinness, 79-54
OOCHY KOOCHY, Baby Ford, 88-58

OOH AAH (G-SPOT), Wayne Marshall, 94-29, 96-50
OOH! AAH! CANTONA, 1300 Drums featuring The Unjustified Ancients Of M U, 96-11
OOH AAH.. JUST A LITTLE BIT, Gina G, 96-1
OOH-AH-AA (I FEEL IT), E.Y.C., 95-33
OOH BABY, Gilbert O'Sullivan, 73-18
OOH BOY, Rose Royce, 80-46
OOH I DO, Lynsey De Paul, 74-25
OOH I LIKE IT, Jonny L, 93-73
OOH LA LA, Joe 'Mr. Piano' Henderson, 60-46
OOH LA LA, Coolio, 97-14
OOH LA LA, Rod Stewart, 98-16
OOH LA LA, Wiseguys, 98-55, 99-2
OOH LA LA LA, Red Raw featuring 007, 95-59
OOH LA LA LA (LET'S GO DANCIN'), Kool And The Gang, 82-6
OOH! MY SOUL, Little Richard, 58-22
OOH TO BE AH, Kajagoogoo, 83-7
OOH-WAKKA-DOO-WAKKA-DAY, Gilbert O'Sullivan, 72-8
OOH! WHAT A LIFE, Gibson Brothers, 79-10
OOHHH BABY, Vida Simpson, 95-70
OOO LA LA LA, Teena Marie, 88-74
OOOIE, OOOIE, OOOIE, Prickly Heat, 98-57
OOOPS, 808 State featuring Bjork, 91-42
OOOPS UP, Snap!, 90-5
OOPS UP SIDE YOUR HEAD, Gap Band, 80-6, 87-20
007 (SHANTY TOWN):
  Desmond Dekker and the Aces, 67-14
  Musical Youth *, 83-26
OPAL MANTRA, Therapy?, 93-13
OPEN ARMS, Mariah Carey, 96-4
OPEN ROAD, Gary Barlow, 97-7
OPEN SESAME, Leila K, 93-23
OPEN UP, Mungo Jerry, 72-21
OPEN UP, Leftfield Lydon, 93-13
OPEN UP THE RED BOX, Simply Red, 86-61
OPEN UP YOUR HEART, Joan Regan, 55-19
OPEN UP YOUR MIND (LET ME IN), Real People, 91-70
OPEN YOUR EYES, Black Box, 91-48
OPEN YOUR HEART, Human League Blue, 81-6
OPEN YOUR HEART, M People, 95-9
OPEN YOUR HEART, Madonna, 86-4
OPEN YOUR MIND, 808 State, 91-38
OPEN YOUR MIND, Usura, 93-7, 97-21
THE OPERA HOUSE, Jack E. Makossa, 87-48
OPERAA HOUSE, Malcolm McLaren presents the World Famous Supreme Team Show, 90-75
OPERATOR, Midnight Star, 85-66
OPERATOR, Little Richard, 86-67
OPPORTUNITIES (LET'S MAKE LOTS OF MONEY), Pet Shop Boys, 86-11
OPPOSITES ATTRACT, Paula Abdul (duet with the Wild Pair), 90-2
OPTIMISTIC, Sounds Of Blackness, 91-45, 92-28
OPUS 40, Mercury Rev, 99-31
OPUS 17 (DON'T YOU WORRY 'BOUT ME), 4 Seasons featuring the "Sound" Of Frankie Valli, 66-20
ORANGE BLOSSOM SPECIAL, Spotnicks, 62-29
ORANGE CRUSH, R.E.M., 89-28
ORCHARD ROAD, Leo Sayer, 83-16

ORDINARY ANGEL, Hue And Cry, 88-42
ORDINARY DAY, Curiosity Killed The Cat, 87-11
ORDINARY GIRL, Alison Moyet, 87-43
ORDINARY LIVES, Bee Gees, 89-54
ORDINARY WORLD, Duran Duran, 93-6
ORIGINAL, Leftfield Halliday, 95-18
THE ORIGINAL BIRD DANCE, Electronica's, 81-22
ORIGINAL NUTTAH, UK Apachi with Shy Fx, 94-39
ORIGINAL SIN (THEME FROM THE SHADOW), Taylor Dayne, 95-63
ORINOCO FLOW (SAIL AWAY), Enya, 88-1
ORVILLE'S SONG, Keith Harris and Orville, 82-4
OSSIE'S DREAM . . . (SPURS ARE ON THEIR WAY TO WEMBLEY), Tottenham Hotspur F.A. Cup Final Squad Season 1980/81, 81-5
THE OTHER MAN'S GRASS (IS ALWAYS GREENER), Petula Clark, 67-20
THE OTHER SIDE, Aerosmith, 90-46
THE OTHER SIDE OF LOVE, Yazoo, 82-13
THE OTHER SIDE OF ME, Andy Williams, 76-42
THE OTHER SIDE OF SUMMER, Elvis Costello, 91-43
THE OTHER SIDE OF THE SUN, Janis Ian, 80-44
THE OTHER SIDE OF YOU, Mighty Lemon Drops, 86-67
THE OTHER WOMAN, THE OTHER MAN, Gerard Kenny, 84-69
OTHERNESS [EP], Cocteau Twins, 95-59
OUIJA BOARD, OUIJA BOARD, Morrissey, 89-18
OUR DAY WILL COME, Ruby and the Romantics, 63-38
OUR FAVOURITE MELODIES, Craig Douglas with Harry Robinson and his Orchestra, 62-9
OUR FRANK, Morrissey, 91-26
OUR HOUSE, Madness, 82-5
OUR LAST SONG TOGETHER, Neil Sedaka, 73-31
OUR LIPS ARE SEALED:
  Go-Go's, 82-47
  Fun Boy Three, 83-7
OUR LOVE, Elkie Brooks, 82-43
(OUR LOVE) DON'T THROW IT ALL AWAY, Andy Gibb, 79-32
OUR RADIO ROCKS, PJ and Duncan AKA, 95-15
OUR WORLD, Blue Mink, 70-17
OUT COME THE FREAKS:
  Was (Not Was), 84-41
  Was (Not Was) *, 88-44
OUT DEMONS OUT, Edgar Broughton Band, 70-39
OUT HERE ON MY OWN, Irene Cara, 82-58
OUT IN THE DARK, Lurkers, 79-72
OUT IN THE FIELDS, Gary Moore and Phil Lynott, 85-5
OUT OF CONTROL, Angelic Upstarts, 80-58
OUT OF CONTROL, Rolling Stones, 98-51
OUT OF CONTROL, Chemical Brothers, 99-21
OUT OF HAND, Mighty Lemon Drops, 87-66
OUT OF MY HEAD, Marradona, 94-38, 97-39
OUT OF MY MIND, Johnny Tillotson, 63-34
OUT OF MY MIND, Duran Duran, 97-21
OUT OF REACH, Vice Squad, 82-68

OUT OF REACH, Primitives, 88-25
OUT OF SEASON, Almighty, 93-41
OUT OF SIGHT.OUT OF MIND, Level 42, 98-49
OUT OF SPACE, Prodigy, 92-6, 96-52
OUT OF TEARS, Rolling Stones, 94-36
OUT OF THE BLUE, Debbie Gibson, 88-19
OUT OF THE BLUE, System F, 99-14
OUT OF THE SINKING:
  Paul Weller, 94-20
  Paul Weller, 96-16
OUT OF THE STORM, Incognito, 96-57
OUT OF THE VOID, Grass-Show, 97-75
OUT OF THIS WORLD, Tony Hatch, 62-50
OUT OF TIME:
  Chris Farlowe, 66-1, 75-44
  Dan McCafferty, 75-41
  Rolling Stones, 75-45
OUT OF TOUCH, Daryl Hall and John Oates, 84-48, 85-62
OUT OF TOWN, Max Bygraves, 56-18
OUT ON THE FLOOR, Dobie Gray, 75-42
OUT THERE, Dinosaur Jr, 93-44
OUT THERE, Friends Of Matthew, 99-61
OUT WITH HER, Blow Monkeys, 87-30
OUTA SPACE, Billy Preston, 72-44
OUTDOOR MINER, Wire, 79-51
OUTERSPACE GIRL, Beloved, 93-38
OUTLAW, Olive, 97-14
OUTRAGEOUS, Stix 'N' Stoned, 96-39
OUTSHINED, Soundgarden, 92-50
OUTSIDE, Omar, 94-43
OUTSIDE, George Michael, 98-2
OUTSIDE IN THE RAIN, Gwen Guthrie, 87-37
OUTSIDE MY WINDOW, Stevie Wonder, 80-52
OUTSIDE OF HEAVEN, Eddie Fisher with Hugo Winterhalter's Orchestra and Chorus, 53-1
OUTSIDE YOUR ROOM [EP] + lead track title, Slowdive, 93-69
OUTSTANDING:
  Gap Band, 83-68
  Kenny Thomas, 91-12
  Andy Cole, 99-68
OVER, Portishead, 97-25
OVER AND OVER, Dave Clark Five, 65-45
OVER AND OVER, James Boys, 73-39
OVER AND OVER, Shalamar, 83-23
OVER & OVER, Plux featuring Georgia Jones, 96-33
OVER AND OVER, Puff Johnson, 97-20
OVER MY SHOULDER, Mike and the Mechanics, 95-12
OVER RISING, Charlatans, 91-15
OVER THE EDGE, Almighty, 93-38
OVER THE HILLS AND FAR AWAY, Gary Moore, 86-20
OVER THE RAINBOW, Sam Harris, 85-67
OVER THE RAINBOW/YOU BELONG TO ME [M], Matchbox, 80-15
OVER THE RIVER, Bitty McLean, 95-27
OVER THE SEA, Jesse Rae, 85-65
OVER THE WEEKEND, Nick Heyward, 86-43
OVER THERE (I DON'T CARE), House Of Pain, 95-20
OVER TO YOU JOHN (HERE WE GO AGAIN) [M], Jive Bunny and the Mastermixers, 91-28
OVER UNDER SIDEWAYS DOWN, Yardbirds, 66-10
OVER YOU, Freddie and the Dreamers, 64-13

A PROMISE, Echo and the
Bunnymen, 81-49
THE PROMISE, Arcadia, 86-37
THE PROMISE, When In Rome,
89-58
PROMISE, Delirious?, 97-20
THE PROMISE, Essence, 98-27
PROMISE ME, Beverley Craven,
91-3
THE PROMISE OF A NEW DAY,
Paula Abdul, 91-52
THE PROMISE YOU MADE,
Cock Robin, 86-28
THE PROMISED LAND:
Chuck Berry, 65-26
Elvis Presley, 75-9
PROMISED LAND:
Joe Smooth, 89-56
Style Council, 89-27
PROMISED YOU A MIRACLE:
Simple Minds, 82-13
Simple Minds Live, 87-19
PROMISES, Ken Dodd with Geoff
Love and his Orchestra, 66-6
PROMISES, Eric Clapton, 78-37
PROMISES, Buzzcocks, 78-20
PROMISES (FRENCH MIX),
Basia, 88-48
PROMISES, Take That, 91-38
PROMISES, Paris Red, 93-59
PROMISES, Cranberries, 99-13
PROMISES, Def Leppard, 99-41
PROPHASE, Transa, 97-65
THE PROPHET, CJ Bolland, 97-19
PROTECT YOUR MIND (FOR
THE LOVE OF A
PRINCESS), DJ Sakin and
Friends, 99-4
PROTECTION, Massive Attack
with Tracey Thorn, 95-14
PROUD MARY:
Creedence Clearwater Revival, 69-8
Checkmates Ltd., featuring Sonny
Charles, 69-30
THE PROUD ONE, Osmonds,
75-5
PROUD TO FALL, Ian McCulloch,
89-51
PROVE IT, Television, 77-25
PROVE YOU WRONG (from
WHOSE FIST IS THIS
ANYWAY [EP]), Prong, 92-58
PROVE YOUR LOVE, Taylor
Dayne, 88-8
PSYCHE ROCK, Pierre
Henry/Michel Colombier, 97-58
PSYCHEDELIC SHACK,
Temptations, 70-33
PSYCHO BASE, Shades Of Rhythm,
97-57
PSYCHONAUT, Fields Of The
Nephilim, 89-35
PSYKO FUNK, Boo-Yaa T.R.I.B.E.,
90-43
A PUB WITH NO BEER, Slim
Dusty with Dick Carr and his
Bushlanders, 59-3
PUBLIC IMAGE, Public Image Ltd,
78-9
PUCKWUDGIE, Charlie Drake,
72-47
PUFF (UP IN SMOKE), Kenny
Lynch, 62-33
PULL THE WIRES FROM THE
WALL, Delgados, 98-69
PULL UP TO THE BUMPER:
Grace Jones, 81-53, 86-12
Patra, 95-50
PULLING MUSSELS (FROM
THE SHELL), Squeeze, 80-44
PULLING PUNCHES, David
Sylvian, 84-56
PULS(T)AR, Ben Liebrand, 90-68
PULVERTURM, Niels Van Gogh,
99-75
PUMP IT UP, Elvis Costello and the
Attractions, 78-24
PUMP ME UP, Grandmaster Melle
Mel and the Furious Five, 85-45
PUMP UP LONDON, Mr. Lee,
88-64
PUMP UP THE BITTER
(BRUTAL MIX), Star Turn On
45 Pints, 88-12
PUMP UP THE JAM, Technotronic
featuring Felly, 89-2, 96-36

PUMP UP THE VOLUME:
M/A/R/R/S, 87-1
Greed featuring Ricardo Da Force,
95-51
PUMPING ON YOUR STEREO,
Supergrass, 99-11
PUMPKIN, Tricky, 95-26
PUNCH AND JUDY, Marillion,
84-29
PUNKA, Kenickie, 96-43, 97-38
PUNKY REGGAE PARTY, Bob
Marley and the Wailers, 77-9
PUPPET MAN, Tom Jones, 71-49
PUPPET ON A STRING, Sandie
Shaw, 67-1
PUPPY LOVE:
Paul Anka, 60-33
Donny Osmonds, 1-72
THE PUPPY SONG, David
Cassidy, 73-1
PURE, Lightning Seeds, 89-16
PURE, G.T.O., 90-57
PURE, 3 Colours Red, 97-28
PURE MASSACRE, Silverchair,
95-71
PURE MORNING, Placebo, 98-4
PURE PLEASURE, Digital
Excitation, 92-37
PURELY BY COINCIDENCE,
Sweet Sensation, 75-11
PURGATORY, Iron Maiden, 81-52
PURITY, New Model Army, 90-61
PURPLE HAZE, Jimi Hendrix
Experience, 67-3
PURPLE HEATHER, Rod Stewart
with the Scottish Euro '96 Squad,
96-16
PURPLE LOVE BALLOON, Cud,
92-27
PURPLE MEDLEY [M], Prince,
95-33
THE PURPLE PEOPLE EATER:
Sheb Wooley, 58-12
Jackie Dennis, 58-29
PURPLE RAIN, Prince and the
Revolution, 84-8
PUSH, Moist, 94-35, 95-20
PUSH, Matchbox 20, 98-38
PUSH IT, Salt-N-Pepa, 88-41, 88-2
PUSH IT, Garbage, 98-9
PUSH THE BEAT, Mirage, 88-67
PUSH THE BEAT/BAUHAUS,
Cappella, 88-60
PUSH THE FEELING ON,
Nightcrawlers, 94-22, 95-3
PUSH UPSTAIRS, Underworld,
99-12
THE PUSHBIKE SONG, Mixtures,
71-2
PUSS, Jesus Lizard, 93-12
PUSS 'N BOOTS, Adam Ant, 83-5
PUSSYCAT, Mulu, 97-50
PUT A LIGHT IN THE
WINDOW, King Brothers with
Geoff Love and his Orchestra,
58-25
PUT A LITTLE LOVE IN YOUR
HEART:
Dave Clark Five, 69-31
Annie Lennox and Al Green,
88-28
PUT HIM OUT OF YOUR
MIND, Dr. Feelgood, 79-73
PUT IT THERE, Paul McCartney,
90-32
PUT MY ARMS AROUND YOU,
Kevin Kitchen, 85-64
PUT OUR HEADS TOGETHER,
O'Jays, 83-45
PUT THE LIGHT ON, Wet Wet
Wet, 91-56
PUT THE MESSAGE IN THE
BOX, Brian Kennedy, 97-37
PUT THE NEEDLE TO THE
RECORD, Criminal Element
Orchestra, 87-63
PUT YOUR ARMS AROUND
ME, Texas, 97-10
PUT YOUR FAITH IN ME,
Alison Limerick, 97-42
PUT YOUR HANDS
TOGETHER, D. Mob
featuring Nuff Juice, 90-7
PUT YOUR HANDS WHERE MY
EYES COULD SEE, Busta
Rhymes, 97-16

PUT YOUR HANDZ UP,
Whooliganz, 94-53
PUT YOUR HEAD ON MY
SHOULDER, Paul Anka, 59-7
PUT YOUR HOUSE IN ORDER
(from TRADE EP 2 [EP]),
Steve Thomas – See Various
Artists (EPs), 98-75
PUT YOUR LOVE IN ME, Hot
Chocolate, 77-10
PUT YOUR MONEY WHERE
YOUR MOUTH IS, Rose
Royce, 77-44
PUT YOURSELF IN MY PLACE:
Isley Brothers, 69-13
Elgins, 71-28
PUT YOURSELF IN MY PLACE,
Kylie Minogue, 94-11
PUTTING ON THE STYLE,
Lonnie Donegan and his Skiffle
Group, 57-1
PYJAMARAMA, Roxy Music, 73-10
QUADROPHONIA, Quadrophonia,
91-14
QUANDO M'INNAMORO (A
MAN WITHOUT LOVE),
Sandpipers, 68-33
QUANDO, QUANDO,
QUANDO:
Pat Boone, 62-41
Engelbert Humperdinck, 99-40
THE QUARTER MOON, V.I.P.'S,
80-55
QUARTER TO THREE, U.S.
Bonds, 61-7
QUE SERA MI VIDA (IF YOU
SHOULD GO), Gibson
Brothers, 79-5
QUE SERA (RERECORDED '88),
Chris Rea, 88-73
QUE SERA SERA, Geno
Washington and the Ram Jam
Band, 66-43
QUE TAL AMERICA, Two Man
Sound, 79-46
QUEEN FOR TONIGHT, Helen
Shapiro with Martin Slavin and
his Orchestra, 63-33
QUEEN JANE, Kingmaker, 93-29
QUEEN OF CLUBS, K C and the
Sunshine Band, 74-7
QUEEN OF HEARTS, Dave
Edmunds, 79-11
QUEEN OF HEARTS, Charlotte,
94-54
QUEEN OF MY SOUL, Average
White Band, 76-23
QUEEN OF NEW ORLEANS,
Jon Bon Jovi, 97-10
THE QUEEN OF 1964, Neil
Sedaka, 75-35
THE QUEEN OF OUTER
SPACE, Wedding Present, 92-23
QUEEN OF RAIN, Roxette, 92-28
QUEEN OF THE HOP, Bobby
Darin, 59-24
QUEEN OF THE NEW YEAR,
Deacon Blue, 90-21
QUEEN OF THE NIGHT,
Whitney Houston, 93-14
QUEEN OF THE RAPPING
SCENE (NOTHING EVER
GOES THE WAY YOU
PLAN), Modern Romance,
82-37
THE QUEEN'S BIRTHDAY
SONG, St. John's College School
Choir and the Band Of The
Grenadier Guards, 86-40
QUEEN'S FIRST EP [EP], Queen,
77-17
QUEER, Garbage, 95-13
QUEST, System 7, 93-74
QUESTION, Moody Blues, 70-2
THE QUESTION, Seven Grand
Housing Authority, 93-70
QUESTION OF FAITH,
Lighthouse Family, 98-21
A QUESTION OF LUST, Depeche
Mode, 86-28
A QUESTION OF TIME, Depeche
Mode, 86-17
QUESTIONS AND ANSWERS,
Sham 69, 79-18
QUESTIONS I CAN'T ANSWER,
Heinz, 64-39

QUICK JOEY SMALL (RUN
JOEY RUN), Kasenetz-Katz
Singing Orchestral Circus, 68-19
QUIEREME MUCHO (YOURS),
Julio Iglesias, 82-3
QUIET LIFE, Japan, 81-19
QUIT PLAYING GAMES (WITH
MY HEART), Backstreet Boys,
97-2
QUIT THIS TOWN, Eddie and the
Hot Rods, 78-36
QUITE A PARTY, Fireballs, 61-29
QUITE RIGHTLY SO, Procol
Harum, 68-50
QUOTE GOODBYE QUOTE,
Carolyne Mas, 80-71
QUOTH, Polygon Window, 93-49
R.I.P. PRODUCTIONS, R.I.P.
Productions, 97-58
R.O.C.K. IN THE U.S.A., John
Cougar Mellencamp, 86-67
R.R. EXPRESS, Rose Royce, 81-52
R.S.V.P., Five Star, 85-45
R.S.V.P., Jason Donovan, 91-17
R.S.V.P./FAMILIUS
HORRIBILUS, Pop Will Eat
Itself, 93-27
R TO THE A, CJ Lewis, 95-34
R U READY, Salt 'N Pepa, 97-24
R U SLEEPING, Indo, 98-31
RABBIT, Chas and Dave, 80-8
THE RACE, Yello, 88-7, 92-55
RACE, Tiger, 96-37
RACE FOR THE PRIZE, Flaming
Lips, 99-39
THE RACE IS ON, Dave Edmunds
and the Stray Cats, 81-34
THE RACE IS ON, Suzi Quatro,
78-43
RACE WITH THE DEVIL, Gene
Vincent and the Blue Caps,
56-28
RACE WITH THE DEVIL:
Gun, 68-8
Girlschool, 80-49
RACHEL, Al Martino, 53-10
RACHMANINOFF'S 18TH
VARIATION ON A THEME
BY PAGANINI, Winifred
Atwell with Wally Stott and his
Orchestra, 54-9
RACIST FRIEND, Special A.K.A.,
83-60
RADANCER, Marmalade, 72-6
RADAR LOVE:
Golden Earring, 73-7
Golden Earring 'Live', 77-44
Oh Well, 90-65
RADIATION VIBE, Fountains Of
Wayne, 97-32
RADICAL YOUR LOVER, Little
Angels featuring The Big Bad
Horns, 90-34
RADICCIO [EP], Orbital, 92-37
RADIO, Shaky featuring Roger
Taylor, 92-37
RADIO, Teenage Fanclub, 93-31
RADIO, Corrs, 99-18
RADIO AFRICA, Latin Quarter,
86-19
RADIO GA GA, Queen, 84-2
RADIO HEAD, Talking Heads,
87-52
RADIO HEART, Radio Heart
featuring Gary Numan, 87-35
RADIO MUSICOLA, Nik Kershaw,
86-43
RADIO ON, Ricky Ross, 96-35
RADIO RADIO, Elvis Costello and
the Attractions, 78-29
RADIO ROMANCE, Tiffany, 88-13
RADIO SONG, R.E.M., 91-28
RADIO WALL OF SOUND, Slade,
91-21
RADIO WAVES, Roger Waters,
87-74
RADIOACTIVE, Gene Simmons,
79-41
RADIOACTIVITY, Kraftwerk,
91-43
RAG DOLL, 4 Seasons featuring the
"Sound" of Frankie Valli, 64-2
RAG DOLL, Aerosmith, 90-42
RAG MAMA RAG, Band, 70-16
RAGAMUFFIN MAN, Manfred
Mann, 69-8

THE SKIN GAME, Gary Numan, 92-68

SKIN O' MY TEETH, Megadeth, 92-13

SKIN ON SKIN, Grace, 96-21

SKIN TRADE, Duran Duran, 87-22

THE SKIN UP [EP], Skin, 93-67

SKINHEAD MOONSTOMP, Symarip, 80-54

SKIP TO MY LU, Lisa Lisa, 94-34

SKUNK FUNK, Galliano, 92-41

SKWEEZE ME, PLEEZE ME, Slade, 73-1

A SKY-BLUE SHIRT AND A RAINBOW TIE, Norman Brooks, 54-17

SKY HIGH:
Jigsaw, 75-9
Newton, 95-56

SKY PILOT, Eric Burdon, 68-40

SKY PLUS, Nylon Moon, 96-43

SKY'S THE LIMIT, Notorious B.I.G. featuring 112, 98-35

SKYDIVE, Freefall featuring Jan Johnston, 98-75

THE SKYE BOAT SONG, Roger Whittaker and Des O'Connor, 86-10

SKYLARK, Michael Holliday with Norrie Paramor and his Orchestra, 60-39

SKYWRITER, Jackson Five, 73-25

SLADE – ALIVE AT READING '80 [EP], Slade, 80-44

SLAIN BY ELF, Urusei Yatsura, 98-63

SLAM, Humanoid, 89-54

SLAM, Onyx, 93-31

SLAM DUNK (DA FUNK), 5, 97-10

SLAM JAM, WWF Superstars, 92-4

SLANG, Def Leppard, 96-64

SLAP & TICKLE, Squeeze, 79-24

SLASH 'N' BURN, Manic Street Preachers, 92-20, 97-54

SLAVE NEW WORLD, Sepultura, 94-46

SLAVE TO LOVE, Bryan Ferry, 85-10

SLAVE TO THE GRIND, Skid Row, 91-43

SLAVE TO THE RHYTHM, Grace Jones, 85-12, 94-28

SLAVE TO THE VIBE, Aftershock, 93-11

SLAVES NO MORE, Blow Monkeys featuring Sylvia Tella, 89-73

SLEAZY BED TRACK, Bluetones, 98-35

SLEDGEHAMMER, Peter Gabriel, 86-4

SLEEP, Marion, 95-53, 96-17

SLEEP ALONE, Wonder Stuff, 91-43

SLEEP FREAK, Heavy Stereo, 95-46

SLEEP ON THE LEFT SIDE, Cornershop, 98-23

SLEEP TALK, Alyson Williams, 89-17

SLEEP WALK, Santo and Johnny, 59-22

SLEEP WELL TONIGHT, Gene, 94-36

SLEEP WITH ME, Birdland, 90-32

SLEEPER, Audioweb, 95-74, 96-50

SLEEPING BAG, ZZ Top, 85-27

SLEEPING IN, Menswear, 95-24

SLEEPING IN MY CAR, Roxette, 94-14

SLEEPING ON THE JOB, Gillan, 80-55

SLEEPING SATELLITE, Tasmin Archer, 92-1

SLEEPING WITH THE LIGHTS ON, Curtis Stigers, 92-53

SLEEPWALK, Ultravox, 80-29

SLEEPY JOE, Herman's Hermits, 68-12

SLEEPY SHORES, Johnny Pearson Orchestra, 71-8

SLID, Fluke, 93-59

SLIDE, Rah Band, 81-50

SLIDE, Goo Goo Dolls, 99-43

SLIGHT RETURN, Bluetones, 96-2

THE SLIGHTEST TOUCH, Five Star, 87-4

SLIP AND DIP, Coffee, 80-57

SLIP AND SLIDE, Medicine Head, 74-22

SLIP SLIDIN' AWAY, Paul Simon, 77-36

SLIP YOUR DISC TO THIS, Heatwave, 77-15

SLIPPERY PEOPLE (LIVE VERSION), Talking Heads, 84-68

SLIPPIN', DMX, 99-30

SLIPPING AWAY, Dave Edmunds, 83-60

SLOOP JOHN B, Beach Boys, 66-2

SLOPPY HEART, Frazier Chorus, 89-73

SLOW AND SEXY, Shabba Ranks (featuring Johnny Gill), 92-17

SLOW DOWN, John Miles, 77-10

SLOW DOWN, Loose Ends, 86-27

SLOW FLOW, Braxtons, 97-26

SLOW HAND, Pointer Sisters, 81-10

SLOW IT DOWN, East 17, 93-13

SLOW MOTION, Ultravox, 81-33

SLOW MOTION REPLAY, The, 93-35

SLOW RIVERS, Elton John and Cliff Richard, 86-44

SLOW TRAIN TO DAWN, The, 87-64

SLOW TRAIN TO PARADISE, Tavares, 78-62

SLOW TWISTIN', Chubby Checker, 62-23

SLOWDIVE, Siouxsie and the Banshees, 82-41

SLY, Massive Attack, 94-24

SMACK MY BITCH UP, Prodigy, 97-8

SMALL ADS, Small Ads, 81-63

SMALL BIT OF LOVE, Saw Doctors, 94-24

SMALL BLUE THING, Suzanne Vega, 86-65

SMALL SAD SAM, Phil McLean, 62-34

SMALL TOWN, John Cougar Mellencamp, 86-53

SMALL TOWN CREED, Kane Gang, 84-60

A SMALL VICTORY, Faith No More, 92-29

SMALLTOWN BOY:
Bronski Beat, 84-3, 91-32
UK, 96-74

SMARTY PANTS, First Choice, 73-9

SMASH IT UP, Damned, 79-35

SMELLS LIKE NIRVANA, "Weird Al" Yankovic, 92-58

SMELLS LIKE TEEN SPIRIT:
Nirvana, 91-7
Abigail, 94-29

SMILE:
Nat "King" Cole, 54-2
Robert Downey Jr., 93-68

SMILE, Pussycat, 76-24

THE SMILE, David Essex, 83-52

SMILE, Audrey Hall featuring Sly Dunbar and Robert Shakespeare, 86-14

SMILE, Aswad featuring Sweetie Irie, 90-53

SMILE, Supernaturals, 97-23

A SMILE IN A WHISPER, Fairground Attraction, 88-75

SMILER, Heavy Stereo, 95-46

SMOKE, Natalie Imbruglia, 98-5

SMOKE GETS IN YOUR EYES:
Platters, 59-1
Blue Haze, 72-32
Bryan Ferry, 74-17
John Alford, 96-13

SMOKE ON THE WATER:
Deep Purple, 77-21
Deep Purple (from New Live and Rare Volume 3 [EP]), 80-48
Rock Aid Armemia, 89-39

SMOKEBELCH II, Sabres Of Paradise, 93-55

SMOKESTACK LIGHTNIN', Howlin' Wolf, 64-42

SMOKEY BLUE'S AWAY, New Generation, 68-38

SMOKIN' IN THE BOY'S ROOM:
Brownsville Station, 74-27
Motley Crue, 85-71, 86-51

SMOKIN' ME OUT, Warren G featuring Ron Isley, 97-14

SMOOTH, Santana featuring Rob Thomas, 99-75

SMOOTH CRIMINAL, Michael Jackson, 88-8

SMOOTH OPERATOR, Sade, 84-19

SMOOTH OPERATOR, Big Daddy Kane, 89-65

SMOOTHIN' GROOVIN', Ingram, 83-56

SMUGGLER'S BLUES, Glenn Frey, 85-22

THE SMURF, Tyrone Brunson, 82-52

THE SMURF SONG, Father Abraham, 78-2

THE SNAKE, Al Wilson, 75-41

SNAKE BITE [EP], David Coverdale's Whitesnake, 78-61

SNAKE IN THE GRASS, Dave Dee, Dozy, Beaky, Mick and Tich, 69-23

SNAKEDRIVER (from SOUND OF SPEED [EP]), Jesus And Mary Chain, 93-30

SNAP MEGAMIX [M], Snap!, 91-10

SNAPPINESS, BBG, 90-28, 96-50

SNEAKIN' SUSPICION, Dr. Feelgood, 77-47

SNEAKING OUT THE BACK DOOR, Matt Bianco, 84-44

SNOBBERY AND DECAY, Act, 87-60

SNOOKER LOOPY, Matchroom Mob with Chas and Dave, 86-6

SNOOP'S UPSIDE YA HEAD, Snoop Doggy Dogg featuring Charlie Wilson, 96-12

SNOOPY VS. THE RED BARON:
Royal Guardsmen, 67-8
Hotshots, 73-4

SNOT RAP, Kenny Everett featuring Sid Snot and Cupid Stunt, 83-9

SNOW, O.R.N., 97-61

SNOW COACH, Russ Conway, 59-7

SNOWBIRD, Anne Murray, 70-23

SNOWBOUND FOR CHRISTMAS, Dickie Valentine, 57-28

THE SNOWS OF NEW YORK, Chris De Burgh, 95-60

SO AMAZING, Luther Vandross, 87-33

SO BEAUTIFUL, Urban Cookie Collective, 95-68

SO BEAUTIFUL, Chris De Burgh, 97-29

SO CALLED FRIEND, Texas, 93-30

SO CLOSE, Diana Ross, 83-43

SO CLOSE, Hall and Oates, 90-69

SO CLOSE, Dina Carroll, 92-20

SO CLOSE TO LOVE, Wendy Moten, 94-35

SO COLD THE NIGHT, Communards, 86-8

SO DAMN COOL, Ugly Kid Joe, 92-44

SO DEEP, Reese Project, 93-54

SO DEEP IS THE NIGHT, Ken Dodd, 64-31

SO DO I, Kenny Ball and his Jazzmen, 62-14

SO EMOTIONAL, Whitney Houston, 87-5

SO FAR AWAY, Dire Straits, 85-20

SO FINE, Howard Johnson, 82-45

SO FINE, Kinane, 98-63

SO GOOD, Roy Orbison, 67-32

SO GOOD, Eternal, 94-13

SO GOOD, Boyzone, 95-3

SO GOOD, Juliet Roberts, 98-15

SO GOOD, SO RIGHT/IN THE THICK OF IT, Brenda Russell, 80-51

SO GOOD TO BE BACK HOME AGAIN, Tourists, 80-8

SO GOOD (TO COME HOME TO), Ivan Matias, 96-69

SO GROOVY, Wendell Williams, 91-74

SO HARD, Pet Shop Boys, 90-4

SO HELP ME GIRL, Gary Barlow, 97-11

SO HERE I AM, UB40, 82-25

SO HOT, J.C., 98-74

SO IN LOVE, Orchestral Manoeuvres In The Dark, 85-27

SO IN LOVE (THE REAL DEAL), Judy Cheeks, 93-27

SO IN LOVE WITH YOU, Freddy Breck, 74-44

SO IN LOVE WITH YOU, Spear Of Destiny, 88-36

SO IN LOVE WITH YOU, Texas, 94-28

SO IN LOVE WITH YOU, Duke, 96-66, 96-22

SO INTO YOU, Michael Watford, 94-53

(SO IT WAS . . . SO IT IS) SO IT WILL ALWAYS BE, Everly Brothers, 63-23

SO LET ME GO FAR, Dodgy, 95-30

SO LITTLE TIME, Arkarna, 97-46

SO LONELY, Police, 80-6

SO LONG, Fischer-Z, 80-72

SO LONG, Fierce, 99-15

SO LONG BABY, Del Shannon, 61-10

SO LOW, Ocean Colour Scene, 99-34

SO MACHO, Sinitta, 86-2

SO MANY WAYS, Braxtons, 97-32

SO MANY WAYS, Ellie Campbell, 99-26

SO MUCH IN LOVE:
Tymes, 63-21
All-4-One, 94-60, 94-49

SO MUCH IN LOVE, Mighty Avengers, 64-46

SO MUCH LOVE, Tony Blackburn, 68-31

SO MUCH TROUBLE IN THE WORLD, Bob Marley and the Wailers, 79-56

SO NATURAL, Lisa Stansfield, 93-15

SO NEAR TO CHRISTMAS, Alvin Stardust, 84-29

SO PURE, Baby D, 96-3

SO PURE, Alanis Morissette, 99-38

SO REAL, Love Decade, 91-14

SO RIGHT, Railway Children, 90-68

SO RIGHT, K-Klass, 92-20

SO SAD THE SONG, Gladys Knight and the Pips, 76-20

SO SAD (TO WATCH GOOD LOVE GO BAD), Everly Brothers, 60-4

SO SORRY, I SAID, Liza Minnelli, 89-62

SO TELL ME WHY, Poison, 91-25

SO THE STORY GOES, Living In A Box, 87-34

SO THIS IS ROMANCE, Linx, 81-15

SO TIRED, Frankie Vaughan with Alyn Ainsworth and his Orchestra, 67-21

SO TIRED, Ozzy Osbourne, 84-20

SO TIRED OF BEING ALONE, Sybil, 96-53

SO WHAT, Gilbert O'Sullivan, 90-70

SO WHAT!, Ronny Jordan, 92-32

SO WHATCHA GONNA DO NOW?, Public Enemy, 95-50

SO YOU WIN AGAIN, Hot Chocolate, 77-1

SO YOU'D LIKE TO SAVE THE WORLD, Lloyd Cole, 93-72

SO YOUNG, Suede, 93-22

SO YOUNG, Corrs, 98-6

SOAPBOX, Little Angels, 93-33

SOBER, Drugstore, 98-68

SOBER, Jennifer Paige, 99-68

SOCKIT2ME, Missy Misdemeanor Elliott featuring Da Brat, 97-33

SOFT AS YOUR FACE, Soup Dragons, 87-66

SOFT TOP, HARD SHOULDER, Chris Rea, 93-53

SOFTLY AS I LEAVE YOU, Matt Monro, 62-10

TEXAS COWBOYS, Grid, 93-21, 94-17

THA CROSSROADS, Bone Thugs-N-Harmony, 96-8

THA DOGGFATHER, Snoop Doggy Dogg, 98-36

THA HORNS OF JERICHO, DJ Supreme, 98-29

THA WILDSTYLE: DJ Supreme, 96-39, 97-24 Porn Kings V's DJ Supreme *, 99-10

THANK ABBA FOR THE MUSIC [M], Steps Tina Cousins Cleopatra B*Witched Billie, 99-4

THANK GOD IT'S CHRISTMAS, Queen, 84-21

THANK GOD IT'S FRIDAY, R. Kelly, 99-68

THANK U, Alanis Morissette, 98-5

THANK U VERY MUCH, Scaffold, 67-4

THANK YOU, Pale Fountains, 82-48

THANK YOU, Boyz II Men, 95-26

THANK YOU FOR A GOOD YEAR, Alexander O'Neal, 88-30

THANK YOU FOR BEING A FRIEND, Andrew Gold, 78-42

THANK YOU FOR HEARING ME, Sinead O'Connor, 94-13

THANK YOU FOR THE MUSIC, Abba, 83-33

THANK YOU FOR THE PARTY, Dukes (Bugatti and Musker), 82-53

THANK YOU MY LOVE, Imagination, 84-22

THANK YOU WORLD, World Party, 91-68

THANKS A LOT, Brenda Lee, 65-41

THANKS FOR GIVING US CHRISTMAS (from SONGS FOR CHRISTMAS '87 [EP]), Minipops, 87-39

THANKS FOR MY CHILD, Cheryl Pepsi Riley, 89-75

THANKS FOR SAVING MY LIFE, Billy Paul, 74-33

THANKS FOR THE MEMORY (WHAM BAM THANK YOU MAM), Slade, 75-7

THANKS FOR THE NIGHT, Damned, 84-43

THAT CERTAIN SMILE, Midge Ure, 85-28

THAT DON'T IMPRESS ME MUCH, Shania Twain, 99-3

THAT GIRL, Stevie Wonder, 82-39

THAT GIRL, Maxi Priest featuring Shaggy, 96-15

THAT GIRL BELONGS TO YESTERDAY, Gene Pitney, 64-7

THAT GIRL (GROOVY SITUATION), Freddie McGregor, 87-47

THAT JOKE ISN'T FUNNY ANYMORE, Smiths, 85-49

THAT LADY, Isley Brothers, 73-14

THAT LOOK, De'lacy, 96-19

THAT LOOK IN YOUR EYE, Ali Campbell, 95-5

THAT LOVING FEELING, Cicero, 92-46

THAT LUCKY OLD SUN, Velvets, 61-46

THAT MAN (HE'S ALL MINE), Inner City, 90-42

THAT MEANS A LOT, P.J. Proby, 65-30

THAT NOISE, Anthony Newley, 62-34

THAT OLD BLACK MAGIC, Sammy Davis, 55-16

THAT OLE DEVIL CALLED LOVE, Alison Moyet, 85-2

THAT SAME OLD FEELING, Pickettywitch, 70-5

THAT SOUND, Michael Moog, 99-32

THAT SOUNDS GOOD TO ME [M], Jive Bunny and the Mastermixers, 90-4

THAT THING YOU DO!, Wonders, 97-22

THAT WAS MY VEIL, John Parish + Polly Jean Harvey, 96-75

THAT WAS THE DAY [RR] (from DIS-INFECTED [EP]), The, 94-17

THAT WAS THEN BUT THIS IS NOW, ABC, 83-18

THAT WAS THEN, THIS IS NOW, Monkees, 86-68

THAT WAS YESTERDAY, Foreigner, 85-28

THAT WOMAN'S GOT ME DRINKING, Shane MacGowan and the Popes, 94-34

THAT'LL BE THE DAY: Crickets, 57-1 Everly Brothers, 65-30

THAT'LL DO NICELY, Bad Manners, 83-49

THAT'S ALL, Genesis, 83-16

THAT'S AMORE, Dean Martin with Dick Stabile and his Orchestra, 54-2, 96-43

THAT'S ENTERTAINMENT, Jam, 81-21, 83-60, 91-57

THAT'S HOW A LOVE SONG WAS BORN, Ray Burns with the Coronets, 55-14

THAT'S HOW I FEEL ABOUT YOU, Londonbeat, 92-69

THAT'S HOW I'M LIVIN', Ice-T, 93-21

THAT'S HOW I'M LIVING, Toni Scott, 89-48, 90-63

THAT'S HOW STRONG MY LOVE IS, In Crowd, 65-48

THAT'S JUST THE WAY IT IS, Phil Collins, 90-26

THAT'S LIFE, Frank Sinatra, 66-46

THAT'S LIVIN' ALRIGHT, Joe Fagin, 84-3

THAT'S LOVE, Billy Fury with the Four Jays, 60-19

THAT'S LOVE, THAT IT IS, Blancmange, 83-33

THAT'S MY DOLL, Frankie Vaughan with Wally Stott and his Orchestra, 59-28

THAT'S MY HOME, Mr. Acker Bilk and his Paramount Jazz Band (Vocal Mr. Acker Bilk), 61-7

THAT'S NICE, Neil Christian, 66-14

THAT'S RIGHT, Deep River Boys, 56-29

THAT'S THE WAY, Honeycombs, 65-12

THAT'S THE WAY GOD PLANNED IT, Billy Preston, 69-11

THAT'S THE WAY (I LIKE IT): K C and the Sunshine Band, 75-4, 91-59 Dead Or Alive, 84-22 Clock, 98-11

THAT'S THE WAY I WANNA ROCK N ROLL, AC/DC, 88-22

THAT'S THE WAY IT FEELS, Two Nations, 87-74

THAT'S THE WAY IT IS, Mel and Kim, 88-10

THAT'S THE WAY IT IS, Celine Dion, 99-12

THAT'S THE WAY LOVE GOES, Charles Dickens, 65-37

THAT'S THE WAY LOVE GOES, Young M.C., 91-65

THAT'S THE WAY LOVE GOES, Janet Jackson, 93-2

THAT'S THE WAY LOVE IS: Ten City, 89-8 Volcano with Sam Cartwright, 95-72

THAT'S THE WAY LOVE IS, Bobby Brown, 93-56

THAT'S THE WAY OF THE WORLD, D Mob featuring Cathy Dennis, 90-48

THAT'S THE WAY THE MONEY GOES, M, 80-45

THAT'S THE WAY YOU DO IT, Purple Kings, 94-26

THAT'S WHAT FRIENDS ARE FOR, Deniece Williams, 77-8

THAT'S WHAT FRIENDS ARE FOR, Dionne and Friends featuring Elton John, Gladys Knight and Stevie Wonder, 85-16

THAT'S WHAT I LIKE [M], Jive Bunny and the Mastermixers, 89-1

THAT'S WHAT I THINK, Cyndi Lauper, 93-31

THAT'S WHAT I WANT, Marauders, 63-43

THAT'S WHAT I WANT TO BE, Neil Reid, 72-45

THAT'S WHAT LIFE IS ALL ABOUT, Bing Crosby with the Pete Moore Orchestra, 75-41

THAT'S WHAT LOVE CAN DO, Toutes Les Filles, 99-44

THAT'S WHAT LOVE IS FOR, Amy Grant, 91-60

THAT'S WHAT LOVE WILL DO, Joe Brown and the Bruvvers, 63-3

THAT'S WHEN I REACH FOR MY REVOLVER, Moby, 96-50

THAT'S WHEN I THINK OF YOU, 1927, 89-46

THAT'S WHEN THE MUSIC TAKES ME, Neil Sedaka, 73-18

THAT'S WHERE MY MIND GOES, Slamm, 94-68

THAT'S WHERE THE HAPPY PEOPLE GO, Trammps, 76-35

THAT'S WHY I LIE, Ray-J, 98-71

THAT'S WHY I'M CRYING, Ivy League, 65-22

THAT'S WHY WE LOSE CONTROL, Young Offenders, 98-60

THAT'S YOU, Nat King Cole with the music of Nelson Riddle, 60-10

THE WAY WE WERE/TRY TO REMEMBER [M], Gladys Knight and the Pips, 75-4

THEM BONES, Alice In Chains, 93-26

THEM GIRLS/THEM GIRLS, Zig and Zag, 94-5

THEM HEAVY PEOPLE (from KATE BUSH ON STAGE [EP]), Kate Bush, 79-10

THEM THERE EYES, Emile Ford; Johnny Keating Music; Babs Knight Group, 60-18

THE THEME, Unique 3, 89-61

THEME, Sabres Of Paradise, 94-56

THE THEME, Dreem Teem, 97-34

THEME FOR A DREAM, Cliff Richard and the Shadows, 61-3

THEME FOR YOUNG LOVERS, Shadows, 64-12

THE THEME FROM "A SUMMER PLACE": Percy Faith and his Orchestra, 60-2 Norrie Paramor and his Orchestra, 60-36

THEME FROM 'CADE'S COUNTY', Henry Mancini and his Orchestra, 72-42

THEME FROM 'CHEERS' (WHERE EVERYBODY KNOWS YOUR NAME), Gary Portnoy, 84-58

THEME FROM "COME SEPTEMBER", Bobby Darin and his Orchestra, 61-50

THEME FROM DIXIE, Duane Eddy, 61-7

THEME FROM DR. KILDARE (THREE STARS WILL SHINE TONIGHT), Richard Chamberlain, 62-12

THEME FROM E.T. (THE EXTRA-TERRESTRIAL), John Williams, 82-17

THEME FROM "EXODUS": Ferrante and Teicher, 61-6 Semprini *, 61-25

THEME FROM FILM "THE LEGION'S LAST PATROL" (CONCERTO DISPERATO), Ken Thorne and his Orchestra; trumpet solo: Ray Davies, 63-4

THE THEME FROM GET CARTER, Roy Budd, 99-68

THEME FROM HARRY'S GAME, Clannad, 82-5

THE THEME FROM HILL STREET BLUES, Mike Post featuring Larry Carlton, 82-25

THEME FROM 'HONG KONG BEAT', Richard Denton and Martin Cook, 78-25

THEME FROM JURASSIC PARK: John Williams, 93-45 Soul City Orchestra *, 93-70

THEME FROM M*A*S*H* (SUICIDE IS PAINLESS): Mash, 80-1 Manic Street Preachers, 92-7

THEME FROM MAHOGANY "DO YOU KNOW WHERE YOU'RE GOING TO", Diana Ross, 76-5

THEME FROM MISSION: IMPOSSIBLE, Adam Clayton and Larry Mullen, 96-7

THEME FROM NEW YORK, NEW YORK, Frank Sinatra, 80-59, 86-4

"THEME FROM P.O.P.", Perfectly Ordinary People, 88-61

THEME FROM S-EXPRESS, S-Express, 88-1, 96-14

THEME FROM "SHAFT": Isaac Hayes, 71-4 Van Twist *, 85-57 Eddy and the Soulband, 85-13

THEME FROM SUPERMAN (MAIN TITLE), London Symphony Orchestra conducted by John Williams, 79-32

THEME FROM 'THE APARTMENT', Ferrante and Teicher, 60-44

THEME FROM THE DEER HUNTER (CAVATINA), Shadows, 79-9

THE THEME FROM THE FILM "LIMELIGHT": Ron Goodwin and his Orchestra, 53-3 Frank Chacksfield and his Orchestra *, 53-2 Jimmy Young *, 53-8

THEME FROM 'THE MAGNIFICENT SEVEN', Al Caiola and his Orchestra, 61-34

THEME FROM "THE PERSUADERS", John Barry, 71-13

THEME FROM THE PROFESSIONALS, Laurie Johnson's London Big Band, 97-36

A THEME FROM THE 'THREEPENNY OPERA' (MACK THE KNIFE): Billy Vaughn and his Orchestra, 56-12 "Unforgettable" sound of the Dick Hyman Trio, 56-9 Louis Armstrong and his All Stars, 56-8, 59-24

THEME FROM TRAVELLING MAN, Duncan Browne, 84-68

THEME FROM TURNPIKE [EP] + lead track title, Deus, 96-68

THEME FROM TV'S "VIETNAM" – CANON IN D MAJOR (PACHEBEL), Orchestre De Chambre Jean-Francois Paillard, 88-61

(THEME FROM) VALLEY OF THE DOLLS, Dionne Warwick, 68-28

THE THEME FROM "WE'LL MEET AGAIN", Denis King and his Orchestra, 82-36

THEME FROM Z-CARS (JOHNNY TODD): Johnny Keating, 62-8 Norrie Paramor Orchestra, 62-33

THE THEME: IT'S PARTY TIME, Tracey Lee, 97-51

THEME MUSIC FROM THE FILM "2001" A SPACE ODYSSEY THUS SPAKE ZARATHUSTRA: Philharmonia Orchestra conducted by Lorin Maazel, 69-33
Deodato arranged and conducted by Eumir Deodato *, 73-7
THEME ONE, Cozy Powell, 79-62
THEME SONG FROM "WHICH WAY IS UP", Stargard, 78-19
THEN, Charlatans, 90-12
THEN CAME YOU: Dionne Warwicke and the Detroit Spinners, 74-29
Junior Giscombe, 92-32
THEN HE KISSED ME: Crystals, 63-2
Beach Boys *, 67-4
Gary Glitter *, 81-39
THEN I FEEL GOOD, Katherine E, 92-56
THEN I KISSED HER, Beach Boys, 67-4
THEN YOU CAN TELL ME GOODBYE, Casinos, 67-28
THEN YOU TURN AWAY, Orchestral Manoeuvres In The Dark, 91-50
THERE AIN'T NOTHIN' LIKE THE LOVE, Montage, 97-64
THERE AIN'T NOTHING LIKE SHAGGIN', Tams, 87-21
THERE ARE MORE QUESTIONS THAN ANSWERS, Johnny Nash, 72-9
THERE ARE MORE SNAKES THAN LADDERS, Captain Sensible, 84-57
THERE BUT FOR FORTUNE, Joan Baez, 65-8
THERE BUT FOR THE GRACE OF GOD, Fire Island featuring: Love Nelson, 94-32
THERE GOES MY EVERYTHING: Engelbert Humperdinck, 67-2
Elvis Presley, 71-6
THERE GOES MY FIRST LOVE, Drifters, 75-3
THERE GOES THAT SONG AGAIN, Gary Miller, 61-32
THERE GOES THE NEIGHBORHOOD, Sheryl Crow, 98-19
THERE I GO AGAIN, Power Of Dreams, 92-65
THERE I GO (SE PER TE C'E SOLTANTO QUELL'UOMO), Vikki Carr, 67-50
THERE I'VE SAID IT AGAIN: Al Saxon and his Orchestra, 61-48
Bobby Vinton, 63-34
THERE IS A LIGHT THAT NEVER GOES OUT, Smiths, 92-25
THERE IS A MOUNTAIN, Donovan, 67-8
THERE IS A STAR, Pharao, 95-43
THERE IS ALWAYS SOMETHING THERE TO REMIND ME, Housemartins, 88-35
THERE IS NO LOVE BETWEEN US ANYMORE, Pop Will Eat Itself, 88-66
THERE IT IS, Shalamar, 82-5
THERE MUST BE A REASON, Frankie Laine with Paul Weston and his Orchestra (Carl Fischer: piano), 54-9
THERE MUST BE A WAY: Joni James, 59-24
Frankie Vaughan with Alyn Ainsworth and his Orchestra, 67-7
THERE MUST BE AN ANGEL (PLAYING WITH MY HEART), Eurythmics, 85-1
THERE MUST BE THOUSANDS, Quads, 79-66
THERE SHE GOES: La's, 89-59, 90-13, 99-65
Sixpence None The Richer, 99-14
THERE SHE GOES AGAIN, Quireboys, 90-37

THERE THERE MY DEAR, Dexy's Midnight Runners, 80-7
THERE WILL NEVER BE ANOTHER TONIGHT, Bryan Adams, 91-32
THERE WILL NEVER BE ANOTHER YOU, Chris Montez, 66-37
THERE WILL NEVER BE ANOTHER YOU, Jimmy Ruffin, 85-68
THERE WON'T BE MANY COMING HOME, Roy Orbison, 66-18
(THERE'LL BE BLUEBIRDS OVER)THE WHITE CLIFFS OF DOVER, Robson Green and Jerome Flynn, 95-1
THERE'LL BE SAD SONGS (TO MAKE YOU CRY), Billy Ocean, 86-1
THERE'S A BRAND NEW WORLD, Five Star, 88-61
THERE'S A GHOST IN MY HOUSE: R. Dean Taylor, 74-3
Fall, 87-30
THERE'S A GOLD MINE IN THE SKY, Pat Boone with Billy Vaughn's Orchestra, 57-23
THERE'S A GUY WORKS DOWN THE CHIP SHOP, SWEARS HE'S ELVIS, Kirsty MacColl, 81-14
THERE'S A HEARTACHE FOLLOWING ME, Jim Reeves, 64-6
THERE'S A HOLE IN THE BUCKET, Harry Belafonte and Odetta, 61-32
THERE'S A KIND OF HUSH (ALL OVER THE WORLD): Herman's Hermits *, 67-7
Carpenters, 76-22
THERE'S A WHOLE LOT OF LOVING, Guys and Dolls, 75-2
(THERE'S) ALWAYS SOMETHING THERE TO REMIND ME: Sandie Shaw, 64-1
(THERE'S GONNA BE) A SHOWDOWN, Archie Bell and the Drells, 73-36
THERE'S GOT TO BE A WAY, Mariah Carey, 91-54
THERE'S MORE TO LOVE, Communards, 88-20
THERE'S NO LIVING WITHOUT YOU, Will Downing, 93-67
THERE'S NO ONE QUITE LIKE GRANDMA, St. Winifred's School Choir, 80-1
THERE'S NO OTHER WAY, Blur, 91-8
THERE'S NOTHING BETTER THAN LOVE, Luther Vandross (Duet with Gregory Hines), 88-72
THERE'S NOTHING I WON'T DO, JX, 96-4
THERE'S NOTHING LIKE THIS, Omar, 91-14
THERE'S SOMETHING WRONG IN PARADISE, Kid Creole and the Coconuts, 83-35
THERE'S THE GIRL, Heart, 87-34
THERE'S YOUR TROUBLE, Dixie Chicks, 99-26
THESE ARE DAYS, 10,000 Maniacs, 92-58
THESE ARE THE DAYS OF OUR LIVES, Queen, 91-1
THESE ARE THE TIMES, Dru Hill, 99-4
THESE ARMS OF MINE, Proclaimers, 94-51
THESE BOOTS ARE MADE FOR WALKIN': Nancy Sinatra, 66-1
Billy Ray Cyrus, 92-63
THESE DAYS, Bon Jovi, 96-7
THESE DREAMS, Heart, 86-62, 88-8
THESE EARLY DAYS, Everything But The Girl, 88-75

THESE THINGS ARE WORTH FIGHTING FOR, Gary Clail On-U Sound System, 93-45
THESE THINGS WILL KEEP ME LOVING YOU, Velvelettes, 71-34
THEY ALL LAUGHED, Frank Sinatra, 99-41
(THEY CALL HER) LA BAMBA, Crickets, 64-21
THEY DON'T CARE ABOUT US, Michael Jackson, 96-4
THEY DON'T KNOW, Tracey Ullman, 83-2
THEY DON'T KNOW, Jon B, 98-32
THEY LONG TO BE CLOSE TO YOU: Carpenters, 70-6, 90-25
Gwen Guthrie, 86-25
THEY SAY IT'S GONNA RAIN, Hazell Dean, 85-58
THEY SHOOT HORSES DON'T THEY?, Racing Cars, 77-14
THEY'RE COMING TO TAKE ME AWAY, HA-HAAA!, Napoleon XIV, 66-4
THEY'RE HERE, EMF, 92-29
THIEVES IN THE TEMPLE, Prince, 90-7
THIEVES LIKE US, New Order, 84-18
THIGHS HIGH (GRIP YOUR HIPS AND MOVE), Tom Browne, 80-45
THIN LINE BETWEEN LOVE AND HATE, Pretenders, 84-49
THE THIN WALL, Ultravox, 81-14
A THING CALLED LOVE, Johnny Cash and the Evangel Temple Choir, 72-4
THE THING I LIKE, Aaliyah, 95-33
THINGS, Bobby Darin, 62-2
THINGS CAN ONLY GET BETTER, Howard Jones, 85-6
THINGS CAN ONLY GET BETTER, D:Ream, 93-24, 94-1, 97-19
THINGS GET BETTER, Eddie Floyd, 67-31
THINGS THAT ARE, Runrig, 95-40
THINGS THAT MAKE YOU GO HMMM . . ., C&C Music Factory (featuring Freedom Williams), 91-4
THE THINGS THE LONELY DO, Amazulu, 86-43
THE THINGS WE DO FOR LOVE, 10cc, 76-6
THINGS WE DO FOR LOVE, Horace Brown, 96-27
THINK, Brenda Lee, 64-26
THINK, Chris Farlowe, 66-37
THINK: Aretha Franklin, 68-26
Aretha Franklin, 90-31
THINK ABOUT . . ., D.J.H. featuring Stefy, 91-22
THINK ABOUT THAT, Dandy Livingstone, 73-26
THINK ABOUT THE WAY (BOM DIGI DIGI BOM . . .), Ice MC, 94-42, 96-38
THINK ABOUT YOUR CHILDREN, Mary Hopkin, 70-19
THINK FOR A MINUTE (NEW VERSION), Housemartins, 86-18
THINK I'M GONNA FALL IN LOVE WITH YOU, Dooleys, 77-13
THINK IT ALL OVER, Sandie Shaw, 69-42
THINK IT OVER, Crickets, 58-11
THINK OF ME (WHEREVER YOU ARE), Ken Dodd, 75-21
THINK OF YOU, Usher, 95-70
THINK OF YOU, Whigfield, 95-7
THINK SOMETIMES ABOUT ME, Sandie Shaw, 66-32
THINK TWICE, Celine Dion, 94-1

THINKIN' ABOUT YOUR BODY: Bobby McFerrin, 88-46
2 Mad, 91-43
THINKIN' AIN'T FOR ME, Paul Jones, 67-32
THINKING ABOUT YOUR LOVE: Skipworth and Turner, 85-24
Phillip Leo, 95-64
THINKING ABOUT YOUR LOVE, Kenny Thomas, 91-4
THINKING OF YOU: Sister Sledge, 84-11, 93-17
Maureen Walsh, 90-11
THINKING OF YOU, Colourfield, 85-12
THINKING OF YOU, Hanson, 98-23
THINKING OF YOU BABY, Dave Clark Five, 64-26
THIRD FINGER, LEFT HAND, Pearls, 72-31
THE THIRD MAN, Shadows, 81-44
THIRD RAIL, Squeeze, 93-39
13 STEPS LEAD DOWN, Elvis Costello, 94-59
THE 13TH, Cure, 96-15
13TH DISCIPLE, Five Thirty, 91-67
30 CENTURY MAN, Catherine Wheel, 93-47
THIRTY THREE, Smashing Pumpkins, 96-21
36D, Beautiful South, 92-46
THIS AIN'T A LOVE SONG, Bon Jovi, 95-6
THIS AND THAT, Tom Jones, 66-44
THIS BEAT IS MINE, Vicky "D", 82-42
THIS BEAT IS TECHNOTRONIC, Technotronic featuring MC Eric, 90-14
THIS BOY, Justin, 98-34
THIS BRUTAL HOUSE, Nitro Deluxe, 87-47, 88-24
THIS CAN BE REAL, Candy Flip, 90-60
THIS CHARMING MAN, Smiths, 83-25, 92-8
THIS CORROSION, Sisters Of Mercy, 87-7
THIS COWBOY SONG, Sting (featuring Pato Banton), 95-15
THIS DJ, Warren G, 94-12
THIS DOOR SWINGS BOTH WAYS, Herman's Hermits, 66-18
THIS FEELIN', Frank Hooker and Positive People, 80-48
THIS FEELING, Puressence, 98-33
THIS FLIGHT TONIGHT, Nazareth, 73-11
THIS GARDEN, Levellers, 93-12
THIS GENERATION, Roachford, 94-38
THIS GOLDEN RING, Fortunes, 66-15
THIS GUY'S IN LOVE WITH YOU, Herb Alpert, 68-3, 69-46
THIS HERE GIRAFFE, Flaming Lips, 96-72
THIS HOUSE, Tracie Spencer, 91-65
THIS HOUSE, Alison Moyet, 91-40
THIS HOUSE IS NOT A HOME, Rembrandts, 96-58
THIS HOUSE (IS WHERE YOUR LOVE STANDS), Big Sound Authority, 85-21
THIS I SWEAR, Richard Darbyshire, 93-50
THIS I SWEAR, Kim Wilde, 96-46
THIS IS A CALL, Foo Fighters, 95-5
THIS IS A REBEL SONG, Sinead O'Connor, 97-60
THIS IS ENGLAND, Clash, 85-24
THIS IS FAKE D.I.Y. (from BIS VS. THE D.I.Y. CORPS [EP]), Bis, 96-45
THIS IS FOR REAL, David Devant And His Spirit Wife, 97-61
THIS IS FOR THE LOVER IN YOU, Babyface featuring LI Cool J, Jody Watley, Howard Hewett and Jeffrey Daniels, 96-12

TILL THE END OF THE DAY,
Kinks, 65-8
TILL THERE WAS YOU, Peggy
Lee with Jack Marshall's Music,
61-30
TILL WE MEET AGAIN, Inner
City, 91-47, 93-55
TILTED, Sugar, 93-48
TIME, Craig Douglas with Harry
Robinson and his Orchestra,
61-9
TIME, Light Of The World, 81-35
TIME, Frida and B.A. Robertson,
83-45
TIME, Freddie Mercury, 86-32
TIME, Kim Wilde, 90-71
TIME, Supergrass, 95-2
TIME, Marion, 96-29
TIME AFTER TIME:
Cyndi Lauper, 84-3
Hyperactive featuring Janey Lee
Grace, 93-71
Changing Faces (featuring Jay-Z),
98-35
TIME AFTER TIME, Beloved,
90-46
TIME ALONE WILL TELL,
Malcolm Roberts, 67-45
A TIME AND A PLACE, Mike and
the Mechanics, 91-58
TIME AND CHANCE, Color Me
Badd, 93-62
TIME AND THE RIVER, Nat
King Cole, 60-23
TIME AND TIDE, Basia, 88-61
TIME BOMB, 808 State, 92-59
TIME BOMB, Rancid, 95-56
**TIME (CLOCK OF THE
HEART),** Culture Club, 82-3
TIME DRAGS BY, Cliff Richard
and the Shadows, 66-10
TIME FOR ACTION, Secret Affair,
79-13
TIME FOR LIVIN', Association,
68-23
TIME FOR LOVE, Kim English,
95-48
THE TIME HAS COME, Adam
Faith, 61-4
THE TIME HAS COME, P.P.
Arnold, 67-47
**TIME HAS TAKEN IT'S TOLL
ON YOU,** Crazyhead, 88-65
THE TIME IN BETWEEN, Cliff
Richard and the Shadows, 65-22
TIME IS ON MY SIDE (LIVE),
Rolling Stones, 82-62
TIME IS TIGHT, Booker T. and the
M.G.'S, 69-4
A TIME LIKE THIS, Haywoode,
83-48
**TIME, LOVE AND
TENDERNESS,** Michael
Bolton, 91-28
TIME OF OUR LIVES, Alison
Limerick, 94-36
**TIME OF YOUR LIFE (GOOD
RIDDANCE),** Green Day,
98-11
TIME SELLER, Spencer Davis
Group, 67-30
TIME STAND STILL, Rush, 87-42
TIME TO GET BACK, Hysteric
Ego, 99-50
TIME TO GET UP, Liquid, 93-46
**TIME TO MAKE THE FLOOR
BURN [M],** Megabass, 90-16
TIME TO MAKE YOU MINE,
Lisa Stansfield, 92-14
TIME TO MOVE ON, Sparkle,
98-40
**TIME TO SAY GOODBYE (CON
TE PARTIRO),** Sarah
Brightman and Andrea Bocelli,
97-2
THE TIME WARP:
Damian, 87-51, 88-64, 89-7
Cast of the New Rocky Horror
Show, 98-57
TIME WILL CRAWL, David
Bowie, 87-33
TIMEBOMB, Chumbawamba,
93-59
TIMELESS, Daniel O'Donnell and
Mary Duff, 96-32
TIMELESS MELODY, La's, 90-57

**THE TIMES THEY ARE
A-CHANGIN':**
Peter, Paul and Mary, 64-44
Bob Dylan, 65-9
Ian Campbell Folk Group, 65-42
TIN MACHINE, Tin Machine,
89-48
TIN SOLDIER, Small Faces, 67-9
TIN SOLDIERS, Stiff Little Fingers,
80-36
TINA MARIE, Perry Como and the
Ray Charles Singers with Mitchell
Ayres and his Orchestra, 55-24
TINGLE, That Petrol Emotion,
91-49
TINSEL TOWN, Ronny Jordan,
94-64
**TINSELTOWN TO THE
BOOGIEDOWN,** Scritti Politti,
99-46
TINY CHILDREN, Teardrop
Explodes, 82-44
TINY DYNAMITE [EP], Cocteau
Twins, 85-52
TINY MACHINE, Darling Buds,
90-60
THE TIP OF MY FINGERS, Des
O'Connor with Alyn Ainsworth
and his Orchestra, 70-15
TIPP CITY, Amps, 95-61
TIRED OF BEING ALONE:
Al Green, 71-4
Texas, 92-19
TIRED OF TOEIN' THE LINE,
Rocky Burnette, 79-58
TIRED OF WAITING FOR YOU,
Kinks, 65-1
TISHBITE, Cocteau Twins, 96-34
**TO A BRIGHTER DAY
(O'HAPPY DAY),** Beat System,
93-70
**TO ALL THE GIRLS I'VE
LOVED BEFORE,** Julio
Iglesias and Willie Nelson, 84-17
TO BE A LOVER, Billy Idol, 86-22
TO BE IN LOVE, MAW presents
India, 99-23
TO BE LOVED:
Jackie Wilson, 58-23
Malcolm Vaughan with the Michael
Sammes Singers, 58-14
TO BE OR NOT TO BE, B.A.
Robertson, 80-9
**TO BE OR NOT TO BE (THE
HITLER RAP),** Mel Brooks,
84-12
TO BE REBORN, Boy George,
87-13
TO BE WITH YOU, Mr. Big, 92-3
TO BE WITH YOU AGAIN, Level
42, 87-10
**TO CUT A LONG STORY
SHORT,** Spandau Ballet, 80-5
TO EARTH WITH LOVE, Gay
Dad, 99-10
TO FRANCE, Mike Oldfield vocals
by Maggie Reilly, 84-48
**TO HAVE AND TO HOLD
(THEME SONG FROM
THE LWT SERIES),** Catherine
Stock, 86-17
TO HERE KNOWS WHEN, My
Bloody Valentine, 91-29
**TO KNOW HIM, IS TO LOVE
HIM:**
Teddy Bears, 58-2, 79-66
Peter and Gordon *, 65-5
**TO KNOW SOMEONE DEEPLY
IS TO KNOW SOMEONE
SOFTLY,** Terence Trent
D'Arby, 90-55
**TO KNOW YOU IS TO LOVE
YOU,** Peter and Gordon, 65-5
TO LIVE & DIE IN LA, Makaveli
(2 Pac is Makaveli), 97-10
TO LOVE ONCE AGAIN, Solid
Harmonic, 98-55
TO LOVE SOMEBODY:
Bee Gees, 67-41
Nina Simone, 69-5
Jimmy Somerville, 90-8
Michael Bolton, 92-16
TO MAKE A BIG MAN CRY, P.J.
Proby, 66-34
**TO THE BEAT OF THE DRUM
(LA LUNA),** Ethics, 95-13

TO THE BIRDS, Suede, 92-49
TO THE END, Blur, 94-16
TO THE LIMIT, Tony De Vit,
95-44
TO THE MOON AND BACK,
Savage Garden, 97-55, 98-3
TO THE WORLD, O.R.G.A.N,
98-33
TO WHOM IT CONCERNS,
Chris Andrews, 65-13
TO WIN JUST ONCE, Saw
Doctors, 96-14
TO YOU I BELONG, B*Witched,
98-1
TO YOU I BESTOW, Mundy, 96-60
TOAST, Streetband, 78-18
TOAST OF LOVE, Three Degrees,
76-36
TOBACCO ROAD, Nashville Teens,
64-6
TOCA ME, Fragma, 99-11
TOCCATA, Sky, 80-5
**TOCCATA AND FUGUE IN D
MINOR,** Vanessa-Mae, 95-16
TODAY, Sandie Shaw, 68-27
TODAY, Talk Talk, 82-14
TODAY, Smashing Pumpkins, 93-44
**TODAY FOREVER [EP] + lead
track title,** Ride, 91-14
TODAY'S THE DAY, Sean
Maguire, 97-27
TODAY'S YOUR LUCKY DAY,
Harold Melvin and the Blue
Notes featuring Nikko, 84-66
TOGETHER:
Connie Francis, 61-6
P.J. Proby, 64-8
TOGETHER, O. C. Smith, 77-25
TOGETHER, Danny Campbell and
Sasha, 93-57
TOGETHER AGAIN, Ray Charles,
66-48
TOGETHER AGAIN, Janet, 97-4
TOGETHER FOREVER, Rick
Astley, 88-2
**TOGETHER IN ELECTRIC
DREAMS,** Giorgio Moroder
with Philip Oakey, 84-3
**TOGETHER WE ARE
BEAUTIFUL:**
Steve Allan, 79-67
Fern Kinney, 80-1
TOGETHERNESS, Mike Preston,
60-41
TOKOLOSHE MAN, John Kongos,
71-4
TOKYO, Classix Nouveaux, 81-67
TOKYO JOE, Bryan Ferry, 77-15
TOKYO MELODY, Helmut
Zacharias and his Orchestra, 64-9
TOKYO STEALTH FIGHTER,
Dave Angel, 97-58
TOKYO STORM WARNING,
Elvis Costello and the
Attractions, 86-73
TOLEDO, Elvis Costello with Burt
Bacharach, 99-72
TOM DOOLEY:
Lonnie Donegan and his Skiffle
Group, 58-3
Kingston Trio, 58-5
TOM HARK:
Elias and his Zig-Zag Jive Flutes,
58-2
Ted Heath and his Music, 58-24
Piranhas, 80-6
TOM PILLIBI, Jacqueline Boyer,
60-33
TOM SAWYER (LIVE), Rush,
81-25
TOM THE PEEPER, Act One,
74-40
TOM-TOM TURNAROUND,
New World, 71-6
**TOM TRAUBERT'S BLUES
(WALTZING MATILDA),**
Rod Stewart, 92-6
TOMB OF MEMORIES, Paul
Young, 85-16
TOMBOY, Perry Como with
Mitchell Ayres Orchestra and the
Ray Charles Singers, 59-10
TOMMY GUN, Clash, 78-19
TOMORROW, Johnny Brandon
with the Phantoms and the
Norman Warren Music, 55-8

TOMORROW, Sandie Shaw, 66-9
TOMORROW, Communards, 87-23
TOMORROW, Tongue 'N' Cheek,
90-20
TOMORROW, Silverchair, 95-59
TOMORROW, James, 97-12
TOMORROW NEVER DIES,
Sheryl Crow, 97-12
TOMORROW NIGHT, Atomic
Rooster, 71-11
TOMORROW PEOPLE, Ziggy
Marley and the Melody Makers,
88-22
TOMORROW RISING, Cliff
Richard, 73-29
**TOMORROW ROBINS WILL
SING,** Stevie Wonder, 95-71
TOMORROW, TOMORROW, Bee
Gees featuring Barry Gibb,
Maurice Gibb and Colin
Peterson, 69-23
TOMORROW'S CLOWN, Marty
Wilde, 61-33
TOMORROW'S GIRLS, U.K. Subs,
79-28
TOMORROW'S GIRLS, Donald
Fagen, 93-46
**TOMORROW'S (JUST ANOTHER
DAY),** Madness, 83-8
TOM'S DINER:
Suzanne Vega, 87-58
DNA featuring Suzanne Vega, 90-2
TOM'S PARTY, T-Spoon, 99-27
**TONES OF HOME [EP] + lead
track title,** Blind Melon, 93-62
TONGUE, R.E.M., 95-13
TONGUE TIED, Cat, 93-17
TONIGHT, Shirley Bassey and the
Rita Williams Singers with Geoff
Love and his Orchestra, 62-21
TONIGHT, Move, 71-11
TONIGHT, Rubettes, 74-12
TONIGHT, Zaine Griff, 80-54
TONIGHT, Modettes, 81-68
TONIGHT, Steve Harvey, 83-63
TONIGHT, Kool And The Gang,
84-2
TONIGHT, Boomtown Rats, 84-73
TONIGHT, David Bowie, 84-53
TONIGHT, New Kids On The
Block, 90-3
TONIGHT, Def Leppard, 93-34
**TONIGHT (COULD BE THE
NIGHT),** Velvets, 61-50
**TONIGHT I CELEBRATE MY
LOVE,** Peabo Bryson and
Roberta Flack, 83-2
TONIGHT I'M ALRIGHT, Narada
Michael Walden, 80-34
TONIGHT I'M FREE, PJ and
Duncan (Byker Grove), 93-62
**TONIGHT I'M GONNA LOVE
YOU ALL OVER,** Four Tops,
82-43
**TONIGHT I'M YOURS (DON'T
HURT ME),** Rod Stewart, 81-8
TONIGHT IN TOKYO, Sandie
Shaw, 67-21
**TONIGHT IS WHAT IT MEANS
TO BE YOUNG,** Jim Steinman
and Fire Inc., 84-67
TONIGHT, TONIGHT, Smashing
Pumpkins, 96-7
**TONIGHT, TONIGHT,
TONIGHT,** Genesis, 87-18
**TONIGHT YOU BELONG TO
ME,** Patience and Prudence,
56-28
TONIGHT'S THE NIGHT, Rod
Stewart, 76-5
TONITE, Supercar, 99-15
TONITE, Phats and Small, 99-11
TOO BEAUTIFUL TO LAST,
Engelbert Humperdinck, 72-14
TOO BIG, Suzi Quatro, 74-14
TOO BLIND TO SEE IT, Kym
Sims, 91-5
**TOO BUSY THINKING ABOUT
MY BABY:**
Marvin Gaye, 69-5
Mardi Gras, 72-19
TOO CLOSE, Next, 98-24
TOO DRUNK TO FUCK, Dead
Kennedys, 81-36
TOO GONE, TOO LONG, En
Vogue, 97-20

WHO'S GONNA RIDE YOUR WILD HORSES, U2, 92-14
WHO'S GONNA ROCK YOU, Nolans, 80-12
WHO'S IN THE HOUSE (THE HIP HOUSE ANTHEM), Beatmasters with Merlin, 89-8
WHO'S IN THE STRAWBERRY PATCH WITH SALLY, Dawn featuring Tony Orlando, 74-37
WHO'S JOHNNY ("SHORT CIRCUIT" THEME), El Debarge, 86-60
WHO'S LEAVING WHO, Hazell Dean, 88-4
WHO'S LOVING MY BABY, Shola Ama, 97-13
WHO'S SORRY NOW:
Johnnie Ray with Paul Weston and his Orchestra, 56-17
Connie Francis, 58-1
WHO'S THAT GIRL?:
Eurythmics, 83-3
Flying Pickets, 84-71
WHO'S THAT GIRL, Madonna, 87-1
WHO'S THAT GIRL? (SHE'S GOT IT), A Flock Of Seagulls, 85-66
WHO'S THAT MIX [M], This Year's Blonde, 87-62
WHO'S THE BAD MAN?, Dee Patten, 99-42
WHO'S THE DARKMAN?, Darkman, 94-46
WHO'S THE MACK!, Mark Morrison, 97-13
WHO'S THE MAN, House Of Pain, 93-23
WHO'S ZOOMIN' WHO, Aretha Franklin, 85-11
WHODUNIT, Tavares, 77-5
WHOLE LOTTA LOVE:
C.C.S., 70-13
Goldbug, 96-3
Led Zeppelin, 97-21
WHOLE LOTTA ROSIE, AC/DC, 80-36
WHOLE LOTTA SHAKIN' GOIN' ON, Jerry Lee Lewis, 57-8
WHOLE LOTTA TROUBLE, Stevie Nicks, 89-62
WHOLE LOTTA WOMAN, Marvin Rainwater, 58-1
WHOLE NEW WORLD, It Bites, 86-54
A WHOLE NEW WORLD (ALADDIN'S THEME), Regina Belle and Peabo Bryson, 93-12
THE WHOLE OF THE MOON:
Waterboys, 85-26, 91-3
Little Caesar, 90-68
THE WHOLE TOWN'S LAUGHING AT ME, Teddy Pendergrass, 77-44
THE WHOLE WORLD LOST IT'S HEAD, Go-Go's, 95-29
WHOOMP! (THERE IT IS):
Tag Team, 94-34, 94-48
Tag Team *, 94-53
Clock, 95-4
WHOOPS NOW, Janet Jackson, 95-9
WHOOSH, Whoosh, 97-72
WHOSE FIST IS THIS ANYWAY [EP], Prong, 92-58
WHOSE LAW (IS IT ANYWAY?), Guru Josh, 90-26
WHOSE PROBLEM?, Motels, 80-42
WHY:
Anthony Newley, 60-1
Frankie Avalon, 60-20
Donny Osmond, 72-3
WHY, Roger Whittaker, 71-47
WHY:
Carly Simon, 82-10, 89-56
Glamma Kid, 99-10
WHY?, Bronski Beat, 84-6
WHY, Annie Lennox, 92-5
WHY, D-Mob with Cathy Dennis, 94-23
WHY, 3T featuring Michael Jackson, 96-2

WHY?, Ricardo Da Force, 96-58
WHY ARE PEOPLE GRUDGEFUL?, Fall, 93-43
WHY ARE YOU BEING SO REASONABLE NOW?, Wedding Present, 88-42
WHY BABY WHY, Pat Boone, 57-17
WHY BELIEVE IN YOU, Texas, 91-66
WHY CAN'T I BE YOU?, Cure, 87-21
WHY CAN'T I WAKE UP WITH YOU?, Take That, 93-2
WHY CAN'T THIS BE LOVE, Van Halen, 86-8
WHY CAN'T WE BE LOVERS, Holland-Dozier featuring Lamont Dozier, 72-29
WHY CAN'T WE LIVE TOGETHER, Timmy Thomas, 73-12, 90-54
WHY CAN'T YOU, Clarence 'Frogman' Henry, 61-42
WHY DID YA, Tony Di Bart, 95-46
WHY DID YOU DO IT, Stretch, 75-16
WHY DO FOOLS FALL IN LOVE:
Teenagers featuring Frankie Lymon, 56-1
Alma Cogan with vocal group, 56-22
Diana Ross, 81-4, 94-36
WHY DO I ALWAYS GET IT WRONG, Live Report, 89-73
WHY DO LOVERS BREAK EACH OTHERS' HEARTS, Showaddywaddy, 80-22
WHY DOES A MAN HAVE TO BE STRONG?, Paul Young, 87-63
WHY DOES IT ALWAYS RAIN ON ME?, Travis, 99-10
WHY DOES MY HEART FEEL SO BAD?, Moby, 99-16
WHY DON'T THEY UNDERSTAND, George Hamilton IV, 58-22
WHY DON'T WE TRY AGAIN, Brian May, 98-44
WHY DON'T YOU, Rage, 93-44
WHY DON'T YOU BELIEVE ME?, Joni James with Lew Douglas and his Orchestra, 53-11
WHY DON'T YOU DANCE WITH ME, Future Breeze, 97-50
WHY DON'T YOU GET A JOB?, Offspring, 99-2
WHY DON'T YOU TAKE ME?, One Dove, 94-30
WHY D'YA LIE TO ME, Spider, 83-65
WHY ME?, Linda Martin, 92-59
WHY ME?, PJ and Duncan (A.K.A. Ant and Declan), 94-27
WHY ME?, A House, 94-52
WHY (MUST WE FALL IN LOVE), Diana Ross and the Supremes and the Temptations, 70-31
WHY MUST WE WAIT UNTIL TONIGHT, Tina Turner, 93-16
WHY NOT NOW, Matt Monro, 61-24
WHY NOT TONIGHT, Mojos, 64-25
WHY OH WHY, Spearhead, 97-45
WHY, OH WHY, OH WHY, Gilbert O'Sullivan, 73-6
WHY SHE'S A GIRL FROM THE CHAINSTORE, Buzzcocks, 80-61
WHY SHOULD I, Bob Marley and the Wailers, 92-42
WHY SHOULD I BE LONELY ?, Tony Brent, 59-24
WHY SHOULD I CRY?, Nona Hendryx, 87-60
WHY SHOULD I LOVE YOU?, Des'ree, 92-44
WHY WHY BYE BYE, Bob Luman, 60-46
WHY? WHY? WHY?, Deja Vu, 94-57

WHY YOU TREAT ME SO BAD, Shaggy featuring Grand Puba, 96-11
WHY'S EVERYBODY ALWAYS PICKIN' ON ME?, Bloodhound Gang, 97-56
WIBBLING RIVALRY, Oas*s, 95-52
WICHITA LINEMAN, Glen Campbell, 69-7
WICKED, Ice Cube, 93-62
WICKED GAME, Chris Isaak, 90-10
WICKED LOVE, Oceanic, 91-25
WICKED WAYS, Blow Monkeys, 86-60
THE WICKEDEST SOUND, Rebel MC (featuring Tenor Fly), 91-43
WICKI WACKY HOUSE PARTY, Team, 88-55
WIDE AWAKE IN A DREAM, Barry Biggs, 81-44
WIDE BOY, Nik Kershaw, 85-9
WIDE EYED AND LEGLESS, Andy Fairweather Low, 75-6
WIDE OPEN SPACE (from FOUR [EP]), Mansun, 96-15
WIDE PRAIRIE, Linda McCartney, 98-74
WIDESHIRE TWO (from SPINDRIFT [EP]), Thousand Yard Stare, 92-58
WIG-WAM BAM:
Sweet, 72-4
Black Lace, 86-63
Damian, 89-49
WIGGLE IT, 2 In A Room, 91-3
WIGGLY WORLD, Mr Jack, 97-32
WIKKA WRAP, Evasions, 81-20
THE WILD AMERICA [EP] + lead track title, Iggy Pop, 93-63
WILD AND WONDERFUL, Almighty, 90-50
THE WILD BOYS, Duran Duran, 84-2
WILD CAT, Gene Vincent, 60-21
WILD CHILD, W.A.S.P., 86-71
WILD FLOWER, Cult, 87-30, 87-24
WILD FRONTIER, Gary Moore, 87-35
WILD HEARTED SON, Cult, 91-40
WILD HEARTED WOMAN, All About Eve, 88-33
WILD HONEY, Beach Boys, 67-29
WILD IN THE COUNTRY, Elvis Presley with the Jordanaires, 61-4
WILD IS THE WIND, David Bowie, 81-24
WILD LOVE, Mungo Jerry, 73-32
WILD LUV, Roach Motel, 94-75
WILD 'N FREE, Rednex, 95-55
WILD NIGHT, John Mellencamp with Me'shell Ndegeocello, 94-34
WILD ONE, Bobby Rydell, 60-7
WILD ONE, Suzi Quatro, 74-7
THE WILD ONES, Suede, 94-18
WILD SIDE, Motley Crue, 88-26
WILD SIDE OF LIFE:
Tommy Quickly, 64-33
Status Quo, 76-9
WILD SURF, Ash, 98-31
WILD THING:
Troggs, 66-2
Goodies, 75-21
Troggs and Wolf, 93-69
WILD THING, Tone Loc, 89-21
WILD WEST HERO, Electric Light Orchestra, 78-6
WILD WILD LIFE, Talking Heads, 86-43
WILD, WILD WEST, Get Ready, 95-65
WILD WILD WEST, Will Smith (featuring Dru Hill), 99-2
WILD WIND, John Leyton, 61-2
WILD WOMEN DO, Natalie Cole, 90-16
WILD WOOD, Paul Weller, 93-14, 99-22
WILD WORLD:
Jimmy Cliff, 70-8
Maxi Priest, 88-5
Mr. Big, 93-59
WILDLIFE [EP], Girlschool, 82-58

WILDSIDE, Marky Mark and the Funky Bunch, 91-42
WILFRED THE WEASEL, Keith Michell Captain Beaky and his Band, 80-5
WILL I WHAT, Mike Sarne featuring Billie Davis with the Charles Blackwell Orchestra, 62-18
WILL SHE ALWAYS BE WAITING, Bluebells, 84-38
WILL THE WOLF SURVIVE, Los Lobos, 85-57
WILL 2K, Will Smith (featuring K-Ci), 99-2
WILL WE BE LOVERS, Deacon Blue, 93-31
WILL YOU?, Hazel O'Connor, 81-8
WILL YOU BE MY BABY?, Infiniti featuring Grand Puba, 96-53
WILL YOU BE THERE, Michael Jackson, 93-9
WILL YOU BE THERE (IN THE MORNING), Heart, 93-19
WILL YOU BE WITH ME, Maria Nayler, 98-65
WILL YOU LOVE ME TOMORROW:
Shirelles, 61-4
Melanie, 74-37
Bryan Ferry, 93-23
WILL YOU MARRY ME?, Paula Abdul, 92-73
WILL YOU SATISFY?, Cherrelle, 86-57
WILL YOU WAIT FOR ME, Kavana, 99-29
WILLIAM, IT WAS REALLY NOTHING, Smiths, 84-17
WILLIE CAN:
Alma Cogan with Desmond Lane – penny whistle, 56-13
Beverley Sisters, 56-23
WILLING TO FORGIVE, Aretha Franklin, 94-17
WILLINGLY (MELODIE PERDUE), Malcolm Vaughan, 59-28
WILLOW TREE, Ivy League, 66-50
WILMOT, Sabres Of Paradise, 94-36
WIMOWEH, Karl Denver, 62-4
WIN, PLACE OR SHOW (SHE'S A WINNER), Intruders, 74-14
WINCHESTER CATHEDRAL, New Vaudeville Band, 66-4
THE WIND, P J Harvey, 99-29
THE WIND BENEATH MY WINGS:
Lee Greenwood, 84-49
Bette Midler, 89-5
Bill Tarmey, 94-40
Steven Houghton, 97-3
THE WIND CRIES MARY, Jimi Hendrix Experience, 67-6
WIND IT UP (REWOUND), Prodigy, 93-11, 96-71
WIND ME UP (LET ME GO), Cliff Richard and the Shadows, 65-2
WIND OF CHANGE, Scorpions, 91-53, 91-2
A WINDMILL IN OLD AMSTERDAM, Ronnie Hilton with the Michael Sammes Singers and Orchestra, 65-23
THE WINDMILLS OF YOUR MIND, Noel Harrison, 69-8
WINDOW PANE [EP] + lead track title, Real People, 91-60
WINDOW SHOPPING, R. Dean Taylor, 74-36
WINDOWLICKER, Aphextwin, 99-16
WINDOWS '98, Sil, 98-58
WINDPOWER, Thomas Dolby, 82-31
THE WINDSOR WALTZ, Vera Lynn with Chorus of Members of HM Forces, 53-11
WINDSWEPT, Bryan Ferry, 85-46
WINGS OF A DOVE, Madness, 83-2
WINGS OF LOVE, Bone, 94-55
THE WINKER'S SONG (MISPRINT), Ivor Biggun and the Red Nosed-Burglars, 78-22

YOU LITTLE TRUSTMAKER, Tymes, 74-18

YOU LOOK SO FINE, Garbage, 99-19

YOU LOVE US, Manic Street Preachers, 91-62, 92-16, 97-49

YOU LOVE YOU, Subcircus, 97-61

YOU MADE ME BELIEVE IN MAGIC, Bay City Rollers, 77-34

YOU MADE ME LOVE YOU, Nat 'King' Cole, 59-22

YOU MADE ME THE THIEF OF YOUR HEART, Sinead O'Connor, 94-42

YOU MAKE IT HEAVEN, Terri Wells, 83-53

YOU MAKE IT MOVE, Dave Dee, Dozy, Beaky, Mick and Tich, 65-26

YOU MAKE LOVING FUN, Fleetwood Mac, 77-45

YOU MAKE ME FEEL BRAND NEW, Stylistics (featuring Airrion Love and Russell Thompkins, Jr.), 74-2

(YOU MAKE ME FEEL LIKE A) NATURAL WOMAN, Mary J. Blige, 95-23

YOU MAKE ME FEEL LIKE DANCING:
Leo Sayer, 76-2
Groove Generation featuring Leo Sayer, 98-32

YOU MAKE ME FEEL (MIGHTY REAL):
Sylvester, 78-8
Jimmy Somerville, 90-5
Dream Frequency, 94-65
Byron Stingily, 98-13

YOU MAKE ME WANNA . . ., Usher, 98-1

YOU MAKE ME WANT TO SCREAM, Dandys, 98-71

YOU MAKE ME WORK, Cameo, 88-74

YOU, ME AND US, Alma Cogan, 57-18

YOU MEAN EVERYTHING TO ME, Neil Sedaka with Stan Applebaum and his Orchestra, 60-45

YOU MEAN THE WORLD TO ME, Toni Braxton, 94-30

YOU MIGHT NEED SOMEBODY:
Randy Crawford, 81-11
Shola Ama, 97-4

YOU MUST BE PREPARED TO DREAM, Ian McNabb featuring Ralph Molina and Billy Talbot of Crazy Horse with Mike 'Tone' Hamilton – rhythm guitar, 94-54

YOU MUST GO ON, Bernard Butler, 99-44

YOU MUST HAVE BEEN A BEAUTIFUL BABY, Bobby Darin, 61-10

YOU MUST LOVE ME, Madonna, 96-10

YOU MY LOVE, Frank Sinatra, 55-13

YOU NEED HANDS, Max Bygraves with the Clarke Brothers and Eric Rodgers and his Orchestra, 58-3

YOU NEED WHEELS, Merton Parkas, 79-40

YOU NEEDED ME:
Anne Murray, 78-22
Boyzone, 99-1

YOU NEVER CAN TELL, Chuck Berry, 64-23

YOU NEVER DONE IT LIKE THAT, Captain and Tennille, 78-63

YOU NEVER KNOW WHAT YOU'VE GOT, Me and You featuring 'We The People Band', 79-31

YOU NEVER LOVE THE SAME WAY TWICE, Rozalla, 94-16

YOU ON MY MIND, Swing Out Sister, 89-28

YOU ONLY LIVE TWICE/ JACKSON, Nancy Sinatra, 67-11

YOU ONLY YOU, Rita Pavone with Geoff Love and his Orchestra, 67-21

YOU OUGHTA KNOW, Alanis Morissette, 95-22

YOU OWE IT ALL TO ME, Texas, 93-39

YOU PLAYED YOURSELF, Ice-T, 90-64

YOU REALLY GOT ME, Kinks, 64-1, 83-47

YOU REMIND ME, Mary J. Blige, 93-48

YOU REMIND ME OF SOMETHING, R. Kelly, 95-24

(YOU SAID) YOU'D GIMME SOME MORE, KC and the Sunshine Band, 83-41

YOU SCARE ME TO DEATH, Marc Bolan, 81-51

YOU SEE THE TROUBLE WITH ME, Barry White, 76-2

YOU SEND ME:
Sam Cooke, 58-29
Rod Stewart, 74-7

YOU SEXY DANCER, Rockford Files, 95-34, 96-59

YOU SEXY SUGAR PLUM (BUT I LIKE IT), Rodger Collins, 76-22

YOU SEXY THING:
Hot Chocolate, 75-2, 87-10, 97-6
T-Shirt, 97-63
Clock *, 97-11

YOU SHOOK ME ALL NIGHT LONG, AC/DC, 80-38, 86-46

YOU SHOULD BE DANCING:
Bee Gees, 76-5
Blockster *, 99-3

YOU SHOULD BE MINE (DON'T WASTE YOUR TIME), Brian McKnight featuring Mase, 98-36

YOU SHOULD HAVE KNOWN BETTER, T. C. Curtis backing vocals by Galaxy, 85-50

YOU SHOWED ME, Salt 'N' Pepa, 91-15

YOU SHOWED ME, Lightning Seeds, 97-8

YOU SPIN ME ROUND (LIKE A RECORD), Dead Or Alive, 84-1

YOU STILL TOUCH ME:
Sting, 96-27
Sting (from Live At T.F.I. Friday [EP]), 96-53

YOU STOLE THE SUN FROM MY HEART, Manic Street Preachers, 99-5

YOU SURE LOOK GOOD TO ME, Phyllis Hyman, 81-56

YOU SURROUND ME, Erasure, 89-15

YOU TAKE ME UP, Thompson Twins, 84-2

YOU TAKE MY HEART AWAY, De Etta Little and Nelson Pigford, 77-35

YOU TALK TOO MUCH, Sultans Of Ping F.C., 93-26

YOU THINK YOU OWN ME, Hinda Hicks, 98-19

YOU THINK YOU'RE A MAN, Divine, 84-16

YOU TO ME ARE EVERYTHING:
Real Thing, 76-1, 86-5
Sonia, 91-13
Sean Maguire, 95-16

YOU TOOK THE WORDS RIGHT OUT OF MY MOUTH, Meat Loaf, 78-33

YOU TRIP ME UP, Jesus And Mary Chain, 85-55

YOU USED TO HOLD ME SO TIGHT, Thelma Houston, 84-44

YOU USED TO LOVE ME, Faith Evans, 95-42

YOU USED TO SALSA, Richie Rich's Salsa House (featuring Ralphi Rosario), 91-52

YOU WANNA KNOW, Thunder, 99-49

YOU WANT IT, YOU GOT IT, Detroit Emeralds, 73-12

YOU WANT THIS, Janet Jackson, 94-14

YOU WEAR IT WELL, Rod Stewart, 72-1

YOU WEAR IT WELL, El Debarge with Debarge, 85-54

(YOU WERE MADE FOR) ALL MY LOVE, Jackie Wilson, 60-33

YOU WERE MADE FOR ME, Freddie and the Dreamers, 63-3

YOU WERE MEANT FOR ME, Jewel, 97-32

YOU WERE ON MY MIND, Crispian St. Peters, 66-2

YOU WERE THERE, Heinz, 64-26

YOU WEREN'T IN LOVE WITH ME, Billy Field, 82-67

YOU WILL RISE, Sweetback featuring Amel Larrieux from Groove Theory, 97-64

YOU WIN AGAIN, Bee Gees, 87-1

YOU WOKE UP MY NEIGHBOURHOOD, Billy Bragg, 91-54

YOU WON'T BE LEAVING, Herman's Hermits, 66-20

YOU WON'T FIND ANOTHER FOOL LIKE ME, New Seekers featuring Lyn Paul, 73-1

YOU WON'T SEE ME CRY, Wilson Phillips, 92-18

YOU WOULDN'T KNOW LOVE, Cher, 90-55

YOU, YOU ROMEO, Shirley Bassey with Wally Stott and his Orchestra, 57-29

YOU YOU YOU, Alvin Stardust, 74-6

YOU'D BETTER COME HOME, Petula Clark, 65-44

YOU'LL ALWAYS BE A FRIEND, Hot Chocolate, 72-23

YOU'LL ALWAYS FIND ME IN THE KITCHEN AT PARTIES, Jona Lewie, 80-16

YOU'LL ANSWER TO ME, Cleo Laine, 61-5

YOU'LL BE IN MY HEART, Phil Collins, 99-17

YOU'LL BE MINE (PARTY TIME), Gloria Estefan, 96-18

YOU'LL NEVER BE SO WRONG, Hot Chocolate, 81-52

YOU'LL NEVER FIND ANOTHER LOVE LIKE MINE, Lou Rawls, 76-10

YOU'LL NEVER GET TO HEAVEN [EP], Stylistics, 76-24

YOU'LL NEVER GET TO HEAVEN (IF YOU BREAK MY HEART):
Dionne Warwick, 64-20
Stylistics (from You'll Never Get To Heaven [EP]), 76-24

YOU'LL NEVER KNOW, Shirley Bassey with the Rita Williams Singers and Geoff Love and his Orchestra, 61-6

YOU'LL NEVER KNOW, Hi-Gloss, 81-12

YOU'LL NEVER KNOW WHAT YOU'RE MISSIN' 'TIL YOU TRY, Emile Ford and the Checkmates, 60-12

YOU'LL NEVER KNOW WHAT YOU'RE MISSING, Real Thing, 77-16

YOU'LL NEVER, NEVER KNOW, Platters, 57-23

YOU'LL NEVER STOP ME LOVING YOU, Sonia, 89-1

YOU'LL NEVER WALK ALONE:
Gerry and the Pacemakers, 63-1
Elvis Presley with the Jordanaires, 68-44
Crowd, 85-1
Robson and Jerome, 96-1
Tibor Rudas presents the 3 Tenors Paris 1988: Jose Carreras, Placido Domingo, Luciano Pavarotti, 98-35

YOU'LL SEE, Madonna, 95-5

YOU'RE A BETTER MAN THAN I, Sham 69, 79-49

YOU'RE A LADY, Peter Skellern, 72-3

YOU'RE A STAR, Aquarian Dream, 79-67

YOU'RE ALL I NEED, Motley Crue, 88-23

YOU'RE ALL I NEED TO GET BY:
Marvin Gaye and Tammi Terrell, 68-19
Johnny Mathis and Deniece Williams, 78-45

YOU'RE ALL THAT MATTERS TO ME, Curtis Stigers, 92-6

YOU'RE BEEN DOING ME WRONG, Delegation, 77-49

YOU'RE BREAKING MY HEART, Keely Smith, 65-14

YOU'RE DRIVING ME CRAZY, Temperance Seven vocal refrain by Mr. Paul MacDowall, 61-1

YOU'RE EVERYTHING TO ME, Boris Gardiner, 86-11

(YOU'RE) FABULOUS BABE, Kenny Williams, 77-35

YOU'RE FREE TO GO, Jim Reeves, 72-48

YOU'RE GONNA GET NEXT TO ME, Bo Kirkland and Ruth Davis, 77-12

YOU'RE GONNA MISS ME, Turntable Orchestra, 89-52

YOU'RE GORGEOUS, Babybird, 96-3

"YOU'RE" HAVING MY BABY, Paul Anka, 74-6

YOU'RE HISTORY, Shakespear's Sister, 89-7

YOU'RE IN A BAD WAY, Saint Etienne, 93-12

YOU'RE IN LOVE, Wilson Phillips, 91-29

YOU'RE IN MY HEART, Rod Stewart, 77-3

YOU'RE IN MY HEART, David Essex, 83-59

YOU'RE INVITED (BUT YOUR FRIEND CAN'T COME), Vince Neil, 92-63

YOU'RE LOOKIN' HOT TONIGHT, Barry Manilow, 83-47

YOU'RE LYING, Linx, 80-15

YOU'RE MAKIN ME HIGH, Toni Braxton, 96-7

YOU'RE MORE THAN A NUMBER IN MY LITTLE RED BOOK, Drifters, 76-5

YOU'RE MOVING OUT TODAY, Carole Bayer Sager, 77-6

YOU'RE MY BEST FRIEND, Queen, 76-7

YOU'RE MY BEST FRIEND, Don Williams, 76-35

YOU'RE MY EVERYTHING, Temptations, 67-26

YOU'RE MY EVERYTHING, Max Bygraves, 69-34

YOU'RE MY EVERYTHING:
Lee Garrett, 76-15
East Side Beat, 93-65

YOU'RE MY GIRL, Rockin' Berries, 65-40

YOU'RE MY HEART, YOU'RE MY SOUL, Modern Talking, 85-56

YOU'RE MY LAST CHANCE, 52nd Street, 86-49

YOU'RE MY LIFE, Barry Biggs, 77-36

YOU'RE MY NUMBER ONE, S Club 7, 99-5

(YOU'RE MY ONE AND ONLY) TRUE LOVE, Ann-Marie Smith, 95-46

(YOU'RE MY) SOUL AND INSPIRATION, Righteous Brothers, 66-15

YOU'RE MY WORLD, Nick Heyward, 88-67

YOU'RE MY WORLD (IL MIO MONDO), Cilla Black, 64-1

YOU'RE NEVER TOO YOUNG, Cool Notes, 84-42

EP INDEX

ALBUM INDEX

ALWAYS & FOREVER, Eternal, 93-2

ALWAYS AND FOREVER – THE COLLECTION, Various Artists: Compilations – Impression, 84-24

ALWAYS AND FOREVER THE LOVE ALBUM, Various Artists: Compilations – Telstar, 87-41

ALWAYS GUARANTEED, Cliff Richard, 87-5

ALWAYS ON MY MIND – ULTIMATE LOVE SONGS, Elvis Presley, 97-3

ALWAYS THERE, Marti Webb, 86-65

AM I NOT YOUR GIRL?, Sinead O'Connor, 92-6

AMADEUS [OST], Neville Marriner and the Academy Of St. Martin In The Fields, 85-64

AMANDA MARSHALL, Amanda Marshall, 96-47

AMANDLA, Miles Davis, 89-49

AMAROK, Mike Oldfield, 90-49

AMAZING, Elkie Brooks with the Royal Philharmonic Orchestra, 96-49

AMAZING DARTS, Darts, 78-8

AMAZING GRACE, Judy Collins, 85-34

THE AMAZING KAMIKAZE SYNDROME, Slade, 83-49

AMAZING THINGS, Runrig, 93-2

AMAZULU, Amazulu, 86-97

AMBIENT DUB VOLUME 2 – EARTH JUICE, Various Artists: Compilations – Beyond, 93-20

AMBIENT 4 ON LAND, Brian Eno, 82-93

AMBIENT MOODS, Various Artists: Compilations – PolyGram TV, 96-7

AMERICA, Herb Alpert and the Tijuana Brass, 71-45

AMERICA, America, 72-14

AMERICA'S LEAST WANTED, Ugly Kid Joe, 92-13

AMERICAN CAESAR, Iggy Pop, 93-43

THE AMERICAN DINER, Various Artists: Compilations – Dino, 95-7

AMERICAN DREAMS, Various Artists: Compilations – Starblend, 85-43

AMERICAN ENGLISH, Wax, 87-59

AMERICAN FOOL, John Cougar, 82-37

AMERICAN GRAFFITI, Various Artists: Films – Original Soundtracks, 74-37

AMERICAN HEARTBEAT, Various Artists: Compilations – Epic, 84-4

AMERICAN PIE, Don McLean, 72-3

AMERICAN STARS 'N' BARS, Neil Young, 77-17

AMERICAN THIGHS, Veruca Salt, 94-47

AMERICANA, Offspring, 98-10

AMERIKKKA'S MOST WANTED, Ice Cube, 90-48

AMIGOS, Santana, 76-21

AMIGOS PARA SIEMPRE (FRIENDS FOR LIFE), Jose Carreras, 92-53

AMMONIA AVENUE, Alan Parsons Project, 84-24

AMNESIA, Richard Thompson, 88-89

AMONG MY SWAN, Mazzy Star, 96-57

AMONG THE LIVING, Anthrax, 87-18

AMOR, Julio Iglesias, 82-14

AMORICA, Black Crowes, 94-8

AMOUR – THE ULTIMATE LOVE COLLECTION, Various Artists: Selected Series – Ultimate, 97-3

AMPLIFIED HEART, Everything But The Girl, 94-20

AMUSED TO DEATH, Roger Waters, 92-8

THE ANALOGUE THEATRE, C.J. Bolland, 96-43

ANAM, Clannad, 90-14

ANARCHY, Chumbawamba, 94-29

ANCIENT HEART, Tanita Tikaram, 88-3

AND, John Martyn, 96-32

AND ALL BECAUSE THE LADY LOVES . . . , Various Artists: Compilations – Dover, 89-2

AND I LOVE YOU SO, Shirley Bassey, 72-24

AND I LOVE YOU SO, Perry Como, 73-1

AND I LOVE YOU SO, Howard Keel, 84-6

. . . AND JUSTICE FOR ALL, Metallica, 88-4

AND NOW THE LEGACY BEGINS, Dream Warriors, 91-18

. . . AND OUT COME THE WOLVES, Rancid, 95-55

AND STILL I RISE, Alison Limerick, 92-53

. . . AND THE BEAT GOES ON, Various Artists: Compilations – Telstar, 88-12

. . . AND THEN THERE WERE THREE . . . , Genesis, 78-3

ANDERSON BRUFORD WAKEMAN HOWE, Anderson Bruford Wakeman Howe, 89-14

ANDREW LLOYD WEBBER: REQUIEM, Placido Domingo, Sarah Brightman, Paul Miles-Kingston, Winchester Cathedral Choir and the English Chamber Orchestra conducted by Lorin Maazel, 85-4

ANDREW LLOYD WEBBER – THE PREMIERE COLLECTION, Various Artists: Compilations – Really Useful/Polydor, 88-1

ANDROMEDA HEIGHTS, Prefab Sprout, 97-7

ANDY STEWART, Andy Stewart, 62-13

ANDY WILLIAMS' GREATEST HITS, Andy Williams, 70-1

ANDY WILLIAMS SHOW, Andy Williams, 70-10

ANDY WILLIAMS' SOUND OF MUSIC, Andy Williams, 70-22

ANGEL CLARE, Art Garfunkel, 73-14

ANGEL DELIGHT, Fairport Convention, 71-8

ANGEL DUST, Faith No More, 92-2

ANGEL STATION, Manfred Mann's Earth Band, 79-30

ANGELIC UPSTARTS, Angelic Upstarts, 81-27

ANGELS & ELECTRICITY, Eddi Reader, 98-49

ANGELS WITH DIRTY FACES, Tricky, 98-23

ANIMAL BOY, Ramones, 86-38

ANIMAL MAGIC, Blow Monkeys, 86-21

ANIMAL MAGNETISM, Scorpions, 80-23

ANIMAL RIGHTS, Moby, 96-38

ANIMAL TRACKS, Animals, 65-6

ANIMALISMS, Animals, 66-4

ANIMALIZE, Kiss, 84-11

THE ANIMALS, Animals, 64-6

ANIMALS, Pink Floyd, 77-2

ANIMATION, Jon Anderson, 82-43

ANNIE, Various Artists: Films – Original Soundtracks, 82-83

ANNIVERSARY – 20 YEARS OF HITS, Tammy Wynette, 87-45

THE ANNUAL, Various Artists: Selected Series – The Annual, 95-13

THE ANNUAL II – PETE TONG & BOY GEORGE, Various Artists: Selected Series – The Annual, 96-1

THE ANNUAL III – PETE TONG & BOY GEORGE, Various Artists: Selected Series – The Annual, 97-1

THE ANNUAL IV – JUDGE JULES & BOY GEORGE, Various Artists: Selected Series – The Annual, 98-1

THE ANNUAL – MILLENNIUM EDITION – MIXED BY JUDGE JULES & TALL PAUL, Various Artists: Selected Series – The Annual, 99-2

ANOMIE & BONHOMIE, Scritti Politti, 99-33

ANOTHER BLACK AND WHITE MINSTREL SHOW, George Mitchell Minstrels, 61-1

ANOTHER GREY AREA, Graham Parker, 82-40

ANOTHER KIND OF BLUES, U.K. Subs, 79-21

ANOTHER LEVEL, Blackstreet, 96-26

ANOTHER LEVEL, Another Level, 98-13

ANOTHER MONTY PYTHON RECORD, Monty Python's Flying Circus, 71-26

ANOTHER MUSIC IN A DIFFERENT KITCHEN, Buzzcocks, 78-15

ANOTHER NIGHT – U.S. ALBUM, Real McCoy, 95-6

ANOTHER PAGE, Christopher Cross, 83-4

ANOTHER PERFECT DAY, Motorhead, 83-20

ANOTHER PERFECT DAY, Various Artists: Compilations – Columbia, 98-13

ANOTHER PLACE AND TIME, Donna Summer, 89-17

ANOTHER SIDE OF BOB DYLAN, Bob Dylan, 64-8

ANOTHER STEP, Kim Wilde, 86-73

ANOTHER STRING OF HITS, Shadows, 80-16

ANOTHER TICKET, Eric Clapton, 81-18

ANOTHER TIME, ANOTHER PLACE, Engelbert Humperdinck, 71-48

ANOTHER TIME, ANOTHER PLACE, Bryan Ferry, 74-4

ANOTHER WORLD, Brian May, 98-23

ANOTHER YEAR, Leo Sayer, 75-8

ANSWERS TO NOTHING, Midge Ure, 88-30

ANTENNA, ZZ Top, 94-3

ANTHEM, Toyah, 81-2

ANTHEM, Black Uhuru, 84-90

THE ANTHEMS '92-'97, Various Artists: Compilations – United Dance, 97-8

THE ANTHOLOGY, Deep Purple, 85-50

ANTHOLOGY 1, Beatles, 95-2

ANTHOLOGY 2, Beatles, 96-1

ANTHOLOGY 3, Beatles, 96-4

ANTHOLOGY – THE SOUNDS OF SCIENCE, Beastie Boys, 99-36

ANTICHRIST SUPERSTAR, Marilyn Manson, 96-73

THE ANTIDOTE, Ronny Jordan, 92-52

ANTMUSIC – THE VERY BEST OF ADAM ANT, Adam Ant/Adam and the Ants, 93-6

ANUTHA ZONE, Dr. John, 98-33

THE ANVIL, Visage, 82-6

ANY LOVE, Luther Vandross, 88-3

ANYMORE FOR ANYMORE, Ronnie Lane and the band Slim Chance, 74-48

ANYTHING, Damned, 86-40

ANYTHING FOR YOU, Gloria Estefan and Miami Sound Machine, 88-1

ANYTHING IS POSSIBLE, Debbie Gibson, 91-69

ANYTIME ANYWHERE, Rita Coolidge, 77-6

ANYWAY, Family, 70-7

ANYWAYAWANNA, Beatmasters, 89-30

ANYWHERE, New Musik, 81-68

APOCALYPSE 91 . . . THE ENEMY STRIKES BLACK, Public Enemy, 91-8

APPETITE FOR DESTRUCTION, Guns N' Roses, 87-5

APPLE VENUS – VOLUME 1, XTC, 99-42

APPOLONIA / FEEL THE DROP, B M Ex, 93-17

APPROVED BY THE MOTORS, Motors, 78-60

APRIL MOON, Sam Brown, 90-38

AQUALUNG, Jethro Tull, 71-4

AQUARIUM, Aqua, 97-6

ARBORESCENCE, Ozric Tentacles, 94-18

ARC OF A DIVER, Steve Winwood, 81-13

ARCHITECTURE AND MORALITY, Orchestral Manoeuvres In The Dark, 81-3

ARCHIVE 1967-75, Genesis, 98-35

ARCHIVE ONE, Dave Clarke, 96-36

ARE YOU EXPERIENCED, Jimi Hendrix Experience, 67-2

ARE YOU GONNA GO MY WAY, Lenny Kravitz, 93-1

ARE YOU NORMAL?, Ned's Atomic Dustbin, 92-13

ARE YOU OKAY?, Was (Not Was), 90-35

ARE YOU READY?, Bucks Fizz, 82-10

ARENA, Duran Duran, 84-6

ARETHA, Aretha Franklin, 86-51

ARETHA NOW, Aretha Franklin, 68-6

ARGUS, Wishbone Ash, 72-3

ARGY BARGY, Squeeze, 80-32

ARIA – THE OPERA ALBUM, Andrea Bocelli, 98-33

ARISE, Sepultura, 91-40

ARKANSAS TRAVELER, Michelle Shocked, 92-46

ARKOLOGY, Lee 'Scratch' Perry, 97-49

ARMAGEDDON, Various Artists: Films – Original Soundtracks, 98-19

ARMCHAIR MELODIES, David Gray and Tommy Tycho, 76-21

ARMCHAIR THEATRE, Jeff Lynne, 90-24

ARMED FORCES, Elvis Costello and the Attractions, 79-2

AROUND THE FUR, Deftones, 97-56

AROUND THE NEXT DREAM, BBM, 94-9

AROUND THE WORLD IN A DAY, Prince and the Revolution, 85-5

AROUND THE WORLD – LIVE IN CONCERT, Osmonds, 76-41

AROUND THE WORLD – THE JOURNEY SO FAR, East 17, 96-3

ARRIVAL, Abba, 76-1

ART AND ILLUSION, Twelfth Night, 84-83

THE ART GARFUNKEL ALBUM, Art Garfunkel, 84-12

THE ART OF CHRIS FARLOWE, Chris Farlowe, 66-37

THE ART OF FALLING APART, Soft Cell, 83-5

THE ART OF WAR, Bone Thugs-N-Harmony, 97-42

ARTIFICIAL INTELLIGENCE II, Various Artists: Compilations – Warp, 94-16

THE ARTISTS VOLUME 1, Earth Wind And Fire/Jean Carn/Rose Royce, 85-65

BANDS OF GOLD – THE ELECTRIC EIGHTIES, Various Artists: Compilations – Stylus, 87-82

BANDS OF GOLD – THE SENSATIONAL SEVENTIES, Various Artists: Compilations – Stylus, 87-75

BANDSTAND, Family, 72-15

BANDWAGONESQUE, Teenage Fanclub, 91-22

BANG!, World Party, 93-2

BANG! – GREATEST HITS OF FRANKIE GOES TO HOLLYWOOD, Frankie Goes To Hollywood, 93-4

BARAFUNDLE, Gorky's Zygotic Mynci, 97-46

THE BARBARA DICKSON ALBUM, Barbara Dickson, 80-7

THE BARBARA DICKSON SONGBOOK, Barbara Dickson, 85-5

BARBED WIRE KISSES, Jesus And Mary Chain, 88-9

BARBOLETTA, Santana, 74-18

BARBRA STREISAND GREATEST HITS VOLUME 2, Barbra Streisand, 79-1

BARBRA STREISAND'S GREATEST HITS, Barbra Streisand, 70-44

BARBRA – THE CONCERT, Barbra Streisand, 94-63

BARCELONA, Freddie Mercury and Montserrat Caballe, 88-15

BARCELONA GOLD, Various Artists: Compilations – Warner Brothers, 92-15

BARCLAY JAMES HARVEST LIVE, Barclay James Harvest, 74-40

BARCLAY JAMES HARVEST XII, Barclay James Harvest, 78-31

BARE WIRES, John Mayall's Blues Breakers, 68-3

BARK, Jefferson Airplane, 71-42

BARK AT THE MOON, Ozzy Osbourne, 83-24

BARRY, Barry Manilow, 80-5

BARRY LIVE IN BRITAIN, Barry Manilow, 82-1

BARRY MANILOW SINGIN' WITH THE BIG BANDS, Barry Manilow, 94-54

BARRY SINGS SINATRA, Barry Manilow, 98-72

BARRY WHITE'S GREATEST HITS VOLUME 2, Barry White, 77-17

THE BASEMENT TAPES, Bob Dylan, 75-8

BASKET OF LIGHT, Pentangle, 69-5

BASS CULTURE, Linton Kwesi Johnson, 80-46

BAT OUT OF HELL, Meat Loaf, 78-9

BAT OUT OF HELL II – BACK INTO HELL, Meat Loaf, 93-1

BATMAN [OST], Prince, 89-1

BATMAN [OST], Danny Elfman, 89-45

BATMAN FOREVER, Various Artists: Films – Original Soundtracks, 95-11

BATTERIES NOT INCLUDED, After The Fire, 82-82

BATTLE HYMNS FOR CHILDREN SINGING, Haysi Fantayzee, 83-53

THE BATTLE OF LOS ANGELES, Rage Against The Machine, 99-23

THE BATTLE RAGES ON . . ., Deep Purple, 93-21

BAY OF KINGS, Steve Hackett, 83-70

BAYOU COUNTRY, Creedence Clearwater Revival, 70-62

THE BBC 1922-1972 (TV AND RADIO EXTRACTS), Various Artists: Television and Radio Combined, 72-16

BBC RADIO 1 LIVE IN CONCERT, New Order, 92-33

BBC SESSIONS, Led Zeppelin, 97-23

BBC SESSIONS, Jimi Hendrix Experience, 98-42

BBC TV'S BEST OF TOP OF THE POPS, Various Artists: Selected Series – Top Of The Pops, 75-21

BE HERE NOW, Oasis, 97-1

BE MY LOVE . . . AN ALBUM OF LOVE, Placido Domingo, 90-14

BE SEEING YOU, Dr. Feelgood, 77-55

BE YOURSELF TONIGHT, Eurythmics, 85-3

THE BEACH BOYS, Beach Boys, 85-60

THE BEACH BOYS LOVE YOU, Beach Boys, 77-28

BEACH BOYS PARTY, Beach Boys, 66-3

BEACH BOYS TODAY, Beach Boys, 66-6

BEACH PARTY 2, James Last, 71-47

BEACHES [OST], Bette Midler, 89-21

A BEARD OF STARS, Tyrannosaurus Rex, 70-21

A BEARD OF STARS / UNICORN [RI], Tyrannosaurus Rex, 72-44

THE BEAST INSIDE, Inspiral Carpets, 91-5

BEASTER, Sugar, 93-3

BEAT, King Crimson, 82-39

BEAT BOY, Visage, 84-79

BEAT BOYS IN THE JET AGE, Lambrettas, 80-28

BEAT CRAZY, Joe Jackson, 80-42

BEAT GIRL [OST], Adam Faith, 61-11

BEAT OF THE BRASS, Herb Alpert and the Tijuana Brass, 68-4

BEAT RUNS WILD, Various Artists: Compilations – Mercury, 86-70

BEAT STREET, Various Artists: Films – Original Soundtracks, 84-30

BEAT THE CARROTT, Jasper Carrott, 81-13

THE BEAT, THE RHYME, THE NOISE, Wee Papa Girl Rappers, 88-39

BEAT THIS – 20 HITS OF RHYTHM KING, Various Artists: Compilations – Stylus, 89-9

BEATLEMANIA, Various Artists: Anonymous - Top Six, 64-19

THE BEATLES AT THE HOLLYWOOD BOWL, Beatles, 77-1

BEATLES BALLADS, Beatles, 80-17

BEATLES CONCERTO, Rostal and Schaefer, 79-61

BEATLES FOR SALE, Beatles, 64-1

THE BEATLES 1962 – 1966, Beatles, 73-3

THE BEATLES 1967 – 1970, Beatles, 73-2

THE BEATLES TAPES, Beatles, 76-45

THE BEATLES (THE WHITE ALBUM), Beatles, 68-1

BEATS RHYMES AND BASSLINES – THE BEST OF RAP, Various Artists: Compilations – PolyGram TV, 92-7

BEATS, RHYMES AND LIFE, A Tribe Called Quest, 96-28

BEATSONGS, Blue Aeroplanes, 91-33

BEAUCOUP FISH, Underworld, 99-3

BEAUTIFUL DREAMS, Chris De Burgh, 95-33

BEAUTIFUL FREAK, Eels, 97-5

THE BEAUTIFUL GAME – EUFA EURO '96, Various Artists: Compilations – RCA, 96-10

BEAUTIFUL INSANE, Electrasy, 98-48

BEAUTIFUL MALADIES 1983-1993: THE ISLAND YEARS, Tom Waits, 98-63

BEAUTIFUL NOISE, Neil Diamond, 76-10

BEAUTIFUL SUNDAY, Lena Martell, 80-23

BEAUTIFUL – THE REMIX ALBUM, Blondie, 95-25

BEAUTIFUL VISION, Van Morrison, 82-31

BEAUTIFUL WASTELAND, Capercaillie, 97-55

BEAUTY AND THE BEAT, Peggy Lee and George Shearing, 60-16

BEAUTY ON A BACK STREET, Daryl Hall and John Oates, 77-40

BEAUTY STAB, ABC, 83-12

BECOME WHAT YOU ARE, Juliana Hatfield Three, 93-44

BECOMING X, Sneaker Pimps, 96-27

BED, Five Thirty, 91-57

BEDTIME STORIES, Judge Dread, 75-26

BEDTIME STORIES, Madonna, 94-2

BEE GEES FIRST, Bee Gees, 67-8

BEE GEES GREATEST, Bee Gees, 79-6

BEEBOP MOPTOP, Danny Wilson, 89-24

BEETHOVEN TRIPLE CONCERTO, Berlin Philharmonic Orchestra conducted by Herbert Von Karajan – soloist: David Oistrakh (violin), Mstislav Rostropovich (cello), Sviatoslau Richter (piano), 70-51

BEETHOVEN VIOLIN CONCERTO, CORIOLAN OVERTURE, Nigel Kennedy with Klaus Tennstedt conducting the North German Radio Symphony Orchestra, 92-40

BEETHOVEN WAS DEAF, Morrissey, 93-13

BEFORE AND AFTER, Tim Finn, 93-29

BEFORE THE CALM, Witness, 99-59

BEFORE THE FLOOD, Bob Dylan, 74-8

BEFORE THE RAIN, Eternal, 97-3

BEGGAR ON A BEACH OF GOLD, Mike and the Mechanics, 95-9

BEGGARS BANQUET, Rolling Stones, 68-3

BEGIN THE BEGUINE, Julio Iglesias, 81-5

BEGINNINGS, Steve Howe, 75-22

BEHAVIOUR, Pet Shop Boys, 90-2

BEHIND CLOSED DOORS, Charlie Rich, 74-4

BEHIND CLOSED DOORS, Secret Affair, 80-48

BEHIND CLOSED DOORS, Thunder, 95-5

BEHIND THE MASK, Fleetwood Mac, 90-1

BEHIND THE SUN, Eric Clapton, 85-8

THE BEIDERBECKE COLLECTION, Frank Ricotti All Stars, 88-14

BEING WITH YOU, Smokey Robinson, 81-17

BELIEF, Innocence, 90-24

BELIEVE, Cher, 98-7

BELIEVE IN ME, Duff McKagan, 93-27

BELIEVE IN MUSIC, Various Artists: Compilations – K-Tel, 73-2

BELIEVE YOU ME, Blancmange, 85-54

BELLA DONNA, Stevie Nicks, 81-11

BELLAMY BROTHERS, Bellamy Brothers, 76-21

THE BELLE STARS, Belle Stars, 83-15

BELOW THE SALT, Steeleye Span, 72-43

BEN, Michael Jackson, 73-17

BEN-HUR, Various Artists: Films – Original Soundtracks, 60-15

BEND SINISTER, Fall, 86-36

THE BENDS, Radiohead, 95-4

BENEATH THE SURFACE, Gza/Genius, 99-56

BENEFIT, Jethro Tull, 70-3

BENNY GOODMAN TODAY, Benny Goodman, 71-49

BENT OUT OF SHAPE, Rainbow, 83-11

BENTLEY RHYTHM ACE, Bentley Rhythm Ace, 97-13

BERLIN, Lou Reed, 73-7

BERNSTEIN IN BERLIN – BEETHOVEN SYMPHONY NO. 9, Orchestra and Chorus conducted by Leonard Bernstein, 90-54

BERSERKER, Gary Numan, 84-45

BERT KAEMPFERT – BEST SELLER, Bert Kaempfert, 67-25

THE BEST . . . I, Smiths, 92-1

THE BEST . . . II, Smiths, 92-29

THE BEST . . . ALBUM IN THE WORLD . . . EVER!, Various Artists: Selected Series – Best . . . Ever!, 95-2

THE BEST . . . ALBUM IN THE WORLD . . . EVER! 2, Various Artists: Selected Series – Best . . . Ever!, 96-1

THE BEST . . . ALBUM IN THE WORLD . . . EVER! 3, Various Artists: Selected Series – Best . . . Ever!, 96-2

THE BEST . . . ALBUM IN THE WORLD . . . EVER! 4, Various Artists: Selected Series – Best . . . Ever!, 96-2

THE BEST . . . ALBUM IN THE WORLD . . . EVER! 5, Various Artists: Selected Series – Best . . . Ever!, 97-1

THE BEST . . . ALBUM IN THE WORLD . . . EVER! 6, Various Artists: Selected Series – Best . . . Ever!, 97-8

THE BEST ALBUM . . . IN THE WORLD . . . EVER! 7, Various Artists: Selected Series – Best . . . Ever!, 98-11

THE BEST . . . AND FRIENDS ALBUM IN THE WORLD . . . EVER!, Various Artists: Selected Series – Best . . . Ever!, 99-8

THE BEST . . . ANTHEMS . . . EVER!, Various Artists: Selected Series – Best . . . Ever!, 97-1

THE BEST . . . ANTHEMS . . . EVER! 2, Various Artists: Selected Series – Best . . . Ever!, 98-3

THE BEST . . . ANTHEMS . . . EVER! 3, Various Artists: Selected Series – Best . . . Ever!, 98-19

THE BEST CHART HITS ALBUM IN THE WORLD . . . EVER!, Various Artists: Selected Series – Best . . . Ever!, 98-1

THE BEST CHART HITS IN THE WORLD . . . EVER! 99, Various Artists: Selected Series – Best . . . Ever!, 99-5

THE BEST CHRISTMAS ALBUM IN THE WORLD . . . EVER!, Various Artists: Selected Series – Best . . . Ever!, 93-2

THE BEST CHRISTMAS ALBUM IN THE WORLD . . . EVER!, Various Artists: Selected Series – Best . . . Ever!, 96-2

THE CULT OF RAY, Frank Black, 96-39

CULTOSAURUS ERECTUS, Blue Oyster Cult, 80-12

CUNNING STUNTS, Caravan, 75-50

CUPID AND PSYCHE 85, Scritti Politti, 85-5

CURE FOR SANITY, Pop Will Eat Itself, 90-33

CURED, Steve Hackett, 81-15

A CURIOUS FEELING, Tony Banks, 79-21

THE CURSE, Throwing Muses, 92-74

CURTAIN UP, Various Artists: Compilations – Pye, 59-4

CURTAINS, Tindersticks, 97-37

CURTIS STIGERS, Curtis Stigers, 92-7

CURVED AIR, Curved Air, 71-11

CUT, Slits, 79-30

CUT THE CAKE, Average White Band, 75-28

CUT THE CRAP, Clash, 85-16

CUTS BOTH WAYS, Gloria Estefan, 89-1

CUTS LIKE A KNIFE, Bryan Adams, 86-21

THE CUTTER AND THE CLAN, Runrig, 95-45

CUTTIN' HERBIE, B Boys, 84-90

CYBERPUNK, Billy Idol, 93-20

CYCLONE, Tangerine Dream, 78-37

CYMANSA GANN, Massed Welsh Choirs, 69-5

CYPRESS HILL III (TEMPLES OF BOOM), Cypress Hill, 95-11

D'EUX – THE FRENCH ALBUM, Celine Dion, 95-7

D-FROST – 20 GLOBAL DANCE WARNINGS, Various Artists: Compilations – Touchdown, 93-8

D:REAM ON VOLUME 1, D:Ream, 93-5

D-TRAIN, D-Train, 82-72

DA GAMES IS TO BE SOLD, NOT TO BE TOLD, Snoop Dogg, 98-28

DA REAL WORLD, Missy Misdemeanor Elliott, 99-40

DADA, Alice Cooper, 83-93

DAMM RIGHT, I'VE GOT THE BLUES, Buddy Guy, 91-43

DAMN THE TORPEDOES, Tom Petty and the Heartbreakers, 79-57

DAMNED DAMNED DAMNED, Damned, 77-36

DANCE, Gary Numan, 81-3

THE DANCE, Fleetwood Mac, 97-15

DANCE ADRENALIN, Various Artists: Compilations – Telstar, 93-1

DANCE BUZZ, Various Artists: Compilations – Global Television, 95-3

THE DANCE CHART, Various Artists: Compilations – Telstar, 87-23

DANCE CLASSICS VOLUME 1, Various Artists: Compilations – Arcade, 91-8

DANCE CLASSICS VOLUME 2, Various Artists: Compilations – Arcade, 91-7

DANCE CRAZE, Various Artists: Films – Original Soundtracks, 81-5

DANCE DANCE DANCE, Various Artists: Compilations – K-Tel, 81-29

DANCE DANCE DANCE, James Last, 88-38

DANCE DECADE – DANCE HITS OF THE 80'S, Various Artists: Compilations – London, 89-8

DANCE DIVAS, Various Artists: Compilations – PolyGram TV, 94-11

DANCE ENERGY, Various Artists: Selected Series – Dance Energy, 91-20

DANCE ENERGY 2, Various Artists: Selected Series – Dance Energy, 91-6

DANCE ENERGY 3, Various Artists: Selected Series – Dance Energy, 91-10

DANCE ENERGY 4 – FEEL THE RHYTHM, Various Artists: Selected Series – Dance Energy, 92-6

DANCE HALL AT LOUSE POINT, John Parish/Polly Jean Harvey, 96-46

DANCE HEAT '95, Various Artists: Compilations – Virgin, 95-8

THE DANCE HITS ALBUM, Various Artists: Compilations – Towerbell, 86-10

DANCE HITS '86, Various Artists: Compilations – K-Tel, 86-35

DANCE HITS II, Various Artists: Compilations – Towerbell, 86-25

DANCE HITS 94 – VOLUME 1, Various Artists: Compilations – Telstar, 94-1

DANCE HITS '94 VOLUME 2, Various Artists: Compilations – Telstar, 94-1

DANCE IN THE MIDNIGHT, Marc Bolan, 83-83

DANCE INTO THE LIGHT, Phil Collins, 96-4

DANCE MANIA 95 – VOLUME 1, Various Artists: Compilations – Pure Music, 95-1

DANCE MANIA 95 – VOLUME 2, Various Artists: Compilations – Pure Music, 95-1

DANCE MANIA 95 – VOLUME 3, Various Artists: Compilations – Pure Music, 95-1

DANCE MANIA 95 -VOLUME 4, Various Artists: Compilations – Pure Music, 95-7

DANCE MANIA VOLUME 1, Various Artists: Compilations – Needle, 87-46

DANCE MANIA VOLUME 2, Various Artists: Compilations – Serious, 88-59

DANCE MASSIVE, Various Artists: Compilations – Dino, 94-3

DANCE MASSIVE 2, Various Artists: Compilations – Dino, 94-8

DANCE MASSIVE '95, Various Artists: Compilations – Dino, 95-2

DANCE MIX – DANCE HITS VOLUME 1, Various Artists: Selected Series – Dance Mix, 83-85

DANCE MIX – DANCE HITS VOLUME 2, Various Artists: Selected Series – Dance Mix, 83-51

DANCE MIX – DANCE HITS VOLUME 3, Various Artists: Selected Series – Dance Mix, 84-70

DANCE MIX – DANCE HITS VOLUME 4, Various Artists: Selected Series – Dance Mix, 84-99

DANCE MIX '87, Various Artists: Compilations – Telstar, 87-39

DANCE MIX UK, Various Artists: Compilations – Global Television, 96-6

DANCE MIX UK 2, Various Artists: Compilations – Global Television, 96-10

DANCE NATION, Various Artists: Selected Series – Dance Nation, 96-5

DANCE NATION 3 – PETE TONG & JUDGE JULES, Various Artists: Selected Series – Dance Nation, 97-1

DANCE NATION 4 – PETE TONG/BOY GEORGE, Various Artists: Selected Series – Dance Nation, 97-2

DANCE NATION SIX – TALL PAUL & BRANDON BLOCK, Various Artists: Selected Series – Dance Nation, 99-1

DANCE NATION '95, Various Artists: Compilations – Vision, 95-6

DANCE '95, Various Artists: Compilations – Virgin, 95-8

DANCE OF THE FLAMES, Incantation, 83-61

DANCE TIP 2000, Various Artists: Compilations – Warner.esp/Global TV, 96-7

DANCE TIP 3, Various Artists: Compilations – Global Television, 95-2

DANCE TIP 4, Various Artists: Compilations – Warner.esp/Global TV, 96-7

DANCE TIP '95, Various Artists: Compilations – Global Television, 95-3

DANCE TO THE HOLY MAN, Silencers, 91-39

DANCE TO THE MAX, Various Artists: Compilations – Virgin, 94-2

DANCE TO THE MAX 2, Various Artists: Compilations – Virgin, 94-4

DANCE TO THE MAX 3, Various Artists: Compilations – Virgin, 94-12

DANCE TO THE MUSIC, Various Artists: Compilations – K-Tel, 77-5

DANCE WARS – JUDGE JULES VS. JOHN KELLY, Various Artists: Compilations – JDJ, 96-11

DANCE WITH THE GUITAR MAN, Duane Eddy, 63-14

DANCE WITH THE SHADOWS, Shadows, 64-2

DANCE! . . . YA KNOW IT!, Bobby Brown, 89-26

DANCE ZONE – LEVEL ONE, Various Artists: Selected Series – Dance Zone, 94-1

DANCE ZONE – LEVEL TWO, Various Artists: Selected Series – Dance Zone, 94-1

DANCE ZONE – LEVEL THREE, Various Artists: Selected Series – Dance Zone, 94-1

DANCE ZONE – LEVEL FOUR, Various Artists: Selected Series – Dance Zone, 95-1

DANCE ZONE – LEVEL FIVE, Various Artists: Selected Series – Dance Zone, 95-1

DANCE ZONE – LEVEL SIX, Various Artists: Selected Series – Dance Zone, 95-1

DANCE ZONE – LEVEL SEVEN, Various Artists: Selected Series – Dance Zone, 96-1

DANCE ZONE – LEVEL EIGHT, Various Artists: Selected Series – Dance Zone, 96-4

DANCE ZONE – LEVEL NINE, Various Artists: Selected Series – Dance Zone, 99-7

DANCE ZONE '94, Various Artists: Selected Series – Dance Zone, 94-2

DANCE ZONE '95, Various Artists: Selected Series – Dance Zone, 95-8

DANCEMIX.UK.V1, Various Artists: Compilations – Warner.esp, 99-13

DANCER WITH BRUISED KNEES, Kate and Anna McGarrigle, 77-35

DANCES WITH WOLVES [OST], John Barry, 91-45

DANCIN' IN THE KEY OF LIFE, Steve Arrington, 85-41

DANCIN' ON THE EDGE, Lita Ford, 84-96

DANCIN' – 20 ORIGINAL MOTOWN MOVERS, Various Artists: Compilations – Telstar, 83-97

DANCING IN THE STREET – 43 MOTOWN DANCE CLASSICS, Various Artists: Compilations – Universal Music TV, 99-13

DANCING ON SUNSHINE, Various Artists: Compilations – PolyGram TV, 92-4

DANCING ON THE CEILING, Lionel Richie, 86-2

DANCING ON THE COUCH, Go West, 87-19

DANCING '68 VOLUME 1, James Last, 69-40

DANCING UNDERCOVER, Ratt, 86-51

DANCING WITH STRANGERS, Chris Rea, 87-2

DANDY IN THE UNDERWORLD, T. Rex, 77-26

DANGER ZONE, Sammy Hagar, 80-25

DANGER ZONE, Various Artists: Compilations – PolyGram TV, 97-15

DANGER ZONE VOLUME 1, Various Artists: Compilations – Quality Television, 92-16

DANGEROUS, Michael Jackson, 91-1

DANGEROUS ACQUAINTANCES, Marianne Faithfull, 81-45

DANGEROUS CURVES, Lita Ford, 92-51

DANGEROUS MINDS, Various Artists: Films – Original Soundtracks, 96-13

DANGEROUS MUSIC, Robin George, 85-65

THE DANIEL O'DONNELL IRISH COLLECTION, Daniel O'Donnell, 96-35

DANNY RAMPLING – LOVE GROOVE DANCE PARTY, Various Artists: Compilations – Metropole Music, 96-10

DANNY RAMPLING – LOVE GROOVE DANCE PARTY, Various Artists: Compilations – Metropole Music, 97-17

DANNY RAMPLING/LOVE GROOVE PARTY 5 & 6, Various Artists: Compilations – Metropole Music, 97-12

DANNY TENAGLIA LIVE IN ATHENS, Various Artists: Compilations – Global Underground, 99-16

DARE, Human League, 81-1

DARE TO LOVE, Jimmy Somerville, 95-38

DARING ADVENTURES, Richard Thompson, 86-92

DARK DAYS IN PARADISE, Gary Moore, 97-43

THE DARK SIDE OF THE MOON, Pink Floyd, 73-2

DARKDANCER, Les Rythmes Digitales, 99-53

DARKLANDS, Jesus And Mary Chain, 87-5

DARKNESS ON THE EDGE OF TOWN, Bruce Springsteen, 78-16

DARREN DAY, Darren Day, 98-62

DART ATTACK, Darts, 79-38

DARTS, Darts, 77-9

A DATE WITH DANIEL – LIVE, Daniel O'Donnell, 93-21

A DATE WITH ELVIS, Elvis Presley, 59-4

A DATE WITH ELVIS, Cramps, 86-34

A DATE WITH THE EVERLY BROTHERS, Everly Brothers, 61-3

DAUGHTER OF TIME, Colosseum, 70-23

DAVE CLARK'S TIME THE ALBUM, Various Artists: Studio Cast, 86-21

DAVE DEE, DOZY, BEAKY, MICK AND TICH, Dave Dee, Dozy, Beaky, Mick and Tich, 66-11

ELEGY, Nice, 71-5

ELEMENTAL, Tears For Fears, 93-5

ELEMENTALZ, Brotherhood, 96-50

ELEMENTS – SEB FONTAINE/TONY DE VIT, Various Artists: Compilations – Westway Dance, 98-15

ELEMENTS – THE BEST OF MIKE OLDFIELD, Mike Oldfield, 93-5

ELEVENTEEN, Daisy Chainsaw, 92-62

THE ELEVENTH HOUR, Magnum, 83-38

ELGAR CELLO CONCERTO, Julian Lloyd Webber with the Royal Philharmonic Orchestra conducted by Sir Yehudi Menuhin, 87-94

ELGAR/PAYNE: SYMPHONY NO. 3, BBC Symphony Orchestra conducted by Andrew Davis, 98-44

ELGAR VIOLIN CONCERTO, Nigel Kennedy with the London Philharmonic Orchestra conducted by Vernon Handley, 86-97

ELIMINATOR, ZZ Top, 83-3

ELITE HOTEL, Emmylou Harris, 76-17

ELITE SYNCOPATIONS, Chris Barber, 60-18

ELIZIUM, Fields Of The Nephilim, 90-22

ELLA AT THE OPERA HOUSE, Ella Fitzgerald, 60-16

ELLA SINGS GERSHWIN, Ella Fitzgerald, 60-13

ELLA SINGS GERSHWIN VOLUME 5, Ella Fitzgerald, 60-18

ELO'S GREATEST HITS, Electric Light Orchestra, 79-7

ELTON JOHN, Elton John, 70-11

ELTON JOHN AND TIM RICE'S AIDA, Elton John and Friends, 99-29

THE ELTON JOHN LIVE ALBUM 17-11-70, Elton John, 71-20

ELTON JOHN'S GREATEST HITS, Elton John, 74-1

ELVIS, Elvis Presley, 73-16

ELVIS – A LEGENDARY PERFORMER VOLUME 1, Elvis Presley, 74-20

ELVIS ARON PRESLEY, Elvis Presley, 80-21

ELVIS AS RECORDED AT MADISON SQUARE GARDEN, Elvis Presley, 72-3

ELVIS AS RECORDED ON STAGE IN MEMPHIS, Elvis Presley, 74-44

ELVIS' CHRISTMAS ALBUM, Elvis Presley, 71-7

ELVIS 56, Elvis Presley, 96-42

ELVIS FOR EVERYONE, Elvis Presley, 65-8

ELVIS FOR EVERYONE, Elvis Presley, 72-48

ELVIS' GOLDEN RECORDS, Elvis Presley, 58-3

ELVIS' GOLDEN RECORDS VOLUME 2, Elvis Presley, 60-4

ELVIS' GOLDEN RECORDS VOLUME 3, Elvis Presley, 64-6

ELVIS IN CONCERT [OST-TV], Elvis Presley, 77-13

ELVIS IN DEMAND, Elvis Presley, 77-12

ELVIS IS BACK!, Elvis Presley, 60-1

ELVIS – NBC TV SPECIAL [OST-TV], Elvis Presley, 69-2

ELVIS NOW, Elvis Presley, 72-12

ELVIS PRESLEY – BALLADS: 18 CLASSIC LOVE SONGS, Elvis Presley, 85-23

ELVIS PRESLEY EP PACK, Elvis Presley, 82-97

ELVIS PRESLEY SINGS LIEBER AND STOLLER, Elvis Presley, 80-32

THE ELVIS PRESLEY SUN COLLECTION, Elvis Presley, 75-16

ELVIS (ROCK 'N' ROLL NO. 1), Elvis Presley, 59-4

ELVIS SINGS FLAMING STAR, Elvis Presley, 69-2

ELVIS'S 40 GREATEST HITS, Elvis Presley, 75-1

EMANCIPATION, Artist, 96-18

EMBRYA, Maxwell, 98-11

EMERALD CLASSICS, Various Artists: Compilations – Stoic, 84-35

EMERALD CLASSICS VOLUMES I AND II, Various Artists: Compilations – Westmoor, 90-14

EMERALD ROCK, Various Artists: Compilations – PolyGram TV, 95-14

EMERGENCY, Kool And The Gang, 84-47

EMERGENCY ON PLANET EARTH, Jamiroquai, 93-1

EMERSON, LAKE AND PALMER, Emerson, Lake and Palmer, 70-4

EMERSON, LAKE AND POWELL, Emerson, Lake and Powell, 86-35

EMMERDANCE, Woolpackers, 96-26

EMOTION, Barbra Streisand, 84-15

AN EMOTIONAL FISH, An Emotional Fish, 90-40

THE EMOTIONAL HOOLIGAN, Gary Clail On-U Sound System, 91-35

EMOTIONAL RESCUE, Rolling Stones, 80-1

EMOTIONS, Various Artists: Compilations – K-Tel, 78-2

EMOTIONS, Mariah Carey, 91-4

EMPEROR TOMATO KETCHUP, Stereolab, 96-27

EMPIRE, Queensryche, 90-13

EMPIRE BURLESQUE, Bob Dylan, 85-11

EMPIRE OF THE SENSELESS, Senseless Things, 93-37

EMPIRES AND DANCE, Simple Minds, 80-41

EMPTY GLASS, Pete Townshend, 80-11

EMPTY ROOMS, John Mayall, 70-9

EN-TACT, Shamen, 90-31

ENCHANTED, Marc Almond, 90-52

ENCORE, Tangerine Dream, 77-55

ENCORE, Marti Webb, 85-55

ENCORE, Elaine Paige, 95-20

THE END COMPLETE, Obituary, 92-52

END HITS, Fugazi, 98-47

END OF MILLENNIUM PSYCHOSIS BLUES, That Petrol Emotion, 88-53

END OF PART ONE (THEIR GREATEST HITS), Wet Wet Wet, 93-1

END OF THE CENTURY, Ramones, 80-14

THE END OF THE INNOCENCE, Don Henley, 89-17

ENDLESS, Heaven 17, 86-70

ENDLESS FLIGHT, Leo Sayer, 76-4

ENDLESS HARMONY SOUNDTRACK, Beach Boys, 98-56

ENDLESS LOVE, Various Artists: Compilations – TV Records, 82-26

ENDLESS LOVE, Various Artists: Compilations – PolyGram TV, 95-3

ENDLESS, NAMELESS, Wildhearts, 97-41

ENDLESS SUMMER – GREATEST HITS, Donna Summer, 94-37

ENDTRODUCING . . ., DJ Shadow, 96-17

ENERGIQUE, Bizarre Inc, 92-41

ENERGY ORCHARD, Energy Orchard, 90-53

ENERGY RUSH, Various Artists: Selected Series – Energy Rush, 92-1

ENERGY RUSH II, Various Artists: Selected Series – Energy Rush, 92-7

ENERGY RUSH 7, Various Artists: Selected Series – Energy Rush, 94-2

ENERGY RUSH DANCE HITS 93 (2ND DIMENSION), Various Artists: Selected Series – Energy Rush, 93-2

ENERGY RUSH DANCE HITS 94, Various Artists: Selected Series – Energy Rush, 94-3

ENERGY RUSH – EURO DANCE HITS 94, Various Artists: Selected Series – Energy Rush, 94-5

ENERGY RUSH FACTOR 5, Various Artists: Selected Series – Energy Rush, 93-3

ENERGY RUSH K9, Various Artists: Selected Series – Energy Rush, 95-3

ENERGY RUSH LEVEL 3, Various Artists: Selected Series – Energy Rush, 93-3

ENERGY RUSH PHASE 4, Various Artists: Selected Series – Energy Rush, 93-2

ENERGY RUSH PRESENTS DANCE HITS 93, Various Artists: Selected Series – Energy Rush, 93-1

ENERGY RUSH PRESENTS DANCE HITS OF THE YEAR, Various Artists: Selected Series – Energy Rush, 93-3

ENERGY RUSH – SAFE SIX, Various Artists: Selected Series – Energy Rush, 93-5

ENERGY RUSH – XTERMIN8, Various Artists: Selected Series – Energy Rush, 94-1

ENGELBERT, Engelbert Humperdinck, 69-3

ENGELBERT HUMPERDINCK, Engelbert Humperdinck, 69-5

THE ENGELBERT HUMPERDINCK COLLECTION, Engelbert Humperdinck, 87-35

ENGELBERT HUMPERDINCK – HIS GREATEST HITS, Engelbert Humperdinck, 74-1

ENGLISH SETTLEMENT, XTC, 82-5

ENJOY YOURSELF, Kylie Minogue, 89-1

ENLIGHTENMENT, Van Morrison, 90-5

ENTER THE DRU, Dru Hill, 98-42

ENTERTAINMENT, Gang Of Four, 79-45

ENTREAT, Cure, 91-10

ENVY OF ANGELS, Mutton Birds, 97-64

ENYA [OST-TV], Enya, 87-69

THE EPIC YEARS, Shaky, 92-57

EPONYMOUS, R.E.M., 88-69

EQUALLY CURSED AND BLESSED, Catatonia, 99-1

EQUALS EXPLOSION, Equals, 68-32

EQUATOR, Uriah Heep, 85-79

EQUINOXE, Jean-Michel Jarre, 78-11

ERASURE, Erasure, 95-14

ERIC BURDON DECLARES WAR, Eric Burdon and War, 70-50

ERIC CARMEN, Eric Carmen, 76-58

ERIC CLAPTON, Eric Clapton, 70-17

EROICA, Wendy and Lisa, 90-33

EROTICA, Madonna, 92-2

ERROL FLYNN, Dogs D'Amour, 89-22

ESCAPE, Journey, 82-32

ESCAPE FROM TV, Jan Hammer, 87-34

ESCM, BT, 97-35

ESPECIALLY FOR YOU, Don Williams, 81-33

ESPECIALLY FOR YOU, Joe Longthorne, 89-22

ESPECIALLY FOR YOU, Daniel O'Donnell, 94-14

ESPECIALLY FOR YOU, Various Artists: Compilations – Columbia, 99-1

ESPRESSO LOGIC, Chris Rea, 93-8

ESSENTIAL BALLET, Various Artists: Compilations – Decca, 92-9

THE ESSENTIAL CHILL, Various Artists: Compilations – Arcade, 92-16

ESSENTIAL CLASSICS, Various Artists: Compilations – Deutsche Grammophon, 90-6

THE ESSENTIAL COLLECTION, Elvis Presley, 94-6

THE ESSENTIAL COLLECTION, Marc Bolan and T. Rex, 95-24

THE ESSENTIAL COLLECTION, Dionne Warwick, 96-58

ESSENTIAL DISCO AND DANCE, Various Artists: Compilations – Nouveau Music, 84-96

THE ESSENTIAL DOMINGO, Placido Domingo, 89-20

ESSENTIAL ELLA, Ella Fitzgerald, 94-35

THE ESSENTIAL GROOVE, Various Artists: Compilations – PolyGram TV, 95-11

ESSENTIAL HARDCORE, Various Artists: Compilations – Dino, 91-1

THE ESSENTIAL JEAN-MICHEL JARRE, Jean-Michel Jarre, 83-14

THE ESSENTIAL JOSE CARRERAS, Jose Carreras, 91-24

THE ESSENTIAL KARAJAN, Herbert Von Karajan, 88-51

THE ESSENTIAL KIRI, Kiri Te Kanawa, 92-23

ESSENTIAL MILLENNIUM – PETE TONG FATBOY SLIM PAUL OAKENFOLD, Various Artists: Selected Series – Essential Selection, 99-10

ESSENTIAL MIX – TONG COX SASHA OAKENFOLD, Various Artists: Compilations – Ffrr, 96-12

ESSENTIAL MIX 2 – TONG, MACKINTOSH . . ., Various Artists: Compilations – Ffrr, 96-6

ESSENTIAL MIX 3 – TONG, SEAMAN, JULES ETC, Various Artists: Compilations – Ffrr, 96-12

THE ESSENTIAL MOZART, Various Artists: Compilations – Decca, 91-1

ESSENTIAL OPERA, Various Artists: Compilations – Decca, 91-2

ESSENTIAL OPERA 2, Various Artists: Compilations – Decca, 93-17

THE ESSENTIAL PAVAROTTI, Luciano Pavarotti, 90-1

ESSENTIAL PAVAROTTI II, Luciano Pavarotti, 91-1

ESSENTIAL SELECTION '98 – PETE TONG/PAUL OAKENFOLD, Various Artists: Selected Series – Essential Selection, 98-11

ESSENTIAL SELECTION '98 – PETE TONG/PAUL OAKENFOLD, Various Artists: Selected Series – Essential Selection, 99-13

ESSENTIAL SOUNDTRACKS, Various Artists: Films – Related Compilations, 99-4

FAREWELL MY SUMMER LOVE, Michael Jackson, 84-9

FAREWELL TO KINGS, Rush, 77-22

FASHION NUGGET, Cake, 97-53

FAST FORWARD, Various Artists: Magazine Related, 91-4

FASTER THAN THE SPEED OF NIGHT, Bonnie Tyler, 83-1

FASTWAY, Fastway, 83-43

FAT DANCE HITS, Various Artists: Compilations – Global Television, 99-5

THE FAT OF THE LAND, Prodigy, 97-1

FAT OUT OF HELL, Roy Chubby Brown, 96-67

FAT POP HITS, Various Artists: Compilations – Global Television, 99-6

FATBACK LIVE, Fatback, 87-80

FATE FOR BREAKFAST, Art Garfunkel, 79-2

FATE OF NATIONS, Robert Plant, 93-6

FATHER ABRAHAM IN SMURFLAND, Father Abraham and the Smurfs, 78-19

FAVOURITES, Peters and Lee, 75-2

FAVOURITES, Daniel O'Donnell, 90-61

FAWLTY TOWERS, Various Artists: Television – Soundtracks, 79-25

FAWLTY TOWERS VOLUME 2, Various Artists: Television – Soundtracks, 81-26

FE REAL, Maxi Priest, 92-60

FEAR OF A BLACK PLANET, Public Enemy, 90-4

FEAR OF FOURS, Lamb, 99-37

FEAR OF MUSIC, Talking Heads, 79-33

FEAR OF THE DARK, Iron Maiden, 92-1

FEARGAL SHARKEY, Feargal Sharkey, 85-12

FEARLESS, Family, 71-14

FEARLESS, Eighth Wonder, 88-47

FEAST, Creatures, 83-17

FEEL, Roachford, 97-19

FEEL LIKE MAKING LOVE, Various Artists: Compilations – The Hit Label, 95-17

FEEL THIS, Jeff Healey Band, 92-72

FEELING FREE, Sydney Youngblood, 89-23

FEELING GOOD – THE VERY BEST OF NINA SIMONE, Nina Simone, 94-9

FEELING STRANGELY FINE, Semisonic, 99-16

FEELINGS, Various Artists: Compilations – K-Tel, 77-3

FEELS LIKE RAIN, Buddy Guy, 93-36

FEETS DON'T FAIL ME NOW, Herbie Hancock, 79-28

FELICIANO, Jose Feliciano, 68-6

FELINE, Stranglers, 83-4

FELIX #1, Felix, 93-26

FELLOW HOODLUMS, Deacon Blue, 91-2

THE FEMALE TOUCH, Various Artists: Compilations – Warner.esp/Global TV, 98-2

THE FEMALE TOUCH 2, Various Artists: Compilations – Warner.esp/Global TV, 99-9

FERMENT, Catherine Wheel, 92-36

FERRY ACROSS THE MERSEY, Gerry and the Pacemakers, 65-19

FESTIVAL, Santana, 77-27

FEVER IN FEVER OUT, Luscious Jackson, 97-55

FFRR – SILVER ON BLACK, Various Artists: Compilations – London, 89-8

FFWD, Ffwd, 94-48

FICTION, Comsat Angels, 82-94

FICTION TALES, Modern Eon, 81-65

FIDDLER ON THE ROOF, Various Artists: Stage Cast – London, 67-4

FIDDLER ON THE ROOF, Various Artists: Films – Original Soundtracks, 72-26

FIELDS OF GOLD – THE BEST OF STING 1984-1994, Sting, 94-2

FIERCE, Various Artists: Compilations – Cooltempo, 87-37

15 BIG ONES, Beach Boys, 76-31

5TH DIMENSION, Byrds, 66-27

THE FIFTH ELEMENT [OST], Eric Serra, 97-58

FIFTY NUMBER ONES OF THE '60S, Various Artists: Compilations – Global Television, 95-8

FIFTY YEARS ON WITH JIMMY SHAND, Jimmy Shand, His Band and Guests, 83-97

52ND STREET, Billy Joel, 78-10

THE '56 SESSIONS VOLUME 1, Elvis Presley, 78-47

FIGHTING, Thin Lizzy, 75-60

FILE UNDER EASY LISTENING, Sugar, 94-7

FILIGREE AND SHADOW, This Mortal Coil, 86-53

FILTH HOUNDS OF HADES, Tank, 82-33

FILTH PIG, Ministry, 96-43

FILTHY LUCRE LIVE, Sex Pistols, 96-26

FIN DE SIECLE, Divine Comedy, 98-9

THE FINAL, Wham!, 86-2

THE FINAL COUNTDOWN, Europe, 86-9

THE FINAL COUNTDOWN – THE VERY BEST OF SOFT METAL, Various Artists: Compilations – Telstar, 90-9

THE FINAL CUT, Pink Floyd, 83-1

THE FINAL FRONTIER, Keel, 86-83

FINALLY, Ce Ce Peniston, 92-10

FINALLY, Blackstreet, 99-27

FIND OUT, Steven Dante, 88-87

FIND YOUR WAY, Gabrielle, 93-9

FINDERS KEEPERS [OST], Cliff Richard and the Shadows, 66-6

THE FINE ART OF SURFACING, Boomtown Rats, 79-7

FINE YOUNG CANNIBALS, Fine Young Cannibals, 85-11

THE FINEST, Fine Young Cannibals, 96-10

FINEST HOUR, Lindisfarne, 75-55

FINGS AIN'T WOT THEY USED TO BE, Various Artists: Stage Cast – London, 60-5

FINN, Finn, 95-15

FINYL VINYL, Rainbow, 86-31

FIRE AND ICE, Yngwie Malmsteen, 92-57

FIRE & SKILL – THE SONGS OF THE JAM, Various Artists: Compilations – Ignition, 99-12

FIRE AND WATER, Free, 70-2

FIRE AND WATER, Dave Greenfield and Jean-Jacques Burnel, 83-94

FIRE DANCES, Killing Joke, 83-29

FIRE GARDEN, Steve Vai, 96-41

THE FIRE INSIDE, Bob Seger and the Silver Bullet Band, 91-54

FIRE OF UNKNOWN ORIGIN, Blue Oyster Cult, 81-29

FIREBALL, Deep Purple, 71-1

FIREWORKS, Jose Feliciano, 70-65

FIRING ON ALL SIX, Lone Star, 77-36

THE FIRM, Firm, 85-15

FIRST AND LAST AND ALWAYS, Sisters Of Mercy, 85-14

FIRST BAND ON THE MOON, Cardigans, 96-18

FIRST BLOOD . . . LAST CUTS, W.A.S.P., 93-69

THE FIRST BORN IS DEAD, Nick Cave and the Bad Seeds, 85-53

THE FIRST CHAPTER, Mission, 87-35

THE FIRST DAY, David Sylvian and Robert Fripp, 93-21

THE FIRST FAMILY, Vaughn Meader, 62-12

FIRST LADIES OF COUNTRY, Various Artists: Compilations – CBS, 80-37

THE FIRST LADY OF SOUL, Aretha Franklin, 86-89

THE FIRST LIVE RECORDINGS, Elvis Presley, 84-69

FIRST LOVE, Various Artists: Compilations – Arcade, 80-58

FIRST LOVE, Michael Ball, 96-4

THE FIRST OF A MILLION KISSES, Fairground Attraction, 88-2

THE FIRST OF TOO MANY, Senseless Things, 91-66

FIRST RAYS OF THE NEW RISING SUN, Jimi Hendrix, 97-37

FIRST STEP, Faces, 70-45

THE FIRST SUMMER OF LOVE, Various Artists: Compilations – PolyGram TV/Sony TV, 97-6

FIRST TAKE, Roberta Flack, 72-47

FIRST TEN YEARS, Joan Baez, 71-41

FIRST (THE SOUND OF MUSIC), Then Jerico, 87-35

FIRST TIME EVER I SAW YOUR FACE, Johnny Mathis, 72-40

THE FISH AND THE TREE AND THE BIRD AND THE BELL, Various Artists: Compilations – Columbia, 91-9

FISH OUT OF WATER, Chris Squire, 75-25

THE FISH PEOPLE TAPES, Alexei Sayle, 84-62

FISH RISING, Steve Hillage, 75-33

FISHERMAN'S BLUES, Waterboys, 88-13

FISHING FOR LUCKIES, Wildhearts, 96-16

5, J.J. Cale, 79-40

5, Lenny Kravitz, 98-18

FIVE, Five, 98-1

FIVE BRIDGES, Nice, 70-2

FIVE FACES OF MANFRED MANN, Manfred Mann, 64-3

FIVE GUYS NAMED MOE, Various Artists: Stage Cast – London, 91-59

FIVE MAN ACOUSTICAL JAM, Tesla, 91-59

FIVE MILES OUT, Mike Oldfield, 82-7

THE FIVE PENNIES, Various Artists: Films – Original Soundtracks, 60-2

5,000 SPIRITS OR THE LAYERS OF THE ONION, Incredible String Band, 67-25

5150, Van Halen, 86-16

FLAG, Yello, 88-56

THE FLAME, Annabel Lamb, 84-84

FLAMENCO GUITAR, Manitas De Plata, 67-40

FLAMING PIE, Paul McCartney, 97-2

FLAMING STAR AND SUMMER KISSES, Elvis Presley, 65-11

FLARED HITS AND PLATFORM SOUL, Various Artists: Compilations – Vision, 95-13

FLASH, Jeff Beck, 85-83

FLASH GORDON [OST], Queen, 80-10

FLASH LIGHT, Tom Verlaine, 87-99

FLASH TRACKS, Various Artists: Compilations – TV Records, 82-19

FLASHDANCE, Various Artists: Films – Original Soundtracks, 83-9

FLASHPOINT, Rolling Stones, 91-6

THE FLAT EARTH, Thomas Dolby, 84-14

FLAUNT IT, Sigue Sigue Sputnik, 86-10

FLAUNT THE IMPERFECTION, China Crisis, 85-9

FLEETWOOD MAC, Peter Green's Fleetwood Mac, 68-4

FLEETWOOD MAC, Fleetwood Mac, 76-23

FLEETWOOD MAC LIVE, Fleetwood Mac, 80-31

FLESH AND BLOOD, Roxy Music, 80-1

FLESH AND BLOOD, Poison, 90-3

FLEX, Lene Lovich, 80-19

FLICK OF THE SWITCH, AC/DC, 83-4

FLIGHT OF ICARUS/THE TROOPER, Iron Maiden, 90-7

FLIGHT OF THE CONDOR, Various Artists: Compilations – Telstar, 97-13

THE FLIGHT OF THE CONDOR [OST-TV], Inti Illimani-Guamary, 83-62

FLIGHTS OF FANCY, Paul Leoni, 83-17

THE FLINTSTONES, Various Artists: Films – Original Soundtracks, 94-18

FLIP, Nils Lofgren, 85-36

FLOATERS, Floaters, 77-17

FLOCK, Flock, 70-59

A FLOCK OF SEAGULLS, A Flock Of Seagulls, 82-32

FLOGGING A DEAD HORSE, Sex Pistols, 80-23

FLOOD, They Might Be Giants, 90-14

FLOODLAND, Sisters Of Mercy, 87-9

FLOORED GENIUS – THE BEST OF JULIAN COPE AND THE TEARDROP EXPLODES, Julian Cope and the Teardrop Explodes, 92-22

FLORAL DANCE, Brighouse and Rastrick Brass Band, 78-10

FLOWER DRUM SONG, Various Artists: Stage Cast – Broadway, 60-2

FLOWER DRUM SONG, Various Artists: Stage Cast – London, 60-10

FLOWERS, Ace Of Base, 98-15

FLOWERS IN THE DIRT, Paul McCartney, 89-1

FLOWERS OF ROMANCE, Public Image Ltd, 81-11

FLUSH THE FASHION, Alice Cooper, 80-56

FLY, Dixie Chicks, 99-38

FLY LIKE AN EAGLE, Steve Miller Band, 76-11

FLY ON THE WALL, AC/DC, 85-7

FLYER, Nanci Griffith, 94-20

FLYING COLOURS, Chris De Burgh, 88-1

FLYING COWBOYS, Rickie Lee Jones, 89-50

FLYING LIZARDS, Flying Lizards, 80-60

FM, Various Artists: Films – Original Soundtracks, 78-37

FOCUS, Focus, 75-23

FOCUS 3, Focus, 72-6

FOCUS AT THE RAINBOW, Focus, 73-23

FOG ON THE TYNE, Lindisfarne, 71-1

FOLK FESTIVAL OF THE BLUES (LIVE RECORDING), Various Artists: Concerts and Festivals, 64-16

FOLLOW THAT GIRL, Various Artists: Stage Cast – London, 60-5

FOLLOW THE LEADER, Eric B. and Rakim, 88-25

FOLLOW THE LEADER, Korn, 98-5

FOLLOW YOUR DREAM, Daniel O'Donnell, 92-17

F1 ROCK, Various Artists: Compilations – Telstar, 96-20

HAWAII, High Llamas, 96-62
HAWAIIAN
PARADISE/CHRISTMAS,
Wout Steenhuis, 81-28
HAWKS AND DOVES, Neil Young,
80-34
HAWKWIND, Hawkwind, 84-75
HE GOT GAME [OST], Public
Enemy, 98-50
HE TOUCHED ME, Elvis Presley,
72-38
HE WALKS BESIDE ME, Elvis
Presley, 78-37
HE WAS BEAUTIFUL, Iris
Williams, 79-69
HE'LL HAVE TO GO, Jim Reeves,
64-16
HE'S THE DJ, I'M THE
RAPPER, DJ Jazzy Jeff and
Fresh Prince, 88-68
HEAD FIRST, Uriah Heep, 83-46
HEAD LIKE A ROCK, Ian
McNabb, 94-29
HEAD MUSIC, Suede, 99-1
HEAD ON, Samson, 80-34
THE HEAD ON THE DOOR,
Cure, 85-7
HEAD OVER HEELS, Cocteau
Twins, 83-51
HEAD OVER HEELS, Various
Artists: Television – Soundtracks,
93-3
HEAD OVER HEELS, Paula
Abdul, 95-61
HEADED FOR THE FUTURE,
Neil Diamond, 86-36
HEADHUNTERS, Krokus, 83-74
THE HEADLESS CHILDREN,
W.A.S.P., 89-8
HEADLESS CROSS, Black Sabbath,
89-31
HEADLINE HITS, Various Artists:
Compilations – K-Tel, 83-5
HEADLINES, Midnight Star,
86-42
HEADLINES AND DEADLINES
– THE HITS OF A-HA, A-Ha,
91-12
HEADQUARTERS, Monkees, 67-2
HEADSTONE – THE BEST OF
UFO, UFO, 83-39
THE HEALER, John Lee Hooker
and Friends, 89-63
THE HEALING GAME, Van
Morrison, 97-10
HEAR IN THE NOW
FRONTIER, Queensryche,
97-46
HEAR MY SONG (THE BEST
OF JOSEF LOCKE), Josef
Locke, 92-7
HEAR 'N' AID, Various Artists:
Compilations – Vertigo, 86-50
HEAR NOTHING, SEE
NOTHING, SAY
NOTHING, Discharge, 82-40
HEARSAY / ALL MIXED UP,
Alexander O'Neal, 87-4
HEART, Heart, 85-19
HEART AND SOUL, Barry White,
85-34
HEART AND SOUL, Edith Piaf,
87-58
HEART & SOUL, Various Artists:
Compilations – PolyGram TV,
97-17
HEART AND SOUL, Joy Division,
98-70
HEART AND SOUL – 18
CLASSIC SOUL CUTS,
Various Artists: Compilations –
Heart and Soul, 89-2
HEART & SOUL – NEW SONGS
FROM ALLY MCBEAL
[OST-TV], Vonda Shepard, 99-9
THE HEART AND SOUL OF
ROCK AND ROLL, Various
Artists: Compilations – Telstar,
88-60
HEART AND SOUL – THE
VERY BEST OF T'PAU,
T'Pau, 93-35
HEART AND SOUL III –
HEART FULL OF SOUL,
Various Artists: Compilations –
Heart and Soul, 90-4

HEART FULL OF SOUL, Various
Artists: Compilations – Dino,
93-9
HEART FULL OF SOUL, Various
Artists: Compilations –
Warner.esp/Global TV, 98-8
HEART FULL OF SOUL – 2,
Various Artists: Compilations –
Warner.esp/Global TV, 99-12
HEART IN MOTION, Amy Grant,
91-25
HEART LIKE A SKY, Spandau
Ballet, 89-31
HEART 'N' SOUL, Tina Charles,
77-35
THE HEART OF A WOMAN,
Johnny Mathis, 75-39
THE HEART OF CHICAGO,
Chicago, 89-6
THE HEART OF CHICAGO –
1967-1997, Chicago, 99-21
A HEART OF GOLD, Various
Artists: Compilations – Telstar,
93-9
THE HEART OF ROCK AND
ROLL – BEST OF HUEY
LEWIS AND THE NEWS,
Huey Lewis and the News,
92-23
HEART OF STONE, Cher, 89-7
THE HEART OF THE 80S & 90S,
Various Artists: Radio – Related
Compilations, 98-9
HEART OVER MIND, Jennifer
Rush, 87-48
HEART, SOUL AND VOICE, Jon
Secada, 94-17
HEART STRINGS, Foster and
Allen, 92-37
HEART TO HEART – 20 HOT
HITS, Ray Charles, 80-29
HEART TO HEART – 24 LOVE
SONG DUETS, Various Artists:
Compilations – K-Tel, 86-8
HEARTBEAT, Hank Marvin, 93-17
HEARTBEAT CITY, Cars, 84-25
HEARTBEAT – FOREVER
YOURS, Various Artists:
Selected Series – Heartbeat, 95-1
HEARTBEAT – LOVE ME
TENDER, Various Artists:
Selected Series – Heartbeat, 97-6
HEARTBEAT (MUSIC FROM
THE TV SERIES), Various
Artists: Selected Series –
Heartbeat, 92-1
HEARTBEAT – NUMBER 1
LOVE SONGS OF THE '60S,
Various Artists: Selected Series –
Heartbeat, 96-2
HEARTBEAT – THE 60'S GOLD
COLLECTION, Various
Artists: Selected Series –
Heartbeat, 98-7
HEARTBEATS, Barbara Dickson,
84-21
HEARTBREAK STATION,
Cinderella, 90-36
HEARTBREAKER, Free, 73-9
HEARTBREAKER, Dionne
Warwick, 82-3
HEARTBREAKERS, Various
Artists: Compilations – K-Tel,
77-2
HEARTBREAKERS, Matt Monro,
80-5
HEARTBEATERS – 18
CLASSIC LOVE HITS,
Various Artists: Compilations –
Starblend, 86-38
HEARTLANDS, Various Artists:
Compilations – Dino, 92-4
HEARTLIGHT, Neil Diamond,
82-43
HEARTS AND BONES, Paul
Simon, 83-34
HEARTS AND FLOWERS, Joan
Armatrading, 90-29
HEARTS OF FORTUNE,
Immaculate Fools, 85-65
HEARTWORK, Carcass, 93-67
THE HEAT, Dan Reed Network,
91-15
THE HEAT IS ON!, Various
Artists: Compilations – Arcade,
91-4

THE HEAT IS ON – 16 TRACKS,
Various Artists: Compilations –
Portrait, 86-9
HEAT OF SOUL VOLUME 1,
Various Artists: Compilations –
Mastersound, 87-96
HEAT TREATMENT, Graham
Parker and the Rumour, 76-52
HEATHCLIFF LIVE (THE
SHOW), Various Artists: Stage
Cast – London, 96-41
HEAVEN AND HELL, Vangelis,
76-31
HEAVEN AND HELL, Black
Sabbath, 80-9
HEAVEN AND HELL, Meat
Loaf/Bonnie Tyler, 89-9
HEAVEN IS WAITING, Danse
Society, 84-39
HEAVEN KNOWS, Jaki Graham,
85-48
HEAVEN ON EARTH, Belinda
Carlisle, 88-4
HEAVEN OR LAS VEGAS,
Cocteau Twins, 90-7
HEAVEN UP HERE, Echo and the
Bunnymen, 81-10
HEAVENLY, Ladysmith Black
Mambazo, 97-53
HEAVENLY HARDCORE,
Various Artists: Compilations –
Dino, 92-2
HEAVY, Various Artists:
Compilations – K-Tel, 83-46
THE HEAVY HEAVY HITS,
Madness, 98-19
HEAVY HORSES, Jethro Tull,
78-20
HEAVY NOVA, Robert Palmer,
88-17
HEAVY PETTING ZOO, Nofx,
96-60
HEAVY RHYME EXPERIENCE
VOLUME 1, Brand New
Heavies, 92-38
HEAVY SOUL, Paul Weller, 97-2
HEAVY WEATHER, Weather
Report, 77-43
THE HEIGHT OF BAD
MANNERS, Bad Manners,
83-23
HEJIRA, Joni Mitchell, 76-11
HELL BENT FOR LEATHER,
Frankie Laine, 61-7
HELL FREEZES OVER, Eagles,
94-18
HELL HATH NO FURY, Rock
Goddess, 83-84
HELL ON EARTH, Mobb Deep,
96-67
HELL TO PAY, Jeff Healey Band,
90-18
HELL'S DITCH, Pogues, 90-12
HELLBILLY DELUXE, Rob
Zombie, 98-37
HELLO, Status Quo, 73-1
HELLO CHILDREN . . .
EVERYWHERE, Various
Artists: Compilations – EMI,
88-59
HELLO DAD . . . I'M IN JAIL,
Was (Not Was), 92-61
HELLO DOLLY, Louis Armstrong,
64-11
HELLO DOLLY!, Barbra Streisand,
70-45
HELLO, I MUST BE GOING!,
Phil Collins, 82-2
HELLO I'M JOHNNY CASH,
Johnny Cash, 70-6
HELLO NASTY, Beastie Boys, 98-1
HELP!, Beatles, 65-1
HELP – WAR CHILD, Various
Artists: Compilations – Go!
Discs, 95-1
HELP YOURSELF, Tom Jones,
68-4
HELP YOURSELF, Julian Lennon,
91-42
HELTER SKELTER, Vow Wow,
89-75
HEMISPHERES, Rush, 78-14
HENDRIX IN THE WEST, Jimi
Hendrix, 72-7
HENRY MANCINI, Henry
Mancini, 76-26

HENRY'S DREAM, Nick Cave and
the Bad Seeds, 92-29
HEPBURN, Hepburn, 99-28
HER BEST SONGS, Emmylou
Harris, 80-36
HERE, Leo Sayer, 79-44
HERE AND THERE, Elton John,
76-6
HERE COME THE
MINSTRELS, George Mitchell
Minstrels, 66-11
HERE COME THE WARM JETS,
Brian Eno, 74-26
HERE COME THE
TREMELOES, Tremeloes,
67-15
HERE THEY COME: THE
GREATEST HITS OF THE
MONKEES, Monkees, 97-15
HERE TODAY, TOMORROW,
NEXT WEEK, Sugarcubes,
89-15
HERE WE COME, A1, 99-20
HERE WHERE THERE IS
LOVE, Dionne Warwick,
67-39
HERE'S SOME THAT GOT
AWAY, Style Council, 93-39
HERE'S TO FUTURE DAYS,
Thompson Twins, 85-5
HERGEST RIDGE, Mike Oldfield,
74-1
HERMAN'S HERMITS, Herman's
Hermits, 65-16
HERMIT OF MINK HOLLOW,
Todd Rundgren, 78-42
HERO AND HEROINE, Strawbs,
74-35
HERO OF THE DAY, Metallica,
96-47
HEROES, David Bowie, 77-3
HEROES, Commodores, 80-50
HEX EDUCATION HOUR, Fall,
82-71
HEY, Glitter Band, 74-13
HEY HEY IT'S THE MONKEES
– GREATEST HITS, Monkees,
89-12
HEY STOOPID, Alice Cooper, 91-4
HI ENERGY, Various Artists:
Compilations – K-Tel, 79-17
HI-FI COMPANION ALBUM,
Ray Conniff, 60-3
HI INFIDELITY, Reo Speedwagon,
81-6
HI LIFE – THE BEST OF AL
GREEN, Al Green, 88-34
HI TENSION, Hi Tension, 79-74
HICKORY HOLLER
REVISITED, O. C. Smith,
68-40
THE HIDDEN CAMERA, Photek,
96-39
HIDDEN TREASURES, Barry
Manilow, 93-36
HIDE YOUR HEART, Bonnie
Tyler, 88-78
HIDEAWAY, De'lacy, 95-53
HIGH AND MIGHTY, Uriah
Heep, 76-55
HIGH CIVILZATION, Bee Gees,
91-24
HIGH CRIME, Al Jarreau, 84-81
HIGH LAND, HARD RAIN,
Aztec Camera, 83-22
HIGH 'N' DRY, Def Leppard, 81-26
HIGH ON A HAPPY VIBE, Urban
Cookie Collective, 94-28
HIGH ON EMOTION – LIVE
FROM DUBLIN, Chris De
Burgh, 90-15
HIGH ON THE HAPPY SIDE,
Wet Wet Wet, 92-1
HIGH PRIORITY, Cherrelle, 86-17
HIGH SOCIETY, Various Artists:
Films – Original Soundtracks,
60-16
HIGHER AND HIGHER – THE
BEST OF HEAVEN 17,
Heaven 17, 93-31
HIGHER GROUND, Barbra
Streisand, 97-12
THE HIGHER THEY CLIMB,
David Cassidy, 75-22
HIGHLIGHTS FROM JEFF
WAYNE'S MUSICAL

MUSIC FOR LIFE, Various Artists: Compilations – warner.esp, 99-17

MUSIC FOR PLEASURE, Monaco, 97-11

MUSIC FOR THE JILTED GENERATION, Prodigy, 94-1

MUSIC FOR THE LAST NIGHT OF THE PROMS, Sir. Charles Groves conducting the Royal Philharmonic Orchestra and Chorus with Sarah Walker (soprano), 90-39

MUSIC FOR THE MASSES, Depeche Mode, 87-10

MUSIC FOR THE PEOPLE, Marky Mark and the Funky Bunch, 91-61

MUSIC FOR THE SEASONS, Various Artists: Compilations – Ronco, 82-41

MUSIC FROM 'EDWARD VII' [OST-TV], London Symphony Orchestra, 75-52

MUSIC FROM RIVERDANCE – THE SHOW, Bill Whelan, 95-31

MUSIC FROM THE BBC-TV SERIES 'THE SINGING DETECTIVE', Various Artists: Television – Soundtracks, 86-10

MUSIC FROM THE TELEVISION SERIES 'MIAMI VICE', Various Artists: Television – Soundtracks, 85-11

MUSIC FROM 'TWIN PEAKS' [OST-TV], Angelo Badalamenti with Julee Cruise and Various Artists, 90-27

MUSIC IN THE DOLLS HOUSE, Family, 68-35

MUSIC MAGIC, Rose Royce, 84-69

MUSIC MAKES MY DAY, Olivia Newton-John, 74-37

MUSIC MAN, Various Artists: Stage Cast – London, 61-8

THE MUSIC MAN, Various Artists: Films – Original Soundtracks, 62-14

MUSIC 'N' MOTION, Christina Gregg, 78-51

MUSIC OF AMERICA, Richmond Strings with the Mike Sammes Singers, 76-18

MUSIC OF GLENN MILLER IN SUPER STEREO, Syd Lawrence, 71-43

THE MUSIC OF JAMES LAST, James Last, 73-19

THE MUSIC OF LOVE, Richard Clayderman, 84-28

MUSIC OF QUALITY AND DISTINCTION (VOLUME 1), Various Artists: Compilations – Virgin, 82-25

THE MUSIC OF RICHARD CLAYDERMAN, Richard Clayderman, 83-21

THE MUSIC OF THE COSMOS, Various Artists: Television – Soundtracks, 81-43

MUSIC OF THE MILLENNIUM, Various Artists: Television – Related Compilations, 99-2

MUSIC OF THE MOUNTAINS, Manuel and his Music Of The Mountains, 60-17

MUSIC OF THE NIGHT, Various Artists: Compilations – PolyGram TV, 98-5

THE MUSIC PEOPLE, Various Artists: Compilations – CBS, 72-10

MUSIC TO WATCH GIRLS BY, Various Artists: Compilations – Columbia, 99-2

THE MUSIC'S BACK, Dominic Kirwan, 97-54

MUSICAL CHAIRS, Hootie And The Blowfish, 98-15

MUSICAL MADNESS, Mantronix, 86-66

THE MUSICALS, Michael Ball, 96-20

MUSIK, Plastik Man, 94-58

MUSIQUE/THE HIGH ROAD, Roxy Music, 83-26

MUSTN'T GRUMBLE, Chas and Dave, 82-35

MUTATIONS, Beck, 98-24

MUTINY (STUDIO CAST RECORDING), David Essex, Frank Finlay and Various Artists, 83-39

MY AIM IS TRUE, Elvis Costello, 77-14

MY BABY JUST CARES FOR ME, Nina Simone, 87-56

MY BROTHER THE COW, Mudhoney, 95-70

MY CATHEDRAL, Jim Reeves, 70-48

MY CHERIE AMOUR, Stevie Wonder, 69-17

MY CLASSIC COLLECTION, Richard Clayderman with the Royal Philharmonic Orchestra, 90-29

MY CONCERTO FOR YOU, Russ Conway, 60-5

MY FAIR LADY, Various Artists: Stage Cast – Broadway, 58-2

MY FAIR LADY, Shelley Manne, 60-20

MY FAIR LADY, Various Artists: Stage Cast – Broadway, 64-19

MY FAIR LADY, Various Artists: Films – Original Soundtracks, 64-9

MY FAIR LADY, Various Artists: Studio Cast, 87-41

MY FIRST ALBUM, Lolly, 99-21

MY FRIEND, Jim Reeves, 72-32

MY GENERATION, Who, 65-5

MY GENERATION, Various Artists: Compilations – Telstar, 92-16

MY GENERATION – THE VERY BEST OF THE WHO, Who, 96-11

MY GIFT TO YOU, Alexander O'Neal, 88-53

MY GIRL, Various Artists: Films – Original Soundtracks, 92-13

MY HEART'S DELIGHT, Luciano Pavarotti with the Royal Philharmonic Orchestra, 94-44

MY HITS AND LOVE SONGS, Glen Campbell, 99-50

MY LIFE, Mary J. Blige, 94-59

MY LIFE FOR A SONG, Placido Domingo, 83-21

MY LIFE IN THE BUSH OF GHOSTS, Brian Eno and David Byrne, 81-29

MY LIFE: THE GREATEST HITS, Julio Iglesias, 98-18

MY LOVE IS YOUR LOVE, Whitney Houston, 98-4

MY NAME IS BARBRA, TWO, Barbra Streisand, 66-6

MY NATION UNDERGROUND, Julian Cope, 88-42

MY ONLY FASCINATION, Demis Roussos, 76-39

MY PEOPLE WERE FAIR AND HAD SKY IN THEIR HAIR BUT NOW THEY'RE CONTENT TO WEAR STARS ON THEIR BROWS, Tyrannosaurus Rex, 68-15

MY PROMISE, No Mercy, 97-17

MY SECRET PASSION – THE ARIAS, Michael Bolton, 98-25

MY SOUL, Coolio, 97-28

MY TRIBUTE – BRYN YEMM INSPIRATIONAL ALBUM, Bryn Yemm and the Gwent Chorale, 85-85

MY WAY, Frank Sinatra, 69-2

MY WAY, Usher, 98-16

MY WAY – THE BEST OF FRANK SINATRA, Frank Sinatra, 97-7

MYSTERIES OF FUNK, Grooverider, 98-50

MYSTERIO, Ian McCulloch, 92-46

MYSTERY, Hot Chocolate, 82-24

MYSTERY, Rah Band, 85-60

MYSTERY GIRL, Roy Orbison, 89-2

THE MYTHS AND LEGENDS OF KING ARTHUR & THE KNIGHTS OF THE ROUND TABLE, Rick Wakeman, 75-2

N.O.R.E., Noreaga, 98-72

NAH=POO-THE ART OF BLUFF, Wah!, 81-33

THE NAIL FILE – THE BEST OF JIMMY NAIL, Jimmy Nail, 97-8

NAKED, Kissing The Pink, 83-54

NAKED, Talking Heads, 88-3

NAKED, Blue Pearl, 90-58

NAKED, Scarlet, 95-59

NAKED, Louise, 96-7

NAKED BABY PHOTOS, Ben Folds Five, 98-65

NAKED THUNDER, Ian Gillan, 90-63

THE NAME OF THIS BAND IS TALKING HEADS, Talking Heads, 82-22

NANCY AND LEE, Nancy Sinatra and Lee Hazlewood, 68-17

NANCY'S GREATEST HITS, Nancy Sinatra, 70-39

NANTUCKET SLEIGHRIDE, Mountain, 71-43

THE NASHVILLE DREAM, Various Artists: Compilations – Quality Television, 93-10

NASHVILLE SKYLINE, Bob Dylan, 69-1

NAT KING COLE SINGS AND THE GEORGE SHEARING QUINTET PLAYS, Nat 'King' Cole and the George Shearing Quintet, 62-8

NATIONAL ANTHEMS 99: MIXED BY RUFF DRIVERZ, Various Artists: Compilations – Telstar, 99-3

NATIONAL ANTHEMS 99 – VOLUME 2, Various Artists: Compilations – Telstar, 99-14

NATIVE PLACE, Railway Children, 91-59

NATIVE TONGUE, Poison, 93-20

NATTY DREAD, Bob Marley and the Wailers, 75-43

NATURAL, Peter Andre, 96-1

NATURAL ACT, Kris Kristofferson and Rita Coolidge, 78-35

NATURAL AVENUE, John Lodge, 77-38

NATURAL BORN KILLERS, Various Artists: Films – Original Soundtracks, 95-10

NATURAL HIGH, Commodores, 78-8

NATURAL MYSTIC, Bob Marley and the Wailers, 95-5

NATURAL THING, Juliet Roberts, 94-65

NATURAL WOMAN, Various Artists: Compilations – Global Television, 95-7

NATURAL WOMAN – VOLUME 2, Various Artists: Compilations – Global Television, 96-10

THE NATURE OF THE BEAST, April Wine, 81-48

NAZARETH LIVE, Nazareth, 81-78

NEAPOLIS, Simple Minds, 98-19

NEARLY GOD – POEMS, Nearly God, 96-10

NEARNESS OF YOU, Glenn Miller and his Orchestra, 69-30

NEBRASKA, Bruce Springsteen, 82-3

NECK AND NECK, Chet Atkins and Mark Knopfler, 90-41

NEED FOR NOT, Levitation, 92-45

NEGOTIATIONS AND LOVE SONGS 1971-1986, Paul Simon, 88-17

NEIL REID, Neil Reid, 72-1

NEITHER FISH NOR FLESH, Terence Trent D'Arby, 89-12

NEITHER WASHINGTON NOR MOSCOW . . ., Redskins, 86-31

NENA, Nena, 84-31

NEO WAVE, Silver Sun, 98-74

NEON BALLROOM, Silverchair, 99-29

THE NEPHILIM, Fields Of The Nephilim, 88-14

NERVE NET, Brian Eno, 92-70

NEVER A DULL MOMENT, Rod Stewart, 72-1

NEVER CAN SAY GOODBYE, Gloria Gaynor, 75-32

NEVER ENDING SONG OF LOVE, New Seekers, 72-35

NEVER ENOUGH, Melissa Etheridge, 92-56

NEVER FELT SO GOOD, James Ingram, 86-72

NEVER FOR EVER, Kate Bush, 80-1

NEVER LET HER GO, David Gates, 75-32

NEVER LET ME DOWN, David Bowie, 87-6

NEVER LET ME GO, Luther Vandross, 93-11

NEVER LOVED ELVIS, Wonder Stuff, 91-3

NEVER MIND THE BOLLOCKS, HERE'S THE SEX PISTOLS, Sex Pistols, 77-1

NEVER NEVER NEVER, Shirley Bassey, 73-10

NEVER, NEVERLAND, Annihilator, 90-48

NEVER ON SUNDAY, Various Artists: Films – Original Soundtracks, 61-17

NEVER S-A-Y NEVER, Brandy, 98-19

NEVER SAY DIE, Black Sabbath, 78-12

NEVER TOO LATE, Status Quo, 81-2

NEVER TOO MUCH, Luther Vandross, 87-41

NEVER TOO YOUNG TO ROCK, Various Artists: Compilations – GTO, 75-30

NEVERLAND, Mission, 95-58

NEVERMIND, Nirvana, 91-7

NEW ADVENTURES IN HI-FI, R.E.M., 96-1

THE NEW AGE OF ATLANTIC, Various Artists: Compilations – Atlantic, 72-25

NEW BEGINNING, SWV, 96-26

NEW BOOTS AND PANTIES!!, Ian Dury, 77-5

NEW CLEAR DAYS, Vapors, 80-44

NEW COLOURS, New Seekers, 72-40

NEW DAY, Jane Harrison, 89-70

NEW DIMENSIONS, Three Degrees, 79-34

NEW ENGLAND, Wishbone Ash, 76-22

A NEW FLAME, Simply Red, 89-1

NEW FORMS, Roni Size Reprazent, 97-8

NEW FRONTIERS [EP], DJ Hype Presents Ganja Kru, 97-56

NEW FUNKY NATION, Boo-Yaa T.R.I.B.E., 90-92

NEW GOLD DREAM (81,82,83,84), Simple Minds, 82-3

THE NEW GOODIES LP, Goodies, 75-25

NEW HITS 96, Various Artists: Selected Series – Hits, 96-1

NEW HITS 1997, Various Artists: Selected Series – Hits, 97-1

NEW HITS 98, Various Artists: Selected Series – Hits, 98-1

NEW HITS 99, Various Artists: Selected Series – Hits, 99-1

NEW HOPE FOR THE WRETCHED, Plasmatics, 80-55

NEW HORIZONS, Don Williams, 79-29

NEW JACK CITY, Various Artists: Films – Original Soundtracks, 91-16

NEW JACK SWING MASTERCUTS VOLUME 1, Various Artists: Compilations – Mastercuts, 92-8

THE SEEKERS, Seekers, 65-16

SEEKERS – SEEN IN GREEN, Seekers, 67-15

THE SEER, Big Country, 86-2

SELECT, Kim Wilde, 82-19

SELECTED AMBIENT WORKS VOLUME II, Aphex Twin, 94-11

SELF, Quintessence, 72-50

SELF ABUSED, S*M*A*S*H, 94-59

SELF CONTROL, Laura Branigan, 84-16

SELF PORTRAIT, Bob Dylan, 70-1

SELLING ENGLAND BY THE POUND, Genesis, 73-3

SEMI-DETACHED, Therapy?, 98-21

SEMI-DETACHED SUBURBAN, Manfred Mann, 79-9

SEMINAL LIVE, Fall, 89-40

SENSATIONAL, Michelle Gayle, 97-17

SENSATIONAL ALEX HARVEY BAND LIVE, Sensational Alex Harvey Band, 75-14

SENSE, Lightning Seeds, 92-53

SENSE AND SENSUALITY, Au Pairs, 82-79

A SENSE OF WONDER, Van Morrison, 85-25

SENSES, Various Artists: Compilations – PolyGram TV, 94-5

SENSUAL CLASSICS, Various Artists: Compilations – Teldec, 92-19

THE SENSUAL WORLD, Kate Bush, 89-2

SENTIMENTAL JOURNEY, Ringo Starr, 70-7

SENTIMENTALLY YOURS, Rose Marie, 87-22

SENTINEL, Pallas, 84-41

SEPTEMBER MORN, Neil Diamond, 80-14

SERENADE, Neil Diamond, 74-11

SERENADE, Juan Martin and the Royal Philharmonic Orchestra, 84-21

SERENITY, Culture Beat, 93-13

SERGEANT PEPPER KNEW MY FATHER, Various Artists: Magazine Related, 88-37

SGT. PEPPER'S LONELY HEARTS CLUB BAND, Beatles, 67-1

SGT. PEPPER'S LONELY HEARTS CLUB BAND, Various Artists: Films – Original Soundtracks, 78-38

SERIOUS HIP-HOP 2, Various Artists: Compilations – Serious, 87-95

SERIOUS HITS . . . LIVE!, Phil Collins, 90-2

SERIOUSLY ORCHESTRAL, Louis Clark conducting the Royal Philharmonic Orchestra, 91-31

SERVE CHILLED, Various Artists: Compilations – Virgin, 95-16

A SESSION WITH THE DAVE CLARK FIVE, Dave Clark Five, 64-3

SESSIONS SEVEN, Various Artists: Compilations – Ministry Of Sound, 97-4

SESSIONS EIGHT – TODD TERRY, Various Artists: Compilations – Ministry Of Sound, 97-11

SESSIONS NINE – ERICK MORILLO, Various Artists: Compilations – Ministry Of Sound, 98-17

SET, Thompson Twins, 82-48

SET THE CONTROLS FOR THE HEART OF THE BASS, Bass-O-Matic, 90-57

SET THE TWILIGHT REELING, Lou Reed, 96-26

SETTING SONS, Jam, 79-4

SEVEN, James, 92-2

SEVEN AGES OF ACKER, Mr. Acker Bilk, 60-6

SEVEN AND THE RAGGED TIGER, Duran Duran, 83-1

SEVEN BRIDES FOR SEVEN BROTHERS, Various Artists: Films – Original Soundtracks, 61-6

777, System 7, 93-30

SEVEN SINGLES DEEP, Icicle Works, 86-52

SEVEN TEARS, Goombay Dance Band, 82-16

SEVEN THE HARD WAY, Pat Benatar, 85-69

SEVENS, Garth Brooks, 97-34

17 SECONDS, Cure, 80-20

THE SEVENTH ONE, Toto, 88-73

SEVENTH SOJOURN, Moody Blues, 72-5

SEVENTH SON OF A SEVENTH SON, Iron Maiden, 88-1

SEVENTH STAR, Black Sabbath featuring Tony Iommi, 86-27

7800 DEGREES FAHRENHEIT, Bon Jovi, 85-28

SEX & JAZZ & ROCK & ROLL, Jools Holland and his R&B Orchestra, 96-38

SEX AND RELIGION, Vai, 93-17

SEX AND TRAVEL, Right Said Fred, 93-35

SEX, CHIPS & ROCK N' ROLL, Various Artists: Television – Soundtracks, 99-12

SEX MACHINE – THE VERY BEST OF JAMES BROWN, James Brown, 91-19

SEX PACKETS, Digital Underground, 90-59

SEX, SWEAT AND BLOOD, Various Artists: Compilations – Beggars Banquet, 82-88

SEXTET, A Certain Ratio, 82-53

SEXUAL HEALING, Various Artists: Compilations – EMI, 91-7

A SHADE OF RED, Redhead Kingpin and the F.B.I., 89-35

SHADES, J.J. Cale, 81-44

SHADES, Shades Of Rhythm, 91-51

SHADES OF GREEN, Foster and Allen, 97-55

SHADES OF ROCK, Shadows, 70-30

SHADES OF SOUL, Various Artists: Compilations – Global Television, 96-15

SHADES OF SOUL, Various Artists: Compilations – Global Television, 98-9

SHADOW DANCING, Andy Gibb, 78-15

SHADOW MUSIC, Shadows, 66-5

SHADOW OF YOUR SMILE, Andy Williams, 66-24

THE SHADOWS, Shadows, 61-1

SHADOWS AND LIGHT, Joni Mitchell, 80-63

SHADOWS AND LIGHT, Wilson Phillips, 92-6

THE SHADOWS' GREATEST HITS, Shadows, 63-2

SHADOWS IN THE NIGHT – 16 CLASSIC TRACKS, Shadows, 93-22

SHADOWS 20 GOLDEN GREATS, Shadows, 77-1

SHAFT, Isaac Hayes, 71-17

SHAKA ZULU, Ladysmith Black Mambazo, 87-34

SHAKE YOU DOWN, Gregory Abbott, 87-53

SHAKE YOUR MONEY MAKER, Black Crowes, 91-36

SHAKEN AND STIRRED, David Arnold, 97-11

SHAKEN 'N' STIRRED, Robert Plant, 85-19

SHAKESPEARE ALABAMA, Diesel Park West, 89-55

SHAKIN' STEVENS, Shakin' Stevens, 81-34

SHAKIN' STEVENS GREATEST HITS, Shakin' Stevens, 84-8

SHAKING THE TREE, Peter Gabriel, 90-11

SHAKY, Shakin' Stevens, 81-1

SHAME, Brad, 93-72

SHAME AND SIN, Robert Cray Band, 93-48

THE SHAMEN COLLECTION, Shamen, 98-26

SHAMROCK DIARIES, Chris Rea, 85-15

SHANGO, Santana, 82-35

SHANGRI-LA, Animal Nightlife, 85-36

SHAPE UP AND DANCE FEATURING ANGELA RIPPON (VOLUME II), Angela Rippon, 82-8

SHAPE UP AND DANCE WITH FELICITY KENDAL (VOLUME ONE), Felicity Kendal, 82-29

SHAPE UP AND DANCE WITH SUZANNE DANDO, Suzanne Dando, 84-87

SHARE MY WORLD, Mary J. Blige, 97-8

SHARPE – OVER THE HILLS & FAR AWAY, Various Artists: Compilations – Virgin, 96-14

SHAVED FISH, John Lennon, 75-8

SHAVING PEACHES, Terrorvision, 98-34

SHE, Harry Connick Jr., 94-21

SHE WAS ONLY A GROCER'S DAUGHTER, Blow Monkeys, 87-20

SHE WEARS MY RING, Solomon King, 68-40

SHE WORKS HARD FOR THE MONEY, Donna Summer, 83-28

SHE'S A LADY, Tom Jones, 71-9

SHE'S JUST AN OLD LOVE TURNED MEMORY, Charley Pride, 77-34

SHE'S SO UNUSUAL, Cyndi Lauper, 84-16

SHE'S THE BOSS, Mick Jagger, 85-6

SHE'S THE ONE [OST], Tom Petty and the Heartbreakers, 96-37

SHEER GREED, Girl, 80-33

SHEER HEART ATTACK, Queen, 74-2

SHEER MAGIC, Mr. Acker Bilk, 77-5

SHEET MUSIC, 10 C.C., 74-9

SHEIK YERBOUTI, Frank Zappa, 79-32

SHELTER, Lone Justice, 86-84

SHELTER, Brand New Heavies, 97-5

SHEPHERD MOONS, Enya, 91-1

SHER-OO, Cilla Black, 68-7

SHERRICK, Sherrick, 87-27

SHERRY, Four Seasons, 63-20

SHERYL CROW, Sheryl Crow, 96-5

SHIFT-WORK, Fall, 91-17

SHINE, Average White Band, 80-14

SHINE, Frida, 84-67

SHINE: 20 BRILLIANT INDIE HITS, Various Artists: Selected Series – Shine, 95-4

SHINE, Mary Black, 97-33

SHINE [OST], David Hirschfelder, 97-46

SHINE TOO, Various Artists: Selected Series – Shine, 95-4

SHINE 3, Various Artists: Selected Series – Shine, 95-13

SHINE FOUR, Various Artists: Selected Series – Shine, 96-3

SHINE 5, Various Artists: Selected Series – Shine, 96-2

SHINE 6, Various Artists: Selected Series – Shine, 96-2

SHINE 7, Various Artists: Selected Series – Shine, 96-13

SHINE 8, Various Artists: Selected Series – Shine, 97-6

SHINE 9, Various Artists: Selected Series – Shine, 97-7

SHINE 10, Various Artists: Selected Series – Shine, 98-10

SHINE – BEST OF 97, Various Artists: Selected Series – Shine, 98-20

SHIP ARRIVING TOO LATE TO SAVE A DROWNING WITCH, Frank Zappa, 82-61

SHIRLEY, Shirley Bassey, 61-9

SHIRLEY BASSEY, Shirley Bassey, 62-14

SHIRLEY BASSEY AT THE PIGALLE, Shirley Bassey, 65-15

THE SHIRLEY BASSEY COLLECTION, Shirley Bassey, 72-37

THE SHIRLEY BASSEY SINGLES ALBUM, Shirley Bassey, 75-2

SHIRLEY BASSEY SINGS ANDREW LLOYD WEBBER, Shirley Bassey, 93-34

SHIRLEY BASSEY SINGS THE MOVIES, Shirley Bassey, 95-24

SHOOT THE BOSS, Monkey Mafia, 98-69

SHOOT THE MOON, Judie Tzuke, 82-19

SHOOTING RUBBERBANDS AT THE STARS, Edie Brickell and New Bohemians, 89-25

SHOOTING STAR, Elkie Brooks, 78-20

SHOOTING STARS, Dollar, 79-36

SHOP ASSISTANTS, Shop Assistants, 86-100

SHOPPING BAG, Partridge Family, 72-28

A SHORT ALBUM ABOUT LOVE, Divine Comedy, 97-13

SHORT BACK 'N' SIDES, Ian Hunter, 81-79

SHORT SHARP SHOCKED, Michelle Shocked, 88-33

SHORT STORIES, Jon and Vangelis, 80-4

SHOT OF LOVE, Bob Dylan, 81-6

SHOULD THE WORLD FAIL TO FALL APART, Peter Murphy, 86-82

THE SHOUTING STAGE, Joan Armatrading, 88-28

SHOVE IT, Cross, 88-58

SHOW, Cure, 93-29

SHOW ME LOVE, Robin S, 93-34

THE SHOW MUST GO ON, Shirley Bassey, 96-47

A SHOW OF HANDS, Rush, 89-12

SHOW PEOPLE, Mari Wilson with the Wilsations, 83-24

SHOW SOME EMOTION, Joan Armatrading, 77-6

THE SHOW, THE AFTER-PARTY, THE HOTEL, Jodeci, 95-4

SHOWADDYWADDY, Showaddywaddy, 74-9

SHOWBIZ, Cud, 94-46

SHOWBIZ, Muse, 99-69

SHOWBOAT, Various Artists: Studio Cast, 60-12

SHOWDOWN, Isley Brothers, 78-50

SHOWSTOPPERS, Barry Manilow, 91-53

SHOWTIME, George Mitchell Minstrels, 67-26

SHUT UP AND DANCE/FUCK OFF AND DIE, Various Artists: Compilations – Shut Up And Dance, 92-20

SHUT UP AND DANCE (THE DANCE MIXES), Paula Abdul, 90-40

SHUT UP AND DIE LIKE AN AVIATOR, Steve Earle and the Dukes, 91-62

SHUTTERED ROOM, Fixx, 82-54

SIAMESE DREAM, Smashing Pumpkins, 93-4

SID SINGS, Sid Vicious, 79-30

SIEZE THE TIME, Fun Da Mental, 94-74

SIGN 'O' THE TIMES, Prince, 87-4

SIGN OF THE HAMMER, Manowar, 84-73

SIGNALS, Rush, 82-3

SIGNIFICANT OTHER, Limp Bizkit, 99-26

SIGNING OFF, UB40, 80-2

SIGNS OF LIFE, Penguin Cafe Orchestra, 87-49

SPEED GARAGE ANTHEMS –
VOLUME 2, Various Artists:
Compilations – Global
Television, 98-5
SPEED GARAGE ANTHEMS IN
IBIZA, Various Artists:
Compilations – Global
Television, 98-7
SPEED GARAGE ANTHEMS 99,
Various Artists: Compilations –
Global Television, 99-13
SPELLBOUND, Tygers Of Pan
Tang, 81-33
SPELLBOUND, Paula Abdul, 91-4
SPICE, Spice Girls, 96-1
SPICE GIRLS PRESENT THE
BEST GIRL POWER
ALBUM IN THE WORLD
. . . EVER!, Various Artists:
Selected Series – Best . . . Ever!..,
97-2
SPICEWORLD, Spice Girls, 97-1
SPIDERS, Space, 96-5
SPIKE, Elvis Costello, 89-5
SPILT MILK, Jellyfish, 93-21
SPINNER, Brian Eno and Jah
Wobble, 95-71
THE SPINNERS ARE IN
TOWN, Spinners, 70-40
SPINNERS LIVE
PERFORMANCE, Spinners,
71-14
SPIRIT, John Denver, 76-9
THE SPIRIT, Magnum, 91-50
SPIRIT, Sean Maguire, 96-43
SPIRIT, Jewel, 98-54
SPIRIT OF EDEN, Talk Talk, 88-19
SPIRIT OF RELAXATION,
Dreamkeeper, 97-71
SPIRIT OF ST. LOUIS, Ellen
Foley, 81-57
SPIRIT OF TRANQUILITY,
Harmonium, 98-25
SPIRITCHASER, Dead Can Dance,
96-43
SPIRITS DANCING IN THE
FLESH, Santana, 90-68
SPIRITS HAVING FLOWN, Bee
Gees, 79-1
SPIRITS OF NATURE, Various
Artists: Compilations – Virgin,
96-5
SPIRITUALLY IBIZA, Various
Artists: Compilations – Dino,
95-17
SPIT IN YOUR EAR, Spitting
Image, 86-55
SPITFIRE, Jefferson Starship, 76-30
SPLINTER GROUP, Peter Green,
97-71
SPLIT, Groundhogs, 71-5
SPLIT, Lush, 94-19
SPOOKY, Lush, 92-7
SPORTS, Huey Lewis and the News,
85-23
SPORTS CAR, Judie Tzuke, 80-7
THE SPOTLIGHT KID, Captain
Beefheart and his Magic Band,
72-44
SPOTLIGHT ON NANA
MOUSKOURI, Nana
Mouskouri, 74-38
SPOTLIGHT ON THE GEORGE
MITCHELL MINSTRELS,
George Mitchell Minstrels, 64-6
SPRAWN – THE ALBUM, Various
Artists: Films – Original
Soundtracks, 97-18
SPYBOY, Emmylou Harris, 98-57
SPYGLASS GUEST, Greenslade,
74-34
SQUARE THE CIRCLE, Joan
Armatrading, 92-34
SQUEEZING OUT SPARKS,
Graham Parker and the Rumour,
79-18
SSSSH, Ten Years After, 69-4
STACKED UP, Senser, 94-4
STAGE, David Bowie, 78-5
STAGE FRIGHT, Band, 70-15
STAGE HEROES, Colm Wilkinson,
89-27
STAGE STRUCK, Rory Gallagher,
80-40
STAGE-STRUCK, David Essex,
82-31

STAGES, Elaine Paige, 83-2
STAIN, Living Colour, 93-19
STAINED GLASS, Judas Priest,
78-27
STAKES IS HIGH, De La Soul,
96-42
STAMPEDE, Doobie Brothers,
75-14
STAND BY ME (THE
ULTIMATE
COLLECTION), Ben E. King
and the Drifters, 87-14
STAND BY YOUR MAN, Tammy
Wynette, 75-13
STAND STRONG STAND
PROUD, Vice Squad, 82-47
STAND UP, Jethro Tull, 69-1
STANDARDS, Alarm, 90-47
STANDING HAMPTON, Sammy
Hagar, 82-84
STANDING IN THE LIGHT,
Level 42, 83-9
STANDING ON A BEACH –
THE SINGLES, Cure, 86-4
STANDING TALL, Crusaders,
81-47
STANLEY ROAD, Paul Weller, 95-1
STAR!, Various Artists: Films –
Original Soundtracks, 68-36
STAR, Belly, 93-2
STAR FLEET PROJECT, Brian
May and Friends, 83-35
A STAR IS BORN [OST],
Barbra Streisand, 77-1
STAR PARTY, Various Artists:
Compilations – K-Tel, 78-4
STAR PORTRAIT, Johnny Cash,
72-16
STAR TRACKIN' 76, Various
Artists: Compilations – Ronco,
76-9
STAR TRACKS, Various Artists:
Compilations – K-Tel, 80-6
STAR WARS [OST], Composed and
conducted by John Williams;
Performed by the London
Symphony Orchestra, 78-21
STAR WARS – THE PHANTOM
MENACE [OST], Composed
and conducted by John Williams;
Performed by the London
Symphony Orchestra, 99-8
STARDUST, Pat Boone, 58-10
STARDUST MEMORIES, Peter
Skellern, 95-50
STARGAZERS, Various Artists:
Compilations – Kasino, 85-69
STARING AT THE SUN, Level 42,
88-2
STARLESS AND BIBLE BLACK,
King Crimson, 74-28
STARLIGHT EXPRESS, Various
Artists: Stage Cast – London,
84-21
STARRY EYED AND BOLLOCK
NAKED, Carter – The
Unstoppable Sex Machine,
94-22
STARRY NIGHT, Julio Iglesias,
90-27
STARS, Simply Red, 91-1
STARS CHARITY FANTASIA
SAVE THE CHILDREN
FUND, Various Artists:
Compilations – Save The
Children Fund, 66-6
STARS CRASH DOWN, Hue And
Cry, 91-10
STARS FROM STARS AND
GARTERS, Various Artists:
Television – Related
Compilations, 64-17
STARS MEDLEY, Star Sound,
82-94
STARS OF '68, Various Artists:
Compilations – Marble Arch,
68-23
STARS ON 45, Star Sound, 81-1
STARS ON 45 VOLUME 2, Star
Sound, 81-18
STARS ON SUNDAY BY
REQUEST, Various Artists:
Television – Related
Compilations, 78-65
THE STARS WE ARE, Marc
Almond, 88-41

STARSKY AND HUTCH
PRESENTS, Various Artists:
Television – Related
Compilations, 98-13
START – THE BEST OF
BRITISH, Various Artists:
Compilations – Dino, 94-13
STARTRAX CLUB DISCO,
Startrax, 81-26
STATE OF EUPHORIA, Anthrax,
88-12
STATE OF OUR UNION, Long
Ryders, 85-66
STATE OF THE WORLD
ADDRESS, Biohazard, 94-72
STATELESS, Lene Lovich, 79-35
STATIC & SILENCE, Sundays,
97-10
STATION TO STATION, David
Bowie, 76-5
STATIONARY TRAVELLER,
Camel, 84-57
STATUS QUO – LIVE, Status Quo,
77-3
STATUS QUO LIVE AT THE
N.E.C., Status Quo, 84-83
STAY HUNGRY, Twisted Sister,
84-34
STAY ON THESE ROADS, A-Ha,
88-2
STAY STICK!, Cramps, 90-62
STAY WITH ME, Regina Belle,
89-62
STAY WITH ME TONIGHT,
Jeffrey Osborne, 84-56
STAY WITH THE HOLLIES,
Hollies, 64-2
STAYING ALIVE, Various Artists:
Films – Original Soundtracks,
83-14
STEADY DIET OF NOTHING,
Fugazi, 91-63
STEAL YOUR FACE, Grateful
Dead, 76-42
STEAM, East 17, 94-3
STEAMIN'! – HARDCORE '92,
Various Artists: Compilations –
Cookie Jar, 91-3
STEEL WHEELS, Rolling Stones,
89-2
STEELTOWN, Big Country, 84-1
STELLA, Yello, 85-92
STEP BY STEP, Jeff Lorber, 85-97
STEP BY STEP, New Kids On The
Block, 90-1
STEP IN THE ARENA, Gang
Starr, 91-36
STEP ONE, Steps, 98-2
STEP TWO, Showaddywaddy, 75-7
STEPHEN STILLS, Stephen Stills,
70-30
STEPHEN STILLS 2, Stephen
Stills, 71-22
STEPPENWOLF, Steppenwolf,
70-59
STEPPENWOLF LIVE,
Steppenwolf, 70-16
STEPPIN' TO THE SHADOWS,
Shadows, 89-11
STEPPING OUT – THE VERY
BEST OF JOE JACKSON, Joe
Jackson, 90-7
STEPS IN TIME, King, 85-6
STEPTACULAR, Steps, 99-1
STEPTOE AND SON, Wilfred
Brambell and Harry H. Corbett,
63-4
STEPTOE AND SON, Wilfred
Brambell and Harry H. Corbett,
64-14
STEREO '57 (ESSENTIAL ELVIS
VOLUME 2), Elvis Presley,
89-60
STEREO MUSICALE
SHOWCASE, Various Artists:
Compilations – Polydor, 66-26
THE STEVE HOWE ALBUM,
Steve Howe, 79-68
STEVE MCQUEEN, Prefab Sprout,
85-21
STEVE MILLER BAND LIVE!,
Steve Miller Band, 83-79
STEVE WINWOOD, Steve
Winwood, 77-12
STEVEN HOUGHTON, Steven
Houghton, 97-21

STEVEN SMITH AND FATHER
AND 16 GREAT SONGS,
Steven Smith and Father, 72-17
STEVIE WONDER'S GREATEST
HITS, Stevie Wonder, 68-25
STICK AROUND FOR JOY,
Sugarcubes, 92-16
STICK TO ME, Graham Parker and
the Rumour, 77-19
STICKY FINGERS, Rolling Stones,
71-1
STIFF'S LIVE STIFFS, Various
Artists: Compilations – Stiff,
78-28
STIGMA, EMF, 92-19
STILETTO, Lita Ford, 90-66
STILL, Joy Division, 81-5
STILL BURNING, Mike Scott,
97-34
STILL CAN'T SAY GOODBYE,
Charlie Landsborough, 99-39
STILL CLIMBING, Brownstone,
97-19
STILL CRAZY AFTER ALL
THESE YEARS, Paul Simon,
75-6
STILL GOT THE BLUES, Gary
Moore, 90-13
STILL IN THE GAME, Keith
Sweat, 98-62
STILL LIFE (AMERICAN
CONCERTS 1981), Rolling
Stones, 82-4
STILL NOT BLACK ENOUGH,
W.A.S.P., 95-52
STILL OUT OF ORDER, Infa
Riot, 82-42
STILL TOGETHER, Gladys
Knight and the Pips, 77-42
STILL WATERS, Bee Gees, 97-2
STILL WATERS RUN DEEP,
Four Tops, 70-29
STILLS, Stephen Stills, 75-31
THE STING, Marvin Hamlisch,
74-7
STOLEN MOMENTS, John Hiatt,
90-72
STOMPIN' AT THE SAVOY,
Rufus and Chaka Khan, 84-64
STOMPIN' PARTY, Various Artists:
Compilations – Dino, 92-10
STONE AGE, Rolling Stones, 71-4
STONE GON', Barry White, 74-18
STONE KILLERS, Prince Charles
and the City Beat Band, 83-84
THE STONE ROSES, Stone Roses,
89-19
STONE ROSES – 10TH
ANNIVERSARY EDITION,
Stone Roses, 99-26
STONED AND DETHRONED,
Jesus And Mary Chain, 94-13
STONEDHENGE, Ten Years
After, 69-6
STONES, Neil Diamond, 71-18
STONES IN THE ROAD, Mary
Chapin Carpenter, 94-26
STONEY END, Barbra Streisand,
71-28
STOOSH, Skunk Anansie, 96-9
STOP!, Sam Brown, 89-4
STOP MAKING SENSE, Talking
Heads, 84-37
STOP THAT TRAIN, Clint
Eastwood and General Saint,
83-98
STOP THE WORLD, Black, Rock
and Ron, 89-72
STOP THE WORLD – I WANT
TO GET OFF, Various Artists:
Stage Cast – London, 61-8
STORIES OF JOHNNY, Marc
Almond, 85-22
STORM, Vanessa-Mae, 97-27
STORM BRINGER, Deep Purple,
74-6
STORM FRONT, Billy Joel, 89-5
A STORM IN HEAVEN, Verve,
93-27
STORM WATCH, Jethro Tull, 79-27
STORMS, Nanci Griffith, 89-38
STORMSVILLE, Johnny and the
Hurricanes, 60-18
THE STORY OF A YOUNG
HEART, A Flock Of Seagulls,
84-30

THE WORLD BEATERS SING THE WORLD BEATERS, England Football World Cup Squad 1970, 70-4

WORLD CLIQUE, Deee-Lite, 90-14

WORLD COMING DOWN, Type O Negative, 99-49

WORLD DANCE – THE DRUM + BASS EXPERIENCE, Various Artists: Compilations – Firm, 97-10

WORLD DEMISE, Obituary, 94-65

WORLD GONE WRONG, Bob Dylan, 93-35

WORLD IN MOTION, Jackson Browne, 89-39

WORLD IN UNION, Union and Various Artists, 91-17

WORLD IN UNION – ANTHEMS, Various Artists: Compilations – PolyGram TV, 95-8

THE WORLD IS FULL OF MARRIED MEN, Various Artists: Films – Original Soundtracks, 79-25

WORLD MACHINE, Level 42, 85-3

WORLD MOODS, Various Artists: Compilations – Virgin/EMI, 98-17

THE WORLD OF BLUES POWER, Various Artists: Selected Series – The World Of, 69-24

THE WORLD OF BRASS BANDS, Various Artists: Selected Series – The World Of, 69-13

THE WORLD OF CHARLIE KUNZ, Charlie Kunz, 69-9

THE WORLD OF CHRISTMAS, Choir Of King's College, Cambridge, 71-38

WORLD OF HIS OWN, Jools Holland, 90-71

THE WORLD OF HITS VOLUME 2, Various Artists: Selected Series – The World Of, 69-7

THE WORLD OF JOHNNY CASH, Johnny Cash, 70-5

THE WORLD OF JOSEF LOCKE TODAY, Josef Locke, 69-29

THE WORLD OF KENNETH MCKELLAR, Kenneth McKellar, 69-27

THE WORLD OF MANTOVANI, Mantovani, 69-6

THE WORLD OF MANTOVANI VOLUME 2, Mantovani, 69-4

WORLD OF MORRISSEY, Morrissey, 95-15

A WORLD OF OUR OWN, Seekers, 65-5

THE WORLD OF PHASE 4 STEREO, Various Artists: Selected Series – The World Of, 69-29

THE WORLD OF PROGRESSIVE MUSIC (WOWIE ZOWIE), Various Artists: Selected Series – The World Of, 69-17

WORLD OF THE BACHELORS, Bachelors, 69-8

WORLD OF THE BACHELORS VOLUME 2, Bachelors, 69-11

THE WORLD OF VAL DOONICAN, Val Doonican, 69-2

THE WORLD OF YOUR 100 BEST TUNES, Various Artists: Radio – Related Compilations, 71-10

THE WORLD OF YOUR 100 BEST TUNES VOLUME 2, Various Artists: Radio – Related Compilations, 71-9

THE WORLD OF YOUR 100 BEST TUNES VOLUME 10, Various Artists: Radio – Related Compilations, 75-41

WORLD OUTSIDE, Psychedelic Furs, 91-68

WORLD POWER, Snap!, 90-10

WORLD RADIO, Leo Sayer, 82-30

WORLD SERVICE, Spear Of Destiny, 85-11

WORLD SHUT YOUR MOUTH, Julian Cope, 84-40

WORLD WIDE LIVE, Scorpions, 85-18

A WORLD WITHOUT DAVE, Carter – The Unstoppable Sex Machine, 97-73

THE WORLD WITHOUT END, Mighty Lemon Drops, 88-34

THE WORLD WON'T LISTEN, Smiths, 87-2

WORLD WRESTLING FEDERATION – THE MUSIC – VOLUME 4, James A. Johnston, 99-44

THE WORLDS OF FOSTER AND ALLEN, Foster and Allen, 88-16

THE WORLD'S WORST RECORD SHOW, Various Artists: Compilations – K-Tel, 78-47

WORLDES BLYSSE, Mediaeval Baebes, 98-73

WORLDWIDE, Everything But The Girl, 91-29

WORLDWIDE 50 GOLD AWARD HITS VOLUME 1 – A TOUCH OF GOLD, Elvis Presley, 70-49

WORRY BOMB, Carter – The Unstoppable Sex Machine, 95-9

THE WORST ALBUM IN THE WORLD EVER . . . EVER!, Shirehorses, 97-22

WOULD YA LIKE MORE SCRATCHIN', Malcolm McLaren and the World's Famous Supreme Team Show, 84-44

WOULD YOU BELIEVE, Hollies, 66-16

WOULDN'T YOU LIKE IT, Bay City Rollers, 75-3

WOW!, Bananarama, 87-26

WOW! – LET THE MUSIC LIFT YOU UP, Various Artists: Compilations – Arcade, 94-13

WOW WHAT A PARTY, Various Artists: Compilations – K-Tel, 87-97

WOWEE ZOWEE, Pavement, 95-18

WOYAYA, Osibisa, 72-11

WRAP YOUR ARMS AROUND ME, Agnetha Faltskog, 83-18

WRECKIN' CREW, Meteors, 83-53

WRECKING BALL, Emmylou Harris, 95-46

WRECKLESS ERIC, Wreckless Eric, 78-46

WRESTLEMANIA – THE ALBUM, WWF Superstars, 93-10

THE WRITING ON THE WALL, Bucks Fizz, 86-89

THE WRITING'S ON THE WALL, Destiny's Child, 99-12

WRITTEN IN RED, Stranglers, 97-52

WU-TANG FOREVER, Wu-Tang Clan, 97-1

X, Inxs, 90-2

X, Beloved, 96-25

THE X FACTOR, Iron Maiden, 95-8

X-TRA NAKED, Shabba Ranks, 93-38

XANADU [OST], Olivianewton-John/Electric Light Orchestra, 80-2

THE XENON CODEX, Hawkwind, 88-79

XL – 1, Pete Shelley, 83-42

XL – RECORDINGS – THE SECOND CHAPTER, Various Artists: Compilations – XL Recordings, 91-5

XXV, Shadows, 83-34

YANG, Fish, 95-52

YARDBIRDS, Yardbirds, 66-20

YEAH YEAH YEAH YEAH/OUR TROUBLED YOUTH, Bikini Kill/Huggy Bear, 93-12

YEAR OF THE CAT, Al Stewart, 77-38

YEAR OF THE HORSE, Neil Young and Crazy Horse, 97-36

YELLOW MOON, Don Williams, 83-52

YELLOW SUBMARINE, Beatles featuring the George Martin Orchestra, 69-3

YELLOW SUBMARINE SONGTRACK [OST], Beatles, 99-8

YEMEN CUTTA CONNECTION, Black Star Liner, 96-66

YENTL [OST], Barbra Streisand, 83-21

THE YES ALBUM, Yes, 71-7

. . . YES PLEASE!, Happy Mondays, 92-14

YESSHOWS, Yes, 81-22

YESSONGS, Yes, 73-7

YESTERDAY ONCE MORE, Carpenters, 84-10

YESTERDAY WENT TOO SOON, Feeder, 99-8

YESTERDAYS, Yes, 75-27

YESTERDAY'S DREAMS, Four Tops, 69-37

YESTERDAY'S MEMORIES, James Last, 71-17

YIELD, Pearl Jam, 98-7

YIN, Fish, 95-58

YOU AND ME BOTH, Yazoo, 83-1

YOU ARE BEAUTIFUL, Stylistics, 75-26

YOU ARE WHAT YOU IS, Frank Zappa, 81-51

YOU BOYZ MAKE BIG NOIZE, Slade, 87-98

YOU BREAK MY HEART IN 17 PLACES, Tracey Ullman, 83-14

YOU CAN ALL JOIN IN, Various Artists: Compilations – Island, 69-18

YOU CAN DANCE, Madonna, 87-5

YOU CAN'T ARGUE WITH A SICK MIND, Joe Walsh, 76-28

YOU CAN'T HIDE YOUR LOVE FOREVER, Orange Juice, 82-21

YOU CAN'T STOP ROCK 'N' ROLL, Twisted Sister, 83-14

YOU CAUGHT ME OUT, Tracey Ullman, 84-92

YOU COULD HAVE BEEN WITH ME, Sheena Easton, 81-33

YOU DON'T BRING ME FLOWERS, Neil Diamond, 79-15

YOU GOTTA SAY YES TO ANOTHER EXCESS, Yello, 83-65

YOU GOTTA SIN TO GET SAVED, Maria McKee, 93-26

YOU KNOW IT'S ME, Barbara Dickson, 81-39

YOU LIGHT UP MY LIFE, Johnny Mathis, 78-3

YOU MAKE ME FEEL LIKE SINGING A SONG, Max Bygraves, 74-39

YOU, ME AND HE, Mtume, 84-85

YOU, ME & US, Martine McCutcheon, 99-2

YOU? ME? US?, Richard Thompson, 96-32

YOU MIGHT BE SURPRISED, Roy Ayers, 85-91

YOU MUST REMEMBER THIS . . . , Various Artists: Compilations – Happy Days, 95-16

YOU NEVER CAN TELL, Chuck Berry, 64-18

YOU SCARE ME TO DEATH, Marc Bolan, 81-88

YOU TAKE MY HEART AWAY, Shirley Bassey, 77-34

YOU WANT IT, YOU GOT IT, Bryan Adams, 85-78

YOU'LL NEVER KNOW, Rodney Franklin, 80-64

YOU'LL NEVER WALK ALONE, Elvis Presley, 71-20

YOU'LL NEVER WALK ALONE, Various Artists: Compilations – V2, 97-18

YOU'RE GONNA GET IT, Tom Petty and the Heartbreakers, 78-34

YOU'RE MY BEST THING, Don Williams, 78-58

YOU'RE NEVER ALONE WITH A SCHIZOPHRENIC, Ian Hunter, 79-49

YOU'RE THE INSPIRATION – 16 ROMATIC LOVE SONGS, Various Artists: Compilations – Columbia, 91-10

YOU'RE UNDER ARREST, Miles Davis, 85-88

YOU'VE COME A LONG WAY, BABY, Fatboy Slim, 98-1

YOU'VE GOT A FRIEND, Barbara Windsor, 99-45

YOU'VE GOT THE POWER, Third World, 82-87

YOU'VE GOT TO LAUGH, Various Artists: Compilations – Towerbell, 86-51

YOUNG AMERICANS, David Bowie, 75-2

YOUNG GODS, Little Angels, 91-17

YOUNG HEARTS RUN FREE, Candi Staton, 76-34

THE YOUNG ONES [OST], Cliff Richard and the Shadows, 61-1

YOUNG TEAM, Mogwai, 97-75

YOUNG WARM AND WONDERFUL, Gene Pitney, 67-39

YOUNGER THAN YESTERDAY, Byrds, 67-37

YOUR ARSENAL, Morrissey, 92-4

YOUR FAVOURITE HYMNS, Ian Tracey with the Liverpool Cathedrals' Choirs, 92-62

YOUR FILTHY LITTLE MOUTH, David Lee Roth, 94-28

YOUR SECRET LOVE, Luther Vandross, 96-14

YOURS SINCERELY, Harry Secombe, 91-46

YOURS SINCERELY, Pasadenas, 92-6

YOURSELF OR SOMEONE LIKE YOU, Matchbox 20, 98-50

THE YOUTH OF TODAY, Musical Youth, 82-24

YOUTHANASIA, Megadeth, 94-6

YOUTHQUAKE, Dead Or Alive, 85-9

ZAGORA, Loose Ends, 86-15

ZAPPA IN NEW YORK, Frank Zappa, 78-55

ZARAGON, John Miles, 78-43

ZAZU, Rosie Vela, 87-20

ZEBOP!, Santana, 81-33

ZEITGEIST, Levellers, 95-1

ZENYATTA MONDATTA, Police, 80-1

ZERO SHE FLIES, Al Stewart, 70-40

ZIGGY STARDUST – THE MOTION PICTURE, David Bowie, 83-17

ZINC ALLOY AND THE HIDDEN RIDERS OF TOMORROW, Marc Bolan and T. Rex, 74-12

ZINGALAMDUNI, Arrested Development, 94-16

ZIP STYLE METHOD, John Cooper Clarke, 82-97

ZONES, Hawkwind, 83-57

ZOOLOOK, Jean-Michel Jarre, 84-47

ZOOROPA, U2, 93-1

ZOOT, Zoot Money and the Big Roll Band, 66-23

ZUCCHERO, Zucchero, 91-29

ZUMA, Neil Young, 75-44